ATHLETICS
2014
THE INTERNATIONAL
TRACK AND FIELD ANNUAL

BY PETER MATTHEWS
ASSOCIATION OF
TRACK & FIELD STATISTICIANS

SPORTS
BOOKS

Published by SportsBooks Ltd

Copyright: SportsBooks Limited and Peter Matthews 2014

SportsBooks Limited
9 St Aubyns Place
York
YO24 1EQ
United Kingdom
Tel: 01904 613475
e-mail   randall@sportsbooks.ltd.uk
Website   www.sportsbooks.ltd.uk

This publication incorporates the ATFS Annual.

Photographs supplied by Mark Shearman, 22 Grovelands Road, Purley, Surrey, CR8 4LA. Tel: 0208 660 0156: mark@athleticsimages.com

British Library Cataloguing in Publication Data

Athletics: the international track and
field annual – 2014
1. Athletics. Track & Field events –
Serials
1. International athletics annual (London)
796.4'2'05

ISBN 9781907524424

Cover design: Kath Grimshaw

Printed arranged by Jellyfish Solutions, UK

CONTENTS

INTRODUCTION

THE CORE OF this International Athletics Annual is, as ever, the deep lists of performances for the past year. It was interesting that standards in depth were down from the previous year, although this is a usual feature of a post-Olympic year. Nonetheless it was still the second best ever year as the steady advance in world athletics continues, despite occurring at a much slower pace than in the early years of the ATFS Annual in the 1950s and 1960s and in an era when world records are broken fairly infrequently. I comment further on these trends in my Notes from the Editor.

The early editions of the ATFS Annuals are slim volumes compared to today's editions of this Annual in which I try to pack as much as I can of the essential statistics of the sport. My thanks to all contributors and as usual I am particularly delighted that the link with those first editions is maintained with an article by the doyen of track statisticians, the redoubtable Dr Roberto Quercetani, and also that Bob Phillips, assistant editor in the days of World Sports as publishers for 20 years (1953-72), also contributes an article. How the sport has changed over the years since then with a proliferation of World and Continental championships and how the sport has spread so that athletes can and do come from all corners of the globe. If you look at world lists for 1950 the only Africans in the lists are those from South Africa apart from two jumpers from West Africa; so nobody from Kenya and Ethiopia – and look now at how runners from these nations dominate the distance lists. Then as now the marvellous US high school and collegiate system generates large numbers of quality athletes even though track and field is a lowly-regarded sport in that country, but the proportion of athletes from Europe has shrunk considerably. There are massive opportunities for international competition now, but I miss the matches between nations that were such an important part of the competitive structure of that era and thus that there are fewer chances of representing one's country by athletes not quite at the elite level.

The slight reduction in standards has meant that the 2013 lists take up a little less space this year and I have been able to expand the 2014 indoor lists. Also fewer international championships than in most years has given me some space to elaborate some themes in my Notes pages and to add a few miscellaneous items. I maintain the inclusion of short lists from 50 years ago, part of my policy of taking some look at the past as well as chronicling the deeds of toady's athletes.

As ever there is much to look forward to in the year ahead, with exciting new talents making progress and lots of major events to savour. As I conclude this Annual we have already had World Championships Indoors and at Half Marathon this year, and next we will have the exciting new IAAF World Relays, then the Commonwealth Games, European Championships, World University Games, Continental Cup, African Championships, Asian Games and so much more quite apart from the Diamond League and other invitation events. All to be processed for ATHLETICS 2015.

Peter Matthews 5 April 2014

Information can be sent to me to 10 Madgeways Close, Great Amwell, Ware, Herts SG12 9RU, England.
Email: p.matthews@btinternet.com
Information or requests re sales, distribution, publication etc. to the publishers, SportsBooks Ltd.
Email: info@ sportsbooks.ltd.uk
www.sportsbooks.ltd.uk

ABBREVIATIONS

The following abbreviations have been used for meetings with, in parentheses, the first year that they were held.

AAU   (USA) Amateur Athletic Union Championships (1888) (later TAC)
Af-AsG Afro-Asian Games (2003)
AfCh African Championships (1979)
AfG African Games (1965)
Af-J African Junior Championships (1994)
AmCp America's Cup (World Cup Trial) (1977)
APM Adriaan Paulen Memorial, Hengelo
AsiC Asian Championships (1973)
AsiG Asian Games (1951)
Asi-J Asian Junior Championships (1990)
ASV Weltklasse in Köln, ASV club meeting (1934)
Athl Athletissima, Lausanne (1976)
Balk Balkan Games (1929), C – Championships
Barr (Cuba) Barrientos Memorial (1946)
BGP Budapest Grand Prix (1978)
Bisl Bislett Games, Oslo (1965) (Bergen 2004)
Bol G Bolivar Games (1938)
BrGP British Grand Prix
CAC Central American and Caribbean Championships (1967)
CAG Central American and Caribbean Games (1926)
CalR California Relays (1942)
C.Asian Central Asian Championships
CAU Inter-counties, GBR (1934)
CISM International Military Championships (1946)
CG Commonwealth Games (1930)
C.Cup Continental Cup (2010)
Déca Décanation, Paris (C) (2005)
DL Diamond League (2010)
DNG DN Galan, Stockholm (1966)
Drake Drake Relays (1910)
EAF European Athletics Festival, Bydgoszcz (2001)
EAsG East Asian Games (1993)
EC European Championships (1934)
ECCp European Clubs Cup (1975)
EChall European Challenge (10,000m 1997, Throws 2001)
ECp European Cup – track & field (1965), multi-events (1973)
EI European Indoor Championships (1970, Games 1966-9)
EICp European Indoor Cup (2003)
EJ European Junior Championships (1970)
ET European Team Championships (replaced European Cup, 2009)
EU23 European Under-23 Championships (1997) and European Under-23 Cup (1992-4)
FBK Fanny Blankers-Koen Games, Hengelo (formerly APM) (1981)
FlaR Florida Relays (1939)
FOT (USA) Final Olympic Trials (1920)
Franc Francophone Games (1989)
Gaz Gaz de France meeting, FRA (was BNP) (1968)
GGala Golden Gala, Roma (from 1980), Verona (1988), Pescara (1989), Bologna (1990)
GL Golden League (1998-2009)

GNR Great North Run – Newcastle to South Shields, GBR (1981)
GP Grand Prix
GPF IAAF Grand Prix Final (1985)
GS Golden Spike, Ostrava (1969)
Gugl Zipfer Gugl Grand Prix, Linz (1988)
GWG Goodwill Games (1986)
Hanz Hanzekovic Memorial, Zagreb
Herc Herculis, Monte Carlo, Monaco (1987)
IAAF International Association of Athletics Federations
IAC IAC meeting (1968), formerly Coca-Cola
IAU International Association of Ultrarunners
IbAm Ibero-American Championships (1983)
ISTAF Internationales Stadionfest, Berlin (1921)
Jenner Bruce Jenner Classic, San Jose (1979)
Jerome Harry Jerome Track Classic (1984)
Jordan Payton Jordan U.S. Track & Field Open, Stanford (2004)
JUCO Junior Colleges Championships, USA
KansR Kansas Relays, Lawrence (1923)
Kuso Janusz Kusocinski Memorial (1954)
Kuts Vladimir Kuts Memorial ((1978))
LGP London Grand Prix, Crystal Palace
MAI Malmö AI Galan, Sweden (formerly Idag) (1958)
Mal Malinowski Memorial, Poland
Mast Masters pole vault, Grenoble (1987)
MedG Mediterranean Games (1951)
Mill Millrose Games, New York indoors (1908)
ModR Modesto Relays
MSR Mt. San Antonio College Relays (1959)
NA Night of Athletics, Heusden (2000) formerly Hechtel
NACAC North American, Central American & Caribbean Ch (2003)
NC National Championships
NC-w National Winter Championships
NCAA National Collegiate Athletic Association Championships, USA (1921)
NCAA-r NCAA Regional Championships (2003)
NCp National Cup
Nebiolo Memorial Primo Nebiolo, Torino (2000), originally 1963)
NG National Games
Nik Nikaïa, Nice (1976)
NM Narodna Mladezhe, Sofia (1955)
N.Sch National Schools
Nurmi Paavo Nurmi Games (1957)
NYG New York Games (1989)
OD Olympischer Tag (Olympic Day)
Oda Mikio Oda Memorial Meeting, Hiroshima
Odlozil Josef Odlozil Memorial, Prague (1994)
OG Olympic Games (1896)
OT Olympic Trials
Owens Jesse Owens Memorial (1981)
PAm Pan American Games (1951)
PArab Pan Arab Championships (1977) (G-Games 1953)
Pedro Pedro's Cup, Poland (2005)
PennR Pennsylvania Relays (1895)
PTS Pravda Televízia Slovnaft, Bratislava (1957) (later GPB)
Pre Steve Prefontaine Memorial (1976)

RdVin	Route du Vin Half Marathon, Luxembourg (1962)
RomIC	Romanian International Championships (1948)
RWC	Race Walking Challenge Final (2007)
SACh	South American Championships (1919)
SAsG	South Asian Games (1984)
SEAG	South East Asia Games (1959)
SEC	Southeast Conference Championships
SGP	IAAF Super Grand Prix
Slovn	Slovnaft, Bratislava (formerly PTS) (1990)
Spark	Sparkassen Cup, Stuttgart (indoor) (1987)
Spart	(URS) Spartakiad (1956)
Spitzen	Spitzen Leichtathletik Luzern (1987)
Stra	Stramilano Half marathon, Milan
Super	Super Meet, Japan (Tokyo, Shizuoka, Yokohama, Kawasaki)
Tsik	Athens Grand Prix Tsiklitiria (1998)
TexR	Texas Relays (1925)
USOF	US Olympic Festival
VD	Ivo Van Damme Memorial, Brussels (1977)
Veniz	Venizélia, Haniá, Crete (1936)
WAC	Western Athletic Conference Championships
WAF	World Athletics Finals (2003)
WCh	World Championships (1983)
WCM	World Challenge Meeting (2010)
WCp	World Cup – track & field (1977), marathon (1985) Walking – Lugano Trophy – men (1961), Eschborn Cup – women (1979)
WCT	World Championships Trial
WG	World Games, Helsinki (1961)
WI	World Indoor Championships (1987), World Indoor Games (1985)
WJ	World Junior Championships (1986)
WK	Weltklasse, Zürich (1962)
WMilG	World Military Games (or CISM) (1995)
WUG	World University Games (1923)
WY	World Youth Championships (1999)
Zat	Emil Zátopek Classic, Melbourne
Znam	Znamenskiy Brothers Memorial (1958)
-j, -y, -23	Junior, Youth or under-23

Dual and triangular matches are indicated by "v" (versus) followed by the name(s) of the opposition. Quadrangular and larger inter-nation matches are denoted by the number of nations and -N; viz 8-N designates an 8-nation meeting.

Events

CC	cross-country
Dec	decathlon
DT	discus
h	hurdles
Hep	heptathlon
HJ	high jump
HMar	half marathon
HT	hammer
JT	javelin
LJ	long jump
Mar	marathon
Pen	pentathlon
PV	pole vault
R	relay
SP	shot
St	steeplechase
TJ	triple jump
W	walk
Wt	weight

Miscellaneous abbreviations

+	Intermediate time in longer race
=	Tie (ex-aequo)
A	Made at an altitude of 1000m or higher
b	date of birth
D	Made in decathlon competition
dnf	did not finish
dnq	did not qualify
dns	did not start
exh	exhibition
h	heat
H	Made in heptathlon competition
hr	hour
i	indoors
kg	kilograms
km	kilometres
m	metres
M	mile
m/s	metres per second
mx	Made in mixed men's and women's race
nh	no height
O	Made in octathlon competition
P	Made in pentathlon competition
pb	personal best
Q	Made in qualifying round
qf	quarter final (or q in lists)
r	Race number in a series of races
sf	semi final (or s in lists)
w	wind assisted
WIR	world indoor record
WR	world record or best
y	yards
*	Converted time from yards to metres: For 200m: 220 yards less 0.11 second For 400m: 440 yards less 0.26 second For 110mh: 120yh plus 0.03 second

Countries

(IAAF membership reached 213 in 2008, back to 212 in 2011). IAAF and IOC abbreviations are now identical.

AFG	Afghanistan
AHO	Netherlands Antilles #
AIA	Anguilla
ALB	Albania
ALG	Algeria
AND	Andorra
ANG	Angola
ANT	Antigua & Barbuda
ARG	Argentina
ARM	Armenia
ARU	Aruba
ASA	American Samoa
AUS	Australia
AUT	Austria
AZE	Azerbaijan
BAH	Bahamas
BAN	Bangladesh
BAR	Barbados
BDI	Burundi
BEL	Belgium
BEN	Benin
BER	Bermuda
BHU	Bhutan
BIH	Bosnia Herzegovina
BIZ	Belize
BLR	Belarus
BOL	Bolivia
BOT	Botswana
BRA	Brazil
BRN	Bahrain
BRU	Brunei
BUL	Bulgaria
BUR	Burkina Faso
CAF	Central African Republic

Code	Country	Code	Country	Code	Country
CAM	Cambodia	ISV	US Virgin Islands	PRK	North Korea (DPR Korea)
CAN	Canada	ITA	Italy	PUR	Puerto Rico
CAY	Cayman Islands	IVB	British Virgin Islands	PYF	French Polynesia
CGO	Congo	JAM	Jamaica	QAT	Qatar
CHA	Chad	JOR	Jordan	ROU	Romania
CHI	Chile	JPN	Japan	RSA	South Africa
CHN	People's Republic of China	KAZ	Kazakhstan	RUS	Russia
CIV	Côte d'Ivoire (Ivory Coast)	KEN	Kenya	RWA	Rwanda
CMR	Cameroon	KGZ	Kyrgyzstan	SAM	Samoa
COD	Democratic Republic of Congo	KIR	Kiribati	SCG	Serbia & Montenegro (to 2006)
COK	Cook Islands	KOR	Korea	SCO	Scotland
COL	Colombia	KSA	Saudi Arabia	SEN	Sénégal
COM	Comoros	KUW	Kuwait	SEY	Seychelles
CPV	Cape Verde Islands	LAO	Laos	SIN	Singapore
CRC	Costa Rica	LAT	Latvia	SKN	St Kitts & Nevis
CRO	Croatia	LBA	Libya	SLE	Sierra Leone
CUB	Cuba	LBR	Liberia	SLO	Slovenia
CUR	Curaçao	LCA	St Lucia	SMR	San Marino
CYP	Cyprus	LES	Lesotho	SOL	Solomon Islands
CZE	Czech Republic	LIB	Lebanon	SOM	Somalia
DEN	Denmark	LIE	Liechtenstein	SRB	Serbia
DJI	Djibouti	LTU	Lithuania	SRI	Sri Lanka
DMA	Dominica	LUX	Luxembourg	STP	São Tomé & Princípe
DOM	Dominican Republic	MAC	Macao	SUD	Sudan
ECU	Ecuador	MAD	Madagascar	SUI	Switzerland
EGY	Egypt	MAR	Morocco	SUR	Surinam
ENG	England	MAS	Malaysia	SVK	Slovakia
ERI	Eritrea	MAW	Malawi	SWE	Sweden
ESA	El Salvador	MDA	Moldova	SWZ	Swaziland
ESP	Spain	MDV	Maldives	SYR	Syria
EST	Estonia	MEX	Mexico	TAN	Tanzania
ETH	Ethiopia	MGL	Mongolia	TCH	Czechoslovakia (to 1991)
FIJ	Fiji	MKD	Former Yugoslav Republic of Macedonia	TGA	Tonga
FIN	Finland	MLI	Mali	THA	Thailand
FRA	France	MLT	Malta	TJK	Tadjikistan
FRG	Federal Republic of Germany (1948-90)	MNE	Montenegro	TKM	Turkmenistan
FSM	Micronesia	MNT	Montserrat	TKS	Turks & Caicos Islands
GAB	Gabon	MON	Monaco	TLS	East Timor
GAM	The Gambia	MOZ	Mozambique	TOG	Togo
GBR	United Kingdom of Great Britain & Northern Ireland	MRI	Mauritius	TPE	Taiwan (Chinese Taipei)
GBS	Guinea-Bissau	MSH	Marshall Islands	TRI	Trinidad & Tobago (now TTO)
GDR	German Democratic Republic (1948-90)	MTN	Mauritania	TUN	Tunisia
GEO	Georgia	MYA	Myanmar	TUR	Turkey
GEQ	Equatorial Guinea	NAM	Namibia	TUV	Tuvalu
GER	Germany (pre 1948 and from 1991)	NCA	Nicaragua	UAE	United Arab Emirates
GHA	Ghana	NED	Netherlands	UGA	Uganda
GIB	Gibraltar	NEP	Nepal	UKR	Ukraine
GRE	Greece	NFI	Norfolk Islands	URS	Soviet Union (to 1991)
GRN	Grenada	NGR	Nigeria	URU	Uruguay
GUA	Guatemala	NGU	Papua New Guinea	USA	United States
GUI	Guinea	NI	Northern Ireland	UZB	Uzbekistan
GUM	Guam	NIG	Niger	VAN	Vanuatu
GUY	Guyana	NMA	Northern Marianas Islands	VEN	Venezuela
HAI	Haiti	NOR	Norway	VIE	Vietnam
HKG	Hong Kong, China	NRU	Nauru	VIN	St Vincent & the Grenadines
HON	Honduras	NZL	New Zealand	WAL	Wales
HUN	Hungary	OMA	Oman	YEM	Republic of Yemen
INA	Indonesia	PAK	Pakistan	YUG	Yugoslavia (to 2002)
IND	India	PAN	Panama	ZAM	Zambia
IRI	Iran	PAR	Paraguay	ZIM	Zimbabwe
IRL	Ireland	PER	Peru		
IRQ	Iraq	PHI	Philippines		
ISL	Iceland	PLE	Palestine		
ISR	Israel	PLW	Palau		
		PNG	Papua New Guinea		
		POL	Poland		
		POR	Portugal		

\# ceased to exist as a separate territory in 2010, and absorbed into the Netherlands.

ACKNOWLEDGEMENTS

ONCE AGAIN I would like to thank all those who have helped me to compile this Annual – whether in a major way or just with a few items of information. As they have throughout the 64-year history of the ATFS Annual, the annual world lists provide the essential core of the book and I have worked up these lists from original compilations by Richard Hymans and Mirko Jalava with reference to those of Marco Buccellato. I refer all who want to follow the results of the sport closely to Mirko's superb web site www.tilastopaja.net. I am indebted to Carlos Fernández for his expertise on the road lists and to Ray Herdt for the walks. I circulate draft lists to a number of ATFS experts and receive much valuable information from a worldwide circle of correspondents. Of the great Spanish group, Juan Mari Iriondo and Miguel Villeseñor checked the biographies and obituaries with great care. Börre Lilloe provided much index data and Ken Nakamura checked distance lists. I am delighted that Bob Phillips and Roberto Quercetani have again provided articles.

After the untimely death of Jirí Havlín in 2010, came the very sad news of the passing of Milan Skocovsky in 2013. These two great Czech experts were at the heart of the ATFS lists for so many years and they are sorely missed, so we will welcome volunteers to fill this gap who might like to compile and check world lists, especially for women and juniors.

Both for this annual and throughout the year with *Athletics International* Winfried Kramer helps with widespread probing for results as do the area experts: *Africa*: Yves Pinaud, *Asia*: Heinrich Hubbeling, *Central and South America*: Eduardo Biscayart and Luis Vinker, and specialists: *Records* György Csiki, *Road racing*: Marty Post, *Ultrarunning* Andy Milroy, *Indoors* Ed Gordon, *Multi events*: Hans van Kuijen.

Australia: Paul Jenes and David Tarbotton; *Austria*: Dr Karl Graf; *Belgium*: André de Hooghe and Alain Monet; *Bulgaria*: Aleksandar Vangelov; *China*: Mirko Jalava; *Cuba*: Alfredo Sánchez; *Czech Republic*: Milan Urban; *Denmark*: Erik Laursen; *Dominican Republic*: Arisnel Rodríguez; *Estonia*: Erlend Teemägi and Enn Endjärv; *Finland*: Juhani Jalava, Mirko Jalava, Mikko Nieminen and Matti Hannus; *France*: Alain Bouillé, Carles Baronet, Patricia Doilin and José Guilloto; *Germany*: Sven Kuus; *Greece*: Thomas Konstas and Nikos Kriezis; *Hungary*: György Csiki; *India*: Ram. Murali Krishnan; *Ireland*: Pierce O'Callaghan; *Israel*: David Eiger; *Italy*: Raul Leoni, *Japan*: Yoshimasa Noguchi,

Akihiro Onishi and Ken Nakamura; *Latvia*: Andris Stagis; *Lithuania*: Stepas Misiunas; *Luxembourg*: Georges Klepper; *Malaysia*: Jad Adrian, *Montenegro*: Ivan Popovic; *New Zealand*: Murray McKinnon and Tony Hunt; *Norway*: Tore Johansen, Ole Petter Sandvig and Børre Lilloe; *Poland*: Zbigniew Jonik, Janusz Rozum and Tadeusz Wolejko; *Portugal*: Manuel Arons Carvalho; *Puerto Rico*: Pedro Anibal Diaz; *Romania*: Alexandru Boriga; *Russia*: Sergey Tikhonov; *Serbia*: Ozren Karamata and Olga Acic; *Slovakia*: Alfons Juck; *Slovenia*: Zdravko Peternelj; *South Africa*: Danie Cornelius, Riël Hauman and Richard Mayer; *Spain*: José Luis Hernández, Carles Baronet and the AEEA team; *Sweden*: Jonas Hedman and Peter Larsson; *Switzerland*: Alberto Bordoli and Antonin Hejda; *Trinidad*: Bernard Linley; *Turkey*: Nejat Kök, *Ukraine*: Paul Rudenko, *UK*: Tony Miller; *USA*: Tom Casacky, Garry Hill, Sieg Lindstrom, Glen McMicken, Marty Post, Jack Shepherd, Mike Kennedy, and *Track Newsletter*.

Also various national federation lists and to those who post results or ranking lists to various web sites.

Also to Mark Butler, Ottavio Castellini (IAAF), Carole Fuchs, José Maria García, Stan Greenberg, Christian Lenz, Alan Lindop, Rooney Magnusson (obituaries), Bill Mallon, Pino Mappa, David Monti, Bob Phillips, Zdenek Procházka (hammer), Roberto Quercetani, Miguel Villaseñor and Rob Whittingham.

My apologies to anybody whose name I may have missed or who have corresponded with other key ATFS personnel, but all help, however small is deeply appreciated.

Keep the results flowing
During the year Mel Watman and I publish marks to ATFS standards (150-200 deep on world lists) in *Athletics International*, of which there are over 35 issues per year by email. This serves as a base from which the lists in this book can be compiled, together with information from web sites, *Track & Field News* (USA) with its email results spin-off *Track Newsletter* and newsletters, especially Alfons Juck's *EME News* and Carles Baronet's *Track in Sun* blog.

In order to ensure that the record of 2014 is as complete as possible I urge results contribution worldwide to *AI*, and then in turn our lists in *Athletics 2015* will be as comprehensive as we can make them.
Peter Matthews

THE ASSOCIATION OF TRACK & FIELD STATISTICIANS

The ATFS was founded in Brussels (at the European Championships) in 1950 and ever since has built upon the work of such key founding members as Roberto Quercetani, Don Potts and Fulvio Regli to produce authoritative ranking lists in the International Athletics Annual and elsewhere.
Current Executive Committee
President: Paul Jenes AUS
Vice-President: A.Lennart Julin SWE

Treasurer: Tom Casacky USA
Secretary: Michael J McLaughlin AUS
Past Presidents: Rooney Magnusson SWE, Dr Roberto Quercetani ITA
Committee: Eduardo Biscayart ARG/USA, Riël Hauman RSA, Nejat Kök TUR, Bernard Linley TRI, Giuseppa Mappa ITA, Peter J Matthews GBR, Yoshimasa Noguchi JPN, Yves Pinaud FRA

Website: www.afts.org

Internet – Websites

IAAF	www.iaaf.org
IAU	www.iau-ultramarathon.org
African AC	www.webcaa.org
Asian AA	www.athleticsasia.org
CAC Confederation.	www.cacacathletics.org
European AA	www.european-athletics.org
NACAC	www.athleticsnacac.org
Oceania AA	www.athletics-oceania.com
S. American Fed.	www.consudatle.org
WMRA	www.wmra.info
World Masters	www.world-masters-athletics.org
Marathon Majors	www.worldmarathonmajors.com
Africa	www.africathle.com
Andorra	www.faa.ad
Argentina	www.cada-atletismo.org
Australia	www.athletics.com.au
Austria	www.oelv.at
Bahamas	www.bahamastrack.com
Bahrain	www.bahrainathletics.org
Belarus	www.bfla.eu
Belgium	www.val.be
Bermuda	www.btfa.bm
Bosnia Hercegovina	www.asbih.org
Brazil	www.cbat.org.br
Bulgaria	www.bfla.org
Canada	www.athletics.ca
Chile	www.fedachi.cl
China	www.athletics.org.cn
Colombia	www.fecodatle.org
Croatia	www.has.hr
Cyprus	www.koeas.org.cy
Czech Republic	www.atletika.cz
Denmark	www.dansk-atletik.dk
Dominican Republic	www.fedomatle.org
England	www.englandathletics.org
Estonia	www.ekjl.ee
Finland	www.sul.fi
France	www.athle.com
Germany	www.deutscher- leichtathletik-verband.de
	www.leichtathletik.de
Great Britain	www.uka.org.uk
deep statistics	www.topsinathletics.info
	www.thepowerof10.info
Greece	www.segas.gr
Hong Kong	www.hkaaa.com
Hungary	www.masz.hu
Iceland	www.fri.is
India	www.indianathletics.org
Indonesia	www.indonesia-athletics.org
Ireland	www.athleticsireland.ie
Israel	www.iaa.co.il
Italy	www.fidal.it
Jamaica	www.trackandfieldja.com
Japan	www.jaaf.or.jp
running news	japanrunningnews.blogspot.co.uk
Kazakhstan	www.kazathletics.kz
Kenya	www.athleticskenya.org.ke

Latvia	http://lat-athletics.lv
Lithuania	www.laf.lengvoji.lt
Luxembourg	www.fla.lu
Macedonia	www.afm.org.mk
Malaysia	www.maf.org.my
results	www.adriansprints.com
Mexico	www.fmaa.mx
Moldova	www.fam.com.md/
Monaco	www.fma.mc
Montenegro	www.ascg.co.me
Morocco	www.moroccanathletics.com
Netherlands	www.atletiekunie.nl
New Zealand	www.athletics.org.nz
Northern Ireland	www.niathletics.org
Norway	www.friidrett.no
Peru	www.feperatle.com
Poland	www.pzla.pl
Portugal	www.fpatletismo.pt
Puerto Rico	www.atletismofapur.com
Qatar	www.qatarathletics.com/en/
Romania	www.fra.ro
Russia	www.rusathletics.com
Scotland	www.scottishathletics.org.uk
	www.scotstats.com
Serbia	www.serbia-athletics.org.rs
Singapore	www.singaporeathletics.org.sg
Slovakia	www.atletikasvk.sk
Slovenia	www.atletska-zveza.si
South Africa	www.athletics.org.za
Spain	www.rfea.es
Sweden	www.friidrott.se
Switzerland	www.swiss-athletics.ch
Taiwan	www.cttfa.org.tw
Trinidad & Tobago	www.ttnaaa.org
Turkey	www.taf.org.tr
Ukraine	www.uaf.org.ua
Uruguay	www.atlecau.org.uy
USA	www.usatf.org (results) www.tfrrs.org
collegiate results	www.ustfccca.org
Wales	www.welshathletics.org
	athleticsstatswales.webeden.co.uk

Other recommended sites for statistics and results

AIMS	www.aimsworldrunning.org
ARRS	www.arrs.net
British historical	www.gbrathletics.com
DGLD (German stats)	www.ladgld.de Marathons
French history etc.	http://cdm.athle.com
Marathons	www.marathonguide.com
Masters Track & Field	www.mastersathletics.net
Mirko Jalava	www.tilastopaja.com
NUTS/Track Stats	www.nuts.org.uk
Rankings etc	www.all-athletics.com
Runners World	www.runnersworld.com
Tracklion (NED/BEL)	sportsjon.net/tracklione.html
Track & Field News	www.trackandfieldnews.com
Track in Sun results	trackinsun.blogspot.co.uk
World Juniors	www.worldjuniorathleticsnewsnzl.co.n
Olympic Games	www.aafla.org
	www.sports-reference.com

DIARY OF 2013
by Peter Matthews

A chronological survey of highlights in major events in the world of track and field athletics.

See Championships or National sections for more details. DL = Samsung Diamond League, WCM = World Challenge Meeting.

January

5 **Edinburgh**, GBR. Bobby Mack, Genzebe Dibaba and Fionnuala Britton were senior winners at the first IAAF Permit race of the year, with Europe beating GBR and USA in an international contest.

13 **Houston**, USA. It was cold and wet but again Ethiopians won the marathons: Bazu Worku 2:10:17 for his first win in ten marathons and Merima Mohammed 2:23:37.

25 **Dubai**, United Arab Emirates. 14th Standard Chartered Dubai Marathon. Once again there was impressive running in this race and five men bettered 2:05 (best ever times for places 3-4-5), four Ethiopians Lelisa Desisa, 11 days after his 21st birthday, 2:04:45, Berhanu Shiferaw 2:04:48 (world age 19 best), Tadesse Tola 2:04:49 and Endeshaw Shum 2:04:52 followed by Kenyan Bernard Koech 2:04:53. Ethiopians took the first six women's places, headed by Tirfe Tsegaye 2:23:23 and Ehitu Kiros, who took 10:42 off her previous best with 2:23:23. Each winner earned $200,000.

26 **Glasgow**, GBR. The annual International match was held in the new Emirates Arena and was won by Russia 58 (6 wins) from USA 58 (four wins), GBR 50, Germany 49 and Commonwealth Select 40. Highlight was the 600m in which Duane Solomon set a US indoor record of 1:15.70 to win from Dai Greene, UK record 1:16.22, and Andrew Osagie 1:16.45.

26 **Boston (Allston)**, USA. Galen Rupp improved his mile best from 3:56.22 to 3:50.92.

27 **Osaka**, Japan. Kayoko Fukushi ran 2:24:01 to take 17 seconds off her marathon pb, but after leading from 30k had to settle for second in the 32nd Osaka Women's Marathon as she was passed with 800m to go by Tetyana Hamera-Shmyrko, who had been 30 secs behind Fukushi at 35k (1:58:44 to 1:59:14) and who won in 2:23:58.

28 **New York** (Madison Square Garden). US Open. Asafa Powell and Veronica Campbell-Brown were 50m winners in 5.64 and 6.08 and Lolo Jones the 50m hurdles in 6.78, the world's fastest times since 2005, 2000 and 2008 respectively.

29 **Trinec**, Czech Republic. 19 year-old Alessia Trost became the 65th woman to clear 2 metres in the high jump.

February

2 **Arnstadt**, Germany. Winners at the 37th indoor "High Jump with Music" were Aleksey Dmitrik 2.36 and Tia Hellebaut 1.96.

2 **Karlsruhe**, Germany. The 3000m races provided the top marks: Bernard Lagat 7:34.71 and Meseret Defar 8:35.28 both having clear wins.

2 **Boston (Roxbury)**, USA. New Balance GP. Hagos Gebrhiwet won the 3000m in a world junior record 7:32.87 from Galen Rupp 7:33.67, and Mary Cain delighted the fans by smashing the US high school record for 2 miles in the last event of the evening. She ran 9:38.68 for 3rd behind Tirunesh Dibaba 9:13.17.

3 **Moscow**. Russian Winter meeting (IAAF Permit). Mutaz Essa Barshim equaled his Asian indoor record with 2.37 and Holly Bleasdale pole vaulted 4.75. Mohammed Aman sped to 1:15.60 for 600m, an Asian record and world junior best.

6 **Banská Bystrica**, Slovakia. Mutaz Essa Barshim maintained his brilliant form with a high jump win at 2.36 over Aleksey Dmitrik 2.32.

7-8 **Volgograd**, Russia. Yekaterina Bolshova retained her Russian pentathlon title with a world season's best of 4851 points.

8 **Düsseldorf**, Germany. Björn Otto, with a world M35 pole vault record of 5.90 and Murielle Ahouré, with 7.08 for 60m, set meeting records at the PSD Bank meeting.

9-10 **UK Indoor Championships**, Sheffield. Holly Bleasdale starred with 4.77 in the pole vault.

9 **Donetsk**, Ukraine. Winners at the Samsung Pole Vault Stars meeting were Renaud Lavillenie 5.85 and Yarisley Silva 4.76, a CAC indoor record.

12-14 **Russian Indoor Championships**, Moscow. Some top names missed the meeting, which served as selection trials for the European Indoors. Current world-leading marks were recorded by Sergey Shubenkov, 60mh 7.50, and Kseniya Ustalova, 400m 51.31.

15 **Ra's Al Khaymah**, United Arab Emirates. In ideal conditions (13°C at the 7 am start) there was unprecedented depth for a half marathon. For the first time three men (all Kenyans: Geoffrey Kipsang 58:54, Stanley Biwott 58:56 and Geoffrey Mutai 58:58) broke 59 minutes and women's records were set with four inside 67 min (Lucy Kabuu 66:09. Priscah Jeptoo 66:11, Rita Jeptoo 66:27 and Meseret Hailu 66:56 Ethiopian record), six inside 68 min and ten inside 69 min – all Kenyans or Ethiopians. There were best ever place marks for men's 3rd and women's 2nd to 11th.

16   Birmingham, GBR. IAAF Permit Meeting. Murielle Ahouré ran the fastest 60m of the indoor season, 6.99 a metre ahead of Shelly-Ann Fraser-Pryce, 7.09 in her first ever indoor meeting. Ahoure's time was a UK all-comers record as was the 4:00.83 run by Genzebe Dibaba for 1500m. Natasha Hastings 50.88 beat Perri Shakes-Drayton 51.36 at 400m.

16   New York (Armory), USA. Three North American records were set at the 106th Millrose Games: Bernard Lagat scored his 10th win at the meeting with 8:09.49 for 2 miles, and at 600m Eric Sowinski ran 1:15.61 and Alysia Montaño 1:23.59. Lopez Lomong won the Wanamaker Mile in 3:51.21 from Matt Centrowitz 3:51.34.

16-17   French   Indoor   Championships, Aubière. Renaud Lavillenie won the pole vault with 5.93.

16-17   Italian   Indoor   Championships, Ancona. National records were set by Michael Tumi, 60m 6.51, Silvario Chisani, HJ 2.33, and Roberta Bruni, PV 4.60.

21   Stockholm, Sweden. XL Galen. Abeba Aregawi, making her first appearance in her adopted nation since gaining Swedish citizenship, missed the world indoor record by just 0.12 with 3:58.40 for 1500m despite a last 200m in 29.5. There were also fine 3000m races, won by Galen Rupp, who took 2.27 off Bernard Lagat's US record with 7:30.16, and by Genzebe Dibaba, whose 8:26.95 took 20.06 off her pb and took her to fourth on the world all-time indoor list. These were matched as world-leading marks by 1:45.05 for 800m by Mohammed Aman and 2:17.05 for 1000m by Ayanleh Souleiman. Shelly-Ann Fraser-Pryce improved at 60m to 7.04.

22-24   Fayetteville, USA. Kimberlyn Duncan ran the fastest 200m of the indoor season, 22.54 at the SEC Championships.

23   Balkan   Indoor   Championships, Istanbul, Turkey. Turkey was the top nation.

23   Russian   Winter   Walks Championships, Sochi. Heading the usual plethora of fast times were winners Pyotr Trofimov, 20k 1:18:28, Sergey Bakulin, 35k 2:26:08, and Yelena Lashmanova, women's 20k 1:25:49.

23-24   German   Indoor   Championships, Karlsruhe. Björn Otto won the pole vault with 5.85 and Christina Schwanitz the women's shot with 19.79.

24   Tokyo, Japan. Times were slowed by cold (4.6°C at start) and windy conditions, but Dennis Kimetto ran a superb second half of 62:28 to win the seventh Tokyo Marathon in 2:06:50. Women's winner Aberu Kebede was just 6 seconds outside the women's course record with 2:25:34. There were 34,832 finishers (27,827 men and 7005 women).

26-28   Russian   Winter   Throws Championships, Adler. Early world-leading marks were set by Dmitriy Tarabin, JT 85.63, and Tatyana Lysenko, HT 74.07.

28- Mar 3   32nd   European   Indoor Championships, Göteborg, Sweden. There were world-leading marks at ten events. Best of these was the 6.01 pole vault by Renaud Lavillenie for his third successive title… and he celebrated going higher than anyone other than Sergey Bukba at 6.07, only to see the red flag raised as the bar shifted off the pegs while staying up in the air. The best women's marks were the 14.88 triple jump by Olga Saladuha and 7.01 long jump by Darya Klishina. Perri Shakes-Drayton had a triumphant final day, as she first won the 400m in great style in 50.85 and then came back to anchor the British 4x400m team to the one championship record of the meeting, 3:27.56. Impressive sprinting depth was headed by the world-leading 60m marks of 6.48 by Jimmy Vicaut and James Dasoulu, and Sergey Shubenkov also went to the top of the world list with 7.49 for 60m hurdles. Aleksandr Menkov long jumped 8.31, just ahead of Michel Tornéus who set Swedish records at 8.27 and 8.29, and there was a huge triple jump of 17.70 by Daniele Greco. The sixth men's world lead came in the heptathlon as Eelco Sintnicolaas scored 6372, adding 31 points to his Dutch record. Ruth Beitia won the high jump with 1.99m for her fifth European Indoor medal and her first gold. Russia topped the points table from Britain and France, as each had four gold medals. *For leading results see Athletics 2013 p. 86-7.*

March

1-2   Taicang, China. The IAAF Race Walk Challenge races were combined with Chinese Championships and had great depth of times with 20k winners being Li Jianbo 1:18:52 and Sun Huanhuan 1:27:36.

2-3   US   Indoor   Championships, Albuquerque. Jenn Suhr won her seventh US indoor title and took Yelena Isinbayeva's world indoor pole vault record with a first time clearance at 5.02. Other top performances included a world leading 21.80 shot put by Ryan Whiting, 6.49 and 7.08 60m times (altitude-aided) by D'Angelo Cherry and Barbara Pierre, and a world age-20 heptathlon best of 6232 by Gunnar Nixon, but entries were thin.

8-9   NCAA   Indoor   Championships, Fayetteville, USA. Lawi Lalang achieved a double for the second successive year as he won the 1 mile in 3:54.74 and 3000m in 7:45.94, both championship records and within the space of one hour and 40 minutes. US collegiate records were set by Tia Brooks, 19.22 in the women's shot, and by Arkansas in the 4x400m relay with 3:03.50. Derek Drouin cleared a Canadian indoor record 2.35 for his third successive high jump title and Ameer Webb ran 20.37 in the heats of the 200m for a world leading time before winning the final in 20.42. Arkansas won the men's title and Oregon the women's for the fourth successive year.

10   **Asian Walks Championships**, Nomi, Japan. Yusuke Suzuki set a Japanese record of 1:18:34 in winning the men's 20k title.

16-17 **14th European Cup Winter Throwing**, Castellón, Spain. Mariya Abakumova produced the third best performance of her career as she threw the javelin 69.34 and a second world-leading mark came in the women's discus, won clearly by Nadine Müller with 66.69.

16-17 **Copa Cuba**, Havana, Cuba. Yarisley Silva won the national pole vault title with a CAC record 4.81.

17   **Lugano**, Switzerland. Wang Zhen won the men's 20k in 1:19:08 and Liu Hong the women's in 1:27:06 in the first races of the EA Walking Circuit for 2013.

23   **New Zealand Championships**, Auckland, Valerie Adams won her 12th national shot title with 20.37 and all six puts over 20m.

23   **Dudince**, Slovakia. Erick Barrondo set a CAC record with 3:41:09 to win the 50k at the 32nd "Dudinska patdesiatka" meeting.

24   **World Cross-Country Championships**, Bydgoszcz, Poland. Kenya had three individual wins, senior men, Japheth Korir, and both women's races – Emily Chebet, senior, and Faith Kipyegon, who defended her junior title. Ethiopia claimed the junior men's winner, Hagos Gebrhiwet, and had victorious teams in both men's races. Just 398 athletes competed, 215 men and 183 women from 41 countries, the lowest figures since the 1980s, while the percentage of European athletes at 25.8% was the lowest ever when the event has been held in Europe. Ben True (USA), 6th in the senior men's race was the best-placed non-African in any race.

27-30 **86th Texas Relays**, Austin, USA. Warm winds blew the sprinters to super fast times, headed by Darvis Patton 100m 9.75w and Brianna Rollins 100mh 12.54w.

31   **Rio de Janeiro**, Brazil. Watched by a crowd of some 20,000 Usain Bolt enjoyed a win at 150m in 14.42 on a blue straight track set up on Copacabana beach.

April

4-6   **Florida Relays**, Gainesville, USA. The Boogie Fast TC team of Nia Ali, Kristi Castlin, Yvette Lewis and Queen Harrison set a world best time for 4x100m hurdles with 50.78.

6   **Melbourne**, Australia (WCM).

6   **Caserta**, Italy. Yadisleidy Pedroso ran the 200m hurdles in 24.8 compared to the previous world best of 25.6 by Patricia Girard in 2011.

6   **Tucson**, USA. Kori Carter made a huge breakthrough by running 54.71 for 400m hurdles from a previous best of 57.10 in 2011.

7   **Paris**, France. Peter Kimeli Some won the annual marathon in 2:05:38, a 2:51 improvement on his pb, and women's winner was Feysa Tadesse in a course record time of 2:21:06, a 2:01 improvement for her. There were a record 38,690 finishers, a total bettered only by New York.

14   **Rotterdam Marathon**, Netherlands. In warm conditions with a headwind in the closing stage, Tilahun Regassa won in 2:05:38 and the women's winner was Jemima Jelagat in 2:23:27, a pb by over 6 minutes.

15   **117th Boston Marathon**, USA. Race winners, Lelisa Desisa 2:10:22 and Rita Jeptoo 2:26:25, each won $150,000, but then, 4:14 after the race started, this event made the world's headlines for all the wrong reasons when two bombs detonated near the densely packed finish line claimed three deaths and 176 injured, many of whom had limbs blown off.

17-20 **Kansas Relays**, Lawrence, USA. Ryan Whiting beat Reese Hoffa 21.65 to 21.60 in the shot.

18-20 **55th Mt SAC Relays**, Walnut, California, USA. This was again a massive meeting, starting with 20 distance races (eight at 10,000m!) on the Thursday, then 46 track and 30 field on the Friday and 91 track and 42 field on the Saturday. Top marks included a 2.34 high jump by Erik Kynard and sharp sprinting from English Gardner, 100m 11.00 pb, Blessing Okagbare, 200m 22.31 pb, and Yvette Lewis, 100mh 12.43w.

21   **Hamburg**, Germany. Eliud Kipchoge made a splendid marathon debut (the seventh fastest ever) as he won the marathon by 2:05 in 2:05:30.

22   **Virgin London Marathon**, GBR. While the men's winner Tsegaye Kedebe split 61:36 and 64:28 for his 2:06:04, women's winner Priscah Jeptoo ran negative splits with 71:49 and 68:26 for 2:20:15. Each won $100,000. Second places were taken by Emmanuel Mutai 2:06:33 and Edna Kiplagat 2:21:32. There were 34,187 finishers (21,968 men and 12,201 women).

23-27 **119th Penn Relays**, Philadelphia, USA. A three-day attendance of 111,834 included 48,817 at Franklin Field for the final day when US teams won all four of the six of the relay races against 'The World'. Shelly-Ann Fraser-Pryce anchored the Jamaican women's 4x100m team to a 42.42 win and Mohammed Aman contributed a 1:44.0 800m to Ethiopia's distance medley win in 9:16.34. The top race for records was the women's 4x800m when five teams smashed their national record, headed by the USA improving from 8:17.91 to 8:04.31, helped by a 1:58.6 anchor by Alysia Montaño.

25-27   104th **Drake Relays**, Des Moines, USA. A sell-out crowd of 14,504 on the final day enjoyed the action that included a 4:03.35 win at 1500m by local star Jenny Simpson and a 17th CAC pole vault record (at 4.85) by Yarisley Silva.

28-29   **Hiroshima**, Japan. 17 year-old Yoshihide Kiryu tied the world junior record (although unable to be ratified due a non-standard wind gauge) in his 100m heat and ran 10.03 in the final at the Mikio Oda Memorial.

May

2-3   **Florence**, Italy. Andrey Kravchenko won the decathlon with 8390, his best score since 2008, at the first IAAF Combined Events Challenge of the year.

4   **Kingston**, Jamaica (WCM). Tyson Gay won the 100m in 9.86, well clear of Nesta Carter 10.03, for his 35th legal mark inside 10.00 and more sharp sprint wins came from Nickel Ashmeade, 200m, 20.00, Veronica Campbell-Brown, 100m 11.01, and Dawn Harper-Nelson, 100mh 12.62.

9   **Georgetown**, Cayman Islands. Usain Bolt won his opening 100m race of 2013 at the 2nd Cayman Invitational, but it was closely run as he had a margin of just 0.006 over Kemar Bailey-Cole, 10.083 to 10.089.

10   **Doha**, Qatar (DL). Brittney Reese long jumped a Diamond League record 7.25 and Blessing Okagbare was 2nd with 7.14w. This opening DL fixture, conducted in ideal conditions of about 30°C and little wind, was again of very high quality. Reese's jump, Ryan Whiting's 22.28 pb in the shot, Hagos Gebrhiwet's 7:30.36 for 3000m, and Abeba Aregawi's Swedish women's record 3:56.60 for 1500m remained the best marks of 2013. Three women beat 3:58 in a 1500m race for the first time since 2006 as 19 year-old Faith Kipyegon was 2nd in a Kenyan record 3:56.98 and Genzebe Dibaba 3rd in 3:57.54. David Rudisha had another majestic victory with 1:43.87 for his season's opener at 800m, and Asbel Kiprop led eleven men under 3:35 in 3:31.13. Alyson Felix had her one 400m race of 2013 and ran 50.19 but was well beaten by Amantle Montsho 49.88, with Christine Ohuruogu 3rd in 50.53. Sandra Perkovic had five discus throws over 65m with a best of 67.37.

11-12   **IAU World 24 Hours Championships**, Steenbergen, Norway. The Unites States met with great success, winning both team titles and Jon Olsen was the men's winner with 269.675k. The women's winner Mami Kudo ran 252.205k, passing 200k en route in 18:45:51, both world road bests.

12   **Belém**, Brazil (WCM). Ana Claúdia Silva ran a South American record 11.05 for 100m.

14   **Brno**, Czech Republic. Zuzana Hejnová ran a world best of 38.75 for 300m hurdles.

16   **Uberlândia**, Brazil. Augusto de Oliveira set a South American pole vault record at 5.81.

18   **Shanghai**, China (DL). Kirani James ran his second fastest ever time, 44.02, in winning clearly from LaShawn Merritt 44.60. Shelly-Ann Fraser-Pryce won the 100m in a world-leading 10.93 from Blessing Okagbare 11.00 and Carmelita Jeter 11.08, but Jeter clutched her right quadricep just before the finish line and was stretchered off. 18 year-old Conselus Kipruto improved his pb to 8:01.16 as Kenyans took the first nine places in the 3000m steeplechase with Paul Koech 2nd in 8:02.63 and Hillary Yego 3rd in 8:03.57, and Asbel Kiprop, seemingly out of it in seventh with 100m to go, scored a thrilling 1500m victory over Mekonnen Gebremedhin in 3:32.39. Genzebe Dibaba's finishing pace in winning the 5000m in 14:45.92 was too much for Meseret Defar. Yelena Isinbayeva opened her season with a 4.70 vault before passing her final attempt at 4.85 because of a problem with her left Achilles; and Christina Schwanitz broke through the 20m shot barrier with efforts of 20.12 and 20.20 from a previous best of 19.79 indoors. Top Chinese result was an 8.34 long jump win by Li Jinzhe.

18   **Ponce**, Puerto Rico (WCM). Johnny Dutch won the 400m hurdles in a world-leading 48.02 from local star Javier Culson 48.36.

19   **European Cup in Race Walking Cup**, Dudince, Slovakia. Yohann Diniz, 3:41:07, won the 50km for the second time and there were Russian wins in the 20k races, from Denis Strelkov 1:21:40 and Anisya Kirdyapkina 1:28:39, as well both junior races and team wins in all five races.

19   **Wiesbaden**, Germany. 18th WLV Throwers Cup. Top mark was 68.31 at discus by Robert Harting.

21   **Beijing**, China (WCM). This was the first athletics meeting held at the Bird's Nest Stadium since the 2008 Olympics and was attended by over 50,000 spectators. Anna Chicherova jumped a world-leading 2.02 for high jump, Justin Gatlin impressed with a 9.91 100m win and Li Jinzhe won the long jump with 8.31.

21-24   **Arab Championships**, Doha, Qatar. Six new championship records included 44.72 for 400m by Youssef Al-Masrahi.

23-25   **NCAA Qualifying**, USA. Preliminary rounds for the NCAA Championships were held in Eastern and Western sections at Greensboro and Austin.

24-25   **European Clubs Cup**, Vila Real de Santo António, Portugal. Luch Moskva achieved their 17th successive win in the women's match, but were beaten by four points by Fiamme Galle of Italy in the men's.

24-25   Götzis, Austria. Winners in cold weather were Damian Warner, 8307 decathlon, and Brianne Theisen, 6376 heptathlon.

25   Halle, Germany. Werfertage. Top marks came in the hammer – a world-leading 80.71 by Dilshod Nazarov and 74.92 by Betty Heidler, from Éva Orbán 73.66 Hungarian record.

25   Manchester, GBR. BT Great City Games. Allyson Felix, 150m 16.36 150m, and Perri Shakes-Drayton, 200mh 25.74, ran world bests on the straight elevated purpose-built track laid in the city centre (although better times have been recorded around a turn).

25   New York (Randall's Island), USA. adidas GP (DL). Dismal weather marred performances. Tyson Gay won the 100m in 10.02, Sandra Perkovic maintained her discus supremacy with 68.48 and Blanka Vlasic won the high jump with 1.94 in her first competition since September 2011.

25-26   Pan-American Race Walking Cup, Guatemala City, Guatemala.

28- Jun 1   Games of Small States of Europe, Luxembourg.

June

1   Eugene, USA. 39th Prefontaine Classic (DL). Best of the ten world-leading marks at an outstanding meeting was a 2.40 Asian record high jump by Mutaz Essa Barshim, who had stiff opposition from Erik Kynard 2nd and Derek Drouin 3rd, both clearing 2.36, a Canadian record for Drouin. Renaud Lavillenie won the pole vault with 5.95 and beat fellow Olympic medallists Björn Otto 5.90 and Raphael Holzdeppe 5.84, and in the women's triple jump Caterine Ibargüen won with 14.93w from Olga Saladuha 14.85. There were three German wins in the throws: Robert Harting, discus 69.75 from Piotr Malachowski 68.19, Betty Heidler, hammer 75.21, and Christina Obergföll, javelin 67.70. Valerie Adams had to come from behind to win the shot by just 3cm from Gong Lijiao, 20.15 to 20.12. Surprise Olympic bronze medallist Hansle Parchment won the 110m hurdles with a Jamaican record 13.05 ahead of Orlando Ortega pb 13.08 and David Oliver 13.10, and LaShawn Merritt beat Kirani James 44.32 to 44.39 at 400m. Assisting winds helped fast sprint times with the 100m races won by Justin Gatlin 9.86w and Shelly-Ann Fraser-Pryce 10.71w from Blessing Osagbare 10.75 and Veronica Campbell-Brown 10.78, the first time three women had beaten 10.80 in one race. Although hoping for some 25 secs quicker, Kenenisa Bekele went to the top of the world 10,000m list with 27:12.08. 20 year-old Francine Niyonsaba won the 800m in a world leading 1:56.72, but she had to share the appreciative crowd's attention with Mary Cain, who, less than a month after her 17th birthday, finished strongly out in lane three for a North American junior record of 1:59.51. Asbel Kiprop won the Bowerman Mile in 3:49.48 from Aman Wote 3:49.88, while in the steeplechase Ezekiel Kemboi was disqualified for pushing rival Conseslus Kipruto off the track close to the finish. The latter had, however, recovered to win by 0.35 in 8:03.59.

2   Comrade's Marathon, South Africa. Claude Moshiywa set a record of 5:32:09 for the 'up' direction of the 86.96k race from Durban to Pietermaritzburg and Yelena Nurgaliyeva had an eighth women's race win.

4   Havana, Cuba. Top mark at the Barrientos Memorial was a 17.69 triple jump by Pedro Pichardo, a world age-19 best.

5-8   NCAA Championships, Eugene, USA. Collegiate records were set by women hurdlers: Brianne Rollins maintained her brilliant run of success with 12.47 in her semi and 12.39 in the final of the 100m hurdles, and Kori Carter (also 2nd at 100mh in 12.79) won the 400mh in 53.21. Florida and Texas A&M tied for the men's title with 53 points with Arkansas 46.5 third, while the women's title was on for the first time by Kansas 60, followed by Texas A&M 44 and Oregon 43. Kimberlyn Duncan ran 22.04w for 200m for her third successive indoor and outdoor 200m double and other top marks came from Charles Silmon 9.89w and English Gardner 10.96 for 100m. As he had at the Indoor championships, Lawi Lalang won a double, in this case 5000m and 10,000m. *See USA section for winners.*

6   Rome, Italy. Golden Gala (DL). Usain Bolt's narrow defeat by Justin Gatlin 9.94 to 9.95 captured the headlines but there were several other surprises, including Murielle Ahouré beating Alyson Felix at 200m 22.36 to 22.64. A crowd of 52,305 in the Olympic Stadium saw world-leading marks by Mohammed Aman, 800m 1:43.61, Yenaw Alamirew, 5000m 12:54.95, and Amantle Montsho, 400m 49.87.

6-9   São Paulo, Brazil. Carlos Eduardo Chinin set a South American decathlon record with 8393 points at the Trofeu Brazil (national championships).

7-9   Japanese Championships, Tokyo. Koji Murofushi won his 19th successive national hammer title with 76.42.

8   European Cup 10,000m, Pravets, Bulgaria.

8   Hengelo, Netherlands. 31st Fanny Blankers-Koen Games (WCM). After 35 successive wins, Robert Harting lost at the discus. He threw 69.91, but had to yield to the Polish record of 71.84 by Pyotr Malachowski. Yarisley Silva raised her world outdoor leading mark from 4.85 to 4.90, her 18th Central American & Caribbean pole vault record.

8   **Turin**, Italy. 14th Primo Nebiolo Memorial (EA Premium). Dayron Robles returned to competition, but was only 6th in 13.82 at 110m hurdles,

9   **Rabat**, Morocco. 6th Mohammed VI meeting (WCM). Three days after his win over Usain Bolt, Justin Gatlin was beaten 9.98w to 10.02, by Christophe Lemaitre at 100m.

10   **Prague**, Czech Republic. 18th Josef Odlozil Memorial. Vitezslav Vesely won the javelin with 86.94.

11   **Moscow Challenge**, Russia (WCM). Top mark, in steady rain, was 65.94 for javelin by Mariya Abakumova.

12   **Dakar**, Sénégal (WCM).

13   **Oslo**, Norway (DL). Exxon Mobil Bislett Games. In the final event on a chilly night Usain Bolt swept to a world leading 19.79 in his first 200m of the year, and another world-leading mark was 14:26.90 for 5000m by Meseret Defar, well ahead of Viola Kibiwot 14:33.48 and Genzebe Dibaba 14:37.56. The Dream Mile was won by Ayanleh Souleiman in 3:50.53.

15   **Szczecin**, Poland. Superb hammer competitions provided the highlights of the 59th annual Janusz Kusocinski Memorial meeting as both Krisztián Pars 81.01, from Lukas Melich 80.28 his first ever 80m throw, and Betty Heidler 76.48 won with world-leading marks.

15-16 **Ratingen**, Germany. Pascal Behrenbruch won the decathlon with 8514 and Julia Mächtig the heptathlon with 6430.

20-23 **Jamaican Championships**, Kingston. There was terrific depth of sprinting. Usain Bolt won his first national title since 2009, 100m in 9.94 with head wind of 1.2 m/s, Warren Weir beat Nickel Ashmeade 19.79 to 20.04 at 200m and Shelly-Ann Fraser-Pryce ran just the 200m, winning in 22.13. Novlene Williams-Mills ran 50.01 for her seventh 400m title in eight years.

20-23 **US Championships**, Des Moines. Three North Americans women's records were set in an outstanding meeting: 12.26 for 100m hurdles by Brianna Rollins (after 12.33w heat and 12.30w semi), 20.24 shot by Michelle Carter and 75.73 hammer by Amanda Bingson. Tyson Gay scored a brilliant sprint double in 9.75 (meet record) and 19.74, until later discredited by his positive drugs test, as Justin Gatlin finished well behind despite running 9.89. Indeed all the sprints produced spectacular times in the hot weather, including English Gardner improving from 10.96 to 10.87 in her semi and 10.85 in the women's 100m final, just 0.02 ahead of Octavious Freeman. Brigetta Barrett's 2.04 high jump clearance was to remain the best of 2013. The time was very slow, but Bernard Lagat won his sixth US 5000m title, while Jenn Suhr won her seventh at pole vault with 4.70 and there were fifth titles for Brad Walker at pole vault,

A.G.Kruger at hammer and Alysia Montaño at 800m (1:58.67).

21-23 **Trinidad & Tobago Championships**, Port of Spain. Sharp sprinting was headed by Keston Bledman 9.85w and Kelly-Ann Baptiste, who ran a world-leading 10.83 for 100m and national record 22.36 for 200m.

22-23 **European Team Championships**, Gateshead, GBR. Russia won a third consecutive title in a close-fought battle from Germany and Britain. It was blustery on day one and rain-soaked on day two, so not conducive to great performances but Perri Shakes-Drayton won the 400m in a pb 50.50 and outstanding on the men's side were Aleksandr Menkov's 8.36 long jump and Dmitriy Tarabin's 85.99 javelin throw. Mo Farah charged around the last lap of the slow 5000m in 50.89. The First League in Dublin was won by the Czech Republic, the Second League in Kaunas by Slovenia and the Third League in Banská Bystrica by Slovakia.

26-29 17th **Mediterranean Games**, Mersin, Turkey. Ilham Tanui Özbilen scored a notable double with 1500m in 3:35.09 and then smashing the Games record with a Turkish record of 1:44.00 for 800m.

27   **Ostrava**, Czech Republic. 52nd Golden Spike (WCM). Two impressive Czech victories headed performances: Vitezslav Vesely threw the javelin 87.58 and Zuzana Hejnová ran 53.32 for 400m hurdles. Another Czech Lukas Melich led the hammer with 80.16 until Krisztián Pars threw 80.75 in the final round and similarly Betty Heidler overtook Anita Wlodarczyk with 75.24 to 74.98 in the women's hammer. Yelena Isinbayeva beat Yarisley Silva in the pole vault 4.78 to 4.72. World leads came from Valerie Adams, 20.88 in the shot, and Tirunesh Dibaba, 30:26.67 for 10,000m.

27   **Sollentuna**, Sweden. Dibaba's 10,000m world lead was short lived as here Meseret Defar ran the distance in 30:08.06 and Dejen Gebremeskel won the men's race in 26:51.02 from Abera Kuma 26:52.85 and Imane Merga 26:57.33, times that were to remain the three fastest of 2013.

28   **Reims**, France, EA Premium. Mahiedine Mekhissi-Benabbad ran 4:56.85 for 2000m.

29-30 **European Cup of Combined Events**. For the first time men's and women's scores were aggregated for this competition and France won the Super League at Tallinn from Russia and Estonia and had the individual decathlon winner in Kevin Mayer 8390. The Netherlands won the First League at Nottwil and Norway the Second League at Ribeira Brava.

30   **Birmingham**, GBR. Sainsbury's Grand Prix (DL). Mo Farah ran the final lap in 53.39 to outkick his main East African rivals in the 5000m as Yenew Alamirew and Hagos Gebrhiwet were 2nd and 3rd. Another British success came as

Christine Ohuruogu 50.63 edged past Amantle Montsho in the 400m. Christian Taylor beat Teddy Tamgho 17.66 to 17.47 in the triple jump and Bohdan Bondarenko improved his high jump best from 2.33 to 2.36 in beating Erik Kynard 2.34.

30   **Zhukovskiy**, Russia. 55th Znamenskiy Memorial. Oksana Kondratyeva won the hammer with a world-leading 77.13.

July

1   **Burnaby**, Canada. Harry Jerome Classic. Duane Solomon ran the third best ever time for 600m with 1:13.28.

3-7   **Asian Championships**, Pune, India. Satomi Kubokura of Japan won her fourth successive title at 400m hurdles and athletes of the meeting were announced as Yousef Al-Masrahi (400m 45.08) and Ruth Chebet, who won the women's 3000m steeplechase in a Bahrain record 9:40.84 at 16 years 230 days. This was one of seven new championship records.

4   **Lausanne**, Switzerland. Athletissima (DL). Bohdan Bondarenko high jumped 2.39 at the first attempt and 2.41 at the third before making reasonable attempts at adding 1cm to Javier Sotomayor's 1993 world record of 2.45, and Erik Kynard was second with 2.37. Other world leads came from David Oliver, who ran his quickest 110m hurdles time for two years with 13.03 and Sandra Perkovic, who won the discus with 68.96 but was pressed by Yarelis Barrios 67.36. Ryan Whiting beat Reese Hoffa 21.88 to 21.58 in the shot and Blessing Okagbare long jumped a pb 6.98 to beat Brittney Reese 6.96. Tyson Gay won the 100m in 9.79 from Asafa Powell 9.88, Mike Rodgers 9.96 and the ever-amazing Kim Collins, who clocked the fastest time of his life, a national record and world age-37 best of 9.97.

5-7   24th **Central American & Caribbean Championships**, Morelia, Mexico. Even with most of the stars missing, there was still excellent sprinting, helped of course by high altitude of 1950m.

5-7   48th   **South   American Championships**, Cartagena, Colombia. With Brazil easily the most successful nation, Thiago da Silva, just 19 years of age, cleared 5.83m to add a centimetre to the South American pole vault record set just two weeks earlier by his compatriot Agusto de Oliveira. Rosibel Garcia achieved the 800m/1500m double for the fourth time and her 1500m win was her fifth in succession at this biennial event, as was the Germán Lauro's in the shot, and he added the discus title for the third time. Alex Quiñónez and Ana Cláudia Silva of Brazil won 100m/200m doubles.

6   **European Mountain Running Championships**, Borovec, Bulgaria. Italy achieved their 18th men's team win in the 19 years of the event

and their 11th women's team win.

6   **Saint-Denis**, France. Areva meeting (DL). Capacity crowd of over 52,000. The best result came in the last race as Usain Bolt won the 200m in 19.73 with Warren Weir second in 19.92. There were three earlier world-leading marks: Kirani James ran 43.86 for 400m to win a great battle with LaShawn Merritt 44.09, Tirunesh Dibaba 14:23.68 for 5000m and Ezekiel Kemboi 7:59.03 steeplechase from Mahiedine Mekhissi-Benabbad's European record 8:00.09. Zuzana Hejnová maintained her steady improvement and unbeaten run with a Czech 400mh record of 53.23 with Perri Shakes-Drayton 2nd in 53.96, while Shelly-Ann Fraser-Pryce just held off Blessing Okagbare at 100m, 10.92 to 10.93.

6-7   **German Championships**, Ulm. Betty Heidler won her ninth successive hammer title with 73.93 and there were seventh titles for Robert Harting 67.95 discus and Markus Esser 76.41 hammer. Sabine Mockenhaupt won her 12th German 5000m title in 13 years from 2001 (and her 30th at all distances).

7-12   **World University Games**, Kazan, Russia. Russians dominated, amassing 20 gold medals (next best South Africa and USA with four apiece), 17 silver and eight bronze. Top marks came in the long jump won by Luis Rivera 8.46 from Aleksandr Menkov 8.42. Other high quality men's winners included a 10.10/20.00w sprint double by Anaso Jobodwana and a 79.99 hammer throw by Pawel Fajdek. The most significant women's result was a world leading heptathlon score of 6623 by Tatyana Chernova.

10   **Budapest**, Hungary. 3rd István Gyulai Memorial Meeting. Kim Collins again broke 10 secs for 100m with a 9.99 win

10   **Liège (Naimette-Xhovément)**, Belgium.

10-14   **European Under-23 Championships**, Tampere, Finland. Top performances included a Serbian 400m hurdles record of 48.76 by Emir Bekric, 8.37 long jump by Eusebio Cáceres, European U23 4x100m record of 38.77 by a British team anchored by 100m champion Adam Gemili, 1.98 high jump by Alessia Trost and multi-event scores of 8366 by Kai Kazmirek and 6215 by Katarina Johnson-Thompson.

10-14   8th **World Youth Championships**, Donetsk, Ukraine. Held in beautiful weather, there were new championship bests in 12 events and three world junior records: Meresa Kassaye, 2000m steeplechase 5:19.99, Jamaica, men's medley relay 1:49.23, and Yanique Thompson, women's 76.2cm 100m hurdles 12.94, with Dior Hall 13.01 also under the previous record. Robert Kiptoo Biwott front-ran the 1500m for 3:36.7, 0.01 inside the championship record. Several athletes made huge breakthroughs such as by 400m winners, Martin Manley 46.95 to 45.89 and Sabrina Bakare 53.98 to 52.77, Jaheel Hyde at 110m hurdles from 13.72 to 13.47 heat and 13.22 semi before winning the final in 13.13, just 0.01 short of Wilhem Belocian's world youth record from 2012, and Marvin Williams 50.39 in the 400m hurdles from an alleged pre-meet best of 53.41. Karsten Warholm enjoyed a marvellous two days as he improved his Norwegian youths octathlon record from 5946 points to 6451, just 40 short of Jake Stein's WYR.

12-13   UK Championships, Birmingham. James Dasaolu sped to an impressive 9.91 for in his semi-final but did not run the final, leaving Dwain Chambers to win in 10.04, his seventh 100m title.

12-14   French   Championships,   Paris (Charléty). Renaud Lavillenie won the pole vault at 5.95 and Jimmy Vicaut twice ran 9.95 for 100m.

13   Heusden-Zolder, Belgium. KBC Night of Athletics. 12 of the 13 finishers in the 5000m set pbs, headed by 12:59.43 from Albert Rop.

13   Kenyan   World   Champs   Trials, Nairobi. Exceptional high altitude times were run at 10,000m won by Bidan Karoki in 27:31.61with eight men under 28 minutes and Conseslus Kipruto won the 3000m steeplechase in 8:13.5, with Ezekiel Kemboi jogging in 6th, Hilary Yego 11th and Paul Kipsiele Koech 12th, while six men led by Silas Kiplagat 3:33.7 broke 3:35 for 1500m.

13   Madrid, Spain (WCM). Nesta Carter took advantage of +1.8 wind and the 640m altitude to run 9.87 for 100m. Brigetta Barrett and Blanka Vlasic matched clearances up to 1.98 and four failures at 2.02 before Vlasic conceded high jump victory to her US rival.

14   Shocking   news   came   through   that both Tyson Gay and Asafa Powell had tested positive for banned substances. In Powell's case he and Sherone Simpson were among five Jamaicans to have samples found to contain an amphetamine at the Jamaican Championships and Gay later admitted that had had tested positive for a steroid. Neither case had been resolved by the end of the year.

15   Moscow, Russia. Kuts Memorial. Antonina Krivoshapka ran a world-leading time of 49.57 for 400m and Sergey Litvinov won the hammer with 80.89.

17   Luzern, Switzerland. The 27th Spitzen Leichtathletik meeting included Yarisley Silva beating a top-class pole vault field with 4.81 from Silke Spiegelburg 4.71.

18-21   European   Junior   Championships, Rieti, Italy. Anita Henriksdóttir (2:01.13 for 800m) and Emel Dereli (18.04 Turkish record in the shot) completed notable World Youth and European Junior doubles. Wilhem Belocian improved the European junior record for 110m hurdles to 13.18, Timofey Chalyy smashed the championships record of 49.70 with a Russian junior record of 49.23 for 400m hurdles and a

third (wind-legal) championship record was set by Malaika Mlhambo with a 6.70 long jump. Russia just came out on top of the points table, but Britain were just 9 points behind and headed the medal table with 9 golds to Russia's 8. The total of 961 athletes competing was a new record high.

19-21   Polish   Championships, Torun. Szymon Ziólkowski won his 14th national hammer title, Tomasz Majewski his eleventh shot title in twelve years and Piotr Malachowski his eighth discus title in nine years.

22-27   Russian   Championships, Moscow. There were world-leading marks in the javelin as Dmitriy Tarabin added 2.85m to his pb with a final round 88.84, and women's hammer as Tatyana Lysenko threw an opening 77.27 before a mighty 78.15 in round two. Yuliya Zaripova passed the steeplechase, but was a notable winner of the 1500m in 4:02.56.

23   Herculis, Monaco (DL). The usual perfect conditions for this meeting helped set up a great 1500m that was won by Asbel Kiprop in 3:27.72 for fourth on the world all-time list and the fastest for nine years. In second place Mo Farah ran 3:28.81, compared to his previous best of 3:33.98 and in so doing took the UK record set by Steve Cram in his world record 3:29.67 in Nice in 1985 and Fermin Cacho's 3:28.95 European record from 1997. Caleb Ndiku was 3rd in a pb 3:29.50. The two fastest times of 2013 came in the 5000m from Edwin Soi 12:51.34 and Albert Rop 12:51.96 with Isiah Koech and Thomas Longosiwa also under 13 minutes. Amantle Montsho took her Botswana 400m record to 49.33 and in the field Renaud Lavillenie pole vaulted 5.96 and Vitezslav Vesely threw the javelin 87.68. Murielle Ahouré set an Ivory Coast 200m record at 22.24 with the surprising Tiffany Townsend 2nd in 22.26 ahead of Shelly-Ann Fraser-Pryce 22.28. Setting up his later World success Jehue Gordon won the 400m hurdles in 48.00 and US 4x100m teams ran world-leading times of 37.58 and 41.75. The meeting ended with the traditional fireworks display and Brigetta Barrett, having won the high jump with 2.01, reappeared as a singer – belting out the Stevie Wonder number 'For Once In My Life' – together with some backing dancers.

25-29   Finnish Championships, Lahti. Tero Pitkämäki, who had previously won in 2004-07, won the javelin with 85.70.

26-27   London, GBR. Sainsbury's Anniversary Games (DL). A year on from the Olympic Games this was an opportunity for one last use of the Olympic Stadium before it was to be re-developed for football and 60,000 capacity crowds, many of whom had not had the chance to come in 2012, came for the two days. Seven Olympic champions won here, including Usain Bolt with 9.85 for 100m.

Shelly-Ann Fraser-Pryce ran a world-leading 10.77 in her heat but eased to 4th in 10.94 in the final, won by Blessing Okagbare, who ran African records of 10.86 in her heat and 10.79 in the final. Renaud Lavillenie cleared a French record 6.02 for a fifth consecutive pole vault win over 5.90, and another mark that remained the best of 2013 was 20.90 by Valerie Adams in the shot. Zuzana Hejnová improved her Czech 400mh record to 53.07 and Augustine Choge won the Emsley Carr Mile for the second time, in 3:50.01.

26-28 Italian Championships, Milan. Nicola Vizzoni won his 13th hammer title from 1998 and shot putter Chiara Rosa her ninth in succession.

27-28 Balkan Championships, Stara Zagora, Bulgaria. In her final season Nicoleta Grasu (41) regained the Balkan discus title she had previously won in 1992 and 1997-9! Also winning after a long gap was Marian Oprea, making a welcome return to form with a 17.24 triple jump win; he was Balkan champion in 2001-03.

27-28 Spanish Championships, Alcobendas. Mario Pestano won his 13th successive Spanish discus title to equal the Spanish record for any event; but with 63.87 he beat Frank Casañas by just 20cms, Berta Castells won her 11th successive women's title, Ruth Beitia her ninth with eight in succession at high jump, and Natalia Rodríguez her ninth at 1500m from 2000.

August

10-18 14th World Championships, Moscow, Russia. Splendidly organised and staged in overwhelmingly good conditions, this was a feast of top-class competition. To start with, however, crowds were disappointing. Usain Bolt again bestrode the Championships, taking his fourth global event triple and he was matched in winning both 100m and 200m by the far-smaller figure of Shelly-Ann Fraser-Pryce. The other double individual victor was Mo Farah, supreme with his driving finishes in 5000m and 10,000m. Tirunesh Dibaba maintained her career unbeaten record at 10,000m and Meseret Defar added a second World 5000m title (and fifth medal at the event) to her double Olympic success. Dibaba was joined as a three-time World champion at one event by Bolt (200m), Ezekiel Kemboi (steeplechase), Robert Harting (discus), Yelena Isinbayeva (pole vault) and Brittney Reese (long jump), while Valerie Adams went one better with a fourth shot title, an all-time women's record. There were three championships records: Bohdan Bondarenko, 2.41 high jump, Tatyana Lysenko, 78.80 hammer, and Jamaica, women's 4x100m 41.29. *See Championships section for reports and results.*

18 Auckland (North Shore), New Zealand. Jacko Gill missed the Worlds due to a foot injury, but made up for that somewhat as he added 27cm to the world junior record with the 6kg shot with 23.00.

21 Dubnica nad Váhom, Slovakia. Great hammer throwing headed performances at the 11th Athletics Bridge (EA Permit) meeting as Krisztián Pars 82.40 beat Pavel Fajdek 82.27 in the men's event and Anita Wlodarczyk won the women's with 78.22.

22 Stockholm, Sweden. 47th DN Galan (DL). Performances were a little disappointing on a chilly evening. Meseret Defar 8:30.29 and Mercy Cherono pb 8:31.23 were 1-2 in the women's 5000m in which seven of the next eight finishers also set lifetime bests. 1 carat diamonds worth $10,000 awarded to athletes setting stadium records went to Zuzana Hejnová, 400mh 53.70, Mariya Abakumova, javelin 68.59, and Valerie Adams also received a diamond as her 20.30 beat Nadezhda Ostapchuk's 20.63 in 2010 that had been annulled because of her doping history.

23-25 Pan-American Junior Championships, Medellín, Colombia (A). The USA, with 15 golds, 16 silvers and 7 bronzes comfortably headed the medal table.

25 Bad Köstritz, Germany. Tero Pitkämäki threw a 2013 javelin world best of 89.03.

25 Berlin (Elstal), Germany. Mariya Abakumova threw 69.75 in a big win over Christina Obergföll 65.82.

28 Zürich, Switzerland. Weltklasse. The first of the two Diamond League finals. In a heralded clash Meseret Defar 14:32.83 beat Tirunesh Dibaba 14:34.82 to secure the DL $40,000 first prize for 5000m. Zuzana Hejnová completed wins at all seven 400mh DL races with 53.32. The shot competitions were again held the day before the main meeting at Zürich's main railway station with wins for Ryan Whiting 22.03 and Valerie Adams 20.98, an Oceania and Commonwealth indoor record and 21.13 best.

28- Sep 1 African Junior Championships, Bambous, Mauritius.

31 DécaNation, Valence, France. Eight teams were headed by the USA 137, Russia 121 and France 118.

September

1 Berlin, Germany. 72nd ISTAF (WCM). Mariya Abakumova produced the best javelin throw of 2013, 70.53 well clear of Linda Stahl 65.35 and Christina Obergföll 63.30. Anita Wlodarczyk won the hammer with 77.15 over 2m ahead of Tatyana Lysenko and Berry Heidler and Yipsi Moreno was fourth with 70.89 in the final competition of her brilliant career. Top German mark came from Robert Harting with 69.02 in the discus. As usual there was an excellent crowd at c.53,000.

3   **Rovereto**, Italy. 49th Palio Citta della Quercia meeting.

3   **Zagreb**, Croatia. 63rd Boris Hanzekovic Memorial (WCM). The capacity crowd had the disappointment of the first loss of the year for discus star Sandra Perkovic, beaten 66.29 to 65.63 by Gia Lewis-Smallwood, and Milcah Chemos was unexpectedly beaten in the 3000m steeplechase by Hiwot Ayalew.

6   **Brussels**, Belgium. 37th Van Damme Memorial (DL). Star of this DL final meeting was Mohammed Aman, whose 1:42.37 Ethiopian record is ninth on the world all-time list and the second best ever by a junior; Nick Symmonds finished well for second in 1:43.03. Yenew Alamirew had a well-judged win at 5000m in 12:58.75 from Bernard Lagat 12:58.99 and Hagos Gebrhiwet 12:59.33. Warren Weir won the 200m in 1987 while Usain Bolt won the non-DL 100m in 9.80 and Renaud Lavillenie returned to top form with a 5.96 vault meeting record. The outstanding performances in the women's events were 10.72 for 100m by Shelly-Ann Fraser-Pryce, winning by nearly three metres, and by Dawn Harper-Nelson who ran a season's best of 12.48 for 100m hurdles.

7-8   **Finland v Sweden**, Gothenburg, Sweden beat Finland clearly in both men's, 234-174, and women's, 213-197, matches in the annual Finnkampen.

7-9   12th **Chinese National Games**, Shenyang. Li Ling added a centimetre to the Asian women's pole vault record with 4.65 at this quadrennial meeting.

8   **Rieti**, Italy (WCM). The 43rd edition of this meeting. Sandra Perkovic, discus 66.12, and Sally Pearson, 100mh 12.64, broke meeting records, and in final leg of the IAAF Hammer Throw Challenge Anita Wlodarczyk sealed a women's win with 76.47 and Krisztián Pars the men's with 79.80. The top nine runners in the 1500m all clocked seasonal or personal bests as Silas Kiplagat won in 3:30.13 from Johan Cronje, who set a South African record of 3:31.93.

8   29th **WMRA World Mountain Running Championships**, Krynica, Poland. The Ugandan quartet, headed by Philip Kiplimo, won the men's team title by taking the first four places and Alice Gaggi led the Italian women's team to victory.

10-14   7th **Francophone Games**, Nice, France. Top performance was 75.62 for hammer by Anita Wlodarczyk. This added 5.36m to the championship record and was her tenth competition over 75m in 2013.

14-15   **Talence**, France. Decastar Multis. Anna Melnychenko followed her World success by winning the heptathlon with 6308, sealing the overall IAAF Combined Events Challenge for the $30.000 first prize. Damian Warner was the decathlon winner beating Willem Coertzen, the leader after the first day, by 43 points with

8161, but this was not quite enough to gain him the overall Challenge, as this went to Andrey Kravchenko (who did not compete here) with a total from his three events that was 104 points more than Warner's.

15   32nd **Great North Run, Newcastle to South Shields**, GBR. In a classic race Kenenisa Bekele, in his first race beyond 15k, held off Mo Farah's thrilling finish by 1 second in 60:09. In third place Haile Gebrselassie set a world masters best of 60:41. The great Ethiopians Meseret Defar, 2nd in 66:09, and Tirunesh Dibaba, 3rd in 66:56, gave best to Priscah Jeptoo who had a brilliant run to win in 65:45, producing a sensational tenth mile of 4:34 and from 10k to 20k in 30:06, to leave the others well behind. The drop of 30.5m overall and point-to-point course meant that this was not eligible for a world record,

22   **5th Avenue Mile, New York**, USA. Winners were Nick Willis 3:52.1 and Jenny Simpson 4:19.3.

25-29   3rd **Islamic Solidarity Games**, Palembang, Indonesia.

29   **Berlin Marathon**, Germany. Wilson Kipsang took 15 seconds off the world record with 2:03:23 at the 40th BMW Berlin marathon with Eliud Kipchoge 2nd in 2:04:05 and Geoffrey Kipsang 3rd in 2:06:26. The winner had 5k splits of 14:33, 29:16, 43:45, 58:20, 61:34 half, 1:13:13, 1:28:01, 1:42:36 and 1:57:12 and he became the first man to break 2:04 twice and 2:05 four times. Florence Kiplagat won the women's race in 2:21:13 from Sharon Cherop 2:22:28.

October

13   **Chicago Marathon**, USA. Running remarkably even splits Dennis Kimetto smashed the course record with 2:03:45 – the fourth-fastest time in history on a record-legal course – from Emmanuel Mutai 2:03:52 pb as they became the first two men every to run every single 5k split in a marathon under 14:50. Sammy Kitwara ran a pb 2:05:16 for third. Women's winner was Rita Jeptoo in 2:19:57, the only women's sub-2:20 marathon in 2013, as she rallied from her narrow defeat here last year, breaking away from training partner Jemima Jelagat 2:20:48 in the final kilometres with Mariya Konovalova third in a pb 2:22:46. Both winners won $100,000 with Jeptoo earning a further $40,000 for breaking 2:20 and Kimetto receiving a $75,000 bonus for his sub-2:04.

18-20   **South American Junior Championships**, Resistencia, Argentina.

20   **Amsterdam**, Netherlands. Wilson Chebet won for the third successive year (2011- 2:05:43 and 2012 – 2:05:41) in a course record time of 2:05:36. Second was Birhanu Girma, who improved his best from 2:12:48 to 2:06:06. 20- year old Valentine Kipketer was a clear women's winner in 2:23:02.

27   Frankfurt-am-Main, Germany. Winning times in the 32nd BMW Frankfurt Marathon – Vincent Kipruto 2:06:15 and Caroline Kilel 2:22:34 (a pb by two seconds) – were remarkable given that stormy (winds of up to 50 km/h) and wet weather severely marred the opportunity for fast times. There were 11,000 finishers.

November

3   New York City Marathon, USA. On a cold and windy day Priscah Jeptoo was the women's winner in 2:25:07, and in addition to her $125.000 first prize added $500,000 as winner of the 2012/13 World Marathon Majors Series title. She became the first woman since Grete Waitz in 1983 and 1986 to win London and New York Marathons in the same year. Geoffrey Mutai, 2:08:24, retained the title he had won in 2011. There were a record 50,304 finishers from 50,740 starters.

23   Chiba, Japan. The annual International Ekiden in which three men and three women run alternate legs of the 42.195k course was won by Kenya in 2:03:59, well ahead of Japan 2:07:13.

26-30   Bolivar Games, Trujillo, Peru. Championship records were set in 23 events. Colombia was the most successful nation, with Rafith Rodríguez winning at 400m in 45.62 and 800m in 1:45.14.

December

1   Fukuoka, Japan. Martin Mathathi won the 67th Fukuoka International race in 2:07:16 by a margin of 1:44; this was his first completed marathon.

8   European Cross-Country Championships, Belgrade, Serbia. Alemayehu Bezabeh (who had also won in 2009) and Sophie Duarte were the senior champions, but the British team was again much the most successful, winning four of the six team titles with Emelia Gorecka winning a record fourth medal in the junior women's race (after 3rd 2010, 1st 2011 and 2nd 2012). In this race Britain had five of the top 13 finishers.

15-19   South East Asia Games, Nay Pyi Taw, Myanmar.

WORLD MARATHON RECORD SPLITS COMPARED

	Gebr'ie	Gebr'ie	Makau	Kipsang
5k	14:44	14:35	14:37	14:33
10k	29:27	29:13	29:17	29:16
15k	44:16	44:03	43:52	43:45
20k	59:10	58:50	58:30	58:20
Half	62:29	62:05	61:44	61:34
25k	1:14:05	1:13:41	1:13:18	1:13:13
30k	1:28:56	1:28:27	1:27:38	1:28:01
35k	1:43:38	1:43:05	1:42:16	1:42:36
40k	1:58:08	1:57:34	1:57:15	1:57:12
Finish	2:04:26	2:03:59	2:03:38	2:03:23

IAAF Combined Events Challenge Winners

Year	Men's decathlon	Women's heptathlon
1998	Erki Nool EST 25,967	Urszula Wlodarczyk POL 19,235
1999	Tomás Dvořák CZE 26,476	Eunice Barber FRA 19,880
2000	Erki Nool EST 26,089	Sabine Braun GER 19,151
2001	Tomás Dvořák CZE 25,943	Yelena Prokhorova RUS 19,624
2002	Roman Sebrle CZE 26,301	Sabine Braun GER 18,987
2003	Tom Pappas USA 28,119	Carolina Klüft SWE 20,295
2004	Roman Sebrle CZE 25,952	Carolina Klüft SWE 20,541
2005	Roman Sebrle CZE 25,381	Carolina Klüft SWE 20,399
2006	Dmitriy Karpov KAZ 25,145	Carolina Klüft SWE 20,124
2007	Roman Sebrle CZE 25,261	Lyudmila Blonska UKR 19,895
2008	Andrey Kravchenko BLR 25,448	Hyleas Fountain USA 19,759
2009	Trey Hardee USA 25,448	Nataliya Dobrynska RUS 19,487
2010	Romain Barras FRA 25,063	Tatyana Chernova RUS 19,537
2011	Leonel Suárez CUB 25,172	Tatyana Chernova RUS 20,332
2012	Hans Van Alphen BEL 25,259	Tatyana Chernova RUS 19,717
2013	Andrey Kravchenko BLR 25,084	Anna Melnychenko UKR 19,310

Scores are for the total of best three events

IAAF Race Walking Challenge Winners

Year	Men's winner	Women's winner
2003	Robert Korzeniowski POL	Gillian O'Sullivan IRL
2004	Robert Korzeniowski POL	Elisa Rigaudo ITA
2005	Francisco J. Fernández ESP	Rita Turova BLR
2006	Francisco J. Fernández ESP	Claudia Stef ROU
2007	Luke Adams AUS	Rita Turova BLR
2008	Jared Tallent AUS	Kjersti Tysse Plätzer NOR
2009	Eder Sánchez MEX	Kjersti Tysse Plätzer NOR
2010	Wang Zhen CHN	Tatyana Sibileva RUS
2011	Valeriy Borchin RUS	Olga Kaniskina RUS
2012	Wang Zhen CHN	Liu Hong CHN
2013	Jared Tallent AUS	Yelena Lashmanova RUS

IAAF Hammer Challenge

Men

2010	Koji Murofushi JPN 238.52m
2011	Krisztián Pars HUN 239.03
2012	Krisztián Pars HUN 242.35
2013	Pawel Fajdek POL 246.23

Women

2010	Betty Heidler GER 225.88m
2011	Bertt Heidler GER 228.09
2012	Betty Heidler GER 230.49
2013	Anita Wlodarczyk POL 233.83

Most successive titles won in major nations:

21	Srecko Stiglic YUG
	HT 1966-86 (and 1988)
21	Terry McHugh IRL
	JT 1984-2004
20	Anna Söderberg SWE
	DT 1993-2012
20	Eha Rünne EST
	W DT 1992-2011 (& 1988-9)
19	Koji Murofushi JPN
	HT 1995-2013
18	Chris Harmse RSA
	HT 1996-2013
17	Eha Rünne EST
	W SP 1992-2008
	(& 1998-9, 2010)
17	Mette Bergmann NOR
	DT 1984-2000

ATHLETES OF 2013
By Peter Matthews

Male Athlete of the Year

USAIN BOLT WAS chosen as the IAAF World Male Athlete of the Year for the fifth time in six years. There is no doubt that he remains the superstar of our sport, his worldwide reputation far above any other athlete. But it could have been a close call over the other shortlisted candidates Bohdan Bondarenko and Mo Farah. Bolt achieved the sprint treble at the World Championships just as he had done in 2009 and at the Olympic Games of 2008 and 2012 and he now has eight gold and tow silver medals from World Championships as well as those six Olympic gold medals. He did not, of course, approach his world record times, but a 9.77 and 19.66 double remains remarkable as he won nine of ten individual finals and the Jamaican 4x100m time in Moscow, to which he contributed the anchor leg, was the sixth fastest ever run.

Mo Farah did not approach his Moscow record times in duplicating his Olympic double at 5000m and 10,000m but his sprint finishing powers are now legendary and there seems no way that his current rivals can beat him at these distances. Only Kenenisa Bekele before him had ever won the Olympic and World 5000/10,000m double double. It remains to be seen whether Farah will continue at these events in major meetings or will be seduced by the challenges of the marathon. Meanwhile his most staggering performance in 2013 was in reducing his 1500m best from 3:33.98 to 3:28.81, sixth on the world all-time list, so that he is now the European record holder at both 1500m and 10,000m and he also ran the fastest ever time by a British athlete for half marathon, 60:10 in the Great North Run, in which he was just beaten in a great race by a resurgent Bekele.

The most extraordinary breakthrough by any world champion in 2013 came in the high jump from Bohdan Bondarenko. He exceeded his pre-season best of 2.31 (2012) by jumping 2.33 in his first two competitions, at Doha and in Shanghai, when Mutaz Essa Barshim beat him on countback. Four competitions at 2.28 then followed before he really got going: 2.34 and 2.36 in the Diamond League meeting in Birmingham, and then 2.39 and 2.41 in Lausanne. After winning with 2.38 at the Anniversary Games in London he had a try at 2.43 and then two at the world record height of 2.47, of which the last was a pretty good attempt to take Javier Sotomayor's 20 year-old record. Then he matched his 2.41 national record on his second attempt at the Worlds, with three failures at the world record height of 2.46. In all he had 13 wins, 1 tie and 1 loss in 2013.

While none of the three top men had unbeaten seasons, Farah won his only race at 10,000m (and both his 3000m races) and Robert Heffernan his only race at 50k walk.

Other world champions who got close to unbeaten seasons were Mohamed Aman who lost just one (his first) of his ten 800m finals, Krisztián Pars won 14 of 15 at hammer, LaShawn Merritt 8 of 10 finals at 400m, Farah 4 of 5 at 5000m. Ryan Whiting won 13 of 16 at shot, and although his win streak was ended at 35, Robert Harting won 10 of 13 at discus. Ashton Eaton won both his completed decathlons but was a non-finisher at Talence. Top ranking contender Dennis Kimetto won both his marathons.

Most successful in the Diamond League (DL) was Ryan Whiting with six wins and Bohdan Bondarenko with five from seven possible.

There were no world records at any standard track and field event in 2013 (or the first time since 1907!), but that for the marathon fell, as Wilson Kipsang ran 2:03:23 in Berlin (although Geoffrey Mutai's 2011 time on the overall downhill and wind-aided Boston course was faster).

100 Metres

SPRINT STANDARDS remained at a very high level in 2013, and Usain Bolt stayed as the top man (for the fourth time), although not approaching his world record times. At 100m

---

Selections for World Top Ten

My selection of the top 10 athletes of 2010 together with the lists compiled by international experts polled by *Track & Field News* and those of *Athletics International* readers:

	PJM	TFN	AI
Bohdan Bondarenko	1	1	3
Usain Bolt	2	2	1
Mo Farah	3	3	2
Robert Harting	4	6	9=
Mohammed Aman	5	4	4
LaShawn Merritt	6	5	9=
Aleksandr Menkov	7	9	-
Renaud Lavillenie	8	8	-
Ashton Eaton	9	7	7
Teddy Tamgho	10	10	5
Wilson Kipsang	-	-	6
Asbel Kiprop	-	(13)	8

he won six of his seven finals, beaten by just 0.01 sec by Justin Gatlin (the American's first ever win over Bolt) in Rome, but beating Gatlin by 0.08 to win the World title in his fastest of the year, 9.77. Bolt had three of the year's six fastest times as Tyson Gay ran the fastest, 9.75 to win the US title from Gatlin 9.89. But shortly after that came the shocking news that Gay had failed a drugs test (later revealed to be for steroids) and also that the former world record holder Asafa Powell had failed a test. In his case, it was for stimulants, and, with other Jamaicans under suspicion, a WADA team investigated the lack of sufficient out-of-competition testing in the Caribbean home of so much sprint talent.

Discounting Gay, Gatlin was clearly the world number two and with Mike Rodgers and Nesta Carter, who took World bronze, had the best depth of times. Rodgers was only 6th at the Worlds and had been 4th at the US Champs, but had win-loss advantage, 6-2 v Carter and 6-1 v Kemar Bailey-Cole although 2-2 v Nickel Ashmeade. Carter in turn was 6-1 v World 4th placer and Jamaican 2nd Bailey-Cole, who was 3-3 against both Ashmeade and Kim Collins. The latter was still, at 37 years old, very much a force to be reckoned with although he did not run at the Worlds as he remains in dispute with his national federation. Ashmeade was 5th at the Worlds and had better times, but Collins beat him clearly when they met, in DL races in Lausanne and Monaco. Two Europeans completed the World final: Christophe Lemaitre 7th and James Dasaolu 8th. The later had three brilliant runs, but was inconsistent and not starting in other finals, and Lemaitre was only 7th (in London) in his one DL race, so rated top European was Jimmy Vicaut (3rd World semi), 1-1 v Dasaolu and 3-3 v Collins. Charles Silmon won the NCAA title and was 3rd in the US Champs but exited in his heat at the Worlds. Dentarius Locke was 2nd and 6th in those US races followed by an excellent 2nd in 9.98 in Monaco behind Gatlin but ahead of Vicaut, Rodgers, Collins and Bailey-Cole. Yohan Blake missed the whole season through a serious leg injury.

The fastest times run indoors at 60 metres were 6.48 by Jimmy Vicaut and Dasaolu 1-2 at the European Indoors, while both US (6.49A) and NCAA (6.54) titles were won by D'Angelo Cherry.

Most times at 10.00/10.05 or faster: Gatlin 10+2w/11+3w, Rodgers 9+4w/13+4w, Carter 8+1w/10+2w, Bolt 8/9, Bailey-Cole 6/12, Ashmeade 4+1w/7+1w, Vicaut 4/7, Dasaolu 4, Gay 3+1w, Collins 2/4+1w, Locke 2+2w/4+2w, Silmon 1+5w/2+5w, Isiah Young 1+2w/1+5w, Powell 1/3, Keston Bledman 1w/2+2.

1. Bolt, 2. Gatlin, 3. Rodgers, 4. Carter, 5. Bailey-Cole, 6, Collins, 7. Ashmeade, 8. Vicaut, 9. Silmon, 10. Dasaolu

200 Metres

THE DISCREDITED Tyson Gay won the US title in 19.75 but otherwise the year's three fastest times were recorded by Usain Bolt in his three finals: successively 19.79 in Oslo, 19.73 in Saint-Denis and 19.66 at the Worlds. Bolt is top for the sixth successive year. A clear second in Moscow was Walter Weir, whose 19.79 matched the time with which he had won the Jamaican title and who won 8 of his 11 finals; his three second places were twice to Bolt and once to Nickel Ashmeade. The latter was 4th at the Worlds between Curtis Mitchell 3rd and Jason Young 5th. Ashmeade was 2-1 v Young and both had generally superior seasons to the US 3rd placer Mitchell. The World 5-6-7-8 were Adam Gemili, who showed immense promise at age 19 but who only ran the event three times including 4th at the European U23s, Anaso Jobodwana, World University Games winner but only 4th at the NCAAs, Churandy Martina and Jaysuma Saidy-Ndure. Of these men Martina had the best depth of performance. Isiah Young was the only other man to break 20 seconds; he had modest runs in his two Diamond League races, but was 2nd in both NCAAs and US Champs and 3rd in his World semi. European Team winner Christophe Lemaitre did not contest this event at the Worlds and was beaten 1-0 by Wallace Spearmon, US 4th placer but 6th in his World semi, but he was 1-0 v Saidy-Ndure, who in turn was 3-0 v Isiah Young and 2-1 v Spearmon and Rasheed Dwyer, 4th Jamaican and 2nd WUG. Walter Dix ran just four 200m races but was 2-0 v Saidy-Ndure and Martina.

Most times at 20.30 or better: Weir 10+1w, J Young 8+1w, Ashmeade 8, Jobodwana 4+3w, Mitchell 4+2w, Dwyer 4+1w, Bolt, Gemili, Martina 4; Spearmon, Lemaitre 3; I Young, Ameer Webb 2+3w, Gay 2+2w, Antoine Adams, Bryshon Nellum 1+2w.

1. Bolt, 2. Weir, 3. Ashmeade, 4. J Young, 5. C Mitchell, 6. Martina, 7. Gemili, 8. Jobodwana, 9. I Young, 10. Dix

400 Metres

FOR THE THIRD YEAR LaShawn Merritt and Kirani James were the top two – sharing the top ten times of 2013 between them, 6-4 to Merritt. They traded wins prior to Moscow, Merritt winning in Eugene and James in Saint-Denis. James was the favourite to defend his World title but faded to 7th in the Moscow final as Merritt, ranked in the top three for the seventh time, won by a huge margin of 0.66 secs from Tony McQuay, who was followed by Luguelín Santos, Jonathan Borlée, Pavel Maslák and Youssef Al-Masrahi. McQuay, 2nd in the US Champs with Arman Hall 3rd and Josh Mance 4th, had a 3-1 advantage over Santos over the season. The next trio were closely matched, with J Borlée 3-2 against Maslák and

Al-Masrahi, who were 3-3 in their duels. Then, although his best of 45.08 was only 16th on the world list, I ranked Mance next due to his most consistent season, including nine sub 45.5 times. It was close for the final two ranking places. Kevin Borlée and Deon Lendore were both 4th in World semis. Trinidad champion Lendore was beaten for the NCAA title by Bryshon Nellum with Hall 3rd, but Nellum was only 6th in his heat at the US Champs. Ânderson Henriques, just beaten by Vladimir Krasnov for the World Universities title, did well to make the Worlds final, but did not get into any Diamond League races, and David Verburg, 6th US Champs and 4th NCAAs, had a good set of times. Lendore, with 45.15, was much the fastest in the indoor season.

Most sub-45.00 times: Merritt 11, James 9, McQuay 5, Santos 4, Al-Masrahi, Maslák 3.
    1. Merritt, 2, James, 3. McQuay, 4. Santos,
    5. J Borlée, 6. Al-Masrahi, 7. Maslák, 8. Mance,
    9. K Borlée, 10. Lendore

800 Metres

DAVID RUDISHA HAS dominated 800m running for several years, but had just two races (wins in Doha and New York) before a knee injury ended his season, so is hard to rank. He was succeeded as world number one by Mohammed Aman, the one man to beat Rudisha in both 2011 and 2012, who, although still a junior, stepped up to win the World title and to record the one sub-1:43 time of the year, 1:42.37 to take the DL final in Brussels ahead of Nick Symmonds 1:43.03 and Ferguson Rotich Cheruiyot 1:43.22, second and third fastest of the year. Aman won nine of his ten races, his one loss being in his first race, 1:44.21 behind Rudisha 1:43.87 in Doha. Symmonds had six wins in ten finals and after third to Aman and Timothy Kitum in Eugene, was 2nd to Duane Solomon at the US Champs and to Aman at the Worlds. Behind him in Moscow the order 3-8 was Ayanleh Souleiman, Marcin Lewandowski, Andrew Osagie, Solomon, Pierre-Ambroise Bosse and Abdulaziz Mohamed. Cheruiyot was disqualified for fifth place in his semi-final.

Souleiman ran just four 800m races and was also 6th in Brussels. While the American had faster times, Lewandowski beat Solomon 3-1, including also 4th to 5th in Brussels. The promising Bosse had DL 2nd places in Rome, Lausanne and Monaco. Andre Olivier had an excellent record, losing only to Aman and Bosse, before injury ended his season at the end of June and he did not meet the US 3rd Brandon Johnson, who was 3rd in his World semi. Olivier was 1-0 against Osagie, who was 1-1 with Johnson. Job Kinyor had five sub 1:45 times, including when winning the Kenyan title and when 4th at the their Trials, but was only 8th in Zürich after that. Abdulrahman Musaeb Balla

was another to be 3rd in his World semi and he then won in Rieti in 1:43.93 and was second to Mohamed in the Islamic Solidarity meeting.

Most times sub-1:44.5: Aman 9, Symmonds, Solomon, Lewandowski 6; Cheruiyot, Bosse, Johnson, Balla, Mohamed 3.
    1. Aman, 2. Symmonds, 3. Lewandowski,
    4. Solomon, 5. Bosse, 6. Cheruiyot, 7.
    Souleiman, 8. Rudisha, 9. Johnson, 10. Olivier

1500 Metres

WE REMAIN IN AN AGE of no one dominating the world of the milers, but Asbel Kiprop surely has the greatest talent of today's top men. He won the World title and returns to the top ranking he held 2009-11. He was only 6th in Stockholm and Zürich after the Championships, but before then had run 3:27.72 in Monaco from Mo Farah's astonishing European record 3:28.81 and Caleb Ndiku 3:29.50. These were the only sub-3:30 times of the year and for Farah it was his only race at the event in 2013. Silas Kiplagat was 6th in the slowly-run World final but overall was 4-3 v Kiprop, including beating him at the Kenyan trials, a race in which Nixon Chepseba was 3rd, followed by Ndiku, Bethwel Birgen and Collins Cheboi. The next ranking places are helped by win-loss as Ayanleh Souleiman was 3-1 v Chepseba, who was 3-1 v Ndiku, who was 4-1 v Birgen. Souleiman was only 11th in his World semi as he tried to return from winning bronze at 800m, but had major wins in Oslo, Saint-Denis and Stockholm plus 2nd in the DL final in Zürich. Johan Cronje was the surprise bronze medallist in Moscow, but was ranked rather lower due to some inconsistency, but nonetheless better than the silver medallist Matt Centrowitz, who won a slow US Champs race but otherwise had 8th in Monaco as his best race. Birgen, 4th in Monaco, was 4-3 v Cheboi, 2-1 v Cronje and 3-2 v Mekonnen Gebremedhin (World 7th). Cheboi was 4-0 v Centrowitz and 2-2 v Cronje. The year's fastest mile times were run at the Prefontaine Classic in Eugene, won by Kiplagat in 3:49.48 with Kiprop 2nd and Aman Wote 3rd in sub-3:50 times. After Farah the top European was ex-Kenyan Ilham Tanui Özbilen, the European Team winner and 5th in Monaco in 3:31:30, but only 9th in his World semi.

Most times sub-3:34 or 3:51M: Kiprop, Kiplagat 6, Birgen 4, Souleiman 7, Chepseba, C Ndiku 3.
    1. Kiprop, 2. Kiplagat, 3. Souleiman, 4. Chepseba,
    5. Ndiku, 6. Birgen, 7. Cronje, 8. Cheboi, 9. Centrowitz,
    10. Wote

3000 Metres/2 Miles

GALEN RUPP RAN the year's fastest time indoors: a North American record 7:30.16 in Stockholm, with Caleb Ndiku 2nd in 7:31.66. Outdoors the five fastest times were run in the Doha DL meeting. Hagos Gebrhiwet, who set a world junior record indoors with a winning 7:32.87 in Boston, won in 7:30.36 from Thomas Longosiwa, Yenew Alamirew, Ndiku and Hayle Ibrahimov. Bernard Lagat set a North American indoor 2 miles record with 8:09.49 in New York and also won his three 3000m races of the year. Ibrahimov won the European Indoor 3000m.

5000 Metres

MO FARAH REPEATED his Olympic 5000m and 10,000m double. In doing so he did not need to run fast until the last extraordinary laps, 53.44 at 5000m and 54.49 at 10,000m. He won four of his five 5000m races and his fastest time, which came in the one race he lost ¬ to Edwin Soi in Eugene on 1 June – was 13:06.88 for only 16th place on the world list. But nobody could doubt that he was capable of running much faster if he had needed to, exemplified by his amazing range from 3:28.81 for 1500m to 60:10 for half marathon and he is top for the third year. The two fastest times of the year came at Monaco from Soi 12:51.36 and Albert Rop 12:51.96 with Isiah Koech and Thomas Longosiwa also breaking 13 minutes. There were three men under 13 minutes in Rome: Yenew Alamirew, Hagos Gebrhiwet and Koech, and in Brussels: Alamirew, Bernard Lagat and Gebrhiwet and this race had the best depth of times with eleven under 13:10. This was almost matched by the Eugene race that had ten. Alamirew, who also won in Lausanne and was second to Farah in Birmingham (0-3 to Farah in all), was only 9th in the Worlds but ranks second, with win-loss of 4-1 over Gebrhiwet, 3-1 v Koech and 2-2 v Soi as these men were 2nd, 3rd and 5th respectively in Moscow. Gebrhiwet was 3-1 against both Koech and Soi, who went 3-3 in their clashes. Longosiwa and Lagat, 4th and 6th at the Worlds, went 2-2 overall. Muktar Edris was 7th and Galen Rupp 8th at the Worlds and Rupp was 2-1 v Rop with these three men were 10th, 11th and 7th in Brussels, although Rop had the faster times. NCAA champion Lawi Lalang ran 13:00.95 for 5th in Monaco, but did not have enough to back this up.

Most times sub 13:08: Longosiwa, Soi 4, Gebrhiwet, I Koech, Edris, Rop 3.
1. Farah, 2. Alamirew, 3. Gebrhiwet, 4. Soi, 5. I Koech, 6. Longosiwa, 7. Lagat, 8. Edris, 9. Rupp, 10. Rop

10,000 Metres

WITH NO 10,000m THIS YEAR at the Van Damme Memorial in Brussels there was a lack of opportunity for the best men to meet outside the World Champs and positions in that race have the major impact on the rankings. Gold and silver medals went to Mo Farah and Ibrahim Jeylan in their only 10,000s of the year while bronze was taken by the prolific Paul Tanui, who ran five more 10,000m races. These three men were 11th, 12th and 10th on the world

lists as the three fastest (and sub 27 min times) came at Sollentuna: Dejen Gebremeskel, Abera Kuma, and Imane Merga, respectively 16th, 5th and 12th at the Worlds. Yigrem Demelesh was 4th in Sollentuna in 27:15.51 but apart from that the next seven best times were run at Eugene on May 31, a race won by Kenenisa Bekele (who won his other 10,000m at Lier), followed by Merga, Kuma, Bidan Karoki (6th Worlds), Birhan Nebebew, Vincent Chepkok and Teklemariam Medhin. Galen Rupp won the US title and was 4th at the Worlds with Kenneth Kipkemoi 7th.
1. Farah, 2. Jeylan, 3. Tanui, 4. Rupp. 5. Kuma, 6. Karoki, 7. K Bekele, 8. Kipkemoi, 9. Merga, 10. Gebremeskel

Half Marathon

HALF MARATHONS continued to be popular, although just 13 men (11 Kenyans and 2 Ethiopians) bettered 1 hour compared to 29 in 2012. The East African domination was also shown by Kenyans taking 40 of the top 60 and 57 of the top 100 places in world lists with Ethiopia 14 and 21 respectively and Eritrea 4 and 5. Geoffrey Kipsang, Stanley Biwott and Geoffrey Mutai ran the three sub-59 times of the year at Ra's Al-Khaymah, and Mutai was second to Atsedu Tsegay at New Delhi, in the race with perhaps the top depth of talent. Wilson Kiprop was third there and had earlier won the Rome-Ostia race. Biwott went on to win in Philadelphia and Mutai in Rio and Udine, all in sub 60 minute times. One of the greatest ever duels at the distance came at the Great North Run, in which Kenenisa Bekele on his debut at the distance just held off a frenzied finish by Mo Farah, while third was Haile Gebrselassie, who won his other two half marathons, in a world over-40 best (on this slightly downhill course) of 60:41.

Marathon

THE ONE WORLD RECORD to be set in 2013 at any standard Olympic event came in the men's marathon as Wilson Kipsang ran 2:03:23 in Berlin, the eighth world best (six for men, two for women) to be set on this fast, flat course from 1998. This was Kipsang's sixth win in nine career marathons from 2010 and he became the first to run twice under 2:04 following his 2:03:42 at Frankfurt in 2011. However he is not ranked top as he was 5th in London in 2:07:47 in his other 2013 marathon. Further sub 2:04 times were recorded in Chicago from Dennis Kimetto 2:03:45 and Emmanuel Mutai 2:03:52. Kimetto has an unbeaten record at the event, having made a sensational debut with a 2:04:16 win in Berlin in 2012 and also winning in 2:06:50 in Tokyo earlier in the year. Mutai had been 2nd in London in 2:06:33 behind Tsegaye Kebede, who went on to World 4th and New York 2nd. The greatest depth of times was in Dubai in January when five men broke 2:05: Lelisa Desisa 2:04:45

followed by Berhanu Shiferaw, Tadesse Tola, Endeshaw Negesse and Bernard Koech. But the greatest depth of talent was probably in London, where other top placings were 3rd Ayele Abshero, 4th Feyisa Lilesa, 5th Wilson Kiprotich and 6th Stephen Kiprotich. The last went on to win the World title in the heat of Moscow but he was only 12th in New York and his best time of 2:08:05 in London leaves him outside the world top 50. Geoffrey Mutai, whose 2:03:02 in Boston 2011 remains the fastest ever marathon (if ineligible for records), won in difficult conditions in New York in 2:08:24, but had been a non-finisher in London, and Desisa won Boston as well as taking the World silver. Eliud Kipchoge, the 2003 world 5000m champion, made a brilliant marathon debut with 2:05:30 in Hamburg and improved to 2:04:05 when second in Berlin. Tola ran four excellent marathons as he followed his third in Dubai with 2nd in Paris behind Peter Some (World 9th), 3rd in the Worlds and 1st in Beijing. Unbeaten in a pair of good races was Vincent Kipruto, in Otsu and Frankfurt.

1. Desisa, 2. Kimetto, 3. E Mutai, 4. Kipsang, 5. Kipchoge, 6. Tola, 7. Kebede, 8. Kiprotich, 9. Some, 10. Shiferaw

3000 Metres Steeplechase

EZEKIEL KEMBOI SHOWED his unprecedented big race ability by adding a third World title to his two Olympic golds, and he also ran the year's fastest time, 7:59.03 in Saint-Denis, when Mahiedine Mekhissi-Benabbad was second in a European record time of 8:00.09. The year's next three fastest times had come in Shanghai in May, when 18 year-old Conseslus Kipruto ran 8:01.16 ahead of Paul Kipsiele Koech and Hillary Yego. C Kipruto went on to win in Eugene (from a disqualified Kemboi), Oslo, Ostrava and at the Kenyan Trials, followed by 2nd in the Worlds and 3rd in Stockholm and Zürich. He takes top ranking with a 5-1 advantage over Kemboi, who after his World triumph was a non-finisher in Stockholm and Berlin and 10th in Zürich. Yego was only 11th at the Kenyan Trials but finished the season brilliantly with wins in Stockholm, Zürich and Berlin and was 4-3 v Koech, 12th at the Kenyan Trials and 4th at the Worlds, a place behind Mekhissi. Koech, ranked for the twelfth year like Kemboi, was 2-0 v Evan Jager, the US champion who ran just three steeplechase finals but was 5th at the Worlds, where he was followed by Matt Hughes, who ran brilliantly there but was otherwise outside 8:20, and Abel Mutai, who was the next best of the Kenyans with win-loss advantage of 2-0 v Brimin Kipruto, 3-2 v Julius Birech and 2-1 v Gilbert Kirui, all of whom were in the world top ten (which had eight Kenyans). Birech was 4-2 v B Kipruto, who was 4-3 v Kirui, although Kirui had better times.

Most times under 8:15: C Kipruto 8, Koech,

Yego, Birech 6, Kirui 5, Mekhissi-Benabbad 4, Kemboi, B Kipruto, Mutai 3.

1. C Kipruto, 2. Kemboi, 3. Mekhissi-Benabbad, 4. Yego, 5. Koech, 6. Jager, 7. Mutai, 8. Birech, 9. B Kipruto, 10. Kirui

110 Metres Hurdles

DAVID OLIVER STARTED the season relatively slowly, but ended as clearly the world's number one as he had been in 2010; in all he won 9 of his 16 finals. He ran the fastest time, 13.00, to win the World title and had 7 of the 13 wind-legal times at 13.13 or better. Ryan Wilson beat him for the US title, and was a clear second at the World Champs and also to Oliver at the DL final in Zürich. Sergey Shubenkov and Jason Richardson were 3rd and 4th in the Worlds and 4th and 3rd in Zürich. Aries Merritt, so dominant in 2012, was 3rd in the US Champs and 6th at the Worlds and in Zürich, but 3-3 v Richardson. Jamaican champion Andrew Riley was 8th in the Worlds, so behind William Sharman 5th and Thomas Martinot-Lagarde 7th, but had better times than those Europeans and on win-loss was 5-1 v Richardson and 4-1 v Ryan Brathwaite, who was 3-1 v Richardson and had DL wins in New York and Birmingham but was 6th in his Worlds semi. Dayron Robles remained in dispute with the Cuban federation, but came back from a short-lived 'retirement' with a good series of races and was 3-0 v Sharman, who in turn was 5-3 v Artur Noga (6th Worlds semi). Oliver had been only third in Eugene in 13.10 behind Hansle Parchment, 13.05 for second on the world list, and Orlando Ortega 13.08, but both were then injured, Parchment suffering a severely sprained left ankle. Younger brother Pascal beat Thomas Martinot-Lagarde 4-0 v Noga 3-1, but was only 5th I his World heat.

Indoors Shubenkov ran the fastest 60m hurdles time: 7.49 to win the European Indoor title.

Most times under 13.30: Oliver 13+2w, Wilson 9+3w, Shubenkov 10+2w, Brathwaite 9+1w, Richardson 7+2w, Merritt 5+4w, Riley 5, Ortega 4, Noga, Parchment 3.

1. Merritt, 2. Richardson, 3. Liu, 4. Oliver, 5. Parchment, 6. Shubenkov, 7. Wilson, 8. Ortega, 9. Robles, 10. Fourie

400 Metres Hurdles

JEHUE GORDON ONLY JUST beat Michael Tinsley to take the World title, 47.69 to 47.70. Those were the fastest times of the year but it was just as close for the top spot. While Gordon beat him 3-2, Tinsley had eleven times under 49 secs to four by Gordon, but Gordon also won the DL final in Brussels from Omar Cisneros and Javier Culson, who were 6th and 4th respectively at the Worlds. Emir Bekric made a major breakthrough for World bronze, taking his Serbian record from 48.83 (with which he won at the Mediterranean Games) to 48.36 and 48.05 in Moscow. Tinsley won the US title from

Kerron Clement, and Bershawn Jackson with Johnny Dutch 4th, but Dutch ranks third with a first, two seconds and a third in his Diamond League races and records of 3-1 v Cisneros and 5-1 v Culson, while Clement was 8th at the Worlds and Jackson a non-finisher in his semi-final. Culson was 4-3 v Cisneros. The US 5th placer Justin Gaymon also had a good season and was 3-1 v Félix Sánchez, who was 5th at the Worlds. Mamadou Kasse Hann was 2-1 v Sánchez and 3-1 v Gaymon.

Most times under 48.60: Culson 10, Tinsley, Dutch 8; Cisneros, Gaymon, Hann 6; Gordon 4, Bekric, Sánchez, Jackson 3.

1. Gordon, 2. Tinsley, 3. Dutch, 4. Cisneros, 5. Culson, 6. Bekric, 7. Hann, 8. Gaymon, 9. Sánchez, 10. Clement

High Jump

BOHDAN BONDARENKO, WHO had never previously ranked in the world top ten, had a wonderful season. He won at all but one of his 15 meetings (a loss on count-back at 2.33 to Mutaz Essa Barshim in Shanghai) and improved his best from 2.31 (2012) to 2.41, a height he cleared both in Lausanne and to win the World title; this was the world's best since Javier Sotomayor's 2.42 in 1994. Barshim at 2.40, Drouin 2.38 and Kynard 2.37 also helped made this the best year for the event since the 1990s. Barshim won 5/6 indoors and 7/11 outdoors; he led the indoor rankings at 2.37 before his 2.40 in Eugene and 2.38 for the World silver and he was 3-0 v Drouin and 2-1 v Kynard, who were 3rd and 5th at the Worlds. These four men dominated the performance lists. Canadian champion Drouin won NCAA titles indoors and out and beat Kynard 3-1 outdoors and 1-0 indoors. Ivan Ukhov had some poor performances but was 4th with 2.35 at the Worlds. Konstadínos Baniótis, who has a possible drugs penalty, had four meetings from 2.34 to 2.32, but was behind on win-loss to Ukhov and Aleksandr Shustov, the Russian 1-2, and also to Donald Thomas. At the Worlds 6th Thomas and 7th Shustov cleared 2.31, while Baniótis was 10= at 2.25, although he returned to form with 2.33 at the DL final in Zürich.

Two more Russians excelled indoors as Sergey Mudrov 2.35 and Aleksey Dmitrik 2.33 were 1st and 2nd at the European Indoors and Dmitrik jumped 2.31 or better (with a best of 2.36) in all his seven competitions. Outdoors Mudrov won the WUG title with 2.31 but had a next best of 2.26, and Dmitrik had a best of 2.30; he beat Ukhov 3-0 indoors but lost 2-1 outdoors. Dusty Jonas jumped 2.34 indoors and had three outdoor jumps at 2.30-2.31 but like Dmitrik did not qualify for the World final. He contests the final ranking spots with Robbie Grabarz, 8th at the Worlds but well down from his 2012 form with a best of 2.31 indoors and out, Danill Tsyplakov, Mihai Donisan and Mickaël Hanany.

Jaroslav Bába was 3rd at the European Indoors, one of two 2.30 plus jumps indoors, but he had an outdoor best of 2.27.

Most competitions over 2.30m (outdoors+in): Drouin 13+3i, Bondarenko 10, Kynard 8+2i, Barshim 7+6i, Baniótis 4+1i, Jonas 3+1i, Hanany 3, Ukhov, Donisan, Tsplyakov 2+1i, Dmitrik 1+7i, Mudrov 1+2i.

1. Bondarenko, 2. Barshim, 3. Drouin, 4. Kynard, 5. Ukhov (6), 6. Baniótis (7), 7. Shustov (8), 8. Thomas (9), 9. Tsyplakov (10), 10. Grabarz (-). – Dmitrik (5) (Including indoors).

Pole Vault

RAPHAEL HOLZDEPPE BEAT Renaud Lavillenie on count-back for the World title after both cleared 5.89, but there is no doubt that Lavillenie remained world number one for the fourth year. He headed the world outdoor list with 6.02 at the London Anniversary Games, but his highpoint had come indoors when after clearing 6.01 to win the European Indoor title he seemed to have been successful at 6.07, a height that only Sergey Bubka had ever bettered, only to see the red flag raised as the bar shifted off the pegs while staying up in the air. Lavillenie won all seven of his competitions indoors and 13 of 19 in the outdoor season (with two competitions actually held indoors) and he had the top four performances indoors and the top seven outdoors, all at 5.92 or higher. Holzdeppe had the next best, at 5.91 in Rome, followed by Björn Otto, 5.90 indoors and out. Otto, who was 2nd at the European Indoors, 3rd at the Worlds and German champion indoors and out, beat Holzdeppe 7-5 outdoors and 7-0 indoors and had the best depth of marks with 9 indoor and 8 outdoor marks at 5,80 or better. Brad Walker was 4th and Maite Mohr 5th at the Worlds, both clearing 5.82, but Mohr was ahead in their other two clashes. Konstadínos Filippídis set Greek records indoors at 5.83 and outdoors at 5.82; although 10th at the Worlds he was 4-4 outdoors against both Holzdeppe and Mohr and 2-3 v Walker. Filippídis also had an excellent indoor season, 3-1 v Mohr, with Mohr beating him 3rd to 4th, both at 5.76 at the European Indoors. Jan Kudlicka, 5th European Indoors and 7th Worlds was clearly next in the rankings. The Brazilians Augusto de Oliveira (5.81 and 5.82) and Thiago Braz da Silva (5.83) set South American records and were 11th and dnq 14 at the Worlds; with the former 10-1 up on win-loss. Although his best of 5.75 was less than all the above, Seito Yamamoto had a consistent year and was 6th at the Worlds, also taking the WUG silver behind Sam Kendricks (both 5.60).

Most competitions over 5.70m (outdoors/in): Otto 16+13i, Kudlicka 11+4i, Lavillenie 10+11i, Holzdeppe 10+2i, Filippídis 9+9i, de Oliveira 8+1i, Mohr 5+5i, Yamamoto 4+1i, Walker 4, Lázaro Borges 3, Yang Yansheng 3i.

1. Lavillenie, 2. Holzdeppe (3), 3. Otto (2), 4. Mohr (5), 5. Walker (6), 6. Filippídis (4), 7. Kudlicka, 8. de Oliveira, 9. Yamamoto, 10. Braz da Silva. (Including indoors).

Long Jump

ALEKSANDR MENKOV WAS clearly the top long jumper of 2013, jumping a world-leading 8.56 to win the World title and winning all three indoor competitions, including the European Indoor title, and 7 of 10 outdoors. He was beaten 8.46 to 8.42 by Luis Rivera at the World University Games and Rivera confirmed his big improvement (from 8.22 in 2012) with 3rd at the Worlds. There Ignisious Gaisah, having just switched from Ghana to the Netherlands, surprised to take the silver, but although a prolific competitor, he was inconsistent and indeed there was little between most of those contending for ranking places. Eusebio Cáceres was third on the world list with 8.37 to win the European U23 title, and was 4th at the Worlds, where he was followed by South American champion Mauro da Silva and European Indoor bronze medallist Christian Reif. Zarck Visser did not qualify (17th) at the Worlds but improved from the 8.29 with which he had won the South African title to 8.32 for a surprise win in the DL final in Zürich. He was 4-3 against compatriot Khotso Mokoena, but the latter, 7th at the Worlds and 4-5 v Gaisah, had generally better big meeting performances. Li Jinzhe was fourth on the World list, jumping 8.34 twice and 8.31 but 12th at the Worlds in his only competition outside China. Damar Forbes had an excellent US season winning the NCAA title (and 2nd indoors) and then won the Jamaican title but after a win in Saint-Denis his European form was poor apart from 8th at the Worlds. Olympic champion Greg Rutherford was a promising 3rd at Eugene with 8.22 but then had injury problems and managed only 7.87 for 14th in the World qualifying; he was beaten 3-0 by World 10th placer Loúis Tsátoumas but beat his British rival Chris Tomlinson 3-1. Michel Tornéus was 2nd at the European Indoors and Marquis Dendy won the NCAA indoor title, but neither did as well outdoors and were 19th and 27th in the World qualifying. Four-time World Champion Dwight Phillips took advantage of his wild card to compete at the World Champs and came 11th. Remarkable there were no US jumpers in the rankings, with US champion George Kitchens no jumping in World qualifying.

Most competitions over 8.15m (outdoors/in): Menkov 8+4i, Cáceres, Visser 5; Reif 4+1i, da Silva 4+1w, Rivera 4, Mokoena, Alyn Camara 3; Forbes 1+1i+2w, Tornéus 3i, Dendy 2i+2w.

1. Menkov, 2. Rivera, 3. Cáceres, 4. da Silva, 5. Reif, 6. Gaisah, 7. Mokoena, 8. Li, 9. Visser, 10. Forbes

Triple Jump

TEDDY TAMGHO HAD missed a year and a half of competition, but returned to confirm his immense promise and reach peak form with 18.04 (third all-time) to win the World title. He also won the DL final in Brussels and the same three men followed him in those two major events. At the Worlds 2-4 were Pedro Pichardo, Will Claye and Christian Taylor and in Brussels 2-4 were Taylor, Claye and Pichardo. Pichardo beat Taylor 3-2 but Claye beat Taylor 2-1. Daniele Greco excelled with 17.70 to win the European Indoor title from Ruslan Samitov and Aleksey Fyodorov, but completed only three outdoor competitions. Those, however, were all over 17m, winning at the Mediterranean Games and 2nd in the DL meetings at Rome and Monaco before he was unable to jump at the World Champs. Ernesto Revé and Yoann Rapinier had better distances outdoors, although Revé was unable to replicate his Cuban form (beating Pichardo twice) in Europe and Rapinier was last in the World final. Fyodorov had only one outdoor 17m jump, but showed fine competitive ability with wins in the European Team, European U23 and Russian Champs, 2nd WUG and 5th Worlds. Martin Oprea was 6th and Gaetan Saku Bafuanga 7th at the Worlds, while Benjamin Compaoré had a 2-0 record against Fyodorov, Saku Bafuanga and World 10th placer Dimítrios Tsiámis before ending his season at the end of June.

Most competitions over 17.00: Pichardo 10, Tamgho, Taylor 9; Claye 5+1w, Revé 5, Greco 3+2i, Oprea 1+1i+1w.

1. Tamgho, 2. Pichardo, 3. Taylor, 4. Claye, 5. Revé (6), 6. Rapinier (7), 7. Greco (5), 8. Fyodorov, 9, Oprea, 10. Compaoré. (Including indoors).

Shot

RYAN WHITING WAS beaten by David Storl for the World title, but had the world's top four marks and threw 21.27 or better in all but one of his outdoor competitions and in 3 of 4 indoors; he won all four competitions indoors and 9 of 11 in the outdoor season (including under a roof in Zürich). His only other loss was to Reese Hoffa in Birmingham and his bests indoors (21.80) and out (22.11) came in winning US titles. Storl was 2-0 v Hoffa, who had better marks and a 3-2 win-loss against Dylan Armstrong, although the latter was 3rd to Hoffa's 4th at the Worlds. Ladislav Prásil made a massive improvement as his every competition, four indoors and 18 outdoors, was better than his best of 20.14 in 2012. He was 3rd in the European Indoors and 5th at the Worlds, beating the World 6th placer Tomasz Majewski (who had surgery in December 2012) 7-0. Germán Lauro, who improved the South American record to 21.26 was 7th and Georgi Ivanov 8th at the Worlds. Lauro beat Ivanov 2-1, although Ivanov was 2nd at the DL final to Lauro's 7th. Although Zach Lloyd was 3rd at the US Champs, he did not have much to back that up, so next best Americans are Cory Martin, 9th in the Worlds, Joe Kovacs, who beat the World 10th Artur Kolasinac in their only meeting but had some poor results, and Kurt Roberts. After ten years in the rankings Christian Cantwell made a slow return to 20m form after elbow surgery.

Most competitions over 20.80: Whiting 11+6i, Prásil 9+1i, Hoffa 8+1i, Storl 7+1i, Armstrong 5+1i, Lauro, Ivanov 5, Majewski 3+1i, Roberts 2+2i.

1. Whiting, 2. Storl, 3. Hoffa, 4. Armstrong, 5. Prásil, 6. Majewski, 7. Lauro, 8. Ivanov, 9. Martin, 10. Kolasinac.

Discus

THE TWO BEST MARKS of the year were set on June 8 in Hengelo. Piotr Malachowski won with 71.84, the seventh best mark of all-time, from Robert Harting 69.91. Thus Harting lost his unbeaten record after 35 successive wins from 2011, and he had two more second places in 2013, to Martin Wierig in Ostrava and to Gerd Kanter in the DL final in Zürich, but he had ten wins and is top for the fifth successive year. Harting had seven and Malachowski three of the year's best performances and 11 and 7 respectively of the 22 over 67m. Kanter was 3rd at the Worlds and 4-6 v Malachowski to make the world top three for the ninth successive season. Ehsan Hadadi did not compete at the Worlds due to a dispute with his national federation but was 4-2 v World 4th placer Wierig. A surprise 5th in Moscow was Victor Hogan, but he lacked the depth of performance of others such as the World 6th Robert Urbanek, 7th Vikas Gowda and 9th Frank Casañas (7th OG). Urbanek was 3-0 v Casañas, 5-1 v Gowda and 5-2 v Erik Cadée, who although dnq 14th at the Worlds, was 4-2 v Casañas and Gowda. Julian Wruck was 11th at the Worlds after an unbeaten season in the USA (winning the NCAA title) and Australia. Also in contention were Cuban champion Jorge Fernández and Mario Pestano, 10th and 12th at the Worlds. Virgilijus Alekna, now aged 41, was 16th in qualifying at the Worlds with a best of 64.66 for 2nd at the European Throws but drops out after 17 successive years in the rankings.

Most competitions over 65m: Malachowski 14, Harting 13, Kanter 10, Wierig 9, Wruck 8, Hadadi, Casañas 5, Cadée 4.

1. Harting, 2. Malachowski, 3. Kanter, 4. Hadadi, 5. Wierig, 6. Urbanek, 7. Cadée, 8. Gowda, 9. Casañas, 10. Wruck

Hammer

KRISZTIÁN PARS IS top ranked for the third successive year (with ten years in the top six); again winning 14 of his 15 competitions. Pavel Fajdek added 58cm to his pb to score an upset win at the World Champs, beating Pars 81.97 to 80.30, and he did even better with 82.27 at Dubnica, but there Pars won with the year's best throw of 82.40. Fajdek beat Pars for the IAAF World Hammer Challenge by just 5 centimetres over their best three competitions.

Lukás Melich was third at the World Champs and in the Challenge, and he had 3 competitions over 80m to 9 by Pars and 2 by Fajdek. Primoz Kozmus competed sparingly, but took 4th at the Worlds, a place ahead of Asian champion Dilshod Nazarov, whom he beat 2-0. Koji Murofushi, as usual making his only other appearance at the Japanese Champs, was 6th in Moscow but his lack of major events make him hard to rank, and next was Nicola Vizzoni, who threw 77.61 in Moscow but had a next best of 76.06, so well below many other men, such as the World 8-9-10: Marcel Lomnicky, Szymon Ziólkowski and Markus Esser, who were clearly separated on win-loss – Lomnicky 4-2 v Ziólkowski, who was 5-1 v Esser. Sergey Litvinov was 11th at the Worlds and 3-1 v Oleksiy Sokryskyy, who was 4-1 v Ziólkowski, indicating the sometimes circular nature of these records.

Most competitions over 80m/78.50m: Pars 9/14, Melich 3/9, Fajdek 2/9, Nazarov 1/6, Kozmus 5, Litvinov 1/3.

1. Pars, 2. Fajdek, 3. Melich, 4. Kozmus, 5. Nazarov, 6. Lomnicky, 7. Ziólkowski, 8. Esser, 9. Litvinov, 10. Sokryskyy

Javelin

VITEZSLAV VESELY RETAINED top ranking with the World title and three Diamond League wins. He beat Tero Pitkämäki 3-2 including by just 10cm in Moscow, and the Finn beat him in the DL final in Brussels in a welcome return to top form that included the year's best throw of 89.03 in Bad Köstritz. Dmitriy Tarabin came to Moscow highly favoured after wins in the European Team Champs and WUG, but had to settle for 3rd Worlds and 4th in Brussels, a place behind World 5th Antti Ruuskanen, who was 2-1 against Julius Yego, who was 4th in the Worlds, when he added 3.31m to his Kenyan record, and 5th in Brussels. Yego and the next group were evenly matched in terms of distances thrown. Andreas Thorkildsen still struggled to get near his best; he was 6th in the Worlds and in Brussels, but ahead in both those meetings of Swedish champion Kim Amb (10th and 8th), who, however, had a 5-4 overall advantage. Ari Mannio, 4th at the Finnish Championship won by Pitkämäki from Ruuskanen and Teemu Wirkkala, was 3-3 against both Thorkildsen and Yego. Thomas Röhler was only 29th in World qualifying, but had been 2nd in the European Throws and Team Champs and 3rd in the European U23s as well as being German champion; he was 3-2 v

Thorkildsen and 1-1 v World 8th Risto Mätas. Olympic champion Keshorn Walcott started with 84.39 in May, but had only one other 80m meeting and was 18th in qualifying at the Worlds, at which the original 5th placer Roman Avramenko was disqualified for drugs abuse.

Most competitions over 84m/82.50m: Pitkämäki 12/12, Vesely 8/8, Tarabin 6/11, Ruuskanen 5/7, Avramenko 4/6, Amb 2/7, Yego, Guillermo Martínez 2/2, Mannio 1/8, Thorkildsen 1/4, Röhler 0/6.

1. Vesely, 2. Pitkämäki, 3. Tarabin, 4. Ruuskanen,
5. Yego, 6. Thorkildsen, 7. Amb, 8. Mannio,
9. Röhler, 10. Mätas

Decathlon

ASHTON EATON DID NOT stretch to attack his world record but, apart from his dnf at Talence, won both his decathlons: 8291 USA Champs and 8809 Worlds. The 2012 number two Trey Hardee did not finish either of those events. The rankings pretty much follow the World Champs result of 2 Michael Schrader 8670 (also 1st at Ulm 8427), 3 Damian Warner (also winner at Götzis, Canadian Champs and Talence), 4 Kevin Mayer (1st European Cup), 5 Eelco Sintnicolaas (1st European Cup First League, 3rd Talence), 6 Carlos Eduardo Chinin (2nd Götzis), 7 Rico Freimuth (2nd Ratingen), 8 Ilya Shkuryenov (1st Russian, 2nd European U23), 9 Willem Coertzen (5th Ratingen, 2nd Talence), 10 Leonel Suárez, 11 Pascal Behrenbruch, 12 Andrey Kravchenko. Mayer, Freimuth, Sintnicolaas and Behrenbruch were non-finishers at Götzis, but Behrenbruch had the year's third highest score with 8514 in Ratingen and Kravchenko, with wins in Firenze 8390 and Kladno 8380 added to his 8314 at the Worlds, won the IAAF Combined Events Challenge from Warner, Behrenbruch, Sintnicolaas and Coertzen. Also at 8350+ were the Ratingen 3-4 Jan Felix Knobel and Kai Kazmirek and the latter won the European U23 title.

The top indoor heptathlon scores came at the European Indoors: Sintnicolaas 6372 and Mayer 6298, and from Gunnar Nixon's 6232A US win.

1. Eaton, 2. Schrader, 3. Warner, 4. Mayer, 5. Chinin, 6. Sintnicolaas, 7. Freimuth,
8. Shkuryenov, 9. Behrenbruch, 10. Kravchenko.

20 Kilometres Walk

IT WAS JUST ABOUT impossible to produce a definitive ranking list for 2013 – such was the conflicting evidence of form by the leading walkers, and none of the top three had ranked before. Aleksandr Ivanov, yet another product of Viktor Chegin's controversial coaching centre in Saransk, was the surprise World champion; his time was a pb of 1:20:58 but that was 32nd on the world list and his previous races were 4th in the Russian Winter Champs and European Cup and 2nd in the European U23s. Then going down the World Champs order we have: 2 Chen Ding, who had one win and a dnf at Taicang, 3

Miguel Ángel López (2nd to Benjamin Sánchez in the Spanish Champs and 2nd European Cup), 4 João Vieira (two wins, 2nd La Coruña to Jared Tallent, 5th Sesto SG and 7th European Cup), 5 Denis Strelkov (3rd Russian Winter, 1st European Cup and 3rd WUG), 6 Takumi Saito (2nd Japanese), 7 Ruslan Dmytrenko (2nd UKR Ch, Lugano and WUG, 5th European Cup). Further down was 12 Yusuke Suzuki, who won the Japanese and Asian titles and was 4th at Sesto SG, 26 Cai Zeliin, 2nd at Taicang and at the Chinese National Games, and 49 Andrey Ruzavin, Russian champion, 2nd at the Russian Winter Champs, 4th WUG and 15th European Cup; disqualified was Wang Zhen, who won at Lugano and in the Chinese National Games. World University Games champion was Andrey Krivov, whose other race was 4th at the Champs, European U23 champion was Pyotr Bogatryev (4th RUS-w, 2nd RUS Champs), The year's fastest time was 1:18:28 by Pyotr Trofimov, who went on to be 17th at the European Cup and 3rd in the Russian Champs. Concentrating on 50k at the Worlds was Matej Tóth, who had an excellent record of 1-2-3-1-3 in his five 20k races, with wins at Dudince and Sesto SG and 3rd in the European Cup.

1. Ivanov, 2 López, 3. Strelkov, 4. Chen Ding,
5. Wang Zhen, 6. Dmytrenko, 7. Tóth, 8. Suzuki,
9. Vieira, 10. Cai Zelin

50 Kilometres Walk

THE WORLD CHAMPIONSHIP race was the year's fastest, providing 8 of the 10 best times (to 3:43:38), with wins by Yohann Diniz, European Cup, and Erick Barrondo, Dudince, slipping into 6th and 7th on the world list. The World 1st Robert Heffernan (3:37:56), 3rd Jared Tallent (helping him to win the IAAF Race Walking Challenge), 5th Matej Tóth and 8th Lukasz Nowak had no other 50k races, while the 2nd Mikhail Ryzhov, 4th Igor Hlavan and 7th Ivan Noskov were 2nd, 4th and 3rd respectively in the European Cup. Diniz was 2nd to Barrondo (no other 50k races) in Dudince and was 10th at the Worlds. Further top World placings were 6th Grzegorz Sudol (dnf Dudince, 5th European Cup), and 9th Takayuki Tanii who also had a fast 3:44:25 to win the Japanese title. Yuri Andronov won the Russian title in 3:43:54 but had no other races.

1. Heffernan, 2. Ryzhov, 3. Tallent, 4. Hlavan,
5. Diniz, 6. Tóth, 7. Noskov, 8. Sudol, 9. Nowak,
10. Tanii

World Champions from:

Ireland: Eamonn Coghlan 5000m 1983, Sonia O'Sullivan W 5000m 1995, Robert Heffernan 50kW 2013

Uganda: Dorcus Inzikuru 3000mSt 2005, Stephen Kirotich Mar 2013

Colombia: Caterine Ibargüen W TJ 2013

Female Athlete of the Year

SHELLEY-ANN FRASER-PRYCE WAS selected as the IAAF Woman Athlete of the year, and it is hard to disagree with that verdict in favour of the treble world sprint champion. She is building up a formidable competitive record as she added her second World titles at both 100m and 4x100m (also in 2009) to her Olympic 100m titles of 2008 and 2012 plus Olympic silver at 200m and 4x100m in 2012 and World 4x100m silver in 2007 (as a reserve) and 2011. She had set CAC and Commonwealth records with 10.73 in 2009 and 10.70 in 2012 and got close to that with 10.71 in Moscow this year.

Fraser-Pryce did not, however, have a perfect record in 2013 as she had a 4th at 100m and a 2nd and 3rd at 200m, in contrast to the two other IAAF short-listed Athlete of the Year candidates: Valerie Adams, in the IAAF top three for the fourth time, who won all her 14 shot competitions, and Zuzana Hejnová, who won all her 15 hurdles races: world bests of 38.75 and 38.16 at 300m, and 11 plus 2 heats at 400m. And a notable number of other world champions also went through the year undefeated at their events: Abeba Aregawi (10 plus 2 heats at 1500m), Brianna Rollins (7 finals and 11 heats at 100mh and all races at other events: 4+4h at 60mh, 4+3h at 200m and 1 at 400m), Shkolina Shkolina (7 including one tie at high jump), Caterine Ibargüen (triple jump), and, with more limited competition Tirunesh Dibaba (2 at 10,000m), Yelena Isinbayeva (four at pole vault) and Yelena Lashmanova (four at 20k walk). Also winning two of two big races were Priscah Jeptoo and Rita Jeptoo at the Marathon. Sandra Perkovic won 11 of 12 at discus, including all seven in the Diamond League, in which Hejnová also won all seven and Aregawi and Ibargüen had six wins.

100 Metres

SHELLY-ANN FRASER-PRYCE RETAINS her top ranking and ran the three fastest times of the year, 10.71 to win the World title, 10.72 in the DL final in Brussels and 10.77 in her heat in London. There, however, probably not really bothered, she was 4th in the final for her only loss in seven 100m finals. Blessing Okagbare won in London in 10.79 and had three second places in DL races (all to Fraser-Pryce), so that although only 6th at the Worlds she ranks second. She was 3-1 v Murielle Ahouré, who was 2nd at the Worlds. Carmelita Jeter was 3rd and English Gardner 4th at the Worlds, with Gardner, NCAA and US champion, having a better set of times. She won at Walnut in April in 11.00 with Jeter last in 11.68, but not too much should be made of that as Jeter was just returning from the injury she sustained when 3rd in the Shanghai GP. Kerron Stewart was 5th in the Worlds and 4th in Zurich and Brussels, where

Selections for World Top Ten			
	PJM	TFN	AI
Shelly-Ann Fraser-Pryce	1	2	1
Zuzana Hejnová	2	4	2
Valerie Adams	3	1	4
Brianna Rollins	4	3	3
Priscah Jeptoo	5	(13)	10
Abeba Aregawi	6	5	5
Sandra Perkovic	7	6	7
Yelena Lashmanova	8	(11)	-
Svetlana Shkolina	9	8	-
Mesaret Defar	10	7	6
Tirunesh Dibaba		10	8
Caterine Ibargüen		9	9

she was a place ahead of US 5th placer Barbara Pierre, who was 4-3 v US 3rd placer and World 7th Alex Anderson (also 2nd in Brussels). US and NCAA 2nd Octavious Freeman completed the World finalists in 8th place, but Carrie Russell, after 5th in the Jamaican Champs, had a better record including a win in Zürich, 3rd in Brussels and 2-1 against Stewart. Five women are new to the rankings. The US Champs was of such standard that Lauryn Williams ran 11.00 in her semi, the fastest ever non-qualifying mark. Fourth in their semis at the Worlds were Ivet Lalova, the best European, and Ana Cláudia Silva of Brazil. Kelly-Ann Baptiste was 3rd in London, but then withdrew from the Worlds with a doping case pending, and similarly Veronica Campbell-Brown was suspended after crossing the line first in Kingston and coming in 3rd in 10.78w in Eugene, behind Fraser-Pryce 10.71w and Okagbare 10.75w, all well clear of 4th Stewart 10.97w. Neither of these suspended athletes was considered for a ranking prior to clarification on their cases.

Ahouré ran the three fastest indoor 60m times and won all her five finals, headed by 6.99 in Birmingham when Fraser-Pryce, who had won in Stockholm in 7.04, was 2nd in 7.09.

Most times under 11.00/11.10: Fraser-Pryce 7+1w, Gardner 5/8+2w, Ahouré 5+1w/8+1w, Pierre 5+1w/7+1w, Jeter 4/6, Okagbare 3+1w/8+1w, Anderson 3/8+1w, Baptiste 3/4+1w, Freeman 2/5, Stewart 1+1w/6+1w, Scott 1/2+2w, Silva 1w/3+3w.

1. Fraser-Pryce, 2. Okagbare, 3. Ahouré.
4. Gardner, 5. Jeter, 6. Stewart, 7. Pierre, 8. Anderson, 9. Russell, 10. Freeman. (8 Baptiste)

200 Metres

SHELLY-ANN FRASER-PRYCE HAD her busiest season at 200m, and moves up a spot to top ranking, winning the World title by 0.15 and the Zürich DL title by 0.26, both from Murielle Ahouré, for an overall record of 5 wins in 7 finals, with the year's fastest time of 22.13 at the Jamaican Champs. Blessing Okagbare beat F-P in Birmingham and was 3rd in the Worlds, and Ahouré and Tiffany Townsend beat her in

Monaco. Allyson Felix tumbled to the ground with an injury to her right hamstring in the World final, having earlier won in Beijing and London with second places in Rome and at the US Champs. In the last she was beaten 21.80w to 21.85 by Kimberlyn Duncan, who was 3rd in her World semi, and Jeneba Tarmoh was 3rd, Shalonda Solomon 4th, Charonda Williams 6th and Townsend 7th. Shanuae Miller, still a junior, took 4th place in the Worlds, with Tarmoh 5th, Williams 6th and Mariya Ryemyen 7th. Ryemyen was 3-1 v Williams and 3-0 v Townsend, Solomon 2-0 v Townsend and Townsend 6-1 v Williams. Antonique Strachan beat Miller at the Bahamas Champs and was 5th in her semi at the Worlds.

Most times under 22.70: Fraser-Pryce 7+1w, Ahouré 7, Felix 5+2w, Ryemyen 4, Miller 3+1w, Townsend 3, Duncan 2+3i+4w, Solomon 2+3w, Aurieyall Scott 2+1i+2w, Baptiste 2+1w.

1. Fraser-Pryce, 2. Okagbare, 3. Ahouré, 4. Felix, 5. Duncan, 6. Miller, 7. Tarmoh. 8. Ryemyen, 9. Solomon, 10. Townsend

400 Metres

CHRISTINE OHURUOGU OUT-DIPPED Amantle Montsho to win the World title in a British record time of 49.41, but whereas she had 4 wins in 10 finals, Montsho had 6 in 10 and crucially beat Ohuruogu 5-2. She headed the world list with 49.33 in Monaco. Antonina Krivoshapka only ran four events but was 3rd at the Worlds and Stephenie Ann McPherson was 4th, but all were beaten in the DL final by the World 5th placer Natasha Hastings, as the order behind her in Brussels was 2 Montsho, 3 Krivoshapka, 4 Francena McCorory (World 6th), 5 Ohuruogu, 6 McPherson. It was close on win-loss as Hastings was 4-4 and McPherson 2-2 v McCorory.

There was a big gap after the top six, with Kseniya Ryzhova 7th and Novlene Williams-Mills 8th in the Worlds and McCorory 7-0 v Williams-Mills, who was 8th and Ryzhova 9th in Brussels. Contenders for the last two ranking places raced very little at 400m. Allyson Felix ran 400m just once, 2nd in Doha in 50.19 behind Montsho, but ahead of Ohuruogu, McCorory and Hastings. Kseniya Zadorina had four wins, including the WUG title before 6th in the Russian Champs. Indoors Perri Shakes-Drayton had the fastest time of 50.85 in winning the European Indoor title, but was 0.49 behind Hastings 50.88 in Birmingham. Shakes-Drayton then ran 50.88 in Loughborough and 50.50, well ahead of Zadorina at the European Team Champs, for wins in her two outdoor races. Ashley Spencer was NCAA champion indoors and out and was 3rd in the US Champs, but 5th in her World semi.

Most times under 50.50: Montsho 10, McPherson, McCorory 7; Hastings 5, Ohuruogu 4, Krivoshapka 3.

1. Montsho, 2. Ohuruogu, 3. Krivoshapka, 4. McPherson, 5. Hastings, 6. McCorory, 7. Williams-Mills, 8. Ryzhova, 9. Spencer (10), 10. Shakes-Drayton (9). (including indoors).

800 Metres

FRANCINE NIYONSABA MADE a wonderful start to her career as in her first season of 2012 she won the African title and ranked third in the world. She looked set to move higher in 2013 as she won her three 800m races, including in the year's fastest times with 1:56.72 in Eugene and 1:57.26 in Saint-Denis, but then was stopped by injury. She would surely have been the favourite in Moscow, but there we had an upset win by Eunice Sum who held off that consummate racer Mariya Savinova to take the gold medal with the Americans Brenda Martinez and Alysia Montaño 3rd and 4th. Sum, not ranked before, had been beaten by Winny Chebet in the Kenyan Championships but won her other five 800m finals, including at Stockholm and Zürich after the Worlds. Savinova also raced sparingly with three wins and second to Sum both at the Worlds and in the DL final in Zürich. Montaño and Martinez went 2-2, with the former winning at the US Champs, where 19 year-old Ajee' Wilson, later 6th at the Worlds, was 3rd. Yekaterina Poistogova had four big race wins and was 5th at the Worlds, with Nataliya Lupu, European Indoor champion, 7th. Janeth Jepkosgei started promisingly but did not run again after 2nd to Sum in the Kenyan Trials, so although she was 2-0 v Malika Akkaoui, the latter, despite only 8th in her semi at the Worlds, rates higher, helped by a 2-1 record v Poistogova and 3-2 v Wilson, with a series of good results including 3rd in Stockholm and Zurich. Yekaterina Kupina ran the only sub-2 minute time indoors and four such times outdoors, including when second to Margarita Mukasheva (7th heat Worlds) at the WUG, but was 5th at the Russian Champs.

Most times under 1:59.5: Montaño 7, Martinez 6, Sum, Savinova, Poistogova 4.

1. Sum, 2. Savinova, 3. Niyonsaba, 4. Martinez, 5. Montaño, 6. Poistogova. 7. Akkaoui, 8. Wilson, 9. Jepkosgei (10), 10. Lupu (9). (including indoors).

1500 Metres

ABEBA AREGAWI WAS clearly the stand-out athlete, from indoor wins in 3:58.40 in Stockholm and 4:04.47 for the European Indoor title, to winning all eight of her outdoor competitions. Jennifer Simpson followed a big win in Monaco in 4:00.48 with World silver, 0.32 behind Aregawi, but was among many who fell over each other in the DL final in Brussels and she came in 10th, way behind Aregawi. The year's three fastest times came early, in the DL meeting in Doha, as Aregawi won in 3:56.60 from Faith Kipyegon 3:56.98 (Commonwealth record) and Genzebe Dibaba 3:57.54, and other sub-4 time was 3:58.58 by Hellen Obiri in Eugene. Obiri had a very strong season, with 5 wins in 9 races, and 2nd in Monaco and 3rd at the Worlds and Brussels. Kipyegon was 2nd in Eugene and in the Kenyan Trials (to Obiri) before 5th at the Worlds, a place behind Hannah England, who was 2-1 with Kipyegon and 5th at the European Team Champs and in Brussels. Dibaba had two big indoor wins in 4:02.25 and 4:00.83 but only three outdoor competitions; after Doha she was 2nd to Aregawi in Rome and 8th at the Worlds. Yekaterina Sharmina was 6th at the Worlds after winning the European Team and WUG races, but was only 7th in Brussels. Eunice Sum had a consistent series of races and was 2-1 v Nancy Langat, while another top 800m runner Brenda Martinez is a little hard to rate with just four 1500m races, but was 3rd in New York (behind Aregawi and Obiri) and Monaco, and was 2-0 v Shannon Rowbury, 4th at the US Champs, Monaco and Brussels, who was 1-1 v Langat (9th Worlds). 17 year-old Mary Cain, who established six US high school records at distances from 800m to 5000m, eschewed the World Youths for the senior Worlds and excelled to make the final and place 10th.

Most times under 4:04 (or 4:23.6 mile): Aregawi 6+1i, Simpson, Obiri 4; Dibaba 2+2i.
1. Aregawi, 2, Simpson, 3. Obiri, 4. Kipyegon, 5. England (6), 6. G Dibaba (5), 7. Sharmina, 8. Martinez, 9. Sum, 10. Langat. (including indoors).

3000 Metres

GENZEBE DIBABA RAN the year's fastest time, 8:26.95 indoors in Stockholm, and it was in that city that the seven fastest outdoor times were run in a race in which Dibaba was 8th in 8:37.00. Winner was Meseret Defar in 8:30.29 from Mercy Cherono, Sifan Hassan, Viola Kibiwot, Gladys Cherono, Hellen Obiri and Shannon Rowbury. Defar also won indoors in Karlsruhe with 8:35.28, and the only other race won in under 8:40 was outdoors in Rieti by Mercy Cherono 8:35.97.

5000 Metres

ORIGINALLY BOTH SELECTED to double at the World Championships, Meseret Defar and Tirunesh Dibaba were directed to run just one event. Defar duly regained her 5000m title, producing a trademark 59.82 last lap while Dibaba won again at 10,000m. But a keenly awaited clash between them happened at the DL final in Zürich and here Defar emerged as the clear winner 14:32.83 to 14:34.82. Dibaba won her other two 5000m races, in Eugene and in Saint-Denis, where she set the year's fastest time of 14:23.68. Defar, who achieved her tenth successive top three ranking, lost her first outdoor race of the year, to Genzebe Dibaba in Shanghai, but then won in Oslo in 14:26.90. Faster than that was Almaz Ayana, with 14:25.84 for second in Saint-Denis and she went on to the World bronze, just behind the Kenyan Trials winner Mercy

Cherono, who was also 4th in Shanghai, 2nd in Eugene, 5th in Oslo and 3rd in Zürich. Viola Kibiwot was 4th in the Worlds and also well-placed in the other major clashes: 3rd Shanghai, 2nd Oslo and Kenyan Trials and 6th Zürich. G Dibaba was 3rd in Oslo, but dnf in Zürich, and compatriot Buze Diriba had a consistent series of races including 5th at the Worlds but was beaten 3-0 by Margaret Muriuki, who, however, was a non-finisher in her heat at the Worlds. Emily Chebet and Gladys Cherono were 9th and 10th on the world list with their 4th and 5th places in Zürich, but had no other major 5000m races. Gelete Burka was slightly quicker with 14:42.07 for 3rd in Saint-Denis, but ran 14:50+ times in Shanghai, Eugene and Hengelo (won by Ayana). The 2011 world champion Vivian Cheruiyot missed the season due to pregnancy.

Most times under 15:05: Cherono, Diriba 6, Defar, Burka, Kibiwot 4; Dibaba, Ayana, Muriuki, Agnes Tirop, Irene Cheptai 3.
1. Defar, 2. T Dibaba, 3. M Cherono, 4. Ayana, 5. Kibiwot, 6. G Dibaba, 7. Muriuki, 8. Diriba, 9. Burka, 10. Tirop

10,000 Metres

MESERET DEFAR RAN easily the year's fastest time, 30:08.06 at Sollentuna, where Afera Godfay was 2nd in 31:08.23. All the other ten sub 31-minute times came in Ostrava or the Worlds. There were also good races in the USA and Japan, but, as is the increasing trend, a general dearth of quality opportunity at the event. Tirunesh Dibaba won in both Ostrava and Moscow so is top for the sixth time in her unbeaten career of eleven track 10k races. Gladys Cherono was 2nd and Belaynesh Oljira 3rd in both these big races. Cherono also won the Kenyan Trials race from Emily Chebet and Selly Chepyego, who were 4th and 7th at the Worlds. Hitomi Niiya won the Japanese title and was 5th at the Worlds, Shitaye Eshete, was World 6th with wins at the Asian Champs and Islamic Solidarity meeting, and Shalane Flanagan followed wins at Stanford and at the US Champs with World 8th. Breaking 31 minutes also were the Ostrava 4-5 Yeshaneh Ababel (World 9th) and Sule Utura.
1. T Dibaba, 2. G Cherono, 3. Oljira, 4. Defar, 5. E Chebet, 6. Niiya, 7. Eshete, 8. Chepyego, 9. Flanagan, 10. Ababel

Half Marathon

PRISCAH JEPTOO HAD a sensational run to win the Great North Run in 65:45, the year's fastest time, leaving Meseret Defar and Tirunesh Dibaba well behind. The year's second fastest time was 66:09 by Lucy Kabuu at Ra's Al-Khaymah, 2 secs ahead of Priscah Jeptoo with Rita Jeptoo, Meseret Hailu, Florence Kiplagat and Helah Kiprop following, all in the 2013 top 11. Of these women, also having fast wins (68 min or better) were Defar in New

Orleans, Kiprop in Berlin and Kiplagat in New Delhi. In that last race Gladys Cherono, winner in Prague in 66:48, Kabuu and Hailu were 2nd, 3rd and 4th

Marathon

AFTER SIX WOMEN had run under 2:20 in 2012 just one did so in 2013 – that was Rita Jeptoo, 2:19:57 in Chicago, when she ran 68:42 for the second half. She completed a US double as she had earlier won in Boston. An even more impressive double was achieved by Priscah Jeptoo, who won in London in 2:20:15 and then added victory in New York, thanks to a spectacular and self-confident 69:07 second half when she made up a halfway deficit of 3:22 down on the two leaders. Edna Kiplagat successfully defended her World title, but she was second in London and later ninth in New York. The year's third fastest time was the 2:20:48 for 2nd in Chicago by Jemima Jelagat, who had earlier won in Rotterdam. The other World medallists were Valeria Straneo, also 5th in New York, and Kayoko Fukushi, also 2nd in Osaka. The best depth of times came in Frankfurt with six at 2:24:06 or better, headed by 2:22:34 by Caroline Kilel, who, however had been 21st in Tokyo, and 2:23:00 by Filomena Chepchirchir, who had won in Seoul. Valentine Kipketer won in both Mumbai and Amsterdam but did not finish at the Worlds, and other major winners were Florence Kiplagat in Berlin after 6th in London, Ryoko Kazaki in Nagoya before 4th in the Worlds, Feysa Tadesse in Paris, but dnf Worlds, Aberu Kebede (12th Worlds) in Tokyo and Shanghai, and Merima Mohamed Hasen in Houston before 2nd in Paris and Shanghai. Others to have two top results included Sharon Cherop, 3rd Boston and 2nd Berlin, and Birhane Dibaba, 2nd in Nagoya and 3rd in Frankfurt,

1. P Jeptoo, 2. E Kiplagat, 3. R Jeptoo,
4. Jelagat, 5. Straneo, 6. Fukushi,
7. F Kiplagat, 8. Kazaki, 9. Kebede, 10. Cherop

3000 Metres Steeplechase

IN 2012 YULIYA ZARIPOVA was Olympic champion and undefeated at the steeplechase, but she ran the event just once in 2013, winning the World Universities title in 9:28.00. Also Olympic silver medallist Habiba Ghribi ran just once, for 7th at Doha in 9:22.20. Meanwhile Milcah Chemos regained the top ranking that she had in 2010, winning 7 of her 9 races (plus one at 2000m steeplechase) and the rest of the top women slotted into their World Championship places, clearly backed up by overall win-loss records, as 2nd Lydia Chepkurui was 4-2 v 3rd Sofia Assefa, who was 5-1 v 4th Hiwot Ayalew, who was 7-0 v Etenesh Diro. Then, however, I rank Purity Kirui ahead of World 6th Hyvin Jepkemoi, as Kirui had far better times despite Jepkemoi being 3rd and Kirui 5th at the

Kenyan Trials, where Gladys Kipkemoi (12th in her heat at the Worlds) was 2nd to Chemos with Lydia Rotich 6th. The top ten in the World list were all Africans, the list completed by Ethiopian champion Almaz Ayana, with Zaripova next as fastest European. Europeans placed 7th to 14th in the World final, headed by Valentyna Zhudina 7th, Antje Möldner-Schmidt 8th and Gesa Felicitas Krause 9th.

Most times under 9:30: Ayalew 10, Diro 9, Chemos, Chepkurui 8, Assefa 6. Kirui 4.

1. Chemos, 2. Chepkurui, 3. Assefa, 4. Ayalew,
5. Diro, 6. Kirui, 7. Jepkemoi, 8. Kipkemoi,
9. Rotich, 10. Ayana

100 Metres Hurdles

BRIANNA ROLLINS IS a newcomer to the world rankings, but while as a US collegian she did not contest any of the Diamond League races, she completed an unbeaten season with the World title. She won that in 12.44 having showed peak form at the US Champs, with successive races of 12.30w, 12.33w and 12.26, the world's fastest time since 1992. Queen Harrison was the year's next fastest with 12.43 for 2nd at those US Champs. Sally Pearson made a late start after a hamstring injury but had a solid year, if not able to emulate her marvellous form of 2011 and 2012, and she took the World silver. She was, however, beaten 4-2 by Dawn Harper-Nelson, 4th at the Worlds, a place behind Tiffany Porter, but going on to win the DL final in Brussels from Pearson, Cindy Billaud (7th Worlds), Porter and Kellie Wells. Harrison was 5th at the Worlds but fared well overall; on win-loss she was 4-1 v Porter and Wells and 1-1 v Pearson. Missing the chance of running in Moscow were Wells 4th and Lolo Jones 5th at the US Olympic Champs; Wells was 4-1 v Jones and 6-3 v Porter and Jones 3-1 v Porter. Jones was also 5-1 v Nia Ali, 3rd at the US Champs and 3rd in her semi at the Worlds. Further US athletes in contention for the rankings were 6th and 7th at their Championships Kristi Castlin and Vashti Thomas (WUG champion), together with Yvette Lewis (1-0 v Billaud). Angela Whyte had four wins in five races in Canada, plus one win in the US before 6th in the Worlds in a light racing programme.

Rollins had also headed the world indoor rankings, with a best of 7.78 from her four finals. She was NCAA champion indoors and out.

Most times at 12.70 or faster: Rollins 9+4w, Harper-Nelson 9+1w, Pearson 9, Porter 5+1w, Harrison, Wells, Jones 4+2w; Ali 3+1w, Castlin, Thomas 2+2w.

1. Roliins, 2. Harper-Nelson, 3. Pearson, 4.
Harrison, 5. Wells, 6. Jones, 7. Porter, 8. Ali,
9. Castlin, 10. Whyte

400 Metres Hurdles

ZUZANA HEJNOVÁ HAD one of the greatest ever seasons at the event. Getting steadily faster, she set three Czech records, 53.23 in Saint-Denis, 53.07 in London and 52.83 at the Worlds as she won all 11 of her competitions, including all seven Diamond League races. A serious injury to her left knee that threatens her future career at the event held Perri Shakes-Drayton back to 7th in the Worlds, but as well as taking the UK title she had a win and three seconds in DL races. Her best of 53.87 in London was bettered by Kori Carter, 53.31 to win the NCAA title, but Carter who had a pre-2013 best of 57.10, was unable to start in her semi at the US Champs and was 4th in London in her only race outside the USA. Dalilah Muhammad improved from 56.04 (2011) six times to 53.83 to win the US title and she was 2nd at the Worlds; only 8th in the DL final, she was also 2-1 down to Shakes-Drayton. Rankings 4th to 12th were close. Lashinda Demus had a quiet year due to a leg injury, but produced her best for 3rd at the Worlds, where Hanna Titimets was 4th and Eildih Child 5th. Child also had four wins, including the European Team race and three thirds in her eight competitions, while Titimets was WUG champion and 4th in Zürich. Much faster, however, were Georganne Moline, US and NCAA 2nd but only 6th in her heat at the Worlds, Kaliese Spencer, who was disqualified in her World heat but was 3-1 v Muhammad and 2-0 v Demus, ending well with 2nd in Stockholm and Zürich, and Angela Morosanu, 6th on the world list with 53.85. Anna Yaroshchuk, 2-4 v Titimets, was 2nd in the European Teams, 6th Worlds and 5th Stockholm and Zürich, while Denisa Rosolová was 3rd in Zürich after 4th in her semi at the Worlds.

Most times under 54.0/55.0: Hejnová 10/12, Shakes-Drayton 4/6, Moline 2/11, Muhammad 2/10, Carter 1/6, Morosanu 1/3, Child 6, Demus 5, Spencer, Titimets 4; Yaroshchuk 3.

1. Hejnová, 2. Shakes-Drayton, 3. Muhammad, 4. Carter, 5. Demus, 6. Child, 7. Moline, 8. Spencer, 9. Titimets, 10. Rosolová

High Jump

SVETLANA SHKOLINA RANKS top for the first time; she won all her seven competitions (tying with Anna Chicherova in Rome) and matched her pb of 2.03 to win the World title. Her four DL wins included the final in Brussels. Chicherova and Brigetta Barrett were 2-2 and Barrett had the slightly better marks as well as out-jumping the Russian, 2.00 to 1.97 at the Worlds. As in 2012 Barrett was NCAA champion indoors and out and she topped the world list with 2.04 at the US Champs. Ruth Beitia tied Chicherova for the World bronze medal and was at her best indoors with 1.99 to win the European Indoor title. She beat Emma Green Tregaro, 3rd European Indoors and 5th Worlds, 3-2 outdoors (with one tie) and 2-0 indoors. Blanka Vlasic was not entirely happy with her form and had

Achilles and heel problems, so called a halt to her comeback season in July, but she had been the fourth woman to clear 2m outdoors in 2013 (her 102nd competition at that height or more) and ended with three 1.98 competitions; she was 2-0 v Beitia. Mariya Kuchina, who jumped 1.98 indoors to win the European Team competition, was 4-1 v Kamila Stepaniuk (7= Worlds) and 3-2 v Irena Gordeyeva. Stepaniuk beat Gordeyeva 3-2 outdoors (although 0-1 indoors) and was 3-3 outdoors (3-0 indoors) v World 6th placer Justyna Kasprzycka, who was only 8th at the WUG (won by Stepaniuk with Kuchina 2nd), but 3-0 v Gordeyeva. Alessia Trost was best indoors, with a 2.00 pb and was 4= at the European Indoors and 7= at the Worlds with an outdoor best of 1.98 to win the European U23 title. Tia Hellebaut had a best of 1.97 indoors but retired before the outdoor season.

Most competitions over 2.00/1.96m outdoors (+indoors): Barrett 3/6, Chicherova 2/8, Shkolina 2/6, Vlasic 1/4, Green Tregaro 2+1i, Beitia, Trost 1+2i.

1. Shkolina, 2. Barrett, 3. Chicherova, 4. Vlasic, 5. Beitia, 6. Green Tregaro, 7. Kuchina, 8. Stepaniuk (9), 9. Kasprzycka (10), 10. Gordeyeva (-), – Trost (8). (Including indoors)

Pole Vault

THE HIGHLIGHT OF the World Championships for the Moscow crowd was the gold medal taken in the vault by Yelena Isinbayeva, following her wins in 2005 and 2007. She won all her four competitions (also Shanghai, Ostrava and Russian Champs), although her Moscow 4.89 was bettered on the world list by Jenn Suhr's 5.02 to win the US indoor title at high-altitude Albuquerque and by Yarisley Silva's 4.90 in Hengelo. Silva ranks second with a 5-2 advantage outdoors over Suhr, although they were 3rd and 2nd respectively at the Worlds, both at 4.82. Silva had a particularly busy year with the best depth of times from 5 wins in 7 indoor events and 7 in 13 outdoors and 7 competitions at 4.80 plus to 4 by Suhr and 1 by Isinbayeva. Silke Spiegelburg, 4th at the Worlds, was a major contender with the top three; she had a season's best of 4.79 to win the DL final in Zürich from Fabiana Murer, Silva and Jirina Svodobová and was 2-2 outdoors v Suhr.

Further World placings were 5= Murer and Anastasiya Savchenko, 7 Angelina Zhuk-Krasnova (European U23 champion), 8= Lisa Ryzih and Svobodová. Although she was 4th in the US Champs, Mary Saxer was the second best US vaulter and was 2-0 v Russian runner-up Savchenko and 2-1 v Svobodová, who was 2-1 (1 tie) v Savchenko, although Savchenko had a 3-1 advantage indoors. Kylie Hutson was 2nd in the US Champs indoors and out, but no heighted in qualifying at the Worlds. Holly Bleasdale won the European Indoor title on count-back from Anna Rogowska and had three indoor clearances from 4.70 to 4.77, but very limited outdoor form before injury ended her season.

Most competitions over 4.60m (outdoors/in): Silva 10+7i, Spiegelburg 9, Murer 8+2i, Suhr 7+5i, Saxer 7+2i, Hutson 5+5i, Svobodová 5+2i, Savchenko 4+5i, Isinbayeva, Strutz 4, Carolin Hingst 3, Bleasdale 1+7i, Rogowska 1+2i.

1. Isinbayeva, 2. Silva, 3. Suhr, 4. Spiegelburg, 5. Murer, 6. Saxer, 7. Svobodová (8), 8. Savchenko (7), 9. Zhuk-Krasnova (10), 10. Hutson (-). – Bleasdale (9). (Including indoors)

Long Jump

BRITTNEY REESE RANKS top for the fifth successive year. She rarely produces a consistent series of jumps but just look at her record. She took her sixth global title with 7.01 in Moscow, having set a pb of 7.25 in Doha. She won 1/2 competitions indoors (beaten by Janay DeLoach Soukop at the Millrose Games) and 5/10 outdoors. There were two 7m jumpers indoors: Darya Klishina (7.01 at the European Indoors) and Olga Kucherenko (7.00) and outdoors these two were 7th and 5th respectively at the Worlds with Klishina winning the WUG title. Three more women jumped 7m outdoors: Sosthene Moguenara, Oksana Zhukovskaya and Blessing Okagbare, but Zhukovskaya had a next best outdoors of 6.40 and Moguenara was 12th at the Worlds, However, Okagbare mixed her brilliant sprinting with quality jumping and took the World silver and was 2nd at the DL final in Zürich behind World bronze medallist and European Indoor 4th Shara Proctor, whom she beat overall 4-1; she was also 2-2 v Reese. Ivana Spanovic excelled with the World bronze medal and was also Balkan champion indoors and out and 3rd in Zürich. She was 2-0 outdoors v Klishina, but the latter is ahead if we include her indoor record. DeLoach Soukop was US champion indoors and out and, although ending her season with 11th at the Worlds as she had to jump off the 'wrong' foot, was 3-1 v Proctor and 1-1 v Klishina. Olga Sudareva had a very limited campaign: three wins in Belarus and 4th at the Worlds. Yelena Sokolova slipped from her 2012 form but was 2nd at the WUG and 8th at the Worlds followed by 6th in Zürich. Éloyse Lesueur was dnq 22nd at the Worlds, but won at the European Teams and was 3-2 v Moguenara and 4-1 v US 2nd placer Tori Polk; she also jumped 6.90 for 2nd in the European Indoors.

Most competitions over 6.70m (outdoors/in): Proctor 10+1i, Klishina 6+3i, Okagbare 6, Reese 5+1w+1i, Sokolova 5, DeLoach 4+2w+4i, Spanovic 4+1i, Polk 4, Sudareva 3+1w, Lesueur 3+2i, Funmi Jimoh 2+2w, Kucherenko 2+4i.

1. Reese, 2. Okagbare, 3. Proctor, 4. Spanovic (6), 5. DeLoach (5), 6. Klishina (4), 7. Sudareva (9), 8. Kucherenko (7), 9. Sokolova (10), 10. Lesueur (8). (including indoors).

Triple Jump

AFTER TWO YEARS ranked second, Caterine Ibargüen was the clear number one in 2013, winning all her nine competitions. She shared top place on the outdoor world list at 14.85 with Olga Saladuha and was joined as achieving three 14.80m jumps by Yekaterina Koneva, to one indoor and one out by Saladuha, although the latter went further with that 14.88 to win the European Indoor title. Ibargüen also had a wind-assisted 14.93. Koneva took silver and Saladuha bronze at the Worlds with Saladuha beating Koneva at the European Teams. Next were the World 4th and 6th placers, Kimberley Williams who beat Hanna Knyazheva-Minenko 6-2. Mabel Gay competed only in Cuba apart from her World 5th place and ranks behind the Russian 1-2 Irina Gumenyuk and Anna Pyatykh with Pyatykh ahead 7th to 8th at the Worlds and 3-1 on win-loss. They were both up on win-loss to World 9th Snezana Rodic. Gumenyuk was also Russian champion indoors, adding European Indoor silver. Dana Veldáková, 11th in the Worlds and 3-2 v Rodic, takes the final ranking spot.

Most competitions over 14.30m: Saladuha 9+4i, Koneva 9+1i, Ibargüen 9, Williams 6+2w, Knyazyeva 6, Gumenyuk 4+5i.

1. Ibargüen, 2. Koneva (3), 3. Saladuha (2), 4. Williams, 5. Knyazyeva (5), 6. Pyatykh, 7. Gumenyuk, 8. Gay, 9. Rodic, 10. Valyukevich. (including indoors)

Shot

VALERIE ADAMS IS top for the seventh time in eight years and extended her winning sequence from 2010 to 42 by winning all her 14 competitions in 2013. Her best mark was 20.98 under the roof in Zürich and in all indoors and out she had the best seven performances of 2013. Gong Lijiao was only 3cm behind Adams, 20.12 to 20.15 at Eugene, but otherwise the only time that anybody got within a metre of Adams was Christina Schwanitz, who set a season's best of 20.41 at the World Championships behind the 20.88 of the New Zealander. Schwanitz had five 20m competitions to 12 by Adams and one each by Gong and Michelle Carter, who were 3rd and 4th at the Worlds with Russian champion Yevgeniya Kolodko 5th. Kolodko was also 2nd in Zürich with Carter 3rd and Schwanitz 4th and was 2-1 v Carter, who was US champion indoors and out. These top five were far superior to the rest, who had a best performance of 19.24 by Alena Kopets, and were closely matched. Kopets had been 3rd at the European Indoors behind Schwanitz and Kolodko, but was only 12th at the Worlds, where the next best were 6th Li Ling, 7th Irina Tarasova (5th European Indoors), and 8th Tia Brooks. Li was Chinese champion but was beaten at the Chinese National Games by Gong and Liu

Xiangrong, who was Asian champion and 2nd to Tarasova at the WUG before 10th at the Worlds. Brooks was NCAA champion indoors and out but was beaten 3-1 by Kopets. Nadine Kleinert did not contest the championships but challenges for a ranking.

Most over 19m: Schwanitz 18+7i, Adams 11+2i, Carter 8+2i, Kolodko 7+3i, Gong 6+1i.

　1. Adams, 2. Schwanitz, 3. Gong, 4. Carter, 5. Kolodko, 6. Tarasova (7), 7. Li Ling (9), 8. Brooks (8), 9. Liu Xiangrong (10), 10. Kopets (6). (Including indoors).).

Discus

SANDRA PERKOVIC HAD an almost identical season to that of 2012 as she won 11 of her 12 competitions including the World title and all seven Diamond League meetings. Her one loss this year was to Gia Lewis-Smallwood in Zagreb. Perkovic had the top five performances of the year, from 68.96 in Lausanne to 67.99 with which she won the World title from Mélina Robert-Michon (who set a French record 66.28), Yarelys Barrios, Nadine Müller, Lewis-Smallwood and Tan Jian. Win-loss helped sort out the rankings from 2-5 as Barrios was 3-1 v Lewis-Smallwood, who was 3-1 v Müller and 4-1 v Robert-Michon, the latter two being 3-3. Zinaida Sendriute, 9th at the Worlds, had the next best record; she was 4-4 v Robert-Michon and 2-2 v Müller. Zaneta Glanc was World 7th but had lesser marks than Tan or the Cuban champion Yaimí Pérez (11th Worlds) and European U23 champion Anna Rüh. The World 10th Dani Samuels was in contention for a ranking place, but Gu Siyu was unable to get close to her early season 67.86 (second on the world lists) and had no throws in qualifying at the Worlds.

Most competitions over 63m: Perkovic 13, Barrios 11, Lewis-Smallwood, Tan, Pérez 7; Müller 6, Robert-Michon, Sendriute, Rüh 5.

　1. Perkovic, 2. Barrios, 3. Lewis-Smallwood, 4. Robert-Michon, 5. Müller, 6. Sendriute, 7. Tan, 8. Glanc, 9. Pérez, 10. Rüh

Hammer

THE SAME THREE WOMEN as in 2012 took the top ranking spots, but the order changed. Tatyana Lysenko won the World title from Anita Wlodarczyk, but Wlodarczyk won at all their other meetings for a 5-1 advantage and she returns to the top ranking that she had in 2009; she was a clear winner of the IAAF World Hammer Challenge. Betty Heidler took her seventh top three ranking, but after winning her first nine competitions of the year had an aberration and did not qualify (18th) at the Worlds. Although she competed sparingly, Zhang Wenxiu produced her seventh global top five position with 3rd at the Worlds. Her compatriot Wang Zheng won the Asian title and was 4th at the Worlds on her only other competition outside China, and the World 5-10

were Anna Bulgakova, Yipsi Moreno, Oksana Kondratyeva, Éva Orbán, Jeneva McCall and Amanda Bingson. Bingson beat McCall and set North American records at 74.92 and 75.73 at the US Champs, but McCall had a 3-2 overall advantage. Orbán was 3-1 v Bingson. Gulfiya Khanafeyeva was 12th at the Worlds after only 4th at the Russian Champs, but was in close contention, 4-3 v Kondratyeva. Kathrin Klaas was 4-2 v Orbán but was let down by her dnq 20th at the Worlds.

Most competitions over 73m: Wlodarczyk 15, Heidler 10, Lysenko 8, Kondratyeva 6, Moreno 5, Zhang W, Bulgakova 4.

　1. Wlodarczyk, 2. Lysenko, 3. Heidler, 4. Zhang, 5. Bulgakova, 6. Wang, 7. Moreno, 8. Kondratyeva, 9. McCall, 10. Orbán

Javelin

MARIYA ABAKUMOVA HAD the top four plus 6th and 7th performances, headed by 70.53 in Berlin, yet she ranks behind Christina Obergföll, as the German produced her best to win the World title with 69.05 and in all beat Abakumova 6-4. The Russian threw 69.09 in qualifying in Moscow but 65.09 in the final, a metre and a half behind silver medallist Kimberley Mickle, who was 2-1 against 4th placer Linda Stahl. Kathryn Mitchell was 5th and Sunette Viljoen 6th in Moscow, but, 2-2 on win-loss, Viljoen had the better marks. Next ranked is Vira Rebryk 11th in the Worlds but 2-1 against the 7th placer Viktoriya Sudarushkina. Lu Huihui was fifth on the world list with 65.62 but only had four competitions, all in China. She beat Li Lingwei three times but the latter won the Asian title and was 8th at the Worlds. Then three non-qualifiers for the World final Katharina Molitor (13th), Martina Ratej (20th) and Madara Palameika (27th), in that order on win-loss record, had the next best series of 60m plus performances, while Sinta Ozolina-Kovale did well early on with 64.38 in Riga and Sofi Flinck, 18 in July, won the European Junior title and was 10th at the Worlds. Barbora Spotáková, top ranked six times in the previous seven years, gave birth to a son in May, but returned to throw 62.33 in September.

Most competitions over 62m: Abakumova 17, Obergföll 13, Stahl 11, Mickle 9, Viljoen 6, Mitchell, Rebryk 4; Lu Huihui 3.

　1. Spotáková, 2. Viljoen, 3. Obergföll, 4, Abakumova, 5. Stahl, 6. Lu. 7. Rebryk, 8. Sayers, 9. Molitor, 10. Ratej

Heptathlon

SUFFERING FROM ACHILLES problems, Olympic champion Jessica Ennis-Hill was unable to contest a heptathlon in 2013, and standards were down , The best mark was 6623 by Tatyana Chernova for gold at the World Universities. Chernova missed the Worlds through a tendon injury and her other heptathlon was

4th with 6284 at Götzis. That renowned meeting was won by Brianne Theisen-Eaton from Nadine Broersen and Dafne Schippers. The two Dutch athletes went on to 3rd and 10th at the Worlds. Anna Melnychenko was only 7th in Götzis but had three wins, at Kladno, Worlds (6586 points) and Talence, plus 2nd to Karolina Tyminska (9th Worlds, 2nd Kladno and Talence) in the European Cup. Her scores meant that she won her IAAF World Combined Events Challenge crown from Theisen-Eaton, Claudia Rath, Broersen and Eliska Klucinová (7th Worlds). Theisen-Eaton was a clear second at the Worlds, where there was a thrilling battle for bronze, with pbs smashed in the 800m before the result came through as 3. Schippers, 4. Rath, 5. Katrina Johnson-Thomson (also European U23 champion). Sixth was Sharon Day, who recorded the year's third best score, 6550 to win the US title, but who had not finished in Götzis. Just missing a ranking was Laura Ikauniece (6th Götzis, 2nd WUG, 11th Worlds).

The best indoor pentathlon scores were achieved by Yekaterina Bolshova, 4851 for the Russian title, and at the European Indoors won by Antoinette Nana Djimou with 4666 from Yana Maksimova 4658 and Melnychenko 4608; Bolshova was a non-finisher with a foot injury. Melnychenko had a slightly higher score of 4623 to win the Ukrainian title.

1. Melnychenko, 2. Theisen-Eaton, 3. Chernova, 4. Schippers, 5. Rath, 6. Day, 7. Johnson-Thompson, 8. Tyminska, 9. Broersen, 10. Klucinová

20 Kilometres Walk

YELENA LASHMANOVA CLEARLY retained her top ranking, winning all her four 20k races. The year's four fastest times came in the Russian Winter Championships where she was followed by Anisya Kirdyapkina, Vera Sokolova and Irina Yumanova. Kirdyapkina won at the European Cup and World Universities before 2nd to Lashmanova at the Worlds. There Liu Hong, winner in Lugano, and Sun Huanhuan, winner in Taicang, were 3rd and 4th, but they had been 2nd and 5th at the Chinese National Games, won by Lu Xiuzhi, who was second in Taicang. Sokolova went on to 2nd in the European Cup, with fellow Russians Marina Pandakova (5th Russian Winter) and Yumanova complet-

ing a Russian 1-2-3-4, but was disqualified at the WUG and Worlds. Yumanova was also 2nd at the WUG. Further World Champs top placings: 5 Elisa Rigaudo (6th Lugano, dnf European Cup), 6 Beatriz Pascual (6th Rio Maior and La Coruña and 9th European Cup), 7 Anezka Drahotová (7th Lugano), 8 Ana Cabacinha (3rd Rio M, 5th European Cup), 9 Julia Takacs (2nd La Coruña, 22nd European Cup). The IAAF World Race Walking Challenge was won by Lashmanova with prolific racer Inês Henriques (11th Worlds, 8th European Cup) 2nd and Cabecinha 3rd.

1. Lashmanova, 2. Kaniskina, 3. Liu Hong, 4. Qieyang, 5. Kirdyapkina, 6. Lu Xiuzhi, 7. Rigaudo, 8. Pascual, 9. Cabecinha, 10. Vasco

Longevity in the World Rankings

Most years in the top ten for those ranked in 2013

Name	Event	No.1	Years
Men			
Ezekiel Kemboi KEN	3000mSt	3	12
Paul K. Koech KEN	3000mSt	3	12
Reese Hoffa USA	SP	3	11
Gerd Kanter EST	DT	2	11
Usain Bolt JAM	200m	6	10
Andreas Thorkildsen NOR	JT	6	10
Krisztián Pars HUN	HT	3	10
Brimin Kipruto KEN	3000mSt	0	10
Kenenisa Bekele ETH	10,000m	6	9
Primoz Kozmus SLO	HT	2	9
Tero Pitkämäki FIN	JT	2	9
Women			
Yelena Isinbayeva RUS	PV	7	13
Yipsi Moreno CUB	HT	1	13
Valerie Adams NZL	SP	7	11
Meseret Defar ETH	5000m	4	11
Blanka Vlasic CRO	HJ	4	11
Tirunesh Dibaba ETH	5000m	5	10
Allyson Felix USA	200m	4	10
Betty Heidler GER	HT	4	10
Lashinda Demus USA	400mh	3	10
Anna Pyatykh RUS	TJ	0	10
Zhang Wenxiu CHN	HT	0	10
Anna Chicherova RUS	HJ	2	9
Janeth Jepkosgei KEN	800m	1	9
Christina Obergföll GER	JT	1	9
Ruth Beitia ESP	HJ	0	9

Also four or more years at No. 1

	Event		Years
Men			
David Rudisha KEN	800m	5	7
Robert Harting GER	DT	5	7
Asbel Kiprop KEN	1500m	4	7
Usain Bolt JAM	100m	4	6
Women			
Tirunesh Dibaba ETH	10,000m	6	6
Brittney Reese USA	LJ	5	6

The greatest all-round distance runners: 1500m – 3000m – 5000m – 10,000m

Mo Farah's 3:28.81 for 1500m took him to fourth place on this table, scoring athletes' pbs on the IAAF tables

Kenenisa Bekele	3:32.35	7:25.79	12:37.35	26:17.73	5089	HMar 60:09
Haile Gebrselassie	3:31.76	7:25.09	12:39,36	26:22.75	5085	HMar 58:55 Mar 2:03:59
Daniel Komen	3:29.46	7:20.67	12:39.74	27:38.32	5021	
Mo Farah	3:28.81	7:34.47	12:53.11	26:46.57	4976	HMar 60:10
Eliud Kipchoge	3:50.40M	7:27.66	12:46.53	26:49.02	4973	HMar 59:25 Mar 2:04:05
Salah Hissou	3:33.95	7:28.93	12:50.80	26:38.08	4960	HMar 61:56, Mar 2:12:15

CROSS-COUNTRY – NATIONAL CHAMPIONS 2013

	Men (long distance)	Women (long distance)
Australia (Aug)	Mitch Brown	Bridey Delaney
Austria	Valentin Pfeil	Andrea Mayr
Belgium	Koen Naert	Almensch Blete
Brazil	Gulmar Lopes	Cruz da Silva
Bulgaria	Yolo Nikolov	Milka Milkhaylova
Canada (Nov)	Lucas Bruchet	Natasha Wodak
China	Su Guoxiong	Ding Changqin
Colombia	Andres Peña	Angela Figueroa
Croatia (Nov)	Dino Bosnjak	Matea Matosevic
Cuba	Henry Jaen	Yudileyvis Castillo
Czech Republic	Milan Kocourek	Lucie Sekanová
Denmark	Morten Muknkholm	Simone Glad
England	Keith Gerrard	Louise Damen
Ethiopia (Trials)	Feyisa Lilesa	Hiwot Ayalew
Finland	Lewis Korir	Sandra Eriksson
France	Yassine Mandour	Clemence Calvin
Germany	Richard Ringer	Sabrina Mockenhaupt
Greece	Dímos Maggínas	Magdalini Gazéa
Hungary (Nov)	Ádám Kovács	Zsófia Erdélyi
India	G.Lakshmanan	O.P.Jaisha
(Dec)	Rat Ram Saini	Preeja Sridharan
Ireland (Nov)	Paul Pollock	Fionnuala Britton
Israel	Girmaw Amare	Azawant Teka
Italy	Gebriele De Nard	Samira Tourla
Kenya	Philemon Rono	Margaret Wangare
Latvia	Edgars Bertuks	Lina Sulgina
Lithuania	Justinas Berzanskis	Milda Vilcinskaite
(autumn)	Marius Diliunas	Remalda Kergyte
Luxembourg	Christian Thielen	Martine Mellina
Morocco	Abdenasir Fathi	Selima El Ouali Alami
Netherlands (Nov)	Khalid Choukoud	Sifan Hassan
New Zealand	Malcolm Hicks	Nicki McFadzien
Northern Ireland	Stephen Scullion	Ganiel O'Neill
Norway (Sep)	Ørjan Grønnevig	Anne Kristine Nevin
Poland	Blazej Brzezinski	Katarzyna Kowalska
Portugal	Manuel Damião	Ana Dulce Félix
Romania	Marius Ionescu	Cristiana Fromuz
Russia	Yuriy Chechun	Gulshat Fazlitdinova
(Sep)	Gleb Sharikov	Yekaterina Sokolenko
Scotland	Wegene Tafese ETH	Beth Potter
Serbia	Mirko Petrovic	Amela Terzic
Slovakia (Nov)	Juraj Vitko	Katarina Beresová
Slovenia	Jan Breznik	Lucia Krkoc
South Africa (Sep)	Elroy Gelant	Lebo Phalula
Spain	Sergio Sánchez	Gema Barrachina
Sweden	Mikael Ekvall	Meraf Bahta
Switzerland	Adriano Engelhardt	Livia Burri
Trinidad & Tobago (Dec)	Kendis Bullard	Jenelle Nedd
Turkey	Cihat Ulus	Senem Çaglan
Uganda	Moses Kipsiro	Viola Chemos
UK (CAU)	Frank Tickner	Louise Damen
Ukraine (Mar)	Oleksandr Matviychuk	Viktoriya Pogorelska
(Oct)	Roman Romanenko	Olga Kotovska
USA	Chris Derrick	Shalane Flanagan
Venezuela	Alexis Peña	Egris Arias
Wales	Dewi Griffiths	Andrea Whitcombe
Arab	Alemu Bekele BRN	Shitaye Eshete BRN
Balkan	Marius Ionescu ROU	Sonja Stolic SRB
European Clubs	Andrea Lalli ITA	Hiwot Ayalew ETH (TUR)
Teams	Fiamme Gialle ITA	Luch Moskva RUS
NACAC	Craig Forys USA	Natasha Fraser CAN
NCAA (Nov)	Edward Cheserek KEN	Abbey D'Agostino USA
Nordic (Nov)	Abdi Hakin Ulad DEN	Charlotta Fougberg SWE
South American	Gilberto Lopes BRA	Cruz da Silva BRA
Southern Africa	Elroy Gelant RSA	Lavinia Haitope NAM
World Military	Zelalem Regasa BRN	Shitaye Eshete BRN

Short course winners	Men	Women
Austria	Christian Steinhammer	
China	Su Guoxiong	Li Zhenzhu
Denmark	Morten Muknkholm	Simone Glad
Finland	Lewis Korir	
Germany	Florian Orth	
Lithuania (Spring)	Justinas Berzanskis	Milda Vilcinskaite
(Autumn)	Priit Aus	Liina Tsernov
Norway	Hans Kristian Fløystad	Ingeborg Kristine Lind
Poland	Krzysztof Zebrowski	Angelika Cichocka
Portugal	Rui Silva	Carla Rocha
Russia	Yegor Nikolayev	Yelene Kobeleva
Scotland (Nov)	Alastair Hay	Laura Muir
Slovakia	Jozef Pelikan	
Slovenia	Mitja Krevs	
South Africa	Elroy Gelant	Thembi Baloyi
Sweden	Andreas Åhwall	Meraf Bahta
Switzerland	Mario Bachtiger	Fabienne Schlumpf
Ukraine	Pavlo Veretskyy	Viktoriya Pogorelska
(Oct)	Oleksandr Borysyuk	Yuliya Shmatenko
World Military	Alemu Bekele BRN	

Winners of EAA and IAAF Permit Cross-Country Races 2013

5 Jan	Edinburgh (IAAF)	Bobby Mack USA	Fionnuala Britton IRL
6 Jan	San Giorgio su Legnano (IAAF)	Muktar Edris ETH	Degefa Worknesh ETH
12 Jan	Antrim (IAAF)	Thomas Ayeko UGA	Fionnuala Britton IRL
13 Jan	Elgóibar (EA)	Conseslus Kipruto KEN	Gelete Burka ETH
20 Jan	Santiponce (IAAF)	Jairus Birech KEN	Mercy Cherono KEN
26 Jan	Belgrade (EA)	Barnabas Bene HUN	Amela Terzic SRB
27 Jan	Diekirch (IAAF)	Albert Rop KEN	Eleni Gebrehiwot ETH
3 Feb	San Vittore Olana (IAAF)	Muktar Edris ETH	Afera Godfay ETH
10 Feb	Chiba (IAAF)	Charles Ndirangu KEN	Ruth Wanjiru KEN
26 Feb	Albufeira (IAAF)	Manuel Damião POR	Gorreti Jepkoech KEN
11 Nov	Soria (IAAF)	Dickson Huru UGA	Marta Tigabea ETH
17 Nov	Atapuerca (IAAF)	Imane Merga ETH	Hiwot Ayalew ETH
24 Nov	Alobendas (EA)	Emmanuel Bett KEN	Sofia Assefa ETH
24 Nov	Leffinckroucke (EA)	Cornelius Kangogo KEN	Hiwot Ayalew ETH
24 Nov	Roeselare (EA)	Bashir Abdi BEL	Almensch Belete BEL
24 Nov	Tilburg (EA)	Dame Tasama BEL	Sifan Hassan NED
15 Dec	Venta de Baños (EA)	Cyprian Kotut KEN	Mercy Cherono KEN

European Cross-Country Championships 2013

At Belgrade, Serbia December 8

Senior Men (10k)
1. Alemayehu Bezabeh ESP 29:11
2. Polat Kemboi Arikan TUR 29:32
3. Andy Vernon GBR 29:35
4. Jeroen D'Hoedt BEL 29:35
5. Hassan Chahdi FRA 29:40
6. Mohamed Marhum ESP 29:46
7. Richard Ringer GER 29:49
8. Bashir Abdi BEL 29:53
9. Koen Naert BEL 29:54
10. Ben Lkhainouch FRA 29:56
11. Iván Fernández ESP 29:58
12. Thomas Farrell GBR 29:59
13. Antonio D Jiménez ESP 30:02
14. Philipp Pflieger GER 30:03
15. Michael Mulhare IRL 30:07
80 of 81 finished.
Teams: 1. ESP 31, 2. BEL 49, 3.
GBR 60, 4. FRA 66, 5. GER 69, 6.
IRL 90, 7. TUR 105, 8. ITA 151, 9.
POR 205, 10. AUT 228, 11. SRB 275.

Under-23 Men (8k)
1. Pieter-Jan Hannes BEL 24:02
2. Mitko Tsenov BUL 24:07
3. Nemanja Cerovac SRB 24:08
4. Ivan Strebkov UKR 24:10
5. Luke Caldwell GBR 24:13
6. Ørjan Grønnevig NOR 24:15
7. Callum Hawkins GBR 24:18
8. Michele Fontana ITA 24:19
84 of 87 finished.
Teams: 1. GBR 40, 2. UKR 72, 3.
FRA 78, 4. IRL 120, 5. RUS 139, 12
completed.

Junior Men (6k)
1. Ali Kaya TUR 17:49
2. Isaac Kimeli BEL 17:51
3. Mikhail Strelkov RUS 18:05
4. Jonathan Davies GBR 18:06
5. Lorenzo Dini ITA 18:06
112 of 114 finished.
Teams: 1. FRA 48, 2. RUS 51, 3.
ITA 55, 4. GBR 67, 5. TUR 114, 21
completed

Senior Women (8k)
1. Sophie Duarte FRA 26:34
2. Gemma Steel GBR 26:39
3. Dulce Félix POR 26:41
4. Fionnuala Britton IRL 26:45
5. Karoline Bjerkeli Grøvdal
NOR 26:52
6. Almensch Belete BEL 27:00
7. Julia Bleasdale GBR 27:02
8. Veronica Inglese ITA 27:12
9. Carla Salomé Rocha POR 27:13
10. Iris M. Fuentes-Pila ESP 27:17
11. Lauren Howarth GBR 27:18
12. Clémence Calvin FRA 27:25
13. Silvia Danekova BUL 27:26
14. Diana Martín ESP 27:26
15. Stephanie Twell GBR 27:27
73 of 74 finished.
Teams: 1. GBR 35, 2. FRA 54, 3.
ESP 61, 4. ITA 97, 5. POR 109, 6.
IRL 115, 7. TUR 117, 8. CZE 197, 9.
DEN 219, 10. ROU 231.

2013 WORLD ROAD RACE REVIEW
By Marty Post

THE ROAD RACE of the year – indeed for many years – took place at the Great North Run in mid-September. Lining up at the start were three of the greatest distance runners (albeit on the track) in recent history and arguably all time. Mo Farah was the home country hero as the Briton had only the month before completed a World Championship gold medal double at 5000 and 10,000 metres to go along with the same golden pair at the 2012 London Olympics and a previous gold at the 2011 WC 5000m. Ethiopian Kenenisa Bekele had a couple of 5000 golds and six more at the 10,000 at the Olympics and World Championships. His countryman, Haile Gebrselassie, also picked up six 10,000m golds at the Olympics and Worlds and was one-time world-record holder at the half-marathon. The trio stuck together for almost 20km when Gebrselassie fell back. Bekele then surged as Farah gave chase, with the Ethiopian holding one for a bare one second victory, 60:09 to 60:10. Both were personal bests, with Farah's time the fastest ever for a British runner. Gebrselassie came through next in 60:43, a world best time for a runner over the age of 40.

History was made at the Ra's Al-Khaymah half marathon on February 15 as for the first time ever three men finished under 59 minutes. A battle to the finish among three Kenyans helped to generate the speedy results as Geoffrey Kipsang 58:54 just prevailed over Stanley Biwott 58:56 and Geoffrey Mutai 58:58. Two others broke one hour. Another Kenyan, Bernard Koech produced the fastest mark of the year – and the third fastest all-time – at 58:41. However he ran it at the non-record quality Rock 'n' Roll Marathon course in San Diego which drops 4 metres/kilometre. Kenyans dominated the 2013 half marathon world list, with 17 of the 19 performances under one hour.

The fastest road 10k of the year, 27:30, was run by Ethiopian, Adugna Bikila, at the Taroudant 10K, an event not previously known for producing fast times. Two other men ran 27:34 and 27:38 there. However, a course that has traditionally yielded fast winners produced another one, as Leonard Patrick Komon led 2013's 15k list at 42:15 at the ABN-AMRO Zevenheuvelenloop (Seven Hills) race. Runner-up Nicholas Kemboi 42:32 had the year's other sub-43 minute finish.

Other male road leaders at distances not frequently contested included Dejene Gebremeskel (13:20, 5k), Neguse Tesfaldet (45:28, 10 miles) and Richard Sigei (1:13:34, 25k).

The 2013 RAK Half-marathon was also the site of an extraordinary number of fast women's times. Kenyan Lucy Kabuu won in 1:06:09, a time bettered by only three women in history, while best times for place were recorded from second through eleventh. Four women broke 67 minutes, six broke 68 and 10 broke 69. Priscah Jeptoo would push Kiptoo down a spot all-time later in the year when she ran a superb 65:45 at the Great North Run, a time just five seconds off Paula Radcliffe's course and world best. (The start to finish has an elevation loss of 30.5m and separation of more than 75%) Meseret Defar, second at 66:09, became the fastest Ethiopian half-marathoner of all-time. Another Kenyan, Gladys Cherono, joined the sub-67 minute club, with a 66:48 win at Praha in April.

Tirunesh Dibaba of Ethiopia also moved up high on the all-time road running lists with a 30:30 for 10k at Tilburg, nine seconds off Radcliffe's world record and the fourth fastest performance ever recorded. Dibaba also won at Manchester in 30:49. Kenyan Joyce Chepkirui and Ethiopian Tadalech Bekele waged a fast battle at Berlin, 30:37 to 38:38, as they became the number seven and eight fastest 10k runners.

Chepkirui was also involved in another extremely close and quick contest at the Dam tot Damloop 10 miles, barely edging countrywoman Flomena Chepchirchir with both timed in a world-leading 51:33. New Zealand's Kim Smith had 2013's fastest time at 5k (15:16), and Lucy Kabuu at 25k (1:21:35, second fastest in history), also on the streets of Berlin.

Leading Road Races 2013

6 Jan	Nice 10k	James Theuri FRA 28:50	Christelle Daunay FRA 32:26
13 Jan	Egmond aan Zee HMar	Abera Kuma ETH 61:20	Helah Kiprop KEN 70:55
13 Jan	Houston HMar	Feyisa Lelisa ETH 60:54	Mamitu Daska ETH 69:53
20 Jan	Alicante HMar	John Mwangangi KEN 61:48	Georgina Rono KEN 70:00
20 Jan	Naples FL HMar	Kiprono Kurgat KEN 63:38	Belainesh Gebre ETH 71:55
25 Jan	Dubai 10k	Samuel Tesfalidet ERI 28:50	Alem Fikre ETH 32:39
27 Jan	Carlsbad HMar	Stephen Sambu KEN 63:02	Belainesh Gebre ETH 72:10
27 Jan	Marrakech HMar	El Hassan el Abbassi MAR 61:09	Waganesh Mekasha ETH 68:48
2 Feb	Edinburg 10k	Alene Emere ETH 28:23	Belainesh Gebre ETH 33:23
3 Feb	Granollers HMar	Stephen Kiprotich UGA 61:15	Jebichi Yator KEN 74:24
3 Feb	Marugame HMar	Collis Birmingham AUS 60:56	Tiki Gelana ETH 68:53
10 Feb	Karatsu 10M/10k	Yuichiro Ueno JPN 46:56	Keiko Nogami JPN 32:54
10 Feb	Schoorl 10k	Abdi Nageeye NED 29:14	Karoline Grøvdal NOR 32:35
15 Feb	Ra's Al-Khaymah HMar	Geoffrey Kipsang KEN 58:54	Lucy Kabuu KEN 66:09
17 Feb	Barcelona HMar	Eliud Kipchoge KEN 60:04	Atsede Baysa ETH 67:34
17 Feb	Guadalajara HMar	Julius Keter KEN 63:44	Marisol Romero MEX 72:18
17 Feb	Kumamoto 30k	Yuki Kawauchi JPN 1:29:31	Yuko Mizuguchi JPN 1:43:46
17 Feb	Ome 30k	Masaki Ito JPN 1:30:21	Asami Kato JPN 1:44:23
17 Feb	Verona HMar	Robert Ndiwa KEN 62:03	Eliana Patelli ITA 76:48
24 Feb	New Orleans HMar	Mo Farah GBR 60:59	Meseret Defar ETH 67:25
24 Feb	San Juan 10k	Sammy Kitwara KEN 28:42	Joyce Chepkirui KEN 31:40
3 Mar	Alphen aan den Rijn 20k	Abdi Negeeye NED 58:51	Ruth van der Meijden NED 70:11
3 Mar	Bath HMar	Tewodros Shiferaw ETH 63:26	Pauline Wanjiru KEN 70:28
3 Mar	Rome-Ostia HMar	Wilson Kiprop KEN 59:15	Flomena Cheyech KEN 67:39
3 Mar	Paris HMar	Abebe Negewo ETH 61:33	Gladys Kipsoi KEN 69:11
9 Mar	Jacksonville 15k NC	Ben True USA 43:38	Janet Bawcom USA 49:44
10 Mar	Den Haag HMar	Edwin Kipyego KEN 60:05	Laurane Picoche FRA 71:45
10 Mar	Stressa-Verbania HMar	Luke Rotich KEN 60:14	Tadalech Bekele ETH 69:31
10 Mar	Taroudant 10k	Adugna Bikila ETH 27:30	Khadija Sammah MAR 32:11
16 Mar	Kerzers 15k	Edwin Kiptoo KEN 43:48	Tabitha Wambui KEN 51:06
17 Mar	New York City HMar	Wilson Kipsang KEN 61:02	Caroline Rotich KEN 69:09
17 Mar	Virginia Beach 8k	Philip Mosima KEN 22:16	Risper Gesabwa KEN 25:40
17 Mar	Yamaguchi HMar	Fumihiro Maruyama JPN 61:15	Yukiko Akaba JPN 68:59
23 Mar	Azpeitia HMar	Mark Kiptoo KEN 60:42	Tsgereda Girma ETH 71:04
23 Mar	Mobile 10k	Elly Sang KEN 28:58	Ogla Kimaiyo KEN 32:33
24 Mar	Lisbon HMar	Bernard Koech KEN 59:54	Edna Kiplagat KEN 68:48
24 Mar	Milano HMar	Kiprop Limo KEN 61:49	Pauline Njeri KEN 71:19
24 Mar	Venlo HMar	Philemon Yator KEN 61:53	Jane Moraa KEN 70:40
30 Mar	Paderborn 10k	Richard Mengich KEN 28:00	Esther Chemtai KEN 31:45
30 Mar	Paderborn HMar	Ghirmay Ghebreslassie ERI 60:09	Eunice Kirono KEN 70:59
30 Mar	Westfield 5k (dh 28m)	Simon Ndirangu KEN 13:16	Kim Smith NZL 14:48
30 Mar	New Orleans 10k	Isiah Koech KEN 27:32	Alice Kimutai KEN 31:51
31 Mar	Berkane HMar	Kennedy Kimutai KEN 61:58	Belaynesh Oljira ETH 71:18
1 Apr	Dongio 10k	Mukhtar Edris ETH 28:11	Ivana Iozzia ITA 35:57
6 Apr	Charleston 10k	Simon Ndirangu KEN 28:06	Hiwot Ayalew ETH 32:18
6 Apr	Praha HMar	Zersenay Tadese ERI 60:10	Gladys Cherono KEN 66:48
7 Apr	Berlin HMar	Jacob Kendagor KEN 59:36	Helah Kiprop KEN 67:54
7 Apr	Brunssum 10k	James Rungaru KEN 28:03	Esther Chemtai KEN 31:53
7 Apr	Carlsbad 5k	Dejen Gebremeskel ETH 13:20	Geleta Burka ETH 15:26
7 Apr	Madrid HMar	Haile Tegegn ETH 62:57	Meseret Kitata ETH 71:31
7 Apr	Poznan HMar	Martin Mukule KEN 63:29	Lucy Macharia KEN 71:10
7 Apr	Rabat HMar	Nicholas Kemboi QAT 60:27	Cynthia Limo KEN 69:59

Date	Race	Men	Women
7 Apr	Washington DC 10M	Daniel Salel KEN 46:06	Caroline Rotich KEN 52:46
14 Apr	Boston 5k	Dejen Gebremeskel ETH 13:37	Kim Smith NZL 15:16
14 Apr	Dublin 10k	Kenenisa Bekele ETH 28:51	Lauren Howarth GBR 33:36
14 Apr	Richmond 10k	Julius Kogo KEN 28:18	Ogla Kimaiyo KEN 32:25
14 Apr	Wien HMar	Haile Gebrselassie ETH 61:14	Tanith Maxwell RSA 77:20
21 Apr	Hilversum 10k	John Kipsang KEN 28:37	Lucy Macharia KEN 32:24
21 Apr	Ivry/Vitry-sur-Seine HMar	Dawit Weldeselasie ERI 61:07	Gladys Kipsoi KEN 70:08
21 Apr	Nice HMar	Dino Sefir ETH 60:30	Elvan Abeylegesse TUR 70:32
21 Apr	Toronto 10k (82m dh)	Kip Kangogo KEN 28:57	Lanni Marchant CAN 31:57
21 Apr	Vancouver 10k	Paul Kimugul KEN 29:04	Natasha Fraser CAN 32:42
21 Apr	Yangzhou HMar	Yakob Jarso ETH 60:39	Worknesh Degefa ETH 68:43
27 Apr	Des Moines 10k	Emmanuel Bett KEN 28:23	Makida Abdela ETH 33:29
27 Apr	Des Moines 20k	Mark Kiptoo KEN 62:27	Belaynesh Gebre ETH 72:08
28 Apr	Würzburg 10k	Japhet Korir KEN 27:52	Agnes Mutune KEN 32:22
1 May	Marseille 10k	Kinde Atanaw ETH 28:12	Christelle Daunay FRA 32:51
5 May	Spokane 12k	Belete Assefa ETH 34:21	Bizunesh Deba ETH 39:53
5 May	Berlin 25k	Richard Sigei KEN 1:13:34	Lucy Kabuu KEN 1:21:37
11 May	Grand Rapids 25k NC	Julius Keter KEN 1:14:07	Chemtai Rionotukei KEN 1:25:45
11 May	New York 10k	Leonard P.Komon KEN 27:58	Aziza Aliyu ETH 34:34
12 May	Sendai HMar	Mekubo Moguso KEN 61:54	Mizuki Noguchi JPN 70:36
18 May	Bern 10M	Haile Gebrselassie ETH 47:00	Cynthia Kosgei KEN 55:43
19 May	Bangalore 10k	Alexander Oleitiptip KEN 28:07	Gladys Cherono KEN 32:03
19 May	Gifu HMar	Zersenay Tadese ERI 60:31	Mestawat Tufa ETH 70:03
19 May	Göteborg HMar	Jackson Kiprop UGA 63:13	Isabella Ochichi KEN 71:29
19 May	San Francisco 12k	Tolossa Gedefa ETH 35:01	Diane Nukuri-Johnson BDI 40:12
19 May	Santos 10k	Edwin Rotich KEN 27:45	Nancy Kipron KEN 32:36
25 May	Ottawa 10k	Hassan El Abbassi MAR 27:37	Malika Assahah MAR 31:46
26 May	Foz do Iguacu HMar	Mark Korir KEN 61:19	Nancy Jepkosgei Kipron KEN 71:40
26 May	Lisboa 5k	women only	Priscah Jeptoo KEN 15:47
26 May	Manchester 10k	Moses Kipsiro UGA 27:52	Tirunesh Dibaba ETH 30:49
27 May	Boulder 10k (A)	Allan Kiprono KEN 29:29	Merima Mohammed ETH 33:59
27 May	London 10k	Mo Farah GBR 29:13	Katrina Wootton GBR 32:37
1 Jun	Albany 5k	women only	Emily Chebet KEN 15:26
1 Jun	Des Moines 20k	Daniel Kipkoech KEN 60:56	Belaynesh Gebre ETH 68:41
2 Jun	Casablanca 10k	Hassan El Abbassi MAR 27:56	Malika Asahasah MAR 31:59
2 Jun	San Diego HMar (dh 84m)	Bernard Koech KEN 58:41	Edna Kiplagat KEN 68:56
7 Jun	Oelde 10k	Philip Langat KEN 28:19	Agnes Mutune KEN 32:25
8 Jun	Ceské Budejovice HMar	Tamirat Tola ETH 62:04	Hurtesa Kedija ETH 72:11
8 Jun	Green Bay 10k	Lani Rutto KEN 29:12	Risper Gesabwa KEN 32:58
8 Jun	New York City 10k	women only	Mamitu Daska ETH 31:47
8 Jun	Zwolle HMar	Edwin Kiptoo KEN 61:19	Agnes Mutune KEN 70:16
15 Jun	Peoria 4M	Shadrack Kosgei KEN 18:05	Risper Gesabwa KEN 20:42
22 Jun	Duluth HMar NC	Mo Trafeh USA 61:17	Adriana Nelson USA 71:19
22 Jun	Langueux 10k	Tesfaye Abera ETH 28:21	Fantu Jimma ETH 32:22
22 Jun	Olomouc HMar	Henry Kiplagat KEN 63:00	Betelem Moges ETH 70:38
23 Jun	Boston 10k	Stephen Sambu KEN 28:06	Mamitu Daska ETH 31:44
23 Jun	Vancouver HMar	Kip Kangogo KEN 63:33	Krista Duchene CAN 70:52
29 Jun	Appingedam 10k	Geoffrey Mutai KEN 27:37	Lilian Jelagat KEN 31:56
4 Jul	Atlanta 10k (dh 34m)	Mosinet Geremew ETH 28:07	Lineth Chepkurui KEN 32:09
14 Jul	Utica 15k	Julius Keter KEN 43:55	Lineth Chepkurui KEN 50:33
26 Jul	Castelbuono 10k	Wilson Kiprop KEN 30:10	men only
27 Jul	Davenport 7M	Leonard Korir KEN 32:15	Sule Utura ETH 36:34
28 Jul	Bogotá HMar (A)	Geoffrey Kosgei KEN 63:46	Priscah Jeptoo KEN 72:24
28 Jul	Corribianco 10k/6.6k	Emmanuel Kipsang KEN 28:06	Mercy Kibarus KEN 21:28
3 Aug	Cape Elizabeth 10k	Micah Kogo KEN 28:04	Joyce Chepkirui KEN 31:24
11 Aug	Sydney 14k	Ben Moreau GBR 41:48	Linda Spencer GBR 48:38
11 Aug	Falmouth 7M	Micah Kogo KEN 32:10	Joyce Chepkirui KEN 36:43
18 Aug	Rio de Janeiro HMar	Geoffrey Mutai KEN 59:57	Nancy Jepkosgei Kipron KEN 71:52
18 Aug	San Diego HMar	Nelson Oyugi KEN 61:59	Wendy Thomas USA 73:15

Date	Race		
24 Aug	Amatrice 8.5k	Ezekiel Kemboi KEN 24:41	Zeddy Limo KEN 28:42
24 Aug	Flint 10M	Julius Kogo KEN 45:55	Aliphine Tuliamuk-Bolton KEN 54:28
31 Aug	Lille HMar	Vincent Kipruto KEN 60:39	Diane Chepkemoi KEN 70:14
1 Sep	Düsseldorf 10k	Frederick Ngeny KEN 28:13	Mary Maina KEN 32:33
1 Sep	Luanda HMar	John Mwangangi KEN 61:29	Guteni Shone ETH 68:59
1 Sep	Tilburg 10M/10k	Tsegay Tuemay ERI 46:06	Tirunesh Dibaba ETH 30:30
2 Sep	New Haven 20k NC	Matt Tegenkamp USA 60:10	Meghan Peyton USA 69:57
7 Sep	Prague 10k	Daniel Chebii KEN 27:35	Josephine Chepkoech KEN 32:00
7 Sep	Stockholm 10k	women only	Isabellah Andersson SWE 33:42
8 Sep	Hamburg 10k	Richard Mengich KEN 28:56	Cynthia Kosgei KEN 32:34
15 Sep	Philadelphia HMar	Stanley Biwott KEN 59:36	Lyudmila Kovalenko UKR 68:59
15 Sep	Porto HMar	Samuel Wanjiku KEN 61:48	Mercy Kibarus KEN 71:11
15 Sep	S.Shields HMar (dh 30.5m)	Kenenisa Bekele ETH 60:09	Priscah Jeptoo KEN 65:45
15 Sep	Ústi nad Labem HMar	Philemon Limo KEN 60:38	Josephine Chepkoech KEN 69:08
15 Sep	Krems HMar	Luka Rotich Lobiwan KEN 61:15	Pauline Wanjiku KEN 70:48
21 Sep	Zürich-Uster HMar	Tadesse Abraham ERI 62:37	Cynthia Kosgei KEN 73:23
22 Sep	New York 5th Avenue 1M	Nick Willis NZL 3:52.1	Jennifer Simpson 4:19.3 (9.2m dh)
22 Sep	Providence 5k NC	Andrew Bumbalough USA 13:46	Molly Huddle USA 15:30
22 Sep	Udine HMar	Geoffrey Mutai KEN 59:06	Gorreti Jepkoech KEN 70:06
22 Sep	Zaandam 10M	Nguse Tesfaldet ERI 45:28	Joyce Chepkirui KEN 51:33
29 Sep	Paris-Versailles 16.3k	Mule Wasihun ETH 47:01	Sarah Chepchirchir KEN 53:28
29 Sep	Remich HMar	Jackson Limo KEN 61:31	Zinash Hayile ETH 72:41
29 Sep	Utrecht 10k	Timothy Kiptoo KEN 28:25	Joyce Chepkirui KEN 31:20
6 Oct	Breda HMar	Emmanuel Oliaulo KEN 61:51	Valentine Kibet KEN 71:50
6 Oct	Glasgow HMar	Haile Gebrselassie ETH 61:09	Susan Partridge GBR 70:40
6 Oct	Lisboa HMar	Wilson Kiprop KEN 60:19	Valeria Straneo ITA 69:23
6 Oct	Nancy HMar	Alfred Cherop KEN 62:52	Gladys Kipsoi KEN 71:14
12 Oct	Trento 10k	Edwin Soi KEN 29:01	men only
13 Oct	Berlin 10k	Leonard P.Komon KEN 27:48	Joyce Chepkirui KEN 30:37
13 Oct	Boston HMar	Lelisa Desisa ETH 60:34	Kim Smith NZL 69:14
13 Oct	Groningen 4M	Yenew Alamirew ETH 17:30	Viola Kibiwott KEN 19:14
13 Oct	Paris 20k	Tebalu Zawude ETH 58:06	Sarah Chepchirchir KEN 65:01
13 Oct	Rennes 10k/5k	Kinde Atanaw ETH 27:45	Buze Diriba ETH 15:22
14 Oct	Boston 10k	women only	Sentayehu Ejigu ETH 31:33
20 Oct	Birmingham HMar	Thomas Ayeko UGA 62:32	Gemma Steel GBR 70:19
20 Oct	Cremona HMar	Taoufique El Barhoumi MAR 62:35	Hellen Jepkurgat KEN 72:41
20 Oct	Saint-Denis HMar	Tebalu Zawude ETH 63:04	Cynthia Jerotich KEN 71:13
20 Oct	Valencia HMar	Jacob Kendagor KEN 59:58	Joyce Chepkirui KEN 68:15
26 Oct	Tulsa 15k	Julius Kogo KEN 43:25	Aliphine Tuliamuk-Bolton KEN 49:24
27 Oct	Marseille-Cassis 20k	Mule Wasihum ETH 60:09	Josephine Chepkoech KEN 70:03
27 Oct	Nairobi HMar (A)	Solomon Mutai UGA 62:55	Corret Jepkoech KEN 71:52
27 Oct	Portsmouth 10M	Emmanuel Bett KEN 48:03	Florence Kiplagat KEN 53:53
2 Nov	New York City 5k	Nick Willis NZL 13:46	Molly Huddle USA 15:27
3 Nov	Pittsburgh 10M	Elijah Karanja KEN 46:50	Sarah Kiptoo KEN 53:56
16 Nov	Bulle 8k/6k	Patrick Ereng KEN 23:45	Cynthia Kosgei KEN 20:10
16 Nov	Richmond 8k	Emmanuel Bor KEN 22:41	Alice Kamunya KEN 24:53
17 Nov	Boulogne-Billancourt HMar	Franklin Chepkwony KEN 60:11	Sarah Jepchirchir KEN 70:33
17 Nov	Istanbul 15k	Birhan Nebebew ETH 43:21	Yenenesh Tilahun ETH 49:52
17 Nov	Monterrey HMar	Jacob Chemtai KEN 62:44	Sarah Kiptoo KEN 71:21
17 Nov	Nijmegen 15k	Leonard P.Komon KEN 42:15	Tirunesh Dibaba ETH 48:43
17 Nov	Philadelphia HMar	Elijah Karanja KEN 62:59	Rkia El Moukim MAR 70:53
24 Nov	Addis Ababa 10k (A)	Atsedu Tsegay ETH 29:22	Netsanet Gudeta ETH 33:24
28 Nov	Manchester USA 4.75M	Sam Chelanga KEN 21:32	Alice Kamunya KEN 25:08
28 Nov	San Jose 5k	David Torrence USA 13:34	Kim Conley USA 15:29
30 Nov	Basel 7.55k/5.9k	Abraham Tadesse ERI 22:10	Jane Muia KEN 19:43
1 Dec	Kosa 10M	Micah Njeru KEN 48:54	men only
1 Dec	's-Heerenberg 15k	Patrick Ereng KEN 43:01	Cynthia Kosgei KEN 49:46
7 Dec	Genève 7.25k/4.79k	Abraham Kipyatich KEN 20:56	Cynthia Kosgei KEN 15:55
7 Dec	Nanning HMar	Abebe Negewo ETH 62:55	Gladys Chemweno KEN 73:01

14 Dec	Sion 7.35k/5.25k	Patrick Ereng KEN 20:07	Jane Muia KEN 16:19
15 Dec	New Delhi HMar	Atsedu Tsegay ETH 59:12	Florence Kiplagat KEN 68:00
15 Dec	Zhuhai HMar	Mosinet Geremew ETH 62:47	Tadelech Bekele Alemu ETH 70:58
15 Dec	Zürich 9k/6.6k	Patrick Ereng KEN 26:13	Cynthia Kosgei KEN 21:33
29 Dec	Houilles 10k	Cornelius Kangogo KEN 27:58	Afera Godfay ETH 32:06
31 Dec	Bolzano 10.05k/5.05k	Imane Merga ETH 28:44	Maryam Yusuf Jamal BRN 16:01
31 Dec	Luanda 10k	Stanley Biwott KEN 28:31	Priscah Jeptoo KEN 32:10
31 Dec	Madrid 10k (dh 55m)	Leonard P.Komon KEN 28:02	Linet Masai KEN 31:33
31 Dec	Peurbach 6.8k/5.1k	Cornelius Kangogo KEN 18:58	Amela Terzic SRB 16:38
31 Dec	Roma 10k	Cyprian Kotut KEN 28:17	Tirunesh Dibaba ETH 32:00
31 Dec	São Paolo 15k	Edwin Rotich KEN 43:48	Nancy Kipron KEN 51:58
31 Dec	Trier 8k/5k	Homiyu Tesfaye ETH 22:39	Corinna Harrer GER 15:53

MARATHON REVIEW – 2013
By Marty Post

THE IAAF CELEBRATED its centenary in 2012 and a point of pride was that it was able to ratify at least one official world record in every year. As the next centennial began, though, it looked like this exceptional streak might end. By the end of the outdoor track and field season, no pending world records had been set in any in-stadium event. The last good chance would come down to the final Sunday in September on the streets of Berlin. In 2011 Patrick Makau Musyoki set the marathon world record of 2:03:38 there. A few weeks later another Kenyan, Wilson Kipsang, narrowly missed that mark, running 2:03:42 in Frankfurt.

On September 29 Kipsang, in top form, would attack the fast Berlin course with the WR fixed in his sights. But at 30 kilometres this quest was in jeopardy. Two years earlier Makau (paced along by Peter Kirui) pushed hard to that point to dispose of then world record-holder Haile Gebrselassie. Makau posted a split of 1:27:38 or 23 seconds faster than Kipsang at that same point. However, Makau backed off over the final 12.2 kms, taking exactly 36 minutes to reach the finish. Kipsang, running a more measured tempo, used only 35 minutes 22 seconds to make up the deficit and a lot more. He broke the tape at 2:03:23, the third consecutive men's marathon world record at Berlin, and the only IAAF world record in 2013.

Two weeks later at Chicago the newly minted world record was threatened. Well into the race Dennis Kimetto was just off pace and he came within 22 seconds at 2:03:45, the fastest record quality time ever run in North America. Kimetto ran splits of 14:46/14:37/14:39/14:38/14:39/14:45/14:35/14:36 to become the first man to run every 5km split in a marathon sub-14:50. Emmanuel Mutai, the runner-up in 2:03:52

that day, also ran a sequence of sub-14:50s and achieved some prominence as the first man to break 2 hours 4 minutes and not win on a standard course. Kimetto and Mutai ran the fourth and fifth fastest times in history. Mutai displaced Eliud Kipchoge, who ran 2:04:05 at Berlin, as the fastest non-winner ever on a record quality course. At Hamburg in April, Kipchoge ran a marathon debut in 2:05:30 (sixth fastest ever) and his one-year combined total of 4:09:35 was the third best double, excluding 2011 times from Boston.

There was a record for a one-year triple by Ethiopian Tadesse Tola. He ran 2:04:49 at Dubai, 2:06:33 at Paris and 2:07:16 at Beijing for a total time of 6:18:38. Tola added in a bronze medal winning time of 2:10:23 at the World Championships giving him an 8:29:01 quadruple. Japan's Yuki Kawauchi was even more prolific with high-end marathoning. In 2013 he ran a record one year four sub-2:10s and six sub-2:12s. In a two week span he ran 2:09:05 at Fukuoka (Dec. 1) and 2:09:15 at Hofu (Dec. 15).

Tsegaye Kebede continued to demonstrate why he is the most consistent elite marathoner of this generation. He won the London Marathon, was fourth at the World Championships and second at the New York City Marathon. Moreover this made him the first man ever to score points within the same calendar year in three different events that comprise the World Marathon Majors Series. It also earned him the $500,000 award as the 2012-13 WMM champion.

Kenyans also dominated the 2013 women's marathon competitions. Edna Kiplagat made history as the first to successfully defend her World Championships gold medal. (Catherine Ndereba also won twice, but not consecutively).

Priscah Jeptoo became just the third woman ever and the first in 24 years with same year wins at the world's two biggest marathons: London and New York City. She joined Wanda Panfil (1989) and Grete Waitz (1983, 1986) and she also earned $500,000 for the 2012-13 WMM title.

For the third time in the past four years, Chicago was the site of the year's fastest time. Halfway through the race, Rita Jeptoo was on 2:22:30 pace, but she covered the last half in just 68 minutes 42 seconds, for a final time of 2:19:57 and the only women's sub-2:20 of 2013. Rita Jeptoo also joined a short list of same year Boston-Chicago double winners: Ingrid Kristiansen (1986), Catherine Ndereba (2000, 2001) and Svetlana Zakharova (2003). Florence Kiplagat won at Berlin for the second time in three years, as Kenyan women swept the six scoring races for the 2012-13 WMM series. However Ethiopian Aberu Kebede won at Tokyo, a new event going forward.

There were two significant world age group records set on German soil within two weeks. Irina Mikitenko became the first woman over 40 to break 2:25, at 2:24:54 at Berlin on September 29, and Helga Miketta lowered her own 70 years plus standard to 3:35:15 at Essen on October 13.

After a cancellation in 2012 because of Super Storm Sandy, the ING New York City Marathon came back in a very big way. It became the first marathon in history with more than 50,000 finishers, smashing the old record of 46,795 from 2011 by 3509, a grand total of 50,304.

Winners of 2013 International Marathons

Date	City	Men's Winner	Time	Women's Winner	Time
5 Jan	Xiamen	Negari Terfa ETH	2:07:32	Fatuma Sado ETH	2:27:35
10 Jan	Tiberias	Pius Dominic Ondoro KEN	2:08:00	Ashete Bekere ETH	2:40:22
13 Jan	Houston	Bazu Worku ETH	2:10:17	Merima Hasen ETH	2:23:37
20 Jan	Mumbai	Jackson Kiprop UGA	2:09:32	Valentine Kipketer KEN	2:24:33
25 Jan	Dubai	Lelisa Desisa ETH	2:04:45	Tirfi Tsegaye ETH	2:23:23
27 Jan	Marrakech	Stephen Tum KEN	2:06:35	Gulume Tollessa ETH	2:36:05
27 Jan	Osaka	women only		Tetyana Hamera-Shmyrko UKR	2:23:58
3 Feb	Beppu-Oita	Yuki Kawauchi JPN	2:08:15	Chiyuki Mochizuki JPN	2:40:11
24 Feb	Hong Kong	Julius Maisei KEN	2:14:18	Misiker Mekonnen ETH	2:30:49
24 Feb	Sevilla	Solomon Busendich KEN	2:10:13	Ehitu Bizuayehu ETH	2:29:52
24 Feb	Tokyo	Dennis Kimetto KEN	2:06:05	Aberu Kebede ETH	2:25:34
3 Mar	Otsu (Lake Biwa)	Vincent Kipruto KEN	2:08:34	men only	
3 Mar	Torreon (A)	Isaac Kemboi KEN	2:13:56	Truphena Tarus KEN	2:37:03
3 Mar	Treviso (dh 106m)	Said Boudalia ITA	2:20:38	Josephine Njoki KEN	2:43:32
10 Mar	Brescia	Daniel Songok KEN	2:11:46	Doreen Kitaka KEN	2:39:30
10 Mar	Nagoya	women only		Ryoko Kizaki JPN	2:23:34
17 Mar	Barcelona	Gezahegn Abera ETH	2:10:17	Lemelem Berha ETH	2:34:38
17 Mar	Los Angeles (dh 122m)	Erick Mose KEN	2:09:44	Aleksandra Duliba BLR	2:26:08
17 Mar	Roma	Negari Terfa ETH	2:07:56	Helena Kirop KEN	2:24:40
17 Mar	Seoul	Franklin Chepkwony KEN	2:06:59	Flomena Chepchirchir KEN	2:25:43
23 Mar	Chongqing	Lema Feyisa ETH	2:10:39	Elfnesh Melaku ETH	2:31:41
31 Mar	Zhengzhou	John Kelai KEN	2:16:28	Yang Fengxia CHN	2:30:38
7 Apr	Debno	Desta Morkama ETH	2:13:48	Agnieszka Gortel POL	2:40:03
7 Apr	Milano	Gemechu Worku ETH	2:09:25	Monica Jepkoech KEN	2:32:54
7 Apr	Paris	Peter Some KEN	2:05:38	Feysa Tadesse ETH	2:21:06
7 Apr	Santiago	Julius Keter KEN	2:11:43	Jacqueline Kiplimo KEN	2:30:52
7 Apr	Zürich	Abraham Tadesse ERI	2:07:45	Lisa Stublic CRO	2:25:44
14 Apr	Brighton	Dominic Kangor KEN	2:10:46	Eunice Kales KEN	2:28:50
14 Apr	Daegu	Abraham Kiprotich KEN	2:08:33	Margaret Agai KEN	2:23:28
14 Apr	Lódz	Belachew Ameta ETH	2:10:02	Karolina Jarzynska POL	2:26:45
14 Apr	Pyongyang	Ketema Bekele ETH	2:13:04	Kim Mi-gyong PRK	2:26:32
14 Apr	Rotterdam	Tilahun Regassa ETH	2:05:38	Jemima Jelagat KEN	2:23:27
14 Apr	Wien	Henry Sugut KEN	2:08:19	Flomena Cheyech KEN	2:24:34
15 Apr	Boston (dh 136m)	Lelisa Desisa ETH	2:10:22	Rita Jeptoo KEN	2:26:25
21 Apr	Beograd	Edwin Kiptum KEN	2:19:33	Olivera Jevtic SRB	2:36:09
21 Apr	Enschede	Isaac Kosgei KEN	2:09:17	Arenda Abbink NED	2:59:52
21 Apr	Hamburg	Eliud Kipchoge KEN	2:05:30	Diana Lobacevske LTU	2:29:17
21 Apr	Linz	Robert Kwambai KEN	2:09:21	Natalia Cherches MDA	2:33:53
21 Apr	London	Tsegaye Kebede ETH	2:06:04	Priscah Jeptoo KEN	2:20:15

Date	City	Men		Women	
21 Apr	Nagano	Yuki Kawauchi JPN	2:14:27	Natalya Puchkova RUS	2:30:40
21 Apr	Padova	Paulo Roberto Paula ITA	2:13:00	Hanane Janat MAR	2:36:18
21 Apr	Warszawa	Sisay Lemma ETH	2:09:02	Milka Jerotich KEN	2:28:23
28 Apr	Düsseldorf	Dereje Debele ETH	2:07:48	Melkam Gizaw ETH	2:26:24
28 Apr	Gunsan	Francis Kipkoech Bowen KEN	2:12:31	Noh Hyun-jin KOR	2:42:12
28 Apr	Madrid	Francis Kiprop KEN	2:10:37	Vanessa Veiga ESP	2:36:38
5 May	Hannover	Lusapho April RSA	2:08:32	Olena Burkovska UKR	2:27:07
5 May	Mont St Michael	Benjamin Bitok KEN	2:12:16	Daketo Ayantu ETH	2:35:56
5 May	Pittsburgh	James Kirwa KEN	2:13:37	Mary Akor USA	2:37:35
5 May	Salzburg	Eliud Kiplagat KEN	2:14:16	Joan Kigen KEN	2:36:10
6 May	Belfast	Joel Kipsang KEN	2:19:28	Natalya Lehonkova RUS	2:36:50
12 May	Lens	Raymond Kemboi KEN	2:14:21	Emily Ngetich KEN	2:41:48
12 May	Mainz	Tola Bane ETH	2:11:20	Valary Aiyabei KEN	2:39:47
12 May	Praha	Nicholas Kemboi QAT	2:08:51	Caroline Rotich KEN	2:27:00
19 May	Riga	Duncan Koech KEN	2:15:35	Aberash Nesga ETH	2:40:31
26 May	Edinburgh	Tola Lema ETH	2:15:32	Risper Kimaiyo KEN	2:35:57
26 May	Ottawa	Tariku Jufar ETH	2:08:05	Yeshi Esayias ETH	2:25:31
1 Jun	Stockholm	Shumi Eticha ETH	2:16:13	Isabellah Andersson SWE	2:33:49
2 Jun	San Diego	Simon Kariuki KEN	2:15:00	Natalya Sergeveya RUS	2:35:05
8 Jun	Luxembourg	Bellor Yator KEN	2:17:51	Shewaye Gemechu ETH	2:43:33
8 Sep	Münster	Evans Taiget KEN	2:15:55	Eleni Gebrehiwot ETH	2:29:12
15 Jun	Lanzhou (A)	Solomon Tsige ETH	2:15:40	Ashu Kasim ETH	2:43:44
22 Jun	Duluth	Bazu Worku ETH	2:11:14	Sarah Kiptoo KEN	2:26:32
7 Jul	Southport, GC	Yuki Kawauchi JPN	2:10:01	Yukiko Akaba JPN	2:27:17
7 Jul	Rio de Janeiro	Giomar da Silva BRA	2:18:03	Hadish Letay ETH	2:40:18
25 Aug	Mexico City (A)	Raul Mendoza PER	2:16:56	Gladys Tejeda PER	2:37:34
25 Aug	Sapporo	Koji Gokaya JPN	2:14:26	Yuko Watanabe JPN	2:29:13
8 Sep	Johannesburg	Shadrack Kemboi KEN	2:14:02	Mapaseka Makhanya RSA	2:37:06
15 Sep	Moscow	Aleksandr Matviychuk UKR	2:19:36	Irina Smoknikova KAZ	2:44:55
21 Sep	Hengshui	Alfred Kering KEN	2:08:42	Aberu Mekuria ETH	2:26:07
22 Sep	Cape Town	Lindikhaya Mthangayi RSA	2:17:03	Samukeliso Moyo ZIM	2:42:47
22 Sep	Odense	Julius Mutai KEN	2:15:12	Anne-Mette Ågaard DEN	2:52:19
22 Sep	Omsk	Ketema Bekele ETH	2:13:23	Meseret Mengistu, ETH	2:32:00*
22 Sep	Karlsruhe	David Kisang KEN	2:12:11	Zherfe Worku ETH	2:34:50
28 Sep	Taiyuan	Botoru Tsegaye ETH	2:11:27	Alice Chelagat CHN	2:30:40
29 Sep	Berlin	Wilson Kipsang KEN	2:03:23	Florence Kiplagat KEN	2:21:13
29 Sep	Kuala Lumpur	Lilan Kennedy Kiprop KEN	2:19:01	Rose Kosgei KEN	2:41:05
29 Sep	Warszawa	Yared Shegumo POL	2:10:34	Goitetom Haftu ETH	2:29:32
6 Oct	Bregenz	Richard Bett KEN	2:12:45	Esther Macharia KEN	2:30:50
6 Oct	Bucuresti	Victor Chelokoi KEN	2:14:05	Tigist Worku ETH	2:37:28
6 Oct	Kosice	Patrick Korir KEN	2:09:36	Ashete Bekere ETH	2:27:47
6 Oct	Lisboa	Paul Lonyangat KEN	2:09:46	Agnes Kiprop KEN	2:31:15
6 Oct	St. Paul	Nicholas Arciniaga USA	2:13:11	Annie Bersagel USA	2:30:53
13 Oct	Budapest	Gábor Józsa HUN	2:22:58	Simona Staicu HUN	2:42:26
13 Oct	Buenos Aires	Julius Nderitu KEN	2:11:02	Lucy Karimi KEN	2:33:36
13 Oct	Chicago	Dennis Kimetto KEN	2:03:45	Rita Jeptoo KEN	2:19:57
13 Oct	Eindhoven	Yemane Tsegay Adhane ETH	2:09:11	Ruth Wanjiru KEN	2:34:48
13 Oct	Graz	Philip Kigen KEN	2:16:04	Rosina Kiboino KEN	2:43:03
13 Oct	Guadalajara (A)	Tomas Dominguez MEX	2:18:03	Gladys Omwenga KEN	2:45:45
13 Oct	Gyeongju	Joel Kimurer KEN	2:07:48	Choi Bo-ra KOR	2:42:40
13 Oct	Köln	Nicholas Chelimo KEN	2:09:45	Janet Rono KEN	2:28:36
13 Oct	Melbourne	Pius Ondoro KEN	2:10:47	Lisa Jane Weightman AUS	2:26:05
13 Oct	Metz	Mark Tanui KEN	2:13:32	Magdaline Chemjor KEN	2:49:29
13 Oct	München	Frank Schauer GER	2:18:56	Silke Optekamp GER	2:41:53
13 Oct	Poznan	David Tarus KEN	2:13:08	Marina Damantsevich BLR	2:36:02
20 Oct	Amsterdam	Wilson Chebet KEN	2:05:36	Valentine Kipketer KEN	2:23:02
20 Oct	Beijing	Tadesse Tola ETH	2:07:16	Zhang Yingying CHN	2:31:19
20 Oct	Reims	Peter Kiplagat KEN	2:11:36	Aberash Nesga ETH	2:35:11
20 Oct	Toronto	Deressa Chimsa ETH	2:07:05	Flomena Cheyech KEN	2:25:13

Date	Location	Men's Winner	Time	Women's Winner	Time
20 Oct	Verbania	Charles Maina KEN	2:16:50	Zeytuna Arba ETH	2:37:17
27 Oct	Casablanca	Milton Rotich KEN	2:08:55	Gulilat Taye ETH	2:34:46
27 Oct	Chunchon	Nickson Kurgat KEN	2:08:29	Park Yu-jin KOR	2:41:30
27 Oct	Frankfurt	Vincent Kipruto KEN	2:06:15	Caroline Kilel KEN	2:22:34
27 Oct	Jakarta	William Chebor KEN	2:14:42	Mulu Seboka ETH	2:42:58
27 Oct	Ljubljana	Mulugeta Wami ETH	2:10:26	Caroline Chepkwony KEN	2:27:27
27 Oct	Nairobi (A)	Kenneth Mungara KEN	2:11:40	Winfrida Kwamboka KEN	2:33:18
27 Oct	Osaka	Jackson Limo KEN	2:12:06	Monica Jepkoech KEN	2:39:23
27 Oct	Podgorica	Elisha Sawe KEN	2:19:23	Sladana Petrunovic MNE	2:42:33
27 Oct	Toulouse	Benjamin Bitok KEN	2:10:54	Corinne Herbreteau-Cante FRA	2:37:50
28 Oct	Venezia	Nixon Machichim KEN	2:13:10	Mercy Kibarus KEN	2:31:14
29 Oct	Dublin	Sean Sehir IRL	2:18:19	Maria McCambridge IRL	2:38:51
3 Nov	New York City	Geoffrey Mutai KEN	2:08:24	Priscah Jeptoo KEN	2:25:07
3 Nov	Porto	Joash Mutau KEN	2:13:04	Chaltu Waka ETH	2:37:47
3 Nov	Rennes	Abrha Asefa ETH	2:09:09	Yestsehay Desaglegn ETH	2:33:08
3 Nov	Seoul	James Kwambai KEN	2:06:25	Park Ho-sun KOR	2:31:32
10 Nov	Athína	Hillary Yego KEN	2:13:55	Joan Rotich KEN	2:41:34
10 Nov	Beirut	William Kipsang KEN	2:13:34	Rehima Kedir ETH	2:33:29
10 Nov	Cannes	Abdisa Sori ETH	2:13:58	Salina Jebet KEN	2:41:34
17 Nov	Istanbul	Siraj Gena ETH	2:13:19	Rebecca Chesire KEN	2:29:05
17 Nov	Torino	Patrick Terer KEN	2:08:52	Ivana Iozzia ITA	2:34:12
17 Nov	Valencia	Felix Keny KEN	2:07:14	Azalech Masresha ETH	2:27:01
17 Nov	Yokohama	*women only*		Albina Mayorova RUS	2:25:55
24 Nov	Firenze	Oleksandr Sitkovskiy UKR	2:09:14	Abeba Tekulu ETH	2:30:37
24 Nov	Guangzhou	Sisay Jisa ETH	2:11:25	Goitetom Haftu ETH	2:39:17
24 Nov	La Rochelle	Isaac Kosgei KEN	2:12:29	Zerfe Boku ETH	2:38:00
1 Dec	Fukuoka	Martin Mathathi KEN	2:07:16	*men only*	
1 Dec	Macau	Julius Maisei KEN	2:12:43	Gyong Kim-mi PRK	2:36:32
1 Dec	Shanghai	Stephen Mokoka RSA	2:09:30	Aberu Kebede ETH	2:23:28
1 Dec	Singapore	Luka Chelimo KEN	2:15:00	Sharon Cherop KEN	2:41:12
8 Dec	Cancun	Erick Mose KEN	2:19:45	Emily Chepkorir KEN	2:42:34
8 Dec	Castellón	Andualem Belay ETH	2:11:59	Marta Markos ETH	2:36:14
8 Dec	Honolulu	Gilbert Chepkwony KEN	2:18:47	Ehitu Kiros ETH	2:36:02
8 Dec	Sacramento (dh 105m)	Weldon Kirui KEN	2:14:34	Becky Wade USA	2:30:41
15 Dec	Hofu	Ser-od Bat-Ochir MGL	2:09:00	Hisae Yoshimatsu JPN	2:37:57
15 Dec	Kisumu	Boaz Kiprono KEN	2:18:08	Joan Rotich KEN	2:42:34
15 Dec	Taipei	Josphat Kamzee KEN	2:14:10	Rebecca Chesire KEN	2:33:20

* Yevgeniya Danilova, RUS, 2:31:50, disqualified, doping violation
** Abraham Kiprotich, FRA, 2:12:28, disqualified, doping violation
A = altitude over 1000m; dh = net downhill >1m/km

REVIEW OF ULTRARUNNING 2013
by Andy Milroy

IN 2013 THE 100k event was hit by the repeated cancellation of the World 100k despite attempts to hold the competition in three different geographical regions – Asia, Africa and the Middle East. However to a degree the partial eclipse of this event was to be compensated for by the revival of a longer event which once had been dominant – the 100 miles – as the track event come back to the fore.

Although the World 100k was cancelled, the European event was held at Belves in France. It was won by Asier Cuevas ESP in 6:53:14 from Michael Boch FRA 6:56:49 and another Spaniard in third José Antonio Requejo 6:57:02. Not surprisingly Spain took the team title from France and Russia. There was the fastest time of the year in the women's race, with the Swede Kajsa Berg clocking 7:38:52 ahead of

Irina Antropova (née Vishnevskaya) of Russia 7:42:52 and Sue Harrison of Britain 7:48:12, Russia took the team title from Sweden with Italy third.

However it was away from international championships that perhaps the highlight of the men's 100k season took place. Running his first ever 100k, and indeed his first ever ultra, Russian mountain runner, Vasiliy Larkin, just 22 years old, set a national record of 6:18:26 in St Petersburg in September. It will be interesting to watch his progress in the event in the future. Selecting the top 100k runner of the year is not straightforward but with Larkin almost twenty minutes faster than the next best runner, the winner of the Yubetsu race in Japan, Hideo Nojo, the Russian would seem to be the logical choice. With Kajsa Berg winning the European title in the fastest time of the year, she seems the obvious choice, especially as she also ran the second fastest time of the year later in Stockholm (7:40:49).

The greatest distance of the year in the 24 hour came late in the year in Taipei when Japan's Yoshikazu Hara covered 273.650k on the track. However in the tough competition of the World 24 hour in Steenbergen in the Netherlands it was the Americans Jon Olsen and John Dennis who emerged as the top two runners with 269.675k and 262.734k respectively. Another major 24 hour mark was set by another Japanese runner, Takayoshi Shigemi in Tokyo, where he ran 269.225k. In the World 24 hours not surprisingly it was the US men's team that came first, from Japan and Germany, whilst in the European 24 hours held at the same time, Germany was first from Russia and Italy. Jon Olsen can probably be regarded as the top male 24 hour performer, although Hara went further in December. However by then Olsen's season was done; he had surpassed the US 100 mile track record with 11:59:28 in September.

The leading woman in the 24 hours at the moment is Mami Kudo and she stamped her authority on the Steenbergen event, setting a new world road best by some eight kilometres with 252.205k as well as setting a new 200k road mark of 18.45.51. Behind the 48 year-old Japanese the US team ran solidly to take the next three places and the team title, Sabrina Little 244 669k and Suzanna Bon 236 228k taking the other medals. Japan and France took the silver and bronze team medals in the World event whilst in the European, France, Great Britain and Germany took the top three positions. The top track mark was by New Zealander Deb Nicholl with 239.564k set in Australia.

For the second year running the 48 hour event did not reach its former heights, but at least in 2013 Kevin Muller of Australia covered over 400km (407.560 km) at Caboolture. In the same event, the Swedish runner Torill Fonn covered 341.559 km to produce the best female 48 hour mark of the year.

At 6 days competition was stronger. Didier Sessegolo of France ran 858.707k on the track at Abingdon in Britain whilst Wolfgang Schwerk of Germany ran 857.769k on the road at Balaton in Hungary. The best women's mark was by France's Christine David with 740.492k at Abingdon. There were some nine 6 day races in 2013 with a tenth spanning the New Year. Focussed primarily in Europe, there were also several races in the United States and one in South Africa.

The best 1000 mile mark looks to be 14 days 04:26:52 by Petr Spacil CZE in New York on the road. It was a split in the longer 3100 mile event which was won by the Russian Nikolay Duzhiy in 47 days 05:39:05. The first woman was Paula Mairer AUT in 50 days 04:57:24.

Points to point courses have deep roots within the sport. The Up run of the Comrades Marathon in South Africa from Durban to Pietermaritzburg was won by by Claude Moshiywa in 5:32:09. Experienced 100k performer Jonas Buud of Sweden was second some way back in 5:41:21 with another South African Mpesela Ntlosoeu in third 5:43:38. The women's race was dominated by runners from Eastern Europe. Yelena Nurgaliyeva won the race for the eighth time from sister Olesya who has also won once, 6:27:09 to 6:28:07. Another Russian Irina Antropova was third in 6:44:36 and fourth was the former Polish runner, now GBR, Joasia Zakrzewski in 6:53:29.

The Spartathlon from Athens to Sparta had a greater mix of nationalities. João Oliveira of Portugal took the title in 23:29:08 with experienced 24 hour performer Florian Reus second in 25:29:54, some two hours behind, and top Italian 24 hour runner, Ivan Cudin timed at 25:54:49 in third. In December Cudin set a new Italian 24 hour track record in Taipei at 266.702k. The Hungarian Szilvia Lubics won the women's race in 28:03:04, once again two hours clear of the opposition, the two Germans, Antje Krause 30:07:15 and Heike Bergmann 30:22:03.

There were two extended stage races in 2013. The Trans Gaule, across France from Roscoff to Gruissan-Plage in 19 stages covering 1190k, was won by Jean-Jacques Moros FRA with an elapsed time of 100:42:27. Carmen Hildebrand GER was the first woman in an elapsed time of 116:33:29. In Taiwan the Tour de Taiwan Ultramarathon lasted 14 stages and covered 1090.5k. Shingo Inoue of Japan won in an elapsed time of 109:25:21, with the local runner Huang Yen-Ling the first woman in 142:42:45.

As I said in the opening paragraph, 2013 featured a revival in the 100 miles event, particularly on the track. One of the oldest of the ultramarathons, this is a fascinating event that attracts both the 100k runners, moving up and the 24 hour runners moving down. In a 24 hour race, some runners may run well to the 100 mile point only to suffer for their early pace in the later stages. There were two US 100 miles track records for men in 2013, both under 12 hours, Zach Bitter running 11:47:21, surpassing Jon Olsen's 11:59:28 earlier in the year, and Pam Smith set a national track record 14:11:26.

The Japanese Mikie Sakane 14:28:44 and Mami Kudo 14:35:36 closed in on Ann Trason's world road mark. The previous year Yoshikazu Hara had set an Asian men's track record under 12 hours. This allied to the ten 6-day races in 2013 show a growing width in events internationally in addition to the standard 100k and 24 hour races.

24 HOURS ALL-TIME LISTS

Men

303.506 t	Yiannis	Kouros	GRE/AUS	13.2.56	1		Adelaide	5 Oct 97
282.282	Denis	Zhalybin	RUS	30.6.80	1	NC	Sankt Peterburg	2 Sep 06
277.543	Michael	Morton	USA	20.10.71	1	WCh	Katowice	9 Sep 12
276.209	Wolfgang	Schwerk	FRG	28.7.55	1		Köln	9 May 87
275.982 t	Anatoliy	Kruglikov	RUS	9.10.57	1	NC	Podolsk	25 Jun 95
274,884 t	Ryoichi	Sekiya	JPN	27.12.56	1		Taipei	25 Nov 07
274.715	Bernard	Gaudin	FRA	18.9.49	1		Niort	14 Nov 82
274.480 t	Dave	Dowdle	GBR	7.11.54	1		Gloucester	23 May 82
274.119	Hans-Martin	Erdmann	FRG	9.9.44	2		Köln	9 May 87
273.828t	Valmir	Nunes (10)	BRA	16.1.64	1		Taipei	11 Mar 03
273.708	Shingo	Inoue	JPN	27.9.80	1	WCh	Brive-la-Gaillarde	14 May 10
273.650 t	Yoshikazu	Hara	JPN	13.8.72	1		Taipei	8 Dec 13
272.624 t	Jean-Gilles	Boussiquet	FRA	26.7.44	1		Lausanne	3 May 81
272.619 t	Eduard	Khirov	RUS	12.7..61	2	NC	Podolsk	25 Jun 95
271.750 t	Masayuki	Otaki	JPN	5.6.65	1		Taipei	28 Mar 04
270.337 t	Lubomir	Hrmo	SVK	5.2.61	2		S.Giovanni Lupatoto	23 Sep 01
270.087	Paul	Beckers	BEL	22.8.62	1	EC	Uden	12 Oct 03
269.675	Jonathan	Olsen	USA	18.8.74	1	WCh	Steenbergen	12 May 13
269.225	Takayoshi	Shigemi	JPN	8.6.82	1		Tokyo	10 Nov 13
268.859	Alain	Prual (20)	FRA	24.9.59	1		Gravigny	12 Aug 99
Indoors								
275.576	Nikolay	Safin ¶	RUS	.58	1		Moskva	28 Feb 93
269.560	Nasibula	Khusnulin	RUS	27.3.55	2		Podolsk	27 Feb 94

Women

255.303k t	Mami	Kudo	JPN	17.7.64	1		Soochow	11 Dec 11
250.106 t	Edit	Bérces	HUN	16.5.64	1		S.Giovanni Lupatoto	22 Sep 02
247.076	Elizabeth	Hawker	GBR	10.3.76	1	Comm	Llandudno	24 Sep 11
244.669	Sabrina	Moran/Little	USA	12.7.86	2	WCh	Steenbergen	12 May 13
244.232	Michaela	Dimitriadu	CZE	23.12.73	1	WCh/EC	Katowice	9 Sep 12
243.657	Sigrid	Lomsky	GER	16.1.42	1	IAU EC	Basel	2 May 93
243.644	Anne-Cécile	Fontaine	FRA	4.11.71	1	IAU Ch	Bergamo	3 May 09
243.381	Mikie	Sakane	JPN	31.7.75	1		Tokyo	8 Oct 12
242.624 t	Irina	Reutovich	RUS	21.1.50	1	NC	Moskva	10 May 98
242,228	Lyudmila	Kalinina (10)	RUS	12.12.68	1	WCh	Wörschach	16 Jul 05
240.385	Connie	Gardner	USA	6.11.63	2	WCh	Katowice	9 Sep 12
240.169 t	Eleanor	Adams/Robinson	GBR	20.11.47	1		Melbourne	20 Aug 89
239.874	Galina	Yeremina	RUS	15.2.53	2	WCh	Wörschach	16 Jul 05
239.685	Anne-Marie	Vernet	FRA	15.12.67	1	WCh	Seoul	19 Oct 08
239.564k t	Deb	Nicholl	NZL	10.2.70	1		Caboolture	21 Jul 13
238.875	Emily	Gelder	GBR	1.4.75	3	WCh/EC	Katowice	9 Sep 12
238.021	Sabrina	Moran	USA	12.7.86	1	NC	Cleveland	7 May 12
237.154	Sumie	Inagaki	JPN	6.4.66	1	WCh	Brno	24 Oct 04
236.453	Hilary	Walker	GBR	9.11.53	1		Preston	28 Aug 88
236.228	Suzanna	Bon	USA	28.7.64	3	WCh	Steenbergen	12 May 13
235.597	Brigitte	Bec (20)	FRA	7.4.64	1		Brive	25 May 06

IAAF WORLD CHAMPIONSHIPS 2013

August 10-18, Moscow, Russia

Splendidly organised and staged in over-whelmingly good conditions, the 14th World Championships provided a feast of top-class competition. Crowds were small for the morning sessions and far from full for most of the evening ones, but lack of numbers was compensated by their enthusiasm for the Russian (and Ukrainian) competitors, with the peak reached for Yelena Isinbayeva's pole vault triumph and major success on day 7 with world-leading performances from Aleksandr Menkov, 8.52m in the long jump, and Tatyana Lysenko, 78.80 hammer. The last was also a Russian record and needed as she had just lost the lead to the Polish record of 78.46 by Anita Wlodarczyk. Russians also won both the 20k walks, the women's high jump and 4x400m relay.

Usain Bolt took his fourth global event triple and the far-smaller figure of Shelly-Ann Fraser-Pryce followed her 100m victory (with a record 0.22 victory margin) with another clear win at 200m, in which Allyson Felix's bid to add to her record tally of eight gold and ten World medals came to grief, and anchoring the Jamaican 4x100m team to an even more decisive win. The other double individual victor was Mo Farah; just as at the Olympic Games nobody had any answer to his tactical acumen and searing finish. The Ethiopian women stars were not permitted to clash, so Tirunesh Dibaba maintained her career unbeaten record at 10,000m and Meseret Defar added a second World title (and fifth medal at the event) to her double Olympic success. Dibaba was joined as a three-time World champion at one event by Bolt (200m), Ezekiel Kemboi (steeplechase), Robert Harting (discus), Isinbayeva and Brittney Reese (long jump), while Valerie Adams went one better with a fourth shot title, an all-time women's record. In all 14 individual Olympic champions won here (with Farah and Bolt each taking two titles) and 10 won again from Daegu 2011.

Bohdan Bondarenko's 2.41, Lysenko's hammer throw and the Jamaican women's 4x100m 41.29 were the only championships records of the meeting, but there were many exciting tussles, such as in the women's 400m in which Christine Ohuruogu's drive and dip finish just got her the verdict over Amantle Montsho, the win by Jehue Gordon over Michael Tinsley in the 400m hurdles, and the thrilling 4x400m win of Russia over the USA, but there were often keen battles for silver and bronze medals, while some winners were well clear of the opposition. Apart from the Jamaican super-star sprinters, in this category were LaShawn Merritt (400m), David Oliver (110m hurdles), Ashton Eaton (decathlon), Zuzana Hejnová (400mh) and Sandra Perkovic (discus). Pavel Fajdek scored an upset hammer win with 81.97, one of 17 world-leading marks, and perhaps the best individual performance came on the final day, as Teddy Tamgho fulfilled his promise with 18.04 in the triple jump.

Russia headed the medal table with 7 golds, although their 17 medals in all was well behind the 25 won by the USA who were well ahead on points. The 6 golds won by the Jamaican sprinters matched the US total, and the Kenyan and Ethiopian distance runners ensured their high

Medals and Points Table

Points: 8 for 1st to 1 for 8th place. 62 nations placed athletes in top eight, 37 won medals, and 10 won gold.

Nation	G	S	B	Points	2011	2009
USA	6	14	5	282	251	230
RUS	7	4	6	182	200.5	153.5
KEN	5	4	3	139	174	120
GER	4	2	1	101.5	83	102
JAM	6	2	1	100	191	136
ETH	3	3	4	97	66	88
GBR	3	-	3	79	70	80
UKR	2	-	1	51	33	29
FRA	1	2	1	50	45	39.5
POL	1	2	-	43.5	44	72
CHN	-	1	3	42	60.5	50
CAN	-	1	4	41	12	12
CZE	2	-	1	37.5	24	12.5
CUB	-	1	2	32	48	51
JPN	-	-	1	31	18	27
AUS	-	2	1	27	34	45
NED	-	1	1	24	4	4.5
ESP	-	-	2	23.5	11	29
NGR	-	1	1	19	7.5	4
ITA	-	1	-	18.5	17	21
BRA	-	-	-	18.5	13	13
RSA	-	-	1	18	34	23
CIV	-	2	0	14	0	0
TRI	1	-	-	13	16	32

SWE (1G), SRB (2B) 12, FIN (1S), DOM (1B) 10, BEL 9, COL, CRO, IRL, NZL, UGA 8 (1G); HUN 8 (1S), MEX 8 (1B), BAH 8, QAT, BOT (1S) 7; DJI, EST 6 (1B); POR 6, BLR, ROU, SLO, SVK 5; KSA, NOR, TJK 4; BRN, ISR, PUR 3; ARG, GRN, IND, SEN 2; BUL, EGY, ERI, PRK 1

In all 18 nations won gold medals, 38 medals and 60 placed athletes in the top eight (respectively 16, 41 and 62 in 2011).

positions. Germany and Britain did well for Western European nations and Ukraine, Netherlands and Nigeria made notable advances, but falling back were Belarus from 25 points to 5, Morocco from 23 to 0, and Latin America. There were first ever World medals for Colombia (gold from Caterine Ibargüen), Ivory Coast and Serbia.

Men

100 Metres (prelim, h 10th, sf, F 11th -0.3)

1. Usain Bolt JAM	9.77
2. Justin Gatlin USA	9.85
3. Nesta Carter JAM	9.95
4. Kemar Bailey-Cole JAM	9.98
5. Nickel Ashmeade JAM	9.98
6. Mike Rodgers USA	10.04
7. Christophe Lemaitre FRA	10.06
8. James Dasaolu GBR	10.21

AFTER RODGERS AND Gatlin broke 10 secs in the first round and seven men, headed by Ashmeade 9.90 did so in the semis, Bolt regained his title, cutting down Gatlin's early lead to pass his rival at 70m and win by 0.08 in a race run in pouring rain (and with lightning bolts!). Zhang Peimeng set Chinese records in heat 10.04 and semi 10.00, when he lost a place in he final very narrowly to Lemaitre, in a time that was the fastest ever non-qualifying mark.

200 Metres (h, sf 16th, F 17th 0.0)

1. Usain Bolt JAM	19.66
2. Warren Weir JAM	19.79
3. Curtis Mitchell USA	20.04
4. Nickel Ashmeade JAM	20.05
5. Adam Gemili GBR	20.08
6. Anaso Jobodwana RSA	20.14
7. Churandy Martina NED	20.35
8. Jaysuma Saidy Ndure NOR	20.37

BOLT WON HIS fifth successive global 200m title, running 10.2 for the first half, a metre ahead of Gemili, Ashmeade and Weir, and raced clear although Weir finished well for second as did Mitchell, who won a close race for third. Gemili (pb) and Jobodwana, both 20.17, were fastest in the heats, and in the semis winners were Mitchell 19.97 and 19 year-old Gemili 19.98 in pbs and Bolt in 20.12. 20.37 by Saidy Ndure was the best ever 8th place time.

400 Metres (h 11th, sf 12th, F 13th)

1. LaShawn Merritt USA	43.74
2. Tony McQuay USA	44.40
3. Luguelín Santos DOM	44.52
4. Jonathan Borlée BEL	44.54
5. Pavel Maslák CZE	44.91
6. Youssef Al-Masrahi KSA	44.97
7. Kirani James GRN	44.99
8. Anderson Henriques BRA	45.03

THE KEENLY-AWAITED duel between Merritt (1st 2009, 2nd 2007 & 2009) and James (1st 2011) proved no contest as Merritt clipped 0.01 from the pb he set when winning the 2008 Olympic title and ran away from the field with 11.1 for 100m, 21.3 for 200m and 32.0 for 300m. At that point James 32.3 and Borlée 32.4 followed, but James drifted back as McQuay and fast-finishing Santos squeezed past Borlée for silver and bronze. All eight finalists bettered 45 secs in the semis, headed by 44.60 by Merritt and a national record 44.61 by Al-Masrahi.

800 Metres (h 10th, sf 11th, F 13th)

1. Mohammed Aman ETH-J	1:43.31
2. Nick Symmonds USA	1:43.55
3. Ayanleh Souleiman DJI	1:43.76
4. Marcin Lewandowski POL	1:44.08
5. Andrew Osagie GBR	1:44.36
6. Duane Solomon USA	1:44.42
7. Pierre-Ambroise Bosse FRA	1:44.79
8. Abdulaziz Mohammed KSA	1:46.57

AMAN WAS EASILY the fastest in the heats with 1:44.93 and in the first semi Solomon blazed through 24.38, 50.67 and 1:17.25 for 1:43.87 from Mohammed 1:44.10. Solomon tried the same tactics in the final, but his opening 23.53 was far too fast and he slowed to 50.28 virtually level with Symmonds 50.26, and still led at 600m in 1:16.73, but he tied up in the straight, when 19 year-old Aman (last 100m 13.35) passed the much more powerfully-built Symmonds in the last 30m and became the first Ethiopian to win an outdoor global title at the distance.

1500 Metres (h 14th, sf 16th, F 18th)

1. Asbel Kiprop KEN	3:36.28
2. Matt Centrowitz USA	3:36.78
3. Johan Cronje RSA	3:36.83
4. Nixon Chepseba KEN	3:36.87
5. Homiyu Tesfaye GER	3:37.03
6. Silas Kiplagat KEN	3:37.11
7. Mekonnen Gebremedhin ETH	3:37.21
8. Henrik Ingebrigtsen NOR	3:37.52
9. Mohamed Moustaoui MAR	3:38.08
10. Nathan Brannen CAN	3:38.09
11. Florian Carvalho FRA	3:39.17
12. Chris O'Hare GBR	3:46.04

KIPROP, THE DEFENDING champion, led at 400m in 59.79 and reached 800m in a slow 2:00.43, leading the pack behind Chepseba who went through in 1:59.35 and who still led at the bell in 2:42.76, followed by Kiprop 2:43.06, and at 1200m in 2:56.41. While Centrowitz and Cronje had a desperate battle for the other medals, Kiprop unwound his long stride and, with 12.52 for the last 100m of a 53.22 lap, eased away to a clear win. After his 800m medal, the fancied Ayanleh Souleiman found a fifth race too much and was only 11th in his semi-final.

5000 Metres (h 13th, F 16th)

1. Mo Farah GBR	13:26.98

2. Hagos Gebrhiwet ETH-J	13:27.26
3. Isiah Koech KEN	13:27.26
4. Thomas Longosiwa KEN	13:27.67
5. Edwin Soi KEN	13:29.01
6. Bernard Lagat USA	13:29.24
7. Muktar Edris ETH-J	13:29.56
8. Galen Rupp USA	13:29.87
9. Yenew Alamirew ETH	13:31.27
10. Ryan Hill USA	13:32.69
11. Dejene Regassa BRN	13:34.54
12. Elroy Gelant RSA	13:43,58
13. Sindre Buraas NOR	13:45.67
14. Zane Robertson NZL	13:46.55
15. Brett Robinson AUS	14:03.77

AFTER HIS 10,000m win surely the only way to beat Farah was to try to run him off his feet, but, although only Farah and Rupp has run the 10, none of his rivals were prepared to do that, and a first lap in the final of 71.48 set the tone. The first kilometre took 2:25.12 and second 2:52.99, as Farah showed briefly in the lead. 3000m was reached in 8:27.79 before, at last, the tempo was upped by Koech with a fourth kilometre of 2:36.91. With Alamirew in furious pursuit, Farah took off with just over 600m to go, covered his 11th lap in 60.28 and reached the bell just ahead of Alamirew and Longosiwa with several others close behind in 12:33.47, that 200m segment taking 28.33. Throughout the last lap Farah fought off every challenge with 26.90 and 26.61 200m sections. He ran the last 400m in 53.44, 800m in 1:50.75 and kilometre in 2:22.12. Gebrhiwet, who snatched second place ahead of the Kenyans, finished even faster with a last 400m of 53.38 and 1000m of 2:21.82. All finalists had run faster in the heats, inside 13:28 headed by Edris 13:20.82.

10,000 Metres (10th)

1. Mo Farah GBR	27:21.71
2. Ibrahim Jeylan ETH	27:22.23
3. Paul Tanui KEN	27:22.61
4. Galen Rupp USA	27:24.39
5. Abera Kuma ETH	27:25.27
6. Bidan Karoki KEN	27:27.17
7. Kenneth Kipkemoi KEN	27:28.50
8. Nguse Tesfaldet ERI	27:29.21
9. Mohammed Ahmed CAN	27:35.76
10. Dathan Ritzenhein USA	27:37.90
11. Thomas Ayeko UGA	27:40.96
12. Imane Merga ETH	27:42.02
13. Moses Kipsiro UGA	27:44.53
14. Cameron Levins CAN	27:47.89
15. Tsuyoshi Ugachi JPN	27:50.79

JUST AS IN 2011 Jeylan chased Farah around the final bend, but this time Farah had the speed and strength to win by half a second as he ran the last lap in 53.36 (26.2 & 27.2), although Jeylan ran 52.8 (26.5 & 26.3). 32 men, of whom 7 did not finish, contested the final. The pace was sedate from the start with kilometres of 2:45.73, 2:49.69, 2:44.53, 2:43.19, 2:46.81 (13:49.95), 2:47.57,

2:48.71, 2:45.17 and 2:44.08 with Tanui doing most of the leading, but Farah, who covered the second half of the race in 13:29.3 (13:52.4 first half) ran the final kilometre in 2:26.23 and had a last lap of 54.49 for his third fastest time of 27:21.71.

Marathon (17th)

1. Stephen Kiprotich UGA	2:09:51
2. Lelisa Desisa ETH	2:10:12
3. Tadesse Tola ETH	2:10:23
4. Tsegay Kebede ETH	2:10:47
5. Kentaro Nakamoto JPN	2:10:50
6. Solonei da Silva BRA	2:11:40
7. Paulo Paula BRA	2:11:40
8. Yemane Tsegay ETH	2:11:43
9. Peter Kimeli Some KEN	2:11:47
10. Jackson Kiprop UGA	2:12:12
11. Beraki Beyene ERI	2:13:40
12. Bernard Kipyego KEN	2:14:01
13. Jeff Eggleston USA	2:14:23
14. Masakazu Fujiwara JPN	2:14:29
15. Javier Guerra ESP	2:14:33

KIPROTICH BECAME ONLY the second man (Gezahegne Abera was the first in 2000/2001) to win both Olympic and World titles. The race started at 3.30 pm in a temperature of 23°C and the runners understandably took it steady in the early stages so that at halfway 17 runners were in the leading pack in 65:12/13. The decisive break came in the 37th kilometre as Kiprotich, Tola and Desisa went clear. Tola was dropped first and Kiprotich went away with a kilometre to go and won by 21 secs. Kenya, so dominant in marathons around the world, had just two finishers, 9th and 12th. 51 of the 69 starters finished.

3000m Steeplechase (h 12th, F 15th)

1. Ezekiel Kemboi KEN	8:06.01
2. Conseslus Kipruto KEN-j	8:06.37
3. Mahiedine Mekhissi Bennabad FRA	8:07.86
4. Paul Kipsiele Koech KEN	8:08.62
5. Evan Jager USA	8:08.67
6. Matthew Hughes CAN	8:11.64
7. Abel Mutai KEN	8:17.04
8. Yoann Kowal FRA	8:17.41
9. Hamid Ezzine MAR	8:19.53
10. Ion Luchianov MDA	8:19.99
11. Ángel Mullera ESP	8:20.93
12. Jacob Araptany UGA	8:25.86
13. Alexandre Genest CAN	8:27.01
14. Benjamin Kiplagat UGA	8:31.09
dnf. Noureddine Smaïl FRA	–

KEMBOI WON HIS third consecutive world title with a strong finish and a last kilometre in 2:34.06 after slow opening kilometres of 2:45.94 and 2:46.01 (Koech 5:31.95) from a most disappointed 18 year-old Kipruto. Mekhissi was fastest, 8:15.43, in the heats.

110 Metres Hurdles (h 11th, sf, F 12th 0.3)

1. David Oliver USA	13.00

2. Ryan Wilson USA	13.13
3. Sergey Shubenkov RUS	13.24
4. Jason Richardson USA	13.27
5. William Sharman GBR	13.30
6. Aries Merritt USA	13.31
7. Thomas Martinot-Lagarde FRA	13.42
8. Andrew Riley JAM	13.51

A REJUVENATED OLIVER won in a world-leading time by a record margin of 0.13 in a World 110mh final after running the fastest ever World Championship heat at 13.05 from Shubenkov 13.16, and these two were also the fastest in the semis: Shubenkov 13.17 from Oliver 13.18. After a ragged start Richardson won the first semi in 13.34, but Merritt only just made it after a terrible start and 2009 world champion Ryan Brathwaite went out. Hansle Parchment fell in the second semi. In the final Wilson finished fast to take silver while Richardson clipped the final hurdle.

400 Metres Hurdles (h 12th, sf 13th, F 15th)

1. Jehue Gordon TRI	47.69
2. Michael Tinsley USA	47.70
3. Emir Bekric SRB	48.05
4. Omar Cisneros CUB	48.12
5. Félix Sánchez DOM	48.22
6. Javier Culson PUR	48.38
7. Mamadou Kassé Hann SEN	48.68
8. Kerron Clement USA	49.08

TINSLEY LED FOR much of the final before Gordon pulled up to level between the final two barriers and just took the verdict with his dip in a thrilling finish to take 0.27 off his national record and Tinsley improving his best by 0.21. There was the fastest ever time for sixth place. Tinsley was fastest in the heats at 49.07 and the semi-final winners were Gordon 48.10m Tinsley 48.31 and Cisneros in a Cuban record 47.93. Bekric set Serbian records with 48.36 semi and 48.05 final. Defending champion Dai Greene was 5th in his semi in 49.25, nowhere bear full fitness, and the 2005 champion Bershawn Jackson tore a hamstring in his heat.

High Jump (Q 2.31 13th, F 5th)

1. Bohdan Bondarenko UKR	2.41*
2. Mutaz Essa Barshim QAT	2.38
3. Derek Drouin CAN	2.38
4. Ivan Ukhov RUS	2.35
5. Erik Kynard USA	2.32
6. Donald Thomas BAH	2.32
7. Aleksandr Shustov RUS	2.32
8. Robbie Grabarz GBR	2.29
9. Zhang Guowei CHN	2.29
10= Konstadínos Baniótis GRE	2.25
10= Kabelo Kgosiemang BOT	2.25
10= Ryan Ingraham BAH	2.25

THREE MEN AT 2.38 or higher tied the record for any competition set at the World Championships indoors and out in 1987 and after

Barshim had cleared first time and Drouin on his second attempt at 2.38, Bondarenko, who had cleared 2.29 and 2.35 first time, passing 2.38, added 1cm to Javier Sotomayor's championship record with 2.41, equalling his recent Ukraine record, on his second attempt. He then had a go at 2.46, coming quite close on his second attempt. Nine men cleared 2.29 in qualifying and three more went through with 2.26.

Pole Vault (Q 5.70m 10th, F 12th)

1. Raphael Holzdeppe GER	5.89
2. Renaud Lavillenie FRA	5.89
3. Björn Otto GER	5.82
4. Brad Walker USA	5.82
5. Malte Mohr GER	5.82
6. Seito Yamamoto JPN	5.75
7. Jan Kudlicka CZE	5.75
8. Sergey Kucheryanu RUS	5.65
9. Alhaji Jeng SWE	5.65
10. Konstadínos Filippídis GRE	5.65
11. Augusto de Oliveira BRA	5.65
12. Xue Changrui CHN	5.50
nh. Valentin Lavillenie FRA	–

LAVILLENIE HAD BEATEN Holzeppe 8-2 in their previous 2013 clashes and had dominated recent major events, but took three attempts to clear 5.89 after the German had gone over first time before both failed at 5.96. Holzdeppe had also had first-time clearances at 5.65 and 5.82, while Lavillenie went over these second time. Count-back settled bronze for Otto from Walker and Mohr at 5.82. Clearances at 5.55 were enough for 13 men to make the final.

Long Jump (Q 8.10m 14th, F 16th)

1. Aleksandr Menkov RUS	8.56/0.2
2. Ignisious Gaisah NED	8.29/0.4
3. Luis Rivera MEX	8.27/0.6
4. Eusebio Cáceres ESP	8.26/0.8
5. Mauro da Silva BRA	8.24/0.6
6. Christian Reif GER	8.22/0.1
7. Khotso Mokoena RSA	8.10/0.4
8. Damar Forbes JAM	8.02/0.1
9. Sebastian Bayer GER	7.98/0.1
10. Loúis Tsátoumas GRE	7.98/0.4
11. Dwight Phillips USA	7.88/0.3
12. Li Jinzhe CHN	7.84/-0.2

THE FOUR-TIME champion Phillips competed due to wild card and exceeded his season's best of 7.89 to qualify for the final with 7.95, but Olympic champion Greg Rutherford managed only 7.87 for 14th as top qualifying mark was 8.25 by Cáceres. In the final Reif led the first round with 8.15, then Cáceres jumped 8.25 in the second before Menkov established his clear superiority with 8.52, 8.43 and 8.56 in rounds 3-5. The ex-Ghanaian Gaisah, who scraped into the final with 7.89, set a Dutch record of 8.29 in the fifth round.

Triple Jump (Q 17.05m 16th, F 18th)

1. Teddy Tamgho FRA — 18.04/0.3
2. Pedro Pablo Pichardo CUB — 17.68/-0.1
3. Will Claye USA — 17.52/0.5
4. Christian Taylor USA — 17.20/0.4
5. Aleksey Fyodorov RUS — 16.90/0.4
6. Marian Oprea ROU — 16.82/-0.9
7. Gaëtan Saku Bafuanga FRA — 16.79/-0.3
8. Fabrizio Schembri ITA — 16.74/0.2
9. Dong Bin CHN — 16.73/-0.1
10. Dimítrios Tsiámis GRE — 16.66/-0.6
11. Samyr Laine HAI — 16.09/-0.8
12. Yoann Rapinier FRA — 15.17/-0.3

TAMGHO LED THE qualifying with 17.41 from Rapinier 17.39, and, after Pichardo had jumped 17.38, leapt to 17.65 in the first round of the final. The Cuban then regained the lead with a second-round 17.68 and Claye went to third with 17.33 and 17.52, while Taylor and Tamgho (twice) had fouls around 18m. In the fourth round Tamgho took the lead by matching Pichardo's 17.68 and he had another foul around 18m in the fifth before producing the world's best jump since 1996 and the third longest of all-time with his final-round 18.04.

Shot (Q 20.65m 15th, F 16th)

1. David Storl GER — 21.73
2. Ryan Whiting USA — 21.57
3. Dylan Armstrong CAN — 21.34
4. Reese Hoffa USA — 21.12
5. Ladislav Prásil CZE — 20.98
6. Tomasz Majewski POL — 20.98
7. Germán Lauro ARG — 20.40
8. Georgi Ivanov BUL — 20.39
9. Cory Martin USA — 20.09
10. Asmir Kolasinac SRB — 19.96
11. Antonín Zalsky CZE — 19.54
12. Martín Stasek CZE — 19.10

THE FAVOURITE WHITING was the only man over 21m with 21.51 in qualifying, and went further with 21.57 in the first round of the final. But Storl once again showed his ability to be at his best in a major championship and started with season's bests of 21.19 and 21.24 with Hoffa third at 21.12. Whiting had three more puts in the 21.20 to 21.35 range, but Stork took gold with a huge fifth round throw of 21.73 (ruled a foul until photographic evidence was consulted). Armstrong took the bronze with his fifth-round 21.34.

Discus (Q 65.00m 12th, F 13th)

1. Robert Harting GER — 69.11
2. Piotr Malachowski POL — 68.36
3. Gerd Kanter EST — 65.19
4. Martin Wierig GER — 65.02
5. Victor Hogan RSA — 64.35
6. Robert Urbanek POL — 64.32
7. Vikas Gowda IND — 64.03
8. Viktor Butenko RUS — 63.38
9. Frank Casañas ESP — 62.89
10. Jorge Fernández CUB — 62.88
11. Julian Wruck AUS — 62.40
12. Mario Pestano ESP — 61.88

THE 1-2-3 WERE the same as in Berlin 2009 and Harting won for the third time, (plus his 2012 Olympic title), leading the qualifying with 66.62 and, after taking the lead with 68.13 in round two, having the two best throws, 69.11 and 69.08 in fourth and sixth rounds in the final. Kanter did not improve on 65.19 in round two, but Malachowski pressed with his last three throws of 67.18, 68.36 and 67.21. Virgilijus Alekna, the 2003 and 2005 champion, now 41, failed to qualify (16th 61.91) for a final he had reached at every World Champs from 1997.

Hammer (Q 77.00m 10th, F 12th)

1. Pawel Fajdek POL — 81.97
2. Krisztián Pars HUN — 80.30
3. Lukas Melich CZE — 79.36
4. Primoz Kozmus SLO — 79.22
5. Dilshod Nazarov TJK — 78.31
6. Koji Murofushi JPN — 78.03
7. Nicola Vizzoni ITA — 77.61
8. Marcel Lomnicky SVK — 77.57
9. Szymon Ziółkowski POL — 76.84
10. Markus Esser GER — 76.25
11. Sergey Litvinov RUS — 75.90
12. Yuriy Shayunov BLR — 73.68

AS EXPECTED PARS, who came to Moscow after 23 successive wins, led the qualifying with 79.06 and started in the final with 80.30, but then, with his first throw, Fajdek added 58cm to his lifetime best with 81.97 and backed that with 80.92 in round two. Murofushi, as usual in only his second competition of the year, started with 78.08, but was passed in round two by Kozmus 79.21 and 79.22 in the next two rounds and by Melich, a third round 79.36. Meanwhile Pars had three 79m plus throws but had to settle for silver as Fajdek, at 24, became the youngest ever world hammer champion.

Javelin (Q 82.50m 15th, F 17th)

1. Vitezslav Vesely CZE — 87.17
2. Tero Pitkämäki FIN — 87.07
3. Dmitriy Tarabin RUS — 86.23
4. Julius Yego KEN — 85.40
5. Antti Ruuskanen FIN — 81.44
6. Andreas Thorkildsen NOR — 81.06
7. Abdelrahman El Sayed EGY — 80.94
8. Risto Mätas EST — 80.03
9. Stuart Farquhar NZL — 79.24
10. Kim Amb SWE — 78.91
11. Ivan Zaytsev UZB — 78.33
drugs dq (5) Roman Avramenko UKR — 82.05

VESELY THREW 87.17 with his first throw in the final. His next best was 83.80, while Pitkämäki started with 83.40 and then had five 85m plus throws topped with 87.07 in round three. Local favourite Tarabin took third place with 84.38 in the second round and after Yego improved his Kenyan record from 82.09 to

85.40 in round five, took the bronze with a final round 86.23. Olympic champion Keshorn Walcott was 19th with 78.78 in qualifying, in which 80.18 sufficed to make the final and the best throw was 84.39 by Pitkämäki.

Decathlon (10th-11th)

1. Ashton Eaton USA	8809
2. Michael Schrader GER	8670
3. Damian Warner CAN	8512
4. Kevin Mayer FRA	8446
5. Eelco Sintnicolaas NED	8391
6. Carlos Eduardo Chinin BRA	8388
7. Rico Freimuth GER	8382
8. Ilya Shkurenyov RUS	8370
9. Willem Coertzen RSA	8343
10. Leonel Suárez CUB	8317
11. Pascal Behrenbruch GER	8316
12. Andrey Kravchenko BLR	8314
13. Gunnar Nixon USA	8312
14. Mihail Dudas SRB	8275
15. Thomas Van Der Plaetsen BEL	8255

EATON BECAME THE first man to hold the three global multi-event titles (Olympic and World decathlon, World Indoor heptathlon) simultaneously. After starting with 10.35 and 7.73 he had disappointing marks at shot and high jump so that he was only third at that stage, but a splendid 46.02 400m took him to a first day lead with 4502 from Nixon 4493 and Schrader 44.27 and a fine second day took him to a win by the clear margin of 139 points. The depth was terrific as best ever marks were set for places 10 to 15 with 7 of the first 13 setting pbs and Coertzen an African record 8343.

4 x 100 Metres Relay (h, F 18th)

1. JAM	37.36	Carter, Bailey-Cole, Ashmeade, Bolt (heat: 3. Weir, 4. O Bailey)
2. USA	37.66	Silmon, Rodgers, Salaam, Gatlin
3. CAN	37.92	Smellie, Brown, Richards-Kwok, J Warner
4. GER	38.04	Jakubczyk, Knipphals, Reus, Keller
5. NED	38.37	Mariano, Martina, Bonevacia, Paulina
6. JPN	38.39	Kiryu, Fujimitsu, Takase, Iizuka
7. TRI	38.57	Taffe, Bledman, Sorillo, Thompson
dq. GBR	(37.80)	Gemili, Aikines-Aryeetey, Ellington, Chambers

JAMAICA ROMPED HOME a good 3m clear of the USA in a world leading 37.36, the sixth fastest ever time. Only one American and four Jamaican teams have ever gone quicker. The USA, who had the fastest heat time of 38.06, were slightly ahead approaching the last change but that was bungled, with Gatlin taking a couple of steps into Jamaica's lane, and Bolt rocketed away from his opponent and won his eighth World Championships gold medal to tie the record. The British squad (heat winners

in 38.12) celebrated wildly after crossing the line third in 37.80 but the second change was made out of their box and they were disqualified for their fifth successive failure at a major championships.

4 x 400 Metres Relay (h 15th, F 16th)

1. USA	2:58.71	Verburg 45.0, McQuay 44.1, Hall 44.87, L Merritt 44.77 (J Harris and Mance ran in ht)
2, JAM	2:59.88	McDonald 46.0, Steele 44.3, O Johnson 45.53, Francis 44.05 (Bell ran in heat)
3. RUS	2:59.90	Dyldin 45.4, Mosin 44.8, Petukhov 45.05, Krasnov 44.67
4. GBR	3:00.88	C Williams 45.3, Rooney 44.5, Bingham 45.65, Levine 45.35
5. BEL	3:01.02	J Borlée 45.50, K Borlée 44.04, D Borlée 45.74, Oyowe 45.74
6. TRI	3:01.74	Quow 45.6, L Gordon 45.3, J Gordon 45.12, Solomon 45.74
7. BRA	3:02.19	P de Oliveira 45.9, Cardoso 45.2, Henriques 45.32, H de Sousa 45.73
8. AUS	3:02.26	Solomon 45.6, Beck 45.8, Burns 45.36, Thomas 45.36

THE US WERE fastest in the heats with a world leading 2:59.85 and led from the start in the final for their fifth successive title at the event as Merritt eased to victory on the final leg. A brilliant final leg of 44.05 by 18 year-old Javon Francis ensued silver for Jamaica by just 0.02 from Russia. Three Borlée brothers ran for Belgium, with Jonathan running a second leg 44.1 and Kévin a final leg 43.90 to qualify in 3:00.81; Kevin's 44.04 was the fastest for any team in the final.

20 Kilometres Walk (11th)

1. Aleksandr Ivanov RUS	1:20:58
2. Chen Ding CHN	1:21:09
3. Miguel Angel López ESP	1:21:21
4. João Vieira POR	1:22:05
5. Denis Strelkov RUS	1:22:06
6. Takumi Saito JPN	1:22:09
7. Ruslan Dmytrenko UKR	1:22:14
8. Iñaki Gómez CAN	1:22:21
9. Christopher Linke GER	1:22:36
10. Kim Hyun-sub KOR	1:22:50
11. Dane Bird-Smith AUS	1:23:06
12. Yusuke Suzuki JPN	1:23:20
13. Jaime Quiyuch GUA	1:23:24
14. Matteo Giupponi ITA	1:23:27
15. Andriy Kovenko UKR	1:23:46

IVANOV WAS PERHAPS the most surprising gold medallist in Moscow and at 20 became the youngest winner of this event; he set a pb despite steamy, hot weather (29°C) and came through in the second half after being 14 sec behind halfway leader Suzuki 40:34. At 15k Ivanov, Chen and Érick Barrondo were 22 sec ahead of López, but Barrondo was disqualified in the 18th kilometre. 53 men finished and 5 were disqualified (including also Wang Zhen) and another 5 did not finish.

50 Kilometres Walk (14th)

1. Robert Heffernan IRL		3:37.56
2, Mikhail Ryzhov RUS		3:38:58
3. Jared Tallent AUS		3:40:03
4. Igor Hlavan UKR		3:40:39
5. Matej Tóth SVK		3:41:07
6. Grzegorz Sudol POL		3:41:20
7. Ivan Noskov RUS		3:41:36
8. Lukasz Nowak POL		3:43:38
9. Takayuki Tanii JPN		3:44:26
10. Yohann Diniz FRA		3:45:18
11. Hiroki Arai JPN		3:45:56
12. Jesús Ángel García ESP		3:46:44
13. Sergiy Budza UKR		3:47:36
14. Ivan Trotskiy BLR		3:47:52
15. Marco De Luca ITA		3:48:05

AFTER THREE CHAMPIONSHIPS fourth places, Heffernan came good at the age of 35 in a time that was just 2 sec outside his Irish record. He shared fifth place for the first 20k, but came from being 16 sec down at 10k and 22 sec at 20k to share the lead with Sudol at halfway after a 21:36 5k split and went on to 1:47:22 for the second half after 1:50:34 for the first half. Crucial were Heffernan's 21:29 and 21:18 splits from 30k to 40k, at which point Ryzhov was 2 sec behind but then a big gap to the rest. Heffernan's next 5k in 21:22 opened up an 18 sec lead and he stretched that to over a minute with a final 21:30. Tallent's bronze was his fifth global champs medal. Fourteen walkers achieved pbs as 36 went inside 4 hours, second only in depth to the London Olympics. Jesús Ángel García, the 1993 champion, worked his way through the field to finish 12th in his 11th World Championship, setting a men's record and tying the overall record set by Portuguese walker Susana Feitor. 46 finished from 60 starters.

Women

100 Metres (h 11th, sf, F 12th -0.3)

1. Shelly-Ann Fraser-Pryce JAM	10.71
2. Murielle Ahouré CIV	10.93
3. Carmelita Jeter USA	10.94
4. English Gardner USA	10.97
5. Kerron Stewart JAM	10.97
6. Blessing Okagbare NGR	11.04
7. Alexandria Anderson USA	11.10
8. Octavious Freeman USA	11.16

FRASER-PRYCE, SPORTING black and pink hair, regained her title by 0.22 sec, easily the biggest World 100m winning margin. Gardner started just the fastest but was caught by F-P at 20m and was passed in the closing 10m by Ahouré and Jeter. Gardner broke 11 secs with 10.94 in her heat and four women did so in the

semis: Fraser-Pryce winning the first in 10.87 from Stewart 10.97 after Jeter and Ahouré had run 10.95 in the second.

200 Metres (h, sf 15th, F 16th -0.3)

1. Shelly-Ann Fraser-Pryce JAM	22.17
2. Murielle Ahouré CIV	22.32
3. Blessing Okagbare NGR	22.32
4. Shaunae Miller BAH-J	22.74
5. Jeneba Tarmoh USA	22.78
6. Charonda Williams USA	22.81
7. Mariya Ryemyen UKR	22.84
dnf. Allyson Felix USA	–

FRASER-PRYCE CELEBRATED her sprint double while Felix, seeking a fourth World 200m title, lay writhing on the curve after c.40m, victim of a tear of her right medial hamstring. Ahouré just held off the fast-finishing Okagbare for the silver. Felix ran fastest in heats 22.59 and semis 22.30.

400 Metres (h 10th, sf 11th, F 12th)

1. Christine Ohuruogu GBR	49.41
2. Amantle Montsho BOT	49.41
3. Antonina Krivoshapka RUS	49.78
4. Stephenie Ann McPherson JAM	49.99
5. Natasha Hastings USA	50.30
6. Francena McCorory USA	50.68
7. Kseniya Ryzhova RUS	50.98
8. Novlene Williams-Mills JAM	51.49

OHURUOGU, THE 2009 champion, was fastest in the heats and Montsho, the 2011 champion, in the semis, heading six women (the eventual 1-6 in the final) under 50 secs with 49.56 as the other semi was won by Ohuruogu 49.75 and McCorory 49.86. In the final Hastings in lane 3 went out fast, as did Montsho in lane 5, and between them Ohuruogu was drawn to a slightly quicker 200m than usual, but was 7th in 23.8 behind McCorory 23.3, Montsho 23.4, Hastings and Krivoshapka 23.5. At 300m Montsho led in 35.7 from McCorory 35.7, Krivoishapka 36.0, Hastings and Ohuruogu 36.1. Montsho ran the last 100m in 13.7 but Ohuruogu's long stride never faltered and she drew almost level a metre or two from the end. Montsho, head up, crossed the finish line upright whereas Ohuruogu lunged forward and won by just 0.004 to take 0.02 off Kathy Cook's British record set at the 1984 Olympic Games.

800 Metres (h 15th, sf 16th, F 18th)

1. Eunice Sum KEN	1:57.38
2. Mariya Savinova RUS	1:57.80
3. Brenda Martinez USA	1:57.91
4. Alysia Montaño USA	1:57.95
5. Yekaterina Poistogova RUS	1:58.05
6. Ajee' Wilson USA-J	1:58.21
7. Nataliya Lupu UKR	1:59.79
8. Lenka Masná CZE	2:00.59

MONTAÑO CHARGED AHEAD in each round, with opening laps of 57.02 in her heat

(1:59.47) and 56.33 in her semi (1:58.92) before blazing through 200m in 26.91 (from Sum 27.58) and 400m in 56.12, well ahead of Sum 57.16 and Masná 57.57. That big lead was maintained through 600m 1:26.49 from Sum 1:27.60, Savinova 1:27.89 and Martinez 1:28.06. Entering the final straight Montaño's lead over Sum was down to 3m with Savinova a close third, and inevitably she began to run out of gas and was passed by the other two and, just before the line, by Martinez as Sum drove hard for the gold medal. Wilson ran a North American junior record in sixth place.

1500 Metres (h 11th, sf 13th, F 15th)

1. Abeba Aregawi	SWE	4:02.67
2. Jennifer Simpson	USA	4:02.99
3. Hellen Obiri	KEN	4:03.86
4. Hannah England	GBR	4:04.98
5. Faith Kipyegon	KEN-J	4:05.08
6. Yekaterina Sharmina	RUS	4:05.49
7. Zoe Buckman	AUS	4:05.77
8. Genzebe Dibaba	ETH	4:05.99
9. Nancy Langat	KEN	4:06.01
10. Mary Cain	USA-Y	4:07.19
11. Siham Hilali	MAR	4:09.16
12. Yelena Korobkina	RUS	4:10.18

AREGAWI WAS A clear favourite and won with a 58.84 last lap, chased hard by defending champion Simpson for Sweden's first ever medal, let alone win, in a middle distance World Champs race. Obiri nipped past on the inside to take the bronze. 17 year-old Cain, who had skipped the World Youths Champs, did well, with 4:05.21 in her semi, to make the final.

5000 Metres (h 14th, F 17th)

1. Meseret Defar	ETH	14:50.19
2. Mercy Cherono	KEN	14:51.22
3. Almaz Ayana	ETH	14:51.33
4. Viola Kibiwot	KEN	15:01.67
5. Buze Diriba	ETH-J	15:05.38
6. Molly Huddle	USA	15:05.73
7. Shannon Rowbury	USA	15:06.10
8. Susan Kuijken	NED	15:14.70
9. Yelena Nagovitsyna	RUS	15:24.83
10. Dolores Checa	ESP	15:30.42
11. Tejitu Daba	BRN	15:33.89
12. Kim Conley	USA	15:36.58
13. Karoline Bjerkeli Grøvdal	NOR	15:48.87
14. Dominika Nowakowska	POL	15:58.26
15. Jackie Areson	AUS	16:08.32

AFTER HEATS, IN which Defar was fastest with 15:22.94, the final was run at a very slow pace through kilometres of 3:10.78, 3:02.24 and 3:04.33 before Ayana took the lead at 3000m 9:18.38. Shadowed by Defar, she ran the fourth kilometre in 2:50.86 and still led at the bell from Defar, Cherono and Kibiwot. Defar then raced away with her usual terrific last lap – 59.82 with 29.31 for the last 200m – and had run 2:40.90

for the last kilometre as she added this title to that won in 2007 and her two Olympic wins at 5000m.

10,000 Metres (11th)

1. Tirunesh Dibaba	ETH	30:43.35
2. Gladys Cherono	KEN	30:45.17
3. Belaynesh Oljira	ETH	30:46.98
4. Emily Chebet	KEN	30:47.02
5. Hitomi Niiya	JPN	30:56.70
6. Shitaye Eshete	BRN	31:13.79
7. Sally Chepyego	KEN	31:22.11
8. Shalane Flanagan	USA	31:34.83
9. Yeshaneh Ababel	ETH	32:02.09
10. Christelle Daunay	FRA	32:04.44
11. Marisol Romero	MEX	32:16.36
12. Jordan Hasay	USA	32:17.93
13. Ana Dulce Félix	POR	32:36.73
14. Amy Hastings	USA	32:51.19
15. Karolina Jarzynska	POL	32:54.15

DIBABA TOOK HER record at 10,000m on the track to 11 wins in 11 races and this was her fifth World gold medal at 5000m or 10,000m. Flanagan led through 1000m 3:07.57, 6:13.92 and 9:20.85, before Niiya took over to lead metronomically through 5000m 15:30.38 and 9000m 29:54.12, by when only four others had kept up with her. Dibaba launched her finishing drive with 500m to go and ran the last lap in 59.96 and Cherono overtook Oljira with 300m to go. Chebet missed bronze by just 0.04 as the plucky Japanese could only come in fifth. 17 of 19 runners finished.

Marathon (10th)

1. Edna Kiplagat	KEN	2:25:44
2. Valeria Straneo	ITA	2:25:58
3. Kayoko Fukushi	JPN	2:27:45
4. Ryoko Kizaki	JPN	2:31:28
5. Alessandra Aguilar	ESP	2:32:38
6. Emma Quaglia	ITA	2:34:16
7. Madai Pérez	MEX	2:34:23
8. Kim Hye-gyong	PRK	2:35:49
9. Deena Kastor	USA	2:36:12
10. Susan Partridge	GBR	2:36:24
11. Jessiva Trengrove	AUS	2:37:11
12. Diana Lobacevske	LTU	2:37:48
13. Aberu Kebede	ETH	2:38:04
14. Kim Hye-song	PRK	2:38:28
15. Lishan Dula	BRN	2:38:47

TIMES FOR THE leading runners were remarkably good considering the hot (27°C) and muggy weather from the 2pm start and 24 of the 70 starters failed to finish. The first half was run in 1:12:59, with Straneo responsible for pushing on, but after that two favourites Lucy Kabuu (24th) and Aberu Kebede (13th) fell back. At 30k Straneo led in 1:44:00 by 1 sec from Melkamu and Kiplagat and 6 sec from Fukushi. Melkamu dropped back from 32k and did not finish, as Straneo ran 17:05 for 5k to 35k and 17:07 to 2:18:22 at 40k, but soon after that Kiplagat ran ahead to retain her title by a

14 sec margin from Straneo, who at 37 became the oldest ever World Champs medallist in an individual running event.

3000m Steeplechase (h 10th, F 13th)

1. Milcah Chemos Cheywa KEN	9:11.65
2. Lydia Chepkurui KEN	9:12.55
3. Sofia Assefa ETH	9:12.84
4. Hiwot Ayalew ETH	9:15.25
5. Etenesh Diro ETH	9:16.97
6. Hyvin Jepkemoi KEN	9:22.05
7. Valentyna Zhudina UKR	9:33.73
8. Antje Möldner-Schmidt GER	9:34.06
9. Gesa Felicitas Krause GER	9:37.11
10. Eilish McColgan GBR	9:37.33
11. Diana Martín ESP	9:38.30
12. Natalya Gorchakova RUS	9:38.57
13. Anuta Bobocel ROU	9:53.35
14. Silvia Danekova BUL	9:58.57
15. Salima El Ouali Alami MAR	10:08.36

ALTHOUGH THIS EVENT was only introduced to the Worlds in 2005, this was the first time that an East African had won the title, as they took the first six places here and Chemos lived up to her billing as favourite. She won her heat in 9:36.36 before Diro won a much faster second heat in 9:24.02, and, after Ayalew had run a quick opening kilometre of 3:01.72 in the final, led for most of the way through a slower second kilometre to 6:11.38 and a final one of 3:00.29, aided perhaps by the fact that Ayalew hit a hurdle and fell with just over 800m to go, although she got up and finished hard for the bronze medal.

100 Metres Hurdles (h 16th, sf, F 17th -0.6)

1. Brianna Rollins USA	12.44
2. Sally Pearson AUS	12.50
3. Tiffany Porter GBR	12.55
4. Dawn Harper-Nelson USA	12.59
5. Queen Harrison USA	12.73
6. Angela Whyte CAN	12.78
7. Cindy Billaud FRA	12.84
8. Yuliya Kondakova RUS	12.86

ROLLINS WAS NOT fazed by this being her first major international championship as she was fastest in the heats with 12.55, won her semi in 12.54, with Pearson 12.50 and Porter 12.63 winning the others, and took the gold medal in beautiful style in 12.44 despite being very slowly away (0.263 reaction time) and nearly 2m down to Pearson at the first hurdle. Porter ran a pb to take the bronze ahead of Harper-Nelson.

400 Metres Hurdles (h 12th, sf 13th, F 15th)

1. Zuzana Hejnová CZE	52.83
2. Dalilah Muhammad USA	54.09
3. Lashinda Demus USA	54.27
4. Anna Titimets UKR	54.72
5. Eilidh Child GBR	54.86
6. Anna Yaroshchuk UKR	55.01
7. Perri Shakes-Drayton GBR	56.25
8. Nickiesha Wilson JAM	57.34

HEJNOVÁ WAS COMPLETELY dominant, winning her semi in 53.52 and streaking to a world-leading and Czech record time of 52.83 in the final. She had a winning margin of 1.26 sec from Muhammad that beat the previous event record of 0.93. Shakes-Drayton had been fastest in the heats with 54.42 and won her semi in 53.92, but sustained an injury to her left knee early in the final. Kaliese Spencer, fourth at the last two World Champs and the 2012 Olympics, won her heat easily in 54.10 only to be disqualified for a trail leg infringement, while in the same heat Georganne Moline fell. Olympic champion Antyukh was 6th in her semi in 55.55.

High Jump (Q 1.95 15th, F 17th)

1. Svetlana Shkolina RUS	2.03
2. Brigetta Barrett USA	2.00
3= Anna Chicherova RUS	1.97
3= Ruth Beitia ESP	1.97
5. Emma Green Tregaro SWE	1.97
6. Justyna Kasprzycka POL	1.97
7= Kamila Stepaniuk POL	1.93
7= Alessia Trost ITA	1.93
9= Irina Gordeyeva RUS	1.93
9= Zheng Xingjuan CHN	1.93
11. Levern Spencer LCA	1.89
12. Airine Palsyte LTU	1.89
nh. Marie-Laurence Jungfleisch GER	–

TWO WOMEN CLEARED 2.00, both at the first attempt as four others went out at that height, Barrett had a clean card while Shkolina had a failure at 1.93. Then the medals were settled as Shkolina equalled her pb of 2.03 on her first try and Barrett failed twice at that height and once at 2.05. 13 women made the final by clearing 1.92 in qualifying.

Pole Vault (Q 4.60m 11th, F 13th)

1. Yelena Isinbayeva RUS	4.89
2. Jennifer Suhr USA	4.82
3. Yarisley Silva CUB	4.82
4. Silke Spiegelburg GER	4.75
5= Anastasiya Savchenko RUS	4.65
5= Fabiana Murer BRA	4.65
7. Angelina Zhuk-Krasnova RUS	4.65
8= Lisa Ryzih GER	4.55
8= Jirina Svobodová CZE	4.55
10. Kristina Gadschiew GER	4.45
11. Li Ling CHN	4.45
12. Marion Lotout FRA	4.45

TO THE DELIGHT of the home crowd Isinbayeva regained the title she had won in 2005 and 2007. 12 women cleared 4.55 in qualifying to make the final, in which seven women were still in at 4.75. Three took their leave, and medals were decided at 4.82, cleared by Suhr and Isinbayeva on their first attempts and by Silva on her third, with Spiegelburg failing. Suhr led as Isinbayeva had a failure on her opening

4.65, but Isinbayeva went over 4.89 on her first attempt for the gold. The heights for third and fourth equalled the best ever for those positions as did seventh (and in qualifying 10th to 12th), and 17 women over 4.45 in qualifying was a record.

Long Jump (Q 6.75m 10th, F 11th)

1.	Brittney Reese USA	7.01/0.2
2.	Blessing Okagbare NGR	6.99/0.2
3.	Ivana Spanovic SRB	6.82/0.1
4.	Olga Sudarova BLR	6.82/-0.1
5.	Olga Kucherenko RUS	6.81/0.1
6.	Shara Proctor GBR	6.79/0.4
7.	Darya Klishina RUS	6.76/-0.1
8.	Tori Polk USA	6.73/0.2
9.	Yelena Sokolova RUS	6.65/0.2
10.	Erica Jarder SWE	6.47/0.3
11.	Janay DeLoach Soukup USA	6.44/0.1
12.	Sosthene Moguenara GER	6.42/0.3

AS AT THE 2012 Olympics Reese managed only 6.57 in qualifying to scrape into the final as Proctor 6.85 and Okagbare 6.83 had the best jumps. It was different in the final, however, as Reese jumped 7.01 in the second round, backed by 6.95 in the fifth, but was pressed hard by Okagbare, who led in the first round with 6.89 and ended with 6.99 and 6.95. Third place changed several times before Spanovic won the bronze on count-back with a Serbian record.

Triple Jump (Q 14.30m 13th, F 15th)

1.	Caterine Ibargüen COL	14.85/0.2
2.	Yekaterina Koneva RUS	14.81/0.9
3.	Olga Saladuha UKR	14.65/0.9
4.	Kimberly Williams JAM	14.62/0.6
5.	Mabel Gay CUB	14.45/1.2
6.	Hanna Knyazyeva-Minenko ISR	14.33/0.1
7.	Anna Pyatykh RUS	14.29/0.5
8.	Irina Gumenyuk RUS	14.15/0.8
9.	Snezana Rodic SLO	14.13/0.2
10.	Anna Jagaciak POL	13.95/0.2
11.	Dana Veldáková SVK	13.84/0.8
12.	Athanasía Pérra GRE	13.75/0.7

SALADUHA, 14.69, AND Ibargüen, 14.52, led the qualifiers, but Saladuha could only manage 14.65 for third in the final as first Koneva jumped 14.81 (14.94 from take-off to landing) and then Ibargüen 14.89 (also 14.94 in all), all these jumps coming in the second round. Ibargüen, who won Colombia's first gold, also had 14.83 in round four.

Shot (Q 18.65m 11th, F 12th)

1.	Valerie Adams NZL	20.88
2.	Christina Schwanitz GER	20.41
3.	Gong Lijiao CHN	19.95
4.	Michelle Carter USA	19.94
5.	Yevgeniya Kolodko RUS	19.81
6.	Li Ling CHN	18.39
7.	Irina Tarasova RUS	18.37
8.	Tia Brooks USA	18.09
9.	Halyna Obleshchuk UKR	18.08
10.	Liu Xiangrong CHN	18.04
11.	Natalia Ducó CHI	18.02
12.	Alena Kopets BLR	17.70

ADAMS WAS A near certainty for the title, and she duly led the qualifying with 19.89 from Carter 19.76, and had the four best puts in the final, starting with 20.61 and improving to 20.88 in round three. Carter started with 19.92 and 19.94, before Gong took over second place with 19.95. Schwanitz had been fifth with 19.74 before delivering a big pb of 20.41 in the final round.

Discus (Q 63.00m 10th, F 11th)

1.	Sandra Perkovic CRO	67.99
2.	Mélina Robert-Michon FRA	66.28
3.	Yarelys Barrios CUB	64.96
4.	Nadine Müller GER	64.47
5.	Gia Lewis-Smallwood USA	64.23
6.	Tan Jian CHN	63.34
7.	Zaneta Glanc POL	62.90
8.	Denia Caballero CUB	62.80
9.	Zinaida Sendriute LTU	62.54
10.	Dani Samuels AUS	62.42
11.	Yaimé Pérez CUB	62.39
12,	Rocío Comba ARG	59.83

PERKOVIC HAD THREE valid throws in the final, all over 67.50, a metre and a half ahead of the best of runner-up Robert-Michon, who threw 65.13 and 65.08 in rounds 3 and 4 and ended with a French record 66.28. Sendriute was best in qualifying with 64.16.

Hammer (Q 73.00m 14th, F 16th)

1.	Tatyana Lysenko RUS	78.80*
2.	Anita Wlodarczyk POL	78.46
3.	Zhang Wenxiu CHN	75.58
4.	Wang Zheng CHN	74.90
5.	Anna Bulgakova RUS	74.62
6.	Yipsi Moreno CUB	74.16
7.	Oksana Kondratyeva RUS	72.76
8.	Éva Orbán HUN	72.70
9.	Jeneva McCall USA	72.65
10.	Amanda Bingson USA	72.56
11.	Bianca Perie ROU	71.25
12.	Gulfiya Khanafeyeva RUS	71.07

THERE WAS A high standard throughout with the best ever marks for 2nd, 10th and 12th places, and, in qualifying, led by Wlodarczyk 76.18 (best ever for a preliminary round), for 14th and 18th (Betty Heidler a surprise non-qualifier at 68.83). In the final Lysenko produced mighty throws of 77.58 and 77.33 in the first two rounds, to which the closest response was a pb of 74.90 by Wang. However, from 74.21 for 4th Wlodarczyk stunned the partisan crowd when she took the lead in the third round with 77.79. Then in the fourth round Lysenko threw 78.80 for a Championship and Russian record, to which Wlodarczyk immediately responded with a Polish record 78.46. Zhang took bronze with 75.08 and 75.58 in rounds 3 and 4.

Javelin (Q 61.50m 16th, F 18th)

1. Christina Obergföll GER	69.05	
2. Kimberley Mickle AUS	66.60	
3. Mariya Abakumova RUS	65.09	
4. Linda Stahl GER	64.78	
5. Kathryn Mitchell AUS	63.77	
6. Sunette Viljoen RSA	63.58	
7. Viktoriya Sudarushkina RUS	62.21	
8. Li Lingwei CHN	61.30	
9. Tatjana Jelaca SRB	60.81	
10. Sofi Flinck SWE-J	59.52	
11. Vira Rebryk UKR	58.33	
12. Nadeeka Lakmali SRI	58.16	

AFTER FIVE SILVERS and a bronze in major championships Obergföll at last won gold. Abakumova threw 69.09 for the best ever mark in a qualifying competition, from Mickle pb 65.73, and led in the first round of the final with 65.09 from Stahl 64.78 and Obergföll 64.63. In round two Mickle took the lead with another pb 66.60 before Obergföll settled the issue with 69.05. After that Abakumova's best was 64.33 as she tried desperately to capture her top form.

Heptathlon (12/13th)

1. Anna Melnychenko UKR	6586	
2. Brianne Theisen Eaton CAN	6530	
3. Dafne Schippers NED	6477	
4. Claudia Rath GER	6462	
5. Katarina Johnson-Thompson GBR		6449
6. Sharon Day USA	6407	
7. Eliska Klucinová CZE	6332	
8. Antoinette Nana Djimou FRA	6326	
9. Karolina Tyminska POL	6270	
10. Nadine Broersen NED	6224	
11. Laura Ikauniece LAT	6159	
12. Yorgelis Rodríguez CUB-J	6148	
13. Ellen Sprunger SUI	6081	
14. Nafissatou Thiam BEL-J	6070	
15. Györgyi Farkas-Zsivoczky HUN	6067	

MISSING THE 2011 1-2 Chernova and Ennis-Hill, the standard was lower this year but Melnychenko took advantage of that to add 141 points to her pb with a consistent series of performances and seven of the top 8 set pbs. There was a remarkable final 800m as the first eight set pbs, many by huge margins, such as Schippers from 2:15.52 to 2:08.62 to hang on to third place and set a Dutch record. Rath improved from 2:08.68 to 2:06.43 to fall 15 points short of bronze and in turn was only 13 ahead of Johnson-Thompson who set her fourth consecutive pb, 2:07.64 from a previous best 2:10.76 – she improved overall by 182 points. Top earlier marks included 1.92 high jump by Thiam and 22.84 for 200m by Schippers on a first day in which Melnychenko led with 3912 from Schippers 3837, Day 3837 and Theisen 3810.

4 x 100 Metres Relay (h & F 18th)

1. JAM	41.29*	Russell, Stewart, Calvert, Fraser-Pryce (heat: 4. Brooks)
2. USA	42.75	Tarmoh, Anderson, Gardner, Freeman
3. GBR	42.87	Asher-Smith, Nelson, Lewis, H Jones
4. GER	42.90	Kwadwo, Weit, Pinto, Sailer
5. RUS	42.93	Belkina, Rusakova, Savlinis, Bolsun
6. CAN	43.28	Emmanuel, Hyacinthe, Davis, Bingham
dnf. BRA	-	E dos Santos, Silva, Krasucki, Gomes
dq. FRA	(42.73)	Distel-Bonnet, Ikuesan, Soumaré, Akakpo

THERE WERE FAST heat wins from USA 41.82 and Jamaica 41.87, with Britain winning the other in 42.75. Missing Carmelita Jeter and Allyson Felix, the US bungled the second change and Fraser-Pryce brought Jamaica home in the second fastest time ever recorded. Their 1.46 margin was the greatest ever in World/Olympic competition. France originally placed second in 42.73 (much slower than their heat time of 42.25) but were subsequently disqualified after a British protest. Brazil set a South American record of 42.29 in their heat but failed to finish in the final,

4 x 400 Metres Relay (h 16th, F 17th)

1. RUS	3:20.19	Gushchina 51.0e, Firova 49.6e, Ryzhova 50.23, Krivoshapka 49.40 (Antukh ran in ht)
2. USA	3:20.41	Beard 50.6, Hastings 50.1, Spencer 50.4, McCorory 49.25 (Atkins ran in ht)
3. GBR	3:22.61	Child 51.9, Cox 50.3, Adeoye 51.01, Ohuruogu 49.43
4. FRA	3:24.21	Gayot 51.54, Guion-Firmin 50.26, Hurtis 51.74, Guei 50.67
5. UKR	3:27.38	Prystyupa 52.5e, Lyakhova 51.2e, Logvynenko 52.50, Pygyda 51.18
6. NGR	3:27.57	Omotosho 52.4e, P George 51.2e, Abogunloko 54.29, R George 49.67
7. ROU	3:28.40	Pastor 52.7e, Lavric 51.8e, Belgyan 53.08, Razor 50.85
dq. ITA	(3:27.39)	Bazzoni 52.2e, Milani 51.4e, Spacca 52.66, Grenot 51.13

IN THE FINAL the lead alternated as Beard led, then Firova took over on the second leg. Ryzhova held that lead for Russia and Krivoshapka, who had gained a vital 3m at the final change, grimly held off McCorory for victory. Britain were an isolated third.

20 Kilometres Walk (13th)

1. Yelena Lashmanova RUS	1:27:08	
2. Anisya Kirdyapkina RUS	1:27:11	
3. Liu Hong CHN	1:28:10	
4. Sun Huanhuan CHN	1:28:32	
5. Elisa Rigaudo ITA	1:28:41	
6. Beatriz Pascual ESP	1:29:00	
7. Anezka Drahotová CZE-J	1:29:05	

8. Ana Cabecinha POR — 1:29:17
9. Júlia Takács ESP — 1:29:25
10. Eleonora Giorgi ITA — 1:30:01
11. Inês Henriques POR — 1:30:28
12. Lyudmyla Olyanovska UKR — 1:30:48
13. Antonella Palmisano ITA — 1:30:50
14. Mayra Herrera GUA — 1:30:59
15. Qieyang Shenjie CHN — 1:31:15

LASHAMANOVA, STILL ONLY 21, added to her series of major titles by walking final 5k splits of 21:27 and 20:15 after Drahotová and Rigaudo had led by six seconds at halfway in 45:20. Kirdyapkina went with her but after Lashmanova's 19th kilometre in 3:58 was actually well behind as they entered the stadium when Lashmanova was confused as to where the finish was and lost a lot of ground to her rival. The third Russian Vera Sokolova, in third place, was disqualified at the stadium. 57 women finished from 61 starters.

Prize money

Individual Events: Winner: US $60,000, 2nd $30,000, 3rd $20,000, 4th $15,000, 5th $10,000, 6th $6000, 7th $5000, 8th $4000.
Relays: Winners $80,000, 2nd $40,000, 3rd $20,000, 4th $16,000, 5th $12,000, 6th $8000, 7th $6000, 8th $4000.

2013 CHAMPIONSHIPS

World Youth Championships

At Donetsk, Ukraine 10-14 July

Boys

100m 1. Ma Youxue CHN 10.35
(-0.4) 2. Ojie Edoburun GBR 10.35
3. Reynier Mena CUB 10.37

200m 1. Michael O'Hara JAM 20.63
(-1.0) 2. Vitor Hugo dos Santos BRA 20.67
3. Reynier Mena CUB 20.79

400m 1. Martin Manley JAM 45.89
2. Ryan Clark USA 46.46
3. Alex Sampao KEN 46.78

800m 1. Alfred Kipketer KEN 1:48.01
2. Konstantin Tolokonnikov RUS 1:48.29
3. Kyle Langford GBR 1:48.32

1500m 1. Robert Kiptoo Biwott KEN 3:36.77*
2. Tesfu Tewelde ERI 3:42.14
3. Titus Kipruto Kibiego KEN 3:42.97

3000m 1. Yomif Kejelcha ETH 7:53.56
2. Vedic Kipkoech KEN 7:56.60
3. Alexander Mutiso Munyao KEN 7:56.86

2000mSt 1. Meresa Kassaye ETH 5:19.99*
2. Nicholas Bett KEN 5:20.92
3. Justus Kipkorir Lagat KEN 5:30.00

110mh 1. Jaheel Hyde JAM 13.13*
(-1.1) 2. Marlon Humphrey USA 13.24
91.4cm 3. Lu Yang CHN 13.33

400mh 1. Marvin Williams JAM 50.39
83.8cm 2. Wang Yang CHN 50.78
3. Kenneth Selmon USA 51.30

HJ 1. Woo Sang-hyeok KOR 2.20
2. Bai Jiaxu CHN 2.18
3. Christoffe Bryan JAM 2.16

PV 1. Harry Coppell GBR 5.25
2. Huang Bokei CHN 5.20
3. Lev Skorish ISR 5.10

LJ 1. Anatoliy Ryapolov RUS 7.79/0.7
2. Fang Yaoqing CHN 7.53/0.2
3. Isaiah Moore USA 7.53/0.1

TJ 1. Lázaro Martínez CUB 16.63/1.8*
2. Fang Yaoqing CHN 16.48/0.7
3. Dimitri Antonov GER 16.02/0.8

5kg SP 1. Patrick Müller GER 22.02
2. Henning Prüfer GER 21.94

1.5kg DT 3. Mohamed Hamza EGY 20.58
1. Matthew Denny AUS 67.54
2. Henning Prüfer GER 65.62
3. Cheng Yulong CHN 62.80

5kg HT 1. Matija Greguric CRO 79.38
2. Pavel Polyakov BLR 79.02
3. Matthew Denny AUS 78.67

JT 700g 1. Matija Muhar SLO 78.84
2. Norbert Rivasz-Tóth HUN 78.27
3. Pablo Bugallo ESP 76.63

Oct 1. Karsten Warholm NOR 6451
2. Feliks Shestopolov RUS 6260
3. Jan Dolezal CZE 6222

Medley R 1. JAM (W Williams, O'Hara, O Williams, Manley) 1:49.23*
2. USA 1:50.14
3. JPN 1:50.52

10,000W 1. Toshikazu Yamanishi JPN 41:53.80
2. Maksim Krasnov RUS 42:03.10
3. Diego García ESP 42:03.32

Girls

100m 1. Ky Westbrook USA 11.33
(-0.8) 2. Ariana Washington USA 11.40
3. Ángela Tenorio ECU 11.41

200m 1. Irene Ekelund ECU 22.92*
(-0.1) 2. Ángela Tenorio ECU 23.13
3. Ariana Washington USA 23.20

400m 1. Sabrina Bakare GBR 52.77
2. Olivia Baker USA 53.38
3. Tiffany James JAM 52.56

800m 1. Anita Hinriksdottir ISL 2:01.13*
2. Sara Dureti Edao ETH 2:03.25
3. Raevyn Rogers USA 2:03.32

1500m 1. Tigist Gashaw ETH 4:14.25
2. Dawit Seyoum ETH 4:15.51
3. Alexa Efraimson USA 4:16.07

3000m 1. Liiian Kasait Rengeruk KEN 8:58.74
2. Berhan Demiesa ETH 9:00.06
3. Silenat Yismaw ETH 9:01.63

2000mSt 1. Rosefline Chepngetich KEN 6:14.60
2. Daisy Jepkemei KEN 6:15.12
3. Woynshet Ansa ETH 6:30.05

100mh 1. Yanique Thompson JAM 12.94*
(0.0) 2. Dior Hall USA 13.01
76.2cm 3. Mikiah Brisco USA 13.29

400mh	1. Helene Swanepoel RSA 58.08	**10,000m**	1. Stephen Mokoka RSA 28:45.96
	2. Tia Adana Belle BAR 58.42		2. Anatoliy Rybakov RUS 28:47.27
	3. Lisa-Marie Jacoby GER 58.75		3. Yevgeniy Rybakov RUS 28:47.28
HJ	1. Eleanor Patterson AUS 1.88	**Half Mar**	1. Gladwin Mzazi RSA 63:37
	2. Erika Furlani ITA 1.82		2. Stephen Mokoka RSA 63:37
	3= Ghizlane Sbia MAR 1.79		3. Shogo Nakamura JPN 64:21
	3= Julia du Plessis RSA 1.79	**3000mSt**	1. Ilgizar Safiulin RUS 8:32.53
PV	1. Robeilys Peinado VEN 4.25		2. Sebastián Martos ESP 8:37.94
	2. Alyona Lutkovskaya RUS 4.15		3. Patrick Nasti ITA 8:38.41
	3. Krista Obizayeva LAT 4.05	**110mh**	1. Eddie Lovett ISV 13.43
LJ	1. Florentina Marincu ROU 6.42/0.3	(1.7)	2. Konstantin Shabanov RUS 13.46
	2. Keturah Orji USA 6.39/1.2		3. Sergey Shubenkov RUS 13.47
	3. Natalia Chacinska POL 6.22/0.4	**400mh**	1. Martin Kucera SVK 49.79
TJ	1. Florentina Marincu ROU 13.75/0.8		2. Amadou Ndiaye SEN 49.90
	2. Wang Rong CHN 13.69/0.5		3. Ian Dewhurst AUS 49.96
	3. Keturah Orji USA 13.69/0.8	**HJ**	1. Sergey Mudrov RUS 2.31
SP 3kg	1. Emel Dereli TUR 20.14*		2. Andriy Protsenko UKR 2.31
	2. Alyona Bugakova RUS 18.60		3. Wang Yu CHN 2.28
	3. Ashlie Blake USA 17.57	**PV**	1. Sam Kendricks USA 5.60
DT	1. Xie Yuchen CHN 56.34*		2. Seito Yamamoto JPN 5.60
	2. Claudine Vita GER 52.59		3. Nikita Filippov KAZ 5.50
	3. Liang Xinjun CHN 51.50	**LJ**	1. Luis Rivera MEX 8.46/1.3
HT 3kg	1. Réka Gyurátz HUN 73.20*		2. Aleksandr Menkov RUS 8.42/0.9
	2. Helga Völgyi HUN 71.95		3. Marcos Chuva POR 8.15/1.2
	3. Valeriya Semenkova UKR 68.62	**TJ**	1. Viktor Kuznyetsov UKR 17.01/1.0
JT 500g	1. Mackenzie Little AUS 61.47*		2. Aleksey Fyodorov RUS 16.89w/2.2
	2. Yulenmis Aguilar CUB 59.94		3. Yevgeniy Ektov KAZ 16.57/0.8
	3. Anete Kocina LAT 54.26	**SP**	1. Aleksandr Lesnoy RUS 20.30
Hep	1. Celina Leffler GER 5747		2. Indrajit Singh IND 19.70
Yth imps	2. Emma Stenlöf SWE 5590		3. Valeriy Kokoyev RUS 19.65
	3. Louisa Grauvogel GER 5581	**DT**	1. Ronald Julião BRA 63.54
Medley R	1. USA (Hall, Westbrook, Rogers, Baker) 2:05.15		2. Giovanni Faloci ITA 62.23
			3. Gleb Sidorchenko RUS 62.16
	2. IVB 2:07.40	**HT**	1. Pawel Fajdek POL 79.99
	3. JPN 2:07.61		2. Marcel Lomnicky SVK 78.73
5000mW	1. Olga Shargina RUS 22:13.91*		3. Sergey Litvinov RUS 78.08
	2. Momoko Mizota JPN 22:42.77	**JT**	1. Dmitriy Tarabin RUS 83.11
	3. Noemi Stella ITA 22:48.95.		2. Robert Oosthuizen RSA 81.63

Medal table leaders: JAM 6-0-2, KEN 4-3-4, ETH 3-3-2, AUS 3-0-1, USA 2-7-8, CHN 2-6-3, RUS 2-5-0, GER 2-3-3, GBR 2-1-1, ROU 2-0-0, HUN 1-2-0, CUB & JPN 1-1-2, SWE 1-1-0
22 nations won gold, 37 medals of any colour.

World University Games

At Kazan, Russia 7-12 July
Men

100m	1. Anaso Jobodwana RSA 10.10		3. Fatih Avan TUR 81.24
(0.5)	2. Ryota Yamagata JPN 10.21	**Dec**	1. Thomas Van der Plaetsen BEL 8164
	3. Hua Wilfried Koffi CIV 10.21		2. Sergey Sviridov RUS 7939
200m	1. Anaso Jobodwana RSA 20.00w		3. Brent Newdick NZL 7611
(2,4)	2. Rasheed Dwyer JAM 20.23	**20kmW**	1. Andrey Krivov RUS 1:20:47
	3. Shota Iizuka JPN 20.33		2. Ruslan Dmytrenko UKR 1:20:54
400m	1. Vladimir Krasnov RUS 45.49		3. Denis Strelkov RUS 1:21:32
	2. Anderson Henriques BRA 45.50	**4x100m**	1. UKR (Perestyuk, Smelyk, Bodrov, Korzh) 38.56
	3. Nicholas Maitland JAM 45.63		
800m	1. Nijel Amos BOT 1:46.53		2. JPN (Yamagata, Hara, Yonaguni, Iizuka) 39.12
	2. Jozef Repcik SVK 1:47.30		
	3. Andreas Vojta AUT 1:47.31		3. POL (Adamski, Kuc, Zaczek, Krynski) 39.29
1500m	1. Valentin Smirnov RUS 3:39.39		
	2. Jeremy Rae CAN 3:39.45	**4x400m**	1. RUS (Dyldin, Buryak, Kashefrazov, Krasnov) 3:03.70
	3. Jerry Motsau RSA 3:39.51		
5000m	1. Hayle Ibrahimov AZE 13:35.89		2. CAN (Ayesu-Attah, Rodney, Robertson, Harper) 3:05.26
	2. Paul Chelimo KEN 13:37.09		
	3. Richard Ringer GER 13:37.18		3. RSA (Conradie, de Swardt, Beneke, van Niekerk) 3:06.19
		Women	
		100m	1. Aurieyall Scott USA 11.28
		(-0.2)	2. Lina Grincikaité LTU 11.32
			3. Andreea Ograzeanu ROU 11.41
		200m	1. Kimberley Hyacinthe CAN 22.78
		(1.6)	2. Hanna-Maari Latvala FIN 22.98
			3. Andreea Ograzeanu ROU 23.10
		400m	1. Kseniya Ustalova RUS 50.60

	2. Alena Tamkova RUS 51.17
	3. Anastacia Le-Roy JAM 51.72
800m	1. Margarita Mukasheva KAZ 1:58.96
	2. Yekaterina Kupina RUS 1:59.57
	3. Eglé Balciunaité LTU 1:59.82
1500m	1. Yekaterina Sharmina RUS 4:05.49
	2. Yelena Korobkina RUS 4:08.13
	3. Luiza Gega ALB 4:08.71
5000m	1. Olga Golovkina RUS 15:43.77
	2. Ayuko Suzuki JPN 15:51.47
	3. Mai Shoji JPN 16:11.90
	drugs dq (1) Roxana Bârcâ ROU 15:39.76
10,000m	1. Ayuko Suzuki JPN 32:54.17
	2. Alina Prokopyeva RUS 33:00.93
	3. Mai Tsuda JPN 33:14.59
HMar	1. Mai Tsuda JPN 73:12
	2. Alina Prokopyeva RUS 73:18
	3. Yukiko Okuono JPN 73:24
3000mSt	1. Yuliya Zaripova RUS 9:28.00
	2. Svitlana Shmidt UKR 9:40.41
	3. Gülcan Mingir TUR 9:45.88
100mh	1. Vashti Thomas USA 12.61
(1.8)	2. Alina Talay BLR 12.78
	3. Danielle Williams JAM 12.84
400mh	1. Hanna Titimets UKR 54.64
	2. Hanna Yaroshchuk UKR 54.77
	3. Irina Davydova RUS 54.79
HJ	1. Kamila Stepaniuk POL 1.96
	2. Mariya Kuchina RUS 1.96
	3. Anna Iljustsenko EST 1.94
PV	1. Anastasiya Savchenko RUS 4.60
	2. Martina Schultze GER 4.40
	3. Fanny Smets BEL 4.30
LJ	1. Darya Klishina RUS 6.90/0.3
	2. Yelena Sokolova RUS 6.73/-1.2
	3. Michelle Weitzel GER 6.56/-0.5
TJ	1. Yekaterina Koneva RUS 14.82/-0.2
	2. Anna Jagaciak POL 14.21/-0.4
	3. Carmen Toma ROU 14.14/0.2
SP	1. Irina Tarasova RUS 18.75
	2. Liu Xiangrong CHN 18.58
	3. Natalia Ducó CHI 17.96
DT	1. Vera Ganeyeva RUS 61.26
	2. Yelena Panova RUS 56.86
	3. Maryke Oberholzer RSA 54.09
HT	1. Jeneva McCall USA 73.75
	2. Oksana Kondratyeva RUS 72.22
	3. Mariya Bespalova RUS 69.20
	drugs dq (3). Zalina Marghieva MDA 71.10
JT	1. Mariya Abakumova RUS 65.12
	2. Viktoriya Sudarushkina RUS 62.68
	3. Elisabeth Eberl AUT 55.02
Hep	1. Tatyana Chernova RUS 6623
	2. Laura Ikauniece LAT 6321
	3. Györgyi Zsivoczky-Farkas HUN 6269
20kW	1. Anisya Kirdyapkina RUS 1:29:30
	2. Irina Yumanova RUS 1:30:41
	3. Lina Bikulova RUS 1:32:30
4x100m	1. UKR (Povh, Pohrebnyak, Ryemyen, Pyatachenko) 42.77
	2. USA (V Thomas, Scott, J Barber, T Johnson) 43.54
	3. POL (Popowicz, Wedler, Ptak, Koldej) 43.81
4x400m	1. RUS (Tamkova, Kotlyarova, Renzhina, Ustalova) 3:26.61

2. CAN (Montcalm, Wells, Croft, Brown) 3:32.93
3. RSA (van der Merwe, Nienaber, Palframan, Ebersohn) 3:36.05

IAAF World Race Walking Challenge

Results of walks at 14 meetings qualified. Walkers needed to compete at three or more of these to qualify and positions were based on the best positions from these races, with a sliding scale of points from three categories. Prize money: 1st $30,000, 2nd $20,000, 3rd $14,000, 4th $9000, 5th $7000, 6th $6000, 7th $4500, 8th $4000, 9th $3000, 10th $2000, 11th $1000, 12th $500.

Overall placings: 1. Jared Tallent 34, 2. João Vieira 28, 3. Matej Tóth 26, 4. Robert Heffernan 20, 5. Dane Bird-Smith 20, 6. Erik Tysse 18, Women – 1. Yelena Lashmanova 38, 2. Inês Henriques 34. 3. Ana Cabecinha 23, 4. Lucie Pelantová 17, 5, Mónica Equihua 16, 6, Julia Takacs 16.

IAAF Hammer Throw Challenge

Final standings, top three meetings to score. Prize money from $30,000 for 1st to $500 for 12th.

Men: 1. Pawel Fajdek 246.23m, 2. Krisztián Pars HUN 244.17, 3. Lukas Melich 239.80, 4. Dilshod Nazarov 236.22, 5. Primoz Kozmus 234.89, 6. Marcel Lomnicky 233.63, 7. Szymon Ziólkowski 233.07, 8. Oleksiy Sokyrskyy 229.71, 9. Markus Esser 229.28, 10. Sergey Litvinov 229.70.

Women: 1. Anita Wlodarczyk 233.83, 2. Tatyana Lysenko 227,59, 3. Betty Heidler 226.93, 4. Yipsi Moreno 220.74, 5. Jeneva McCall 218.76, 6. Éva Orbán 218.24, 7. Kathrin Klaas GER 214.10, 8. Martina Hrasnová 212.57, 9. Gulfiya Khanafeyeva 208.06; drugs dq (9) Zalina Marghieva 212.51.

World Marathon Majors 2012–13 Final Standings

Men: 1. Tsegaye Kebede ETH 75 points (3rd 2012 London, 1st 2012 Chicago, 1st 2013 London, 2nd 2013 New York), 2. Wilson Kipsang KEN 61 (1st 2012 London, 3rd 2012 OG, 5th 2013 London, 1st 2013 Berlin), 3= Stephen Kiprotich UGA & Geoffrey Mutai KEN 50, 5= Lelisa Desisa ETH & Dennis Kimetto KEN 40; **Women**: 1. Priscah Jeptoo KEN 75 (3rd 2012 London, 2nd 2012 OG, 1st 2013 London, 1st 2013 New York), 2, Rita Jeptoo KEN 65 (2nd 2012 Chicago, 1st 2013 Boston, 1st 2013 Chicago), 3. Edna Kiplagat KEN 55, 4. Sharon Cherop KEN 50, 5. Atsede Baysa ETH 31.

African Combined Events & Walks Championships

At Bambous, Mauritius 18-19 April
Men Dec: Guillaume Thierry MRI 7043, **20kW**: Lebogang Shange RSA 1:28:31; **Women Hep**: Nafisatou Thiam BEL 6021, **10kW**: Chahinez Nasri TUN 51:15.

IAAF World Combined Events Challenge

Based on the sum of the best scores achieved in any three of the 13 designated competitions during the year.

Men Decathlon

1	Andrey Kravchenko BLR	25.084	8390 Florence	8380 Talence	8314 World Ch
2	Damian Warner CAN	24,980	8307 Götzis	8512 World Ch	8161 Talence
3	Pascal Behrenbruch GER	24,768	8514 Ratingen	8316 World Ch	7938 Talence
4	Eelco Sintnicolaas NED	24,731	8322 Eur Cup F	8391 World Ch	8018 Talence
5	Willem Coertzen RSA	24,676	8215 Ratingen	8343 World Ch	8118 Talence
6	Gunnar Nixon USA	24,646	8136 Götzis	8198 USA Ch	8313 World Ch
7	Eduard Mikhan BLR	24,068	7975 Götzis	8125 Eur Cup	7968 World Ch
8	Artem Lukyanenko RUS	23,865	8067 Eur Cup	8177 World Ch	7621 Talence

Women Heptathlon

1	Anna Melnychenko UKR	19,310	6416 Kladno	6586 World Ch	6308 Talence
2	Brianne Theisen-Eaton CAN	19,158	6376 Götzis	6520 World Ch	6252 Talence
3	Claudia Rath GER	19,014	6317 Ratingen	6462 World Ch	6235 Talence
4	Karolina Tyminska POL	18,995	6360 Kladno	6347 Eur Cup	6288 Talence
5	Nadine Broersen NED	18,807	6345 Götzis	6238 Eur Cup F	6224 World Ch
6	Eliska Klucinová CZE	18,745	6190 Kladno	6332 World Ch	6223 Talence
7	Laura Ikauniece LAT	18,666	6186 Götzis	6321 WUG	6159 World Ch
8	Antoinette Djimou Ida FRA	18,488	6058 Götzis	6104 Eur Cup	6326 World Ch

Prize Money: 1st $30,000, 2nd $20,000, 3rd $15,000, 4th $10,000, 5th $8000, 6th $7000, 7th $6000, 8th $5000.

11th African Junior Championships

At Bambous, Mauritius 29 August – 1 September
Men: **100m**: Harry Chukwudike NGR 10.54. **200m**: Divine Oduduru NGR 21.19, **400m**: Denis Opio UGA 46.94, **800m**: Berke Kahsay ETH 1:46.94, **1500m**: Matthew Kiptanui KEN 3:39.91, **5000m**: Moses Mukono KEN 13:54.36, **10,000m**: Moses Kurong UGA 28:31.80, **3000mSt**: Festus Kiprono KEN 8:38.99, **110mh**: Mohamed Koussi MAR 14.14, **400mh**: Constant Pretorius RSA 51.08, **HJ**: Omar Kaseb ALG 2.11, **LJ**: Andrew Boer RSA 7.58w, **TJ**: Ntokozo Ndlovu RSA 15.92, 6kg **SP**: Ahmed Hassan EGY 19.59, 1.75kg **DT**: Gerhard De Beer RSA 55.58, 6kg **HT**: Eslam Ibrahim EGY 74.49, **JT**: Alex Kiprotich KEN 71.43, **4x100m/4x400m**: NGR 40.36/3:14.50, **10,000mW**: Aymene Sabri ALG 45:58.52. **Women**: **100m**: Thebogo Mamathu RSA 11.98, **200m**: Nkiruka Uwakwe NGR 24.21, **400m**: Ada Benjamin NGR 52.87, **800m**: Alem Gereziher ETH 2:03.78, **1500m**: Dawit Seyaum ETH 4:09.00, **3000m**: Haylu Haftamnesh ETH 9:32.33, **5000m**: Ruti Aga ETH 16:00.98, **3000mSt**: Weynshet Ansa ETH 9.59.46, **100mh**: Marthe Koala BUR 14.09, **400mh**: Dihia Haddar ALG 58.82, **HJ**: Rhizlane Siba MAR 1.75, **LJ**: Ese Brume NGR 6.33w, **TJ**: Lerato Sechele LES 12.62, **SP**: Lezaan Jordaan RSA 15.07, **DT**: Fadya Kasaby EGY 42.71, **HT**: Ayah Ibrahim EGY 53.88, **JT**: Megan Wilke RSA 47.42, **4x100m/4x400m**: NGR 46.28/3:37.93, **5000mW**: Askale Tiksa ETH 25:30.90. **Medal table**: NGR 9G-7S-3B, RSA 7-9-8, ETH 7-7-8, EGY 5-4-2, KEN 4-9-4; 15 of 29 competing nations won medals.

African Youth Championships

At Warri, Nigeria 28-31 March
Men: **100m/200m**: Divine Oduduru NGR 10.62/21.56, **400m**: Keita Tijani GAM 47.39, **800m/1500m**: Robert Biwott KEN 1:47.01/3:41.96, **3000m**: Awet Nftalem ERI 8:17.28, **2000mSt**: Edwin Koskei KEN 5:42.18, **110mh** 91.4cm: Ifeanyichukwu NGR 14.00, **LJ**: Joseph Oreva-Oghene NGR 6.91. **TJ**: Fabian Edoki NGR 15.18, **SP** 5kg: Hamza Mohamed EGY 20.17, **DT** 1.5kg: Salem Elghoba EGY 60.46, **JT** 700g: Ubang Ubang ETH 64.67, **Oct**: Moustafa Mohamed EGY 5360, **Medley R**: GAM 1:53.35, **10,000mW**: Gonfa Bonsa ETH 52:25.34.
Women: **100m/200m**: Deborah Adewale NGR 11.87/24.13, **400m**: Ofonime Odiong NGR 54.46, **800m**: Zeytuna Mohammed ETH 2:05.05, **1500m**: Dureto Idai ETH 4:27.61. **3000m**: Mercy Chepwogen KEN 9:17.52, **2000mSt**: Daisy Jepkemei KEN 6:24.52, **100mh** 76.2cm: Gaber Omar EGY 14.04, **400mh**: Nathaniel Onome NGR 62.04, **HJ**: Ghizlane Siba MAR 1.80, **LJ**: Samir Esraa EGY 5.63, **TJ**: Veronica Ugeh NGR 12.56, **SP** 3kg: Judith Aniefung NGR 14.46, **DT**: Khaled Mahmoud NGR 42.40, **HT** 3kg: Mostafa Mohamed EGY 61.52, **JT**: Veronica Ugeh NGR 44.33, **Hep**: Riham Hamdy Kamal EGY 4604, **MedleyR**: NGR 2:09.36, **10,000mW**: Sisay Ginfa ETH 52:25.34. **Medal table leaders**: NGR 13G-10S-12B, EGY 8-6-2, ETH 6-13-6, KEN 5-4-2, GAM 2-0-0, ERI 1-1-1.

18th Arab Championships

At Doha, Qatar 21-24 May
Men: **100m**: Samuel Francis QAT 10.31. **200m**: Aziz Ouhadi MAR 20.46w, **400m**: Youssef Al-Masrahi KSA 44.72*, **800m**: Musaeb Abdulrahman Balla QAT 1:45.90, **1500m**: Ayanleh Souleiman DJI 3:39.44, **5000m**: Albert Rop BRN 13:52.54, **10,000m**: Alemu Bekele BRN 29:45.43, **HMar**: Bilal Mohamed MAR 67:02, **3000mSt**: Abdelmajed Touil ALG 8:57.92, **110mh**: Lyès Mokdel ALG 13.63*, **400mh**: Miloud Rahmani ALG 50.52, **HJ**: Mutaz Essa Barshim QAT 2.30, **PV**: Mouhcine Cheaouri MAR 5.00, **LJ**: Hussein Taher Al-Sabee KSA 7.99, **TJ**: Issam Nima ALG 17.01w, **SP**: Meshari Suroor

Saad KUW 19.37, **DT**: Rashid Al-Dosari QAT 61.91, **HT**: Ali Mohamed Al-Zankawi KUW 74.28, **JT**: Ihab Abdulrahman Al-Sayed EGY 79.17*, **Dec**: Mourad Souissi ALG 7317, **4x100m**: OMA 39.83, **4x400m**: KSA 3:06.23, **20kmW**: Hassanine Sbai TUN 1:30:30. **Women: 100m**: Souhair Bouali ALG 11.95, **200m**: Danah Abdulrazak IRQ 23.83w, **400m**: Greta Taslakian LIB 53.63, **800m**: Genzeb Shami BRN 2:09.30, **1500m**: Rabab Arrafi MAR 4:53.92, **5000m**: Betlhem Desalegn UAE 15:48.59, **10,000m**: Shitaye Eshete BRN 34:25.82, **HMar**: Lishan Dula BRN 1:21:53, **3000mSt**: Salima El Ouali Alami MAR 9:47.33*, **100mh/LJ**: Yamina Hajjaji MAR 13.62/6.05, **400mh**: Hayat Lambarki MAR 57.79, **HJ**: Ghizlane Siba MAR 1.76, **PV**: Sirini Ebondo TUN 4.10*, **TJ**: Baya Rahouli ALG 14.29, **SP**: Fadhia Said Ibrahim EGY 14.05, **DT**: Ilham Dahba EGY 49.44, **HT**: Rana Ahmed Ibrahim EGY 59.40, **JT**: Rada Adel Ahmad Toufik EGY 47.49, **Hep**: Yasmina Omrani ALG 5573*, **4x100m/4x400m**: MAR 46.59*/3:42.10, **10kmW**: Olfa Lafi TUN 50:34. **Medal table**: MAR 11G-5S-5B, ALG 8-6-5, BRN 5-10-7, EGY 4-6-7, QAT 4-5-2, TUN 4-3-2, KSA 3-4-4, KUW 2-1-1. IRQ 1-2-2. OMA 1-0-3, DJI 1-0-2, LIB 1-0-1. UAE 1-0-1. SUD 0-4-2, JOR 0-0-2.

Asian Championships

At Pune, India 3-7 July

100m	1. Su Bingtian CHN 10.17	
(-0.3)	2. Samuel Francis QAT 10.27	
	3. Barakat Al-Harthi BRN 10.30	
200m	1. Xie Zhenye CHN 20.87	
(0.7)	2. Fahad Al-Subaie KSA 20.92	
	3. Kei Takase JPN 20.92	
400m	1. Youssef Al-Masrahi KSA 45.08	
	2. Ali Khamis Abbas BRN 45.65	
	3. Yuzo Kanemaru JPN 45.95	
800m	1. Abdulrahman Musaeb Balla QAT 1:46.92	
	2. Abdulaziz Mohamed KSA 1:47.01	
	3. Bilal Mansour Ali BRN 1:48.56	
1500m	1. Emad Hamed Noor KSA 3:39.51	
	2. Mohamed Al-Garni QAT 3:40.75	
	3. Bilal Mansour Ali BRN 3:40.86	
5000m	1. Dejene Regassa BRN 13:53.25	
	2. Alemu Bekele BRN 13:57.23	
	3. Emad Hamed Noor KSA 14:05.88	
10,000m	1. Alemu Bekele BRN 28:47.26	
	2. Bilisuma Shugi BRN 28:58.67	
	3. Ram Saini IND 29:35.42	
3000mSt	1. Tarek Mubarak Taher BRN 8:34.77	
	2. Dejene Regassa BRN 8:37.40	
	3. Tsuyoshi Takeda JPN 8:48.48	
110mh	1. Jiang Fan CHN 13.61	
(0.1)	2. Abdulaziz Al-Mandeel KUW 13.78	
	3. Wataru Yazawa JPN 13.88	
400mh	1. Yasuhiro Fueki JPN 49.86	
	2. Cheng Wen CHN 50.07	
	3. Satinder Singh IND 50.35	
HJ	1. Bi Xiaoliang CHN 2.21	
	2= Jithin Thomas IND 2.21	
	2= Keyvan Ghanbarzadeh IRI 2.21	
PV	1. Xue Changrui CHN 5.60	
	2. Lu Yao CHN 5.20	
	3. Jin Min-sub KOR 5.20	
LJ	1. Wang Jianan CHN-Y 7.95/1.4	
	2. Prem Kumar IND 7.92/0.0	

	3. Tang Gongchen CHN 7.89w/2.1	
TJ	1. Cao Shuo CHN 16.77/0.1	
	2. Renjith Maheshwary IND 16.76w/2.1	
	3. Arpinder Singh IND 16.58/1.2	
SP	1. Sultan Al-Hebshi KSA 19.68	
	2. Chang Ming-Huang TPE 19.61	
	3. Om Prakash Singh IND 19.45	
DT	1. Vikas Gowda IND 64.90	
	2. Mohammed Samimi IRI 61.93	
	3. Ahmed Mohamed Dheeb QAT 60.82	
HT	1. Dilshod Nazarov TJK 78.32	
	2. Mohamed Ali Al-Zankawi KUW 74.70	
	3. Qi Dakai CHN 74.19	
JT	1. Ivan Zaytsev UZB 79.76	
	2. Sachith Madhuranga SRI 79.62	
	3. Samarjeet Singh IND 75.03	
Dec	1. Dmitriy Karpov KAZ 8037*	
	2. Akihiko Nakamura JPN 7720	
	3. Leonid Andreyev UZB 7383	
4x100m	1. HKG 38.94	
	2. JPN 39.11	
	3. CHN 39.17	
4x400m	1. KSA 3:02.53	
	2. JPN 3:04.46	
	3. SRI 3:04.92	
Women		
100m	1. Wei Yongli CHN 11.29	
(1.9)	2. Chisato Fukushima JPN 11.53	
	3. Tao Yujia CHN 11.63	
200m	1. Viktoriya Zyabkina KAZ 23.62	
(-0.6)	2. Asha Roy IND 23.71	
	3. Dutee Chand IND	
400m	1. Zhao Yanmin CHN 52.49	
	2. Machettira Raju Poovamma IND 53.37	
	3. Gerta Taslakian LIB 53.43	
800m	1. Wang Chenyu CHN 2:02.47	
	2. Genzebe G Shumi BRN 2:04.16	
	3. Tintu Luka IND 2:04.48	
1500m	1. Betlhem Desalegn UAE 4:13.67	
	2. Mimi Belete BRN 4:14.04	
	3. Ajako Jinnouchi JPN 4:16.73	
5000m	1. Betlhem Desalegn UAE 15:12.84*	
	2. Shitaye Eshete BRN 15:22.17	
	3. Tejeto Daba BRN 15:38.63	
10,000m	1. Shitaye Eshete BRN 32:17.29*	
	2. Alia Mohamed Saeed UAE 32:39.39	
	3. Ayumi Hagiwara JPN 32:47.44	
3000mSt	1. Ruth Chebet BRN 9:40.84*	
	2. Sudha Singh IND 9:56.27	
	3. Pak Kum-hyang PRK 10:09.80	
100mh	1. Ayaka Kimura JPN 13.25	
(-0.5)	2. Anastasiya Soprunova KAZ 13.44	
	3. Jayapal Hemasree IND 14.01	
400mh	1. Satomi Kubokura JPN 56.82	
	2. Manami Kira JPN 57.78	
	3. Jo Eun-ju KOR 58.21	
HJ	1. Nadia Dusanova UZB 1.90	
	2. Svetlana Radvizil UZB 1.88	
	3. Marina Aitova KAZ 1.88	
PV	1. Li Ling CHN 4.54*	
	2. Ren Mengqian CHN 4.40	
	3. Sukanya Chomchuendee THA 4.15	
LJ	1. Sachiko Masumi JPN 6.55/0.0	
	2. Anastasiya Juravleva UZB 6.36/-0.1	
	3. Mayookha Johny IND 6.30/0.0	

TJ 1. Anastasiya Juravleva UZB 14.18/1.8
2. Aleksandra Kotlyarova KAZ 13.89/0.8
3. Irina Ektova KAZ 13.75/1.8
SP 1. Liu Xiangrong CHN 18.67
2. Leyla Rajabi IRI 18.18
3. Gao Yang CHN 17.76
DT 1. Su Xinyue CHN 55.88
2. Jiang Fengjing CHN 55.70
3. Li Tsai-Yi TPE 55.32
HT 1. Wang Zheng CHN 72.78*
2. Liu Tingting CHN 67.16
3. Masumi Aya JPN 63.41
JT 1. Li Lingwei CHN 60.65*
2. Nadeeka Lakmali SRI 60.16
3. Risa Miyashita JPN 55.30
Hep 1. Wassana Winatho THA 5818
2. Yekaterina Voronina UZB 5599
3. Chie Kiriyama JPN 5451
4x100m 1. CHN 44.01
2. JPN 44.38
3. THA 44.44
4x400m 1. IND 3:32.26
2. CHN 3:35.31
3. JPN 3:35.72
Medal table leaders: CHN 16G-6S-5B; BRN 5-7-3, JPN 4-6-10, KSA 4-2-1, UZB 3-4-1. IND 2-6-9, KAZ 2-1-2, UAE 2-1-0, QAT 2-1-2; 12 nations won gold and 20 of 43 won medals

Asian Walks Championships

At Nomi City, Japan 10 March
Men 20k: 1. Yusuke Suzuki 1:18:34, 2. Li Tianlei CHN 1:21:28, 3. Gurmeet Singh IND 1:21:38; **Women 20k:** 1. Kumi Otoshi 1:33:49, 2. Nguyen Thi Thanh Phuc VIE 1:35:26, 3. Jeon Yong-eun KOR 1:35:49.

67th Balkan Championships

At Stara Zagora, Bulgaria 27-28 July
Men: TUR 192, ROU 187, BUL 181, GRE 178, SRB 152, CRO 142, MDA131, BIY 102, MKD 39, ARM 31, ALB 19. **100m**: Denis Dimitrov BUL 10.32w, **200m**: Petar Kremenski 20.79, **400m**: Yavuz Can TUR 46.66, **800m**: Konstadínos Nakapoúlos GRE 1:49.93, **1500m**: Goran Nava SRB 3:44.89, **3000m**: Jasmin Ljacic SRB 8:12.36, **5000m**: Dina Bosnjak CRO 14:36.96, **3000mSt**: Mitko Tsenov BUL 8:46.69, **110mh**: Konstadínos Douvalídis GRE 13.44w/2.3, **400mh**: Emir Bekric SRB 48.96*, **HJ**: Mihai Donisan ROU 2.31, **PV**: Panayiótis Láskaris GRE 5.40, **LJ**: Alper Kulaksiz TUR-Y 7.86w, **TJ**: Marian Oprea ROU 17.24, **SP**: Georgi Ivanov 20.71, **DT**: Irfan Yildirim TUR 63.01, **HT**: Sergey Marghiev MDA 73.77, **JT**: Dejan Mileusnic BIH 76.34, **4x100m**: ROU 40.03, **4x400m**: CRO 3:08.66. **Women**: ROU 202, BUL 195, TUR 187, GRE & SRB 168, CRO 127, BIH 120, MDA 88, MKD 41, MNE 14, ARM 11. **100m**: Ivet Lalova BUL 11.15, **200m**: Grigoría-Emmanouéla Keramidá GRE 23.68, **400m**: Adelina Pastor ROU 52.76, **800m**: Dorina Korozi ROU 2:05.60, **1500m/3000m**: Amela Terzic SRB 4:16.27/9:18.60, **5000m**: Roxana Bârca ROU 15:40.61, **3000mSt**: Silvia Danekova BUL 9:43.81, **100mh**: Olibia Petsoúdi GRE 13.55, **400mh**: Vanya Stambolova BUL 56.21, **HJ**: Adonía Steryíou GRE 1.95, **PV**: Loréla Mánou GRE 4.45*, **LJ**: Ivana Spanovic SRB 6.76, **TJ**: Cristina Toma ROU 14.56w, **SP**: Radoslava Mavrodieva 18.08, **DT**:

Nicoleta Grasu ROU 56.05, **HT**: Bianca Perie ROU 68.76, **JT**: Tatjana Jelaca SRB 56.54, **4x100m**: BUL 45.41, **4x400m**: ROU 3:29.13.
Half Marathon *at Oradea, ROU 15 September*. **Men**: Nicolae Soare ROU 64:26, **Women**: Olivera Jevtic SRB 74:39.
Marathon *at Podgorica, Montenegro 27 October*. **Men**: Yolo Nikolov BUL 2:19:31, **Women**: Sladana Perunovic MNE 2:42:28.
Walks *at Ayvalik – Balikesie, Turkey 27 March*. **Men 20k**: Vladimir Savanovic SRB 1:28:42, **Women 20k**: Adriana Enache ROU 1:39:17.

17th Bolivar(ianos) Games

At Trujillo, Peru 25-30 Npvember
Men: 100m/200m: Alex Quiñónez ECU 10.52/20.47*, **400m/800m:** Rafith Rodríguez COL 45.62/1:45.14*, **1500m:** Freddy Espinoza COL 3:48.97, **5000m/10,000m:** Leslie Encina CHI 13:54.6*/28:59.79*, **HMar:** Diego Colorado COL 66:16*, **3000mSt:** José Gregorio Peña VEN 8:26.6*, **110mh/LJ:** Jorge Armando McFarlane PER 13.76/7.80, **400mh:** Lucirio Francisco Garrido VEN 49.74*, **HJ:** Arturo Chávez PER 2.17, **PV:** Daniel Zupeuc CHI 5.00, **TJ:** Jhon Freddy Murillo COL 16.75w, **SP:** Aldo González BOL 18.23, **DT:** Mauricio Ortega COL 59.67*, **HT:** Pedro Muñoz VEN 68.35*, **JT:** Víctor Fatecha PAR 74.49; **Dec:** Oscar Campos VEN 7204, **4x100m:** VEN 39.34, **4x400m:** COL 3:05.43*, **20kmW:** Erick Barrondo GUA 1:23:25; **50kW:** Andrés Chocho ECU 3:58:50. **Women: 100m:** Ángela Tenorio ECU 11.60, **200m/400m:** Nercely Soto VEN 23.46/51.94*, **800m/1500m:** Rosibel García COL 2:01.98/4:09.75*, **5000m/10,000m:** Inés Melchor PER 15:30.63*/33:52.9*, **HMar:** Gladys Lucy Tejeda PER 72:53; **3000mSt:** Muriel Coneo COL 10:00.09*, **100mh:** Lina Florez COL 13.12*, **400mh:** Yadira Moreno COL 57.17*, **HJ:** Kashani Ríos PAN 1.79, **PV:** Robeilys Peinado VEN 4.30*, **LJ:** Paola Mautino PER 6.32, **TJ:** Yorsiris Urrutia COL 14.08, **SP:** Ahymara Espinoza VEN 18.15*, **DT:** Karen Gallardo CHI 56.77*, **HT:** Rosa Rodríguez VEN 73.36*, **JT:** Flor Ruiz COL 58.18*, **Hep:** Ana Camila Pirelli PAR 5733 NR*, **4x100m/4x400m:** COL 43.90/3:34.35*, **20kmW:** Mirna Ortiz GUA 1:34:07*. **Medal table:** COL 16G-19S-11B, VEN 10-12-10, PER 7-4-8, CHI 4-5-5, ECU 4-4-8, GUA & PAR 2-0-1, PAN 1-2-3, BOL 1-0-0, DOM 0-1-0.

24th Central American & Caribbean Championships

At Morelia, Mexico (A) 5-7 July
Men: 100m: Andrew Fisher JAM 10.14, **200m:** Antoine Adams SKN 20.13, **400m:** Jarrin Solomon TRI 45.54, **800m:** Andy González CUB 1:49.54, **1500m:** Christopher Sandoval MEX 3:52.94, **5000m:** Juan Luis Barrios MEX 14:08.19, **10,000m:** Juan Carlos Romero MEX 30:11.84, **3000mSt:** Javier Quintana MEX 9:17.56, **110mh:** Shane Brathwaite BAR 13.70, **400mh:** Emanuel Mayers TRI 49.72, **HJ:** Darrell Garwood JAM 2.22, **PV:** Raúl Ríos MEX 5.10, **LJ:** Alberto Álvarez MEX 7.85, **TJ:** Yordanis Durañona DMA 16.45, **SP:** O'Dayne Richards JAM 20.97*, **DT:** Chad Wright JAM 60.79, **HT:** Roberto Sawyers CRC 68.92, **JT:** Carlos Armenta MEX 72.49, **Dec:** Rodrigo Armando Sagaon MEX 7011, **4x100m:** BAH (Griffith, J Rolle, Mackey,

Hart) 38.77, **4x400m**: TRI (Quow, Mayers, Cedenio, Solomon) 3:02.19, **20kW**: Jorge Alejandro Martínez MEX 1:27:17. **Women: 100m**: Sheri-Ann Brooks JAM 11.21, **200m**: Kineke Alexander VIN 23.00, **400m**: Kadecia Baird GUY 51.32, **800m**: Natoya Goule JAM 2:02.02, **1500m**: Brenda Flores MEX 4:27.55, **5000m**: Marisol Romero MEX 16:04.93, **10,000m**: Kathya García MEX 35:19.92, **3000mSt**: Azucena Ríos MEX 10:56.55, **100mh**: Monique Morgan JAM 13.25, **400mh**: Danielle Dowie JAM 56.39, **HJ**: Levern Spencer LCA 1.95, **PV**: Carmelita Correa MEX 3.95, **LJ**: Francine Simpson JAM 6.49, **TJ**: Tamara Myers BAH 13.18, **SP**: Cleopatra Borel TRI 17.56, **DT**: Allison Randall JAM 55.26, **HT**: Samantha Hernández MEX 54.27, **JT**: Carolys Ortiz PUR 57.48, **Hrp**: Chrystal Ruíz 5467, **4x100m**: JAM (Thompson, Palmer, Bailey, Brooks) 43.58, **4x400m**: TRI (Fermin, McKnight, Modeste, A Brooks) 3:30.64. **Medal Table Leaders**: MEX 17G-19-11, JAM 11-6-4, TRI 5-4-4, BAH 2-3-3, BAR 1-2-1, CUB 1-1-3, CRC 1-1-1, LCA 1-1-0, PUR & VIN 1-0-1; in all 19 countries won medals.

10th Central American Games

At San José, Costa Rica (A) 9-12 March
Men: 100m: Rolando Palacios HON 10.39, **200m**: Alonso Edward PAN 20.52, **400m**: Jarlex Lynch CRC 47.16, **800m**: Jenner Pellico GUA 1:51.16, **1500m/5000m/10,000m**: Víctor Manuel González 3:58.00/14:49.30/31:10.38, **3000mSt**: Miguel Ángel Chan GUA 9:34.72, **110mh**: Ronald Bennett HON 14.43, **400mh**: Kenneth Medwood BIZ 51.14, **HJ**: William Ríos PAN 2.05, **LJ**: Irving Saladino PAN 7.99, **TJ**: Jason Castro HON 15.39, **SP**: Luis Pedro Folgar GUA 15.62, **DT**: Winston Campbell HON 51.64, **JT**: Lusia Taracena GUA 64.31. **4x100m**: HON 41.61. **4x400m**: CRC 3:11.15, **20kW**: Allan Segura CRC 1:28:43. **Women: 100m**: Ruth Hunt PAN 11.88w, **200m**: Shantely Scott CRC 23.84, **400m**: Desirée Bermúdez CRC 54.90, **800m/1500m**: Andrea Ferris PAN 2:06.39/4:31.62, **5000m/10,000m**: Elida Hernández GUA 17:08.62/36:04.41. **3000mSt**: Rolanda Bell PAN 11:07.77, **100mh**: Jeimmy Bernárdez HON 14.42, **400mh**: Sharolyn Scott CRC 59.57, **LJ/Hep**: Ana María Porras CRC 5.67/4785, **TJ**: Ana Lucía Camargo GUA 12.17, **SP**: Natyan Catano PAN 12.58, **DT**: Aixa Middleton PAN 49.08, **HT**: Sabrina Gaitán GUA 53.30, **4x100m**: PAN 46.66, **4x400m**: CRC 3:48.90, **20kW**: Cristina López ESA 1:48:12.

6th East Asian Games

At Tianjin, China 7-9 October
100m: Su Bingtian CHN 10.31, **200m**: Asuka Cambridge JPN 20.93, **400m**: Lim Chan-ho KOR 46.58, **800m**: Sho Kawamoto JPN 1:53.18, **1500m**: Zhang Haikun CHN 3:52.85, **5000m**: Sota Hoshi JPN 14:25.00, **110mh**: Jiang Fan CHN 13.58, **400mh**: Cheng Wen CHN 49.66, **PV**: Seito Yamamoto JPN 5.50, **LJ**: Kim Sang-su KOR 7.71, **TJ**: Fu Haitao CHN 16.21, **SP**: Wang Guangfu CHN 19.34, **HT**: Wan Yong CHN 69.26, **JT**: Zhao Qinggang CHN 82.97, **4x100m**: JPN 38.44, **4x400m**: CHN 3:07.27, **Women: 100m/200m**: Wei Yongli CHN 11.57/23.71, **400m**: Chen Jingwen CHN 53.76, **800m**: Song Tingting CHN

2:08.89, **1500m**: Zhao Jing CHN 4:17.87, **5000m**: Riki Matsuzaki JPN 16:09.72, **10,000m**: Yuko Shimizu JPN 32:50.42, **3000mSt**: Li Zhenzhu CHN 9:53.17, **100mh**: Wu Shujiao CHN 12.93, **400mh**: Xiao Xia CHN 56.97, **SP**: Liu Xiangrong CHN 18.40, **4x100m/4x400m**: CHN 43.66/3:35.65. **Medal table leaders**: CHN 20G-11S-5B, JPN 7-9-9, KOR 2-3-6, TPE 0-3-7

European Junior (U20) Championships

At Rieti, Italy 18-21 July
Men

100m		1. Chijindu Ujah GBR 10.40
		2. Denis Dimitrov BUL 10.46
		3. Robert Polkowski GER 10.53
200m		1. Nethanee Mitchell-Blake GBR 20.60
(-0.7)		2. Leon Reid GBR 20.92
		3. Matthew Hudson-Smith GBR 20.94
400m		1. Pavel Ivashko RUS 45.81
		2. Patryk Dobek POL 46.15
		3. Thomas Jordier FRA 46.21
800m		1. Patrick Zwicker GER 1:49.58
		2. Aaron Botterman BEL 1:49.80
		3. Leo Morgana FRA 1:50.04
1500m		1. Jake Wightman GBR 3:44.14
		2. Süleyman Bekmezci TUR 3:44.45
		3. Julius Lawnik GBR 3:45.43
5000m		1. Ali Kaya TUR 13:49.76
		2. Samuele Dini ITA 14:36.25
		3. Jonathan Davies GBR 14:26.62
10,000m		1. Ali Kaya TUR 28:31.16*
		2. Loronzo Dini ITA 29:31.11
		3. Dino Bosnjak CRO 29:59.07
3000mSt		1. Zak Seddon GBR 8:45.91
		2. Viktor Bakharev RUS 8:47.81
		3. Ersin Tekal TUR 8:54.54

Medal and placing table

	G	S	B	Pts
RUS	8	7	7	195.5
GBR	9	6	4	187
GER	4	1	6	134
FRA	2	3	4	111.5
ITA	1	4	2	95
POL	2	4	1	76
UKR	2	2	3	70
TUR	3	2	1	58
FIN	1	2	0	53
ESP	0	0	2	52
SWE	1	1	0	46
HUN	1	2	1	45
BEL	1	2	1	43
NED	1	1	2	41
IRL	0	1	0	35
CZE	1	0	2	30
NOR	1	0	1	28
ROU	0	2	0	28
CRO	0	1	2	27
BLR	1	1	0	23
SUI	1	0	1	22
LTU	0	0	0	18

EST (1B) 15, BIH & ISL (1G) 13, DEN (1B) 11, GRE 10.5, BUL (1S) & POR 10, ARM (1G), & SLO 8, SRB 6, LAT, AUT & SVK 5, CYP 4.5, AZE 3.

110mh	1.	Wilhem Belocian FRA 13.18*
(0.9)	2.	Lorenzo Perini ITA 13.30
99cm	3.	Brahian Peña SUI 13.31
400mh	1.	Timofey Chalyy RUS 49.23*
	2.	Aleksandr Skorobogatko RUS 50.13
	3.	Jacob Paul GBR 50.71
HJ	1.	Tobias Potye GER 2.20
	2.	Andrey Skobeyko BLR 2.18
	3.	Mikhail Akimenko RUS 2.18
PV	1.	Eirik Greibrokk Dolve NOR 5.30
	2=	Leonid Kobelev RUS 5.25
	2=	Axel Chapelle FRA 5.25
LJ	1.	Elliot Safo GBR 7.86/-0.3
	2.	Mathias Broothaerts BEL 7.84/-1.0
	3.	Guy-Elphège Anouman FRA 7.60/-0.4
TJ	1,	Levon Aghasyan ARM 16.01/1.4
	2.	Kristian Pulli FIN 15.88/-0.1
	3.	Vladimir Kozlov BLR 15.85/-0.1
SP 6kg	1.	Mesud Pezer BIH 20.44
	2.	Filip Mihaljevic CRO 20.23
	3.	Andrzej Regin POL 20.07
DT 1.75kg	1.	Róbert Szikszai HUN 64.75
	2.	Nicholas Percy GBR 62.04
	3.	Aleksandr Dobrenshkiy RUS 61.54
HT 6kg	1.	Valeriy Pronkin RUS 78.34
	2.	Bence Pásztor HUN 77.35
	3.	Marco Bortolato ITA 73.43
JT	1.	Julian Weber GER 79.68
	2.	Maksym Bohdan UKR 78.77
	3.	German Komarov RUS 73.95
Dec Jnr	1.	Yevgeniy Likhanov RUS 7975
	2.	Aleksey Cherkasov RUS 7790
	3.	Tim Nowak GER 7778
10,000W	1.	Pavel Parshin RUS 41:01.55
	2.	Vito Minei ITA 41:08.76
	3.	Alvaro Martín ESP 41:13.95
4x100m	1.	POL (Mudlaff, Kabacinski, Kalandyk, Jablonski) 39.80
	2.	GER 39.96
	3.	ITA 40.00
4x400m	1.	RUS (Peremetov, Savin, Khasanov, Ivashko) 3:04.87
	2.	POL 3:05.07
	3.	GBR 3:05.14
Women		
100m	1.	Stella Akakpo FRA 11.52
(-1.0)	2.	Sophie Papps GBR 11.72
	3.	Klára Seidlová CZE 11.88
200m	1.	Dina Asher-Smith GBR 23.29
(-2.2)	2.	Desiree Henry GBR 23.56
	3.	Tessa van Schagen NED 23.65
400m	1.	Patrycja Wyciszkiewicz POL 51.56
	2.	Bianca Razor ROU 51.82
	3.	Yekaterina Renzhina RUS 52.27
800m	1.	Anita Henriksdóttir ISL-Y 2:01.14
	2.	Olena Sidorska UKR 2:01.46
	3.	Christina Hering GER 2:03.11
1500m	1.	Nataliya Pryshchepa UKR 4:18.51
	2.	Sofia Ennaoui POL 4:20.20
	3.	Aurora Dybedokken NOR 4:21.27
3000m	1.	Emelia Gorecka GBR 9:12.53
	2.	Emine Hatun Tuna TUR 9:25.83
	3.	Anna Petrova RUS 9:30.00
5000m	1.	Jip Vastenberg NED 16:03.31
	2.	Oona Kettunen FIN 16:03.79
	3.	Yelena Kudashkina RUS 16:08.12

3000mSt	1.	Oona Kettunen FIN 9:45.51
	2.	Marusa Mismas SLO 9:51.15
	3.	Maya Rehberg GER 10:00.04
100H	1.	Noemi Zbären SUI 13.17
(1.3)	2.	Sarah Lavin IRL 13.34
	3.	Heloise Kane FRA 13.36
400H	1.	Hayley McLean GBR 57.26
	2.	Joan Medjid FRA 57.34
	3.	Stine Troest DEN 57.41
HJ	1.	Kateryna Tabashnyk UKR 1.90
	2.	Aleksandra Yaryshkina RUS 1.88
	3.	Iryna Herashchenko UKR 1.84
PV	1.	Alena Lutkovskaya RUS-Y 4.30
	2.	Femke Pluin NED 4.25
	3.	Sonia Malavisi ITA 4.20
LJ	1.	Malaika Mlhambo GER 6.70/0.9*
	2.	Jazmin Sawyers GBR 6.63/0.5
	3.	Maryna Bekh UKR 6.44/-0.3
TJ	1.	Ottavio Cestonaro ITA 13.41/-0.5
	2.	Elena A. Panturoui ROU 13.36/-0.6
	3.	Ana Peleteiro ESP 13.29/-0.1
SP	1.	Emel Dereli TUR-Y 18.04
	2.	Sophie McKinna GBR 17.09
	3.	Katlin Piirimäe EST 16.80
DT	1.	Nataliya Shirobokova RUS 54.21
	2.	Karolina Makul POL 53.25
	3.	Tetyana Yuryeva UKR 53.15
HT	1.	Hanna Zinchuk BLR 65.44
	2.	Réka Gyurátz HUN-Y 65.01
	3.	Beatrix Banga HUN 63.89
JT	1.	Sofi Flinck SWE 57.91
	2.	Christin Hussing GER 57.90
	3.	Sara Kolak CRO 57.79
Hep	1.	Nafissatou Thiam BEL 6298
	2.	Sofia Linde SWE 6081
	3.	Marjolein Lindemans BEL 5831
10,000W	1.	Anezka Drahotová CZE 44:15.87
	2.	Oksana Golyatkina RUS 44:21.03
	3.	Eliska Drahotová CZE 44:45.27
4x100m	1.	GBR (Miller, Asher-Smith, S Wilson, Henry) 43.81
	2.	FRA 44.00
	3.	NED 44.22
4x400m	1.	POL (Curylo, Dabrowska, Janowicz, Wyciszkiewicz) 3:32.63
	2.	RUS 3:33.36
	3.	GER 3:33.40

European U23 Championships

At Tampere, Finland 10-14 July

100m	1.	Adam Gemili GBR 10.20
(-0.3)	2.	Deji Tobais GBR 10.29
	3.	Hensley Paulina NED 10.48
200m	1.	Karol Zalewski POL 20.41
(-0.3)	2.	Dan Talbot GBR 20.46
	3.	Pavel Maslák CZE 20.49
400m	1.	Lev Mosin RUS 45.51
	2.	Vitaliy Butrym UKR 45.88
	3.	Nikita Uglov RUS 46.04
800m	1.	Pierre-Ambroise Bosse FRA 1:45.79
	2.	Taras Bybyk UKR 1:46.20
	3.	Amel Tuka BIH 1:46.29

1500m
1. Pieter-Jan Hannes BEL 3:43.83
2. Charlie Grice GBR 3:44.41
3. Alberto Imedio ESP 3:44.65

5000m
1. Henrik Ingebrigtsen NOR 14:19.39
2. Tom Farrell GBR 14:19.94
3. Aitor Fernández ESP 14:20.65

10,000m
1. Gabriel Navarro ESP 29:43.22
2. Nicolae Alexandru Soare ROU 29:43.76
3. Abdi Hakin Ulad DEN 29:44.78

3000mSt
1. Abdelaziz Merzoughi ESP 8:34.64
2. Giuseppe Gerratana ITA 8:35.55
3. Tanguy Pepiot FRA 8:38.07

110mh
(-0.4)
1. Simon Krauss FRA 13.55
2. Koen Smet NED 13.58
3. Gregor Traber GER 13.66

400mh
1. Emir Bekric SRB 48.76
2. Sebastian Rodger GBR 49.19
3. Rasmus Mägi EST 49.19

HJ
1. Douwe Amels NED 2.28
2. Daniyil Tsyplakov RUS 2.28
3= Adónios Mástoras GRE 2.26
3= Allan Smith GBR 2.26

PV
1. Anton Ivakin RUS 5.60
2. Robert Sobera POL 5.60
3= Valentin Lavillenie FRA 5.50
3= Daniel Clemens GER 5.50

LJ
1. Eusebio Cáceres ESP 8.37/1.1*
2. Sergey Morgunov RUS 8.01/1.1
3. Kirill Sukharev RUS 7.90/1.1

TJ
1. Aleksey Fyodorov RUS 17.13/-0.1
2. Gaetan Saku Bafuanga FRA 16.57/0.6
3. Artyom Primak RUS 16.49/0.3

SP
1. Jakub Szyszkowski POL 19.78
2. Dominik Witczak POL 19.63
3. Mikhal Abramchuk BLR 19.42

DT
1. Andrius Gudzius LTU 62.40
2. Viktor Butenko RUS 62.27
3. Danijel Furtula MNE 61.61

Medal and placing table

	G	S	B	Pts
RUS	9	7	5	207
GER	5	6	6	183.5
GBR	5	7	3	155.5
FRA	3	2	5	115.5
POL	3	4	1	106.5
UKR	1	6	2	100m
ITA	1	2	4	75
ESP	3	0	3	67
NED	2	2	2	67
ROU	1	3	0	52
CZE	0	0	2	45
SWE	0	0	1	34
BEL	1	1	0	33
BLR	1	0	1	29
FIN	0	0	1	28
NOR	2	0	0	26
LAT	2	0	0	25
SRB	2	0	1	22
HUN	0	1	0	22
GRE	0	0	2	19.5

LTU (1-1-0) 16, SUI (1B) 16. IRL 16, TUR (1G) 13, SLO (0-1-1) 13, EST (1B) 13, AZE (1S) 12, BUL (1G) 11. CRO 10.5, BIH (1B) 9, AUT 7, DEN, MNE & POR (1B) 6, MDA 4, CYP 3, ISR 2

HT
1. Zakhar Makhrosenko BLR 74.63
2. Akos Hudi HUN 74.09
3. Quentin Bigot FRA 74.00

JT
1. Zigismunds Sirmais LAT 82.77
2. Bernhard Seifert GER 82.42
3. Thomas Röhler GER 81.74

Dec
1. Kai Kazmirek GER 8366
2. Ilya Shkurenyov RUS 8279
3. Adam Helcelet CZE 8252

20kmW
1. Pyotr Bogatyrev RUS 1:21:31
2. Aleksandr Ivanov RUS 1:21:34
3. Hagen Pohle GER 1:25:04

4x100m
1. GBR (Tobais, Talbot, Walker-Khan, Gemili) 38.77*
2. POL (Olszewski, Slowikowski, Zalewski, Zimniewicz) 38.81
3. ESP (Viles, Burriel, Hortelano, Cáceres) 38.87

4x400m
1. RUS (Mosin, Nesmashnyi, Vazhov, Uglov) 3:04.63
2. BEL (Thijs, D Borlée, Vanhaeren, Watrin) 3:04.90
3. ITA (Incantalupo, Valentini, Lorenzi, Tricca) 3:05.10

Women
100m
(-0.7)
1. Dafne Schippers NED 11.13
2. Jodie Williams GBR 11.42
3. Tatjana Pinto GER 11.50

200m
(-0.5)
1. Jodie Williams GBR 22.92
2. Lenora Guion Firmin FRA 22.96
3. Gloria Hooper ITA 23.24

400m
1. Lenora Guion Firmin FRA 51.68
2. Mirela Lavric ROU 52.06
3. Justyna Swiety POL 52.22

800m
1. Mirela Lavric ROU 2:01.56
2. Olha Lyakhova UKR 2:01.90
3. Selina Büchel SUI 2:02.74

1500m
1. Amela Terzic SRB 4:05.69*
2. Corinna Harrer GER 4:07.71
3. Laura Muir GBR 4:08.19

5000m
1. Gamze Bulut TUR 15:45.03
2. Layes Abdullayeva AZE 15:51.72
3. Kate Avery GBR 15:54.07

10,000m
1. Gulshat Fazlitdinova RUS 32:53.93
2. Viktoriya Khapilina UKR 33:56.85
3. Anastasia Karakatsáni GRE 33:57.74

3000mSt
1. Gesa-Felicitas Krause GER 9:38.91*
2. Yekaterina Sokolenko RUS 9:49.34
3. Yevdokiya Bukina RUS 10:03.41

100mh
(-0.1)
1. Isabelle Pedersen NOR 13.12
2. Karolina Koleczek POL 13.30
3. Nooralotta Neziri FIN 13.39

400mh
1. Vera Rudakova RUS 55.92
2. Bianca Baak NED 56.75
3. Anastasiya Lebid UKR 56.92

HJ
1. Alessia Trost ITA 1.98*
2. Airine Palsyté LTU 1.92
3. Oksana Krasnokutskaya RUS 1.90

PV
1. Angelina Zhuk-Krasnova RUS 4.70*
2. Anzhelika Sidorova RUS 4.60
3. Angelica Bengtsson SWE 4.55

LJ
1. Lena Malkus GER 6.76/1.0
2. Krystyna Hryshutyna UKR 6.61/1.6
3. Dafne Schippers NED 6.59/1.6

TJ
1. Gabriela Petrova BUL 13.91/0.6
2. Daria Derkach ITA 13.56/1.5

3. Maja Bratkic SLO 13.52/-0.2
SP 1. Olha Holodna UKR 18.11
2. Shanice Craft GER 17.29
3. Lena Urbaniak GER 16.98
DT 1. Anna Rüh GER 61.45
2. Shanice Craft GER 58.64
3. Irina Rodrigues POR 56.80
HT 1. Sophie Hitchon GBR 70.72
2. Barbara Spiler SLO 69.69
3. Alexia Sedykh FRA 66.67
JT 1. Lina Muze LAT 58.61
2. Sarah Mayer GER 55.43
3. Marija Vucenovic SRB 54.43
Hep 1. Katarina Johnson-Thompson GBR 6215
2. Kira Biesenbach GER 5946
3. Anastasiya Mokhnyuk UKR 5898
20kmW 1. Svetlana Vasilyeva RUS 1:30:07
2. Lyudmyla Olyanovska UKR 1:30:37
3. Antonella Palmisano ITA 1:30:59
4x100m 1. GER (Hollender, Günther, Pinto,
         Grompe) 43.29*
2. GBR (Tagoe, Humphreys, Johncock,
         J Williams) 43.83
3. ITA (Gamba, Siragusa, Amidei, Hooper)
         43.86
4x400m 1. POL (Gorzkowska, Holub,
         Karczmarczyk, Swiety) 3:29.74
2. ROU (Gal, Lavric, Belgyan, Pastor)
         3:30.28
3. FRA (Guion Firmin, Fedronic, Bertheau,
         Raharolahy) 3:30.64

European Winter Throwing Cup

At Castellón, Spain 16-17 March
Men: SP: 1. Borja Vivas ESP 20.00, 2. Georgi Ivanov BUL 19,68, 3, Andriy Semenov UKR 19.55; **DT**: 1. Daniel Jasinski GER 64.69, 2. Virgilijus Alekna LTU 64.66, 3. Erik Cadée NED 64.38; **HT**: 1. Kristztián Pars HUN 77.24, 2. Pavel Krivitskiy BLR 75.89, 3. Pawel Fahdek POL 75.52; **JT**: 1. Zigismunds Sirmais LAT 82.51, 2. Thomas Röhler GER 81.87, 3. Risto Mätas EST 79.10; **U23: JT**: Valeriy Iordan RUS 82.89; **Women: SP**: 1. Yevgeniya Kolodko RUS 19.04, 2. Alena Kopets BLR 18.18, 3. Irina Tarasova RUS 17.98; **DT**: 1. Nadine Müller GER 66.69, 2. Mélina Robert-Michon FRA 61.26, 3. Dragana Tomasevic SRB 61.12; **HT**: 1. Tatyana Lysenko RUS 71.54, 2. Kathrin Klaas GER 71.07, 3. Tracey Andersson SWE 70.82; drugs dq (1) Zalina Marghieva MDA 71.98; **JT**: 1. Mariya Abakumova RUS 69.34, 2. Vira Rebryuk UKR 63.42, 3. Linda Stahl GER 61.97.

European Cup Race Walking

At Dudince, Slovakia 19 May
Men 20km: 1. Denis Strelkov RUS 1:21:40, 2. Miguel Ángel López ESP 1:21:48, 3. Matej Tóth SVK 1:21:51. 4. Aleksandr Ivanov RUS 1:22:15, 5. Ruslan Dmytrenko UKR 1:22:30, 6. Erik Tysse NOR 1:22:43, 7. João Vieira POR 1:23:03, 8. Rafal Augustyn POL 1:23:16, 9. Robert Heffernan IRL 1:23:26, 10. Christopher Linke GER 1:23:28, 62 of 75 finished. Team: 1. RUS 20, 2. UKR 30, 3. POL 44, 4. BLR 52, 5. ESP 68, 6. ITA 71. 14 teams scored.
Men 50km: . Yohann Diniz FRA 3:41:07, 2. Mikhail Ryzhov RUS 3:44:41. 3. Ivan Noskov RUS 3:45:31.

4. Igor Hlavan UKR 3:46:09, 5. Grzegorz Sudol POL 3:46:41. 6. Ivan Banzeruk UKR 3:47:35, 7. Konstantin Maksimov RUS 3:47:48, 8. Rafal Sikora POL 3:48:13, 9. Sergiy Budza UKR 3:49:24, 10. Aléxandros Papamihaíl GRE 3:51:05. 34 of 49 finished. Team: 1. RUS 12, 2. UKR 19, 3. POL 31. 4. ESP 37, 5. FRA 46, 6. ITA 51. 9 teams scored.
U20 Men 10km: 1. Pavel Parshin RUS 41:13, 2. Nikolay Markov RUS 41:13, 3. Vito Minei ITA 41:26, 48 of 54 finished. Team: 1. RUS 3, 2. ITA 12, 3. ESP 13, 18 teams scored.
Women 20 km: 1. Anisya Kirdyapkina RUS 1:28:39, 2. Vera Sokolova RUS 1:29:18, 3. Marina Pandakova RUS 1:29:25, 4. Irina Yumanova 1:29:37, 5. Ana Cabecinha POR 1:31:48, 6. Eleonora Giorgi ITA 1:32:09, 7. Lyudmyle Olyanovska UKR 1:32:30, 8. Inês Henriques POR 1:32:39, 9. Beatriz Pascual ESP 1:32:53, 10. Vera Santos POR 1:32:54, 49 of 58 finished. Team: 1. RUS 6, 2. POR 23, 3. ESP 39, 4. UKR 44, 5. BLR 50, 6. POL 56, 9 teams scored.
U20 Women 10km: 1. Nadezhda Leontyeva RUS 46:14, 2. Anezka Drahotová CZE 46:29, 3. Oksana Golyatkina RUS 47:04, drugs dq (1), Yekaterina Medvedeva RUS 44:45, 2. 44 of 46 finished. Team: (pre drugs dq) 1. RUS 3, 2. CZE 11. 3. BLR 15, 14 teams scored.

European Cup 10,000m

At Pravets, Bulgaria 8 June
Men: 1. Sergio Sánchez ESP 28:31.75, 2. Halil Akkas TUR 28:31.82, 3. Ahmed El Mazoury ITA 28:36.40; **Team**: 1. ITA 1:26:32.92, 2. ESP 1:27:23.76. **Women**: 1. Sabrina Mockenhaupt GER 32:13.54, 2. Christelle Daunay FRA 32:46.39, 3. Olivera Jevtic SRB 32:52.56; **Team**: 1. ESP 1:42:00.90, 2. GBR 1:42:07.44, 3. BLR 1:43:03.61.

European Cup Combined Events

For the first time men's and women's scores were combined/
Super League *At Tallinn, Estonia 29-30 June*
1. FRA 41,421. 2. RUS 41,032, 3. EST 41,027, 4. BLR 40,175, 5. POL 38,763, 6. GBR 38,653, 7. UKR 37,850, 8. ITA 37,617. **Dec**: 1. Kevin Mayer FRA 8390, 2. Eduard Mikhon BLR 8125, 3. Mikk Pahapill EST 8099, 4. Artem Lukyanenko RUS 8067, 5. Florian Geffrouais FRA 7990
Women Hep: 1. Karolina Tyminska POL 6347, 2. Anna Melnychenko UKR 6260, 3. Grit Sadeiko EST 6221. 4. Antoinette Nana Djimou FRA 6104, 5. Yana Maksimova BLR 6027.
First League *At Nottwil, Switzerland 29-30 June*
1. NED 40,749, 2. SUI 38,767, 3. CZE 38,291. 4. SWE 38,274, 5. FIN 37,362, 6. ESP 36,885, 7. HUN 32,283. **Dec**: 1. Eelco Sintnicolaas NED 8322, 2. Nicklas Wiberg SWE 7678, 3. Bas Markies NED 7457
Women Hep: 1. Nadine Broersen NED 6238, 2. Eliska Klucinová CZE 6013, 3. Ellen Sprunger SUI 5987.
Second League. *At Ribeira Brava, Portugal 29-30 June*
1. NOR 37,928, 2. POR 36,250, 3. ROU 34,895. **Dec**: Lars Viken Rise NOR 7621
W Hep: Lucija Cvitanovic CRO 5547.

European Team Championships

Super League at Gateshead, GBR 22-23 June
1. RUS 354.5, 2. GER 347.5, 3. GBR 338, 4. FRA 310.5, 5. POL 305.5, 6. UKR 291.5, 7. ITA 260.5, 8. ESP 251. 9. TUR 197.5, 10. BLR 155.5, 11. GRE 152, 12. NOR 137.

Men

100m	1.	Jimmy Vicaut FRA 10.28
(-4.1/-0.5)	2.	Jaysuma Saidy Ndure NOR 10.37
	3 (1B).	Kamil Krynski POL 10.40
200m	1.	Christophe Lemaitre FRA 20.27w
(2.4/1.7)	2.	Jaysuma Saidy Ndure NOR 20.47w
	3 (1B).	Sergiy Smelyk UKR 20.62
400m	1.	Vladimir Krasnov RUS 45.69
	2.	Nigel Levine GBR 45.88
	3.	David Gollnow GER 45.90
800m	1.	Adam Kszczot POL 1:47.27
	2.	Ilham Tanui Özbilen TUR 1:47.39
	3.	Andrew Osagie GBR 1:47.41
1500m	1.	Ilham Tanui Özbilen TUR 3:38.57
	2.	Charlie Grice GBR 3:39.76
	3.	Marcin Lewandowski POL 3:39.82
3000m	1.	Bouabdellah Tahri FRA 8:05.31
	2.	Halil Akkas TUR 8:05.50
	3.	Valentin Smirnov RUS 8:05.77
5000m	1.	Mohamed Farah GBR 14:10.00
	2.	Bouabdellah Tahri FRA 14:12.91
	3.	Kemal Koyuncu TUR 14:14.18
3000mSt	1.	Tarik Langat Akdag TUR 8:36.25
	2.	Abdelaziz Merzoughi ESP 8:37.22
	3.	Yoann Kowal FRA 8:38.76
110mh	1.	Sergey Shubenkov RUS 13.19w
(2.4)	2.	Pascal Martinot Lagarde FRA 13.28w
	3.	Artur Noga POL 13.33w
400mh	1.	Silvio Schirrmeister GER 49.15
	2.	David Greene GBR 49.39
	3.	Mickaël François FRA 49.79
HJ	1.	Bohdan Bondarenko UKR 2.28
	2.	Mickaël Hanany FRA 2.28
	3.	Tom Parsons GBR 2.24
PV	1.	Renaud Lavillenie FRA 5.77
	2.	Giuseppe Gibilisco ITA 5.60
	3.	Björn Otto GER 5.50
LJ	1.	Aleksandr Menkov RUS 8.36/1.9
	2.	Loúis Tsátoumas GRE 8.12/0.8
	3.	Gerg Rutherford GBR 8.02w/2.6
TJ	1.	Aleksey Fyodorov RUS 16.70/-1.3
	2.	Teddy Tamgho FRA 16.62/-2.0
	3.	Nathan Douglas GBR 16.45/-1.0
SP	1.	David Storl GER 20.47
	2.	Tomasz Majewski POL 20.29
	3.	Aleksandr Lesnoy RUS 20.27
DT	1.	Robert Harting GER 64.25
	2.	Mario Pestano ESP 61.34
	3.	Ercüment Olgundeniz TUR 61.32
HT	1.	Pawel Fajdek POL 77.00
	2.	Markus Esser GER 75.32
	3.	Quentin Bigot FRA 75.22
	drugs dq (3)	Esref Apak TUR 76.29
JT	1.	Dmitriy Tarabin RUS 85.99
	2.	Thomas Röhler GER 83.31
	3.	Roman Avramenko UKR 81.74

4x100m	1.	GBR (Gemili, Aikines-Aryeetey, Ellington, Dasaolu) 38.39
	2.	GER (Schmidt, Knipphals, Reus, Keller) 38.69
	3.	POL (Zaczek, Zimniewicz, Zalewski, Krynski) 38.71
4x400m	1.	GBR (Bingham, C Williams, R Williams, Buck) 3:05.37
	2.	RUS (Kenig, Kashefrazov, Buriak, Krasnov) 3:06.09
	3.	POL (Marciniszyn, Omelko, Pietrzak, Kozlowski) 3:06.18

Women

100m	1.	Olesya Povh UKR 11.51
(-4.3/-4.6)	2 (1B).	Myriam Soumaré FRA 11.66
	3 (2A).	Tatjana Pinto GER 11.72
200m	1.	Mariya Ryemyen UKR 22.80
(0.7)	2.	Myriam Soumaré FRA 23.05
	3.	Anyika Onuora GBR 23.12
400m	1.	Perri Shakes-Drayton GBR 50.50
	2.	Kseniya Zadorina RUS 51.07
	3.	Marie Gayot FRA 51.54
800m	1.	Jessica Judd GBR 2:00.82
	2.	Yekaterina Sharmina RUS 2:00.86
	3.	Olga Lyakhova UKR 2:02.30
1500m	1.	Yekaterina Sharmina RUS 408.86
	2.	Isabel Macías ESP 4:09.95
	3.	Renata Plis POL 4:10.73
3000m	1.	Yelena Korobkina RUS 9:01.45
	2.	Laura Weightman GBR 9:03.11
	3.	Iris Fuentes-Pila ESP 9:03.20
5000m	1.	Olga Golovkina RUS 15:32.45
	2.	Emelia Gorecka GBR 15:40.52
	3.	Sabrina Mockenhaupt GER 15:40.94
3000mSt	1.	Natalya Aristarkhova RUS 9:30.64
	2.	Valentyna Zhudina UKR 9:34.90
	3.	Antje Möldner-Schmidt GER 9:35.67
100mh	1.	Tiffany Porter GBR 12.62w
(2.6)	2.	Tatyana Dektyareva RUS 12,88w
	3.	Anna Plotitsyna UKR 12.91
400mh	1.	Eilidh Child GBR 54.42
	2.	Hanna Yaroshchuk UKR 55.27
	3.	Vera Rudakova RUS 56.20
HJ	1.	Mariya Kuchina RUS 1.98
(indoors)	2=	Kamila Stepaniuk POL 1.92
	2=	Alessia Trost ITA 1.92
PV	1.	Silke Spiegelburg GER 4.60
	2.	Anzhelika Sidorova RUS 4.55
	3.	Anna Rogowska POL 4.40
LJ	1.	Éloyse Lesueur FRA 6.44/0.1
	2.	Darya Klishina RUS 6.43/-0.7
	3.	Shara Proctor GBR 6.43/-0.3
TJ	1.	Olga Saladuha UKR 14.49/0.9
	2.	Yekaterina Koneva RUS 14.10w/2.6
	3.	Simona La Mantia ITA 13.99w/2.5
SP	1.	Christina Schwanitz GER 19.30
	2.	Halyna Obleshchuk UKR 18.05
	3.	Emel Dereli TUR 17.50
DT	1.	Mélina Robert-Michon FRA 63.75
	2.	Julia Fischer GER 62.67
	3.	Zaneta Glanc POL 61.70
HT	1.	Betty Heidler GER 74.31
	2.	Anita Wlodarczyk POL 74.14
	3.	Sophie Hitchon GBR 72.97
JT	1.	Christina Obergföll GER 62.64

2. Mercedes Chilla ESP 58.55
3. Vira Rebryk UKR 57.92
4x100m 1. UKR (Povh, Pyatachenko, Ryemyen, Pohrebnyak) 42.62
2. GER (Kwadwo, Weit, Pinto, Sailer) 43.15
3. RUS (Katsura, Kashina, Savlinis, Kuzina) 43.23
4x400m 1. GBR (Child, Cox, Beesley, Ohuruogu) 3:28.60
2. RUS (Gusarova, Terekhova, Firova, Zadorina) 3:29.46
3. FRA (Gayot, Guion Firmin, Anacharsis, Guei) 3:29.55

First League at Dublin, Ireland 22-23 June
1. CZE 351.5, 2. SWE 311. 3. NED 299, 4. ROU 297.5, 5. POR 269, 6. FIN 251.5, 7. IRL 242, 8. BEL 236.5, 9. HUN 226, 10. EST 211. 11. BUL 206, 12. SUI 206.
Winners: **Men**: **100m**: Churandy Martina NED 10.46, **200m**: Pavel Máslak CZE 21.20, **400m**: Kevin Borlée BEL 45.61. **800m**: Brian Gregan IRL 46.32, **1500m**: Pieter-Jan Hannes BEL 3:45.05, **3000m**: Niclas Sandells FIN 8:17.78, **5000m**: Bashir Abdi BEL 14:52.78, **3000mSt**: Mitko Tsenov BUL 8:45.16, **110mh**: Balázs Baji HUN 13.45, **400mh**: Rasmus Mägi EST 51.07, **HJ**: Jaroslav Bába CZE 2.20, **PV**: Jan Kudlicka CZE 5.50, **LJ**: Eero Haapala FIN 7.96w, **TJ**: Fabian Florant NED 16.49, **SP**: Ladislav Prasil CZE 20.62, **DT**: Sergiu Ursu ROU 63.02, **HT**: Krisztián Pars HUN 76.56, **JT**: Vitezslav Vesely CZE 80.44, **4x100m**: NED 39.14, **4x400m**: IRL 3:08.12
Women: **100m**: Ivet Lalova BUL 11.79. **200m**: Angela Morosanu ROU 23.48, **400m**: Zuzana Hejnová CZE 51.90, **800m**: Mirela Lavric ROU 2:03.44, **1500m**: Maureen Koster NED 4:22.66, **3000m**: Susan Kuijken NED 9:07.04, **5000m**: Jip Vastenburg NED 16:12.88, **3000mSt**: Sandra Eriksson FIN 9:47.76, **100mh**: Rosina Hodde NED 13.17, **400mh**: Denisa Rosolová CZE 55.34, **HJ**: Nafissatou Thiam BEL 1.89, **PV**: Jirina Svodobová CZE 4.40, **LJ**: Grit Sadeiko EST 6.26, **TJ**: Gabriela Petrova BUL 13.55w, **SP**: Radoslava Mavrodieva BUL 18.35, **DT**: Nicoleta Grasu ROU 57.34, **HT**: Éva Orbán HUN 68.57, **JT**: Oona Sormunen FIN 56.04, **4x100m**: CZE 44.20, **4x400m**: ROU 3:30.77.

Second League at Kaunas, Lithuania 22-23 June
1. SLO 221. 2. LTU 209, 3. SRB 192, 4. CRO 178.5, 5. DEN 171.5, 6. AUT 171.5, 7. CYP 155, 8. ISR 150.
Winners: **100m**: Rytis Sakalauskas LTU 10.44, **200m**: Jan Zumer SLO 21.22, **400m**: Nick Ekelund-Arenander DEN 45.93, **800m**: Nick Jensen DEN 1:52.40, **1500m**: Andrteas Vojta AUT 3:50.53, **3000m**: Mirko Petrovic SRB 8:27.75, **5000m**: Brenton Rowe AUT 14:09.30, **3000mSt**: Ole Hesselbjerg DEN 8:44.55, **110mh**: Milan Trajkovic CYP 13.67, **400mh**: Emir Bekric SRB 49.98, **HJ**: Raivydas Stanys LTU 2.21. **PV**: Rasmus Jørgensen DEN 5.65, **LJ**: Marius Rudys LTU 7.74, **TJ**: Yochai Halevi ISR 16.73, **SP**: Asmir Kolasinac SRB 20.37, **DT**: Apostolos Parellis CYP 60.17, **HT**: Primoz Kozmus SLO 72.92, **JT**: Matija Kranjc SLO 73.36, **4x100m**: LTU 39.83, **4x400m**: SRB 3:08.73
Women: **100m**: Lina Grincikaite LTU 11.31. **200m**: Eleni Artymata 23.15, **400m**: Agne Serksniene LTU 52.81. **800m**: Egle Balciunaite LTU 2:03.05, **1500m**:

Amela Terzic SRB 4:26.73, **3000m**: Sonja Stolic SRB 9:27.69, **5000m**: Olivera Jevtic SRB 15:50.94, **3000mSt**: Marusa Mismas SLO 9:58.93, **100m**: Marina Tomic SLO 13.28, **400mh**: Egle Staisiunaite LTU 57.75, **HJ**: Ana Simic CRO 1.93, **PV**: Tina Sutej SLO 4.30, **LJ**: Nektaria Panagi CYP 6.46, **TJ**: Snezana Rodic 14.07, **SP**: Valentina Muzaric CRO 17.29, **DT**: Sandra Perkovic CRO 65.77, **HT**: Barbara Spiler SLO 68.22, **JT**: Martina Ratej SLO 62.60, **4x100m**: SLO 44.73, **4x400m**: LTU 3:35.11.

Third League at Banská Bystrica, Slovakia 22-23 June
1. SVK 531.5. 2. LAT 484.5. 3. MDA 455.5, 4. ISL 430.5, 5. LUX 396.5, 6. BIH 352, 7. GEO 338, 8. AZE 312.5, 9. ARM 301. 10. MNE 275, 11. MLT 243.5, 12. MKD 190.5, 13. AND 149, 14. Small States of Europe 130.5, 15. ALB 65.5.

7th Francophone Games

At Nice, France 10-14 September
Men: **100m**: Emmanuel Biron FRA 10.41, **200m**: Segun Makinde CAN 20.80, **400m**: Antoine Gillet BEL 46.64, **800m**: Abdulrahman Musaeb Balla QAT 1:46.57, **1500m**: Ayanleh Soulieiman DJI 3:57.35, **5000m**: Othmane El Goumri MAR 13:48.76, **10,000m**: Hicham Bellani MAR 28:49.09, **3000mSt**: Hamid Ezzine MAR 8:43,41, **110mh**: Sekou Kaba CAN 13.84, **400mh**: Mamadou Kasse Hann SEN 49.48, **HJ**: Derek Drouin CAN 2.30, **PV**: Valentin Lavillenie FRA 5.50, **LJ**: Adrian Strzalkowski POL 7.99w, **TJ**: Yoann Rapinier FRA 17.11, **SP**: Tomasz Majewski POL 20.18*, **DT**: Sergiu Ursu ROU 62.87, **HT**: Pawel Fajdek POL 78.28, **JT**: Lukasz Grzeszczuk POL 78.62*, **Dec**: Bastien Auzeil FRA 7780, **4x100m**: CAN 39.14, **4x400m**: FRA 3:05.22, **20kmW**: Kevin Campion FRA 1:24:32.
Women: **100m**: Ayodelé Ikuesan FRA 11.72, **200m**: Crystal Emmanuel CAN 23.63, **400m**: Floria Guel FRA 52.31, **800m**: Mirela Lavric ROU 2:02.27, **1500m**: Rabab Arrafi MAR 4:18.70, **10,000m**: Diane Nukuri-Johnson BDI 32:29.14*, **3000mSt**: Ancuta Bobocel ROU 9:46.82, **100m**: Anne Zagré BEL 13.41, **400m**: Hayat Lambarki MAR 57.22, **HJ**: Mélanie Skotnik FRA 1.86, **PV**: Marion Lotout FRA 4.40, **LJ/TJ**: Anna Jagaciak POL 6.68/13.92, **SP**: Anca Heltne ROU 17.14, **DT**: Suzanne Kragbé CIV 55.58, **HT**: Anita Wlodarczyk POL 75.62*, **JT**: Krista Woodward 52.82, **Hep**: Laura Arteil FRA 5534, **4x100m**: BEL 44.70, **4x400m**: ROU 3:29.81, **20kW**: Laura Polti SUI 1:37:23.

17th Mediterranean Games

At Mersin, Turkey 26-29 June
Men: **100m**: Emmanuel Biron FRA 10.22, **200m**: Likoúrgos-Stéfanos Tsákonas GRE 20.45, **400m**: Matteo Galvan ITA 45.59, **800m/1500m**: Ilham Tanui Özbilen TUR 1:44.00*/3:35.09, **5000m**: Rabah Aboud ALG 13:38.01, **10,000m**: Polat Kemboi Arikan TUR 28:17.26, **HMar**: Ahmed Baday MAR 66:54, **3000mSt**: Amor Benyahia TUN 8:14.05, **110mh**: Konstadínos Douvalídis GRE 13.45*, **400mh**: Emir Bekric SRB 48.83*, **HJ**: Konstadínos Baniótis GRE 2.34*, **PV**: Giuseppe Gibilisco ITA 5.70, **LJ**: Loúis Tsátoumas GRE 8.14, **TJ**: Daniele Greco ITA 17.13, **SP**: Borje Vivas ESP 19.99, **DT**: Martin Maric CRO 61.46, **HT**: Mostafa Al-Gamal EGY 76.68, **JT**: Fatih Avan TUR 83.84, **4x100m/4x400m**: ITA 39.06/3:04.61.

Women: 100m: Ilenia Draisci ITA 11.53, **200m:** Eleni Artymata CYP 23.18, **400m:** Chiara Bazzoni ITA 52.08, **800m:** Malika Akkaoui MASR 2:00.72, **1500m:** Siham Hilali MAR 4:04.06*, **5000m:** Christine Bardelle FRA 15:39.54, **10,000m:** Kenza Dahmani ALG 32:42.47, **HMar:** Valeria Straneo ITA 71:00*, **3000mSt:** Amina Betiche ALG 9:40.71*, **100mh:** Marzia Caravelli ITA 12.98, **400mh:** Hayat Lambarki MAR 55.27, **HJ:** Burcu Yüksel-Ayhan TUR & Ana Simic CRO 1.92, **PV:** Stélla-Iró Ledáki GRE 4.50*, **LJ:** Nektaria Panagi CYP 6.51, **TJ:** Athanasía Pérra GRE 14.48, **DT:** Sandra Perkovic CRO 66.21*, **HT:** Jessika Guehaseim FRA 67.14, **JT:** Martina Ratej SLO 60.28, **Hep:** Yasmina Omrani ALG 5802, **4x100m/4x400m:** ITA 44.66/ 3:32.44, **20kW:** Eleonora Giorgi ITA 1:39:13. **Medal Table:** ITA 12G-6S-9B, GRE 6-4-6, TUR 5-7-7, MAR 4-7-3, FRA 4-2-5, CRO 3-1-0, CYP 2-1-1, ESP 1-5-2, EGY 1-3-1, SLO 1-2-1, SRB 1-2-0, TUN 1-0-2, ALB 0-1-0, BIH & MNE 0-0-1.

Pan-American Combined Events Cup

At Ottawa, Canada 1-2 June
Men Dec: 1. Yordani García CUB 8141, 2. José Ángel Mendieta CUB 7766, 3, Gray Horn USA 7581. **Women Hep:** 1. Yorgelis Rodríguez CUB 5947, 2. Ana Camila Pirelli PAR 5683, 3. Lindsay Schwartz USA 5645.

Pan-American Junior Championships

At Medellín, Colombia (A) 23-25 August
100m: Zhamel Hughes AIA 10.31, **200m:** Reynier Mena CUB 20.63, **400m:** Brandon McBride CAN 45.89, **800m:** Bryan Antonio Martínez MEX 1:50.35, **1500m:** Craig Engels USA 3:53.13, **5000m:** Edgar García MEX 14:44.54, **10,000m:** Matthew McClintock USA 31:12.39, **3000mSt:** Yuber Echeverry COL 9:16.37, Jnr **110mh:** Juan Carlos Moreno COL 13.42, **400mh:** Khallifah Rosser USA 50.75, **HJ:** Wally Ellerson USA 2.16, **PV:** Shawn Barber CAN 5.35, **LJ:** Higor Alves BRA 7.95w, **TJ:** Lázaro Martínez CUB 16.49, **6kg SP:** Josh Freeman USA 20.20, 1.75kg, **DT:** Hayden Reed USA 62.49, **6kg HT:** Diego del Real MEX 72.99, **JT:** Alex Pascal CAY 72.82, Jnr **Dec:** Felipe Vinícius dos Santos BRA 7762, **4x100m/4x400m:** USA 39.17/3:06.57, **10,000mW:** Erwin González MEX 40:36.85, **Women: 100m/200m:** Arialis Gandulla CUB 11.32w/23.27, **400m:** Courtney Okolo USA 52.19, **800m:** Jenna Westaway CAN 2:06.94, **1500m:** Julia Zrinyi CAN 4:36.88, **3000m/3000mSt:** Zulema Arenas PER 9:42.70/10:28.94, **5000m:** Hetaira Palacios PER 18:11.57, **100mh:** Alexis Perry USA 13.56, **400mh:** Sage Watson CAN 56.81, **PV:** Alysha Newman CAN 4.40*, **LJ:** Alexis Faulkner USA 6.24, **TJ:** Paula Álvarez CUB 13.57, **SP:** Stamatia Scarvelis USA 15.46, **DT:** Izabela da Silva BRA 54.15, **HT:** Hassana Divó CUB 60.54, **JT:** Megan Glasmann USA 53.93*, **Hep:** Yusleidys Mendieta CUB 5627, **4x100m/4x400m:** USA 43.97/3:36.48. **Medal table leaders,** USA 15G-16S-7B, CUB 8-3-0, CAN 6-6-7, BRA 4-6-4, MEX 4-1-4, PER 3-0-2, COL 2-4-6, 9 nations won gold, 21 won medals.

Pan-American Race Walking Cup

At Guatemala City, Guatemala (A) 25-26 May
Men: 20kW: 1. Diego Flores MEX 1:24:16, 2. Eider Arevalo COL 1:24:35, 3. Caio Bonfim BRA 1:25:27; **50kW:** 1. Omar Zepeda MEX 3:57:52, 2, Horacio Nava MEX 3:58:00, 3, Omar Segura MEX 4:03:11; **Junior 10kW:** Manuel Soto COL 41:19; **Women 20kmW:** 1. Kimberley García PER 1:35:01. 2. Lorena Arenas COL 1:35:14, 3. Yanelli Caballero MEX 1:35:19; **Junior 10kmW:** Alejandra Ortega MEX 49:13.

Games of the Small States of Europe

At Luxemburg May 28- 1 June
Men: 100m: Christos Hatziaggelídis CYP 10.77, **200m:** Ivar Kristinn Jasonarson ISL 21.88, **400m:** Kevin Moore MLT 47.53, **800m/1500m:** Amine Khadiri CYP 1:53.15/3:54.20, **5000m:** Pol Mellina LUX 14:29.82, **10,000m:** Marcos Sanza Arranz AND 30:17.47, **3000mSt:** Zouhair El Ouardi MON 9:18.71. **110mh:** Milan Trajkovic CYP 14.03, **400mh:** Jacques Frisch LUX 52.28, **HJ:** Vasilios Konstantinou CYP 2.12, **PV:** Nikandros Stylianou CYP 5.15, **LJ:** Christodoulos Theofilou CYP 7.28, **TJ:** Panagiotis Volou CYP 15.93, **SP/DT:** Danijel Furtula MNE 18.43/62.83*, **JT:** Gudmundur Sverrisson ISL 74.38, **4x100m/4x400m:** CYP 41.71/3:13.55. **Women: 100m:** Ramona Papaioannou CYP 11.57/23.40, **400m/800m:** Anítxa Hinriksdóttir ISL 54.29/2:04.60, **1500m:** Martine Nobili LUX 4:27.08, **5000m/10,000m:** Sladana Perunovic MNE 16:53.20/35:21.21. **100mh:** Natalia Christofi CYP 14.32, **400mh:** Kim Reuland LUX 59.80, **HJ:** Marija Vukovic MNE 1.77, **PV:** Gina Reuland LUX 4.00, **LJ:** Nektaria Panayi CYP 6.07, **TJ:** Eleftheria Christofi CYP 13.20, **SP:** Florentia Kappa CYP 15.36, **JT:** Asdis Hjálmsdóttir ISL 56.15, **4x100m:** CYP 46.02, **4x400m:** ISL 3:40.97.

South American Championships

At Cartagena, Colombia 5-7 July
Men

100m	1. Alex Quiñónez ECU	10.22
(1.3)	2. Bruno de Barros BRA	10.33
	3. Isidro Montoya COL	10.38
200m	1. Alex Quiñónez ECU	20.44*
(1.9)	2. Bernardo Baloyes COL	20.71
	3. Jorge Henrique Vides BRA	20.71
400m	1. José Meléndez VEN	46.31
	2. Wagner Cardozo BRA	46.38
	3. Stephan James GUY	46.47
800m	1. Rafith Rodríguez COL	1:46.34
	2. Diego Gomes BRA	1:48.17
	3. Lutimar Paes BRA	1:48.50
1500m	1. Jean Carlos Machado BRA	3:45.94
	2. Federico Bruno ARG	3:45.94
	3. Iván López CHI	3:46.00
5000m	1. Bayron Piedra ECU	14:15.35
	2. Víctor Aravena CHI	14:17.97
	3. Javier Guarín COL	14:19.82

10,000m	1. Solonei da Silva BRA 29:51.79		2. Muriel Coneo COL 4:15.84
	2. José Luis Rojas PER 30:13.10		3. Andrea Ferris PAN 4:21.34
	3. William Naranjo COL 30:19.29	**5000m**	1. Carolina Tabares COL 16:09.82
3000mSt	1. José Gregorio Peña VEN 8:32.01		2. Gladys Tejeda PER 16:19.39
	2. Mauricio Valdivia CHI 8:44.36		3. Wilma Arizapana PER 16:22.82
	3. Gládson Barbosa BRA 8:45.10	**10,000m**	1. Cruz da Silva BRA 34:44.14
110mh	1. Jorge McFarlane PER 13.61		2. Carolina Tabares COL 34:47.59
(1.0)	2. Matheus Inocêncio BRA 13.67		3. Diana Landi ECU 35:12.53
	3. Jonathan Mendes BRA 13.84	**3000mSt**	1. Erika Lima BRA 9:54.97
400mh	1. Mahau Suguimati BRA 49.86		2. Rolanda Bell PAN 10:04.01
	2. Andrés Silva URU 50.52		3. Muriel Coneo COL 10:09.91
	3. Yeison Rivas COL 51.01	**100mh**	1. Lina Florez COL 13.09
HJ	1. Talles Silva BRA 2.22	(2.0)	2. Briggit Merlano COL 13.20
	2= Wanner Miller COL 2.19		3. Fabiana dos Santos BRA 13.21
	2= Guilherme Cobbo BRA 2.19	**400mh**	1. Liliane Barbosa BRA 58.03
PV	1. Thiago da Silva BRA 5.83*		2. Déborah Rodríguez URU 58.06
	2. Germán Chiaraviglio ARG 5.40		3. Fernanda Tavares BRA 58.83
	3. João Gabriel Sousa BRA 5.40	**HJ**	1. Mônica de Freitas BRA 1.79
LJ	1. Mauricio Vinicius da Silva BRA		2. Anyi García COL 1.76
	8.24*/1.8		3= Kashani Rios PAN 1.73
	2. Jorge McFarlane PER 8.01w/2.6		3= Aline Fernanda Santos BRA 1.73
	3. Irving Saladino PAN 7.94/1.5	**PV**	1. Karla da Silva BRA 4.20
TJ	1. Jefferson Dias Sabino BRA 16.73/1.1		2. Valeria Chiaraviglio ARG 4.15
	2. Jhon Murillo COL 16.36w/2.1		3. Milena Agudelo COL 3.90
	3. Jonathan Silva BRA 16.35/1.6	**LJ**	1. Macarena Reyes CHI 6.54w/2.9
SP	1. Germán Lauro ARG 20.87*		2. Keila Costa BRA 6.49/1.4
	2. Darlan Romani BRA 19.64		3. Jéssica dos Reis BRA 6.49w/2.5
	3. Michael Putman PER 18.73	**TJ**	1. Keila Costa BRA 14.21w/3.4
DT	1. Germán Lauro ARG 60./45		2. Yorsiris Urrutia COL 13.92/1.6
	2. Andrés Rossini ARG 57.77		3. Giselly Landázuri COL 13.71/1.3
	3. Mauricio Ortega COL 57.76	**SP**	1. Geisa Arcanjo BRA 18.27
HT	1. Wágner Domingos BRA 71.36		2. Sandra Lemus COL 17.72
	2. Juan Ignacio Cerra ARG 69.33		3. Ahymará Espinoza VEN 17.47
	3. Allan Wolski BRA 66.25	**DT**	1. Fernanda Borges BRA 60.79*
JT	1. Víctor Fatecha PAR 76.14		2. Rocío Comba ARG 58.75
	2. Arley Ibargüen COL 76.13		3. Karen Gallardo CHI 57.04
	3. Braian Toledo ARG 75.33	**HT**	1. Rosa Rodríguez VEN 68.38
Dec	1. Román Gastaldi ARG 7273		2. Eli Johana Moreno COL 67.22
	2. Renato Câmara BRA 7175		3. Jennifer Dahlgren ARG 65.82
	3. Oscar Campos VEN 7000	**JT**	1. Flor Ruiz COL 60.23*
4x100m	1. BRA (Moreira, Vides, Lucindo, Firmiano) 39.47		2. Laila e Silva BRA 58.80
	2. COL 39.76		3. Jucilene de Lima BRA 57.73
	3. VEN 39.81	**Hep**	1. Tamara de Souza BRA 5685
4x400m	1. VEN (Ramírez, Bravo, Meléndez, Mezones) 3:03.64		2. Ana Camila Pirelli PAR 5610
	2. COL 3:06.25		3. Agustina Zerboni ARG 5317
	3. BRA 3:08.60	**4x100m**	1. BRA (Silva, Krasucki, J de Lima, E dos Santos) 43.37
20000mW	1. Caio Bonfim BRA 1:24:28.4		2. COL 44.01
	2. Eider Arévalo COL 1:24:36.4		3. CHI 46.42
	3. Andrés Chocho ECU 1:26:20.2	**4x400m**	1. BRA (J Sousa, E dos Santos, Barbosa, J de Lima) 3:35.37
Women			2. COL 3:36.29
100m	1. Ana Cláudia Silva BRA 11.21		3. ECU 3:43.01
(0.1)	2. Franciela Krasucki BRA 11.27	**20000mW**	1. Lorena Arenas COL 1:37:46.2
	3. Eliecet Palacios COL 11.56		2. Arabelly Orjuela COL 1:38:59.8
200m	1. Ana Cláudia Silva BRA 22.70w		3. Wendy Cornejo BOL 1:39:43.9
(3.4)	2. Nercely Soto VEN 23.05		
	3. Erika Chávez ECU 23.10		
400m	1. Joelma Sousa BRA 52.25		
	2. Nercely Soto VEN 53.96		
	3. Yenifer Padilla COIL 54.28		
800m	1. Rosibel García COL 2:02.45		
	2. Flávia de Lima BRA 2:02.94		
	3. Andrea Ferris PAN 2:03.57		
1500m	1. Rosibel García COL 4:15.84		

Medal table

	G	S	B	Points
BRA	24	10	13	449
COL	7	17	10	292
VEN	4	2	4	136
ARG	3	6	3	119

ECU	3	-	4	78
CHI	1	2	2	59
PER	1	3	2	53
PAR	1	1	-	30
PAN	-	1	4	28

URU (2S) 12, BOL (1B) 7, GUY (1B) 6

27th South East Asia Games

At Nay Pyi Taw, Myanmar 15-19 December

Men: **100m/200m**: Jirapong Meenapra THA 10.48/21.29, **400m**: Archand C.Bagsit PHI 47.22, **800m**: Mohd Jironi Ruduan MAS 1:50.98, **1500m**: Duong Van Thai VIE & Mohd Jironi Riduan MAS 3:58.02, **5000m/10,000m**: Nguyen Van Lai VIE 14:19.35/29:44.82, **Mar**: Mok Ying Ren SIN 2:28:36, **3000mSt**: Christopher Ulboc PHI 9:01.59, **110mh**: Jumrus Rittidet THA 13.72*, **400mh**: Eric Cray PHI 51.29, **HJ**: Nauraj Singh Randhawa MAS 2.17, **PV**: Kreeta Sinthawacheewa THA 5.15, **LJ**: Henry Dagmil PHI 7.80, **TJ**: Nguyen Van Hung VIE 16.67*, **SP**: Thawat Khachin THA 17.54, **DT**: Muhammad Irfan Shamsuddin MAS 53.16, **HT**: Tantipong Phetchaiya THA 62.23*, **JT**: Peerachet Janthra THA 76.30*, **Dec**: Jesson Ramil Cid PHI 7038, **4x100m**: THA 39.75, **4x400m**: PHI 3:09.32, **20kmW**: Hendro INA 1:29:41. **Women**: **100m/200m**: Vu Thi Huong VIE 11.59/23.55, **400m**: Treewadee Yongphan THA 53.11, **800m/1500m**: Do Thi Thao VIE 2:05.52/4:22.64, **5000m**: Phyu War Thet MYA 16:06.01, **10,000m**: Triyaningsih INA 34:32.68, **Mar**: Pham Thi Binh VIE 2:45:34, **3000mSt**: Rina Budiarti INA 10:04.54 **100mh**: Dedeh Erawati INA 13.53, **400mh/Hep**: Wassana Winatho THA 58.85/5556, **HJ**: Duong Thi Viet Anh VIE 1.84, **PV**: Sukanya Chomchuendee THA 4.21*, **LJ/TJ**: Maria Natalia Londa INA 6.39/14.17*, **SP**: Zhang Guirong SIN 14.99, **DT**: Subenrat Insaeng THA 56.77, **HT**: Panwat Gimsrang THA 54.96, **JT**: Saowalak Phetthong THA 52.96, **4x100m/4x400m**: THA 44.42/3:36.58, **20kmW**: Saw Mar Lar Nwe MYA 1:35:03. **Medals**: THA 14G-8S-10B, INA 13-12-11, VIE 9-9-14, MAS 6-2-3, PHI 2-9-5, SIN 2-3-2, MYA 0-3-1.

IAU 100km European Championships

Ay Belves, France 27 April

Men: 1. Asier Cuevas ESP 6:53:14, 2. Michael Boch FRA 6:56:49, 3. José Antonio Requejo ESP 6:57:02; Team: 1. ESP 20:54:52, 2. FRA 21:15:57, 3. RUS 21:25:58

Women: 1. Kajsa Berg SWE 7:38:52, 2. Irina Antropova RUS 7:42:52, 3. Sue Harrison GBR 7:48:12; Team: 1. RUS 23:28:22, 2. SWE 24:04:25, 3. ITA 25:24:24.

26th IAU World 24 Hours Championships

At Steenbergen, Norway 11-12 May. Incorporated European Championships.

Men: 1. Jon Olsen USA 269.675k, 2. John Dennis USA 262.734, 3. Florian Reus GER (1 EUR) 259.939, 4. Anatoliy Kruglikov RUS (2 EUR) 257.040, 5. Timur Ponomarev RUS (3 EUR) 256.666, 6. Toshiro Naraki JPN 255.940, 7. Shuhei Odani JPN 250.327; Team: 1. USA 780.552k, 2. JPN 752.567, 3. GER (1 EUR)

752.007, 4. RUS (2 EUR) 748.162, 5. ITA (3 EUR) 715.739, 6. GBR 696.401

Women: 11. Mami Kudo JPN 252.205, 2. Sabrina Little USA 244.669k, 3. Suzanna Bon USA 236.228, 4. Traci Falbo USA 229.702, 5. Anne-Marie Vernet FRA (1 EUR) 229.393, 6. Sayuri Oka JPN 228.907, 7. Cécile Nissen FRA (2 EUR) 227.618, 8. Sharon Law GBR (3 EUR) 226.107; **Team**: 1. USA 710.599k, 2. JPN 705.582, 3. FRA (1 EUR) 670.698, 4. GBR (2 EUR) 658.357, 5. GER (3 EUR) 651.117, 6. SWE 648.852.

European Mountain Racing Championships

At Borovec, Bulgaria 6 July. **Men** 11.8k (1027m height difference): 1. Bernard De Matteis ITA 56:30, 2. Alex Baldaccini ITA 57:35, 3. Ahmet Arslan TUR 57:47; Team: 1. ITA 7, 2. GBR 31. 3. TUR 51. **Junior Men** 8.8k (1027m HD): Ramazan Karagoz TUR 48:51; Team: TUR 21. **Women** 8.8k (1027m HD): 1. Andrea Mayr AUT 51:49, 2. Valentina Belotti ITA 52:54, 3. Mateja Kosovelj SLO 53:08; Team: 1. ITA 11. 2. SUI 36, 3. GBR 52. **Junior Women** 3.5k (530m HD): Melanie Albrecht GER 25:49, Team: RUS 24.

* *Indicates Championships or Games record*

IAAF DIAMOND LEAGUE

The IAAF's successor to the Golden League, the expanded and more globally widespread Diamond League, was launched in 2010 with 14 meetings spread across Asia, Europe, the Middle East and the USA. The total prize money was increased from $6.63 million (with a $50,000 bonus for any new world record) in 2010 to $8 million from 2011 winners of each Race received a Diamond Trophy (4 carats of diamonds) and a $40,000 cash prize.

SAMSUNG DIAMOND LEAGUE – winners 2013

D Doha May 10, **Sh** Shanghai May 18, **NY** New York May 25, **E** Eugene Jun 1, **R** Rome Jun 6, **O** Oslo Jun 13, **Bi** Birmingham Jun 30, **L** Lausanne Jul 4, **P** Paris Saint-Denis Jul 6, **M** Monaco Jul 19, **CP** London (CP) Jul 26-27; **St** Stockholm Aug 22; Finals with double points at: **Z** Zürich Aug 29, **Br** Brussels Sep 6.

Men:

100m: Justin Gatlin D- 9.97, R- 9.94, M- 9.94; Tyson Gay NY- 10.02, L- 9.79; Nesta Carter Bi- 9.99; Usain Bolt Z- 9.90

200m: Warren Weir Sh- 20.18, M- 19.89, Br- 19.87, CP- 19.89; Nickel Ashmeade E- 20.14; Usain Bolt P- 19.73; Sergiy Smelyk St- 20.54

400m: Kirani James D- 44.02, P- 43.96, CP- 44.65; LaShawn Merrit NY- 44.32, St- 44.69, Z- 44.13; Youssef Al-Masrahi O- 45.33

800m: David Rudisha D- 1:43.87, NY 1:45.14; Mohammed Aman R- 1:43.61, Bi- 1:45.18, L- 1:45.33, Br- 1:42.37; Duane Solomon M- 1:43.72

1500m/1M: Asbel Kiprop Sh- 3:32.39; Silas Kiplagat E 3:49.48M, Z- 3:30.97; Ayanleh Souleiman O- 3:50.53M, P- 3:32.55, St- 3:33.59; L- Augustine Choge CP- 3:50.01

3/5000m: Hagos Gebrehiwot D- 7:30.36, NY- 13:10.03; Yenew Alamirew R- 12:54.95, L- 13:06.69, Br- 12:58.75; Mo Farah Bi- 13:14.24; Edwin Soi M- 12:52.34
3000mSt: Conseslus Kipruto Sh- 8:01.16, E- 8:03.59, O- 8:04.48, CP- 8:06.86; Ezekiel Kemboi P- 7:59.03; Hilary Yego St- 8:09.81, Z- 8:08.03
110mh: Jason Richardson Sh- 13.23; Hansle Parchment E- 13.05; Ryan Brathwaite NY- 13.19, Aries Merritt P- 13.09; David Oliver CP- 13.20, St- 13.21, Z- 13.12
400mh: Michael Tinsley D- 48.92; Johnny Dutch R- 48.31; Javier Culson Bi- 48.59, L- 48.14; Jehue Gordon M- 48.00
HJ: Bohdan Bondarenko D- 2.33, Bi- 2.36, L- 2.41, CP- 2.38, Z- 2.33; Mutaz Essa Barshim Sh- 2.33, E- 2.40
PV: Konstadínos Filippídis D- 5.82, L- 5.72; Renaud Lavillenie E- 5.95, P- 5.92, M- 5.96, Br- 5.96; Raphael Holzdeppe R- 5.91
LJ: Li Jinzhe Sh- 8.34; Aleksandr Menkov E- 8.39, Bi- 8.27, CP- 8.31, St- 8.18; Damar Forbes P- 8.11; Zarck Visser- Z 8.32
TJ: Christian Taylor D- 17.25, R- 17.08, Bi- 17.66, M- 17.30; Benjamin Compaoré NY- 16.45; Pedro Pichardo L- 17.58; Teddy Tamgho Br- 17.30
SP: Ryan Whiting D- 22.28, NY- 21.27, L- 21.88, Z- 22.03i, Br- 21.45; David Storl R- 20.70; Reese Hoffa Bi- 21.31
DT: Piotr Malachowski Sh- 67.34, CP- 67.35, St- 65.86; Robert Harting E- 69.75, P- 67.04; Gerd Kanter O- 66.52, Z- 67.02
JT: Vitezslav Vesely D- 85.09, O- 85.96, M- 87.68; Tero Pitkämäki Sh- 87.60, Br- 87.32; Andrea Thorkildsen Bi- 83.94; Kim Amb L- 82.65

Women
100m: Shelly-Ann Fraser-Pryce Sh- 10.93, E- 10.71w, P- 10.92, Br- 10.72; Ivet Lalova O- 11.04; Blessing Okagbare L- 10.79; Kerron Stewart St- 11.24
200m: Shelly-Ann Fraser-Pryce D- 22.48w, Z- 22.40; Veronica Campbell-Brown NY- 22.53, Murielle Ahouré R- 22.36, M- 22.24; Blessing Okagbare Bi- 22.55; Mariya Ryemyen L- 22.61
400m: Amantle Montsho D- 49.88, NY- 49.91, R- 49.87, M- 49.33; Christine Ohuruogu Bi- 50.83; Francine McCorory L- 50.36, Natasha Hastings Br- 50.36
800m: Francine Niyonsaba Sh- 2:00.33, E- 1:56.72, P- 1:57.26; Yekaterina Poistogova O- 1:59.39; Brenda Martinez CP- 1:58.29; Eunice Sum St- 1:58.84, Z- 1:58.82
1500m: Abeba Aregawi D- 3:56.60, NY- 4:03.69, R- 4:00.23, Bi- 4:03.70, L- 4:02.11, Br- 4:05.41; Jennifer Simpson M- 4:00.48
3/5000m: Genzebe Dibaba Sh- 14:45.92; Tirunesh Dibaba NY- 14:42.01, P- 14:23.68; Meseret Defar O- 14:26.90, St- 8:30.29, Z- 14:32.83; Shannon Rowbury CP- 8:41.46
3000mSt: Lidya Chepkurui D- 9:13.75, NY- 9:30.82; Milcah Chemos R- 9:16.14, Bi- 9:17.43, M- 9:14.17, Br- 9:15.06; Hiwot Ayalew L- 9:17.66
100mh: Dawn Harper-Nelson D- 12.60, R- 12.65, Bi- 12.64, L- 12.53, Br- 12.48; Tiffany Porter O- 12.76; Queen Harrison M- 12.64
400mh: Zuzana Hejnová Sh- 53.79, E- 53.70, O-

53.60, P- 53.23, CP- 53.07, St- 53.70, Z- 53.32
HJ: Blanka Vlasic NY- 1.94; Anna Chicherova R- 1.98 (=), P- 2.01; Svetlana Shkolina R- 1.98 (=), O- 1.97, St- 1.98, Br- 2.00; Brigetta Barrett M- 2.01
PV: Yelena Isinbayeva Sh- 4.70; Jennifer Suhr NY- 4.63; Silke Spiegelburg O- 4.65, St- 4.69, Z- 4.79; Yarisley Silva Bi- 4.73, CP- 4.83
LJ: Britney Reese D- 7.25, R- 6.99; Janay DeLoach NY- 6.79; Shara Proctor O- 6.89, Z- 6.88; Blessing Okagbare L- 6.98, M- 7.04w
TJ: Caterine Ibargüen Sh- 14.49, E- 14.93, B- 14.93, Br- 14.49, O- 14.81, P- 14.69; Yekaterina Koneva CP- 14.52
SP: Christina Schwanitz Sh- 20.20, O- 20.10; Valerie Adams E- 20.15, P- 20.62, CP- 20.90, St- 20.30, Z- 20.98
DT: Sandra Perkovic D- 68.23, NY- 68.48, R- 68.25, Bi- 64.32, L- 68.96, M- 65.30, Br- 67.04
JT: Christine Obergföll NY- 65.33, E- 67.70, R- 66.45, P- 64.74, CP- 65.61; Mariya Abakumova St- 68.59, Z- 68.94

FINAL PLACINGS

Men: 100m: 1. Gatlin 14, 2. Bolt 10, 3. Carter 5; **200m:** 1. Weir 18, 2. Ashmeade 8, 3. Smelyk 4; **400m:** 1. Merritt 20, 2. James 18, 3. Al-Masrahi 4; **800m:** 1. Aman 22, 2. Solomon 4, 3. Nick Symmonds 4; **1500m:** 1. Souleiman 18, 2. Kiplagat 14, 3. Kiprop 6; **5000m:** 1. Alamirew 19, 1. Gebrhiwet 15, 3. Soi 4; **3000mSt:** 1. C Kipruto 15, 2. Yego 3, 3. Kemboi 6; **110mh:** 1. Oliver 18, 2. Richardson 6, 3. Ryan Wilson 6; **400mh:** 1. Culson 15, 2. Gordon 12, 3. Tinsley 9; **HJ:** 1. Bondarenko 26, 2. Barshim 13, 3. Baniótis 4; **PV:** 1. Lavillenie 22, 2. Filippídis 13, 3. Augusto de Oliveira 3; **LJ:** 11. Menkov 18, 2. Visser 8, 3. Khotso Mokoena 6; **TJ:** 1. Taylor 23, 2. Tamgho 13, 3. Pichardo 5; **SP:** 1. Whiting 26, 2. Georgi Ivanov 4, 3. Ladislav Prásil 3; **DT:** 1. Kanter 16, 2. Malachowski 14, 3. Harting 12; **JT:** 1. Vesely 18, 2. Pitkämäki 16, 3. Thorkildsen 8. **Women: 100m:** 1. Fraser-Pryce 20, 2. Alex Anderson 6, 3. Stewart 4; **200m:** 1. Fraser-Pryce 15, 2. Ahouré 12, 3. Ryemyen 6; **400m:** 1. Montsho 24, 2. Hastings 11, 3. McCorory 8; **800m:** 1. Sum 12, 2. Malika Akkaoui 6, 3. Poistogova 4; **1500m:** 1. Aregawi 28, 2, Hellen Obiri 6, Simpson 5; **5000m:** 1. Defar 18; 2. T Dibaba 12, 3. Mercy Cherono 6; **3000mSt:** 1. Chemos 20, 2. Chepkurui 12, Sofia Assefa 12; **100mh:** 1. Harper-Nelson 22, 2. Kellie Wells 7, 3. Porter 5; **400H:** 1. Hejnová 32, 2. Kaliese Spencer 7, 3. Denisa Rosolová 2; **HJ:** 1. Shkolina 20, Chircherova 17, 3. Emma Green Tregaro 6; **PV:** 1. Spiegelburg 12, 2. Silva 13, 3. Fabiana Murer 10; **LJ:** 1. Proctor 17, 2. Okagbare 14, 3. Reese 10; **TJ:** 1. Ibargüen 28, Olga Saladuha 11, Kimberly Williams 7; **SP:** 1. Adams 24, 2. Schwanitz 12, 3. Michelle Carter 6; **DT:** 1. Perkovic 32, 2. Gia Lewis-Smallwood 9, 3. Yarelys Barrios 6; **JT:** 1. Obergföll 25, 2. Abakumova 18, 3. Linda Stahl 4.

IAAF Diamond League fixtures for 2014: May 9 Doha, May 17 Shanghai, May 31 Eugene, Jun 5 Rome, Jun 11 Oslo, Jun 14 New York, Jul 3 Lausanne, Jul 5 Paris, Jul 11-12 Glasgow, Jul 18 Monaco, Aug 21 Stockholm, Aug 24 Birmingham, Finals: Aug 28 Zürich, Sep 5 Brussels.

MAJOR MEETINGS 2013-2014

Diamond League, World Challenge and European Athletics Premium Meetings

DL – Diamond League, WC – World Challenge, EAP European Premium Meeting (EAC Classic).

2013 date		Meeting	2014 date	
6 Apr	WC	Telstra Melbourne Track Classic, AUS	22 Mar	WC
4 May	WC	Jamaica International, KIngston JAM	3 May	WC
10 May	DL	Qatar Super Grand Prix, Doha, QAT	9 May	DL
5 May	WC	Golden Grand Prix, Tokyo, JPN	11 May	WC
18 May	WC	Ponce Grand Prix, PUR	17 May	WC
18 May	DL	Shanghai Golden Grand Prix, CHN	18 May	DL
21 May	WC	Bejing, CHN	21 May	WC
1 Jun	DL	Prefontaine Classic, Eugene, Oregon, USA	31 May	DL
6 Jun	DL	Golden Gala, Rome, ITA	5 Jun	DL
8 Jun	WC	Fanny Blankers-Koen Games, Hengelo, NED	8 Jun	WC
9 Jun	WC	Mohammed VI d'Athlétisme, Rabat, MAR Marrakech in 2014	9 Jun	WC
10 Jun	EAP	Josef Odlozil Memorial, Prague, CZE	9 Jun	EAP
13 Jun	DL	ExxonMobil Bislett Games, Oslo, NOR	11 Jun	DL
11 Jun	WC	Moscow Challenge, RUS	12 Jun	WC
9 Jun	EAP	Memorial Primo Nebiolo, Turin, ITA	13 Jun	EAP
25 May	DL	adidas Grand Prix, New York (RI), USA	14 Jun	DL
15 Jun	WC	Dakar, SEN	28 Jun	WC
27 Jun	WC	Golden Spike, Ostrava, CZE	17 Jun	WC
(16 Jun)	–	Paavo Nurmi Games, Turku, Finland	25 Jun	EAP
4 Jul	DL	Athletissima, Lausanne, SUI	3 Jul	DL
6 Jul	DL	Meeting AREVA Paris Saint-Denis, FRA	5 Jul	DL
26/27 Jul	DL	Anniversary Games, London (OS) 2013, Grand Prix, Glasgow 2014	11/12 Jul	DL
23 Jul	DL	Herculis, Monaco, MON	18 Jul	DL
13 Jul		Atletismo Madrid, ESP	19 Jul	WC
13 Jul	EAP	KBC Night of Athletics, Heusden-Zolder, BEL	19 Jul	EAC
12 May	WC	GP Brasil de Atletismo, Bélem BRA	10 Aug	WC
22 Aug	DL	DN Galan, Stockholm, SWE	21 Aug	DL
30 Jun	DL	British Grand Prix, Birmingham, GBR	24 Aug	DL
29 Aug	DL	Weltklasse, Zürich, SUI	28 Aug	DL
8 Jul	EAP	Meeting Stanislas, Nancy (Tomblaine), FRA	2 Jul	EAC
23-25 Aug	–	Internationales Hochsprun, Eberstadt, Germany	22-24 Aug	EAP
18-19 Aug	–	Hochsprung-Meeting, Eberstadt, GER	23-25 Aug	EPM
20 Aug	EAC	Gugl Games, Linz, AUT	26 Aug	EPM
1 Sep	WC	ISTAF, Berlin, GER	31 Aug	WC
3 Sep	WC	Zagreb, CRO	2 Sep	WC
3 Sep	EAP	Palio Citta della Quercia, Rovereto, ITA	2 Sep	EAP
6 Sep	DL	Memorial Van Damme, Brussels, BEL	5 Sep	DL
8 Sep	WC	Rieti, ITA	7 Sep	WC

INDOORS

IAAF and EAA – respective indoor permit meetings; US USATF series in USA.

2013 date		Meeting	2014 date	
8 Feb	EAA	International PSD Bank, Düsseldorf, GER	30 Jan	EAA
12 Feb	EAA	Pedro's Cup, Bydgoszcz, POL	31 Jan	EAA
19 Jan	EAA	International Games, Reykjavik, ISL	1 Feb	IAAF
3/4 Feb		International Combined Events, Tallinn, EST	1/2 Feb	EAA
4 Feb	US	New Balance Indoor GP, Boston (Roxbury), USA	2 Feb	US
2 Feb	IAAF	BW-Bank Meeting, Karlsruhe, GER	1 Feb	IAAF
3 Feb	IAAF	Russian Winter, Moscow, RUS	2 Feb	IAAF
21 Feb	IAAF	XL-Galan, Stockholm, SWE	6 Feb	IAAF
8 Feb		Europa HJ Meeting, Banská Bystrica, CZE	6 Feb	EAA
2 Feb		New Balance Indoor DP, Boston, USA	8 Feb	IAAF/US
10 Feb		Flanders Indoor, Gent, BEL	9 Feb	IAAF
16 Feb		Millrose Games, New York (Armory), USA	15 Feb	US
15 Feb	IAAF	British Indoor Grand Prix, Birmingham, GBR	15 Feb	IAAF
9 Feb	EAA	Pole Vault Stars, Donetsk, UKR	15 Feb	EAA
1-3 Mar	US	USA Indoor Championships. Albuquerque	22-23 Feb	US
–		Praha, CZE	25 Feb	EAA

IAAF WORLD COMBINED EVENTS CHALLENGE 2013 & 2014

	Oceania Combined Events Champs. Melbourne, AUS	3/4 Apr
4/5 May	Multistars, Firenze, ITA	2/3 May
25/26 May	Hypo-Mehrkampf Meeting, Götzis, AUT	31 May-1 Jun
8/9 Jun	TNT Express Meeting, Kladno, CZE	14/15 Jun
15/16 Jun	Erdgas DLV Mehrkampf, Ratingen, GER	28/29 Jun
14/15 Sep	Decastars, Talence, FRA	20/21 Sep

Plus International Championships

IAAF WORLD RACE WALKING CHALLENGE 2013 & 2014

23 Feb	Chihuahua MEX	22 Feb
1 Mar	Taicang, CHN	–
–	Dudince, SVK	22 Mar
7 Apr	Rio Maior, POR	5 Apr
(13 Apr)	Podebrady, CZE	12 Apr
1 May	Coppa Città di Sesto San Giovanni, ITA	–
1 Jun	Gran Premio Cantones de La Coruña, ESP	31 May

Plus International Championships

IAAF HAMMER THROW CHALLENGE 2014

Above meetings at Kingston, Tokyo, Ponce, Beijing, Szczecin, Marrakech, Moskva, Ostrava, Turku, Dakar, Velenje, Budapest, Karlstad, Madrid, Berlin

AFRICA 2014 CAA Golden Events

Brazzaville CGO 15 or 22 Jun, Warri NGR ?

ASIAN AA Grands Prix

2013: Bangkok THA 4 May, Chonburi THA 8 May, Colombo SRI 12 May
2014: Coimbatore IND 7 Jun and others

EUROPEAN AA CLASSIC MEETINGS 2014

(with 2013 dates of these meetings first). See also above for EAP Meetings 2013 that are EAC 2014.
Riga LAT 30/29 May, Kalamáta GRE 1 Jun/31 May, Bydgoszcz POL 8/3 Jun, Szczecin POL (Kusocinski) 15/7 Jun, Dessau GER 31 May/11 Jun, Huelva ESP (Iberoamerican) 12/12 Jun, Sotteville-lès-Rouen FRA 8 Jul/14 Jun, Göteborg SWE 15/14 Jun, Sollentuna SWE 27/26 Jun, Zhukovskiy RUS (Znamenskiy Memorial) 30/27 Jun, Tomblaine FRA (2 Jul)/27 Jun, Velenje SLO 4 Jun/1 Jul, Padua ITA 1 Sep/6 Jul, Linz Aut (Gugl) 26 Aug/7 Jul, Montreuil-sous-Bois FRA 3 Jun/7 Jul, Budapest HUN (István Gyulai Memorial) 10/8 Jul, Luzern SUI (Spitzen) 17/15 Jul, Karlstad SWE 23/16 Jul, Malmö SWE -/5 Aug, Cagliari ITA (Terra Sarda) 1 Jun/6 Sep
2013: Dubnica nad Váhom SVK (Athletic Bridge) 24/(30) Aug

NORTH AMERICA NACAC MEETINGS 2013/2014 dates

George Town CAY 8/7 May, Tortola IVB -/7 Jun, Toronto CAN 11/11 Jun, Halifax CAN 9/14 Jun, Edmonton CAN 29 Jun/5 Jul, Victoria CAN 5/8 Jul, Vancouver CAN (Harry Jerome International) 1/11 Jul

SOUTH AMERICA 2013/2014 dates

São Paulo BRA 19/2 May, Uberlândia BRA 16/7 May, Caracas VEN (Brigido Iriarte) -/9 May

MAJOR INTERNATIONAL EVENTS 2013–2019
2014

Asian Indoor Championships – Hangzhou, China (15-16 Feb)
IAAF World Indoor Championships – Sopot, Poland (7-9 March)
IAAF World Half Marathon Championships – Copenhagen, Denmark (29 Mar)
IAAF World Race Walking Cup – Taicang, China (3-4 May)
IAAF World Relays – Nassau, Bahamas (24-25 May)
European Cup 10,000m – Skopje, Macedonia (7 Jun)
Asian Junior Championships – Taipei City, Taiwan (12-15 Jun)
European Team Championships – Braunschweig, GER (21-22 Jun)
    1st League Tallinn EST, 2nd League Riga LAT, 3rd League Tbilisi GEO
World University Games – Gwangju, Korea (July)
European Cup Combined Events – Torun, Poland (5-6 July)
    1st and 2nd League Donetsk, Ukraine
IAAF World Junior Championships – Eugene, USA (22-27 July)
Commonwealth Games – Glasgow, GBR (23 Jul – 3 Aug)
NACAC U23 Championships – Kamloops, Canada (8-10 Aug)
African Championships – Marrakech, Morocco (10-14 Aug)
European Championships – Zürich, Switzerland (12-17 Aug)
Youth Olympic Games – Nanjing, China (20-26 Aug)

WMRA World Mountain Running Championships – Casette de Massa, Italy (13 Sep)
IAAF Continental Cup – Marrakech, Morocco (13-14 Sep)
Asian Games – Incheon, Korea (19 Sep–4 Oct)
Central American & Caribbean Games – Veracruz, Mexico (23-30 Nov)
European Cross Country Championships – Samokov, Bulgaria (14 Dec)

2015

European Indoor Championships – Praha (Prague,) Czech Republic (6-8 Mar)
IAAF World Cross Country Championships – Guiyang (A), China (28 Mar)
IAAF World Relays – Nassau, Bahamas (May)
European Cup of Race Walking – Ivano-Frankivsk, Ukraine (17 May)
European Team Championships – Cheboksary, Russia (20-21 June)
Asian Championships – Wuhan, China (June)
World University Games – Gwangju, Korea (3-14 July)
IAAF World Youth Championships – Cali (A), Colombia (15-19 July)
European U23 Championships – Tallinn, Estonia (9-12 July)
European Junior Championships – Eskilstuna, Sweden (16-19 July)
Pan-American Games – Toronto, Canada (10-26 July)
All-Africa Games – Brazzaville, Congo
IAAF World Championships – Beijing, China (22-30 Aug)
European Cross Country Championships – Paray-le-Monial, France (13 Dec)

2016

IAAF World Indoor Championships – Portland, Oregon, USA (March)
IAAF World Race Walking Cup – Cheboksary, Russia
European Championships – Amsterdam, Netherlands (5-10 July)
European Youth Championships (14-19 July)
Olympic Games – Rio de Janeiro, Brazil (5-12 Aug)
IAAF World Half Marathon Championships – Cardiff, GBR (26 March)

2017

IAAF World Championships – London, GBR (5-13 August)

2018

IAAF World Indoor Championships – Birmingham, GBR (March)
Commonwealth Games – Gold Coast, Australia (4-15 April)
IAAF World Race Walking Cup – Cheboksary, Russia
Central American & Caribbean Games –
European Championships – Berlin, Germany
Youth Olympic Games – Buenos Aires, Argentina (11-23 Sep)

2019

Asian Games – Hanoi, Vietnam
Pan-American Games ¬ Lima, Peru
World University Games – Brasilia, Brazil

Athletes who retired in 2013/14

Men: Larry Achike GBR, Ralf Bartels GER, Abdul Buhari GBR, Richard Davenport GBR, Marlon Devonish GBR, Stefan Eberhardt GER, Mark Frank GER, Anson Henry CAN, Marcin Jedrusinski POL, Olli-Pekka Karjalainen FIN, Sachith Maduranga SRI, José Manuel Martínez ESP, Romain Mesnil FRA, Mbulaeni Mulaudzi RSA, Tim Nelson USA, Jamie Nieto USA, André Niklaus GER, Marcin Nowak POL, Darvis Patton USA, Josef Prorok CZE, Jarred Rome USA, Yaroslav Rybakov RUS, Atsushi Sato JPN, Roman Sebrle CZE, Petr Svoboda CZE, Dariusz Trafas POL, Marcel van der Westen NED
Women: Phyllis Agbo GBR, Vera Cechlová CZE, Lidia Chojecka POL, Zoë Derham GBR, Nataliya Dobrynska UKR, Anne-Kathrin Elbe GER, Delloreen Ennis JAM, Perdita Felicien CAN, Debbie Ferguson McKenzie BAH, Manuela Gentili ITA, Nicoleta Grasu ROU, Anna Jakubczak POL, Anna Jesien POL, Olga Kaniskina RUS, Nadine Kleinert GER, Daria Korczynska POL, Jeanette Kwakye GBR, Tatyana Ledebeva RUS, Kaire Leibak LTU, Kerri-Ann Mitchell CAN, Yipsi Moreno CUB, Hitomi Niiya JPN, Abi Oyepitan GBR, Emily Pidgeon GBR, Roslinda Samsu MAS, Aretha Thurmond USA, Maria Vasco ESP, Lauryn Williams USA, Mary Wineberg USA

WORLD INDOOR CHAMPIONSHIPS 2014

Ergo Arena Sopot, Poland 7-9 March
THE 15th EDITION of the IAAF World Indoor Championships was a great success – well organised with much excellent athletics and enthusiastic crowds filling the 11,000-seat Ergo Arena on the last two days.

The final event, the men's 4x400m relay produced the one world indoor and championship record as the US team took 0.70 off the old official mark. But the performance of the meeting was perhaps the 6.98 win at 60m by the ever-smiling Shelly-Ann Fraser-Pryce. She was up against Murielle Ahouré, who was not only the world-leader at 7.03 but had also run the fastest times in both heat and semi-finals and again excelled with 7.01 but still could not match the flying Jamaican. The male athlete of the meeting was surely Ashton Eaton, who missed his world record in the heptathlon by just a second over 1000m.

Some champions won easily as the star of the indoor season Genzebe Dibaba flowed away from the field after a very slow start to the 3000m with c.4:04 for the second 1500m, and Abeba Aregawi was simply a class apart in the 1500m. Similarly out on their own were two more super-stars of our sport – Ashton Eaton and Valerie Adams, who won her ninth global shot title. The last two were among five athletes who defended their titles, the others being Ryan Whiting, again over 22m in the shot, Mohammed Aman at 800m and Mauro da Silva at long jump. But it was a major surprise that

Sally Pearson lost her title to a fine run by Nia Ali as the Australian's bid went wrong with her first stride. Another 2012 world champion who gained a silver medal was magnificent as at 39 Bernard Lagat was again the oldest ever World Indoor male medallist. Others to excel included Pavel Maslák, who gave a command performance to win the 400m, and splendid middle distance front-running wins by Ayanleh Souleiman 1500m and Chanelle Price 800m. Top field event in depth was the men's high jump in which Mutaz Essa Barshim beat Ivan Ukhov on count-back at 2.38. and the women's pole vault matched records with seven women over 4.65 and ten over 4.55. In all world leading marks for 2014 were set in 12 events.

There were many shocks, typical of true championship action, and some delightful breakthroughs such as by the 22 year-old New Zealand shot putter Tom Walsh, who took shot bronze with his fourth national indoor record of the meeting, and the British pair of Richard Kilty, who came clear of a seemingly very open 60m field to win in 6.49 after pbs at 6.53 and 6.52 in the rounds, and Katarina Johnson-Thompson, who produced a pb of 6.81 for long jump silver after being unable to contest the pentathlon that she could well have won.

On the downside there were some unfortunate (lane) disqualifications, perhaps inevitable on 200m indoor tracks, such as Marcin Lewandowski losing 800m bronze and Nick Willis after crossing the line 4th in the 1500m.

MEN

60 Metres (a-b-b)
1. Richard Kilty GBR	6.49
2. Marvin Bracy USA	6.51
3. Femi Ogunode QAT	6.52
4. Su Bingtian CHN	6.52
5. Gerald Phiri ZAM	6.52
6. Dwain Chambers GBR	6.53
7. Nesta Carter JAM	6.57
8, Kimmari Roach JAM	6.58

400 Metres (a-a-b)
1. Pavel Maslák CZE	45.24
2. Chris Brown BAH	45.58
3. Kyle Clemons USA	45.74
4. David Verburg USA	46.21
5. Lalonde Gordon TTO	46.39
6. Nery Brenes CRC	47.32

800 Metres (a-c)
1. Mohammed Aman ETH	1:46.40
2. Adam Kszczot POL	1:46.76
3. Andrew Osagie GBR	1:47.10
4. André Olivier RSA	1:47.31
5. Thijmen Kupers NED	1:47.74
dq. Marcin Lewandowski POL	(1:47.09)

1500 Metres (a-b)
1. Ayanleh Souleiman DJI	3:37.52
2. Aman Wote ETH	3:38.08

3. Abdelaati Iguider MAR	3:38.21
4. Ilham Tanui Özbilen TUR	3:39.10
5. Jakub Holusa CZE	3:39.23
6. Will Leer USA	3:39.60
7. Homiyu Tesfaye GER	3:39.90
8. Bethwell Birgen KEN	3:40.66
lane dq (4) Nick Willis NZL	(3:38.47)

3000 Metres (a-c)
1. Caleb Ndiku KEN	7:54.94
2. Bernard Lagat USA	7:55.22
3. Dejen Gebremeskel ETH	7:55.39
4. Galen Rupp USA	7:55.84
5. Hagos Gebrhiwet ETH	7:56.34
6. Hayle Ibrahimov AZE	7:56.37
7. Elroy Gelant RSA	7:57.31
8. Cam Levins CAN	7:57.37
9. Augustine Choge KEN	7:57.46
10. Collis Birmingham AUS	7:57.55
11. Andy Vernon GBR	7:58.25
12. Zane Robertson NZL	8:01.81

60 Metres Hurdles (b-c-c)
1. Omo Osaghae USA	7.45
2. Pascal Martinot Lagarde FRA	7.46
3. Garfield Darien FRA	7.47
4. Andrew Pozzi GBR	7.53
5. Gregor Traber GER	7.56
6. Erik Balnuweit GER	7.56
7. William Sharman GBR	7.60

dns. Andrew Rlley JAM	–

High Jump (b-c)
1. Mutaz Essa Barshim QAT	2.38
2. Ivan Ukhov RUS	2.38
3. Andriy Protsenko UKR	2.36
4. Erik Kynard USA	2.34
5. Daniil Tsyplakov RUS	2.32
6. Marco Fassinotti ITA	2.29
7. Zhang Guowei CHN	2.29
8. Michael Mason CAN	2.25

Pole Vault (b-c) No qualifying round
1. Konstadínos Filippídis GRE	5.80
2. Malte Mohr GER	5.80
3. Jan Kudlicka CZE	5.80
4. Thiago Braz da Silva BRA	5.75
5. Xue Changrui CHN	5.75
6. Robert Sobera POL	5.65
7. Augusto D de Oliveira BRA	5.65
8. Luke Cutts GBR	5.65
9. Yang Yancheng CHN	5.55
10. Jérôme Clavier FRA	5.55
11. Kévin Menaldo FRA	5.55
12. Pawel Wojciechowski POL	5.40

Long Jump (a-b)
1. Mauro da Silva BRA	8.28
2. Li Jinzhe CHN	8.23
3. Michel Tornéus SWE	8.21
4. Loúis Tsátoumas GRE	8.13

5. Aleksandr Menkov RUS   8.08
6. Adrian Strzalkowski POL   7.96
7. Luis Rivera MEX   7.93
8. Christian Reif GER   7.75
Triple Jump (b-c)
1. Lyukman Adams RUS   17.37
2. Ernesto Revé CUB   17.33
3. Pedro Pichardo CUB   17.24
4. Marian Oprea ROU   17.21
5. Karol Hoffmann POL   16.89
6. Chris Carter USA   16.74
7. Cao Shuo CHN   16.55
8, Viktor Kuznetsov UKR   16.51
Shot (a)
1. Ryan Whiting USA   22.05
2. David Storl GER   21.79
3. Tomas Walsh NZL   21.26
4. Tomasz Majewski POL   21.04
5. Georgi Ivanov BUL   21.02
6. Germán Lauro ARG   20.50
7. Orazio Cremona RSA   20.49
8. Aleksandr Lesnoy RUS   20.16
Heptathlon (a/b)
1. Ashton Eaton USA   6632
   (6.66. 7.78, 14.88, 2.06, 7.64, 5.20
   2:34.72
2. Andrey Kravchenko BLR   6303
3. Thomas Van Der Plaetsen BEL
                                6259
4. Eelco Sintnicolaas NED   6198
5. Oleksiy Kasyanov UKR   6176
6. Kai Kazmirek GER   6173
7. Damian Warner CAN   6129
8. Pascal Behrenbruch GER   (4983)
4 x 400 Metres (b-c)
1. USA   3:02.13
   K Clemons 46.10, D Verburg 45.46,
   K Butler 45.43, C Smith 45.14
   C Parros and R Babineaux in heat
2. GBR   3:03.49C Williams 45.91, J
   Bowie 45.92, L Lennon-Ford 45.83,
   N Levine 45.83. M Bingjam ran in
   heat.
3. JAM   3:03.69
   E Nolan 46.34, A Fothergill 45.92,
   A Gauntlett 45.52, E Steele 45.91
   D Hyatt and J Brown ran in heat
4. POL   3:04.39
5. RUS   3:07.12
6. UKR   3:08.79
WOMEN
60 Metres (b-c-c)
1. Shelley-Ann Fraser-Pryce JAM
                                6.98
2. Murielle Ahouré CIV   7.01
3. Tianna Bartoletta USA   7.06
4. Asha Philip GBR   7.11
5. Veronica Campbell-Brown JAM
                                7.13
6. Michelle Lee Ahye TTO   7.16
7. Gloria Asumnu NGR   7.18
8. Verena Sailer GER   7.18
400 Metres (a-a-b)
1. Francena McCorory USA   51.12
2. Kaliese Spencer JAM   51.54
3. Shaunae Miller BAH   52.06
4, Justyna Swiety POL   52.20
5. Patricia Hall JAM   52.51
6. Joanna Atkins USA   52.55

800 Metres (a-c)
1. Chanelle Price USA   2:00.09
2. Angelika Cichocka POL   2:00.45
3. Marina Arzamasova BLR   2:00.79
4. Selina Büchel SUI   2:01.06
5. Natalia Lupu UKR   2:01.17
6. Lenka Masná CZE   2:02.46
1500 Metres (a-b)
1. Abeba Aregawi SWE   4:00.61
2. Axumawit Embaye ETH   4:07.12
3. Nicole Sifuentes CAN   4:07.61
4. Siham Hilali MAR   4:07;62
5. Treniere Moser USA   4:07.84
6. Luiza Gega ALB   4:08.24
7. Svetlana Karamasheva RUS
                              4:13.89
dq (3). Rababe Arrafi MAR (4:07.53)
dq (8). Heather Kampf USA(4:21.78)
3000 Metres (a-c)
1. Genzebe Dibaba ETH   8:55.04
2. Hellen Obiri KEN   8:57.72
3. Maryam Jamal BRN   8:59.16
4. Irene Jelagat KEN   9:02.67
5. Sifan Hassan NED   9:03.22
6. Betlhem Desalegn UAE   9:04.06
7. Renata Plis POL   9:07.05
8. Shannon Rowbury USA   9:07.82
9. Margherita Magnani ITA   9:10.13
10. Gabrielle Grunewald USA   9:11.76
11. Hiwot Ayalew ETH   9:12.51
12. Alia Saeed Mohammed UAE
                              9:21.23
60 Metres Hurdles (a-b-b)
1. Nia Ali USA   7.80
2. Sally Pearson AUS   7.85
3. Tiffany Porter GBR   7.86
4. Cindy Billaud FRA   7.89
5. Janay DeLoach Soukup USA   7.90
6. Cindy Roleder GER   8.01
7. Nadine HIldebrand GER   8.02
8. Yuliya Kondakova RUS   8.08
High Jump (a-b)
1= Mariya Kuchina RUS   2.00
1= Kamila Licwinko POL   2.00
3. Ruth Beitia ESP   2.00
4. Justyna Kasprzycka POL   1.97
5. Emma Green Tregaro SWE   1.94
6. Blanka Vlasic CRO   1.94
7. Levern Spencer LCA   1.94
8= Marie-Laurence Jungfleisch
   GER   1.90
8= Nafassatou Thiam BEL   1.90
Pole Vault (c) No qualifying round
1, Yarisley Silva CUB   4.70
2= Anzhelika Sidorova RUS   4.70
2= Jirína Svobodová CZE   4.70
4. Fabiana Murer BRA   4.70
5= Jennifer Suhr USA   4.65
5= Anna Rogowska POL   4.65
7. Silke Spiegelburg GER   4.65
8. Mary Saxer USA   4.55
9. Holly Bleasdale GBR   4.55
10. Tina Sutej SLO   4.55
11. Anastasia Savchenko RUS   4.45
12. Nikoléta Kiriakapoúlou GRE   4.30
Long Jump (b-c)
1. Éloyse Lesueur FRA   6.85
2. Katarina Johnson-Thompson
   GBR   6.81
3. Ivana Spanovic SRB   6.77
4. Shara Proctor GBR   6.68

5. Tori Polk USA   6.61
6. Teresa Dobija POL   6.52
7. Darya Klishina RUS   6.51
8. Erica Jarder SWE   6.36
Triple Jump (a-b)
1. Yekaterina Koneva RUS   14.46
2. Olga Saladuha UKR   14.45
3. Kimberly Williams JAM   14.39
4. Patricia Mamona POR   14.26
5. Li Yanmei CHN   14.19
6. Ksenia Detsuk BLR   14.13
7. Yarianna Martínez CUB   13.99
8. Dana Veldáková SVK   13.75
Shot (b)
1. Valerie Adams NZL   20.67
2. Christina Schwanitz GER   19.94
3. Gong Lijiao CHN   19.24
4. Yevgeniya Kolodko RUS   19.11
5. Michelle Carter USA   19.10
6. Anita Márton HUN   18.17
7. Yuliya Leontyuk BLR   18.16
8. Jeneva McCall USA   18.05
Pentathlon (a)
1. Nadine Broersen NED   4830
   (8.32, 1.93, 14.59, 6.17, 2:14.97)
2. Brianne Theisen-Eaton CAN   4768
3. Alla Fyodorova UKR   4724
4. Sharon Day-Monroe USA   4718
5. Claudia Rath GER   4681
6. Yana Maksimova BLR   4651
7. Anna Melnychenko UKR   4587
8. Karolina Tyminska POL   4557
4 x 400 Metres (c)
1. USA   3:24.83
   N Hastings 51.89, J Atkins 50.91,
   F McCorory 50.33, C Tate 51.70.
   J Hayes & M Hargrove ran in heat.
2. JAM   3:26.54
   P Hall 52.80, A McLaughlin 51.25.
   K Spencer 51.13, S A McPherson
   51.36. V Chambers & N Goule ran
   in heat.
3. GBR   3:27.90
   E Child 52.25, S Cox 51.80, M
   Adeoye 51.33, C Ohuruogu 52.52.
   V Ohuruogu ran in heat.
4. RUS   3:28.89
   Kseniya Ryzhova last leg of 49.83
5. POL   3:29.89
6. NGR   3:31.59
Leading Nations – Medals & Points

Nation	G	S		Points
USA	8	3	2	141.5
RUS	3	2	-	65
POL	1	2	-	65
GBR	1	2	3	61
GER	-	3	-	48
JAM	1	2	2	45
ETH	2	5	1	40
UKR	-	1	2	33
CHN	-	1	1	30
CZE	1	1	1	27.5
FRA	1	1	1	26
CUB	1	1	1	23
KEN	1	1	-	21
BLR	-	1	1	21
NED	1	-	-	21
BRA	1	-	1	20
SWE	1	-	1	19

17 nations won gold, 30 medals and
50 placed athletes in top 8.

EUROPEAN CHAMPIONSHIPS 2014

The first European Championships were staged at the Stadio Comunale, Torino, Italy in 1934 for men only. Women's championships were held separately in 1938, but men's and women's events were combined at one venue from 1946. The championships are held at four-yearly intervals, although there was a break in that pattern when they were held in 1969 and 1971, until a biennial pattern was set in 2012. The 22nd Championships will be held in Zürich, Switzerland on 12-17 August 2014.

Championship Records

Men

100m	9.99	Francis Obikwelu POR	2006
	(9.96dq	Dwain Chambers GBR	2002)
200m	19.85	Konstadinos Kedéris GRE	2002
400m	44.52	Iwan Thomas GBR	1998
800m	1:43.84	Olaf Beyer GDR	1978
1500m	3:35.27	Fermín Cacho ESP	1994
5000m	13:10.15	Jack Buckner GBR	1986
10000m	27:30.99	Martti Vainio FIN	1978
Mar	2:10:31	Martín Fiz ESP	1994
3000mSt	8:07.87	Mahieddine Mekhissi FRA	2010
110mh	13.02	Colin Jackson GBR (s/F)	1998
400mh	47.48	Harald Schmid FRG	1982
HJ	2.36	Andrey Silnov RUS	2006
PV	6.00	Rodion Gataullin URS	1994
LJ	8.47	Christian Reif GER	2010
TJ	17.99	Jonathan Edwards GBR	1998
SP	22.22	Werner Günthör SUI	1986
DT	68.87	Piotr Malachowski POL	2010
HT	86.74	Yuriy Sedykh URS	1986
JT	89.72	Steve Backley GBR	1998
Dec	8811	Daley Thompson GBR	1986
4x100m	37.79	France	1990
4x400m	2:58.22	GBR	1990
20 kmW	1:18:37	Franc. J. Fernández ESP	2002
50 kmW	3:36:39	Rob. Korzeniowski POL	2002

Women

100m	10.73	Christine Arron FRA	1998
200m	21.71	Heike Drechsler GDR	1986
400m	48.15	Marita Koch GDR	1982
800m	1:55.41	Olga Minayeva URS	1982
1500m	3:56.91	Tatyana Tomashova RUS	2006
3000m	8:30.28	Svetlana Ulmasova URS	1982
5000m	14:52.20	Alemitu Bekele TUR	2010
10000m	30:01.09	Paula Radcliffe GBR	2002
Mar	2:26:05	Maria Guida ITA	2002
3000mSt	9:17.57	Yuliya Zarudneva RUS	2010
100mh	12.38	Yordanka Donkova BUL	1986
400mh	52.92	Natalya Antyukh URS	2010
HJ	2.03	Tia Hellebaut BEL	2006
	2.03	Venelina Veneva BUL	2006
	2.03	Blanka Vlasic CRO	2010
PV	4.80	Yelena Isinbayeva RUS	2006
LJ	7.30	Heike Drechsler GDR	1990
TJ	15.15	Tatyana Lebedeva RUS	2006
SP	21.69	Viktoriya Pavlysh UKR	1998
DT	71.36	Diane Sachse GDR	1986
HT	76.67	Tatyana Lysenko RUS	2006
JT	77.44	Fatima Whitbread GBR	q1986
new spec	67.47	Miréla Manjani GRE	2002
Hep	6823	Jessica Ennis GBR	2010
4x100m	41.68	GDR	1990
4x400m	3:16.87	GDR	1986
20kmW	1:26:42	Olimpiada Ivanova RUS	2002

Four Successive Titles

Men
4 Janis Lusis URS JT 1962-66-69-71
4 Steve Backley GBR JT 1990-94-98-2002
4 Colin Jackson GBR 110mh 1990-94-98-2002

Women
4 Nadezhda Chizhova URS SP 1966-69-71-74
4 Heike Drechsler GDR/GER 1986-90-94-98

Most Gold Medals at all events

Men: 5 Harald Schmid FRG, Roger Black GBR
Women: 6 Marita Koch GDR, 5 Fanny Blankers-Koen NED, Irena Szewinska POL, Marlies Göhr GDR, Heike Drechsler GDR/GER, Grit Breuer GDR/GER

Most Medals

Men: 6 Harald Schmid FRG 1978-86, Pietro Mennea ITA 1971-4, Roger Black GBR 1986-94
Women: 10 Irena Szewinska POL 1966-78, 8 Fanny Blankers-Koen NED 1938-50, Renate Stecher GDR 1969-74; 7 Marlies Göhr GBR 1978-86; 7 Yevgeniya Sechenova USS 1946-50, Marita Koch GDR 1978-86, Heike Drechsler GDR/GER 1986-98, Irina Privalova RUS 1994-8, Grit Breuer GDR/GER 1990-2002

Medals By Nation 1934-2012

Nation	Men			Women			Total
	G	S	B	G	S	B	
USSR	65	69	60	54	41	43	332
UK	78	53	51	16	21	28	247
GDR	39	37	32	51	45	33	237
France	42	38	32	13	10	14	149
Russia	15	14	12	34	35	33	143
Germany *	26	24	22	22	25	21	140
FR Germany	27	24	37	9	20	18	135
Poland	23	29	26	15	9	27	129
Italy	30	34	22	5	7	18	116
Sweden	21	32	33	6	4	4	100
Finland	27	27	32	4	2	5	97

30 other nations have won medals
* Germany - 1934 and 1938 Championships. The Federal Republic took part from 1954 and the GDR from 1958. Germany again from 1994.
The European nations from the ex-USSR, Czech Republic and Slovakia from Czechoslovakia and the ex-constituent nations of Yugoslavia competed from 1994.

Timetable and Qualifying Standards

QUALIFYING standards must be achieved in bona fide competition (indoors or outdoors) between 1 January 2013 to 3 August 2014. Each country can enter up to three athletes per event provided all of them have achieved the qualifying standard or one per event where the standard has not been achieved. 16 natauional teams are permitted for each relay event. The first three in the European Cup 10,000m in 2013 and 2014 automatically qualify for entry. European Atletiucs will consider additional athletes if target numbers of entries are not met. Marathon Cups are incorporated; minimum of three and maximum of six per team. Six days of competition are scheduled. Dates of successive rounds (July-August)

Event	Days	Qual. standards
Men		
100m	12-13-13	10.38
200m	14-14-15	20.95
400m	12-13-15	46.75
800m	12-13-15	1:47.80
1500m	15-17	3:40.50
5000m	15-17	13:40.00
10,000m	13	28:55.00
Mar	17	none
3000mSt	12-14	8:37.50
110mh	13-14-14	13.90
400mh	12-13-15	51.10
HJ	13-15	2.26
PV	14-16	5.52
LJ	15-17	7.95
TJ	12-14	16.55
SP	13-12	19.70
DT	12-13	62.30
HT	14-16	73.50
JT	14-17	78.80
Dec	12/13	7820
4x100m	16-17	none
4x400m	16-17	none
20 kmW	13	1:26:30
50 kmW	15	4:10:00

Event	Days	Qual. standards
Women		
100m	12-13-13	11.60
200m	14-14-15	23.65
400m	12-13-15	53.40
800m	13-14-16	2:03.00
1500m	12-15	4:12.00
5000m	14-16	15:45.00
10,000m	12	33:30.00
Mar	16	none
3000mSt	15-17	9:55.00
100mh	12-12-13	13.38
400mh	13-14-16	57.90
HJ	15-17	1.90
PV	12-14	4.35
LJ	12-13	6.55
TJ	13-11	13.95
SP	15-17	16.30
DT	15-16	56.00
HT	13-15	68.00
JT	12-14	57.40
Hep	14/15	5920
4x100m	16-17	none
4x400m	16-17	none
20kmW	14	1:37:00

Most Championships Contested

6 Ludvik Danek TCH 1962-78
6 Abdon Pamich ITA 1954-71
6 Nenad Stekic YUG 1971-90
6 Fern. Ribeiro POR 1986-2010
6 Fel. Moldovan ROU 1990-2010

Most Medals at One Event

5 Igor Ter-Ovanesyan URS long jump 3/2/0 1958-71

Most Medals at one Championship

Men
4 John Regis GBR 2/1/1 1990
Women
4 Fanny Blankers-Koen HOL 3/1/0 1950
4 Irena Kirszenstein/Szewinska POL 3/1/0 1966
4 Stanislawa Walasiewicz POL 2/2/0 1938

COMMONWEALTH GAMES 2014

The 20th Commonwealth Games are due to be staged in Glasgow, Scotland, with the tracke events at Hampden Park from 27 July to 2 August. These multi-sport competitions are held every four years, and contested by athletes representing the nations of the British Commonwealth. They were first staged as the British Empire Games at Hamilton, Canada in 1930. They became the British Empire and Commonwealth Games in 1954, and the British Commonwealth Games in 1970. The last Games were held in New Delhi, India in October 2010. The walks events have been dropped from the usual timetable.

Games Records

Men							
100m	9.88	Ato Boldon TRI	1998		8.22	Peter Burge AUS	1998
200m	19.97	Frank Fredericks NAM	1994		8.22	Jai Taurima AUS	1998
400m	44.52	Iwan Thomas WAL	1998	TJ	17.86	Jonathan Edwards ENG	2002
800m	1:43.22	Steve Cram ENG	1986	SP	21.02	Dylan Armstrong CAN	2010
1500m	3:32.16	Filbert Bayi TAN	1974	DT	66.39	Frantz Kruger RSA	2002
5000m	12:56.41	Augustine Choge KEN	2006	HT	77.53	Stuart Rendell AUS	2006
10000m	27:45.39	Wilberforce Talel KEN	2002	JT	88.75	Marius Corbett RSA	1998
Mar	2:09:12	Ian Thompson ENG	1974	(old)	89.48	Michael O'Rourke NZL	1982
3000mSt	8:14.72	Johnstone Kipkoech KEN	1994	Dec	8663	Daley Thompson ENG	1986
110mh	13.08	Colin Jackson WAL	1990/94	4x100m	38.20	England	1998
400mh	48.05	Louis van Zyl RSA	2006	4x400m	2:59.03	Jamaica	1998
HJ	2.36	Nick Saunders BAH	1990	20kmW	1:19:55	Nathan Deakes AUS	2006
PV	5.80	Steve Hooker AUS	2006	30kmW	2:07:47	Simon Baker AUS	1986
LJ	8.39w	Yusuf Alli NGR	1990	50kmW	3:42:53	Nathan Deakes AUS	2006
	8.30	Fabrice Lapierre AUS	2010	**Women**			
				100m	10.91	Debbie Ferguson BAH	2002

200m	22.20	Debbie Ferguson BAH	2002
	22.19w	Merlene Ottey JAM	1982
400m	50.17	Sandie Richards JAM	1998
800m	1:57.35	Maria Mutola MOZ	2002
1500m	4:05.26	Nancy Langat KEN	2010
3000m	8:32.17	Angela Chalmers CAN	1994
500m	14:31.42	Paula Radcliffe GBR	2002
10000m	31:27.83	Salina Kosgei KEN	2002
3000mSt	9:19.51	Dorcus Inzikuru UGA	2006
Mar	2:25:28	Lisa Martin AUS	1990
100mh	12.65	Brigitte Foster-Hylton JAM	
			2006 (h)
400mh	53.82	Jana Pittman AUS	2006
HJ	1.96	Hestrie Cloete RSA	2002
PV	4.62	Kym Howe-Nadin AUS	2006
LJ	6.97	Bronwyn Thompson AUS	2006
TJ	14.86	Ashia Hansen ENG	2002
SP	20.47	Valerie Adams NZL	2010
DT	65.92	Beatrice Faumuina NZL	1998
HT	68.57	Sultana Frizell CAN	2010
JT	62.34	Sunette Viljoen RSA	2010
old	69.80	Tessa Sanderson ENG	1986
Hep	6695	Jane Flemming AUS	1990
4x100m	42.44	Bahamas	2002
4x400m	3:25.63	Australia	2002
10kmW	43:57	Jane Saville AUS	1998
20kmW	1:32:46	Jane Saville AUS	2006

Most gold medals at all events
Men

6 Don Quarrie JAM 100m 1970-74-78, 200m 1970-74, 4x100mR 1970

Women

7 Marjorie Jackson AUS 100y 1950-54, 220y 1950-54, 4x110yR 1954, 440yR and 660yR 1950

7 Raelene Boyle AUS 100m 1970-74, 200m 1970-74, 400m 1982, 4x100mR 1970-74

6 Pam Kilborn/Ryan AUS 80mh 1962-66-70, LJ 1962, 4x100mR 1966-70

Most Medals – all events
Men: 6 Don Quarrie 1970-78, Harry Hart 1930-34. Allan Wells 1978-82

Women: 9 Raelene Boyle 1970-8. 8 Denise Robertson/Boyd AUS 1974-8; 7 Marjorie Jackson 1950-54, Valerie Young 1958-72, Kathy Cook ENG 1978-86, Angella Issajenko CAN 1982-86, Debbie Flintoff AUS 1982-90

Most Medals at one Games
Men 4 Keith Gardner 1958 2G, 1S, 1B

Women 5 Decima Norman 1938 5G; 5 Shirley Strickland 1950 3G, 2S

Most Games Contested
6 Robin Tait NZL 1962-82, successively 4-3-6-1-4-8 at men's discus, Judy Oakes ENG 1978-98, successively 3-1-2-2-1-1 at women's shot.

Record medal-winning span of 20 years by Oakes and by Robert Weir (winner of hammer 1982, and at discus 5-3-1-3 in 1982-94-98-02).

WORLD JUNIOR CHAMPIONSHIPS

The World Junior Championmships have been held bienially from 1988 when they were staged in Athens, Greece. The 15th edition of the meeting will be held in Eugene, Ortegon 22-27 July 2014.

Championship Records after 2012

Men

100m	10.05	Adam Gemili GBR	2012
200m	20.28	Andrew Howe ITA	2004
400m	44.66	Hamdam Al-Bishi KSA	2000
800m	1:43.79	Nijel Amos BOT	2012
1500m	3:35.53	Abdelati Iguider MAR	2004
5000m	13:08.57	Abreham Cherkos ETH	2008
10000m	27:30.85	Josphat Bett KEN	2008
3000mSt	8:06.10	Conseslus Kiprono KEN	2012
110mh 3'3"	13.18	Yordan O'Ferrill CUB	2012
400mh	48.51	Kerron Clement USA	2004
HJ	2.37	Dragutin Topic YUG	1990
	2.37	Steve Smith GBR	1992
PV	5.71	Germán Chiaraviglio ARG	2006
LJ	8.20	James Stallworth USA q	1990
TJ	17.04	Yoelbi Quesada CUB	1992
SP 6kg	22.20	Jacko Gill NZL	2012
DT 1.75kg	67.32	Margus Hunt EST	2006
HT 6kg	85.97	Ashraf Amjad El-Seify QAT	2012
JT	83.07	Robert Oosthuizen RSA	2006
Dec jnr	8126	Andrey Kravchenko BLR	2004
4x100m	38.92	USA	2002
4x400m	3:01.90	USA	1986
10kmW	39:35.01	Stanis. Yemelyanov URS	2008

Women

100m	11.12	Veronica Campbell JAM	2000
200m	22.53	Anthonique Strachan BAH	2012
400m	50.50	Ashley Spencer USA	2012
800m	2:00.06	Elena Mirela Lavric ROU	2008
1500m	4:04.96	Faith Kipyegon KEN	2012
3000m	8:46.86	Zhang Linli CHN	1992
5000m	15:21.52	Meselech Melkamu ETH	2004
3000mSt	9:31.35	Christine Muyanga KEN	2008
100mh	12.96	Aliuska López CUB sf	1988
400mh	54.70	Lashinda Demus USA	2002
HJ	2.00	Galina Astafei ROM	1988
PV	4.50	Angelica Bengtsson SWE	2012
LJ	6.82	Fiona May GBR	1988
TJ	14.62	Tereza Marinova BUL	1996
SP	18.76	Cheng Xiaoyan CHN	1994
DT	68.24	Ilke Wyludda GDR	1988
HT	70.62	Alexandra Tavernier FRA	2012
JT	63.01	Vira Rebryk UKR	2008
Hep	6470	Carolina Klüft SWE	2002
4x100m	43.40	Jamaica	2002
4x400m	3:28.39	GDR	1988
10kmW	43:24.72	Tatyana Mineyeva RUS	2008

OBITUARY 2013

See ATHLETICS 2013 for obituaries from early 2013: Hartmut Briesenick, Nel Büch, Charles Capozzoli, Cummin Clancy, Roger Dunkley, Jack Emery, Abderrahim Goumri, Noé Hernández, Karl-Erik Israelsson, Lennart Karlsson, Samson Kimobwa, Ann-Britt Leyman-Olsson, Teddy Mccook, Elaine Martyn, Pietro Mennea, Rita Ridley, Alemayehu Shumye, Éva Szigeti-Tóth, John Thomas.

Olof Viktor **'Olle' ÅBERG** (Sweden) (b. 24 Jan 1925 Hofors) on 30 December. He was 7th at 1500m at the 1952 Olympic Games after being ranked third in the world in 1951, when he was Swedish champion. He set the world record for 1000m with 2:21.3 in 1952 and ran on four WR relay teams for his club Gefle IF: two at 4x1500m and two at 4x1 mile. Pbs: 800m 1:49.3 (1953), 1500m 3:45.4 (1951), 1M 4:04.2 (1952). 17 internationals 1947-56.

Fernando AGUILAR Camacho (Spain) (b. 14 Feb 1938 Frailes, Jaén) on 20 June in Torrevieja. He competed at the 1964 Olympic Games (12th heat 5000m, dnf 10,000m) and was Spanish champion at 1500m in 1965, 5000m 1963, 10,000m 1963 and 1967, and cross-country 1966-7. He set four Spanish records: 5000m 14:02.2 (1963), 14:02.0 (1964); 10,000m 29:22.2 (1963) and 28:59.0 (1964). Other pbs: 1500m 3:46.3 (1964), 3000m 8:11.2 (1964), 5000m 13:54.4 (1967). 42 internationals.

Erik Torsten **AHLDÉN** (Sweden) (b. 4 Sep 1923 Ramsjö, Ljusdal) on 6 July in Nacka, Stockholm. In 1948 he ranked second in the world with pbs at 3000m 8:09.6 and 5000m 14:13.2 (behind Emil Zátopek 8:07.8 and 14:10.0) and that year was 4th at 5000m at the Olympic Games. Other pbs: 1500m 3:48.2 (1945), 1M 4:09.4 (1946), 2000m 5:12.0 (1948), 2M 8:54.1i (1949). He also won Swedish titles at 5000m in 1948 and 4k cross-country in 1946; 4 internationals. He became Swedish team manager.

André ALBERTY (France) (b. 29 Nov 1931) on 1 March. He was a member of the ATFS from 1966 and co-founder of the French statistical organisation (ASFA – Association des Statisticiens français d'athlétisme) in 1965, He was a compiler for the first two editions (1964 and 1968) of National Athletics of All Countries in the World and helped compile French lists 1966-75 for the FFA (French Federation), also helping to reconstruct old French lists with particular interest in the French Caribbean.

Pedro APELLÁNIZ (Spain) (b. 8 Feb 1924 Iberluce, Galdácano) on 22 April in Usánsolo.

He threw the javelin at the 1948 Olympic Games, won 13 Spanish titles 1944-8, 1950-5 and 1957-8 and was 3rd at the Mediterranean Games in 1955. He set seven Spanish records from 56.42 in 1946 to 63.62 (just outside the world top 50 that year) in 1948. 22 Internationals.

Helga ARENDT (Germany) (b. 24 Apr 1964 Köln) on 11 March at Pulheim-Brauweiler. At 400m she was World Indoor champion in 1989 and European Indoor silver medallist in 1988 (4th in 1987), also FRG champion in 1988-9 outdoors and indoors 1987-9. She was 7th at the Olympic Games in 1988 (4th 4x100m) and a relay reserve in 1992, and was a 400m semi-finalist at the 1987 Worlds and 1990 Europeans (5th and 4th respectively in the relay). Pbs: 100m 11.82/11.3 (1988), 200m 23.13 (1988), 300m 36.49i (1988), 400m 50.36 (1988), 400mh 60.33 (1984). She ran on the team that set a world indoor 4x200m best of 1:32.55 in 1988; 17 internationals 1984-93. She worked as a lawyer.

Ilkka Kullervo **AUER** (Finland) (b. 16 Mar 1930 Viipuri) on 16 August in Helsinki. He was 5= on the world list for 3000m steeplechase in 1956 with a pb and Finnish record of 8:42.4, but went out in his heat at the Olympic Games. He was Finnish champion in 1957 (and at 5k cross-country in 1956). Other pbs: 1500m 3:48.8 (1956), 3000m 8:15.8 (1957), 5000m 14:10.4 (1957), 10,000m 29:50.6 (1956).

Laslo BABITS (Canada) (b. 17 Apr 1958 Oliver, British Columbia) on 12 June in Vancouver. A javelin thrower, he had a best of 86.90 after he was 8th at the Olympic Games in 1984. In 1982 he had been 2nd in the Commonwealth Games and at the NCAAs (for Washington State University), and in 1983 won the Pan-American Games title with a non-qualifying 16th at the World Champs. He was Canadian champion in 1984-5 (2nd 1981-3).

Emmanuel McDonald BAILEY (Trinidad & Tobago) (b. 8 Dec 1920 Williamsville, Trinidad) on 4 December at his home in Port of Spain, Trinidad. A beautiful stylist, he represented Britain at the Olympic Games of 1948 and 1952, rather than his native country. He had first run in the AAAs in 1939 before war service in the RAF and he was also champion of Trinidad during the war before dominating British sprinting in the late 1940s and early 1950s and was a huge favourite with the British public. He collected a record 14 AAA titles (plus one at sprint relay) by winning the 100y and 220y each year 1946-53, except for 1948. That year Bailey was well below form, running only 3rd in the AAA 100y, before, suffering from a throat infection, he was 6th in the Olympic 100m. In 1952 he took the Olympic 100m bronze in a blanket finish, adding 4th at 200m. Although resident in Britain he was not permitted to compete at the European Championships, but he competed in nine international matches for Britain, winning 20 of his 22 races 1946-52. In that period he set British records at 100y (14 at 9.7 and 9.6), 100m (5 from 10.4 to a world record 10.2 at Belgrade on 25 Aug 1951), 200m (7 from 21.2 to 20.9) and had wind assisted bests for 100y of 9.4 and 220y of 20.5 on a straight track. In 1953 he became a professional rugby league player, but only played one friendly match for Leigh. He returned to his native Trinidad, where he became a leading administrator, retaining his enthusiastic interest in the sport throughout his life.

Progress at 100y/100m, 200m (y = 220y): 1939- 10.2y, 21.6y; 1940- 9.8y, 22.0y; 1941- 9.8y, 21.8y; 1942- 9.8y, 21.4; 1943- 9.8y, 22.1y; 1944- 9.8y, 21.2y; 1945- 9.8y, 22.4y, 1946- 9.7y/10.3, 21.3; 1947- 9.7y, 10.3, 21.2; 1948- 9.7y/10.4, 21.7; 1949- 9.6y/10.3/10.2w, 21.1y; 1950- 9.6y/10.3, 20.9; 1951- 9.6y/10.2, 21.0/20.5wySt; 1952- 10.4, 20.9; 1953- 9.7y/10.7, 21.3y/21.0ySt.

Hal BATEMAN (USA) (b. 28 Nov 1931 Staten Island, New York) on 10 April in Corpus Christi, Texas. He attended Rutgers University and, after two years in the US Army, earned a degree in journalism from Michigan State University. He was the first managing editor of *Track & Field News* 1960-3 and then sports information director at Western Michigan University 1963-9 and then at the U.S. Air Force Academy 1969-84. He also worked for the U.S. Olympic Committee, and was the USOC press officer at the Olympic Games of 1984 and 1988, and for USA Track & Field until 2002 as the organisation's historian, editor of media guides and press officer at many major events. A long-time member of the ATFS and FAST, he compiled *America's Best – A compilation of U.S. Olympic and International Track and Field Stars 1896-1987.*

David **'Dave'** Russell **BATTEN** (New Zealand) (b. 1927?) on 11 September in Christchurch at the age of 86. He won bronze medals at the 1950 Empire Games at 440y and 4x440y and was a semi-finalist at 220y. He went to Canterbury University and was NZ champion at 100y 1947, 220y 1948-51 and 440y 1949-50. A smooth stylist, he set a NZ record 21.2 for 220y in 1950 and had other pbs of 100y 9.9 (1947) and 440y 48.6 (1950).

Naomi BEINART (South Africa) (b. 9 Jun 1937 Johannesburg) on 8 January in Vancouver, Canada. She supported her husband Harry (d.1991) in his vital work on South African athletics statistics and continued after his death as a member of the Executive Committee of the South African Athletics Statisticians (SAAS).

Todd BENNETT (GBR) (b. 6 Jul 1962 Southampton) at his home in Bartley, Hampshire on 16 July after a 6-month battle with cancer. He was dedicated to the sport as an athlete, coach and team manager and was an inspiration to a huge number of young athletes and school children that he coached and supported.

Coached by Mike Smith, having first competed in the English Schools at 1500m steeplechase in 1977, he won the European Junior 400m (2nd 4x400m) in 1981 and competed in 34 senior internationals for Britain 1981-9. Just 1.70m tall, he excelled indoors – he won the European 400m title in 1985 (in a world indoor best of 45.56) and 1987 and was 2nd in the Worlds in 1985. Outdoors he was 5th in 1982 and 9th in 1990 at 400m plus a 200m silver in 1986 and 4x400m relay gold in 1982 and 1986 at the Commonwealth Games. At 400m: qf Olympics 1984 and 1988, sf Europeans 1982 and Worlds 1983. A very fine relay runner, he won 4x400m silver medals at the 1982 Europeans and 1984 Olympics and bronze at the 1983 Worlds. He won UK and AAA titles at 200m in 1984 and the AAA indoor 400m in 1985 and 1987.

He set a Commonwealth and European 300m best of 32.14 in 1984 and other pbs were 100m 10.46 (1986), 200m 20.36 (1984), 400m 45.27 (1988), 400mh 51.5 (1985), LJ 7.01 (1982).

Marianne Claire **BLACK** (née **DEW**) (GBR) (b. 8 Sep 1938 Tooting, London) on 16 September. In 1958 she competed at the Commonwealth Games (dq semi-final 220y after 24.42 in heat) and European Championships (4th semifinal 200m and silver medal at 4x100m) and in all in 7 UK internationals 1958-62. Pbs: 60y 7.2i (1959), 60m 7.7i (1958), 100y 10.9 (1962), 100m 11.9 (1961), 220y 24.2 (UK record in WAAA semi 1958), 440y 59.0 (1961). A member of Selsonia Ladies, she was 3rd in 1958 and 2nd in 1959 at 220y at the WAAA Championships. A schoolteacher, she later married Alan Black.

Pyotr Grigarevich **BOLOTNIKOV** (USSR) (b. 8 Mar 1930 Zinovkino, Russia) on 20 December at the age of 83. Olympic champion at 10,000m in 1960 when he took 26 secs off his best with 28:32.18, he went on to break the world record with 28:18.8 at Kiev on 15 Oct 1960, taking 11.6 secs off the record set by Vladimir Kuts in 1956, and improved that to 28:18.2 in Moscow on 11 Aug 1962 for his sixth successive USSR title. His first had been in 1957 when he beat the great Kuts by 0.2 in a then pb 29:09.8 and he won a further 10,000m title in 1964 and at 5000m was champion each year 1958-62 and cross-country champion in 1958. He had only started in athletics at the age of 20 when he joined the Red Army and he first broke 30 minutes in 1956, placing 9th at 5000m and 16th at 10,000m at the Olympic Games. In 1962 he won the 10,000m and was 3rd at 5000m at the European Championships and at his third Olympics was 25th at 10,000m in 1964. Other pbs: 1500m 3:46.0 (1961), 3000m 8:00.8 (1959, USSR record), 5000m 13:38.1 (1960), 3000mSt 8:56.7 (1961). From 1965-85 he worked as an athletics coach with Spartak Moskva, was their president in 1990-2 and was made honorary president in 1996.

Annual progress (year list ranking) at 5000m, 10,000,: 1954- 15:15.0, 31:40.0; 1955- 14:35.2 (97), 30:05.4 (36); 1956- 14:10.0 (30), 29:27.0 (12); 1957- 13:54.4 (5), 29:09.8 (2); 1958- 13:58.8 (9), 29:04.4 (7); 1959- 13:52.8 (9), 29:03.0 (1); 1960- 13:38.1 (1), 28:18.8 (1); 1961- 13:53.8 (9), 29:04.4 (7); 1962- 13:50.6 (6=), 28:18.1 (1); 1963- 14:09.2 (73), 29:16.4 (15); 1964- 13:38.6 (2), 28:39.6 (6); 1965- 13:43.0 (15), 28:58.6 (17).

Gerardo (né Gerhard) **BÖNNHOFF** (Argentina) (b. 24 Jun 1926 Berlin) on 26 December in El Palomar. He was 6th at 200m at the 1952 Olympic Games after being a quarter-finalist at 100m and 200m in 1948, and was 4th at 200m and 3rd at 4x100m in the 1951 Pan-American Games. At South American Championships he won the 100m in 1947 (2nd 1952 and 1956), the 200m in 1952 (2nd 1947, 3rd 1956) and 4x100m in 1947 and 1952 (2nd 1949 and 1956). He set a world junior record and South American record for 100m with 10.3 (1945) and ran 10.2w in 1946. He tied the Argentine record for 200m with 21.3 (1947). Argentinian champion at 100m 1945, 1947-50 and 1953; and 200m 1945. 1947-53 and 1960. Originally German, he arrived in Argentina at the age of ten and became an Argentine citizen in 1947. He was an ATFS member and wrote *A sus marcas*.

Lars Göte BOUDRIE (Sweden) (b. 3 May 1928 Vallentuna) on 14 September. At 3000m steeplechase – four internationals, pb 9:00.0 (1954). Other pbs: 3000m 8:24.2 (1954), 5000m 14:41.8 (1954).

Attilio BRAVI (Italy) (b. 9 Sep 1936 Bra, Cuneo) on 27 November in Bra. He had a best long jump of 7.66 in 1958 and was 10th at the 1960 Olympics, and 7th in 1954 (at age 18) and 4th in 1958 at the European Championships. He won the World Universities title in 1959 and three World Military Championships. He set an Italian youth record with 7.14 in 1952, and that year, at 16, won his first senior national title, going on to win seven more 1954-60. He taught for 25 years at ISEF (University Institute of Physical Education) and was a provincial chairman of the Italian Olympic National Committee (CONI) until January 2013.

Dr. Craig BRIGHAM (USA) (b. 6 May 1954) on 22 April in Charlotte, North Carolina. He set a US high school record for decathlon of 7359 points in 1972 that lasted until Curtis Beach beat it in 2009, and his pb was 8017 points (7934 on current tables) when 9th in the USA-USSR-Poland match for 11th in the world list in 1975,

when he was also 2nd in the AAUs and the NCAAs. He was 7th in the 1977 World University Games. Other pbs: 100m 10.9 (1972), 11.01 (1973); 400m 50.1 (1975), 1500m 4:35.4 (1975), 110mh 15.06 (1975), HJ 2.10 (1975), PV 4.98 (1973), LJ 6.90 (1975), SP 15.31 (1972), DT 49.78 (1976), JT 67.24 (1975). He went to the University of Oregon and earned a medical degree from Northwestern University before working as an orthopaedic spine surgeon.

Marco BUCCI (Italy) (b. 29 Nov 1960 Ferrara) on 6 August in Velletri. A discus thrower, he set four Italian records in 1984 from 65.16 to 66.96, but had to withdraw from the Olympic Games that year due to a muscle strain. He was third at the 1983 World University Games and Italian champion in 1982 and 1984; 14 internationals 1982-5. pb SP 18.38 (1985).

Lesley CANTWELL (New Zealand) (b. 22 Feb 1987) on 6 June in Papeete, Tahiti, just three days after winning the Oceania women's 5000m walk title in a personal best time of 25:39.79. She felt unwell and collapsed two hours after completing the race. Other pbs: 3000mW 14:35.40, 20kmW 1:51:26 (both 2013). Her mother, Judith, won the NZ 1500m title in 1989.

Lennart CARLSSON (Sweden) (b. 30 Dec 1932) on 16 January at the age of 80. At 20k walk he was 14th at the 1960 Olympic Games.

Taisia CHENCHIK (Russia/USSR) (b. 30 Jan 1936 Pryluky, Ukraine) on 19 November. She grew up in Chelyabinsk, Russia and had a most distinguished career at the high jump. She won the 1964 Olympic bronze after 5th in 1960, and at the European Championships won in 1966 after 2nd in 1958 and 6th in 1962. She also won at the World University Games in 1963 and European Cup in 1965 and six times in the celebrated USSR v USA matches. She was USSR champion 1957-9 and 1963, 2nd in 1962 and 1964-5, and 3rd in 1960-1 and 1967. Her first Russian records were 1.74 and 1.75 in 1957 with the built-up shoe that was made illegal at the end of that year, and then she set five records from 1.74 in 1958 to 1.78 (second on the all-time list to Iolanda Balas) at the 1964 Olympics. She graduated with an electrical engineering degree and lectured at the Moscow Power Engineering Institute.

Annual progress (year list ranking): 1954- 1.55 (66=), 1955- 1.60 (23=), 1956- 1.66 (11=), 1957- 1.75 (3), 1958- 1.76 (2), 1959- 1.78 (2), 1960- 1.75 (3=), 1961- 1.74 (3=), 1962- 1.76 (3=), 1963- 1.74 (7), 1964- 1.78 (4), 1965- 1.76 (5=), 1966- 1.75 (4=), 1967- 1.76 (3=), 1968- 1.75 (21=), 1969- 1.74 (31=).

Jon Frederic **COLE (USA)** (b. 4 Jan 1943 Chicago) on 10 January in Arizona. He won the US discus title in 1969 and was 6th at shot in 1966. He went to Arizona State University and was 2nd in the NCAA discus in 1965. Pbs

SP 19.18 (1968), DT 65.91 (1972, 4th in the world that year), JT 62.23 (1963). He set many world records in powerlifting and won US titles in 1968, 1970 and 1972.

David Robert **COLEMAN (GBR)** (b. 26 April 1926, Alderley Edge, Cheshire) on 21 December. For some 40 years he was the voice of athletics with BBC Television, commentating on every Olympics from 1960 to 2000, when he became the first broadcaster or journalist to be awarded the Olympic Order. He had been awarded the OBE in 1992. A useful miler, he was a successful journalist before joining the BBC in Birmingham as a news assistant and sports editor in 1954. He presented *Grandstand* from 1958 to 1968 and *Sportsnight with Coleman* 1968-72, and hosted *A Question of Sport* for 18 years from 1979.

Michael John **DENLEY (GBR)** (b. 21 Nov 1931) on 31 December. A member of Thames Valley Harriers, in 1952 he set British javelin records with 65.42 and 65.86. His dnq 19th at the Olympic Games was one of 8 UK internationals 1950-3. AAA champion 1950 and 1952-3. He was a quantity surveyor.

John **Basil** Charles **DICKINSON** (Australia) (b. 25 Apr 1915 Queenbeyan, New South Wales) on 7 October at his home in the Blue Mountains, New South Wales. He won bronze medals at both long jump and triple jump at the Empire Games in 1938, having won Australian titles at triple jump in 1934 and 1936 and long jump in 1937. He was ranked second on the world triple jump list in 1935 with 15.63 in Sydney behind compatriot Jack Metcalfe's world record of 15.78, but was injured at the 1936 Olympic Games, and came 16th. He won the New South Wales decathlon in 1939 and was the chief judge for the jumps at the 1956 Olympic Games in Melbourne. Pb LJ 7.48 (1938).

Lynnette E. **DONALDSON** (née Fisher) (New Zealand) on 24 February in Christchurch at the age of 67. She won the NZ 880y title in 1967 and 1968. Pbs: 880y 2:08.87 (1967), 1M 5:03.1 (1968).

Arieh **'Arik' EINSTEIN** (Israel) (b. 3 Jan 1939 Tel Aviv) on 26 November in Tel Aviv. He cleared 1.85m in 1956 and was the national HJ champion as a 17-year-old, before dedicating himself to the stage and becoming the greatest Israeli singer over half a century.

Mario ELEUSIPPI (Argentina) (b. 25 Sep 1934) on 7 December. At pole vault he was South American champion in 1963, set national records with 4.15 in 1962 (breaking a NR from 1933) and 4.20 in 1963, and was national champion in 1958-1960 and 1962. He became a famous coach, like his elder brother Enrique (died in 2012).

György ERDÉLYI (Hungary) (b. 15 Jul 1947, Atkár) on 24 June in Budapest. A javelin thrower, he was 10th at the European Champs, was Hungarian champion in 1974, and had five internationals 1974-7. Pbs: JT (old) 85.48 (1976), (new) 63.20 (1992).

Patrick ETOLU (Uganda) (b.17 Mar 1935 Asingei) on 23 December in Soroti. He tied for 12th at high jump at the 1956 Olympic Games after winning the silver medal in 1954 and going on to 4= in 1958 and 9th in 1962 at the Empire/Commonwealth Games. His final Ugandan record was 2.03 in 1956.

Thomas Jefferson **'Tommy' FULTON** (USA) (b.31 Dec 1951) on 8 August in Port Charlotte, Florida. He was 8th in the 1972 US Olympic Trials 800m in his pb of 1:47.3 while at Texas Southern University, and also had bests for 1500m 3:40.4 (1974) and 1 mile 3:57.8 (1973).

Olga GYARMATI-ACZEL (Hungary) (b. 5 Oct 1924 Debrecen) on 27 October in Greenfield, Massachusetts, USA. She was Hungary's second female Olympic champion in athletics with the 1948 long jump (also 10th in 1952 and 11th in 1956). She won World University Games titles in 1949 at long jump and 1951 at 200 metres, adding four silvers and two bronzes at the Universiade in 1949 and 1951. She won 23 Hungarian titles at individual events: 100m 1941, 1949 and 1951, 200m 1951-2, 80mh 1948-49 and 1951-5, high jump 1942 and 1949, long jump 1948-9 and 1951-6, and pentathlon 1950 and 1955, plus four national relay titles. She competed in 31 internationals 1942-56 and set 23 national records at six events. Pbs: 60m 7.8 (1950), 100m 11.9 (1951), 200m 24.8 (1951), 80mh 11.1 (1956), HJ 1.60 (1950), LJ 6.23 (1953), SP 11.12 (1952), JT 25.22 (1949), Pen 4160 (1955, 1954 tables).

After the 1956 Olympics, she left Hungary, as did many Hungarian athletes in response to the Soviet invasion of their country. She first settled in England and became a British citizen. She married Hungarian writer Tamás Aczél (her second marriage), and they later lived in Orange, Massachusetts in the United States.

Anthony Miles **'Tony' HARPER** (Bermuda) (b. 6 Dec 1938 Batu Gajah, Malaysia) on 17 April. He ran at 400m in the 1968 Olympic Games and 440y/400m and 440y/400mh at the 1966 and 1970 Commonwealth Games. Pbs: 400m 47.3, 880y 1:52.4 and 440yh 52.2, all Bermudan records in 1966 when at Loughborough College in England. He had British parents.

Arquímedes HERRERA (Venezuela) (b. 8 Aug 1935 Sucre) on 30 May in Maracaibo. He was a semi-finalist at both 100m and 200m and 6th at 4x100m at the 1964 Olympic Games. At the 1963 Pan-American Games he was 2nd at 100m and 4x100m and 3rd at 200, he was 2nd at 200m and 3rd at 100m at the 1962 CAC Games, and South American champion at 100m and 4x100m in 1961 (2nd 200m) and 100m and 200m in 1963, plus second at 4x100m in 1965. He set South American and CAC records (hand timed) for 100m at 10.2 (1963) and 10.1 (1964) and 200m 20.5 (!964), plus South American record 20.8 (1963). Auto timed pbs: 100m 10.32 (1963), 200m 21.09 (1964).

Tamás HOMONNAY (Hungary) (b. 2 Jan 1926 Budapest) in May in Monroe, Connecticut, USA. At pole vault he was 11th at the 1952 Olympic Games, 4th at the 1954 Europeans and 4th in 1951 and 1st in 1954 at the World Youth Games. He set 8 national records from 4.14 (1949) to 4.35 (1956), was Hungarian champion 1949-56 and had 31 internationals at HJ/PV 1943-56. Pb HJ 1.84 (1943). He fled to the USA after the 1956 revolution.

Ari HUUMONEN (Finland) (b. 5 Mar 1956 Hämeenlinna) on 20 May in Hämeenlinna. A discus thrower with nerves of steel, he threw a best of 65.44 when fourth at home in Helsinki at the 1983 World Championships. A colourful character, he is remembered from his habit of competing just a few times every summer (almost never abroad, because he hated flying) and arriving at the last moment with no warm-up. After four Finnish silvers 1979-82 he was Finnish champion in 1983, 1985 and 1987, and third in 1988 in his farewell competition. He threw over 60 m 1979-85 and 1987, and had two wins in 12 international matches 1979-84.

Yuriy Borisovich **ISAKOV** (Russia) (b. 30 Dec 1949 Yekaterinburg) on 29 September. He ranked in the world's top ten for pole vault in four years in the early 1970s. He no-heighted in qualifying at the 1976 Olympic Games, but had more success at the Europeans: 1969- nh, 1971-7th, 1974- 3rd; and 3rd in 1971, and 4th in 1972 at the European Indoors. He also tied for silver at the 1973 World University Games, and was 1= in 1973 and 3rd in 1975 at the European Cup. He set an unofficial European Junior record with 5.02 in 1968 and USSR records with 5.36 in 1971 and 5.41 in 1973 before his pb 5.50 in 1977, and was USSR champion in 1969 and 1973.

Wilton JACKSON (Trinidad and Tobago) (b. 15 Nov 1935) on 10 March in San Fernando. In his best year of 1959 he won the 200m at the British West Indies Championships, the national 200m and 400m titles, and the 4x100m silver medal at the Pan American Games (where he also reached the 100m and 200m semifinals), also setting career best times for 100m 10.3 and 220y half-turn 20.8. He was also Trinidad 100m and 200m champion in 1960 and represented TRI at the 1958 CG (hts 440 and both relays), 1962 CAC Games (2nd 200m, 4x100m, 4x400m), 1964 Olympics and 1967 Pan American Games. He studied at Morgan State University in the early sixties, coached Hasely Crawford in the seventies, and was president of the national association 1983-6. Other pbs: 100y 9.5 (1962), 220yt 21.1 (1961), 440y 47.6 (1960) and 400mh 55.4 (1958).

Jan JASKÓLSKI (Poland) (b. 29 Oct 1939 Inowroclaw) on 22 June in Inowroclaw. A triple jumper, with a best of 16.76 (1966), he competed at three Olympic Games 1960-8, making the final once, 12th in 1964, and was 4th at the European Championships in both 1962 and 1966. He was 2nd in the Polish Championships seven times (1960, 1963-4, 1966-9), five times to the great Józef Schmidt. Pb LJ 7.64/7.69w (1962). He was an economist as well as a coach and judge in track and field.

Roine Sven Torbjörn KARLSSON (Sweden) (b. 12 Nov 1943 Uppsala) on 17 February in Uppsala. At 20km walk he was 20th at the 1964 Olympic Games and had 8 more internationals for Sweden; pbs: 20kW 1:34:05 (1968), 50kW 4:30:21 (1969).

Olavi KAUHANEN (Finland) (b. 23 Jun 1926 Äyräpää, Karelia, now Russia) on 30 December in Tampere. A fireman and somewhat unlucky javelin thrower, he missed 1956 and 1960 Olympic selection partly for political reasons, being a member of TUL (Worker's Sports Federation). Finnish champion in 1956 and 1959 with two silvers, he had nine international dual matches in 1954-9 with five wins, pb 79.63 (1959). He did an M40 world best of 72.88 in 1966 and threw 64.68 aged 45. He was a member of Finnish volleyball team in the 1952 World Championships. On 13 Sep 1959 he won Finnish volleyball and TUL javelin titles on the same day

Alexandra Phyllis '**Sandra**' **KNOTT** (USA) (b. 9 Oct 1937 Worcester, Massachusetts) on 26 June in Springfield, Oregon. A member of the Cleveland Recreation Club, at 800m she set a US record in 1963 with 2:09.7 and won the US Olympic Trials in 1964 before placing 6th in her heat at the Games in Tokyo. She won five AAU titles: 440y 1962-3 and 880y/800m in 1963-4 plus 880y indoors in 1964. Pb 1500m 4:36.7 (1965). She later earned graduate and masters degrees in nursing and specialised in the treatment of diabetes.

Nadezhda Leonidovna **KOLESNIKOVA-ILYINA** (Russia) (b. 24 Jan 1949 Zelenokumsk, Stavropol Kray) was killed in a car crash in Moscow on 7 December. At the Olympic Games she won 4x400m bronze in 1976 and was a semi-finalist in 1972 and 1976. She also won 4x400m bronze medals at the Europeans in 1971 and 1974 and was 4th at 400m in 1974 after 5th in her heat in 1971. She was 2nd in the European Indoors at 400m in 1974 (after a world indoor best 52.44 in her semi-final) and 1975, was World Universities champion in 1973, 3rd in 1973 and 5th in 1975 at the European Cup, and USSR champion in 1973-5, having started with 6th at 800m at the 1966 European Juniors. She set four USSR records at 400m with hand timing from 52.1 (1973) to 51.3 (1976) and four with auto-timing from 52.29 (1972) to 51.19 (1976). Other pbs 200m 23.6 (1976),

23.90 (1973); 800m 2:04.1 (1970). Her daughter Nadiya Petrova (b. 8 Jun 1982) is a top tennis player, winning 13 WTA singles tournaments 2003-12 and 24 doubles, including the WTA Championship in 2004 and 2012, reaching a career high of world number three in 2006.

Waclaw KUZMICKI (Poland) (b. 27 Apr 1921 Bialystok) on 19 August in Katowice. At the decathlon he was 10th at the 1946 Europeans and 16th at the 1948 Olympic Games (6153 points). Polish champion at pentathlon 1947 and 1950, triple jump 1947. He was married to Irene Hejducka (1929-2008), who competed at 100m and 4x100m at the 1946 Europeans.

Robert Henry 'Bob' LAWSON (USA) (b. 5 Jan 1935) on 3 April in Ocean Shores, Washington. He was the world's third ranked decathlete in 1955 with 7063 points on the 1952 scoring tables (7086 current tables) and narrowly missed Olympic selection in 1956 when fourth in the US Trials. He went to the University of Southern California, and was successively 2nd, 4th, 3rd and 5th in the AAU decathlon 1955-8 and 4th in the NCAA 120yh in 1958. Other pbs: 120yh 14.1 (1958), 220yhSt 23.3/23.0w (1957), LJ 7.51 (1958). He became a highly respected coach and was still competing in masters throwing events in his mid-seventies.

Meskerem LEGESSE (Ethiopia) (b. 28 Sep 1986) on collapsing at lunch in a Chinese restaurant in Hamden, USA on 17 July. She was due to give birth to a second child that was delivered successfully by staff at the hospital to which she was taken. When just 15 years old she was 4th at 1500m at the 2002 African Championships and she ran at the 2004 Olympics (ht 1500m). Pbs: 800m 2:01.11 (2003), 2:01.03i (world junior indoor record 2004); 1500m 4:03.96 (2003), 1M 4:34.07i (2007), road: 10km 32:59 (2009), HMar 75:51 (2009).

Ferdinand Andries **'Ferdie' LE GRANGE** (South Africa) (b. 26 Aug 1948 Molteno) on 29 October. At the marathon he set six South African records from the first sub 2:20 time run in Africa, 2:19:02.2 on his debut at the event at Durbanville in 1971 and 2:17:51.4 on the same course two months later, then 2:16:10 for 8th in Manchester and 2:15:34.6 for a win in Brussels a mere week later in 1972. He followed that with 2:13:58 for 4th in Manchester in 1973 and finally 2:12:47 at Port Elizabeth in 1974 to retain the RSA title that he had won the previous year. He also set South African records for 10 miles in 47:58.6 and 1 hour with 20,158m at Bellville in 1974. Other pbs: 3000m 8:21.0 (1969), 2M 8:59.2 (1972), 5000m 13:46.6 (1973), 10,000m 28:55.0 (1973). He became a plastic surgeon in Germiston.

Gert LE ROUX (South Africa) (b. July 1935 Theunissen) on 17 August. A long-time ATFS member and Executive Committee member for Africa, he was a giant in South African athletics, a hugely committed administrator and meticulous historian. He was Secretary of the SAAAU from 1971 to 1994 and involved in the production of the South African Athletics Annual for 50 consecutive years. A graduate of the University of the Orange Free State and state under-19 rugby player, he began his career as a news reporter at the SA Broadcasting Corporation, later concentrating on sports reporting.

Doris LORENZ (née MÜLLER) (Germany) (b. 25 Feb 1935 Massenei/bei Waldheim) on 25 February in Leipzig. The European silver medallist at discus in 1962 after 6th in 1958, she competed at two Olympic Games (nt 1960 and 14th 1964) and was GDR champion each year 1957-61. She set nine GDR records from 49.04 (1957) to 56.39 (1962), 31 internationals 1955-64, and married javelin thrower Günter Lorenz on 15 Dec 1962.

Ulf Bertil LUNDH (Norway) (b. 11 Oct 1932) on 15 June. A middle distance runner who competed in 12 internationals for Norway 1956-9, he was 9th in the European 1500m in 1958 and had pbs of 800m 1:47.8, 1000m 2:21.8, 1500m 3:42.1 (with an earlier Norwegian record of 3:43.1) and 1M 4:05.0 (all 1958).

Gordon Edmund **McKENZIE** (USA) (b. 26 Jun 1927 Fort Totten, New York) on 21 July. AAU cross-country champion in 1954, he was 4th at 5000m at the 1955 Pan-American Games and in 1956 was 18th in the Olympic 10,000m. At the marathon he was second at Boston and 48th at the Olympic Games in 1960 and won the Pan-American Games silver medal in 1963. Pbs: 1M 4:12.9i (1954), 2M 8:58.8i (1955), 3M 14:02.9 (1955), 6M 29:31.7 (1958), 10,000m 30:34.4 (1956), Mar 2:22:18 (1960). He went to New York University and ran for the New York Pioneer Club. He was married for 59 years to the former Christina Slemon, who in 1953 was a member of the British team that set a world record of 6:49.0 for the 3x880y relay.

Josef MALEK (Czech Republic) (b. 12 Mar 1933 Prague) on 13 March in Prague. Czechoslovak hammer champion 1958 and 1960-2 with national records of 62.37 (1958) and 63.01 (1959) and pb 64.92 (1963). 23 internationals 1954-63, dnq European Champs 1962.

Maurice **'Moss' Lane MARSHALL** (New Zealand) (b. 12 Jan 1927 Thames, Waikato) on 16 May in Hamilton. He was third at 1 mile at the 1950 Empire Games and ran at the 1952 Olympics (heats 800m and 1500m). NZ champion 1M 1951-2 (2nd 1946-50), pbs: 880y 1:53.5 (1951), 1M 4:11.8 (1952). A teacher, headmaster of Southwell School in Hamilton 1972-88, and awarded the MBE in 1989.

Imre MÁTRAHÁZI Sr. (Hungary) (b. 23 Jul 1928) on 20 March. A mechanical engineer by profession, he was an emblematic figure in Hungarian Athletics, a much respected competition organiser and technical official; a member of the board of the Hungarian Federation for 27 years and chair of the federation's technical committee. His son Imre Jr. is Technical Manager of the IAAF Competitions Department.

Heather Simpson Mitchell **MAY** (New Zealand) (née Wright) (b. 4 Aug 1922 Reefton) on 28 July in Wellington. Having been a tap dancer and contortionist, she only started in athletics at the age of 28, and won the NZ high jump title in 1951 (2nd 80mh, 3rd LJ) and in 1954. Pbs: HJ 1.58 (1958), LJ 5.50 (1951), Pen 3577 (1956), From the 1980s she won several World Masters titles and set world age group records.

Alain MIMOUN O'Kacha (France) (b. 1 Jan 1921 Le Telagh, Algeria) on 27 June in Saint-Mandé, Île-de-France. A fine distance runner, he achieved his greatest success at cross-country, at which he was International champion in 1949, 1952-3 and 1956 (and 2nd 1950 and 1958). On the track he seemed the perennial runner-up to Emil Zátopek, taking silver medals at the Olympics in 1948 at 10,000m, and in 1952 at both 5000m and 10,000m and at the Europeans at both those events in 1950. He came into his own, however, with Olympic gold in 1956, when after a disappointing 12th at 10,000m he ran his first ever marathon and took the gold medal, with Zátopek in sixth place. His wife had given birth to a child on the eve of the race. He was also 34th in the 1960 Olympic marathon. He won both 5000m and 10,000m at the Mediterranean Games in 1951 and 1955. He won 32 national titles, 12 at 10,000m, 8 at 5000m, 6 each at cross-country and marathon, and had 85 international appearances 1947-66. His 11 French records included his bests for 5000m 14:07.58 (1952), 10,000m 29:13.4 (1956), 1 Hour 19,364m (1956), 20,000m 1:01:56.4 (1956) and 25.000m 1:21:39.6 (1959), and his fastest marathon was 2:25:29.3 (1958) plus 2:23:41 for his first French title in 1959 but probably short at 41.7km. He continued to run as a veteran, setting numerous age-group records over many years.

Progress at 5000m, 10,000m, Mar: 1941- 32:42.6, 1946- 15:09.7, 32:05.7; 1947- 14:47.4, 31:21.0; 1948- 14:39.8, 30:47.4; 1949- 14:26.0, 29:53.0; 1950- 14:26.0, 30:21.0; 1951- 14:23.0, 30:01.4; 1952- 14:07.4, 29:29.4; 1953- 14:08.4, 29:51.0; 1954- 14:31.66, 30:21.8; 1955- 14:27.9, 29:49.0; 1956- 14:23.4, 29:13.4, 2:25:00; 1957- 14:10.6, 29:53.2; 1958- 14:16.4, 29:30.6, 2:25:29.3; 1959- 14:19.8, 30:24.8, 2:23:41sh; 1960- 14:24.4, 30:18.8, 2:31:20; 1961- 14:42.8, 30:27.6; 1962- 14:37.8, 30:15.4; 1963- 14:52.0, 30:39.8, 2:33:19; 1964- 14:22.0, 29:57.4, 2:28:55; 1965- 14:50.2, 30:32.6, 2:30:19; 1966- 14:56.4, 30:16.8, 2:25:41; etc.

Ottavio 'Tai' MISSONI (Italy) (b. 11 Feb 1921 Ragusa di Dalmazia, now in Croatia) on 9 May in Sumirago. A 400m hurdler, he was 6th at the 1948 Olympic Games and 4th in the European Championships in 1950 (having competed in the heats of the 400m flat in 1938). He won the World Student Games 400m in 1939 and was Italian champion at 400m 1939 and 400mh 1947-8; 22 internationals 1937-53. After WWII, in which he was a prisoner of war, he began creating wool tracksuits (worn by the Italian team at the 1948 Games) and founded his eponymous label and fashion house (internationally known for its colourful knitwear designs) with his wife Rosita in 1953. Pbs: 400m 47.8 (1939), 400mh 53.1 (1948).

Eleanor Inez **MONTGOMERY** (USA) (b. 13 Nov 1946) on 28 December in Cleveland. She won the high jump as a 16 year-old at the Pan-American Games in 1963 and again in 1967, when she set a US record at 1.78 and ranked second in the world. She improved the US record to 5ft 11in/1.80m in 1969. She was 8th at the 1964 Olympic Games and did not qualify (19th) in 1968. She won the US high jump in 1963-7 and 1969, and indoors each year 1963-9, and the Olympic Trials in 1964, having won her first national title with the US girls long jump in 1962 (pb 5.52). She attended Tennessee State University.

Motsapi MOOROSI (Lesotho) (b. 4 May 1945) on 8 February in Maseru. He became the first Lesotho athlete to run at the Olympic Games in 1972 (ht 100m, qf 200m) and also ran at the 1974 Commonwealth Games (ht 200m and 400m). He set national records with 100m 10.2 (1971), 200m 20.90 (1972) and 400m 47.7 (1971).

Patrick John Anthony **MORRISON** (GBR) (b. 16 Nov 1945 Cork, Ireland) on 20 December. Having moved to England with his family at the age of 13, he began running in 1961 and made rapid progress to be AAA junior champion at 100y and 220y in 1964 and AAA champion at 220y in 1965. That year, at the age of 19, he made four international appearances for Britain and also competed for Ireland against England. He went to Stanford University in USA on an athletic scholarship and there in 1966 ran pbs of 9.6 for 100y (to tie the Irish record he had set in 1965 in Dublin) and 21.2 for 220y (matching the 21.1 for 200m from 1965). At Stanford he refused to cut his long hair and coach Peyton Jordan dropped him from the team. Although the University gave him an academic scholarship and he graduated in English literature, he did not compete again. Instead he took up art and was awarded a scholarship by San Francisco Art Institute. As well as his painting he became custodian of the Cotton Exchange in Los Angeles. Other pbs: 100m 10.7/10.5w (1964), 400m 49.0 (1964), LJ 7.13 (1964).

Ahmed Ishtiaq MUBARAK (Malaysia) (b. 6 Feb (1948) on 9 August in Hulu Kelang Selangor. He was a three-time Olympian (heats 1968, 1972, 1976), won bronze in 1966 and silver in 1974 at the Asian Games, was the silver medallist at the Asian Championships in 1973 and 1975 and also ran in the heats at the 1974 and 1978 Commonwealth Games – all at 110m hurdles, at which his 14.08 in 1976 (after a hand-timed 13.8 two weeks earlier) stood as the Malaysian record for 15 years. He also won the SEA Games 110mh in 1969, 1971, 1973 and 1977.

Donna-Marie Louise MURRAY (later Hartley-Wass) (GBR) (b. 1 May 1955 Southampton) on 8 June in Elsecar, South Yorkshire. She was the golden girl of British athletics in the 1970s. Coached by Mike Smith at Southampton AAC, she first competed at a major championship at the age of 17, reaching the semi-finals of the Olympic Games 200m in 1972. She was 7th at 200m and won 4x100m bronze at the 1973 European Juniors, before taking up the 400m seriously in 1974. Her greatest success came in 1978 when she won gold medals at 400m and 4 x 400m at the Commonwealth Games, and in that year she was 6th in the European 400m. At the Olympics she was a 400m quarter-finalist in 1976 and won a relay bronze medal in 1980. She won the WAAA 200m in 1972, 400m 1975, and the UK 400m 1977. She ran on the British team which set a world record for 4 x 200m in 1977 and set British records at 200m 22.75 (1978), 300m 36.2 (1974) and 400m 51.77 (1974), 51.28 (1975) and 51.2 (1978). Other bests: 100m 11.46 (1975), 800m 2:07.8 (1976). She was awarded the MBE in 1979. She took up bodybuilding on retiring from athletics, and became UK champion and runner-up in Miss Universe in 1988. In 1977 she had married Bill Hartley, who won a relay silver at the Commonwealth Games and gold at the European Championships in 1978. He ran his best 400m hurdles time, 49.65, to win the 1975 AAA title, and also won UK titles in 1978 and 1981. After that marriage was dissolved Donna married comedian Bobby Knutt (real name Wass) in 1987.

Progress at 400m: 1971- 59,7m 1973- 56.9, 1974- 51.77, 1975- 51.28, 1976- 51.29, 1977- 51.5/51.62, 1978- 51.2/51.43, 1979- 51.47, 1980- 52.33, 1982- 56.56.

Johanna Katarina **NILSSON** (Sweden) (b. 27 Mar 1983 Kalmar) on 25 June in Sweden. From a distinguished athletics family, she competed for Sweden at 1500m, 10th in 1999 and 9th in 2001 at the European Juniors, and 5th in 2003 and 12th in 2005 at the European U23s and was 3rd in the 2005 European Cross-country (and 3rd junior team 1999), but achieved her greatest successes in the USA. For the University of Northern Arizona she won NCAA titles indoors at 1 mile in 2003 (in a Swedish indoor record 4:32.49) and 2006 and 3000m in 2006 and at cross-country in 2005. Other pbs: 800m 2:05.11 (2003), 1500m 4:10.72 (2003), 3000m 9:06.61i (2006).

Fritz NUSSBAUM (Switzerland) (b. 1 Jan 1924 Uster) on 11 September in Langenthal. At the decathlon he was 23rd at the 1948 Olympic Games, was Swiss champion in 1948 and 1953 and had a pb of 6566 points (1934 tables) in 1953.

Bengt Asbjörn **PERSSON** later WIDMARK (Sweden) (b. 31 Oct 1939 Lövånger) on 14 November in Visby. At 3000m steeplechase he was 10th at the 1968 Olympic Games and at the Europeans was 9th in 1966 and 11th in 1969. He was Swedish champion at steeplechase in 1963-9, 5000m and 10,000m 1965, and 12k cross-country in 1964-6. Pbs: 1500m 3:46.1 (1965), 2000m 5:13.8 (1965), 3000m 7:57.8 (1968), 2M 8:41.2 (1968), 5000m 13:48.6 (1968), 10,000m 29:36.2 (1965), 3000mSt 8:33.8 (1968); 35 internationals.

Lionel PETERS (GBR) (b. 15 May 1937 Southend-on-Sea) on 18 July in Harrow, London. A chartered accountant and a member of the NUTS and ATFS from the 1980s, he set up World Junior Athletics News and published a series of World Junior Annuals.

Jean Catherine **PICKERING**, née Desforges. (GBR) (b. 4 Jul 1929 Forest Gate, London) on 25 March at her home in Welwyn, Hertfordshire. Starting athletics seriously in 1947 she became a highly talented all-rounder, winning the European long jump title in 1954, when she also ran on the 4th placed British sprint relay team. She was 6th at 80m hurdles at the 1950 Europeans and competed at the Empire Games of 1950 and 1954, with bronze medals at 80m hurdles and long jump in 1954. Britain's woman athlete of the year in 1953, when she set British records at long jump (6.10m) and pentathlon (3997 points, 1954 tables), she was WAAA champion at 80m hurdles in 1949, 1952-4, long jump and pentathlon 1953-4. She considered her finest performance to be the wind assisted 10.9 that she ran in the semi-final of the 80m hurdles at the 1952 Olympics, but she only managed 11.6 for 5th in the final, when she was hampered by an ill Fanny Blankers-Koen smashing into the first two hurdles in the adjoining lane; she also gained a bronze medal in the 4x100m in 46.2, a UK record which was inside the pre-Games world record. Her 'legal' best 80mh time was 11.1 (1954). 100y flat best: 10.9w (1952). Jean was awarded the MBE in the 2010 New Year's Honours for her work for the Ron Pickering Memorial Trust that has now given a remarkable £1.3 million to aid young athletes.

She met her husband to be Ron Pickering OBE (1930-91) at school, Stratford Grammar. Ron became an inspirational National Coach for Wales before moving on to become an athletics commentator for BBC Television. Their son Shaun Pickering (b. 14 Nov 1961) was a multiple Welsh record holder with bests of shot 20.45 (1997), discus 54.38 (1988) and hammer 68.64 (1984), ultimately gaining most success at the shot at which he won the Commonwealth bronze medal in 1998 and competed at the 1996 Olympic Games.

Baldassare PORTO (Italy) (b. 19 Jan 1923 Catania) on 1 December. For several seasons he was Italy's 4x400m first leg-man, including silver medals at the 1950 Europeans and 1952 Mediterranean Games, dnf 1952 Olympic Games. Italian champion at 400m 1950, 14 internationals 1948-55. Pbs: 100m 10.7 (1949), 400m 47.8 (1950).

Henry M. **REBELLO** (India) (b. 17 Nov 1928 Lucknow) on 27 August in Gurgaon, Haryana. He competed in the triple jump at the 1948 Olympic Games (no jump in the final) and that year set an Indian record of 15.29 for fifth on the world list. He was a Group Captain in the Indian Air Force and first Director in Sports Authority of India.

Giovanni 'Gianni' ROCCA (Italy) (b. 13 Jun 1929 Milan) in Milan on 11 August. He competed at 4x400m at the Olympic Games of 1948 and 1952 and at 400m in 1952. Pbs: 200m 21.9 (1952), 400m 48.4 (1952), 8 internationals 1948-53.

Frank George John **SALVAT** (GBR) (b. 30 Oct 1934 Edgware, London) on 24 June in Brighton. A member of Finchley Harriers, after winning the AAA 3 miles title, he ran twice for Britain at 5000m in 1960, 2nd against France in a pb 13:54.8 and in the heats at the Olympic Games. Other pbs 1M 4:02.3, 3000m 8:00.4, 2M 8:52.2, 3M 13:28.2+ (all 1960). He first came to prominence when 3rd in the National Junior CC in 1956.

Mark Gavin **SESAY** (GBR) (b. 13 Dec 1972) on 20 November in Leeds. He showed great talent at 800m as a teenager, setting a UK youths record of 1:49.9 in 1989 and winning four English Schools titles. He then ran 1:48.30 at 17 in 1990 and was a semi-finalist at the World Juniors. He was 3rd in the 1991 European Juniors, but did not improve further due to illness and injury until 1:46.05 and 46.22 for 400m in 1997. He was 3rd in the 1997 European Cup but missed the 1998 season due to a stress fracture. Returning, he was AAA champion and ran his pb of 1:45.68 in 1999 but drifted away from the sport after 2000. He ran (heats) at the 1997 and 1999 World Champs. Other pbs: 200m 22.0w (1997), 600m 1:16.61 (1997), 1500m 3:49.5 (1997). A member of Leeds City AC, he went to Loughborough University.

Dr. Isobel Blanche Armitage BARBER (née **'Quita' SHIVAS**) (GBR) (b. 19 Apr 1925) on 18 March at Melrose in the Scottish Borders. A graduate of Aberdeen University, she made one international appearance, running in the 100m heats at the 1952 Olympic Games. She was WAAA champion at 60m in 1950 and 2nd at 100m in 1950 and 1952 and had pbs: 100y 11.2 (1951), 11.0uw (1950); 100m 12.4 (1952), 220y straight 25.5 (1950).

Milan SKOCOVSKY (Czech Republic) (b. 25 Feb 1937 Prerov) on 24 November. A teacher, he was a founder member of the Czechoslovak Association of Athletics Statisticians in 1960 and a member of the ATFS from 1968. He was the key compiler of world junior statistics for some 40 years and attended eight World Junior Championships as a statistician for the IAAF. He was co-author of the *Small Encyclopedia of Athletics* and of *Who Was Who in Czech Athletics.* He was chairman of his club Lokomotiva Nymburk and from 1973 a member of the Czech federation's technical committee. Up to his death he had been issuing bulletins with detailed results of Czech meetings and athletes around the world.

Ronald **'Ronnie' Ray SMITH (USA)** (b. 28 Mar 1949 Los Angeles) on 31 March in Los Angeles. A student at San Jose State University under coach Bud Winter in the 'Speed City' days, he ran the third leg on the US team that won the 1968 Olympic title in a world record time of 38.24 at high altitude in Mexico City. He had been 4th in the US Olympic Trials 100m, 0.02 behind Mel Pender, having earlier in the year being 5th in the AAU Championships (and 3rd at 200m), after tying the world record with a hand-time 9.9 in his semi-final behind Jim Hines 9.9, although the auto timing showed them a metre apart with Hines 10.03 and Smith 10.14 (his pb and world junior best). All this at the age of 19, but it was his only year in the world top ten. Other pbs: 100y 9.3 (1969), 9.2w (1968), 200m 20.4/20.75, 20.2w (1968).

Charel **'Charles' SOWA** (Luxembourg) (b. 17 Apr 1933 Schifflange) on 7 July in Schifflange. A fine race walker, he competed at four Olympic Games: 20km/50km: 1960- 18/21, 1964- 16/9, 1968- 19/16, 1972- 18/10, and four European Championships: 1962- 10/dnf, 1966- 12/10, 1969- dq/7, 1971- 12/10. Luxembourg records and best: track 5000m (2) 20:43.2 (1992), 10,000m (43:44.0 1961), 20,000m (3) 1:32:46.4 (1964), 1 hour (6) 13,291m (1972); road: 20km (3) 1:27:32 (1972), 50km (2) 4:12:05 (1969). LUX champion 20kmW (10) 1960-2, 1964, 1967-8, 1970-2, 1974; 30kmW 1958-9.

Irina STASYUK, née Chernushenko (Belarus) (b. 9 Mar 1979 Slutsk) on 5 December. She had a long jump best of 6.74 in her final year of competition 2008, in which year she was a non-qualifier (18th) at the Olympic Games. She was also dnq 20th at the 2006 Europeans and was BLR champion each year 2001-03 and indoors 2003 and 2006-08.

Brian Douglas **STERNBERG** (USA) (b. 21 Jun 1943 Seattle) on 23 May in Seattle. He broke the world junior record twice (4.64 and 4.77m) in 1962 and then, as a 19 year-old student at the University of Washington, set three world pole vault records in 1963: 5.00 (the first outdoor 5m clearance) at Philadelphia on 27 April, 5.05 (unratified) at Modesto on 25 May and 5.08 at Compton on 7 June. He won the NCAA and AAU titles and was undefeated, but his brilliant career, with huge promise for the future, was cut short on July 2 as, demonstrating a double-back somersault with twist on a trampoline. he lost control and landed on his neck. This accident left him a quadriplegic and wheelchair-bound for life.
Progress: 1957- 2.59, 1958- 3.05, 1959- 3.58, 1960- 3.81, 1961- 4.36, 1962- 4.77, 1963- 5.08.

Henry Robert H. **STINSON** (GBR) (b. 15 Mar 1931) on 3 April. A solicitor by profession and a Cambridge University 'blue' at 220 yards hurdles with a pb of 25.5 (1954), he was a driving force behind the Achilles Club as team manager and later chairman. He was the inaugural chairman of the British Athletics League 1968-72, and, as General Secretary of the British Amateur Athletic Board 1977-9 and the chairman of its Finance Committee 1979-87, prepared the way for British athletics to move from amateurism to today's professional sport. His great service to athletics culminated in his careful and astute work for the IAAF as their Treasurer from 1984 to 2003; he was then a Life Vice-President of the IAAF from 2003. Awarded the MBE.

Glenn STOJANOVIC (Australia) (b. 3 Feb 1974) in a road accident on 25 October. He set an Oceania junior record of 8:40.62 when 5th in the 3000m steeplechase at the 1992 World Junior Championships, and, still a junior in 1993, won the Australian senior 1 mile title in his pb of 4:00.80 and ran 3:45.4 for 1500m.

Calum STUART (New Zealand) (b. 2 Jul 1975) on 8 May in Hamilton. At 400mh he was national champion in 1996 and in 1999 (in his pb of 50.43).

César SUÁREZ de CENTI (Spain) (b. 10 Mar 1946 La Coruña) on 15 April. He was Spanish triple jump champion in 1969 with a pb of 15.91 and won indoor titles at LJ 1967 and TJ 1969

Dominik SUCHENSKI (Poland) (b. 8 Sep 1926) on 20 May in Brodnicy. He ran in the heats of the 4x100m relay at the 1952 Olympics and had pbs of 100m 10.6 (1950), 220y 22.6 (1950), LJ 6.98 (1949).

Edward Ignacy **SZKLARCZYK** (Poland) (b. 31 Jul 1941 Sucha Beskidzka) on 26 April in Bydgoszcz. At 3000m steeplechase he ran at the 1964 Olympics (heats), was 3rd in the European

Cup in 1965 and Polish champion 1963-6, with a best of 8:34.6 (1970).

Albert George 'Albie' THOMAS (Australia) (b. 8 Feb 1935 Hurstville, New South Wales) on 27 October in Sydney. He set three world records: 2 miles 8:32.0 Dublin 7 Aug 1958 (the day after he had set the pace and come 5th in 3:58.6 behind Herb Elliott's world record 3:54.5 for the mile), 3 miles 13:10.8 Dublin 9 Jul 1958 and at 4 x 1 mile for Australia 16:25.6 Melbourne 22 Mar 1959. He also set a world indoor best for 3 miles with 13:26.4 (1964). He won silver at 3 miles and bronze at 1 mile at the 1958 Empire & Commonwealth Games and was also fifth at both 1 and 3 miles in 1962. His record at three Olympic Games was: 1956- 5th 5000m; 1960- 11th 5000m, ht 1500m; 1964- ht 1500m & 5000m; and he was Australian champion at 1 mile 1962-5 and 3 miles 1957-60. Other pbs: 1500m 3:42.6 (1964), 1M 3:58.3 (1964), 2000m 5:10.0 (1964), 3000m 8:01.4 (1960), 5000m 13:50.0 (1964), 6M 28:30.4 (1957), 10,000m 29:21.0 (1956), Mar 2:29:04 (1963), having set Australian records with 3000m 8:05.2 (1958), 3M 13:25.9 (1957) and 5000m 13:51.4 (1963). He also won the 1500m and 3000m at the first World Masters Championships in 1975.

Wilbur Marvin 'Moose' **THOMPSON** (USA) (b. 6 Apr 1921 Frankfurt, South Dakota) on 25 December in Long Beach. He won the 1948 Olympic title at shot with an Olympic record and career best 17.12, 44cm ahead of James Delaney, who had narrowly beaten him at the US Olympic Trials. He won the National Junior College title in 1939 and 1940 before going to the University of Southern California. After war service, he was 2nd in the NCAAs in 1946 (after 5th in 1942) but never won an AAU title, placing 4th in 1945-6 and 3rd in 1948-9 in seven top six placings to 1952.
Progress at SP (year list ranking): 1939- 15.24 (40), 1940- 15.42 (22), 1942- 15.31 (4), 1943- 14.68 (33), 1945- 15.43 (9), 1946- 16.22 (4), 1947- 16.70 (3), 1948- 17.12 (2), 1949- 16.80 (4=), 1950- 16.90 (4), 1952- 16.52 (13). Pb DT 48.33 (1951).

Viktor Sergiyovych **TSYBULENKO** (USSR/ Ukraine) (b. 13 Jul 1930 Vyepriki, near Kiev) on 19 October. He won the Olympic javelin title in 1960 with his personal best throw of 84.64 (the fifth all-time) after 4th place in 1952 and taking bronze in 1956. He was also 4th in 1954 and 2nd in 1962 at the European Championships and was World University Games champion in 1957 after 2nd in 1953. He was USSR champion in 1952, 1955-7 and 1959 (2nd in 1953-4 and 1960 and 3rd in 1958 and 1962). He set USSR records with 73.37 (1950), 79.89 (1956) and 83.34 (1957) and ranked in the world top ten in 10 of the 11 years 1952-62. Pb SP 16.45 (1958).
Progress (year list ranking): 1948- 52.59, 1949- 64.71 (43), 1950- 73.37 (2), 1951- 70.28 (13),

1952- 72.26 (8), 1953- 74.93 (7), 1954- 73.98 (14), 1955- 75.85 (10), 1956- 79.89 (7), 1957- 83.34 (4), 1958- 77.78 (13), 1959- 79.66 (11), 1960- 84.64 (2), 1961- 83.12 (5), 1962- 80.73 (9), 1963- 78.70 (22).

Stanley Frank 'Stan' VICKERS (GBR) (b. 18 Jun 1932 Lewisham, London) on 17 April in Seaford, East Sussex. At 20km walk he was European champion in 1958, and at the Olympics was 5th in 1956 (in a British record time of 1:32:34.2) and 3rd in 1960. He was succeeded as Britain's number one by Ken Matthews, and the two had some great contests, not least the AAA 2 miles championship of 1960, a race in which both men broke the British record that Vickers had equalled two weeks earlier, having stood at 13:11.4 to George Larner since 1904. Vickers won in 13:02.4 with Matthews 2nd in 13:09.6. Vickers was regarded by walking experts as one of the most stylish of the great walkers. His other best times: track: 5M 35:24.2 (1960), 10,000m 43:43.6 (1960), 7M 50:09.0 (1958), 10M 1:14:31.4 (1957), 1 hour 13,517m (UK record 1958), road 20km 1:31:43 (1960). A member of Belgrave Harriers, he won the RWA 10 miles in 1957-8 and the 20 miles in 1960, and was AAA champion at 2M 1957-8 and 1960 and at 7M 1957-8.

John VISLOCKY (USA) (b. 18 Apr 1921 Manhattan, NY) on 2 May in Colchester, Vermont. A member of New York AC, he was AAU indoor champion at high jump in 1946-8 and 1950 and outdoors 5th in 1941 before 2nd, 3rd and 5th in 1947-9, when he ranked in the world's top ten in each of those years. Pb 2.03 (1949). He worked in insurance and was an active Masters competitor at throws as well as high jump.

Angela VOIGT (GDR/Germany) née Schmalfeld (b. 18 May 1951 Weferlingen) on 10 April in Magdeburg. At long jump she was the European Cup winner in 1973 (and 4th at pentathlon) and in 1974 was 2nd at the European Indoors and 4th outdoors. After 3rd in the European Cup in 1975, in 1976 she set a world indoor best of 6.76 and then the outdoor world record of 6.92 at Dresden on 9 May, before going on to win the Olympic title at long jump. After giving birth to a baby in 1977 she returned to win the European silver medal with 6.79 in 1978. 24 internationals for GDR 1973-8. GDR LJ champion 1973, 1975-6 and 1978-9 and indoors LJ 1973-4, 1976 and 1982, and Pen 1973. Other pbs: 100m 11.63 (1975), 11.5 (1974); 200m 23.6 (1973), 100mh 13.2 (1973), SP 13.81 (1974), Pen 4647 (1973).

Annual progression at LJ: 1967- 5.39, 1968- 5.57, 1969- 5.60, 1970- 5.73, 1971- 5.78, 1972- 6.23, 1973- 6.76, 1974- 6.77, 1975- 6.61, 1976- 6.92, 1978- 6.79, 1979- 6.77, 1980- 6.72, 1981- 6.52, 1982- 6.39.

Carl B. 'Berny' WAGNER (USA) (b. 30 Sep 1924 Fresno, California) on 27 May at Corvallis, Oregon. After war service in the Navy he graduated from Stanford and began his coaching career at high school level. He became head track and cross country coach at Oregon State University in 1965 and supported Dick Fosbury in developing the Flop. He was men's jumps coach for the 1976 US Olympic team and later appointments included Executive Director of the Track & Field Association USA (1978-81) and National Coach Coordinator for The Athletics Congress (then the US governing body) 1981-9.

Hans-Joachim WALDE (Germany) (b. 28 Jun 1942 Gläsersdorf, now Szklary Górne, Poland) on 18 April in Jever, Niedersachsen. He was twice an Olympic medallist at the decathlon: bronze in 1964 and silver in 1968 with his pb of 8111 points (8094 on current tables) before dnf 1972, and was the European bronze medallist in 1971. He was FRG decathlon champion in 1964 and 1969 (2nd 1968 and 1971). Individual event pbs: 100m 10.97A (1968), 10.8 (1969); 200m 22.1 (1971), 400m 49.03A (1968), 1500m 4:31.9 (1971), 110mh 14.87A (1968), 14.7 (1971); 400mh 55.8, HJ 2.01 (1967), PV 4.30A (1968), LJ 7.64A (1968), TJ 14.31)1961), SP 15.71 (1968), DT 48.54 (1964), JT 71.62 (1968). Having specialised in shoulder surgery, he became director of sports medicine at Northwest hospital in Frisian Sande, Lower Saxony.

Annual progression at Dec (1985 tables): 1961- 6875, 1962- 6974, 1963- 7530, 1964- 7720, 1966- 7088, 1967- 7902, 1968- 8094A, 1969- 7822, 1970- 7340, 1971- 7986, 1972- 7876.

Roger Wilfred WALTERS (GBR) (b. 16 Nov 1948 West Bromwich) on 10 August. He competed in six internationals for Britain 1969-73, and had pbs of 60m 6.8i (1970), 100y 9.7 (1971), 100m 10.5/10.3w (1969), auto 10.68/10.63w (1972); 200m 21.2 (1969), 21.42 (1972). A member of Wolverhampton & Bilston, he was a reserve for the 1972 Olympic 4x100m squad. He became a leading sprint coach, including of the UK team at the 2008 Olympic Games.

Owen WARNER (New Zealand) on 25 September in Hamilton at the age of 75. He won New Zealand walking titles at 20k 1969-72, 20 miles 1969 and 1971, and 50k 1970-2.

Amelia WERSHOVEN (USA) (b. 11 Dec 1930 Ridgefield Park, New Jersey) (née Bert, later Wood) on 7 June in Mattitick, New York. A javelin thrower, she won three medals at the Pan-American Games silver in 1951 (5th shot) and bronze in 1955 and 1959 (each time with a different name!), and was 14th at the 1956 Olympic Games. She was AAU champion at javelin in 1953 (2nd 1951-2, 1954-9) and also in 1955 at baseball throw, setting a women's world record for this activity with 76.92m in August 1957.She also won the AAU indoor basketball throw in 1955, 1957 and 1959. Pb JT 47.22 (1958).

Bengt Hardley **WIKNER** (Sweden) (b, 21 Mar 1923 Orsa) on 6 February. Swedish discus champion in 1949, 5 internationals including 7th at 1946 Europeans, pb 49.00 (1946, 8th world list that year).

Charles WILLIAMS (Trinidad & Tobago) (b. 15 Nov 1930) in August. He was national champion at 100y in Trinidad in 1953 before moving to Britain two years later. He had a 100m best of 10.5 (1957) and ran at the 1958 Empire Games (heats 100y and 4x110y). Later he became a highly successful veteran athlete, from winning the M45 100m and 200m at the first World Veterans Championships in 1975 and set numerous records from M45 to M75 and winning World, European and national Masters titles into his 80s.

Marianna ZACHARIADI (Cyprus) (b. 25 Feb 1990 Athens) on 29 April in Athens, having suffered from the cancer Hodgkin's Lymphoma for two years. She had a Cypriot father and a Greek mother. A promising pole vaulter, she was 5th in the World Youths and 9th in the European Juniors in 2007 and Greek U23 and Junior champion in 2008. Opting to compete for Cyprus, she set national records indoors at 4.41 (to win the Balkan title) and outdoors at 4.45 (for 2nd at the Mediterranean Games) in 2009, going on to 5th at the European Juniors and a non-qualifying 24= at the World Champs. In what proved to be the last competition of her career, she cleared 4.40 to win the Commonwealth Games silver medal in October 2010, losing on count-back to Alana Boyd. She was Cypriot champion 2009-10.

Died in early 2014

Prince **Adedoyin** Folaranmi **ADEGBOYEGA** (Nigeria) (b. 11 Sep 1922 Shagamu) in January in Abeokuta. He starred in Britain while studying medicine from 1942 at Queen's University, Belfast, where his coach was Franz Stampfl. He competed for Britain v France in 1946 and 1947 and at the 1948 Olympic Games (5th LJ, 12th HJ), was AAA champion at high jump 1947, and won ten Northern Irish titles, including at four events in 1947. Pbs: 120yh 14.9 (1949), HJ 1.96 (1949), LJ 7.35 (1947), TJ 13.95 (1948).

Randhawa Ranjit BHATIA (India) (b. 27 May 1938 London) on 9 February in New Delhi. A Rhodes scholar at Jesus College, Oxford, in 1960 he won the UAU (British Universities) 3 miles title and represented India at 5000m and marathon at the Rome Olympics. A member of London's Belgrave Harriers, he set best times of 4:08.7 for the mile, 9:02.8 for 2M, 13:56.0 for 3M, 14:28.0 for 5000m and 29:50.4 for 6M (all 1960). Awarded the OBE for his services to

athletics, he spent his working life as Reader in Mathematics at St Stephen's College, Delhi, but also wrote the *Reebok Handbook of Indian Athletics* in 1999, was a long-time member of the ATFS and covered seven Olympics for Indian newspapers.

Georges BREITMAN (France) (b. 27 Mar 1920 Paris) on 27 January in Paris. The French pole vault champion in 1943-6 and 1953, he set a French record of 4.11 (1949) with a pb of 4.13 (1952) and represented France in 35 Internationals 1945-56. These included the European Champs of 1946 (6th) and 1950 (9th) and Olympic Games of 1948 (dnq 13th) and 1952 (dnf decathlon). He was a physician and later a renowned radiologist and in 1954 married actress and singer Colette Deréal.

Rt. Hon Sir **Christopher** John **CHATAWAY** (GBR) (b. 31 Jan 1931 Chelsea, London) on 19 January. The 'Red Fox' was a charismatic athlete who went on to distinguished careers in several fields. He was a friend and Oxford colleague of Roger Bannister, whom he helped to the first sub-four minute mile in 1954. Two months later he was 2nd in the AAA 3 miles, sharing the world record of 13:32.2 with winner Fred Green, before going on to beat Green to win the Empire Games 3 miles. He took the silver medal behind Vladimir Kuts in the European 5000m, running 14:08.8 to the world record of 13:56.6 by Kuts. In an epic race under the floodlights of the White City in October 1954, both men smashed that record as Chataway gained his revenge and just won 13:51.6 to 13:51.7. Fittingly he ended that year by being voted the first BBC Sports Personality of the Year. In Olympic 5000m finals Chataway led for much of the last lap in 1952 but fell after being passed by Emil Zátopek and staggered home in 5th place; he was 11th in 1956. He also set a world record running the first leg for the British team that ran 16:41.0 for 4x1 mile in 1953. He was AAA 3 miles champion in 1952 and 1955, when he ran a world record 13:23.2. He set British records also at 2000m 5:09.4 (1955), two at 3000m to 8:06.2 (1954) and three at 2 miles to 8:41.0 (1954) and had other best times: 1500m 3:43.6 (1955), 1 mile 3:59.8 (1955 to become the world's fourth 4-minute miler). For Oxford University he won the mile in 1951-3 and 3 miles in 1952 in the Varsity Match against Cambridge and the Varsity cross-country in 1950-2.

On 25 Sep 1955 he became the first newscaster on Independent Television and he was a Conservative MP 1959-66 and 1969-74, with ministerial positions from 1970-4 before retiring from politics to further a business career. He was managing director of Orion Bank 1974-88 and then chairman of the Civil Aviation Authority. He was knighted in 1995 for his services to the aviation industry.

Jiří DADAK (Czech Republic) (b. 7 Mar 1946 Valasské Meziříčí) on 14 March. At the hammer he was 4th at the 1952 Olympic Games and at the European Championships was 3rd in 1950 and 9th in 1954, competing in 13 internationals 1949-54,. He was national champion in 1949 and 1951 and set three Czechoslovak records from 55.89 in 1950 to 57.60 in 1951 with a pb of 58.54 (1955), and DT 46.71 (1950).

Jaroslav HALVA (Slovakia) (b. 20 May 1942 Modrý Kameň) on 12 March. He competed in 13 internationals for Czechoslovakia 1970-6 as a javelin thrower and set a national record with 80.06 in 1970. He became a successful coach in Slovakia and in the Czech Republic.

Professor **Jerzy HAUSLEBER** (Poland/ Mexico) (b. 1 Aug 1930 Vilnius, now Lithuania) on 13 March in Mexico City. He won five Polish walks titles: outdoors 10k 1954-5, 20k 1959 and 30k 1955 and indoor 10k 1956. He was 12th at 20k in the 1958 European Championships and set Polish records for 20k with 1:34:49 (1958) and 1:34:45.6 (1959), 30k 2:36:52.6 (1955) and 2 hours 23,089m (1955) as well as at 10k (pb 44:15.6 in 1958) and 1 hour. He became a coach and was invited to Mexico in 1966. There he coached José Pedraza to Olympic silver in 1968. He remained as head coach of Mexican walkers with great success to 2004 and he became a Mexican citizen in 1984.

Erling HELLE (Norway) (b. 14 Feb 1936) on 31 January 31. Norwegian shot champion in 1958, he competed in 17 international matches 1955-60 and has pbs: SP 15.89 and DT 48.71 (both 1960).

Rolf Lennart **HESSELVALL** (Sweden) (b. 27 Apr 1946 Stockholm) on January 10. Swedish champion at 5000m and 10000m 1948-9; 14 internationals; pbs: 3000m 8:04.2 (1969), 5000m 14:00.4 (1969), 10000m 29:12.37 (1974).

John **Andrew HOLDEN** (GBR) (b. 22 Oct 1948 Preston) during the night of 4/5 January. A most popular runner and loyal member of Tipton Harriers (formerly running for Preston Harriers), he set a British record for 3000m steeplechase of 8:26.4 when winning at the IAC meeting at Crystal Palace on 15 Sep 1972. Just a couple of weeks earlier he had been 5th in his heat at the Olympic Games. While at Birmingham University he was 2nd in the World University Games and 5th at the Commonwealth Games in 1970, and he went out in the heats of the 1971 Europeans. He was AAA steeplechase champion in 1970 and 1971 and later 3rd in 1980 and 2nd in 1981 at the marathon. He was National Junior cross-country champion in 1969 and has a best senior placing of 7th in 1971 with five appearances for England in the International/World CC (including on the winning England team in

1971, 1976 and 1979) after 5th in the Juniors in 1968. Other pbs: 1500m 3:52.6 (1972), 1M 4:07.2 (1970), 2000m 5:12.6 (1970), 3000m 8:01.6i (1970), 8:03.0 (1973); 2M 8:36.4 (1973), 5000m 13:59.8 (1976), 10,000m 29:03.2 (1973), 1 Hour 19,160m (1973), Mar 2:15:18 (1980), 2000mSC 5:35.21 (1976). Continuing running into veteran ranks, he was a dentist and also coached.

Michal JOACHIMOWSKI (Poland) (b. 26 Sep 1950 Znin) on 19 January in Torun. Immediately after the years of domination by Josef Schmidt, he was Polish triple jump champion 1972-6 and 1978. At the Olympic Games he was 7th in 1972 and dnq 13th in 1976, 5th at the European Championships in 1974 and World University Games champion in 1975. He achieved greatest success at the European Indoors, winning in 1974 and 2bd in 1973 and 1975. He was third in the world lists in 1973 with 17.06 (Polish record) and 1974 with 17.03.

Paavo KOTILA (Finland) (b. 26 Aug 1927 Veteli) on 26 January in Oulu. At the marathon he won at Boston in 1960 and was 2nd in Fukuoka 1957 & 1960, Kosice 1955 and Athens 1957, plus winning the Nordic title in 1957. He was Finnish champion in 1955, 1956 (a great race partly on dirt roads at Pieksämäki when he ran 2:18:04.8, at the time the fastest ever on an out-and-back course) and 1961 After leading the first 10k, he was 13th in the 1956 Olympics. Pb 10 000 m 30:45.0 (1960).

Pierre LACAZE (France) (b. 14 June 1925, Pontacq near Pau) on 6 February in Lourdes. A high jumper who was equal ninth at the 1948 Olympics and had five internationals 1946-8 with a pb of 1.95 (1948).

Pamela Chesopich **LISORENG** (Kenya) (b. 5 Aug 1988) collapsed and died after completing a training run in Eldoret on 1 March. She was 8th in the World Junior Cross-Country in 2006 and had a best performance of 70:09 for 7th in the Prague Half Marathon in 2013. Other pbs: 1500m 4:17.7A (2012), 3000m 9:19.74 (2010), 5000m 15:56.321 (2010), Mar 2:34:13 (2013). She was married to Boniface Kirui, 5000m 13:27.26 (2009), 10km 27:41 (2009), HMar 61:07 (2011), Mar 2:12:50 (2012), and they had a young son.

Amadou MEITÉ (Ivory Coast) (b. 28 Nov 1949) on 11 February in Abidjan. He was African champion at 100m (and 5th at 200m) in 1978 and ran at 100m and 4x100m at the Olympic Games of 1972 and 1976, reaching quarter- and semi-finals respectively of the 100m. He was 7th at 100m in the 1977 World Cup. Pbs: 100m 10.32 (1980), 10.1 (1979); 200m 21.00 (1978), 20.7 (1971). He coached his sons, sprinters Ibrahim (10.24 in 2000) and Ben Youssef (10.06 NR in 2012).

David William 'Dave' POWER (Australia) (b. 14 Jul 1928 Maitland, New South Wales) on 2 February on the Sunshine Coast in Queensland One of Australia's greatest distance runners, he won Commonwealth gold at both 6 miles and marathon in 1958 and silver medals at both events in 1962 (as well as 7th at 3 miles in 1958). At the Olympic Games he was 7th at 10,000m in 1956 and then was 5th at 5000m and won the bronze medal at 10,000m in 1960. He was Australian champion at 3 miles in 1960-2, 6 miles in 1958-60 and 1962, and cross-country in 1955-6 and 1958. He set multiple Australian records: 5000m 13:51.8 (1960), 6M 27:52.8 (1960), 10,000m 28:37.64 (1960), 10M 50:21.2 (1956) and 1Hr 19,211m (1956). Other pbs: 1M 4:00.2 (1960), 2M 8:37.2 (1963), 3M 13:24.0 (1961), Mar 2:22:15.4 (1962). He worked in the banking industry for over 30 years, then moved to the Sunshine Coast managing a holiday motel with his wife.

Peter Alan WILKINSON (GBR) (b. 27 Jun 1933 Chesterfield) in February. At the marathon in 1958 he was bronze medallist at the Commonwealth Games and fourth at the European Champs. He ran his fastest time of 2:19:54 in 1960 and the following year won the Polytechnic and Enschede Marathons. In the International Cross Country Champs he was 26th in 1959 and 20th in 1961 (with team silver for England) after his best National CC placings of 9th in 1959 and 10th in 1961.

William Gale 'Bill' WOODHOUSE (USA) (b. 11 Dec 1936 Mason City, Iowa) on 9 January in Corpus Christi, Texas. Although only ranked tenth in the world that year by Track & Field News (but 4th at 200m) he tied the world record for 100 yards with 9.3 at Abilene on 5 May 1959, having run 9.1w and 19.9w for 220y straight there on 18 April. Later that year he ran the third leg on the winning US 4x100m team at the Pan-American Games. He ran the second leg on the Abilene Christian College team anchored by Bobby Morrow that set world records for 4x110y of 39.9 in 1957 and 39.7 in 1958 and at 4x220y with 1:24.0 in 1956 and the first leg on the 1:22.6 for 4x220y in 1958. He was 3rd in the AAU 100m in 1959 and 1960, 4th in the NCAA 100y and 220y in 1958, and 5th at 100m in the US Olympic Trials in 1960. Other pbs: 100m 10.2 (1960), 220y turn 20.7 (1959).

Died in 2009

Elly DAMMERS (Netherlands) (b. 15 Aug 1921 Amsterdam) on 3 Jan in Houten. At the javelin she was 4th at the 1946 Europeans and 8th at the 1948 Olympics, setting Dutch records of 41.08 (19430 `and 41.99 (1946). Dutch champion 1940 and 1942-4

Georges GAILLOT (France) (b. 27 Apr 1917 Châtellerault) on 14 April at Châtellerault. He was French champion at 10,000m in 1939 and 1946 and set a French record of 1:06:00.0 for 20,000m in 1947. Pb 10,000m 30:36.4 (1942). His daughter and grand-daughter became French walks internationals.

André OSTERBERGER (France) (b. 26 Oct 1920 Saignes) on 18 January in Yssingeaux. At hammer in 1952 he won the French title, set a French record at 52.95 and competed in the Olympic Games. He also competed at the 1950 Europeans in 12 internationals 1950-2, with his career ended by a traffic accident in May 2013.

Randolf PEUKERT (Germany/ GDR) (b. 21 Mar 1929 Liberec, CZE) on 18 February in Halle. Five internationals at pole vault for GDR 1953-7 with three national records 4.15 and 4.20 (1954) and 4.28 (1955), and pb 4.32 (1957). Second in GDR Champs in 1953-6 and 1958, third 1957.

In 2010: Robert PHELPS (USA) (b. 14 Feb 1923) on 15 October. While at the University of Illinois he was NCAA champion in 1944 (joint) and 1945, and tied for first in 1945 AAUs. Pb 4.24i/4.19 (1945).

In 2011: Alfred PROKSCH (Austria) (b. 11 Dec 1908 Vienna) on 3 January in Vienna at the age of 102. He tied for 6th at pole vault at the 1936 Olympic Games, set eight Austrian records from 3.72 in 1933 to 4.115 in 1937, was national champion in 1933, 1937 and 1950 and competed successfully as a Masters athlete. He was a commercial artist.

Wolfgang REINHARDT (Germany/FRG) (b. 6 May 1943 Göppingen) on 11 June in Munich. He was the Olympic silver medallist at pole vault with 5.05 in 1964 after setting European records at 5.04 and 5.11 earlier in the year (3rd on the world list that year). His only other years over 5m were 1965 (5.00i) and 1969 (5.07), He had set seven previous FRG records from 4.56 (1962) to 4.93 (1964). FRG champion 1963-5 and indoors 1963 and 1968.

Died in 2012

René CUCUAT (France) (b. 29 Apr 1942 Hayange) on 21 July in Clermont-Ferrand. Ten internationals at long jump 1954-60; pbs 100m 10.6w (195), LJ 7.24 (1957) Good rugby player.

Jean-Paul JEANNET (France) (b. 22 Dec 1942 Lacave near St-Girons) on 27 August in a car crash. Six internationals at 110mh 1964-6, 5th WUG 1964, pbs: 110mh 14.1 (1965), 200mh 23.5w (1966).

Raymond MAHAUT (France) (b. 14 Aug 1926 Paris) on 28 June in Paris. In 1952 he set a French record of 9:07.6 behind Gaston Reiff WR 8:40.4. Ten internationals at 10,000m 1952-6, pb 30:43.8 (1952).

DRUG BANS 2013

As announced by IAAF or national governing bodies. Suspension: L - life ban, y = years, m = months, W = warning and disqualification, P = pending hearing.

Leading athletes

Men	Name	Date	Ban
Hussain Al-Hamdah KSA			2.5y
Denis Alekseyev RUS		27 Jun	2y
Anthony Alozie AUS		13 Sep	20m
Esref Apak TUR		8 Jun	2y
Roman Avramenko UKR		17 Aug	2y
Konstadínos Baniótis GRE		28 Nov	P
Jarrod Bannister AUS		19 Jun	20m
Pyotr Bogatyrev RUS			P
Oleksandr Drygol UKR		13 Jul	2y
Fatih Eryildirim TUR		7 Jun	2.5y
Miguel Ángel Gamonal ESP		29 Sep	2y
Tyson Gay USA		23 May	P
Oleg Istominov KAZ		15 Jun	2y
Pavel Karavayev RUS		18 Feb	2y
Abraham Kiprotich FRA		17 Nov	P
Valentin Kruglyakov RUS		13 & 18 Feb	4y
Wilson Loyanae KEN		4 Jan	2y
Alberto Lozano ESP		27 Jul	2y
Trevorvano Mackey BAH		Jun	P
Angel Mullera ESP		28 Jul	??
Maksym Obrubanskyy ITA		17 Feb	4y
Asafa Powell JAM		Jun	P
José Rocha POR		11 Dec	2y
Sergey Sánchez ESP		27 Jul	2y
Benjamin Kiprop Serem KEN		10 Nov	2y
Kaan Sencan TUR		1 Jun	2.5y
Mohamed Shahween KSA			3y
Dmitriy Sivakov BLR		31 May	2y
Traves Smikle JAM		Jun	P
Attila Szabó HUN		1 Oct	1y
Yevgeniy Ustavshchikov RUS		22 Dec	P
Igor Vinichenko RUS		27 Feb & 6 Mar	2y
Yuriy Voronchuk BLR		7 May	2y
Andrey Vorontsov BLR		18 Jan 4y & 3 Dec	L

Women

Name	Date	Ban
Semra Akdogan TUR	1 May	2y
Esther Akinsulie CAN	6 Feb	6m
Tatyana Akulinushkina RUS	8 Jun	6m
Cagdas Arslan TUR	1 Jun	2y
Anna Avdeyeva RUS	30 Jul	2y
Yuliya Balykina BLR	11 Jun	2y
Kelly-Ann Baptiste TRI		P
Roxana Bârca ROU	11 Jul	2y
Dominique Blake JAM	1 Jul	6y
Yelizaveta Bryzgina UKR	15 Aug	2y
Jill Camarena-Williams USA	1 Jul	6m
Veronica Campbell-Brown JAM	4 May	W
Yelena Churakova RUS	26 Jan	2y
Yevgeniya Danilova RUS	22 Sep	2y
Alice Decaux FRA	22 Jun	6m
Yunna Dmitriyeva RUS	9 May	2y
Viktoriya Dolgacheva RUS	26 Jun	2y
Cecilia Dzul MEX	24 Apr	2y
Dilek Esmer TUR	2 Jun	2.5y
Olga Golovkina RUS	16 Jul	2y
Emel Güngör TUR	30 May	2.5y
Semoy Hackett TRI		P
Sabine Heitling BRA	7 Jun	1y

Name	Date	Ban
Lilian Jelagat KEN	29 Jun	2y
Esen Kale-Kizildag TUR	1 Jun	2y
Anastasiya Korshunova RUS	27 Jun	2y
Ayman Kozhakhmetova KAZ	13 Aug	2y
Eyerusalem Kuma ETH	20 Oct	2y
Yeliz Kurt TUR	7 Jun	2y
Yekaterina Medvedyeva RUS	19 May	2y
Natalya Mikhnevich BLR	12 Apr	2y
Tezdzhan Naimova BUL	3 Mar	L
Darya Pizhankova UKR	14 Aug	L
Allison Randall JAM	Jun	P
Salome Rigishvili GEO	23 Jun	2y
Tugce Sahutoglu TUR	1 May	27
Kivilcim Salman-Kaya TUR	1 Jun	2y
Yekaterina Shlyakhova RUS	30 Mar	2y
Sherone Simpson JAM	Jun	P
Yevgeniya Solovyova RUS	13 Feb	6m
Sun Juan CHN	26 Apr	2y
Natalya Volgina RUS	30 Mar	2y
Mariya Yakovenko RUS	19 Feb	2y
Nevin Yanit TUR	8 Feb	P
Elif Yildorim TUR	8 Jun	2y
Lyudmila Yosypenko UKR	25 Aug	4y
Olena Zhushman UKR	2 Jul	9m
Yekaterina Zyuganova RUS	5 Mar	2y

L?: Udaya Lazmi IND; **8y**: André Koekemoer RSA (23 Jul), **4y**: Simona Maxim ROU (1 Aug); **3y**: Devis Licciardi ITA (21 Sep); **2.5y**: Isa Can TUR (25 May); **2y**: Umut Aday TUR (1 Jun), Elif Akbas TUR (12 May), Burcu Akmazoglu TUR (12 May), M Alameen IND (10 Sep), Ghina Al Asir LIB (10 Nov), Mubarak Al-Bishi KSA (13 Feb), Rashed Al Failkawi & Ibrahim Alenizi KUW (24 Mar), Emrah Altunkalem TUR (26 May), Daniela Alonso Arreola MEX (6 Jul), Abdullah Al-Asseri KSA (13 Feb), Shola Anota NGR (14 Jun), Massoud Azizi AFG (10 Aug), Adewummi Bamhi-hiybin TUR (12 May), Busra Bas TUR (2 Jun), Sarik Bilgin TUR (12 May), Hassan Birinci TUR (2 Jun), Marina Buchelnikova RUS (9 Feb), Gokce Celenk TUR (12 May), Emrah Coban TUR (1 May), Fatumata Coly SEN (12 Jun), Marta Caroline Costa POR (10 Feb), Lorenzo Dalavalle ITA (11 May), Kubra Danis TUR (12 May), Deepa IND (31 Jan), Burak Demit TUR (8 Jun), Oguzhan Demir TUR (1 Jun), J R Divyasree IND (13 Mar), Anna Domentyeva RUS (16 Apr), Pari-naz Ebrahimi IRI (3 May), Hicham El Ghazi BEL (10 Mar), Mohammed El Mounim ITA (9 Jul), Batuhan Eruygun TUR (1 Jun), Anton Fisun RUS (29 May), Wendoli Flanders DOM (4 Apr), Jimmy Fontaine FRA (22 Jun), Artur Grigoryev RUS (21 Apr), Al;eksandr Gulyayeva RUS (22 Dec), Ahmad Hazer LIB (11 Jun), J Jayaraj IND (15 Mar), Peris Jepkorir KEN (5 May), Lucky Iyoha NGR (21 Jun), Ümmuhani Karacadir TUR (2 Jun), Sarbjeet Kaur IND (13 Mar), Durgesh Khare IND (14 Jun), Valeriya Kharitonova RUS (9 Feb), Khalid Kidallah KSA (13 Feb), Svetlana Komarova RUS (22 Dec) (Cansu Korur TUR (11 Jun), Shalendra Kumar IND (14 Mar), Osga Kurtes TUR (15 May), Shine Kutti IND (13 Mar), Serkan Lapcin TUR (8 Jun), Natalya Logutenkova RUS (Mar 30), Marco Morgado POR, Omar Morad KUW (27 Apr), Majed Mohamed KSA (14 Feb), Ramzi Naim LIB (6 Jun), Simge Olcun TUR (12 Jun), Alan de Oliveira BRA (7 Jul), Gulslum Ozdemir Gunes TUR (1 May), Urfan Ozolan TUR (12

Jun), Sachin Pal IND (12 Mar), Ebrahim Rahimian IRI (9 Aug), Naim Ramzy LIB (7 Jun), Tomas Tomas Rauktys LTU (27 Jul), Olga Rezkaya BLR (31 Oct), Idalto Rodrigues BRA (5 May), Yelena Ryabova TKM (11 Aug), Narim Saglam TUR (5 Jun), Sonu Saini IND (6 Jun), Marwa Salah Salem BRN (28 Oct), Jeremias Saloj GUA (17 Aug), Camila dos Santos BRA, Saurabh IND (31 Jan), Furkan Sen TUR (5 Jun), Olena Serdyuk UKR (14 Apr), Viktoriya Shevchuk BLR (30 May), Jagmohan Singh IND (12 Aug), Sergat Soyer TUR (13 Jun), Karim Tahri FRA (14 Jul), Serdat Tamaç TUR (8 Jun), Rui Teixeira POR (24 Sep), Shraddha Tiwari IND (7 Dec), Berkay Tolun TUR (12 May), Dmitriy Tsyganov RUS (23 May), Rinat Valiyev KAZ (17 Apr), Ebru Yurddas TUR (8 Jun); **1y:** Cecilia Francis NGR (29 Mar), Pauline Kahenya KEN (3 Mar), Sarbjeet Kaur IND (1 Mar); Corrado Mortillaro ITA (17 Mar), Paulo Santos de Jesus BRA (24 Aug); **9m:** Muriel Deguilhem FRA (30 Jun), **6m:** Camila A dos Santos BRA (25 Aug), Mario Jurjevic CRO (16 Feb), Maksim Kachanov RUS-Y (19 Sep), Sandrine Prisse FRA (24 Aug), Kevin Tatard FRA (10 Feb), Julia Zappettini Vasquez CHI (29 Mar); **4m:** Hirut Beyene ETH; **3m:** Edrees Hawsawi KSA (16 Apr), Helga Mathee RSA (2 Jun), Esmael Mosadegh IRI (2 Apr), Spencer Walden USA (28 Jul); **W:** Hammod Alahmad KUW (24 Mar), Guillaume Lecoq FRA, Zohar Zemiro ISR.

Add to Drugs Bans 2012
Men

Jynocel Basweti KEN	22 Jan	2y
Shawn Crawford USA	17 Nov	2y
Matt Davies AUS	11 Feb	2y
Ivan Gertlyn RUS	15 Oct	2y
Hasan Heidarpoor IRI	19 Jan	8y
Hassan Hirt FRA	3 Aug	2y
Dimitríos Hondrokoúkis GRE	4 Jul	2y
Kirill Ikonnikov RUS	8 Oct	2y
Nahashon Kimaiyo KEN	25 Nov	1y
Amine Laâlou MAR	20 Jul	2y
Cameron Ostrowski USA	7 Jun	1y
Alex Schwazer ITA	30 Jul	3.5y
Anthony Wairuri KEN	28 Oct	2y

Women

Mary Akor USA	16 Dec	2y
Salome Biwott KEN	28 Oct	2y
Ail Cakir TUR		P
Nadezhda Ostapchuk BLR	8 Aug	4y
Nilgun Öztürk TUR	19 May	2y
Darya Pishchalnikova ESP	20 May	10y
Irina Titova RUS	20 Dec	2y
Tshilofelo Thipe RSA	6 Jul	2y
Wang Jiali CHN	29 May	2y
Tameka Williams SKN	21 Jul	3y
Kaori Yoshida JPN	9 Dec	1y

L: Henry Azike NGR (5 Dec); **2y:** Malik Abhishek IND (27 Dec), Yosin Adeloye NGR (6 Dec), Ammar Ali Makki IRQ (12 Dec), Amerjeet IND (15 Mar), Veysi Aslan TUR (11 Nov), Hussein Awaba LIB (11 Dec), Margaret Benson NGR (5 Dec), M A Bibin IND (26 Jun), Mbatha Bonsumuso RSA (19 May), Rachna Dahiya IND (31 Oct), S.Dhamalingam IND ((31 Oct), Alisher Eshbekov TJK/RUS (4 Dec), Rita Rani Gandua IND (15 Mar), Dulu Gogoi IND (21 Mar), Amr Hossein Hosseini EGY (11 Jun), Mohd Firdaus Jamen MAS (12 Jul), Ali Ekber Kayas TUR (19 May), Ibrahim Kerem IRQ (16 Jun), Shakil Khan IND (7 Aug). Pierre Adrien Lods FRA (2 Dec), Lu Sun CHN (28 Dec), José Magno Mota BRA (1 Apr), Marco Murgado POR (17 Dec),

Niketa IND (21 Jan), Fatima Pichot FRA (29 Sep), Poonam Singh IND (29 Oct), P Pushparaju IND (25 Jun), Jean Pierre Serafini LUX (19 May), Harmilan Bains Singh IND (28 Dec), Harpreet Singh IND (13 Mar), Surinder Pal Singh IND, Roger Wenzel USA (4 Aug); Luigi Zullo ITA (16 Sep); **19m:** Trey Downing USA (14 Nov); **1.5y:** Euriclidis Varela CPV; **1y:** Andrew Kimutai KEN (18 Nov), Yolima Mena Valencia COL (12 Nov); Rami Ivamar de Oliveira BRA (30 Jun); **9m:** Wociech Cwik POL (23 Sep); **6m:** Elisabeth Etchart FRA (29 Jul).

Add to Drugs Bans 2011
Men

Agustin Félix ESP	31 May	2y
Igor Yerokhin RUS	25 Feb	L

Women

Yekaterina Ishova (Gorbunova) RUS	12 Jul	2y

8y: Fernando Silva POR (29 Oct), **4y:** Marco Morgado POR (29 Oct), **2y:** Situ Zubaidah, Mohamad Noor Imran Hadi, Noorjannah Jamaludin, Nural Sarah Abdul Kadir, Yee Li Ling (all MAS, 24 May), Harun Rasheed MAS (12 Sep); **8m:** Siti Fatimah MAS (24 May)

Add to Drugs Bans 2010

Men: José Rocha POR	11 Dec	2y
Women: Pinar Saka TUR	18 Jun	3y

2y: Stéphane Joly SUI (14 Oct)

Add to Drugs Bans 2009   all results annulled from then). **Women**

Olena Antonova UKR	21 Aug	2y
Yelizaveta Grechishnikova RUS	18 Aug	2y
Zalina Marghieva MDA	20 Aug	2y

Add to Drugs Bans 2008

Women: Susanne Pumper AUT	9 Mar	8y

From IAAF Athlete Biological Passport programme:
The Athlete Biological Passport involves measuring and monitoring an athlete's blood variables over time and establishes an individual longitudinal profile which can indicate the use of prohibited substances or prohibited methods.
Women: 2-year ban, all results annulled from:

Yelena Arzhakova RUS:	12 Jul 11
Tetyana Petlyuk UKR	18 Aug 09
Anzhela Shevchenko UKR	2 Jul 11

The IAAF confirmed that five of the world's leading throwers received 2-year bans following the re-testing of anti-doping samples taken at the 2004 Olympics and 2005 World Champs. **From 2004:** Yuriy Bilonog UKR forfeited results between 10.8.2004 and 17.8.2006 and Svetlana Krivelyova RUS and Irina Yatchenko BLR results 18.8.2004 to 17.8.2006. **From 2005:** Olga Kuzenkova RUS) loses results between 12.8.2005 and 11.8.2007. For Bilonog and Krivelyova, the sanctions under IAAF rules were in addition to those previously imposed by the IOC to disqualify both athletes from the 2004 Olympics and to withdraw their respective medals. Andrey Mikhnevich BLR received a lifetime ban with all results annulled from the World Champs on 6 August 2005, at which he was originally 6th. This caused widespread chaos for shot results – and redistribution of medals at 2007 and 2011 Worlds, 2006 and 2010 World, 2008 Olympics, and 2006 and 2010 Europeans etc.
Although Crystal Cox, who ran in the heats, received a drugs ban and was stripped of her gold medal, the US team that ran in the final of the 4x400m at the 2004 Olympic Games retain their gold medals.

WORLD LISTS 1964

! = world record.
Auto times are shown after the hand times where known

MEN – 100 YARDS

9.1!	Bob Hayes USA	1	Coral Gables	1 Jan
9.2	Edwin Roberts TRI	2	Orangeburg	18 Apr
9.2	Darel Newman USA	1h	Fresno	9 May
9.3	Anthony Watson USA	1	Norman	11 Apr
9.3	Harry Jerome CAN	1	Eugene	11 Apr
9.3	Richard Stebbins USA	1	Houston	9 May
9.3	John Roderick USA	1	Lubbock	9 May
9.3	Travis Williams USA	1h	Fresno	9 May
9.3	Dave Morris USA	2h	Fresno	9 May
9.3	Mel Pender USA	1	Fort Campbell	19 May
9.3A	Henry Carr USA	1	Salt Lake C	23 May

50th best 9.5, 100th 9.6

9.2Aw	Bernie Rivers USA	1	Albuquerque	21 Mar

100 METRES

10.0/10.06!	Bob Hayes USA	1	Tokyo	15 Oct
9.91w 5.3		1s1	Tokyo	15 Oct
10.0!	Horacio Esteves VEN	1	Caracas	15 Aug
10.1	Arquimedes Herrera VEN	1	Caracas	2 Aug
10.1	Hideo Iijima JPN	1	Berlin	14 Jun
10.1	Trenton Jackson USA	1s	Eugene	19 Jun
10.1	Harry Jerome CAN	1s	Eugene	19 Jun
10.1	Enrique Figuerola CUB	1	Tartu	21 Jun
10.2	(A) Leroy McAllister USA, Dennis Johnson JAM, Richard Stebbins USA, Henry Carr USA, Dave Blunt USA, Darel Newman USA, Marian Dudziak POL, Nikolay Politiko URS, Michael Ahey GHA.			

50th best 10.3, 100th 10.4

9.9w	R.L.Lasater USA	1	Commerce	17 Apr
10.1w	Darel Newman USA	1	Walnut	25 Apr
10.1w	Fritz Obersiebrasse GER	1	Hamburg	24 May
10.1w	Gerry Ashworth USA	2	New York	3 Jul
10.1w	Paul Genevay FRA	1	Valence	1 Aug
10.1w	Wieslaw Maniak POL	2s1	Tokyo	15 Oct

200 METRES (* 220y less 0.1 sec.)

20.1*!	Henry Carr USA	1	Tempe	4 Apr
20.36		1	Tokyo	17 Oct
20.3*	Edwin Roberts TRI	1	Toronto	7 Sep
20.4=	Paul Drayton USA	1	Quantico	6 Jun
20.4*	Bob Hayes USA	1	Fresno	13 Jun
20.3w		1s	Eugene	19 Jun
20.4	Sergio Ottolina ITA	1	Saarbrücken	21 Jun
20.4*A	Seraphino Antao KEN	1	Kisumu	5 Sep
20.5*	Richard Stebbins USA	1	Grambling	18 Apr
20.5*	Bernie Rivers USA	1	Sunnyvale	18 Apr
20.5	Arquimedes Herrera VEN	1	Caracas	2 Aug
20.6A	T.J.Bell USA	1	C. de México	2 May

50th best 20.9, 100th 21.1

20.4w	Harry Jerome CAN	2s	Eugene	19 Jun

220 YARDS Straight Track (* 200m +0.1)

20.1	Edwin Roberts TRI	1	Raleigh	16 May
20.1w	Bob Hayes USA	1	Coral Gables	1 Jan

400 METRES (* 440y less 0.3 sec.)

44.9!	Mike Larrabee USA	1	Los Angeles	12 Sep
45.15		1	Tokyo	19 Oct
45.0	Ulis Williams USA	2	Los Angeles	12 Sep
45.2/24	Wendell Mottley TRI	2	Tokyo	19 Oct
45.6	Ollan Cassell USA	3	Los Angeles	12 Sep
45.6/64	Andrej Badenski POL	3	Tokyo	19 Oct
45.6+	Henry Carr USA	1	Melbourne	7 Nov
45.7*	Kent Bernard USA	1h	Evanston	30 May
45.7A*	Bob Tobler USA	1	Salt Lake C	23 May
45.7	Josef Trousil CZE	1	Praha	26 Jun
45.7/79	Robbie Brightwell GBR	1s1	Tokyo	18 Oct
45.7/75		4	Tokyo	19 Oct

50th best 46.7, 100th 47.0

800 METRES (* 880y less 0.7 sec.)

1:45.1	Peter Snell NZL	1	Tokyo	16 Oct
1:45.6	Bill Crothers CAN	2	Tokyo	16 Oct
1:45.7*	Morgan Groth USA	1	Kingston	15 Aug
1:45.8*	George Kerr JAM	2	Kingston	15 Aug
1:45.9	Wilson Kiprugut KEN	4	Tokyo	16 Oct
1:46.5*	Neville Myton JAM	3	Kingston	15 Aug
1:46.6	Tom Farrell USA	5	Tokyo	16 Oct
1:46.8*	Jery Siebert USA	1	San Diego	13 Jun
1:46.9	Valeriy Bulishev URS	1	Kyiv	14 Au
1:46.9	Dieter Bogatzki FRG	3s	Tokyo	15 Oct

50th best 1:48.5, 100th 1:49.2

1000 METRES

2:16.6!	Peter Snell NZL	1	Auckland	12 Nov
2:18.6	Jean Wadoux FRA	1	St.Maur	3 Jun
2:18.8	John Boulter GBR	1	Oxford	4 Jul
2:19.3	John Davies NZL	2	Auckland	12 Nov

1500 METRES

3:37.6+	Peter Snell NZL	1	Auckland	17 Nov
3:38.1	Tom O'Hara USA	1	New Brusnwick	28 Jun
3:38.8	Dyrol Burleson USA	2	New Brusnwick	28 Jun
3:38.9	Jim Grelle USA	3	New Brusnwick	28 Jun
3:38.9	Witold Baran POL	2s	Tokyo	17 Oct
3:39.0	Jim Ryun USA	4	New Brusnwick	28 Jun
3:39.10	Alan Simpson GBR	1	London (WC)	15 Aug
3:39.3	Josef Odlozil TCH	3s	Tokyo	17 Oct
3:39.6	John Davies NZL	1	Dunedin	8 Feb
3:39.7	Michel Bernard FRA	4s	Tokyo	17 Oct

50th best 3:43.6, 100th 3:46.2

1 MILE

3:54.1!	Peter Snell NZL	1	Auckland	17 Nov
3:56.0	Witold Baran POL	1	London (WC)	3 Aug
3:56.4	Josef Odlozil TCH	2	Auckland	17 Nov
3:56.8	John Davies NZL	3	Auckland	17 Nov
3:57.4	Dyrol Burleson USA	1	Compton	5 Jun
3:57.6	Tom O'Hara USA	2	Compton	5 Jun
3:56.4i		1	Chicago	6 Mar
3:57.6	Archie San Romani USA	3	Compton	5 Jun

10th best 3:58.3, 100th 4:06.9

3000 METRES

7:56.4	Witold Baran POL	1	Warszawa	23 Aug
7:57.6	Lech Boguszewicz POL	2	Warszawa	23 Aug
7:57.2i	Michel Jazy FRA	1	Paris	8 Feb

2 MILES

8:26.4!	Bob Schul USA	1	Los Angeles	29 Aug
8:31.9i	Bill Baillie NZL	1	Portland	25 Jan

5000 METRES

13:38.0	Bob Schul USA	1	Compton	5 Jun
13:38.6	Pyotr Bolotnikov URS	1	Zürich	23 Jun
13:39.0	Ron Clarke AUS	2	Zürich	23 Jun
13:40.0	Bill Baillie NZL	2	Compton	5 Jun
13:43.0	Ron Larrieu USA	3	Compton	5 Jun
13:43.4	Gaston Roelants BEL	3	Zürich	23 Jun
13:44.0	Gerry Loindgren USA	4	Compton	5 Jun
13:45.0	Kestutis Orentas URS	1	Moskva	4 Jul
13:45.6	Mike Wiggs GBR	2	Moskva	4 Jul
13:46.6	Neville Scott NZL	2	Napier	5 Feb

50th best 13:57.4, 100th 14:08.0

3 MILES

13:07.6	Ron Clarke AUS	1	Melbourne	3 Dec
13:15.6+	Bob Schul USA	1	Compton	5 Jun
13:15.8+	Bill Baillie NZL	2	Compton	5 Jun

10,000 METRES

28:24.4	Billy Mills USA	1	Tokyo	14 Oct
28:24.8	Mohamed Gammoudi TUN	2	Tokyo	14 Oct
28:25.8	Ron Clarke AUS	3	Tokyo	14 Oct
28:31.8	Mamo Wolde ETH	4	Tokyo	14 Oct
28:33.0	Murray Halberg NZL	2	Auckland	17 Nov

28:39.6	Pyotr Bolotnikov URS	1	Kyiv	27 Aug
28:40.0	Nikolay Dutov URS	2	Kyiv	27 Aug
28:40.6	Leonid Ivanov URS	3	Kyiv	27 Aug
28:41.6	Anatoliy Skripnik URS	4	Kyiv	27 Aug
28:41.8	Gaston Roelants BEL	1	Bruxelles	29 Aug

50th best 29:25.0, 100th 29:52.0

6 Miles

27:26.44	Mike Bullivant GBR	1	London (WC)	10 Jul
27:27.01	Ron Hill GBR	2	London (WC)	10 Jul
27:32.8	Murray Halberg NZL	1	Auckland	23 Mar
27:35.03	Jim Hogan IRL	3	London (WC)	10 Jul
27:36.09	Martin Hyman GBR	4	London (WC)	10 Jul
27:36.8+	Ron Clarke AUS	1	Auckland	17 Nov
27:37.35	Mike Freary GBR	5	London (WC)	10 Jul

MARATHON

2:12:11.2!	Abebe Bikila ETH	1	Tokyo	21 Oct
2:13:55!	Basil Heatley GBR	1	Chiswick	13 Jun
2:14:12	Ron Hill GBR	2	Chiswick	13 Jun
2:14:48	Toru Terasawa JPN	1	Fukuoka	6 Dec
2:15:26	Vaclav Chudomel TCH	3	Chiswick	13 Jun
2:15:37	Juan Taylor GBR	1	Port Talbot	27 Jun
2:15:42	Takayuki Nakao JPN	2	Fukuoka	6 Dec
2:16:10.2A	Mamo Wolde ETH	1	Addis Ababa	3 Aug
2:16:22.8	Kokichi Tsuburaya JPN	3	Tokyo	21 Oct
2:17:02.4	Brian Kilby GBR	4	Tokyo	21 Oct

50th best 2:21:25, 100th 2:24:25

3000m STEEPLECHASE

8:30.8	Gaston Roelants BEL	1	Tokyo	17 Oct
8:31.8	Adolfas Aleksiejunas URS	1h	Tokyo	15 Oct
8:32.4	Maurice Herriott GBR	2	Tokyo	17 Oct
8:33.8	Ivan Belyayev URS	3	Tokyo	17 Oct
8:34.2	Lars-Erik Gustafsson SWE	2h	Tokyo	15 Oct
8:34.2	George Young USA	3h	Tokyo	15 Oct
8:34.6	Guy Texereau FRA	4h	Tokyo	15 Oct
8:35.3	Slavko Span YUG	1	Ljubljana	3 Aug
8:35.6	Lazar Naroditskiy URS	2	Kyiv	29 Aug
8:35.6	Vladimir Komarov URS	3	Kyiv	29 Aug

50th best 8:48.0, 100th 8:55.8

110 METRES HURDLES (y = 120yh)

13.4	Hayes Jones USA	1	New York	4 Jul
13.4y	Roy Hicks USA	1	Corpus Christi	25 Mar
13.6	Blaine Lindgren USA	1	Los Angeles	25 Jul
13.6	Willie Davenport USA	1	Los Angeles	25 Sep
13.7	Bobby May USA	1	Eugene	20 Jun
13.7	Anatoliy Mikhailov URS	3	Tokyo	18 Oct
13.7y	Roger Morgan USA	1	Monroe	2 May
13.7y	John Bethea USA	1	Baltimore	13 Jun
13.7y	Elias Gilbert USA	2	Baltimore	13 Jun
13.8	Gerry Cerulla USA	3	Compton	5 Jun
13.8	Eddy Ottoz ITA	1	Modena	30 Aug
13.8y	Russ Rogers USA	1	Quantico	2 May

50th best 14.1, 100th 14.2

200 METRES HURDLES

| 22.8 | Vasiliy Anisimov | 1 | Kyiv | 30 Aug |

400 METRES HURDLES (* 440y less 0.3 sec.)

49.1!	Rex Cawley USA	1	Los Angeles	13 Sep
49.4	Jay Luck USA	1	New York	3 Jul
49.6	Roberto Frinolli ITA	1	Roma	19 Sep
49.8	Bill Hardin USA	2	Los Angeles	13 Sep
50.1	Chris Stauffer USA	3	New York	3 Jul
50.1	Salvatore Morale ITA	2	Roma	19 Sep
50.2	John Ciooper GBR	2	Tokyo	16 Oct
50.2	Willie Atterberry USA	1	Compton	5 Jun
50.3	Vasiliy Anisimov URS	1	Kyiv	29 Aug
50.4*	Ken Roche AUS	1	San Diego	13 Jun
50.4	Jaako Tuominen FIN	2	Oslo	11 Aug
50.4	Gary Knoke AUS	4	Tokyo	16 Oct

50th best 501.5, 100th 52.2

HIGH JUMP

2.24	Valeriy Brumel URS	1	Zürich	23 Jun
2.21	Ni Zhiqin CHN	1	Shanghai	11 Oct
2.20i	John Thomas USA	1	Baltimore	29 Feb
2.18		2	Tokyo	21 Oct
2.20	Eduard Czernil POL	1	Hässleholm	30 Jul
2.17	Robert Shavlakadze URS	1	Kyiv	28 Aug
2.165	John Rambo USA	1	Long Beach	2 May
2.16i	Lew Hoyt USA	1	New York	13 Feb
2.16	Mahamat Idriss CHA	1	Fort Lamy	28 Mar
2.16	Richard Ross USA	1	Houston	8 May
2.16	Ed Carruthers USA	1	New Brunswick	28 Jun
2.15	Andrey Khmarskiy URS	2	Leselidze	16 May

50th best 2.08, 100th 2.06

2.175 et John Rambo USA   -   Fresno   13 Jun

POLE VAULT

5.28!	Fred Hansen USA	1	Los Angeles	25 Jul
5.15	Manfred Preusger GDR	1	Leipzig	27 Aug
5.11	Wolfgang Reinhardt FRG	1	Leverkusen	6 Jul
5.10	Don Meyers USA	1	Compton	5 Jun
5.09	John Pennel USA	2	San Diego	13 Jun
5.18 et		-	Los Angeles	29 Aug
5.08	Dave Tork USA	2	New Brunswick	27 Jun
5.02	Wlodz. Sokolowski POL	1	Spala	12 Jul
5.01	Wolfgang Nordwig GDR	1	Berlin	24 Sep
5.00	Mel Hein USA	3	San Diego	13 Jun
5.00	Rudolf Tomasek TCH	1	Oslo	3 Sep
5.00	Klaus Lehnertz FRG	3	Tokyo	17 Oct

50th best 4.75, 100th 4.61

LONG JUMP

8.34!	Ralph Boston USA	*	Los Angeles	12 Sep
8.42w			Los Angeles	12 Sep
8.18	Igor Ter-Ovanesyan URS	1	Kyiv	30 Aug
8.16	Gayle Hopkins USA	1	Eugene	19 Jun
8.09	Godfrey Moore USA	1	Baltimore	20 Jun
8.07	Lynn Davies GBR	1	Tokyo	18 Oct
8.03	Leonid Barkhovskiy URS	1	Los Angeles	25 Jul
8.01	Charlie Mays USA	2	Modesto	23 May
8.02w		4	New York	3 Jul
8.01	Antanas Vaupshas URS	2	Kyiv	12 Sep
8.01	Phil Shinnick USA	3	Los Angeles	12 Sep
7.98	Sid Nicodlas USA	3	Modesto	23 May

50th best 7.66, 100th 7.51

8.22w Darrell Horn USA   2   New York   3 Jul
8.09w Bill Miller USA   3   New York   3 Jul

TRIPLE JUMP

16.85	Józef Schmidt POL	1	Tokyo	16 Oct
16.58	Tien Chao-Chung CHN	1	Beijing	3 Jun
16.58	Oleg Fyedoseyev URS	2	Tokyo	16 Oct
16.57	Viktor Kravchenko URS	3	Tokyo	16 Oct
16.48	Takayuki Okazaki JPN	1	Kita-Kyushu	19 Apr
16.47	Adil Dementyev URS	1	Krasnodar	15 Oct
16.46	Fred Alsop GBR	4	Tokyo	16 Oct
16.43	Ira Davis USA	1	Los Angeles	26 Jul
16.35	Günter Krivec FRG	1	Berlin	23 Aug
16.28	Serban Ciochina ROU	1	Budapest	19 Aug

50th best 15.90, 100th 15.54

16.29w Ian Tomlinson AUS   1   Melbourne   4 Jan

SHOT

20.68!	Dallas Long USA	1	Los Angeles	25 Jul
20.20	Randy Matson USA	2	Tokyo	17 Oct
19.50	Wladyslaw Komar POL	1	Budapest	21 Jun
19.45	Parry O'Brien USA	2	Los Angeles	19 May
19.39	Vilmos Varju HUN	3	Tokyo	17 Oct
19.35	Viktor Lipsnis URS	2	Los Angeles	25 Jul
19.26i	Gary Gubner USA	1	New York	13 Feb
19.20	Dave Davis USA	1	Los Angeles	5 Aug
19.09	Nikolay Karasyov URS	1	Kyiv	29 Aug
19.09	Dieter Urbach FRG	1	München	8 Sep

50th best 18.06, 100th 17.29

DISCUS

64.55!	Ludvik Danek TCH	1	Turnov	2 Aug
62.94!	Al Oerter USA	1	Walnut	25 Apr
61.66	Rink Babka USA	1	Oxnard	1 Aug
61.19	Jay Silvester USA	1	Osaka	25 Oct
61.05	Dave Weill USA	2	Osaka	25 Oct
60.12	Edmund Piatkowski POL	1	Warszawa	27 Sep
59.97	Bill Neville USA	1	Long Beach	5 Sep
50.95	Lars Haglund SWE	2	Stockholm	30 Aug
59.94	Zenon Begier POL	1	Warszawa	22 Aug
59.76	Jerzy Klockowski POL	1	Gdansk	23 May

50th best 55.74, 100th 53.23

HAMMER

70.53	Hal Connolly USA	1	Walnut	26 Sep
69.74	Romuald Klim URS	1	Tokyo	18 Oct
69.55	Yuriy Bakarinov URS	1	Kyiv	28 Aug
69.09	Gyula Zsivótzky HUN	2	Tokyo	18 Oct
69.01	Heinrich Thun AUT	1	Leoben	19 Jul
68.50	Sándor Eckschmidt HUN	1	Praha	19 Sep
68.37	Yuriy Nikulin URS	1	Kyiv	16 Aug
68.26	Gennadiy Kondrashov URS	2	Los Angeles	25 Jul
68.09	Uwe Beyer FRG	3	Tokyo	18 Oct
67.89	Aleksey Baltovskiy URS	2	Kyiv	13 Sep

50th best 63.20, 100th 59.64

JAVELIN

91.72!	Terje Pedersen NOR	1	Oslo	1 Sep
85.09	Janusz Sidlo POL	1	Roma	27 Sep
84.89	Wladyslaw Nikiciuk POL	1	Warszawa	20 Aug
84.63	Jorma Kinnunen FIN	1	Jyväskylä	3 Sep
83.95	Willy Rasmussen NOR	2	Oslo	2 Sep
82.66	Pauli Nevala FIN	1	Tokyo	14 Oct
82.64	Vladimir Kuznyetsov URS	1	Moskva	27 Sep
82.59	Janis Lusis URS	1	Los Angeles	26 Sep
82.32	Gergely Kulcsar HUN	2	Tokyo	14 Oct
81.90	Hermann Saloman FRG	1	Leverkusen	4 Jul

50th best 77.14, 100th 73.78

DECATHLON (1962 tables)

7950	Manfred Bock FRG	1	Liestal	7 Jun
7887	Willi Holdorf FRG	1	Tokyo	20 Oct
7854	Horst Beyer FRG	1	Karlsruhe	19 Jul
7853	Yang Chuan-Kwang TPE	1	Walnut	27 Jun
7852	Hans-Joachim Walde FRG	2	Karlsruhe	19 Jul
7842	Rein Aun URS	2	Tokyo	20 Oct
7787	Paul Herman USA	4	Tokyo	20 Oct
7772	Mikhail Storozhenko URS	2	Kyiv	30 Aug
7740	Russ Hodge USA	1	Walnut	26 Apr
7728	Dick Emberger USA	1	Los Angeles	13 Sep

50th best 7074

20 KILOMETRES WALK

1:27:46.8	Hans-Georg Reimann GDR	1	Jena	12 Jul
1:28:06	Abdon Pamich ITA	1	Carate Brianza	5 Jul
1:28:37.0	Gerhard Adolph GDR	2	Jena	12 Jul
1:28:45.8t	Ken Matthews GBR	1	Walton-on-Th.	6 Jun
1:29:00.8	Dieter Lindner GDR	3	Jena	12 Jul
1:29:42	Zigurds Irbe URS	1	Riga	12 May
1:29:45.2	Aleksandr Basylyenko URS	1	Orscha	17 May
1:29:54.0	Albert Kotov URS	2	Orscha	17 May
1:29:59.0	Ed. Salmanavicius URS	3	Orscha	17 May
1:30:09	Gennadiy Agapov URS	4	Moskva	4 Jul

50th best 1:32:43

50 KILOMETRES WALK

4:08:30	Abdon Pamich ITA	1	Calolziocorte	14 Jun
4:09:56.4t	Grigoriy Klimov URS	1	Moskva	26 Sep
4:11:31.2	Paul Nihill GBR	3	Tokyo	18 Oct
4:12:49.2	Christophe Höhne GDR	2	Moskva	5 Jul
4:13:15.0	Yevgeniy Lyungin URS	3	Moskva	5 Jul
4:14:17.4	Ingvar Pettersson SWE	3	Tokyo	18 Oct
4:15:26.8	Burkhard Leuschke GDR	4	Tokyo	18 Oct
4:17:06.8	Robert Gardiner AUS	5	Tokyo	18 Oct
4:17:48.6	Helmut Wilke GDR	2	Podebrady	2 Aug
4:19:55.8	Anatoliy Vedyakov URS	7	Tokyo	18 Oct

4 x 100 METRES

39.0/06!	USA	1	Tokyo	21 Oct
39.2	France	1	Annecy	18 Jul
39.3	Italy	2	Annecy	18 Jul
39.3/36	Poland	2	Tokyo	21 Oct
39.4	GDR	1	Berlin	23 Aug
39.4/49	Jamaica	4	Tokyo	21 Oct
39.4/50	USSR	5	Tokyo	21 Oct
39.5/53	Venezuela	6	Tokyo	21 Oct
39.6	FR Germany	1	Fulda	2 Aug
39.6/69	Great Britain	8	Tokyo	21 Oct

4 x 400 METRES

3:00.7!	USA	1	Tokyo	21 Oct
3:03.5	FR	2	Hannover	1 Aug
3:01.6	Great Britain	2	Tokyo	21 Oct
3:01.7	Trinidad & Tobago	3	Tokyo	21 Oct
3:02.3	Jamaica	4	Tokyo	21 Oct
3:04,3	Germany (FRG & GDR)	5	Tokyo	21 Oct
3:05.3	Poland	6	Tokyo	21 Oct
3:05.9	USSR	7	Tokyo	21 Oct
3:06.1	FR Germany	2	Köln	13 Sep

WOMEN

100 YARDS

10.5	Diane Bowering AUS	1	Murray Bridge	25 Jan
10.5	Margaret Burvill AUS	1	Sydney	25 Jan
10.5	Marilyn Black AUS	1	Sydney	14 Mar
	10.3w		Sydney	19 Dec
10.5	Edith McGuire USA	1	Nashville	2 May
10.5	Betty Cuthbert AUS	1	Sydney	2 Aug

10th best 10.6, 50th 10.9

10.2w	Debbie Thompson USA	1	Baltimore	6 Jun
10.4w	Doreen Porter NZL	1	Walnut	25 Apr
10.4w	Marilyn White USA	1	Walnut	17 May

100 METRES

11.2/23!	Wyomia Tyus USA	1q1	Tokyo	15 Oct
11.3	Ewa Klobukowska	1	Budapest	6 Sep
11.4	Miguelina Cobian CUB	1	La Habana	26 Apr
11.4	Renate Meyer FRG	1	Lübeck	26 Jul
11.4	Margit Nemeshazine HUN	2	Budapest	6 Sep
11.4	Irena Piotrowski CAN	1	Vancouver	19 Sep
11.4/47	Edith McGuire USA	1h	Tokyo	15 Oct
11.4	Marilyn Black AUS	1q	Tokyo	15 Oct
11.4	Hannelore Raepke GDR	1	Varna	5 Oct

11.5 eleven women, 50th best 11.7

11.2w	Marilyn Black AUS	1	Sydney	13 Sep
11.3w	Edith McGuire USA	1h	New York	7 Aug
11.3w	Rosie Bonds USA	2h	New York	7 Aug
11.3w	Betty Cuthbert AUS	2	Sydney	13 Sep

11.4w seven women

200 METRES (* 220y less 0.1 sec.)

22.8*!	Margaret Burvill AUS	1	Perth	22 Feb
23.0/05	Edith McGuire USA	1	Tokyo	19 Oct
23.1/13	Irena Kirszenstein POL	2	Tokyo	19 Oct
23.1/18	Marilyn Black AUS	3	Tokyo	19 Oct
23.3*	Joyce Bennett AUS	2	Perth	22 Feb
23.3	Lyudmila Samotyesova URS	1	Tokyo	3 Nov
23.4	Karin Balzer GDR	1P	Leipzig	24 May
23.5*	Daphne Arden GBR	1	London (WC)	4 Jul
23.5/58	Una Morris JAM	4	Tokyo	19 Oct
23.6*	Janet Simpson GBR	1	Welwyn GC	13 Aug
23.6	Miguelina Cobian CUB	1	Warszawa	23 Aug
23.6	Halina Gorecka POL	1	Lódz	13 Sep
23.6	Barbara Sobotta POL	2	Lódz	13 Sep

50th best 24.3

400 METRES

51.2!	Shin Keum-dan PRK	1	Pyongyang	21 Oct
52.0/01	Betty Cuthbert AUS	1	Tokyo	17 Oct
52.20	Ann Packer GBR	2	Tokyo	17 Oct
53.0	Maria Itkina URS	1	Kyiv	29 Aug
53.3/39	Judy Amoore AUS	1s	Tokyo	16 Oct

53.4*	Dixie Willis AUS	1	Melbourne	29 Feb
53.8	Joy Grieveson GBR	2	London (WC)	3 Aug
54.0	Antonia Munkácsi HUN	3s	Tokyo	16 Oct
54.1	Tilly van der Zwaard NED	3s	Tokyo	16 Oct
54.2	Gertriud Schmidt GDR	1	Liberec	19 Jul
54.2	Antje Gleichfeld FRG	1	Odawara	31 Oct
50th best 55.8	* 440y less 0.3 sec.			

800 METRES

1:58.0!	Shin Keum-dan PRK	1	Pyongyang	5 Sep
2:01.1	Ann Packer GBR	1	Tokyo	17 Oct
2:01.9	Maryvonne Dupureur FRA	2	Tokyo	20 Oct
2:02.8	Marise Chamberlain NZL	3	Tokyo	20 Oct
2:03.5	Zsuzsa Nagy HUN	4	Tokyo	20 Oct
2:03.7	Zoya Skobtsova URS	1	Kyiv	13 Sep
2:03.9	Antje Gleichfeld FRG	5	Tokyo	20 Oct
2:04.0	Tamara Dmitriyeva URS	2	Kyiv	13 Sep
2:04.1	Laine Eerik URS	3	Kyiv	13 Sep
2:04.2	Vyera Mukhanova URS	4	Kyiv	13 Sep
50th best 2:09.4				

1 MILE

4:56.0	Alison Noble GBR	1	London (WC)	4 Jul
4:56.9	Penelope Gardner GBR	2	London (WC)	4 Jul

80 METRES HURDLES

10.5!	Karin Balzer GDR	1P	Leipzig	23 May
	10.54w	1	Tokyo	19 Oct
10.5!	Irina Press URS	1	Kyiv	9 Aug
	10.62w	4	Tokyo	19 Oct
10.5!	Draga Stamejcic YUD	1	Celje	5 Sep
10.5!	Pamela Kilborn AUS	1	Osaka	25 Oct
	10.56w	3	Tokyo	19 Oct
10.6	Ikuko Yoda JPN	1	Tachikawa	5 Apr
10.6	Nilia Kulkova URS	1h	Riga	12 Jun
10.6	Zenta Kop FRG	1h	Berlin	8 Aug
10.6	Tereza Ciepla POL	1	Okayama	29 Oct
	10.55w	2	Tokyo	19 Oct
10.7	Nine women. 50th best 10.7, 50th 11.0			
10.6w	Avis McIntosh NZL	1	Tauranga	29 Mar
10.6w	Maria Piatkowska POL	1h	Tokyo	18 Oct
10.6w	Rosie Bonds USA	1h	Tokyo	18 Oct

100 METRES HURDLES (2'6")

13.4	Patricia Pryce	1	Watford	11 Jul

HIGH JUMP

1.90	Iolanda Balas ROM	1	Bucuresti	19 Aug
1.835	Michele Brown AUS	1	Sydney	1 Nov
1.79	Wu Fu-shan CHN	1	Taiyuan	9 Jun
1.78	Taisia Chenchik URS	3	Tokyo	15 Oct
1.77	Cheng Feng-jung CHN	1	Dalian	22 Aug
	1.80 et	-	Beijing	25 Sep
1.76	Karin Ruger GDR	1	Potsdam	15 Aug
1.76	Wu Yun-hsin CHN	1=p	Beijing	25 Sep
1.76	Frances Slaap GBR	1	Portsmouth	26 Sep
1.75	Diana Gerace CAN	1	Vancouver	9 May
1.75	Gerda Kupferschmid GDR	1	Jena	11 Jul
1.75	Jaroslawa Bieda POL	1	Warszawa	16 Jul
50th best 1.675				

LONG JUMP

6.76!	Mary Rand GBR	1	Tokyo	14 Oct
6.70!	Tatyana Shchelkanova URS	1	Moskva	4 Jul
6.60	Irena Kirszenstein POL	2	Tokyo	14 Oct
6.55	Willye White USA	*	Los Angeles	26 Jul
	6.60w	2	Los Angeles	26 Ju
6.49	Aida Chuyko URS	1	Kyiv	12 Sep
6.48	Hildrun Laufer (Claus) GDR	1	Liberec	18 Jul
6.46	Berit Berthelsen NOR	2	London (WC)	4 Jul
6.46	Viorica Viscopoleanu ROU	1	Bucuresti	12 Sep
6.45	Helga Hoffmann FRG	1	Lódz	13 Sep
6.40	Ingrid Becker FRG	1	Kassel	28 May
50th best 6.08				
6.47w	Martha Watson USA	2	New York	8 Aug

SHOT

18.40	Tamara Press URS	1	Minsk	21 Sep
17.61	Renaye Garisch GDR	2	Tokyo	20 Oct
17.54	Margarita Helmboldt GDR	1	Regis-Breit	16 Aug
17.50	Galina Zybina URS	2	Kyiv	7 Aug
17.26	Valerie Young NZL	4	Tokyo	20 Oct
17.21	Irina Press URS	3	Minsk	31 May
16.98	Valentina Nazarova URS	1	Tartu	26 Jun
16.82	Johanna Hübner GDR	2	Regis-Breit	16 Aug
16.60	Nadezhda Chizhova URS	1	Warszawa	18 Sep
1653	Ana Salagean ROU	1	Poiana Brasov	2 Sep
50th best 14.87				

DISCUS

58.82	Tamara Press URS	1	Budapest	28 Jun
57.21	Ingrid Lotz GDR	2	Tokyo	19 Oct
57.19	Yevgeniya Kuznyetsova	1	Khabarovsk	28 Sep
56.97	Lia Manoliu ROU	1	Tokyo	19 Oct
56.70	Verzhinia Mikhailova BUL	4	Tokyo	19 Oct
56.30	Jirina Nemcová TCH	1	Praha	18 Sep
55.86	Kriemhild Limberg GDR	1	Jena	30 Aug
55.30	Antonia Popova URS	Q	Kyiv	30 Aug
55.22	Jolán Kleiber HUN	1	Budapest	9 Mat
54.88	Doris Lorenz GDR	2	Jena	30 Aug
50th best 49.91				

JAVELIN

62.40!	Yelena Gorchakova URS	Q	Tokyo	16 Oct
61.38!	Elvira Ozolina URS	1	Kyiv	27 Aug
60.54	Mihaela Penes ROU	1	Tokyo	16 Oct
58.27	Márta Rudás HUN	2	Tokyo	16 Oct
57.66	Anneliese Gerhards FRG	1	Ludwigshafen	27 Sep
57.42	Inge Schwalbe GDR	2	Berin	23 Aug
57.18	Mariya Moskalenko URS	Q	Kyiv	27 Aug
56.61	Birute Kalediene URS	1	Kyiv	9 Aug
56.08	Maria Diaconescu ROU	1	Bucuresti	21 Aug
55.66	Marion Graefe GDR	1	Berlin	30 Sep
50th best 50.70				

PENTATHLON (1954 tables)

5246!	Irina Press URS	1	Tokyo	17 Oct
5035	Mary Rand GBR	2	Tokyo	17 Oct
4995	Galina Bystrova URS	1	Kyiv	30 Aug
4823	Mary Peters GBR	1	Belfast	19 Aug
4790	Karin Balzer GDR	1	Leipzig	24 May
4790	Draga Stamejcic YUG	5	Tokyo	17 Oct
4775	Valentina Tikhomirova URS	1	Krasnodar	19 Oct
4772	Mariya Sizyakova URS	2	Moskva	5 Jul
4768	Inge Exner GDR	2	Leipzig	24 May
4767	Helen Frith AUS	1	Melbourne	28 Feb
4737	Helga Hoffmann FRG	6	Tokyo	17 Oct
50th best 4416				

4 x 100 METRES

43.6 /69(!)	Poland	1	Tokyo	21 Oct

Poland kept the gold medal but lost the WR later when
Ewa Kobukowska failed a sex chromosome test in 1966

43.9/92	USA	2	Tokyo	21 Oct
44.00/09	Great Britain	3	Tokyo	21 Oct
44.4/44	USSR	4	Tokyo	21 Oct
44.5	FR Germany	2	Lódz	13 Sep
45.0	Ausralia	6	Tokyo	21 Oct
45.1	Hungary	2	Budapest	5 Sep

The first organised meeting of the modern era: Oxford v Cambridge in 1864

By Bob Phillips

IT'S A NEAT coincidence that the 150th anniversary of the first organised meeting of the modern athletics era should come about in this same year of 2014 as the 60th anniversary of the first sub-four-minute mile. Oxford was the setting for both of these historic occasions: not quite on the same track, but only a stone's throw apart. One tangible difference is that whilst Roger Bannister was thinking of breaking four minutes, his predecessors of 90 years before mostly regarded five minutes as being the benchmark for an exceptional mile performance.

There had been other meetings prior to 1864; in particular at the Royal Military Academy at Sandhurst during the years 1849 to 1853 and from 1850 onwards at Exeter College, Oxford, among whose future athletic notabilities would be Bannister himself. However, the first competitive match to be arranged between Oxford and Cambridge Universities was a much more formal affair and laid the foundations for a series which still continues in 2014. Though the inaugural chosen venue was the Christ Church ground at Oxford, the credit for devising the idea rests mainly with Richard Webster, an undergraduate at Cambridge who himself took part in the encounter and was later to become Lord Alverstone, Lord Chief Justice of England and president of the Amateur Athletic Association.

Amateur athletics was still very much in its formative years, as the sport had been entirely dominated by professionals, and Montague Shearman, who was the pre-eminent contemporary historian of athletics in the 19th Century, was to write in 1887 that an upsurge of interest among the middle and upper classes of society 'was the natural product of the over-pressure of commercial and professional life … hours of work being long, there comes a craving amongst adults for violent exercise'. Shearman – arch-proponent, though he was, of amateur ideals – was generous enough to admit also that 'there can be little doubt that the first amateur athletic sports were suggested by the performance of the professional "pedestrians", and that whenever there was an unusual galaxy of pedestrian ability the amateurs began to imitate them'. In this context 'pedestrian' was the

term used to describe both runners and walkers.

Such imitation of the pedestrians had been no more than a pale copy through the 1850s and early 1860s. A dozen amateurs – all but three from Oxford or Cambridge – had run 10 seconds flat for 100 yards and one had even been timed in 9½ sec, though officiating, understandably, was a rough-and-ready business in those days. So among them might or might not have been someone to match the greatest professional sprinter of those years, George Seward. But by the beginning of 1864 the amateur best for 880 yards was only 2min 3sec, as against the fastest professional time of 1:58.0, and the respective 'record' mile times were 4:33 for the amateurs and 4:21¾ for the professionals.

Not that the 28 athletes who gathered together for the eight events which formed that pioneering Inter-Varsity meeting would have concerned themselves at all with such comparisons. The idea of competing against professionals or anyone from the working-classes would have scandalised these gentlemen amateurs, and Shearman – who knew very well about these matters because he was to win the Inter-Varsity 100 yards for Oxford in 1876 – paints a delightful picture of their indolent attitude: 'At Oxford after luncheon the athletes in twos and threes may be observed wending their way over Magdalen Bridge to the ground. Before long they may be seen scampering also in twos and threes over the path or over the hurdles, or essaying the hurling of weight or hammer. You run "spins" with your friends, or take the long-distance runner a lap upon his way; then, perhaps, a try at the long jump or the weight … oh, glorious days of youth and training before the race of life has begun!'

This first Oxford-v-Cambridge match of 1864 took place on Saturday 5 March, and that sort of date, despite the likelihood of typically English inclement weather, became set as the fixture progressed over the years – for as much a reason as any other because when the venue was soon moved to London, in 1867, its location and the timing provided an opportunity to witness the Boat Race on the River Thames. Equally vital was the fact that athletics was to be got out of the way by springtime at Oxford and Cambridge to allow the rather more serious business of cricket to begin. Reason eventually prevailed after a century or so and May became the chosen month for the athletes to show their paces in some degree of warmth.

On that Saturday morning of the mid-Victorian era *The Times* had previewed the meeting with a 'form guide' which seemed largely to be based on intuition rather than inside knowledge, save for the confident assertion that 'the mile race engrosses most attention, and from the time taken by the champions of both Universities, it looks a good thing for Mr Lawes, whose partisans are backing him freely'. Amateur principles in no way deterred the supporters of both sides from staking their money with the bookmakers, and maybe the Mr Lawes in question placed a bet or two on himself. He could well afford to do so because his father, Sir John Lawes, had made his fortune as an agricultural scientist who owned his own factories manufacturing chemically-based manure.

The order of events was 100 yards, high jump, 440 yards, 120 yards hurdles, 200 yards hurdles, long jump, one mile and a steeplechase of about two miles. *The Times* reported that there was an enthusiastic attendance by 'a vast number of persons, including many of the college authorities and some hundreds of ladies, who took a very keen interest in the proceedings; everything was carried out in the most satisfactory manner'. Ensuring such decorum was a bevy of clerics: the Reverend Leslie Stephen, father of the novelist Virginia Woolf, was the referee and the Reverends AH Faber and HM Luckock were the judges. Charles Lawes, in addition to starting as favourite for the mile, acted as one of the stewards. The Reverend Stephen was the very personification of 'muscular christianity', having set a Cambridge record for the mile and later to become one of the very first Alpine mountaineers.

The 100 yards and 440 yards were won for Oxford by Benjamin Derbyshire, who had been responsible for that speculative 9½-second clocking at his college sports the previous November, but on this occasion he was not nearly as fleet-footed as before and his margin of success in the 100 was a mere half-a-yard over Alban Harrison, of Cambridge, in 10½ seconds. Derbyshire led Harrison home again in the 440 in 56.0. The Cambridge man had run another of that ever-growing number of 10-flat 100-yard clockings in December. There might have been a stronger Cambridge challenge in the quarter-mile, but their other representative, Percy Thornton, who was to equal and then beat the amateur best for 880 yards in a single afternoon in 1865, was not in the best of health and finished last.

Both hurdle races were won by Cambridge, and AWT Daniel would have completed the double but for the fact that 'at the end there was a drop of about two feet' and his team-mate, E Wynne Finch, emulated his ornithological namesake by ungraciously flying through the air and snatching victory. Daniel, in any case, was rather more noted among his peers for his skills with the cricket-bat while at school, having scored 112 not out in 1860 for Harrow against Eton. By the time that the eagerly-anticipated mile race was to begin, Oxford led by four events to two as FH Gooch, also renowned on the cricket field, won the high jump and long jump, helped in the latter event by both Cambridge athletes suffering 'accidents on the hard ground that incapacitated them'.

Lawes duly won the mile for Cambridge from Oxford's AH Hannam. 'Lawes looked back two or three times over his left shoulder, his opponent being on his right', reported the correspondent for *The Times* of the closing stages of the race, and he then continued, 'On seeing Hannam up with him, Lawes bounded away and in 20 yards more was again quite three yards ahead. So he kept to the end, winning a fine race, Hannam falling exhausted after passing the judges'. The winning time was a mere 4min 56sec, but with 'the last lap, 26 yards less than a quarter-of-a-mile, only occupying 51 seconds'. Lawes was also to become the first English national title-holder, winning at the Amateur Athletic Club championships of 1866 in a much faster 4:39. He was to lead an eventful life, indulging himself as a rich man's son of independent means by pursuing a career as a sculptor, of which one obituarist was to say somewhat unkindly that 'his success was never quite equal to his ambitions'. Like so many others representing Oxford or Cambridge in that 1864 match, athletics was of secondary interest as a pastime to Lawes as he was also one of the very finest oarsmen in the country, winning the Diamond Sculls at Henley in 1865.

The closing event, the steeplechase, was also won for Cambridge to end the match in a 4-4 draw. The victor here was Richard Garnett, ahead of the man whose idea the match had been, the future Lord Alverstone. Garnett was to set the best performances on record for an amateur at two miles later in 1864 and at three miles in 1866, but as the respective times were 10:15½ and 16:27, whereas the fastest professionals had run 9:11½ (William Lang) and 14:36 (Jack White), both in 1863, Garnett's level of ability only proved to show once again that the divide between the two classes of athlete remained very wide.

Naturally, standards at the Inter-Varsity match were to improve dramatically over the years. Olympic champions from Oxford or Cambridge in the first half of the 20th Century would include Arnold Jackson from pre-World War I; Bevil Rudd (for South Africa), Guy Butler, Harold Abrahams, Douglas Lowe and Lord Burghley from the 1920s; and then Tommy Hampson, Robert Tisdall (Ireland), Jack Lovelock (New Zealand) and Godfrey Brown in the 1930s. Roger Bannister and Chris Chataway improved the match mile record for Oxford to 4:14.8 and 4:08.4 in 1950 and 1953 respectively, though it was their Cambridge contemporary, Chris Brasher, who would win Olympic gold. Another Olympic champion, Herb Elliott, of Australia failed to break the mile record but ran the fastest 880 yards so far of 1:49.9 in 1961. Somewhat perversely, the 1500 metres now alternates with the mile on the match schedule and the record for the latter distance stands to Simon Mugglestone, of Oxford, at 3:58.9 in 1989. Recent years have been far less productive of Olympic winners; the only one in athletics being David Hemery, but even then it was his brother, John, who made a longer lasting impression in the record-books by winning three hurdles races for Oxford in 1972 and then ten years later two more for Cambridge. A women's Inter-Varsity match was introduced in 1975, and Stephanie Cook eventually put her athletic skills to perfect use in winning the 2000 Olympic modern pentathlon title, though she had previously been a rower at Cambridge rather than a runner; but she did set a Varsity match record in 1997 for 5000m when she had moved on to Lincoln College, Oxford.

The field events, reflecting characteristic British disdain over many years for anything too technically demanding, have been of nowhere near the same calibre as those on the track, and the high-jump record, for example, lasted from 1876 until 1948, when it was beaten at long last by a Cambridge undergraduate from Denmark, Ívar Vind, who did not take matters too seriously, nonchalantly smoking a cigarette between leaps. The closest any winner in the Inter-Varsity jumps or throws has got to Olympic gold was the future Sir George Stuart Robertson, who arrived in Athens in 1896 to find that there was no competition for him in the hammer, which he had won against Cambridge for the previous three years, but was instead awarded the laurel leaves of a victor for reciting a poem in ancient Greek. Again reflecting the occasionally contrary nature of the Inter-Varsity organisers, the hammer was dropped from the match for 54 years from 1921 onwards despite having just been won by the man who remains to this day Britain's best ever Olympic exponent of the event, Malcolm Nokes, bronze-medallist at the Games of 1924.

The standards are considerably lower in the 21st Century, as illustrated by the hammer event in last year's match – the 139th in the series twice interrupted by World Wars – which was won at 39.66m. In 1921 Nokes threw 148ft exactly, which is equivalent to 45.12 metres. The outstanding athlete in 2013 was Nadine Prill, captain of the Oxford women's team, who won the 100, 200 and 400 metres and shared in both relay successes, but you will seek in vain either her name, or those of any other Inter-Varsity winners that day, elsewhere in the pages of this annual. Ms Prill will, no doubt, worry not one jot about that – still in 2014, just as 150 years before, a win against the 'other' university, let alone as many wins as hers, will remain a personal athletics memory to savour for a lifetime.

The Varsity Match

From 1864 to 2013: Oxford have 72 wins, Cambridge 59, with 7 drawn matches. Scoring was by event 1864 to 1937 and on points from 1938. The women's match has been won 28 times by Cambridge and 11 by Oxford from its introduction in 1975.

The 1866 and 1868 matches were held in Oxford and that of 1865 in Cambridge, but from 1867 the sports moved to London, where they stayed until 1977, when they again reverted to alternating between Oxford and Cambridge.

Most individual wins: 18 Phyllis Agbo (Cambridge) – 5 in 2005 (100m, 200m, 100mh, LJ, SP), 6 in 2006 (100m, 200m, LJ, TJ, SP, JT) and a record 7 in 2007 (100m, 200m, 100mh, LJ, TJ, SP, JT).

Men's record: 13 Dwayne Heard (Oxford) in 7 years: 200m 1986, LJ 1983-9 and TJ 1984-5 and 1987-9; 12 Pierre Faber (Oxford, RSA) in 4 years: HJ 1996, PV 1996-7, SP & DT 1996-9, HT 1999.

Most individual wins in one match by a man: 5 Jon Ridgeon (Cambridge) 100m, 200m, 400m, 110mh and 200mh in 1988.

Distinguished athletes to have held previous records for most wins in the series include:
8 Harold Abrahams (Cambridge) (100y 1920-3, 220y 1923, LJ 1920, 1922-3)
9 Adrian Metcalfe (Oxford) (100y 1962, 1064; 220y 1961-2, 1964; 440y 1961-4)

Winning doubles for three successive years were: Lord Burghley (Cambridge) 120yh and 220yh 1925-7 and Derek Johnson (Oxford) 440y and 880y 1954-6.

The first international inter-university match was when Oxford beat Yale 5½ to 3½ at Queen's Club, Kensington, London. Yale met Cambridge at Manhattan Field, New York on 5 October 1895, winning 8 events to 3, and the first of the series of matches between the combined Oxford/Cambridge and Harvard/Yale took place on 22 July 1899 at Queen's Club. The 44th match in this series was held in 2013 and Oxford/Cambridge teams have also met other Ivy League combined US university teams in their American Series.

Track & Field Statistics – As it was Sixty-Plus Years Ago and as it is Now

by Roberto L Quercetani

IT IS CERTAINLY not easy to remember when I first caught 'the bug'. Yet my memory seems to have settled on an episode which occurred on an August day in 1932 while I was walking in the centre of Firenze in the company of my father. In the Piazza Vittorio Emanuele (now Piazza della Repubblica) my sight was attracted to a large screen mounted on top of a building on which a newsreel was unfolding, and I was excited more than somewhat by the announcement that 'Luigi Beccali ha vinto i 1500 metri ai Giochi Olimpici di Los Angeles'. (... won the 1500 ...).

I was a ten-year-old schoolboy at the time and the oldest newspaper clippings to be found in my scrapbooks date from that year. What's more, my earliest recollection of a major event seen 'de visu' again concerns 'Nini' Beccali, setting a new Italian 800 metres record of 1:50.6 in a handicap race in Firenze during the halftime intermission of a soccer match in 1933 (I think this was Fiorentina vs. Roma, but please don't ask me about the result). Incidentally, Marquis Luigi Ridolfi, then a magnate of both sports, was the man responsible for staging such a vagary.

Whether these first experiences were responsible or not, it is a fact that in later years the peak of my passion for athletics was often associated with middle distance running, and 800 and 1500-metre races have always been the ones to send a special tingle down my spine.

As far as I can remember there has always been a curious link between 'les deux amours' of my life: studying foreign languages and following track and field events. The former was for years my main concern at school and elsewhere, whereas in the practice of the latter I never went beyond the recreational level (racing with my friends up and down the hills and along the stretches of beautiful Boboli Garden, not far from my home). As far as athletics was concerned I chose instead to become an avid recorder – and, in due time, analyser – of track action from far and wide. Foreign languages helped me to 'widen the walls of my prison'. In those days my country happened to live under a dictatorship and it was not easy to have access to current foreign publications. Fortunately, I happened to live in the central area of Florence, traditionally inhabited by a fair amount of foreigners. Two of them gave me lessons in English and French.

Already as a teenager I was a dedicated reader of *La Gazzetta dello Sport*, a pink coloured daily published in Milano. Now and then I bought *L'Auto*, a yellow Paris daily which was the predecessor of *L'Equipe*. In the summer of 1938 I chanced upon a copy of *Der Leichtathlet*, a German weekly which in terms of worldwide coverage was probably the leader at that time. I managed to talk my good father into paying for a subscription for me for six months. Using whatever German I could master, I wrote a letter addressed to their column 'Sie fragen, wir antworten' ('They ask, we answer'), in which I listed questions such as 'Who were the US 1500-metre champions of the last five years?' To my amazement, I got a reply in due time. That was the first time my 'by-line' appeared in a paper– not bad, in those days, for a 16-year old fan.

Then World War 2 broke out, the ravages of which I witnessed and partly suffered. When it was over, however, I found an employment as a technical interpreter with the British army for five months and later with the American army for over three years. Later on I acquired new track friends, mostly through correspondence. Fulvio Regli of Switzerland and Don Potts, a mathematics professor from USA, were foremost among them. Both were keen track statisticians and I still remember them as the best friends I have ever had. In 1948, shortly before the London Olympics, Don and I published a book, in a photo-processed form – *A Handbook on Olympic Games Track and Field Athletics*. It contained 50-deep World All Time Lists for Olympic (and English) events as at the end of 1947, together with 20-deep lists for 1947 and a summary of Olympic track and field results from 1896 to 1936. To the best of our knowledge, it was the first book ever published with detailed (i.e. with date and place) All-Time lists of best performers. As such it received wide acclaim, notably from Harold Abrahams, the Olympic 100 metres champion of 1924, who once wrote: 'This book proved invaluable in helping with the seeding for the Olympic events '.

At the start of 1950 Fulvio Regli, with whom I had started to publish European years lists, launched a bold proposal in a letter to me: 'Why not form an international association of track and field statisticians?' My reaction to the idea was very enthusiastic and we immediately brought our plan to the attention of Don and our European friends. Of course, the main reason for our proposal was not so much to make the 'family' which already existed into something 'official' but rather to have a suitable platform for stirring interest in and promoting knowledge of track statistics among the media ad the public. Our aim was to be established in the course of time on a truly worldwide basis.

Fulvio and I – by then a pretty good multi-lingual couple – got together with seven other European statisticians on 26 August 1950 at the Café de la Madeleine, rue de la Montagne, in Bruxelles. We all happened to be in the Belgian capital to witness the European Championships (later in the same day Emil Zátopek won a thrilling 5000m race, defeating local hero Gaston Reiff among others). The first ATFS meeting was organized by André Greuze, a Belgian sport journalist and statistician. In attendance that Saturday morning were the following, in alphabetical order: Bruno Bonomelli (Italy), André Greuze, Erich Kamper (Austria), Norris McWhirter (GB), Roberto L Quercetani (Italy), Fulvio Regli (Switzerland), André Senay (France), Björn-Johan Weckman (Finland) and Ekkehard zur Megede (West Germany). Two other friends, Donald Potts, the only non-European, and Wolfgang Wünsche (West Germany) were not there. But they had given their assent and were to be considered as founder members like the rest of us.

During the meeting in Brussels it was relatively easy to exchange views because everyone had at least one language in common with one other at the table. We thus founded the Association of Track and Field Statisticians (ATFS). Our declared aims were the following:

1) To rationalise the work of track statisticians the world over by means of close international co-operation.

2) To produce detailed world, continental and national all-time and year lists for both men and women from which an accurate and reliable basis could be derived for the making of analyses.

Needless to say, all events in the Olympic programme were to receive due attention, and that obviously included the women's section which until then had been neglected by most if not all of us. An impromptu vote among those present resulted in the election of myself as President, Fulvio Regli as Secretary, and André Greuze as Treasurer. Our first decision was to choose Harold Abrahams as Honorary President.

In 1951 the first ATFS publication appeared in Lugano, Switzerland – *The 1951 ATFS International Athletics Annual*, with Fulvio and myself as editors. Detailed World and European lists for 1950 were the main features of its 128 pages. The following year the annual carried the first women's All-Time World List – 30 to 50 deep in each event – ever to be published, which was compiled by Zoltán Subert of Hungary and Fulvio Regli.

We realized that we were setting foot in what was generally – if not entirely – a 'no man's land'. True, national year lists had occasionally appeared in some countries even much earlier – e.g. in USA (AAU Handbooks) since the beginning of the century. But as regards 'global' compilations nothing of the kind had ever been done, with only one notable exception as far as I know – the *Internationales Leichtathletik-Jahrbuch*, edited in 1922 by a young Swiss, Maurice Loesch, then working as an interpreter at 'Bureau International de Travail' (the International Labour Office) in Geneva. This book had short World Year lists for 1921, as well as national records for a good number of European countries. The author was only 20 at the time. As dire destiny would have it, he died only two years later. And the history of track statistics was put back by several decades ... In the Thirties and early Forties, Hans Borowik of Germany used to publish 50-deep world year lists (without details) in the afore-mentioned *Der Leichtathlet*.

In 1953 Harold Abrahams was instrumental in providing for us a steadier platform through the medium of *World Sports* magazine in London, which was to publish the ATFS Annual for 20 years. Step by step the book became a more refined affair from every standpoint. Peter Matthews took over with the 1985 edition and has been at the 'wheel' ever since, doing a magnificent job, with the valid help of old and new members. In the meantime the book has grown in every respect and is now the 'vade-mecum' of all those who love our sport. For example, some sport journalists in Italy use to refer to it as 'Il Matthews'.

Quite understandably, many things have changed in the world in the last 60 years. First of all, computers have replaced letters and typewriters. In the Fifties it was very difficult to contact adequate sources – especially in some countries. That notably included USSR. In 1950 I wrote a letter to the athletics federation of that vast country, then a major problem for us. A reply reached me more than two months later ... from the USSR Embassy in Rome. They relayed the data I had asked for – written in Cyrillic characters. Nowadays. through the internet and the likes, similar information can be obtained in much quicker ways.

In 1973 my countryman Luigi Mengoni edited a book by the title *World and National Leaders in T. & F. Athletics, 1860–1972*, in which for every country he gave each year's leader in all events, The first statistician who tried to 'discover' Africa, a most difficult continent for us, was Yves Pinaud of France. Nowadays he compiles detailed African year lists, 100-deep in every event.

In the early days of the ATFS, lists of best performances (not performers) began to appear here and there. In 1987 my friend and countryman Pino Mappa produced an *All Time World List of Best Performances* which was 1000-deep in every Olympic event. In later years I joined him in this 'game'. Lest you think that may be the last world in terms of 'depth', let me tell you that in 2013 Pino Mappa, helped by the AEEA (the association of Spanish statisticians, possibly the most active of national bodies in our sphere), a book devoted exclusively to men's 100-meter marks made throughout the world as at the end of 2012. – it contained no less than *6604 marks made by 588 performers (10.20 or*

better)! Add that he gives wind readings for each and every mark!

In this field statisticians go hand in hand with historians. Back in 1986 an 'équipe' consisting of Rooney Magnusson (Sweden), Don Potts, Fulvio Regli, Luigi Mengoni, Wally Donovan (USA) and yours truly edited the first of 4 volumes with detailed World Year Lists covering the period 1921 to 1950. Even though some of the above-mentioned friends are no longer with us, such a project has not been abandoned and lists from earlier years are being prepared.

Even in the once neglected women's section great progress has been made recently. John Brant of Britain and Janusz Wasko of Poland recently edited a book with 100-deep world lists for the period 1921-1962.

Needless to say, the athletics world – not least the IAAF – has derived great benefits from the countless hours of work put in by members of the ATFS, for many years at least on a quasi-amateur basis.

May we wish our successors from all corners of the globe the best of enjoyment.

International Athletics Annuals 1951–2014

Years, names of the annual and publishers from the first edition of the ATFS Annual as mentioned in the above article.

International Athletics Annual 1951 and 1952 *A.T.F.S. International Athletic Annual.* Tipographia 'la Commerciale', S.A. Lugano, Switzerland
1953 to 1972 *World Sports International Athletics Annual.* World Sports, London
The 1972 edition was the last of the series of World Sports annuals with the ATFS lists, but smaller annuals (128 pages) were published in 1973 and 1974 by them under their new name of Sportsworld. These, however, did not contain the full ATFS lists, which appeared in the German-published book below.
1973 and 1974 *Athletic Track and Field Statistics Annual.* Verlag Bartels & Wernitz, Berlin, FRG. The main list co-ordinator in 1973 was Vladimir Visek and in the 1974 Annual he was joined by Jan Popper.
1975–8 *Association of Track and Field Statisticians Annual.* Track & Field News, Los Altos, California, USA. These contained men's lists and indexes only in slim volumes of 96–128 pages.
Information on women's athletics was well catered for in the first two years, as Peter Pozzoli's *Women's World Athletics Yearbook* (annual from 1969 to 1976) contained very deep lists (chief compiler, Jan Popper), but unfortunately that was the last of the series, and deep annual women's lists for 1977 and 1978 were published only in the Czechoslovak Bulletins START.
1979–84 *Association of Track and Field Statisticians Annual.* ATFS, published in Denmark.
From 1985 deep annual lists, as originally compiled by the ATFS, have been included in an Annual which was expanded to over 600 pages to include articles, results, reviews, biographies etc. so as to provide a comprehensive 'bible of the sport'.
1985–6 *International Athletics Annual.* Sports World Publications Ltd, a division of London & International Publishers.
1987–89 *Athletics '8x'.* Sports World Publications Ltd.
1990 *Athletics 1990.* London & Continental Communications Ltd.
1991–4 *Athletics 199x.* Burlington Publishing Ltd (later Harmsworth Active).
1995– 2014 *Athletics xxxx.* SportsBooks Ltd.

General Editors: RL Quercetani 1951–69, Fulvio Regli 1951–5, Rooney Magnusson 1970–2, Don Potts 1975–8, Palle Lassen 1979–84, Peter Matthews 1985–date
Assistant Editor: Bob Phillips 1966–72; **Principal compiler**: Nejat Kök 1979–84

NOTES FROM THE EDITOR

The Post-Olympic Year

IT WAS NOT surprising in a post-Olympic year that worldwide standards in depth fell and indeed there was a clear decline across most of the events. For men the 10th best performer in the world in 2012 was better than in 2013 in 17 events to 4 with one tie, and even more markedly at 100th best – 19 events to 1 (2 ties) and at my base level standards for the lists (for which I also include the half marathon) by 20 events to 2 (1 tie). This was a much sharper decline than in the previous post-Olympic year when the men's figures for 2008 compared to 2009 were 11-10 (1=), 15-6 (1=) and 15-7 (1=). The only men's events that were better in 2013 than in 2012 were at 10th best: 3000m steeple, high jump, pole vault and decathlon (with 200m equal), and at 100th best: 800m and 20km walk (with high jump and pole vault equal).

The situation is very similar for women as the 10th best performer in the world in 2012 was better than in 2013 in 17 events to 4 with one tie, and totally at 100th – 20 events to 0 (1 tie, high jump). At my base level standards for the lists (for which I also include the half marathon) by 2012 was ahead 19 events to 3 (200m, marathon and 20km walk).

Overall the number of performers across all events making my base standards was 4386 men and 4270 women in 2012 to 4006 men and 3884 women in 2013. While that showed a big decline, the 2013 figures were nonetheless the second highest ever in each case. *See my Trends pages 524 and 525 for the detail.*

Note that the 10th best standards for all the men's field events were set prior to 2000 as indeed they were for the 'old' field events for women.

World Records

I FIRST BECAME interested in sporting records in the mid-1950s and that was the beginning of an era in which records in athletics were broken very regularly with scores of new world records in athletics every year. The effects of the Second World War were massive in that it took 15 years from 1939 before pre-war standards were generally exceeded, but then the floodgates opened, the celebrated first sub-4 minute mile being the most famous of the avalanche of records that went at every event.

The 8.13m long jump set by Jesse Owens on his day-of-days at Ann Arbor on 25 May 1935 set the record for the longest lasting of all world records at standard events with 25 years 79 days

until Ralph Boston jumped 8.12m at Walnut on 12 August 1960, but that was very much an exception as the only world record not to be broken during the 1950s

Standards of athletics improved very rapidly as we advanced into a more peaceful era and one in which people all over the world were able, due to economic and social reasons, to participate in sport so much more widely than they had been in times when only those from developed nations who were able to find the leisure time took part regularly. There were also rapid advances in coaching, medicinal support and equipment. The long jump record, after eight world marks in 1961-7 was given the huge boost of Bob Beamon's sensational world record at the 1968 Olympic Games when he improved the record from 8.35 to 8.90. The freak combination of favourable factors (including a wind reading of +2.0 as well as 2247m altitude) meant that Beanon's record was very long-lived but even that went in the greatest ever field event duel, Mike Powell against Carl Lewis in the World Championships on 30 August 1991 in Tokyo, as Powell jumped 8.95m. Top competition at the very high altitude of Mexico City in October 1968 produced other very long-lasting records for men: Lee Evans 400m 43.86 to 1988 and the US 4x400m team's 2:56.16, equalled in 1988 and not broken until 1992, but these were exceptions to the trend of rapid turnover in records.

From the mid 1980s, and accelerated later by the collapse of the old regimes in Eastern Europe, and of course by the clampdown on drug abuse, the number of records set each year slowed steadily to today's trickle so that in 2013 we had only one world record in a standard event - the men's marathon. On 15 February 2014 Renaud Lavillenie set an absolute world record in the pole vault with his 6.16m in Donetsk and that removed Sergey Bubka's indoor 6.15 set 20 years and 359 days earlier.

So Bubka's record has gone but we are in an unprecedented era in which many records have lasted a very long time, and of those in the list below surely many, perhaps most, will last for many more years to come.

50 years ago in 1964 world records were set in 12 of the 24 men's events and 9 of the (then) 12 women's events.

It can also be noted that on 8 June 2014 Kenenisa Bekele is likely to have held both 5000m and 10,000m world records for ten years, having already passed Paavo Nurmi's 'record' for holding both marks simultaneously.

The oldest (still standing) world records in Olympic events (as at 1 April 2014)

MEN

27 years 299 days	Jürgen Schult (GDR) 74.08 discus 74.08 6 Jun 1986	
27 years 213 days	Yuriy Sedykh (USSR) 86.74 hammer 30 Aug 1986	
23 years 316 days	Randy Barnes (USA) 23.12 shot 20 May 1990	
22 years 213 days	Mike Powell (USA) 8.95 long jump 30 Aug 1991	
21 years 237 days	Kevin Young (USA) 46.78 400m hurdles 6 Aug 1992	
20 years 247 days	J.avier Sotomayor (Cuba) 2.45 high jump 27 Jul 1993	
20 years 221 days	USA 2:54.29 4x400m relay 22 Aug 1993	

WOMEN

30 years 239 days	Jarmila Kratochvílová (TCH/CZE) 1:53.28 800m 26 Jul 1983	
28 years 177 days	Marita Koch (GDR) 47.60 400m 6 Oct 1985	
	GDR 41.37 4x100m relay 6 Oct 1985	
26 years 298 days	Natalya Lisovskaya (USSR) 22.63 shot 7 Jun 1987	
26 years 213 days	Stefka Kostadinova (Bulgaria) 2.09 high jump 30 Aug 1987	
25 years 294 days	Galina Chistyakova (USSR) 7.52 long jump 11 Jun 1988	
22 years 265 days	Gabriele Reinsch (GDR) 76.80 discus 9 Jul 1988	
22 years 258 days	Florence Griffith-Joyner (USA) 10.49 100m 16 Jul 1988	
22 years 223 days	Yordanka Donkova (Bulgaria) 12.21 100m hurdles 20 Aug 1988	
22 years 188 days	Jackie Joyner-Kersee (USA) 7291 heptathlon 24 Sep 1988	
22 years 183 days	F.lorence Griffith-Joyner (USA) 21.34 200m 29 Sep 1988	
22 years 181 days	USSR 3:15.17 4x400m relay 1 Oct 1988	

No. of Olympic events in which world records have been set outdoors each year: men/women:

Year	m/w	Year	m/w	Year	m/w	Year	m/w	Year	m/w
2000	2/4	2003	3/3	2006	3/2	2009	2/1	2012	3/1
2001	1/4	2004	5/3	2007	3/2	2010	1/1	2013	1/0
2002	5/2	2005	2/4	2008	7/5	2011	2/2		

Note: figures above include records set by athletes subsequently disqualified for drugs abuse

Rule Changes

COMPETITION RULE CHANGES effective from November 1, 2013: The decathlon (with the same order of events as the men's decathlon) will replace the current octathlon for youths to better provide for the transition of young male athletes in combined events.

Two world records for women in road races: for mixed gender races and for single gender races will be recognised. Thus Paula Radcliffe will hold the mixed gender marathon record with 2:15:25 in 2003 and the single gender record with 2:17:42 in 2005. The medley relay (currently 100-200-300-400m) may be run with the legs in a different order. The women's 4x1500m relay will be added (in line with the introduction of the IAAF World Relays) to the list of events for which world records are recognised. The best legal performance as at 31 Dec 2014 shall be the initial world record mark.

Also announced by the IAAF in 2013 was a new qualification system for the Olympics and World Championships. Effective for the 2015 IAAF World Champs in Beijing, there will be a fixed number of athletes per event with the combined total of 2000 athletes competing (2231 athletes competed at London 2012). Instead of 'A' and 'B' standards, there will be a single qualification standard for each event, which aims to fill 75% of the quota for that discipline. The rest of the places will be filled by the top-ranked athletes in each event. All other existing qualification elements – such as the three athletes per nation rule and wild card entries – will remain generally unchanged. In future this qualification format may be extended to youth and junior championships. My one comment on this is that I hope that the cut (compared to 2012) will be from the non-qualified athletes such as the one-per-nation quotas allowed to compete particularly in the preliminary round of the 100m rather than from further reductions to field events that would mean the lack of some of the world's best competitors (as happened at the 2014 World Indoors with a very high qualification standard in, for instance, the men's triple jump).

While on the subject of rule changes I have not commented before on the recent IAAF reduction of the weights for shot, discus, hammer and javelin, but I did not and do not see any necessity for this. Such changes contrast with the lack over the years of any change to two senior specifications that are surely inappropriate. Women's hurdles for 100m have long been generally agreed to be too low at 2ft 9in (84cm) as a height of 3ft (91cm) would be a much better test of hurdling ability, and comparable to the 3'6" (1.067m) used for men's high hurdling. Also for the women's hammer an increase from 4kg to 5kg could be more appropriate. But it is, of course, hard to change such established specifications.

The greatest all-round distance runners

	1500m	3000m	5000m	10,000m	Points	HMar	Marathon
1. Kenenisa Bekele	3:32.35	7:25.79	12:37.35	26:17.73	5066	60:09	
2. Haile Gebrselassie	3:31.76	7:25.09	12:39.36	26:22.75	5064	58:55	2:03:59
3. Daniel Komen	3:29.46	7:20.67	12:39.74	27:38.32	5001		
4. Mo Farah	3:28.81	7:34.47	12:53.11	26:46.57	4956	60:10	
5. Eliud Kipchoge	3:50.40M	7:27.66	12:46.53	26:49.02	4953	59:25	2:04:05
6. Salah Hissou	3:33.95	7:28.93	12:50.80	26:38.08	4951	61:56	2:12:15
7. Saïd Aouita	3:29.46	7:29.45	12:58.39	27:26.11	4896		
8. Galen Rupp	3:50.92iM	7:30.16i	12:58.90	26:48.00	4886	60:30	
9. Mohammed Mourhit	3:36.14	7:26.62	12:58.45	26:52.30	4874	60:18	
10. Paul Tergat	3:58.4M	7:28.70	12:49.87	26:27.85	4866	59:06	2:04:55
11. Dieter Baumann	3:33.51	7:30.50	12:54.70	27:21.53	4852		
12. Luke Kipkosgei	3:35.48	7:27.59	12:56.50	27:12.37	4850	61:18	
13. Tariku Bekele	3:37.26	7:28.70	12:53.45	27:03.54	4848		
14. Moses Kipsiro	3:37.6	7:30.95	12:50.72	27:04.48	4835	63:15	

M = 1 mile time

If we add scores for the marathon to those for 1500, 3000, 5000 and 10,000 then the wonderful Haile Gebrselassie is of course top, the order being:

1. Haile Gebrselassie	6338	5. Abderrahim Goumri	6005	9. Benjamin Maiyo	5928
2. Eliud Kipchoge	6223	6. Hailu Mekonnen	5986	10= Matt Tegenkamp	5925
3. Paul Tergat	6120	7. Richard Limo	5972	10= Arturo Barrios	5925
4. Salah Hissou	6073	8. Ismail Sghyr	5953	12. Mark Carroll	5923

IN 2012 MO FARAH achieved the remarkable feat of winning Olympic gold medals at both 5000m and 10,000m. In 2013 he emulated Kenenisa Bekele in doing the same feat at the World Championships.

He did not, however, run especially fast at either distance as he was 16th on the 2013 world list at 5000m with 13:05.88 and 11th at 10,000m with 27:21.71. However, just weeks before going to Moscow he had run a remarkable 3:28.81 European record for 1500m. This took him up to fourth place on a table, scoring athletes' pbs on the IAAF tables for distances from 1500m to 10,000m.

Mo Farah is due to make his marathon debut in London before this book is in stock, but after we go to press – so it will be fascinating to see how he rates on the above list after that.

Prolific marathoner

The most prolific marathoner in 2013 was Yuki Kawauchi of Japan. He had a best time of 2:08:14 for 4th at Seoul in March and in all he ran 11 marathons in the year, winning five of them and running 4 times under 2:10, 9 under 2:15 and all 11 under 2:19. That followed 9 marathons in 2012 (five wins), 5 in 2011, 2 in 2010 and 3 in 2009. He went on to run marathons in February and March 2014. In his 32 marathons he has only once run slower then 2:22 (when winning in 2:22:38 in April 2012).

Straight in at No. 1

Bohdan Bondarenko was my choice (and that of *Track & Field News*) as the male World Athlete of the year in 2013. Looking back over the years I can find only two men in the past 50 years to have achieved that distinction without even ranking in the world top ten at any event before heading the world ratings. They were Lasse Viren in 1972, when he was world number one at both 5000m and 10,000m, and Michael Johnson in 1990, when he topped the rankings at both 200m and 400m. Bondarenko was not, of course, a complete unknown as he had high jumped over 2.30 in 2011 and 2012 and

he had been 7th at the 2012 Olympic Games. Nonetheless just to come straight in at no.1 at any event having never achieved a world top ten ranking at any event before is fairly rare – but three men and two women did so in 2013. In the past 20 years of my rankings in this Annual those who have done so are:

Men

1994: Wilson Kipketer 800m

1995: John Godina SP, Michele Didoni 20kW

1996: Lee Bong-ju Mar, Joseph Keter 3kmSt, Jefferson Pérez 20kW

1997: Abel Antón Mar

1998: Japheth Kimutai 800m, Ronaldo da Costa Mar, Adam Nelson SP

1999: Vyacheslav Voronin HJ

2000: Szymon Ziólkowski HT

2001: Félix Sánchez 400mh, Yaroslav Rybakov HJ

2002: Michael Blackwood 400m

2003: Elid Kipchoge 5000m

2004: Jeremy Wariner 400m, Andreas Thorkildsen JT

2005: Brad Walker PV, Sergey Kirdyapkin 50kW

2006: Micah Kogo 10,000m, Andrey Silnov HJ, Steve Hooker PV

2007: David Rudisha 800m

2008: Abubaker Kaki 800m
2010: Teddy Tamgho TJ, Stanislav Yemelyanov
20kW
2011: Mo Farah 5000m, Christian Taylor TJ
2013: Lelisa Desisa Mar, Bohdan Bondarenko
HJ, Aleksandr Ivanov 20kW
Women
1995: Ghada Shouaa Hep, Irina Stankina 10kW
1996: Fatuma Roba Mar
1997: Marion Jones 100m & 200m, Beatrice
Faumuiná DT
1998: Naoko Takahashi Mar, Glory Alozie 100mh
1999: Paraskevi Tsiamita TJ, Mirela Tzelili JT
2002: Sureyya Ayhan 1500m, Alesya Turova
3000mSt, Carolina Klüft Hep
2003: Anastasiya Kapachinskaya 200m,
Tirunesh Dibaba 5000m, Gulnara
Samitova 3000mSt
2004: Yuliya Nesterenko 100m, Joanna Hayes
100mh, Faní Halkía 400mh
2005: Maryam Jamal 1500m, Michelle Perry
100mh
2006: Inga Abitova 10,000m
2008: Shelly-Ann Fraser-Pryce 100m, Pamela
Jelimo 800m, Oksana Menkova HT
2009: Caster Semenya 800m
2011: Morgan Uceny 2011
2012: Aslo Cakir 1500m, Tiki Gelana Mar,
Yelena Lashmanova Hep
2013: Eunice Sum 800m, Brianna Rollins 100mh

Father and son World Record holders

There aren't too many cases of father and son both breaking official world records but the Calvin Smiths can now claim that distinction. Calvin Smith the father set a 100m world record of 9.93 at altitude in 1983 as well as contributing to 4x100m records in 1983 and 1984; Calvin Smith II was a member of the US team which broke the indoor 4x400m record in Sopot.
Previous examples:
Imre (HT 1948-50) and Miklos (JT 1976) Németh of Hungary.
Archie San Romani (USA) – the senior at 2000m 1937 and 4x1M 1936, and junior at 4 x 1M 1962.
Charles Jenkins (4x440y 1956) and Charles 'Chip' Jenkins (4x400m indoor 1989) from USA.
Arthur (walks from 5000m to 50km 1927-35) and Fritz (1 hour walk 1941) Schwab of Switzerland.
Then with fathers setting world bests before official IAAF ratification, there are"
The Järvinen's (Finland) – Verner (DT 1901-09) and his sons with official world records: Matti (JT 1930-6) and Akilles (Dec 1928-32).
Bernie Wefers (USA) – senior 100y, 220y and 4x440y 1895-7 and junior 4x110y 1921.
There are no examples of mother-daughter, mother-son or father-daughter world record setters as yet.

Presentation

I HAVE BEEN fortunate to be able to go to many of the world's major meetings for many years. As so often in the past, so with the World Championships outdoors in Moscow and the World Indoor Championships in Sopot, I came away exhilarated from seeing not just top-class athletics, but, with all the attendant thrills and spills, real competitive action. That comes especially from the championships format, having the full range of events and a real purpose for each and every competitor.

Now one can certainly get that from seeing the super-elite in action in one-day meetings, and one generally gets a superb range of talents at the highest level of such events. But it is not necessarily the best of the best, for sometimes one gets the feeling that for some it may be just another meeting, just another payday, whereas at the major Championship that is the one that really matters.

Over the years the IAAF has done much to encourage the promoters of the one-day meetings, and the most recent development of Diamond League fixtures (and the next tier, the World Challenge meetings) has made sure that all standard events get a fair share and that athletes at the less obviously attractive events have appropriate opportunities. So the rapid decline in the number of field events at such meetings has been halted, but they still get short shrift at some events. Some argue for a reduction in the number of events at one-day meetings, but that reflects a very condescending attitude to spectators, many of whom thoroughly enjoy having many simultaneous events to watch. Also the likes of meeting organisers or even presentation teams sometimes fail to understand just how much many people follow and enjoy the field events. After all an hour-long field event in which individuals can be followed for a series of attempts, with the competition building, is often far more rewarding than a race lasting less than a minute.

Top-class athletics needs to be well presented and one must bear in mind that there will be vastly varying levels of understanding of the sport in the crowds that are attracted to meetings. I am concerned, however, that with the perceived need to attract younger audiences and the idea that such people have short attention spans as well as lack of knowledge of the sport, that some of the major one-day meetings are being spoiled by the razzmatazz of presentation. I therefore repeat the piece that I wrote for *Athletics International* after sitting watching the Anniversary Games meeting in the Olympic Stadium in London in July 2013.

Simon Barnes, chief sportswriter at *The Times* wrote after this meeting on Monday July 29:

"I seem to have lost the battle for live sporting events that keep faith with live sport as a spectacle. I now have to accept that at certain big events, such as the athletics at the Olympic Stadium over the weekend, it is essential to have a hysterical disc jockey yelling inanities into a microphone. Since we have to have such people, is it not possible to adjust the public-address system so that we can hear something more than an overwrought counter-tenor bray? Communications technology in modern stadiums does, I think, run to a volume button. Volume ten is surely quite loud enough even for the most fastidious. Joy, we might be able to distinguish the actual words."

I responded: "Hear! Hear! I have spent 45 years presenting athletics to the public and believe very strongly in the need to guide and inform the public at athletics meetings, but increasingly the athletics has been secondary to excessively loud music (which surely distracts many of the field event athletes) and to shouting announcers seeking to stir up the noise. I have sat and watched the Diamond League meetings in Britain this year and both have, to my mind, been seriously damaged by the presentation. The crowd, as in the Olympic Stadium this past weekend, can be trusted to generate their own excitement, benefitting from informed guidance."

I would add that a friend of mine – a sports enthusiast, but not specifically an athletics fan – went for the first time to such a meeting, attracted as were most of the crowd by the opportunity to experience the Olympic Stadium at the Anniversary Games, since so many people were unable to get tickets for any of the events there in 2012. He told me that he had enjoyed the athletics, but, because of the above, would not go again. What the presentation team fail to appreciate was that sitting for hours bombarded by excessively loud music is actually unpleasant.

The use of music for such occasions as a 'High Jump with Music' event is fine because one can tailor it to the athlete and his or her attempt, but blanket use of it for multi-event competitions is surely distracting to many of the athletes, especially when it is targeted at the current track event, as well as extremely annoying to many spectators – or at least those who actually want to watch the action. The latest pop music has, for decades, rung out in football stadiums, and this certainly helps to create the atmosphere – BUT it is not played during the action, just as a game of football is shown uninterrupted in television coverage, a far cry from the sort of coverage given to athletics by the BBC in Britain, where banal chat is presented to viewers instead of live action and field events are hardly ever shown live.

Doping Bans

IT IS VERY sad to see that the list of Doping Bans in this Annual (see pages 100-101) is the longest that we have ever published. This is, of course, partly a measure of how the authorities are better at catching would-be cheats, but so many obviously think they can get away with it or are in the hands of unscrupulous agents and coaches. Particularly noticeable are the large number of athletes caught in India, Russia and Turkey with a disconcerting number of big names, particularly from Russia, But the In 2013 the Turkish Athletics Federation (TAF) banned 31 of its athletes for two years for drug violations (with probably more to add) and three of these athletes competed at the London Olympic Games. The positive tests are "part of a concerted and much more aggressive anti-policy in Turkey" that had been in place for 6 months according to the President of Turkey's National Olympic Committee, Ugur Erderner.

Real progress seems to be being made in the honing of methods to identify illegal substances, and the IAAF's Athlete Biological Passport programme in partnership with the World Anti-Doping Agency (WADA) has led the way in finding culprits.

At the 2013 World Championships a total of 1919 blood samples were collected from the athletes located at four different hotels, and these were analysed daily in the WADA-accredited laboratory in Moscow for haematological screening. The corresponding serum samples were transferred to the Lausanne Laboratory for further analyses of various blood bio markers. In addition to the blood sampling, all urine samples collected at the IAAF World Championships were analysed by the Moscow Anti-Doping laboratory, including the numerous specialised analyses such as EPO and IRMS. A total of 538 athletes were urine tested during the competition and 132 during the pre-competition period. All urine samples collected in Moscow were to be transferred to long-term storage facilities provided by the Lausanne laboratory for eventual re-analyses at a later stage. From the urine testing conducted, the IAAF found seven athletes, including one finalist, with adverse findings.

A by-product of the programme is that samples from past championships have been re-tested, so medallists from, for instance, the 2004 Olympics and 2005 World Championships have received bans and lost their results. This has meant massive re-writing of results and lists for many years – a problem for us statisticians. One just hopes that lessons are being learnt by the athletes and their mentors, but sadly one fears that long lists of banned athletes are likely to continue to be the norm. Unfortunately a culture of clean sport and antipathy to cheating is not something that pertains in many societies around the world.

Lists of athletes receiving bans are posted in the IAAF list "Athletes currently suspended from all competitions in athletics following an Anti-Doping Rule Violation" that is available on their website. New athletes to this lists were also included in the regular IAAF newsletters, but unfortunately this practice stopped with their March 2014 issue – and this is a pity as it makes it much harder for us to keep up with newly banned athletes and thus to amend results..

Winter Olympic Games 2014

With silver at the 2-man bobsleigh at Sochi 2014, Lauryn Williams became the fifth person to have won a medal at both the Summer and Winter Olympic Games and the first of these to have done so in athletics, having won gold at 4x100m in 2012 and silver at 100m in 2004. Five other Olympic athletes (one man and four women) competed in the bobsleigh events in Sochi:

Other 2014 bobsleigh competitors with athletics credentials

Men 2m
2nd   Beat Hefti SUI. 60m 6.70i 03
6th   Bryan Barnett CAN. 200m 20.31 '07, dnf ht OG 2008. Also 13th 4m
19th   Edwin van Calker 19th NED. Dec 7089 5 WJ '98. Also 11th 4m
26th   Duncan Harvey AUS. 110mh 14.14 3 AUS Ch '04. Also 22nd 26th 4m
28th   Hisashi Miyazaki JPN. 200m 20.53 '03, qf/6R WCh '03. Also 4m

Men 4m
2nd   Janis Strenga LAT. JT 71.96 '10, dnq WJ '10
4th   Aleksey Pushkarev RUS. 100m 10.53 '09
5th   Joel Fearon GBR. 100m 10.10 '13
5th   Bruce Tasker GBR. 400m 47.69 '07, won England U20 indoor 2007
5th   Stuart Benson GBR. 100m 10.49 '08
6th   Marko Hübenbecker GER. SP 18.05 '06, dnq WY '03
6th   Alexander Rödiger GER. SP 16.25 '05, dnq WJ '04
9th   Neville Wright CAN-2. 100m 10.30A '07, 3 WUG '07, ht 4x100m WCh '07.
10th   Thorsten Margis GER-2. Dec 7707 '11, 4 WJ '08
19th   Andrew Matthews GBR-2. 100m 10.36 '05, 4 EJ '03, 8/4R E23 '05.
William Frullani ITA was sent home from Sochi after a positive drugs test. Dec 7984 '02, 1 ECp '04.

Women 2m
3rd   Aja Evans USA. SP 17.08i/16.99 '10
3rd   Jamie Greubel USA. Hep 5465 '06
4th   Judith Vis NED. Hep 5743 '00

6th   Hanna Mariën BEL. 200m 22.68 '06, 2nd 4x100m OG 2008; 3rd WUG '07.
9th   Olga Stulneva (née Fyodorova) RUS. 100m 11.21 2 ECp '05, 2nd 4x100m OG 2004; 3 4x100m WCh '03
11th   Lolo Jones USA. 100mh 12.43/12.29w '08. OG: 2008 7th, 2012 4th.1 WI 60mh 2008 & 2010.
14th   Jana Pittman AUS. 400mh 53.22 '03, 1 WCh 2003 & 2007; OG: 2000 ht, 2004

Skeleton Bob
The gold medallist Lizzie Yarnold GBR had pbs: SP 12.61 and JT 43.68 in 2009 when she was 20. She placed 5th/4th/4th in English U23 javelin 2008-10, 3rd England SP 2010.

Other Sports
American Football
British discus record holder **Lawrence Okoye** signed for the NFL's San Francisco 49ers as an undrafted free agent ... although he had never played American football. **Margus Hunt** of Estonia, the 2.03m (6ft 8in) tall 2006 World Junior shot & discus champion, was drafted by the Cincinnati Bengals as a defensive end, while **Marquise Goodwin**, 8.33 long jumper, world junior champion in 2008 and NCAA champion 2010 and 2012, was drafted by the Buffalo Bills and plays for them as a wide receiver and kick-off returner.

Cycling
Anzeka Drahotová is making rapid progress at walking as she won the European Junior 10,000m title in 2013 and, still a junior, set a Czech record for 20k with 1:28:13. But she also competed at the junior women's world road race at cycling in 2013, coming 19th.
Emma Pooley (GBR), the 2008 Olympic silver medallist and 2010 world champion at cycling road time trial, won the Lausanne marathon in 2:44:29 in 2013.

Triathlon
With the 10km race being an integral part, with swimming and cycling, of triathlon, it must be expected that many men and women have top form at both athletics and triathlon.
Alistair Brownlee, Olympic triathlon champion in 2012 and world champion in 2009 and 2011 was Britain's third fastest man at 10,000m in 2013, running 28:32.48 at Stanford in April.
Non Stanford won the ITU World Triathlon series for women in 2013. She ran 32:41 for 10km at Manchester in March, returning to a sport in which she had shown exceptional promise as a teenager, running a Welsh U20 record of 4:23.55 at 1500m and 9:22.84 for 3000m at 15 in 2004, placing 5th in the European Youth Olympics 3000m in 2005, and competing in the 2006 World Junior Cross-country. **Anne Haug** (Ger), 3rd in the ITU World series also ran 74:29 for half marathon in 2013.

The Geography of World Athletics

THIS IS THE 30th edition of the International Athletics Annual that I have compiled. It is fascinating to consider the changes that there have been in the sport over the past 30 years. Perhaps most noticeable has been the worldwide spread of the sport. Here is an analysis of the athletes that I have featured in the biographical profiles section of the 1985 Annual and in this 2014 Annual. While the selection of athletes is to some extent subjective, as the super elite of the sport they give a useful picture of the spread of such athletes worldwide. In 1985 there were 574 athletes included (358 men and 216 women)

and in 2014 there are 797 athletes (421 men and 376 women). I analyse these by continental areas and by the major nations. I have been able to expand the numbers included each year and the proportion of women has increased considerably due to the increase in events for them: in 1984 the 10,000m and walk had still to be added to the women's Olympic programme and we did not have the steeplechase, pole vault, triple jump and hammer as standard women's events. So I show both the number of athletes and their percentages of the total for that year.

	1984 Men No.	%	1984 Women No.	%	2014 Men No.	%	2014 Women No.	%
Africa	30	8%	2	1%	115	27%	71	19%
Ethiopia	5		0		26		27	
Kenya	13		0		64		34	
Asia	8	2%	5	2%	26	6%	24	6%
China	3		4		11		14	
CAC	15	4%	6	3%	42	10%	25	7%
Cuba	8		6		10		6	
Jamaica	2		2		13		15	
Europe	219	61%	159	74%	160	38%	179	48%
Czechoslovakia*	11		7		7		9	
France	8		4		13		7	
Germany*	48		46		16		22	
Italy	14		4		4		6	
Poland	10		4		12		7	
Russia	included in USSR				33		60	
UK	23		18		16		11	
Ukraine	included in USSR				8		11	
USSR	49		45					
N. America	77	22%	34	16%	60	14%	66	18%
USA	72		26		57		62	
Oceania	9	3%	10	5%	8	2%	7	2%
Australia	6		8		5		5	
S. America	0	0%	0	1%	10	2%	4	1%

Note that in 1984 the whole of the USSR was included in the figures for Europe, although a few of their athletes were from the Asian part of the Soviet Union.
In 1984 FRG 21/10, GDR 27/36. In 2014 Czech Republic 5/6, Slovakia 2/3.

The marked relative decline of Europe can be seen readily, and even more marked has been the ascent of athletes from African nations, headed by the super distance runners from Ethiopia and Kenya. Jamaican athletes have led the way for big advances from the Central American and Caribbean nations, while even the USA, still easily the world's top power, has featured a decline in the relative strength of their men, but a big increase in women's athletics.

Medal tables at Global Championships   The number of nations to have won medals

Olympic Games

	M	W	All
1984	21	14	26
1988	19	11	23
1992	25	21	35
1996	31	29	45
2000	29	33	44
2004	34	25	40
2008	31	26	42
2012	30	21	41

World Championships

	M	W	All
1983	22	12	27
1987	23	13	27
1991	23	17	29
1993	25	25	36
1995	34	26	43
1997	29	27	41
1999	34	28	42
2001	32	29	42

	M	W	All
2003	35	28	43
2005	36	21	41
2007	35	29	48
2009	29	25	37
2011	29	25	41
2013	27	26	38

Win Streaks

THE GREATEST CURRENT win streak in athletics is that of the New Zealand shot putter Valerie Adams. She has won 46 successive competitions from August 2010 to the end of March 2014, and there is every likelihood that she will add substantially to that sequence. Before that she had lost eight times in 2010 to Nadezhda Ostapchuk, later to receive a drugs ban after she had finished ahead of Adams at the 2012 Olympic Games. But before those 2010 losses Adams had 28 successive shot wins from 2nd to Ostapchuk at the World Athletics Final on 23 Sep 2007, her only loss in 12 competitions that year. She had also won 7 of 8 competitions in 2006, coming 2nd to Natalya Khoronenko at the World Athletics Final on 10 September. But Khoronenko (later Mikhnevich) is another athlete later to receive a drugs ban. Going back another year, Adams won 16 of 17 shot competitions in 2005, her one loss coming in her twelfth competition that year when she was second to Olga Ryabinkina in the World Championships (after removing the original winner Ostapchuk, who belatedly received her first drugs ban from that event). So if we were to call those 2nd places to Khoronenko and Ostapchuk wins, Adams would have 94 successive 'wins' from that World Champs loss on 13 Aug 2005. This is a record of sustained excellence with few parallels.

The greatest ever "win streak" was that achieved by Romanian Iolanda Balas who won 150 successive high jump competitions from 1957 to 1976/

A list of notable win streaks at one event:
Men
116 Parry O'Brien USA SP 1952-6
107 Edwin Moses USA 400mh 1977-87
    (122 including heats)
88 Jim Fuchs USA SP 1949-51
73 Imre Németh HUN HT 1946-50
68 Jiri Skobla TCH SP 1952-5
65 Carl Lewis USA LJ 1981-91
60 Adhemar Ferreira da Silva BRA TJ 1950-6
Women
150 Iolanda Balas ROM 1957-67
86+ Gisela Mauermayer GER DT 1935-49
    (or 65 2.6.1935 to 2.8.1942)
At various events
Men
82 Harrison Dillard USA sprints & hurdles
    1947-8
70 Manfred Germar FRG sprints 1956-8
69 Emil Zatopek TCH all distances 1949-51
65 Greg Rice USA all distances 1940-3
Women
90 Renate Stecher GDR 100m & 200m 1970-4
86 Merlene Ottey JAM sprints (inc 13 heats)
    1989-91
83 Chi Cheng TPE all events 1970

IAAF World Half Marathon Championships 2014
At Kavarna, Bulgaria 7 October

Men			Women		
1. Geoffrey Kipsang KEN	59:08		1. Gladys Cherono KEN	67:29	
2. Samuel Tsegay ERI	59:21		2. Mary Ngugi KEN	67:44	
3. Guye Adola ETH	59:21		3. Selly Chepyego Kaptich KN	67:52	
4. Zersenay Tadese ERI	59:38		4. Lucy Kabuu KEN	68:37	
5. Nguse Amsolom ERI	60:00		5. Mercy Kibarus KEN	68:42	
6. Wilson Kiprop KEN	60:01		6. Netsanet Gudeta ETH	68:46	
7. Ghirmay Ghebreslassie ERI	60:10		7. Christelle Daunay FRA	68:48	
8. Samsom Gebreyohannes ERI	60:13		8. Valeria Straneo ITA	68:55	
9. Adugna Tekele ETH	60:15		9. Tsehay Desalegn ETH	69:04	
10. Kenneth Kipkemoi KEN	60:29		10. Genet Yalew ETH	69:15	
11. Geoffrey Kusuro UGA	60:41		11. Krisztina Papp HUN	70:08	
12. Stephen Mokoka RSA	60:47		12. Mame Feyisa ETH	70:08	
13. Elroy Gelant RSA	61:10		13. Annie Bersagel USA	70:10	
14. Bonsa Dida ETH	61:12		14. Lauren Kleppin USA	70:16	
15. Lusapho April RSA	61:16		15. Sayo Nomura JPN	70:18	
16. Polat Arikan TUR	61:22		16. Hitrut Alemayehu ETH	70:25	
17. Ayad Lamdassem ESP	61:22		17. Risa Takenaka JPN	70:30	
18. Masato Kikuchi JPN	61:23		18. Alyson Dixon GBR	70:38	
19. Fikre Assefa ETH	61:30		19. Reia Iwade JPN	70:45	
20. El Hassane Ben Lkhainouch FRA	61:31		120. Karoline Bjerkeli Grøvdal NOR	70:53	

109 of 114 finished

Teams: 1. ERI 2:58:59, 2. KEN 2:59:38, 3. ETH 3:00:48, 4. RSA 3:03:13, 5. UGA 3:04:39, 6. JPN 3:05:45, 7. USA 3:06:18, 8. BRN 3:06:27, 9. FRA 3:07:28, 10. ESP 3:08:01, 18 teams scored.

88 of 89 finished

Teams: 1. KEN 3:23:05, 2. ETH 3:27:05, 3. JPN 331:33, 4. ITA 3:31:57, 5. USA 3:32:48, 6. FRA 3:36:21, 7. CHN 3:37:43, 8. ERI 3:41:58, 9. Nor 3:42:43, 10. RSA 3:43:23, 15 teams scored.

REFERENCE BOOKS 2013–14

British Athletics 1951 (A4 121 pages) and **British Athletics 1952** (A4 125 pages) by Michael Sheridan. Published by the author, 27 Yew Tree Park, Congresbury, Somerset BS49 5ER, UK. Deep year lists for each year. Price £20 each or £38 if purchased together.

African Athletics 1957 by Yves Pinaud A5 26pp. This is the eighth in a series of booklets reconstructing annual lists of performers from the earliest years of African athletics by Yves Pinaud. **African Athletics 1976** and **African Athletics 1975** follow in the series. Each: Price 10 euro, or US $15, including postage (banknotes possible) from Polymédias, 46 rue des Bordeaux, 94220 Charenton-le-Pont, France.

Athletics in Yugoslavia 1941-1945 by Ozren Karamata. Hardback 476 pages. The book deals with the athletic life (mostly competitions, but other topics as well) in the five regions of divided Yugoslavia in the years of WWII. Text is in Serbian, but detailed results and lists take up much of the book. We know the area as a war zone but a surprising amount of athletics took place in 1941-4. 35 euros including postage, contact the author at ozrenk@bio.bg.ac.rs

Metedo Fermín Cacho. This is an attractive 238-page paperback book by José Luis Hernández, Ignacio Mansilla and Daniel Mostaza, with plenty of colour photographs, on the career on Fermín Cacho, the 1992 Olympic and 1994 European champion at 1500m. The text is in Spanish and there are lists of all his races year-by-year for his career 1984-2003, which is surveyed chronologically with a statistical appendix. The book comes with a DVD of the best moments from his career. There are forewords by Hicham El Guerrouj and Abel Antón. Cost 21 euros from José Luis Hernández at estadistica@rfea.es

Mo Farah's autobiography, **"Twin Ambitions"**, 370 pp. published by Hodder & Stoughton (www.hodder.co.uk) £20. This is an absorbing 370-page read, documenting his ups and downs en route to his gold medal triumphs at the Olympics and World Champs and has a 17 page analysis by Peter Matthews of Mo's career with details of all his documented races from April 1995 (aged 12) to September 2013.

The 1912 Stockholm Olympics. Essays on the Competitions, the People, The City. Edited by Leif Yttergren and Hans Boling. 286 pages. Translated from the Swedish, this is a fascinating collection of studies of the Games of 1912 that did so much to set the Olympics on the way to their modern status. The editors state: "One aim of this book is to deepen the understanding of the 1912 Stockholm Olympics by studying them from a range of perspectives". They succeed in doing this and it is interesting to see how some of the problems of the modern age were addressed over a century ago. Published by McFarland & Co. Inc. £39.53 from Eurospanbookstore.com

The Past is a Foreign Country. The History of Scottish Athletics by Colin Shields and Arnold Black. 284 pages, lavishly illustrated with almost 200 photographs. 12 chapters with career biographies of the great names of Scottish athletics and a further 100 profiles plus the story of the Commonwealth Games. Published April 2014. £12 plus postage, contact Arnold Black at satsbook@aol.com

The Greatest Athletes of the Modern Era, Statistics from Early Years to the Present – Men's Long Jump and Triple Jump. A4 164p. This is the ninth in the series by Ari Törmä with very detailed statistics from all-time lists as at 31.12.1868 to 75 deep all-time lists at four-yearly intervals to 31.12.2012 plus yearly progressions for top three men on Törmä's scoring system and profiles of Carl Lewis and Vilho Tuulos. Published by the Finnish Athletics Archive Society, Suomen Yleisurheiluarkisto, membership of which is euros 65 with 3-5 booklets plus newsletters each year, The price of one book for non-members is 25 euros including postage. Payments to Suomen Yleisurheiluarkisto. IBAN: FI82 1572 3000 406017. SWIFT: NDEAFIHH on in cash or by PayPal. Payment information from mikko.nieminen@dlc.fi. Book information from athletics@aritorma.net

Balkan All Times Athletics 2nd Edition November 2013 by Karolos Sargolos contains 50 performers and 20 performances for all standard events. A4. Contact Karolos at ksargologos@yahoo.gr. Price 12 euros plus postage.

Japanese and World All-time Lists. A4 size (landscape), 340pp. 100-deep performance and 300-deep performers for all standard events and shorter lists for non-standard events for Japan (by Yoshimasa Noguchi) and for the world (by Tatsumi Senda), the lists are in small point-size and the names and venues are in Japanese characters, but performances, dates of birth and marks, plus heights and weights of the athletes are in Roman numerals so enthusiasts can readily identify the athletes etc. From Tatsumi

Senda, 3-4-33 Shioe, Hyogo 661-0976, Japan for US $15 or 10 Euros by SAL postage.

World All-Time Lists. Luis Leite has updated to October 2013 his world lists – now up to 1000 deep for all men's and 800 deep for all women's Olympic events with top 50 performances. Contact him at leite.luis1@gmail.com

Annuals

European Athletics Yearbook 2013. This was once again split into three parts this year: The first is the Athletics Review 2013 – a beautifully illustrated 156-page A4 review of the year packed with illustrations and features on competitions and developments. The second is the Statistics Yearbook 2013, A5 480pp with records, championship bests and 100-deep European lists with 50-deep lists for U23s and U20s, 30-deep indoor lists in 2013 and 50-deep all-time lists compiled as usual by Mirko Jalava. The third is a 92-page pocket sized Directory. Statistics Yearbook (with free Athletics Review) 25 euro in Europe, 30 euro elsewhere – see www.European-athletics.org

Combined Events Annual 2013 by Hans van Kuijen. A5, 208pp. The 21st edition of this attractively produced annual included top 200 men's decathlon and women's heptathlon lists for 2013 and all scores over 7550 and 5600 respectively with deep all-time world lists (to 8000 and 6000) plus indoor year and all-time lists. Also results of major events, records, profiles and complete career details for the world's top multi-eventers with a special profile of the great Roman Sebrle. In Europe: 30 euro or £30 sterling cash (no cheques). Outside Europe: US $50 cash – from Hans van Kuijen, de Bergen 66, 5706 RZ Helmond, Netherlands. Email: j.kuijen4@upcmail.nl. Back numbers 2005-11: €15 each.

L'Athlétisme Africain/African Athletics 2013. A5, 152 pages. By Yves Pinaud. Published by Éditions Polymédias for the Confederation of African Athletics with support from the IAAF, the 32nd edition in this splendid series has 100 deep men's and women's lists for Africa for 2012, with all-time lists, national championships and major results. 20 euro, £18 or US $30 inc. postage from La Mémoire du Sport, 46 rue des Bordeaux, 94220 Charenton-le-pont, France. (Also available: booklist with very extensive list of athletics books and magazines for sale).

Asian Athletics 2012 Rankings. A5 96 pages. Heinrich Hubbeling continues his magnificent annual job of compiling Asian statistics. The booklet contains top 30s for 2012 for athletes from Asian nations, with continuation lists for countries other than China and Japan, indicating new national records, and full lists of Asian records. Euro 15/US $22 in cash or by International Money Order from the author, Haydnstrasse 8, 48691 Vreden, Germany. email hhubbeling@t-online.de. Copies also available for 1998, 2005-11 at €10/US $15 each.

Athlérama 2012. A5 688pp. The 50th edition of the French Annual, edited by Patricia Doilin with a strong team of compilers, is again a superb reference book. Packed with information on French athletics – records, profiles of 81 top athletes, results, deep year lists for 2012 for all age groups plus all-time lists and indexes. Maintaining the sequence these are French top ten lists for 1912 and 1962. 28 euros from the FFA, 33 avenue Pierre de Coubertin, 7540 Paris Cedex 13, France. email Patricia.Doilin@athle.org

British Athletics 2013. A5 408 pages. The 55th NUTS Annual, edited by Rob Whittingham, Peter Matthews, and Tony Miller. Deep UK ranking lists for all age groups in 2012, top 12 merit rankings, all-time lists, results etc. £18 plus postage (£2 UK & Europe, £5 outside Europe); from Rob Whittingham, 7 Birch Green, Croft Manor, Glossop, Derbyshire SK13 8PR, UK. Cash or sterling cheques.

Eesti Kergejõustiku Aastaraamat 2014. 280pp. An attractively produced annual with comprehensive Estonian ranking lists indoors and out for 2013, with results and records and many colour photographs. From the Estonian Athletic Federation, Maakri 23, Tallinn 10145, Estonia. ejkl@ejkl.ee

Israeli Athletics Annual 2012/13. 240 x 170mm, 54pp, illustrated. By David Eiger. Records, championship results, 2012 top 20s and all-time lists, with profiles of leading Israeli athletes. 7 euro or US $10 from David Eiger, 10 Ezra Hozsofer Str, Herzliya 46 371, Israel. Back numbers also available.

Latvijas Vieglatletikas Gadagramata 2013. A5 560 pp. Comprehensive coverage of Latvian athletics for 2012, including records, results, athlete profiles and year and all-time lists with some colour photos, compiled by Andris Stagis. From the Latvian Athletic Association, Augsiela 1, Riga LV-1009, Latvia.

Annuaire FLA 2013. A4 256p. The Luxembourg Annual, edited by Georges Klepper, is again a magnificent and extraordinarily comprehensive volume, with reviews, results, 2012 and all-time lists, plus many colour photographs. 15 euros locally, by post €18 in Luxembourg, €27 elsewhere to account no. LU32 1111 0200 0321 0000. See www.fla.lu.

Malaysian Athletics Annual Best Performances 2013 by Jad Adrian Washif. 82pp with 2013 Malaysian Rankings, All-Time Rankings, National Records, and results of major Malaysian meets in 2013. Contact the author at: info@adriansprints.com

Athletics New Zealand 2012 Almanac. A5 148pp. Edited by Steve Hollings and Simon Holroyd. The third annual from Athletics NZ includes national ranking lists for 2012 up to 50 deep for seniors plus lists for juniors and youths, all-time top 20s, records for the various age groups and results of championships and other major events. For details, see www.athletics.org. nz and go to "Shop". Price including postage: $NZ50 international, $40 Australia & Pacific, $30 New Zealand.

Friidrott 2013. 170 x 240 mm 508pp, 371 pictures, hardback. Edited by Jonas Hedman, text in Swedish. A high quality production which covers world and Scandinavian athletics, including detailed championships and major events results with narrative, world outdoor top 50 year and all-time-lists, top 25 Scandinavian and Swedish year and all-time lists plus indoor top tens and record lists for World, Europe, Scandinavia and Sweden. 495 kronor from TextoGraf Förlag, Jonas Hedman, Springarvägen 14, 142 61 Trångsund, Sweden. See www.textograf.com. *Info in English*

Southeast Asia Athletics Annual 2012/13. A5, 165 pages. This second annual for the region by ATFS member Jad Adrian Washif contains results of major meetings, 2012 and all-time ranking lists, national records (outdoor & indoor) for all countries and statistical profiles for 56 men and 44 women. Price EUR 10 (SEA), EUR 15 (outside SEA) inc. shipping and handling fees. Payment in cash or cheque, bank transfers, credit card, debit card, paypal, and western union to: Jad Adrian Washif, L7, Kolej 12 UPM, 43400 Serdang Selangor, Malaysia. See: www. adriansprints.com. Email: jad_adrianwashif@ yahoo.com

Sverige Bästa 2012. A5 288 pages. Edited by Jonas Hedman. Detailed Swedish lists for seniors (100 deep), juniors and youth (20 deep). $20 (plus postage and shipping) from the Swedish Athletic Association: Svenska Friidrottsförbundet, Heliosgatan 3, 120 30 Stockholm, Sweden. Email: info@friidrott.se

Anuario Athlético Español 2012/2013. This massive publication with results, 2013 year and all-time lists, with all-time Spanish champions, current biographies and much more is available for downloading in sections at http://www. rfea.es/revista/libros/rfea_rankingAL.htm

2013 USA Track & Field Media Guide & FAST Annual (general editors: Jared Slinde for USATF and Tom Casacky for FAST). A5 819pp. The first 274 pages is the USATF Media Guide with detailed profiles of top US athletes, published for the 19th year with the 35th FAST Annual, containing records, 50-deep US lists for 2012 and all-time, with 15-deep junior and college all-time lists. The massive final index section includes annual progressions and championships details for top American athletes. $25 post paid in the USA or $42 or 30 Euros airmail from Tom Casacky, PO Box 192252, San Francisco, CA 94119-2252, USA. Payment is easiest by PayPal (to tom@interis.com); also cash, postal money orders and Western Union transfers.

Yleisurheilu 2013. A5 672pp. The Finnish Yearbook, published by Suomen Urheilulitto (Finnish Athletics) and compiled by Juhani and Mirko Jalava, contains every conceivable statistic for Finnish athletics (with results and deep year lists) in 2013 and also world indoor, outdoor and junior lists for the year as known at November. 19 euros plus 10 euros for postage and packaging. Orders by e-mail to juhani@ tilastopaja.fi.

Statistical Bulletins

TRACK STATS. The NUTS quarterly bulletin, edited by Bob Phillips, includes a wealth of fascinating statistics and articles. A5, 68-80 pages. Annual subscription (4 issues) is £20 (UK), £25 (rest of Europe) or £28 (elsewhere); contact Liz Sissons, 9 Fairoak Lane, Chessington, Surrey KT9 2NS, UK. lizsissons9@gmail.com

Contents of recent issues have included:
April 2013: comprehensive review by editor Bob Phillips of the career of Harry Whittle; career record of Ann Packer 1957-64; features on Harold Whitlock and Sam Mussabini by Dave Terry

July 2013: complete career of Mary Rand, memories of Maureen Gardner, the 'Gateshead Clipper'; Jack Potts, part 1 of a study of early distance running by Andy Milroy, the Hägg-Andersson rivalry and pole vaulting pioneers.

October 2013: Six articles on the steeplechase including a survey of Americans of the 1930s; national records as at the end of 1939, 1959 and 1969; and descriptions of the 1920 Olympic race and its winner, Guernsey-born Percy Hodge. Career record (1929-1945) of Cyril Holmes by Neil Shuttleworth and a profile/interview with Clive Williams of a later British sprinter, Ron Jones.

January 2014: a comprehensive career record for Paula Radcliffe, more in the series of progressive UK all-comers records lists, and a wide variety of fascinating historical articles.

Don Turner (donturner@btinternet.com) also has stocks of NUTS publications, including back issues of Track Stats from 1998.

Each £5: Event booklets (detailed statistics on UK athletes including results of championships and very detailed all-time lists, profiles etc.): UK women's hurdles (2004), Long Jump (2005), Shot Put (2006), Pole Vault (2008). Also 1930-39 UK men's ranking lists. And the two most recent publications: **Hammer** by Ian Tempest (2011),

88pp at £8 including postage. **Decathlon** (2011) 120pp by Alan Lindop £9 including postage.

The **DGLD** – **the German** statistical group, Deutsche Gesellschaft für Leichtathletik-Dokumentation produces annual national ranking lists (**Deutsche Bestenliste**, 208 pages) for Germany and impressive bulletins of up to 292 pages, packed with historical articles and statistical compilations. Each issue (three per year) includes statistical profiles of athletes born 70, 75, 80, 85, 90 years ago etc. Membership, with free Deutsche Bestenliste – euro 55 per year. Contact Hans Waynberg, Liebigstrasse 9, 41464 Neuss, Germany; hans.waynberg@t-online.de. Website: www.leichtathletik-dgld.de

No. 65 1 Mar 2013 had 274 pages with contents including: Complete career record of Luz Long 1929-42 with world, European and German year lists for LJ/TJ for his best years; Olympic marathons of 1920 and 1924 with history of the event in that era; Year lists for Saxony 1919-25; Women's pentathlon all-time lists – world to end 1945 and German to end 1949; Part 2 of extensive GDR Juniors index 1949-90; German all-time list for women's TJ; Top 50 German lists for women's HJ each age 13-19; Udo Beyer profile including his 118 competitions over 20.85m.

No. 66 1 Jun 2013 had 284 pages including: Olympic marathons 1896 and 1904, Saxony lists 1926-30, German men's sprint lists at end 1945, Part 3 of the GDR Juniors index 1949-90; Top 50 German lists for women's LJ each age 13-19.

No. 67 1 Nov 2013 had 266 pages including a long article by Hubert Hamacher on 'The Start' by sprinters, the Olympic Marathon 1928 with details of races leading up to it and career details of all participants, year lists 1931-45 for Saxony, German all-time lists at 31.12.45 for men's non-standard distances, German women's 800m top 40s for each age 13 to 19 and 100k all-times for senior age groups from 30+.

The DGLD has also published **Das war die DDR-Leichtathletik 1945-1990 (Band 1** has results of GDR championships, top ten lists for each event and each year 1946-90, GDR athletes in major championships etc. **Band 2** has progressive records, indoor lists, indoor and junior championships etc. Each 30 euros from Hans Waynberg.

The **Spanish group, the AEEA** continues to produce magnificent publications. Membership (four bulletins per year) is 55 euros per year (€61 outside Europe) from AEEA secretary Ignacio Mansilla, C/Encinar del Rey, 18 - 28450 Collado Mediano, Madrid, Spain. email: ranking@rfea.es

Bulletin No. 92 (A5 386 pages) featured a massive compilation by Pino Mappa of men's 100m all-time lists with 6604 wind-legal and 2563 wind assisted performances to 10.20, top ten averages and an index of 958 athletes in these lists. Then followed sprint careers for Usain Bolt, Carl Lewis and, Pietro Mennea; records and all-time lists for women from the Canary Islands, and part one of Hungarian Athletics Statistics by Gábor Szabó 1875-1914.

Bulletin No. 93 (A5 388 pages) featured the 'Historia del Atletismo Madrileño' (190 pages), the Madrid region from 1903 to 1945 with results and record progressions. Then the 'Anuario Atlético Español 2012-2013' (153 pages) with Spanish ranking lists for 2013 and the complete career record of retiring María Vasco; also Spanish yearly bests for each event from 1961 and a career profile of Josep Molins.

Lista Española de todos los tiempos contained Spanish all-time lists as at 31 October 2013. See http://www.rfea.es/ranking/altt/alltimeESP_2013.pdf.

The AEEA have produced a CD containing all 93 issues of their bulletin, from 1987 to January 2014 – a fantastic volume of Spanish and world statistical and historical material at over 20,000 pages. Just 25 euros including postage.

The Spanish athletics magazine "**Atletismo Español**" is now free and digital. See it at: http://issuu.com/atlemoesp/docs

IAAF Handbooks

The **Statistics Handbook** for the **IAAF World Youth Championships**, Donetsk 2013, 139 pages by Ottavio Castellini and Félix Capilla, can be downloaded from www.iaaf.org.

The **IAAF Statistics Book** for the Moscow World Champs 2013, produced in collaboration with the ATFS and edited by Mark Butler and replicating the style of previous editions, ran to 800 pages. It is available to download from the IAAF website (www.iaaf.org).

Sopot 2014 Statistics Handbook for the World Indoor Championships. 371 pages. Edited by Mark Butler as another magnificent work with the usual features. Again available for downloading.

The **IAAF Yearbook for 2013**, edited by Laura Arcoleo and full of articles, reviews and colour photos in its 104 pages, is downloadable free as a PDF. http://www.iaaf.org/about-iaaf/documents/iaaf-newsletter

See www.iaaf.org/about-iaaf/publications for their extensive list of publications and videos for sale at 17 rue Princesse Florestine, BP 359, MC 98007, Monaco. Prices include postage by airmail. Email to: headquarters@iaaf.org. Payment by credit card (Visa, Mastercard or eurocard only), quoting name on card, number of card, expiry date, name and address and signature.

AMENDMENTS TO ATHLETICS 2013

p.52-9 **Olympic Games.** Drugs dqs: 50km walk: (5) Yerokhin, Move up the rest and add 15. Horacio Nava MEX 3:46:59; W 800m: Drugs dq for (6). Arzhakova; DT: dq for: (2). Pishchalnikova confirmed, so move up all from 2. Liu Yanfeng; HT: (8) Marghieva, move rest up; Hep: (4) Yosypenko, move rest up. Medal table and points to: USA 305, RUS 8-4-5 169.5, KEN 113, GER 95, CHN 1-1-4 75, UKR 42, FRA 41, CUB 1-1-2 26, CAN 22.5, POL 22, LTU 10, LAT 7, IND 4, BDI , SVK 3

p.69 **European Championships.** 800m: Drugs dq for (1). Arzhakova, move up 1. Sharp etc.; LJ: Drugs dq for (5). Melis Mey, move up Radevica etc., add 8. Svetlana Denyayeva RUS 6.40/0.3; Hep: Drugs dq for (2(. Yosypenko, move up Ikauniece etc. add 8. Ida Marcussen NOR 6073. Medal table and points to: GER 200.5, RUS 4-5-5 148.5, UKR 4-6-6 136.5, GBR 4-2-1 96, CZE 68.5, TUR 66.5, ESP 64, BLR 0-2-4 47, NOR 39, SWE 36, LAT 0-1-1 26, SVK 19.5, SUI 10. LTU 15, MDA 3

p.75 **Race Walking World Cup: 50k:** Drugs dq for (2). Igor Yerokhin, so move up the rest from Jared Tallent to 2nd, 15. Sergiy Budza UKR 3:53:02; **Teams**: 1. RUS 22, 2. CHN 33, 3. UKR 37, 4. MEX 49, 5. ESP 77, 6. KOR 82, 7. ITA 88, 8. POR 118, 9. BLR 122, 10. IND 122, 11. KAZ 154.

p.79 **European Cup Winter Throwing:** W HT: drugs dq (1). Z Marghieva.

p.87 **European Indoor Championships.** Women's 60m: (1). Naimova drugs dq, so 2-8 move up to 1-7; 60m hurdles: (1). Yanit drugs dq so move rest up 1-7. Medals and points: RUS 145, GBR 99.5, GER 61, FRA 4-3-2-91, UKR 3-0-1-55, ITA 1-2-2-52.5, BLR 1-1-2-40, IRL 0-0-3-21, NED 1-0-0-20, remove BUL from list; 13 nations won gold.

p.109 **1963 Lists:** 5000m 100th best 14:15.0.

p.138 **AUSTRALIA:** Champion 200m: Sean Wroe 21.44 (Davies drugs dq).

p.140 **BAHAMAS:** Champion 200m: Mackey 20.68.

p.189 **JAPAN:** Champion Mar: Horoyuki Horibata 2:08:24.

p.214 **RUSSIA.** Champion 10000m: Natalya Popkova 31:55.83 (drugs dq Grechishnikova).

p.241 **USA.** NCAA champion: HT: Alexander Ziegler GER 75.78.

2012 World Lists

Men
60m: 6.59 drugs dq Heidarpoor
100m: 10.27 Laryea-Airong
200m: 20.71w Seymour 2.9.89
800m: 1:43.81 Melly 24.3.94, 1:46.74 Mohammed Mainy MAR-J 12.11.93, 1:47.40 Homiyu Tesfaye, 1:47.43 Ahmed Mainy MAR 20.8.86 17 Aug, 1:47.45 Souleiman
1500m: 3:31.61 Seurei 27.3.84 (& 800m 1:45.67, 1000m 2:16.39), 3:36.65 Kamal Majdoubi; to drugs dq: 3:30.54 Laâlou (best to then 3:35.02+ 5 in 1M Oslo 7 Jun)
3000m: 7:43,50 Rop b. 17.7.92 so NOT Junior (and 5000m 13:01.91); 7:44.09 Conseslus Kipruto (and 3000mSt 8:03.49)
5000m: 13:22.46dq El Hachimi # 5.5.80 (and 10km 28:04, Mar 2:09:49)
10,000m: 28:14.36A Nicholas Togom KEN 17.2.92 14 Jun (from 28:27.1A), 28:33.35 Emerick 1.3.89

10km: 28:21 Abdosh 25.8.87
HMar: 59:11 at 20k 56:02 Kenneth Kipkemoi; (50) to (90) wrongly numbered; 61:15 Kendagor 19.9.84, 61:38 Joseph Aperumoi, 61:40 Hillary Bii KEN .85 21 Oct, 61:54 Phillip Kiplimo UGA 23.3.90 2 Sep
Mar: 2:07:01 Kimaiyo 2.9.90, 2:07:35 Kebede b. 17.2.81, 2:07:39 Getachew b. 30.4.90, 2:07:41 Tolossa 13.9.80 (and 25k/30k list), 2:07:57 Kiyeng 22.4.83. 2:10:14 Desta Gebrehiwet
3000mSt: delete 8:34.1A Hillary Kemboi
110mh: 13.78w Solomon Williams
HJ: 2.26i Siverio, 2.20 Ostrowski 15.6.92; Best out: 2.20 D Edwards. Juniors: 2.21i Dergachev add as best out: 2.20 2 NC Almaty 19 Jun, add 2.20 Muamer Aissa Barshim QAT-J 3.1.94 11 DL Doha 11 May, delete 2.20 Chen Hangqi not junior
PV: 5.70 Yang Yancheng
LJ: (31+2w/18) perfs. 8.10 Kuznetsov 17.7.86, L Williams 20.12.87, 7.94 Kumar 6.2.93; Juniors: 7.76w Anouman; delete 7.88w Kim Sang-su
TJ: 16.86i Tsapik 1 Mogilyov 26 Feb (16.82 best out), 16.28 1.1 Charles le Roux 25 Feb & 16.34Aw 3.3 17 Mar, 16.27 DeJongh 12.3.90
SP: 19.11 Davis 11.9.90, 18.96 Garrett 21.12.90, 18.51 Irwin 2.6.92 (& DT 58.18)
DT: 61.25 Cuesta 1 Miranda Ebro 21 Jun, 59.05 Plummer 19.8.90
JT: 81.84 Amb 31.7.90
4x400m: delete 3:04.05 VEN
10,000m: 40:12.90 Ivanov 25.4.93
30km/35kmW: Move to drugs disqualification Igor Yerokhin 2:08:19/2:32:24 and adjust placings to 6/7/8 at NC-w Sochi for Yargunkin etc.
50kmW: Move to drugs disqualification Igor Yerokhin 3:37:54 and 3:38:10, and adjust all placings in WCp from 3rd and OG from 6th up a place. 3:58:57 Moreno 10 Dudince 24 Mar.

Women
100m: 11.18/11.05w T Williams ¶ (& 200m 22.45), 11.30A R Thomas (best la 11.41 23 Jun, 11.32w 4.8 2 Wichita 14 Apr), 11.37A K Thomas (& Jnrs), 11.37A Allen
200m: delete 23.26w Purvis
400m: 51.60 drugs dq Saka
600m/800m/1000m/1500m: drugs dq Arzhakova 1:26.9 /1:57.67/2:36.69i/4:00/82.
800m: 1:58.55 Markelova 1h4, 1:59.03 Cherkasova 3, 1:59.54 Akkaoui 6, 1:59.90 Soboleva 8, 2:00.24 Martynova 9=, 2:00.52 Sharp 1, move (70) to (90) down a position
1500m: (31/20), 4:13.08 Winslow 10.12.90; to drugs dq 3:59.89 Gorbunova & 4:00.82 Arzhakova
5000m: 15:21.36 mx Aga, 15:43.0A Wanjiku 29.9.88
10000m: 32:25.43 Wellings 20, 32:58.73 Kellner 4.8.91, 33:01.03 Gregg 21.1.87; 31:07.88 Grechishnikova to drugs dq, move up rest in this NC
HMar: 71:12 Chepkemoi
Mar: 2:24:17 Agai 10.6.88 (& 10,000m 32:47.67A), 2:24:27 Barsosio 5.8.82 (& 10k 31:51, HMar 70:25), 2:26L:41A Biwott move to drugs dq
3000mSt: 10:06.58 Mattox 27.11.88; & Jnrs: 10:11.2A Phanice Chemutai UGA-Y 2.2.95 1 Kitale 7 Apr. 10:14.8A Betaw Y 27.12.96
400m: 57.14 Adekoya 16.1.93, so remove from Juniors; delete 58.03 K Harrison
PV: 4.31 Riebold, 4.15 Karlee Coffee 25.1.81; best out: 4.21A Bartnovskaya

LJ: 6.49 Morrison 5.8.90, 6.45i Marincu 8.4.96
SP: 16.58 Öztürk ¶
DT: (31/6), 64.45 Tan Jian CHN 20.1.88 2 Werfer
Wiesbaden 12 May; Drugs disqualification confirmed
for Pishchalnikova (from 20 May)
HT: drugs dq 74.47 Z Marghieva; 71.16 Safránlová 3
JT: 56.96 Andraud 1 Lons-le-Saunier 2 Jun (from 56.52)
4x100m: 44.57 NOR 24 May
4x400m: delete 3:34.36 LBR
20kW: (30/22) after 1:28:30 Vasilyeva, 1:33:41 Pinedo
14 Lugano 18 Mar (not 1:33:15 but 1:35:12 on 4 Mar)

Amendments to World Indoor Lists 2013
2000m: 5:02.06+ Caleb Ndiku, 5:02.27+ Galen Rupp
21 Feb; **3000m**: 7:39.59 Rop b. 17.7.92; **60mh**: 7.57
Balnuweit 2s2 1 Mar, 7.67 Swift 24 Feb; **5000mW**:
19:15.50 Pyotr Trofimov 12 Jan; **Women: 60m**: drugs
dq 7.10 Naimova, 7.12 Lalova 3, 7.14 Schippers 4,
400m: 51.27 Hejnová & 52.12 Rosolová 2 Mar; **800-
1500m**: delete Arzhakova 800m 2:01.04,1000m 2:36.69,
1500m 4:09.15 (loses 7th World Indoor 1500m); **1000m**:
drugs dq 2:38.86 Shevchenko; **60mh**: 7.89 drugs dq
Yanit, amend Talay, Borsi, O'Rourke to 1-2-3 at EI, but
Talay's time was 7.94 and she has 7.94 1 Val-de-Reuil
12 Feb; 7.96 Tiffani McReynolds. **PV**: 4.45 Riebold, 4.42
Malácová 2 Feb; **3000mW**: 21:37.09 Olga Suranova
RUS 7.12.86 2 & 21:40.41 Marina Pandakova 3 both
Novocheboksarsk 12 Jan
Change from 1 Mar to 2 Mar: 400m o/s: 45.92 Spratling,
46.05 Giesting; 3000m: 7:47.91# Lelei; HJ: 2,26 Harris.

Amendments to Previous World Lists
2011: LJ: 7.84 Vasiliy Kopeykin RUS 9.3.88 1 Jun;
Drugs dq for Igor Yerokhin, so move to footnote his
35kP 2:26:36 and 50kW 3:49:05 (and loses European
Cup 2nd place, p.76); W 200m: 22.94 -0.6 Montsho;
400m: 51.53 drugs dq Saka; Yelena Arzhakova: drugs
dq 800m 1:58.77 (replace by 1:59.56 1h3 NC-23
Yerino 24 Jun & 1:59.35i 2 NC Moskva 17 Feb), 1500m
4:07.69 (replace by 4:10.88 2 Znam Zhukovskiy 3 Jul &
4:08.81i 2 NC Moskva 18 Feb); Yeketerina Gorbunova:
drugs dq 4:01.02 (replace by 4:07.04 4 Moskva 9 Jul);
5000: 15:02.38 drugs dq Grechishnikova; HT: drugs dq
72.93 Z Marghieva; move up to 71.33 1 Orbán, 69.37
Hao 3;
2010: 100: 9.88 1.0 Dix; PV: 5.50 Dmitriy Golovtsov
1 Yaroslavl 15 May (from 5.40); 10,000mW: 40:38.74
Érick Barrondo GUA 14.6.91 19 Nov; 20kmW: 1:23:16A
Barrondo 1 Ciudad de Guatemala 19 Dec; W 5000:
15:14.19 drugs dq Grechishnikova; HT: drugs dq 71.50
Z Marghieva
2009: W 3000m indoor: 8:42.56+i Meskerem Assefa
ETH 20.9.85 2 in 5k Stockholm 18 Feb 09
2008: HJ: Best outdoors: 2.27 Mason 1 Kalamáta 4 Jun
(delete at 2.30)
2007: W LJ: 6.90 drugs dq Kotova 6.90 on 29 Jun, but
6.90 on 28 Aug OK, 7.10w drugs dq; 6.72 Pyatykh (4),

6.54 Chernushenko (6), HT: Drugs dq: Kuzenkova 72.36
(after ban 66.56 22q WCh Osaka 28 Aug)
2006: Drugs dq: Bilonog SP 20.84 (after ban 19.96 2
Padova 1 Sep), DT 62.67; W LJ: drugs dq Kotova all
marks, 6.71 Trybanska (2)
2006 Indoor lists: W LJ: Drugs dq 7.00 Kotova
(Madison, Gomes and Montaner to 1-2-3)
2005: Drugs dq: Bilonog SP 20.93, DT 64.97; W SP:
Krivelyova 20.24, DT: Yatchenko 60.25; W LJ: Drugs dq:
Kotova LJ perfs 6.87, 6.83 & 6.79; Udmurtova 6.81 (1),
Barber 6.76w (2), 6.75 George (1)
2004: SP: 21.18 drugs dq Bilonog (earlier 20.88 1 ECCp
Moskva 29 May); W SP: Krivelyova her 19.49 dq
1993: 4x800m: 7:11.42 BLR team was: Andrew Sudnik,
Azat Rakipi, Anatoly Makarevich, Ivan Komar 1 EurR
Portsmouth 5 Jun

Championships Medal Changes
Drugs dqs – move rest up accordingly
2012: Europeans: W 1500m: (4) Gorbunova
2011: European U23: Arzakova from 1st 800m & 1500m,
move up 2/3 to 1/2 and add 800m: 3. Aleksandra
Bulanova RUS 2:01.40, 1500m: add 3. Katarzyna
Broniatowska POL 4:22.06; 5000m: (2) Gorbunova, so
2. Stockton, 3. Clémence Calvin FRA 16:02.07; **Worlds**:
SP: (3) Mikhnevich; W 5000m: (14) Grechishnikova; HT:
(8) Z Marghieva; **European Team**: SP: (3) Mikhnevich;
World University Games: W 1500m: dq Gorbunova so
3. Denise Krebs GER 4:07.70; HT: dq Marghieva, so 1
Orbán, 2 Perie, 3 Hao Shuai CHN 69.37
2010: World Indoors: SP: (2) Mikhnevich; **Europeans**:
SP: (1) Mikhnevich, W 5000m: (8/6) Grechishnikova
2008: Olympics SP: (3) Mikhnevich
2007: Worlds: SP: (3) Mikhnevich; **European Cup**: W LJ:
(2) Kotova (p.77)
2006: World Indoors: SP: (2) Mikhnevich; W LJ: dq
(1) Kotova move 2-8 up to 1-7 on p.605 2006 Annual);
Europeans: SP: (2) Mikhnevich; **European Cup**: W LJ:
(1) Kotova (p.83)
2005: World Champs: W LJ: (2) Kotova (p.68), SP (1)
Ostapchuk; **World Athletics Final**: W LJ: (1) Kotova
(p.89)
2004: Olympics: HT: (2) Tikhon.

*Thanks to José María García, Ed Gordon, Juan Mari
Iriondo, Winfried Kramer, Yves Pinaud, Bernt Solaas*

Add to banned/suspended athletes
To add to pages 100-101 (Drugs bans)
Leading athletes noted in early 2014 as being suspended:
Men
William Frulliani ITA	18 Feb	
Abdellah Haidane ITA	26 Feb	P
Women		
Svetlana Biryukova RUS	26 Feb	P
Anca Heltne ROU	16 Feb	P

Add to Records set outdoors in 2014
MEN
100	W20=	10.01	Trayvon BROMELL	USA	Austin		29 Mar 14
WOMEN							
20kW	NAm	1:30:41	Rachel SEAMAN	CAN	Manchester USA		30 Mar 14

EVENT DOMINANCE

AT THE END of 2014, Sergey Bubka had the top 15 marks on the world all-time performance list for pole vault, those marks, the last of them 20 years ago, sitting above Steve Hooker's 6.06i in 2009. This was the greatest current dominance currently for any athletics event. But in the 2014 indoor season Renaud Lavillenie jumped first 6.08 and then took Bubka's world record with a clearance at 6.16. But Bubka maintains his dominance as of the 29 performances at 6.05 or higher he has 24, Laveillenie 2 and Hooker, Maksim Tarasov and Dmitriy Markov 1 each.

The greatest ever dominance at a track and field event is that established by Iolanda Balas of Romania, who won 150 successive women's high jump competitions from 1957 to 1967 and set 14 world records from 1.75 in 1956 to 1.91 in 1961. On 22 June 1958 at Cluj she became the first women to clear 1.80m and before the next women – Michele Brown on 27 Sep 1964 – cleared that height, Balas had 80 competitions at that height or higher.

Before Bubka, the greatest ever domination at a men's event was also in the pole vault – by Cornelius 'Dutch' Warmerdam. On 12 April 1940 at Berkeley, California he became the first man to clear 15ft/4.57m (from the previous world record of 4.54). This was the first of his seven world records (three ratified) outdoors up to 4.77 on 23 May 1942 and five indoor world bests, two of which were absolute records, up to his final mark of 4.79 on 20 March 1943 in Chicago, a mark that remained the best with a bamboo pole. From 1941 to 1944 he totalled 43 clearances at 15ft or higher in 33 competitions and nobody else vaulted that height until Bob Richards went over 4.59/15ft 1in indoors in New York on 27 Jun 1951.

The table below shows, event by event, the athletes with the most marks in the current top 100 world all-time lists. Also shown are athletes particularly dominant at the top of the lists – thus Usain Bolt has 7 of the top 15 100m marks and Natalya Lisovskaya the best four in the women's shot. As can be seen, Yelena Isinbayeva has the greatest dominance at her event, with Heike Drechsler, Sergey Bubka and Ilona Slupianek all having 40 or more marks in their event top 100s, even long after the end of their careers.

Most performances in the top 100 (about) all-time performances at each event as at 28 February 2014.

Men

Event	To	No.	Leading athlete (s)
100m	9.86	105	Asafa Powell 26, Usain Bolt 25 (7 of top 15)
200m	19.87	103	Usain Bolt 21 (12 of 22)
400m	44.18	102	Michael Johnson 26 (12 of 20), Jeremy Wariner 20
800m	1:43.09	103	Wilson Kipketer 20, David Rudisha 15 (6 of 9)
1500m	3:30.22	100	Hicham El Guerrouj 36
5000m	13:54.83	100	Kenenisa Bekele 11
10000m	27:02.59	100	Kenenisa Bekele 11
Mar	2:06:08	102	Haile Gebrselassie 6
3000mSt	8:03.17	100	Paul K.Koech 27
110mh	13.03	102	Allen Johnson 15
400mh	47.69	104	Edwin Moses 26
HJ	2.38	108	Javier Sotomayor 30 (21 of 41 at 2.40 or more)
PV	5.98	99	Sergey Bubka 45 (all of these at 6m or more)
LJ	8.54	105	Carl Lewis 31 (6 of 9)
TJ	17.68	107	Jonathan Edwards 21 (5 of 7)
SP	22.04	103	Ulf Timmermann 17
DT	69.91	102	Virgilijus Alekna 22
HT	82.92	100	Yuriy Sedykh 19 (9 of 14), Sergey Litvinov I 18
JT (new)	89.60	100	Jan Zelezny (top 5, 17 of 29)
Dec	8607	100	Dan O'Brien 12
20kW	1:18:45	100	Francisco J. Fernández 7
50kW	3:41:20	101	Denis Nizhegorodov 6

Track events - outdoors only. Wind-legal marks only

Women

Event	To	No.	Leading athlete (s)
100m	10.84	109	Marion Jones 25
200m	22.01	104	Merlene Ottey 17
400m	49.34	101	Marita Koch 22 (5 of 7)
800m	1:56.36	101	Maria Mutola 15
1500m	3:58.3	100	Maricica Puica 5
5000m	14:37.20	100	Meseret Defar & Tirunesh Dibaba 14
10000m	30:48.51	100	Tirunesh Dibaba 7
Mar	2:22:36	100	Paula Radcliffe 5 (1st 3), Catherine Ndereba 5
3000mSt	9:17.85	100	Milcah Chemos 15
100mh	12.47	103	Yordanka Donkova 22 (13 of 28)
400mh	53.36	103	Lashinda Demus, Kim Batten & Deon Hemmings 12
HJ	2.04	109	Stefa Kostadinova 33, Blanka Vlasic 27
PV	4.81	99	Yelena Isinbayeva 54 (24 of 30 4.90 or more)
LJ	7.21	105	Heike Drechsler 47
TJ	14.99	105	Tatyana Lebedeva 29
SP	21.54	101	Ilona Slupianek 41, Natalya Lisovskaya 22 (top 4), Helena Fibingerová 21
DT	70.88	101	Diana Gansky 22
HT	75.73	100	Betty Heidler 24, Tatyana Lysenko 22
JT (new)	66.91	102	Christina Obergföll 26, Barbora Spotáková 23
Hep	6667	100	Jackie Joyner-Kersee 16 (top 6)
20kW	1:27:34	101	Olympiada Ivanova 9

HALL OF FAME 2014

WE STARTED a Hall of Fame in ATHLETICS 2001. Five athletes are added each year – a mix of past and current stars. Prior to this year 86 athletes have been included (there was a bumper selection in ATHLETICS 2003 following a survey of the best athletes for each event).

Current stars are only included if they have already had at least ten years in international competition and this year we include two who fulfil that criteria. Meseret Defar follows our inclusion last year of her great rival Tirunesh Dibaba and the head-to-head record of these two marvellous women distance runners is shown. Usain Bolt has also now celebrated a decade in world class, as he was first ranked in the world top ten for 200m in 2003, having won the World Junior gold medal in 2002. Surely no one can doubt his pre-eminence amongst the great sprinters of all-time. To accompany these modern stars we include Janis Lusis, who was ranked number one in the world for javelin nine times, was European champion four times and won the 1968 Olympic title and two great women sprinters of the 1980s and 1990s, Evelyn Ashford and Marie-José Pérec.

Evelyn ASHFORD (USA) (b. 15 April 1957 Shreveport, Louisiana) The diminutive (1.65m 52kg) Ashford was in the forefront of women's sprinting for a time unparalleled until Merlene Ottey, her span of Olympic competition running from 1976, when she was fifth in the 100m, to 1992 when she was a semi-finalist and won a third successive sprint relay gold medal. She won the individual 100m in 1984 and the silver medal in 1988; and her four Olympic gold medals tied the then US Olympic record for any sport. At 100m with auto timing she ran 33 sub-11 second times (including 10 wind assisted), with five US records and world records of 10.79 at Colorado Springs in 1983 and 10.76 at Zürich in 1984 (when she beat her great rival Marlies Göhr 10.84).

She ran the 200m less often, but set four US records to 21.83 in 1979, and had seven years in the world top ten, with 27 successive finals wins 1978-86. She won the 100m and 200m double at the 1979 Pan-American Games and at the World Cups of 1979 and 1981. She was third at 100m in the World Championships of 1991, but had previously met with misfortune at this event, pulling up with a hamstring injury in the 1983 100m final and having to withdraw through injury in 1987 after qualifying at 200m. She studied at UCLA and was US champion at 100m 1977, 1979 and 1981-3; 200m 1977-9, 1981 and 1983.

World indoor bests: 50y: 5.77 and 5.74 (1983), 60y: 6.54 (1982). Other bests: 60m 7.15i (1990), 400m 51.08 (1984).

Janis Voldemarovits **LUSIS** (USSR/Latvia) b. 19 May 1939 Jelgava). Lusis was an outstanding javelin thrower who won four European titles between 1962 and 1971 and a complete set of Olympic medals – gold 1968, silver 1972, bronze 1964, before placing eighth in 1976. He won 12 USSR titles between 1962 and 1976, the World Student Games title in 1963, and in four European Cup Finals was first twice and second twice, for an outstandingly consistent record in a notoriously inconsistent event. A fine all-rounder, who was also a world-ranked decathlete (best of 7486 points in 1962 on the 1985 tables), he married the 1960 Olympic javelin champion, Elvira Ozolina.

He set his first Latvian record with 77.48m in 1961 and six USSR records from 86.04 in 1962 to world records of 91.98 in 1968 and 93.80 in 1972. He became a coach of javelin throwers in Latvia and the USSR, and with Elvira spent three years in Madagascar 1987-90. He was an Olympic team coach in 1980, 1992 and 2000, when his son Voldemars (b. 7 Dec 1974, pb new javelin 84.19 in 2003) competed for Latvia, as he did in 2004.

Marie-José PÉREC (France) (b. 9 May 1968 Basse Terre, Guadeloupe). Pérec won gold medals in each of her three Olympic finals in the 1990s and in the two World Championships finals she attempted. At her peak this superbly built sprinter (1.80m, 60kg) was a winner, but she had fragile legs, which hindered her in both 1993 and 1997, and, with five different coaches, the reputation of being a "diva". Nevertheless she is best remembered for her long raking stride and her championship dominance in the years from 1991 to 1996.

She won the Olympic 400m title at Barcelona 1992 in 48.82 and in Atlanta 1996 she preceded Michael Johnson by becoming the first person to win Olympic titles at both 200m and 400m at the same Games. She smashed her best time and the Olympic record with 48.25 in the 400m and three days later surprised the specialist sprinters by winning the 200m.

Born in the Caribbean, she moved to Paris with her mother at the age of 16, and made her Olympic debut at 200m in 1988. She won the European Indoor 200m in 1989 but was disqualified for breaking lane when winning the World Cup 400m in 50.30. She took European bronze at 200m in 1990, and had a great year at 400m in 1991 with French records of 50.53 and 49.32 in her first two races, then 49.76 to win in Nice and then 49.13 to win the world title. After her 1992 Olympic success she concentrated on 200m in 1993 when she was 4th in the World Champs. In 1994 she won European gold at 400m and 4x400m and regained her World

400m title in 1995. That year she also tried the 400m hurdles and showed immense potential with four French records to 53.25 and a win in the European Cup. By then she was training in Los Angeles with the celebrated John Smith. She ran a few sprints in 1997 and did not compete in 1998 due to the effects of a virus illness but returned in 1999, although not regaining enough form to go to the World Championships. Training for a while with Marita Koch's husband Wolfgang Meier, Pérec had just one race at 200m and one at 400m (3rd in Nice, her first at 400m for three years) in 2000 and went to Sydney but fled from there when confronted with the pressure of the much-hyped intended clash with Cathy Freeman at 400m.

French titles: 100m 1991, 200m 1992, 1995; 400m 1988, 400m hurdles 1989. Other best times: 60m 7.29i (1992), 100m 10.96 (1991), 200m 21.99 (1993).

Usain St. Leo **BOLT** (Jamaica) (b. 21 Aug 1986 Sherwood Content, Trelawny). "Lightning Bolt", an imposing figure at 1.96m tall and 86kg,

Meseret Defar v Tirunesh Dibaba

Date	Meet	Venue	Defar	Dibaba
3000m				
30.8.02	VD	Bruxelles	8:40.28- 10	8:41.86- 11
1.2.03		Boston (R)	8:57.22- 1	8:58.75- 3
1.7.03	Athl	Lausanne	8:43.36- 2	8:50.20- 5
20.2.04	GP	Birmingham	8:33.44- 1	8:33.56- 2
10.9.06	WAF	Stuttgart	8:34.22- 1	8:34.74- 2
5000m				
21.7.02	WJ	Kingston	15:54.94- 1	15:55.99- 2
25.1.03		Boston	15:36.69- 1	15:40.68- 2
10.5.03	NC	Addis Ababa	16:17.5A- 2	16:01.5A- 1
17.5.03	adidas	Gresham	14:59.88- 1	15:01.44- 2
27.6.03	Bisl	Oslo	14:43.46- 4	14:39.94- 3
11.7.03	GGala	Roma	14:40.34- 1	14:41.97- 4
11.10.03	AfG	Abuja	16:42.0- 1	16:43.4- 4
30.10.03	AfAsG	Hyderabad	15:47.69- 1	15:48.21- 2
31.1.04	BIG	Boston	14:53.14- 1	14:53.99- 2
11.6.04	Bisl	Oslo	14:58.79- 6	14:30.88- 2
2.7.04	GGala	Roma	14:44.81- 3	14:47.43- 4
23.8.04	OG	Athína	14:45.65- 1	14:51.83- 3
8.7.05	GGala	Roma	14:32.90- 3	14:32.57- 1
13.8.05	WCh	Helsinki	14:39.54- 2	14:38.59- 1
9.9.05	WAF	Monaco	14:45.87- 1	14:46.84- 2
8.7.06	GL	Saint-Denis	14:54.30- 2	14:54.24- 1
14.7.06	GGala	Roma	14:53.51- 2	14:52.37- 1
10.8.06	AfCh	Bambous	15:56.00- 1	15:56.04- 2
25.8.06	VD	Bruxelles	14:33.78- 2	14:30.63- 1
3.9.06	ISTAF	Berlin	15:02.51- 1	15:02.87- 2
9.9.06	WAF	Stuttgart	16:04.78- 2	16:04.76- 1
22.8.08	OG	Beijing	15:44.12- 3	15:41.40- 1
12.9.09	WAF	Thessaloníki	15:25.31- 1	15:25.92- 2
9.6.12	DL	New York	14:57.02- 2	14:50.80- 1
10.8.12	OG	London	15:04.25- 1	15:05.15- 3
29.8.13	WK	Zürich	14:32.83- 1	14:34.82- 2
5km road				
7.4.02		Carlsbad	15:58- 11	15:19- 2
13.4.03		Carlsbad	15:19- 5	15:00- 3
Half Marathon				
15.9.13	GNR	South Shields	66:09- 2	66:56- 3

Overall 21-13 to Defar: Defar 5-0 at 3000m, 15-11 at 5000m, 1-0 at Half Mar; Dibaba 2-0 at 5km.

was a junior phenomenon and in 2008 proved to be the super-star of the Beijing Olympic Games as he swept to the unique feat of winning the sprint treble with world records in each final. He has gone on to transcend the world of track and field athletics to be a world superstar, adding eight World titles and repeating his Olympic treble in 2012.

He won the IAAF 'Rising Star' award for men in 2002 and in 2003. From a best time for 200m of 21.73 in 2001, he ran 20.61 to win the 2002 CAC U17 title and became the youngest ever male world junior champion at 15 years 332 days, having set a world age best with 20.58 in his heat. In 2003 he was undefeated and ran a 2003 world U18 record of 20.13 to win the Pan-American Junior title after taking the World Youth title; he was Jamaican senior champion but did not meet any of the world elite. He also ran a startling 45.35 in his only major race at 400m in 2003 and has run a 44.4 400m relay leg. Still only 17 years of age, he set a world junior record of 19.93 to win the Caribbean Junior title in April 2004. He was then injured and did not compete again until the Olympics, when he went out in his heat. Still a junior he won the CAC title in 20.01 and ran 19.99 in 2005 just before the World Championships but there came in 8th in the 200m final after pulling up with an injury. From then it has been a triumphant progress.

Meseret DEFAR (Ethiopia) has won more Global titles over 3000/5000 than any other athlete. To go with her 2004 Olympic title and World titles in 2007 and 2013, she won the World indoor title four times between 2004 and 2010. Having won a silver medal in the 2000 World Junior 5000m, Defar dominated the junior ranks in 2002 with gold medals in the 3000 and 5000. Failure to qualify for the final of the 2003 World Championships meant that Defar was first reserve for the Olympic 5000 team for Ethiopia until Ejegayehu Dibaba opted for the 10,000m. She proceeded to win a bizarrely paced race which enabled her to win by 20m with a last lap of 68.5 seconds. Defar next won gold at the 2007 Worlds with a final lap of 58.2 seconds, having taken silver behind Dibaba in 2005.

At 1.55m Defar has found indoor racing with its sharp turns very much to her liking. Forays into 10,000m running have been less successful, although she did produce the world's fastest time in 2009 before having her legs turn to glue in the last 50m of the World Championships, and she was easily the fastest again in 2013. She turned to the half marathon in 2010, running 67:45, improving to 66:09 in 2013. She has also won a record nine World Athletics Finals races: six at 3000m and three at 5000m.

See Biographies for details of Bolt and Defar.

Bohdan Bondarenko.

Aleksandr Menkov.

Hall
of
Fame

Yelena Isinbayeva won her ninth global title and entered our Hall of Fame.

Zuzana Hejnová was perfect over the hurdles in 2013.

Brianna Rollins won all her 34 races in 2013.

Mohammed Aman takes World 800m gold. Immediately behind him are Nick Symmonds (USA, 2nd) and Ayanleh Souleiman (3rd).

Priscah Jeptoo won both London and New York Marathons and was seen at her best in winning the Great North Run.

Teddy Tamgho

Svetlana Shkolina

Caterine Ibargüen.

NATIONAL CHAMPIONS 2013
and BIOGRAPHIES OF LEADING ATHLETES
By Peter Matthews

THIS SECTION incorporates biographical profiles of 796 of the world's top athletes, 420 men and 376 women, listed by nation. Also listed are national champions at standard events in 2013 for the leading countries prominent in athletics (for which I have such details).

The athletes profiled have, as usual, changed quite considerably from the previous year , not only that all entries have been updated, but also that many newcomers have been included to replace those who have retired or faded a little from the spotlight. The choice of who to include is always invidious, but I have concentrated on those who are currently in the world's top 10-15 per event, those who have the best championship records and some up-and-coming athletes who I consider may make notable impact during the coming year.

Since this section was introduced in the 1985 Annual, biographies have been given for a total of 4409 different athletes (2509 men and 1900 women).

The ever continuing high turnover in our sport is reflected in the fact that there are many newcomers to this section (135 in all, 71 men, 64 women), as well as 12 athletes (5 men, 7 women) reinstated from previous Annuals. So, as even bigger change than usual. The athletes to have had the longest continuous stretch herein are Haile Gebrselassie 21 years, Jesús Ángel García 20 years, Virgilijus Alekna and Szymon Ziółkowski 18 years. Athletes who have retired have generally been omitted.

No doubt some of those dropped from this compilation will also again make their presence felt; the keen reader can look up their credentials in previous Annuals, and, of course, basic details may be in the athletes' index at the end of this book.

Athletes included in these biographies are identified in the index at the end of this Annual by * for those profiled in this section and by ^ for those who were included in previous Annuals.

The biographical information includes:
a)   Name, date and place of birth, height (in metres), weight (in kilograms).
b)   Previous name(s) for married women; club or university; occupation.
c)   Major championships record – all placings in such events as the Olympic Games, World Championships, European Championships, Commonwealth Games, World Cup and Continental Cup; leading placings in finals of the World Indoor Championships, European or World Junior Championships, European Under-23 Championships and other Continental Championships; and first three to six in European Indoors or World University Games. European Cup/Team Champs and IAAF Grand Prix first three at each event or overall. World Athletics Final (WAF) and Diamond League series (DL) winners
d)   National (outdoor) titles won or successes in other major events.
e)   Records set: world, continental and national; indoor world records/bests (WIR/WIB).
f)   Progression of best marks over the years at each athlete's main event(s).
g)   Personal best performances at other events.
h)   Other comments.
See Introduction to this Annual for lists of abbreviations used for events and championships.

Information given is as known at 1 April 2014 (to include performances at the World Indoor Championships and some other early indoor and outdoor events of 2014).

I am most grateful to various ATFS members who have helped check these details. Additional information or corrections would be welcomed for next year's Annual.

Peter Matthews

ALGERIA

Governing body: Fédération Algerienne d'Athlétisme, BP n°61, Dely-Ibrahim 160410, Alger. Founded 1963.
National Champions 2013: Men: 100m/LJ: Ali Bouguesba 10.66/7.43, 200m/400m: Miloud Laaredj 21.43/46.89. 800m: Mohamed Belbachir 1:49.50, 1500m: Abderrahmane Anou 3:42.66, 5000m: Abdelghani Bensaadi 14:04.04, 3000mSt: Bilal Tabti 8:32.32, 110mh: Othman Hadj Lazib 14.01, 400mh: Admelmalik Lahoulou 51.30, HJ: Kamel Rabia 2.13, TJ: Lauhab Kafia 16.47, 20kW: Hicham Medjber 1:26:01; **Women**: 100m/200m: Souheir Bouali 11.79/23.88, 400m/400mh: Dihia Haddar 55.18/59.01, 800m/1500m: Amina Betiche 2:09.54/4:21.62, 5000m: Souiad Aït Salem 16:07.58, 3000mSt: Hadjer Soukhal 10:39.57, LJ: Khadidja Ammour 6.02, TJ: Baya Rahouli 13.83, HT: Zouina Bouzebra 56.92, 20kW: Bariza Ghezalani 1:49:01.

Taoufik MAKHLOUFI b. 29 Apr 1988 Souk Ahras 1.76m 70kg.
At (800m)/1500m: OG: '12- 1; WCh: '09/11- sf; AfG: '11- 1/3; AfCh: '10- h, '12- (1).
Progress at 800m, 1500m: 2008- 3:43.4, 2009- 1:49.40, 3:34.34; 2010- 1:48.39, 3:32.94; 2011- 1:46.32, 3:34.4; 2012- 1:43.71, 3:30.80; 2013- 3:36.30. pb 1M 3:52.94 '13.

ARGENTINA

Governing body: Confederación Argentina de Atletismo, 21 de Noviembre No. 207. 3260 Concepción del Uruguay, Entre Ríos. Founded 1954 (original governing body founded 1919).
National Championships first held in 1920 (men), 1939 (women). **2013 Champions: Men**: 100m/200m: Lucas Semino 10.84/21.90, 400m: Fabio Martínez 48.12, 800m: Franco Díaz 1:50.82, 1500m: Federico Bruno 3:51.72, 5000m: Miguel Ángel Bárzola 14:24.27, 10,000m/HMar: Mariano Mastromarino 29:47.69/67:02, Mar: Luis Ariel Molina 2:22:34, 3000mSt: Joaquín Arbe 9:04.59, 110mh: Agustín Carrera 14.65, 400mh: Emiliano Suárez 53.16, HJ: Carlos Layoy 2.10, PV: Germán Chiaraviglio 5.20, LJ: Mauricio Romero 7.07, TJ: Maximiliano Díaz 16.09, SP/DT: Germán Lauro 20.56/58.57, HT: Juan Cerra 67.86, JT: Braian Toledo 78.11, Dec: Román Andrés Gastaldi 7262, 20,000W: Juan Manuel Cano 1:22:46.5. **Women**: 100m/200m: Victoria Woodward 12.09/25.05, 400m: María Ayelén Diogo 56.57, 800m: Mariana Borelli 2:08.51, 1500m: Belén Casetta 4:30.04, 5000m: Rosa Godoy 16:44.23, 10,000m: Nadia Rodríguez 33:41.20, HMar: María Peralta 78:16, Mar: Karina Neipán 2:45:10, 3000St: Carolina Lozano 11:15.94, 100mh: Noelina Madarieta 14.97, 400mh: Belén Casetta 62.59, HJ: Valeria Paz 1.60, PV: Valeria Chiaraviglio 4.10, LJ: Fiorella Chiappe 5.61, TJ: Paula Pitzinger 11.75, SP/DT: Rocío

Comba 14.21/54.41, HT: Daniela Gómez 55.49, JT: Bárbara López 54.02, Hep: Augustina Zerboni 5243, 20,000W: Florencia Thomas 1:56:57.2.

Germán LAURO b. 2 Apr 1984 Trenque Lauquen, Buenos Aires 1.85m 127kg. Ferro Carril Oeste.
At SP/(DT): OG: '08- dnq 31, '12- 6/dnq 37; WCh: '07-09-11: dnq 23/ nt/20; 13- 7; WI: '12- 6; PAm: '07- 5/4, '11- 3; SACh: '05-06-07-09-11-13: 4/1/1&1/1&1/1&2/1&1. Won S.AmG 2014, IbAm SP & DT 2012; ARG SP 2005-13, DT 2007-13.
Shot Records: 6 South American indoor 2012-14; 13 Argentinian 2006-13.
Progress at SP: 2001- 15.24, 2002- 15.14, 2003- 16.87, 2004- 17.79, 2005- 18.17, 2006- 19.78, 2007- 19.67, 2008- 19.88, 2009- 19.20, 2010- 20.43, 2011- 20.42, 2012- 20.84, 2013- 21.26, 2014- 21.04i. pb DT 63.55 '12. 6th in 2012 was best Argentinian placing at Olympics for 56 years.

Women

Jennifer DAHLGREN b. 21 Apr 1984 Buenos Aires 1.80m 115kg. Studied English teaching at the University of Georgia
At HT: OG: '04-08-12: dnq 22/29/nt; WCh: '05-07-09-13: dnq nm/24/17/17, '11- 9; WJ: '00- dnq 23, 02- 5; WY: '01- 4; PAm: '07- 3, '11- 6; SACh: '05-06-09-11-13: 1/1/3/1/3; CCp: '10- 5; Won SAm-J 2000, PAm-J 2003, NCAA 2006-07, IbAm 2010, ARG 2008-09, 2011-12.
14 South American hammer records 2004-10.
Progress at HT: 1999- 46.36, 2000- 56.68, 2001- 57.18, 2002- 59.48, 2003- 61.60, 2004- 66.12, 2005- 67.07, 2006- 72.01, 2007- 72.94, 2008- 66.38, 2009- 72.79, 2010- 73.74, 2011- 73.44, 2012- 72.79, 2013- 72.74. pbs: SP 15.54i '04, 15.03 '03; DT 44.28 '03, Wt 24.04i '06 (S.Am rec).
Her mother Irene Fitzner competed at 100m at the 1972 Olympics and was 2nd in the South American 100m in 1971.

AUSTRALIA

Governing body: Athletics Australia, Suite 22, Fawkner Towers, 431 St.Kilda Rd, Melbourne, Victoria 3004. Founded 1897.
National Championships first held in 1893 (men) (Australasian until 1927), 1930 (women). **2013 Champions: Men**: 100m/200m: Joshua Ross 10.34/20.57, 400m: Alex Beck 46.18, 800m: Alex Rowe 1:50.25, 1500m: James Kaan 3:46.29, 5000m: Cameron Page 13:29.45, 10,000m: Collis Birmingham 27:56.22, HMar: Martin Dent 63:56, Mar: Matthew Cox 2:29:13, 3000mSt: James Nipperess 8:49.39, 110mh: Justin Merlano 13.76, 400mh: Tristan Thomas 49.68, HJ: Brandon Starc 2.28, PV: Joel Pocklington 5.20, LJ: Fabrice Lapierre 8.00, TJ: Alwyn Jones 16.37, SP: Damien Birkenhead 19.27, DT: Julien Wruck 66.32, HT: Timothy Driesen 69.68, JT: Jarrod Bannister

79.68, Dec: Kyle McCarthy 7391, 5000mW/20kW: Dane Bird-Smith 19:25.21/1:25:43, 20kW: Jared Tallent 1:22:10, 50kW: Kim Mottram 4:28:12. **Women:** 100m: Ashleigh Whittaker 11.53, 200m: Monica Brennan 23.41, 400m: Caitlin Sargent 52.66, 800m: Kelly Hetherington 2:01.22, 1500m: Zoe Buckman 4:09.79, 5000m: Kaila McKnight 15:53.91, 10,000m/HMar: Nikki Chapple 32:56.25/71:00, Mar: Sharon Ryder 3:01:43, 3000mSt: Genevieve LaCaze 10:01.20, 100mh: Shannon McCann 13.41, 400mh: Lauren Boden 56.47, HJ: Eleanor Patterson 1.85, PV: Alana Boyd 4.30, LJ: Kerrie Perkins 6.43, TJ: Linda Leverton 13.68, SP: Kimberley Mulhall 14.99, DT: Alix Kennedy 55.76, HT: Lara Nielsen 58.25, JT: Kimberley Mickle 62.26, Hep: Ashleigh Hamilton 5369, 5000mW: Jess Rothwell 21:37.81, 20kW: Tanya Holliday 1:34:32/Kelly Ruddick 1:33:15.

Benn HARRADINE b. 14 Oct 1982 Newcastle, NSW 1.98m 115kg. Ringwood. Personal trainer.
At DT: OG: '08- dnq 31, '12- 9; WCh: '09- dnq 15, '11- 5, '13- dnq 20; CG: '06- 8, '10- 1; CCp: '10- 2. AUS champion 2007-08, 2010-12.
Five Oceania discus records 2008-13.
Progress at DT: 2000- 51.50, 2001- 54.76, 2002- 57.78, 2003- 55.25, 2004- 57.68, 2005- 63.65, 2006- 60.70, 2007- 62.99, 2008- 66.37, 2009- 64.97, 2010- 66.45, 2011- 66.07, 2012- 67.53, 2013- 68.20. pb SP 15.17 '05.

Steve HOOKER b. 16 Jul 1982 Melbourne 1.87m 85kg. Perth.
At PV: OG: '04- dnq 28=, '08- 1, '12- nh; WCh: '05-07-09-11: dnq 17=/9/1/dnq nh; CG: '06- 1, '10- 1; WJ: '00- 4; WI: '08- 3, '10- 1; WCp: '06- 1, '10- 1. AUS champion 2008, 2010.
Three Oceania indoor records 2007-09, two Commonwealth indoor records 2009.
Progress at PV: 1999- 5.00, 2000- 5.20, 2001- 5.30, 2002- 5.25, 2003- 5.45, 2004- 5.65, 2005- 5.87, 2006- 5.96, 2007- 5.91, 2008- 6.00, 2009- 6.06i/5.95, 2010- 6.01i/5.95, 2011- 5.60, 2012- 5.72, 2013- 5.40. pbs: 100m 10.82 '10, 10.6, 10.68w '05; 200m 21.1 '05, LJ 7.10 '05.
Suffering from an adductor injury, he took just one jump to qualify for the World final in 2009, and then was able to take just two jumps in the final, but he cleared 5.90 for the gold. Played Australian Rules football before taking up pole vaulting. Married Russian runner Yekaterina Kostetskaya (1 WJ 400mh 2004, 5 WCh 800m 2011) in 2012. His father Bill was 6th CG 800m 1974, pbs: 800m 1:45.36 '73, 400mh pb 50.6 '69, and his mother Erica (née Nixon) was 6th LJ, 4th Pen 1974 and 2nd LJ 1978 (in pb 6.58) at CG.

Jared TALLENT b. 17 Oct 1984 Ballarat 1.78m 60kg. Ballarat YCW. Graduate of University of Canberra.
At 20kW(/50kW): OG: '08- 3/2, '12- 7/2; WCh: '05- 18, '07- dq, '09- 6/7, '11- 26/3, 13- (3); CG: '06- 3, '10- 1; WCp: '06-08-10-12: 14/10/(3)/(2). At

10,000mW: WJ: '02- 19; WY: '01- 7. Won AUS 5000mW 2012, 20kW 2008-11, 2013; 30kW 2004, 50kW 2007, 2009, 2011.
Commonwealth 5000m walk record 2009.
Progress at 20kW, 50kW: 2002- 1:40:21, 2003- 1:31:24, 2004- 1:27:02, 2005- 1:22:53, 2006- 1:21:36, 3:55:08; 2007- 1:21:25, 3:44:45, 2008- 1:19:41, 3:39:27; 2009- 1:19:42, 3:38:56; 2010- 1:19:15, 3:54:55; 2011- 1:19:57, 3:43:36; 2012- 1:20:02, 3:36:53; 2013- 1:20:41, 3:40:03. pbs: 3000mW 11:15.07 '09, 5000mW 18:41.83 '09, 10,000mW 40:41.5 '06, 10kW 38:29 '10, 30kW 2:10:52 '13, 35kW; 2:32:37 '12.
Won IAAF Walks Challenge 2008 and 2013.
Married Claire Woods on 30 Aug 2008, she has 20kW pb 1:28:53 '12, 2 CG '10.

Mitchell WATT b. 25 Mar 1988 Bendigo, Victoria 1.84m 83kg. QE2 Track Club. Studying law and commerce at University of Queensland.
At LJ: OG: '12- 2; WCh: '09- 3, '11- 2; WI: '10- 3. Won AUS 2011, DL 2011.
Oceania long jump record 2011.
Progress at LJ: 2001- 6.32, 2002- 6.98, 2008- 7.97, 2009- 8.43, 2010- 8.16, 2011- 8.54, 2012- 8.28, 2013- 8.01. pb 100m 10.31 '11.
After playing Australian Rules football and rugby, he returned to athletics in 2008 and made rapid advance.

Julian WRUCK b. 6 Jul 1991 Brisbane 1.98m 125kg. Sports student at UCLA, previously Texas Tech, USA.
At DT: OG: '12- dnq 13; WCh: '13- 11; CG: '10- 8; WJ: '10- 3. AUS champion 2013, NCAA 2011 and 2013.
Progress at DT: 2008- 51.89, 2009- 54.74, 2010- 61.02, 2011- 65.74, 2012- 64.84, 2013- 68.16. pb SP 17.01 '13

Women

Zoe BUCKMAN b. 21 Dec 1988 Grafton, Melbourne 1.72m 55kg. Was at University of Oregon, USA.
At 1500m: OG: '12- sf; WCh: 13- 7; WJ: '06- 11 (sf 800m). AUS champion 2011, 2013.
Australian 1000m record 2012
Progress at 1500m: 2004- 4:31.47, 2005- 4:27.51mx/4:27.58, 2006- 4:19.96mx/4:20.24, 2007- 4:24.68, 2008- 4:20.57, 2009- 4:15.66, 2010- 4:12.80, 2011- 4:05.06, 2012- 4:05.03, 2013- 4:04.82. pbs: 400m 54.62 '04, 800m 2:00.93 '13, 1000m 2:37.84 '12, 1M 4:30.86 '12, 4:30.75 irr. '13; 2000m 5:39.17 '13, 3000m 8:58.0 '13.

Kimberley MICKLE b. 28 Dec 1984 Perth 1.69m 69kg. Mandurah/Rockingham.
At JT: OG: '12- dnq 17; WCh: '09- dnq 15, '11- 6, '13- 2; CG: '06- 4, '10- 2; WJ: '02- 9; WY: '01- 1; WCp: '06- 5, '10- 3. AUS champion 2005-07, 2009-13. Oceania javelin record 2014.
Progress at JT: 1999- 45.13, 2000- 45.76, 2001- 51.83, 2002- 52.77, 2003- 48.03, 2004- 50.38, 2005- 58.16, 2006- 58.56, 2007- 59.36, 2008- 57.64, 2009-

63.49, 2010- 61.36, 2011- 63.82, 2012- 64.12, 2013-66.60, 2014- 66.83.

Kathryn MITCHELL b. 10 Jul 1982 Hamilton, Victoria 1.68m 75kg. Eureka AC.
At JT: OG: '12- 9; WCh: '13- 5; CG: '06- 6, '10- 5; AUS champion 2008.
Progress at JT: 1999- 43.17, 2000- 51.44, 2001-54.98, 2002- 54.72, 2003- 57.11, 2004- 48.10, 2005-54.87, 2006- 58.81, 2007- 58.61, 2008- 58.77, 2010-59.68, 2011- 59.47, 2012- 64.34, 2013- 63.77, 2014-66.10.

Sally PEARSON b. 19 Sep 1986 Sydney 1.66m 60kg. née McLellan. Gold Coast Victory. Griffith University.
At (100m)/100mh: OG: '08- 2, '12- 1; WCh: '03-hR, '07- sf/sf, '09-11-13: 5/1/2; CG: '06- 7/fell/3R, '10- dq/1; WJ: '04- 3/4; WY: '03- 1; WCp: '06- 8/4, '10- 1. At 60mh: WI: '12- 1, '14- 2. AUS champion 100m & 100mh 2005-7, 2009, 2011; 200m 2011.
Records: Oceania 100mh (8) 2007-11, 60m 2009 & 60mh indoors (3) 2009-12; Commonwealth 100mh (2) 2011.
Progress at 100mh: 2003- 14.01, 2004- 13.30, 2005- 13.01, 2006- 12.95, 2007- 12.71, 2008- 12.53, 2009- 12.50, 2010- 12.57, 2011- 12.28, 2012- 12.35, 2013- 12.50. pbs: 60m 7.16 '11, 100m 11.14 '07, 150m 16.86 '10, 200m 23.02/22.66w '09, 300m 38.34 '09, 400m 53.86mx '11, 200mh 27.54 '06, 60mh 7.73i '12, 200mh 26.96 '09, 400mh 62.98 '07. Married Kieran Pearson on 3 April 2010. IAAF female Athlete of the Year 2011.

Dani SAMUELS b. 26 May 1988 Fairfield, Sydney 1.82m 82kg. Westfields, University of Western Sydney.
At DT/(SP): OG: '08- 9, '12- 11; WCh: '07-09-11-13: dnq 13/1/10/10; CG: '06- 3/12; WJ: '06- 1/7; WY: '05- 1/3; WCp: '06- 6; WUG: '07- 2, '09- 1; CCp: '10- 4. AUS champion SP 2006-07, 2009, 2012; DT 2005-11.
Progress at DT: 2001- 39.17, 2002- 45.52, 2003-47.29, 2004- 52.21, 2005- 58.52, 2006- 60.63, 2007-60.47, 2008- 62.95, 2009- 65.44, 2010- 65.84, 2011-62.33, 2012- 63.97, 2013- 64.46, 2014- 65.59. pbs: SP 17.05 '14, HT 45.39 '05.
Sisters Jamie and Casey played basketball for Australia.

AUSTRIA

Governing body: Österreichischer Leichtathletik Verband (OLV), 1040 Vienna, Prinz Eugenstrasse 12. Founded 1902.
National Championships first held in 1911 (men), 1918 (women). **2013 Champions: Men:** Benjamin Grill 10.56, 200m: Ekemini Bassey 21.69, 400m: Dominik Hufnagl 48.63, 800m: Günther Matzinger 1:51.78, 1500m: Andreas Vojta 4:02.21, 5000m: Christian Steinhammer 14:50.76, 10,000m: Thomas Rossmann 31:30.82, HMar: Günther Weidlinger 63:40, Mar: Roman Weger 2:20:09, 3000mSt: Christoph Sander 8:53.21, 110mh: Manuel Prazak 14.40, 400mh:

Thomas Kain 51.47, HJ: Manuel Leitner 2.00, PV: Paul Kilbertus 5.15, LJ: James Beckford JAM 7.56, TJ: Roman Schmied 15.48, SP: Lukas Weisshaidinger 18.24, DT: Gerhard Mayer 60.00, HT: Michael Hofer 54.33, JT: Matthias Kaserer 69.38, Dec: Severin Chum 6684, 20kW: Dietmar Hirschmugl 1:57:29, 50kW: Franz Kropik 5:09:27. **Women:** 100m/200m: Doris Röser 11.73/24.24, 400m/400mh: Verena Menapace 56.03/59.84, 800m: Elisabeth Niedereder 2:11.46, 1500m/5000m: Anita Baierl 4:40.87/17:11.64, 10,000m: Isabelle Heers GER 37:25.11, HMar: Andrea Mayr 75:07, Mar: Karin Freitag 2:46:04, 3000mSt: Stefanie Huber 10:42.88, 100mh: Linda Thoms 14.19, HJ: Monika Gollner 1.80, PV: Kira Grünberg 4.00, LJ: Marina Kraushofer 6.18, TJ: Michaele Egger 12.19, SP: Djeneba Touré 13.56, DT: Sonja Spendelhofer 46.43, HT: Claudia Stern 50.80, JT: Elisabeth Eberl 52.11, Hep: Stefanie Waldkircher 5154, 10kW/20kW: Kathrin Schultze 56:28/1:51:32.

Beate SCHROTT b. 15 Apr 1988 St. Pölten 1.77m 68kg. Union St. Pölten. Student.
At 100mh: OG: '12- 8; WCh: '11- sf; EC: '10- h, '12- 4; EU23: '09- sf; EJ: '07- h, At LJ: WJ: '06- dnq 23. At 60mh: WI: '12- 7. Won Austrian 100mh 2009-12.
Four Austrian 100mh records 2011-12.
Progress at 100mh: 2004- 15.55, 2005- 14.79, 2006- 14.34, 2007- 13.90, 2008- 13.72, 2009- 13.29, 2010- 13.55, 2011- 12.95, 2012- 12.82, 2013-12.87/12.84w. pbs: 60m 7.61i '11, 200m 25.59 '07, 300m 38.34 '09, 60mh 7.96i '13, LJ 6.10 '06.

AZERBAIJAN

Hayle IBRAHIMOV b. 18 Jan 1990 Mek'ele, Tigray, Ethiopia 1.68m 58kg. Baku.
At 5000m: OG: '12- 9; EC: '10- 3, '12- 6; EJ: '09- 1 (1 10,000m); WUG: '13- 1. At 3000m: WI: '14- 6; EI: '11- 2, '13- 1. Eur U23 CC: '12- 8.
AZE records: 3000m (2) 2012-13, 5000m (4) 2010-12.
Progress at 5000m: 2009- 13:53.60, 2010- 13:32.98, 2011- 13:34.54, 2012- 13:11.54, 2013- 13:23.59. pbs: 1500m 3:44.76 '10, 3000m 7:34.57 '13, 10,000m 30:03.57 '11. Formerly Haile Desta Hagos of Ethiopia, switched to AZE 1 Feb 2009..

BAHAMAS

Governing body: Bahamas Association of Athletics Associations, P.O.Box SS 5517, Nassau. Founded 1952.
National Champions 2013: Men: 100m: Derrick Atkins 10.20, 200m: Trevorvany Mackey 20.71, 400m: Ramon Miller 44.93, 800m: Andre Colebrook 1:51.67, 1500m: O'Neil Williams 3:58.15, 5000m: Keithrell Hanna 16:33.54, 110mh: Shamar Sands 13.97, 400mh: Jeffrey Gibson 51.10, HJ: Trevor Barry 2.29, LJ: Raymond Higgs 7.88, TJ: Cameron Parker 15.75, SP/HT: Delron Inniss 13.91/41.79, DT: Gerrad Burrows

45.38, JT: Wilfred Ferguson 39.70. **Women**: 100m: Sheniqua Ferguson 11.18, 200m: Anthonique Strachan 22.32, 400m: Laniece Clarke 53.03, 800m: Te'shon Adderley 2:11.86, 100mh: Krystal Bodie 13.57, 400mh: Carlissa Russell 63.45, LJ: Bianca Stuart 6.61, TJ: Tamara Myers 12.92, SP: Racquel Williams 13.22, DT: Juliana Duncanson 42.03, JT: Carlene Johnson 40.49.

Trevor BARRY b. 14 Jun 1983 Nassau 1.90m 77kg. NoDak.
At HJ: OG: '12- dnq 16=; WCh: '09- dnq 17, '11- 3; CG: '10- 2; PAm: '07- 7; WI: '12- 8. Won CAC 2011, BAH 2004-06, 2009, 2012.
Progress at HJ: 2002- 2.14, 2004- 2.13, 2005- 2.20, 2006- 2.19, 2007- 2.26, 2008- 2.25A, 2009- 2.28, 2010- 2.29, 2011- 2.32, 2012- 2.31, 2013- 2.25. pb LJ 7.78/7.82w '06.

Christopher BROWN b. 15 Oct 1978 Nassau 1.78m 68kg. Was at Norfolk State University.
At 400m/4x400mR: OG: '00- qf/3R, '04- sf, '08- 4/2R, '12- 4/1R; WCh: '01-03-05-07-09-11-13: h&1R/sf&3R/4&2R/4&2R/5/sf/sf; CG: '02- 7/3R, '06- 4; PAm: '07- 1/1R. '11- 7; PAm-J: '97- 2R; CAG: '98- 3R, '99- 1R, '03- 2/1R; WI: '06-08-10-12-14: 3/3/1/3/2; BAH champion 2002, 2004, 2007-09. At 800m: CG: '98- h.
Bahamas records 400m 2007 & 2008, 800m 1998. CAC & Commonwealth 4x400m record 2012. World M35 400m record indoors 2014.
Progress at 400m: 1997- 47.46, 1998- 46.44, 1999- 45.96, 2000- 45.08, 2001- 45.45, 2002- 45.11, 2003- 44.94A/45.16, 2004- 45.09, 2005- 44.48, 2006- 44.80, 2007- 44.45, 2008- 44.40, 2009- 44.81, 2010- 45.05, 2011- 44.79, 2012- 44.67, 2013- 45.18. pbs: 200m 21.05 '03, 20.56w '06; 300m 32.4+ '12, 800m 1:49.54 '98.
Fourth at four global championships outdoors. Had fastest split (43.42 anchor leg) in 2005 World 4x400m.

Demetrius PINDER b. 13 Feb 1989 Grand Bahama 1.78m 70kg. Studied theatre at Texas A&M University, USA.
At 400m: OG: '12- 7/1R; WCh: '11- sf; WI: '12- 2; BAH champion 2010-12.
CAC & Commonwealth 4x400m record 2012.
Progress at 400m: 2006- 49.03, 2007- 47.48, 2008- 47.34, 2009- 48.21i, 2010- 44.93, 2011- 44.78, 2012- 44.77. pbs: 200m 20.23 '12, 300m 32.3+ '12.

Donald THOMAS b. 1 Jul 1984 Freeport 1.90m 75kg. Lindenwood University, USA.
At HJ: OG: '08/12- dnq 21=/30=; WCh: '07-09-11-13: 1/dnq 15/11/6; CG: '06- 4, '10- 1; PAm: '07- 2, '11- 1; CAG: '06- 4=, '10- 1; CCp: '10- 2. Won WAF & NCAA indoors 2007, BAH 2007, 2010-11.
Progress at HJ: 2006- 2.24, 2007- 2.35, 2008- 2.28i/ 2.26, 2009- 2.30, 2010- 2.32, 2011- 2.32, 2012- 2.27, 2013- 2.32.
A basketball player, he made a sensational start by clearing 2.22 indoors in January 2006 with no high jump training since he had jumped at school five years earlier. 19 months later he was world champion.

Women

Shaunae MILLER b. 15 Apr 1994 Nassau 1.85m 69kg. University of Georgia, USA.
At (200m)/400m: OG: '12- ht; WCh: '13- (4); WJ: '10- 1, '12- 4; WY: '11- 1; WI: '14- 3. Won BAH 400m 2010-11, NCAA indoor 400m 2013.
CAC junior records 200m 2013, 400m 2013.
Progress at 200m, 400m: 2009- 55.52, 2010- 24.09, 52.45; 2011- 23.70, 51.84; 2012- 22.70, 51.25; 2013- 22.45/22.41w, 50.70. Pbs: 60m 7.59i '13, 100m 11.41 '12, 300m 36.40i '14.
Great-uncle Leslie Miller set BAH 400m record of 46.99 at 1968 Olympics.

Anthonique STRACHAN b. 22 Aug 1993 Nassau 1.68m 57kg. Student at Southern Union, Alabama, USA.
At (100m)/200m: OG: '12- sf; WCh: '11/13- sf; WJ: '10- sf, '12- 1/1; PAm-J: '11- 1. Won BAH 200m 2013.
Two CAC junior 200m records 2011-12.
Progress at 200m: 2009- 23.95, 2010- 23.66, 2011- 22.70, 2012- 22.53, 2013- 22.32. Pbs: 100m 11.20 '12, 400m 54.48 '10.
Won IAAF Female Rising Star Award 2012.

BAHRAIN

Governing body: Bahrain Athletics Association, PO Box 29269, Isa Twon-Manama. Founded 1974.

Albert Kibichii **ROP** b. 17 Jul 1992 Kapsabet, Kenya 1.76m 55kg.
Records: 1 Asian, 2 Bahrain 5000m and Bahrain 3000m 2013.; 2 Asian indoor 3000m 2014 (if eligible).
Progress at 5000m: 2010- 14:15.81A, 2011- 13:03.70, 2012- 13:01.91, 2013- 12:51.96. Pbs: 1500m 3:45.7A '13, 3000m 7:35.53 '13.
Bahrain citizen from 2 Apr 2013, international eligibility 1 Apr 2014.

Abraham Kipchirchir **ROTICH** b. 26 Sep 1993 Kenya 1.81m 62kg.
Progress at 800m: 2010- 1:50.76A, 2011- 1:46.4A, 2012- 1:43.13, 2013- 1:44.57. pb 1000m 2:17.08 '12.
Transferred from Kenya to Bahrain 2 Apr 2013, international eligibility 1 Apr 2014.

Women

Mimi BELETE b. 9 Jun 1988 Ethiopia 1.64m 62kg.
At 1500m/(5000m): OG: '12- sf; WCh: '09- sf, '11- 7, '13- sf; AsiG: '10- 3/1; AsiC: '09- 6, '13- 2; CCp: '10- 4; won W.Asian 2010.
Progress at 1500m: 2007- 4:13.55, 2008- 4:06.84, 2009- 4:04.36, 2010- 4:00.25, 2011- 4:03.13, 2012- 4:01.72, 2013- 4:03.63. pbs: 800m 2:04.63 '10, 2000m 5:38.53 '13, 3000m 8:32.18 '10, 5000m 15:15.59 '10.
From Ethiopia, has lived in Belgium from 2005;

BRN from 2009. Younger sister Almensch Belete BEL pbs 1500m 4:06.87 '10, 5000m 15:03.63 '11; 5 EI 3000m 2013.

Shitaye ESHETE Habtegebrei b. 21 May 1990 Ethiopia 1.59m 46kg.
At (5000m/)10,000m: OG: '12- 10/6; WCh: '11- 6, '13- 6; AsiG: '10- 3; AsiC: '11- 1, '13- 1; AfC: '09- (6); CCp: '10- (6). At 3000m: WI: '12- 5. World CC: '10-11-13: 11/12/4. Won Arab 10,000m 2013, CC 2010, 2013; Asian CC 2012, Asian indoor 3000m 2012.
Three BRN 10,000m records 2010-12.
Progress at 10,000m: 2010- 31:53.27, 2011- 31:21.57, 2012- 30:47.25, 2013- 31:13.79. pbs: 3000m 8:49.27i '12, 5000m 15:03.13 '13.

Maryam Yusuf **JAMAL** b. 16 Sep 1984 Alkesa, Arsi Province, Ethiopia 1.70m 54kg. Stade Lausanne, Switzerland.
At (800m)/1500m: OG: '08- 5, '12- 3; WCh: '05- 07-09-11: 5/1/1/11; WI: '06- 3, '08- 2; AsiG: '06- 1/1, '10- 6/1; WCp: '06- 1. At 3000m: WI: '14- 3. World CC: '09- 9, '11- 23; Won WAF 2005-08, Swiss CC 2003, P.Arab 800m, 1500m & 5000m 2005, Arab 4k CC 2006, Asian indoor 1500m & 3000m 2014, CC 2007, 2009.
Records: Two Asian 1M 2007, 2000m 2009, Bahrain 800m (3), 1500m (3), 2000m, 3000m (3), 5000m 2005-09. Asian indoor 1500m 2006 & 2008, 1M (4:24.71) 2010.
Progress at 800m, 1500m, 5000m: 2003- 4:18.12, 2004- 2:02.18, 4:07.78, 15:19.45mx; 2005- 1:59.69, 3:56.79, 14:51.68; 2006- 1:59.04, 3:56.18, 2007- 3:58.75, 15:20.28; 2008- 1:57.80, 3:59.79i/3:59.84; 2009- 1:59.98, 3:56.55; 2010- 1:59.89, 3:58.93; 2011- 4:00.33, 2012- 2:00.44, 4:01.19; 2013- 4:07.31. pbs: 1M 4:17.75 '07, 2000m 5:31.88 '09, 3000m 8:28.87 '05, HMar 71:43 '04.
Has a record 16 sub-4 min 1500m times. Formerly Ethiopian Zenebech Kotu Tola, based in Switzerland, ran series of fast times after converting to Jamal of Bahrain in 2005. First Olympic medallist for Bahrain at any sport. Married to Mnashu Taye (now Tareq Yaqoob BRN).

BARBADOS

Governing body: Amateur Athletic Association of Barbados, P.O.Box 46, Bridgetown. Founded 1947.
National Champions 2013: Men: 100m: Ramon Gittens 10.18, 200m: Burkheart Ellis 20.65, 400m/800m: Fabian Norgrove 47.06/1:53.34, 1500m: Joshua Hunte 4:04.95, 5000m: Elliott Peterson 16:30.51, 110mh: Ryan Brathwaite 13.25, 400mh: Kion Joseph 51.31, HJ: Henderson Dottin 2.10, LJ: Lutalo Boyce 7.76, TJ: Barry Batson 15.70, SP/DT: Kemar Holder-Edghill 12.99/43.74, JT: Janeil Craigg 67.52. **Women**: 100m: Jade Bailey 11.59, 200m: Ariel Jackson 23.48, 400m: Sade Sealy 53.05, 800m: Shani Adams 2:14.56, 5000m: Christina Laurent 18:05.11, 100mh: Kierre Beckles 13.34 (1h 13.32/nwi), 400mh: Tia-Adana Belle 59.79, HJ: Yuriko Harewood 1.60, LJ: Jalisa Burrowes 5.80, SP/DT: Leah Bannister 10.92/37.48, JT: Jenila Atherley 40.47.

Ryan BRATHWAITE b. 6 Aug 1988 Bridgetown 1.86m 75kg. Sociology graduate of the University of Mississippi.
At 110mh: OG: '08- sf, '12- 5; WCh: '07-09-11-13: sf/1/h/sf; WY: '05- 2; WJ: '06- h; PAm: '07- 4; CAG: '10- 1; PAm-J: '07- 3; won WAF 2009, CAC-J 2006, BAR 2008-09, 2011, 2013.
Eight Barbados 110mh records 2008-13.
Progress at 110mh: 2005- 14.64, 2006- 14.14, 2007- 13.61, 2008- 13.38, 2009- 13.14/13.05w, 2010- 13.34/13.10w, 2011- 13.54, 2012- 13.23, 2013- 13.14/13.13w. pbs: 60m 7.02i '08, 55mh 7.18i '09, 60mh 7.61i '10.
First world medallist for Barbados in athletics. Namesake, but no relation Shane (b. 8 Feb 1990) has 110mh pb 13.31A/13.43w '12, 13.44 '13 and was world youth octathlon champion 2007 and CAC 110mh champ[ion 2013.

BELARUS

Governing body: Belarus Athletic Federation, Kalinovskogo Street 111A, Minsk 220119. Founded 1991.
National Champions 2013: Men: 100m: Aleksey Chigorevskiy 10.58, 200m/110mh: Aleksandr Linnik 21.22/13.53, 400m: Aleksandr Krasovskiy 48.61, 800m: Maksim Yuschenko 1:51.01, 1500m: Anis Ananenko 3:53.20, 5000m: Sergey Platonov 14:13.48, 10,000m: Stepan Rogavtsov 29:32.48, 3000mSt: Aleksandr Tereshenko 8:46.38, 400mh: Nikita Yakovlev 51.13, HJ: Artyom Zaytsev 2.20, PV: Stanislav Tikonchik 5.20, LJ: Konstantin Boritsevskiy 7.68, TJ: Aleksey Tsapik 16.45w, SP/DT: Pavel Lyzhin 20.12/59.47, HT: Yuriy Shayunov 76.36, JT: Pavel Melshko 76.96, Dec: Anatoliy Koshar 7346, 20kW: Ivan Trotskiy 1:23:52, 50kW: Dmitriy Dyubin 4:22:23. **Women**: 100m: Yeketerina Gonchar 11.53, 200m: Olga Ostyashko 23.81, 400m: Yuliya Uremya 53.01, 800m: Marina Arzamasova 2:01.63, 1500m: Natalya Koreyvo 4:16.26, 5000m/10,000m: Olga Mazurenok 16:36.74/34:19.66, 3000mSt: Anastasiya Puzakova 10:06.33, 100mh: Alina Talay 12.97, 400mh: Martina Boyko 59.46, HJ: Valeriya Bogdanovich 1.80, PV: Irina Yakoltsevich 4.00, LJ: Olga Sudareva 6.74w, TJ: Natalya Vyatkina 14.10, SP: Alena Kopets 18.62, DT: Svetlana Serova 56.76, HT: Alena Krechik 65.77, JT: Tatyana Kholodovich 58.37, Hep: Anna Kulinich 5254, 20kW: Anastasiya Yatsevich 1:35:16.

Andrey KRAVCHENKO b. 4 Jan 1986 Petrikov, Gomel region 1.87m 84kg.
At Dec: OG: '08- 2; WCh: '07- dq 100m, '09- 10, 13- 12; EC: '10- 3; WJ: '04- 1; EU23: '07- 1; EJ: '05-

1; ECp: '08-09: 1/1. At Oct: WY: '03- 2. At Hep: WI: '08-10-12-14: 2/4/6/2; EI: '07- 3, '11- 1. World youth record for octathlon (6415) 2003. Progress at Dec: 2005- 7833, 2006- 8013, 2007- 8617, 2008- 8585, 2009- 8336, 2010- 8370, 2011- 8023, 2013- 8390. pbs: 60m 7.03i '08, 100m 10.86 '07, 400m 47.17 '07, 1000m 2:39.80i '11, 1500m 4:24.44 '06, 60mh 7.90i '10, 110mh 13.93 '07, HJ 2.21i '14, 2.16 '04; PV 5.30i/5.20 '08, LJ 7.90 '07, SP 15.42i '14, 14.96 '13; DT 47.11 '13, JT 64.35 '07, Hep 6303i '13.
Added 604 points to pb to win with European U23 record at Götzis 2007. Won IAAF Combined Events Challenge 2008 and 2013.

Pavel KRIVITSKIY b. 17 Apr 1984 Grodno 1.84m 115kg.
At HT: OG: '12- dnq 28; WCh: '09- 8, '11- 5, '13- dnq 14; EC: '10- dnq 16, '12- 9; EU23: '05- 1; ET: '10- 1. Won BLR 2007, 2010-12.
Progress at HT: 2004- 72.05, 2005- 77.51, 2006- 78.62, 2007- 78.61, 2008- 80.02, 2009- 79.48, 2010- 80.44, 2011- 80.67, 2012- 80.25, 2013- 79.36.

Pavel LYZHIN b. 24 Mar 1981 Voronok, Russia 1.89m 110kg. Mogilyov. Army.
At SP(/DT): OG: '04- dnq 16, '08- 4, '12- 8; WCh: '03-05-07-09-11-13: dnq 14/nt/19/6/dnq 15/dnq nt; EC: '02- dnq, '06- 8, '10- 6; WJ: '00- 4/7; EU23: '01- 8, '03- 1; EJ: '99- 4/2; WI: '10- 5; EI: '02- 6, '07- 2; WUG: '03- 2, '05- 5. Won BLR SP 2001, 2004, 2009, 2011-13; DT 2013.
Progress at SP: 1999- 17.98, 2000- 19.12, 2001- 20.12, 2002- 20.15, 2003- 20.86, 2004- 20.92, 2005- 20.38, 2006- 20.85, 2007- 20.82i/20.02, 2008- 20.98, 2009- 20.98, 2010- 21.21, 2011- 20.85, 2012- 20.69, 2013- 20.12, 2014- 20.20i. pb DT 61.72 '07.

Yuriy SHAYUNOV b. 22 Oct 1987 Minsk 1.89m 120kg.
At HT: WCh: '09- dnq 26, '11- nt, '13- 12; EC: '10- 12: dnq 20/17; WJ: '04- dnq 13, '06- 4; EU23: '07- 1, '09- 1; EJ: '05- 3; WUG: '09- 1, '13- 4. BLR champion 2009, 2013.
Progress at HT: 2007- 74.92, 2008- 77.32, 2009- 80.72, 2010- 78.73, 2011- 78.70, 2012- 79.00, 2013- 78.99.

Women

Marina ARZAMASOVA b. 17 Dec 1987 Minsk 1.73m 57kg. née Kotovich. Minsk.
At 800m: OG: '12- 5; WCh: '11/13- sf; EC: '12- 3: dnq 20/17; WJ: '06- h; WI: '14- 3; EI: '13- 3. Won W.MilG 2011, BLR 800m 2008, 2013, 1500m 2013.
Progress at 800m: 2004- 2:09.37, 2005- 2:07.24, 2006- 2:06.39, 2007- 2:04.33, 2008- 2:02.67, 2009- 2:05.53i, 2011- 1:59.30, 2012- 1:59.63, 2013- 1:59.60. pbs: 400m 52.81 '12, 600m 1:27.28i '13, 1000m 2:37.93 '11, 1500m 4:15.99 '12..

Alena KOPETS b. 14 Feb 1988 1.78m 84kg.
At SP: WCh: '13- 12; WJ: '06- dnq 17 (DT dnq 19); EU23: '09- 3; EJ: '07- 2 (DT dnq 14); WUG: '09- 3; EI: '13- 3. BLR champion 2013.
Progress at SP: 2006- 15.88, 2007- 16.32i/16.21,

2008- 16.71i/16.69, 2009- 17.97, 2010- 17.99, 2011- 18.82i/17.71, 2012- 18.90i/17.83, 2013- 19.24. pb DT 52.83 '11.

Oksana MENKOVA b. 28 Mar 1982 Krichev, Mogilev region 1.83m 91kg.
At HT: OG: '08- 1, '12- 7; WCh: '03-07-09-13: dnq 23/nt/13/22; EC: '02/06: dnq 27/23; EU23: 03- 2; EJ: '01- 5; WUG: '05- 5; ECp: '07- 2, '08- 1. Five Belarus hammer records 2006-12.
Progress at HT: 1999- 47.87, 2000- 56.50, 2001- 59.24, 2002- 66.42, 2003- 67.58, 2004- 70.23, 2005- 70.15, 2006- 76.86, 2007- 73.94, 2008- 77.32, 2009- 76.32, 2010- 67.27, 2011- 67.78, 2012- 78.69, 2013- 75.45.
Had a terrible record at major events and only 11th in qualifying, but took gold with Olympic record 76.34 in 2008. Daughter Anna born on 25 Sep 2010.

Anastasiya MIRONCHIK-IVANOVA b. 13 Apr 1989 Slutsk 1.71m 54kg. Minsk.
At LJ: OG: '12- 7; WCh: '09- 11, '11- 4; EC: '10- 6; WJ: '08- 2; WY: '05- 8; EU23: '09- 2, '11- 6; WI: '12- 5; EI: '11- 6. BLR champion 2007, 2010-12.
Progress at LJ: 2004- 5.90, 2005- 6.10/6.13w, 2007- 6.03i/5.89, 2008- 6.71, 2009- 6.65/6.76w, 2010- 6.84, 2011- 6.85/6.92w, 2012- 7.08/7.22w, 2013- 6.60. pb TJ 14.29 '11.

Olga SUDAREVA b. 22 Feb 1984 Gomel 1.76m 63kg. née Serygeyenko. Gomel.
At LJ: OG: '08/12- dnq 32/13; WCh: '13- 4; EC: '12- 2; BLR champion 2008, 2011, 2013.
Progress at LJ: 2005- 6.01i/6.00, 2006- 6.33, 2007- 6.46, 2008- 6.72, 2011- 6.40, 2012- 6.85, 2013- 6.82. pbs: 60m 7.86i '08, 200m 24.86 '08.

Alina TALAY b. 14 May 1989 Orsha, Vitebsk 1.64m 54kg.
At 100mh: OG: '12- sf; WCh: '13- sf; EC: '10- sf, '12- 2; WJ: '08- 4; EU23: '09- 3, '11- 1; WUG: '13- 2; ET: '11- 2; won W.MilG 2011, BLR 2009-10, 2013. At 60mh: WI: '12- 3; EI: '11-5, '13- 1.
Progress at 100mh: 2007- 14.38/14.01w, 2008- 13.31, 2009- 13.07, 2010- 12.87, 2011- 12.91, 2012- 12.71, 2013- 12.78. pbs: 60m 7.35i '13, 100m 11.48 '11, 200m 23.59 '11, 50mh 6.89i '11, 60mh 7.94i '13.

BELGIUM

Governing bodies: Ligue Royale Belge d'Athlétisme, Stade Roi Baudouin, avenue du Marathon 199B, 1020 Bruxelles (KBAB/LRBA). Vlaamse Atletiekliga (VAL); Ligue Belge Francophone d'Athlétisme (LBFA). Original governing body founded 1889.
National Championships first held in 1889 (women 1921). **2013 Champions: Men**: 100m: Damien Broothaerts 10.51, 200m: Jonathan Borlée 20.38, 400m: Kevin Borlée 44.73, 800m: Jan Van Den Broeck 1:49.30, 1500m: Kim Ruell 3:54.50, 5000m/10,000m/HMar: Abdelhadi El Hachimi 13:59.33/29:00.02/68:28, Mar: Stijn

Fincioen 2:23:56, 3000mSt: Krijn Van Koolwyk 9:05.21, 110mh: Adrien Deghelt 13.55, 400mh: Tim Rummens 50.23, HJ: Bram Ghuys 2.20, PV: Thomas Van Der Plaetsen 5.35, LJ: Corentin Campener 7.51, TJ: Leopold Kapeta 15.28, SP: Jurgen Verbrugghe 17.42; DT: Philip Milanov 58.86, HT: Nicolas Pierre 63.15, JT: Thomas Smet 73.55, Dec: Frédéric Xhonneux 7500. **Women:** 100m/100mh: Anne Zagré 11.46/12.85, 200m: Hanne Claes 23.33, 400m: Laetitia Liebert 53.69, 800m: Sofie Lauwers 2:09.01, 1500m: Sofie Van Accom 4:20.76, 5000m: Veerle Van Linden 17:12.17, 10,000m/Mar: Els Rens 35:14.84/2:46:30, HMar: Hanna Vandenbussche 1:20:29; 3000mSt: , 400mh: Axelle Dauwens 55.96, HJ: Hanne Van Hessche 1.85, PV: Fanny Smets 4.25, LJ: Camille Laus 6.03, TJ: Linda Onana 12.90, SP/HT: Jolien Boumkwo 14.74/57.29, DT: Annelies Peetroons 51.24, JT: Alice Fleury 45.74, Hep: Jesse Vercruysse 5038.

Jonathan BORLÉE b. 22 Feb 1988 Woluwe-Saint Lambert 1.80m 70kg. Was at Florida State University.
At 400m: OG: '08- sf/5R, '12- 6; WCh: '11- 5, '13-4; EC: '10- 7/3R, '12- 1R; WJ: '06- 4; WY: '05- 5; EJ: '07- h; WI: '10- 2R; EI: '11- 3R. Won NCAA 2009.
At 200m: EC: '12- 4. Won BEL 200m 2012-13, 400m 2006, 2011
Four Belgian 400m records 2009-12, 300m 2012.
Progress at 400m: 2005- 47.50, 2006- 46.06, 2007-47.85, 2008- 45.11, 2009- 44.78, 2010- 44.71, 2011-44.78, 2012- 44.43, 2013- 44.54. pbs: 60m 6.81i '07, 100m 10.78 '07, 200m 20.31 '12, 300m 31.87 '12, 600m 1:18.60i '11.
Twin brother of Kevin Borlée, their sister Olivia (b. 10 Apr 1986) has pbs 100m 11.39 '07, 200m 22.98 '06, 3 WCh '07, 2 OG '08 at 4x100mR. Younger brother Dylan pb 45.80 '13 (the three brothers ran on BEL 4x400m team 5th WCh 2013). Their father Jacques was an international 400m runner (45.4 '79), mother Edith Demartelaere had pbs 200m 23.89 and 400m 54.09 in 1984.

Kévin BORLÉE b. 22 Feb 1988 Woluwe-Saint Lambert 1.80m 71kg. WS. Was at Florida State University.
At 400m: OG: '08- sf/5R, '12- 5; WCh: '09- sf/4R, '11- 3, '13- sf; EC: '10- 1/3R, '12- 1R; WJ: '06- sf; WI: '10- 2R; EI: '11- 3R; CCp: '10- 4/2R. At 200m: WY: '05- sf. Won DL 2012, BEL 200m 2009, 2011; 400m 2007, 2013.
Belgian 400m records 2008 and 2012.
Progress at 400m: 2005- 47.86, 2006- 46.63, 2007-46.38, 2008- 44.88, 2009- 45.28, 2010- 45.01, 2011-44.74, 2012- 44.56, 2013- 44.73. pbs: 60m 6.85i '13, 100m 10.62 '07, 200m 20.72 '11, 300m 32.72i '13, 32.76 '08; 600m 1:15.65i '11.

Hans VAN ALPHEN b. 12 Jan 1982 Turnhout 1.91m 91kg. ZWAT.
At Dec: OG: '08- dnf, '12- 4; WCh: '07- 11; EC: '10- 5; WUG: '07- 2. Won BEL Dec 2005.

Three Belgian decathlon records 2007-12.
Progress at Dec: 2002- 6840, 2004- 7054, 2005-7064, 2006- 7411, 2007- 8047, 2008- 7634, 2009- 8070, 2010- 8091, 2011- 8200, 2012- 8519. pbs: 60m 7.08i '08, 100m 10.96 '12, 400m 48.25 '07, 1000m 2:37.06i '11, 1500m 4:17.51 '09, 60mh 8.19i '06, 110mh 14.55 '12, HJ 2.06 '12, PV 4.96 '12, LJ 7.64 '12, SP 15.68 '10, DT 51.89 '12, JT 67.59 '12, Hep 5938i '11.
Improved by 319 points to win at Götzis 2012; Won at Talence 2011 and 2012. Won IAAF Combined Events Challenge 2012.

Thomas VAN DER PLAETSEN b. 24 Dec 1990 Gent 1.88m 82kg. AAC Deinze.
At Dec: WCh: '11- 13, '13- 15; EU23: '11- 1; EJ: '09- 1; WUG: '13- 1; Won BEL PV 2011, 2013; Dec 2010. At Hep: WI: '14- 3; EI: '11- 6.
Belgian decathlon record 2011.
Progress at Dec: 2010- 7564, 2011- 8157, 2013-8255. pbs: 60m 7.13i '14, 100m 11.09 '13, 200m 22.34 '10, 400m 48.64 '11, 1000m 2:40.50i '14, 1500m 4:32.52 '11, 60mh 8.06i '14, 110mh 14.45 '11, HJ 2.17 '11, PV 5.35 '13, LJ 7.80 '13, SP 14.32i '14, 13.57 '13; DT 41.32 '13, JT 65.31 '13, Hep 6259i '14.

BOTSWANA

Governing body: Botswana Athletics Association, PO Box 2399, Gaborone. Founded 1972.

Nijel AMOS b. 15 Mar 1994 Marobela 1.79m 60kg.
At 800m: OG: '12- 2; WJ: '12- 1, WY: '11- 5; WUG: '13- 1.
World junior 800m and two Botswana 800m records 2012.
Progress at 800m: 2011- 1:47.28, 2012- 1:41.73, 2013- 1:44.71. pbs: 400m 45.66A '13, 45.94 '12; 600m 1:15.0+ 12.

Women

Amantle MONTSHO b. 4 Jul 1983 Mabudutsa 1.73m 64kg.
At 400m: OG: '04- h, '08- 8, '12- 4; WCh: '05-07-09-11-13: h/sf/8/1/2; CG: '06- sf, '10- 1; AfG: '03-07-11: h/1/1; AfCh: '04-06-08-10-12: h/2/1/1/1/1; WI: '10- 4; CCp: '10- 1/3R. Won DL 2011-13.
Botswana records 100m 2011, 200m 2001-12, 400m 2003-12.
Progress at 400m: 2003- 55.03, 2004- 53.77, 2005-52.59, 2006- 52.14, 2007- 50.90, 2008- 49.83A/50.54, 2009- 49.89, 2010- 49.89, 2011- 49.56, 2012- 49.54, 2013- 49.33. pbs: 100m 11.60 '11, 200m 22.89 '12, 22.88w '11, 300m 36.33i '10 (African record).
First Botswana woman to win a major title.

BRAZIL

Governing body: Confederação Brasileira de Atletismo (CBAt), Avenida Rio Purus No. 103 - Conj. Vieiralves, Bairro N.Sra das Graças, Manaus, AM 69053-050. Founded 1914 (Confederação 1977).

National Championships first held in 1925. **2013 Champions**: **Men**: 100m: José Carlos Moreira 10.16, 200m: Bruno de Barros 20.33, 400m: Ânderson Henriques 45.64, 800m: Diego Gomes 1:46.41, 1500m: Lutimar Paes 3:45.51, 5000m: Éderson Perela 13:54.16, 10,000m: Marílson dos Santos 28:37.71, 3000mSt: Gládson Barbosa 8:43.19, 110mh: Matheus Inocêncio 13.43w, 400mh: Mahau Suguimati 49.59, HJ: Guilherme Cobbo 2.22, PV: Augusto de Oliveira 5.70, LJ: Mauro da Silva 8.31, TJ: Jefferson Dias Sabino 16.94 , SP: Darlan Romani 18.53, DT: Ronald Julião 61.62, HT: Wágner Domingos 69.17, JT: Paulo da Silva 74.28, Dec: Carlos Eduardo Chinin 8393, 20kW: Caio Bonfim 1:26:19, 50kW: Cláudio dos Santos 4:14:18. **Women**: 100m: Ana Cláudia Silva 11.07, 200m: Franciela Krasucki 22.76. 400m: Joelma Sousa 52.32, 800m: Flavia de Lima 2:03.31, 1500m: Christiane dos Santos 4:23.30, 5000m: Adriana da Silva 16:12.88, 10,000m: Cruz da Silva 33:05.92, 3000mSt: Érika Lima 10:08.09, 100mh: Fabiana dos Santos 13.28, 400mh: Liliana Barbosa 58.09, HJ: Aline Santos 1.83, PV: Fabiana Murer 4.73 LJ/TJ: Keila Costa 6.51/14.58, SP: Geisa Arcanjo 17.55, DT: Andressa de Morais 58.78, HT: Carla Michel 58.42, JT: Jucilene de Lima 61.98, Hep: Tamara de Souza 5814, 20000mW: Érica de Sena 1:33:37.

Bruno de BARROS b. 7 Jan 1987 Maceió 1.78m 70kg. AD Criciuma.
At 200m/4x100mR: OG: '08- h, '12- sf; WCh: '11- 6, '13- h; PAm: '11- 3/1R. At 100m: SACh:'13- 2. Won BRA 100m 2011, 200m 2011-13.
Progress at 200m: 2006- 21.15, 2007- 21.05, 2008- 20.47, 2009- 20.48, 2011- 20.16, 2012- 20.37, 2013- 20.24. pb 100m 10.16 '09, 10.1 '06.
Two year drugs ban 2009-11.

Carlos Eduardo CHININ b. 3 May 1985 São Paulo 1.95m 83kg. BM&F Atletismo.
At Dec: OG: '08- dnf; WCh: '07- dnf '13- 6; PAm: '07- 3; SACh: '05-06-09: 4/1/1; WUG: '07- 3; BRA champion 2008, 2010, 2013.
South American records: decathlon 2013, indoor heptathlon 2014.
Progress at Dec: 2005- 7426, 2006- 7261, 2007- 7977, 2008- 7850 2009- 7690, 2010- 7641, 2011- 8068, 2013- 8393. pbs: 60m 7.01i '14, 100m 10.78 '13, 400m 48.18 '07, 1000m 2:44.88i '14, 1500m 4:23.99 '07, 60mh 7.99i '14. 110mh 14.05 '13, HJ 2.13 '07, PV 5.10 '13, LJ 7.76 '07, SP 15.28 '13, DT 48.38 '11, JT 59.98 '13, Hep 5951i '14.

Augusto Dutra de OLIVEIRA b. 16 Jul 1990 Marília, São Paulo 1.80m 70kg. BMF Bovespa.
At PV: WCh: '13- 11; WI: '14- 7; SACh: '11- 4; won SAmG 2014, SAm-J '2009.
Two South American pole vault records and two indoors 2013.
Progress at PV: 2008- 4.60, 2009- 5.00, 2010- 5.40, 2011- 5.32, 2012- 5.45, 2013- 5.82.

Anderson Freitas **HENRIQUES** b. 3 Mar 1992 Caçapava do Sul 1.87m 80kg. SOGIPA.
At 400m: WCh: '13- 8; PAm: '11- 8; WUG: '13- 2; won IbAm 2012, SAmG 2014, SAm-J 2011, BRA 2011, 2013.
Progress at 400m: 2010- 46.24, 2011- 45.71A/45.81, 2012- 45.59, 2013- 44.95, 2014- 45.03. pb 200m 21.02 '13.

Marílson Gomes **dos SANTOS** b. 6 Aug 1977 Brasília, DF 1.74m 58kg. BM&F Atletismo.
At Mar: OG: '08- dnf, '12- 5; WCh: '05- 10, '09- 16. At 5000m(/10,000m): PAm: '03- 3/2, '07- (2), '11- (1); SAm: '03- 1; WJ: '96- dnq; WCp: '06- 5. At HMar: WCh: '07- 7, '08- 8; WUG: '97- 1, '99- 1. Won IbAm 5000m 2006, BRA 5000m 2003, 2007-09; 10,000m 2003-04, 2006-11, 2013; SAm HMar 2011, CC 2008.
South American records 5000m 2006, 10,000m, 15km, 20km & HMar 2007, 30km 2010; two BRA 10,000m records 2006-07.
Progress at 5000m, 10,000m, Mar: 1995- 14:29.7, 30:19.05; 1996- 14:18.3, 29:52.5; 1997- 14:08.1, 29:30.41; 1998- 14:20.08, 29:12.05; 1999- 14:05.35, 28:54.9; 2000- 13:52.19, 28:39.87; 2001- 14:03.47, 29:02.89; 2002- 14:00.68, 28:34.59; 2003- 13:48.52, 28:22.58; 2004- 13:48.07, 28:21.38, 2:08:48; 2005- 13:40.8, 29:05.42, 2:13:40; 2006- 13:19.43, 27:48.49, 2:09:58; 2007- 13:22.11, 27:28.12, 2:08:37; 2008- 27:35.05, 2:08:43; 2009- 13:34.79, 27:58.83, 2:15:13; 2010- 13:34.92, 28:44.59; 2:08:46; 2011- 28:09:24, 2:06:34; 2012- 2:08:03, 2013- 13:47.22, 28:24.20, 2:09:24. Road pbs: 15k 42:15 '07, 20k 56:32 '07, HMar 59:33 '07, 30k 1:29:23+ '10.
Won New York City Marathon 2006 and 2008. Married to Juliana de Azevedo (3rd WJ 800m 2002. At 1500m: SACh: '03- 1, '06- 1 (1 4x400m); PAm: '05- 1; pbs 800m 2:01.35 '05, 1500m 4:11.39 '07).

Mauro Vinícius da SILVA b. 26 Dec 1986 Presidente Prudente 1.83m 69kg.
At LJ: OG: '08- dnq 26, '12- 7; WCh: '13- 5; WI: '12- 1, '14- 1; SACh: '13- 1. BRA champion 2010, 2012-13.
Progress at LJ: 2005- 7.35/7.73w, 2006- 7.61, 2007- 7.66, 2008- 8.10/8.20w?, 2009- 8.04i/7.94, 2010- 8.12, 2011- 8.27, 2012- 8.28i/8.11, 2013- 8.31, 2014- 8.28i. pbs: 60m 6.76i '09, 100m 10.40 '07, 200m 21.02 '07.
Won World Indoor title with 8.23 but took off behind the board with 24cm to spare.

Thiago Braz da SILVA b. 16 Dec 1993 Marília 1.93m 84kg. BMF Bovespa
At PV: WCh: '13- dnq 14=; WJ: '12- 1; WI: '14- 4; SACh: '13- 1; won Yth Oly 2010, PAm-J '2011.
South American pole vault record 2013, indoors (2) 2014.
Progress at PV: 2009- 4.60, 2010- 5.10, 2011- 5.31, 2012- 5.55, 2013- 5.83, 2014- 5.76i.

Women

Fabiana de Almeida **MURER** b. 16 Mar 1981

Campinas, São Paulo 1.72m 64kg. BM&F
Atletismo. Degree in physiotherapy.
At PV: OG: '08- 10=, '12- dnq 14; WCh: '05-07-09-
11-13: dnq 15/6=/5/1/5=; WJ: '98- dnq 14=, '00-
10; PAm: '99-07-11: 9/1/2; WI: '08-10-14: 3=/1/4;
SACh: '99-01-05-06-07-09-11:   3/6/2/1/1/1/1;
WCp: '06- 2, '10- 3. Won DL 2010, IbAm 2006,
2010; SAmG 2014; SAm-J 1998-2000, BRA 2005-
07, 2010, 2013.
13 South American pole vault records, 15
indoors 2006-11, 29 BRA records 1998-2011.
Progress at PV: 1998- 3.66, 1999- 3.81, 2000- 3.90,
2001- 3.91, 2002- 3.70, 2003- 4.06, 2004- 4.25,
2005- 4.40, 2006- 4.66, 2007- 4.66i/4.65, 2008-
4.80, 2009- 4.82, 2010- 4.85, 2011- 4.85, 2012- 4.77,
2013- 4.75.
Married to coach Élson de Souza (pb 5.02 '89).

BULGARIA

Governing body: Bulgarian Athletics
Federation, 75 bl. Vassil Levski, Sofia 1000.
Founded 1924.
National Championships first held in 1926
(men), 1938 (women). **2013 Champions: Men:**
100m: Denis Dimitrov 10.16, 200m: Peter
Kremenski 20.73, 400m: Radoslav Stefanov 48.49,
800m: Sava Todorov 1:51.74, 1500m: Ivan Popov
3:49.42, 5000m/10,000m/HMar/Mar: Yolo
Nikolov 14:40.89/30:13.63/69:26/2:23:25, 3000mSt:
Mitko Tsenov 8:27.09, 110mh: Martin Arnaudov
13.91, 400mh: Milan Volkanov 54.05, HJ: Viktor
Ninov 2.24, PV: Spas Bukhalov 5.20, LJ: Zlatozar
Atanasov 7.84, TJ: Rumen Dimitrov 16.61w, SP/
DT: Rosen Karamfilov 16.49/55.47, HT: Zdravko
Dimitrov 66.66, JT: Kolio Neshev 67.06, Dec:
Kiril Zagorski 5434, 20kW: Bozhidar Vasilev
1:52:43. **Women:** 100m/200m: Gabriela Laleva
11.69/23.81, 400m: Nikolina Nikolova 52.61,
800m: Teodora Kolarova 2:03.65,
1500m/10,000m/ HMar/Mar/3000mSt: Silvia
Danekova 4:36.07/38:44.39/1:20:00/2:52:27/9:46.
54, 5000m: Iveta Sotirova-Mitsova 18:51.15,
100mh/LJ: Kristina Damyanova 14.15/6.24,
400mh: Iva Dimova 60.46, HJ: Mirela Demireva
1.90, PV: Temenuga Atanasova 3.50, TJ: Gabriela
Petrova 13.96w, SP: Radoslava Mavrodieva
18.48, DT: Atanaska Angelova-Dimitrova 47.39,
HT: Mikhaela Metodieva 51.27, JT: Khristina
Georgieva 49.79, Hep: Elena Uzunova 3208,
20kW: Radosveta Simeonova 1:58:10.

Georgi IVANOV b. 13 Mar 1985 1.87m 130kg.
Dukla Praha.
At SP: OG: '08- dnq, '12- dnq 22; WCh: '09- dnq
33, '13- 8; EC: '10/12- dnq 21/16; WJ: '02- dnq,
'04- 1; WY: '01- 1; WI: '14- 5; EU23: '07- 4; EJ: '03-
3, BUL champion 2007-09, 2011-12; Balkan 2013.
Two Bulgarian shot records 2013.
Progress at SP: 2002- 17.98i/16.37, 2003-
18.42i/16.73, 2005- 19.51, 2006- 19.04i/18.96,
2007- 19.42, 2008- 20.02, 2009- 19.41, 2010-
19.90i/19.12, 2011- 19.23i/18.90, 2012- 20.33, 2013-

21.09, 2014- 21.02i. pb DT 51.96 '04.
Engaged to Andriana Banova (TJ 14.34 '11);
their son was born in 2013.

Women

Ivet LALOVA-COLLIO b. 18 May 1984 Sofia
1.68m 56kg. née Lalova. Levski Sofia,
Panellínios GRE.
At 100m/(200m): OG: '04- 4/5, '08- sf/qf, '12- sf/
sf; WCh: '07- qf, '09- qf/h, '11- 7/sf, '13- sf/sf; EC:
'10- h, '12- 1/sf; WJ: '02- sf; WY: '01- h/sf; EJ: '03:
1/1; EI: '05- (1). At 60m: WI: '12- 8; EI: '13- 3. Won
BUL 100m 2004-05, 200m 2004; Balkan 100m
2011, 2013.
Bulgarian 100m record 2004.
Progress at 100m, 200m: 1998- 13.0, 27.2; 1999-
12.71, 2000- 12.14, 25.24; 2001- 11.72, 24.03; 2002-
11.59, 24.4; 2003- 11.14, 22.55; 2004- 10.77,
22.51/22.36w; 2005- 11.03, 22.76; 2007- 11.26/
11.15w, 23.00; 2008- 11.31/11.28w, 23.13; 2009-
11.48/11.24w, 23.60; 2010- 11.43, 23.71; 2011-
10.96, 22.66; 2012- 11.06/11.01w, 22.98; 2013-
11.04, 22.78. pbs: 50m 6.23i+ '12, 60m 7.12i '13.
Broke her leg in a collision with another athlete
on 14 Jun 2005. Married Simone Collio (Italy,
60m 6.55 ITA record 2008, 100m 10.06 in 2009)
on 20 Sep 2013. Her father Miroslav Lalov had
100m best of 10.4 and was BUL 200m champion
in 1966, her mother Liliya was a heptathlete.

Vania STAMBOLOVA b. 28 Nov 1983 Varna
1.75m 63kg. Cehrno more Atletik Varna.
Student at the Sports Academy of Sofia.
At 400m: EC: '06- 1; WI: '06-10-12: 2/3/4; EI: '11-
4; WCp: '06- 2. At 400mh: OG: '12- h; WCh: '05-
09-11-13: h/sf/6/sf; EC: '10- 2; WUG: '09- 1; CCp:
'10- 3. Won Balkan 400mh 2005, 2011, 2013;
400m 2011; BUL 400mh 2009, 400mh 2002, 2005-
06. Bulgarian Records: 400m (5) 2006, 400mh
(2) 2006-10.
Progress at 400m. 400mh: 1998- 57.91, 64.34;
1999- 57.45, 63.53; 2000- 58.82, 62.72; 2001- 57.86,
61.38; 2002- 58.30, 61.11; 2005- 52.99, 56.29; 2006-
49.53, 54.55; 2009- 51.47, 55.14; 2010- 50.88, 53.82;
2011- 50.98, 53.68; 2012- 50.87, 54.04; 2013- 54.77.
pb 200m 22.81 '06, 22.7 '10; 300m 36.81i '12,
800m 2:02.03i '12, 1000m 2:42.76i '14.
Former footballer. Two-year drugs ban 2007-09.

Venelina VENEVA-MATEEVA b. 13 Jun 1974
Ruse 1.79m 61kg. Dunav Ruse.
At HJ: OG: '96-04-12: dnq 29=/15/20=, '00- 9=;
WCh: '91-5-9-09-11: dnq 21=/14/14=/15/21, '01-
03-05: 4/4/10; EC: '98-06-0-12: 5/2/dnq 22=/12;
EJ: '91- 2; WI: '01- 3, '04- 7; EI: '00-05-07-11-13:
4/3/dq3/7=/6. BUL champion 1995, 2004, 2009-
10; Balkan 2003.
Progress at HJ: 1987- 1.68, 1988- 1.80, 1989- 1.86,
1990- 1.93i/1.90, 1991- 1.91, 1992- 1.91, 1993-
1.89i/1.85, 1994- 1.90, 1995- 1.94, 1996- 1.94i/1.88,
1998- 2.03, 1999- 1.90, 2000- 2.01, 2001- 2.04,
2002- 2.02i, 2003- 2.01, 2004- 2.01, 2005- 1.98,
2006- 2.04, 2007- 1.96i/2.02idq, 2009- 1.95, 2010-

1.95, 2011- 1.98, 2012- 1.95, 2013- 1.93i/1.90. pbs: LJ 6.17 '90, TJ 12.51 '95.
Daughter Neapola born in 1997. World age-15 best of 1.93i in 1990. Two year drugs ban from positive test 24 Jan 2007.

BURUNDI

Francine NIYONSABA b. 5 May 1993 Nkanda Bweru, Ruyiqi 1.61m 56kg.
At 800m: OG: '12- 6; AfCh: '12- 1.
Five Burundi 800m records 2012.
Progress at 800m: 2012- 1:56.59, 2013- 1:56.72. pb 600m 1:27.6 '12.

CANADA

Governing body: Athletics Canada, Suite B1-110, 2445 S-Laurent Drive, Ottawa, Ontario K1G 6C3. Formed as Canadian AAU in 1884.
National Championships first held in 1884 (men), 1925 (women). **2013 Champions: Men:** 100m: Aaron Brown 10.25, 200m: Tremaine Harris 21.18, 400m: Philip Osei 46.47, 800m: Geoff Harris 1:47.75, 1500m: Nathan Brannen 3:51.10, 5000m: Cam Levins 14:11.63, 10,000m: Mohammed Ahmed 29:22.04, HMar: Eric Gillis 65:56, Mar: Rob Watson 2:18:33, 3000mSt: Matt Hughes 8:29.50, 110mh: Ingvar Moseley 14.01, 400mh: Tait Nystuen 51.36, HJ: Derek Drouin 2.31, PV: Shawn Barber 5.40, LJ: Taylor Stewart 7.76, TJ: Kurt McCormack 14.47, SP/DT: Tim Nedow 20.72/55.35, HT: James Steacy 72.96, JT: Kyle Nielsen 76.23, Dec: Damian Warner 8145, 10,000mW: Iñaki Gómez 40:01, 20kW: Bruno Carrière 1:35:19. **Women:** 100m: Crystal Emmanuel 11.48, 200m: Kimberley Hyacinthe 22.91, 400m: Alicia Brown 52.92, 800m: Melissa Bishop 2:02.84, 1500m: Kate Van Buskirk 4:16.45, 5000m: Andrea Seccafien 16:25.30, 10,000m: Natasha Fraser 33:21.43, HMar: Krista Duchene 72:27, Mar: Lioudmila Kortchaguina 2:33:10, 3000mSt: Jessica Furlan 9:59.62, 100mh: Angela Whyte 12.99, 400mh: Noelle Montcalm 56.43, HJ: Michele Kinsella 1.83, PV: Heather Hamilton 4.20, LJ: Christabel Nettey 6.49, TJ: Carolina Eberhardt 12.71, SP/DT: Julie Labonté 17.63/52.81, HT: Sultana Frizell 68.23, JT: Krista Woodward 58.59, Hep: Brianne Theisen 6233, 10000W: Katelynn Ramage 54:36.

Dylan ARMSTRONG b. 15 Jan 1981 Kamloop, British Columbia 1.90m 125kg. Dylan BC Athletics. Was at University of Texas.
At SP: OG: '08- 3, '12- 5; WCh: '07-09-11-13: 8/dnq 17/2/3; CG: '10- 1; WI: '10- 3; PAm: '07- 1, '11- 1; PAm-J: '99- 2 (1 HT, 3 DT); CCp: '10- 5. At HT: WCh: '01- dnq 31; WJ: '00- 2 (dnq DT). Won Canadian HT 2001-02, SP 2005-10, 2012; DL SP 2011.
Seven Canadian shot records 2008-11.
Progress at SP: 1999- 16.16, 2000- 16.30, 2001- 18.07, 2004- 19.55, 2005- 19.83, 2006- 20.62, 2007- 20.72, 2008- 21.04, 2009- 20.92, 2010- 21.58, 2011-

22.21, 2012- 21.50, 2013- 21.45. pbs: DT 54.60 '00, HT 71.51 '03, Wt 22.78i '03.

Derek DROUIN b. 6 Mar 1990 Sarnia, Ontario 1.95m 80kg. Student of exercise science at Indiana University.
At HJ: OG: '12- 3=; WCh: '13- 3WY: '07- 10. Won PAmJ 2009, CAN 2012-13, NCAA 2013, Franc G 2013.
Two Canadian high jump records 2013.
Progress at HJ: 2007- 2.07, 2008- 2.11, 2009- 2.27, 2010- 2.28i/2.26, 2011- 2.33i/2.23, 2012- 2.31, 2013- 2.38. pbs: 60mh 7.98i '12, 1000m 2:45.06i '13, 110mh 14.04 '13, PV 4.15i '13. 3.65 '11; LJ 7.20i '13, 6.85 '11; Hep 5817i '13.

Damian WARNER b. 4 Nov 1989 London, Ontario 1.85m 83kg.
At Dec: OG: '12- 5; WCh: '11- 18, '13- 3. Canadian champion 2011-13. At Hep: WI: '14- 7.
Progress at Dec: 2010- 7449, 2011- 8102A/7832, 2012- 8442, 2013- 8512. pbs: 60m 6.74i '10, 100m 10.34 '13, 200m 20.96 '13, 400m 47.63 '13, 1000m 2:37.98i '14, 1500m 4:29.85 '12, 60mh 7.69i '14, 110mh 13.61 '12, HJ 2.09 '13, PV 4.80A '12, LJ 7.54 '12, TJ 14.75w '08, SP 14.23 '13, DT 45.90 '12, JT 64.67 '13, Hep: 6129 14.
Made 340 points improvement on pb when 5th at 2012 Olympics, setting six pbs, and 70 more at 2013 Worlds, with thrtee pbs. Won Götzis & Talence 2013.

Women

Sultana FRIZELL b. 24 Oct 1984 Perth, Ontario 1.83m 110kg. Was at University of Georgia.
At HT: OG: '08/12- dnq 33/25; WCh: '09- 10, '13- dnq 16; CG: '10- 1; PAm: '07- 7, '11- 2; PAm-J: '03- 4; Canadian champion 2007-08, 2010, 2013. Four Commonwealth hammer records 2009-12, North American 2012, seven Canadian 2008-12. Progress at HT: 2002- 54.75, 2003- 57.95, 2004- 63.36, 2005- 66.42, 2006- 63.39, 2007- 67.92, 2008- 70.94, 2009- 72.07, 2010- 72.24, 2011- 71.46, 2012- 75.04, 2013- 71.57. pbs: SP 15.82 '06, Wt 20.37i '05, JT 46.58 '04.

Brianne THEISEN-EATON b. 18 Dec 1988 Humboldt 1.80m 64kg. Sasketchewan. Student at University of Oregon
At Hep: OG: '12- 10; WCh: '09- 15, '13- 2; WJ: '06- 17. Won CAN 2013, PAm-J 2007, NCAA 2009-10, 2012. At Pen: WI: '14- 2.
Progress at Hep: 2005- 5181, 2006- 5240, 2007- 5413, 2008- 5738, 2010- 6094, 2012- 6440, 2013- 6530. pbs: 200m 23.77 '13, 400m 53.72 '12, 800m 2:09.03 '13, 60mh 8.13i '14, 100mh 13.09A '12, 13.13 '13; HJ 1.88i '12, 1.86 '10; LJ 6.37/6.39w '13, SP 13.86i '14, 13.28 '13; JT 46.47 '12, Pen 4766i '14.
Won Götzis 2013. Married Ashton Eaton on 15 July 2013.

Angela WHYTE b. 22 May 1980 Edmonton 1.70m 56kg. Graduate in crime and justice studies from University of Idaho, USA.
At 100mh: OG: '04- 6, '08- h; WCh: '01-03-05-07-

09-13: h/sf/sf/8/h/6; CG: '02-06-10: 5/2/2; PAm: '03- 5, '07- 3, '11- 2. Canadian champion 2001, 2013.
Progress at 100mh: 1999- 13.97/13.43Aw, 2000- 13.37A/13.58, 2001- 13.09/12.82w, 2002- 13.03 /13.00w, 2003- 12.78, 2004- 12.69, 2005- 12.88, 2006- 12.69, 2007- 12.63/12.55w, 2008- 12.96, 2009- 12.93, 2010- 12.98/12.93w, 2011- 12.88/12.76w, 2012- 12.83/12.75w, 2013- 12.66A/12.76/12.52w. pbs: 60m 7.36i '08, 100m 11.63 '03, 11.37w '04; 200m 23.60 '07, 800m 2:19.91 '03, 55mh 7.48iA '03, 60mh 7.92i '08, 400mh 58.74 '01, HJ 1.68 '03, LJ 6.21i '08, 6.15 '07; SP 11.98 '03, JT 37.79 '03, Hep 5745 '03.

Jessica ZELINKA b. 3 Sep 1981 London, Ontario 1.72m 62kg. Calgary AB.
At Hep(/100mh): OG: '08- 5, '12- 6/7; WCh: '05- 11, '11- 9, '13- (sf); CG: '06- 4, '10- 2; PAm: '07- 1; WJ: '00- 5/h. Won CAN Hep 2001, 2004-06, 2008, 2010, 2012; 100mh 2012.
Six Canadian heptathlon records 2006-12.
Progress at 100mh. Hep: 1996- 4700, 1997- 4586, 1998- 14.18/14.13w, 4859; 1999- 14.18, 5059; 2000- 13.81, 5583; 2001- 13.67, 5702; 2002- 5962, 2003- 13.52, 6031; 2004- 13.26/13.10w, 6296; 2005- 13.42/13.15w, 6137; 2006- 13.08, 6314; 2007- 13.25, 6343; 2008- 12.97, 6490; 2010- 13.19, 6204; 2011- 13.01, 6353; 2012- 12.65, 6599A/6480; 2013- 12.86/ 12.66w. pbs: 50m 6.56i '02, 60m 7.53i '04, 100m 11.63 '14, 11.36w '13; 200m 23.32 '12, 800m 2:07.95 '08, 60mh 8.19i '06, HJ 1.79 '07, LJ 6.19/6.23w '06, SP 14.97 '07, JT 46.60A '12, Pen 4386i '07.

CHILE

Governing body: Federación Atlética de Chile, Calle Santo Toribio No 660, Ñuñoa, Santiago de Chile. Founded 1914.
National Champions 2013: Men: 100m/200m: Cristián Reyes 10.68/21.25, 400m: Sergio Germain 47.84, 800m: Aquiles Zúñiga 1:52.35, 1500m: Iván López 3:41.47, 5000m/10,000m: Leslie Encina 14:22.48/30:45.45, 3000mSt: Mauricio Valdivia 9:07.15, 110mh: Diego Lyon 14.29, 400mh: Gustavo Gutiérrez 52.04, HJ: Rodrigo Arriagada 1.99, PV: Daniel Zupeuc 5.00, LJ: Daniel Pineda 7.50, TJ: Sandro Corona 14.84, SP: José Joaquín Ballivián 16.72, DT: Nicolás Laso 51.16, HT: Roberto Sáez 61.02, JT: Tomás Labarca 60.87, 20kW: Yerko Araya 1:29:14. Women: 100m: Viviana Olivares 11.97, 200m: María Ignacia Montt 24.67, 400m/400mh: Javiera Errázuriz 55.34/60.39, 800m: Nicole Manríquez 2:13.99, 1500m: Javiera Faletto 4:46.21, 5000m: Clara Morales 17:34.97, 10,000m: Jennifer González 35:27.67, 3000m St: Margarita Masías 11:27.43, 100mh: Carolina Castillo 14.52, HJ: Javiera Lazo 1.64, PV: Macarena Fuica 3.40, LJ: Daniela Pavez 6.16, TJ: Javiera Jorquera 12.50, SP: Ivana Gallardo 14.95, DT: Karen Gallardo 53.27, HT: Constanza Ávila 51.05, JT: María Paz Ríos 45.91, 20kW: Wendy Cornejo BOL 1:40:24.

CHINA

Governing body: Athletic Association of the People's Republic of China, 2 Tiyuguan Road, Beijing 100763.
National Championships first held in 1910 (men), 1959 (women). **2013 Champions: Men**: 100m: Su Bingtian 10.17, 200m: Xie Zhenye 20.67, 400m: Wang Weihai 47.17, 800m: Yang Xiaofei 1:50.58, 1500m: Li Lei 3:46.88, 5000m: Su Guoxiong 14:13.20, 10,000m: Ren Longyun 29:58.66, Mar: Yang Changjia 2:25:20, 3000mSt: Zhang Zhongji 8:52.74, 110mh: Shi Dongpeng 13.54, 400mh: Cheng Wen 50.74, HJ: Wang Chen 2.15, PV: Lu Yao 5.30, LJ: Tang Gongchen 7.85, TJ: Cao Shuo 17.58, SP: Ding Weiye 19.47, DT: Xin Jia 57.88, HT: Wan Yong 73.28, JT: Zhao Qinggang 78.55, Dec: Zhu Hengjun 7405, 20kW: Li Jianbo 1:18:52, 50kW: Niu Wenbin 3:56:56. **Women**: 100m/200m: Wei Yongli 11.39/23.55, 400m: Cheng Chong 53.54, 800m: Song Tingting 2:04.49, 1500m: Liu Fang 4:16.71, 5000m: Wei Xiaojie 15:30.61, 10,000m: Liu Ruihian 32:08.76, Mar: Zhang Yingying 2:31:19, 3000mSt: Fang Xiaoyu 10:06.52, 100mh: Wu Shujiao 13.09, 400mh: Xiao Xia 57.54, HJ: Zheng Xingjuan 1.84, PV: Li Ling 4.40, LJ: Wang Rong 6.33, TJ: Xie Limei 14.17, SP: Li Ling 17.80, DT: Sun Taifeng 58.73, HT: Hao Shuai 67.96, JT: Liu Shiying 59.58, Hep: Wang Qingling 5619, 20kW: Sun Huanhuan 1:27:36.
National Games 2013: Men: 100m/200m: Zhang Peimeng 10.08/20.47, 400m: Chen Jianxin 46.19, 1500m: Zhang Haikun 3:41.27, 10,000m: Ren Longyun 29:03.83, 3000mSt: Wang Yashuan 8:37.66, 110mh Xie Wenjun 13.38, 400mh: Cheng Wen 50.08, HJ: Wang Yu 2.29, PV: Xue Changrui 5.60, LJ: Li Jinzhe 8.34, TJ: Cao Shuo 17.26, SP: Wang Guangfu 20.12, DT: Wu Jian 60.98, HT: Wang Shizhu 75.20, JT: Zhao Qinggang 83.14, Dec: Zhu Hengjun 7662, 20kmW: Wang Zhen 1:19:54, 50kmW: Wu Qianlong 3:51:35. **Women**: 100m: Tao Yujia 11.48, 200m: Jiang Lan 23.31, 400m: Zhao Yanmin 52.15, 800m/1500m: Zhao Jing 2:02.36/4:12.32, 5000m: Jiang Xiaoli 15:49.14, 10,000m: Cao Mojie 31:55.66, 100mh: Wu Shujiao 12.96, 400mh: Xiao Xia 56.25, HJ: Zheng Xingjuan 1.92, PV: Li Ling 4.65, LJ: Xu Xiaoling 6.48, TJ: Xie Limei 14.39, SP: Gong Lijiao 18.75, DT: Tan Jian 64.11, HT: Zhang Wenxiu 73.68, JT: Li Lingwei 63.06, Hep: Wang Qingling 5785, 20kmW: Lu Xiuzhi 1:27:53.

CAI Zelin b. 11 Apr 1991 Dali, Yunnan 1.72m 55kg.
At 20kW: OG: '12- 4; WCh: '13- 26. At 10,000mW: WJ: '10- 2; WCp: '10- 2J Wwon CHN 20kW 2012.
Progress at 20kW: 2010- 1:22:28, 2011- 1:21:07, 2012- 1:18:47, 2013- 1:18:55. Pbs: 10,000W 38:59.98 '12, 30kmW 2:45:13 '09.

CHEN Ding b. 5 Aug 1992 Dali, Yunnan 1.80m 62kg. Guangdong.

At 20kW: OG: '12- 1; WCh: '13- 2; WCp: '10- 5, '12- 8. At 10,000mW: WJ: '08- 2; WCp: '08- 2J. World youth 10,000m walk record 2008.
Progress at 20kW: 2008- 1:20:16, 2009- 1:21:21, 2010- 1:21:59, 2011- 1:18:52, 2012- 1:17:40, 2013- 1:21:09. Pbs: 10kW 38:23 '10, 39:47.20t '08; 30kmW 2:12:16 '10.

CHU Yafei b. 5 Sep 1988 Haikou 1.72m 55kg. Inner Mongolia.
At 20kW: OG: '08- 10; WCh: '09- 13, '11- 11; WCp: '10- 2; AsiG: '10- 2; AsiC: '09- 2; WUG: '07- 1. 2nd RWC 2011.
At 10km road walk records: Asian junior (39:00) 2006, Asian (38:40) 2010.
Progress at 20kW: 2004- 1:27:23, 2005- 1:22:18, 2006- 1:18:44, 2007- 1:24:37, 2008- 1:21:04, 2009- 1:19:51, 2010- 1:21:11, 2011- 1:18:38, 2012- 1:24:48, 2013- 1:21:52. Pbs: 10,000mW 39:22.47 '12, 37:57R '10; 30kW 2:14:46 '06.

LI Jianbo b. 14 Nov 1986 Qujing, Yunnan 1.76m 57kg.
At 50kW: OG: '08- 14, '12- 6; WCh: '11- 25, '13- 26.
At 20kW: WCh: '09- 12; AsiC: '09- 1. Won Asian walks 50k 2009, Asi-J 10kW 2004, CHN 20kW 2013, 50kW 2012.
Progress at 20kW, 50kW: 2003- 1:26:37, 4:03:08; 2004- 1:26:21, 2005- 1:19:34, 3:45:13; 2006- 1:19:38, 3:43:02; 2007- 1:23:23, 3:53:24; 2008- 1:20:47, 3:52:12; 2009- 1:19:10, 3:44:59; 2010- 1:21:08, 2011- 1:25:45, 3:43:38; 2012- 1:20:55, 3:39:01; 2013- 1:18:52, 3:52:12. pb 35kW 2:34:42 '13.

LI Jinzhe b. 1 Sep 1989 Beijing 1.88m 64kg.
At LJ: OG: '12- dnq 20; WCh: '09- dnq 13, '13- 12; WI: '14- 2; AsiC: '09- 1; CCp: '10- 4; won E.Asian 2009, Asian indoors 2012, CHN 2009, CHN NG 2013.
Progress at LJ: 2006- 7.19i, 2007- 7.85, 2008- 7.79, 2009- 8.18, 2010- 8.12/8.29w, 2011- 8.02, 2012- 8.25, 2013- 8.34.

LIU Xiang b. 13 Jul 1983 Shanghai 1.89m 74kg.
At 110mh: OG: '04- 1, '08/'12- h; WCh: '01-03-05-07-11: sf/3/2/1/2; WJ: '00- 4; WUG: '01- 1; AsiG: '02-06-10: 1/1/1; AsiC: '02-05-09: 1/1/1; WCp: '02- dnf, '06- 2. Won WAF 2006, CHN 2002, 2004-06; CHN NG 2005, E.Asian 2001, 2005, 2009. At 60mh: WI: '03-04-08-10-12: 3/2/1/7/2.
World 110mh records 2004 & 2006, five Asian & CHN records 2002-06; World junior records 110mh 2002, indoors 50mh (6.53 and 6.52) & 60mh (7.61 and 7.55). Eight Asian indoor 60mh records 2002-12.
Progress at 110mh: 1999- 14.19, 2000- 13.75, 2001- 13.32, 2002- 13.12, 2003- 13.17, 2004- 12.91, 2005- 13.05, 2006- 12.88, 2007- 12.92, 2008- 13.18, 2009- 13.15, 2010- 13.09, 2011- 13.00, 2012- 12.97/12.87w. pbs: 200m 21.27 '02. 50mh 6.52i '02, 60mh 7.41i '12, HJ 2.04 '98.
With his brilliant Olympic 110mh win in 2004 he tied the world record of 12.91 and become the first Chinese man to win a global athletics

gold medal. Took world record to 12.88 at Lausanne 2006. World age records 16 (13.94)-17-18 2000-02. Injured at 2008 and 2012 Olympics.

SI Tianfeng b. 17 Jun 1984 Xintai, Shandong 1.81m 67kg. Shandong
At 50kW: OG: '08- 17, '12- 3; WCh: '11- 4, '13- dnf; AsiG '10- 1; WCp: '10- 4, '12- 3. Won CHN 2008.
Progress at 50kW: 2003- 3:59:23, 2004- 3:55:37, 2005- 3:42:55, 2006- 3:52:06, 2007- 3:58:27, 2008- 3:45:13, 2009- 3:44:15, 2010- 3:47:04, 2011- 3:38:48, 2012- 3:37:16, 2013- 3:53:19. pb 20kW 1:20:05 '05, 30k 2:11:07 '12, 35k 2:32:16 '12.

WANG Hao b. 16 Aug 1989 Qiqihaer, Inner Mongolia 1.80m 65kg. Heilongjiang.
At 20kW: OG: '08- 4; WCh: '09- 2, '11- 12; WCp: '10- 1; AsiG: '10- 1; won CHN 2007, CHN NG 2009.
Progress at 20kW, 50kW: 2007- 1:21:20.69t, 2008- 1:19:47, 2009- 1:18:13, 3:41:55; 2010- 1:20:50, 2011- 1:21:03, 2012- 1:23:40, 2013- 1:22:40, 4:02:56. Pbs: 10,000mW 41:42.08 '07, 10kW 38:00 '10, 30kW 2:20:47 '07, 50kW 4:10:45 '12.

WANG Zhen b. 24 Aug 1991 Changzhou 1.80m 62kg. Heilongjiang.
At 20kW: OG: '12- 3; WCh: 11- 4, '13- dq; WCp: '12- 1; CHN champion 2011, NG 2013. Won World Race Walking Challenge Final 10k 2010, 2012 (2nd 2011).
Walks records: World junior 10k 2010, Asian 20k & 10,000m track 2012.
Progress at 20kW: 2008- 1:28:01, 2009- 1:22:10, 2010- 1:20:42, 2011- 1:18:30, 2012- 1:17:36, 2013- 1:19:08. Pbs: 5000mW 20:16.04 '09, 10kW 37:44 '10, 38:30.38 '12; 30kmW 2:08:46 '08, 50kmW 3:53:00 '09.

XUE Changrui b. 31 May 1991 Shandong prov.1.83m 60kg
At PV: WCh: '13- 12; WI: '14- 5, AsiC: '13- 1. Won CHN NG 2013.
Progress at PV: 2011- 5.30, 2012- 5.60, 2013- 5.75i/5.65, 2014- 5.76i. pb LJ 7.15 '08

ZHANG Peimeng b. 13 Mar 1987 Beijing 1.86m 78kg.
At 100m: WCh: '13- sf; AsiC: '09-1. WUG: '07- 2/3R. At 200m: OG: '08- h; WJ: '06- sf. Won Chinese 100m 2007, 200m 2011.
Chinese records 100m (3) and 200m 2013.
Progress at 100m: 2004- 10.80, 2005- 10.53, 2006- 10.64, 2007- 10.27, 2008- 10.23, 2009- 10.28, 2010- 10.31, 2011- 10.21, 2012- 10.28, 2013- 10.00. pbs: 60m 6.58i '13, 200m 20.47 '13.

Women

GONG Lijiao b. 24 Jan 1989 Luquan, Hebei Prov. 1.74m 110kg. Hebei.
At SP: OG: '08- 5, '12- 3; WCh: '07-09-11-13: 7/3/4/3; WI: '10- 8, '14- 3; AsiG: '10- 2; AsiC: '09- 1; CCp: '10- 3. Chinese champion 2007-12, NG 2009, 2013; Asian indoor 2008.
Progress at SP: 2005- 15.41i, 2006- 17.92, 2007-

19.13, 2008- 19.46, 2009- 20.35, 2010- 20.13, 2011-
20.11, 2012- 20.22, 2013- 20.12. pb JT 53.94 '07.

GU Siyu b. 11 Feb 1993 1.82m 80kg.
At DT: WCh: '13- dnq.
Progress at DT: 2008- 47.85, 2009- 50.02, 2010-
53.79, 2011- 56.12, 2012- 60.59, 2013- 67.86. pb SP
16.59 '11.

LI Ling b. 7 Feb 1985 Shenyang, Liaoning Prov.
1.83m 84kg. Liaoning.
At SP: OG: '08- 14, '12- 4; WCh: '07- 4, '11- 6, '13-
6; AsiG: '06- 1, '10- 1; AsiC: '05- 3; AsJ: '04- 1;
WCp: '06- 5. Chinese champion 2006, 2013.
Progress at SP: 2002- 15.45, 2003- 16.55, 2004-
17.34, 2005- 18.68, 2006- 19.05, 2007- 19.38, 2008-
18.86, 2009- 18.97, 2010- 19.94, 2011- 19.72, 2012-
19.95, 2013- 19.15.

LI Yanfeng b. 15 May 1979 Suihua City,
Heilongjiang 1.79m 90kg.
At DT: OG: '04- 8, '08- 7, '12- 2; WCh: '11- 1;
AsiG: '10- 1; AsiC: '00-02-03-07: 3/1/1/2; WUG:
'01- 2, '03- 2; WCp: '02- 4, '10- 1. Won E.Asian G
& CHN NG 2009, CHN 2010-11.
Progress at DT: 1997- 56.68, 1998- 57.30, 1999-
63.67, 2000- 60.84, 2001- 61.77, 2002- 62.52, 2003-
61.87, 2004- 64.34, 2005- 61.61, 2007- 62.24, 2008-
63.79, 2009- 66.40, 2010- 66.18, 2011- 67.98, 2012-
67.84, 2013- 63.91.
Married on 6 Oct 2013.

LIU Hong b. 12 May 1987 Anfu, Jiangxi Prov.
1.61m 48kg. Guangdong.
At 20kW: OG: '08- 4, '12- 4; WCh: '07-09-11-13:
19/3,/2/3; WCp: '06- 6; AsiG: '06- 1, '10- 1; won
CHN 2010-11, NG 2009. At 10,000mW: WJ: '06- 1;
won World Race Walking Challenge Final 10k
2012 (2nd 2011).
Asian records 5000m & 20k walk 2012.
Progress at 20kW: 2004- 1:35:04, 2005- 1:29:39,
2006- 1:28:26, 2007- 1:29:41, 2008- 1:27:17, 2009-
1:28:11, 2010- 1:30:06, 2011- 1:27:17, 2012- 1:25:46,
2013- 1:27:06, 2014- 1:27:25. pbs: 3000mW 12:18.18
'05, 5000mW 20:34.76 '12, 10kW 42:30R '10,
43:16.68t '12.

LIU Xiangrong b. 6 Jun 1988 Hohhot, Nei
Mongol region 1.85m 119kg.
At SP: OG: '12- 6; WCh: '09- 10, '11- dnq 17, '13-
10; WI: '12- 6; AsiC: '07-09-11-13: 1/2/2/1; WUG:
'13- 2; Won Asian Indoor 2012, E.Asian 2013.
Progress at SP: 2006- 16.94, 2007- 18.58, 2008-
18.69, 2009- 18.69, 2010- 18.49, 2011- 18.74, 2012-
19.24, 2013- 18.81i/18.73. pb DT 47.77 '06.

LU Huihui b. 26 Jun 1989 Huwan, Henan 1.71m
68kg.
At JT: OG: '12- 5.
Two Asian javelin records 2012-13.
Progress at JT: 2005- 49.62, 2006- 49.96, 2010-
55.35, 2011- 58.72, 2012- 64.95, 2013- 65.62.

LU Xiuzhi b. 26 Oct 1993 Chuzhou 1.67m 52kg.
At 20kW: OG: '12- 6; WCp: '12- 4; 3rd RWC 2012,
won CHN NG 2013, Champs 2014.

Asian junior 20k walk record 2012.
Progress at 20kW: 2011- 1:29:50, 2012- 1:27:01,
2013- 1:27:53, 2014- 1:28:57. pb 10kW 43:16 '12.

QIEYANG Shenjie b. 11 Nov 1990 Haiyan,
Qinghai Prov. 1.60m 50kg.
At 20kW: OG: '12- 3; WCh: '11- 5, '13- 15; WCp:
'12- 15.
Asian 20k walk record 2012.
Progress at 20kW: 2009- 1:35:54, 2010- 1:30:33,
2011- 1:28:04, 2012- 1:25:16, 2013- 1:28:05. pbs:
5000mW 20:42.67 '12, 10kW 43:16 '12.
First athlete from Tibet to win an Olympic
medal.

SUN Huanhuan b. 15 Mar 1990 1.61m 50kg.
At 20kW: WCh: '13- 4.
Progress at 20kW: 2008- 1:32:11, 2009- 1:32:51,
2010- 1:30:35, 2011- 1:29:46, 2012- 1:30:21, 2013-
1:27:36.

TAN Jian b. 20 Jan 1988 Chengdu 1.79m 80kg.
Sichuan,
At DT: OG: '12- dnq; WCh: '11- 6, '13- 6; WJ: '06-
3. Chinese champion 2012, NG 2013.
Progress at DT: 2004- 56.00, 2005- 57.01, 2007-
56.99, 2008- 55.04, 2009- 57.40, 2010- 59.65, 2011-
63.72, 2012- 64.45, 2013- 64.40.

WANG Zheng b. 14 Dec 1987 Xian, Shanxi
Province 1.74m 108kg.
At HT: OG: '08- dnq 32; WCh: '13- 4; WJ: '06- 9;
AsiG: '10- 2; AsiC: '13- 1; won As-J 2006, E.Asian
2009
Asian hammer record 2014.
Progress at HT: 2000- 60.30, 2001- 66.30, 2002-
67.13, 2003- 70.60, 2004- 72.42, 2005- 73.24, 2006-
74.15, 2007- 74.86, 2008- 74.32, 2009- 74.25, 2010-
73.83, 2011- 75.65, 2012- 75.72, 2012- 76.99, 2013-
75.58, 2014- 77.68.

XIE Limei b. 27 Jun 1986 Fujian Prov. 1.73m
57kg. Fujian.
At TJ: OG: '08- 12, '12- dnq 23; WCh: '07- 8, '09-
9, '11- dnq 25; WJ: '04- 2; AsiG: '06- 1, '10- 2;
AsiC: '05- 1, '11- 1; WI: '08- 8, '10- 7; CCp: '10- 4.
Won Asian indoors 2012, CHN 2006-07, 2009-11,
2013; NG 2013.
Asian TJ record 2007.
Progress at TJ: 2002- 13.51, 2003- 13.89, 2004-
14.08, 2005- 14.38, 2006- 14.54, 2007- 14.90, 2008-
14.39, 2009- 14.62, 2010- 14.35, 2011- 14.54/14.62w,
2012- 14.21i/13.82, 2013- 14.39. pb LJ 6.41 '06.

ZHANG Wenxiu b. 22 Mar 1986 Dalian 1.82m
108kg. Army.
At HT: OG: '04- 7, '08- 3, '12- 4; WCh: '01-03-05-
07-09-11-13: 11/dnq 14/4/3/5/3/3; WJ: '02- dnq
20; AsiG: '06- 1, '10- 1; AsiC: '05- 1, '09- 1; WCp:
'06- 4, '10- 2. Won Asi-J 2002, CHN 2004, 2006-
10, 2012; NG 2003, 2009, 2013.
Nine Asian hammer records 2001-12, world
youth 2003, two world junior 2004-05.
Progress at HT: 2000- 60.30, 2001- 66.30, 2002-
67.13, 2003- 70.60, 2004- 72.42, 2005- 73.24, 2006-
74.15, 2007- 74.86, 2008- 74.32, 2009- 74.25, 2010-

73.83, 2011- 75.65, 2012- 75.72, 2012- 76.99, 2013-
75.58. World age bests at 15-16-18.

COLOMBIA

Governing body: Federación Colombiana de
Atletismo, Calle 27° No. 25-18, Apartado Aéreo
6024, Santafé de Bogotá. Founded 1937.
National Games Champions 2013: Men: 100m:
Isidro Montoya 10.40, 200m 400m: Bernardo
Baloyes 20.54w/46.88, 800m: Rafith Rodríguez
1:49.73, 1500m/3000mSt: Gerald Giraldo 3:47.44
/8:52.36, 5000m/10,000m: Javier Akexander
Guarin 14:25.23/30:22.89, 110mh: Paulo César
Villar 14.07, 400mh: Yeison Rivas 51.37, HJ:
Wanner Miller 2.14, PV: César Lucumi 4.95, LJ:
Edwin Murillo 7.81, TJ: Jhon Freddy Murillo
16.68, SP: Edder Moreno 17.60, DT: Mauricio
Ortega 53.37, HT: Jacobo de León 62.13, JT: Arley
Ibargüen 75.70, Dec: José Gregorio Lemus 6848,
10,000mW: Jorge Díaz 40:30.60, 20kW: Eider
Arévalo 1:25:00, 35kW: Jorge Ruiz 2:42:15.
Women: 100m: María Alejandra Idrobo 11.64,
200m: Merlin Palacios 23.76, 400m: Yenifer Padilla
53.76, 800m/1500m: Rosibel García 2:07.00/4:21.97,
5000m/10,000m: Carolina Tabares 16:20.57/
35:33.64, 3000mSt: Muriel Coneo 10:50.06, 100mh:
Briggit Merlano 13.12, 400mh: Princesa Oliveros
59.32, HJ: Anyi Paola García 1.76, PV: Milena
Agudelo 3.70, LJ: Yorsiris Urrutia 6.25, TJ: Giselly
Landázuri 13.81, SP: Sandra Lemus 16.13, DT:
Johana Martínez 55.87, HT: Johana Moreno 66.50,
JT: Flor Ruiz 54.51, Hep: Sandra Milena Denis
4691, 10,000mW: Lorena Arenas 46:00.54, 20kW:
Arabelly Orjuela 1:37:36.

Luis Fernando LÓPEZ b. 3 Jun 1979 Pasto,
Nariño 1.73m 60kg.
At 20kW: OG: '04- 24, '08- 9, '12- dq; WCh: '05-
07-09-11-13: 12/22/5/3/dnf; PAm: '03-07-11: 4/
dq/3; SACh: '08/09- 1; CAG: '06- 1; WCp: '10- 4.
Won PAm Cup 2011.
Walk records: South American 20,000m
(1:20:53.6) 2009 and 10km 2010; Colombian
20km walk 2009.
Progress at 20kW: 2001- 1:26:31A, 2002- 1:26:47.6t,
2003- 1:25:09, 2004- 1:22:52, 2005- 1:20:26, 2006-
1:24:11, 2007- 1:24:22.7tA, 2008- 1:20:59, 2009-
1:20:03, 2010- 1:21:12, 2011- 1:20:38, 2012- 1:23:41,
2013- 1:21:51. pb 10kW Rd 38:10 '10.
Won Colombia's first ever medal at the World
Championships in 2011.

Women

Caterine IBARGÜEN b. 12 Feb 1984 Apartadó,
Antioquia 1.81m 65kg. Studying nursing.
At TJ/(LJ): OG: '12- 2; WCh: '11- 3, '13- 1; WJ: '02:
dnq 17; PAm: '11- 1/3; SACh: '03- 3/2, '05- 3/3,
'06- 2/2, '07- (3), '09- 1, '11- 1/3; CAG: '02- 2, '06-
(2), '10- 2. At HJ: OG: '04- dnq 28=; WCh: '09-
dnq 28=; PAm: '07- 4; SACh: '99-05-06-07-09:
3/1/1/1/1; CAG: '02- 2, '06- 2. Won DL 20-13,
COL HJ 1999, 2001-03, 2005-12; LJ 2003-04, 2006-

08, 2011-12; TJ 2002-05, 2007-12.
Records: South American triple jump (6) 2011,
junior HJ 2004. Colombia HJ (7) 2002-05, LJ (7)
2004-11, TJ (14) 2004-11
Progress at TJ: 2001- 12.90, 2002- 13.38A, 2003-
13.23A, 2004- 13.64A, 2005- 13.66A, 2006-
13.91A/13.98Aw, 2007- 12.66A, 2008- 13.79A,
2009- 13.96A/13.93, 2010- 14.29, 2011- 14.99A/
14.84, 2012- 14.95A/ 14.85, 2013- 14.85/14.93w.
pbs: 200m 25.34 '08, 100mh 14.09 '11, HJ 1.93A
'05, LJ 6.73A/6.87Aw/6.63/6.66w '12, SP 13.79
'10, JT 44.81 '09, Hep 5742 '09.
Formely a high jumper, concentrating fully on
TJ from 2010. First Colombian woman to win a
medal in world champs. Unbeaten in eight
competitions in 2013. She lives in Puerto Rico.

CROATIA

Governing body: Hrvatski Atletski Savez, Trg
kralja Petra Svacica 17, 10000 Zagreb. Founded
1912.
National Champions 2013 Men: 100m:
Tomislav Kasnar 10.67, 200m: Zvonimir
Ivaskovic 22.04, 400m: Zeljko Vioncek 47.26,
800m: Rudolf Kralj 1:51.74, 1500m: Jure Bozinovic
3:56.96, 5000m/10,000m: Goran Grdenic 15:26.75
/32:22.04, Mar: Milorad Vojvodic 2:36:18,
3000mSt: Jure Josipovic 9:27.68, 110mh: Sanjin
Simic 14.77, 400mh: Milan Kotur 53.62, HJ: Alen
Melon 2.14, PV: Hrvoje Sedlar 4.60, LJ: Marko
Prugovecki 7.74, TJ: Andro Duzevic 15.21, SP:
Marin Premeru 20.06, DT: Filip Mihaljevic
56.87, HT: Andras Haklits 70.88, JT: Ante-Roko
Zemunik 68.02, Dec: Nikola Andjelic 5221,
20kmW: Zelimir Haubrih 1:51:18. **Women**:
100m/100mh: Ivana Loncarek 12.03/13.45,
200m/400m: Anita Banovic 24.41/53.68, 800m:
Katarina Smiljanec 2:13.78, 1500m: Sanda Kocis
4:38.95, 3000m/5000m: Lisa Stubic 9:29.47
/16:30.83, 10,000m: Barbara Belusic 36:08.27,
Mar: Marija Vrajic 2:52:38, 3000mSt: Kristina
Bozic 10:49.70, 400mh: Nikolina Horvat 63.02,
HJ: Lucija Zubcic 1.74, PV: Petra Malkoc 3.81, LJ:
Mirjana Gagic 6.18, TJ: Sonja Krnjeta 13.11, SP/
DT: Ivana Muzaric 13.05/44.42, HT: Petra
Jakelici 57.73, JT: Sara Kolak 55.93, Hep: Tihana
Jeletic 4428, 10kmW: Hana Hajsok 65:53.

Women

Sandra PERKOVIC b. 21 Jun 1990 Zagreb
1.83m 80kg. Zagreb.
At DT(/SP): OG: '12- 1; WCh: '09- 9, '13- 1; EC:
'10- 1, '12- 1; WJ: '06- dnq 21, '08- 3/dnq 13; WY:
'07- 2/dnq 13; EJ: '07- 2, '09- 1/5; CCp: '10- 2.
Won DL 2012-13, Med G 2013; CRO SP 2008-10,
DT 2010, 2012.
Eight Croatian DT records 2009-14, two SP
2010-11.
Progress at DT: 2006- 50.11, 2007- 55.42, 2008-
55.89, 2009- 62.79, 2010- 66.93, 2011- 67.96/69.99dq,
2012- 69.11, 2013- 68.96, 2014- 70.51. pb SP
16.99i/16.40 '11.

First woman to win European and Olympic gold for Croatia. Won 11 of 12 competitions in both 2012 and 2013. 70.51m in March 2014 was women's world's best discus throw since 1992. Six months drugs ban 2011.

Blanka VLASIC b. 8 Nov 1983 Split 1.92m 75kg. ASK Split.
At HJ: OG: '00- dnq 17, '04- 11, '08- 2; WCh: '01-03-05-07-09-11: 6/7/dnq 19=/1/1/2; EC: '02- 5=, '06- 4, 10- 1; WJ: '00- 1, '02- 1; WY: '99- 8; EU23: '03- 1; EJ: '01- 7; WI: '03-04-06-08-10-14: 4/3/2/1/1/6; EI: '07- 4, '09- 5=; CCp: '10- 1. Won DL 2010, WAF 2007-09, DL 2011, MedG 2001, CRO 2001-02, 2005.
Ten Croatian high jump records 2003-09.
Progress at HJ: 1998- 1.68, 1999- 1.80, 2000- 1.93, 2001- 1.95, 2002- 1.96, 2003- 2.01, 2004- 2.03, 2005- 1.95, 2006- 2.05i/2.03, 2007- 2.07, 2008- 2.06, 2009- 2.08, 2010- 2.06i/2.05, 2011- 2.03, 2013- 2.00. 2014- 2.00i.
IAAF Woman Athlete of the Year 2010. Won 5/6 Golden League HJs in both 2007 and 2008. She has had 103 competitions at 2m or higher to Feb 2014 (and 171 jumps over 2m), including 42 successive Jul 2007- Feb 2009, but in 2008 lost on count-back both at Olympic Games (when she won first ever athletics medal for Croatia) and in the final Golden League meeting, thus losing her share of the Jackpot. She had 60 attempts at the world record 2007-10. Her father Josko set the Croatian decathlon record with 7659 (1983) and named his daughter after Casablanca, where he won Mediterranean Games title.

CUBA

Governing body: Federación Cubana de Atletismo, Calle 13 y C Vedado 601, Zona Postal 4, La Habana 10400. Founded 1922.
National Champions 2013: Men: 100m: Yaniel Carrero 10.0h, 200m: Yoandys Lescay 21.13, 400m: Oreste Rodríguez 46.87, 800m/1500m: Andy González 1:50.04/3:54.38, Mar: Henrry Jaen 2:30:30, 110mh: Ignacio Morales 13.54, 400mh: Omar Cisneros 50.07, HJ: Víctor Moya 2.16, PV: Lázaro Borges 5.40, LJ: Junior Díaz 8.02, TJ: Ernesto Revé 17.46, SP: Isidro Portuondo 16.90, DT: Jorge Fernández 62.12, HT: Reinier Mejías 74.95, JT: Guillermo Martínez 85.59, Dec: José Angel Mendieta 7953, 20kW: Rubén Goliat 1:25:06. **Women**: 100m/200m: Dulaimi Débora Odelín 11.50/23.77, 400m: Daysiurami Bonne 53.18, 800m: Sahily Diago 2:04.46, 1500m: Rose Marie Almanza 4:22.03, Mar: Yailén García 3:00:28, 100mh: Belkis Milanés 13.21, 400mh: *none*, HJ: Lesyaní Mayor 1.80, PV: Yarisley Silva 4.81, LJ: Paula Álvarez 6.04, TJ: Mabel Gay 14.09, SP: Yaniuvis López 17.48, DT: Yaimé Pérez 66.01, HT: Yipsi Moreno 72.36, JT: Lismania Muñoz 59.29, Hep: Yorgelis Rodríguez 6186.

Lázaro BORGES b. 19 Jun 1986 La Habana 1.73m 70kg.
At TJ: OG: '08/12- dnq nh/16=; WCh: '11- 2, '13-dnq 21=; WI: '12- 5=; PAm: '07- nh, '11- 1; Won IbAm 2010, CAC 2008, Cuban 2005-07, 2009-10, 2013.
Pole vault records: two CAC 2011, 7 Cuban 2011, CAC indoor 2012.
Progress at TJ: 2002- 3.60, 2003- 4.25, 2004- 4.80, 2005- 5.10, 2006- 5.30, 2007- 5.50, 2008- 5.70, 2009- 5.65, 2010- 5.60, 2011- 5.90, 2012- 5.72i/5.60, 2013- 5.71.
Breakthrough season in 2011, when he improved national record by 25cm from six occasions, and became first Cuban ever to medal at PV in a World Championship, and first ever Cuban male PV gold at Pan-American Games.

Omar CISNEROS b. 19 Nov 1989 Camagüey 1.86m 80kg.
At 400mh: OG: '12- sf; WCh: '09/11- sf, '13- 4; PAmG: '11- 1/1R. Won IbAm 2010, Cuban 2009-10, 2013. At 400m: PAm: '07- sf.
Four Cuban 400mh records 2010-13.
Progress at 400mh: 2007- 49.57, 2008- 50.1, 2009- 48.87, 2010- 48.21, 2011- 47.99A/49.26, 2012- 48.23, 2013- 47.93. pbs: 200m 21.36 '07, 400m 45.47 '12, 600m 1:17.61 '13.

Jorge FERNÁNDEZ b. 2 Dec 1987 Matanzas 1.90m 100kg. MTZ.
At DT: OG: '08- dnq 27, '12- 11; WCh: '11- 8, '13-10; PAmG: '11- 1; WJ: '06- 5. Won CAC 2008-09, Cuban 2009-14 (& SP 2014).
Progress at DT: 2005- 53.69, 2006- 54.77, 2007- 57.57, 2008- 63.31, 2009- 63.92, 2010- 66.00, 2011- 65.89, 2012- 66.05, 2013- 65.09. pb SP 16.94 '14.

Yordani GARCÍA b. 21 Nov 1988 San Luis, Pinar del Río 1.93m 88kg.
At Dec: OG: '08- 15, '12- 14; WCh: '07- 8, '09- 8, '11- dnf; PAm: '07- 2, '11- 3; WJ: '06- 2. At Oct: WY: '05- 1. At Hep: WI: '12- 7. Won Cuban Dec 2006-07, 2010; PV 2011; PAmG 2009, 2013. Cuban & CAC junior decathlon record 2007. World youth octathlon record (6482) 2005.
Progress at Dec: 2005- 6765, 2006- 7879h, 2007- 8257, 2008- 7992, 2009- 8496, 2010- 8381h, 2011- 8397, 2012- 8061, 2013- 8157h, 2014- 8337. pbs: 60m 6.89i '09, 6.6 '13; 100m 10.60 '09, 10.5dt '10, 300m 34.4 '13, 400m 48.34 '09, 1000m 2:50.21i '12, 1500m 4:31.40 '11, 60mh 7.80i '10, 110mh 13.89 '09, HJ 2.10 '09, PV 4.90 '10, LJ 7.36 '09, SP 16.50 '09, DT 47.70 '08, JT 69.37 '09, Hep 5905i '09.

Guillermo MARTÍNEZ b. 28 Jun 1981 Camagüey 1.85m 100kg.
At JT: OG: '12- dnq 16; WCh: '05-07-09-11-13: 10/9/2/3/dnq 15; PAm: '07- 1, '11- 1; CAG: '06- 1. Won CAC 2009, 2011; IbAm 2010, Cuban 2004-07, 2009-14.
Cuban & CAC javelin records 2006 & 2011.
Progress at JT: 1999- 64.66, 2000- 70.82, 2001-

73.50, 2002- 75.90, 2003- 75.35, 2004- 81.45, 2005-
84.06, 2006- 87.17, 2007- 85.93, 2009- 86.41, 2010-
86.38, 2011- 87.20A, 2012- 82.72, 2013- 85.59.

Orlando ORTEGA b. 29 Jul 1991 La Habana
1.85m 70kg.
At 110mh: OG: '12- 6; WCh: '13- h; WJ: '10- h;
PAm: '11- 3. Cuban champion 2011.
Progress at 110mh: 2009- 14.11, 2010- 13.99, 2011-
13.29/13.1w, 2012- 13.09, 2013- 13.08. pbs: 100m
10.62 '11, 400m 47.84 '09, 50mh 6.66+i '12, 60mh
7.54i '13.

Pedro Pablo PICHARDO b. 30 Jun 1993
Santiago de Cuba 1.85m 71kg.
At TJ: WCh: '13- 2; WJ: '12- 1; WI: '14- 3. Won
CAC-J 2012, CUB 2014.
Progress at TJ: 2009- 14.55, 2010- 15.35/15.45w,
2011- 16.09, 2012- 16.79, 2013- 17.69, 2014- 17.76.

Ernesto REVÉ b. 26 Feb 1992 Guantánamo
1.81m 65kg.
At TJ: WJ: '10- 2; WI: '14- 2. Cuban champion
2012-13. CAC junior triple jump record (=) 2011.
Progress at TJ: 2006- 14.97, 2007- 15.22, 2008-
16.32, 2009- 16.56, 2010- 16.73, 2011- 17.40, 2012-
17.13, 2013- 17.46, 2014- 17.58. pb LJ 7.00 '03.

Dayron ROBLES b. 19 Nov 1986 Guantánamo
1.91m 91kg. AS Monaco.
At 110mh: OG: '08- 1, '12- dq; WCh: '05-07-09-11:
sf/4/sf/dq(1); WJ: '04- 2, WY: '03- 6; CAG: '06- 1;
PAm: '07- 1, '11- 1; WCp: '06- 3; won PAm-J 2005,
WAF 2007, CAC 2009, Cuban 2006-07, DL 2011.
At 60mh: WI: '06- 2, '10- 1.
World 110mh record 2008, three Cuban & CAC
2006-08, CAC junior record 2005. Two CAC
60mh indoor records 2008.
Progress at 110mh: 2002- 15.01, 2003- 14.30, 2004-
13.75, 2005- 13.46/13.2/13.41w, 2006- 13.00, 2007-
12.92, 2008- 12.87, 2009- 13.04, 2010- 13.01, 2011-
13.00, 2012- 13.10, 2013- 13.18. pbs: 100m 10.70 '06,
200m 21.85 '06, 50mh 6.39i '08, 60mh 7.33i '08.
Season's record 7 sub-13 second times in 2008.
Disqualified for obstructing Liu Xiang after
finishing first at 2011 Worlds. Pulled muscle in
2012 Olympic final. Left Cuba in 2013, becoming
ineligible to represent the country internationally.

Leonel SUÁREZ b. 1 Sep 1987 Holguín 1.81m
76kg.
At Dec: OG: '08- 3, '12- 3; WCh: '09- 2, '11- 3, '13-
10; PAm: '07- 4, '11- 1. CAC and Cuban champion 2009. At Hep: WI: '10- 7.
CAC decathlon record 2009, four Cuban records
2008-09.
Progress at Dec: 2005- 7267, 2006- 7357, 2007-
8156, 2008- 8527, 2009- 8654, 2010- 8328, 2011-
8501, 2012- 8523, 2013- 8317. pbs: 60m 7.11i '09,
100m 10.90 '08, 10.6w '06; 400m 47.65 '09, 1000m
2:36.12i '10, 1500m 4:16.70 '08, 60mh 7.90i '10,
110mh 14.12 '08, HJ 2.17 '08, PV 5.00 '08, LJ 7.52
'11, SP 15.20 '09, DT 47.32 '11, JT 77.47 '09, Hep
5964i '10.

Won at Talence 2010. Won IAAF Combined
Events Challenge 2011.

Women

Yarelys BARRIOS b. 12 Jul 1983 Pinar del Río
1.72m 98kg.
At DT: OG: '08- 2, '12- 3; WCh: '07-09-11-13:
2/2/3/3; WJ: '02- 7; PAm: '07- 1, '11- 1; CAG: '06-
2; WUG: '07- 1; CCp: '10- 3. Won DL 2010-11,
WAF 2008-09, CAC 2005, 2008-09; CUB 2009-12.
Progress at DT: 1999- 44.45, 2000- 50.22, 2001-
48.92, 2002- 54.10, 2003- 58.37, 2004- 59.51, 2005-
60.61, 2006- 61.01, 2007- 63.90/66.68ex, 2008-
66.13, 2009- 65.86, 2010- 65.96, 2011- 66.40A,
2012- 68.03, 2013- 67.36.

Mabel GAY b. 5 May 1983 Santiago de Cuba
1.85m 69kg.
At TJ: OG: '08- dnq 15; WCh: '03-05-09-11-13: 5/
dnq 18/2/4/5; WJ: '00- 4,'02- 1; WY: '99- 1; PAm:
'03-07-11: 1/3/3; PAm-J: '01- 1; CAG: '06- 1; WI:
'04-10-12: 9/5/3; Won WAF 2009. CAC 2008,
CAC-J 2002, IbAm 2002, Cuban 2003-04, 2006,
2013. CAC junior TJ record 2002.
Progress at TJ: 1997- 13.00, 1998- 13.48, 1999-
13.82, 2000- 14.02, 2001- 14.05, 2002- 14.29, 2003-
14.52, 2004- 14.57i/14.20, 2005- 14.21/14.44w,
2006- 14.27, 2007- 14.66, 2008- 14.41A/14.39,
2009-14.64, 2010- 14.30i/14.06, 2011- 14.67, 2012-
14.40, 2013- 14.45. pb LJ 6.28 '09.
World age 17 record in 1999.

Yipsi MORENO b. 19 Nov 1980 Camagüey
1.71m 81kg.
At HT: OG: '00- 4, '04- 2, '08- 2, '12- 6; WCh: '99-
01-03-05-07-11-13: 18/1/1/1/2/4/6; WJ: '98- 4;
PAm: '99-03-07-11: 2/1/1/1; CAG: '06- 1; WUG:
'01- 2; WCp: '02-06-10: 2/3/3. Won WAF 2003,
2005, 2007-08, PAm-J 1997, IbAm 2004, Cuban
2000-04, 2007, 2012-13.
World junior hammer record 1999, 22 CAC
records 1999-2008.
Progress at HT: 1996- 53.94, 1997- 61.96, 1998-
61.00, 1999- 66.34, 2000- 69.36, 2001- 70.65, 2002-
71.47, 2003- 75.14, 2004- 75.18, 2005- 74.95, 2006-
74.69, 2007- 76.36, 2008- 76.62, 2010- 75.19, 2011-
75.62, 2012- 75.59, 2013- 74.16.
Married to hammer thrower Abdel Murguía
(pb 61.73 '02). Their son (Abdel Murguía
Moreno) born in August 2009.

Yaimé PÉREZ b. 29 May 1991 Santiago de Cuba
1.74m 78kg.
At DT: OG: '12- dnq 29; WCh: '13- 11; WJ: '10- 1.
Cuban champion 2013-14.
Progress at DT: 2007- 46.29, 2008- 51.80, 2009-
55.23, 2010- 59.30, 2011- 59.26, 2012- 62.50, 2013-
66.01. 2014- 65.13. pbs SP 13.88 '08.

Yargeris SAVIGNE b. 13 Nov 1984 Niceto
Pérez, Guantánamo 1.68m 59kg.
At (LJ)/TJ: OG: '08- dnq 17/5, '12- 9; WCh: '05-
3/2, '07- 1, '09- 1, '11- 6; WJ: '02- (dnq); PAm:
'03- (3), '07- 3/1, '11- 2; WI: '06- 5/5, '08- 1, '10- 2,
'12- 4; CCp: '10- 2/3 Won DL 2010, WAF 2007,

CAC TJ 2005, 2009 (LJ 2005,); IbAm 2010, Cuban TJ 2007, 2009, 2011 (LJ 2006-07).
Records: three Cuban TJ 2005-07, two CAC indoor 2008.
Progress at LJ, TJ: 1998- 12.13, 1999- 5.60, 12.65; 2000- 5.92, 12.70; 2001- 6.24, 13.03; 2002- 6.46, 2003- 6.63, 2004- 6.60A/6.52, 2005- 6.77/6.88w, 14.82; 2006- 6.67/6.81w, 14.91; 2007- 6.79i/6.66 /6.81w, 15.28; 2008- 6.77i/6.49, 15.20; 2009- 6.77, 15.00; 2010- 6.91, 15.09; 2011- 14.99, 2012- 6.30, 14.55i/14.35; 2013- 14.05.

Yarisley SILVA b. 1 Jun 1987 Pinar del Rio 1.69m 68kg.
At PV: OG: '08- dnq 27=, '12- 2; WCh: '11- 5, '13- 3; WI: '12- 7, '14- 1; WJ: '06- dnq; PAm: '07- 3, '11- 1; Won CAC 2009, Cuban 2004, 2006-07, 2009, 2012-13.
Pole vault records: 18 Cuban & CAC 2007-13 (9 in 2011), 8 CAC indoor 2012 & 2013 (to 4.82).
Progress at PV: 2001- 2.50, 2002- 3.10, 2003- 3.70, 2004- 4.00, 2005- 4.10, 2006- 4.20, 2007- 4.30, 2008- 4.50, 2009- 4.50, 2010- 4.40, 2011- 4.75A/4.70, 2012- 4.75, 2013- 4.90.

CYPRUS

Governing body: Amateur Athletic Association of Cyprus, Olympic House, 2025 Strovolos, Nicosia. Founded 1983. **National Championships** first held in 1896, 1952 (women). **2013 Champions: Men**: 100m/200m: Panayiotis Ioannou 10.47/21.75w, 400m: Reginos Menelaou 48.30, 800m/1500m: Christos Demetriou 1:52.45/4:00.52, 5000m: Nicolaos Frangou 15:28.07, 10,000m: Rafael Nicodimou 33:05.64, HMar/Mar: Michael Keenan 78:19/2:42:54, 3000mSt: Christoforos Protopapas 9:33.53, 110mh: Milan Trajkovic 13.83, 400mh: Neophytos Georgiou 54.52, HJ: Ioannis Ananiades 2.00, PV: Nicandros Stylianou 4.90, LJ: Periklis Cleovoulou 7.56w, TJ: Panayiotis Volou 15.97, SP: Georgios Arestis 17.77, DT: Apostolos Parellis 59.91, HT: Constantinos Stathelakos 68.61, JT: Constant-inos Stavrou 62.42, Dec: Elvis Kryoukov 6561. **Women**: 100m: Ramona-Anna Papaioannou 11.62, 200m: Eleni Artymata 23.20, 400m: Kalliopi Kountouri 56.30, 800m/ 1500m: Natalia Evangelidou 2:08.01/4:22.37, 5000m/10,000m: Marilena Sophocleous 17:44.95 /36:57.26, HMar/Mar: Panayiota Andreou 1:25:16/3:20:33, 3000mSt: Elpida Christodoulidou 11:27.44, 100mh: Angeliki Athanasopoulou 14.53, 400mh: Elena Stephanou 62.31, HJ: Leontia Kallenou 1.81, PV: Anna Fitidou 3.60, LJ: Nectaria Panayi 6.41, TJ: Eleftheria Christofi 13.35, SP: Florentia Kappa 15.68, DT: Zacharoula Georgiade 52.41, HT: Paraskevi Theodorou 61.24, JT: Alex-andra Tsisiou 50.04, Hep: Rafaella Ioannou 4531w.

CZECH REPUBLIC

Governing body: Cesky atleticky svaz, Diskarská 100, 16900 Praha 6 -Strahov, PO Box

40. AAU of Bohemia founded in 1897. **National Championships** first held in 1907 (Bohemia), 1919 (Czechoslovakia), 1993 CZE. **2013 Champions: Men**: 100m: Zdenek Stromsik 10.32, 200m: Pavel Maslák 20.67, 400m: Jan Tesar 46.77, 800m: Tomas Vystrk 1:53.17, 1500m: Milan Kocourek 3:55.07, 5000m: Lukás Kourek 14:42.64, 10,000m: Milan Kocourek 29:30.20, HMar: Vít Pavlista 65:35, Mar: Jirí Homolác 2:21:37, 3000mSt: Lukás Olejnicek 8:59.13, 110mh: Martin Mazác 13.48, 400mh: Václav Barák 49.95, HJ: Jaroslav Bába 2.25, PV: Jan Kudlicka 5.76, LJ: Jirí Sykora 7.64, TJ: Martin Vachata 15.44, SP: Ladislav Prásil 21.04, DT: Tomás Vonavka 60.38, HT: Lukas Melich 78.04, JT: Petr Frydrych 75.46, Dec: Marek Lukas 7518, 20kW: Pavel Schrom 1:28:32, 50kW: Lukás Gdula 4:12:55. **Women**: 100m: Katerina Cechová 11.37, 200m: Denisa Rosolová 23.25, 400m: Jitka Bartonicková 52.87, 800m: Eliska Kutrová 2:11.14, 1500m: Lucie Sekanová 4:18.96, 5000m: Kristiina Mäki 16:42.00, 10,000m: Monika Preibischová 34:19.05, HMar: Ivana Sekyrová 74:06, Mar: Petra Pastorová 2:26:44, 3000mSt: Michaela Drábková 11:00;.97, 100mh: Lucie Skrobáková 12.79, 400mh: Katerina Hálová 58.69, HJ: Romana Dubnova 1.86, PV: Jirina Svobodová 4.35, LJ: Jana Koresová 6.65, TJ: Lucie Májková 13.23, SP: Jana Kárníková 16.65, DT: Jitka Kubelová 57.54, HT: Tereza Králová 67.15, JT: Petra Andrejsková 53.28, Hep: Katerina Cachová 5702, 20kW: Lucie Pelantová 1:32:08.

Jan KUDLICKA b. 29 Apr 1988 Opava 1.84m 76kg. Dukla Praha.
At PV: OG: '08- 10, '12- 8; WCh: '09: dnq 23=, '11- 9, '13- 7; EC: '10- 10, '12- 6; WJ: '06- 5=; WY: '05- 6; EU23: '09- 8=; WI: '14- 3; EI: '13- 5; Won CZE 2008, 2010-13.
Progress at PV: 2003- 4.21, 2004- 4.80, 2005- 5.09, 2006- 5.30, 2007- 5.61/5.62ex, 2008- 5.70, 2009- 5.62, 2010- 5.65, 2011- 5.81ex/5.65, 2012- 5.73, 2013- 5.83ex/5.77i/5.76, 2014- 5.80i. pbs: 60m 7.11i '07, HJ 2.05i/2.03 '07, LJ 7.55 '07, TJ 14.41 '07.

Pavel MASLÁK b. 21 Feb 1991 Havírov 1.76m 67kg. Dukla Praha.
At 400m: OG: '12- sf (h 200m); WCh: '13- 5; EC: '12- 1; WY: '07- h; WI: '12- 5, '14- 1; EI: '13- 1/3R. At 200m: WJ: '10- 7; EU23: '11- 3, '13- 3; EJ: '09- 5/2R. At 100m: WJ: '08- h. Won CZE 200m 2012-13, 400m 2011.
European indoor 300m & 500m bests 2014. CZE records: 200m (4) 2012-13, 400m (4) 2012-13.
Progress at 400m: 2006- 50.41, 2007- 48.30, 2008- 47.60, 2009- 47.44, 2010- 46.89, 2011- 47.05i/47.43, 2012- 44.91, 2013- 44.84. pbs: 60m 6.65i '14, 100m 10.36 '13, 200m 20.49 '13, 300m 32.15i '14, 32.34 '13; 500m 1:00.35 '13.
European Athletics Rising Star Award 2012.

Lukás MELICH b. 16 Sep 1980 Jilemnice, Liberecky kraj 1.86m 110kg. Dukla Praha.
At HT: OG: '08- dnq 29, '12- 6; WCh: '05-09: dnq

14/14, '13- 3; WJ: '98- 10; EC: '06/12: dnq 16/28; EU23: '01- 11; EJ: '99- 5. CZE champion 2003, 2006-10, 2012-13.
Progress at HT: 1996- 52.02, 1997- 59.90, 1998- 64.64, 1999- 68.73, 2000- 69.08, 2001- 71.47, 2002- 70.82, 2003- 76.38, 2004- 76.22, 2005- 79.36, 2006- 77.91, 2007- 74.74, 2008- 76.97, 2009- 78.91, 2010- 73.24, 2011- 75.40, 2012- 79.44, 2013- 80.28. pbs: DT 51.56 '03, Wt 24.75 '06.

Ladislav PRÁSIL b. 17 May 1990 Sternberk 1.98m 125kg. Dukla Praha.
At SP: WCh: '13- 5; EC: '12- dnq 19; EU23: '11- 5; EJ: '09- 7; EI: '13- 3; Czech champion 2012-13.
Progress at SP: 2007- 14.32i, 2008- 16.82, 2009- 17.67, 2010- 18.26, 2011- 18.41, 2012- 20.14, 2013- 21.47.

Vitezslav VESELY b. 27 Feb 1983 Hodonin 1.86m 94kg. Dukla Praha.
At JT: OG: '08- 12, '12- 4; WCh: '09- dnq 28, '11- 4, '13- 1; EC: '10- 9, '12- 1; WJ: '02- 9. Won DL 2012- 13, CZE 2008, 2010-12.
Progress at JT: 2001- 66.18, 2002- 73.22, 2003- 66.95, 2004- 72.32, 2005- injured, 2006- 75.98, 2007- 79.45, 2008- 81.20, 2009- 80.35, 2010- 86.45, 2011- 84.11, 2012- 88.34, 2013- 87.68.

Women

Anezka DRAHOTOVÁ b. 22 Jul 1995 Rumburk. USK Praha.
At 20kW: WCh: '13- 7. At 10,000mW: WJ: '12- 6; EJ: '11- 13, '13- 1 (9 3000mSt); ECp: '13- 2J. At 5000mW: WY: '11- 6. World Mountain Running: '12- 7J.
Czech records 10,000m 2013, 20km walk (2) 2013-14.
Progress at 20kW: 2013- 1:29:05, 2014- 1:28:13. pbs: 1500m 4:24.46i '14, 4:24.89 '13; 3000m 9:26.28 '13, 5000m 16:47.24 '13, 3000mSt 10:10.45 '13, 10kmRd 33:59 '13, 10,000mW 44:15.87 '13, 44:14+R '14.
19th in junior women's world road race at cycling in 2013. Twin Eliska 4/3 EJ 10,000mW 2011/2013.

Zuzana HEJNOVÁ b. 19 Dec 1986 Liberec 1.70m 54kg. Dukla Praha.
At 400mh/4x400mR: OG: '08- 7, '12- 3; WCh: '05-07-09- sf, '11- 7, '13- 1; EC: '06- sf, '10- 4, 12- 4/3R; EU23: '07- 3; WJ: '02- 5, '04- 2; EJ: '03- 3; '05- 1; WY: '03- 1; WI: '10- 3R; ET: '09- 3, '11- 1. Won DL 2013. At 400m: EI: '13- 4/3R. At Pen: EI: '11- 7. Won CZE 400mh 2006, 2009.
12 Czech 400mh records 2005-13. Three world bests 300mh 2011 (38.91) and 2013 (38.75 & 38.16).
Progress at 400mh: 2002- 58.42, 2003- 57.54, 2004- 57.44, 2005- 55.89, 2006- 55.83, 2007- 55.04, 2008- 54.96, 2009- 54.90, 2010- 54.13, 2011- 53.29, 2012- 53.38, 2013- 52.83. pbs: 150m 17.66 '13, 200m 23.65 '13, 300m 37.49A/37.80 '13, 400m 51.90/51.27i '13, 800m 2:07.99i '11, 60mh 8.25i '11, 100mh 13.36 '11, 13.18w '10; 300mh 38.16 '13, HJ

1.80i '11, 1.74 '04; LJ 5.96i '11, 5.76 '07, SP 12.11i '11, JT 36.11 '10, Pen 4453i '11.
Unbeaten season at hurdles in 2013. Sister of Michaela Hejnová (b. 10 Apr 1980) pb Hep 6174w/6065 '04; OG: '04- 26; EC '02- 7; EU23: '01- 5; WJ: '98- 5; EJ: '97- 6/'99- 6 (100mh); WUG: '01- 5, '03- 3.

Eliska KLUCINOVÁ b. 14 Apr 1988 Prague 1.77m 69kg. USK Praha.
At Hep: OG: '12- 17; WCh: '09- 23, '13- 7; EC: '10- 7, '12- 7; WJ: '06- 8; WY: '05- 8; EU23: '09- 4, EJ: '07- 2; WUG: '13- 4. Won CZE LJ 2012, Hep 2008-09.
Three CZE heptathlon records 2010-13.
Progress at Hep: 2004- 5006, 2005- 5074, 2006- 5468, 2007- 5844, 2008- 5728, 2009- 6015, 2010- 6268, 2012- 6283, 2013- 6332. pbs: 200m 24.56 '12, 800m 2:12.50 '13, 60mh 8.67i '13, 100mh 13.97 '13, HJ 1.89 '13, LJ 6.30 '10, SP 14.49i/14.48 '10, JT 50.75 '10, Pen 4291i '11.

Denisa ROSOLOVÁ b. 21 Aug 1986 Karvina 1.75m 63kg. née Scerbová. USK Praha.
At 400m/4x400mR: WCh: '11- sf; EC: '10- 5; WI: '10- 3R, '12- 6; EI: '11- 1, '13- 5/3R; ET: '11- 2. At 400mh: OG: '12- 7; WCh: '13- sf; EC: '12- 2/3R.
At LJ: OG: '04/08- dnq 24/20; WCh: '07- dnq 13; WJ: '04- 1; WY: '01- 10, '03- 2; EJ: '03- 4, '05- 1; EI: '07- 3. At Hep: OG: '08- dnf; EC: '06- dnf. Won CZE LJ 2004, 2007-08; 200m 2008, 2010-11, 2013; 400mh 2012.
Progress at 400m, 400mh: 2001- 57.26, 2002- 55.55, 2004- 60.09H, 2007- 54.05i, 2008- 53.61i, 2009- 55.63i, 2010- 50.85, 2011- 50.84, 2012- 52.07, 54.24; 2013- 52.12i, 54.38. pbs: 60m 7.44i '11, 100m 11.61/11.32w '10, 200m 23.03 '10, 300m 36.94i/37.09 '10, 800m 2:11.70 '08, 60mh 8.20i '08, 100mh 13.32 '08, HJ 1.80i/1.77 '06, LJ 6.68 '04, TJ 13.10 '05, SP 12.48 '08, JT 35.12 '07, Pen 4632i '06, Hep 6104 '08.
Divorced from husband tennis player Lukas Rosol, who achieved top fame in 2012 by beating Rafael Nadal at Wimbledon.

Barbora SPOTÁKOVÁ b. 30 Jun 1981 Jablonec nad Nisou 1.82m 80kg. Dukla Praha.
At JT: OG: '04- dnq 23, '08- 1, '12- 1; WCh: '05-07-09-11: dnq 13/1/2/2; EC: '02- dnq 17, '06- 2, '10- 3; EU23: '03- 6; WUG: '03- 4, '05- 1; ET: '09- 2, '11- 3; won DL 2010, 2012; WAF 2006-08, Czech 2003, 2005-12. At Hep: WJ: '00- 4.
World javelin record 2008, two European records 2008, 11 Czech records 2006-08. World heptathlon javelin best (60.90) in 2012.
Progress at JT: 1996- 31.32, 1997- 37.28, 1998- 44.56, new: 1999- 41.69, 2000- 54.15, 2001- 51.97, 2002- 56.76, 2003- 56.65, 2004- 60.95, 2005- 65.74, 2006- 66.21, 2007- 67.12, 2008- 72.28, 2009- 68.23, 2010- 68.66, 2011- 71.58, 2012- 69.55, 2013- 62.33. pbs: 200m 25.33/25.11w '00, 800m 2:18.29 '00, 60mh 8.68i '07, 100mh 13.99 '00, 400mh 62.68 '98, HJ 1.78 '00, LJ 5.65 '00, SP 14.53 '07, DT 36.80 '02, Hep 5880 '12, Dec 6749 '04.

Son Janek born 24 May 2013.
Jirina SVOBODOVÁ b. 20 May 1986 Plzen 1.75m 69kg. née Ptácníková. USK Praha.
At PV: OG: '12- 6=; WCh: '09- dnq 16=, '11- 7, '13- 8=; EC: '06- dnq 27, '10- 5, '12- 1; WJ: '02/04- nh; EJ: '03- 6, '05- 4; WY: '03- 5; WUG: '09- 1; WI: '10-12-14: 5/6/2=; EI: '11- 4=, '13- 4; ET: '09- 5, '11- 3. CZE champion 2009-11, 2013.
Czech pole vault record 2013.
Progress at PV: 2001- 3.20, 2002- 4.00, 2003- 4.02, 2004- 4.11i/3.90, 2005- 4.15, 2006- 4.27, 2007- 4.22i/ 4.00, 2008- 4.28, 2009- 4.55, 2010- 4.66, 2011- 4.65, 2012- 4.72, 2013- 4.76. pb LJ 5.85 '10, 5.95i '11.
Married Petr Svoboda (1 EI 60mh 2011, CZE 110mh record 13.27 '10) on 19 Sep 2012.

DENMARK

Governing body: Dansk Athletik Forbund, Idraettens Hus, Brøndby Stadion 20, DK-2605 Brøndby. Founded 1907.
National Championships first held in 1894.
2013 Champions: Men: 100m: Kristoffer Hari 10.62, 200m/400m: Nick Ekelund-Arenander 20.98/46.23, 800m: Nick Jensen 1:50.66, 1500m: Andreas Bueno 3:55.79, 5000m: Jesper Faurschou 14:34.30, 10,000m: Abdi Hakim Ulad 29:39.09, HMar: Lars Budolfsen 66:17, Mar: Henrik Them Andersen 2:18:02, 3000mSt: Ole Hesselbjerg 9:14.10, 110mh: Andreas Martinsen 13.77, 400mh: Christian Laugesen 52.85, HJ/Dec: Andreas Jeppesen 2.09/5714, PV: Rasmus Jørgensen 5.05, LJ: Benjamin Gabrielsen 7,21, TJ: Peder Nielsen 15.91, SP: Kim Christensen 19.26, DT: Emil Mikkelsen 52.60, HT: Torben Wolf 61.83, JT: Lukas Björnvad 65.49, 5000mW/ 10,000mW: Andreas W. Nielsen 23:23.58/51:46.3, 30kW: Jacob Sørensen 2:44:42. **Women:** 100m: Anna Olsson 12.07, 200m/100mh: Mette Graversgaard 24.99/14.76, 400m: Anne Sofie Kirkegaard 55.36, 800m: Dagmar Olsen 2:09.45, 1500m: Line Schulz 4:26.57, 5000m/3000mSt: Simone Glad 17:22.17/10:43.58, 10,000m: Anna Holm-Baumeister 34:36.29, HMar: Jessica Draskau-Petersson 74:16, Mar: Anne-Mette Aagaard 2:44:14, 400mh: Helene Wellm 64.74, HJ: Sandra Christensen 1.74, PV: Caroline Bonde Holm 4.35, LJ Jessie Ipsen 5.95, TJ: Janne Nielsen 12.62, SP: Trine Mulbjerg 14.85, DT: Kathrine Bebe 48.66, HT: Meiken Greve 57.70, JT: Nina Otto 49.95, Hep: Mathilde Deikema 4213, 3000mW/5000mW: Birgit Klaproth 21:36.32 40:52.6.

DJIBOUTI

Hassan Ayanleh SOULEIMAN b. 3 Dec 1992 Somalia 1.72m 80kg.
At (800m)/1500m: WCh: '13- 3/sf; WI: '12- 5; AfG: '11- 6; AfCh: '12- 2; WI: '14- 1; won DL 2013, ArabG 2011, FrancG 2013. At 3000m: WY: '09- h.
DJI records: 800m (3) 2012-13, 1000m 2013, 1500m (2) 2011-12, 1M (2) 2012-13, 3000m 2012.
Progress at 800m, 1500m: 2011- 1:51.78A, 3:34.32;

2012- 1:47.45, 3:30.31; 2013- 1:43.63, 3:31.64. pbs: 1000m 2:15.77 '13, 1M 3:50.07 '13, 3000m 7:39.81i '13, 7:42.22 '12.
In 2014 became Djibouti's first ever world champion.

DOMINICAN REPUBLIC

Governing body: Federación Dominicana de Asociaciones de Atletismo. Avenida J.F. Kennedy, Centro Olímpico "Juan Pablo Duarte". Santo Domingo. Founded 1953.

Félix SÁNCHEZ b. 30 Aug 1977 New York, USA 1.78m 73kg. Was at University of Southern California.
At 400mh: OG: '00- sf, '04- 1, '08- h, '12- 1; WCh: '99-01-03-05-07-09-11-13: ht/1/1/dnf/2/8/4/5; PAm: '99- 4, '03- 1/3R, '07- 4/3R, '11- 3; CAG: '02- 1R, '10- 4; WCp: '02- 1R. Won NCAA 2000, GWG 2001, GP 2002 (3rd overall), WAF 2003.
Three CAC 400mh records 2001-03. DOM records: 400mh (11) 1997-2003, 400m (3) 2001-02.
Progress at 400mh: 1995- 51.33, 1996- 51.19, 1997- 50.01, 1998- 51.30, 1999- 48.60, 2000- 48.33, 2001- 47.38, 2002- 47.35, 2003- 47.25, 2004- 47.63, 2005- 48.24, 2006- 49.10, 2007- 48.01, 2008- 51.10, 2009- 48.34, 2010- 48.17, 2011- 48.74, 2012- 47.63, 2013- 48.10. pbs: 100m 10.45 '05, 200m 20.87 '01, 400m 44.90 '01, 800m 1:49.36 '04, 200mSt 22.68 '13.
Born in New York and raised in California, he first competed for the Dominican Republic, where his parents were born, in 1999 after placing 6th in US 400m. He took a share of the Golden League jackpot in 2002 and won 43 successive 400mh races (including 7 heats) from loss to Dai Tamesue on 2 Jul 2001 until he pulled up in Brussels on 3 Sep 2004. Ran his fastest time for eight years to regain Olympic title in 2012, the same time (47.63) with which he had won in 2004.

Luguelín SANTOS b. 12 Nov 1993 Bayaguana 1.73m 61kg. Universidad Interamericana de San Germán, Puerto Rico.
At 400m: OG: '12- 2; WCh: '13- 3 (h 200m); WJ: '10- 6, '12- 1; PAm: '11- 2/2R; YthOG: '10- 1.
DOM records 200m 2013, 400m (3) 2011-12.
Progress at 400m: 2009- 47.88, 2010- 46.19, 2011- 44.71A, 2012- 44.45, 2013- 44.52. pbs: 200m 20.55A '13, 20.73 '12; 300m 32.4+/32.56 '12, 600m 1:16.90i '14, 800m 1:49.18 '14.

ERITREA

Governing body: Eritrean National Athletics Federation, PO Box 1117, Asmara. F'd 1992.
Teklemariam MEDHIN Weldeselassie b. 24 Jun 1989 Hazega 1.78m 57kg.
At (5000m)/10,000m: OG: '08- 32,'12- 7; WCh: '09- 15/12, '13- dnf; WJ: '06- (12). World CC: 2006-07-08-09-10-11-13:   13J/14J/23/9/2/14/3. African CC: '12- 2.
Progress at 5000m, 10,000m: 2006- 14:13.9, 2008-

13:48.18, 27:46.50; 2009- 13:11.01, 27:58.89; 2010-
13:04.55, 28:50.63A; 2011- 13:16.53, 27:37.21; 2012-
13:17.25, 27:16.69; 2013- 13:32.86, 27:19.97. pbs:
3000m 7:48.6+ '11, Road 10M 47:11 '09, HMar
61:55 '13.

Zersenay TADESE b. 8 Feb 1982 Adi Bana
1.60m 56kg. C.A. Adidas. Madrid, Spain.
At (5000m)/10,000m: OG: '04- 7/3, '08- 5, '12- 6;
WCh: '03- (8), '05- 14/6, '07- 4, '09- 2, '11- 4;
AfCh: '02- 6, AfG: '07- 1. World CC: 2002-03-04-
05-06-07-08-09: 30/9/6/2/4/1/3/3; 20k: '06- 1;
HMar: '02-03-07-08-09-10-12-14: 21/7/1/1/1/2/1/4.
Records: World 20km and half marathon 2010.
Eritrean 3000m (2), 2M, 5000m (4), 10,000m (5)
HMar (3) 2003-10.
Progress at 5000m, 10,000m, HMar: 2002-
13:48.79, 28:47.29, 63:05; 2003- 13:05.57, 28:42.79,
61:26; 2004- 13:13.74, 27:22.57; 2005- 13:12.23,
27:04.70, 59:05; 2006- 12:59.27, 26:37.25, 59:16;
2007- 27:00.30, 58:59; 2008- 27:05.11, 59:56; 2009-
13:07.02, 26:50.12, 59:35; 2010- 58:23, 2011-
12:59.32, 26:51.09, 58:30; 2012- 27:33.51, 59:34;
2013- 60:10. pbs: 3000m 7:39.93 '05, 2M 8:19.34
'07, Road: 15k 41:27 '05, 10M 45:52 '07, 20k 55:21+
'10, Mar 2:10:41 '12.
Won Eritrea's first medal at Olympics in 2004
and World CC in 2005 and first gold in the
World 20k in 2006 before four more at half marathon. At half marathon had 15 wins in 18 races
2002-13; ran 59:05 for the fastest ever half marathon to win the Great North Run (slightly
downhill overall) in 2005 and won Lisbon 2010-
11 in two fastest ever times. Won a national
road cycling title in 2001 before taking up athletics.
His younger brother **Kidane** (b. 31 Aug 1987)
has pbs 5000m 13:11.85 '10, 10,000m 27:06.16 '08;
at 5000m/(10,000m): OG: '08- 10/12, WCh: '09-
h/9; World CC: '12- 6.

ESTONIA

Governing body: Eesti Kergejõustikuliit,
Maakri 23, Tallinn 10145. Founded 1920.
National Championships first held in 1917.
2013 Champions: Men: 100m: Timo Tiismaa
10.79, 200m/400m: Marek Niit 20.89/46.23,
800m: Allar Lamp 1:52.75, 1500m: Nikolai
Vedehin 3:54.37, 5000m/10,000m: Sergei
Tserepannikov 14:26.67/30:12.21, HMar/Mar:
Roman Fosti 66:58/2:20:48, 3000mSt: Priit Aus
9:02.99, 110mh: Andres Raja 13.96, 400mh:
Aarne Nirk 53.11, HJ: Karl Lumi 2.16, PV:
Veiko Kriisk 5.00, LJ: Henrik Kutberg 7.51, TJ:
Igor Syunin 15.76, SP: Kristo Galeta 19.15, DT:
Gerd Kanter 65.99, HT: Martin Lehemets
64.20, JT: Risto Mätas 80.78, Dec: Andres Raja
7960, 20000mW: Lauri Lelumees 1:38:35.99,
50kW: Margus Luik 4:27.19. **Women:**
100m/200m: Ksenija Balta 11.62/23.58 400m:
Helin Meier 56.16, 800m/1500m: Liina
Tsernov 2:11.72/ 4:20.15, 5000m: Jekaterina

Patjuk 17:19.05, 10,000m/HMar/Mar: Lily
Luik 36:29.13/79:02/ 2:50:17, 3000mSt: Kelly
Nevolihhin 11:25.17, 100mh/LJ: Grit Sadeiko
13.57/6.20, 400mh: Maris Mägi 56.56, HJ:
Anna Iljustsenko 1.88, PV: Lembi Vaher 4.00,
TJ: Liane Pintsaar 12.83, SP: Kätlin Piirimäe
15.08, DT: Anu Teesaar 49.74, HT: Kati Ojaloo
60.07, JT: Liina Laasma 57.12, Hep: Terje
Kaunissaar 5181, 10,000mW/ 20kW: Margarita
Kozlova 62:43.16/2:06:40.

Gerd KANTER b. 6 May 1979 Tallinn 1.96m
125kg. Tallinna SS Kalev. Business management graduate.
At DT: OG: '04- dnq 19, '08- 1, '12- 3; WCh: '03-05-
07-09-11-13: dnq 25/2/1/3/2/3; EC: '02-06-10-12:
12/2/4/2; EU23: '01- 5; WUG: '05- 1. Won WAF
2007-08, DL 2012-13, Estonian 2004-09, 2011-13.
Five Estonian discus records 2004-06.
Progress at DT: 1998- 47.37, 1999- 49.65, 2000-
57.68, 2001- 60.47, 2002- 66.31, 2003- 67.13, 2004-
68.50, 2005- 70.10, 2006- 73.38, 2007- 72.02, 2008-
71.88, 2009- 71.64, 2010- 71.45, 2011- 67.99, 2012-
68.03, 2013- 67.59. pb SP 17.31i '04, 16.11 '00.
Threw over 70m in four rounds at Helsingborg
on 4 Sep 2006; a feat matched only by Virgilijus
Alekna. Six successive seasons over 70m.

Risto MÄTAS b. 30 Apr 1984 Tartu 1.90m 87kg.
Audentese SK.
At JT: OG: '12- dnq 21; WCh: '13- 8; EC: '06- dnq
19, '12- 10; EJ: '03- 12. Estonian champion 2007,
2012-13.
Progress at JT: 2003- 64.45, 2004- 73.31, 2005-
79.68, 2006- 80.53, 2007- 77.29, 2008- 79.38, 2009-
73.56, 2010- 69.12, 2011- 81.56, 2012- 82.10, 2013-
83.48.

Women

Anna ILJUSTSENKO b. 12 Oct 1985 Sillamäe
1.68m 49kg. Orthodontist, graduate of dental
medicine from University of Tartu. Tartu
Ülikooli Akadeemiline SK.
At HJ: OG: '08/12- dnq 21/15=; WCh: '09 dnq
17=, '11- 12, '13- dnq 16-; EC: '06-10-12: dnq
20/11/dnq 15=; WJ: '04- dnq; EU23: '05-11, '07-
dnq 13; EI: '13- 4=; WUG: '11- 3, '13- 3; Estonian
champion 2005-11, 2013.
Eight Estonian high jump records 2008-11.
Progress at HJ: 2002- 1.80i, 2003- 1.77, 2004- 1.82,
2005- 1.85, 2006- 1.89, 2007- 1.85, 2008- 1.91,
2009- 1.93i/1.91, 2010- 1.95, 2011- 1.96, 2012-
1.93i/1.91, 2013- 1.94.

ETHIOPIA

Governing body: Ethiopian Athletic
Federation, Addis Ababa Stadium, PO Box
3241, Addis Ababa. Founded 1961. **2013
National Champions: Men:** 100m/200m:
Amanuel Abebe 10.6/21.34, 400m: Mohamed
Gemechu 47.5, 800m: Esrael Aweke 1:47.8,
1500m: Aman Kedi 3:39.92, 5000m/10,000m:
Belete Assefa 13:42.7/28:28.6, Mar: Dereje

Tesfaye 2:13:05, 3000mSt: Tafesse Seboka 8:49.2, 110mh: Behilu Alemeshet 14.5, 400mh: Mezemure H'Mariyam 52.6, HJ: Garwich Ose 1.95, PV: Samson Besha 3.80, LJ: Lingo Ubang 7.81, TJ: Tesfaye Nedasa 15.23, SP: Desta Abera 13.09, DT/JT: Miteku Tilahun 43.56/64.50, HT: Biruke Abreham 44.84, 10,000mW: Cherenet Mekori 46:39.16. **Women**: 100m: Neima Seffa 12.0, 200m: Selam Abrhaley 23.9, 400m: Kore Tola 55.5, 800m: Mantegbosh Melese 2:02.3, 1500m: Sofiya Shemsu 4:17.4, 5000m: Senbere Teferi 16:21.0, 10,000m: Yebregual Melese 33:32.7, Mar: Ehete Bizuayehu 2:43:52, 3000mSt: Almaz Ayana 10:02.6, 100mh: Konjit Teshome 14.9, 400mh: Meaza Kebede 61.5, HJ: Areayat Dibo 1.67, LJ: Zeyeba Zeyene 5.61, TJ: Nibolo Uguda 12.56, SP: Zurga Usman 11.64, DT: Meresit G/Egzabhereb 41.48, JT: Hiwot Girma 41.81, 10,000mW: Askale Tikesa 50:55.75.

Ayele ABSHERO Biza b. 28 Dec 1990 Yeboda 1.67m 52kg.
At 5000m: Af-J: '09- 4. At Mar: OG: '12- dnf. World CC: '08- 2J, '09- 1J.
Progress at 10,000m, Mar: 2009- 27:54.29, 2011- 27:48.94, 2012- 2:04:23, 2013- 2:06:57. pbs: 3000m 7:40.08 '10, 5000m 13:11.38 '09; Road: 15k 42:02 '10, 10M 45:33 '10, HMar 59:42 '11.
Second fastest ever debut marathon to win at Dubai in 2012, 3rd London 2013. Elder brother Tessema has marathon pb 2:08:26 '08.

Yenew ALAMIREW b. 27 May 1990 Tilili 1.75m 57kg.
At 5000m: OG: '12- 12; WCh: '13- 9; AfG: '11- 2; won DL 2013. At 3000m: WI: '12- 9.
Progress at 5000m: 2010- 13:16.53, 2011- 13:00.46, 2012- 12:48.77, 2013- 12:54.95. pbs: 1500m 3:35.09+ '11, 1M 3:50.43 '11, 3000m 7:27.26 '11, 10kmRd 29:26A '10.

Mohammed AMAN Geleto b. 10 Jan 1994 Asella 1.69m 55kg.
At 800m: OG: '12- 6; WCh: '11- 8, '13- 1; WY: '11-2; WI: '12- 1, '14- 1; won DL 2012-13, Afr-J 800m 2011, Yth OG 1000m 2010.
Records: Ethiopian (6) 2011-13, world youth 800m indoors and out 2011, world junior 600m indoor 2013 (1:15.60), African indoor 800m 2014.
Progress at 800m: 2008- 1:50.29, 2009- 1:46.34, 2010- 1:48.5A, 2011- 1:43.37, 2012- 1:42.53, 2013- 1:42.37. pbs: 600m 1:15.0+ '12, 1000m 2:19.54 '10, 1500m 3:43.52 '11, 1M 3:57.14 '11.
Was disqualified from taking the African Junior 800m gold in 2009 for being under-age (at 15). Youngest ever World Indoor champion at 18 years 60 days in 2012. Beat David Rudishsa in the latter's last races in both 2011 and 2012.

Kenenisa BEKELE b. 13 Jun 1982 near Bekoji, Arsi Province 1.62m 54kg.
At 5000m(/10,000m): OG: '04- 2/1, '08- 1/1, '12- (4); WCh: '03- 3/1, '05- (1), '07- (1), '09- 1/1; WJ: '00- 2; AfG: '03- 1; AfCh: '06- 1, '08- 1. At 3000m:

WY: '99- 2; WI: '06- 1; WCp: '06- 2. World CC: '99- 9J, 4k: '01- 1J/2 4k, '02-03-04-05-06: all 1/1, '08- 1. Won WAF 3000m 2003, 2009; 5000m 2006.
World records: 5000m 2004, 10,000m 2004 & 2005, indoor 5000m (12:49.60) 2004, 2000m 2007, 2M 2008; World junior record 3000m 2001.
Progress at 5000m, 10,000m: 2000- 13:20.57, 2001- 13:13.33, 2002- 13:26.58, 2003- 12:52.26, 26:49.57; 2004- 12:37.35, 26:20.31; 2005- 12:40.18, 26:17.53; 2006- 12:48.09, 2007- 12:49.53, 26:46.19; 2008- 12:50.18, 26:25.97; 2009- 12:52.32, 26:46.31; 2011- 13:27e+, 26:43.16; 2012- 12:55.79, 27:02.59; 2013- 13:07.88, 27:12.08. pbs: 1000m 2:21.9+ '07, 1500m 3:32.35 '07, 1M 3:56.2+ '07, 2000m 4:49.99i '07, 4:58.40 '09, 3000m 7:25.79 '07, 2M 8:04.35i '08, 8:13.51 '07; Rd 15k 42:42 '01, 10M 46:06 '13, 20k 57:19 '13, HMar 60:09 '13.
At cross-country has a record 20 (12 individual, 8 team) world gold medals from his record winning margin of 33 seconds for the World Juniors in 2001, a day after second in senior 4km. The only man to win both World senior races in the same year, he did this five times. Unbeaten in 27 races from Dec 2001 to March 2007 when he did not finish in the Worlds. After winning all his 12 10,000m track races including five major gold medals, from a brilliant debut win over Haile Gebrselassie at Hengelo in June 2003, he had two years out through injury and then dropped out of World 10,000 in 2011 before running the year's fastest time to win at Brussels. 17 successive wins at 5000m 2006-09. Shared Golden League jackpot in 2009. Won Great North Run on half marathon debut 2013. IAAF Athlete of the Year 2004-05.
His fiancée Alem Techale (b. 13.12.87, the 2003 World Youth 1500m champion) died of a heart attack on 4 Jan 2005. He married film actress Danawit Gebregziabher on 18 Nov 2007.

Tariku BEKELE b. 21 Jan 1987 near Bekoji 1.68m 52kg.
At 5000m: OG: '08- 6; WCh: '05- 7, '07- 5; WJ: '04- 3, '06- 1; AfG: '07- 3; AfCh: '08- 4, '10- 6. At 10,000m: OG: '12- 3. At 3000m: WY: '03- 2; WI: '06-08-10: 6/1/4; CCp: '10- 4; won WAF 3000m 2006. World CC: '05- 6J, '06- 3J.
World junior indoor 2M best 2006.
Progress at 5000m, 10,000m: 2004- 13:11.97, 2005- 12:59.03, 2006- 12:53.81, 2007- 13:01.60, 2008- 12:52.45, 2010- 12:53.97, 2011- 12:59.25, 2012- 12:54.13, 27:03.24; 2013- 13:13.61, 27:38.15. pbs: 1500m 3:37.26 '08, 2000m 5:00.1 '06, 3000m 7:28.70 '10, 2M 8:04.83 '07, Road: 15k 43:35 '11, 10M 46:33 '10.
Younger brother of Kenenisa Bekele.

Deressa CHIMSA Edae b. 21 Nov 1986 Koreodo 1.75m 62kg.
At Mar: WC: '09- dnf. World HMar: '12- 2. Won ETH HMar 2009.

Progress at Mar: 2008- 2:10:16, 2009- 2:07:54, 2010- 2:08:45, 2011- 2:07:39, 2012- 2:05:42, 2013- 2:07:05. pbs: HMar 60:51 '12. Marathon wins: Daegu 2010, Prague 2012, Toronto 2013.

Yigrem DEMELASH b. 28 Jan 1994 1.67m 52kg. At 10,000m: WJ: '12- 1.
Progress at 5000m, 10,000m: 2012- 13:03.30, 26:57.56; 2013- 13:13.18, 27:15.51.

Lelisa DESISA Benti b. 14 Jan 1990 Shewa 1.70m 52kg.
At 10,000m: Af-J: '09- 1. At: HMar: WCh: '10- 7, AfG: '11- 1. At Mar: WCh: '13- 2.
Progress at 10,000m, HMar, Mar: 2009- 28:46.74, 2010- 59:39; 2011- 59:30, 2012- 27:11.98, 62:50; 2013 -60:34, 2:04:45. pbs: 5000m 13:22.91 '12, Road: 10k 28:15 '13, 15k 42:25 '10, 10M 45:36 '11.
Brilliant marathon debut to win Dubai 2013 and then won Boston and 2nd Worlds.

Muktar EDRIS Awel b. 14 Jan 1994 Adio 1.72m 57kg.
At 5000m: WCh: '13- 7; WJ: '12- 1. At 10,000m: Af-J: '11- 4. World CC: '11- 7J, '13- 3J. Won African Junior CC 2012.
Progress at 5000m: 2012- 13:04.34, 2013- 13:03.69. ps: 10,000m 28:44.95 '13, 10k Rd 28:11 '13.

Roba GARI Chebute b. 12 Apr 1982 Wera Jarso. Oromiya region 1.81m 60kg.
At 3000mSt: OG: '08- h, '12- 4; WCh: '07-09-11-13: 10/6/5/h; AfG: '07- 5, '11- 2; AfCh: '10- 3; CCp: '10- 2; ETH champion 2005, 2007, 2010.
Five Ethiopian 3000mSt records 2009-12.
Progress at 3000mSt: 2007- 8:15.05, 2008- 8:22.07, 2009- 8:11.32, 2010- 8:09.87, 2011- 8:10.03, 2012- 8:06.16, 2013- 8:12.22. pbs: 3000m 7:42.12i '08, 7:43.38 '10; 5000m 13:33.17 '08, 2000mSt 5:19.96 '07.

Gebre-egziabher GEBREMARIAM b. 10 Sep 1984 Shere, Tigray region 1.78m 56kg.
At 10,000m (5000m): OG: '04- (4), '12- 8; WCh: '03- (6), '05- 15, '07- 6, '09- 10; WJ: '02- 1 (3); AfG: '03- 2, '07- 3; AfCh: '08- 1. At Mar: WCh: '11- dnf.
World CC: '02-03-04-05-06-08-09-10: 1J/3/2&2/ 9(4k)/13/17/1/10. Won ETH CC 2003 & 2009, 5000m 2005, 10,000m 2005., 2009; E.Afr 2004.
Progress at 5000m, 10,000m, Mar: 2001- 14:13.74A, 31:04.61A; 2002- 13:12.14, 27:25.61; 2003- 12:58.08, 28:03.03; 2004- 12:55.59, 26:53.73; 2005- 12:52.80, 27:11.57; 2006- 13:30.95, 27:03.95; 2007- 13:10.29, 26:52.33; 2008- 13:36.67, 27:20.65; 2009- 13:13.20, 27:44.04; 2010- 2:08:14, 2011- 2:04:53wdh/2:08:00, 2012- 13:33.2+, 27:03.58, 2:22:56; 2013- 2:10:28. pbs: 3000m 7:39.48 '05, 2M 9:34.82i '06, HMar 60:25 '10, 3000mSt 8:57.7A '02.
Won New York 2010 on marathon debut, 3rd Boston 2011 and 2013. Married Worknesh Kidane on 4 Feb 2006. She has 21 World CC medals, he has 16.

Mekonnen GEBREMEDHIN Woldegiorgis b. 11 Oct 1988 Addis Ababa 1.80m 64kg.
At 1500m: OG: '12- 6; WCh: '07-09-11-13: sf/h/7/7; WI: '08-10-12: 6/4/3; AfCh: '10- 3; CCp:

'10- 2. At 800m: WJ: '06- sf.
Progress at 1500m: 2004- 3:47.1A, 2006- 3:41.00, 2007- 3:36.04, 2008- 3:35.68, 2009- 3:34.49, 2010- 3:31.57, 2011- 3:31.90, 2012- 3:31.45, 2013- 3:32.43. pbs: 800m 1:46.63 '12, 1M 3:49.70 '11, 3000m 7:41.42 '11, 3000mSt 8:59.06 '12.

Dejen GEBREMESKEL b. 24 Nov 1989 Adiqrat, Tigray region 1.78m 53kg.
At 5000m: OG: '12- 2; WCh: '11- 3; WJ: '08- 3; Af-J: '07- 2. At 10,000m: WCh: '13- 16. At 3000m: WI: '10- 12-14: 10/5/3. World CC: '08- 18J.
Progress at 5000m, 10,000m: 2007- 13:21.05, 2008- 13:08.96, 2009- 13:03.13, 2010- 12:53.56, 2011- 12:55.89, 2012- 12:46.81, 2013- 13:31.02, 26:51.02. pbs: 3000m 7:34.14i '12, 7:45.9+ '10.
Fastest ever debut 10,000m at Sollentuna 2013.

Hagos GEBRHIWET Berhe b. 11 May 1994 Tsaedaenba, Tigray region 1.67m 65kg. Mesfen Engineering
At 5000m: OG: '12- 11; WCh: '13- 2. At 3000m: WY: '11- 5; WI: '14- 5. World CC: '13- 1J, African CC: '12- 4J.
World junior records 5000m 2012, indoor 3000m 2013.
Progress at 5000m: 2011- 14:10.0A, 2012- 12:47.53, 2013- 12:55.73. pbs: 3000m 7:30.36 '13, 10k Rd 27:57dh '11.

Haile GEBRSELASSIE b. 18 Apr 1973 Arsi 1.64m 53kg.
At 10,000m (5000m): OG: '96- 1, '00- 1, '04- 5, '08- 6; WCh: '93- 1 (2), '95- 1, '97- 1, '99- 1, '01- 3, '03- 2; WJ: '92- 1 (1); AfG: '93- 3 (2). At 3000m: WI: '97- 1, '99- 1 (1 1500m), '03- 1. Won GP 3000m 1995, 1998. World CC: '91-2-3-4-5-6: 8J/2J/7/3/4/5; HMar: '01- 1; Rd Rly team: '94- 2.
World records 5000m (4) 1994-8, 10,000m (3) 1995-8, 20000m & 1Hr 2007; 10km road (27:02) 2002, 15km & 10M road 2005, 20km, HMar & 25km 2006, Marathon 2007 & 2008, 30km road 2009; Indoors 2000m 1998, 3000m (7:30.72 '96, 7:26.15 '98), 5000m (13:10.98 '96, 12:59.04 '97, 12:50.38 '99); World best 2M 1995 (8:07.46) & 1997, indoors 8:04.69 (2003). ETH records 1993- 9: 1500m (3), 1M (1), 3000m (6), 5000m (6), 10,000m (3), marathon (5) 2002-08. World M35 bests 10,000m & Mar 2008, M40 HMar 2013.
Progress at 5000m, 10,000m, Mar: 1992- 13:36.06, 28:03.99; 1993- 13:03.17, 27:30.17; 1994- 12:56.96, 27:15.00; 1995- 12:44.39, 26:43.53; 1996- 12:52.70, 27:07.34; 1997- 12:41.86, 26:31.32; 1998- 12:39.36, 26:22.75; 1999- 12:49.64, 27:57.27; 2000- 12:57.95, 27:18.20; 2001- 27:54.41, 2002- 28:16.50, 2:06:35; 2003- 12:54.36, 26:29.22; 2004- 12:55.51, 26:41.58; 2005- 2:06:20, 2006- 2:05:56, 2007- 26:52.81, 2:04:26; 2008- 26:51.20, 2:03:59; 2009- 28:22.3+, 2:05:29, 2010- 2:06:09, 2011- dnf, 2012- 13:33.6+, 27:20.39, 2:08:17. pbs: 800m 1:49.35i '97, 1000m 2:20.3+i '98, 1500m 3:31.76i '98, 3:33.73 '99; 1M 3:52.39 '99, 2000m 4:52.86i '98, 4:56.1 '97; 3000m 7:25.09 '98, 2M 8:01.08 '97, 10M 45:23.80 '07, 20000m 56:25.98 '07, 1Hr 21285m '07; Road: 15k

41:22 '05, 10M 44:24 '05, 20k 55:48 '06, HMar 58:55 '06, 25k 1:11:37 '06, 30k 1:27:49 '09.

He set the first of his 27 world records (20 officially ratified) in Hengelo in 1994 at 5000m From 1992 to 2004 he had 13 wins in 19 races at 10,000m, 26/28 at 3000m/2M, and 28/36 at 5000 including 16 successive 1996 to 2000. He has 12/14 wins at half marathon 2001-11, including the 2010 Great North Run. After missing the 2002 summer season through injury he set a world 10km road record of 27:02 at Doha, Qatar in December for a reward of $1 million.

He had run c.2:48 for the marathon at the age of 15, but made his senior debut at the distance at London 2002, when he was third in 2:06:35 and won at Amsterdam in 2:06:20 in 2005. In 2006 he was 9th in London, then won the Berlin and Fukuoka marathons, but dnf London 2007. He smashed the world record with 2:04:26 to win the Berlin Marathon in 2007 and in 2008 he won in Dubai in 2:04:53 before another WR at Berlin – 2:03:59. He won again in Dubai and Berlin in 2009 and in Dubai 2010. IAAF Athlete of the Year 1998.

His brother Tekeye had marathon pb 2:11:45 '94 and was 13th in 1991 World Cup.

Markos GENETI b. 30 May 1984 Walega 1.75m 55kg.
At 5000m: WJ: '02- 2; AfG: '03- 4. At 3000m: WY: '01- 1; WI: '04- 3. At 1500m: WCh: '05- sf. World CC: '07- 15.
Progress at 5000m: 2001- 13:50.14, 2002- 13:28.83, 2003- 13:11.87, 2004- 13:17.57, 2005- 13:00.25, 2006- 13:13.98, 2007- 13:07.65, 2008- 13:08.22, 2009- 13:31.71i, 2010- 13:18.64i/13:21.99. At Mar: 2011- 2:06:35, 2012- 2:04:54, 2013- 2:12:44, 2014- 2:05:13. pbs: 1500m 3:33.83 '05, 1M 4:08.8 '10, 3000m 7:32.69i '07, 7:38.11 '05; 2M 8:08.39i '04, 8:19.61 '06, Road: 10k 29:38 '11, HMar 62:01 '11 Won in Los Angeles 2011 in sixth fastest ever debut marathon time. 3/2 Dubai 2012/2014.

Yakob JARSO b. 5 Feb 1988 Assela 1.73m 54kg. Honda, Japan.
At 3000mSt: OG: '08-4; WCh: '09- 5; Af-J: '07- 2. At 10,000m: AfCh: '10- 5.
Ethiopian 3000mSt record 2008.
Progress at 10.000m, 3000mSt: 2007- 8:29.99, 2008- 27:32.52, 8:13.47; 2009- 27:30.08, 8:12.13; 2010- 28:20.66A. At Mar: 2011- 2:11:13, 2014- 2:05:37. pbs: 1500m 3:38.54 '09, 5000m 13:19.20 '09, 15km Rd 43:15 '10, HMar 60:07 '10, Mar 2:11:13 '12.

Ibrahim JEYLAN Gashu b. 12 Jun 1989 Bale Province 1.68m 57kg. Muger Cement.
At 10,000m: WCh: '11- 1, '13- 2; WJ: '06- 1, '08- 3; AfG: '11- 1; AfCh: '08- 2. At 3000m: WY: '05- 2. World CC: '06- 5J, '08- 1J. ETH 10,000m 2006.
Two world youth 10,000m records 2006.
Progress at 5000m, 10,000m: 2006- 13:09.38, 27:02.81; 2007- 13:17.99, 27:50.53; 2008- 13:15.12, 27:13.85; 2009- 13:19.70, 27:22.19; 2010- 13:21.29,

27:12.43; 2011- 13:09.95, 27:09.02; 2013- 13:09.16, 27:22.23. pbs: 3000m 8:04.21 '05, 15k 43:38 '08, HMar 61:47 '14.

Tsegaye KEBEDE Wordofa b. 15 Jan 1987 Gerar Ber 1.58m 50kg.
At Mar: OG: '08- 3; WCh: '09- 3, '13- 4.
Progress at Mar: 2007- 2:08:16, 2008- 2:06:10, 2009- 2:05:18, 2010- 2:05:19, 2011- 2:07:48, 2012- 2:04:38, 2013- 2:06:04. pbs: Road: 10k 28:10 '08, HMar 59:35 '08.
Marathon wins: Addis Ababa 2007, Paris 2008, Fukuoka 2008-09, London 2010 & 2013, Chicago 2012; 2nd London 2009 and Chicago 2010, New York 2013 (3rd 2011); 3rd London 2012. World Marathon Majors winner 2012/13. Has record 11 sub-2:08 times. Won Great Ethiopian Run 2007, Great North Run 2008.

Abera KUMA Lema b. 31 Aug 1990 Ambo 1.60m 50kg.
At 5000m: WCh: '11- 5, '13- 5; Af-J: '09- 1. At 3000m: WY: '07- 5.
Progress at 5000m, 10,000m: 2009- 13:29.40, 2010- 13:07.83, 2011- 13:00.15, 27:22.54; 2012- 13:09.32, 27:18.39; 2013- 26:52.85. pbs: 1500m 3:48.73 '09, 3000m 7:39.09i/7:40.85 '12, Road: 15k 42:01 '10, 10M 45:28 '11, HMar 60:19 '12.

Feyisa LILESA b. 1 Feb 1990 Tullu Bultuma 1.58m 50kg.
At Mar: WCh: '11- 3, '13- dnf, World CC: 2008- 09-10-11-13: 14J/12/25/17/9. ETH CC champion 2013.
Progress at Mar: 2009- 2:09:12, 2010- 2:05:23, 2011- 2:10:32, 2012- 2:04:52, 2013- 2:07:46. pbs: 5000m 13:34.80 '08, 10,000m 27:46.97 '08; Road: 15k 42:15+ '13, 20k 56:19+ '12, HMar 59:22 '12, 25k 1:13:22 '13, 30k 1:28:05 '13.
Marathons won: Dublin 2009, Xiamen 2010. 3rd/2nd Chicago 2010/2012, 4th Rotterdam 2010 in then fastest ever by 20 year-old, 4th London 2013.

Imane MERGA Jida b. 15 Oct 1988 Tulu Bolo, Oromia region 1.74m 61kg. Defence.
At 5000m/(10,000m): WCh: '09- (4), '11- dq/3, '13- (12); AfCh: '10- 5; Af-J: '07- (3); CCp: '10- 5; won DL 2010-11, WAF 2009. World CC: '07-11-13: 7J/1/2.
Progress at 5000m, 10,000m: 2007- 13:33.52, 30:12.03; 2008- 13:08.20, 27:33.53, 2009- 12:55.66, 27:15.94; 2010- 12:53.58; 2011- 12:54.21, 26:48.35; 2012- 12:59.77, 27:14.02; 2013- 13:09.17, 26:57.33. pbs: 3000m 7:45.8+ '10, HMar 59:56 '12.
Disqualified for running inside the kerb after finishing 3rd in World 5000m 2011.

Dino SEFIR Kemal b. 28 May 1988 Shoa 1.72m 59kg.
At 10,000m: AfG: '11- 5. At Mar: OG: '12- dnf. World CC: '09- 15, '11- 12.
Progress at Mar: 2010- 2:20:36, 2011- 2:10:33, 2012- 2:04:50, 2013- 2:09:13. pbs: 3000m 7:44.37 '09, 5000m 13:11.69 '08, 10,000m 28:23.40 '11;

Road: 15k 43:57 '11, HMar 59:42 '11.
2nd Dubai Marathon 2012.
Berhanu SHIFERAW Tolcha b. 31 May 1993 1.65m 52kg.
At 2000mSt: WY: '09- 5.
Progress at Mar: 2011- 2:09:11, 2012- 2:08:51, 2013- 2:04:48. pbs: HMar 61:41 '10, 2000mSt 5:37.32 '09, 3000mSt 8:36.02 '12.
Won Taiyuan and Ljubljana marathons 2012, fastest by 19 year-old when 2nd Dubai 2013.
Tadesse TOLA Woldegeberal b. 31 Oct 1987 Addis Ababa 1.78m 60kg.
At Mar: '13- 3. At 10,000m: WCh: '07- 13; AfCh: '06- 5; AfG: '07- 2. World 20k: '06- 7; World CC: '06- 10J, '07- 7, '09- 17.
Progress at 10,000m, Mar: 2006- 28:15.16, 2007- 27:04.89, 2008- 27:15.17, 2009- 28:51.4A, 2:15:48; 2010- 2:06:31, 2011- 2:07:13, 2012- 2:05:10, 2013- 2:04:49, 2014- 2:05:57. pbs: 3000m 7:43.70 '07, 5000m 13:18.82 '07, 10,000m 27:04.89 '07; Road: 15k 43:49 '08, 20k 57:27 '06, HMar 59:49 '10.
Won Paris Marathon 2010 (2nd 2013), Beijing 2013; 2nd Frankfurt 2010 & Tokyo 2014. Pb when 3rd at Dubai 2013.
Aman WOTE Fete b. 18 Apr 1984 Kabete 1.81m 64kg.
At 1500m: OG: '12- ht; WCh: 13- sf; AfG: '11- 5; AfCh: '10- 7; WI: '12- 4, '14- 2.
Progress at 1500m: 2010- 3:38.89A 2011- 3:35.61, 2012- 3:35:38, 2013- 3:32.65. pbs: 800m 1:44.99 '13, 1M 3:49.88 '13; 3000m 7:43.99i '13.

Women

Sofia ASSEFA Abebe b. 14 Nov 1987 Tenta District, south Wello 1.71m 58kg. Ethiopian Bank.
At 3000mSt: OG: '08- h, '12- 3; WCh: '09- 13, '11- 6,'13- 3; AfCh: '08- 4, '10- 2; CCp: '10- 3.
Ethiopian 3000mSt records 2011 and 2012.
Progress at 3000mSt: 2006- 10:17.48, 2007- 9:48.46, 2008- 9:31.58, 2009- 9:19.91, 2010- 9:20.72, 2011- 9:15.04, 2012- 9:09.00, 2013- 9:12.84. pbs: 1000m 2:49.79 '07, 5000m 15:59.74 '07, 2000mSt 6:33.49 '07.
Hiwot AYALEW Yemer b. 6 Mar 1990 Gojam, Amhara 1.73m 51kg. Commercial Bank.
At 3000mSt: OG: '12- 5; WCh: '13- 4; AfG: '11- 2. At 3000m: WI: '14-11. World CC: '11- 11, '13- 2.
Progress at 3000mSt: 2011- 9:23.88, 2012- 9:09.61, 2013- 9:15.25. pbs: 3000m 8:43.29i '14, 2M: 9:21.59i '14, 5000m 14:49.36 '12, 10k Rd 33:22A '11.
Younger sister of Wude Ayalew.
Wude AYALEW Yimer b. 4 Jul 1987 Sekela, Amhara region 1.50m 44kg.
At 10,000m: WCh: '09- 3; AfG: '11- 2; AfCh: '08- 3, '10- 4. At 5000m: WJ: '06- 5. World CC: '06-07-09-11: 5/10/5/6. Won ETH CC 2009.
Progress at 5000m, 10,000m: 2006- 14:57.23, 33:57.0; 2008- 15:07.65, 31:06.84; 2009- 14:38.44, 30:11.87; 2010- 15:02.47, 32:29.92A; 2011- 14:59.71, 31:24.09; 2013- 31:16.68. pbs: 1500m 4:14.85 '07,

3000m 8:30.93 '09; Road: 10k 31:41+ '08, 15k 48:52 '11, HMar 67:58 '09.
Won Great Ethiopian Run 2008. Older sister of Hiyot Ayalew.
Almaz AYANA Eba b. 21 Nov 1991 1.65m 50kg.
At 5000m: WCh: '13- 3. At 3000mSt: WJ: '10- 5; ETH champion 2013.
World junior 3000m steeplechase record 2010.
Progress at 5000m, 3000mSt: 2009- 10:03.75, 2010- 9:22.51, 2011- 15:12.24, 9:30.23; 2012- 14:57.97, 9:38.62; 2013- 14:25.84, 9:27.49. pbs: 3000m 8:40.53+ '13, 10k rd 32:19 '10.
Atsede BAYSA Tesema **(or BAYISA)** b. 16 Apr 1987 1.60m 42kg.
At Mar: WCh: '09- 26, '11- 14. At HMar: WCh: '07- 11; AfG: '07- 2.
Progress at Mar: 2006- 2:37:48, 2007- 2:29:08, 2008- 2:33:07, 2009- 2:24:42, 2010- 2:22:04, 2011- 2:23:50, 2012- 2:22:03, 2013- 2:25:14. pbs: Road: 10k 33:14 '09, 15k 49:15 '12, HMar 67:34 '13.
Marathon wins: Istanbul 2007, Paris 2009-10, Xiamen 2010, Chicago 2012 (2nd 2010).
Gelete BURKA Bati b. 15 Feb 1986 Kofele 1.65m 45kg.
At 1500m: OG: '08- h; WCh: '05- 8, '09- 10 (fell), '11- sf, '13- h; WI: '08- 1, '10- 3; AfCh: '07- 1; AfCh: '08- 1, '10- 2; CCp: '10- 7. At 3000m: WI: '12- 3. At 5000m: OG: '12- 5; WCh: '07- 10. World CC: '03-05-06-07-08-09: 3J/1J/1 4k/4/6/8. Won ETH 800m 2011, 1500m 2004-05, 2007; 5000m 2005, 4k CC 2006.
African records: 1M 2008, 200m 2009, indoor 1500m 2008, junior 1500m 2005. World youth 1M best (4:30.81) 2003.
Progress at 1500m, 5000m: 2003- 4:10.82, 16:23.8A, 2004- 4:06.10, 2005- 3:59.60, 14:51.47; 2006- 4:02.68, 14:40.92; 2007- 4:00.48, 14:31.20; 2008- 3:59.75i/4:00.44, 14:45.84; 2009- 3:58.79, 2010- 3:59.28, 2011- 4:03.28, 2012- 14:41.43, 2013- 4:04.36, 14:42.07. pbs: 800m 2:02.89 '10, 1M 4:18.23 '10, 2000m 5:30.19 '09, 3000m 8:25.92 '06; Rd: 10k 32:38+ '12, 15k 49:26 '12, HMar 71:10+ 13, Mar 2:26:03 '14.
Married Taddele Gebrmehden in 2007.
Firehiwot DADO Tufa b. 9 Jan 1984 Arsi 1.65m.
Progress at Mar: 2008- 2:37:34, 2009- 2:27:08, 2010- 2:25:28, 2011- 2:23:15, 2012- 2:34:56dh, 2014- 2:25:53. pbs: Road: 10k 31:49 '13, 15k 48:32+ '12, 20k 65:06+ '12, HMar 68:35 '12, 30k 1:40:45 '11.
Marathon wins: New York 2011, Rome 2009-11, Florence 2010. 3rd Dubai 2014.
Mamitu DASKA Molisa b. 16 Oct 1983 Liteshoa 1.64m 45kg.
At HMar: AfrG: '11- 2. World CC: '09- 12, '10- 8.
Progress at Mar: 2009- 2:26:38, 2010- 2:24:19, 2011- 2:21:59, 2012- 2:23:52, 2013- 2:23:23. pbs: 10,000m 31:36.88 '09. Road: HMar 68:07 '09, 30k 1:39:46 '11.
Marathon wins: Dubai 2010, Houston and Frankfurt 2011.

Bizunesh DEBA b. 8 Sep 1987 1.62m 45kg.
Progress at Mar: 2009- 2:32:17, 2010- 2:27:24,
2011- 2:23:19, 2013- 2:24:26. pbs: 5000m 15:52.33
'04, Road: 10k 32:10 '10, HMar 68:59 '14.
Married Worku Bayi in 2005, lives in Bronx,
New York. Marathon wins: Sacramento 2009,
Jacksonville, Duluth, St.Paul & Sacramento
2010, Los Angeles & San Diego 2011. 2nd New
York 2011, Houston 2013.

Meseret DEFAR b. 19 Nov 1983 Addis Ababa
1.55m 42kg.
At 5000m(/10,000m): OG: '04- 1, '08- 3, '12- 1;
WCh: '03- h, '05- 2, '07- 1, '09- 3/5, '11- 3/dnf,
'13- 1; WJ: '00- 2, '02- 1; AfG: '03- 1, '07- 1; AfCh:
'00-06-08-10: 2/1/2/2; WCp: '06- 1. At 3000m:
WJ: '02- 1; WY: '99- 2; WI: '03-04-06-08-10-12:
3/1/1/1/1/2; CCp: '10- 1. Won WAF 3000m
2004-09, 5000m 2005, 2008-09; DL 5000m 2013.
World CC: '02- 13J.
Records: World 5000m 2006 & 2007, 2M 2007 (2);
indoor 3000m 2007, 2M 2008 (9:10.50) & 2009
(9:06.26), 5000m 2009; African 5000m 2005,
Ethiopian 3000m (2) 2006-07. World 5k road
best 14:46 Carlsbad 2006.
Progress at 3000m, 5000m, 10,000m: 1999-
9:02.08, 33:54.9A; 2000- 8:59.90, 15:08.36; 2001-
8:52.47, 15:08.65; 2002- 8:40.28, 15:26.45; 2003-
8:38.31, 14:40.34; 2004- 8:33.44i/8:36.46, 14:44.81;
2005- 8:30.05i/8:33.57, 14:28.98; 2006- 8:24.66,
14:24.53; 2007- 8:23.72i/8:24.51, 14:16.63; 2008-
8:27.93i/8:34.53, 14:12.88; 2009- 8:26.99i/8:30.15,
14:24.37i/14:36.38, 29:59.20; 2010- 8:24.46i/8:36.09,
14:24.79i/14:38.87; 2011- 8:36.91i/8:50.36+, 14:29.52,
31:05.05; 2012- 8:31.56i/8:46.49, 14:35.85; 2013-
8:30.29, 14:26.90, 30:08.06. pbs: 1500m 4:02.00 '10,
1M: 4:28.5ei '06, 4:33.07+ '07; 2000m 5:34.74i/
5:38.0 '06, 2M 8:58.58 '07, road 15k 47:30 '13,
HMar 66:09 '13.
Married to Teodros Hailu. IAAF woman athlete of the year 2007. Record nine WAF wins.
Expecting a baby in June 2014.

Berhane DIBABA b. 11 Sep 1993 1.59m 44kg.
Progress at Mar: 2012- 2:29:22, 2013- 2:23:01,
2014- 2:22:30. pb HMar 71:13 '13.
Won Valencia marathon 2012; 2nd São Paulo
2012, Nagoya 2013, Tokyo 2014; 3rd Frankfurt
2013.

Genzebe DIBABA b. 8 Feb 1991 Bekoji. Muger
Cement. 1.68m 52kg.
At 1500m: OG: '12- h; WCh: '13- 8; WI: '12- 1. At
3000m: WI: '14- 1. At 5000m: WCh: '09 -8, '11- 8;
WJ: '08- 2, '10- 1; Af-J: '09- 1. World CC: '07-08-
09-10-11: 5J/1J/1J/11J/9. Won ETH 1500m 2010.
World indoor records 1500m, 3000m & 2M
2014. Ethiopian 1500m record 2012.
Progress at 1500m, 5000m: 2007- 15:53.46, 2008-
15:02.41, 2009- 14:55.52, 2010- 4:04.80i/4:06.10,
15:08.06; 2011- 4:05.90, 14:37.56; 2012- 3:57.77,
2013- 3:57.54, 14:37.68; 2014- 3:55.17i. pbs: 1500m
5:34.35i '13, 3000m 8:16.60i '14, 8:37.00 '13; 2M
9:00.48i '14.

Younger sister of Ejegayehu (2 OG 10,000m
2004, 3 WCh 5000 & 10,000m 2005) and Tirunesh
Dibaba.

Mare DIBABA Hurssa b. 20 Oct 1989 Sululta
1.60m 42kg.
At Mar: OG: '12- 23. At HMar: AfG: '11- 1. Won
AZE 3000m and 5000m 2009.
AZE records (as Mare Ibrahimova) at 3000m
and 5000m 2009.
Progress at HMar, Mar: 2008- 70:28, 2009- 68:45,
2010- 67:13, 2:25:27, 2011- 68:39, 2:23:25; 2012-
67:44, 2:19:52; 2014- 2:21:36. pbs: 3000m 9:16.94
'09, 5000m 15:42.83 '09, Road: 10k 31:55+ '10, 15k
48:04+ '10, 10M 51:29+ '10, 20k 63:47+ '10.
She switched to Azerbaijan in December 2008
but back to Ethiopia as of 1 Feb 2010. Third
Dubal Marathon 2012, won at Xiamen 2014.

Tirunesh DIBABA Kenene b. 1 Oct 1985 Chefa
near Bekoji, Arsi region 1.60m 47kg.
At 5000m(/10,000m): OG: '04- 3, '08- 1/1, '12-
3/1; WCh: '03- 1, '05- 1/1, '07- (1), '13- (1); WJ:
'02- 2; AfG: '03- 4; AfCh: '06- 2, '08- (1), '10- (1).
At 3000m: WCp: '06- 1. World CC: '01-02-03-05-
06-07-08-10: 5J/2J/1J/1/1/2/1/4; 4k: '03-04-05:
7/2/1. Won WAF 5000m 2006, ETH 4k CC &
5000m 2003. 8k CC 2005.
World records: 5000m 2008, indoor 5000m 2005
(14:32.93) & 2007, junior 5000m 2003-04, indoor
3000m & 5000m 2004, world road 5k best 14:51
2005, 15k 2009. African 10,000m record 2008.
Progress at 5000m: 2002- 14:49.90, 2003- 14:39.94,
2004- 14:30.88, 2005- 14:32.42, 30:15.67; 2006-
14:30.40, 2007- 14:27.42i/14:35.67, 31:55.41; 2008-
14:11.15, 29:54.66; 2009- 14:33.65, 2010- 14:34.07,
31:51.39A; 2012- 14:50.80, 30:20.75; 2013- 14:23.68,
30:26.67. pbs: 2000m 5:42.7 '05, 3000m 8:29.55
'06, 2M 9:12.23i '10, road 15k 46:28 '09, HMar
66:56 '13.
In 2003 she became, at 17 years 333 days, the
youngest ever world champion at an individual event and in 2005 the first woman to win
the 5000m/10,000m double (with last laps of
58.19 and 58.4) at a global event after earlier in
the year winning both World CC titles. Now
has women's record 21 World CC medals.
Married Sileshi Sihine on 26 Oct 2008. Due to
injuries, did not compete in 2011 until the
final day of the year when she won a 10k road
race in Madrid in 31:30. Then she retained the
Olympic 10,000m title and won the Great
North Run on half marathon debut in 2012.
She has run eleven 10,000m track races – and
won them all.

Buze DIRIBA Kejela b. 9 Feb 1994 Arsi 1.60m
43kg.
At 5000m: WCh: '13- 5; WJ: '12- 1. World CC:
'11- 10J, '13- 9J
Progress at 35000m: 2012- 14:53.06, 2013-
14:50.02. pbs: 1500m 4:10.96 '12, 3000m 8:39.65
'12, 10k Rd 33:52 '12.

Etenesh DIRO Neda b. 10 May 1991 Jeidu, Oromiya 1.69m 47kg.
At 3000mSt: OG: '12- 6; WCh: '13- 5.
Progress at 3000mSt: 2011- 9:49.18, 2012- 9:14.07, 2013- 9:16.97. pbs: 3000m 9:00.39 '11, 5000m 15:19.77 '12, Road: 10k 33:32A '11, 15k 51:21 '09, HMar 71:35 '10.

Erba Tiki GELANA b. 22 Oct 1987 Bekoji, Oromiya 1.65m 48kg.
At Mar: OG: '12- 1; WCh: '13- dnf.
Ethiopian marathon record 2012.
Progress at Mar: 2009- 2:33:49, 2010- 2:28:28, 2011- 2:22:08, 2012- 2:18:58, 2013- 2:36:55. pbs: 3000m 8:55.88 '08, 5000m 15:17.74 '08, 10,000m 31:27.80 '08; Road: 15k 48:09 '12, 20k 65:06+ '12, HMar 67:48 '12, 30k 1:40:45 '11.
Won Amsterdam Marathon 2011, Rotterdam 2012.

Kalkidan GEZAHEGNE b. 8 May 1991 Addis Ababa 1.63m 44kg.
At 1500m: WCh: '09- 9, '11- 5; WJ: '08- 2; WI: '10- 1; Af-J: '09- 2. At 800m: AfCh: '08- h.
World junior indoor records 1500m & 1M 2010.
Progress at 1500m: 2008- 4:10.14, 2009- 4:02.98, 2010- 4:03.28i, 2011- 4:00.97, 2013- 4:06.19. pbs: 800m 2:06.2 '08, 1M 4:24.10i '10, 4:37.76 '08; 3000m 8:47.37i '11, 8:38.61 '09.

Meseret HAILU b. 12 Sep 1990 Oromia region 1.68m 54kg.
At Mar: WCh: '13- dnf. World HMar: '12- 1.
Progress at Mar: 2009- 2:43:29, 2010- 2:30:42, 2011- 2:34:38, 2012- 2:21:09, 2013- 2:26:58, 2014- 2:26:20. pbs: 10k 31:18 '13, HMar 66:56 '13, 30k 1:41:06 '12.
Won Amsterdam Marathon 2012, 2nd Boston 2013.

Aberu KEBEDE Shewaye b. 12 Sep 1989 Shewa 1.63m 50kg.
At Mar: WCh: '11- 12, '13- 13. World HMar: '09- 3; CC: '07- 16J. Won ETH 10,000m 2009.
Progress at 10,000m, Mar: 2009- 30:48.26, 2010- 32:17.74, 2:23:58; 2011- 2:24:34, 2012- 31:09.28, 2:20:30; 2013- 2:23:28. pbs: 5km Rd 15:13 '09, HMar 67:39 '09.
Won Rotterdam and Berlin marathons 2010 after 2nd Dubai on debut, won Berlin again in 2012 and Tokyo and Shanghai 2013.

Werknesh KIDANE b. 21 Nov 1981 Mayshie district, Tigray region 1.58m 42kg.
At 10,000m: OG: '04- 4, '12- 4; WCh: '03- 2, '05- 6; AfG: '03- 2; At 5000m: OG: '00- 7; WCh: '01- h; WJ: '98- 6; AfG: '99- 4. At 3000m: WI: '01- 9. World CC: '97-8-9-00-01-03-04-05-10: 13J/3J/1J/ 9J/1/3/3/9; 4k: '01-02-03-04-05: 5/2/2/4/2. Won ETH 10,000m 2003, 2005; 4k CC 2001-02, E.Afr 4k & 8k CC 2004.
Progress at 5000m, 10,000m: 1998- 15:50.10, 1999- 15:24.56, 2000- 14:47.40, 33:48.7A; 2001- 15:29.96, 31:43.41; 2002- 14:43.53, 2003- 14:33.04, 30:07.15; 2004- 14:38.05, 30:28.30; 2005- 15:01.6,

30:19.39; 2009- 31:19.00, 2011- 31:08.92, 2012- 15:04.65, 30:39.38. pbs: 1500m 4:17.0A '03, 3000m 8:36.39 '05, Road: 15k 47:37 '11, 10M 51:03 '11, HMar 67:28 '11, Mar 2:26:15dh/2:27:15 '11.
Has won women's record 21 team and individual medals at World CC. Married Gebre Gebremariam on 4 Feb 2006, sons Nathaniel born 2 May 2006, Muse born 2 Aug 2007.

Fantu MAGISO Manedo b. 9 Jun 1992 Hosana Lenchicho 1.78m 60kg.
At 800m: WCh: '11- sf, '13- h; WI: '12- 4; AfG: '11- 2. At 400m/400mR: WCh; '09- sf; AfCh: '10- 2R; Af-J: '11- 1/3R (2 200m).
Ethiopian records: 200m (4) 2010-11, 400m 2011, 800m (4) 2011-12.
Progress at 800m: 2011- 1:59.17, 2012- 1:57.48, 2013- 2:00.25. pbs: 200m 23.90A '11, 400m 52.09A, 52.23 '11.

Meselech MELKAMU b. 27 Apr 1985 Debre Markos, Amhara region 1.58m 47kg.
At 5000m(/10,000m): OG: '08- 8; WCh: '05- 4, '07- 6, '09- 5/2, '11- (5); AfG: '07- 2, '11- (dnf); AfCh: '06- 6, '08- 1, '10- (2); WJ: '04- 1. At Mar: WCh: '13- dnf. At 3000m: WI: '08- 2. World CC: '03-04-05-06-07-08-09-10-11: 4J/1J/4 & 6/3 & 3/3/9/3/3/4 (17 medals). Won ETH 5000m 2004, 4k CC 2005, CC 2006-07.
African 10,000m record 2009.
Progress at 5000m, 10,000m, Mar: 2003- 15:27.93, 2004- 15:00.02, 2005- 14:38.97, 2006- 14:37.44, 2007- 14:33.83, 2008- 14:38.78, 31:04.93; 2009- 14:34.17, 29:53.80; 2010- 14:31.91, 31:04.52; 2011- 14:39.44, 30:56.55m 2012- 2:21:01, 2013- 2:25:46. pbs: 1500m 4:07.52 '07, 1M 4:33.94 '03, 2000m 5:39.2i+, 5:46.3+ '07; 3000m 8:23.74i '07, 8:34.73 '05, Road: HMar 68:05 '13, 25k 1:23:23 '12, 30k 1:39:58 '12.
Third fastest ever marathon debut to win at Frankfurt 2012. 2nd Dubai 2014.

Aselefech MERGIA b. 23 Jan 1985 Woliso 1.68m 45kg.
At Mar: OG: '12- 42; WCh: '09- 3, '11- dnf. HMar: WCh: '08- 2. World CC: '08- 16.
Ethiopian marathon record 2012.
Progress at HMar, Mar: 2006- 74:13, 2007- 74:50, 2008- 68:17, 2009- 67:48, 2:25:02; 2010- 67:22, 2:22:38; 2011- 67:21, 2:22:45; 2012- 69:42+, 2:19:31. pbs: 1500m 4:14.85 '07, 3000m 8:54.42 '08; Road: 10k 31:25+ '08, 15k 47:53 '09, 20k 64:13 '09, 30k 1:41:52 '09.
2nd Paris Marathon 2009 on debut, 2nd London 2010, won Dubai 2011-12. Daughter Sin born in 2013.

Belaynesh OLJIRA Jemane b. 26 Jun 1990 Welek'a, Amhara 1.65m 49kg.
At 10,000m: OG: '12- 5; WCh: '13- 3. World CC: '11- 16, '13- 3; AfCC: '12- 5. Won ETH 10,000m 2011. Ethiopian 1500m record 2012.
Progress at 10,000m, Mar: 2011- 31:17.80, 2012- 30:26.70, 2013- 30:31.44, 2:25:01. pbs: 1500m

4:33.14 '12, 3000m 8:40.73 '10, 5000m 14:58.16 '10, Road: 15k 49:46 '10, HMar 67:27 '11.
Feysa TADESSE Boru b. 19 Nov 1988 1.67m 53kg.
At Mar: WCh: '13- dnf. World HMar: '10- 4, '12- 2; CC: '10- 7.
Progress at Mar: 2009- 2:36:57, 2011- 2:25:20, 2012- 2:23:07, 2013- 2:21:06. pbs: 10,000m 32:29.07 '10, Road: 10k 32:21 '13, 15k 48:51 '12, 20k 65:41 '12, HMar 68:35 '13.
Three wins in seven marathons: Seoul and Shanghai 2012. Paris 2013.
Tirfi TSEGAYE Beyene b. 25 Nov 1984 Bokoji 1.65m 54kg.
World HMar: '09- 6.
Progress at Mar: 2008- 2:35:32, 2009- 2:28:16, 2010- 2:22:44, 2011- 2:24:12, 2012- 2:21:19, 2013- 2:23:23, 2014- 2:22:23. pbs: HMar 67:42 '12.
Marathon wins: Porto 2008, Paris 2012, Dubai 2013, Tokyo 2014

FINLAND
Governing body: Suomen Urheiluliitto, Radiokatu 20, SF-00240 Helsinki. Founded 1906.
National Championships first held in 1907 (men), 1913 (women). **2013 Champions: Men:** 100m/200m: Jonathan Åstrand 10.57/20.77, 400m: Christoffer Envall 48.32, 800m: Niclas Sandells 1:51.93, 1500m Niclas Sandells 4:03.27, 5000m/10,000m/HMar: Lewis Korir KEN 14:00.02/28:37.14/65:03, Mar: Miika Takala 2:27:22, 3000mSt: Jukka Keskisalo 8:53.18, 110mh: Jussi Kanervo 13.98, 400mh: Petteri Monni 51.35, HJ: Jussi Viita 2.20, PV: Eemeli Salomäki 5.40, LJ: Tommi Evilä 7.92w, TJ: Aleksi Tammentie 16.49, SP: Arttu Kangas 19.07, DT: Jouni Waldén 57.65, HT: David Söderberg 74.08, JT: Tero Pitkämäki 85.70, Dec: Mauri Kaattari 7333, 20kW: Veli-Matti Partanen 1:29:40.
Women: 100m/200m: Hanna-Maari Latvala 11.42/23.31, 400m: Sanna Aaltonen 54.45, 800m: Johanna Matintalo 2:08.71, 1500m: Johanna Lehtinen 4:22.02, 5000m: Minna Lamminen 16:12.91, 10,000m: Oona Kettunen 34:38.89, HMar: Suvi Miettinen 75:13, Mar: Elina Lindgren 2:45:56, 3000mSt: Sandra Eriksson 9:43.34, 100mh: Nooralotta Neziri 13.16, 400mh: Venla Paunonen 57.44, HJ: Laura Rautanen 1.84, PV: Minna Nikkanen 4.30, LJ: Matilda Bogdanoff 6.22, TJ: Elina Torro 13.66, SP: Katri Hirvonen 15.33, DT: Sanna Kämäräinen 53.46, HT: Merja Korpela 69.38, JT: Oona Sormunen 58.00, Hep: Miia Kurppa 5410, 10kW/20kW: Anne Halkivaha 47:06/1:37:48.
Ari MANNIO b. 23 Jul 1987 Lehtimäki 1.85m 104kg. Lehtimäen Jyske.
At JT: OG: '12- 11; WCh: '11- dnq 14; EC: '12- 3; WJ: '04- 6, '06- 2; EU23: '07- 4, '09- 1; EJ: '05- 3; ET: '10- 3. Finnish champion 2011.
Progress at JT: 2004- 70.83, 2005- 76.40, 2006-

79.68, 2007- 80.31, 2008- 81.54, 2009- 85.70, 2010- 85.12. 2011- 85.12, 2012- 84.62, 2013- 84.65.
Tero PITKÄMÄKI b. 19 Dec 1982 Ilmajoki 1.95m 92kg. Nurmon Urheilijat. Electrical engineer.
At JT: OG: '04- 8, '08- 3, '12- 5; WCh: '05-07-09- 11-13: 4/1/5/dnq 17/2; EC: '06- 2, '10- 3, '12- 11; EU23: '03- 3; EJ: '01- 6; ECp: '06- 1. Won WAF 2005, 2007; Finnish 2004-07, 2013.
Progress at JT: 1999- 66.83, 2000- 73.75, 2001- 74.89, 2002- 77.24, 2003- 80.45, 2004- 84.64, 2005- 91.53, 2006- 91.11, 2007- 91.23, 2008- 87.70, 2009- 87.79, 2010- 86.92, 2011- 85.33, 2012- 86.98, 2013- 89.03.
Partner is Niina Kelo (b. 26 Mar 1980) pb Hep 5956 (15 EC 2006).
Antti RUUSKANEN b. 21 Feb 1984 Kokkola 1.89m 86kg. Pielaveden Sampo.
At JT: OG: '12- 3; WCh: '09-11-13: 6/9/5; EU23: '05- 2; EJ: '03- 3. Finnish chmpion 2012.
Progress at JT: 2002- 66.08, 2003- 72.87, 2004- 75.84, 2005- 79.75, 2006- 84.10, 2007- 82.71/ 87.88dh, 2008- 87.33, 2009- 85.39, 2010- 83.45, 2011- 82.29, 2012- 87.79, 2013- 85.70.
Teemu WIRKKALA b. 14 Jan 1984 Pielavesi 1.87m 85kg. Toholammin Urheilijat.
At JT: OG: '08- 5; WCh: '07-09-13: 12/9/dnq 17; EC: '06- dnq 13, '10- 5, '12- dnq; WJ: '02- 7; WY: '01- 1; EU23: '05- 6; EJ: '03- 1. Finnish champion 2009.
Progress at JT: 2001- 69.22, 2002- 74.56, 2003- 80.57, 2004- 80.87, 2005- 80.68, 2006- 82.82, 2007- 84.06, 2008- 84.10, 2009- 87.23, 2010- 86.53, 2011- 82.39, 2012- 83.73, 2013- 82.91.

FRANCE
Governing body: Fédération Française d'Athlétisme, 33 avenue Pierre de Coubertin, 75640 Paris cedex 13. Founded 1920.
National Championships first held in 1888 (men), 1918 (women). **2013 Champions: Men:** 100m: Jimmy Vicaut 9.95, 200m: Christophe Lemaitre 20.34, 400m: Mame-Ibra Anne 46.05, 800m: Hamid Oualich 1:47.87, 1500m: Florian Carvalho 3:47.85, 5000m: Noureddine Smaïl 13:49.68, 10,000m: Riad Guerfi 29:04.20, HMar: Abdellatif Meftah 64:20, Mar: Ruben Iindongo 2:17:44, 3000mSt: Mahiédine Mekhissi-Benabbad 8:46.57, 110mh: Thomas Martinot-Lagarde 13.30, 400mh: Yoann Décimus 49.52, HJ: Mickaël Hanany 2.31, PV: Renaud Lavillenie 5.95, LJ: Salim Sdiri 8.10w, TJ: Teddy Tamgho 17.49w, SP: Gaëtan Bucki 19.33, DT: Jean-François Aurokiom 58.48, HT: Jérôme Bortoluzzi 72.49, JT: Vitolio Tipotio 71.74, Dec: Gaël Quérin 8146, 10,000mW/20kW: Kevin Campion 38:37.02/ 1:28:06, 50kW: Xavier Le Coz 4:09:41. **Women:** 100m/200m: Myriam Soumaré 11.30/22.96, 400m: Floria Guei 52.05, 800m: Clarisse Moh 2:04.47, 1500m: Laurane Picoche 4:25.88, 5000m: Sophie Duarte 15:49.24, HMar: Aline Camboulives

77:10, Mar: Corinne Herbreteau-Cante 2:37:50, 3000mSt: Claire Perraux 10:00.80, 100mh: Cindy Billaud 12.59, 400mh: Phara Anacharsis 56.07, HJ: Mélanie Skotnik 1.85, PV: Marion Lotout 4.50, LJ: Éloyse Lesueur 6.49, TJ: Teresa Nzola Neso Ba 13.95w, SP: Jessica Cérival 16.88, DT: Mélina Robert-Michon 59.55, HT: Stéphanie Falzon 69.78, JT: Mathilde Andraud 56.02, Hep: Camille Le Joly 5560, 10,000mW: Violaine Averous 48:16.97, 20kW: Emilie Tissot 1:37:23.

Pierre-Ambroise BOSSE b. 11 May 1992 Nantes 1.85m 68kg. UA Gujan Mestras.
At 800m: OG: '12- sf; WCh: '13- 7; EC:'12- 3; WJ: '10- 8; EU23: '13- 1; EJ: '11- 1. Won FRA 2012.
Progress at 800m: 2007- 2:02.81, 2008- 1:56.05, 2010- 1:48.38, 2011- 1:46.18, 2012- 1:44.97, 2013- 1:43.76. pbs: 400m 48.54 '11, 600m 1:15.63i '13, 1000m 2:17.63i '14, 2:18.20 '13; 1500m 3:54.81 '09.

Benjamin COMPAORÉ b. 5 Aug 1987 Bar-le-Duc 1.89m 86kg. Strasbourg AA.
At TJ: OG: '12- 6; WCh: '11- 8; EC: '10- 5; WJ: '06- 1; EJ: '05- 9.; WI: '12- 6.
Progress at TJ: 2003- 14.50, 2004- 15.48, 2005- 16.00/16.12w, 2006- 16.61, 2007- 16.62, 2008- 17.05, 2009- 16.98, 2010- 17.21/17.28w, 2011- 17.31, 2012- 17.17, 2013- 17.07. pbs: 60m 7.13i '08, 100m 10.76 '13, 400m 48.69 '12, 1500m 4:44.43 '12, 110mh 15.72 '12, HJ 1.98 '12, LJ 7.88 '08, Dec 6704 '12.

Garfield DARIEN b. 22 Dec 1987 Lyon 1.87m 76kg. EA Chambéry.
At 110mh: OG: '12- sf; WCh: '09- sf; EC: '10- 2, '12- 2; WJ: '04- 7; EJ: '05- 1; CCp: '10- 4; ET: '11- 2; French champion 2012. At 60mh: WI: '14- 3; EI: '09- 6, '11- 2.
Progress at 110mh: 2004- 14.03/13.98w, 2005- 13.73, 2006- 13.94/13.92w, 2008- 13.50/13.43w, 2009- 13.36, 2010- 13.34, 2011- 13.37, 2012- 13.15, 2013- 14.47. pbs: 200m 22.05 '06, 60mh 7.47i '14, HJ 1.84 '03.
Father Daniel Darien had 110mh pb 13.76 '87.

Yohann DINIZ b. 1 Jan 1978 Epernay 1.85m 69kg. EFS Reims Athlétisme.
At 20kW: ECp: '07- 1; At 50kW: OG: '08- dnf, '12- dq; WCh: '05-07-09-11-13: dq/2/12/dq/10; EC: '06- 1, '10- 1; ECp: '05- 4, '13- 1. Won French 10,000mW 2010, 2012; 20kW 2007-09, 50kW 2005. World record 50,000m track walk 2011. French records 5000mW (3) 2006-08, 20kW (3) 2005-12, 50kW 2006 & 2009, 1 Hr 2010.
Progress at 20kW, 50kW: 2001- 1:35:05.0t, 2002- 1:30:40, 2003- 1:26:54.99t, 2004- 1:24:25, 3:52:11.0t; 2005- 1:20:20, 3:45:17; 2006- 1:23:19, 3:41:39; 2007- 1:18:58, 3:44:22; 2008- 1:22:31, 2009- 1:22:50, 3:38:45; 2010- 1:20:23, 3:40:37; 2011- 3:35:27.2t, 2012- 1:17:43, 2013- 1:23:17, 3:41:07. pbs: 3000mW 10:52.44 '08, 5000mW 18:18.01 '08, 10,000mW 38:44.97 '11, 1HrW 15,395m '10, 35kW 2:32:24 '12.

Renaud LAVILLENIE b. 18 Sep 1986 Barbezieux-Saint-Hilaire 1.77m 69kg. Clermont Athl. Auvergne.
At PV: OG: '12- 1; WCh: '09- 3, '11- 3, '13- 2; WI: '12- 1; EC: '10- 1, '12- 1; EU23: '07- 10; EI: '09-11-13: 1/1/1; CCp: '10- 2; ET: '09-10-13: 1/1/1. Won DL 2010-13, French 2010, 2012-13.
World indoor pole vault record 2014. French record (indoors) 2011 and outdoors 2013.
Progress at PV: 2002- 3.40, 2003- 4.30, 2004- 4.60, 2005- 4.81i/4.70, 2006- 5.25i/5.22, 2007- 5.58i/5.45, 2008- 5.81i/5.65, 2009- 6.01, 2010- 5.94, 2011- 6.03i/5.90, 2012- 5.97, 2013- 6.02, 2014- 6.16i. pbs: 60m 7.23i '08, 100m 11.04 '11, 60mh 8.41i '08, 100m 11.20 '11, 110mh 14.51 '10, HJ 1.89i '08, 1.87 '07; LJ 7.31 '10, Hep 5363i '08.
Broke Sergey Bubka's 21 year-old absolute world pole vault record indoors in 2014. His brother Valentin (b. 16 Jul 1991) has PV pb 5.70i/5.65 '13 and was 3rd at the European U23s and nh in World final in 2013.

Christophe LEMAITRE b. 11 Jun 1990 Annecy 1.89m 74kg. AS Aix-les-Bains.
At 100m/(200m): OG: '12- (6); WCh: '09- qf, '11- 4/3/2R, '13- 7; EC: '10- 1/1/1R, '12- 1/3R; WJ: '08- (1); WY: '07- 4/5; EJ: '09- 1; CCp: '10- 1; ET: '10- 2, '11- 1/1, '13- (1). At 60m: EI: '11- 3. Won French 100m 2010-12, 200m 2010-13.
French records 100m (7) 2010-11, 200m (2) 2010-11, European junior 100m 2009. U23 2010-11.
Progress at 100m, 200m: 2005- 11.46, 2006- 10.96, 2007- 10.53, 21.08; 2008- 10.26, 20.83; 2009- 10.04/10.03w, 20.68; 2010- 9.97, 20.16; 2011- 9.92, 19.80; 2012- 10.04/9.94w, 19.91; 2013- 10.00/9.98w, 20.07. pbs: 60m 6.55i '10, 150m St 14.90 '13.
First Caucasian sub-10.00 100m runner and first to win sprint treble at European Champs.

Pascal MARTINOT-LAGARDE b. 22 Sep 1991 St Maur-des-Fossés 1.90m 80kg. Neuilly Plaisance Sport.
At 110mh: WCh: '13- h; WJ: '10- 1; EU23: '11- h; EJ: '09- 4; ET: '13- 2. At 60mh: WI: '12- 3, '14- 2; EI: '13- 3.
Progress at 110mh: 2008- 15.03, 2009- 14.13, 2010- 13.74, 2011- 13.94, 2012- 13.41/13.30w, 2013- 13.12. pbs: 60m 7.07i '10, 100m 10.94 '13, 60mh 7.45i '14.
His brother **Thomas** (b. 7 Feb 1988) has 110mh pb 13.26, 7 WCh and French champion in 2013.

Kevin MAYER b. 10 Feb 1992 Argenteuil 1.86m 77kg. EA Tain-Tournon.
At Dec: OG: '12- 15; WCh: '13- 4; EC: '12- dnf; WJ: '10- 1; EJ: '11- 1; ECp: '13- 1. At Oct: WY: '09- 1. At Hep: EI: '13- 2.
Progress at Dec: 2011- 7992, 2012- 8447w/8415, 2013- 8446. pbs: 60m 7.10i '13, 100m 11.04 '13, 400m 48.66 '11, 1000m 2:37.30i '13, 1500m 4:18.04 '12, 60mh 8.01i '13, 110mh 14.21 '12, HJ 2.10i '10, 2.09 '12; PV 5.20 '12, LJ 7.63 '13, SP 15.16i/14.95 '13, DT 45.37 '13, JT 66.09 '13, Hep 6297i '13.

Mahiédine MEKHISSI-BENABBAD b. 15 Mar 1985 Reims 1.90m 75kg. EFS Reims.

At 3000mSt: OG: '08- 2, '12- 2; WCh: '07/09- h, '11- 3, '13- 3; EC: '10- 1, '12- 1; WJ: '04- h; EU23: '05- h, '07- 1; CCp: '10- 3; ECp: '07- 2, '08- 1; French champion 2008, 2012-13. At 1500m: WI: '10- 8; EI: '13- 1; WCp: '06- 7.
World best 2000m steeplechase 2010. European 3000mSt record 2013,
Progress at 3000mSt: 2003- 9:52.07, 2004- 9:01.01, 2005- 8:34.45, 2006- 8:28.25, 2007- 8:14.22, 2008- 8:08.95, 2009- 8:06.98, 2010- 8:02.52, 2011- 8:02.09, 2012- 8:10.90, 2013- 8:00.09. pbs: 800m 1:53.61 '04, 1000m 2:17.14 '09, 1500m 3:33.12 '13, 2000m 4:56.85 '13, 3000m 7:43.72i '13, 7:44.98 '10; 5000m 14:32.9 '05, 2000mSt 5:10.68 '10.

Yoann RAPINIER b. 29 Sep 1989 Pontoise 1.82m 70kg. Franconville Ermont.
At TJ: WCh: '13- 12; EU23: '09- 9; EI: '11- 4. Won Franc G 2013.
Progress at TJ: 2004- 12.56i, 2005- 12.83, 2007- 14.04i, 2008- 15.69, 2009- 16.24, 2010- 16.58/16.73w, 2011- 17.23i/16.39/16.46w, 2012- 16.76, 2013- 17.07. pbs: 100m 10.85 '10, 200m 22.16 '10, 400m 47.80 '10, 400mh 54.17 '07, HJ 2.15i/2.08 '08, LJ 7.30 '10.

Bouabdellah 'Bob' TAHRI b. 20 Dec 1978 Metz 1.91m 68kg. Athlétisme Metz Métropole.
At 3000mSt: OG: '00- h, '04- 7, '08- 5; WCh: '99-01-03-05-07-09-11: 12/5/4/8/5/3/4; EC: '98-02-06-10: 10/4/3/2; WJ: '96- 7; WCp: '06- 3; ECp: '00-01-02-04: 1/1/1/1. At 5000m: EJ: '97- 1; CCp: '10- 3; ECp: '05- 2, '13- 2. At 3000m: WI: '01- 11; EI: '98-07-09: 8/2/2; ECp: '07- 1, '13- 1. At 1500m: WCh: '13- sf. World CC: '97- 22J, '04- 15 4k; Eur CC: '05- 4, '08- 6. Won FRA 1500m 2004, 2006; 3000mSt 1998, 2010-11.
Three European records 3000mSt 2003-09, indoor 5000m (13:11.13) 2010; best 2000mSt 2002 & 2009. World best 2000mSt 2010.
Progress at 3000mSt: 1996- 8:44.65, 1998- 8:19.75, 1999- 8:12.24, 2000- 8:16.14, 2001- 8:09.23, 2002- 8:10.83, 2003- 8:06.91, 2004- 8:14.26, 2005- 8:09.58, 2006- 8:09.53, 2007- 8:09.06, 2008- 8:12.72, 2009- 8:01.18, 2010- 8:03.72, 2011- 8:05.72. pbs: 800m 1:48.96 '01, 1000m 2:20.34 '05, 1500m 3:32.73 '13, 1M 3:52.95 '02, 2000m 4:57.58 '02, 3000m 7:33.18 '09, 5000m 13:12.29 '07, 10,000m 27:31.46 '11, 15k Rd 43:49 '12, HMar 63:38 '13, Mar 2:18:16 '13, 2000mSt 5:13.47 '10.
Missed 2012 season through injury.

Teddy TAMGHO b. 15 Jun 1989 Paris 1.87m 82kg. CA Montreuil.
At TJ: WCh: '09- 11, '13- 1; EC: '10- 3; WI: '10- 1; WJ: '08- 1; EJ: '07- 4; EI: '11- 1 (4 LJ); ET: '10- 3, '13- 2. Won DL 2010, French 2009-10, 2013.
Four World indoor triple jump records 2010 (17.90) & 2011, four absolute French records 2009-13; three Eur U23 records 2010.
Progress at TJ: 2004- 12.56, 2005- 14.89, 2006- 15.58, 2007- 16.53i/16.35/16.42w, 2008- 17.19/17.33w, 2009- 17.58i/17.11, 2010- 17.98, 2011- 17.92i/17.91, 2013- 18.04. pbs: 60m 6.92i '06, 100m 10.60 '09, LJ

8.01i '11, 7.81 '13.
2011 season ended when broke ankle in warm-up for European U23s and also missed all of 2012. His 18.04 to win 2013 World title was third best ever and world's best for 17 years. Fractured his shin in November 2013 and will miss all the 2014 season.

Jimmy VICAUT b. 27 Feb 1992 Bondy 1.88m 83kg. Paris Avenir Athletic.
At 100m/(200m)/4x100mR: OG: '12- sf; WCh: '11- 6/2R, '13- sf/sf; EC: '10- 1R, '12- 2/3R (res); WJ: '10- 3; WY: '09- 7; EJ: '11- 1/1R; ET: '13- 1. At 60m: EI: '13- 1. Won French 100m 2013.
Progress at 100m: 2005- 13.0, 2006- 12.50, 2007- 11.0, 2008- 10.75/10.69w, 2009- 10.56, 2010- 10.16, 2011- 10.07, 2012- 10.02, 2013- 9.95. pbs: 60m 6.48i '13, 200m 20.30 '13.
His brother Willi was French U17 shot champion in 2012 and has senior pb of 16.28 '13.

Women

Cindy BILLAUD b. 11 Mar 1986 Nogent-sur-Marne 1.67m 59kg. US Créteil.
At 100mh: WCh: '09- sf, '11- h, '13- 7; WJ: '04- sf; EU23: '07- sf; EJ: '05- 3; FRA champion 2013. At 60mh: WI: '14- 4; EI: '09- 7.
Progress at 100mh: 2004- 13.48, 2005- 13.57, 2006- 13.49/13.46w, 2007- 13.25, 2008- 12.99/12.97w, 2009- 12.97, 2010- 13.11, 2011- 12.93, 2012- 12.97, 2013- 12.59. pbs: 60m 7.64i '08, 100m 12.00 '05, 200m 24.68 '08, 50mh 7.14+i '12, 60mh 7.89i '14.

Sophie DUARTE b. 31 Jul 1981 Rodez 1.70m 54kg. AC Paris Joinville.
At 3000mSt: OG: '08- h; WCh: '07- 5, '09- 15; EC: '10- 7; EU23: '03- 9; CCp: '10- 9; ECp: '07-09-10: 2/2/5. At 5000m: WCh: '13- h. Won French 5000m 2013, 3000mSt 2007-08, 2010-11. Eur CC: '08-11-12-13: 15/6/6/1.
Three French 3000mSt records 2007-09.
Progress at 3000mSt: 2003- 10:17.76, 2004- 10:29.13, 2005- 10:07.73, 2006- 10:14.36, 2007- 9:27.51, 2008- 9:35.35, 2009- 9:25.62, 2010- 9:35.52, 2011- 9:44.18, 2012- 9:46.60. pbs: 800m 2:14.26 '04, 1500m: 4:13.60 '09, 3000m 9:07.78i '08, 9:26.43 '07; 5000m 15:14.57 '13, 10k Rd 31:53 '14.

Stéphanie FALZON b. 7 Jan 1983 Bordeaux 1.70m 75kg. B. Sud Médoc Athlé.
At HT: OG: '08- dnq 14, '12- 8; WCh: '07- dnq 16, '09- 9, '11- 11; EC: '06/10- dnq 15/17, '12- 6; WJ: '00- dnq 28, '02- 6; EU23: '03- dnq, '05- 8; EJ: '01- 8; French champion 2006, 2008-10, 2012-13.
Progress at HT: 2000- 53.71, 2001- 57.31, 2002- 59.98, 2003- 64.16, 2004- 65.21, 2005- 65.12, 2006- 68.84, 2007- 71.11, 2008- 73.40, 2009- 72.54, 2010- 73.40, 2011- 71.53, 2012- 73.06, 2013- 69.78.

Éloyse LESUEUR b. 15 Jul 1988 Créteil 1.79m 65kg. Saint Denis Emotion.
At LJ: OG: '12- 8; WCh: '09- 11-13: dnq 18/26/22; WI: '08- 4, '12- 1; WY: '05- 2 (7 100m); EC: '12- 1; EU23: '09- 3; EJ: '07- 2; EI: '11- 4, '13- 2; ET: '10-11-

13: 1/3/1. French champion 2006, 2010-13. At Hep: WJ: '06- dnf.
Progress at LJ: 2002- 5.72, 2003- 5.50, 2004- 5.68, 2005- 6.40, 2006- 6.30/6.47w, 2007- 6.47, 2008- 6.84i/6.50, 2009- 6.64/6.72w, 2010- 6.78, 2011- 6.91, 2012- 6.81/7.04w, 2013- 6.90i/6.78, 2014- 6.86i. pbs: 60m 7.34i '12, 100m 11.57 '06, 200m 24.11 '06, 800m 2:21.67 '06, 100mh 13.89 '06, HJ 1.75 '06, Hep 5370w/5320 '06.

Antoinette NANA DJIMOU Ida b. 2 Aug 1985 Douala, Cameroon 1.74m 69kg. CA Montreuil.
At Hep: OG: '08- 18, '12- 5; WCh: '07-09-11-13: dnf/7/7/8; EC: '06-10-12: 21/dnf/1; WJ: '04- 4; EU23: '05- 5, '07- 7; ECp: '08- 2. At Pen: WI: '10- 5; EI: '09- 11-13: 3/1/1. Won French LJ 2008, Hep 2006-07.
CMR heptathlon record 2003, French indoor pentathlon record 2011.
Progress at Hep: 2003- 5360, 2004- 5649, 2005- 6089w/5792, 2006- 5981, 2007- 5982, 2008- 6204, 2009- 6323, 2010- 5994, 2011- 6409, 2012- 6576, 2013- 6326. pbs: 60m 7.51i '11, 100m 11.78 '08, 200m 24.36 '11, 800m 2:15.94 '12, 60mh 8.11i '10, 100mh 12.96 '12, HJ 1.84i '10, 1.83 '11; LJ 6.44i '09, 6.42 '12, 6.61w '08; SP 15.41i/14.84 '13, JT 57.27 '12, Pen 4723i '11.
Came to France at age 14, naturalised French citizen in 2004. Three pbs when winning European gold in 2012.

Mélina ROBERT-MICHON b. 18 Jul 1979 Voiron 1.80m 85kg. Lyon Athlétisme
At DT: OG: '00/04- dnq 29/30, '08- 8, '12- 5; WCh: '01-03-07-09-13: dnq 20/11/11/8/2; EC: '98-02-06-12: dnq 29/12/dnq 16/6; WJ: '98- 2; EU23: '99-12, '01- 1; WUG: '01- 3; ECp: '00-01-02-03-04-06-07-08-09-13: 5/6/8/2/4/7/5/4/2/1.
French champion 2000-09, 2011-13; MedG 2009.
Five French discus records 2000-13.
Progress at DT: 1997- 49.10, 1998- 59.27, 1999- 60.17, 2000- 63.19/63.61dh, 2001- 63.87, 2002- 65.78, 2003- 64.27, 2004- 64.54, 2005- 58.01, 2006- 59.89, 2007- 63.48, 2008- 62.21, 2009- 63.04, 2010- 56.52, 2011- 61.07, 2012- 63.98, 2013- 66.28, 2014- 64.20. pbs: SP 15.23 '07, HT 47.92 '02.
Daughter Elyssa born in 2010. Broke her 11 year-old French record in winning 2013 World silver.

Myriam SOUMARÉ b. 29 Oct 1986 Paris 1.67m 57kg. AA Pays de France Athlé 95.
At 100m/(200m): OG: '12- sf/7; WCh: '09- qf, '11- 13: sf/sf; EC: '10- 3/1/2R, '12- (3); EU23: '07- 3; ET: '13- 2/2. At 4x400m: EJ: '05- 7. At 60m: WI: '10- 7; EI: '11- 7, '13- 2. Won FRA 100m 2009, 2012-13; 200m 2011-13.
Progress at 100m: 2004- 24.66i, 2005- 12.07/11.98w, 24.05; 2006- 11.68, 23.78; 2007- 11.50/11.39w, 23.44; 2008- 11.43, 23.64/23.40w; 2009- 11.34, 23.34; 2010- 11.18/11.13w, 22.32; 2011- 11.17/11.12w, 22.71; 2012- 11.07, 22.56; 2013- 11.30, 22.83/22.81w. pbs: 50m 6.22i '10, 55m 6.86i '13, 60m 7.07i '13, 400m 53.44'11, LJ 6.08 '13.

Astonishing breakthrough in final of European 200m 2010 when she improved pb from 23.01 to win in 22.32. Daughter Elyssa born in 2010. Parents came from Mauritania.

GERMANY

Governing body: Deutscher Leichtathletik Verband (DLV), Alsfelder Str. 27, 64289 Darmstadt. Founded 1898.
National Championships first held in 1891.
2013 Champions: Men: 100m/200m: Julian Reus 10.14/20.36, 400m: David Gollnow 46.07, 800m: Robin Schembra 1:47.05, 1500m: Carsten Schlangen 3:43.38, 5000m: Arne Gabius 14:01.76, 10,000m: Philipp Pflieger 29:09.65, HMar: Jan Fitschen 63:22, Mar: Frank Schauer 2:18:54, 3000mSt: Steffen Uliczka 8:40.62, 110mh: Matthias Bühler 13.49, 400mh: Silvio Schirrmeister 49.24, HJ: Matthias Haverney 2.22, PV: Björn Otto 5.80, LJ: Alyn Camara 8.15, TJ: Andreas Pohle 16.35, SP: David Storl 21.04, DT: Robert Harting 67.95, HT: Markus Esser 76.41, JT: Thomas Röhler 83.56, Dec: Arthur Abele 8251, 20kW: Hagen Pohle 1:22:37, 50kW: Carl Dohmann 3:57:58. **Women**: 100m: Verena Sailer 11.09, 200m: Inna Weit 23.16, 400m: Esther Cremer 51.93, 800m: Fabienne Kohlmann 2:04.00, 1500m: Corrinna Harrer 4:12.12, 5000m: Sabrina Mockenhaupt 15:32.73, 10,000m/HMar: Eleni Gebrehiwot ETH 32:26.92/73:15, Mar: Silke Optekamp 2:41:50, 3000mSt: Antje Möldner-Schmidt 9:46.80, 100mh: Nadine Hildebrand 12.90, 400mh: Claudia Wehrsen 57.78, HJ: Marie-Laurence Jungfleisch 1.92, PV: Martina Strutz 4.65, LJ: Sosthene Moguenara 6.69, TJ: Jenny Elbe 13.58, SP: Nadine Kleinert 19.76, DT: Nadine Müller 64.17, HT: Betty Heidler 73.93, JT: Linda Stahl 63.70, Hep: Carolin Schäfer 5804, 20kW: Bianca Schenker 1:44:36.

Sebastian BAYER b. 11 Jun 1986 Aachen 1.89m 79kg. Hamburger SV. Soldier.
At LJ: OG: '08- dnq 23, '12- 5; WCh: '09- dnq 19, '11- 8, '13- 8; EC: '06- dnq 20, '12- 1; WJ: '04- dnq 17; EJ: '05- 2; EI: '09- 1, '11- 1. German champion 2006, 2008-09, 2011-12.
Progress at LJ: 2000- 5.65, 2001- 6.14, 2002- 6.57, 2003- 7.27, 2004- 7.57, 2005- 7.82i/7.73, 2006- 7.95, 2007- 7.88i, 2008- 8.15, 2009- 8.71i/8.49, 2010- 8.06, 2011- 8.17, 2012- 8.34, 2013- 8.04. pbs: 60m 6.80i '09, 100m 10.73 '09, HJ 1.83 '03.
Sensational improvement at 2009 European Indoors – from pb of 8.17 to 8.29 and then European record 8.71 with final jump.

Pascal BEHRENBRUCH b. 19 Jan 1985 Offenbach 1.96m 94kg. LG Eintracht Frankfurt.
At Dec: OG: '12- 10; WCh: '09- 6, '11- 7, '13- 11; EC: '06- 5, '12- 1; EJ: '03- 10; EU23: '07- 2. At Hep: WI: '14- 8.
Progress at Dec: 2005- 7842, 2006- 8209, 2007- 8239, 2008- 8242, 2009- 8439, 2010- 8202, 2011- 8232, 2012- 8558, 2013- 8514. pbs: 60m 7.08i '10,

100m 10.84 '07, 10.73w '13; 400m 48.40 '13, 1000m 2:53.39i '06, 1500m 4:24.16 '06, 60mh 8.10i '10, 110mh 14.02 '09, HJ 2.03 '08, PV 5.00 '12, LJ 7.21 '11, 7.32w '07, SP 16.89 '12, DT 51.31 '09, JT 71.40 '11, Hep 5604i '06.

Matthias de ZORDO b. 21 Feb 1988 Bad Kreuznach 1.90m 97kg. SC Magdeburg.
At JT: OG: '12- dnq; WCh: '11- 1; EC: '10- 2; EU23: '09- 8; EJ: '07- 1, CCp: '10- 3; ET: '10- 1, '11-3. Won DL 2011, German 2010-11.
Progress at JT: 2006- 71.67, 2007- 78.67, 2008-82.51, 2009- 80.15, 2010- 87.81, 2011- 88.36, 2012-81.62, 2013- 81.49. Left-handed.

Markus ESSER b. 3 Feb 1980 Leverkusen 1.80m 105kg. TSV Bayer 04 Leverkusen. Army lieutenant.
At HT: OG: '00-04-08: dnq 35/10/9; WCh: '05-07-09-11-13: 4/8/6/4/10; EC: '02-06-10-12: dnq 29/4/dnq 19/7; WJ: '98- 12; EJ: '99- 3; EU23: '01- 7; ECp: '04-05-07-08-09-10-11-13: 2/3/2/3/3/1/2. German champion 2006-08, 2010-13.
Progress at HT: 1997- 64.78, 1998- 73.10, 1999-70.29, 2000- 76.66, 2001- 75.69, 2002- 76.94, 2003-78.13, 2004- 79.01, 2005- 80.00, 2006- 81.10, 2007-80.68, 2008- 79.97, 2009- 79.43, 2010- 78.87, 2011-79.69, 2012- 77.93, 2013- 77.99.

Rico FREIMUTH b. 14 Mar 1988 Potsdam 1.96m 92kg. Hallesche LA-Freunde.
At Dec: OG: '12- 6; WCh: '11- dnf, '13- 7; EU23: 09- 10; EJ: '07- 3.
Progress at Dec: 2009- 7689, 2010- 7826, 2011-8287, 2012- 8322, 2013- 8488w/8382. pbs: 60m 6.98i '12, 100m 10.54/10.36w '13, 200m 21.39 '12, 400m 47.51 '12, 1000m 2:48.22i '12, 1500m 4:34.60 '13, 60mh 7.84i '14, 110mh 13.79 '12, HJ 1.99 '13, PV 4.90 '12, LJ 7.55 '13, SP 15.14 '12, DT 49.11 '12, JT 65.04 '11, Hep 5715i '12.
His father Uwe had decathlon best of 8794 (1984), and was 4th at 1983 Worlds and 1986 Europeans and twice winner at Götzis. Uwe and Rico are the highest scoring father-son combination. His uncle Jörg won the high jump bronze medal at the 1980 Olympic Games in a pb of 2.31.

Robert HARTING b. 18 Oct 1984 Cottbus 2.01m 126kg. SCC Berlin.
At DT: OG: 08- 4, '12- 1; WCh: '07-09-11-13: 2/1/1/1; ECh: '06- dnq 13, '10- 2, '12- 1; CCp: '10- 1; ECp: '07-08-09-10-11-13: 2/2/2/1/1/1; WJ: '02- dnq 13; WY: '01- 2; EU23: '05- 1. German champion 2007-13.
Progress at DT: 2002- 54.25, 2003- 59.54, 2004-64.05, 2005- 66.02, 2006- 65.22, 2007- 66.93, 2008-68.65, 2009- 69.43, 2010- 69.69, 2011- 68.99, 2012-70.66, 2013- 69.91. pb SP 18.63 '07.
35 successive wins 2011-13. His brother Christoph (b. 4 Oct 1990) has pb 64.99 '13, dnq 13 WCh '13.

Raphael HOLZDEPPE b. 28 Sep 1989 Kaiserslautern 1.81 m78kg. LAZ Zweibrücken.

At PV: OG: 08- 8, '12- 3; WCh: '11- dnq 20, '13- 1; EC '10- 9, '12- 3; WJ: '06- 5, '08- 1; EU23: '09- 1; EJ: '07- dnq; EI: '13- 8.
World junior pole vault record (=) 2008 (and indoors 5.68).
Progress at PV: 2002- 3.45, 2003- 4.25, 2004- 4.50, 2005- 5.00, 2006- 5.42, 2007- 5.50, 2008- 5.80, 2009- 5.65, 2010- 5.80, 2011- 5.72, 2012- 5.91, 2013-5.91.

Kai KAZMIREK b. 28 Jan 1991 Torgau 1.89m 86kg. LG Rhein-Wied.
At Dec: WJ: '10- 6; EU23: '11- 6, '13- 1; EJ: '09- 3. German champion 2012. At Hep: WI: '14- 6.
Progress at Dec: 2011- 7802, 2012- 8130, 2013-8366. pbs: 60m 7.02i '14, 100m 10.81/10.61w '13, 200m 21.40 12, 400m 46.75 '11, 1000m 2:39.51i '14, 1500m 4:34.46 '13, 60mh 8.00i '13, 110mh 14.15 '11, HJ 2.13 '12, PV 5.20 '13, LJ 7.64i 14, 7.58 '13; SP 14.06i '14, 13.65 '13; DT 44.77 '13, JT 59.39 '12, Hep 6173i '13.

Jan Felix KNOBEL b. 16 Jan 1989 Bad Homburg 1.92m 91kg. LG Eintracht Frankfurt. Architecture student.
At Dec: OG: '12- dnf; WCh: '11- 8; WJ: '06- 1; EU23: '11- 19. German champion 2009. At Oct: WY: 05- 5.
Progress at Dec: 2009- 7758, 2010- dnf, 2011-8288, 2012- 8228, 2013- 8396w. pbs: 60m 7.18i '10, 100m 11.04 '12, 10.85w '13; 400m 48.89 '12, 1000m 2:49.22i '10, 1500m 4:43.12 '11, 60mh 8.24i '13, 110mh 14.59 '13, HJ 2.01 '11, PV 5.03 '12, LJ 7.36 '13, SP 16.06 '11, DT 50.87 '13, JT 76.36 '13, Hep 5778i '10.

Malte MOHR b. 24 Jul 1986 Bochum 1.92m 84kg. TV Wattenscheid.
At PV: OG: '12- 9=; WCh: '09- 14, '11- 5, '13- 5; EC: '10- dnq 17=, '12- 4; WI: '10-12-14: 2/4/2; EI: '11- 3, 13- 3; ET: '09- 2, '11- 2. German champion 2010-12.
Progress at PV: 2003- 4.81, 2004- 5.11i, 2005-5.30, 2006- 5.71, 2007- 5.31, 2008- 5.76, 2009- 5.80, 2010- 5.90, 2011- 5.86i/5.85, 2012- 5.91, 2013- 5.86, 2014- 5.90i.
His father (and coach) Wolfgang Mohr had a best of 5.41 in 1976 and his mother Gisela Derksen was a good junior multi-eventer.

Björn OTTO b. 16 Oct 1977 Frechen 1.91m 90kg. ASV Köln. Studied biology at University of Cologne.
At PV: OG: '12- 2; WCh: '07- 5, '09- dnq 18=, '13-3; EC: '12- 2; WI: '12- 2; EI: '00-05-07-13: 6/4/3/2; WUG: '99-01-03-05: 8/7/3=/1; ET: '13- 3. German champion 2013.
German pole vault record 2012. Two world over-35 records 2013.
Progress at PV: 1991- 3.20, 1992- 3.20, 1993- 4.10, 1994- 4.71, 1995- 5.00, 1996- 5.30i/5.20, 1997- 5.40, 1998- 5.52sq/5.40, 1999- 5.55/5.60ex, 2000-

Chris Chataway, who died aged 82 this year, is pictured at the moment of his greatest triumph, his world 5000m record victory over Vladimir Kuts at White City in 1954.
(courtesy Track & Field News)

Robert Heffernan at last won a medal – and it was gold at 50km in Moscow.

Abeba Aregawi beats Jenny Simpson to win the Moscow 1500m.

Genzebe Dibaba was the star of the 2014 indoor season with world records at 1500m, 3000m and 2 miles and World Indoor gold at 3000m.

Mo Farah celebrates winning the World 10,000m from his 2011 conqueror Ibrahim Jeylan.

Ezekiel Kemboi after his fifth global steeplechase title.

David Storl

It could hardly have been closer – Christine Ohuruogu dips to beat Amantle Montsho for the World 400m title in a British record time of 49.41

Tatyana Lysenko produced a Championship and Russian record of 78.80 to win the World hammer title.

5.65/5.71ex, 2001- 5.51/5.63ex, 2002- 5.63sq/5.60, 2003- 5.72i/5.70, 2004- 5.82i/5.70, 2005- 5.80, 2006- 5.85, 2007- 5.90, 2008- 5.70, 2009- 5.71, 2010- 5.60i/5.41, 2011- 5.75/5.80ex, 2012- 6.01, 2013- 5.90.

Christian REIF b. 24 Oct 1984 Speyer 1.96m 84kg. LC Rehlingen. Sports student.
At LJ: OG: '12- dnq 13; WCh: '07- 9, '11- 7, '13- 6; EC: '10- 1; WI: '10- 5, '14- 8; EI: '13- 3; CCp: '10- 3. German champion 2010.
Progress at LJ: 2001- 7.15, 2002- 7.55, 2004- 7.83, 2005- 7.64i, 2006- 7.90, 2007- 8.19, 2008- 7.80, 2009- 8.18, 2010- 8.47, 2011- 8.26/8.38w, 2012- 8.26, 2013- 8.27. pbs: 60m 6.86i '06, 100m 10.68 '06, 200m 21.90 '06.
Tied pb of 8.27 in qualifying, then 8.47 in final of Europeans 2010.

Thomas RÖHLER b. 30 Sep 1991 Jena 1.95m 83kg. LC Jena.
At JT: WCh: '13- dnq 29; EC: '12- dnq 13; WJ: '10- 9; EU23: '11- 7, '13- 3; ET: '13- 2. German champion 2012-13.
Progress at JT: 2009- 61.26, 2010- 76.37, 2011- 78.20, 2012- 80.79, 2013- 83.95.

Michael SCHRADER b. 1 Jul 1987 Duisberg-Homburg 1.86m 84kg. TSV Bayer 04 Leverkusen.
At Dec: OG: '08- 10; WCh: '13- 2; EU23: '07- 6. German champion 2010.
Progress at Dec: 2007- 7947, 2008- 8248, 2009- 8522, 2010- 8003, 2013- 8670. pbs: 100m 10.51 '11, 200m 21.70 '09, 400m 47.66 '13, 1500m 4:19.32 '08, 110mh 14.02 '13, HJ 2.00 '12, PV 5.10 '13, LJ 8.05 '09, SP 14.74 '13, DT 46.44 '13, JT 65.67 '13.
Won Götzis decathlon with seven pbs 2009, set three pbs when adding 148 points to pb for World silver 2013.

David STORL b. 21 Jul 1990 Rochlitz 1.99m 115kg. LAC Erdgas Chemnitz. Federal police officer.
At SP: OG: '12- 2; WCh: '09- dnq 27. '11- 1, '13- 1; EC: '10- 4, '12- 1; WJ: '08- 1; WY: '07- 1; EU23: '11- 1; EJ: '09- 1; WI: '10-13-14: 6/2/2; EI: '11- 2; ET: '11- 1, '13- 1. German champion 2011-13.
World junior shot record and three with 6kg (to 22.73) 2009.
Progress at SP: 2008- 18.46, 2009- 20.43, 2010- 20.77, 2011- 21.78, 2012- 21.88i/21.86, 2013- 21.73, 2014- 21.79i.

Martin WIERIG b. 10 Jun 1987 Neindorf 2.02m 108kg. SC Magdeburg. Federal police officer.
At DT: OG: '12- 6; WCh: '11- dnq 18, '13- 4; EC: '10- 7, '12- dnq 14; WJ: '04- 8, '06- 3; EU23: '07- 1, '09- 3; EJ: '05- 3 (dnq SP).
Progress at DT: 2005- 57.44, 2006- 57.37, 2007- 61.10, 2008- 63.09, 2009- 63.90, 2010- 64.93, 2011- 67.21, 2012- 68.33, 2013- 67.46. pb SP 17.30 '11.

Women

Julia FISCHER b. 1 Apr 1990 Berlin 1.92m 95kg. SC Charlottenburg.

At DT: OG: '12- dnq 20; WCh: '13- dnq 13; EC: '12- 5; WJ: '08- 2; WY: '07- 1; EU23: '11- 1; EJ: '09- 2; ET: '13- 2.
Progress at DT: 2005- 45.69, 2006- 50.23, 2007- 51.39, 2008- 55.92, 2009- 56.74, 2010- 57.49, 2011- 59.60, 2012- 64.22, 2013- 66.04.

Kristina GADSCHIEW b. 3 Jul 1984 Vassilyevka, Kyrgyzstan 1.70m 62kg. LAZ Zweibrücken.
At PV: WCh: '09- 10, '11- 10=, '13- 10; WUG: '07- 2, '09- 3; WI: '10- 7; EI: '09-11-13: 5/3/7.
Progress at PV: 1999- 3.50, 2000- 3.65, 2001- 3.90i/3.70, 2005- 4.22, 2006- 4.35, 2007- 4.40, 2008- 4.52, 2009- 4.58, 2010- 4.60, 2011- 4.66i/4.60, 2012- 4.60, 2013- 4.61.
Moved to Germany as a child.

Betty HEIDLER b. 14 Oct 1983 Berlin 1.75m 80kg. LG Eintracht Frankfurt. Federal police officer.
At HT: OG: '04- 4, '08- 9, '12- 3; WCh: '03-05-07-09-11-13: 11/dnq 29/1/2/2/dnq 18; EC: '06-10-12: 5/1/dnq 16; EU23: '03- 4, '05- 2; WJ: '00/02- dnq 19/17; EJ: '01- 9, WUG: '09- 1; CCp: '10- 4; ECp: '04-07-09-10-11-13: 3/1/2/1/1/1. Won WAF 2006, 2009; World HT challenge 2010-12, German 2005-13.
World hammer record 2011, seven German records 2004-11.
Progress at HT: 1999- 42.07, 2000- 56.02, 2001- 60.54, 2002- 63.38, 2003- 70.42, 2004- 72.73, 2005- 72.19, 2006- 76.55, 2007- 75.77, 2008- 74.11, 2009- 77.12, 2010- 76.38, 2011- 79.42, 2012- 78.07, 2013- 76.48.

Carolin HINGST b. 18 Sep 1980 Donauwörth 1.74m 60kg. USC Mainz.
At PV: OG: '04- dnq 22=, '08- 6; WCh: '01-03-05-07-13: 10/dnq 15=/10/dnq 17=/dnq 17; EC: '02- dnq 13=, '10- 11; EU23: '01- 3; WI: '04- dnq 9; EI: '05- 4; ECp: '05- 2; GER champion 2004, 2008.
Progress at PV: 1999- 3.60, 2000- 4.01, 2001- 4.50, 2002- 4.50, 2003- 4.51, 2004- 4.66, 2005- 4.65i/4.50, 2006- 4.52, 2007- 4.70i/4.61, 2008- 4.65, 2009- 4.60i/4.53, 2010- 4.72, 2011- 4.65, 2012- 4.40, 2013- 4.71. pbs: 100mh 14.54 '98, HJ 1.75 '98, LJ 5.81 '98.

Kathrin KLAAS b. 6 Feb 1984 Haiger 1.68m 72kg. LG Eintracht Frankfurt.
At HT: OG: '08- dnq 24, '12- 5; WCh: '05-07-13: dnq -/ 27/20, '09- 4, '11- 7; EC: '06-10-12: 6/dnq 15/4; EJ: '03-8, EU23: '05- 4; WUG: '09- 3.
Progress at HT: 2000- 44.24, 2001- 50.10, 2002- 57.74, 2003- 63.72, 2004- 68.01, 2005- 70.91, 2006- 71.67, 2007- 73.45, 2008- 70.39, 2009- 74.23, 2010- 74.53, 2011- 75.48, 2012- 76.05, 2013- 72.57.

Nadine KLEINERT b. 20 Oct 1975 Magdeburg 1.90m 90kg. SC Magdeburg. Soldier.
At SP: OG: '00- 8, '04- 2, '08- 7, '12- dnq 13; WCh: '97-99-01-03-05-07-09-11: 7/2/2/2/7/3/3/2/8; EC: '98-02-06-10-12: 6/6/6/7/1; WJ: '92- 12, '94- 6; EU23: '94- 3Cp, '97- 1; EJ: '93- 2; WI: '99-01-04-

06-10-12: 5/4/3/2/5/5; EI: '96-98-00: 5/5/2; ECp: '99-01-04-05-09-11: 2/1/3/2/1/1. Won GP 1999. German champion 1998, 2000-01, 2005, 2008, 2010, 2012 (& 7 indoors).
Progress at SP: 1990- 13.85, 1991- 15.08, 1992- 16.32, 1993- 17.07, 1994- 17.44, 1995- 17.13, 1996- 18.37, 1997- 18.91, 1998- 19.22, 1999- 19.61, 2000- 19.81, 2001- 19.86, 2002- 19.24, 2003- 19.33i/19.14, 2004- 19.55, 2005- 20.06, 2006- 19.64i/19.15, 2007- 19.77, 2008- 19.89, 2009- 20.20, 2010- 19.64, 2011- 19.26, 2012- 19.67, 2013- 18.76. pb DT 50.99 '01.
Made all 24 major World and European finals she contested from 1997 until missing Olympic final by one place in 2012.

Gesa Felicitas KRAUSE b. 3 Aug 1992 Ehringshausen 1.67m 55kg. LG Eintracht Frankfurt. Student.
At 3000mSt: OG: '12- 8; WCh: '11- 9, '13- 9; EC: '12- 4; WJ: '10- 4; EU23: '13- 1; EJ: '11- 1. At 2000mSt: WY: '09- 7.
European junior 3000mSt record 2011.
Progress at 3000mSt: 2010- 9:47.78, 2011- 9:32.74, 2012- 9:23.52, 2013- 9:37.11. pbs: 800m 2:05.25 '11, 1000m 2:44.68 '10, 1500m 4:11.94 '12, 3000m 9:01.16i '12, 5km Rd 16:15 '11, 2000mSt 6:22.45 '11.

Irina MIKITENKO b. 23 Aug 1972 Bakanas, Kazakhstan 1.58m 49kg. née Volynskaya. TV Wattenscheid 01.
At 5000m: OG: '96- h, '00- 5, '04- 7; WCh: '99- 4, '01- 5, '03- h; ECp: '99-00: 2/2. At 10,000m: EC: '98- 8, '06- 9; WCp: '98- 5. At Mar: OG: '12- 14. 3rd GP 3000m 1999. World 4k CC: '00- 19. Won Central Asian 1500m 1995; German 10,000m 1998, 2006, 2008; 5000m 1999-2000, 2006.
Marathon bests W35 2008, W40 2013; German records 3000m 2000, 5000m (3) 1999, marathon 2008.
Progress at 5000m, 10,000m, Mar: 1995- 15:47.85, 1996- 15:49.59, 1997- 15:48.29, 1998- 15:18.86, 32:10.61; 1999- 14:42.03, 31:38.68; 2000- 14:43.59; 2001- 14:53.00, 31:29.55; 2003- 14:56.64, 31:38.48; 2004- 14:55.43, 32:04.86; 2006- 15:28.00, 31:44.82; 2007- 32:42.95, 2:24.51; 2008- 31:57.71, 2:19:19; 2009- 2:22:11, 2010- 32:48.69, 2:26:40; 2011- 2:22:18, 2012- 2:24:53, 2013- 2:24:54. pbs: 800m 2:09.97 '98, 1500m 4:06.08 '01, 2000m 5:40.6 '01, 3000m 8:30.39 '00, Road: 10k 30:57 '08, HMar 68:51 '08, 25k 1:23:08 '08, 30k 1:39:36 '08.
Made fine marathon debut with 2nd Berlin 2007 and in 2008 won London in pb 2:24:14, improving by 4:55 when she won in Berlin. Won again in London and 2nd Chicago 2009. She won the Marathon Majors prize for 2007-08 and 2008-09. 2nd Berlin 2011. German parents; changed nationality from Kazakhstan to Germany in March 1998. Her husband Alexander had 5000m pb of 13:39.95 (1994); son Alexander, and daughter Vanessa (born in July 2005). Her father-in-law Leonid Mikitenko won the 1966 European bronze medal at 10,000m

with pbs 13.36.4 for 5000m, 28:12.4 at 10,000m.

Sosthene Taroum **MOGUENARA** b. 17 Oct 1989 Sarh, Moyen-Chari, Chad 1.82m 68kg. TV Wattenscheid 01.
At LJ: OG: '12- dnq 20; WCh: '11- dnq 31, '13- 12; EC: '12- 4; EU23: '09- 4, '11- 3. German champion 2013.
Progress at LJ: 2007- 6.22, 2008- 6.37, 2009- 6.61/6.69w, 2010- 6.65, 2011- 6,83, 2012- 6.88, 2013- 7.04. pbs: 60m 7.66i '08, 100m 11.94 '10, 200m 24.85 '07.
Has lived in Germany from the age of nine.

Antje MÖLDNER-SCHMIDT b. 13 Jun 1984 Babelsberg 1.73m 56kg. SC Potsdam. Police officer.
At 3000mSt: OG: '08- h, '12- 7; WCh: '09- 9, '13- 8; EC: '12- 3; ECp: '09- 1, '13- 3. At 1500m: WJ: '02- h, EU23: '05- 3, EJ: '03- 6; EI: '05- 6. Won GER 1500m 2005, 2007; 3000mSt 2008-09, 2012-13. GER records 3000mSt (2) 2008-09.
Progress at 3000mSt: 2008- 9:29.86, 2009- 9:18.54, 2012- 9:21.78, 2013- 9:29.27. pbs: 800m 2:04.34 '05, 1000m 2:48.36 '07, 1500m 4:08.81 '05, 2000m 5:47.66 '06, 3000m 9:00.74 '05, 5000m 16:05.82 '07, 2000mSt 6:15.90 '09.
Unable to compete in 2010 due to a lymphoid cells disorder.

Katharina MOLITOR b. 8 Nov 1983 Bedurg, Erft 1.82m 76kg. TSV Bayer 04 Leverkusen.
At JT: OG: '08- 8, 12- 6; WCh: '11- 5, "13- dnq 13; EC: '10- 4, '12- 5; EU23: '05- 2; WUG: '07- 6, '08- 4. German champion 2010.
Progress at JT: 2000- 42.94, 2001- 48.53, 2002- 49.01, 2003- 48.03, 2004- 50.04, 2005- 57.01, 2006- 57.58, 2007- 58.87, 2008- 61.74, 2009- 62.69, 2010- 64.53, 2011- 64.67, 2012- 63.20, 2013- 63.55.
Played volleyball in the Bundesliga.

Nadine MÜLLER b. 21 Nov 1985 Leipzig 1.93m 90kg. Hallesche LA-Freunde. Federal police officer.
At DT: OG: '12- 4; WCh: '07-09-11-13: dnq 23/6/2/4; EC: '10- 8, '12- 2; WJ: '04- 3; EU23: '05- 10, '07- 8; EJ: '03- 2; ET: '10- 1. German champion 2010-13.
Progress at DT: 2000- 36.10, 2001- 46,27, 2002- 48.90, 2003- 53.44, 2004- 57.85, 2005- 59.35, 2006- 58.46, 2007- 62.93, 2008- 61.36, 2009- 63.46, 2010- 67.78, 2011- 66.99, 2012- 68.89, 2013- 66.89.

Christina OBERGFÖLL b. 22 Aug 1981 Lahr (Baden) 1.75m 79kg. LG Offenburg.
At JT: OG: '04- dnq 15, '08- 3, '12- 2; WCh: '05-07-09-11-13: 2/2/5/4/1; EC: '06-10-12: 4/2/2; EU23: '01- 9, '03- 8; WJ: '00- 8; ECp: '07-09-10-11-13: 1/1/1/1/1. Won DL 2011, 2013; German 2007-08, 2011-12.
European javelin records 2005 & 2007.
Progress at JT: 1997- 49.20, 1998- 48.52, new: 1999- 50.57, 2000- 54.50, 2001- 56.83, 2002- 60.61, 2003- 57.40, 2004- 63.34, 2005- 70.03, 2006- 66.91, 2007- 70.20, 2008- 69.81, 2009- 68.59, 2010- 68.63,

2011- 69.57, 2012- 67.04, 2013- 69.05.
Made a great breakthrough at the 2005 World
Champs to take her pb from 64.59 to a European
record 70.03 and the silver medal. Married her
coach Boris Henry (JT: 90.44 '97; 3rd Worlds
1995 & 2003, Europeans 2002) on 14 Sep 2013;
expecting a baby in 2014.

Claudia RATH b. 25 Apr 1986 Hadamar,
Hessen 1.75m 65kg. LG Eintracht Frankfurt.
At Hep: WCh: '11- 4; EC: '10- 11, '12- 6. German
champion 2010-11. At WI: '14- 5.
Progress at Hep: 2003- 5231, 2004- 5353, 2005-
5323, 2007- 5274, 2008- 5697, 2009- 5941, 2010-
6107, 2011- 6098, 2012- 6210, 2013- 6462. pbs:
200m 24.22 '10, 800m 2:06.43 '13, 60mh 8.43i '14,
100mh 13.46 '13, HJ 1.83 '13, LJ 6.67 '13, SP 13.66i
'14, 13.27 '12; JT 41.57 '12, Pen 4681i '14.

Anna RÜH b. 17 Jun 1993 Greifswald 1.86m
78kg. SC Neubrandenburg.
At SP: DT: '12- 9; EC: '12- 4; WJ: '10- dnq 21, '12-
1; EU23: '13- 1; EJ: '11- 2 (3 SP).
Progress at DT: 2009- 44.43, 2010- 51.67, 2011-
59.97, 2012- 63.38, 2013- 64.33, 2014- 63.21. pb SP
16.53i '12, 16.01 '11.

Elisaveta **'Lisa' RYZIH** b. 27 Sep 1988 Omsk,
Russia 1.79m 59kg. Formerly Ryshich. ABC
Ludwigshafen. Psychology student.
At PV: OG: '12- 6=; WCh: '13- 8=; EC: '10- 3, '12-
7; WJ: '04- 1, '06- nh; WY: '03- 1; EU23: '09- 1; EJ:
'07- 4; EI: '11- 7; CCp: '10- 2.
Progress at PV: 2002- 3.92, 2003- 4.10, 2004- 4.30,
2005- 4.15, 2006- 4.35, 2007- 4.35, 2008- 4.52i/4.50,
2009- 4.50, 2010- 4.65, 2011- 4.65i, 2012- 4.65,
2013- 4.55, 2014- 4.61i. pb LJ 5.38w '06.
Set world age bests at 13 in 2002 and 15 in 2004.
Her sister 'Nastja' was World Indoor champion
in 1999 and set four world junior and five
European junior PV records in 1996 to 4.15, and
three German records in 1999 to 4.50i/4.44 and
had a pb of 4.63 in 2006. Their family left Omsk
in Siberia in 1992 to live in Ulm; mother
Yekaterina Ryzhikh (née Yefimova b. 20 Jan
1959) had HJ pb 1.91i '85 and 1.89 '81, and father
Vladimir is a pole vault coach.

Verena SAILER b. 16 Oct 1985 Illertissen 1.66m
57kg. MTG Mannheim
At 100m: OG: '08- 5R, '12- sf; WCh: '07- qf, '09-
sf/3R, '13- sf; EC: '06- sf, '10- 1, '12- 6/1R; WJ:
'04- 5; EU23: '05- 3, '07- 1; EJ: '03- 6; CCp: '10- 4;
ECp: '07- 2. At 60m: WI: '14- 8; EI: '09- 3, '13- 7.
Won German 100m 2006-10, 2012-13.
Progress at 100m: 2001- 12.13, 2002- 11.88, 2003-
11.58, 2004- 11.49. 2005- 11.51, 2006- 11.43, 2007-
11.31, 2008- 11.28, 2009- 11.18/11.11w, 2010-
11.10/11.06w, 2011- 11.63/11.46w, 2012- 11.05,
2013- 11.02. pbs: 60m 7.12i '13, 200m 24.01 '06.
Former gymnast.

Christina SCHWANITZ b. 24 Dec 1985
Dresden 1.80m 103kg. LV 90 Erzebirge. Soldier.
At SP: OG: '08- 11, '12- 10; WCh: '05-09-11-13:

7/12/12/2; EC: '12- 5; WJ: '04- 3; EU23: '05- 2; WI:
'08- 6, '14- 2; EI: '11- 2, '13- 1; ECp: '08- 1, '13- 1.
German champion 2011. 2013.
Progress at SP: 2001- 13.57, 2002- 14.26, 2003-
15.25, 2004- 16.98, 2005- 18.84, 2007- 17.06, 2008-
19.68i/19.31, 2009- 19.06, 2010- 18.28, 2011- 19.20,
2012- 19.15i/19.05, 2013- 20.41, 2014- 20.05i. pb
DT 47.27 '03.

Lilli SCHWARZKOPF b. 28 Aug 1983 Novo
Pokrovka, Kyrgyzhstan 1.74m 65kg. LG Rhein-
Wied. Student.
At Hep: OG: '08- 8, '12- 2; WCh: '05-07-09-11:
13/5/dnf/6; EC: '06- 3; WJ: '02- 5; EU23: '05- 2.
German champion 2004.
Progress at Hep: 2001- 5079, 2002- 5597, 2003-
5735, 2004- 6161, 2005- 6146, 2006- 6420, 2007-
6439, 2008- 6536, 2009- 6355, 2010- 6386, 2011-
6370, 2012- 6649. pbs: 100m 12.22 '10, 200m 24.72
'11, 800m 2:09.63 '06, 60mh 8.46i '10, 100mh
13.26 '12, HJ 1.83 '07, LJ 6.35i/6.34 '07, SP 14.89
'11, JT 55.25 '09, Pen 4641i '08.
Has lived in Germany from age 7.

Silke SPIEGELBURG b. 17 Mar 1986
Georgsmarienhütte 1.73m 64kg. TSV Bayer 04
Leverkusen. Economics student.
At PV: OG: '04- 13, '08- 7, '12- 4; WCh: '07-09-11-
13: nh/4/9/4; EC: '06-10-12: 6/2/4=; WJ: '02- 8;
WY: '01- 1; EU23: '07- 4; EJ: '03- 1, '05- 1; WI:
'06-12-14: 8/4/7; EI: '07-09-11: 5/2/2; ECp: '08-09-
10-11-13: 3/3/2/2/1; Won WAF 2008, DL 2012-13,
German 2005-10, 2012.
PV records: World junior 2005, German 2012.
Progress at PV: 1998- 2.75, 1999- 3.30, 2000- 3.75,
2001- 4.00, 2002- 4.20, 2003- 4.20i/4.15, 2004-
4.40, 2005- 4.48i/4.42, 2006- 4.56, 2007- 4.60,
2008- 4.70, 2009- 4.75i/4.70, 2010- 4.71, 2011-
4.76i/4.75, 2012- 4.82, 2013- 4.79.
Brothers: Henrik PV pb 4.80, Christian (b. 15
Apr 1976) 5.51 '98; **Richard** (b. 12 Aug 1977) 5.85
'01; 6= WCh 01, 1 WUG 99.

Linda STAHL b. 2 Oct 1985 Steinheim 1.74m
72kg. TSV Bayer 04 Leverkusen. Medical student.
At JT: OG: '12- 3; WCh: '07-09-11-13: 8/6/dns/4;
EC: '10- 1, '12- 3; EU23: '07- 1; CCp: '10- 4.
German champion 2013.
Progress at JT: 2000- 42.94, 2001- 43.96, 2002-
47.23, 2003- 47.32, 2004- 50.11, 2005- 53.94, 2006-
57.17, 2007- 62.80, 2008- 66.06, 2009- 63.86, 2010-
66.81, 2011- 60.78, 2012- 64.91, 2013- 65.76. pb SP
13.91i '06.

Martina STRUTZ b. 4 Nov 1981 Schwerin
1.60m 57kg. SC Neubrandenburg. Police officer.
At PV: OG: '12- 5; WCh: '11- 2; EC: '06- 5, '12- 2;
WJ: '00- 5; EU23: '01- 4, '03- 9=; WCp: '06- 4.
German champion 2011, 2013.
Two German pole vault records 2011.
Progress at PV: 1996- 3.30, 1997- 3.60i/3.50,
1998- 3.80, 1999- 4.10, 2000- 4.20, 2001- 4.42,
2002- 4.30, 2003- 4.20, 2004- 4.31, 2005- 4.40i/4.35,

2006- 4.50, 2007- 4.45, 2008- 4.52, 2009- 4.40, 2010- 4.30, 2011- 4.80, 2012- 4.60, 2013- 4.65.

GREECE

Governing body: Hellenic Amateur Athletic Association (SEGAS), 137 Siggroú Avenue, 171 21 Nea Smirni, Athens. Founded 1897.
National Championships first held in 1896 (men), 1930 (women). **2013 Champions**: 100m/200m: Likoúrgos-Stéfanos Tsákonas 10.24w/20.57, 400m: Mihaíl Dardaneliótis 47.05, 800m: Konstadínos Nakópoulos 1:48.34, 1500m: Andréas Dimitrákis 3:39.32, 5000m: Konstadínos Gelaoúzos 14:53.54, 10,000m: Dímos Maggínas 30:28.28, HMar Konstadínos Poúlios 69:07, Mar: Hristóforos Meroúsis 2:23:59, 3000mSt: Yeóryios Míno Órgges 9:11.03, 110mh: Konstadínos Douvalídis 13.34, 400mh: Ioánnis Loulás 51.11, HJ: Konstadínos Baniótis 2.32, PV: Konstadínos Filippídis 5.80, LJ: Loúis Tsátoumas 8.23, TJ: Dimítrios Tsiámis 17.05, SP: Mihaíl Stamatóyiannis 19.11, DT: Yeóryios Trémos 57.01, HT: Aléxandros Papadimitríou 67.35 (record 16th consecutive win), JT: Konstadínos Vertoúdos 72.42, Dec: Kiriákos Pilídis 6623, 20kW: Aléxandros Papamihaíl 1:26:25, 50kW: Konstadínos Stamélos 4:44:02.
Women: 100m/200m: Grigoría-Emmanouéla Keramidá 11.46w/23.33, 400m: Agní Dervéni 53.64, 800m: María Kládou 2:02.30, 1500m: Eléni Theodorakopoúlou 4:23.59, 5000m: Anastasia Karakatsáni 16:14.23, 10,000m: Ouranía Reboúli 34:26.56, HMar/Mar: Magdaliní Gazéa 77:54/ 2:46:04, 3000mSt: María Pardaloú 10:07.08, 100mh: Olibía Petsoúdi 13.47, 400mh: Hristína Hantzí-Neag 58.38, HJ: Ekateríni Kiriakopoúlou 1.82, PV: Nikoléta Kiriakopoúlou 4.65, LJ: Evaggelía Galéni 6.62, TJ: Athanasía Pérra 14.38, SP: Evaggelía Sofáni 15.55, DT: Hrisoúla Anagnostopoúlou 54.01, HT: Agápi Proskinito-poúlou 61.46, JT: Sávva Líka 55.98, Hep: Iríni Daniíl 4874, 20kW: Antigóni Drisbióti 1:37:31.

Konstadínos BANIÓTIS b. 6 Nov 1986 Komotini, Rhodope 2.02m 80kg. PMS Olympiada Komotinis (Thrace).
At HJ: OG: '08/12- dnq 37=/25=; WCh: '09/11- dnq 16/15=, '13- 10=; EC: '10- 8, '12- dnq 16=; WI: '12- 4=; EU23: '07- 12; EI: '09- 6, '11- 4. Greek champion 2008-11, 2013; MedG 2013.
Progress at HJ: 2002- 1.98, 2003- 2.02, 2004- 1.90, 2005- 2.07, 2006- 2.17, 2007- 2.23, 2008- 2.27, 2009- 2.29i/2.28, 2010- 2.28, 2011- 2.32i/2.28, 2012- 2.31i/2.25, 2013- 2.34.

Konstadínos FILIPÍDDIS b. 26 Nov 1986 Athens 1.90m 78kg. Panellínios YS Athens. Postgraduate student at Athens University of Economics and Business.
At PV: OG: '12- 7; WCh: '05-09-11-13: dnq 14=/ dnq 17/6/10; EC: '06-10: dnq 26/21=, '12- 5; WJ: '04- 4; WY: '03- 4; EJ: '05- 2; WI: '10-12-14: 4=/7/1; EI: '11- 5, '13- 4; WUG: '05- 2; ET: '09/10- 4; Won

MedG 2005; Greek champion 2005, 2009-13. Nine Greek pole vault records 2005-13.
Progress at PV: 2001- 3.70, 2002- 4.80, 2003- 5.22, 2004- 5.50, 2005- 5.75, 2006- 5.55, 2007- 5.35i/5.30/5.40dq, 2009- 5.65, 2010- 5.70i/5.55, 2011- 5.75, 2012- 5.80, 2013- 5.83i/5.82, 2014- 5.80i.
Two-year drugs ban (reduced to 18 months) from positive test on 16 June 2007.

Loúis TSÁTOUMAS b. 12 Feb 1982 Messíni 1.87m 76kg. Messiniakós YS (Kalamáta).
At LJ: OG: '04-08-12: dnq 22/nj/dnq 29; WCh: '03-09-11-13: 12/11/dnq 14/10; EC: '06- 8, '10- 6; WJ: '00- dnq 21; WY: '99- 4; EU23: '03- 1; EJ: '01- 1; WI: '06-12-14: 4/6/4; EI: '07- 2, '13- 5; WCp: '06- nj; ECp: '03-07-08-09-13: 1/1/1/3/2; Greek champion 2003-08, 2010-11. 2013 (& 8 indoors); MedG 2013. Greek long jump record 2007.
Progress at LJ: 1996- 6.56, 1997- 7.07, 1998- 7.41/7.43w, 1999- 7.64, 2000- 7.52, 2001- 7.93/7.98w, 2002- 8.17, 2003- 8.34, 2004- 8.19/8.37w, 2005- 8.15i/8.14, 2006- 8.30, 2007- 8.66, 2008- 8.44, 2009- 8.21, 2010- 8.09/8.17w, 2011- 8.26, 2012- 8.05i/7.98, 2013- 8.23/8.24w, 2014- 8.23i. pb 200m 22.3 '98.
8.66 is best outdoors by European at sea-level.

Women

Nikoléta KIRIAKOPOÚLOU b. 21 Mar 1986 Athens 1.67m 54kg. AYES Kámiros Rhodes.
At PV: OG: '08/12- dnq 27=/19=; WCh: '09- dnq 19, '11- 8, '13- dnq 13=; EC: '10- dnq 13, '12- 3; WJ: '04- 6; EJ: '05- 7; EI: '11- 9. Balkan champion 2008, Med G 2009, Greek 2009, 2011-13.
Five Greek pole vault records 2010-11.
Progress at PV: 2001- 2.90, 2002- 3.10, 2003- 3.70, 2004- 4.00, 2005- 4.10, 2006- 3.60, 2007- 4.00i/3.90, 2008- 4.45, 2009- 4.50, 2010- 4.55, 2011- 4.71, 2012- 4.60, 2013- 4.65, 2014- 4.72i.

Paraskeví 'Voula' PAPAHRÍSTOU b. 17 Apr 1989 Athens 1.70m 53kg. AEK (Athens).
At TJ: WCh: '09/11- dnq 29/16; EC: '12- 11; WJ: '08- 3; EU23: '09/11- 1/1. Won Greek LJ 2011-12, TJ 2009, 2011.
Progress at TJ: 2005- 12.75, 2006- 12.81/13.13w, 2007- 12.98i/12.92, 2008- 13.86i/13.79/13.94w, 2009- 14.47i/14.35, 2010- 13.94i/13.85, 2011- 14.72, 2012- 14.58/14.77w, 2013- 14.21. pb LJ 6.60 '12.

GRENADA

Governing body: Grenada Athletic Assocation, PO Box 419, St George's. Founded 1924.

Kirani JAMES b. 1 Sep 1992 St George's 1.85m 74kg. Student at University of Alabama, USA
At (200m)/400m: OG: '12- 1; WCh: '11- 1, '13- 7; WJ: '08- 2, '10- 1; WY: '07- 2, '09- 1/1; WI: '12- 6. Won DL 2011, PAm-J 400m 2009, 200m 2011; NCAA 2010-11.
Records: CAC & Commonwealth 400m 2012, GRN 200m 2011, 400m (2) 2011-12; Indoor 400m: CAC & Commonwealth 2010 (45.24) & 2011; World Junior (44.80) 2011.

Progress at 400m: 2007- 46.96, 2008- 45.70, 2009- 45.24, 2010- 45.01, 2011- 44.36, 2012- 43.94, 2013- 43.96. pbs: 200m 20.41A/20.53w '11, 20.76 '10; 300m: 32.0+ '12.
He set world age bests at 14 and 15. In 2011 he became the youngest ever World or Olympic champion at 400m and in 2012 the first Olympic medallist for Grenada at any sport. In January 2012 the 'Kirani James Boulevard' was opened in the Grenadan capital St.George. IAAF Rising Star award 2011.

GUATEMALA

Governing body: Federación Nacional de Atletismo, Palacio de los Deportes, 26 Calle 9-31, Zona 5, Ciudad de Guatemala. Fd 1896.

Érick BARRONDO b. 14 Jun 1991 San Cristóbal Verapaz 1.72m 60kg.
At 20kW(/50kW): OG: '12- 2/dq; WCh: '11- 10, '13- dq; PAm: '11- 1. Won Bol G 20kW 2013, GUA 50kW 2012.
50k walk records: CAC 2013, GUA 2012-13.
Progress at 20kW, 50kW: 2010- 1:23:16A, 2011- 1:20:58, 2012- 1:18:25, 3:44:59; 2013- 1:20:25, 3:41:09. pb 10,000mW 40:10.73A '13.
Won Guatemala's first Olympic medal at any sport in 2012. His cousin José Alejandro Barrondo has 10,000mW pb 42:00.98 '13.

HUNGARY

Governing body: Magyar Atlétikai Szövetség, 1146 Budapest, Istvánmezei út 1-3. Fd 1897.
National Championships first held in 1896 (men), 1932 (women). **2013 Champions. Men**: 100m: Roland Németh 10.51, 200m: Gyözö Móré 21.44, 400m: Tibor Kása 46.71, 800m/1500m: Tamás Kazi 1:48.7/3:46.67, 5000m: Barnabás Bene 15:22.2, 10,000m/Mar: Gábor Józsa 30:17.61/ 2:22:58, HMar: Tamás Kovács 66:08, 3000mSt: Áron Dani 9:03.04, 110mh: Balázs Baji 13.62, 400mh: Tibor Koroknai 51.04, HJ: Péter Bakosi 2.18, PV: Dezsö Szabó 5.25, LJ: Mark Szabó 7.49, TJ: Tibor Galambos 15.84, SP: Lajos Kürthy 18.16, DT: András Seres 58.96, HT: Krisztián 480.41, JT: Krisztián Török 72.92, Dec: Attila Zsivoczky-Pandel 7569, 20kW/50kW: Sándor Rácz 1:30:21/4:11:48. **Women**: 100m/200m: Éva Kaptur 11.47/24.2h, 400m: Natália Zsigovics 54.05, 800m: Bernadett Aradi 2:12.41, 1500m /10,000m/HMar: Krisztina Papp 4:17.24/ 32:42.40/72:32, 5000m: Zsófia Erdélyi 17:00.3, Mar: Simona Juhász-Staicu 2:42:26, 3000mSt: Zita Kácser 10:44.10, 100mh/Hep: Xénia Krizsán 13.82/5725, 400mh: Dóra Szarvas 59.75, HJ: Barbara Szabó 1.84, PV: Zsófia Siskó 4.00, LJ: Fanni Schmelcz 6.54w, TJ: Krisztina Hoffer 13.18, SP/DT: Anita Márton 17.82/54.71, HT: Éva Orbán 68.06, JT: Vanda Juhász 58.97, 20kW: Viktória Madarász 1:39:07.

Krisztián PARS b. 18 Feb 1982 Körmend 1.88m 113kg. Dobó SE.

At HT: OG: '04- 5, '08- 4, '12- 1; WCh: '05-07-09-11-13: 7/5/4/2/2; EC: '06- 6, '10- 3, '12- 1; WY: '99- 1; EJ: '01- 1; EU23: '03- 1. Won HUN 2005-12; World HT challenge 2011-12.
World junior records with 6kg hammer: 80.64 & 81.34 in 2001.
Progress at HT: 1998- 54.00, 1999- 61.92, 2000- 66.80, 2001- 73.09, 2002- 74.18, 2003- 78.81, 2004- 80.90, 2005- 80.03, 2006- 82.45, 2007- 81.40, 2008- 81.96, 2009- 81.43, 2010- 79.64, 2011- 81.89, 2012- 82.28, 2013- 82.40. pbs: SP 15.60 '05, DT 53.80 '06.

Women

Éva ORBÁN b. 29 Nov 1984 Pápa, Veszprém 1.73m 75kg. VEDAC, Was at University of Southern California, USA.
At HT: OG: '04-08-12: dnq 24/34/16; WCh: '05-09-11: dnq 20/14/12, '13- 8; EC: '06- dnq 25, '10- 11, '12- 7; WY: '01- 11; EU23: '05- 11; EJ: '03- 6, WUG: '11- 1. HUN champion 2005-06, 2008-11, 2013; NCAA 2008..
Three Hungarian hammer records 2011-13.
Progress at HT: 1999- 47.70, 2000- 50.53, 2001- 58.04, 2002- 62.00, 2003- 65.77, 2004- 67.60, 2005- 68.70, 2006- 69.10, 2007- 66.98, 2008- 70.18, 2009- 70.16, 2010- 69.73, 2011- 71.33, 2012- 69.03, 2013- 73.44. pbs: SP 12.93 '05, DT 45.40 '05.

ICELAND

Governing body: Frjálsíthróttasamband Islands, Engjavegur 6, IS-104 Reykjavik. Founded 1947.
National Championships first held in 1927. **2013 National champions: Men**: 100m/200m /400m: Kolbeinn Hödur Gunnarsson 10.65w/ 21.68w/49.78, 800m: Kristin Thór Kristinsson 1:53.02, 1500m/5000m: Hlynur Andrésson 4:02.03/15:26.68, 3000mSt: Haraldur Tómas Hallgrimsson 10:58.46, 110mh: Ólafur Gudmundsson 15.92w, 400mh: Kristinn Jasonarson 56.42, HJ: Hermann Thór Haraldsson 1.87, PV: Mark Johnson 5.15, LJ: Kristinn Torfason 7.45w, TJ: Bjarki Gislason 14.63w, SP: Ódinn Björn Thorsteinsson 17.53, DT: Blake Thomas Jakobsson 50.98, HT: Hilmar Örn Jónsson 57.04, JT: Gudmundur Sverrison 80.66. **Women**: 100m/ 200m/LJ: Hafdís Sigurdardóttir 11.75w/24.18/ 6.36w, 400m: Hafdís Sigurdardóttir 54.46, 800m: Thórdis Eva Steinsdóttir 2:19.52, 1500m/ 3000m: Arndis Yr Hafthorsdóttir 4:49.18/ 10:30.26, 100mh: Arna Stefania Gudmundsdóttir 14.11, 400mh: Fjóla Signy Hannesdóttir 61.37, HJ/SP: Sveinbjörg Zophoníasdóttir 1.67/12.78, PV: Bogey Ragnheidur Leósdóttir 3.56, TJ: Thelma Lind Kristjansdóttir 11.51w, DT: Jófrídur Ísdís Skaftadóttir 38.42, HT: Adalheidur María Vigfísdóttir 43.49, JT: Ásdis Hjálmsdóttir 56.16.

INDIA

Governing body: Athletics Federation of India, WZ-72, Todapur Main Road, Dev Prakash

Shastri Marg, New Delhi - 110012. Fd 1946.
National Championships first held as Indian
Games in 1924. **2013 Champions: Men:** 100m:
Anirudda Kalidas Gujar 10.46, 200m Amiya
Kumar Mallick 21.22, 400m: P.P.Kunhu
Mohammed 46.51, 800m: Sajeesh Joseph 1:49.50,
1500m: Sandeep Karan Singh 3:46.97, 5000m:
G.Lakshmanan 13:58.53, 10,000m: Kheta Ram
29:47.92, 3000mSt: Jaiveer Singh 9:00.41, 110mh:
A.Suresh 14.19, 400mh Durgesh Kumar Pal
50.89, HJ: Jithin C.Thomas 2.21, PV: K.P.Bimin
5.00, LJ: Ankit Sharma 7.73, TJ: Arpinder Singh
16.70, SP Om Prakash Singh 18.67, DT: Arjun
Kumar 54.10, HT: Chandrodaya Narayan Singh
67.75, JT: Ravinder Singh 75.47, Dec: Daya Ram
6812, 20000mW: Ganpati 1:27:18.15, 20kW:
Gurmeet Singh 1:21:17, 50kW: Sandeep Kumar
4:02:19. **Women:** 100m/200m: Dutee Chand
11.73/24.02, 400m: M.R.Poovamma 53.96, 800m:
Tintu Luka 2:01.87, 1500m: Sini A. Markose
4:29.72, 5000m/10,000m: Suriya Loganathan
16:24.58/34:07.45, 3000mSt: Sudha Singh 10:09.04,
100mh: Gayathri Govindaraj 13.70, 400mh:
Rajan Elavarasi 60.80, HJ: Reena Singh 1.70, PV:
Vakharia Khyati 3.70, LJ/TJ: Maliakhal A.
Prajusha 6.25/12.91, SP: Manpreet Kaur 15.03,
DT: Parmila 48.10, HT: Poonam Devi 54.14, JT:
Annu Rani 54.35, Hep: Sushmita Singha Roy
5183, 20000mW/20kW: Kushbir Kaur 1:45:21.47
/1:38:52.

Vikas GOWDA b. 5 Jul 1983 Mysore, Karnataka
1.96m 115kg. Studied statistics at University of
North Carolina, USA.
At DT: OG: '04/08- 14/22, '12- 8; WCh: '05/07-
dnq 14/17, '11- 7, '13- 7; CG: '06- 6, '10- 2; AsiG:
'06- 6, '10- 3; AsiC: 05- 2, '11- 2, '13- 1. Won
NCAA 2006.
Three Indian discus records 2005-12
Progress at DT: 2002- 55.28, 2003- 59.32, 2004-
64.35, 2005- 64.69, 2006- 61.76, 2007- 64.96, 2008-
64.83, 2010- 63.69, 2011- 64.91, 2012- 66.28, 2013-
65.82. pb SP 19.62 '06.

IRAN

Governing body: Amateur Athletic Federation
of Islamic Republic of Iran, Shahid Keshvari
Sports Complex, Razaneh Junibi St Mirdamad
Ave, Tehran. Founded 1936.

Ehsan HADADI b. 21 Jan 1985 Ahvaz 1.93m
125kg.
At DT: OG: '08- dnq 17, '12- 2; WCh: '07- 7, '11- 3;
WJ: '04- 1; AsiG: '06- 1, '10- 1; AsiC: '03-05-07-09-
11: 8/1/1/1/1; AsiJ: '04- 1; WCp: '06- 2, '10- 3.
W.Asian champion 2005.
Eight Asian discus records 2005-08.
Progress at DT: 2002- 53.66, 2003- 54.40, 2004-
54.96, 2005- 65.25, 2006- 63.79, 2007- 67.95, 2008-
69.32, 2009- 66.19, 2010- 68.45, 2011- 66.08, 2012-
68.20, 2013- 66.98. pb SP 17.82i '08, 16.00 '06.
First Iranian athlete to win an Olympic medal.

IRELAND

Governing Body: The Athletic Association of
Ireland (AAI), Unit 19, Northwood Court,
Northwood Business Campus, Santry, Dublin
9. Founded in 1999. Original Irish federation
(Irish Champions AC) founded in 1873.
National Championships first held in 1873.
2013 Champions: Men: 100m: David Hynes
10.64, 200m: Steven Colvert 21.13, 400m: Brian
Murphy 47.14, 800m: Paul Robinson 1:48.92,
1500m: Eoin Everard 3:44.58, 5000: Mark
Christie 14:07.18, 10,000m: Mark Kenneally
29:21.69, HMar: Mark Christie 66:09, Mar: Sean
Hehir 2:18:19, 3000mSt: Rory Chesser 9:08.65,
110mh: Tom Carey 14.77, 400mh: Thomas Barr
49.78, HJ: Barry Pender 2.05, PV: David
Donegan 4.65, LJ: Eamonn Fahey 7.20, TJ:
Denis Finnegan 15.07, SP: Seán Breathnach
15.60, DT: Marco Pons 47.77, HT: Conor
McCullough 70.75, JT: Rory Gunning 56.58,
Dec: David McCarthy 5644, 10,000mW:
Brendan Boyce 42:40.19, 20kW: Michael Doyle
1:37:43, 30kW: Alex Wright 2:13:57. **Women:**
100m/200m/LJ: Kelly Proper 11.78/23.64/6.25,
400m: Jennifer Carey 53.46, 800m: Aislinn
Crossey 2:07.49, 1500m: Laura Crowe 4:13.96,
5000m/Mar: Maria McCambridge 15:55.44
/2:38:51, HMar: Lizzie Lee 74:48, 3000mSt:
Michelle Finn 10:16.90, 100mh: Sarah Lavin
13.61, 400mh: Jessie Barr 57.48, HJ: Shannen
Dawkins 1.65, PV: Tori Pena 4.40, TJ: Caoimhe
King 12.41w, SP/DT: Claire Fitzgerald
13.80/48.22, HT: Cara Kennedy 51.94, JT: Anita
Fitzgibbon 54.92, Hep: Kelly Proper 5418,
5000mW: Sinead Burke 25:27.11, 20kW:
Michelle Turner 1:45:38.

Robert HEFFERNAN b. 20 Feb 1978 Cork City
1.73m 55kg. Togher AC.
At 20kW/(50kW): OG: '00- 28, '04- dq, '08- 8, '12-
9/4; WCh: '01-05-07-09-13: 14/dq/6/15/(1); EC:
'02- 8, '10- 4/4; WCp: '08- 9, '12- 11; ECp: '07-09-
13: 5/4/9. At 10,000mW: EJ: '97- 14; EU23: '99- 13.
Won Irish 10,000mW 2001-02, 2004-5, 2007-11;
20kW 2000-02, 2004, 2009; 30kW 2008.
Irish records: 3000mW 2013, 20kW (4) 2001-08,
50kW (3) 2010-12. World M35 3000mW 2013.
Progress at 20kW, 50kW: 1999- 1:26:45, 2000-
1:22:43, 2001- 1:21:11, 2002- 1:20:25, 2003- 1:23:03,
2004- 1:20:55, 2005- 1:24:20, 2006- 1:22:24, 2007-
1:20:15, 2008- 1:19:22, 2009- 1:22:09, 2010- 1:20:45,
3:45:30; 2011- 1:20:54, 3:49:28; 2012- 1:20:18,
3:37.54; 2013- 1:21:59, 3:37.56. pbs: 3000mW
11:10.02i '02, 11:11.94 '13; 5000mW 18:51.46i '08,
18:59.37 '07; 10,000mW 38:27.57 '08, 30kW 2:07:48
'11, 35kW 2:31:19 '00.
Married to Marian Andrews (b. 16 Apr 1982,
Irish 400m champion 2008-09, pb 53.10 '11).

Women

Fionnuala BRITTON b. 24 Sep 1984 Wicklow
1.58m 45kg. Kilcoole.

At 10,000m: OG: '12- 15 (h 5000m); EC: '12- 4. At 3000m: EI: '13- 3. At 3000mSt: OG: '08- h; WCh: '07- 12, '11- h; EC: '06- h, '10- 11; EU23: 05- 9. World CC: '13- 14; Eur CC: '07-09-10-11-12-13: 7/11/4/1/1/4. Won Irish 3000mSt 2008-9, CC 2007-08.

Progress at 10,000m, 3000mSt: 2004- 10:33.10, 2005- 10:06.26, 2006- 9:49.20, 2007- 9:41.36, 2008- 9:43.57, 2009- 9:54.10, 2010- 9:42.49, 2011- 9:37.60, 2012- 31:29.22. pbs: 1500m 4:13.96i '13, 4:18.03 '11; 3000m 8:54.37i '13, 8:55.01mx '12; 5000m 15:12.97 '12.

ISRAEL

Governing body: Israeli Athletic Association, PO Box 24190, Tel Aviv 61241. Founded as Federation for Amateur Sport in Palestine 1931.
National Championships first held in 1935. **2013 Champions: Men**: 100m: Asaf Malka 10.66, 200m: Amit Cohen 21.36, 400m: Donald Sanford 46.23, 800m: Mokat Fatana 1:51.65, 1500m: Yimer Getahun 3:44.48, 5000m: Aimeru Almeya 14:00.19, 10,000m/HMar (7 Dec 2012): Tasama Moogas 28:12.58/64:40, Mar: Assrat Mamo 2:22:28, 3000mSt: Noam Ne'eman 9:00.40, 110mh: Tomer Almogi 14.48, 400mh: Maor Szeged 52.46, HJ: Niki Palli 2.02, PV: Lev Skorish 5.02, LJ/TJ: Yochai Halevi 7.57/16.45, SP: Itamar Levi 18.15, DT: Mark Alterman 57.75, HT: Viktor Zaginaiko 59.43, JT: Assa'el Arad 60.23, Dec: Konstantin Krinitzkiy 6038. **Women**: 100m/200m: Olga Lenskiy 11.57/24.01, 400m/ 800m: Shanie Landen 55.61/ 2:09.21, 1500m /5000m: Maor Tiyouri 4:31.15/ 16:55.57, 10,000m: Azawant Teka 36:44.81, HMar/ Mar: Ricki Salem 1:22:11/2:54:31, 3000mSt: Roni Gaddish 11:17.02, 100mh: Irina Lenskiy (12th title) 14.89, 400mh: Kristina Vanusheva 64.83, HJ/Hep: Maayan Shahaf 1.83/3762, PV: Na'ama Bernstein 3.25, LJ: Yulia Pushkaryov 5.68, TJ: Hanna Knyazyeva-Minenko 14.50, SP/DT: Anastasia Muchkaev 15.40/49.69, HT: Yevgeniya Zabolotniy (10th successive title) 51.95, JT: Dorit Naor 44.75 (17th title).

Hanna KNYAZYEVA-MINENKO b. 25 Sep 1989 Periaslav-Khmelnytskyi 1.78m 61kg. Kiev. At TJ: OG: '12- 4; WCh: '13- 6; WJ: '08- 4; EJ: '07- 2; EU23: '11- 5. UKR champion 2012, ISR 2013. Five Israeli triple jump records 2013.
Progress at TJ: 2005- 12.87, 2006- 13.28, 2007- 13.85, 2009- 13.81, 2010- 13.65, 2011- 14.20, 2012- 14.71, 2013- 14.58. pb LJ 6.40 '12.
Married Anatoliy Minenko (Dec 7046 '10) in 2013; switched from Ukraine to Israel 12 May 13.

ITALY

Governing Body: Federazione Italiana di Atletica Leggera (FIDAL), Via Flaminia Nuova 830, 00191 Roma. Constituted 1926. First governing body formed 1896.
National Championships first held in 1897 (one event)/1906 (men), 1927 (women). 2013

Champions: **Men**: 100m: Delmas Obou 10.37, 200m: Diego Marani 20.77, 400m: Matteo Galvan 45.71, 800m: Michele Oberti 1:51.41, 1500m: Merihun Crespi 3:42.67, 5000m: Stefano La Rosa 14:11.34, 10,000m/3000mSt: Jamel Chatbi 28:56.27/8:40.76, HMar: Gianmarco Buttazzo 63:25, Mar: Ruggero Pertile 2:16:20, 110mh: Hassane Fofana 13.93, 400mh: Eusebio Haliti 49.85, HJ: Marco Fassinotti 2.27, PV: Claudio Michel Stecchi 5.50, LJ: Alessio Guarini 8.00, TJ: Fabrizio Schembri 16.98, SP: Marco Dodoni 18.39, DT: Giovanmi Faloci 62.56, HT: Nicola Vizzoni 74.10, JT: Norbert Bonvecchio 75.36, Dec: Michele Calvi 7460, 10,000mW: Matteo Giupponi 40:40.42, 20kW: Vito Di Bari 1:27:01, 50kW: *2014* Matteo Giupponi 3:51:49. **Women**: 100m: Gloria Hooper 11.54, 200m /100mh: Marzia Caravelli 23.16/13.01, 400m: Chiara Bazzoni 52.57, 800m: Marta Milani 2:04.08, 1500m/5000m: Giulia Viola 4:14.26/ 16:05.39, 10,000m: Valeria Straneo 32:30.56, HMar: Claudia Pinna 72:41, Mar: Elisa Stefani 2:40:53, 3000mSt: Nicole Reina 10:13.89, 400mh: Yadisleidy Pedroso 55.26, HJ: Alessia Trost 1.90, PV: Giorgia Benecchia 4.20, LJ: Tania Vicenzino 6.47, TJ: Simona La Mantia 13.86, SP: Chiara Rosa 17.47, DT: Valentina Aniballi 56.10, HT: Micaela Mariani 63.14, JT: Sara Jemai 53.45, Hep: Carolina Bianchi 5259, 10,000mW: Elisa Rigaudo 43:44.96, 20kW: Federica Ferraro 1:36:23.

Fabrizio DONATO b. 14 Aug 1976 Latina 1.89m 82kg. Fiamme Gialle.
At TJ: OG: '00/04/08: dnq 25/21/21, '12- 3; WCh: '03/07-09-13: dnq 13/32/41/15, '11- 10; EC: '02- 06-10-12: 4,/dnq 16/9/1; EJ: '95- 5; WI: '01-08-10- 12: 6/4/5/4; EI: '00-02-09-11: 6/4/1/2; ECp: '00- 02-03-04-06: 2/2/1/6/1. Won MedG 2001, Italian 2000, 2004, 2006-08, 2010-11.
Italian triple jump record 2000.
Progress at TJ: 1992- 12.88, 1993- 14.36, 1994- 15.27, 1995- 15.81, 1996- 16.35, 1997- 16.40A, 1998- 16.73, 1999- 16.66i/16.53w, 2000- 17.60, 2001- 17.05, 2002- 17.17, 2003- 17.16, 2004- 16.90, 2005- 16.65/16.68w, 2006- 17.33i/17.24, 2007- 16.97/ 17.06w, 2008- 17.27i/16.91/17.29w, 2009- 17.59i/ 15.81, 2010- 17.39i/17.08, 2011- 17.73i/17.17, 2012- 17.53/17.63w, 2013- 16.86. pb LJ 8.03i '11, 8.00 '06. Italian indoor record to win 2009 European Indoor title. Married Patrizia Spuri (400m 51.74 '98, 8 EC 98, 800m 1:59.96 '98) on 27 Sep 2003.

Daniele GRECO b. 1 Mar 1989 Nardó, Apulia 1.84m 75kg. Fiamme Oro, Padova.
At TJ: OG: '12- 4; WCh: '09-13: dnq 34/nj; EC: '10-12: dnq 17/24; WJ: '08- 4; EU23: '09- 1, '11- 4; EJ: '07- 12; WI: '12- 5; EI: '13- 1. Won Italian 2012, Med G 2013.
Progress at TJ: 2005- 15.01, 2006- 15.45, 2007- 15.58i/15.54, 2008- 16.41, 2009- 17.20, 2010- 16.95i/16.57, 2011- 16.89, 2012- 17.47/17.67w, 2013- 17.70i/17.25. pbs: 60m 6.75i '09, 100m 10.38 '08, 200m 21.17 '12, LJ 7.44i '14, 7.20 '09.

Engaged to Francesca Lanciano (b. 3 Apr 1994), 11 WY '11, 12 WJ '12, NJR 13.59 '12.

Giorgio RUBINO b. 15 Apr 1986 Roma 1.76m 55kg. Fiamme Gialle.
At 20kW: OG: '08- 18, '12- 42; WCh: '07-09-11-13: 5/4/dq/2828; EC: '06- 8, '10- 5; EU23: '07- dq; ECp: '09- 1, '11- 5. At 10,000mW: WJ: '04- 10; WY: '03- 4; EJ: '05- 3. Won Italian 10kW 2012, 20kW 2005, 2014.
Progress at 20kW: 2005- 1:23:58, 2006- 1:22:05, 2007- 1:21:17, 2008- 1:22:11, 2009- 1:19:37, 2010- 1:22:12, 2011- 1:20:44, 2012- 1:20:10, 2013- 1:21:07.
pbs: 5000mW 19:14.33i '08, 19:38.5 '06; 10,000mW 39:43.20 '11, 38:00R '10; 35kW 2:36:50 '09.

Nicola VIZZONI b. 4 Nov 1973 Pietrasanta, Lucca 1.93m 126kg. Fiamme Gialle.
At HT: OG: '00- 2, '04- 10, '08- dnq 13, '12- 8; WCh:'99-01-09-11-13: 7/4/9/8/7, '97-03-05-07- dnq 22/15/25/17; EC: '98-02-06-10-12: dnq 17/ dnq 13/9/2/5; WJ: '92- 5; EJ: '91- 8; WUG: '97- 5, '99- 5, '01- 1; WCp: '10- 4; ECp: '99-01-02-03-04- 05-08-09-10: 4/2/7/5/3/4/2/1/2; EU23Cp: '92- 5. Won Med G 2009, ITA 1998, 2000-07, 2009-11, 2013.
Progress at HT: 1991- 66.62, 1992- 69.32, 1993- 70.76, 1994- 71.78, 1995- 74.48, 1996- 75.30, 1997- 77.10, 1998- 77.89, 1999- 79.59, 2000- 79.64, 2001- 80.50, 2002- 78.80, 2003- 77.69, 2004- 76.95, 2005- 74.82, 2006- 76.89, 2007- 78.21, 2008- 78.79, 2009- 79.74, 2010- 79.12, 2011- 80.29, 2012- 76.42, 2013- 77.61.
Left-handed thrower. Engaged to Claudia Coslovich (ITA javelin record 65.30 '00).

Women

Eleanora GIORGI b. 17 Jun 1980 Cuneo 1.68m 56kg. Fiamme Gialle.
At 20kW: OG: '12- 14; WCh: '13- 10; EU23: '09- 11, '11- 4; WCp: '12- 14; ECp: '13- 6. At 10,000mW: WJ: '08- 18.
Progress at 20kW: 2009- 1:34:27, 2010- 1:34:00, 2011- 1:33:46, 2012- 1:29:48, 2013- 1:30:01, 2014- 1:27:28. pbs: 3000mW 11:50.08i '13, 5000mW 20:46.12 '13, 10kW 44:33.56t '13, 44:14R '14.

Libania GRENOT b. 12 Jul 1983 Santiago de Cuba 1.75m 65kg. Fiamme Galle.
At 400m: OG: '08/12- sf; WCh: '01- hR, '05- h, '09/13- sf; EC: '10- 4, '12- 6; WY: '99- 5; PAm: '03- 4; CCp: '10- 6/2R; ET: '10- 1. Won MedG 2009, CUB 2003-05, ITA 400m 2009-10, 200m 2012.
Four Italian 400m records 2008-09.
Progress at 400m: 1997- 56.2, 1998- 54.9, 1999- 53.87, 2000- 53.79, 2001- 52.91, 2002- 53.34A, 2003- 52.20, 2004- 51.68, 2005- 51.51, 2007- 54.21, 2008- 50.83, 2009- 50.30, 2010- 50.43, 2011- 52.17, 2012- 50.55, 2013- 50.47. pbs: 200m 22.85 '12, 500m 1:08.26 '09.
Switched from Cuba to Italy after she married Silvio Scaffetti in 2006 and gained Italian citizenship on 18 Mar 2008.

Simone LA MANTIA b. 14 Apr 1983 Palermo 1.77m 65kg. Fiamme Gialle. Studied PE at Palermo University.
At TJ: OG: '04/12- dnq 17/18; WCh: '03-05-11-13: dnq 17/14/15/14; EC: '06-10-12: dnq/2/4; WJ: '02- 8; EJ: '01- 10; EU23: '03- 2, '05- 1; WI: '04- 11, '06- dnq 16; EI: '05-11-13: 8/1/3; CCp: '10- 5; ET: '11- 2, '13- 3. Italian champion 2004-06, 2010-12; W.Mil G 2011.
Progress at TJ: 1998- 12.71, 1999- 12.03, 2000- 12.50, 2001- 13.51/13.63w, 2002- 13.33, 2003- 14.31, 2004- 14.49/14.71w, 2005- 14.69, 2006- 14.21, 2007- 13.89, 2008- 13.79, 2009- 13.79/13.83w, 2010- 14.56, 2011- 14.60i/14.43, 2012- 14.29, 2013- 14.26i/13.97/13.99w. pb LJ 6.48 '05.
Her father Antonino La Mantia had 3000mSt pb 8:42.2 '74 and mother Monica Mutschlechner 800m 2:08.3 '77.

Elisa RIGAUDO b. 17 Jun 1980 Cuneo 1.68m 56kg. Fiamme Gialle.
At 20kW: OG: '04- 6, '08- 3, '12- 7; WCh: '03-05- 07-09-11-13: 10/7/dnf/9/4/5; EC: '06- 3; EU23: '01- 1; WCp: '02-04-06-12: 16/5/10/7; ECp: '05-07- 11: 3/4/3. At 5000mW: WJ: '98- 7; EJ: '99-6. Won MedG 20kW 2005, Italian 5000mW 2004, 2007; 10,000mW 2013, 20kW 2004-05, 2008.
Progress at 20kW: 1999- 1:42:40. 2000- 1:32:50, 2001- 1:29:54, 2002- 1:30:42, 2003- 1:30:34, 2004- 1:27:49, 2005- 1:29:26, 2006- 1:28:37, 2007- 1:29:15, 2008- 1:27:12, 2009- 1:29:04, 2011- 1:30:44, 2012- 1:27:36, 2013- 1:28:41. pbs: 3000mW 11:57.00i '04, 12:28.92 '02; 5000mW 20:56.29 '02, 10kW 42:29.06t '13.
Won IAAF Walks Challenge 2004. Daughter Elena born in September 2010.

Valeria STRANEO b. 5 Apr 1976 Alessandria 1.68m 44kg. SBV Runner Team 99, Turin.
At Mar: OG: '12- 8; WCh: 13- 2. World HMar: '14- 8. Eur CC: '11- 10. Won MedG HMar 2013, ITA 10,000m 2013, HMar 2012, 2014.
Italian marathon record 2012.
Progress at Mar: 2009- 2:41:15, 2011- 2:26:33, 2012- 2:23:44, 2013- 2:25:58. pbs: 3000m 9:31.10 '11, 10,000m 32:15.87 '12; Road: 10k 32:07 '11, HMar 67:46 '12.
2nd Rotterdam Marathon 2012. Won Stramilano 2011. Children Leonardo born 2006 and Arianna 2007. Reached national standard after removal of spleen in 2010.

Alessia TROST b. 8 Mar 1993 Pordenone 1.88m 66kg. Fiamme Gialle.
At HJ: WCh: '13- 7=; WJ: '12- 1; WY: '09- 1; EU23: '13- 1; EJ: '11- 4; EI: '13- 4=; ET: '13- 2; YthOly: '10- 2. Italian champion 2013.
Progress at HJ: 2003- 1.37, 2004- 1.55, 2005- 1.62, 2006- 1.68, 2008- 1.81, 2009- 1.89, 2010- 1.90, 2011- 1.87, 2012- 1.92, 2013- 2.00i/1.98. pbs: 100mh 15.5 '11, LJ 5.96 '10, SP 10.76i '14, Pen 4035i '14.

IVORY COAST

Governing Body: Fédération Ivoirienne d'Athlétisme, Abidjan. Founded 1960.

Murielle AHOURÉ b. 23 Aug 1987 Abidjan 1.67m 57kg. Graduated in criminal law from the University of Miami, USA
At 100m/200m: OG: '12- 7/6; WCh: '13- 2/2. At 60m: WI: '12- 2, 14- 2. Won NCAA Indoor 200m 2009.
Two African 60m indoor records 2013. CIV records 100m (3) 2009-11, 200m (3) 2012-13.
Progress at 100m: 2005- 11.96, 2006- 11.42, 23.33; 2007- 11.41/11.28w, 23.34; 2008- 11.45, 23.50; 2009- 11.09, 22.78; 2010- 11.41, 2011- 11.06/10.86w, 2012- 10.99, 22.42; 2013- 10.91, 22.24. pbs: 60m 6.99i '13, 300m 38.09i '07, 400m 54.77 '08.
Lived in Paris from age 2, then USA from age 12. Won first medals for Ivory Coast at World Champs.

JAMAICA

Governing body: Jamaica Athletics Administrative Association, PO Box 272, Kingston 5. Founded 1932.
2013 Champions: Men: 100m: Usian Bolt 9.94, 200m: Warren Weir 19.79, 400m: Javere Bell 45.08, 800m: Jo-Wayne Hibbert 1:47.76, 1500m: Rayan Lawrence 3:51.60, 5000m: Kemoy Campbell 13:43.20, 3000mSt: Kirk Brown 9:21.37, 110mh: Andrew Riley 13.35, 400mh: Leford Green 49.20, HJ: Christoffe Bryan 2.15, PV: Xavier Boland 4.30, LJ: Damar Forbes 8.25, TJ: Wilbert Walker 16.40w, SP: O'Dayne Richards 20.00, DT: Chad Wright 62.35, HT: Caniggia Raynor 56.31, JT: Orrin Powell 68.96. **Women:** 100m: Kerron Stewart 10.96, 200m: Shelly-Ann Fraser 22.13, 400m: Novlene Williams-Mills 50.01, 800m: Natoya Goule 1:59.93, 1500m: Chante Roberts 4:39.37, 3000mSt: Koreen Hinds 9:46.46, 100mh: Danielle Williams 12.69, 400mh: Ristanna Tracey 54.52, HJ: Saniel Atkinson Grier BAH 1.85, LJ: Francine Simpson 6.35w, TJ: Kimberly Williams 14.52, SP: Alyssa Wisdom 16.09, DT: Allison Randall 58.97, HT: Daina Levy 64.30, JT: Kateema Riettie 54.31.

Nickel ASHMEADE b. 7 Apr 1990 Ocho Rios, Saint-Ann 1.84m 87kg.
At 200m/4x100mR (100m): WCh: '11- 5, '13- 4/1R (5); WJ: '08- 2/2R (2 4x400m); WY: '07- 3 (2, 3 MedR); PAm-J: '09- 1; won DL 2012, CAC 2009.
Progress at 100m, 200m: 2006- 10.60, 21.30; 2007- 10.39, 20.76; 2008- 10.34, 20.80/20.16w; 2009- 10.37/10.21w, 20.40; 2010- 10.39, 20.63; 2011- 9.96, 19.91; 2012- 9.93, 19.85; 2013- 9.90, 19.93. pbs: 60m 6.92i '09, 400m 47.19 '12.

Kemar BAILEY-COLE b. 10 Jan 1992 St. Catherine 1.93m 83kg. Racers TC.
At 100m/4x100mR (200m): OG: '12- res (1)R; WCh: '13- 4/1R; WY: '09- sf/sf.
Progress at 100m: 2008- 10.85, 2009- 10.41/

10.38w, 2010- 10.53, 2011- 10.28, 2012- 9.97, 2013- 9.93. pbs: 200m 20.83 '12, 400m 47.36 '14.

Yohan BLAKE b. 26 Dec 1989 St. James 1.81m 79kg. Racers TC.
At 100m/4x100mR: OG: '12- 2/2/1R; WCh: '11- 1/1R; WJ: '06- 3/1R, '08- 4/2R; WY: '05- 7; PAm-J: '07- 2 (3 4x400m); won CAC-J 100m & 200m 2006; JAM 100m & 200m 2012.
World record 4x100m 2012.
Progress at 100m, 200m: 2005- 10.56, 22.10; 2006- 10.33, 20.92; 2007- 10.11, 20.62; 2008- 10.27/10.20w, 21.06; 2009- 10.07/9.93dq, 20.60; 2010- 9.89, 19.78; 2011- 9.82/9.80w, 19.26; 2012- 9.69, 19.44; 2013- 20.72. pbs: 60m 6.75i '08, 400m 46.32 '13.
3-month drugs ban from positive test at Jamaican Champs 25 Jun 2009. Cut 200m pb from 20.60 to 19.78 in Monaco 2010 and then to 19.26 in Brussels 2011. Youngest ever World 100m champion at 21 in 2011.

Usain BOLT b. 21 Aug 1986 Sherwood Content, Trelawny 1.96m 88kg. Racers TC.
At (100m)/200m/4x100mR: OG: '04- h, '08 & '12- 1/1/1R; WCh: '05- 8, '07- 2/2R, '09- 1/1/1R, '11- dq/1/1R, '13- 1/1/1R; WJ: 02- 1/2R/2R; WY: '01- sf, '03- 1; PAm-J: '03- 1/2R; WCp: '06- 2; won WAF 200m 2009, DL 100m 2012, CAC 200m 2005, JAM 100m 2008-09, 2013; 200m 2005, 2007-09.
World records: 100m (3), 200m (2), 4x100m (4) 2008-12, best low altitude 300m 2010, CAC records 100m (4) 2008-09, 200m (3) 2007-09, WJR 200m 2003 & 2004, World U18 100m record 2003.
Progress at 100m, 200m, 400m: 2000- 51.7; 2001- 21.73, 48.28; 2002- 20.58, 47.12; 2003- 20.13, 45.35; 2004- 19.93, 2005- 19.99, 2006- 19.88, 2007- 10.03, 19.75, 45.28; 2008- 9.69, 19.30, 46.94; 2009- 9.58, 19.19, 45.54; 2010- 9.82, 19.56, 45.87; 2011- 9.76, 19.40; 2012- 9.63, 19.32; 2013- 9.77, 19.66, 46.44. pbs: 60m 6.31+ '09, 100y 9.14+ '11, 150m 14.35 straight & 14.44+ turn '09 (world bests), 300m 30.97 '10 (world low altitude best).
Bolt was the sensational superstar of the 2008 Olympics when he won triple gold – all in world records. In 2009 he smashed both the 100m and 200m WRs at the World Champs and after two more golds at the 2011 Worlds (dq for false start at 100m) he repeated his Olympic treble in 2012 and won a further World treble in 2013. Ten World Champs medals matches Carl Lewis In 2002, after running 20.61 to win the CAC U17 200m title, he became the youngest ever male world junior champion at 15y 332d and set a world age best with 20.58, with further age records for 16 and 17 in 2003-04. Won IAAF 'Rising Star' award for men in 2002 and 2003 and male Athlete of the Year Award 2008-09, 2011-12. He has won 37 of his 41 100m finals 2007-13. He was appointed an Ambassador-at-Large for Jamaica.

Nesta CARTER b. 11 Oct 1985 Banana Ground 1.78m 70kg. MVP TC.
At 100m/4x100mR: OG: '08/12- 1R; WCh: '07-

sf/2R, '11- 7/1R, '13- 3/1R. At 200m: WJ: '04- sf/
res (2)R. At 60m: WI: '10-12-14: 7/2/7.
Three world 4x100m records 2008-12.
Progress at 100m: 2004- 10.0/10.56/10.52w,
2005- 10.59, 2006- 10.20, 2007- 10.11, 2008- 9.98,
2009- 9.91, 2010- 9.78, 2011- 9.89, 2012- 9.95, 2013-
9.87. pbs: 50m 5.67i '12, 60m 6.49i '12, 200m 20.25
'11, 400m 47.82 '09.

Damar FORBES b. 18 Sep 1990 Saint Ann
1.87m 77kg. Sports administration degree from
Louisiana State University.
At LJ: OG: '12- dnq 19; WCh: '11- dnq 20, '13- 8.
Jamaican champion 2012-13, NCAA 2013.
Progress at LJ: 2009- 7.51i/7.48, 2010- 9.93, 2011-
8.23, 2012- 8.13, 2013- 8.25/8.35w. Pbs: 60m 6.73i
'13, 100m 10.51 '13, 55mh 7.48i '09, 60mh 8.12i
'09, TJ 16.11i '12, 15.85 '10.

Leford GREEN b. 14 Nov 1986 St. Catherine
1.86m 79kg.
At 400mh: OG: '12- 7; WCh: '11- sf/3R, '13- sf;
CAG: 10- 1; Won CAC 2011, JAM 2009-13. At
400m/4x400m: WCh: '07- 4R; CAG: '06- sf/1R;
PAm: '07- sf.
At 400m: 2004- 48.14, 2005- 46.68, 53.01; 2006-
45.82, 50.81; 2007- 45.71, 52.69; 2008- 45.56, 50.51;
2009- 46.19; 2010- 45.68, 48.47; 2011- 45.46, 49.03;
2012- 46.76, 48.61; 2013- 48.84. pbs: 200m 20.61
'11, 20.41w '09; 600m 1:19.41i '12.

Hansle PARCHMENT b. 17 Jun 1990 Saint
Thomas 1.96m 90kg. Student of psychology at
University of the West Indies.
At 110mh: OG: '12- 3; WCh: '13- sf; CG: '10- 5;
WY: '07- sf; WUG: '11- 1. JAM champion 2012.
Three Jamaican 110mh records 2012-13.
Progress at 110mh: 2010- 13.71, 2011- 13.24, 2012-
13.12, 2013- 13.05. Pb 400mh 53.74 '08.

Asafa POWELL b. 23 Nov 1982 St Catherine
1.90m 88kg. MVP. Studied sports medicine at
Kingston University of Technology.
At 100m/4x100mR: OG: '04- 5 (dns 200), '08-
5/1R, '12- 8; WCh: '03- qf, '07- 3/2R, '09- 3/1R;
CG: '02- sf/2R, '06- 1/1R; PAm-J: '01- 2R. Won
JAM 100m 2003-05, 2007, 2011; 200m 2006, 2010;
WAF 100m 2004, 2006-08; 200m 2004; DL 100m
2011, GL 2006.
Four world 100m records, five CAC &
Commonwealth 2005-07, seven JAM 2004-7;
WR 4x100m 2008. Two world bests 100y 2010.
Progress at 100m, 200m: 2001- 10.50, 2002- 10.12,
20.48; 2003- 10.02/9.9, 2004- 9.87, 20.06; 2005-
9.77, 2006- 9.77, 19.90; 2007- 9.74, 20.00; 2008- 9.72,
2009- 9.82, 2010- 9.82/9.72w, 19.97; 2011- 9.78, 20.55;
2012- 9.85, 2013- 9.88. pbs: 50m 5.64i '12, 60m
6.42+ '09, 6.50i '12; 100y 9.07+ '10, 400m 45.94 '09.
Disqualified for false start in World quarters
2003 after fastest time (10.05) in heats. In 2004
he tied the record of nine sub-10 second times
in a season and in 2005 he took the world
record for 100m at Athens, tying that at
Gateshead and Zürich in 2006, when he ran a

record 12 sub-10 times and was world athlete of
the year. Took record to 9.74 in Rieti 2007 and
ran 15 sub-10 times in 2008, including seven
sub-9.90 in succession after 5th place at
Olympics. Now has record 81 sub-10 times
(plus 7w). Withdrew from 2011 Worlds through
injury. IAAF Athlete of the Year 2006. In July
2013 it was announced that he had tested positive for a banned stimulant and his case is
pending. Elder brother Donovan (b. 31 Oct
1971): at 60m: 6.51i '96 (won US indoors '96, 6
WI '99; 100m 10.07/9.7 '95).

Andrew RILEY b. 6 Sep 1988 Saint Thomas
1.88m 80kg. Economics graduate of University
of Illinois.
At 110mh: OG: '12- h; WCh: '11- sf, '13- 8. JAM
champion 2011, 2013; won NCAA 100m 2012,
110mh 2010 & 2012. At 60mh: WI: '14 dns final.
Progress at 110mh: 2009- 13.74/13.61w, 2010-
13.45, 2011- 13.32, 2012- 13.19, 2013- 13.14. Pbs:
60m 6.57i '12, 100m 10.02 '12, 200m 21.25w '12,
60mh 7.53i '12, HJ 2.10 '08.
First to win NCAA 100m and 110mh double 2012.

Dwight THOMAS b. 23 Sep 1980 Kingston
1.85m 82kg. adidas.
At 110mh: WCh: '09- 7, '11- dns. At 100m/4x-
100mR: OG: '04- sf, '08- res 1R; WCh: '03- sf,
'05- 5, '07- res 2R, '09- res 1R; CG: '02- 4=/2R;
PAm: '99- 3R; WJ: '98- 3/1R. At 200m: OG: '00-
qf/4R. At 60m: WI: '03- sf. At 60mh: WI: '04- 8.
Won CAC-J 110mh 1998, PAm-J 100m & 200m
1999, Jamaican 100m & 200m 2002.
Jamaican 110mh records 2009 & 2011.
Progress at 100m, 110mh: 1998- 10.38, 14.40/
13.86w; 1999- 10.37, 2000- 10.12, 2001- 10.19, 2002-
10.15, 13.74; 2003- 10.19, 2004- 10.12, 13.34; 2005-
10.00, 2006- 10.11, 2007- 10.15/10.07w, 14.25;
2008- 10.20/10.14w; 2009- 10.33, 13.16; 2010-
13.25/13.1w, 2011- 13.15, 2012- 13.36/13.17w, 2013-
13.27. pbs: 55m 6.27i '01, 60m 6.61i '03, 200m
20.32 '07, 60mh 7.59i '04.

Warren WEIR b. 31 Oct 1989 Trelawny 1.78m
75kg. Racers TC.
At 200m/4x100mR: OG: '12- 3; WCh: '13- 2/res
1R; won DL 2013, JAM 2013. At 110mh: WJ: '08- sf.
Progress at 200m: 2008- 22.26, 2009- 21.46w,
2010- 21.52, 2011- 20.43, 2012- 19.84, 2013- 19.79.
pbs: 100m 10.02 '13, 400m 46.23 '13, 110mh 13.65
'07, 13.45w '08; 400mh 53.28 '09.

Jason YOUNG b. 21 Mar 1991 1.80m 68kg.
Racers TC.
At 200m: WUG: '11- 2.
Progress at 200m: 2007- 22.10, 2008- 21.61, 2009-
21.57, 2011- 20.53, 2012- 19.86, 2013- 19.98/19.96w.
pb 100m 10.06 '12.

Women

Schillonie CALVERT b. 27 Jul 1988 Saint James
1.66m 57kg. Racers TC. University of
Technology.
At 100m/4x100R: OG: '12- res (2)R; WCh: '13-

sf/1R; WJ: '04- 7, '06- sf/3/3R; WY: '05- 3; PAm-J '05- 2, '07-1 (2 200m).
CAC & Commonwealth 4x100m record 2013.
Progress at 100m: 2004- 11.44/11.33w, 2005- 11.40, 2006- 11.21, 2007- 11.35, 2008- 11.23, 2009- 11.19, 2010- 11.36, 2011- 11.05, 2012- 11.05, 2013- 11.07. pbs: 200m 22.55 '11, 400m 53.50 '12.

Veronica CAMPBELL-BROWN b. 15 May 1982 Clarks Town, Trelawny 1.63m 61kg. Adidas. Was at University of Arkansas, USA.
At (100m)/200m/4x100mR: OG: '00- 2R, '04- 3/1/1R, '08- 1, '12- 3/4/2R; WCh: '05- 2/4/2R, '07- 1/2/2R, '09- 4/2, '11- 2/1/2R; CG: '02- (2)/2R, '06- 2; WJ: '98- (qf), '00- 1/1/2R; WY: '99- (1)/1R; PAm-J: '99- 2R. At 60m: WI: '10-12- 14: 1/1/5. Won WAF 100m 2004-05, 200m 2004, CAC-J 100m 2000, JAM 100m 2002, 2004-05, 2007, 2011; 200m 2004-05, 2007-09, 2011.
Three CAC & Commonwealth 4x100m records 2004-12. CAC junior 100m record 2000.
Progress at 100m, 200m: 1999- 11.49, 23.73; 2000- 11.12/11.1, 22.87; 2001- 11.13/22.92; 2002- 11.00, 22.39; 2004- 10.91, 22.05; 2005- 10.85, 22.35/22.29w; 2006- 10.99, 22.51; 2007- 10.89, 22.34; 2008- 10.87/10.85w, 21.74; 2009- 10.89/10.81w, 22.29; 2010- 10.78, 21.98; 2011- 10.76, 22.22; 2012- 10.81, 22.32; 2013- 11.01/10.78w, 22.53/22.18w.
pbs: 50m 6.08i '12, 60m 7.00i '10, 100y 9.91+ '11 (world best), 400m 52.24i '05, 52.25 '11.
In 2000 became the first woman to become World Junior champion at both 100m and 200m. Unbeaten at 200m in 28 finals (42 races in all) from 11 March 2000 to 22 July 2005 (lost to Allyson Felix). Married Omar Brown (1 CG 200m 2006) on 3 Nov 2007. She received a public warning for a positive test for a banned diuretic on 4 May 2013 and was suspended for the season, but the Court of Arbitration for Sport upheld her appeal against the suspension in February 2014.

Shelly-Ann FRASER-PRYCE b. 27 Dec 1986 Kingston 1.60m 52kg. MVP. Graduate of the University of Technology. née Fraser. Married Jason Pryce on 7 Jan 2011.
At 100m/4x100mR: OG: '08- 1, '12- 1/2/2R; WCh: '07- res (2)R, '09- 1/1R, '11- 4/2R, '13- 1/1/1R. SAt 60m: WI: '14- 1. Won WAF 2008, DL 100m 2012-13, 200m 2013; JAM 100m 2009, 2012; 200m 2012-13.
CAC and Commonwealth records 100m 2009 & 2012, 4x100m (3) 2011-13.
Progress at 100m, 200m: 2002- 11.8, 2003- 11.57, 2004- 11.72, 24.08; 2005- 11.72; 2006- 11.74, 24.8; 2007- 11.31/11.21w, 23.5; 2008- 10.78, 22.15; 2009- 10.73, 22.58; 2010- 10.82dq, 22.47dq; 2011- 10.95, 22.59/22.10w; 2012- 10.70, 22.09; 2013- 10.71, 22.13. pb 60m 6.98i '14.
Double World and Olympic champion. Huge improvement in 2008 and moved to joint third on world all-time list for 100m when winning 2009 world 100m title. 6-month ban for positive

test for a non-performance enhancing drug on 23 May 2010.

Anneisha McLAUGHLIN b. 6 Jan 1986 Manchester 1.63m 54kg. University of Technology.
At 200m/4x100mR: WCh: '09- 5, '13- sf; WJ: '02- 2/1R, '04- 2/2R; WY: '03- 1 (2 MedR); WUG: '11- 1/3R; PAm-J: '03- 2/2R, '05- 1. At 400m/4x-400mR: WJ: '00- 2R; WY: '01- 3 (2 MedR); WI: 14- 2R. Won CAC-J 400m 2000, 100m & 200m 2002' JAM 200m 2010.
Progress at 200m: 2000- 24.33w, 2001- 23.11, 2002- 22.94, 2003- 23.19, 2004- 23.21, 2005- 23.00, 2006- 23.47, 2007- 23.28/23.27w, 2008- 23.34, 2009- 22.55, 2010- 22.54, 2011- 22.54, 2012- 22.61, 2013- 22.58. pbs: 100m 11.23 '13, 400m 51.89 '12.

Stephenie Ann McPHERSON b. 25 Nov 1988 1.68m 55kg. MVP. Was at Kingston University of Technology.
At 400m: WCh: '13- 4; WI: 14- 2R.
Progress at 400m: 2006- 56.42, 2007- 55.77, 2008- 52.80, 2009- 51.95, 2010- 51.64, 2012- 52.98, 2013- 49.92. pb 100m 11.44 '10, 200m 23.04 '10, 800m 2:15.24 '12, 400mh 57.46 '12.

Carrie RUSSELL b. 18 Oct 1990 1.71m 68kg. University of Technology.
At 100m/4x100mR: WCh: '13- 1R; WJ: '06- 3/3R; WUG: '11- 1/3R.
CAC & Commonwealth 4x100m record 2013.
Progress at 100m: 2006- 11.36, 2007- 11.72, 2008- 11.44/11.39w, 2009- 11.27/11.21w, 2010- 11.14, 2011- 11.05, 2012- 11.24, 2013- 10.98. pb: 60m 7.28 '14, 200m 22.62 '13.

Sherone SIMPSON b. 12 Aug 1984 Manchester, Jamaica 1.75m 59kg. MVP. Graduate of Kingston University of Technology.
At 100m/(200m)/4x100mR: OG: '04- 6/1R, '08- 2=/6, '12- (sf)/2R; WCh: '05- 6/2R, '11- (8)/2R; CG: '06- (1)/1R; WJ: '02- 1R; PAm-J: '03- 2/2R; WCp: '06- 1/1R. Won WAF 100m 2006, JAM 100m 2006, 2010; 200m 2006.
Three CAC& Commonwealth 4x100m records 2004-12.
Progress at 100m, 200m: 2000- 12.54, 2001- 12.17, 25.01; 2002- 11.60, 24.21; 2003- 11.37/11.1, 23.60; 2004- 11.01, 22.70; 2005- 10.97, 22.54; 2006- 10.82, 22.00; 2007- 11.43, 22.76; 2008- 10.87, 22.11; 2009- 11.15/11.04w; 2010- 11.02, 22.65/22.64w; 2011- 11.00, 22.73; 2012- 11.01, 22.37; 2013- 11.03, 22.55. pbs: 400m 51.25 '08, 100mh 14.10 '02.

Kenia SINCLAIR b. 14 July 1980 St Catherine 1.67m 54kg. Was at Seton Hall University, USA.
At 800m: OG: '08- 6; WCh: '05/07/09- sf, '11- 7; CG: '06- 2; WI: '06- 2; CCp: '10- 2. Won JAM 800m 2005-09, 2011-12; 1500m 2006-07, 2011.
Five Jamaican 800m records 2005-06. CAC indoor 1000m record (2:38.62) 2010.
Progress at 800m: 2002- 2:05.26i/2:07.39, 2003- 2:03.21, 2005- 1:58.88, 2006- 1:57.88, 2007- 1:58.61, 2008- 1:58.24, 2009- 1:59.13, 2010- 1:58.16, 2011-

1-58.21, 2012- 2:01.55, 2013- 2:03.62. pbs: 400m 56.84 '03, 600m 1:25.6+ '09, 1000m 2:37.37 '05, 1500m 4:05.56 '07, 1M 4:32.33i '05, 3000m 9:52.71i '02, 10kmRd 34:27 '11.
Based in Gainesville, Florida.

Kerron STEWART b. 16 Apr 1984 Kingston 1.75m 61kg. Adult education student at Auburn University, USA.
At 100m/(200m)/4x100mR: OG: '08- 2=/3, '12- sf/2R; WCh: '07- 7/2R, '09- 2/1R, '11- 6/5/2R, '13- 5/1R; WJ: '02- 4/1R; WY: '01- 2/2R. Won NCAA 200m 2007, indoor 60m & 200m 2007; JAM 100m 2008, 2013.
Three CAC & Commonwealth 4x100m records 2011-13.
Progress at 100m, 200m: 2000- 11.89, 24.09w; 2001- 11.70, 23.90; 2002- 11.46, 24.21; 2003- 11.34, 23.50; 2004- 11.40, 23.63i/23.66; 2005- 11.63, 23.77i/24.22/23.46w; 2006- 11.03, 22.65; 2007- 11.03, 22.41; 2008- 10.80, 21.99; 2009- 10.75, 22.42; 2010- 10.96, 22.57/22.34w; 2011- 10.87, 22.63.; 2012- 10.92, 22.70; 2013- 10.96, 22.71. pbs: 55m 6.71i '06, 60m 7.14i '07, 400m 51.83 '13.

Melaine WALKER b. 1 Jan 1983 Kingston 1.73m 58kg. Racers TC. Social work graduate of University of Texas, USA.
At 400mh/4x400mR: OG: '08- 1, '12- sf; WCh: '01-07-09-11: h/sf/1/2; CG: '02- 4; WJ: '00- 3/2R, '02- 2 (5 100mh); CAG: '06- 3/2R; Jamaican champion 2006-09, 2012; WAF 2008-09. At 200m: WJ: '98- 5/3 4x100R; WY: '99- 2.
Two CAC 400mh records 2008-09.
Progress at 400mh: 1999- 58.99, 2000- 56.96, 2001- 55.62, 2002- 55.84, 2003- 57.24, 2004- 56.62, 2005- 55.09, 2006- 54.87, 2007- 54.14, 2008- 52.64, 2009- 52.42, 2010- 55.33, 2011- 52.73, 2012- 53.74. pbs: 60m 7.40i '05, 100m 11.63 '99, 200m 23.46 '12, 400m 51.61 '08, 800m 2:11.96 '11, 60mh 8.05i '06, 100mh 12.75 '06.

Rosemarie WHYTE b. 8 Sep 1986 Trelawny 1.75m 66kg. Racers TC.
At 400m/4x400mR: OG: '08- 7/3R, '12- 8/3R; WCh: '09- 2R, '11- sf/2R, '13- hR. Won JAM 400m 2008.
Progress at 400m: 2002- 55.51, 2007- 53.47, 2008- 50.05, 2009- 51.55, 2010- 50.67, 2011- 49.84, 2012- 50.08, 2013- 50.86. pbs: 100m 11.60/11.4 '06, 200m 22.74 '09, 800m 2:12.60 '14, 100mh 14.27/14.2 '06, 400mh 59.89 '09, HJ 1.65 '06, LJ 6.35 '06, TJ 13.04 '06, JT 31.15 '06, Hep 5262 '06.

Kimberly WILLIAMS b. 3 Nov 1988 Saint Thomas 1.69m 66kg. Florida State University, USA.
At TJ: OG: '12- 6; WCh: '09/11 dnq 15/14, '13- 4; WJ: '06- dnq 15; WY: '05- dnq; CAG: '10- 1; PAm-J: '07- 2; WI: '12- 5, '14- 3. Won NCAA LJ & TJ 2009, JAM TJ 2010, 2012-13.
Progress at TJ: 2004- 12.53/12.65w, 2005- 12.63/13.09w, 2006- 13.18, 2007- 13.52, 2008- 13.82i/13.69/13.83w, 2009- 14.08/14.38w, 2010- 14.23, 2011- 14.25,

2012- 14.53, 2013- 14.62/14.78w. pbs: 100m 11.76 '12, 200m 24.55 '11, LJ 6.55i 11, 6.42/6.66w '09.

Novlene WILLIAMS-MILLS b. 26 Apr 1982 Saint Ann 1.70m 57kg. Studied recreation at University of Florida, USA.
At 400m/4x400mR: OG: '04- sf/3R, '08- sf/3R, '12- 5/3R; WCh: '05- 2R, '07- 3/2R, '09- 4/2R, '11- 8/2R, '13- 8; CG: '06- 3; PAm: '03- 6/2R; WI: '06- 5; WCp: '06- 3/1R. Won JAM 400m 2006-07, 2009-13.
Progress at 400m: 1999- 55.62, 2000- 53.90, 2001- 54.99, 2002- 52.05, 2003- 51.93, 2004- 50.59, 2005- 51.09, 2006- 49.63, 2007- 49.66, 2008- 50.11, 2009- 49.77, 2010- 50.04, 2011- 50.05, 2012- 49.78, 2013- 50.01. pbs: 200m 23.25 '10, 500m 1:11.83i '03.
Married 2007. Younger sister Clora Williams (b. 26.11.83) joined her on JAM's 3rd place 4x400m team at 2010 WI; she has 400m pb 51.06 and won NCAA 2006.

Shericka WILLIAMS b. 17 Sep 1985 Black River, St. Elizabeth 1.70m 64kg. MVP. Kingston University of Technology.
At 400m/4x400mR: OG: '08- 2/3R, '12- 3R; WCh: '05- sf/2R, '07- sf/2R, '09- 2/2R, '11- 6/2R; CG: '06- 5; WCp: '06- 1R, '10- 4/1R; won JAM 400m 2005.
Progress at 200m, 400m: 2001- 24.74, 2003- 23.90, 55.44; 2004- 23.96/23.70w, 53.52; 2005- 23.08, 50.97; 2006- 22.55, 50.24; 2007- 23.32, 50.37; 2008- 22.50, 49.69; 2009- 22.57, 49.32; 2010- 23.25, 50.04; 2011- 23.49/23.16w, 50.45; 2012- 23.12, 50.34; 2013- 51.86. pb 100m 11.34 '07, 800m 2:09.17 '07.

Nickiesha WILSON b. 28 Jul 1986 Kingston 1.73m 64kg. Racers TC. Was at Louisiana State University, USA.
At 400mh: OG: '08/12- sf/sf; WCh: '07- 4, '09/11- sf, 13- 8; CG: '10- 3; PAm: '07- 2; PAm-J: '05-1; CAG: '10- 1; CCp: '10- 1/1R; won NCAA 2008, CAC 2009, JAM 2010.
Progress at 100mh, 400mh: 2005- 13.98, 57.38; 2006- 13.64/13.44w, 56.77; 2007- 12.93, 53.97; 2008- 12.85/12.63w, 54.45; 2009- 12.79/12.72w, 54.89; 2010- 13.17, 54.52; 2011- 13.23, 55.57; 2012- 13.00, 55.50; 2013- 54.94. pbs: 60m 7.55i '10, 200m 23.59i '08, 400m 53.66i '08, 60mh 8.01i '07, LJ 6.26 '11.

JAPAN

Governing body: Nippon Rikujo-Kyogi Renmei, 1-1-1 Jinnan, Shibuya-Ku, Tokyo 150-8050. Founded 1911.
National Championships first held in 1914 (men), 1925 (women). **2013 Champions: Men:** 100m: Ryota Yamagata 10.11, 200m: Shota Iizuka 20.31, 400m: Yuzo Kanemaru 45.56, 800m: Sho Kawamoto 1:47.43, 1500m: Yuki Akimoto 4:02.32, 5000m: Sota Hoshi 13:49.57, 10,000m: Yuki Sato 28:24.94, Mar: Masakazu Fujiwara 2:08:51, 3000mSt: Minato Yamashita 8:33.57, 110mh: Wataru Yazawa 13.59, 400mh: Takayuki Kishimoto 49.08, HJ: Hiromi Takahari

2.25, PV: Seito Yamamoto 5.70, LJ: Kosuke Inoue 7.76, TJ: Yohei Kajikawa 16.36, SP: Satoshi Hatase 18.30, DT: Shigeo Hatakeyama 56.90, HT: Koji Murofushi 76.42, JT: Yukifumi Murakami 81.04, Dec: Keisuke Ushiro 7808, 20kW: Yusuke Suzuki 1:19:02, 50kW: Takayuki Tanii 3:44:25. **Women**: 100m/200m: Chisato Fukushima 11.45/23.35, 400m: Haruka Sugiura 52.52, 800m: Miho Ito 2:05.30, 1500m: Ayako Jinnouchi 4:16.17, 5000m: Felista Wanjugu KEN 15:21.57. 10,000m: Hitomi Niiya 31:06.67, Mar: Ryoko Kizaki 2:23:34, 3000mSt: Yoshika Arai 9:58.22, 100mh: Hitomi Shimura 13.02, 400mh: Satomi Kubokura 56.62, HJ: Miyuki Fukumoto 1.90, PV: Kanae Tatsuta 4.10, LJ: Saeko Okayama 6.59, TJ: Fumiyo Yoshida 13.14, SP: Yukiko Shirai 15.65, DT: Ai Shikimoto 52.86, HT: Masumi Aya 64.20, JT: Yuki Ebihara 60.41, Hep: Chie Kiriyama 5564, 20kW: Kumi Otoshi 1:30:45.

Yukifumi MURAKAMI b. 23 Dec 1979 Ueshima, Ehime 1.86m 102kg. Suzuki Motor, Was at Nihon University.
At JT: OG: '04/08/12- dnq 18/15/24; WCh: '05-07-11-13: dnq 27/21/15/21, '09- 3; WJ: '98- 3; AsiG: 02-06-10: 2/2/1; AsiC: '09- 1, '11- 1; Asi-J: '97- 2; JPN champion 2000-11, 2013.
Progress at JT: 1995- 56.60, 1996- 68.00, 1997- 76.54, 1998- 73.62, 1999- 71.70, 2000- 78.57, 2001- 80.59, 2002- 78.77, 2003- 78.98, 2004- 81.71, 2005- 79.79, 2006- 78.54, 2007- 79.85, 2008- 79.71, 2009- 83.10, 2010- 83.15, 2011- 83.53, 2012- 83.95, 2013- 85.96.

Koji MUROFUSHI b. 8 Oct 1974 Shizuoka 1.87m 103kg. Graduate of Chukyo University. Mizuno.
At HT: OG: '00- 9, '04- 1, '08- 5, '12- 3; WCh: '95-97-99-01-03-07-11-13: dnq/10/dnq 14/2/3/6/1/6; WJ: '92- 8; AsiG: '94- 2, '98- 1, '02- 1; AsiC: '93-5-8-02: 2/2/2/1; WCp: '02- 2 (9 DT), '06- 1. Won GWG 2010, GP 2002 (2nd 2000), WAF 2006, World HT challenge 2010, E.Asian 1997, 2001; Japanese 1995-2013.
18 Japanese hammer records 1998-2003, Asian records 2001 & 2003.
Progress at HT: 1991- 61.76, 1992- 66.30, 1993- 68.00, 1994- 69.54, 1995- 72.32, 1996- 73.82, 1997- 75.72, 1998- 78.57, 1999- 79.17, 2000- 81.08, 2001- 83.47, 2002- 83.33, 2003- 84.86, 2004- 83.15, 2005- 76.47, 8006- 82.01, 2007- 82.62, 2008- 81.87, 2009- 78.36, 2010- 80.99, 2011- 81.24, 2012- 78.71, 2013- 78.03. pb DT 44.64 '96.
Won IAAF HT Challenge 2010. His father Shigenobu Murofushi won a record five Asian Games gold medals 1970-86 and held the Japanese hammer record with 75.96 (Los Angeles 1984) until Koji broke it for the first time on 26 Apr 1998. His mother was the 1968 European Junior javelin champion, Serafina Moritz (Romania). His sister **Yuka** (b. 11 Feb 77) holds Japanese records: DT 58.62 '07 and HT 67.77 '04; 6th WJ DT 1996.

Kentaro NAKAMOTO b. 7 Dec 1982 Shimonoseki, Yamaguchi 1.73m 58kg. Yaskawa Electric Corporation.
At Mar: OG: '12- 6; WCh: '11- 10, '13- 5.
Progress at Mar: 2008- 2:13:54, 2009- 2:13:53, 2010- 2:11:42, 2011- 2:09:31, 2012- 2:98:53, 2013- 2:08:35. pbs: 5000m 14:04.31 '11, 10,000m 28:54.59 '12, HMar 62:29 '09.
2nd Beppu Marathon 2013.

Yusuke SUZUKI b. 1 Feb 1988 Yokohama 1.69m 56kg. Fujitsu.
At 20kW: OG: '12- 36; WCh: '09- 42, '11- 8, '13- 12; AsiG: '10- 5; Asian champion 2013, JPN 2011, 2013. At 10,000mW: WJ: 04- 17, '06- 3; WY: '05- 3.
Two Japanese 20k walk records 2013-14.
Progress at 20kW: 2007- 1:24:40, 2008- 1:22:34, 2009- 1:22:05, 2010- 1:20:06, 2011- 1:21:13, 2012- 1:22:30, 2013- 1:18:34, 2014- 1:18:17. pb 10kW 39:02 '14, 39:38.8t '09.

Yuki YAMAZAKI b. 16 Jan 1984 Toyama 1.77m 65kg. Was at Juntendo University.
At (20kW)/50kW: OG: '04- 16, '08- 11/7, '12- dq; WCh: '05-07-09: 8/dnf/dq; WCp: '10- 6; AsiG: '02- dq/dq, '06- (4); AsiC: '03- (2), '07- 2. At 10,000mW: WJ: '00- 20, '02- 5; WY: '01- 4. Won JPN 20kW 2002, 50kW 2004-10, 2012.
Four Japanese 50k walk records 2006-09. World youth 5000m walk best 2001.
Progress at 50kW: 2004- 3:55:20, 2005- 3:50:40, 2006- 3:43:38, 2007- 3:47:40, 2008- 3:41:29, 2009- 3:40:12, 2010- 3:46:46, 2011- 3:44:03, 2012- 3:41:47. pbs: 5000mW 19:35.79 '01, 10,000mW 39:48.52 '08, 20kW 1:20:38 '03.

Women

Kayoko FUKUSHI b. 25 Mar 1982 Itayanagi, Aiomori pref. 1.60m 45kg. Wacoal.
At Mar: WCh: '13- 3. At 5000m/(10,000m): OG: '04- (26), '08- h/11, '12- h/10; WCh: '03- h/11, '05-12/11, '07- 14/10, '09- (9); WJ: '00- 4; AsiG: '02- 2/2, '06- (1), '10- 5/4; WCp: '06- 3 (5 3000m). World 20km: '06- 6; CC: '02- 15, '06- 6. Won JPN 5000m 2002, 2004-07, 2010; 10,000m 2002-07, 2010.
World 15km record & Asian 20km & HMar records 2006, Japanese records: 3000m 2002, 5000m (4) 2002-05.
Progress at 5000m, 10,000m, Mar: 1998- 16:56.35, 1999- 16:38.69, 35:37.54; 2000- 15:29.70, 2001- 15:10.23, 31:42.05; 2002- 14:55.19, 30:51.81; 2003- 15:09.02, 31:10.57; 2004- 14:57.73, 31:05.68; 2005- 14:53.22, 31:03.75; 2006- 15:03.17, 30:57.90; 2007- 15:05.73, 32:13.58; 2008- 15:12.7, 31:01.14, 2:40:54; 2009- 15:23.44mx, 31:23.49; 2010- 15:17.86, 31:29.03; 2011- 30:54.29, 2:24:38; 2012- 15:09.31, 31:10.35; 2013- 32:42.56, 2:24:21. pbs: 3000m 8:44.40 '02, 15k 46:55 '06, 20k 63:41 '06, HMar 67:26 '06, 30k 1:41:25 '08.
Set Japanese junior records at 3000m, 5000m and 10,000m in 2001. 2nd Osaka marathon 2013.

Ryoko KIZAKI b. 21 Jun 1985 Yosano, Kyoto Pref. 1.57m 44kg. Daihatsu.
At Mar: OG: '12- 16; WCh: 13- 4; JPN champion 2013. At HMar: WUG: '05- 2; WCh: '09-10: 12/10, At 10,000m: WUG: '07- 2 (4 5000m).
Progress at Mar: 2010- 2:27:34, 2011- 2:26:32, 2012- 2:27:16, 2013- 2:23:34, 2014- 2:25:26. pbs: 1500m 4:23.36 '04, 3000m 9:16.3 '08, 5000m 15:22.87 '11, 10,000m 31:38.71 '10, HMar 70:16 '09.
Marathon wins: Yokohama 2011, Nagoya 2013 (3rd 2014).

Hitomi NIIYA b. 26 Feb 1988 Soja, Okayama pref. 1.64m 45kg.
At (5000m)/10,000m: OG: '12- h/9; WCh: '11- (13), '13- 5; AsiC: '11- (2). At 3000m: WY: '05- 3. Won JPN 5000m 2012, 10,000m 2013.
Progress at 10,000m: 2012- 30:59.19, 2013- 30:56.70. pbs: 3000m 9:10.34 '05, 5000m 15:10.20 '12, HMar 71:41 '08, Mar 2:30:58 '09.
Led for much of 10,000m races at OG 2012 and WCh 201s.

Mizuki NOGUCHI b. 3 Jul 1978 Kanagawa 1.50m 41kg. Globary.
At 10,000m: WCh: '01- 13. At Mar: OG: '04- 1; WCh: '03- 2, '13- dnf. World HMar: '99-00-01- 02: 2/4/4/9. Won Asian CC 1999, E.Asian HMar 2001, JPN Mar 2003.
Asian marathon record 2005. World road records 25km 1:22:12 & 30km 1:38:48 in 2005 Berlin Marathon.
Progress at 10,000m, Mar: 1999- 33:09.98, 2000- 32:05.23, 2001- 31:51.13, 2002- 31:50.18, 2:25:35; 2003- 31:59.28, 2:21:18; 2004- 31:21.03, 2:26:20, 2005- 31:44.29, 2:19:12; 2006- 31:50.13, 2007- 2:21:37, 2013- 2:24:05. pbs: 3000m 9:24.51 '98, 5000m 15:34.36 '99, Rd: 15k 48:11 '01, HMar 67:43 '06, 30k 1:39:09 '04.
Formerly excelling at half marathon, she won the Nagoya marathon on debut in 2002 and again at Osaka in January 2003, at the Olympics in 2004, in Berlin 2005 and Tokyo 2007. 3rd Nagoya 2013.

KAZAKHSTAN

Governing body: Athletic Federation of the Republic of Kazakhstan, Abai Street 48, 480072 Almaty. Founded 1959.
2013 National Champions: Men: 100m: Vyacheslav Muravyev 10.80, 200m: Vladislav Leshin 21.30w, 400m: Sergey Zaykov 46.76, 800m/1500m: Ivan Obeyshik 1:51.78/3:57.57, 5000m/10,000m: Andrey Leymenov 15:04.04 /31:18.34, 3000mSt: Amir Baytukanov 9:40.11, 110mh: Nikkita Kozyrev 14.87, 400mh: Anton Khoroshev 51.13, HJ: Anton Bodnar 2.20, PV: Baurzhan Serikbayev 5.00, LJ: Kirill Agoyev 8.04w, TJ: Roman Valiyev 17.02, SP/DT: Ivan Ivanov 18.25/53.02, HT: Niko Palkin 48.04, JT: Nursultan Tagayev 46.28, Dec: Alexandr Martirosov 6471, 20kW: Stanislav Borisov 1:32:44; **Women**: 100m: Svetlana Ivanchukova

11.86, 200m: Viktoriya Zyabkina 23.64, 400m: Marina Maslenko 53.72, 800m: Tatyana Yurchenko 2:09.11, 1500m: Gulzhanat Zhanatbek 4:24.12, 5000m/10,000m: Irina Smolnikova 17:36.44/37:04.46, 3000mSt: Bolnura Asylbek 12:25.06, 100mh: Anastasiya Soprunova 13.09, 400mh: Marina Zayko 59.58, HJ: Regina Sarsekova 1.75, PV: Olga Lapina 3.80, LJ/TJ: Irina Ektova 6.15w/14.23, SP: Alexandra Fisher 14.51, DT: Yelena Bykova 36.60, JT: Asiya Rabayeva 38.17.

Dmitriy KARPOV b. 23 Jul 1981 Karaganda 1.98m 94kg.
At Dec: OG: '04- 3, '08- dnf, '12- 18; WCh: '03-05- 07-09-11-13: 3/dnf/3/21/21/dnf; WJ: '00- 4; AsiG: '02-06-10: 2/1/1; AsiC: '13- 1; won E.Asian 2001. At Hep: WI: '04- 4, '08- 3; won Asian indoors 2012, 2014. At 110mh: AsiC: '02- 5. Won KAZ 200m 2003, Dec 1999.
Two Asian decathlon records 2004 (& four KAZ 2003-04), three indoor heptathlon 2004-08.
Progress at Dec: 1999- 7105, 2000- 7620, 2001- 7567, 2002- 7995, 2003- 8374, 2004- 8725, 2006- 8438, 2007- 8586, 2008- 8504, 2009- 8029, 2010- 8026, 2011- 8089, 2012- 8173, 2013- 8037. pbs: 60m 7.04i '04, 100m 10.69 '06, 10.50w '04; 200m 21.65 '03, 400m 46.81 '04, 1000m 2:42.34i '04, 1500m 4:32.34 '06, 60mh 7.79i '03, 110mh 13.93 '02, HJ 2.12 '03, PV 5.30 '08, LJ 8.05 '02, SP 16.95 '10, DT 52.80 '04, JT 60.31 '06, Hep 6229i '08.
Set national record of 8253 to win at Desenzano in 2003 from previous best 7995. Then three pbs en route to World bronze and KAZ record 8374. In 2004 he was third at Götzis with 8512 and set three pbs in his 8725 for Olympic bronze. Did not compete in 2005 apart from two false starts in World Champs decathlon 100m, but won at Ratingen and Talence after 2nd Götzis in 2006 to win the IAAF Combined Events Challenge. Won at Götzis 2008. His wife Irina (née Naumenko) has Hep pb 6140 '03.

Women

Marina AITOVA b. 13 Sep 1982 Karaganda 1.80m 60kg. née Korzhova.
At HJ: OG: '04- dnq 31=, '08- 10=, '12- dnq; WCh: '03-09-11-13: dnq 22=/13=/19=/25, '07- 7=; AsiG: '02- 2, '06- 1; AsiC: '00- 02-11-13: 2/3/3/3; WJ: '00- 9=; WY: '99- 4; WI: '08- 5, '10- 7=; WUG: '07- 1; WCp: '06- 3. Won Asi-J 2001, Af-AsG & C.Asian G 2003, Asian indoor 2006, 2010; KAZ 2002-04, 2011.
Two Asian high jump records 2008-09.
Progress at HJ: 1999- 1.86, 2000- 1.90, 2001- 1.86i/1.85, 2002- 1.94, 2003- 1.89, 2004- 1.91i/1.89, 2005- 1.75, 2006- 1.95, 2007- 1.96, 2008- 1.97, 2009- 1.99, 2010- 1.94i, 2011- 1.94, 2012- 1.95, 2013- 1.95. pb LJ 6.00 '01.

Olga RYPAKOVA b. 30 Nov 1984 Kamenogorsk 1.83m 62kg. née Alekseyeva.
At TJ/(LJ): OG: '08- 4 (dnq 29), '12- 1; WCh: '07- 11, '09- 10, '11- 2; WJ: '00- (dnq 23); AsiG: '06- (3),

'10- 1/2; AsiC: '07- 1/1, '09- 1; WI: '08-10-12: 4/1/2; WUG: '07- (1); WCp: '06- (8), '10: 1/3; won DL TJ 2012, Asian Indoor LJ & TJ 2009. At Hep: WJ: '02- 2; WY: '01- 4; AsiG: '06- 1; won C.Asian 2003. Won KAZ LJ 2005, 2008, 2011; TJ 2008, 2011; Hep 2006.
Four Asian TJ records 2008-10, five indoors 2008-10, seven KAZ records 2007-10.
Progress at LJ, TJ: 2000- 6.23, 2001- 6.00, 2002- 6.26, 2003- 6.34i/6.14, 2004- 6.53i, 2005- 6.60, 2006- 6.63, 2007- 6.85, 14.69; 2008- 6.52/6.58w, 15.11; 2009- 6.58i/6.42, 14.53/14.69w; 2010- 6.60, 15.25; 2011- 6.56, 14.96; 2012- 14.98. pbs: 200m 24.83 '02, 800m 2:20.12 '02, 60mh 8.67i '06, 100mh 14.02 '06, HJ 1.92 '06, SP 13.04 '06, JT 41.60 '03, Hep 6122 '06, Pen 4582i '06 (Asian rec).
Former heptathlete, concentrated on long jump after birth of daughter. Four KAZ and three Asian TJ records with successive jumps in Olympic final 2008, three Asian indoor records when won World Indoor gold in 2010. Son born June 2013.

KENYA

Governing body: Kenya Amateur Athletic Association, PO Box 46722, 00100 Nairobi. Founded 1951.
2013 National Champions: Men: 100m: Tonny Chirchir 10.45, 200m: Mike Nyangau 20.69, 400m: Alpha Kishoyan 45.5, 800m: Job Kinyor 1:44.9, 1500m: Augustine Choge 3:34.3, 5000m: Isiah Koech 13:30.4, 10,000m: Geoffrey Mutai 27:55.3, 3000mSt: John Koech 8:21.5, 110mh: Samuel Korir 14.46, 400mh: William Mutunga 49.82, HJ: Mathew Sawe 2.15, LJ/TJ: Elijah Kimitei 7.87/16.45, JT: Julius Yego 76.49, 20kW: David Kimutai 1:27:52. **Women**: 100m/200m: Milicent Ndoro 11.86/24.43, 400m: Maureen Maiyo 52.2, 800m: Winnie Chebet 2:00.04, 1500m: Hellen Obiri 4:05.3, 5000m: Mary Ngugi 16:03.7, 10,000m: Lucy Kabuu 32:44.1, 3000mSt: Lydia Chepkurui 9:38.6, 20kW: Grace Wanjiru 1:38:15.

Leonard BARSOTON b. 21 Oct 1994 1.66m 56kg.
World CC: '13- 2J. Won Afr CC 2014.
Progress at 10,000m: 2013- 27:33.13. pb 5000m 13:19.04 '13.

Emmanuel Kipkemei **BETT** b. 30 Mar 83 1.70m 55kg.
Progress at 10,000m: 2011- 26:51.95, 2012- 26:51.16, 2013- 27:28.71. pbs: 5000m 13:08.35 '12, 15k 43:00+ '11, HMar 60:56 '12.

Josphat Kipkoech **BETT** b. 12 Jun 1990 Kericho 1.73m 60kg.
At 10,000m: WJ: '10- 1.
Progress at 5000m, 10,000m: 2008- 13:44.51, 27:30.85; 2009- 12:57.43, 28:21.51; 2010- 13:11.60, 28:05.46A; 2011- 13:11.29, 26:48.99; 2012- 13:32.20i, 27:39.65; 2013- 13:19.46, 27:44.26A. pbs: 3000m 7:42.38 '09, HMar 61:01 '12.

Jairus Kipchoge **BIRECH** b. 14 Dec 1992 1.68m 54kg.
At 3000mSt: AfG: '11- 4; Af-J: '11- 2.
Progress at 3000mSt: 2010- 8:50.0A, 2011- 8:11.31, 2012- 8:03.43, 2013- 8:08.72. pbs: 2000m 4:58.76 '11, 3000m 7:41.83 '13, 5000m 14:01.4A '12.

Bethwel BIRGEN b. 6 Aug 1988 Eldoret 1.78m 64kg.
At 1500m: WCh: '13- sf; WI: '14- 8.
Progress at 1500m: 2010- 3:35.60, 2011- 3:34.59, 2012- 3:31.00, 2013- 3:30.77. pbs: 800m 1:48.32 '11, 1M 3:50.42 '13, 3000m 7:37.15 '13, 5000m 14:01.0A '12.

Stanley Kipleting **BIWOTT** b. 21 Apr 1986 1.76m 60kg.
Progress HMar, Mar: 2006- 214:265, 2007- 61:20, 2010- 2:09:41, 2011- 60:23, 2:07:03; 2012- 59:44, 2:05:12; 2013- 58:56. Road pbs: 10k 28:00 '12, 15k 42:13 '13, 20k 56:02 '13, 30k 1:28:06 '12.
Marathon wins: São Paulo 2010, Chunchon 2011, Paris 2012.

Wilson Kwambai **CHEBET** b. 12 Jul 1985 Marakwet 1.74m 59kg.
World HMar: '09- 6.
Progress at HMar, Mar: 2005- 62:19, 2006- 62:38, 2007- 60:13, 2008- 59:33, 2009- 59:15, 2010- 60:31. 2:06:12; 2011- 2:05:27, 2012- 2:05:41, 2013- 2:05:36. pbs: 5000m 13:38.4A '11, Road: 10k 27:33 '09, 15k 41:44 '09, 20k 57:33 '09.
Second fastest debut marathon for 2nd Amsterdam 2010; won Rotterdam 2011 and Amsterdam 2011-13. His elder brother Joseph Biwott has marathon pb 2:09:40 '11.

Collins CHEBOI b. 25 Sep 1987 1.75m 64kg.
At 1500m: AfG: '11- 2.
Progress at 1500m: 2007- 3:490A, 2009- 3:36.24, 2010- 3:34.17, 2011- 3:32.45, 2012- 3:32.08, 2013- 3:31.53. pbs: 1M 3:51.44 '12, 2000m 5:00.30+ '12, 3000m 7:51.41 '10, 5000m 13:51.3A '13.

Vincent Kiprop **CHEPKOK** b. 5 Jul 1988 Kapkitony, Keiyo district 1.74m 60kg.
At 5000m: WCh: '09- 9. World CC: '07- 2J, '11- 3.
African CC: '12- 5.
Progress at 5000m, 10,000m: 2006- 13:17.57, 28:23.46; 2008- 13:06.41, 2009- 12:55.98, 2010- 12:51.45, 2011- 12:55.29, 2012- 12:59.28, 26:51.68; 2013- 13:15.51, 27:17.30. pbs: 1500m 3:40.47 '08, 3000m 7:30.15 '11, Road: 10k 28:12 '12, HMar 61:46 '14.

Nixon Kiplimo **CHEPSEBA** b. 12 Dec 1990 Keiyo 1.85m 66kg.
At 1500m: OG: '12- 11; WCh: '13- 4; Af-J: '09- 2.
Won DL 2011.
Progress at 1500m: 2009- 3:37.2A, 2010- 3:32.42, 2011- 3:30.94, 2012- 3:29.77, 2013- 3:33.15. pbs: 800m 1:45.6A '12, 1000m 2:18.61 '09, 1M 3:50.95 '13, 3000m 7:37.64i '11.

Ferguson Rotich **CHERUIYOT** b. 30 Nov 1989 1.83m 73kg.

At 800m: WCh: '13- sf.
Progress at 800m: 2013- 1:43.22.

Augustine Kiprono **CHOGE** b. 21 Jan 1987 Kipsigat, Nandi 1.62m 53kg.
At 5000m: CG: '06- 1; WJ: '04- 1. At 3000m: WY: '03- 1; WI: '10-12-14: 11/2/9. At 1500m: OG: '08- 9; WCh: '05- h, '09- 5. World CC: '03-05-06-08: 4J/1J/7 (4k)/12. Won KEN 1500m 2013, E. African Youth 800m/1500m/3000m 2003, Junior 1500m 2004.
Records: World 4x1500m 2009, world youth 5000m 2004, world junior 3000m 2005.
Progress at 1500m, 5000m: 2003- 3:37.48, 13:20.08; 2004- 3:36.64, 12:57.01; 2005- 3:33.99, 12:53.66; 2006- 3:32.48, 12:56.41; 2007- 3:31.73, 2008- 3:31.57, 13:09.75; 2009- 3:29.47, 2010- 3:30.22, 13:04.64; 2011- 3:31.14, 13:21.24; 2012- 3:37.47, 13:15.50; 2013- 3:33.21, 13:05.31. pbs: 800m 1:44.86 '09, 1000m 2:17.79i '09, 1M 3:50.01 '13, 2000m 4:56.30i '07, 3000m 7:28.00i/7:28.76 '11, 10,000m 29:06.5A '02.
At 17 in 2004 he become youngest to break 13 minutes for 5000m.

Dickson Kiptolo **CHUMBA** b. 27 Oct 1986 1.67m 50kg. Nandi.
Progress at Mar: 2010- 2:09:20dh, 2011- 2:07:23, 2012- 2:05:46, 2013- 2:10:15, 2014- 2:05:42. pbs: 1500m 3:44.33 '10, 5000m 13:41.34 '10, road: 10k 28:09 '13, HMar 61:34 '12, 30k 1:28:36 '12.
Marathon wins: Rome 2011, Eindhoven 2012, Tokyo 2014.

Bidan KAROKI Muchiri b. 21 Aug 1990 Nyandarua 1.67m 65kg. S&B Foods, Japan.
At 10,000m: OG: '12- 5; WCh: '13- 6; AfG: '11- 2. Won Kenyan CC 2012.
Progress at 10,000m: 2010- 27:23.62, 2011- 27:13.67, 2012- 27:05.50; 2013- 27:13.12. pbs: 1500m 3:50.91 '08, 3000m 7:37.68 '13, 5000m 13:15.75 '13, HMar 59:58 '14.
Went to Japan in 2007.

Ezekiel KEMBOI Cheboi b. 25 May 1982 Matira, near Kapsowar, Marakwet District 1.75m 62kg.
At 3000mSt: OG: '04- 1, '08- 7, '12- 1; WCh: '03-05-07-09-11-13: 2/2/2/1/1/1; CG: '02-06-10: 2/1/2; AfG: '03- 1, '07- 2; AfCh: '02- 4, '06- dq, '10- 2; Af-J: '01- 1. Won WAF 2009, Kenyan 2003, 2006-07.
Progress at 3000mSt: 2001- 8:23.66, 2002- 8:06.65, 2003- 8:02.49, 2004- 8:02.98, 2005- 8:09.04, 2006- 8:09.29, 2007- 8:05.50, 2008- 8:09.25, 2009- 7:58.85, 2010- 8:01.74, 2011- 7:55.76, 2012- 8:10.55, 2013- 7:59.03. pbs: 1500m 3:40.8A '04, 3000m 7:44.24 '12, 5000m 13:50.61 '11, 10k Rd 28:38 '11.
Five gold and three silver medals from global 3000m steeplechase races.

Stephen Kipkosgei **KIBET** b. 9 Nov 1986.
At HMar: WCh: '12- 5.
Progress at HMar: 2009- 60:34, 2010- 60:09, 2011- 60:20, 2012- 58:54, 2013- 59:59. road pbs: 10k

27:51+ '12, 15k 42:01+ '12, 20k 55:55+ '12, Mar 2:08:05 '12.
Six successive half marathon wins 2009-12

Mike Kipruto **KIGEN** b. 15 Jan 1986 Keiyo district 1.70m 54kg.
At 5000m/(10,000m): AfCh: '06- 2/2; WCp: '06- 2. World CC: '06- 5. Won Kenyan 5000m 2006.
Progress at 5000m, 10,000m: 2005- 13:22.48, 2006- 12:58.58, 28:03.70; 2008- 13:09.84, 2009- 13:04.38, 2011- 13:11.65, 27:30.53; 2012- 13:21.55A, 27:03.49; 2013- 13:36.51. pbs: 3000m 7:35.87 '06, 2M 8:20.09 '05, HMar 59:58 '11, Mar 2:08:24 '13.

Dennis Kipruto **KIMETTO** b. 22 Jan 1984.
World 25km road record 2012.
Progress at Mar: 2012- 2:04:16, 2013- 2:03:45. Road pbs: 10k 28:21 '12, 15k 42:46 '11, HMar 59:14 '12, 25k 1:11:18 '12.
Second Berlin 2012 in fastest ever marathon debut after earlier major road wins at half marathon and 25k in Berlin in 2012. Won Tokyo and Chaicago marathons 2013.

Eliud KIPCHOGE b. 5 Nov 1984 Kapsisiywa, Nandi 1.67m 52kg.
At 5000m: OG: '04- 3, '08- 2; WCh: '03-05-07-09-11: 1/4/2/5/7; CG: '10- 2. At 3000m: WI: '06- 3. World CC: '02-03-04-05: 5J/1J/4/5; HMar: '12- 6. Won WAF 5000m 2003, 3000m 2004, Kenyan CC 2005.
World junior 5000m record 2003. World road best 4M 17:10 '05.
Progress at 1500m, 5000m, 10,000m, Mar: 2002- 13:13.03, 2003- 3:36.17, 12:52.61; 2004- 3:33.20, 12:46.53; 2005- 3:33.80, 12:50.22; 2006- 3:36.25i, 12:54.94; 2007- 3:39.98, 12:50.38, 26:49.02; 2008- 13:02.06, 26:54.32; 2009- 12:56.46, 2010- 3:38.36, 12:51.21; 2011- 12:55.72i/12:59.01, 26:53.27; 2012- 12:55.34, 27:11.93; 2013- 2:04:05. pbs: 1M 3:50.40 '04, 2000m 4:59.?+ '04, 3000m 7:27.66 '11, 2M 8:07.39i '12, 8:07.68 '05; 10k Rd 26:55dh '06, 27:34 '05; HMar 59:25 '12.
Kenyan Junior CC champion 2002-03, followed World Junior CC win by winning the World 5000m title, becoming at 18 years 298 days the second youngest world champion. Age 19 bests for 3000m & 5000m 2004. Ran 26:49.02 in 10,000m debut at Hengelo in 2007. Won Hamburg Marathon on debut (2:05:30) then 2nd Berlin in 2013.

Kenneth Kiprop **KIPKEMOI** b. 2 Aug 1984 1.65m 52kg.
At 10,000m: WCh: '13- 7; AfCh: '12- 1. Kenyan champion 2012. World HMar: '14- 10.
Progress at 10,000m, HMar: 2009- 62:59A, 2011- 27:48.5A, 59:47; 2012- 26:52.65, 59:11; 2013- 27:28.50, 60:45. pbs: 3000m 7:49.28+ '11, 5000m 13:03.37 '12, 15k 43:22 '12.

John KIPKOECH (also CHEPKWONY) b. 29 Dec 1991 1.60m 52kg.
At 5000m: WCh: '13- h;WJ: '10- 2. World CC: '09- 9J.

Progress at 5000m: 2010- 13:26.03, 2012- 12:49.50, 2013- 13:01.64. pb 3000m 7:32.72 '10.

Silas KIPLAGAT b. 20 Aug 1989 Siboh village, Marakwet 1.70m 57kg.
At 1500m: OG: '12- 7; WCh: '11- 2, '13- 6; CG: '10- 1; AfCh: '10- 4; WI: '12- 6. Won DL 2012, Kenyan 2011.
Progress at 1500m: 2009- 3:39.1A, 2010- 3:29.27, 2011- 3:30.47, 2012- 3:29.63, 2013- 3:30.13. pbs: 800m 1:44.8A '12, 1M 3:49.39 '11, 3000m 7:39.94 '10, 5000m 13:55.0A '13, 10k Rd 28:00 '09.

Asbel Kipruto **KIPROP** b. 30 Jun 1989 Uasin Gishu, Eldoret. North Rift 1.86m 70kg.
At (800m)/1500m: OG: '08- 1, '12- 12; WCh: '07- 4, '09- sf/4, '11- 1, '13- 1; AfG: '07- 1; AfCh: '10- 1; CCp: '10- 6; Won DL 2010, Kenyan 2007, 2010. At 800m: AfCh: '08- 3. World CC: '07- 1J.
Progress at 800m, 1500m: 2007- 3:35.24, 2008- 1:44.71, 3:31.64; 2009- 1:43.17, 3:31.20; 2010- 1:43.45, 3:31.78; 2011- 1:43.15, 3:30.46; 2012- 1:45.91, 3:28.88; 2013- 1:44.8A, 3:27.72. pbs: 1M 3:48.50 '09, 3000m 7:42.32 '07, 5000m 13:59.7A '10.
Father David Kebenei was a 1500m runner.

Wilson KIPROP b. 14 Apr 1987 Soi, Uasin Gishu 1.72m 62kg.
At 10,000m: OG: '12- dnf; AfCh: '10- 1. World HMar: '10- 1, '14- 6. Won KEN 10,000m 2010, CC 2014.
Progress at 10,000m, Mar: 2010- 27:26.93A, 2:09:09; 2011- 27:32.9A; 2012- 27:01.98, 2013- 28:18.0A. pbs: 5000m 13:30.13i '09, 13:45.38 '08; 1Hr 20756m '09; 15k Rd 43:50 '08, HMar 59:15 '12.

Brimin KIPRUTO b. 31 Jul 1985 Korkitony, Marakwet District 1.76m 54kg.
At 3000mSt: OG: '04- 2, '08- 1 '12- 5; WCh: '05- 07-09-11: 3/1/7/2; CG: '10- 3; Af-J: '03- 2; KEN champion 2011. At 1500m: WJ: '04- 3. At 2000St: WY: '01- 2. World 4k CC: '06- 18.
Commonwealth & African 3000mSt record 2011.
Progress at 3000mSt: 2002- 8:33.0A, 2003- 8:34.5A, 2004- 8:05.52, 2005- 8:04.22, 2006- 8:08.32, 2007- 8:02.89, 2008- 8:10.26, 2009- 8:03.17, 2010- 8:00.90, 2011- 7:53.64, 2012- 8:01.73, 2013- 8:06.86. pbs: 1500m 3:35.23 '06, 2000m 4:58.76i '07, 3000m 7:39.07i '12, 7:47.33 '06; 5000m 13:58.82 '04, 2000mSt 5:36.81 '01.
First name is actually Firmin, but he stayed with the clerical error of Brimin, written when he applied for a birth certificate in 2001.

Conseslus KIPRUTO b. 8 Dec 1994 1.74m 55kg.
At 3000mSt: WCh: '13- 2; WJ: '12- 1; won DL 2013. At 2000St: WY: '11- 1. World CC: 2013- 5J.
Progress at 3000mSt: 2011- 8:27.30, 2012- 8:03.49, 2013- 8:01.16. pbs: 1000m 2:19.85 '12, 1500m 3:39.57 '13, 3000m 7:44.09 '12, 2000mSt 5:28.65 '11.

Geoffrey Kamworer **KIPSANG** b. 28 Nov 1992 1.76m 60kg.
World CC: '11- 1J; HMar: '14- 1.
Progress at 10,000m, HMar, Mar: 2011- 27:06.35, 59:31; 2012- 59:26, 2:06:12; 2013- 28:17.0A, 58:54,

2:06:26; 2014- 59:08, 2:07:37. pbs: 1500m 3:48.15 '10, 3000m 7:54.15 '10. 5000m 13:12:23 '11; Road: 15k 42:05 '12, 20k 56:02 '13.
3rd in Berlin Marathon 2012 (on debut) and 2013. Won RAK half marathon 2013.

Wilson KIPSANG Kiprotich b. 15 Mar 1982 Keiyo district 1.82m 62kg.
At Mar: OG: '12- 3; HMar: WCh: '09- 4.
World marathon record 2013.
Progress at HMar, Mar: 2008- 59:16, 2009- 58:59, 2010- 60:04, 2:04:57; 2011- 60:49, 2:03:42; 2012- 59:06, 2:04:44; 2013- 61:02, 2:03:23. pbs: 5000m 13:55.7A '09, 10,000m 28:37.0A '07; Road: 10k 27:42 '09, 15k 41:51+ '11, 10M 44:59+ '11, 20k 56:10+ '12, 25k 1:12:58, 30k 1:28:02 '13.
At marathon: third in Paris in 2:07:13 on debut, and won Frankfurt in 2010 and 2011, Lake Biwa 2011, London and Honolulu 2012, Berlin 2013. Won Great North Run 2012.

Mark Kosgei **KIPTOO** b. 21 Jun 1976 Lugafri 1.75m 64kg. Kenyan Air Force.
At 5000m: CG: '10- 3; AfG: '07- 9; AfCh: '10- 3, '12- 1 (2 10,000m). World CC: '08- 14, '09- 7. Won World Military 5000m & 2nd 10,000m 2007, KEN 5000m 2008.
Progress at 5000m, 10,000m: 2007- 13:12.60, 28:22.62; 2008- 13:06.60, 27:14.67; 2009- 12:57.62, 2010- 12:53.46, 28:37.4A; 2011- 12:59.91, 26:54.64; 2012- 13:06.23, 27:18.22; 2013- 13:20.51, 28:24.04A. pbs: 1500m 3:48.0A '05, 3000m 7:32.97 '09, 2M 8:29.96 '12, HMar 60:29 '11, Mar 2:06:16 '13 (2nd Frankfurt on debut).

Bernard KIPYEGO Kiprop b. 16 Jul 1986 Kapkitony, Keiyo district 1.60m 50kg.
At 10,000m: WCh: '09- 5; Af-J: '03- 3. At Mar: WCh: '13- 12. World CC: '05-07-08: 2J/3/10; HMar: '09- 2.
Progress at 10,000m, Mar: 2003- 29:29.09, 2004- 28:18.94, 2005- 27:04.45, 2006- 27:19.45, 2007- 26:59.51, 2008- 27:08.06, 2009- 27:18.47, 2010- 2:07:01, 2011- 2:06:29, 2012- 2:06:40, 2013- 2:07:19. pbs: 3000m 7:54.91 '05, 5000m 13:09.96 '05, Road: 15k 42:34 '11, 10M 45:44 '11, HMar 59:10 '09.
Won in Berlin on half marathon debut in 59:34 in 2009, 5th Rotterdam on marathon debut 2010, 2nd Paris 2011 and Beijing 2013; 3rd Chicago 2011 and Tokyo 2013.

Michael Kipkorir **KIPYEGO** b. 2 Oct 1983 Kemeloi, Marakwet 1.68m 59kg.
At 3000mSt: WCh: '03- h; WJ: '02- 1; AfCh: '08- 2. At 3000m: WY: '99- 8; Af-J: '01- 2. At Mar: WCh: '13- 25. World CC: '02-03-07: 12J/4 4k/6.
Progress at 3000mSt: 2001- 8:41.26, 2002- 8:22.90, 2003- 8:13.02, 2004- 8:23.14, 2005- 8:10.66, 2006- 8:14.99, 2007- 8:11.62, 2008- 8:09.05, 2009- 8:08.48, 2010- 8:16.46. At Mar: 2011- 2:06:48, 2012- 2:07:37, 2013- 2:06:58, 2014- 2:06:58. pbs: 1500m 3:39.93 '05, 3000m 7:50.03 '09.
Won Tokyo Marathon 2012, 2nd 2013, 4th 2014. Brother of Sally Kipyego.

Abel KIRUI b. 4 Jun 1982 Bornet, Rift Valley 1.77m 62kg. Police.
At Mar: OG: '12- 2; WCh: '09- 1, '11- 1.
Progress at Mar: 2006- 2:15:22, 2007- 2:06:51, 2008- 2:07:38, 2009- 2:05:04, 2010- 2:08:04, 2011- 2:07:38, 2012- 2:07:56. pbs: 1500m 3:46.10 '05, 3000m 7:55.90 '06, 5000m 13:52.71 '05, 10,000m 28:16.86A '08; Road: 10k 27:59 '09, 15k 42:22 '07, 10M 46:40 '11, HMar 60:11 '07, 25k: 1:13:41 '08, 30k 1:28:25 '08.
Brilliantly retained World marathon title with halves of 65:07 and 62:31 and a fastest 5k split of 14:18. Won Vienna Marathon 2008, 2nd Berlin 2007, 3rd Rotterdam 2009. Uncle Mike Rotich has marathon pb 2:06:33 '03.

Gilbert Kiplangat **KIRUI** b. 22 Jan 1994 1.72m 55kg.
At 3000mSt: WJ: '12- 2; won Af-J 2011. At 2000St: WY: '11- 2.
Progress at 3000mSt: 2010- 8:40.1A, 2011- 8:25.03, 2012- 8:11.27, 2013- 8:06.96. pbs: 2000mSt 5:30.49 '11.

Alfred KIRWA YEGO b. 28 Nov 1986 Eldoret 1.75m 56kg. Cento Torri Pavia, Italy.
At 800m: OG: '08- 3; WCh: '05- h, '07- 1, '09- 2, '11- 7; WJ: '04- 2; AfCh: '06- 3, '10- 2. Won WAF 2008.
Progress at 800m, 1500m: 2004- 1:47.39, 3:37.95; 2005- 1:44.45, 3:50.14; 2006- 1:43.89, 3:38.55; 2007- 1:44.50, 2008- 1:44.01, 3:33.69; 2009- 1:42.67, 3:33.68; 2010- 1:43.97, 2011- 1:44.07, 2012- 1:44.49, 2013- 1:46.43. pbs: 1000m 2:17.60 '10, 1M 3:55.18 '11. Ran 24.6 last 200m to win 2007 World 800m.

Timothy KITUM b. 20 Nov 1994 Marakwet 1.72m 60kg.
At 800m: OG: '12- 3; WJ: '12- 2; WY: '11- 3.
Progress at 800m: 2011- 1:44.98, 2012- 1:42.53, 2013- 1:44.45. pbs: 600m 1:14.4A '12, 1000m 2:17.96 '12.

Sammy Kiprop **KITWARA** b. 26 Nov 1986 Sagat village, Marakwet district 1.77m 54kg.
At 10,000m: Kenyan champion 2009. World HMar: '09- 10, '10- 3.
Progress at 10,000m, HMar, Mar: 2007- 28:11.6A, 2008- 28:12.26A, 60:54; 2009- 27:44.46A, 58:58; 2010- 28:32.77A, 59:34; 2011- 58:47, 2012- 2:05:54, 2013- 61:53, 2:05:16; 2014- 2:06:30. pbs: 5000m 13:34.0A '08, Road: 10k 27:11 '10, 15k 41:54 '09, 10M 45:17 '08, 20k 57:42 '08.
4th Chicago marathon 2012, 3rd Rotterdam & Chicago 2013, Tokyo 2014

Bernard Kiprop **KOECH** b. 31 Jan 1988 1.65m 50kg.
At Mar: WCh: '13- dnf.
Progress at Mar: 2013- 2:04:53. pbs: 1500m 3:44.33 '10, 5000m 13:41.34 '10, road: 10k 27:54 '12, 15k 42:32 '12, 20k 56:54 '13, HMar 59:10 '12, 58:41dh '13.
Fifth in Dubai on marathon debut (6th fastest ever) and third in Amsterdam in 2013.

Isiah Kiplangat **KOECH** b. 19 Dec 1993 Kericho 1.78m 60kg.
At 5000m: OG: '12- 5; WCh: '11- 4, '13- 3; won DL 5000m 2012, Kenyan 2011, 2013. At 3000m: WY: '09- 1. World CC: '10- 4J, '11- 10J.
World junior records indoors: 5000m 2011, 3000m 2011 & 2012.
Progress at 5000m, 10,000m: 2010- 13:07.70, 2011- 12:53.29i/12:54.18, 2012- 12:48.64, 27:17.03; 2013- 12:56.08. pbs: 1500m 3:38.7A '12, 3000m 7:30.43 '12, 2M 8:14.16 '11.

Paul Kipsiele **KOECH** b. 10 Nov 1981 Cheplanget, Buret District 1.68m 57kg.
At 3000mSt: OG: '04- 3; WCh: '05- 7, '09- 4, '13- 4; AfG: '03- 2; AfCh: '06- 1; WCp: '06- 2; won DL 2010-12, WAF 2005-08. At 3000m: WI: '08- 2.
Progress at 3000mSt: 2001- 8:15.92, 2002- 8:05.44, 2003- 7:57.42, 2004- 7:59.65, 2005- 7:56.37, 2006- 7:59.94, 2007- 7:58.80, 2008- 8:00.57, 2009- 8:01.26, 2010- 8:02.07, 2011- 7:57.32, 2012- 7:54.31, 2013- 8:02.63. pbs: 1500m 3:37.92 '07, 2000m 5:00.9+i '08, 3000m 7:32.78i '10, 7:33.93 '05; 2M 8:06.48i/ 8:13.31 '08, 5000m 13:02.69i 12, 13:05.18 '10.

Micah Kemboi **KOGO** b. 3 Jun 1986 Burnt Forest, Uasin Gishu 1.70m 60kg.
At 10,000m: OG: '08- 3; WCh: '09- 7.
World 10k road record (27:01) 2009.
Progress at 5000m, 10,000m: 2004- 14:02.99, 2005- 13:16.31, 2006- 13:00.07, 26:35.63; 2007- 13:10.68, 26:58.42; 2008- 13:03.71, 27:04.11; 2009- 13:01.30, 27:26.33; 2010- 13:07.62, 2011- 13:46.01, 27:50.50. At Mar: 2013- 2:06:56. pbs: 2000m 5:03.05 '06, 3000m 7:38.67 '07, 2M 8:20.88 '05; Road: 15k 41:51+ '11, 10M 44:59+ '11, 20k 56:10+ '12, HMar 59:07 '12.
Won Van Damme 10,000m in Brussels in 2006 for 6th world all-time. 2nd Boston on marathon debut 2013, then 4th Chicago.

Daniel Kipchirchir **KOMEN** b. 27 Nov 1984 Chemorgong, Kolbatek district 1.75m 60kg.
At 1500m: WCh: '05- h, '07/11- sf; WI: '06- 2, '08- 2; won WAF 2007. At 5000m: Af-J: '03- 2.
Progress at 1500m, 5000m: 2003- 13:49.20, 2004- 3:34.66, 13:16.26; 2005- 3:29.72, 2006- 3:29.02, 2007- 3:31.75, 2008- 3:31.49, 13:24.39; 2009- 3:34.86i, 2010- 3:32.16, 13:04.02; 2011- 3:32.47A, 13:20.80; 2012- 3:32.98, 13:09.90; 2013- 3:33.05.
pbs: 800m 1:47.3A '05, 1000m 2:16.9+ '06, 1M 3:48.28 '07, 3000m 7:31.41 '11.

Leonard Patrick **KOMON** b. 10 Jan 1988 Korungotuny Village, Mt. Eldon District 1.75m 52kg.
World CC: '06-07-08-09-10: 2J/4J/2/4/4.
World road records 10km and 15km 2010.
Progress at 5000m, 10,000m: 2006- 13:04.12, 2007- 13:04.79, 2008- 13:17.48, 26:57.08; 2009- 12:58.24, 28:02.24A; 2010- 12:59.15, 2011- 26:55.29, 2012- 27:01.58. pbs: 2000m 5:04.0+ '07, 3000m 7:33.27 '09, 2M 8:22.56 '07, road 10k 26:44 '10, 15k 41:13 '10, 10M 44:27 '11, HMar 59:14 '14 (fastest ever debut at Berlin).

Japheth Kipyegon **KORIR** b. 30 Jun 1993 Sotik 1.68m 55kg.
At 5000m: 3rd Comm YthG 2008. World CC: 09-10-13: 5J/3J/1; Af-J CC: 11- 1, 12- 2.
Progress at 5000m: 2008- 13:57.2A, 2010- 13:19.43, 2011- 13:17.18, 2012- 13:11.44i, 2013- 13:31.94 pbs: 3000m 7:40.37 '12, 10k Rd 28:43 '12.
Became youngest ever senior men's world cross-country champion in 2013.

Leonard Kirwa **KOSENCHA** b. 21 Aug 1994 Trans Mara 1.76m 62kg.
At 800m: WY: 11- 1.
World youth 800m record 2011.
Progress at 800m: 2011- 1:44.08, 2012- 1:43.40, 2013- 1:48.82.

James Kipsang **KWAMBAI** b. 28 Feb 1983 Marakwet East district 1.62m 52kg
Commonwealth marathon record 2009.
Progress at Mar: 2006- 2:10:20, 2007- 2:12:25, 2008- 2:05:36, 2009- 2:04:27, 2010- 2:11:31, 2011- 2:08:50, 2012- 2:05:50, 2013- 2:06:25. pbs: Road: 10k 28:17 '02, 20k 58:51 '08, HMar 59:09 '09, 30k 1:28:27 '08.
Won Brescia and Beijing marathons 2006, took 4:44 off pb when 2nd in Berlin 2008 and went to joint second all-time when 2nd in Rotterdam 2009. Won Joongang Seoul Marathon 2011-13.

Lawi LALANG b. 15 Jun 1991 Eldoret 1.70m 58kg. University of Arizona.
Won NCAA CC 2011, 5000m 2013 & 10,000m 2013; indoor 3000m & 5000m 2013, 1M and 3000m 2013.
Progress at 5000m: 2011- 13:30.64, 2012- 13:18.55, 2013- 13:00.95. pbs: 800m 1:48.88 '11, 1500m 3:33.20 '13, 1M 3:52.88i '14, 3000m 7:42.79i '13, 8:00.07 '11; 10,000m 28:14.63 '13.
Older brother **Boaz** (b. 8 Fen 1989) won CG 800m '10, pb 1:42.95 '10.

Martin Kiptolo **LEL** b. 29 Oct 1978 Kapsabet 1.71m 54kg.
At Mar: OG: '08- 5. World HMar: '03- 1.
African record 30km 2008.
Progress at Mar: 2002- 2:10:02, 2003- 2:10:30, 2004- 2:13:38, 2005- 2:07:26, 2006- 2:06:41, 2007- 2:07:41, 2008- 2:05:15, 2011- 2:05:45, 2012- 2:06:51. pbs: 10k 27:25 '06, 15k 42:41 '07, 10M 45:40 '07, HMar 59:30 '06, 30k 1:28:30 '08.
Exclusively a road runner. Marathons: dnf Prague and 2nd in Venice 2002, 3rd Boston 2003-04, 1st New York 2003 and 2007 and London 2005, 2007 and 2008 (2nd 2006 and 2011-12). He won the Marathon Majors prize for 2007-08. Won Great North Run 2007, 2009.

Thomas Pkemei **LONGOSIWA** b. 14 Jan 1982 West Pokot 1.75m 57kg. North Rift.
At 5000m: OG: '08- 12, '12- 3; WCh: '11- 6, '13- 4; AfG: '07- 6. World CC: '06- 13J (but dq after birthdate found to be 1982). Won Kenyan 5000m 2007.
Progress at 5000m: 2006- 13:35.3A, 2007-

12:51.95, 2008- 13:14.36, 2009- 13:03.43, 2010- 13:05.60, 2011- 12:56.08, 2012- 12:49.04, 2013- 12:59.81. pbs: 1500m 3:41.92 '13, 2000m 5:01.6+ '10, 3000m 7:30.09 '09, 10,000m 28:11.3A '06.

Patrick MAKAU Musyoki b. 2 Mar 1985 Manyanzwani, Tala Kangundo district 1.73m 57kg.
World HMar: '07- 2, '08- 2.
World 30km and marathon records 2011.
Progress at HMar, Mar: 2005- 62:00, 2006- 62:42, 2007- 58:56, 2008- 59:29, 2009- 58:52, 2:06:14; 2010- 59:51, 2:04:48; 2011- 2:03:38, 2012- 2:06:08. pbs: 3000m 7:54.50 '07, 5000m 13:42.84 '06. Road: 10k 27:27 '07, 15k 41:30 '09, 10M 45:41 '12, 20k 55:53 '07, 30k 1:27:38 '11.
Second fastest ever debut marathon when 4th Rotterdam 2009 and won there a year later in 2:04:48 for fourth world all-time. Won Berlin 2010 and 2011, Frankfurt 2012.

Moses Ndiema **MASAI** b. 1 Jun 1986 Kapsogom 1.72m 57kg.
At 10,000m: OG: '08- 4, '12- 12; WCh: '09- 3; WJ: '04- 10. World CC: '04-05-08: 16J/7J/5. Won Afr-J 5000 & 10,000m 2005, Kenyan CC 2006.
World junior marathon record 2005.
Progress at 5000m, 10,000m: 2004- 13:25.5+e, 27:07.29; 2005- 13:24.36, 28:08.6A; 2006- 13:13.28, 27:03.20; 2007- 13:08.81, 26:49.20; 2008- 12:50.55, 27:04.11; 2009- 13:06.16, 26:57.39; 2010- 13:02.45, 2011- 13:13.03, 27:10.05; 2012- 12:59.21, 27:02.25. pbs: 1500m 3:37.3A '08, 3000m 7:44.75 '09; Road: 15k 45:18 '09, 10M 45:16 '09, Mar 2:10:13 '05.
Marathon wins (while a junior) at Hannover 2004 and Essen 2005. His sister is **Linet Masai** (qv) and their younger brother **Dennis** won the World Junior 10,000m in pb 27:53.88 in 2010. His partner **Doris Changeiywo** was 4th in the 2008 World CC, 2nd CG 10,000m 2010.

Richard Kipkemboi **MATEELONG** b. 14 Oct 1983 Lenape, Narok District 1.79m 65g. Police.
At 3000mSt: OG: '08- 3; WCh: '07- 3, '09- 2, '11- 7; CG: '10- 1; AfCh: '04-08-10: 2/1/1; CCp: '10- 1. World CC: '10- 7. Won Kenyan CC 2007, 3000mSt 2009.
Progress at 3000mSt: 2004- 8:05.96, 2005- 8:10.97, 2006- 8:07.50, 2007- 8:06.66, 2008- 8:07.64, 2009- 8:00.89, 2010- 8:06.44, 2011- 8:07.41, 2013- 8:40.47. pbs: 1500m 3:41.2A '05, 3000m 7:48.71 '05, 5000m 13:30.4A '06, 10,000m 28:18.4A '07.

Martin Irungu **MATHATHI** b. 25 Dec 1985 Nyahururu 1.67m 52kg. Suzuki, Japan.
At 10,000m: OG: '08- 7; WCh: '05- 5, '07- 3, '11- 5. World CC: '06- 3.
Progress at 5000m, 10,000m: 2003- 14:09.3A, 27:43.16; 2004- 13:03.84, 27:22.46; 2005- 13:05.99, 27:08.42; 2006- 13:05.55, 27:10.51; 2007- 13:22.13, 27:09.90; 2008- 13:46.87, 27:08.25; 2009- 13:11.46, 26:59.88; 2010- 13:10.94, 2011- 13:15.93, 27:23.85; 2012- 13:27.06, 27:35.16; 2013- 27:52.65. pbs: 1500m 3:38.57 '06, Road: 10M 44:51 '04 (world junior best), 15k 42:14 '10, 20k 56:44 '10, HMar

58:56 '11, Mar 2:07:16 '13.
Won Great North Run 2011. Won Fukuoka Marathon 2013.

Bernard Nganga MBUGUA b. 17 Jan 1985 1.70m 55kg.
Progress at 3000mSt: 2007- 8:43.0A, 2009- 8:17.94, 2010- 8:16.22, 2011- 8:05.88, 2012- 8:08.33, 2013- 8:19.14. pbs: 1500m 3:40.29 '13, 5000m 13:49.19 '11, 2000mSt 5:25.70 '10.

Josphat Kiprono MENJO b. 20 Aug 1979 Kapsabet 1.68m 50kg.
At 5000m: AfG: '07- 2; AfCh: '06- 5, '08- 5. At 10,000m: WCh: '07- 8; won W.Mil G 2011.
Progress at 5000m, 10,000m: 2004- 13:48.7A, 2005- 13:14.38, 2006- 13:09.24, 27:29.45; 2007- 13:06.69, 27:04.61; 2008- 13:06.17, 27:09.37; 2010- 12:55.95, 26:56.74; 2011- 13:21.10, 27:55.81; 2012- 13:10.55, 2013- 28:03.0A. pbs: 1500m 3:38.40 '10, 1M 3:53.62 '10. 3000m 7:42.6+ '10, 2M 8:18.96 '07, HMar 61:42 '10.

Moses Cheruiyot **MOSOP** b. 17 Jul 1985 Kamasia, Marakwet 1.72m 57kg. Police officer.
At 10,000m: OG: '04- 7; WCh: '05- 3. World CC: '02-03-05-07-09: 10J/7J/18/2/11; HMar: '10- 10. Won KEN 10,000m 2006, CC 2009.
World records 25,000m and 30,000m 2011.
Progress at 5000m, 10,000m: 2002- 29:38.6A, 2003- 13:11.75, 27:13.66; 2004- 13:09.68, 27:30.66; 2005- 13:06.83, 27:08.96; 2006- 12:54.46, 27:17.00; 2007- 13:07.89, 26:49.55. At Mar: 2011- 2:03:06wdh/ 2:05:37, 2012- 2:05:03, 2013- 2:11:19. pbs: 3000m 7:36.88 '06, 15k Rd 42:25+ '10, HMar 59:20 '10, 20000m 58:02.2 '11, 25000m 1:12:25.4 '11, 30000m 1:26:47.4 '11.
Second with fastest ever marathon debut at Boston and won Chicago 2011. 3rd Rotterdam 2012. Married to Florence Kiplagat (qv).

Abel Kiprop **MUTAI** b. 2 Oct 1988 Nandi 1.72m 73kg.
At 3000mSt: OG: '12- 3; WCh: '13- 7; Af-J: '07- 1; Kenyan champion 2012. At 2000mSt: WY: '05- 1.
Progress at 3000mSt: 2006- 8:35.38, 2007- 8:29.76, 2009- 8:11.40, 2011- 8:21.02, 2012- 8:01.67, 2013- 8:08.83. pbs: 3000m 8:05.16 '06, 5000m 14:07.80 '06, 2000mSt 5:24.69 '05.

Emmanuel Kipchirchir **MUTAI** b. 12 Oct 1984 Tulwet, Rift Valley 1.68m 54kg.
At Mar: OG: '12- 17; WCh: '09- 2.
Progress at Mar: 2007- 2:06:29, 2008- 2:06:15, 2009- 2:06:53, 2010- 2:06:23, 2011- 2:04:40, 2012- 2:08:01, 2013- 2:03:52. pbs: 10,000m 28:21.14 '06, Road: 10k 27:51 '06, 15k 42:11 '10, 20k 56:44 '10, HMar 59:52 '11, 30k 1:28:04 '13.
Made marathon debut with 7th in Rotterdam in 2:13:06 in 2007, then won in Amsterdam. London: 4th 2008 & 2009, 2nd 2010 & 2013, 1st 2011. 2nd New York 2010-11, Chicago 2013. World Marathon Majors winner 2010/11.

Geoffrey Kiprono **MUTAI** b. 7 Oct 1981 Koibatek District 1.83m 56kg. Policeman.

At 10,000m: AfCh: '10- 3. World CC: '11- 5. Won Kenyan 10,000m 2013, CC 2011.
Progress at 10,000m, Mar: 2007- 2:12:50sh?, 2008- 28:01.74, 2:07:50; 2009- 2:07:01, 2010- 27:27.79A, 2:04:55; 2011- 2:03:02wdh/2:05:06, 2012- 28:23.0A, 2:04:15; 2013- 27:55.3A, 2:08:24. pbs: 15k 42:12+ '13, 20k 56:02 '13, HMar 58:58 '13, 30k 1:28:49+ '13.
Marathons: Won Monte Carlo 2008, Eindhoven 2008 & 2009, Boston 2011, New York 2011 & 2013, Berlin 2012; 2nd Rotterdam and Berlin 2010. World Marathon Majors winner 2011/12.

Caleb Mwangangi **NDIKU** b. 9 Oct 1992 1.83m 68kg.
At 1500m: WJ: '10- 1; WY: '09- 2; AfG: '11- 1; AfCh: '12- 1; Kenyan champion 2012. At 3000m: WI: '14- 1. World CC: '10- 1J.
Progress at 1500m: 2009- 3:38.2A, 2010- 3:37.30, 2011- 3:32.02, 2012- 3:32.39, 2013- 3:29.50. pbs: 800m 1:52.6A '07, 1M 3:49.77 '11, 3000m 7:30.99 '12, 5000m 13:03.80 '13, 10,000m 28:39.8A '13.

Lucas Kimeli **ROTICH** b. 16 Apr 1990 1.71m 57kg.
At 3000mSt: WY: '07- 2. World CC: '08- 3J, '10- 18.
Progress at 5000m, 10,000m: 2007- 29:12.5A, 2008- 13:15.54, 2009- 12:58.70, 28:15.0A; 2010- 12:55.06, 27:33.59; 2011- 13:00.02, 26:43.98; 2012- 13:09.58, 27:09.38. pbs: 1500m 3:43.64 '08, 3000m 7:35.57 '11, HMar 59:44 '11, Mar 2:08:12 '13.

David Lekuta **RUDISHA** b. 17 Dec 1988 Kilgoris 1.89m 73kg. Masai.
At 800m: OG: '12- 1; WCh: '09- sf, '11- 1; WJ: '06- 1/4R; AfCh: '08- 1, '10- 1; Af-J: '07- 1; CCp: '10- 1. Won DL 2010-11, WAF 2009, Kenyan 2009-11.
Three world 800m records 2010-12, four African records 2009-10.
Progress at 800m: 2006- 1:46.3A, 2007- 1:44.15, 2008- 1:43.72, 2009- 1:42.01, 2010- 1:41.01, 2011- 1:41.33, 2012- 1:40.91, 2013- 1:43.87. pbs: 400m 45.50 '10, 600m 1:14.28+ '11.
IAAF Male Athlete of the Year 2010, won 26 successive 800m finals 2009-11. His father Daniel won 4x400m silver medal at 1968 Olympics with 440y pb 45.5A '67.

Edwin Cheruiyot **SOI** b. 3 Mar 1986 Kericho 1.68m 53kg.
At 5000m: OG: '08- 3, '12- h; WCh: '13- 5; AfCh: '10- 1; CCp: '10- 4. At 3000m: WI: '08- 4, '12- 3; won WAF 3000m 2007, 5000m 2007-08. World CC: '06- 8 4k, '07- 9.
Progress at 5000m, 10,000m: 2002- 29:06.5A, 2004- 13:22.57, 2005- 13:10.78, 2006- 12:52.40, 27:14.83; 2007- 13:10.21, 2008- 13:06.22, 2009- 12:55.03, 2010- 12:58.91, 2011- 12:59.15, 2012- 12:55.99, 2013- 12:51.34. pbs: 1500m 3:44.76 '05, 2000m 5:01.4+ '10, 3000m 7:27.55 '11, 2M 8:14.10 '11, 10k Rd 28:13 '08.

Paul Kipngetich **TANUI** b. 22 Dec 1990 Chesubeno village, Moio district 1.72m 54kg. Kyudenko Corporation, Japan.

At 10,000m: WCh: '11- 9, '13- 3. World CC: '09-10-11: 4J/8/2. Won Kenyan CC 2010.
Progress at 10,000m: 2009- 27:25.24, 2010- 27:17.61, 2011- 26:50.63, 2012- 27:27.56, 2013- 27:21.50. pbs: 1500m 3:43.97 '10, 3000m 7:50.88 '11, 5000m 13:04.65 '11.

Hillary Kipsang **YEGO** b. 2 Apr 1992 1.78m 60kg.
At 2000mSt: WY: '09- 1.
Progress at 3000mSt: 2009- 8:46.8A, 2010- 8:19.50, 2011- 8:07.71, 2012- 8:11.83. 2013- 8:03:57. pbs: 1500m 3:43.3 '10, 3000m 7:53.18 '10, 2000mSt 5:25.33 '09, 10k Rd 29:10 '11, Mar 2:13:59 '13.
Won 2013 Athens Classic Marathon on debut at the distance.

Julius Kiplagat **YEGO** b. 4 Jan 1989 1.75m 85kg.
At JT: OG: '12- 12; WCh: '13- 4; CG: '10- 7; AfG: '11- 1; AfCh: '10- 3, '12- 1. Kenyan champion 2008-13.
Five Kenyan javelin records 2011-13.
Progress at JT: 2008- 72.18A, 2009- 74.00A, 2010- 75.44, 2011- 78.34A, 2012- 81.81; 2013- 85.40.

Women

Emily CHEBET Muge b. 18 Feb 1986 Bornet 1.57m 45kg.
At 10,000m: WCh: '07- 9, '13- 4; AfCh: '06- 3. World CC: '03-10-13: 5J/1/1.
Progress at 5000m, 10,000m: 2006- 31:33.39, 2007- 32:31.21, 2010- 32:49.43A. 2011- 31:30.22, 2013- 14:46.89, 30:47.02. pbs: 1500m 4:18.75 '05, 3000m 8:53.46 '05; Road 10k 30:58 '12, HMar 68:20 '13.
Has daughter Emily. Married to Edward Muge (Kenyan 10,000m champion 2008 in pb 27:52.09A).

Milcah CHEMOS Cheywa b. 24 Feb 1986 Bugaa Village, Mt. Elgon district 1.63m 48kg. Police.
At 3000mSt: OG: '12- 4; WCh: '09- 3, '11- 3, '13- 1; CG: '10- 1; AfCh: '10- 1; CCp: '10- 2. Won DL 2010-13, KEN 2010-11.
Commonwealth & African 3000mSt record 2012.
Progress at 3000mSt: 2009- 9:08.57, 2010- 9:11.71, 2011- 9:12.89, 2012- 9:07.14, 2013- 9:11.65. pbs: 800m 2:04.35A '11, 1500m 4:12.3A '09, 2000m 5:41.64 '09, 3000m 8:43.92 '09, 2000mSt 6:16.95 '13.
Married to Alex Sang (pb 800m 1:46.84 '08). Started athletics seriously after birth of daughter Lavine Jemutai and in first season, 2008, was 4th in Kenyan 800m. Rapid progress from first steeplechase in April 2009.

Joyce CHEPKIRUI b. 20 Aug 1988. Buret district.
At 10,000m: OG: '12- dnf. At 1500m: AfG: '11- 2; Af-J: '07- 5. At HMar: WCh: '10- 5. African CC: '12- 1. Won Kenyan CC 2012.
Progress at 10,000m, HMar: 2007- 75:11, 2009- 71:47, 2010- 69:25, 2011- 31:26.10, 69:04; 2012- 32:34.71A, 67:03; 2013- 68:15. pbs: 1500m 4:08.80A '11, 3000mSt 10:26.7A '08; Road: 10k 30:37 '11, 10M 51:33 '13.

Lydia Tum **CHEPKURUI** b. 23 Aug 1984 1.70m 52kg.
At 3000mSt: WCh: '13- 2; AfG: '11- 4, Kenyan champion 2013.
Progress at 3000mSt: 2011- 9:30.73, 2012- 9:14.98, 2013- 9:12.55. pbs: 1500m 4:14.97 '12, 3000m 8:56.43i '14, 2M 9:45.97i '14.

Gladys CHERONO b. 18 Feb 1986 Bornet 1.58m 46kg.
At 10,000m: WCh: '13- 2; AfCh: '12- 1 (1 5000m). World HMar: '14- 1. Won Kenyan 5000m 2012.
Progress at 5000m, 10,000m: 2005- 16:16.8A, 2007- 16:03.8A, 2008- 15:56.0A, 2012- 15:39.5A, 32:41.40; 2013- 14:47.12, 30:29.23. pbs: 1500m 4:25.13 '04, 3000m 8:34.05 '13, HMar 66:48 '13.

Mercy CHERONO b. 7 May 1991 Kericho 1.68m 54kg.
At (3000m)/5000m: WCh: '11- 5, '13- 2; WJ: '08-(1), '10- 1/2; WY: '07- (1); Af-J: '09- 1/2. World CC: '07-09-10: 23J/2J/1J. Won Afr CC 2011.
Progress at 5000m: 2007- 16:49.13A, 2009- 15:46.74A, 2010- 14:47.13, 2011- 14:35.13, 2012- 14:47.18, 2013- 14:40.33. pbs: 800m 2:05.7A '13, 1500m 4:02.31 '11, 2000m 5:35.65 '10, 3000m 8:31.23 '13, 10,000m 34:33.4A '06.

Sharon Jemutai **CHEROP** b. 16 Mar 1984 Marakwet district 1.57m 45kg.
At Mar: WCh: '11- 3. At 10,000m: AfG: '99- 5. At 5000m: WJ: '00- 3. World CC: '02- 10J.
Progress at Mar: 2007- 2:38:45, 2008- 2:39:52, 2009- 2:33:53, 2010- 2:22:43, 2011- 2:22:42wdh/2:29:14, 2012- 2:22:39, 2013- 2:22:28. pbs: 3000m 9:09.23 '04, 5000m 15:40.7A '00, 10,000m 32:03.0A '11, HMar 67:08 '11.
Marathon wins: Toronto and Hamburg 2010, Boston and Turin 2012, Singapore 2013; 2nd Berlin 2013, 3rd Boston 2011, 2013.

Vivian CHERUIYOT b. 11 Sep 1983 Keiyo 1.55m 38kg.
At 5000m (/10,000m): OG: '00- 14, '08- 5, '12- 2/3; WCh: '07- 2, '09- 1, '11- 1/1; CG: '10- 1; WJ: '02- 3; AfG '99- 3; AfCh: '10- 1; CCp: '10- 1; won DL 2010-12. At 3000m: WY: '99- 3; WI: '10- 2. World CC: '98-9-00-01-02-04-06-07-11: 5J/2J/1J/4J/3J/8 4k/8 4k/8/1. Won KEN 1500m 2009, 5000m 2010-11, 10,000m 2011-12.
African 2000m record 2009, Commonwealth 5000m 2009 & 2011, indoor 3000m (8:30.53) 2009; Kenyan 5000m 2007 & 2011.
Progress at 5000m, 10,000m: 1999- 15:42.79A, 2000- 15:11.11, 2001- 15:59.4A, 2002- 15:49.7A, 2003- 15:44.8A, 2004- 15:13.26, 2006- 14:47.43, 2007- 14:22.51, 2008- 14:25.43, 2009- 14:37.01, 2010- 14:27.41, 2011- 14:20.87, 30:48.98; 2012- 14:35.62, 30:30.44. pbs: 1500m 4:06.6A '12, 2000m 5:31.52 '09, 3000m 8:28.66 '07, 2M 9:12.35i '10.
Laureus Sportswomen of the Year for 2011. Married Moses Kirui on 14 Apr 2012; son born 19 Oct 2013.

Irene JELAGAT b. 10 Dec 1988 Samutet, Nyanza 1.62m 45kg.
At 1500m: OG: '08- h; WCh: '09- h; CG: '10- 6; AfG: '11- 1; AfCh: '08- 5, '10- 4; WJ: '06- 1; WY: '05- dns; WI: '10- 5. At 3000m: WI: 13- 4.
Progress at 1500m: 2005- 4:21.3A, 2006- 4:08.88, 2007- 4:10.27, 2008- 4:04.59, 2009- 4:03.62, 2010- 4:03.76, 2011- 4:02.59. pb 800m 2:02.99 '06, 3000m 8:40.75i '14, 5000m 16:08.2A '13.

Jemima JELAGAT Sumgony b. 21 Dec 1984
Progress at Mar: 2006- 2:35:22, 2007- 2:29:41, 2008- 2:30:18, 2010- 2:32:34, 2011- 2:28:32, 2012- 2:31:52, 2013- 2:20:48. pbs: 5000m 16:51.0A '13, 10,000m 33:08.0A '13, Road: 10k 31:15 '06, 15k 47:14 '13, 10M 50:38 '13, 20k 62:32 '13, HMar 68:35 '13.
2nd Chicago Marathon 2013.

Pamela JELIMO b. 5 Dec 1989 Kapsabet 1.75m 60kg.
At 800m: OG: '08- 1, '12- 4; WCh: '09- sf; WI: '12- 1; AfCh: '08- 1/2R. At 400m: Af-J: '07- 1 (7 200m). Won WAF 800m 2008, DL 2012, Kenyan 400m 2008.
Five world junior and four African & Commonwealth 800m records 2008. Kenyan 600m records 2008 & 2012.
Progress at 800m: 2007- c.2:14, 2008- 1:54.01, 2009- 1:59.49A, 2010- 2:01.52, 2011- 2:09.12, 2012- 1:56.76. pbs: 200m 24.68 '07, 400m 52.14A '12, 600m 1:23.36 '12, 1500m (4:07.11i dq '12).
Set world junior records in just third and fourth major 800m finals. Won Golden League jackpot 2008, when in her first season of 800m running she won all 13 finals and three heats. Married Peter Kiprotich Murrey in November 2007.

Hyvin Kiyeng **JEPKEMOI** b. 13 Jan 1992 1.56m 45kg.
At 3000mSt: WCh: '13- 6; AfG: '11- 1 (4 5000m); AfCh: '12- 3.
Progress at 3000mSt: 2011- 10:00.50, 2012- 9:23.53, 2013- 9:22.05. pbs: 1500m 4:19.44 '11, 3000m 9:07.51 '11, 5000m 15:42.64 '11.

Janeth JEPKOSGEI b. 13 Dec 1983 Kabirirsang, near Kapsabet 1.67m 47kg. North Rift.
At 800m: OG: '08- 2, '12- 7; WCh: '07- 1, '09- 2, '11- 3; CG: '06- 1; AfCh: '06- 1, '10- 2; WJ: '02- 1; WY: '99- h; WCp: '06- 2, '10- 1; won DL 2010, WAF 2007, KEN 2011.
Five Kenyan 800m records 2005-07.
Progress at 800m, 1500m: 1999- 2:11.0A, 2001- 2:06.21, 2002- 2:00.80, 2003- 2:03.05, 2004- 2:00.52, 4:11.91; 2005- 1:57.82, 4:15.77; 2006- 1:56.66, 4:15.43; 2007- 1:56.04, 4:14.70; 2008- 1:56.07, 4:08.48; 2009- 1:57.90, 4:13.87; 2010- 1:57.84, 4:04.17; 2011- 1:57.42, 4:02.32; 2012- 1:57.79, 4:07.34; 2013- 1:58.71, 4:12.61. pbs: 400m 54.06A '10, 600m 1:25.0+ '08, 1000m 2:37.98 '02, 1M 4:28.72 '08.
Brilliant front-running victory at 2007 Worlds.

Priscah JEPTOO b. 26 Jun 1984 Nandi, Rift Valley 1.65m 49kg.
At Mar: OG: '12- 2; WCh: '11- 2. At 10,000m: AfG: '99- 5. At 5000m: WJ: '00- 3. Won KEN CC 2014.
Progress at Mar: 2009- 2:30:40, 2010- 2:27:02, 2011- 2:22:55, 2012- 2:20:14, 2013- 2:20:15. Road pbs: 10k 31:18 '13, 15k 47:14 '13, 10M 50:38 '13, 20k 62:32 '13, HMar 65:45 '13.
Marathon wins: Porto 2009, Turin 2010, Paris 2011, London 2013 (3rd 2012), New York 2013. World Marathon Majors winner 2012/13. Won Great North Run 2013. Married to Douglas Chepsiro, son born 20 Feb 2009.

Rita Sitienei **JEPTOO** b. 15 Feb 1981 Eldoret 1.65m 48kg.
At Mar: WCh: '05- 7, '07- 7; World 20k: '06- 3; HMar: '04- 14.
African record 20km road 2006.
Progress at Mar: 2004- 2:28:11, 2005- 2:24:22, 2006- 2:23:38, 2007- 2:32:03, 2008- 2:26:34, 2011- 2:25:44, 2012- 2:22:04, 2013- 2:19:57. pbs: 3000m 9:38.13 '98, 5000m 15:56.90 '02, 10,000m 33:23.04A '05; Road: 10k 31:17 '13, 15k 47:13+ '13, 20k 63:11 '13, HMar 66:27 '11.
Won marathons at Stockholm and Milan 2004, Boston 2006 & 2013 (3rd 2008), Eldoret 2011; Chicago 2013 (2nd 2012).

Lucy Wangui KABUU b. 24 Mar 1984 Ichamara, Nyeri region 1.55m 41kg. Suzuki, Japan.
At (5000m)/10,000m: OG: '04- 9, '08- 7; CG: '06- 3/1; AfCh: '08- 4. At Mar: WCh: '13- 24. World 4k CC: '05- 5; HMar: '14- 4. Won KEN 10,000m 2013.
Progress at 5000m, 10,000m, HMar: 2001- 15:45.04, 2002- 15:33.03, 32:54.70; 2003- 15:10.23, 31:06.20; 2004- 14:47.09, 31:05.90, 69:47; 2005- 15:00.20, 31:22.37; 2006- 14:56.09, 31:29.66; 2007- 14:57.55, 31:32.52; 2008- 14:33.49, 30:39.96; 2009- 16:50.3A, 2011- 67:04, 2013- 32:44.1A, 66:09;. At Mar: 2012- 2:19:34, 2013- 2:24:06, 2014- 2:24:16. pbs: 1500m 4:08.6A '12, 3000m 8:46.15 '08. Road 15k 47:13+ 13, 20k 62:48 '13, 25k 1:21:37 '13.
At the marathon set the pace in Osaka 2007, but at her first proper try was 2nd in 2:19:34 at Dubai 2012. 3rd Chicago 2012 and Tokyo 2014. Won Great North Run 2011, RAK half marathon 2013.

Mary Jepkosgei **KEITANY** b. 18 Jan 1982 Kisok, Kabarnet 1.68m 53kg.
At Mar: OG: '12- 4. World HMar: '07- 2, '09- 1.
Records: World 25km 2010, 10M, 20km, half marathon 2011. African and two Kenyan half marathon 2009. Kenyan marathon 2012.
Progress at HMar: Mar: 2000- 72:53, 2002- 73:01, 2003- 73:25, 2004- 71:32, 2005- 70:18, 2006- 69:06, 2007- 66:48, 2009- 66:36, 2010- 67:14, 2:29:01; 2011- 65:50, 2:19:19; 2012- 66:49, 2:18:37. pbs: 1500m 4:24.33 '99, 10,000m 32:18.07 '07; Road: 5k 15:25 '11, 10k 30:45 '11, 15k 46:40 '11, 10M 50:05 '11, 20k 62:36 '11, 25k 1:19:53 '10.
11 wins in 12 half marathons 2006-12.

Marathons: 3rd New York 2010-11, won London 2011-12. Married to Charles Koech (pbs 10k 27:56 & HMar 61:27 '07), son Jared born in June 2008 and daughter Samantha on 5 Apr 2013.

Sylvia Chibiwott **KIBET** b. 28 Mar 1984 Kapchorwa, Keiyo district 1.57m 44kg. Kenya Police.
At 5000m: OG: '08- 4; WCh: '07- 4, '09- 2, '11- 2; CG: '10- 2; AfG: '07- 3; AfCh: '06- 3. At 3000m: WI: '08-10-12: 4/4/4, won Afr-Y 1998. At 1500m: WY: '99- 2. World CC: '11- 13. Won KEN 5000m 2011.
Progress at 5000m, 10,000m: 2006- 15:02.54, 31:39.34; 2007- 14:57.37, 2008- 15:00.03, 2009- 14:37.77, 30:47.20; 2010- 14:31.91, 2011- 14:35.43, 2012- 14:46.73, 2013- 14:58.26. pbs: 1500m 4:05.33i/4:07.87 '10, 3000m 8:37.47 '13, 2M 9:16.62 '07, Road: 15k 48:24 '12, 10M 51:42 '12, HMar 69:51 '09.
Did not compete in 2001-02. Married Erastus Limo in 2003, daughter Britney Jepkosgei born in 2004. Older sister is Hilda Kibet NED and cousin of Lornah Kiplagat NED.

Viola Jelagat **KIBIWOT** b. 22 Dec 1983 Keiyo 1.57m 45kg.
At 1500m: OG: '08- h; WCh: '07- 5, '09/11- sf; CG: '06- 7, '10- 7; WJ: '02- 1. At 5000m: OG: '12- 6; WCh: '13- 4. World CC: '00-01-02-13: 3J/1J/1J/7; AfCC: '11-2.
Progress at 1500m, 5000m: 2003- 15:32.87, 2004- 4:06.64, 2006- 4:08.74, 2007- 4:02.10, 2008- 4:04.17, 14:51.59; 2009- 4:02.70, 2010- 4:03.39, 14:48.57; 2011- 4:05.51, 14:34.86; 2012- 3:59.25, 14:39.53; 2013- 4:00.76, 14:33.48. pbs: 800m 2:04.7A '12, 2000m 5:42.57 '09, 3000m 8:33.97 '13, 2M 9:18.26 '07.

Valentine KIPKETER b. 5 Jan 1993 1.50m 40kg.
Progress at Mar: 2012- 2:28:02, 2013- 2:23:02.
Pbs: 3000m 9:17.12 '10, 5000m 16:22.83 '10, Road: 10k 33:07 11, HMar 68:21 '11.
Won Mumbai and Amsterdam marathons 2013.

Edna Ngeringwony **KIPLAGAT** b. 15 Nov 1979 Eldoret 1.71m 54kg. Corporal in Kenyan Police.
At Mar: OG: '12- 20; WCh: '11- 1, '13- 1. At 3000m: WJ: '96- 2, '98- 3. World CC: '96-97-06: 5J/4J/13.
African record 30km 2008.
Progress at Mar: 2005- 2:50:20, 2010- 2:25:38, 2011- 2:20:46, 2012- 2:19:50, 2013- 2:21:32. pbs: 3000m 8:53.06 '96, 5000m 15:57.3A '06, 10,000m 33:27.0A '07; Road: 5k 15:20 '10, 10k 31:18 '10, 15k 47:57 '10, 10M 54:56 '09, HMar 67:41 '12.
Won Los Angeles and New York Marathons 2010, 2nd London 2012-13 (3rd 2011). Married to Gilbert Koech (10,000m 27:55.30 '01, 10k 27:32 '01, Mar 2:13:45 dh '05, 2:14:39 '09); two children.

Florence Jebet **KIPLAGAT** b. 27 Feb 1987 Kapkitony, Keiyo district 1.55m 42kg.
At 5000m: WJ: '06- 2. At 10,000m: WCh: '09- 12. World CC: '07- 5, '09- 1; HMar: '10- 1. Won Kenyan 1500m 2007, CC 2007 & 2009.

World records 20km and half marathon 2014. Kenyan 10,000m record 2009.
Progress at 5000m, 10,000m, HMar, Mar: 2006- 15:32.34, 2007- 14:40.74, 31:06.20; 2009- 14:40.14, 30:11.53; 2010- 14:52.64, 32:46.99A, 67:40; 2011- 68:02, 2:19:44; 2012- 30:24.85, 66:38, 2:20:57; 2013- 67:13, 2:21:13; 2014- 65:12. pbs: 1500m 4:09.0A '07, 3000m 8:40.72 '10, Road: 15k 46:35 '14, 20k 61:56 '14, 30k 1:39:38 '13.
Won half marathon debut in Lille in 2010, followed a month later by World title. Did not finish in Boston on marathon debut in 2011; won Berlin 2011 and 2013. Formerly married to Moses Mosop, daughter Aisha Chelagat born April 2008. Niece of William Kiplagat (Mar 2:06:50 '99, 8 WCh '07).

Sally Jepkosgei **KIPYEGO** b. 19 Dec 1985 Kapsowar, Marakwet district 1.68m 52kg. Was at Texas Tech University, USA.
At (5000m)/10,000m: OG: '12- 4/2; WCh: '11- 2, '13- 7. World CC: '01- 8J. Won record equalling nine NCAA titles 5000m 2008, 10,000m 2007, CC 2006-08, indoor 3000m 2007, 5000m 2007-09.
Progress at 5000m, 10,000m: 2005- 16:34.90, 2006- 16:13.39, 2007- 15:19.72, 31:56.72; 2008- 15:11.88, 31:25.48; 2009- 15:09.03, 33:44.7A; 2010- 14:38.64, 2011- 14:30.42, 30:38.35; 2012- 14:43.11, 30:26.37. pbs: 800m 2:08.26 '08, 1500m 4:06.23 '11, 1M 4:27.19i/4:29.64 '09, 2000m 5:35.20 '09, 3000m 8:35.89 '12, 2M 9:21.04i '14, HMar 68:31 '14.
Married to Kevin Chelimo (5000m 13:14.57 '12). One of her eight brothers is Mike Kipyego (3000mSt 8:08.48).

Faith Chepngetich **KIPYEGON** b. 10 Jan 1994 Bornet 1.57m 42kg.
At 1500m: OG: '12- h; WCh: '13- 5; WJ: '12- 1; WY: '10- 1. World CC: '10-11-13: 4J/1J/1J, Won African CC 2014, Jnr 2012.
African junior & Kenyan 1500m record 2013.
Progress at 1500m: 2010- 4:17.1A, 2011- 4:09.48, 2012- 4:03.82, 2013- 3:56.98. pb 800m 2:02.8A '13. Older sister is Beatrice Mutai (b. 19 Apr 1987) 11 World CC 2013.

Purity Cherotich **KIRUI** b. 13 Aug 1991 1.66m 50kg.
At 3000mSt: WJ: '10- 1.
Progress at 3000mSt: 2008- 10:27.19A, 2009- 10:05.1A, 2010- 9:36.34, 2011- 9:37.85, 2012- 9:35.61, 2013- 9:19.42. pbs: 1500m 4:31.83 '08, 5000m 16:13.42 '11.

Nancy Chebet **LANGAT** (or LAGAT) b. 22 Aug 1981 Eldoret 1.53m 49kg.
At (800m)/1500m: OG: '04- sf, '08- 1; WCh: '05- h, '09/11- sf, '13- 7; CG: '10- 1/1; AfCh: '04-08-10: 1/4/1; CCp: '10- 8; won DL 2010, WAF 2009, KEN 2010. At 800m: WJ: '96- 3, '98- 2, '00- 1; Af-J: '95/97- 1. World 4k CC: '05- 8.
Progress at 800m, 1500m: 1996- 2:03.10A, 4:22.93; 1997- 2:01.6A, 1998- 2:03.88A, 1999- 2:04.7A, 2000- 2:01.26, 4:23.78; 2001- 4:23.78, 2004- 2:05.63,

4:04.76; 2005- 2:02.51, 4:02.31; 2008- 2:05.84, 4:00.23; 2009- 1:59.17, 4:01.64; 2010- 1:57.75, 4:00.13; 2011- 2:02.8A, 4:03.66; 2012- 4:09.10, 2013- 4:01.41. pbs: 1000m 2:45.5+ '08, 1M 4:28.50 '13, 3000m 9:12.64 '12, 5000m 16:33.9A '08.
Married to Kenneth Cheruiyot (Mar 2:07:18 '01, 3 WCh HMar 1997 in pb 60:00). Sons Keith (b. 2002) and Klein (b. 2006).

Linet Chepkwemoi **MASAI** b. 5 Dec 1989 Kapsokwony, Mount Elgon district 1.70m 55kg.
At (5000m)/10,000m: OG: '08- 4; WCh: '09- 1, '11- 6/3; AfCh: '10- 3. World CC: '07-08-09-10-11: 1J/3/2/2/2. Won KEN 10,000m 2010, CC 2010-11.
World junior record and Kenyan record at 10,000m 2008, World 10 miles road record 2009.
Progress at 5000m, 10,000m: 2007- 14:55.50, 2008- 14:47.14, 30:26.50; 2009- 14:34.36, 30:51.24; 2010- 14:31.14, 31:59.36A; 2011- 14:32.95, 30:53.59; 2012- 14:53.93, 2013- 15:02.98, 31:02.89. pbs: 1500m 4:12.26 '09, 2000m 5:33.43 '09, 3000m 8:38.97 '07. Road: 15k 47:21 '09, 10M 50:39 '09.
Younger sister of Moses (qv) and Dennis Masai. Younger sister Magdalene has 5000m pb 15:17.15 "13.

Margaret Wangere **MURIUKI** b. 21 Mar 1986 1.58m 45kg.
At 1500m: AfG: '07- 7; AfCh: '12- 3, At 5000m: WCh: '13- h; World CC: 08-10-13: 8/6/5. Won KEN CC 2013
Progress at 5000m: 2003- 16:55.7A, 2005- 16:39.6A, 2010- 14:48.94, 2011- 15:19.89, 2013- 14:40.48. pbs: 10kmRd 31:05 '10, HMar 69:21 '12.

Mercy Wanjiru **NJOROGE** b. 10 Jun 1986 Njabini, Nyandarua District 1.58m 46kg.
At 3000mSt: OG: '12- 10; WCh: '11- 4; CG: '10- 2; AfG: '07- 5; AfCh: '08- 5, '10- 4; WJ: '04- 4; Kenyan champion 2012. Won Afr-J 3000m & 3000mSt 2005. World CC: '05- 4J, '06- 12.
Progress at 3000mSt: 2004- 9:52.25, 2005- 9:50.63, 2007- 9:43.02, 2008- 9:42.99, 2010- 9:26.64, 2011- 9:16.94, 2012- 9:25.21. pbs: 1500m 4:19.08 '11, 2000m 5:55.62+ '12, 3000m 8:39.70i '11, 8:48.16 '06; 5000m 15:17.03 '11, 10kmRd 33:52 '06.

Veronica Wanjiru **NYARUAI** b. 29 Oct 1989 Nyahururu 1.65m 43kg.
At 5000m: AfCh: '08- 5, '12- 2. At 1500m: AfG: '07- 2; WCh: '07- sf. At 3000m: WJ: '06- 1, WY: '05- 1. At 3000mSt: OG: '08- h. World CC: '05- 06-07: 2J/2J/3J.
Progress at 5000m: 2004- 16:05.7A, 2005- 15:13.1A. 2006- 15:42.1A, 2007- 15:23.37, 2008- 15:05.38. 2012- 14:44.82. pbs: 1500m 4:08.22 '06, 2000m 5:54.68+ 12, 3000m 8:40.81 '12, 3000mSt 9:37.11 '08. Road: 10k 32:32 '09, HMar 73:55 '11.

Hellen Onsando **OBIRI** b. 13 Dec 1989 Nyangusu, Kisii 1.55m 45kg.
At 1500m: OG: '12- 12; WCh: '11- 10 (fell), '13- 3. At 3000m: WI: '12- 1, '14- 2. Won Kenyan 1500m 2011-13.
Progress at 1500m: 2011- 4:02.42, 2012- 3:59.68,

2013- 3:58.58. pbs: 800m 2:00.54 '11, 1000m 2:46.00i '12, 2000m 5:44.8+i '12, 3000m 8:29.99i '14, 8:34.25 '13; 5000m 15:49.7A '13.

Philes ONGORI b. 19 Jul 1986 Chironge, Kisii district 1.58m 47kg. Based in Sapporo, Japan.
At 10,000m: WCh: '07- 8. World HMar: '09- 2.
Progress at 5000m, 10,000m, Mar: 2003- 16:11.32, 2004- 15:08.3mx/15:25.50, 2005- 15:09.49, 32:30.83; 2006- 15:19.90, 31:18.85; 2007- 14:50.15, 31:39.11; 2008- 14:46.20mx/14:46.06, 30:29.21mx /31:19.73; 2009- 15:12.15, 31:53.46; 2011- 2:24:20, 2013- 2:28:53. pbs: 800m 2:05.56 '04, 1500m 4:11.90 '04, 3000m 8:47.88 '07, Road: 15k 47:38 '08, HMar 67:38 '09.
Won Japanese High School 3000m 2004. Won Rotterdam Marathon 2011 on debut.

Lydia Chebet **ROTICH** b. 8 Aug 1988 Kipkilot, Keiyo District 1.58m 45kg. Kenya Police traffic officer.
At 3000mSt: OG: '12- h; WCh: '11- 5; AfCh: 10- 3.
Progress at 3000mSt: 2007- 10:44.3A, 2008- 9:55.62, 2009- 9:26.51, 2010- 9:18.03, 2011- 9:19.20, 2012- 9:31.09, 2013- 9:26.31. pb 5000m 16:01.0A '12.

Eunice Jepkoech **SUM** b. 2 Sep 1988 Burnt Forest, Uasin Gishu 1.68m 54kg. Police.
At 800m: WCh: '11- sf, '13- 1; AfCh: '10- h,'12- 2; won DL 2013. At 1500m: OG: '12- h, Won Kenyan 800m 2012.
Progress at 800m, 1500m: 2009- 2:07.4A, 2010- 2:00.28, 2011- 1:59.66A, 4:12.41; 2012- 1:59.13, 4:04.26; 2013- 1:57.38, 4:02.05. pb 3000m 8:53.12 '12.
Daughter Diana Cheruto born in 2008.

KOREA

Governing body: Korea Athletics Federation, 10 Chamshil Dong, Songpa-Gu, Seoul. Founded 1945. **National Champions 2013**:
Men: 100m: Kim Min-kyun 10.49, 200m: Cho Kyu-won 21.18, 400m: Park Bong-ko 46.65, 800m: Choi Hyun-gi 1:51.04, 1500m: Park Tae-sung 3:49.47, 5000m: Yuk Gun-tae 14:27.55, 10,000m: Kim Hyo-su 30:48.10, 3000mSt: Kwon Jae-woo 9:14.78, 110mh: Kim Byung-jun 13.85, 400mh: Kim Dae-hong 52.19, HJ: Lee Sung 2.19, PV: Jim Min-sup 5.53, LJ: Kim Duk-hyung 7.75, TJ: Yoo Jae-hyuk 16.00, SP: Jung Il-woo 17.91, DT: Choi Jong-bum 59.68, HT: Lee Yun-chul 70.14, JT: Kim Yee-lam 74.46, Dec: Kim Kun-woo 7268, 20kW: Kim Hyun-sub 1:23:32.
Women: 100m/200m: Jung Han-sol 12.07/24.61, 400m: Choi Eun-ju 55.42, 800m: Huh Yeon-jung 2:10.50, 1500m: Hyun Suh-yong 4:36.21, 5000m/10,000m: Lee Su-min 16:42.14/35:10.54, 3000mSt: Lee Se-jung 10:50.11, 100mh: Lee Ji-min 13.95, 400mh: Kim Shin-ae 60.78, HJ: Han Da-rye 1.76, PV: Choi Yea-eun 3.70, LJ/TJ: Cho Eun-jung 6.17/13.04, SP: Lee Mi-young 16.33, DT: Cho Hye-rim 49.26, HT: Kang Na-ru

62.77, JT: Kim Kyong-ae 53.94, Hep: Chung Yeon-jin 4956, 20kW: Weon Ases-byeol 1:43:11.
KIM Hyun-sub b. 31 May 1985 Sokcho 1.75m 53kg.
At 20kW: OG: '08- 23, '12- 17; WCh: '07-09-11-13: 20/34/6/10; AsiG: '06- 2, '10- 3; WUG: '05-07-09: 2/6/5. Asian champion 2011, 2014; KOR 2005-06, 2008-13. At 10,000m/10kmW: WJ: '04- 3; WCp: '04- 8.
Four Korean 20km road walk records 2008-14.
Progress at 20kW: 2004- 1:24:58, 2005- 1:22:15, 2006- 1:21:45, 2007- 1:20:54, 2008- 1:19:41, 2009- 1:22:00, 2010- 1:19:36, 2011- 1:19:31, 2012- 1:21:36, 2013- 1:21:22, 2014- 1:19:24. Pb 10,000mW 39:30.56 '09, 38:13R '10.

KUWAIT

Governing body: Kuwait Association of Athletic Federation, PO Box 5499, 13055 Safat, Kuwait. Founded 1957.

Ali **Mohammed AL-ZINKAWI** b. 27 Feb 1984 Kuwait City 1.86m 97kg.
At HT: OG: '04/08/12- dnq 29/18/18; WCh: '05/09/11- dnq 21/13/13, '07- 12; WJ: '02- 2; AsiG: '06- 2; AsiC: '03-05-07-09-11-12: 1/1/1/2/1/4; CCp: '10- 3. Pan-Arab champion 2004-05, 2007, 2009, 2011, 2013; West Asian 2005, 2010, Asian-J 2002.
13 Kuwait hammer records 2004-09, Asian junior record 2003.
Progress at HT: 2001- 64.66, 2002- 66.88, 2003- 72.70, 2004- 76.54, 2005- 76.25, 2006- 76.97, 2007- 77.14, 2008- 77.25, 2009- 79.74, 2010- 78.40, 2011- 79.27, 2012- 75.28, 2013- 76.68.
His father Mohamed Al-Zinkawi competed at 1976, 1980 and 1988 Olympics at shot, best 18.65 '81.

LATVIA

Governing body: Latvian Athletic Association, 1 Augsiela Str, Riga LV-1009. Founded 1921.
National Championships first held in 1920 (men), 1922 (women). **2013 Champions: Men**: 100m/200m: Janis Mezitis 10.69/21.42, 400m/400mh: Janis Baltuss 47.69/52.53, 800m: Renars Stepins 1:52.20, 1500m: Pauls Arents 3:51.33, 3000m: JanisViskers 8:20.22, 5000m Dmitrijs Serjogins 14:51.05, HMar: Valerijs Zolnerovics 66:53, Mar: Kristaps Berzins 2:30:36, 3000mSt: Konstantins Dinars 9:20.91, 110mh/Dec: Janis Jansons 14.27w/7647, HJ: Janis Vaivods 1.98, PV: Mareks Arents 5.35, LJ/TJ: Elvijs Misans 7.86/16.10, SP/DT: Oskars Vaisjuns 16.50/54.18, HT: Igors Sokolovs 72.30, JT: Rolands Strobinders 80.35. **Women**: 100m/200m: Laura Ikauniece 12.00/24.27, 400m: Aleksandra Koblence 56.80, 800m: Liga Jansone 2:17.34, 1500m/3000mSt: Valerija Linkevica 4:35.15/11:13.84, 3000m: Diana Jakubjaneca 10:12.14, 5000m: Valtere Kitioja 18:55.39, HMar: Jelena Prokopcuka 72:52, Mar:

Dace Lina 2:55:06, 100mh/Hep: Ilona Dramacenoka 14.85w/4879, 400mh: Liga Velvere 58.65, HJ: Madara Onuzane 1.80, PV: Ildze Bortascenoka 4.13, LJ: Mara Griva 6.20, TJ: Santa Matule 13.16, SP: Inga Mikelsone 13.31, DT: Dace Steinerte 49.55, HT: Vaira Kumermane 52.56, JT: Lina Muze 61.97, 10,000mW: Agnese Pastare 45:11.4.

Zigismunds SIRMAIS b. 6 May 1992 Riga 1.91m 90kg.
At JT: OG: '12- dnq; WCh: '11: dnq 32; EC: '12- dnq 23; WJ: '10- 7; EU23: '13- 1; EJ: '11- 1.
Two world junior javelin records 2011.
Progress at JT: 2009- 65.03, 2010- 82.27, 2011- 84.69, 2012- 84.06, 2013- 82.77.
Sister Katrina Sirma (b. 31 Mar 1994) pb JT 51.69 '11.

Vadims VASILEVSKIS b. 5 Jan 1982 Riga 1.88m 101kg. Jekabpils.
At JT: OG: '04- 2, '08- 9, '12- dnq 37; WCh: '05-07-09-11-13: dnq 16/4/dnq 25/dnq 14; EC: '02-06-10-12: dnq 16/4/dnq 23/dnq; WJ: '00- 8; EU23: '03- 7; EJ: '01- 7; WUG: '07- 1. Latvian champion 2008, 2011; WAF 2008.
Three Latvian javelin records 2006-07.
Progress at JT: 1998- 59.17, 1999- 63.82, 2000- 73.07, 2001- 73.25, 2002- 81.92, 2003- 77.81, 2004- 84.95, 2005- 81.30, 2006- 90.43, 2007- 90.73, 2008- 86.65, 2009- 90.71, 2010- 84.08, 2011- 88.22, 2012- 86.50, 2013- 82.79.
Set personal bests in qualifying (84.43) and final at 2004 Olympics.

Women

Laura IKAUNIECE b. 31 May 1992 Jürmala 1.79m 60kg. Jürmalas SS.
At Hep: OG: '12- 8; WCh: '13- 11; EC: '12- 2; WJ: '10- 6; WY: '09- 2; EJ: '11- 3; WUG: '13- 2. Won LAT 100m 2012-13, 200m 2009, 2013; 100mh & HJ 2010.
Latvian heptathlon record 2012.
Progress at Hep: 2008- 5175, 2010- 5618, 2011- 6063, 2012- 6414, 2013- 6321. Pbs: 60m 7.65i '14, 200m 24.08 '13, 800m 2:12.13 '12, 60mh 8.38i '14, 100mh 13.44 '13, HJ 1.85i/1.83 '12, LJ 6.31 '12, SP 13.06i '14, 12.88 '13; JT 53.73 '12, Hep 4496i '14.
Her mother Vineta Ikauniece set current Latvian records at 100m 11.34A '87, 200m 22.49A '87 and 400m 50.71 '88, and her father Aivars Ikaunieks had 110mh bests of 13.71A '87 and 13.4 '84.

Madara PALAMEIKA b. 18 Jun 1987 Valdemarpils 1.85m 76kg. Ventspils.
At JT: OG: '12- 8; WCh: '09-13: dnq 27/27, '11- 11; EC: '10- 8, '12- 8; WJ: '06- dnq 16; EU23: '07- 3, '09- 1; EJ: '05- dnq 17. Latvian champion 2009-11.
Latvian javelin record 2009.
Progress at JT: 2002- 42.31, 2003- 49.11, 2004- 51.50, 2005- 51.75, 2006- 54.19, 2007- 57.98, 2008- 53.45, 2009- 64.51, 2010- 62.02, 2011- 63.46, 2012- 62.74, 2013- 62.72.

LITHUANIA

Governing body: Athletic Federation of Lithuania, Kareiviu 6, LT-09117 Vilnius. Founded 1921.
National Championships first held in 1921 (women 1922). **2013 Champions: Men:** 100m/200m: Rytis Sakalauskas 10.37/20.91, 400m: Gediminas Kucinskas 48.36, 800m: Vitalij Kozlov 1:51.06, 1500m: Petras Gliebus 3:52.63, 5000m/10,000m: Remigijus Kancys 15:07.3/31:34.10, HMar/Mar: Tomas Venckunas 72:26/2:27:01, 3000mSt: Dominykas Butkevicius 9:44.33, 110mh/400mh: Arturas Janauskas 14.45/53.19, HJ: Raivydas Stanys 2.24, PV/Dec: Benas Kentra 4.40/7278, LJ: Povilas Mykolaitis 7.82, TJ: Andrius Griucevicius 15.25, SP: Sarunas Banevicius 18.68, DT: Andrius Guzdzius 61.02, HT: Martynas Sedys 62.52, JT: Skirmantas Simoliunas 62.16, 20kW: Tadas Suskevicius 1:25:39. **Women:** 100m: Lina Grincikaite 11.69, 200m: Eva Misiunaite 24.48, 400m: Agne Serksniene 52.63, 800m/1500m: Rasa Batuleviciute 2:08.06/4:28.68, 5000m: Loreta Kancyte 17:42.64, 10,000m: Milda Vilcinskaite 36:12.94, HMar/Mar: Renata Siliuk 1:33:39/3:11.05, 100mh: Sonata Tamosaityte 13.63, 400mh: Egle Staisiunaite 57.67, HJ: Airine Palsyte 1.95, PV: Vitalija Dejeva 3.40, LJ: Lina Andrijauskaite 6.03, TJ: Dovile Dzindzaletaite 13.52, SP: Laura Gedminaité 14.50, DT: Zinaida Sendriute 60.76, HT: Sandra Miseikyte 47.32, JT: Liveta Jasiunaite 50.83, Hep: Juste Rinkeviciute 4572, 10kW: Kristina Saltanovic 46:03, 20kW: Brigita Virbalyte 1:30:55.

Virgilijus ALEKNA b. 13 Feb 1972 Terpeikiai, Kupiskis 2.00m 130kg. Graduate of Lithuanian Academy of Physical Culture. Guard of the Lithuanian president 1995-2010, advisor to the Lithuanian Ministry of the Interior from 2011.
At DT: OG: '96-00-04-08-12: 5/1/1/3/4; WCh: '95-97-99-01-03-05-07-09-11-13: dnq 19/2/4/2/1/1/4/4/6/dnq 16; EC: '98-02-06-10: 3/2/1/5; WCp: '98- 1, '06- 1. Won WAF 2003, 2005-06, 2009; GP 2001 (2nd 1999); DL 2011. LTU champion 1998, 2000-05, 2008-09, 2011-12.
Four Lithuanian discus records 2000. World over-40 record 2012.
Progress at DT: 1990- 52.84, 1991- 57.16, 1992- 60.86, 1993- 62.84, 1994- 64.20, 1995- 62.78, 1996- 67.82, 1997- 67.70, 1998- 69.66A, 1999- 68.25, 2000- 73.88, 2001- 70.99, 2002- 66.90, 2003- 69.69, 2004- 70.97, 2005- 70.67, 2006- 71.08, 2007- 71.56, 2008- 71.25, 2009- 69.59, 2010- 65.33, 2011- 67.90, 2012- 70.28, 2013- 64.66. pb SP: 19.99 '97.
His 72.35 and 73.88 at the 2000 LTU Championships were the second and third longest ever discus throws. His 70.17 to win the 2005 World title (coming from 2nd at 68.10 with the last throw) was the first ever 70m throw at a global championships. He has 20 competitions and 31 throws over 70m. 37 successive wins from August 2005 to 4th at Worlds August 2007.

Married on 4 Mar 2000 Kristina Sablovskyte (pb LJ 6.14 '96, TJ 12.90 '97, sister of Remigija Nazaroviene).

Women

Zinaida SENDRIUTE b. 10 Jun 1984 Skuodas 1.88m 89kg. Skuodo.
At DT: OG: '08- dnq 33, '12- 8; WCh: '09- dnq 31, '11- 12, '13- 9; EC: '06-10-12: dnq 17/5/dnq 17; EJ: '03- 7; EU23: '05- 6; WUG: '11-2; Lithuanian champion 2003, 2005-08, 2010-13.
Progress at DT: 2000- 33.37, 2001- 40.55, 2002- 48.66, 2003- 50.62, 2004- 51.38, 2005- 55.25, 2006- 57.26, 2007- 56.74, 2008- 59.42, 2009- 60.21, 2010- 60.70, 2011- 62.49, 2012- 64.03, 2013- 65.97. pb SP 14.15 '10.

Austra SKUJYTE b. 12 Aug 1979 Birzai 1.88m 80kg. Graduated in kinesiology from Kansas State University, USA. Masters degree from the Lithuanian Academy of Physical Culture.
At Hep: OG: '00- 12, '04- 2, '08- dnf, '12- 5; WCh: '01-03-05-07-11: 6/10/4/6/8; EC: '02- 4; WJ: '98- 6; EU23: '99- 6, '01- 3. At Pen: WI: '04-08-12: 3/5/3; EI: '07- 4, '11- 2. At SP: WCh: '09- dnq 17; EC: '10- 12, '12- 11 (dnq 13= HJ). Won NCAA 2001-02; LTU 100mh 2000, 2005, 2012; HJ 2005, LJ 2005, 2007, 2012; SP 2001-02, 2004-05, 2007, 2009-11; DT 2009; Hep 1997.
World decathlon record 2005.
Progress at Hep: 1997- 4930, 1998- 5606, 1999- 5724, 2000- 6104, 2001- 6150w, 2002- 6275, 2003- 6213, 2004- 6435, 2005- 6386, 2007- 6380, 2008- 6235, 2011- 6338, 2012- 6599. pbs: 100m 12.49 '05, 200m 24.82 '04, 24.79w '07; 400m 57.19 '05, 800m 2:15.92 '04, 1500m 5:15.86 '05, 60mh 8.57i '12, 100mh 13.96 '11, 13.83w '04; HJ 1.92 '12, PV 3.20 '06, LJ 6.39i '05, 6.34 '12, 6.43w '12; SP 17.86 '09, DT 53.89 '10, JT 52.63 '07, Pen 4802i '12, Dec 8358 '05.
Set three pbs in 2004 Olympics, including two seconds off 800m best to secure silver. Returned to multi-events in 2011 after two years concentrating on shot.

LUXEMBOURG

Governing body: Fédération Luxembourgeoise d'Athlétisme, 3 Route d'Arlon, L-8009 Strassen, Luxembourg. Founded 1928.
2013 National Champions: Men: 100m: Festus Geraldo 11.23, 200m: Vincent Karger 22.39, 400m: Tom Scholer 48.83, 800m: Charles Grethen 1:51.98, 1500m: Christophe Bestgen 4:09.09, 5000m: Eric Durrer 16:25.79, 10,000m/HMar: Pol Mellina 30:38.10/68:10, Mar: Frank Schweitzer 2:31:44, 3000mSt: Luc Scheller 10:31.4, 110mh: Claude Godart 14.66, 400mh: Gil Nicola 60.05, HJ: Quentin Bebon & Ben Kiffer 1.90, PV: Joe Seil 4.60, LJ: Tom Hutmacher 6.71, TJ: Asmir Mirascic 14.00, SP: Bob Bertemes 17.69, DT: Sven Forster 48.68, HT: Steve Tonizzo 49.82, JT: Mykyta Thill 52.08, Dec: Wesley

Charlet 5951. **Women**: 100m: Tiffany Tshilumba 12.17, 200m: Shanila Mutumba 25.45, 400m: Charline Mathias 55.18, 800m/1500m: Jenny Gloden 2:18.54/4:51.42, 3000m/10,000m: Pascale Schmoetten 10:21.21/37:24.97, HMar: Annette Jaffke 1:24:27, Mar: Karin Schank 3:08:46, 3000mSt: Liz Weiler 12:28.2, 100m: Victoria Rausch 15.32, 400mh: Kim Reuland 62.06, HJ: Elodie Tshilumba 1.71, PV: Gina Reuland 4.11, LJ: Laurence Jones 5.79, TJ: Nita Bokomba 11.65, SP: Stéphanie Krumlovsky 12.76, DT: Sandy Debra 33.27, HT: Mireille Tonizzo 39.96, JT: Véronique Michel 37.93.

MEXICO

Governing body: Federación Mexicana de Atletismo, Anillo Periférico y Av. del Conscripto, 11200 México D.F. Founded 1933.
National Champions 2013: Men: 100m: Alexis Viera 10.74, 200m: José Carlos Herrera 21.00, 400m: José Martínez 47.26, 800m: James Eichberger 1:51.65, 1500m: Christopher Sandoval 3:51.14, 5000m: Juan Luis Barrios 13:59.29, 10,000m: Juan Carlos Romero 29:55.15, 3000mSt: Luis Ibarra 9:05.93, 110mh: José Antonio Flores 14.15, 400mh: Sergio Rios 51.15, HJ: Edgar Rivera 2.22, PV: Victor Manuel Castillero 5.20, LJ: Luis Rivera 8.17, TJ: Alberto Álvarez 16.21, SP/DT: Mario Cota 17.62/55.44, HT: Diego del Real 66.63, JT: Juan José Méndez 78.43, Dec: Román Garibay 7372, 20000mW: Horacio Nava 1:25:24.13, 20kW: Diego Flores 1:22:16. **Women**: 100m/200m: Iza Daniela Flores 12.07/23.80, 400m/800m: Gabriela Medina 52.47/2:04.35, 1500m: Cristina Guevara 4:20.98, 5000m: Marisol Romero 15:50.01, 10,000m: Kathya García 35:01.11, 3000mSt: Azucena Ríos 10:41.63, 100m: Georgina Támez 13.87, 400mh: Zudikey Rodríguez 58.13, HJ: Romary Rifka 1.80, PV: Carmelita Correa 4.00, LJ: Ivonne Treviño 6.19, TJ: Rita Rosado 12.99w, SP: Cecilia Dzul 15.89, DT: Iraís Estrada 52.48, HT: Abril Hernández 54.59, JT: Betzabet Menéndez 51.86, Hep: Christal Ruiz 5354, 10,000mW: María Guadalupe González 48:38.86, 20kW: Yabelli Caballero 1:34:58.

Luis RIVERA Morales b. 21 Jun 1987 Agua Prieta, Sonora 1.83m 79kg. Degree in engineering from University of Arizona.
At LJ: OG: '12- dnq 32; WCh: '13- 3; WI: '14- 7; WUG: '13- 1. Won Mexican LJ 2006-07, 2009-10, 2012-13; TJ 2005-07.
Two Mexican long jump records 2013.
Progress at LJ: 2006- 7.31/7.47w, 2007- 7.60, 2008- 7.84i/7.61, 2009- 7.99i/7.95, 2010- 7.93, 2011- 7.77Ai/7.32, 2012- 8.22, 2013- 8.46. pbs: 110mh 15.02 '07, TJ 15.97 '09.
Brother Edgar (b. 13 Feb 1991) has HJ pb 2.28 '11 (5 WY 07, 6 WJ 10).

Éder SÁNCHEZ b. 21 May 1986 Toluca 1.76m 67kg. Mexican army sergeant.

At 20kW: OG: '08- 15, '12- 6; WCh: '05-07-09-11: 8/4/3/14; WCp: '08-10-12: 3/6/7; PAm: '11- 6; CAG: '06- 2, '10- 1; won MEX 2006. At 10,000mW: WJ: '04- 4; PAm-J: '03- 2; WCp: '04- 2J.
CAC 5000mW record 2009, junior 20kW 2005.
Progress at 20kW: 2005- 1:19:02, 2006- 1:23:24A, 2007- 1:20:08, 2008- 1:18:34, 2009- 1:19:22, 2010- 1:21:16, 2011- 1:19:36, 2012- 1:19:52. pbs: 3000mW 11:13.45 '09, 5000mW 18:40.11 '09, 10,000mW 40:46.29 '04, 10k Rd 38:31 '09, 50kW 3:53:19 '11.
Won IAAF Race Walking Challenge 2009.
Nephew of Rosario Sánchez (2nd PAm 20kW 1999 & 2003) and of Joel Sánchez (3rd OG 50kW 2000).

MOROCCO

Governing Body: Fédération Royale Marocaine d'Athlétisme, Complex Sportif Prince Moulay Abdellah, PO Box 1778 R/P, Rabat. Fd. 1957.
2013 National Champions: Men: 100m/200m: Abdelghani Zaghali 10.97/21.48, 400m/400mh: Abdelhadi Massaoudi 47.44/51.96, 800m: Nader Belhanbel 1:45.69; 1500m: Othmane El Goumri 3:37.79, 5000m: Aziz Lahbadi 13:31.78, 10,000m: Hicham Bellani 28:31.06, 3000mSt: Brahim Taleb 8:30.05, 110mh: Lohamed Koussi 14.74, 400mh: Hassan Akabbou 52.02, LJ: Abdelhakim Mlaab 7.57, TJ: Abderrahim Zahouani 15.59, SP: Mohamed Gharrous 17.43, DT: Nabil Kiram 53.63, HT: Driss Barid 64.95, JT: Mohamed Driouch 64.19. **Women**: 400m: Hasna Grioui 55.40, 800m: Halima Hachlaf 2:00.93, 1500m: Ibtissam Aït Elbatoui 4:20.66, 5000m/10,000m: Khadija Sammah 15:54.21/34:57.29, 3000mSt: Salima El Ouali Alami 9:49.09, 100mh: Yamina Hajjaji 13.94, 400mh: Lamia Lhabz 58.06, HJ: Ghiziane Siba 1.73, LJ: Jamaa Chnaïk 6.13, TJ: Jihad Bakhechi 13.18, DT: Amina Moudden 48.04, HT: Fatine Oubourogaa 54.08.

Hamid EZZINE b. 5 Dec 1983 Aït Ali 1.74m 60kg.
At 3000mSt: OG: '08- h. '12- 7; WCh: '05-07-11-13: h/h/9/9; AfCh: 04- 4, '06- 5. Won Franc G 2013.
Progress at 3000mSt: 2004- 8:25.10, 2005- 8:21.38, 2006- 8:19.37, 2007- 8:09.72, 2008- 8:13.20, 2011- 8:11.81, 2012- 8:16.93, 2013- 8:13.27. pbs: 1500m 3:43.03 '12, 3000m 7:54.65 '11, 5000m 14:28.68 '02.
Two-year drugs ban 2009-11. Older brother Ali set MAR 300mSt record 8:03.57 '00; OG: '00- 3, '04- 8; WCh: '99- 3, '01- 2, '03- 10; WJ: '96- 3.

Abdelaati IGUIDER b. 25 Mar 1987 Errachidia 1.70m 52kg.
At 1500m(/5000m): OG: '08- 5, '12- 3/6; WCh: '07-09-11-13: h/11/5/sf; WJ: '04- 1, '06- 6; WI: '10-12-14: 2/1/3.
Progress at 1500m, 5000m: 2004- 3:35.53, 2005- 3:35.63, 2006- 3:32.68, 2007- 3:32.75, 2008- 3:31.88, 2009- 3:31.47, 2010- 3:34.25, 2011- 3:31.60, 2012- 3:33.99, 13:09.17; 2013- 3:33.29. pbs: 800m 1:47.14 '07, 1000m 2:19.14 '07, 1M 3:51.78 '12, 3000m 7:34.92i '13, 7:41.95 '07.

Mohamed MOUSTAOUI b. 2 Apr 1985 Khouribga 1.74m 60kg.
At 1500m: OG: '08/12- sf; WCh: '07-09-11-13: sf/6/ 6/9; AfCh: '06- 5; WJ: '04- 4; AfJ: '03- 2; Arab champion 2007. World CC: '04- 14J, '05- 14 4k.
Progress at 1500m: 2003- 3:42.9, 2004- 3:37.44, 2005- 3:36.20, 2006- 3:32.51, 2007- 3:32.67, 2008- 3:32.06, 2009- 3:32.60, 2010- 3:36.92+, 2011- 3:31.84, 2012- 3:35.46, 2013- 3:32.08. pbs: 800m 1:45.44 '09, 1000m 2:20.00i '08, 1M 3:50.08 '08, 2000m 5:00.98i '07, 3000m 7:43.08i '09, 7:43.99 '11; 2M 8:26.49i '05, 5000m 13:22.61 '05.

Women

Malika AKKAOUI b. 25 Dec 1987 Zaida, Meknès-Tafilalet 1.60m 46kg.
At 800m: OG: '12- sf; WCh: '13: sf; AfCh: 10- 3, '12- 3; WJ: '06- h. At 1500m: WCh: '11- h. Won MAR 800m 2007-08, MedG 2013.
Progress at 800m: 2004- 2:09.2, 2005- 2:08.1, 2006- 2:06.29, 2007- 2:05.04, 2008- 2:04.25, 2009- 2:02.10, 2010- 2:00.6, 2011- 1:59.75, 2012- 1:59.01i/ 1:59.54, 2013- 1:57.64. pbs: 400m 53.94 '11, 1000m 2:39.86 '13, 1500m 4:04.96 '11.

Halima HACHLAF b. 6 Sep 1988 Boumia, Meknès-Tafilalet 1.68m 56kg.
At 800m: OG: '12- sf; WCh: '09-11-13: h/sf/ sf; AfCh: '07- 2 (3 1500m), '08- 4; WJ: '04- 9, '06- sf; WY: '03- sf, '05- 4.
Progress at 800m: 2004- 2:06.06, 2005- 2:06.91, 2006- 2:05.75, 2007- 2:02.60, 2008- 2:04.05, 2009- 2:00.91, 2010- 1:58.40, 2011- 1:58.27, 2012- 1:58.84, 2013- 1:59.38. pbs: 400m 54.96 '11, 600m 1:28.22 '07, 1500m 4:06.69 '13.
Older brother Abdelkader Hachlaf had pbs 1500m 3:33.59 '01, 3000mSt 8:08.76 '06.

Siham HILALI b. 2 May 1986 Oued Zem 1.61m 58kg.
At 1500m: OG: '08-10, '12- sf; WCh: '07-09-11-13: h/h/sf/11; AfCh: 10- 10; WJ: '04- 3 (3 3000m); WI: '08- 5, '14- 4. Won MedG 2013. At 3000m: WY: '03- 1.
Progress at 1500m: 2003- 4:15.1, 2004- 4:08.15, 2006- 4:25.82, 2007- 4:04.03, 2008- 4:05.36, 2009- 4:03.74, 2010- 4:03.89, 2011- 4:01.33, 2012- 4:02.59, 2013- 4:02.16. pbs: 800m 2:00.15 '13, 2000m 5:47.93 '09, 3000m 8:46.17i '12, 9:03.16 '04.

Btissam Boucif LAKHOUAD b. 7 Dec 1980 Khouribga 1.72m 55kg.
At 1500m: OG: '08- 12, '12- h; WCh: '09- sf, '11- 4, '13- sf; AfCh: '10- 3 (4 800m); CCp: '10- dnf.
Moroccan 1500m record 2010.
Progress at 1500m: 2004- 4:11.26, 2005- 4:18.01, 2006- 4:08.22, 2007- 4:03.4, 2008- 4:06.37, 2009- 4:03.23, 2010- 3:59.35, 2011- 4:01.09, 2012- 3:59.65, 2013- 4:04.63. pbs: 800m 2:00.22 '12, 1000m 2:38.14i '12, 1M 4:25.35 '07, 3000m 9:08.02 '07, 10k Rd 33:22 '06.

NETHERLANDS

Governing body: Koninklijke Nederlandse Atletiek Unie (KNAU), Postbus 60100, NL-6800

JC Arnhem. Founded 1901.
National Championships first held in 1910 (men), 1921 (women). **2013 Champions: Men**: 100m: Churandy Martina 10.04, 200m: Dennis Spillekom 20.96, 400m: Jürgen Wielart 45.83, 800m: Thijmen Kupers 1:52.54, 1500m: Mark Nouws 3:52.61, 5000m: Jesper van der Wielen 14:08.73, 10,000m: Michael Butter 29:52.65, HMar: Khalid Choukoud 63:27, Mar: Patrick Stitzinger 2:18:53, 3000mSt: Simon Vroemen 9:13.22, 110mh: Koen Smet 13.52w, 400mh: Jesper Arts 51.01, HJ: Douwe Amels 2.21, PV: Rutger Koppelaar 5.42, LJ: Ignisious Gaisah 7.85, TJ: Fabian Florant 16.30, SP: Erik van Vreumingen 18.85, DT: Erik Cadée 65.61, HT: Vincent Onos 67.89, JT: Bjorn Blommerde 71.31, Dec: Bas Markies 7234, 20kW: Harold van Beek 1:48:41, 50kW: Rob Tersteeg 5:09:41. Women: 100: Madiea Ghafoor 11.58w, 200m: Anouk Hagen 24.98, 400m: Nicky van Leuveren 52.14, 800m: Yvonne Hak 2:07.77, 1500m: Sifan Hassan 4:21.87?/Maureen Koster 4:23.11, 5000m: Helen Hofstede 16:20.06, 10,000m: Miranda Boonstra 35:29.20, HMar: Ruth van der Meijden 74:07, Mar: Andrea Deelstra 2:35:39, 3000mSt: Jolande Verrstarten 11:43.27, 100mh: Rosina Hodde 13.02, 400mh: Bianca Baak 59.51, HJ: Sietske Noorman 1.85, PV: Rianna Galiart 4.11, LJ/TJ: Brenda Baar 6.26/13.05, SP: Melissa Boekelman 17.60, DT: Corinne Nugter 51.87, HT: Eva Reinders 60.34, JT: Nadine Broersen 52.52, Hep: Amanda Spiljard 5382.

Erik CADÉE b. 15 Feb 1984 s'Hertogenbosch 2.01m 120kg. Prins Hendrik, Vught.
At DT: OG: '12- 10; WCh: '07-09-11-13: dnq 23/19/19/14; EC: '10- nt, '12- 10; WJ: '02- dnq 22; EU23: '05- 5; EJ: '03- 1; EYth: '01- 2. Dutch champion 2010, 2012-13.
Progress at DT: 2002- 50.63, 2003- 54.05, 2004- 56.59, 2005- 60.27, 2006- 61.36, 2007- 62.68, 2008- 61.75, 2009- 65.61, 2010- 66.20, 2011- 66.95, 2012- 67.30, 2013- 65.92. pb SP 18.99i, 17.70 '09.

Ignisious GAISAH b. 20 Jun 1983 Kumasi 1.86m 70kg. Formerly known as Anthony Essuman.
At LJ: OG: '04- 6, '12- dnq 18; WCh: '03-05-11-13: 4/2/dnq 17/2; CG: '06- 1, '10- 3; AfG: '03- 1, '11- 2; AfCh: '06- 1, '12- 3; WI: '06-10-12: 1/7/7; WCp: '06- 4. Won WAF 2004, Dutch 2013.
Long jump records: Ghana (9) 2003-06, NED 2013, African junior 2002, indoor 2006.
Progress at LJ: 1998- 7.35, 1999- 7.42, 2000- 7.40, 2002- 8.12, 2003- 8.30, 2004- 8.32, 2005- 8.34, 2006- 8.43/8.51w, 2007- 8.08, 2008- 7.78i, 2009- 7.78, 2010- 8.12, 2011- 8.26. 2012- 8.04, 2013- 8.29. pb 100m 11.04 09.
Changed from Ghana to Netherlands, where he has lived since 2002, in 2013.

Churandy MARTINA b. 3 Jul 1984 Willemstad, Curaçao 1.80m 68kg. Rotterdam Atletiek. Studied civil engineering at University of Texas

at El Paso, USA.
At 100m/(200m): OG: '04- qf, '08- 4/dq, '12- 6/5; WCh: '03- h, '05- qf, '07- 5/5, '09- qf, '11- sf/sf, '13- sf/7; WJ: '00- h/h, '02- qf; WY: '99- sf; EC: '12- (1)/1R; PAm: '03- sf, '07- 1; CAG: '06- 1/1R, '10- 1/1/3R; CCp: '10- (2)/1R. Won PAm-J 2003; NED 100m 2011-13, 200m 2011. Records: AHO 100m (8) 2004-08, 200m (6) 2005-10, 400m 2007; NED 100m (2) 2011-12, 200m (2) 2012.
Progress at 100m, 200m: 2000- 10.73, 21.73; 2001- 10.64A, 21.55; 2002- 10.30, 20.81; 2003- 10.29/10.26w, 20.71; 2004- 10.13, 20.75; 2005- 10.13/9.93Aw, 20.32/20.31w; 2006- 10.04A/10.06/ 9.76Aw 9.99w, 20.27A; 2007- 10.06, 20.20; 2008- 9.93, 20.11; 2009- 9.97, 20.76; 2010- 10.03A/10.07/ 9.92w, 20.08; 2011- 10.10, 20.38; 2012- 9.91, 19.85; 2013- 10.03, 20.01. pbs: 60m 6.58i '10, 400m 46.13A '07.
At 2008 Olympics set three national records at 100m and one at 200m before crossing line in second place in final in 19.82 only to be disqualified for running out of his lane. Competed for Netherlands Antilles until 2010.

Eelco SINTNICOLAAS b. 7 Apr 1987 Dordrecht 1.86m 81kg. AV '34 (Apeldoorn). Economics student.
At Dec: OG: '12- 11; WCh: '09- dnf, '11- 5, '13- 5; EC: '10- 2; WJ: '06- 8; EU23: '09- 1; EJ: '05- 14. At Hep: WI: '14- 4; EI: '11- 4, '13- 1.
Dutch decathlon record 2012.
Progress at Dec: 2007- 7466, 2008- 7507w, 2009- 8112, 2010- 8436, 2011- 8304, 2012- 8506, 2013- 8391. pbs: 60m 6.88i '13, 100m 10.71 '10, 10.69w '08; 200m 21.62 '10, 400m 47.88 '10, 1000m 2:37.42i '06, 1500m 4:22.29 '11, 60mh 7.88i '13, 110mh 13.92/13.89w '13, 400mh 51.59 '10, HJ 2.08i/2.02 '13, PV 5.52i '11, 5.45 '10; LJ 7.65i, 7.76w '09, 7.65 '12; SP 14.66i '14, 14.31 '11; DT 43.18 '12, JT 63.59 '12, Hep 6372i '13.
Set six pbs in improving pb by 277 points for European silver 2010.

Rutger SMITH b. 9 Jul 1981 Groningen 1.97m 130kg. Groningen Atletiek.
At SP (/DT): OG: '04- dnq 13/16, '08- 8/7, '12- dnq 14/16; WCh: '03- dnq 25/15, '05- 2, '07- 3/3, '11- (dnq 15); EC: '02- 8, '06- 3/7, '12- 2/3; WJ: '00- 1/3; EU23: '03- 3/1; EJ: '99- 1/1; WI: '03-08-12: dnq 10/4/7; EI: '05- 2; ECp: '04- 2/2. Won NED SP 2000, 2002-08; DT 2002-08, 2011.
Three Dutch shot records 2005-06.
Progress at SP, DT: 1998- 15.23, 51.18; 1999- 18.27, 53.81; 2000- 19.48, 58.74; 2001- 18.92i/18.21, 59.96; 2002- 20.39, 64.69; 2003- 20.52, 62.70; 2004- 20.94, 63.79; 2005- 21.41, 65.51; 2006- 21.62, 64.60; 2007- 21.19, 67.63; 2008- 20.89i/20.80, 66.85, 2011- 19.95i, 67.77; 2012- 20.56i/20.55, 66.97; 2013- 65.91.
First athlete to win World Championships medals in shot and discus.

Women

Nadine BROERSEN b. 29 Apr 1990 Hoorn 1.71m 62kg. AV Sprint Breda.

At Hep: OG: '12- 12; WCh: '13- 10; EU23: '11- 9; EJ: '09- 5. At Pen: 14- 1. Won NED HJ 2010-11, JT 2013.
Two Dutch high jump records 2013 and indoors 2014.
Progress at Hep: 2009- 5507, 2010- 5967, 2011- 5932(w)/5854, 2012- 6319, 2013- 6345. pbs: 200m 25.01 '13, 800m 2:12.89 '13, 60mh 8.32i '13, 100mh 13.50 '13, HJ 1.93i '14, 1.90 '13; LJ 6.20 '13, SP 14.93i '14, 14.34 '13; JT 54.97 '12, Pen 4830i '14.
Lost c.200 points in stumbling at last hurdle in first event of 2013 World heptathlon.

Sifan HASSAN b. '1 Jan' 1993 Adama, Ethiopia 1.66m 52kg. Eindhoven Atletiek.
At 3000m: WI: '14- 5. Eur CC: 13- 1 U23.
Progress at 1500m: 2011- 4:20.13, 2012- 4:08.74, 2013- 4:03.73. pbs: 800m 2:00.86 '13, 1M 4:29.85 '12, 3000m 8:32.53 '13, 10kRd 34:28 '12, HMar 77:10 '11.
Came to the Netherlands as a refugee at age 15. Dutch eligibility from 18 Nov 2013.

Dafne SCHIPPERS b. 15 Jun 1992 Utrecht 1.79m 68kg. Hellas.
At Hep: OG: '12- 11; WCh: '13- 3; WJ: '10- 1; EJ: '09- 4, '11- 1. At 100m/LJ: EU23: '13- 1/3. At 200m/4x100mR: WCh: '11- sf; EC: 12- 5/2R; WJ: '10- 3R. At 60m: EI: '13- 4. Won NED 100m 2011-12, LJ 2012.
Dutch records 200m 2011, Hep 2013.
Progress at Hep: 2009- 5507, 2010- 5967, 2011- 6172, 2012- 6360, 2013- 6477. pbs: 60m 7.14i '13, 100m 11.19. 11.13w '11; 150m 16.93 '13, 200m 22.69 '11, 800m 2:08.62 '13, 60mh 8.18i '12, 100mh 13.27 '11, HJ 1.80 '12, LJ 6.59 '13, SP 14.19 '11, JT 41.80 '11.
Added 117 points to pb and reduced 800m best from 2:15.52 to 2:08.62 in taking 2013 World heptathlon bronze.

NEW ZEALAND

Governing body: Athletics New Zealand, PO Box 305 504, Triton Plaza, Auckland.
National Championships first held in 1887 (men), 1926 (women). **2013 Champions: Men:** 100m/200m: Joseph Millar 10.32/21.38, 400m: Andrew Whyte 46.52, 800m: Brad Mathas 1:50.71, 1500m/HMar: Hamish Carson 3:46.26/68:52, 3000m: Nick Willis 7:57.63, 5000m: Hugo Beamish 14:01.09, 10,000m: Caden Shields 31:32.85, Mar: Dougal Thorburn 2:25:33, 3000mSt: Daniel Balchin 9:37.17, 110mh: Mike Cochrane 14.27, 400mh: Daniel O'Shea 50.64, HJ: William Crayford 2.09, PV: Nicholas Southgate 4.85, LJ: Matthew Wyatt 7.53, TJ: Phillip Wyatt 15.06, SP/DT: Tom Walsh 19.42/50.27, HT: Philip Jensen (19th title) 60.73, JT: Stuart Farquhar 80.17, Dec: Scott McLaren 7750, 3000mW: Michael Parker 13:28.64, 20kW: Graeme Jones 1:44:35, 50kW: *no finishers*. **Women:** 100m/LJ: Mariah Ririnui 11.84/6.01, 200m/ Hep: Portia Bing 24.59/5774w, 400m: Monique Williams 54.40, 800m: Angela

Smit 2:06.97, 1500m: Lucy Van Dalen 4:16.80, 3000m: Camille Buscomb 9:17.05, 5000m: Becky Wade 16:25.66, 10,000m: Kelly Hurung 38:23.20, HMar: Alex Williams 78:17, Mar: Shireen Crumpton 2:55:04, 3000mSt: Sarah McSweeney 10:33.44, 100mh: Fiona Morrison 13.64, 400mh: Zoe Ballantyne 62.10, HJ: Elizabeth Lamb 1.82, PV: Valerie Chan 3.43, TJ: Nneka Okpala 12.06, SP: Valerie Adams 20.37, DT: Siositina Hakeai 57.52, HT: Nicole Bradley 56.81, JT: Madeleine Chapman 47.63, 3000mW/20kW: Roseanne Robinson 14:09.92/1:47:42.

Jacko GILL b. 20 Dec 1994 Auckland 1.90m 118kg. Takapuna.
At SP: WJ: '10- 1, '12- 1; WY: '11- 1, YthOG: '10- 2. Five World youth shot records 5kg 23.86 '10, 24.35 and 24.45 '11; 6kg (4) 21.34 to 22.31, 7.26kg (3) in 2011. World junior 6kg record 23.00 '13. Three NZL records 2011.
Progress at SP: 2010- 18.57, 2011- 20.38, 2012- 20.05.
World age 15 and 16 bests for 5kg, 6kg and 7.26kg shot. His father Walter was NZ champion at SP 1987 & 1989, DT 1975, pbs 16.57 '86 & 53.78 (1975); his mother Nerida (née Morris) had discus best of 51.32 and was NZ champion in 1990.

Tomas WALSH b. 1 Mar 1992 Timaru 1.86m 123kg. South Canterbury.
At SP: WJ: '10- dnq 16; WY: '09- 6 (dnq 31 DT), WI: '14- 3. NZ champion SP 2010-14, DT 2013.
Two New Zealand shot records 2013-14 and two Oceania indoor records 2014.
Progress at SP: 2010- 17.57, 2011- 18.83, 2012- 19.33, 2013- 20.61, 2014- 21.28i/21.16. pb DT 53.58 '14. Set four NZ indoor shot records at 2014 World Indoors.

Nick WILLIS b. 25 Apr 1983 Lower Hutt 1.83m 68kg. Economics graduate of University of Michigan, USA.
At 1500m: OG: '04- sf, '08- 2, '12- 9; WCh: '05- 07-11-13: sf/10/12/sf; CG: '06-1, '10- 3; WJ: '02- 4; WI: '08/14- dq; WCp: '06- 3. Won NCAA indoor 2005, NZ 1500m 2006, 3000m 2013, 5000m 2011-12.
Four NZ 1500m records 2005-12. Oceania 1500m record 2012 and indoors (3:35.80) 2010.
Progress at 1500m: 2001- 3:43.54, 2002- 3:42.69, 2003- 3:36.58, 2004- 3:32.64, 2005- 3:32.38, 2006- 3:32.17, 2007- 3:35.85, 2008- 3:33.51, 2009- 3:38.85i, 2010- 3:35.17, 2011- 3:31.79, 2012- 3:30.35, 2013- 3:32.57. pbs: 800m 1:45.54 '04, 1000m 2:16.58 '12, 1M 3:50.66 '08, 3000m 7:40.62 '13, 5000m 13:27.54 '05.
His brother Steve (b. 25 Apr 1975) had pbs: 1500m 3:40.29 '99, 1M 3:59.04 '00.

Women

Valerie ADAMS b. 6 Oct 1984 Rotorua 1.93m 123kg. Auckland City.
At SP: OG: '04- 7, '08- 1, '12- 1; WCh: '03-05-07-09-11-13: 5/2/1/1/1/1; CG: '02-06-10: 2/1/1; WJ:

'02- 1; WY: '99- 10, '01- 1; WI: '04-08-10-12-14: dnq 10/1/2/1/1; WCp: '02- 6, '06- 1, '10- 1. Won WAF 2008-09, DL 2011-13, NZL SP 2001-11, 2013-14; DT 2004, HT 2003.
Nine Oceania & Commonwealth shot records 2005-11, 22 NZ 2002-11, 10 OCE indoor 2004-13. Progress at SP: 1999- 14.83, 2000- 15.72, 2001- 17.08, 2002- 18.40, 2003- 18.93, 2004- 19.29, 2005- 19.87, 2006- 20.20, 2007- 20.54, 2008- 20.56, 2009- 21.07, 2010- 20.86, 2011- 21.24, 2012- 21.11, 2013- 20.98i/20.90, 2014- 20.67i. pbs: DT 58.12 '04, HT 58.75 '02.
NIne senior global shot titles. Matched her age with metres at the shot from 14 to 18 and missed that at 19 by only two months. 28 successive shot wins from September 2007 to World Indoor silver in March 2010, and another 46 from August 2010 to March 2014. Her father came from England and her mother from Tonga. Married New Caledonia thrower Bertrand Vili (SP 17.81 '02, DT 63.66 '09, 4 ECp '07 for France) in November 2004 (divorced in 2010).

Kimberley SMITH b. 19 Nov 1981 Papakura 1.66m 49kg. Social science graduate of Providence College.
At 5000m: OG: '04- h; WUG: '05- 1; WCp: '06- 4. At 10,000m: OG: '08- 9; WCh: '05- 15, '07- 5, '09- 8. At 3000m: WI: '08- 6. At Mar: OG: '12- 15. World CC: '05- 12, '09- 13; HMar: '09- 7. Won NCAA 5000m and indoor 3000m & 5000m 2004; NZ 5000m 2002, 2006, 2008; CC 2002.
Oceania records: 3000m 2007, 5000m & 10,000m 2008; indoor 1M 2008, 3000m 2007, 5000m 2005 & 2009. NZ records 5000m (3) 2005-07, 10,000m (3) 2005-08, HMar (4) 2009-11, Mar 2010.
Progress at 5000m, 10,000m, Mar: 2002- 16:30.10, 2003- 15:47.92, 2004- 15:09.72, 33:45.81; 2005- 14:50.46i/15:05.68, 31:21.00, 2006- 14:56.58, 2007- 14:49.41, 31:20.63; 2008- 14:45.93, 30:35.54; 2009- 14:39.89i/14:52.49, 31:21.42; 2010- 2:25:21, 2011- 15:14.02, 2:25:46; 2012- 2:26:59, 2013- 31:46.37, 2:28:36. pbs: 1500m 4:11.25 '04, 1M 4:24.14i '04, 3000m 8:35.31 '07, 2M 9:13.94i '08, Rd: 15k 47:37 '11, 10M 53:10 '10, 20k 63:38+ '11, HMar 67:11 '11. Did not finish on marathon debut in New York 2008. Married Pat Tarpy on 1 Sep 2012.

NIGERIA

Governing body: The Athletic Federation of Nigeria, P.O.Box 18793, Garki, Abuja. F'd 1944.
2013 National Champions: Men: 100m: Egwero Ogho-Oghene 10.18, 200m: Elvis Ukale 21.16, 400m: Noah Akwu 45.59, 800m/1500m/ 3000mSt: Hamajan Soudi 1:49.19/3:48.93/9:14.32, 5000m/10,000m: Kefas Williams 14:52.30/ 31:19.96, HMar: Gideon Goyet 66+, 110mh: Selim Nurudeen 13.64, 400mh: Henry Okorie 51.30, HJ: Okpara Theddus 2.10, PV: Edwin Emmanuel 3.70, LJ: Oluwashola Anoya 7.61, TJ: Tosin Oke 16.64, SP: Ezeofor Kenechukwu 16.00, DT:

Augustine Nwoye 51.01, HT: Ibrahim Bada 55.10, JT: Kenechukwu Ezeofor 68.03, 20000mW: Oluwaseyi Lawal 1:28+ distance?. **Women**: 100m/200m/LJ: Blessing Okagbare 11.25/22.65/ 6.68, 400m: Regina George 50.99, 800m/1500m: David Abiye 2:05.63/4:50.17, 5000m: Amoinat Olowora 17:47.16, 10,000m: Janet Dung 37:22.02, HMar: Pam Deborah 1:20+, 100mh: Ugonna Ndu 13.47, 400mh: Ajoke Odumosu 56.35, HJ: Doreen Amata 1.90, PV: Moreen Williams 2.90, TJ: Blessing Ibrahim 13.37, SP: Nkechi Chime 13.69, DT: Celestina Efobi 40.65, HT: Queen Obisesan 62.06, JT/Hep: Patience Okoro 41.87/5238, 20000mW: Queensly Asedo 1:31:36 distance?

Women

Ajoke ODUMOSU b. 27 Oct 1987 Lagos 1.68m 59kg. Was at University of South Alabama, USA. At 400mh: OG: '12- 8; WCh: '07-09-11-13: h/sf/ sf/h; CG: '10- 1; AfG: '07- 3, '11- 1; AfCh: '08-10-12: 1/2/1 ; WJ: '06- 5/2R; CCp: '10- 2. Won Af-J 2003, Nigerian 2009-13. At 400m: OG: '08- sf. Four Nigerian 400mh records 2009-12. Progress at 400mh: 2003- 60.03, 2004- 57.33, 2006- 56.09, 2007- 55.37, 2008- 55.92A, 2009- 54.80, 2010- 54.59, 2011- 56.23, 2012- 54.40, 2013- 55.10. pbs: 100m 11.71 '09, 200m 23.42 '10, 400m 51.39 '08, 50.46dt '07.

Blessing OKAGBARE b. 9 Oct 1988 Sapele 1.80m 68kg. Student at University of Texas at El Paso, USA. At LJ/(100m): OG: '08- 3, '12- dnq 17/8; WCh: '11- dnq 18/5, '13- 2/6 (3 200m); AfG: '07- 2 (4 TJ), '11- 1/2; AfCh: '10- 1/1/1R, '12- 1/2; WJ: '06- 16 (dnq 17 TJ); CCp: '10- 6/3/3R; Won Nigerian 100m 2009-13, 200m 2013, LJ 2008-09, 2011-13; TJ 2008; NCAA 100m & LJ 2010. Two African 100m records 2013, Nigerian & African junior TJ record 2007. Progress at 100m, 200m, LJ: 2004- 5.85 irreg, 2006- 6.16, 2007- 6.51, 2008- 23.76A, 6.91; 2009- 11.16, 6.73/6.90w; 2010- 11.00/10.98w/10.7Aw, 22.71, 6.88; 2011- 11.08/11.01w, 22.94, 6.78/6.84w; 2012- 10.92, 22.63, 6.97; 2013- 10.79/10.75w, 22.31, 7.00/7.14w. pbs: 60m 7.18i '10, 300m 37.04 '13, TJ 14.13 '07.

NORWAY

Governing body: Norges Friidrettsforbund, Serviceboks 1, Ullevaal Stadium, 0840 Oslo. Founded 1896.

National Championships first held in 1896 (men), 1947 (women, walks 1937). **2013 Champions**: **Men**: 100m: Anders Erlend Idås 10.68, 200m: Øyvind Kjerpeset 21.10, 400m: Andreas Roth 47.37, 800m: Henrik Ingebrigtsen 1:48.25, 1500m: Filip Ingebrigtsen 3:55.18, 5000m/10,000m: Ørjan Grønnevig 14:16.44/ 29:55.31/66:58, Mar: John Henry Strupstad 2:30:22, 3000mSt: Tom Erling Kårbø 8:56.41, 110mh: Karsten Warholm 14.70, 400mh: Øyvind

Kjerpeset 50.38, HJ: Brede Raa Ellingsen 2.14, PV: Eirik Greibrokk Dolve 5.00, LJ: Mateusz Parlicki 7.47, TJ: Sindre Almsengen 15.58, SP: Stian Andersen 16.50, DT: Fredrik Amundgård 56.89, HT: Eivind Henriksen 72.16, JT: Andreas Thorkildsen 80.91, Dec: Lars Vikan Rise 7608, 10,000mW/20kW: Erik Tysse 41:56.3/1:26:35, 50kW: none. **Women**: 100m: Ezinne Okparaebo 11.30, 200m/400m: Line Kloster 23.72/53.41, 800m: Trine Mjåland 2:04.86, 1500m: Karoline Bjerkeli Grøvdal 4:18.90, 5000m: Hilde Aasheim 16:27.31, 10,000m: Runa Skrove Falch 35:18.60, HMar: Marthe Katrine Myhre 1:20:01, Mar: Maria Venås 2:48:26, 3000mSt: Karoline E. Skatteboe 10:47.26, 100mh: Isabelle Pedersen 13.25, 400mh: Vilde Svortevik 58.82, HJ: Katarina Mögenburg 1.75, PV: Cathrine Larsåsen 4.30, LJ: Ida Marcussen 6.24, TJ: Inger Anne Frøysedal 12.95, SP: Kristin Sundsteigen 15.41, DT: Grete Etholm 51.48, HT: Trude Raad 60.61, JT: Tove Beate Dahle 52.20, Hep: Frida Thorsås 5371, 3000mW: Merete Helgheim 14:19.62, 10kW: not held

Henrik INGEBRIGTSEN b. 24 Feb 1991 Stavanger 1.80m 69kg. Sandnes IL At 1500m: OG: '12- 5; WCh: 13- 8; EC: '10- h, '12- 1; WJ: '10- h; EU23: '11- h; EJ: '09- h. At 5000m: EU23: '13- 1. Won NOR 800m 20.13, 1500m 2010, 2012. Eur U23 CC: '12- 1. Norwegian records: 1500m (2) 2012-13, 1M 2012. Progress at 1500m: 2004- 4:30.63, 2005- 4:22.48, 2006- 4:04.15, 2007- 3:54.08, 2008- 3:50.63, 2009- 3:44.53, 2010- 3:38.61, 2011- 3:39.50, 2012- 3:35.43, 2013- 3:33.95. pbs: 800m 1:48.25 '13, 1M 3:54.28 '12, 3000m 7:42.19 '13, 5000m 14:19.39 '13, 2000mSt 5:41.03 '09, 3000mSt 8:52.56 '09. Younger brother Filip (b. 20 Apr 1993) 1500m pb 3:38.76 '13 (10 WJ '12, 6 EU23 '13).

Jaysuma SAIDY NDURE b. 1 Jan 1984 Bakau, The Gambia 1.92m 72kg. IL i BUL, Oslo. At (100m)/200m: OG: '04- qf/qf, '08- qf/sf, '12- h/sf; WCh: '03- h, '05- sf, '09- (sf), '11- sf/4, '13- 8; EC: '10- 6/5, '12- (3); CG: '02- qf, '06- sf; WJ: '02- h; AfG: '03- h/sf; AfCh: '04- 3/6; CCp: '10- dnf, ET: '13- 2/2. At 60m: EI: '13- 1. Won WAF 200m 2007, Norwegian 100m 2007-08, 2011; 200m 2007, 2010, 2012. Records: Gambian 100m & 200m 2001-06, Norwegian 100m (6) 2007-11, 200m 2007. Progress at 100m, 200m: 2001- 10.66, 21.27; 2002- 10.73/10.59w, 21.20; 2003- 10.52/10.51w, 21.18; 2004- 10.26, 20.69; 2005- 10.31/10.18w, 20.51/ 20.14w, 2006- 10.27, 20.47; 2007- 10.06, 19.89; 2008- 10.01, 20.45; 2009- 10.10/10.07w, 20.55; 2010- 10.00/9.98w, 20.29; 2011- 9.99, 19.95; 2012- 10.13, 20.34; 2013- 10.07/9.95w, 20.23/20.12w. pbs: 60m 6.55i '08, 300m 33.76 '09, 400m 48.71 '09. Having lived in Oslo from 2001, became a Norwegian citizen in November 2006.

Andreas THORKILDSEN b. 1 Apr 1982 Kristiansand 1.88m 90kg. Kristiansands IF. At JT: OG: '04- 1, '08- 1, '12- 6; WCh: '01-03-05-

07-09-11-13: dnq 26/11/2/2/1/2/6; EC: '02-06-10-
12: dnq 15/1/1/4; WJ: '00- 2; EU23: '03- 4; EJ:
'99- 7, '01- 2; EY: '97- 1; WCp: '06- 1;CCp: '10- 1;
ET: '10- 2. Won DL 2010, WAF 2006, 2009; NOR
2001-06, 2009-11, 2013.
World junior javelin record 2001, seven
Norwegian records 2005-06.
Progress at JT: 1996- 53.82, 1998- 61.57, 1999-
72.11, 2000- 77.48, 2001- 83.87, 2002- 83.43, 2003-
85.72, 2004- 86.50, 2005- 89.60, 2006- 91.59, 2007-
89.51, 2008- 90.57, 2009- 91.28, 2010- 90.37, 2011-
90.61, 2012- 84.72, 2013- 84.64. pbs: SP 9.96 '01,
DT 38.02 '01.
His mother Bente Amundsen was a Norwegian
champion at 100mh (pb 14.6), father Tomm was
a junior international with bests of 100m 10.9
and javelin 71.64.

PANAMA

Governing body: Federación Panameña de
Atletismo, Apartado 0860-00684, Villa Lucre,
Ciudad de Panamá. Founded 1945.

Irving SALADINO b. 23 Jan 1983 Ciudad de
Colón 1.83m 70kg. Studied electrical engineering at University of São Paulo.
At LJ: OG: '04- dnq 36, '08- 1, '12- dnq; WCh:
'05-07-09-11: 6/1/nj/dnq 22; WJ: '02- dnq; PAm:
'07- 1; CAG: '06- 1; SACh: '03- 3, '13- 3; WI: '06- 2;
WCp: '06- 1; won WAF & IbAm 2006, CAG 2013,
SAm U23 2004, SAmG 2014.
Three South American LJ records 2006-08,
indoors (7) 2006-08, 12 Panama 2002-08.
Progress at LJ: 2001- 7.11, 2002- 7.51A/7.39, 2003-
7.46, 2004- 8.12A/7.79, 2005- 8.29/8.51w, 2006-
8.56/8.65w, 2007- 8.57, 2008- 8.73, 2009- 8.63,
2010- 8.30/8.46w, 2011- 8.40, 2012- 8.16, 2013-
7.99A/7.94, 2014- 8.16. pbs: 100m 10.4 '04, TJ 14.47
'04.
Set South American indoor record in qualifying and four more in final of WI 2006 for the
first medal ever for Panama at World
Championships. Clear world number one in
2006, winning 15/16 outdoors and in 2007
when he won all nine competitions, 21 successive wins to June 2008. Based in Brazil 2005-09
and from 2014.

Women

Yvette LEWIS b. 16 Mar 1985 Germany 1.73m
62kg. Norfolk Read Deal. Was at Hampton
University, where now an assistant coach.
At 100mh(/TJ): PAm: '07- 8/6, '11- 1/7; WJ: '04-
(dnq); won SAmG 2014, NCAA TJ 2007.
South American records: 100mh and six 60mh
indoors 2013.
Progress at 100mh: 2005- 13.53, 2006- 13.14,
2007- 13.06, 2008- 12.85, 2009- 12.85, 2010- 13.19,
2011- 12.76/12.74w, 2012- 12.84/12.74w, 2013-
12.67. pbs: 55m 6.96i '07, 60m 7.40i '06, 100m
11.56 '07, 200m 23.50 '06, 400m 56.63i '09, 50mh
7.06+i '09, 60mh 7.84i '13, HJ 1.78i '05, 1.78 '07; LJ

6.29i '09, 6.24 '07, 6.46w '12; TJ 13.84 '08, Hep
5378 '12, Pen 3852i '07.
Switched from USA to Panama 25 Oct 2012.

POLAND

Governing body: Polski Zwiazek Lekkiej
Atletyki (PZLA), ul. Myslowicka 4, 01-612
Warszawa. Founded 1919.
National Championships first held in 1920
(men), 1922 (women). **2013 Champions: Men:**
100m/200m: Karol Zalewski 10.31/20.49, 400m:
Marcin Marciniszyn 45.98, 800m: Artur
Kuciapski 1:49.98, 1500m: Krzysztof Zebrowski
3:38.94, 5000m: Artur Kozlowski 14:30.77,
10,000m: Tomasz Szymkowiak 29:32.95, HMar:
Marcin Blazinski 65:04, Mar: Arkadiusz
Gardzielewski 2:13:43, 3000mSt: Mateusz
Demczyszak 8:26.30, 110mh: Artur Noga 13.29,
400mh: Damian Krupa 51.40, HJ: Szymon
Kiecana 2.25, PV: Lukasz Michalski 5.60, LJ:
Adrian Strzalkowski 7.76, TJ: Michal Lewan-
dowski 16.54, SP: Tomasz Majewski 20.69, DT:
Piotr Malachowski 66.87, HT: Szymon
Ziólkowski 77.74, JT: Hubert Chmielak 80.28,
Dec: Marcin Przybyl 7241, 20kW: Artur Brzozo-
wski 1:22:16, 50kW: Adrian Blocki 3:50:48.
Women: 100m/200m: Marika Popowicz 11.29/
23.24, 400m: Justyna Swiety 53.06, 800m:
Angelika Cichocka 2:03.26, 1500m: Renata Plis
4:09.30, 5000m: Karolina Jarzyniszyn 15:47.31,
10,000m: Agnieszka Mierzejewska 34:14.17, HMar:
Olga Kalendarowa-Ochal 74:04, Mar: Agnieszka
Gortel-Maciuk 2:40:03, 3000mSt: Katarzyna
Kowalska 10:00.34, 100mh: Karolina Koleczek
13.21, 400mh: Joanna Linkiewicz 56.86, HJ:
Justyna Kasprzycka 1.92, PV: Anna Rogowska
4.55, LJ: Teresa Dobija 6.58, TJ: Anna Jagaciak
14.20, SP: Agnieszka Dudzinska 16.94, DT: Zaneta
Glanc 59.13, HT: Anna Wlodarczyk 76.93, JT:
Barbara Madejczyk 57.69, Hep: Agnieszka Bor-
owska 5481, 20kW: Agnieszka Dygacz 1:30:58.

Pawel FAJDEK b. 4 Jun 1989 Swiebodzice
1.86m 120kg. KS Agros Zamosc.
At HT: OG: '12- dnq; WCh: '11- 11, '13- 1; WJ:
'08- 4; EU23: '09- 8, '11- 1; WUG: '11- 1, '13- 1; ET:
'11- 2, '13- 1. Won POL 2012, Franc G 2013,
World HT challenge 2013.
Progress at HT: 2008- 64.58, 2009- 72.36, 2010-
76.07, 2011- 78.54, 2012- 81.39, 2013- 82.27. pb Wt
23.22i '14

Adam KSZCZOT b. 2 Sep 1989 Opoczno 1.78m
68kg. RKS Lódz. Studied organisation and
management.
At 800m: OG: '12- sf; WCh: '09/13- sf, '11- 6; EC:
'10- 3; WJ: '08- 4; EU23: '09/11- 1; EJ: '07- 3; WI:
'10- 3, '14- 2; EI: '09-11-13: 4/1/1; ET: '11/13- 1.
Polish champion 2009, 2010, 2012.
Polish 1000m record 2011.
Progress at 800m: 2005- 1:59.57, 2006- 1:51.09,
2007- 1:48.10, 2008- 1:47.16, 2009- 1:45.72, 2010-
1:45.07, 2011- 1:43.30, 2012- 1:43.83, 2013- 1:44.76,

pbs: 400m 46.51 '11, 600m 1:14.55 '10, 1000m 2:16.99 '11, 1500m 3:46.53 '10.

Marcin LEWANDOWSKI b. 13 Jun 1987 Szczecin 1.79m 64kg. SL WKS Zawisza Bydgoszcz. PE student.
At 800m: OG: '08/12- sf; WCh: '09- 8, '11- 4, '13- 4; EC: '10- 1; WJ: '06- 4; EU23: '07- 1, '09- 2; WI: '14- dq; EI: '09- 6, '11- 2; CCp: '10- 2; ECp: '08- 2, '10- 3; won World Military 2011. At 1500m: EJ: '05- 7; EI: '13- 4; ET: '13- 3. Won Polish 800m 2011, 1500m 2008, 2010.
Polish 1000m record 2011.
Progress at 800m: 2004- 1:51.73, 2005- 1:48.86, 2006- 1:46.69, 2007- 1:45.52, 2008- 1:45.84, 2009- 1:43.84, 2010- 1:44.10, 2011- 1:44.53, 2012- 1:44.34, 2013- 1:43.79. pbs: 400m 47.76 '09, 600m 1:15.77 '10, 1000m 2:15.76 '11, 1500m 3:37.37i '14, 3:38.98 '13. Coached by brother Tomasz (1:51.00 '03).

Tomasz MAJEWSKI b. 30 Aug 1981 Nasielsk 2.04m 142kg. AZS-AWF Warszawa. Graduated in political science from Cardinal Wyszynski University.
At SP: OG: '04- dnq 17, '08- 1, '12- 1; WCh: '05- 07-09-11-13: 7/4/2/8/6; EC: '06- 6, '10- 1; EU23: '03- 4; WI: '04-06-08-10-12-14: 4/6/3/4/3/4; EI: '09- 1; WUG: '03- 5, '05- 1; CCp: '10- 2; ECp: '07- 08-09-10-11-13: 3/2/1/1/2/2. Won WAF 2008, Polish 2002-05, 2007-13; Franc G 2013.
Polish shot record 2009.
Progress at SP: 1998- 12.91, 1999- 15.77, 2000- 17.77, 2001- 18.34, 2002- 19.33, 2003- 20.09, 2004- 20.83i/20.52, 2005- 20.64, 2006- 20.66, 2007- 20.87, 2008- 21.51, 2009- 21.95, 2010- 21.44, 2011- 21.60, 2012- 21.89, 2013- 20.98. pb DT 51.79 '07.
Improved pb every year of his career to 2009. Went from 20.97 to 21.04 in qualifying and 21.21 and 21.51 in final to win Olympic gold in 2008.

Piotr MALACHOWSKI b. 7 Jun 1983 Zuromin 1.93m 130kg. WKS Slask Wroclaw. Army corporal.
At DT: OG: '08- 2, '12- 5; WCh: '07-09-11-13: 12,/2/9/2; EC: '06- 6, '10- 1; WJ: '02- 6; EU23: '03- 9, '05- 2; EJ: '01- 5; CCp: '10- 4; ECp: '06-07-08-09-10-11: 1/1/3/1/2/3. Won DL 2010, POL 2005-10, 2012-13.
Nine Polish discus records 2006-13.
Progress at DT: 2000- 52.04, 2001- 54.19, 2002- 56.84, 2003- 57.83, 2004- 62.04, 2005- 64.74, 2006- 66.21, 2007- 66.61, 2008- 68.65, 2009- 69.15, 2010- 69.83, 2011- 68.49, 2012- 68.94, 2013- 71.84.

Lukasz MICHALSKI b. 2 Aug 1988 Bydgoszcz 1.90m 85kg. SL WKS Zawisza Bydgoszcz. Studied medicine.
At PV: OG: '12- 11; WCh: '09- dnq 22=, '11- 4; EC: '10- 7; WJ: '06- 8; WY: '05- 4; EU23: '09- 5; EJ: '07- 3; WUG: '11- 1; WI: '10- 9; EI: '09- 6; ET: '09- 3; Polish champion 2010, 2011 (tie), 2012-13.
Progress at PV: 2004- 4.80, 2005- 5.25, 2006- 5.30, 2007- 5.50, 2008- 5.51, 2009- 5.71, 2010- 5.80, 2011- 5.85, 2012- 5.72, 2013- 5.60. pb LJ 6.95 '08.

Artur NOGA b. 2 May 1988 Racibórz 1.96m 82kg. KS AZS-AWF Kraków.

At 110mh: OG: '08- 5, '12- h; WCh: '09/13- sf; EC: '10- 5, '12- 3; WJ: '06- 1; EU23: '09- 1; EJ: '07- 1; ET: '10- 2, '13- 3. Polish champion 2008, 2010, 2012- 13. At 60mh: WI: '12- 8.
Polish 110mh record 2012.
Progress at 110mh: 2007- 14.08, 2008- 13.34, 2009- 13.35, 2010- 13.29/13.20w, 2011- 13.57, 2012- 13.27, 2013- 13.26. pbs: 100m 10.68 '07, 200m 21.33 '07, 60mh 7.64i '08.

Lukasz NOWAK b. 18 Dec 1988 Poznan 1.94m 77kg. AZS Poznan.
At 50kW: OG: '12- 8; WCh: '13- 8; EC: '10- 8. At 20kW: EU23: '09- 13. Won POL 50kW 2012.
Progress at 50kW: 2009- 3:58:57, 2010- 3:50:30, 2011- 3:46:40, 2012- 3:42:47, 2013- 3:43:38. pbs: 3000mW 11:41.30 '11; 5000mW 19:13.08i '14, 19:24.57 '11; 10kW 40:30 '13; 20kW 1:20:48 '13; 30kW 2:13:07 '13; 35kW 2:35:17 '13.

Grzegorz SUDOL b. 28 Aug 1978 Nowa Deba 1.75m 64kg. KS AZS-AWF Kraków. PE graduate.
At 50kW: OG: '04- 7, '08- 9; WCh: '03-05-07-09- 11-13: dq/dq/21/4/dnf/6; EC: '02- 10, '06- 10, '10- 2; ECp: '13- 5. At 20kW: OG: '12- 24. At 10,000mW: WJ: '96- 7, EJ: '97- 10. Won POL 20kW 2008-09, 2012; 50kW 2002, 2007-08.
Unratified Polish 30,000m record 2011.
Progress at 50kW: 2002- 3:50:37, 2003- 3:55:40, 2004- 3:49:09, 2006- 3:50:24, 2007- 3:55:22, 2008- 3:45:47, 2009- 3:42:34, 2010- 3:42:24, 2012- 3:46:01, 2013- 3:41:20. pbs: 3000mW 11:21.90 '12, 5000mW 18:55.01i '05, 19:06.07 '12; 10kW 39:01 '05, 20kW 1:20:46 '13, 30kW 2:11:12.0t '11, 35kW 2:33:53 '13. Three times Polish 50k champion – each event held in different countries (CZE, AUT, SVK).

Robert URBANEK b. 29 Apr 1987 Leczyca 2.00m 120kg. MKS Aleksandrów Lódzki
At DT: OG: '12- dnq 32; WCh: '13- 6; EC: '12- 6.
Progress at PV: 2004- 47.09, 2005- 47.83, 2006- 50.84, 2007- 56.18, 2008- 62.22, 2009- 60.54, 2010- 60.74, 2011- 64.37, 2012- 66.93, 2013- 65.30. pb SP 16.21 '07.

Pawel WOJCIECHOWSKI b. 6 Jun 1989 Bydgoszcz 1.90m 85kg. SL WKS Zawisza Bydgoszcz. PE student.
At PV: OG: '12- dnq; WCh: '11- 1; WJ: '08- 2; EU23: '11- 1; EJ: '07- dnq 16; EI: '11- 4. Won W.Military 2011. Polish pole vault record 2011.
Progress at PV: 2001- 2.50, 2002- 2.70, 2003- 3.10, 2004- 3.50, 2005- 4.10, 2006- 4.70, 2007- 5.00, 2008- 5.51, 2009- 5.40i/5.22, 2010- 5.60, 2011- 5.91, 2012- 5.62, 2014- 5.76i.

Szymon ZIÓLKOWSKI b. 1 Jul 1976 Poznan 1.92m 120kg. OS AZS Poznan.
At HT: OG: '96-00-04-08-12: 10/1/dnq 12/7/7; WCh: '95-99-01-05-07-09-11-13: dnq 22/dnq 23/1/3/7/2/7/9; EC: '98-02-06-10-12: 5/dnq 15/5/5/3; WJ: '94- 1; EJ: '93- 7, '95- 1; EU23: '97- 2; ECp: '96-99-01-04-05-06-07-08-09: 2/2/1/1/1/1/ 1/1/2. Polish champion 1996-7, 1999-2002, 2004- 09, 2011, 2013.

Six Polish hammer records 2000-01.
Progress at HT: 1991- 55.96, 1992- 63.84, 1993-
67.34, 1994- 72.48, 1995- 75.42, 1996- 79.52, 1997-
79.14, 1998- 79.58, 1999- 79.01, 2000- 81.42, 2001-
83.38, 2002- 79.78, 2003- 76.97, 2004- 79.41, 2005-
79.35, 2006- 82.31, 2007- 80.70, 2008- 79.55, 2009-
79.30, 2010- 77.99, 2011- 79.02, 2012- 78.51, 2013-
78.79. pbs: SP 15.25 '95, DT 49.58 '00, Wt 21.10i '14.
His sister Michalina (b. 1983) was second in the
2000 Polish U18 Championships, pb 58.33 '04.
Married javelin thrower (50.90 '98 (old), 50.64 '99)
Joanna Domagala in December 2000 and after
divorce Iwona Dorobisz (100m 11.47 '09) in 2008.

Women

Zaneta GLANC b. 11 Mar 1983 Poznan 1.87m
96kg. OS AZS Poznan. Studied sociology.
At DT: OG: '08/12- dnq nt/23; WCh: '09- 4, '11-
4, '13- 7; EC: '10- dnq 13; EJ: '05- dnq; WUG:
'09- 2, '11- 1; ET: '11- 3, '13- 3. Won POL 2009,
2013.
Progress at DT: 2003- 47.03, 2004- 51.30, 2005-
56.15, 2006- 56.00, 2007- 59.36, 2008- 61.42, 2009-
63.96, 2010- 62.16, 2011- 63.99, 2012- 65.34, 2013-
62.90.

Joanna FIODOROW b. 4 Mar 1989 Augustów
1.69m 89kg. AZS Poznan.
At HT: OG: '12- 10; WCh: '11- dnq 21; WJ: '08-
dnq 19; EU23: '09- 4, '11- 2.
Progress at HT: 2005- 40.96, 2006- 50.18, 2007-
55.93, 2008- 61.22, 2009- 62.80, 2010- 64.66, 2011-
70.06, 2012- 74.18, 2013- 68.92, 2014- 72.70. pbs:
SP 12.87 '10, JT 35.56 '09.

Justyna KASPRZYCKA b. 20 Aug 1987
Glubczyce 1.83m 62kg. AZS-AWF Wroclaw
At HJ: WCh: '13- 6; EU23: '07- 9=, '09- 9; WI: '12-
4; Polish champion 2013.
Progress at HJ: 2001- 1.58, 2002- 1.67, 2003- 1.77,
2004- 1.76i/1.72, 2005- 1.74, 2006- 1.78, 2007- 1.86,
2008- 1.79i/1.74, 2009- 1.87, 2010- 1.88, 2011-
1.84i, 2012- 1.84, 2013- 1.97, 2014- 1.97i.

Kamila LICWINKO b. 22 Mar 1986 1.83m
59kg. née Stepaniuk. KS Podlasie Bialystok.
At HJ: WCh: '09- dnq 16, '13- 7=; EU23: '07- 4; EJ:
'05- 7; WIO: '14- 1=, EI: '09- 8; ET: '13- 2; WUG:
'13- 1. Polish champion 2007-09.
Polish high jump records 2013 & 2014.
Progress at HJ: 1999- 1.46, 2000- 1.61, 2001- 1.66,
2002- 1.75, 2003- 1.75, 2004- 1.84, 2005- 1.86,
2006- 1.85i/1.84, 2007- 1.90, 2008- 1.91, 2009- 1.93,
2010- 1.92i/1.89, 2011- 1.88i, 2012- 1.89, 2013- 1.99,
2014- 2.00i.
Married Michal Licwinko in 2013.

Anna ROGOWSKA b. 21 May 1981 Gdynia
1.71m 57kg. SKLA Sopot. PE student.
At PV: OG: '04- 3, '08- 10=, '12- nh; WCh: '03-05-
07-09-11-13: 7/6=/8/1/10=/dnq; EC: '02- 7=;
EU23: '03- 3; WI: '03-04-06-08-10-14: 6=/7/2/6
/3/5=; EI: '05-07-11-13: 2/3/1/2; ECp: '05-08-10-
11-13: 1/2/3/1/3. Polish champion 2009, 2011,
2013.

Nine Polish pole vault records 2004-05, indoors
(2) 2010-11.
Progress at PV: 1997- 2.60, 1998- 2.90, 1999- 3.40,
2000- 3.60, 2001- 3.90, 2002- 4.40, 2003- 4.47i/4.45,
2004- 4.71, 2005- 4.83, 2006- 4.80i/4.70, 2007-
4.72i/4.60, 2008- 4.66, 2009- 4.80, 2010- 4.81i/4.71,
2011- 4.85i/4.75, 2012- 4.71i/4.70, 2013- 4.67i/4.60.
Coached by husband Jacek Torlinski (PV 4.85
'97).

Karolina TYMINSKA b. 4 Oct 1984 Swiebodzin
1.75m 69kg. SKLA Sopot.
At Hep: OG: '08- 7, '12- dnf; WCh: '07-09-11-13:
15/dnf/4/9; EC: '06- dnf (dnq LJ), '10- 5; EU23:
'05- dnf (LJ dnq 17); ECp: '06-09-13: 2/3/1. At
Pen: WI: '08-10-12-14: 6/6/4/8; EI: '05-07-09-11:
8/7/5/4. Won POL 100mh 2011, Hep 2006-07,
2011.
Progress at Hep: 2002- 5147, 2004- 5787, 2005-
6026, 2006- 6402, 2007- 6200, 2008- 6428, 2009-
6191, 2010- 6230, 2011- 6544, 2012- dnf, 2013-
6360. pbs: 60m 7.61i '09, 100m 12.15 '05, 200m
23.32 '06, 800m 2:05.21 '11, 60mh 8.34i '10,
100mh 13.12 '11, HJ 1.78 '11, LJ 6.63 '08, SP
15.11i/14.82 '08, JT 42.40 '13, Pen 4769i '08.

Anita WLODARCZYK b. 8 Aug 1985 Rawicz
1.78m 95kg. RKS Skra Warszawa. PE student.
At HT: OG: '08- 6, '12- 2; WCh: '09- 1, '11- 5, '13-
2; EC: '10- 3, '12- 1; EU23: '07- 9; ET: '09- 1, '13- 2.
Won POL 2009, 2011-12, Franc G 2013, World HT
challenge 2013.
Two world hammer records 2009-10, four Polish
records 2009-13.
Progress at HT: 2003- 43.24, 2004- 54.74, 2005-
60.51, 2006- 65.53, 2007- 69.07, 2008- 72.80, 2009-
77.96, 2010- 78.30, 2011- 75.33, 2012- 77.60, 2013-
78.46. pbs: SP 13.25 '06, DT 52.26 '08, Wt 20.09i '14.

PORTUGAL

Governing body: Federação Portuguesa de
Atletismo, Largo da Lagoa, 1799-538 Linda-a-
Velha. Founded in 1921.
National Championships first held in 1910
(men), 1937 (women). **2013 Champions: Men:**
100m/200m: Yazaldes Nascimento 10.44/21.00,
400m: António Rodrigues 48.80, 800m: Miguel
Moreira 1:51.18, 1500m: Hélio Gomes 3:41.02,
5000m: Paulo Pinheiro 14:26.72, 10,000m:
Daniel Pinheiro 29:59.27, Mar: Rui Pedro Silva
2:13:11, 3000mSt: Daniel Gregório 8:58.39,
110mh: Rasul Dabó 13.57, 400mh: Jorge Paula
50.47, HJ: Paulo Conceição 2.16, PV: Edi Maia
5.45, LJ: Marcos Chuva 7.65, TJ: Nelson Évora
16.41, SP: Marco Fortes 19.57, DT: Filipe Vital e
Silva 56.91, HT: Dário Manso 69.15, JT: Tiago
Aperta 69.88, Dec: Tiago Marto 7184,
10,000mW/20kW: João Vieira 40:02.78/1:26:36,
50kW: Luís Gil 4:12:31. **Women**: 100m: Carla
Tavares 11.66, 200m: Sónia Tavares 23.93, 400m:
Joceline Monteiro 55.35, 800m/ 1500m: Sandra
Teixeira 2:08.29/4:27.41, 5000m /3000mSt:
Salomé Rocha 16:14.15/10:01.41, 10,000m: Ana

Dulce Félix 35:17.70, Mar (held Dec 2012): Anabela Tavares 2:45:44, 100mh: Eva Vital 13.52, 400mh: Vera Barbosa 58.18, HJ: Liliana Viana 1.83, PV: Marta Onofre 4.22, LJ: Teresa Carvalho 6.23, TJ: Patricia Mamona 13.86, SP: Isabel Ribeiro 13.58, DT: Irina Rodrigues 55.06, HT: Vânia Silva 60.34, JT: Sílvia Cruz 53.54, Hep: Cláudia Rodrigues 5125, 10,000mW/20kW: Inês Henriques 43:31.29, 20kW: Ana Cabecinha 1:30:49.

Nelson ÉVORA b. 20 Apr 1984 Abidjan, Côte d'Ivoire 1.81m 64kg. Sport Lisboa e Benfica.
At (LJ/)TJ: OG: '04- dnq 40, '08- 1; WCh: '05-07-09-11: dnq 14/1/2/5; EC: '06- 6/4; WJ: '02- dnq 18/6; EU23: '05- 3; EJ: '03- 1/1; WUG: '09- 1, '11-1; WI: '06- 6, '08- 3; EI: '07- 5; ECp: '09- 2/1; Won WAF TJ 2008, POR LJ 2006-07, TJ 2003-04, 2006-07, 2009-11, 2013.
Six Portuguese triple jump records 2006-07, Cape Verde LJ & TJ records 2001-02.
Progress at TJ: 1999- 14.35, 2000- 14.93i, 2001-16.15, 2002- 15.87, 2003- 16.43, 2004- 16.85i/16.04, 2005- 16.89, 2006- 17.23, 2007- 17.74, 2008- 17.67, 2009- 17.66/17.82w, 2010- 16.36, 2011- 17.35, 2013-16.68. pbs: HJ 2.07i '05, 1.98 '99; LJ 8.10 '07.
Portugal's first male world champion in 2007. He suffered a serious injury in right tibia (in same place where he had an operation in February 2010) in January 2012 and missed season. Father from Cape Verde, mother from Côte d'Ivoire, relocating to Portugal when he was five. Switched nationality in 2002. Sister Dorothé (b. 28 May 1991) 400m pb 55.11 '13.

Marco FORTES b. 26 Sep 1982 Lisboa 1.89m 139kg. Sport Lisboa e Benfica.
At SP: OG: '08/12: dnq 37/15; WCh: '09-13: dnq 17/16, '11- 5; EC: '10- dnq 12, '12-5; WJ: '00- dnq 18 (dnq 26 DT); EU23: '03- 12; EJ: '01- 3; EI: '11- 8, '13- 5; Won IbAm 2010, POR SP 2002-13 (& 12 indoor), DT 2009, 2011
Five Portuguese shot records 2008-12.
Progress at SP: 2000- 17.31, 2001- 18.02, 2002-18.76, 2003- 18.57, 2004- 18.19, 2005- 17.89, 2006-18.74, 2007- 19.18, 2008- 20.13, 2009- 20.52, 2010-20.69, 2011- 20.89, 2012- 21.02, 2013- 20.22, 2014-21.01. pb DT 58.32 '09.

João VIEIRA b. 20 Feb 1976 Portimão 1.74m 58kg. Sporting Clube de Portugal.
At 20kW: OG: '04- 10, '08- 32, '12- 11 (dnf 50k); WCh: '99-01-03-05-07-09-11-13: dq/dq/17/dnf/25/10/15/4; EC: '98-02-06-10: 20/12/3/3; WCp: '02- 11, '06- 8; ECp: '03-07-13: 4/7/7. At 10,000mW: WJ: '94- 11; Won POR 10,000mW 2011-13, 20kW 1996, 1999-2007, 2009, 2011-14; 50kW 2004, 2008, 2012.
Portuguese records: 5000mW 2000, 10,000mW 2011, 20kW (3) 2002-06, 50kW 2004 & 2012.
Progress at 20kW: 1995- 1:33:51, 1996- 1:23:49, 1997- 1:20:59, 1998- 1:22:50, 1999- 1:22:46, 2000-1:22:53, 2001- 1:22:52, 2002- 1:20:44, 2003- 1:20:30, 2004- 1:20:48, 2005- 1:21:56, 2006- 1:20:09, 2007-1:20:42, 2008- 1:21:13, 2009- 1:21:43, 2010- 1:20:49, 2011- 1:22:44, 2012- 1:20:41, 2013- 1:21:08. pbs: 5000m 18:33.16 '00, 10,000mW 39:44.91 '11, 39:06R '10; 30kW 2:09:49 '04, 50kW 3:45:17 '12. Twin brother Sergio has 20kW pb 1:20:58 '97.

Women

Jéssica AUGUSTO b. 8 Nov 1981 Paris, France 1.65m 46kg. Nike.
At Mar: OG: '12- 7. At 3000mSt: OG: '08- h (h 5000); WCh: '09- 11. At 5000m/(10,000m): WCh: '05- h, '07- 15, '11- (10); EC: '10- 3/2; EU23: '03-dnf; WUG: '07- 1; CCp: '10- 7. At 3000m (1500m): WJ: '00- 8; EU23: '01- (10); EJ: '99- 6 (12); WI: '08-8, '10- 7; EI: '09- 10. World CC: '07- 12, '10- 21; Eur CC: '98-99-00-02-04-05-06-07-08-09-10: 12J/8J/1J/16/18/30/9/11/2/4/1. Won POR 1500m 2007, 2011; 5000m 2006, IbAm 3000m 2004, 2006, 2010.
Two Portuguese 3000m steeplechase records 2008-10, European indoor 2M best 2010.
Progress at 5000m, 10,000m, Mar, 3000mSt: 2003- 15:51.63, 2004- 15:15.76, 2005- 15:20.45, 2006- 15:37.55, 2007- 14:56.39, 2008- 15:19.67, 9:22.50; 2009- 9:25.25, 2010- 14:37.07, 31:19.15, 9:18.54; 2011- 15:19.60, 32:06.68, 2:24:33; 2012-2:24:59, 2013- 15:38.73, 2:29:11. pbs: 800m 2:07.97i '02, 1500m 4:07.89i/4:08.32 '10, 1M 4:32.58i '09, 4:42.15 '99, 2000m 5:45.6i '09, 3000m 8:41.53 '07, 2M 9:19.39i '10, 9:22.89 '07; road 15k 48:40 '08, 10M 53:15 '08, HMar 69:08 '09.
Won Great North Run 2009.

Ana CABECINHA b. 29 Apr 1984 Beja 1.68m 52kg. CO Pechão.
At 20kW: OG: '08- 8, '12- 9; WCh: '11- 7, '13- 8; EC: '10- 8; EU23: '05- 4; WCp '08-10-12: 11/8/9; ECp: '13- 5. At 5000mW: WY: '01- 10. At 10,000mW: WJ: '02- 12; EJ: '03- 3; won IbAm 2006, 2010; 2nd RWC 2012; POR 10,000mW 2005, 2008, 2010, 2012, 20kW 2012-14.
POR records 10,000m and 20km walk 2008.
Progress at 20kW: 2004- 1:37:39, 2005- 1:34:13, 2006- 1:31:02, 2007- 1:32:46, 2008- 1:27:46, 2009-1:33:05, 2010- 1:31:14, 2011- 1:31:08, 2012- 1:28:03, 2013- 1:29:17. pbs: 3000mW 12:21.56i '13, 12:31.86 '12; 5000mW 21:31.06 '14, 21:21R '12; 10,000mW 43:08.17 '08; running 1500m 4:31.73 '07, 3000m 9:46.08 '13, 5000m 17:57.34 '12.

Inês HENRIQUES b 1 May 1980 Santarém 1.56m 48kg. CN Rio Maior.
At 20kW: OG: '04- 25, '12- 15; WCh: '01-05-07-09-11-13: dq/27/7/11/10/11; EC: '02-06-10: 15/12/9; EU23: '01- 10; WCp: '06-10-12: 13/3/10; ECp: '07-7, '13- 8; Won POR 10,000mW 2006, 2009, 2011, 2013; 20kmW 2009, 2011. At 5000mW: EJ: '99- 12.
Progress at 20kW: 2000- 1:41:09, 2001- 1:34:49, 2002- 1:34:46.5t, 2003- 1:36:03, 2004- 1:31:23.7t, 2005- 1:33:24, 2006- 1:30:28, 2007- 1:30:24, 2008-1:31:06, 2009- 1:30:34, 2010- 1:29:36, 2011- 1:30:29, 2012- 1:29:54, 2013- 1:29:30. pbs: 3000mW 12:25.36i '13, 12:38.75 '07; 5000mW 21:38.05 '10, 10,000mW 43:22.05 '08, 43:09R '10.

Patrícia MAMONA b. 21 Nov 1988 Lisbon 1.68m 53kg. Sporting CP. Was at Clemson Universoty.
At TJ: OG: '12- dnq 13; WCh: '11- dnq 27; WJ: '06- 6; WY: '05- 7; EC: '10- 8, '12- 2; EU23: '09- 5; EJ: '07- dnq 15; WI: '14- 4; EI: '13- 8; WUG: '11- 2. POR champion 2008-13, NCAA 2010-11.
Seven Portuguese triple jump records 2009-12.
Progress at TJ: 2004- 12.71, 2005- 12.87, 2006- 13.37/13.38w, 2007- 13.24, 2008- 13.51, 2009- 13.83, 2010- 14.12, 2011- 14.42, 2012- 14.52, 2013- 14.02/14.07w, 2014- 14.36i. pbs: 200m 24.42 '10, 800m 2:19.70i '09, 60mh 8.41i '09, 100mh 13.53/13.49w '10, HJ 1.69i '09, 1.69 '11; LJ 6.21i '09, 6.16 '05; Pen 4081i '09, Hep 5293 '11.

Vera SANTOS b. 3 Dec 1981 Santarém 1.64m 57kg. Sporting Clube de Portugal.
At 20kW: OG: '08- 9, '12- 49; WCh: '03-05-07-09-13: 15/15/11/5/17; EC: '02- 17, '06- 8, '10- 6; EU23: '01- 12, '03- 2; WUG: '05- 2; WCp '08- 3, '10- 2; ECp: '05- 7, '13- 10. At 10,000mW: WJ: '00- 5. Won POR 20kW 2005, 2010.
Progress at 20kW: 2000- 1:39:20.5t, 2001- 1:35:51, 2002- 1:34:46.6t, 2003- 1:32:43, 2004- 1:33:00, 2005- 1:31:30, 2006- 1:30:41, 2007- 1:32:53, 2008- 1:28:14, 2009- 1:29:27, 2010- 1:28:29, 2011- 1:29:55, 2012- 1:32:48, 2013- 1:31:00. pbs: 3000mW 12:17.59 '10, 5000mW 21:01.43 '10, 10,000mW 43:52.73 '10.

PUERTO RICO

Governing body: Federación de Atletismo Amateur de Puerto Rico, 90, Ave. Río Hondo, Bayamón, PR 00961-3113. Founded 1947.
National Champions 2013: Men: 100m: Miguel Lopez 10.46, 200m: Carlos Rodríguez 21.60, 400m: Félix Martínez 46.70, 800m: ?, 1500m/ 5000m: Alfredo Santana 3:54.31/15:25.87, 110mh: Héctor Cotto 14.30, 400mh: Erick Alejandro 49.80, HJ: Ruben Rosa 1.90, PV: Yeisel Cintrón 4.70, LJ: Abdel Merced 7.18w, TJ: Julio Pagán 14.02, SP: Carlos Martínez 15.86, DT: Alfredo Romero 49.39, HT: Alexis Figueroa 61.59, JT: Felipe Ortíz 62.17. **Women**: 100m/200m: Genoxika Cancel 11.70/24.59, 400m: Carol Rodríguez 53.22, 800m: Beverly Ramos 2:06.65, 1500m: Angelín Figueroa 4:45.99, 5000m/3000mSt: ?, 100m: Natshalie Isaac 14.07, 400mh: Keyshaliz Dumeng 64.95, HJ: Alysbeth Félix 1.70, PV: Diamara Planell 3.80, LJ: Leila Reyes 5.92w, TJ: Frances López 11.46, SP: Ambar Pertez 11.62, DT: Ashley Arroyo 43.79, HT: Keyshla Luna 54.06, JT: Coraly Ortíz 55.93.

Javier CULSON b. 25 Jul 1984 Ponce 1.98m 79kg.
At 400mh: OG: '08- sf, '12- 3; WCh: '07-09-11-13: sf/2/2/6; PAm: '07- 6; CAG: '06- 5, '10- 2; PAm-J: '03- 3; WUG: '07- 3; CCp: '10- 2; won DL 2012-13, IbAm 2006, CAC 2009.
Seven Puerto Rican 400mh records 2007-10.
Progress at 400mh: 2002- 54.47, 2003- 51.10, 2004- 50.77, 2005- 50.62, 2006- 49.48, 2007- 49.07,

2008- 48.87, 2009- 48.09, 2010- 47.72. 2011- 48.32, 2012- 47.78, 2013- 48.14. pbs: 200m 21.64w '07, 400m 45.99 '12, 800m 1:49.83 '14, 110mh 13.84 '07.

QATAR

Governing body: Qatar Association of Athletics Federation, PO Box 8139, Doha. Founded 1963.

Mutaz Essa BARSHIM Ahmed b. 24 Jun 1991 Doha 1.92m 70kg. Team Aspire.
At HJ: OG: '12- 3=; WCh: '11- 7, '13- 2; WJ: '10- 1; AsiG: '10- 1; AsiC: '11- 1; WI: '12- 9=, '14- 1; won Asian indoors 2012. 2014; Asi-J 2010, W.Mil G 2011, Arab 2011, 2013; Gulf 2013.
Two Asian high jump records 2012-13 and indoors 2013-14, 14 Qatar records 2010-13.
Progress at HJ: 2008- 2.07, 2009- 2.14, 2010- 2.31, 2011- 2.35, 2012- 2.39, 2013- 2.40, 2014- 2.38i.
Qatari father, Sudanese mother. Younger brother Muamer Aissa Barshim has HJ pb 2.20 (2012).

ROMANIA

Governing body: Federatia Romana de Atletism, 2 Primo Nebiolo Str, 011349 Bucuresti. Founded 1912.
National Championships first held in 1914 (men), 1925 (women). **2013 Champions: Men**: 100m: Bogdan Madaras 10.53, 200m: Doru Teofilescu 22.05, 400m: Florin Purcea 47.67, 800m: Valentin Voicu 1:50.72, 1500m: Alexandru Staicu 3:54.55, 3000m: Andrei Stefana 8:18.98, 5000m/10,000m: Ilie Corneschi 15:07.08/ 30:54.34, HMar: Marius Ionescu 64:58, Mar: Stefan Lupulescu 2:25:25, 3000mSt: Daniel Betej 8:54.90, 110mh: Cornel Bananau 14.42 400mh: Gabriel Tudorache 54.86, HJ: Alexandru Tufa 2.20, PV: Valentin Stanciu 4.40, LJ: Ionut Grecu 6.94, TJ: Marian Oprea 17.32w, SP: Vlad Zinca 16.32, DT: Sergiu Ursu 63.32, HT: Ion Sorescu 62.74, JT: Levente Bartha 70.33, Dec: Ionut Feniuc 6700, 20kW: Marius Cocioran 1:27:33/Narcis Mihaila 1:36:00. **Women**: 100m: Andreea Ograzeanu 11.37, 200m: Simina Rizea 25.26, 400m: Bianca Razor 52.40, 800m: Dorina Korozsi 2:03.50, 1500m: Florina Pierdevara 4:21.96, 3000m: Mihaela Petrea 10:03.33, 5000m/10,000m: Nicoleta Petrescu 16:56.65/35:10.00, HMar: Cristiana Frumuz 73:39, Mar: Liliana Danci 2:48:54, 3000mSt: Claudia Prisecaru 10:59.03, 100mh: Anamaria Nesteriuc 13.81w, 400mh: Sanda Belgyan 61.38, HJ: Daniela Stanciu 1.90, PV: Ana Maria Antonencu 3.20, LJ: Ciornelia Deiac 6.49, TJ: Cristina Bujin 13.68, SP: Andreea Huzum-Vitan 15.47, DT: Nicoleta Grasu 57.46 (18th title), HT: Bianca Perie 68.80, JT: Nicoleta Anghelescu 53.01, Hep: Beatrice Puiu 5814, 20kW: Claudia Stef 1:36:50/Ana Rodean 1:39:51.

Marian OPREA b. 6 Jun 1982 Pitesti 1.90m 80kg. Rapid Bucuresti & Dinamo Bucuresti. Sports teacher.

At TJ: OG: '04- 2, '08- 5; WCh: '01-03-13: dnq 13/17/15, '05- 3, '13- 6; EC: '02-06-10-12: dnq 14/3/2/dnq 21; WJ: '00- 1; WY: '99- 4; EU23: '03-2; EJ: '99- 3, '01- 1; WI: '03-04-06-14: 8/5/4/4; EI: '02- 2, '11- 3; WUG: '01- 2; WCp: '06- 3, '10- 1. ROU champion 2001, 2003-08, 2013; Balkan 2001-03, 2013.
Romanian TJ records 2003 and 2005.
Progress at TJ: 1997- 14.37, 1998- 14.78, 1999-15.98, 2000- 16.49, 2001- 17.11/17.13w, 2002-17.29i/17.11/17.39w, 2003- 17.63, 2004- 17.55, 2005- 17.81, 2006- 17.74i/17.56, 2007- 17.32, 2008-17.28, 2010- 17.51, 2011- 17.62i/17.19, 2012-16.97i/16.56/16.68w, 2013- 17.24/17.32w, 2014-17.30i. pb LJ 7.73 '05, 8.06w '11.
Silver medal in 2004 was best ever Olympic placing by a Romanian male. Major surgery on his left knee in October 2008 meant that he did not compete in 2009.

Women

Angela MOROSANU b. 26 Jul 1986 Iasi 1.78m 57kg. Dinamo Bucuresti & Enka SC, TUR.
At (200m)/400mh: OG: '08- sf, '12- h; WCh: '09-8; EC: '06- 8/sf, '10- 5, '12- sf; WJ: '04- 8; EU23: '07- 1; ECp: '06- 2/4. At 100m: ECp: '05- 5. At 400m: EJ: '05- 1 (3 200m); WI: '04- 3R, '08- 5; EI: '07- 4. Won ROU 100m 2005-06, 200m 2003-06, 2012; 400m 2005-07, 400mh 2009-10, 2012.
Progress at 400mh: 2004- 58.30, 2005- 59.28, 2006- 55.37, 2007- 54.40, 2008- 56.07, 2009- 53.95, 2010- 54.58, 2011- 58.05, 2012- 54.81, 2013- 53.85. pbs: 60m 7.30i '05, 100m 11.47 '05, 200m 22.91 '06, 400m 51.93i '07, 52.48 '05; 60mh 8.11i '12.

Bianca-Florentina **PERIE** b. 1 Jun 1990 Roman, Neamt district 1.70m 70kg. S.C.M. Bacau. Student.
At HT: OG: '08/12- dnq 18/21; WCh: '07/09- dnq 26/19, '11-13- 6/11; EC: '10-4, '12- 9; WJ: '06/08- 1; WY: '05/07- 1; EU23: '11- 1; EJ: '07/09- 1; WUG: '11- 2, '13- 4; Won ROU 2009-13, Balkan 2013.
Progress at HT: 2003- 47.14, 2004- 57.67, 2005-65.13, 2006- 67.38, 2007- 67.24, 2008- 69.59, 2009-69.63, 2010- 73.52, 2011- 72.04, 2012- 70.05, 2013-71.57. pb SP 13.04i '07.
World age 14 best of 65.13 in 2005. Her younger sister Roxana won the bronze medal in the 2011 World Youth hammer.

RUSSIA

Governing body: All-Russia Athletic Federation, Luzhnetskaya Nab. 8, Moscow 119992. Founded 1911.
National Championships first held 1908, USSR women from 1922. **2013 Champions: Men**: 100m: Aleksandr Brednev 10.38, 200m: Aleksandr Khyutte 20.94, 400m: Maksim Dyldin 45.55, 800m: Yuriy Borzakovskiy 1:46.98, 1500m: Valentin Smirnov 3:47.09, 5000m: Rinas Akhmadiyev 13:49.73, 10,000m: Yevgeniy Rybakov 28:34.59, HMar: Sergey Rybin 64:31,

Mar: Artyom Aplachkin 2:15:23, 3000mSt: Ilgizar Safiulin 8:28.87, 110mh: Sergey Shubenkov 13.19, 400mh: Denis Kudryavtsev 49.40, HJ: Ivan Ukhov 2.30, PV: Sergey Kucheryanu 5.60, LJ: Sergey Morgunov 8.06, TJ: Alelksey Fyodorov 16.81, SP: Maksim Sidorov 20.45, DT: Nikolay Sedyuk 61.39, HT: Sergey Litvinov 77.77, JT: Dmitriy Tarabin 88.84, Dec: Ilya Shkurenyov 8354, 20kW: Andrey Ruzavin 1:19:08, 50kW: Yuriy Andronov 3:43:54.
Women: 100m: Olga Kharitonova 11.51, 200m: Yelena Bolsun 23.38, 400m: Kseniya Zadorina 50.55, 800m: Yelena Kotulskaya 1:59.56, 1500m: Yuliya Zaripova 4:02.56, 5000m: Yelena Nagovitsyna 15:23.17, 10,000m: Gulshat Fazlitdinova 32:01.83, HMar: Alla Kulyatina 73:16, Mar: Marina Kovalyova 2:35:03, 3000mSt: Natalya Aristarkova 9:34.33, 100mh: Yuliya Kondakova 12.81, 400mh: Irina Davydova 55.49, HJ: Svetlana Shkolina 1.97, PV: Yelena Isinbayeva 4.75, LJ: Lyudmila Kolchanova 6.89, TJ: Irina Gumenyuk 14.50, SP: Yevgeniya Kolodko 19.86, DT: Yekaterina Strokova 61.34, HT: Tatyana Lysenko 78.15, JT: Mariya Abakumova 65.99, Hep: Kristina Savitskaya 6210, 20kW: Lina Bikulova 1:28:42.
Note: Clubs abbreviations: Dyn – Dynamo, VS – Trade Union sports society, YR – Army, YR – Yunest Rossii.

Lyukman ADAMS b. 24 Sep 1988 St. Petersburg 1.94m 87kg.
At TJ: OG: '12- 9; EC: '10- 6; EJ: '07- 1; WI: '12- 3, '14- 1. Russian champion 2012.
Progress at TJ: 2005- 15.97, 2006- 15.16, 2007-16.75, 2008- 16.86i/16.78, 2009- 16.22i/16.20, 2010-17.17/17.21w, 2011- 17.32i/15.60, 2012- 17.53, 2013-16.82, 2014- 17..37i. pb LJ 7.47i '05, 7.42 '07.
Married to Yevgeniya Polyakova (60m 7.09 '08, 1 EI '09; 100m 11.09 '07; 4x100m 1 OG '08).

Yuriy ANDRONOV b. 6 Nov 1971 Samara 1.80m 68kg. Samara VS.
At 50kW: OG: '04- 9; WCh: '09- dnf; EC: '02-06-10: dq/3/10; WCp: '04- 3, '06- 3; ECp: '05-07-09: 3/5/3; RUS champion 2010, 2012-13.
World M40 50k walk record 2012.
Progress at 50kW: 1991- 4:06:49, 1993- 3:59:28, 1994- 3:52:30, 1995- 3:57:54, 1996- 3:47:04, 1997-3:54:52, 1999- 3:50:34, 2001- 3:52:57, 2002- 3:42:06, 2003- 3:48:26, 2004- 3:46:49, 2005- 3:42:34, 2006-3:42:38, 2007- 3:42:55, 2009- 3:49:09, 2010- 3:54:22, 2011- 3:42:25, 2012- 3:40:46, 2013- 3:43:54. pbs: 5000mW 19:09.7i '02, 20kW: 1:22:42.0t '02, 30kW 2:07:23 '04, 35kW 2:28:01 '03.

Sergey BAKULIN b. 13 Nov 1986 Insar, Mordoviya. 1.69m 58kg. Mordoviya VS.
At 20kW: EC: '06- 5; EU23: '07- 3; WCp: '06- 6, '10- 7; WUG: '09- 1. At 50kW: OG: '12- 5; WCh: '11- 1; EC: '10- 3; WCp: '12- 4; ECp: '09- 4; Russian champion 2011.
Progress at 20kW, 50kW: 2006- 1:19:54, 2007-1:19:14, 2008- 1:18:18, 3:52:38; 2010- 1:24:05, 3:43:26; 2011- 3:38:46, 2012- 3:38:55. pbs: 5000mW 18:26.82i '12, 10kW: 39:03 '06, 35kW 2:24:25 '09.

Valeriy BORCHIN b. 11 Sep 1986 Povodimovo, Mordoviya 1.78m 63kg. Saransk VS.
At 20kW: OG: '08- 1, '12- dnf; WCh: '07- dnf, '09- 1, '11- 1; EC: '06- 2; EU23: '07- 1; WCp: '08- 2, '12- 9; ECp: '07- 9; Russian champion 2006.
Progress at 20kW: 2006- 1:20:00, 2007- 1:18:56, 2008- 1:17:55, 2009- 1:17:38, 2011- 1:18:55, 2012- 1:21:29. pbs: 3000mW 18:11.8i '10, 5000mW 18:16.54 '12, 10kW: 38:42 '11.
Served one year drugs ban 2005-06.

Yuriy BORZAKOVSKIY b. 12 Apr 1981 Kratovo, Moskva reg. 1.82m 72kg. Moskva Dyn.
At 800m/4x400mR: OG: '00-04-08-12: 6/1/sf/sf; WCh: '03-05-07-09-11: 2/2/3/4/3; EC: '02- 2R, '12- 1; EJ: '99- 1; WI: '01- 1, '06- 3; EI: '00- 1, '09- 1; ECp: '99-02-10: 1/1/1; 2nd GP 2001. At 400m: EC: '02- sf; EU23: '01- 1; At 1500m: ECp: '03- 3. Won Russian 800m 2004, 2009-11, 2013; 1500m 2005, 2007-08.
Records: Two world junior indoor 800m 2000, European Junior 800m (2) & 1000m 2000; Russian: 800m (4) 2001, 1000m 2008.
Progress at 800m: 1997- 1:52.8i/1:53.69, 1998- 1:47.71, 1999- 1:46.13, 2000- 1:44.33, 2001- 1:42.47, 2002- 1:44.20, 2003- 1:43.68, 2004- 1:43.92, 2005- 1:44.18, 2006- 1:43.42, 2007- 1:44:38, 2008- 1:42.79, 2009- 1:43.58, 2010- 1:44.65, 2011- 1:43.99, 2012- 1:45.09, 2013- 1:45.24. pbs: 200m 22.56 '99, 400m 45.84 '00, 600m 1:16.02i '10, 1000m 2:15.50 '08, 1500m 3:40.28 '05, 3000m 8:32 '99.
He won at the World Youth Games in 1998, and at 18 had a startling victory in sprinting to victory in the European Cup 800m. In 2000 he set a hugely impressive Russian senior and world junior record 1:44.38 in Dortmund. He did not compete at the 2001 Worlds or 2002 Europeans at 800m, although he ran a 44.75 last leg in the European 4x400m. He typically leaves himself a tremendous amount to do on the second lap of his 800m races but Olympic success in 2004 came from a remarkably even-paced race.

Aleksey DMITRIK b. 12 Apr 1984 Slantsy. Leningrad reg, 1.91m 69kg. St Petersburg YR.
At HJ: WCh: '11- 2, '13- dnq 25=; EC: '10- 7; WJ: '02- 14; WY: '01- 1; EJ: '03- 2; EU23: '05- 6; EI: '09- 2=, '13- 2; ECp: '05- 1, '11- 2. Won RUS 2011.
Progress at HJ: 2000- 2.08, 2001- 2.23, 2002- 2.26, 2003- 2.28, 2004- 2.30, 2005- 2.34i/2.30, 2006- 2.28, 2007- 2.30, 2008- 2.33i/2.27, 2009- 2.33, 2010- 2.32i/2.31, 2011- 2.36, 2012- 2.35i/2.33, 2013- 2.36i/2.30, 2014- 2.40i.
Mother Yelana was a 1.75m high jumper.

Aleksey FYODOROV b. 25 May 1991 Smolensk 1.84m 73kg. Mosoovskaya Smolenskaya.
At TJ: WCh: '11- dnq 18, 13- 5; EC: '12- 4; WY: '07- 2; EU23: '11-2/, '13- 1; EJ: '09- 1; EI: '13- 3; WUG: '13- 2; ET: '13- 1. won RUS 2011, 2013.
Progress at TJ: 2007- 15.59, 2008- 16.08, 2009- 16.62, 2010- 17.12/17.18w, 2011- 17.05i/17.01, 2012- 17.19, 2013- 17.13.
Parents Leonid and Tatyana were triple jumpers

Aleksandr IVANOV b. 26 Jun 1994 Nizhny Tagiul, Sverdlovsk 1.70m 55kg. Mordoviya VS.
At 20kW: WCh: '13- 1; EU23: '13- 2; ECp: '13- 4. At 10,000W: WJ: '12- 2; WCp: 'EJ: '11- 6; 12- 2J.
Progress at 20kW: 2013- 1:20:58, 2014- 1:20:44. pbs: 5000mW 19:35.0 '12, 10,000W: 40:12.90 '12, 39:29R '13.

Vladimir KANAYKIN b. 21 Mar 1985 Atyuryevo, Mordoviya 1.70m 65kg. Saransk VS.
At 20kW: '12- dq; WCh: '11- 2; WCp: '12- 3; ECp: '11- 6. At 50kW: WCh: '05- dq, '07- dnf; EC: '06- 9; WCp: '08- dq (2); ECp: '07- 1; Won RWC 30kW 2007, RUS 20km 2007, 50km 2005-06. At 10,000mW: WJ: '02- 1, '04- 2; WY: '01- 1.
World record 20km walk 2007, three world bests 30km & 35km walk 2004-06 (each to win Russian winter 35k).
Progress at 20kW, 50kW: 2003- 1:21:23, 2004- 1:22:00, 3:40:40; 2005- 1:21:11, 3:40:40; 2006- 1:21:20, 3:45:57; 2007- 1:17:16, 3:40:57; 2008- 1:16:53dq, 3:36:55dq; 2010- 1:22:23. 2011- 1:19:14, 2012- 1:19:43. pbs: 5000mW 18:17.13i '12, 20:20.26 '03; 10,000mW: 40:58.48 '04, 10kW: 38:16 '04, 30kW 2:01:13 '06, 35kW 2:21:31 '06.
Disqualified when well clear of field in 2004 at World Cup junior 10km. 2-year drugs ban after positive EPO test 20 Apr 2008.

Sergey KIRDYAPKIN b. 18 Jun 1980 Insar, Mordoviya Rep. 1.78m 67kg. Saransk VS.
At 50kW: OG: '08- dnf, '12- 1; WCh: '05-07-09-11: 1/dnf/1/dnf; EC: '10- dnf; WCp: '08- 6, '12- 1; ECp: '05- 2. Won RUS 50kW 2009.
Progress at 50kW: 2001- 4:08:16, 2002- 3:52:19, 2004- 3:43:20, 2005- 3:38:08, 2006- 4:23:27, 2008- 3:48:29, 2009- 3:38:35, 2012- 3:35:59. pbs: 5000mW 19:28.35i '13, 10kW 40:23 '10, 20kW 1:23:57 '11, 30kW 2:05:06 '03, 35kW 2:25:42 '12.
Married to Anisya Kirdyapkina (qv).

Andrey KRIVOV b. 14 Nov 1985 Komsomolsky, Mordovia 1.85m 72kg. Mordovia. Sports student.
At 20kW: OG: '12- 37; WCh: '09- 17; EC: '10- 6; EU23: '07- 2; WCp: '08-10-12: 5/3/2; ECp: '11- 8; WUG: '11- 1, '13- 1. Won RUS 2009, 2011.
Progress at 20kW: 2005- 1:22:21, 2007- 1:20:12, 2008- 1:19:06, 2009- 1:19:55, 2010- 1:22:20, 2011- 1:20:16, 2012- 1:18:25, 2013- 1:20:47. pbs: 10,000mW: 40:35.2 '05, 35kW 2:29:44 '06.

Aleksandr LESNOY b. 28 Jul 1988 1.94m 116kg.
At SP: WCh: '13: dnq 21; WUG: '13- 1; WI: '14- 8.
Progress at SP: 2008- 16.46, 2009- 16.80, 2010- 19.09, 2011- 19.60, 2012- 20.05, 2013- 20.60, 2014- 21.23. pb DT 58.80 '12.

Sergey LITVINOV b. 27 Jan 1986 Rostov-on-Don, Russia 1.85m 105kg.
At HT: WCh: '09- 5, '11- dnq 15, '13- 11; WJ: '04- 9; EU23: '07- 11; EJ: '05- 9; WUG: '13- 3. German champion 2009, Russian 2013.
Progress at HT: 2004- 60.00, 2005- 73.98, 2006- 66.46, 2007- 74.80, 2008- 75.35, 2009- 77.88, 2010-

78.98, 2011- 78.90, 2012- 80.98, 2013- 80.89.
Switched from Belarus to Germany 15 Jul 2008, but from 1 Jan 2011 had moved to Russia. His father Sergey Litvinov (USSR) set three world records at hammer 1980-3 with a pb of 86.04 '86; he was Olympic champion 1988 (2nd 1980) and World champion 1983 and 1987. His mother was born in Germany.

Aleksandr MENKOV b. 7 Dec 1990 Minusinsk, Krasnoyarsk reg. 1.78m 74kg. Krasnoyarsk VS. Krasnoyarsk State University.
At LJ: OG: '12- 11; WCh: '09- dnq 32, '11- 6, '13- 1; WI: '12- 3, '14- 5; EU23: '11- 1; EJ: '09- 1; EI: '13- 1; WUG: '13- 2; ET: '11- 1, '13- 1. Won DL 2012-13, Russian 2012. Two Russian records 2013.
Progress at LJ: 2008- 6.98, 2009- 8.16, 2010- 8.10, 2011- 8.28, 2012- 8.29, 2013- 8.56. pbs: HJ 2.15 '10, TJ 15.20 '09.

Sergey MORGUNOV b. 9 Feb 1993 Shakhty, Rostov 1.78m 70kg..
At LJ: OG: '12- dnq 16; WJ: '12- 1; EU23: '13- 2; EJ: '11- 1. Russian champion 2013.
World junior long jump record 2012.
Progress at LJ: 2010- 7.66, 2011- 8.10/8.18w, 2012- 8.35, 2013- 8.06.

Sergey MUDROV b. 8 Sep 1990 Kineshma, Ivanova reg. 1.88m 79kg. Luch Moskva Reg
At HJ: EC: '12- 4; WJ: '08- 4; WY: '07- 2; EU23: '11- 2; EJ: '09- 1; EI: '13- 1; WUG: '11- 3, '13- 1.
Progress at HJ: 2006- 2.10, 2007- 2.22, 2008- 2.18, 2009- 2.25, 2010- 2.30i/2.27, 2011- 2.30, 2012- 2.31, 2013- 2.35i/2.31, 2014- 2.32i.

Ivan NOSKOV b. 17 Jul 1988 Mordoviya 1.77m 62kg.
At 50kW: WCh: '13- 7; ECp: '13- 3.
Progress at 50kW: 2012- 3:55:16, 2013- 3:44:41. pbs: 20kW: 1:23:49 '11, 30kW 2:05:56 '12, 35kW 2:26:33 '12.

Andrey RUZAVIN b. 28 Mar 1986 1.75m 70kg. Mordoviya.
At 20kW: WCh: '13- 49; WCp: '12- 5; WUG: '09- 2; won RUS 2008, 2012-13. At 10,000m/10kW: WJ: '04- 1; EJ: '05- 1; WCp: '04- 6J; ECp: '05- 1J.
Progress at 20kW: 2004- 1:25:48, 2005- 1:21:51, 2006- 1:24:24, 2007- 1:20:07, 2009- 1:21:08, 2010- 1:21:01, 2011- 1:21:09, 2012- 1:17:47, 2013- 1:19:06. pbs: 5000mW 18:15.54i '14, 10,000mW 38:48.03 '08, 10kW 38:17 '09, 35kW 2:25:19 '09.

Mikhail RYZHOV b. 17 Dec 1991 1.80m 65kg. Mordoviya.
At 50kW: WCh: '13- 2; ECp: '13- 2, At 20kW: WUG: '11- 2.
Progress at 50kW: 2012- 3:53:49, 2013- 3:38:58. pbs: 5000mW 19:09.86i '14, 10kmW 39:11 '12, 20kW: 1:21:49 '11, 30kW 2:05:39 '12, 35kW 2:25:59 '12.

Ruslan SAMITOV b. 11 Jul 1991 Kazan 1.87m 77kg. Tatarstan.
At TJ: EC: '12: dnq 15; EJ: '09- 4; EI: '13- 2.
Progress at TJ: 2008- 15.09, 2009- 16.02, 2010-

16.51i/16.42, 2011- 16.90, 2012- 17.25, 2013- 17.30i/ 16.39.
Ilya SHKURENYOV b. 11 Jan 1991 Linevo, Volgograd reg. 1.91m 82kg.
At Dec: OG: '12- 16; WCh: '13- 8; EC: '12- 3; WJ: '10- 2; EU23: '11- 5. Russian champion 2013. At Hep: WI: '12- 4; EI: '13- 5.
Progress at Dec: 2011- 7894, 2012- 8219, 2013- 8370. pbs: 60m 7.04i '12, 100m 10.91 '13, 400m 48.39 '13, 1000m 2:41.65i '13, 1500m 4:30.41 '12, 60mh 8.06i '12, 110mh 14.13 '13, HJ 2.06 '10, PV 5.40 '13, LJ 7.54 '13, SP 14.84i '11, 13.98 '13; DT 45.28 '13, JT 59.46 '13, Hep 6018i '13.

Sergey SHUBENKOV b. 4 Oct 1990 Barnaul, Altay Kray 1.90m 75kg. Tumen State University.
At 110mh: OG: '12- sf; WCh: '11- h, '13- 3; EC: '12- 1; EU23: '11- 1; EJ: '09- 2, WUG: '13- 3; ET: '13- 1. RUS champion 2013. At 60mh: EI: '13- 1.
Four Russian 110mh records 2012.
Progress at 110mh: 2010- 13.54, 2011- 13.46, 2012- 13.09, 2013- 13.16/13.10w. pb 60mh 7.49i '13.
Mother Natalya Shubenkova had heptathlon pb 6859 '04; 4th 1988 OG and 3rd 1986 EC.

Aleksandr SHUSTOV b. 29 Jun 1984 Karaganda, Kazakhstan 1.99m 85kg. Moskva VS.
At HJ: OG: '12- dnq 15; WCh: '11- 8, '13- 7; EC: '10- 1; EU23: '05- 12; WUG: '07- 1; EI: '09- 4=, '11- 3; ET: '09-10: 3/1. Russian champion 2010.
Progress at HJ: 2002- 2.10, 2003- 2.11, 2004- 2.15, 2005- 2.23, 2006- 2.28, 2007- 2.31, 2008- 2.30, 2009- 2.32i, 2010- 2.33, 2011- 2.36, 2012- 2.35, 2013- 2.35. pbs: LJ 7.18i '12, Hep 4564i '12.
Married to Yekaterina Kondratyeva (200m 22.64 '04, 2 WUG '03, 6 EC '06).

Maksim SIDOROV b. 13 May 1986 Moskva 1.90m 126kg. Moskva Reg. Dyn.
At SP: OG: '12- 11; WCh: '09-11-13: dnq 30/14/13; EU23: '07- 8; EJ: '05- 3; WUG: '07- 1; WI: '12- 5; EI: '11- 3. Russian champion 2009, 2011-13.
Progress at SP: 2006- 18.52, 2007- 20.01, 2008- 19.98, 2009- 20.92, 2010- 20.50, 2011- 21.45, 2012- 21.51, 2013- 20.98. pb DT 50.71 '06.

Andrey SILNOV b. 9 Sep 1984 Shakhty, Rostov region 1.98m 83kg. Moskva Reg. VS.
At HJ: OG: '08- 1, '12- 12; WCh: '07- 11=; EC: '06- 1; EU23: '05- 9; WI: '12- 2; WCp: '06- 2; ECp: '06- 1, '08- 1. Won WAF 2008, Russian 2006.
Progress at HJ: 2002- 2.10, 2003- 2.10, 2004- 2.15, 2005- 2.28, 2006- 2.37, 2007- 2.36i/2.30, 2008- 2.38, 2009- 2.21, 2010- 2.33, 2011- 2.36, 2012- 2.37, 2013- 2.32i/2.18.

Dmitriy STARODUBTSEV b. 3 Jan 1986 Chelyabinsk region 1.91m 79kg. Moskva TU.
At PV: OG: '08- 5, '10- 4; WCh: '11- 12=; EC: '06- dnq 21=, '10- nh; WJ: '04- 1; WY: '03- 2; EU23: '07- 4; EJ: '05- 1; WI: '10- 6=, '12- 9; EI: '07- 6=; WUG: '07- 3; WCp: '06- 9. RUS champion 2010.
Progress at PV: 2003- 5.10, 2004- 5.50, 2005- 5.50, 2006- 5.65i/5.61, 2007- 5.70, 2008- 5.75, 2009- 5.70, 2010- 5.70i/5.65, 2011- 5.90i/5.72, 2012- 5.80i/5.75, 2013- 5.70i/5.30. pb Dec 7412 '07.

Denis STRELKOV b. 26 Oct 1990. Mordoviya 1.85m 75kg.
At 20kW: WCh: '13- 5; EU23: '11- 3; ECp: '13- 1; WUG: '13- 3. At 10,000m/10kW: WY: '07- 8; EJ: '09- 2; WCp: '08- 3J; ECp: '09- 10J.
Progress at 20kW: 2010- 1:20:19, 2011- 1:24:25, 2012- 1:20:31, 2013- 1:19:53. pbs: 10,000mW 40:24.97 '09, 10kW 39:16 '08, 50kW 4:04:36 '11.

Sergey SVIRIDOV b. 20 Oct 1990 Yekaterinburg 1.92m 85kg. Moskva YU.
At Dec: OG: '12- 8; WCh: '13- 20' EJ: '09- 15; WG: '13- 2. Russian champion 2012.
Progress at Dec: 2010- 7449, 2011- 8102A/7832, 2012- 8365, 2013- 7939. pbs: 60m 6.98i '12, 100m 10.78 '12, 400m 48.28 '12, 1000m 2:43.52i '12, 1500m 4:25.15 '12, 60mh 8.26i '12, 110mh 14.83 '12, HJ 2.04i '13, 1.99 '12; PV 4.60 '12, LJ 7.55i '13, 7.52 '12; SP 15.03 '12, DT 50.02 '12, JT 69.38 '13, Hep 5855i '12.

Dmitriy TARABIN b. 29 Oct 1991 Berlin, Germany 1.76m 85kg. Student at Russian State University of Physical Education, Moscow
At JT: WCh: '11- 10, '13- 3; WJ: '09- 3; WY: '07- dnq 23; EU23: '11- 3; EJ: '09- dnq 13; WUG: '13- 1; ET: '13- 1. Russian champion 2013.
Progress at JT: 2007- 55.18, 2008- 67.39, 2009- 69.63, 2010- 77.65, 2011- 85.10, 2012- 82.75; 2013- 88.84.
Switched from Moldova to Russia 9 June 2010. Married Mariya Abakumova on 12 Oct 2012.

Daniyil TSYPLAKOV b. 29 Jul 1992 Khabarovsk reg. 1.78m 70kg. Khabarovskiy.
At HJ: WY: '09- 3; EU23: '13- 2; EJ: '11- 4; WI: '14- 5.
Progress at HJ: 2008- 2.11, 2009- 2.21, 2010- 2.21, 2011- 2.26, 2012- 2.31, 2013- 2.30, 2014- 2.34i.

Ivan UKHOV b. 29 Mar 1986 Chelyabinsk 1.92m 83kg. Sverdlovsk TU.
At HJ: OG: '12- 1; WCh: '09- 10, '11- 5=, '13- 4; EC: '06- 12=, '10- 2; WJ: '04- dnq 13; EJ: '05- 1; WUG: '05- 4; WI: '10-12-14: 1/3/2; EI: '09- 1, '11- 1. Won DL 2010, Russian 2009, 2012-13.
Progress at HJ: 2004- 2.15, 2005- 2.30, 2006- 2.37i/2.33, 2007- 2.39i/2.20, 2008- 2.36i/2.30, 2009- 2.40i/2.35, 2010- 2.38i/2.36, 2011- 2.38i/2.34, 2012- 2.39, 2013- 2.35, 2014- 2.42i.
Former discus thrower.

Stanislav YEMELYANOV b. 23 Oct 1990 Pavlovo, Nizhni Novgorod Reg. 1.75m 62kg. Mordoviya VS. Law student.
At 20kmW: WCh: '11- 5; EC: '10- 1; ECp: '11- 1; RUS champion 2010. At 10,000m: WJ: '08- 1; WY: '07- 1; EJ: '09- 1; ECp: '09- 1J.
World junior 10k walk record 2009.
Progress at 20kW: 2010- 1:19:43, 2011- 1:19:33, 2012- 1:18:29. pbs: 10kW 38:28 '09, 39:35.01t '08; 30kW 2:24:25 '09.

Aleksey ZAGORNYI b. 31 May 1978 Yaroslavl 1.97m 135kg. Luch Moskva.
At HT: OG: '00-12: dnq 22/23; WCh: '03-07-13: dnq 22/25/nt; '09- 3; EC: '02- 11, '12- 2; EJ: '97- 5;

EU23: '99- 7; WUG: '01- 4. Russian champion 2007, 2009.
Progress at HT: 1994- 59.90, 1995- 71.00, 1996- 71.94, 1997- 71.30, 1998- 77.03, 1999- 77.20, 2000- 79.68, 2001- 80.80, 2002- 83.43, 2003- 80.13, 2004- 78.79, 2005- 80.81, 2006- 78.18, 2007- 79.12, 2008- 81.39, 2009- 80.10, 2010- 78.22, 2011- 81.73, 2012- 78.40, 2013- 79.26.

Women

Mariya ABAKUMOVA b. 15 Jan 1986 Stavropol 1.78m 85kg. Krasnodar VS.
At JT: OG: '08- 2, '12- 10; WCh: '07- 09-11-13: 7/3/1/3; EC: '10- 5; WJ: '04- dnq 25; WY: '03- 4; EU23: '07- 6; EJ: '05- 1; WUG: '13- 1; CCp: '10- 1; ECp: '08-09-10: 2/3/3. Won WAF 2009, Russian 2008, 2011-13.
European javelin record 2008, four Russian 2008-11.
Progress at JT: 2002- 51.81, 2003- 51.41, 2004- 58.26, 2005- 59.53, 2006- 60.12, 2007- 64.28, 2008- 70.78, 2009- 68.92, 2010- 68.89, 2011- 71.99, 2012- 66.86, 2013- 70.53.
Married Dmitriy Tarabin on 12 Oct 2012

Elmira ALEMBEKOVA b. 30 Jun 1990 Saransk. Mordoviya.
At 10,000m/10kmW: WJ: '08- 2; EJ: '09- 1; WCp: '08- 3J, At 5000mW: WY: '05- 2.
Progress at 20kW: 2010- 1:35:53, 2011- 1:27:35, 2012- 1:25:27. pbs: 10,000mW: 43:45.26 '08.

Natalya ANTYUKH b. 26 Jun 1981 Leningrad 1.82m 73kg. Moskva VS.
At 400m/4x400mR: OG: '04- 3/2R; WCh: '01- h, '05- sf/1R, '07- 6; EC: '02- 2R; WI: '03-04-06: 1R/res1R/1R; EI: '02- 1, '07- 2R, '09- 4/1R; WCp: '02- 3R; ECp: '01- 3/1R, '05- 1/1R, '06- 1R. At 200m: ECp: '04- 2. At 400mh: OG: '12- 1/2R; WCh: '09- 6/res 3R, '11- 3/3R, '13- sf/res1R; EC: '10- 1; CCp: '10- 4; ET: '10- 1&1R, '11- 2. Won Russian 400m 2007, 400mh 2010-12.
Progress at 400m: 2000- 54.79, 2001- 51.19, 2002- 51.17i/51.24, 2003- 51.73i/52.28, 2004- 49.85, 2005- 50.67, 2006- 50.37i/50.47, 2007- 49.93, 2008- 51.19, 2009- 50.90, 2011- 50.73, 2012- 51.27. At 400mh: 1996- 60.11, 1997- 59.75, 1998- 59.94, 2000- 58.30, 2009- 54.11, 2010- 52.92, 2011- 53.75, 2012- 52.70, 2013- 55.20. pbs: 200m 22.73 '12, 300m 36.0+ '04, 200mhSt 26.23 '13.

Tatyana ARKHIPOVA b. 8 Apr 1983 Cheboksary 1.60m 53kg. née Petrova. Moskva VS.
At Mar: OG: '12- 3. At 3000mSt: OG: '08- 4; WCh: '07- 2; EC: '06- 2; WCp: '06- 5. At 3000m/5000m: WJ: '02- 4/6. At 5000m/10,000m: EU23: '05- 2/1. Eur CC: '01- 19J, '02- 4J.
World best indoor 3000mSt 9:07.00 '06.
Progress at 10,000m, Mar, 3000mSt: 2003- 10:05.70, 2004- 32:37.88, 2:36:44; 2005- 32:17.49, 2:31:03; 2006- 9:22.82, 2007- 9:09.19, 2008- 9:12.33, 2009- 2:25:53, 10:00.36; 2011- 32:18.88, 2:25:01; 2012- 2:23:29. pbs: 1500m 4:23.95i '02, 3000m 8:44.13 '06, 5000m 15:46.58 '03, 10k Rd 32:10 '07.

Won Los Angeles marathon 2009. Pregnant in 2013.

Mariya BESPALOVA b. 21 May 1986 Leningrad 1.83m 85kg. Mordovia VS.
At HT: OG: '12- 10; WJ: '04- dnq; WY: '03- 2; WUG: '13- 3.
Progress at HT: 2002- 52.62, 2003- 58.47, 2004- 59.72, 2005- 61.73, 2006- 62.58, 2007- 63.50, 2008- 67.08, 2009- 69.02, 2010- 64.92, 2011- 71.93, 2012- 76.72, 2013- 71.70. pb DT 44.19 '06.

Lina BIKULOVA b. 1 Oct 1988. Moskva
At 20kmW: WUG: '13- 3; Russian champion 2013. World junior 20km walk best 2008.
Progress at 20kW: 2005- 1:48:36, 2008- 1:42:59, 2009- 1:32:39, 2010- 1:35:33, 2011- 1:32:45, 2012- 1:31:01, 2013- 1:28:42. pbs: 5000mW 22:09.8i '13, 10kW 44:24 '13.

Svetlana BIRYUKOVA b. 12 May 1991 Sankt-Peterburg 1.80m 72kg. née Denyayeva. Vborgskaya..
At LJ: ECh: '12- 8; EU23: '11- dnq 15 (8 TJ).
Progress at LJ: 2007- 6.18, 2008- 6.05i/5.93, 2009- 5.88, 2010- 6.28i/6.26, 2011- 6.48, 2012- 6.72/6.85w, 2013- 6.76i/6.68, 2014- 6.98i. pbs: 60m 7.50i '13, TJ 13.96i '13, 13.68 '11, 14.00w '12. Faces doping ban for test on 26 Feb 2014.

Yekaterina BOLSHOVA b. 4 Feb 1988 St. Peterburg 1.78m 66kg. St. Petersburg.
At Hep: EC: '12- 4. At Pen: WI: '12- 6. At HJ: WY: '05- 8.
Progress at Hep: 2007- 5297, 2008- 4940, 2009- 5590, 2010- 5738, 2011- 5050, 2012- 6466. pbs: 200m 24.17 '12, 800m 2:10.10 '12, 60mh 8.14i '12, 100mh 13.50 '12, HJ 1.92i/1.91 '12, LJ 6.57i '13, 6.45 '12, SP 13.98 '12, JT 40.47 '12, Pen 4896i '12.

Anna BULGAKOVA b. 17 Jan 1988 Stavropol 1.73m 90kg. Stavropol VS.
At HT: OG: '08- dnq 20; WCh: '13- 5; EC: '12- 3; WJ: '04- 4, '06- 2; WY: '05- 2; EJ: '07- 4.
Progress at HT: 2003- 57.24, 2004- 63.83, 2005- 64.43, 2006- 67.79, 2007- 68.49, 2008- 73.79, 2010- 66.29, 2011- 69.10, 2012- 74.02, 2013- 76.17, 2014- 73.00. pb DT 44.19 '06.

Tatyana CHERNOVA b. 29 Jan 1988 Krasnodar 1.90m 70kg. Krasnodar VS.
At Hep: OG: '08- 3, '12- 3; WCh: '07- dnf, '09- 8, '11- 1; EC: '10- 4; WJ: '06- 1; WY: '05- 1; WUG: '13- 1. At Pen: WI: '08-10-12: 7/3/5.
Progress at Hep: 2006- 6227, 2007- 6768w, 2008- 6618, 2009- 6386, 2010- 6572, 2011- 6880, 2012- 6774, 2013- 6623. pbs: 200m 23.49 '12, 23.32w '11; 800m 2:06.50 '08, 60mh 8.02i '12, 100mh 13.32 '11, 13.04w '07, 400mh 56.14 '07, HJ 1.87 '07, LJ 6.82 '11, SP 14.54i '10, 14.17 '11, JT 54.49 '06, Pen 4855i '10.
Won at Talence 2010-11 and IAAF Combined Events Challenge 2010-12. Her mother Lyudmila (née Zenina) won a 4x400m Olympic gold medal (ran in heats) for 4x400m in 1980, pbs: 200m 22.9 '82, 400m 50.91 '83.

Anna CHICHEROVA b. 22 Jul 1982 Yerevan, Armenia 1.80m 57kg. Moskva VS. Physical culture graduate.
At HJ: OG: '04- 6, '08- 3, '12- 1; WCh: '03-05-07-09-11-13: 6/4/2=/2/1/3=; EC: '06- 7=; WJ: '00- 4; WY: '99- 1; EJ: '01- 2; WUG: '05- 1; WI: '03-04-12: 3/2/2=; EI: '05- 1, '07- 5=; ECp: '06- 3. Russian champion 2004, 2007-09, 2011-12.
Progress at HJ: 1998- 1.80, 1999- 1.89, 2000- 1.90, 2001- 1.92, 2002- 2.00i/1.89, 2003- 2.04i/2.00, 2004- 2.04i/1.98, 2005- 2.01i/1.99, 2006- 1.96i/1.95, 2007- 2.03, 2008- 2.04, 2009- 2.02, 2011- 2.07, 2012- 2.06i/2.05, 2013- 2.02.
Moved with family to Russia at the beginning of the 1990s. Married to Gennadiy Chernoval KAZ, pbs 100m 10.18, 200m 20.44 (both 2002), 2 WUG 100m & 200m 2001, 2 AsiG 2002 2002; their daughter Nika born on 7 Sep 2010.

Irina DAVYDOVA b. 27 May 1988 Alexandrov, Vladimir reg. 1.70m 65kg. Moskva SC.
At 400mh: OG: '12- sf; WCh: '13- sf; EC: '12- 1; EU23: '09-5; WUG: '11- 2, '13- 3. Won RUS 2013.
Progress at 400mh: 2006- 60.27, 2007- 58.55, 2008- 58.62, 2009- 56.14, 2010- 55.74, 2011- 55.48, 2012- 53.77, 2013- 54.79. pbs: 200m 24.53i '11, 400m 51.94i '12, 53.12 '11; 500m 1:10.54i '12.

Tatyana DEKTYAREVA b. 5 Aug 1981 Yekaterinburg 1.74m 60kg. Finpromko.
At 100mh: OG: '08- h, '12- sf; WCh: '09- h, '11- 5, '13- sf; EC: '10- 6; ET: '10- 11-13: 1/1/2; Russian champion 2011-12. At 60mh: WI: '10- 8.
Progress at 100mh: 2004- 13.98, 2005- 13.36/13.30w, 2006- 13.04, 2007- 13.30/13.10w, 2008- 12.84/12.81w, 2009- 12.96, 2010- 12.68, 2011- 12.76, 2012- 12.75, 2013- 12.91/12.88w. pbs: 60m 7.42i '08, 100m 11.76 '08, 200m 23.59 '06, 300m 37.93i '06, 800m 2:05.87 '04, 60mh 7.94i '10.

Aleksandra FEDORIVA b. 13 Sep 1988 Moskva 1.75m 60kg. SC Luch Moskva. Student of advertising at Moscow University of Humanitarian Studies.
At 400m/4x400m: WI: '12- 2/3R. At 200m/4x-100mR: OG: '08- sf/1R, '12- sf; EC: '10- 3; EU23: '09- 1; CCp: '10- 1; ECp: '10- 1R, '11- 3/2R. At 100m: WCh: '11- sf; ET: '11- 3. At 100mh: WJ: '06- 4; WY: '05- sf; EJ: '07- 1. Won RUS 200m 2011-12.
Progress at 200m: 2007- 23.29, 2008- 22.56, 2009- 22.97, 2010- 22.41, 2011- 23.17, 2012- 22.19. pbs: 60m 7.24i '10, 100m 11.28, 11.09w '11; 300m 36.54i '12, 400m 51.18i '12, 60mh 7.91i '10, 100mh 12.90 '08.
Her mother Lyudmila Belova/Fedoriva had 400m best 50.63 '84, father Andrey Fedoriv 200m 3rd EC and 20.53 '86; ran at five Worlds and two Olympics. Married Aleksandr Shpayer (RUS 60m indoor champion 6.63 '11) in 2012; daughter Varvara born 31 July 2013.

Svetlana FEOFANOVA b. 16 Jul 1980 Moskva 1.64m 53kg. Moskva TU.

At PV: OG: '00- dnq, '04- 2, '08- 3, '12- dnq; WCh: '01-03-07-11: 2/1/3/3; EC: '02- 1, '06- 4, '10- 1; WI: '01-03-04-06-08-10: 2=/1/3/3/5/2; EI: '02- 1, '07- 1; WCp: '02- 2, '10- 1; ECp: '00-01-02-10: 1/1/1/1; 2nd GP 2001. Won RUS 2001, 2006, 2008, 2011-12.
Pole vault records: World 2004, 9 European 2001-04, 11 Russian 2000-04, 9 world indoor 2002-04 (4.71-4.85), 13 European indoor 2001-04.
Progress at PV: 1998- 3.90, 1999- 4.10, 2000- 4.50, 2001- 4.75, 2002- 4.78, 2003- 4.80i/4.75, 2004- 4.88, 2005- 4.70i, 2006- 4.70, 2007- 4.82, 2008- 4.75, 2009- 4.70, 2010- 4.80i/4.75, 2011- 4.75, 2012- 4.65, 2013- 4.60.
Was a top gymnast, winning Russian titles at youth, junior and U23 level at asymmetric bars and floor exercises. Set five indoor world records in a month in 2002.

Tatyana FIROVA b. 10 Oct 1982 Sarov, Nizhegorodskaya region 1.78m 68kg. Moskva Reg. Dyn.
At 400m/4x400m: OG: '04- res 2R, 08- 6/2R, '12- 2R; WCh: '05- res 1R, '09- 3R, '13- 1R; EC: '06- res 1R, '10- 1/1R; EU23: '03- 3/1R; EJ: '01- 1; WI: '10- 2/2R; WUG: '03- 1; CCp: '10- 3/2R; ECp: '03- 1R, '13- 2R.
Progress at 400m: 2000- 53.69, 2001- 52.94, 2002- 53.72, 2003- 51.43, 2004- 50.44, 2005- 50.41, 2006- 50.08, 2007- 50.98, 2008- 50.11, 2009- 50.59, 2010- 49.89, 2011- 50.84, 2012- 49.72, 2013- 50.71. pbs: 200m 23.27 '11, 500m 1:09.41i '08, 600m 1:25.23i '08.

Gulnara GALKINA b. 9 Jul 1978 Naberezhnye Chelny, Tatarstan 1.75m 55kg. née Samitova. Naberezhnye Chelny Dyn.
At 3000mSt (5000m): OG: '04- (6), '08- 1 (12), '12- dnf; WCh: '03- (7), '07- 7, '09- 4; ECp: '03-08-11: 1/1/1. At 1500m: WI: '04- 3. At 3000m: ECp: '04-07-09: 1/1/1. Eur CC: '08- 12. Won WAF 3000mSt 2008, RUS 1500m 2004, 5000m 2003-04, 3000mSt 2003, 2008; indoor 1500m & 3000m 2004.
Three world and five Russian records 3000m steeplechase 2003-08.
Progress at 5000m, 3000mSt: 2003- 14:54.38, 9:08.33; 2004- 14:53.70, 9:01.59; 2006- 9:53.83, 2007- 9:11.68, 2008- 14:33.13, 8:58.81; 2009- 9:11.09, 2011- 16:06.09, 9:29.75; 2012- 15:39.97, 9:24.60; 2013- 9:30.72. pbs: 800m 2:00.29 '09, 1000m 2:35.91i '04, 1500m 4:01.29 '04, 1M 4:20.23 '07, 2000m 5:31.03 '07, 3000m 8:41.72i '04, 8:42.96 '08; 10kRd 32:43 '12, HMar 75:50 '13.
Great breakthrough in 2003, starting with world indoor 3000mSt best of 9:29.54. Married Anton Galkin (400m 44.83 '04) in 2004. Daughter Alina born 24 Jun 2010.

Irina GORDEYEVA b. 9 Oct 1986 Leningrad 1.85m 55kg. Yunost Rossii.
At HJ: OG: '12- 10; WCh: '13- 9=; EC: '10- dnq 13=, '12- 3=; WJ: '04- 9; WY: '03- 7=; EJ: '05- 4; EI: '09- 5=.

Progress at HJ: 2001- 1.75, 2002- 1.82, 2003- 1.84, 2004- 1.88, 2005- 1.88, 2006- 1.88, 2007- 1.87i/1.83, 2008- 1.95, 2009- 2.02, 2010- 1.97, 2011- 1.94, 2012- 2.04, 2013- 1.99.

Irina GUMENYUK b. 6 Jan 1988 Sankt-Peterburg 1.76m 59kg. St.Petersburg.
At TJ: WCh: '13- 8; EJ: '07- 9; EI: '13- 2. Russian champion 2013.
Progress at TJ: 2006- 13.06, 2007- 13.52, 2008- 13.65, 2009- 13.49i, 2010- 13.33, 2011- 14.14, 2012- 14.24i/14.03, 2013- 14.58. pb LJ 6.38 '11.

Yuliya GUSHCHINA b. 4 Mar 1983 Novocherkask 1.75m 63kg. Moskva reg. VS.
At 200m(/100m)/4x100mR: OG: '08- 1R; WCh: '05- 6, '07- 5R, '09/11- sf; EC: '06- 2/5/1R, '10- 4R; EU23: '03- 5; WCp: '06- 4/5/1R; ECp: '05-06-07-10-11: 1R/(1)&1R/1R/1R/2R. At 400m/4x400mR: OG: '08- 4/2R, '12- sf/2R; WCh: '13- 1R; WI: '06-08-12: res1R/1R/3R; ECp: '05/07/08- 1R. Won RUS 100m 2011, 200m 2005, 2009; 400m 2008.
World indoor records 4x200m 2005, 4x400m 2006.
Progress at 200m, 400m: 1997- 25.96, 1998- 25.32, 1999- 58.18, 2000- 25.01, 55.85; 2001- 24.24, 55.91; 2002- 23.92/23.88w, 53.26; 2003- 23.58, 51.94; 2004- 23.06, 2005- 22.53, 53.81i; 2006- 22.69/22.52w, 51.26i; 2007- 22.75, 2008- 22.58, 50.01; 2009- 22.63, 51.06; 2010- 22.80/22.79w, 52.04i; 2011- 22.88/22.69w, 52.18; 2012- 22.95, 49.28; 2013- 23.32, 51.06. pbs: 60m 7.24i '07, 7.2i '03; 100m 11.13 '06, 300m 36.93i '10.
Married Ivan Buzolin (400m 46.24 '08, 2R EI '07) on 12 Sep 2010.

Yelena ISINBAYEVA b. 3 Jun 1982 Volgograd 1.74m 66kg. Volgograd Dyn.
At PV: OG: '00- dnq, '04- 1, '08- 1, '12- 3; WCh: '03-05-07-09-11-13: 3/1/1/nh/6/1; EC: '02- 2, '06- 1; WJ: '98- 9, '00- 1, WY: '99- 1; EU23: '03- 1; EJ: '99- 5, '01- 1; WI: '01-03-04-06-08-10-12: 7/2/1/1/1/4/1; EI: '05- 1; WCp: '06- 1. Won WAF 2004-07, 2009; Russian 2002, 2013.
15 outdoor world pole vault records 2003-09, 13 indoor 2004-12 (inc. 3 absolute WR), world junior indoor records 2000 and 2001.
Progress at PV: 1997- 3.30, 1998- 4.00, 1999- 4.20, 2000- 4.45i/4.40, 2001- 4.47i/4.46, 2002- 4.60/4.65ex, 2003- 4.82, 2004- 4.92, 2005- 5.01, 2006- 4.91, 2007- 4.93i/4.91, 2008- 5.05, 2009- 5.06, 2010- 4.85i, 2011- 4.85i/4.76, 2012- 5.01i/4.75, 2013- 4.89. Former gymnast. World age bests at 17-18-19 in 2000-02, world titles as Youth, junior and senior. World indoor records in all four competitions 2005 and a further five outdoors in 2005. These included the first 5m vault by a woman (at the London GP) followed by 5.01 to win the World title by 41 cm. Shared Golden League jackpot in 2007 and 2009. Passed 2010 summer season. IAAF female Athlete of the Year 2004-05 & 2008. Expecting a baby in May 2041 and plans to marry Nikita Petinov (b. 29 Aug 1990. JT 74.88 '13) in July.

Anastasiya KAPACHINSKAYA b. 21 Nov 1979 Moskva 1.76m 65kg. Luch Moskva.
At 200m/4x400mR: OG: '12- res(2)R; WCh: '03- 1; EC: '10- 4/1R; WI: '03- 2, '04- dq (1); ECp: '03- 1. At 400m: OG: '08- 5/2R; WCh: '01- sf/3R, '03- 2R, '09- 7/3R, '11- 3/3R; EC: '02- 5/2R. Won Russian 200m 2008, 400m 2011.
Progress at 200m, 400m: 1999- 23.85, 2000- 23.66, 53.32; 2001- 23.24i/22.6, 50.97; 2002- 23.41, 51.39; 2003- 22.38, 50.59; 2004- 22.71i, 2006- 22.80, 51.16; 2007- 23.73, 52.14; 2008- 22.48, 50.02; 2009- 22.92, 49.97; 2010- 22.47, 50.16; 2011- 22.55, 49.35; 2012- 50.37, 2013- 22.39, 50.91 pbs: 100m 11.79 '99, 300m 36.61 '02, 800m 2:09.75i '07.
She served a 2-year drugs ban after finishing first in the World Indoor 200m in 2004.

Gulfiya KHANAFEYEVA b. 4 Jun 1982 Chelyabinsk 1.73m 84kg. Moskva TU.
At HT: OG: '12- dnq 15; WCh: '07- dq(10), '13- 12; EC: '06- 2; EU23: '03- 3; EJ: '01- 10; WUG: '03- 2; ECp: '05- 3. Russian champion 2006.
World hammer record 2006.
Progress at HT: 1998- 51.10, 1999- 53.80, 2000- 57.20, 2001- 61.10, 2002- 62.19/64.50dq, 2003- 68.92, 2004- 72.71, 2005- 70.76, 2006- 77.26, 2007- 72.10/77.36dq, 2008- 75.07dq, 2011- 71.11, 2012- 77.08, 2013- 75.02.
She had a 3-month ban in 2002 after testing positive for a stimulant and 2 year drugs ban from 9 May 2007.

Anisya KIRDYAPKINA b. 23 Oct 1989 Saransk, Mordoviya 1.65m 51kg. née Kornikova. Mordovia TU.
At 20kmW: OG: '12- 5; WCh: '09- 4. '11- 3, '13- 2; EC: '10- 2; WCp: '10- 6, '12- 6; ECp: '09-11-13: 2/2/1; WUG: '13- 1; RUS champion 2010, 2012.
At 10,000mW: EJ: '07- 1; ECp: '07- 1J.
World junior 20km walk best 2008.
Progress at 20kW: 2007- 1:28:00, 2008- 1:25:30, 2009- 1:25:26, 2010- 1:25:11, 2011- 1:25:09, 2012- 1:26:26. 2013- 1:25:59. pbs: 3000mW 11:44.10i '12, 5000mW 21:06.3 '06, 10,000mW 43:27.30 '06, 42:04R '11.
Married to Sergey Kirdyapkin (qv).

Aleksandra KIRYASHOVA b. 21 Aug 1985 Leningrad 1.68m 55kg. Luch Moskva.
At PV: WCh: '09- 9; EC: '12- 8; WJ: '04- nh; WY: '01- 2; EU23: '07- 1; EJ: '03- 3; WUG: '07- 1, '11- 1; EI: '09- 4, '11- 6.
Progress at PV: 2000- 3.70, 2001- 4.00, 2002- 4.21, 2003- 4.21i/4.15, 2004- 4.25i/4.20, 2005- 4.30, 2006- 4.30i/4.20, 2007- 4.50, 2008- 4.50, 2009- 4.65, 2010- 4.65i/4.54, 2011- 4.65, 2012- 4.58, 2013- 4.56i/4.50.

Darya KLISHINA b. 15 Jan 1991 Tver 1.80m 57kg. Moskva. Model.
At LJ: WCh: '11- 7, '13- 7; WY: '07- 1; EU23: '11- 1; EJ: '09- 1; WI: '10- 5, '12- 4; EI: '11- 1, '13- 1, WUG: '13- 1; ET: '11- 1, '13- 2.
Progress at LJ: 2005- 5.83, 2006- 6.33/6.47w,

2007- 6.49, 2008- 6.52i/6.20, 2009- 6.80, 2010- 7.03, 2011- 7.05, 2012- 6.93, 2013- 7.01i/6.90/6.98w.

Lyudmila KOLCHANOVA b. 1 Oct 1979 Sharya, Kostroma 1.75m 60kg. Kostroma TU.
At LJ: OG: '12- 6; WCh: '07- 2, '13- dnq 15; EC: '06- 1, '10- 5; WUG: '05- 1; EI: '05- 5; WCp: '06- 1; ECp: '08- 1. Russian champion 2007, 2010, 2013.
Progress at LJ: 2000- 6.20, 2001- 6.12i/6.07, 2002- 6.32, 2003- 6.09i/6.07, 2004- 6.54, 2005- 6.79, 2006- 7.11, 2007- 7.21, 2008- 7.04, 2009- 6.72, 2010- 7.01, 2011- 6.84/7.06w, 2012- 6.87, 2013- 6.89. pbs: HJ 1.82 ?, TJ 13.88 '04.
Having been a high jumper, she played basketball before returning to athletics in 2000.

Yevgeniya KOLODKO b. 2 Jul 1990 Neryungi, Yakutia 1.88m 85kg.
At SP: OG: '12- 2; WCh: '11- 5, '13- 5; WI: '12- 7, '14- 4; EU23: '11- 1; EJ: '09- 9; EI: '13- 2. Russian champion 2012-13.
Progress at SP: 2007- 14.26, 2008- 15.04i/14.87, 2009- 15.38, 2010- 16.73, 2011- 19.78, 2012- 20.48, 2013- 19.97i/19.86.

Oksana KONDRATYEVA b. 22 Nov 1985 1.80m 80kg. Moskva. Moscow State University of PE.
At HT: WCh: '13- 7; WUG: '13- 2.
Progress at HT: 2004- 57.36, 2005- 62.24, 2006- 61.81, 2007- 64.09, 2008- 66.08, 2009- 67.84, 2010- 71.90, 2011- 69.87, 2012- 73.31, 2013- 77.13.
Mother Lydmila Kondratyeva (1980 Olympic 100m champion) and father Yuriy Sedykh (hammer world record holder).

Yekaterina KONEVA b. 25 Sep 1988 Khabarovsk 1.69m 55kg. Khabarovskiy.
At TJ: WCh: '13-2; WI: '14- 1; WUG: '11- 1, '13- 1; ET: '13- 2.
Progress at TJ: 2010- 13.93/14.00w, 2011- 14.46, 2012- 14.60i/14.36, 2013- 14.82. pbs: 60m 7.39i '07, 100m 11.76 '09, 200m 23.89 '09, LJ 6.70/6.80w '11.
Two-year drugs ban 2007-09.

Mariya KONOVALOVA b. 14 Aug 1974 Angarsk 1.78m 62kg. née Pantyukhova. Moskva VS.
At 10,000m: OG: '08- 5; WCh: '09- 11. At 5000m: WCh: '95- 6, '99- 7, '07- 11; EC: '10- 4. At 3000m: WI: '95- 12; EI: '96- 5. Eur CC: '05-06-08: 10/2/4. Won RUS 5000m 2009-10.
Progress at 5000m, 10,000m, Mar: 1995- 15:01.23, 1997- 16:10.4/32:53.69; 1998- 15:13.22, 1999- 14:58.60, 2000- 15:49.04, 2007- 15:02.96, 2008- 14:38.09, 30:35.84; 2009- 14:42.06, 30:31.03; 2010- 14:49.68, 2:23:50; 2011- 2:25:18, 2012- 15:27.54, 2:25:38; 2013- 15:27.16, 2:22:46; 2014- 2:23:43. pbs: 1500m 4:05.10 '98, 2000m 5:38.98i '10, 3000m 8:30.18 '99, 15km 49:58+ '10, HMar 69:56 '12, 30km 1:41:18+ '10.
Won Nagoya Marathon 2014, 3rd Chicago 2010 & 20 1t

Yelena KOTULSKAYA b. 8 Aug 1988 Moskva 1.74m 61kg. née Kofanova. Moskva.

At 800m: WCh: '09/13- sf; WI: '12- 5; EU23: '09-1; EJ: '07- h; EI: '13- 2; WUG: '11- 2, '13- 5. Russian champion 2013.
World indoor 4x800m record 2010 & 2011.
Progress at 800m: 2003- 2:13.11, 2005- 2:08.61, 2006- 2:05.82i, 2007- 2:02.66, 2008- 2:01.80, 2009-1:58.60, 2010- 1:58.50, 2011- 1:58.04, 2012- 1:57.77, 2013- 1:59.56. pbs: 400m 53.19 '09, 500m 1:13.23i '06, 600m 1:26.38i '11, 1000m 2:37.01i '13, 1500m 4:15.49 '09.

Angelina KRASNOVA b. 7 Feb 1991 Moskva 1.68m 55kg. née Zhuk. Irkutskaya.
At PV: WCh: '13- 7; EU23: '13- 1; EI: '13- 5.
Progress at PV: 2007- 3.60i, 2008- 3.80, 2010- 4.10, 2011- 4.30i/4.25, 2012- 4.40, 2013- 4.70.

Antonina KRIVOSHAPKA b. 21 Jul 1987 Volgograd 1.68m 60kg. Rostov-na-Donu VS.
At 400m/4x400m: OG: '12- 6/2R; WCh: '09-3/3R, '11- 5/3R, '13- 3/1R; EC: '10- 3/1R; WJ: '04- h; WY: '03- 2; EI: '09- 1/1R; CCp: '10- 2R. Won RUS 2009, 2012.
Progress at 400m: 2002- 54.35, 2003- 53.09, 2004-53.67, 2005- 55.03i/55.63, 2006- 55.40i, 2007-52.32, 2008- 51.24, 2009- 49.29, 2010- 50.10, 2011-49.92, 2012- 49.16, 2013- 49.57. pbs: 200m 23.01 '13, 300m 36.38i '09.

Anna KRYLOVA b. 3 Oct 1985. née Kuropatkina. Luch Moskva.
At TJ: WCh: '11- 7; WI: '12- 6; EU23: '07- 4.
Progress at TJ: 2001- 12.85, 2002- 12.75, 2003-12.86, 2004- 13.34/13.62w, 2005- 13.25, 2006-14.13, 2007- 14.20, 2008- 13.84i/13.32, 2009-14.14i/13.27, 2010- 14.02i/13.69/13.77w, 2011-14.35, 2012- 14.40, 2013- 14.27. pb LJ 6.45 '06.
Cousin of Denis Kapustin, TJ 1 EC 94, 3 OG 00.

Olga KUCHERENKO b. 5 Nov 1985 Sidory, Volgograd region 1.72m 59kg. Lokomotiv Penza.
At LJ: WCh: '09- 5, '11- 2, '13- 5; EC: '10- 3; EU23: '07- 12; EI: '09-3, '13- 6; ET: '09-10: 2/2.
Progress at LJ: 2002- 6.08, 2004- 6.30, 2005- 6.34, 2006- 6.72/6.80w, 2007- 6.41/6.70w, 2008-6.87i/6.70, 2009- 6.91, 2010- 7.13, 2011- 6.86, 2012-7.03, 2013- 7.00i/6.81.

Mariya KUCHINA b. 14 Jan 1993 Prokhladny, Kabardino-Balkar 1.82m 60kg. Moskovskaya.
At HJ: WJ: '12- 3; WY: '09- 2; EJ: '11- 1; WI: '14- 1=; WUG: '13- 2; ET: '13- 1. Won Yth Oly 2010.
World junior indoor high jump record 2011.
Progress at HJ: 2009- 1.87, 2010- 1.91, 2011- 1.97i/1.95, 2012- 1.96i/1.89, 2013- 1.98i/1.96., 2014- 2.01i.

Yelena LASHMANOVA b. 9 Apr 1992 Saransk 1.70m 48kg. Biology student at Mordovia State University.
At 20kmW: OG: '12- 1; WCh: '13- 1; WCp: '12- 1.
At 10,000mW: WJ: '10- 1; EJ: '11- 1; ECp: '11- 1J.
At 5000mW: WY: '09- 1.
Official world 20km walk record 2012, world junior 10,000m walk record 2011.
Progress at 20kW: 2012- 1:25:02, 2013- 1:25:49. pbs: 5000mW 20:44.37i '10, 10,000mW 42:59.48 '11.

Best ever debut at 20k walk (1:26:30 in 2012) and has won all seven of her career 20k walks 2012-3. Won IAAF Walks Challenge 2013.

Tatyana LYSENKO b. 9 Oct 1983 Bataisk, Rostov region 1.86m 81kg. Bataisk VS.
At HT: OG: '04- dnq 19, '12- 1; WCh: '05-09-11-13: 2/6/1/1; EC: '06- 1, '10- 2; EU23: '03- 5; WUG: '03- 5; WCp: '06- 2, '10- 1; ECp: '06-07-10-11: 1/dq1/2/2. Won RUS 2005, 2009-13.
Three world hammer records, nine Russian records 2005-13.
Progress at HT: 2000- 49.08, 2001- 55.73, 2002-61.85, 2003- 67.19, 2004- 71.54, 2005- 77.06, 2006-77.80, 2007- 77.30/78.61dq, 2009- 76.41, 2010-76.03, 2011- 77.13, 2012- 78.51, 2013- 78.80.
Two-year drugs ban after positive test on 9 May 2007.

Anna NAZAROVA b. 3 Feb 1986 St. Petersburg 1.72m 58kg.
At LJ: OG: '12- 5; WJ: '04- dnq; EJ: '05- 3; EU23: '07- 1; WUG: '11- 1; WI: '10- 6.
Progress at LJ: 2003- 6.00/6.12w, 2004- 6.48, 2005- 6.50i/6.31, 2006- 6.66, 2007- 6.81, 2008-6.71/6.75w, 2009- 6.60, 2010- 6.75i/6.54, 2011-6.89i/6.88, 2012- 7.11. pb TJ 13.80i '07, 13.39 '10.
Daughter born April 2013.

Yekaterina POISTOGOVA b. 1 Mar 1991 Arzamas, Nizhny Novgorod reg. 1.75m 65kg. née Zavyalova. Ural State Forestry University.
At 800m: OG: '12- 3; WCh: '13- 5; WJ: '08- sf, '10-8; WY: '07- sf; EJ: '09- 3 (10 1500m). Russian champion 2012.
Progress at 800m, 1500m: 2007- 2:06.96, 2008-2:04.96, 2009- 2:02.11, 4:18.82; 2010- 2:04.33, 4:27.68; 2011- 2:02.2, 4:17.9; 2012- 1:57.53, 4:00.11; 2013- 1:58.05, 4:14.63. pbs: 600 1:26.6+ '12, 1000m 2:36.97i '13.
Husband Stepan Poistogov 800m pb 1:46.02 '12.

Anna PYATYKH b. 4 Apr 1981 Moskva 1.76m 64kg. Moskva VS.
At TJ: OG: '04- 8, '08- 8; WCh: '03-05-07-09-13: 4/3/4/3/7; EC: '02- 8, '06- 3; WJ: '00- 2; EJ: '99-3; WI: '03-06-10: 4/2/3; ECp: '02-03-04-05-09: 1/1/1/1/2. Won WAF 2008, Russian 2004, 2006.
Progress at TJ: 1998- 12.98, 1999- 13.59, 2000-14.19, 2001- 14.21/14.22w, 2002- 14.67, 2003-14.79, 2004- 14.85, 2005- 14.88, 2006- 15.02/15.17w, 2007- 14.88, 2008- 14.91, 2009- 14.67/14.84w, 2010- 14.68, 2011- 14.24, 2013- 14.40. pb LJ 6.72 '07.
Married to Yuriy Abramov (won Russian marathon 2010 in pb 2:11:39); twin daughters born January 2011.

Kseniya RYZHOVA b. 19 Apr 1987 Lipetsk 1.72m 62kg. née Vdovina. Moskva Dyn.
At 400m/4x400m: WCh: '11- res 3R, '13- 7/1R; WJ: '06- sf; EU23: '07- sf (1 4x100mR), '09- 1R; WI: '10-2R; EI: '11- 1R.

Progress at 400m: 2009- 52.22, 2010- 51.41, 2011- 50.67, 2012- 50.43, 2013- 49.80. pbs: 60m 7.38i '07, 100m 11.55 '08, 200m 22.91/22.85w '10, 300m 36.3+ '13, TJ 13.18 '04.
Married Yevgeniy Ryzhov (5000m 14:16.67 '09) in January 2013. Ran brilliant final leg in 49.83 for 4th place in WI 4x400m 2014.

Anastasiya SAVCHENKO b. 15 Nov 1989 Omsk 1.75m 65kg. Luch Moskva.
At PV: OG: '12- dnq 26-; WCh: '13- 5=; EC: '12- 4; EU23: '09- 8, '11- 6; WUG: '13- 1; WI: '14- 11; EI: '13- 5=.
Progress at PV: 2005- 3.80, 2006- 3.80i/3.70, 2007- 3.90, 2008- 4.20i/4.10, 2009- 4.30i/4.20, 2010- 4.30, 2011- 4.40, 2012- 4.60, 2013- 4.73.

Mariya SAVINOVA b. 13 Aug 1985 Chelyabinsk 1.72m 60kg. Sverdlovsk Dyn.
At 800m: OG: '12- 1; WCh: '09- 5, '11- 1, '13- 2; EC: '10- 1; WI: '10- 1; EI: '09- 1; CCp: '10- 3; ET: '11- 1. Won Russian 800m 2009, 2011.
World indoor 4x800m record 2008.
Progress at 800m: 2002- 2:09.68, 2003- 2:08.38, 2004- 2:07.43, 2005- 2:07.03, 2006- 2:05.91, 2007- 2:00.78, 2008- 2:01.07, 2009- 1:57.90, 2010- 1:57.56, 2011- 1:55.87, 2012- 1:56.19, 2013- 1:57.80. pbs: 400m 51.43 '12, 600m 1:26.11i '09, 1:26.6+ '12; 1000m 2:34.56i '09, 1500m 4:08.2i, 4:10.25 '10.
Married Aleksey Farnosov (1500m 3:41.69i '11) on 10 Sep 2010.

Kristina SAVITSKAYA b. 10 Jun 1991 Krasnoyarsk 1.80m 72kg. Student at the Krasnoyarsk Academy of Summer Sports.
At Hep: OG: '12- 7; WCh: '13- dnf; WY: '07- 16; EU23: '11- 7, EJ: '09- 6; WUG: '13- 5; Russian champion 2012-13.
Progress at Hep: 2009- 5642, 2011- 5989, 2012- 6681, 2013- 6210. pbs: 200m 24.46 '12, 800m 2:12.27 '12, 60mh 8.37i '12, 100mh 13.37 '12, HJ 1.88 '12, LJ 6.65 '12, SP 15.27 '12, JT 46.83 '12, Pen 4590i '12.

Yekaterina SHARMINA b. 6 Aug 1986 Bryansk 1.72m 59kg. née Martynova. Sverdlovsk Dyn.
At 1500m: OG: '12- h; WCh: '11- sf, '13- 6; EJ: '05- 2; EI: '11- 3; WUG: '13- 1; ET: '11- 2, '13- 1 (2 800m). At 800m: WJ: '04- sf; WY: '03- 4; EU23: '07- 7. Won Russian 1500m 2011, short CC 2010.
World indoor 4x800m record 2011.
Progress at 1500m: 2004- 4:24.71i, 2005- 4:15.46, 2006- 4:15.09, 2007- 4:15.81, 2008- 4:03.68i/4:05.06, 2009- 4:05.40, 2010- 4:09.46, 2011- 4:01.68, 2012- 3:59.49, 2013- 4:04.55. pbs: 400m 55.97i '08, 56.59 '06; 800m 1:59.17 '11, 1000m 2:37.63i '08.
Married Yevgeniy Sharmin (800m 1:47.40 '12) in September 2011.

Svetlana SHKOLINA b. 9 Mar 1986 Yartsevo, Smolensk reg. 1.87m 66kg. Luch Moskva.
At HJ: OG: '08- 14, '12- 3; WCh: '09- 6, '11- 5, 13- 1; EC: '10- 4; WJ: '04- 2; WY: '03- 2=; EU23: '07- 1; EJ: '05- 1; WI: '10- 4; EI: '09- 4=, '11- 4=; WUG:

'05-4, '07- 4; ECp: '10: 2. Won DL 2013, Russian 2010, 2013.
Progress at HJ: 2001- 1.75, 2002- 1.84, 2003- 1.88, 2004- 1.91, 2005- 1.92, 2006- 1.92, 2007- 1.96, 2008- 1.98, 2009- 1.98, 2010- 2.00i/1.98, 2011- 2.00i/1.99, 2012- 2.03, 2013- 2.03.

Liliya SHOBUKHOVA b. 13 Nov 1977 Beloretsk, Bashkortostan 1.69m 50kg. née Volkova. Beloretsk VS.
At 5000m: OG: '04- 13, '08- 6, '12- dnf; WCh: '05- 9; EC: '02- 17, '06- 2; WCp: '06- 2; ECp: '04- 05-06: 2/1/1. At 10,000m: WCh: '09- 19; EC: '10- dnf. At Mar: OG: '12- dnf. At 3000m: WI: '06- 2; EI: '02- 5, '05- 5. World 4km CC: '02- 23. Eur CC: '02- 17, '04- 11. Won Russian 5000m 2002, 2005, 2008; 10,000m 2009.
Records: European 5000m 2008, World indoor 3000m 2006, world 30km road 2011; 3 Russian marathon records 2010-11.
Progress at 5000m, 10,000m, Mar: 1998- 16:50.64, 2001- 15:42.0, 2002- 15:25.00, 2004- 14:52.19, 2005- 14:47.07, 2006- 14:56.57, 2007- 15:51.53, 2008- 14:23.75, 2009- 30:29.36, 2:24:24; 2010- 2:20:25, 2011- 2:18:20, 2012- 2:22:59. pbs: 800m 2:03.18 '06, 1000m 2:39.81i '06, 1500m 4:03.78 '04, 1M 4:22.14 '04, 2000m 5:35.80 '07, 3000m 8:27.86i '06, 8:34.85 '04; Road: 10k 33:11 '01, HMar 69:25+ '11, 30k 1:38:23+ '11.
Marathons: London 3rd on marathon debut 2009, 1st 2010, 2nd 2011; won Chicago 2009-11 and the World Marathon Majors Series 2009/10 and 2010/11. Daughters Anna born in 2003, Yelizaveta in 2013.

Tatyana SIBILEVA b. 17 May 1980 Chelyabinsk 1.59m 42kg. Chelyabinsk VS.
At 20kW: OG: '08- 11; WCh: '07- 9; EU23: '01- 4; WUG: '03- 1, '05- 3; WCp: '08- 2; ECp: '07- 6.
Progress at 20kW: 1998- 1:29:53, 2000- 1:30:51, 2001- 1:27:33, 2002- 1:32:17, 2003- 1:27:54, 2004- 1:29:12, 2005- 1:31:18, 2006- 1:28:58, 2007- 1:28:51, 2008- 1:26:16, 2009- 1:31:59, 2010- 1:25:52, 2011- 1:30:37, 2012- 1:26:59. pbs: 10kW 42:15+ '08, 45:09.3t '06; 30000mW 2:24:56 '04 (world best).
Won IAAF Race Walking Challenge 2010.

Anzhelika SIDOROVA b. 28 Jun 1991 Moskva 1.70m 52kg. Moskva.
At PV: WJ: '10- 4; EU23: '13- 2; WI: '14- 2=; EI: '13- 3; ET: '13- 2.
Progress at PV: 2007- 3.80, 2008- 4.00, 2009- 4.10i/4.00, 2010- 4.30, 2011- 4.40i/4.30, 2012- 4.50, 2013- 4.62i/4.60, 2014- 4.72i.

Yelena SLESARENKO b. 28 Feb 1982 Volgograd 1.78m 57kg. née Sivushenko. Volgograd VS.
At HJ: OG: '04- 1, '08- 4; WCh: '07-09-11-13: 4/10/4/dnq 20=; EC: '06- 5; EU23: '03- 2; EJ: '01- 4; WUG: '03- 3; WI: '04-06-08: 1/1/2; EI: '02- 5=; WCp: '06- 1; ECp: '04- 1, '07- 1. Won WAF 2004, Russian 2005.

Progress at HJ: 1999- 1.82, 2000- 1.88, 2001-
1.94i/1.88, 2002- 1.97, 2003- 1.98i/1.96, 2004-
2.06, 2005- 2.00, 2006- 2.02i/2.00, 2007- 2.02,
2008- 2.03, 2009- 1.96, 2010- 1.88i, 2011- 1.97,
2013- 1.92.
Tied Russian indoor record to win gold at 2004
World Indoors and set a Russian record of 2.06
to win Olympic gold. Daughter Liza born on 20
July 2012.

Yelena SOBOLEVA b. 3 Oct 1982 Bryansk
1.76m 66kg. Lokomotiv Moskva.
At 1500m: WCh: '05- 4, '07- dq (2); EC: '06- 4;
EU23: '03- 6; WI: '06- 2, '08- dq (1); EI: '13- 6.
Won Russian 1500m 2006.
WIR 1500m 3:58.28 2006 (two cancelled in
2008).
Progress at 800m, 1500m: 2002- 2:04.43, 2003-
2:01.65, 4:12.02; 2004- 4:11.98, 2005- 2:00.59,
4:01.14; 2006- 1:57.28, 3:56.43; 2007dq- 1:59.49,
3:57.30; 2008dq- 1:54.85, 3:56.59; 2011- 2:03.45.
4:06.64; 2012- 1:59.90, 4:00.09; 2013- 2:00.17.
4:04.30. pbs: 1000m 2:32.40i '06, 2:36.50 '05; 1M
4:15.63dq '07, 4:33.88i '13; 2000m 5:36.43 '07,
3000m 8:55.89 '05.
Two-year drugs ban with results cancelled
from 26 Apr 2007. Son born in July 2010.

Vera SOKOLOVA b. 8 Jun 1987 Solianoy,
Chuvashiya 1.51m 51kg. Mordovia VS.
At 20kmW: WCh: '09- 14, '11- 11, '13- dq; EC:
'10- 3; WCp: '10- 4; ECp: '09-11-13: 10/1/2;
Russian champion 2009. At 10,000mW: WJ: '02-
04-06: 9/3/4; EJ: '05- 1; WCp: '04/06- 1J; ECp:
'03- 2J, '05- 1J. At 5000mW: WY: '03- 1.
Walks records: World 20km 2011, world junior
10,000m and 5000m indoors 2005.
Progress at 20kW: 2006- 1:40:03, 2007- 1:32:56,
2008- 1:30:11, 2009- 1:25:26, 2010- 1:25:35, 2011-
1:25:08, 2012- 1:28:06. 2013- 1:26:00. pbs: 3000m
11:58.44i '14, 12:51.96 '04, 5000mW 20:10.3i '10,
10kW 42:04+ '11, 43:11.34t '05.

Yelena SOKOLOVA b. 23 Jul 1986 Staryi Oskol,
Belgorod reg. 1.70m 61kg. née Kremneva.
Krasnodarsk krai.
At LJ: OG: '12- 2; WCh: '09- dnq 13, '13- 9; EU23:
'07- 3; EI: '07- 5, '09- 2; WUG: '07- 2, '13- 2. Won
DL 2012, Russian 2009, 2012.
Progress at LJ: 2002- 6.33, 2003- 6.39i?/6.31,
2006- 6.53, 2007- 6.71, 2008- 6.74, 2009- 6.92,
2010- 6.72/6.90w, 2011- 6.76, 2012- 7.07, 2013-
6.91. pbs: 60m 7.34i '12, 100m 11.61 '12, TJ
13.15i/12.93 '03.

Irina TARASOVA b. 15 Apr 1987 Kovrov
1.83m 110kg.
At SP: OG: '12- 8; WCh: '13- 7; ECh: '12- 2; WI:
'12- 8; WJ: '04- 5, '06- 3; WY: '03- 5; EU23: '07- 1;
EJ: '05- 2; EI: '13- 5; WUG: '07- 1, '13- 1.
Progress at SP: 2002- 14.01, 2003- 15.04, 2004-
16.16, 2005- 16.79i/16.53, 2006- 17.11, 2007- 18.27,
2008- 18.45, 2009- 18.21, 2010- 18.18, 2011- 18.72,
2012- 19.35, 2013- 19.20.

Kseniya USTALOVA b. 14 Jan 1988 Sverdlovsk
1.77m 65kg. Sverdlovsk. Engineering student.
At 400m/4x400m: EC: '10- 2/1R; EU23: '09-
1/1R; EJ: '07- 2/1R; WUG: '11- 1R, '13- 1/1R;
CCp: '10- 2R; WI: '12- 3R; ET: '10- 1/1R. Russian
champion 2010.
Progress at 400m: 2005- 55.51, 2006- 54.00i.
2007- 52.90, 2008- 54.57, 2009- 51.45, 2010- 49.92,
2011- 52.03, 2012- 50.48, 2013- 50.60. pbs: 200m
24.09 '10, 300m 36.76i '13.

Viktoriya VALYUKEVICH b. 22 May 1982
Sochi 1.78m 63kg. née Gurova. Krasnodar
TU.
At TJ: OG: '04- dnq 21, '08- 7, '12- 8; WCh: '05- 10;
EU23: '03- 1; EJ: '01- 3; WUG: '03- 2; EI: '05- 1;
ECp: '06- 2, '07- 3.
Progress at TJ: 1998- 12.56, 1999- 13.02, 2000-
13.44, 2001- 13.75/13.92w, 2002- 14.22, 2003-
14.37, 2004- 14.65, 2005- 14.74i/14.38, 2006- 14.60,
2007- 14.46, 2008- 14.85, 2009- 14.40, 2012- 14.64,
2013- 14.36. pb LJ 6.72 '07.
Married Dmitrij Valukevic (BLR/SVK triple
jumper) in September 2008. Son Georgiy born
in June 2010.

Kseniya ZADORINA b. 2 Mar 1987 Moskva
1.73m 59kg. Moskva Dyn.
At 400m/4x400m: WCh: '11- res (3)R; EC: '10-
res1R, '12- 2; WJ: '06- 4; EU23: '07- 3/1R, 09-
2/1R; EJ: '05- 2/1R; WUG: '07- 3/2R; EI: '11-
3/1R, '13- 2R; ET: '10- 1R, '13- 2/2R. Russian
champion 2013.
Progress at 400m: 2005- 52.64, 2006- 51.81, 2007-
51.06, 2008- 51.48, 2009- 51.41, 2010- 50.87, 2011-
50.92, 2012- 51.16, 2013- 50.55. pbs: 200m 23.66i
'11, 24.15 '08; 500m 1:08.94i '06 (WJR).

Yuliya ZARIPOVA b. 26 Apr 1986 Sbetlyi Yar,
Volgograd reg. née Zarudneva. 1.72m 54kg.
Volgograd Dyn.
At 3000mSt: OG: '12- 1; WCh: '09- 2, '11- 1; EC:
'10- 1; WUG: '13- 1; CCp: '10- 1; ET: '10- 1. At
800m: EJ: '05- h. At 3000m: EI: '09- 7. Eur CC:
'05- 8J, '08- 3 U23. Won Russian 1500m 2013,
3000mSt 2009, 2011-12.
Progress at 3000mSt: 2008- 9:54.9, 2009-
9:08.39, 2010- 9:17.57, 2011- 9:07.03, 2012-
9:05.02. 2013- 9:28.00. pbs: 800m 2:05.44 '05,
1500m 4:01.70 '12, 3000m 8:54.50i '09, 5000m
16:02.81i '10.

SAINT KITTS & NEVIS

Governing body: Saint Kitts Amateur Athletic
Association, PO Box 932, Basseterre, St Kitts.
Founded 1961.

Kim COLLINS b. 5 Apr 1976 Ogees, Saint-Peter
1.75m 64kg. Studied sociology at Texas
Christian University, USA.
At 100m (/200m): OG: '96- qf, 00- 7/sf, '04- 6,
'08- sf/6; WCh: '97- h, '99- h/h, '01- 5/3=, '03- 1,
'05- 3, '07- sf, '09- qf/qf, '11- 3/sf/3R; CG: '02- 1;
PAm: '07- 5, '11- 2; PAm-J: '95- 2; CAC: '99- 2,

'01- 1/1, '03- 1; WCp: '02- 2/2R. At 60m: WI: '03-2, '08- 2=. Won NCAA indoor 60m & 200m 2001. SKN records: 100m from 1996 to 2013, 200m from 1998, 400m 2000. M35 world indoor 60m record 2014.
Progress at 100m, 200m: 1995- 10.63, 21.85; 1996- 10.27, 21.06; 1998- 10.18/10.16w, 20.88/20.78w; 1999- 10.21, 20.43, 2000- 10.13A/10.15/10.02w, 20.31A/20.18w; 2001- 10.04A/10.00?/9.99w, 20.20 /20.08w; 2002- 9.98, 20.49; 2003- 9.99/9.92w, 20.40w; 2004- 10.00, 20.98; 2005- 10.00, 2006- 10.33, 21.53; 2007- 10.14, 2008- 10.05, 20.25; 2009- 10.15/10.08w, 20.45; 2010- 10.20, 21.35/20.76w; 2011- 10.00A/10.01, 20.52; 2012- 10.01/9.96w, 2013- 9.97, 21.37i. pbs: 60m 6.49i '14, 400m 46.93 '00.
The first athlete from his country to make Olympic and World finals and in 2003 the first to win a World Indoor medal and a World title; won a further medal in his 8th World Champs. There is a 'Kim Collins Highway' in St Kitts.

ST. LUCIA

Governing body: Saint Lucia Athletics Association, Olympic House, Barnard Hill P.O.GM 697 Gable Woods Mall, Castries.

Levern SPENCER b. 23 Jun 1984 Port of Spain, Trinidad 1.80m 54kg. Was at University of Georgia.
At HJ: OG: '08/12- dnq 27/19; WCh: '05-07-09-11-13: dnq 22/15=/dnq 24=/dnq 13/11; CG: '02-06-10: 12=/5/3; WJ: '02- 8; WY: '01- 3; PAm: '03-5, '07- 3; CAG: '06- 3, '10- 1; WI: '14- 7; CCp: '10-3=. CAC champion 2005, 2008-09, 2011.
Nine St. Lucia high jump records 2004-10.
Progress at HJ: 2000- 1.80, 2001- 1.81, 2002- 1.83, 2003- 1.86, 2004- 1.88, 2005- 1.94, 2006- 1.90, 2007- 1.94, 2008- 1.93, 2009- 1.95, 2010- 1.98, 2011- 1.94, 2012- 1.91, 2013- 1.95A, 2014- 1.95i. pbs: 200m 24.22 '05, LJ 5.95 '05.

SAUDI ARABIA

Governing body: Saudi Arabian Athletics Federation, PO Box 5802, Riyadh 11432. Founded 1963.

Youssef Ahmed **AL-MASRAHI** b. 31 Dec 1987 Njaran 1.76m 76kg.
At 400m: OG: 12- sf; WCh: '09- h, '13- 6; AsiG: '08- 1R, '10- 3/1R; AsiC: '11- 1, '13- 1/1R; Gulf champion 2009, Arab 2011, 2013- 1.
KSA 400m record 2013.
Progress at 400m/4x400mR: 2007- 48.89, 2008- 46.45, 2009- 45.84, 2010- 45.48, 2011- 45.44, 2012- 45.43, 2013- 44.61. pbs: 200m 21.14 '12, 800m 1:54.14 '07.

SENEGAL

Governing body: Fédération Sénégalaise d'Athlétisme, BP 1737, Stade Iba Mar DIOP, Dakar. Founded 1960.

Mamadou Kassé **HANN** b. 6 Mar 1988 Pikine,

Dakar 1.90m 73kg. Lives in France.
At 400mh OG: '12- sf; WCh: '13- 7; AfG: '07- h; AfCh: '06-08-10-12: h/h&3R/3/2; CCp: '10- 4.
Progress at 400mh: 2005- 54.41, 2006- 51.82, 2007- 51.26, 2008- 50.22, 2009- 50.63, 2010- 48.89, 2011- 50.38, 2012- 48.80, 2013- 48.50. pbs: 200m 21.23 '10, 400m 46.13 '10.

SERBIA

Governing body: Athletic Federation of Serbia, Strahinjica Bana 73a, 11000 Beograd. Founded in 1921 (as Yugoslav Athletic Federation).
National Championships (Yugoslav) first held in 1920 (men) and 1923 (women). **2013 Champions: Men:** 100m/200m: Marko Antic 10.74/21.48, 400m/400mh: Emira Bekric 46.58/49.32, 800m: Nemanja Kojic 1:50.06, 1500m: Goran Nava 3:48.37, 3000m: Mirko Petrovic 8:30.37, 5000m/10,000m: Jasmin Ljajic 14:38.96/30:12.21, HMar: Milos Milovanovic 1:13:14, Mar: Ognjen Stojanovic 2:46:29, 3000mSt: Darko Zivanovic 9:18.83, 110mh: Milan Ristic 14.20, HJ: Milos Todosijevic 2.16, PV/Dec: Dino Dogic 3.60/7454, LJ: Aleksandar Bundalo 7.66, TJ: Petar Djuric 15.39, SP: Asmir Kolasinac 20.64, DT: Milos Markovic 54.56, HT: Zoran Loncar 58.45, JT: Vedran Samac 73.19, 10kW/10,000mW: Vladimir Savanovic 41:42/42:08.28. **Women:** 100m/200m: Katarina Sirmic 11.99/24.50, 400m: Tamara Markovic 55.10, 800m/1500m: Amela Terzic 2:06.58/4:26.16, 3000m: Teodora Simovic 9:59.93, 5000m: Sonja Stolic 16:36.27, 10,000m: Olivera Jevtic 32:58.80, HMar: Ksenija Bubnjevic 1:22:04, Mar: *not held*, 3000mSt: Ana Subotic 10:40.76, 100mh: Ivana Petkovic 14.43, 400mh: Jelena Grujic 61.08, HJ: Zorana Bukvic 1.78, PV: Jelena Radinovic Vasic 3.60, LJ: Ivana Spanovic 6.48, TJ: Aleksandra Radic 12.52, SP: Dijana Sefcic 14.35, DT: Dragana Tomasevic 62.54, HT: Sara Savatovic 61.36, JT: Tatjana Jelaca 60.01, Hep: *not held*, 5kW Rd: Milica Stojanovic 28:10, 5000mW: Biljana Popovic 28:07.41.

Emir BEKRIC b. 14 Mar 1991 Belgrade 1.96m 87kg. AC Partizan, Belgrade.
At 400mh: OG: '12- sf; WCh: '11- sf, '13- 3; WJ: '10- 7; EC: '12- 2; EU23: '11- 3, '13- 1; EJ: '09- sf. Won MedG 2013, Balkan 2011, 2013; SRB 400m 2012-13, 400mh 2009, 2012-13.
Eight Serbian 400mh records 2011-13.
Progress at 400mh: 2007- 57.10, 2008- 53.46, 2009- 52.85, 2010- 50.67, 2011- 49.55, 2012- 49.21, 2013- 48.05. pb 400m 46.49 '13.

Mihail DUDAS b. 1 Nov 1989 Novi Sad 1.82m 85 kg. AC Vojvodina, Novi Sad.
At Dec: OG: '12- dnf; WCh: '11- 6, '13- 14; EC: '10- dnf, '12- 4; WJ: '08- 3; Eur23: '09- 3, '11- 3; EJ: '07- 15. At Hep: EI: '13- 3. Won SRB PV 2012. LJ & Dec 2011.
Three Serbian decathlon records 2011-13.
Progress at Dec: 2009- 7855, 2010- 7966, 2011- 8256, 2012- 8154, 2013- 8275. pbs: 60m 6.90 '11,

100m 10.67 '13, 400m 47.47 '11, 1000m 2:39.04i
'13, 1500m 4:24.30 '09, 60mh 8.13i '13, 110mh
14.59/14.52w '13, HJ 2.04 '09, PV 4.90 '11, LJ 7.63
'10, SP 14.39i '12, 13.85 '10, DT 46.90 '12, JT 59.98
'12, Hep 6099i '13.

Asmir KOLASINAC b. 15 Oct 1984 Skopje,
Macedonia 1.85m 130kg. AC Partizan, Belgrade.
At SP: OG: '08- dnq 32, '12- 7; WCh: '09- dnq 21,
'11- 10, '13- 10; EC: '10- 8, '12- 3; EU23: '05- dnq;
EI: '13- 1; Won Balkan 2011; SRB 2008, 2010-13.
Progress at SP: 2003- 14.43, 2004- 15.64, 2005-
17.88, 2006- 17.85, 2007- 19.30, 2008- 19.99, 2009-
20.41, 2010- 20.52i/20.38, 2011- 20.50, 2012- 20.85,
2013- 20.80, 2014- 20.67i.

Women

Ivana SPANOVIC b. 10 May 1990 Zrenjanin
1.76m 65kg. AK Vojvodina, Novi Sad.
At LJ: OG: '08- dnq 30, '12- 11; WCh: '13- 3; WJ:
'06- 7, '08- 1; WY: '05- dnq, '07- 2; EC: '10- 8, '12-
dnq 14; EU23: '11- 2; EJ: '07- 5, '09- 2; WI: '14- 3;
EI: '13- 5; WUG: '09- 1. Serbian champion 2006,
2008, 2011-13, Balkan 2011, 2013.
Three Serbian long jump records 2009-13
Progress at LJ: 2003- 5.36, 2004- 5.91, 2005- 6.43,
2006- 6.48i/6.38, 2007- 6.53i/6.41, 2008- 6.65,
2009- 6.71, 2010- 6.78, 2011- 6.71/6.74w, 2012-
6.64, 2013- 6.82, 2014- 6.92i. pbs: 60m 7.41i '13,
100m 11.90 '13, 60mh 8.59i '11, TJ 13.54 '11, Pen
4240i '13.
Won first medal for Serbia at World Champs.

Dragana TOMASEVIC b. 4 Jun 1982 Sremska
Mitrovica 1.75m 80kg. AK Sirmijum, Sremska
Mitrovica.
At DT: OG: '04/08/12- dnq 37/13/18; WCh: '05-
7, '07/09/13- dnq 19/19.14, '11- 7; EC: '06- 8, '10- 6,
'12- 9; EU23: '03- 11; EJ: '01- 10; WUG: '05- 3,
'07- 3; Won Balkan 2005, 2007, 2011; MedG 2005,
SCG 2001-03, SRB 2006-07, 2013.
Four SCG/SRB discus records 2005-06.
Progress at DT: 1999- 34.93, 2000- 45.87/47.04dh,
2001-52.80/53.00dh, 2002- 54.41/55.33dh, 2003-
56.24/56.74dh, 2004- 59.52, 2005- 62.43, 2006-
63.63, 2007- 61.52, 2008- 62.70, 2009- 61.89, 2010-
62.55, 2011- 62.48, 2012- 61.92, 2013- 63.04. pb SP
14.81 '04.

SLOVAKIA

Governing body: Slovak Athletic Federation,
Junácka 6, 832 80 Bratislava. Founded 1939.
National Championships first held in 1939.
2013 Champions: Men: 100m: Adam Zavacky
10.26w, 200m/110mh: Viliam Papso 21.40w/
13.89w, 400m: Martin Kucera 47.46, 800m: Jozef
Repcík 1:51.88, 1500m: Jozef Pelikán 3:58.40,
5000m: Juraj Vitko 15:10.31, 10,000m/Mar: Jozef
Urban 31:29.22/2:23:51, HMar: Tibor Sahadja
70:04, 3000mSt: Ján Domeny 10:02.66, 400mh:
Roman Olejnik 55.09, HJ/Dec: Peter Horák
2.20/6040, PV: Ján Zmoray 5.00, LJ: Tomás
Veszelka 7.33w, TJ: Martin Koch 15.58w, SP:

Matus Olej 18.15, DT: Matej Gasaj 56.38, HT:
Marcel Lomnicky 77.89, JT: Patrik Zenúch 73.87,
20kW: Anton Kucmin 1:25:28, 50kW: Dusan
Majdan 4:03.37. **Women**: 100m: Lenka Krsáková
11.40w, 200m: Alexandra Bezeková 24.02w,
400m: Iveta Putalová 54.69, 800m: Zofia Nanova
2:16.83, 1500m: Viktória Malceková 4:40.27.
5000m: Lucia Janecková 17:48.53, 10,000m/
HMar: Katarina Beresová 35:11.77/77:49, Mar:
Ingrid Petnuchová 2:50:38, 3000mSt: Katarina
Pokorná 11:38.20, 100mh: Lucia Mokrásová
14.12, 400mh: Andrea Holleyová 61.91, HJ: Iveta
Srnková 1.69, PV: Slovomira Slúková 4.00, LJ:
Renata Medgyesová 6.63w, TJ: Dana Veldáková
13.94w, SP: Ivana Kristofícová 15.76, DT: Ivona
Tomanová 49.23, HT: Martina Hrasnová 69.90,
JT: Jana Licáková 44.82, Hep: Lenka Ponistová
4459, 20kW: Mária Gáliková 1:42:00.

Marcel LOMNICKY b. 6 Jul 1987 Nitra 1.77m
106kg. TJ Stavbár Nitra. Was at Virginia Tech
University, USA.
At HT: OG: '12- dnq 15; WCh: '11: dnq 21, '13- 8;
WJ: '04- dnq 17, '06- 3; EC: '10: dnq 24, '12- 11;
EU23: '07- 3, '09- 6; EJ: '05- 8; WUG: '11- 2, '13- 2.
SVK champion 2012-13, won NCAA HT 2009,
indoor Wt 2012.
Progress at HT: 2005- 64.27, 2006- 69.53, 2007-
72.17, 2008- 72.66, 2009- 71.78, 2010- 74.83, 2011-
75.84, 2012- 77.43, 2013- 78.73. pbs: SP 15.73 '07,
DT 43.82 '08, Wt 23.05i '12.
Sister Nikola Lomnicka (b. 16 Sep 1988) has
hammer best 68.15 '14 and won NCAA 2010.

Matej TÓTH b. 10 Feb 1983 Nitra 1.85m 73kg.
Dukla Banská Bystrica.
At 20kW/(50kW): OG: '04- 32, '08- 26, '12- (7);
WCh: '05- 21, 07- 14, '09- 9/10, '11- 13/dnf, '13-
(5); EC: '06- 6, '10- 7, EU23: '03- 6; WCp: '10- (1);
ECp: '09-11-13: 9/2/3. At 10,000mW: WJ: '02- 16,
WY: '99- 8; EJ: '01- 6. Won SVK 20kW 2005-08,
2010-12; 50kW 2011.
SVK 50k walk records 2009 & 2011.
Progress at 20kW, 50kW: 1999- 1:34:29, 2000-
1:30:28, 2001- 1:29:33, 2003- 1:13:17, 2004- 1:23:18,
2005- 1:21:38, 2006- 1:21:39, 2007- 1:25:10, 2008-
1:21:24, 2009- 1:20:53, 3:41:32; 2010- 1:22:04,
3:53:30; 2011- 1:20:16, 3:39:46; 2012- 1:20:25,
3:41:24; 2013- 1:20:14, 3:41:07; 2014- 1:19:48. pbs:
3000BINGSON
mW 10:57.32i '11, 11:05.95 '12; 5000mW 18:34.56i
'12, 18:54.39 '11; 10000W 39:45.03 '06, 39:07R '10;
30kW 2:12:44 '13, '13- 2:34:23 '13.

Women

Martina HRASNOVÁ b. 21 Mar 1983 Bratislava
1.77m 88kg. née Danisová. Dukla Banská
Bystrica.
At HT: OG: '08- 8, '12- dnq 19; WCh: '01-07-13:
dnq 23/12/21, '09- 3; EC: '02 & '06- dnq 26, '12-
2; WJ: '00- 5, '02- 2; EJ: '99- 4, '01- 2; WUG: '07- 5,
'09- 2. Won SVK SP 2003, 2006; HT 2000-01,
2006, 2008-09, 2011-13.

14 Slovakian hammer records 2001-09.
Progress at HT: 1999- 58.61, 2000- 61.62, 2001-
68.50, 2002- 68.22, 2003- 66.36, 2005- 69.24, 2006-
73.84, 2007- 69.22, 2008- 76.82, 2009- 76.90, 2011-
72.47, 2012- 73.34, 2013- 72.41. pbs: 60m 7.96i '12,
SP 15.02 '06, DT 43.15 '06, Wt 21.74i '11.
Two-year drugs ban (nandrolone) from July
2003. Daughter Rebeka born on 4 July 2010.
Brother of Branislav Danis (HT 69.20 '06), who
is now her coach.

Lucia KLOCOVÁ b. 20 Nov 1983 Martin, Zilina
1.71m 58kg. AK ZTS Martin.
At 800m: OG: '04/08- sf; WCh: '03/05/07/09/11-
sf; EC: '06- sf, '10- 4, '12- 5; WJ: '00- 3, '02- 2;
EU23: '03- 2, '05- 5; EJ: '01- 1. At 1500m: OG:
'12- 8. Won SVK 400m 2007, 800m 2004, 2006,
2010-12; 1500m 2010-11.
SVK records: 1000m 2012, 1500m (4) 2010-12.
Progress at 800m, 1500m: 1998- 2:11.63, 2000-
2:04.00, 2001- 2:03.06, 2002- 2:01.59, 2003- 2:00.60,
2004- 2:00.79, 2005- 2:00.64, 2006- 2:00.28, 2007-
1:58.62, 2008- 1:58.51, 2009- 1:59.79, 4:30.65; 2010-
1:59.31, 4:08.86; 2011- 1:59.48, 4:30.95; 2012-
2:00.16, 4:02.99. pbs: 400m 52.98 '07, 600m 1:26.96
'08, 1000m 2:38.72 '12.
Seven successive 800m semi-finals at World
and Olympics, then Olympic 1500m finalist at
1500m in 2012. Son Adam born on 29 June 2013.

Dana VELDÁKOVÁ b. 3 Jun 1981 Roznava
1.79m 60kg. Dukla Banská Bystrica.
At (LJ/)TJ: OG: '08- dnq, '12- 12; WCh: '05- dnq
17, '07-09-11-13: 12/8/11/11; EC: '02/06- dnq
15/24, '10- 7, '12- 5; WJ: '98- 6, '00- 4/3; EU23:
'01- 5, '03- 4; EJ: '99- 8; WI: '06-10-12-14: 8/6/8/8;
EI: '07-09-11:; WUG: '03- 5, '07- 2. Won SVK
100mh 2003, TJ 2002-05, 2007-13, Hep 2001, 2004.
Two SVK triple jump records 2007-08.
Progress at TJ: 1998- 13.12, 1999- 13.13/13.19w,
2000- 13.92, 2001- 13.73, 2002- 13.99, 2003- 14.02,
2004- 13.96A, 2005- 14.16, 2006- 14.19, 2007- 14.41,
2008- 14.51, 2009- 14.43, 2010- 14.32/14.59w,
2011- 14.48, 2012- 14.36, 2013- 14.31. pbs: 60m
7.73i '06, 60mh 8.82i '03, 100mh 14.38 '01, HJ 1.75
'01, LJ 6.56 '08, SP 11.56i '04, Hep 5191 '01, Pen
3746i '03.
Twin **Jana** LJ 6.72 '08, 6.88w '10; TJ 13.40 '04.

SLOVENIA

Governing body: Atletska Zveza Slovenije,
Letaliska cesta 33c, 1122 Ljubljana. Current
organisation founded 1948.
2013 National Champions: Men: 100m: Gregor
Kokalovic 10.48, 200m: Jan Zumer 20.96, 400m:
Luka Janezic 47.18, 800m: Zan Rudolf 1:51.92,
1500m/3000m: Mitja Krevs 3:47.95/9:00.97,
5000m/10,000m: Jan Breznik 15:39.79/31:23.47,
HMar/Mar: Anton Kosmac 67:45/2:24:57,
3000mSt: Blaz Grad 10:17.77, 110mh/400mh:
Peter Hribarsek 14.85/53.82, HJ: Rozle Prezelj
2.28, PV: Andrej Poljanec 5.00, LJ: Rok Viler 7.27,
TJ: Martin Gradisek 15.75w, SP: Marko Spiler

18.23, DT: Tadej Hribar 51.99, HT: Primoz 5us
79.70, JT: Matija Kranjc 78.42, Dec: Luka Krizaj
5333. **Women**: 100m/200m: Kristina Zumer
11.55/23.51, 400m: Liona Rebernik 54.51, 800m:
Sonja Roman 2:11.78, 1500m: Marusa Mismas
4:28.65, 3000m/5000m: Mojca Grandovec
10:53.21 18:33.97, 10,000m: Mateja Simic 36:48.32,
HMar: Mateja Kosovelj 79:06, Mar: Zana Jereb
2:42:09, 3000mSt: *not held*, 100mh: Marina Tomic
13.12, 400mh: Marusa Berlot 65.74, HJ: Marusa
Novak 1.76, PV: Tina Sutej 4.35, LJ: Snezana
Rodic 6.41w, TJ: Maja Bratkic 13.35/0.0, SP:
Monika Lebenicnik 13.74, DT: Veronika Domjan
46.71, HT: Barbara Spiler 68.20, JT: Martina
Ratej 57.55, Hep: Klementina Kleideric 4066.

Primoz KOZMUS b. 30 Sep 1979 Novo mesto
1.88m 106kg. AK Brezice.
At HT: OG: '00- dnq 38, '04- 6, '08- 1, '12- 2;
WCh: '03-07-09-11-13: 5/2/1/3/4; EC: '02- dnq
25, '06- 7; EU23: '99- 12, '01- 14; WJ: '98- dnq.
SLO champion 1999-2004, 2006, 2008-09, 2011,
2013; WAF 2008-09.
Ten SLO hammer records 2000-09.
Progress at HT: 1995- 45.82, 1996- 54.10, 1997-
61.08, 1998- 66.28, 1999- 70.11, 2000- 76.84, 2001-
71.17, 2002- 75.87, 2003- 81.21, 2004- 79.34, 2006-
80.38, 2007- 82.30, 2008- 82.02, 2009- 82.58,
2011- 80.28, 2012- 79.36, 2013- 79.70.
First Slovenian Olympic champion. Older sister
Simona set Slovenian women's hammer record
(58.60 '01).

Women

Martina RATEJ b. 2 Nov 1981 Celje 1.78m 69kg.
AD Kladivar Celje.
At JT: OG: '08- dnq 37, '12- 7; WCh: '09- 11, '11- 7,
'13- dnq 20; EC: '06- dnq 21, '10- 7, '12- dnq 21;
WJ: '00- dnq 15. Won SLO 2005-13, MedG 2013.
Five SLO javelin records 2008-10.
Progress at JT: 1999- 48.74, 2000- 46.83, 2005-
50.86, 2006- 57.49, 2007- 58.49, 2008- 63.44, 2009-
63.42, 2010- 67.16, 2011- 65.89, 2012- 65.24, 2013-
62.60.

Snezana RODIC b. 19 Aug 1982 Koper 1.80m
66kg. née Vukmirovic. AD MASS Ljubljana.
At TJ: WCh: '05/09- dnq 16/19, '13- 9; EC: '10- 6,
'12- dnq 15; EU23: '03- 11 (dq LJ); EI: '09- 6, '11- 4.
Won SLO LJ 2004, 2013; TJ 2003-04, 2008, 2010.
Progress at TJ: 2003- 13.47, 2004- 13.97, 2005-
14.18, 2007- 14.03, 2008- 14.06/14.29w, 2009-
14.18i/14.10, 2010- 14.47/14.52w, 2011- 14.35i/
14.23, 2012- 14.20, 2013- 14.58. pbs: 60m 7.92i '03,
60mh 8.27i '05, 100mh 14.27 '03, LJ 6.53 '13, Hep
4897 '00.
Married to international footballer Aleksander
Rodic.

Tina SUTEJ b. 7 Nov 1988 Ljubljana 1.73m
58kg. Mass Ljubljana. Biology student at
University of Arkansas, USA.
At PV: OG: '12- dnq 19=; WCh: '11= dnq 12; EC:
'10- 10, '12- dnq 24; WJ: '06- 2; WY: '05- 8; EU23:

'09- 5; WUG: '11- 2; WI: '14- 10. SLO champion 2006, 2008-13.
Nine SLO pole vault records 2010-11.
Progress at PV: 2004- 3.81, 2005- 4.10, 2006- 4.25, 2007- 4.17i/4.10, 2008- 4.20, 2009- 4.25, 2010- 4.50, 2011- 4.61, 2012- 4.55, 2013- 4.35, 2014- 4.71i.

SOUTH AFRICA

Governing body: Athletics South Africa, PO Box 2712, Houghton 2041. Original body founded 1894.
National Championships first held in 1894 (men), 1929 (women). **2013 Champions: Men**: 100m/200m: Simon Magakwe 10.45/20.74, 400m: Wade van Niekerk 45.99, 800m: André Olivier 1:46.50, 1500m: Johan Cronje 3:38.13, 5000m/ 10,000m/HMar: Stephen Mokoka 13:25.94/ 28:22.50/62:45, Mar: Benedict Moeng 2:17:32, 3000mSt: Edwin Molepo 8:33.06, 110mh: Antonio Alkana 14.11, 400mh: Cornel Fredericks 48.78, HJ: Ruan Claasen 2.10, PV: Eben Beukes 5.20, LJ: Zarck Visser 8.29, TJ: Roger Haitengi 16.12, SP: Orazio Cremona 19.84, DT: Victor Hogan 61.68, HT: Chris Harmse 72.40 (19th successive title), JT: Robert Oosthuizen 76.41, Dec: Gert Swanepoel 6886, 20kW: Lebogang Shange 1:26:06.
Women: 100m: Alyssa Conley 11.72, 200m: Justine Palframan 23.28, 400m: Rorisang Rammonye 53.41, 800m: Gena Lofstrand 2:04.60, 1500m/5000m: Mapaseka Makhanya 4:16.08/ 15:53.61, 10,000m: Mpho Mabuza 34:31.28, HMar: René Kalmer 75:18, Mar: Cornelia Joubert 2:46:13, 3000mSt: Nolene Conrad 10:44.42, 100mh: Rikenette Steenkamp 13.64, 400mh: Annerie Ebersohn 56.04, HJ/Hep: Bianca Erwee 1.85/5715, PV: Deoné Joubert 3.80, LJ: Lynique Prinsloo 6.81, TJ: Matsi Dltotla 13.09, SP: Lezaan Jordaan 15.38, DT: Maryke Oberholzer 57.24, HT: Nanette Stapelberg 53.29, JT: Sunette Viljoen 61.87, 20kW: Anel Oosthuizen 1:44:40.

Willem COERTZEN b. 30 Dec 1982 Nigel, Gauteng 1.86m 80kg. Shaftesbury Barnet H, GBR.
At Dec: OG: '12- 9; WCh: '09-11-13: 14/dnf/9; AfCh: '08- 2; RSA champion 2008, 2011-12.
Two African decathlon records 2009-13, four RSA records 2009-13.
Progress at Dec: 2007- 7245, 2008- 7721 2009- 8146, 2012- 8244, 2013- 8343. pbs: 100m 10.89 '09, 10.74w '13; 400m 48.32 '13, 1500m 4:23.75 '12, 110mh 14.13 '13, 14.11w '09; HJ 2.08 '13, PV 4.63 '12, LJ 7.58 '09, 7.64w '11; SP 14.08 '11, DT 43.61 '13, JT 69.35 '13.

Johan CRONJE b. 13 Apr 1982 Bloemfontein 1.82m 69kg.
At 1500m: OG: '04- sf; WCh: '05- sf, '09- h, '13- 3; WJ: '00- 5; WY: '99- 5; AfCh: '04-06-10-12: 5/6/9/5; Won RSA 2002, 2004, 2008-09, 2012-13.
Two South African 1500m records 2013.
Progress at 1500m: 1998- 3:53.5A, 1999- 3:46.45, 2000- 3:41.21, 2001- 3:40.29, 2002- 3:37.28, 2003-

3:43.85, 2004- 3:37.83, 2005- 3:35.58, 2006- 3:36.73, 2007- 3:37.67, 2008- 3:38.37, 2009- 3:33.63, 2010- 3:35.24, 2012- 3:35.23, 2013- 3:31.93. pbs: 800m 1:45.64 '13, 1000m 2:18.48i '08, 2:18.56 '10; 1M 3:54.84 '09, 3000m 8:02.14 '04, 5000m 13:59.52 '09.

Cornel FREDERICKS b. 3 Mar 1990 Caledon 1.78m 70kg.
At 400mh/4x400mR: OG: '12- h; WCh: '11- 5, "13- sf; WJ: '08- 4; WY: '07- 5; AfCh: '10- 2; Won RSA 2010, 2012-13; Af-J 110mh & 400mh 2009.
Progress at 400mh: 2008- 50.39, 2009- 49.92, 2010- 48.79A/48.99, 2011- 48.14, 2012- 48.91, 2013- 48.78. pbs: 400m 46.95 '10, 300mh 35.15 '10.

Victor HOGAN b. 25 Jul 1989 Vredenburg, Western Cape 1.98m 108kg.
At DT: WCh: '13- 5; WJ: '08- 4; AfG: '11- 2; AfCh: '10- 3, '12- 1; CCp: '10- 8; Af-J: '07- 1; RSA champion 2010-13.
Progress at DT: 2008- 59.21, 2009- 57.67A, 2010- 58.30, 2011- 62.60, 2012- 62.76, 2013- 65.33.

Anaso JOBODWANA b. 30 Jul 1992 Aberdeen, Eastern Cape 1.87m 71kg. Student at Jacksonville State University, USA.
At (100m)/200m: OG: '12- 8; WCh: '13- sf/6; WUG: '13- 1/1.
Progress at 100m/200m: 2009- 21.68A, 2010- 20.95A, 2012- 10.34/10.24w, 20.27; 2013- 10.10, 20.13/20.00w. pb 60m 6.66i 13.

Godfrey Khotso MOKOENA b. 6 Mar 1985 Heidelberg, Gauteng 1.90m 73kg. Tuks AC, Pretoria.
At LJ/(TJ): OG: '04- (dnq 29), '08- 2, '12- 8; WCh: '05-07-09-11-13: 7/5/2/dnq 15=/7; CG: '06- 4/2; WJ: '02- 12, '04- 2/1; AfG: '03- 3/2, '07- 3; AfCh: '06- 2/2, '10- 1; WI: '06-08-10: 5/1/2. At HJ: WY: '01- 5. Won RSA LJ 2005-07, 2009-11; TJ 2004-06.
Records: Three African LJ 2009, RSA LJ (5) 2005-09, TJ (2) 2004-05, African junior TJ 2004.
Progress at LJ, TJ: 2001- 7.17A, 2002- 7.82A, 16.03A; 2003- 7.84A/7.83, 16.28; 2004- 8.09, 16.96A/16.77; 2005- 8.37A/8.22, 17.25; 2006- 8.39/8.45w, 16.95; 2007- 8.34A/8.28/8.32w, 16.75; 2008- 8.25/8.35w, 2009- 8.50, 2010- 8.23A/8.15/ 8.22w, 2011- 8.25/8.31w, 2012- 8.29A/8.24, 2013- 8.30. pbs: 100m 10.7A '09, HJ 2.10 '01.
Plans to return to triple jumping in 2014.

André OLIVIER b. 29 Dec 1989 Pietermaritzburg 1.92m 72kg.
At 800m: OG: '12- sf; WJ: '08- 3; WI: '14- 4; AfCh: '12- 3; Af-J: '07- 4; RSA champion 2013. At 1500m: WY: '05- 11. At 4x400m: WUG: '11- 3.
Progress at 800m: 2004- 1:57.7A, 2005- 1:52.2A, 2006- 1:49.58A, 2007- 1:47.92, 2008- 1:46.85, 2009- 1:45.41, 2011- 1:46.84, 2012- 1:44.29, 2013- 1:44.37, 2014- 1:44.99i. pbs: 400m 46.95A '08, 1500m 3:39.40 '09.

Louis J. van ZYL b. 20 Jul 1985 Bloemfontein 1.86m 75kg. Tuks AC, Pretoria.
At 400mh/4x400mR: OG: '08- 5, '12- h; WCh: '05-07-09-11-13: 6/h/sf/3&2R/h; CG: '06- 1/2R,

'10- 2; AfG: '07- 1; AfCh: '06- 1, '08- 1/1R, '10- 1;
WJ: '02- 1, '04- 4/2R; WY: '01- 3; WCp: '06- 2, '10-
5; RSA champion 2003, 2005-06, 2008, 2011.
Two RSA 400m hurdles records 2011.
Progress at 400mh: 2001- 51.14A, 2002- 48.89,
2003- 49.22, 2004- 49.06, 2005- 48.11, 2006- 48.05,
2007- 48.24, 2008- 48.22, 2009- 47.94, 2010- 48.51A/
48.63, 2011- 47.66, 2012- 49,42A, 2013- 49.11. pbs:
100m 10.62 '07, 10.3Aw '03, 10.5A '01; 200m 21.02A
'09, 21.0A '03; 300m 32.32 '09, 400m 44.86A '11,
46.02 '08; 200mhSt 22.63 '13, 300mh 35.76 '04.
Ran world U18 record of 48.89 to win World
Junior title in 2002 after world age record at 15
in 2001. Commonwealth Games record to win
400mh gold and ran brilliant final leg in
4x400m to take RSA from fifth to second in
2006. Married Irvette van Blerk (pbs HMar
70:56 '11, Mar 2:33:41 '12) on 29 Sep 2012.

Zarck VISSER b. 15 Sep 1989 Welkom 1.78m 70kg.
At LJ: WCh: 13- dnq 13; AfCh: '12- 2; South
African champion 2012-13.
Progress at LJ: 2007- 7.21A, 2008- 7.62A, 2009-
7.77, 2010- 7.76A/7.79Aw, 2011- 7.85, 2012-
8.15A/8.07/8.21w, 2013- 8.32. pb TJ 15.66A '08.

Women

Caster SEMENYA b. 7 Jan 1991 Polokwane,
Limpopo Province 1.70m 64kg. Tuks AC,
Pretoria. Student of sports science at University
of Pretoria.
At 800m: OG: '12- 2; WCh: ' 09- 1, '11- 2; WJ: '08-
h; Afr-J: '09- 1 (1 1500m), won RSA 800m 2011-
12, 1500m 2011, Southern Africa 800m 2009.
Two RSA 800m records 2009, 600m 2012.
Progress at 800m: 2007- 2:09.35, 2008- 2:04.23,
2009- 1:55.45, 2010- 1:58.16, 2011- 1:56.35, 2012-
1:57.23, 2013- 1:58.92. pbs: 400m 52.54A, 53.16
'11, 600m 1:25.56 '12, 1500m 4:08.01 '09.
Questions over her gender arose at the African
Junior and World Champs in 2009, and she was
barred from competing by Athletics South
Africa until the IAAF determined whether she
was free to compete again. They did so in July
2010 but saying that the medical details of her
case remained confidential.

Sunette VILJOEN b. 6 Oct 1983 Johannesburg
1.70m 70kg. University of North West,
Potchefstroom.
At JT: OG: '04/08- dnq 35/33, '12- 4; WCh:
'03/09- dnq 16/18, '11- 3, '13- 6; CG: '06- 1, '10- 1;
AfG: '03- 3, '07- 3; AfCh: '04-06-08-10: 1/2/1/1;
WUG: '07- 5, '09- 1, '11- 1; CCp: '10- 2. Won Afro-
Asian Games 2003, RSA 2003-04, 2006, 2009-13.
Four African javelin records 2009-12, two
Commonwealth 2011-12.
Progress at JT: 1999- 43.89A, 2000- 45.50A, 2001-
50.70A, 2002- 58.33A, 2003- 61.59, 2004- 61.15A,
2005- 57.31, 2006- 60.72, 2007- 58.39, 2008-
62.24A, 2009- 65.43, 2010- 66.38, 2011- 68.38,
2012- 69.35, 2013- 64.51.
Son Hervé born in 2005.

SPAIN

Governing body: Real Federación Española de
Atletismo (RFEA), Avda. Valladolid, 81 - 1°,
28008 Madrid, Spain. Founded 1918.
National Championships first held in 1917
(men), 1931 (women). **2013 Champions: Men**:
100m: Ángel David Rodríguez 10.26, 200m:
Bruno Hortelano 20.58, 400m: Samuel García
46.43, 800m: Kevin López 1:47.98, 1500m: David
Bustos 3:47.11, 5000m: Alemayehu Bezabeh
13:35.59 (drugs dq: Sergio Sánchez 13:32.68),
10,000m: Carles Castillejo 27:57.92, HMar: Ayad
Lamdassem 63:56, Mar: Javier Guerra 2:12:21/
Carles Castillejo 2:12:43, 3000mSt: Ángel
Mullera 8:29.61, 110mh: Francisco Javier López
13.82, 400mh: Diego Cabello 50.28, HJ: Simón
Siverio 2.20, PV: Igor Bychkov 5.65, LJ: Jean
Marie Okutu 7.76, TJ: Pablo Torrijos 16.71w, SP:
Borja Vivas 19.92, DT: Mario Pestano 63.28
(13th successive title), HT: Javier Cienfuegos
76.08, JT: Manuel Uriz 69.60, Dec: David Gómez
7484, 10,000mW: Miguel Ángel López 39:07.58,
20kW: Benjamín Sánchez 1:22:33, 50kW:
Claudio Villanueva 3:55:13. **Women**:
100m/200m: Estela García 11.61/23.90, 400m:
Aauri Lorena Bokesa 51.77, 800m: Adriana
Cagigas 2:08.75, 1500m: Natalia Rodríguez
4:24.13, 5000m: Dolores Checa 15:41.79, 10,000m:
Lidia Rodríguez 32:50.34, HMar Alessandra
Aguilar 72:55, Mar: María Jesús Gestido
2:40:22/Estela Navascués 2:32:38, 3000mSt:
Diana Martín 9:54.37, 100mh: Olatz Arrieta
13.96, 400mh: Laura Natali Sotomayor 59.12,
HJ: Ruth Beitia 1.93, PV: Naroa Agirre 4.40, LJ:
María del Mar Jover 6.55, TJ: Patricia Sarrapio
13.50, SP: Úrsula Ruiz 16.50, DT: Sabina Asenjo
52.58, HT: Berta Castells 66.88 (11th successive
title), JT: Nora Aida Bicet 55.96, Hep: Estrella
Estefanía Fortes 5340, 10,000mW/20kW: Julia
Takacs 42:32.74/1:28:44.

Eusebio CÁCERES b. 10 Sep 1991 Onil,
Alicante 1.76m 69kg. Centre Esportiu Colivenc.
At LJ: OG: '12- dnq 14; WCh: '11- dnq 19, '13- 4;
EC: '10- 8, '12- 5; WJ: '08- '3, '10- 2; EJ: '09- 6;
EU23: '11- 8, '13- 1; ECp: '09- 1. Won ESP 2012.
European junior long jump record 2010. World
junior indoor heptathlon best 5984 '10.
Progress at LJ: 2002- 4.39, 2003- 4.93, 2004-
5.57/5.60w, 2005- 6.77, 2006- 7.36, 2007- 7.57,
2008- 7.86, 2009- 8.00/8.17w, 2010- 8.27, 2011-
8.23, 2012- 8.06/8.31w, 2013- 8.37. pbs: 60m 6.77i
'12, 100m 10.43 '11, 10.34w '09; 200m 21.43 '13,
60mh 8.29i '11, 110mh 14.93w '11, HJ 1.96i '10,
1.93 '09; PV 4.60i '10, 4.30 '09; JT 53.32 '11, Hep
5667i '11, Dec 7273w '11.

Frank Yennifer **CASAÑAS** b. 18 Oct 1978 La
Habana, Cuba 1.87m 115kg. Playas de Castellón.
At DT: OG: '00/04- dnq 24/17, '08- 5, '12- 7;
WCh: '03-05-09-13: dnq 21/21/16;/9 EC: '10- 11,
'12- 5; WJ: '96- 3; PAm: '99- 4, '03- 2; CAG: '98- 2;

PAm-J: '97- 1; ET: '11- 2; won IbAm 2000, Cuban 2003-05, MedG 2009.
Progress at DT: 1995- 50.08, 1996- 54.86, 1997- 57.36, 1998- 60.52, 1999- 63.90, 2000- 63.32, 2002- 64.04, 2003- 65.08, 2004- 64.20, 2005- 65.32, 2006- 67.14, 2007- 64.68, 2008- 67.91, 2009- 67.17, 2010- 66.95, 2010- 66.62, 2011- 67.18, 2012- 67.74, 2013- 66.16. pb SP 17.68 '07.
Spanish citizen from 27 May 2008. Married to Dolores Pedrares (HT pb 67.14 '04).

Jesús Ángel GARCÍA b. 17 Oct 1969 Madrid 1.72m 64kg. Canal de Isabel II.
At 50kW: OG: '92-96-00-04-08-12: 10/dnf/12/ 5/4/19; WCh: '93-5-7-9-01-03-05-07-09-11-13: 1/ 5/2/dnf/2/6/dq/dq/3/dq/12; EC: '94-98-02-06- 10: 4/dq/3/2/5; WCp: '93-5-7-9-02-04-06-08-10- 12: 2/2/1/4/dq/6/6/14/5/6; ECp: '96-8-00-01-09: 1/2/1/1/2. At 20kW: WUG: '91- 5. Won Spanish 50kW 1997, 2000, 2007, 2012.
World M40 50km walk record 2010.
Progress at 50kW: 1991- 4:05:10, 1992- 3:48:24, 1993- 3:41:41, 1994- 3:41:28, 1995- 3:41:54, 1996- 3:46:59, 1997- 3:39.54, 1998- 3:43:17, 1999- 3:40:40, 2000- 3:42:51, 2001- 3:43:07, 2002- 3:44:33, 2003- 3:43:56, 2004- 3:44:42, 2005- 3:48:19, 2006- 3:42:48, 2007- 3:46:08, 2008- 3:44:08, 2009- 3:41:37, 2010- 3:47:56, 2011- 3:48:11, 2012- 3:48.15, 2013- 3:46:44.
pbs: 5000mW 19:33.3 '01, 10,000mW 40:38.86 '09, road: 5kW 20:07 '04, 10kW 40:25 '99, 20kW 1:23:00 '09, 30kW 2:08:47 '01, 35km 2:31:06 '94; running Mar 2:47:43 '09.
Competed in all major champs 1992-2013, inc. tying men's record of six Olympic Games and setting men's record of 11 World Champs; has 55 races under 4 hours and 41 sub 3:50 for 50km and 22 years walking sub 3:50. In 1997 he married Carmen Acedo, who won a rhythmic gymnastics world title in 1993.

Miguel Ángel LÓPEZ b. 3 Jul 1988 Murcia 1.81m 70kg. UCAM Athleo Cieza.
At 20kW: OG: '12- 5; WCh: '11- 16, '13- 3; EC: '10- 14; EU23: '09- 1; WCp: '10- 12; ECp: '11- 7, '13- 2. At 10kW: WJ: '06- 14; WY: '05- 6; EJ: '05- 9, '07- 8; WCp: '06- 2J; ECp: '07- 2J. Won Spanish 10,000mW 2010, 2012-13; 20kW 2010, 2012.
Progress at 20kW: 2008- 1:23:44, 2009- 1:22:23, 2010- 1:23:08, 2011- 1:21:41, 2012- 1:19:49, 2013- 1:21:21. pbs: 3000mW 11:39.92 '13, 5000mW 19:20.50 '13, 10,000mW 39:07.58 '13.

Mario PESTANO b. 8 Apr 1978 Santa Cruz de Tenerife 1.95m 120kg. Unicaja Jaén.
At DT: OG: '04- dnq 12, '08- 9, '12- dnq 14; WCh: '99-01-03-05-07-09-11-13:   dnq   30/dnq 22/8/11/10/10/11/12; EC: '02-06-10-12: 4/4/6/4; EU23: '99- 3; EJ: '97- 11; WCp: '02- 3; ECp: '01-05- 06-08-09-13: 2/1/3/1/3/2. Won WAF 2004, IbAm 2004, 2010; MedG 2005, Spanish 2001-13.
Eight Spanish discus records 2001-08.
Progress at DT: 1995- 49.36, 1996- 50.56, 1997- 53.68, 1998- 54.96, 1999- 61.73, 2000- 61.63, 2001- 67.92, 2002- 64.46, 2003- 64.99, 2004- 68.00, 2005-

66.57, 2006- 66.31, 2007- 68.26, 2008- 69.50, 2009- 66.63, 2010- 66.90, 2011- 67.97, 2012- 67.15, 2013- 65.79. pb SP 18.75i '00, 18.64 '02.

Women

Ruth BEITIA b. 1 Apr 1979 Santander 1.92m 71kg. Piélagos Inelecma. Graduate of physical therapy at University of Santander.
At HJ: OG: '04- dnq 16=, '08- 7=, '12- 4; WCh: '03-05-07-09-11-13: 11=/dnq 19=/6/5/dnq 16/3=; EC: '02-06-10-12: 11/9/6=/1; WJ: '96- dnq, '98- 8, EU23: '01- 1; EJ: '97- 9; WI: '01-03-06-08-10-12-14: 7/5=/3/4/2/6/3; EI: '05-07-09-11-13: 2/3/2/2/1; WCp: '02- 6=; ECp: '03-06-07-09-11: 2/2/2/2/3; Won IbAm 2010, Med G 2005, Spanish 2003, 2006-13 (and 13 indoors 2002-14).
Nine Spanish HJ records 1998-2007 (and eight indoors 2001-07).
Progress at HJ: 1989- 1.29, 1990- 1.39, 1991- 1.50, 1992- 1.55, 1993- 1.66, 1994- 1.74, 1995- 1.80, 1996- 1.85, 1997- 1.87i/1.86, 1998- 1.89, 1999- 1.83, 2000- 1.86i/1.85, 2001- 1.94i/1.91, 2002- 1.94, 2003- 2.00, 2004- 2.00i/1.96, 2005- 1.99i/1.97, 2006- 1.98i/1.97, 2007- 2.02, 2008- 2.01, 2009- 2.01, 2010- 2.00, 2011- 1.96i/1.95, 2012- 2.00, 2013- 1.99i/1.97, 2014- 2.00i. pbs: 200m 25.26 '02, 100mh 14.95 '97, 14.93w '00; LJ 6.04 '03, TJ 12.43/12.73w '11.
She is a deputy of the Parliament of Cantabria, her autonomous community. Her sister Inmaculada (b. 8 Sep 1975) had TJ pb 13.43 '00.

Beatriz PASCUAL b. 9 May 1982 Barcelona 1.63m 64kg. Valencia Terra i Mar.
At 20kW: OG: '08- 6, '12- 8; WCh: '07-09-11-13: 13/6/9/6; EC: '02- 12, '06- 20, '10- 5; EU23: '03- 4; WCp: '10- 11, '12- 5; ECp: '09- 6, '13- 9. At 10kW: WJ: '00- 6; EJ: '01- 3. Won Spanish 10,000mW 2008, 2010, 2012; 20kW 2006, 2008-09, 2011.
Spanish walk records 5000m (3) 2008-12, 10,000m 2010.
Progress at 20kW: 2002- 1:32:38, 2003- 1:31:31, 2004- 1:30:22, 2005- 1:32:49, 2006- 1:33:55, 2007- 1:30:37, 2008- 1:27:44, 2009- 1:29:54, 2010- 1:28:05, 2011- 1:28:51, 2012- 1:27:56, 2013- 1:29:00. pbs: 3000mW 13:06.48 '04, 5000mW 20:45:11 '12, 10,000mW 42:40.33 '10; HMar (run) 82:43 '08.

Natalia RODRÍGUEZ b. 2 Jun 1979 Tarragona 1.64m 49kg. C.G.Tarragona.
At 1500m: OG: '00- h, '04- 10, '08- 6, '12- h; WCh: '01-03-09-11-13: 6/sf/6/dq (1)/3/sf, EC: '02- 6, '10- 3; EU23: '99- 4, '01- 2, WJ: '98- 6, EJ: '97- 5; WI: '10- 2; EI: '09- 2; ECp: '03- 1. At 800m: WJ: '96- h. At 3000m: ET: '11- 2. Won Spanish 1500m 2000-05, 2009-10, 2012.
Spanish 1500m record 2005.
Progress at 1500m: 1995- 4:42.4, 1996- 4:38.40, 1997- 4:17.28, 1998- 4:16.20, 1999- 4:10.65, 2000- 4:04.24, 2001- 4:06.32, 2002- 4:02.84, 2003- 4:01.30, 2004- 4:03.01, 2005- 3:59.51, 2008- 4:03.19, 2009- 4:03.73/4:03.36 dq, 2010- 4:01.30, 2011- 4:01.50, 2012- 4:09.25, 2013- 4:06.20. pbs: 800m 2:01.35 '01, 1M 4:21.92 '08, 3000m 8:35.86 '09, 5000m

16:15.21 '11, 10k Rd 34:12 '09.
Finished first but disqualified for pushing through on inside and knocking Gelete Burka over in World 1500m 2009. Daughter Guadalupe born in November 2007.

Julia TAKACS b. 29 Jun 1989 Budapest, Hungary 1.71m 55kg. Independiente.
At 20kW: WCh: '13: 9; EU23: '09- 5, '11- 2; WCp: '12- 11; ECp: '09- 11, '11- 10; WUG: '11- 1. At 10,000mW: WJ: '08- 6. Won Spanish 10,000mW 2009, 2011; 20kW 2013-14.
Spanish 10,000m walk record 2013.
Progress at 20kW: 2006- 1:43:49, 2007- 1:38:57, 2008- 1:39:12, 2009- 1:35:04, 2010- 1:30:14, 2011- 1:31:32, 2012- 1:30:37, 2013- 1:28:44, 2014- 1:29:08.
pbs: 5000mW 21:07.97 '13, 10,000mW 42:32.74 '13
She has lived in Spain from the ge of 14 and switched from Hungary to Spain 19 June 2008.

SRI LANKA
Governing body: Athletic Association of Sri Lanka, n°33 Torrington Avenue, Colombo 7. Founded 1922.
National Champions 2013: Men: 100m: Umanga Sanjeewa 10.62, 200m/400m: Kasun Senevirathne 21.60/46.65, 800m: Indunil Herath 1:51.11, 1500m: Punchi Chamal 3:54.40, 5000m: D.Lionel Samarajeewa 14:38.24, 10,000m: Saman Kumara 30:57.42, 3000mSt: R.M.S.Pushpakumara 9:01.09, 110mh: Hasitha Nirmal 14.41, 400mh: Jagath Gunathilake 52.19, HJ: Manjula Wijesekara 2.20, PV: Ishara Sandaruwan 4.60, LJ: Janaka Wimalasiri 7.46, TJ: Dinesh Fernando 15.92, SP: Joy Perera 15.07, DT: Gayan Jayawardana 43.45, HT: H.P.S.J.Abeywardena 45.23, JT: Sampath Ranasinghe 70.85, Dec: W.K.D.S.Perera 5956.
Women: 100m/200m: Jani De Silva 11.92/24.85, 400m: Chandrika Rasnayake 53.05, 800m: W.K.L.A.Nimali 2:04.32, 1500m: Gayanthika Abeyrathne 4:21.00, 5000m: Geethani Rajasekara 16:58.13, 10,000m: Chaturika Hemamali 35:36.47, 3000mSt: Nilani Ratnayake 10:41.76, 100mh: Amali Wijesinghe 14.51, 400mh: T.G.N.D. Wickramesinghe 60.29, HJ: Shayamali Sooriyampola 1.78, PV: Anoma Karunawansa 3.30, LJ: N.C.D.Priyadharshani 5.97, TJ: Sachantha Dulanjali 12.48, SP: Kumudumali Fernando 14.26, DT: Amanthi Silva 43.40, HT: A.W.A.C.Amarasinghe 38.78, JT: Nadeeka Lakmali 59.12, Hep: K.M.K.N.A.Fernando 3741.

SUDAN
Governing body: Sudan Athletic Association, PO Box 13274, 11 111 Khartoum. Founded 1959.

Abubaker KAKI Khamis b. 21 Jun 1989 Elmuglad 1.76m 63kg.
At 800m: OG: '08- sf, '12- 7; WCh: '07- h, '09- sf, '11- 2; WJ: '06- 6, '08- 1; WI: '08- 1, '10- 1; AfG: '07- 1. At 1500m: WY: '05- 3. At 4x400m: AfCh: '08- 2R. Won Pan Arab G 800m & 1500m 2007.
World junior records 800m & 1000m (& indoor

1000m) 2008. SUD records 800m (3), 1000m (2) 2008-10, 1500m 2011.
Progress at 800m, 1500m: 2005- 1:48.43, 3:45.06; 2006- 1:45.78, 3:47.58; 2007- 1:43.90, 3:47.92; 2008- 1:42.69, 3:39.71; 2009- 1:43.09, 3:39.89; 2010- 1:42.23, 2011- 1:43.13, 3:31.76; 2012- 1:43.32, 3:34.34; 2013- 1:46.57i. pbs: 1000m 2:13.62 '10, 10k Rd 30:18 '07.
Ran world's fastest 800m (WJR) for five years at Oslo 2008.

SWEDEN
Governing body: Svenska Friidrottsförbundet, Heliosgaten 3, 120 30 Stockholm. Founded 1895.
National Championships first held in 1896 (men), 1927 (women). **2013 Champions: Men**: 100m: Tom Kling Baptiste 10.50, 200m: Johan Wissman 21.15, 400m: Nick Ekelund-Arenander (has dual citizenship DEN/SWE), 800m/1500m: Johan Rogestedt 1:48.89/3:47.14, 5000m: Musael Temesghen 14:20.41, 10,000m: Adil Bouafif 29:11.26, HMar: Mikael Ekvall 66:08, Mar: Mustafa Mohamed 2:20:08, 3000mSt: Napoleon Solomon 8:57.36, 110mh: Philip Nossmy 13.68, 400mh: Jonathan Carbe 51.69, HJ: Mehdi Alkhatib 2.12, PV: Carl Sténson 5.09, LJ: Michel Tornéus 7.88, TJ: Mathias Ström 15.87, SP: Leif Arrhenius 19.58, DT: Niklas Arrhenius 64.07, HT: Mattias Jons 75.24, JT: Kim Amb 81.48, Dec: Petter Olson 7643, 10,000mW: Anatole Ibáñez 40:50.5, 20kW/50kW: Perseus Karlström 1:25:15/3:52:43. **Women**: 100m/200m: Irene Ekelund 11.63/23.26, 400m: Moa Hjelmer 53.68, 800m: Sofia Öberg 2:08.21, 1500m: Linn Nilsson 4:33.60, 5000m/3000mSt: Charlotta Fougberg 16:07.44/10:12.01, 10,000m/HMar/Mar: Isabellah Andersson 33:22.95/75:17/2:33:49, 100mh: Emma Tuvesson 13.74, 400mh: Frida Persson 58.10, HJ: Emma Green Tregaro 1.90, PV: Malin Dahlström 4.18, LJ: Erica Jarder 6.54w, TJ: Lynn Johnson 13.14, SP: Frida Åkerström 15.92, DT: Sofia Larsson 55.44, HT: Tracey Andersson 68.74, JT: Sofi Flink 57.42, Hep: Victoria Joäng 5426, 5000mW: Mari Olsson 23:07.6, 20kW: Siw Karlström 1:47:23.

Kim AMB b. 31 Jul 1990 Solna 1.80m 85kg. F Bålsta IK.
At JT: OG: '12- dnq 18; WCh: '13- 10; EC: '12- 7; WJ: '08- dnq 13; EU23: '11- 4. Swedish champion 2011-13.
Progress at JT: 2007- 55.01, 2008- 69.34, 2009- 66.06, 2010- 77.81, 2011- 80.09, 2012- 81.84, 2013- 84.61. pb PV 3.45 '06.
His father Björn had a best with the old javelin of 62.60 '79.

Michel TORNÉUS b. 26 May 1986 Botkyrka 1.84m 70kg. Hammarby IF.
At LJ: OG: '12- 4; WCh: '09-11-13: dnq 28/27/19; EC: '10- 9, '12- 3; EU23: '07- 10; EJ: '05- 4; WI: '14- 3; EI: '11- 7, '13- 2; ET: '11- 2. Won Swedish LJ

2005, 2007-10, 2012-13; TJ 2012.
Swedish long jump record 2012.
Progress at LJ: 2001- 6.48, 2002- 6.74/6.86w,
2003- 7.07, 2004- 7.41, 2005- 7.94, 2006- 7.68, 2007-
7.85, 2008- 7.86, 2009- 8.11, 2010- 8.12/8.21w,
2011- 8.19, 2012- 8.22, 2013- 8.29i/8.00/8.12w.
pbs: 60m 6.93i '12, 100m 10.71/10.63w '11, 400mh
55.48 '04, HJ 1.99i '05, 1.92 '04; TJ 15.90 '12, Dec
6115 '04. Father came from DR of Congo.

Women

Abeba AREGAWI b. 5 Jul 1990 Adigrat, Tigray
1.69m 48kg. Hammarby IF.
At 1500m: OG: '12- 5; WCh: '13- 1; WI: 14- 1; EI:
'13- 1; won DL 2012-13. At 800m: Af-J: '09- 3.
Won ETH 800m 2009.
1500m records: Ethiopian 2012, Swedish 2013,
European indoor 2014.
Progress at 1500m: 2010- 4:01.96, 2011- 4:01.47i/
4:10.30, 2012- 3:56.54, 2013- 3:56.60, 2014- 3:57.91i.
pbs: 800m 1:59.20 '13.
Lived in Stockholm from 2009; granted Swedish
citizenship on 28 Jun 2012 and accepted by the
IAAF to compete for Sweden from 10 Dec 2012
but from then has lived in Ethiopia and
divorced from her husband and coach Henok
Weldegebriel. Unbeaten at 1500m in 2013.

Angelica BENGTSSON b. 8 July 1993
Väckelsång 1.64m 51kg. Hässelby SK.
At PV: OG: '12- dnq 19=, WCh: '13- dnq 16; EC:
'12- 10; WJ: '10- 1, '12- 1; WY: '09- 1; EU23: '13- 3;
EJ: '11- 1; YthOG: '10- 1.
Pole vault records: Two world youth 2010; four
world junior indoors 2011, two world junior
outdoor bests, three Swedish 2011-12.
Progress at PV: 2005- 3.10, 2006- 3.40, 2007- 3.90,
2008- 4.12, 2009- 4.37, 2010- 4.47, 2011- 4.63i/4.57.
2012- 4.58, 2013- 4.55, 2014- 4.62i.
Rising Star Awards: IAAF 2010, European
Athletics 2012. Her father Glenn had JT pb 67.08
'82, sister Victoria PV 4.00 '09.

Emma GREEN TREGARO b. 8 Dec 1984
Bergsjön Göteborg 1.80m 62kg. Örgryte IS.
At HJ: OG: '08- 9, '12- 8; WCh: '05-07-09-11-13:
3/7=/7=/11/5; EC: '06-10-12: 11/2/3=; WJ: '02- 9;
EU23: '05- 2; EJ: '03- 3; WI: '10- 5=, '14- 5; EI: '05-
8, '13- 3; CCp: '10- 2; ET: '09- 5, '11- 1. At 200m:
ECp: '06- 5. Won Swedish HJ 2005, 2007-11, 2013
(& 9 indoors); LJ 2005.
Progress at HJ: 1998- 1.66i, 1999- 1.71, 2000-
1.75i/1.73, 2001- 1.82, 2002- 1.82, 2003- 1.86,
2004- 1.90, 2005- 1.97, 2006- 1.96i/1.92, 2007- 1.95,
2008- 1.98i/1.96, 2009- 1.96, 2010- 2.01, 2011- 1.95,
2012- 1.95i/1.93, 2013- 1.97, 2014- 1.97i. pbs: 60m
7.42i '06, 100m 11.58 '06, 200m 23.02 '06, 400m
54.95 '06, LJ 6.41 '05, TJ 13.69i '06, 13.39 '07.
Her uncle Göte Green ran 47.9 for 400m in 1977.
Married coach Yannick Tregaro in March 2011.

Ebba JUNGMARK b. 10 Mar 1987 Onsala
1.79m 57 kg. Mölndals AIK. Was at Washington
State University, USA.

At HJ: OG: '12- dnq 20=; WCh: '07/11- dnq
23/17; EC: '10- dnq 17, '12- 10; WJ: '06- 5; EU23:
'07- 3; EJ: '05- 12; WI: '12- 2=; EI: '11- 3, '13- 2.
Won NCAA indoors 2008.
Progress at HJ: 2000- 1.50, 2001- 1.60, 2002- 1.73,
2003- 1.78, 2004- 1.77i/1.75, 2005- 1.80, 2006-
1.85i/1.84, 2007- 1.92, 2008- 1.89i/1.84, 2009-
1.86, 2010- 1.90, 2011- 1.96i/1.94, 2012- 1.95i/1.91,
2013- 1.96i/1.89. pbs: LJ 5.59i '09, TJ 12.98 '12,
Pen 3642i '09.

SWITZERLAND

Governing body: Schweizerischer
Leichtathletikverband (SLV), Haus des Sports,
Postfach 606, 3000 Bern 22. Formed 1905 as
Athletischer Ausschuss des Schweizerischen
Fussball-Verbandes.
National Championships first held in 1906
(men), 1934 (women). **2013 Champions: Men:**
100m: Reto Schenkel 10.33, 200m: Silvan Wicki
21.36, 400m: Philipp Weissenberger 46.62,
800m: Hugo Santacruz 1:51.43, 1500m: Mario
Bächtiger 3:55.70, 5000m: Adsriano Engelhardt
14:33.24, 10,000m/HMar: Christian Kreienbühl
29:44.57/68:02, Mar: Michael Ott 2:16:53, 3000mSt:
Marco Kern 9:02.57, 110mh: Tobias Furer 13.94,
400mh: Kariem Hussein 49.78, HJ: Roman
Sieber 2.12, PV: Patrick Schütz 5.00, LJ: Yves
Zellweger 7.67, TJ: Andreas Graber 16.44, SP:
Yannis Croci 15.51, DT: Lukas Jost 53.19, HT:
Martim Bingisser 62.09, JT: Lukas Wieland 75.11,
Dec: Michael Bucher 7308, 20kW: Alex Florez
1:33.52. **Women:** 100m/200m: Mujinga Kambundji
11.66/23.29, 400m: Simone Werner 54.85, 800m:
Selina Büchel 2:05.11, 1500m: Lisa Kurmann
4:25.08, 5000m: Sabine Fischer 16:08.85, 10,000m
/HMar: Maja Neuenschwander 34:50.92/73:44,
Mar: Renate Wyss 2:40:54, 3000mSt: -, 100mh:
Noemi Zbären 13.32, 400mh: Petra Fontanive
58.00, HJ: Giovanna Demo 1.74, PV: Nicole
Büchler 4.40, LJ: Irène Pusterla 6.52, TJ: Barbara
Leuthard 13.12, SP: Jasmin Lukas 13.76, DT:
Elisabeth Graf 48.26, HT: Nicole Zihlmann
61.54, JT: Nathalie Meier 51.83, Hep: Valérie
Reggel 5856, 5000mW/20kW: Laura Polli
23:20/1:43:12, 10kW: Marie Polli 47:28.

TADJIKISTAN

Governing body: Athletics Federation of
Tadjikistan, Rudski Avenue 62, Dushanbe
734025. Founded 1932.

Dilshod NAZAROV b. 6 May 1982 Dushanbe
1.87m 115kg.
At HT: OG: '08- 11, '12- 10; WCh: '05-07-09-11-13:
dnq 16/dnq 21/11/10/5; WJ: '98- dnq 15, '00- 5,
AsiG: '98-02-06-10: 7/9/1/1; AsiC: '03-05-07-09-
13: 3/2/2/1/1; CCp: '10- 2. Won Asi-J 1999, 2001,
C.Asian 2003.
Progress at HT: 1998- 63.91, 1999- 63,56, 2000-
66.50, 2001- 68.08, 2002- 69.86, 2003- 75.56, 2004-
76.58, 2005- 77.63, 2006- 74.43, 2007- 78.89, 2008-

79.05, 2009- 79.28, 2010- 80.11, 2011- 80.30, 2012-
77.70, 2013- 80.71.
President of national federation.

TRINIDAD & TOBAGO

Governing body: National Association of
Athletics Administrations of Trinidad &
Tobago, PO Box 605, Port of Spain, Trinidad.
Founded 1945, reformed 1971.
National Champions 2013: Men: 100m: Keston
Bledman 9.86w, 200m: Lalonde Gordon 20.26,
400m: Deon Lendore 45.29, 800m: Jamaal James
1:49.22, 1500m: Matthew Hagley 3:59.02, 5000m:
Denzel Ramirez 15:23.41, 10,000m: Richard
Jones 30:58.33, 110mh: Mikel Thomas 13.29w;
400mh Jehue Gordon 49.25, HJ: Omari Benoit
2.01, LJ: Kyron Blaise 7.87w, TJ: Chris Hercules
16.21, SP: Akeem Stewart 18.59, DT: Quincy
Wilson 57.15, JT: Shakiel Waithe 65.63. **Women**:
100m/200m: Kelly-Ann Baptiste 10.83/22.36,
400m: Shawna Fermin 53.25, 800m: Alena
Brooks 2:05.25, 1500m: Pilar McShine 4:19.69,
100mh: Aleesha Barber 13.20, 400mh: Sparkle
McKnight 56.59, HJ: Deandra Daniel 1.65, LJ:
Dorane McNee 5.45w, TJ: Ayanna Alexander
13.72, SP: Portious Warren 12.87, DT: Sharisse
Downey 42.78, JT: Darlene Lewis 40.50, Hep:
Kechell Douglas 3125.

Keston BLEDMAN b. 8 Mar 1988 San Fernando
1.83m 75kg. Simplex.
At 100m/4x100mR: OG: '08- 2R, '12- sf/3R;
WCh: '07- qf, '09- res(2)R, '11/13- sf; WJ: '06- 7 (h
200m); WY: '05- 3; PAm: '07- sf; CAG: '10- 7/1R.
Won PAm-J 2007, CAC 2011, TRI 2012-13.
Progress at 100m: 2005- 10.48, 2006- 10.32, 2007-
10.14/10.05w, 2008- 10.18, 2009- 10.10/10.0, 2010-
10.01/9.93w, 2011- 9.93, 2012- 9.86/9.85w, 2013-
10.02/9.86w. pbs: 60m 6.62i '12, 200m 20.73 '08.

Jehue GORDON b. 15 Dec 1991 Port of Spain
1.90m 80kg. adidas. Sports management student at University of West Indies, Trinidad.
At 400mh: OG: '12- 6; WCh: '09- 4, '11- sf, '13- 1;
WJ: '08- sf, '10- 1; PAm-J: '09- 2. TTO champion
2008-11, 2013.
Three TRI 400mh records 2009-13.
Progress at 400mh: 2008- 51.39, 2009- 48.26,
2010- 48.47, 2011- 48.66, 2012- 47.96, 2013- 47.69.
pbs: 400m 46.43 '10, 600m 1:20.65 '14, 800m
1:53.32 '10, 110mh 13.82 '12, 200mhSt 23.00 '12.

Lalonde GORDON b. 25 Nov 1988 Lowlands,
Tobago 1.79m 83kg. Tigers. Studied at Mohawk
Valley CC.
At 400m/4x400mR: OG: '12- 3/3R; CG: '10- sf;
CAG: '10- 3R; WI: '12- 3R, '14- 5. At 200m: WCh:
'13- sf. Won TTO 200m 2013. 400m 2012.
Progress at 400m: 2009- 49.47, 2010- 46.33, 2011-
45.51, 2012- 44.52, 2013- 45.67, 2014- 45.17i. pbs:
100m 10.45 '12, 200m 20.26 '13, 300m 32.47i '14
(CAC record), 32.5+ '12.
Moved with his family to New York at the age

of seven, and still lives there.
Deon LENDORE b. 28 Oct 1992 Arima 1.79m
75kg. Student at Texas A&M University, USA.
At 400m/4x400mR: OG: '12- h/3R; WCh: '13- sf;
WJ: '10- sf; WY: '09- sf. TTO champion 2013.
Progress at 400m: 2009- 47.61, 2010- 46.59, 2011-
46.50, 2012- 45.13, 2013- 44.94, 2014- 45.03i. pb
200m 20.68i '14, 21.20 '11.

Richard THOMPSON b. 7 Jun 1985 Cascade
1.87m 79kg. Memphis. Was at Louisiana State
University.
At 100m: OG: '08- 2/2R, '12- 7/3R; WCh: '07- qf,
'09- 5/2R, '11/13- sf; PAm: '07- h. Won TRI 100m
2009-11, 200m 2010; NCAC 100m 2007, NCAA
100m & 60m indoor 2008.
Progress at 100m, 200m: 2004- 10.65, 2005- 10.47,
21.73; 2006- 10.27/10.26w, 21.24; 2007- 10.09/9.95w,
20.90; 2008- 9.89, 20.18; 2009- 9.93, 20.65; 2010-
10.01/9.89w, 20.37; 2011- 9.85, 20.85; 2012- 9.96,
20.80; 2013- 10.14/9.91w, 21.06. pbs: 60m 6.45+
'09, 6.51i '08.

Keshorn WALCOTT b. 2 Apr 1993 Toco 1.83m
90kg. Toco tafac.
At JT: OG: '12- 1; WCh: '13- dnq 19; WJ: '10- dnq,
'12- 1; WY: '09- dnq 13; PAm: '11- 7. Won CAC-J
2010, 2012; TTO 2012.
Five Trinidad javelin records 2012, eight CAC
junior 2011-12.
Progress at JT: 2009- 60.02, 2010- 67.01, 2011-
75.77A, 2012- 84.58, 2013- 84.39. pb TJ 14.28 '10.
First Caribbean Olympic champion and youngest ever Olympic champion in throwing events.
Won IAAF Rising Star Award 2012. Elder
brother Elton TJ pb 16.43/16.51w '11 & 4 WY '09,
aunt Anna Lee Walcott Hep pb 5224 '00.

Women

Kelly-Ann BAPTISTE b. 14 Oct 1986 Plymouth,
Tobago 1.60m 54kg. Zenith. Studied psychology at Louisiana State University.
At 100m/(200m): OG: '08- qf, '12- 6; WCh: '05-
qf, '09- sf/sf, '11- 3; WJ: '02- sf, '04- (4); WY: '03- 3;
PAm: '03- h; CCp: '10- 1/1R. Won NCAA 100m
& indoor 60m 2008, TTO 100m 2005-06, 2008-10,
2012-13; 200m 2005, 2013.
TRI records: 100m (6) 2005-14, 200m (5) 2005-13.
Progress at 100m, 200m: 2002- 11.71, 24.03; 2003-
11.48, 23.22; 2004- 11.40, 23.41/22.99w; 2005-
11.17/11.04w, 22.93; 2006- 11.08, 22.73; 2007-
11.22, 22.90i/22.95; 2008- 11.06/10.97w, 22.67; 2009-
10.94/10.91w, 22.60; 2010- 10.84, 22.78/22.58w;
2011- 10.90, 2012- 10.86, 22.33w; 2013- 10.83, 22.36.
pbs: 55m 6.73i '06, 60m 7.13i '08.
She was withdrawn from 2013 World Champs
team after failing a drugs test, but CAS decision awaited on her case.

TUNISIA

Governing body: Fédération Tunisienne
d'Athlétisme, B.P. 264, Cité Mahrajane 1082,
Tunis. Founded 1957.

Women

Habiba GHRIBI–Boudraa b. 9 Apr 1984 Kairouan 1.70m 57kg.
At 3000mSt: OG: '08- 13, '12- 2; WCh: '05- h, '09- 6, '11- 2; AfCh: '06- 2. At 5000m: AfCh: '02- 11.
Tunisian records: 3000m (3) 2008-13, 3000mSt (9) 2005-12.
Progress at 3000mSt: 2005- 9:51.49, 2006- 10:14.36, 2007- 9:50.04, 2008- 9:25.50, 2009- 9:12.52, 2011- 9:11.97, 2012- 9:08.37. pbs: 1500m: 4:12.37 '09, 3000m 8:52.06 '13, 5000m 16:12.9 '03, 10,000m 35:03.83 '05, 10kRd 33:30 '04.
Missed 2010 season after toe surgery. Won first Olympic medal for a woman from Tunisia.

TURKEY

Governing body: Türkiye Atletizm Federasyonu, 19 Mayis Spor Kompleksi, Ulus-Ankara. Founded 1922.
National Champions 2013: Men: 100m/200m: Izzet Safer 10.50/21.01, 400m: Yavuz Can 46.60, 800m: Levent Ates 1:53.31, 1500m/5000m: Kemal Koyuncu 3:44.95/13:51.72, 3000m: Halil Akkas 7:52.07, 1000m: Meymet Çaglayan 29:52.01, Mar: Bekir Karayel 2:20:27, 3000mSt: Hakan Duvar 8:43.30, 110mh: Mustafa Günes 14.26, 400mh: Enis Ünsal 52.16, HJ: Serhat Birinci 2.16, PV: Cihan Güç 4.60, LJ: Alper Kulaksiz 7.60, TJ: Askin Karaca 15.45, SP: Hüseyin Atici 18.73, DT: Ercüment Olgundeniz 61.33, HT: Esref Apak 76.94, JT: Mustafa Tan 72.80, Dec: Yusuf Pehlevan 6238, 15kW: Ersin Tacir 1:08:53, 20kW: Ozan Pamuk 1:30:45. **Women**: 100m/200m: Nimet Karakus 11.73/23.63, 400m: Birsen Engin 53.86, 800m/1500m: Tugba Koyuncu-Karakaya 2:01.65/4:13.73, 3000m: Emine Hatun Tuna 9:29.56, 5000m: Esma Aydemir 16:34.76, 10,000m: Bahar Dogan 34:52.81, Mar: Elvan Abeylegesse 2:29:30, 3000mSt: Binnaz Uslu 9:45.22, 100mh: Esen Kale-Kizildag 14.23, 400mh: Özge Akin 58.08, HJ: Burcu Yüksel-Ayhan 1.87, PV: Seda Firtina 3.90, LJ: Serpil Koçak 6.11, TJ: Sevim Serbest-Sinmez 13.57, SP: Filiz Gül-Kadogan 14.02, DT: Elcin Kaya 47.27, HT: Aysegül Alniaçik 62.08, JT: Berivan Sakir 50.71, Hep: Pinar Aday 5048, 15kW: Gamez Özgör 1:17:04, 20kW: Gülsen Kilinç 1:56:22.

Tarik Langat AKDAG (ex Patrick Kipkurui LANGAT) b. 16 Jun 1988 Nandi, Kenya 1.76m 60kg. ENKA.
At 3000mSt: OG: '12- 9; WCh: '13- h; EC: '12- 2; ET: '13- 1.
Turkish 3000m steeplechase record 2012.
Progress at 3000mSt: 2004- 8:53.6A, 2005- 8:40.3A, 2006- 8:37.4A, 2007- 8:46.8A, 2008- 8:19.13, 2009- 8:21.38, 2010- 8:09.12, 2011- 8:08.59, 2012- 8:17.85, 2013- 8:20.08. pbs: 3000m 7:47.68 '10, 2M 8:26.96 '10, 5000m 13:45.21A '06, 10,000m 29:03.1 '06.
Switched from Kenya to Turkey 22 Jun 2011.

Polat Kemboi ARIKAN (ex Paul KEMBOI) b.

12 Dec 1990 Cheptirte, Kenya 1.73m 62kg.
At (5000m)/10,000m: OG: '12- h/9; WCh: '13- dnf; EC: '12- 3/1; ECp: '12- 1; won Med G 2013.
At 3000m: EI: '13- 10. Eur CC: '12- 7, '13- 2.
World HMar: 14- 16
Turkish records 3000m 2012, 5000m 2011, HMar 2014.
Progress at 5000m, 10,000m: 2006- 14:23.4A, 2009- 13:24.25, 2010- 13:18.12, 2011- 13:05.98, 2012- 13:12.55i/13:27.21, 27:38.81; 2013- 28:17.26.
pbs: 1500m 3:47.05 '12, 3000m 7:42.31 '12, HMar 61:21 146.
Became a Turkish citizen 9 Jun 2011, originally with 2-year wait for international eligibility, but waiting period ended in February 2012.

Fatih AVAN b. 1 Jan 1989 Kahraman Maras 1.83m 90kg. Fenerbahçe Spor Kulubu.
At JT: OG: '12- dnq 20; WCh: '09: dnq 19, '11- 5, '13- dnq 12; EC: '12- dnq 14; EU23: '09- 7, '11- 2; WUG: '11- 1, '13- 3. Won Med G 2009, 2013; TUR 2008.
Eight Turkish javelin records 2009-12.
Progress at JT: 2005- 55.88, 2006- 61.40, 2007- 66.28, 2008- 71.73, 2009- 79.78, 2010- 79.13, 2011- 84.79, 2012- 85.60, 2013- 84.58.

Seref OSMANOGLOU Ex Sheryf El-Sheryf UKR b. 2 Jan 1989 Simpheropol 1.83m 74kg. Dnipropetrovskaya. Student.
At TJ: OG: '12- dnq 13; WCh: '11- 12; EC: '12- 2; WJ: '06- 5, '08- 9; WY: '05- 5; EU23: '11- 1; EJ: '07- 6.
Progress at TJ: 2004- 15.53, 2005- 16.18, 2006- 16.30, 2007- 16.10, 2008- 16.60i/16.35, 2009- 15.90i/15.52, 2010- 16.56i/16.42, 2011- 17.72, 2012- 17.04/17.28w, 2013- 16.43. pb LJ 8.05 '12.
Huge breakthrough at 2011 European U23s, improving pb from 16.92 to 16.99, 17.04 and then 17.72. Acquired Turkish citizenship 3 Jun 2013. His father, a gynaecologist, comes from Sudan.

Ilham Tanui ÖZBILEN (formerly William Biwott Tanui KEN) b. 5 Mar 1990 Kocholwo, Keiyo, Kenya 1.77m 61kg. ENKA.
At 1500m: OG: '12- 8; WCh: '13- sf; EC: '12- 2; WI: '12- 2, '14- 4; EI: '13- 2; ET: '13- 1 (2 800m); won WAF 2009, MedG 2013 (& 800m).
Records: World 4x1500m & world junior 1M 2009; Turkish 800m (6), 1500m (2) 2011-13, 1M 2013.
Progress at 800m, 1500m: 2008- 3:42.5A, 2009- 3:31.70, 2010- 3:33.67, 2011- 1:44.25, 3:31.37; 2012- 3:33.32, 2013- 1:44.00, 3:31.30. pbs: 1000m 2:15.96i '14, 2:17.08 '11; 1M 3:49.29 '09, 3000m 7:50.61i '12.
Became a Turkish citizen on 9 Jun 2011.

Women

Elvan ABEYLEGESSE b. 11 Sep 1982 Addis Ababa, Ethiopia 1.59m 40kg. ENKA.
At 5000m/(10,000m): OG: '04- 12 (8 1500m), '08- 2/2; WCh: '01- h, '03- 5, '07- 5/2, '09- (dnf); EC: '02- 7, '06- 3/dnf, '10- 1/1; WU: '06- 6 (6 1500m); WY: '99- (5 3000m); EU23: '03- 1; EJ: '99- 2, '01- 1 (1 3000m); CCp: '10- 4; ECp: '06-07-08: (1/1/1).

Won WAF 5000m 2003-04, Med G 10,000m 2009. World CC: '99- 9J; Eur CC: '00-01-02-03: 3J/1J/ 3/2. Won TUR Mar 2013.
Records: World 5000m 2004, European 10,000m 2008. Turkish 2000m 2003, 3000m 2002, 5000m 2004, 10,000m 2006 & 2008, HMar 2010.
Progress at 1500m, 5000m, 10,000m: 1999- 4:24.1, 16:06.40; 2000- 4:18.7, 16:33.77; 2001- 4:11.31, 15:21.12, 33:29.20; 2002- 4:11.00, 15:00.49; 2003- 4:07.25, 14:53.56; 2004- 3:58.28, 14:24.68; 2005- 15:08.59; 2006- 4:11.61, 14:59.29, 30:21.67; 2007- 15:00.88, 31:25.15; 2008- 14:58.79, 29:56.34; 2009- 15:30.47, 31:51.98; 2010- 4:15.23, 14:31.52, 31:10.23; 2013- 32:59.30. pbs: 800m 2:07.10 '04, 2000m 5:33.83 '03, 3000m 8:31.94 '02; Rd: 15k 49:29 '12, HMar 67:07 '10, Mar 2:29:30 '13.
Known as Hewan Abeye ETH, then Elvan Can on move to Turkey. She became the first Turkish athlete to set a world record in 2004 and the first Turkish woman to win an Olympic medal in 2008. Married Semeneh Debelie ETH on 25 Feb 2011, their daughter Arsema was born on 28 July 2011.

UGANDA

Governing body: Uganda Athletics Federation, PO Box 22726, Kampala. Founded 1925.

Jacob ARAPTANY b. 11 Feb 1992 Kaproron 1.68m 58kg.
At 3000mSt: OG: '12- h; WCh: '11- 6, '13- 12; WJ: '10- 3; AfG: '11- 5; AfCh: '12- 8; Af-J: '11- 3. World CC: '11- 9J.
Progress at 3000mSt: 2009- 8:26.4A, 2010- 8:28.14, 2011- 8:15.72A, 2012- 8:14.48, 2013- 8:16.43. pbs: 800m 1:49.95A '11, 1500m 3:36.16A '11, 2000mSt 5:28.48 '11.

Benjamin KIPLAGAT b. 4 Mar 1989 Magoro 1.86m 61kg.
At 3000mSt: OG: '08- 9,'12- dq; WCh: '07-09-11- 13: h/11/10/14; CG: '10- 4; WJ: '06- 6, '08- 2; AfG: '07- 7; AfCh: '10- 5, '12- 3; CCp: '10- 4. World CC: '07- 5J, '08- 4J.
Six Ugandan 3000mSt records 2007-10.
Progress at 3000mSt: 2005- 8:39.1A, 2006- 8:34.14, 2007- 8:21.73, 2008- 8:14.29, 2009- 8:12.98, 2010- 8:03.81, 2011- 8:08.43, 2012- 8:17.55, 2013- 8:13.07. pbs: 1500m 3:38.86 '09, 3000m 7:46.50 '10, 5000m 13:22.67 '07, 10,000m 29:03.1 '06.

Stephen KIPROTICH b. 27 Feb 1989 Kapchorwa 1.72m 56kg.
At Mar: OG: '12- 1; WCh: '11- 9, '13- 1. At 5000m: WCh: '07- h. At 10,000m: WCh: '10- 5, AfCh: '10- 6, World CC: '08- 12J, '11- 6; AfrCC: '11- 2.
Ugandan marathon record 2011.
Progress at Mar: 2011- 2:07:20, 2012- 2:07:50, 2013- 2:08:05. Pbs: 5000m 13:23.70 '08, 10,000m 27:58.03 '10, HMar 61:15 '13, 3000mSt 8:26.66 '10.
Won Enschede marathon on debut 2011. Became the second man ever to win Olympic and World titles at marathon.

Moses KIPSIRO b. 2 Sep 1986 Chesimat 1.74m 59kg.
At 5000m(/10,000m): OG: '08- 4, '12- 15/10; WCh: '05- h, '07- 3, '09- 4, '13- (13); CG: '06- 7, '10- 1/1; AfG: '07- 1, '11- 1; Af Ch: '06- 3/1, '10- 4/2; CCp: '10- 2 (2 3000m). At 3000m: WI: '12- 7. World CC: '03-05-08-09-10-11-13: 18J/20J/13/2/3/11/4.
UGA records: 3000m (4) 2005-09, 5000m 2007.
Progress at 5000m: 2005- 13:13.81, 2006- 13:01.88, 28:03.46; 2007- 12:50.72, 2008- 12:54.70, 2009- 12:59.27, 2010- 13:00.15, 27:33.37A; 2011- 13:09.17, 2012- 13:00.68, 27:04.48; 2013- 13:11.56, 27:44.53. pbs: 1500m 3:37.6 '08, 2000m 5:00.66+ '11, 3000m 7:30.95 '09, 2M 8:08.16i '12, HMar 63:15A '14.
Sealed brilliant 5k/10k double at 2010 CG with last laps of 53.01 and 53.96.

UKRAINE

Governing body: Ukrainian Athletic Federation, P.O. Box 607, Kiev 01019. Founded 1991. **National Champions 2013: Men**: 100m: Vitaliy Korzh 10.51, 200m: Sergiy Smelyk 20.52, 400m: Vitaliy Butrym 46.24, 800m: Viktor Tyumentsev 1:50.71, 1500m/5000m: Oleksandr Borysyuk 3:39.38/13:51.67, HMar: Igor Russ 66:05, Mar: Igor Olefirenko 2:14:10, 3000mSt: Pavlo Oliynyk 8:53.82, 110mh: Sergiy Kopanayko 13.89, 400mh: Denys Nechyporenko 51.36, HJ: Yuroy Krymarenko 2.28, PV: Oleksandr Korchmid 5.60, LJ: Taras Neledya 7.58, TJ: Viktor Yastrebov 16.62, SP: Andriy Borodkin 19.53, DT: Mykyta Nesterenko 58.74, HT: Yevgen Vynogradov 76.70, JT: Yuriy Kushniruk 73.62, 20kW: Andriy Kovenko 1:20:22/Oleksiy Kazanin 1:23:30; 50kW: Igor Sakharuk 3:57:24. **Women**: 100m: Nataliya Pogrebnyak 11.54, 200m: Yelizaveta Bryzgina 22.72, 400m: Nataliya Pygyda 51.37, 800m: Liliya Lobanova 2:03.46, 1500m: Nataliya Pryshchepa 4:18.55, 5000m: Viktoriya Pogoryelska 15:48.43, HMar: Tetyana Vernigor 76:40, Mar: Svitlana Stanko 2:40:05, 3000mSt: Valeriya Mara 9:57.64, 100mh: Anna Plotitsyna 13.05, 400mh: Anna Titimets 56.02, HJ: Oksana Okuneva 1.92, PV: Kateryna Kozlova 4.20, LJ: Anastasiya Mokhnyuk 6.47, TJ: Nataliya Yastrebova 14.15w, SP: Halyna Obleshchuk 18.40, DT: Natalya Semenova 59.34, HT: Nataliya Zolotuhina 67.00, JT: Margaryta Dorozhon 62.01, 20kW: Lyudmyla Olyanovska 1:30:26/Inna Kashyna 1:34:59.

Bohdan BONDARENKO b. 30 Aug 1989 Kharkiv 1.97m 80kg.
At TJ: OG: '12- 7; WCh: '11- dnq 15=, '13- 1; EC: '12- 11; WJ: '06- 3, '08- 1; EU23: '11- 1; EJ: '07- 9; WUG: '11- 1, ET: '13- 1. Won DL 2013.
UKR high jump record 2013.
Progress at HJ: 2005- 2.15, 2006- 2.26, 2007- 2.25i/2.19, 2008- 2.26, 2009- 2.27/2.15, 2010- 2.10, 2011- 2.30, 2012- 2.31, 2013- 2.41.
His father Viktor had decathlon pb of 7480 '87.

Ruslan DMYTRENKO b. 22 Mar 1986 Kyiv 1.80m 62kg. Donetsk.
At 20kW: WCh: '09- 33, '11- 7, '13- 7; EC: '10- 12; WCp: '12- 4; EU23: '07- 6; ECp: '13- 5; WUG: '13- 2; UKR champion 2009, 2011. At 10,000m/10kW: EJ: '05- 11; ECp: '05- 6J.
Progress at 20kW: 2006- 1:27:16, 2007- 1:23:31, 2008- 1:25:26, 2009- 1:21:21, 2010- 1:21:54, 2011- 1:21:31, 2012- 1:20:17, 2013- 1:20:38, 2014- 1:20:08. pbs: 5000mW 18:21.76i '14, 10,000mW 39:26.90i '12, 39:33.91 '10.

Igor HLAVAN b. 25 Sep 1990 Nazarivka, Kirovgrad 1.72m 62kg.
At 50kW: OG: '12- 18; WCh: '13- 4; WCp: '12- 12; ECp: '13- 4. Won UKR 35kW 2013
UKR 50km walk record 2013.
Progress at 50kW: 2010- 4:08:08, 2011- 4:03:18, 2012- 3:48:07, 2013- 3:40:39. pbs: 5000mW 19:24.37i '13, 10,000mW 41:52.5i '11, 20kW 1:22:32 '13, 35k 2:31:15 '13.

Oleksiy KASYANOV b. 26 Aug 1985 Stakhanov, Lugansk 1.91m 84kg. Spartak Zaporozhye.
At Dec: OG: '08- 7, '12- 7; WCh: '09- 4, '11- 12, '13- dnf; EC: '10- dnf, '12- 2; EU23: '07- 4; WUG: '07- 4; ECp: '09- 3. UKR champion 2008. At Hep: WI: '10-12-14: 6/2/5; EI: '09- 2.
Progress at Dec: 2006- 7599, 2007- 7964, 2008- 8238, 2009- 8479, 2010- 8381, 2011- 8251, 2012- 8312. pbs: 60m 6.83i '09, 100m 10.50 '11, 400m 47.46 '08, 1000m 2:39.44i '14, 1500m 4:22.27 '08, 60mh 7.85i '13, 110mh 14.01 '12, HJ 2.08i 14, 2.05 '09; PV 4.82 '09, LJ 8.04i/7.97 '10, SP 15.72 '09, DT 51.95 '10, JT 55.84 '07, Hep 6254i '10.
Won Talence decathlon 2009.

Viktor KUZNETSOV b. 17 Jul 1986 Zaporozhye 1.90m 67kg. Kiev Dynamo.
At TJ (LJ): OG: '08- 8, '12- (dnq 31); WCh: '09- (dnq 17), '13- dnq 14; EC: '06- (4), '10- 4; WJ: '04- 3; WI: '14- 8; EI: '07- 7, '13- 4; WUG: '07-11-13: 2/2/1; ET: '10- 1, '11- 3.
World junior long jump best (indoors) 2005.
Progress at LJ, TJ: 2002- 6.89, 2003- 8.12i, 15.17; 2004- 16.84i/16.58, 2005- 8.22i, 16.51i; 2006- 7.96/8.25w, 16.35i/16.17; 2007- 7.74, 16.94; 2008- 17.16, 2009- 8.09, 2010- 8.11i, 17.29; 2011- 17.01, 2012- 8.10, 2013- 17.02i/17.01.

Andriy PROTSENKO b. 20 May 1988 Kherson 1.90m 65kg. Khersonskaya. Biotechnology graduate.
At HJ: OG: '12- 9; WCh: '09/11/13- dnq 25/27/23=; EC: '10- dnq 17, '12- dnq 13=; EU23: '09- 3; EJ: '07- 2; WUG: '13- 2; ET: '10- 3. UKR champion 2012.
Progress at HJ: 2005- 2.10, 2006- 2.18i/2.10, 2007- 2.21, 2008- 2.30, 2009- 2.25, 2010- 2.25, 2011- 2.31, 2012- 2.31, 2013- 2.32, 2014- 2.36i.

Oleksandr PYATNYTSYA b. 14 Jul 1985 Dnipropetrovsk 1.86m 90kg.
At JT: OG: '12- 2; WCh: '09/11- dnq 25/27/29; EC: '10- 4, '12- 5; EU23: '07- 3. UKR champion

2009, 2011. UKR javelin records 2010 & 2012.
Progress at JT: 2005- 65.63, 2006- 72.20, 2007- 76.28, 2008- 78.54, 2009- 81.96, 2010- 84.11, 2011- 82.61, 2012- 86.12, 2013- 77.46.

Oleksiy SOKYRSKYY b. 16 Mar 1985 Gorlivka 1.85m 108kg.
At HT: OG: '12- 4; WCh: '09-11: dnq 22/17; EC: '10- 6, '12- nt; WJ: '04- 8, EU23: '07- 6; WUG: '09- 3; ET: '11- 3. UKR champion 2010-11.
Progress at HT: 2005- 70.23, 2006- 71.95, 2007- 73.44, 2008- 75.54, 2009- 76.50, 2010- 76.62, 2011- 78.33, 2012- 78.91, 2013- 77.38.

Women

Alina FYODOROVA b. 13 Jul 1989 Kniazhychi 1.74m 63kg.
At Hep: WCh: '11- 21; WJ: '08- 18; EU23: '11- 6; ECp: 11- 5. At Pen: WI: '14- 3; WI: '13- 8.
Progress at Hep: 2006- 5193, 2007- 5437, 2008- 5475, 2009- 5742, 2010- 5760, 2011- 6008, 2012- 6126, 2013- 5792. pbs: 200m 25.12 '12, 800m 2:15.31i 14, 2:15.78 '12; 60mh 8.52i '14, 100mh 14.06 '11, HJ 1.90 '13, LJ 6.34i '14, 6.33 '12; SP 15.34i '14, 14.71 '12; JT 40.60 '11, Pen 4724i '11.

Tetyana HAMERA-SHMYRKO b. 1 Jun 1983 Hrada, Ternopil 1.65m 52kg.
At Mar: OG: '12- 5; WCh: '11- 15.
Two UKR marathon records 2012.
Progression at marathon: 2011- 2:28:14, 2012- 2:24:32, 2013- 2:23:58, 2014- 2:24:37. Pbs: 800m 2:08.81 '04, 1500m 4:26.61 '08, 3000m 9:32.06 '09, 5000m 16:16.55 '10, 10,000m 32:50.13 '12, HMar 71:40 '13.
Won Kraków marathon on debut 2011, won Osaka 2013-14 (2nd 2012).

Nataliya LUPU b. 4 Nov 1987 Marshyntsi 1.70m 50kg. Cherniyevskaya.
At 800m: OG: '12- sf; WCh: '09- h, '13- 7; EC: '10- h; WI: '12- 2, '14- 5; EU23: '07- h, '09- 2; WJ: '06- 4; EJ: '05- 1/3R; EI: '13- 1; ET: '10- 1. Won UKR 2012.
Progress at 800m: 2002- 2:10.99, 2003- 2:07.75, 2004- 2:05.08, 2005- 2:02.66, 2006- 2:03.24, 2007- 2:04.62, 2008- 2:00.96, 2009- 2:00.32, 2010- 1:59.59, 2011- 1:59.12, 2012- 1:58.46, 2013- 1:59.43. pbs: 400m 52.91 '11, 1000m 2:42.58i '13, 1500m 4:20.93 '03.

Anna MELNYCHENKO b. 24 Apr 1983 Tbilisi, Georgia 1.78m 59kg.
At Hep: OG: '08- 14, '12- 9; WCh: '07- dnf, '09- 6, '13- 1; EC: '06- 16, '10- dnf; EU23: '05- 13; WUG: '07- 3; ECp: '07-08-09-10-13: 3/1/1/1/2. UKR champion 2003, 2012. At Pen: WI: '14- 7; EI: '13- 3.
Progress at Hep: 2001- 4907, 2002- 5083, 2003- 5523, 2004- 5720, 2005- 5809, 2006- 6055w, 2007- 6143, 2008- 6306/6349u, 2009- 6445, 2010- 6098, 2012- 6407, 2013- 6586. pbs: 200m 23.85 '13, 800m 2:09.85 '13, 60mh 8.18i '14, 100mh 13.26 '13, HJ 1.86 '07, LJ 6.74 '12, TJ 13.21/13.40w '03, SP 14.09 '13, JT 45.11 '09, Pen 4748i '12.
Won IAAF Combined Events Challenge 2013. Formerly married to William Frullani ITA (Dec

7984 '02, Hep 5972 rec 6th EI '09).

Anna MISHCHENKO b. 25 Aug 1983 Sumy 1.66m 51kg. Kharkov Dyn.
At 1500m: OG: '08- 9, '12- h; WCh: '09/11- sf; EC: '10- 11, '12- 3; WUG: '11- 2; ET: '10- 1, '11- 3; UKR champion 2010.
Progress at 1500m: 2003- 4:21.41, 2004- 4:14.09, 2005- 4:19.74, 2006- 4:12.17, 2007- 4:14.57, 2008- 4:05.13, 2009- 4:06.45, 2010- 4:03.14, 2011- 4:01.73, 2012- 4:01.16. pbs: 800m 2:00.92 '12, 1000m 2:39.00 '08, 2000m 5:46.36 '09, 3000m 9:11.09i '11, 9:17.99 '07.
Daughter Alexandra born 25 Aug 2013.

Olesya POVH b. 18 Oct 1987 Dnipropetrovsk 1.69m 63kg. Zaporizhye.
At 100m/4x100mR: OG: '12- sf/3R; WCh: '11- sf/3R, '132- sf; EC: '10- sf/1R, '12- 2; WUG: '13- 1R; ET: '13- 1/1R. At 60m: EI: '11- 1. Won UKR 100m 2010, 2012.
Progress at 100m: 2005- 12.19, 2006- 11.81, 2007- 11.85, 2008- 11.76, 2009- 11.70, 2010- 11.29, 2011- 11.24, 2012- 11.08, 2013- 11.14. pbs: 50m 6.21i '12, 60m 7.13i '11, 200m 22.58 '11.

Vira REBRYK b. 25 Feb 1989 Yalta 1.76m 65kg.
At JT: OG: '08/12- dnq 16/19; WCh: '09- 9, '11- dnq 16, '13- 11; EC: '10- dnq 17, '12- 1; WJ: '06- 2, '08- 1; WY: '05- 2; EU23: '09- 2, '11- 2; EJ: '07- 1; WUG: '09- 2. '11- 4; ET: '13- 3. Won UKR 2010-12. World junior javelin record 2008; three UKR records 2012.
Progress at JT: 2003- 44.94, 2004- 52.47, 2005- 57.48, 2006- 59.64, 2007- 58.48, 2008- 63.01, 2009- 62.26, 2010- 63.36, 2011- 61.60, 2012- 66.86, 2013- 64.30.

Mariya RYEMYEN b. 2 Aug 1987 Lugansk 1.72m 56kg. Student at Lugansk National teachers' training institute.
At (100m)/200m/4x100mR: OG: '12- sf/3R; WCh: '11- sf/3R, '13- 7; EC: '10- (5)/1R, '12- 1; EU23: '07- h/5, '09- 7/8; WUG: '13- 1R; ET: '11- 1, '13- 1/1R. At 60m: EI: '11- 2, '13- 1. Won UKR 200m 2009-10.
Progress at 200m: 2006- 24.35, 2007- 24.08, 2008- 24.02, 2009- 23.56, 2010- 23.16, 2011- 22.68, 2012- 22.58, 2013- 22.61. pbs: 50m 6.19i '12, 60m 7.10i '13, 100m 11.20 '12, 11.18w '11; 150m 16.73 '13.
Older brother Oleksiy has pbs 100m 10.43 and 200m 21.11 '11; 400m 46.79 '12.

Anna RYZHYKOVA b. 24 Nov 1989 Dnipropetrovsk 1.76m 67kg. née Yaroshchuk.
At 400mh/4x400mR: OG: '12- sf; WCh: '11- sf, '13- 6; EC: '10- sf, '12- 3; WJ: '08- 6/2R; EU23: '09- 8, '11- 1/2R; WUG: '11- 1, '13- 2; ET: '13- 2. At 200m: EJ: '07- h/2 4x100m.
Progress at 400mh: 2006- 57.52, 2007- 56.46, 2008- 56.09, 2009- 57.23, 2010- 55.60, 2011- 54.77, 2012- 54.35, 2013- 54.77. pbs: 60m 7.74i '06, 200m 23.49 '10, 400m 53.31 '11, LJ 6.05 '13.

Olga SALADUHA b. 4 Jun 1983 Donetsk 1.75m 55kg.

At TJ: OG: '08- 9, '12- 3; WCh: '07- 7, '11- 1, '13- 3; EC: '06- 4, '10- 1, '12- 1; WJ: '02- 5; EU23: '05- 4; EJ: '01- 9; WI: '08- 6, '14- 2; EI: '13- 1; WUG: '05- 2, '07- 1; WCp: '06- 6, '10- 2; ECp: '06-08-10-11-13: 1/1/1/1/1. Won DL 2011, UKR 2007-08.
Progress at TJ: 1998- 13.32, 1999- 12.86, 2000- 13.26, 2001- 13.48, 2002- 13.66i/13.63, 2003- 13.26i/ 13.03, 2004- 13.22, 2005- 14.04, 2006- 14.41/14.50w, 2007- 14.79, 2008- 14.84, 2010- 14.81, 2011- 14.98/ 15.06w, 2012- 14.99, 2013- 14.88i/14.85. pb LJ 6.37 '06.
Married to professional road cyclist Denys Kostyuk.

Hanna TITIMETS b. 5 Mar 1989 Pavlograd, Dnipropetrovsk 1.73m 62kg. Dnipropetrovsk.
At 400mh: OG: '12- sf; WCh: '09- h, '11- sf, '13- 4; EC: '10/12- sf; WJ: '08- 4; EU23: '09- 4, '11- 2; EJ: '07- 8 (2 4x100m); WUG: '11- 1 4x100m, '13- 1. UKR champion 2010, 2012-13.
Progress at 400mh: 2006- 59.79, 2007- 58.35, 2008- 57.22, 2009- 55.95, 2010- 55.58, 2011- 54.69, 2012- 54.98, 2013- 54.63. pbs: 60m 7.46i '11, 200m 23.60 '09, 400m 52.73 '11, 60mh 8.50i '13.

UNITED KINGDOM

Governing body: UK Athletics, Alexander Stadium, Walsall, Perry Barr, Birmingham B42 2LR. Founded 1999 (replacing British Athletics, founded 1991, which succeeded BAAB, founded 1932). The Amateur Athletic Association was founded in 1880 and the Women's Amateur Athletic Association in 1922.
National Championships (first were English Championships 1866-79, then AAA 1880-2006, WAAA from 1922). **2013 UK Champions: Men**: 100m: Dwain Chambers 10.04, 200m: James Ellington 20.45w, 400m: Nigel Levine 45.23, 800m: Michael Rimmer 1:47.79, 1500m: Chris O'Hare 3:51.36, 5000m: Andrew Vernon 13:43.17, 10,000m: Andrew Lemoncello 29:28.72, Mar: Derek Hawkins 2:16:50, 3000mSt: James Wilkinson 8:42.45, 110mh: William Sharman 13.44, 400mh: David Greene 48,66, HJ: Robbie Grabarz 2.28, PV: Luke Cutts 5.65, LJ: Chris Tomlinson 8.03, TJ: Julian Reid 16.79, SP: Greg Beard 18.29, DT: Brett Morse 62.05, HT: Andy Frost 72.28, JT: Lee Doran 70.77, Dec: Osman Muskwe 7229, 5000mW: Alex Wright 19:27.39, 10kW/20kW: Tom Bosworth 41:56/1:27:49.
Women: 100m: Asha Philip 11.20, 200m: Anyika Onuora 22.71w, 400m: Christine Ohuruogu 50.98, 800m: Marilyn Okoro 2:02.60, 1500m: Hannah England 4:10.99, 5000m: Stephanie Twell 15:55.01, 10,000m: Alyson Dixon 34:46.75, Mar: Susan Partridge 2:30:46, 3000mSt: Eilish McColgan 9:56.02, 100mh: Tiffany Porter 12.68, 400mh: Perri Shakes-Drayton 54.36, HJ: Emma Nuttall 1.87, PV: Sally Peake 4.23, LJ: Shara Proctor 6.84, TJ: Laura Samuel 13.75w, SP: Rachel Wallader 15.96, DT: Jade Lally 60.23, HT: Shaunagh Brown 62.71, JT: Rosie Semenytsh

49.76, Hep: Jessica Tappin 5676, 5000mW/20kW: Bethan Davies 23:21.08/1:44:15.

Lawrence CLARKE b. 13 Jan 1990 London 1.86m 75kg. Windsor, Slough, Eton & Hounslow. Bristol University.
At 110mh: OG: '12- 4; WCh: '11- h; CG: '10- 3; E23: '11- 3; EJ: '09- 1. UK champion 2011.
Progress at 110mh: 2008- 15.3, 2009- 13.91/13.82w, 2010- 13.69/13.51w, 2011- 13.58, 2012- 13.31/13.14w, 2013- 13.81. Pbs: 100m 10.64 '12, 60mh 7.67i '12.

Luke CUTTS b. 13 Feb 1988 Doncaster 1.92m 82kg. The Dearne.
At PV: WCh: '09- dnq 23=; CG: '10- nh; WJ: '06- 9; EC: '12- dnq 20; EU23: '09- 2; EJ: '07- dnq; WI: '14- 8. UK champion 2009, 2013.
UK pole vault record (indoor) 2014.
Progress at PV: 2001- 3.30, 2002- 3.40, 2003- 4.00i/ 3.90, 2004- 4.70, 2005- 4.90i/4.70, 2006- 5.30, 2007- 5.40i/5.30, 2008- 5.50i/5.30, 2009- 5.62i/ 5.60, 2010- 5.53i/5.45, 2011- 5.60i/5.20, 2012- 5.45i/ 5.43, 2013- 5.71i/5.70, 2014- 5.83i. pbs: 60m 7.16i '08, HJ 1.95 '08, LJ 7.07 '12, 7.12w '11.

James DASAOLU b. 5 Sep 1987 Dulwich, London 1.80m 75kg. Croydon H. Graduate of Loughborough University.
At 100m: OG: '12- sf; WCh: '13- 8; EC: '10- sf; ET: '13- 1R. At 60m: EI: '13- 2.
Progress at 100m: 2006- 10.75/10.7/10.61w, 2007- 10.33, 2008- 10.26, 2009- 10.09, 2010- 10.23/10.06w, 2011- 10.11, 2012- 10.13, 2013- 9.91. pbs: 60m 6.47i '14, 200m 21.9 '07.

Mohamed FARAH b. 23 March 1983 Mogadishu, Somalia 1.71m 65kg. Newham & Essex Beagles.
At 5000m (/10,000m): OG: '08- h, '12- 1/1; WCh: '07- 6, '09- 7, '11- 1/2, '13- 1/1; EC: '06- 2, '10- 1/1, '12- 1; CG: '06- 9; WJ: '00- 10; EJ: '01- 1; EU23: '03 & '05- 2; ECp: '08-09-10-13: 1/1/1 &(1)/1. At 3000m: WY: '99- 6; WI: '08- 6, '12- 4; EI: '05-07- 09-11: 6/5/1/1; ECp: '05-06: 2/2. World CC: '07- 11, '10- 20; Eur CC: '99-00-01-04-05-06-08-09: 5J/ 7J/2J/15/21/1/2/2. Won UK 5000m 2007, 2011.
Records: European 10,000m & indoor 5000m 2011, 1500m 2013; indoor 2M 2012; UK 5000m 2010 & 2011, half marathon 2011 & 2013.
Progress at 1500m, 5000m, 10,000m: 1996- 4:43.9, 1997- 4:06.41, 1998- 3:57.67, 1999- 3:55.78, 2000- 3:49.60, 14:05.72; 2001- 3:46.1, 13:56.31; 2002- 3:47.78, 14:00.5; 2003-3:43.17, 13:38.41; 2004- 3:43.4, c.14:25; 2005- 3:38.62, 13:30.53; 2006- 3:38.02, 13:09.40; 2007- 3:45.2i+, 3:46.50, 13:07.00; 2008- 3:39.66, 13:08.11, 27:44.54; 2009- 3:33.98, 13:09.14; 2010- 12:57.94, 27:28.86; 2011- 12:53.11, 26:46.57; 2012- 3:34.66, 12:56.98, 27:30.42; 2013- 3:28.81, 13:05.88, 27:21.71. pbs: 800m 1:48.69 '03, 1M 3:56.49 '05, 2000m 5:06.34 '06, 3000m 7:34.47i '09, 7:36.85 '13; 2M 8:08.07i '12, 8:20.47 '07; 2000mSt 5:55.72 '00; road 15k 43:13 '09, 10M 46:25 '09, HMar 60:10 '13.

Sixth man ever to win Olympic 5000m/10,000m double at same Games; first British athlete to win either title. In 2013 became third man to win World 5000m/10,000m double. Joined his father in England in 1993. Won in New York on half marathon debut 2011.

Adam GEMILI b. 6 Oct 1993 London 1.78m 73kg. Blackheath & Bromley.
At 100m/(200m).4x100mR: OG: '12- sf; WCh: '13- (5); WJ: '12- 1; EU23: '13- 1/4/1R; EJ: '11- 2/2R; ET: '13- 1R.
Progress at 100m, 200m: 2009- 11.2, 2010- 10.80/ 10.72w, 21.87w; 2011- 10.35/10.23w, 20.98; 2012- 10.05, 20.38; 2013- 10.06, 19.98. Pb 60m 6.68i '12.
Sixth equal all-time junior list 10.05 to win World Junior 100m in 2012, improved 200m best from 20.30 to 20.17 and 19.98 at 2013 Worlds before 5th in final in 20.08. As a footballer he was a member of the youth academy at Chelsea before playing for Dagenham & Redbridge and then making a huge impact as a sprinter from 2011.

Robbie GRABARZ b. 3 Oct 1987 Enfield 1.92m 87kg. Newham & Essex Beagles.
At HJ: OG: '12- 3=; WCh: '13- 8; EC: '12- 1; WJ: '06- 12; EU23: '09- 11; WI: '12- 6=; EI: '13- 6; won DL 2012, UK 2012-13.
UK high jump record 2012.
Progress at HJ: 2002- 1.75, 2004- 2.00, 2005- 2.22, 2006- 2.20i/2.14, 2007- 2.21, 2008- 2.27, 2009- 2.23i/2.22, 2010- 2.28, 2011- 2.28, 2012- 2.37, 2013- 2.31. pb TJ 14.40 '09.

David 'Dai' GREENE b. 11 Apr 1986 Llanelli 1.83m 75kg. Swansea Harriers.
At 400mh: OG: '12- 4; WCh: '09- 7 (res (2)R), '11- 1, '13- sf; EC: '06- h, '10- 1; CG: '10- 1; EU23: '07- 1; EJ: '05- 2; CCp: '10- 1; ET: '09-10-11-13: 1/1/1/2.
UK champion 2009-10, 2012-13; won DL 2011.
Progress at 400mh: 2003- 55.0/55.06, 2004- 53.42, 2005- 51.14, 2006- 49.91, 2007- 49.58, 2008- 49.53, 2009- 48.27, 2010- 47.88, 2011- 48.20, 2012- 47.84, 2013- 48.66. pbs: 100m 11.1 '06, 200m 22.1 '05, 21.73w '08; 400m 45.82 '11, 600m 1:16.22i '13.

Richard KILTY b. 2 Sep 1989 Middlesbrough 1.84m 80kg. Gateshead H.
At 200m/4x100mR: WCh: '13- hR; EU23: '09- 1; '11- 2R; WJ: '08- sf. At 60m: WI: '14- 1.
Progress at 100m, 200m: 2004- 11.43/11.3w, 2005- 10.96/10.90w, 22.60; 2006- 10.76/10.75w, 21.96; 2007- 10.61, 21.37; 2008- 10.60/10.5/10.51w, 21.19; 2009- 10.43, 20.80; 2010- 10.44, 21.41i; 2011- 10.32, 20.53; 2012- 10.23/10.15w, 20.50; 2013- 10.10, 20.34. pbs: 60m 6.49i '14, 400m 48.58 '13.

Steve LEWIS b. 20 May 1986 Stoke-on-Trent 1.91m 83kg. Newham & Essex Beagles. Studied sports science at Loughborough University.
At PV: OG: '08- dnq, '12- 5=; WCh: '07- dnq, '09- 7=, '11- 9=, '13- dnq; CG: '06- 3, '10- 2; WJ: '04- 9; WY: '03- 3; EU23: '07- 7; EJ: '05- 5; WI: '10- 6=; '12- 5=; EI: '09- 4, '13- 6=; ECp: '08- 3. Won AAA

2006, UK 2007-08, 2011-12.
UK pole vault record 2012.
Progress at PV: 1999- 3.20, 2000- 3.70, 2001-
4.30i/4.20, 2002- 4.65, 2003- 5.05, 2004- 5.20,
2005- 5.35, 2006- 5.50, 2007- 5.61, 2008- 5.71,
2009- 5.75i/5.72, 2010- 5.72i/5.65, 2011- 5.65,
2012- 5.82, 2013- 5.71i/5.70.

Andrew OSAGIE b. 19 Feb 1988 Harlow 1.89m
72kg. Harlow. St Mary's University College..
At 800m: OG: '12- 8; WCh: '11- sf, '13- 5; CG: '10-
sf; EU23: '09- h; WI: '12- 3, '14- 3; EI: '11- 4; ET:
'13- 3. Won UK 2011-12.
Progress at 800m: 2004- 1:56.0, 2005- 1:52.90,
2006- 1:52.51, 2007- 1:47.34, 2008- 1:53.12, 2009-
1:47.15, 2010- 1:46.41, 2011- 1:45.36, 2012- 1:43.77,
2013- 1:44.36. pbs: 400m 48.8 '09, 600m 1:16.45i
'13, 1000m 2:18.56i '11, 1500m 3:48.99 '09.

Andrew POZZI b. 15 May 1992 Leamington
Spa 1.86m 79kg. Startford-upon-Avon. Bristol
University.
At 110mh: OG: '12- h; EJ: '11- 2. UK champion
2012. At 60mh: WI: '12- 4, '14- 4.
Progress at 110mh: 2009- 14.8, 2011- 13.73/13.66w,
2012- 13.34. pbs: 100m 10.9 '11, 60mh 7.53i '14, LJ
6.73 '09.

Martyn ROONEY b. 3 Apr 1987 Croydon 1.98m
78kg. Croydon H. Was at Loughborough
University.
At 400m/4x400mR: OG: '08- 6, '12- sf; WCh: '07-
h, '09- sf/2R, '11- sf, '13- 4R; EC: '10- 3/2R; CG:
'06- 5; WJ: '06- 3/3R; EJ: '05- 2/1R; ECp: '07-08-
10: 3/1&2R/1. Won UK 2008, 2010-12.
Progress at 400m: 2003- 49.4, 2004- 47.46, 2005-
46.44, 2006- 45.35, 2007- 45.47, 2008- 44.60, 2009-
45.35, 2010- 44.99, 2011- 45.30, 2012- 44.92, 2013-
45.05. pbs: 60m 7.12i '09, 200m 21.08 '13, 20.87w
'11; 600m 1:16.9 '05, 800m 1:50.55 '05.
Ran anchor leg in 43.73 on 4x400m at 2008
Olympics.

Greg RUTHERFORD b. 17 Nov 1986 Milton
Keynes 1.88m 84kg. Marshall Milton Keynes.
At LJ: OG: '08- 10, '12- 1; WCh: '09- 5, '07-11-13-
dnq 21/15=/14; EC: '06- 2; CG: '06- 8, '10- 2; EJ:
'05- 1; EI: '09- 6; ET: '13- 3. Won AAA 2005-06,
UK 2008, 2012.
UK Long jump records 2009 and 2012.
Progress at LJ: 1999- 5.04, 2001- 6.16, 2003- 7.04,
2004- 7.28, 2005- 8.14, 2006- 8.26, 2007- 7.96, 2008-
8.20, 2009- 8.30, 2010- 8.22, 2011- 8.27/8.32w,
2012- 8.35, 2013- 8.22. pbs: 60m 6.68i '09, 100m
10.26 '10.
Great-grandfather Jock Rutherford played 11
internationals for England at football 1904-08.

William SHARMAN b. 12 Sep 1984 Lagos,
Nigeria 1.88m 82kg. Belgrave Harriers.
Economics graduate of University of Leicester.
At 110mh: WCh: '09- 4, '11- 5=, '13- 5; EC: '06- h,
'10/12- sf; CG: '10- 2; EU23: '05- 4; EJ: '03- 5. Won
UK 2010, 2013. At 60mh: WI: '14- 7.
Progress at 110mh: 2003- 14.31, 2004- 13.94/

13.86w, 2005- 13.88/13.72w, 2006- 13.49/13.45w,
2007- 13.68, 2008- 13.67/13.6/13.59w, 2009- 13.30,
2010- 13.39/13.35w/12.9w, 2011- 13.47, 2012- 13.50,
2013- 13.26. pbs: 60m 6.89i '07, 100m 10.86 '05,
10.66w '13; 200m 21.59 '06, 400m 48.53 '05,
1500m 4:45.25 '05, 60mh 7.53i '14, HJ 2.08 '05, PV
4.00 '05, LJ 7.14 '04, 7.15w '05; SP 12.99 '05, DT
33.99 '03, JT 43.45 '05, Dec 7384 '05, Hep 5278i
'05.
National junior decathlon champion 2003.
Improved pb from 13.44 to 13.38 and 13.30 at
2009 Worlds.

Chris TOMLINSON b. 15 Sep 1981 Middlesbrough 1.97m 84kg. Newham & Essex Beagles.
At LJ: OG: '04- 5, '08- dnq 27, '12- 6; WCh: '03- 9,
'05/07- dnq 14/16, '09- 8, '11- 11; EC: '02-06-10-12:
6/9/3/dnq 13; CG: '02-06-10: 6/6/nj; WJ: '00- 12;
WI: '04- 6, '08- 2; EI: '07- 5, '13- 7; WCp: '02- 6;
ECp: '01-02-04-10-11: 2/1/1/3/3; AAA champion 2004, UK 2009-10, 2013.
Three British long jump records 2002-2011.
Progress at LJ: 1996- 5.91/6.09w, 1997-
6.82w/6.44, 1998- 7.23i, 1999- 7.44i/7.40, 2000-
7.62, 2001- 7.75, 2002- 8.27, 2003- 8.16, 2004-
8.25/8.28w, 2005- 7.95i/7.82/7.83w, 2006- 8.09,
2007- 8.29, 2008- 8.18i/7.95/8.09w, 2009- 8.23,
2010- 8.23, 2011- 8.35, 2012- 8.26, 2013- 8.21. pbs:
60m 6.84i '09, 100m 10.69 '02, 10.61w/10.6 '01;
200m 21.73 '02, 21.43w '10; TJ 15.35 '01.
Jumped 8.27 at Tallahassee in April 2002, from
a previous best of 7.87 (and 8.19w), to break the
34-year-old British record set by Lynn Davies.

Rhys WILLIAMS b. 27 Feb 1982 Cardiff 1.83m
73kg. Cardiff AAC. Was at Loughborough
University.
At 400mh: OG: '12- sf; WCh: '05- sf, '09- h, '13-
sf; EC: '06- 3/2R, '10- 2, '12- 1; CG: '06- 4, '10- 3;
WJ: '02- sf; EU23: '05- 1; EJ: '03- 1. AAA champion
2006.
Progress at 400mh: 2001- 53.0/53.42; 2002- 51.68,
2003- 51.15, 2004- 51.64, 2005- 50.57, 2005- 49.60,
2006- 49.09, 2009- 49.38, 2010- 48.96, 2011- 49.59,
2012- 49.17, 2013- 48.84. pbs: 100m 10.91 '12,
200m 21.54 '12, 400m 46.69 '13.
His father J.J.Williams was a famous Welsh
rugby wing and was 4th at 4x100m at the 1970
Commonwealth Games, pb 100m 10.5/10.4w in
1970.

Women

Holly BLEASDALE b. 2 Nov 1991 Preston
1.75m 68kg. Blackburn Harriers.
At PV: OG: '12- 6=; WCh: '11- dnq; WI: '12- 3,
'14- 9; WJ: '10- 3; EU23: '11- 1; EI: '13- 1. UK
champion 2011-12.
Three UK pole vault records 2011-12, five
indoors 2011-12.
Progress at PV: 2007- 2.30, 2008- 3.10i, 2009-
4.05, 2010- 4.35, 2011- 4.71i/4.70, 2012- 4.87i/4.71,
2013- 4.77i/4.60, 2014- 4.73i. pbs: SP 11.32 '11, JT
37.60 '11.

World age-19 best 2011, age-20 best 2012. Engaged to 800m runner Paul Bradshaw (1:47.37 '09).

Eilidh CHILD b. 20 Feb 1987 Perth 1.72m 59kg. Pitreavie.
At 400mh/4x400mR: OG: '12- sf; WCh: '09/11-sf, '13- 5/3R; EC: '10- 8, '12- 4R; CG: '10- 2; EU23: '07- 5, '09- 2; ET: '09-10-13: 3R/2/1&1R. At 400m: WI: '14- 3R; EI: '13- 2/1R.
Progress at 400mh: 2003- 59.8mx, 2004- 59.53, 2005- 59.78, 2006- 59.7/60.05, 2007- 57.11, 2008-56.84, 2009- 55.32, 2010- 55.16, 2011- 55.67, 2012-54.96, 2013- 54.22. pbs: 200m 24.51i '13, 24.56 '08; 300m 37.1i '13, 400m 51.45i/51.83 '13, 800m 2:24.2 '04, 60mh 8.89i '06, 100mh 14.51 '04, 14.38w '07, 200mhSt 26.27 '13.

Hannah ENGLAND b. 6 Mar 1987 Oxford 1.77m 54kg. Oxford City, Graduate of Birmingham and Florida State Universities.
At 1500m (800m): OG: '12- sf; WCh: '11- 2, '13- 4; EC: '10- 10; CG: '10- 4 (5); WJ: '06- h; EU23: '07- 5; ECp: '09- 4 (4), '10- 2. Won UK 2010-11, 2013; NCAA 2008.
Progress at 1500m: 2000- 4:46.81, 2001- 4:39.37, 2002- 4:33.05, 2003- 4:28.22, 2004- 4:25.86, 2005-4:26.16, 2006- 4:17.31, 2007- 4:12.44, 2008- 4:06.19, 2009- 4:04.29, 2010- 4:04.33, 2011- 4:01.89, 2012-4:04.05, 2013- 4:03.38. pbs: 800m 1:59.66 '12, 1M 4:30.29i '09, 4:40.22 '08; 3000m 8:56.72i '10.
Married Luke Gunn (3000mSt 8:28.48 '08) in January 2013.

Jessica ENNIS-HILL b. 28 Jan 1986 Sheffield 1.64m 57kg. Sheffield. Studied psychology at University of Sheffield.
At Hep: OG: '12- 1; WCh: '07- 4, '09- 1, '11- 2; EC: '06- 8, '10- 1; CG: '06- 3; WJ: '04- 8; WY: '03- 5; EJ: '05- 1; WUG: '05- 3; ECp: '07- 1. At Pen: WI: '10- 1, '12- 2; EI: '07- 6. At 100mh: EU23: '07- 3. Won UK 100mh 2007, 2009, 2012; HJ 2007, 2009, 2011-12.
Records: Commonwealth heptathlon (2) 2012, indoor pentathlon 2010 & 2012, UK high jump 2007, 100mh 2012, indoor 60mh 2010.
Progress at Hep: 2001- 4801, 2002- 5194, 2003-5116, 2004- 5542, 2005- 5910, 2006- 6287, 2007-6469, 2009- 6731, 2010- 6823, 2011- 6790, 2012-6955. pbs: 60m 7.36i '10, 100m 11.39+ '10, 150mStr 16.99 '10, 200m 22.83 '12, 800m 2:07.81 '11, 60mh 7.87i '12, 100mh 12.54 '12, HJ 1.95 '07, LJ 6.51 '10, 6.54w '07; SP 14.79i '12, 14.67 '11; JT 48.33 '13, Pen 4965i '12.
Set four pbs in adding 359 points to best score for third at 2006 Commonwealth Games. Stress fracture ended 2008 season in May. Set SP pb when winning 2009 World title and three indoor bests when winning 2010 World Indoor gold. Three pbs en route to Olympic gold 2012. Won Götzis heptathlon 2010-12. Laureus World Sportswoman of the Year 2013. Married Andy Hill on 18 May 2013. Expecting a baby in 2014.

Katarina JOHNSON-THOMPSON b. 9 Jan 1993 Liverpool 1.83m 70kg. Liverpool H.
At Hep: OG: '12- 14; WCh: '13- 5; WY: '09- 1; EU23: '13- 1; EJ: '09- 8, '11- 6. At LJ: WJ: '12- 1 (sf 100mh); WI: '14- 2.
UK high jump record (indoors) 2014.
Progress at Hep: 2008- 5343, 2009- 5481, 2011-5787, 2012- 6267, 2013- 6449. pbs: 60m 7.50i '14, 100m 12.35 '08, 12.2 '09, 12.1w '10; 200m 23.37 '13, 300m 38.56i '08, 800m 2:07.64 '13, 60mh 8.40i '14, 100mh 13.48 '12, 400mh 61.0 '13, HJ 1.96i '14, 1.89 '12; LJ 6.81i '14, 6.56 '13, 6.81w '12; TJ 12.56i '12, 12.49 '10; SP 12.49i '14, 11.92 '13; JT 40.86 '13, Pen 4526i '12.
Set pbs in the each of the last four events when adding 182 points to her pb for 5th at the 2013 Worlds. Has all all-time record 27 English age-group titles U15 to U23.

Jennifer MEADOWS b. 17 Apr 1981 Billinge, Wigan 1.56m 48kg. Wigan.
At 800m/4x400mR: OG: '08- sf; WCh: '03- 6R; '07- sf, '09- 3, '11- sf; EC: '10- 3; CG: '10- 2; SR; WI: '08- 5, '10- 2; EI: '07-09-11-13: 5/4/1&2R/4; CCp: '10- 4; ECp: '07-08-09-11: 1R/1/3R/2. At 400m: WJ: '00- sf/1R; EU23: '01- 6/1R, '03- 7/2R; WUG: '01- 2R. Won DL 800m 2011, UK 800m 2011.
Progress at 800m: 1994- 2:16.80, 1995- 2:14.88, 1996- 2:16.4, 1997- 2:16.03, 1999- 2:11.5, 2000-2:10.7, 2001- 2:05.8, 2002- 2:04.46/2:03.35i, 2003-2:06.82mx/2:08.0, 2004- 2:06.84i, 2005- 2:02.05, 2006- 2:00.16, 2007- 1:59.39, 2008- 1:59.11, 2009-1:57.93, 2010- 1:58.43i/1:58.88, 2011- 1:58.60, 2013-2:01.02i. pbs: 100m 11.94/11.8w '01, 11.9 '02; 200m 24.32 '00, 24.0 '02, 23.90w '01; 400m 52.50mx '05, 52.67 '03; 600m 1:25.81i '07, 1000m 2:39.84 '07, 1500m 4:19.36 '06.

Christine OHURUOGU b. 17 May 1984 Forest Gate, London 1.75m 70kg. Newham & Essex Beagles. Studied linguistics at University College, London.
At 400m/4x400mR: OG: '04- sf/4R, '08- 1, '12- 2; WCh: '05- sf/3R, '07- 1/3R, '09- 5, '11- h, '13-1/3R; CG: '06- 1; EU23: '05- 2/2R; EJ: '03- 3/3R; WI: '12- 1R, '14- 3R; EI: '13- 1R; ET: '13- 1R. At 200m: ECp: '08- 2, '09- 3. Won AAA 400m 2004, UK 2009, 2012-13.
UK 400m record 2013.
Progress at 400m: 2000- 59.0, 2001- 55.29, 2003-54.21, 2004- 50.50, 2005- 50.73, 2006- 50.28, 2007-49.61, 2008- 49.62, 2009- 50.21, 2010- 50.88, 2011-50.85, 2012- 49.70, 2013- 49.41. pbs: 60m 7.39i '06, 100m 11.35 '08, 150mStr 16.94 '09, 200m 22.85 '09, 300m 36.76+ '09.
Played for England U17 and U19 at netball. Withdrawn from GB European Champs team in 2006 after missing three drugs tests, resulted in a one-year ban. Her younger sister Victoria (b. 28 Feb 1993) has 400m pb 52.62 '13; res 3R WI '14.

Tiffany PORTER b. 13 Nov 1987 Ypsilanti, USA 1.72m 62kg. née Ofili. Doctorate in pharmacy from University of Michigan.

At 100mh: OG: '12- sf; WCh: '11- 4, '13- 3; WJ: '06- 3 (for USA); ET: '13- 1. At 60mh: WI: '12- 2, '14- 3; EI: '11- 2. Won UK 100mh 2011, 2013; NCAA 100mh & 60mh indoors 2009.
Three British 100mh records 2011.
Progress at 100mh: 2005- 14.19, 2006- 13.37/13.15w, 2007- 12.80, 2008- 12.73, 2009- 12.77/12.57w, 2010- 12.85, 2011- 12.56, 2012- 12.65/12.47w, 2013- 12.55. pbs: 60m 7.41i '11, 100m 11.70 '09, 11.63w '08; 200m 23.90 '08, 400mh 61.96 '06, LJ 6.48 '09; UK records: 50mh 6.83i '12, 55mh 7.38i '12, 60mh 7.80i '11.
Opted for British nationality in September 2010 through her mother being born in London (father born in Nigeria). Married US hurdler Jeff Porter (qv) in May 2011. Sister Cindy Ofili (b. 5 Aug 1994) USA has pbs: 60mh 8.07Ai/8.08i '14, 100mh 13.34/13.30w '13.

Shara PROCTOR b. 16 Sep 1988 The Valley, Anguilla 1.74m 56kg. Birchfield H. Was at University of Florida, USA.
At LJ: OG: '12- 9; WCh: '07-09-11-13: dnq 29/6/dnq 20/6; WI: '12- 3, '14- 4; CG: '06- dnq 13; WJ: '06- dnq 16; WY: '05- 6; EI: '13- 4; ET: '13- 3. Won DL 2013, CAC 2009, UK 2011-13.
Records: Anguilla: LJ 2005-09, TJ 2007-09; UK LJ 2012.
Progress at LJ: 2003- 5.64, 2004- 5.99A. 2005- 6.24, 2006- 6.17, 2007- 6.17, 2008- 6.54A/6.52/6.61w, 2009- 6.71, 2010- 6.69, 2011- 6.81, 2012- 6.95, 2013- 6.92. pbs: 60m 7.49i '13, 100m 12.27 '08, 12.10w '10; TJ 13.88i '10, 13.74 '09.
Switched from Anguilla (a British Dependent Territory without a National Olympic Committee) to Britain from 16 Nov 2010. Younger sister Shinelle (b. 27 Jun 91) set Anguillan high jump records at 1.70 in 2009 and 2010 and 1.72i in 2014.

Goldie SAYERS b. 16 Jul 1982 Newmarket 1.71m 70kg. Belgrave H.
At OG: '04- dnq 20, '08- 4, '12- dnq; WCh: '05- 12, '07/09- dnq 18/13, '11- 10; EC: '06- 12, '12- 4; CG: '02- 6, '06- 5; WJ: '00- 6; WY: '99- 5; EJ: '01- 2; EU23: '03- 11; WUG: '03- 5, '05- 4; ECp: '10- 2, '11- 2. AAA champion 2003-06, UK 2007-12.
Three UK javelin records 2007-12.
Progress at JT: 1996- 41.56, 1997- 45.10, 1998- 51.92, new: 1999- 51.06, 2000- 54.48, 2001- 55.40, 2002- 58.20, 2003- 56.29, 2004- 60.85, 2005- 61.45, 2006- 60.41, 2007- 65.05, 2008- 65.75, 2009- 59.82, 2010- 63.15, 2011- 64.46, 2012- 66.17.
Did not compete in 2013 due to necessity for an elbow operation.

Perri SHAKES-DRAYTON b. 21 Dec 1988 London 1.70m 67kg. Victoria Park & Tower Hamlets, Brunel University.
At 400mh/4x400mR: OG: '12- sf; WCh: '09- sf, '11- sf, '13- 7; EC: '10- 3/3R; WI: '12- 1R; WJ: '06- 8; EU23: '09-1; EJ: '07- 2/2R; ET: '11- 3. At 400m: EI: '13- 1/1R; ET: '13- 1/1R. Won UK 400m 2011, 400mh 2008, 2010-13.
Progress at 400mh: 2006- 57.52, 2007- 56.46, 2008- 56.09, 2009- 55.26, 2010- 54.18, 2011- 54.62, 2012- 53.77, 2013- 53.67. pbs: 60m 7.44i '09, 100m 11.78 '09, 11.7w '07; 200m 23.71mx '10, 300m 36.9+i '13, 400m 50.50 '13, 800m 2:08.35mx/2:08.6 '11, 100mh 14.07 '08, 200mhSt 25.74 '13.

USA

Governing body: USA Track and Field, One RCA Dome, Suite #140, Indianapolis, IN 46225. Founded 1979 as The Athletics Congress, when it replaced the AAU (founded 1888) as the governing body.
National Championships first held in 1876 (men), 1923 (women). **2013 Champions: Men**: 100m/200m: Tyson Gay 9.75/19.75 dq?, 400m: LaShawn Merritt 44.21, 800m: Duane Solomon 1:43.27, 1500m: Matthew Centrowitz 3:45.17, 5000m: Barnard Lagat 14:54.16, 10,000m: Galen Rupp 28:47.32, HMar: Mohamed Trafeh 61:17, Mar: Nick Arcianaga 2:13:11, 3000mSt: Evan Jager 8:20.67, 110mh: Aries Merritt 12.93, 400mh: Michael Tinsley 47.96, HJ: Erik Kynard 2.28, PV: Brad Walker 5.65, LJ: George Kitchens 8.23w, TJ: Omar Craddock 17.15w, SP: Ryan Whiting 22.11, DT: Lance Brooks 62.29, HT: A.G.Kruger 75.52, JT: Riley Dolezal 83.50, Dec: Ashley Eaton 8291, 20000W: Tim Seaman 1:30:13.1, 50kW: Patrick Stroupe 4:25:06. **Women**: 100m: English Gardner 10.85, 200m: Kimberlyn Duncan 21.80w, 400m: Natasha Hastings 49.94, 800m: Alysia Montaño 1:58.67, 1500m: Treniere Moser 4:28.62, 5000m: Jenny Simpson 15:33.77, 10,000m: Shalane Flanagan 31:43.20, HMar: Adriana Nelson 71:19, Mar: Annie Bersagel 2:30:53, 3000mSt: Nicole Bush 9:44.53, 100mh: Brianna Rollins 12.26, 400mh: Dalilah Muhammad 53.83, HJ: Brigetta Barrett 2.04, PV: Jenn Suhr 4.70, LJ: Janay DeLoach Soukup 6.89w, TJ: Andrea Geubelle 14.03w, SP: Michelle Carter 20.24, DT: Gia Lewis-Smallwood 65.13, HT: Amanda Bingson 75.73, JT: Brittany Borman 60.91, Hep: Sharon Day 6550, 20,000mW: Maria Michta 1:37:34.46, 50kW: Erin Taylor-Talcott 4:50:40.
NCAA Championships first held in 1921 (men), 1982 (women). **2013 Champions: Men**: 100m: Charles Silmon 9.89w, 200m: Ameer Webb 20.10w, 400m: Bryshon Nellum 44.73, 800m: Elijah Greer 1:46.58, 1500m: Mac Fleet 3:50.25, 5000m/10,000m: Lawi Lalang KEN 13:35.19/29:29.65, 3000mSt: Anthony Rotich KEN 8:21.19, 110mh: Wayne Davis TRI 13.14w, 400mh: Reggie Wyatt 48.58, HJ: Derek Drouin CAN 2.34, PV: Sam Kendricks 5.70, LJ: Damar Forbes JAM 8.35w, TJ: Omar Craddock 16.92, SP: Ryan Crouser 20.31, DT: Julian Wruck AUS 64.94, HT: Tomás Kruzliak SVK 69.26, JT: Sam Humphreys 77.95, Dec: Johannes Hock GER 8267. **Women**: 100m: English Gardner 10.96, 200m: Kimberlyn Duncan 22.04w, 400m: Ashley Spencer 50.28, 800m: Natoya Goule

JAM 2:00.06, 1500m: Natalija Pillusina LTU 4:13.25, 5000m: Abbey D'Agostino 15:43.68, 10,000m: Betsy Saina KEN 33:08.85, 3000mSt: Emma Coburn 9:35.38, 100mh: Brianna Rollins 12.39, 400mh: Kori Carter 53.21, HJ: Brigetta Barrett 1.95, PV: Bethany Buell 4.45, LJ: Lorraine Ugen GBR 6.77, TJ: Shenieka Thomas JAM 14.14, SP: Tia Brooks 18.91, DT: Anna Jelmini 57.95, HT: Chelsea Cassulo 69.12, JT: Freya Jones GBR 54.95, Hep: Lindsay Vollmer 6086.

Jeshua ANDERSON b. 22 Jun 1989 Mission Hills, California 1.88m 84kg. Was at Washington State University.
At 400mh/4x400mR: WCh: '11- sf; WJ: '08- 1/1R; WUG: '11- 1. Won US 2011; NCAA 2008-09, 2011.
Progress at 400mh: 2008- 48.68, 2009- 48.47, 2010- 48.63, 2011- 47.93, 2012- 48.88, 2013- 49.14.
pbs: 400m 46.08 '09, 500m 1:10.86i '12, 60mh 7.98i '11, 110mh 13.78 '11.
Broke 22 year-old US high school 300mh record with 35.28 in 2007. Played as wide receiver at American Football.

Ryan BAILEY b. 13 Apr 1989 Portland, Oregon 1.93m 100kg. Nike.
At 100m/4x100mR: OG: '12- 5/2R. At 4x400m: WJ: '08- res (1)R.
N.American 4x100m record 2012.
Progress at 100m, 200m: 2007- 10.48/10.45w, 21.13/21.11w; 2008- 10.28, 20.69; 2009- 10.05, 20.45; 2010- 9.88, 20.10; 2012- 9.88, 20.43; 2013- 10.10/10.00w. pbs: 55m 6.20i '09, 60m 6.58A/6.61i '10, 300m 33.50 '07, 400m 47.05 '08, 60mh 7.97i '08, 110mh 14.13 '08.
His nephew Eric Bailey 400mh pb 50.04 '11.

Marvin BRACY b 15 Dec 1993 1.88m 74kg. Student at Florida State University.
At 100m/4x100mR: WJ: '10- res 1R; PAm-J: 11-1. At 60m: WI: '14- 2.
Progress at 100m: 2009- 48.72, 2010- 10.42/10.19w, 2011- 10.28/10.05w, 2012- 10.25/10.06w, 2013-10.09. pbs: 60m 6.48Ai/6.51i '14, 200m 21.02 '12.
Wide receiver at American Football.

Christian CANTWELL b. 30 Sep 1980 Jefferson City, Missouri 1.93m 154kg. Nike. Studied hotel and restaurant management at University of Missouri.
At SP: OG: '08- 2, '12- 4; WCh: '05- 4, '09- 1, '11- 3; WI: '04-08-10: 1/1/1; CCp: '10- 1; won DL 2010, WAF 2003, 2009; US 2005, 2009-10. At DT: PAm-J: '99- 2.
Progress at SP: 1999- 15.85, 2000- 19.67, 2001-19.71, 2002- 21.45, 2003- 21.62, 2004- 22.54, 2005-21.67, 2006- 22.45, 2007- 21.96, 2008- 22.18i/21.76, 2009- 22.16, 2010- 22.41, 2011- 22.07, 2012- 22.31, 2013- 20.13i/19.86. pbs: DT 59.32 '01, HT 57.18 '01, Wt 22.04i '03.
Three competitions over 22m in 2004, then 4th in US Olympic Trials. Married Teri Steer (b. 3 Oct 1975, SP pb 19.21 '01, 3 WI 1999) 29 Oct 2005.

Matthew CENTROWITZ b. 18 Nov 1989 Beltsville, Maryland 1.76m 61kg. Nike. Studied sociology at the University of Oregon.
At 1500m: OG: '12- 4; WCh: '11- 3, '12- 2; WI: '12- 7. At 5000m WJ: '08- 11. Won US 2011, 2013; NCAA 2011, PAm-J 2007.
Progress at 1500m: 2007- 3:49.54, 2008- 3:44.98, 2009- 3:36.92, 2010- 3:40.14, 2011- 3:34.46, 2012-3:31.96, 2013- 3:33.58. pbs: 800m 1:45.86 '13, 1000m 2:19.56i '13, 1M 3:51.34i/3:51.79 '13, 3000m 7:46.19i '12, 2M 8:40.55 '07, 5000m 13:47.73 '10.
Father Matt pbs: 1500m 3:36.60 '76, 3:54.94 '82, 5000m US record 13:12.91 '82, 10,000m 28:32.7 '83; h OG 1500m 1976; 1 PAm 5000m 1979. Sister Lauren (b. 25 Sep 1986) 1500m pb 4:10.23 '09.

Will CLAYE b. 13 Jun 1991 Phoenix 1.80m 68kg. Nike. Was at University of Oklahoma, then Florida.
At (LJ)/TJ: OG: '12- 3/2; WCh: '11- 9/3, '13- 3; WI: '12- 4/1; won PAm-J and NCAA 2009.
Progress at LJ, TJ: 2007- 14.91/15.19w, 2008-7.39/7.48w, 15.97; 2009- 7.89/8.00w, 17.19/17.24w; 2010- 7.30w, 16.30; 2011- 8.29, 17.50/17.62w; 2012-8.25, 17.70i/17.62; 2013- 8.10, 17.52. pb 100m 10.64/10.53w '12.
Possibly youngest ever NCAA champion – he won 2009 title on his 18th birthday with 17.24w (and US junior record 17.19). First athlete to win Olympic medals at both LJ and TJ since 1936.

Kerron CLEMENT b. 31 Oct 1985 Port of Spain, Trinidad 1.88m 84kg. Nike. Was at University of Florida.
At 400mh/4x400mR: OG: '08- 2/res1R, '12- 8; WCh: '05- 4, '07- 1/res 1R, '09- 1/1R, '11- sf, '13-8; WJ: '04- 1/1R; WI: '10- res 1R; WCp: '06- 1. Won WAF 2008-09, US 2005-06, NCAA 2004-05. World junior 4x400m record 2004, world indoor records: 400m 2005, 4x400m 2006.
Progress at 400m, 400mh: 2002- 49.77H, 2003-50.13H, 2004- 45.90, 48.51; 2005- 44.57i, 47.24; 2006- 44.71, 47.39; 2007- 44.48, 47.61; 2008- 45.10, 47.79; 2009- 45.08, 47.91; 2010- 46.01, 47.86; 2011-45.42, 48.74; 2012- 46.49, 48.12; 2013- 45.74, 48.06. pbs: 60m 6.89i '10, 100m 10.23 '07, 200m 20.40i '05, 20.49 '07; 300m 31.94i '06, 55mh 7.28i '05, 60mh 7.80i '04, 110mh 13.78 '04.
Born in Trinidad, moved to Texas in 1998, US citizenship confirmed in 2005. Ran world-leading 47.24, the world's fastest time since 1998, to win 2005 US 400mh title.

Ryan CROUSER b. 18 Dec 1992 Portland 2.01m 109kg. Student at Texas University.
At SP/DT: WY: '09- 1/2. Won NCAA shot 2013, indoors 2014.
Progress at SP: 2011- 19.48i, 2012- 20.29i/19.32, 2013- 21.09, 2014- 21.27. pbs: DT 59.77 '12, JT 61.16 '09.
Set High School 1.62kg DT record 72.40 '11. His father Mitch SP 20.04i '83, 19.94 '82, DT 67.22 '85; uncle Dean SP 21.07 '82, DT 65.88 '83; uncle Brian JT 83.00 '87, old JT 95.10 '85, won NCAA

1982 & 1985, dnq OG 1988 & 1992; Dean's children: Sam SP 17.62 '13, JT 80.80 '12, US junior & HS record '10; Haley US junior JT record 55.22 '12, 4 WY '11.

Walter DIX b. 31 Jan 1986 Coral Springs, Florida 1.78m 84kg. Nike. Studied social science at Florida State University.
At 100m/200m: OG: '08- 3/3; WCh: '11- 2/2; won US 100m 2010-11, 200m 2008, 2011; NCAA 100m 2005, 2007; 200m 2006-08; DL 200m 2011. World junior 200m indoor record (20.37) 2005.
Progress at 100m, 200m: 2002- 10.72/10.67w, 2003- 10.41/10.29w, 21.04/20.94w; 2004- 10.28, 20.62/20.54w; 2005- 10.06/9.96w, 20.18; 2006- 10.12, 20.25; 2007- 9.93, 19.69; 2008- 9.91/9.80w, 19.86; 2009- 10.00, 2010- 9.88, 19.72; 2011- 9.94, 19.53; 2012- 10.03/9.85w, 20.02; 2013- 9.99, 20.12. pbs: 55m 6.19i '07, 60m 6.59i '06, 150mSt 14.65 '11, 400m 46.75 '10, LJ 7.39 '04.

Johnny DUTCH b. 20 Jan 1989 Clayton NC 1.80m 82kg. Nike. Studied media arts at University of South Carolina.
At 400mh: WCh: '09- sf; WJ: '08- 2; PAm-J: '07- 1/2R. Won NCAA 2010.
Progress at 400mh: 2005- 52.06, 2006- 52.37, 2007- 50.07, 2008- 48.52, 2009- 48.18, 2010- 47.63, 2011- 48.47, 2012- 48.90, 2013- 48.02. pbs: 400m 46.75 '13, 55mh 7.31i '10, 60mh 7.71i '09, 110mh 13.50/13.30w '10.

Ashton EATON b. 21 Jan 1988 Portland, Oregon 1.86m 86kg. Oregon TC. Graduate of University of Oregon.
At Dec: OG: '12- 1; WCh: '09- 18, '11- 2; won US 2012-13, NCAA 2008-10. At Hep: WI: '12- 1, 14- 1. World decathlon record 2012, indoor heptathlon records 2010 (6499), 2011 (6568) and 2012.
Progress at Dec: 2007- 7123, 2008- 8122, 2009- 8241w/8091, 2010- 8457, 2011- 8729, 2012- 9039, 2013- 8809. pbs: 60m 6.66i '11, 100m 10.21 '12, 10.19w '10; 200m 20.76 '13, 400m 45.64 '13, 800m 1:55.90i '10, 1000m 2:32.67i '10, 1500m 4:14.48 '12, 60mh 7.60i '11, 110mh 13.35 '11, 13.34w '12; HJ 2.11i '10, 2.11 '12; PV 5.35i '14, 5.30 '12; LJ 8.23 '12, SP 15.40 '13, DT 47.36 '11, JT 66.64 '13, Hep 6645i '12.
Set best ever marks in decathlons with 100m 10.21 and LJ 8.23 in WR in Eugene 22/23 June 2012. Married Brianne Theisen CAN on 15 July 2013.

Justin GATLIN b. 10 Feb 1982 Brooklyn, NY 1.85m 79kg. XTEP. Was at University of Tennessee.
At 100m/(200m)/4x100mR: OG: '04- 1/3/2R, '12- 3/2R; WCh: '05- 1/1, '11- sf, '13- 2/2R. At 60m: WI: '03- 1, '12- 1. Won DL 100m 2013, US 100m 2005-06, 2012; 200m 2005 (indoor 60m 2003), NCAA 100m & 200m 2001-02 (& indoor 60m/200m 2002).
N.American 4x100m record 2012.
Progress at 100m, 200m: 2000- 10.36, 2001- 10.08,

20.29/19.86w; 2002: under international suspension 10.05/10.00w, 19.86; 2003- 9.97, 20.04; 2004- 9.85, 20.01; 2005- 9.88/9.84w, 20.00; 2006- 9.77dq, 2010- 10.09, 20.63; 2011- 9.95, 20.20; 2012- 9.79, 20.11; 2013- 9.85, 20.21. pbs: 60m 6.45i '03, 55mh 7.39i '02, 60mh 7.86i '01, 110mh 13.41dq '02, 13.78/13.74w '01; LJ 7.34i '01, 7.21 '00.
Top hurdler in high school (110mh 13.66 and 300mh 36.74 on junior hurdles). Retained NCAA sprint titles while ineligible for international competition in 2002 after failing a drugs test in 2001 (when he won 100m, 200m and 110mh at the US Juniors) for a prescribed medication to treat Attention Deficit Disorder. Reinstated by IAAF in July 2002. Won 2005 World 100m title by biggest ever winning margin of 0.17. Won all five 100m competitions in 2006, including tying the world record with 9.77 in Doha and taking the US title, but had tested positive for testosterone before these performances. He received a four-year drugs ban but returned to competition in August 2010.

Tyson GAY b. 9 Aug 1982 Lexington 1.83m 73kg. adidas. Studied marketing at University of Arkansas.
At 100m/(200m)/4x100mR: OG: '08- sf, '12- 4/2R; WCh: '05- (4), '07- 1/1/1R, '09- 2; WCp: '06- 1/1R, '10- 1R. Won DL 2010, WAF 100m 2009, 200m 2005-06, US 100m 2007-08, 2013; 200m 2007, 2013; NCAA 100m 2004.
Five N.American 100m records 2008-12.
Progress at 100m, 200m: 2000- 10.56, 21.27; 2001- 10.28, 21.23; 2002- 10.27/10.08w, 20.88/20.21w; 2003- 10.01Aw/10.14w, 21.15/20.31w; 2004- 10.06/10.10w, 20.07; 2005- 10.08, 19.93; 2006- 9.84, 19.68; 2007- 9.84/9.76w, 19.62; 2008- 9.77/9.68w, 20.00; 2009- 9.69, 19.58; 2010- 9.78, 19.76; 2011- 9.79, 2012- 9.80, 20.21; 2013- 9.75dq, 19.74dq. pbs: 60m 6.39+ '09, 6.55i '05; 150mSt 14.51 '11, 200m/220ySt 19.41/19.54 '10, 400m 44.89 '10.
Ran four 200m races in under 19.85 in 2006. Then greatest ever sprint double (9.84 and 19.62) at 2007 US Champs and ran fastest ever 100m 9.68w/+4.1 (after US record in qf) to win US Olympic Trials in 2008 but pulled hamstring in 200m qf and unable to compete again until Olympics, where he was not back to top form. IAAF Athlete of the Year 2006. He tested positive for a banned substance (later reported as a steroid) in May 2013 and he withdrew from the World Championships; case still to be resolved.

Justin GAYMON b. 13 Dec 1986 Stewartsville, New Jersey 1.75m 70kg. Graduiate in advertising from University of Georgia.
At 400mh: won NACAC 2008.
Progress at 400mh: 2004- 52.87, 2005- 50.84, 2006- 50.20, 2007- 49.25, 2008- 48.46, 2009- 48.86, 2010- 48.65, 2011- 48.58, 2012- 48.97, 2013- 48.46. pbs: 200m 21.28 '08, 400m 45.94i/46.17 '08, 55mh 7.47i '07, 60mh 7.86i '09, 110mh 13.90 '06, 13.85w '07.

Arman HALL b 14 Feb 1994 Florida 1.88m 77kg. Student at University of Florida.
At 400m/4x400mR: WCh: '13- sf/1R; WJ: '12-2/1R; WY: '11- 1/1 medley R.
Progress at 400m: 2009- 48.72, 2010- 47.43, 2011-46.01, 2012- 45.39, 2013- 44.82. pb 200m 20.55Ai/20.58i '14, 20.73 '13.

James Edward 'Trey' HARDEE b. 7 Feb 1984 Birmingham, Alabama 1.96m 95kg. Nike. Was at Mississippi State University and University of Texas.
At Dec: OG: '08- dnf, '12- 2; WCh: '09- 1, '11- 1, '13- dnf; won NCAA 2005, US 2009. At Hep: WI: '10- 2.
Progress at Dec: 2003- 7544, 2004- 8041, 2005-7881, 2006- 8465, 2008- 8534, 2009- 8790, 2011-8689, 2012- 8671, 2013- dnf. pbs: 55m 6.30i '06, 60m 6.71i '06, 100m 10.39 '10, 10.28w '06; 200m 20.98 '06, 400m 47.51 '06, 1000m 2:45.67i '12, 1500m 4:40.94 '12, 60mh 7.70i '10, 110mh 13.54 '12; HJ 2.06i '10, 2.05 '08; PV 5.30Ai '06, 5.25 '08; LJ 7.88 '11, SP 15.94i '09, 15.72 '12; DT 52.68 '08, JT 68.99 '11, Hep 6208Ai '06.
Won IAAF Combined Events Challenge 2009. Engaged to Chelsea Johnson (PV 4.73 '08, 2= WCh 2009); her father Jan Johnson set a world indoor PV best 5.36 '70, won at the 1971 Pan-Ams and was the 1972 Olympic bronze medallist.

Antwon HICKS b. 12 Mar 1983 Hot Springs, Arkansas 1.87m 79kg. adidas. Sociology graduate of the University of Mississippi.
At 110mh: WJ: '02- 1; won NCAA indoor 60mh 2004-05.
Progress at 110mh: 2002- 13.59/13.42w, 2003-13.49/13.46w, 2004- 13.45, 2005- 13.35, 2006-13.49/13.37w, 2007- 13.36, 2008- 13.09, 2009-13.24, 2010- 13.29, 2011- 13.35, 2012- 13.14, 2013-13.25. pbs: 60m 6.80i '08, 100m 10.94 '07, 200m 21.39 '05, 55mh 7.15i '04, 60mh 7.53i '08, HJ 2.08/2.16i '01.

Reese HOFFA b. 8 Oct 1977 Evans, Georgia 1.82m 133kg. New York AC. Was at University of Georgia.
At SP: OG: '04- dnq 21, '08- 6, '12- 3; WCh: '03-07-09-11-13: dnq/1/4/4/4; PAm: '03- 1; WI: '04-06-08-12: 2/1/2/4; WUG: '01- 9; WCp: '06- 2; won WAF 2006-07, DL 2012, USA 2007-08, 2012.
Progress at SP: 1998- 19.08, 1999- 19.35, 2000-19.79, 2001- 20.22, 2002- 20.47, 2003- 20.95, 2004-21.67, 2005- 21.74i/21.29, 2006- 22.11i/21.96, 2007-22.43, 2008- 22.10, 2009- 21.89, 2010- 22.16, 2011-22.09, 2012- 22.00, 2013- 21.71. pbs: DT 58.46 '99, HT 60.05 '02.
Added 37cm to his best to win World Indoor gold 2006. Married Renata Foerst (HT 55.49 '04) in 2005.

Bershawn JACKSON b. 8 May 1983 Miami 1.73m 69kg. Nike. Studied accountancy at St Augustine's University, Raleigh.

At 400mh/4x400mR: OG: '08- 3; WCh: '03- h (dq), '05- 1, '07- sf/res 1R, '09- 3/res 1R, '11-6/1R, '13- sf; WJ: '02- 3/1R; CCp: '10- 3/1R; won DL 2010, WAF 2004-05, US 2003, 2008-10. At 400m: WI: '10- 5/1R; won US indoor 2005, 2010.
Progress at 400mh: 2000- 52.17, 2001- 50.86, 2002- 50.00, 2003- 48.23, 2004- 47.86, 2005- 47.30, 2006- 47.48, 2007- 48.13, 2008- 48.02, 2009- 47.98, 2010- 47.32, 2011- 47.93, 2012- 48.20, 2013- 48.09.
pbs: 200m 21.03/20.46w '04, 400m 45.06 '07, 500m 1:01.99i '14, 600m 1:18.65i '06, 800m 1:53.40 '11, 200mhSt 22.26 '11.

Evan JAGER b. 8 Mar 1989 Algonquin, Illinois 1.86m 66kg. Oregon TC. Was at University of Wisconsin.
At 3000mSt: OG: '12- 6; WCh: '13- 5; US champion 2012-13. At 1500m: WJ: '08- 8. At 5000m: WCh: '09- h.
N.American 3000m steeplechase record 2012.
Progress at 5000m, 3000mSt: 20009- 13:22.18, 2012- 8:06.81, 2013- 13:02.40, 8:08.60. pbs: 800m 1:50.10i '10, 1:51.04 '08; 1500m 3:36.34 '13, 1M 3:54.35 '09, 2000m 4:47.56i '14, 3000m 7:35.16 '12, 2M 8:14.95i '13.
Set US record in only his fifth steeplechase race, improving pb by 10.59 secs. In 2009 he had come 3rd in the US Champs in only his second race at 5000m.

Brandon JOHNSON b. 6 Mar 1985 Mannheim, Germany 1.75m 68kg Was at UCLA.
At 800m: WCh: '13. At 400mh: WJ: 04- 2/1 4x400mR.
Progress at 400mh, 800m: 2004- 48.62, 2005-48.59, 2006- 50.12, 2007- 49.02, 1:50.85; 2008-48.68, 2009- 50.12, 2012- 1:46.73, 2013- 1:43.84.
pbs: 60m 6.82i '06, 100m 10.60/10.44w '03, 10.2w '02; 200m 21.29 '05, 20.9w '03; 400m 46.34 '05, 1500m 3:53.95 '13.

Dustin 'Dusty' JONAS b. 19 Apr 1986 Floresville, Texas 1.98m 84kg. Nike. Was at University of Nebraska.
At HJ: OG: '08- dnq 26=; WCh: '11/13- dnq 30/16=; WI: '10- 3; PAm-J: '05- 1; CCp: '10- 6. Won NCAA indoor 2008.
Progress at HJ: 2002- 2.16, 2003- 2.22, 2004- 2.13, 2005- 2.24, 2006- 2.28, 2007- 2.25i/2.24, 2008-2.36A, 2009- 2.26i/2.24, 2010- 2.33, 2011- 2.31, 2012- 2.25i, 2013- 2.34i/2.31. pb LJ 7.47/7.76w '07; TJ 15.15i '12, 15.07 '07.

Trell KIMMONS b. 13 Jul 1985 Coldwater, Mississippi 1.78m 77kg. adidas. Was at Mississippi State University.
At 100m/4x100mR: OG: '12- 2R; WCh: '11- sf; WJ: '04- 1R. At 60m: WI: '10- 4, '12- 4.
N.American 4x100m record 2012.
Progress at 100m: 2003- 10.3w, 2004- 10.39/10.34w/10.0w, 2005- 10.22/10.16Aw, 2006- 10.17, 2007- 10.31/10.25w, 2008- 10.30, 2009- 10.16, 2010-9.95/9.92w, 2011- 10.04/9.97w, 2012- 10.02/10.00w, 2013- 10.22/10.02w. pbs: 50m 5.68i '12, 60m

USA 243

6.45Ai '12, 6.53i '06; 100y 9.37+ '10, 200m 20.37
'10, 20.3 '06, 20.32Aw '05; 400m 47.53 '10.
Standout football player in high school.
Joe KOVACS b. 28 Jun 1989 Nazareth,
Pennsylvania 1.88m 114kg. Was at Penn State
University.
Progress at SP: 2007- 16.49, 2008- 16.86i, 2009-
18.53, 2010- 19.36i/18.73, 2011- 19.84i/19.15, 2012-
21.08, 2013- 20.82, 2014- 21.46i. pbs: DT 56.08 '11,
HT 61.50 '11, Wt 19.07i '11.
Erik KYNARD b. 3 Feb 1991 Toledo, Ohio
1.93m 86kg. Kansas State University.
At HJ: OG: '12- 2; WCh: '11- dnq 14, '13- 5; WJ:
'08- dnq 19=; WI: '14- 4; Won US 2013, NCAA
2011-12.
Progress at HJ: 2007- 2.13i, 2008- 2.23i/2.15,
2009- 2.24i/2.22, 2010- 2.25, 2011- 2.33i/2.31,
2012- 2.34, 2013- 2.37, 2014- 2.34i. pb LJ 7.15i '09.
Bernard LAGAT b. 12 Dec 1974 Kapsabet,
Kenya 1.75m 61kg. Nike. Studied business management at Washington State University, USA.
At 1500m (/5000m): OG: '00- 3, '04- 2, '08- sf/9,
'12- (4); WCh: '01- 2, '05- sf, '07- 1/1, '09- 3/2, '11-
(2), '13- (6); WI: '03- 2; AfCh: '02- 1; WUG: '99- 1;
WCp: '02- 1; 2nd GP 1999-2000-02, WAF 2005-
06. At 3000m: WI: '01-04-10-12-14: 6/1/1/1/2;
CCp: '10- 1/(1). Won WAF 3000m 2005, 2008;
KEN 1500m 2002, US 1500m 2006, 2008; 5000m
2006-08, 2010-11, 2013; NCAA 5000m 1999 (and
indoor 1M/3000m).
Records: Commonwealth and KEN 1500m
2001, N.American 1500m 2005, 3000m 2010,
5000m 2010 & 2011, indoor 2000m 2014, 3000m
2007, 2M 2011 & 2013, 5000m 2010, 2012. World
M35 3000m & 5000m 2010, 1M and 5000m 2011,
2000m (i) 2014.
Progress at 1500m, 5000m: 1996- 3:37.7A, 1997-
3:41.19, 13:50.33; 1998- 3:34.48, 13:42.73; 1999-
3:30.56, 13:36.12; 2000- 3:28.51, 13:23.46; 2001-
3:26.34, 13:30.54; 2002- 3:27.91, 13:19.14; 2003-
3:30.55, 2004- 3:27.40, 2005- 3:29.30, 12:59.29;
2006- 3:29.68, 12:59.22; 2007- 3:33.85, 13:30.73;
2008- 3:32.75, 13:16.29; 2009- 3:32.56, 13:03.06;
2010- 3:32.51, 12:54.12; 2011- 3:33.11, 12:53.60;
2012- 3:34.63, 12:59.92; 2013- 3:36.36, 12:58.99.
pbs: 800m 1:46.00 '03, 1000m 2:16.18 '08, 1M
3:47.28 '01, 2000m 4:54.74i '14, 4:55.49 '99; 3000m
7:29.00 '10, 2M 8:09.49i '13, 8:12.45 '08, HMar
62:33 '13.
Gave up his final year of scholastic eligibility
(as under NCAA rules no payments can be
received) at his university in order to compete
(for money) in the 1999 GP Final, in which he
was 2nd. He was 2nd to Hicham El Guerrouj
six times in 2001, including his 3:26.34 at
Brussels for 2nd on the world all-time list, and
six times in 2002. Withdrew from 2003 Worlds
after testing positive for EPO, but this was later
repudiated. Lives in Tucson, Arizona, gained
US citizenship 2005. First man ever to win
1500m/5000m double at the US Champs in

2006 and at World Champs in 2007. Oldest ever
male World Indoor champion and medallist at
39y 87d in 2014.
A sister **Mary Chepkemboi** competed at the
1982 Commonwealth Games and won African
3000m in 1984, and another **Evelyne Jerotich
Langat** has 71:35 half marathon pb. Of his
brothers **William Cheseret** has a marathon pb
of 2:12:09 '04 and **Robert Cheseret** won NCAA
5000m in 2004 and 10,000m in 2005, pbs 5000m
13:13.23 & 10,000m 28:20.11 '05.
Tony McQUAY b. 16 Apr 1990 West Palm
Beach, Florida 1.80m 70kg. adidas. Was at
University of Florida.
At 400m: OG: '12- sf/2R; WCh: '11- h, '13- 2/1R;
US champion 2011, NCAA 2012.
Progress at 400m: 2008- 48.09, 2009- 46.84, 2010-
45.37, 2011- 44.68, 2012- 44.49, 2013- 44.40. pbs:
100m 10.22 '13, 200m 20.60 '12, 300m 32.40 '13.
Josh MANCE b. 21 Mar 1992 Los Angeles
1.91m 82kg. Was at University of Southern
California.
At 400m/4x400mR: OG: '12- res 2R; WCh: '13-
res 1R; WJ: '10- 5/1R; WY: '09- 2/1 Med R; PAm-
J: '11- 1/1R; US champion 2011, NCAA 2012.
Progress at 400m: 2007- 48.36, 2008- 46.61, 2009-
46.22, 2010- 45.90, 2011- 45.29, 2012- 44.83, 2013-
45.08. pbs: 200m 21.20 '11, 21.18w '10; 800m
1:51.16 '12.
Leonel MANZANO b. 12 Sep 1984 Dolores
Hidalgo, Guanajuato, Mexico 1.65m 57kg. Nike.
Was at the University of Texas.
At 1500m: OG: '08- sf,'12- 2; WCh: '07- h, '09- 12,
'11/13- sf; CCp: '10- 3. Won US 2012, NCAA
2005, 2008.
Progress at 1500m: 2003- 4:07.83M, 2005- 3:37.13,
2006- 3:39.49, 2007- 3:35.29, 2008- 3:36.67, 2009-
3:33.33, 2010- 3:32.37, 2011- 3:33.66, 2012- 3:34.08,
2013- 3:33.14. pbs: 800m 1:44.56 '10, 1000m
2:19.73 '09, 1M 3:50.64 '10, 3000m 8:14.59i '06.
Has lived in the USA from the age of 4.
Cory MARTIN b. 22 May 1985 Bloomington,
Indiana 1.96m 125kg. Nike. Was at Auburn
University.
At SP: WCh: '13- 9; WJ: '04- 11 (dnq 15 HT); Won
NCAA SP & HT 2008.
Progress at SP: 2004- 17.95i/17.60, 2005- 18.85,
2006- 18.42i, 2007- 19.63, 2008- 20.35, 2009- 20.43,
2010- 22.10, 2011- 20.72, 2012- 21.31, 2013- 20.67.
pbs: DT 58.59 '08, HT 75.06 '09, 35lbWt 24.38i '10.
Aries MERRITT b. 24 Jul 1985 Marietta,
Georgia 1.83m 74kg. Nike. Studied sports man-
agement at University of Tennessee.
At 110mh: OG: '12- 1; WCh: '09- h, '11- 5=, '13- 6;
WJ: '04- 1. At 60mh: WI: '12-1, Won DL 110mh
2012, NCAA 60mh indoors & 110mh 2006, US
indoor 60mh & 110mh 2012.
World 110mh record 2012.
Progress at 110mh: 2004- 13.47, 2005- 13.38/
13.34w, 2006- 13.12, 2007- 13.09, 2008- 13.24,

2009- 13.15, 2010- 13.61, 2011- 13.12, 2012- 12.80, 2013- 13.09. pbs: 55m 6.43i '05, 60m 6.90i '10, 200m 21.31 '05, 50mh 6.54i '12, 55mh 7.02+i '12, 60mh 7.43Ai/7.44i '12, 400mh 51.94 '04.
Record 8 (and 2w) sub-13 second times in 2012.

LaShawn MERRITT b. 27 Jun 1986 Portsmouth, Virginia 1.88m 82kg. Nike. Studied sports management at Old Dominion University, Norfolk, Virginia.
At 400m/4x400mR: OG: '08- 1/1R, '12- dnf ht; WCh: '05- res(1)R, '07- 2/1R, '09- 1/1R, '11- 2/1R. '13- 1/1R; WJ: '04- 1/1R (1 at 4x100); WI: '06- 1R; WCp: '06- 1/1R; won WAF 2007-09, DL 2013; US 2008-09, 2012-13.
World junior records 4x100m and 4x400m 2004, World indoor 400m junior best (44.93) 2005.
Progress at 200m, 400m: 2002- 21.46, 2003- 21.33, 47.9?; 2004- 20.72/20.69w, 45.25; 2005- 20.38, 44.66; 2006- 20.10, 44.14; 2007- 19.98, 43.96; 2008- 20.08/19.80w, 43.75; 2009- 20.07, 44.06; 2011- 20.13, 44.63; 2012- 20.16, 44.12; 2013- 20.26, 43.74. pbs: 55m 6.33i '04, 60m 6.68i '06, 100m 10.47/10.38w '04, 300m 31.30 '09, 500m 1:01.39i '12.
World age-18 400m record with 44.66 in 2005 and world low-altitude 300m best 2006 and 2009. Spent a year at East Carolina University before signing for Nike and returning home to Portsmouth. Two-year drugs ban for three positive tests from October 2009, reduced by three months after US arbitration panel declared that he had taken the steroid accidentally in buying a product intended for sexual enhancement; successfully challenged IOC rule preventing anyone serving 6 months or more from a drugs offence from competing in the next Games. Injured, he had to pull up in 2012 Olympic heat.

Curtis MITCHELL b. 11 Mar 1989 Daytona Beach 1.88m 79kg. Was at Texas A&M University.
At 200m: WCh: '13- 3; WJ: '08- 4; Won NCAA indoors 2010, NACC 2010.
Progress at 200m: 2007- 21.62, 2008- 20.74, 2009- 20.58, 2010- 19.99, 2011- 20.98, 2012- 20.89/20.24w, 2013- 19.97. pbs: 60m 6.85i '10, 100m 10.25 '10, 10.23w '08.

Maurice MITCHELL b. 22 Dec 1989 Kansas City, Missouri 1.78m 73kg. Nike. Studied social sciences at Florida State University.
At 200m: OG: '12- sf; Won NCAA 2011-12. At 4x100m: WCh: '11- h.
Progress at 200m: 2007- 20.77, 2008- 21.40/21.23w/20.5w, 2009- 20.64, 2010- 20.24, 2011- 20.19/19.99w, 2012- 20.13/20.08w, 2013- 20.32. pbs: 60m 6.55i '11, 100m 10.00 '11, 400m 47.60.

Bryshon NELLUM b. 1 May 1989 Los Angeles 1.83m 79kg. Was at University of Southern California.
At 400m/4x400mR: OG: '12- sf/2R; WJ: '06- 1R; WY: '05- 3; PAm-J: '07- 1. Won NCAA 2013.
Progress at 400m: 2004- 47.27, 2005- 46.81, 2006- 46.20, 2007- 45.38, 2010- 45.94, 2011- 45.56, 2012-

44.80, 2013- 44.73. pb 200m 20.23/19.99w '13.
Career seriously threatened when he was shot three times in the leg by gang in 2009.

Gunnar NIXON b. 13 Jan 1993 Waetherford, Oklahoma 1.90m 77kg.
At Dec: WCh: '13- 13; WJ: '12- 1; PAm-J '11- 2.
Unrtatified world heptathlon indoor record & N.American junior decathlon record 2012.
Progress at Dec: 2007- 7245, 2008- 7721 2009- 8146, 2012- 7892, 2013- 8312. pbs: 60m 6,86A '13. 100m 10.80 '13, 10.74w '13; 400m 48.56 '13, 1500m 4:22.36 '12, 160mh 7.93Ai '13, 10mh 14.51 '12, HJ 2.17 '12, PV 4.80A/4.66 '13, LJ 7.80 '13. SP 14.08 '11, DT 42.23 '12, JT 60.44 '13., Hep 6232A '13

David OLIVER b. 24 Apr 1982 Orlando 1.88m 93kg. Nike. Marketing graduate of Howard University.
At 110mh: OG: '08- 3; WCh: '07- sf, '11- 4, '13- 1; CCp: '10- 1. Won DL 2010, 2013; WAF 2008, US 2008, 2010-11. At 60mh: WI: '10- 3.
Two North American 110mh records 2010.
Progress at 110mh: 2001- 14.04, 2002- 13.92/13.88w, 2003- 13.60, 2004- 13.55, 2005- 13.29/13.23w, 2006- 13.20, 2007- 13.14, 2008- 12.95/12.89w, 2009- 13.09, 2010- 12.89, 2011- 12.94, 2012- 13.07, 2013- 13.00. pbs: 60m 6.88i '04, 50mh 6.50i '12, 55mh 7.01+i '12, 60mh 7.37i '11.
Mother, Brenda Chambers, 400mh pb 58.54 '80.

Omoghan OSAGHAE b. 18 May 1988 Lubbock 1.84m 75kg. Was at Texas Tech University.
At 60mh: WI: '14- 1; US indoor champion 2011, 2013-14.
Progress at 110mh: 2007- 13.99, 2008- 13.65, 2009- 13.51/13.42w, 2011- 13.23/13.22w, 2012- 13.24, 2013- 13.35/13.31w. pbs: 100m 10.62 '11, 60m 7.01i '08, 100m 10.64 '11, 200m 21.13 '09, 50mh 6.52i '12, 55mh 7.07i '11. 60mh 7.45i '14.
His father played soccer for Nigeria.

David PAYNE b. 24 Jul 1982 Cincinnati 1.85m 81kg. Was at University of Cincinnati.
At 110mh: OG: '08- 2; WCh: '07- 3, '09- 3; PAm: '07- 2. US champion 2009.
Progress at 110mh: 2002- 13.92, 2003- 13.53, 2004- 13.48/13.42w, 2005- 13.33, 2006- 13.31, 2007- 13.02, 2008- 13.17/13.06w, 2009- 13.12, 2010- 13.22, 2011- 13.63, 2012- 13.32/13.22w, 2013- 13.30/13.22w. pbs: 100m 10.56 '07, 200m 21.15 '07, 60mh 7.51i '07, 400mh 51.16 '04.

Jeff PORTER b. 27 Nov 1985 Summit, New Jersey 1.83m 84kg. Sports management degree from University of Michigan.
At 110mh: OG: '12- sf; PAm: '11- 4. Won NCAA indoor 60mh 2007.
Progress at 110mh: 2004- 14.08, 2005- 14.12, 2006- 13.93/13.92w, 2007- 13.57, 2008- 13.47, 2009- 13.37, 2010- 13.45, 2011- 13.26, 2012- 13.08, 2013- 13.35. pbs: 60m 6.77i '14, 100m 10.56 '11, 50mh 6.50i '12, 60mh 7.46i '14.
Married to Tiffany Porter (see UK). His twin brother Joe played in the NFL.

Jason RICHARDSON b. 4 Apr 1986 Houston 1.86m 73kg. Nike. Was at University of South Carolina.
At 110mh: OG: '12- 2; WCh: '11- 1, '13- 4; WY: '03- 1 (1 400mh); won NCAA 2008.
Progress at 110mh: 2004- 13.76, 2005- 13.50, 2006- 13.43/13.36w, 2008- 13.21, 2009- 13.29, 2010- 13.34, 2011- 13.04, 2012- 12.98, 2013- 13.20/13.17w.
pbs: 100m 10.90 '03, 200m 21.13 '03, 400m 46.96 '12, 60mh 7.53i '08, 400mh 49.79 '04.

Kurt ROBERTS b. 20 Feb 1988 Lancaster, Ohio 1.91m 127kg. Was at Ashland University.
Progress at SP: 2007- 16.39, 2008- 17.81, 2009- 18.78, 2010- 19.80i/18.76, 2011- 19.55, 2012- 21.14, 2013- 20.98, 2014- 21.50i.

Michael RODGERS b. 24 Apr 1985 Brenham, Texas 1.78m 73kg. Nike. Studied kinesiology at Oklahoma Baptist University.
At 100m/4x100mR: WCh: '09- sf, '13- 6/2R; At 60m: WI: '08- 4, '10- 2. Won US 100m 2009, indoor 60m 2008.
Progress at 100m: 2004- 10.55/10.31w, 2005- 10.30/10.25w, 2006- 10.29/10.18w, 2007- 10.10, 10.07w, 2008- 10.06/10.01w, 2009- 9.94/9.9/9.85w, 2010- 10.00/9.99w, 2011- 9.85, 2012- 9.94, 2013- 9.90. pbs: 60m 6.48Ai/6.50i '11, 200m 20.24 '09.
Dropped out of US World Champs team after positive test for stimulant on 19 July 2011, for which he subsequently received a 9-month suspension. Younger sister Alishea Usery won US junior 400m 2009, pb 53.27 '09.

Galen RUPP b. 8 May 1986 Portland 1.80m 62kg. Nike. Studied business at University of Oregon.
At (5000/)10,000m: OG: '08- 13, '12- 7/2; WCh: '07- 11, '09- 8, '11- 9/7, '13- 8/4. At 5000m: WJ: '04- 9; PAm-J: '03- 1. At 3000m: WI: '10- 5, '14- 4; WY: '03- 7. Won US 5000m 2012, 10,000m 2009- 13, NCAA 5000m & 10,000m (& indoor 3000m & 5000m) 2009, CC 2008.
North American records: 10,000m 2011, junior 5000m 2004, 10,000m 2005; indoor 5000m (13:11.44) 2011 & 2014, 3000m 2013, 2M 2012, 2014.
Progress at 5000m, 10,000m: 2002- 14:34.05, 2003- 14:20.29, 2004- 13:37.91, 29:09.56; 2005- 13:44.72. 28:15.52; 2006- 13:47.04, 30:42.10; 2007- 13:30.49, 27:33.48; 2008- 13:59.14, 27:36.99; 2009- 13:18.12i/13:42.59+, 27:37.99; 2010- 13:07.35, 27:10.74; 2011- 13:06.86, 26:48.00; 2012- 12:58.90, 27:25.33; 2013- 13:01.37, 27:24.39; 2014- 13:01.26i.
pbs: 800m 1:49.87i/1:50.00 '09, 1500m 3:34.75 '12, 1M 3:50.92i/3:52.11 '13, 3000m 7:30.16i '13, 7:43.24 '10, 2M 8:07.41i '14, HMar 60:30 '11.

Charles SILMON b. 4 Jul 1991 Waco, Texas 1.75m 72kg. Student at Texas Christian University.
At 100m/4x100mR: WCh: '13- h/2R; WJ: 2/1R; won NCAA 2013.
Progress at 100m, 200m: 2007- 10.60, 21.53; 2008- 10.56/10.47w, 21.02; 2009- 10.41/10.24w, 2010-

10.23, 20.65A/20.58w; 2011- 10.20A/10.24/10.18w, 20.56A/20.60; 2012- 10.05/10.04w, 20.65; 2013- 9.98/9.85w, 20.23. pbs: 60m 6.60i '13.

Duane SOLOMON b. 28 Dec 1984 Lompoc, California 1.91m 77kg. Sociology graduate of University of Southern California.
At 800m: OG: '12- 4; WCh: '07- h, '13- 6; PAm: '07- h. Won US 2013, US indoor 2011.
World indoor 4x800m record 2014.
Progress at 800m: 2002- 1:51.76, 2003- 1:49.79, 2005- 1:47.84, 2006- 1:47.45, 2007- 1:45.69, 2008- 1:45.71, 2009- 1:46.82, 2010- 1:45.23, 2011- 1:45.86, 2012- 1:42.82, 2013- 1:43.27. pbs: 400m 45.98 '12, 600m 1:13.28 '13, 1000m 2:17.84 '10, 1500m 3:48.29 '08, 1M 4:03.26 '10.

Wallace SPEARMON b. 24 Dec 1984 Chicago 1.90m 80kg. Saucony. Was at University of Arkansas.
At 200m/4x100mR: OG: '08- dq, '12- 4; WCh: '05-07-09-13: 2/3&1R/3/sf; WCp: '06- 1/1R, '10- 1/1R. Won DL 2006, US 2006, 2010, 2012; NCAA 2004-05. At 4x400m: WI: '06- 1R.
WIR 4x400m and world indoor best 300m 2006.
Two US indoor 200m records 2005.
Progress at 100m, 200m: 2003- 21.05, 2004- 10.38, 20.25/20.12w; 2005- 10.35/10.21w, 19.89; 2006- 10.11, 19.65; 2007- 9.96, 19.82; 2008- 10.07, 19.90; 2009- 10.18, 19.85; 2010- 10.15, 19.79/19.77w; 2011- 20.18; 2012- 10.26/10.06w, 19.90/19.82w; 2013- 10.29/9.92w, 20.10. pbs: 60m 6.66i '12, 150mSt 14.87 '12, 300m 31.88i '06, 32.14 '09; 400m 45.22 '06.
Disqualified for running out of his lane after crossing the line in 3rd place at the 2008 Olympics. His father (also Wallace, b. 3 Sep 1962) had pbs: 100m 10.19 '87, 10.05w '86, 10.0w '81; 200m 20.27/20.20w '87; 1 WUG 200/4x100m, 3 PAm 200m 1987.

Nick SYMMONDS b. 30 Dec 1983 Blytheville, Arkansas 1.78m 73kg. Brooks Beasts TC. Biochemistry graduate of Willamette University.
At 800m: OG: '08- sf, '12- 5; WCh: '07-09-11-13: sf/6/5/2; WI: '08- 6; CCp: '10- 5. US champion 2008-12.
Progress at 800m: 2003- 1:49.51, 2004- 1:50.87, 2005- 1:48.82, 2006- 1:45.83, 2007- 1:44.54, 2008- 1:44.10, 2009- 1:43.83, 2010- 1:43.76, 2011- 1:43.83, 2012- 1:42.95, 2013- 1:43.03. pbs: 400m 48.84 '04, 600m 1:14.47 '08, 1000m 2:16.35 '10, 1000m 2:18.87i '14, 2:20.52 '09; 1500m 3:34.55 '13, 1M 3:56.72i '07, 4:00.21 '13.

Angelo TAYLOR b. 29 Dec 1978 Albany, Georgia 1.88m 84kg. Nike. Was at Georgia Tech University. Electrician.
At 400mh/4x400mR: OG: '00- 1/dq (res 1)R, '04- sf, '08- 1/1R, 12- 5/2R; WCh: '99- h/dq(1)R, '01- sf/dq(1)R, '07- (3 400m)/1R, '09- h/1R, '11- 7/1R; WJ: '96- 3; PAm-J: '97- 1/1R; won GP 2000 (and overall), NCAA 1998, US 400mh 1999-2001, 400m 2007, indoor 400m 1999

Progress at 400m, 400mh: 1995- -, 52.76, 1996-46.7, 50.18; 1997- 46.19i/46.81, 48.72; 1998- 45.14, 47.90; 1999- 45.50i, 48.15; 2000- 44.89, 47.50; 2001-44.68, 47.95; 2002- 44.85, 48.87; 2003- 46.32, 48.94; 2004- 45.85, 48.03; 2006- 45.24, 49.44; 2007- 44.05, 48.45; 2008- 44.38, 47.25; 2009- 45.15, 48.30; 2010-44.72, 47.79; 2011- 44.82, 47.94; 2012- 44.93, 47.95; 2013- 46.80, 51.55. pbs: 100m 10.58 '08, 200m 20.23 '10, 300m 32.67 '02, TJ 14.76 '96.
Brilliant year in 1998, with fastest ever time by a 19 year-old and losing just twice (to Bryan Bronson) at 400mh. Went out in his heat (misjudging the finish) when favourite for 1999 World 400mh, but made amends with relay gold, and, after winning Olympic gold in 2000, stumbled off the last hurdle in 2001 World 400mh semi. Regained Olympic title in 2008.

Christian TAYLOR b. 18 Jun 1990 Fayetteville 1.90m 75kg. Student at University of Florida.
At (LJ/)TJ: OG: '12- 1; WCh: '11- 1, '13- 4; WI: '12- 2; WJ: '08- 7/8 (res 1 4x400m); WY: '07- 3/1. Won DL 2012-13, NACAC 2010-11, US 2011-12, NCAA indoor 2009-10.
Progress at TJ: 2007- 15.98, 2008- 16.05, 2009-16.98i/16.65/16.91w, 2010- 17.18i/17.02/17.09w, 2011- 17.96, 2012- 17.81, 2013- 17.66. pbs: 60m 6.79i '11, 200m 20.70 '13, 400m 45.34 '09, LJ 8.19 '10.
Both parents came from Barbados.

Michael TINSLEY b. 21 Apr 1984 Little Rock, Arkansas 1.85m 74kg. adidas. Studied criminal justice at Jackson State University.
At 400mh: OG: '12- 2; WCh: '13- 2; won NCAA 2008, US 2012-13.
Progress at 400mh: 2002- 52.5, 2004- 50.87, 2005-48.55, 2006- 48.25, 2007- 48.02, 2008- 48.84, 2009-48.53, 2010- 48.46, 2011- 48.45, 2012- 47.91, 2013-47.70. pbs: 60m 6.92i '05, 200m 20.66 '09, 20/34w '13; 400m 46.02i '06, 46.05 '07; 55mh 7.39i '04, 60mh 7.84i '06, 110mh 13.86 '04.

Brad WALKER b. 21 Jun 1981 Aberdeen, South Dakota 1.88m 86kg. New York AC. Graduated in business administration from University of Washington
At PV: OG: '08- dnq nh, '12- nh; WCh: '05- 2, '07- 1, '13- 4; WI: '06-08-12: 1/2/3; Won WAF 2005, 2007; US 2005, 2007, 2009, 2012-13; indoors 2005-06, NCAA indoor 2003-04.
North American pole vault record 2008.
Progress at PV: 1999- 4.80, 2000- 5.12, 2001- 5.48i/5.36, 2002- 5.64, 2003- 5.80i/5.65, 2004- 5.82, 2005-5.96, 2006- 6.00, 2007- 5.95, 2008- 6.04, 2009- 5.80, 2010- 5.61, 2011- 5.84, 2012- 5.90, 2013- 5.83.

Jeremy WARINER b. 31 Jan 1984 Irving, Texas 1.83m 70kg. adidas. Studied outdoor recreation at Baylor University.
At 400m/4x400mR: OG: '04- 1/1R, '08- 2/1R; WCh: '05- 1/1R, '07- 1/1R, '09- 2/1R; PAm-J: '03-2/1R; CCp: '10- 1. Won DL 2010, US 2004-05, NCAA 2004, WAF 2006.
WIR 4x400m 2006.

Progress at 200m, 400m: 2001- 21.33/21.23w, 46.68; 2002- 21.17/20.8/20.41w, 45.57; 2003- 20.78, 45.13; 2004- 20.59, 44.00; 2005- 20.52w, 43.93; 2006- 20.19, 43.62; 2007- 20.35, 43.45; 2008- 20.37, 43.82; 2009- 20.30, 44.60; 2010- 44.13. 2011- 20.71, 44.88; 2012- 20.53, 44.96; 2013- 20.99Ai, 45.35. pbs: 100m 10.52w '02, 300m 31.58+ '07.
His 43.93 to win 2005 World title was world's fastest 400m time for five years, his 43.62 to win Rome GP in 2006 the fastest for seven years and his 43.45 to win the 2007 World title took him to third on the world all-time list. He shared the Golden League jackpot and won all eleven 400m races in 2006 with three sub-44 times (a record seven sub-44.25s and 10 sub 44.50s) until he dropped out in Shanghai. Won all 10 races in 2007 apart from failure to start in Sheffield.

Ryan WHITING b. 24 Nov 1986 Harrisburg PA 1.91m 131kg. Nike. Studied civil engineering at Arizona State University.
At SP: OG: '12- 9; WCh: '11- 6, '13- 2; WI: '12- 1, '14- 1; PAm-J: '05- 1 (1 DT); Won DL 2013, US 2013, NACAC 2009, NCAA 2009-10, indoor 2008-10, DT 2010.
Progress at SP: 2006- 19.75, 2007- 20.35, 2008-21.73i/20.60, 2009- 20.99, 2010- 21.97, 2011- 21.76, 2012- 22.00i/21.66, 2013- 22.28, 2014- 22.23i. pb DT 61.11 '08, Wt 18.94i '10.

Jesse WILLIAMS b. 27 Dec 1983 Modesto 1.84m 75kg. Oregon TC. Graduate of University of Southern California, formerly at North Carolina State.
At HJ: OG: '08- dnq 19=, '12- 9=; WCh: '05/07-dnq 15/26, '11- 1, '13- dnq 23=; WJ: '02- 4=; WI: '08-10-12: 6=/5/6=; Won US 2008, 2010-11; NCAA indoors and out 2005-06; DL 2011.
Progress at HJ: 2001- 2.16, 2002- 2.21, 2003- 2.24, 2004- 2.24, 2005- 2.30, 2006- 2.32, 2007- 2.33, 2008- 2.32i/2.30, 2009- 2.36i/2.34, 2010- 2.34Ai/2.30, 2011- 2.37, 2012- 2.36, 2013- 2.31. pb LJ 7.53 '06. Also a wrestler in high school.

Ryan WILSON b. 19 Dec 1980 Columbus, Ohio 1.88m 81kg. Nike. Graduate (art) of University of Southern California.
At 110mh: WCh: '13- 2; won NCAA 2003.
Progress at 110mh: 2000- 14.00/13.79w, 2001-13.69, 2002- 13.55, 2003- 13.35, 2004- 13.65/13.58w, 2005- 13.99, 2006- 13.22, 2007- 13.02, 2008- 13.28, 2009- 13.21, 2010- 13.12, 2011- 13.36/13.35w, 2012-13.18, 2013- 13.08. pbs: 400m 48.52 '01, 50mh 6.78i '02, 55mh 7.18+i '12, 60mh 7.75i '12, 400mh 49.33 '03, LJ 7.29 '02.

Isiah YOUNG b. 5 Jan 1990 Manhattan, Kansas 1.83m 75kg. Student at University of Mississippi.
At 200m: OG: '12- sf; WCh: '13- sf.
Progress at 100m, 200m: 2008- 10.96; 2009- 10.44, 21.50/21.33w; 2010- 10.32, 20.98; 2011- 10.31, 20.81; 2012- 10.09/10.08w, 20.33/20.16w; 2013-9.99/9.93w, 19.86. pbs: 60m 6.61i '12.

Women

Nia ALI b. 23 Oct 1988 Philadelphia 1.70m 64kg. Nike. Was at University of Southern California. At 100mh: WCh: '13- sf; WUG: '11- 1. Won NCAA 2011=. At 60mh: WI: '14- 1, won US indoor 2013-14.
Progress at 100mh: 2005- 14.20, 2006- 13.63/13.55w, 2007- 13.25, 2008- 13.14, 2009- 13.17, 2011- 12.73/12.63w, 2012- 12.78, 2013- 12.48. pbs: 60m 7.43i '14, 200m 23.90 '09, 800m 2:24.55 '07, 60mh 7.80i '14, HJ 1.86 '11, LJ 5.89 '09, SP 13.61 '09, JT 39.24 '09, Hep 5824 '09.

Alexandria ANDERSON b. 28 Jan 1987 Chicago 1.75m 60kg. Nike. Was at University of Texas. At 100m/4x100mR: WCh: '11- res (1)R, '13- 7/2R; WJ: '04- 1R, '06- 5/1R. At 200m: PAm-J: '05- 2. Won NCAA 100m 2009.
Progress at 100m, 200m: 2002- 11.81, 24.10w; 2003- 11.62, 23.48; 2004- 11.41, 23.45; 2005- 11.39/ 11.38w, 22.96; 2006- 11.12/11.10w, 23.16/23.14w; 2007- 11.21/11.11w, 22.67; 2008- 11.07/10.98w, 22.75; 2009- 11.02/10.92w, 22.60; 2010- 11.04, 22.83; 2011- 11.01/10.91w, 22.87; 2012- 11.12/10.88w, 22.98/22.84w; 2013- 10.91, 22.67w. pbs: 50m 6.28i '12, 55m 6.88i '06, 60m 7.12Ai '11, 7.17i '08; 400m 52.63 '05, 60mh 8.83Ai '06, LJ 6.32 '05, TJ 11.68 '07.

Brigetta BARRETT b. 24 Dec 1990 Valhalla, New York 1.83m 64kg. Student at University of Arizona.
At HJ: OG: '12- 2; WCh: '11- 10, "13- 2; WUG: '11- 1. Won US 2011, 2013; NCAA 2011-13.
Progress at HJ: 2007- 1.72, 2008- 1.83A, 2009- 1.83, 2010- 1.91, 2011- 1.96, 2012- 2.03, 2013- 2.04. pb 400m 55.04 '13.

Tianna BARTOLETTA b. 30 Aug 1985 Elyria, Ohio 1.68m 60kg. née Madison. Nike. Studied biology at University of Central Florida, formerly at University of Tennessee.
At 100m/4x100mR: OG: '12- 4/1R. At LJ: WCh: '05- 1, '07- 10; WI: '06- 1; PAm-J: '03- 4, NCAA champion indoors and out 2005. At 60m: WI: '12- 3, '14- 3; won US indoor 2012.
Progress at 100m, LJ: 2000- 5.73, 2001- 6.07, 2002- 11.98/11.91w, 6.20; 2003- 11.68, 6.28; 2004- 11.50/ 11.35w, 6.60; 2005- 11.41, 6.89/6.92w; 2006- 11.52/ 11.50w, 6.80i/6.60; 2007- 6.60/6.61w; 2008- 11.54, 6.53/6.58w; 2009- 11.05, 6.48; 2010- 11.20, 6.44; 2011- 11.29, 6.21/6.58w; 2012- 10.85, 6.48; 2013- 11.41, 23.30. pbs: 55m 6.69i '09, 60m 7.02i '12, 200m 22.37/22.33w '12.
Set long jump pbs in qualifying and final of 2005 Worlds. Now concentrating on sprinting, but also competed on the US bobsled team in 2012/13. Married John Bartoletta in 2012.

Jessica BEARD b. 8 Jan 1989 Euclid, Ohio 1.68m 57kg. adidas. Psychology student at Texas A&M University.
At 400m/4x400mR: WCh: '09- sf/res (1)R, '11- sf/1R, '13- 2R; WJ: '06- 5/1R, '08- 2/1R; PAm-J: '07- 3; won NCAA 2011.

Progress at 400m: 2004- 55.22, 2005- 52.39, 2006- 51.89, 2007- 51.63, 2008- 51.09A/51.47, 2009- 50.56, 2010- 51.02, 2011- 51.06, 2012- 51.19, 2013- 51.05. pbs: 60m 7.52i '11, 100m 11.86 '09, 11.49w '11; 200m 22.81 '13.

Amanda BINGSON b. 20 Feb 1990 Victorville, Calfornia 1.70m 89kg. New York AC. Sports psychology graduate of University of Nevada, Las Vegas.
At HT: OG: '12- dnq 27; WCh: '13- 10. US champion 2013; NACAC 2012.
North American hammer record 2013.
Progress at SP: 2009- 55.19, 2010- 64.07, 2011- 69.79, 2012- 71.78, 2013- 75.73, 2014- 75.12. pbs: DT 46.08A '11, Wt 22.42i '14. Former gymnast.

Tia BROOKS b. 2 Aug 1990 Saginaw, Michigan 1.83m 109kg. University of Oklahoma.
At SP: OG: '12- dnq 19, WCh: '13- 8. NCAA champion indoors and out 2012-13.
Progress at SP: 2008- 14.64, 2009- 14.13i/14.09. 2010- 17.37, 2011- 18.00, 2012- 19.00i/18.47, 2013- 19.22i/18.96. pb DT 43.71 '08.

Stephanie BROWN TRAFTON b. 1 Dec 1979 San Luis Obispo, California 1.93m 102kg. née Brown. Nike. Engineering graduate of Cal Poly San Luis Obispo.
At DT: OG: '04- dnq 21, '08- 1, '12- 7; WCh: '09- 12, '11- 5. US champion 2009, 2011-12.
US discus record 2012.
Progress at DT: 1997- 45.78, 1998- 55.24, 1999- 52.79, 2001- 51.46, 2002- 54.11, 2003- 57.78, 2004- 61.90, 2005- 55.35, 2006- 59.03, 2007- 61.40, 2008- 66.17, 2009- 66.21, 2010- 65.11, 2011- 64.13, 2012- 67.74, 2013- 55.11. pb SP 17.86 '04.
Former basketball player. Married Jerry Trafton in March 2005, daughter Juliana born September 2013.

T'Erea BROWN b. 24 Oct 1989 Charleston, Missouri 1.78m 59kg. adidas. Studied advertising at University of Miami.
At 400mh: OG: '12- 6. US champion 2010, NCAA 2011.
Progress at 400mh: 2005- 60.60, 2006- 60.45, 2007- 62.60, 2008- 56.72, 2009- 55.98. 2010- 54.74, 2011- 55.59, 2012- 54.21, 2013- 54.83. pbs: 200m 24.81 '08, 400m 53.25i '11, 60mh 8.00i '10, 100mh 12.84/12.70w '10.

Mary CAIN b. 3 May 1996 New York 1.70m 50kg. Bronxville HS, New York.
At 1500m: WCh: '13- 10; WJ: '12- 6.
Two world junior indoor 1000m records 2014; North American junior records: 800m, 1500m, indoor 1500m 2013-14, 1M 2014.
Progress at 1500m: 2011- 4:23.59, 2012- 4:11.01, 2013- 4:04.62. pbs: 800m 1:59.51 '13, 1000m 2:25.80i '14, 1M 4:24.11i '14, 4:39.28 '12; 3000m 9:02.10i '13, 2M 9:38.68Mi '13, 5000m 15:45.46 '13.

Amber CAMPBELL b. 5 Jun 1981 Indianapolis 1.70m 91kg. Nike. Was at Coastal Carolina University.

At HT: OG: '08/12- dnq 21/12; WCh: '05-11-13: dnq 18/13/13, '09- 11; PAm: '11- 3. Won US HT 2012, indoor Wt 2007-11.
Progress at HT: 2000- 49.16, 2001- 62.08, 2002- 63.76, 2003- 64.58, 2004- 67.23, 2005- 69.52, 2006- 67.52, 2007- 70.33, 2008- 70.19, 2009- 70.61, 2010- 71.94, 2011- 72.59, 2012- 71.80, 2013- 73.03. pbs: SP 14.81i '02, 14.42 '04; 20lb Wt 24.70i '10.

Kori CARTER b. 6 Mar 1992 Pasadena 1.65m 57kg. Nike. Human biology student at Stanford University.
At 4000mh: WJ: '08- h; Won NCAA 2013. At 100mh: WY: '09- 2.
Progress at 400mh: 2007- 62.21, 2008- 60.22, 2009- 59.89, 2010- 60.47, 2011- 57.10, 2012- 57.60, 2013- 53.21. pbs: 100m 11.57 '11, 200m 23.67 '12. 60mh 8.17Ai '13, 100mh 12.76 '13.

Michelle CARTER b. 12 Oct 1985 San Jose 1.75m 110kg. Nike. Liberal arts graduate from University of Texas.
At SP: OG: '08- 15, '12- 5; WCh: '09- 6, '11- 9, '13- 4; WI: '12- 3, '14- 5; WJ: '04- 1; WY: '01- 2; PAm: '11- 3; PAm-J: '03- 1. US champion 2008-09, 2011, 2013; NCAA indoor 2006.
North American shot record 2013.
Progress at SP: 2000- 14.76, 2001- 15.23, 2002- 16.25, 2003- 16.73, 2004- 17.55, 2005- 18.26, 2006- 17.98, 2007- 17.57, 2008- 18.85, 2009- 19.13, 2010- 18.80, 2011- 19.86, 2012- 19.60, 2013- 20.24. pbs: DT 54.06 '07.
Her father Mike set a world junior shot record in 1970 and won the Olympic silver in 1984, seven NCAA titles (4 in, 3 out) (for a unique father-daughter double) and WUG gold in 1981 and 1983, pb 21.76 '84. Her younger sister D'Andra (b. 17 Jun 1987) won the NCAA discus in 2009, pb 57.73 '08.

Kristi CASTLIN b. 7 Jul 1988 Douglasville, Georgia 1.70m 79kg. adidas. Political science graduate of Virginia Tech University.
At 100mh: Won PAm-J 2007. At 60mh: WI: '12- dq/false start ht; won US indoors 2012.
Progress at 100mh: 2005- 13.85, 2006- 13.73, 2007- 12.91/12.82w, 2008- 12.81, 2009- 12.89, 2010- 12.83/12.59w, 2011- 12.83/12.68w, 2012- 12.56/12.48w, 2013- 12.61. pbs: 55m 7.04i '08, 60m 7.47i '08, 100m 11.60 '12, 11.49w '11; 200m 23.46 '12, 50mh 6.81+i '12, 55mh 7.37i '12, 60mh 7.84Ai/7.91i '12. 400mh 60.44 '07.

Jessica COSBY TORUGA b. 31 May 1982 Reseda, California 1.73m 77kg. Nike. Was at UCLA (now strength coach there).
At HT: OG: '08/12- dnq nt/13; WCh: '07: dnq 14, '09- 7, '11- 10; won NACAC 2007, US 2006, 2008- 09, 2011. At SP: WJ: '00- 9, won NCAA 2002.
US hammer record 2012.
Progress at HT: 2001- 55.73, 2002- 59.54, 2003- 61.15, 2005- 66.88, 2006- 70.78, 2007- 68.34, 2008- 70.72, 2009- 72.21, 2010- 71.24, 2011- 72.65, 2012- 74.19, 2013- 73.58. pbs: SP 17.63 '05, 20lb Wt

20.40i '04. 4 months drugs ban from August 2009. Left-handed thrower. Married David Toruga on 25 Aug 2012.

Virginia CRAWFORD b. 7 Sep 1983 Seattle 1.78m 63kg. née Powell. Nike. Was at University of Southern California.
At 100mh: WCh: '05- sf, '07- 5, '09- 6; WY: '99- 8/2R; WCp: '06- 3. At 60mh: WI: '10- 5. Won US 100mh 2006-07, NCAA 100mh & indoor 60mh 2005-06.
Progress at 100mh: 2000- 14.07, 2001- 13.39, 2002- 13.62, 2003- 13.07, 2004- 13.07, 2005- 12.61, 2006- 12.48, 2007- 12.45, 2008- 12.75/12.74w, 2009- 12.64/12.47w, 2010- 12.63, 2011- 12.73/12.65w, 2012- 12.59, 2013- 12.67. pbs: 60m 7.21i '06, 100m 11.10/10.93Aw '06, 200m 23.29 '06, 50mh 6.90i '12, 60mh 7.84i '06.
Married Shawn Crawford (200m 1/2 OG 2004/- 8, 3=/4 WCh 2001/09, 1 WI 2001, 19.79 '04) on 16 Apr 2010.

Sharon DAY-MONROE b. 9 Jun 1985 Brooklyn, New York 1.75m 70kg. née Day. Asics. Was at Cal Poly State University.
At Hep: OG: '12- 15; WCh: '09- 10, '11- 17, '13- 6. US champion 2011, 2013. At Hep: WI: '14- 4. At HJ: OG: '08- dnq 24=; WCh: '09- dnq 17=; WJ: '04- 3; PAm: '07- 6; won PAm-J 2003, NCAA 2005.
US indoor heptahlon record 2014.
Progress at Hep: 2007- 5244, 2008- 5642, 2009- 6177, 2010- 6006(w), 2011- 6058, 2012- 6343, 2013- 6550. pbs: 200m 24.02 '13, 400m 56.54 '07, 800m 2:08.94 '13, 55mh 7.98i '12, 60mh 8.43i '14, 100mh 13.51 '13, HJ 1.95 '08, LJ 6.15 '12, 6.16w '13; SP 15.59i '14, 14.77 '13; JT 47.38 '13, Pen 4805Ai '14.
Married Dan Monroe on 1 Sep 2014.

Cynthia 'Janay' DeLOACH SOUKUP b. 12 Oct 1985 Panama City, Florida 1.65m 59kg. Nike. Psychology graduate of Colorado State University.
At LJ: OG: '12- 3; WCh: '11- 6, '13- 11; WI: '12- 2; PAm: '07- 10. Won US 2013, US indoor 2011-13.
At 60mh: WI: '14- 5.
Progress at LJ: 2004- 6.14Ai/6.05/6.14w, 2005- 6.27A/6.43w, 2006- 6.21Ai, 2007- 6.42Ai/6.41/6.45w, 2008- 6.48/6.51w, 2009- 6.33i/6.04, 2010- 6.61, 2011- 6.99Ai/6.97, 2012- 7.03/7.15w, 2013- 6.99/7.08w. pb 55m 6.85Ai '05, 60m 7.31Ai '06, 100m 11.45 '08, 200m 24.60 '07, 24.26Aw '08; 60mh 7.82Ai/7.90i '14, 100mh 12.97 '13, HJ 1.73i '11, SP 12.67i '11, Pen 4289i '11.
Married Patrick Soukup in September 2012.

Lashinda DEMUS b. 10 Mar 1983 Palmdale, California 1.70m 62kg. Nike. Student at University of South Carolina.
At 400mh/4x400mR: OG: '04- sf, '12- 2; WCh: '05- 2, '09- 2/1R, '11- 1, '13- 3; WJ: '02- 1/1R; WCp: '06- 2/2R. Won WAF 2005-06, PAm-J 1999, US 2005-06, 2009, 2011; NCAA 2002.
Two world junior records 400mh 2002.
Progress at 400mh: 1998- 64.61, 1999- 57.04,

2001- 55.76, 2002- 54.70, 2003- 55.65, 2004- 53.43, 2005- 53.27, 2006- 53.02, 2008- 53.99, 2009- 52.63, 2010- 52.82, 2011- 52.47, 2012- 52.77, 2013- 54.22. pbs: 50m 6.64i '01, 60m 7.73i '01, 100m 11.5 '01, 200m 23.99 '14, 23.50w '05; 400m 51.09 '10, 500y 1:05.8i '01, 800m 2:07.49 '12, 55mh 7.65i '04, 60mh 8.11i '04, 100mh 12.96 '11, 12.93w '05.

Twin sons Duane and Donte born 5 Jun 2007. Her mother, Yolanda Rich, had a 400m best of 52.19 in 1980.

Kimberlyn DUNCAN b. 2 Aug 1991 Katy, Texas 1.73m 59kg. Louisiana State University.
At 200m: WCh: '13- sf; won US 2013, NCAA 2011-13 (and indoors).
Progress at 100m, 200m: 2007- 24.54, 2008- 24.33, 2009- 23.46, 2010- 11.84, 23.08/22.96w; 2011- 11.09/11.02w, 22.24/22.18w, 2012- 10.96/10.94, 22.22; 2013- 11.08/11.02w, 22.35/21.80w. pb 60m 7.16i '13.

Allyson FELIX b. 18 Nov 1985 Los Angeles 1.68m 57kg. Nike. Elementary education graduate of University of Southern California.
At 200m/4x400mR: OG: '04- 2, '08- 2/1R, '12- 1/1R (4 x400m); WCh: '03- qf, '05- 1, '07- 1/1 4x100mR/1R, '09- 1/1R, '11- 3/1R (2 400m, 1 4x100m), '13- dnf; WJ: '02- 5; PAm: '03- 3; WI: '10- 1R. At 100m: OG: '12- 5; WY: '01- 1 (1 Medley R). Won DL 200m & 400m 2010, WAF 200m 2005-06, 2009; US 100m 2010, 200m 2004-05, 2007-09, 2012; 400m 2011.
World junior record 200m 2004 after unratified (no doping test) at age 17 in 2003.
Progress at 100m, 200m, 400m: 2000- 12.19/11.99w, 23.90; 2001- 11.53, 23.31/23.27w; 2002- 11.40, 22.83/22.69w, 55.01; 2003- 11.29/ 11.12w, 22.11A/22.51, 52.26; 2004- 11.16, 22.18, 51.83A; 2005- 11.05, 22.13, 51.12; 2006- 11.04, 22.11; 2007- 11.01, 21.81, 49.70; 2008- 10.93, 21.93 /21.82w, 49.83; 2009- 11.08, 21.88, 49.83; 2010- 11.27, 22.03, 50.15; 2011- 11.26+, 22.32, 49.59; 2012- 10.89, 21.69; 2013- 11.06+, 22.30, 50.19. pbs: 50m 6.43i '02, 60m 7.10i '12, 150mSt 16.36 '13 (world best), 300m 36.33i '07.
First teenager to won a World sprint title. Unbeaten in ten 200m competitions 2005 and in five 2007. Has women's record eight world gold medals including three in 2007 when she had a record 0.53 winning margin at 200m and ran a 48.0 400m relay leg, and four Olympic gold medals. IAAF female Athlete of the Year 2012. Older brother Wes Felix won World Junior bronze at 200m and gold in WJR at 4x100m in 2002, pbs: 100m 10.23 '05, 200m 20.43 '04.

Shalane FLANAGAN b. 8 Jul 1981 Boulder 1.65m 50kg. Nike. Was at University of North Carolina.
At 5000m/(10,000m): OG: '04- h, '08- 10/3; WCh: '05- h, '07- 8, '09- (14), '11- (7), '13- (8). At Mar: OG: '10. World CC: '10- 12, '11-3; 4k: '05- 14, 05- 20. Won US 5000m 2005, 10,000m 2008, 2011, 2013; HMar 2010, Mar 2012, CC 2008, 2010-11,

2013; 4km CC 2004-05, indoor 3000m 2007, NCAA CC 2002-03, indoor 3000m 2003.
North American records: 5000m and indoor 3000m 2007, 10,000m (2) 2008, 15km road 2014.
Progress at 5000m, 10,000m, Mar: 2001- 16:29.68, 2003- 15:20.54, 2004- 15:05.08, 2005- 15:10.96, 2007- 14:44.80, 2008- 14:59.69, 30:22.22; 2009- 14:47.62i/15:10.86, 31:23.43; 2010- 14:49.08, 2:28:40; 2011- 14:45.20, 30:39.57; 2012- 31:59.69, 2:25:38; 2013- 31:04.85, 2:27:08. pbs: 800m 2:09.28 '02, 1500m 4:05.86 '07, 1M 4:33.81i '11, 4:48.47 '00; 3000m 8:33.25i/8:35.34 '07, Road: 15k 47:03 '14, 10M 51:45 '10, HMar 68:37 '10.
2nd New York 2010 on marathon debut and won Olympic Trials 2012. Married to Steve Edwards. Mother, Cheryl Bridges, set marathon world best with 2:49:40 in 1971 and was 4th in 1969 International CC, father Steve ran in World Cross 1976-7, 1979.

Hyleas FOUNTAIN b. 14 Jan 1981 Columbus, Georgia 1.70m 64kg. Nike. University of Georgia.
At Hep: OG: '08- 2, '12- dnf; WCh: '05- 12, '07- dnf, '11- 24. At Pen: WI: '06- 8, '10- 4. Won NCAA Hep 2003, LJ 2004; US Hep 2005, 2007-08, 2010, 2012.
N.American indoor pentathlon record 2010.
Progress at Hep: 2001- 4905, 2002- 5673w, 2003- 5999, 2004- 6035, 2005- 6502, 2006- 6148, 2007- 6090, 2008- 6667, 2010- 6735w, 2012- 6419. pbs: 60m 7.47i '11, 200m 23.21 '08, 800m 2:15.32 '08, 55mh 7.61i '05, 60mh 7.98i '09, 100mh 12.70 '12, 12.65w '08; HJ 1.90 '10, LJ 6.89/6.95w '09; TJ 13.40 '04, SP 14.26i '10, 13.81 '09; JT 48.15 '08, Pen 4753i '10.
Won Talence and IAAF Combined Events Challenge 2008. Pulled out after five events with a neck injury when on line for a big pb at the 2009 US Champs. US bobsled international 2012.

Octavious FREEMAN b. 20 Apr 1992 Lake Wales, Florida 1.69m 57kg. Student at University of Central Florida.
At 100m/4x100mR: WCh: '13- 8/2R.
Progress at 100m, 200m: 2008- 11.64/11.59w, 23.95/23.71w; 2009- 11.48/11.20Aw, 23.20; 2010- 11.18/11.11Aw, 23.24/23.19Aw; 2011- 11.21, 22.96; 2012- 11.09, 22.74; 2013- 10.87, 22.55. pbs: 60m 7.15i '12, LJ 6.05 '12.

English GARDNER b. 22 Apr 1992 Philadelphia 1.62m 50kg. Student at University of Oregon.
At 100m/4x100mR: WCh: '13- 4/2R; Won NCAA 100m 2013, indoor 60m 2012.
Progress at 100m, 200m: 2005- 11.99, 24.53; 2007- 11.61, 24.01; 2008- 11.82/11.49w, 24.27/24.19w; 2011- 11.03, 23.02; 2012- 11.10/11.00w, 22.82; 2013- 10.85, 22.62. pbs: 60m 7.12i '12, 400m 53.73 '12.

Kara GOUCHER b. 9 Jul 1978 Queens, New York 1.70m 58kg. née Grgas-Wheeler. Nike. Studied psychology at Colorado State University.

At (5000m)/10,000m: OG: '08- 9/10; WCh: '07- 3, '11- 13. At Mar: OG: '12- 11; WCh: '09- 9. At 3000m: WCp: '06- 3. World 4k CC: '06- 21. Won US 5000m 2008-09, HMar 2012; NCAA 3000m, 5000m & CC 2000.

Progress at 5000m, 10,000m: 1999- 16:57.31, 2000- 15:28.78, 2001- 15:31.77, 2003- 15:42.97, 33:44.86; 2004- 16:30.35, 2005- 15:17.55, 2006- 15:08.13, 31:17.12; 2007- 14:55.02, 32:02.05; 2008- 14:58.10, 30:55.16; 2009- 15:20.94, 2:27:48; 2011- 15:11.47, 31:16.65, 2:24:52wdh; 2012- 2:26:06, 2013- 31:46.64. pbs: 800m 2:06.79 '09, 1500m 4:05.14 '06, 1M 4:33.19i/4:37.58 '09, 2000m 5:41.28 '09, 3000m 8:34.99 '07, 2M 9:41.32 '07, Road: 15k 47:36 '07, 10M 50:59 '07, HMar 66:57 '07, 30k 1:43:33 '08, Mar 2:25:53 '08.

After surprise World 10,000m bronze, made brilliant half marathon debut to win Great North Run 2007 with American best. Third New York Marathon 2008, with fastest ever US women's debut, and Boston 2009.

Married (2001) **Adam Goucher** (18 Feb 1975) (pbs: 1500m 3:36.64 '01, 1M 3:54.17 '99, 2000m 4:58.92 '99, 3000m 7:34.96 '01, 2M 8:12.73 '06, 5000m 13:10.00 '06, 10,000m 27:59.41 '06). Their son Colton born on 24 Sep 2010.

Dawn HARPER-NELSON b. 13 May 1984 Norman, Oklahoma 1.68m 61kg. Nike. Studied psychology at UCLA.

At 100mh: OG: '08- 1, '12- 2; WCh: '09- 7, '11- 3, '13- 4; won DL 2012-13, PAm-J 2003, US 2009.

Progress at 100mh: 2002- 13.63, 2003- 13.33/13.21w, 2004- 13.16/12.91w, 2005- 12.91, 2006- 12.80A/12.86, 2007- 12.67, 2008- 12.54, 2009- 12.48/12.36w, 2010- 12.77w, 2011- 12.47, 2012- 12.37, 2013- 12.48. pbs: 60m 7.70i '05, 100m 11.66 '07, 200m 23.97 '06, 50mh 6.96i '12, 60mh 7.98i '06.

Married Craig Everhart (b. 13 Sep 1983, 400m 44.89 '04) in October 2007, and then Alonzo Nelson on 27 March 2013.

Queen HARRISON b. 10 Sep 1988 Loch Sheldrake, New York 1.70m 60kg. Saucony. Student of business marketing at Virginia Tech.

At 100mh: WCh: '13- 5; At 400mh: OG: '08- sf; WCh: '11- sf; PAm-J: '07- 1 (2 100mh); won NCAA 100mh, 400mh & 60mh indoors 2010.

Progress at 100mh, 400mh: 2007- 12.98, 55.81; 2008- 12.70, 54.60; 2009- 13.14/12.98w, 56.03; 2010- 12.61/12.44w, 54.55; 2011- 12.88, 54.78; 2012- 12.62, 55.32; 2013- 12.43. pbs: 400m 52.88 '08, 60mh 7.94i '10, LJ 5.82i '06.

Natasha HASTINGS b. 23 Jul 1986 Brooklyn, NY 1.73m 63kg. Under Armour. Studied exercise science at University of South Carolina.

At 400m/4x400m: OG: '08- res 1R; WCh: '07- sf/res 1R, '09/11- res 1R, '13- 5/2R; WJ: '04- 1/1R; WY: '03- 1; WI: '10- 1R, '12- 3/2R; PAm-J: '03- 1R, '05- 1/1R. Won US 2013, NCAA indoors and out 2007.

World junior 500m indoor best 2005, North American indoor 4x400m record 2014.

Progress at 400m: 2000- 54.21, 2001- 55.06, 2002- 53.42, 2003- 52.09, 2004- 52.04, 2005- 51.34, 2006- 51.45, 2007- 49.84, 2008- 50.80, 2009- 50.89, 2010- 50.53, 2011- 50.83Ai/50.97, 2012- 50.72, 2013- 49.94. pbs: 55m 7.08i '02, 60m 7.26i '13, 100m 11.24 '13, 200m 22.61 '07, 300m 35.9+ '07, 500m 1:10.05i '05.

Father from Jamaica, mother Joanne Gardner was British (ran 11.89 to win WAAA U15 100m at 14 in 1977).

Molly HUDDLE b. 31 Aug 1984 Elmira, New York 1.63m 48kg. Saucony. Was at University of Notre Dame.

At 5000m: OG: '12- 11; WCh: '11- h, '13- 6; CCp: '10- 3; won US 2011. World CC: '10- 19, '11- 17. North American 5000m record 2010.

Progress at 5000m, 10,000m: 2003- 15:36.95, 2004- 15:32.55, 2005- 16:12.17i, 2006- 15:40.41, 32:37.871 2007- 15:17.13, 33:09.27; 2008- 15:25.47, 33:17.73; 2009- 15:53.91, 32:42.11; 2010- 14:44.76, 31:27.12; 2011- 15:10.01, 31:28.66; 2012- 15:01.32, 2013- 14:58.15. pbs: 1000m 4:08.09 '13, 1M 4:41.91i '04, 4:46.70 '07; 3000m 8:42.99 '13, 10M Rd 54:01 '09, HMar 69:04 '14.

Married to Kurt Benninger CAN (pbs 1500m 3:38.03 '08, 1M 3:56.99 '08, 5000m 13:30.27 '09).

Kylie HUTSON b. 27 Nov 1987 Terre Haute 1.65m 57kg. Nike. Was at Indiana State University.

At PV: WCh: '11/13- dnq 15/nh; won US 2011, NCAA 2009, 2011.

Progress at PV: 2006- 3.58, 2007- 4.10i/3.96, 2008- 4.30, 2009- 4.40, 2010- 4.51, 2011- 4.70i/4.65, 2012- 4.52Ai/4.40, 2013- 4.75Ai/4.70.

Carmelita JETER b. 24 Nov 1979 Los Angeles 1.63m 53kg. Nike. Was at California State University, Dominguez Hills.

At 100m/(200m)/4x100mR: OG: '12- 2/3/1R; WCh: '07- 3/res 1R, '09- 3, '11- 1/2/1R, '13- 3; won DL 100m 2010-11, 200m 2011; WAF 100m 2007, 2009; US 100m 2009, 2011-12. At 60m: WI: '10- 2.

Progress at 100m, 200m: 1998- 11.88, 2000- 11.69, 23.65/23.99w; 2001- 11.82, 24.20; 2002- 11.77/11.46w, 24.10; 2003- 11.61/11.43w, 23.67; 2004- 11.56, 23.98; 2005- 12.00/11.72w, 2006- 11.48, 23.54; 2007- 11.02, 22.82; 2008- 10.97, 22.47/22.35w; 2009- 10.64, 22.59; 2010- 10.82, 22.54; 2011- 10.70, 22.20; 2012- 10.78, 22.11; 2013- 10.93, 22.77. pbs: 60m 7.02Ai/7.05i '10, 300m 37.52 '13, 400m 53.08 '09. Second fastest woman of all-time at 100m.

Oluwafunmilayo 'Funmi' JIMOH b. 29 May 1984 Seattle 1.73m 64kg. Nike. Was at Rice University.

At LJ: OG: '08- 12; WCh: '09/11/13- dnq 21/nj/dnq 13; won US 2008-09, NCAA 2008.

Progress at LJ: 2004- 6.14, 2005- 6.31, 2006- 6.44, 2007- 6.46/6.62w, 2008- 6.91, 2009- 6.96, 2010- 6.81/6.87w, 2011- 6.88, 2012- 6.82, 2013- 6.92. pbs: 60m 7.67i '04, 100m 12.03 '08, 11.65w '11; 200m 23.91A '11, 24.28 '08, 23.65w '06; 400m 59.57i '09,

60mh 8.32i '07, 100mh 13.51 '05, 13.39w '07; HJ 1.75i '05, 1.66 '07; SP 10.68i '06, Pen 3937i '06, Hep 5335 '07.

Lori 'Lolo' JONES b. 5 Aug 1982 Des Moines 1.75m 60kg. Asics. Spanish & economic graduate of Louisiana State University.
At 100mh: OG: '08- 7, '12- 4; WCh: '07- 6; CCp: '10- 2; Won US 2008, 2010; NACAC 2004. At 60mh: WI: '08- 1, '10- 1; won NCAA indoor 2003, US indoor 2007-09.
N.American indoor 60m hurdles record 2010.
Progress at 100mh: 2000- 14.04, 2001- 13.31/13.17w/12.7w, 2002- 12.84, 2003- 12.90, 2004- 12.77, 2005- 12.76, 2006- 12.56, 2007- 12.57, 2008- 12.43/12.29w, 2009- 12.47, 2010- 12.55, 2011- 12.67, 2012- 12.58, 2013- 12.50/12.44w. pbs: 55m 6.87i '03, 60m 7.27i '03, 100m 11.24 '06, 200m 23.76 '04, 23.50w '03; 50mh 6.78i '12, 55mh 7.57i '03, 60mh 7.72i '10, 400mh 59.95 '00.
Crashed into 9th hurdle when leading Olympic final after pb 12.43 in semi in 2008. Won gold in the 2-man bobsled as brakeman on the US team at the 2013 World Championships and was 11th at the 2014 Winter Olympics.

Bianca KNIGHT b. 2 Jan 1989 Ridgeland, Mississippi 1.63m 60kg. adidas. Psychology student at University of Texas.
At (100m)/200m: OG: '12- 1R; WCh: '11- 1R; WY: '05- 1/2/1 Med R; PAm-J: '07- 1. Won NCAA indoor 2008.
World junior indoor 200m record 2008.
Progress at 100m, 200m: 2002- 12.07, 24.37; 2003- 11.80, 23.81; 2004- 11.56, 23.06; 2005- 11.38, 23.33; 2006- 11.26, 22.94; 2007- 11.36/11.28w, 22.97Ai/23.17A/22.93w; 2008- 11.07, 22.40i/22.43/22.25w; 2009- 11.17/11.12w, 22.50; 2010- 11.40, 22.59; 2011- 11.22, 22.35; 2012- 11.13, 22.46/22.34w, 2013- 11.49, 23.16/22.86w. pbs: 50m 6.28i '12, 55m 6.75+i '12, 60m 7.16i '08, 300m 36.41i '11, 400m 52.55 '11.

Gia LEWIS-SMALLWOOD b. 1 Apr 1979 Urbana, Illinois 1.83m 93kg. Nike. Was at University of Illinois.
At DT: OG: '12- dnq 15; WCh: '11- dnq 15, '13- 5; PAm: '11- 4. US champion 2013.
US discus record 2012.
Progress at DT: 2000- 53.52, 2001- 57.76, 2002- 52.28, 2003- 54.95, 2004- 57.88, 2005- 50.85, 2006- 49.95, 2007- 52.02, 2008- 59.96, 2009- 60.32, 2010- 65.58, 2011- 62.26, 2012- 63.97, 2013- 66.29. pb Wt 18.91i '02.

Chaunté LOWE b. 12 Jan 1984 Templeton, California 1.75m 59kg. née Howard. Nike. Economics gradate of Georgia Tech University.
At HJ: OG: '04- dnq 26=, '08- 6, '12- 6; WCh: '05- 2, '09- 7=; PAm-J: '03- 3; WI: '06-10-12: 8/3/1; Won DL 2012, US 2006, 2008-10, 2012; NCAA 2004, indoors 2004-05.
3 N.American HJ records 2010, indoors 2012.
Progress at HJ: 2000- 1.75, 2001- 1.84, 2002- 1.87, 2003- 1.89, 2004- 1.98A, 2005- 2.00, 2006- 2.01,

2008- 2.00, 2009- 1.98, 2010- 2.05, 2011- 1.78, 2012- 2.02Ai/2.01. pbs: 100m 11.83 '05, 100mh 13.78 '04, LJ 6.90 '10, TJ 12.93 '04, 12.98w '05.
Married Mario Lowe (b. 20 Apr 1980, TJ pb 16.15 '02) in 2005, daughters Jasmine born 30 Jul 2007 and Aurora in 4 Apr 2011 and son Mario Josiah in August 2013.

Brenda MARTINEZ b. 8 Sep 1987 Upland, California 1.63m 52kg. New Balance. Stidied sociology and law at University of California - Riverside.
At 800m: WCh: '13- 3.
Progress at 800m, 1500m: 2007- 2:04.22, 4:21.18; 2008- 2:02.34, 4:17.09; 2009- 2:00.85, 4:09.52; 2010- 2:04.76, 4:18.17; 2011- 2:01.07, 4:10.77; 2012- 1:59.14, 4:06.96; 2013- 1:57.91, 4:00.94. pbs: 1000m 2:38.48 '12, 1M 4:26.76 '12, 3000m 9:07.99+i '13, 2M 9:51.91i '13, 5000m 15:30.89mx '13, 5kmRd 15:24 '14. Married Carlos Handler in October 2012.

Jeneva McCALL b. 28 Oct 1989 Dolton, Illinois 1.78m 102kg. Was at Southern Illinois University.
At HT: WCh: '11- dnq 14, '13- 9; WUG: '13- 1. At SP: WI: '14- 8. Won NCAA DT 2010, HT 2012.
Progress at HT: 2009- 55.83, 2010- 64.17, 2011- 69.55, 2012- 69.38, 2013- 74.77. pbs: SP 19.10i '12, 18.47 '13, DT 59.45 '12, Wt 23.94i '13.

Francena McCORORY b. 20 Oct 1988 Hampton, VA 1.70m 60kg. adidas. Psychology graduate of Hampton University.
At 400m/4x400mR: OG: '12- 7/1R; WCh: '11- 4/1R, '13- 6/2R; WI: '14- 1/1R won NCAA indoors 2009-10, out 2010.
World junior indoor 300m best 2007, North American indoor 4x400m record 2014.
Progress at 400m: 2004- 54.54, 2006- 51.93i, 2008- 51.54, 2009- 50.58, 2010- 50.52, 2011- 50.24, 2012- 50.06, 2013- 49.86. pbs: 55m 6.86i '06, 60m 7.43i '07, 100m 11.68 '05, 11.56w '10; 200m 22.92 '10, 300m 35.7+ '13, 500m 1:09.01i '12, 600m 1:29.07i '13, 800m 2:20.25i '07.

Georganne MOLINE b. 6 Mar 1990 Phoenix, Arizona 1.78m 59kg. Psychology and communication student at University of Arizona.
At 400mh: OG: '12- 5; WCh: '13- h.
Progress at 400mh: 2010- 57.88, 2011- 57.41, 2012- 53.92, 2013- 53.72. pbs: 200m 23.37 '13, 400m 52.09i '13, 52.92 '12; 800m 2:09.58 '14.
53.92 in Olympic final was seventh 400mh pb of her 2012 season.

Alysia MONTAÑO b. 26 Apr 1986 Queens, New York 1.70m 61kg. née Johnson. Triangle Champions TC. Was at University of California.
At 800m: OG: '12- 5; WCh: '07- h, '11- 4, '13- 4; PAm: '07- 6; WI: '10- 3; CCp: '10- 8; won US 2007, 2010-13; NCAA 2007.
North American indoor 600m record 2013.
Progress at 800m: 2004- 2:08.97, 2005- 2:05.49, 2006- 2:01.80, 2007- 1:59.29, 2008- 2:00.57, 2009- 2:01.09, 2010- 1:57.34, 2011- 1:57.48, 2012- 1:57.37, 2013- 1:57.75. pbs: 200m 24.41iA '13, 400m 52.09

'10, 600m 1:23.59i '13, 1:26.7+ '12; 1500m 4:28.43 '09.

Always runs with a flower in her hair. Marred Louis Montaño on 19 Mar 2011, exepcting a baby in August 2014.

LaShaunte'a MOORE b. 31 Jul 1983 Akron, Ohio 1.70m 62kg. adidas. Was at University of Arkansas. Training to be a nurse.

At 200m: OG: '04- sf, WCh: '07- 7; WY: '99- 4/1 MedR; won NCAA 2004.

Progress at 100m, 200m: 1997- 11.93, 1998- 11.67w, 23.86w; 1999- 11.66, 23.26; 2001- 11.64/ 11.57w, 23.59/23.40w; 2002- 11.47, 23.13/22.89w; 2003- 11.33/11.27w, 23.09/22.81Aw; 2004- 11.26, 22.63/22.37w; 2005- 11.39/11.25w, 22.93; 2006- 11.40, 22.89/22.64w; 2007- 11.26/11.10w, 22.46; 2008- 11.03, 22.70; 2009- 11.21, 22.57; 2010- 10.97, 22.46; 2011- 11.17/11.04w, 22.58; 2012- 11.11/ 10.93w, 22.71; 2013- 11.26/10.98w, 22.40. pbs: 60m 7.36i '03, 400m 54.92 '07.

Dalilah MUHAMMAD b. 7 Feb 1990 Jamaica, New York 1.70m 62kg. Business graduate of University of Southern Califormia.

At 400mh: WCh: '13- 2; WY: '07- 1; PAm-J: '09- 2; US champion 2013.

Progress at 400mh: 2005- 61.25, 2006- 59.82, 2007- 57.09, 2008- 57.81, 2009- 56.49, 2010- 57.14, 2011- 56.04, 2012- 56.19, 2013- 53.83. pbs: 60m 7.64i '10, 100m 11.42 '13, 200m 23.62 '09, 400m 52.75 '13, 60mh 8.23i '12, 100mh 13.33 '12, HJ 1.75 '10.

Barbara PIERRE b. 28 Apr 1987 Port-au-Prince, Haiti 1.75m 60kg. Was at St. Augustine's College.

At 100m/4x100mR: OG: '08- qf; PAm: '11- 2/2R.

At 60m: WI: '12-4.

Haiti records at 100m 2009, 200m 2008-09.

Progress at 100m: 2003- 11.98, 2005- 11.78, 2006- 11.66, 2007- 11.30, 2008- 11.40A, 2009- 11.18, 2010- 11.35, 2011- 11.14, 2012- 11.34, 2013- 10.85. pbs: 50m 6.22+i '12, 55m 6.89i '07, 60m 7.06Ai '12, 7.09 '13; 100y 10.38y '11, 200m 23.23 '10, 400m 57.04 '08.

With dual citizenship, she switched from US to Haiti 31 Dec 2007, and back to US 24 Mar 2010.

Tori POLK b. 21 Sep 1983 Hewitt, Texas 1.73m 24kg. Studied accountancy at Texas Tech University.

At LJ: WCh: '11- dnq 33, '13- 8; PAm: '11- 7; WI: '14- 5.

Progress at LJ: 2000- 5.87, 2001- 6.06, 2002- 5.84/ 6.11w, 2004- 5.99i/6.06Aw, 2005- 6.29/6.33w, 2006- 6.47Ai, 2007- 5.95, 2008- 6.54, 2009- 6.58A/ 6.62Aw, 2010- 6.56, 2011- 6.75, 2012- 6.54, 2013- 6.75/6.80w, 2014- 6.70i. pbs: 60m 7.66i '14, 100m 11.02w '09, 200m 24.19A '05, 24.21 '02; 400m 55.13 '04.

Brittney REESE b. 9 Sep 1986 Gulfport, Mississippi 1.73m 64kg. Nike. English graduate of University of Mississippi.

At LJ: OG: '08- 5, '12- 1; WCh: '07-09-11-13:

8/1/1/1; WI: '10- 1, '12- 1; won DL 2010-11, WAF 2009, US 2008-12, NCAA 2007-08.

North American indoor long jump record 2012. Progress at LJ: 2004- 6.31, 2006- 5.94, 2007- 6.83, 2008- 6.95, 2009- 7.10, 2010- 6.94/7.05w, 2011- 7.19, 2012- 7.23i/7.15, 2013- 7.25. pbs: 50m 6.23i '12, 60m 7.24i '11, 100m 11.63 '09, 11.20w '11; HJ 1.88i/1.84 '08, TJ 13.16 '08.

Concentrated on basketball at Gulf Coast Community College in 2005-06. Has won six successive global titles.

Sanya RICHARDS-ROSS b. 26 Feb 1985 Kingston, Jamaica 1.73m 61kg. Nike. University of Texas.

At (200m)/400m/4x400m: OG: '04- 6/1R, '08- 3/1R, '12- 5/1/1R; WCh: '03- sf/1R, '05- 2, '07- (5)/1R, '09- 1/1R, '11- 7/1R; WJ: '02- 3/2; WCp: '06- 1/1; WI: '12- 1/2R. Won WAF 200m 2008, 400m 2005-09, US 2003, 2005-06, 2008-09, 2012; NCAA 2003.

US & N.American 400m record 2006, world junior indoor bests 200m, 400m (2) 2004.

Progress at 200m, 400m: 1999- 23.84, 2000- 23.57, 54.34; 2001- 23.09, 53.49; 2002- 23.01, 50.69; 2003- 22.80i/22.86, 50.58; 2004- 22.49i/22.73, 49.89; 2005- 22.53, 48.92; 2006- 22.17, 48.70; 2007- 22.31, 49.27; 2008- 22.49, 49.74; 2009- 22.29, 48.83; 2010- 51.82; 2011- 22.63, 49.66; 2012- 22.09, 49.28; 2013- 51.43. pbs: 60m 7.21i '04, 100m 10.97 '07, 10.89w '12; 300m 35.6 '05, 800m 2:10.74 '10, LJ 6.08 '01.

Left Jamaica at the age of 12 and gained US citizenship on 20 May 2002. Her 48.92 at Zürich in 2005 and then 48.70 at the World Cup in 2006 (to beat 22 year-old US record) were the world's fastest 400m times since 1996. Unbeaten in 13 finals outdoors at 400m in 2006 and after WAF win scored 200m/400m double at World Cup. Record 46 times sub-50 secs for 400m. Shared Golden League jackpot 2006, 2007 and 2009. IAAF female Athlete of the Year 2006 & 2009. Married New York Giants cornerback Aaron Ross on 26 Feb 2010.

Brianna ROLLINS b. 18 Aug 1991 Miami 1.64m 55kg. Student at Clemson University.

At 100mh: WCh: '13- 1; Won US 2013, NACAC 2012. Won NCAA 100mh 2013, indoor 60mh 2011 & 2013.

North American 100n hurdles record 2013.

Progress at 100mh: 2007- 14.48, 2008- 13.93, 2009- 13.83, 2011- 12.99/12.88w, 2012- 12.70/12.60Aw, 2013- 12.26. pbs: 200m 23.04/23.02w '13, 300m 37.90i '10, 400m 53.93 '13, 60mh 7.78i '13, 400mh 60.58 '09.

Undefeated in 2013: inc. heats 200m- 7, 400m- 1, 60mh- 8, 100mh- 18.

Shannon ROWBURY b. 19 Sep 1984 San Francisco 1.65m 52kg. Nike. Was at Duke University.

At 1500m: OG: '08- 7, '12- 6; WCh: '09- 3, '11- sf; Won US 2008-09, NCAA indoor mile 2007. At

3000m: WI: '14- 8; CCp: '10- 2. At 5000m: WCh: '13- 7.
Progress at 1500m: 2004- 4:17.41, 2005- 4:14.81, 2006- 4:12.31, 2008- 4:00.33, 2009- 4:00.81, 2010- 4:01.30, 2011- 4:05.73, 2012- 4:03.15, 2013- 4:01.28. pbs: 800m 2:00.47 '10, 1M 4:20.34 '08, 3000m 8:31.38 '10, 2M 9:52.16i '14, 5000m 15:00.51 '10, 3000mSt 9:59.4 '06.
Engaged to Pablo Solares (Mexican 1500m record 3:36.67 '09).

Mary SAXER b. 21 Jun 1987 Buffalo, NY 1.66m 57kg. Nike. Marketing graduate of University of Notre Dame.
At PV: WI: '12- 4, 14- 8.
Progress at PV: 2004- 3.81, 2005- 4.32i/4.19, 2006- 4.05i/3.90, 2007- 3.86i/3.80, 2008- 4.06, 2009- 4.30, 2010- 4.50, 2011- 4.60, 2012- 4.62Ai/4.53, 2013- 4.70, 2014- 4.71Ai.

Jennifer SIMPSON b. 23 Aug 1986 Webster City, Iowa 1.65m 50kg. née Barringer. New Balance. Studied political science at University of Colorado.
At 1500m: OG: '12- sf; WCh: '11- 1, '13- 2. At 3000mSt: OG: '08- 9; WCh: '07- h, '09- 5; won NCAA 2006, 2008-09. Won US 5000m 2013, 3000mSt 2009.
Three North American 3000m steeplechase records 2008-09.
Progress at 1500m, 5000m, 3000mSt: 2006- 16:15.23, 9:53.04, 2007- 4:21.53, 15:48.24, 9:33.95; 2008- 4:11.36, 9:22.26; 2009- 3:59.90, 15:01.70i/15:05.25, 9:12.50; 2010- 4:03.63, 15:33.33; 2011- 4:03.54, 15:11.49; 2012- 4:04.07, 2013- 4:00.48, 14:56.26. pbs: 800m 2:00.45 '13, 1M 4:25.91i '09, 3000m 8:42.03i '09, 8:48.72 '12, 2M 9:26.19i '14.
Married Jason Simpson on 8 Oct 2010. Won 5th Avenue Mile 2011.

Shalonda SOLOMON b. 19 Dec 1985 Inglewood, California 1.69m 56kg. Reebok. Student at University of South Carolina.
At (100m)/200m/4x100m: WCh: '11- 4/res (1)R; WJ: '04- 1/1R; PAm-J: '03- 1/1/1R; CCj: '10- (2)/1R. Won NCAA 200m 2006, NCAAC 100m & 200m 2006.
Progress at 100m, 200m: 2001- 11.57/11.37w, 23.65/23.22w; 2002- 11.51/11.46w, 23.31; 2003- 11.35/11.25w, 22.93; 2004- 11.41/11.32w, 22.82; 2005- 11.29, 22.74/22.72w; 2006- 11.09/11.07w, 22.36/22.30w; 2007- 11.33, 22.77; 2008- 11.16, 22.48/22.36w; 2009- 11.04/11.00w, 22.41; 2010- 10.90, 22.47; 2011- 11.08/10.90w, 22.15; 2012- 11.26, 22.82; 2013- 11.04/10.97w, 22.41/22.33w. pbs: 55m 6.72i '09, 60m 7.15Ai '11, 7.21i '06; 300m 36.45i '09, 400m 53.47 '08.

Ashley SPENCER b. 8 Jun 1993 Indianapolis 1.68m 54kg. Student at University of Texas, firmerly Illinois
At 400m/4x400mR: WCh: '13- sf/2R; WJ: '12- 1/1R. Won NCAA 2012-13.

Progress at 400m: 2012- 50.50, 2013- 50.28. pbs: 60m 7.42i '13, 100m 11.46 '13, 200m 22.99 '12, 100mh 14.40/14.28w '11, 400mh 56.32 '13.

Jennifer SUHR b. 6 Feb 1982 Fredonia, New York 1.80m 64kg. adidas. née Stuczynski. Graduate of Roberts Wesleyan University, now studying child psychology.
At PV: OG: '08- 2, '12- 1; WCh: '07- 10, '11- 4, '13- 2; WI: '08- 2, '14- 5=; WCp: '06- nh; US champion 2006-10, 2012-13; indoors 2005, 2007-09, 2011-12.
Records: world indoors 2013, four North American pole vault records 2007-08, four indoors 2009-13.
Progress at PV: 2002- 2.75, 2004- 3.49, 2005- 4.57i/4.26, 2006- 4.68i/4.66, 2007- 4.88, 2008- 4.92, 2009- 4.83i/4.81, 2010- 4.89, 2011- 4.91, 2012- 4.88i/4.81, 2013- 5.02A/4.91. pbs: 55mh 8.07i '05, JT 46.82 '05.
All-time top scorer at basketball at her university, then very rapid progress at vaulting.

Jeneba TARMOH b. 27 Sep 1989 San Jose CA 1.67m 59kg. Student at Texas A&M University.
At (100m)/200m/4x100m: OG: '12- res (1)R; WCh: '11- h, '13- 5/2R; WJ: '06- 7/1R, '08- (1)/1R. Won NCAAC 100m 2010.
Progress at 100m, 200m: 2004- 12.07w, 2005- 11.81/11.61w, 24.04/23.56w; 2006- 11.24, 23.14; 2007- 11.27, 23.34/23.20w; 2008- 11.21, 22.94; 2009- 11.31, 23.31i/23.43/23.16w; 2010- 11.19/11.00w, 22.65; 2011- 11.23/10.94w, 22.28; 2012- 11.07, 22.35/22.30w; 2013-10.93, 22.70/22.15w. pbs: 50m 6.14+i '12. 55m 6.86Ai '06, 60m 7.22i '12.

Vashti THOMAS b. 21 Apr 1990 San Jose, California 1.75m 60kg. Academy of Art. Was at Texas A&M University.
At 100mh:WJ: '08- h; (dnq 28 TJ) WUG: '13- 1/2R.
Progress at 100mh. LJ: 2005- 14.16, 2006- 14.51, 2007- 13.03, 5.88/6.13w; 2008- 13.44, 6.22; 2009- 13.31/13.05w, 6.32i/5.98/6.26w; 2010- 13.08, 6.45; 2011- 13.14, 6.20; 2012- 13.31/13.02w, 6.97; 2013- 12.61/12.56w, 6.68. pbs: 60m 7.40Ai '13, 100m 11.70 '13, 11.63w '08; 200m 22.75A/23.33 '13, 60mh 8.13i '13, TJ 13.28i '09, 13.14 '08.

De'Hashia 'Deedee' TROTTER b. 8 Dec 1982 Twentynine Palms, California 1.78m 60kg. Saucony. Degree in criminal justice from University of Tennessee.
At 400m/4x400mR: OG: '04- 5/1R, '08- sf, '12- 3/1R; WCh: '03- sf/res (1)R, '05- 5, '07- 5/1R; WI: '10- 1R; PAm: '03- 1R; WCp: '06- 2R. Won US 2007, NCAA 2004.
Progress at 400m: 1998- 58.61, 1999- 59.12, 2000- 56.82, 2001- 56.02, 2002- 53.66, 2003- 50.66, 2004- 50.00, 2005- 49.88, 2006- 49.80, 2007- 49.64, 2008- 50.88, 2009- 52.00, 2010- 51.23Ai/51.52, 2011- 51.17, 2012- 49.72, 2013- 51.67. pbs: 55m 6.93i '04, 60m 7.46i '05, 100m 11.65 '02, 200m 22.85/22.54w '13, 300m 35.8+ '07, LJ 6.00 '02.

Morgan UCENY b. 10 Mar 1985 Plymouth, Indiana 1.68m 57kg. adidas. Was at Cornell University.
At 800m: PAm: '07- h. At 1500m: OG: '12- dnf; WCh: '11- 9; won DL 2011, US 2011-12.
Progress at 800m, 1500m: 2002- 2:13.04, 2004- 2:19.73, 2005- 2:06.26, 2006- 2:04.32, 2007- 2:01.75, 4:17.18; 2008- 2:00.01, 4:06.93; 2009- 2:00.06, 4:09.95; 2010- 1:58.67, 4:02.40; 2011- 1:58.37, 4:00.06; 2012- 2:02.46, 4:01.59; 2013- 2:02.51, 4:08.49. pbs: 400m 55.50 '06, 600m 1:27.70i '07, 1000m 2:37.61 '13, 1M 4:38.87i '08.
Brought down at 950m in World 1500m in 2011, and fell at start of last lap in 2012 Olympics.

Kellie WELLS b. 16 Jul 1982 Richmond, Virginia 1.63m 57kg. Nike. Was at Hampton University.
At 100mh: OG: '12- 3; WCh: '11- dnf. US champion 2011.
Progress at 100mh: 2003- 13.96, 2004- 13.25, 2005- 13.57/13.29w, 2006- 13.25/13.17w, 2007- 12.93, 2008- 12.58, 2009- 13.01, 2010- 12.68, 2011- 12.50/12.35w, 2012- 12.48, 2013- 12.54/12.47w. pbs: 50m 7.33i '06, 100m 11.50 '08, 200m 23.53 '06, 50mh 6.84i '12, 55mh 7.37i '11, 60mh 7.79Ai/ 7.82i '11.
Suffered a serious hamstring injury after finishing the 2008 Olympic Trials semi in a pb 12.58 and struggled for two years until brilliant indoor season in 2011.

Charonda WILLIAMS b. 27 Mar 1987 Richmond, California 1.67m 55kg. adidas. Was at Arizona State University.
At 200m: WCh: '09- sf, '13- 6. Won DL 2012.
Progress at 200m: 2006- 24.19/24.08w, 2007- 23.53, 2008- 23.09, 2009- 22.55/22.39w, 2010- 22.97, 2011- 22.85/22.78w, 2012- 22.52, 2013- 22.71. pbs: 55m 6.99Ai '08, 60m 7.29Ai '09, 7.36i '11; 100m 11.07 '13, 10.95w '12; 300m 37.04i '11, 400m 52.71 '11, LJ 5.91 '07, 6.03w '00.

Ajee' WILSON b. 8 May 1994 1.69m 55kg. Juventis TC. Student of kinesiology at Temple University, Philadelphia.
At 800m: WCh: '13- 6; WJ: '10- 5, '12- 1; WY: '11- 1; won US indoor 2013.
Records: world junior 600m & N.American junior 800m 2013.
Progress at 800m: 2008- 2:11.43, 2009- 2:07.08, 2010- 2:04.18, 2011- 2:02.64, 2012- 2:00.91, 2013- 1:58.21. pbs: 400m 54.35 '12, 600m 1:26.45 '13, 1000m 2:48.88i '14, 1500m 4:24.56 '13, 3000m 10:13.41 '07.
Elder sister Jade has 400mh pb 59.90 '12.

UZBEKISTAN

Governing body: Athletic Federation of Uzbekistan, Navoi str. 30, 100129 Tashkent.

Svetlana RADZIVIL b. 17 Jan 1987 Tashkent 1.84m 61kg
At HJ: OG: '08- dnq 18, '12- 7; WCh: '09- dnq 21=,

'11- 8=; AsiG: '06- 7, '10- 1; AsiC: '09-11-13: 3/2/2; WJ: '02- dnq, '04- 13, '06- 1; WY: '03- dnq; WI: '12- 8. Won Asi-J 2006, Asian indoor 2014.
Progress at HJ: 2002- 1.84, 2003- 1.78, 2004- 1.88, 2005- 1.85, 2006- 1.91, 2007- 1.91, 2008- 1.93, 2009- 1.91, 2010- 1.95, 2011- 1.95, 2012- 1.97, 2013- 1.94, 2014- 1.96i.

VENEZUELA

Governing body: Federación Venezolana de Atletismo, Apartado Postal 29059, Caracas. Founded 1948.

National Champions 2013: Men: 100m: Diego Armando Rivas 10.39, 200m: Jermaine David Chirinos 20.94, 400m: Noel Campos 46.44, 800m: Lucirio Antonio Garrido 1:48.09, 1500m: Alexis Darbel Peña 3:47.95, 5000m: Marvin Francisco Blanco 14:22.31, 10,000m: Walter Suárez 31:15.25, 3000mSt: William Díaz 9:11.70, 110mh/HJ: Albert Idel Bravo 14.43w/2.05, 400mh: Luccirio Garrido 50.65, PV: César González 4.60, LJ: Santiago Luis Cova 7.50, TJ: Yender Cardona 15.54, SP/DT: Mario Enrique González 16.03/47.18, HT: Prinston Quailey 60.04, JT: Alejandro Bell 64.64, Dec: Ricardo Herrada 7168, 20kmW: Richard Vargas 1:29:20. **Women**: 100m: Andra Purica 11.78, 200m: Wilmary Álvarez 24.16, 400m/400mh: Magdalena Mendoza 55.58/59.12, 800m: Idamis Navas 2:12.55, 1500m: María Osorio 4:37.08, 5000m/ 3000mSt: Yeisi Alvarez 17:03.04/10:56.19, 10,000m: Reismer Romero 40:34.16, 100mh: Génesis Romero 13.66, 400mh: Estephany Balladares 62.84, HJ: Yolimar Rojas 1.70, PV: Robeilys Peinado 3.90, LJ: Munich Tovar 6.27, TJ: Yudelis González 12.82, SP: Gioanny Rojas 15.44, DT: Yulimar Monagas 42.48, HT: Diurkina Freyte 53.23, JT: Estephany Chacón 49.01, Hep: Guillercy González 5398, 20000mW: Milángela Rosales 1:44:14.

ZIMBABWE

Governing body: Amateur Athletic Association of Zimbabwe, PO Box MP 187, Mount Pleasant, Harare. Founded in 1912.

Ngonidzashe MAKUSHA b. 11 Mar 1987 Chitungwiza, Harare 1.78m 73kg. Student at Florida State University, USA.
At LJ (100m): OG: '08- 4; WCh: '11- 3 (sf); WJ: '06- 12 (sf); AfG: '07- 3R (sf). Won NCAA 100m 2011, LJ 2008-09, 2011; ZIM LJ 2006-07.
Zimbabwe records 100 (2) 2011, long jump (5) 2006-11.
Progress at 100m. LJ: 2005- 7.34?, 2006- 10.64Aw, 7.87A; 2007- 10.52, 7.69; 2008- 8.30, 2009- 8.21i/7.73/8.11w, 2010- 7.71i/7.54, 2011- 9.89, 8.40; 2012- 7.86, 2013- 8.04/8.20w. pbs: 55m 6.30i '08, 60m 6.60i '09, 200m 21.38A '06, TJ 14.90A '06.
Superb unique treble at 2011 NCAAs with 100m 9.89 and LJ 8.40 plus 4x100m leg. Suffered ruptured Achilles in May 2012.

INTRODUCTION TO WORLD LISTS AND INDEX

Records

World, World U20 and U18, Olympic, Area and Continental records are listed for standard events. In running events up to and including 400 metres, only fully automatic times are shown. Marks listed are those which are considered statistically acceptable by the ATFS, and thus may differ from official records. These are followed by 'odd events', road bests and bests by over 35/40 masters.

World All-time and Year Lists

Lists are presented in the following format: Mark, Wind reading (where appropriate), Name, Nationality (abbreviated), Date of birth, Position in competition, Meeting name (if significant), Venue, Date of performance.

In standard events the best 30 or so performances are listed followed by the best marks for other athletes. Position, meet and venue details have been omitted beyond 100th in year lists.

In the all-time lists performances which have been world records (or world bests, thus including some unratified marks) are shown with WR against them (or WIR for world indoor records).

Juniors (U20) are shown with-J after date of birth, and Youths (U18) with -Y.

Indexes

These contain the names of all athletes ranked with full details in the world year lists for standard events (and others such as half marathon). The format of the index is as follows: Family name, First name, Nationality, Birthdate, Height (cm) and Weight (kg), 2013 best mark, Lifetime best (with year) as at the end of 2012.

* indicates an athlete who is profiled in the Biographies section, and ^ one who has been profiled in previous editions.

General Notes

Altitude aid

Marks set at an altitude of 1000m or higher have been suffixed by the letter "A" in events where altitude may be of significance.

Although there are no separate world records for altitude assisted events, it is understood by experts that in all events up to 400m in length (with the possible exclusion of the 110m hurdles), and in the horizontal jumps, altitude gives a material benefit to performances. For events beyond 800m, however, the thinner air of high altitude has a detrimental effect.

Supplementary lists are included in relevant events for athletes with seasonal bests at altitude who have low altitude marks qualifying for the main list.

Some leading venues over 1000m

Addis Ababa ETH	2365m
Air Force Academy USA	2194
Albuquerque USA	1555
Antananarivo MAD	1350
Ávila ESP	1128
Bloemfontein RSA	1392
Bogotá COL	2644
Boulder USA	1655
Bozeman USA	1467
Calgary CAN	1045
Cali COL	1046
Ciudad de Guatemala GUA	1402
Ciudad de México MEX	2247
Cochabamba BOL	2558
Colorado Springs USA	1823
Cuenca ECU	2561
Denver USA	1609
El Paso USA	1187
Flagstaff USA	2107
Fort Collins USA	1521
Gabarone BOT	1006
Germiston RSA	1661
Guadalajara MEX	1567
Harare ZIM	1473
Johannesburg RSA	1748
Kampala UGA	1189
Krugersdorp RSA	1740
La Paz BOL	3630
Levelland USA	1069
Logan USA	1372
Medellín COL	1541
Monachil ESP	2302
Nairobi KEN	1675
Pietersburg RSA	1230
Pocatello USA	1361
Potchefstroom RSA	1351
Pretoria RSA	1400
Provo USA	1380
Pueblo USA	1487
Reno USA	1369
Roodepoort RSA	1720
Rustenburg RSA	1157
Salt Lake City USA	1321
Secunda RSA	1628
Sestriere ITA	2050
Soría ESP	1056
South Lake Tahoe USA	1909
Sucre BOL	2750
Tunja COL	2810
Windhoek NAM	1725
Xalapa MEX	1420

Some others over 500m

Albertville FRA	550
Almaty KZK	847
Ankara TUR	902
Bangalore, IND	949
Bern SUI	555
Blacksburg USA	634
Boise USA	818
Canberra AUS	581
La Chaux de Fonds SUI	997
Caracas VEN	922
Edmonton CAN	652

Jablonec CZE	598
Las Vegas USA	619
Lausanne SUI	597
Lubbock USA	988
Madrid ESP	640
Magglingen SUI	751
Malles ITA	980
Moscow, Idaho USA	787
München GER	520
Nampa, Idaho USA	760
Salamanca ESP	806
Santiago de Chile CHI	520
São Paulo BRA	725
Sofia BUL	564
Spokane USA	576
Trípoli GRE	655
Tucson USA	728
Uberlândia BRA	852
350m-500m	
Annecy FRA	448
Banská Bystrica SVK	362
Fayetteville USA	407
Genève SUI	385
Götzis AUS	448
Johnson City USA	499
Rieti ITA	402
Sindelfingen GER	440
Stuttgart GER	415
Tashkent UZB	477
Zürich SUI	410

Automatic timing
In the main lists for sprints and hurdles, only times recorded by fully automatic timing devices are included.

Hand timing
In the sprints and hurdles supplementary lists are included for races which are hand timed. Athletes with a hand timed best 0.01 seconds or more better than his or her automatically timed best has been included, but hand timed lists have been terminated close to the differential levels considered by the IAAF to be equivalent to automatic times, i.e. 0.24 sec. for 100m, 200m, 100mh, 110mh, and 0.14 sec. for 400m and 400mh. It should be noted that this effectively recognises bad hand timekeeping, for there should be no material difference between hand and auto times, but badly trained timekeepers anticipate the finish, having reacted to the flash at the start.

In events beyond 400m, auto times are integrated with hand timed marks, the latter identifiable by times being shown to tenths. All-time lists also include some auto times in tenths of a second, identified with '.

Indoor marks
Indoor marks are included in the main lists for field events and straightway track events, but not for other track events as track sizes vary in circumference (200m is the international standard) and banking, while outdoor tracks are standardised at 400m. Outdoor marks for athletes with indoor bests are shown in a supplemental list.

Mixed races
For record purposes athletes may not, except in road races, compete in mixed sex races. Statistically there would not appear to be any particular logic in this, and women's marks set in such races are shown in our lists – annotated with mx. In such cases the athlete's best mark in single sex competition is appended.

Field event series
Field event series are given (where known) for marks in the top 30 performances lists.

Tracks and Courses
As well as climatic conditions, the type and composition of tracks and runways will affect standards of performance, as will the variations in road race courses.

Wind assistance
Anemometer readings have been shown for sprints and horizontal jumps in metres per second to one decimal place. If the figure was given to two decimal places, it has been rounded to the next tenth upwards, e.g. a wind reading of +2.01m/s, beyond the IAAF legal limit of 2.0, is rounded to +2.1; or -1.22m/s is rounded up to -1.2.

For multi-events a wind-assisted mark is one in which the average of the three wind-measured events is > 2m/s.

Drugs bans
The IAAF Council may decertify an athlete's records, titles and results if he or she is found to have used a banned substance before those performances. Performances at or after such a positive finding are shown in footnotes. Such athletes are shown with ¶ after their name in year lists, and in all-time lists if at any stage of their career they have served a drugs suspension of a year or more (thus not including athletes receiving public warnings or 3 month bans for stimulants etc., which for that year only are indicated with a #). This should not be taken as implying that the athlete was using drugs at that time. Nor have those athletes who have subsequently unofficially admitted to using banned substances been indicated; the ¶ is used only for those who have been caught.

Venues
Place names occasionally change. Our policy is to use names in force at the time that the performance was set. Thus Leningrad prior to 1991, Sankt-Peterburg from its re-naming.

Amendments
Keen observers may spot errors in the lists. They are invited to send corrections as well as news and results for 2014.

Peter Matthews
Email p.matthews121@btinternet.com

WORLD & CONTINENTAL RECORDS

As at 1 April 2014. **Key:** W = World, Afr = Africa, Asi = Asia, CAC = Central America & Caribbean, Eur = Europe, NAm = North America, Oce = Oceania, SAm = South America, Com = Commonwealth, W20 = World Junior (U20), W18 = World Youth (U18, not officially ratified by IAAF). h hand timed.
Successive columns show: World or Continent, performance, name, nationality, venue, date.
A altitude over 1000m, + timing by photo-electric-cell, # awaiting ratification, § not officially ratified

100 METRES

W,CAC,Com	9.58	Usain BOLT	JAM	Berlin	16 Aug 2009
NAm	9.69	Tyson GAY	USA	Shanghai	20 Sep 2009
Afr	9.85	Olusoji FASUBA	NGR	Doha	12 May 2006
Eur	9.86	Francis OBIKWELU	POR	Athína	22 Aug 2004
Oce	9.93	Patrick JOHNSON	AUS	Mito	5 May 2003
Asi	9.99	Samuel FRANCIS	QAT	Amman	26 Jul 2007
SAm	10.00A	Róbson da SILVA	BRA	Ciudad de México	22 Jul 1988
W20	10.01	Darrel BROWN	TRI	Saint-Denis	24 Aug 2003
	10.01 §	Jeffery DEMPS	USA	Eugene	28 Jun 2008
	10.01 §	Yoshihide KIRYU	JPN	Hiroshima	29 Apr 2013
W18	10.19	Yoshihide KIRYU	JPN	Fukuroi	3 Nov 2012

200 METRES

W,CAC,Com	19.19	Usain BOLT	JAM	Berlin	20 Aug 2009
NAm	19.32	Michael JOHNSON	USA	Atlanta	1 Aug 1996
Afr	19.68	Frank FREDERICKS	NAM	Atlanta	1 Aug 1996
Eur	19.72A	Pietro MENNEA	ITA	Ciudad de México	12 Sep 1979
SAm	19.81	Alonso EDWARD	PAN	Berlin	20 Aug 2009
Asi	20.03	Shingo SUETSUGU	JPN	Yokohama	7 Jun 2003
Oce	20.06A	Peter NORMAN	AUS	Ciudad de México	16 Oct 1968
W20	19.93	Usain BOLT	JAM	Hamilton, BER	11 Apr 2004
W18	20.13	Usain BOLT	JAM	Bridgetown	20 Jul 2003

400 METRES

W, NAm	43.18	Michael JOHNSON	USA	Sevilla	26 Aug 1999
Com, CAC	43.94	Kirani JAMES	GRN	London (OS)	6 Aug 2012
Afr	44.10	Gary KIKAYA	COD	Stuttgart	9 Sep 2006
SAm	44.29	Sanderlei PARRELA	BRA	Sevilla	26 Aug 1999
Eur	44.33	Thomas SCHÖNLEBE	GER	Roma	3 Sep 1987
Oce	44.38	Darren CLARK	AUS	Seoul	26 Sep 1988
Asi	44.56	Mohamed AL-MALKY	OMN	Budapest	12 Aug 1988
W20	43.87	Steve LEWIS	USA	Seoul	28 Sep 1988
W18	45.14	Obea MOORE	USA	Santiago de Chile	2 Sep 1995

800 METRES

W, Afr, Com	1:40.91	David RUDISHA	KEN	London (OS)	9 Aug 2012
Eur	1:41.11	Wilson KIPKETER	DEN	Köln	24 Aug 1997
SAm	1:41.77	Joaquim CRUZ	BRA	Köln	26 Aug 1984
NAm	1:42.60	Johnny GRAY	USA	Koblenz	28 Aug 1985
Asi	1:42.79	Youssef Saad KAMEL	BRN	Monaco	29 Jul 2008
CAC	1:42.85	Norberto TELLEZ	CUB	Atlanta	31 Jul 1996
Oce	1:44.3+ h	Peter SNELL	NZL	Christchurch	3 Feb 1962
W20	1:41.73	Nijel AMOS	BOT	London (OS)	9 Aug 2012
W18	1:43.37	Mohamed AMAN	ETH	Rieti	10 Sep 2011

1000 METRES

W, Afr, Com	2:11.96	Noah NGENY	KEN	Rieti	5 Sep 1999
Eur	2:12.18	Sebastian COE	GBR	Oslo	11 Jul 1981
NAm	2:13.9	Rick WOHLHUTER	USA	Oslo	30 Jul 1974
SAm	2:14.09	Joaquim CRUZ	BRA	Nice	20 Aug 1984
Asi	2:14.72	Youssef Saad KAMEL	BRN	Stockholm	22 Jul 2008
Oce	2:16.57	John WALKER	NZL	Oslo	1 Jul 1980
CAC	2:17.0	Byron DYCE	JAM	København	15 Aug 1973
W20	2:13.93 §	Abubaker KAKI	SUD	Stockholm	22 Jul 2008
W18	2:17.44	Hamza DRIOUCH	QAT	Sollentuna	9 Aug 2011

1500 METRES

W, Afr	3:26.00	Hicham EL GUERROUJ	MAR	Roma	14 Jul 1998
Com	3:26.34	Bernard LAGAT	KEN	Bruxelles	24 Aug 2001
Eur	3:28.81	Mo FARAH	GBR	Monaco	19 Jul 2013
Asi	3:29.14	Rashid RAMZI	BRN	Roma	14 Jul 2006

NAm	3:29.30	Bernard LAGAT	USA	Rieti	28 Aug 2005
Oce	3:30.35	Nick WILLIS	NZL	Monaco	20 Jul 2012
SAm	3:33.25	Hudson Santos de SOUZA	BRA	Rieti	28 Aug 2005
CAC	3:35.03	Maurys CASTILLO	CUB	Huelva	7 Jun 2012
W20	3:30.24	Cornelius CHIRCHIR	KEN	Monaco	19 Jul 2002
W18	3:33.72	Nicholas KEMBOI	KEN	Zürich	18 Aug 2006

1 MILE

W, Afr	3:43.13	Hicham El GUERROUJ	MAR	Roma	7 Jul 1999
Com	3:43.40	Noah NGENY	KEN	Roma	7 Jul 1999
Eur	3:46.32	Steve CRAM	GBR	Oslo	27 Jul 1985
NAm	3:46.91	Alan WEBB	USA	Brasschaat	21 Jul 2007
Asi	3:47.97	Daham Najim BASHIR	QAT	Oslo	29 Jul 2005
Oce	3:48.98	Craig MOTTRAM	AUS	Oslo	29 Jul 2005
SAm	3:51.05	Hudson de SOUZA	BRA	Oslo	29 Jul 2005
CAC	3:57.34	Byron DYCE	JAM	Stockholm	1 Jul 1974
	3:57.34	Juan Luis BARRIOS	MEX	Dublin	17 Jul 2013
W20	3:49.29	William BIWOTT TANUI	KEN	Oslo	3 Jul 2009
W18	3:54.56	Isaac SONGOK	KEN	Linz	20 Aug 2001

2000 METRES

W, Afr	4:44.79	Hicham EL GUERROUJ	MAR	Berlin	7 Sep 1999
Com	4:48.74	John KIBOWEN	KEN	Hechtel	1 Aug 1998
Oce	4:50.76	Craig MOTTRAM	AUS	Melbourne	9 Mar 2006
Eur	4:51.39	Steve CRAM	GBR	Budapest	4 Aug 1985
NAm	4:52.44	Jim SPIVEY	USA	Lausanne	15 Sep 1987
Asi	4:55.57	Mohammed SULEIMAN	QAT	Roma	8 Jun 1995
SAm	5:03.34	Hudson Santos de SOUZA	BRA	Manaus	6 Apr 2002
CAC	5:03.4	Arturo BARRIOS	MEX	Nice	10 Jul 1989
W20	4:56.25	Tesfaye CHERU	ETH	Reims	5 Jul 2011
W18	4:56.86	Isaac SONGOK	KEN	Berlin	31 Aug 2001

3000 METRES

W, Afr, Com	7:20.67	Daniel KOMEN	KEN	Rieti	1 Sep 1996
Eur	7:26.62	Mohammed MOURHIT	BEL	Monaco	18 Aug 2000
NAm	7:29.00	Bernard LAGAT	USA	Rieti	29 Aug 2010
Asi	7:30.76	Jamal Bilal SALEM	QAT	Doha	13 May 2005
Oce	7:32.19	Craig MOTTRAM	AUS	Athína	17 Sep 2006
CAC	7:35.71	Arturo BARRIOS	MEX	Nice	10 Jul 1989
SAm	7:39.70	Hudson Santos de SOUZA	BRA	Lausanne	2 Jul 2002
W20	7:28.78	Augustine CHOGE	KEN	Doha	13 May 2005
W18	7:32.37	Abreham CHERKOS Feleke	ETH	Lausanne	11 Jul 2006

5000 METRES

W, Afr	12:37.35	Kenenisa BEKELE	ETH	Hengelo	31 May 2004
Com	12:39.74	Daniel KOMEN	KEN	Bruxelles	22 Aug 1997
Eur	12:49.71	Mohammed MOURHIT	BEL	Bruxelles	25 Aug 2000
Asi	12:51.96 §	Albert ROP	BRN	Monaco	19 Jul 2013
	12:51.98	Saif Saaeed SHAHEEN	QAT	Roma	14 Jul 2006
NAm	12:53.60	Bernard LAGAT	USA	Monaco	22 Jul 2011
Oce	12:55.76	Craig MOTTRAM	AUS	London	30 Jul 2004
CAC	13:07.79	Arturo BARRIOS	MEX	London (CP)	14 Jul 1989
SAm	13:19.43	Marilson DOS SANTOS	BRA	Kassel	8 Jun 2006
W20	12:47.53	Hagos GEBRHIWET	ETH	Saint-Denis	6 Jul 2012
W18	12:54.19	Abreham CHERKOS Feleke	ETH	Roma	14 Jul 2006

10,000 METRES

W, Afr	26:17.53	Kenenisa BEKELE	ETH	Bruxelles	26 Aug 2005
Com	26:27.85	Paul TERGAT	KEN	Bruxelles	22 Aug 1997
Asi	26:38.76	Abdullah Ahmad HASSAN	QAT	Bruxelles	5 Sep 2003
Eur	26:46.57	Mohamed FARAH	GBR	Eugene	3 Jun 2011
NAm	26:48.00	Galen RUPP	USA	Bruxelles	16 Sep 2011
CAC	27:08.23	Arturo BARRIOS	MEX	Berlin	18 Aug 1989
Oce	27:24.95	Ben ST LAWRENCE	AUS	Stanford	1 May 2011
SAm	27:28.12	Marilson DOS SANTOS	BRA	Neerpelt	2 Jun 2007
W20	26:41.75	Samuel WANJIRU	KEN	Bruxelles	26 Aug 2005
W18	27:02.81	Ibrahim JAYLAN Gashu	ETH	Bruxelles	25 Aug 2006

HALF MARATHON

| W, Afr | 58:23 | Zersenay TADESE | ERI | Lisboa | 21 Mar 2010 |
| Com | 58:33 | Samuel WANJIRU | KEN | Den Haag | 17 Mar 2007 |

SAm	59:33	Marilson DOS SANTOS	BRA	Udine	14 Oct 2007
NAm	59:43	Ryan HALL	USA	Houston	14 Jan 2007
Eur	59:52	Fabian RONCERO	ESP	Berlin	1 Apr 2001
Oce	60:02 §	Darren WILSON	AUS	Tokyo	19 Jan 1997
	60:56	Collis BIRMINGHAM	AUS	Marugame	3 Feb 2013
Asi	60:25	Atsushi SATO	JPN	Udine	14 Oct 2007
CAC	60:14	Armando QUINTANILLA	MEX	Tokyo	21 Jan 1996
W20	59:16	Samuel WANJIRU	KEN	Rotterdam	11 Sep 2005
W18	60:38	Faustin BAHA Sulle	TAN	Lille	4 Sep 1999

MARATHON

W, Afr, Com	2:03:23	Wilson KIPSANG	KEN	Berlin	29 Sep 2013
NAm	2:05:38	Khalid KHANNOUCHI (ex MAR)	USA	London	14 Apr 2002
SAm	2:06:05	Ronaldo da COSTA	BRA	Berlin	20 Sep 1998
Asi	2:06:16	Toshinari TAKAOKA	JPN	Chicago	13 Oct 2002
Eur	2:06:36 §	António PINTO	POR	London	16 Apr 2000
	2:06:36	Benoît ZWIERZCHIEWSKI	FRA	Paris	6 Apr 2003
Oce	2:04:32	Tsegaye MEKONNEN	ETH	Dubai	24 Jan 2014
CAC	2:08:30	Dionicio CERÓN	MEX	London	2 Apr 1995
W20	2:06:07	Edic NDIEMA	KEN	Amsterdam	16 Oct 2011
W18	2:11:43	LI He	CHN	Beijing	14 Oct 2001

3000 METRES STEEPLECHASE

W, Asi	7:53.63	Saïf Saaeed SHAHEEN	QAT	Bruxelles	3 Sep 2004
Afr	7:53.64	Brimin KIPRUTO	KEN	Monaco	22 Jul 2011
Com	7:55.72	Bernard BARMASAI	KEN	Köln	24 Aug 1997
Eur	8:00.09	Mahiedine MEKHISSI-BENABBAD	FRA	Saint-Denis	6 Jul 2013
NAm	8:06.81	Evan JAGER	USA	Monaco	20 Jul 2012
Oce	8:14.05	Peter RENNER	NZL	Koblenz	29 Aug 1984
SAm	8:14.14	Wander MOURA	BRA	Mar del Plata	22 Mar 1995
CAC	8:25.69	Salvador MIRANDA	MEX	Barakaldo	9 Jul 2000
W20	7:58.66	Stephen CHERONO (now Shaheen)	KEN	Bruxelles	24 Aug 2001
W18	8:17.28 §	Jonathan NDIKU	KEN	Bydgoszcz	13 Jul 2008

110 METRES HURDLES

W, NAm	12.80	Aries MERRITT	USA	Bruxelles	7 Sep 2012
CAC	12.87	Dayron ROBLES	CUB	Ostrava	12 Jun 2008
Asi	12.88	LIU Xiang	CHN	Lausanne	11 Jul 2006
NAm	12.89	David OLIVER	USA	Saint-Denis	16 Jul 2010
Eur, Com	12.91	Colin JACKSON	GBR/Wal	Stuttgart	20 Aug 1993
Afr	13.24	Lehann FOURIE	RSA	Bruxelles	7 Sep 2012
SAm	13.27A	Paulo César VILLAR	COL	Guadalajara	28 Oct 2011
Oce	13.29	Kyle VANDER-KUYP	AUS	Göteborg	11 Aug 1995
W20	13.12	LIU Xiang (with 3'6" hurdles)	CHN	Lausanne	2 Jul 2002
W20 99cm h	13.08 §	Wayne DAVIS	USA	Port of Spain	31 Jul 2009
W18	13.43	SHI Dongpeng	CHN	Shanghai	6 May 2001
W18 91cm h	13.18	Wayne DAVIS	USA	Ostrava	12 Jul 2007

400 METRES HURDLES

W, NAm	46.78	Kevin YOUNG	USA	Barcelona	6 Aug 1992
Afr, Com	47.10	Samuel MATETE	ZAM	Zürich	7 Aug 1991
CAC	47.25	Felix SÁNCHEZ	DOM	Saint-Denis	29 Aug 2003
Eur	47.37	Stéphane DIAGANA	FRA	Lausanne	5 Jul 1995
Asi	47.53	Hadi Soua'an AL-SOMAILY	KSA	Sydney	27 Sep 2000
SAm	47.84	Bayano KAMANI	PAN	Helsinki	7 Aug 2005
Oce	48.28	Rohan ROBINSON	AUS	Atlanta	31 Jul 1996
W20	48.02	Danny HARRIS	USA	Los Angeles	17 Jun 1984
W18	48.89	L.J. VAN ZYL	RSA	Kingston	19 Jul 2002

HIGH JUMP

W, CAC	2.45	Javier SOTOMAYOR	CUB	Salamanca	27 Jul 1993
Eur	2.42	Patrik SJÖBERG	SWE	Stockholm	30 Jun 1987
	2.42 i§	Carlo THRÄNHARDT	FRG	Berlin	26 Feb 1988
NAm	2.40 i§	Hollis CONWAY	USA	Sevilla	10 Mar 1991
		Charles AUSTIN	USA	Zürich	7 Aug 1991
Asi	2.40	Mutaz Essa BARSHIM	QAT	Eugene	1 Jun 2013
Com	2.38i	Steve SMITH	GBR/Eng	Wuppertal	4 Feb 1994
	2.38	Troy KEMP	BAH	Nice	12 Jul 1995
	2.38	Derek DROUIN	CAN	Moskva	15 Aug 2013
Afr, Com	2.38	Jacques FREITAG	RSA	Oudtshoorn	5 Mar 2005

Oce	2.36	Tim FORSYTH	AUS	Melbourne	2 Mar 1997
SAm	2.33	Gilmar MAYO	COL	Pereira	17 Oct 1994
W20	2.37	Dragutin TOPIC	YUG	Plovdiv	12 Aug 1990
		Steve SMITH	GBR	Seoul	20 Sep 1992
W18	2.33	Javier SOTOMAYOR	CUB	La Habana	19 May 1984

POLE VAULT

W, Eur	6.16 i	Renaud LAVILLENIE	FRA	Donetsk	15 Feb 2014
	6.14 A	Sergey BUBKA	UKR	Sestriere	31 Jul 1994
Oce, Com	6.05	Dmitriy MARKOV	AUS	Edmonton	9 Aug 2001
NAm	6.04	Brad WALKER	USA	Eugene	8 Jun 2008
Afr	6.03	Okkert BRITS	RSA	Köln	18 Aug 1995
Asi	5.92i	Igor POTAPOVICH	KAZ	Stockholm	19 Feb 1998
	5.90	Grigoriy YEGOROV	KAZ Stuttgart 19 Aug 1993 & London (CP)		10 Sep 1993
	5.90	Igor POTAPOVICH	KAZ	Nice	10 Jul 1996
CAC	5.90	Lázaro BORGES	CUB	Daegu	29 Aug 2011
SAm	5.83	Thiago Braz da SILVA	BRA	Cartagena	5 Jul 2013
W20	5.80	Maksim TARASOV	RUS	Bryansk	14 Jul 1989
	5.80	Raphael HOLZDEPPE	GER	Biberach	28 Jun 2008
W18	5.51	Germán CHIARAVIGLIO	ARG	Pôrto Alegre	1 May 2004

LONG JUMP

W, NAm	8.95	Mike POWELL	USA	Tokyo	30 Aug 1991
Eur	8.86 A	Robert EMMIYAN	ARM	Tsakhkadzor	22 May 1987
SAm	8.73	Irving SALADINO	PAN	Hengelo	24 May 2008
CAC	8.71	Iván PEDROSO	CUB	Salamanca	18 Jul 1995
Com	8.62	James BECKFORD	JAM	Orlando	5 Apr 1997
Oce	8.54	Mitchell WATT	AUS	Stockholm	29 Jul 2011
Afr	8.50	Khotso MOKOENA	RSA	Madrid	4 Jul 2009
Asi	8.48	Mohamed Salim AL-KHUWALIDI	KSA	Sotteville	2 Jul 2006
W20	8.35	Sergey MORGUNOV	RUS	Cheboksary	20 Jun 2012
W18	8.25	Luis Alberto BUENO	CUB	La Habana	28 Sep 1986

TRIPLE JUMP

W, Eur, Com	18.29	Jonathan EDWARDS	GBR/Eng	Göteborg	7 Aug 1995
NAm	18.09	Kenny HARRISON	USA	Atlanta	27 Jul 1996
CAC	17.92	James BECKFORD	JAM	Odessa, Texas	20 May 1995
SAm	17.90	Jadel GREGÓRIO	BRA	Belém	20 May 2007
Asi	17.59	LI Yanxi	CHN	Jinan	26 Oct 2009
Oce	17.46	Ken LORRAWAY	AUS	London (CP)	7 Aug 1982
Afr	17.37	Tareq BOUGTAÏB	MAR	Khémisset	14 Jul 2007
W20	17.50	Volker MAI	GDR	Erfurt	23 Jun 1985
W18	17.24	Lazaro MARTÍNEZ	CUB	La Habana	1 Feb 2014

SHOT

W, NAm	23.12	Randy BARNES	USA	Westwood	20 May 1990
Eur	23.06	Ulf TIMMERMANN	GER	Haniá	22 May 1988
Com	22.21	Dylan ARMSTRONG	CAN	Calgary	25 Jun 2011
Afr	21.97	Janus ROBBERTS	RSA	Eugene	2 Jun 2001
CAC	21.45	Dorian SCOTT	JAM	Tallahassee	28 Mar 2008
Oce	21.26	Scott MARTIN	AUS	Melbourne	21 Feb 2008
SAm	21.26	Germán LAURO	ARG	Doha	10 May 2013
Asi	21.13	Sultan Abdulmajeed AL-HEBSHI	KSA	Doha	8 May 2009
W20	21.05 i§	Terry ALBRITTON	USA	New York	22 Feb 1974
	20.65 §	Mike CARTER	USA	Boston	4 Jul 1979
	20.43	David STORL	GER	Gerlingen	6 Jul 2009
W18	20.38	Jacko GILL	NZL	Auckland (North Shore)	5 Dec 2011
W20 6kg	23.00	Jacko GILL	NZL	Auckland (North Shore)	18 Aug 2013
W18 5kg	24.45	Jacko GILL	NZL	Auckland (North Shore)	19 Dec 2011

DISCUS

W, Eur	74.08	Jürgen SCHULT	GDR	Neubrandenburg	6 Jun 1986
NAm	72.34 ¶	Ben PLUCKNETT	USA	Stockholm	7 Jul 1981
	71.32 §	Ben PLUCKNETT	USA	Eugene	4 Jun 1983
CAC	71.06	Luis DELIS	CUB	La Habana	21 May 1983
Afr, Com	70.32	Frantz KRUGER	RSA	Salon-de-Provence	26 May 2002
Asi	69.32	Ehsan HADADI	IRI	Tallinn	3 Jun 2008
Oce	68.20	Benn HARRADINE	AUS	Townsville	10 May 2013
SAm	66.32	Jorge BALLIENGO	ARG	Rosario	15 Apr 2006
W20	65.62 §	Werner REITERER	AUS	Melbourne	15 Dec 1987

W18/20	65.31	Mykyta NESTERENKO	UKR	Tallinn	3 Jun 2008
W20 1.75kg	70.13	Mykyta NESTERENKO	UKR	Halle	24 May 2008
W18 1.5kg	77.50	Mykyta NESTERNKO	UKR	Koncha Zaspa	19 May 2008

¶ Disallowed by the IAAF following retrospective disqualification for drug abuse, but ratified by the AAU/TAC

HAMMER

W, Eur	86.74	Yuriy SEDYKH	UKR/RUS	Stuttgart	30 Aug 1986
Asi	84.86	Koji MUROFUSHI	JPN	Praha	29 Jun 2003
NAm	82.52	Lance DEAL	USA	Milano	7 Sep 1996
Afr	81.29	Mostafa Hicham AL-GAMAL	EGY	Al-Qáhira	21 Mar 2014
Com	80.63	Chris HARMSE	RSA	Durban	15 Apr 2005
Oce	79.29	Stuart RENDELL	AUS	Varazdin	6 Jul 2002
CAC	77.78	Alberto SANCHEZ	CUB	La Habana	15 May 1998
SAm	76.42	Juan CERRA	ARG	Trieste	25 Jul 2001
W20	78.33	Olli-Pekka KARJALAINEN	FIN	Seinäjoki	5 Aug 1999
W18	73.66	Vladislav PISKUNOV	UKR	Kyiv	11 Jun 1994
W20 6kg	85.57	Ashraf Amgad EL-SEIFY	QAT	Barcelona	14 Jul 2012
W18 5kg	85.38	Joaquin GÓMEZ	ARG	Buenos Aires	30 Nov 2013

JAVELIN

W, Eur	98.48	Jan ZELEZNY	CZE	Jena	25 May 1996
Com	91.46	Steve BACKLEY	GBR/Eng	Auckland (NS)	25 Jan 1992
NAm	91.29	Breaux GREER	USA	Indianapolis	21 Jun 2007
Oce	89.02	Jarrod BANNISTER	AUS	Brisbane	29 Feb 2008
Afr	88.75	Marius CORBETT	RSA	Kuala Lumpur	21 Sep 1998
Asi	87.60	Kazuhiro MIZOGUCHI	JPN	San José	27 May 1989
CAC	87.20A	Guillermo MARTÍNEZ	CUB	Guadalajara	28 Oct 2011
SAm	84.70	Edgar BAUMANN	PAR	San Marcos	17 Oct 1999
W20	84.69	Zigismunds SIRMAIS	LAT	Bauska	22 Jun 2011
W18 700g	89.34	Braian Ezequiel TOLEDO	ARG	Mar del Plata	6 Mar 2010

DECATHLON

W, NAm	9039	Ashton EATON	USA	Eugene	23 Jun 2012
Eur	9026	Roman SEBRLE	CZE	Götzis	27 May 2001
Com	8847	Daley THOMPSON	GBR/Eng	Los Angeles	9 Aug 1984
Asi	8725	Dmitriy KARPOV	KAZ	Athína	24 Aug 2004
CAC	8654	Leonel SUÁREZ	CUB	La Habana	4 Jul 2009
Oce	8490	Jagan HAMES	AUS	Kuala Lumpur	18 Sep 1998
SAm	8393	Carlos Eduardo CHININ	BRA	São Paulo	8 Jun 2013
Afr	8343	Willem COERTZEN	RSA	Moskva	11 Aug 2013
W20	8397	Torsten VOSS (with 3'6" hurdles)	GDR	Erfurt	7 Jul 1982
W18	8104h	Valter KÜLVET	EST	Viimsi	23 Aug 1981
	7829	Valter KÜLVET	EST	Stockholm	13 Sep 1981

4 X 100 METRES RELAY

W, CAC, Com	36.84	JAM (Carter, Frater, Blake, Bolt)		London (OS)	11 Aug 2012
NAm	37.04	USA (Kimmons, Gatlin, Gay, R Bailey)		London (OS)	11 Aug 2012
Eur	37.73	GBR (Gardener, Campbell, Devonish, Chambers)		Sevilla	29 Aug 1999
SAm	37.90	BRA (V Lima, Ribeiro, A da Silva, CI da Silva)		Sydney	30 Sep 2000
Afr	37.94	NGR (O Ezinwa, Adeniken, Obikwelu, D Ezinwa)		Athína	9 Aug 1997
Asi	38.03	JPN (Tsukahara, Suetsugu, Takahira, Asahara)		Osaka	1 Sep 2007
Oce	38.17	AUS (Henderson, Jackson, Brimacombe, Marsh)		Göteborg	12 Aug 1995
W20	38.66	USA (Kimmons, Omole, Williams, Merritt)		Grosseto	18 Jul 2004
W18	40.03	JAM (W Smith, M Frater, Spence, O Brown)		Bydgoszcz	18 Jul 1999

4 X 400 METRES RELAY

W, NAm	2:54.29	USA (Valmon, Watts, Reynolds, Johnson)		Stuttgart	22 Aug1993
Eur	2:56.60	GBR (Thomas, Baulch, Richardson, Black)		Atlanta	3 Aug 1996
CAC, Com	2:56.72	BAH (Brown, Pinder, Mathieu, Miller)		London (OS)	10 Aug 2012
SAm	2:58.56	BRA (C da Silva, A J dosSantos, de Araújo, Parrela)		Winnipeg	30 Jul 1999
Afr	2:58.68	NGR (Chukwu, Monye, Nada, Udo-Obong)		Sydney	30 Sep 2000
Oce	2:59.70	AUS (Frayne, Clark, Minihan, Mitchell)		Los Angeles	11 Aug 1984
Asi	3:00.76	JPN (Karube, K Ito, Osakada, Omori)		Atlanta	3 Aug 1996
W20	3:01.09	USA (Johnson, Merritt, Craig, Clement)		Grosseto	18 Jul 2004
W18	3:12.05	POL (Zrada, Kedzia, Grzegorczyk, Kowalski)		Kaunas	5 Aug 2001

20 KILOMETRES WALK

W, Eur	1:17:16	Vladimir KANAYKIN	RUS	Saransk	29 Sep 2007
	1:16:43 §	Sergey MOROZOV	RUS	Saransk	8 Jun 2008
SAm	1:17:21	Jefferson PÉREZ	ECU	Saint-Denis	23 Aug 2003
CAC	1:17:25.6 t	Bernardo SEGURA	MEX	Bergen (Fana)	7 May 1994

Oce, Com	1:17:33	Nathan DEAKES	AUS	Cixi	23 Apr 2005
Asi	1:17:36	WANG Zhen	CHN	Taicang	30 Mar 2012
Afr	1:19:02	Hatem GHOULA	TUN	Eisenhüttenstadt	10 May 1997
NAm	1:20:58	Iñaki GÓMEZ	CAN	London	4 Aug 2012
W20	1:18:06 §	Viktor BURAYEV	RUS	Adler	4 Mar 2001
W18	1:18:07	LI Gaobo	CHN	Cixi	23 Apr 2005

20,000 METRES TRACK WALK

W, CAC	1:17:25.6	Bernardo SEGURA	MEX	Bergen (Fana)	7 May 1994
Asi	1:18:03.3	BU Lingtang	CHN	Beijing	7 Apr 1994
Eur	1:18:35.2	Stefan JOHANSSON	SWE	Bergen (Fana)	15 May 1992
Oce, Com	1:19:48.1	Nathan DEAKES	AUS	Brisbane	4 Sep 2001
SAm	1:20:23.8	Andrés CHOCHO	ECU	Buenos Aires	5 Jun 2011
NAm	1:22:27.0	Tim BERRETT	CAN	Edmonds, WA	9 Jun 1996
Afr	1:22:51.84	Hatem GHOULA	TUN	Leutkirch	8 Sep 1994
W20	1:20:11.72	LI Gaobo	CHN	Wuhan	2 Nov 2007
W18	1:24:28.3	ZHU Hongjun	CHN	Xian	15 Sep 1999

50 KILOMETRES WALK

W, Eur	3:34:14	Denis NIZHEGORODOV	RUS	Cheboksary	11 May 2008
Oce, Com	3:35:47	Nathan DEAKES	AUS	Geelong	2 Dec 2006
Asi	3:36:06	YU Chaohong	CHN	Nanjing	22 Oct 2005
CAC	3:41:09	Erick BARRONDO	GUA	Dudince	23 Mar 2013
NAm	3:47:48	Marcel JOBIN	CAN	Québec	20 Jun 1981
SAm	3:49:26	Andrés CHOCHO	ECU	Valley Cottage	28 Oct 2012
Afr	3:55:32	Marc MUNDELL	RSA	London	11 Aug 2012
W20	3:41:10	ZHAO Jianguo	CHN	Wajima	16 Apr 2006
W18	3:45:46	YU Guoping	CHN	Guangzhou	23 Nov 2001

50,000 METRES TRACK WALK

W, Eur	3:35:27.2	Yoahnn DINIZ	FRA	Reims	12 Mar 2011
CAC	3:41:38.4	Raúl GONZÁLEZ	MEX	Bergen (Fana)	25 May 1979
Oce, Com	3:43:50.0	Simon BAKER	AUS	Melbourne	9 Sep 1990
Asi	3:48:13.7	ZHAO Yongshen	CHN	Bergen (Fana)	7 May 1994
NAm	3:56:13.0	Tim BERRETT	CAN	Saskatoon	21 Jul 1991
SAm	3:57:58.0	Claudio dos SANTOS	BRA	Blumenau	20 Sep 2008
Afr	4:21:44.5	Abdelwahab FERGUÈNE	ALG	Toulouse	25 Mar 1984

World Records at other men's events recognised by the IAAF

20,000m	56:25.98+	Haile GEBRSELASSIE	ETH	Ostrava	27 Jun 2007
1 Hour	21,285 m	Haile GEBRSELASSIE	ETH	Ostrava	27 Jun 2007
25,000m	1:12:25.4	Moses MOSOP	KEN	Eugene	3 Jun 2011
30,000m	1:26:47.4	Moses MOSOP	KEN	Eugene	3 Jun 2011
U18 Octathlon	6491	Jake STEIN	AUS	Villeneuve d'Ascq	7 Jul 2011
4 x 200m	1:18.68	Santa Monica Track Club	USA	Walnut	17 Apr 1994
		(Michael Marsh, Leroy Burrell, Floyd Heard, Carl Lewis)			
4 x 800m	7:02.43	Kenya Team	KEN	Bruxelles	25 Aug 2006
		(Joseph Mutua, William Yiampoy, Ismael Kombich, Wilfred Bungei)			
4 x l500m	14:36.23	W Biwott, Gathimba, G Rono, Choge	KEN	Bruxelles	4 Sep 2009

Walking

2 Hours track	29,572m+	Maurizio DAMILANO	ITA	Cuneo	3 Oct 1992
30km track	2:01:44.1	Maurizio DAMILANO	ITA	Cuneo	3 Oct 1992
U20 10,000m track	38:46.4	Viktor BURAYEV	RUS	Moskva	20 May 2000
U20 10km road	37:44	WANG Zhen	CHN	Beijing	18 Sep 2010
W18 10km road	38:57	LI Tianlei	CHN	Beijing	18 Sep 2010

WOMEN

100 METRES

W, NAm	10.49	Florence GRIFFITH JOYNER	USA	Indianapolis	16 Jul 1988
CAC, Com	10.70	Shelly-Ann FRASER	JAM	Kingstobn	29 Jun 2012
Eur	10.73	Christine ARRON	FRA	Budapest	19 Aug 1998
Asi	10.79	LI Xuemei	CHN	Shanghai	18 Oct 1997
Afr	10.79	Blessing OKAGBARE	NGR	London (OS)	27 Jul 2013
SAm	11.05	Ana Cláudia SILVA	BRA	Belém	12 May 2013
Oce	11.11	Melissa BREEN	AUS	Canberra	9 Feb 2014
W20	10.88	Marlies OELSNER/GÖHR	GDR	Dresden	1 Jul 1977
W18	11.13	Chandra CHEESEBOROUGH	USA	Eugene	21 Jun 1976

200 METRES

W, NAm	21.34	Florence GRIFFITH JOYNER	USA	Seoul	29 Sep 1988
CAC, Com	21.64	Merlene OTTEY	JAM	Bruxelles	13 Sep 1991

Eur	21.71	Marita KOCH	GDR	Chemnitz	10 Jun 1979
	21.71 §	Marita KOCH	GDR	Potsdam	21 Jul 1984
	21.71	Heike DRECHSLER	GDR	Jena	29 Jun 1986
	21.71 §	Heike DRECHSLER	GDR	Stuttgart	29 Aug 1986
Asi	22.01	LI Xuemei	CHN	Shanghai	22 Oct 1997
Afr	22.06 A§	Evette DE KLERK	RSA	Pietersburg	8 Apr 1989
	22.07	Mary ONYALI	NGR	Zürich	14 Aug 1996
Oce	22.23	Melinda GAINSFORD-TAYLOR	AUS	Stuttgart	13 Jul 1997
SAm	22.48	Ana Cláudia da SILVA	BRA	São Paulo	6 Aug 2011
W20	22.18	Allyson FELIX	USA	Athína	25 Aug 2004
	22.11A	Allyson FELIX (no doping control)	USA	Ciudad de México	3 May 2003
W18	22.58	Marion JONES	USA	New Orleans	28 Jun 1992

400 METRES

W, Eur	47.60	Marita KOCH	GDR	Canberra	6 Oct 1985
Oce, Com	48.63	Cathy FREEMAN	AUS	Atlanta	29 Jul 1996
NAm	48.70	Sanya RICHARDS	USA	Athína	16 Sep 2006
CAC	48.89	Ana GUEVARA	MEX	Saint-Denis	27 Aug 2003
Afr	49.10	Falilat OGUNKOYA	NGR	Atlanta	29 Jul 1996
SAm	49.64	Ximena RESTREPO	COL	Barcelona	5 Aug 1992
Asi	49.81	MA Yuqin	CHN	Beijing	11 Sep 1993
W20	49.42	Grit BREUER	GER	Tokyo	27 Aug 1991
W18	50.01	LI Jing	CHN	Shanghai	18 Oct 1997

800 METRES

W, Eur	1:53.28	Jarmila KRATOCHVÍLOVÁ	CZE	München	26 Jul 1983
Afr,W20,Com	1:54.01	Pamela JELIMO	KEN	Zürich	29 Aug 2008
CAC	1:54.44	Ana Fidelia QUIROT	CUB	Barcelona	9 Sep 1989
Asi	1:55.54	LIU Dong	CHN	Beijing	9 Sep 1993
NAm	1:56.40	Jearl MILES CLARK	USA	Zürich	11 Aug 1999
SAm	1:56.68	Letitia VRIESDE	SUR	Göteborg	13 Aug 1995
Oce	1:58.25	Toni HODGKINSON	NZL	Atlanta	27 Jul 1996
W18	1:57.18	WANG Yuan	CHN	Beijing	8 Sep 1993

1000 METRES

W, Eur	2:28.98	Svetlana MASTERKOVA	RUS	Bruxelles	23 Aug 1996
Afr	2:29.34	Maria Lurdes MUTOLA	MOZ	Bruxelles	25 Aug 1995
Com	2:29.66	Maria Lurdes MUTOLA	MOZ	Bruxelles	23 Aug 1996
NAm	2:31.80	Regina JACOBS	USA	Brunswick	3 Jul 1999
SAm	2:32.25	Letitia VRIESDE	SUR	Berlin	10 Sep 1991
CAC	2:33.21	Ana Fidelia QUIROT	CUB	Jerez de la Frontera	13 Sep 1989
Asi	2:33.6 §	Svetlana ULMASOVA	UZB	Podolsk	5 Aug 1979
Oce	2:37.84	Zoe BUCKMAN	AUS	Oslo	24 May 2012
W20	2:35.4a	Irina NIKITINA	RUS	Podolsk	5 Aug 1979
	2:35.4	Katrin WÜHN	GDR	Potsdam	12 Jul 1984
W18	2:38.58	Jo WHITE	GBR	London (CP)	9 Sep 1977

1500 METRES

W, Asi	3:50.46	QU Yunxia	CHN	Beijing	11 Sep 1993
Eur	3:52.47	Tatyana KAZANKINA	RUS	Zürich	13 Aug 1980
Afr	3:55.30	Hassiba BOULMERKA	ALG	Barcelona	8 Aug 1992
Com	3:56.98	Faith KIPYEGON	KEN	Doha	10 May 2013
NAm	3:57.12	Mary DECKER/SLANEY	USA	Stockholm	26 Jul 1983
Oce	4:00.93	Sarah JAMIESON	AUS	Stockholm	25 Jul 2006
CAC	4:01.84	Yvonne GRAHAM	JAM	Monaco	25 Jul 1995
SAm	4:05.67	Letitia VRIESDE	SUR	Tokyo	31 Aug 1991
W20	3:51.34	LANG Yinglai	CHN	Shanghai	18 Oct 1997
W18	3:54.52	ZHANG Ling	CHN	Shanghai	18 Oct 1997

1 MILE

W, Eur	4:12.56	Svetlana MASTERKOVA	RUS	Zürich	14 Aug 1996
NAm	4:16.71	Mary SLANEY	USA	Zürich	21 Aug 1985
Com	4:17.57	Zola BUDD	GBR/Eng	Zürich	21 Aug 1985
Asi	4:17.75	Maryam Yusuf JAMAL	BRN	Bruxelles	14 Sep 2007
Afr	4:18.23	Gelete BURKA	ETH	Rieti	7 Sep 2008
Oce	4:22.66	Lisa CORRIGAN	AUS	Melbourne	2 Mar 2007
CAC	4:24.64	Yvonne GRAHAM	JAM	Zürich	17 Aug 1994
SAm	4:30.05	Soraya TELLES	BRA	Praha	9 Jun 1988
W20	4:17.57	Zola BUDD	GBR	Zürich	21 Aug 1985
W18	4:30.81	Gelete BURKA	ETH	Heusden	2 Aug 2003

2000 METRES

W, Eur	5:25.36	Sonia O'SULLIVAN	IRL	Edinburgh	8 Jul 1994
Com	5:26.93	Yvonne MURRAY	GBR/Sco	Edinburgh	8 Jul 1994
Asi	5:29.43+§	WANG Junxia	CHN	Beijing	12 Sep 1993
	5:31.88	Maryam Yusuf JAMAL	BRN	Eugene	7 Jun 2009
NAm	5:32.7	Mary SLANEY	USA	Eugene	3 Aug 1984
Afr	5:30.19	Gelete BURKA	ETH	Bruxelles	4 Sep 2009
Oce	5:37.71	Benita JOHNSON	AUS	Ostrava	12 Jun 2003
W20	5:33.15	Zola BUDD	GBR	London (CP)	13 Jul 1984
W18	5:46.5+	Sally BARSOSIO	KEN	Zürich	16 Aug 1995

3000 METRES

W, Asi	8:06.11	WANG Junxia	CHN	Beijing	13 Sep 1993
Eur	8:21.42	Gabriela SZABO	ROM	Monaco	19 Jul 2002
Com	8:22.20	Paula RADCLIFFE	Eng	Monaco	19 Jul 2002
Afr	8:23.23	Edith MASAI	KEN	Monaco	19 Jul 2002
NAm	8:25.83	Mary SLANEY	USA	Roma	7 Sep 1985
Oce	8:35.31	Kimberley SMITH	NZL	Monaco	25 Jul 2007
CAC	8:37.07	Yvonne GRAHAM	JAM	Zürich	16 Aug 1995
SAm	9:02.37	Delirde BERNARDI	BRA	Linz	4 Jul 1994
W20	8:28.83	Zola BUDD	GBR	Roma	7 Sep 1985
W18	8:36.45	MA Ningning	CHN	Jinan	6 Jun 1993

5000 METRES

W, Afr	14:11.15	Tirunesh DIBABA	ETH	Oslo	6 Jun 2008
Com	14:20.87	Vivian CHERUIYOT	KEN	Stockho;lm	29 Jul 2011
Eur	14:23.75	Liliya SHOBUKHOVA	RUS	Kazan	19 Jul 2008
Asi	14:28.09	JIANG Bo	CHN	Shanghai	23 Oct 1997
NAm	14:44.76	Molly HUDDLE	USA	Bruxelles	27 Aug 2010
Oce	14:45.93	Kimberley SMITH	NZL	Roma	11 Jul 2008
CAC	15:04.32	Adriana FERNÁNDEZ	MEX	Gresham	17 May 2003
SAm	15:18.85	Simone Alves da SILVA	BRA	São Paulo	20 May 2011
W20	14:30.88	Tirunesh DIBABA	ETH	Bergen (Fana)	11 Jun 2004
W18	14:45.71	SONG Liqing	CHN	Shanghai	21 Oct 1997

10,000 METRES

W, Asi	29:31.78	WANG Junxia	CHN	Beijing	8 Sep 1993
Afr	29:53.80	Meselech MELKAMU	ETH	Utrecht	14 Jun 2009
Eur	29:56.34	Elvan ABEYLEGESSE	TUR	Beijing	15 Aug 2008
Com	30:01.09	Paula RADCLIFFE	GBR/Eng	München	6 Aug 2002
NAm	30:22.22	Shalane FLANAGAN	USA	Beijing	15 Aug 2008
Oce	30:35.54	Kimberley SMITH	NZL	Stanford	4 May 2008
CAC	31:10.12	Adriana FERNANDEZ	MEX	Brunswick	1 Jul 2000
SAm	31:47.76	Carmen de OLIVEIRA	BRA	Stuttgart	21 Aug 1993
W20	30:26.50	Linet MASAI	KEN	Beijing	15 Aug 2008
W18	31:11.26	SONG Liqing	CHN	Shanghai	19 Oct 1997

HALF MARATHON

W, Afr, Com	65:12	Florence KIPLAGAT	KEN	Barcelona	16 Feb 2014
Eur	66:25	Lornah KIPLAGAT	NED	Udine	14 Oct 2007
Oce	67:11	Kimberley SMITH	NZL	Philadelphia	18 Sep 2011
Asi	67:26	Kayoko FUKUSHI	JPN	Marugame	5 Feb 2006
NAm	67:34	Deena KASTOR	USA	Berrlin	2 Apr 2006
CAC	68:34 dh	Olga APPELL	MEX	Tokyo	24 Jan 1993
	69:28	Adrian FERNÁNDEZ	MEX	Kyoto	9 Mar 2003
SAm	70:30	Yolanda CABALLERO	COL	New York	17 Mar 2013
W20	67:57	Abebu GELAN	ETH	Ra's Al Khaymah	20 Feb 2009
W18	72:31	LIU Zhuang	CHN	Yangzhou	24 Apr 2011

MARATHON

W, Eur, Com	2:15:25	Paula RADCLIFFE	GBR/Eng	London	13 Apr 2003
Afr	2:18:37	Mary KEITANY	KEN	London	22 Apr 2012
Asi	2:19:12	Mizuki NOGUCHI	JPN	Berlin	25 Sep 2005
NAm	2:19:36	Deena KASTOR	USA	London	23 Apr 2006
Oce	2:22:36	Benita JOHNSON	AUS	Chicago	22 Oct 2006
CAC	2:22:59	Madai PÉREZ	MEX	Chicago	22 Oct 2006
SAm	2:29:17	Adriana da SILVA	BRA	Tokyo	26 Feb 2012
W20	2:22:38	ZHANG Yingying	CHN	Xiamen	5 Jan 2008

3000 METRES STEEPLECHASE

W, Eur	8:58.81	Gulnara GALKINA	RUS	Beijing	17 Aug 2008
Afr, Com	9:07.14	Milcah CHEMOS Cheywa	KEN	Oslo	7 Jun 2012
NAm	9:12.50	Jennifer BARRINGER	USA	Berlin	17 Aug 2009
Oce	9:18.35	Donna MacFARLANE	AUS	Oslo	6 Jun 2008
Asi	9:26.25	LIU Nian	CHN	Wuhan	2 Nov 2007
CAC	9:27.21	Mardrea HYMAN	JAM	Monaco	9 Sep 2005
SAm	9:41.22	Sabine HEITLING	BRA	London	25 Jul 2009
W20	9:20.37	Birtukan ADAMU	ETH	Roma	26 May 2011
W18	9:29.52	Korahubish ITA'A	ETH	Huelva	10 Jun 2009

100 METRES HURDLES

W, Eur	12.21	Yordanka DONKOVA	BUL	Stara Zagora	20 Aug 1988
NAm	12.26	Brianna ROLLINS	USA	Des Moines	22 Jun 2013
Oce, Com	12.28	Sally PEARSON	AUS	Daegu	3 Sep 2011
Asi	12.44	Olga SHISHIGINA	KAZ	Luzern	27 Jun 1995
Afr	12.44	Glory ALOZIE	NGR	Monaco	8 Aug 1998
	12.44	Glory ALOZIE	NGR	Bruxelles	28 Aug 1998
	12.44	Glory ALOZIE	NGR	Sevilla	28 Aug 1999
CAC	12.45	Brigitte FOSTER	JAM	Eugene	24 May 2003
SAm	12.67	Yvette LEWIS	PAN	Lahti	17 Jul 2013
W20	12.84	Aliuska LÓPEZ	CUB	Zagreb	16 Jul 1987
W18	12.95	Candy YOUNG	USA	Walnut	16 Jun 1979

400 METRES HURDLES

Eur, W	52.34	Yuliya PECHONKINA	RUS	Tula	8 Aug 2003
CAC, Com	52.42	Melaine WALKER	JAM	Berlin	20 Aug 2009
NAm	52.47	Lashinda DEMUS	USA	Daegu	1 Sep 2011
Afr	52.90	Nezha BIDOUANE	MAR	Sevilla	25 Aug 1999
Oce	53.17	Debbie FLINTOFF-KING	AUS	Seoul	28 Sep 1988
Asi	53.96	HAN Qing	CHN	Beijing	9 Sep 1993
	53.96	SONG Yinglan	CHN	Guangzhou	22 Nov 2001
SAm	55.84	Lucimar TEODORO	BRA	Belém	24 May 2009
W20	54.40	WANG Xing	CHN	Nanjing	21 Oct 2005
W18	55.20	Leslie MAXIE	USA	San Jose	9 Jun 1984

HIGH JUMP

W, Eur	2.09	Stefka KOSTADINOVA	BUL	Roma	30 Aug 1987
Afr, Com	2.06	Hestrie CLOETE	RSA	Saint-Denis	31 Aug 2003
NAm	2.05	Chaunté HOWARD-LOWE	USA	Des Moines	26 Jun 2010
CAC	2.04	Silvia COSTA	CUB	Barcelona	9 Sep 1989
Asi	1.99	Marina AITOVA	KAZ	Athína	13 Jul 2009
Oce	1 98	Vanessa WARD	AUS	Perth	12 Feb 1989
	1.98	Alison INVERARITY	AUS	Ingolstadt	17 Jul 1994
SAm	1.96	Solange WITTEVEEN	ARG	Oristano	8 Sep 1997
W20	2.01	Olga TURCHAK	KAZ	Moskva	7 Jul 1986
	2.01	Heike BALCK	GDR	Chemnitz	18 Jun 1989
W18	1.96A	Charmaine GALE	RSA	Bloemfontein	4 Apr 1981
	1.96	Olga TURCHAK	UKR	Donetsk	7 Sep 1984
	1.96	Eleanor PATTERSON	AUS	Townsville	7 Dec 2013

POLE VAULT

W, Eur	5.06	Yelena ISINBAYEVA	RUS	Zürich	28 Aug 2009
NAm	4.92	Jennifer STUCZYNSKI	USA	Eugene	6 Jul 2008
CAC	4.90	Yarisley SILVA	CUB	Hengelo	8 Jun 2013
Com	4.87i	Holly BLEASDALE	GBR	Villeurbanne	21 Jan 2012
SAm	4.85	Fabiana MURER	BRA	San Fernando	4 Jun 2010
	4.85	Fabiana MURER	BRA	Daegu	30 Aug 2011
Oce, Com	4.76	Alana BOYD	AUS	Perth	24 Feb 2012
Asi	4.65	LI Ling	CHN	Shenyang	8 Sep 2013
Afr	4.42	Elmarie GERRYTS	RSA	Wesel	12 Jun 2000
W20	4.63i	Angelica BENGTSSON	SWE	Stockholm	25 Feb 2011
	4.58	Angelica BENGTSSON	SWE	Sollentuna	5 Jul 2012
W18	4.47	Angelica BENGTSSON	SWE	Moskva	22 May 2010

LONG JUMP

W, Eur	7.52	Galina CHISTYAKOVA	RUS	Sankt-Peterburg	11 Jun 1988
NAm	7.49	Jackie JOYNER-KERSEE	USA	New York	22 May 1994
	7.49A §	Jackie JOYNER-KERSEE	USA	Sestriere	31 Jul 1994
SAm	7.26A	Maurren MAGGI	BRA	Bogotá	26 Jun 1999

CAC, Com	7.16A	Elva GOULBOURNE	JAM	Ciudad de México	22 May 2004
Afr	7.12	Chioma AJUNWA	NGR	Atlanta	1 Aug 1996
Asi	7.01	YAO Weili	CHN	Jinan	5 Jun 1993
Oce	7.00	Bronwyn THOMPSON	AUS	Melbourne	7 Mar 2002
W20	7.14	Heike DAUTE/Drechsler	GDR	Bratislava	4 Jun 1983
W18	6.91	Heike DAUTE/Drechsler	GDR	Jena	9 Aug 1981

TRIPLE JUMP

W, Eur	15.50	Inessa KRAVETS	UKR	Göteborg	10 Aug 1995
Afr, Com	15.39	Françoise MBANGO ETONE	CMR	Beijing	17 Aug 2008
CAC	15.29	Yamilé ALDAMA	CUB	Roma	11 Jul 2003
Asi	15.25	Olga RYPAKOVA	KAZ	Split	4 Sep 2010
SAm	14.99A	Caterine IBARGÜEN	COL	Bogotá	13 Aug 2011
NAm	14.45	Tiombé HURD	USA	Sacramento	11 Jul 2004
Oce	14.04	Nicole MLADENIS	AUS	Hobart	9 Mar 2002
	14.04	Nicole MLADENIS	AUS	Perth	7 Dec 2003
W20	14.62	Tereza MARINOVA	BUL	Sydney	25 Aug 1996
W18	14.57	HUANG Qiuyan	CHN	Shanghai	19 Oct 1997

SHOT

W, Eur	22.63	Natalya LISOVSKAYA	RUS	Moskva	7 Jun 1987
Asi	21.76	LI Meisu	CHN	Shijiazhuang	23 Apr 1988
Oce, Com	21.24	Valerie ADAMS	NZL	Daegu	29 Aug 2011
CAC	20.96	Belsy LAZA	CUB	Ciudad de México	2 May 1992
NAm	20.24	Michelle CARTER	USA	Des Moines	22 Jun 2013
SAm	19.30	Elisângela ADRIANO	BRA	Tunja	14 Jul 2001
Afr	18.35	Vivian CHUKWUEMEKA	NGR	Ijebu Ode	17 Apr 2006
	18.43 §	Vivian CHUKWUEMEKA	NGR	Walnut	19 Apr 2003
W20	20.54	Astrid KUMBERNUSS	GDR	Orimattila	1 Jul 1989
W18	19.08	Ilke WYLUDDA	GDR	Karl-Marx-Stadt	9 Aug 1986

DISCUS

W, Eur	76.80	Gabriele REINSCH	GDR	Neubrandenburg	9 Jul 1988
Asi	71.68	XIAO Yanling	CHN	Beijing	14 Mar 1992
CAC	70.88	Hilda RAMOS	CUB	La Habana	8 May 1992
Oce, Com	68.72	Daniela COSTIAN	AUS	Auckland	22 Jan 1994
NAm	67.74	Stephanie TRAFTON-BROWN	USA	Wailuku	4 May 2012
Afr	64.87	Elizna NAUDE	RSA	Stellenbosch	2 Mar 2007
SAm	64.21	Andressa de MORAIS	BRA	Barquisimeto	10 Jun 2012
W20	74.40	Ilke WYLUDDA	GDR	Berlin	13 Sep 1988
W18	65.86	Ilke WYLUDDA	GDR	Neubrandenburg	1 Aug 1986

HAMMER

W, Eur	79.42	Betty HEIDLER	GER	Halle	21 May 2011
CAC	76.62	Yipsi MORENO	CUB	Zagreb	9 Sep 2008
Asi	76.99	ZHANG Wenxiu	CHN	Ostrava	24 May 2012
NAm	75.73	Amanda BINGSON	USA	Des Moines	22 Jun 2013
Com	75.04	Sultana FRIZELL	CAN	Tucson	16 Mar 2012
SAm	73.74	Jennifer DAHLGREN	ARG	Buenos Aires	10 Apr 2010
Oce	71.12	Bronwyn EAGLES	AUS	Adelaide	6 Feb 2003
Afr	69.20	Amy SÈNE	SEN	Chateauroux	9 Mar 2014
W20	73.24	ZHANG Wenxiu	CHN	Changsha	24 Jun 2005
W18	70.60	ZHANG Wenxiu	CHN	Nanning	5 Apr 2003
W18 3kg	76.04	Réka GYURÁTZ	HUN	Zalaegerszeg	23 Jun 2013

JAVELIN

W, Eur	72.28	Barbora SPOTÁKOVÁ	CZE	Stuttgart	13 Sep 2008
CAC	71.70	Osleidys MENÉNDEZ	CUB	Helsinki	14 Aug 2005
Afr, Com	69.35	Sunette VILJOEN	RSA	New York	9 Jun 2012
Oce	66.83	Kim MICKLE	AUS	Melbourne	22 Mar 2014
NAm	66.67	Kara PATTERSON	USA	Des Moines	25 Jun 2010
Asi	65.62	LU Huihui	CHN	Zhaoqing	27 Apr 2013
SAm	62.62A	Sabina MOYA	COL	Ciudad de Guatemala	12 May 2002
W20	63.01	Vira REBRYK	UKR	Bydgoszcz	10 Jul 2008
W18	62.93	XUE Juan	CHN	Changsha	27 Oct 2003

HEPTATHLON

W, NAm	7291	Jackie JOYNER-KERSEE	USA	Seoul	24 Sep 1988
Eur	7032	Carolina KLÜFT	RUS	Osaka	26 Aug 2007
Com	6955	Jeccica ENNIS	GBR/Eng	London (OS)	4 Aug 2012

Asi	6942	Ghada SHOUAA	SYR	Götzis	26 May 1996
Oce	6695	Jane FLEMMING	AUS	Auckland	28 Jan 1990
CAC	6527	Diane GUTHRIE-GRESHAM	JAM	Knoxville	3 Jun 1995
Afr	6423	Margaret SIMPSON	GHA	Götzis	29 May 2005
SAm	6160	Lucimara DA SILVA	BRA	Barquisimeto	10 Jun 2012
W20	6542	Carolina KLÜFT	SWE	München	10 Aug 2002
W18	6185	SHEN Shengfei	CHN	Shanghai	18 Oct 1997

DECATHLON

W, Eur	8358	Austra SKUJYTE	LTU	Columbia, MO	15 Apr 2005
Asi	7798 §	Irina NAUMENKO	KAZ	Talence	26 Sep 2004
NAm	7577 §	Tiffany LOTT-HOGAN	USA	Lage	10 Sep 2000
CAC	7245 §	Magalys GARCÍA	CUB	Wien	29 Jun 2002
Afr, Com	6915	Margaret SIMPSON	GHA	Réduit	19 Apr 2007
SAm	6570	Andrea BORDALEJO	ARG	Rosario	28 Nov 2004
Oce	5740	Preya CAREY	AUS	Brisbane	6 Sep 2001

4 X 100 METRES RELAY

W, NAm	40.82	USA (Madison, Felix, Knight, Jeter)		London (OS)	10 Aug 2012
CAC, Com	41.29	JAM (Russell, Stewart, Calvert, Fraser-Pryce)		Moskva	18 Aug 2013
Eur	41.37	GDR (Gladisch, Rieger, Auerswald, Göhr)		Canberra	6 Oct 1985
Asi	42.23	Sichuan CHN (Xiao Lin, Li Yali, Liu Xiaomei, Li Xuemei)	Shanghai	23 Oct 1997
SAm	42.29	BRA (E dos Santos, Silva, Krasucki, R Santos)		Moskva	18 Aug 2013
Afr	42.39	NGR (Utondu, Idehen, Opara-Thompson, Onyali)		Barcelona	7 Aug 1992
Oce	42.99A	AUS (Massey, Broadrick, Lambert, Gainsford-Taylor)		Pietersburg	18 Mar 2000
W20	43.29	USA (Knight, Tarmoh, Olear, Mayo)		Eugene	8 Aug 2006
W18	44.05	GDR (Koppetsch, Oelsner, Sinzel, Brehmer)		Athína	24 Aug 1975

4 X 400 METRES RELAY

W, Eur	3:15.17	URS (Ledovskaya, Nazarova, Pinigina, Bryzgina)		Seoul	1 Oct 1988
NAm	3:15.51	USA (D.Howard, Dixon, Brisco, Griffith Joyner)		Seoul	1 Oct 1988
CAC, Com	3:18.71	JAM (Whyte, Prendergast, N Williams-Mills, S Williams)	Daegu	3 Sep 2011
Afr	3:21.04	NGR (Bisi Afolabi, Yusuf, Opara, Ogunkoya)		Atlanta	3 Aug 1996
Oce	3:23.81	AUS (Peris, Lewis, Gainsford-Taylor, Freeman)		Sydney	30 Sep 2000
Asi	3:24.28	Hebei CHN (An X, Bai X, Cao C, Ma Y)		Beijing	13 Sep 1993
SAm	3:26.68	BRA (Coutinho, de Oliveira, Souza, de Lima)		São Paulo	7 Aug 2011
W20	3:27.60	USA (Anderson, Kidd, Smith, Hastings)		Grosseto	18 Jul 2004
W18	3:36.98	GBR (Ravenscroft, E McMeekin, Kennedy, Pettett)		Duisburg	26 Aug 1973

10 KILOMETRES WALK

W, Eur	41:04	Yelena NIKOLAYEVA	RUS	Sochi	20 Apr 1996
Asi	41:16	WANG Yan	CHN	Eisenhüttenstadt	8 May 1999
Oce, Com	41:30	Kerry SAXBY-JUNNA	AUS	Canberra	27 Aug 1988
CAC	42:42	Graciela MENDOZA	MEX	Naumburg	25 May 1997
NAm	44:17	Michelle ROHL	USA	Göteborg	7 Aug 1995
SAm	45:03	Geovanna IRUSTA	BOL	Podebrady	19 Apr 1997
Afr	45:06A	Susan VERMEULEN	RSA	Bloemfontein	17 Apr 1999
W20	41:52 §	Tatyana MINEYEVA	RUS	Penza	5 Sep 2009
	41:57 §	GAO Hongmiao	CHN	Beijing	8 Sep 1993
W18	43:28	Aleksandra KUDRYASHOVA	RUS	Adler	19 Feb 2006

10,000 METRES TRACK WALK

W, Asi	41:37.9 §	GAO Hongmiao	CHN	Beijing	7 Apr 1994
W, Eur	41:56.23	Nadyezhda RYASHKINA	RUS	Seattle	24 Jul 1990
Oce, Com	41:57.22	Kerry SAXBY-JUNNA	AUS	Seattle	24 Jul 1990
NAm	44:30.1 m	Alison BAKER	CAN	Bergen (Fana)	15 May 1992
	44:06 no kerb	Michelle ROHL	USA	Kenosha	2 Jun 1996
CAC	44:16.21	Cristina LÓPEZ	ESA	San Salvador	13 Jul 2007
SAm	45:11.2A	Lorena ARENAS	COL	Medellín	15 Apr 2012
Afr	47:30.28	Chahinez AL-NASRI	TUN	Amman	16 May 2012
W20	42:49.7 §	GAO Hongmiao	CHN	Jinan	15 Mar 1992
	42:59.48	Yelena LASHMANOVA	RUS	Tallinn	21 Jul 2011
W18	42:56.09	GAO Hongmiao	CHN	Tangshan	27 Sep 1991

20,000 METRES TRACK WALK

W, Eur	1:26:52.3	Olimpiada IVANOVA	RUS	Brisbane	6 Sep 2001
Asi, W20	1:29:32.4 §	SONG Hongjuan	CHN	Changsha	24 Oct 2003
SAm	1:31:46.9	Sandra Lorena ARENAS	COL	Santiago de Chile	13 Mar 2014
NAm	1:33:28.2	Teresa VAILL	USA	Carson	25 Jun 2005
Oce, Com	1:33:40.2	Kerry SAXBY-JUNNA	AUS	Brisbane	6 Sep 2001

CAC	1:34:56.7A	Maria del Rosario SÁNCHEZ	MEX	Xalapa	16 Jul 2000
Afr	1:36:43.43A	Nicolene CRONJE	RSA	Germiston	20 Mar 2004
W18	1:34:21.56	WANG Xue	CHN	Wuhan	1 Nov 2007

20 KILOMETRES WALK

W, Eur	1:24:50 §	Olimpiada IVANOVA	RUS	Adler	4 Mar 2001
	1:25:02	Yeoena LASHMANOVA	RUS	London	11 Aug 2012
Asi	1:25:16	QIEYANG Shenjie	CHN	London	11 Aug 2012
Oce, Com	1:27:44	Jane SAVILLE	AUS	Naumburg	2 May 2004
CAC	1:28:31	Mima ORTIZ	GUA	Rio Maior	6 Apr 2013
SAm	1:31:25	Miriam RAMÓN	ECU	Lima	7 May 2005
NAm	1:31:40	Rachel SEAMAN	CAN	Lugano	16 Mar 2014
Afr	1:34:19 §	Grace WANJIRU-NJUE	KEN	Nairobi	1 Aug 2010
W20	1:25:30	Anisya KIRDYAPKINA	RUS	Adler	23 Feb 2008
W18	1:30:28	ZHOU Tongmei	CHN	Cixi	23 Apr 2005

World Records at other track & field events recognised by the IAAF

1 Hour	18,517 m	Dire TUNE	ETH	Ostrava	12 Jun 2008
20,000m	1:05:26.6	Tegla LOROUPE	KEN	Borgholzhausen	3 Sep 2000
25,000m	1:27:05.84	Tegla LOROUPE	KEN	Mengerskirchen	21 Sep 2002
30,000m	1:45:50.0	Tegla LOROUPE	KEN	Warstein	6 Jun 2003
4x200m	1:27.46	USA (L Jenkins, L Colander, N Perry, M Jones)		Philadelphia	29 Apr 2000
4x800m	7:50.17	USSR (Olizarenko, Gurina, Borisova, Podyalovskaya)		Moskva	5 Aug 1984

WORLD BESTS AT NON-STANDARD EVENTS

Men

50m	5.47+e	Usain Bolt	JAM	Berlin (in 100m)	16 Aug 2009
60m	6.31+	Usain Bolt	JAM	Berlin (in 100m)	16 Aug 2009
100 yards	9.07	Asafa Powell	JAM	Ostrava	27 May 2010
150m turn	14.44+	Usain Bolt	JAM	Berlin (in 200m)	20 Aug 2009
150m straight	14.35	Usain Bolt	JAM	Manchester	17 May 2009
300m	30.85A	Michael Johnson	USA	Pretoria	24 Mar 2000
	30.97	Usain Bolt	JAM	Ostrava	27 May 2010
500m	59.32	Orestes Rodríguez	CUB	La Habana	15 Feb 2013
600m	1:12.81	Johnny Gray	USA	Santa Monica	24 May 1986
2 miles	7:58.61	Daniel Komen	KEN	Hechtel	19 Jul 1997
2000m Steeple	5:10.68	Mahiedine Mekhissi	FRA	Reims	30 Jun 2010
200mh	22.55	Laurent Ottoz	ITA	Milano	31 May 1995
(hand time)	22.5	Martin Lauer	FRG	Zürich	7 Jul 1959
200mh straight	22.10	Andrew Turner	GBR	Manchester	15 May 2011
220yh straight	21.9	Don Styron	USA	Baton Rouge	2 Apr 1960
300mh	34.48	Chris Rawlinson	GBR	Sheffield	30 Jun 2002
35lb weight	25.41	Lance Deal	USA	Azusa	20 Feb 1993
Pentathlon	4282 points	Bill Toomey	USA	London (CP)	16 Aug 1969
(1985 tables)		(7.58, 66.18, 21.3, 44.52, 4:20.3)			
Double decathlon	14,571 points	Joe Detmer	USA	Lynchburg	24/25 Sep 2010

10.93w, 7.30, 200mh 24.25w, 12.27, 5k 18:25.32, 2:02.23, 1.98, 400m 50.43, HT 31.82, 3kSt 11:22.47
15.01, DT 40.73, 200m 22.58, 4.85, 3k 10:25.99, 400mh 53.83, 51.95, 4:26.66, TJ 13.67, 10k 40:27.26

3000m track walk	10:47.11	Giovanni De Benedictis	ITA	San Giovanni Valdarno	19 May 1990
5000m track walk	18:05.49	Hatem Ghoula	TUN	Tunis	1 May 1997
10,000m track walk	37:53.09	Francisco Javier Fernández	ESP	Santa Cruz de Tenerife	27 Jul 2008
10 km road walk	37:11	Roman Rasskazov	RUS	Saransk	28 May 2000
30 km road walk	2:01:13+	Vladimir Kanaykin	RUS	Adler	19 Feb 2006
35 km road walk	2:21:31	Vladimir Kanaykin	RUS	Adler	19 Feb 2006
100 km road walk	8:38:07	Viktor Ginko	BLR	Scanzorosciate	27 Oct 2002

Women

50m	5.93+	Marion Jones	USA	Sevilla (in 100m)	22 Aug 1999
60m	6.85+	Marion Jones	USA	Sevilla (in 100m)	22 Aug 1999
100 yards	9.91	Veronica-Campbell-Brown	JAM	Ostrava	31 May 2011
150m	16.10+	Florence Griffith-Joyner	USA	Seoul (in 200m)	29 Sep 1988
300m	34.1+	Marita Koch	GDR	Canberra (in 400m)	6 Oct 1985
500m	1:05.9	Tatána Kocembová	CZE	Ostrava	2 Aug 1984
600m	1:22.63	Ana Fidelia Quirot	CUB	Guadalajara, ESP	25 Jul 1997
2 miles	8:58.58	Meseret Defar	ETH	Bruxelles	14 Sep 2007
2000m Steeple	6:03.38	Wioletta Janowska	POL	Gdansk	15 Jul 2006
200mh	24.8	Yadisleidis Pedroso	ITA	Caserta	6 Apr 2013
	25.82	Patricia Girard	FRA	Nantes	22 Sep 1999
300mh	38.16	Zuzana Hejnová	CZE	Cheb	2 Aug 2013
4 x 1500m	17:08.34	Tennesse University	USA	Philadelphia	24 Apr 2009
		(Price, Wright, Bell, Bowman)			

Double heptathlon	10,798 pts	Milla Kelo	FIN	Turku	7/8 Sep 2002
	100mh 14.89, HJ 1.51, 1500m 5:03.74, 400mh 62.18, SP 12.73, 200m 25.16, 100m 12.59				
	LJ 5.73w, 400m 56.10, JT 32.69, 800m 2:23.94, 200mh 28.72, DT 47.86, 3000m 11:48.68				
3000m track walk	11:48.24	Ileana Salvador	ITA	Padova	29 Aug 1993
5000m track walk	20:02.60	Gillian O'Sullivan	IRL	Dublin	13 Jul 2002
50 km road walk	4:10:59	Monica Svensson	SWE	Scanzorosciate	21 Oct 2007
100km road walk	10:04:50	Jolanta Dukure	LAT	Scanzorosciate	21 Oct 2007

LONG DISTANCE WORLD BESTS – MEN TRACK

	hr:min:sec	Name	Nat	Venue	Date
15,000m	0:42:18.7+	Haile Gebrselassie	ETH	Ostrava	27 Jun 2007
10 miles	0:45:23.8+	Haile Gebrselassie	ETH	Ostrava	27 Jun 2007
15 miles	1:11:43.1	Bill Rodgers	USA	Saratoga, Cal.	21 Feb 1979
20 miles	1:39:14.4	Jack Foster	NZL	Hamilton, NZ	15 Aug 1971
30 miles	2:42:00+	Jeff Norman	GBR	Timperley, Cheshire	7 Jun 1980
50 km	2:48:06	Jeff Norman	GBR	Timperley, Cheshire	7 Jun 1980
40 miles	3:48:35	Don Ritchie	GBR	London (Hendon)	16 Oct 1982
50 miles	4:51:49	Don Ritchie	GBR	London (Hendon)	12 Mar 1983
100 km	6:10:20	Don Ritchie	GBR	London (CP)	28 Oct 1978
150 km	10:34:30	Denis Zhalybin	RUS	London (CP)	20 Oct 2002
100 miles	11:28:03	Oleg Kharitonov	RUS	London (CP)	20 Oct 2002
200 km	15:10:27+	Yiannis Kouros	AUS	Adelaide	4-5 Oct 1997
200 miles	27:48:35	Yiannis Kouros	GRE	Montauban	15-16 Mar 1985
500 km	60:23.00+ ??	Yiannis Kouros	GRE	Colac, Aus	26-29 Nov 1984
500 miles	105:42:09+	Yiannis Kouros	GRE	Colac, Aus	26-30 Nov 1984
1000 km	136:17:00	Yiannis Kouros	GRE	Colac, Aus	26-31 Nov 1984
1500 km	10d 17:28:26	Petrus Silkinas	LTU	Nanango, Qld	11-21 Mar 1998
1000 mile	11d 13:54:58+	Petrus Silkinas	LTU	Nanango, Qld	11-22 Mar 1998
2 hrs	37.994 km	Jim Alder	GBR	Walton-on-Thames	17 Oct 1964
12 hrs	162.400 km +	Yiannis Kouros	GRE	Montauban	15 Mar 1985
24 hrs	303.506 km	Yiannis Kouros	AUS	Adelaide	4-5 Oct 1997
48 hrs	473.797 km	Yiannis Kouros	AUS	Surgères	3-5 May 1996
6 days	1036.8 km	Yiannis Kouros	GRE	Colac, Aus	20-26 Nov 2005

LONG DISTANCE ROAD RECORDS & BESTS – MEN

Where superior to track bests (over 10km) and run on properly measured road courses. (I) IAAF recognition.

10 km (I)	0:26:44	Leonard Patrick Komon	KEN	Utrecht	26 Sep 2010
15 km (I)	0:41:13	Leonard Patrick Komon	KEN	Nijmegen	21 Nov 2010
10 miles	0:44:24 §	Haile Gebrselassie	ETH	Tilburg	4 Sep 2005
	0:44:45	Paul Koech	KEN	Amsterdam-Zaandam	21 Sep 1997
20 km (I)	0:55:21+	Zersenay Tadese	ERI	Lisboa	21 Mar 2010
25 km (I)	1:11:18	Dennis Kimetto	KEN	Berlin	6 May 2012
30 km (I)	1:27:38	Patrick Makau	KEN	Berlin	25 Sep 2011
	1:27:37 §	Peter Kirui	KEN	Berlin (dnf Mar)	25 Sep 2011
20 miles	1:35:22+	Steve Jones	GBR	Chicago	10 Oct 1985
30 miles	2:37:31+	Thompson Magawana	RSA	Claremont-Kirstenbosch	12 Apr 1988
50km	2:43:38+	Thompson Magawana	RSA	Claremont-Kirstenbosch	12 Apr 1988
40 miles	3:45:39	Andy Jones	CAN	Houston	23 Feb 1991
50 miles	4:50:21	Bruce Fordyce	RSA	London-Brighton	25 Sep 1983
100 km (I)	6:13:33	Takahiro Sunada	JPN	Yubetsu	21 Jun 1998
1000 miles	10d:10:30:35	Yiannis Kouros	GRE	New York	21-30 May 1988
Ekiden (6) (I)	1:57:06 #	Kenya	KEN	Chiba	23 Nov 2005
5 stages	1:55:59	Ethiopia	ETH	Chiba	24 Nov 2003
10k Dejene Birhanu, 5k Hailu Mekonnen, 10k Gebr. Gebremariam, 5k Markos Geneti, 12.195k Sileshi Sihine					
12 hrs	162.543 km	Yiannis Kouros	GRE	Queen's, New York	7 Nov 1984

LONG DISTANCE WORLD BESTS – WOMEN TRACK

15 km	0:48:54.91+	Dire Tune	ETH	Ostrava	12 Jun 2008
10 miles	0:54:21.8	Lorraine Moller	NZL	Auckland	9 Jan 1993
20 miles	1:59:09 !	Chantal Langlacé	FRA	Amiens	3 Sep 1983
30 miles	3:12:25+	Carolyn Hunter-Rowe	GBR	Barry, Wales	3 Mar 1996
50 km	3:18:52+	Carolyn Hunter-Rowe	GBR	Barry, Wales	3 Mar 1996
40 miles	4:26:43	Carolyn Hunter-Rowe	GBR	Barry, Wales	7 Mar 1993
50 miles	5:48:12.0+	Norimi Sakurai	JPN	San Giovanni Lupatoto	27 Sep 2003
100 km	7:14:05.8	Norimi Sakurai	JPN	San Giovanni Lupatoto	27 Sep 2003
150 km	13:45:54	Hilary Walker	GBR	Blackpool	5-6 Nov 1988
100 miles	13:52.02+	Mami Kudo	JPN	Soochow	10-11 Dec 2011
200 km	17:52.18+	Mami Kudo	JPN	Soochow	10-11 Dec 2011
200 miles	39:09:03	Hilary Walker	GBR	Blackpool	5-7 Nov 1988
500 km	77:53:46	Eleanor Adams	GBR	Colac, Aus.	13-16 Nov 1989

500 miles	130:59:58+	Sandra Barwick	NZL	Campbelltown, AUS	18-23 Nov 1990
1000 km	8d 00:27:06+	Eleanor Robinson	GBR	Nanango, Qld	11-19 Mar 1998
1500 km	12d 06:52:12+	Eleanor Robinson	GBR	Nanango, Qld	11-23 Mar 1998
1000 miles	13d 02:16:49	Eleanor Robinson	GBR	Nanango, Qld	11-24 Mar 1998
2 hrs	32.652 km	Chantal Langlacé	FRA	Amiens	3 Sep 1983
12 hrs	147.600 km	Ann Trason	USA	Hayward, Cal	3-4 Aug 1991
24 hours	255.303 km	Mami Kudo	JPN	Soochow	10-11 Dec 2011
48 hrs	385.130 km	Mami Kudo	JPN	Surgères	22-24 May 2010
6 days	883.631 km	Sandra Barwick	NZL	Campbelltown, AUS	18-24 Nov 1990

! Timed on one running watch only

LONG DISTANCE ROAD RECORDS & BESTS - WOMEN

	hr:min:sec	Name	Nat	Venue	Date
10 km (l)	0:30:21	Paula Radcliffe	GBR	San Juan	23 Feb 2003
15 km (l)	46:28	Tirunesh Dibaba	ETH	Nijmegen	15 Nov 2009
10 miles	0:50:05+	Mary Keitany	KEN	Ra's Al-Khaymah	18 Feb 2011
	0:50:01+ dh	Paula Radcliffe	GBR	Newcastle	21 Sep 2003
20 km (l)	1:02:36+	Mary Keitany	KEN	Ra's Al-Khaymah	18 Feb 2011
	1:02:21+ dh	Paula Radcliffe	GBR	Newcastle	21 Sep 2003
Half mar (l) qv +	1:05:50	Mary Keitany	KEN	Ra's Al-Khaymah	18 Feb 2011
	1:05:40 dh	Paula Radcliffe	GBR	South Shields	21 Sep 2003
25 km (l)	1:19:53	Mary Keitany	KEN	Berlin	9 May 2010
30 km (l)	1:38:23+ §	Liliya Shobukhova	RUS	Chicago	9 Oct 2011
	1:36:36+ dh	Paula Radcliffe	GBR	London	13 Apr 2003
20 miles	1:43:33+	Paula Radcliffe	GBR	London	13 Apr 2003
30 miles	3:01:16+	Frith van der Merwe	RSA	Claremont-Kirstenbosch	25 Mar 1989
50 km	3:08:39	Frith van der Merwe	RSA	Claremont-Kirstenbosch	25 Mar 1989
40 miles	4:26:13+	Ann Trason	USA	Houston	23 Feb 1991
50 miles	5:40:18	Ann Trason	USA	Houston	23 Feb 1991
100 km (l)	6:33:11	Tomoe Abe	JPN	Yubetsu	25 Jun 2000
100 miles	13:47:41	Ann Trason	USA	Queen's, New York	4 May 1991
200 km	18:45:51	Mami Kudo	JPN	Steenbergen	11-12 May 2013
1000 km	7d 01:11:00+	Sandra Barwick	NZL	New York	16-23 Sep 1991
1000 miles	12d 14:38:40	Sandra Barwick	NZL	New York	16-29 Sep 1991
Ekiden (6 stages)	2:11:22	(l)	ETH	Chiba	24 Nov 2003

Berhane Adere, Tirunesh Dibaba, Eyerusalem Kuma, Ejegayou Dibaba, Meseret Defar, Werknesh Kidane

| 12 hours | 144.840 km | Ann Trason | USA | Queen's, New York | 4 May 1991 |
| 24 hours | 252.205 km | Mami KUDO | JPN | Steenbergen | 12 May 2013 |

100 KILOMETRES CONTINENTAL RECORDS

Men
W, Asi	6:13:33	Takahiro SUNADA	JPN	Yubetsu	21 Jun 1998
Eur	6:16:41	Jean-Paul PRAET	BEL	Torhout	24 Jun 1989
SAm	6:18:09	Valmir NUNES	BRA	Winschoten	16 Sep 1995
Afr	6:25:07	Bruce FORDYCE	RSA	Stellenbosch	4 Feb 1989
Oce	6:29:23	Tim SLOAN	AUS	Ross-Richmond	23 Apr 1995
NAm	6:30:11	Tom JOHNSON	USA	Winschoten	16 Sep 1995

Women
W, Asi	6:33:11	Tomoe ABE	JPN	Yubetsu	25 Jun 2000
NAm	7:00:48	Ann TRASON	USA	Winschoten	16 Sep 1995
Eur	7:10:32	Tatyana ZHYRKOVA	RUS	Winschoten	11 Sep 2004
SAm	7:20:22	Maria VENÂNCIO	BRA	Cubatão	8 Aug 1998
Afr	7:31:47	Helena JOUBERT	RSA	Winschoten	16 Sep 1995
Oce	7:40:58	Linda MEADOWS	AUS	North Otago	18 Nov 1995

WORLD INDOOR RECORDS

Men   to March 2014
50 metres	5.56A	Donovan Bailey	CAN	Reno	9 Feb 1996
60 metres	6.39	Maurice Greene	USA	Madrid	3 Feb 1998
	6.39	Maurice Greene	USA	Atlanta	3 Mar 2001
200 metres	19.92	Frank Fredericks	NAM	Liévin	18 Feb 1996
400 metres	44.57	Kerron Clement	USA	Fayetteville	12 Mar 2005
800 metres	1:42.67	Wilson Kipketer	KEN	Paris (Bercy)	9 Mar 1997
1000 metres	2:14.96	Wilson Kipketer	KEN	Birmingham	20 Feb 2000
1500 metres	3:31.18	Hicham El Guerrouj	MAR	Stuttgart	2 Feb 1997
1 mile	3:48.45	Hicham El Guerrouj	MAR	Gent	12 Feb 1997
2000 metres #	4:49.99	Kenenisa Bekele	ETH	Birmingham	17 Feb 2007
3000 metres	7:24.90	Daniel Komen	KEN	Budapest	6 Feb 1998
2 miles #	8:04.35	Kenenisa Bekele	ETH	Birmingham	16 Feb 2008

5000 metres	12:49.60	Kenenisa Bekele	ETH	Birmingham	20 Feb 2004
10000 metres #	27:50.29	Mark Bett	KEN	Gent	10 Feb 2002
50 m hurdles	6.25	Mark McKoy	CAN	Kobe	5 Mar 1986
60 m hurdles	7.30	Colin Jackson	GBR	Sindelfingen	6 Mar 1994
High jump	2.43	Javier Sotomayor	CUB	Budapest	4 Mar 1989
Pole vault	6.16	Renaud Lavillenie	FRA	Donetsk	15 Feb 2014
Long jump	8.79	Carl Lewis	USA	New York	27 Jan 1984
Triple jump	17.92	Teddy Tamgho	FRA	Paris (Bercy)	6 Mar 2011
Shot	22.66	Randy Barnes	USA	Los Angeles	20 Jan 1989
Javelin #	85.78	Matti Närhi	FIN	Kajaani	3 Mar 1996
35 lb weight #	25.86	Lance Deal	USA	Atlanta	4 Mar 1995
3000m walk #	10:31.42	Andreas Erm	GER	Halle	4 Feb 2001
5000m walk	18:07.08	Mikhail Shchennikov	RUS	Moskva	14 Feb 1995
10000m walk #	38:31.4	Werner Heyer	GDR	Berlin	12 Jan 1980
4 x 200m	1:22.11	United Kingdom		Glasgow	3 Mar 1991
		(Linford Christie, Darren Braithwaite, Ade Mafe, John Regis)			
4 x 400m	3:02.13	USA		Sopot	9 Mar 2014
		(Kyle Clemons, David Verburg, Kind Butler, Calvin Smith)			
	3:01.96 §	USA (not ratified – no EPO analysis)		Fayetteville	11 Feb 2006
		(Kerron Clement, Wallace Spearmon, Darold Williamson, Jeremy Wariner)			
4 x 800m	7:13.11	USA All-Stars		Boston (Roxbury)	8 Feb 2014
		(Richard Jones, David Torrence, Duane Solomon, Erik Sowinski)			
Heptathlon	6645 points	Ashton Eaton	USA	Istanbul	9/10 Mar 2012
		(6.79 60m, 8.16 LJ, 14.56 SP, 2.03 HJ, 7.68 60mh, 5.20 PV, 2:32.77 1000m)			

Women

50 metres	5.96+	Irina Privalova	RUS	Madrid	9 Feb 1995
60 metres	6.92	Irina Privalova	RUS	Madrid	11 Feb 1993 & 9 Feb 1995
200 metres	21.87	Merlene Ottey	JAM	Liévin	13 Feb 1993
400 metres	49.59	Jarmila Kratochvílová	CZE	Milano	7 Mar 1982
800 metres	1:55.82	Jolanda Ceplak	SLO	Wien	3 Mar 2002
1000 metres	2:30.94	Maria Lurdes Mutola	MOZ	Stockholm	25 Feb 1999
1500 metres	3:55.17	Genzebe Dibaba	ETH	Karlsruhe	1 Feb 2014
1 mile	4:17.14	Doina Melinte	ROM	East Rutherford	9 Feb 1990
2000 metres #	5:30.53	Gabriela Szabo	ROM	Sindelfingen	8 Mar 1998
3000 metres	8:16.60	Genzebe Dibaba	ETH	Stockholm	6 Feb 2014
2 miles #	9:00.48	Genzebe Dibaba	ETH	Birmingham	15 Feb 2014
5000 metres	14:24.37	Meseret Defar	ETH	Stockholm	18 Feb 2009
50 m hurdles	6.58	Cornelia Oschkenat	GDR	Berlin	20 Feb 1988
60 m hurdles	7.68	Susanna Kallur	SWE	Karlsruhe	10 Feb 2008
High jump	2.08	Kajsa Bergqvist	SWE	Arnstadt	4 Feb 2006
Pole vault	5.02A	Jenn Suhr	USA	Albuquerque	2 Mar 2013
Long jump	7.37	Heike Drechsler	GDR	Wien	13 Feb 1988
Triple jump	15.36	Tatyana Lebedeva	RUS	Budapest	5 Mar 2004
Shot	22.50	Helena Fibingerová	CZE	Jablonec	19 Feb 1977
Javelin #	61.29	Taina Uppa/Kolkkala	FIN	Mustasaari	28 Feb 1999
20 lb weight #	25.56	Brittany Riley	USA	Fayetteville	10 Mar 2007
3000m walk	11:35.34 un	Gillian O'Sullivan	IRL	Belfast	15 Feb 2003
	11:40.33	Claudia Iovan/Stef	ROM	Bucuresti	30 Jan 1999
5000m walk #	20:37.77	Margarita Turova	BLR	Minsk	13 Feb 2005
10000m walk	43:54.63	Yelena Ginko	BLR	Mogilyov	22 Feb 2008
4 x 200m	1:32.41	Russia		Glasgow	29 Jan 2005
		(Yekaterina Kondratyeva, Irina Khabarova, Yuliya Pechonkina, Yuliya Gushchina)			
4 x 400m	3:23.37	Russia		Glasgow	28 Jan 2006
		(Yuliya Gushchina, Olga Kotlyarova, Olga Zaytseva, Olesya Krasnomovets)			
4 x 800m	8:06.24	Moskva	RUS	Moskva	18 Feb 2011
		(Aleksandra Bulanova, Yekaterina Martynova, Yelena Kofanova , Anna Balakshina)			
Pentathlon	5013 points	Nataliya Dobrynska	UKR	Istanbul	9 Mar 2012
		(8.38 60mh, 1.84 HJ, 16.51 SP, 6.57 LJ, 2:11.15 800m)			

events not officially recognised by the IAAF

WORLD INDOOR JUNIOR (U20) RECORDS

First approved by IAAF Council in 2011. **Men**

60 metres	6.51	Mark Lewis-Francis	GBR	Lisboa	11 Mar 2001
200 metres	20.37	Walter Dix	USA	Fayetteville	11 Mar 2005
400 metres	44.80	Kirani James	GRN	Fayetteville	27 Feb 2011
800 metres	1:44.35	Yuriy Borzakovskiy	RUS	Dortmund	30 Jan 2000
1000 metres	2:15.77	Abubaker Kaki	SUD	Stockholm	21 Feb 2008
1500 metres	3:36.28	Belal Mansoor Ali (overage!)	BRN	Stockholm	20 Feb 2007
One mile	3:55.02	German Fernandez	USA	College Station	28 Feb 2009
3000 metres	7:32.87	Hagos Gebrhiwet	ETH	Boston (Roxbury)	2 Feb 2013

5000 metres	12:53.29	Isiah Koech	KEN	Düsseldorf	11 Feb 2011
60mh (99cm)	7.48	Wilhem Belocian	FRA	Val-de-Reuil	9 Mar 2014
High jump	2.35	Volodymyr Yashchenko	URS	Milano	12 Mar 1978
Pole vault	5.68	Raphael Holzdeppe	GER	Halle	1 Mar 2008
Long jump	8.22	Viktor Kuznetsov	UKR	Brovary	22 Jan 2005
Triple jump	17.14	Volker Mai	GDR	Piréas	2 Mar 1985
Shot (6kg)	22.35	David Storl	GER	Rochlitz	20 Dec 2009
Heptathlon	6022	Gunnar Nixon	USA	Fayetteville	27/28 Jan 2012
(jnr imps)		(6.94, 7.96, 13.19, 1.96, 7.90, 4.60, 2:51.42)			

Women

60 metres	7.09	Joan Uduak Ekah	NGR	Maebashi	7 Mar 1999
200 metres	22.40	Bianca Knight	USA	Fayetteville	14 Mar 2008
400 metres	50.82	Sanya Richards	USA	Fayetteville	13 Mar 2004
800 metres	2:01.03	Meskerem Legesse	ETH	Fayetteville	14 Feb 2004
1000 metres	2:35.80	Mary Cain	USA	Boston (Roxbury)	8 Feb 2014
1500 metres	4:03.28	Kalkidan Gezahegne	ETH	Stockholm	10 Feb 2010
One mile	4:24.10	Kalkidan Gezahegne	ETH	Birmingham	20 Feb 2010
3000 metres	8:33.56	Tirunesh Dibaba	ETH	Birmingham	20 Feb 2004
5000 metres	14:53.99	Tirunesh Dibaba	ETH	Boston	31 Jan 2004
60m hurdles	8.06	Ulrike Denk	FRG	Dortmund	19 Feb 1983
	8.06	Monique Ewanje Épée	FRA	Madrid	22 Feb 1986
High jump	1.97	Mariya Kuchina	RUS	Trinec	26 Jan 2011
Pole vault	4.63	Angelica Bengtsson	SWE	Stockholm	22 Feb 2011
Long jump	6.88	Heike Daute	GDR	Berlin	1 Feb 1983
Triple jump	14.37	Ren Ruiping	CHN	Barcelona	11 Mar 1995
Shot	20.51	Heidi Krieger	GDR	Budapest	8 Feb 1984
Pentathlon	4635A	Kendell Williams	USA	Albuquerque	15 Mar 2014
		(8.21, 1.88, 12.05, 6.32, 2:17.31)			
	4558	Nafissatou Thiam	BLE	Gent	3 Feb 2013
		(8.65, 1.84, 14.00, 6.30, 2:21.18)			

WORLD VETERANS/MASTERS RECORDS

MEN – aged 35 or over

100 metres	9.97A	Linford Christie (2.4.60)	GBR	Johannesburg	23 Sep 1995
	9.97	Kim Collins (5.4.76)	SKN	Lausanne	4 Jul 2013
200 metres	20.11	Linford Christie (2.4.60)	GBR	Villeneuve d'Ascq	25 Jun 1995
400 metres	45.68	Alvin Harrison (20.1.74)	DOM	San Juan	5 Apr 2009
	45.58i	Chris Brown (15.10.78)	BAH	Sopot	8 Mar 2014
800 metres	1:43.36	Johnny Gray (19.6.60)	USA	Zürich	16 Aug 1995
1000 metres	2:18.8+	William Tanui (22.2.64)	KEN	Rome	7 Jul 1999
1500 metres	3:32.45	William Tanui (22.2.64)	KEN	Athína	16 Jun 1999
1 mile	3:51.38	Bernard Lagat (12.12.74)	USA	London (CP)	6 Aug 2011
2000 metres	4:58.3+ e	William Tanui (22.2.64	KEN	Monaco	4 Aug 1999
	4:54.74i	Bernard Lagat (12.12.74)	USA	New York	15 Feb 14
3000 metres	7:29.00	Bernard Lagat (12.12.74)	USA	Rieti	29 Aug 2010
5000 metres	12:53.60	Bernard Lagat (12.12.74)	USA	Monaco	22 Jul 2011
10000 metres	26:51.20	Haile Gebrselassie (18.4.73)	ETH	Hengelo	24 May 2008
20000 metres	57:44.4+	Gaston Roelants (5.2.37)	BEL	Bruxelles	20 Sep 1972
1 Hour	20,822m	Haile Gebrselassie (18.4.73)	ETH	Hengelo	1 Jun 2009
Half Marathon	59:10 dh	Paul Tergat (17.6.69)	KEN	Lisboa	13 Mar 2005
	59:50	Haile Gebrselassie (18.4.73)	ETH	Den Haag	14 Mar 2009
Marathon	2:03:59	Haile Gebrselassie (18.4.73)	ETH	Berlin	28 Sep 2008
3000m steeple	8:04.95	Simon Vroemen (11.5.69)	NED	Bruxelles	26 Aug 2005
110m hurdles	12.96	Allen Johnson (1.3.71)	USA	Athína	17 Sep 2006
400m hurdles	48.10	Felix Sánchez (30.8.77)	DOM	Moskva	13 Aug 2013
High jump	2.31	Dragutin Topic (12.3.71)	SRB	Kragujevac	28 Jul 2009
	2.31	Jamie Nieto (2.11.76)	USA	New York	9 Jun 2012
Pole vault	5.90i	Björn Otto (16.10.77)	GER	Cottbus	30 Jan 2013
	5.90i	Björn Otto		Düsseldorf	8 Feb 2013
	5.90	Björn Otto		Eugene	1 Jun 2013
	5.85 sq	Derek miles (28.9.72)	USA	Berlin	7 Sep 2008
Long jump	8.50	Larry Myricks (10.3.56)	USA	New York	15 Jun 1991
	8.50	Carl Lewis (1.7.61)	USA	Atlanta	29 Jul 1996
Triple jump	17.92	Jonathan Edwards (10.5.66)	GBR	Edmonton	6 Aug 2001
Shot	22.67	Kevin Toth ¶ (29.12.67)	USA	Lawrence	19 Apr 2003
Discus	71.56	Virgilijus Alekna (13.2.72)	LTU	Kaunas	25 Jul 2007
Hammer	83.62	Igor Astapkovich (4.1.63)	BLR	Staiki	20 Jun 1998
Javelin	92.80	Jan Zelezny (16.6.66)	CZE	Edmonton	12 Aug 2001
Decathlon	8241	Kip Janvrin (8.7.65)	USA	Eugene	22 Jun 2001
		(10.98, 7.01, 14.21, 1.89, 48.41, 14.72, 45.59, 5.20, 60.41, 4:14.96)			

20 km walk	1:18:44	Vladimir Andreyev (7.9.66)	RUS	Cheboksary	12 Jun 2004
20000m t walk	1:20:55.4+	Maurizio Damilano (6.4.57)	ITA	Cuneo	3 Oct 1992
50 km walk	3:36:03	Robert Korzeniowski (30.7.68)	POL	Saint-Denis	27 Aug 2003
50000m t walk	3:49:29.7	Alain Lemercier (11.1.57)	FRA	Franconville	3 Apr 1994

MEN – aged 40 or over

100 metres	10.29	Troy Douglas (30.11.62)	NED	Leiden	7 Jun 2003
200 metres	20.64	Troy Douglas (30.11.62)	NED	Utrecht	9 Aug 2003
400 metres	47.82	Enrico Saraceni (19.5.64)	ITA	Århus	25 Jul 2004
	47.5u	Lee Evans (25.2.47)	USA		Apr 1989
800 metres	1:48.22	Anthony Whiteman (13.11.71)	GBR	Indianapolis	6 Jun 2012
1000 metres	2:24.93i	Vyacheslav Shabunin (27.9.69)	RUS	Moskva	10 Jan 2010
1500 metres	3:42.02	Anthony Whiteman (13.11.71)	GBR	Manchester (Stretford)	7 Jul 2012
1 mile	3:58.79	Anthony Whiteman (13.11.71)	GBR	Nashville	2 Jun 2012
	3:58.15i	Eamonn Coghlan (21.11.52)	IRL	Boston	20 Feb 1994
3000 metres	8:02.54	Vyacheslav Shabunin (27.9.69)	RUS	Moskva	7 Jun 2010
	8:01.44i	Vyacheslav Shabunin (27.9.69)	RUS	Moskva	7 Feb 2010
5000 metres	13:43.15	Mohamed Ezzher (26.4.60)	FRA	Sotteville	3 Jul 2000
10000 metres	28:30.88	Martti Vainio (30.12.50)	FIN	Hengelo	25 Jun 1991
10 km road	28:00	Haile Gebrselassie (18.4.73)	ETH	Manchester	25 May 2013
1 Hour	19.710k	Steve Moneghetti (26.9.62)	AUS	Geelong	17 Dec 2005
Half marathon	60:41 dh	Haile Gebrselassie (18.4.73)	ETH	South Shields	15 Sep 2013
	61:09	Haile Gebrselassie		Glasgow	6 Oct 2013
Marathon	2:08:46	Andrés Espinosa (4.2.63)	MEX	Berlin	28 Sep 2003
3000m steeple	8:38.40	Angelo Carosi (20.1.64)	ITA	Firenze	11 Jul 2004
110m hurdles	13.97	David Ashford (24.1.63)	USA	Indianapolis	3 Jul 2004
	13.79 ?	Roger Kingdom (26.8.62)	USA	Slippery Rock	23 Jun 2004
400m hurdles	48.10	Félix Sánchez (30.8.77)	DOM	Moskva	13 Aug 2013
High jump	2.28	Dragutin Topic (12.3.71)	SRB	Beograd	20 May 2012
Pole vault	5.71i	Jeff Hartwig (25.9.67)	USA	Jonesboro	31 May 2008
	5.70	Jeff Hartwig		Eugene	29 Jun 2008
Long jump	7.68A	Aaron Sampson (20.9.61)	USA	Cedar City, UT	21 Jun 2002
	7.59i	Mattias Sunneborn (27.9.70)	SWE	Sätra	3 Feb 2013
	7.57	Hans Schicker (3.10.47)	FRG	Kitzingen	16 Jul 1989
Triple jump	16.58	Ray Kimble (19.4.53)	USA	Edinburgh	2 Jul 1993
Shot	21.71	Rees Hoffa (8.10.77)	USA	Des Moines	27 Apr 2013
Discus	70.28	Virgilijus Alekna (13.2.72)	LTU	Klaipeda	23 Jun 2012
Hammer	82.23	Igor Astapkovich (4.1.63)	BLR	Minsk	10 Jul 2004
Javelin	85.92	Jan Zelezny (16.6.66)	CZE	Göteborg	9 Aug 2006
Pentathlon	3510 pts	Werner Schallau (8.9.38)	FRG	Gelsenkirchen	24 Sep 1978
		6.74, 59.20, 23.0, 43.76, 5:05.7			
Decathlon	7525 pts	Kip Janvrin (8.7.65)	USA	San Sebastián	24 Aug 2005
		11.56, 6.78, 14.01, 1.80, 49.46, 15.40, 42.70, 4.70, 58.43, 4:25.87			
20 km walk	1:21:36	Willi Sawall (7.11.41)	AUS	Melbourne	4 Jul 1982
20000m t walk	1:24:58.8	Marcel Jobin (3.1.42)	CAN	Sept Isles	12 May 1984
50 km walk	3:40:46	Yuriy Andronov (6.11.71)	RUS	Moskva	11 Jun 2012
50000m t walk	3:51:54.5	José Marín (21.1.50)	ESP	Manresa	7 Apr 1990
4x100m	42.20	SpeedWest TC	USA	Irvine	2 May 2004
		(Frank Strong, Cornell Stephenson, Kettrell Berry, Willie Gault)			
4x400m	3:20.83	S Allah, K Morning, E Gonera, R Blackwell USA Philadelphia			27 Apr 2001

WOMEN – aged 35 or over

100 metres	10.74	Merlene Ottey (10.5.60)	JAM	Milano	7 Sep 1996
200 metres	21.93	Merlene Ottey (10.5.60)	JAM	Bruxelles	25 Aug 1995
400 metres	50.27	Jearl Miles Clark (4.9.66)	USA	Madrid	20 Sep 2002
800 metres	1:56.53	Lyubov Gurina (6.8.57)	RUS	Hechtel	30 Jul 1994
1000 metres	2:31.5	Maricica Puica (29.7.50)	ROM	Poiana Brasov	1 Jun 1986
1500 metres	3:57.73	Maricica Puica (29.7.50)	ROM	Bruxelles	30 Aug 1985
1 mile	4:17.33	Maricica Puica (29.7.50)	ROM	Zürich	21 Aug 1985
2000 metres	5:28.69	Maricica Puica (29.7.50)	ROM	London (CP)	11 Jul 1986
3000 metres	8:23.23	Edith Masai (4.4.67)	KEN	Monaco	19 Jul 2002
5000 metres	14:33.84	Edith Masai (4.4.67)	KEN	Oslo	2 Jun 2006
10000 metres	30:30.26	Edith Masai (4.4.67)	KEN	Helsinki	6 Aug 2005
Half Marathon	67:16	Edith Masai (4.4.67)	KEN	Berlin	2 Apr 2006
Marathon	2:19:19	Irina Mikitenko (23.8.72)	GER	Berlin	28 Sep 2008
3000m steeple	9:24.26	Marta Domínguez (3.11.75)	ESP	Huelva	7 Jun 2012
100m hurdles	12.40	Gail Devers (19.11.66)	USA	Lausanne	2 Jul 2002
400m hurdles	52.94	Marina Styepanova (1.5.50)	RUS	Tashkent	17 Sep 1986
High jump	2.01	Inga Babakova (27.6.67)	UKR	Oslo	27 Jun 2003
Pole vault	4.70	Stacy Dragila (25.3.71)	USA	Chula Vista	22 Jun 2008
Long jump	6.99	Heike Drechsler (16.12.64)	GER	Sydney	29 Sep 2000
Triple jump	14.68	Tatyana Lebedeva (21.7.76)	RUS	Cheboksary	3 Jul 2012

	14.82i	Yamilé Aldama (14.8.72)	GBR	Istanbul	19 Mar 2012
Shot	21.46	Larisa Peleshenko (29.2.64)	RUS	Moskva	26 Aug 2000
	21.47i	Helena Fibingerová (13.7.49)	CZE	Jablonec	9 Feb 1985
Discus	69.60	Faina Melnik (9.7.45)	RUS	Donetsk	9 Sep 1980
Hammer	72.42	Iryna Sekyachova (21.7.76)	UKR	Yalta	4 Jun 2012
Javelin	68.34	Steffi Nerius (1.7.72)	GER	Berlin (Elstal)	31 Aug 2008
Heptathlon	6533 pts	Jane Frederick (7.4.52)	USA	Talence	27 Sep 1987
	13.60, 1.82, 15.50, 24.73; 6.29, 49.70, 2:14.88				
5000m walk	20:12.41	Elisabetta Perrone (9.7.68)	ITA	Rieti	2 Aug 2003
10km walk	41:41	Kjersti Tysse Plätzer (18.1.72)	NOR	Kraków	30 May 2009
10000m t walk	43:26.5	Elisabetta Perrone (9.7.68)	ITA	Saluzzo	4 Aug 2004
20km walk	1:25:59	Tamara Kovalenko (5.6.64)	RUS	Moskva	19 May 2000
20000m t walk	1:27:49.3	Yelena Nikolayeva (1.2.66)	RUS	Brisbane	6 Sep 2001
4x100m	48.63	Desmier, Sulter, Andreas, Apavou	FRA	Eugene	8 Jun 1989
4x400m	3:50.80	Mitchell, Mathews, Beadnall, Gabriel	GBR	Gateshead	8 Aug 1999

WOMEN – aged 40 or over

Event	Mark	Athlete	Nat	Venue	Date
100 metres	10.99	Merlene Ottey (10.5.60)	JAM	Thessaloniki	30 Aug 2000
200 metres	22.72	Merlene Ottey (10.5.60)	SLO	Athína	23 Aug 2004
400 metres	53.05A	María Figueirêdo (11.11.63)	BRA	Bogotá	10 Jul 2004
	53.14	María Figueirêdo (11.11.63)	BRA	San Carlos, VEN	19 Jun 2004
800 metres	1:59.25	Yekaterina Podkopayeva (11.6.52)	RUS	Luxembourg	30 Jun 1994
1000 metres	2:36.16	Yekaterina Podkopayeva (11.6.52)	RUS	Nancy	14 Sep 1994
	2:36.08i	Yekaterina Podkopayeva	RUS	Liévin	13 Feb 1993
1500 metres	3:59.78	Yekaterina Podkopayeva (11.6.52)	RUS	Nice	18 Jul 1994
1 mile	4:23.78	Yekaterina Podkopayeva (11.6.52)	RUS	Roma	9 Jun 1993
3000 metres	9:11.2	Joyce Smith (26.10.37)	GBR	London	30 Apr 1978
	9:02.83i	Lyubov Kremlyova (21.12.61)	RUS	Moskva	22 Jan 2002
5000 metres	15:20.59	Elena Fidatov (24.7.60)	ROM	Bucuresti	7 Aug 2000
10000 metres	31:31.18	Edith Masai (4.4.67)	KEN	Alger	21 Jul 2007
1 hour	16.056k	Jackie Fairweather (10.11.67)	AUS	Canberra	24 Jan 2008
Half Marathon	69:56	Irina Permitina (3.2.68)	RUS	Novosibirsk	13 Sep 2008
Marathon	2:24:54	Irina Mikitenko (23.8.2)	GER	Berlin	29 Sep 2013
3000m steeple	10:00.75	Minori Hayakari (29.11.72)	JPN	Kumagaya	22 Sep 2013
100 m hurdles	13.20	Patricia Girard (8.4.68)	FRA	Paris	14 Jul 2008
400 m hurdles	58.35	Barbara Gähling (20.3.65)	GER	Erfurt	21 Jul 2007
	58.3 h	Gowry Retchakan (21.6.60)	GBR	Hoo	3 Sep 2000
High jump	1.87	Iryna Mikhalchenko (20.1.72)	UKR	Yalta	13 Jun 2012
Pole vault	4.10	Doris Auer (10.5.71)	AUT	Innsbruck	6 Aug 2011
	4.11 §	Doris Auer (10.5.71)	AUT	Wien	5 Jul 2011
Long jump	6.64	Tatyana Ter-Mesrobian (12.5.68)	RUS	Sankt-Peterburg	31 May 2008
	6.64i	Tatyana Ter-Mesrobian	RUS	Sankt-Peterburg	5 Jan 2010
Triple jump	14.06	Yamilé Aldama (14.8.72)	GBR	Eugene	1 Jun 2013
Shot	19.05	Antonina Ivanova (25.12.32)	RUS	Oryol	28 Aug 1973
	19.16i	Antonina Ivanova	RUS	Moskva	24 Feb 1974
Discus	67.89	Iryna Yatchenko (31.10.65)	BLR	Staiki	29 Jun 2008
Hammer	59.29	Oneithea Lewis (11.6.60)	USA	Princeton	10 May 2003
Javelin	61.96	Laverne Eve (16.6.65)	BAH	Monaco	9 Sep 2005
Heptathlon	5449 pts	Tatyana Alisevich (22.1.69)	BLR	Staiki	3 Jun 2010
	14.80, 1.62, 13.92, 26.18, 5.55, 45.44, 2:24.39				
5000m walk	21:57.40	Kelly Ruddick (19.4.73)	AUS	Geelong	10 Oct 2013
10km walk	45:09+	Kerry Saxby-Junna (2.6.61)	AUS	Edmonton	9 Aug 2001
10000m t walk	46:43.94	Graciela Mendoza (23.3.63)	MEX	Iquique	14 Jun 2008
20km walk	1:33:04	Graciela Mendoza (23.3.63)	MEX	Lima	7 May 2005
20000m t walk	1:33:28.15t	Teresa Vaill (20.11.62)	USA	Carson	25 Jun 2005
4x100m	48.22	Cadinot, Barilly, Valouvin, Lapierre	FRA	Le Touquet	24 Jun 2006
4x400m	3:57.28	Loizou, Kay, Smithe, Cearns	AUS	Brisbane	14 Jul 2001

WORLD AND CONTINENTAL RECORDS SET IN 2013

OUTDOORS – MEN

100	W20	10.01 §	Yoshihide KIRYU	JPN	Hiroshima	29 Apr 13
	W35 =	9.97	Kim COLLINS	SKN	Lausanne	4 Jul 13
500	W, CAC	59.32	Orestes RODRÍGUEZ	CUB	La Habana	5 Feb 13
1500	Eur	3:28.81	Mo FARAH	GBR	Monaco	19 Jul 13
1 Mile	CAC =	3:57.34	Juan Luis BARRIOS	MEX	Dublin	17 Jul 13
5000	Asi	12:51.96 §	Albert ROP	BRN	Monaco	19 Jul 13
10k	W40	28:00	Haile GEBRSELASSIE	ETH	Manchester	25 May 13
15k	Oce	42:59+	Collis BIRMINGHAM	AUS	Marugame	3 Feb 13
10 Miles	W40	47:00	Haile GEBRSELASSIE	ETH	Bern	18 May 13
20k	Oce	57:38+	Collis BIRMINGHAM	AUS	Marugame	3 Feb 13

Event	Region	Mark	Name	Country	Place	Date
HMar	Oce	60:56	Collis BIRMINGHAM	AUS	Marugame	3 Feb 13
	W40	60:41 dh	Haile GEBRSELASSIE	ETH	South Shields	15 Sep 13
	W40	61:09	Haile GEBRSELASSIE	ETH	Glasgow	6 Oct 13
30k	NAm	1:28:35+	Bolota ASMEROM	USA	London	21 Apr 13
Mar	W,Afr,Com	2:03:23	Wilson KIPSANG	KEN	Berlin	29 Sep 13
2000SC	W18, W20	5:19.99	Meresa KAHSAY	ETH	Donetsk	12 Jul 13
3000SC	Eur	8:00.09	Mahiedine MEKHISSI-BENABBAD	FRA	Saint-Denis	6 Jul 13
400H	W35	48.10	Felix SÁNCHEZ	DOM	Moskva	13 Aug 13
HJ	Asi	2.40	Mutaz Essa BARSHIM	QAT	Eugene	1 Jun 13
	Com =	2.38	Derek DROUIN	CAN	Moskva	15 Aug 13
PV	SAm	5.81	Augusto Dutra de OLIVEIRA	BRA	Uberlândia	16 May 13
	W35	5.90	Björn OTTO	GER	Eugene	1 Jun 13
	SAm	5.82	Augusto Dutra de OLIVEIRA	BRA	Hof	22 Jun 13
	SAm	5.83	Thiago Braz da SILVA	BRA	Cartagena	5 Jul 13
SP/6kg	W20	23.00	Jacko GILL	NZL	Auckland (NS)	18 Aug 13
SP	SAm	21.26	Germán LAURO	ARG	Doha	10 May 13
DT	Oce	68.20	Benn HARRADINE	AUS	Townsville	10 May 13
HT/5kg	W18	85.38	Joaquin GOMEZ	ARG	Buenos Aires	30 Nov 13
Dec	SAm	8393	Carlos Eduardo CHININ	BRA	São Paulo	8 Jun 13
		(10.85, 7.55, 15.28, 2.04, 48.18 / 14.08, 42.46, 4.90, 59.58, 4:34.77)				
	Afr	8343	Willem COERTZEN	RSA	Moskva	11 Aug 13
		(10.95, 7.44, 13.88, 2.05, 48.32 / 14.30, 43.25, 4.50, 69.35, 4:24.60)				
Medley R	W18	1:49.23	W.Williams, O'Hara, O.Williams, Manley	JAM	Donetsk	14 Jul 13
3000W	W35	11:11.94	Robert HEFFERNAN	IRL	Cork	2 Jul 13
50kW	CAC	3:41:09	Erick BARRONDO	GUA	Dudince	23 Mar 13

OUTDOORS – WOMEN

Event	Region	Mark	Name	Country	Place	Date
100	SAm =	11.15	Franciela KRASUCKI	BRA	São Paulo	6 Apr 13
	SAm	11.13	Ana Cláudia SILVA	BRA	Campinas	4 May 13
	SAm	11.05	Ana Cláudia SILVA	BRA	Belém	12 May 13
	Afr	10.86	Blessing OKAGBARE	NGR	London (OS)	27 Jul 13
	Afr	10.79	Blessing OKAGBARE	NGR	London (OS)	27 Jul 13
1500	Com	3:56.98	Faith KIPYEGON	KEN	Doha	10 May 13
HMar	SAm	70:30	Yolanda CABALLERO	COL	New York	17 Mar 13
Mar	W40	2:24:54	Irina MIKITENKO	GER	Berlin	29 Sep 13
200k	W, Asi	18:45:51	Mami KUDO	JPN	Steenbergen	12 May 13
24Hr	W, Asi	252.205k	Mami KUDO	JPN	Steenbergen	12 May 13
2000SC	NAm	6:19.09	Bridget FRANEK	USA	Eugene	16 Mar 13
3000SC	W40	10:06.70	Minori HAYAKARI	JPN	Los Angeles (ER)	17 May 13
	W40	10:00.75	Minori HAYAKARI	JPN	Kumagaya	22 Sep 13
100H/76	W18	12.94	Yanique THOMPSON	JAM	Donetsk	11 Jul 13
100H	NAm	12.26	Brianna ROLLINS	USA	Des Moines	22 Jun 13
	SAm	12.67	Yvette LEWIS	PAN	Lahti	17 Jul 13
200H	W, Eur	24.8	Yadisleidis Pedroso	ITA	Caserta	6 Apr 13
200H St	W, Eur	25.74	Perri SHAKES-DRAYTON	GBR	Manchester	25 May 13
300H	W, Eur	38.75	Zuzana HEJNOVÁ	CZE	Susice	14 May 13
	W, Eur	38.16	Zuzana HEJNOVÁ	CZE	Cheb	2 Aug 13
HJ	W18 =	1.96	Eleanor PATTERSON	AUS	Townsville	7 Dec 13
PV	CAC	4.81	Yarisley SILVA	CUB	La Habana	16 Mar 13
	CAC	4.85	Yarisley SILVA	CUB	Des Moines	26 Apr 13
	CAC	4.90	Yarisley SILVA	CUB	Hengelo	8 Jun 13
	Asi	4.65	LI Ling	CHN	Shenyang	8 Sep 13
TJ	W40	14.06	Yamilé ALDAMA	GBR	Eugene	1 Jun 13
SP	NAm	20.24	Michelle CARTER	USA	Des Moines	22 Jun 13
HT/3kg	W18	73.44	Réka GYURÁTZ	HUN	Budapest	18 May 13
	W18	73.62	Helga VÖLGYI	HUN	Szombathely	12 Jun 13
	W18	73.91 & 76.04	Réka GYURÁTZ	HUN	Zalaegerszeg	23 Jun 13
HT	NAm	75.73	Amanda BINGSON	USA	Des Moines	22 Jun 13
JT	Asi	65.62	LU Huihui	CHN	Zhaoqing	27 Apr 13
4x100 R	SAm	42.29	dos Santos, Silva, Krasucki, R Santos	BRA	Moskva	18 Aug 13
	CAC, Com	41.29	Russell, Stewart, Calvert, Fraser-Pryce	JAM	Moskva	18 Aug 13
4x800 R	NAm	8:04.31	Wallace, Martinez, Wilson, Montaño	USA	Philadelphia	27 Apr 13
	Afr	8:07.58	Chebet, Sum, Obiri, J Jepkosgei	KEN	Philadelphia	27 Apr 13
	Oce	8:18.96	Buckman, Laman, Gregson, Kajan	AUS	Philadelphia	27 Apr 13
4x100H R	W, NAm	50.78	Ali, Castlin, Lewis, Q Harrison	USA	Gainesville	6 Apr 13
5000W	Afr	22:37.78	Chahinez NASRI	TUN	Balma	1 May 13
	W40	21:57.40	Kelly RUDDACK	AUS	Geelong	10 Oct 13
20kW	CAC =	1:28:54	Mirna ORTIZ	GUA	Lugano	17 Mar 13
	CAC	1:28:31	Mirna ORTIZ	GUA	Rio Maior	6 Apr 13

See ATHLETICS 2012 for Indoor Records set in January - March 2013 – and add

INDOORS – MEN

SP/5kg	W18	21.56	Patrick MÜLLER	GER	Neubrandenburg	22 Dec 13
SP	W35	21.60	Reese HOFFA	USA	Lawrence	17 Apr 13
	SAm	20.44 & 20.53	Germán LAURO	ARG	Zürich	28 Aug 13

INDOORS – WOMEN

60H	SAm	8.05	Yvette LEWIS	PAN	State College	25 Jan 13
	SAm=	8.05	Yvette LEWIS	PAN	Linz	31 Jan 13
	SAm	8.02	Yvette LEWIS	PAN	Moskva	3 Feb 13
	SAm	7.95 & 7.94	Yvette LEWIS	PAN	Düsseldorf	8 Feb 13
	SAm	7.84	Yvette LEWIS	PAN	New York	16 Feb 13
PV	CAC	4.82	Yarisley SILVA	CUB	Des Moines	24 Apr 13
SP	Oce,Com	20.97 & 20.98	Valerie ADAMS	NZL	Zürich	28 Aug 13
	W18	17.31	Emel DERELI	TUR	Istanbul	21 Dec 13
	W18	17.58	Emel DERELI	TUR	Istanbul	28 Dec 13

WORLD AND CONTINENTAL RECORDS SET IN JAN – MAR 2014

INDOORS – MEN   # on oversized track

60	Asi	6.50A §	Tosin OGUNODE	QAT	Flagstaff	25 Jan 14
	Asi=	6.51A	Femi OGUNODE	QAT	Flagstaff	25 Jan 14
	W35	6.49	Kim COLLINS	SKN	Praha	25 Feb 14
200	W18=	21.13	Thomas SOMERS	GBR	Sheffield	2 Mar 14
300	Eur	32.15	Pavel MASLÁK	CZE	Gent	9 Feb 14
	CAC	32.47	Lalonde GORDON	TTO	New York	15 Feb 14
400	W35	45.93	Chris BROWN	BAH	Glasgow	25 Jan 14
	W35	45.84	Chris BROWN	BAH	Sopot	7 Mar 14
	W35	45.58	Chris BROWN	BAH	Sopot	8 Mar 14
600	Afr	1:15.31	Mohamed AMAN	ETH	Moskva	2 Feb 14
	Asi	1:15.83	Abdulrahman Musaeb BALLA	QAT	Moskva	2 Feb 14
800	Afr	1:44.52	Mohamed AMAN	ETH	Birmingham	15 Feb 14
1000	NAm	2:16.76	David TORRENCE	USA	Boston (Allston)	2 Mar 14
2000	NAm, W35	4:54.74	Bernard LAGAT	USA	New York	15 Feb 14
	Com	4:55.35	Cameron LEVINS	CAN	New York	15 Feb 14
3000	W18	7:42.05	Yomif KEJELCHA	ETH	Bordeaux	26 Jan 14
	Asi	7:39.24 §	Albert ROP	BRN	Düsseldorf	30 Jan 14
	Asi	7:38.77 §	Albert ROP	BRN	Gent	9 Feb 14
2M	NAm	8:07.41	Galen RUPP	USA	Boston (Allston)	25 Jan 14
5000	NAm	13:01.26	Galen RUPP	USA	Boston (Allston)	16 Jan 14
60H/99	W20	7.48	Wilhem BELOCIAN	FRA	Val-de-Reuil	9 Mar 14
HJ	Eur=	2.42	Ivan UKHOV	RUS	Praha	25 Feb 14
	Asi	2.38	Mutaz Essa BARSHIM	QAT	Sopot	9 Mar 14
PV	SAm	5.72	Thiago Braz DA SILVA	BRA	Malmö	8 Feb 14
	SAm	5.76	Thiago Braz DA SILVA	BRA	Donetsk	15 Feb 14
	W, Eur	6.16	Renaud LAVILLENIE	FRA	Donetsk	15 Feb 14
SP/5kg	W18	21.89	Konrad BUKOWIECKI	POL	Aleksandrów Lódz	4 Jan 14
	W18	22.24	Konrad BUKOWIECKI	POL	Bydgoszcz	31 Jan 14
SP/6kg	W18	20.22	Konrad BUKOWIECKI	POL	Spala	19 Jan 14
SP	SAm	20.68 & 21.04	Germán LAURO	ARG	Praha	25 Feb 14
	Oce	20.88 & 21.26	Tomas WALSH	NZL	Sopot	7 Mar 14
Hep	SAm=	5951	Carlos CHININ	BRA	Tallinn	8 Feb 14
			(7.01, 7.41, 14.27, 2.01 / 8.01, 4.64, 2:44.88)			
4x400 R	Afr	3:07.95	Ogunmola, Akwu, Isah, Morton	NGR	Sopot	8 Mar 14
	W, NAm	3:02.13	Clemons, Verburg, Butler, Smith	USA	Sopot	9 Mar 14
	CAC, Com	3:03.69	Nolan, Fothergill, Gauntlett, Steele	JAM	Sopot	9 Mar 14
4x800 R	W, NAm	7:13.11	Jones, Torrence, Solomon, Sowinski	USA	Boston (Roxbury)	8 Feb 14
3000W	W40	11:51.60	Mikel ODRIOZOLA	ESP	San Sebastián	25 Jan 14
5000W	W35	18:29.44	Yohann Diniz	FRA	Reims	26 Jan 14
	W40	19:40.17	Yuriy ANDRONOV	RUS	Samara	30 Jan 14
	Afr	19:51.36	Hedi TÉRAOUI	TUN	Bordeaux	23 Feb 14

INDOORS – WOMEN

60	SAm	7.23 & 7.19	Franciela KRASUCKI	BRA	São Caetano do Sul	16 Feb 14
400	NAm	50.46A	Phyllis FRANCIS	USA	Albuquerque	15 Mar 14
600	Afr	1:25.76	Regina GEORGE	NGR	Fayetteville	10 Jan 14
1000	W20	2:39.25	Mary CAIN	USA	Boston (Allston)	16 Jan 14
	W20	2:35.80	Mary CAIN	USA	Boston (Roxbury)	8 Feb 14
1500	W, Afr	3:55.17	Genzebe DIBABA	ETH	Karlsruhe	1 Feb 14
	Eur	3:57.91	Abeba AREGAWI	SWE	Stockholm	6 Feb 14
	W18	4:08.47	Gudaf TSEGAY	ETH	Stockholm	6 Feb 14
2000	Oce	5:47.62	Lucy VAN DALEN	NZL	Boston	8 Feb 14

Event	Cat	Mark	Name	Nat	Venue	Date
3000	W, Afr	8:16.60	Genzebe DIBABA	ETH	Stockholm	6 Feb 14
	Com	8:29.99	Hellen OBIRI	KEN	Stockholm	6 Feb 14
2M	W, Afr	9:00.48	Genzebe DIBABA	ETH	Birmingham	15 Feb 14
HJ	W40	1.80	Oana PANTELIMON	ROU	Budapest	27 Mar 14
Hep	W18	4284	Morgan LAKE	GBR	Växjö	9 Feb 14
			(8.97, 1.85, 13.38, 5.87, 2:24.48)			
	NAm	4805A	Sharon DAY-MONROE	USA	Albuquerque	21 Feb 14
			(8.44, 1.88, 15.59, 6.09, 2:13.19)			
	W20	4635A	Kendall Williams	USA	Albuquerque	15 Mar 14
			(8.21, 1.88, 12.05, 6.32, 2:17.31)			
4x400 R	CAC	3:29.43	Chambers, McLaughlin, Goule, McPherson	JAM	Sopot	8 Mar 14
	Afr	3:29.67	Omotoso, George, Abogunloko, Abugan	NGR	Sopot	8 Mar 14
	CAC, Com	3:26.54	Hall, McLaughlin, Spencer, McPherson	JAM	Sopot	9 Mar 14
3000W	Afr	15:03.84	Olfa LAFI	TUN	Nantes	15 Feb 14
	W35	12:23.46	Maria José POVES	ESP	Zaragoza	9 Mar 14

OUTDOORS – MEN

Event	Cat	Mark	Name	Nat	Venue	Date
Mar	W20	2:04:32	Tsegaye MEKONNEN	ETH	Dubai	24 Jan 14
TJ	W18	17.24	Lazaro MARTÍNEZ	CUB	La Habana	1 Feb 14
HT	Afr	81.29	Mostafa Hicham AL-GAMAL	EGY	Al-Qáhira	21 Mar 14

OUTDOORS – WOMEN

Event	Cat	Mark	Name	Nat	Venue	Date
100	Oce	11.11	Melissa BREEN	AUS	Canberra	9 Feb 14
15k	NAm	47:03	Shalane FLANAGAN	USA	Jacksonville	15 Mar 14
20k	SAm	67:02+	Yolanda CABALLERO	COL	Marugame	2 Feb 14
	W,Afr,Com	61:56+	Florence KIPLAGAT	KEN	Barcelona	16 Feb 14
HMar	W,Afr,Com	65:12	Florence KIPLAGAT	KEN	Barcelona	16 Feb 14
HT	Afr	69.20	Amy SÈNE	SEN	Chateauroux	9 Mar 14
	Asi	77.68	WANG Zheng	CHN	Chengdu	29 Mar 14
JT	Oce	66.83	Kim MICKLE	AUS	Melbourne	22 Mar 14
20000W	SAm	1:31:46.9	Sandra Lorena ARENAS	COL	Santiago de Chile	13 Mar 14
20kW	NAm	1:31:40	Rachel SEAMAN	CAN	Lugano	16 Mar 14

SPLIT TIMES IN WORLD RECORDS

Men

			400m	800m	1200m	1600m	2000m	2400m	2800m
800m	1:40.91	Rudisha 2010	49.28	1:40.91	(600m 1:14.30)				
1000m	2:11.96	Ngeny 1999	49.66	1:44.62	(200m 24.12, 600m 1:17.14)				
1500m	3:26.00	El Guerrouj 1998	54.3	1:50.7	2:46.4	(1000m 2:18.8)			
1M	3:43.13	El Guerrouj 1999	55.2	1:51.2	2:47.0	(1000m 2:19.2)			
2000m	4:44.79	El Guerrouj 1999	57.1	1:55.4	2:52.4	3:49.60			
3000m	7:20.67	Komen 1996	57.6	1:57.0	2:54.9	3:53.6	4:53.4	5:51.3	6:51.2 (1500m 3:38.6)
2M	7:58.61	Komen 1997	58.6	2:00.4		3:58.4	4:58.2	5:56.7	6:57.5 (1M 3:59.2)
5000m	12:37.35	Bekele 2004	kms:	2:33.24, 5:05.47, 7:37.34, 10:07.93, last 400m 57.9					
10,000m	26:17.53	Bekele 2005	kms:	2:40.6, 5:16.4, 7:53.3, 10:30.4, 13:09.4, 15:44.66, 18:23.98, 21:04.63, 23:45.09, 26:17.53, last 400m 57.1					
3kmSt	7:53.63	Shaheen 2004	1000m 2:36.13, 2000m 5:18.09						

Women

			400m	800m	1200m	1600m	2000m
800m	1:53.28	Kratochvílová 1983	56.1	1:53.28	(600m 1:25.0)		
1000m	2:28.98	Masterkova 1996	58.3	1:59.8	(200m 28.4, 600m 1:29.1)		
1500m	3:50.46	Qu Yunxia 1993	57.2	2:00.8	3:05.2		
1M	4:12.56	Masterkova 1996	62.0	2:06.7	3:12.2	(1000m 2:39.5, 1500m 3:56.77)	
2000m	5:25.36	O'Sullivan 1994	64.9	2:07.8	3:14.8	4:23.5	5:25.36

			1km	2km	3km	4km	5km	6km	7km	8km	9km
3000m	8:06.11	Wang J 1993	2:42.0	5:29.7	(last 400m 62.7)						
2M	8:58.58	Defar 2007	2:48.4	5:37.5	8:24.51	(1M 4:33.07, last 400m 62.6)					
5000m	14:11.15	Dibaba 2008	2:48.3	5:43.8	8:39.0	11:28.44	14:11.15				
10000m	29:31.78	Wang J 1993	2:54.7	5:56.6	8:59.2	12:02.8	15:05.7	18:10.1	21:14.4	23:59.9	26:44.8
3kmSt	8:58.81	Galkina 2008	1000m 2:58.63, 2000m 6:01.20								

Most World Records: Sergey Bubka USR/UKR set a total of 35 at pole vault: 17 outdoors from 5.85 (1984) to 6.14 (1994) and 18 indoors (9 ratified by IAAF) from 5.81 (1844) to 6.15 (1993). Paavi Nurmi FIN set 22 official and 13 unofficial world records at distances from 1500m to 20,000m between 1921 and 1931. The most world records by a woman at one event is 28 at pole vault (15 outdoors, 13 indoors) by Yelena Isinbayeva RUS 2003-09.

Oldest: 41y 238d Yekaterina Podkopayeva RUS women's 4x800m indoor 8:18.71 Moskva 4 Feb 1994.

Youngest: 14y 334d Wang Yan CHN 5000m walk 21:33.8 Jian 9 Mar 1986 (unratified).

Youngest male: 17y 198d Thomas Ray PV 3.42m Ulverston 19 Sep 1879 (prior to IAAF jurisdiction (from 1913)).

Most world records set in one day: 6 Jesse Owens USA at Ann Arbor 23 May 1935: 100y 9.4, LJ 8.13m, 220y straight (& 200m) 20.3, 220y hurdles straight (& 220yh) 22.6.

Record span of setting world records: Men: 15 years Haile Gebrselassie ETH 1994-2009

Mark	Wind	Name		Nat	Born	Pos	Meet	Venue	Date

WORLD MEN'S ALL-TIME LISTS

100 METRES

Mark	Wind	Name		Nat	Born	Pos	Meet	Venue	Date
9.58 WR	0.9	Usain	Bolt	JAM	21.8.86	1	WCh	Berlin	16 Aug 09
9.63	1.5		Bolt			1	OG	London (OS)	5 Aug 12
9.69 WR	0.0		Bolt			1	OG	Beijing	16 Aug 08
9.69	2.0	Tyson	Gay ¶	USA	9.8.82	1		Shanghai	20 Sep 09
9.69	-0.1	Yohan	Blake	JAM	26.12.89	1	Athl	Lausanne	23 Aug 12
9.71	0.9		Gay			2	WCh	Berlin	16 Aug 09
9.72 WR	1.7		Bolt			1	Reebok	New York (RI)	31 May 08
9.72	0.2	Asafa	Powell	JAM	23.11.82	1rA	Athl	Lausanne	2 Sep 08
9.74 WR	1.7		Powell			1h2	GP	Rieti	9 Sep 07
9.75	1.1		Blake			1	NC	Kingston	29 Jun 12
9.75	1.5		Blake			2	OG	London (OS)	5 Aug 12
9.76	1.8		Bolt			1		Kingston	3 May 08
9.76	1.3		Bolt			1	VD	Bruxelles	16 Sep 11
9.76	-0.1		Bolt			1	GGala	Roma	31 May 12
9.76	1.4		Blake			1	WK	Zürich	30 Aug 12
9.77 WR	1.6		Powell			1	Tsik	Athína	14 Jun 05
9.77 WR	1.5		Powell			1	BrGP	Gateshead	11 Jun 06
9.77 WR	1.0		Powell			1rA	WK	Zürich	18 Aug 06
9.77	1.6		Gay			1q1	NC/OT	Eugene	28 Jun 08
9.77	-1.3		Bolt			1	VD	Bruxelles	5 Sep 08
9.77	0.9		Powell			1h1	GP	Rieti	7 Sep 08
9.77	0.4		Gay			1	GGala	Roma	10 Jul 09
9.77	-0.3		Bolt			1	WCh	Moskva	11 Aug 13
9.78	0.0		Powell			1	GP	Rieti	9 Sep 07
9.78	-0.4		Gay			1	LGP	London (CP)	13 Aug 10
9.78	0.9	Nesta	Carter	JAM	10.11.85	1		Rieti	29 Aug 10
9.78	1.0		Powell			1	Athl	Lausanne	30 Jun 11
9.79 WR	0.1	Maurice	Greene	USA	23.7.74	1rA	Tsik	Athína	16 Jun 99
9.79	-0.2		Bolt			1	GL	Saint-Denis	17 Jul 09
9.79	0.1		Gay			1	VD	Bruxelles	27 Aug 10
9.79	1.1		Gay			1h1		Clermont	4 Jun 11
9.79	0.6		Bolt			1	Bisl	Oslo	7 Jun 12
9.79	1.5	Justin	Gatlin ¶	USA	10.2.82	3	OG	London (OS)	5 Aug 12
		(33 performances by 7 athletes)							
9.80	0.4	Steve	Mullings ¶	JAM	29.11.82	1	Pre	Eugene	4 Jun 11
9.84 WR	0.7	Donovan	Bailey	CAN	16.12.67	1	OG	Atlanta	27 Jul 96
9.84	0.2	Bruny	Surin	CAN	12.7.67	2	WCh	Sevilla	22 Aug 99
		(10)							
9.85 WR	1.2	Leroy	Burrell	USA	21.2.67	1rA	Athl	Lausanne	6 Jul 94
9.85	1.7	Olusoji	Fasuba	NGR	9.7.84	2	SGP	Doha	12 May 06
9.85	1.3	Michael	Rodgers	USA	24.4.85	2	Pre	Eugene	4 Jun 11
9.85	1.0	Richard	Thompson	TRI	7.6.85	1	NC	Port of Spain	13 Aug 11
9.86 WR	1.2	Carl	Lewis	USA	1.7.61	1	WCh	Tokyo	25 Aug 91
9.86	-0.4	Frank	Fredericks	NAM	2.10.67	1	Athl	Lausanne	3 Jul 96
9.86	1.8	Ato	Boldon	TRI	30.12.73	1rA	MSR	Walnut	19 Apr 98
9.86	1.4	Keston	Bledman	TRI	8.3.88	1	NC	Port-of-Spain	23 Jun 12
9.86	0.6	Francis	Obikwelu	NGR/POR	22.11.78	2	OG	Athína	22 Aug 04
9.87	0.3	Linford	Christie ¶	GBR	2.4.60	1	WCh	Stuttgart	15 Aug 93
		(20)							
9.87A	-0.2	Obadele	Thompson	BAR	30.3.76	1	WCp	Johannesburg	11 Sep 98
9.88	1.8	Shawn	Crawford ¶	USA	14.1.78	1	Pre	Eugene	19 Jun 04
9.88	0.6	Walter	Dix	USA	31.1.86	2		Nottwil	8 Aug 10
9.88	0.9	Ryan	Bailey	USA	13.4.89	2		Rieti	29 Aug 10
9.88	1.0	Michael	Frater	JAM	6.10.82	2	Athl	Lausanne	30 Jun 11
9.89	1.6	Travis	Padgett	USA	13.12.86	1q2	NC/OT	Eugene	28 Jun 08
9.89	1.6	Darvis	Patton	USA	4.12.77	1q3	NC/OT	Eugene	28 Jun 08
9.89	1.3	Ngonidzashe	Makusha	ZIM	11.3.87	1	NCAA	Des Moines	10 Jun 11
9.90	0.4	Nickel	Ashmeade	JAM	7.4.90	1s2	WCh	Moskva	11 Aug 13
9.91	1.2	Dennis	Mitchell ¶	USA	20.2.66	3	WCh	Tokyo	25 Aug 91
		(30)							
9.91	0.9	Leonard	Scott	USA	19.1.80	2	WAF	Stuttgart	9 Sep 06
9.91	-0.5	Derrick	Atkins	BAH	5.1.84	2	WCh	Osaka	26 Aug 07
9.91	-0.2	Daniel	Bailey	ANT	9.9.86	2	GL	Saint-Denis	17 Jul 09
9.91	0.7	Churandy	Martina	NED	3.7.84	2s1	OG	London (OS)	5 Aug 12
9.91	1.1	James	Dasaolu	GBR	5.9.87	1s2	NC	Birmingham	13 Jul 13
9.92	0.3	Andre	Cason	USA	20.1.69	2	WCh	Stuttgart	15 Aug 93

Mark	Wind	Name		Nat	Born	Pos	Meet	Venue	Date
9.92	0.8	Jon	Drummond	USA	9.9.68	1h3	NC	Indianapolis	12 Jun 97
9.92	0.2	Tim	Montgomery ¶	USA	28.1.75	2	NC	Indianapolis	13 Jun 97
9.92A	-0.2	Seun	Ogunkoya	NGR	28.12.77	2	WCp	Johannesburg	11 Sep 98
9.92	1.0	Tim	Harden	USA	27.1.74	1	Spitzen	Luzern	5 Jul 99
		(40)							
9.92	2.0	Christophe	Lemaitre	FRA	11.6.90	1	NC	Albi	29 Jul 11
9.93A	WR1.4	Calvin	Smith	USA	8.1.61	1	USOF	USAF Academy	3 Jul 83
9.93	-0.6	Michael	Marsh	USA	4.8.67	1	MSR	Walnut	18 Apr 92
9.93	1.8	Patrick	Johnson	AUS	26.9.72	1		Mito	5 May 03
9.93	1.1	Ivory	Williams #	USA	2.5.85	1rA		Réthimno	20 Jul 09
9.93	1.3	Nickel	Ashmeade	JAM	4.7.90	2	Pre	Eugene	2 Jun 12
9.94	0.2	Davidson	Ezinwa ¶	NGR	22.11.71	1	Gugl	Linz	4 Jul 94
9.94	-0.2	Bernard	Williams	USA	19.1.78	2	WCh	Edmonton	5 Aug 01
		(48)							
9.95A	WR0.3	Jim	Hines	USA	10.9.46	1	OG	Ciudad de México	14 Oct 68
9.95		a further ten men. 100th man 10.00, 200th 10.07, 300th 10.11, 400th 10.15, 500th 10.18							

Doubtful wind reading

9.91	-2.3	Davidson	Ezinwa ¶	NGR	22.11.71	1		Azusa	11 Apr 92

Low altitude best 9.94 0.1 Ogunkoya 1 AfCh Dakar 19 Aug 98

Wind-assisted – performances to 9.78, performers listed to 9.92

9.68	4.1	Tyson	Gay	USA	9.8.82	1	NC/OT	Eugene	29 Jun 08
9.69A	5+	Obadele	Thompson	BAR	30.3.76	1		El Paso	13 Apr 96
9.72	2.1		Powell			1	Bisl	Oslo	4 Jun 10
9.75	3.4		Gay			1h1	NC	Eugene	25 Jun 09
9.75	2.6		Powell			1h2	DL	Doha	14 May 10
9.75	4.3	Darvis	Patton	USA	4.12.77	1rA	TexR	Austin	30 Mar 13
9.76A	6.1	Churandy	Martina	AHO	3.7.84	1		El Paso	13 May 06
		9.92w				3	Bisl	Oslo	4 Jun 10
9.76	2.2		Gay			1	GP	New York	2 Jun 07
9.77	2.1		Bolt			1	GS	Ostrava	17 Jun 09
9.78	5.2	Carl	Lewis	USA	1.7.61	1	NC/OT	Indianapolis	16 Jul 88
9.78	3.7	Maurice	Greene	USA	23.7.74	1	GP II	Stanford	31 May 04
9.79	5.3	Andre	Cason	USA	20.1.69	1h4	NC	Eugene	16 Jun 93
9.80	4.1	Walter	Dix	USA	31.1.86	2	NC/OT	Eugene	29 Jun 08
9.83	7.1	Leonard	Scott	USA	19.1.80	1r1	Sea Ray	Knoxville	9 Apr 99
9.83	2.2	Derrick	Atkins	BAH	5.1.84	2	GP	New York	2 Jun 07
9.84	5.4	Francis	Obikwelu	NGR/POR	22.11.78	1		Zaragoza	3 Jun 06
9.85	4.8	Dennis	Mitchell ¶	USA	20.2.66	2	NC	Eugene	17 Jun 93
9.85A	3.0	Frank	Fredericks	NAM	2.10.67	1		Nairobi	18 May 02
9.85	4.1	Travis	Padgett	USA	13.12.86	4	NC/OT	Eugene	29 Jun 08
9.85	3.6	Keston	Bledman	TRI	8.3.88	1rA		Clermont	2 Jun 12
9.85	3.2	Charles	Silmon	USA	4.7.91	1s1	NC	Des Moines	21 Jun 13
9.86	2.6	Shawn	Crawford ¶	USA	14.1.78	1	GP	Doha	14 May 04
9.86	3.6	Michael	Frater	JAM	6.10.82	2h4	NC	Kingston	23 Jun 11
9.86	3.2	Rakieem "Mookie"	Salaam	USA	5.4.90	2s1	NC	Des Moines	21 Jun 13
9.87	11.2	William	Snoddy	USA	6.12.57	1		Dallas	1 Apr 78
9.87	4.9	Calvin	Smith	USA	8.1.61	1s2	NC/OT	Indianapolis	16 Jul 88
9.87	2.4	Michael	Marsh	USA	4.8.67	1rA	MSR	Walnut	20 Apr 97
9.88	2.3	James	Sanford	USA	27.12.57	1		Los Angeles (Ww)	3 May 80
9.88	5.2	Albert	Robinson	USA	28.11.64	4	NC/OT	Indianapolis	16 Jul 88
9.88	4.9	Tim	Harden	USA	27.1.74	1	NC	New Orleans	20 Jun 98
9.88	4.5	Coby	Miller	USA	19.10.76	1		Auburn	1 Apr 00
9.88	3.6	Patrick	Johnson	AUS	26.9.72	1		Perth	8 Feb 03
9.88	3.0	Darrel	Brown	TRI	11.10.84	1	NC	Port of Spain	23 Jun 07
9.88	3.7	Ivory	Williams #	USA	2.5.85	1	TexR	Austin	3 Apr 10
9.89	4.2	Ray	Stewart	JAM	18.3.65	1s1	PAm	Indianapolis	9 Aug 87
9.90	5.2	Joe	DeLoach	USA	5.6.67	5	NC/OT	Indianapolis	16 Jul 88
9.90	7.1	Kenny	Brokenburr	USA	29.10.68	2r1	Sea Ray	Knoxville	9 Apr 99
9.90A	7.8	Teddy	Williams	USA	3.7.88	1		El Paso	11 Apr 09
9.90	2.8	Lerone	Clarke	JAM	2.10.81	1		Clermont	11 Jun 11
9.91	5.3	Bob	Hayes	USA	20.12.42	1s1	OG	Tokyo	15 Oct 64
9.91	4.2	Mark	Witherspoon	USA	3.9.63	2s1	PAm	Indianapolis	9 Aug 87
9.91	3.7	Nicolas	Macrozonaris	CAN	22.8.80	1	NC	Edmonton	22 Jun 02
9.91	3.2	Dentarius	Locke	USA	12.12.89	2	NCAA	Eugene	7 Jun 13
9.92A	4.4	Chidi	Imo ¶	NGR	27.8.63	1s1	AfG	Nairobi	8 Aug 87
9.92A	2.8	Olapade	Adeniken	NGR	19.8.69	1rA		Sestriere	29 Jul 95
9.92	2.8	Kim	Collins	SKN	5.4.76	1rA	Tex R	Austin	5 Apr 03
9.92	3.7	Joshua 'J.J.'	Johnson	USA	10.5.76	2	Aragón	Zaragoza	28 Jul 07
9.92	3.7	Clement	Campbell	JAM	19.2.75	3	Aragón	Zaragoza	28 Jul 07
9.92	2.4	Trell	Kimmons	USA	13.7.85	4	DL	New York	12 Jun 10

Mark	Wind	Name		Nat	Born	Pos	Meet	Venue	Date
9.92	4.3	Wallace	Spearmon	USA	24.12.84	2rA	TexR	Austin	30 Mar 13
Rolling start:	9.89w	3.7 Patrick	Jarrett ¶	JAM	2.10.77	1	Pre	Eugene	27 May 01
Hand timing	and three men at 9.7w								
9.7	1.9	Donovan	Powell ¶	JAM	31.10.71	1rA		Houston	19 May 95
9.7	1.9	Carl	Lewis	USA	1.7.61	2rA		Houston	19 May 95
9.7	1.9	Olapade	Adeniken	NGR	19.8.69	3rA		Houston	19 May 95
Drugs disqualification									
9.77	1.7	Justin	Gatlin ¶	USA	10.2.82	(1)	SGP	Doha	12 May 06
9.78	2.0	Tim	Montgomery ¶	USA	28.1.75	(1)	GPF	Paris (C)	14 Sep 02
9.79	1.1	Ben	Johnson ¶	CAN	30.12.61	(1)	OG	Seoul	24 Sep 88
9.87	2.0	Dwain	Chambers ¶	GBR	5.4.78	(2)	GPF	Paris (C)	14 Sep 02
9.7w ht	3.5		Johnson	CAN	30.12.61	(1)		Perth	24 Jan 87

200 METRES

Mark	Wind	Name		Nat	Born	Pos	Meet	Venue	Date
19.19	WR-0.3	Usain	Bolt	JAM	21.8.86	1	WCh	Berlin	20 Aug 09
19.26	0.7	Yohan	Blake	JAM	26.12.89	1	VD	Bruxelles	16 Sep 11
19.30	WR-0.9		Bolt			1	OG	Beijing	20 Aug 08
19.32	WR0.4	Michael	Johnson	USA	13.9.67	1	OG	Atlanta	1 Aug 96
19.32	0.4		Bolt			1	OG	London (OS)	9 Aug 12
19.40	0.8		Bolt			1	WCh	Daegu	3 Sep 11
19.44	0.4		Blake			2	OG	London (OS)	9 Aug 12
19.53	0.7	Walter	Dix	USA	31.1.86	2	VD	Bruxelles	16 Sep 11
19.54	0.0		Blake			1	VD	Bruxelles	7 Sep 12
19.56	-0.8		Bolt			1		Kingston	1 May 10
19.57	0.0		Bolt			1	VD	Bruxelles	4 Sep 09
19.58	1.3	Tyson	Gay	USA	9.8.82	1	Reebok	New York	30 May 09
19.58	1.4		Bolt			1	Athl	Lausanne	23 Aug 12
19.59	-0.9		Bolt			1	Athl	Lausanne	7 Jul 09
19.62	-0.3		Gay			1	NC	Indianapolis	24 Jun 07
19.63	0.4	Xavier	Carter	USA	8.12.85	1	Athl	Lausanne	11 Jul 06
19.63	-0.9		Bolt			1	Athl	Lausanne	2 Sep 08
19.65	0.0	Wallace	Spearmon	USA	24.12.84	1		Daegu	28 Sep 06
19.66	WR1.7		M Johnson			1	NC	Atlanta	23 Jun 96
19.66	0.0		Bolt			1	WK	Zürich	30 Aug 12
19.66	0.0		Bolt			1	WCh	Moskva	17 Aug 13
19.67	-0.5		Bolt			1	GP	Athína	13 Jul 08
19.68	0.4	Frank	Fredericks	NAM	2.10.67	2	OG	Atlanta	1 Aug 96
19.68	-0.1		Gay			1	WAF	Stuttgart	10 Sep 06
19.68	-0.1		Bolt			1	WAF	Thessaloníki	13 Sep 09
19.69	0.9		Dix			1	NCAA-r	Gainesville	26 May 07
19.70	0.4		Gay			2	Athl	Lausanne	11 Jul 06
19.70	0.8		Dix			2	WCh	Daegu	3 Sep 11
19.71A	1.8		M Johnson			1rA		Pietersburg	18 Mar 00
19.72A	WR 1.8	Pietro	Mennea	ITA	28.6.52	1	WUG	Ciudad de México	12 Sep 79
19.72	1.8		Dix			1	Pre	Eugene	3 Jul 10
19.72	0.1		Gay			1	Herc	Monaco	22 Jul 10
	(32/9)								
19.73	-0.2	Michael	Marsh (10)	USA	4.8.67	1s1	OG	Barcelona	5 Aug 92
19.75	1.5	Carl	Lewis	USA	1.7.61	1	NC	Indianapolis	19 Jun 83
19.75	1.7	Joe	DeLoach	USA	5.6.67	1	OG	Seoul	28 Sep 88
19.77	0.7	Ato	Boldon	TRI	30.12.73	1rA		Stuttgart	13 Jul 97
19.79	1.2	Shawn	Crawford ¶	USA	14.1.78	1	OG	Athína	26 Aug 04
19.79	0.9	Warren	Weir	JAM	31.10.89	1	NC	Kingston	23 Jun 13
19.80	0.8	Christophe	Lemaitre	FRA	11.6.90	3	WCh	Daegu	3 Sep 11
19.81	-0.3	Alonso	Edward	PAN	8.12.89	2	WCh	Berlin	20 Aug 09
19.83A	WR 0.9	Tommie	Smith	USA	6.6.44	1	OG	Ciudad de México	16 Oct 68
19.84	1.7	Francis	Obikwelu	NGR/POR	22.11.78	1s2	WCh	Sevilla	25 Aug 99
19.85	-0.3	John	Capel ¶	USA	27.10.78	1	NC	Sacramento	23 Jul 00
	(20)								
19.85	-0.5	Konstadínos	Kedéris ¶	GRE	11.7.73	1	EC	München	9 Aug 02
19.85	1.4	Churandy	Martina	NED	3.7.84	2	Athl	Lausanne	23 Aug 12
19.85	0.0	Nickel	Ashmeade	JAM	4.7.90	2	WK	Zürich	30 Aug 12
19.86A	1.0	Don	Quarrie	JAM	25.2.51	1	PAm	Cali	3 Aug 71
19.86	1.6	Maurice	Greene	USA	23.7.74	2rA	DNG	Stockholm	7 Jul 97
19.86	1.5	Jason	Young	JAM	21.3.91	1	Spitzen	Luzern	17 Jul 12
19.86	1.6	Isiah	Young	USA	5.1.90	1	NC	Des Moines	23 Jun 13
19.87	0.8	Lorenzo	Daniel	USA	23.3.66	1	NCAA	Eugene	3 Jun 88
19.87A	1.8	John	Regis	GBR	13.10.66	1		Sestriere	31 Jul 94
19.87	1.2	Jeff	Williams	USA	31.12.65	1		Fresno	13 Apr 96
	(30)								

Mark	Wind	Name		Nat	Born	Pos	Meet	Venue	Date
19.88	-0.3	Floyd	Heard	USA	24.3.66	2	NC	Sacramento	23 Jul 00
19.88	0.1	Joshua 'J.J'	Johnson	USA	10.5.76	1	VD	Bruxelles	24 Aug 01
19.89	-0.8	Claudinei	da Silva	BRA	19.11.70	1	GPF	München	11 Sep 99
19.89	1.3	Jaysuma	Saidy Ndure	NOR	1.1.84	1	WAF	Stuttgart	23 Sep 07
19.90	1.3	Asafa	Powell	JAM	23.11.82	1	NC	Kingston	25 Jun 06
19.92A	WR1.9	John	Carlos	USA	5.6.45	1	FOT	Echo Summit	12 Sep 68
19.96	-0.9	Kirk	Baptiste	USA	20.6.63	2	OG	Los Angeles	8 Aug 84
19.96	0.4	Robson	da Silva	BRA	4.9.64	1	VD	Bruxelles	25 Aug 89
19.96	-0.3	Coby	Miller	USA	19.10.76	3	NC	Sacramento	23 Jul 00
19.97	-0.9	Obadele	Thompson	BAR	30.3.76	1	Super	Yokohama	9 Sep 00
		(40)							
19.97	0.0	Curtis	Mitchell	USA	11.3.89	1s1	WCh	Moskva	16 Aug 13
19.98	1.7	Marcin	Urbas	POL	17.9.76	2s2	WCh	Sevilla	25 Aug 99
19.98	0.3	Jordan	Vaden ¶	USA	15.9.78	2	NC	Indianapolis	25 Jun 06
19.98	1.4	LaShawn	Merritt ¶	USA	27.6.86	2	adidas	Carson	20 May 07
19.98	-0.3	Steve	Mullings ¶	JAM	29.11.82	5	WCh	Berlin	20 Aug 09
19.99	0.6	Calvin	Smith	USA	8.1.61	1	WK	Zürich	24 Aug 83
19.98	-0.3	Adam	Gemili	GBR	6.10.93	1s3	WCh	Moskva	16 Aug 13
19.99	1.7	Rodney	Martin	USA	22.12.82	4	NC/OT	Eugene	6 Jul 08
20.00	0.0	Valeriy	Borzov	UKR	20.10.49	1	OG	München	4 Sep 72
20.00	0.0	Justin	Gatlin ¶	USA	10.2.82	1		Monterrey	11 Jun 05
		(50)							

100th man 20.15, 200th 20.27, 300th 20.35, 400th 20.41, 500th 20.46

Wind-assisted 2 performances to 19.73, performers listed to 19.99

19.61	>4.0	Leroy	Burrell	USA	21.2.67	1	SWC	College Station	19 May 90
19.70	2.7		Johnson			1s1	NC	Atlanta	22 Jun 96
19.73	3.3	Shawn	Crawford ¶	USA	14.1.78	1	NC	Eugene	28 Jun 09
19.80	3.2	LaShawn	Merritt ¶	USA	27.6.86	1		Greensboro	19 Apr 08
19.83	9.2	Bobby	Cruse	USA	20.3.78	1r2	Sea Ray	Knoxville	9 Apr 99
19.86	4.6	Roy	Martin	USA	25.12.66	1	SWC	Houston	18 May 86
19.86	4.0	Justin	Gatlin ¶	USA	10.2.82	1h2	NCAA	Eugene	30 May 01
19.90	3.8	Steve	Mullings ¶	JAM	29.11.82	1		Fort Worth	17 Apr 04
19.91		James	Jett	USA	28.12.70	1		Morgantown	18 Apr 92
19.93	2.4	Sebastián	Keitel	CHI	14.2.73	1		São Leopoldo	26 Apr 98
19.94	4.0	James	Sanford	USA	27.12.57	1s1	NCAA	Austin	7 Jun 80
19.94	3.7	Chris	Nelloms	USA	14.8.71	1	Big 10	Minneapolis	23 May 92
19.94	2.3	Kevin	Little	USA	3.4.68	1s3	NC	Sacramento	17 Jun 95
19.95	3.4	Mike	Roberson	USA	25.3.56	1h3	NCAA	Austin	5 Jun 80
19.96	2.2	Rohsaan	Griffin	USA	21.2.74	1s1	NC	Eugene	26 Jun 99
19.98	2.1	Aaron	Armstrong	TRI	14.10.77	1	NC	Port of Spain	26 Jun 05
19.98	2.1	Brendan	Christian	ANT	11.12.83	1		Austin	2 May 09
19.98	2.4	Darvis	Patton	USA	4.12.77	2	NC	Eugene	26 Jun 11
19.99	2.7	Ramon	Clay ¶	USA	29.6.75	2s1	NC	Atlanta	22 Jun 96
19.99	2.6	Maurice	Mitchell	USA	22.12.89	1	NCAA	Des Moines	11 Jun 11
19.99	3.2	Bryshon	Nellum	USA	1.5.89	1s2	NCAA	Eugene	6 Jun 13

Low altitude mark for athletes with lifetime bests at high altitude

19.94	0.3	Regis		2	WCh	Stuttgart	20 Aug 93	19.96 0.0 Mennea	1 Barletta	17 Aug 80

Suspended under IAAF rules

19.86	1.5	Justin	Gatlin ¶	USA	10.2.82	1	SEC	Starkville	12 May 02

Hand timing

19.7A		James	Sanford	USA	27.12.57	1		El Paso	19 Apr 80
19.7A	0.2	Robson C.	da Silva	BRA	4.9.64	1	AmCp	Bogotá	13 Aug 89

300 METRES

In 300m races only, not including intermediate times in 400m races

30.85A		Michael	Johnson	USA	13.9.67	1		Pretoria	24 Mar 00
30.97		Usain	Bolt	JAM	21.8.86	1	GS	Ostrava	27 May 10
31.30		LaShawn	Merritt	USA	27.6.86	1	Pre	Eugene	7 Jun 09
31.31			Merritt			1		Eugene	8 Aug 06
31.48		Danny	Everett	USA	1.11.66	1		Jerez de la Frontera	3 Sep 90
31.48		Roberto	Hernández	CUB	6.3.67	2		Jerez de la Frontera	3 Sep 90
31.56		Doug	Walker ¶	GBR	28.7.73	1		Gateshead	19 Jul 98
31.61		Anthuan	Maybank	USA	30.12.69	1		Durham	13 Jul 96
31.67		John	Regis	GBR	13.10.66	1	Vaux	Gateshead	17 Jul 92
31.70		Kirk	Baptiste	USA	20.6.63	1	Nike	London (CP)	18 Aug 84
31.72		Jeremy	Wariner	USA	31.1.84	1	GS	Ostrava	12 Jun 08

400 METRES

43.18	WR	Michael	Johnson	USA	13.9.67	1	WCh	Sevilla	26 Aug 99
43.29	WR	Butch	Reynolds ¶	USA	8.6.64	1	WK	Zürich	17 Aug 88
43.39			Johnson			1	WCh	Göteborg	9 Aug 95
43.44			Johnson			1	NC	Atlanta	19 Jun 96
43.45		Jeremy	Wariner	USA	31.1.84	1	WCh	Osaka	31 Aug 07

MEN All-time

Mark	Wind	Name		Nat	Born	Pos	Meet	Venue	Date
43.49			Johnson			1	OG	Atlanta	29 Jul 96
43.50		Quincy	Watts	USA	19.6.70	1	OG	Barcelona	5 Aug 92
43.50			Wariner			1	DNG	Stockholm	7 Aug 07
43.62			Wariner			1rA	GGala	Roma	14 Jul 06
43.65			Johnson			1	WCh	Stuttgart	17 Aug 93
43.66			Johnson			1	NC	Sacramento	16 Jun 95
43.66			Johnson			1rA	Athl	Lausanne	3 Jul 96
43.68			Johnson			1	WK	Zürich	12 Aug 98
43.68			Johnson			1	NC	Sacramento	16 Jul 00
43.71			Watts			1s2	OG	Barcelona	3 Aug 92
43.74			Johnson			1	NC	Eugene	19 Jun 93
43.74		LaShawn	Merritt ¶	USA	27.6.86	1	WCh	Moskva	13 Aug 13
43.75			Johnson			1		Waco	19 Apr 97
43.75			Merritt			1	OG	Beijing	21 Aug 08
43.76			Johnson			1	GWG	Uniondale, NY	22 Jul 98
43.81		Danny	Everett	USA	1.11.66	1	NC/OT	New Orleans	26 Jun 92
43.82			Wariner			1	WK	Zürich	29 Aug 08
43.83			Watts			1	WK	Zürich	19 Aug 92
43.84			Johnson			1	OG	Sydney	25 Sep 00
43.86A	WR	Lee	Evans	USA	25.2.47	1	OG	Ciudad de México	18 Oct 68
43.86			Johnson			1	Bisl	Oslo	21 Jul 95
43.86			Wariner			1	Gaz	Saint-Denis	18 Jul 08
43.87		Steve	Lewis	USA	16.5.69	1	OG	Seoul	28 Sep 88
43.88			Johnson			1	WK	Zürich	16 Aug 95
43.90			Johnson			1		Madrid	6 Sep 94
		(30/8)							
43.94		Kirani	James	GRN	1.9.92	1	OG	London (OS)	6 Aug 12
43.97A		Larry	James	USA	6.11.47	2	OG	Ciudad de México	18 Oct 68
		(10)							
44.05		Angelo	Taylor	USA	29.12.78	1	NC	Indianapolis	23 Jun 07
44.09		Alvin	Harrison ¶	USA/DOM	20.1.74	3	NC	Atlanta	19 Jun 96
44.09		Jerome	Young ¶	USA	14.8.76	1	NC	New Orleans	21 Jun 98
44.10		Gary	Kikaya	COD	4.2.78	2	WAF	Stuttgart	9 Sep 06
44.13		Derek	Mills	USA	9.7.72	1	Pre	Eugene	4 Jun 95
44.14		Roberto	Hernández	CUB	6.3.67	2		Sevilla	30 May 90
44.15		Anthuan	Maybank	USA	30.12.69	1rB	Athl	Lausanne	3 Jul 96
44.16		Otis	Harris	USA	30.6.82	2	OG	Athína	23 Aug 04
44.17		Innocent	Egbunike	NGR	30.11.61	1rA	WK	Zürich	19 Aug 87
44.18		Samson	Kitur	KEN	25.2.66	2s2	OG	Barcelona	3 Aug 92
		(20)							
44.20A		Charles	Gitonga	KEN	5.10.71	1	NC	Nairobi	29 Jun 96
44.21		Ian	Morris	TRI	30.11.61	3s2	OG	Barcelona	3 Aug 92
44.26		Alberto	Juantorena	CUB	21.11.50	1	OG	Montreal	29 Jul 76
44.27		Alonzo	Babers	USA	31.10.61	1	OG	Los Angeles	8 Aug 84
44.27		Antonio	Pettigrew ¶	USA	3.11.67	1	NC	Houston	17 Jun 89
44.27		Darold	Williamson	USA	19.2.83	1s1	NCAA	Sacramento	10 Jun 05
44.28		Andrew	Valmon	USA	1.1.65	4	NC	Eugene	19 Jun 93
44.28		Tyree	Washington	USA	28.8.76	1		Los Angeles (ER)	12 May 01
44.29		Derrick	Brew	USA	28.12.77	1	SEC	Athens, GA	16 May 99
44.29		Sanderlei	Parrela	BRA	7.10.74	2	WCh	Sevilla	26 Aug 99
		(30)							
44.30		Gabriel	Tiacoh	CIV	10.9.63	1	NCAA	Indianapolis	7 Jun 86
44.30		Lamont	Smith	USA	11.12.72	4	NC	Atlanta	19 Jun 96
44.31		Alejandro	Cárdenas	MEX	4.10.74	3	WCh	Sevilla	26 Aug 99
44.33		Thomas	Schönlebe	GDR	6.8.65	1	WCh	Roma	3 Sep 87
44.34		Darnell	Hall	USA	26.9.71	1	Athl	Lausanne	5 Jul 95
44.35		Andrew	Rock	USA	23.1.82	2	WCh	Helsinki	12 Aug 05
44.36		Iwan	Thomas	GBR	5.1.74	1	NC	Birmingham	13 Jul 97
44.37		Roger	Black	GBR	31.3.66	2rA	Athl	Lausanne	3 Jul 96
44.37		Davis	Kamoga	UGA	17.7.68	2	WCh	Athína	5 Aug 97
44.37		Mark	Richardson	GBR	26.7.72	1	Bisl	Oslo	9 Jul 98
		(40)							
44.38		Darren	Clark	AUS	6.9.65	3s1	OG	Seoul	26 Sep 88
44.40		Fred	Newhouse	USA	8.11.48	2	OG	Montreal	29 Jul 76
44.40		Chris	Brown	BAH	15.10.78	2	Bisl	Oslo	6 Jun 08
44.40		Jermaine	Gonzales	JAM	26.11.84	1	Herc	Monaco	22 Jul 10
44.40		Tony	McQuay	USA	16.4.90	2	WCh	Moskva	13 Aug 13
44.41A		Ron	Freeman	USA	12.6.47	3	OG	Ciudad de México	18 Oct 68
44.43A		Ezra	Sambu	KEN	4.9.78	1	WCT	Nairobi	26 Jul 03

Mark	Wind	Name		Nat	Born	Pos	Meet	Venue	Date
44.43		Jonathan	Borlée	BEL	22.2.88	1h3	OG	London (OS)	4 Aug 12
44.44		Tyler	Christopher	CAN	3.10.83	3	WCh	Helsinki	12 Aug 05
44.45A		Ronnie	Ray	USA	2.1.54	1	PAm	Ciudad de México	18 Oct 75
44.45		Darrell	Robinson	USA	23.12.63	2	Pepsi	Los Angeles (Ww)	17 May 86
44.45		Avard	Moncur	BAH	2.11.78	1		Madrid	7 Jul 01
44.45		Leonard	Byrd	USA	17.3.75	1	GP	Belém	5 May 02
44.45		Luguelin	Santos	DOM	12.11.93	1	FBK	Hengelo	27 May 12

(54)
100th man 44.64, 200th 44.89, 300th 45.11, 400th 45.27, 500th 45.40

Mark	Wind	Name		Nat	Born	Pos	Meet	Venue	Date
Drugs dq: 44.21		Antonio	Pettigrew ¶	USA	3.11.67	1		Nassau	26 May 99

Hand timing   * 440 yards time less 0.3 secs

Mark	Wind	Name		Nat	Born	Pos	Meet	Venue	Date
44.1		Wayne	Collett	USA	20.10.49	1	OT	Eugene	9 Jul 72
44.2*		John	Smith	USA	5.8.50	1	AAU	Eugene	26 Jun 71
44.2		Fred	Newhouse	USA	8.11.48	1s1	OT	Eugene	7 Jul 72

600 METRES

Mark	Wind	Name		Nat	Born	Pos	Meet	Venue	Date
1:12.81		Johnny	Gray	USA	19.6.60	1		Santa Monica	24 May 86
1:13.2 + ?		John	Kipkurgat	KEN	16.3.44	1		Pointe-à-Pierre	23 Mar 74
1:13.28		Duane	Solomon	USA	28.12.84	1		Burnaby	1 Jul 13
1:13.49		Joseph	Mutua	KEN	10.12.78	1		Liège (NX)	27 Aug 02
1:13.80		Earl	Jones	USA	17.7.64	2		Santa Monica	24 May 86

800 METRES

Mark	Wind	Name		Nat	Born	Pos	Meet	Venue	Date
1:40.91 WR		David	Rudisha	KEN	17.12.88	1	OG	London (OS)	9 Aug 12
1:41.01 WR			Rudisha			1rA		Rieti	29 Aug 10
1:41.09 WR			Rudisha			1	ISTAF	Berlin	22 Aug 10
1:41.11 WR		Wilson	Kipketer	DEN	12.12.70	1	ASV	Köln	24 Aug 97
1:41.24 WR			Kipketer			1rA	WK	Zürich	13 Aug 97
1:41.33			Rudisha			1		Rieti	10 Sep 11
1:41.51			Rudisha			1	NA	Heusden-Zolder	10 Jul 10
1:41.54			Rudisha			1	DL	Saint-Denis	6 Jul 12
1:41.73 !WR		Sebastian	Coe	GBR	29.9.56	1		Firenze	10 Jun 81
1:41.73 WR			Kipketer			1rA	DNG	Stockholm	7 Jul 97
1:41.73		Nijel	Amos	BOT	15.3.94	2	OG	London (OS)	9 Aug 12
1:41.74			Rudisha			1	adidas	New York	9 Jun 12
1:41.77		Joaquim	Cruz	BRA	12.3.63	1	ASV	Köln	26 Aug 84
1:41.83			Kipketer			1	GP II	Rieti	1 Sep 96
1:42.01			Rudisha			1	GP	Rieti	6 Sep 09
1:42.04			Rudisha			1	Bisl	Oslo	4 Jun 10
1:42.12A			Rudisha			1	OT	Nairobi	23 Jun 12
1:42.17			Kipketer			1	TOTO	Tokyo	16 Sep 96
1:42.20			Kipketer			1	VD	Bruxelles	22 Aug 97
1:42.23		Abubaker	Kaki	SUD	21.6.89	2	Bisl	Oslo	4 Jun 10
1:42.27			Kipketer			1	VD	Bruxelles	3 Sep 99
1:42.28		Sammy	Koskei	KEN	14.5.61	2	ASV	Köln	26 Aug 84
1:42.32			Kipketer			1	GP II	Rieti	8 Sep 02
1:42.33 WR			Coe			1	Bisl	Oslo	5 Jul 79
1:42.34			Cruz			1r1	WK	Zürich	22 Aug 84
1:42.34		Wilfred	Bungei	KEN	24.7.80	2	GP II	Rieti	8 Sep 02
1:42.37		Mohammed	Aman	ETH	10.1.94	1	VD	Bruxelles	6 Sep 13
1:42.41			Cruz			1	VD	Bruxelles	24 Aug 84
1:42.47		Yuriy	Borzakovskiy	RUS	12.4.81	1	VD	Bruxelles	24 Aug 01
1:42.49			Cruz			1		Koblenz	28 Aug 85

(30/10)
! photo-electric cell time

Mark	Wind	Name		Nat	Born	Pos	Meet	Venue	Date
1:42.53		Timothy	Kitum	KEN	20.11.94	3	OG	London (OS)	9 Aug 12
1:42.55		André	Bucher	SUI	19.10.76	1rA	WK	Zürich	17 Aug 01
1:42.58		Vebjørn	Rodal	NOR	16.9.72	1	OG	Atlanta	31 Jul 96
1:42.60		Johnny	Gray	USA	19.6.60	2r1		Koblenz	28 Aug 85
1:42.62		Patrick	Ndururi	KEN	12.1.69	2rA	WK	Zürich	13 Aug 97
1:42.67		Alfred	Kirwa Yego	KEN	28.11.86	2	GP	Rieti	6 Sep 09
1:42.69		Hezekiél	Sepeng ¶	RSA	30.6.74	2	VD	Bruxelles	3 Sep 99
1:42.69		Japheth	Kimutai	KEN	20.12.78	3	VD	Bruxelles	3 Sep 99
1:42.79		Fred	Onyancha	KEN	25.12.69	3	OG	Atlanta	31 Jul 96
1:42.79		Youssef Saad	Kamel	KEN/BRN	29.3.83	2	Herc	Monaco	29 Jul 08

(20)

Mark	Wind	Name		Nat	Born	Pos	Meet	Venue	Date
1:42.81		Jean-Patrick	Nduwimana	BDI	9.5.78	2rA	WK	Zürich	17 Aug 01
1:42.82		Duane	Solomon	USA	28.12.84	4	OG	London (OS)	9 Aug 12
1:42.85		Norberto	Téllez	CUB	22.1.72	4	OG	Atlanta	31 Jul 96
1:42.86		Mbulaeni	Mulaudzi	RSA	8.9.80	3	GP	Rieti	6 Sep 09
1:42.88		Steve	Cram	GBR	14.10.60	1rA	WK	Zürich	21 Aug 85
1:42.91		William	Yiampoy	KEN	17.5.74	3	GP II	Rieti	8 Sep 02

MEN All-time

Mark	Wind	Name		Nat	Born	Pos	Meet	Venue	Date
1:42.95		Boaz	Lalang	KEN	8.2.89	2rA		Rieti	29 Aug 10
1:42.97		Peter	Elliott	GBR	9.10.62	1		Sevilla	30 May 90
1:42.95		Nick	Symmonds	USA	30.12.83	5	OG	London (OS)	9 Aug 12
1:42.98		Patrick	Konchellah	KEN	20.4.68	2	ASV	Köln	24 Aug 97
		(30)							
1:43.03		Kennedy/Kenneth	Kimwetich	KEN	1.1.73	2		Stuttgart	19 Jul 98
1:43.06		Billy	Konchellah	KEN	20.10.62	1	WCh	Roma	1 Sep 87
1:43.07		Yeimer	López	CUB	20.8.82	1		Jerez de la Frontera	24 Jun 08
1:43.08		José Luiz	Barbosa	BRA	27.5.61	1		Rieti	6 Sep 91
1:43.09		Djabir	Saïd-Guerni	ALG	29.3.77	5	VD	Bruxelles	3 Sep 99
1:43.13		Abraham Kipchirchir	Rotich	KEN	26.6.93	1	Herc	Monaco	20 Jul 12
1:43.15		Mehdi	Baala	FRA	17.8.78	5	GP II	Rieti	8 Sep 02
1:43.15		Asbel	Kiprop	KEN	30.6.89	2	Herc	Monaco	22 Jul 11
1:43.16		Paul	Ereng	KEN	22.8.67	1	WK	Zürich	16 Aug 89
1:43.17		Benson	Koech	KEN	10.11.74	1		Rieti	28 Aug 94
		(40)							
1:43.20		Mark	Everett	USA	2.9.68	1rA	Gugl	Linz	9 Jul 97
1:43.22		Pawel	Czapiewski	POL	30.3.78	5rA	WK	Zürich	17 Aug 01
1:43.22		Ferguson	Cheruiyot	KEN	30.11.89	3	VD	Bruxelles	6 Sep 13
1:43.25		Amine	Laâlou	MAR	13.5.82	1	GGala	Roma	14 Jul 06
1:43.26		Sammy	Langat (Kibet)	KEN	24.1.70	1rB	WK	Zürich	14 Aug 96
1:43.30		William	Tanui	KEN	22.2.64	2		Rieti	6 Sep 91
1:43.30		Adam	Kszczot	POL	2.9.89	2		Rieti	10 Sep 11
1:43.31		Nixon	Kiprotich	KEN	4.12.62	1		Rieti	6 Sep 92
1:43.33		Robert	Chirchir	KEN	26.11.72	3		Stuttgart	19 Jul 98
1:43.33		William	Chirchir	KEN	6.2.79	6	VD	Bruxelles	3 Sep 99
1:43.33		Joseph Mwengi	Mutua	KEN	10.12.78	1rA	WK	Zürich	16 Aug 02
		(51)		100th man 1:43.88, 200th 1:44.66, 300th 1:45.08, 400th 1:45.42, 500th 1:45.73					

1000 METRES

Mark	Wind	Name		Nat	Born	Pos	Meet	Venue	Date
2:11.96	WR	Noah	Ngeny	KEN	2.11.78	1	GP II	Rieti	5 Sep 99
2:12.18	WR	Sebastian	Coe	GBR	29.9.56	1	OsloG	Oslo	11 Jul 81
2:12.66			Ngeny			1	Nik	Nice	17 Jul 99
2:12.88		Steve	Cram	GBR	14.10.60	1		Gateshead	9 Aug 85
2:13.40	WR		Coe			1	Bisl	Oslo	1 Jul 80
2:13.56		Kennedy/Kenneth	Kimwetich	KEN	1.1.73	2	Nik	Nice	17 Jul 99
2:13.62		Abubaker	Kaki	SUD	21.6.89	1	Pre	Eugene	3 Jul 10
2:13.73		Noureddine	Morceli	ALG	28.2.70	1	BNP	Villeneuve d'Ascq	2 Jul 93
2:13.9	WR	Rick	Wohlhuter	USA	23.12.48	1	King	Oslo	30 Jul 74
2:13.96		Mehdi	Baala	FRA	17.8.78	1		Strasbourg	26 Jun 03
2:14.09		Joaquim	Cruz	BRA	12.3.63	1	Nik	Nice	20 Aug 84
2:14.28		Japheth	Kimutai	KEN	20.12.78	1	DNG	Stockholm	1 Aug 00

1500 METRES

Mark	Wind	Name		Nat	Born	Pos	Meet	Venue	Date
3:26.00	WR	Hicham	El Guerrouj	MAR	14.9.74	1	GGala	Roma	14 Jul 98
3:26.12			El Guerrouj			1	VD	Bruxelles	24 Aug 01
3:26.34		Bernard	Lagat	KEN/USA	12.12.74	2	VD	Bruxelles	24 Aug 01
3:26.45			El Guerrouj			1 rA	WK	Zürich	12 Aug 98
3:26.89			El Guerrouj			1	WK	Zürich	16 Aug 02
3:26.96			El Guerrouj			1	GP II	Rieti	8 Sep 02
3:27.21			El Guerrouj			1	WK	Zürich	11 Aug 00
3:27.34			El Guerrouj			1	Herc	Monaco	19 Jul 02
3:27.37	WR	Noureddine	Morceli	ALG	28.2.70	1	Nik	Nice	12 Jul 95
3:27.40			Lagat			1rA	WK	Zürich	6 Aug 04
3:27.52			Morceli			1	Herc	Monaco	25 Jul 95
3:27.64			El Guerrouj			2rA	WK	Zürich	6 Aug 04
3:27.65			El Guerrouj			1	WCh	Sevilla	24 Aug 99
3:27.72		Asbel	Kiprop	KEN	30.6.89	1	Herc	Monaco	19 Jul 13
3:27.91			Lagat			2	Herc	Monaco	19 Jul 02
3:28.12		Noah	Ngeny	KEN	2.11.78	2	WK	Zürich	11 Aug 00
3:28.21+			El Guerrouj			1	in 1M	Roma	7 Jul 99
3:28.37			Morceli			1	GPF	Monaco	9 Sep 95
3:28.37			El Guerrouj			1	Herc	Monaco	8 Aug 98
3:28.38			El Guerrouj			1	GP	Saint-Denis	6 Jul 01
3:28.40			El Guerrouj			1	VD	Bruxelles	5 Sep 03
3:28.51			Lagat			3	WK	Zürich	11 Aug 00
3:28.57			El Guerrouj			1rA	WK	Zürich	11 Aug 99
3:28.6+			Ngeny			2	in 1M	Roma	7 Jul 99
3:28.73			Ngeny			2	WCh	Sevilla	24 Aug 99
3:28.81		Mohamed	Farah	GBR	23.3.83	2	Herc	Monaco	19 Jul 13

Mark	Wind	Name		Nat	Born	Pos	Meet	Venue	Date
3:28.84			Ngeny			1	GP	Paris (C)	21 Jul 99
3:28.86	WR		Morceli			1		Rieti	6 Sep 92
3:28.88		Asbel	Kiprop	KEN	30.6.89	1	Herc	Monaco	20 Jul 12
3:28.91			El Guerrouj			1rA	WK	Zürich	13 Aug 97
		(30/6))							
3:28.95		Fermín	Cacho	ESP	16.2.69	2rA	WK	Zürich	13 Aug 97
3:28.98		Mehdi	Baala	FRA	17.8.78	2	VD	Bruxelles	5 Sep 03
3:29.02		Daniel Kipchirchir	Komen	KEN	27.11.84	1	GGala	Roma	14 Jul 06
3:29.14		Rashid	Ramzi ¶	MAR/BRN	17.7.80	2	GGala	Roma	14 Jul 06
		(10)							
3:29.18		Vénuste	Niyongabo	BDI	9.12.73	2	VD	Bruxelles	22 Aug 97
3:29.27		Silas	Kiplagat	KEN	20.8.89	1	Herc	Monaco	22 Jul 10
3:29.29		William	Chirchir	KEN	6.2.79	3	VD	Bruxelles	24 Aug 01
3:29.46	WR	Saïd	Aouita	MAR	2.11.59	1	ISTAF	Berlin	23 Aug 85
3:29.46		Daniel	Komen	KEN	17.5.76	1	Herc	Monaco	16 Aug 97
3:29.47		Augustine	Choge	KEN	21.1.87	1	ISTAF	Berlin	14 Jun 09
3:29.50		Caleb	Ndiku	KEN	9.10.92	3	Herc	Monaco	19 Jul 13
3:29.51		Ali	Saïdi-Sief ¶	ALG	15.3.78	1	Athl	Lausanne	4 Jul 01
3:29.53		Amine	Laâlou	MAR	13.5.82	2	Herc	Monaco	22 Jul 10
3:29.67	WR	Steve	Cram	GBR	14.10.60	1	Nik	Nice	16 Jul 85
3:29.77		Sydney	Maree	USA	9.9.56	1	ASV	Köln	25 Aug 85
		(20)							
3:29.77		Sebastian	Coe	GBR	29.9.56	1		Rieti	7 Sep 86
3:29.77		Nixon	Chepseba	KEN	12.12.90	2	Herc	Monaco	20 Jul 12
3:29.91		Laban	Rotich	KEN	20.1.69	2rA	WK	Zürich	12 Aug 98
3:30.04		Timothy	Kiptanui	KEN	5.1.80	2	GP	Saint-Denis	23 Jul 04
3:30.07		Rui	Silva	POR	3.8.77	3	Herc	Monaco	19 Jul 02
3:30.18		John	Kibowen	KEN	21.4.69	3rA	WK	Zürich	12 Aug 98
3:30.20		Haron	Keitany	KEN	17.12.83	2	ISTAF	Berlin	14 Jun 09
3:30.24		Cornelius	Chirchir	KEN	5.6.83	4	Herc	Monaco	19 Jul 02
3:30.31		Ayanleh	Souleiman	DJI	3.12.92	2	FBK	Hengelo	27 May 12
3:30.33		Ivan	Heshko	UKR	19.8.79	2	VD	Bruxelles	3 Sep 04
		(30)							
3:30.35		Nick	Willis	NZL	25.4.83	3	Herc	Monaco	20 Jul 12
3:30.46		Alex	Kipchirchir	KEN	26.11.84	3	VD	Bruxelles	3 Sep 04
3:30.54		Alan	Webb	USA	13.1.83	1	Gaz	Saint-Denis	6 Jul 07
3:30.55		Abdi	Bile	SOM	28.12.62	1		Rieti	3 Sep 89
3:30.57		Reyes	Estévez	ESP	2.8.76	3	WCh	Sevilla	24 Aug 99
3:30.58		William	Tanui	KEN	22.2.64	3	Herc	Monaco	16 Aug 97
3:30.67		Benjamin	Kipkurui	KEN	28.12.80	2	Herc	Monaco	20 Jul 01
3:30.72		Paul	Korir	KEN	15.7.77	3	VD	Bruxelles	5 Sep 03
3:30.77	WR	Steve	Ovett	GBR	9.10.55	1		Rieti	4 Sep 83
3:30.77		Bethwel	Birgen	KEN	6.8.88	4	Herc	Monaco	19 Jul 13
		(40)							
3:30.80		Taoufik	Makhloufi	ALG	29.4.88	5	Herc	Monaco	20 Jul 12
3:30.83		Fouad	Chouki ¶	FRA	15.10.78	3	WK	Zürich	15 Aug 03
3:30.90		Andrew	Wheating	USA	21.11.87	4	Herc	Monaco	22 Jul 10
3:30.92		José Luis	González	ESP	8.12.57	3	Nik	Nice	16 Jul 85
3:30.92		Tarek	Boukensa	ALG	19.11.81	1	GGala	Roma	13 Jul 07
3:30.94		Isaac	Viciosa	ESP	26.12.69	5	Herc	Monaco	8 Aug 98
3:30.99		Robert	Rono	KEN	11.10.74	3	VD	Bruxelles	30 Aug 02
3:30.99		Isaac	Songok	KEN	25.4.84	3rA	WK	Zürich	6 Aug 04
3:31.01		Jim	Spivey	USA	7.3.60	1	R-W	Koblenz	28 Aug 88
3:31.04		Daham Najim	Bashir	KEN/QAT	8.11.78	2	SGP	Doha	13 May 05
		(50)							

100th man 3:32.13, 200th 3:33.96, 300th 3:35.02, 400th 3:35.80, 500th 3:36.50

Drugs disqualification: 3:30.77 Adil Kaouch ¶   MAR   1.1.79   1   GGala   Roma   13 Jul 07

1 MILE

Mark	Wind	Name		Nat	Born	Pos	Meet	Venue	Date
3:43.13	WR	Hicham	El Guerrouj	MAR	14.9.74	1	GGala	Roma	7 Jul 99
3:43.40		Noah	Ngeny	KEN	2.11.78	2	GGala	Roma	7 Jul 99
3:44.39	WR	Noureddine	Morceli	ALG	28.2.70	1		Rieti	5 Sep 93
3:44.60			El Guerrouj			1	Nik	Nice	16 Jul 98
3:44.90			El Guerrouj			1	Bisl	Oslo	4 Jul 97
3:44.95			El Guerrouj			1	GGala	Roma	29 Jun 01
3:45.19			Morceli			1	WK	Zürich	16 Aug 95
3:45.64			El Guerrouj			1	ISTAF	Berlin	26 Aug 97
3:45.96			El Guerrouj			1	BrGP	London (CP)	5 Aug 00
3:46.24			El Guerrouj			1	Bisl	Oslo	28 Jul 00
3:46.32	WR	Steve	Cram	GBR	14.10.60	1	Bisl	Oslo	27 Jul 85
3:46.38		Daniel	Komen	KEN	17.5.76	2	ISTAF	Berlin	26 Aug 97
3:46.70		Vénuste	Niyongabo	BDI	9.12.73	3	ISTAF	Berlin	26 Aug 97

Mark	Wind	Name		Nat	Born	Pos	Meet	Venue	Date
3:46.76		Saïd	Aouita	MAR	2.11.59	1	WG	Helsinki	2 Jul 87
3:46.78			Morceli			1	ISTAF	Berlin	27 Aug 93
3:46.91		Alan	Webb	USA	13.1.83	1		Brasschaat	21 Jul 07
3:46.92			Aouita			1	WK	Zürich	21 Aug 85
3:47.10			El Guerrouj			1	BrGP	London (CP)	7 Aug 99
3:47.28		Bernard	Lagat	KEN/USA	12.12.74	2	GGala	Roma	29 Jun 01
3:47.30			Morceli			1	VD	Bruxelles	3 Sep 93
3:47.33	WR	Sebastian	Coe	GBR	29.9.56	1	VD	Bruxelles	28 Aug 81
		(21/10)							
3:47.65		Laban	Rotich	KEN	20.1.69	2	Bisl	Oslo	4 Jul 97
3:47.69		Steve	Scott	USA	5.5.56	1	OsloG	Oslo	7 Jul 82
3:47.79		José Luis	González	ESP	8.12.57	2	Bisl	Oslo	27 Jul 85
3:47.88		John	Kibowen	KEN	21.4.69	3	Bisl	Oslo	4 Jul 97
3:47.94		William	Chirchir	KEN	6.2.79	2	Bisl	Oslo	28 Jul 00
3:47.97		Daham Najim	Bashir	KEN/QAT	8.11.78	1	Bisl	Oslo	29 Jul 05
3:48.17		Paul	Korir	KEN	15.7.77	1	GP	London (CP)	8 Aug 03
3:48.23		Ali	Saïdi-Sief ¶	ALG	15.3.78	1	Bisl	Oslo	13 Jul 01
3:48.28		Daniel Kipchirchir	Komen	KEN	27.11.84	1	Pre	Eugene	10 Jun 07
3:48.38		Andrés Manuel	Díaz	ESP	12.7.69	3	GGala	Roma	29 Jun 01
		(20)							
3:48.40	WR	Steve	Ovett	GBR	9.10.55	1	R-W	Koblenz	26 Aug 81
3:48.50		Asbel	Kiprop	KEN	30.6.89	1	Pre	Eugene	7 Jun 09
3:48.78		Haron	Keitany	KEN	17.12.83	2	Pre	Eugene	7 Jun 09
3:48.80		William	Kemei	KEN	22.2.69	1	ISTAF	Berlin	21 Aug 92
3:48.83		Sydney	Maree	USA	9.9.56	1		Rieti	9 Sep 81
3:48.95		Deresse	Mekonnen	ETH	20.10.87	1	Bisl	Oslo	3 Jul 09
3:48.98		Craig	Mottram	AUS	18.6.80	5	Bisl	Oslo	29 Jul 05
3:49.08		John	Walker	NZL	12.1.52	2	OsloG	Oslo	7 Jul 82
3:49.20		Peter	Elliott	GBR	9.10.62	2	Bisl	Oslo	2 Jul 88
3:49.22		Jens-Peter	Herold	GDR	2.6.65	3	Bisl	Oslo	2 Jul 88
		(30)							
3:49.29		William	Biwott/Özbilen	KEN/TUR	5.3.90	2	Bisl	Oslo	3 Jul 09
3:49.31		Joe	Falcon	USA	23.6.66	1	Bisl	Oslo	14 Jul 90
3:49.34		David	Moorcroft	GBR	10.4.53	3	Bisl	Oslo	26 Jun 82
3:49.34		Benjamin	Kipkurui	KEN	28.12.80	3	VD	Bruxelles	25 Aug 00
3:49.38		Andrew	Baddeley	GBR	20.6.82	1	Bisl	Oslo	6 Jun 08
3:49.39		Silas	Kiplagat	KEN	20.8.89	2	Pre	Eugene	4 Jun 11
3:49.40		Abdi	Bile	SOM	28.12.62	4	Bisl	Oslo	2 Jul 88
3:49.45		Mike	Boit	KEN	6.1.49	2	VD	Bruxelles	28 Aug 81
3:49.50		Rui	Silva	POR	3.8.77	3	GGala	Roma	12 Jul 02
3:49.56		Fermín	Cacho	ESP	16.2.69	2	Bisl	Oslo	5 Jul 96
		(40)							
3:49.60		José Antonio	Redolat	ESP	17.2.76	4	GGala	Roma	29 Jun 01
3:49.70		Mekonnen	Gebremedhin	ETH	11.10.88	4	Pre	Eugene	4 Jun 11
3:49.75		Leonard	Mucheru	KEN/BRN	13.6.78	5	GGala	Roma	29 Jun 01
3:49.77		Ray	Flynn	IRL	22.1.57	3	OsloG	Oslo	7 Jul 82
3:49.77		Wilfred	Kirochi	KEN	12.12.69	2	Bisl	Oslo	6 Jul 91
3:49.77		Caleb	Ndiku	KEN	9.10.92	5	Pre	Eugene	4 Jun 11
3:49.80		Jim	Spivey	USA	7.3.60	3	Bisl	Oslo	5 Jul 86
3:49.83		Vyacheslav	Shabunin	RUS	27.9.69	6	GGala	Roma	29 Jun 01
3:49.88		Aman	Wote	ETH	18.4.84	3	Pre	Eugene	1 Jun 13
3:49.91		Simon	Doyle	AUS	9.11.66	4	Bisl	Oslo	6 Jul 91
		(50)							
			100th 3:51.25, 200th 3:53.39, 300th 3:54.96						
Indoors: 3:49.78		Eamonn	Coghlan	IRL	24.11.52	1		East Rutherford	27 Feb 83

2000 METRES

Mark	Wind	Name		Nat	Born	Pos	Meet	Venue	Date
4:44.79	WR	Hicham	El Guerrouj	MAR	14.9.74	1	ISTAF	Berlin	7 Sep 99
4:46.88		Ali	Saïdi-Sief ¶	ALG	15.3.78	1		Strasbourg	19 Jun 01
4:47.88	WR	Noureddine	Morceli	ALG	28.2.70	1		Paris (JB)	3 Jul 95
4:48.36			El Guerrouj			1		Gateshead	19 Jul 98
4:48.69		Vénuste	Niyongabo	BDI	9.12.73	1	Nik	Nice	12 Jul 95
4:48.74		John	Kibowen	KEN	21.4.69	1		Hechtel	1 Aug 98
4:49.00			Niyongabo			1		Rieti	3 Sep 97
4:49.55			Morceli			1	Nik	Nice	10 Jul 95
4:50.08		Noah	Ngeny	KEN	2.11.78	1	DNG	Stockholm	30 Jul 99
4:50.76		Craig	Mottram	AUS	18.6.80	1		Melbourne (OP)	9 Mar 06
4:50.81	WR	Saïd	Aouita	MAR	2.11.59	1	BNP	Paris (JB)	16 Jul 87
4:51.30		Daniel	Komen	KEN	17.5.76	1		Milano	5 Jun 98
4:51.39	WR	Steve	Cram (10)	GBR	14.10.60	1	BGP	Budapest	4 Aug 85
Indoors									
4:49.99		Kenenisa	Bekele	ETH	13.6.82	1		Birmingham	17 Feb 07

3000 METRES

Mark	Wind	Name		Nat	Born	Pos	Meet	Venue	Date
7:20.67	wr	Daniel	Komen	KEN	17.5.76	1		Rieti	1 Sep 96
7:23.09		Hicham	El Guerrouj	MAR	14.9.74	1	VD	Bruxelles	3 Sep 99
7:25.02		Ali	Saïdi-Sief ¶	ALG	15.3.78	1	Herc	Monaco	18 Aug 00
7:25.09		Haile	Gebrselassie	ETH	18.4.73	1	VD	Bruxelles	28 Aug 98
7:25.11	wr	Noureddine	Morceli	ALG	28.2.70	1	Herc	Monaco	2 Aug 94
7:25.16			Komen			1	Herc	Monaco	10 Aug 96
7:25.54			Gebrselassie			1	Herc	Monaco	8 Aug 98
7:25.79		Kenenisa	Bekele	ETH	13.6.82	1	DNG	Stockholm	7 Aug 07
7:25.87			Komen			1	VD	Bruxelles	23 Aug 96
7:26.02			Gebrselassie			1	VD	Bruxelles	22 Aug 97
7:26.03			Gebrselassie			1	GP II	Helsinki	10 Jun 99
7:26.5	e		Komen			1	in 2M	Sydney	28 Feb 98
7:26.62		Mohammed	Mourhit ¶	BEL	10.10.70	2	Herc	Monaco	18 Aug 00
7:26.69			K Bekele			1	BrGP	Sheffield	15 Jul 07
7:27.18		Moses	Kiptanui	KEN	1.10.70	1	Herc	Monaco	25 Jul 95
7:27.26		Yenew	Alamirew	ETH	27.5.90	1	DL	Doha	6 May 11
7:27.3+			Komen			1	in 2M	Hechtel	19 Jul 97
7:27.42			Gebrselassie			1	Bisl	Oslo	9 Jul 98
7:27.50			Morceli			1	VD	Bruxelles	25 Aug 95
7:27.55		Edwin	Soi (10)	KEN	3.3.86	2	DL	Doha	6 May 11
7:27.59		Luke	Kipkosgei	KEN	27.11.75	2	Herc	Monaco	8 Aug 98
7:27.66		Eliud	Kipchoge	KEN	5.11.84	3	DL	Doha	6 May 11
7:27.67			Saïdi-Sief			1	Gaz	Saint-Denis	23 Jun 00
7:27.72			Kipchoge			1	VD	Bruxelles	3 Sep 04
7:27.75		Thomas	Nyariki	KEN	27.9.71	2	Herc	Monaco	10 Aug 96
7.28.04			Kiptanui			1	ASV	Köln	18 Aug 95
7.28.28			Kipkosgei			2	Bisl	Oslo	9 Jul 98
7.28.28		James	Kwalia	KEN/QAT	12.6.84	2	VD	Bruxelles	3 Sep 04
7:28.37			Kipchoge			1	SGP	Doha	8 May 09
7:28.41		Paul (30/15)	Bitok	KEN	26.6.70	3	Herc	Monaco	10 Aug 96
7:28.45		Assefa	Mezegebu	ETH	19.6.78	3	Herc	Monaco	8 Aug 98
7:28.67		Benjamin	Limo	KEN	23.8.74	1	Herc	Monaco	4 Aug 99
7:28.70		Paul	Tergat	KEN	17.6.69	4	Herc	Monaco	10 Aug 96
7:28.70		Tariku	Bekele	ETH	21.1.87	1		Rieti	29 Aug 10
7:28.72		Isaac K. (20)	Songok	KEN	25.4.84	1	GP	Rieti	27 Aug 06
7:28.76		Augustine	Choge	KEN	21.1.87	4	DL	Doha	6 May 11
7:28.93		Salah	Hissou	MAR	16.1.72	2	Herc	Monaco	4 Aug 99
7:28.94		Brahim	Lahlafi	FRA/MAR	15.4.68	3	Herc	Monaco	4 Aug 99
7:29.00		Bernard	Lagat	USA	12.12.74	2		Rieti	29 Aug 10
7:29.09		John	Kibowen	KEN	21.4.69	3	Bisl	Oslo	9 Jul 98
7:29.34		Isaac	Viciosa	ESP	26.12.69	4	Bisl	Oslo	9 Jul 98
7:29.45	wr	Saïd	Aouita	MAR	2.11.59	1	ASV	Köln	20 Aug 89
7:29.92		Sileshi	Sihine	ETH	29.1.83	1	GP	Rieti	28 Aug 05
7:30.09		Ismaïl	Sghyr	MAR/FRA	16.3.72	2	Herc	Monaco	25 Jul 95
7:30.09		Thomas (30)	Longosiwa	KEN	14.1.82	2	SGP	Doha	8 May 09
7:30.15		Vincent	Chepkok	KEN	5.7.88	5	DL	Doha	6 May 11
7:30.36		Mark	Carroll	IRL	15.1.72	5	Herc	Monaco	4 Aug 99
7:30.36		Hagos	Gebrhiwet	ETH	11.5.94	1	DL	Doha	10 May 13
7:30.43		Isiah	Koech	KEN	19.12.93	1	DNG	Stockholm	17 Aug 12
7:30.50		Dieter	Baumann ¶	GER	9.2.65	6	Herc	Monaco	8 Aug 98
7:30.53		El Hassan	Lahssini	MAR/FRA	1.1.75	6	Herc	Monaco	10 Aug 96
7:30.53		Hailu	Mekonnen	ETH	4.4.80	1	VD	Bruxelles	24 Aug 01
7:30.62		Boniface	Songok	KEN	25.12.80	3	VD	Bruxelles	3 Sep 04
7:30.76		Jamal Bilal	Salem	KEN/QAT	12.9.78	4	SGP	Doha	13 May 05
7:30.78		Mustapha (40)	Essaïd	FRA	20.1.70	7	Herc	Monaco	8 Aug 98
7:30.84		Bob	Kennedy	USA	18.8.70	8	Herc	Monaco	8 Aug 98
7:30.95		Moses	Kipsiro	UGA	2.9.86	1	Herc	Monaco	28 Jul 09
7:30.99		Khalid	Boulami	MAR	7.8.69	1	Nik	Nice	16 Jul 97
7:30.99		Caleb	Ndiku	KEN	9.10.92	2	DNG	Stockholm	17 Aug 12
7:31.13		Julius	Gitahi	KEN	29.4.78	6	Bisl	Oslo	9 Jul 98
7:31.14		William	Kalya	KEN	4.8.74	3	Herc	Monaco	16 Aug 97
7:31.20		Joseph	Kiplimo	KEN	20.7.88	1	GP	Rieti	6 Sep 09
7:31.41		Sammy Alex	Mutahi	KEN	1.6.89	2	GP	Rieti	6 Sep 09
7:31.41		Daniel Kipchirchir	Komen	KEN	27.11.84	6	DL	Doha	6 May 11

Mark	Wind	Name		Nat	Born	Pos	Meet	Venue	Date
7:31.59		Manuel	Pancorbo	ESP	7.7.66	7	Bisl	Oslo	9 Jul 98
		(50)							

100th man 7:35.16, 200th man 7:39.52, 300th 7:42.1, 400th 7:43.90, 500th 7:45.67

Indoors

Mark	Wind	Name		Nat	Born	Pos	Meet	Venue	Date
7:24.90			Komen			1		Budapest	6 Feb 98
7:26.15			Gebrselassie			1		Karlsruhe	25 Jan 98
7:26.80			Gebrselassie			1		Karlsruhe	24 Jan 99
7:27.80			Alamirew			1	Spark	Stuttgart	5 Feb 11
7:27.93			Komen			1	Spark	Stuttgart	1 Feb 98
7:28.00		Augustine	Choge	KEN	21.1.87	2	Spark	Stuttgart	5 Feb 11
7:30.16		Galen	Rupp	USA	8.5.86	1		Stockholm	21 Feb 13

2 MILES

Mark	Wind	Name		Nat	Born	Pos	Meet	Venue	Date
7:58.61 WR		Daniel	Komen	KEN	17.5.76	1		Hechtel	19 Jul 97
7:58.91			Komen			1		Sydney	28 Feb 98
8:01.08 WR		Haile	Gebrselassie	ETH	18.4.73	1	APM	Hengelo	31 May 97
8:01.72			Gebrselassie			1	BrGP	London (CP)	7 Aug 99
8:01.86			Gebrselassie			1	APM	Hengelo	30 May 99
8:03.50		Craig	Mottram	AUS	18.6.80	1	Pre	Eugene	10 Jun 07
8:04.83		Tariku	Bekele	ETH	21.1.87	2	Pre	Eugene	10 Jun 07

Indoors

Mark	Wind	Name		Nat	Born	Pos	Meet	Venue	Date
8:04.35		Kenenisa	Bekele	ETH	13.6.82	1	GP	Birmingham	16 Feb 08
8:06.48		Paul Kipsiele	Koech	KEN	10.11.81	2	GP	Birmingham	16 Feb 08

5000 METRES

Mark	Wind	Name		Nat	Born	Pos	Meet	Venue	Date
12:37.35 WR		Kenenisa	Bekele	ETH	13.6.82	1	FBK	Hengelo	31 May 04
12:39.36 WR		Haile	Gebrselassie	ETH	18.4.73	1	GP II	Helsinki	13 Jun 98
12:39.74 WR		Daniel	Komen	KEN	17.5.76	1	VD	Bruxelles	22 Aug 97
12:40.18			K Bekele			1	Gaz	Saint-Denis	1 Jul 05
12:41.86 WR			Gebrselassie			1	WK	Zürich	13 Aug 97
12:44.39 WR			Gebrselassie			1	WK	Zürich	16 Aug 95
12:44.90			Komen			2	WK	Zürich	13 Aug 97
12:45.09			Komen			1	WK	Zürich	14 Aug 96
12:46.53		Eliud	Kipchoge	KEN	5.11.84	1	GGala	Roma	2 Jul 04
12:46.81		Dejen	Gebremeskel	ETH	24.11.89	1	DL	Saint-Denis	6 Jul 12
12:47.04		Sileshi	Sihine	ETH	29.9.83	2	GGala	Roma	2 Jul 04
12:47.53		Hagos	Gebrhiwet	ETH	11.5.94	2	DL	Saint-Denis	6 Jul 12
12:48.09			K Bekele			1	VD	Bruxelles	25 Aug 06
12:48.25			K Bekele			1	WK	Zürich	18 Aug 06
12:48.64		Isiah	Koech	KEN	19.12.93	3	DL	Saint-Denis	6 Jul 12
12:48.66		Isaac K.	Songok	KEN	25.4.84	2	WK	Zürich	18 Aug 06
12:48.77		Yenew	Alamirew (10)	ETH	27.5.90	4	DL	Saint-Denis	6 Jul 12
12:48.81		Stephen	Cherono/Shaheen	KEN/QAT	15.10.82	1	GS	Ostrava	12 Jun 03
12:48.98			Komen			1	GGala	Roma	5 Jun 97
12:49.04		Thomas	Longosiwa	KEN	14.1.82	5	DL	Saint-Denis	6 Jul 12
12:49.28		Brahim	Lahlafi	MAR	15.4.68	1	VD	Bruxelles	25 Aug 00
12:49.50		John	Kipkoech	KEN	29.12.91	6	DL	Saint-Denis	6 Jul 12
12:49.53			K Bekele			1	Aragón	Zaragoza	28 Jul 07
12:49.64			Gebrselassie			1	WK	Zürich	11 Aug 99
12:49.71		Mohammed	Mourhit ¶	BEL	10.10.70	2	VD	Bruxelles	25 Aug 00
12:49.87		Paul	Tergat	KEN	17.6.69	3	WK	Zürich	13 Aug 97
12:50.16			Sihine			1	VD	Bruxelles	14 Sep 07
12:50.18			K Bekele			1	WK	Zürich	29 Aug 08
12:50.22			Kipchoge			1	VD	Bruxelles	26 Aug 05
12:50.24		Hicham	El Guerrouj	MAR	14.9.74	2	GS	Ostrava	12 Jun 03
		(30/17)							
12:50.25		Abderrahim	Goumri ¶	MAR	21.5.76	2	VD	Bruxelles	26 Aug 05
12:50.55		Moses	Masai	KEN	1.6.86	1	ISTAF	Berlin	1 Jun 08
12:50.72		Moses	Kipsiro	UGA	2.9.86	3	VD	Bruxelles	14 Sep 07
		(20)							
12:50.80		Salah	Hissou	MAR	16.1.72	1	GGala	Roma	5 Jun 96
12:50.86		Ali	Saïdi-Sief ¶	ALG	15.3.78	1	GGala	Roma	30 Jun 00
12:51.00		Joseph	Ebuya	KEN	20.6.87	4	VD	Bruxelles	14 Sep 07
12:51.34		Edwin	Soi	KEN	3.3.86	3	Herc	Monaco	19 Jul 13
12:51.45		Vincent	Chepkok	KEN	5.7.88	2	DL	Doha	14 May 10
12:51.96		Albert	Rop	KEN/BRN	17.7.92	2	Herc	Monaco	19 Jul 13
12:52.33		Sammy	Kipketer	KEN	29.9.81	2	Bisl	Oslo	27 Jun 03
12:52.45		Tariku	Bekele	ETH	21.1.87	2	ISTAF	Berlin	1 Jun 08
12:52.80		Gebre-egziabher	Gebremariam	ETH	10.9.84	3	GGala	Roma	8 Jul 05
12:52.99		Abraham	Chebii	KEN	23.12.79	4	Bisl	Oslo	27 Jun 03
		(30)							

Mark Wind	Name		Nat	Born	Pos	Meet	Venue	Date
12:53.11	Mohamed	Farah	GBR	23.3.83	1	Herc	Monaco	22 Jul 11
12:53.41	Khalid	Boulami	MAR	7.8.69	4	WK	Zürich	13 Aug 97
12:53.46	Mark	Kiptoo	KEN	21.6.76	1	DNG	Stockholm	6 Aug 10
12:53.58	Imane	Merga	ETH	15.10.88	3	DNG	Stockholm	6 Aug 10
12:53.60	Bernard	Lagat	USA	12.12.74	2	Herc	Monaco	22 Jul 11
12:53.66	Augustine	Choge	KEN	21.1.87	4	GGala	Roma	8 Jul 05
12:53.72	Philip	Mosima	KEN	2.1.77	2	GGala	Roma	5 Jun 96
12:53.84	Assefa	Mezegebu	ETH	19.6.78	1	VD	Bruxelles	28 Aug 98
12:54.07	John	Kibowen	KEN	21.4.69	4	WCh	Saint-Denis	31 Aug 03
12:54.15	Dejene	Berhanu	ETH	12.12.80	3	GGala	Roma	2 Jul 04
	(40)							
12:54.19	Abreham	Cherkos	ETH	23.9.89	5	GGala	Roma	14 Jul 06
12:54.46	Moses	Mosop	KEN	17.7.85	3	Gaz	Saint-Denis	8 Jul 06
12:54.58	James	Kwalia	KEN/QAT	12.6.84	5	Bisl	Oslo	27 Jun 03
12:54.70	Dieter	Baumann ¶	GER	9.2.65	5	WK	Zürich	13 Aug 97
12:54.85	Moses	Kiptanui	KEN	1.10.70	3	GGala	Roma	5 Jun 96
12:54.99	Benjamin	Limo	KEN	23.8.74	3	Gaz	Saint-Denis	4 Jul 03
12:55.06	Lucas	Rotich	KEN	16.4.90	4	Bisl	Oslo	4 Jun 10
12:55.52	Hicham	Bellani	MAR	15.9.79	7	GGala	Roma	14 Jul 06
12:55.53	Chris	Solinsky	USA	5.12.84	5	DNG	Stockholm	6 Aug 10
12:55.58	Abebe	Dinkesa	ETH	6.3.84	2	Gaz	Saint-Denis	1 Jul 05
	(50)	100th man 13:01.82, 200th 13:09.62, 300th 13:13.20, 400th 13:17.21, 500th 13:19.73						
Indoors: 12:49.60		K Bekele			1		Birmingham	20 Feb 04

10,000 METRES

Mark Wind	Name		Nat	Born	Pos	Meet	Venue	Date
26:17.53wr	Kenenisa	Bekele	ETH	13.6.82	1	VD	Bruxelles	26 Aug 05
26:20.31wr		K Bekele			1	GS	Ostrava	8 Jun 04
26:22.75wr	Haile	Gebrselassie	ETH	18.4.73	1	APM	Hengelo	1 Jun 98
26:25.97		K Bekele			1	Pre	Eugene	8 Jun 08
26:27.85wr	Paul	Tergat	KEN	17.6.69	1	VD	Bruxelles	22 Aug 97
26:28.72		K Bekele			1	FBK	Hengelo	29 May 05
26:29.22		Gebrselassie			1	VD	Bruxelles	5 Sep 03
26:30.03	Nicholas	Kemboi	KEN/QAT	25.11.83	2	VD	Bruxelles	5 Sep 03
26:30.74	Abebe	Dinkesa	ETH	6.3.84	2	FBK	Hengelo	29 May 05
26:31.32wr		Gebrselassie			1	Bisl	Oslo	4 Jul 97
26:35.63	Micah	Kogo	KEN	3.6.86	1	VD	Bruxelles	25 Aug 06
26:36.26	Paul	Koech	KEN	25.6.69	2	VD	Bruxelles	22 Aug 97
26:37.25	Zersenay	Tadese	ERI	8.2.82	2	VD	Bruxelles	25 Aug 06
26:38.08wr	Salah	Hissou	MAR	16.1.72	1	VD	Bruxelles	23 Aug 96
26:38.76	Abdullah Ahmad	Hassan (10)	QAT	4.4.81	3	VD	Bruxelles	5 Sep 03
	(Formerly Albert Chepkurui KEN)							
26:39.69	Sileshi	Sihine	ETH	29.9.83	1	FBK	Hengelo	31 May 04
26:39.77	Boniface	Kiprop	UGA	12.10.85	2	VD	Bruxelles	26 Aug 05
26:41.58		Gebrselassie			2	FBK	Hengelo	31 May 04
26:41.75	Samuel	Wanjiru	KEN	10.11.86	3	VD	Bruxelles	26 Aug 05
26:41.95		Kiprop			3	VD	Bruxelles	25 Aug 06
26:43.16		K Bekele			1	VD	Bruxelles	16 Sep 11
26:43.53wr		Gebrselassie			1	APM	Hengelo	5 Jun 95
26:43.98	Lucas	Rotich	KEN	16.4.90	2	VD	Bruxelles	16 Sep 11
26:46.19		K Bekele			1	VD	Bruxelles	14 Sep 07
26:46.31		K Bekele			1	WCh	Berlin	17 Aug 09
26:46.44		Tergat			1	VD	Bruxelles	28 Aug 98
26:46.57	Mohamed	Farah	GBR	23.3.83	1	Pre	Eugene	3 Jun 11
26:47.89		Koech			2	VD	Bruxelles	28 Aug 98
26:48.00	Galen	Rupp	USA	8.5.86	3	VD	Bruxelles	16 Sep 11
26:48.35	Imane	Merga	ETH	15.10.88	2	Pre	Eugene	3 Jun 11
	(30/17)							
26:48.99	Josphat	Bett	KEN	12.6.90	3	Pre	Eugene	3 Jun 11
26:49.02	Eliud	Kipchoge	KEN	5.11.84	2	FBK	Hengelo	26 May 07
26:49.20	Moses	Masai	KEN	1.6.86	2	VD	Bruxelles	14 Sep 07
	(20)							
26:49.38	Sammy	Kipketer	KEN	29.9.81	1	VD	Bruxelles	30 Aug 02
26:49.55	Moses	Mosop	KEN	17.7.85	3	FBK	Hengelo	26 May 07
26:49.90	Assefa	Mezegebu	ETH	19.6.78	2	VD	Bruxelles	30 Aug 02
26:50.20	Richard	Limo	KEN	18.11.80	3	VD	Bruxelles	30 Aug 02
26:50.63	Paul	Tanui	KEN	22.12.90	4	Pre	Eugene	3 Jun 11
26:51.02	Dejen	Gebremeskel	ETH	24.11.89	1		Sollentuna	27 Jun 13
26:51.16	Emmanuel	Bett	KEN	30.3.83	1	VD	Bruxelles	7 Sep 12
26:51.49	Charles	Kamathi	KEN	18.5.78	1	VD	Bruxelles	3 Sep 99
26:51.68	Vincent	Chepkok	KEN	5.7.88	2	VD	Bruxelles	7 Sep 12

Mark	Wind	Name		Nat	Born	Pos	Meet	Venue	Date
26:52.23	WR	William	Sigei	KEN	14.10.69	1	Bisl	Oslo	22 Jul 94
		(30)							
26:52.30		Mohammed	Mourhit ¶	BEL	10.10.70	2	VD	Bruxelles	3 Sep 99
26:52.33		Gebre-egziabher	Gebremariam	ETH	10.9.84	4	FBK	Hengelo	26 May 07
26:52.65		Kenneth	Kipkemoi	KEN	2.8.84	3	VD	Bruxelles	7 Sep 12
26:52.85		Abera	Kuma	ETH	31.8.90	2		Sollentuna	27 Jun 13
26:52.87		John Cheruiyot	Korir	KEN	13.12.81	5	VD	Bruxelles	30 Aug 02
26:52.93		Mark	Bett	KEN	22.12.76	6	VD	Bruxelles	26 Aug 05
26:54.25		Mathew	Kisorio ¶	KEN	16.5.89	7	Pre	Eugene	3 Jun 11
26:54.64		Mark	Kiptoo	KEN	21.6.76	8	Pre	Eugene	3 Jun 11
26:55.29		Leonard Patrick	Komon	KEN	10.1.88	9	Pre	Eugene	3 Jun 11
26:55.73		Geoffrey	Kirui	KEN	16.2.93	6	VD	Bruxelles	16 Sep 11
		(40)							
26:56.74		Josphat	Menjo	KEN	20.8.79	1		Turku	29 Aug 10
26:57.36		Josphat	Muchiri Ndambiri	KEN	12.2.85	1		Fukuroi	3 May 09
26:57.56		Yigrem	Dimelash	ETH	28.1.94	4	VD	Bruxelles	7 Sep 12
26:58.38	WR	Yobes	Ondieki	KEN	21.2.61	1	Bisl	Oslo	10 Jul 93
26:59.51		Bernard	Kipyego	KEN	16.7.86	4	VD	Bruxelles	14 Sep 07
26:59.60		Chris	Solinsky	USA	5.12.84	1		Stanford	1 May 10
26:59.81		Titus	Mbishei	KEN	28.10.90	7	VD	Bruxelles	16 Sep 11
26:59.88		Martin Irungu	Mathathi	KEN	25.12.85	2		Fukuroi	3 May 09
27:01.83		Gideon	Ngatuny	KEN	10.10.86	2		Tendo	16 May 09
27:01.98		Wilson	Kiprop	KEN	14.4.87	1	OT	Eugene/USA	1 Jun 12
		(50)							

100th man 27:16.49, 200th 27:31.16, 300th 27:40.08, 400th 27:46.12, 500th 27:54.28

20,000 METRES & 1 HOUR

Mark		Name		Nat	Born	Pos	Meet	Venue	Date
56:25.98+	21 285m	Haile	Gebrselassie	ETH	18.4.73	1	GS	Ostrava	27 Jun 07
56:55.6+	21 101	Arturo	Barrios	MEX	12.12.63	1		La Flèche	30 Mar 91
57:24.19+	20 944	Jos	Hermens	NED	8.1.50	1		Papendal	1 May 76
57:18.4+	20 943	Dionísio	Castro	POR	22.11.63	1		La Flèche	31 Mar 90

HALF MARATHON

Included are the slightly downhill courses: Newcastle to South Shields 30.5m, Tokyo 33m, Lisboa (Spring to 2008) 69m

Mark	Wind	Name		Nat	Born	Pos	Meet	Venue	Date
58:23	WR	Zersenay	Tadese	ERI	8.2.82	1		Lisboa	21 Mar 10
58:30			Z Tadese			1		Lisboa	20 Mar 11
58:33	WR	Samuel	Wanjiru	KEN	10.11.86	1		Den Haag	17 Mar 07
58:46		Mathew	Kisorio ¶	KEN	16.5.89	1		Philadelphia	18 Sep 11
58:47		Atsedu	Tsegay	ETH	17.12.91	1		Praha	31 Mar 12
58:48		Sammy	Kitwara	KEN	26.11.86	2		Philadelphia	18 Sep 11
58:52		Patrick	Makau	KEN	2.3.85	1		Ra's Al Khaymah	20 Feb 09
58:53	WR		Wanjiru			1		Ra's Al Khaymah	9 Feb 07
58:54		Stephen	Kibet	KEN	9.11.86	1		Den Haag	11 Mar 12
58:54		Geoffrey	Kipsang	KEN	28.11.92	1		Ra's Al-Khaymah	15 Feb 13
58:55	WR	Haile	Gebrselassie	ETH	18.4.73	1		Tempe	15 Jan 06
58:56			Makau			1		Berlin	1 Apr 07
58:56	dh	Martin	Mathathi (10)	KEN	25.12.85	1	GNR	South Shields	18 Sep 11
58:56		Stanley	Biwott	KEN	21.4.86	2		Ra's Al-Khaymah	15 Feb 13
58:58			Kitwara			1		Rotterdam	13 Sep 09
58:58		Geoffrey	Mutai	KEN	7.10.81	3		Ra's Al-Khaymah	15 Feb 13
58:59			Z Tadese			1	WCh	Udine	14 Oct 07
58:59		Wilson	Kipsang	KEN	15.3.82	2		Ra's Al Khaymah	20 Feb 09
59:02			Makau			2	WCh	Udine	14 Oct 07
59:02		Jonathan	Maiyo	KEN	.88	2		Den Haag	11 Mar 12
59:05	dh		Tadese			1	GNR	South Shields	18 Sep 05
59:05		Evans	Cheruiyot	KEN	10.5.82	3	WCh	Udine	14 Oct 07
59:05		Ezekiel	Chebii	KEN	3.1.91	1		Lille	1 Sep 12
59:06	dh	Paul	Tergat	KEN	17.6.69	1		Lisboa	26 Mar 00
59:06	dh		Kipsang			1	GNR	South Shields	16 Sep 12
59:06			G Mutai			1		Udine	22 Sep 13
59:07		Paul	Kosgei	KEN	22.4.78	1		Berlin	2 Apr 06
59:07	dh	Micah	Kogo	KEN	3.6.86	2	GNR	South Shields	16 Sep 12
59:08			Maiyo			2		Rotterdam	13 Sep 09
59:09		James Kipsang	Kwambai	KEN	28.2.83	3		Rotterdam	13 Sep 09
		(30/20)							
59:10		Bernard	Kipyego	KEN	16.7.86	4		Rotterdam	13 Sep 09
59:10		Bernard	Koech	KEN	31.1.88	2		Lille	1 Sep 12
59:11		Kenneth	Kipkemoi	KEN	2.8.84	3		Den Haag	11 Mar 12
59:14		Dennis	Kimetto	KEN	22.4.84	1		Berlin	1 Apr 12
59:15		Deriba	Merga	ETH	26.10.80	1		New Delhi	9 Nov 08

Mark	Wind	Name		Nat	Born	Pos	Meet	Venue	Date
59:15		Wilson	Chebet	KEN	12.7.85	5		Rotterdam	13 Sep 09
59:15		Wilson	Kiprop	KEN	14.4.87	2		Berlin	1 Apr 12
59:19		Tilahun	Regassa	ETH	18.1.90	1		Abu Dhabi	7 Jan 10
59:19		Robert	Chemosin	KEN	1.2.89	2		Ostia	3 Mar 13
59:20	dh	Hendrick	Ramaala	RSA	2.2.72	2		Lisboa	26 Mar 00
		(30)							
59:20		Moses	Mosop	KEN	17.7.85	1	Stra	Milano	21 Mar 10
59:20		Simon	Cheprot	KEN	2.7.93	3		Ostia	3 Mar 13
59:21	dh	Robert Kipkoech	Cheruiyot	KEN	26.9.78	2		Lisboa	13 Mar 05
59:22		Feyisa	Lilesa	ETH	1.2.90	1		Houston	15 Jan 12
59:23		John	Kiprotich	KEN	.89	6		Rotterdam	13 Sep 09
59:25		Eliud	Kipchoge	KEN	5.11.84	3		Lille	1 Sep 12
59:25		Pius	Kirop	KEN	8.1.90	4		Berlin	1 Apr 12
59:26		Francis	Kibiwott	KEN	15.9.78	2		Berlin	1 Apr 07
59:27	dh	Wilson	Kiprotich Kebenei	KEN	20.7.80	3		Lisboa	13 Mar 05
59:27		Patrick	Ivuti	KEN	30.6.78	4		Rotterdam	9 Sep 07
		(40)							
59:28		Robert	Kipchumba	KEN	24.2.84	2		Rotterdam	10 Sep 06
59:30	dh	Martin	Lel	KEN	29.10.78	1		Lisboa	26 Mar 06
59:30		Yonas	Kifle	ERI	24.3.77	5	WCh	Udine	14 Oct 07
59:30		Geoffrey	Mutai	KEN	7.10.81	1		Valencia	22 Nov 09
59:30		Philemon	Limo	KEN	2.8.85	1		Praha	2 Apr 11
59:30		Lelisa	Desisa	ETH	14.1.90	1		New Delhi	27 Nov 11
59:31		Victor	Kipchirchir	KEN	5.12.87	5		Den Haag	11 Mar 12
59:32		Dieudonné	Disi	RWA	24.4.78	6	WCh	Udine	14 Oct 07
59:33		Marílson	dos Santos	BRA	6.8.77	7	WCh	Udine	14 Oct 07
59:35		Tsegaye	Kebede	ETH	15.1.87	2		Ra's Al Khaymah	8 Feb 08
59:36		Sammy	Kosgei	KEN	20.1.86	2		Berlin	5 Apr 09
59:36		Joel	Kimurer	KEN	21.1.88	2		Valencia	21 Oct 12
		(52)							

100th man 59:57, 200th man 60:33, 300th 60:53, 400th 61:96, 500th 61:17

Short course: 58:51 Paul Tergat KEN 17.6.69 1 Stra Milano 49m sh 30 Mar 96

Mark	Wind	Name		Nat	Born	Pos	Meet	Venue	Date
58:51		Paul	Tergat	KEN	17.6.69	1	Stra	Milano 49m sh	30 Mar 96

MARATHON

In second column: P = point-to-point or start/finish more than 30% apart, D = point-to-point and downhill over 1/1000

Mark	Wind	Name		Nat	Born	Pos	Meet	Venue	Date
2:03:23	WR	Wilson	Kipsang	KEN	15.3.82	1		Berlin	29 Sep 13
2:03:38	WR	Patrick	Makau	KEN	2.3.85	1		Berlin	25 Sep 11
2:03:42			W Kipsang			1		Frankfurt	30 Oct 11
2:03:45		Dennis	Kimetto	KEN	22.1.84	1		Chicago	13 Oct 13
2:03:52		Emmanuel	Mutai	KEN	12.10.84	2		Chicago	13 Oct 13
2:03:59	WR	Haile	Gebrselassie	ETH	18.4.73	1		Berlin	28 Sep 08
2:04:05		Eliud	Kipchoge	KEN	5.11.84	2		Berlin	29 Sep 13
2:04:15		Geoffrey	Mutai	KEN	7.10.81	1		Berlin	30 Sep 12
2:04:16			Kimetto			2		Berlin	30 Sep 12
2:04:23		Ayele	Abshero	ETH	28.12.90	1		Dubai	27 Jan 12
2:04:26	WR		Gebrselassie			1		Berlin	30 Sep 07
2:04:27		Duncan	Kibet	KEN	25.4.78	1		Rotterdam	5 Apr 09
2:04:27		James Kipsang	Kwambai (10)	KEN	28.2.83	2		Rotterdam	5 Apr 09
2:04:38		Tsegaye	Kebede	ETH	15.1.87	1		Chicago	7 Oct 12
2:04:40			E Mutai			1		London	17 Apr 11
2:04:44			W Kipsang			1		London	22 Apr 12
2:04:45		Lelisa	Desisa	ETH	14.1.90	1		Dubai	25 Jan 13
2:04:48			Makau			1		Rotterdam	11 Apr 10
2:04:48		Yemane	Tsegay	ETH	8.4.85	1		Rotterdam	15 Apr 12
2:04:48		Berhanu	Shiferaw	ETH	31.5.93	2		Dubai	25 Jan 13
2:04:49		Tadesse	Tola	ETH	31.10.87	3		Dubai	25 Jan 13
2:04:50		Dino	Sefir	ETH	28.5.88	2		Dubai	27 Jan 12
2:04:50		Getu	Feleke	ETH	28.11.86	2		Rotterdam	15 Apr 12
2:04:52		Feyisa	Lilesa	ETH	1.2.90	2		Chicago	7 Oct 12
2:04:52		Endeshaw	Shumi	ETH	.90	4		Dubai	25 Jan 13
2:04:53			Gebrselassie			1		Dubai	18 Jan 08
2:04:53		Bernard	Koech (20)	KEN	31.1.88	5		Dubai	25 Jan 13
2:04:54		Markos	Geneti	ETH	30.5.84	3		Dubai	27 Jan 12
2:04:55	WR	Paul	Tergat	KEN	17.6.69	1		Berlin	28 Sep 03
2:04:55			G Mutai			2		Rotterdam	11 Apr 10
		(30/22)							
2:04:56		Sammy	Korir	KEN	12.12.71	2		Berlin	28 Sep 03
2:04:56		Jonathan	Maiyo	KEN	.88	4		Dubai	27 Jan 12
2:05:03		Moses	Mosop	KEN	17.7.85	3		Rotterdam	15 Apr 12
2:05:04		Abel	Kirui	KEN	4.6.82	3		Rotterdam	5 Apr 09
2:05:10		Samuel	Wanjiru	KEN	10.11.86	1		London	26 Apr 09

MEN All-time

Mark	Wind	Name		Nat	Born	Pos	Meet	Venue	Date
2:05:12		Stanley	Biwott	KEN	21.4.86	1		Paris	15 Apr 12
2:05:13		Vincent	Kipruto	KEN	13.9.87	3		Rotterdam	11 Apr 10
2:05:15		Martin	Lel	KEN	29.10.78	1		London	13 Apr 08
		(30)							
2:05:16		Levi	Matebo Omari	KEN	3.11.89	2		Frankfurt	30 Oct 11
2:05:16		Sammy	Kitwara	KEN	26.11.86	3		Chicago	13 Oct 13
2:05:25		Bazu	Worku	ETH	15.9.90	3		Berlin	26 Sep 10
2:05:25		Albert	Matebor	KEN	20.12.80	3		Frankfurt	30 Oct 11
2:05:27		Jaouad	Gharib	MAR	22.5.72	3		London	26 Apr 09
2:05:27		Wilson	Chebet	KEN	12.7.85	1		Rotterdam	10 Apr 11
2:05:27		Tilahun	Regassa	ETH	18.1.90	3		Chicago	7 Oct 12
2:05:30		Abderrahim	Goumri ¶	MAR	21.5.76	3		London	13 Apr 08
2:05:37	P	Wilson	Loyanei ¶	KEN	86	1		Seoul	18 Mar 12
2:05:38	WR	Khalid	Khannouchi	MAR/USA	22.12.71	1		London	14 Apr 02
		(40)							
2:05:38		Peter	Some	KEN	5.6.90	1		Paris	7 Apr 13
2:05:39		Eliud	Kiptanui	KEN	6.6.89	1		Praha	9 May 10
2:05:41		Yami	Dadi	ETH	82	6		Dubai	27 Jan 12
2:05:42		Abdullah Dawit	Shami	ETH	16.7.84	7		Dubai	27 Jan 12
2:05:42		Deresse	Chimsa	ETH	21.11.76	8		Dubai	27 Jan 12
2:05:46		Dickson	Chumba	KEN	27.10.86	1		Eindhoven	14 Oct 12
2:05:48		Jafred	Kipchumba	KEN	8.8.83	1		Eindhoven	9 Oct 11
2:05:49		William	Kipsang	KEN	26.6.77	1		Rotterdam	13 Apr 08
2:05:50		Evans	Rutto	KEN	8.4.78	1		Chicago	12 Oct 03
2:06:05	WR	Ronaldo da	Costa	BRA	7.6.70	1		Berlin	20 Sep 98
2:06:05		Laban	Korir	KEN	30.12.85	2		Amsterdam	16 Oct 11
2:06:05		Mariko	Kipchumba	KEN	.75	1		Reims	21 Oct 12
		(52)		100th man 2:06:48, 200th 2:07:41, 300th 2:08:17, 400th 2:08:47, 500th 2:09:23					

Downhill point-to-point course – Boston marathon is downhill overall (139m) and sometimes strongly wind-aided.

Mark	Wind	Name		Nat	Born	Pos	Meet	Venue	Date
2:03:02		Geoffrey	Mutai	KEN	7.10.81	1		Boston	18 Apr 11
2:03:06		Moses	Mosop	KEN	17.7.85	2		Boston	18 Apr 11
2:04:53		Gebre-egziabher	Gebremariam	ETH	10.9.84	3		Boston	18 Apr 11
2:04:58		Ryan	Hall	USA	14.10.82	4		Boston	18 Apr 11
2:05:52		Robert Kiprono	Cheruiyot	KEN	10.8.88	1		Boston	19 Apr 10

2000 METRES STEEPLECHASE

Mark	Name		Nat	Born	Pos	Meet	Venue	Date
5:10.68	Mahiedine	Mekhissi	FRA	15.3.85	1		Reims	30 Jun 10
5:13.47	Bouabdellah	Tahri	FRA	20.12.78	1		Tomblaine	25 Jun 10
5:14.43	Julius	Kariuki	KEN	12.6.61	1		Rovereto	21 Aug 90
5:14.53	Saïf Saaeed	Shaheen	QAT	15.10.82	1	SGP	Doha	13 May 05
5:16.22	Phillip	Barkutwo	KEN	6.10.66	2		Rovereto	21 Aug 90
5:16.46	Wesley	Kiprotich	KEN	31.7.79	2	SGP	Doha	13 May 05
5:16.85	Eliud	Barngetuny	KEN	20.5.73	1		Parma	13 Jun 95

3000 METRES STEEPLECHASE

Mark	Wind	Name		Nat	Born	Pos	Meet	Venue	Date
7:53.63	WR	Saïf Saaeed	Shaheen	KEN/QAT	15.10.82	1	VD	Bruxelles	3 Sep 04
7:53.64		Brimin	Kipruto	KEN	31.7.85	1	Herc	Monaco	22 Jul 11
7:54.31		Paul Kipsiele	Koech	KEN	10.11.81	1	GGala	Roma	31 May 12
7:55.28	WR	Brahim	Boulami ¶	MAR	20.4.72	1	VD	Bruxelles	24 Aug 01
7:55.51			Shaheen			1	VD	Bruxelles	26 Aug 05
7:55.72	WR	Bernard	Barmasai	KEN	6.5.74	1	ASV	Köln	24 Aug 97
7:55.76		Ezekiel	Kemboi	KEN	25.5.82	2	Herc	Monaco	22 Jul 11
7:56.16		Moses	Kiptanui	KEN	1.10.70	2	ASV	Köln	24 Aug 97
7:56.32			Shaheen			1	Tsik	Athína	3 Jul 06
7:56.34			Shaheen			1	GGala	Roma	8 Jul 05
7:56.37			P K Koech			2	GGala	Roma	8 Jul 05
7:56.54			Shaheen			1	WK	Zürich	18 Aug 06
7:56.58			Koech			1	DL	Doha	11 May 12
7:56.81		Richard	Mateelong	KEN	14.10.83	2	DL	Doha	11 May 12
7:56.94			Shaheen			1	WAF	Monaco	19 Sep 04
7:57.28			Shaheen			1	Tsik	Athína	14 Jun 05
7:57.29		Reuben	Kosgei	KEN	2.8.79	2	VD	Bruxelles	24 Aug 01
7:57.32			P K Koech			3	Herc	Monaco	22 Jul 11
7:57.38			Shaheen			1	WAF	Monaco	14 Sep 03
7:57.42			P K Koech			2	WAF	Monaco	14 Sep 03
7:58.09			Boulami			1	Herc	Monaco	19 Jul 02
7:58.10			S Cherono			2	Herc	Monaco	19 Jul 02
7:58.50			Boulami			1	WK	Zürich	17 Aug 01
7:58.66			S Cherono			3	VD	Bruxelles	24 Aug 01
7:58.80			P K Koech			1	VD	Bruxelles	14 Sep 07

Mark	Wind	Name		Nat	Born	Pos	Meet	Venue	Date
7:58.85			Kemboi			1	SGP	Doha	8 May 09
7:58.98			Barmasai			1	Herc	Monaco	4 Aug 99
7:59.03			Kemboi			1	DL	Saint-Denis	6 Jul 13
7:59.08 WR	Wilson		Boit Kipketer	KEN	6.10.73	1	WK	Zürich	13 Aug 97
7:59.18 WR			Kiptanui			1	WK	Zürich	16 Aug 95
	(30/10)								
8:00.09	Mahiedine	Mekhissi-Benabbad		FRA	15.3.85	2	DL	Saint-Denis	6 Jul 13
8:01.18	Bouabdellah	Tahri		FRA	20.12.78	3	WCh	Berlin	18 Aug 09
8:01.16	Conseslus	Kipruto		KEN	8.12.94	1	DL	Shanghai	18 May 13
8:01.67	Abel	Mutai		KEN	2.10.88	2	GGala	Roma	31 May 12
8:01.69	Kipkirui	Misoi		KEN	23.12.78	4	VD	Bruxelles	24 Aug 01
8:03.41	Patrick	Sang		KEN	11.4.64	3	ASV	Köln	24 Aug 97
8:03.43	Jairus	Birech		KEN	14.12.92	4	DL	Saint-Denis	6 Jul 12
8:03.57	Ali	Ezzine		MAR	3.9.78	1	Gaz	Saint-Denis	23 Jun 00
8:03.57	Hillary	Yego		KEN	2.4.92	3	DL	Shanghai	18 May 13
8:03.74	Raymond	Yator		KEN	7.4.81	3	Herc	Monaco	18 Aug 00
	(20)								
8:03.81	Benjamin	Kiplagat		UGA	4.3.89	2	Athl	Lausanne	8 Jul 10
8:03.89	John	Kosgei		KEN	13.7.73	3	Herc	Monaco	16 Aug 97
8:04.95	Simon	Vroemen ¶		NED	11.5.69	2	VD	Bruxelles	26 Aug 05
8:05.01	Eliud	Barngetuny		KEN	20.5.73	1	Herc	Monaco	25 Jul 95
8:05.35 WR	Peter	Koech		KEN	18.2.58	1	DNG	Stockholm	3 Jul 89
8:05.37	Philip	Barkutwo		KEN	6.10.66	2		Rieti	6 Sep 92
8:05.4 WR	Henry	Rono		KEN	12.2.52	1		Seattle	13 May 78
8:05.43	Christopher	Kosgei		KEN	14.8.74	2	WK	Zürich	11 Aug 99
8:05.51	Julius	Kariuki		KEN	12.6.61	1	OG	Seoul	30 Sep 88
8:05.68	Wesley	Kiprotich		KEN	1.8.79	4	VD	Bruxelles	3 Sep 04
	(30)								
8:05.75	Mustafa	Mohamed		SWE	1.3.79	1	NA	Heusden-Zolder	28 Jul 07
8:05.88	Bernard	Nganga (Mbugua)		KEN	.85	2	ISTAF	Berlin	11 Sep 11
8:05.99	Joseph	Keter		KEN	13.6.69	1	Herc	Monaco	10 Aug 96
8:06.13	Tareq Mubarak	Taher		BRN	24.3.84	3	Tsik	Athína	13 Jul 09
8:06.16	Roba	Gari		ETH	12.4.82	3	DL	Doha	11 May 12
8:06.81	Evan	Jager		USA	8.3.89	3	Herc	Monaco	20 Jul 12
8:06.77	Gideon	Chirchir		KEN	24.2.66	2	WK	Zürich	16 Aug 95
8:06.88	Richard	Kosgei		KEN	29.12.70	2	GPF	Monaco	9 Sep 95
8:06.96	Gilbert	Kirui		KEN	22.1.94	2	DL	London (OS)	27 Jul 13
8:07.02	Brahim	Taleb		MAR	16.2.85	2	NA	Heusden-Zolder	28 Jul 07
	(40)								
8:07.13	Paul	Kosgei		KEN	22.4.78	2	GP II	Saint-Denis	3 Jul 99
8:07.18	Obaid Moussa	Amer ¶		KEN/QAT	18.4.85	4	OG	Athína	24 Aug 04
8:07.44	Luis Miguel	Martín		ESP	11.1.72	2	VD	Bruxelles	30 Aug 02
8:07.59	Julius	Nyamu		KEN	1.12.77	5	VD	Bruxelles	24 Aug 01
8:07.62	Joseph	Mahmoud		FRA	13.12.55	1	VD	Bruxelles	24 Aug 84
8:07.75	Jonathan	Ndiku Muia		KEN	18.9.91	6	Herc	Monaco	22 Jul 11
8:07.96	Mark	Rowland		GBR	7.3.63	3	OG	Seoul	30 Sep 88
8:08.02 WR	Anders	Gärderud		SWE	28.8.46	1	OG	Montreal	28 Jul 76
8:08.12	Matthew	Birir		KEN	5.7.72	3	GGala	Roma	8 Jun 95
8:08.14	Sa'ad Shaddad	Al-Asmari		KSA	24.9.68	4	DNG	Stockholm	16 Jul 02
	(50)								

100th man 8:12.25, 200th 8:18.23, 300th 8:21.90, 400th 8:24.12, 500th 8:26.4

Drugs disqualification: 7:53.17 Brahim Boulami ¶ MAR 20.4.72 1 WK Zürich 16 Aug 02

110 METRES HURDLES

Mark	Wind	Name		Nat	Born	Pos	Meet	Venue	Date
12.80 WR	0.3	Aries	Merritt	USA	24.7.85	1	VD	Bruxelles	7 Sep 12
12.87 WR	0.9	Dayron	Robles	CUB	19.11.86	1	GS	Ostrava	12 Jun 08
12.88 WR	1.1		Liu Xiang	CHN	13.7.83	1rA	Athl	Lausanne	11 Jul 06
12.88	0.5		Robles			1	Gaz	Saint-Denis	18 Jul 08
12.89	0.5	David	Oliver	USA	24.4.82	1	DL	Saint-Denis	16 Jul 10
12.90	1.1	Dominique	Arnold	USA	14.9.73	2rA	Athl	Lausanne	11 Jul 06
12.90	1.6		Oliver			1	Pre	Eugene	3 Jul 10
12.91 WR	0.5	Colin	Jackson	GBR	18.2.67	1	WCh	Stuttgart	20 Aug 93
12.91 WR	0.3		Liu Xiang			1	OG	Athína	27 Aug 04
12.91	0.2		Robles			1	DNG	Stockholm	22 Jul 08
12.92 WR	-0.1	Roger	Kingdom	USA	26.8.62	1	WK	Zürich	16 Aug 89
12.92	0.9	Allen	Johnson	USA	1.3.71	1	NC	Atlanta	23 Jun 96
12.92	0.2		Johnson			1	VD	Bruxelles	23 Aug 96
12.92	1.5		Liu Xiang			1	GP	New York	2 Jun 07
12.92	0.0		Robles			1	WAF	Stuttgart	23 Sep 07
12.92	-0.3		Merritt			1	OG	London (OS)	8 Aug 12
12.93 WR	-0.2	Renaldo	Nehemiah	USA	24.3.59	1	WK	Zürich	19 Aug 81

MEN All-time

Mark	Wind	Name		Nat	Born	Pos	Meet	Venue	Date
12.93	0.0		Johnson			1	WCh	Athína	7 Aug 97
12.93	-0.6		Liu Xiang			1	WAF	Stuttgart	9 Sep 06
12.93	0.1		Robles			1	OG	Beijing	21 Aug 08
12.93	1.7		Oliver			1	NC	Des Moines	27 Jun 10
12.93	-0.3		Oliver			1	WK	Zürich	19 Aug 10
12.93	1.2		Merritt			1	NC/OT	Eugene	30 Jun 12
12.93	0.6		Merritt			1	LGP	London(CP)	13 Jul 12
12.93	0.0		Merritt			1	Herc	Monaco	20 Jul 12
12.94	1.6	Jack	Pierce (10)	USA	23.9.62	1s2	NC	Atlanta	22 Jun 96
12.94	1.8		Oliver			1	Pre	Eugene	4 Jun 11
12.94	0.1		Merritt			1s2	OG	London (OS)	8 Aug 12
12.95	0.6		Johnson			1	OG	Atlanta	29 Jul 96
12.95	1.5	Terrence	Trammell	USA	23.11.78	2	GP	New York	2 Jun 07
12.95	1.7		Liu Xiang			1	WCh	Osaka	31 Aug 07
12.95	2.0		Oliver			1	SGP	Doha	9 May 08
12.95	-1.7		Robles			1		Dubnica nad Váhom	7 Sep 08
12.95	-0.9		Merritt			1	DL	Birmingham	26 Aug 12
		(34/11)							
12.97	1.0	Ladji	Doucouré	FRA	28.3.83	1	NC	Angers	15 Jul 05
12.98	0.6	Mark	Crear	USA	2.10.68	1		Zagreb	5 Jul 99
12.98	1.5	Jason	Richardson	USA	4.4.86	1s3	NC/OT	Eugene	30 Jun 12
13.00	0.5	Anthony	Jarrett	GBR	13.8.68	2	WCh	Stuttgart	20 Aug 93
13.00	0.6	Anier	García	CUB	9.3.76	1	OG	Sydney	25 Sep 00
13.01	0.3	Larry	Wade ¶	USA	22.11.74	1rA	Athl	Lausanne	2 Jul 99
13.02	1.5	Ryan	Wilson	USA	19.12.80	3	GP	New York	2 Jun 07
13.02	1.7	David	Payne	USA	24.7.82	3	WCh	Osaka	31 Aug 07
13.03	-0.2	Greg	Foster	USA	4.8.58	2	WK	Zürich	19 Aug 81
		(20)							
13.03	1.0	Reggie	Torian	USA	22.4.75	1	NC	New Orleans	21 Jun 98
13.05	1.4	Tony	Dees ¶	USA	6.8.63	1		Vigo	23 Jul 91
13.05	-0.8	Florian	Schwarthoff	GER	7.5.68	1	NC	Bremen	2 Jul 95
13.05	0.9	Hansle	Parchment	JAM	17.6.90	1	Pre	Eugene	1 Jun 13
13.08	1.2	Mark	McKoy	CAN	10.12.61	1	BNP	Villeneuve-d'Ascq	2 Jul 93
13.08	0.0	Stanislav	Olijar	LAT	22.3.79	2	Athl	Lausanne	1 Jul 03
13.08	1.2	Jeff	Porter	USA	27.11.85	3	NC/OT	Eugene	30 Jun 12
13.08	0.9	Orlando	Ortega	CUB	29.7.91	2	Pre	Eugene	1 Jun 13
13.09	2.0	Antwon	Hicks	USA	12.3.83	2s2	NC/OT	Eugene	6 Jul 08
13.09	-1.1	Sergey	Shubenkov	RUS	4.10.90	1s2	EC	Helsinki	1 Jul 12
		(30)							
13.12	1.5	Falk	Balzer ¶	GER	14.12.73	2	EC	Budapest	22 Aug 98
13.12	1.0	Duane	Ross ¶	USA	5.12.72	3	WCh	Sevilla	25 Aug 99
13.12	1.9	Anwar	Moore	USA	5.3.79	1	ModR	Modesto	5 May 07
13.12	0.0	Pascal	Martinot Lagarde	FRA	22.9.91	2	DL	Saint-Denis	6 Jul 13
13.13	1.6	Igor	Kovác	SVK	12.5.69	1	DNG	Stockholm	7 Jul 97
13.13	2.0	Dexter	Faulk	USA	14.4.84	2	GS	Ostrava	17 Jun 09
13.14	0.1	Ryan	Brathwaite	BAR	6.6.88	1	WCh	Berlin	20 Aug 09
13.14	0.0	Andrew	Riley	JAM	6.9.88	4	DL	Saint-Denis	6 Jul 13
13.15	0.3	Robin	Korving	NED	29.7.74	5rA	Athl	Lausanne	2 Jul 99
13.15	0.1	Dwight	Thomas	JAM	23.9.80	2	Bisl	Oslo	9 Jun 11
		(40)							
13.15	-0.3	Garfield	Darien	FRA	22.12.87	1s3	EC	Helsinki	1 Jul 12
13.17	-0.4	Sam	Turner	USA	17.6.57	2	Pepsi	Los Angeles (Ww)	15 May 83
13.17	0.0	Tonie	Campbell	USA	14.6.60	3	WK	Zürich	17 Aug 88
13.17	0.5	Courtney	Hawkins	USA	11.7.67	1		Ingolstadt	26 Jul 98
13.17	0.4	Mike	Fenner	GER	24.4.71	1		Leverkusen	9 Aug 98
13.17	-0.1	Maurice	Wignall	JAM	17.4.76	1s1	OG	Athína	26 Aug 04
13.18	0.5	Emilio	Valle	CUB	21.4.67	3s1	OG	Atlanta	29 Jul 96
13.19	1.9	Steve	Brown	USA/TRI	6.1.69	1h4	NC	Atlanta	21 Jun 96
13.19	1.7		Shi Dongpeng	CHN	6.1.84	5	WCh	Osaka	31 Aug 07
13.19	1.7	Ronnie	Ash	USA	2.7.88	3	NC	Des Moines	27 Jun 10
13.19	1.2	Mikel	Thomas	TRI	23.11.87	1		Montverde, FL	8 Jun 13
		(51)							

100th man 13.29, 200th 13.42, 300th 13.50, 400th 13.57, 500th 13.63

Rolling start but accepted by race officials

13.10A	2.0	Falk	Balzer ¶	GER	14.12.73	1	WCp	Johannesburg	13 Sep 98

Doubtful timing: Scheessel 4 Jun 95 +1.3 1. Mike Fenner GER 24.4.71 13.06, 2. Eric Kaiser ¶ GER 7.3.71 13.08

Wind-assisted marks   *Performances to 12.94, performers to 13.17*

12.87	2.6	Roger	Kingdom	USA	26.8.62	1	WCp	Barcelona	10 Sep 89
12.87	2.4		Liu Xiang	CHN	13.7.83	1	Pre	Eugene	2 Jun 12
12.89	3.2	David	Oliver	USA	24.4.82	1s1	NC/OT	Eugene	6 Jul 08
12.91	3.5	Renaldo	Nehemiah	USA	24.3.59	1	NCAA	Champaign	1 Jun 79

Mark	Wind	Name		Nat	Born	Pos	Meet	Venue	Date
12.94A	2.8		Jackson			1rA		Sestriere	31 Jul 94
12.98	3.1	Ronnie	Ash	USA	2.7.88	1	NACAC	Miramar	9 Jul 10
13.00	2.6	Anwar	Moore	USA	5.3.79	1	DrakeR	Des Moines	28 Apr 07
13.05	3.6	Ryan	Brathwaite	BAR	6.6.88	1		Austin	2 May 09
13.06	2.1	Mark	McKoy	CAN	10.12.61	1	Gugl	Linz	13 Aug 92
13.12	2.4	Dexter	Faulk	USA	14.4.84	4	Pre	Eugene	2 Jun 12
13.14	2.9	Igor	Kazanov	LAT	24.9.63	1r1	Znam	Leningrad	8 Jun 86
13.14	4.7	Lawrence	Clarke	GBR	12.3.90	1		Madrid	7 Jul 12
13.14	3.8	Wayne	Davis	TRI	22.8.91	1	NCAA	Eugene	8 Jun 13
13.14	2.6		Oliver			1h3	NC	Des Moines	22 Jun 13
13.15	2.1	Courtney	Hawkins	USA	11.7.67	1		Salamanca	10 Jul 98
Hand timing: 12.8 1.0 Renaldo			Nehemiah	USA	24.3.59	1		Kingston	11 May 79
Wind-assisted									
12.8	2.4	Colin	Jackson	GBR	18.2.67	1		Sydney	10 Jan 90
12.9	4.1	Mark	Crear	USA	2.10.68	1rA	S&W	Modesto	8 May 93
12.9	3.1	William	Sharman	GBR	12.9.84	1r2		Madrid	2 Jul 10

400 METRES HURDLES

Mark		Name		Nat	Born	Pos	Meet	Venue	Date
46.78 WR		Kevin	Young	USA	16.9.66	1	OG	Barcelona	6 Aug 92
47.02 WR		Edwin	Moses	USA	31.8.55	1		Koblenz	31 Aug 83
47.03		Bryan	Bronson ¶	USA	9.9.72	1	NC	New Orleans	21 Jun 98
47.10		Samuel	Matete	ZAM	27.7.68	1rA	WK	Zürich	7 Aug 91
47.13 WR			Moses			1		Milano	3 Jul 80
47.14			Moses			1	Athl	Lausanne	14 Jul 81
47.17			Moses			1	ISTAF	Berlin	8 Aug 80
47.18			Young			1	WCh	Stuttgart	19 Aug 93
47.19		Andre	Phillips	USA	5.9.59	1	OG	Seoul	25 Sep 88
47.23		Amadou	Dia Bâ	SEN	22.9.58	2	OG	Seoul	25 Sep 88
47.24		Kerron	Clement	USA	31.10.85	1	NC	Carson	26 Jun 05
47.25		Félix	Sánchez	DOM	30.8.77	1	WCh	Saint-Denis	29 Aug 03
47.25		Angelo	Taylor	USA	29.12.78	1	OG	Beijing	18 Aug 08
47.27			Moses			1	ISTAF	Berlin	21 Aug 81
47.30		Bershawn	Jackson (10)	USA	8.5.83	1	WCh	Helsinki	9 Aug 05
47.32			Moses			1		Koblenz	29 Aug 84
47.32			Jackson			1	NC	Des Moines	26 Jun 10
47.35			Sánchez			1rA	WK	Zürich	16 Aug 02
47.37			Moses			1	WCp	Roma	4 Sep 81
47.37			Moses			1	WK	Zürich	24 Aug 83
47.37			Moses			1	NC/OT	Indianapolis	17 Jul 88
47.37			Young			1	Athl	Lausanne	7 Jul 93
47.37		Stéphane	Diagana	FRA	23.7.69	1	Athl	Lausanne	5 Jul 95
47.38			Moses			1	Athl	Lausanne	2 Sep 86
47.38		Danny	Harris ¶	USA	7.9.65	1	Athl	Lausanne	10 Jul 91
47.38			Sánchez			1rA	WK	Zürich	17 Aug 01
47.39			Clement			1	NC	Indianapolis	24 Jun 06
47.40			Young			1	WK	Zürich	19 Aug 92
47.42			Young			1	ASV	Köln	16 Aug 92
47.43			Moses			1	ASV	Köln	28 Aug 83
47.43		James	Carter	USA	7.5.78	2	WCh	Helsinki	9 Aug 05
		(31/13)							
47.48		Harald	Schmid	FRG	29.9.57	1	EC	Athína	8 Sep 82
47.53		Hadi Soua'an	Al-Somaily	KSA	21.8.76	2	OG	Sydney	27 Sep 00
47.54		Derrick	Adkins	USA	2.7.70	2	Athl	Lausanne	5 Jul 95
47.54		Fabrizio	Mori	ITA	28.6.69	2	WCh	Edmonton	10 Aug 01
47.60		Winthrop	Graham	JAM	17.11.65	1	WK	Zürich	4 Aug 93
47.63		Johnny	Dutch	USA	20.1.89	2	NC	Des Moines	26 Jun 10
47.66A		L.J. 'Louis'	van Zyl	RSA	20.7.85	1		Pretoria	25 Feb 11
		(20)							
47.67		Bennie	Brazell	USA	2.6.82	2	NCAA	Sacramento	11 Jun 05
47.69		Jehue	Gordon	TRI	15.12.91	1	WCh	Moskva	15 Aug 13
47.70		Michael	Tinsley	USA	21.4.84	2	WCh	Moskva	15 Aug 13
47.72		Javier	Culson	PUR	25.7.84	1		Ponce	8 May 10
47.75		David	Patrick	USA	12.6.60	4	NC/OT	Indianapolis	17 Jul 88
47.81		Llewellyn	Herbert	RSA	21.7.77	3	OG	Sydney	27 Sep 00
47.82 WR		John	Akii-Bua	UGA	3.12.49	1	OG	München	2 Sep 72
47.82		Kriss	Akabusi	GBR	28.11.58	3	OG	Barcelona	6 Aug 92
47.82		Periklis	Iakovákis	GRE	24.3.79	2	GP	Osaka	6 May 06
47.84		Bayano	Kamani	PAN	17.4.80	2s1	WCh	Helsinki	7 Aug 05
		(30)							

MEN All-time

Mark	Wind	Name		Nat	Born	Pos	Meet	Venue	Date
47.84		David	Greene	GBR	11.4.86	2	DL	Saint Denis	6 Jul 12
47.89		Dai	Tamesue	JPN	3.5.78	3	WCh	Edmonton	10 Aug 01
47.91		Calvin	Davis	USA	2.4.72	1s2	OG	Atlanta	31 Jul 96
47.92		Aleksandr	Vasilyev	BLR	26.7.61	2	ECp	Moskva	17 Aug 85
47.93		Kenji	Narisako	JPN	25.7.84	3	GP	Osaka	6 May 06
47.93		Jeshua	Anderson	USA	22.6.89	1	NC	Eugene	26 Jun 11
47.93		Omar	Cisneros	CUB	19.11.89	1s3	WCh	Moskva	13 Aug 13
47.94		Eric	Thomas	USA	1.12.73	1	GGala	Roma	30 Jun 00
47.97		Maurice	Mitchell	USA	14.5.71	2rA	WK	Zürich	14 Aug 96
47.97		Joey	Woody	USA	22.5.73	3	NC	New Orleans	21 Jun 98
		(40)							
47.98		Sven	Nylander	SWE	1.1.62	4	OG	Atlanta	1 Aug 96
48.00		Danny	McFarlane	JAM	14.2.72	1s2	OG	Athína	24 Aug 04
48.02A		Ockert	Cilliers	RSA	21.4.81	1		Pretoria	20 Feb 04
48.04		Eronilde	de Araújo	BRA	31.12.70	2	Nik	Nice	12 Jul 95
48.05		Ken	Harnden	ZIM	31.3.73	1	GP	Paris (C)	29 Jul 98
48.05		Kemel	Thompson	JAM	25.9.74	1	GP	London (CP)	8 Aug 03
48.05		Isa	Phillips	JAM	22.4.84	1	NC	Kingston	27 Jun 09
48.05		Emir	Bekric	SRB	14.3.91	3	WCh	Moskva	15 Aug 13
48.06		Oleg	Tverdokhleb	UKR	3.11.69	1	EC	Helsinki	10 Aug 94
48.06		Ruslan	Mashchenko	RUS	11.11.71	1	GP II	Helsinki	13 Jun 98
		(50)	100th man 48.50, 200th man 49.04, 300th man 49.29, 400th 49.51, 500th 49.68						
Best at low altitude:		47.66	van Zyl	1	GS		Ostrava		31 May 11
Drugs Disqualification		47.15	Bronson ¶	1	GWG		Uniondale, NY		19 Jul 98

HIGH JUMP

Mark	Wind	Name		Nat	Born	Pos	Meet	Venue	Date
2.45 WR		Javier	Sotomayor ¶	CUB	13.10.67	1		Salamanca	27 Jul 93
2.44 WR			Sotomayor			1	CAC	San Juan	29 Jul 89
2.43 WR			Sotomayor			1		Salamanca	8 Sep 88
2.43i			Sotomayor			1	WI	Budapest	4 Mar 89
2.42 WR		Patrik	Sjöberg	SWE	5.1.65	1	DNG	Stockholm	30 Jun 87
2.42i WR		Carlo	Thränhardt	FRG	5.7.57	1		Berlin	26 Feb 88
2.42			Sotomayor			1		Sevilla	5 Jun 94
2.41 WR		Igor	Paklin	KGZ	15.6.63	1	WUG	Kobe	4 Sep 85
2.41i			Sjöberg			1		Pireás	1 Feb 87
2.41i			Sotomayor			1	WI	Toronto	14 Mar 93
2.41			Sotomayor			1	NC	La Habana	25 Jun 94
2.41			Sotomayor			1	TSB	London (CP)	15 Jul 94
2.41		Bogdan	Bondarenko	UKR	30.8.89	1	Athl	Lausanne	4 Jul 13
2.41			Bondarenko			1	WCh	Moskva	15 Aug 13
2.40 WR		Rudolf	Povarnitsyn	UKR	13.6.62	1		Donetsk	11 Aug 85
2.40i			Thränhardt			1		Simmerath	16 Jan 87
2.40i			Sjöberg			1		Berlin	27 Feb 87
2.40			Sotomayor			1	NC	La Habana	12 Mar 89
2.40			Sjöberg			1	ECp-B	Bruxelles	5 Aug 89
2.40			Sotomayor			1	AmCp	Bogota	13 Aug 89
2.40		Sorin	Matei	ROU	6.7.63	1	PTS	Bratislava	20 Jun 90
2.40i		Hollis	Conway	USA	8.1.67	1	WI	Sevilla	10 Mar 91
2.40			Sotomayor			1		Saint Denis	19 Jul 91
2.40		Charles	Austin	USA	19.12.67	1	WK	Zürich	7 Aug 91
2.40			Sotomayor			1	Barr	La Habana	22 May 93
2.40			Sotomayor			1	TSB	London (CP)	23 Jul 93
2.40			Sotomayor			1	WCh	Stuttgart	22 Aug 93
2.40i			Sotomayor			1		Wuppertal	4 Feb 94
2.40i			Sotomayor			1	TSB	Birmingham	26 Feb 94
2.40			Sotomayor			1		Eberstadt	10 Jul 94
2.40			Sotomayor			1	Nik	Nice	18 Jul 94
2.40			Sotomayor			1	GWG	Sankt-Peterburg	29 Jul 94
2.40			Sotomayor			1	WCp	London (CP)	11 Sep 94
2.40			Sotomayor			1	PAm	Mar del Plata	25 Mar 95
2.40		Vyacheslav	Voronin (10)	RUS	5.4.74	1	BrGP	London (CP)	5 Aug 00
2.40i		Stefan	Holm	SWE	25.5.76	1	EI	Madrid	6 Mar 05
2.40i		Ivan	Ukhov	RUS	29.3.86	1		Pireás	25 Feb 09
2.40		Mutaz Essa	Barshim	QAT	24.6.91	1	Pre	Eugene	1 Jun 13
		(38/13)							
2.39 WR			Zhu Jianhua	CHN	29.5.63	1		Eberstadt	10 Jun 84
2.39i		Dietmar	Mögenburg	FRG	15.8.61	1		Köln	24 Aug 85
2.39i		Ralf	Sonn	GER	17.1.67	1		Berlin	1 Mar 91
2.38i		Gennadiy	Avdeyenko	UKR	4.11.63	2	WI	Indianapolis	7 Mar 87

Mark	Wind	Name		Nat	Born	Pos	Meet	Venue	Date
2.38		Sergey	Malchenko	RUS	2.11.63	1		Banská Bystrica	4 Sep 88
2.38		Dragutin	Topic ¶	YUG	12.3.71	1		Beograd	1 Aug 93
2.38i		Steve	Smith	GBR	29.3.73	2		Wuppertal	4 Feb 94
		(20)							
2.38i		Wolf-Hendrik	Beyer	GER	14.2.72	1		Weinheim	18 Mar 94
2.38		Troy	Kemp	BAH	18.6.66	1	Nik	Nice	12 Jul 95
2.38		Artur	Partyka	POL	25.7.69	1		Eberstadt	18 Aug 96
2.38i		Matt	Hemingway	USA	24.10.72	1	NC	Atlanta	4 Mar 00
2.38i		Yaroslav	Rybakov	RUS	22.11.80	1		Stockholm	15 Feb 05
2.38		Jacques	Freitag	RSA	11.6.82	1		Oudtshoorn	5 Mar 05
2.38		Andriy	Sokolovskyy	UKR	16.7.78	1	GGala	Roma	8 Jul 05
2.38i		Linus	Thörnblad	SWE	6.3.85	2	NC	Göteborg	25 Feb 07
2.38		Andrey	Silnov	RUS	9.9.84	1	LGP	London (CP)	25 Jul 08
2.38		Derek	Drouin	CAN	6.3.90	3	WCh	Moskva	15 Aug
13		(30)							
2.37		Valeriy	Sereda	RUS	30.6.59	1		Rieti	2 Sep 84
2.37		Tom	McCants	USA	27.11.62	1	Owens	Columbus	8 May 88
2.37		Jerome	Carter	USA	25.3.63	2	Owens	Columbus	8 May 88
2.37		Sergey	Dymchenko	UKR	23.8.67	1		Kiyev	16 Sep 90
2.37i		Dalton	Grant	GBR	8.4.66	1	EI	Paris	13 Mar 94
2.37i		Jaroslav	Bába	CZE	2.9.84	2		Arnstadt	5 Feb 05
2.37		Jesse	Williams	USA	27.12.83	1	NC	Eugene	26 Jun 11
2.37		Robbie	Grabarz	GBR	3.10.87	3	Athl	Lausanne	23 Aug 12
2.37		Eric	Kynard	USA	3.2.91	2	Athl	Lausanne	4 Jul 13
2.36 WR		Gerd	Wessig	GDR	16.7.59	1	OG	Moskva	1 Aug 80
		(40)							
2.36		Sergey	Zasimovich	KZK	6.9.62	1		Tashkent	5 May 84
2.36		Eddy	Annys	BEL	15.12.58	1		Gent	26 May 85
2.36i		Jim	Howard	USA	11.9.59	1		Albuquerque	25 Jan 86
2.36i		Jan	Zvara	CZE	12.2.63	1	vGDR	Jablonec	14 Feb 87
2.36i		Gerd	Nagel	FRG	22.10.57	1		Sulingen	17 Mar 89
2.36		Nick	Saunders	BER	14.9.63	1	CG	Auckland	1 Feb 90
2.36		Doug	Nordquist	USA	20.12.58	2	NC	Norwalk	15 Jun 90
2.36		Georgi	Dakov	BUL	21.10.67	2	VD	Bruxelles	10 Aug 90
2.36		Lábros	Papakóstas	GRE	20.10.69	1	NC	Athína	21 Jun 92
2.36i		Steinar	Hoen	NOR	8.2.71	1		Balingen	12 Feb 94
		(50)							
2.36		Tim	Forsyth	AUS	17.8.73	1	NC	Melbourne	2 Mar 97
2.36		Sergey	Klyugin	RUS	24.3.74	1	WK	Zürich	12 Aug 98
2.36		Konstantin	Matusevich	ISR	25.2.71	1		Perth	5 Feb 00
2.36		Martin	Buss	GER	7.4.76	1	WCh	Edmonton	8 Aug 01
2.36		Aleksander	Walerianczyk	POL	1.9.82	1	EU23	Bydgoszcz	20 Jul 03
2.36		Michal	Bieniek	POL	17.5.84	1		Biala Podlaska	28 May 05
2.36i		Andrey	Tereshin	RUS	15.12.82	1	NC	Moskva	17 Feb 06
2.36A		Dusty	Jonas	USA	19.4.86	1	Big 12	Boulder	18 May 08
2.36		Aleksey	Dmitrik	RUS	12.4.84	1	NC	Cheboksary	23 Jul 11
2.36		Aleksandr	Shustov	RUS	29.6.84	2	NC	Cheboksary	23 Jul 11
		(60)		100th man 2.34, 200th 2.31, 300th 2.29, 400th 2.28, 500th 2.26					

Best outdoor marks for athletes with indoor bests

2.39	Conway	1	USOF	Norman	30 Jul 89	2.36	Mögenburg	3		Eberstadt	10 Jun 84
2.39	Ukhov	1	NC	Cheboksary	5 Jul 12	2.36	Howard	1		Rehlingen	8 Jun 87
2.38	Avdeyenko	2=	WCh	Roma	6 Sep 87	2.36	Zvara	1		Praha	23 Aug 87
2.37	Thränhardt	2		Rieti	2 Sep 84	2.36	Grant	4	WCh	Tokyo	1 Sep 91
2.37	Smith	1	WJ	Seoul	20 Sep 92	2.36	Hoen	1		Oslo	1 Jul 97
2.37	Holm	1		Athína	13 Jul 08	2.36	Bába	2=	GGala	Roma	8 Jul 05

Ancillary jumps – en route to final marks

2.40	Sotomayor		8 Sep 88	2.40	Sotomayor		29 Jul 89	2.40	Sotomayor	5 Jun 94

POLE VAULT

Mark		Name		Nat	Born	Pos	Meet	Venue	Date
6.15i		Sergey	Bubka	UKR	4.12.63	1		Donetsk	21 Feb 93
6.14i			Bubka			1		Liévin	13 Feb 93
6.14A WR			Bubka			1		Sestriere	31 Jul 94
6.13i			Bubka			1		Berlin	21 Feb 92
6.13 WR			Bubka			1	TOTO	Tokyo	19 Sep 92
6.12i			Bubka			1	Mast	Grenoble	23 Mar 91
6.12 WR			Bubka			1		Padova	30 Aug 92
6.11i			Bubka			1		Donetsk	19 Mar 91
6.11 WR			Bubka			1		Dijon	13 Jun 92
6.10i			Bubka			1		San Sebastián	15 Mar 91
6.10 WR			Bubka			1	MAI	Malmö	5 Aug 91
6.09 WR			Bubka			1		Formia	8 Jul 91

Mark	Wind	Name		Nat	Born	Pos	Meet	Venue	Date
6.08i			Bubka			1	NC	Volgograd	9 Feb 91
6.08	WR		Bubka			1	Znam	Moskva	9 Jun 91
6.07	WR		Bubka			1	Super	Shizuoka	6 May 91
6.06	WR		Bubka			1	Nik	Nice	10 Jul 88
6.06i		Steve	Hooker	AUS	16.7.82	1		Boston (R)	7 Feb 09
6.05	WR		Bubka			1	PTS	Bratislava	9 Jun 88
6.05i			Bubka			1		Donetsk	17 Mar 90
6.05i			Bubka			1		Berlin	5 Mar 93
6.05			Bubka			1	GPF	London (CP)	10 Sep 93
6.05i			Bubka			1	Mast	Grenoble	6 Feb 94
6.05			Bubka			1	ISTAF	Berlin	30 Aug 94
6.05			Bubka			1	GPF	Fukuoka	13 Sep 97
6.05		Maksim	Tarasov	RUS	2.12.70	1	GP II	Athína	16 Jun 99
6.05		Dmitriy	Markov	BLR/AUS	14.3.75	1	WCh	Edmonton	9 Aug 01
6.04		Brad	Walker	USA	21.6.81	1	Pre	Eugene	8 Jun 08
6.03	WR		Bubka			1	Ros	Praha	23 Jun 87
6.03i			Bubka			1		Osaka	11 Feb 89
6.03		Okkert	Brits	RSA	22.8.73	1	ASV	Köln	18 Aug 95
6.03		Jeff	Hartwig	USA	25.9.67	1		Jonesboro	14 Jun 00
6.03i		Renaud	Lavillenie	FRA	18.9.86	1	EI	Paris (Bercy)	5 Mar 11
		(32/8)							
6.02i		Rodion	Gataullin	RUS	23.11.65	1	NC	Gomel	4 Feb 89
6.01		Igor	Trandenkov (10)	RUS	17.8.66	1	NC	Sankt Peterburg	4 Jul 96
		Hiit bar hard, but kept it on with his hand illegally. Next best 5.95				1		Dijon	26 May 96
6.01		Tim	Mack	USA	15.9.72	1	WAF	Monaco	18 Sep 04
6.01		Yevgeniy	Lukyanenko	RUS	23.1.85	1	EAF	Bydgoszcz	1 Jul 08
6.01	sq	Björn	Otto	GER	16.10.77	1		Aachen	5 Sep 12
6.00		Tim	Lobinger	GER	3.9.72	1	ASV	Köln	24 Aug 97
6.00i		Jean	Galfione	FRA	9.6.71	1	WI	Maebashi	6 Mar 99
6.00i		Danny	Ecker	GER	21.7.77	1		Dortmund	11 Feb 01
6.00		Toby	Stevenson	USA	19.11.76	1eA	CalR	Modesto	8 May 04
6.00		Paul	Burgess	AUS	14.8.79	1		Perth	25 Feb 05
Most competitions at 6 metres or more: S Bubka 44, Hartwig 8, Gataullin & Tarasov 7, Hooker 4, Brits & Walker 3									
5.98		Lawrence	Johnson	USA	7.5.74	1		Knoxville	25 May 96
5.97		Scott	Huffman	USA	30.11.64	1	NC	Knoxville	18 Jun 94
		(20)							
5.96		Joe	Dial	USA	26.10.62	1		Norman	18 Jun 87
5.95		Andrei	Tivontchik	GER	13.7.70	1	ASV	Köln	16 Aug 96
5.95		Michael	Stolle	GER	17.12.74	1	Herc	Monaco	18 Aug 00
5.95		Romain	Mesnil	FRA	13.6.77	1		Castres	6 Aug 03
5.94i		Philippe	Collet	FRA	13.12.63	1	Mast	Grenoble	10 Mar 90
5.93i	WIR	Billy	Olson	USA	19.7.58	1		East Rutherford	8 Feb 86
5.93i		Tye	Harvey	USA	25.9.74	2	NC	Atlanta	3 Mar 01
5.93		Alex	Averbukh	ISR	1.10.74	1	GP	Madrid (C)	19 Jul 03
5.92		István	Bagyula	HUN	2.1.69	1	Gugl	Linz	5 Jul 91
5.92		Igor	Potapovich	KAZ	6.9.67	2		Dijon	13 Jun 92
		(30)							
5.92		Dean	Starkey	USA	27.3.67	1	Banes	São Paulo	21 May 94
5.91	WR	Thierry	Vigneron	FRA	9.3.60	2	GGala	Roma	31 Aug 84
5.91i		Viktor	Ryzhenkov	UZB	25.8.66	2		San Sebastián	15 Mar 91
5.91A		Riaan	Botha	RSA	8.11.70	1		Pretoria	2 Apr 97
5.91		Pawel	Wojciechowski	POL	6.6.89	1		Szczecin	15 Aug 11
5.91		Malte	Mohr	GER	24.7.86	1		Ingolstadt	22 Jun 12
5.91		Raphael	Holzdeppe	GER	28.9.89	3	OG	London (OS)	10 Aug 12
5.90		Pierre	Quinon	FRA	20.2.62	2	Nik	Nice	16 Jul 85
5.90i		Ferenc	Salbert	HUN/FRA	5.8.60	1	Mast	Grenoble	14 Mar 87
5.90		Miroslaw	Chmara	POL	9.5.64	1	BNP	Villeneuve d'Ascq	27 Jun 88
		(40)							
5.90i		Grigoriy	Yegorov	KAZ	12.1.67	1		Yokohama	11 Mar 90
5.90		Denis	Petushinskiy ¶	RUS	28.6.67	1	Znam	Moskva	13 Jun 93
5.90i		Pyotr	Bochkaryov	RUS	3.11.67	1	EI	Paris (B)	12 Mar 94
5.90		Jacob	Davis	USA	29.4.78	1	TexR	Austin	4 Apr 98
5.90		Viktor	Chistyakov	RUS/AUS	9.2.75	1		Salamanca	15 Jul 99
5.90		Pavel	Gerasimov	RUS	29.5.79	1		Rüdlingen	12 Aug 00
5.90		Nick	Hysong	USA	9.12.71	1	OG	Sydney	29 Sep 00
5.90		Giuseppe	Gibilisco	ITA	5.1.79	1	WCh	Saint-Denis	28 Aug 03
5.90i		Igor	Pavlov	RUS	18.7.79	1	EI	Madrid	5 Mar 05
5.90		Lázaro	Borges	CUB	19.6.86	2	WCh	Daegu	29 Aug 11
5.90i		Dmitriy	Starodubtsev	RUS	3.1.86	1		Chelyabinsk	18 Dec 11
		(51)		100th man 5.81, 200th 5.71, 300th 5.65, 400th 5.60, 500th 5.55					

Mark	Wind	Name		Nat	Born	Pos	Meet	Venue	Date

Best outdoor marks for athletes with lifetime bests indoors

Mark	Wind	Name		Nat	Born	Pos	Meet	Venue	Date
6.02		Lavillenie	1 DL		London (OS) 27 Jul 13	5.98		Galfione	1	Amiens	23 Jul 99
6.00		Gataullin	1		Tokyo	16 Sep 89	5.93		Ecker	1	Ingolstadt	26 Jul 98
6.00		Hooker	1		Perth	27 Jan 08	5.90		Yegorov	2	WCh Stuttgart	19 Aug 93

Ancillary jump: 6.05i Bubka   13 Feb 93
Outdoors on built-up runway: 5.90 Pyotr Bochkaryov RUS 3.11.67 1   Karlskrona   28 Jun 96
Exhibition or Market Square competitions

| 6.00 | | Jean | Galfione | FRA | 9.6.71 | 1 | | Besançon | 23 May 97 |
| 5.95 | | Viktor | Chistiakov | RUS/AUS | 9.2.75 | 1 | | Chiari | 8 Sep 99 |

LONG JUMP

Mark	Wind	Name	Surname	Nat	Born	Pos	Meet	Venue	Date
8.95	WR 0.3	Mike	Powell	USA	10.11.63	1	WCh	Tokyo	30 Aug 91
8.90A	WR2.0	Bob	Beamon	USA	29.8.46	1	OG	Ciudad de México	18 Oct 68
8.87	-0.2	Carl	Lewis	USA	1.7.61	*	WCh	Tokyo	30 Aug 91
8.86A	1.9	Robert	Emmiyan	ARM	16.2.65	1		Tsakhkadzor	22 May 87
8.79	1.9		Lewis			1	TAC	Indianapolis	19 Jun 83
8.79i	–		Lewis			1		New York	27 Jan 84
8.76	1.0		Lewis			1	USOF	Indianapolis	24 Jul 82
8.76	0.8		Lewis			1	NC/OT	Indianapolis	18 Jul 88
8.75	1.7		Lewis			1	PAm	Indianapolis	16 Aug 87
8.74	1.4	Larry	Myricks ¶	USA	10.3.56	2	NC/OT	Indianapolis	18 Jul 88
8.74A	2.0	Erick	Walder	USA	5.11.71	1		El Paso	2 Apr 94
8.74	1.2	Dwight	Phillips	USA	1.10.77	1	Pre	Eugene	7 Jun 09
8.73	1.2	Irving	Saladino	PAN	23.1.83	1	FBK	Hengelo	24 May 08
8.72	-0.2		Lewis			1	OG	Seoul	26 Sep 88
8.71	-0.4		Lewis			1	Pepsi	Los Angeles (Ww)	13 May 84
8.71	0.1		Lewis			1	OT	Los Angeles	19 Jun 84
8.71	1.9	Iván	Pedroso	CUB	17.12.72	1		Salamanca	18 Jul 95
8.71i		Sebastian	Bayer (10)	GER	11.6.86	1	EI	Torino	8 Mar 09
8.70	0.8		Myricks			1	NC	Houston	17 Jun 89
8.70	0.7		Powell			1		Salamanca	27 Jul 93
8.70	1.6		Pedroso			1	WCh	Göteborg	12 Aug 95
8.68	1.0		Lewis			Q	OG	Barcelona	5 Aug 92
8.68	1.6		Pedroso			1		Lisboa	17 Jun 95
8.67	0.4		Lewis			1	WCh	Roma	5 Sep 87
8.67	-0.7		Lewis			1	OG	Barcelona	6 Aug 92
8.66	0.8		Lewis			*	MSR	Walnut	26 Apr 87
8.66	1.0		Myricks			1		Tokyo	23 Sep 87
8.66	0.9		Powell			1	BNP	Villeneuve d'Ascq	29 Jun 90
8.66A	1.4		Lewis			*		Sestriere	31 Jul 94
8.66	0.3		Pedroso			1		Linz	22 Aug 95
8.66	1.6	Loúis	Tsátoumas	GRE	12.2.82	1		Kalamáta	2 Jun 07
		(31/11)							
8.63	0.5	Kareem	Streete-Thompson	CAY/USA	30.3.73	1	GP II	Linz	4 Jul 94
8.62	0.7	James	Beckford	JAM	9.1.75	1		Orlando	5 Apr 97
8.59i		Miguel	Pate	USA	13.6.79	1	NC	New York	1 Mar 02
8.56i	–	Yago	Lamela	ESP	24.7.77	2	WI	Maebashi	7 Mar 99
8.56	0.2	Aleksandr	Menkov	RUS	7.12.90	1	WCh	Moskva	16 Aug 13
8.54	0.9	Lutz	Dombrowski	GDR	25.6.59	1	OG	Moskva	28 Jul 80
8.54	1.7	Mitchell	Watt	AUS	25.3.88	1	DNG	Stockholm	29 Jul 11
8.53	1.2	Jaime	Jefferson	CUB	17.1.62	1	Barr	La Habana	12 May 90
8.52	0.7	Savanté	Stringfellow	USA	6.11.78	1	NC	Stanford	21 Jun 02
		(20)							
8.51	1.7	Roland	McGhee	USA	15.10.71	2		São Paulo	14 May 95
8.50	0.2	Llewellyn	Starks	USA	10.2.67	2		Rhede	7 Jul 91
8.50	1.3	Godfrey Khotso	Mokoena	RSA	6.3.85	2	GP	Madrid	4 Jul 09
8.49	2.0	Melvin	Lister	USA	29.8.77	1	SEC	Baton Rouge	13 May 00
8.49	0.6	Jai	Taurima	AUS	26.6.72	2	OG	Sydney	28 Sep 00
8.48	0.8	Joe	Greene	USA	17.2.67	3		São Paulo	14 May 95
8.48	0.6	Mohamed Salim	Al-Khuwalidi	KSA	19.6.81	1		Sotteville-lès-Rouen	2 Jul 06
8.47	1.9	Kevin	Dilworth	USA	14.2.74	1		Abilene	9 May 96
8.47	0.9	John	Moffitt	USA	12.12.80	2	OG	Athína	26 Aug 04
8.47	-0.2	Andrew	Howe	ITA	12.5.85	2	WCh	Osaka	30 Aug 07
		(30)							
8.47	1.6	Christian	Reif	GER	24.10.84	1	EC	Barcelona	1 Aug 10
8.46	1.2	Leonid	Voloshin	RUS	30.3.66	1	NC	Tallinn	5 Jul 88
8.46	1.6	Mike	Conley	USA	5.10.62	2		Springfield	4 May 96
8.46	1.8	Cheikh Tidiane	Touré	SEN/FRA	25.1.70	1		Bad Langensalza	15 Jun 97
8.46	0.3	Ibrahin	Camejo	CUB	28.6.82	1		Bilbao	21 Jun 08
8.46	1.3	Luis	Rivera	MEX	21.6.87	1	WUG	Kazan	12 Jul 13 8.45

Mark	Wind	Name		Nat	Born	Pos	Meet	Venue	Date
2.0	Nenad	Stekic	YUG	7.3.51		1	PO	Montreal	25 Jul 75
8.44	1.7	Eric	Metcalf	USA	23.1.68	1	NC	Tampa	17 Jun 88
8.43	0.8	Jason	Grimes	USA	10.9.59	*	NC	Indianapolis	16 Jun 85
8.43	1.8	Giovanni	Evangelisti	ITA	11.9.61	1		San Giovanni Valdarno	16 May 87
		(40)							
8.43i	–	Stanislav	Tarasenko	RUS	23.7.66	1		Moskva	26 Jan 94
8.43	0.1	Luis Felipe	Méliz	CUB/ESP	11.8.79	2	OD	Jena	3 Jun 00
8.43	-0.2	Ignisious	Gaisah	GHA/NED	20.6.83	2	GGala	Roma	14 Jul 06
8.42	0.4	Salim	Sdiri	FRA	26.10.78	1		Pierre-Bénite	12 Jun 09
8.41	1.5	Craig	Hepburn	BAH	10.12.69	1	NC	Nassau	17 Jun 93
8.41i	–	Kirill	Sosunov	RUS	1.11.75	2	WI	Paris (B)	8 Mar 97
8.40	1.4	Douglas de	Souza	BRA	6.8.72	1		São Paulo	15 Feb 95
8.40	0.4	Robert	Howard	USA	26.11.75	1	SEC	Auburn	17 May 97
8.40	2.0	Gregor	Cankar	SLO	25.1.75	1		Celje	18 May 97
8.40	0.0		Lao Jianfeng	CHN	24.5.75	1	NC	Zhaoqing	28 May 97
8.40	1.0	Yahya	Berrabah	MAR	13.10.81	1	Franc	Beirut	2 Oct 09
8.40	0.5	Fabrice	Lapierre	AUS	17.10.83	1		Nuoro	14 Jul 10
8.40	0.0	Ngonidzashe	Makusha	ZIM	11.3.87	1	NCAA	Des Moines	9 Jun 11
		(53)	100th man 8.32, 200th 8.22, 300th 8.17, 400th 8.11, 500th 8.08						

Best at low altitude: 8.61 1.3 Emmiyan 1 GWG Moskva 6 Jul 86   8.58 1.8 Walder 1 Springfield 4 May 86

Wind-assisted marks performances to 8.70, performers to 8.42

Mark	Wind	Name		Nat	Born	Pos	Meet	Venue	Date
8.99A	4.4	Mike	Powell	USA	10.11.63	1		Sestriere	21 Jul 92
8.96A	1.2+	Iván	Pedroso	CUB	17.12.72	1		Sestriere	29 Jul 95
8.95A	3.9		Powell			1		Sestriere	31 Jul 94
8.91	2.9	Carl	Lewis	USA	1.7.61	2	WCh	Tokyo	30 Aug 91
8.90	3.7		Powell			1	S&W	Modesto	16 May 92
8.79	3.0		Pedroso			1	Barr	La Habana	21 May 92
8.78	3.1	Fabrice	Lapierre	AUS	17.10.83	1	NC	Perth	18 Apr 10
8.77	3.9		Lewis			1	Pepsi	Los Angeles (Ww)	18 May 85
8.77	3.4		Lewis			1	MSR	Walnut	26 Apr 87
8.73	4.6		Lewis			Q	NC	Sacramento	19 Jun 81
8.73	3.2		Lewis			Q	NC	Indianapolis	17 Jun 83
8.73A	2.6		Powell			1		Sestriere	31 Jul 91
8.73	4.8		Pedroso			1		Madrid	20 Jun 95
8.72	2.2		Lewis			1	NYG	New York	24 May 92
8.72A	3.9		Lewis			2		Sestriere	31 Jul 94
8.70	2.5		Pedroso			1		Padova	16 Jul 95
8.68	4.9	James	Beckford	JAM	9.1.75	1	JUCO	Odessa, Tx	19 May 95
8.66A	4.0	Joe	Greene	USA	17.2.67	2		Sestriere	21 Jul 92
8.64	3.5	Kareem	Streete-Thompson	CAY/USA	30.3.73	2	NC	Knoxville	18 Jun 94
8.63	3.9	Mike	Conley	USA	5.10.62	2	NC	Eugene	20 Jun 86
8.57	5.2	Jason	Grimes	USA	10.9.59	1	vFRG,AFR	Durham	27 Jun 82
8.53	4.9	Kevin	Dilworth	USA	14.2.74	1		Fort-de-France	27 Apr 02
8.51	3.7	Ignisious	Gaisah	GHA	20.6.83	1	AfCh	Bambous	9 Aug 06
8.49	2.6	Ralph	Boston	USA	9.5.39	1	OT	Los Angeles	12 Sep 64
8.49	4.5	Stanislav	Tarasenko	RUS	23.7.66	2		Madrid	20 Jun 95
8.48	2.8	Kirill	Sosunov	RUS	1.11.75	1		Oristano	18 Sep 95
8.48	3.4	Peter	Burge	AUS	3.7.74	1		Gold Coast (RB)	10 Sep 00
8.48	2.1	Brian	Johnson	USA	25.3.80	1	Conseil	Fort-de-France	8 May 08
8.46	3.4	Randy	Williams	USA	23.8.53	1		Eugene	18 May 73
8.46		Vernon	George	USA	6.10.64	1		Houston	21 May 89
8.44		Keith	Talley	USA	28.1.64	Q		Odessa, Tx	16 May 85
8.42		Anthony	Bailous	USA	6.4.65	Q		Odessa, Tx	16 May 85
8.42A	4.5	Milan	Gombala	CZE	29.1.68	3		Sestriere	21 Jul 92

Exhibition: 8.46 Yuriy Naumkin RUS 4.11.68 1   Iglesias   6 Sep 96

Best outdoors

8.56 1.3 Lamela 1   Torino 24 Jun 99   8.49 1.6 Bayer 1 NC Ulm   4 Jul 09
8.46A 0.0 Pate 1 Cd. de México 3 May 03 and 8.45 1.5 2 NC Stanford 21 Jun 02, 8.48w 5.6 1 Fort Worth 21 Apr 01

Ancillary marks – other marks during series (to 8.67/8.70w)

8.84	1.7	Lewis	30 Aug 87	8.89Aw	2.4	Pedroso	29 Jul 95	8.75w	2.1	Lewis	16 Aug 87
8.71	0.6	Lewis	19 Jun 83	8.84Aw	3.8	Powell	21 Jul 92	8.75Aw	3.4	Powell	21 Jul 92
8.68	0.3	Lewis	18 Jul 88	8.83w	2.3	Lewis	30 Aug 91	8.73w	2.4	Lewis	18 May 85
8.68	0.0	Lewis	30 Aug 91	8.80Aw	4.0	Powell	21 Jul 92	8.73w		Powell	16 May 92
8.67	-0.2	Lewis	5 Sep 87	8.78Aw		Powell	21 Jul 92	8.71Aw		Powell	31 Jul 91

TRIPLE JUMP

Mark	Wind	Name		Nat	Born	Pos	Meet	Venue	Date
18.29	WR 1.3	Jonathan	Edwards	GBR	10.5.66	1	WCh	Göteborg	7 Aug 95
18.09	-0.4	Kenny	Harrison	USA	13.2.65	1	OG	Atlanta	27 Jul 96
18.04	0.3	Teddy	Tamgho	FRA	15.6.89	1	WCh	Moskva	18 Aug 13
18.01	0.4		Edwards			1	Bisl	Oslo	9 Jul 98
18.00	1.3		Edwards			1	McD	London (CP)	27 Aug 95

Mark	Wind	Name		Nat	Born	Pos	Meet	Venue	Date
17.99	0.5		Edwards			1	EC	Budapest	23 Aug 98
17.98	WR 1.8		Edwards			1		Salamanca	18 Jul 95
17.98	1.2		Tamgho			1	DL	New York	12 Jun 10
17.97	WR 1.5	Willie	Banks	USA	11.3.56	1	TAC	Indianapolis	16 Jun 85
17.96	0.1	Christian	Taylor	USA	18.6.90	1	WCh	Daegu	4 Sep 11
17.93	1.6		Harrison			1	DNG	Stockholm	2 Jul 90
17.92	1.6	Khristo	Markov	BUL	27.1.65	1	WCh	Roma	31 Aug 87
17.92	1.9	James	Beckford	JAM	9.1.75	1	JUCO	Odessa, TX	20 May 95
17.92i	WIR -		Tamgho			1	EI	Paris (Bercy)	6 Mar 11
17.92	0.7		Edwards			1	WCh	Edmonton	6 Aug 01
17.91i	WIR -		Tamgho			1	NC	Aubière	20 Feb 11
17.91	1.4		Tamgho			1	Athl	Lausanne	30 Jun 11
17.90	1.0	Vladimir	Inozemtsev	UKR	25.5.64	1	PTS	Bratislava	20 Jun 90
17.90	0.4	Jadel	Gregório	BRA	16.9.80	1	GP	Belém	20 May 07
17.90i			Tamgho			1	WI	Doha	14 Mar 10
17.89A	WR 0.0	João Carlos	de Oliveira (10)	BRA	28.5.54	1	PAm	Ciudad de México	15 Oct 75
17.88	0.9		Edwards			2	OG	Atlanta	27 Jul 96
17.87	1.7	Mike	Conley	USA	5.10.62	1	NC	San José	27 Jun 87
17.86	1.3	Charles	Simpkins	USA	19.10.63	1	WUG	Kobe	2 Sep 85
17.86	0.3		Conley			1	WCh	Stuttgart	16 Aug 93
17.86	0.7		Edwards			1	CG	Manchester	28 Jul 02
17.85	0.9	Yoelbi	Quesada	CUB	4.8.73	1	WCh	Athína	8 Aug 97
17.84	0.7		Conley			1		Bad Cannstatt	4 Jul 93
17.83i	WIR -	Aliecer	Urrutia	CUB	22.9.74	1		Sindelfingen	1 Mar 97
17.83i	WIR -	Christian	Olsson (30/15)	SWE	25.1.80	1	WI	Budapest	7 Mar 04
17.81	1.0	Marian	Oprea	ROU	6.6.82	1	Athl	Lausanne	5 Jul 05
17.81	0.1	Phillips	Idowu	GBR	30.12.78	1	EC	Barcelona	29 Jul 10
17.78	1.0	Nikolay	Musiyenko	UKR	16.12.59	1	Znam	Leningrad	7 Jun 86
17.78	0.6	Lázaro	Betancourt ¶	CUB	18.3.63	1	Barr	La Habana	15 Jun 86
17.78	0.8	Melvin	Lister (20)	USA	29.8.77	1	NC/OT	Sacramento	17 Jul 04
17.77	1.0	Aleksandr	Kovalenko	RUS	8.5.63	1	NC	Bryansk	18 Jul 87
17.77i	-	Leonid	Voloshin	RUS	30.3.66	1		Grenoble	6 Feb 94
17.75	0.3	Oleg	Protsenko	RUS	11.8.63	1	Znam	Moskva	10 Jun 90
17.74	1.4	Nelson	Évora	POR	20.4.84	1	WCh	Osaka	27 Aug 07
17.73i		Walter	Davis	USA	2.7.79	1	WI	Moskva	12 Mar 06
17.73i	-	Fabrizio	Donato	ITA	14.8.76	2	EI	Paris (Bercy)	6 Mar 11
17.72i		Brian	Wellman	BER	8.9.67	1	WI	Barcelona	12 Mar 95
17.72	1.3	Sheryf	El-Sheryf	UKR	2.1.89	1	EU23	Ostrava	17 Jul 11
17.70i	-	Will	Claye	USA	13.6.91	1	WI	Istanbul	11 Mar 12
17.70i		Daniele	Greco (30)	ITA	1.3.89	1	EI	Göteborg	2 Mar 13
17.69	1.5	Igor	Lapshin	BLR	8.8.63	1		Stayki	31 Jul 88
17.69i		Yoandri	Betanzos	CUB	15.2.82	2	WI	Doha	14 Mar 10
17.69	2.0	Pedro Pablo	Pichardo	CUB	30.6.93	1	Barr	La Habana	4 Jun 13
17.68	0.4	Danil	Burkenya	RUS	20.7.78	1	NC	Tula	31 Jul 04
17.68A	1.6	Alexis	Copello	CUB	12.8.85	1		Ávila	17 Jul 11
17.66	1.7	Ralf	Jaros	GER	13.12.65	1	ECp	Frankfurt-am-Main	30 Jun 91
17.65	1.0	Aleksandr	Yakovlev	UKR	8.9.57	1	Znam	Moskva	6 Jun 87
17.65	0.8	Denis	Kapustin	RUS	5.10.70	2	Bisl	Oslo	9 Jul 98
17.64	1.4	Nathan	Douglas	GBR	4.12.82	1	NC	Manchester (SC)	10 Jul 05
17.63	0.9	Kenta	Bell	USA	16.3.77	1c2	MSR	Walnut	21 Apr 02
			(40)						
17.62i	-	Yoel	García	CUB	25.11.73	2		Sindelfingen	1 Mar 97
17.62	-0.2	Arne David	Girat	CUB	26.8.84	3	ALBA	La Habana	25 Apr 09
17.60	0.6	Vladimir	Plekhanov	RUS	11.4.58	2	NC	Leningrad	4 Aug 85
17.59i	-	Pierre	Camara	FRA	10.9.65	1	WI	Toronto	13 Mar 93
17.59	0.3	Vasiliy	Sokov	RUS	7.4.68	1	NC	Moskva	19 Jun 93
17.59	0.8	Charles	Friedek	GER	26.8.71	1		Hamburg	23 Jul 97
17.59	0.9	Leevan	Sands	BAH	16.8.81	3	OG	Beijing	21 Aug 08
17.59	0.0		Li Yanxi	CHN	26.6.84	1	NG	Jinan	26 Oct 09
17.58	1.5	Oleg	Sakirkin	KZK	23.1.66	2	NC	Gorkiy	23 Jul 89
17.58	1.6	Aarik	Wilson (50)	USA	25.10.82	1	LGP	London (CP)	3 Aug 07

Wind-assisted marks – performances to 17.86, performers to 17.59

Mark	Wind	Name		Nat	Born	Pos	Meet	Venue	Date
18.43	2.4	Jonathan	Edwards	GBR	10.5.66	1	ECp	Villeneuve d'Ascq	25 Jun 95
18.20	5.2	Willie	Banks	USA	11.3.56	1	NC/OT	Indianapolis	16 Jul 88
18.17	2.1	Mike	Conley	USA	5.10.62	1	OG	Barcelona	3 Aug 92
18.08	2.5		Edwards			1	BrGP	Sheffield	23 Jul 95

100th man 17.38, 200th 17.18, 300th 17.01, 400th 16.87, 500th 16.76

Mark	Wind	Name		Nat	Born	Pos	Meet	Venue	Date
18.03	2.9		Edwards			1	GhG	Gateshead	2 Jul 9!
18.01	3.7		Harrison			1	NC	Atlanta	15 Jun 9(
17.97	7.5	Yoelbi	Quesada	CUB	4.8.73	1		Madrid	20 Jun 9!
17.93	5.2	Charles	Simpkins	USA	19.10.63	2	NC/OT	Indianapolis	16 Jul 8£
17.92	3.4	Christian	Olsson	SWE	25.1.80	1	GP	Gateshead	13 Jul 0:
17.91	3.2		Simpkins			1	NC	Eugene	21 Jun 8€
17.86	3.9		Simpkins			1	NC/OT	New Orleans	21 Jun 9:
17.86	5.7	Denis	Kapustin	RUS	5.10.70	1		Sevilla	5 Jun 9₄
17.82	2.5	Nelson	Évora	POR	20.4.84	1	NC	Seixal	26 Jul 0£
17.81	4.6	Keith	Connor	GBR	16.9.57	1	CG	Brisbane	9 Oct 8:
17.76A	2.2	Kenta	Bell	USA	16.3.77	1		El Paso	10 Apr 0₄
17.75		Gennadiy	Valyukevich	BLR	1.6.58	1		Uzhgorod	27 Apr 8€
17.75	7.1	Brian	Wellman	BER	8.9.67	2		Madrid	20 Jun 9!
17.73	4.1	Vasiliy	Sokov	RUS	7.4.68	1		Riga	3 Jun 8£
17.69	3.9	Alexis	Copello	CUB	12.8.85	1	ALBA	La Habana	25 Apr 0£
17.67	3.4	Daniele	Greco	ITA	1.3.89	1	NC	Bressanone	8 Jul 1:
17.63	4.3	Robert	Cannon	USA		1	NC/OT	Indianapolis	16 Jul 8£
17.59	2.1	Jerome	Romain	DMA/FRA	12.6.71	3	WCh	Göteborg	7 Aug 9!

Best outdoor marks for athletes with indoor bests | 17.65 1.4 Betanzos 2 ALBA La Habana 25 Apr 09

17.79	1.4	Olsson	1	OG	Athína	22 Aug 04		17.67w	5.4	1		Bilbao	1 Jul 06
17.75	1.0	Voloshin	1	WCh	Tokyo	26 Aug 91	17.62A0.1	Wellman	1		El Paso	15 Apr 95
17.71	-0.7	Davis	1	NC	Indianapolis	25 Jun 06	17.62	0.6	Claye	2	OG	London (OS)	9 Aug 12
17.70	1.7	Urrutia	1	GP II	Sevilla	6 Jun 96	17.60	1.9	Donato	1		Milano	7 Jun 00

Low altitude best: 17.65 0.1 Copello 1 Barr La Habana 30 May 09 | 17.63w 2.8 1 EC Helsinki 30 Jun 12

Ancillary marks – other marks during series (to 17.78/17.84w)

									18.06w	4.9	Banks	16 Jul 88
18.16 WR	1.3	Edwards	7 Aug 95	17.84	1.7	Tamgho	12 Jun 10	17.90w	2.5	Edwards	25 Jun 95
17.99	0.1	Harrison	27 Jul 96	18.39w	3.7	Edwards	25 Jun 95	17.84w	2.1	Edwards	23 Aug 98

SHOT

Mark		Name		Nat	Born	Pos	Meet	Venue	Date
23.12 WR		Randy	Barnes ¶	USA	16.6.66	1		Los Angeles (Ww)	20 May 9(
23.10			Barnes			1	Jenner	San José	26 May 9(
23.06 WR		Ulf	Timmermann	GDR	1.11.62	1	Veniz	Haniá	22 May 88
22.91 WR		Alessandro	Andrei	ITA	3.1.59	1		Viareggio	12 Aug 87
22.86		Brian	Oldfield	USA	1.6.45	1	ITA	El Paso	10 May 7£
22.75		Werner	Günthör	SUI	1.6.61	1		Bern	23 Aug 88
22.67		Kevin	Toth ¶	USA	29.12.67	1	KansR	Lawrence	19 Apr 0:
22.66i			Barnes			1	Sunkist	Los Angeles	20 Jan 8£
22.64 WR		Udo	Beyer	GDR	9.8.55	1		Berlin	20 Aug 8€
22.62 WR			Timmermann			1		Berlin	22 Sep 8£
22.61			Timmermann			1		Potsdam	8 Sep 88
22.60			Timmermann			1	vURS	Tallinn	21 Jun 8€
22.56			Timmermann			1		Berlin	13 Sep 88
22.55i			Timmermann			1	NC	Senftenberg	11 Feb 8£
22.54		Christian	Cantwell	USA	30.9.80	1	GP II	Gresham	5 Jun 04
22.52		John	Brenner	USA	4.1.61	1	MSR	Walnut	26 Apr 87
22.51			Timmermann			1		Erfurt	1 Jun 8€
22.51		Adam	Nelson (10)	USA	7.7.75	1		Gresham	18 May 0:
22.47			Timmermann			1		Dresden	17 Aug 8€
22.47			Günthör			1	WG	Helsinki	2 Jul 87
22.47			Timmermann			1	OG	Seoul	23 Sep 88
22.45			Oldfield			1	ITA	El Paso	22 May 7€
22.45			Cantwell			1	GP	Gateshead	11 Jun 0€
22.43			Günthör			1	v3-N	Lüdenscheid	18 Jun 87
22.43		Reese	Hoffa	USA	8.10.77	1	LGP	London (CP)	3 Aug 07
22.42			Barnes			1	WK	Zürich	17 Aug 88
22.41			Cantwell			1	Pre	Eugene	3 Jul 1(
22.40			Barnes			1		Rüdlingen	13 Jul 9€
22.40i			Nelson			1		Fayetteville	15 Feb 08
22.39			Barnes			2	OG	Seoul	23 Sep 88
		(30/11)							
22.28		Ryan	Whiting	USA	24.11.86	1	DL	Doha	10 May 1:
22.24		Sergey	Smirnov	RUS	17.9.60	2	vGDR	Tallinn	21 Jun 8€
22.21		Dylan	Armstrong	CAN	15.1.81	1	NC	Calgary	25 Jun 11
22.20		John	Godina	USA	31.5.72	1		Carson	22 May 05
22.10		Sergey	Gavryushin	RUS	27.6.59	1		Tbilisi	31 Aug 8€
22.10		Cory	Martin	USA	22.5.85	1		Tucson	22 May 1(
22.10		Andrey	Mikhnevich ¶	BLR	12.7.76	1		Minsk	11 Aug 11
22.09		Sergey	Kasnauskas	BLR	20.4.61	1		Stayki	23 Aug 84
22.09i		Mika	Halvari	FIN	13.2.70	1		Tampere	7 Feb 00
		(20)							

Mark	Wind	Name		Nat	Born	Pos	Meet	Venue	Date
22.02i		George	Woods	USA	11.2.43	1	LAT	Inglewood	8 Feb 74
22.02		Dave	Laut	USA	21.12.56	1		Koblenz	25 Aug 82
22.00	WR	Aleksandr	Baryshnikov	RUS	11.11.48	1	vFRA	Colombes	10 Jul 76
21.98		Gregg	Tafralis ¶	USA	9.4.58	1		Los Gatos	13 Jun 92
21.97		Janus	Robberts	RSA	10.3.79	1	NCAA	Eugene	2 Jun 01
21.96		Mikhail	Kostin	RUS	10.5.59	1		Vitebsk	20 Jul 86
21.95		Tomasz	Majewski	POL	30.8.81	1	DNG	Stockholm	30 Jul 09
21.93		Remigius	Machura ¶	CZE	3.7.60	1		Praha	23 Aug 87
21.92		Carl	Myerscough ¶	GBR	21.10.79	1	NCAA	Sacramento	13 Jun 03
21.88i		David	Storl	GER	27.7.90	2	WI	Istanbul	9 Mar 12
	(30)								
21.87		C.J.	Hunter ¶	USA	14.12.68	2	NC	Sacramento	15 Jul 00
21.85	WR	Terry	Albritton	USA	14.1.55	1		Honolulu	21 Feb 76
21.83i		Aleksandr	Bagach ¶	UKR	21.11.66	1		Brovary	21 Feb 99
21.82	WR	Al	Feuerbach	USA	14.1.48	1		San José	5 May 73
21.82		Andy	Bloom	USA	11.8.73	1	GPF	Doha	5 Oct 00
21.81		Yuriy	Bilonog ¶	UKR	9.3.74	1	NC	Kiev	3 Jul 03
21.78	WR	Randy	Matson	USA	5.3.45	1		College Station	22 Apr 67
21.78		Dan	Taylor	USA	12.5.82	1		Tucson	23 May 09
21.77i		Mike	Stulce ¶	USA	21.7.69	1	v GBR	Birmingham	13 Feb 93
21.77		Dragan	Peric	YUG	8.5.64	1		Bar	25 Apr 98
	(40)								
21.76		Michael	Carter	USA	29.10.60	2	NCAA	Eugene	2 Jun 84
21.74		Janis	Bojars	LAT	12.5.56	1		Riga	14 Jul 84
21.73		Augie	Wolf ¶	USA	3.9.61	1		Leverkusen	12 Apr 84
21.69		Reijo	Ståhlberg	FIN	21.9.52	1	WCR	Fresno	5 May 79
21.68		Geoff	Capes	GBR	23.8.49	1	4-N	Cwmbrân	18 May 80
21.68		Edward	Sarul	POL	16.11.58	1		Sopot	31 Jul 83
21.67		Hartmut	Briesenick	GDR	17.3.49	1		Potsdam	1 Sep 73
21.63i		Joachim	Olsen	DEN	31.5.77	1		Tallinn	25 Feb 04
21.63		Maris	Urtans	LAT	9.2.81	1	ET-2	Beograd	19 Jun 10
21.62		Rutger	Smith	NED	9.7.81	1		Leiden	10 Jun 06

(50) 100th man 21.12, 200th 20.70, 300th 20.36, 400th 20.06, 500th 19.84

Not recognised by GDR authorities

22.11		Rolf	Oesterreich	GDR	24.8.49	1		Zschopau	12 Sep 76

Drugs disqualification

22.84			Barnes			1		Malmö	7 Aug 90
21.82		Mike	Stulce ¶	USA	21.7.69	1		Brenham	9 May 90

Best outdoor marks for athletes with lifetime bests indoors

21.97	Whiting	1	NCAA	Eugene	12 Jun 10	21.61	Olsen	1		Köbenhavn	13 Jun 07
21.63	Woods	2	CalR	Modesto	22 May 76	21.70	Stulce ¶	1	OG	Barcelona	31 Jul 92
21.86	Storl	2	OG	London (OS)	3 Aug 12						

Ancillary marks – other marks during series (to 22.45)

22.84 WR	Andrei	12 Aug 87	22.72 WR	Andrei	12 Aug 87	22.55	Barnes	20 May 90
22.76	Barnes	20 May 90	22.70	Günthör	23 Aug 88	22.49	Nelson	18 May 02
22.74	Andrei	12 Aug 87	22.58	Beyer	20 Aug 86	22.45	Timmermann	22 May 88

DISCUS

Mark	Wind	Name		Nat	Born	Pos	Meet	Venue	Date
74.08	WR	Jürgen	Schult	GDR	11.5.60	1		Neubrandenburg	6 Jun 86
73.88		Virgilijus	Alekna	LTU	13.2.72	1	NC	Kaunas	3 Aug 00
73.38		Gerd	Kanter	EST	6.5.79	1		Helsingborg	4 Sep 06
72.02			Kanter			1eA		Salinas	3 May 07
71.88			Kanter			1eA		Salinas	8 May 08
71.86	WR	Yuriy	Dumchev	RUS	5.8.58	1		Moskva	29 May 83
71.84		Piotr	Malachowski	POL	7.6.83	1	FBK	Hengelo	8 Jun 13
71.70		Róbert	Fazekas ¶	HUN	18.8.75	1		Szombathely	14 Jul 02
71.64			Kanter			1		Kohila	25 Jun 09
71.56			Alekna			1		Kaunas	25 Jul 07
71.50		Lars	Riedel	GER	28.6.67	1		Wiesbaden	3 May 97
71.45			Kanter			1		Chula Vista	29 Apr 10
71.32		Ben	Plucknett ¶	USA	13.4.54	1	Pre	Eugene	4 Jun 83
71.26		John	Powell	USA	25.6.47	1	NC	San José	9 Jun 84
71.26		Rickard	Bruch	SWE	2.7.46	1		Malmö	15 Nov 84
71.26		Imrich	Bugár (10)	CZE	14.4.55	1	Jenner	San José	25 May 85
71.25			Fazekas			1	WCp	Madrid (C)	21 Sep 02
71.25			Alekna			1	Danek	Turnov	20 May 08
71.18		Art	Burns	USA	19.7.54	1		San José	19 Jul 83
71.16	WR	Wolfgang	Schmidt	GDR	16.1.54	1		Berlin	9 Aug 78
71.14			Plucknett			1		Berkeley	12 Jun 83
71.14		Anthony	Washington	USA	16.1.66	1eA		Salinas	22 May 96

Mark	Wind	Name		Nat	Born	Pos	Meet	Venue	Date
71.12			Alekna			1	WK	Zürich	11 Aug 00
71.08			Alekna			1		Réthimno	21 Jul 06
71.06		Luis Mariano	Delís ¶	CUB	12.12.57	1	Barr	La Habana	21 May 83
71.06			Riedel			1	WK	Zürich	14 Aug 96
71.00			Bruch			1		Malmö	14 Oct 84
70.99			Alekna			1		Stellenbosch	30 Mar 01
70.98		Mac	Wilkins	USA	15.11.50	1	WG	Helsinki	9 Jul 80
70.98			Burns			1	Pre	Eugene	21 Jul 84
		(30/16)							
70.82		Aleksander	Tammert	EST	2.2.73	1		Denton	15 Apr 06
70.66		Robert	Harting	GER	18.10.84	1	Danek	Turnov	22 May 12
70.54		Dmitriy	Shevchenko ¶	RUS	13.5.68	1		Krasnodar	7 May 02
70.38	WRU	Jay	Silvester	USA	27.8.37	1		Lancaster	16 May 71
		(20)							
70.32		Frantz	Kruger	RSA/FIN	22.5.75	1		Salon-de-Provence	26 May 02
70.06		Romas	Ubartas ¶	LTU	26.5.60	1		Smalininkay	8 May 88
70.00		Juan	Martínez ¶	CUB	17.5.58	2	Barr	La Habana	21 May 83
69.95		Zoltán	Kövágó	HUN	10.4.79	1		Salon-de-Provence	25 May 06
69.91		John	Godina	USA	31.5.72	1		Salinas	19 May 98
69.90		Jason	Young	USA	27.5.81	1		Lubbock	26 Mar 10
69.70		Géjza	Valent	CZE	3.10.53	2		Nitra	26 Aug 84
69.62		Knut	Hjeltnes ¶	NOR	8.12.51	2	Jen	San José	25 May 85
69.62		Timo	Tompuri	FIN	9.6.69	1		Helsingborg	8 Jul 01
69.50		Mario	Pestano	ESP	8.4.78	1	NC	Santa Cruz de Tenerife	27 Jul 08
		(30)							
69.46		Al	Oerter	USA	19.9.36	1	TFA	Wichita	31 May 80
69.44		Georgiy	Kolnootchenko	BLR	7.5.59	1	vUSA	Indianapolis	3 Jul 82
69.40		Art	Swarts ¶	USA	14.2.45	1		Scotch Plains	8 Dec 79
69.36		Mike	Buncic	USA	25.7.62	1		Fresno	6 Apr 91
69.32		Ehsan	Hadadi	IRI	21.1.85	1		Tallinn	3 Jun 08
69.28		Vladimir	Dubrovshchik	BLR	7.1.72	1	NC	Stayki	3 Jun 00
69.26		Ken	Stadel	USA	19.2.52	2	AAU	Walnut	16 Jun 79
68.94		Adam	Setliff	USA	15.12.69	1		Atascadero	25 Jul 01
68.91		Ian	Waltz	USA	15.4.77	1		Salinas	24 May 06
68.90		Jean-Claude	Retel	FRA	11.2.68	1		Salon-de-Provence	17 Jul 02
		(40)							
68.88		Vladimir	Zinchenko	UKR	25.7.59	1		Dnepropetrovsk	16 Jul 88
68.76		Jarred	Rome	USA	21.12.76	2cA		Chula Vista	6 Aug 11
68.64		Dmitriy	Kovtsun ¶	UKR	29.9.55	1		Riga	6 Jul 84
68.58		Attila	Horváth	HUN	28.7.67	1		Budapest	24 Jun 94
68.52		Igor	Duginyets	UKR	20.5.56	1	NC	Kyiv	21 Aug 82
68.50		Armin	Lemme	GDR	28.10.55	1	vUSA	Karl-Marx-Stadt	10 Jul 82
68.49A		Casey	Malone	USA	6.4.77	1		Fort Collins	20 Jun 09
68.48	WR	John	van Reenen	RSA	26.3.47	1		Stellenbosch	14 Mar 75
68.44		Vaclovas	Kidykas	LTU	17.10.61	1		Sochi	1 Jun 88
68.33		Martin	Wierig	GER	10.6.87	1		Schönebeck	26 Jul 12
		(50)	100th man 66.98, 200th 65.16, 300th 64.18, 400th 62.96, 500th 61.79						

Subsequent to or at drugs disqualification   ! recognised as US record

72.34!		Ben	Plucknett ¶	USA	13.4.54	(1)	DNG	Stockholm	7 Jul 81
71.20			Plucknett			(1)	CalR	Modesto	16 May 81
70.84		Kamy	Keshmiri ¶	USA	23.1.69	(1)		Salinas	27 May 92

Sloping ground

72.08		John	Powell	USA	25.6.47	1		Klagshamn	11 Sep 87
69.80		Stefan	Fernholm	SWE	2.7.59	1		Klagshamn	13 Aug 87
69.44		Adam	Setliff	USA	15.12.69	1		La Jolla	21 Jul 01
68.46		Andy	Bloom	USA	11.8.73	2cA		La Jolla	25 Mar 00

Ancillary marks – other marks during series (to 70.96)
72.35 Alekna 3 Aug 00   72.30 Kanter 4 Sep 06   71.08 Plucknett 4 Jun 83

HAMMER

Mark	Wind	Name		Nat	Born	Pos	Meet	Venue	Date
86.74	WR	Yuriy	Sedykh	RUS	11.6.55	1	EC	Stuttgart	30 Aug 86
86.73		Ivan	Tikhon ¶	BLR	24.7.76	1	NC	Brest	3 Jul 05
86.66	WR		Sedykh			1	vGDR	Tallinn	22 Jun 86
86.34	WR		Sedykh			1		Cork	3 Jul 84
86.04		Sergey	Litvinov	RUS	23.1.58	1	OD	Dresden	3 Jul 86
85.74			Litvinov			2	EC	Stuttgart	30 Aug 86
85.68			Sedykh			1	BGP	Budapest	11 Aug 86
85.60			Sedykh			1	PTG	London (CP)	13 Jul 84
85.60			Sedykh			1	Drz	Moskva	17 Aug 84
85.20			Litvinov			2		Cork	3 Jul 84
85.14			Litvinov			1	PTG	London	11 Jul 86

Mark	Wind	Name		Nat	Born	Pos	Meet	Venue	Date
85.14			Sedykh			1	Kuts	Moskva	4 Sep 88
85.02			Sedykh			1	BGP	Budapest	20 Aug 84
84.92			Sedykh			2	OD	Dresden	3 Jul 86
84.90		Vadim	Devyatovskiy ¶	BLR	20.3.77	1		Staiki	21 Jul 05
84.88			Litvinov			1	GP-GG	Roma	10 Sep 86
84.86		Koji	Murofushi	JPN	8.10.74	1	Odlozil	Praha	29 Jun 03
84.80			Litvinov			1	OG	Seoul	26 Sep 88
84.72			Sedykh			1	GWG	Moskva	9 Jul 86
84.64			Litvinov			2	GWG	Moskva	9 Jul 86
84.62		Igor	Astapkovich	BLR	4.1.63	1	Expo	Sevilla	6 Jun 92
84.60			Sedykh			1	8-N	Tokyo	14 Sep 84
84.58			Sedykh			1	Znam	Leningrad	8 Jun 86
84.51			Tikhon			1	NC	Grodno	9 Jul 08
84.48		Igor	Nikulin	RUS	14.8.60	1	Athl	Lausanne	12 Jul 90
84.46			Sedykh			1		Vladivostok	14 Sep 88
84.46			Tikhon			1		Minsk	7 May 04
84.40		Jüri	Tamm	EST	5.2.57	1		Banská Bystrica	9 Sep 84
84.36			Litvinov			2	vGDR	Tallinn	22 Jun 86
84.32			Tikhon			1		Staiki	8 Aug 03
		(30/8)							
84.19		Adrián	Annus ¶	HUN	28.6.73	1		Szombathely	10 Aug 03
83.68		Tibor	Gécsek ¶	HUN	22.9.64	1		Zalaegerszeg	19 Sep 98
		(10)							
83.46		Andrey	Abduvaliyev	TJK/UZB	30.6.66	1		Adler	26 May 90
83.43		Aleksey	Zagornyi	RUS	31.5.78	1		Adler	10 Feb 02
83.40 @		Ralf	Haber	GDR	18.8.62	1		Athína	16 May 88
	82.54					1		Potsdam	9 Sep 88
83.38		Szymon	Ziółkowski	POL	1.7.76	1	WCh	Edmonton	5 Aug 01
83.30		Olli-Pekka	Karjalainen	FIN	7.3.80	1		Lahti	14 Jul 04
83.04		Heinz	Weis	GER	14.7.63	1	NC	Frankfurt	29 Jun 97
83.00		Balázs	Kiss	HUN	21.3.72	1	GP II	Saint-Denis	4 Jun 98
82.78		Karsten	Kobs	GER	16.9.71	1		Dortmund	26 Jun 99
82.64		Günther	Rodehau	GDR	6.7.59	1		Dresden	3 Aug 85
82.62		Sergey	Kirmasov ¶	RUS	25.3.70	1		Bryansk	30 May 98
		(20)	@ competitive meeting but unsanctioned by GDR federation						
82.62		Andrey	Skvaruk	UKR	9.3.67	1		Koncha-Zaspa	27 Apr 02
82.58		Primoz	Kozmus	SLO	30.9.79	1		Celje	2 Sep 09
82.54		Vasiliy	Sidorenko	RUS	1.5.61	1		Krasnodar	13 May 92
82.52		Lance	Deal	USA	21.8.61	1	GPF	Milano	7 Sep 96
82.45		Krisztián	Pars	HUN	18.2.82	1		Celje	13 Sep 06
82.40		Plamen	Minev	BUL	28.4.65	1	NM	Plovdiv	1 Jun 91
82.38		Gilles	Dupray	FRA	2.1.70	1		Chelles	21 Jun 00
82.28		Ilya	Konovalov ¶	RUS	4.3.71	1	NC	Tula	10 Aug 03
82.27		Pawel	Fajdek	POL	4.6.89	2		Dubnica nad Váhom	21 Aug 13
82.24		Benjaminas	Viluckis	LIT	20.3.61	1		Klaipeda	24 Aug 86
		(30)							
82.24		Vyacheslav	Korovin	RUS	8.9.62	1		Chelyabinsk	20 Jun 87
82.23		Vladislav	Piskunov ¶	UKR	7.6.78	2		Koncha-Zaspa	27 Apr 02
82.22		Holger	Klose	GER	5.12.72	1		Dortmund	2 May 98
82.16		Vitaliy	Alisevich	BLR	15.6.67	1		Parnu	13 Jul 88
82.08		Ivan	Tanev	BUL	1.5.57	1	NC	Sofia	3 Sep 88
82.00		Sergey	Alay	BLR	11.6.65	1		Stayki	12 May 92
81.88		Jud	Logan ¶	USA	19.7.59	1		State College	22 Apr 88
81.81		Libor	Charfreitag	SVK	11.9.77	3	Odlozil	Praha	29 Jun 03
81.79		Christophe	Épalle	FRA	23.1.69	1		Clermont-Ferrand	30 Jun 00
81.79		Christoph	Sahner	FRG	23.9.63	1		Wemmetsweiler	11 Sep 88
		(40)							
81.70		Aleksandr	Seleznyov	RUS	25.1.63	2		Sochi	22 May 93
81.66		Aleksandr	Krykun	UKR	1.3.68	1		Kiev	29 May 04
81.64		Enrico	Sgrulletti	ITA	24.4.65	1		Ostia	9 Mar 97
81.56		Sergey	Gavrilov	RUS	22.5.70	1	Army	Rostov	16 Jun 96
81.56		Zsolt	Németh	HUN	9.11.71	1		Veszprém	14 Aug 99
81.52		Juha	Tiainen	FIN	5.12.55	1		Tampere	11 Jun 84
81.49		Valeriy	Svyatokho	BLR	20.7.81	1	NCp	Brest	27 May 06
81.45		Esref	Apak	TUR	3.1.82	1	Cezmi	Istanbul	4 Jun 05
81.44		Yuriy	Tarasyuk	BLR	11.4.57	1		Minsk	10 Aug 84
81.35		Wojciech	Kondratowicz	POL	18.4.80	1		Bydgoszczcz	13 Jul 03
		(50)	100th man 80.02, 200th 77.54, 300th 75.62, 400th 74.30, 500th 72.80						

A – mark made at an altitude of 1000m or higher, i – indoors, Q – in qualifying competition, WR – world record

MEN All-time

Mark	Wind	Name		Nat	Born	Pos	Meet	Venue	Date

Ancillary marks – other marks during series (to 84.85)

86.68	Sedykh	30 Aug 86	85.82	Sedykh	22 Jun 86	85.42	Litvinov	3 Jul 86	85.20	Sedykh	3 Jul 84
86.62	Sedykh	30 Aug 86	85.52	Sedykh	13 Jul 84	85.28	Sedykh	30 Aug 86	85.04	Sedykh	13 Jul 84
86.00	Sedykh	3 Jul 84	85.46	Sedykh	30 Aug 86	85.26	Sedykh	11 Aug 86	84.98	Sedykh	4 Sep 88
86.00	Sedykh	22 Jun 86	85.42	Sedykh	11 Aug 86	85.24	Sedykh	11 Aug 86	84.92	Litvinov	3 Jul 86

JAVELIN

Mark	Wind	Name		Nat	Born	Pos	Meet	Venue	Date
98.48 WR		Jan	Zelezny	CZE	16.6.66	1		Jena	25 May 96
95.66 WR			Zelezny			1	McD	Sheffield	29 Aug 93
95.54A WR			Zelezny			1		Pietersburg	6 Apr 93
94.64			Zelezny			1	GS	Ostrava	31 May 96
94.02			Zelezny			1		Stellenbosch	26 Mar 97
93.09		Aki	Parviainen	FIN	26.10.74	1		Kuortane	26 Jun 99
92.80			Zelezny			1	WCh	Edmonton	12 Aug 01
92.61		Sergey	Makarov	RUS	19.3.73	1		Sheffield	30 Jun 02
92.60		Raymond	Hecht	GER	11.11.68	1	Bisl	Oslo	21 Jul 95
92.42			Zelezny			1	GS	Ostrava	28 May 97
92.41			Parviainen			1	ECp-1A	Vaasa	24 Jun 01
92.28			Zelezny			1	GPF	Monaco	9 Sep 95
92.28			Hecht			1	WK	Zürich	14 Aug 96
92.12			Zelezny			1	McD	London (CP)	27 Aug 95
92.12			Zelezny			1	TOTO	Tokyo	15 Sep 95
91.82			Zelezny			1	McD	Sheffield	4 Sep 94
91.69		Kostadínos	Gatsioúdis	GRE	17.12.73	1		Kuortane	24 Jun 00
91.68			Zelezny			1	GP	Gateshead	1 Jul 94
91.59		Andreas	Thorkildsen	NOR	1.4.82	1	Bisl	Oslo	2 Jun 06
91.53		Tero	Pitkämäki	FIN	19.12.82	1		Kuortane	26 Jun 05
91.50			Zelezny			1	Kuso	Lublin	4 Jun 94
91.50A			Zelezny			1		Pretoria	8 Apr 96
91.50			Hecht			1		Gengenbach	1 Sep 96
91.46 WR		Steve	Backley	GBR	12.2.69	1		Auckland (NS)	25 Jan 92
91.40			Zelezny			1	BNP	Villeneuve d'Ascq	2 Jul 93
91.34			Zelezny			1		Cape Town	8 Apr 97
91.33			Pitkämäki			1	WAF	Monaco	10 Sep 05
91.31			Parviainen			2	WCh	Edmonton	12 Aug 01
91.30			Zelezny			1	ISTAF	Berlin	1 Sep 95
91.29		Breaux	Greer	USA	19.10.76	1	NC	Indianapolis	21 Jun 07
	(30/9)	71 over 90m (most: Zelezny 35, Parviainen 8, Hecht, Pitkämäki & Thorkildsen 6, Makarov 5)							
90.73		Vadims	Vasilevskis	LAT	5.1.82	1		Tallinn	22 Jul 07
	(10)								
90.60		Seppo	Räty	FIN	27.4.62	1		Nurmijärvi	20 Jul 92
90.44		Boris	Henry	GER	14.12.73	1	Gugl	Linz	9 Jul 97
89.16A		Tom	Petranoff	USA	8.4.58	1		Potchefstroom	1 Mar 91
89.10 WR		Patrik	Bodén	SWE	30.6.67	1		Austin	24 Mar 90
89.02		Jarrod	Bannister	AUS	3.10.84	1	NC	Brisbane	29 Feb 08
88.90		Aleksandr	Ivanov	RUS	25.5.82	1	Znam	Tula	7 Jun 03
88.84		Dmitriy	Tarabin	RUS	29.10.91	1	NC	Moskva	24 Jul 13
88.75		Marius	Corbett	RSA	26.9.75	1	CG	Kuala Lumpur	21 Sep 98
88.70		Peter	Blank	GER	10.4.62	1	NC	Stuttgart	30 Jun 01
88.36		Matthias	de Zordo	GER	21.2.88	1	VD	Bruxelles	16 Sep 11
	(20)								
88.34		Vitezslav	Vesely	CZE	27.2.83	Q	OG	London (OS)	8 Aug 12
88.24		Matti	Närhi	FIN	17.8.75	1		Soini	27 Jul 97
88.23		Petr	Frydrych	CZE	13.1.88	1	GS	Ostrava	27 May 10
88.22		Juha	Laukkanen	FIN	6.1.69	1		Kuortane	20 Jul 92
88.20		Gavin	Lovegrove	NZL	21.10.67	1	Bisl	Oslo	5 Jul 96
88.00		Vladimir	Ovchinnikov	RUS	2.8.70	1		Tolyatti	14 May 95
87.83		Andrus	Värnik	EST	27.9.77	1		Valga	19 Aug 03
87.82		Harri	Hakkarainen	FIN	16.10.69	1		Kuortane	24 Jun 95
87.79		Antti	Ruuskanen	FIN	21.2.84	1		Lahti	26 Aug 12
87.60		Kazuhiro	Mizoguchi	JPN	18.3.62	1	Jenner	San José	27 May 89
	(30)								
87.40		Vladimir	Sasimovich ¶	BLR	14.9.68	2		Kuortane	24 Jun 95
87.34		Andrey	Moruyev	RUS	6.5.70	1	ECp	Birmingham	25 Jun 94
87.23		Teemu	Wirkkala	FIN	14.1.84	1		Joensuu	22 Jul 09
87.20		Viktor	Zaytsev	UZB	6.6.66	1	OT	Moskva	23 Jun 92
87.20		Peter	Esenwein	GER	7.12.67	1		Rehlingen	31 May 04
87.20A		Guillermo	Martínez	CUB	28.6.81	1	PAm	Guadalajara	28 Oct 11
87.17		Dariusz	Trafas	POL	16.5.72	1		Gold Coast (RB)	17 Sep 00
87.12		Tom	Pukstys	USA	28.5.68	2	OD	Jena	25 May 97

Mark	Wind	Name		Nat	Born	Pos	Meet	Venue	Date
87.12		Emeterio	González	CUB	11.4.73	1	OD	Jena	3 Jun 00
86.98		Yuriy	Rybin	RUS	5.3.63	1		Nitra	26 Aug 95
	(40)								
86.94		Mick	Hill	GBR	22.10.64	1	NC	London (CP)	13 Jun 93
86.80		Einar	Vihljálmsson	ISL	1.6.60	1		Reykjavik	29 Aug 92
86.80		Robert	Oosthuizen	RSA	23.1.87	1		Oudtshoorn	1 Mar 08
86.74		Pål Arne	Fagernes	NOR	8.6.74	Q	OG	Sydney	22 Sep 00
86.68		Tero	Järvenpää	FIN	2.10.84	1	NC	Tampere	27 Jul 08
86.67		Andrew	Currey	AUS	7.2.71	1		Wollongong	22 Jul 01
86.64		Klaus	Tafelmeier	FRG	12.4.58	1	NC	Gelsenkirchen	12 Jul 87
86.64		Ainars	Kovals	LAT	21.11.81	2	OG	Beijing	23 Aug 08
86.63		Harri	Haatainen	FIN	5.1.78	2	GP II	Gateshead	19 Aug 01
86.50		Tapio	Korjus	FIN	10.2.61	1		Lahti	25 Aug 88
	(50)	100th man 84.28, 200th 81.70, 300th 80.03, 400th 78.90						new javelin introduced in 1986	

Ancillary marks – other marks during series (to 91.40)

95.34	Zelezny		29 Aug 93		92.26	Zelezny		26 Mar 97		91.44	Zelezny	25 May 96
92.88	Zelezny		25 May 96		91.88	Zelezny		27 Aug 95		91.44	Zelezny	26 Mar 97
92.30	Zelezny		26 Mar 97		91.48	Zelezny		15 Sep 95				

Javelins with roughened tails, now banned by the IAAF

96.96	WR	Seppo	Räty	FIN	27.4.62	1		Punkalaidun	2 Jun 91
94.74	Irreg		Zelezny			1	Bisl	Oslo	4 Jul 92
91.98	WR		Räty			1	Super	Shizuoka	6 May 91
90.82		Kimmo	Kinnunen	FIN	31.3.68	1	WCh	Tokyo	26 Aug 91
87.00		Peter	Borglund	SWE	29.1.64	1	vFIN	Stockholm	13 Aug 91
Downhill: 87.88		Antti	Ruuskanen	FIN	21.2.84	1		Savonlinna	16 Sep 07

DECATHLON

9039	WR	Ashton		Eaton		USA	21.1.88	1	NC/OT	Eugene		23 Jun 12
		10.21/0.4	8.23/0.8	14.20	2.05	46.70		13.70/-0.8	42.81	5.30	58.87	4:14.48
9026	WR	Roman		Sebrle		CZE	26.11.74	1		Götzis		27 May 01
		10.64/0.0	8.11/1.9	15.33	2.12	47.79		13.92/-0.2	47.92	4.80	70.16	4:21.98
8994	WR	Tomás		Dvorák		CZE	11.5.72	1	ECp	Praha		4 Jul 99
		10.54/-0.1	7.90/1.1	16.78	2.04	48.08		13.73/0.0	48.33	4.90	72.32	4:37.20
8902				Dvorák				1	WCh	Edmonton		7 Aug 01
		10.62/1.5	8.07/0.9	16.57	2.00	47.74		13.80/-0.4	45.51	5.00	68.53	4:35.13
8900				Dvorák				1		Götzis		4 Jun 00
		10.54/1.3	8.03/0.0	16.68	2.09	48.36		13.89/-1.0	47.89	4.85	67.21	4:42.33
8893				Sebrle				1	OG	Athína		24 Aug 04
		10.85/1.5	7.84/0.3	16.36	2.12	48.36		14.05/1.5	48.72	5.00	70.52	4:40.01
8891	WR	Dan		O'Brien		USA	18.7.66	1		Talence		5 Sep 92
		10.43w/2.1	8.08/1.8	16.69	2.07	48.51		13.98/-0.5	48.56	5.00	62.58	4:42.10
8869				Eaton				1	OG	London (OS)		9 Aug 12
		10.35/0.4	8.03/0.8	14.66	2.05	46.90		13.56/0.1	42.53	5.20	61.96	4:33.59
8847	WR	Daley		Thompson		GBR	30.7.58	1	OG	Los Angeles		9 Aug 84
		10.44/-1.0	8.01/0.4	15.72	2.03	46.97		14.33/-1.1	46.56	5.00	65.24	4:35.00
8844w				O'Brien				1	TAC	New York		13 Jun 91
		10.23	7.96	16.06	2.08	47.70		13.95W/4.2	48.08	5.10	57.40	4:45.54
8842				Sebrle				1		Götzis		30 May 04
		10.92/0.5	7.86w/3.3	16.22	2.09	48.59		14.15/0.3	47.44	5.00	71.10	4:34.09
8837				Dvorák				1	WCh	Athína		6 Aug 97
		10.60/0.8	7.64/-0.7	16.32	2.00	47.56		13.61/0.8	45.16	5.00	70.34	4:35.40
8832	WR	Jürgen		Hingsen		FRG	25.1.58	1	OT	Mannheim		9 Jun 84
		10.70w/2.9	7.76/-1.6	16.42	2.07	48.05		14.07/0.2	49.36	4.90	59.86	4:19.75
8832		Bryan		Clay		USA	3.1.80	1	NC/OT	Eugene		30 Jun 08
		10.39/-0.4	7.39/-1.6	15.17	2.08	48.41		13.75/1.9	52.74	5.00	70.55	4:50.97
8825	WR			Hingsen				1		Bernhausen		5 Jun 83
		10.92/0.0	7.74	15.94	2.15	47.89		14.10	46.80	4.70	67.26	4:19.74
8824				O'Brien				1	OG	Atlanta		1 Aug 96
		10.50/0.7	7.57/1.4	15.66	2.07	46.82		13.87/0.3	48.78	5.00	66.90	4:45.89
8820				Clay				2	OG	Athína		24 Aug 04
		10.44w/2.2	7.96/0.2	15.23	2.06	49.19		14.13/1.5	50.11	4.90	69.71	4:41.65
8817				O'Brien				1	WCh	Stuttgart		20 Aug 93
		10.57/0.9	7.99/0.4	15.41	2.03	47.46		14.08/0.0	47.92	5.20	62.56	4:40.08
8815		Erki		Nool		EST	25.6.70	2	WCh	Edmonton		7 Aug 01
		10.60/1.5	7.63/2.0	14.90	2.03	46.23		14.40/0.0	43.40	5.40	67.01	4:29.58
8812				O'Brien				1	WCh	Tokyo		30 Aug 91
		10.41/-1.6	7.90/0.8	16.24	1.91	46.53		13.94/-1.2	47.20	5.20	60.66	4:37.50
8811				Thompson				1	EC	Stuttgart		28 Aug 86
		10.26/2.0	7.72/1.0	15.73	2.00	47.02		14.04/-0.3	43.38	5.10	62.78	4:26.16

Mark	Wind	Name	Nat	Born	Pos	Meet	Venue	Date
8809		Eaton			1	WCh	Moskva	11 Aug 13
	10.35/-0.5 7.73/0.3 14.39	1.93 46.02	13.72/0.4	45.00 5.20 64.83				4:29.80
8807		Sebrle			1		Götzis	1 Jun 03
	10.78/-0.2 7.86/1.2 15.41	2.12 47.83	13.96/0.0	43.42 4.90 69.22				4:28.63
8800		Sebrle			1		Götzis	2 Jun 02
	10.95/0.5 7.79/1.8 15.50	2.12 48.35	13.89/1.6	48.02 5.00 68.97				4:38.16
8800		Sebrle			1	EC	München	8 Aug 02
	10.83/1.3 7.92/0.8 15.41	2.12 48.48	14.04/0.0	46.88 5.10 68.51				4:42.94
8792	Uwe	Freimuth	GDR	10.9.61	1	OD	Potsdam	21 Jul 84
	11.06/ 7.79/ 16.30	2.03 48.43	14.66/	46.58 5.15 72.42				4:25.19
8791		Clay			1	OG	Beijing	22 Aug 08
	10.44/0.3 7.78/0.0 16.27	1.99 48.92	13.93/-0.5	53.79 5.00 70.97				5:06.59
8790	Trey	Hardee (10)	USA	7.2.84	1	WCh	Berlin	20 Aug 09
	10.45/0.2 7.83/1.9 15.33	1.99 48.13	13.86/0.3	48.08 5.20 68.00				4:48.91
8784	Tom	Pappas	USA	6.9.76	1	NC	Stanford	22 Jun 03
	10.78/0.2 7.96/1.4 16.28	2.17 48.22	14.13/1.7	45.84 5.20 60.77				4:48.12
8774 WR		Thompson			1	EC	Athína	8 Sep 82
	10.51/0.3 7.80/0.8 15.44	2.03 47.11	14.39/0.9	45.48 5.00 63.56				4:23.71
(30/11)								
8762	Siegfried	Wentz	FRG	7.3.60	2		Bernhausen	5 Jun 83
	10.89 7.49/ 15.35	2.09 47.38	14.00	46.90 4.80 70.68				4:24.90
8735	Eduard	Hämäläinen	FIN/BLR	21.1.69	1		Götzis	29 May 94
	10.50w/2.1 7.26/1.0 16.05	2.11 47.63	13.82/-3.0	49.70 4.90 60.32				4:35.09
8727	Dave	Johnson	USA	7.4.63	1		Azusa	24 Apr 92
	10.96/0.4 7.52w/4.5 14.61	2.04 48.19	14.17/0.3	49.88 5.28 66.96				4:29.38
8725	Dmitriy	Karpov	KAZ	23.7.81	3	OG	Athína	24 Aug 04
	10.50w/2.2 7.81/-0.9 15.93	2.09 46.81	13.97/1.5	51.65 4.60 55.54				4:38.11
8709	Aleksandr	Apaychev	UKR	6.5.61	1	vGDR	Neubrandenburg	3 Jun 84
	10.96/ 7.57/ 16.00	1.97 48.72	13.93/	48.00 4.90 72.24				4:26.51
8706	Frank	Busemann	GER	26.2.75	2	OG	Atlanta	1 Aug 96
	10.60/0.7 8.07/0.8 13.60	2.04 48.34	13.47/0.3	45.04 4.80 66.86				4:31.41
8698	Grigoriy	Degtyaryov	RUS	16.8.58	1	NC	Kiyev	22 Jun 84
	10.87/0.7 7.42/0.1 16.03	2.10 49.75	14.53/0.3	51.20 4.90 67.08				4:23.09
8694	Chris	Huffins	USA	15.4.70	1	NC	New Orleans	20 Jun 98
	10.31w/3.5 7.76w/2.5 15.43	2.18 49.02	14.02/1.0	53.22 4.60 61.59				4:59.43
8680	Torsten	Voss	GDR	24.3.63	1	WCh	Roma	4 Sep 87
	10.69/-0.3 7.88/1.2 14.98	2.10 47.96	14.13/0.1	43.96 5.10 58.02				4:25.93
(20)								
8670	Michael	Schrader	GER	1.7.87	2	WCh	Moskva	11 Aug 13
	10.73/-0.5 7.85/0.2 14.56	1.99 47.66	14.29/0.4	46.44 5.00 65.67				4:25.38
8667 WR	Guido	Kratschmer	FRG	10.1.53	1		Bernhausen	14 Jun 80
	10.58w/2.4 7.80/ 15.47	2.00 48.04	13.92/	45.52 4.60 66.50				4:24.15
8654	Leonel	Suárez	CUB	1.9.87	1	CAC	La Habana	4 Jul 09
	11.07/0.7 7.42/0.8 14.39	2.09 47.65	14.15/-0.6	46.07 4.70 77.47				4:27.29
8644	Steve	Fritz	USA	1.11.67	4	OG	Atlanta	1 Aug 96
	10.90/0.8 7.77/0.9 15.31	2.04 50.13	13.97/0.3	49.84 5.10 65.70				4:38.26
8644	Maurice	Smith	JAM	28.9.80	2	WCh	Osaka	1 Sep 07
	10.62/0.7 7.50/0.0 17.32	1.97 47.48	13.91/-0.2	52.36 4.80 53.61				4:33.52
8634 WR	Bruce	Jenner	USA	28.10.49	1	OG	Montreal	30 Jul 76
	10.94/0.0 7.22/0.0 15.35	2.03 47.51	14.84/0.0	50.04 4.80 68.52				4:12.61
8627	Robert	Zmelík	CZE	18.4.69	1		Götzis	31 May 92
	10.62w/2.1 8.02/0.2 13.93	2.05 48.73	13.84/1.2	44.44 4.90 61.26				4:24.83
8626	Michael	Smith	CAN	16.9.67	1		Götzis	26 May 96
	11.23/-0.6 7.72/0.6 16.94	1.97 48.69	14.77/-2.4	52.90 4.90 71.22				4:41.95
8617	Andrey	Kravchenko	BLR	4.1.86	1		Götzis	27 May 07
	10.86/0.2 7.90/0.9 13.89	2.15 47.46	14.05/-0.1	39.63 5.00 64.35				4:29.10
8603	Dean	Macey	GBR	12.12.77	3	WCh	Edmonton	7 Aug 01
	10.72/-0.7 7.59/0.4 15.41	2.15 46.21	14.34/0.0	46.96 4.70 54.61				4:29.05
(30)								
8583w	Jón Arnar	Magnússon	ISL	28.7.69	1	ECp-2	Reykjavik	5 Jul 98
	10.68/2.0 7.63/2.0 15.57	2.07 47.78	14.33W/5.2	44.53 5.00 64.16				4:41.60
8573					3		Götzis	31 May 98
	10.74/0.5 7.60/-0.2 16.03	2.03 47.66	14.24/0.7	47.82 5.10 59.77				4:46.43
8574	Christian	Plaziat	FRA	28.10.63	1	EC	Split	29 Aug 90
	10.72/-0.6 7.77/1.1 14.19	2.10 47.10	13.98/0.7	44.36 5.00 54.72				4:27.83
8574	Aleksandr	Yurkov	UKR	21.7.75	4		Götzis	4 Jun 00
	10.69/0.9 7.93/1.8 15.26	2.03 49.74	14.56/-0.9	47.85 5.15 58.92				4:32.49
8571	Lev	Lobodin	RUS	1.4.69	3	EC	Budapest	20 Aug 98
	10.66w/2.2 7.42/0.2 15.67	2.03 48.65	13.97/0.9	46.55 5.20 56.55				4:30.27
8566	Sebastian	Chmara	POL	21.11.71	1		Alhama de Murcia	17 May 98
	10.97w/2.9 7.56/1.2 16.03	2.10 48.27	14.32/1.8	44.39 5.20 57.25				4:29.66

Mark	Wind	Name		Nat	Born	Pos	Meet	Venue			Date
8558		Pascal	Behrenbruch	GER	19.1.85	1	EC	Helsinki			28 Jun 12
	10.93/0.8	7.15/-0.8	16.89	1.97	48.54		14.16/0.2	48.24	5.00	67.45	4:34.02
8554		Attila	Zsivoczky	HUN	29.4.77	5		Götzis			4 Jun 00
	10.64w/2.1	7.24/-1.0	15.72	2.18	48.13		14.87/-0.9	45.64	4.65	63.57	4:23.13
8548		Paul	Meier	GER	27.7.71	3	WCh	Stuttgart			20 Aug 93
	10.57/0.9	7.57/1.1	15.45	2.15	47.73		14.63/0.0	45.72	4.60	61.22	4:32.05
8547		Igor	Sobolevskiy	UKR	4.5.62	2	NC	Kiyev			22 Jun 84
	10.64/0.7	7.71/0.2	15.93	2.01	48.24		14.82/0.3	50.54	4.40	67.40	4:32.84
8534		Siegfried	Stark	GDR	12.6.55	1	OT	Halle			4 May 80
	11.10w	7.64	15.81	2.03	49.53		14.86w	47.20	5.00	68.70	4:27.7
	(40)		Peñalver below	(7.19w/4.0)							
8534w/8478		Antonio	Peñalver	ESP	1.12.68	1		Alhama de Murcia			24 May 92
	10.76w/3.9	7.42W/6.2	16.50	2.12	49.50		14.32/0.8	47.38	5.00	59.32	4:39.94
8528		Aleksandr	Pogorelov	RUS	10.1.80	3	WCh	Berlin			20 Aug 09
	10.95/-0.3	7.49/-0.4	16.65	2.08	50.27		14.19/0.3	48.46	5.10	63.95	4:48.70
8526		Francisco Javier	Benet	ESP	25.3.68	2		Alhama de Murcia			17 May 98
	10.72w/2.9	7.45/-1.2	14.57	1.92	48.10		13.83/1.8	46.12	5.00	65.37	4:26.81
8526		Kristjan	Rahnu	EST	29.8.79	1		Arles			5 Jun 05
	10.52w/2.2	7.58/1.6	15.51	1.99	48.60		14.04w/3.1	50.81	4.95	60.71	4:52.18
8524		Sébastien	Levicq	FRA	25.6.71	4	WCh	Sevilla			25 Aug 99
	11.05/0.2	7.52/-0.4	14.22	2.00	50.13		14.48/0.6	44.65	5.50	69.01	4:26.81
8519		Yuriy	Kutsenko	RUS	5.3.52	3	NC	Kiyev			22 Jun 84
	11.07/0.5	7.54/-0.1	15.11	2.13	49.07		14.94/0.3	50.38	4.60	61.70	4:12.68
8519		Hans	Van Alphen	BEL	12.1.82	1		Götzis			27 May 12
	10.96/1.0	7.62/1.1	15.23	2.06	49.54		14.55/0.4	45.45	4.96	64.15	4:20.87
8512		Damian	Warner	CAN	4.11.89	3	WCh	Moskva			11 Aug 13
	10.43/-0.5	7.39/0.3	14.23	2.05	48.41		13.96/0.4	44.13	4.80	64.67	4:29.97
8506		Valter	Külvet	EST	19.2.64	1		Staiki			3 Jul 88
	11.05/-1.4	7.35/0.4	15.78	2.00	48.08		14.55/-0.8	52.04	4.60	61.72	4:15.93
8506		Eelco	Sintnicolaas	NED	7.4.87	2		Götzis			27 May 12
	10.77/-0.7	7.27/-1.6	14.20	2.00	48.02		14.10/0.8	42.81	5.36	63.59	4:30.08
	(50)		100th man 8334, 200th 8171, 300th 8063, 400th 7972, 500th 7889								

MEN All-time

4 x 100 METRES RELAY

Mark		Nat	Team	Pos	Meet	Venue	Date
36.84	WR	JAM	N Carter 10.1, Frater 8.9, Blake 9.0, Bolt 8.8	1	OG	London (OS)	11 Aug 12
37.04	WR	JAM	N Carter, Frater, Blake, Bolt	1	WCh	Daegu	4 Sep 11
37.04		USA	Kimmons 10.1, Gatlin 8.9, Gay 9.0, Bailey 9.0	2	OG	London (OS)	11 Aug 12
37.10	WR	JAM	N Carter, Frater, Bolt, Powell	1	OG	Beijing	22 Aug 08
37.31		JAM	Mullings, Frater, Bolt, Powell	1	WCh	Berlin	22 Aug 09
37.36		JAM	Carter, Bailey Cole, Ashmeade, Bolt	1	WCh	Moskva	18 Aug 13
37.38		USA	Demps, Patton, Kimmons, Gatlin	1h2	OG	London (OS)	10 Aug 12
37.39		JAM	Carter, Frater, Blake, Bailey-Cole	1h1	OG	London (OS)	10 Aug 12
37.40	WR	USA	Marsh, Burrell, Mitchell, C Lewis	1	OG	Barcelona	8 Aug 92
37.40	WR	USA	Drummond, Cason, D Mitchell, L Burrell	1s1	WCh	Stuttgart	21 Aug 93
37.45		USA	Kimmons, Spearmon, Gay, Rodgers	1	WK	Zürich	19 Aug 10
37.48		USA	Drummond, Cason, D Mitchell, L Burrell	1	WCh	Stuttgart	22 Aug 93
37.50	WR	USA	Cason, Burrell, Mitchell, C Lewis	1	WCh	Tokyo	1 Sep 91
37.58		USA	'Red': Silmon, Rodgers, Salaam, Gatlin	1	Herc	Monaco	19 Jul 13
37.59		USA	Drummond, Montgomery, B Lewis, Greene	1	WCh	Sevilla	29 Aug 99
37.59		USA	Conwright, Spearmon, Gay, Smoots	1	WCp	Athína	16 Sep 06
37.61		USA	Drummond, Williams, B Lewis, Greene	1	OG	Sydney	30 Sep 00
37.61		USA	Kimmons, Gatlin, Gay, Bailey	1	Herc	Monaco	20 Jul 12
37.62		TRI	Brown, Burns, Callander, Thompson	2	WCh	Berlin	22 Aug 09
37.65		USA	Drummond, Williams, C Johnson, Greene	1	ISTAF	Berlin	1 Sep 00
37.66		USA	Silmon, Rodgers, Salaam, Gatlin	2	WCh	Moskva	18 Aug 13
37.67	WR	USA	Marsh, Burrell, Mitchell, C Lewis	1	WK	Zürich	7 Aug 91
37.69		CAN	Esmie 10.47, Gilbert 9.02, Surin 9.25, Bailey 8.95	1	OG	Atlanta	3 Aug 96
37.70		JAM	Clarke, Frater, Mullins, Bolt	1	WK	Zürich	28 Aug 09
37.73		GBR	Gardener, Campbell, Devonish, Chambers	2	WCh	Sevilla	29 Aug 99
37.73		USA	Trammell, Rodgers, Patton, Spearmon	2	WK	Zürich	28 Aug 09
37.75		USA	Cason, Burrell, Mitchell, Marsh	1h2	WCh	Tokyo	31 Aug 91
37.75		JAM	Forsythe, Bailey Cole, Weir, Bolt	1	DL	London (OS)	27 Jul 13
37.76		JAM	Forsythe, Frater, S Mullings, Blake	2	WK	Zürich	19 Aug 10
37.77		GBR	Jackson, Jarrett, Regis, Christie	2	WCh	Stuttgart	22 Aug 93
37.77		USA	A Drummond, B Williams, Patton, Greene	1	ISTAF	Berlin (P)	10 Aug 03
			(31 performances by teams from 5 nations) Further bests by nations:				
37.79	w	FRA	Morinière, Sangouma 8.90, Trouabal, Marie-Rose	1	EC	Split	1 Sep 90
37.90		BRA	de Lima, Ribeiro, A da Silva, Cl da Silva	2	OG	Sydney	30 Sep 00
37.94		NGR	O Ezinwa, Adeniken, Obikwelu, D Ezinwa	1s2	WCh	Athína	9 Aug 97
38.00		CUB	Simón, Lamela, Isasi, Aguilera	3	OG	Barcelona	8 Aug 92

Mark	Wind	Name	Nat	Born	Pos	Meet	Venue	Date
38.02	URS	Yevgenyev, Bryzgin, Muravyov, Krylov			2	WCh	Roma	6 Sep 87
	(10)							
38.02	GER	Reus, Unger, Kosenkow, Jakubczyk			1		Weinheim	27 Jul 12
38.03	JPN	Tsukahara, Suetsugu 9.08, Takahira, Asahara			5	WCh	Osaka	1 Sep 07
38.12	GHA	Duah, Nkansah, Zakari, Tuffour			1s1	WCh	Athína	9 Aug 97
38.17	AUS	Henderson, Jackson, Brimacombe, Marsh			1s2	WCh	Göteborg	12 Aug 95
38.17	ITA	Donati, Collio, Di Gregorio, Checcucci			2	EC	Barcelona	1 Aug 10
38.29	NED	Mariano, Martina, Codrington, van Luijk			3h1	OG	London (OS)	10 Aug 12
38.31	POL	Masztak, Kuc, Kubaczyk, Krynski			6h2	OG	London (OS)	10 Aug 12
38.38	CHN	Guo Fan, Liang Jiahong, Su Bingtiang, Zhang Peimeng			5h1	OG	London (OS)	10 Aug 12
38.41	SKN	Lestrod, Rogers, Adams, Lawrence			6h1	OG	London (OS)	10 Aug 12
38.45	AHO	Goeloe, Raffaela, Duzant, Martina			6	WCh	Helsinki	13 Aug 05
	(20, with RUS and UKR for USSR)							
38.46	URS/RUS	Zharov, Krylov, Fatun, Goremykin			4	EC	Split	1 Sep 90
38.46	ESP	Viles, Ruiz, Hortelano, Rodríguez			4h1	WCh	Moskva	18 Aug 13
38.47	RSA	Nagel, du Plessis, Newton, Quinn			1	WCh	Edmonton	12 Aug 01
38.47	HKG	Tang Yik Chun, Lai Chun Ho, Ng Ka Fung, Tsui Chi Ho			1		Taipei	26 May 12
38.53	UKR	Rurak, Osovich, Kramarenko, Dologodin			1	ECp	Madrid	1 Jun 96
38.60	CIV	Meité, Douhou, Sonan, N'Dri			3s1	WCh	Edmonton	12 Aug 01
38.61	GRE	Séggos, Alexópoulos, Panayiotópoulos, Hoídis			2	ECp	Paris (C)	19 Jun 99
38.62	SUI	Mancini, Schenkel, Wilson, Schneeberger			3	WK	Zürich	8 Sep 11
38.63	SWE	Karlsson, Mårtensson, Hedner, Strenius			3s2	OG	Atlanta	2 Aug 96
38.67	HUN	Karaffa, Nagy, Tatár, Kovács			1	BGP	Budapest	11 Aug 86
Multi-nation team								
37.46		Racers TC Bailey/ANT, Blake JAM, Forsythe JAM, Bolt JAM			1	LGP	London (CP)	25 Jul 09
37.82		Drummond/USA, Jarrett/GBR, Regis/GBR, Mitchell/USA			2	MSR	Walnut	17 Apr 94
One man disqualified for drugs								
37.91	NGR	Asonze ¶, Obikwelu, Effiong, Aliu			(3)	WCh	Sevilla	29 Aug 99

4 x 200 METRES RELAY

Mark	Wind	Name	Pos	Meet	Venue	Date
1:18.68	WR	USA – Santa Monica Track Cluc				
		Marsh 20.0, Burrell 19.6, Heard 19.7, C Lewis 19.4	1	MSR	Walnut	17 Apr 94
1:19.10		World All-Stars	2	MSR	Walnut	17 Apr 94
		Drummond USA 20.4, Mitchell USA 19.3, Bridgewater USA 20.3, Regis GBR 19.1				
1:19.11	WR	Santa Monica TC/USA M.Marsh, L Burrell, Heard, C Lewis	1	Penn	Philadelphia	25 Apr 92
1:19.16		USA Red Team Crawford, Clay, Patton, Gatlin	1	PennR	Philadelphia	26 Apr 03
1:19.38	WR	Santa Monica TC/USA Everett, Burrell, Heard, C Lewis	1	R-W	Koblenz	23 Aug 89
1:19.39		USA Blue Drummond, Crawford, B Williams, Greene	1	PennR	Philadelphia	28 Apr 01
1:19.45		Santa Monica TC/USA DeLoach, Burrell, C.Lewis, Heard	1	Penn	Philadelphia	27 Apr 91
1:19.47		Nike Int./USA Brokenburr, A Harrison, Greene, M Johnson	1	Penn	Philadelphia	24 Apr 99
Best non-US nations						
1:20.79		Central Arizona DC/Jamaica	1	MSR	Walnut	24 Apr 88
		Bucknor, Campbell, O'Connor, Davis)				
1:21.10	ITA	Tilli, Simionato, Bongiorno, Mennea	1		Cagliari	29 Sep 83
1:21.22	POL	Tulin, Balcerzak, Pilarczyk, Urbas	2		Gdansk	14 Jul 01
1:21.29	GBR	Adam, Mafe, Christie, Regis	1	vURS	Birmingham	23 Jun 89

4 x 400 METRES RELAY

Mark	Wind	Name	Pos	Meet	Venue	Date
2:54.29	WR	USA Valmon 44.5, Watts 43.6, Reynolds 43.23, Johnson 42.94	1	WCh	Stuttgart	22 Aug 93
2:55.39		USA Merritt 44.4, Taylor 43.7, Neville 44.16, Wariner 43.18	1	OG	Beijing	23 Aug 08
2:55.56		USA Merritt 44.4, Taylor 43.7, Williamson 44.32, Wariner 43.10	1	WCh	Osaka	2 Sep 07
2:55.74	WR	USA Valmon 44.6, Watts 43.00, M.Johnson 44.73, S Lewis 43.41	1	OG	Barcelona	8 Aug 92
2:55.91		USA O Harris 44.5, Brew 43.6, Wariner 43.98, Williamson 43.83	1	OG	Athína	28 Aug 04
2:55.99		USA L Smith 44.62, A Harrison 43.84, Mills 43.66, Maybank 43.87	1	OG	Atlanta	3 Aug 96
2:56.16A	WR	USA Matthews 45.0, Freeman 43.2, James 43.9, Evans 44.1	1	OG	Ciu. México	20 Oct 68
2:56.16	WR	USA Everett 43.79, S Lewis 43.69, Robinzine 44.74, Reynolds 43.94	1	OG	Seoul	1 Oct 88
2:56.60	GBR	I Thomas 44.92, Baulch 44.19, Richardson 43.62, Black 43.87	2	OG	Atlanta	3 Aug 96
2:56.65	GBR	Thomas 44.8, Black 44.2, Baulch 44.08, Richardson 43.57	2	WCh	Athína	10 Aug 97
2:56.72	BAH	Brown 44.9, Pinder 43.5, Mathieu 44.25, Miller 44.01	1	OG	London (OS)	10 Aug 12
2:56.75	JAM	McDonald 44.5, Haughton 44.4, McFarlane 44.37, Clarke 43.51	3	WCh	Athína	10 Aug 97
2:56.91		USA Rock 44.7, Brew 44.3, Williamson 44.40, Wariner 43.49	1	WCh	Helsinki	14 Aug 05
2:57.05		USA Nellum 45.2, Mance 43.5, McQuay 43.41, Taylor 44.85	2	OG	London (OS)	10 Aug 12
2:57.29		USA Everett 45.1, Haley 44.0, McKay 44.20, Reynolds 44.00	1	WCh	Roma	6 Sep 87
2:57.32		USA Ramsey 44.9, Mills 44.6, Reynolds 43.74, Johnson 44.11	1	WCh	Göteborg	13 Aug 95
2:57.32	BAH	McKinney 44.9, Moncur 44.6, A.Williams 44.43, Brown 43.42	2	WCh	Helsinki	14 Aug 05
2:57.53	GBR	Black 44.7, Redmond 44.0, Regis 44.22, Akabusi 44.59	1	WCh	Tokyo	1 Sep 91
2:57.57		USA Valmon 44.9, Watts 43.4, D.Everett 44.31, Pettigrew 44.93	2	WCh	Tokyo	1 Sep 91
2:57.86		USA Taylor 45.4, Wariner 43.6, Clement 44.72, Merritt 44.16	1	WCh	Berlin	23 Aug 09
2:57.87		USA L Smith 44.59, Rouser 44.33, Mills 44.32, Maybank 44.63	1s2	OG	Atlanta	2 Aug 96
2:57.91		USA Nix 45.59, Armstead 43.97, Babers 43.75, McKay 44.60	1	OG	Los Angeles	11 Aug 84

Mark	Wind	Name	Nat	Born Pos	Meet	Venue	Date
2:57.97		McDonald , Haughton , McFarlane, D Clarke	JAM	1	PAm	Winnipeg	30 Jul 99
2:58.00		Rysiukiewicz 45.6, Czubak 44.2, Haczek 44.0, Mackowiak 44.2	POL	2	GWG	Uniondale, NY	22 Jul 98
2:58.03		Bain 45.9, Mathieu 44.1, A Williams 44.02, Brown 44.05	BAH	2	OG	Beijing	23 Aug 08
2:58.06		Dyldin 45.5, Frolov 44.6, Kokorin 44.34, Alekseyev 43.56	RUS	3	OG	Beijing	23 Aug 08
2:58.07		Ayre 44.9, Simpson 44.9, Spence 44.48, Clarke 43.81	JAM	3	WCh	Helsinki	14 Aug 05
2:58.19		Moncur 45.1, C Brown 44.5, McIntosh 44.42, Munnings 44.13	BAH	2	WCh	Edmonton	12 Aug 01
	(28/6)	plus six times for teams that contained an athlete who was subsequently banned for drugs abuse					
2:58.56		Cl. da Silva 44.6, A dos Santos 45.1, de Araújo 45.0, Parrela 43.9	BRA	2	PAm	Winnipeg	30 Jul 99
2:58.68		Chukwu 45.18, Monye 44.49, Bada 44.70, Udo-Obong 44.31	NGR	1	OG	Sydney	30 Sep 00
2:58.96		Djhone 45.4, Keita 44.7, Diagana 44.69, Raquil 44.15	FRA	2	WCh	Saint-Denis	31 Aug 03
2:59.13		Martínez 45.6, Herrera 44.38, Tellez 44.81, Hernández 44.34	CUB	1h2	OG	Barcelona	7 Aug 92
	(10)						
2:59.21		Pistorius 45.58, Mogawane 43.97, de Beer 44.46, Victor 45.20	RSA	3h1	WCh	Daegu	1 Sep 11
2:59.37		K Borlée 45.4, J Borlée 43.6, Van Branteghem 44.44, Ghislain 45.88	BEL	5	OG	Beijing	23 Aug 08
2:59.40		L.Gordon 45.1, Solomon 43.9, Alleyne-Forte 45.51, Lendore 44.75	TRI	3	OG	London (OS)	10 Aug 12
2:59.63		D Kitur 45.4, S Kitur 45.13, Kipkemboi 44.76, Kemboi 44.34	KEN	3h2	OG	Barcelona	7 Aug 92
2:59.70		Frayne 45.38, Clark 43.86, Minihan 45.07, Mitchell 45.39	AUS	4	OG	Los Angeles	11 Aug 84
2:59.86		Möller 45.8, Schersing 44.8, Carlowitz 45.3, Schönlebe 44.1	GDR	1	vURS	Erfurt	23 Jun 85
2:59.95		Jovkovic, Djurovic, Macev, Brankovic 44.3	YUG	2h3	WCh	Tokyo	31 Aug 91
2:59.96		Dobeleit 45.7, Henrich 44.3, Itt 45.12, Schmid 44.93	FRG	4	WCh	Roma	6 Sep 87
3:00.44A		Cuesta 46.2, Peguero 44.6, Tapia 45.2, L Santos 44.5	DOM	2	PAm	Guadalajara	28 Oct 11
		3:02.02 Peguero, Santa, Vidal, Sánchez		3	PAm	Santo Domingo	9 Aug 03
3:00.64		Diarra 46.53, Dia 44.94, Ndiaye 44.70, Faye 44.47	SEN	4	OG	Atlanta	3 Aug 96
	(20)						
3:00.76		Karube 45.88, Ito 44.86, Osakada 45.08, Omori 44.94	JPN	5	OG	Atlanta	3 Aug 96
3:00.79		Chiwira 46.2, Mukomana 44.6, Ngidhi 45.79, Harnden 44.20	ZIM	2h3	WCh	Athína	9 Aug 97
3:00.82A		A Ramírez 45.7, Aguilar 45.3, Acevedo 44.7, Longart 45.2	VEN	3	PAm	Guadalajara	28 Oct 11
		3:01.70 Ramírez, Bravo, Meléndez, Longart		2	IbAmC	Barquisimeto	10 Jun 12
3:01.12		Lönnqvist 46.7, Salin 45.1, Karttunen 44.8, Kukkoaho 44.5	FIN	6	OG	München	10 Sep 72
3:01.37		Bongiorni 46.2, Zuliani 45.0, Petrella 45.3, Ribaud 44.9	ITA	4	EC	Stuttgart	31 Aug 86
3:01.42		I Rodríguez 46.0, Canal 44.1, Andrés 45.88, Reina 45.48	ESP	4h1	WCh	Edmonton	11 Aug 01
3:01.60		Louis 46.67, Peltier 44.97, Edwards 45.04, Forde 44.92	BAR	6	OG	Los Angeles	11 Aug 84
3:01.61		Georgiev 45.9, Stankulov 46.0, Raykov 45.07, Ivanov 44.66	BUL	2h1	WCh	Stuttgart	21 Aug 93
3:02.09		Govile 46.72, Kyeswa 44.60, Rwamuhanda 46.40, Okot 44.37	UGA	7	OG	Los Angeles	11 Aug 84
3:02.11		Kasbane, Dahane, Belcaid, Lahlou 44.5	MAR	1h2	WCh	Tokyo	31 Aug 91
	(30)						

Including subsequently banned athlete

Mark	Wind	Name	Nat	Pos	Meet	Venue	Date
2:54.20(WR)		Young 44.3, Pettigrew ¶ 43.2, Washington 43.5, Johnson 43.2	USA	(1)	GWG	Uniondale, NY	22 Jul 98
2:56.35		A Harrison 44.36, Pettigrew 44.17, C Harrison 43.53, Johnson 44.29	USA	(1)	OG	Sydney	30 Sep 00
2:56.45		J Davis 45.2, Pettigrew 43.9, Taylor 43.92, M Johnson 43.49	USA	(1)	WCh	Sevilla	29 Aug 99
2:56.47		Young 44.6, Pettigrew 43.1, Jones 44.80, Washington 44.80	USA	(1)	WCh	Athína	10 Aug 97
2:56.60		Red Taylor 45.0, Pettigrew 44.2, Washington 43.7, Johnson 43.7	USA	(1)	PennR	Philadelphia	29 Apr 00
2:57.54		Byrd 45.9, Pettigrew 43.9, Brew 44.03, Taylor 43.71	USA	1	WCh	Edmonton	12 Aug 01

4 x 800 METRES RELAY

Mark		Name	Nat	Pos	Meet	Venue	Date
7:02.43		Mutua 1:46.73, Yiampoy 1:44.38, Kombich 1:45.92, Bungei 1:45.40	KEN	1	VD	Bruxelles	25 Aug 06
7:02.82			USA	2	VD	Bruxelles	25 Aug 06
		J Harris 1:47.05, Robinson 1:44.03, Burley 1:46.05, Krummenacker 1:45.69					
7:03.89	WR	Elliott 1:49.14, Cook 1:46.20, Cram 1:44.54, Coe 1:44.01	GBR	1		London (CP)	30 Aug 82
7:04.70		van Oudtshoorn 1:46.9, Sepeng 1:45.2, Kotze 1:48.3, J Botha 1:44.3	RSA	1		Stuttgart	6 Jun 99
7:06.66		Sultan 1:45.81, Al-Badri 1:46.71, Suleiman 1:45.89, Ali Kamal 1:48.25	QAT	4	VD	Bruxelles	25 Aug 06
7:07.40		Masunov, Kostetskiy, Matvetev, Kalinkin	URS	1		Moskva	5 Aug 84
7:08.5	WR	Kinder 1:46.9, Adams 1:47.5, Bogatzki 1:47.9, Kemper 1:46.2	FRG	1		Wiesbaden	13 Aug 66

4 x 1500 METRES RELAY

Mark		Name	Nat	Pos	Meet	Venue	Date
14:36.23	WR	W Biwott 3:38.5, Gathimba 3:39.5, G Rono 3:41.4, Choge 3:36.9	KEN	1	VD	Bruxelles	4 Sep 09
14:38.8	WR	Wessinghage 3:38.8, Hudak 3:39.1, Lederer 3:44.6, Fleschen 3:36.3	FRG	1		Köln	16 Aug 77
14:40.4	WR	Polhill 3:42.9, Walker 3:40.4, Dixon 3:41.2, Quax 3:35.9	NZL	1		Oslo	22 Aug 73
14:45.63		Kalutskiy, Yakovlev, Legeda, Lotarev	URS	1		Leningrad	4 Aug 85
14:46.16		Larios, ESP Jiménez 3:40.9, Pancorbo 3:41.2, A García 3:43.9, Viciosa 3:40.2		1		Madrid	5 Sep 91
14:46.3		Aldridge, Clifford, Harbour, Duits	USA	1		Bourges	23 Jun 79
14:46.92		Birmingham 3:39.2, Gregson 3:44.2, Kealey 3:43.3, Bromlet 3:40.3	AUS	3	VD	Bruxelles	4 Sep 09
14:48.2		Bégouin 3:44.5, Lequement 3:44.3, Philippe 3:42.2, Dien 3:37.2	FRA	2		Bourges	23 Jun 79
14:50.2		Melville, Dixon, Quax, Walker	NZL	1		Auckland	17 May 75

Mixed Team

Mark		Name	Pos	Meet	Venue	Date
14:44.31		Ali BRN 3:38.1, Birgen KEN 3:43.3, N Kemboi KEN 3:40.0, Campbell IRL 3:43.0	2	VD	Bruxelles	4 Sep 09

4 x 1 MILE RELAY

Mark		Name	Nat	Pos	Venue	Date
15:49.08		Coghlan 4:00.2, O'Sullivan 3:55.3, O'Mara 3:56.6, Flynn 3:56.98	IRL	1	Dublin	17 Aug 85
15:59.57		Rogers 3:57.2, Bowden 4:02.5, Gilchrist 4:02.8, Walker 3:57.07	NZL	1	Auckland	2 Mar 83

MEN All-time

Mark	Wind	Name		Nat	Born	Pos	Meet	Venue	Date

3000 METRES TRACK WALK

Mark	Wind			Nat	Born	Pos	Meet	Venue	Date
10:47.11		Giovanni	De Benedictis	ITA	8.1.68	1		S.Giovanni Valdarno	19 May 90
10:52.44+		Yohann	Diniz	FRA	1.1.78	1	in 5k	Villeneuve d'Ascq	27 Jun 08
10:56.22		Andrew	Jachno	AUS	13.4.62	1		Melbourne	7 Feb 91
10:56.34+		Roman	Mrázek	SVK	21.1.62	1k	PTS	Bratislava	14 Jun 89
10:59.04		Luke	Adams	AUS	22.10.76	1		Cork	3 Jul 10
11:00.2+		Jozef	Pribilinec	SVK	6.7.60	1k		Banská Bystrica	30 Aug 85
11:00.50+		Francisco Javier	Fernández ¶	ESP	6.3.77	1	in 5k	Villeneuve d'Ascq	8 Jun 07
11:00.56		David	Smith	AUS	24.7.55	1		Perth	24 Jan 87
11:03.01		Vladimir	Andreyev	RUS	7.9.66	2		Formia	13 Jul 97
Indoors									
10:31.42		Andreas	Erm	GER	12.3.76	1		Halle	4 Feb 01
10:54.61		Carlo	Mattioli	ITA	23.10.54	1		Milano	6 Feb 80
10:56.77+		Ivano	Brugnetti	ITA	1.9.76	1	in 5k	Torino	21 Feb 09
10:56.88		Reima	Salonen	FIN	19.11.55	1		Turku	5 Feb 84
10:57.32		Matej	Tóth	SVK	10.2.83	1		Wien	12 Feb 11
11:00.86+		Frants	Kostyukevich	BLR	4.4.63	1k	EI	Genova	28 Feb 92

5000 METRES TRACK WALK

Mark	Wind			Nat	Born	Pos	Meet	Venue	Date
18:05.49		Hatem	Ghoula	TUN	7.6.73	1		Tunis	1 May 97
18:17.22		Robert	Korzeniowski	POL	30.7.68	1		Reims	3 Jul 92
18:18.01		Yohann	Diniz	FRA	1.1.78	1		Villeneuve d'Ascq	27 Jun 08
18:27.34		Francisco Javier	Fernández ¶	ESP	6.3.77	1		Villeneuve d'Ascq	8 Jun 07
18:28.80		Roman	Mrázek	SVK	21.1.62	1	PTS	Bratislava	14 Jun 89
18:30.43		Maurizio	Damilano	ITA	6.4.57	1		Caserta	11 Jun 92
ndoors									
18:07.08		Mikhail	Shchennikov	RUS	24.12.67	1		Moskva	14 Feb 95
18:08.86		Ivano	Brugnetti	ITA	1.9.76	1	NC	Ancona	17 Feb 07
18:11.41		Ronald	Weigel	GDR	8.8.59	1mx		Wien	13 Feb 88
18:11.8		Valeriy	Borchin ¶	RUS	11.9.86	1		Saransk	30 Dec 10
18:15.25		Grigoriy	Kornev	RUS	14.3.61	1		Moskva	7 Feb 92
18:16.54 ?		Frants	Kostyukevich	BLR	4.4.63	2	NC	Gomel	4 Feb 89
18:17.13		Vladimir	Kanaykin ¶	RUS	21.3.85	2	Winter	Moskva	5 Feb 12
18:19.97		Giovanni	De Benedictis	ITA	8.1.68	1	EI	Genova	28 Feb 92
18:22.25		Andreas	Erm	GER	12.3.76	1	NC	Dortmund	25 Feb 01
18:23.18		Rishat	Shafikov	RUS	23.1.70	1		Samara	1 Mar 97
18:24.13		Francisco Javier	Fernández ¶	ESP	6.3.77	1		Belfast	17 Feb 07
18:26.82		Sergey	Bakulin	RUS	13.11.86	3	Winter	Moskva	5 Feb 12
18:27.15		Alessandro	Gandellini	ITA	30.4.73	1	NC	Genova	12 Feb 00
18:27.80		Jozef	Pribilinec	SVK	6.7.60	2	WI	Indianapolis	7 Mar 87
18:27.95		Stefan	Johansson	SWE	11.4.67	3	EI	Genova	28 Feb 92
18:28.54		Igor	Yerokhin	RUS	4.9.85	1		Samara	31 Jan 13

10,000 METRES TRACK WALK

Mark	Wind			Nat	Born	Pos	Meet	Venue	Date
37:53.09		Francisco Javier	Fernández ¶	ESP	6.3.77	1	NC	Santa Cruz de Tenerife	27 Jul 08
37:58.6		Ivano	Brugnetti	ITA	1.9.76	1		Sesto San Gioavnni	23 Jul 05
38:02.60		Jozef	Pribilinec	SVK	6.7.60	1		Banská Bystrica	30 Aug 85
38:06.6		David	Smith	AUS	24.7.55	1		Sydney	25 Sep 86
38:12.13		Ronald	Weigel	GDR	8.8.59	1		Potsdam	10 May 86
38:18.0+		Valdas	Kazlauskas	LTU	23.2.58	1		Moskva	18 Sep 83
38:20.0		Moacir	Zimmermann	BRA	30.12.83	1		Blumenau	7 Jun 08
38:24 0+		Bernardo	Segura	MEX	11.2.70	1	SGP	Fana	7 May 94
38:24.31		Hatem	Ghoula	TUN	7.6.73	1		Tunis	30 May 98
38:26.4		Daniel	García	MEX	28.10.71	1		Sdr Omme	17 May 97
38:26.53		Robert	Korzeniowski	POL	30.7.68	1		Riga	31 May 02
38:27.57		Robert	Heffernan	IRL	20.2.78	1	NC	Dublin	20 Jul 08
38:30.38			Wang Zhen	CHN	24.8.91	1		Tianjin	16 Sep 12
38:32.0		Erik	Tysse	NOR	4.12.80	1	NC	Bergen (Fana)	13 Jun 08
38:37.6+		Jefferson	Pérez	ECU	1.7.74	1	in 20k	Fana	9 May 98
38:38.0		Walter	Arena	ITA	30.5.64	1		Catania	13 Apr 90
Indoors									
38:31.4		Werner	Heyer	GDR	14.11.56	1		Berlin	12 Jan 80

20 KILOMETRES WALK

Mark	Wind			Nat	Born	Pos	Meet	Venue	Date
1:16:43		Sergey	Morozov ¶	RUS	21.3.88	1	NC	Saransk	8 Jun 08
1:17:16		Vladimir	Kanaykin ¶	RUS	21.3.85	1	RWC	Saransk	29 Sep 07
1:17:21	WR	Jefferson	Pérez	ECU	1.7.74	1	WCh	Saint-Denis	23 Aug 03
1:17:22	WR	Francisco Javier	Fernández ¶	ESP	6.3.77	1		Turku	28 Apr 02
1:17:23		Vladimir	Stankin	RUS	2.1.74	1	NC-w	Adler	8 Feb 04
1:17:25.6t		Bernardo	Segura	MEX	11.2.70	1	SGP	Bergen (Fana)	7 May 94

Mark	Wind	Name		Nat	Born	Pos	Meet	Venue	Date
1:17:30		Alex	Schwazer ¶	ITA	26.12.84	1		Lugano	18 Mar 12
1:17:33		Nathan	Deakes	AUS	17.8.77	1		Cixi	23 Apr 05
1:17:36			Kanaykin			1	NC	Cheboksary	17 Jun 07
1:17:36			Wang Zhen	CHN	24.8.91	1		Taicang	30 Mar 12
1:17:38		Valeriy	Borchin ¶ (10)	RUS	11.9.86	1	NC-w	Adler	28 Feb 09
1:17:40			Chen Ding	CHN	5.8.92	2		Taicang	30 Mar 12
1:17:41			Zhu Hongjun	CHN	18.8.83	2		Cixi	23 Apr 05
1:17:43		Yohann	Diniz	FRA	1.1.78	2		Lugano	18 Mar 12
1:17:46		Julio	Martínez	GUA	27.9.73	1		Eisenhüttenstadt	8 May 99
1:17:46		Roman	Rasskazov	RUS	28.4.79	1	NC	Moskva	19 May 00
1:17:47		Andrey	Ruzavin	RUS	28.3.86	1	NC-w	Sochi	18 Feb 12
1:17:52			Fernández			1		La Coruña	4 Jun 05
1:17:53			Cui Zhide	CHN	11.1.83	3		Cixi	23 Apr 05
1:17:55			Borchin			1	NC-w	Adler	23 Feb 08
1:17:56		Alejandro	López	MEX	9.2.75	2		Eisenhüttenstadt	8 May 99
1:18:00			Fernández			2	WCh	Saint-Denis	23 Aug 03
1:18:03.3twR			Bo Lingtang	CHN	12.8.70	1	NC	Beijing	7 Apr 94
1:18:05		Dmitriy	Yesipchuk (20)	RUS	17.11.74	1	NC-w	Adler	4 Mar 01
1:18:06		Viktor	Burayev ¶	RUS	23.8.82	2	NC-w	Adler	4 Mar 01
1:18:06		Vladimir	Parvatkin	RUS	10.10.84	1	NC-w	Adler	12 Mar 05
1:18:07			Rasskazov			1	NC-w	Adler	20 Feb 00
1:18:07			Rasskazov			3	WCh	Saint-Denis	23 Aug 03
1:18:07			Li Gaobo	CHN	4.5.89	4		Cixi	23 Apr 05
1:18:12		Artur	Meleshkevich	BLR	11.4.75	1		Brest	10 Mar 01
		(30/24)							
1:18:13wR		Pavol	Blazek	SVK	9.7.58	1		Hildesheim	16 Sep 90
1:18:13			Wang Hao	CHN	16.8.89	1	NG	Jinan	22 Oct 09
1:18:14		Mikhail	Khmelnitskiy	BLR	24.7.69	1	NC	Soligorsk	13 May 00
1:18:14		Noé	Hernández	MEX	15.3.78	4	WCh	Saint-Denis	23 Aug 03
1:18:16		Vladimir	Andreyev	RUS	7.9.66	2	NC	Moskva	19 May 00
1:18:17		Ilya	Markov	RUS	19.6.72	2	NC-w	Adler	12 Mar 05
		(30)							
1:18:18		Yevgeniy	Misyulya	BLR	13.3.64	1		Eisenhüttenstadt	11 May 96
1:18:18		Sergey	Bakulin	RUS	13.11.86	2	NC-w	Adler	23 Feb 08
1:18:20wR		Andrey	Perlov	RUS	12.12.61	1	NC	Moskva	26 May 90
1:18:20		Denis	Nizhegorodov	RUS	26.7.80	3	NC-w	Adler	4 Mar 01
1:18:22		Robert	Korzeniowski	POL	30.7.68	1		Hildesheim	9 Jul 00
1:18:23		Andrey	Makarov	BLR	2.1.71	2	NC	Soligorsk	13 May 00
1:18:25		Andrey	Krivov	RUS	14.11.85	3	NC-w	Sochi	18 Feb 12
1:18:25		Erick	Barrondo	GUA	14.6.91	3		Lugano	18 Mar 12
1:18:27		Daniel	García	MEX	28.10.71	2	WCp	Podebrady	19 Apr 97
1:18:27			Xing Shucai	CHN	4.8.84	5		Cixi	23 Apr 05
		(40)							
1:18:29		Stanislav	Yemelyanov	RUS	23.10.90	4	NC-w	Sochi	18 Feb 12
1:18:28		Pyotr	Trofimov	RUS	28.11.83	1	NC-w	Sochi	23 Feb 13
1:18:30			Yu Chaohong	CHN	12.12.76	6		Cixi	23 Apr 05
1:18:31			Han Yucheng	CHN	16.12.78	7		Cixi	23 Apr 05
1:18:32			Li Zewen	CHN	5.12.73	4	WCp	Podebrady	19 Apr 97
1:18:33			Liu Yunfeng ¶	CHN	3.8.79	8		Cixi	23 Apr 05
1:18:34		Eder	Sánchez	MEX	21.5.86	3	WCp	Cheboksary	10 May 08
1:18:34		Yusuke	Suzuki	JPN	2.1.88	1	AsiC	Nomi	10 Mar 13
1:18:35.2t		Stefan	Johansson	SWE	11.4.67	1	SGP	Bergen (Fana)	15 May 92
1:18:36		Mikhail	Shchennikov	RUS	24.12.67	1	NC	Sochi	20 Apr 96
		(50)							

100th man 1:19:32, 200th 1:20:37, 300th 1:21:23, 400th 1:21:59, 500th 1:2227

Probable short course

1:18:33		Mikhail	Shchennikov	RUS	24.12.67	1	4-N	Livorno	10 Jul 93

Drugs disqualification

1:16:53dq		Vladimir	Kanaykin ¶	RUS	21.3.85	2	NC	Saransk	8 Jun 08
1:17:52			Morozov ¶			2	NC-w	Sochi	18 Feb 12

30 KILOMETRES WALK

2:01:13+		Vladimir	Kanaykin ¶	RUS	21.3.85	1	in 35k	Adler	19 Feb 06
2:01:44.1t		Maurizio	Damilano	ITA	6.4.57	1		Cuneo	3 Oct 92
2:01:47+			Kanaykin			1	in 35k	Adler	13 Mar 05
2:02:27+			Kanaykin			1	in 35k	Adler	8 Feb 04
2:02:41		Andrey	Perlov	RUS	12.12.61	1	NC-w	Sochi	19 Feb 89
2:02:45		Yevgeniy	Misyulya	BLR	13.3.64	1		Mogilyov	28 Apr 91
2:03:06		Daniel	Bautista	MEX	4.8.52	1		Cherkassy	27 Apr 80
2:03:50+		Vladimir	Parvatkin	RUS	10.10.84	2	in 35k	Adler	19 Feb 06

MEN All-time

Mark	Wind	Name		Nat	Born	Pos	Meet	Venue	Date
2:03:56.5t		Thierry	Toutain	FRA	14.2.62	1		Héricourt	24 Mar 91
2:04:00		Aleksandr	Potashov	BLR	12.3.62	1		Adler	14 Feb 93
2:04:24		Valeriy	Spitsyn	RUS	5.12.65	1	NC-w	Sochi	22 Feb 92
2:04:30		Vitaliy	Matsko (10)	RUS	8.6.60	2	NC-w	Sochi	19 Feb 89
2:04:49+		Semyon	Lovkin	RUS	14.7.77	1=	in 35k	Adler	1 Mar 03
2:04:49+		Stepan	Yudin	RUS	3.4.80	1=	in 35k	Adler	1 Mar 03
2:04:50+		Sergey	Kirdyapkin	RUS	16.1.80	2	in 35k	Adler	13 Mar 05
2:04:55.5t		Guillaume	Leblanc	CAN	14.4.62	1		Sept-Iles	16 Jun 90
2:05:01		Sergey	Katureyev	RUS	29.9.67	2	NC-w	Sochi	22 Feb 92
2:05:05		Pyotr	Pochenchuk	UKR	26.7.54	2		Cherkassy	27 Apr 80
2:05:06		Nathan	Deakes	AUS	17.8.77	1	NC	Hobart	27 Aug 06
2:05:08+		Denis	Nizhegorodov	RUS	26.7.80	3	in 35k	Adler	19 Feb 06
2:05:09		Mikhail	Shchennikov	RUS	24.12.67	1	NC-w	Adler	11 Feb 96
2:05:12		Valeriy	Suntsov (20)	RUS	10.7.55	3		Cherkassy	27 Apr 80

35 KILOMETRES WALK

Mark	Wind	Name		Nat	Born	Pos	Meet	Venue	Date
2:21:31		Vladimir	Kanaykin ¶	RUS	21.3.85	1	NC-w	Adler	19 Feb 06
2:23:17			Kanaykin			1	NC-w	Adler	8 Feb 04
2:23:17			Kanaykin			1	NC-w	Adler	13 Mar 05
2:24:25		Semyon	Lovkin	RUS	14.7.77	1	NC-w	Adler	1 Mar 03
2:24:25		Sergey	Bakulin	RUS	13.11.86	1	NC-w	Adler	1 Mar 09
2:24:50		Denis	Nizhegorodov	RUS	26.7.80	2	NC-w	Adler	19 Feb 06
2:24:56			Nizhegorodov			2	NC-w	Adler	1 Mar 09
2:25:19		Andrey	Ruzavin	RUS	28.3.86	3	NC-w	Adler	1 Mar 09
2:25:38		Stepan	Yudin	RUS	3.4.80	2	NC-w	Adler	1 Mar 03
2:25:42		Sergey	Kirdyapkin	RUS	18.6.80	1	NC-w	Sochi	18 Feb 12
2:25:57			Kirdyapkin			2	NC-w	Adler	13 Mar 05
2:25:58		German	Skurygin ¶	RUS	15.9.63	1	NC-w	Adler	20 Feb 98
2:25:59			Kanaykin ¶			1	NC-w	Adler	23 Feb 08
2:25:59		Mikhail	Ryzhov	RUS	17.12.91	2	NC-w	Sochi	26 Feb 12
		(14/9)							
2:26:16		Alex	Schwazer ¶ (10)	ITA	26.12.84	1		Montalto Di Castro	24 Jan 10
2:26:25		Aleksey	Voyevodin ¶	RUS	9.8.70	2	NC-w	Adler	8 Feb 04
2:26:29		Yuriy	Andronov	RUS	6.11.71	4	NC-w	Adler	1 Mar 09
2:26:33		Ivan	Noskov	RUS	16.7.88	3	NC-w	Sochi	26 Feb 12
2:26:36		Igor	Yerokhin ¶	RUS	4.9.85	1	NC-w	Sochi	26 Feb 11
2:26:46		Oleg	Ishutkin	RUS	22.7.75	1	NC-w	Adler	9 Feb 97
2:27:02		Yevgeniy	Shmalyuk	RUS	14.1.76	1	NC-w	Adler	20 Feb 00
2:27:07		Dmitriy	Dolnikov	RUS	19.11.72	2	NC-w	Adler	20 Feb 98
2:27:21		Pavel	Nikolayev	RUS	18.12.77	3	NC-w	Adler	20 Feb 98
2:27:29		Nikolay	Matyukhin	RUS	13.12.68	2	NC-w	Adler	9 Feb 97
2:27:42		Aleksey	Bartsaykin (20)	RUS	22.3.89	2	NC-w	Sochi	23 Feb 13

50 KILOMETRES WALK

Mark	Wind	Name		Nat	Born	Pos	Meet	Venue	Date
3:34:14	WR	Denis	Nizhegorodov	RUS	26.7.80	1	WCp	Cheboksary	11 May 08
3:35:27.2t	WR	Yohann	Diniz	FRA	1.1.78	1		Reims	12 Mar 11
3:35:29			Nizhegorodov			1	NC	Cheboksary	13 Jun 04
3:35:47		Nathan	Deakes	AUS	17.8.77	1	NC	Geelong	2 Dec 06
3:35:59		Sergey	Kirdyapkin	RUS	16.1.80	1	OG	London	11 Aug 12
3:36:03	WR	Robert	Korzeniowski	POL	30.7.68	1	WCh	Saint-Denis	27 Aug 03
3:36:04		Alex	Schwazer ¶	ITA	26.12.84	1	NC	Rosignano Solvay	11 Feb 07
3:36:06			Yu Chaohong	CHN	12.12.76	1	NG	Nanjing	22 Oct 05
3:36:13			Zhao Chengliang	CHN	1.6.84	2	NG	Nanjing	22 Oct 05
3:36:20			Han Yucheng	CHN	16.12.78	1	NC	Nanning	27 Feb 05
3:36:39	WR		Korzeniowski			1	EC	München	8 Aug 02
3:36:42		German	Skurygin ¶ (10)	RUS	15.9.63	2	WCh	Saint-Denis	27 Aug 03
3:36:53		Jared	Tallent	AUS	17.10.84	2	OG	London	11 Aug 12
3:37:04			Schwazer			2	WCp	Cheboksary	11 May 08
3:37:09			Schwazer			1	OG	Beijing	22 Aug 08
3:37:16			Si Tianfeng	CHN	17.6.84	3	OG	London	11 Aug 12
3:37:26	WR	Valeriy	Spitsyn	RUS	5.12.65	1	NC	Moskva	21 May 00
3:37:41	WR	Andrey	Perlov	RUS	12.12.61	1	NC	Leningrad	5 Aug 89
3:37:46		Andreas	Erm	GER	12.3.76	3	WCh	Saint-Denis	27 Aug 03
3:37:54		Robert	Heffernan	IRL	20.2.78	4	OG	London	11 Aug 12
3:37:56			Heffernan			1	WCh	Moskva	14 Aug 13
3:37:58			Xing Shucai	CHN	4.8.84	2	NC	Nanning	27 Feb 05
3:38:01		Aleksey	Voyevodin ¶	RUS	9.8.70	4	WCh	Saint-Denis	27 Aug 03
3:38:02			Nizhegorodov			1	WCp	La Coruña	14 May 06
3:38:08			Kirdyapkin			1	WCh	Helsinki	12 Aug 05
3:38:08		Igor	Yerokhin ¶	RUS	4.9.85	1	NC	Saransk	8 Jun 08

Mark	Wind	Name		Nat	Born	Pos	Meet	Venue	Date
3:38:08			Kirdyapkin			1	WCp	Saransk	13 May 12
3:38:17	WR	Ronald	Weigel	GDR	8.8.59	1	IM	Potsdam	25 May 86
3:38:23			Nizhegorodov			5	WCh	Saint-Denis	27 Aug 03
3:38:29		Vyacheslav	Ivanenko	RUS	3.3.61	1	OG	Seoul	30 Sep 88
		(30/21)							
3:38:43		Valentí	Massana	ESP	5.7.70	1	NC	Orense	20 Mar 94
3:38:46		Sergey	Bakulin	RUS	13.11.86	1	NC	Saransk	12 Jun 11
3:38:58		Mikhail	Ryzhov	RUS	17.12.91	2	WCh	Moskva	14 Aug 13
3:39:01			Li Jianbo	CHN	14.11.86	7	OG	London	11 Aug 12
3:39:17			Dong Jimin	CHN	10.10.83	4	NC	Nanning	27 Feb 05
3:39:21		Vladimir	Potemin	RUS	15.1.80	2	NC	Moskva	21 May 00
3:39:22		Sergey	Korepanov	KAZ	9.5.64	1	WCp	Mézidon-Canon	2 May 99
3:39:34		Valentin	Kononen	FIN	7.3.69	1		Dudince	25 Mar 00
3:39:45		Hartwig	Gauder	GDR	10.11.54	3	OG	Seoul	30 Sep 88
		(30)							
3:39:46		Matej	Tóth	SVK	10.2.83	1	NC	Dudince	26 Mar 11
3:39:54		Jesús Angel	García	ESP	17.10.69	1	WCp	Podebrady	20 Apr 97
3:40:02		Aleksandr	Potashov	BLR	12.3.62	1	NC	Moskva	27 May 90
3:40:07		Andrey	Plotnikov	RUS	12.8.67	2	NC	Moskva	27 May 90
3:40:08		Tomasz	Lipiec ¶	POL	10.5.71	2	WCp	Mézidon-Canon	2 May 99
3:40:12		Oleg	Ishutkin	RUS	22.7.75	2	WCp	Podebrady	20 Apr 97
3:40:12		Yuki	Yamazaki	JPN	16.1.84	1		Wajima	12 Apr 09
3:40:13		Nikolay	Matyukhin	RUS	13.12.68	3	WCp	Mézidon-Canon	2 May 99
3:40:23			Gadasu Alatan	CHN	27.1.84	3	NG	Nanjing	22 Oct 05
3:40:39		Igor	Hlavan	UKR	25.9.90	4	WCh	Moskva	14 Aug 13
		(40)							
3:40:40		Vladimir	Kanaykin ¶	RUS	21.3.85	1	NC	Saransk	12 Jun 05
3:40:46	WR	José	Marin	ESP	21.1.50	1	NC	Valencia	13 Mar 83
3:40:46		Yuriy	Andronov	RUS	6.11.71	1		Moskva	11 Jun 12
3:40:57.9t		Thierry	Toutain	FRA	14.2.62	1		Héricourt	29 Sep 96
3:41:02		Francisco Javier	Fernández ¶	ESP	6.3.77	1	NC	San Pedro del Pinatar	1 Mar 09
3:41:09		Érick	Barrondo	GUA	14.6.91	1		Dudince	23 Mar 13
3:41:10			Zhao Jianguo	CHN	19.1.88	1	AsiC	Wajima	16 Apr 06
3:41:16		Trond	Nymark	NOR	28.12.76	2	WCh	Berlin	21 Aug 09
3:41:20	WR	Raúl	González	MEX	29.2.52	1		Podebrady	11 Jun 78
3:41:20			Zhao Yongsheng	CHN	16.4.70	1	WCp	Beijing	30 Apr 95
3:41:20		Grzegorz	Sudol	POL	28.8.78	6	WCh	Moskva	14 Aug 13
		(51)							

100th man 3:44:53, 200th 3:49:50, 300th 3:52:31, 400th 3:55:07. 500th 3:57:47

Drugs disqualification

3:36:55		Vladimir	Kanaykin ¶	RUS	21.3.85	(2)	WCp	Cheboksary	11 May 08
3:37:54		Igor	Yerokhin ¶	RUS	4.9.85	(5)	OG	London	11 Aug 12
3:38:10			Yerokhin			(2)	WCp	Saransk	13 May 12

100 KILOMETRES WALK

8:38.07	Viktor	Ginko	BLR	7.12.65	1		Scanzorosciate	27 Oct 02
8:43:30		Ginko			1		Scanzorosciate	29 Oct 00
8:44:28		Ginko			1		Scanzorosciate	19 Oct 03
8:48:28	Modris	Liepins	LAT	30.8.66	1		Scanzorosciate	28 Oct 01
8:54:35	Aleksey	Rodionov	RUS	5.3.57	1		Scanzorosciate	15 Nov 98
8:55:12	Pascal	Kieffer	FRA	6.5.61	1		Besançon	18 Oct 92
8:55:40	Vitaliy	Popovich	UKR	22.10.62	1		Scanzorosciate	31 Oct 99
8:58:12	Gérard	Lelièvre	FRA	13.11.49	1		Laval	7 Oct 84
8:58:47	Zóltan	Czukor	HUN	18.12.62	2		Scanzorosciate	27 Oct 02

Some notes on all-time lists at end of 2013

Deep all-time lists (generally 100 performances and 500 performers for all standard men's and women's events) have been compiled by Richard Hymans and Peter Matthews to be published next year by Jonas Hedman in a book that also includes the author's selections of the all-time top ten greats for each event (delayed from last year).

Oldest mark in top 50 World Lists: Men: in wind assisted sections: LJ 8.49w Ralph Boston USA 2 Sep 1964, 100m 9.91w Bob Hayes USA 15 Oct 1964; in main lists: SP: 37= 21.78 Randy Matson USA 22 Apr 1967. Women: by an individual 100mh 48= 12.59 Anneliese Ehrhardt GDR 8 Sep 1972.

Oldest marks in top 500s: LJ : 364= 8.13 Jesse Owens 25 May 35, then 800m: 486= 1:45.7 Roger Moens 3 Aug 1955

Changes in 2013: Many events had considerable changes to deep all-time lists, but those changing least were:
Women: No change to 200m for legal wind top 50s, or to 800m
Highest changes in: women's SP Schwanitz to 51st, DT: Gu Siyu to 50th, Hep: Melnychenko to 44th

50 years ago – end of 1963 world 100th best all-time marks included (note hand times): **Men**: 100m 10.1, 200m 20.5, 400m 45.6, 800m 1:46.5, 1500m 3:39.3, 1M 3:57.2, 5000m 13:44.2, 10000m 28:48.6, 3000mSt 8:35.4, 110m 13.5, 400mh 50.0, HJ 2.15, PV 4.91, LJ 8.01, TJ 16.51, SP 18.96, DT 59.28, HT 67.73, JT 83.90, 50k 4:10:27.
Women: 100m 11.4, 200m 23.4, 400m 53.9, 800m 2:05.0, 80mh 10.6, HJ 1.75, LJ 6.35, SP 16.59, DT 55.01, JT 55.76

MEN All-time

Mark	Wind	Name		Nat	Born	Pos	Meet	Venue	Date

WOMEN'S ALL-TIME WORLD LISTS

100 METRES

Mark	Wind	Name		Nat	Born	Pos	Meet	Venue	Date
10.49WR	0.0	Florence	Griffith-Joyner	USA	21.12.59	1q1	NC/OT	Indianapolis	16 Jul 88
		@ Probably strongly wind-assisted, but recognised as a US and world record							
10.61	1.2		Griffith-Joyner			1	NC/OT	Indianapolis	17 Jul 88
10.62	1.0		Griffith-Joyner			1q3	OG	Seoul	24 Sep 88
10.64	1.2	Carmelita	Jeter	USA	24.11.79	1		Shanghai	20 Sep 09
10.65A	1.1	Marion	Jones ¶	USA	12.10.75	1	WCp	Johannesburg	12 Sep 98
10.67	-0.1		Jeter			1	WAF	Thessaloníki	13 Sep 09
10.70 (WR)	1.6		Griffith-Joyner			1s1	NC/OT	Indianapolis	17 Jul 88
10.70	-0.1		Jones			1	WCh	Sevilla	22 Aug 99
10.70	2.0		Jeter			1	Pre	Eugene	4 Jun 11
10.70	0.6	Shelly-Ann	Fraser-Pryce	JAM	27.12.86	1	NC	Kingston	29 Jun 12
10.71	0.1		Jones			1		Chengdu	12 May 98
10.71	2.0		Jones			1s2	NC	New Orleans	19 Jun 98
10.72	2.0		Jones			1	NC	New Orleans	20 Jun 98
10.72	0.0		Jones			1	Herc	Monaco	8 Aug 98
10.72	0.0		Jones			1	Athl	Lausanne	25 Aug 98
10.73	2.0	Christine	Arron	FRA	13.9.73	1	EC	Budapest	19 Aug 98
10.73	0.1		Fraser-Pryce			1	WCh	Berlin	17 Aug 09
10.74	1.3	Merlene	Ottey	JAM/SLO	10.5.60	1	GPF	Milano	7 Sep 96
10.75	0.6		Jones			1	GGala	Roma	14 Jul 98
10.75	0.4	Kerron	Stewart	JAM	16.4.84	1	GGala	Roma	10 Jul 09
10.75	0.1		Stewart			2	WCh	Berlin	17 Aug 09
10.75	1.5		Fraser-Pryce			1	OG	London (OS)	4 Aug 12
10.76 WR	1.7	Evelyn	Ashford	USA	15.4.57	1	WK	Zürich	22 Aug 84
10.76	0.9		Jones			1	VD	Bruxelles	22 Aug 97
10.76	0.3		Jones			1q4	WCh	Sevilla	21 Aug 99
10.76	1.1	Veronica	Campbell-Brown	JAM	15.5.82	1	GS	Ostrava	31 May 11
10.77	0.9	Irina	Privalova (10)	RUS	22.11.68	1rA	Athl	Lausanne	6 Jul 94
10.77	-0.9		Jones			1rA	WK	Zürich	12 Aug 98
10.77	0.7	Ivet	Lalova	BUL	18.5.84	1	ECp-1A	Plovdiv	19 Jun 04
10.78A	1.0	Dawn	Sowell	USA	27.3.66	1	NCAA	Provo	3 Jun 89
10.78	1.7		Ottey			1	Expo	Sevilla	30 May 90
10.78	0.4		Ottey			1	GPF	Paris	3 Sep 94
10.78	1.1		Jones			1	BrGP	London (CP)	5 Aug 00
10.78	1.8	Torri	Edwards ¶	USA	31.1.77	1s2	OT	Eugene	28 Jun 08
10.78	0.0		Fraser			1	OG	Beijing	17 Aug 08
10.78	0.8		Campbell-Brown			1	Pre	Eugene	3 Jul 10
10.78	0.4		Jeter			1	VD	Bruxelles	16 Sep 11
10.78	1.5		Jeter			2	OG	London (OS)	4 Aug 12
		(37 performances by 13 athletes)							
10.79	0.0		Li Xuemei	CHN	5.1.77	1	NG	Shanghai	18 Oct 97
10.79	-0.1	Inger	Miller	USA	12.6.72	2	WCh	Sevilla	22 Aug 99
10.81 WR	1.7	Marlies	Göhr'	GDR	21.3.58	1	OD	Berlin	8 Jun 83
10.82	-1.0	Gail	Devers	USA	19.11.66	1	OG	Barcelona	1 Aug 92
10.82	0.4	Gwen	Torrence	USA	12.6.65	2	GPF	Paris	3 Sep 94
10.82	-0.3	Zhanna	Pintusevich-Block ¶	UKR	6.7.72	1	WCh	Edmonton	6 Aug 01
10.82	-0.7	Sherone	Simpson	JAM	12.8.84	1	NC	Kingston	24 Jun 06
		(20)							
10.83	1.7	Marita	Koch	GDR	18.2.57	2	OD	Berlin	8 Jun 83
10.83	-1.0	Juliet	Cuthbert	JAM	9.4.64	2	OG	Barcelona	1 Aug 92
10.83	0.1	Ekateríni	Thánou ¶	GRE	1.2.75	2s1	WCh	Sevilla	22 Aug 99
10.84	1.3	Chioma	Ajunwa ¶	NGR	25.12.70	1		Lagos	11 Apr 92
10.84	1.9	Chandra	Sturrup	BAH	12.9.71	1	Athl	Lausanne	5 Jul 05
10.84	1.8	Kelly-Ann	Baptiste	TRI	14.10.86	1		Clermont	5 Jun 10
10.85	2.0	Anelia	Nuneva	BUL	30.6.62	1h1	NC	Sofia	2 Sep 88
10.85	1.0	Muna	Lee	USA	30.10.81	1	OT	Eugene	28 Jun 08
10.85	1.5	Tianna	Madison	USA	30.8.85	4	OG	London (OS)	4 Aug 12
10.86	0.6	Silke	Gladisch'	GDR	20.6.64	1	NC	Potsdam	20 Aug 87
		(30)							
10.86	1.2	Chryste	Gaines ¶	USA	14.9.70	1	WAF	Monaco	14 Sep 03
10.86	2.0	Marshevet	Myers	USA	25.9.84	2	Pre	Eugene	4 Jun 11
10.88	0.4	Lauryn	Williams	USA	11.9.83	2	WK	Zürich	19 Aug 05
10.89	1.8	Katrin	Krabbe ¶	GDR	22.11.69	1		Berlin	20 Jul 88
10.89	0.0		Liu Xiaomei	CHN	11.1.72	2	NG	Shanghai	18 Oct 97
10.89	1.5	Allyson	Felix	USA	18.11.85	5	OG	London (OS)	4 Aug 12
10.90	1.4	Glory	Alozie	NGR/ESP	30.12.77	1		La Laguna	5 Jun 99

Mark	Wind	Name		Nat	Born	Pos	Meet	Venue	Date
10.90	1.8	Shalonda	Solomon	USA	19.12.85	2		Clermont	5 Jun 10
10.91	0.2	Heike	Drechsler'	GDR/GER	16.12.64	2	GWG	Moskva	6 Jul 86
10.91	1.1	Savatheda	Fynes	BAH	17.10.74	2	Athl	Lausanne	2 Jul 99
		(40)							
10.91	1.5	Debbie	Ferguson McKenzie	BAH	16.1.76	1	CG	Manchester	27 Jul 02
10.92	0.0	Alice	Brown	USA	20.9.60	2q2	NC/OT	Indianapolis	16 Jul 88
10.92	1.1	D'Andre	Hill	USA	19.4.73	3	NC	Atlanta	15 Jun 96
10.92	0.1	Yuliya	Nesterenko	BLR	15.6.79	1s1	OG	Athína	21 Aug 04
10.92	1.0	Blessing	Okagbare	NGR	9.10.88	1s3	OG	London (OS)	4 Aug 12
10.93	1.8	Ewa	Kasprzyk	POL	7.9.57	1	NC	Grudziadz	27 Jun 86
10.93	1.0	Tayna	Lawrence	JAM	17.9.75	3	VD	Bruxelles	30 Aug 02
10.94A	0.6	Diane	Williams	USA	14.12.60	2	USOF	USAF Academy	3 Jul 83
10.94	1.0	Carlette	Guidry	USA	4.9.68	1	NC	New York	14 Jun 91
10.95	1.0	Bärbel	Wöckel'	GDR	21.3.55	2	NC	Dresden	1 Jul 82
10.95	2.0	Me'Lisa	Barber	USA	4.10.80	2	adidas	Carson	20 May 07
10.95A	1.8	Simone	Facey	JAM	7.5.85	1	Big 12	Boulder	18 May 08
		(52)	100th women 11.04, 200th 11.14, 300th 11.20, 400th 11.26, 500th 11.30						
Doubtful wind reading									
10.83	0.0	Sheila	Echols	USA	2.10.64	1q2	NC/OT	Indianapolis	16 Jul 88
10.86	0.0	Diane	Williams	USA	14.12.60	2q1	NC/OT	Indianapolis	16 Jul 88
Probably semi-automatic timing									
10.87	1.9	Lyudmila	Kondratyeva	RUS	11.4.58	1		Leningrad	3 Jun 80
Low altitude best: 10.91 1.6		Sowell				1	NC	Houston	16 Jun 89
Wind-assisted to 10.76 performances and 10.90 performers									
10.54	3.0		Griffith-Joyner			1	OG	Seoul	25 Sep 88
10.60	3.2		Griffith-Joyner			1h1	NC/OT	Indianapolis	16 Jul 88
10.68	2.2		Jones			1	DNG	Stockholm	1 Aug 00
10.70	2.6		Griffith-Joyner			1s2	OG	Seoul	25 Sep 88
10.72	3.0		Jeter			1s1	NC	Eugene	26 Jun 09
10.74	2.7		Jeter			1	NC	Eugene	24 Jun 11
10.75	4.1		Jones			1h3	NC	New Orleans	19 Jun 98
10.76	3.4	Marshevet	Hooker/Myers	USA	25.9.84	1q1	NC/OT	Eugene	27 Jun 08
10.77	2.3	Gail	Devers	USA	19.11.66	1	Jen	San José	28 May 94
10.77	2.3	Ekateríni	Thánou ¶	GRE	1.2.75	1		Rethymno	28 May 99
10.78	5.0	Gwen	Torrence	USA	12.6.65	1q3	NC/OT	Indianapolis	16 Jul 88
10.78	3.3	Muna	Lee	USA	30.10.81	2	NC	Eugene	26 Jun 09
10.79	3.3	Marlies	Göhr'	GDR	21.3.58	1	NC	Cottbus	16 Jul 80
10.80	2.9	Pam	Marshall	USA	16.8.60	1	NC	Eugene	20 Jun 86
10.80	2.8	Heike	Drechsler'	GDR	16.12.64	1	Bisl	Oslo	5 Jul 86
10.82	2.2	Silke	Gladisch/Möller	GDR	20.6.64	1s1	WCh	Roma	30 Aug 87
10.84	2.9	Alice	Brown	USA	20.9.60	2	NC	Eugene	20 Jun 86
10.86	3.4	Lauryn	Williams	USA	11.9.83	2q1	NC/OT	Eugene	27 Jun 08
10.86	2.9	Murielle	Ahouré	CIV	23.8.87	1		Clermont	4 Jun 11
10.87	3.0	Me'Lisa	Barber	USA	4.10.80	1s1	NC	Carson	25 Jun 05
10.88	5.9	Alexandria	Anderson	USA	28.1.87	1		Austin	14 Apr 12
10.89	3.1	Kerstin	Behrendt	GDR	2.9.67	2		Berlin	13 Sep 88
10.90	2.5	Damola	Osayomi ¶	NGR	26.6.86	1	AfrG	Maputo	12 Sep 11
10.89	2.9	Sanya	Richards-Ross	USA	26.2.85	1	TexR	Austin	31 Mar 12
Hand timing									
10.6	0.1	Zhanna	Pintusevich ¶	UKR	6.7.72	1		Kiev	12 Jun 97
10.7		Merlene	Ottey	JAM	10.5.60	1h	NC	Kingston	15 Jul 88
10.7	1.1	Juliet	Cuthbert	JAM	9.4.64	1	NC	Kingston	4 Jul 92
10.7		Mary	Onyali	NGR	3.2.68	1	NC	Lagos	22 Jun 96
10.7	-0.2	Svetlana	Goncharenko	RUS	28.5.71	1		Rostov-na-Donu	30 May 98
10.7A	1.3	Blessing	Okagbare	NGR	9.10.86	1		El Paso	10 Apr 10
10.7w	2.6	Savatheda	Fynes	BAH	17.10.74	1	NC	Nassau	22 Jun 95
Drugs disqualification									
10.75	-0.4		Jones			1	OG	Sydney	23 Sep 00
10.78	0.1		Jones			1	ISTAF	Berlin	1 Sep 00
10.85	0.9	Kelli	White ¶	USA	1.4.77	1	WCh	Saint-Denis	24 Aug 03
10.79w	2.3	Kelli	White ¶	USA	1.4.77	1		Carson	1 Jun 03

200 METRES

Mark	Wind	Name		Nat	Born	Pos	Meet	Venue	Date
21.34wR	1.3	Florence	Griffith-Joyner	USA	21.12.59	1	OG	Seoul	29 Sep 88
21.56wR	1.7		Griffith-Joyner			1s1	OG	Seoul	29 Sep 88
21.62A	-0.6	Marion	Jones ¶	USA	12.10.75	1	WCp	Johannesburg	11 Sep 98
21.64	0.8	Merlene	Ottey	JAM	10.5.60	1	VD	Bruxelles	13 Sep 91
21.66	-1.0		Ottey			1	WK	Zürich	15 Aug 90
21.69	1.0	Allyson	Felix	USA	18.11.85	1	NC/OT	Eugene	30 Jun 12
21.71wR	0.7	Marita	Koch	GDR	18.2.57	1	v CAN	Karl-Marx-Stadt	10 Jun 79
21.71wR	0.3		Koch			1	OD	Potsdam	21 Jul 84

Mark	Wind	Name			Nat	Born	Pos	Meet	Venue	Date
21.71WR	1.2	Heike	Drechsler'		GDR	16.12.64	1	NC	Jena	29 Jun 86
21.71WR	-0.8		Drechsler				1	EC	Stuttgart	29 Aug 86
21.72	1.3	Grace	Jackson		JAM	14.6.61	2	OG	Seoul	29 Sep 88
21.72	-0.1	Gwen	Torrence		USA	12.6.65	1s2	OG	Barcelona	5 Aug 92
21.74	0.4	Marlies	Göhr'		GDR	21.3.58	1	NC	Erfurt	3 Jun 84
21.74	1.2	Silke	Gladisch'		GDR	20.6.64	1	WCh	Roma	3 Sep 87
21.74	0.6	Veronica	Campbell-Brown	(10)	JAM	15.5.82	1	OG	Beijing	21 Aug 08
21.75	-0.1	Juliet	Cuthbert		JAM	9.4.64	2s2	OG	Barcelona	5 Aug 92
21.76	0.3		Koch				1	NC	Dresden	3 Jul 82
21.76	0.7		Griffith-Joyner				1q1	OG	Seoul	28 Sep 88
21.76	-0.8		Jones				1	WK	Zürich	13 Aug 97
21.77	-0.1		Griffith-Joyner				1q2	NC/OT	Indianapolis	22 Jul 88
21.77	1.0		Ottey				1	Herc	Monaco	7 Aug 93
21.77	-0.3		Torrence				1	ASV	Köln	18 Aug 95
21.77	0.6	Inger	Miller		USA	12.6.72	1	WCh	Sevilla	27 Aug 99
21.78	-1.3		Koch				1	NC	Leipzig	11 Aug 85
21.79	1.7		Gladisch				1	NC	Potsdam	22 Aug 87
21.80	-1.1		Ottey				1	Nik	Nice	10 Jul 90
21.80	0.4		Jones				1	GWG	Uniondale, NY	20 Jul 98
21.81	-0.1	Valerie	Brisco		USA	6.7.60	1	OG	Los Angeles	9 Aug 84
21.81	0.4		Ottey				1	ASV	Köln	19 Aug 90
21.81	-0.6		Torrence				1	OG	Barcelona	6 Aug 92
21.81	0.0		Torrence				1	Herc	Monaco	25 Jul 95
21.81	1.6		Jones				1	Pre	Eugene	30 May 99
21.81	1.7		Felix				1	WCh	Osaka	31 Aug 07
		(33/14)								
21.83	-0.2	Evelyn	Ashford		USA	15.4.57	1	WCp	Montreal	24 Aug 79
21.85	0.3	Bärbel	Wöckel'		GDR	21.3.55	2	OD	Potsdam	21 Jul 84
21.87	0.0	Irina	Privalova		RUS	22.11.68	2	Herc	Monaco	25 Jul 95
21.93	1.3	Pam	Marshall		USA	16.8.60	2	NC/OT	Indianapolis	23 Jul 88
21.95	0.3	Katrin	Krabbe ¶		GDR	22.11.69	1	EC	Split	30 Aug 90
21.97	1.9	Jarmila	Kratochvílová		CZE	26.1.51	1	PTS	Bratislava	6 Jun 81
		(20)								
21.99	0.9	Chandra	Cheeseborough		USA	10.1.59	2	NC	Indianapolis	19 Jun 83
21.99	1.1	Marie-José	Pérec		FRA	9.5.68	1	BNP	Villeneuve d'Ascq	2 Jul 93
21.99	1.1	Kerron	Stewart		JAM	16.4.84	2	NC	Kingston	29 Jun 08
22.00	1.3	Sherone	Simpson		JAM	12.8.84	1	NC	Kingston	25 Jun 06
22.01	-0.5	Anelia	Nuneva'		BUL	30.6.62	1	NC	Sofiya	16 Aug 87
22.01	0.0		Li Xuemei		CHN	5.1.77	1	NG	Shanghai	22 Oct 97
22.01	0.6	Muna	Lee		USA	30.10.81	4	OG	Beijing	21 Aug 08
22.04A	0.7	Dawn	Sowell		USA	27.3.66	1	NCAA	Provo	2 Jun 89
22.06A	0.7	Evette	de Klerk'		RSA	21.8.65	1		Pietersburg	8 Apr 89
22.07	-0.1	Mary	Onyali		NGR	3.2.68	1	WK	Zürich	14 Aug 96
		(30)								
22.09	-0.3	Sanya	Richards-Ross		USA	26.2.85	1	DL	New York	9 Jun 12
22.09	-0.2	Shelly-Ann	Fraser-Pryce		JAM	27.12.86	2	OG	London (OS)	8 Aug 12
22.10	-0.1	Kathy	Cook'		GBR	3.5.60	4	OG	Los Angeles	9 Aug 84
22.11	1.0	Carmelita	Jeter		USA	24.11.79	2	NC/OT	Eugene	30 Jun 12
22.13	1.2	Ewa	Kasprzyk		POL	7.9.57	2	GWG	Moskva	8 Jul 86
22.14	-0.6	Carlette	Guidry		USA	4.9.68	1	NC	Atlanta	23 Jun 96
22.15	1.0	Shalonda	Solomon		USA	19.12.85	1	NC	Eugene	26 Jun 11
22.17A	-2.3	Zhanna	Pintusevich-Block ¶		UKR	6.7.72	1		Monachil	9 Jul 97
	22.24			-0.3			2	VD	Bruxelles	30 Aug 02
22.18	-0.6	Dannette	Young-Stone		USA	6.10.64	2	NC	Atlanta	23 Jun 96
22.18	0.9	Galina	Malchugina		RUS	17.12.62	1s2	NC	Sankt Peterburg	4 Jul 96
		(40)								
22.18	0.5	Merlene	Frazer		JAM	27.12.73	1s2	WCh	Sevilla	25 Aug 99
22.19	1.5	Natalya	Bochina		RUS	4.1.62	2	OG	Moskva	30 Jul 80
22.19	0.0	Debbie	Ferguson McKenzie		BAH	16.1.76	1	GP II	Saint-Denis	3 Jul 99
22.19	1.9	Kimberlyn	Duncan		USA	2.8.91	1s2	NCAA	Des Moines	7 Jun 12
22.19	1.0	Aleksandra	Fedoriva		RUS	13.9.88	1	NC	Cheboksary	6 Jul 12
22.20	2.0	Kim	Gevaert		BEL	5.8.78	1	NC	Bruxelles	9 Jul 06
22.21 WR	1.9	Irena	Szewinska'		POL	24.5.46	1		Potsdam	13 Jun 74
22.22	-0.9	Falilat	Ogunkoya		NGR	12.5.68	1	AfCh	Dakar	22 Aug 98
22.22	0.6	Beverly	McDonald		JAM	15.2.70	2	WCh	Sevilla	27 Aug 99
22.22	0.3	Rachelle	Smith (Boone)		USA	30.6.81	2	NC	Carson	26 Jun 05
		(50)	100th woman 22.38, 200th 22.63, 300th 22.77, 4th 22.87, 500th 22.97							

Wind-assisted   Performers listed to 22.20

| 21.82 | 3.1 | Irina | Privalova | | RUS | 22.11.68 | 1 | Athl | Lausanne | 6 Jul 94 |
| 21.91 | 2.8 | Muna | Lee | | USA | 30.10.81 | 1 | | Fort-de-France | 10 May 08 |

Mark	Wind	Name		Nat	Born	Pos	Meet	Venue	Date
22.12	2.6	Kimberlyn	Duncan	USA	2.8.91	1	SEC	Baton Rouge	13 May 12
22.16	3.1	Dannette	Young-Stone	USA	6.10.64	2	Athl	Lausanne	6 Jul 94
22.16	3.2	Nanceen	Perry	USA	19.4.77	1		Austin	6 May 00
22.18A	2.8	Melinda	Gainsford-Taylor	AUS	1.10.71	1		Pietersburg	18 Mar 00
22.18	3.2	Kimberlyn	Duncan	USA	2.8.91	1		Baton Rouge	23 Apr 11
22.19A	3.1	Angella	Taylor'	CAN	28.9.58	1		Colorado Springs	21 Jul 82
22.20	5.6	Marshevet	Hooker/Myers	USA	25.9.84	3	NC/OT	Eugene	6 Jul 08
Hand timing									
21.9	-0.1	Svetlana	Goncharenko	RUS	28.5.71	1		Rostov-na-Donu	31 May 98
21.6w	2.5	Pam	Marshall	USA	16.8.60	1	NC	San José	26 Jun 87
Drugs disqualification									
22.05	-0.3	Kelli	White ¶	USA	1.4.77	1	WCh	Saint-Denis	28 Aug 03
22.18i		Michelle	Collins ¶	USA	12.2.71	1	WI	Birmingham	15 Mar 03

300 METRES

Times in 300m races only

Mark		Name		Nat	Born	Pos	Meet	Venue	Date
35.30A		Ana Gabriela	Guevara	MEX	4.3.77	1		Ciudad de México	3 May 03
35.46		Kathy	Cook'	GBR	3.5.60	1	Nike	London (CP)	18 Aug 84
35.46		Chandra	Cheeseborough	USA	10.1.59	2	Nike	London (CP)	18 Aug 84
Indoors									
35.45		Irina	Privalova	RUS	22.11.68	1		Moskva	17 Jan 93
35.48	#	Svetlana	Goncharenko	RUS	28.5.71	1		Tampere	4 Feb 98

400 METRES

Mark		Name		Nat	Born	Pos	Meet	Venue	Date
47.60 WR		Marita	Koch	GDR	18.2.57	1	WCp	Canberra	6 Oct 85
47.99 WR		Jarmila	Kratochvílová	CZE	26.1.51	1	WCh	Helsinki	10 Aug 83
48.16 WR			Koch			1	EC	Athína	8 Sep 82
48.16			Koch			1	Drz	Praha	16 Aug 84
48.22			Koch			1	EC	Stuttgart	28 Aug 86
48.25		Marie-José	Pérec	FRA	9.5.68	1	OG	Atlanta	29 Jul 96
48.26			Koch			1	GO	Dresden	27 Jul 84
48.27		Olga	Vladykina'	UKR	30.6.63	2	WCp	Canberra	6 Oct 85
48.45			Kratochvílová			1	NC	Praha	23 Jul 83
48.59		Tatána	Kocembová'	CZE	2.5.62	2	WCh	Helsinki	10 Aug 83
48.60 WR			Koch			1	ECp	Torino	4 Aug 79
48.60			Vladykina			1	ECp	Moskva	17 Aug 85
48.61			Kratochvílová			1	WCp	Roma	6 Sep 81
48.63		Cathy	Freeman	AUS	16.2.73	2	OG	Atlanta	29 Jul 96
48.65			Bryzgina'			1	OG	Seoul	26 Sep 88
48.70		Sanya	Richards	USA	26.2.85	1	WCp	Athína	16 Sep 06
48.73			Kocembová			2	Drz	Praha	16 Aug 84
48.77			Koch			1	v USA	Karl-Marx-Stadt	9 Jul 82
48.82			Kratochvílová			1	Ros	Praha	23 Jun 83
48.83		Valerie	Brisco	USA	6.7.60	1	OG	Los Angeles	6 Aug 84
48.83			Pérec			1	OG	Barcelona	5 Aug 92
48.83			Richards			1	VD	Bruxelles	4 Sep 09
48.85			Kratochvílová			2	EC	Athína	8 Sep 82
48.86			Kratochvílová			1	WK	Zürich	18 Aug 82
48.86			Koch			1	NC	Erfurt	2 Jun 84
48.87			Koch			1	VD	Bruxelles	27 Aug 82
48.88			Koch			1	OG	Moskva	28 Jul 80
48.89 WR			Koch			1		Potsdam	29 Jul 79
48.89			Koch			1		Berlin	15 Jul 84
48.89		Ana Gabriela	Guevara	MEX	4.3.77	1	WCh	Saint-Denis	27 Aug 03
		(30/9)							
49.05		Chandra (10)	Cheeseborough	USA	10.1.59	2	OG	Los Angeles	6 Aug 84
49.07		Tonique	Williams-Darling	BAH	17.1.76	1	ISTAF	Berlin	12 Sep 04
49.10		Falilat	Ogunkoya	NGR	12.5.68	3	OG	Atlanta	29 Jul 96
49.11		Olga	Nazarova ¶	RUS	1.6.65	1s1	OG	Seoul	25 Sep 88
49.16		Antonina	Krivoshapka	RUS	21.7.87	1	NC	Cheboksary	5 Jul 12
49.19		Mariya	Pinigina'	UKR	9.2.58	3	WCh	Helsinki	10 Aug 83
49.24		Sabine	Busch	GDR	21.11.62	2	NC	Erfurt	2 Jun 84
49.28 WR		Irena	Szewinska'	POL	24.5.46	1	OG	Montreal	29 Jul 76
49.28		Pauline	Davis-Thompson	BAH	9.7.66	4	OG	Atlanta	29 Jul 96
49.28		Yuliya	Gushchina	RUS	4.3.83	2	NC	Cheboksary	5 Jul 12
49.29		Charity	Opara ¶	NGR	20.5.72	1	GGala	Roma	14 Jul 98
		(20)							
49.30		Petra	Müller'	GDR	18.7.65	1		Jena	3 Jun 88
49.30		Lorraine	Fenton'	JAM	8.9.73	2	Herc	Monaco	19 Jul 02
49.32		Shericka	Williams	JAM	17.9.85	2	WCh	Berlin	18 Aug 09
49.35		Anastasiya	Kapachinskaya ¶	RUS	21.11.79	1	NC	Cheboksary	22 Jul 11

Mark	Wind	Name		Nat	Born	Pos	Meet	Venue	Date
49.40		Jearl	Miles-Clark	USA	4.9.66	1	NC	Indianapolis	14 Jun 97
49.42		Grit	Breuer ¶	GER	16.2.72	2	WCh	Tokyo	27 Aug 91
49.43		Kathy	Cook'	GBR	3.5.60	3	OG	Los Angeles	6 Aug 84
49.43A		Fatima	Yusuf	NGR	2.5.71	1	AfG	Harare	15 Sep 95
49.47		Aelita	Yurchenko	UKR	1.1.65	2	Kuts	Moskva	4 Sep 88
49.49		Olga	Zaytseva	RUS	10.11.84	1	NCp	Tula	16 Jul 06
		(30)							
49.53		Vanya	Stambolova ¶	BUL	28.11.83	1	GP	Rieti	27 Aug 06
49.54		Amantle	Montsho	BOT	4.7.83	1	AfrC	Porto Novo	28 Jun 12
49.56		Bärbel	Wöckel'	GDR	21.3.55	1		Erfurt	30 May 82
49.56		Monique	Hennagan	USA	26.5.76	1	NC/OT	Sacramento	17 Jul 04
49.57		Grace	Jackson	JAM	14.6.61	1	Nik	Nice	10 Jul 88
49.58		Dagmar	Rübsam'	GDR	3.6.62	3	NC	Erfurt	2 Jun 84
49.59		Marion	Jones ¶	USA	12.10.75	1r6	MSR	Walnut	16 Apr 00
49.59		Katharine	Merry	GBR	21.9.74	1	GP	Athína	11 Jun 01
49.59		Allyson	Felix	USA	18.11.85	2	WCh	Daegu	29 Aug 11
49.61		Ana Fidelia	Quirot	CUB	23.3.63	1	PAm	La Habana	5 Aug 91
		(40)							
49.61		Christine	Ohuruogu ¶	GBR	17.5.84	1	WCh	Osaka	29 Aug 07
49.63		Novlene	Williams-Mills	JAM	26.4.82	1		Shanghai	23 Sep 06
49.64		Gwen	Torrence	USA	12.6.65	2	Nik	Nice	15 Jul 92
49.64		Ximena	Restrepo	COL	10.3.69	3	OG	Barcelona	5 Aug 92
49.64		Deedee	Trotter	USA	8.12.82	1	NC	Indianapolis	23 Jun 07
49.64		Debbie	Dunn	USA	26.3.78	1	NC	Des Moines	26 Jun 10
49.65		Natalya	Nazarova	RUS	26.5.79	1	NC	Tula	31 Jul 04
49.65		Nicola	Sanders	GBR	23.6.82	2	WCh	Osaka	29 Aug 07
49.66		Christina	Brehmer/Lathan	GDR	28.2.58	3	OG	Moskva	28 Jul 80
49.66		Lillie	Leatherwood	USA	6.7.64	1	NC	New York	15 Jun 91
		(50)							

100th woman 50.23, 200th 50.85, 300th 51.18, 400th 51.44, 500th 51.67

Mark	Wind	Name		Nat	Born	Pos	Meet	Venue	Date
Hand timing									
48.9		Olga	Nazarova ¶	RUS	1.6.65	1	NP	Vladivostok	13 Sep 88
49.2A		Ana Fidelia	Quirot	CUB	23.3.63	1	AmCp	Bogotá	13 Aug 89

600 METRES

Mark		Name		Nat	Born	Pos	Meet	Venue	Date
1:22.63		Ana Fidelia	Quirot	CUB	23.3.63	1		Guadalajara, ESP	25 Jul 97
1:22.87		Maria Lurdes	Mutola	MOZ	27.10.72	1		Liège (NX)	27 Aug 02
1:23.35		Pamela	Jelimo	KEN	5.12.89	1		Liège (NX)	5 Jul 12

800 METRES

Mark		Name		Nat	Born	Pos	Meet	Venue	Date
1:53.28 wr		Jarmila	Kratochvílová	CZE	26.1.51	1		München	26 Jul 83
1:53.43 wr		Nadezhda	Olizarenko'	UKR	28.11.53	1	OG	Moskva	27 Jul 80
1:54.01		Pamela	Jelimo	KEN	5.12.89	1	WK	Zürich	29 Aug 08
1:54.44		Ana Fidelia	Quirot	CUB	23.3.63	1	WCp	Barcelona	9 Sep 89
1:54.68			Kratochvílová			1	WCh	Helsinki	9 Aug 83
1:54.81		Olga	Mineyeva	RUS	1.9.52	2	OG	Moskva	27 Jul 80
1:54.82			Quirot			1	ASV	Köln	24 Aug 97
1:54.85 wr			Olizarenko			1	Prav	Moskva	12 Jun 80
1:54.87			Jelimo			1	OG	Beijing	18 Aug 08
1:54.94 wr		Tatyana	Kazankina ¶	RUS	17.12.51	1	OG	Montreal	26 Jul 76
1:54.97			Jelimo			1	Gaz	Saint-Denis	18 Jul 08
1:54.99			Jelimo			1	ISTAF	Berlin	1 Jun 08
1:55.04			Kratochvílová			1	OsloG	Oslo	23 Aug 83
1:55.05		Doina	Melinte	ROU	27.12.56	1	NC	Bucuresti	1 Aug 82
1:55.1 '			Mineyeva			1	Znam	Moskva	6 Jul 80
1:55.16			Jelimo			1	VD	Bruxelles	5 Sep 08
1:55.19		Maria Lurdes	Mutola	MOZ	27.10.72	1	WK	Zürich	17 Aug 94
1:55.19		Jolanda	Ceplak ¶	SLO	12.9.76	1rA	NA	Heusden	20 Jul 02
1:55.26		Sigrun	Wodars/Grau (10)	GDR	7.11.65	1	WCh	Roma	31 Aug 87
1:55.29			Mutola			2	ASV	Köln	24 Aug 97
1:55.32		Christine	Wachtel	GDR	6.1.65	2	WCh	Roma	31 Aug 87
1:55.41			Mineyeva			1	EC	Athína	8 Sep 82
1:55.41			Jelimo			1	Bisl	Oslo	6 Jun 08
1:55.42		Nikolina	Shtereva	BUL	25.1.55	2	OG	Montreal	26 Jul 76
1:55.43			Mutola			1	WCh	Stuttgart	17 Aug 93
1:55.45		Caster	Semenya	RSA	7.1.91	1	WCh	Berlin	19 Aug 09
1:55.46		Tatyana	Providokhina	RUS	26.3.53	3	OG	Moskva	27 Jul 80
1:55.5			Mineyeva			1	Kuts	Podolsk	21 Aug 82
1:55.54		Ellen	van Langen	NED	9.2.66	1	OG	Barcelona	3 Aug 92
1:55.54			Liu Dong	CHN	24.12.73	1	NG	Beijing	9 Sep 93
		(30/16)							

Mark	Wind	Name		Nat	Born	Pos	Meet	Venue	Date
1:55.56		Lyubov	Gurina	RUS	6.8.57	3	WCh	Roma	31 Aug 87
1:55.60		Elfi	Zinn	GDR	24.8.53	3	OG	Montreal	26 Jul 76
1:55.68		Ella	Kovacs	ROU	11.12.64	1	RomIC	Bucuresti	2 Jun 85
1:55.69		Irina	Podyalovskaya	RUS	19.10.59	1	Izv	Kyiv	22 Jun 84
	(20)								
1:55.74		Anita	Weiss'	GDR	16.7.55	4	OG	Montreal	26 Jul 76
1:55.87		Svetlana	Masterkova	RUS	17.1.68	1	Kuts	Moskva	18 Jun 99
1:55.87		Mariya	Savinova	RUS	13.8.85	1	WCh	Daegu	4 Sep 11
1:55.96		Lyudmila	Veselkova	RUS	25.10.50	2	EC	Athína	8 Sep 82
1:55.96		Yekaterina	Podkopayeva'	RUS	11.6.52	1		Leningrad	27 Jul 83
1:55.99		Liliya	Nurutdinova ¶	RUS	15.12.63	2	OG	Barcelona	3 Aug 92
1:56.00		Tatyana	Andrianova	RUS	10.12.79	1	NC	Kazan	18 Jul 08
1:56.0 WR		Valentina	Gerasimova	KAZ	15.5.48	1	NC	Kyiv	12 Jun 76
1:56.0		Inna	Yevseyeva	UKR	14.8.64	1		Kyiv	25 Jun 88
1:56.04		Janeth	Jepkosgei	KEN	13.12.83	1	WCh	Osaka	28 Aug 07
	(30)								
1:56.09		Zulia	Calatayud	CUB	9.11.79	1	Herc	Monaco	19 Jul 02
1:56.1		Ravilya	Agletdinova'	BLR	10.2.60	2	Kuts	Podolsk	21 Aug 82
1:56.2 '		Totka	Petrova ¶	BUL	17.12.56	1		Paris (C)	6 Jul 79
1:56.2		Tatyana	Mishkel	UKR	10.6.52	3	Kuts	Podolsk	21 Aug 82
1:56.21		Martina	Kämpfert'	GDR	11.11.59	4	OG	Moskva	27 Jul 80
1:56.21		Zamira	Zaytseva	UZB	16.2.53	2		Leningrad	27 Jul 83
1:56.21		Kelly	Holmes	GBR	19.4.70	2	GPF	Monaco	9 Sep 95
1:56.24			Qu Yunxia	CHN	8.12.72	2	NG	Beijing	9 Sep 93
1:56.40		Jearl	Miles-Clark	USA	4.9.66	3	WK	Zürich	11 Aug 99
1:56.42		Paula	Ivan	ROU	20.7.63	1	Balk	Ankara	16 Jul 88
	(40)								
1:56.43		Hasna	Benhassi	MAR	1.6.78	2	OG	Athína	23 Aug 04
1:56.44		Svetlana	Styrkina	RUS	1.1.49	5	OG	Montreal	26 Jul 76
1:56.51		Slobodanka	Colovic	YUG	10.1.65	1		Beograd	17 Jun 87
1:56.53		Patricia	Djaté	FRA	3.1.71	3	GPF	Monaco	9 Sep 95
1:56.56		Ludmila	Formanová	CZE	2.1.74	4	WK	Zürich	11 Aug 99
1:56.57		Zoya	Rigel	RUS	15.10.52	3	EC	Praha	31 Aug 78
1:56.59		Natalya	Khrushchelyova	RUS	30.5.73	2	NC	Tula	31 Jul 04
1:56.59		Francine	Niyonsaba	BDI	5.5.93	1	VD	Bruxelles	7 Sep 12
1:56.60		Natalya	Tsyganova	RUS	7.2.71	1	NC	Tula	25 Jul 00
1:56.6		Tamara	Sorokina'	RUS	15.8.50	5	Kuts	Podolsk	21 Aug 82
	(50)								

100th woman 1:57.5, 200th 1:58.59, 300th 1:59.35, 400th 1:59.85, 500th 2:00.45

Indoors: 1:55.85 Stephanie Graf   AUT   26.4.73   2   EI   Wien   3 Mar 02
Drugs disqualification
1:54.85   Yelena   Soboleva ¶   RUS   3.10.82   (1)   NC   Kazan   18 Jul 08

1000 METRES

Mark	Wind	Name		Nat	Born	Pos	Meet	Venue	Date
2:28.98 WR		Svetlana	Masterkova	RUS	17.1.68	1	VD	Bruxelles	23 Aug 96
2:29.34 WR		Maria Lurdes	Mutola	MOZ	27.10.72	1	VD	Bruxelles	25 Aug 95
2:30.6 WR		Tatyana	Providokhina	RUS	26.3.53	1		Podolsk	20 Aug 78
2:30.67 WR		Christine	Wachtel	GDR	6.1.65	1	ISTAF	Berlin	17 Aug 90
2:30.85		Martina	Kämpfert'	GDR	11.11.59	1		Berlin	9 Jul 80
2:31.50		Natalya	Artyomova ¶	RUS	5.1.63	1	ISTAF	Berlin	10 Sep 91
2:31.5 A		Maricica	Puica	ROU	29.7.50	1		Poiana Brasov	1 Jun 86
2:31.51		Sandra	Gasser ¶	SUI	27.7.62	1		Jerez de la Frontera	13 Sep 89

1500 METRES

Mark	Wind	Name		Nat	Born	Pos	Meet	Venue	Date
3:50.46 WR			Qu Yunxia	CHN	8.12.72	1	NG	Beijing	11 Sep 93
3:50.98			Jiang Bo	CHN	13.3.77	1	NG	Shanghai	18 Oct 97
3:51.34			Lang Yinglai	CHN	22.8.79	2	NG	Shanghai	18 Oct 97
3:51.92			Wang Junxia	CHN	9.1.73	2	NG	Beijing	11 Sep 93
3:52.47 WR		Tatyana	Kazankina ¶	RUS	17.12.51	1	WK	Zürich	13 Aug 80
3:53.91			Yin Lili ¶	CHN	11.11.79	3	NG	Shanghai	18 Oct 97
3:53.96		Paula	Ivan'	ROU	20.7.63	1	OG	Seoul	1 Oct 88
3:53.97			Lan Lixin	CHN	14.2.79	4	NG	Shanghai	18 Oct 97
3:54.23		Olga	Dvirna	RUS	11.2.53	1	NC	Kyiv	27 Jul 82
3:54.52			Zhang Ling (10)	CHN	13.4.80	5	NG	Shanghai	18 Oct 97
3:55.0 ' WR			Kazankina ¶			1	Znam	Moskva	6 Jul 80
3:55.01			Lan Lixin			1h2	NG	Shanghai	17 Oct 97
3:55.07			Dong Yanmei	CHN	16.2.77	6	NG	Shanghai	18 Oct 97
3:55.30		Hassiba	Boulmerka	ALG	10.7.68	1	OG	Barcelona	8 Aug 92
3:55.33		Süreyya	Ayhan ¶	TUR	6.9.78	1	VD	Bruxelles	5 Sep 03
3:55.38			Qu Yunxia			2h2	NG	Shanghai	17 Oct 97
3:55.47			Zhang Ling			3h2	NG	Shanghai	17 Oct 97
3:55.60			Ayhan			1	WK	Zürich	15 Aug 03

Mark	Wind	Name		Nat	Born	Pos	Meet	Venue	Date
3:55.68	Yuliya	Chizhenko ¶		RUS	30.8.79	1	Gaz	Saint-Denis	8 Jul 06
3:55.82		Dong Yanmei				4h2	NG	Shanghai	17 Oct 97
3:56.0 wr		Kazankina ¶				1		Podolsk	28 Jun 76
3:56.14	Zamira	Zaytseva		UZB	16.2.53	2	NC	Kyiv	27 Jul 82
3:56.18	Maryam	Jamal		BRN	16.9.84	1	GP	Rieti	27 Aug 06
3:56.22		Ivan				1	WK	Zürich	17 Aug 88
3:56.31		Liu Dong		CHN	24.12.73	5h2	NG	Shanghai	17 Oct 97
3:56.43	Yelena	Soboleva ¶		RUS	3.10.82	2	Gaz	Saint-Denis	8 Jul 06
3:56.50	Tatyana	Pozdnyakova		RUS	4.3.56	3	NC	Kyiv	27 Jul 82
3:56.54	Abeba	Aregawi		ETH	5.7.90	1	GGala	Roma	31 May 12
3:56.55		Jamal				1	GGala	Roma	10 Jul 09
3:56.56		Kazankina ¶				1	OG	Moskva	1 Aug 80
	(30/20)								
3:56.62	Asli	Çakir Alptekin		TUR	20.8.85	1	DL	Saint-Denis	6 Jul 12
3:56.63	Nadezhda	Ralldugina		UKR	15.11.57	1	Drz	Praha	18 Aug 84
3:56.65	Yekaterina	Podkopayeva'		RUS	11.6.52	1		Rieti	2 Sep 84
3:56.7 '	Lyubov	Smolka		UKR	29.11.52	2	Znam	Moskva	6 Jul 80
3:56.7	Doina	Melinte		ROU	27.12.56	1		Bucuresti	12 Jul 86
3:56.77+	Svetlana	Masterkova		RUS	17.1.68	1	WK	Zürich	14 Aug 96
3:56.8 '	Nadezhda	Olizarenko'		UKR	28.11.53	3	Znam	Moskva	6 Jul 80
3:56.91	Lyudmila	Rogachova		RUS	30.10.66	2	OG	Barcelona	8 Aug 92
3:56.91	Tatyana	Tomashova ¶		RUS	1.7.75	1	EC	Göteborg	13 Aug 06
3:56.97	Gabriela	Szabo		ROU	14.11.75	1	Herc	Monaco	8 Aug 98
	(30)								
3:56.98	Faith	Kipyegon		KEN	10.1.94	2	DL	Doha	10 May 13
3:57.03		Liu Jing		CHN	3.2.71	6h2	NG	Shanghai	17 Oct 97
3:57.05	Svetlana	Guskova		MDA	19.8.59	4	NC	Kyiv	27 Jul 82
3:57.12	Mary	Decker/Slaney		USA	4.8.58	1	vNord	Stockholm	26 Jul 83
3:57.22	Maricica	Puica		ROU	29.7.50	1		Bucuresti	1 Jul 84
3:57.40	Suzy	Favor Hamilton		USA	8.8.68	1	Bisl	Oslo	28 Jul 00
3:57.4 '	Totka	Petrova ¶		BUL	17.12.56	1	Balk	Athína	11 Aug 79
3:57.41	Jackline	Maranga		KEN	16.12.77	3	Herc	Monaco	8 Aug 98
3:57.46		Zhang Linli		CHN	6.3.73	3	NG	Beijing	11 Sep 93
3:57.54	Genzebe	Dibaba		ETH	8.2.91	3	DL	Doha	10 May 13
	(40)								
3:57.65	Anna	Alminova #		RUS	17.1.85	1	DL	Saint-Denis	16 Jul 10
3:57.71	Christiane	Wartenberg'		GDR	27.10.56	2	OG	Moskva	1 Aug 80
3:57.71	Carla	Sacramento		POR	10.12.71	4	Herc	Monaco	8 Aug 98
3:57.72	Galina	Zakharova		RUS	7.9.56	1	NP	Baku	14 Sep 84
3:57.73	Natalya	Yevdokimova		RUS	17.3.78	2	GP	Rieti	28 Aug 05
3:57.90	Kelly	Holmes		GBR	19.4.70	1	OG	Athína	28 Aug 04
3:57.92	Tatyana	Samolenko/Dorovskikh		UKR	12.8.61	4	OG	Barcelona	8 Aug 92
3:58.12	Naomi	Mugo		KEN	2.1.77	5	Herc	Monaco	8 Aug 98
3:58.20	Anita	Weyermann		SUI	8.12.77	6	Herc	Monaco	8 Aug 98
3:58.2 '	Natalia	Marasescu' ¶		ROU	3.10.52	1	NC	Bucuresti	13 Jul 79
	(50)								

Drugs disqualification: 3:56.15 Mariem Alaoui Selsouli ¶ MAR 8.4.84 1   DL   Saint-Denis   6 Jul 12

100th woman 3:59.95, 200th 4:02.37, 300th 4:04.55, 400th 4:05.86, 500th 4:06.81

1 MILE

Mark	Wind	Name		Nat	Born	Pos	Meet	Venue	Date
4:12.56 wr	Svetlana	Masterkova		RUS	17.1.68	1	WK	Zürich	14 Aug 96
4:15.61 wr	Paula	Ivan'		ROU	20.7.63	1	Nik	Nice	10 Jul 89
4:15.8	Natalya	Artyomova ¶		RUS	5.1.63	1		Leningrad	5 Aug 84
4:16.71 wr	Mary	Slaney (Decker)		USA	4.8.58	1	WK	Zürich	21 Aug 85
4:17.25	Sonia	O'Sullivan		IRL	28.11.69	1	Bisl	Oslo	22 Jul 94
4:17.33	Maricica	Puica		ROU	29.7.50	2	WK	Zürich	21 Aug 85
4:17.57	Zola	Budd'		GBR	26.5.66	3	WK	Zürich	21 Aug 85
4:17.14 **indoor**	Doina	Melinte		ROU	27.12.56	1		East Rutherford	9 Feb 90

Drugs dq: 4:15.63   Yelena   Soboleva ¶   RUS   3.10.82   1   Moskva   29 Jun 07

2000 METRES

Mark	Wind	Name		Nat	Born	Pos	Meet	Venue	Date
5:25.36 wr	Sonia	O'Sullivan		IRL	28.11.69	1	TSB	Edinburgh	8 Jul 94
5:26.93	Yvonne	Murray		GBR	4.10.64	2	TSB	Edinburgh	8 Jul 94
5:28.69 wr	Maricica	Puica		ROU	29.7.50	1	PTG	London (CP)	11 Jul 86
5:28.72 wr	Tatyana	Kazankina ¶		RUS	17.12.51	1		Moskva	4 Aug 84
5:29.43+		Wang Junxia		CHN	9.1.73	1h2	NG	Beijing	12 Sep 93
5:29.64	Tatyana	Pozdnyakova		UKR	4.3.56	2		Moskva	4 Aug 84
5:30.19	Zola	Budd'		GBR	26.5.66	3	PTG	London (CP)	11 Jul 86
5:30.19	Gelete	Burka		ETH	15.2.86	1	VD	Bruxelles	4 Sep 09
5:30.92	Galina	Zakharova		RUS	7.9.56	3		Moskva	4 Aug 84
5:31.03	Gulnara	Samitova/Galkina		RUS	9.7.78	1		Sochi	27 May 07

Indoors: 5:30.53   Gabriela   Szabo   ROU   14.11.75   1   Sindelfingen   8 Mar 98

Mark	Wind	Name		Nat	Born	Pos	Meet	Venue	Date

3000 METRES

Mark	Wind	Name		Nat	Born	Pos	Meet	Venue	Date
8:06.11	WR		Wang Junxia	CHN	9.1.73	1	NG	Beijing	13 Sep 93
8:12.18			Qu Yunxia	CHN	8.12.72	2	NG	Beijing	13 Sep 93
8:12.19	WR		Wang Junxia			1h2	NG	Beijing	12 Sep 93
8:12.27			Qu Yunxia			2h2	NG	Beijing	12 Sep 93
8:16.50			Zhang Linli	CHN	6.3.73	3	NG	Beijing	13 Sep 93
8:19.78			Ma Liyan	CHN	6.9.68	3h2	NG	Beijing	12 Sep 93
8:21.26			Ma Liyan			4	NG	Beijing	13 Sep 93
8:21.42		Gabriela	Szabo	ROU	14.11.75	1	Herc	Monaco	19 Jul 02
8:21.64		Sonia	O'Sullivan	IRL	28.11.69	1	TSB	London (CP)	15 Jul 94
8:21.84			Zhang Lirong	CHN	3.3.73	5	NG	Beijing	13 Sep 93
8:22.06	WR		Zhang Linli			1h1	NG	Beijing	12 Sep 93
8:22.20		Paula	Radcliffe	GBR	17.12.73	2	Herc	Monaco	19 Jul 02
8:22.44			Zhang Lirong			2h1	NG	Beijing	12 Sep 93
8:22.62	WR	Tatyana	Kazankina ¶	RUS	17.12.51	1		Leningrad	26 Aug 84
8:23.23		Edith	Masai (10)	KEN	4.4.67	3	Herc	Monaco	19 Jul 02
8:23.26		Olga	Yegorova	RUS	28.3.72	1	WK	Zürich	17 Aug 01
8:23.75			Yegorova			1	GP	Saint-Denis	6 Jul 01
8:23.96			Yegorova			1	GGala	Roma	29 Jun 01
8:24.19			Szabo			2	WK	Zürich	17 Aug 01
8:24.31			Szabo			1	GP	Paris (C)	29 Jul 98
8:24.51	+	Meseret	Defar	ETH	19.11.83	1	in 2M	Bruxelles	14 Sep 07
8:24.66			Defar			1	DNG	Stockholm	25 Jul 06
8:25.03			Szabo			1	WK	Zürich	11 Aug 99
8:25.40		Yelena	Zadorozhnaya	RUS	3.12.77	2	GGala	Roma	29 Jun 01
8:25.56		Tatyana	Tomashova ¶	RUS	1.7.75	3	GGala	Roma	29 Jun 01
8:25.59			Szabo			1	GP	Paris (C)	21 Jul 99
8:25.62		Berhane	Adere	ETH	21.7.73	3	WK	Zürich	17 Aug 01
8:25.82			Szabo			1	VD	Bruxelles	3 Sep 99
8:25.83		Mary	Slaney	USA	4.8.58	1	GGala	Roma	7 Sep 85
8:25.92		Gelete	Burka	ETH	15.2.86	2	DNG	Stockholm	25 Jul 06
		(30/17)							
8:26.48		Zahra	Ouaziz	MAR	20.12.69	2	WK	Zürich	11 Aug 99
8:26.53		Tatyana	Samolenko' ¶	UKR	12.8.61	1	OG	Seoul	25 Sep 88
8:26.78	WR	Svetlana	Ulmasova	UZB	4.2.53	1	NC	Kyiv	25 Jul 82
		(20)							
8:27.12	WR	Lyudmila	Bragina	RUS	24.7.43	1	v USA	College Park	7 Aug 76
8:27.15		Paula	Ivan'	ROU	20.7.63	2	OG	Seoul	25 Sep 88
8:27.62		Getenesh	Wami	ETH	11.12.74	4	WK	Zürich	17 Aug 01
8:27.83		Maricica	Puica	ROU	29.7.50	2	GGala	Roma	7 Sep 85
8:28.41		Sentayehu	Ejigu	ETH	21.6.85	1	Herc	Monaco	22 Jul 10
8:28.66		Vivian	Cheruiyot	KEN	11.9.83	2	WAF	Stuttgart	23 Sep 07
8:28.80		Marta	Domínguez	ESP	3.11.75	3	WK	Zürich	11 Aug 00
8:28.83		Zola	Budd'	GBR	26.5.66	3	GGala	Roma	7 Sep 85
8:28.87		Maryam	Jamal	BRN	16.9.84	1	Bisl	Oslo	29 Jul 05
8:29.02		Yvonne	Murray	GBR	4.10.64	3	OG	Seoul	25 Sep 88
		(30)							
8:29.06		Priscah	Cherono	KEN	27.6.80	3	WAF	Stuttgart	23 Sep 07
8:29.14		Lydia	Cheromei	KEN	11.5.77	5	WK	Zürich	11 Aug 00
8:29.36		Svetlana	Guskova	MDA	19.8.59	2	NC	Kyiv	25 Jul 82
8:29.52		Mariem Alaoui	Selsouli ¶	MAR	8.4.84	1	Herc	Monaco	25 Jul 07
8:29.55		Tirunesh	Dibaba	ETH	1.10.85	1	LGP	London (CP)	28 Jul 06
8:30.18		Mariya	Pantyukhova	RUS	14.8.74	4	WK	Zürich	11 Aug 99
8:30.22		Carla	Sacramento	POR	10.12.71	2	Herc	Monaco	4 Aug 99
8:30.39		Irina	Mikitenko	GER	23.8.72	6	WK	Zürich	11 Aug 00
8:30.45		Yelena	Romanova	RUS	20.3.63	4	OG	Seoul	25 Sep 88
8:30.59		Daniela	Yordanova ¶	BUL	8.3.76	5	GP	Saint-Denis	6 Jul 01
		(40)							
8:30.66		Fernanda	Ribeiro	POR	23.6.69	3	Herc	Monaco	4 Aug 99
8:30.93		Wude	Ayalew	ETH	4.7.87	3	WAF	Thessaloníki	13 Sep 09
8:30.95		Tegla	Loroupe	KEN	9.5.73	2	Herc	Monaco	18 Aug 00
8:31.23		Mercy	Cherono	KEN	7.5.91	2	DNG	Stockholm	22 Aug 13
8:31.27		Joanne	Pavey	GBR	20.9.73	4	VD	Bruxelles	30 Aug 02
8:31.32		Isabella	Ochichi	KEN	28.10.79	1	Gaz	Saint-Denis	23 Jul 04
8:31.38		Shannon	Rowbury	USA	19.9.84	3	Herc	Monaco	22 Jul 10
8:31.67		Natalya	Artyomova ¶	RUS	5.1.63	5	OG	Seoul	25 Sep 88
8:31.69		Lidia	Chojecka	POL	25.1.77	5	VD	Bruxelles	30 Aug 02
8:31.75		Grete	Waitz'	NOR	1.10.53	1	OsloG	Oslo	17 Jul 79
		(50)							

100th woman 8:37.30, 200th 8:43.74, 300th 8:48.16

Mark	Wind	Name		Nat	Born	Pos	Meet	Venue	Date
Indoors:									
8:23.72		Meseret	Defar	ETH	19.11.83	1	Spark	Stuttgart	3 Feb 07
8:23.74		Meselech	Melkamu	ETH	27.4.85	2	Spark	Stuttgart	3 Feb 07
8:25.27		Sentayehu	Ejigu	ETH	21.6.85	2	Spark	Stuttgart	6 Feb 10
8:26.95		Genzebe	Dibaba	ETH	8.2.91	1		Stockholm	21 Feb 13
8:27.86		Liliya	Shobukhova	RUS	13.11.77	1	NC	Moskva	17 Feb 06
8:28.49		Anna	Alminova	RUS	17.1.85	2	Spark	Stuttgart	7 Feb 09
8:29.00		Olesya	Syreva ¶	RUS	25.11.83	2	NC	Moskva	17 Feb 06

5000 METRES

Mark	Wind	Name		Nat	Born	Pos	Meet	Venue	Date
14:11.15	WR	Tirunesh	Dibaba	ETH	1.10.85	1	Bisl	Oslo	6 Jun 08
14:12.88		Meseret	Defar	ETH	19.11.83	1	DNG	Stockholm	22 Jul 08
14:16.63	WR		Defar			1	Bisl	Oslo	15 Jun 07
14:20.87		Vivian	Cheruiyot	KEN	11.9.83	1	DNG	Stockholm	29 Jul 11
14:22.51			Cheruiyot			2	Bisl	Oslo	15 Jun 07
14:23.46			T Dibaba			1	GP	Rieti	7 Sep 08
14:23.68			T Dibaba			1	DL	Saint-Denis	6 Jul 13
14:23.75		Liliya	Shobukhova	RUS	13.11.77	1	NC	Kazan	19 Jul 08
14:24.53	WR		Defar			1		New York (RI)	3 Jun 06
14:24.68	WR	Elvan	Abeylegesse	TUR	11.9.82	1	Bisl	Bergen (Fana)	11 Jun 04
14:25.43			Cheruiyot			1	VD	Bruxelles	5 Sep 08
14:25.52			Defar			2	VD	Bruxelles	5 Sep 08
14:25.84		Almaz	Ayana	ETH	21.11.91	2	DL	Saint-Denis	6 Jul 13
14:26.90			Defar			1	Bisl	Oslo	13 Jun 13
14:27.41			Cheruiyot			1	DL	Saint-Denis	16 Jul 10
14:28.09	WR		Jiang Bo	CHN	13.3.77	1	NG	Shanghai	23 Oct 97
14:28.39		Sentayehu	Ejigu	ETH	21.6.85	2	DL	Saint-Denis	16 Jul 10
14:28.98			Defar			1	VD	Bruxelles	26 Aug 05
14:29.11		Paula	Radcliffe	GBR	17.12.73	1	ECpS	Bydgoszcz	20 Jun 04
14:29.32		Olga	Yegorova (10)	RUS	28.3.72	1	ISTAF	Berlin	31 Aug 01
14:29.32		Berhane	Adere	ETH	21.7.73	1	Bisl	Oslo	27 Jun 03
14:29.52			Defar			1	DL	Saint-Denis	8 Jul 11
14:29.82			Dong Yanmei	CHN	16.2.77	2	NG	Shanghai	23 Oct 97
14:30.10			Cheruiyot			1	WK	Zürich	8 Sep 11
14:30.18			Defar			1	GS	Ostrava	27 Jun 07
14:30.40			T Dibaba			1	Bisl	Oslo	2 Jun 06
14:30.42		Sally	Kipyego	KEN	19.12.85	2	WK	Zürich	8 Sep 11
14:30.63			T Dibaba			1	VD	Bruxelles	25 Aug 06
14:30.88		Getenesh	Wami	ETH	11.12.74	1	NA	Heusden-Zolder	5 Aug 00
14:30.88			T Dibaba			2	Bisl	Bergen (Fana)	11 Jun 04
		(30/14)							
14:31.14		Linet	Masai	KEN	5.12.89	2	DL	Shanghai	23 May 10
14:31.20		Gelete	Burka	ETH	15.2.86	2	GS	Ostrava	27 Jun 07
14:31.48		Gabriela	Szabo	ROU	14.11.75	1	ISTAF	Berlin	1 Sep 98
14:31.91		Meselech	Melkamu	ETH	27.4.85	3	DL	Shanghai	23 May 10
14:31.91		Sylvia	Kibet	KEN	28.3.84	4	DL	Shanghai	23 May 10
14:32.08		Zahra	Ouaziz	MAR	20.12.69	2	ISTAF	Berlin	1 Sep 98
		(20)							
14:32.33			Liu Shixiang ¶	CHN	13.1.71	3h1	NG	Shanghai	21 Oct 97
14:32.74		Ejagayehu	Dibaba	ETH	25.6.82	3	Bisl	Bergen (Fana)	11 Jun 04
14:33.04		Werknesh	Kidane	ETH	21.11.81	2	Bisl	Oslo	19 Jul 08
14:33.13		Gulnara	Galkina	RUS	9.7.78	2	NC	Kazan	13 Jun 13
14:33.48		Viola	Kibiwot	KEN	22.12.83	2	Bisl	Oslo	6 Jun 08
14:33.49		Lucy	Wangui Kabuu	KEN	24.3.84	2	Bisl	Oslo	2 Jun 06
14:33.84		Edith	Masai	KEN	4.4.67	3	Bisl	Oslo	2 Jun 06
14:35.13		Mercy	Cherono	KEN	7.5.91	3	DL	Saint-Denis	8 Jul 11
14:35.30		Priscah	Jepleting/Cherono	KEN	27.6.80	4	Bisl	Oslo	2 Jun 06
14:36.45	WR	Fernanda	Ribeiro	POR	23.6.69	1		Hechtel	22 Jul 95
		(30)							
14:36.52		Mariem Alaoui	Selsouli ¶	MAR	8.4.84	1	G Gala	Roma	13 Jul 07
14:37.07		Jéssica	Augusto	POR	8.11.81	5	DL	Saint-Denis	16 Jul 10
14:37.33	WR	Ingrid	Kristiansen'	NOR	21.3.56	1		Stockholm	5 Aug 86
14:37.56		Genzebe	Dibaba	ETH	8.2.91	3	Bisl	Oslo	9 Jun 11
14:38.09		Mariya	Konovalova	RUS	14.8.74	3	NC	Kazan	19 Jul 08
14:38.21		Isabella	Ochichi	KEN	28.10.79	4	VD	Bruxelles	26 Aug 05
14:38.44		Wude	Ayalew	ETH	4.7.87	5	Bisl	Oslo	3 Jul 09
14:39.19		Ines	Chenonge	KEN	1.2.82	6	DL	Saint-Denis	16 Jul 11
14:39.22		Tatyana	Tomashova ¶	RUS	1.7.75	4	ISTAF	Berlin	31 Aug 07
14:39.83		Leah	Malot	KEN	7.6.72	1	ISTAF	Berlin	1 Sep 00
		(40)							

Mark	Wind	Name		Nat	Born	Pos	Meet	Venue	Date
14:39.96			Yin Lili ¶	CHN	11.11.79	4	NG	Shanghai	23 Oct 97
14:39.96	Jo		Pavey	GBR	20.9.73	3	VD	Bruxelles	25 Aug 06
14:40.14	Florence		Kiplagat	KEN	27.2.87	6	Bisl	Oslo	3 Jul 09
14:40.41			Sun Yingjie ¶	CHN	3.10.77	1	AsiG	Busan	12 Oct 02
14:40.47	Yelena		Zadorozhnaya	RUS	3.12.77	1	ECp-S	Bremen	24 Jun 01
14:40.48	Margaret		Muriuki	KEN	21.3.86	4	Bisl	Oslo	13 Jun 13
14:41.02	Sonia		O'Sullivan	IRL	28.11.69	2	OG	Sydney	25 Sep 00
14:41.23	Ayelech		Worku	ETH	12.6.79	1	BrGP	London (CP)	5 Aug 00
14:41.28	Pauline		Korikwiang	KEN	1.3.88	7	DL	Shanghai	15 May 11
14:42.03	Irina		Mikitenko	GER	23.8.72	3	ISTAF	Berlin	7 Sep 99
	(50)								

Indoors: 14:24.37 — 100th woman 14:51.68, 200th 15:05.69, 300th 15:12.75, 400th 15:18.72, 500th 15:22.87

Mark	Wind	Name		Nat	Born	Pos	Meet	Venue	Date
Indoors:	14:24.37		Defar			1		Stockholm	18 Feb 09
14:24.79			Defar			1	GE Galan	Stockholm	10 Feb 10
14:27.42			T Dibaba			1	BIG	Boston (R)	27 Jan 07
14:39.89	Kimberley		Smith	NZL	19.11.73	1		New York (Arm)	27 Feb 09

Drugs disqualification: 14:36.79 Alemitu Bekele ¶ TUR 17.9.77 4 VD Bruxelles 27 Aug 10

10,000 METRES

Mark	Wind	Name		Nat	Born	Pos	Meet	Venue	Date
29:31.78 WR			Wang Junxia	CHN	9.1.73	1	NG	Beijing	8 Sep 93
29:53.80	Meselech		Melkamu	ETH	27.4.85	1		Utrecht	14 Jun 09
29:54.66	Tirunesh		Dibaba	ETH	1.10.85	1	OG	Beijing	15 Aug 08
29:56.34	Elvan		Abeylegesse	TUR	11.9.82	2	OG	Beijing	15 Aug 08
29:59.20	Meseret		Defar	ETH	19.11.83	1	NC	Birmingham	11 Jul 09
30:01.09	Paula		Radcliffe	GBR	17.12.73	1	EC	München	6 Aug 02
30:04.18	Berhane		Adere	ETH	21.7.73	1	WCh	Saint-Denis	23 Aug 03
30:07.15	Werknesh		Kidane	ETH	21.11.81	2	WCh	Saint-Denis	23 Aug 03
30:07.20			Sun Yingjie ¶	CHN	3.10.77	3	WCh	Saint-Denis	23 Aug 03
30:08.06			Defar			1		Sollentuna	27 Jun 13
30:11.53	Florence		Kiplagat (10)	KEN	27.2.87	2		Utrecht	14 Jun 09
30:11.87	Wude		Ayalew	ETH	4.7.87	3		Utrecht	14 Jun 09
30:12.53	Lornah		Kiplagat (KEN)	NED	1.5.74	4	WCh	Saint-Denis	23 Aug 03
30:13.37			Zhong Huandi	CHN	28.6.67	2	NG	Beijing	8 Sep 93
30:13.74 WR	Ingrid		Kristiansen'	NOR	21.3.56	1	Bisl	Oslo	5 Jul 86
30:15.67			T Dibaba			1		Sollentuna	28 Jun 05
30:17.15			Radcliffe			1	GP	Gateshead	27 Jun 04
30:17.49	Derartu		Tulu	ETH	21.3.72	1	OG	Sydney	30 Sep 00
30:18.39	Ejegayehu		Dibaba	ETH	25.6.82	2		Sollentuna	28 Jun 05
30:19.39			Kidane			1	GP II	Stanford	29 May 05
30:20.75			T Dibaba			1	OG	London (OS)	3 Aug 12
30:21.67			Abeylegesse			1	ECp	Antalya	15 Apr 06
30:22.22	Shalane		Flanagan	USA	8.7.81	3	OG	Beijing	15 Aug 08
30:22.48	Getenesh		Wami	ETH	11.12.74	2	OG	Sydney	30 Sep 00
30:22.88	Fernanda		Ribeiro	POR	23.6.69	3	OG	Sydney	30 Sep 00
30:23.07	Alla		Zhilyayeva (20)	RUS	5.2.69	5	WCh	Saint-Denis	23 Aug 03
30:23.25			Kristiansen			1	EC	Stuttgart	30 Aug 86
30:24.02			T Dibaba			1	WCh	Helsinki	6 Aug 05
30:24.36			Xing Huina	CHN	25.2.84	1	OG	Athína	27 Aug 04
30:24.39			Dibaba			1	Pre	Eugene	1 Jun 12
	(30/21)								
30:26.20	Galina		Bogomolova	RUS	15.10.77	6	WCh	Saint-Denis	23 Aug 03
30:26.37	Sally		Kipyego	KEN	19.12.85	2	OG	London (OS)	3 Aug 12
30:26.50	Linet		Masai	KEN	5.12.89	4	OG	Beijing	15 Aug 08
30:26.70	Belaynesh		Oljira	ETH	26.6.90	3	Pre	Eugene	1 Jun 12
30:29.21mx	Philes		Ongori	KEN	19.7.86	1mx		Yokohama	23 Nov 08
30:29.23	Gladys		Cherono	KEN	12.5.83	2	GS	Ostrava	27 Jun 13
30:29.36	Liliya		Shobukhova	RUS	13.11.77	1	NC	Cheboksary	23 Jul 09
30:30.26	Edith		Masai	KEN	4.4.67	5	WCh	Helsinki	6 Aug 05
30:30.44	Vivian		Cheruiyot	KEN	11.9.83	3	OG	London (OS)	3 Aug 12
	(30)								
30:31.03	Mariya		Konovalova	RUS	14.8.74	2	NC	Cheboksary	23 Jul 09
30:31.42	Inga		Abitova ¶	RUS	6.3.82	1	EC	Göteborg	7 Aug 06
30:32.03	Tegla		Loroupe	KEN	9.5.73	3	WCh	Sevilla	26 Aug 99
30:32.36	Susanne		Wigene	NOR	12.2.78	2	EC	Göteborg	7 Aug 06
30:32.72	Lidiya		Grigoryeva	RUS	21.1.74	3	EC	Göteborg	7 Aug 06
30:35.54	Kimberley		Smith	NZL	19.11.81	2		Stanford	4 May 08
30:35.91	Birhane		Ababel	ETH	10.6.90	4	GS	Ostrava	27 Jun 13
30:37.68	Benita		Johnson	AUS	6.5.79	8	WCh	Saint-Denis	23 Aug 03
30:38.09			Dong Yanmei	CHN	16.2.77	1	NG	Shanghai	19 Oct 97
30:38.33	Mestawat		Tufa	ETH	14.9.83	1		Nijmegen	25 Jun 08
	(40)								

Mark	Wind	Name		Nat	Born	Pos	Meet	Venue	Date
30:38.78		Jelena	Prokopcuka	LAT	21.9.76	6	EC	Göteborg	7 Aug 06
30:39.41			Lan Lixin	CHN	14.2.79	2	NG	Shanghai	19 Oct 97
30:39.96		Lucy Wangui	Kabuu	KEN	24.3.84	7	OG	Beijing	15 Aug 08
30:39.98			Yin Lili ¶	CHN	11.11.79	3	NG	Shanghai	19 Oct 97
30:47.02		Emily	Chebet	KEN	18.2.86	4	WCh	Moskva	11 Aug 13
30:47.20		Sylvia	Kibet	KEN	28.3.84	4		Utrecht	14 Jun 09
30:47.22			Dong Zhaoxia	CHN	13.11.74	4	NG	Shanghai	19 Oct 97
30:47.25		Shitaye	Eshete	BRN	21.5.90	6	OG	London (OS)	3 Aug 12
30:47.59		Sonia	O'Sullivan	IRL	28.11.69	2	EC	München	6 Aug 02
30:47.72			Wang Dongmei	CHN	3.12.72	5	NG	Shanghai	19 Oct 97
		(50)							

100th woman 31:12.57, 200th 31:34.01, 300th 31:50.39, 400th 32:00.95, 500th 32:16.50

HALF MARATHON

Slightly downhill courses included: Newcastle-South Shields 30.5m, Tokyo 33m (to 1998), Lisboa (Spring to 2008) 69m

Mark	Wind	Name		Nat	Born	Pos	Meet	Venue	Date
65:40	dh	Paula	Radcliffe	GBR	17.12.73	1	GNR	South Shields	21 Sep 03
65:44	dh	Susan	Chepkemei	KEN	25.6.75	1		Lisboa	1 Apr 01
65:45	dh	Priscah	Jeptoo	KEN	26.6.84	1	GNR	South Shields	15 Sep 13
65:50	WR	Mary	Keitany	KEN	18.1.82	1		Ra's Al Khaymah	18 Feb 11
66:09		Lucy	Kabuu	KEN	24.3.84	1		Ra's Al-Khaymah	15 Feb 13
66:09	dh	Meseret	Defar	ETH	19.11.83	2	GNR	South Shields	15 Sep 13
66:11			P Jeptoo			2		Ra's Al-Khaymah	15 Feb 13
66:25		Lornah	Kiplagat	NED	1.5.74	1	WCh	Udine	14 Oct 07
66:27		Rita	Jeptoo	KEN	15.2.81	3		Ra's Al-Khaymah	15 Feb 13
66:34	dh		Kiplagat			2		Lisboa	1 Apr 01
66:36			Keitany			1	WCh	Birmingham	11 Oct 09
66:38		Florence	Kiplagat	KEN	27.2.87	1		Ostia	26 Feb 12
66:40*		Ingrid	Kristiansen (10)	NOR	21.3.56	1	NC	Sandnes	5 Apr 87
66:43	dh	Masako	Chiba	JPN	18.7.76	1		Tokyo	19 Jan 97
66:44		Elana	Meyer	RSA	10.10.66	1		Tokyo	15 Jan 99
66:47			Radcliffe			1	WCh	Bristol	7 Oct 01
66:48			Keitany			2	WCh	Udine	14 Oct 07
66:48		Gladys	Cherono	KEN	12.5.83	1		Praha	6 Apr 13
66:49		Esther	Wanjiru	KEN	27.3.77	2		Tokyo	15 Jan 99
66:49			Keitany			1		Ra's Al-Khaymah	17 Feb 12
66:54			Keitany			1		New Delhi	1 Nov 09
66:56			L Kiplagat			1	City-Pier	Den Haag	25 Mar 00
66:56		Meseret	Hailu	ETH	12.9.90	4		Ra's Al-Khaymah	15 Feb 13
66:56	dh	Tirunesh	Dibaba	ETH	1.10.85	3	GNR	South Shields	15 Sep 13
66:57	dh	Kara	Goucher	USA	9.7.78	1	GNR	South Shields	30 Sep 07
67:00			Keitany			1		Lille	5 Sep 09
67:03	dh	Derartu	Tulu	ETH	21.3.72	3		Lisboa	1 Apr 01
67:03		Joyce	Chepkirui	KEN	10.8.88	1		Praha	31 Mar 12
67:04			Kabuu			1		New Delhi	27 Nov 11
67:06	dh		Kabuu			1	GNR	South Shields	18 Sep 11
		(30/19)							

* uncertain course measurement

Mark	Wind	Name		Nat	Born	Pos	Meet	Venue	Date
67:07		Elvan	Abeylegesse (20)	TUR	11.9.82	1		Ra's Al Khaymah	19 Feb 10
67:08		Sharon	Cherop	KEN	16.3.84	2		New Delhi	21 Nov 11
67:11	dh	Liz	McColgan	GBR	24.5.64	1		Tokyo	26 Jan 92
67:11		Kim	Smith	NZL	19.11.81	1		Philadelphia	18 Sep 11
67:12	dh	Tegla	Loroupe	KEN	9.5.73	1		Lisboa	10 Mar 96
67:13		Mare	Dibaba	ETH	20.10.89	2		Ra's Al Khaymah	19 Feb 10
67:16		Edith	Masai	KEN	4.4.67	1		Berlin	2 Apr 06
67:17		Pasalia	Kipkoech	KEN	22.12.88	1		Rio de Janeiro	19 Aug 12
67:18		Dire	Tune	ETH	19.6.85	1		R'as Al Khaymah	20 Feb 09
67:19	dh	Sonia	O'Sullivan	IRL	28.11.69	1	GNR	South Shields	6 Oct 02
67:21		Aselefech	Mergia	ETH	23.1.85	3		New Delhi	21 Nov 11
		(30)							
67:22		Agnes	Kiprop	KEN	12.12.79	2		Ostia	26 Feb 12
67:23		Margaret	Okayo	KEN	30.5.76	1		Udine	28 Sep 02
67:26		Kayoko	Fukushi	JPN	25.3.82	1		Marugame	5 Feb 12
67:26		Lydia	Cheromei ¶	KEN	11.5.77	2		Praha	31 Mar 13
67:27		Belaynesh	Oljira	ETH	26.6.90	4		New Delhi	27 Nov 11
67:28		Worknesh	Kidane	ETH	21.11.81	2		Philadelphia	18 Sep 11
67:32	dh	Berhane	Adere	ETH	21.7.73	2	GNR	South Shields	21 Sep 03
67:34		Deena	Kastor	USA	14.2.73	2		Berlin	2 Apr 06
67:34		Atsede	Baysa	ETH	16.4.87	1		Barcelona	17 Feb 13
67:38		Philes	Ongori	KEN	19.7.86	2	WCh	Birmingham	11 Oct 09
		(40)							
67:39		Aberu	Kebede	ETH	12.9.89	3	WCh	Birmingham	11 Oct 09
67:39		Helah	Kiprop	KEN	7.4.85	6		Ra's Al-Khaymah	15 Feb 13

Mark	Wind	Name		Nat	Born	Pos	Meet	Venue	Date
67:39		Filomena	Cheyech	KEN	5.7.82	1		Ostia	3 Mar 13
67:41		Teyiba	Erkesso	ETH	30.10.82	4		Ra's Al Khaymah	19 Feb 10
67:41dh		Edna	Kiplagat	KEN	15.9.79	2	GNR	South Shields	16 Sep 12
67:42		Tirfe	Tsegaye	ETH	25.11.84	3		Ostia	26 Feb 12
67:43		Mizuki	Noguchi	JPN	3.7.78	2		Marugame	5 Feb 06
67:46		Valeria	Straneo	ITA	5.4.76	4		Ostia	26 Feb 12
67:47		Lineth	Chepkurui	KEN	23.2.88	2		Philadelphia	19 Sep 10
67:48		Kerryn	McCann	AUS	2.5.67	3		Tokyo	10 Jan 00
67:48		Peninah	Arusei	KEN	23.2.79	2		Lille	4 Sep 10
67:48dh		Tiki	Gelana	ETH	22.10.87	3	GNR	South Shields	16 Sep 12
		(52)							

100th woman 68:34, 200th 69:22, 300th 69:53, 400th 70:17, 500th 70:40

MARATHON

L = loop course or start and finish within 30%, P = point-to-point or start and finish more than 30% apart, D + point-to-point and downhill over 1/1000. 2nd column: M mixed marathon (men and women), W women only race

Mark	Wind	Name		Nat	Born	Pos	Meet	Venue	Date
2:15:25	LM	Paula	Radcliffe	GBR	17.12.73	1		London	13 Apr 03
2:17:18	LM		Radcliffe			1		Chicago	13 Oct 02
2:17:42	LW		Radcliffe			1		London	17 Apr 05
2:18:20	LM	Liliya	Shobukhova	RUS	13.11.77	1		Chicago	9 Oct 11
2:18:37	LW	Mary	Keitany	KEN	18.1.82	1		London	22 Apr 12
2:18:47	LM	Catherine	Ndereba	KEN	21.7.72	1		Chicago	7 Oct 01
2:18:56	LW		Radcliffe			1		London	14 Apr 02
2:18:58	LW	Tiki	Gelana	ETH	22.10.87	1		Rotterdam	15 Apr 12
2:19:12	LM	Mizuki	Noguchi	JPN	3.7.78	1		Berlin	25 Sep 05
2:19:19	LM	Irina	Mikitenko	GER	23.8.72	1		Berlin	28 Sep 08
2:19:19	LW		Keitany			1		London	17 Apr 11
2:19:26	LM		Ndereba			2		Chicago	13 Oct 02
2:19:31	LM	Aselefech	Mergia	ETH	23.1.85	1		Dubai	27 Jan 12
2:19:34	LM	Lucy Wangui	Kabuu	KEN	24.3.84	2		Dubai	27 Jan 12
2:19:36	LW	Deena	Kastor (10)	USA	14.2.73	1		London	23 Apr 06
2:19:39	LM		Sun Yingjie ¶	CHN	3.10.77	1		Beijing	19 Oct 03
2:19:41	LM	Yoko	Shibui	JPN	14.3.79	1		Berlin	26 Sep 04
2:19:44	LM	Florence	Kiplagat	KEN	27.2.87	1		Berlin	25 Sep 11
2:19:46	LM	Naoko	Takahashi	JPN	6.5.72	1		Berlin	30 Sep 01
2:19:50	LW	Edna	Kiplagat	KEN	15.9.79	2		London	22 Apr 12
2:19:51	PM		Zhou Chunxiu	CHN	15.11.78	1	Dong-A	Seoul	12 Mar 06
2:19:52	LM	Mare	Dibaba	ETH	20.10.89	3		Dubai	27 Jan 12
2:19:55	LM		Ndereba			2		London	13 Apr 03
2:19:57	L	Rita	Jeptoo	KEN	15.2.81	1		Chicago	13 Oct 13
2:20:14	LW	Priscah	Jeptoo	KEN	24.6.84	3		London	22 Apr 12
2:20:15	LW	Liliya	Shobukhova			2		London	17 Apr 11
2:20:15	LW		P Jeptoo			1		London	21 Apr 13
2:20:25	LM		Shobukhova			1		Chicago	10 Oct 10
2:20:30	LM	Bezunesh	Bekele (20)	ETH	18.9.83	4		Dubai	27 Jan 12
2:20:30	LM	Aberu	Kebede	ETH	12.9.89	1		Berlin	30 Sep 12
		(30/21)							
2:20:42	LM	Berhane	Adere	ETH	21.7.73	1		Chicago	22 Oct 06
2:20:43	LM	Tegla	Loroupe	KEN	9.5.73	1		Berlin	26 Sep 99
2:20:47	LM	Galina	Bogomolova	RUS	15.10.77	2		Chicago	22 Oct 06
2:20:48	L	Jemima	Jelagat	KEN	21.12.84	2		Chicago	13 Oct 13
2:21:01		Meselech	Melkamu	ETH	27.4.85	1		Frankfurt	28 Oct 12
2:21:06	LM	Ingrid	Kristiansen	NOR	21.3.56	1		London	21 Apr 85
2:21:06		Feyse	Tadesse	ETH	19.11.88	1		Paris	7 Apr 13
2:21:09		Meseret	Hailu	ETH	12.9.90	1		Amsterdam	21 Oct 12
2:21:19		Tirfe	Tsegaye	ETH	25.11.84	2		Berlin	30 Sep 12
		(30)							
2:21:21	LM	Joan	Benoit'	USA	16.5.57	1		Chicago	20 Oct 85
2:21:29	LW	Lyudmila	Petrova	RUS	7.10.68	2		London	23 Apr 06
2:21:30	LM	Constantina	Dita	ROU	23.1.70	2		Chicago	9 Oct 05
2:21:30		Lydia	Cheromei ¶	KEN	11.5.77	6		Dubai	27 Jan 12
2:21:31	LM	Svetlana	Zakharova	RUS	15.9.70	4		Chicago	13 Oct 02
2:21:31	LM	Askale	Tafa	ETH	27.9.84	2		Berlin	28 Sep 08
2:21:34	LM	Getenesh	Wami	ETH	11.12.74	1		Berlin	25 Sep 06
2:21:39		Georgina	Rono	KEN	19.5.84	2		Frankfurt	28 Oct 12
2:21:41		Eunice	Jepkirui	KEN	20.5.84	2		Amsterdam	21 Oct 12
2:21:45	LW	Masako	Chiba	JPN	18.7.76	2		Osaka	26 Jan 03
		(40)							
2:21:46	LW	Susan	Chepkemei ¶	KEN	25.6.75	3		London	23 Apr 06
2:21:51	LW	Naoko	Sakamoto	JPN	14.11.80	3		Osaka	26 Jan 03
2:21:59	LM	Mamitu	Daska	ETH	16.10.83	1		Frankfurt	30 Oct 11

WOMEN All-time

Mark	Wind	Name		Nat	Born	Pos	Meet	Venue	Date
2:22:03		Atsede	Baysa	ETH	16.4.87	1		Chicago	7 Oct 12
2:22:09	LM	Ejegayehu	Dibaba	ETH	25.6.82	2		Chicago	9 Oct 11
2:22:12	LW	Eri	Yamaguchi	JPN	14.1.73	1		Tokyo	21 Nov 99
2:22:22	LW	Lornah	Kiplagat	KEN/NED	1.5.74	4		Osaka	26 Jan 03
2:22:23	LM	Catherina	McKiernan	IRL	30.11.69	1		Amsterdam	1 Nov 98
2:22:28	L	Sharon	Cherop	KEN	16.3.84	2		Berlin	29 Sep 13
2:22:34		Caroline	Kilel	KEN	21.3.81	1		Frankfurt	27 Oct 13
	(50)								
100th woman 2:23:50, 200th 2:25:53, 300th 2:27:00, 400th 2:28:02, 500th 2:28:56									
Drugs dq: 2:20:23	LM	Wei Yanan ¶		CHN	6.12.81	1		Beijing	20 Oct 02
2:22:19	LW	Inga	Abitova ¶	RUS	6.3.82	2		London	25 Apr 10
Downhill point-to-point course – Boston marathon is downhill overall (139m) and sometimes strongly wind-aided.									
2:20:43	DM	Margaret	Okayo	KEN	30.5.76	1		Boston	15 Apr 02
2:21:45	DM	Uta	Pippig ¶	GER	7.9.65	1		Boston	18 Apr 94

2000 METRES STEEPLECHASE

Mark		Name		Nat	Born	Pos	Meet	Venue	Date
6:03.38		Wioletta	Janowska	POL	9.6.77	1		Gdansk	15 Jul 06
6:04.46		Dorcus	Inzikuru	UGA	2.2.82	1	GP II	Milano	1 Jun 05
6:11.63		Livia	Tóth	HUN	7.1.80	2		Gdansk	15 Jul 06
6:11.83		Korahubish	Itaa	KEN	28.2.92	1	WY	Bressanone	10 Jul 09
6:11.84		Marina	Pluzhnikova	RUS	25.2.63	1	GWG	Sankt-Peterburg	25 Jul 94

3000 METRES STEEPLECHASE

Mark		Name		Nat	Born	Pos	Meet	Venue	Date
8:58.81	WR	Gulnara	Samitova/Galkina	RUS	9.7.78	1	OG	Beijing	17 Aug 08
9:01.59	WR		Samitova/Galkina			1		Iráklio	4 Jul 04
9:05.02		Yuliya	Zaripova	RUS	26.4.86	1	DNG	Stockholm	17 Aug 12
9:06.57		Yekaterina	Volkova	RUS	16.2.78	1	WCh	Osaka	27 Aug 07
9:06.72			Zaripova			1	OG	London (OS)	6 Aug 12
9:07.03			Zaripova (Zarudneva)			1	WCh	Daegu	30 Aug 11
9:07.14		Milcah	Chemos Cheywa	KEN	24.2.86	1	Bisl	Oslo	7 Jun 12
9:07.32		Marta	Domínguez	ESP	3.11.75	1	WCh	Berlin	17 Aug 09
9:07.41		Eunice	Jepkorir	KEN	17.2.82	2	OG	Beijing	17 Aug 08
9:07.64			Volkova			3	OG	Beijing	17 Aug 08
9:08.21			Galkina			1	NC	Kazan	18 Jul 08
9:08.33	WR		Samitova			1	NC	Tula	10 Aug 03
9:08.37		Habiba	Ghribi	TUN	9.4.84	2	OG	London (OS)	6 Aug 12
9:08.39			Zarudneva			2	WCh	Berlin	17 Aug 09
9:08.57			Chemos			3	WCh	Berlin	17 Aug 09
9:09.00		Sofia	Assefa	ETH	14.11.87	2	Bisl	Oslo	7 Jun 12
9:09.19		Tatyana	Petrova	RUS	8.4.83	2	WCh	Osaka	27 Aug 07
9:09.39			Domínguez			1		Barcelona	25 Jul 09
9:09.61		Hiwot	Ayalew	ETH	6.3.90	3	Bisl	Oslo	7 Jun 12
9:09.84			Samitova			1		Réthimno	23 Jun 04
9:09.84			Assefa			3	OG	London (OS)	6 Aug 12
9:09.88			Chemos			4	OG	London (OS)	6 Aug 12
9:09.99			Zaripova			1	NC	Cheboksary	3 Jul 12
9:10.36			Ghribi			2	DNG	Stockholm	17 Aug 12
9:11.09			Galkina			4	WCh	Berlin	17 Aug 09
9:11.18			Jepkorir			1		Huelva	13 Jun 08
9:11.58			Galkina			1	GGala	Roma	10 Jul 09
9:11.65			Chemos			1	WCh	Moskva	13 Aug 13
9:11.68			Galkina			1	GP	Athína	2 Jul 07
9:11.71			Chemos			1	GGala	Roma	10 Jun 10
	(30/10)								
9:12.55		Lydia	Chepkurui	KEN	23.8.84	2	WCh	Moskva	13 Aug 13
9:12.50		Jennifer	Barringer/Simpson	USA	23.8.86	5	WCh	Berlin	17 Aug 09
9:13.16		Ruth	Bisibori	KEN	2.1.88	7	WCh	Berlin	17 Aug 09
9:13.22		Gladys	Kipkemboi	KEN	15.10.86	2	GGala	Roma	10 Jun 11
9:13.53		Gülcan	Mingir	TUR	21.5.89	1	Pavlov	Sofia	9 Jun 11
9:14.07		Etenesh	Diro	ETH	10.5.91	3	DNG	Stockholm	17 Aug 11
9:15.04		Dorcus	Inzikuru	UGA	2.2.82	1	SGP	Athína	14 Jun 05
9:16.51	WR	Alesya	Turova	BLR	6.12.79	1		Gdansk	27 Jul 02
9:16.85		Cristina	Casandra	ROU	21.10.77	5	OG	Beijing	17 Aug 08
9:16.94		Mercy	Njoroge	KEN	10.6.86	2	DL	Doha	6 May 11
	(20)								
9:17.15		Wioletta	Frankiewicz/Janowska	POL	9.6.77	1	SGP	Athína	3 Jul 05
9:17.85		Zemzem	Ahmed	ETH	27.12.84	7	OG	Beijing	17 Aug 08
9:18.03		Lydia	Rotich	KEN	8.8.88	3	Bisl	Oslo	4 Jun 09
9:18.35		Donna	MacFarlane	AUS	18.6.77	3	Bisl	Oslo	6 Jun 08
9:18.54		Antje	Möldner-Schmidt	GER	13.6.84	9	WCh	Berlin	17 Aug 09
9:18.54		Jéssica	Augusto	POR	8.11.81	1		Huelva	9 Jun 09

Mark	Wind	Name		Nat	Born	Pos	Meet	Venue	Date
9:19.42		Purity	Kirui	KEN	13.8.91	6	DL	Doha	10 May 13
9:20.23		Mekdes	Bekele	ETH	20.1.87	2		Huelva	13 Jun 08
9:20.37		Birtukan	Adamu	ETH	29.4.92	4	GGala	Roma	26 May 11
9:21.94		Lyubov	Ivanova' ¶	RUS	2.3.81	2	Tsik	Athína	3 Jul 06
		(30)							
9:22.05		Hyvin	Jepkemoi	KEN	13.1.92	6	WCh	Moskva	13 Aug 13
9:22.12		Hanane	Ouhaddou	MAR	.82	1	NA	Heusden-Zolder	18 Jul 09
9:22.15		Yelena	Sidorchenkova	RUS	30.5.80	2	NC	Cheboksary	23 Jul 09
9:22.29 WR		Justyna	Bak	POL	1.8.74	1		Milano	5 Jun 02
9:22.51		Almaz	Ayana	ETH	21.11.91	3	VD	Bruxelles	27 Aug 10
9:22.76		Anna	Willard/Pierce	USA	31.3.84	2	NA	Heusden-Zolder	20 Jul 08
9:23.35		Jeruto	Kiptum	KEN	12.12.81	2	GP	Rieti	27 Aug 06
9:23.52		Gesa-Felicitas	Krause	GER	3.8.92	8	OG	London (OS)	6 Aug 12
9:23.54		Emma	Coburn	USA	19.10.90	9	OG	London (OS)	6 Aug 12
9:24.06		Binnaz	Uslu ¶	TUR	12.3.85	1h1	WCh	Daegu	27 Aug 11
		(40)							
9:24.24		Barbara	Parker	GBR	8.11.82	4	Pre	Eugene	2 Jun 12
9:24.29		Melissa	Rollison	AUS	13.4.83	2	CG	Melbourne	22 Mar 06
9:24.84		Lisa	Aguilera	USA	30.11.79	5	VD	Bruxelles	27 Aug 10
9:25.14		Eva	Arias	ESP	8.10.80	5h1	WCh	Berlin	15 Aug 09
9:25.62		Sophie	Duarte	FRA	31.7.81	6	GGala	Roma	10 Jul 09
9:25.70		Ancuta	Bobocel	ROU	3.10.87	5	DNG	Stockholm	17 Aug 12
9:26.03		Lyudmila	Kuzmina	RUS	13.8.87	2	NC	Cheboksary	23 Jul 11
9:26.07		Salome	Chepchumba	KEN	29.9.82	3	GP	Rieti	27 Aug 06
9:26.23		Rosa María	Morató	ESP	19.6.79	2	NA	Heusden-Zolder	28 Jul 07
9:26.25			Liu Nian	CHN	26.4.88	1		Wuhan	2 Nov 07
		(50)							

100th woman 9:35.51, 200th 9:47.61, 300th 9:55.75

100 METRES HURDLES

Mark	Wind	Name		Nat	Born	Pos	Meet	Venue	Date
12.21 WR	0.7	Yordanka	Donkova	BUL	28.9.61	1		Stara Zagora	20 Aug 88
12.24	0.9		Donkova			1h		Stara Zagora	28 Aug 88
12.25 WR	1.4	Ginka	Zagorcheva	BUL	12.4.58	1	v TCH,GRE	Drama	8 Aug 87
12.26 WR	1.5		Donkova			1	Balk	Ljubljana	7 Sep 86
12.26	1.7	Lyudmila	Narozhilenko ¶	RUS	21.4.64	1rB		Sevilla	6 Jun 92
		(now Ludmila Engquist SWE)							
12.26	1.2	Brianna	Rollins	USA	18.8.91	1	NC	Des Moines	22 Jun 13
12.27	-1.2		Donkova			1		Stara Zagora	28 Aug 88
12.28	1.8		Narozhilenko			1	NC	Kyiv	11 Jul 91
12.28	0.9		Narozhilenko			1rA		Sevilla	6 Jun 92
12.28	1.1	Sally	Pearson'	AUS	19.9.86	1	WCh	Daegu	3 Sep 11
12.29 WR	-0.4		Donkova			1	ASV	Köln	17 Aug 86
12.32	1.6		Narozhilenko			1		Saint-Denis	4 Jun 92
12.33	1.4		Donkova			1		Fürth	14 Jun 87
12.33	-0.3	Gail	Devers	USA	19.11.66	1	NC	Sacramento	23 Jul 00
12.34	-0.5		Zagorcheva			1	WCh	Roma	4 Sep 87
12.35 WR	0.1		Donkova			1h2	ASV	Köln	17 Aug 86
12.35	-0.2		Pearson			1	OG	London (OS)	7 Aug 12
12.36 WR	1.9	Grazyna	Rabsztyn	POL	20.9.52	1	Kuso	Warszawa	13 Jun 80
12.36 WR	-0.6		Donkova			1	NC	Sofiya	13 Aug 86
12.36	1.1		Donkova			1		Schwechat	15 Jun 88
12.36	0.3		Pearson			1s2	WCh	Daegu	3 Sep 11
12.37	1.4		Donkova			1	ISTAF	Berlin	15 Aug 86
12.37	0.7		Devers			1	WCh	Sevilla	28 Aug 99
12.37	1.5	Joanna	Hayes	USA	23.12.76	1	OG	Athína	24 Aug 04
12.37	-0.2	Dawn	Harper-Nelson	USA	13.5.84	2	OG	London (OS)	7 Aug 12
12.38	0.0		Donkova			1	BGP	Budapest	11 Aug 86
12.38	-0.7		Donkova			1	EC	Stuttgart	29 Aug 86
12.38	0.2		Donkova			1	OG	Seoul	30 Sep 88
12.39	1.5	Vera	Komisova' (10)	RUS	11.6.53	1	GGala	Roma	5 Aug 80
12.39	1.5		Zagorcheva			2	Balk	Ljubljana	7 Sep 86
12.39	1.8	Natalya	Grigoryeva ¶	UKR	3.12.62	2	NC	Kyiv	11 Jul 91
12.39	-0.7		Devers			1	WK	Zürich	11 Aug 00
12.39	1.3		Pearson			1s2	OG	London (OS)	7 Aug 12
12.39	1.7		Rollins			1	NCAA	Eugene	8 Jun 13
		(34/11)							
12.42	1.8	Bettine	Jahn	GDR	3.8.58	1	OD	Berlin	8 Jun 83
12.42	2.0	Anjanette	Kirkland	USA	24.2.74	1	WCh	Edmonton	11 Aug 01
12.43	-0.9	Lucyna	Kalek (Langer)	POL	9.1.56	1		Hannover	19 Aug 84
12.43	-0.3	Michelle	Perry	USA	1.5.79	1s1	NC	Carson	26 Jun 05
12.43	0.2	Lolo	Jones	USA	5.8.82	1s1	OG	Beijing	18 Aug 08

WOMEN All-time

Mark	Wind	Name		Nat	Born	Pos	Meet	Venue	Date
12.43	1.2	Queen	Harrison	USA	10.9.88	2	NC	Des Moines	22 Jun 13
12.44	-0.5	Gloria	Uibel (-Siebert)	GDR	13.1.64	2	WCh	Roma	4 Sep 87
12.44	-0.8	Olga	Shishigina ¶	KAZ	23.12.68	1	Spitzen	Luzern	27 Jun 95
12.44	0.4	Glory	Alozie	NGR/ESP	30.12.77	1	Herc	Monaco	8 Aug 98
	(20)								
12.44	0.6	Damu	Cherry ¶	USA	29.11.77	2rA	Athl	Lausanne	11 Jul 06
12.45	1.3	Cornelia	Oschkenat'	GDR	29.10.61	1		Neubrandenburg	11 Jun 87
12.45	1.4	Brigitte	Foster-Hylton	JAM	7.11.74	1	Pre	Eugene	24 May 03
12.45	1.5	Olena	Krasovska	UKR	17.8.76	2	OG	Athína	24 Aug 04
12.45	1.4	Virginia	Powell/Crawford	USA	7.9.83	1	GP	New York	2 Jun 07
12.46	0.7	Perdita	Felicien	CAN	29.8.80	1	Pre	Eugene	19 Jun 04
12.47	1.1	Marina	Azyabina	RUS	15.6.63	1s2	NC	Moskva	19 Jun 93
12.47	1.1	Danielle	Carruthers	USA	22.12.79	2	WCh	Daegu	3 Sep 11
12.48	-0.2	Kellie	Wells	USA	16.7.82	3	OG	London (OS)	7 Aug 12
12.48	1.2	Nia	Ali	USA	23.10.88	3	NC	Des Moines	22 Jun 13
	(30)								
12.49	0.9	Susanna	Kallur	SWE	16.2.81	1	ISTAF	Berlin	16 Sep 07
12.49	1.0	Priscilla	Lopes-Schliep	CAN	26.8.82	2	VD	Bruxelles	4 Sep 09
12.50	0.0	Vera	Akimova'	RUS	5.6.59	1		Sochi	19 May 84
12.50	-0.1	Delloreen	Ennis-London	JAM	5.3.75	3	WCh	Osaka	29 Aug 07
12.50	0.8	Josephine	Onyia ¶	NGR/ESP	15.7.86	1	ISTAF	Berlin	1 Jun 08
12.51	1.4	Miesha	McKelvy	USA	26.7.76	2	Pre	Eugene	24 May 03
12.52	-0.4	Michelle	Freeman	JAM	5.5.69	1s1	WCh	Athína	10 Aug 97
12.53	0.2	Tatyana	Reshetnikova	RUS	14.10.66	1rA	GP II	Linz	4 Jul 94
12.53	-0.4	Svetla	Dimitrova ¶	BUL	27.1.70	1	Herc	Stara Zagora	16 Jul 94
12.53	1.0	Melissa	Morrison	USA	9.7.71	1	DNG	Stockholm	5 Aug 98
	(40)								
12.54	0.4	Kerstin	Knabe	GDR	7.7.59	3	EC	Athína	9 Sep 82
12.54	0.9	Sabine	Paetz/John'	GDR	16.10.57	1		Berlin	15 Jul 84
12.54	1.7	Nichole	Denby	USA	10.10.82	2s2	OT	Eugene	6 Jul 08
12.54	1.3	Jessica	Ennis	GBR	28.1.86	1H5	OG	London (OS)	3 Aug 12
12.56	1.2	Johanna	Klier'	GDR	13.9.52	1r2		Cottbus	17 Jul 80
12.56	1.2	Monique	Ewanjé-Epée	FRA	11.7.67	1	BNP	Villeneuve d'Ascq	29 Jun 90
12.56	0.7	Tiffany	Ofili/Porter	USA/GBR	13.11.87	1s3	WCh	Daegu	3 Sep 11
12.56	0.7	Kristi	Castlin	USA	7.7.88	2	Bisl	Oslo	7 Jun 12
12.57	0.3	Carolin	Nytra	GER	26.2.85	2	Athl	Lausanne	8 Jul 10
12.58	0.6	Nevin	Yanit ¶	TUR	16.2.86	2s3	OG	London (OS)	7 Aug 12
	(50)								

100th woman 12.69, 200th 12.85, 300th 12.96, 400th 13.05, 500th 13.13

Wind assisted performances to 12.37, performers to 12.56

Mark	Wind	Name		Nat	Born	Pos	Meet	Venue	Date
12.28	2.7	Cornelia	Oschkenat'	GDR	29.10.61	1		Berlin	25 Aug 87
12.29	3.5		Donkova			1	Athl	Lausanne	24 Jun 88
12.29	2.7	Gail	Devers	USA	19.11.66	1	Pre	Eugene	26 May 02
12.29	3.8	Lolo	Jones	USA	5.8.82	1	NC/OT	Eugene	6 Jul 08
12.30	2.8		Rollins			1s1	NC	Des Moines	22 Jun 13
12.33	2.3		Rollins			1h3	NC	Des Moines	21 Jun 13
12.35	2.4	Bettine	Jahn	GDR	3.8.58	1	WCh	Helsinki	13 Aug 83
12.35	3.7	Kellie	Wells	USA	16.7.82	1		Gainesville	16 Apr 11
12.36	2.2	Dawn	Harper	USA	13.5.84	1	NC	Eugene	28 Jun 09
12.37	2.7	Gloria	Uibel/Siebert'	GDR	13.1.64	2		Berlin	25 Aug 87
12.37	3.4	Danielle	Carruthers	USA	22.12.79	1s1	NC	Eugene	26 Jun 11
12.40	2.1	Michelle	Freeman	JAM	5.5.69	1	GPF	Fukuoka	13 Sep 97
12.41	2.2	Olga	Shishigina ¶	KAZ	23.12.68	1rA	Athl	Lausanne	5 Jul 95
12.42	2.4	Kerstin	Knabe	GDR	7.7.59	2	WCh	Helsinki	13 Aug 83
12.43	2.7	Yvette	Lewis	USA/PAN	16.3.85	1	MSR	Walnut	20 Apr 13
12.44	2.6	Melissa	Morrison	USA	9.7.71	1		Carson	22 May 04
12.45	2.1	Perdita	Felicien	CAN	29.8.80	1	NC	Victoria	10 Jul 04
12.47	3.0	Tiffany	Porter	USA/GBR	13.11.87	1		Gainesville	21 Apr 12
12.48	3.8	Kristi	Castlin	USA	7.7.88	1		Clermont	2 Jun 13
12.50	2.7	Svetla	Dimitrova ¶	BUL	27.1.70	1		Saint-Denis	10 Jun 94
12.51	3.2	Johanna	Klier'	GDR	13.9.52	1	NC	Cottbus	17 Jul 80
12.51	3.6	Sabine	Paetz/John'	GDR	16.10.57	1		Dresden	27 Jul 84
12.51A	3.3	Yuliya	Graudyn	RUS	13.11.70	1		Sestriere	31 Jul 94
12.52	3.1	Angela	Whyte	CAN	22.5.80	2		Edmonton	29 Jun 11
12.53	2.2	Mihaela	Pogacian	ROU	21.7.58	1	IAC	Edinburgh	6 Jul 91
12.56	2.7	Vashti	Thomas	USA	21.4.90	2	MSR	Walnut	20 Apr 13

Probably hand timed Officially 12.36, but subsequent investigations showed this unlikely to have been auto-timed

Mark	Wind	Name		Nat	Born	Pos	Meet	Venue	Date
12.4	0.7	Svetla	Dimitrova ¶	BUL	27.1.70	1		Stara Zagora	9 Jul 94

Hand timed

Mark	Wind	Name		Nat	Born	Pos	Meet	Venue	Date
12.3 WR	1.5	Anneliese	Ehrhardt	GDR	18.6.50	1	NC	Dresden	22 Jul 73
12.3		Marina	Azyabina	RUS	15.6.63	1		Yekaterinburg	30 May 93

Mark	Wind	Name		Nat	Born	Pos	Meet	Venue	Date
12.0w	2.1	Yordanka	Donkova	BUL	28.9.61	1		Sofiya	3 Aug 86
12.1w	2.1	Ginka	Zagorcheva	BUL	12.4.58	2		Sofiya	3 Aug 86

400 METRES HURDLES

Mark	Wind	Name		Nat	Born	Pos	Meet	Venue	Date
52.34 WR		Yuliya	Nosova-Pechonkina'	RUS	21.4.78	1	NC	Tula	8 Aug 03
52.42		Melaine	Walker	JAM	1.1.83	1	WCh	Berlin	20 Aug 09
52.47		Lashinda	Demus	USA	10.3.83	1	WCh	Daegu	1 Sep 11
52.61 WR		Kim	Batten	USA	29.3.69	1	WCh	Göteborg	11 Aug 95
52.62		Tonja	Buford-Bailey	USA	13.12.70	2	WCh	Göteborg	11 Aug 95
52.63			Demus			1	Herc	Monaco	28 Jul 09
52.64			Walker			1	OG	Beijing	20 Aug 08
52.70		Natalya	Antyukh	RUS	26.6.81	1	OG	London (OS)	8 Aug 12
52.73			Walker			2	WCh	Daegu	1 Sep 11
52.74 WR		Sally	Gunnell	GBR	29.7.66	1	WCh	Stuttgart	19 Aug 93
52.74			Batten			1	Herc	Monaco	8 Aug 98
52.77		Faní	Halkiá	GRE	2.2.79	1s2	OG	Athína	22 Aug 04
52.77			Demus			2	OG	London (OS)	8 Aug 12
52.79		Sandra	Farmer-Patrick	USA	18.8.62	2	WCh	Stuttgart	19 Aug 93
52.79		Kaliese	Spencer (10)	JAM	6.5.87	1	LGP	London (CP)	5 Aug 11
52.82		Deon	Hemmings	JAM	9.10.68	1	OG	Atlanta	31 Jul 96
52.82			Halkiá			1	OG	Athína	25 Aug 04
52.82			Demus			1	GGala	Roma	10 Jun 10
52.83		Zuzana	Hejnová	CZE	19.12.86	1	WCh	Moskva	15 Aug 13
52.84			Batten			1	WK	Zürich	12 Aug 98
52.89		Daimí	Pernía	CUB	27.12.76	1	WCh	Sevilla	25 Aug 99
52.90			Buford			1	WK	Zürich	16 Aug 95
52.90		Nezha	Bidouane	MAR	18.9.69	2	WCh	Sevilla	25 Aug 99
52.90			Pechonkina			1	WCh	Helsinki	13 Aug 05
52.92			Antyukh			1	EC	Barcelona	30 Jul 10
52.94 WR		Marina	Styepanova'	RUS	1.5.50	1s	Spart	Tashkent	17 Sep 86
52.95		Sheena	Johnson/Tosta	USA	1.10.82	1	NC/OT	Sacramento	11 Jul 04
52.96A			Bidouane			1	WCp	Johannesburg	11 Sep 98
52.96			Demus			2	WCh	Berlin	20 Aug 09
52.97			Batten			1	NC	Indianapolis	14 Jun 97
52.97			Bidouane			1	WCh	Athína	8 Aug 97
		(31/16)							
53.02		Irina	Privalova	RUS	22.11.68	1	OG	Sydney	27 Sep 00
53.11		Tatyana	Ledovskaya	BLR	21.5.66	1	WCh	Tokyo	29 Aug 91
53.17		Debbie	Flintoff-King	AUS	20.4.60	1	OG	Seoul	28 Sep 88
53.20		Josanne	Lucas	TRI	14.5.84	3	WCh	Berlin	20 Aug 09
		(20)							
53.21		Marie-José	Pérec	FRA	9.5.68	2	WK	Zürich	16 Aug 95
53.21		Kori	Carter	USA	6.3.92	1	NCAA	Eugene	7 Jun 13
53.22		Jana	Pittman/Rawlinson	AUS	9.11.82	1	WCh	Saint-Denis	28 Aug 03
53.24		Sabine	Busch	GDR	21.11.62	1	NC	Potsdam	21 Aug 87
53.25		Ionela	Târlea-Manolache	ROU	9.2.76	2	GGala	Roma	7 Jul 99
53.28		Tiffany	Ross-Williams	USA	5.2.83	1	NC	Indianapolis	24 Jun 07
53.32		Sandra	Glover	USA	30.12.68	3	WCh	Helsinki	13 Aug 05
53.36		Andrea	Blackett	BAR	24.1.76	4	WCh	Sevilla	25 Aug 99
53.36		Brenda	Taylor	USA	9.2.79	2	NC/OT	Sacramento	11 Jul 04
53.37		Tetyana	Tereshchuk	UKR	11.10.69	3s2	OG	Athína	22 Aug 04
		(30)							
53.47		Janeene	Vickers	USA	3.10.68	3	WCh	Tokyo	29 Aug 91
53.48		Margarita	Ponomaryova'	RUS	19.6.63	3	WCh	Stuttgart	19 Aug 93
53.58		Cornelia	Ullrich'	GDR	26.4.63	2	NC	Potsdam	21 Aug 87
53.63		Ellen	Fiedler'	GDR	26.11.58	3	OG	Seoul	28 Sep 88
53.65A mx		Myrtle	Bothma'	RSA	18.2.64	mx		Pretoria	12 Mar 90
53.74A						1		Johannesburg	18 Apr 86
53.67		Perri	Shakes-Drayton	GBR	21.12.88	2	DL	London (OS)	26 Jul 13
53.68		Vania	Stambolova ¶	BUL	28.11.83	1		Rabat	5 Jun 11
53.72		Yekaterina	Bikert	RUS	13.5.80	2	NC	Tula	30 Jul 04
53.72		Georgeanne	Moline	USA	6.3.90	2	NCAA	Eugene	7 Jun 13
53.77		Irina	Davydova	RUS	27.5.88	1	EC	Helsinki	29 Jun 12
		(40)							
53.83		Dalilah	Muhammad	USA	7.2.90	1	NC	Des Moines	23 Jun 13
53.84		Natasha	Danvers	GBR	19.9.77	3	OG	Beijing	20 Aug 08
53.85		Angela	Morosanu	ROU	26.7.86	2	DL	Shanghai	18 May 13
53.86		Anna	Jesien	POL	10.12.78	1s3	WCh	Osaka	28 Aug 07
53.88		Debbie-Ann	Parris	JAM	24.3.73	3s1	WCh	Edmonton	6 Aug 01
53.93		Yevgeniya	Isakova	RUS	27.11.78	1	EC	Göteborg	9 Aug 06

Mark	Wind	Name		Nat	Born	Pos	Meet	Venue	Date
53.96			Han Qing ¶	CHN	4.3.70	1	NG	Beijing	9 Sep 93
53.96			Song Yinglan	CHN	14.9.75	1	NG	Guangzhou	22 Nov 01
53.96		Anastasiya	Rabchenyuk	UKR	14.9.83	4	OG	Beijing	20 Aug 08
53.97		Nickiesha	Wilson	JAM	28.7.86	2s3	WCh	Osaka	28 Aug 07
(50)									

100th woman 54.61, 200th 55.46, 300th 55.92, 400th 56.26, 500th 56.57

Drugs disqualification: 53.38 Jiang Limei ¶ CHN .3.70 (1) 89 Shanghai 22 Oct 97

HIGH JUMP

Mark	Wind	Name		Nat	Born	Pos	Meet	Venue	Date
2.09 WR		Stefka	Kostadinova	BUL	25.3.65	1	WCh	Roma	30 Aug 87
2.08 WR			Kostadinova			1	NM	Sofiya	31 May 86
2.08i		Kajsa	Bergqvist	SWE	12.10.76	1		Arnstadt	4 Feb 06
2.08		Blanka	Vlasic	CRO	8.11.83	1	Hanz	Zagreb	31 Aug 09
2.07 WR		Lyudmila	Andonova ¶	BUL	6.5.60	1	OD	Berlin	20 Jul 84
2.07 WR			Kostadinova			1		Sofiya	25 May 86
2.07			Kostadinova			1		Cagliari	16 Sep 87
2.07			Kostadinova			1	NC	Sofiya	3 Sep 88
2.07i		Heike	Henkel'	GER	5.5.64	1	NC	Karlsruhe	8 Feb 92
2.07			Vlasic			1	DNG	Stockholm	7 Aug 07
2.07		Anna	Chicherova	RUS	22.7.82	1	NC	Cheboksary	22 Jul 11
2.06			Kostadinova			1	ECp	Moskva	18 Aug 85
2.06			Kostadinova			1		Fürth	15 Jun 86
2.06			Kostadinova			1		Cagliari	14 Sep 86
2.06			Kostadinova			1		Wörrstadt	6 Jun 87
2.06			Kostadinova			1		Rieti	8 Sep 87
2.06i			Kostadinova			1		Pireás	20 Feb 88
2.06			Bergqvist			1		Eberstadt	26 Jul 03
2.06		Hestrie	Cloete	RSA	26.8.78	1	WCh	Saint-Denis	31 Aug 03
2.06		Yelena	Slesarenko	RUS	28.2.82	1	OG	Athína	28 Aug 04
2.06			Vlasic			1		Thessaloníki	30 Jul 07
2.06			Vlasic			1	ECp-1B	Istanbul	22 Jun 08
2.06			Vlasic			1	GP	Madrid	5 Jul 08
2.06		Ariane	Friedrich	GER	10.1.84	1	ISTAF	Berlin	14 Jun 09
2.06i			Vlasic			1		Arnstadt	6 Feb 10
2.06i			Chicherova			1		Arnstadt	4 Feb 12
2.05 WR		Tamara	Bykova (10)	RUS	21.12.58	1	Izv	Kyiv	22 Jun 84
2.05		Inga	Babakova	UKR	27.6.67	1		Tokyo	15 Sep 95
2.05i		Tia	Hellebaut	BEL	16.2.78	1	EI	Birmingham	3 Mar 07
2.05			Hellebaut			1	OG	Beijing	23 Aug 08
2.05		Chaunté	Lowe'	USA	12.1.84	1	NC	Des Moines	26 Jun 10

Further 2.05 performances: Kostadinova 10, Vlasic 10, Bergqvist, Chicherova 2, Henkel, Cloete, Freidrich 1
(58/13)

Mark	Wind	Name		Nat	Born	Pos	Meet	Venue	Date
2.04		Silvia	Costa	CUB	4.5.64	1	WCp	Barcelona	9 Sep 89
2.04i		Alina	Astafei	GER	7.6.69	1		Berlin	3 Mar 95
2.04		Venelina	Veneva ¶	BUL	13.6.74	1		Kalamáta	2 Jun 01
2.04i		Antonietta	Di Martino	ITA	1.6.78	1		Banská Bystrica	9 Feb 11
2.04		Irina	Gordeyeva	RUS	9.10.86	1		Eberstadt	19 Aug 12
2.04		Brigetta	Barrett	USA	24.12.90	1	NC	Des Moines	22 Jun 13
2.03 WR		Ulrike	Meyfarth	FRG	4.5.56	1	ECp	London (CP)	21 Aug 83
(20)									
2.03		Louise	Ritter	USA	18.2.58	1		Austin	8 Jul 88
2.03		Tatyana	Motkova	RUS	23.11.68	2		Bratislava	30 May 95
2.03		Níki	Bakoyiánni	GRE	9.6.68	2	OG	Atlanta	3 Aug 96
2.03i		Monica	Iagar/Dinescu	ROU	2.4.73	1		Bucuresti	23 Jan 99
2.03i		Marina	Kuptsova	RUS	22.12.81	1	EI	Wien	2 Mar 02
2.03		Svetlana	Shkolina	RUS	9.3.86	3	OG	London (OS)	11 Aug 12
2.02i		Susanne	Beyer'	GDR	24.6.61	2	WI	Indianapolis	8 Mar 87
2.02		Yelena	Yelesina	RUS	4.4.70	1	GWG	Seattle	23 Jul 90
2.02		Viktoriya	Styopina	UKR	21.2.76	3	OG	Athína	28 Aug 04
2.02		Ruth	Beitia	ESP	1.4.79	1	NC	San Sebastián	4 Aug 07
(30)									
2.01 WR		Sara	Simeoni	ITA	19.4.53	1	v Pol	Brescia	4 Aug 78
2.01		Olga	Turchak	UKR	5.3.67	2	GWG	Moskva	7 Jul 86
2.01		Desiré	du Plessis	RSA	20.5.65	1		Johannesburg	16 Sep 86
2.01i		Gabriele	Günz	GDR	8.9.61	2		Stuttgart	31 Jan 88
2.01		Heike	Balck	GDR	19.8.70	1	vUSSR-j	Karl-Marx-Stadt	18 Jun 89
2.01i		Ioamnet	Quintero	CUB	8.9.72	1		Berlin	5 Mar 93
2.01		Hanne	Haugland	NOR	14.12.67	1	WK	Zürich	13 Aug 97
2.01i		Tisha	Waller	USA	1.12.70	1	NC	Atlanta	28 Feb 98
2.01		Yelena	Gulyayeva	RUS	14.8.67	2		Kalamata	23 May 98
2.01		Vita	Palamar	UKR	12.10.77	2=	WK	Zürich	15 Aug 03
(40)									

Mark	Wind	Name		Nat	Born	Pos	Meet	Venue	Date
2.01		Amy	Acuff	USA	14.7.75	4	WK	Zürich	15 Aug 03
2.01		Iryna	Myhalchenko	UKR	20.1.72	1		Eberstadt	18 Jul 04
2.01		Emma	Green Tregaro	SWE	8.12.84	2	EC	Barcelona	1 Aug 10
2.00 WR		Rosemarie	Ackermann'	GDR	4.4.52	1	ISTAF	Berlin	26 Aug 77
2.00i		Coleen	Sommer'	USA	6.6.60	1		Ottawa	14 Feb 82
2.00		Charmaine	Gale/Weavers	RSA	27.2.64	1		Pretoria	25 Mar 85
2.00i		Emilia	Dragieva'	BUL	11.1.65	3	WI	Indianapolis	8 Mar 87
2.00		Lyudmila	Avdyeyenko'	UKR	14.12.63	1	NC	Bryansk	17 Jul 87
2.00		Svetlana	Isaeva/Leseva	BUL	18.3.67	2	v TCH,GRE	Drama	8 Aug 87
2.00i		Larisa	Kositsyna	RUS	14.12.63	2	NC	Volgograd	11 Feb 88
		(50)							

2.00 also by Jan Wohlschlag' USA 1 Jul 89 Yolanda Henry USA 30 May 90, Biljana Petrovic ¶ 22 Jun 90, Tatyana Shevchik ¶ BLR Gomel 14 May 93, Britta Vörös/Bilac GDR/SLO 9 Feb 94 (i), Yuliya Lyakhova RUS 15 Feb 99 (i), Zuzana Hlavonová CZE 5 Jun 00, Dóra Györffy HUN 26 Jul 01, Viktoriya Seryogina RUS 11 Jun 02, Svetlana Lapina RUS/ AZE 26 Feb 03 (i), Daniela Rath GER 22 Jun 03, Yekaterina Savchenko' 1 Jul 07, Viktoriya Klyugina RUS 7 Feb 09 (i), Meike Kröger GER 28 Feb 10 (i), Alessia Trost ITA 29 Jan 13 (i)

(64)   100th woman 1.97, 200th 1.94, 300th 1.92, 400th 1.91, 500th 1.90

Best outdoor marks						2.01		Astafei	2		Wörrstadt	27 May 95
2.05	Henkel	1	WCh	Tokyo	31 Aug 91	2.00		Quintero	1	Herc	Monaco	7 Aug 93
2.03	Di Martino	1	ECp-1B	Milano	24 Jun 07	2.00		Kositsyna	1		Chelyabinsk	16 Jul 88
2.02	Iagar/Dinescu	1		Budapest	6 Jun 98	2.00		Bilac	1	EC	Helsinki	14 Aug 94
2.02	Kuptsova	1	FBK	Hengelo	1 Jun 03	2.00		Waller	1	MSR	Walnut	18 Apr 99

Ancillary jumps: 2.06 Kostadinova 30 Aug 87, 2.05i Henkel 8 Feb 92, 2.05i Bergqvist 4 Feb 06, 2.05 Vlasic 31 Aug 09

POLE VAULT

Mark		Name		Nat	Born	Pos	Meet	Venue	Date
5.06 WR		Yelena	Isinbayeva	RUS	3.6.82	1	WK	Zürich	28 Aug 09
5.05 WR			Isinbayeva			1	OG	Beijing	18 Aug 08
5.04 WR			Isinbayeva			1	Herc	Monaco	29 Jul 08
5.03 WR			Isinbayeva			1	GGala	Roma	11 Jul 08
5.02Ai		Jennifer	Suhr	USA	5.2.82	1	NC	Albuquerque	2 Mar 13
5.01 WR			Isinbayeva			2	1	WCh	Helsinki	12 Aug 05
5.01i			Isinbayeva			1	XL Galan	Stockholm	23 Feb 12
5.00 WR			Isinbayeva			1	LGP	London (CP)	22 Jul 05
5.00i			Isinbayeva			1		Donetsk	15 Feb 09
4.95 WR			Isinbayeva			1	GP	Madrid	16 Jul 05
4.95i			Isinbayeva			1		Donetsk	16 Feb 08
4.93 WR			Isinbayeva			1	Athl	Lausanne	5 Jul 05
4.93			Isinbayeva			1	VD	Bruxelles	26 Aug 05
4.93i			Isinbayeva			1		Donetsk	10 Feb 07
4.93			Isinbayeva			1	LGP	London (CP)	25 Jul 08
4.92 WR			Isinbayeva			1	VD	Bruxelles	3 Sep 04
4.92			Stuczynski/Suhr			1	NC/OT	Eugene	6 Jul 08
4.91 WR			Isinbayeva (this jump on 25 Aug)			1	OG	Athína	25 Aug 04
4.91i			Isinbayeva			1		Donetsk	12 Feb 06
4.91			Isinbayeva			1	LGP	London (CP)	28 Jul 06
4.91			Isinbayeva			1	Gaz	Saint-Denis	6 Jul 07
4.91			Suhr			1		Rochester, NY	26 Jul 11
4.91			Suhr			1		Lyndonville	14 Jun 13
4.90 WR			Isinbayeva			1	GP	London (CP)	30 Jul 04
4.90i			Isinbayeva			1	EI	Madrid	6 Mar 05
4.90			Isinbayeva			1	Athl	Lausanne	11 Jul 06
4.90			Isinbayeva			1	GGala	Roma	13 Jul 07
4.90			Stuczynski			1	adidas	Carson	18 May 08
4.90i			Isinbayeva			1		Praha (O2)	26 Feb 09
4.90		Yarisley	Silva	CUB	1.6.87	1	FBK	Hengelo	8 Jun 13
		(30/3)							
4.88 WR		Svetlana	Feofanova	RUS	16.7.80	1		Iráklio	4 Jul 04
4.87i		Holly	Bleasdale	GBR	2.11.91	1		Villeurbanne	20 Jan 12
4.85		Fabiana	Murer	BRA	16.3.81	1	IbAm	San Fernando	4 Jun 10
4.85i		Anna	Rogowska	POL	21.5.81	1	EI	Paris (Bercy)	6 Mar 11
4.83		Stacy	Dragila	USA	25.3.71	1	GS	Ostrava	8 Jun 04
4.82		Monika	Pyrek	POL	11.8.80	2	WAF	Stuttgart	22 Sep 07
4.82		Silke	Spiegelburg	GER	17.3.86	1	Herc	Monaco	20 Jul 12
4.80		Martina	Strutz	GER	4.11.81	2	WCh	Daegu	30 Aug 11
		(10)							
4.78		Tatyana	Polnova	RUS	20.4.79	2	WAF	Monaco	19 Sep 04
4.77		Annika	Becker	GER	12.11.81	1	NC	Wattenscheid	7 Jul 02
4.76		Alana	Boyd	AUS	10.5.84	1		Perth	24 Feb 12
4.75		Katerina	Badurová	CZE	18.12.82	2	WCh	Osaka	28 Aug 07
4.76		Jirina	Svobodová'	CZE	20.5.86	1		Plzen	4 Sep 13

Mark	Wind	Name		Nat	Born	Pos	Meet	Venue	Date
4.75i		Yuliya	Golubchikova	RUS	27.3.83	1		Athína (P)	13 Feb 08
4.75Ai		Kylie	Hutson	USA	27.11.87	2	NC	Albuquerque	2 Mar 13
4.73		Chelsea	Johnson	USA	20.12.83	1		Los Gatos	26 Jun 08
4.73		Anastasiya	Savchenko	RUS	15.11.89	1	NCp	Yerino	15 Jun 13
		(20)							
4.72i		Kym	Howe	AUS	12.6.80	2		Donetsk	10 Feb 07
4.72i		Jillian	Schwartz	USA/ISR	19.9.79	1		Jonesboro	15 Jun 08
4.72		Carolin	Hingst	GER	18.9.80	1		Biberach	9 Jul 10
4.71		Nikolía	Kiriakopoúlou	GRE	21.3.86	4	LGP	London (CP)	5 Aug 11
4.70		Yvonne	Buschbaum	GER	14.7.80	1	NC	Ulm	29 Jun 03
4.70		Vanessa	Boslak	FRA	11.6.82	2	ECp-S	Málaga	28 Jun 06
4.70		Mary	Saxer	USA	21.6.87	1		Chula Vista	6 Jun 13
4.70		Angelina	Zhuk/Krasnova	RUS	7.2.91	1	EU23	Tampere	13 Jul 13
4.68		Anna	Battke	GER	3.1.85	5	ISTAF	Berlin	14 Jun 09
4.67i		Kellie	Suttle	USA	9.5.73	1		Jonesboro	16 Jun 04
		(30)							
4.66i		Christine	Adams	GER	28.2.74	1	IHS	Sindelfingen	10 Mar 02
4.66i		Lacy	Janson	USA	20.2.83	1		Fayetteville	12 Feb 10
4.66i		Kristina	Gadschiew	GER	3.7.84	1		Potsdam	18 Feb 11
4.65		Mary	Sauer/Vincent	USA	31.10.75	2		Madrid (C)	3 Jul 02
4.65		Anastasiya	Ivanova/Shvedova	RUS/BLR	3.5.79	1	Odlozil	Praha	13 Jun 07
4.65		Aleksandra	Kiryashova	RUS	21.8.85	1	NCp	Tula	1 Aug 09
4.65		Lisa	Ryzih	GER	27.9.88	3	EC	Barcelona	30 Jul 10
4.65		Li Ling		CHN	6.7.89	1	NG	Shenyang	8 Sep 13
4.64i		Pavla	Hamácková/Rybová	CZE	20.5.78	4		Bydgoszcz	14 Feb 07
4.64			Gao Shuying	CHN	28.10.79	2	GP	New York	2 Jun 07
		(40)							
4.63		Nastja	Ryshich	GER	19.9.77	1		Nürnberg	29 Jul 06
4.63		April	Steiner-Bennett	USA	22.4.80	1		Norman	12 Apr 08
4.63i		Angelica	Bengtsson	SWE	8.7.93	2		Stockholm	22 Feb 11
4.62b		Melissa	Mueller	USA	16.11.72	1		Clovis	4 Aug 01
		4.60Ai				1		Flagstaff	9 Feb 02
4.62i		Anzhelika	Sidorova	RUS	28.6.91	3	EI	Göteborg	2 Mar 13
4.61		Tina	Sutej	SLO	7.11.88	1	SEC	Athens, GA	14 May 11
4.61		Kate	Dennison	GBR	7.5.84	2		Barcelona	22 Jul 11
4.61		Nicole	Büchler	SUI	17.12.83	3	Spitz	Luzern	17 Jul 13
		(48)							
		100th woman 4.50, 200th 4.36, 300th 4.27, 400th 4.20, 500th 4.15							
4.60 WR		Emma	George	AUS	1.11.74	1		Sydney	20 Feb 99
4.60		15 other women							

Outdoor bests

4.75	Golubchikova	4	OG	Beijing	18 Aug 08	4.65	Howe	1	Saulheim	30 Jun 07
4.70	Hutson	1		Terre Haute	15 Jun 13	4.61	Gadschiew	1	Rovereto	3 Sep 13

Ancillary jumps: Isinbayeva: 4.97 15 Feb 09, 4.96 WR 22 Jul 05, 4.95 18 Aug 08, 4.93 29 Jul 08, 4.92i 23 Feb 12
Exhibition: 4.72 Anastasiya   Shvedova   RUS   3.5.79 1   Aosta   5 Jul 08

LONG JUMP

Mark	Wind	Name		Nat	Born	Pos	Meet	Venue	Date
7.52 WR	1.4	Galina	Chistyakova	RUS	26.7.62	1	Znam	Leningrad	11 Jun 88
7.49	1.3	Jackie	Joyner-Kersee	USA	3.3.62	1	NYG	New York	22 May 94
7.49A	1.7		Joyner-Kersee			1		Sestriere	31 Jul 94
7.48	1.2	Heike	Drechsler	GER	16.12.64	1	v ITA	Neubrandenburg	9 Jul 88
7.48	0.4		Drechsler			1	Athl	Lausanne	8 Jul 92
7.45 WR	0.9		Drechsler'			1	v USSR	Tallinn	21 Jun 86
7.45 WR	1.1		Drechsler			1	OD	Dresden	3 Jul 86
7.45 WR	0.6		Joyner-Kersee			1	PAm	Indianapolis	13 Aug 87
7.45	1.6		Chistyakova			1	BGP	Budapest	12 Aug 88
7.44 WR	2.0		Drechsler			1		Berlin	22 Sep 85
7.43 WR	1.4	Anisoara	Cusmir/Stanciu	ROU	28.6.62	1	RomIC	Bucuresti	4 Jun 83
7.42	2.0	Tatyana	Kotova ¶	RUS	11.12.76	1	ECp-S	Annecy	23 Jun 02
7.40	1.8		Daute' (Drechsler)			1		Dresden	26 Jul 84
7.40	0.7		Drechsler			1	NC	Potsdam	21 Aug 87
7.40	0.9		Joyner-Kersee			1	OG	Seoul	29 Sep 88
7.39	0.3		Drechsler			1	WK	Zürich	21 Aug 85
7.39	0.5	Yelena	Byelevskaya'	BLR	11.10.63	1	NC	Bryansk	18 Jul 87
7.39			Joyner-Kersee			1		San Diego	25 Jun 88
7.37i	–		Drechsler			1	v2N	Wien	13 Feb 88
7.37A	1.8		Drechsler			1		Sestriere	31 Jul 91
7.37		Inessa	Kravets ¶	UKR	5.10.66	1		Kyiv	13 Jun 92
7.36	0.4		Joyner			1	WCh	Roma	4 Sep 87
7.36	1.8		Byelevskaya			2	Znam	Leningrad	11 Jun 88
7.36	1.8		Drechsler			1		Jena	28 May 92

WOMEN All-time

Mark	Wind		Name	Nat	Born	Pos	Meet	Venue	Date
7.35	1.9		Chistyakova			1	GPB	Bratislava	20 Jun 90
7.34	1.6		Daute'			1		Dresden	19 May 84
7.34	1.4		Chistyakova			2	v GDR	Tallinn	21 Jun 86
7.34			Byelevskaya			1		Sukhumi	17 May 87
7.34	0.7		Drechsler			1	v USSR	Karl-Marx-Stadt	20 Jun 87
7.33	0.4		Drechsler			1	v USSR	Erfurt	22 Jun 85
7.33	2.0		Drechsler			1		Dresden	2 Aug 85
7.33	-0.3		Drechsler			1	Herc	Monaco	11 Aug 92
7.33	0.4	Tatyana	Lebedeva	RUS	21.7.76	1	NC	Tula	31 Jul 04
		(33/8)							
7.31	1.5	Yelena	Kokonova'	UKR	4.8.63	1	NP	Alma-Ata	12 Sep 85
7.31	1.9	Marion	Jones ¶	USA	12.10.75	1	Pre	Eugene	31 May 98
		(10)							
7.27	-0.4	Irina	Simagina/Meleshina	RUS	25.5.82	2	NC	Tula	31 Jul 04
7.26A	1.8	Maurren	Maggi ¶	BRA	25.6.76	1	SACh	Bogotá	26 Jun 99
7.25	1.6	Brittney	Reese	USA	9.9.86	1	DL	Doha	10 May 13
7.24	1.0	Larisa	Berezhnaya	UKR	28.2.61	1		Granada	25 May 91
7.21	1.6	Helga	Radtke	GDR	16.5.62	2		Dresden	26 Jul 84
7.21	1.9	Lyudmila	Kolchanova	RUS	1.10.79	1		Sochi	27 May 07
7.20 WR	-0.5	Valy	Ionescu	ROU	31.8.60	1	NC	Bucuresti	1 Aug 82
7.20	2.0	Irena	Ozhenko'	LTU	13.11.62	1		Budapest	12 Sep 86
7.20	0.8	Yelena	Sinchukova'	RUS	23.1.61	1	BGP	Budapest	20 Jun 91
7.20	0.7	Irina	Mushayilova	RUS	6.1.67	1	NC	Sankt-Peterburg	14 Jul 94
		(20)							
7.17	1.8	Irina	Valyukevich	BLR	19.11.59	2	NC	Bryansk	18 Jul 87
7.16		Iolanda	Chen	RUS	26.7.61	1		Moskva	30 Jul 88
7.16A	-0.1	Elva	Goulbourne	JAM	21.1.80	1		Ciudad de México	22 May 04
7.14	1.8	Nijole	Medvedeva ¶	LTU	20.10.60	1		Riga	4 Jun 88
7.14	1.2	Mirela	Dulgheru	ROU	5.10.66	1	Balk G	Sofia	5 Jul 92
7.13	2.0	Olga	Kucherenko	RUS	5.11.85	1		Sochi	27 May 10
7.12	1.6	Sabine	Paetz/John'	GDR	16.10.57	2		Dresden	19 May 84
7.12	0.9	Chioma	Ajunwa ¶	NGR	25.12.70	1	OG	Atlanta	2 Aug 96
7.12	1.3	Naide	Gomes	CPV/POR	10.11.79	1	Herc	Monaco	29 Jul 08
7.11	0.8	Fiona	May	GBR/ITA	12.12.69	2	EC	Budapest	22 Aug 98
		(30)							
7.11	1.3	Anna	Nazarova	RUS	3.2.86	1	Mosc Ch	Moskva	20 Jun 12
7.10	1.6	Chelsea	Hayes	USA	9.2.88	2	NC/OT	Eugene	1 Jul 12
7.09 WR	0.0	Vilhelmina	Bardauskiené	LTU	15.6.53	Q	EC	Praha	29 Aug 78
7.09	1.5	Ljudmila	Ninova	AUT	25.6.60	1	GP II	Sevilla	5 Jun 94
7.08	0.5	Marieta	Ilcu ¶	ROU	16.10.62	1	RumIC	Pitesti	25 Jun 89
7.08	1.9	Anastasiya	Mironchik-Ivanova	BLR	13.4.89	1		Minsk	12 Jun 12
7.07	0.0	Svetlana	Zorina	RUS	2.2.60	1		Krasnodar	15 Aug 87
7.07	0.5	Yelena	Sokolova	RUS	23.7.86	2	OG	London (OS)	8 Aug 12
7.06	0.4	Tatyana	Kolpakova	KGZ	18.10.59	1	OG	Moskva	31 Jul 80
7.06	-0.1	Niurka	Montalvo	CUB/ESP	4.6.68	1	WCh	Sevilla	23 Aug 99
		(40)							
7.06		Tatyana	Ter-Mesrobyan	RUS	12.5.68	1		Sankt Peterburg	22 May 02
7.05	0.6	Lyudmila	Galkina	RUS	20.1.72	1	WCh	Athína	9 Aug 97
7.05	-0.4	Eunice	Barber	FRA	17.11.74	1	WAF	Monaco	14 Sep 03
7.05	1.1	Darya	Klishina	RUS	15.1.91	1	EU23	Ostrava	17 Jul 11
7.04	0.5	Brigitte	Wujak'	GDR	6.3.55	2	OG	Moskva	31 Jul 80
7.04	0.9	Tatyana	Proskuryakova'	RUS	13.1.56	1		Kyiv	25 Aug 83
7.04	2.0	Yelena	Yatsuk	UKR	16.3.61	1	Znam	Moskva	8 Jun 85
7.04	0.3	Carol	Lewis	USA	8.8.63	5	WK	Zürich	21 Aug 85
7.04	1.5	Sosthene	Moguenara	GER	17.10.89	1		Weinheim	2 Aug 13
7.03	0.6	Niki	Xánthou	GRE	11.10.73	1		Bellinzona	18 Aug 97
7.03i	-	Dawn	Burrell	USA	1.11.73	1	WI	Lisboa	10 Mar 01
7.03	1.7	Janay	DeLoach-Soukup	USA	12.10.85	*	NC/OT	Eugene	1 Jul 12
		(52)							

100th woman 6.92, 200th 6.81, 300th 6.75, 400th 6.69, 500th 6.64

Drugs disquailification

7.03	0.1		Xiong Qiying ¶	CHN	14.10.67	Q	NG	Shanghai	21 Oct 97

Wind assisted
Performances to 7.35, performers to 7.05

7.63A	2.1	Heike	Drechsler	GER	16.12.64	1		Sestriere	21 Jul 92
7.45	2.6		Joyner-Kersee			1	NC/OT	Indianapolis	23 Jul 88
7.39	2.6		Drechsler			1		Padova	15 Sep 91
7.39	2.9		Drechsler			1	Expo	Sevilla	6 Jun 92
7.39A	3.3		Drechsler			2		Sestriere	31 Jul 94
7.36	2.2		Chistyakova			1	Znam	Volgograd	11 Jun 89
7.35	3.4		Drechsler			1	NC	Jena	29 Jun 86
7.23A	4.3	Fiona	May	ITA	12.12.69	1		Sestriere	29 Jul 95
7.22	4.3	Anastasiya	Mironchik-Ivanova	BLR	13.4.89	1	NC	Grodno	6 Jul 12

Mark	Wind		Name	Nat	Born	Pos	Meet	Venue	Date
7.19A	3.7	Susen	Tiedtke ¶	GER	23.1.69	1		Sestriere	28 Jul 9⁣
7.17	3.6	Eva	Murková	SVK	29.5.62	1		Nitra	26 Aug 84
7.15	2.8	Janay	DeLoach	USA	12.10.85	Q	NC/OT	Eugene	29 Jun 1⁣
7.14A	4.5	Marieke	Veltman	USA	18.9.71	2		Sestriere	29 Jul 9⁣
7.14	2.2	Blessing	Okagbare	NGR	9.10.88	2	DL	Doha	10 May 1⁣
7.12A	5.8	Níki	Xánthou	GRE	11.10.73	3		Sestriere	29 Jul 9⁣
7.12A	4.3	Nicole	Boegman	AUS	5.3.67	4		Sestriere	29 Jul 9⁣
7.09	2.9	Renata	Nielsen	DEN	18.5.66	2		Sevilla	5 Jun 9⁣
7.08	2.2	Lyudmila	Galkina	RUS	20.1.72	1		Thessaloniki	23 Jun 9⁣
7.07A	5.6	Valentina	Uccheddu	ITA	26.10.66	5		Sestriere	29 Jul 9⁣
7.07A	2.7	Sharon	Couch	USA	13.9.67	1		El Paso	12 Apr 97
7.07A	w	Erica	Johansson	SWE	5.2.74	1		Vygieskraal	15 Jan 0⁣
7.06	3.4		Ma Miaolan	CHN	18.1.70	1	NG	Beijing	10 Sep 9⁣

Best outdoor mark for athlete with all-time best indoors:
Best at low altitude:

| 7.06 | 0.8 | Maggi ¶ | 1 | Milano | 3 Jun 03 | 7.12w | 3.4 May | 1 | NC | Bologna | 25 May 96⁣ |
| | | 7.17w | 2.6 | 1 | São Paulo | 13 Apr 02 |

Ancillary marks – other marks during series (to 7.34/7.36w)
7.45   1.0 Chistyakova 11 Jun 88   7.47Aw 3.1 Drechsler   21 Jul 92   7.38w 2.2 Chistyakova 11 Jun 88
7.37   Drechsler   9 Jul 88   7.39Aw 3.1 Drechsler   21 Jul 92   7.36w   Joyner-Kersee 31 Jul 94

TRIPLE JUMP

Mark	Wind		Name	Nat	Born	Pos	Meet	Venue	Date
15.50 WR	0.9	Inessa	Kravets ¶	UKR	5.10.66	1	WCh	Göteborg	10 Aug 9⁣
15.39	0.5	Françoise	Mbango	CMR	14.4.76	1	OG	Beijing	17 Aug 0⁣
15.36i		Tatyana	Lebedeva	RUS	21.7.76	1	WI	Budapest	6 Mar 04
15.34	-0.5		Lebedeva			1		Iráklio	4 Jul 04
15.33	-0.1		Kravets			1	OG	Atlanta	31 Jul 9⁣
15.33	1.2		Lebedeva			1	Athl	Lausanne	6 Jul 04
15.32	0.5		Lebedeva			1	Super	Yokohama	9 Sep 0⁣
15.32	0.9	Hrisopiyi	Devetzí ¶	GRE	2.1.76	Q	OG	Athína	21 Aug 04
15.32	0.5		Lebedeva			2	OG	Beijing	17 Aug 0⁣
15.30	0.6		Mbango			1	OG	Athína	23 Aug 0⁣
15.29	0.3	Yamilé	Aldama	CUB/SUD/GBR	14.8.72	1	GGala	Roma	11 Jul 0⁣
15.28	0.3		Aldama			1	GP	Linz	2 Aug 04
15.28	0.9	Yargelis	Savigne	CUB	13.11.84	1	WCh	Osaka	31 Aug 07
15.27	1.3		Aldama			1	GP	London (CP)	8 Aug 0⁣
15.25	-0.8		Lebedeva			1	WCh	Edmonton	10 Aug 0⁣
15.25	-0.1		Devetzí			2	OG	Athína	23 Aug 04
15.25	1.7	Olga	Rypakova	KAZ	30.11.84	1	C.Cup	Split	4 Sep 1⁣
15.23	0.8		Lebedeva			1		Réthimno	23 Jun 04
15.23	0.6		Lebedeva			1	Tsik	Athína	3 Jul 0⁣
15.23	1.6		Devetzí			3	OG	Beijing	17 Aug 0⁣
15.22	1.5		Devetzí			1		Thessaloníki	9 Jul 0⁣
15.21	1.2		Aldama			2		Réthimno	23 Jun 04
15.20	0.0	Sarka	Kaspárková	CZE	20.5.71	1	WCh	Athína	4 Aug 97
15.20	-0.3	Tereza	Marinova	BUL	5.9.77	1	OG	Sydney	24 Sep 0⁣
15.20	1.3		Savigne			1	Vard	Réthimno	14 Jul 0⁣
15.19	0.5		Lebedeva			1	Athl	Lausanne	11 Jul 0⁣
15.18	0.3	Iva	Prandzheva ¶ (10)	BUL	15.2.72	2	WCh	Göteborg	10 Aug 9⁣
15.18	-0.2		Lebedeva			1	WCh	Saint-Denis	26 Aug 0⁣
15.16	0.1	Rodica	Mateescu ¶	ROU	13.3.71	2	WCh	Athína	4 Aug 97
15.16i WIR	-	Ashia	Hansen	GBR	5.12.71	1	EI	Valencia	28 Feb 9⁣
15.16	0.7	Trecia	Smith	JAM	5.11.75	2	GP	Linz	2 Aug 04
			(31/13)						
15.14	1.9	Nadezhda	Alekhina	RUS	22.9.78	1	NC	Cheboksary	26 Jul 0⁣
15.09 WR	0.5	Anna	Biryukova	RUS	27.9.67	1	WCh	Stuttgart	21 Aug 93
15.09	-0.5	Inna	Lasovskaya	RUS	17.12.69	1	ECCp-A	Valencia	31 May 97
15.08i		Marija	Sestak	SLO	17.4.79	1		Athína (P)	13 Feb 0⁣
15.07	-0.6	Paraskeví	Tsiamíta	GRE	10.3.72	Q	WCh	Sevilla	22 Aug 9⁣
15.03i		Iolanda	Chen	RUS	26.7.61	1	WI	Barcelona	11 Mar 9⁣
15.03	1.9	Magdelin	Martinez	ITA	10.2.76	1		Roma	26 Jun 04
			(20)						
15.02	0.9	Anna	Pyatykh	RUS	4.4.81	3	EC	Göteborg	8 Sep 0⁣
15.00	1.2	Kène	Ndoye	SEN	20.11.78	2		Iráklio	4 Jul 04
14.99A	1.7	Caterine	Ibargüen	COL	12.2.84	1		Bogotá	13 Aug 1⁣
14.99	0.2	Olha	Saladuha	UKR	4.6.83	1	EC	Helsinki	29 Jun 1⁣
14.98	1.8	Sofia	Bozhanova ¶	BUL	4.10.67	1		Stara Zagora	16 Jul 94
14.98	0.2	Baya	Rahouli	ALG	27.7.79	1	MedG	Almería	1 Jul 0⁣
14.96	0.7	Yelena	Hovorova	UKR	18.9.73	4	OG	Sydney	24 Sep 0⁣

Mark	Wind	Name		Nat	Born	Pos	Meet	Venue	Date
14.94i	–	Cristina	Nicolau	ROU	9.8.77	1	NC	Bucuresti	5 Feb 00
14.94i		Oksana	Udmurtova	RUS	1.2.82	1		Tartu	20 Feb 08
14.90	1.0	Xie Limei		CHN	27.6.86	1		Urumqi	20 Sep 07
		(30)							
14.85	1.2	Viktoriya	Gurova	RUS	22.5.82	3	NC	Kazan	19 Jul 08
14.83i	-	Yelena	Lebedenko	RUS	16.1.71	1		Samara	1 Feb 01
14.83	0.5	Yelena	Oleynikova	RUS	9.12.76	1	Odlozil	Praha	17 Jun 02
14.82	-0.2	Yekaterina	Koneva	RUS	25.9.88	1	WUG	Kazan	11 Jul 13
14.79	1.7	Irina	Mushayilova	RUS	6.1.67	1	DNG	Stockholm	5 Jul 93
14.78i		Adelina	Gavrila	ROU	26.11.78	1		Bucuresti	3 Feb 08
14.76	0.9	Galina	Chistyakova	RUS	26.7.62	1	Spitzen	Luzern	27 Jun 95
14.76	1.1	Gundega	Sproge ¶	LAT	12.12.72	3		Sheffield	29 Jun 97
14.76	0.4	Kseniya	Detsuk	BLR	23.4.86	*	NCp	Brest	26 May 12
14.72	1.8	Huang Qiuyan		CHN	25.1.80	1	NG	Guangzhou	22 Nov 01
		(40)							
14.72		Paraskeví	Papahrístou	GRE	17.4.89	1	Veniz	Haniá	11 Jun 11
14.71	2.0	Hanna	Knyazyeva-Minenko	UKR	25.9.89	1	NC	Yalta	15 Jun 12
14.71	1.4	Athanasía	Pérra	GRE	2.2.83	1	NC	Athína	16 Jun 12
14.70i		Oksana	Rogova	RUS	7.10.78	1		Volgograd	6 Feb 02
14.69	1.2	Anja	Valant	SLO	8.9.77	3		Kalamáta	4 Jun 00
14.69	1.2	Simona	La Mantia	ITA	14.4.83	1		Palermo	22 May 05
14.69	2.0	Teresa	N'zola Meso	ANG/FRA	30.11.83	1	ECp-S	München	23 Jun 07
14.68i		Anastasiya	Taranova-Potapova	RUS	6.9.85	1	EI	Torino	8 Mar 09
14.67	1.2	Ólga	Vasdéki	GRE	26.9.73	1	Veniz	Haniá	28 Jul 99
14.67	1.5	Natalya	Kutyakova	RUS	28.11.86	1		Huelva	2 Jun 11
14.67	0.4	Mabel	Gay	CUB	5.5.83	4	WCh	Daegu	1 Sep 11
		(51)							

100th woman 14.43, 200th 14.12, 300th 13.93, 400th 13.78, 500th 13.65

Wind assisted   *Performances to 15.14, performers to 14.68*

Mark	Wind	Name		Nat	Born	Pos	Meet	Venue	Date
15.24A	4.2	Magdelin	Martinez	ITA	10.2.76	1		Sestriere	1 Aug 04
15.17	2.4	Anna	Pyatykh	RUS	4.4.81	2	SGP	Athína	3 Jul 06
15.10	2.7	Keila	Costa	BRA	6.2.83	1		Uberlandia	6 May 07
15.06	2.6	Olga	Saladuha	UKR	4.6.83	1	DNG	Stockholm	29 Jul 11
14.99	6.8	Yelena	Hovorova	UKR	18.9.73	1	WUG	Palma de Mallorca	11 Jul 99
14.84	4.1	Galina	Chistyakova	RUS	26.7.62	1		Innsbruck	28 Jun 95
14.83	8.3		Ren Ruiping	CHN	1.2.76	1	NC	Taiyuan	21 May 95
14.83	2.2	Heli	Koivula-Kruger	FIN	27.6.75	2	EC	München	10 Aug 02
14.81	2.4	Kseniya	Detsuk	BLR	23.4.86	1	NCp	Brest	26 May 12
14.78	2.7	Kimberly	Williams	JAM	3.11.88	3	Pre	Eugene	1 Jun 13
14.77	2.3	Paraskeví	Papahrístou	GRE	17.4.89	1		Ankara	5 Jun 12
14.75	4.2	Jelena	Blazevica	LAT	11.5.70	1	v2N	Kaunas	23 Aug 97
14.71	2.5	Simona	La Mantia	ITA	14.4.83	1		Roma	25 Jun 04

Best outdoor mark for athlete with all-time best indoors

15.15	1.7	Hansen	1	GPF	Fukuoka	13 Sep 97	14.85	1.4	Udmurtova	1		Padova	31 Aug 08
15.03	1.1	Sestak	6	OG	Beijing	17 Aug 08	14.75	1.1	Gavrila	3	GP II	Rieti	7 Sep 03
14.97w	0.9	Chen	1	NC	Moskva	18 Jun 93	14.70	1.3	Nicolau	1	EU23	Göteborg	1 Aug 99

Ancillary marks – other marks during series (to 15.19)

15.30	0.5	Mbango	23 Aug 04	15.28	-0.3	Ledebeva	4 Jul 04	15.25i		Ledebeva	6 Mar 04
15.21	-0.2	Mbango	23 Aug 04	15.19	1.0	Lebedeva	3 Jul 06	15.19	1.3	Mbango	17 Aug 08

Best al low altitude

14.85   -0.1   Ibargüen   1   Herc   Monaco   20 Jul 12   &   14.93w   2.1   1   Pre   Eugene   1 Jun 13

SHOT

Mark		Name		Nat	Born	Pos	Meet	Venue	Date
22.63 WR		Natalya	Lisovskaya	RUS	16.7.62	1	Znam	Moskva	7 Jun 87
22.55			Lisovskaya			1	NC	Tallinn	5 Jul 88
22.53 WR			Lisovskaya			1		Sochi	27 May 84
22.53			Lisovskaya			1		Kyiv	14 Aug 88
22.50i		Helena	Fibingerová	CZE	13.7.49	1		Jablonec	19 Feb 77
22.45 WR		Ilona	Slupianek' ¶	GDR	24.9.56	1		Potsdam	11 May 80
22.41			Slupianek			1	OG	Moskva	24 Jul 80
22.40			Slupianek			1		Berlin	3 Jun 83
22.38			Slupianek			1		Karl-Marx-Stadt	25 May 80
22.36 WR			Slupianek			1		Celje	2 May 80
22.34			Slupianek			1		Berlin	7 May 80
22.34			Slupianek			1	NC	Cottbus	18 Jul 80
22.32 WR			Fibingerová			1		Nitra	20 Aug 77
22.24			Lisovskaya			1	OG	Seoul	1 Oct 88
22.22			Slupianek			1		Potsdam	13 Jul 80
22.19		Claudia	Losch	FRG	10.1.60	1		Hainfeld	23 Aug 87
22.14i			Lisovskaya			1	NC	Penza	7 Feb 87
22.13			Slupianek			1		Split	29 Apr 80

WOMEN All-time

Mark	Wind	Name		Nat	Born	Pos	Meet	Venue	Date
22.06		Slupianek				1		Berlin	15 Aug 78
22.06		Lisovskaya				1		Moskva	6 Aug 88
22.05		Slupianek				1	OD	Berlin	28 May 80
22.05		Slupianek				1		Potsdam	31 May 80
22.04		Slupianek				1		Potsdam	4 Jul 79
22.04		Slupianek				1		Potsdam	29 Jul 79
21.99 WR		Fibingerová				1		Opava	26 Sep 76
21.98		Slupianek				1		Berlin	17 Jul 79
21.96		Fibingerová				1	GS	Ostrava	8 Jun 77
21.96		Lisovskaya				1	Drz	Praha	16 Aug 84
21.96		Lisovskaya				1		Vilnius	28 Aug 88
21.95		Lisovskaya				1	IAC	Edinburgh	29 Jul 88
		(30/4)							
21.89 WR		Ivanka	Khristova	BUL	19.11.41	1		Belmeken	4 Jul 76
21.86		Marianne	Adam	GDR	19.9.51	1	v URS	Leipzig	23 Jun 79
21.76			Li Meisu	CHN	17.4.59	1		Shijiazhuang	23 Apr 88
21.73		Natalya	Akhrimenko	RUS	12.5.55	1		Leselidze	21 May 88
21.70i		Nadezhda	Ostapchuk ¶	BLR	12.10.80	1	NC	Mogilyov	12 Feb 10
21.69		Viktoriya	Pavlysh ¶	UKR	15.1.69	1	EC	Budapest	20 Aug 98
		(10)							
21.66			Sui Xinmei ¶	CHN	29.1.65	1		Beijing	9 Jun 90
21.61		Verzhinia	Veselinova	BUL	18.11.57	1		Sofiya	21 Aug 82
21.60i		Valentina	Fedyushina	UKR	18.2.65	1		Simferopol	28 Dec 91
21.58		Margitta	Droese/Pufe	GDR	10.9.52	1		Erfurt	28 May 78
21.57 @		Ines	Müller'	GDR	2.1.59	1		Athína	16 May 88
21.45						1		Schwerin	4 Jun 86
21.53		Nunu	Abashidze ¶	UKR	27.3.55	2	Izv	Kyiv	20 Jun 84
21.52			Huang Zhihong	CHN	7.5.65	1	NC	Beijing	27 Jun 90
21.46		Larisa	Peleshenko ¶	RUS	29.2.64	1	Kuts	Moskva	26 Aug 00
21.45 WR		Nadezhda	Chizhova	RUS	29.9.45	1		Varna	29 Sep 73
21.43		Eva	Wilms	FRG	28.7.52	2	HB	München	17 Jun 77
		(20)							
			@ competitive meeting, but unsanctioned by GDR federation						
21.42		Svetlana	Krachevskaya'	RUS	23.11.44	2	OG	Moskva	24 Jul 80
21.31 @		Heike	Hartwig'	GDR	30.12.62	2		Athína	16 May 88
21.27						1		Haniá	22 May 88
21.27		Liane	Schmuhl	GDR	29.6.61	1		Cottbus	26 Jun 82
21.24		Valerie	Adams	NZL	6.10.84	1	WCh	Daegu	29 Aug 11
21.22		Astrid	Kumbernuss	GDR/GER	5.2.70	1	WCh	Göteborg	5 Aug 95
21.21		Kathrin	Neimke	GDR	18.7.66	2	WCh	Roma	5 Sep 87
21.19		Helma	Knorscheidt	GDR	31.12.56	1		Berlin	24 May 84
21.15i		Irina	Korzhanenko ¶	RUS	16.5.74	1	NC	Moskva	18 Feb 99
21.10		Heidi	Krieger	GDR	20.7.65	1	EC	Stuttgart	26 Aug 86
21.06		Svetlana	Krivelyova ¶	RUS	13.6.69	1	OG	Barcelona	7 Aug 92
		(30)							
21.05		Zdenka	Silhavá' ¶	CZE	15.6.54	2	NC	Praha	23 Jul 83
21.01		Ivanka	Petrova-Stoycheva	BUL	3.2.51	1	NC	Sofiya	28 Jul 79
21.00		Mihaela	Loghin	ROU	1.6.52	1		Formia	30 Jun 84
21.00		Cordula	Schulze	GDR	11.9.59	4	OD	Potsdam	21 Jul 84
20.96		Belsy	Laza	CUB	5.6.67	1		Ciudad de México	2 May 92
20.95		Elena	Stoyanova ¶	BUL	23.1.52	2	Balk	Sofiya	14 Jun 80
20.91		Svetla	Mitkova	BUL	17.6.64	1		Sofiya	24 May 87
20.80		Sona	Vasícková	CZE	14.3.62	1		Praha	2 Jun 88
20.72		Grit	Haupt/Hammer	GDR	4.6.66	3		Neubrandenburg	11 Jun 87
20.70		Natalya	Mikhnevich	BLR	25.5.82	2	NC	Grodno	8 Jul 08
		(40)							
20.61		María Elena	Sarría	CUB	14.9.54	1		La Habana	22 Jul 82
20.61		Yanina	Korolchik ¶	BLR	26.12.76	1	WCh	Edmonton	5 Aug 01
20.60		Marina	Antonyuk	RUS	12.5.62	1		Chelyabinsk	10 Aug 86
20.54			Zhang Liuhong	CHN	16.1.69	1	NC	Beijing	5 Jun 94
20.53		Iris	Plotzitzka	FRG	7.1.66	1	ASV	Köln	21 Aug 88
20.50i		Christa	Wiese	GDR	25.12.67	2	NC	Senftenberg	12 Feb 89
20.48		Yevgeniya	Kolodko	RUS	2.7.90	2	OG	London (OS)	6 Aug 12
20.47		Nina	Isayeva	RUS	6.7.50	1		Bryansk	28 Aug 92
20.47			Cong Yuzhen	CHN	22.1.63	2	IntC	Tianjin	3 Sep 88
20.44		Tatyana	Orlova	BLR	19.7.55	1		Staiki	28 May 83
		(50)							

100th woman 19.69, 200th 18.80, 300th 18.15, 400th 17.70, 500th 17.41

Best outdoor marks

21.58	Ostapchuk ¶	1	Minsk	18 Jul 12	20.82 Korzhanenko ¶ 1 Rostov na Donu 30 May 98
21.08	Fedyushina	1	Leselidze	15 May 88	21.06 drugs dq (1) OG Athína 18 Aug 04

Mark	Wind	Name		Nat	Born	Pos	Meet	Venue	Date

Ancillary marks – other marks during series (to 22.09)

22.60	Lisovskaya (WR)	7 Jun 87	22.20	Slupianek	13 Jul 80
22.40	Lisovskaya	14 Aug 88	22.19	Lisovskaya	5 Jul 88
22.34	Slupianek	11 May 80	22.14	Slupianek	25 May 80
22.33	Slupianek	2 May 80	22.14	Slupianek	13 Jul 80

22.12	Slupianek	13 Jul 80
22.11	Slupianek	7 May 80
22.10	Slupianek	25 May 80
22.09	Slupianek	7 May 80

DISCUS

Mark	Wind	Name	Surname	Nat	Born	Pos	Meet	Venue	Date
76.80 WR		Gabriele	Reinsch	GDR	23.9.63	1	v ITA	Neubrandenburg	9 Jul 88
74.56 WR		Zdenka	Silhavá' ¶	CZE	15.6.54	1		Nitra	26 Aug 84
74.56		Ilke	Wyludda	GDR	28.3.69	1	NC	Neubrandenburg	23 Jul 89
74.44			Reinsch			1		Berlin	13 Sep 88
74.40			Wyludda			2		Berlin	13 Sep 88
74.08		Diana	Gansky'	GDR	14.12.63	1	v USSR	Karl-Marx-Stadt	20 Jun 87
73.90			Gansky			1	ECp	Praha	27 Jun 87
73.84		Daniela	Costian ¶	ROU	30.4.65	1		Bucuresti	30 Apr 88
73.78			Costian			1		Bucuresti	24 Apr 88
73.42			Reinsch			1		Karl-Marx-Stadt	12 Jun 88
73.36 WR		Irina	Meszynski	GDR	24.3.62	1	Drz	Praha	17 Aug 84
73.32			Gansky			1		Neubrandenburg	11 Jun 87
73.28		Galina	Savinkova'	RUS	15.7.53	1	NC	Donetsk	8 Sep 84
73.26 WR			Savinkova			1		Leselidze	21 May 83
73.26			Sachse/Gansky			1		Neubrandenburg	6 Jun 86
73.24			Gansky			1		Leipzig	29 May 87
73.22		Tsvetanka	Khristova ¶	BUL	14.3.62	1		Kazanlak	19 Apr 87
73.10		Gisela	Beyer	GDR	16.7.60	1	OD	Berlin	20 Jul 84
73.04			Gansky			1		Potsdam	6 Jun 87
73.04			Wyludda			1	ECp	Gateshead	5 Aug 89
72.96			Savinkova			1	v GDR	Erfurt	23 Jun 85
72.94			Gansky			2	v ITA	Neubrandenburg	9 Jul 88
72.92		Martina	Opitz/Hellmann	GDR	12.12.60	1	NC	Potsdam	20 Aug 87
72.90			Costian			1		Bucuresti	14 May 88
72.78			Hellmann			2		Neubrandenburg	11 Jun 87
72.78			Reinsch			1	OD	Berlin	29 Jun 88
72.72			Wyludda			1		Neubrandenburg	23 Jun 89
72.70			Wyludda			1	NC-j	Karl-Marx-Stadt	15 Jul 88
72.54			Gansky			1	NC	Rostock	25 Jun 88
72.52			Hellmann			1		Frohburg	15 Jun 86
72.52			Khristova			1	BGP	Budapest	11 Aug 86
		(31/10)							
72.14		Galina	Murashova	LTU	22.12.55	2	Drz	Praha	17 Aug 84
71.80 WR		Maria	Vergova/Petkova	BUL	3.11.50	1	NC	Sofiya	13 Jul 80
71.68			Xiao Yanling ¶	CHN	27.3.68	1		Beijing	14 Mar 92
71.58		Ellina	Zvereva' ¶	BLR	16.11.60	1	Znam	Leningrad	12 Jun 88
71.50 WR		Evelin	Schlaak/Jahl	GDR	28.3.56	1		Potsdam	10 May 80
71.30		Larisa	Korotkevich	RUS	3.1.67	1	RusCp	Sochi	29 May 92
71.22		Ria	Stalman	NED	11.12.51	1		Walnut	15 Jul 84
70.88		Hilda Elia	Ramos ¶	CUB	1.9.64	1		La Habana	8 May 92
70.80		Larisa	Mikhalchenko	UKR	16.5.63	1		Kharkov	18 Jun 88
70.68		Maritza	Martén	CUB	16.8.63	1	Ib Am	Sevilla	18 Jul 92
		(20)							
70.50 WR		Faina	Melnik	RUS	9.6.45	1	Znam	Sochi	24 Apr 76
70.34 @		Silvia	Madetzky	GDR	24.6.62	3		Athína	16 May 88
69.34						1		Halle	26 Jun 87
70.02		Natalya	Sadova ¶	RUS	15.7.72	1		Thessaloniki	23 Jun 99
69.86		Valentina	Kharchenko	RUS	.49	1		Feodosiya	16 May 81
69.72		Svetla	Mitkova	BUL	17.6.64	2	NC	Sofiya	15 Aug 87
69.68		Mette	Bergmann	NOR	9.11.62	1		Florø	27 May 95
69.51		Franka	Dietzsch	GER	22.1.68	1		Wiesbaden	8 May 99
69.50		Florenta	Craciunescu'	ROU	7.5.55	1	Balk	Stara Zagora	2 Aug 85
69.14		Irina	Yatchenko ¶	BLR	31.10.65	1		Staiki	31 Jul 04
69.11		Sandra	Perkovic	CRO	21.6.90	1	OG	London (OS)	4 Aug 12
		(30)							
69.08		Carmen	Romero	CUB	6.10.50	1	NC	La Habana	17 Apr 76
69.08		Mariana	Ionescu/Lengyel	ROU	14.4.53	1		Constanta	19 Apr 86
68.92		Sabine	Engel	GDR	21.4.54	1	v URS,POL	Karl-Marx-Stadt	25 Jun 77
68.89		Nadine	Müller	GER	21.11.85	1	ECp-w	Bar	18 Mar 12
68.80A		Nicoleta	Grasu	ROU	11.9.71	1		Poiana Brasov	7 Aug 99
68.64		Margitta	Pufe'	GDR	10.9.52	1	ISTAF	Berlin	17 Aug 79
68.62			Yu Hourun	CHN	9.7.64	1		Beijing	6 May 88
68.62			Hou Xuemei	CHN	27.2.62	1	IntC	Tianjin	4 Sep 88
68.60		Nadezhda	Kugayevskikh	RUS	19.4.60	1		Oryol	30 Aug 83

WOMEN All-time

Mark	Wind	Name		Nat	Born	Pos	Meet	Venue	Date
68.58		Lyubov	Zverkova	RUS	14.6.55	1	Izv	Kyiv	22 Jun 84
		(40)							
68.52		Beatrice	Faumuiná	NZL	23.10.74	1	Bisl	Oslo	4 Jul 97
68.38		Olga	Burova'	RUS	17.9.63	2	RusCp	Sochi	29 May 92
68.18		Tatyana	Lesovaya	KAZ	24.4.56	1		Alma-Ata	23 Sep 82
68.18		Irina	Khval	RUS	17.5.62	1		Moskva	8 Jul 88
68.18		Barbara	Hechevarría	CUB	6.8.66	2		La Habana	17 Feb 89
68.03		Yarelis	Barrios	CUB	12.7.83	1	NC	La Habana	22 Mar 12
67.98			Li Yanfeng	CHN	15.5.79	1		Schönebeck	5 Jun 11
67.96		Argentina	Menis	ROU	19.7.48	1	RomIC	Bucuresti	15 May 76
67.90		Petra	Sziegaud	GDR	17.10.58	1		Berlin	19 May 82
67.86			Gu Siyu	CHN	11.2.93	1		Wiesbaden	19 May 13
		(50)							

100th woman 65.86, 200th 63.64, 300th 61.74, 400th 59.89, 500th 58.70

Unofficial meeting: Berlin 6 Sep 88: 1. Martina Hellmann 78.14, 2. Ilke Wyludda 75.36

Downhill: 69.44 Suzy Powell USA 3.9.76 1 La Jolla 27 Apr 02

Downhill:	69.44	Suzy	Powell	USA	3.9.76	1		La Jolla	27 Apr 02

Drugs disqualification:

70.69		Darya	Pishchalnikova ¶	RUS	19.7.85	(1)	NC	Cheboksary	5 Jul 12
69.99		Sandra	Perkovic #	CRO	21.6.90	(1)		Varazdin	4 Jun 11

Ancillary marks – other marks during series (to 72.92)

73.32	Reinsch	13 Sep 88	73.28	Gansky	27 Jun 87	73.10	Reinsch	9 Jul 88
73.28	Gansky	11 Jun 87	73.16	Wyludda	13 Sep 88	73.06	Gansky	27 Jun 87
						72.92	Hellmann	20 Aug 87

HAMMER

Mark	Wind	Name		Nat	Born	Pos	Meet	Venue	Date
79.42	WR	Betty	Heidler	GER	14.10.83	1		Halle	21 May 11
78.80		Tatyana	Lysenko ¶	RUS	9.10.83	1	WCh	Moskva	16 Aug 13
78.69		Oksana	Menkova	BLR	28.3.82	1		Minsk	18 Jul 12
78.51			Lysenko			1	NC	Cheboksary	5 Jul 12
78.46		Anita	Wlodarczyk	POL	8.8.85	2	WCh	Moskva	16 Aug 13
78.30	WR		Wlodarczyk			1	EAF	Bydgoszcz	6 Jun 10
78.22			Wlodarczyk			1		Dubnica nad Vahom	21 Aug 13
78.19			Menkova			1		Brest	28 Apr 12
78.19			Menkova			1		Minsk	12 Jun 12
78.18			Lysenko			1	OG	London (OS)	10 Aug 12
78.15			Lysenko			1	NC	Moskva	24 Jul 13
78.07			Heidler			1	GS	Ostrava	24 May 12
77.96	WR		Wlodarczyk			1	WCh	Berlin	22 Aug 09
77.80	WR		Lysenko			1		Tallinn	15 Aug 06
77.53			Heidler			1		Fränkisch-Crumbach	12 Jun 11
77.60			Wlodarczyk			2	OG	London (OS)	10 Aug 12
77.53			Heidler			1		Elstal	9 Sep 11
77.41	WR		Lysenko			1	Znam	Zhukovskiy	24 Jun 06
77.40			Heidler			1	ISTAF	Berlin	11 Sep 11
77.32			Menkova			1		Staiki	29 Jun 08
77.30			Lysenko			1		Adler	22 Apr 07
77.26	WR	Gulfiya	Khanafeyeva ¶	RUS	4.6.82	1	NC	Tula	12 Jun 06
77.24			Heidler			1	Colorful	Daegu	16 May 12
77.22			Heidler			1	GS	Ostrava	30 May 11
77.20			Wlodarczyk			1		Cottbus	8 Aug 09
77.20			Lysenko			1		Yerino	22 Jul 12
77.15			Wlodarczyk			1	ISTAF	Berlin	1 Sep 13
77.13			Lysenko			1	WCh	Daegu	4 Sep 11
77.13		Oksana	Kondratyeva	RUS	22.11.85	1	Znam	Zhukovskiy	30 Jun 13
77.12			Heidler			2	WCh	Berlin	22 Aug 09
77.12			Heidler			3	OG	London (OS)	10 Aug 12
		(30/6)							
76.99			Zhang Wenxiu	CHN	22.3.86	2	GS	Ostrava	24 May 12
76.90		Martina	Hrasnová' ¶	SVK	21.3.83	1		Trnava	16 May 09
76.83		Kamila	Skolimowska	POL	4.11.82	1	SGP	Doha	11 May 07
76.72		Mariya	Bespalova	RUS	21.5.86	2		Zhukovskiy	23 Jun 12
		(10)							
76.66		Olga	Tsander	BLR	18.5.76	1		Staiki	21 Jul 05
76.63		Yekaterina	Khoroshikh ¶	RUS	21.1.83	2	Znam	Moskva	24 Jun 06
76.62		Yipsi	Moreno	CUB	19.11.80	1	GP	Zagreb	9 Sep 08
76.56		Alena	Matoshko	BLR	23.6.82	2		Minsk	12 Jun 12
76.33		Darya	Pchelnik	BLR	20.12.81	2		Staiki	29 Jun 08
76.21		Yelena	Konevtsova	RUS	11.3.81	3		Sochi	26 May 07
76.17		Anna	Bulgakova	RUS	17.1.88	2	NC	Moskva	24 Jul 13
76.07	WR	Mihaela	Melinte ¶	ROU	27.3.75	1		Rüdlingen	29 Aug 99
76.05		Kathrin	Klaas	GER	6.2.84	5	OG	London (OS)	10 Aug 12

Mark	Wind	Name		Nat	Born	Pos	Meet	Venue	Date
75.73		Amanda (20)	Bingson	USA	20.2.90	1	NC	Des Moines	22 Jun 13
75.68		Olga	Kuzenkova ¶	RUS	4.10.70	1	NCp	Tula	4 Jun 00
75.09		Yelena	Rigert'	RUS	2.12.83	1	Kuts	Moskva	15 Jul 13
75.08		Ivana	Brkljacic	CRO	25.1.83	2	Kuso	Waszawa	17 Jun 07
75.04		Sultana	Frizell	CAN	24.10.84	1		Tucson	16 Mar 12
74.90			Wang Zheng	CHN	14.12.87	4	WCh	Moskva	16 Aug 13
74.77		Jeneva	McCall	USA	28.10.89	2		Dubnica nad Vahom	21 Aug 13
74.66		Manuèla	Montebrun	FRA	13.11.79	1	GP II	Zagreb	11 Jul 05
74.65		Mariya	Smolyachkova	BLR	10.2.85	2		Staiki	19 Jul 08
74.52		Iryna	Sekachova	UKR	21.7.76	1	NC	Kyiv	2 Jul 08
74.47		Zalina (30)	Marghieva	MDA	5.2.88	1	Univ Ch	Chisinau	7 May 12
74.21		Hanna	Skydan	UKR	14.5.92	1	NC	Yalta	14 Jun 12
74.19		Jessica	Cosby Toruga	USA	31.5.82	4	Pre	Eugene	1 Jun 12
74.18		Joanna	Fiodorow	POL	4.3.89	1	EAF	Bydgoszcz	3 Jun 12
74.17		Tuğçe	Sahutoglu ¶	TUR	1.5.88	1		Izmir	19 May 12
74.10		Iryna	Novozhylova	UKR	7.1.86	1		Kyiv	19 May 12
73.90		Arasay	Thondike	CUB	28.5.86	1		La Habana	18 Jun 09
73.87		Erin	Gilreath	USA	11.10.80	1	NC	Carson	25 Jun 05
73.81		Gwen	Berry	USA	29.6.89	1		Lisle	8 Jun 13
73.74		Jennifer	Dahlgren	ARG	21.4.84	1		Buenos Aires	10 Apr 10
73.64		Rosa (40)	Rodríguez	VEN	2.7.86	1		Barquisimeto	16 May 13
73.59		Ester	Balassini	ITA	20.10.77	1	NC	Bressanone	25 Jun 05
73.52		Bianca	Perie	ROU	1.6.90	1	NC	Bucuresti	16 Jul 10
73.44		Éva	Orbán	HUN	29.11.84	2	Werfer	Halle	25 May 13
73.40		Stéphanie	Falzon	FRA	7.1.83	1	NC	Albi	26 Jul 08
73.21		Eileen	O'Keeffe	IRL	31.5.81	1	NC	Dublin	21 Jul 07
73.16		Yunaika	Crawford	CUB	2.11.82	3	OG	Athína	25 Aug 04
73.03		Amber	Campbell	USA	5.6.81	3	NC	Des Moines	22 Jun 13
72.97		Sophie	Hitchon	GBR	11.7.91	3	ET	Gateshead	23 Jun 13
72.74		Susanne	Keil	GER	18.5.78	1		Nikiti	15 Jul 05
72.55		Kivilcim (50)	Salman-Kaya ¶	TUR	27.3.92	1	NC	Izmir	5 Jul 12

100th woman 69.59, 200th 66.58, 300th 63.97, 400th 62.68, 500th 61.58

Downhill: 75.20 Manuéla Montebrun FRA 13.11.79 1 Vineuil 18 May 03

Ancillary marks – other marks during series to 77.19

77.79	Wlodarczyk	16 Aug 13	77.56	Lysenko	10 Aug 12	77.28	Lysenko	10 Aug 12
77.67	Wlodarczyk	6 Jun 10	77.37	Lysenko	5 Jul 12	77.27	Lysenko	24 Jul 13
77.58	Lysenko	16 Aug 13	77.33	Lysenko	16 Aug 13	77.26	Lysenko	5 Jul 12

Drugs disqualification

78.61		Lysenko				(1)		Sochi	26 May 07
77.71		Lysenko				(1)	GS	Ostrava	27 Jun 07
77.36	Gulfiya	Khanafeyeva ¶	RUS	4.6.82		(2)		Sochi	26 May 07

Ancillary mark: Lysenko: 77.32 27 Jun 07

JAVELIN

Mark		Name		Nat	Born	Pos	Meet	Venue	Date
72.28 WR		Barbora	Spotáková	CZE	30.6.81	1	WAF	Stuttgart	13 Sep 08
71.99		Mariya	Abakumova	RUS	15.1.86	1	WCh	Daegu	2 Sep 11
71.70 WR		Osleidys	Menéndez	CUB	14.11.79	1	WCh	Helsinki	14 Aug 05
71.58			Spotáková			2	WCh	Daegu	2 Sep 11
71.54 WR			Menéndez			1		Réthimno	1 Jul 01
71.53			Menéndez			1	OG	Athína	27 Aug 04
71.42			Spotáková			1	OG	Beijing	21 Aug 08
70.78			Abakumova			2	OG	Beijing	21 Aug 08
70.53			Abakumova			1	ISTAF	Berlin	1 Sep 13
70.20		Christina	Obergföll	GER	22.8.81	1	ECp-S	München	23 Jun 07
70.03			Obergföll			2	WCh	Helsinki	14 Aug 05
69.82			Menéndez			1	WUG	Beijing	29 Aug 01
69.81			Obergföll			1		Berlin (Elstal)	31 Aug 08
69.75			Abakumova			1		Berlin (Elstal)	25 Aug 13
69.57			Obergföll			1	WK	Zürich	8 Sep 11
69.55			Spotáková			1	OG	London (OS)	9 Aug 12
69.53			Menéndez			1	WCh	Edmonton	7 Aug 01
69.48 WR		Trine	Hattestad	NOR	18.4.66	1	Bisl	Oslo	28 Jul 00
69.45			Spotáková			1	Herc	Monaco	22 Jul 11
69.35		Sunette	Viljoen	RSA	6.1.83	1	DL	New York	9 Jun 12
69.34			Abakumova			1	ECp-w	Castellón	16 Mar 13
69.15			Spotáková			1		Zaragoza	31 May 08
69.09			Abakumova			Q	WCh	Moskva	16 Aug 13

Mark	Wind	Name		Nat	Born	Pos	Meet	Venue	Date
69.05		Obergföll				1	WCh	Moskva	18 Aug 13
68.94		Abakumova				1	WK	Zürich	29 Aug 13
68.92		Abakumova				Q	WCh	Berlin	16 Aug 09
68.91		Hattestad				1	OG	Sydney	30 Sep 00
68.89		Abakumova				1	DL	Doha	14 May 10
68.86		Obergföll				1	NC	Kassel	24 Jul 11
68.81		Spotáková				1	Odlozil	Praha	16 Jun 08
	(30/6)								
68.34		Steffi	Nerius	GER	1.7.72	2		Berlin (Elstal)	31 Aug 08
67.67		Sonia	Bisset	CUB	1.4.71	1		Salamanca	6 Jul 05
67.51		Miréla	Manjani/Tzelíli	GRE	21.12.76	2	OG	Sydney	30 Sep 00
67.20		Tatyana	Shikolenko	RUS	10.5.68	1	Herc	Monaco	18 Aug 00
	(10)								
67.16		Martina	Ratej	SLO	2.11.81	3	DL	Doha	14 May 10
66.91		Tanja	Damaske	GER	16.11.71	1	NC	Erfurt	4 Jul 99
66.86		Vira	Rebryk	UKR	25.2.89	1	EC	Helsinki	29 Jun 12
66.81		Linda	Stahl	GER	2.10.85	1	EC	Barcelona	29 Jul 10
66.80		Louise	McPaul/Currey	AUS	24.1.69	1		Gold Coast (RB)	5 Aug 00
66.67		Kara	Patterson	USA	10.4.86	1	NC	Des Moines	25 Jun 10
66.60		Kimberley	Mickle	AUS	28.12.84	2	WCh	Moskva	18 Aug 13
66.17		Goldie	Sayers	GBR	16.7.82	1	LGP	London (CP)	14 Jul 12
65.91		Nikola	Brejchová'	CZE	25.6.74	1	GP	Linz	2 Aug 04
65.62			Lu Huihui	CHN	26.6.89	1		Zhaoqing	27 Apr 13
	(20)								
65.30		Claudia	Coslovich	ITA	26.4.72	1		Ljubljana	10 Jun 00
65.29		Xiomara	Rivero	CUB	22.11.68	1		Santiago de Cuba	17 Mar 01
65.17		Karen	Forkel	GER	24.9.70	2	NC	Erfurt	4 Jul 99
65.11			Li Lingwei	CHN	26.1.89	1		Fuzhou	23 Jun 1210
65.08		Ana Mirela	Termure ¶	ROU	13.1.75	1	NC	Bucuresti	10 Jun 01
64.90		Paula	Huhtaniemi'	FIN	17.2.73	1	NC	Helsinki	10 Aug 03
64.89		Yekaterina	Ivakina	RUS	4.12.64	4	Bisl	Oslo	28 Jul 00
64.87		Kelly	Morgan	GBR	17.6.80	1	NC	Birmingham	14 Jul 02
64.83		Christina	Scherwin	DEN	11.7.76	3	WAF	Stuttgart	9 Sep 06
64.74			Zhang Li	CHN	17.1.89	1		Wuhan	28 Apr 12
	(30)								
64.67		Katharina	Molitor	GER	8.11.83	2	NC	Kassel	24 Jul 11
64.62		Joanna	Stone	AUS	4.10.72	2		Gold Coast (RB)	5 Aug 00
64.62		Nikolett	Szabó	HUN	3.3.80	1		Pátra	22 Jul 01
64.61		Oksana	Makarova	RUS	21.7.71	2	ECp	Paris (C)	19 Jun 99
64.51		Madara	Palameika	LAT	18.6.87	1	EU23	Kaunas	19 Jul 09
64.51		Monica	Stoian	ROU	25.8.82	4	WCh	Berlin	18 Aug 09
64.49		Valeriya	Zabruskova	RUS	29.7.75	1	Znam	Tula	7 Jun 03
64.46		Dörthe	Friedrich	GER	21.6.73	1	NC	Wattenscheid	7 Jul 02
64.38		Sinta	Ozolina-Kovale	LAT	26.2.88	1		Riga	30 May 13
64.34		Kathryn	Mitchell	AUS	10.7.82	3	GS	Ostrava	25 May 12
	(40)								
64.19		Kim	Kreiner	USA	26.7.77	1		Fortaleza	16 May 07
64.08		Barbara	Madejczyk	POL	30.9.76	1	ECp-S	Málaga	28 Jun 09
64.07		Mercedes	Chilla	ESP	19.1.80	1		Valencia	12 Jun 10
64.06		Taina	Uppa/Kolkkala	FIN	24.10.76	1		Pihtipudas	23 Jul 00
64.03		Mikaela	Ingberg	FIN	29.7.74	6	ISTAF	Berlin	1 Sep 00
63.92			Wei Jianhua	CHN	23.3.79	1		Beijing	18 Aug 00
63.89		Felicia	Tilea-Moldovan ¶	ROU	29.9.67	2	WK	Zürich	16 Aug 02
63.73		Laverne	Eve	BAH	16.6.65	1		Nashville	22 Apr 00
63.69			Li Lei	CHN	4.5.74	1	OT	Jinzhou	8 Jun 00
63.65		Indre	Jakubaityté	LTU	24.1.76	1		Kaunas	14 Sep 07
	(50)		100th woman 61.43, 200th 58.04, 300th 56.28						

Ancillary marks – other marks during series (to 68.80)

71.25	Abakumova	2 Sep 11	69.32	Abakumova	21 Aug 08	68.82 Abakumova	1 Sep 13
69.42	Menéndez	7 Aug 01	69.22	Spotáková	21 Aug 08	68.95 Obergföll	8 Sep 11
69.35	Abakumova	25 Aug 13	69.08	Abakumova	21 Aug 08		

Specification changed from 1 May 1999. See ATHLETICS 2000 for Old specification all-time list.

| 80.00 WR | | Petra | Felke | GDR | 30.7.59 | 1 | | Potsdam | 9 Sep 88 |

HEPTATHLON

7291 WR	Jackie	Joyner-Kersee	USA	3.3.62	1	OG	Seoul	24 Sep 88
	12.69/0.5	1.86	15.80	22.56/1.6	7.27/0.7	45.66	2:08.51	
7215 WR		Joyner-Kersee			1	NC/OT	Indianapolis	16 Jul 88
	12.71/-0.9	1.93	15.65	22.30/ 0.0	7.00/-1.3	50.08	2:20.70	
7158 WR		Joyner-Kersee			1	USOF	Houston	2 Aug 86
	13.18/-0.5	1.88	15.20	22.85/1.2	7.03w/2.9	50.12	2:09.69	

Mark	Wind	Name	Nat	Born	Pos	Meet	Venue		Date
7148 WR		Joyner-Kersee			1	GWG	Moskva		7 Jul 86
	12.85/0.2	1.88	14.76	23.00/0.3	7.01/-0.5	49.86		2:10.02	
7128		Joyner-Kersee			1	WCh	Roma		1 Sep 87
	12.91/0.2	1.90	16.00	22.95/1.2	7.14/0.9	45.68		2:16.29	
7044		Joyner-Kersee			1	OG	Barcelona		2 Aug 92
	12.85/-0.9	1.91	14.13	23.12/0.7	7.10/1.3	44.98		2:11.78	
7032		Carolina Klüft	SWE	2.2.83	1	WCh	Osaka		26 Aug 07
	13.15/0.1	1.95	14.81	23.38/0.3	6.85/1.0	47.98		2:12.56	
7007		Larisa Nikitina ¶	RUS	29.4.65	1	NC	Bryansk		11 Jun 89
	13.40/1.4	1.89	16.45	23.97/1.1	6.73w/4.0	53.94		2:15.31	
7001		Klüft			1	WCh	Saint-Denis		24 Aug 03
	13.18/-0.4	1.94	14.19	22.98/1.1	6.68/1.0	49.90		2:12.12	
6985		Sabine Braun	GER	19.6.65	1		Götzis		31 May 92
	13.11/-0.4	1.93	14.84	23.65/2.0	6.63w/2.9	51.62		2:12.67	
6979		Joyner-Kersee			1	NC	San José		24 Jun 87
	12.90/2.0	1.85	15.17	23.02/0.4	7.25/2.3	40.24		2:13.07	
6955		Jessica Ennis	GBR	28.1.86	1	OG	London (OS)		4 Aug 12
	12.54/1.3	1.86	14.28	22.83/-0.3	6.48/-0.6	47.49		2:08.65	
6952		Klüft			1	OG	Athina		21 Aug 04
	13.21/0.2	1.91	14.77	23.27/-0.1	6.78/0.4	48.89		2:14.15	
6946 WR		Sabine Paetz'	GDR	16.10.57	1	NC	Potsdam		6 May 84
	12.64/0.3	1.80	15.37	23.37/0.7	6.86/-0.2	44.62		2:08.93	
6942		Ghada Shouaa	SYR	10.9.72	1		Götzis		26 May 96
	13.78/0.3	1.87	15.64	23.78/0.6	6.77/0.6	54.74		2:13.61	
6935 WR		Ramona Neubert	GDR	26.7.58	1	v USSR	Moskva		19 Jun 83
	13.42/1.7	1.82	15.25	23.49/0.5	6.79/0.7	49.94		2:07.51	
6910		Joyner			1	MSR	Walnut		25 Apr 86
	12.9/0.0	1.86	14.75	23.24w/2.8	6.85/2.1	48.30		2:14.11	
6906		Ennis			1		Götzis		27 May 12
	12.81/0.0	1.85	14.51	22.88/1.9	6.51/0.8	47.11		2:09.00	
6897		John'			2	wOG	Seoul		24 Sep 88
	12.85/0.5	1.80	16.23	23.65/1.6	6.71/0.0	42.56		2:06.14	
6889		Eunice Barber	FRA	17.11.74	1		Arles		5 Jun 05
	12.62w/2.9	1.91	12.61	24.12/1.2	6.78w/3.4	53.07		2:14.66	
6887		Klüft			1	WCh	Helsinki		7 Aug 05
	13.19/-0.4	1.82	15.02	23.70/-2.5	6.87/0.2	47.20		2:08.89	
6880		Tatyana Chernova (10)	RUS	29.1.88	1	WCh	Daegu		30 Aug 11
	13.32/0.9	1.83	14.17	23.50/-1.5	6.61/-0.7	52.95		2:08.04	
6878		Joyner-Kersee			1	NC	New York		13 Jun 91
	12.77	1.89	15.62	23.42	6.97/0.4	43.28		2:22.12	
6875		Nikitina			1	ECp-A	Helmond		16 Jul 89
	13.55/-2.1	1.84	15.99	24.29/-2.1	6.75/-2.5	56.78		2:18.67	
6861		Barber			1	WCh	Sevilla		22 Aug 99
	12.89/-0.5	1.93	12.37	23.57/0.5	6.86/-0.3	49.88		2:15.65	
6859		Natalya Shubenkova	RUS	25.9.57	1	NC	Kyiv		21 Jun 84
	12.93/1.0	1.83	13.66	23.57/-0.3	6.73/0.4	46.26		2:04.60	
6858		Anke Vater/Behmer	GDR	5.6.61	3	OG	Seoul		24 Sep 88
	13.20/0.5	1.83	14.20	23.10/1.6	6.68/0.1	44.54		2:04.20	
6847		Nikitina			1	WUG	Duisburg		29 Aug 89
	13.47	1.81	16.12	24.12	6.66	59.28		2:22.07	
6845 WR		Neubert			1	v URS	Halle		20 Jun 82
	13.58/1.8	1.83	15.10	23.14/1.4	6.84w/2.3	42.54		2:06.16	
6845		Irina Belova ¶	RUS	27.3.68	2	OG	Barcelona		2 Aug 92
	13.25/-0.1	1.88	13.77	23.34/0.2	6.82/0.0	41.90		2:05.08	
(30/13)									
6832		Lyudmila Blonska ¶	UKR	9.11.77	2	WCh	Osaka		26 Aug 07
	13.25/0.1	1.92	14.44	24.09/0.3	6.88/1.0	47.77		2:16.68	
6831		Denise Lewis	GBR	27.8.72	1		Talence		30 Jul 00
	13.13/1.0	1.84	15.07	24.04w/3.6	6.69/-0.4	49.42		2:12.20	
6803		Jane Frederick	USA	7.4.52	1		Talence		16 Sep 84
	13.27/1.2	1.87	15.49	24.15/1.6	6.43/0.2	51.74		2:13.55	
6778		Nataliya Dobrynska	UKR	29.5.82	2	EC	Barcelona		31 Jul 10
	13.59/-1.6	1.86	15.88	24.23/-0.2	6.56/0.3	49.25		2:12.06	
6765		Yelena Prokhorova	RUS	16.4.78	1	NC	Tula		23 Jul 00
	13.54/-2.8	1.82	14.30	23.37/-0.2	6.72/1.0	43.40		2:04.27	
6750		Ma Miaolan	CHN	18.1.70	1	NG	Beijing		12 Sep 93
	13.28/1.5	1.89	14.98	23.86/	6.64/	45.82		2:15.33	
6741		Heike Drechsler	GER	16.12.64	1		Talence		11 Sep 94
	13.34/-0.3	1.84	13.58	22.84/-1.1	6.95/1.0	40.64		2:11.53	
(20)									

WOMEN All-time

Mark	Wind	Name		Nat	Born	Pos	Meet	Venue		Date
6735(w)		Hyleas	Fountain	USA	14.1.81	1	NC	Des Moines		26 Jun 10
	12.93w/2.6	1.90	13.73		23.28w/3.3	6.79w/2.7		42.26	2:17.80	
6703		Tatyana	Blokhina	RUS	12.3.70	1		Talence		11 Sep 93
	13.69/-0.6	1.91	14.94		23.95/-0.4	5.99/-0.3		52.16	2:09.65	
6702		Chantal	Beaugeant ¶	FRA	16.2.61	2		Götzis		19 Jun 88
	13.10/1.6	1.78	13.74		23.96w/3.5	6.45/0.2		50.96	2:07.09	
6695		Jane	Flemming	AUS	14.4.65	1	CG	Auckland		28 Jan 90
	13.21/1.4	1.82	13.76		23.62w/2.4	6.57/1.6		49.28	2:12.53	
6683		Jennifer	Oeser	GER	29.11.83	3	EC	Barcelona		31 Jul 10
	13.37/-1.0	1.83	13.82		24.07/-0.3	6.68/-0.3		49.17	2:12.28	
6681		Kristina	Savitskaya	RUS	10.6.91	1	NC	Cheboksary		3 Jun 12
	13.52/0.0	1.88	15.27		24.61/0.0	6.65/0.0		46.83	2:14.73	
6660		Ines	Schulz	GDR	10.7.65	3		Götzis		19 Jun 88
	13.56/0.4	1.84	13.95		23.93w/2.8	6.70/0.7		42.82	2:06.31	
6658		Svetla	Dimitrova ¶	BUL	27.1.70	2		Götzis		31 May 92
	13.41/-0.7	1.75	14.72		23.06w/2.4	6.64/1.9		43.84	2:09.60	
6649		Lilli	Schwarzkopf	GER	28.8.83	2	OG	London (OS)		4 Aug 12
	13.26/0.9	1.83	14.77		24.77/0.9	6.30/-0.7		51.73	2:10.50	
6646		Natalya	Grachova	UKR	21.2.52	1	NC	Moskva		2 Aug 82
	13.80	1.80	16.18		23.86	6.65w/3.5		39.42	2:06.59	
(30)										
6635		Sibylle	Thiele	GDR	6.3.65	2	GWG	Moskva		7 Jul 86
	13.14/0.6	1.76	16.00		24.18	6.62/1.0		45.74	2:15.30	
6635		Svetlana	Buraga	BLR	4.9.65	3	WCh	Stuttgart		17 Aug 93
	12.95/0.1	1.84	14.55		23.69/0.0	6.58/-0.2		41.04	2:13.65	
6633		Natalya	Roshchupkina	RUS	13.1.78	2	NC	Tula		23 Jul 00
	14.05/-2.8	1.88	14.28		23.47/-0.2	6.45/0.4		44.34	2:07.93	
6623		Judy	Simpson'	GBR	14.11.60	3	EC	Stuttgart		30 Aug 86
	13.05/0.8	1.92	14.73		25.09/0.0	6.56w/2.5		40.92	2:11.70	
6619		Liliana	Nastase	ROU	1.8.62	4	OG	Barcelona		2 Aug 92
	12.86/-0.9	1.82	14.34		23.70/0.2	6.49/-0.3		41.30	2:11.22	
6616		Malgorzata	Nowak'	POL	9.2.59	1	WUG	Kobe		31 Aug 85
	13.27w/4.0	1.95	15.35		24.20/0.0	6.37w/3.9		43.36	2:20.39	
6604		Remigija	Nazaroviene'	LTU	2.6.67	2	URSCh	Bryansk		11 Jun 89
	13.26/1.4	1.86	14.27		24.12/0.7	6.58/0.9		40.94	2:09.98	
6604		Irina	Tyukhay	RUS	14.1.67	3		Götzis		28 May 95
	13.20/-0.7	1.84 14.97			24.33/1.7	6.71/0.5		43.84	2:17.64	
6599A		Jessica	Zelinka	CAN	3.9.81	1	NC	Calgary		28 Jun 12
	12.76/-0.6	1.77	14.74		23.42w/2.1	5.98w/2.9		46.60	2:08.95	
6599		Austra	Skujytė	LTU	12.8.79	5	OG	London (OS)		4 Aug 12
	14.00/0.7	1.92	17.31		25.43/0.9	6.25/-0.6		51.13	2:20.59	
(40)										
6598		Svetlana	Moskalets	RUS	22.1.69	1	NC	Vladimir		17 Jun 94
	13.20/0.8	1.82	13.78		23.56/0.1	6.74/0.8		42.48	2:14.54	
6591		Svetlana	Sokolova	RUS	9.1.81	1	NC	Tula		23 Jun 04
	13.56/1.1	1.82	15.09		24.02/0.6	6.26/0.3		45.07	2:07.23	
6586		Anna	Melnychenko	UKR	24.4.83	1	WCh	Moskva		13 Aug 13
	13.29/-0.6	1.86	13.85		23.87/0.0	6.49/0.2		41.87	2:09.85	
6577		DeDee	Nathan	USA	20.4.68	1		Götzis		30 May 99
	13.28/-0.1	1.76	14.74		24.23/0.2	6.59/1.6		50.08	2:16.92	
6576		Antoinette	Nana Djimou	FRA	2.8.85	5	OG	London (OS)		4 Aug 12
	12.96/1.3	1.80	14.26		24.72/0.3	6.13/-0.2		55.87	2:15.94	
6573		Rita	Ináncsi	HUN	6.1.71	3		Götzis		29 May 94
	13.66/2.0	1.84	13.94		24.20w/2.5	6.78/1.4		46.28	2:16.02	
6572		Heike	Tischler	GDR	4.2.64	2	EC	Split		31 Aug 90
	14.08/-0.9	1.82	13.73		24.29/0.9	6.22/-0.7		53.24	2:05.50	
6563		Natalya	Sazanovich	BLR	15.8.73	2	OG	Atlanta		28 Jul 96
	13.56/-1.6	1.80	14.52		23.72/-0.3	6.70/1.1		46.00	2:17.92	
6559		Olga	Kurban	RUS	16.12.87	1	NC	Chelyabinsk		16 Jun 08
	13.29/0.6	1.77	13.71		24.04/0.5	6.51/0.1		49.23	2:12.42	
6552		Nadezhda	Vinogradova'	RUS	1.5.58	2	NC	Kyiv		21 Jun 84
	13.92/1.0	1.80	15.19		23.84/0.2	6.67/0.1		38.60	2:06.80	
(50)			100th woman 6394, 200th 6194, 300th 6074, 400th 5979, 500th 5859								

Drugs disqualification

6618		Lyudmyla	Yosypenko ¶	UKR	24.9.84	4	OG	London (OS)		4 Aug 12
	13.25/0.9	1.83	13.90		23.68/0.6	6.31/-0.6		49.63	2:13.28	

DECATHLON
IAAF approved order: 100m, DT, PV, JT, 400m / 100mh, LJ, SP, HJ, 1500m, 1997 men's order

8358 WR		Austra	Skujyte	LTU	12.8.79	1		Columbia, MO		15 Apr 05
	12.49/1.6	46.19	3.10	48.78	57.19	14.22w/2.4	6.12/1.6	16.42	1.78	5:15.86

Mark	Wind	Name	Nat	Born	Pos	Meet	Venue	Date

4 x 100 METRES RELAY

Mark		Name	Nat	Pos	Meet	Venue	Date
40.82		Madison, Felix, Knight, Jeter	USA	1	OG	London (OS)	10 Aug 12
41.29		Russell, Stewart, Calvert, Fraser-Pryce	JAM	1	WCh	Moskva	18 Aug 13
41.37	WR	Gladisch, Rieger, Auerswald, Göhr	GDR	1	WCp	Canberra	6 Oct 85
41.41		Fraser-Pryce, Simpson, Campbell-Brown, Stewart	JAM	2	OG	London (OS)	10 Aug 12
41.47		Gaines, Jones, Miller, Devers	USA	1	WCh	Athína	9 Aug 97
41.49		Bogoslovskaya, Malchugina, Voronova, Privalova	RUS	1	WCh	Stuttgart	22 Aug 93
41.49		Finn, Torrence, Vereen, Devers	USA	2	WCh	Stuttgart	22 Aug 93
41.52		Gaines, Jones, Miller, Devers	USA	1h1	WCh	Athína	8 Aug 97
41.53	WR	Gladisch, Koch, Auerswald, Göhr	GDR	1		Berlin	31 Jul 83
41.55		Brown, Williams, Griffith, Marshall	USA	1	ISTAF	Berlin	21 Aug 87
41.56		B Knight, Felix, Myers, Jeter	USA	1	WCh	Daegu	4 Sep 11
41.58		Brown, Williams, Griffith, Marshall	USA	1	WCh	Roma	6 Sep 87
41.58		L.Williams, Felix, Lee, Jeter	USA	1		Cottbus	8 Aug 09
41.60	WR	Müller, Wöckel, Auerswald, Göhr	GDR	1	OG	Moskva	1 Aug 80
41.61A		Brown, Williams, Cheeseborough, Ashford	USA	1	USOF	USAF Academy	3 Jul 83
41.63		Brown, Williams, Cheeseborough, Ashford	USA	1	v GDR	Los Angeles	25 Jun 83
41.64		Madison, Tarmoh, Knight, L Williams	USA	1h1	OG	London (OS)	9 Aug 12
41.65		Brown, Bolden, Cheeseborough, Ashford	USA	1	OG	Los Angeles	11 Aug 84
41.65		Gladisch, Koch, Auerswald, Göhr	GDR	1	ECp	Moskva	17 Aug 85
41.67		Pierre, Anderson, Townsend, C Williams	USA	1	WK	Zürich	29 Aug 13
		(20 performances by 4 nations) from here just best by nation					
41.78		Girard, Hurtis, Félix, Arron	FRA	1	WCh	Saint-Denis	30 Aug 03
41.92		Fynes, Sturrup, Davis-Thompson, Ferguson	BAH	1	WCh	Sevilla	29 Aug 99
42.04		Povh, Stuy, Ryemyen, Bryzgina	UKR	3	OG	London (OS)	10 Aug 12
42.08mx		Pavlova, Nuneva, Georgieva, Ivanova	BUL	mx		Sofiya	8 Aug 84
42.29		Pencheva, Nuneva, Georgieva, Donkova		1		Sofiya	26 Jun 88
42.23		(Sichuan) Xiao Lin, Li Yali, Liu Xiaomei, Li Xuemei	CHN	1	NG	Shanghai	23 Oct 97
42.29		E dos Santos, Silva, Krasucki, R Santos (10)	BRA	2h3	WCh	Moskva	18 Aug 13
42.39		Utondu, Idehen, Opara-Thompson, Onyali	NGR	2h2	OG	Barcelona	7 Aug 92
42.43		Hunte, Smallwood, Goddard, Lannaman	GBR	3	OG	Moskva	1 Aug 80
42.45		Vassell, Schippers, Lubbers, Samuel	NED	3h1	OG	London (OS)	9 Aug 12
42.54		Borlée, Mariën, Ouédraogo, Gevaert	BEL	2	OG	Beijing	22 Aug 08
42.56		Nesterenko, Sologub, Nevmerzhitskaya, Dragun	BLR	3	WCh	Helsinki	13 Aug 05
42.59		Possekel, Helten, Richter, Kroniger	FRG	2	OG	Montreal	31 Jul 76
42.68		Popowicz, Korczynska, Jeschke, Wedler	POL	3	EC	Barcelona	1 Aug 10
42.77		Bailey, Payne, Taylor, Gareau	CAN	2	OG	Los Angeles	11 Aug 84
42.89		Ferrer, López, Duporty, Allen	CUB	6	WCh	Stuttgart	22 Aug 93
42.98		Sokolová, Soborová, Kocembová, Kratochvílová	CZE/TCH	1	WK	Zürich	18 Aug 82
		(20)					
42.99A		Massey, Broadrick, Lambert, Gainsford-Taylor	AUS	1		Pietersburg	18 Mar 00
43.03A		M.Murillo, Palacios, Obregón, D Murillo	COL	2	SAm-r	Bogotá	10 Jul 04
43.01		Durant, Ayhe, R Thomas, Selvon	TRI	4h3	WCh	Moskva	18 Aug 13
43.04		Pistone, Calí, Arcioni, Alloh	ITA	3	ECp-S	Annecy	21 Jun 08
43.07		Tsóni, Kóffa, Vasarmídou, Thánou	GRE	2	MedG	Bari	18 Jun 97
43.19		Akoto, Twum, Anim, Nsiah	GHA	5s1	OG	Sydney	29 Sep 00
43.21		Kambundji, Lavanchy, E.Sprunger, L.Sprunger	SUI	3h2	WCh	Moskva	18 Aug 13
43.25A		Hartman, Moropane, Holtshausen, Seyerling	RSA	2		Pietersburg	18 Mar 00
43.28		M Sánchez, Chala, Mejía, Manzueta	DOM	5h1	WCh	Moskva	18 Aug 13
43.35		Aleksandrova, Kvast, Miljauskiene, Sevalnikova (30)	KAZ	2	SPART	Taskent	16 Sep 86
Best at low altitude							
43.03		M.Murillo, Palacios, Obregón, N.González	COL	3h2	WCh	Helsinki	12 Aug 05
43.18		Wilson, Wells, Robertson, Boyle	AUS	5	OG	Montreal	31 Jul 76
One or more athlete susbsequently drugs dq							
41.67		A Williams, Jones ¶, L Williams, Colander	USA	(1)	3-N	München	8 Aug 04
41.67		A Williams, Jones ¶, L Williams, Colander	USA	(1h1)	OG	Athína	26 Aug 04
41.71		White ¶, Gaines, Miller, Jones ¶	USA	(1)	WCh	Edmonton	11 Aug 01
42.31		Ahye, Baptiste, Selvon, Hackett #	TRI	2h1	OG	London (OS)	9 Aug 12

4 x 200 METRES RELAY

1:27.46	WR	USA Blue Jenkins, Colander-Richardson, Perry, M Jones		1	PennR	Philadelphia	29 Apr 00
1:28.15	WR	GDR Göhr, R.Müller, Wöckel, Koch		1		Jena	9 Aug 80
1:29.42		Texas A & M (USA) Tarmoh, Mayo, Beard, Lucas		1	Penn R	Philadelphia	24 Apr 10
Drugs dq:		1:29.40 USA Red Colander, Gaines, Miller, M Jones ¶		1	Penn	Philadelphia	24 Apr 04

4 x 400 METRES RELAY

3:15.17	WR	URS	1	OG	Seoul	1 Oct 88
		Ledovskaya 50.12, O.Nazarova 47.82, Pinigina 49.43, Bryzgina 47.80				
3:15.51		USA	2	OG	Seoul	1 Oct 88
		D.Howard 49.82, Dixon 49.17, Brisco 48.44, Griffith-Joyner 48.08				

WOMEN All-time

Mark	Wind	Name	Nat	Born	Pos	Meet	Venue	Date
3:15.92	WR	GDR G.Walther 49.8, Busch 48.9, Rübsam 49.4, Koch 47.8			1	NC	Erfurt	3 Jun 84
3:16.71		USA Torrence 49.0, Malone 49.4, Kaiser-Brown 49.48, Miles 48.78			1	WCh	Stuttgart	22 Aug 93
3:16.87		GDR Emmelmann 50.9, Busch 48.8, Müller 48.9, Koch 48.21			1	EC	Stuttgart	31 Aug 86
3:16.87		USA Trotter 50.3, Felix 48.1, McCorory 49.39, Richards-Ross 49.10			1	OG	London (OS)	11 Aug 12
3:17.83		USA Dunn 50.5, Felix 48.8, Demus 50.14, Richards 48.44			1	WCh	Berlin	23 Aug 09
3:18.09		USA Richards-Ross 49.3, Felix 49.4, Beard 49.84, McCorory 49.52			1	WCh	Daegu	3 Sep 11
3:18.29		USA			1	OG	Los Angeles	11 Aug 84
		Leatherwood 50.50, S.Howard 48.83, Brisco-Hooks 49.23, Cheeseborough 49.73						
3:18.29		GDR Neubauer 50.58, Emmelmann 49.89, Busch 48.81, Müller 48.99			3	OG	Seoul	1 Oct 88
3:18.38		RUS			2	WCh	Stuttgart	22 Aug 93
		Ruzina 50.8, Alekseyeva 49.3, Ponomaryova 49.78, Privalova 48.47						
3:18.43		URS			1	WCh	Tokyo	1 Sep 91
		Ledovskaya 51.7, Dzhigalova 49.2, Nazarova 48.87, Bryzgina 48.67						
3:18.54		USA Wineberg 51.0, Felix 48.6, Henderson 50.06, Richards 48.93			1	OG	Beijing	23 Aug 08
3:18.55		USA Trotter 51.2, Felix 48.0, Wineberg 50.24, Richards 49.07			1	WCh	Osaka	2 Sep 07
3:18.58		URS I.Nazarova, Olizarenko, Pinigina, Vladykina			1	ECp	Moskva	18 Aug 85
3:18.63		GDR Neubauer 51.4, Emmelmann 49.1, Müller 48.64, Busch 49.48			1	WCh	Roma	6 Sep 87
3:18.71		JAM Whyte 50.0, Prendergast 49.6, Williams-Mills 49.84, Williams 49.22			2	WCh	Daegu	3 Sep 11
3:18.82		RUS Gushchina 50.6, Litvinova 49.2, Firova 49.20, Kapachinskaya 49.82			2	OG	Beijing	23 Aug 08
3:19.01		USA Trotter 49.8, Henderson 49.7, Richards 49.81, Hennagan 49.73			(1)	OG	Athína	28 Aug 04
		Note team was disqualified as Crystal Cox (subject of retrospective drugs ban) ran for them in the heat						
3:19.04	WR	GDR Siemon' 51.0, Busch 50.0, Rübsam 50.2, Koch 47.9			1	EC	Athína	11 Sep 82
3:19.12		URS Baskakova, I.Nazarova, Pinigina, Vladykina			1	Drz	Praha	18 Aug 84
3:19.23	WR	GDR Maletzki 50.05, Rohde 49.00, Streidt 49.51, Brehmer 49.79			1	OG	Montreal	31 Jul 76
3:19.36		RUS			3	WCh	Daegu	3 Sep 11
		Krivoshapka 50.3, Antyukh 50.0, Litvinova 49.96, Kapachinskaya 49.22						
3:19.49		GDR Emmelmann, Busch, Neubauer, Koch 47.9			1	WCp	Canberra	4 Oct 85
3:19.50		URS Yurchenko 51.2, O.Nazarova 50.2, Pinigina 49.09, Bryzgina 49.03			2	WCh	Roma	6 Sep 87
3:19.60		USA Leatherwood 50.7 , S.Howard 50.0, Brisco-Hooks 48.7, Cheeseborough 50.2			1	Walnut		25 Jul 84
3:19.62		GDR Kotte, Brehmer, Köhn, Koch 48.3			1	ECp	Torino	5 Aug 79
		(26/4 with USSR and Russia counted separately)						
3:19.73		JAM S Williams 50.5, Lloyd 50.1, Prendergast 50.18, NWilliams 48.93			2	WCh	Osaka	2 Sep 07
3:20.04		GBR Ohuruogu 50.6, Okoro 50.9, McConnell 49.79, Sanders 48.76			3	WCh	Osaka	2 Sep 07
3:20.32		CZE/TCH			2	WCh	Helsinki	14 Aug 83
		Kocembová 48.93, Matejkovicová 52.13, Moravcíková 51.51, Kratochvílová 47.75						
3:21.04		NGR Afolabi 51.13, Yusuf 49.72, Opara 51.29, Ogunkoya 48.90			2	OG	Atlanta	3 Aug 96
3:21.21		CAN Crooks 50.30, Richardson 50.22, Killingbeck ¶ 50.62, Payne 50.07			2	OG	Los Angeles	11 Aug 84
3:21.85		BLR Kozak 52.0, Khlyustova 50.3, I Usovich 49.85, S Usovich 49.69			4	OG	Beijing	23 Aug 08
		(10)						
3:21.94		UKR Dzhigalova, Olizarenko, Pinigina, Vladykina			1	URSCh	Kyiv	17 Jul 86
3:22.34		FRA Landre 51.3, Dorsile 51.1, Elien 50.54, Pérec 49.36			1	EC	Helsinki	14 Aug 94
3:22.49		FRG Thimm 50.81, Arendt 49.95, Thomas 51.50, Abt 50.23			4	OG	Seoul	1 Oct 88
3:23.21		CUB Díaz 51.1, Calatayud 51.2, Clement 50.47, Terrero 50.46			6	OG	Beijing	23 Aug 08
3:23.81		AUS Peris-K 51.71, Lewis 51.69, Gainsford-T 51.06, Freeman 49.35			4	OG	Sydney	30 Sep 00
3:24.28		CHN (Hebei) An X, Bai X, Cao C, Ma Y			1	NG	Beijing	13 Sep 93
3:24.49		POL Guzowska 52.2, Bejnar 50.2, Prokopek 50.47, Jesien 51.59			4	WCh	Helsinki	14 Aug 05
3:25.68		ROU Ruicu 52.69, Rîpanu 51.09, Barbu 52.64, Tîrlea 49.26			2	ECp	Paris (C)	20 Jun 97
3:25.7a		FIN Eklund 53.6, Pursiainen 50.6, Wilmi 51.6, Salin 49.9			2	EC	Roma	8 Sep 74
3:25.71		ITA Bazzoni 53.7, Milani 50.8, Spacca 51.64, Grenot 49.61			4	EC	Barcelona	1 Aug 10
		(20)						
3:25.81		BUL Ilieva, Stamenova, Penkova, Damyanova			1	v Hun,Pol Sofiya		24 Jul 83
3:26.33		GRE Kaidantzi 53.2, Goudenoúdi 51.6, Boudá 51.76, Halkiá 49.75			3	ECpS	Bydgoszcz	20 Jun 04
3:26.68		BRA (Bovespa) Coutinho, de Oliveira, Sousa, de Lima			1	NC	São Paulo	7 Aug 11
3:26.89		IND R Kaur 53.1, Beenamol 51.4, Soman 52.51, M Kaur 49.85			3h2	OG	Athína	27 Aug 04
3:27.08		CMR Nguimgo 51.7, Kaboud 52.1, Atangana 51.98, Béwouda 51.35			7	WCh	Saint-Denis	31 Aug 03
3:27.14		MEX Rodríguez 53.3, Medina 51.2, Vela 52.94, Guevara 49.70			4h2	WCh	Osaka	1 Sep 07
3:27.48		IRL Andrews 53.4, Cuddihy 49.9, Bergin 52.60, Carey 51.54			4h3	WCh	Daegu	2 Sep 11
3:27.54		LTU Navickaite, Valiuliene, Mendzoryte, Ambraziene			3	SPART	Moskva	22 Jun 83
3:27.57		ESP Merino 52.2, Lacambra 52.0, Myers 50.85, Ferrer 52.56			7	WCh	Tokyo	1 Sep 91
3:27.86		HUN Orosz, Forgács, Tóth, Pál (30)			5	OG	Moskva	1 Aug 80

5000 METRES WALK (TRACK)

Mark		Name		Nat	Born	Pos	Meet	Venue	Date
20:02.60	WR	Gillian	O'Sullivan	IRL	21.8.76	1	NC	Dublin (S)	13 Jul 02
20:03.0	WR	Kerry	Saxby-Junna	AUS	2.6.61	1		Sydney	11 Feb 96
20:07.52	WR	Beate	Anders/Gummelt	GDR	4.2.68	1	vURS	Rostock	23 Jun 90
20:11.45		Sabine	Zimmer	GER	6.2.81	1	NC	Wattenscheid	2 Jul 05
20:12.41		Elisabetta	Perrone	ITA	9.7.68	1	NC	Rieti	2 Aug 03
20:18.87		Melanie	Seeger	GER	8.1.77	1	NC	Braunschweig	10 Jul 04
20:21.69		Annarita	Sidoti	ITA	25.7.69	1	NC	Cesenatico	1 Jul 95
20:27.59	WR	Ileana	Salvador	ITA	16.1.62	1		Trento	3 Jun 89

Mark	Wind	Name		Nat	Born	Pos	Meet	Venue	Date
20:28.05		Tatyana	Kalmykova	RUS	10.1.90	1	WY	Ostrava	12 Jul 0
20:28.62		Sari	Essayah	FIN	21.2.67	1	NC	Tuusula	9 Jul 94 7

10 KILOMETRES WALK

Mark	Wind	Name		Nat	Born	Pos	Meet	Venue	Date
41:04 WR		Yelena	Nikolayeva	RUS	1.2.66	1	NC	Sochi	20 Apr 96
41:16			Wang Yan	CHN	3.5.71	1		Eisenhüttenstadt	8 May 99
41:16		Kjersti	Plätzer (Tysse)	NOR	18.1.72	1	NC	Os	11 May 02
41:17		Irina	Stankina	RUS	25.3.77	1	NC-w	Adler	9 Feb 97
41:24		Olimpiada	Ivanova ¶	RUS	26.8.70	2	NC-w	Adler	9 Feb 97
41:29 WR		Larisa	Ramazanova	RUS	23.9.71	1	NC	Izhevsk	4 Jun 95
41:30 WR		Kerry	Saxby-Junna	AUS	2.6.61	1	NC	Canberra	27 Aug 88
41:30			O Ivanova			2	NC	Izhevsk	4 Jun 95
41:31		Yelena	Gruzinova	RUS	24.12.67	2	NC	Sochi	20 Apr 96
41:37.9t			Gao Hongmiao	CHN	17.3.74	1	NC	Beijing	7 Apr 94
41:38		Rossella	Giordano (10)	ITA	1.12.72	1		Naumburg	25 May 97
41:41			Nikolayeva			2		Naumburg	25 May 97
41:41			Tysse Plätzer			1		Kraków	30 May 09
41:42		Olga	Kaniskina	RUS	19.1.85	2		Kraków	30 May 09
41:45			Liu Hongyu	CHN	11.1.75	2		Eisenhüttenstadt	8 May 99
41:46		Annarita	Sidoti	ITA	25.7.69	1		Livorno	12 Jun 94
41:46			O Ivanova			1	NC/w	Adler	11 Feb 96
41:47			Saxby-Junna			1		Eisenhüttenstadt	11 May 96
41:48			Li Chunxiu	CHN	13.8.69	1	NG	Beijing	8 Sep 93
41:49			Ramazanova			3	NC	Sochi	20 Apr 96
41:49			Nikolayeva			1	OG	Atlanta	29 Jul 96
41:50		Yelena	Arshintseva	RUS	5.4.71	1	NC-w	Adler	11 Feb 95
		(22/15)							
41:51		Beate	Anders/Gummelt	GER	4.2.68	2		Eisenhüttenstadt	11 May 96
41:52		Tatyana	Mineyeva ¶	RUS	10.8.90	1	NCp-j	Penza	5 Sep 09
41:52		Tatyana	Korotkova	RUS	24.4.80	1		Buy	19 Sep 10
41:53		Tatyana	Sibileva	RUS	17.5.80	1	RWC-F	Beijing	18 Sep 10
41:56		Yelena	Sayko	RUS	24.12.67	2	NC/w	Adler	11 Feb 96
		(20)							
41:56.23t		Nadezhda	Ryashkina	RUS	22.1.67	1	GWG	Seattle	24 Jul 90
42:01		Tamara	Kovalenko	RUS	5.6.64	3	NC-w	Adler	11 Feb 95
42:01		Olga	Panfyorova	RUS	21.8.77	1	NC-23	Izhevsk	16 May 98
42:04+		Vera	Sokolova	RUS	8.6.87	1=	in 20k	Sochi	26 Feb 11
42:04+		Anisya	Kirdyapkina	RUS	23.10.89	1=	in 20k	Sochi	26 Feb 11
42:04+		Tatyana	Shemyakina	RUS	3.9.87	1=	in 20k	Sochi	26 Feb 11
42:05+		Margarita	Turova	BLR	28.12.80	1+	in 20k	Adler	12 Mar 05
42:06		Valentina	Tsybulskaya	BLR	19.2.68	4		Eisenhüttenstadt	8 May 99
42:07		Ileana	Salvador	ITA	16.1.62	1		Sesto San Giovanni	1 May 92
42:09		Elisabetta	Perrone	ITA	9.7.68	4		Eisenhüttenstadt	11 May 96
		(30)							
42:11		Nina	Alyushenko	RUS	29.5.68	3	NC	Izhevsk	4 Jun 95
42:13		Natalya	Misyulya	BLR	16.4.66	5		Eisenhüttenstadt	8 May 99
42:13.7t		Madelein	Svensson	SWE	20.7.69	2	SGP	Fana	15 May 92
42:15			Gu Yan	CHN	17.3.74	3	WCp	Podebrady	19 Apr 97
42:15		Erica	Alfridi	ITA	22.2.68	5		Naumburg	25 May 97
42:15		Jane	Saville	AUS	5.11.74	6		Eisenhüttenstadt	8 May 99
42:16		Alina	Ivanova	RUS	16.3.69	1		Novopolotsk	27 May 89
42:16		Norica	Cîmpean	ROU	22.3.72	1		Calella	9 May 99
42:17		Katarzyna	Radtke	POL	31.8.69	5		Eisenhüttenstadt	11 May 96
42:19+		Iraida	Pudovkina	RUS	2.11.80	2	in 20k	Adler	12 Mar 05
		(40)							

50th woman 42:34, 100th 43:13, 200th 44:06, 300th 44:41
Probable short course: Livorno 10 Jul 93: 1. Ileana Salvador ITA 16.1.62 41:30, 2. Elisabeta Perrone 9.7.68 41:56
Best track times

41:57.22		Kerry	Saxby-Junna	AUS	2.6.61	2	GWG	Seattle	24 Jul 90
42:11.5		Beate	Anders/Gummelt	GER	4.2.68	1	SGP	Fana	15 May 92

20 KILOMETRES WALK

Mark	Wind	Name		Nat	Born	Pos	Meet	Venue	Date
1:24:50		Olimpiada	Ivanova ¶	RUS	26.8.70	1	NC-w	Adler	4 Mar 01
1:24:56		Olga	Kaniskina	RUS	19.1.85	1	NC-w	Adler	28 Feb 09
1:25:02		Yelena	Lashmanova	RUS	9.4.92	1	OG	London	11 Aug 12
1:25:08 WR		Vera	Sokolova	RUS	8.6.87	1	NC-w	Sochi	26 Feb 11
1:25:09		Anisya	Kirdyapkina	RUS	23.10.89	2	NC-w	Sochi	26 Feb 11
1:25:09			Kaniskina			2	OG	London	11 Aug 12
1:25:11			Kaniskina			1	NC-w	Adler	23 Feb 08
1:25:11			Kirdyapkina			1	NC-w	Sochi	20 Feb 10
1:25:16			Qieyang Shenjie	CHN	11.11.90	3	OG	London	11 Aug 12

Mark	Wind	Name		Nat	Born	Pos	Meet	Venue	Date
1:25:18		Tatyana	Gudkova	RUS	23.1.78	1	NC	Moskva	19 May 00
1:25:20		Olga	Polyakova	RUS	23.9.80	2	NC	Moskva	19 May 00
1:25:26			Sokolova			2	NC-w	Adler	28 Feb 09
1:25:26			Kirdyapkina			3	NC-w	Adler	28 Feb 09
1:25:27		Elmira	Alembekova	RUS	30.6.90	1	NC-w	Sochi	18 Feb 12
1:25:29		Irina	Stankina (10)	RUS	25.3.77	3	NC	Moskva	19 May 00
1:25:30			Kirdyapkina			2	NC-w	Adler	23 Feb 08
1:25:32		Yelena	Shumkina	RUS	24.1.88	4	NC-w	Adler	28 Feb 09
1:25:35			Sokolova			2	NC-w	Sochi	20 Feb 10
1:25:41	WR		O Ivanova			1	WCh	Helsinki	7 Aug 05
1:25:42			Kaniskina			1	WCp	Cheboksary	11 May 08
1:25:46		Tatyana	Shemyakina	RUS	3.9.87	3	NC-w	Adler	23 Feb 08
1:25:46			Liu Hong	CHN	12.5.87	1		Taicang	30 Mar 12
1:25:49			Lashmanova			1	NC-w	Sochi	23 Feb 13
1:25:52		Larisa	Yemelyanova	RUS	6.1.80	5	NC-w	Adler	28 Feb 09
1:25:52		Tatyana	Sibileva	RUS	17.5.80	3	NC-w	Sochi	20 Feb 10
1:25:59		Tamara	Kovalenko	RUS	5.6.64	4	NC	Moskva	19 May 00
1:25:59			Kirdyapkina			2	NC-w	Sochi	23 Feb 13
1:26:00			Liu Hong			4	OG	London	11 Aug 12
1:26:00			Sokolova			3	NC-w	Sochi	23 Feb 13
1:26:02			Kaniskina			1	NC-w	Adler	19 Feb 06
		(30/16)							
1:26:11		Margarita	Turova	BLR	28.12.80	1	NC	Nesvizh	15 Apr 06
1:26:14		Irina	Petrova	RUS	26.5.85	2	NC-w	Adler	19 Feb 06
1:26:16		Lyudmila	Arkhipova	RUS	25.11.78	5	NC-w	Adler	23 Feb 08
1:26:22	WR		Wang Yan (20)	CHN	3.5.71	1	NG	Guangzhou	19 Nov 01
1:26:22	WR	Yelena	Nikolayeva	RUS	1.2.66	1	ECp	Cheboksary	18 May 03
1:26:23			Wang Liping	CHN	8.7.76	2	NG	Guangzhou	19 Nov 01
1:26:28		Iraida	Pudovkina	RUS	2.11.80	1	NC-w	Adler	12 Mar 05
1:26:34		Tatyana	Kalmykova	RUS	10.1.90	1	NC	Saransk	8 Jun 08
1:26:35			Liu Hongyu	CHN	11.1.75	3	NG	Guangzhou	19 Nov 01
1:26:46			Song Hongjuan	CHN	4.7.84	1	NC	Guangzhou	20 Mar 04
1:26:47		Irina	Yumanova	RUS	6.11.90	3	NC-w	Sochi	18 Feb 12
1:26:50		Natalya	Fedoskina	RUS	25.6.80	2	ECp	Dudince	19 May 01
1:26:57		Lyudmila	Yefimkina	RUS	22.8.81	3	NC-w	Adler	19 Feb 06
1:27:01			Lu Xiuzhi	CHN	26.10.93	2		Taicang	30 Mar 12
		(30)							
1:27:07		Kjersti	Tysse Plätzer	NOR	18.1.72	2	OG	Beijing	21 Aug 08
1:27:08		Anna	Lukyanova	RUS	23.4.91	5	NC-w	Sochi	18 Feb 12
1:27:09		Elisabetta	Perrone	ITA	9.7.68	3	ECp	Dudince	19 May 01
1:27:12		Elisa	Rigaudo	ITA	17.6.80	3	OG	Beijing	21 Aug 08
1:27:14		Antonina	Petrova	RUS	1.5.77	1	NC-w	Adler	1 Mar 03
1:27:18		Alena	Nartova	RUS	1.1.82	6	NC-w	Adler	23 Feb 08
1:27:19			Jiang Jing	CHN	23.10.85	1	NC	Nanning	25 Feb 05
1:27:22		Gillian	O'Sullivan	IRL	21.8.76	1		Sesto San Giovanni	1 May 03
1:27:25		María	Vasco	ESP	26.12.75	5	OG	Beijing	21 Aug 08
1:27:27		Vira	Zozulya	UKR	31.8.70	1	eNC	Sumy	7 Jun 08
		(40)							
1:27:29		Erica	Alfridi	ITA	22.2.68	4	ECp	Dudince	19 May 01
1:27:30	WB	Nadezhda	Ryashkina	RUS	22.1.67	1	NC-w	Adler	7 Feb 99
1:27:30		Tatyana	Kozlova	RUS	2.9.83	2	NC-w	Adler	12 Mar 05
1:27:35		Tatyana	Korotkova	RUS	24.4.80	2	NC	Cheboksary	12 Jun 04
1:27:36			Sun Huanhuan	CHN	15.3.90	1	NC	Taicang	1 Mar 13
1:27:37			Bo Yanmin	CHN	29.6.87	3	NG	Nanjing	20 Oct 05
1:27:39		Marina	Pandakova	RUS	1.3.89	5	NC-w	Sochi	23 Feb 13
1:27:40			Li Yanfei	CHN	12.1.90	2	NC	Taicang	1 Mar 13
1:27:41		Claudia	Iovan/Stef ¶	ROU	25.2.78	1		La Coruña	5 Jun 04
1:27:42			He Qin	CHN	23.3.92	3	NC	Taicang	1 Mar 13
		(50)		100th best woman 1:29:11, 200th 1:31:03, 300th 1:32:46, 400th 1:34:25					

50 KILOMETRES WALK

Mark		Name		Nat	Born	Pos	Venue	Date
4:10:59		Monica	Svensson	SWE	26.12.78	1	Scanzorosciate	21 Oct 07
4:12:16		Yelena	Ginko	BLR	30.7.76	1	Scanzorosciate	17 Oct 04
4:16:27		Jolanta	Dukure	LAT	20.9.79	1	Paralepa	9 Sep 06
4:25:22		Brigita	Virbalyte	LTU	1.2.85	1	Villa di Serio	17 Oct 10
4:28:13		Evaggelía	Xinoú	GRE	22.11.81	2	Scanzorosciate	17 Oct 04
4:28:53		Neringa	Aidietité	LTU	5.6.83	1	Ivano-Frankivsk	1 Oct 06
4:28:59		Kara	Boufflert	FRA	23.4.66	1	Charly-sur-Marne	18 Feb 07
4:29:56		Natalia	Bruniko	ITA	23.2.73	2	Scanzorosciate	27 Oct 02
4:32:25		Lyudmyla	Shelest	UKR	4.10.74	3	Scanzorosciate	18 Oct 09

Mark	Wind	Name		Nat	Born	Pos	Meet	Venue	Date

JUNIOR MEN'S ALL-TIME LISTS

100 METRES

Mark	Wind	Name		Nat	Born	Pos	Meet	Venue	Date
10.01	0.0	Darrel	Brown	TRI	11.10.84	1q3	WCh	Saint-Denis	24 Aug 03
10.01	1.6	Jeffery	Demps	USA	8.1.90	2q1	NC/OT	Eugene	28 Jun 08
10.01	0.9	Yoshihide	Kiryu	JPN	15.12.95	1h3	Oda	Hiroshima	29 Apr 13
10.03	0.7	Marcus	Rowland	USA	11.3.90	1	PAm-J	Port of Spain	31 Jul 09
10.04	1.7	DeAngelo	Cherry	USA	1.8.90	1h4	NCAA	Fayetteville	10 Jun 09
10.04	0.2	Christoph	Lemaitre	FRA	11.6.90	1	EJ	Novi Sad	24 Jul 09
10.05		Davidson	Ezinwa	NGR	22.11.71	1		Bauchi	4 Jan 90
10.05	0.1	Adam	Gemili	GBR	6.10.93	1	WJ	Barcelona	11 Jul 12
10.06	2.0	Dwain	Chambers	GBR	5.4.78	1	EJ	Ljubljana	25 Jul 97
10.06	1.5	Walter	Dix	USA	31.1.86	1h1	NCAA-r	New York	27 May 05

10.07 Stanley Floyd USA 1980, DaBryan Blanton USA 2003, Tamunosiki Atorudibo HNR 2004, Jimmy Vicaut FRA 2011

Wind assisted to 10.03

Mark	Wind	Name		Nat	Born	Pos	Meet	Venue	Date
9.83	7.1	Leonard	Scott	USA	19.1.80	1		Knoxville	9 Apr 99
9.96	4.5	Walter	Dix	USA	31.1.86	1rA	TexR	Austin	9 Apr 05
9.97	??	Mark	Lewis-Francis	GBR	4.9.82	1q3	WCh	Edmonton	4 Aug 01
9.96	5.0	André	De Grasse	CAN	10.11.94	1	JUCO	Hutchinson, KS	18 May 13
9.98	5.0	Tyreek	Hill	USA	1.3.94	2	JUCO	Hutchinson, KS	18 May 13
9.99A	4.0	Trayvon	Bromell	USA	10.7.95	1		Albuquerque	8 Jun 13
10.02	2.8	DeAngelo	Cherry	USA	1.8.90	1h2	NC-j	Eugene	26 Jun 09
10.02	2.4	Marcus	Rowland	USA	11.3.90	1	NC-j	Eugene	26 Jun 09
10.03	4.9	Christoph	Lemaitre	FRA-	11.6.90	1		Forbach	31 May 09

200 METRES

Mark	Wind	Name		Nat	Born	Pos	Meet	Venue	Date
19.93	1.4	Usain	Bolt	JAM	21.8.86	1		Hamilton, BER	11 Apr 04
20.04	0.1	Ramil	Guliyev	AZE	29.5.90	1	WUG	Beograd	10 Jul 09
20.07	1.5	Lorenzo	Daniel	USA	23.3.66	1	SEC	Starkville	18 May 85
20.13	1.7	Roy	Martin	USA	25.12.66	1		Austin	11 May 85
20.14	1.8	Tyreek	Hill	USA	1.3.94	1		Orlando	26 May 12
20.16A	-0.2	Riaan	Dempers	RSA	4.3.77	1	NC-j	Germiston	7 Apr 95
20.18	1.0	Walter	Dix	USA	31.1.86	1s2	NCAA	Sacramento	9 Jun 05
20.22	1.7	Dwayne	Evans	USA	13.10.58	2	OT	Eugene	22 Jun 76
20.23	0.5	Michael	Timpson	USA	6.6.67	1		State College	16 May 86
20.24	0.2	Joe	DeLoach	USA	5.6.67	3		Los Angeles	8 Jun 85
20.24	0.2	Francis	Obikwelu	NGR	22.11.78	2rB		Granada	29 May 96
20.24	1.4	Roberto	Skyers	CUB	12.11.91	1h5		Camagüey	14 Mar 09

Wind assisted

Mark	Wind	Name		Nat	Born	Pos	Meet	Venue	Date
19.86	4.0	Justin	Gatlin	USA	10.2.82	1h2	NCAA	Eugene	30 May 01
20.01	2.5	Derald	Harris	USA	5.4.58	1		San José	9 Apr 77
20.08	9.2	Leonard	Scott	USA	19.1.80	2r2		Knoxville	9 Apr 99
20.10	4.6	Stanley	Kerr	USA	19.6.67	2r2	SWC	Houston	18 May 86
20.16	5.2	Nickel	Ashmeade	JAM	4.7.90	1	Carifta	Basseterre	24 Mar 08

Hand timing: 19.9 Davidson Ezinwa NGR 22.11.71 1 Bauchi 18 Mar 89

400 METRES

Mark	Name		Nat	Born	Pos	Meet	Venue	Date
43.87	Steve	Lewis	USA	16.5.69	1	OG	Seoul	28 Sep 88
44.36	Kirani	James	GRN	1.9.92	1	WK	Zürich	8 Sep 11
44.45	Luguelín	Santos	DOM	12.11.93	1	FBK	Hengelo	27 May 12
44.66	Hamdam Odha	Al-Bishi	KSA	5.5.81	1	WJ	Santiago de Chile	20 Oct 00
44.66	LaShawn	Merritt	USA	27.6.86	1		Kingston	7 May 05
44.69	Darrell	Robinson	USA	23.12.63	2	USOF	Indianapolis	24 Jul 82
44.73A	James	Rolle	USA	2.2.64	1	USOF	USAF Academy	2 Jul 83
44.75	Darren	Clark	AUS	6.9.65	4	OG	Los Angeles	8 Aug 84
44.75	Deon	Minor	USA	22.1.73	1s1	NCAA	Austin	5 Jun 92
44.82	Arman	Hall	USA	14.2.94	4s1	NC	Des Moines	21 Jun 13
44.93	Nagmeldin	El Abubakr	SUD	22.2.86	1	Is.Sol	Makkah	14 Apr 05

800 METRES

Mark	Name		Nat	Born	Pos	Meet	Venue	Date
1:41.73	Nijel	Amos	BOT	15.3.94	2	OG	London (OS)	9 Aug 12
1:42.37	Mohammed	Aman	ETH	10.1.94	1	VD	Bruxelles	6 Sep 13
1:42.53	Timothy	Kitum	KEN	20.11.94	3	OG	London (OS)	9 Aug 12
1:42.69	Abubaker	Kaki	SUD	21.6.89	1	Bisl	Oslo	6 Jun 08
1:43.13	Abraham Kipchirchir	Rotich	KEN	26.6.93	1	Herc	Monaco	20 Jul 12
1:43.40	Leonard	Kosencha	KEN	21.8.94	2	Herc	Monaco	20 Jul 12
1:43.64	Japheth	Kimutai	KEN	20.12.78	3rB	WK	Zürich	13 Aug 97
1:43.81	Edwin	Melly	KEN	24.3.94	2		Rieti	9 Sep 12
1:43.99	David	Mutua	KEN	20.4.92	4	Herc	Monaco	22 Jul 11
1:44.15	David	Rudisha	KEN	17.12.88	1	VD	Bruxelles	14 Sep 07
1:44.27	Majid Saeed	Sultan	QAT	3.11.86	1	AsiC	Inchon	4 Sep 05

Jnr MEN All-time

Mark	Wind	Name		Nat	Born	Pos	Meet	Venue	Date

1000 METRES
2:13.93		Abubaker	Kaki	SUD	21.6.89	1	DNG	Stockholm	22 Jul 08
2:15.00		Benjamin	Kipkurui	KEN	28.12.80	5	Nik	Nice	17 Jul 99

1500 METRES
3:30.24		Cornelius	Chirchir	KEN	5.6.83	4	Herc	Monaco	19 Jul 02
3:31.13		Mulugueta	Wondimu	ETH	28.2.85	2rA	NA	Heusden	31 Jul 04
3:31.42		Alex	Kipchirchir	KEN	26.11.84	5	VD	Bruxelles	5 Sep 03
3:31.54		Isaac	Songok	KEN	25.4.84	1	NA	Heusden	2 Aug 03
3:31.64		Asbel	Kiprop	KEN	30.6.89	1	GGala	Roma	11 Jul 08
3:31.70		William	Biwott	KEN	5.3.90	3	GGala	Roma	10 Jul 09
3:32.02		Caleb	Ndiku	KEN	9.10.92	4	FBK	Hengelo	29 May 11
3:32.48		Augustine	Choge	KEN	21.1.87	1	ISTAF	Berlin	3 Sep 06
3:32.68		Abdelaati	Iguider	MAR	25.3.87	5	VD	Bruxelles	25 Aug 06
3:32.91		Noah	Ngeny	KEN	2.11.78	9	Herc	Monaco	16 Aug 97
3:33.16		Benjamin	Kipkurui	KEN	28.12.80	1rB	WK	Zürich	11 Aug 99

1 MILE
3:49.29		William	Biwott	KEN	5.3.90	2	Bisl	Oslo	3 Jul 09
3:49.77		Caleb	Ndiku	KEN	9.10.92	5	Pre	Eugene	4 Jun 11
3:50.25		Alex	Kipchirchir	KEN	26.11.84	2	GP II	Rieti	7 Sep 03
3:50.39		James	Kwalia	KEN	12.6.84	1	FBK	Hengelo	1 Jun 03
3:50.41		Noah	Ngeny	KEN	2.11.78	2	Nik	Nice	16 Jul 97
3:50.69		Cornelius	Chirchir	KEN	5.6.83	5	GGala	Roma	12 Jul 02
3:50.83		Nicholas	Kemboi	KEN	18.12.89	6	Bisl	Oslo	6 Jun 08

2000 METRES
4:56.25		Tesfaye	Cheru	ETH	2.3.93	1		Reims	5 Jul 11
4:56.86		Isaac	Songok	KEN	25.4.84	6	ISTAF	Berlin	31 Aug 01
4:58.18		Soresa	Fida	ETH	27.5.93	4		Reims	5 Jul 11
4:58.76		Jairus	Kipchoge	KEN	15.12.92	7		Reims	5 Jul 11

3000 METRES
7:28.78		Augustine	Choge	KEN	21.1.87	2	SGP	Doha	13 May 05
7:29.11		Tariku	Bekele	ETH	21.1.87	2	GP	Rieti	27 Aug 06
7:30.36		Hagos	Gebrhiwet	ETH	11.5.94	1	DL	Doha	10 May 13
7:30.43		Isiah	Koech	KEN	19.12.93	1	DNG	Stockholm	17 Aug 12
7:30.67		Kenenisa	Bekele	ETH	13.6.82	2	VD	Bruxelles	24 Aug 01
7:30.91		Eliud	Kipchoge	KEN	5.11.84	2	VD	Bruxelles	5 Sep 03
7:32.37		Abreham	Cherkos	ETH	23.9.89	2	Athl	Lausanne	11 Jul 06
7:32.72		John	Kipkoech	KEN	29.12.91	4		Rieti	29 Aug 10
7:33.00		Hailu	Mekonnen	ETH	4.4.80	2		Stuttgart	6 Jun 99
7:33.01		Levy	Matebo	KEN	3.11.89	2	GP	Rieti	7 Sep 08
7:34.32		Richard	Limo	KEN	18.11.80	4	VD	Bruxelles	3 Sep 99

5000 METRES
12:47.53		Hagos	Gebrhiwet	ETH	11.5.94	2	DL	Saint-Denis	6 Jul 12
12:48.64		Isiah	Koech	KEN	19.12.93	3	DL	Saint-Denis	6 Jul 12
12:52.61		Eliud	Kipchoge	KEN	5.11.84	3	Bisl	Oslo	27 Jun 03
12:53.66		Augustine	Choge	KEN	21.1.87	4	GGala	Roma	8 Jul 05
12:53.72		Philip	Mosima	KEN	2.1.77	2	GGala	Roma	5 Jun 96
12:53.81		Tariku	Bekele	ETH	21.1.87	4	GGala	Roma	14 Jul 06
12:54.07		Sammy	Kipketer	KEN	29.9.81	2	GGala	Roma	30 Jun 00
12:54.19		Abreham	Cherkos	ETH	23.9.89	5	GGala	Roma	14 Jul 06
12:54.58		James	Kwalia	KEN	12.6.84	5	Bisl	Oslo	27 Jun 03
12:56.15		Daniel	Komen	KEN	17.5.76	2	GG	Roma	8 Jun 95
12:57.05		Mulugueta	Wondimu	ETH	28.2.85	2	ISTAF	Berlin	12 Sep 04

10,000 METRES
26:41.75		Samuel	Wanjiru	KEN	10.11.86	3	VD	Bruxelles	26 Aug 05
26:55.73		Geoffrey	Kirui	KEN	16.2.93	6	VD	Bruxelles	16 Sep 11
26:57.56		Yigrem	Demelash	ETH	28.1.94	4	VD	Bruxelles	7 Sep 12
27:02.81		Ibrahim	Jeylan	ETH	12.6.89	4	VD	Bruxelles	25 Aug 06
27:04.00		Boniface	Kiprop	UGA	12.10.85	5	VD	Bruxelles	3 Sep 04
27:04.45		Bernard	Kipyego	KEN	16.7.86	1	FBK	Hengelo	29 May 05
27:06.35		Geoffrey	Kipsang	KEN	28.11.92	10	Pre	Eugene	3 Jun 11
27:06.47		Habtanu	Fikadu	ETH	13.3.88	8	FBK	Hengelo	26 May 07
27:07.29		Moses	Masai	KEN	1.6.86	7	VD	Bruxelles	3 Sep 04
27:11.18		Richard	Chelimo	KEN	21.4.72	1	APM	Hengelo	25 Jun 91
27:12.42		Sammy Alex	Mutahi	KEN	1.6.89	1		Tokamchi	29 Sep 07
27:13.66		Moses	Mosop	KEN	17.7.85	7	VD	Bruxelles	5 Sep 03

Mark	Wind	Name		Nat	Born	Pos	Meet	Venue	Date

3000 METRES STEEPLECHASE

Mark	Wind	Name		Nat	Born	Pos	Meet	Venue	Date
7:58.66		Stephen	Cherono	KEN	15.10.82	3	VD	Bruxelles	24 Aug 01
8:01.16		Conseslus	Kipruto	KEN	8.12.94	1	DL	Shanghai	18 May 13
8:03.74		Raymond	Yator	KEN	7.4.81	3	Herc	Monaco	18 Aug 00
8:05.52		Brimin	Kipruto	KEN	31.7.85	1	FBK	Hengelo	31 May 04
8:06.96		Gilbert	Kirui	KEN	22.1.94	2	DL	London (OS)	27 Jul 13
8:07.18		Moussa	Omar Obaid	QAT	18.4.85	4	OG	Athína	24 Aug 04
8:07.69		Paul	Kosgei	KEN	22.4.78	5	DNG	Stockholm	7 Jul 97
8:07.71		Hillary	Yego	KEN	2.4.92	3	DL	Shanghai	15 May 11
8:09.37		Abel	Cheruiyot/Yugut	KEN	26.12.84	2	NA	Heusden	2 Aug 03
8:11.31		Jairus	Birech	KEN	15.12.92	5	DL	Saint Denis	8 Jul 11
8:12.91		Thomas	Kiplitan	KEN	15.6.83	7	GP	Doha	15 May 02

110 METRES HURDLES (106cm)

Mark	Wind	Name		Nat	Born	Pos	Meet	Venue	Date
13.12	1.6		Liu Xiang	CHN	13.7.83	1rB	Athl	Lausanne	2 Jul 02
13.23	0.0	Renaldo	Nehemiah	USA	24.3.59	1r2	WK	Zürich	16 Aug 78
13.40	-1.0		Shi Dongpeng	CHN	6.1.84	1	NC	Shanghai	14 Sep 03
13.44	-0.8	Colin	Jackson	GBR	18.2.67	1	WJ	Athína	19 Jul 86
13.46	1.8	Jon	Ridgeon	GBR	14.2.67	1	EJ	Cottbus	23 Aug 85
13.46	-1.6	Dayron	Robles	CUB	19.11.86	1	PAm-J	Windsor	29 Jul 05
13.47	1.9	Holger	Pohland	GDR	5.4.63	2	vUSA	Karl-Marx-Stadt	10 Jul 82
13.47	1.2	Aries	Merritt	USA	24.7.85	4	NCAA	Austin	12 Jun 04
13.47	0.2		Xie Wenjun	CHN	11.7.90	2	GP	Shanghai	20 Sep 08
13.49	0.6	Stanislav	Olijar	LAT	22.3.79	1		Valmiera	11 Jul 98
13.49	1.2	Booker	Nunley	USA	2.7.90	2	SEC	Gainesville	17 May 09

Wind assisted

Mark	Wind	Name		Nat	Born	Pos	Meet	Venue	Date
13.41	2.6	Dayron	Robles	CUB	19.11.86	2	CAC	Nassau	10 Jul 05
13.42	4.5	Colin	Jackson	GBR	18.2.67	2	CG	Edinburgh	27 Jul 86
13.42	2.6	Antwon	Hicks	USA	12.3.83	1	WJ	Kingston	21 Jul 02
13.47	2.1	Frank	Busemann	GER	26.2.75	1	WJ	Lisboa	22 Jul 94

99 cm Hurdles

Mark	Wind	Name		Nat	Born	Pos	Meet	Venue	Date
13.08	2.0	Wayne	Davis	USA	2.7.90	1	PAm-J	Port of Spain	31 Jul 09
13.14	1.6	Eddie	Lovett	USA	25.6.92	1	PAm-J	Miramar	23 Jul 11
13.18	1.0	Yordan	O'Farrill	CUB	9.2.93	1	WJ	Barcelona	12 Jul 12
13.18	0.9	Wilhem	Belocian	FRA	22.6.95	1	EJ	Rieti	20 Jul 13
13.23	1.5	Artur	Noga	POL	2.5.88	1	WJ	Beijing	20 Aug 06
13.24	1.6	Roy	Smith	USA	12.4.92	2	PAm-J	Miramar	23 Jul 11

Wind assisted to 13.20

Mark	Wind	Name		Nat	Born	Pos	Meet	Venue	Date
13.03	2.9	Eddie	Lovett	USA	25.6.92	1h1	PAm-J	Miramar	23 Jul 11
13.15	2.7	Brendan	Ames	USA	6.10.88	1	NC-j	Indianapolis	21 Jun 07
13.18		Arthur	Blake	USA	19.8.66	1	GWest	Sacramento	9 Jun 84

Hand timed: 12.9y Renaldo Nehemiah USA 24.3.59 1 Jamaica, NY 30 May 77

400 METRES HURDLES

Mark	Wind	Name		Nat	Born	Pos	Meet	Venue	Date
48.02		Danny	Harris	USA	7.9.65	2s1	OT	Los Angeles	17 Jun 84
48.26		Jehue	Gordon	TRI	15.12.91	4	WCh	Berlin	18 Aug 09
48.51		Kerron	Clement	USA	31.10.85	1	WJ	Grosseto	16 Jul 04
48.52		Johnny	Dutch	USA	20.1.89	5	NC/OT	Eugene	29 Jun 08
48.62		Brandon	Johnson	USA	6.3.85	2	WJ	Grosseto	16 Jul 04
48.68		Bayano	Kamani	USA	17.4.80	1	NCAA	Boise	4 Jun 99
48.68		Jeshua	Anderson	USA	22.6.89	1	WJ	Bydgoszcz	11 Jul 08
48.72		Angelo	Taylor	USA	29.12.78	2	NCAA	Bloomington	6 Jun 97
48.74		Vladimir	Budko	BLR	4.2.65	2	DRZ	Moskva	18 Aug 84
48.76A		Llewellyn	Herbert	RSA	21.7.77	1		Pretoria	7 Apr 96

HIGH JUMP

Mark	Wind	Name		Nat	Born	Pos	Meet	Venue	Date
2.37		Dragutin	Topic	YUG	12.3.71	1	WJ	Plovdiv	12 Aug 90
2.37		Steve	Smith	GBR	29.3.73	1	WJ	Seoul	20 Sep 92
2.36		Javier	Sotomayor	CUB	13.10.67	1		Santiago de Cuba	23 Feb 86
2.35i		Vladimir	Yashchenko	UKR	12.1.59	1	EI	Milano	12 Mar 78
2.34						1	Prv	Tbilisi	16 Jun 78
2.35		Dietmar	Mögenburg	FRG	15.8.61	1		Rehlingen	26 May 80
2.34		Tim	Forsyth	AUS	17.8.73	1	Bisl	Oslo	4 Jul 92
2.33			Zhu Jianhua	CHN	29.5.63	1	AsiG	New Delhi	1 Dec 82
2.33		Patrik	Sjöberg	SWE	5.1.65	1	OsloG	Oslo	9 Jul 83
2.32i		Jaroslav	Bába	CZE	2.9.84	3		Arnstadt	8 Feb 03
2.32			Huang Haiqiang	CHN	8.2.88	1	WJ	Beijing	17 Aug 06

POLE VAULT

Mark	Wind	Name		Nat	Born	Pos	Meet	Venue	Date
5.80		Maksim	Tarasov	RUS	2.12.70	1	vGDR-j	Bryansk	14 Jul 89

Mark	Wind	Name		Nat	Born	Pos	Meet	Venue	Date
5.80		Raphael	Holzdeppe	GER	28.9.89	2		Biberach	28 Jun 08
5.75		Konstadínos	Filippídis	GRE	26.11.86	2	WUG	Izmir	18 Aug 05
5.72		Andrew	Irwin	USA	23.1.93	1	SEC	Baton Rouge	13 May 12
5.71		Lawrence	Johnson	USA	7.5.74	1		Knoxville	12 Jun 93
5.71		Germán	Chiaraviglio	ARG	16.4.87	1	WJ	Beijing	19 Aug 06
5.71		Shawn	Barber	CAN	27.5.94	2	TexR	Austin	29 Mar 13
5.70		Viktor	Chistyakov	RUS	9.2.75	1		Leppävirta	7 Jun 94
5.70		Artyom	Kuptsov	RUS	22.4.84	1	Znam	Tula	7 Jun 03
5.67i		Leonid	Kivalov	RUS	1.4.88	1	NC-j	Penza	1 Feb 07
5.65		3 men: Rodion	Gataullin UZB 1984, István Bagyula HUN					2.1988, Jacob Davis USA 1997 (i)		

LONG JUMP

Mark	Wind	Name		Nat	Born	Pos	Meet	Venue	Date
8.35	1.1	Sergey	Morgunov	RUS	9.2.93	1	NC-j	Cheboksary	19 Jun 12
8.34	0.0	Randy	Williams	USA	23.8.53	Q	OG	München	8 Sep 72
8.28	0.8	Luis Alberto	Bueno	CUB	22.5.69	1		La Habana	16 Jul 88
8.27	1.7	Eusebio	Cáceres	ESP	10.9.91	Q	EC	Barcelona	30 Jul 10
8.24	0.2	Eric	Metcalf	USA	23.1.68	1	NCAA	Indianapolis	6 Jun 86
8.24	1.8	Vladimir	Ochkan	UKR	13.1.68	1	vGDR-j	Leningrad	21 Jun 87
8.22		Larry	Doubley	USA	15.3.58	1	NCAA	Champaign	3 Jun 77
8.22		Iván	Pedroso	CUB	17.12.72	1		Santiago de Cuba	3 May 91
8.22i		Viktor	Kuznetsov	UKR	14.7.86	1		Brovary	22 Jan 05
8.21A	2.0	Vance	Johnson	USA	13.3.63	1	NCAA	Provo	4 Jun 82
8.20	1.5	James	Stallworth	USA	29.4.71	Q	WJ	Plovdiv	9 Aug 90
Wind assisted									
8.40	3.2	Kareem	Streete-Thompson	CAY	30.3.73	1		Houston	5 May 91
8.35	2.2	Carl	Lewis	USA	1.7.61	1	NCAA	Austin	6 Jun 80
8.29	2.3	James	Beckford	JAM	9.1.75	1		Tempe	2 Apr 94
8.23	4.4	Peller	Phillips	USA	23.6.70	1		Sacramento	11 Jun 88
8.21	2.8	Masaki	Morinaga	JPN	27.3.72	1		Hamamatsu	7 Sep 91

TRIPLE JUMP

Mark	Wind	Name		Nat	Born	Pos	Meet	Venue	Date
17.50	0.4	Volker	Mai	GDR	3.5.66	1	vURS	Erfurt	23 Jun 85
17.42	1.3	Khristo	Markov	BUL	27.1.65	1	Nar	Sofiya	19 May 84
17.40A	0.4	Pedro	Pérez	CUB	23.2.52	1	PAm	Cali	5 Aug 71
17.40	0.8	Ernesto	Revé	CUB	26.2.92	1		La Habana	10 Jun 11
17.31	-0.2	David	Girat Jr.	CUB	26.8.84	Q	WCh	Saint-Denis	23 Aug 03
17.29	1.3	James	Beckford	JAM	9.1.75	1		Tempe	2 Apr 94
17.27		Aliecer	Urrutia	CUB	22.9.74	1		Artemisa	23 Apr 93
17.23	0.2	Yoelbi	Quesada	CUB	4.8.73	1	NC	La Habana	13 May 92
17.19	-0.4	Teddy	Tamgho	FRA	15.6.89	4	Herc	Monaco	29 Jul 08
17.19	2.0	Will	Claye	USA	13.6.91	*	NCAA	Fayetteville	13 Jun 09
Wind assisted to 17.15									
17.33	2.1	Teddy	Tamgho	FRA	15.6.89	1	WJ	Bydgoszcz	11 Jul 08
17.24	2.5	Will	Claye	USA	13.6.91	1	NCAA	Fayetteville	13 Jun 09

SHOT

Mark	Wind	Name		Nat	Born	Pos	Meet	Venue	Date
21.05i		Terry	Albritton	USA	14.1.55	1	AAU	New York	22 Feb 74
20.38						2	MSR	Walnut	27 Apr 74
20.65		Mike	Carter	USA	29.10.60	1	vSU-j	Boston	4 Jul 79
20.43		David	Storl	GER	27.7.90	2		Gerlingen	6 Jul 09
20.39		Janus	Robberts	RSA	10.3.79	1	NC	Germiston	7 Mar 98
20.38		Jacko	Gill	NZL	10.12.94	1		Auckland (NS)	5 Dec 11
20.20		Randy	Matson	USA	5.3.45	2	OG	Tokyo	17 Oct 64
20.20		Udo	Beyer	GDR	9.8.55	2	NC	Leipzig	6 Jul 74
20.13		Jeff	Chakouian	USA	20.4.82	2		Atlanta	18 May 01
19.99		Karl	Salb	USA	19.5.49	4	OT	Echo Summit	10 Sep 68
19.95		Edis	Elkasevic	CRO	18.2.83	1		Velenje	15 Jun 02
6 kg Shot									
23.00		Jacko	Gill	NZL	10.12.94	1		Auckland	18 Aug 13
22.73		David	Storl	GER	27.7.90	1		Osterode	14 Jul 09
21.96		Edis	Elkasevic	CRO	18.2.83	1	NC-j	Zagreb	29 Jun 02
21.78		Krzysztof	Brzozowski	POL	15.7.93	2	WJ	Barcelona	11 Jul 12
21.68		Marin	Premeru	CRO	29.8.90	1		Rijeka	19 May 09
21.24		Georgi	Ivanov	BUL	13.3.85	1	NC-j	Sofia	12 Jun 04
21.14		Damien	Birkinhead	AUS	8.4.93	3	WJ	Barcelona	11 Jul 12

DISCUS

Mark	Wind	Name		Nat	Born	Pos	Meet	Venue	Date
65.62		Werner	Reiterer	AUS	27.1.68	1		Melbourne	15 Dec 87
65.31		Mykyta	Nesterenko	UKR	15.4.91	3		Tallinn	3 Jun 08
63.64		Werner	Hartmann	FRG	20.4.59	1	vFRA	Strasbourg	25 Jun 78
63.26		Sergey	Pachin	UKR	24.5.68	2		Moskva	25 Jul 87

Mark	Wind	Name		Nat	Born	Pos	Meet	Venue	Date
63.22		Brian	Milne	USA	7.1.73	1		State College	28 Mar 92
62.52		John	Nichols	USA	23.8.69	1		Baton Rouge	23 Apr 88
62.36		Tulake	Nuermaimaiti	CHN	8.3.82	2	NG	Guangzhou	21 Nov 01
62.16		Zoltán	Kővágó	HUN	10.4.79	1		Budapest	9 May 97
62.04		Kenth	Gardenkrans	SWE	2.10.55	2		Helsingborg	11 Aug 74
62.04			Wu Tao	CHN	3.10.83	1	NGP	Shanghai	18 May 02

1.75kg Discus

Mark	Wind	Name		Nat	Born	Pos	Meet	Venue	Date
70.13		Mykyta	Nesterenko	UKR	15.4.91	1		Halle	24 May 08
67.32		Margus	Hunt	EST	14.7.87	1	WJ	Beijing	16 Aug 06
66.88		Traves	Smikle	JAM	7.5.92	1		Kingston	31 Mar 11
66.45		Gordon	Wolf	GER	17.1.90	1		Halle	23 May 09
65.88		Omar	El-Ghazaly	EGY	9.2.84	1		Cairo	7 Nov 03
65.71		Marin	Premeru	CRO	29.8.90	1		Split	31 May 09
65.55		Mihai	Grasu	ROM	21.4.87	1	NC	Bucuresti	23 Jul 06
65.52A		Victor	Hogan	RSA	25.7.89	1		Potchefstroom	3 Jul 08
65.51		Andrius	Gudzius	LTU	14.2.91	1		Siauliai	30 Jun 10

HAMMER

Mark	Wind	Name		Nat	Born	Pos	Meet	Venue	Date
78.33		Olli-Pekka	Karjalainen	FIN	7.3.80	1	NC	Seinäjoki	5 Aug 99
78.14		Roland	Steuk	GDR	5.3.59	1	NC	Leipzig	30 Jun 78
78.00		Sergey	Dorozhon	UKR	17.2.64	1		Moskva	7 Aug 83
76.54		Valeriy	Gubkin	BLR	3.9.67	2		Minsk	27 Jun 86
76.42		Ruslan	Dikiy	TJK	18.1.72	1		Togliatti	7 Sep 91
76.37		Ashraf Amjad	El-Seify	QAT	20.2.95	1		Doha	10 Apr 13
75.52		Sergey	Kirmasov	RUS	25.3.70	1		Kharkov	4 Jun 89
75.42		Szymon	Ziolkowski	POL	1.7.76	1	EJ	Nyíregyházá	30 Jul 95
75.24		Christoph	Sahner	FRG	23.9.63	1	vPOL-j	Göttingen	26 Jun 82

6kg Hammer

Mark	Wind	Name		Nat	Born	Pos	Meet	Venue	Date
85.57		Ashraf Amgad	El-Seify	QAT-Y	20.2.95	1	WJ	Barcelona	14 Jul 12
82.97		Javier	Cienfuegos	ESP	15.7.90	1		Madrid	17 Jun 09
82.84		Quentin	Bigot	FRA	1.12.92	1		Bondoufle	16 Oct 11
82.62		Yevgeniy	Aydamirov	RUS	11.5.87	1	NC-j	Tula	22 Jul 06
81.34		Krisztián	Pars	HUN	18.2.82	1		Szombathely	2 Sep 01
81.15		Ákos	Hudi	HUN	10.8.91	1		Veszprém	7 Jul 10
81.16		Özkan	Baltaci	TUR	13.2.94	1		Ankara	31 Jul 13
81.04		Werner	Smit	RSA	14.9.84	1		Bellville	29 Mar 03

JAVELIN

Mark	Wind	Name		Nat	Born	Pos	Meet	Venue	Date
84.69		Zigismunds	Sirmais	LAT	6.5.92	2		Bauska	22 Jun 11
84.58		Keshorn	Walcott	TRI	2.4.93	1	OG	London (OS)	11 Aug 12
83.87		Andreas	Thorkildsen	NOR	1.4.82	1		Fana	7 Jun 01
83.55		Aleksandr	Ivanov	RUS	25.5.82	2	NC	Tula	14 Jul 01
83.07		Robert	Oosthuizen	RSA	23.1.87	1	WJ	Beijing	19 Aug 06
82.52		Harri	Haatainen	FIN	5.1.78	4		Leppävirta	25 May 96
82.52		Till	Wöschler	GER	9.6.91	1	WJ	Moncton	23 Jul 10
81.95		Jakub	Vadlejch	CZE	10.10.90	1		Domazlice	26 Sep 09
81.80		Sergey	Voynov	UZB	26.2.77	1		Tashkent	6 Jun 96
80.94		Aki	Parviainen	FIN	26.10.74	4	NC	Jyväskylä	5 Jul 92
80.57		Teemu	Wirkkala	FIN	14.1.84	1		Espoo	14 Sep 03

DECATHLON

8397		Torsten	Voss	GDR	24.3.63	1	NC	Erfurt	7 Jul 82
	10.76	7.66	14.41	2.09	48.37		14.37	41.76 4.80 62.90	4:34.04
8257		Yordani	Garcia	CUB	21.11.88	8	WCh	Osaka	1 Sep 07
	10.73/0.7	7.15/0.2	14.94	2.09	49.25		14.08/-0.2	42.91 4.70 68.74	4:55.42
8114		Michael	Kohnle	FRG	3.5.70	1	EJ	Varazdin	26 Aug 89
	10.95	7.09/0.1	15.27	2.02	49.91		14.40	45.82 4.90 60.82	4:49.43
8104		Valter	Külvet	EST	19.2.64	1		Viimsi	23 Aug 81
	10.7	7.26	13.86	2.09	48.5		14.8	47.92 4.50 60.34	4:37.8
8082		Daley	Thompson	GBR	30.7.58	1	ECp/s	Sittard	31 Jul 77
	10.70/0.8	7.54/0.7	13.84	2.01	47.31		15.26/2.0	41.70 4.70 54.48	4:30.4
8041		Qi Haifeng		CHN	7.8.83	1	AsiG	Busan	10 Oct 02
	11.09/0.2	7.22/0.0	13.05	2.06	49.09		14.54/0.0	43.16 4.80 61.04	4:35.17
8036		Christian	Schenk	GDR	9.2.65	5		Potsdam	21 Jul 84
	11.54	7.18	14.26	2.16	49.23		15.06	44.74 4.20 65.98	4:24.11
7992		Kevin	Mayer	FRA	10.2.92	8		Kladno	16 Jun 11
	11.23/0.1	7.34/0.2	12.44	2.01	48.66		14.74/-2.0	38.64 4.90 60.96	4:19.79
7938		Frank	Busemann	GER	26.2.75	1		Zeven	2 Oct 94
	10.68/1.6	7.37/1.1	13.08	2.03	50.41		14.34/-1.1	43.44 4.40 63.00	4:37.31
7913		Raul	Duany	CUB	4.1.75	2		La Habana	26 May 94
	11.50	7.13	13.99	2.10	49.70		14.77	37.76 4.50 65.58	4:24.03

Mark	Wind	Name		Nat	Born	Pos	Meet	Venue			Date

IAAF Junior specification with 99cm 110mh, 6kg shot, 1.75kg Discus

8131		Arkadiy	Vasilyev	RUS	19.1.87	1		Sochi			27 May 06
	11.28/-0.8	7.70/2.0	14.59	2.00	49.17		14.67/0.6	46.30	4.70	56.96	4:32.10
8126		Andrey	Kravchenko	BLR	4.1.86	1	WJ	Grosseto			15 Jul 04
	11.09/-0.5	7.46-0.2	14.51	2.16	48.98		14.55*/0.4	43.41	4.50	52.84	4:28.46
8124		Kévin	Mayer	FRA	10.2.92	1	EJ	Tallin			24 Jul 11
	11.40/-1.7	7.52/1.5	14.65	2.04	49.41		14.09/0.7	41.00	4.80	56.60	4:25.23

10,000 METRES WALK

38:46.4	Viktor	Burayev	RUS	23.8.82	1	NC-j	Moskva	20 May 00
38:54.75	Ralf	Kowalsky	GDR	22.3.62	1		Cottbus	24 Jun 81
39:08.23	Daisuke	Matsunaga	JPN	24.3.95	1		Tama	14 Dec 13
39:28.45	Andrey	Ruzavin	RUS	28.3.86	1	EJ	Kaunas	23 Jul 05
39:35.01	Stanislav	Yemelyanov	RUS	23.10.90	1	WJ	Bydgoszcz	11 Jul 08
39:44.71	Giovanni	De Benedictis	ITA	8.1.68	1	EJ	Birmingham	7 Aug 87
39:47.20		Chen Ding	CHN	5.8.92	2	WJ	Bydgoszcz	11 Jul 08
39:49.22		Pei Chuang	CHN	5.12.81	2	NSG	Chengdu	8 Sep 00
39:49.44		Li Tianlei	CHN	13.1.95	4		Tianjin	16 Sep 12
39:50.32		Cui Jin	CHN	1.12.87	2		Jinzhou	30 Aug 06

20 KILOMETRES WALK

1:18:06	Viktor	Burayev	RUS	23.8.82	2	NC-w	Adler	4 Mar 01
1:18:07		Li Gaobo	CHN	23.7.89	4		Cixi	23 Apr 05
1:18:44		Chu Yafei	CHN	5.9.88	5		Yangzhou	22 Apr 06
1:18:52		Chen Ding	CHN	5.8.92	3		Taicang	22 Apr 11
1:18:57		Bai Xuejin	CHN	6.6.87	7		Yangzhou	22 Apr 06
1:19:02	Éder	Sánchez	MEX	21.5.86	11		Cixi	23 Apr 05
1:19:14		Xu Xingde	CHN	12.6.84	3	NC	Yangzhou	12 Apr 03
1:19:34		Li Jianbo	CHN	14.11.86	16		Cixi	23 Apr 05
1:19:38		Yu Guohui	CHN	30.4.77	2	NC	Zhuhai	10 Mar 96
1:19:47		Wang Hao	CHN	16.8.89	4	OG	Beijing	16 Aug 08

4 x 100 METRES RELAY

38.66	USA	Kimmons, Omole, I Williams, L Merritt	1	WJ	Grosseto	18 Jun 04
38.97	JAM	Tracey, Skeen, Minzie, Murphy	2	WJ	Barcelona	14 Jul 12
39.01	JPN	Oseto, Hashimoto, Cambridge, Kanamori	1h1	WJ	Barcelona	13 Jul 12
39.05	GBR	Edgar, Grant, Benjamin, Lewis-Francis	1	WJ	Santiago de Chile	22 Oct 00
39.17	TRI	Simpson, Burns, Holder, Brown	3	WJ	Kingston	21 Jul 02
39.25	FRG	Dobeleit, Klameth, Evers, Lübke	1	EJ	Schwechat	28 Aug 83
39.29	BRA	de Araújo, Monteiro, R dos Santos Jnr, Rocha	2h1	WJ	Barcelona	13 Jul 12
39.31	POL	Bijowski, Slowikowski, Zalewski, Jabłonski	3h1	WJ	Barcelona	13 Jul 12

4 x 400 METRES RELAY

3:01.09	USA	B Johnson, L Merritt, Craig, Clement	1	WJ	Grosseto	18 Jul 04
3:03.80	GBR	Grindley, Patrick, Winrow, Richardson	2	WJ	Plovdiv	12 Aug 90
3:04.06	JAM	S Clarke, Bolt, Myers, Gonzales	2	WJ	Kingston	21 Jul 02
3:04.22	CUB	Cadogan, Mordoche, González, Hernández	2	WJ	Athína	20 Jul 86
3:04.50	RSA	le Roux, Gebhardt, Julius, van Zyl	2	WJ	Grosseto	18 Jul 04
3:04.58	GDR	Preusche, Löper, Trylus, Carlowitz	1	EJ	Utrecht	23 Aug 81
3:04.74	AUS	McFarlane, Batman, Thom, Vincent	1	WJ	Annecy	2 Aug 98
3:04.87	RUS	Peremetov, Savin, Khasanov, Ivashko	1	EJ	Rieti	21 Jul 13

JUNIOR WOMEN'S ALL-TIME LISTS

100 METRES

10.88	2.0	Marlies	Oelsner	GDR	21.3.58	1	NC	Dresden	1 Jul 77
10.89	1.8	Katrin	Krabbe	GDR	22.11.69	1rB		Berlin	20 Jul 88
11.03	1.7	Silke	Gladisch	GDR	20.6.64	3	OD	Berlin	8 Jun 83
11.03	0.6	English	Gardner	USA	22.4.92	1	Pac10	Tucson	14 May 11
11.04	1.4	Angela	Williams	USA	30.1.80	1	NCAA	Boise	5 Jun 99
11.07	0.7	Bianca	Knight	USA	2.1.89	4q2	NC/OT	Eugene	27 Jun 08
11.08	2.0	Brenda	Morehead	USA	5.10.57	1	OT	Eugene	21 Jun 76
11.11	0.2	Shakedia	Jones	USA	15.3.79	1		Los Angeles (Ww)	2 May 98
11.11	1.1	Joan Uduak	Ekah	NGR	16.12.80	5	Athl	Lausanne	2 Jul 99
11.12	2.0	Veronica	Campbell	JAM	15.5.82	1	WJ	Santiago de Chile	18 Oct 00
11.12	1.2	Alexandria	Anderson	USA	28.1.87	1	NC-j	Indianapolis	22 Jun 06
11.12	1.1	Aurieyall	Scott	USA	18.5.92	1	NC-j	Eugene	24 Jun 11

Uncertain timing: 10.99 1.9 Natalya Bochina RUS 4.1.62 2 Leningrad 3 Jun 80
Wind assisted to 11.11

10.96	3.7	Angela	Williams	USA	30.1.80	1		Las Vegas	3 Apr 99
10.97	3.3	Gesine	Walther	GDR	6.10.62	4	NC	Cottbus	16 Jul 80

Mark	Wind	Name		Nat	Born	Pos	Meet	Venue	Date
11.02	2.1	Nikole	Mitchell	JAM	5.6.74	1	Mutual	Kingston	1 May 93
11.04	5.6	Kelly-Ann	Baptiste	TRI	14.10.86	1rB	TexR	Austin	9 Apr 05
11.06	2.2	Brenda	Morehead	USA	5.10.57	1s2	OT	Eugene	21 Jun 76
11.09		Angela	Williams	TRI	15.5.65	1		Nashville	14 Apr 84

200 METRES

Mark	Wind	Name		Nat	Born	Pos	Meet	Venue	Date
22.11A	-0.5	Allyson	Felix	USA	18.11.85	1		Ciudad de México	3 May 03
22.18			0.8			2	OG	Athína	25 Aug 04
22.19	1.5	Natalya	Bochina	RUS	4.1.62	2	OG	Moskva	30 Jul 80
22.37	1.3	Sabine	Rieger	GDR	6.11.63	2	vURS	Cottbus	26 Jun 82
22.42	0.4	Gesine	Walther	GDR	6.10.62	1		Potsdam	29 Aug 81
22.43	0.8	Bianca	Knight	USA	2.1.89	1	Reebok	New York (RI)	31 May 08
22.45	0.5	Grit	Breuer	GER	16.2.72	2	ASV	Köln	8 Sep 91
22.45	0.9	Shaunae	Miller	BAH	15.4.94	2	NC	Freeport	22 Jun 13
22.51	2.0	Katrin	Krabbe	GDR	22.11.69	3		Berlin	13 Sep 88
22.52	1.2	Mary	Onyali	NGR	3.2.68	6	WCh	Roma	3 Sep 87
22.53	0.2	Anthonique	Strachan	BAH	22.8.93	1	WJ	Barcelona	13 Jul 12
22.58	0.8	Marion	Jones	USA	12.10.75	4	TAC	New Orleans	28 Jun 92
Indoors									
22.40		Bianca	Knight	USA	2.1.89	1r2	NCAA	Fayetteville	15 Mar 08
22.49		Sanya	Richards	USA	26.2.85	2rA	NCAA	Fayetteville	12 Mar 04
Wind assisted									
22.25	5.6	Bianca	Knight	USA	2.1.89	5	NC/OT	Eugene	6 Jul 08
22.34	2.3	Katrin	Krabbe	GDR	22.11.69	1	WJ	Sudbury	30 Jul 88
22.41	3.1	Shaunae	Miller	BAH	15.4.94	1		Athens, GA	13 Apr 13
22.49	2.3	Brenda	Morehead	USA	5.10.57	1	OT	Eugene	24 Jun 76
22.53	2.5	Valerie	Brisco	USA	6.7.60	2	AAU	Walnut	17 Jun 79

400 METRES

Mark	Wind	Name		Nat	Born	Pos	Meet	Venue	Date
49.42		Grit	Breuer	GER	16.2.72	2	WCh	Tokyo	27 Aug 91
49.77		Christina	Brehmer	GDR	28.2.58	1		Dresden	9 May 76
49.89		Sanya	Richards	USA	26.2.85	2	NC/OT	Sacramento	17 Jul 04
50.01			Li Jing	CHN	14.2.80	1	NG	Shanghai	18 Oct 97
50.19		Marita	Koch	GDR	18.2.57	3	OD	Berlin	10 Jul 76
50.50		Ashley	Spencer	USA	8.6.93	1	WJ	Barcelona	13 Jul 12
50.59		Fatima	Yusuf	NGR	2.5.71	1	HGP	Budapest	5 Aug 90
50.70		Shaunae	Miller	BAH	15.4.94	2	NCAA	Eugene	7 Jun 13
50.74		Monique	Henderson	USA	18.2.83	1		Norwalk	3 Jun 00
50.78		Danijela	Grgic	CRO	28.9.88	1	WJ	Beijing	17 Aug 06
50.86		Charity	Opara	NGR	20.5.72	2		Bologna	7 Sep 91

800 METRES

Mark	Wind	Name		Nat	Born	Pos	Meet	Venue	Date
1:54.01		Pamela	Jelimo	KEN	5.12.89	1	WK	Zürich	29 Aug 08
1:55.45		Caster	Semenya	RSA	7.1.91	1	WCh	Berlin	19 Aug 09
1:56.59		Francine	Niyonsaba	BDI	5.5.93	1	VD	Bruxelles	7 Sep 12
1:57.18			Wang Yuan	CHN	8.4.76	2h2	NG	Beijing	8 Sep 93
1:57.45		Hildegard	Ullrich	GDR	20.12.59	5	EC	Praha	31 Aug 78
1:57.62			Lang Yinglai	CHN	22.8.79	1	NG	Shanghai	22 Oct 97
1:57.63		Maria	Mutola	MOZ	27.10.72	4	WCh	Tokyo	26 Aug 91
1:57.77			Lu Yi	CHN	10.4.74	4	NG	Beijing	9 Sep 93
1:57.86		Katrin	Wühn	GDR	19.11.65	1		Celje	5 May 84
1:58.16			Lin Nuo	CHN	18.1.80	3	NG	Shanghai	22 Oct 97
1:58.18		Marion	Hübner	GDR	29.9.62	2		Erfurt	2 Aug 81
1:58.21		Ajee'	Wilson	USA	8.5.94	6	WCh	Moskva	18 Aug 13

1500 METRES

Mark	Wind	Name		Nat	Born	Pos	Meet	Venue	Date
3:51.34			Lang Yinglai	CHN	22.8.79	2	NG	Shanghai	18 Oct 97
3:53.91			Yin Lili	CHN	11.11.79	3	NG	Shanghai	18 Oct 97
3:53.97			Lan Lixin	CHN	14.2.79	4	NG	Shanghai	18 Oct 97
3:54.52			Zhang Ling	CHN	13.4.80	5	NG	Shanghai	18 Oct 97
3:56.98		Faith	Kipyegon	KEN	10.1.94	2	DL	Doha	10 May 13
3:59.60		Gelete	Burka	ETH	15.2.86	5	GP	Rieti	28 Aug 05
3:59.81			Wang Yuan	CHN	8.4.76	7	NG	Beijing	11 Sep 93
3:59.96		Zola	Budd	GBR	26.5.66	3	VD	Bruxelles	30 Aug 85
4:00.05			Lu Yi	CHN	10.4.74	8	NG	Beijing	11 Sep 93
4:01.71			Li Ying	CHN	24.6.75	4h2	NG	Beijing	10 Sep 93
4:02.98		Kalkedan	Gezahegn	ETH	8.5.91	3	Tsik	Athína	13 Jul 09
4:03.45		Anita	Weyermann	SUI	8.12.77	1	Athl	Lausanne	3 Jul 96

1 MILE: 4:17.57 Zola   Budd   GBR   26.5.66   3   WK   Zürich   21 Aug 85

2000 METRES: 5:33.15 Zola   Budd   GBR   26.5.66   1   London   13 Jul 84

Mark	Wind	Name		Nat	Born	Pos	Meet	Venue	Date

3000 METRES

Mark	Wind	Name		Nat	Born	Pos	Meet	Venue	Date
8:28.83		Zola	Budd	GBR	26.5.66	3	GG	Roma	7 Sep 85
8:35.89		Sally	Barsosio	KEN	21.3.78	2	Herc	Monaco	16 Aug 97
8:36.45			Ma Ningning	CHN	1.6.76	4	NC	Jinan	6 Jun 93
8:38.61		Kalkedan	Gezahegn	ETH	8.5.91	5	WAF	Thessaloníki	13 Sep 09
8:38.97		Linet	Masai	KEN	5.12.89	5	GP	Rieti	9 Sep 07
8:39.13		Agnes	Tirop	KEN	23.10.95	3		Rieti	8 Sep 13
8:39.65		Buze	Diriba	ETH-	9.2.94	3	Herc	Monaco	20 Jul 12
8:39.90		Gelete	Burka	ETH	15.2.86	3	SGP	Doha	13 May 05
8:40.08		Gabriela	Szabo	ROM	14.11.75	3	EC	Helsinki	10 Aug 94
8:40.28		Meseret	Defar	ETH	19.11.83	10	VD	Bruxelles	30 Aug 02
8:41.86		Tirunesh	Dibaba	ETH	2.6.85	11	VD	Bruxelles	30 Aug 02

5000 METRES

Mark	Wind	Name		Nat	Born	Pos	Meet	Venue	Date
14:30.88		Tirunesh	Dibaba	ETH	1.10.85	2	Bisl	Bergen (Fana)	11 Jun 04
14:35.18		Sentayehu	Ejigu	ETH	21.6.85	4	Bisl	Bergen (Fana)	11 Jun 04
14:39.96			Yin Lili	CHN	11.11.79	4	NG	Shanghai	23 Oct 97
14:43.29		Emebet	Anteneh	ETH	13.1.92	5	Bisl	Oslo	9 Jun 11
14:45.33			Lan Lixin	CHN	14.2.79	2h2	NG	Shanghai	21 Oct 97
14:45.71			Song Liqing	CHN	20.1.80	3h2	NG	Shanghai	21 Oct 97
14:45.90			Jiang Bo	CHN	13.3.77	1		Nanjing	24 Oct 95
14:45.98		Pauline	Korikwiang	KEN	1.3.88	7	Bisl	Oslo	2 Jun 06
14:46.71		Sally	Barsosio	KEN	21.3.78	3	VD	Bruxelles	22 Aug 97
14:47.13		Mercy	Cherono	KEN	7.5.91	7	DL	Shanghai	23 May 10
14:47.14		Linet	Masai	KEN	5.12.89	4	FBK	Hengelo	24 May 08

10,000 METRES

Mark	Wind	Name		Nat	Born	Pos	Meet	Venue	Date
30:26.50		Linet	Masai	KEN	5.12.89	4	OG	Beijing	15 Aug 08
30:31.55			Xing Huina	CHN	25.2.84	7	WCh	Saint-Denis	23 Aug 03
30:39.41			Lan Lixin	CHN	14.2.79	2	NG	Shanghai	19 Oct 97
30:39.98			Yin Lili	CHN	11.11.79	3	NG	Shanghai	19 Oct 97
30:59.92		Merima	Hashim	ETH	.81	3	NA	Heusden-Zolder	5 Aug 00
31:06.20		Lucy	Wangui	KEN	24.3.84	1rA		Okayama	27 Sep 03
31:11.26			Song Liqing	CHN	20.1.80	7	NG	Shanghai	19 Oct 97
31:15.38		Sally	Barsosio	KEN	21.3.78	3	WCh	Stuttgart	21 Aug 93
31:16.50		Evelyne	Kimwei	KEN	25.8.87	1		Kobe	21 Oct 06
31:17.30			Zhang Yingying	CHN	4.1.90	1		Wuhan	2 Nov 07
31:20.38		Tigist	Kiros	ETH	8.6.92	4	GS	Ostrava	31 May 11

MARATHON

Mark	Wind	Name		Nat	Born	Pos	Meet	Venue	Date
2:22:38			Zhang Yingying	CHN	4.1.90	1	NC	Xiamen	5 Jan 08
2:23:06		Merima	Mohamed	ETH	10.6.92	3		Toronto	26 Sep 10
2:23:37			Liu Min	CHN	29.11.83	1		Beijing	14 Oct 01
2:23:57			Zhu Xiaolin	CHN	20.4.84	4		Beijing	20 Oct 02
2:25:48			Jin Li	CHN	29.5.83	6		Beijing	14 Oct 01
2:26:34			Wei Yanan	CHN	6.12.81	1		Beijing	15 Oct 00
2:27:05			Chen Rong	CHN	18.5.88	1		Beijing	21 Oct 07
2:27:30			Ai Dongmei	CHN	15.10.79	3	NG	Beijing	4 Oct 97

3000 METRES STEEPLECHASE

Mark	Wind	Name		Nat	Born	Pos	Meet	Venue	Date
9:20.37		Birtukan	Adamu	ETH	29.4.92	4	GGala	Roma	26 May 11
9:22.51		Almaz	Ayana	ETH	21.11.91	3	VD	Bruxelles	27 Aug 10
9:24.51		Ruth	Bisibori	KEN	2.1.88	1		Daegu	3 Oct 07
9:26.25			Liu Nian	CHN	26.4.88	1		Wuhan	2 Nov 07
9:29.52		Korahubish	Itaa	ETH	28.2.92	1		Huelva	10 Jun 09
9:30.70		Melissa	Rollison	AUS	13.4.83	1	GWG	Brisbane	4 Sep 01
9:31.35		Christine	Muyanga	KEN	21.3.91	1	WJ	Bydgoszcz	10 Jul 08
9:32.74		Gesa-Felicitas	Krause	GER	3.8.92	9	WCh	Daegu	30 Aug 11
9:33.19		Karoline Bjerkeli	Grøvdal	NOR	14.6.90	4		Neerpelt	2 Jun 07
9:33.49		Elizabeth	Mueni	KEN	28.12.91	5	Bisl	Oslo	3 Jul 09

100 METRES HURDLES

Mark	Wind	Name		Nat	Born	Pos	Meet	Venue	Date
12.84	1.5	Aliuska	López	CUB	29.8.69	2	WUG	Zagreb	16 Jul 87
12.88	1.5	Yelena	Ovcharova	UKR	17.6.76	2	ECp	Villeneuve d'Ascq	25 Jun 95
12.89	1.3	Anay	Tejeda	CUB	3.4.83	1		Padova	1 Sep 02
12.91	1.8	Kristina	Castlin	USA	7.7.88	1	NCAA-r	Gainesville	26 May 07
12.92	0.0		Sun Hongwei	CHN	24.11.79	6	NG	Shanghai	18 Oct 97
12.95	1.5	Candy	Young	USA	21.5.62	2	AAU	Walnut	16 Jun 79
12.95A	1.5	Cinnamon	Sheffield	USA	8.3.70	2	NCAA	Provo	3 Jun 89
12.98	1.8	Queen	Harrison	USA	10.9.88	5	NCAA	Sacramento	8 Jun 07
13.00	0.7	Gloria	Kovarik	GDR	13.1.64	3h2	NC	Karl-Marx-Stadt	16 Jun 83

Mark	Wind	Name		Nat	Born	Pos	Meet	Venue	Date
13.00	2.0	Lyudmila	Khristosenko	UKR	14.10.66	1	NC-j	Krasnodar	16 Jul 85
13.01	0.4	Sally	McLellan	AUS	19.9.86	1		Brisbane	27 Nov 05

Wind assisted to 12.99

Mark	Wind	Name		Nat	Born	Pos	Meet	Venue	Date
12.81	3.4	Anay	Tejeda	CUB	3.4.83	1	WJ	Kingston	21 Jul 02
12.82	2.1	Kristina	Castlin	USA	7.7.88	1		College Park	21 Apr 07
12.90	3.0	Adrianna	Lamalle	FRA	27.9.82	1		Fort-de-France	28 Apr 01
12.95	2.4	Shermaine	Williams	JAM	4.2.90	1	NCAA II	San Angelo	23 May 09

400 METRES HURDLES

Mark	Name		Nat	Born	Pos	Meet	Venue	Date
54.40		Wang Xing	CHN	30.11.86	2	NG	Nanjing	21 Oct 05
54.58	Ristananna	Tracey	JAM	5.9.92	2	NC	Kingston	24 Jun 11
54.70	Lashinda	Demus	USA	10.3.83	1	WJ	Kingston	19 Jul 02
54.93		Li Rui	CHN	22.11.79	1	NG	Shanghai	22 Oct 97
55.11	Kaliese	Spencer	JAM	6.4.87	1	WJ	Beijing	17 Aug 06
55.15		Huang Xiaoxiao	CHN	3.3.83	2	NG	Guangzhou	22 Nov 01
55.20	Lesley	Maxie	USA	4.1.67	2	TAC	San Jose	9 Jun 84
55.20A	Jana	Pittman	AUS	9.11.82	1		Pietersburg	18 Mar 00
55.22	Tiffany	Ross	USA	5.2.83	2	NCAA	Baton Rouge	31 May 02
55.26	Ionela	Tirlea	ROM	9.2.76	1	Nik	Nice	12 Jul 95

Drugs disqualification: 54.54 Peng Yinghua ¶ CHN 21.2.79 (2) NG Shanghai 22 Oct 97

HIGH JUMP

Mark	Name		Nat	Born	Pos	Meet	Venue	Date
2.01	Olga	Turchak	UKR	5.3.67	2	GWG	Moskva	7 Jul 86
2.01	Heike	Balck	GDR	19.8.70	1	vURS-j	Karl-Marx-Stadt	18 Jun 89
2.00	Stefka	Kostadinova	BUL	25.3.65	1		Sofiya	25 Aug 84
2.00	Alina	Astafei	ROM	7.6.69	1	WJ	Sudbury	29 Jul 88
1.98	Silvia	Costa	CUB	4.5.64	2	WUG	Edmonton	11 Jul 83
1.98	Yelena	Yelesina	RUS	5.4.70	1	Druzh	Nyiregyháza	13 Aug 88
1.97	Svetlana	Isaeva	BUL	18.3.67	2		Sofiya	25 May 86
1.97i	Mariya	Kuchina	RUS	14.1.93	1		Trinec	26 Jan 11
1.96A	Charmaine	Gale	RSA	27.2.64	1	NC-j	Bloemfontein	4 Apr 81
1.96i	Desislava	Aleksandrova	BUL	27.10.75	2	EI	Paris (B)	12 Mar 94
1.96	Marina	Kuptsova	RUS	22.12.81	1	NC	Tula	26 Jul 00
1.96	Blanka	Vlasic	CRO	8.11.83	1	WJ	Kingston	20 Jul 02
1.96	Airine	Palsyte	LTU	13.7.92	2	WUG	Shenzhen	21 Aug 11
1.96	Eleanor	Patterson	AUS	22.5.96	1	N.Sch	Townsville	7 Dec 13

POLE VAULT

Mark	Name		Nat	Born	Pos	Meet	Venue	Date
4.63i	Angelica	Bengtsson	SWE	8.7.93	2		Stockholm	22 Feb 11
4.58					1		Sollentuna	5 Jul 12
4.60i	Hanna	Sheleh	UKR	14.7.93	3		Donetsk	11 Feb 12
4.60i	Roberta	Bruni	ITA	8.3.94	1	NC	Ancona	17 Feb 13
4.52i	Katie	Byres	GBR	11.9.93	2		Nevers	18 Feb 12
4.50	Valeriya	Volik	RUS	11.5.89	1		Krasnodar	4 Jun 08
4.50	Liz	Parnov	AUS	9.5.94	1		Perth	17 Feb 12
4.48i	Silke	Spiegelburg	GER	17.3.86	2		Münster	25 Aug 05
4.47i	Yelena	Isinbayeva	RUS	3.6.82	1		Budapest	10 Feb 01
4.46					2	ISTAF	Berlin	31 Aug 01
4.46i		Zhang Yingning	CHN	6.1.90	1		Shanghai	15 Mar 07
4.45					1		Changsha	29 Oct 06

4.45i Zhao Yingying CHN 15.2.86 3 Madrid 24 Feb 05; 4.45i Li Ling CHN 6.7.89 1 Beijing 26 Feb 08 (& 4.45 1 Hangzhou 12 Apr 08; 4.45 Marianna Zachariadi CYP 25.2.90 2MedG Pescara 30 Jun 09; 4.45i Joana Kraft GER 27.7.91 4 NC Karlsruhe 28 Feb 10; **Exhibition:** 4.45 Yvonne Buschbaum GER 14.7.80 1 Zeiskam 17 Jul 99

LONG JUMP

Mark	Wind	Name		Nat	Born	Pos	Meet	Venue	Date
7.14	1.1	Heike	Daute	GDR	16.12.64	1	PTS	Bratislava	4 Jun 83
7.03	1.3	Darya	Klishina	RUS	15.1.91	1	Znam	Zhukovskiy	26 Jun 10
7.00	-0.2	Birgit	Grosshennig	GDR	21.2.65	2		Berlin	9 Jun 84
6.94	-0.5	Magdalena	Khristova	BUL	25.2.77	2		Kalamáta	22 Jun 96
6.91	0.0	Anisoara	Cusmir	ROM	28.6.62	1		Bucuresti	23 May 81
6.90	1.4	Beverly	Kinch	GBR	14.1.64	*	WCh	Helsinki	14 Aug 83
6.88	0.6	Natalya	Shevchenko	RUS	28.12.66	2		Sochi	26 May 84
6.84		Larisa	Baluta	UKR	13.8.65	2		Krasnodar	6 Aug 83
6.82	1.8	Fiona	May	GBR	12.12.69	*	WJ	Sudbury	30 Jul 88
6.81	1.6	Carol	Lewis	USA	8.8.63	1	TAC	Knoxville	20 Jun 82
6.81	1.4	Yelena	Davydova	KZK	16.11.67	1	NC-j	Krasnodar	17 Jul 85

Wind assisted

Mark	Wind	Name		Nat	Born	Pos	Meet	Venue	Date
7.27	2.2	Heike	Daute	GDR	16.12.64	1	WCh	Helsinki	14 Aug 83
6.93	4.6	Beverly	Kinch	GBR	14.1.64	5	WCh	Helsinki	14 Aug 83
6.88	2.1	Fiona	May	GBR	12.12.69	1	WJ	Sudbury	30 Jul 88
6.84	2.8	Anu	Kaljurand	EST	16.4.69	2		Riga	4 Jun 88

Jnr WOMEN All-time

Mark	Wind	Name		Nat	Born	Pos	Meet	Venue	Date

TRIPLE JUMP

Mark	Wind	Name		Nat	Born	Pos	Meet	Venue	Date
14.62	1.0	Tereza	Marinova	BUL	5.9.77	1	WC	Sydney	25 Aug 96
14.57	0.2		Huang Qiuyan	CHN	25.1.80	1	NG	Shanghai	19 Oct 97
14.52	0.6	Anastasiya	Ilyina	RUS	16.1.82	q	WJ	Santiago de Chile	20 Oct 00
14.46	1.0		Peng Fengmei	CHN	2.7.79	1		Chengdu	18 Apr 98
14.43	0.6	Kaire	Leibak	EST	21.5.88	1	WJ	Beijing	17 Aug 06
14.38	-0.7		Xie Limei	CHN	27.6.86	1	AsiC	Inchon	1 Sep 05
14.37i	-		Ren Ruiping	CHN	1.2.76	3	WI	Barcelona	11 Mar 95
	14.36		0.0			1	NC	Beijing	1 Jun 94
14.36	0.0	Dailenys	Alcántara	CUB	10.8.91	3	Barr/NC	La Habana	29 May 09
14.35		Yana	Borodina	RUS	21.4.92	1J	Mosc Ch	Moskva	15 Jun 11
14.32	-0.1	Yelena	Lysak ¶	RUS	19.10.75	1		Voronezh	18 Jun 94
14.29	1.2	Mabel	Gay	CUB	5.5.83	1		La Habana	5 Apr 02
Wind assisted									
14.83	8.3		Ren Ruiping	CHN	1.2.76	1	NC	Taiyuan	21 May 95
14.43	2.7	Yelena	Lysak ¶	RUS	19.10.75	1	WJ	Lisboa	21 Jul 94

SHOT

Mark	Wind	Name		Nat	Born	Pos	Meet	Venue	Date
20.54		Astrid	Kumbernuss	GDR	5.2.70	1	vFIN-j	Orimattila	1 Jul 89
20.51i		Heidi	Krieger	GDR	20.7.65	2		Budapest	8 Feb 84
	20.24					5		Split	30 Apr 84
20.23		Ilke	Wyludda	GDR	28.3.69	1	NC-j	Karl-Marx-Stadt	16 Jul 88
20.12		Ilona	Schoknecht	GDR	24.9.56	2	NC	Erfurt	23 Aug 75
20.02			Cheng Xiaoyan	CHN	30.11.75	3	NC	Beijing	5 Jun 94
19.90		Stephanie	Storp	FRG	28.11.68	1		Hamburg	16 Aug 87
19.63			Wang Yawen	CHN	23.8.73	1		Shijiazhuang	25 Apr 92
19.57		Grit	Haupt	GDR	4.6.66	1		Gera	7 Jul 84
19.48		Ines	Wittich	GDR	14.11.69	5		Leipzig	29 Jul 87
19.46			Gong Lijiao	CHN	24.1.89	Q	OG	Beijing	16 Aug 08
19.42		Simone	Michel	GDR	18.12.60	3	vSU	Leipzig	23 Jun 79

DISCUS

Mark	Wind	Name		Nat	Born	Pos	Meet	Venue	Date
74.40		Ilke	Wyludda	GDR	28.3.69	2		Berlin	13 Sep 88
	75.36	unofficial meeting				2		Berlin	6 Sep 88
67.38		Irina	Meszynski	GDR	24.3.62	1		Berlin	14 Aug 81
67.00		Jana	Günther	GDR	7.1.68	6	NC	Potsdam	20 Aug 87
66.80		Svetla	Mitkova	BUL	17.6.64	1		Sofiya	2 Aug 83
66.60		Astrid	Kumbernuss	GDR	5.2.70	1		Berlin	20 Jul 88
66.34		Franka	Dietzsch	GDR	22.1.68	2		Saint-Denis	11 Jun 87
66.30		Jana	Lauren	GDR	28.6.70	1	vURS-j	Karl-Marx-Stadt	18 Jun 89
66.08			Cao Qi	CHN	15.1.74	1	NG	Beijing	12 Sep 93
65.96		Grit	Haupt	GDR	4.6.66	3		Leipzig	13 Jul 84
65.22		Daniela	Costian	ROM	30.4.65	3		Nitra	26 Aug 84

HAMMER

Mark	Wind	Name		Nat	Born	Pos	Meet	Venue	Date
73.24			Zhang Wenxiu	CHN	22.3.86	1	NC	Changsha	24 Jun 05
71.71		Kamila	Skolimowska	POL	4.11.82	1	GPF	Melbourne	9 Sep 01
70.39		Mariya	Smolyachkova	BLR	10.2.85	1		Staiki	26 Jun 04
70.62		Alexandra	Tavernier	FRA	13.12.93	1	WJ	Barcelona	14 Jul 12
69.73		Natalya	Zolotukhina	UKR	4.1.85	1		Kiev	24 Jul 04
69.63		Bianca	Perie	ROU	1.6.90	1	NC-j	Bucuresti	14 Aug 09
68.74		Arasay	Thondike	CUB	28.5.86	2	Barr	La Habana	2 May 05
68.50		Martina	Danisová	SVK	21.3.83	1		Kladno	16 Jun 01
68.49		Anna	Bulgakova	RUS	17.1.88	6		Sochi	26 May 07
68.40		Bianca	Achilles	GER	17.4.81	1		Dortmund	25 Sep 99
68.26		Katerina	Safránková	CZE	8.6.89	1		Pardubice	7 May 08

JAVELIN

Mark	Wind	Name		Nat	Born	Pos	Meet	Venue	Date
63.01		Vira	Rebryk	UKR	25.2.89	1	WJ	Bydgoszcz	10 Jul 08
62.93			Xue Juan	CHN	10.2.86	1	NG	Changsha	27 Oct 03
62.09			Zhang Li	CHN	17.1.89	1		Beijing	25 May 08
61.99			Wang Yaning	CHN	4.1.80	1	NC	Huizhou	14 Oct 99
61.96		Sofi	Flink	SWE	8.7.95	Q	WCh	Moskva	16 Aug 13
61.79		Nikolett	Szabó	HUN	3.3.80	1		Schwechat	23 May 99
61.61			Chang Chunfeng	CHN	4.5.88	1	NC-j	Chengdu	4 Jun 07
61.49			Liang Lili	CHN	16.11.83	1	NC	Benxi	1 Jun 02
61.40		Sofi	Flinck	SWE	8.7.95	1	WJ	Barcelona	11 Jul 12
61.38		Annika	Suthe	GER	15.10.85	1-j		Halle	23 May 04
Pre 1999 specification									
71.88		Antoaneta	Todorova	BUL	8.6.63	1	ECp	Zagreb	15 Aug 81
71.82		Ivonne	Leal	CUB	27.2.66	1	WUG	Kobe	30 Aug 85

Mark	Wind	Name		Nat	Born	Pos	Meet	Venue	Date
70.12		Karen	Forkel	GDR	24.9.70	1	EJ	Varazdin	26 Aug 89
68.94		Trine	Solberg	NOR	18.4.66	1	vURS	Oslo	16 Jul 85

HEPTATHLON

6768w		Tatyana	Chernova	RUS	29.1.88	1		Arles	3 Jun 07
13.04w/6.1	1.82	13.57	23.59w/5.2	6.61/1.2	53.43	2:15.05
6227						1	WJ	Beijing	19 Aug 06
13.70/1.6	1.80	12.18	24.05/0.3	6.35/-0.4	50.51	2:25.49
6542		Carolina	Klüft	SWE	2.2.83	1	EC	München	10 Aug 02
13.33/-0.3	1.89	13.16	23.71/-0.3	6.36/1.1	47.61	2:17.99
6465		Sibylle	Thiele	GDR	6.3.65	1	EJ	Schwechat	28 Aug 83
13.49	1.90	14.63	24.07	6.65	36.22	2:18.36
6436		Sabine	Braun	FRG	19.6.65	1	vBUL	Mannheim	9 Jun 84
13.68	1.78	13.09	23.88	6.03	52.14	2:09.41
6428		Svetla	Dimitrova ¶	BUL	27.1.70	1	NC	Sofiya	18 Jun 89
13.49/-0.7	1.77	13.98	23.59/-0.2	6.49/0.7	40.10	2:11.10
6403		Emilia	Dimitrova	BUL	13.11.67	6	GWG	Moskva	7 Jul 86
13.73	1.76	13.46	23.17	6.29	43.30	2:09.85
6298		Nafissatou	Thiam	BEL	19.8.94	1	EJ	Rieti	19 Jul 13
13.87/1.2	1.89	14.26	25.15/-0.6	6.37/0.1	46.94	2:24.89
6276		Larisa	Nikitina	RUS	29.4.65	8	URS Ch	Kiyev	21 Jun 84
13.87/1.6	1.86	14.04	25.26/-0.7	6.31/0.1	48.62	2:22.76
6267		Katarina	Johnson-Thompson	GBR	9.1.93	15	OG	London (OS)	4 Aug 12
13.48/0.9	1.89	11.32	23.73/-0.3	6.19/-0.4	38.37	2:10.76
6218		Jana	Sobotka	GDR	3.10.65	6	OD	Potsdam	21 Jul 84
14.40	1.74	13.28	24.19	6.27	43.64	2:06.83
Drugs disqualification: 6534 Svetla Dimitrova	BUL	27.1.70	(3)	ECp	Helmond	16 Jul 89
13.30/1.0	1.84	14.35	23.33/-2.2	6.47/-1.4	39.20	2:13.56

10 KILOMETRES WALK

41:52		Tatyana	Mineyeva	RUS	10.8.90	1	NCp-j	Penza	5 Sep 09
41:55		Irina	Stankina	RUS	25.3.77	1	NC-wj	Adler	11 Feb 95
41:57			Gao Hongmiao	CHN	17.3.74	2	NG	Beijing	8 Sep 93
42:15+		Anisya	Kirdyapkina	RUS	23.10.89	1=	in 20k	Adler	23 Feb 08
42:29		Tatyana	Kalmykova	RUS	10.1.90	1	NC-wj	Adler	23 Feb 08
42:31		Irina	Yumanova	RUS	17.6.90	2	NC-wj	Adler	23 Feb 08
42:43.0	t	Svetlana	Vasilyeva	RUS	24.7.92	1	NC-wj	Sochi	27 Feb 11
42:44			Long Yuwen	CHN	1.8.75	3	NC	Shenzen	18 Feb 93
42:45			Li Yuxin	CHN	4.12.74	4		Shenzhen	18 Feb 93
42:45		Kseniya	Trifonova	RUS	7.5.90	2	NC-wj	Adler	28 Feb 09

20 KILOMETRES WALK

1:25:30		Anisya	Kirdyapkina	RUS	23.10.89	2	NC-w	Adler	23 Feb 08
1:26:36		Tatyana	Kalmykova	RUS	10.1.90	1	NC	Saransk	8 Jun 08
1:27:01			Lu Xiuzhi	CHN	26.10.93	2		Taicang	30 Mar 12
1:27:16			Song Hongjuan	CHN	4.7.84	1	NC	Yangzhou	14 Apr 03
1:27:34			Jiang Jing	CHN	23.10.85	2	WCp	Naumburg	2 May 04
1:27:35		Natalya	Fedoskina	RUS	25.6.80	2	WCp	Mézidon-Canon	2 May 99

4 X 100 METRES RELAY

43.29	USA (Blue)	Knight, Tarmoh, Olear, Mayo			1		Eugene	8 Aug 06
43.40	JAM	Simpson, Stewart, McLaughlin, Facey			1	WJ	Kingston	20 Jul 02
43.42	GER	Burghardt, Grompe, Pinto, Frese			1	EJ	Tallinn	24 Jul 11
43.44A	NGR	Utondu, Iheagwam, Onyali, Ogunkoya			1	AfrG	Nairobi	9 Aug 87
43.48	GDR	Breuer, Krabbe, Dietz, Henke			1	WJ	Sudbury	31 Jul 88
		Unsanctioned race 43.33 Breuer, Krabbe, Dietz, Henke			1		Berlin	20 Jul 88
43.68	FRA	Vouaux, Jacques-Sebastien, Kamga, Banco			3	WJ	Grosseto	18 Jul 04
43.81	GBR	Miller, Asher-Smith, S Wilson, Henry			1	EJ	Rieti	21 Jul 13
43.87	URS	Lapshina, Doronina, Bulatova, Kovalyova			1	vGDR-j	Leningrad	20 Jun 87
43.98	BRA	Silva, Leoncio, Krasucki, Santos			2	PAm-J	São Paulo	7 Jul 07
44.04	CUB	Riquelme, Allen, López, Valdivia			2	WJ	Sudbury	31 Jul 88

4 X 400 METRES RELAY

3:27.60	USA	Anderson, Kidd, Smith, Hastings			1	WJ	Grosseto	18 Jul 04
3:28.39	GDR	Derr, Fabert, Wöhlk, Breuer			1	WJ	Sudbury	31 Jul 88
3:29.66	JAM	Stewart, Morgan, Walker, Hall			1	PennR	Philadelphia	28 Apr 01
3:30.03	RUS	Talko, Shapayeva, Soldatova, Kostetskaya			2	WJ	Grosseto	18 Jul 04
3:30.38	AUS	Scamps, R Poetschka, Hanigan, Andrews			1	WJ	Plovdiv	12 Aug 90
3:30.46	GBR	Wall, Spencer, James,. Miller			2	WJ	Kingston	21 Jul 02
3:30.72	BUL	Kireva, Angelova, Rashova, Dimitrova			3	v2N	Sofiya	24 Jul 83
3:30.84	NGR	Abugan, Odumosu, Eze, Adesanya			2	WJ	Beijing	20 Aug 06

Mark	Name		Nat	Born	Pos	Meet	Venue	Date	

MEN'S WORLD LISTS 2013

60 METRES INDOORS

Mark	Name		Nat	Born	Pos	Meet	Venue	Date	
6.48	Jimmy	Vicaut	FRA	27.2.92	1	EI	Göteborg	2	Mar
6.48	James	Dasaolu	GBR	5.9.87	2	EI	Göteborg	2	Mar
6.49A	DeAngelo	Cherry	USA	1.8.90	1	NC	Albuquerque	3	Mar
6.53					1h1	NCAA	Fayetteville	8	Mar
6.50	Darvis	Patton	USA	4.12.77	1	Mill	New York (Armory)	16	Feb
6.51	Yuniel	PérFez	CUB	16.2.85	1		Mondeville	2	Feb
6.51	Michael	Tumi	ITA	12.2.90	1	NC	Ancona	17	Feb
6.52	Lerone	Clarke	JAM	2.10.81	1		Düsseldorf	8	Feb
6.52		Dasaolu			1s2	EI	Göteborg	2	Mar
6.52		Tumi			3	EI	Göteborg	2	Mar
(9/7)									
6.53	Michael	Rodgers	USA	24.4.85	1	GP	Birmingham	16	Feb
6.53	Kim	Collins	SKN	5.4.76	1		Metz	24	Feb
6.54	Marvin	Bracy	USA	15.12.93	1	Tyson	Fayetteville	8	Feb
(10)									
6.54A	Reginald	Dixon	USA	7.6.88	2	NC	Albuquerque	3	Mar
6.55	Ángel David	Rodríguez	ESP	25.4.80	3		Düsseldorf	8	Feb
6.55	Su Bingtian		CHN	29.8.89	1rA		Nanjing	6	Mar
6.55	Marcus	Rowland	USA	11.3.90	2	NCAA	Fayetteville	9	Mar
6.56	Dentarius	Locke	USA	12.12.89	2	Tyson	Fayetteville	8	Feb
6.56	Nesta	Carter	JAM	11.10.85	2	GP	Birmingham	16	Feb
6.56	Julian	Reus	GER	29.4.88	1	NC	Dortmund	23	Feb
6.56A	Joe	Morris	USA	4.10.89	1		Air Force Academy	13	Dec
6.57	Darrell	Wesh	USA	21.1.92	2h1	NCAA	Fayetteville	8	Mar
6.58	Dwain	Chambers	GBR	5.4.78	1	v4N	Glasgow	26	Jan
(20)									
6.58A	Jeremy	Dodson	USA	30.8.87	3	NC	Albuquerque	3	Mar
6.58	Zhang Peimeng		CHN	13.3.87	1		Beijing	29	Mar
6.59	Jaysuma	Saidy Ndure	NOR	1.1.84	2s1	EI	Göteborg	2	Mar
6.59	Keith	Ricks	USA	9.10.90	1		Newport News	7	Dec
6.60	Yevgeniy	Ustavshchikov	RUS	20.7.88	1		Orenburg	1	Feb
6.60	Catalin	Cîmpeanu	ROU	10.3.85	1	NC	Bucuresti	9	Feb
6.60	Antoine	Adams	SKN	31.8.88	3	GP	Birmingham	16	Feb
6.60	Marquesh	Woodson	USA	6.9.93	1	SEC	Fayetteville	24	Feb
6.60	Charles	Silmon	USA	4.7.91	1h2	NCAA	Fayetteville	8	Mar
6.61	Sean	Safo-Antwi	GBR	31.10.90	1rB		London (Nh)	23	Jan
(30)									
6.61	Bryce	Robinson	USA	13.11.93	1h2		Lincoln	1	Feb
6.61	Cameron	Burrell	USA-J	11.9.94	1		Seattle	24	Feb
6.61	Harry	Adams	USA	27.11.89	4	NCAA	Fayetteville	9	Mar
6.62	Mark	Jelks	USA	10.4.84	1		Lawrence	25	Jan
6.62	Patrick	Chinedu	NGR	26.4.84	2		Orenburg	1	Feb
6.62	Egwero	Ogho-Oghene	NGR	26.11.88	2		Gent	10	Feb
6.62	Reza	Ghasemi	IRI	24.7.87	1		Tehran	14	Feb
6.62	Richard	Kilty	GBR	2.9.89	1		Gateshead	17	Feb
6.62	Odain	Rose	SWE	19.7.92	5	EI	Göteborg	2	Mar
6.62A	Cordero	Gray	USA	9.5.89	4	NC	Albuquerque	3	Mar
(40)									
6.63	Rion	Pierre	GBR	24.11.87	1rA2		London (LV)	26	Jan
6.63	Clayton	Vaughn	USA	15.5.92	1s3	Tyson	Fayetteville	8	Feb
6.63	Emmanuel	Biron	FRA	29.7.88	3	NC	Aubière	16	Feb
6.63	Tatum	Taylor	USA-J	8.9.94	2		Seattle	24	Feb
6.63	Harry	Aikines-Aryeetey	GBR	29.8.88	7	EI	Göteborg	2	Mar
6.64	Prezel	Hardy	USA	1.6.92	1		College Station	12	Jan
6.64	Jason	Rogers	SKN	31.8.91	1		Toronto	10	Feb
6.64	Christophe	Lemaitre	FRA	11.6.90	4		Gent	10	Feb
6.64	Gerald	Phiri	ZAM	6.10.88	2	Mill	New York (Armory)	16	Feb
6.64	Hugh	Graham	USA	10.10.92	1h5	SEC	Fayetteville	23	Feb
(50)									
6.64	Tevin	Hester	USA-J	10.1.94	3	ACC	Blacksburg	23	Feb
6.64	Levonte	Whitfield	USA	8.10.93	1h2		Seattle	24	Feb
6.64	Isaiah	Brandt-Sims	USA	26.4.89	3		Seattle	24	Feb
6.64A	Shane	Crawford	USA	4.6.88	6	NC	Albuquerque	3	Mar
6.65	five men								

+ intermediate time in longer race, A made at an altitude of 1000m or higher, D made in a decathlon, h made in a heat, qf quarter-final, sf semi-final, i indoors, Q qualifying round, r race number, -J juniors, -Y youths (b. 1996 or later)

Mark	Wind	Name		Nat	Born	Pos	Meet	Venue	Date

100 METRES

Mark	Wind	Name		Nat	Born	Pos	Meet	Venue	Date
9.77	-0.3	Usain	Bolt	JAM	21.8.86	1	WCh	Moskva	11 Aug
9.80	0.6		Bolt			1	VD	Bruxelles	6 Sep
9.85	0.2		Bolt			1rA	DL	London (OS)	26 Jul
9.85	-0.3	Justin	Gatlin	USA	10.2.82	2	WCh	Moskva	11 Aug
9.86	0.2	Tyson	Gay ¶?	USA	9.8.82	1		Kingston	4 May
9.87	1.5	Nesta	Carter	JAM	11.10.85	1		Madrid	13 Jul
9.89	1.1		Gatlin			2	NC	Des Moines	21 Jun
9.90	0.4	Nickel	Ashmeade	JAM	7.4.90	1s2	WCh	Moskva	11 Aug
9.90	-0.3		Bolt			1	WK	Zürich	29 Aug
9.90	0.6	Michael	Rodgers	USA	24.4.85	2	VD	Bruxelles	6 Sep
9.91	0.1		Gatlin			1		Beijing	21 May
9.91	1.1	James	Dasaolu	GBR	5.9.87	1s2	NC	Birmingham	13 Jul
9.92	0.1		Bolt			1s3	WCh	Moskva	11 Aug
9.93	0.1		Rodgers			2s3	WCh	Moskva	11 Aug
9.93	0.4	Kemar	Bailey-Cole	JAM	10.1.92	2s2	WCh	Moskva	11 Aug
9.94	0.8		Gatlin			1rA	GGala	Roma	6 Jun
9.94	-1.2		Bolt			1	NC	Kingston	21 Jun
9.94	-0.4		Gatlin			1	Herc	Monaco	19 Jul
9.94	-0.2		Gatlin			1s1	WCh	Moskva	11 Aug
9.94	-0.3		Ashmeade			2	WK	Zürich	29 Aug
9.94	0.6		Carter			3	VD	Bruxelles	6 Sep
9.94	0.6		Gatlin			4	VD	Bruxelles	6 Sep
9.95	0.8		Bolt			2rA	GGala	Roma	6 Jun
9.95	0.9	Jimmy	Vicaut	FRA	27.2.92	1h2	NC	Paris (C)	13 Jul
9.95	0.3		Vicaut			1	NC	Paris (C)	13 Jul
9.95	-0.4		Carter			3	WCh	Moskva	11 Aug
9.96	0.1		Rodgers			2		Beijing	21 May
9.96	1.5		Bailey-Cole			1		Kingston	8 Jun
9.96	2.0		Rodgers			3	Athl	Lausanne	4 Jul
9.96	-0.4	Dentarius	Locke	USA	12.12.89	2	Herc	Monaco	19 Jul
9.96	-0.3		Gatlin			3	WK	Zürich	29 Aug
		(31/10)							
9.97	2.0	Kim	Collins	SKN	5.4.76	4	Athl	Lausanne	4 Jul
9.98	1.9	Gabriel	Mvumvure	ZIM	23.4.88	1		Montverde, FL	8 Jun
9.98	1.1	Charles	Silmon	USA	4.7.91	3	NC	Des Moines	21 Jun
9.99	0.3	Isiah	Young	USA	5.1.90	1h3	NCAA-E	Greensboro	23 May
9.99	0.7	Walter	Dix	USA	31.1.86	1		Rieti	8 Sep
10.00	0.4	Christophe	Lemaitre	FRA	11.6.90	4s2	WCh	Moskva	11 Aug
10.00	0.4		Zhang Peimeng	CHN	13.3.87	5s2	WCh	Moskva	11 Aug
10.01	0.9	Yoshihide	Kiryu	JPN-J	15.12.95	1h3	Oda	Hiroshima	29 Apr
10.01	2.0	Antoine	Adams	SKN	31.8.88	1	NC	Basseterre	16 Jun
10.01	2.0	Jason	Rogers	SKN	31.8.91	2	NC	Basseterre	16 Jun
		(20)							
10.01	1.1	Rakieem 'Mookie'	Salaam	USA	5.4.90	5	NC	Des Moines	21 Jun
10.02	1.9	Ramon	Gittens	BAR	20.7.87	2		Montverde, FL	8 Jun
10.02	1.5	Warren	Weir	JAM	31.10.89	2		Kingston	8 Jun
10.02	2.0	Kemar	Hyman	CAY	11.10.89	1		La Chaux-de-Fonds	7 Jul
10.02	-0.3	Keston	Bledman	TTO	8.3.88	2h3	WCh	Moskva	10 Aug
10.03	1.7	Churandy	Martina	NED	3.7.84	1rB	Athl	Lausanne	4 Jul
10.04	1.9	Dwain	Chambers	GBR	5.4.78	1	NC	Birmingham	13 Jul
10.04	1.7	Jacques	Harvey	JAM	5.4.89	1		Ankara	24 Aug
10.05	1.9	Aaron	Brown	CAN	27.5.92	2s1	NCAA	Eugene	5 Jun
10.06	1.9	Diondre	Batson	USA	13.7.92	1		Athens, GA	13 Apr
		(30)							
10.06	0.1		Su Bingtian	CHN	29.8.89	3		Beijing	21 May
10.06	1.9	Derrick	Atkins	BAH	5.1.84	3		Montverde, FL	8 Jun
10.06	-0.3	Adam	Gemili	GBR	6.10.93	8	WK	Zürich	29 Aug
10.07	0.2	Darvis	Patton	USA	4.12.77	3		Kingston	4 May
10.07	1.6	Beejay	Lee	USA	5.3.93	1	Pac-12	Los Angeles	12 May
10.07	0.5	Jason	Livermore	JAM	25.4.88	3h1	NC	Kingston	20 Jun
10.07A	1.7	Andrew	Fisher	JAM	15.12.91	1h2	CAC	Morelia	5 Jul
10.07	0.0	Jaysuma	Saidy Ndure	NOR	1.1.84	1		Luzern	17 Jul
10.07	1.0	Martin	Keller	GER	26.9.86	1r6		Weinheim	2 Aug
10.08	1.2	Samuel	Francis	QAT	27.3.87	5	DL	Doha	10 May
		(40)							
10.08	0.1	Calesio	Newman	USA	20.8.86	4		Beijing	21 May
10.08	1.9	Harry	Aikines-Aryeetey	GBR	29.8.88	2	NC	Birmingham	13 Jul
10.08	0.5	Julian	Reus	GER	29.4.88	1r8		Weinheim	2 Aug

MEN 2013

Mark	Wind	Name		Nat	Born	Pos	Meet	Venue	Date
10.09A	2.0	Alex	Quiñónez	ECU	11.8.89	1		Medellín	25 May
10.09	1.8	Marvin	Bracy	USA	15.12.93	1		Lapinlahti	21 Jul
10.10	1.7	Anaso	Jobodwana	RSA	30.7.92	2q3	NCAA-E	Greensboro	24 May
10.10	0.1	Joel	Fearon	GBR	11.10.88	1h2		La Chaux-de-Fonds	7 Jul
10.10	0.0	Richard	Kilty	GBR	2.9.89	1		Hexham	31 Aug
10.10	0.7	Ryan	Bailey	USA	13.4.89	3		Rieti	8 Sep
10.11	0.7	Ryota	Yamagata	JPN	10.6.92	1	NC	Tokyo [Chofu]	8 Jun
		(50)							
10.11	1.7	Jeffrey	Demps	USA	8.1.90	1h5		Montverde, FL	8 Jun
10.11	1.0	Sheldon	Mitchell	JAM	19.7.90	1h3	NC	Kingston	20 Jun
10.12	1.0	Oshane	Bailey	JAM	9.8.89	2h3	NC	Kingston	20 Jun
10.12	1.8	Alex	Wilson	SUI	19.9.90	1		Bulle	6 Jul
10.12	0.8	Dontae	Richards-Kwok	CAN	1.3.89	1r9		Weinheim	2 Aug
10.12	2.0	Julian	Forte	JAM	1.7.93	1rB		Dubnica nad Váhom	21 Aug
10.13	1.9	Alonso	Edward	PAN	8.12.89	1h3		Clermont, FL	11 May
10.13	0.1	Keith	Ricks	USA	9.10.90	6		Beijing	21 May
10.13A	1.4	Andrew	Hinds	BAR	25.4.84	1h4	CAC	Morelia	5 Jul
10.14	1.6	Ameer	Webb	USA	19.3.91	1rB	TexR	Austin	30 Mar
		(60)							
10.14	0.9	Darrell	Wesh	USA	21.1.92	2	ACC	Raleigh	20 Apr
10.14	1.0	Sam	Effah	CAN	29.12.88	2		Los Angeles (ER)	4 May
10.14	1.9	Richard	Thompson	TTO	7.6.85	4		Montverde, FL	8 Jun
10.14	0.5	Winston	Barnes	JAM	7.11.88	4h1	NC	Kingston	20 Jun
10.14	1.9	Andrew	Robertson	GBR	17.12.90	3	NC	Birmingham	13 Jul
10.15	0.3	Jermaine	Hamilton	JAM	22.10.84	1		Montego Bay	9 Feb
10.15	0.2	Hassan	Taftian	IRI	4.5.93	1		Almaty	15 Jun
10.15	1.5	Kimmari	Roach	JAM	21.9.90	2		Sotteville-lès-Rouen	8 Jul
10.15	1.8	Ángel David	Rodríguez	ESP	25.4.80	5=		Madrid	13 Jul
10.16	1.1	Su'Waibou	Sanneh	GAM	30.10.90	1		New York	30 May
		(70)							
10.16	0.7	José Carlos	Moreira	BRA	28.9.83	1	NC	São Paulo	6 Jun
10.16	0.8	Adam	Harris	GUY	21.7.87	1		Colts Neck, NJ	8 Jun
10.16	-0.1	Egweru	Ogho-Oghene	NGR	26.11.88	1		Warri	14 Jun
10.16	1.5	Denis	Dimitrov	BUL-J	10.2.94	1	NC	Pravets	15 Jun
10.16	0.2	Reza	Ghasemi	IRI	24.7.87	2		Almaty	15 Jun
10.16	0.9	Kenroy	Anderson	JAM	27.6.87	2h2	NC	Kingston	20 Jun
10.16A	1.2	Shavez	Hart	BAH	9.6.92	1h3	CAC	Morelia	5 Jul
10.17	0.0	Jefferson	Lucindo	BRA	17.10.90	1		São Paulo	29 Jun
10.17	0.8	James	Ellington	GBR	6.9.85	6	DL	Birmingham	30 Jun
10.18	1.6	Aaron	Ernest	USA	8.11.93	2rB	TexR	Austin	30 Mar
		(80)							
10.18	0.5	Markesh	Woodson	USA	6.9.93	3	SEC	Columbia, MO	12 May
10.18A	-0.4	Jeff	Henderson	USA	19.2.89	1	NCAA-2	Pueblo, CO	25 May
10.18	1.5	Jason	Young	JAM	21.3.91	3=		Kingston	8 Jun
10.19	0.0	Ryan	Milus	USA	19.9.90	1		Tempe	27 Apr
10.19	0.1	Michael	Tumi	ITA	12.2.90	1		Gavardo	19 May
10.19	1.0	Dexter	Lee	JAM	18.1.91	3h4	NC	Kingston	20 Jun
10.19	1.9	Mark	Lewis-Francis	GBR	4.9.82	4	NC	Birmingham	13 Jul
10.19	0.4	Justyn	Warner	CAN	28.6.87	1r7		Weinheim	2 Aug
10.19	0.3	Takumi	Kuki	JPN	18.5.92	1s2		Tokyo	6 Sep
10.20	1.5	Dario	Horvat	CRO	25.2.92	1		Azusa	11 May
		(90)							
10.20	1.4	Rasheed	Dwyer	JAM	29.1.89	3		Kingston	18 May
10.20	0.5	Taffawee	Johnson	JAM	10.3.88	5h1	NC	Kingston	20 Jun
10.20	0.7	Gavin	Smellie	CAN	26.6.86	1h		Toronto	7 Jul
10.20	1.9	Josh	Swaray	GBR	2.2.86	5	NC	Birmingham	13 Jul
10.20	0.5	Sven	Knipphals	GER	20.9.85	2r8		Weinheim	2 Aug
10.21	0.3	Everton	Clarke	JAM	.92	2		Montego Bay	9 Feb
10.21	0.2	Rondell	Sorrillo	TTO	21.1.86	1		Baie Mahault	8 May
10.21	1.1	Adam	Zavacky	SVK	27.6.88	1		Hodonín	18 May
10.21	1.3	Tevin	Hester	USA-J	10.1.94	1h4	NCAA-E	Greensboro	23 May
10.21	0.9	Ramone	McKenzie	JAM	15.11.90	3h2	NC	Kingston	20 Jun
		(100)							
10.21	1.2	Hannes	Dreyer	RSA	13.1.85	1		Castres	30 Jun
10.21	0.5	Wilfried	Koffi Hua	CIV	24.9.85	3	WUG	Kazan	8 Jul
10.21	0.5	Sergiy	Smelyk	UKR	19.4.87	4	WUG	Kazan	8 Jul
10.21	0.4	Lucas	Jakubczyk	GER	28.4.85	2r7		Weinheim	2 Aug

Mark	Wind	Name		Nat	Born	Pos	Date		Mark	Wind	Name		Nat	Born	Pos	Date
10.22	1.3	Tony	McQuay	USA	16.4.90	5 Apr			10.22	1.9	Reggie	Lewis	USA	18.8.93	23 May
10.22	1.4	Trell	Kimmons	USA	13.7.85	20 Apr			10.22	0.8	Nicholas	Watson	JAM	16.9.89	25 May
10.22	-0.3	Bruno	de Barros	BRA	7.1.87	16 May			10.22	1.9	Carl	Horsley	USA	17.6.92	5 Jun
10.22	1.4	Harry	Adams	USA	27.11.89	23 May			10.22	1.9	Brian	Witherspoon	USA	5.6.85	8 Jun

Mark	Wind	Name		Nat	Born	Pos	Meet	Venue		Date
10.22	0.2	Emmanuel	Biron	FRA	29.7.88					27 Jun
10.22	1.2	Arnaud	Rémy	FRA	19.8.86					30 Jun
10.22	1.2	Roscoe	Engel	RSA	6.3.89					30 Jun
10.22	0.3	Shota	Iizuka	JPN	25.6.91					6 Sep
10.23	0.0	Ahmed	Ali	USA	15.11.93					6 Apr
10.23	1.9	Johnathan	Smith	USA	15.9.92					13 Apr
10.23 w?		Tyreek	Hill	USA-J	1.3.94					19 Apr
10.28										14 Mar
10.23	1.1	Fred	Taylor	USA	17.8.89					27 Apr
10.23	0.9	Kei	Takase	JPN	25.11.88					29 Apr
10.23	1.0	Kind	Butler	USA	8.4.88					3 May
10.23	0.3	Daniel	Bailey	ANT	9.9.86					8 May
10.23	1.5	Ahmad	Rashad	USA	12.12.87					11 May
10.23	1.1	Maxwell	Dyce	USA	25.4.91					11 May
10.23	0.2	Ramil	Guliyev	TUR	29.5.90					21 Jun
10.23A	1.7	Zharnel	Hughes	AIA-J	13.7.95					5 Jul
10.23	2.0	Simon	Magakwe	RSA	25.5.85					7 Jul
10.24	2.0	Tim	Leathart	AUS	22.9.89					9 Mar
10.24	1.5	Mickey	Grimes	USA	10.10.76					11 May
10.24	1.4	Ainsley	Waugh	JAM	17.9.81					18 May
10.24	0.3	Warren	Fraser	BAH	8.7.91					23 May
10.24A	2.0	Daniel	Grueso	COL	30.7.85					25 May
10.24	1.1	Reginald	Dixon	USA	7.6.88					30 May
10.24	1.9	Joe	Morris	USA	4.10.89					5 Jun
10.24	2.0	Federico	Raguni	ITA	21.11.90					19 Jun
10.24	1.4	Jamol	James	TTO	16.7.92					21 Jun
10.24A	1.7	Miguel	López	PUR	9.4.90					5 Jul
10.24	1.6	Amaru "Reto"	Schenkel	SUI	28.4.88					6 Jul
10.24	0.1	Greg	Cackett	GBR	14.11.89					7 Jul
10.24	1.0	Peter	Emelieze	NGR	19.4.88					2 Aug
10.24	1.3	Sota	Kawatsura	JPN	19.6.89					22 Sep
10.25	2.0	Joshua	Ross	AUS	9.2.81					9 Mar
10.25	1.6	Mitchell	Williams-Swain	AUS	5.1.92					6 Apr
10.25A	1.3	Jeremy	Dodson	USA	30.8.87					3 May
10.25A	2.0	Isidro	Montoya	COL	3.11.90					25 May
10.25	1.1	Brijesh "BJ"	Lawrence	SKN	27.12.89					30 May
10.25	1.8	Jazeel	Murphy	JAM-J	27.2.94					15 Jun
10.25	1.2	André	De Grasse	CAN-J	10.11.94					29 Jun
10.25	0.9	Karol	Zalewski	POL	7.8.93					29 Jun
10.26	1.7	Romel	Lewis	JAM	28.1.88					5 May
10.26	1.1	Jacques	Riparelli	ITA	27.3.83					19 May
10.26	1.1	Jeremy	Bascom	GUY	15.10.83					30 May
10.26	1.9	Nil	de Oliveira	SWE	3.9.86					6 Jun
10.26	1.8	Titus	Kafunda	ZAM	3.8.93					6 Jul
10.26	2.0	Mosito	Lehata	LES	8.4.89					7 Jul
10.27	1.4	Remontay	McClain	USA	21.9.92					13 Apr
10.27	0.7	Leroy	Dixon	USA	20.6.83					4 May
10.27	1.9	Justin	Austin	USA	8.10.89					12 May
10.27	0.9	Trayvon	Bromell	USA-J	10.7.95					18 May
10.27	2.0	John	Teeters	USA	19.5.93					23 May
10.27	0.6	Delmas	Obou	ITA	25.10.91					14 Jun
10.27	-1.5	DeAngelo	Cherry	USA	1.8.90					20 Jun
10.27	0.2	Aziz	Ouhadi	MAR	24.7.84					27 Jun
10.27	-0.5	Barakat	Al-Harthi	OMA	15.6.88					4 Jul
		and 10.27 nwi 1 Doha 16 Apr								
10.27	2.0	Obinna	Metu	NGR	12.7.88					7 Jul
10.27	-1.1	Deji	Tobais	GBR	31.10.91					11 Jul
10.27	0.7	Fabio	Cerutti	ITA	26.9.85					7 Sep
10.28	-0.7	Delano	Williams	TKS/GBR	23.12.93					19 Mar
10.28	1.4	Levonte	Whitfield	USA	8.10.93					5 Apr
10.28	1.6	Anthony	Alozie	AUS	18.8.86					6 Apr
10.28	1.5	Kendal	Williams	USA-J	23.9.95					25 Apr
10.28	0.3	Mark	Jelks	USA	10.4.84					8 May
10.28	1.4	Igor	Bodrov	UKR	9.7.87					5 Jun
10.28	0.1	Levi	Cadogan	BAR-J	8.11.95					22 Jun
10.28	0.6	Alexander	Kosenkow	GER	14.3.77					2 Aug
10.28	1.6	Wallace	Spearmon	USA	24.12.84					6 Apr
10.29	1.6	Chen Qiang		CHN	12.6.90					27 Apr
10.29	1.9	Ifrish	Alberg	SUR	13.7.88					11 May
10.29	0.0w?	Lamar	Hicks	USA	1.1.87					12 May
10.29	1.6	Craig	Pickering	GBR	16.10.86					27 May
10.29	0.7	Aldemir	da Silva	BRA	8.6.92					6 Jun
10.29	1.6	Adrian	Griffith	BAH	11.11.84					8 Jun
10.29	0.1	Mikhail	Idrisov	RUS	21.6.88					15 Jun
10.29	0.5	Adolphus	Nevers	JAM	.91					20 Jun
10.29	0.6	Masashi	Eriguchi	JPN	17.12.88					19 Jul
		(188)								

Wind assisted

Mark	Wind	Name		Nat	Born	Pos	Meet	Venue	Date
9.75	4.3	Darvis	Patton	USA	4.12.77	1rA	TexR	Austin	30 Mar
9.85	3.2	Charles	Silmon	USA	4.7.91	1s1	NC	Des Moines	21 Jun
9.86	3.2	Rakieem "Mookie"	Salaam	USA	5.4.90	2s1	NC	Des Moines	21 Jun
9.86	3.2	Keston	Bledman	TTO	8.3.88	1	NC	Port of Spain	22 Jun
9.88	2.6		Gatlin			1	Pre	Eugene	1 Jun
9.89	3.2		Silmon			1	NCAA	Eugene	7 Jun
9.89	2.4		Gatlin			2s2	NC	Des Moines	21 Jun
9.90	2.4		Rodgers			3s2	NC	Des Moines	21 Jun
9.90	2.5		Rodgers			1rA		Dubnica nad Váhom	21 Aug
9.91	3.8		Ashmeade			1h2		Clermont, FL	11 May
9.91	3.2	Dentarius	Locke	USA	12.12.89	2	NCAA	Eugene	7 Jun
9.91	3.2	Richard	Thompson	TTO	7.6.85	2	NC	Port of Spain	22 Jun
9.92	4.3	Wallace	Spearmon	USA	24.12.84	2rA	TexR	Austin	30 Mar
9.92	3.0		Silmon			1s3	NCAA	Eugene	5 Jun
9.93	4.3		Rodgers			3rA	TexR	Austin	30 Mar
9.93	2.4	Isiah	Young	USA	5.1.90	4s2	NC	Des Moines	21 Jun
9.94	4.3		Silmon			4rA	TexR	Austin	30 Mar
9.94	2.6		Rodgers			2	Pre	Eugene	1 Jun
9.95	3.0	Jaysuma	Saidy Ndure	NOR	1.1.84	1		Sundsvall	28 Jul
		(19/12)							
9.96	5.0	André	De Grasse	CAN-J	10.11.94	1	JUCO	Hutchinson, KS	18 May
9.97	3.0	Harry	Adams	USA	27.11.89	1h4		Montverde, FL	1 Jun
9.98	5.0	Tyreek	Hill	USA-J	1.3.94	2	JUCO	Hutchinson, KS	18 May
9.98	2.9	Christophe	Lemaitre	FRA	11.6.90	1		Rabat	9 Jun
9.98	3.0	Julian	Forte	JAM	1.7.93	2		Sundsvall	28 Jul
9.99	3.7	Martin	Keller	GER	26.9.86	1		Clermont, FL	11 May
9.99	4.1	Jeffrey	Demps	USA	8.1.90	1rA		Montverde, FL	1 Jun
9.99	4.1	Terrell	Wilks	USA	30.12.89	1rB		Montverde, FL	1 Jun
9.99A	4.0	Trayvon	Bromell	USA-J	10.7.95	1		Albuquerque	8 Jun
9.99	3.2	Rondell	Sorrillo	TTO	21.1.86	3	NC	Port of Spain	22 Jun
10.00A	4.5	Jeremy	Dodson	USA	30.8.87	1		Fort Collins, CO	27 Apr
10.00	3.7	Julian	Reus	GER	29.4.88	2		Clermont, FL	11 May
10.00	2.6	Ryan	Bailey	USA	13.4.89	3	Pre	Eugene	1 Jun
10.00	4.1	Gerald	Phiri	ZAM	6.10.88	2rA		Montverde, FL	1 Jun
10.00	2.8	Antoine	Adams	SKN	31.8.88	1rA		Edmonton	29 Jun
10.01	3.2	Diondre	Batson	USA	13.7.92	4	NCAA	Eugene	7 Jun

Mark	Wind	Name		Nat	Born	Pos	Meet	Venue	Date
10.01	3.2	Aaron	Brown	CAN	27.5.92	5	NCAA	Eugene	7 Jun
10.02	2.6	Ramone	McKenzie	JAM	15.11.90	1rB		Montverde, FL	8 Jun
10.02	3.2	Trell	Kimmons	USA	13.7.85	4s1	NC	Des Moines	21 Jun
10.02	3.4	Dwain	Chambers	GBR	5.4.78	1s3	NC	Birmingham	13 Jul
10.04	2.7	Ryota	Yamagata	JPN	10.6.92	2	Oda	Hiroshima	29 Apr
10.04	3.8	Kawayne	Fisher	JAM	25.10.86	1		Emporia, KS	11 May
10.04	3.6	Aaron	Ernest	USA	8.11.93	1h2	SEC	Columbia, MO	11 May
10.05	3.9	Innocent	Bologo	BUR	5.9.89	1		Dakar	25 May
10.05	2.4	Calesio	Newman	USA	20.8.86	6s2	NC	Des Moines	21 Jun
10.06	4.9	Henricho	Bruintjies	RSA	16.7.93	1		Durban	27 Apr
10.07	3.2	Cameron	Burrell	USA-J	11.9.94	1-HSTexR		Austin	30 Mar
10.07	3.0	Reggie	Lewis	USA	18.8.93	3s3	NCAA	Eugene	5 Jun
10.07	2.7	Ameer	Webb	USA	19.3.91	2s2	NCAA	Eugene	5 Jun
10.08	5.0	Shavez	Hart	BAH	9.6.92	3	JUCO	Hutchinson, KS	18 May
10.08	3.2	Jamol	James	TTO	16.7.92	4	NC	Port of Spain	22 Jun
10.09	4.3	Cordero	Gray	USA	9.5.89	5rA	TexR	Austin	30 Mar
10.09A	4.5	Joe	Morris	USA	4.10.89	2		Fort Collins, CO	27 Apr
10.09	4.1	Adam	Harris	GUY	21.7.87	4rA		Montverde, FL	1 Jun
10.09	4.1	Adrian	Griffith	BAH	11.11.84	5rA		Montverde, FL	1 Jun
10.09	2.3	Sam	Effah	CAN	29.12.88	1rB		Edmonton	29 Jun
10.10	3.7	Trevorvano	Mackey ¶	BAH	5.1.92	2		Lubbock	25 Apr
10.10	5.8	Sean	Safo-Antwi	GBR	31.10.90	1		London (LV)	8 May
10.11	4.6	Markesh	Woodson	USA	6.9.93	2h1	SEC	Columbia, MO	11 May
10.11	3.0	Prezel	Hardy	USA	1.6.92	4s3	NCAA	Eugene	5 Jun
10.12	5.0	Ahmed	Ali	USA	15.11.93	4	JUCO	Hutchinson, KS	18 May
10.12	2.3	Aziz	Ouhadi	MAR	24.7.84	2		Dakar	12 Jun
10.13	4.3	Clayton	Vaughn	USA	15.5.92	1		Fort Worth	15 Mar
10.13	2.6	Lerone	Clarke	JAM	2.10.81	2rB		Montverde, FL	8 Jun
10.14	4.1	James	Law	USA	8.10.80	2rB		Montverde, FL	1 Jun
10.14	3.0	Ryan	Milus	USA	19.9.90	6s3	NCAA	Eugene	5 Jun
10.15	2.4	Levonte	Whitfield	USA	8.10.93	1		Jacksonville	16 Mar
10.15	2.7	Masashi	Eriguchi	JPN	17.12.88	3	Oda	Hiroshima	29 Apr
10.15	2.4	Jared	Connaughton	CAN	20.7.85	1		Ottawa	10 Jul
10.16	3.2	Kenny	Jackson	USA	.91	1		Amarillo	4 May
10.16	2.5	Justyn	Warner	CAN	28.6.87	3rB	DL	Doha	10 May
10.16		Frederick	Agbaje	NGR	26.6.88	1		Dickinson, ND	10 May
10.17	2.6	Bruno	de Barros	BRA	7.1.87	1h1		Campinas	4 May
10.17	4.6	Chris	Royster	USA	26.1.92	3h1	SEC	Columbia, MO	11 May
10.17	4.1	Jeremy	Hardy	USA	10.8.89	3rB		Montverde, FL	1 Jun
10.17	2.3	Gavin	Smellie	CAN	26.6.86	1		Toronto	7 Jul
10.18	2.4	Kendal	Williams	USA-J	23.9.95	2		Jacksonville	16 Mar
10.18	2.1	Dario	Horvat	CRO	25.2.92	2rD	TexR	Austin	30 Mar
10.19	5.3	Brien	Berry	USA	23.4.93	3		Great Bend, KS	3 May
10.19	2.1	Ailson	Feitosa	BRA	13.8.88	1		Campinas	4 May
10.19	4.1	Taffawee	Johnson	JAM	10.3.88	4=rB		Montverde, FL	1 Jun
10.19	3.2	Ayodele	Taffe	TTO-J	13.9.94	5	NC	Port of Spain	22 Jun
10.19A	3.0	Warren	Fraser	BAH	8.7.91	2h1	CAC	Morelia	5 Jul

Mark	Wind	Name		Nat	Born	Date
10.20	2.3	Johnathan	Smith	USA	15.9.92	16 Mar
10.20	2.2	Maurice	Mitchell	USA	22.12.89	30 Mar
10.20	2.3		Kim Kuk-young	KOR	19.4.91	29 Apr
10.20	2.5	Joshua	Ross	AUS	9.2.81	10 May
10.20	2.9	Michael	Frater	JAM	6.10.82	1 Jun
10.20	2.6	Jamial	Rolle	BAH	16.4.80	8 Jun
10.20	2.9	Emmanuel	Callender	TTO	22.6.85	22 Jun
10.20	3.0	Sergiy	Smelyk	UKR	19.4.87	30 Jun
10.20	3.8	Masafumi	Naoki	JPN	19.11.93	15 Jul
10.20	3.0	Roscoe	Engel	RSA	6.3.89	28 Jul
10.21	5.6	Joseph	Millar	NZL	24.9.92	2 Mar
10.21	3.2	Kyle	Fulks	USA	12.12.93	30 Mar
10.21	3.2	Tommy	Brown	USA	29.3.90	4 May
10.22	2.1	Justin	Austin	USA	8.10.89	27 Apr
10.22	3.8	Brijesh "BJ"	Lawrence	SKN	27.12.89	11 May
10.22	3.9	James	Alaka	GBR	8.9.89	12 May
10.22	3.9	Adama	Jammeh	GAM	10.6.93	25 May
10.22	2.1	Khalfani	Muhammad	PUR-J	26.9.94	25 May
10.23	4.5	Michael	Mathieu	BAH	24.6.83	15 Mar
10.23	4.5	Evan	Emery	USA	22.12.91	19 Apr
10.23	5.1	Justin	Anderson	USA	8.2.91	1 Jun
10.23	4.1	Marcus	Rowland	USA	11.3.90	1 Jun
10.24	3.7	Allan	Burton	JAM	25.2.92	16 Feb
10.24	4.9	Akani	Simbine	RSA	21.9.93	27 Apr
10.24	2.7	Yusuke	Kotani	JPN	23.9.89	29 Apr
10.24	3.9	Quentin	Butler	USA	18.9.92	11 May
10.24	2.8	Dariusz	Kuc	POL	24.4.86	8 Jun
10.24	2.6	Jason	Smyth	IRL	4.7.87	8 Jun
10.24	2.9	John	Constantine	TTO-J	.95	22 Jun
10.24A	3.0	Rolando	Palacios	HON	3.5.87	5 Jul
10.24	2.4	Karol	Zalewski	POL	7.8.93	19 Jul
10.24	2.4	Likoúrgos-Stéfanos	Tsákonas	GRE	8.3.90	20 Jul
10.25	4.8	Antonio	Alkana	RSA	12.4.90	16 Feb
10.25	2.4	Remontay	McClain	USA	21.9.92	20 Apr
10.25	3.7	Rhoan	Sterling	CAN	27.7.80	11 May
10.25	2.8	Alexander	Kosenkow	GER	14.3.77	11 May
10.25	2.7	Justin	Walker	USA	30.11.90	12 May
10.25	2.7	Will	Henry	USA	5.9.90	5 Jun
10.26A	4.5	Jeremy	Rankin	USA	23.9.90	27 Apr
10.26	5.3	David	Winters	USA-J	19.2.94	3 May
10.26	4.0	Tatum	Taylor	USA-J	8.9.94	4 May
10.26	3.8	Jon	Juin	HAI	17.12.89	11 May
10.26	2.7	Elijah	Hall-Thompson	USA-J	22.8.94	11 May
10.26A	2.2	Jermaine	Jones	USA	24.5.91	23 May
10.26	2.9	DeAngelo	Cherry	USA	1.8.90	8 Jun
10.26	4.3	Takashi	Masuda	JPN	25.1.93	12 Oct
10.27	4.5	Deneko	Brown	BAH	15.6.90	4 May
10.27	5.1	David	Bolarinwa	GBR	20.10.93	8 May
10.27	5.9	Johnathan	Farquharson	BAH	3.2.93	8 May
10.27	3.4	Tim	Young	USA	24.8.91	11 May
10.27	4.1	Rodney	Green	BAH	8.12.85	1 Jun
10.27	2.6	Kenneth	Turner	USA	28.8.91	8 Jun
10.28	2.7	Alex	Schaf	GER	28.4.87	25 May

Mark	Wind	Name		Nat	Born	Pos	Meet	Venue		Date
10.28	3.2	Aaron	Armstrong	TTO	14.10.77	22 Jun				
10.29A	4.0	Jerrell	Hancock	USA	6.7.89	23 May				
10.29	2.9	Sharif	Nash	USA	30.3.85	8 Jun				

10.29	2.3	Amr Ibrahim	Seoud	EGY	10.6.86	12 Jun
10.29	3.0	Rytis	Sakalauskas	LTU	27.6.87	20 Jun

Doubtful timing

10.24Aw		Hanno		Engelbrecht	RSA	12.11.87	9 Feb

Low altitude bests

10.22	1.3	Quiñónez	5 Jul
10.24	0.8	Hinds	25 May
	10.22w	2.3	12 Jun

10.24	0.8	S Hart	21 Jun
10.25	1.8	J Henderson	20 Apr
	10.20w	4.5	16 Mar

10.28	-0.4	Fisher	27 Apr
	10.16w	3.0	28 Jul

Hand timed

9.9		Simon	Magakwe	RSA	25.5.85	1	NC	Stellenbosch	15 Apr
10.0	-0.7	Yaniel	Carrero	CUB-J	17.8.95	16 Mar			
10.0		Samuel	Francis	QAT	27.3.87	8 Apr			
10.0	-0.3	Alex	Quiñónez	ECU	11.8.89	15 May			
10.0	0.0	Adetoyi	Durotoye	NGR	9.5.86	18 May			

10.0	0.0	Nicholas	Imhoaperamhe	NGR	18.4.92	18 May
10.0		Onyeaku	Chukwuma	NGR	3.10.91	25 May
10.0		Jonathan	Nmaju	NGR	9.1.93	25 May
10.0		Winston	George	GUY	19.5.87	15 Nov
9.9w dt	5.6	Anculam	Lopes	GBS	6.3.91	2 Jun

Drugs disqualification subject to confirmation

9.75	1.1	Tyson	Gay ¶ ?	USA		9.8.82	1	NC	Des Moines	21 Jun
9.79	2.0		Gay				1	Athl	Lausanne	4 Jul
9.88	2.0	Asafa	Powell	JAM	23.11.82		2	Athl	Lausanne	4 Jul
10.25	0.8	Trevorvano	Mackey ¶	BAH	5.1.92		3	NC	Freeport	21 Jun
9.75w	2.4		Gay				1s2	NC	Des Moines	21 Jun

JUNIORS

See main list for top 3 juniors. 10 performances by 5 men to 10.24. Additional marks and further juniors:

Kiryu		10.17	-0.2	1		Mara		14 Jun	10.22	0.1	1		Tokyo (Chofu)	4 Oct
		10.19	0.1	1		Oita		31 Jul						
Hester		10.22	0.9	3	ACC	Raleigh		20 Apr	10.24	1.9	4h1	NCAA	Eugene	5 Jun
10.23	w?	Tyreek				Hill	USA	1.3.94			1		Sterling, KS	19 Apr
		10.28									1		Winfield	14 Mar
10.23A	1.7	Zharnel				Hughes	AIA	13.7.95	3h2	CAC			Morelia	5 Jul
10.25	1.8	Jazeel				Murphy	JAM	27.2.94	1	NC-j			Kingston	15 Jun
10.25	1.2	André				De Grasse	CAN	10.11.94	1r2				Windsor	29 Jun
10.27	0.9	Trayvon				Bromell	USA	10.7.95	1				Orlando	18 May
10.28	1.5	Kendal				Williams	USA	23.9.95	1				Tallahassee	25 Apr
10.28	0.1	Levi				Cadogan (10)	BAR	8.11.95	3	NC			Bridgetown	22 Jun
10.30	0.6	Ayodele				Taffe	TTO	13.9.94	1	NC-j			Port of Spain	1 Jun
10.31	1.2	Mustaq'eem				Williams	USA	24.8.95	1	Jnr Oly			Greensboro	28 Jul
10.32	0.8	Zdenek				Stromsík	CZE	25.11.94	1	NC			Tábor	15 Jun
10.32	0.5	Chijindu				Ujah	GBR	5.3.94	1h5	EJ			Rieti	18 Jul
10.33	0.7	Khalfani				Muhammad	PUR	26.9.94	1				Clovis	1 Jun
10.34	0.3	Kazuma				Oseto	JPN	5.8.94	3h1	NC			Tokyo (Chofu)	7 Jun
10.34	1.8	Jevaughn				Minzie	JAM	20.7.95	2	NC-j			Kingston	15 Jun
10.35	-0.4	Mo				Youxue	CHN-Y	10.2.96	1	WY			Donetsk	11 Jul
10.35	-0.4	Ojie				Edoburun	GBR-Y	2.6.96	2	WY			Donetsk	11 Jul
10.36	0.5	Cameron				Burrell (20)	USA	11.9.94	1				Austin	10 May
10.36	1.7	Henry				Chukwudike	NGR	9.1.94	1				Port Harcourt	5 Jun
10.36	1.5	Tatum				Bernard-Taylor	USA	8.9.94	1	GWest			Berkeley	9 Jun
10.36	1.4	Vítor				dos Santos	BRA-Y	1.2.96	1				Belém	9 Nov

Wind assisted

See main list for top 4 juniors. 10 performances by 5 men to 10.14. Additional marks and further juniors:

De Grasse		10.08w	5.3	1		Great Bend		4 May	10.12w	3.6	1h1		Great Bend	4 May
Bromell		10.14w		1		Puinta Gorda		25 Apr						
10.30	2.7	Yaniel				Carrero	CUB	17.8.95	1				Camagüey	22 Feb
10.30	4.0	Vitor Hugo				dos Santos	BRA	1.2.95	1h3	NC-J			São Paulo	21 Sep
10.32	3.0	Luís Gabriel				Silva	BRA	28.7.94	1	NC-J			São Paulo	21 Sep
10.33	2.1	Myles				Valentine	USA		2				Norwalk	24 May

Hand timed

10.1	-0.7	César	Ruíz	CUB	18.1.95	2	NC	La Habana	16 Mar
10.1	-0.7	Reynier	Mena	CUB-Y	21.11.96	3	NC	La Habana	16 Mar
10.1	0.0	Henry	Chukwudike	NGR	9,1.94	3		Port Harcourt	18 May

150 METRES STRAIGHT

14.42	1.4	Usain	Bolt	JAM	21.8.86	1		Rio de Janeiro	31 Mar
14.88	1.4	Daniel	Bailey	ANT	9.9.87	2		Rio de Janeiro	31 Mar
14.90	-1.0	Christoph	Lemaitre	FRA	11.6.90	1		Manchester	25 May
14.90	-0.2	Michael	Rodgers	USA	24.4.85	1		Gateshead (Q)	14 Sep

200 METRES

19.66	0.0	Usain	Bolt	JAM	21.8.86	1	WCh	Moskva	17 Aug
19.73	0.2		Bolt			1	DL	Saint-Denis	6 Jul
19.79	1.7		Bolt			1	Bisl	Oslo	13 Jun
19.79	0.9	Warren	Weir	JAM	31.10.89	1	NC	Kingston	23 Jun
19.79	0.0		Weir			2	WCh	Moskva	17 Aug

MEN 2013

Mark	Wind	Name		Nat	Born	Pos	Meet	Venue	Date	
19.86	1.6	Isiah	Young	USA	5.1.90	1	NC	Des Moines	23	Jun
19.87	-0.2		Weir			1	VD	Bruxelles	6	Sep
19.89	0.2		Weir			1	DL	London (OS)	26	Ju
19.92	0.2		Weir			2	DL	Saint-Denis	6	Ju
19.93	-0.2	Nickel	Ashmeade	JAM	7.4.90	2	VD	Bruxelles	6	Sep
19.97	0.0	Curtis	Mitchell	USA	11.3.89	1s1	WCh	Moskva	16	Aug
19.98	-0.3	Jason	Young	JAM	21.3.91	1		Luzern	17	Ju
19.98	-0.3	Adam	Gemili	GBR	6.10.93	1s3	WCh	Moskva	16	Aug
19.99	1.6		Mitchell			2	NC	Des Moines	23	Jun
19.99	0.2		J Young			2	DL	London (OS)	26	Ju
20.00	-0.3		Ashmeade			1		Kingston	4	May
20.00	-0.3		Ashmeade			2s3	WCh	Moskva	16	Aug
20.01	1.4	Churandy	Martina	NED	3.7.84	1	Athl	Lausanne	4	Ju
20.01	0.4		Weir			1	Gyulai	Budapest	10	Ju
20.04	0.0		Mitchell			3	WCh	Moskva	17	Aug
20.05	0.0		Ashmeade			4	WCh	Moskva	17	Aug
20.06	0.9		Ashmeade			2	NC	Kingston	23	Jun
20.07	1.6		Ashmeade			1s1	NC	Kingston	22	Jun
20.07	0.2	Christophe	Lemaitre	FRA	11.6.90	3	DL	Saint-Denis	6	Ju
20.07	0.4		J Young			2	Gyulai	Budapest	10	Ju
20.08	0.0		Gemili			5	WCh	Moskva	17	Aug
20.10	1.6	Wallace	Spearmon (10)	USA	24.12.84	3	NC	Des Moines	23	Jun
20.11	0.9		Weir			1	adidas	New York	25	May
20.12	0.2		J Young			4	DL	Saint-Denis	6	Ju
20.12	0.0		Bolt			1s2	WCh	Moskva	16	Aug
20.12	-0.2	Walter	Dix	USA	31.1.86	3	VD	Bruxelles	6	Sep
		(31/11)								
20.13	1.7	Anaso	Jobodwana	RSA	30.7.92	1q1	NCAA-E	Greensboro	25	May
20.13	0.9	Jason	Livermore	JAM	25.4.88	3	NC	Kingston	23	Jun
20.13A	0.5	Antoine	Adams	SKN	31.8.88	1	CAC	Morelia	7	Ju
20.15	0.4	Rasheed	Dwyer	JAM	29.1.89	1r1	Skol	Warszawa	25	Aug
20.20	1.6	Ameer	Webb	USA	19.3.91	5	NC	Des Moines	23	Jun
20.21	1.4	Shota	Iizuka	JPN	25.6.91	1		Fukuroi	3	May
20.21	0.0	Justin	Gatlin	USA	10.2.82	2	DL	Shanghai	18	May
20.21	0.1	Isaac	Makwala	BOT	29.9.86	1r2		La Chaux-de-Fonds	7	Ju
20.22	-1.3	Chris	Clarke	GBR	25.1.90	1	CAU	Bedford	25	Aug
		(20)								
20.23	1.5	Bryshon	Nellum	USA	1.5.89	1	Pac-12	Los Angeles	12	May
20.23	0.6	Charles	Silmon	USA	4.7.91	1q2	NCAA-W	Austin	25	May
20.23	-0.2	Jaysuma	Saidy Ndure	NOR	1.1.84	5	VD	Bruxelles	6	Sep
20.24	0.7	Bruno	de Barros	BRA	7.1.87	1		São Paulo	19	May
20.26	0.7	LaShawn	Merritt	USA	27.6.86	1		George Town, CAY	8	May
20.26	0.5	Lalonde	Gordon	TTO	25.11.88	1	NC	Port of Spain	23	Jun
20.27	0.9	Delano	Williams	TKS/GBR	23.12.93	1		Kingston	16	Mar
20.27	0.7	Mario	Forsythe	JAM	30.10.85	2		São Paulo	19	May
20.30	0.2	Jimmy	Vicaut	FRA	27.2.92	6	DL	Saint-Denis	6	Ju
20.32	1.5	Carvin	Nkanata	USA	6.5.91	1	IC4A	Princeton	12	May
		(30)								
20.32	1.6	Maurice	Mitchell	USA	22.12.89	6	NC	Des Moines	23	Jun
20.34	-0.1	Richard	Kilty	GBR	2.9.89	1r1		La Chaux-de-Fonds	7	Jul
20.35	-0.3	Akiyuki	Hashimoto	JPN-J	18.11.94	1r3		Fukuroi	3	May
20.35	0.7	Michael	Mathieu	BAH	24.6.83	3		São Paulo	19	May
20.36	-0.4	Julian	Reus	GER	29.4.88	1	NC	Ulm	7	Jul
20.37	1.6	Calesio	Newman	USA	20.8.86	7	NC	Des Moines	23	Jun
20.37	1.8	Mosito	Lehata	LES	8.4.89	1		Sollentuna	27	Jun
20.37	0.3	Alonso	Edward	PAN	8.12.89	1rB		Luzern	17	Jul
20.38	1.2	Aaron	Ernest	USA	8.11.93	1q2	NCAA-E	Greensboro	25	May
20.38	-0.4	Jonathan	Borlée	BEL	22.2.88	1	NC	Bruxelles	21	Jul
		(40)								
20.39	1.3	Edino	Steele	JAM	6.1.87	1r2	Skol	Warszawa	25	Aug
20.39	0.2	Sergiy	Smelyk	UKR	19.4.87	2		Rieti	8	Sep
20.41	-0.5	Ryota	Yamagata	JPN	10.6.92	2		Yokohama	26	May
20.41	-0.5	Yoshihide	Kiryu	JPN-J	15.12.95	1		Nara	15	Jun
20.41	-0.3	Karol	Zalewski	POL	7.8.93	1	EU23	Tampere	13	Jul
20.42	2.0	James	Ellington	GBR	6.9.85	2	FBK	Hengelo	8	Jun
20.44	1.6	Aldemir	da Silva	BRA	8.6.92	2		Belém	12	May
20.44	1.8	Alex	Quiñónez	ECU	11.8.89	1	SAmC	Cartagena	6	Jul
20.44	0.6	Jacques	Harvey	JAM	5.4.89	1		Kortrijk	14	Jul
20.44	0.8	Aaron	Brown	CAN	27.5.92	1r3		Weinheim	2	Aug
		(50)								

Mark	Wind	Name	Nat	Born	Pos	Meet	Venue	Date
20.45	-0.2	Danny Talbot	GBR	1.5.91	1		Genève	1 Jun
20.45	1.6	Dedric Dukes	USA	4.2.92	8	NC	Des Moines	23 Jun
20.45	-0.7	Likoúrgos-Stéfanos Tsákonas	GRE	8.3.90	1	Med G	Mersin	26 Jun
20.45	0.1	Enrico Demonte	ITA	25.9.88	2r2		La Chaux-de-Fonds	7 Jul
20.46	0.9	Yuichi Kobayashi	JPN	25.8.89	2	NC	Tokyo [Chofu]	9 Jun
20.46A	0.4	Bernardo Baloyes	COL-J	6.1.94	1		Cali	23 Jun
20.46	-0.7	Ramil Guliyev	TUR	29.5.90	2	Med G	Mersin	26 Jun
20.47	0.0	Zhang Peimeng	CHN	13.3.87	4	DL	Shanghai	18 May
20.47	0.0	Bruno Hortelano	ESP	18.9.91	2h2	WCh	Moskva	16 Aug
20.48	0.9	Kenji Fujimutsu	JPN	1.5.86	3=	NC	Tokyo [Chofu]	9 Jun
(60)								
20.48	0.9	Kei Takase	JPN	25.11.88	3=	NC	Tokyo [Chofu]	9 Jun
20.49	1.6	Jeremy Dodson	USA	30.8.87	1	MSR	Walnut	20 Apr
20.49	2.0	Trey Hadnot	USA	7.3.92	1	WAC	Arlington	11 May
20.49	1.1	Jerrell Hancock	USA	7.6.89	1		Sioux Falls	11 May
20.49	0.9	Jermaine Brown	JAM	4.7.91	6	NC	Kingston	23 Jun
20.49	-0.3	Pavel Maslák	CZE	21.2.91	3	EU23	Tampere	13 Jul
20.50	0.2	Matteo Galvan	ITA	24.8.88	4		Rieti	8 Sep
20.51	2.0	Jamial Rolle	BAH	16.4.80	1rB		Montverde, FL	8 Jun
20.51	1.4	Sergio Ruíz	ESP	21.10.89	1		Salamanca	12 Jun
20.52	1.4	Blake Heriot	USA	26.9.91	2	Big 12	Waco	5 May
(70)								
20.52	0.9	Diondre Batson	USA	13.7.92	3	SEC	Columbia, MO	12 May
20.52	1.3	Charles Clark	USA	10.8.87	2rA		Montverde, FL	8 Jun
20.52	0.9	Shinji Takahira	JPN	18.7.84	5	NC	Tokyo [Chofu]	9 Jun
20.53	0.6	Davion Collins	USA	3.10.92	1		Las Vegas	11 May
20.53	1.2	Justin Austin	USA	8.10.89	2q1	NCAA-W	Austin	25 May
20.53	1.8	Nil de Oliveira	SWE	3.9.86	2		Sollentuna	27 Jun
20.54	1.9	Remontay McClain	USA	21.9.92	1		Azusa	19 Apr
20.54	0.7	Tremaine Harris	CAN	10.2.92	4		São Paulo	19 May
20.54	1.3	Brandon Byram	USA	11.9.88	3rA		Montverde, FL	8 Jun
20.55	2.0	Akheem Gauntlett	JAM	26.8.90	1		Eugene	20 Apr
(80)								
20.55	-2.8	Xie Zhenye	CHN	17.8.93	1		Jinan	12 May
20.55A	0.5	Luguelín Santos	DOM	12.11.93	4	CAC	Morelia	7 Jul
20.55	0.6	Obinna Metu	NGR	12.7.88	2		Kortrijk	14 Jul
20.56	1.4	Hitoshi Saito	JPN	9.10.86	4		Fukuroi	3 May
20.57	1.5	Joshua Ross	AUS	9.2.81	1	NC	Sydney	14 Apr
20.57	0.5	Wilfried Koffi Hua	CIV	24.9.89	1		Abidjan	27 Apr
20.57A	0.2	Jermaine Jones	USA	24.5.91	1	NCAA-2	Pueblo, CO	25 May
20.57	0.5	Kyle Greaux	TTO	26.4.88	2	NC	Port of Spain	23 Jun
20.58	1.7	Adolphus Nevers	JAM	19.3.90	2		Ljubljana	13 Jul
20.59	0.4	Winston George	GUY	19.5.87	1		Colts Neck, NJ	8 Jun
(90)								
20.59	1.7	Jan Zumer	SLO	9.6.82	3		Ljubljana	13 Jul
20.60	2.0	Greg Nixon	USA	12.9.81	1rB	MSR	Walnut	20 Apr
20.60	1.0	Elijah Hall-Thompson	USA-J	22.8.94	1		Austin	11 May
20.60	-0.5	Tony McQuay	USA	16.4.90	1		St Martin	11 May
20.60	1.5	Brendon Rodney	CAN	9.4.92	2	IC4A	Princeton	12 May
20.60	0.0	Davide Manenti	ITA	16.4.89	1		Rieti	1 Jun
20.60	0.1	Miguel Francis	ANT-J	28.2.95	1	NC	St. John's	2 Jun
20.60	-0.7	David Bolarinwa	GBR	20.10.93	1r2		Regensburg	8 Jun
20.60	1.8	Lestrod Roland	SKN	5.9.92	2h2		Basseterre	9 Jun
20.60	1.5	Alex Wilson	SUI	19.9.90	1		Bulle	6 Jul
(100)								
20.60A	0.5	Adam Harris	GUY	21.7.87	6	CAC	Morelia	7 Jul

20.61	0.0	Darvis	Patton	USA	4.12.77	18 May			
20.62	0.7	Jefferson	Lucindo	BRA	17.10.90	8 Jun			
20.62	1.6	Gil	Roberts	USA	15.3.89	8 Jun			
20.62	0.5	Jorge Henrique	Vides	BRA	24.11.92	9 Jun			
20.62	0.9	Asuka	Cambridge	JPN	31.5.93	9 Jun			
20.62	1.8	Leon	Reid	GBR-J	26.7.94	20 Jul			
20.62	-0.7	Nethaneel	Mitchell-Blake	GBR-J	2.4.94	20 Jul			
20.62	0.7	Oluwasegun	Makinde	CAN	6.7.91	2 Aug			
20.63	0.2	Dentarius	Locke	USA	12.12.89	3 May			
20.63	1.7	James	Taylor	USA	30.6.90	25 May			
20.63	2.0	Ramon	Miller	BAH	17.2.87	8 Jun			
20.63	1.8	Kotaro	Taniguchi	JPN-J	3.11.94	7 Jul			
20.63	-1.0	Michael	O'Hara	JAM-Y	29.9.96	14 Jul			
20.63A	0.0	Reynier	Mena	CUB-Y	21.11.96	24 Aug			
20.64	-0.3	Kazuya	Tajima	JPN	14.9.90	3 May			
20.64	-1.1	Kendal	Williams	USA-J	23.9.95	18 May			
20.64	-1.8	Mustaq'eem	Williams	USA-J	24.8.95	27 Jul			
20.65A	0.8	Josh	Edmonds	USA	23.7.91	24 May			
20.65A	0.2	Jeff	Henderson	USA	19.2.89	25 May			
20.65	0.2	Ellis	Burkheart	BAR	16.9.92	23 Jun			
20.65	1.7	Konstantin	Petryashov	RUS	16.12.84	2 Jul			
20.66	1.5	Nicholas	Hough	AUS	20.10.93	14 Apr			
20.66	2.0	Brian	Witherspoon	USA	5.6.85	8 Jun			
20.66	0.3	Kenroy	Anderson	JAM	27.6.87	17 Jul			
20.66	-0.8	Michael	Rodgers	USA	24.4.85	26 Aug			
20.67	1.9	Hanoj	Carter	USA-J	26.6.94	6 Apr			
20.67	1.5	Daniel	Bailey	ANT	9.9.86	13 Apr			
20.67	1.5	Nick	Boylett	AUS	19.9.86	14 Apr			
20.67A	0.9	Sibusiso	Matsenjwa	SWZ	2.5.88	17 Jun			
20.67	-1.0	Vitor Hugo	dos Santos	BRA-Y	1.2.96	14 Jul			
20.67	0.1	Aleixo Platini	Menga	GER	29.9.87	2 Aug			
20.68	1.5	Tucker	Peabody	USA	14.8.92	11 May			
20.68	1.6	Jared	Connaughton	CAN	20.7.85	12 May			
20.68A	0.8	Taffawee	Johnson	JAM	10.3.88	24 May			

MEN 2013

Mark	Wind	Name		Nat	Born	Pos	Meet	Venue	Date
20.68	0.9	Kind	Butler	USA	8.4.89				25 May
20.69A	0.2	Hitjivirue	Kaanjuka	NAM	29.12.87				23 Feb
20.69	1.5	Innocent	Bologo	BUR	5.9.89				25 May
20.69A		Mike	Mokamba	KEN-J	28.8.94				22 Jun
20.69	0.7	Roscoe	Engel	RSA	6.3.89				30 Jun
20.70	0.9	Christian	Taylor	USA	18.6.90				30 Mar
20.70	-0.4	Darrell	Wesh	USA	21.1.92				20 Apr
20.70	0.7	Ailson	Feitosa	BRA	13.8.88				19 May
20.70	-1.0	Deji	Tobais	GBR	31.10.91				8 Jun
20.70	1.3	Kamil	Krynski	POL	12.5.87				25 Aug
20.71	0.2	Tim	Leathart	AUS	22.9.89				9 Mar
20.71	-1.4	Kavean	Smith	JAM	12.5.91				4 May
20.71	2.0	Devin	Spann	USA	26.10.92				12 May
20.71A	-0.3	Gideon	Trotter	RSA	3.3.92				25 May
20.71	1.4	Akeem	Williams	JAM	7.11.90				25 May
20.71	0.2		Zhang Feng	CHN	29.1.89				16 Jun
20.71	-0.9	Amr Ibrahim	Seoud	EGY	10.6.86				26 Jun
20.72	2.0	Manteo	Mitchell	USA	6.7.87				6 Apr
20.72	-1.5	Carlos	Rodríguez	PUR	7.2.92				7 Apr
20.72	-0.1	Yohan	Blake	JAM	26.12.89				8 Jun
20.72	0.5	Jereem	Richards	TTO-J	13.1.94				23 Jun
20.72	1.8	Arturo	Ramírez	VEN	19.4.91				6 Jul
20.73	1.6	Arman	Hall	USA-J	14.2.94				20 Apr
20.73	2.0	Khalfani	Muhammad	PUR-J	26.9.94				24 May
20.73	1.3	Carl	Horsley	USA	17.6.92				24 May
20.73	2.0	Masafumi	Naoki	JPN	19.11.93				26 May
20.73	0.3	Petar	Kremenski	BUL	14.1.91				16 Jun
20.73	-0.4	Sven	Knipphals	GER	20.9.85				7 Jul
20.74	1.8	Leonardo	Seymore	USA	2.9.89				5 Apr
20.74	0.3	Simon	Magakwe	RSA	25.5.85				13 Apr
20.74	1.3	Deun	White	USA	13.7.85				27 Apr
20.74	2.0	Clement	Campbell	JAM	19.2.75				30 May
20.74	1.6	Mickael-Meba	Zézé	FRA-J	19.5.94				7 Jun
20.74	-0.1	David	Alerte	FRA	18.9.84				14 Jul
20.74A	0.0	André	De Grasse	CAN-J	10.11.94				24 Aug
20.74	-0.4	Fahad Moh'd	Al-Subaie	KSA-J	4.2.94				27 Sep
20.75	0.0	Renny	Quow	TTO	25.8.87				6 Apr
20.75	1.1	Fred	Taylor	USA	17.8.89				27 Apr
20.75	0.3		Gao Dongshi	CHN	14.5.89				21 May
20.75	0.9	Johan	Wissman	SWE	2.11.82				6 Jun
20.75	0.4	Robin	Erewa	GER	24.6.91				2 Aug
20.76	0.0	Armanti	Hayes	USA	23.9.87				13 Apr
20.76	1.5	Craig	Burns	AUS	7.10.88				14 Apr
20.76	1.8	Ashton	Eaton	USA	21.1.88				19 Apr
20.76	1.1	Andrew	Robertson	GBR	17.12.90				19 May
20.77	0.0	Ryan	Milus	USA	19.9.90				27 Apr
20.77	0.9	Ramone	McKenzie	JAM	15.11.90				25 May
20.77	1.0	Aleksandr	Khyutte	RUS	29.9.88				30 May
20.77	-0.4	Maximilian	Kessler	GER	6.4.89				7 Jul
20.77	0.1	Hannes	Dreyer	RSA	13.1.85				7 Jul
20.77	0.0	Jordan	Kirby-Polidore	GBR	26.1.93				23 Jul
20.77	0.1	Jonathan	Åstrand	FIN	9.9.85				28 Jul
20.77	-0.6	Diego	Marani	ITA	27.4.90				28 Jul
20.78	0.9	Odail	Todd	JAM-J	9.6.94				16 Mar
20.78	-1.1	Ceolamar	Ways	USA-J	22.11.94				18 May
20.78	1.2	Prezel	Hardy	USA	1.6.92				25 May
20.78	-0.3	Ainsley	Waugh	JAM	17.9.81				22 Jun
20.78		Greg	Cackett	GBR	14.11.89				14 Jul
20.79A	0.8	Akani	Simbine	RSA	21.9.93				9 Mar
20.79	-0.3	Julian	Forte	JAM	1.7.93				4 May
20.79	1.7	Waymon	Storey	USA	10.5.92				4 May
20.79		Zharnel	Hughes	AIA-J	13.7.95				25 May
20.79	2.0	Brijesh "BJ"	Lawrence	SKN	27.12.89				30 May

(198)

Hand timed

20.5		Winston	George	GUY	19.5.87				10 Mar

Wind assisted

Mark	Wind	Name		Nat	Born	Pos	Meet	Venue	Date
19.79	2.5	Tyson	Gay ¶?	USA	9.8.82	1		Clermont	11 May
19.90	4.4		Weir			1		Edmonton	29 Jun
19.96	4.4	Jason	Young	JAM	21.3.91	2		Edmonton	29 Jun
19.99	3.2	Bryshon	Nellum	USA	1.5.89	1s2	NCAA	Eugene	6 Jun
20.00	2.4	Anaso	Jobodwana	RSA	30.7.92	1	WUG	Kazan	10 Ju
20.02	3.1		Jobodwana			1s3	NCAA	Eugene	6 Jun
20.05	4.3	Ameer	Webb	USA	19.3.91	1s1	NCAA	Eugene	6 Jun
20.09			I Young			1h4	NC	Des Moines	22 Jun
			(8/7)						
20.12	2.2	Jaysuma	Saidy Ndure	NOR	1.1.84	1rA		Sundsvall	28 Ju
20.21	4.5	Brandon	Byram	USA	11.9.88	1h3	NC	Des Moines	22 Jun
20.22	3.1	Julian	Forte	JAM	1.7.93	1rB		Sundsvall	28 Jun
20.25	3.1	Antoine	Adams	SKN	31.8.88	1	NC	Basseterre	16 Jun
20.26	3.1	Aaron	Brown	CAN	27.5.92	2s3	NCAA	Eugene	6 Jun
20.29	3.1	Carvin	Nkanata	USA	6.5.91	3s3	NCAA	Eugene	6 Jun
20.32	4.5	Remontay	McClain	USA	21.9.92	3h3	NC	Des Moines	22 Jun
20.32	2.1	Alonso	Edward	PAN	8.12.89	2		Sotteville-lès-Rouen	8 Ju
20.33	4.3	Justin	Austin	USA	8.10.89	3s1	NCAA	Eugene	6 Jun
20.33	3.7	Calesio	Newman	USA	20.8.86	2h4	NC	Des Moines	22 Jun
20.33	3.1	Gil	Roberts	USA	15.3.89	2h5	NC	Des Moines	22 Jun
20.34	5.6	Michael	Tinsley	USA	21.4.84	1		San Marcos	6 Apr
20.34	4.5	Dedric	Dukes	USA	4.2.92	4h3	NC	Des Moines	22 Jun
20.35	3.2	Diondre	Batson	USA	13.7.92	3s2	NCAA	Eugene	6 Jun
20.36	4.5	Aaron	Ernest	USA	8.11.93	5h3	NC	Des Moines	22 Jun
20.37A	3.2	Jeremy	Dodson	USA	30.8.87	1		Fort Collins	27 Apr
20.41	4.3	Akeem	Williams	JAM	7.11.90	4s1	NCAA	Eugene	6 Jun
20.41	3.1	Terrel	Cotton	USA	19.7.88	4h5	NC	Des Moines	22 Jun
20.42	3.2	Davion	Collins	USA	3.10.92	4s2	NCAA	Eugene	1 Jun
20.44	3.6	Harry	Adams	USA	27.11.89	2rA		Montverde, FL	1 Jun
20.45A	3.2	Joe	Morris	USA	4.10.89	2		Fort Collins	27 Apr
20.46	4.9	Aziz	Ouhadi	MAR	24.7.84	1	ArabC	Doha	24 May
20.48	2.6	Omar	Johnson	JAM	25.11.88	1		Amarillo	16 Mar
20.48	2.2	Oluwasegun	Makinde	CAN	6.7.91	3s1	WUG	Kazan	10 Ju
20.50	3.7	LaShawn	Butler	USA	3.2.87	3h4	NC	Des Moines	22 Jun
20.52	2.7	Ángel David	Rodríguez	ESP	25.4.80	1		Vitoria	6 Ju
20.53	4.7	Brijesh "BJ"	Lawrence	SKN	27.12.89	2		Basseterre	9 Jun
20.53	4.4	Tremaine	Harris	CAN	10.2.92	4		Edmonton	29 Jun
20.54	6.9	Jamil	Hubbard	USA	12.5.86	1		Fort Worth	15 Mar
20.54	2.5	Ryan	Carter	USA	24.7.89	1		Greensboro	4 May
20.54	3.2	Prezel	Hardy	USA	1.6.92	5s2	NCAA	Eugene	6 Jun
20.55	4.9	Fahad Mohamed	Al-Subaie	KSA-J	4.2.94	2	ArabC	Doha	24 May

Mark	Wind	Name		Nat	Born	Pos	Meet	Venue	Date
20.56	2.9	Shavez	Hart	BAH	9.6.92	1h1	JUCO	Hutchinson, KS	17 May
20.56	4.1	Kotaro	Taniguchi	JPN-J	3.11.94	1s1		Hiratsuka	7 Jul
20.56	2.3	Greg	Cackett	GBR	14.11.89	1r3		La Chaux-de-Fonds	7 Jul
20.57	3.4	André	De Grasse	CAN-J	10.11.94	2h3	JUCO	Hutchinson, KS	17 May
20.57A	2.1	Fred	Taylor	USA	17.8.89	1h1	NCAA-2	Pueblo, CO	24 May
20.57	2.6	Shota	Hara	JPN	18.7.92	1		Yokohama	26 May
20.58	3.4	Teray	Smith	BAH-J	28.9.94	1		Nassau	1 Apr
20.58	3.2	Brendon	Rodney	CAN	9.4.92	6s2	NCAA	Eugene	6 Jun
20.58	3.1	James	Taylor	USA	30.6.90	4s3	NCAA	Eugene	6 Jun
20.58	4.7	Miguel	Francis	ANT-J	28.2.95	3		Basseterre	9 Jun
20.59	4.6	David	Winters	USA-J	19.2.94	1		Wichita	13 Apr
20.59A	2.1	Joe	Horn	USA		2h1	NCAA-2	Pueblo, CO	24 May
20.59	4.2	Johan	Wissman	SWE	2.11.82	1rJ		Sundsvall	28 Jul

Mark	Wind	Name		Nat	Born	Date
20.60	4.3	Marcus	Rowland	USA	11.3.90	22 Jun
20.61	6.9	Cordero	Gray	USA	9.5.89	15 Mar
20.61	3.7	Tucker	Peabody	USA	14.8.92	22 Jun
20.61	4.0	Just'n	Thymes	USA-J	24.1.94	22 Jun
20.62	4.1	Hanoj	Carter	USA-J	26.6.94	16 Mar
20.62	3.3	Josh	Edmonds	USA	23.7.91	1 Jun
20.63A	2.1	Roland	Palacios	HON	5.5.87	10 Mar
20.63	3.5	Kendal	Williams	USA-J	23.9.95	16 Mar
20.63	5.0	Brien	Berry	USA	23.4.93	3 May
20.63	5.1	Deji	Tobais	GBR	31.10.91	19 May
20.64	6.9	Sam	Watts	GBR	14.2.92	15 Mar
20.64	3.4	Jevaughn	Minzie	JAM-J	20.7.95	1 Apr
20.65	3.7	Manteo	Mitchell	USA	6.7.87	5 May
20.66	6.9	Mychal	Dungey	USA	13.10.88	15 Mar
20.66	3.5	Levonte	Whitfield	USA	8.10.93	16 Mar
20.66	3.5	Kind	Butler	USA	8.4.89	22 Jun
20.67	2.1	Anthony	Bynum	USA	3.11.92	4 May
20.68	3.5	Kerron	Clement	USA	31.10.85	1 Jun
20.68	3.1	Michael	Bryan	USA	9.6.91	6 Jun
20.68	2.2	Roscoe	Engel	RSA	6.3.89	28 Jul
20.69	3.4	Jereem	Richards	TTO-J	13.1.94	1 Apr
20.69	2.9	Tommy	Brown	USA	29.3.90	4 May
20.69	2.7	David	Verburg	USA	14.5.91	4 May
20.70	3.2	Tim	Faust	USA	11.8.92	6 Jun
20.71	3.5	Arman	Hall	USA-J	14.2.94	5 Apr
20.71	3.7	Ricco	Hall	USA	24.11.92	13 Apr
20.71	3.0	Kenny	Jackson	USA	.91	13 Apr
20.72	3.6	James	Law	USA	8.10.80	1 Jun
20.73	4.6	Johnathan	Smith	USA	15.9.92	20 Apr
20.73	2.5	Darrius	Baker	USA	18.11.90	4 May
20.73	4.0	Tyreek	Hill	USA-J	1.3.94	18 May
20.74	2.5	Rhoan	Sterling	CAN	27.7.80	11 May
20.74	2.3	Titus	Kafunda	ZAM	3.8.93	7 Jul
20.75	2.5	Alexander	Kosenkow	GER	14.3.77	11 May
20.75	3.1	Tom	Kling-Baptiste	SWE	29.8.90	28 Jul
20.76	2.1	Calvin	Smith	USA	10.12.87	8 Jul
20.77	3.4	Zharnel	Hughes	AIA-J	13.7.95	1 Apr
20.77	w?	Ayodelle	Taffe	TTO-J	13.9.94	6 Apr
20.77	2.4	Antillio	Bastian	BAH	20.5.88	8 Jun
20.78	2.5	Trevorvano	Mackey ¶	BAH	5.1.92	25 Apr
20.78	3.2	Akani	Simbine	RSA	21.9.93	28 Apr
20.78	4.0	Tatum	Taylor	USA-J	8.9.94	4 May
20.78	3.7	Rubin	Williams	USA	9.7.83	4 May
20.78A	3.5	Jerimy	Strainge	USA-J	17.2.94	8 Jun
20.78A	2.6	Kenneth	Chibwana	ZIM-J	.94	20 Aug

Indoors

Mark	Wind	Name		Nat	Born	Pos	Meet	Venue	Date
20.48		Trey	Hadnot	USA	7.3.92	2r2	NCAA	Fayetteville	8 Mar
20.72		Jonathan	Åstrand	FIN	9.9.85				9 Feb
20.73	#	Omar	Johnson	JAM	25.11.88				2 Mar
20.76		Marek	Niit	EST	9.8.87				1 Mar

Low altitude bests

Mark	Wind	Name		Pos	Meet	Venue	Date
20.47	0.0	A Adams		6s1	WCh	Moskva	16 Aug
20.25w	3.1				NC	Basseterre	9 Jun
20.40w	3.1	Dodson		3h5	NC	Des Moines	22 Jun
20.71	1.8	Baloyes					6 Jul
20.54w	2.8						15 Jun
20.72	-0.6	Mena					28 Jun

Drugs disqualification subject to confirmation

Mark	Wind	Name		Nat	Born	Pos	Meet	Venue	Date
19.74	1.6	Tyson	Gay	USA	9.8.82	1	NC	Des Moines	23 Jun
20.07	-0.8		Gay			1s2	NC	Des Moines	23 Jun
20.60	-0.4	Trevorvano	Mackey ¶	BAH	5.1.92	1h1	NC	Freeport	22 Jun

JUNIORS

See main list for top 5 juniors. 9 performances by 7 men to 20.62. Additional marks and further juniors:

Kiryu   20.57   0.0   1   NC-j   Nagoya   20 Oct   20.59   1.6   1   Kyoto   19 May

Mark	Wind	Name		Nat	Born	Pos	Meet	Venue	Date
20.62	1.8	Leon	Reid	GBR	26.7.94	1s1	EJ	Rieti	20 Jul
20.62	-0.7	Nethaneel	Mitchell-Blake	GBR	2.4.94	1	EJ	Rieti	20 Jul
20.63	1.8	Kotaro	Taniguchi	JPN	3.11.94	1		Hiratsuka	7 Jul
20.63	-1.0	Michael	O'Hara	JAM-Y	29.9.96	1	WY	Donetsk	14 Jul
20.63A	0.0	Reynier	Mena (10)	CUB-Y	21.11.96	1	PAm-J	Medellín	24 Aug
20.64	-1.1	Kendal	Williams	USA	23.9.95	1		Orlando	18 May
20.64	-1.8	Mustaq'eem	Williams	USA	24.8.95	1		Greensboro	27 Jul
20.67	1.9	Hanoj	Carter	USA	26.6.94	1		Nacogdoches	6 Apr
20.67	-1.0	Vitor Hugo	dos Santos	BRA-Y	1.2.96	2	WY	Donetsk	14 Jul
20.69A		Mike	Mokamba	KEN	28.8.94	1	NC	Nairobi	22 Jun
20.72	0.5	Jereem	Richards	TTO	13.1.94	3	NC	Port of Spain	23 Jun
20.73	1.6	Arman	Hall	USA	14.2.94	1rB		Gainesville	20 Apr
20.73	2.0	Khalfani	Muhammad	PUR	26.9.94	1		Norwalk	24 May
20.74	1.6	Mickael-Meba	Zézé	FRA	19.5.94	1		Bonneuil-sur-Marne	7 Jun
20.74A	0.0	André	De Grasse (20)	CAN	10.11.94	3	PAm-J	Medellín	24 Aud
20.74A	-0.4	Fahad Mohamed	Al-Subaie	KSA	4.2.94	1	Is.Sol	Palembang	27 Sep

Hand: 20.6   0.0   Yaniel   Carrero   CUB   17.8.95   1   NC-j   Las Tunas   19 Jul

Wind assisted. See main list for top 6 juniors. 7 performances by 6 men to 20.59. Additional mark and further juniors:

Baloyes   20.58w   2.8   1   NC   Cartagena   15 Jun

Mark	Wind	Name		Nat	Born	Pos	Venue	Date
20.61	4.0	Just'n	Thymes	USA	24.1.94	1	Des Moines	22 Jun
20.62	4.1	Hanoj	Carter	USA	26.6.94	1	Ruston	16 Mar
20.63	3.5	Kendal	Williams	USA	23.9.95	1	Jacksonville	16 Mar
20.64	3.4	Jevaughn	Minzie	JAM	20.7.95	2	Nassau	1 Apr
20.69	3.4	Jereem	Richards	TTO	13.1.94	3	Nassau	1 Apr

Mark		Name	Nat	Born	Pos	Meet	Venue	Date
20.71	3.5	Arman	Hall	USA	14.2.94	2	FlaR	Gainesville	5 Apr
20.73	4.0	Tyreek	Hill	USA	1.3.94	3	JUCO	Hutchinson, KS	18 May

300 METRES

Mark	Name		Nat	Born	Pos	Meet	Venue	Date
31.97	Rusheen	McDonald	JAM	17.8.92	1		Rieti	8 Sep
32.31	Jonathan	Borlée	BEL	22.2.88	1		Liège (NX)	10 Jul
32.32	Edino	Steele	JAM	6.1.87	1		Lahti	17 Jul
32.34	Greg	Nixon	USA	12.9.81	1		Pasadena	23 Mar
32.34	Pavel	Maslák	CZE	21.2.91	1		Turnov	28 May
32.39	Kind	Butler	USA	8.4.88	2		Liège (NX)	10 Jul
32.40	Tony	McQuay	USA	16.4.90	3		Liège (NX)	10 Jul
32.40	Ramon	Miller	BAH	17.2.87	2		Lahti	17 Jul
32.57	Luguelín	Santos	DOM	12.11.93	1		Mölndal	3 Aug
32.85	Diego	Marani	ITA	27.4.90	2		Rieti	8 Sep

Hand timing

| 32.7 | Orestes | Rodríguez | CUB | 3.6.89 | 1 | | La Habana | 20 Dec |

Indoors

32.48	Lalonde	Gordon	TTO	25.11.88	1		New York (Armory)	11 Jan
32.60	Calvin	Nkanata	USA	6.5.91	1		Kent	7 Dec
32.72	Kévin	Borlée	BEL	22.2.88	2		Gent	10 Feb

In World Champs 400m Moskva 13 Aug: Merritt 32.0, James 32.3

400 METRES

Mark	Name		Nat	Born	Pos	Meet	Venue	Date
43.74	LaShawn	Merritt	USA	27.6.86	1	WCh	Moskva	13 Aug
43.96	Kirani	James	GRN	1.9.92	1	DL	Saint-Denis	6 Jul
44.02		James			1	DL	Shanghai	18 May
44.09		Merritt			2	DL	Saint-Denis	6 Jul
44.13		Merritt			1	WK	Zürich	29 Aug
44.21		Merritt			1	NC	Des Moines	22 Jun
44.32		Merritt			1	Pre	Eugene	1 Jun
44.32		James			2	WK	Zürich	29 Aug
44.36		Merritt			1s1	NC	Des Moines	21 Jun
44.39		James			2	Pre	Eugene	1 Jun
44.40	Tony	McQuay	USA	16.4.90	2	WCh	Moskva	13 Aug
44.49		James			1	GS	Ostrava	27 Jun
44.52	Luguelín	Santos	DOM	12.11.93	3	WCh	Moskva	13 Aug
44.54	Jonathan	Borlée	BEL	22.2.88	4	WCh	Moskva	13 Aug
44.60		Merritt			2	DL	Shanghai	18 May
44.60		Merritt			1s2	WCh	Moskva	12 Aug
44.61	Youssef	Al-Masrahi	KSA	31.12.87	1s1	WCh	Moskva	12 Aug
44.65		James			1	DL	London (OS)	26 Jul
44.66		McQuay			2s1	WChT	Moskva	12 Aug
44.69		Merritt			1	DNG	Stockholm	22 Aug
44.72		James			1		Nassau	13 Apr
44.72		Al-Masrahi			1	ArabC	Doha	22 May
44.72		McQuay			2s1	NC	Des Moines	21 Jun
44.73	Bryshon	Nellum	USA	1.5.89	1	NCAA	Eugene	7 Jun
44.73	Kévin	Borlée	BEL	22.2.88	1	NC	Bruxelles	21 Jul
44.74		Santos			1	Drake	Des Moines	26 Apr
44.74		McQuay			2	NC	Des Moines	22 Jun
44.75	David	Verburg	USA	14.5.91	3s1	NC	Des Moines	21 Jun
44.76		Nellum			1	Pac-12	Los Angeles	12 May
44.81		James			1s3	WCh	Moskva	12 Aug
44.82	Arman	Hall	USA-J	14.2.94	4s1	NC	Des Moines	21 Jun
	(31/10)							
44.84	Pavel	Maslák	CZE	21.2.91	3s3	WCh	Moskva	12 Aug
44.93	Ramon	Miller	BAH	17.2.87	1	NC	Freeport	22 Jun
44.94	Deon	Lendore	TTO	28.10.92	2	NCAA	Eugene	7 Jun
44.95	Anderson	Henriques	BRA	3.3.92	3s1	WCh	Moskva	12 Aug
45.05	Martyn	Rooney	GBR	3.4.87	1	VD	Bruxelles	6 Sep
45.08	Josh	Mance	USA	21.3.92	1		Los Angeles (ER)	4 May
45.08	Javere	Bell	JAM	20.9.92	1	NC	Kingston	23 Jun
45.09	Wayde	van Niekerk	RSA	15.7.92	2	GS	Ostrava	27 Jun
45.10	Kyle	Clemons	USA	27.8.90	1	Big 12	Waco	5 May
45.14	Michael	Berry	USA	10.12.91	2	Pac-12	Los Angeles	12 May
	(20)							
45.18	Chris	Brown	BAH	15.10.78	3s2	WCh	Moskva	12 Aug
45.19	Hugh	Graham	USA	10.10.92	5s1	NC	Des Moines	21 Jun
45.19	Jarrin	Solomon	TTO	11.1.86	2h5	WCh	Moskva	11 Aug

Mark	Name		Nat	Born	Pos	Meet	Venue	Date	
45.21	Michael	Mathieu	BAH	24.6.83	1		Montverde, FL	8	Jun
45.23	James	Harris	USA	19.9.91	2s1	NCAA	Eugene	5	Jun
45.23	Nigel	Levine	GBR	30.4.89	1	NC	Birmingham	14	Jul
45.24	Javon	Francis	JAM-J	14.12.94	2	NC	Kingston	23	Jun
45.25	Manteo	Mitchell	USA	6.7.87	2		Madrid	13	Jul
45.26	LaToy	Williams	BAH	28.5.88	2	NC	Freeport	22	Jun
45.28	Rusheen	McDonald	JAM	17.8.92	1		Lignano	16	Jul
(30)									
45.29	Yoandys	Lescay	CUB-J	5.1.94	1rA		La Habana	28	Jun
45.31	Hugo	de Sousa	BRA	5.3.87	2		São Paulo	11	May
45.33	Torrin	Lawrence	USA	11.4.89	1		Atlanta	11	May
45.33	Calvin	Smith	USA	10.12.87	7	DL	Saint-Denis	6	Jul
45.35	Jeremy	Wariner	USA	31.1.84	2	Drake	Des Moines	26	Apr
45.35	Matteo	Galvan	ITA	24.8.88	3	VD	Bruxelles	6	Sep
45.37	Michael	Bingham	GBR	13.4.86	1		Atlanta	17	May
45.41A	Dane	Hyatt	JAM	22.1.84	1	NCAA-2	Pueblo, CO	25	May
45.45A	Gustavo	Cuesta	DOM	14.11.88	1		Medellín	25	May
45.46	Blake	Heriot	USA	26.9.91	2	Big 12	Waco	5	May
(40)									
45.47	Daundre	Barnaby	CAN	9.12.90	1h1	NCAA-E	Greensboro	23	May
45.48	Akheem	Gauntlett	JAM	26.8.90	3	NC	Kingston	23	Jun
45.48	Richard	Strachan	GBR	18.11.86	1rA		La Chaux-de-Fonds	7	Jul
45.49	Vladimir	Krasnov	RUS	19.8.90	1	WUG	Kazan	9	Jul
45.50	Omar	Johnson	JAM	25.11.88	4	NC	Kingston	23	Jun
45.50	Nick	Ekelund-Arenander	DEN	23.1.89	4		Madrid	13	Jul
45.50	Kind	Butler	USA	8.4.89	2	NA	Heusden-Zolder	13	Jul
45.51	Lev	Mosin	RUS	7.12.92	1	EU23	Tampere	12	Jul
45.53	Brian	Gregan	IRL	31.12.89	1		Huelva	12	Jun
45.53	Edino	Steele	JAM	6.1.87	5	NC	Kingston	23	Jun
(50)									
45.54	Wesley	Neymour	BAH	1.9.88	4	NC	Freeport	22	Jun
45.55	Maksim	Dyldin	RUS	19.5.87	1	NC	Moskva	24	Jul
45.56A	Vernon	Norwood	USA	10.4.92	1		El Paso	13	Apr
45.56	Yuzo	Kanemaru	JPN	18.9.87	1	NC	Tokyo [Chofu]	8	Jun
45.59	Conrad	Williams	GBR	20.3.82	2	NC	Birmingham	14	Jul
45.59	Noah	Akwu	NGR	23.9.90	1	NC	Calabar	20	Jun
45.62	Hiroyuki	Nakano	JPN	9.12.88	1r3		Fukuroi	3	May
45.62	Pedro	de Oliveira	BRA	17.2.92	3		São Paulo	11	May
45.62	Cass	Brown-Stewart	USA	2.8.92	3s1	NCAA	Eugene	5	Jun
45.62	Rafith	Rodríguez	COL	1.6.89	1	Bol G	Trujillo	26	Nov
(60)									
45.63	Nicholas	Maitland	JAM	27.11.89	3	WUG	Kazan	9	Jul
45.64	Ashton	Eaton	USA	21.1.88	1D		Santa Barbara	5	Apr
45.65	Renny	Quow	TTO	25.8.87	3	NC	Port of Spain	22	Jun
45.65	Ali Khamis	Abbas	BRN-J	30.6.95	2	AsiC	Pune	4	Jul
45.65	Donald	Sanford	ISR	5.2.87	1	Macc G	Tel Aviv	24	Jul
45.66A	Nijel	Amos	BOT-J	15.3.94	1		Potchefstroom	19	Mar
45.67	Riker	Hylton	JAM	13.12.88	1rB		Kingston	4	May
45.67	Lalonde	Gordon	TTO	25.11.88	6	Pre	Eugene	1	Jun
45.69	Marcus	Boyd	USA	3.3.89	3	Drake	Des Moines	26	Apr
45.69	Rafal	Omelko	POL	16.1.89	4	WUG	Kazan	9	Jul
(70)									
45.69	Nobuya	Kato	JPN-J	16.4.95	1		Fukuroi	2	Nov
45.71	Najee	Glass	USA-J	12.6.94	2	FlaR	Gainesville	5	Apr
45.71	Kazuya	Watanabe	JPN	20.7.88	1r2		Fukuroi	3	May
45.71	Brycen	Spratling	USA	10.3.92	5s2	NC	Des Moines	21	Jun
45.71	Philip	Osei	CAN	30.10.90	4	Jerome	Burnaby	1	Jul
45.72	Quentin	Iglehart-Summers	USA	15.6.87	1		Houston	30	May
45.72	David	Gollnow	GER	8.4.89	1		Regensburg	8	Jun
45.73	Gil	Roberts	USA	15.3.89	3	MSR	Walnut	20	Apr
45.73	Clayton	Parros	USA	11.12.90	2h6	NCAA-E	Greensboro	23	May
45.73	Mame-Ibra	Anne	FRA	7.11.89	8	DL	Saint-Denis	6	Jul
(80)									
45.74	Kerron	Clement	USA	31.10.85	1		Montverde, FL	1	Jun
45.75	DeWayne	Barrett	JAM	26.9.81	7	NC	Kingston	23	Jun
45.76A	Alphas	Kishoyan	KEN-J	12.10.94	1	WChT	Nairobi	13	Jul
45.77	Eric	Krüger	GER	21.3.88	2		Regensburg	8	Jun
45.79	Abiola	Onakoya	NGR	10.10.90	2	NC	Calabar	20	Jun
45.79	Anas	Beshir	EGY	19.7.93	2	Med G	Mersin	28	Jun
45.80	Wágner	Cardoso	BRA	20.3.89	3	NC	São Paulo	7	Jun
45.80	Dylan	Borlée	BEL	20.9.92	2	NC	Bruxelles	21	Jul

Mark	Name		Nat	Born	Pos	Meet	Venue	Date
45.81	Pavel	Ivashko	RUS-J	16.11.94	1	EJ	Rieti	19 Jul
45.82	Emmnuel	Tugumisirize	UGA	30.11.88	2h1	NCAA-E	Greensboro	23 May
(90)								
45.82A	Rolando	Berch	JAM	8.9.90	2	NCAA-2	Pueblo, CO	25 May
45.82	José	Meléndez	VEN	19.5.93	4h3	WChT	Moskva	11 Aug
45.83	Jürgen	Wielart	NED	17.1.92	1	NC	Amsterdam	21 Jul
45.84	Liemarvin	Bonavacia	CUR	5.4.89	1		Ponce	20 Apr
45.84	Joey	Hughes	USA	26.10.90	1		Westwood	1 Jun
45.84	Toumany	Coulibaly	FRA	6.1.88	2rA		La Chaux-de-Fonds	7 Jul
45.85	Jamaal	Torrance	USA	20.7.83	2		Montverde, FL	1 Jun
45.86	Brunson	Miller	USA	10.2.91	3h1	NCAA-E	Greensboro	23 May
45.86	Isaac	Makwala	BOT	29.9.86	3rA		La Chaux-de-Fonds	7 Jul
45.87A	Jacques	de Swardt	RSA	12.8.92	2		Potchefstroom	19 Mar
(100)								
45.87	Yusuke	Ishitsuka	JPN	19.6.87	2r3		Fukuroi	3 May
45.87	Quincy	Downing	USA	16.1.93	4s3	NCAA	Eugene	5 Jun

Mark		Name	Nat	Born	Date		Mark		Name	Nat	Born	Date
45.88	Errol	Nolan	JAM	18.8.91	12 May		46.09A	Arizmendi	Peguero	DOM	7.8.80	25 May
45.88	Richard	Buck	GBR	14.11.86	1 Jun		46.09	Mamadou-Elimane	Hanné	FRA	6.3.88	22 Jun
45.88	Vitaliy	Butrym	UKR	10.1.91	12 Jul		46.09	Alex	Beck	AUS	7.2.92	21 Jul
45.88	William	Oyowe	BEL	28.10.87	21 Jul		46.10A	Daniel	Harper	CAN	28.8.89	13 Apr
45.89	Thomas	Schneider	GER	7.11.88	8 Jun		46.10	Yoan	Décimus	FRA	30.11.87	7 Jun
45.89	Martin	Manley	JAM-Y	10.3.97	12 Jul		46.10	Peter	Matthews	JAM	13.11.89	20 Jun
45.89A	Brandon	McBride	CAN-J	15.6.94	15 Aug		46.10	Winston	George	GUY	19.5.87	26 Sep
45.90	Chris	Giesting	USA	10.12.92	5 May		46.11	Akino	Ming	JAM	29.11.90	11 May
45.90	Raidel	Acea	CUB	31.10.90	28 Jun		46.12	Steven	Solomon	AUS	16.5.93	12 May
45.90	Luke	Lennon-Ford	GBR	5.5.89	14 Jul		46.12	Johan	Delasse	FRA	14.11.84	6 Jul
45.92	Greg	Nixon	USA	12.9.81	11 May		46.12A	Moses	Kertich	KEN	24.12.85	13 Jul
45.93	Machel	Cedenio	TTO-J	6.9.95	30 Mar		46.13	Ricardo	Chambers	JAM	7.10.84	22 Jun
45.93	Ofentse	Mogawane	RSA	20.2.82	18 Apr		46.13	Lukasz	Krawczuk	POL	15.6.89	20 Jul
45.94	Stephen	Newbold	BAH-J	5.8.94	30 Mar		46.14	Alonzo	Russell	BAH	8.2.92	20 Apr
45.94	Bram	Peters	NED	6.2.92	6 Jul		46.15	Darrell	Bush	USA	13.5.93	13 Apr
45.95	Tyson	Gay ¶?	USA	9.8.82	20 Apr		46.15	Tewado	Latty	JAM	13.6.90	12 May
45.97	Sergey	Petukhov	RUS	22.12.83	24 Jul		46.15	Hideyuki	Hirose	JPN	20.7.89	7 Jun
45.98A	Bernardo	Baloyes	COL-J	6.1.94	25 May		46.15	Patryk	Dobek	POL-J	13.2.94	19 Jul
45.98	Marcin	Marciniszyn	POL	7.9.82	20 Jul		46.15	Teddy	Atine-Venel	FRA	16.3.85	24 Jul
45.98	Antoine	Gillet	BEL	22.3.88	21 Jul		46.15	Dayon	de Oliveira	BRA	4.9.89	14 Sep
45.99A	Burkheart	Ellis	BAR	18.9.92	25 May		46.17	Arturo	Ramirez	VEN	19.4.91	5 Apr
45.99	Marc	Macédon	FRA	15.9.88	7 Jun		46.17	Elvyonn	Bailey	USA	.92	12 May
46.00	Stephon	Pamilton	USA	18.9.91	20 Apr		46.17	David	Dickens	USA	19.3.85	17 May
46.00	Jun	Kimura	JPN	26.5.91	3 May		46.18	Payton	Hazzard	USA	6.9.93	20 Apr
46.00	Kengo	Yamazaki	JPN	30.7.92	8 Jun		46.18	Ronnie	Baker	USA	15.10.93	5 May
46.00	Allodin	Fothergill	JAM	7.2.87	22 Jun		46.18	Juan	Green	USA-J	12.7.94	5 Jun
46.01	Steven	Gayle	JAM-J	19.3.94	18 May		46.18	Isah	Salihu	NGR	2.11.91	14 Jun
46.01A	William	Shell	USA	.92	25 May		46.18	Aleksey	Kenig	RUS	15.8.90	24 Jul
46.01	Kacper	Kozlowski	POL	7.12.86	20 Jul		46.19	Akeem	Williams	JAM	7.11.90	21 Apr
46.02	Oral	Thompson	JAM	11.12.82	18 May		46.19	Patrick	Feeney	USA	29.12.91	23 May
46.02	Michael	Cherry	USA-Y	23.3.95	1 Jun		46.19	Kegan	Campbell	JAM	.93	25 May
46.03	Armon	Owens	USA	18.1.93	6 Apr		46.19A	Josh	Edmonds	USA	23.7.91	25 May
46.03A	Nery	Brenes	CRC	25.9.85	20 Jul		46.19	Mamadou	Kassé Hann	SEN	10.10.86	23 Jun
46.04	Freddy	Mezones	VEN	24.9.87	4 May		46.19		Chen Jianxin	CHN	10.7.87	8 Sep
46.04	Jonathan Henrique da Silva		BRA	17.8.90	6 Jun		46.20	Jereem	Richards	TTO-J	13.1.94	3 May
46.04	Nikita	Uglov	RUS	11.10.93	12 Jul		46.20	Nick	Efkamp	USA	19.9.92	5 May
46.06	Rabah	Yousif	SUD	11.12.86	18 May		46.20	Ryan	Carter	USA	24.7.89	12 May
46.06A	James	Quarles	USA	9.9.90	25 May		46.21	Lamar	Bruton	USA-J	26.5.95	16 Jun
46.06	Jamie	Bowie	GBR	1.4.89	27 Jul		46.21	Thomas	Jordier	FRA-J	12.8.94	19 Jul
46.08	Zack	Bilderback	USA-J	15.7.94	5 May		46.22	Javier	Culson	PUR	25.7.84	6 Apr
46.08	Ismail	Al-Sabyani	KSA	25.4.89	22 May		46.22	Angel	Chelala	FRA	23.8.89	6 Jul
46.08	Duane	Solomon	USA	28.12.84	3 Sep		(185)					

Best at low altitude

45.67	Norwood	1		Lubbock	25 Apr	45.87	Cuesta	1	Tortola	1 Jun
45.99	Hyatt	20 Jun	46.16	Brenes	11 Aug	46.18	McBride	15 Aug		

Indoors

45.72	Errol	Nolan	JAM	18.8.91	1h2	NCAA	Fayetteville	8 Mar
45.92	Patrick	Feeney	USA	29.12.91	8 Mar	46.00 Pavel Trenikhin RUS 24.3.86	2 Mar	
						46.09 Anton Kokorin RUS 5.4.87	9 Mar	

Hand timed

45.2A	David	Rudisha	KEN	17.12.88	1		Nairobi	3 May
45.5	William	Collazo	CUB	31.8.86	1		La Habana	20 Apr
45.5A	Alphas	Kishoyan	KEN	12.10.94	1	NC	Nairobi	22 Jun
46.0A	Moses	Kertich	KEN	24.12.85	22 Jun	46.0A	Boniface Mweresa KEN 13.11.93	15 Mar

JUNIORS

See main list for top 8 juniors. 12 performances by 3 men to 45.54. Additional marks and further juniors:

Hall	45.01	3	NC	Des Moines	22 Jun	45.45	5h2	WCh	Moskva	11 Aug
	45.02	3	NCAA	Eugene	7 Jun	45.50	2h3	NCAA	Eugene	5 Jun
	45.30	3		Madrid	13 Jul	45.54	5s3	WCh	Moskva	11 Aug
Francis	45.37	2h2	WCh	Moskva	11 Aug	45.42	1		Kingston	25 May

Mark	Name		Nat	Born	Pos	Meet	Venue	Date
Lescay	45.36	1 Barr La Habana			4	Jun		
45.89	Martin	Manley	JAM-Y	10.3.97	1	WY	Donetsk	12 Jul
45.89A	Brandon	McBride (10)	CAN	15.6.94	1	PAm-J	Medellín	15 Aug
45.93	Machel	Cedenio	TTO	6.9.95	1		Nassau	30 Mar
45.94	Stephen	Newbold	BAH	5.8.94	1h2		Nassau	30 Mar
45.98A	Bernardo	Baloyes	COL	6.1.94	2		Medellín	25 May
46.01	Steven	Gayle	JAM	19.3.94	3	JUCO	Hutchinson, KS	18 May
46.02	Michael	Cherry	USA-Y	23.3.95	1		Newport News, VA	1 Jun
46.08	Zack	Bilderback	USA	15.7.94	3	Big 12	Waco	5 May
46.15	Patryk	Dobek	POL	13.2.94	2	EJ	Rieti	19 Jul
46.18	Juan	Green	USA	12.7.94	6s3	NCAA	Eugene	5 Jun
46.20	Jereem	Richards	TTO	13.1.94	3		Port of Spain	3 May
46.20	Nick	Efkamp	USA	19.9.92	5	Big12	Waco	5 May
46.20	Ryan	Carter	USA	24.7.89	3	IC4A	Princeton	12 May
46.21	Lamar	Bruton (20)	USA	26.5.95	2	N.Sch	Greensboro	16 Jun
46.21	Thomas	Jordier	FRA	12.8.94	3	EJ	Rieti	19 Jul

500 METRES

Mark	Name		Nat	Born	Pos	Meet	Venue	Date
59.32	Orestes	Rodríguez	CUB	3.6.89	1		La Habana	5 Feb
60.02	William	Collazo	CUB	31.8.86	2		La Habana	5 Feb
60.10	Osmaidel	Pellicier	CUB	30.3.92	3		La Habana	5 Feb
60.15	Amaury	Valle	CUB	18.1.90	4		La Habana	5 Feb
60.35	Pavel	Maslák	CZE	21.2.91	1		Cheb	2 Aug
60.49	Daniel	Nemecek	CZE	11.8.91	2		Cheb	2 Aug

600 METRES

Mark	Name		Nat	Born	Pos	Meet	Venue	Date
1:13.28	Duane	Solomon	USA	28.12.84	1		Burnaby	1 Jul
1:13.9	Raidel	Acea	CUB	31.10.90	1		La Habana	20 Apr
1:14.84	Casimir	Loxsom	USA	17.3.91	2		Burnaby	1 Jul
1:15:27+	Ayanleh	Souleiman	DJI	3.12.92	1	in 800m	Bruxelles	6 Sep
1:15.5+	Mohammed	Aman	ETH	10.1.94	2	in 800m	Bruxelles	6 Sep
1:15.99	Abdulrahman Musaeb Balla		QAT	19.3.89	22 Aug	1:16.09	Anthony Chemut	KEN	17.12.92 22 Aug

Indoors

Mark	Name		Nat	Born	Pos	Meet	Venue	Date
1:15.61	Erik	Sowinski	USA	21.12.89	1	Mill	New York (Armory)	16 Feb
1:15.63	Pierre-Ambroise	Bosse	FRA	11.5.92	1rB		Moskva	3 Feb
1:16.19	Jarrin Solomon	TTO	11.1.86	16 Feb	1:16.43	Timothy Kitum	KEN-J 20.11.94	3 Feb
1:16.22	David Greene	GBR	11.4.86	26 Jan	1:16.45	Andrew Osagie	GBR	19.2.88 26 Jan
1:16.27	Yuriy Borzakovskiy	RUS	12.4.81	3 Feb				

800 METRES

Mark	Name		Nat	Born	Pos	Meet	Venue	Date
1:42.37	Mohammed	Aman	ETH-J	10.1.94	1	VD	Bruxelles	6 Sep
1:43.03	Nick	Symmonds	USA	30.12.83	2	VD	Bruxelles	6 Sep
1:43.22	Ferguson	Cheruiyot	KEN	30.11.89	3	VD	Bruxelles	6 Sep
1:43.27	Duane	Solomon	USA	28.12.84	1	NC	Des Moines	23 Jun
1:43.31		Aman			1	WCh	Moskva	13 Aug
1:43.33		Aman			1	Athl	Lausanne	4 Jul
1:43.55		Symmonds			2	WCh	Moskva	13 Aug
1:43.56		Symmonds			1	WK	Zürich	29 Aug
1:43.61		Aman			1	GGala	Roma	6 Jun
1:43.63	Ayanleh	Souleiman	DJI	3.12.92	1		Sollentuna	27 Jun
1:43.67		Symmonds			1	DL	London (OS)	26 Jul
1:43.70		Symmonds			2	NC	Des Moines	23 Jun
1:43.72		Solomon			1	Herc	Monaco	19 Jul
1:43.76	Pierre-Ambroise	Bosse	FRA	11.5.92	2	Herc	Monaco	19 Jul
1:43.76		Souleiman			3	WCh	Moskva	13 Aug
1:43.78		Aman			1	GS	Ostrava	27 Jun
1:43.79	Marcin	Lewandowski	POL	13.6.87	2	WK	Zürich	29 Aug
1:43.83		Lewandowski			4	VD	Bruxelles	6 Sep
1:43.84	Brandon	Johnson	USA	6.3.85	1		Madrid	13 Jul
1:43.86	Abdulaziz	Mohamed	KSA	7.1.91	1	Is.Sol	Palembang	26 Sep
1:43.87	David	Rudisha (10)	KEN	17.12.88	1	DL	Doha	10 May
1:43.87		Solomon			1s1	WCh	Moskva	11 Aug
1:43.9 A	Jeremiah	Mutai	KEN	27.12.92	1		Nairobi	25 May
1:43.91		Bosse			2	GGala	Roma	6 Jun
1:43.93	Kevin	López	ESP	12.6.90	3	Herc	Monaco	19 Jul
1:43.93	Abdulrahman Musaeb Balla		QAT	19.3.89	1		Rieti	8 Sep
1:43.97		Johnson			3	NC	Des Moines	23 Jun
1:43.97		Aman			1	ISTAF	Berlin	1 Sep
1:44.00	Ilham Tanui	Özbilen	TUR	5.3.90	1	Med G	Mersin	29 Jun

MEN 2013

Mark	Name		Nat	Born	Pos	Meet	Venue	Date
1:44.08		Lewandowski			4	WCh	Moskva	13 Aug
	(30/14)							
1:44.24	Job	Kinyor	KEN	2.9.90	3	DL	Doha	10 May
1:44.33A	Anthony	Chemut	KEN	17.12.92	1	WChT	Nairobi	13 Jul
1:44.33	Rafith	Rodríguez	COL	1.6.89	5	Herc	Monaco	19 Jul
1:44.34	Tyler	Mulder	USA	15.2.87	6	Herc	Monaco	19 Jul
1:44.36	Andrew	Osagie	GBR	19.2.88	5	WCh	Moskva	13 Aug
1:44.37	André	Olivier	RSA	29.12.89	3	GGala	Roma	6 Jun
	(20)							
1:44.43	Anis	Ananenko	BLR	29.11.85	1	Gyulai	Budapest	10 Jul
1:44.45	Timothy	Kitum	KEN-J	20.11.94	7	Herc	Monaco	19 Jul
1:44.49	Edwin	Melly	KEN-J	23.4.94	2		Rieti	8 Sep
1:44.57	Abraham	Rotich	BRN	26.6.93	2	Gyulai	Budapest	10 Jul
1:44.67	Giordano	Benedetti	ITA	22.5.89	4	GGala	Roma	6 Jun
1:44.71	Nijel	Amos	BOT-J	15.3.94	4	Athl	Lausanne	4 Jul
1:44.76	Adam	Kszczot	POL	2.9.89	6	GGala	Roma	6 Jun
1:44.8 A	Asbel	Kiprop	KEN	30.6.89	1		Nairobi	3 May
1:44.84	Kléberson	Davide	BRA	20.7.85	1		São Paulo	27 Mar
1:44.84	Mark	English	IRL	18.3.93	6	DL	London (OS)	26 Jul
	(30)							
1:44.96	Amine	El Manaoui	MAR	20.11.91	1		Rabat	25 Jul
1:44.97	Michael	Rimmer	GBR	3.2.86	6	DL	Doha	10 May
1:44.99	Aman	Wote	ETH	18.4.84	1		Tomblaine	2 Jul
1:45.0 A	Geoffrey	Rono	KEN	21.4.87	2		Nairobi	25 May
1:45.01	Charles	Jock	USA	23.11.89	2		Los Angeles (ER)	17 May
1:45.04	Elijah	Greer	USA	24.10.90	4	NC	Des Moines	23 Jun
1:45.04	Joe	Abbott	USA	3.3.90	7	DL	London (OS)	26 Jul
1:45.08	Michael	Rutt	USA	28.10.87	3		Los Angeles (ER)	17 May
1:45.10	Maurys Surel	Castillo	CUB	19.10.84	5		Madrid	13 Jul
1:45.13	Felix	Kitur	KEN	17.4.87	1		Oordegem	6 Jul
	(40)							
1:45.21	Erik	Sowinski	USA	21.12.89	6	NC	Des Moines	23 Jun
1:45.24	Yuriy	Borzakovskiy	RUS	12.4.81	2	Chall	Moskva	11 Jun
1:45.36	Mark	Wieczorek	USA	25.12.84	4		Los Angeles (ER)	17 May
1:45.37	Tamás	Kazi	HUN	16.5.85	5		Rieti	8 Sep
1:45.38	Sammy	Kirongo	KEN-J	4.2.94	1	Gyulai	Budapest	10 Jul
1:45.39	Antoine	Gakémé	BDI	24.12.91	5s1	WCh	Moskva	11 Aug
1:45.44	Alex	Rowe	AUS	8.7.92	2		Oordegem	6 Jul
1:45.44	Luis Alberto	Marco	ESP	20.8.86	1		Huelva	24 Jul
1:45.45	Brian	Gagnon	USA	8.5.87	5s1	NC	Des Moines	21 Jun
1:45.47	Samir	Jamaa	MAR	9.2.90	2	Med G	Mersin	29 Jun
	(50)							
1:45.47A	Cornelius	Kiplangat	KEN	21.12.92	5	WChT	Nairobi	13 Jul
1:45.49A	Abednego	Chesebe	KEN	20.6.82	1h3		Kampala	18 Jul
1:45.60	Anthony	Romaniw	CAN	15.9.91	3		Ninove	27 Jul
1:45.64	Johan	Cronje	RSA	13.4.82	7	ISTAF	Berlin	1 Sep
1:45.67	Mukhtar	Mohammed	GBR	1.12.90	10	DL	London (OS)	26 Jul
1:45.69	Andreas	Lange	GER	29.1.91	1		Regensburg	8 Jun
1:45.69	Nader	Benhanbel	MAR-J	1.7.94	1	NC	Casablanca	6 Jul
1:45.71	Mohamed Ahmed	Hamada	EGY	22.10.92	3	Med G	Mersin	29 Jun
1:45.71	Abraham	Kiplagat	KEN	8.9.84	5	Gyulai	Budapest	10 Jul
1:45.71A	Ronald	Musagala	UGA	16.12.92	2h3		Kampala	18 Jul
	(60)							
1:45.72	Andy	González	CUB	17.10.87	1	Barr	La Habana	4 Jun
1:45.75	Casimir	Loxsom	USA	17.3.91	2		Dublin	17 Jul
1:45.83	Moses	Kibet	KEN-J	20.11.94	2		Regensburg	8 Jun
1:45.86	Matthew	Centrowitz	USA	18.10.89	4		Portland	8 Jun
1:45.86	Paul	Robinson	IRL	24.5.91	4		Dublin (S)	17 Jul
1:45.88	Diego	Gomes	BRA	19.4.85	2		São Paulo	7 Apr
1:45.88	James	Eichberger	MEX	4.8.90	5		Ninove	27 Jul
1:45.91	Hamid	Oualich	FRA	26.4.88	3		Tomblaine	2 Jul
1:45.94	Wesley	Vázquez	PUR-J	27.3.94	1=		Huelva	25 Jun
1:45.97	Alejandro	Rodríguez	ESP	1.5.89	6		Madrid	13 Jul
	(70)							
1:46.0 A	Bernard	Kipyegon	KEN-J	.94	6	NC	Nairobi	22 Jun
1:46.00	Alejandro	Estévez	ESP	21.1.92	2		Huelva	24 Jun
1:46.01	Robin	Schembera	GER	1.10.88	8	ISTAF	Berlin	1 Sep
1:46.04	Patrick	Zwicker	GER-J	13.7.94	3		Regensburg	8 Jun
1:46.05	Raidel	Acea	CUB	31.10.90	2	Barr	La Habana	4 Jun
1:46.07	Mohamed Amine	Benferare	MAR	16.2.91	1		Alger	13 Jun
1:46.09	Yassine	Hathat	MAR	30.7.91	2		Alger	13 Jun

Mark	Name		Nat	Born	Pos	Meet	Venue	Date
1:46.09	Evans	Kipkorir	KEN	.85	4		Tomblaine	2 Jul
1:46.11	Jozef	Repcík	SVK	3.8.86	1		Tábor	24 Jul
1:46.16	Ján	Kubista	CZE	23.9.90	8	GS	Ostrava	27 Jun
(80)								
1:46.18	Sebastian	Keiner	GER	22.8.89	4		Regensburg	8 Jun
1:46.18	Benson	Seurei	BRN	27.3.84	1		Kortrijk	14 Jul
1:46.20	Prince	Mumba	ZAM	28.8.84	2		Westwood	1 Jun
1:46.2 A	Alfred	Kipketer	KEN-Y	26.12.96	1		Nairobi	11 Jun
1:46.20	Taras	Bybyk	UKR	27.3.92	2	EU23	Tampere	12 Jul
1:46.25	Ahmed	Mainy	MAR	20.8.86	3		Casablanca	6 Jul
1:46.28	Leonel	Manzano	USA	12.9.84	6		Tomblaine	2 Jul
1:46.29	Amel	Tuka	BIH	9.1.91	3	EU23	Tampere	12 Jul
1:46.30A	Fredrick	Korir	KEN	17.4.87	2		Nairobi	11 May
1:46.3 A	Jackson	Kivuva	KEN	11.8.88	7	NC	Nairobi	22 Jun
(90)								
1:46.32	Mac	Fleet	USA	17.10.90	2		Victoria	5 Jul
1:46.32	Mohammed Ayoub	Tiouali	MAR	26.5.91	4	NC	Casablanca	6 Jul
1:46.38	Harun	Abda	USA	1.1.90	6s2	NC	Des Moines	21 Jun
1:46.38	Gideon	Kipngetich	KEN	.90	2rB	NA	Heusden-Zolder	13 Jul
1:46.38	Brandon	McBride	CAN-J	15.6.94	1	NG	Sherbrooke	16 Aug
1:46.40	Homiyu	Tesfaye	ETH/GER	23.6.93	1		Pfungstadt	5 Jun
1:46.40	Reuben	Bett	KEN	6.11.84	4	Skol	Warszawa	25 Aug
1:46.42	Paul	Renaudie	FRA	2.4.90	3	Kuso	Szczecin	15 Jun
1:46.43	Alfred	Kirwa Yego	KEN	28.11.86	1		Beijing	21 May
1:46.44	Jan	Van Den Broeck	BEL	11.3.89	5	NA	Heusden-Zolder	13 Jul
(100)								

Mark	Name		Nat	Born	Date
1:46.46	Abdelhadi	Labâli	MAR	26.4.93	25 Jul
1:46.49	Patrick	Rono	KEN	8.4.92	24 May
1:46.49	Abiyot	Abinet	ETH	10.5.89	8 Jul
1:46.5 A	Joshua	Masikonde	KEN-Y	16.8.96	19 Apr
1:46.53	Ivan	Nesterov	RUS	10.2.85	16 Jun
1:46.57	Jamaal	James	TTO	4.9.88	27 Jul
1:46.59	Andreas	Vojta	AUT	9.6.89	15 Jun
1:46.6 A	Richard	Kiplagat	KEN	3.7.84	14 May
1:46.6 A	Patrick Kiprotich	Rono	KEN-Y	9.4.96	11 Jun
1:46.63	Andrew	Wheating	USA	21.11.87	3 Sep
1:46.68	Lutimar	Paes	BRA	14.12.88	9 Jun
1:46.71	Ryan	Martin	USA	23.3.89	13 Jul
1:46.73	Gareth	Warburton	GBR	23.4.83	15 Jun
1:46.75	Radouane	Baaziri	MAR	23.7.93	6 Jul
1:46.77	Declan	Murray	USA	4.6.91	20 Apr
1:46.77	Mohammed	Moustaoui	MAR	2.4.85	8 Jul
1:46.84	Geoffrey	Harris	CAN	30.1.87	27 Jul
1:46.86A	Geoffrey	Matum	KEN	22.11.87	11 May
1:46.87	Brannon	Kidder	USA	18.11.93	20 Jun
1:46.9 A	Isaac	Kipketer	KEN	29.9.83	17 May
1:46.90	Yeimer	López	CUB	30.5.84	30 May
1:46.94	Kahsay	Berehe	ETH-J	16.5.95	1 Sep
1:46.98	Robert	Biwott	KEN-Y	28.1.96	5 May
1:47.0 A	Daniel	Karweni	KEN-J	12.10.94	19 Apr
1:47.01	Dey Tuach	Dey	USA	15.7.89	20 Jun
1:47.03	Sofiane	Selmouni	FRA	22.9.89	6 Jun
1:47.07	Danyil	Strelnikov	RUS	3.5.92	16 Jun
1:47.09A	Moses	Kipchirchir	KEN	.86	10 May
1:47.09	Kirill	Simakov	RUS	5.3.88	16 Jun
1:47.12	Joshua	Ralph	AUS	27.10.91	12 Dec
1:47.13	Nick	Guarino	USA	24.5.89	15 Jun
1:47.14	Nicholas	Kipkoech	KEN	22.10.92	11 Jun
1:47.15	Tetlo	Emmen	USA	24.1.84	1 Jun
1:47.15	Thijmen	Kupers	NED	4.10.91	12 Jul
1:47.15	Johan	Svensson	SWE	16.5.89	23 Jul
1:47.16	Ahmed	Ismail	SUD	10.9.84	10 May
1:47.18A	Hosea	Kandie	KEN	.85	11 May
1:47.19A	Rynhardt	van Rensburg	RSA	23.3.92	25 May
1:47.19A	Khaled	Benmehdi	ALG	22.10.88	6 Jun
1:47.2 A	Nathan	Kibiwott	KEN	.92	16 Mar
1:47.20	Richard	Jones	USA	15.7.88	20 Apr
1:47.20	Dennis	Krüger	GER	24.4.93	31 May
1:47.22	Charlie	Grice	GBR	7.11.93	7 Aug
1:47.24	Joe	Thomas	GBR	29.1.88	6 Jul
1:47.24	Ignacio	Laguna	ESP	18.5.87	24 Jul
1:47.24	Johan	Rogestedt	SWE	27.1.93	24 Aug
1:47.25A	Jacob	Rozani	RSA	24.1.84	25 May
1:47.26	Ricardo	Cunningham	JAM	3.10.80	1 Jun
1:47.27	Lance	Roller	USA	24.5.90	15 Jun
1:47.30	Pieter Jan	Hannes	BEL	30.10.92	6 Jul
1:47.30	Salah	Echichbani	MAR	1.7.91	6 Jul
1:47.30	Stepan	Poistogov	RUS	14.12.86	25 Jul
1:47.31	Kevin	Stadler	GER	3.4.93	8 Jun
1:47.31	Guy	Learmonth	GBR	24.4.92	24 Aug
1:47.32	Sadiki	White	USA	6.2.91	17 May
1:47.32	Lucirio	Garrido	VEN	8.4.92	28 Nov
1:47.33	Kyle	Smith	CAN	25.1.85	1 Jul
1:47.35	Josh	Guarino	USA	24.5.89	15 Jun
1:47.37	Pablo	Solares	MEX	22.12.84	13 Jul
1:47.38	James	Gilreath	USA	7.8.89	20 Apr
1:47.38	Fouad	El Kaam	MAR	27.5.88	11 May
1:47.38	Viktor	Tyumentsev	UKR	12.3.92	6 Jun
1:47.38	Arturo	Casado	ESP	26.1.83	13 Jun
1:47.42	Joseílton	Cunha	BRA	1.3.93	9 Jun
1:47.43	Sho	Kawamoto	JPN	1.3.93	9 Jun
1:47.44A	Otlaadisa	Segosebe	BOT	12.1.92	25 May
1:47.44	Leoman	Momoh	NGR	30.3.91	5 Jun
1:47.45	Thomas	Riva	CAN	.92	1 Jul
1:47.46	Mbulaeni	Mulaudzi	RSA	8.9.80	25 May
1:47.47A	Emmanuel	Sasia	UGA	10.10.92	20 Jul
1:47.50	Sharif	Webb	USA	9.6.89	1 Jun
1:47.51	David	Mokone	RSA	1.2.91	20 Apr
1:47.51	Ivan	Tukhtachev	RUS	12.7.89	16 Jun
1:47.51	Rickard	Gunnarsson	SWE	19.9.91	23 Jul
1:47.52	Azzine	Boudjemaa	FRA	17.9.82	6 Jun
1:47.52	Jacopo	Lahbi	ITA	1.6.93	5 Jul
1:47.52	Victor José	Corrales	ESP	12.3.89	24 Jul
1:47.53	Andreas	Rapatz	AUT	5.9.86	15 Jun
1:47.54	Artur	Ostrowski	POL	10.7.88	15 Jun
1:47.54	Dmitrijs	Jurkevics	LAT	7.1.87	20 Jul
1:47.54	Rory	Graham-Watson	GBR	3.6.90	4 Sep
1:47.55	Esreal	Awoke	ETH-J	5.4.94	6 Jun
1:47.56	José Alberto	Esteso	ESP	25.8.90	12 Jun
1:47.56	Charel	Grethen	LUX	22.6.92	20 Apr
1:47.56	Travis	Burkstrand	USA	22.7.89	12 May
1:47.56	Mark	Husted	USA	4.6.87	17 May
1:47.56	Amine	Khadiri	CYP	20.11.88	6 Jul
1:47.56	Timo	Benitz	GER	1.12.91	4 Aug
(188)					

Indoors

Mark	Name		Nat	Born	Pos	Meet	Venue	Date
1:46.07	Leoman	Momoh	NGR	30.3.91	1		Fayetteville	1 Mar
1:46.53 #	Lopez	Lomong	USA	1.1.85				9 Feb
1:46.57	Abubaker	Kaki	SUD	21.6.89				16 Feb
1:46.76	Tomás	Squella	CHI	18.10.91				1 Mar
1:46.96	Zan	Rudolf	SLO	9.5.93				31 Jan
1:47.13	Robby	Andrews	USA	29.3.91				3 Mar
1:47.19	Francisco	Roldán	ESP	26.5.90				27 Jan
1:47.42	Boru	Guyota	ETH/USA	1.1.90				23 Feb
1:47.43	Edward	Kemboi	KEN	12.12.91				26 Jan

MEN 2013

Mark	Name		Nat	Born	Pos	Meet	Venue	Date

JUNIORS

See main list for top 12 juniors. 13 performances by 4 men to 1:44.8. Additional marks and further juniors:

Mark	Name		Nat	Born	Pos	Meet	Venue	Date
Aman 6+								
1:44.21					2	DL	Doha	10 May
1:44.42					1	Pre	Eugene	1 Jun
1:44.37					1		Rabat	9 Jun
1:44.71					1s2	WCh	Moskva	11 Aug
1:46.5 A	Joshua	Masikonde	KEN-Y	16.8.96	1		Nairobi	19 Apr
1:46.6 A	Patrick Kiprotich	Rono	KEN-Y	9.4.96	2		Nairobi	11 Jun
1:46.94	Kahsay	Berehe	ETH	16.5.95	1	Af-J	Bambous	1 Sep
1:46.98	Robert	Biwott	KEN-Y	28.1.96	2		Tokyo	5 May
1:47.0 A	Daniel	Karweni	KEN	22.10.94	2		Nairobi	19 Apr
1:47.55	Esreal	Awoke	ETH	5.4.94	4		Montbéliard	6 Jun
1:47.64	Leonard	Kosencha	KEN	21.8.94	9		Rovereto	3 Sep
1:47.70	Undessa	Abdi Uya (20)	ETH	.95	2		Pfungstadt	5 Jun

1000 METRES

Mark	Name		Nat	Born	Pos	Meet	Venue	Date
2:15.77	Ayanleh	Souleiman	DJI	3.12.92	1		Sollentuna	5 Aug
2:16.44	Benson	Seurei	BRN	27.3.84	1		Dillingen	21 Jul
2:17.33	Silas	Too	KEN	.89	2		Dillingen	21 Jul
2:18.20	Pierre-Ambroise	Bosse	FRA	11.5.92				31 May
2:18.70	Job	Kinyor	KEN	2.9.90				26 Aug
2:18.29	Paul	Robinson	IRL	24.5.91				26 Aug
2:18.84	Anthony	Chemut	KEN	17.12.92				26 Aug
2:18.36	Andrew	Wheating	USA	21.11.87				26 Aug
2:18.99	Dickson	Tuwei	KEN	31.10.92				12 May
2:18.99	Michael	Rimmer	GBR	3.2.86				26 Aug

Indoors

Mark	Name		Nat	Born	Pos	Meet	Venue	Date
2:17.77	Marcin	Lewandowski	POL	13.6.87	2		Stockholm	21 Feb
2:17.90	Robby	Andrews	USA	29.3.91	1 Feb			
2:18.27	Michael	Rutt	USA	28.10.87				1 Mar
2:18.26	Brian	Gagnon	USA	8.5.87	1 Mar			
2:18.78	Andrew	Osagie	GBR	19.2.88				21 Feb

1500 METRES

Mark	Name		Nat	Born	Pos	Meet	Venue	Date
3:27.72	Asbel	Kiprop	KEN	30.6.89	1	Herc	Monaco	19 Jul
3:28.81	Mohamed	Farah	GBR	23.3.83	2	Herc	Monaco	19 Jul
3:29.50	Caleb	Ndiku	KEN	9.10.92	3	Herc	Monaco	19 Jul
3:30.13	Silas	Kiplagat	KEN	20.8.89	1		Rieti	8 Sep
3:30.77	Bethwel	Birgen	KEN	6.8.88	4	Herc	Monaco	19 Jul
3:30.97		Kiplagat			1	WK	Zürich	29 Aug
3:31.13		Kiprop			1	DL	Doha	10 May
3:31.30	Ilham Tanui	Özbilen	TUR	5.3.90	5	Herc	Monaco	19 Jul
3:31.53	Collins	Cheboi	KEN	25.9.87	6	Herc	Monaco	19 Jul
3:31.64	Ayanleh	Souleiman	DJI	3.12.92	1	WK	Zürich	29 Aug
3:31.90		Birgen			2	DL	Doha	10 May
3:31.93	Johan	Cronje	RSA	13.4.82	2		Rieti	8 Sep
3:31.94	Zakaria	Maazouzi (10)	MAR	15.6.85	1		Marrakech	20 Apr
3:32.08	Mohammed	Moustaoui	MAR	2.4.85	3		Rieti	8 Sep
3:32.39		Kiprop			1	DL	Shanghai	18 May
3:32.43	Mekonnen	Gebremedhin	ETH	11.10.88	2	DL	Shanghai	18 May
3:32.55		Souleiman			1	DL	Saint-Denis	6 Jul
3:32.57	Nick	Willis	NZL	25.4.83	4		Rieti	8 Sep
3:32.59		Souleiman			3	DL	Doha	10 May
3:32.65	Aman	Wote	ETH	18.4.84	2	DL	Saint-Denis	6 Jul
3:32.73	Bouabdellah	Tahri	FRA	20.12.78	7	Herc	Monaco	19 Jul
3:32.85		Cheboi			4	DL	Doha	10 May
3:32.89		Maazouzi			1rA		Oordegem	6 Jul
3:32.96		Cheboi			3	DL	Shanghai	18 May
3:33.04	Benson	Seurei	BRN	27.3.84	5	DL	Doha	10 May
3:33.05	Daniel Kipchirchir	Komen	KEN	27.11.84	6	DL	Doha	10 May
3:33.13	Mahiedine	Mekhissi-Benabbad	FRA	15.3.85	1		Tomblaine	2 Jul
3:33.14	Leonel	Manzano	USA	12.9.84	3	DL	Saint-Denis	6 Jul
3:33.15	Nixon	Chepseba	KEN	12.12.90	3	WK	Zürich	29 Aug
3:33.18		Moustaoui			4	DL	Saint-Denis	6 Jul
	(30/20)							
3:33.20	Lawi	Lalang	KEN	15.6.91	5	DL	Saint-Denis	6 Jul
3:33.21	Augustine	Choge	KEN	21.1.87	5		Rieti	8 Sep
3:33.23	David	Torrence	USA	26.11.85	6		Rieti	8 Sep
3:33.29	Abdelati	Iguider	MAR	25.3.87	4	DL	Shanghai	18 May
3:33.31	Sadik	Mikhou	MAR	25.7.90	2		Marrakech	20 Apr
3:33.47	Florian	Carvalho	FRA	9.3.89	7	DL	Saint-Denis	6 Jul
3:33.58	Matthew	Centrowitz	USA	18.10.89	8	Herc	Monaco	19 Jul
3:33.71	Fouad	El Kaam	MAR	27.5.88	2		Oordegem	6 Jul
3:33.73	Zebene	Alemayehu	ETH	4.9.92	3		Oordegem	6 Jul
3:33.95	Henrik	Ingebrigtsen	NOR	24.2.91	7	WK	Zürich	29 Aug
	(30)							
3:34.00	Jordan	McNamara	USA	7.3.87	4		Oordegem	6 Jul

Mark	Name		Nat	Born	Pos	Meet	Venue	Date	
3:34.06	Abiyot	Abinet	ETH	10.5.89	2		Tomblaine	2	Jul
3:34.12	Garrett	Heath	USA	3.11.85	5		Oordegem	6	Jul
3:34.18	Homiyu	Tesfaye	GER	23.6.93	9	WK	Zürich	29	Aug
3:34.47	Andrew	Bayer	USA	3.2.90	6		Oordegem	6	Jul
3:34.54	Simon	Denissel	FRA	22.5.90	9	DL	Saint-Denis	6	Jul
3:34.55	Lopez	Lomong	USA	1.1.85	10	DL	Saint-Denis	6	Jul
3:34.55	Nick	Symmonds	USA	30.12.83	10	Herc	Monaco	19	Jul
3:34.64	Dawit	Wolde	ETH	19.5.91	11	DL	Doha	10	May
3:34.93	Cory	Leslie	USA	24.10.89	7		Oordegem	6	Jul
	(40)								
3:35.07	Carsten	Schlangen	GER	31.12.80	2		Rabat	9	Jun
3:35.07	Krzysztof	Zebrowski	POL	9.7.90	7		Rieti	8	Sep
3:35.2 A	James	Magut	KEN	20.7.90	2	NC	Nairobi	22	Jun
3:35.22	Paul	Robinson	IRL	24.5.91	8		Rieti	8	Sep
3:35.25	Ryan	Gregson	AUS	26.4.90	2		Sydney	9	Mar
3:35.27	Will	Leer	USA	15.4.85	8		Oordegem	6	Jul
3:35.37	Chris	O'Hare	GBR	23.11.90	9		Oordegem	6	Jul
3:35.45	Zane	Robertson	NZL	14.11.89	9		Rieti	8	Sep
3:35.47	Teshome	Dirisa	ETH-J	25.4.94	2		Karlsruhe	2	Feb
3:35.48	Craig	Miller	USA	3.8.87	11		Oordegem	6	Jul
	(50)								
3:35.51	Yassine	Bensghir	MAR	3.1.83	1		Rabat	1	Jun
3:35.52	Younès	Essalhi	MAR	20.2.93	1		Sollentuna	27	Jun
3:35.54	John	Bolas	USA	1.11.87	12		Oordegem	6	Jul
3:35.62	Vincent	Kibet	KEN	.91	2		Sollentuna	27	Jun
3:35.67	Tesfaye	Cheru	ETH	2.3.93	2		Dakar	12	Jun
3:35.69	David	Bustos	ESP	25.8.90	2rA	NA	Heusden-Zolder	13	Jul
3:35.87	Hillary	Ngetich	KEN-J	15.9.95	3		Dakar	12	Jun
3:35.88	Mohamed	Al-Garni	QAT	1.7.92	13	DL	Doha	10	May
3:35.93	Othmane	Belharbazi	FRA	3.11.88	13		Oordegem	6	Jul
3:35.95	Abdelhadi	Labäli	MAR	26.4.93	4		Dakar	12	Jun
	(60)								
3:35.97	Pieter Jan	Hannes	BEL	30.10.92	5		Rabat	9	Jun
3:36.30+	Taoufik	Makhloufi	ALG	29.4.88	9	Pre	Eugene	1	Jun
3:36.33	Arturo	Casado	ESP	26.1.83	12	DL	Saint-Denis	6	Jul
3:36.34	Evan	Jager	USA	8.3.89	2r2		Los Angeles (ER)	17	May
3:36.35	Abednego	Chesebe	KEN	20.6.82	1		Dessau	31	May
3:36.36	Andreas	Vojta	AUT	9.6.89	2	FBK	Hengelo	8	Jun
3:36.36	Bernard	Lagat	USA	12.12.74	13	DL	Saint-Denis	6	Jul
3:36.55	Lee	Emanuel	GBR	24.1.85	14		Oordegem	6	Jul
3:36.59	Nathan	Brannen	CAN	8.9.82	7s2	WCh	Moskva	16	Aug
3:36.61	Matt	Elliott	USA	8.9.85	2		Ninove	27	Jul
	(70)								
3:36.69+	Galen	Rupp	USA	8.5.86	5+	DL	London (OS)	26	Jul
3:36.71	Imad	Touil	ALG	11.2.89	3	Med G	Mersin	27	Jun
3:36.73	Soresa	Fida	ETH	27.5.93	1		Montbéliard	6	Jun
3:36.77	Robert	Biwott	KEN-Y	28.1.96	1	WY	Donetsk	14	Jul
3:36.78	Adel	Mechaal	ESP	5.12.90	1		Huelva	12	Jun
3:36.79	Russell	Brown	USA	3.3.85	3r2		Los Angeles (ER)	17	May
3:36.80	Ahmed	Mainy	MAR	20.8.86	3		Rabat	1	Jun
3:36.84	Juan	van Deventer	RSA	26.3.83	3		Dessau	31	May
3:36.88	Cameron	Levins	CAN	28.3.89	4r1		Los Angeles (ER)	17	May
3:36.90	Abderrahmane	Anou	ALG	29.1.91	2		Huelva	12	Jun
	(80)								
3:36.98	Mohammed Ayoub	Tiouali	MAR	26.5.91	7		Tomblaine	2	Jul
3:37.02	James	Kaan	AUS	17.9.90	3		Sydney	9	Mar
3:37.03	Andrew	Wheating	USA	21.11.87	3r2		Los Angeles (ER)	17	May
3:37.03	Ben	Blankenship	USA	15.12.88	1		Lignano	16	Jul
3:37.05	Geoffrey	Barusei	KEN-J	.94	4	ISTAF	Berlin	1	Sep
3:37.10	Josh	Wright	AUS	3.5.91	4		Sydney	9	Mar
3:37.18	Collis	Birmingham	AUS	27.12.84	1		Belfast	25	Jun
3:37.25	Jeroen	D'Hoedt	BEL	10.1.90	7rA	NA	Heusden-Zolder	13	Jul
3:37.31	Liam	Boylan-Pett	USA	11.9.85	16		Oordegem	6	Jul
3:37.45	Sami	Lafi	ALG	25.4.90	2		Alger	18	Jun
	(90)								
3:37.50	Hélio	Gomes	POR	27.12.84	5		Huelva	12	Jun
3:37.5 A	Vincent	Letting	KEN	.93	9	WChT	Nairobi	13	Jul
3:37.51	Maurys Surel	Castillo	CUB	19.10.84	6		Huelva	12	Jun
3:37.54	Jeff	See	USA	6.6.86	6r2		Los Angeles (ER)	17	May
3:37.54	Aman	Kedi	ETH	.93	2rB	NA	Heusden-Zolder	13	Jul
3:37.62	Kim	Ruell	BEL	27.4.87	3rB	NA	Heusden-Zolder	13	Jul

Mark	Name	Nat	Born	Pos	Meet	Venue	Date
3:37.67	Richard Peters	GBR	18.2.90	3		Ninove	27 Jul
3:37.68	Alberto Imedio	ESP	24.5.91	7		Huelva	12 Jun
3:37.75	Sebastian Keiner	GER	22.8.89	8rA	NA	Heusden-Zolder	13 Jul
3:37.77	Carlos Alonso	ESP	15.9.89	8		Huelva	12 Jun
(100)							
3:37.79	Othmane El Goumri	MAR	28.5.92	7			Jul
3:37.82	Linus Kiplagat	KEN-J	23.12.94	13			Jul
3:37.91	Reuben Bett	KEN	6.11.84	8			Jun
3:37.95	Mohamed Al-Azimi	KUW	16.6.82	12			Jun
3:37.96	Mohammed Abid	MAR-J	18.3.95	7			Jul
3:37.97	Lyès Belkhier	ALG	5.10.87	13			Jun
3:38.00	Diego Ruiz	ESP	5.2.82	2			Jul
3:38.13	Charlie Grice	GBR	7.11.93	8			Jun
3:38.13	Bartosz Nowicki	POL	26.2.84	8			Jun
3:38.27	Cameron Page	AUS	12.6.91	9			Jun
3:38.29	Jeremy Rae	CAN	19.5.91	1			Jul
3:38.30	Kevin López	ESP	12.6.90	12			Jun
3:38.31	Dmitrijs Jurkevics	LAT	7.1.87	27			Jun
3:38.34	Rob Finnerty	USA	4.2.90	15			Jun
3:38.35	Mac Fleet	USA	17.10.90	1			Jul
3:38.35	Bryan Cantero	FRA	28.4.91	27			Jul
3:38.36	Cornelius Kangogo	KEN	31.12.93	31			May
3:38.38	Trevor Dunbar	USA	29.4.91	5			Jul
3:38.49	Jamal Hitrane	MAR	1.9.89	2			Jul
3:38.56	Teklit Teweldebrhan	ERI	1.10.93	21			Jul
3:38.57	Ryan Hill	USA	31.1.90	6			Jul
3:38.59	Julian Matthews	NZL	21.7.88	13			Jul
3:38.61	Jonathan Sawe	KEN-J	22.5.95	31			May
3:38.69	Martin Sperlich	GER	28.8.91	31			May
3:38.69	Jerry Motsau	RSA	12.3.90	12			Jun
3:38.71	Jakub Holusa	CZE	20.2.88	18			May
3:38.71	Bader Rassioui	MAR	8.6.85	9			Jun
3:38.72	David Bishop	GBR	9.5.87	17			May
3:38.72	Florian Orth	GER	24.7.89	19			Jul
3:38.76	Filip Ingebrigtsen	NOR	20.4.93	27			Jul
3:38.77	James Shane	GBR	18.12.89	8			Jun
3:38.79	Riley Masters	USA	5.4.90	28			Apr
3:38.8 A	Nicholas Kipchumba	KEN	.89	20			Jul
3:38.8 A	Bernard Kaptingei	KEN	.86	22			Jun
3:38.81	Yegor Nikolayev	RUS	12.2.88	9			Jun
3:38.85	Tony Jordanek	USA	27.12.86	17			May
3:38.89	Bilal Ali Mansour	BRN	17.10.83	10			May
3:38.89A	Ronald Musagala	UGA-J	16.12.94	19			Jul
3:38.91	Brett Johnson	USA	27.9.90	17			May
3:38.91	Victor José Corrales	ESP	12.3.89	19			Jul
3:38.92	Adam Palamar	CAN-J	12.3.94	1			Jul
3:38.98	Marcin Lewandowski	POL	13.6.87	21			Jul
3:39.04	Andrew Bumbalough	USA	14.3.87	6			Jul
3:39.06	De'Sean Turner	USA	16.9.88	16			Jul
3:39.08	Salah Echichbani	MAR	1.7.91	7			Jul
3:39.1 A	Eliah Kiptoo	KEN	9.6.86	13			Jul
3:39.14	Hamza Driouch	QAT-J	16.11.94	19			Jul
3:39.14	Pablo Solares	MEX	22.12.84	1			Jul
3:39.16	Enoch Omwamba	KEN	4.4.93	18			May
3:39.21	Necerddine Hallil	ALG	10.4.88	18			Jun
3:39.21	Valentin Smirnov	RUS	13.2.86	14			Aug
3:39.24	Duncan Phillips	USA	7.6.89	17			May
3:39.27	Elliott Heath	USA	4.2.89	6			Jul
3:39.28	Dan Huling	USA	16.7.83	17			May
3:39.29	Chris Gowell	GBR	26.9.85	17			May
3:39.32	Andréas Dimitrákis	GRE	8.9.90	20			Jul
3:39.33	Francisco Javier Abad	ESP	18.8.81	12			Jun
3:39.33	Ioan Zaizan	ROU	21.7.83	13			Jul
3:39.37	Mohamed Hajjaj	MAR	22.3.83	5			May
3:39.38	Oleksandr Borysyuk	UKR	9.12.85	25			Jul
3:39.41	Flavio Siholhe	MOZ	14.10.90	13			Apr
3:39.45	Chris Derrick	USA	17.10.90	17			May
3:39.51	Imed Hamed Mohamed Nour	KSA	21.4.90	5			Jul
3:39.51	Craig Huffer	AUS	27.10.89	13			Jul
3:39.53	Dumisani Hlaselo	RSA	8.6.89	13			Apr
3:39.54A	Moses Kipsiro	UGA	2.9.86	18			Jul
3:39.57	Michael Atchoo	USA	16.8.91	28			Apr
3:39.57	Conseslus Kipruto	KEN-J	8.12.94	8			Jun
3:39.59	Tarik Moukrime	BEL	2.11.89	27			Jul
3:39.6 A	Paul K. Koech	KEN	10.11.81	25			May
3:39.61	Jordan Williamsz	AUS	21.8.92	1			Jul
3:39.7 A	Titus Kipruto	KEN-Y	3.5.96	11			Jun
3:39.72	Joe Stilin	USA	5.12.89	6			Jul
3:39.77	Eric Harasyn	USA	16.1.89	17			May
3:39.80	Alistair Hamdi	BEL	2.11.89	1			Jul
3:39.80	Tomasz Osmulski	POL	13.3.82	21			Jul
3:39.81	Mack McLain	USA	17.5.88	15			Jun
3:39.84	Volodomyr Kuts	UKR	15.1.87	25			Jul
3:39.87	Alex Hatz	USA	24.2.92	28			Apr
3:39.87	Dan Clark	USA	6.9.86	8			Jun
3:39.89	Adam Czerwinski	POL	2.10.88	1			Jun
3:39.91	Mack Chaffee	USA	4.9.86	28			Apr
3:39.91	Matthew Kiptanui	KEN-J	20.10.94	31			Aug
3:39.95	Stanislav Maslov	UKR	19.1.89	25			Jul
3:39.98	Pavel Khvorostukhin	RUS	18.6.86	15			Jun
3:40.00	Szymon Krawczyk	POL	29.12.88	21			Jun
3:40.0A	Robert Maritim	KEN	.87	25			May
(187)							

Indoors

Mark	Name	Nat	Born	Pos	Meet	Venue	Date
3:34.78	Galen Rupp	USA	8.5.86	1+		Boston (Allston)	26 Jan
3:36.85	Ciarán O'Lionáird	IRL	11.4.88	3+	Millrose	New York (Armory)	16 Feb
3:37.55	Valentin Smirnov	RUS	13.2.86	4		Moskva	3 Feb
3:38.34	Marcin Lewandowski	POL	13.6.87	16 Feb			
3:40.00	Cornelius Ndiwa	KEN	17.12.84				29 Jan
3:38.36	Yegor Nikolayev	RUS	12.2.88	3 Feb			

JUNIORS

See main list for top 4 juniors. 10 performances by 6 men to 3:38.03. Additional marks and further juniors:

Name	Mark	Pos	Meet	Venue	Date
Dirisa	3:36.98	4	FBK	Hengelo	8 Jun
	3:37.64i	2		Karlsruhe	2 Feb
	3:38.03	7		Dakar	12 Jun
Barusei	3:37.13	6	FBK	Hengelo	8 Jun

Mark	Name	Nat	Born	Pos	Meet	Venue	Date
3:37.82	Linus Kiplagat	KEN	23.12.94	9rA	NA	Heusden-Zolder	13 Jul
3:37.96	Mohammed Abid	MAR	18.3.95	2	NC	Casablanca	7 Jul
3:38.61	Jonathan Sawe	KEN	22.5.95	2	Pre	Eugene	31 May
3:38.89A	Ronald Musagala	UGA	16.12.94	1	NC	Kampala	19 Jul
3:38.92	Adam Palamar	CAN	12.3.94	7	Jerome	Burnaby	1 Jul
3:39.13	Hamza Driouch (10)	QAT	16.11.94	12	Herc	Monaco	19 Jul
3:39.57	Conseslus Kipruto	KEN	8.12.94	14	FBK	Hengelo	8 Jun
3:39.7 A	Titus Kipruto	KEN-Y	3.5.96	2		Nairobi	11 Jun
3:39.91	Matthew Kiptanui	KEN	20.10.94	1	Af-J	Bambous	31 Aug
3:40.39	Hassan Ghachoui	MAR	.95	7	NC	Casablanca	6 Jul
3:40.4A	Jonah Rotich	KEN	7.5.94	5h1	NC	Nairobi	20 Jun
3:41.3A	Yenew Tebikew	ETH-Y	14.3.96	3	NC	Assela	30 Jul
3:41.87	Vincent Mutai	KEN	3.11.94	3		Melbourne	5 Apr
3:42.14	Tesfu Tewelde	ERI-J	21.7.97	2	WY	Donetsk	14 Jul
3:42.2A	Timothy Kipchirchir	KEN-Y	20.11.97	1		Nairobi	19 Apr
3:42.25	Elkana Yego (20)	KEN	7.12.94	10		Tomblaine	2 Jul

Mark	Name		Nat	Born	Pos	Meet	Venue	Date	

1 MILE

Mark	Name		Nat	Born	Pos	Meet	Venue	Date	
3:49.48	Silas	Kiplagat	KEN	20.8.89	1	Pre	Eugene	1	Jun
3:49.53	Asbel	Kiprop	KEN	30.6.89	2	Pre	Eugene	1	Jun
3:49.88	Aman	Wote	ETH	18.4.84	3	Pre	Eugene	1	Jun
3:50.01	Augustine	Choge	KEN	21.1.87	1	DL	London (OS)	27	Jul
3:50.07	Ayanleh	Souleiman	DJI	3.12.92	2	DL	London (OS)	27	Jul
3:50.40		Souleiman			4	Pre	Eugene	1	Jun
3:50.42	Bethwel	Birgen	KEN	6.8.88	5	Pre	Eugene	1	Jun
3:50.46	Caleb	Ndiku	KEN	9.10.92	6	Pre	Eugene	1	Jun
3:50.53		Souleiman			1	Bisl	Oslo	13	Jun
3:50.93	James	Magut	KEN	20.7.90	3	DL	London (OS)	27	Jul
3:50.95	Nixon	Chepseba	KEN	12.12.90	2	Bisl	Oslo	13	Jun
3:51.11		Magut			3	Bisl	Oslo	13	Jun
3:51.28	Daniel Kipchirchir	Komen	KEN	27.11.84	4	DL	London (OS)	27	Jul
	(13/10)								
3:51.44	Collins	Cheboi	KEN	25.9.87	8	Pre	Eugene	1	Jun
3:51.45	Lopez	Lomong	USA	1.1.85	9	Pre	Eugene	1	Jun
3:51.79	Matthew	Centrowitz	USA	18.10.89	10	Pre	Eugene	1	Jun
3:52.11	Galen	Rupp	USA	8.5.86	5	DL	London (OS)	27	Jul
3:52.30	Ilham Tanui	Özbilen	TUR	5.3.90	4	Bisl	Oslo	13	Jun
3:52.42	Mohammed	Moustaoui	MAR	2.4.85	6	DL	London (OS)	27	Jul
3:52.42	Jordan	McNamara	USA	7.3.87	7	DL	London (OS)	27	Jul
3:52.74	David	Torrence	USA	26.11.85	8	DL	London (OS)	27	Jul
3:52.90	Andrew	Bayer	USA	3.2.90	9	DL	London (OS)	27	Jul
3:52.94	Taoufik	Makhloufi	ALG	29.4.88	11	Pre	Eugene	1	Jun
	(20)								
3:53.15	Garrett	Heath	USA	3.11.85	10	DL	London (OS)	27	Jul
3:53.40	David	Bustos	ESP	25.8.90	6	Bisl	Oslo	13	Jun
3:53.95	Andreas	Vojta	AUT	9.6.89	8	Bisl	Oslo	13	Jun
3:54.04	Mekonnen	Gebremedhin	ETH	11.10.88	12	Pre	Eugene	1	Jun
3:54.51	Dawit	Wolde	ETH	19.5.91	13	Bisl	Oslo	13	Jun
3:54.53	Henrik	Ingebrigtsen	NOR	24.2.91	12	DL	London (OS)	27	Jul
3:54.61	Charlie	Grice	GBR	7.11.93	13	DL	London (OS)	27	Jul
3:54.75	Lee	Emanuel	GBR	24.1.85	14	DL	London (OS)	27	Jul
3:54.77	Cameron	Page	AUS	12.6.91	1		Cork	2	Jul
3:54.86	Johan	Cronje	RSA	13.4.82	9	Bisl	Oslo	13	Jun
	(30)								

Mark	Name		Nat	Born	Pos		Mark	Name		Nat	Born	Pos
3:55.70	Nick	Willis	NZL	25.4.83	27 Apr		3:57.08	Ryan	Gregson	AUS	26.4.90	1 Jun
3:55.85	Cory	Leslie	USA	24.10.89	17 Jul		3:57.16	Matt	Elliott	USA	8.9.85	1 Jun
3:55.93	Abdelati	Iguider	MAR	25.3.87	1 Jun		3:57.18	Michael	Rutt	USA	28.10.87	27 Apr
3:56.18	Paul	Robinson	IRL	24.5.91	2 Jul		3:57.34	Juan Luis	Barrios	MEX	24.6.83	17 Jul
3:56.27	Duncan	Phillips	USA	7.6.89	17 Jul		3:57.35	Craig	Miller	USA	3.8.87	17 Jul
3:56.39	Will	Leer	USA	15.4.85	31 May		3:57.37	Tyler	Mulder	USA	15.2.87	27 Apr
3:56.66	Ben	Blankenship	USA	15.12.88	2 Jul		3:57.40	Dan	Clark	USA	6.9.86	4 Aug
3:56.78	Benson	Seurei	BRN	27.3.84	15 Jun		3:57.45	Jeff	See	USA	6.6.86	13 Apr
3:57.02	Andrew	Wheating	USA	21.11.87	31 May		**Irregular curb**					
3:57.03	Jonathan	Sawe	KEN-J	22.5.95	27 Apr		3:56.27	Ben	Blankenship	USA	15.12.88	10 Aug
							3:57.49	John	Bolas	USA	1.11.87	10 Aug

Indoors

Mark	Name		Nat	Born	Pos	Meet	Venue	Date	
3:50.92	Galen	Rupp	USA	8.5.86	1r1		Boston (Allston)	26	Jan
3:51.21	Lopez	Lomong	USA	1.1.85	1	Millrose	New York (Armory)	16	Feb
3:51.34	Matthew	Centrowitz	USA	18.10.89	2	Millrose	New York (Armory)	16	Feb
3:52.10	Ciarán	O'Lionáird	IRL	11.4.88	3	Millrose	New York (Armory)	16	Feb
3:52.98	Chris	O'Hare	GBR	23.11.90	4	Millrose	New York (Armory)	16	Feb
3:54.56	Lawi	Lalang	KEN	15.6.91	5	Millrose	New York (Armory)	17	Feb
3:54.89	Ryan	Hill	USA	31.1.90	6	Millrose	New York (Armory)	16	Feb

Mark	Name		Nat	Born	Pos		Mark	Name		Nat	Born	Pos
3:55.97	Ryan	Gregson	AUS	26.4.90	16 Feb		3:56.41 #	Donn	Cabral	USA	12.12.89	9 Feb
3:56.04	Richard	Peters	GBR	18.2.90	26 Jan		3:56.85	Craig	Miller	USA	3.8.87	2 Feb
3:56.12 #	Andrew	Bumbalough	USA	14.3.87	9 Feb		3:57.11 #	Robert	Creese	USA	30.8.93	9 Feb
3:56.14 #	Evan	Jager	USA	8.3.89	9 Feb		3:57.14 #	Michael	Atchoo	USA	16.8.91	23 Feb
3:56.25	Riley	Masters	USA	5.4.90	8 Feb		3:57.22	David	McCarthy	IRL	3.8.88	26 Jan
3:56.28	Patrick	Casey	USA	23.5.90	26 Jan		3:57.43	Jeff	See	USA	6.6.86	2 Feb
3:56.35	Will	Leer	USA	15.4.85	2 Feb							

JUNIORS

Mark	Name		Nat	Born	Pos	Meet	Venue	Date	
3:57.03	Jonathan	Sawe	KEN-J	22.5.95	1	Penn R	Philadelphia	27	Apr
4:00.62	Jake	Wightman	GBR	11.7.94	17	DL	London (OS)	27	Jul

2000 METRES

Mark	Name		Nat	Born	Pos	Meet	Venue	Date	
4:56.85	Mahiedine	Mekhissi-Benabbad	FRA	15.3.85	1		Reims	28	Jun
4:59.52	Geoffrey	Barusei	KEN-J	.94	2		Reims	28	Jun
4:59.56	Nathan	Brannen	CAN	8.9.82	1		Roronto	9	Jul
4:59.97	Jamal	Hitrane	MAR	1.9.89	3		Reims	28	Jun

Mark	Name		Nat	Born	Pos	Meet	Venue		Date
4:59.99	Andrew	Bayer	USA	3.2.90	4		Reims		28 Jun
5:00.60	Benson	Seurei	KEN	27.3.84	5		Reims		28 Jun
5:02.01	Lee	Emanuel	GBR	24.1.85	6		Reims		28 Jun

Indoors

Mark	Name		Nat	Born	Pos		Venue		Date
5:00.59	Soresa	Fida	ETH	27.5.93	1		Metz		24 Feb
5:00.69	Bouabdallah	Tahri	FRA	20.12.78	2		Metz		24 Feb
5:02.06+	Caleb	Ndiku	KEN	9.10.92	21 Feb	5:02.16	Bernard	Kiptum	KEN	8.10.86 26 Jan
5:02.13	Abiyot	Abinet	ETH	10.5.89	26 Jan	5:02.27+	Galen	Rupp	USA	8.5.86 21 Feb

3000 METRES

Mark	Name		Nat	Born	Pos	Meet	Venue	Date
7:30.36	Hagos	Gebrhiwet	ETH-J	11.5.94	1	DL	Doha	10 May
7:32.01	Thomas	Longosiwa	KEN	14.1.82	2	DL	Doha	10 May
7:32.64	Yenew	Alamirew	ETH	27.5.90	3	DL	Doha	10 May
7:33.92	Caleb	Ndiku	KEN	9.10.92	4	DL	Doha	10 May
7:34.57	Hayle	Ibrahimov	AZE	18.1.90	5	DL	Doha	10 May
7:35.06		Ndiku			1		Zagreb	3 Sep
7:35.53	Albert	Rop	KEN/BRN	17.7.92	2		Zagreb	3 Sep
7:36.28	Isiah	Koech	KEN	19.12.93	6	DL	Doha	10 May
7:36.53	Edwin	Soi	KEN	3.3.86	1		Rieti	8 Sep
7:36.59	Ben	True	USA	29.12.85	2		Rieti	8 Sep
7:36.85	Mohamed (11/10)	Farah	GBR	23.3.83	1	DL	London (OS)	27 Jul
7:36.96	Bouabdellah	Tahri	FRA	20.12.78	3		Zagreb	3 Sep
7:37.15	Bethwell	Birgen	KEN	6.8.88	4		Zagreb	3 Sep
7:37.40	John	Kipkoech	KEN	29.12.91	5		Zagreb	3 Sep
7:37.57	Cyrus	Rutto	KEN	21.4.92	3		Rieti	8 Sep
7:37.68	Bidan	Karoki	KEN	21.8.90	6		Zagreb	3 Sep
7:37.70	Augustine	Choge	KEN	21.1.87	7	DL	Doha	10 May
7:39.38	Will	Leer	USA	15.4.85	7		Zagreb	3 Sep
7:39.70	Abrar	Osman	ERI-J	1.1.94	8	DL	Doha	10 May
7:40.02	Andrew	Bumbalough	USA	14.3.87	8		Zagreb	3 Sep
7:40.48	Ben (20)	St. Lawrence	AUS	7.11.81	6		Rieti	8 Sep
7:40.56	Benson	Seurei	BRN	27.3.84	9		Zagreb	3 Sep
7:40.62	Nick	Willis	NZL	25.4.83	10		Zagreb	3 Sep
7:40.78	David	Torrence	USA	26.11.85	11		Zagreb	3 Sep
7:41.02	Collis	Birmingham	AUS	27.12.84	1		Sotteville-lès-Rouen	8 Jul
7:41.83	Jairus	Birech	KEN	15.12.92	9	DL	Doha	10 May
7:41.90	Cornelius	Kangogo	KEN	31.12.93	2		Sotteville-lès-Rouen	8 Jul
7:41.9+	Lawi	Lalang	KEN	15.6.91	3+	Herc	Monaco	19 Jul
7:42.18	Gideon	Gathimba	KEN	9.3.80	3		Sotteville-lès-Rouen	8 Jul
7:42.19	Henrik	Ingebrigtsen	NOR	24.2.91	7		Rieti	8 Sep
7:42.21	Daniel Kipchirchir (30)	Komen	KEN	27.11.84	12		Zagreb	3 Sep
7:42.26	Geoffrey	Kirui	KEN	16.2.93	10	DL	Doha	10 May
7:42.32	Ryan	Hill	USA	31.1.90	2	DL	London (OS)	27 Jul
7:43.36	Evan	Jager	USA	8.3.89	2		Luzern	17 Jul
7:43.84	Andrew	Bayer	USA	3.2.90	13		Zagreb	3 Sep
7:43.98	Tariku	Bekele	ETH	21.1.87	4	DL	London (OS)	27 Jul
7:44.01	Chris	Derrick	USA	17.10.90	4		Luzern	17 Jul
7:44.32+	Geoffrey	Barusei	KEN-J	.94	1	GGala	Roma	6 Jun
7:44.42	Dan	Huling	USA	16.7.83	5		Luzern	17 Jul
7:44.61	Moses	Mukono	KEN-J	27.11.95	4		Sotteville-lès-Rouen	8 Jul
7:44.68	Dathan (40)	Ritzenhein	USA	30.12.82	5	DL	London (OS)	27 Jul
7:44.83	Elroy	Gelant	RSA	25.8.86	5		Sotteville-lès-Rouen	8 Jul
7:44.87	Garrett	Heath	USA	3.11.85	6		Sotteville-lès-Rouen	8 Jul
7:45.1+	Galen	Rupp	USA	8.5.86		in 5k	Monaco	19 Jul
7:45.12	Juan Luis	Barrios	MEX	24.6.83	1		Dublin (S)	17 Jul
7:45.31	Daniele	Meucci	ITA	7.10.85	6	DL	London (OS)	27 Jul
7:45.52	Chris	Thompson	GBR	17.4.81	7	DL	London (OS)	27 Jul
7:45.75	Andrew	Vernon	GBR	7.1.86	2		Dublin	17 Jul
7:46.18	Hassan	Mead	USA	28.8.89	3		Dublin (S)	17 Jul
7:46.39	Bernard	Lagat	USA	12.12.74	1		Linz	26 Aug
7:47.02	Edward (50)	Waweru	KEN	3.10.90	1		Shibetsu	26 Jun

Mark	Name		Nat	Born	Pos		Mark	Name		Nat	Born	Pos	
7:47.07	Ben	Blankenship	USA	15.12.88	8	Jul	7:48.98	Nathan	Brannen	CAN	8.9.82	27	Jul
7:47.77	Diego	Estrada	MEX	12.12.89	17	Jul	7:49.05	Mohammed	Moustaoui	MAR	2.4.85	10	Ma
7:48.03	Eric	Tirop	KEN		13	Jul	7:49.09	Degefa	Deribe	ETH	9.6.87	3	May
7:48.31	Karemi	Thuku	KEN-J	7.7.94	26	Jun	7:49.45+	Vincent	Rono	KEN	.82	8	Jun
7:48.57	Sergio	Sánchez ¶	ESP	1.10.82	13	Jul	7:49.64	Joseph	Stilin	USA	5.12.89	14	Jul
7:48.95	Othmane	El Goumri	MAR	28.5.92	13	Jul	7:49.89	Iván	Fernández	ESP	10.6.88	13	Jul

Mark	Name		Nat	Born	Pos	Meet	Venue	Date
7:50.23	Hicham	Sigueni	MAR	30.1.93				20 May
7:50.50	John	Bolas	USA	1.11.87				27 Jul
7:50.62	Andrew	Poore	USA	3.12.88				14 Jul
7:50.96	Youssouf	Hiss Bachir	DJI	.87				23 Jul
7:51.01	Richard	Ringer	GER	27.2.89				20 May
7:51.01	Illias	Fifa	MAR	16.5.89				13 Jul
7:51.49	Tiidrek	Nurme	EST	18.11.85				23 Jul
7:51.88	Jonathan	Mellor	GBR	27.12.86				27 Jul
7:51.94	Alberto	Lozano ¶	ESP	23.2.87				13 Jul
7:51.99	Soufiyan	Bouqantar	MAR	30.8.93				11 May
7:51.99	Brett	Robinson	AUS	8.5.91				8 Jul
7:52.0 A	Vedic	Cheruiyot	KEN-Y	5.3.96				11 Jun
7:52.05	Dmitrijs	Jurkevics	LAT	7.1.87				3 Aug
7:52.07	Halil	Akkas	TUR	1..7.83				1 Jun

Indoors

Mark	Name		Nat	Born	Pos	Meet	Venue	Date
7:30.16	Galen	Rupp	USA	8.5.86	1		Stockholm	21 Feb
7:31.66	Caleb	Ndiku	KEN	9.10.92	2		Stockholm	21 Feb
7:32.87		Gebrhiwet			1		Boston (Roxbury)	2 Feb
7:33.67		Rupp			2		Boston (Roxbury)	2 Feb
7:34.71	Bernard	Lagat	USA	12.12.74	1		Karlsruhe	2 Feb
7:34.92	Abdelati	Iguider	MAR	25.3.87	3		Stockholm	21 Feb
7:38.35	Paul K.	Koech	KEN	10.11.81	4		Stockholm	21 Feb
7:39.81	Ayanleh	Souleiman	DJI	3.12.92	3		Gent	10 Feb
7:39.98+	Evan	Jager	USA	8.3.89	2+	in 2M	New York (Armory)	16 Feb
7:41.16	Daniel Kipchirchir	Komen	KEN	27.11.84	4		Gent	10 Feb
7:41.59	Mekonnen	Gebremedhin	ETH	11.10.88	5		Gent	10 Feb
7:41.74+	Cameron	Levins	CAN	28.3.89	4+	in 2M	New York (Armory)	16 Feb
7:43.32	Dejen	Gebremeskel	ETH	24.11.89	3		Boston (Roxbury)	2 Feb
7:43.47	Tesfaye	Cheru	ETH	2.3.93	7		Stockholm	21 Feb
7:43.72	Mahiedine	Mekhissi-Benabbad	FRA	15.3.85	3		Düsseldorf	8 Feb
7:43.99	Aman	Wote	ETH	18.4.84	8		Stockholm	21 Feb
7:45.77	Florian	Carvalho	FRA	9.3.89	2		Birmingham	16 Feb
7:46.72	Yoann	Kowal	FRA	28.5.87	4		Karlsruhe	2 Feb
7:46.95	Kemoy	Campbell	JAM	14.1.91	2	NCAA	Fayetteville	9 Mar
7:47.01	Valentin	Smirnov	RUS	13.2.86	1	NC	Moskva	12 Feb

Mark	Name		Nat	Born	Date		Mark	Name	Nat	Born	Date
7:47.16	Simon	Denissel	FRA	22.5.90	10 Feb		7:50.40	Ciarán O'Lionáird	IRL	11.4.88	2 Mar
7:47.57	Yegor	Nikolayev	RUS	12.2.88	12 Feb		7:50.44 #	Eric Jenkins	USA	24.11.91	9 Feb
7:47.91 #	Henry	Lelei	KEN	31.12.88	2 Mar		7:50.97 #	Maverick Darling	USA	9.6.89	22 Feb
7:48.20	Stephen	Kiprotich	KEN	25.11.90	23 Feb		7:51.24	David McCarthy	IRL	3.8.88	14 Feb
7:48.49	Andrey	Safronov	RUS	16.12.85	12 Feb		7:51.46	Lee Emanuel	GBR	24.1.85	16 Feb
7:49.17	Kirubel	Erassa	USA	17.6.93	9 Mar		7:51.61	Zachary Mayhew	USA	27.11.89	9 Feb
7:49.55	Juan Carlos	Higuero	ESP	3.8.78	2 Feb		7:51.77 #	Thomas Farrell	GBR	23.3.91	9 Feb
7:49.98+	Leonard	Korir	KEN	10.12.86	16 Feb		7:51.84	Polat Kemboi Arikan	TUR	12.12.90	23 Feb
7:50.26 #	Kennedy	Kithuka	KEN	4.6.89	2 Feb		7:52.07	Necerddine Hallil	ALG	10.4.88	21 Feb

Disqualified for impeding

Mark	Name		Nat	Born	Pos	Meet	Venue	Date
7:46.21	Eric	Jenkins	USA	24.11.91	-	NCAA	Fayetteville	9 Mar

JUNIORS

See main list for top 4 juniors. 7 performances by 5 men to 7:48.0. Additional mark and further juniors:
Gebrhiwet 2+ 7:44.5+ in 5k Rome 6 Jun

Mark	Name		Nat	Born	Pos	Meet	Venue	Date
7:48.31	Karemi	Thuku	KEN	7.7.94	2		Shibetsu	26 Jun
7:52.0 A	Vedic	Cheruiyot	KEN-Y	5.3.96	1		Nairobi	11 Jun
7:53.56	Yomif	Kejelcha	ETH-Y	1.8.97	1	WY	Donetsk	14 Jul
7:55.40	Mohammed	Abid	MAR	18.3.95	3		Fès	11 May
7:56.86	Alexander	Mutiso	KEN-Y	10.9.96	3	WY	Donetsk	14 Jul
7:57.28	Nicholas	Chepseba (10)	KEN	12.10.84	5		Rehlingen	20 May
7:57,7A	Festus	Kiprono	KEN	29.12.95	1		Nairobi	18 Apr
7:58.4A	Meshack	Letim	KEN-Y	30.11.97	1		Nairobi	16 Mar
7:58.76	Ali	Kaya	TUR	20.4.94	1		Mersin	8 Sep
7:58.84	Paul	Kamaysi	KEN-Y	24.10.96	2		Fukuyama	21 Apr
7:59.0A	Edwin	Melly	KEN-Y	10.8.96	2		Nairobi	16 Mar

2 MILES INDOORS

Mark	Name		Nat	Born	Pos	Meet	Venue	Date
8:09.49	Bernard	Lagat	USA	12.12.74	1	Millrose	New York (Armory)	16 Feb
8:13.02	Andrew	Bumbalough	USA	14.3.87	2	Millrose	New York (Armory)	16 Feb
8:14.69	Cameron	Levins	CAN	28.3.89	3	Millrose	New York (Armory)	16 Feb
8:14.95	Evan	Jager	USA	8.3.89	4	Millrose	New York (Armory)	16 Feb

5000 METRES

Mark	Name		Nat	Born	Pos	Meet	Venue	Date
12:51.34	Edwin	Soi	KEN	3.3.86	1	Herc	Monaco	19 Jul
12:51.96	Albert	Rop	KEN/BRN	17.7.92	2	Herc	Monaco	19 Jul
12:54.95	Yenew	Alamirew	ETH	27.5.90	1	GGala	Roma	6 Ju
12:55.73	Hagos	Gebrhiwet	ETH-J	11.5.94	2	GGala	Roma	6 Ju
12:56.08	Isiah	Koech	KEN	19.12.92	3	Herc	Monaco	19 Jul
12:58.75		Alamirew			1	VD	Bruxelles	6 Sep
12:58.85		I Koech			3	GGala	Roma	6 Jun
12:58.99	Bernard	Lagat	USA	12.12.74	2	VD	Bruxelles	6 Sep
12:59.33		Gebrehiwet			3	VD	Bruxelles	6 Sep
12:59.43		Rop			1rA	NA	Heusden-Zolder	13 Jul

MEN 2013

Mark	Name		Nat	Born	Pos	Meet	Venue	Date	
12:59.81	Thomas	Longosiwa	KEN	14.1.82	4	Herc	Monaco	19	Jul
13:00.95	Lawi	Lalang	KEN	15.6.91	5	Herc	Monaco	19	Jul
13:01.00		Soi			4	VD	Bruxelles	6	Sep
13:01.37	Galen	Rupp	USA	8.5.86	5	VD	Bruxelles	6	Sep
13:01.64	John	Kipkoech (10)	KEN	29.12.91	4	GGala	Roma	6	Jun
13:01.74		Longosiwa			6	VD	Bruxelles	6	Sep
13:02.31		Rop			7	VD	Bruxelles	6	Sep
13:02.40	Evan	Jager	USA	8.3.89	8	VD	Bruxelles	6	Sep
13:02.54		Soi			5	GGala	Roma	6	Jun
13:03.58		Longosiwa			1		Rabat	9	Jun
13:03.69	Muktar	Edris	ETH-J	14.1.94	1	GS	Ostrava	27	Jun
13:03.80	Caleb	Ndiku	KEN	9.10.92	6	GGala	Roma	6	Jun
13:03.98		I Koech			9	VD	Bruxelles	6	Sep
13:04.65		Edris			1	FBK	Hengelo	8	Jun
13:04.75		Soi			1	Pre	Eugene	1	Jun
13:05.00	Aweke	Ayalew	BRN	233.93	2		Rabat	9	Jun
13:05.17		Rupp			6	Herc	Monaco	19	Jul
13:05.31	Augustine	Choge	KEN	21.1.87	2	FBK	Hengelo	8	Jun
13:05.88	Mohamed	Farah	GBR	23.3.83	2	Pre	Eugene	1	Jun
13:06.37		Choge			2	GS	Ostrava	27	Jun
	(30/16)								
13:07.88	Kenenisa	Bekele	ETH	13.6.82	4	GS	Ostrava	27	Jun
13:08.04	Chris	Derrick	USA	17.10.90	11	VD	Bruxelles	6	Sep
13:09.16	Ibrahim	Jeylan	ETH	12.6.89	8	Pre	Eugene	1	Jun
13:09.17	Imane	Merga	ETH	15.10.88	7	GGala	Roma	6	Jun
	(20)								
13:09.45	Aziz	Lahbabi	MAR	3.2.91	3		Rabat	9	Jun
13:09.53	Dathan	Ritzenhein	USA	30.12.82	9	Pre	Eugene	1	Jun
13:10.83	Ben	St. Lawrence	AUS	7.11.81	2rA	NA	Heusden-Zolder	13	Jul
13:11.56	Moses	Kipsiro	UGA	2.9.86	4	Athl	Lausanne	4	Jul
13:11.59	Ben	True	USA	29.12.85	3rA	NA	Heusden-Zolder	13	Jul
13:11.80	Hassan	Mead	USA	28.8.89	4rA	NA	Heusden-Zolder	13	Jul
13:12.01	Andrew	Bumbalough	USA	14.3.87	5rA	NA	Heusden-Zolder	13	Jul
13:12.50	Arne	Gabius	GER	22.3.81	6rA	NA	Heusden-Zolder	13	Jul
13:12.64	Tasama	Dame	ETH	12.10.87	7rA	NA	Heusden-Zolder	13	Jul
13:12.91	Cyrus	Rutto	KEN	21.4.92	3	FBK	Hengelo	8	Jun
	(30)								
13:12.97	Sergio	Sánchez ¶	ESP	1.10.82	5	GS	Ostrava	27	Jun
13:13.18	Yigrem	Demelash	ETH-J	28.1.94	9	GGala	Roma	6	Jun
13:13.60	Yuki	Sato	JPN	26.11.86	8rA	NA	Heusden-Zolder	13	Jul
13:13.61	Tariku	Bekele	ETH	21.1.87	6	Athl	Lausanne	4	Jul
13:13.72	Othmane	El Goumri	MAR	28.5.92	5		Rabat	9	Jun
13:13.83	Zane	Robertson	NZL	14.11.89	9rA	NA	Heusden-Zolder	13	Jul
13:13.91	Kenneth	Kipkemoi	KEN	2.8.84	12	Pre	Eugene	1	Jun
13:14.22	Ryan	Hill	USA	31.1.90	10rA	NA	Heusden-Zolder	13	Jul
13:14.60	Birhan	Nebebew	ETH-J	14.8.94	7	Athl	Lausanne	4	Jul
13:14.91	Alemayehu	Bezabeh	ESP	22.9.86	1		Huelva	12	Jun
	(40)								
13:14.97	Jonathan	Ndiku	KEN	18.9.91	1		Yokohama	16	Nov
13:15.19	Cameron	Levins	CAN	28.3.89	13	Pre	Eugene	1	Jun
13:15.26	Cornelius	Kangogo	KEN	31.12.93	6		Rabat	9	Jun
13:15.32	Berhanu	Legesse	ETH	.93	4	FBK	Hengelo	8	Jun
13:15.33	Diego	Estrada	MEX	12.12.89	3	Jordan	Stanford	28	Apr
13:15.45	Leonard	Korir	KEN	10.12.86	4	Jordan	Stanford	28	Apr
13:15.51	Vincent	Chepkok	KEN	5.7.88	2	adidas	New York	25	May
13:15.54	Jake	Robertson	NZL	14.11.89	11rA	NA	Heusden-Zolder	13	Jul
13:15.75	Bidan	Karoki	KEN	21.8.90	2		Yokohama	16	Nov
13:15.87	Elroy	Gelant	RSA	25.8.86	12rA	NA	Heusden-Zolder	13	Jul
	(50)								
13:15.91	Sindre	Buraas	NOR	8.5.89	13rA	NA	Heusden-Zolder	13	Jul
13:16.07	Younès	Essalhi	MAR	20.2.93	7		Rabat	9	Jun
13:16.57	Paul	Tanui	KEN	22.12.90	1	Oda	Hiroshima	28	Apr
13:16.68	Geoffrey	Kirui	KEN	16.2.93	14	Pre	Eugene	1	Jun
13:16.92	Phillip	Kipyeko	UGA-J	10.1.95	5	FBK	Hengelo	8	Jun
13:17.42	Bouabdellah	Tahri	FRA	20.12.78	9	Athl	Lausanne	4	Jul
13:17.89	Zelalem	Bacha	BRN	10.1.88	7	GS	Ostrava	27	Jun
13:18.00	Alemu	Bekele	BRN	23.3.90	8		Rabat	9	Jun
13:18.42	Dan	Huling	USA	16.7.83	6	Jordan	Stanford	28	Apr
13:18.57	Eric	Jenkins	USA	24.11.91	7	Jordan	Stanford	28	Apr
	(60)								
13:18.72	Demma	Daba	ETH	18.7.89	1		Nobeoka	11	May

Mark	Name		Nat	Born	Pos	Meet	Venue	Date	
13:18.96	Brett	Robinson	AUS	8.5.91	8	GS	Ostrava	27	Jun
13:19.04	Leonard	Barsoton	KEN-J	21.10.94	3		Yokohama	16	Nov
13:19.45	Yitayal	Atnafu	ETH	20.1.93	1		Nijmegen	12	Jun
13:19.46	Josphat	Bett	KEN	12.6.90	9		Rabat	9	Jun
13:19.83	William	Malel	KEN-J	1.3.94	4		Yokohama	16	Nov
13:19.96	Patrick	Mutunga	KEN-J	20.11.94	3	Oda	Hiroshima	28	Apr
13:20.01	Garrett	Heath	USA	3.11.85	8	Jordan	Stanford	28	Apr
13:20.07	Samuel	Chelanga	KEN	23.2.85	9	Jordan	Stanford	28	Apr
13:20.34	Alberto	Lozano ¶	ESP	23.2.87	9	GS	Ostrava	27	Jun
(70)									
13:20.51	Mark	Kiptoo	KEN	21.6.76	5	DL	Birmingham	30	Jun
13:20.57	Alex	Kibet	KEN/QAT	20.10.90	4		Nijmegen	12	Jun
13:20.73	Zewdie	Milion	ETH	24.1.89	2		Nobeoka	11	May
13:20.79	Abrar	Osman	ERI-J	1.1.94	7	FBK	Hengelo	8	Jun
13:20.80	Suguru	Osako	JPN	23.5.91	5		Yokohama	16	Nov
13:20.89	Tsegay	Tuemay	ERI-J	20.12.95	5		Nijmegen	12	Jun
13:20.98	Soufiyan	Bouqantar	MAR	30.8.93	10		Rabat	9	Jun
13:21.55	Will	Leer	USA	15.4.85	1	MSR	Walnut	19	Apr
13:22.15	Bernard	Kimani	KEN	10.9.93	3		Nobeoka	11	May
13:22.37	Aaron	Braun	USA	28.5.87	5		Los Angeles (ER)	17	May
(80)									
13:22.96	Edward	Waweru	KEN	3.10.90	1		Nagoya	8	Jun
13:23.20	Patrick	Mwaka	KEN	2.11.92	2		Nagoya	8	Jun
13:23.32	Denis	Masai	KEN	1.12.91	7		Nijmegen	12	Jun
13:23.59	Hayle	Ibrahimov	AZE	18.1.90	16	Pre	Eugene	1	Jun
13:23.62	Chris	Solinsky	USA	5.12.84	11	Jordan	Stanford	28	Apr
13:24.06	Chris	Thompson	GBR	17.4.81	7	DL	Birmingham	30	Jun
13:24.07	Rory	Fraser	GBR	25.4.87	2	MSR	Walnut	19	Apr
13:24.08	Rabah	Aboud	ALG	1.1.81	11		Rabat	9	Jun
13:24.15	Bobby	Curtis	USA	28.11.84	6		Los Angeles (ER)	17	May
13:24.50	Karemi	Thuku	KEN-J	7.7.94	4		Nobeoka	11	May
(90)									
13:25.21	Dejene	Regassa	BRN	18.4.89	6h2	WCh	Moskva	13	Aug
13:25.62	Illias	Fifa	MAR	16.5.89	3		Huelva	12	Jun
13:25.94	Stephen	Mokoka	RSA	31.1.85	1	NC	Stellenbosch	13	Apr
13:26.31	Hicham	Bellani	MAR	15.9.79	3		Alger	18	Jun
13:26.57	Haron	Lagat	KEN	15.8.83	16rA	NA	Heusden-Zolder	13	Jul
13:26.67	Noureddine	Smaïl	FRA	6.2.87	1rB	Jordan	Stanford	28	Apr
13:26.73	Hiram	Ngatia	KEN-Y	.96	1		Yokohama	29	Sep
13:27.08	Jamel	Chatbi	ITA	30.4.84	1		Oordegem	1	Jun
13:27.10	Dawit	Weldesilasie	ERI-J	10.12.94	5		Alger	18	Jun
13:27.29	Richard	Ringer	GER	27.2.89	2		Oordegem	1	Jun
(100)									

Mark			Nat	Born	Date			Mark			Nat	Born	Date	
13:27.32	Juan Luis	Barrios	MEX	24.6.83	27	Jul		13:31.54	Enoch	Omwamba	KEN	4.4.93	26 May
13:27.33	Meshack	Letim	KEN-Y	30.11.97	13	Jul		13:31.56	Sean	Quigley	USA	8.2.85	19 Apr
13:27.35	Collis	Birmingham	AUS	27.12.84	23	Feb		13:31.70	Parker	Stinson	USA	3.3.92	28 Apr
13:27.38	Paul	Kuira	KEN	25.1.90	17	Nov		13:31.81	Azmeraw	Mengistu	ETH	15.9.92	14 Apr
13:27.60	Elliott	Heath	USA	4.2.89	13	Jul		13:31.88	Luke	Puskedra	USA	8.2.90	17 May
13:27.93	Maverick	Darling	USA	9.6.89	13	Jul		13:31.94	Japheth	Korir	KEN	30.6.93	6 Apr
13:28.05	Mohammed	El Hachimi	BEL	15.12.74	13	Jul		13:32.0A	Peter	Mwololo	KEN	.92	3 May
13:28.08	Marouan	Razine	MAR	9.4.91	1	Jun		13:32.09	Eric	Tirop	KEN		8 Jun
13:28.20	Youssouf	Hiss Bachir	DJI	.87	27	Jul		13:32.14	Joseph	Onsarigo	KEN	.93	16 Jun
13:28.79	Genki	Yagisawa	JPN	4.3.93	29	Sep		13:32.21	Timothy	Toroitich	UGA	10.10.91	9 Jun
13:28.81	Bayron	Piedra	ECU	19.8.82	19	Apr		13:32.22	Hiromitsu	Kakuage	JPN	14.9.90	13 Jul
13:29.08	Jeff	See	USA	6.6.86	28	Apr		13:32.24	Peter	Ndegwa	KEN		8 Jun
13:29.45	Cameron	Page	AUS	12.6.91	13	Apr		13:32.44	Mauricio	González	COL	14.10.88	19 Apr
13:29.55	George	Alex	USA	20.1.90	28	Apr		13:32.76	Charles	Ndirangu	KEN	8.2.93	6 Apr
13:29.55	Richard	Mengich	KEN	.89	15	Jun		13:32.82	Kemoy	Campbell	JAM	14.1.91	29 Mar
13:29.87	Awole	Kedir	ETH	24.5.93	29	Jun		13:32.86	Teklemariam	Medhin	ERI	24.6.89	4 Jul
13:29.94	Luke	Caldwell	GBR	2.8.91	28	Apr		13:32.92	Goltom	Kifle	ERI	3.12.93	12 Jun
13:30.16	Moses	Kibet	UGA	23.3.91	27	Jun		13:33.03	Andrew	Poore	USA	3.12.88	29 Mar
13:30.77	Tsuyoshi	Ugachi	JPN	27.4.87	29	Jun		13:33.04	Vincent	Rono	KEN	.82	3 Jun
13:30.79	Benjamin	Bruce	USA	10.9.82	19	Apr		13:33.13	Joseph	Stilin	USA	5.12.89	17 May
13:30.91	Bashir	Abdi	BEL	10.2.89	19	Apr		13:33.20	Andrew	Vernon	GBR	7.1.86	3 Sep
13:30.96	Nuguse	Hirsuato	ETH	13.2.82	27	Jun		13:33.23	Mulaku	Abera	ETH-J	20.4.94	11 May
13:30.96A	Abdallah	Mande	UGA-J	10.5.95	19	Jul		13:33.57A	Geoffrey	Kusuro	UGA	12.2.89	19 Jul
13:31.02	Dejen	Gebremeskel	ETH	24.11.89	25	May		13:33.77	Nassir	Dawud	ERI	.91	14 Jun
13:31.10	Clement	Langat	KEN	18.12.91	29	Sep		13:33.80A	Solomon	Mutai	UGA	.89	19 Jul
13:31.12	Joilson	da Silva	BRA	29.8.87	12	Jun		13:34.0 A	Ezekiel	Cherop	KEN	.83	11 May
13:31.19	Leul	Gebrselassie	ETH	20.9.93	29	Sep		13:34.0 A	Timothy	Kiptoo	KEN	2.8.84	17 Jun
13:31.21	Liam	Adams	AUS	4.9.86	19	Apr		13:34.30	Elliott	Krause	USA	12.6.90	19 Apr
13:31.39	Ali	Kaya	KEN/TUR-J	20.4.94	1	Jun		13:34.31	Koen	Naert	BEL	3.9.89	27 Jul
13:31.45	Mosinet	Geremew	ETH	12.2.92	14	Jun		13:34.54	Philipp	Pflieger	GER	16.7.87	13 Jul
								13:34.72	Nick	McCormick	GBR	11.9.81	23 Feb

Mark	Name		Nat	Born	Pos	Meet	Venue	Date
13:34.74	Olle	Walleräng	SWE	5.2.85	27	Jul		
13:34.82	Andrew	Bayer	USA	3.2.90	29	Mar		
13:34.84	Anthony	Rotich	KEN		29	Mar		
13:34.95	Jacob	Wanjuki	KEN	16.1.86	14	Apr		
13:35.0A	Douglas	Kipserem	KEN	.87	3	May		
13:35.0A	Peter	Mwololo	KEN	.92	4	May		
13:35.20	Jamal	Hitrane	MAR	1.9.89	9	Jun		
13:35.21	Daniel	Kitonyi	KEN-J	12.1.94	26	May		
13:35.51	Craig	Miller	USA	3.8.87	29	Mar		
13:35.97	Ben	Hubers	CAN	22.12.88	29	Mar		
13:36.26	Abayneh	Abele	ETH	4.11.87	1	Jun		
13:36.27	Paul	Chelimo	KEN	27.10.90		28 Apr		
13:36.46	Ezekiel	Meli	KEN	21.4.84		8 Jun		
13:36.5A	Moses	Mukuno	KEN-J	27.11.95		20 Jun		
13:36.51	Mike	Kigen	KEN	15.1.86		30 Jun		
13:36.64	Iván	Fernández	ESP	10.6.88		21 Jun		
13:36.79	Bolota	Asmerom	USA	12.10.78		19 Apr		
13:36.79	Aritaka	Kajiwara	JPN	16.6.88		29 Sep		
13:36.8A	Josephat	Menjo	KEN	20.8.79		11 May		
13:36.81	Monder	Rizki	BEL	16.8.79		27 Jun		
13:36.98	Alberto	Sánchez	ESP	19.10.88		1 Jun		
	(180)							

Indoors

13:07.00	Lopez	Lomong	USA	1.1.85	1		New York (Armory)	1 Mar
13:25.38	Kennedy	Kithuka	KEN	4.6.89	1		Fayetteville	8 Mar
13:35.46	Matt	Tegenkamp	USA	19.1.82	6		New York (Armory)	1 Mar

JUNIORS

See main list for top 13 juniors. 16 performances by 8 men to 13:20.0. Additional marks and further juniors:

Gebrhiwet 2+	13:07.11		2	Athl	Lausanne	4	Jul	13:17.11	3	DL	Birmingham	30 Jun
	13:10.03		1	DL	New York	25	May				
Edris 2+	13:06.44		10	VD	Bruxelles	6	Sep	13:08.23	3	Athl	Lausanne	4 Jul
Demelesh	13:16.84		8	Athl	Lausanne	4	Jul				

13:27.33	Meshack	Letim	KEN-Y	30.11.97	1rB	NA	Heusden-Zolder	13 Jul
13:30.96A	Abdallah	Mande	UGA	10.5.95	1	NC	Kampala	19 Jul
13:31.39	Ali	Kaya	KEN/TUR	20.4.94	4		Oordegem	1 Jun
13:33.23	Mulaku	Abera	ETH	20.4.94	6		Nobeoka	11 May
13:35.21	Daniel	Kitonyi	KEN	12.1.94	3		Yokohama	26 May
13:36.5A	Moses	Mukuno	KEN	27.11.95	4h2	NC	Nairobi	20 Jun
13:38.0A	Bernard	Kipkemoi	KEN	3..5.94	6h2	NC	Nairobi	20 Jun
13:39.84	Peter	Limo (20)	KEN	.94	11	FBK	Hengelo	8 Jun

Best non-African: 13:46.19 Hideto Yamanaka   JPN   17.3.94   11   Yokohama   29 Sep
Best European: 14:09.46 Jonathan Davies   GBR   28.10.94   4   Solihull   18 May
Note: Albert Rop had been shown with a birth year of 1994, but this is now more generally thought to be 1992.

10,000 METRES

26:51.02	Dejen	Gebremeskel	ETH	24.11.89	1		Sollentuna	27 Jun
26:52.85	Abera	Kuma	ETH	31.8.90	2		Sollentuna	27 Jun
26:57.33	Imane	Merga	ETH	15.10.88	3		Sollentuna	27 Jun
27:12.08	Kenenisa	Bekele	ETH	13.6.82	1	Pre	Eugene	31 Ma
27:12.37		Merga			2	Pre	Eugene	31 May
27:13.10		Kuma			3	Pre	Eugene	31 May
27:13.12	Bidan	Karoki	KEN	21.8.90	4	Pre	Eugene	31 May
27:14.34	Birhan	Tesfaye Nebebew	ETH-J	14.8.94	5	Pre	Eugene	31 May
27:15.51	Yigrem	Demelash	ETH-J	28.1.94	4		Sollentuna	27 Jun
27:17.30	Vincent	Chepkok	KEN	5.7.88	6	Pre	Eugene	31 May
27:19.97	Teklemariam	Medhin	ERI	24.6.89	7	Pre	Eugene	31 May
27:21.50	Paul	Tanui (10)	KEN	22.12.90	1		Kitakyushu	18 May
27:21.71	Mohamed	Farah	GBR	23.3.83	1	WCh	Moskva	10 Aug
27:22.23	Ibrahim	Jeylan	ETH	12.6.89	2	WCh	Moskva	10 Aug
27:22.61		Tanui			3	WCh	Moskva	10 Aug
27:24.39	Galen	Rupp	USA	8.5.86	4	WCh	Moskva	10 Aug
27:24.65		Demelash			8	Pre	Eugene	31 May
27:25.27		Kuma			5	WCh	Moskva	10 Aug
27:26.43		Tanui			1		Kumagaya	20 Sep
27:27.17		Karoki			6	WCh	Moskva	10 Aug
27:28.11	Atsedu	Tsegay	ETH	17.12.91	5		Sollentuna	27 Jun
27:28.50	Kenneth	Kipkemoi	KEN	2.8.84	7	WCh	Moskva	10 Aug
27:28.67	Patrick	Mutunga	KEN-J	20.11.94	1		Tajimi	14 Oct
27:28.71	Emmanuel	Bett	KEN	30.3.83	9	Pre	Eugene	31 May
27:29.21	Nguse	Tesfaldet	ERI	10.11.86	8	WCh	Moskva	10 Aug
27:30.51	Edward	Waweru	KEN	3.10.90	2		Kumagaya	20 Sep
27:30.65		Karoki			1		Naka	18 May
27:31.07	Timothy	Toroitich	UGA	10.10.91	10	Pre	Eugene	31 May
27:31.13		Waweru			2		Tajimi	14 Oct
27:31.61A		Karoki			1	WChT	Nairobi	13 Jul
	(30/20)							
27:32.00	Goitom	Kifle	ERI	3.12.93	11	Pre	Eugene	31 May
27:32.76A		Tanui			2	WChT	Nairobi	13 Jul
27:33.13	Leonard	Barsoton	KEN-J	21.10.94	1		Fukagawa	29 Jun
27:33.38	Karemi	Thuku	KEN-J	7.7.94	2		Fukagawa	29 Jun
27:35.76	Mohammed	Ahmed	CAN	5.1.91	9	WCh	Moskva	10 Aug

Mark	Name		Nat	Born	Pos	Meet	Venue	Date	
27:37.55	Ben	St. Lawrence	AUS	7.11.81	1	Jordan	Stanford	28	Apr
27:37.90	Dathan	Ritzenhein	USA	30.12.82	10	WCh	Moskva	10	Aug
27:38.15	Tariku	Bekele	ETH	21.1.87	12	Pre	Eugene	31	May
27:38.31	Suguru	Osako	JPN	23.5.91	2	Jordan	Stanford	28	Apr
27:39.50	Yuki	Sato	JPN	26.11.86	3	Jordan	Stanford	28	Apr
	(30)								
27:40.81	Chris	Thompson	GBR	17.4.81	4	Jordan	Stanford	28	Apr
27:40.96	Thomas	Ayeko	UGA	10.2.92	11	WCh	Moskva	10	Aug
27:41.30	Elroy	Gelant	RSA	25.8.86	1		Durban	26	Apr
27:43.99	Bashir	Abdi	BEL	10.2.89	5	Jordan	Stanford	28	Apr
27:44.05	Ryan	Vail	USA	19.3.86	6	Jordan	Stanford	28	Apr
27:44.26A	Josphat	Bett	KEN	12.6.90	5	WChT	Nairobi	13	Jul
27:44.53	Moses	Kipsiro	UGA	2.9.86	13	WCh	Moskva	10	Aug
27:44.58	Aaron	Braun	USA	28.5.87	7	Jordan	Stanford	28	Apr
27:45.46	Jake	Robertson	NZL	14.11.89	8	Jordan	Stanford	28	Apr
27:46.06	Samuel	Chelanga	KEN	23.2.85	1	Zátopek	Melbourne	12	Dec
	(40)								
27:46.35	Agato	Yashin Hasen	ETH	19.1.86	1r1		Kawasaki	30	Nov
27:47.89	Cameron	Levins	CAN	28.3.89	14	WCh	Moskva	10	Aug
27:48.55	William	Malel	KEN-J	1.3.94	1		Yokohama	28	Sep
27:50.07	Jacob	Wanjuki	KEN	16.1.86	2r1		Kawasaki	30	Nov
27:50.78	Sean	Quigley	USA	8.2.85	9	Jordan	Stanford	28	Apr
27:50.79	Tsuyoshi	Ugachi	JPN	27.4.87	15	WCh	Moskva	10	Aug
27:51.10	Patrick	Mwaka	KEN	2.11.92	3r1		Kawasaki	30	Nov
27:51.54	Keita	Shitara	JPN	18.12.91	1		Nobeoka	11	May
27:52.38	Girma	Mecheso	ETH/USA	16.1.88	10	Jordan	Stanford	28	Apr
27:52.65	Martin	Mathathi	KEN	25.12.85	2		Nobeoka	11	May
	(50)								
27:53.34	Tetsuya	Yoroizaka	JPN	20.3.90	4r1		Kawasaki	30	Nov
27:53.85A	Leonard Patrick	Komon	KEN	10.1.88	6	WChT	Nairobi	13	Jul
27:54.00	Paul	Kuira	KEN	25.1.90	5r1		Kawasaki	30	Nov
27:54.35	Daniel	Gitau	KEN	1.10.87	3		Fukagawa	29	Jun
27:54.74	Mulaku	Abera	ETH-J	20.4.94	3		Kumagaya	20	Sep
27:54.82	Yuta	Shitara	JPN	18.12.91	3		Nobeoka	11	May
27:55.07	Tony	Okello	UGA	26.12.83	11	Jordan	Stanford	28	Apr
27:55.3 A	Geoffrey	Mutai	KEN	7.10.81	1	NC	Nairobi	22	Jun
27:56.22	Collis	Birmingham	AUS	27.12.84	2	Zát 1 NC	Melbourne	12	Dec
27:56.78	Andrew	Bumbalough	USA	14.3.87	13	Jordan	Stanford	28	Apr
	(60)								
27:57.51	Abayneh	Ayele	ETH	4.11,87	1rB		Fukagawa	29	Jun
27:57.69	Juan Luis	Barrios	MEX	24.6.83	14	Pre	Eugene	31	May
27:57.90	Chihiro	Miyawaki	JPN	28.8.91	6r1		Kawasaki	30	Nov
27:57.92	Carles	Castillejo	ESP	18.8.78	1	NC	Mataró	6	Apr
27:58.02	Alex	Mwangi	KEN	14.6.90	4		Fukagawa	29	Jun
27:59.11	Macharia	Ndirangu	KEN-J	9.9.94	5		Fukagawa	29	Jun
27:59.22	Christopher	Landry	USA	29.4.86	14	Jordan	Stanford	28	Apr
27:59.7 A	Emmanuel	Kipsang	KEN	13.6.91	3	NC	Nairobi	22	Jun
27:59.96	Azmeraw	Mengistu	ETH	15.9.92	2		Naka	18	May
28:01.01	Kassa	Mekashaw	ETH	19.3.84	2rB		Fukagawa	29	Jun
	(70)								
28:01.87	Johnson	Kiumbani	KEN	27.1.93	3		Naka	18	May
28:02.79	Daniel	Kitonyi	KEN-J	12.1.94	1		Yokohama	30	Nov
28:02.86	Zewdie	Milion	ETH	24.1.89	3rB		Fukagawa	29	Jun
28:03.0 A	Josephat Kiprono	Menjo	KEN	20.8.79	4	NC	Nairobi	22	Jun
28:03.5 A	Hosea	Macharinyang	KEN	12.6.85	5	NC	Nairobi	22	Jun
28:04.54	Chris	Derrick	USA	17.10.90	18	WCh	Moskva	10	Aug
28:05.13	Johana	Maina	KEN	24.12.90	8r1		Kawasaki	30	Nov
28:05.66	Leul	Gebrselassie	ETH	20.9.93	2		Kitami	6	Jul
28:05.79	Shogo	Nakamura	JPN	16.9.92	4		Nobeoka	11	May
28:06.74	Daniele	Meucci	ITA	7.10.85	19	WCh	Moskva	10	Aug
	(80)								
28:07.54	Shinobu	Kubota	JPN	12.12.91	10r1		Kawasaki	30	Nov
28:08.5 A	John	Mwangangi	KEN	1.11.90	6	NC	Nairobi	22	Jun
28:09.56	Yuichiro	Ueno	JPN	29.7.85	5		Nobeoka	11	May
28:09.70	Stephen	Mokoka	RSA	31.1.85	2		Durban	26	Apr
28:11.81	Cyrus	Njui	KEN	11.2.86	2		Yokohama	28	Sep
28:12.58	Tasama	Moogas	ISR	2.2.88	1	NC	Tel Aviv	9	May
28:13.23	Ryo	Yamamoto	JPN	18.5.84	8		Fukagawa	29	Jun
28:13.23	Maina	Karukawa	KEN	19.6.91	1r1		Kawasaki	30	Nov
28:14.63	Lawi	Lalang	KEN	15.6.91	1	Pac-12	Los Angeles	11	May
28:15.80	Enoch	Omwamba	KEN	4.4.93	1		Tokyo	19	May
	(90)								

MEN 2013

Mark	Name		Nat	Born	Pos	Meet	Venue	Date
28:15.92	Sota	Hoshi	JPN	6.1.88	9		Fukagawa	29 Jun
28:16.05	Harry	Summers	AUS	19.5.90	3	Zát 2 NC	Melbourne	12 Dec
28:16.18	Liam	Adams	AUS	4.9.86	15	Jordan	Stanford	28 Apr
28:16.27	Joseph	Kamathi	KEN-Y	23.11.96	14r1		Kawasaki	30 Nov
28:16.99	Akihiko	Tsumurai	JPN	10.7.84	10		Fukagawa	29 Jun
28:17.0 A	Geoffrey	Kipsang	KEN	28.11.92	1		Nairobi	24 May
28:17.26	Polat Kemboi	Arikan	TUR	12.12.90	1	Med G	Mersin	27 Jun
28:17.85	James	Rungaru	KEN	14.1.93	2	Isr Ch	Tel Aviv	9 May
28:18.0 A	Wilson	Kiprop	KEN	14.4.87	1		Eldoret	31 May
28:18.11	Kenta	Murayama	JPN	23.2.93	1		Kobe	20 Apr
28:18.26	Chris	Hamer	AUS	2.8.88	4	Zát 3 NC	Melbourne	12 Dec
(100)								

Mark	Name		Nat	Born	Date
28:18.3 A	Elkana	Terer	KEN		31 May
28:18.5 A	Philemon	Rono	KEN	8.2.91	24 May
28:18.73	Minato	Oishi	JPN	19.5.88	30 Nov
28:18.91	Hiroyuki	Ono	JPN	3.10.86	29 Jun
28:20.0 A	Philemon	Limo	KEN	2.8.85	24 May
28:20.43	Josephat	Onsarigo	KEN	.93 3	Jul
28:20.6 A	Charles	Toroitich	KEN	.88	16 May
28:20.71	Tatsuya	Oike	JPN	18.5.90	30 Nov
28:21.12	Sergey	Lebid	UKR	15.7.75	6 Jun
28:21.29	Abdi	Nageeye	NED	2.3.89	31 May
28:22.18	Aritaka	Kajiwara	JPN	16.6.88	30 Nov
28:22.43	Yuma	Hattori	JPN	13.11.93	6 Jul
28:22.47	Tsubasa	Hayakawa	JPN	2.7.90	30 Nov
28:22.7 A	Silas	Cheprot	KEN	2.7.93	22 Jun
28:22.79	Shota	Hattori	JPN	28.10.91	20 Apr
28:23.89	Giovani	dos Santos	BRA	1.7.81	21 Apr
28:23.95	Tomoya	Onishi	JPN	28.3.87	20 Sep
28:24.04A	Mark	Kiptoo	KEN	21.6.76	13 Jul
28:24.20	Marílson	dos Santos	BRA	6.8.77	21 Apr
28:24.26	Naoki	Okamoto	JPN	26.5.84	21 Apr
28:24.31	Tomohiro	Tanigawa	JPN	4.3.89	30 Nov
28:24.74	Lewis	Korir	KEN	11.6.86	30 May
28:25.53	Takuya	Fujimoto	JPN	11.9.89	30 Nov
28:26.0 A	Paul	Lonyangat	KEN	12.12.92	24 May
28:26.03	Hideto	Yamanaka	JPN-J	17.3.94	29 Jun
28:26.04	Yoshinori	Oda	JPN	5.12.80	29 Jun
28:26.20A	Peter	Kibet	UGA	18.6.92	18 Jul
28:26.59	Keita	Baba	JPN	28.4.86	30 Nov
28:26.91	Yuji	Osuda	JPN	18.11.90	30 Nov
28:27.02	Takuya	Noguchi	JPN	2.7.88	30 Nov
28:27.04	Kohei	Matsumura	JPN	25.11.86	29 Jun
28:27.67	Charles	Ndirangu	KEN	8.2.93	18 May
28:27.67	Kenji	Yamamoto	JPN	17.11.89	29 Jun
28:27.69	Masato	Imai	JPN	2.4.84	8 Jun
28:28.40	Ryotaro	Nitta	JPN	14.12.89	21 Apr
28:28.6 A	Belete	Assefa	ETH	3.3.91	26 Jun
28:29.51	Yuya	Konishi	JPN	22.8.90	29 Jun
28:29.87	John	Kariuki	KEN	10.11.86	14 Apr
28:30.25	Benjamin	Gandu	KEN	21.5.90	18 May
28:30.35	John	Gilbertson	USA	7.6.91	29 Mar
28:30.80	José Antonio	Uribe	MEX	3.1.86	28 Apr
28:31.06	Hicham	Bellani	MAR	15.9.79	6 Jul
28:31.14	Bobby	Mack	USA	30.12.84	28 Apr
28:31.16	Ali	Kaya	TUR-J	20.4.94	18 Jul
28:31.43	Takuya	Fukatsu	JPN	10.11.87	29 Jun
28:31.5 A	Simon	Chirchir	KEN-J	.94	4 May
28:31.72	Keiji	Akutsu	JPN	20.3.87	16 Nov
28:31.75	Sergio	Sánchez ¶	ESP	1.10.82	8 Jun
28:31.80	Moses	Kurong	UGA-J	7.7.94	30 Aug
28:31.82	Halil	Akkas	TUR	1.7.83	8 Jun
28:32.23	Kazuhiro	Maeda	JPN	19.4.81	21 Apr
28:32.48	Alistair	Brownlee	GBR	23.4.88	28 Apr
28:32.5 A	Emmanuel	Bor	KEN-J	.95	22 Jun
28:32.54	Atsushi	Yamazaki	JPN	7.10.86	16 Nov
28:33.4 A	John	Kyui	KEN	20.10.84	22 Jun
28:33.50	Masaya	Kakihara	JPN	16.1.93	16 Nov
28:33.66	Yuki	Iwai	JPN	30.12.82	28 Sep
28:34.0A	Tebelu	Zewede	ETH	10.7.93	26 Jun
28:34.29	Chiharu	Takada	JPN	9.7.81	16 Nov
28:34.39	Kenshi	Sawano	JPN	.91	16 Nov
28:34.4	Hassan	Chani	MAR	8.10.91	7 Jul
28:34.59	Yevgeniy	Rybakov	RUS	27.2.85	11 Jun
28:34.59	Mekubo	Mogusu	KEN	25.12.86	29 Jun
28:34.71	Parker	Stinson	USA	3.3.92	29 Mar
28:34.71A	Phillip	Kiplimo	UGA	23.3.90	18 Jul
28:34.79	Mustapha	El Aziz	MAR	.85	6 Jul
28:35.00	Shohei	Kurata	JPN	5.8.92	16 Nov
28:35.72	Takuya	Fujikawa	JPN	17.12.92	23 Nov
28:36.15	Jared	Ward	USA	9.9.88	29 Mar
28:36.28	Elvis	Cheboi	KEN-J	.95	29 Aug
28:36.34	Takanori	Ichikawa	JPN	3.11.90	6 Jul
28:36.38	Kazuya	Namera	JPN	8.3.87	18 Nov
28:36.40	Almed	El Mazoury	ITA	15.3.90	8 Jun
28:36.56	Taichi	Takase	JPN	6.11.89	30 Nov
28:36.88	Anatoliy	Rybakov	RUS	27.2.85	11 Jun
28:36.92	Ryo	Matsumoto	JPN	19.10.90	21 Apr
28:37.0 A	Peter	Kirui	KEN	2.1.88	22 Jun
(177)					

JUNIORS

See main list for top 9 juniors. 11 performances by 8 men to 28:00.0. Additional marks and further juniors:

Mark	Name		Nat	Born	Pos	Meet	Venue	Date
Mutunga	27:40.44	1					Kobe	21 Apr
Malel	27:55.75A	7				WCT	Nairobi	13 Jul
28:26.03	Hideto	Yamanaka (10)	JPN	17.3.94	6rB		Fukagawa	29 Jun
28:31.16	Ali	Kaya	TUR	20.4.94	1	EJ	Rieti	18 Jul
28:31.5 A	Simon	Chirchir	KEN	.94	2		Nairobi	4 May
28:31.80	Moses	Kurong	UGA	7.7.94	1	Af-J	Bambous	30 Aug
28:32.5 A	Emmanuel	Bor	KEN	.95	10	NC	Nairobi	22 Jun
28:36.28	Elvis	Cheboi	KEN	.95	2	Af-J	Bambous	29 Aug
28:37.15	Titus	Waruru	KEN	29.3.94	2rC		Fukagawa	29 Jun
28:37.2	Louis	Ndiema	KEN	.94	4		Nairobi	4 May
28:37.2 A	Hillary	Langat	KEN	14.8.95	13	NC	Nairobi	22 Jun
28:38.81	Kazuma	Tashiro	JPN	2.2.94	3		Tokyo	23 Nov
28:40.00	Abdallah	Mande (20)	UGA	10.5.94	4	Af-J	Bambous	30 Aug

10 KILOMETRES ROAD

Mark	Name		Nat	Born	Pos	Meet	Venue	Date
27:30	Adugna	Bikila	ETH	26.2.89	4		Taroudant	20 Mar
27:33	Isiah	Koech	KEN	19.12.92	1	CresC	New Orleans	30 Mar
27:34	Berhanu	Legesse	ETH	.93	2		Taroudant	20 Mar
27:35	Daniel	Chebii	KEN	28.5.85	1		Praha	8 Sep

Where superior to track best

Mark	Name		Nat	Born	Pos	Meet	Venue	Date
27:36	Kinde	Atanaw	ETH	14.4.93	2		Praha	8 Sep

Mark	Name		Nat	Born	Pos	Meet	Venue	Date
27:37	El Hassan	El Abbassi	MAR	15.7.79	1		Ottawa	25 May
27:37	Geoffrey	Mutai	KEN	7.10.81	1		Appingedam	29 Jun
27:38	Edwin	Mokua	KEN	.93	3		Taroudant	20 Mar
27:42	Najim	El Gady	MAR	31.12.80	4		Ottawa	25 May
27:42	Julius Arile	Lomerinyang	KEN	15.7.83	3		Praha	8 Sep
27:44	Lani	Rutto	KEN		2	CresC	New Orleans	30 Mar
27:45	Edwin	Rotich	KEN		1		Santos	19 May
27:46	Jacob	Kendagor	KEN	19.9.84	1		Marrakech	6 Oct
27:46	Allan	Kiprono	KEN	15.2.90	3	CresC	New Orleans	30 Mar
27:48	Leonard Patrick	Komon	KEN	10.1.88	1		Berlin	13 Oct
27:49	Peter	Mateelong	KEN	.90	4		Taroudant	20 Mar
27:51	Azmeraw	Bekele	ETH	22.1.86	2		Rennes	13 Oct
27:51	Azmeraw	Mengistu	ETH	15.9.92	3		Rennes	13 Oct
27:52	Japhet	Korir	KEN	30.6.93	1		Würzburg	28 Apr
27:52	Wilson	Kipsang	KEN	15.3.82	2		Manchester	26 May
27:53+	Henry	Kiplagat	KEN	16.12.92		in HMar	Den Haag	10 Mar
27:53+	Edwin	Kipyego	KEN	16.11.90		in HMar	Den Haag	10 Mar
27:56	Richard	Mengich	KEN	.89	2		Würzburg	28 Apr
27:56+	John	Mwangangi	KEN	1.11.90		in 10M	Zaandam	22 Sep
27:57	Mule	Wasihun	ETH	.93	4		Rennes	13 Oct
27:58	Emmanuel	Oliaulo	KEN	10.10.92	3		Würzburg	28 Apr
27:58	Cornelius	Kangogo	KEN	15.12.93	1		Houilles	29 Dec
27:59+	Alfers	Lagat	KEN	7.8.86		in HMar	Den Haag	10 Mar
27:59+	Ezekiel	Chebii	KEN	3.1.91		in HMar	Den Haag	10 Mar
27:59+	Kennedy	Kimutai	KEN	18.6.90		in HMar	Den Haag	10 Mar
27:59+	Shimelis	Belay	ETH			in HMar	Den Haag	10 Mar
27:59+	Alfred	Cherop	KEN	2.3.86		in HMar	Den Haag	10 Mar
28:00	Haile	Gebrselassie	ETH	18.4.73	3		Manchester	26 May
28:00	Mustapha	El Aziz	MAR	.85	2		Casablanca	3 Jun
28:00+	Stanley	Biwott	KEN	21.4.86		in HMar	Philadelphia	15 Sep
28:02	Frederick	Ngeny	KEN	.88	2		Paderborn	30 Mar
28:02	Stephen	Sambu	KEN	3.7.88	3		New York	10 May
28:02	David	Kosgei	KEN	.85	2		Appingedam	25 Jun
28:03	James	Rungaru	KEN	14.1.93	1		Brunssum	7 Apr
28:03	Geoffrey	Terer	KEN	.81	1		Tessenderlo	8 Jul
28:03	John Kipsang	Lotiang	KEN	.91	4		Praha	8 Sep
28:04	Elisha	Rotich	KEN	.90	3		Paderborn	30 Mar
28:04	Charles	Toroitich	KEN	.88	2		Brunssum	7 Apr
28:04	Samuel	Tsegay	ERI	24.2.88	1		Wierden	6 Jul
28:04	Micah	Kogo	KEN	3.6.86	1		Cape Elizabeth	4 Aug
28:04	Samir	Jouhar	MAR	29.4.85	3		Marrakech	6 Oct
28:05	Youssef	Kamali	MAR	.79	4		Marrakech	6 Oct
28:06+	Tesfalem	Mehari	ETH	.93		in HMar	Den Haag	10 Mar
28:06	Simon	Ndirangu	KEN	1.11.85	1		Charleston	6 Apr
28:06+	Cyprian	Kotut	KEN	.92		in HMar	Philadelphia	15 Sep
28:07	Alex	Oleitiptip	KEN	22.9.82	1		Bangalore	19 May
28:07 dh 34m	Mosinet	Geremew	ETH	12.2.92	1	Peach	Atlanta	4 Jul
28:07	Wilson	Kiprop	KEN	14.4.87	2		Boianco	28 Jul
28:08	Clement	Langat	KEN	18.12.91	6		Taroudant	20 Mar
28:08	Abdi	Nageeye	NED	2.3.89	4		Brunssum	7 Apr
28:08	Philip	Yego	KEN	.79	5		Brunssum	7 Apr
28:09	Linus	Chumba	KEN	9.2.80	4	CresC	New Orleans	30 Mar
28:09d h 34m	Belete	Assefa	ETH	3.3.91	2	Peach	Atlanta	4 Jul
28:09	Silas	Kipruto	KEN	26.9.84	2		Cape Elizabeth	4 Aug
28:09	Dawit	Weldesilasie	ERI-J	10.12.94	4		Houilles	29 Dec
28:11	Muktar	Edris	ETH-J	14.1.94	1		Dionglo	1 Apr
28:11	Mark	Korir	KEN	10.1.85	2		Santos	19 May
28:11 dh 34m	Peter	Kirui	KEN	2.1.88	3	Peach	Atlanta	4 Jul

Mark	Name		Nat	Born	Date		Mark	Name		Nat	Born	Date
28:12+	Feyisa	Lilesa	ETH	1.2.90	15 Feb		28:14+	Daniel Kiprop	Limo	KEN	10.12.83	3 Mar
28:12+	Geoffrey	Kipsang	KEN	28.11.92	15 Feb		28:14+	Ketema	Behailu	ETH		3 Mar
28:12+	Pius	Kirop	KEN	8.1.90	6 Apr		28:14+	Vincent	Yator	KEN	11.7.89	10 Mar
28:12+	Zersenay	Tadese	ERI	8.2.82	6 Apr		28:14+	Fikadu	Haftu	ETH-J	21.2.94	10 Mar
28:12	Nicholas	Kipkemboi	KEN	5.7.86	19 May		28:14+	Tebalu	Zawude	ETH	2.11.87	10 Mar
28:13+	Getu	Feleke	ETH	28.11.86	15 Feb		28:14+	Abrar	Osman	ERI-J	.94	22 Sep
28:13+	Stephen	Kibet	KEN	9.11.86	15 Feb		28:15+	Sahle	Warga	ETH	30.1.84	3 Mar
28:13	Tsegay	Tuemay	ERI-J	20.12.95	30 Mar		28:15+	Simon	Cheprot	KEN	2.7.93	3 Mar
28:13+	Amanuel	Mesel	ERI	29.12.90	6 Apr		28:15+	Birhanu	Shumie	ETH		3 Mar
28:13+	Hillary Bett	Kiplagat	KEN	.80	6 Apr		28:15	Anis	Selmouni	MAR	15.3.79	10 Mar
28:13	Yitayal	Atnafu	ETH	20.1.93	13 Oct		28:15	Lelisa	Desisa	ETH	14.1.90	23 Jun
28:13	Yomif	Kejelcha	ETH-Y	1.8.97	13 Oct		28:16	David	Bett	KEN		30 Mar
28:14+	Daniel	Wanjiru	KEN	26.5.92	15 Feb		28:16	Leonard	Langat	KEN	7.8.90	26 May
28:14+	Joel	Kimurer	KEN	21.1.88	15 Feb		28:16	Bonsa	Dida	ETH-J	21.1.95	6 Jul
28:14+	Robert	Chemosin	KEN	1.2.89	3 Mar		28:16	Mamiyo	Nuguse	ETH	13.2.82	13 Oct

Mark	Name		Nat	Born	Pos Meet	Venue	Date
28:17	Eliud	Tarus	KEN	3.3.93	26 May		
28:17dh3 4m	Sammy	Kitwara	KEN	26.11.86	4 Jul		
28:17+	Peter	Kibet	KEN	18.6.92	22 Sep		
28:18	Philemon	Yator	KEN	2.4.92	30 Mar		
28:18	Julius	Kogo	KEN	12.8.85	14 Apr		
28:18	Phillip	Kipyeko	KEN-J	1.1.95	2 Nov		
28:19	Pius	Nyantika	KEN	.87	14 Apr		
28:19	Philemon	Cheboi	KEN	8.11.93	13 Oct		
28:20	James	Lagat	KEN		30 Mar		
28:20+	Philemon	Limo	KEN	2.8.85	6 Apr		
28:20+	Tigabu	Gebremariam	ETH	3.11.90	6 Apr		
28:20+	Abere	Kassaw	ETH-J	8.12.94	6 Apr		
28:20	Timothy	Kiptoo	KEN	2.8.84	26 May		
28:20	Dawit	Wolde	ETH	19.5.91	13 Oct		
28:20	Leon	Ndiema	KEN	.90	29 Dec		
28:21	Hassan	Chani	MAR	5.5.88	10 Mar		
28:21	Tesfaye	Abera	ETH	31.3.92	22 Jun		
28:22	Toufik	Al Allam	MAR	30.4.89	3 Jun		
28:22	Emmanuel	Mutai	KEN	12.10.84	4 Aug		
28:23	Alene	Emere	ETH	5.3.82	2 Feb		
28:23+	Victor	Kipchirchir	KEN	5.12.87	7 Apr		
28:23	Henry	Sang	KEN		7 Apr		
28:23	Milton	Rotich	KEN	.84	22 Jun		

Mark	Name		Nat	Born	Pos Meet	Venue	Date
28:23dh 34m	Mike	Kigen	KEN	15.1.86	4 Jul		
28:23	Hicham	Laqouahi	MAR	13,6,89	6 Oct		
28:23+	David	Maru	KEN		20 Oct		
28:24	Philip	Mosima	KEN	1.2.77	30 Mar		
28:24	Evans	Taiget	KEN	.85	30 Mar		
28:24	Tola	Aderat	ETH		22 Jun		
28:24+	Abraham	Cheroben	KEN	10.11.92	20 Oct		
28:25dh 34m	Matt	Tegenkamp	USA	19.1.82	4 Jul		
28:25	Hassan	Ouazzin	MAR	.90	3 Jun		
28:26	Gilbert	Okari	KEN	2.7.78	30 Mar		
28:26	Isaac	Mwangi	KEN	.87	7 Apr		
28:26	Samson	Gebreyohannes	ERI	7.2.92	22 Jun		
28:26	Pius	Ondoro	KEN	.88	25 Aug		
28:28	Abraham	Tadese	ERI	12.8.86	23 Mar		
28:29	Dickson	Marwa	TAN	9.3.82	1 Mar		
28:29	Mike	Kigen	KEN	15.1.86	19 May		
28:29+	Silas	Ngetich	KEN		15 Sep		
28:29+	Tamirat	Tola	ETH		15 Sep		
28:30	Daniel	Salel	KEN	11.12.90	23 Jun		
28:30dh 34m	Moses	Masai	KEN	1.6.85	4 Jul		
28:30+	Nicholas	Bor	KEN		15 Sep		
28:30+	Abebe	Negewo	ETH	20.5.84	15 Sep		
28:30	Yimer	Aweke	ETH	23.2.93	13 Oct		

15/20 KILOMETRES ROAD

See also Half Marathon lists

15k	20k	Name		Nat	Born	Pos	Meet	Venue	Date
42:15		Leonard Patrick	Komon	KEN	10.1.88	1		Nijmegen	17 Nov
42:28+	(57:40)	Henry	Kiplagat	KEN	16.12.82		in HMar	Den Haag	10 Mar
42:32		Nicholas	Kipkemboi	KEN	5.7.86	2		Nijmegen	17 Nov
42:37+	57:14	Hillary Bett	Kiplagat	KEN	.80		in HMar	Praha	6 Apr
(43:26)	57:57	Enock	Omwamba	KEN	4.4.93	1		Tachikawa	19 Oct
42:48+	57:59	Ezekiel	Chebii	KEN	3.1.91		in HMar	Den Haag	10 Mar
43:26	58:00	Daniel	Kitonyi	KEN	12.1.94	2		Tachikawa	19 Oct
42:56+		Alfred	Cherop	KEN	2.3.86		in HMar	Den Haag	10 Mar
42:56+	58:22	Adugna	Bikila	ETH	26.2.89		in HMar	Valencia	20 Oct
43:01+		Daniel	Chebii	KEN	28.5.85		in HMar	Praha	6 Apr
43:01+	58:01	Abere	Kassaw	ETH-J	8.12.94		in HMar	Praha	6 Apr
43:01		Patrick	Ereng	KEN	.87	1		s'Heerenberg	17 Nov
43:02		Ezrah	Sang	KEN-J	.94	2		s'Heerenberg	17 Nov
	58:06	Tebalu	Zewede	ETH	10.7.93	1		Paris	13 Oct
	58:08	Charles	Ogari	KEN		2		Paris	13 Oct
43:11		Kibet	Soyekwo	UGA	6.6.92	3		s'Heerenberg	17 Nov

10 MILES ROAD

10M	15k	Name		Nat	Born	Pos	Meet	Venue	Date
45:17+		Stanley	Biwott	KEN	21.4.86		in HMar	Philadelphia	15 Sep
45:28	42:31	Niguse	Tesfaldet	ERI	10.11.86	1		Zaandam	22 Sep
45:30	42:31	John	Mwangangi	KEN	1.11.90	2		Zaandam	22 Sep
45:31		Peter	Kirui	KEN	2.1.88	3		Zaandam	22 Sep
45:31	42:30	Abera	Kuma	ETH	31.8.90	4		Zaandam	22 Sep
45:33+		Cyprian	Kotut	KEN	.92		in HMar	Philadelphia	15 Sep
45:33+		Edwin	Kipyego	KEN	16.11.90		in HMar	Philadelphia	15 Sep
45:55		Julius	Kogo	KEN	12.8.85	1		Flint	24 Aug
46:04+		Stephen	Sambu	KEN	3.7.88		in HMar	Boston	13 Oct
46:04+		Daniel	Salel	KEN	11.12.90		in HMar	Boston	13 Oct
46:05+		Lelisa	Desisa	ETH	14.1.90		in HMar	Boston	13 Oct
46:05+		Samuel	Chelanga	KEN	23.2.85		in HMar	Boston	13 Oct
46:06	42:58	Tsegay	Tuemay	ERI-J	20.12.95	1		Tilburg	1 Sep
46:06+		Kenenisa	Bekele	ETH	13.6.82	1=	in HMar	Newcastle	15 Sep
46:06+		Mohamed	Farah	GBR	23.3.83	1=	in HMar	Newcastle	15 Sep
46:06+		Haile	Gebrselassie	ETH	18.4.73	1=	in HMar	Newcastle	15 Sep
46:07		Allan	Kiprono	KEN	15.2.90	2		Washington	7 Apr
46:18	43:07	Raymond	Yator	KEN	7.4.81	2		Tilburg	1 Sep
46:26	43:11	Wilson	Chebet	KEN	12.7.85	3		Tilburg	1 Sep
46:30+		Lani	Rutto	KEN		13 Oct			
46:32		Leonard Patrick	Komon	KEN	10.1.88	22 Sep			
46:33	43:22	Peter	Kamais	KEN	7.11.76	1 Sep			

46:34	Julius	Koskei	KEN	6.4.82	24 Aug
46:36	Abrar	Osman	ERI-J	.94	22 Sep
46:39	Stephen	Kiplagat	KEN		1 Sep

HALF MARATHON

Slighly downhill race: 30.5m South Shields

HMar	20k	15k	Name		Nat	Born	Pos	Venue	Date
58:54	56:02	42:13	Geoffrey	Kipsang	KEN	28.11.92	1	Ra's Al-Khaymah	15 Feb
58:56	56:03	42:13	Stanley	Biwott	KEN	21.4.86	2	Ra's Al-Khaymah	15 Feb
58:58	56:05	42:15	Geoffrey	Mutai	KEN	7.10.81	3	Ra's Al-Khaymah	15 Feb

Mark			Name		Nat	Born	Pos	Meet	Venue	Date
59:06				G Mutai			1		Udine	22 Sep
59:12			Atsedu	Tsegay	ETH	17.12.91	1		New Delhi	15 Dec
59:15		42:11	Wilson	Kiprop	KEN	14.4.87	1		Ostia	3 Mar
59:19		42:11	Robert	Chemosin	KEN	1.2.89	2		Ostia	3 Mar
59:20		42:11	Simon	Cheprot	KEN	2.7.93	3		Ostia	3 Mar
59:25	56:19	42:15	Feyisa	Lilesa	ETH	1.2.90	4		Ra's Al-Khaymah	15 Feb
59:30				G Kipsang			2		New Delhi	54 Dec
59:36			Jacob	Kendagor	KEN	19.9.84	1		Berlin	7 Apr
59:36				Biwott			1		Philadelphia	15 Sep
59:49				W Kiprop			3		New Delhi	14 Dec
59:54	56:54		Bernard	Koech (10)	KEN	31.1.88	1		Lisboa	24 Mar
59:55			Kenneth	Kipkemoi	KEN	2.8.84	4		New Delhi	15 Dec
59:57				G Mutai			1		Rio de Janeiro	18 Aug
59:58		42:46		Kendagor			1		Valencia	20 Oct
59:59	57:01	42:35	Stephen	Kibet	KEN	9.11.86	5		Ra's Al-Khaymah	15 Feb
59:59			Cyprian	Kotut	KEN	.92	2		Philadelphia	15 Sep
60:02	57:02	42:36	Joel	Kimurer	KEN	21.1.88	6		Ra's Al-Khaymah	15 Feb
60:03	56:49	42:46		Kipkemoi			2		Valencia	20 Oct
60:04	57:12	43:02	Eliud	Kipchoge	KEN	5.11.84	1		Barcelona	17 Feb
60:04			Edwin	Kipyego	KEN	16.11.90	3		Philadelphia	15 Sep
60:05	56:58	42:17		Kipyego			2		Den Haag	5 Mar
60:09			Ghirmay	Ghebrselassie	ERI-J	14.11.95	1		Paderborn	30 Mar
60:09		dh	43:03 Kenenisa	Bekele	ETH	13.6.82	1	GNR	South Shields	15 Sep
60:10	57:14	42:37	Zersenay	Tadese	ERI	8.2.82	1		Praha	6 Apr
60:10	57:14	42:37	Amanuel	Mesel (20)	ERI	29.12.90	2		Praha	6 Apr
60:10		dh	43:02 Mohamed	Farah	GBR	23.3.83	2	GNR	South Shields	15 Sep
60:11			Frankline	Chepkwony	KEN	15.6.84	1		Boulogne-Billancourt	17 Nov
			(30/22)							
60:12			Silas	Kipruto	KEN	26.9.84	2		Berlin	7 Apr
60:14			Luka	Rotich	KEN	7.8.88	1		Verbania	10 Mar
60:16	57:14	42:38	John Kipsang	Lotiang	KEN	.91	3		Praha	6 Apr
60:18	57:14	42:37	Pius	Kirop	KEN	8.1.90	4		Praha	6 Apr
60:21	57:18		Peter	Some	KEN	5.6.90	2		Lisboa	24 Mar
60:21	57:14	42:28	Henry	Kiplagat	KEN	16.12.82	5		Praha	6 Apr
60:24			Nicholas	Kipkemboi	KEN	5.7.86	5		New Delhi	15 Dec
60:26	57:19	42:35	Getu	Feleke	ETH	28.11.86	7		Ra's Al-Khaymah	15 Feb
			(30)							
60:27			Victor	Kipchirchir	KEN	5.12.87	3		Berlin	7 Apr
60:27			Nicholas	Kemboi	QAT	25.11.83	1		Rabat	7 Apr
60:28			Evans	Kiplagat	KEN	5.3.88	2		Rabat	7 Apr
60:30			Dino	Sefir	ETH	28.5.88	1		Nice	21 Apr
60:31			Robert	Kwambai	KEN	22.11.85	2		Verbania	10 Mar
60:33			Tebalu	Zawude	ETH	2.11.87	3		Rabat	7 Apr
60:33			Yusuf	Biwott	KEN	12.11.86	2		Nice	21 Apr
60:34			Lelisa	Desisa	ETH	14.1.90	1		Boston	13 Oct
60:35			Mule	Wasehun	ETH	.93	3		Nice	21 Apr
60:35			Adugna	Tekele	ETH	26.12.89	4		Nice	21 Apr
			(40)							
60:37	57:28		John	Mwangangi	KEN	1.11.90	3		Valencia	20 Oct
60:38		42:56	Philemon	Limo	KEN	2.8.85	1		Ústí nad Labem	15 Sep
60:38	57:41	43:01	Abreham	Cheroben	KEN	10.11.92	4		Valencia	20 Oct
60:39		43:06	Sahle	Warga	ETH	30.1.84	1		Ostia	3 Mar
60:39			Yakob	Jarso	ETH	5.2.88	1		Yangzhou	21 Apr
60:39			Vincent	Kipruto	KEN	13.9.87	1		Lille	31 Aug
60:39			Philemon	Rono	KEN	8.2.91	2		Lille	31 Aug
60:40		42:58	Abebe	Negewo	ETH	20.5.84	2		Ústí nad Labem	15 Sep
60:41		dh	43:01 Haile	Gebrselassie	ETH	18.4.73	3	GNR	South Shields	15 Sep
60:41			Daniel	Salel	KEN	11.12.90	2		Boston	13 Oct
			(50)							
60:41			Stephen	Sambu	KEN	3.7.88	3		Boston	13 Oct
60:41	57:41	42:47	David	Maru	KEN		5		Valencia	20 Oct
60:42		42:48	Daniel Kiprop	Limo	KEN	10.12.83	5		Ostia	3 Mar
60:42			Mark	Kiptoo	KEN	21.6.76	1		Azkoitia	23 Mar
60:46			Nguse	Tesfaldet	ERI	10.11.86	3		Yangzhou	21 Apr
60:49			Mark	Korir	KEN	10.1.85	2		Rio de Janeiro	18 Aug
60:50	57:41	42:49	David	Kosgei	KEN	.85	6		Valencia	20 Oct
60:53		43:06	Ketema	Behailu	ETH		6		Ostia	3 Mar
60:53			Ruben	Limaa	KEN	.87	3		Verbania	10 Mar
60:54	57:48	43:23	Martin	Mathathi	KEN	25.12.85	2		Gifu	19 May
			(60)							

MEN 2013

Mark			Name		Nat	Born	Pos	Meet	Venue	Date
60:55	57:49	43:23	Jacob	Wanjuki	KEN	16.1.86	3		Gifu	19 May
60:56	57:38	42:59	Collis	Birmingham	AUS	27.12.84	1		Marugame	3 Feb
60:58	57:48	42:48	Shimelis	Belay	ETH		3		Den Haag	10 Mar
61:00			Gebre-egziabher	Gebremariam	ETH	10.9.84	2		New Orleans	24 Feb
61:00	57:50	42:47	Kennedy	Kimutai	KEN	18.6.90	4		Den Haag	10 Mar
61:00			Ezekiel	Chebii	KEN	3.1.91	5		Nice	21 Apr
61:02			Hillary	Kipchumba	KEN	25.11.92	4		Verbania	10 Mar
61:02			Wilson	Kipsang	KEN	15.3.82	1		New York	17 Mar
61:02			Nicholas	Togom	KEN	17.2.92	2		Udine	22 Sep
61:04			Samuel	Chelanga	KEN	23.2.85	4		Boston	13 Oct
61:05			Habtamu	Assefa	ETH	29.3.85	3		Lille	31 Aug
61:06			Daniele	Meucci	ITA	7.10.85	2		New York	17 Mar
61:06			Tesfaye	Abera	ETH	31.3.92	4		Rabat	7 Apr
61:07			Dawit	Weldesilasie	ERI-J	10.12.94	1		Vitry-sur-Seine	21 Apr
61:07			Abere	Kassaw	ETH-J	8.12.94	2		Boulogne-Billancourt	17 Nov
61:08	57:54	43:23	Cyrus	Njui	KEN	11.2.86	4		Gifu	19 May
61:09			El Hassan	El Abbassi	MAR	15.7.79	1		Marrakech	27 Jan
61:09	57:46		Abera	Kuma	ETH	31.8.90	3		Lisboa	24 Mar
61:10	57:54	43:01	Daniel	Wanjiru	KEN	26.5.92	9		Ra's Al-Khaymah	15 Feb
61:10			Dathan	Ritzenhein	USA	30.12.82	3		New York	17 Mar
61:12			Gladwin	Mzazi	RSA	28.8.88	7		New Delhi	15 Dec
61:15	(58:10)	43:09	Enoch	Omwamba	KEN	4.4.93	2		Marugame	3 Feb
61:15			Stephen	Kiprotich	UGA	27.2.89	1		Granollers	3 Feb
61:15	58:06	43:28	Fumihiro	Maruyama	JPN	1.7.90	1		Yamaguchi	17 Mar
61:15		43:12	Julius	Lomerinyang	KEN	15.7.83	3		Ústí nad Labem	15 Sep
61:16	58:10	43:06	Tsuyoshi	Ugachi	JPN	27.4.87	3		Marugame	3 Feb
61:16			Benson	Oloisunga	KEN	.86	2		Krems	15 Sep
61:17			Mohamed	Trafeh	USA	1.5.85	1	NC	Duluth	22 Jun
61:17			Abraraw	Misganaw	ETH	.90	3		Boulogne-Billancourt	17 Nov
61:18			Carles	Castillejo	ESP	18.8.78	2		Granollers	3 Feb
61:18		42:26	Goitom	Kifle	ERI	3.12.93	2		Lisboa	6 Oct
61:19	58:10	43:08	Kenta	Murayama	JPN	23.2.93	4		Marugame	3 Feb
61:19			Leonard	Korir	KEN	10.12.86	4		New York	17 Mar
61:19			Edwin	Kiptoo	KEN	28.12.87	1		Zwolle	8 Jun
61:21	58:10	43:08	Benjamin	Gandu	KEN	21.5.90	5		Marugame	3 Feb
61:21			Juan Luis	Barrios	MEX	24.6.83	5		New York	17 Mar
61:21			Geoffrey	Kenesi	KEN	.90	2		Vitry-sur-Seine	21 Apr
61:22			Mebrahtom	Keflezighi	USA	5.5.75	2		Duluth	22 Jun
61:24			Anthony	Maritim	KEN	.86	2		Azkoitia	23 Mar
61:25			Edwin	Rotich	KEN		2		Foz do Iguaçu	26 May

(100)

Mark		Name		Nat	Born	Date
61:26		Silas	Limo	KEN	.92	1 Sep
61:27		Joseph	Kimeli	KEN	8.10.86	17 Feb
61:27	42:47	Tamirat	Tola	ETH		15 Sep
61:27		Richard	Mengich	KEN	.89	15 Dec
61:28		Johana	Maina	KEN	24.12.90	17 Mar
61:28	43:01	Tigabu	Gebremariam	ETH	3.11.90	6 Apr
61:28		Robert	Langat	KEN	11.2.88	15 Sep
61:29		Jackson	Limo	KEN	.88	21 Apr
61:32		Emmanuel	Mutai	KEN	12.10.84	15 Feb
61:32	43:15	Tesfalem	Mehari	ETH	.93	10 Mar
61:32A		Joseph	Mwenga	KEN		7 Jul
61:32+		Wilfred	Kigen	KEN	21.1.86	29 Sep
61:32		Lani	Rutto	KEN		13 Oct
61:33	43:08	Micah	Njeru	KEN	5.8.88	3 Feb
61:33		Mohammed	Burka	ETH	.90	21 Apr
61:33+		Negari	Terfa	ETH	12.6.83	29 Sep
61:33+		Stephen	Chemlany	KEN	9.8.82	29 Sep
61:34	43:06	Birhanu	Shumie	ETH		3 Mar
61:34		Stephen	Kiprotich	KEN	25.11.90	3 Mar
61:34	42:48	Alfers	Lagat	KEN	7.8.86	10 Mar
61:34		Alex	Oleitiptip	KEN	22.9.82	1 Sep
61:35		Simon	Ndirangu	KEN	1.11.85	22 Sep
61:37		Deriba	Merga	ETH	26.10.80	3 Mar
61:37		Aschalew	Meketa	ETH		3 Mar
61:37		Frederick	Ngeny	KEN	.88	7 Apr
61:37		Robert	Kajuga	RWA	.85	21 Apr
61:37		Giovani	dos Santos	BRA	1.7.81	26 May
61:37		Emmanuel	Sikuku	KEN	12.5.93	22 Sep
61:38		John	Ndungu	KEN		15 Feb
61:38		Gilbert	Masai	KEN	20.5.81	3 Mar
61:38		Joseph	Kiptum	KEN	25.9.87	7 Apr
61:38		Leonard	Langat	KEN	7.8.90	7 Apr
61:40		Emmanuel	Bett	KEN	30.3.83	6 Oct
61:41		Ahme	Baday	MAR	12.1.74	27 Jan
61:42		Fikadu	Seboka	ETH		27 Jan
61:43	43:28	Gideon	Ngatuny	KEN	10.10.86	17 Mar
61:43		Abayneh	Ayele	ETH	4.11.87	19 May
61:44		Daniel	Chebii	KEN	28.5.85	20 Oct
61:45		Pius	Ondoro	KEN	.88	31 Aug
61:46		Tsegay	Tuemay	ERI-J	20.12.95	15 Sep
61:48		Bernard	Kitur	KEN	10.1.90	24 Mar
61:48		Asrat	Demissie	ETH		21 Apr
61:48		Samuel	Ndungu	KEN	4.4.88	15 Sep
61:51		Jason	Hartmann	USA	21.3.81	17 Mar
61:51		Bernard	Muthoni	KEN		1 Sep
61:51		Loitarakwai	Olengurisi	KEN		6 Oct
61:51		Emmanuel	Oliaulo	KEN	10.10.92	6 Oct
61:51		James	Rungaru	KEN	14.1.93	17 Nov
61:52+		Dennis	Kimetto	KEN	22.1.84	13 Oct
61:52+		Shadrack	Kosgei	KEN	24.11.84	13 Oct
61:52+		Moses	Mosop	KEN	17.7.85	13 Oct
61:53		Bonse	Dida	ETH-J		13 Jan
61:53		Philemon	Yator	KEN	2.4.92	24 Mar
61:53		Khalid	Choukoud	NED	23.3.86	6 Oct
61:53+		Ayele	Abshero	ETH	28.12.90	13 Oct
61:53+		Tariku	Jufar	ETH	18.7.84	13 Oct
61:53+		Mike	Kigen	KEN	15.1.86	13 Oct
61:53+		Sammy	Kitwara	KEN	26.11.86	13 Oct
61:53+		Micah	Kogo	KEN	3.6.86	13 Oct
61:54		Mekubo	Mogusu	KEN	25.12.86	12 May
61:54+		Merkebu	Birke	ETH	20.1.88	13 Oct
61:55		Teklemariam	Medhin	ERI	24.6.89	6 Apr
61:55		Kiflum	Slum	ERI	9.6.87	7 Apr
61:55		Evans	Korir	KEN	.87	31 Aug
61:56		Alene	Emere	ETH	5.3.82	11 Aug
61:56		Solomon	Kirka	KEN		29 Sep
61:57		Patrick	Mwaka	KEN	2.11.92	19 May
61:57		Wilfred	Murgor	KEN	12.12.88	13 Oct

Mark	Name		Nat	Born	Pos Meet	Venue	Date
61:58A	Julius	Keter	KEN	20.10.88 24 Nov	61:59 Ayad	Lamdassem ESP 11.10.81	6 Oct
61:59dh 34m	Nelson	Oyugi	KEN	.93 18 Aug	(171)		

Downhill

Mark	Name		Nat	Born	Pos Meet	Venue	Date
58:42 dh 86.5m	Bernard	Koech	KEN	31.1.88	1	San Diego	2 Jun

JUNIORS

See main list for top 3 juniors. 7 performances by 5 men to 62:00. Additional marks and further juniors:

Mark	Name		Nat	Born	Pos	Venue	Date
Kassaw	61:17	6			Praha		6 Apr
Diba	61:54	7			Lille		1 Sep
61:46	Tsegay	Tuemay	ERI	20.12.95	6	Krems	15 Sep
61:53	Bonse	Dida	ETH	21.1.95	3	Egmond Aan Zee	13 Jan
62:06	Fikadu	Haftu	ETH	21.2.94	1	Wuzhong	8 Sep
62:26	Solomon	Deksisa	ETH	11.3.94	12	Lille	1 Sep
62:41	Tsegaye	Mekonnen	ETH	15.6.95	3	Porto	15 Sep
62:52	Samuel	Rutto	KEN	.95	3	Warszawa	24 Mar
62:54	Yusuke	Nishiyama	JPN	7.11.94	9	Ageo	17 Nov
62:54	Hazuma	Hattori	JPN	7.2.95	10	Ageo	17 Nov
62:59	Koki	Ido	JPN	10.7.94	17	Ageo	17 Nov
63:05	Joshua	Munywoki	KEN	.94	1	Pila	8 Sep
63:18	Isaac	Langat	KEN	18.12.94	6	Boulogne-Billancourt	17 Nov
63:28	Rintaro	Takeda	JPN	5.4.94	24	Ageo	17 Nov
63:32	Takumi	Ichida	JPN	12.12.94	26	Ageo	17 Nov
63:42	Panuel	Mkungo	KEN	.94	5	Nancy	6 Oct
63:43	Hajime	Sakamoto	JPN	25.10.94	31	Ageo	17 Nov
63:49	Hiroto	Kanamori	JPN	10.2.94	34	Ageo	17 Nov

In addition to those shown in Marathon listing

25 – 30 KILOMETRES ROAD

25k	30k	Name		Nat	Born	Pos Meet	Venue	Date
1:13:13	1:28:01+	Victor	Kipchirchir	KEN	5.12.87	in Mar	Berlin	29 Sep
1:13:13	1:28:01+	Philemon	Rono	KEN	8.2.91	in Mar	Berlin	29 Sep
1:13:13+		Edwin	Kiptoo	KEN	28.12.87	in Mar	Berlin	29 Sep
1:13:14	1:28:02+	Wilfred	Kirwa	KEN	21.1.86	in Mar	Berlin	29 Sep
1:13:17	1:28:06+	Moses	Mosop	KEN	17.7.85	in Mar	Chicago	13 Oct
1:13:17+		Ayele	Abshero	ETH	28.12.90	in Mar	Chicago	13 Oct
1:13:18	1:28:08+	Mike	Kigen	KEN	15.1.86	in Mar	Chicago	13 Oct
1:12:58	1:28:14+	Wilson	Kipsang	KEN	15.3.82	in Mar	London	21 Apr
1:12:58+		Mike	Kigen			in Mar	London	21 Apr
1:13:19	1:28:15+	Tariku	Jufar	ETH	18.7.84	in Mar	Chicago	13 Oct
1:13:34	1:28:20+	Richard	Sigei	KEN	11.5.84	in Mar	Rotterdam	14 Apr
1:13:34	1:28:20+	Ezekiel	Chebii	KEN	3.1.91	in Mar	Rotterdam	14 Apr
1:13:15	1:28:22+	Negari	Terfa	ETH	12.6.83	in Mar	Berlin	29 Sep
1:13:36	1:28:22+	John	Mwangangi	KEN	1.11.90	in Mar	Rotterdam	14 Apr
1:13:00	1:28:49+	Geoffrey	Mutai	KEN	7.10.81	in Mar	London	21 Apr
1:13:16		Simon	Ndirangu	KEN	1.11.85	in Mar	Chicago	13 Oct
1:13:34	1:29:05+	Eliud	Kiplagat	KEN	.85	in Mar	Rotterdam	14 Apr
1:14:11	1:29:12+	Dickson	Chumba (1:14:11)	KEN	27.10.86	in Mar	Amsterdam	20 Oct
	1:29:13+	Yekeber	Bayabel	ETH	10.11.91	in Mar	Amsterdam	20 Oct
	1:29:13+	Abrha	Gebretsadik	ETH		in Mar	Amsterdam	20 Oct
	1:29:13+	Frankline	Chepkwony	KEN	15.6.84	in Mar	Amsterdam	20 Oct
1:14:07		Julius	Keter	KEN	20.10.88	1	Grand Rapids	11 May

MARATHON

	25k	30k	Name		Nat	Born	Pos	Venue	Date
2:03:23	1:13:13	1:28:01	Wilson	Kipsang	KEN	15.3.82	1	Berlin	29 Sep
2:03:45	1:13:19	1:28:04	Dennis	Kimetto	KEN	22.1.84	1	Chicago	13 Oct
2:03:52	1:13:18	1:28:04	Emmanuel	Mutai	KEN	12.10.84	2	Chicago	13 Oct
2:04:05	1:13:13	1:28:01	Eliud	Kipchoge	KEN	5.11.84	2	Berlin	29 Sep
2:04:45			Lelisa	Desisa	ETH	14.1.90	1	Dubai	25 Jan
2:04:48			Berhanu	Shiferaw	ETH	31.5.93	2	Dubai	25 Jan
2:04:49			Tadesse	Tola	ETH	31.10.87	3	Dubai	25 Jan
2:04:52			Endeshaw	Negesse	ETH	13.3.88	4	Dubai	25 Jan
2:04:53			Bernard	Koech	KEN	31.1.88	5	Dubai	25 Jan
2:05:16	1:13:17	1:28:05	Sammy	Kitwara (10)	KEN	26.11.86	3	Chicago	13 Oct
2:05:30		1:29:45		Kipchoge			1	Hamburg	21 Apr
2:05:36	1:14:11	1:29:13	Wilson	Chebet	KEN	12.7.85	1	Amsterdam	20 Oct
2:05:38	1:14:19	1:29:55	Peter	Some	KEN	5.6.90	1	Paris	7 Apr
2:05:38	1:13:35	1:28:21	Tilahun	Regassa	ETH	18.1.90	1	Rotterdam	14 Apr
2:06:04	1:12:59	1:28:08	Tsegaye	Kebede	ETH	15.1.87	1	London	21 Apr
2:06:06	1:14:12	1:29:13	Berhanu	Girma	ETH	22.11.86	2	Amsterdam	20 Oct
2:06:15	1:14:34	1:29:21	Vincent	Kipruto	KEN	13.9.87	1	Frankfurt	27 Oct
2:06:16	1:14:34	1:29:22	Mark	Kiptoo	KEN	21.6.76	2	Frankfurt	27 Oct
2:06:25			James	Kwambai	KEN	28.2.83	1	Seoul	3 Nov

MEN 2013

Mark			Name		Nat	Born	Pos	Meet	Venue	Date
2:06:26	1:13:13	1:28:01	Geoffrey	Kipsang	KEN	28.11.92	3		Berlin	29 Sep
2:06:29	1:14:12	1:29:13		B Koech			3		Amsterdam	20 Oc
2:06:33			Nicholas	Kipkemboi (20)	KEN	5.7.86	6		Dubai	25 Jan
2:06:33	1:14:19	1:29:35		Tola			2		Paris	7 Ap
2:06:33	1:12:58	1:27:49		E Mutai			2		London	21 Ap
2:06:34	1:14:19	1:29:35	Eric	Ndiema	KEN	28.12.92	3		Paris	7 Ap
2:06:35			Stephen	Tum	KEN	12.7.86	1		Marrakech	27 Jan
2:06:45	1:13:35	1:28:21	Getu	Feleke	ETH	28.11.86	2		Rotterdam	14 Ap
2:06:50				Kimetto			1		Tokyo	24 Feb
2:06:56	1:14:19	1:29:35	Megersa	Bacha	ETH	18.1.85	4		Paris	7 Ap
2:06:56	1:13:18	1:28:05	Micah	Kogo	KEN	3.6.86	4		Chicago	13 Oc
2:06:57	1:14:19	1:29:35	Philip Sanga	Kimutai	KEN	10.9.83	5		Paris	7 Ap
2:06:57	1:12:59	1:27:50	Ayele	Abshero	ETH	28.12.90	3		London	21 Ap
2:06:58			Michael	Kipyego	KEN	2.10.83	2		Tokyo	24 Feb
2:06:59			Frankline (34/29)	Chepkwony	KEN	15.6.84	1		Seoul	17 Ma
2:07:05			Deressa	Chimsa	ETH	21.11.86	1		Toronto	20 Oc
2:07:08			Mark	Korir	KEN	10.1.85	2		Seoul	3 Nov
2:07:11			Shumi	Dechase	ETH	28.5.89	2		Seoul	17 Ma
2:07:14			Felix	Keny	KEN	25.12.85	1		Valencia	17 Nov
2:07:16			Martin	Mathathi	KEN	25.12.85	1		Fukuoka	1 Dec
2:07:19			Bernard	Kipyego	KEN	16.7.86	2		Beijing	20 Oc
2:07:20			Daniel	Rono	KEN	13.7.78	3		Beijing	20 Oc
2:07:26			Seboka	Tola	ETH	10.11.87	3		Seoul	17 Ma
2:07:32			Negari	Terfa	ETH	12.6.83	1		Xiamen	5 Jan
2:07:34	1:14:27	1:29:34	Elijah	Kemboi	KEN	10.9.84	3		Frankfurt	27 Oc
2:07:35			Limenih	Getachew	ETH	30.4.90	2		Hamburg	21 Ap
2:07:41			Gezahegn	Girma	ETH	28.11.83	2		Marrakech	27 Jan
2:07:44			Paul	Lonyangat	KEN	12.12.92	2		Xiamen	5 Jan
2:07:44	1:13:16	1:28:22	Stephen	Chemlany	KEN	9.8.82	4		Berlin	29 Sep
2:07:45			Abraham	Tadesse	ERI	12.8.86	1		Zürich	7 Ap
2:07:46		1:27:50	Feyisa	Lilesa	ETH	1.2.90	4		London	21 Ap
2:07:46	1:14:35	1:29:22	Jacob	Chesari	KEN	6.4.84	4		Frankfurt	27 Oc
2:07:48			Dereje	Debele	ETH	26.7.86	1		Düsseldorf	28 Ap
2:07:48			Joel	Kimurer	KEN	21.1.88	1		Gyeongju	13 Oc
2:07:55			Dadi	Yami	ETH	.82	7		Dubai	25 Jan
2:07:55			Mustapha	El Aziz	MAR	.85	3		Seoul	3 Nov
2:08:00			Pius	Ondoro	KEN	.88	1		Tiberias	10 Jan
2:08:00			Kazuhiro	Maeda	JPN	19.4.81	4		Tokyo	24 Feb
2:08:02	1:14:13	1:29:13	Abdullah Dawit	Shami	ETH	16.7.84	4		Amsterdam	20 Oc
2:08:05	1:13:41	1:29:24	Stephen	Kiprotich	UGA	27.2.89	6		London	21 Ap
2:08:05			Tariku	Jufar	ETH	18.7.84	1		Ottawa	26 May
2:08:10			Deribe	Robi	ETH	26.9.84	2		Tiberias	10 Jan
2:08:12			Luka	Rotich	KEN	7.8.88	2		Ottawa	26 May
2:08:14			Yuki	Kawauchi	JPN	5.3.87	4		Seoul	17 Ma
2:08:15			Sylvester Kimeli	Teimet	KEN	4.6.84	6		Paris	7 Ap
2:08:17			Gilbert	Kirwa	KEN	20.12.85	6		Tokyo	24 Feb
2:08:17	1:14:44	1:29:53	Albert	Matebor	KEN	20.12.80	5		Frankfurt	27 Oc
2:08:17			Amanuel	Mesel	ERI	29.12.90	2		Valencia	17 Nov
2:08:19			Sahle	Warga	ETH	30.1.84	7		Paris	7 Ap
2:08:19			Henry	Sugut	KEN	4.5.85	1		Wien	14 Ap
2:08:20			Abraham	Girma	ETH	.86	8		Paris	7 Ap
2:08:22	1:13:00	1:28:35	Yared	Asmerom	ERI	3.2.79	7		London	21 Ap
2:08:24			Mike	Kigen	KEN	15.1.86	8		Dubai	25 Jan
2:08:24			Geoffrey	Mutai	KEN	7.10.81	1		New York	3 Nov
2:08:28			Habtamu	Assefa	ETH	29.3.85	9		Dubai	25 Jan
2:08:29			Nixson	Kurgat	KEN	7.11.87	1		Chuncheon	27 Oct
2:08:30			David	Kiyeng	KEN	22.4.83	2		Chuncheon	27 Oct
2:08:31			Francis	Kibiwott	KEN	15.9.78	3		Tiberias	10 Jan
2:08:32			Lusapho	April	RSA	24.5.82	1		Hannover	5 May
2:08:33			Abraham	Kiprotich ¶	FRA	17.8.85	1		Daegu	14 Ap
2:08:34			Solomon	Kiptoo	KEN	27.8.87	2		Wien	14 Ap
2:08:35			Kentaro	Nakamoto	JPN	7.12.82	2		Oita	3 Feb
2:08:35			Haile	Gemeda	ETH	22.10.88	4		Roma	17 Ma
2:08:39	1:12:59	1:27:50	Stanley	Biwott	KEN	21.4.86	8		London	21 Ap
2:08:42	Geoffrey		Ndungu		KEN	11.3.87	3		Wien	14 Ap
2:08:42	Alfred		Kering		KEN	.80	1		Hengshui	21 Sep
2:08:46	Dereje		Tadesse		ETH	24.1.87	4		Tiberias	10 Jan
2:08:46	Abebe		Degefa		ETH	20.5.84	4		Beijing	20 Oct
2:08:48	James		Mwangi		KEN	23.6.84	3		Otsu	3 Ma

Mark	Name		Nat	Born	Pos	Meet	Venue	Date
2:08:50	Sammy	Kibet	KEN	2.2.82	3		Marrakech	27 Jan
2:08:50	Lukas	Kanda	KEN	.87	5		Roma	17 Mar
2:08:51	Masakazu	Fujiwara	JPN	6.3.81	4	1 NC	Otsu	3 Mar
2:08:51	Nicholas	Kemboi	QAT	25.11.83	1		Praha	12 Ma
2:08:52	Samuel	Maswai	KEN	29.3.88	5		Berlin	29 Sep
2:08:52	Patrick	Terer	KEN	6.7.89	1		Torino	17 Nov
2:08:53	Gemechu	Worku	ETH	.85	10		Dubai	25 Jan
2:08:53	Francis K.	Bowen	KEN	12.10.73	3		Chuncheon	27 Oct
2:08:55	Milton	Rotich	KEN	.84	1		Casablanca	27 Oct
2:09:00	Gebretsadik	Adhana	ETH	16.7.92	4		Xiamen	5 Jan
2:09:00	Abrhe Milaw	Assefa	ETH	.88	1		Rennes	3 Nov
2:09:00	Joseph	Gitau	KEN	3.1.88	2		Fukuoka	1 Dec
2:09:00	Serod	Bat-Ochir	MGL	7.10.81	1		Hofu	15 Dec
2:09:02	Sisay	Lemma	ETH	12.12.90	1		Warszawa	21 Apr
2:09:05	Feyisa	Bekele	ETH	4.8.83	7		Tokyo	24 Feb
2:09:06	Ryo	Yamamoto	JPN	18.5.84	5		Otsu	3 Mar
2:09:06	Boniface	Mbuvi	KEN	20.12.86	2		Gyeongju	13 Oct

(100)

Mark	Name		Nat	Born	Date
2:09:08	Julius	Muriuki	KEN	3.7.85	10 Jan
2:09:10	Suehiro	Ishikawa	JPN	27.9.79	3 Mar
2:09:10	Duncan	Koech	KEN	28.12.81	28 Apr
2:09:11	Hafid	Chani	MAR	12.2.86	12 Feb
2:09:11	Yemane	Tsegay Adhane	ETH	8.4.85	13 Oct
2:09:13	Dino	Sefir	ETH	28.5.88	24 Feb
2:09:14	Takayuki	Matsumiya	JPN	21.2.80	24 Feb
2:09:14	Oleksandr	Sitkovskiy	UKR	9.6.78	24 Nov
2:09:17	Isaac	Kosgei	KEN	.81	21 Apr
2:09:19	Bazu	Worku	ETH	15.9.90	13 Oct
2:09:20	Stephen	Chebogut	KEN	.84	25 Jan
2:09:21	Robert	Kwambai	KEN	22.11.85	21 Apr
2:09:24	Marilson	dos Santos	BRA	6.8.77	29 Sep
2:09:28	Ayad	Lamdassem	ESP	11.10.81	21 Apr
2:09:30	Stephen	Mokoka	RSA	31.1.85	1 Dec
2:09:31	Bentayehu	Assefa	ETH	17.6.92	13 Oct
2:09:32	Jackson	Kiprop	UGA	20.10.86	20 Jan
2:09:32	John	Mwangangi	KEN	1.11.90	14 Apr
2:09:34	Josphat	Kiprono	KEN	.88	21 Apr
2:09:36	Gosha	Girma	ETH	.81	7 Apr
2:09:36	Patrick	Korir	KEN	10.9.77	6 Oct
2:09:37	Henryk	Szost	POL	20.1.82	1 Dec
2:09:39	Yekeber	Bayabel	ETH	10.11.91	20 Oct
2:09:42	Gezahegn	Alemayehu	ETH	.87	6 Oct
2:09:43	Felix	Kiprotich	KEN	.88	3 Nov
2:09:44	Josphat	Keiyo	KEN	.80	17 Mar
2:09:45	Elisha	Kiprop	KEN	.85	6 Oct
2:09:45	Nicholas	Chelimo	KEN	8.1.83	13 Oct
2:09:45	Dathan	Ritzenhein	USA	30.12.82	13 Oct
2:09:47	Samson	Barmao	KEN	17.4.82	17 Mar
2:09:48	Patrick	Cheruiyot	KEN	.90	21 Apr
2:09:48	Jason	Mbote	KEN	5.1.77	3 Nov
2:09:48	Beraki	Beyene	ERI	6.2.80	1 Dec
2:09:49	Afewerk	Mesfin	ETH	12.10.92	25 Jan
2:09:49	Elias	Kemboi	KEN	10.3.84	21 Apr
2:09:49	Jonathan	Maiyo	KEN	5.5.88	13 Oct
2:09:49	Gilbert	Koech	KEN	.81	20 Oct
2:09:50	Marius	Kipserem	KEN	.88	7 Apr
2:09:50	Benjamin	Kiptoo	KEN	.79	17 Nov
2:09:52	Teferi	Kebede	ETH	17.2.81	1 Dec
2:09:53	Peter	Kamais	KEN	7.11.76	5 Jan
2:09:53	Elijah	Keitany	KEN	18.10.83	17 Mar
2:09:53	Shengo	Kebede	ETH		28 Apr
2:09:54	Henry	Chirchir	KEN	14.5.85	13 Oct
2:09:55	Evans	Ruto	KEN	14.1.84	13 Oct
2:09:55	Dejene	Yirdaw	ETH	21.8.78	17 Nov
2:09:55	Samuel	Ndungu	KEN	4.4.88	1 Dec
2:09:56	Asmare	Workneh	ETH	.85	28 Apr
2:09:57	Evans	Cheruiyot	KEN	10.5.82	21 Apr
2:09:58	Daniel	Chepyegon	UGA	1.6.86	17 Mar
2:09:58	Michael	Chege	KEN		1 Dec
2:10:00	Botoru	Tsegaye	ETH	25.10.85	17 Mar
2:10:01	Lani	Rutto	KEN		27 Oct
2:10:02	Alemayehu	Ameta	ETH	.85	14 Apr
2:10:03	Julius	Lomerinyang	KEN	15.7.83	3 Nov
2:10:04	Stephen	Kibiwott	KEN	3.4.80	14 Apr
2:10:05	Mekuant	Ayenew	ETH	.91	5 Ma
2:10:06	Mutai	Kipkemei	KEN		13 Oct
2:10:08	John	Kiprotich	KEN	5.6.83	17 Mar
2:10:11	Jaouad	Gharib	MAR	22.5.72	21 Apr
2:10:12	Kohei	Matsumura	JPN	25.11.86	3 Mar
2:10:13	Solomon	Busendich	KEN	10.1.84	24 Feb
2:10:15	Dickson	Chumba	KEN	27.10.86	20 Oct
2:10:17	Gezahegne	Abera	ETH	.85	17 Mar
2:10:18	Viktor	Röthlin	SUI	14.10.74	3 Mar
2:10:22	Tomoya	Adachi	JPN	18.12.85	3 Mar
2:10:23	Debebe	Tolossa	ETH	13.9.90	14 Apr
2:10:23	Fikre	Assefa	ETH	18.1.89	21 Apr
2:10:23	Richard	Sigei	KEN	11.5.84	27 Oct
2:10:24	Gashaw	Melese	ETH	26.9.78	26 May
2:10:26	Edwin	Korir	KEN	2.8.87	7 Apr
2:10:26	Worknesh	Tiruneh	ETH	.84	13 Oct
2:10:26	Mulugueta	Wami	ETH	12.7.82	27 Oct
2:10:27	Philemon	Kisang	KEN	9.6.82	17 Mar
2:10:27	Gilbert	Masai	KEN	20.5.81	7 Apr
2:10:27	Lawrence	Kimaiyo	KEN	2.9.90	21 Apr
2:10:28	Mariko	Kiplagat	KEN	10.1.82	5 Jan
2:10:29	Masato	Imai	JPN	2.4.84	24 Feb
2:10:29	Hiroaki	Sano	JPN	28.2.88	13 Oct
2:10:31	Edeo	Mamo	ETH	.90	10 Jan
2:10:31	Julius	Chepkwony	KEN	.88	27 Oct
2:10:32	Ismael Bushendich	Chemtan	KEN	7.7.91	27 Oct
2:10:33	Nicholas	Kamakya	KEN	2.3.85	21 Apr
2:10:34	Yared	Shegumo	POL	11.1.83	29 Sep
2:10:36	Julius Kiplagat	Korir	KEN	10.1.82	21 Apr
2:10:37	Jairus	Chanchaima	KEN	5.12.84	5 Jan
2:10:37	Francis	Kiprop	KEN	4.6.82	28 Apr
2:10:38	Weldu	Negash	ETH	12.11.86	29 Sep
2:10:38	Samson	Kagia	KEN	11.10.84	17 Nov
2:10:39	Lemma	Debele	ETH	23.1.85	23 Mar
2:10:39	Solomon	Molla	ETH	20.1.87	29 Sep
2:10:39	Chiharu	Takada	JPN	9.7.81	1 Dec
2:10:41	Gideon	Kipketer	KEN	10.11.92	24 Feb
2:10:45	Eliud Kiplagat	Barngetuny	KEN	.85	6 Oct
2:10:46	Dominic	Kangor	KEN		14 Apr
2:10:47	Denis	Ndiso	KEN	31.12.83	23 Mar
2:10:48	Abraham	Keter	KEN		17 Mar
2:10:49	Jepkopol	Kamzee	KEN	11.2.84	14 Apr
2:10:50	Dereje	Tesfaye	ETH	30.9.85	25 Jan
2:10:50	Raymond	Bett	KEN	.84	28 Apr
2:10:51	Herpasa	Negasa	ETH	.93	25 Jan
2:10:51	Bernard	Rotich	KEN	11.8.86	14 Apr
2:10:54	Hideaki	Tamura	JPN	21.7.88	3 Mar
2:10:54	Teferi	Regasa	ETH		23 Mar
2:10:54	Benjamin	Bitok	KEN	.82	27 Oct
2:10:55	Laban	Moiben	KEN	30.10.83	20 Jan
2:10:56	David	Cherono	KEN	.84	21 Apr
2:10:56	Wosen	Zeleke	ETH	.92	29 Sep
2:10:57	Matthew	Bowen	KEN	.88	3 Nov
2:10:58	Samson	Bungei	KEN	.82	17 Nov
2:10:59	Soji	Ikeda	JPN	22.12.86	24 Feb
2:10:59	Ryosuke	Fukuyama	JPN	25.9.80	3 Mar

(212)

Excessively downhill Los Angeles 17 Mar, Boston 15 Apr

Mark	Name		Nat	Born	Date
2:09:44	Erick	Mose	KEN	3.2.87	17 Mar
2:10:28	Gebre-egziabher	Gebremariam	ETH	10.9.84	15 Apr
2:10:31	Julius	Keter	KEN	20.10.88	17 Mar
2:10:51	Weldon	Kirui	KEN	2.12.88	17 Mar

MEN 2013

Mark	Name		Nat	Born	Pos	Meet	Venue		Date

JUNIORS

Mark	Name		Nat	Born	Pos	Meet	Venue		Date
2:16:12	Ernest	Ngeno	KEN	20.5.95	12		Eindhoven		13 Ocr
2:16:29	Peter	Limo	KEN	.94	3		Wuzhong		8 Sep

100 KILOMETRES

Mark	Name		Nat	Born	Pos	Meet	Venue		Date
6:18:26	Vasiliy	Larkin	RUS	19.8.91	1		Sankt-Peterburg		7 Sep
6:37:16	Hideo	Nojo	JPN	24.12.76	1		Yubetsu		30 Jun
6:39:59	Giorgio	Calcaterra	ITA	11.2.72	1		Faenza		26 May
6:40:14	Steven	Way	GBR	6.7.74	1		Stockholm		4 Aug
6:41:44	Takayoshi	Shigemi	JPN	8.6.82	2		Yubetsu		30 Jun
6:44:33	Tsutomu	Nagata	JPN	20.2.84	3		Yubetsu		30 Jun
6:46:25	Michael	Boch	FRA	11.10.81	1		Winschoten		14 Sep
6:47:41	Jérôme	Bellanca	FRA	25.9.77	1		Amiens		12 Oct
6:48:44	Yoshikazu	Hara	JPN	13.8.72	1		Nakamura		20 Oct
6:49:53	Yevgeniy	Glyva (10)	UKR	10.11.83	2		Faenza		26 May
6:49:53	Yoshiki	Takada	JPN	18.7.83	4		Yubetsu		30 Jun

6:53:14	Asier	Cuevas	ESP	16.1.73	28 Apr
6:55:09	Erick	Wainaina	KEN	19.12.73	30 Jun
6:56:14	Kosuke	Yamazoe	JPN	76	30 Jun
6:56:22	Andre	Collet	GER	21..9.71	13 Apr
6:57:02	José Antonio	Requejo	ESP	12.12.82	28 Apr
6:58:01	Hermann	Achmüller	ITA	17.2.71	26 May
6:58:06	Pieter	Vermeesch	BEL	6.7.76	28 Apr
6:58:16	Vladimir	Burzak	RUS	31.1.83	7 Sep
6:58:27	Oleksandr	Holovnytsky	UKR	29.6.75	22 Jun
6:58:53	Masakazu	Takahashi	JPN	23.12.73	30 Jun
6:59:10	Makoto	Imakoga	JPN	.75	30 Jun
6:59:42	Jörg	Heiner	GER	24.8.73	13 Apr

Best track times
6:58:07 t	Pieter	Vermeesch	BEL	6.7.76	10 Sep

Indoors
6:56:57	Dmitry	Pavlov	RUS	30.5.85	16 Feb

24 HOURS

Mark	Name		Nat	Born	Pos	Meet	Venue	Date
273.650 t	Yoshikazu	Hara	JPN	13.8.72	1		Taipei	8 Dec
269.675	Jonathan	Olsen	USA	18.8.74	1	WCh	Steenbergen	12 May
269.225	Takayoshi	Shigemi	JPN	8.6.82	1		Tokyo	10 Nov
266.702 t	Ivan	Cudin	ITA	15.2.75	2		Taipei	8 Dec
262.734	John	Dennis	USA	4.8.80	2	WCh	Steenbergen	12 May
259.939	Florian	Reus	GER	2.3.84	3	WCh	Steenbergen	12 May
259.708	Tetsuo	Kiso	JPN	1.5.68	2		Tokyo	10 Nov
258.064 t	Johan van der	Merwe	RSA	24.2.72	3		Taipei	8 Dec
257.040	Anatoliy	Kruglikov	RUS	9.10.57	4	WCh	Steenbergen	12 May
256.666	Timur	Ponomarev (10)	RUS	3.2.88	5	WCh	Steenbergen	12 May
255.940	Toshiro	Naraki	JPN	10.8.76	6	WCh	Steenbergen	12 May
255.872	Lionel	Ozanne	FRA	4.7.70	1		Grenoble	6 Oct
254.553	Christian	Dilmi	FRA	15.6.66	2		Grenoble	6 Oct
252.324	Yuya	Fujita	JPN	5.6.76	3		Tokyo	10 Nov
251.113	Andrzej	Radzikowski	POL	1.4.81	1		Katowice	20 Oct
250.327	Shuhei	Kotani	JPN	25.8.88	7	WCh	Steenbergen	12 May

249.320	Patrick	Hösl	GER	18.7.73	12 May
248.143	Joseph	Fejes	USA	14.12.65	12 May
248.079 t	Marco	Consani	GBR	15.11.74	22 Sep
247.996	Thierry	Douriez	FRA	28.4.64	6 Oct
247.318	Ryuta	Yoshida	JPN	11.5.80	10 Nov
247.187	Lojze	Primozic	SLO	1.5.69	12 May
246.548	Kenji	Takeda	JPN	1.6.65	10 Nov
246.300	Ryo	Abiko	JPN	16.1.75	12 May
246.155	Steve	Holyoak	GBR	8.9.64	12 May
245.929	Seiyo	Ogawara	JPN	30.4.80	10 Nov
245.676	Vincent	Rivoire	FRA	25.9.61	7 Apr
245.505 t	Olivier	Leblond	USA	30.4.72	15 Dec
244.664 t	Eoin	Keith	IRL	11.10.68	20 Jul
244.334	Tiziano	Marchesi	ITA	2.3.69	12 May
243.991	Janis	Actins	LAT	9.9.72	12 May
243.781	Kaishu	Akaba	JPN	3.6.70	10 Nov
243.777 t	Barry	Loveday	GBR	5.10.77	14 Apr
243.772	Stefan Stu	Thoms	GER	18.10.66	14 Jul
243.010	Serge	Arbona	USA	13.3.65	19 May
242.749	Oliver	Leu	GER	5.8.74	12 May
242.345	Harvey	Lewis	USA	13.4.76	22 Sep

Best track time: 252.211 Toshiro Naraki JPN 10.8.76 4 Taipei 8 Dec

Indoors
247.797	Bjørn	Taranger Kronen	NOR	23.4.79	1 Dec
242.401	Johan	Steene	SWE	25.12.73	1 Dec

2000 METRES STEEPLECHASE

Mark	Name		Nat	Born	Pos	Meet	Venue	Date
5:19.99	Meresa	Kassaye	ETH-Y	23.5.96	1	WY	Donetsk	12 Jul
5:20.92	Nicholas	Bett	KEN-Y	20.12.96	2	WY	Donetsk	12 Jul
5:29.85	Steffen	Uliczka	GER	17.7.84	1		Kiel	28 Jul
5:30.00	Justus	Lagat	KEN-Y	20.5.96	3	WY	Donetsk	12 Jul

JUNIORS
4 performances by 3 men to 5:30.0. Additional mark and further juniors:

Bett	5:29.2A	1		Nairobi	11 Jun
5:32.92	Hicham	Chemlal	MAR-Y	2.12.97	4	WY	Donetsk	12 Jul
5:36.64	Michaele	Atsbaha	ETH-Y	26.6.97	5	WY	Donetsk	12 Jul

3000 METRES STEEPLECHASE

Mark	Name		Nat	Born	Pos	Meet	Venue	Date
7:59.03	Ezekiel	Kemboi	KEN	25.5.82	1	DL	Saint-Denis	6 Jul
8:00.09	Mahiedine	Mekhissi-Benabbad	FRA	15.3.85	2	DL	Saint-Denis	6 Jul
8:01.16	Conseslus	Kipruto	KEN-J	8.12.94	1	DL	Shanghai	18 May
8:02.63	Paul K.	Koech	KEN	10.11.81	2	DL	Shanghai	18 May

Mark	Name		Nat	Born	Pos	Meet	Venue	Date
8:03.57	Hillary	Yego	KEN	2.4.92	3	DL	Shanghai	18 May
8:03.59		C Kipruto			1	Pre	Eugene	1 Jun
8:04.48		C Kipruto			1	Bisl	Oslo	13 Jun
8:05.86		Koech			2	Pre	Eugene	1 Jun
8:06.01		Kemboi			1	WCh	Moskva	15 Aug
8:06.37		C Kipruto			2	WCh	Moskva	15 Aug
8:06.60		Mekhissi			3	Pre	Eugene	1 Jun
8:06.86	Brimin	Kipruto	KEN	31.7.85	1	DL	London (OS)	27 Jul
8:06.96	Gilbert	Kirui	KEN-J	22.1.94	2	DL	London (OS)	27 Jul
8:07.00		Kemboi			2	Bisl	Oslo	13 Jun
8:07.86		Mekhissi			3	WCh	Moskva	15 Aug
8:08.03		Yego			1	WK	Zürich	29 Aug
8:08.60	Evan	Jager	USA	8.3.89	4	Pre	Eugene	1 Jun
8:08.62		Koech			4	WCh	Moskva	15 Aug
8:08.67		Jager			5	WCh	Moskva	15 Aug
8:08.72	Jairus	Birech	KEN	15.12.92	2	WK	Zürich	29 Aug
8:08.83	Abel	Mutai	KEN	2.10.88	4	DL	Shanghai	18 May
8:08.84		Yego			1	ISTAF	Berlin	1 Sep
8:09.01		Yego			3	Bidl	Oslo	13 Jun
8:09.17		Yego			1		Beijing	21 May
8:09.17		Koech			3	DL	Saint-Denis	6 Jul
8:09.31		Koech			2	ISTAF	Berlin	1 Sep
8:09.50		Kirui			5	DL	Shanghai	18 May
8:09.81		Yego			1	DNG	Stockholm	22 Aug
8:09.84		Yego			5	Pre	Eugene	1 Jun
8:10.04		Mutai			6	Pre	Eugene	1 Jun
8:10.27		Birech			6	DL	Shanghai	18 May
	(31/10)							
8:11.64	Matt	Hughes	CAN	3.8.89	6	WCh	Moskva	15 Aug
8:12.22	Roba	Gari	ETH	12.4.82	4	DL	Saint-Denis	6 Jul
8:12.53	Yoann	Kowal	FRA	28.5.87	1		Rabat	9 Jun
8:13.07	Benjamin	Kiplagat	UGA	4.3.89	5	DL	Saint-Denis	6 Jul
8:13.27	Hamid	Ezzine	MAR	5.10.83	2		Rabat	9 Jun
8:14.05	Amor	Ben-Yahia	TUN	1.7.85	1	Med G	Mersin	28 Jun
8:15.89	Noureddine	Smaïl	FRA	6.2.87	6	DL	Saint-Denis	6 Jul
8:15.93	Abdelmadjed	Touil	ALG	11.2.89	4		Rabat	9 Jun
8:16.43	Jacob	Araptany	UGA	11.2.92	1	Gyulai	Budapest	10 Jul
8:16.96	John	Koech	KEN-J	23.8.95	6	DNG	Stockholm	22 Aug
	(20)							
8:17.18	Clement	Kemboi	KEN	1.2.92	2	Gyulai	Budapest	10 Jul
8:18.78	Jonathan	Ndiku	KEN	18.9.91	5		Rabat	9 Jun
8:19.07	Elijah	Chelimo	KEN	10.3.84	3	Gyulai	Budapest	10 Jul
8:19.14	Bernard Mbugua	Nganga	KEN	17.1.85	4		Beijing	21 May
8:19.22	Jaouad	Chemlal	MAR-J	11.4.94	6		Rabat	9 Jun
8:19.26 drugs?	Angel	Mullera	ESP	20.4.84	4h1	WCh	Moskva	12 Aug
8:19.64	Ion	Luchianov	MDA	31.1.81	5h1	WCh	Moskva	12 Aug
8:20.08	Cory	Leslie	USA	24.10.89	4		Tokyo	5 May
8:20.08	Tarik Langat	Akdag	TUR	16.6.88	2	Med G	Mersin	28 Jun
8:20.11	Hichem	Bouchicha	ALG	19.5.89	2		Rabat	1 Jun
	(30)							
8:20.87	José Gregorio	Peña	VEN	12.1.87	7	ISTAF	Berlin	1 Sep
8:21.19	Anthony	Rotich	KEN	.93	1	NCAA	Eugene	7 Jun
8:21.62	Mohammed	Boulama	MAR	31.12.93	3		Rabat	1 Jun
8:21.92	Dan	Huling	USA	16.7.83	7	DNG	Stockholm	22 Aug
8:22.68	Abdelaziz	Merzougui	MAR	30.8.91	1		Huelva	12 Jun
8:22.95	Haron	Lagat	KEN	15.8.83	8	ISTAF	Berlin	1 Sep
8:22.97	Sebastián	Martos	ESP	20.6.89	2		Huelva	12 Jun
8:23.16	Henry	Lelei	KEN	31.12.88	2	NCAA	Eugene	7 Jun
8:23.31	Krystian	Zalewski	POL	11.4.89	9		Rabat	9 Jun
8:23.43	Alexandre	Genest	CAN	30.6.86	3	Jordan	Stanford	28 Apr
	(40)							
8:23.57	Steffen	Uliczka	GER	17.7.84	3		Huelva	12 Jun
8:23.84	Mounatcer	Zaghou	MAR	1.1.89	10		Rabat	9 Jun
8:24.45	Stanley	Kebenei	KEN	6.11.89	3	NCAA	Eugene	7 Jun
8:24.59	Timothy	Toroitich	UGA	10.10.91	5	Gyulai	Budapest	10 Jul
8:24.62	Yuri	Floriani	ITA	25.12.81	4		Huelva	12 Jun
8:24.90	Habtamu	Jaleta	ETH	19.4.93	11		Rabat	9 Jun
8:25.0 A	Lawrence	Kemboi	KEN	.93	2	NC	Nairobi	22 Jun
8:25.01	Lukasz	Parszczynski	POL	4.5.85	9	Bisl	Oslo	13 Jun
8:25.2 A	Edwin	Kirwa	KEN		3	NC	Nairobi	22 Jun

MEN 2013

Mark	Name		Nat	Born	Pos	Meet	Venue	Date	
8:25.34	Roberto (50)	Alaiz	ESP	20.7.90	6	Gyulai	Budapest	10	Jul
8:25.37	Jamel	Chatbi	ITA	30.4.84	13		Rabat	9	Jun
8:25.56	De'Sean	Turner	USA	16.9.88	3	NC	Des Moines	23	Jun
8:25.96	Abdelhamid	Zerrifi	ALG	20.6.86	13	DL	Saint-Denis	6	Jul
8:26.24	Vadym	Slobodenyuk	UKR	17.3.81	1		Yalta	6	Jun
8:26.30	Mateusz	Demczyszak	POL	18.1.86	1	NC	Torun	19	Jul
8:26.77	Tomasz	Szymkowiak	POL	5.7.83	7		Huelva	12	Jun
8:26.82	Andrew	Poore	USA	3.12.88	4	NC	Des Moines	23	Jun
8:27.09	Mitko	Tsenov	BUL	13.6.93	1	NC	Pravets	15	Jun
8:27.36	Silas	Kitum	KEN	25.5.90	7		Beijing	21	May
8:28.21	Wilson (60)	Maraba	KEN	2.12.86	4	GS	Ostrava	27	Jun
8:28.6	Gerald	Giraldo	COL	21.3.89	2	Bol G	Trujillo	29	Nov
8:28.65	Ilgizar	Safiulin	RUS	9.12.92	8h1	WCh	Moskva	12	Aug
8:28.74	James	Wilkinson	GBR	13.7.90	6	GS	Ostrava	27	Jun
8:28.92	Chris	Winter	CAN	22.7.86	1		Lapinlahti	21	Jul
8:29.10	Billy	Nelson	USA	11.9.84	2		Los Angeles (ER)	17	May
8:29.2 A	Hillary	Kemboi	KEN	.86	2		Nairobi	11	May
8:29.5 A	Peter	Mateelong	KEN	26.11.89	4	NC	Nairobi	22	Jun
8:29.82	Hicham	Sigueni	MAR	30.1.93	10	Pre	Eugene	1	Jun
8:29.92	Meresa	Kassaye	ETH-Y	23.5.96	11	DNG	Stockholm	22	Aug
8:30.02	Donnie (70)	Cowart	USA	24.10.85	3		Los Angeles (ER)	17	May
8:30.05	Brahim	Taleb	MAR	16.2.85	1	NC	Casablanca	7	Jul
8:30.28	Patrick	Nasti	ITA	30.8.89	4		Dessau	31	May
8:30.78	Devis	Licciardi	ITA	21.7.86	1		Brugnera	7	Sep
8:30.87	Travis	Mahoney	USA	25.7.90	4		Los Angeles (ER)	17	May
8:31.28	Matt	Cleaver	USA	7.11.89	5		Los Angeles (ER)	17	May
8:31.34	Andrey	Farnosov	RUS	9.7.80	9		Huelva	12	Jun
8:31.4 A	Kennedy	Njiru	KEN	.87	3		Nairobi	11	May
8:31.48	Taylor	Milne	CAN	14.6.81	6		Los Angeles (ER)	17	May
8:31.75	Josphat	Koech	KEN	.82	2		Brugnera	7	Sep
8:31.84	Nikolay (80)	Chavkin	RUS	22.4.84	1r1	NC	Moskva	23	Jul
8:32.32	Bilal	Tabti	ALG	7.6.93	1		Alger	3	Jul
8:32.37	Willy	Komen	KEN	22.12.87	4		Bellinzona	11	Jun
8:32.41	Hillary	Bor	KEN	22.11.89	7	Jordan	Stanford	28	Apr
8:32.51	Tomás	Tajadura	ESP	25.6.85	10		Huelva	12	Jun
8:32.57	Cameron	Bean	USA	17.12.86	8	Jordan	Stanford	28	Apr
8:32.68	Rob	Mullett	GBR	31.7.87	6		Dessau	31	May
8:32.72	Nelson	Kipkosgei	KEN	9.3.93	6		Alger	18	Jun
8:32.89	Jun	Shinoto	JPN	2.4.85	10	Jordan	Stanford	28	Apr
8:33.06	Edwin	Molepo	RSA	31.5.87	1	NC	Stellenbosch	12	Apr
8:33.09	Alberto (90)	Paulo	POR	3.10.85	11		Huelva	12	Jun
8:33.18	Alex	Kibet	KEN/QAT?	20.10.90	1		Doha	30	Apr
8:33.22	Craig	Forys	USA	13.7.89	1		Baie Mahault	8	May
8:33.48	Tsuyoshi	Takeda	JPN	22.1.87	7		Tokyo	5	May
8:33.57	Minato	Yamashita	JPN	15.11.88	1	NC	Tokyo [Chofu]	7	Jun
8:33.72	Benabbad	Redouane	MAR	9.10.91	3	NC	Casablanca	7	Jul
8:33.74	Youcef	Abdi	AUS	7.12.77	1		Melbourne	6	Apr
8:33.82	Aoi	Matsumoto	JPN	7.9.87	2	NC	Tokyo [Chofu]	7	Jun
8:34.23	Donn	Cabral	USA	12.12.89	7		Los Angeles (ER)	17	May
8:34.32	Tareq Mubarak	Taher	BRN	24.3.84	10h1	WCh	Moskva	12	Aug
8:34.42	Zak (100)	Seddon	GBR-J	28.6.94	11	Jordan	Stanford	28	Apr

8:34.55	Luis Enrique	Ibarra	MEX	4.7.80	17 May		8:36.82	Benjamin	Bruce	USA	10.9.82	23	Jun
8:34.87	Ildar	Minshin	RUS	5.2.85	15 Jun		8:36.91	Mustapha	Ferrane	ALG	22.3.84	5	Jul
8:34.87	James	Nipperess	AUS	21.5.90	27 Jun		8:37.40	Dejene	Regassa	BRN	18.4.89	5	Jul
8:35.0 A	Kennedy	Kosgei	KEN	.85	11 May		8:37.44A	Nathan	Ayeko	UGA	10.10.93	19	Jul
8:35.39	Albert	Minczér	HUN	1.10.86	8 Jun		8:37.66		Wang Yashuan	CHN	26.6.88	8	Sep
8:35.46	Silas	Too	KEN	.89	31 May		8:38.0 A	Linus	Chumba	KEN	9.2.80	11	May
8:35.53	Yuriy	Klopstov	RUS	22.12.89	25 May		8:38.07	Tanguy	Pépiot	FRA	6.7.91	14	Jul
8:35.55	Giuseppe	Gerratana	ITA	8.11.92	14 Jul		8:38.16	Nahom	Mesfin	ETH	3.6.89	1	Jun
8:35.59	Yegor	Nikolayev	RUS	12.2.88	25 May		8:38.28	Aric	Van Halen	USA	6.10.89	24	May
8:35.65	Tolossa	Nurgi	ETH	29.3.90	27 Jun		8:38.5 A	Isaac	Yego	KEN		27	Apr
8:35.99	Ilya	Sukharev	UKR	17.6.86	27 Jun		8:38.61	Ibrahim	Ezzaydouny	MAR	28.4.91	12	Jun
8:36.10	Dmitriy	Balashov	RUS	19.1.89	23 Jul		8:38.65	Marcos	Peón	ESP	11.1.83	12	Jun
8:36.3 A	Peter	Kipkorir	KEN		4 May		8:38.71	Ryan	Brockerville	CAN	29.7.89	17	May
8:36.4 A	Festus	Kiprono	KEN-J	29.12.95	19 Apr		8:38.76	Radhouane	Majdoub	MAR		1	Jun
8:36.46	Jared	Bassett	USA	6.5.90	24 Jun		8:38.96	Brian	Himelright	USA	30.3.90	28	Apr
8:36.51	Stanislav	Anishchenkov	RUS	21.8.82	15 Jun		8:38.97		Zhang Zhongji	CHN	27.10.87	8	Sep

Mark	Name		Nat	Born	Pos	Meet	Venue	Date
8:39.08	Sisay	Korme	ETH	9.1.85	15 Jun			
8:39.14	Najibe Marco	Salami	ITA	7.7.85	5 Jul			
8:39.27	Pavlo	Oliynyk	UKR	9.5.88	6 Jun			
8:39.52	Alex	Brill	USA	23.9.90	24 May			
8:39.65		Yang Tao	CHN	23.3.87	8 Sep			

Disqualified for obstruction: 8:03.94 Kemboi

Mark	Name		Nat	Born	Pos	Meet	Venue	Date
8:39.85	Lloyd	Bosman	RSA	25.2.88	12 Apr			
8:39.86	Lyle	Weese	USA	26.10.79	8 Jun			
8:39.98	Jukka	Keskisalo	FIN	27.3.81	31 Aug			
8:39.99	Mauricio	Valdivia	CHI	11.10.89	7 Jun			
					(2)	Pre	Eugene	1 Jun

JUNIORS

See main list for top 6 juniors. 15 performances by 3 men to 8:17.00. Additional marks and further juniors:

C Kipruto 4+	8:10.76	3	WK	Zürich	29 Aug	8:12.35	3	DNG Stockholm 22 Aug
	8:11.27	1	GS	Ostrava	27 Jun	8:13.5A	1	WCT Naitrobi 13 Jul
G Kirui 2+	8:11.55	2	DNG	Stockholm	22 Aug	8:12.93	5	WK Zürich 29 Aug
	8:12.36	5	Bisl	Oslo	13 Jun	8:15.67	3	Beijing 21 May

Mark	Name		Nat	Born	Pos	Meet	Venue	Date
8:36.4 A	Festus	Kiprono	KEN	29.12.95	1		Nairobi	19 Apr
8:41.8A	Abraham	Kapsis	KEN-Y	.96	7		Mumias	27 Apr
8:43.0A	James	Maina	KEN	.94	9	NC	Nairobi	22 Jun
8:44.45	Viktor	Bakharev (10)	RUS	5.5.94	6		Sochi	25 May
8:44.57	Rantso	Mokopane	RSA	9.8.94	1		Durban	27 Apr
8:44.90	Hicham	Chemlal	MAR-Y	2.12.97	7		Rabat	1 Jun
8:45.93	Abraham	Habte	ERI		10		Beijing	21 May
8:46.94A	Vincent	Rutoh	KEN	17.9.95	3		Nairobi	13 Aug
8:48.23	Yasutaka	Ishibashi	JPN	24.8.94	5		Yokohama	25 May
8:49.0A	Edwin	Melly	KEN-Y	10.8.96	1		Kericho	30 May
8:49.2A	Zewedu	Mola	ETH	20.5.95	1		Addis Ababa	17 Mar
8:49.8A	Gigsa	Tolosa	ETH-Y	29.3.96	2		Addis Ababa	17 Mar
8:49.90A	Justine	Wakeri (20)	KEN	.94	4		Nairobi	13 Aug

60 METRES HURDLES INDOORS

Mark	Name		Nat	Born	Pos	Meet	Venue	Date
7.49	Sergey	Shubenkov	RUS	4.10.90	1	EI	Göteborg	1 Mar
7.50	Kevin	Craddock	USA	25.6.87	1		Düsseldorf	8 Feb
7.50		Shubenkov			1	NC	Moskva	12 Feb
7.50	Eddie	Lovett	USA/ISV	25.6.92	1	NCAA	Fayetteville	9 Mar
7.51	Omo	Osaghae	USA	18.5.88	1	GP	Birmingham	16 Feb
7.51	Paolo	Dal Molin	ITA	31.7.87	2	EI	Göteborg	1 Mar
7.52	Osaghae				2		Düsseldorf	8 Feb
7.52		Shubenkov			1s2	EI	Göteborg	1 Mar
7.52		Shubenkov			1h3	EI	Göteborg	1 Mar
	(9/5)							
7.53	Pascal	Martinot-Lagarde	FRA	22.9.91	1	NC	Aubière	16 Feb
7.54	Orlando	Ortega	CUB	29.7.91	1h2		Karlsruhe	2 Feb
7.56	Dimitri	Bascou	FRA	20.7.87	2	NC	Aubière	16 Feb
7.56	Balázs	Baji	HUN	9.6.89	4	EI	Göteborg	1 Mar
7.57	Erik	Balnuweit	GER	21.9.88	2s2	EI	Göteborg	1 Mar
	(10)							
7.58	Andrew	Pozzi	GBR	15.5.92	1h2		Birmingham	3 Feb
7.58	Maksim	Lynsha	BLR	6.4.85	6	EI	Göteborg	1 Mar
7.59	Spencer	Adams	USA	10.9.89	1r1		New York (Armory)	1 Feb
7.59	Konstantin	Shabanov	RUS	17.11.89	1		Moskva	3 Feb
7.59	Jeff	Porter	USA	27.11.85	1	Mill	New York (Armory)	16 Feb
7.59	Wayne	Davis II	TTO	22.8.91	2	NCAA	Fayetteville	9 Mar
7.60		Xie Wenjun	CHN	11.7.90	3	GP	Birmingham	16 Feb
7.60	Andrew	Riley	JAM	6.9.88	2	Mill	New York (Armory)	16 Feb
7.62A	Brendan	Ames	USA	6.10.88	1		Albuquerque	1 Feb
7.63	Aries	Merritt	USA	24.7.85	1		Houston	26 Jan
	(20)							
7.63	Jarret	Eaton	USA	24.6.89	3	Mill	New York (Armory)	16 Feb
7.63	Keiron	Stewart	JAM	21.11.89	2h2	NCAA	Fayetteville	8 Mar
7.64	Konstadínos	Douvalídis	GRE	10.3.87	4s1	EI	Göteborg	1 Mar
7.65	Caleb	Cross	USA	31.5.91	1	Tyson	Fayetteville	8 Feb
7.65	Yordan	O'Farrill	CUB-J	9.2.93	5h1		Düsseldorf	8 Feb
7.66	Barrett	Nugent	USA	29.1.90	3h2		Düsseldorf	8 Feb
7.66	Garfield	Darien	FRA	22.12.87	1h2		Lyon	21 Dec
7.67	Gianni	Frankis	GBR	16.4.88	1		Wien	29 Jan
7.68	Greggmar	Swift	BAR	16.2.91	3	Tyson	Fayetteville	8 Feb
7.68	Ray	Stewart	USA	5.4.89	1h3		Seattle	22 Feb
	(30)							
7.68	Gregor	Traber	GER	2.12.92	2	NC	Dortmund	23 Feb
7.68	Rasul	Dabó	POR	14.2.89	2h3	EI	Göteborg	1 Mar
7.69	Koen	Smet	NED	9.8.92	1r2		Amsterdam	13 Jan
7.69	Terence	Somerville	USA	5.11.89	1		Columbus	15 Feb
7.69	Matthias	Bühler	GER	2.9.86	3	NC	Dortmund	23 Feb

MEN 2013

Mark	Name		Nat	Born	Pos	Meet	Venue	Date
7.69	Vladimir	Vukicevic	NOR	6.5.91	5s2	EI	Göteborg	1 Mar
7.69	Keith	Hayes	USA	16.2.90	3h2	NCAA	Fayetteville	8 Mar
7.70	Devon	Hill	USA	26.10.89	1h		Blacksburg	8 Feb
7.70	Jordan	Mullen	USA	6.4.90	1	Big 10	Geneva, OH	23 Feb
7.70	Dominik	Bochenek	POL	14.5.87	2h4	EI	Göteborg	1 Mar
(40)								
7.70	Jackson	Quiñónez	ESP	12.6.80	3h2	EI	Göteborg	1 Mar
7.71A	Demoye	Bogle	USA	8.11.91	1		Albuquerque	8 Feb
7.71	Jason	Richardson	USA	4.4.86	5	Mill	New York (Armory)	16 Feb
7.72	Nick	Gayle	GBR	4.1.85	3h1		Wien	29 Jan
7.72	Dániel	Kiss	HUN	12.2.82	2h2		Moskva	3 Feb
7.73	Eric	Keddo	JAM	1.7.85	1		Winston-Salem	19 Jan
7.73	Alexander	Brorsson	SWE	29.5.90	1		Malmö	27 Jan
7.73	Allan	Scott	GBR	27.12.82	3		Wien	29 Jan
7.73	Antwon	Hicks	USA	12.3.83	1		Saskatoon	1 Feb
7.73	Helge	Schwarzer	GER	26.11.85	1h2	NC	Dortmund	23 Feb
(50)								
7.73	Jonathan	Cabral	USA	31.12.92	5h1	NCAA	Fayetteville	8 Mar

110 METRES HURDLES

Mark		Name		Nat	Born	Pos	Meet	Venue	Date
13.00	0.3	David	Oliver	USA	24.4.82	1	WCh	Moskva	12 Aug
13.03	0.9		Oliver			1	Athl	Lausanne	4 Jul
13.05	0.9	Hansle	Parchment	JAM	17.6.90	1	Pre	Eugene	1 Jun
13.05	-0.6		Oliver			1h4	WCh	Moskva	11 Aug
13.08	0.9	Orlando	Ortega	CUB	29.7.91	2	Pre	Eugene	1 Jun
13.08	1.4	Ryan	Wilson	USA	19.12.80	1	NC	Des Moines	23 Jun
13.09	0.0	Aries	Merritt	USA	24.7.85	1	DL	Saint-Denis	6 Jul
13.10	0.9		Oliver			3	Pre	Eugene	1 Jun
13.11	1.4		Oliver			2	NC	Des Moines	23 Jun
13.12	0.0	Pascal	Martinot-Lagarde	FRA	22.9.91	2	DL	Saint-Denis	6 Jul
13.12	-0.5		Oliver			1	WK	Zürich	29 Aug
13.13	0.0		Oliver			3	DL	Saint-Denis	6 Jul
13.13	0.3		Wilson			2	WCh	Moskva	12 Aug
13.14	0.0	Andrew	Riley	JAM	6.9.88	4	DL	Saint-Denis	6 Jul
13.14	0.0	Ryan	Brathwaite	BAR	6.6.88	5	DL	Saint-Denis	6 Jul
13.14	1.3		Merritt			1h2	DL	London (OS)	27 Jul
13.15	0.0		Wilson			6	DL	Saint-Denis	6 Jul
13.16	0.3		Oliver			1		Beijing	21 May
13.16	-0.6	Sergey	Shubenkov	RUS	4.10.90	2h4	WCh	Moskva	11 Aug
13.17	0.3		Ortega			1		Baie Mahault	8 May
13.17	-0.6		Shubenkov			1s2	WCh	Moskva	12 Aug
13.18	0.9		Wilson			4	Pre	Eugene	1 Jun
13.18	1.8	Dayron	Robles (10)	CUB	19.11.86	1		Sotteville-lès-Rouen	8 Jul
13.18	-0.6		Oliver			2s2	WCh	Moskva	12 Aug
13.19	1.2		Brathwaite			1	adidas	New York	25 May
13.19	1.2	Mikel	Thomas	TTO	23.11.87	1		Montverde, FL	8 Jun
13.19	-0.1		Shubenkov			1	NC	Moskva	24 Jul
13.20	0.9		Riley			5	Pre	Eugene	1 Jun
13.20	0.9		Shubenkov			1	GGala	Roma	6 Jun
13.20	0.9	Jason	Richardson	USA	4.4.86	2	Athl	Lausanne	4 Jul
13.20	0.3		Oliver			1	DL	London (OS)	27 Jul
13.20	-0.6		Wilson			3s2	WCh	Moskva	12 Aug
(32/12)									
13.25	0.3	Antwon	Hicks	USA	12.3.83	1		Kingston	4 May
13.26	0.0	Thomas	Martinot-Lagarde	FRA	7.2.88	8	DL	Saint-Denis	6 Jul
13.26	0.3	William	Sharman	GBR	12.9.84	2	DL	London (OS)	27 Jul
13.26	0.2	Artur	Noga	POL	2.5.88	1	Skol	Warszawa	25 Aug
13.27	1.2	Dwight	Thomas	JAM	23.9.80	2		Montverde, FL	8 Jun
13.28	-0.5		Xie Wenjun	CHN	11.7.90	3	DL	Shanghai	18 May
13.30	0.9	David	Payne	USA	24.7.82	4	Athl	Lausanne	4 Jul
13.34	1.4	Konstadínos	Douvalídis	GRE	10.3.87	1	NC	Athína	20 Jul
(20)									
13.35	0.9	Jeff	Porter	USA	27.11.85	7	Pre	Eugene	1 Jun
13.35	1.8	Omo	Osaghae	USA	18.5.88	3		Sotteville-lès-Rouen	8 Jul
13.36	0.5	Balázs	Baji	HUN	9.6.89	3h3	WCh	Moskva	11 Aug
13.38	1.2	Devon	Hill	USA	26.10.89	3		Montverde, FL	8 Jun
13.38	0.5	Konstantin	Shabanov	RUS	17.11.89	2h1	WCh	Moskva	11 Aug
13.38	-0.3	Wayne	Davis	TTO	22.8.91	2h2	WCh	Moskva	11 Aug
13.39	0.6	Eddie	Lovett	USA/ISV	25.6.92	1q3	NCAA-E	Greensboro	25 May

Mark	Wind	Name		Nat	Born	Pos	Meet	Venue	Date	
13.40	-0.2	Spencer	Adams	USA	10.9.89	1		Auburn	6	Apr
13.42	0.0	Kevin	Craddock	USA	25.6.87	3	Gyulai	Budapest	10	Jul
13.43	1.0	Ray	Stewart	USA	5.4.89	1	Pac-12	Los Angeles	12	May
		(30)								
13.43	0.9	Lehann	Fourie	RSA	16.2.87	6	Athl	Lausanne	4	Jul
13.43	0.0	Adrien	Deghelt	BEL	10.5.85	1		Ninove	27	Jul
13.44	1.2	Ryan	Fontenot	USA	4.5.86	1		San Marcos, TX	27	Apr
13.44	0.5	Shane	Brathwaite	BAR	8.2.90	1		George Town, CAY	8	May
13.44	0.0	Yordan	O'Farrill	CUB	9.2.93	1	Barr	La Habana	4	Jun
13.44	0.7	Dominic	Berger	USA	19.5.86	1		Colts Neck, NJ	8	Jun
13.44	1.7	Erik	Balnuweit	GER	21.9.88	1		Mannheim	30	Jun
13.45	1.5	Matthias	Bühler	GER	2.9.86	1h1		Bottrop	19	Jul
13.46	0.0	Jhoanis	Portilla	CUB	24.7.90	2	Barr	La Habana	4	Jun
13.47	1.4	Johnathan	Cabral	USA	31.12.92	1q2	NCAA-W	Austin	25	May
		(40)								
13.48	0.0	Ignacio	Morales	CUB	28.1.87	3	Barr	La Habana	4	Jun
13.48	0.4	Martin	Mazác	CZE	6.5.90	1	NC	Tábor	15	Jun
13.48	-0.1		Shi Dongpeng	CHN	6.1.84	1		Shenyang	16	Jun
13.48	-0.4	Greggmar	Swift	BAR	16.2.91	2	NC	Bridgetown	22	Jun
13.48	1.5	Barrett	Nugent	USA	29.1.90	4h1	DL	Birmingham	30	Jun
13.49	0.5	Terence	Somerville	USA	5.11.89	1q2	NCAA-E	Greensboro	25	May
13.49	1.3	Emanuele	Abate	ITA	8.7.85	1rB	ET	Gateshead	23	Jun
13.49	1.9	Ben	Reynolds	IRL	26.9.90	1		Belfast	25	Jun
13.49	1.7	Gregor	Traber	GER	2.12.92	2		Mannheim	30	Jun
13.49	-1.2	Alexander	John	GER	3.5.86	2	NC	Ulm	6	Jul
		(50)								
13.49	1.7	Philip	Nossmy	SWE	6.12.82	1rA		Sundsvall	28	Jul
13.50	0.7	Othman	Hadj Lazib	ALG	10.5.83	2		Besançon	15	Jun
13.50	-0.1		Jiang Fan	CHN	16.9.89	2		Shenyang	16	Jun
13.50	0.8	Gregory	Sedoc	NED	16.10.81	2	ET-1	Dublin	23	Jun
13.50	-0.8	Tyrone	Akins	USA	6.1.86	2		Lignano	16	Jul
13.51	1.4	Johnny	Dutch	USA	20.1.89	1		Coral Gables, FL	16	Mar
13.51	0.5	Joel	Brown	USA	31.1.80	1		Bellinzona	11	Jun
13.51	0.7	Dimitri	Bascou	FRA	20.7.87	1h2	NC	Paris (C)	14	Jul
13.52	0.6	Selim	Nurudeen	NGR	1.2.83	2h1		Clermont, FL	11	May
13.52	1.0	Rasul	Dabo	POR	14.2.89	2		La Chaux-de-Fonds	7	Jul
		(60)								
13.53	0.3	Deuce	Carter	JAM	28.9.90	4		Kingston	4	May
13.53	0.2	Aleksandr	Linnik	BLR	28.1.91	1	NC	Grodno	27	Jul
13.53	1.7	Fred	Townsend	USA	19.2.82	2rA		Sundsvall	28	Jul
13.54	2.0	Gianni	Frankis	GBR	16.4.88	1		London (Nh)	26	Jun
13.55	-0.4	Simon	Krauss	FRA	12.2.92	1	EU23	Tampere	13	Jul
13.56	-0.8	Enrique	Llanos	PUR	7.5.80	5		Ponce	18	May
13.57	1.2	Malcolm	Anderson	USA	18.9.89	4		Montverde, FL	8	Jun
13.58	0.8	Matheus	Inocêncio	BRA	17.5.81	1h3	NC	São Paulo	8	Jun
13.58	1.5	Hideki	Omuro	JPN	25.7.90	1s1	NC	Tokyo [Chofu]	9	Jun
13.58	-0.4	Koen	Smet	NED	9.8.92	2	EU23	Tampere	13	Jul
		(70)								
13.59A	-0.1	Ruan	de Vries	RSA	1.2.86	1		Potchefstroom	20	Apr
13.59	-1.3	Vanier	Joseph	USA	9.9.91	1	Drake	Des Moines	27	Apr
13.59	1.3	Wataru	Yazawa	JPN	2.7.91	1	NC	Tokyo (Chofu)	9	Jun
13.59	-0.1	Dario	De Borger (Seghers)	BEL	20.3.92	3h1		Fribourg	3	Aug
13.60	-0.2	Ladji	Doucouré	FRA	28.3.83	1		Bruxelles	6	Jul
13.61	0.3	Jonathan	Mendes	BRA	14.4.90	1h1	NC	São Paulo	8	Jun
13.61	1.7	Ronald	Brookins	USA	5.7.89	1		Chula Vista	8	Jun
13.61	1.3	Hiroyuki	Sato	JPN	6.8.90	3	NC	Tokyo [Chofu]	9	Jun
13.61	1.0	Jorge	McFarlane	PER	20.2.88	1	SAmC	Cartagena	5	Jul
13.61	-0.2		Kim Byung-jun	KOR	15.8.91	2	EAsG	Tianjin	9	Oct
		(80)								
13.62A	1.0	Brendan	Ames	USA	6.10.88	1		Air Force Academy	3	May
13.62A	1.1	Eric	Keddo	JAM	1.7.84	2h2	CAC	Morelia	5	Jul
13.62	0.2	Maksim	Lynsha	BLR	6.4.85	2	NC	Grodno	27	Jul
13.63	0.1	Lyès	Mokdel	ALG	20.6.90	1	Arab C	Doha	22	May
13.63	0.5	Keith	Nkrumah	GHA	28.11.90	2q2	NCAA-E	Greensboro	25	May
13.64	-0.4	Ashton	Eaton	USA	21.1.88	1D		Santa Barbara	6	Apr
13.64	-0.4	Damian	Warner	CAN	4.11.89	2D		Santa Barbara	6	Apr
13.64	-1.0	Don	Pollitt	USA	1.10.91	1	IC4A	Princeton	12	May
13.64	0.1	Francisco Javier	López	ESP	29.12.89	1		Zaragoza	8	Jun
13.65	1.0	Gerkenz	Senesca	USA	6.4.90	2rB	FlaR	Gainesville	5	Apr
		(90)								
13.65	1.7	Ronald	Forbes	CAY	5.4.85	2		Miramar, FL	29	Apr

Mark	Wind	Name		Nat	Born	Pos	Meet	Venue	Date
13.65	0.0	Dániel	Kiss	HUN	12.2.82	6		Budapest	10 Jul
13.65	0.3	Ji Wei		CHN	5.2.84	3	NG	Shenyang	9 Sep
13.65	-1.2	Yutaro	Furukawa	JPN	3.6.85	1		Tokyo (Chofu)	7 Oct
13.66	-0.1	Abdulaziz	Al-Mandeel	KUW	22.5.89	1		Bangkok	4 May
13.66A	-0.7	Sabiel	Anderson	JAM	21.6.88	1	NCAA-2	Pueblo, CO	25 May
13.66	0.5	Keith	Hayes	USA	16.2.90	3q2	NCAA-E	Greensboro	25 May
13.67	0.1	Lu Anye		CHN	12.3.90	3		Zhaoqing	28 Apr
13.67	1.8	Chris	Thomas	USA	9.2.81	2		New York	30 May
13.67	0.8	Milan	Trajkovic	CYP	17.9.92	1	ET-2	Kaunas	23 Jun
(100)									
13.67A	1.9	Jeffrey	Julmis	HAI	6.1.87	2h1	CAC	Morelia	5 Jul
13.68	0.8	Andreas	Martinsen	DEN	17.7.90				22 Jun
13.69	1.5	Aleec	Harris	USA	31.10.90				27 Apr
13.69	0.7	Brandon	Winters	USA	11.12.91				25 May
13.69	0.1	Jackson	Quiñónez	ESP	12.6.80				8 Jun
13.69		Vladimir	Vukicevic	NOR	6.5.91				30 Jun
13.69	1.2	Samuel	Coco-Viloin	FRA	19.10.87				14 Jul
13.70	1.0	Tre	Lathan	USA	15.7.92				5 May
13.70	1.5	Moussa	Dembélé	SEN	30.10.88				29 Jun
13.70	1.0	Damien	Broothaerts	BEL	12.11.84				14 Jul
13.70	0.2	Trey	Hardee	USA	7.2.84				27 Jul
13.71	1.8	Jarret	Eaton	USA	24.6.89				28 Apr
13.71	0.7	Akeem	Smith	JAM	15.10.87				25 May
13.71	0.7	James	Gladman	GBR	3.6.93				30 Jun
13.72	-5.1?	Ahmad	Al-Moualed	KSA	16.2.88				17 Apr
13.72	0.5	Marcus	Maxey	USA	9.10.90				25 May
13.72	-0.7	Dominik	Bochenek	POL	14.5.87				8 Jun
13.72	1.7	Logan	Taylor	USA	3.4.86				8 Jun
13.72	1.3	Masanori	Nishizawa	JPN	16.7.87				9 Jun
13.72	-0.1		Yin Jing	CHN	23.5.88				16 Jun
13.72	1.3	Nick	Gayle	GBR	4.1.85				29 Jun
13.72	-0.3	Jamras	Rittidet	THA	1.2.89				19 Dec
13.73	0.0	Andrew	Brunson	USA	4.4.86				4 May
13.73	w?	Matthew	Brisson	CAN	21.9.88				10 May
13.74	0.3	Éder Antônio	de Souza	BRA	15.10.86				29 Jun
13.75	-0.1	Fabio	dos Santos	BRA	11.10.83				29 Jun
13.75	-0.4	Thingalaya	Siddhanth	IND	1.3.91				23 Jul
13.75	0.3	David	Ilariani	GEO	20.1.81				25 Jul
13.76	0.4	Jordan	Mullen	USA	6.4.90				12 May
13.77	-1.2	Ethan	Holmes	USA	16.3.91				6 Apr
13.77	1.5	Kenji	Yahata	JPN	4.11.80				29 Apr
13.77	-0.8	Adams	Abdulrazaaq	USA	27.4.88				11 May
13.77	1.5	Genta	Masuno	JPN	24.5.93				9 Jun
13.77	0.4	Petr	Penáz	CZE	27.8.91				15 Jun
13.77	0.0		Lei Yiwen	CHN	11.12.93				8 Sep
13.78	1.6	Trevor	Brown	USA	24.3.92				11 May
13.78	-1.0	Helge	Schwarzer	GER	26.11.85				8 Jun
13.78	1.2	Bano	Traoré	FRA	25.4.85				14 Jul
13.78	0.4		Zhang Jianxin	CHN	29.10.87				8 Sep
13.79	0.0	Vincent	Wyatt	USA	18.10.92				4 May
13.79	-1.0	Amadou	Guèye	SEN	12.10.90				12 May
13.79	0.7	Carrington	Queen	USA	21.9.87				8 Jun
13.79	0.0		Zhu Haibao	CHN	6.1.90				16 Jun
13.80	0.3	Caleb	Cross	USA	31.5.91				20 Apr
13.80	0.8	Solomon	Williams	USA	1.6.91				25 May
13.80	0.8	Amir	Shaker	IRQ	18.10.89				28 Jul
13.80	-0.4	Paulo César	Villar	COL	28.7.78				26 Nov
13.81	1.7	Héctor	Cotto	PUR	8.8.84				29 Apr
13.81	1.9	Tim	Young	USA	24.8.91				10 May
13.81	0.6	Trey	Holloway	USA-J	7.7.94				25 May
13.81	1.5	Aleksey	Dryomin	RUS	10.5.89				2 Jun
13.81	1.3	Hassane	Fofana	ITA	28.4.92				15 Jun
13.81	-0.1	Lawrence	Clarke	GBR	12.3.90				14 Jul
13.81	1.2	Julian	Marquardt	GER	2.4.91				19 Jul
13.82	0.7	Cedrique	Smith	USA	18.9.90				20 Apr
13.82	0.7	Demoye	Bogle	USA	8.11.91				25 May
13.82	0.8	Chris	Williams	USA-J	5.3.94				25 May
13.82	1.5	Hideki	Nomoto	JPN	13.3.84				9 Jun
13.82	-0.5		Lee Jung-joon	KOR	26.3.84				28 Jun
13.83	1.2	Gonzalo	Barroilhet	CHI	19.8.86				13 Apr
13.83	-0.1		Ma Lei	CHN	29.6.89				16 Jun
13.83		Rouhollah	Ashgari	IRI	8.1.82				21 Jun
13.83	1.0	Pedro	García	ESP	4.4.92				28 Jul
13.84	-1.3	Durrell	Busby	TTO	23.12.89				27 Apr
13.84	0.8	Sebastian	Barth	GER	1.2.93				8 Jun
13.84	1.2	Yuta	Notoya	JPN	8.7.89				9 Jun
13.84	-0.3	Yidiel	Contreras	CUB	27.11.91				28 Jul
13.84	-0.2	Sekou	Kaba	CAN	25.8.90				11 Sep
13.85	0.4	Rashard	Marshall	JAM	.87				18 May
13.85	-1.5	Joseph	Hylton	GBR	17.11.89				27 May
13.85	0.9	Rico	Freimuth	GER	14.3.88				16 Jun
13.85	1.0	Javier	McFarlane	PER	21.10.91				5 Jul
13.85	0.8	Chris	Kinney	USA	9.11.88				1 Sep
13.85	0.4		Park Tae-kyong	KOR	30.7.80				20 Oct
13.86	-0.6	Isaac	Williams	USA	30.11.93				12 May
13.86	-0.2	Marlon	Odom	GER	4.12.82				8 Jun
13.86	0.1	Kyohei	Hayakawa	JPN	20.11.91				8 Jun
13.86	1.2	Terrence	Trammell	USA	23.11.78				8 Jun
13.86	0.3	Rayzam Shah	Wan Sofian	MAS	11.1.88				3 Sep
13.87	0.7	Ahmad	Hazer	LIB	4.9.89				7 Jun
13.87	1.5	Akitoshi	Igo	JPN	.91				9 Jun
13.87	-0.1		Chen Shuyan	CHN	26.1.93				16 Jun
13.88	2.0	Milan	Ristic	SRB	8.8.91				29 Mar
13.88	1.2	Ken	Taylor	USA	8.5.90				13 Apr
13.88	1.0	Tarique	Hill	USA	31.12.90				5 May
13.88	1.2	Kyohei	Mita	JPN	16.8.91				9 Jun
13.88	1.5	Akira	Sasaki	JPN	21.8.91				9 Jun
13.88	0.7	Jussi	Kanervo	FIN	1.2.93				27 Jun
13.88		Tobias	Furer	SUI	8.8.87				30 Jun
13.88	-0.2		Li Haifeng	CHN	20.11.89				8 Sep
13.89	-1.3	Tyler	Sipes	USA	9.1.90				27 Apr
13.89	1.9	Artem	Lukyanenko	RUS	30.1.90				25 May
13.89	0.6	Cameron	Hall	USA	12.5.93				25 May
13.89	0.8	Davon	Wilson-Angel	USA	8.5.91				25 May
13.89A	1.9	Genaro	Rodríguez	MEX	10.12.90				5 Jul
13.89	0.0	Alex	Al-Ameen	GBR	2.3.89				14 Jul
13.89	1.5	Sergiy	Kopanayko	UKR	5.11.88				24 Jul
13.89	1.6	Andres	Raja	EST	2.6.82				28 Jul
13.89	1.5	Kotaro	Miyau	JPN	12.7.91				7 Sep
(199)									

Wind assisted

Mark	Wind	Name		Nat	Born	Pos	Meet	Venue	Date
13.05	2.6		Oliver			1s1	NC	Des Moines	22 Jun
13.09	2.6		Merritt			2s1	NC	Des Moines	22 Jun
13.10	2.2	Sergey	Shubenkov	RUS	4.10.90	1h1	WUG	Kazan	11 Jul
13.13	2.6	Ryan	Brathwaite	BAR	6.6.88	1	DL	Birmingham	30 Jun
13.14	3.8	Wayne	Davis	TTO	22.8.91	1	NCAA	Eugene	8 Jun
13.14	2.6		Oliver			1h3	NC	Des Moines	22 Jun
13.17	2.6	Jason	Richardson	USA	4.4.86	3s1	NC	Des Moines	22 Jun
13.19	2.4		Shubenkov			1	ET	Gateshead	23 Jun
(8/6)									
13.22	4.1	David	Payne	USA	24.7.82	1h4	NC	Des Moines	22 Jun
13.24	2.1	Spencer	Adams	USA	10.9.89	1h3	NCAA	Eugene	6 Jun
13.29	2.1	Eddie	Lovett	USA/ISV	25.6.92	1	NCAA-E	Eugene	6 Jun
13.30	4.1	Keith	Hayes	USA	16.2.90	2h4	NC	Des Moines	22 Jun
13.31	2.1	Ronald	Forbes	CAY	5.4.85	1		Clermont, FL	11 May
13.31	2.6	Omo	Osaghae	USA	18.5.88	4s1	NC	Des Moines	22 Jun

Mark	Wind	Name		Nat	Born	Pos	Meet	Venue	Date
13.32	2.1	Erik	Balnuweit	GER	21.9.88	2		Clermont, FL	11 May
13.32	2.5	Devon	Hill	USA	26.10.89	2h2	NC	Des Moines	22 Jun
13.33	2.6	Johnathan	Cabral	USA	31.12.92	1rB	TexR	Austin	30 Mar
13.33	2.5	Dominic	Berger	USA	19.5.86	3h2	NC	Des Moines	22 Jun
13.37	2.7	Ashton	Eaton	USA	21.1.88	3	MSR	Walnut	20 Apr
13.37	2.3	Terence	Somerville	USA	5.11.89	1h4	NCAA-E	Greensboro	24 May
13.40	3.6	Brendan	Ames	USA	6.10.88	3h1	NC	Des Moines	22 Jun
13.41	3.0	Simon	Krauss	FRA	12.2.92	1		Castres	30 Jun
13.41	2.7	Rasul	Dabo	POR	14.2.89	2h1		La Chaux-de-Fonds	7 Jul
13.43	2.2	Matheus	Inocêncio	BRA	17.5.81	1	NC	São Paulo	9 Jun
13.43	2.9	Shane	Brathwaite	BAR	8.2.90	1		Liège (NX)	10 Jul
13.44	2.9	Joel	Brown	USA	31.1.80	2		Liège (NX)	10 Jul
13.49	2.9	Tyrone	Akins	USA	6.1.86	3		Liège (NX)	10 Jul
13.50	3.6	Andrew	Brunson	USA	4.4.86	4h1	NC	Des Moines	22 Jun
13.51	2.6	Keiron	Stewart	JAM	21.11.89	4rB	TexR	Austin	30 Mar
13.52	3.8	Don	Pollitt	USA	1.10.91	6	NCAA	Eugene	8 Jun
13.52	2.1	Koen	Smet	NED	9.8.92	1	NC	Amsterdam	21 Jul
13.53A	3.0	Jorge	McFarlane	PER	20.2.88	1		Medellín	25 May
13.53	2.7	Gianni	Frankis	GBR	16.4.88	3h1		La Chaux-de-Fonds	7 Jul
13.54	3.3	Gerkenz	Senesca	USA	6.4.90	1		Montverde, FL	1 Jun
13.55	3.3	Aleec	Harris	USA	31.10.90	1rB	MSR	Walnut	20 Apr
13.55	3.0	Trevor	Brown	USA	24.3.92	4h1	NCAA	Eugene	6 Jun
13.55	2.2	Jonathan	Mendes	BRA	14.4.90	2	NC	São Paulo	9 Jun
13.55	2.5	Chris	Thomas	USA	9.2.81	5h2	NC	Des Moines	22 Jun
13.60	4.1	Terrence	Trammell	USA	23.11.78	6h4	NC	Des Moines	22 Jun
13.62	2.2	Francisco Javier	López	ESP	29.12.89	2h1	WUG	Kazan	11 Jul
13.62	6.7	Yutaro	Furukawa	JPN	3.6.85	2		Hiratsuka	19 Oct
13.63	4.5	Jeffrey	Julmis	HAI	6.1.87	1		Manhattan, KS	11 May
13.63	2.9	Damien	Broothaerts	BEL	12.11.84	6		Liège (NX)	10 Jul
13.65	3.2	Dominik	Bochenek	POL	14.5.87	1h2		Katowice	29 May

Mark	Wind	Name		Nat	Born	Date		Mark	Wind	Name		Nat	Born	Date
13.67	3.5	Marcus	Maxey	USA	9.10.90	19 Apr		13.77	2.4	Kyohei	Mita	JPN	16.8.91	29 Apr
13.67A	2.6	Jamras	Rittidet	THA	1.2.89	27 Apr		13.77	2.6	Trey	Holloway	USA-J	7.7.94	24 May
13.68	2.1	Tre	Lathan	USA	15.7.92	13 Apr		13.78	4.5	Antonio	Alkana	RSA	12.4.90	16 Feb
13.68	2.7	Petr	Penáz	CZE	27.8.91	29 Jun		13.78	3.0	Milan	Ristic	SRB	8.8.91	20 Apr
13.69	2.1	Caleb	Cross	USA	31.5.91	13 Apr		13.78	3.6	Yuki	Matsushita	JPN	9.9.91	7 Jul
13.69	3.8	Lawson	Montgomery	USA	9.7.90	11 May		13.79	3.0	Aurel	Manga	FRA	24.7.92	24 Jun
13.71	6.7	Genta	Masuno	JPN	24.5.93	19 Oct		13.80	2.6	Joseph	Hylton	GBR	17.11.89	14 Aug
13.72	2.2	Thingalaya	Siddhanth	IND	1.3.91	14 Apr		13.81	2.1	Tjendo	Samuel	NED	19.12.89	21 Jul
13.72	3.3	Demetrius	Lindo	USA	28.3.92	20 Apr		13.81	3.9	Allan	Scott	GBR	27.12.82	11 Aug
13.72	3.8	Keith	Hopkins	USA	14.4.86	11 May		13.82	2.1	Herman	Washington	USA	29.3.92	13 Apr
13.72A	4.1	Andre	Collins	JAM	28.9.88	24 May		13.82	3.5	Jeffrey	Artis-Gray	USA	13.8.90	19 Apr
13.73A	3.0	Paulo César	Villar	COL	28.7.78	25 May		13.83	2.7	Aramis	Massenberg	USA	6.3.91	3 May
13.73	2.9	Sekou	Kaba	CAN	25.8.90	29 Jun		13.83	2.5	Maurice	Lyke	USA	6.8.89	12 May
13.75A	4.1	Ty'reak	Murray	USA	.92	24 May		13.84	3.0	Yoann	Kamara	FRA	7.4.91	30 Jun
13.76	2.2	Justin	Merlino	AUS	10.12.86	14 Apr		13.85A	4.3	Andrew	Etheridge	USA	10.7.91	24 May
13.76A	3.8	Darius	Reed	USA	2.1.88	24 May		13.86	2.6	Alex	Al-Ameen	GBR	2.3.89	14 Aug
								13.87 to 13.89w ten men						

Best at low altitude

13.67	1.4	de Vries		30 Jun		13.72	1.1	Keddo		22 Jun	
						13.77	0.0	Ames		6 Apr	

Hand timed

Mark	Wind	Name		Nat	Born	Pos	Meet	Venue	Date
13.4		Ignacio	Morales	CUB	28.1.87	1		La Habana	25 May
13.5	-1.8	Jorge	McFarlane	PER	20.2.88	31 May		13.5	Abdulaziz Al-Mandeel KUW 22.5.89 8 Apr
13.5	1.6	Milan	Trajkovic	CYP	17.9.92	8 Jun		13.5	Aleksandr Linnik BLR 28.1.91 18 Jul
								13.5	0.0 Jonathan Mendes BRA 14.4.90 20 Apr

JUNIORS

Mark	Wind	Name		Nat	Born	Pos	Meet	Venue	Date
13.81	0.6	Trey	Holloway	USA	7.7.94	3q3	NCAA-E	Greensboro	25 May
	13.77w	2.6				2h1	NCAA-E	Greensboro	24 May
13.82	0.8	Chris	Williams	USA	5.3.94	3q3	NCAA-W	Austin	25 May
13.90	-0.6		Yang Wei-Ting	TPE	22.9.94	1h2		Taipei	27 May
13.92	0.4	Takumu	Furuya	JPN-Y	12.3.97	1		Oita	2 Aug
13.93	1.2	Fredrick	Ekholm	SWE	15.6.94	1		Göteborg	30 Jun
13.94	0.9	Bryce	Grace	USA	18.7.94	2		Austin	13 Apr
13.94	1.7	Tramaoine	Maloney	BAR	1.6.94	1rB	MSR	Walnut	19 Apr
13.98	0.0	Gen	Yada	JPN	2.4.94	1	NC-j	Nagoya	18 Oct
14.03	0.4		Huang Kun-Yu	TPE	24.10.94	2	NG	Taipei	21 Oct
14.05	-0.1	Ryan	Billian (10)	USA	29.10.94	1		Akron	11 May

110 Metres Hurdles – 99 cm hurdles

Mark	Wind	Name		Nat	Born	Pos	Meet	Venue	Date
13.18	0.9	Wilhem	Belocian	FRA	6.6.95	1	EJ	Rieti	20 Jul
13.24	0.5	Omar	McLeod	JAM	25.4.94	1	N.Sch	Kingston	16 Mar
13.30	0.9	Lorenzo	Perini	ITA	22.7.94	2	EJ	Rieti	20 Jul
	13.39	1.6	1	NC-j	Rieti	15 Jun			
13.31	0.9	Brahian	Peña	SUI	3.4.94	3	EJ	Rieti	20 Jul

MEN 2013

Mark	Wind	Name		Nat	Born	Pos	Meet	Venue	Date
13.38	0.9	Tony	Brown	USA	13.7.95	1	TexR	Austin	30 Mar
	13.40	0.9 1	Austin		10 May	10 performances by 8 men to 13.40			
13.38	1.5	Marlon	Humphrey	USA-Y	8.7.96	1		Mountain Brook	13 Apr
13.40	0.9	Remy	Robillart	FRA	14.9.94	4	EJ	Rieti	20 Jul
13.42A	0.8	Juan Carlos	Moreno	COL	13.1.94	1	PAm-J	Medellín	24 Aug
13.45	0.1	David	Omoregie	GBR	1.11.95	1h3	EJ	Rieti	20 Jul
13.45	1.6	Jules	de Bont (10)	NED	23.12.94	2h2	EJ	Rieti	20 Jul
13.48	-0.1	Devon	Allen	USA	12.12.94	1	G.West	Berkeley	9 Jun
13.51	0.5	Tyler	Mason	JAM	15.1.95	2	N.Sch	Kingston	16 Mar
13.51A	0.0	Tiaan	Smit	RSA	14.3.95	1	NC-j	Pretoria	6 Apr
13.52	1.9		Huang Kun-Yu	TPE	24.10.94	1		Taipei	8 Mar
13.54	-1.2	Wellington	Zaza	USA	20.1.95	1	N.Sch	Greensboro	15 Jun
13.59	-0.1	Roger	Iribarne	CUB-Y	2.1.96	1		La Habana	1 Feb
13.61A	0.8	Daviod	Franco	VEN	12.7.95	3	PAm-J	Medellín	24 Aug
13.64	0.4	David	King	GBR	13.6.94	1	NC-j	Bedford	16 Jun
13.64	1.3	Isaiah	Moore	USA-Y	12.6.96	1	Jnr Oly	Greensboro	28 Jul
13.66	1.9		Yang Wei-Ting (20)	TPE	22.9.94	2		Taipei	8 Mar
13.66	1.0	Ruebin	Walterrs	TTO	2.4.95	1		Port of Spain	24 Mar
Wind assisted									
13.30	4.1	Marlon	Humphrey	USA-Y	8.7.96	1		Mobile	6 Apr
13.62	3.6	Benjamin	Sedecias	FRA	18.1.95	1r2		Montgeron	23 Jun

200 METRES HURDLES STRAIGHT

Mark	Wind	Name		Nat	Born	Pos	Meet	Venue	Date
22.63	-0.3	Louis 'L.J.'	van Zyl	RSA	20.7.85	1		Manchester	25 May
22.64	-0.3	Jack	Green	GBR	6.10.91	2		Manchester	25 May
22.68	-0.3	Félix	Sánchez	DOM	30.8.77	3		Manchester	25 May

400 METRES HURDLES

Mark	Name		Nat	Born	Pos	Meet	Venue	Date
47.69	Jehue	Gordon	TTO	15.12.91	1	WCh	Moskva	15 Aug
47.70	Michael	Tinsley	USA	21.4.84	2	WCh	Moskva	15 Aug
47.93	Omar	Cisneros	CUB	19.11.89	1s3	WCh	Moskva	13 Aug
47.96		Tinsley			1	NC	Des Moines	22 Jun
47.98		Tinsley			1	DL	London (OS)	27 Jul
48.00		Gordon			1	Herc	Monaco	19 Jul
48.02	Johnny	Dutch	USA	20.1.89	1		Ponce	18 May
48.05	Emir	Bekric	SRB	14.3.91	3	WCh	Moskva	15 Aug
48.06	Kerron	Clement	USA	31.10.85	2	NC	Des Moines	22 Jun
48.09	Bershawn	Jackson	USA	8.5.83	3	NC	Des Moines	22 Jun
48.10		Gordon			1s1	WCh	Moskva	13 Aug
48.10	Félix	Sánchez	DOM	30.8.77	2s3	WCh	Moskva	13 Aug
48.12		Cisneros			4	WCh	Moskva	15 Aug
48.14	Javier	Culson	PUR	25.7.84	1	Athl	Lausanne	4 Jul
48.20		Dutch			2	Herc	Monaco	19 Jul
48.21		Dutch			4	NC	Des Moines	22 Jun
48.21		Clement			3s3	WCh	Moskva	13 Aug
48.22		Sánchez			5	WCh	Moskva	15 Aug
48.31		Dutch			1	GGala	Roma	6 Jun
48.31		Tinsley			1s2	WCh	Moskva	13 Aug
48.32		Gordon			1	VD	Bruxelles	6 Sep
48.35		Culson			3	Herc	Monaco	19 Jul
48.36		Culson			2		Ponce	18 May
48.36		Culson			2	GGala	Roma	6 Jun
48.36		Bekric			2s2	WCh	Moskva	13 Aug
48.38		Culson			6	WCh	Moskva	15 Aug
48.40		Dutch			2	DL	London (OS)	27 Jul
48.42		Culson			2s1	WCh	Moskva	13 Aug
48.43		Tinsley			1	adidas	New York	25 May
48.44		Cisneros			1h1	ESP Ch	Alcobendas	27 Jul
	(30/9)							
48.46	Justin	Gaymon	USA	13.12.86	3	DL	London (OS)	27 Jul
48.50	Mamadou Kassé	Hann	SEN	10.10.86	4	Herc	Monaco	19 Jul
48.58	Reggie	Wyatt	USA	17.9.90	1	NCAA	Eugene	7 Jun
48.66	Dai	Greene	GBR	11.4.86	1	NC	Birmingham	13 Jul
48.78	Cornel	Fredericks	RSA	3.3.90	1	NC	Stellenbosch	13 Apr
48.79	Mahau	Suguimati	BRA	13.11.84	1r3		Fukuroi	3 May
48.84	Rhys	Williams	GBR	27.2.84	3rA		Luzern	17 Jul
48.84	Leford	Green	JAM	14.11.86	5	VD	Bruxelles	6 Sep
49.08	Takayuki	Kishimoto	JPN	6.5.90	1	NC	Tokyo [Chofu]	9 Jun
49.11	Louis 'L.J'	van Zyl	RSA	20.7.85	1		Velenje	4 Jun

Mark	Wind	Name		Nat	Born	Pos	Meet	Venue	Date
49.14		Jeshua (20)	Anderson	USA	22.6.89	1	MSR	Walnut	20 Apr
49.15		Roxroy	Cato	JAM	1.5.88	1		Raleigh	30 Mar
49.15		Silvio	Schirrmeister	GER	7.12.88	1	ET	Gateshead	22 Jun
49.17		Annsert	Whyte	JAM	10.4.87	4s3	WCh	Moskva	13 Aug
49.18		Piet C	Beneke	RSA	18.7.90	2	NC	Stellenbosch	13 Apr
49.19		Michael	Stigler	USA	5.4.92	2	NCAA	Eugene	7 Jun
49.19		Sebastian	Rodger	GBR	29.6.91	2	EU23	Tampere	13 Jul
49.19		Rasmus	Mägi	EST	4.5.92	3	EU23	Tampere	13 Jul
49.23		Timothy	Chalyy	RUS-J	7.4.94	1	EJ	Rieti	21 Jul
49.28		Isa	Phillips	JAM	22.4.84	5s1	WCh	Moskva	13 Aug
49.31		Yasuhiro (30)	Fueki	JPN	20.12.85	2	NC	Tokyo [Chofu]	9 Jun
49.32		Steven	White	USA	27.7.91	3	NCAA	Eugene	7 Jun
49.34		Miloud	Rahmani	ALG	13.12.83	2	Med G	Mersin	29 Jun
49.35		Mickaël	François	FRA	12.3.88	1		Ninove	27 Jul
49.37		Ali	Arastu	USA	18.6.92	4	NCAA	Eugene	7 Jun
49.39		Jeffrey	Gibson	BAH	15.8.90	5	NCAA	Eugene	7 Jun
49.40		Denis	Kudryavtsev	RUS	13.4.92	1	NC	Moskva	24 Jul
49.42		Yuta	Imazeki	JPN	6.11.87	2r3		Fukuroi	3 May
49.44		Eric	Alejandro	PUR	15.4.86	7s3	WCh	Moskva	13 Aug
49.47		Vladimir	Antmanis	RUS	12.3.84	2	NC	Moskva	24 Jul
49.49A		Sabiel (40)	Anderson	JAM	21.6.88	1	NCAA-2	Pueblo, CO	25 May
49.49		Richard	Yates	GBR	26.1.86	3	NC	Birmingham	13 Jul
49.52		Yoan	Décimus	FRA	30.11.87	2	NC	Paris (C)	14 Jul
49.56		Tristan	Thomas	AUS	23.5.86	4		Tokyo	5 May
49.57		Miles	Ukaoma	USA	21.7.92	6	NCAA	Eugene	7 Jun
49.57		Takatoshi	Abe	JPN	12.11.91	3	NC	Tokyo [Chofu]	9 Jun
49.58		Ben	Sumner	GBR	16.8.83	1		Chambéry	30 Jun
49.59A		Boniface	Mucheru	KEN	2.5.92	1	WChT	Nairobi	13 Jul
49.62		Niall	Flannery	GBR	26.4.91	2		Chambéry	30 Jun
49.62		Varg	Königsmark	GER	28.4.92	1	WK	Zürich	29 Aug
49.65		Ivan (50)	Shablyuyev	RUS	17.4.88	3	NC	Moskva	24 Jul
49.66		Winder	Cuevas	DOM	1.8.88	6		Ponce	18 May
49.66			Cheng Wen	CHN	18.3.92	1	EAsG	Tianjin	7 Oct
49.70A		Nicholas	Bett	KEN	.92	2	WChT	Nairobi	13 Jul
49.71		Yuki	Matsushita	JPN	9.9.91	3		Tokyo [Chofu]	5 Oct
49.72A		Emanuel	Mayers	TTO	9.3.89	1	CAC	Morelia	7 Jul
49.73		Georg	Fleischhauer	GER	21.10.88	1r2		Weinheim	2 Aug
49.74		Amadou	Ndiaye	SEN	6.12.92	1s2	WUG	Kazan	9 Jul
49.74		Lucirio	Garrido	VEN	4.10.88	1	Bol G	Trujillo	28 Nov
49.75		Reuben	McCoy	USA	16.3.86	1		Atlanta	17 May
49.76		Javan (60)	Gallimore	JAM	7.8.93	2h1	NC	Kingston	21 Jun
49.76		Emerson	Chalá	ECU	2.8.91	2	Bol G	Trujillo	28 Nov
49.77		Akihiko	Nakamura	JPN	23.10.90	3s1	NC	Tokyo [Chofu]	8 Jun
49.77		Artur	Langowski	BRA	8.5.91	2	NC	São Paulo	9 Jun
49.78		Thomas	Barr	IRL	24.7.92	3s2	EU23	Tampere	12 Jul
49.78		Michal	Broz	CZE	16.6.92	5	EU23	Tampere	13 Jul
49.78		Kariem	Hussein	SUI	1.4.89	1	NC	Luzern	27 Jul
49.79		Martin	Kucera	SVK	10.5.90	1	WUG	Kazan	10 Jul
49.82A		William	Mutunga	KEN	17.9.93	1	NC	Nairobi	22 Jun
49.82		Mohamed	Sghaier	TUN	18.7.88	3		Chambéry	30 Jun
49.85A		Wouter (70)	le Roux	RSA	17.1.86	1		Potchefstroom	20 Apr
49.85		Eusebio	Haliti	ITA	1.1.91	1	NC	Milano	28 Jul
49.86A		El Hadji Seth	Mbow	SEN	2.4.85	2	NCAA-2	Pueblo, CO	25 May
49.86		Keisuke	Nozawa	JPN	7.6.91	4	NC	Tokyo [Chofu]	9 Jun
49.88		Adam	Durham	USA	30.8.85	4s1	NC	Des Moines	21 Jun
49.89		Yasmani	Copello	CUB	15.4.87	2		Hérouville	13 Jun
49.89		Ian	Dewhurst	AUS	13.11.90	3s2	WUG	Kazan	9 Jul
49.90			Chen Chieh	TPE	8.5.92	2	EAsG	Tianjin	7 Oct
49.92		Hugo	Grillas	FRA	28.2.89	3	Med G	Mersin	29 Jun
49.93		Aleksandr	Skorobogatko	RUS-J	7.8.94	2	NC-j	Kazan	15 Jun
49.94		Tomoharu (80)	Kino	JPN	4.8.89	4r3		Fukuroi	3 May
49.94		Yuta	Konishi	JPN	31.7.90	4s1	NC	Tokyo [Chofu]	8 Jun
49.95		Václav	Barák	CZE	22.10.90	1	NC	Tábor	16 Jun
49.95		Øyvind	Kjerpeset	NOR	12.12.91	1		Göteborg	28 Jun

MEN 2013

Mark	Name		Nat	Born	Pos	Meet	Venue	Date
49.96	Atsushi	Yamada	JPN	3.7.91	1r2		Fukuroi	3 May
49.96	Diego	Cabello	ESP	14.1.88	1		Huelva	12 Jun
49.96		Li Zhilong	CHN	9.3.88	1		Shenyang	16 Jun
49.98	Omar	McLeod	JAM-J	25.4.94	1		Kingston	15 Mar
50.02A	Amaurys	Valle	CUB	18.1.90	3	CAC	Morelia	7 Jul
50.06	Leonardo	Capotosti	ITA	24.7.88	1		Orvieto	5 Jul
50.07	Mike	Cochrane	NZL	13.8.91	1		Sydney	9 Mar
	(90)							
50.08	Aleksandr	Derevyagin	RUS	24.3.79	4	NC	Moskva	24 Jul
50.09	Kazuaki	Yoshida	JPN	31.8.87	2		Osaka	30 Jun
50.10	Kotaro	Miyao	JPN	12.7.91	4		Tokyo (Chofu)	5 Oct
50.11	Jordin	Andrade	USA	5.5.92	1		Las Vegas	11 May
50.11		Chen Ke	CHN	14.9.89	2		Jinan	12 May
50.12	Jamele	Mason	PUR	19.10.89	8		Ponce	18 May
50.13	Jason	Harvey	IRL	9.8.91	2	NC	Dublin	28 Jul
50.14	Caleb	Cross	USA	31.5.91	3q1	NCAA-W	Austin	24 May
50.16	Daniel	O'Shea	NZL	11.2.89	3	NC	Sydney	14 Apr
50.16	Jodi-Rae	Blackwood	JAM	6.3.91	4q1	NCAA-W	Austin	24 May
	(100)							

Mark	Name		Nat	Born	Pos	Date		Mark	Name		Nat	Born	Pos	Date
50.17	David	Gollnow	GER	8.4.89	4	Jun		50.56	Dmitriy	Koblov	KAZ	30.11.92	16	May
50.22	Giacomo	Panizza	ITA	30.7.89	28	Jul		50.57	Seiya	Kato	JPN	22.11.92	8	Sep
50.23	Jesper	Arts	NED	2.4.92	30	Jun		50.58	Tatsuhiko	Mizuno	JPN	25.10.90	3	May
50.23	Tim	Rummens	BEL	16.12.87	21	Jul		50.58	Oleg	Mironov	RUS	5.3.93	26	May
50.24	Keyunta	Hayes	USA	15.2.92	21	Jun		50.58	Víctor	Solarte	VEN	6.1.86	28	Nov
50.25	Josef	Robertson	JAM	14.5.87	17	May		50.60	Drew	Branch	USA	13.5.93	13	Apr
50.25	Ludovic	Dubois	FRA	13.4.86	1	Jun		50.60	Jack	Green	GBR	6.10.91	16	Jun
50.25	Marlon	Humphrey	USA-Y	8.7.96	16	Jun		50.61	Timothy	Holmes	USA-J	22.5.94	16	Jun
50.25A	Vincent	Kosgei	KEN	11.11.85	13	Jul		50.61	Tibor	Koroknai	HUN	24.1.90	9	Jul
50.27	Kei	Maeno	JPN	10.5.91	23	Aug		50.63	Denys	Nechyporenko	UKR	7.1.90	6	Jun
50.30	Mehdi	Omara Besson	FRA	8.4.88	30	Jun		50.63	Kenta	Takeda	JPN	27.4.86	8	Jun
50.31	Hederson	Estefani	BRA	11.9.91	9	Jun		50.63	Stef	Vanhaeren	BEL	15.1.92	21	Jul
50.34	Paulo César	Villar	COL	28.7.78	28	Nov		50.64	Constant	Pretorius	RSA-J	26.1.94	13	Apr
50.35	Isaiah	Gill	USA	20.6.90	24	May		50.65	Ricardo	Lima	POR	2.1.85	12	Jun
50.35	Satinder	Singh	IND	7.2.87	7	Jul		50.65	Tom	Burton	GBR	29.10.88	13	Jul
50.35	Felix	Franz	GER	6.5.93	2	Aug		50.65		Wang Guozhong	CHN-J	31.1.95	10	Sep
50.35	Aramis	Díaz	ITA	22.11.74	3	Aug		50.66	Eric	Futch	USA	25.4.93	24	May
50.37	Takaoki	Hashimoto	JPN	18.7.92	3	May		50.66	Jack	Houghton	GBR	3.9.93	16	Jun
50.38	Yuichi	Nagano	JPN	11.1.93	3	May		50.67	Quentin	Seigel	GER	7.4.88	2	Aug
50.41	Vladimir	Guziy	RUS	3.8.88	8	Jun		50.67	Patryk	Dobek	POL-J	13.2.94	21	Sep
50.41	Alvin	Miles	USA	15.4.84	21	Jun		50.69	Yeison	Rivas	COL	24.9.87	28	Nov
50.43	Tatsuya	Hirose	JPN	13.10.91	12	May		50.70	Jonathan	Puemi	SUI	7.4.91	27	Jul
50.44	Konstantin	Andreyev	RUS	10.8.90	22	Jul		50.71	Abdelmadik	Lahoulou	ALG	7.5.92	8	Jul
50.45	Tait	Nystuen	CAN	29.5.91	8	Jul		50.71	Jacob	Paul	GBR-J	6.2.95	21	Jul
50.45	Sohei	Okada	JPN	17.9.93	20	Jul		50.72	Le Roux	Hamman	RSA	6.1.92	13	Apr
50.46	LaRon	Bennett	USA	25.11.82	17	May		50.72	Aleksey	Pogorelov	RUS	26.3.83	24	Jul
50.46	Michaël	Bultheel	BEL	30.6.86	8	Jun		50.74	Eric	Cray	PHI	6.11.88	5	Apr
50.47	Jorge	Paula	POR	8.10.84	28	Jul		50.74	Joshua	Smith	USA	.92	24	May
50.48	Andrés	Silva	URU	27.3.86	12	Aug		50.75	Yusuf	Muhammad	USA	14.1.92	11	May
50.49	Tobias	Giehl	GER	25.7.91	7	Jul		50.75A	Khallifah	Rosser	USA-J	13.7.95	24	Aug
50.50	Johnathan	Cabral	USA	31.12.92	12	May		50.76	Mirko	Schmidt	GER	16.9.88	8	Jun
50.50	Greg	Coleman	USA	24.7.93	24	May		50.77	Slater	Ezell	USA	22.11.90	19	Apr
50.51		Chen Dayu	CHN	11.1.88	12	May		50.77	Kenneth	Medwood	BIZ	14.12.87	4	May
50.51	Ethan	Holmes	USA	16.3.91	24	May		50.77	Jibri	Victorian	USA	26.6.91	4	May
50.53	Hideki	Yano	JPN	13.12.85	3	May		50.78	Andre	Peart	JAM	14.9.89	12	May
50.54	Cam	Viney	USA	6.9.93	24	May		50.78A	Daniel	Ross	USA	.91	23	May
50.54	Tatsuya	Tateno	JPN	5.8.91	4	Oct		50.78	Erik	Heggen	BEL	5.5.92	21	Jul
50.56	Cameron	French	NZL	17.5.92	6	Apr		50.79	James	Forman	GBR	12.12.91	1	Jun
50.56	Scottie	Hearns	USA-J	3.1.94	12	May			(177)					

Low altitude bests

50.06	le Roux	4		Chambéry	30 Jun		50.28	Kosgei	11 May	50.34	Mayers	11 May
50.09	Mbow	2		Charlottesville	10 May		50.34	S Anderson	27 Apr	50.45	Valle	28 Jun

JUNIORS

See main list for top 3 juniors. 10 performances by 4 men to 50.25. Additional marks and further juniors:

Chalyy	49.33	3h1	WCh	Moskva	12 Aug	50.06	5s2 WCh	Moskva	13 Aug
	49.78	1	NC-j	Kazan	15 Jun				
Skorogogatko	50.12	1s1	EJ	Rieti	20 Jul	50.20	1	Krasnodar	17 May
	50.13	2	EJ	Rieti	21 Jul				

50.25	Marlon	Humphrey	USA-Y	8.7.96	1	N.Sch	Greensboro	16 Jun
50.56	Scottie	Hearns	USA	3.1.94	2	SEC	Columbia, MO	12 May
50.61	Timothy	Holmes	USA	22.5.94	2	N.Sch	Greensboro	16 Jun
50.64	Constant	Pretorius	RSA	26.1.94	3	NC	Stellenbosch	13 Apr
50.65		Wang Guozhong	CHN	31.1.95	1h3	NG	Shenyang	10 Sep
50.67	Patryk	Dobek	POL	13.2.94	1		Gdansk	21 Sep
50.71	Jacob	Paul (10)	GBR	6.2.95	3	EJ	Rieti	21 Jul
50.75A	Khallifah	Rosser	USA	13.7.95	1		Medellín	24 Aug

Mark	Name		Nat	Born	Pos	Meet	Venue	Date	
50.83	Mitsuru	Sugai	JPN	.94	2		Hiratsuka	23	Jun
50.84	Durgesh	Kumar Pal	IND	20.4.94	1		Hyderabad	14	Aug
50.89	Patryk	Adamczyk	POL	5.1.94	4	EJ	Rieti	21	Jul
50.98	Pavel	Agafonov	RUS	28.8.95	5	EJ	Rieti	21	Jul
51.01	Byron	Robinson	USA	10.5.95	3		Greensboro	15	Jun
51.07		Wang Yang	CHN-Y	20.9.96	4		Shenyang	16	Jun
51.11	Ramfis	Vega	PUR	7.1.94	2		Ponce	20	Apr
51.16	Takumu	Furuya	JPN-Y	12.3.97	1		Oita	1	Aug
51.20	Kei	Sakamoto (20)	JPN	27.6.95	1s3		Oita	1	Aug

HIGH JUMP

Mark	Name		Nat	Born	Pos	Meet	Venue	Date	
2.41	Bogdan	Bondarenko	UKR	30.8.89	1	Athl	Lausanne	4	Jul

2.24/1 2.30/1 2.35/1 2.39/1 2.41/3 2.46/xxx

	2.41	1	WCh	Moskva		15	Aug	2.29/1 2.35/1 2.41/2 2.46/xxx
	2.38	1	DL	London (OS)		26	Jul	2.28/1 2.34/1 2.38/1 2.43/x 2.47/xx
	2.36	1	DL	Birmingham		30	Jun	2.21/1 2.28/1 2.31/1 2.34/1 2.36/1
	2.34	1=		Berdichev		6	Sep	2.20/1 2.34/2 2.37/xxx

2.40	Mutaz Essa	Barshim	QAT	24.6.91	1	Pre	Eugene	1	Jun

2.16/1 2.21/1 2.26/1 2.30/1 2.33/1 2.36/1 2.39/xx 2.40/1

	2.38	2	WCh	Moskva		15	Aug	2.20/1 2.25/1 2.29/1 2.32/2 2.35/1 2.38/1 2.41/x 2.44/xx
	2.37i	1		Moskva		3	Feb	2.20/1 2.24/1 2.27/1 2.30/1 2.37/1 2.40/xxx
	2.36i	1		Banská Bystrica		6	Feb	2.15/1 2.30/1 2.36/3
	2.34i	1		Trinec		29	Jan	2.15/1 2.20/1 2.24/1 2.28/1 2.31/3 2.34/1 2.36/x 2.38/xx

2.38	Derek	Drouin	CAN	6.3.90	3	WCh	Moskva	15	Aug

2.20/1 2.25/1 2.29/1 2.32/1 2.35/1 2.38/2 2.41/xxx

	2.36	3	Pre	Eugene		1	Jun	2.16/1 2.21/1 2.26/1 2.30/1 2.33/1 2.36/3 2.39/xxx
	2.35i	1	NCAA	Fayetteville		9	Mar	2.15/1 2.20/1 2.23/1 2.26/1 2.29/1 2.32/1 2.35/1 2.38/xxx
	2.35	1		Ninove		27	Jul	2.14/1 2.20/1 2.25/1 2.30/2 2.33/1 2.37/xxx
	2.34	1	NCAA	Eugene		7	Jun	2.15/1 2.20/1 2.24/1 2.28/1 2.31/x 2.34/2 2.39/xxx

2.37	Eric	Kynard	USA	3.2.91	2	Athl	Lausanne	4	Jul

2.20/1 2.24/1 2.27/1 2.30/1 2.33/1 2.35/x 2.37/1 2.39/x 2.41/xx

	2.36	2	Pre	Eugene		1	Jun	2.16/1 2.21/1 2.26/1 2.30/1 2.33/1 2.36/2 2.39/xxx
	2.36	2	DL	London (OS)		26	Jul	2.16/1 2.20/1 2.24/1 2.28/1 2.34/1 2.36/1 2.40/xxx
	2.34	1	MSR	Walnut		20	Apr	2.13/1 2.18/1 2.23/1 2.28/1 2.31/1 2.34/3 2.37/xxx
	2.34	2	DL	Birmingham		30	Jun	2.16/1 2.21/1 2.25/1 2.28/2 2.31/3 2.34/3 2.36/x

2.36i	Aleksey	Dmitrik	RUS	12.4.84	1		Arnstadt	2	Feb

2.27/1 2.30/1 2.33/2 2.36/1

2.35i	Sergey	Mudrov	RUS	8.9.90	1	EI	Göteborg	2	Mar

2.19/1 2.23/1 2.27/1 2.31/2 2.33/1 2.35/1 2.37/xxx

	2.34i	1	NC	Moskva		13	Feb	2.20/1 2.24/1 2.30/1 2.34/1 2.37/xxx

2.35	Ivan	Ukhov	RUS	29.3.86	4	WCh	Moskva	15	Aug

2.20/1 2.25/1 2.29/1 2.32/1 2.35/1 2.38/xxx

2.34i	Dusty	Jonas	USA	19.4.86	1		Lincoln	2	Feb

2.10/1 2.18/1 2.25/2 2.28/2 2.31/2 2.34/3

2.34	Konstadínos	Baniótis	GRE	6.11.86	1	Med G	Mersin	27	Jun

2.15/1 2.21/1 2.24/2 2.28/1 2.30/1 2.32/1 2.34/2 2.37/xxx

2.34	Yuriy	Krimarenko	UKR	11.8.83	1=		Berdichev	6	Sep
	(27/10)								

2.10/1 2.15/1 2.20/1 2.25/1 2.30/1 2.32/1 2.34/2 2.37/xxx

17 performances at 2.33: Barshim 4, Bondarenko, Drouin 3; Baniótis, Dmitrik 2; Kynard, Chesani, Wang 1

2.33i	Silvano	Chesani	ITA	17.7.88	1	NC	Ancona	17	Feb
2.33		Wang Yu	CHN	18.8.91	1		Beijing	21	May
2.32i		Zhang Guowei	CHN	4.6.91	1		Nanjing	7	Mar
2.32	Donald	Thomas	BAH	1.7.84	6	WCh	Moskva	15	Aug
2.32	Aleksandr	Shustov	RUS	29.6.84	7	WCh	Moskva	15	Aug
2.32	Andriy	Protsenko	UKR	20.5.88	3		Berdichev	6	Sep
2.32i	Andrey	Silnov	RUS	9.9.84	1		Rostov	21	Dec
2.31i	Robbie	Grabarz	GBR	3.10.87	1	NC	Sheffield	10	Feb
2.31i	Jaroslav	Bába	CZE	2.9.84	3	EI	Göteborg	2	Mar
2.31	Michael	Mason	CAN	30.9.86	2=	MSR	Walnut	20	Apr
	(20)								
2.31	Jesse	Williams	USA	27.12.83	2=	MSR	Walnut	20	Apr
2.31	Szymon	Kiecana	POL	26.3.89	2		Opole	9	Jun
2.31	Mickaël	Hanany	FRA	25.3.83	1	NC	Paris (C)	14	Jul
2.31	Mihai	Donisan	ROU	24.7.88	1	Balk C	Stara Zagora	27	Jul
2.30i	Gianmarco	Tamberi	ITA	1.6.92	3		Banská Bystrica	6	Feb
2.30i	Viktor	Ninov	BUL	19.6.88	1		Praha	14	Feb
2.30i	Dmitriy	Semyonov	RUS	2.8.92	2	NC	Moskva	13	Feb
2.30i	Daniyil	Tsyplakov	RUS	29.7.92	3	NC	Moskva	13	Feb
2.30	Ryan	Ingraham	BAH	2.11.93	1		Edmonton	29	Jun
2.29i	Ricky	Robertson	USA	19.9.90	1		Jonesboro	25	Jan
	(30)								

MEN 2013

Mark	Name		Nat	Born	Pos	Meet	Venue	Date
2.29i	Adónios	Mástoras	GRE	6.1.91	4	EI	Göteborg	2 Mar
2.29A	Kabelo Mmono	Kgosimang	BOT	7.1.86	1		Potchefstroom	6 Mar
2.29i	Marcus	Jackson	USA	8.7.91	2	NCAA	Fayetteville	9 Mar
2.29	Liam	Zamel-Paez	AUS	4.8.88	1		Perth	16 Mar
2.28	Brandon	Starc	AUS	24.11.93	1	NC	Sydney	13 Apr
2.28	Keith	Moffatt	USA	20.6.84	1		Nassau	13 Apr
2.28	Jamal	Wilson	BAH	1.9.88	3		Nassau	13 Apr
2.28	Edgar	Rivera	MEX	13.2.91	1		Tempe	27 Apr
2.28	Tom	Parsons	GBR	5.5.84	1	LI	Loughborough	19 May
2.28	Nick	Ross	USA	8.8.91	1		Westwood	1 Jun
	(40)							
2.28	Diego	Ferrín	ECU	21.3.88	1		La Habana	13 Jun
2.28	Wojciech	Theiner	POL	25.6.86	1		Iława	21 Jun
2.28	Piotr	Sleboda	POL	22.1.87	2		Iława	21 Jun
2.28	Nik	Bojic	AUS	18.1.92	4	WUG	Kazan	9 Jul
2.28	Douwe	Amels	NED	16.9.91	1	EU23	Tampere	14 Jul
2.28	Rozle	Prezelj	SLO	26.9.79	1	NC	Celje	28 Jul
2.28	Raivydas	Stanys	LTU	3.2.87	2		Rovereto	3 Sep
2.28	Naoto	Tobe	JPN	31.3.92	1		Tokyo	8 Sep
2.27i	James	White	USA	22.1.92	1		Lincoln	12 Jan
2.27i	Montez	Blair	USA	23.10.90	1		Ithaca	19 Jan
	(50)							
2.27i	Marco	Fassinotti	ITA	29.4.89	1		London (LV)	26 Jan
2.27i	Alexandru	Tufa	ROU	28.5.89	1		Bucuresti	26 Jan
2.27i	Ilya	Ivanyuk	RUS	9.3.93	2		Moskva	31 Jan
2.27i	Ivan	Ilyichev	RUS	14.10.86	2		Moskva	3 Feb
2.27i	Andrey	Patrakov	RUS	7.11.89	6	NC	Moskva	13 Feb
2.27	Takashi	Eto	JPN	5.2.91	1		Tokyo (Chofu)	6 Oct
2.26i	Ed	Wright	USA	3.3.86	1		Clemson	11 Jan
2.26i	Torian	Ware	USA	17.12.92	2		Clemson	11 Jan
2.26i	Matus	Bubeniík	SVK	14.11.89	2		Ostrava	22 Jan
2.26i	Matthias	Haverney	GER	21.7.85	3		Dresden	25 Jan
	(60)							
2.26i	Osku	Torro	FIN	21.8.79	3		Hustopece	26 Jan
2.26i	Michal	Kabelka	SVK	4.2.85	6		Hustopece	26 Jan
2.26i	Geoffrey	Davis	USA	8.8.90	1		West Lafayette	16 Feb
2.26i	James	Harris	USA	19.9.91	1		Notre Dame	2 Mar
2.26i	Ronnie	Black	USA	2.8.90	4	NCAA	Fayetteville	9 Mar
2.26	Jeron	Robinson	USA	30.4.91	1		Kingsville, TX	13 Apr
2.26	Allan	Smith	GBR	6.11.92	3=	EC-2	Tampere	14 Jul
2.26	Lev	Missirov	RUS	4.8.90	1		Moskva	15 Jul
2.26		Pai Long	CHN	8.10.89	2	NG	Shenyang	10 Sep
2.25i	Jeremy	Taiwo	USA	15.1.90	1H		Nampa	8 Jan
	(70)							
2.25i	Nikita	Anishchenkov	RUS	25.7.92	1		Volgograd	26 Jan
2.25i	Dmytro	Demyanyuk	UKR	30.6.83	2=	NC	Sumy	14 Feb
2.25i	Vitaliy	Samoylenko	UKR	22.5.84	2=	NC	Sumy	14 Feb
2.25	Trevor	Barry	BAH	14.6.83	3	Drake	Des Moines	26 Apr
2.25	Guilherme	Cobbo	BRA	1.10.87	1	da Silva	São Paulo	5 May
2.25	Eure	Yáñez	VEN	20.5.93	1		São Paulo	12 May
2.25		Wang Chen	CHN	27.2.90	4		Beijing	21 May
2.25	Miguel Ángel	Sancho	ESP	24.4.90	1	ECCp	Vila Real de S.António	25 May
2.25	Andrey	Churyla	BLR	19.5.93	1		Minsk	7 Jun
2.25	Artyom	Naumovich	BLR	19.2.91	2		Minsk	7 Jun
	(80)							
2.25	Hiromi	Takahari	JPN	13.11.87	1	NC	Tokyo [Chofu]	9 Jun
2.25	Ali Mohamed Younes	Idris	SUD	15.9.89	2		Bühl	21 Jun
2.25	Rafael	dos Santos	BRA	10.10.91	1		São Paulo	30 Jun
2.25	Donte	Nall	USA	27.1.88	1		Hilversum	7 Jul
2.25	Fabrice	Saint-Jean	FRA	21.11.80	2	NC	Paris (C)	14 Jul
2.25	Luis Joel	Castro	PUR	28.1.91	1		Köln	17 Jul
2.25	Arturo	Chávez	PER	12.1.90	1		Lima	10 Nov
2.25i	Mikhail	Veryovkin	RUS	28.6.91	1		Kineshma	8 Dec
2.24i	Sergey	Zasimovich	KAZ	11.3.86	1		Yekaterinburg	7 Jan
2.24i	Dmytro	Yakovenko	UKR	17.9.92	2		Zaporozhnye	30 Jan
	(90)							
2.24i	Kris	Kornegay-Gober	USA	6.10.91	2		Blacksburg	26 Jan
2.24i	Peter	Horák	SVK	7.12.83	6		Trinec	29 Jan
2.24i	Viktor	Shapoval	UKR	17.10.79	1		Zaporozhnye	30 Jan
2.24i	Abdoulaye	Diarra	FRA/MLI	27.5.88	2	NC	Aubière	17 Feb
2.24i		Sun Zhao	CHN	8.2.90	2		Nanjing	7 Mar

Mark	Name		Nat	Born	Pos	Meet	Venue	Date
2.24	Manjula Kumara	Wijesekara	SRI	30.1.84	1		Colombo	12 May
2.24	Martin	Günther	GER	8.10.86	1		Eppingen	30 May
2.24	Andriy	Kovalyov	UKR	11.6.92	1		Yalta	5 Jun
2.24	Anthony	May	USA	19.9.90	4	NCAA	Eugene	7 Jun
2.24	Zurab	Gogochuri	GEO	22.3.90	1	NC	Tbilisi	8 Jun
	(100)							
2.24	Vadim	Vrublevskiy	RUS	18.3.93	2		Istanbul	8 Jun
2.24	Jeffery	Herron	USA	22.4.90	1=		Ames	11 Jun
2.24	Cameron	Ostrowski	USA	15.6.92	1=		Ames	11 Jun
2.24	Mateusz	Przybylko	GER	9.3.92	5	EU23	Tampere	14 Jul
2.24i	Garrett	Huyler	USA	15.1.87	1		Ithaca	7 Dec

2.23i	Briar	Ploude	USA	9.3.91	25 Jan		2.21	Hoova	Taylor	USA	11.6.87	30 May
2.23i	Sergey	Goleshev	BLR	30.6.84	5 Feb		2.21	Jithin	Thomas	IND	1.6.90	8 May
2.23i	Justin	Frick	USA	3.8.88	16 Feb		2.21		Jin Qichao	CHN	24.11.91	8 May
2.23i	Bryan	McBride	USA	10.12.91	9 Mar		2.21	Brandon	Williams	DMA	14.12.87	8 May
2.23	Jon	Hill	USA	11.12.91	20 Apr		2.21	C.Nikhil	Chittarasu	IND	24.8.90	12 May
2.23	Talles	Souza	BRA	20.8.91	27 Apr		2.21	Randall	Cunningham	USA-Y	4.1.96	18 May
2.23	Andrea	Bettinelli	ITA	6.10.78	25 May		2.21	Nawaf Ahmed	Al-Yami	KSA	21.7.91	15 Jun
2.23	Marius	Dumitrache	ROU	15.6.89	20 Jul		2.21	Semen	Pozdnyakov	RUS	28.11.92	26 Jun
2.23		Li Peng	CHN	18.1.80	10 Sep		2.21		Bi Xiaoliang	CHN	26.12.92	7 Jul
2.23i	Andriy	Rubel	UKR	24.5.89	14 Dec		2.21	Ryo	Sato	JPN-J	21.7.94	21 Jul
2.22i	Alen	Melon	CRO	25.10.91	19 Jan		2.20i	Janis	Vanags	LAT	16.6.92	5 Jan
2.22i	Yaroslav	Rybakov	RUS	22.11.80	19 Jan		2.20i	Falk	Wendrich	GER-J	12.6.95	6 Jan
2.22i	Serhat	Birinci	TUR	13.5.90	19 Jan		2.20i	Eduard	Malchenko	RUS	24.10.86	7 Jan
2.22i	Yevgeniy	Korshunov	RUS	11.4.86	19 Jan		2.20i	Zack	Riley	USA	20.5.92	11 Jan
2.22i	Samson	Oni	GBR	25.6.81	26 Jan		2.20i	Javier	Bermejo	ESP	23.12.78	19 Jan
2.22Ai	Jules	Sharpe	USA	11.10.91	8 Feb		2.20i	Artyom	Zaytsev	BLR	7.12.84	26 Jan
2.22Ai	Deante	Kemper	USA	27.3.93	8 Feb		2.20i	Konstantin	Karpov	BLR	4.4.92	5 Feb
2.22i	Alexander	Bowen	USA	3.4.93	12 Feb		2.20	Sergio	Mestre	CUB	30.8.91	22 Feb
2.22i	Tanner	Anderson	USA	4.5.92	16 Feb		2.20	Víctor	Moya	CUB	24.10.82	22 Feb
2.22	Talles	Silva	BRA	20.8.91	27 Apr		2.20i		Yi Shisuo	CHN	20.2.90	7 Mar
2.22	Jon	Hendershot	USA	12.11.91	3 May		2.20	Mitchell	Haag	USA	24.4.91	30 Mar
2.22	Edward	Dudley	USA	21.6.92	10 May		2.20	Carlos	Layoy	ARG	26.2.91	20 Apr
2.22	Chris	Baker	GBR	2.2.91	27 May		2.20	Mohamed	Koita	FRA	8.1.90	26 Apr
2.22	Fernand	Djoumessi	CMR	5.9.89	9 Jun		2.20	Brian	Carmichael	USA	6.7.90	27 Apr
2.22	Maciej	Lepiato	POL	18.8.88	9 Jun		2.20		Lee Sung	KOR	6.5.88	3 May
2.22		Lee Hup Wei	MAS	5.5.87	21 Jun		2.20	Mark	Jones	USA	14.10.92	12 May
2.22A	Darrel	Garwood	JAM	19.9.85	7 Jul		2.20	Maalik	Reynolds	USA	26.4.92	12 May
2.22	Piotr	Milewski	POL	2.10.91	21 Jul		2.20	Angel	Kararadev	BUL	18.4.79	19 May
2.22	Tairo	Omata	JPN	12.9.89	28 Jul		2.20	Jacorian	Duffield	USA	2.9.92	7 Jun
2.22	Majed El Dein	Ghazal	SYR	21.4.87	13 Aug		2.20	Wally	Ellenson	USA-J	4.5.94	7 Jun
2.22	Josué	da Costa	BRA	15.3.93	31 Aug		2.20	Takuya	Tomiyama	JPN	7.4.85	9 Jun
2.22	Sylwester	Bednarek	POL	28.4.89	31 Aug		2.20	Ferrante	Graselli	ITA	4.4.91	14 Jun
2.22		Yoon Sung-hyun	KOR-J	1.6.94	22 Oct		2.20	Sergey	Milokumov	RUS	13.11.87	16 Jun
2.21i	Anton	Bodnar	KAZ	12.4.92	23 Jan		2.20	Vladislav	Lomidze	RUS	20.1.89	16 Jun
2.21i	Roman	Yevgenyev	RUS	6.2.88	25 Jan		2.20	Dmitriy	Pokidov	RUS	20.12.90	16 Jun
2.21i	Corey	Thomas	USA	17.7.91	25 Jan		2.20	Matt	Roberts	GBR	22.12.84	6 Jul
2.21i	Lukás	Beer	SVK	23.8.89	31 Jan		2.20		Woo Sang-hyuk	KOR-Y	23.4.96	13 Jul
2.21i	Arseniy	Rasov	RUS	23.6.92	2 Feb		2.20	Tobias	Potye	GER-J	16.3.95	20 Jul
2.21i	Simón	Siverio	ESP	2.8.88	9 Feb		2.20	Bram	Ghuys	BEL	14.2.93	21 Jul
2.21i	Keyvan	Ghanbarzadeh	IRI	26.5.90	14 Feb		2.20	Muamer Essa	Barshim	QAT-J	1.2..94	27 Jul
2.21i	Amir	Hosseinzadeh	IRI	23.3.87	14 Feb		2.20	Niki	Palli	ISR	28.5.87	29 Jul
2.21i	Jan-Peter	Larsen	NED	18.3.79	16 Feb		2.20	Davis	Smith	GBR	14.7.91	3 Aug
2.21i	Jussi	Viita	FIN	26.9.85	23 Feb		2.20	Marco	Gelati	ITA	14.2.90	29 Sep
2.21i	Nick	Ridge	USA	14.11.92	23 Feb		2.20	Nauraj Singh	Randhawa	MAS	27.9.92	20 Oct
2.21	Logan	Brittain	USA-J	30.3.94	2 Mar		2.20i	Mikhail	Akimenko	RUS-J	6.12.95	15 Dec
2.21	David	Smith	USA	2.5.92	30 Mar		2.20i	Sebastián	Deschamps	FRA	12.4.87	21 Dec
								(197)				

Best outdoors

2.31	Jonas	1	Drake	Des Moines	26 Apr		2.25	Black	3=	NC	Des Moines	23 Jun
2.31	Chesani	1		Modena	1 Jun		2.25	Blair	3=	NC	Des Moines	23 Jun
2.31	Grabarz	3	DL	Birmingham	30 Jun		2.25	Demyanyuk	2	NC	Donetsk	24 Jul
2.31	Mudrov	1	WUG	Kazan	8 Jul		2.25	Tamberi	2	NC	Milano	28 Jul
2.30	Dmitrik	4	Pre	Eugene	1 Jun		2.24	Harris	4	TexR	Austin	30 Mar
2.30	Tsyplakov	1	NC-23	Cheboksary	26 Jun		2.24	Davis	1		Knoxville	13 Apr
2.29	Zhang Guowei	Q	WCh	Moskva	13 Aug		2.24	Horák	1		Brno	14 May
2.27	Jackson	3	TexR	Austin	30 Mar		2.24	Sun Zhao	2		Shenyang	15 Jun
2.27	Fassinotti	1	NC	Milano	28 Jul		2.24	Ninov	1	NC	Pravets	16 Jun
2.27	Bába	3		Sillamäe	20 Aug		2.24	Semyonov	3	NC-23	Cheboksary	26 Jun
2.26	Ilyichev	3		Opole	9 Jun		2.24	Bubeník	3		Tábor	24 Jul
2.26	Ivanyuk	2	NC-23	Cheboksary	26 Jun		2.24	Patrakov	4	NC	Moskva	25 Jul
2.26	Mástoras	3=	EU23	Tampere	14 Jul							

2.22	Frick	20 Apr	2.21	Bodnar	8 May		2.20	Yi Shisuo	15 Jun	2.20	Melon	12 Jul
2.22	Bowen	5 May	2.21	Yakovenko	17 May		2.20	Rubel	16 Jun	2.20	Rasov	25 Jul
2.22	Korshunov	29 May	2.21	Birinci	8 Jun		2.20	Kornegay-Gober	23 Jun	2.20	Siverio	27 Jul
2.22	Tufa	9 Jun	2.21	Torro	21 Jul		2.20	Tufa	28 Jun	2.20	Diarra	14 Sep
2.22	Haverney	7 Jul	2.20	Zasimovich	16 May		2.20	Viita	7 Jul	2.20	Beer	14 Sep
2.21	Ghanbarzadeh	25 Apr	2.20	Zaitsev	7 Jun		2.20	Shapoval	9 Jul			

Mark	Name			Nat	Born	Pos	Meet	Venue		Date

JUNIORS

Mark	Name			Nat	Born	Pos	Meet	Venue		Date
2.22		Yoon Sung-hyun		KOR	1.6.94	1	NG	Incheon		22 Oct
	2.21	1	Yeongju		14 Sep			5 performances by 4 men to 2.21		
2.21	Logan	Brittain		USA	30.3.94	1		Canyon		2 Mar
2.21	Randall	Cunningham		USA-Y	4.1.96	1		Las Vegas		18 May
2.21	Ryo	Sato		JPN	21.7.94	1		Chiba		21 Jul
2.20i	Falk	Wendrich		GER	12.6.95	1		Clarholz		6 Jan
	2.18					4		Garbsen		19 May
2.20	Wally	Ellenson		USA	4.5.94	8	NCAA	Eugene		7 Jun
2.20		Woo Sang-hyuk		KOR-Y	23.4.96	1	WY	Donetsk		13 Jul
2.20	Tobias	Potye		GER	16.3.95	1	EJ	Rieti		20 Jul
2.20	Muamer Essa	Barshim		QAT	1.2..94	1		Hässleholm		27 Jul
2.20i	Mikhail	Akimenko (10)		RUS-J	6.12.95	1		Moskva		15 Dec
	2.18					1	NC-J	Kazan		16 Jun
2.19i	Yuriy	Dergachev		KAZ	8.11.94	1	NC	Shimkent		2 Feb
2.19	Chrsitoffe	Bryan		JAM-Y	26.4.96	1	N.Schj	Kingston		16 Mar
2.19	Justin	Fondren		USA	2.2.94	2	SEC	Columbia MO		12 May
2.18	Chris	Kandu		GBR	10.9.95	1	NC-J	Bedgford		16 Jun
2.18	Usman	Usmanov		RUS	26.10.95	2	NC-J	Kazan		16 Jun
2.18	Tihomir Ivaylo	Ivanov		BUL	11.7.94	2	NC	Pravets		16 Jun
2.18	Vladyslav	Dorofyeyev		UKR	22.4.94	1	NC-J	Kharkiv		17 Jun
2.18	Andrey	Skobeyko		BLR	11.6.95	1		Minsk		28 Jun
2.18	Ignacio	Vigo		ESP	11.5.94	1	NC-j	Castellón		7 Jul
2.18		Bai Jiaxu		CHN-Y	1.11.97	2	WY	Donestsk		13 Jul
2.18	Dábniel	Jankovics		HUN	1.3.95	2	NC	Budapest		27 Jul
2.18	Yohan Camilo	Chaverra		COL	21.3.95	1	SAm-J	Resistencia		20 Oct

POLE VAULT

Mark	Name			Nat	Born	Pos	Meet	Venue		Date
6.02	Renaud	Lavillenie		FRA	18.9.86	1	DL	London (OS)		27 Jul
				5.70/1	5.84/1	5.91/1	5.97/x	6.02/1	6.16/xxx	
	6.01i	1	EI	Göteborg	3 Mar	5.76/1	5.86/1	5.91/1	5.96/1 6.01/1 6.07/xxx	
	5.96	1	Herc	Monaco	19 Jul	5.86/1	5.96/1	6.02/xxx		
	5.96	1	VD	Bruxelles	6 Sep	5.67/1	5.74/1	5.81/1	5.86/1 5.96/2 6.04/xxx	
	5.95	1	Pre	Eugene	1 Jun	5.71/3	5.84/1	5.90/3	5.95/2 6.00/xxx	
	5.95	1	NC	Paris (C)	14 Jul	5.80/3	5.95/1	6.05/x		
	5.94i	1		Metz	24 Feb	5.76/1	5.82/1	5.94/1	6.00/xx	
	5.93i	1	NC	Aubière	17 Feb	5.77/3	5.87/1	5.93/3	6.00/xxx	
	5.93i	1		Aulnay-sous-Bois	21 Dec	5.75/2	5.83/1	5.93/1	6.04/xxx	
	5.92i	1eA		Rouen	26 Jan	5.70/1	5.82/1	5.87/1	5.92/3 6.00/xxx	
	5.92	1	GS	Ostrava	27 Jun	5.82/1	5.92/1	6.00/xxx		
	5.92	1	DL	Saint-Denis	6 Jul	5.77/1	5.82/1	5.92/1	6.02/xxx	
	5.89	2	WCh	Moskva	12 Aug	5.82/2	5.89/3	5.96/xxx		
	5.86i	1		Reno	18 Jan	5.70/1	5.86/2	5.92/xxx		
	5.86	2	GGala	Roma	6 Jun	5.80/2	5.86/2	5.91/xxx		
	5.85i	1		Donetsk	9 Feb	5.75/1	5.85/1	5.93/xxx		
	5.83i	1		Aubière	12 Jan	5.63/1	5.73/1	5.83/3	5.93/xxx	
	5.83i	1		Karlsruhe	2 Feb	5.83/1	5.93/xxx			
5.91	Raphael	Holzdeppe		GER	28.9.89	1	GGala	Roma		6 Jun
				5.50/2	5.70/2	5.80/1	5.91/3	5.96/xxx		
	5.89	1	WCh	Moskva	12 Aug	5.65/1	5.82/1	5.89/1	5.96/xxx	
	5.84	3	Pre	Eugene	1 Jun	5.78/2	5.84/1	5.90/xxx		
5.90i	Björn	Otto		GER	16.10.77	1		Cottbus		30 Jan
				5.50/1	5.70/2	5.80/1	5.90/3			
	5.90i	1		Düsseldorf	8 Feb	5.50/1	5.70/1	5.80/2	5.90/2	
	5.90	2	Pre	Eugene	1 Jun	5.51/2	5.71/1	5.84/x	5.90/2 5.95/xxx	
	5.85i	1	NC	Dortmund	24 Feb	5.55/1	5.70/3	5.80/x	5.85/1 6.01/xxx	
	5.85i	1		Dessau	6 Mar					
	5.83i	1		Pardubice	5 Feb	5.65/1	5.73/2	5.83/2	5.93/xx	
	5.83i	1		Potsdam	16 Feb	5.63/1	5.83/3	6.01/xxx		
	5.83	1		Athina	18 May	5.53/1	5.73/2	5.83/3	5.93/xxx	
5.86	Malte	Mohr		GER	24.7.86	3	GGala	Roma		6 Jun
				5.50/1	5.70/2	5.86/3	5.96/xxx			
	5.84	4	Pre	Eugene	1 Jun	5.51/1	5.71/3	5.84/1	5.90/xxx	
5.83i	Konstadinos	Filippídis		GRE	26.11.86	1		Linz		31 Jan
				5.45/1	5.55/1	5.63/1	5.70/1	5.77/2	5.83/3 5.91/xxx	
5.83	Brad	Walker		USA	21.6.81	1		Phoenix		17 May
				5.50/1	5.70/2	5.83/2	6.00/xxx			
5.83	Thiago	Braz da Silva		BRA	16.12.93	1	SACh	Cartagena		5 Jul
				5.20/1	5.30/1	5.40/1	5.50/1	5.65/2	5.70/2 5.83/3
	(34/7)									

Mark	Name		Nat	Born	Pos	Meet	Venue	Date	
5.82	Augusto	Dutra de Oliveira	BRA	16.7.90	1		Hof	22	Jun
5.81	Sam	Kendricks	USA	7.9.92	1	TexR	Austin	29	Mar
5.80i		Yang Yancheng	CHN	5.1.88	2		Düsseldorf	8	Feb
	(10)								
5.77i	Jan	Kudlicka	CZE	29.4.88	1	NC	Praha (Strom)	17	Feb
5.75i		Xue Changrui	CHN	31.5.91	2		Nevers	23	Feb
5.75i	Hendrik	Gruber	GER	28.9.86	3	NC	Dortmund	24	Feb
5.75i	Tobias	Scherbarth	GER	17.8.85	4	NC	Dortmund	24	Feb
5.75	Seito	Yamamoto	JPN	11.3.92	1		Hiratsuka	23	Jun
5.72	Karsten	Dilla	GER	17.7.89	1		Rottach-Egern	13	Jul
5.71i	Steve	Lewis	GBR	20.5.86	6=	EI	Göteborg	3	Mar
5.71i	Robert	Sobera	POL	19.1.91	6=	EI	Göteborg	3	Mar
5.71	Shawn	Barber	CAN-J	27.5.94	2	TexR	Austin	29	Mar
5.71	Lázaro	Borges	CUB	19.6.86	1		Madrid	13	Jul
	(20)								
5.71	Sergey	Kucheranyu	RUS	30.6.85	2		Madrid	13	Jul
5.71i	Luke	Cutts	GBR	13.2.88	1		Villeurbanne	14	Dec
5.70i	Fábio Gomes da	Silva	BRA	4.8.83	1		São Caetano do Sul	23	Feb
5.70i	Valentin	Lavillenie	FRA	16.7.91	3		Metz	24	Feb
5.70i	Andrew	Irwin	USA	23.1.93	1	NCAA	Fayetteville	8	Mar
5.70	Hiroki	Ogita	JPN	30.12.87	1	MSR	Walnut	20	Apr
5.70	Jack	Whitt	USA	12.4.90	1		Tulsa	18	May
5.70	Edi	Maia	POR	10.11.87	1		Lisboa	2	Jun
5.70	Oleksandr	Korchmid	UKR	22.1.82	1		Kyiv	14	Jun
5.70	Vladislav	Revenko	UKR	15.11.84	2		Kyiv	14	Jun
	(30)								
5.70	Giuseppe	Gibilisco	ITA	5.1.79	1	Med G	Mersin	28	Jun
5.70	Mike	Arnold	USA	13.8.90	1		Grand Rapids	10	Jul
5.70i	Dmitriy	Starodubtsev	RUS	3.1.86	1		Chelyabinsk	15	Dec
5.68	Michal	Balner	CZE	12.9.82	2		Dubnica nad Váhom	21	Aug
5.67	John	Prader	USA	10.2.91	1		San Luis Obispo	27	Apr
5.65i	Anton	Ivakin	RUS	3.2.91	1	NC	Moskva	14	Feb
5.65	Jeremy	Scott	USA	21.5.81	2	NC	Des Moines	21	Jun
5.65	Rasmus W	Jørgensen	DEN	23.1.89	1	ET-2	Kaunas	22	Jun
5.65	Igor	Bychkov	ESP	7.3.87	1	NC	Alcobendas	28	Jul
5.65	Alhaji	Jeng	SWE	13.12.81	9	WCh	Moskva	12	Aug
	(40)								
5.65i	Kévin	Menaldo	FRA	12.7.92	2		Aulnay-sous-Bois	21	Dec
5.64		Jin Min-sup	KOR	2.9.92	1		Taipei	28	May
5.62i	Jérôme	Clavier	FRA	3.5.83	2eA		Orleans	12	Jan
5.62i	Émile	Denecker	FRA	28.3.92	3eA		Rouen	26	Jan
5.62i		Zhang Wei	CHN-J	22.3.94	1		Lyon	7	Feb
5.62i	Stanley	Joseph	FRA	24.10.91	2		Villeurbanne	10	Feb
5.62i	Romain	Mesnil	FRA	13.6.77	3		Villeurbanne	10	Feb
5.62i	Robert	Renner	SLO-J	8.3.94	4		Villeurbanne	10	Feb
5.62	Ivan	Horvat	CRO	17.8.93	1		Koper	29	Jun
5.62	Mareks	Arents	LAT	6.6.86	1=		Plzen	4	Sep
	(50)								
5.61	Cale	Simmons	USA	5.2.91	3	TexR	Austin	29	Mar
5.61	Jake	Blankenship	USA-J	15.3.94	4	TexR	Austin	29	Mar
5.61	Jordan	Scott	USA	22.2.88	1		Louisville	8	Jun
5.61	João Gabriel	Sousa	BRA	6.11.84	1		São Paulo	29	Jun
5.60Ai	Mike	Woepse	USA	29.5.91	1		Albuquerque	8	Feb
5.60i	Jason	Wurster	CAN	23.9.84	1		Blacksburg	2	Mar
5.60i	Ivan	Yeryomin	UKR	30.5.89	Q	EI	Göteborg	2	Mar
5.60i	Daichi	Sawano	JPN	16.9.80	1		Taipei	15	Mar
5.60		Kim Yoo-suk	KOR	19.1.82	2	MSR	Walnut	20	Apr
5.60	Nick	Mossberg	USA	5.4.86	1		Chula Vista	2	May
	(60)								
5.60	Aleksandr	Gripich	RUS	21.9.86	1		Sochi	25	May
5.60	Artem	Burya	RUS	11.4.86	2	Chall	Moskva	11	Jun
5.60	Nikita	Filippov	KAZ	7.10.91	1		Almaty	15	Jun
5.60	Piotr	Lisek	POL	16.8.92	2	Kuso	Szczecin	15	Jun
5.60	Jeff	Coover	USA	1.12.87	4	NC	Des Moines	21	Jun
5.60	Dustin	DeLeo	USA	3.1.86	5	NC	Des Moines	21	Jun
5.60	Vincent	Favretto	FRA	5.4.84	1		Vénissieux	23	Jun
5.60	Claudio Michel	Stecchi	ITA	23.11.91	1		Rieti	5	Jul
5.60	Jere	Bergius	FIN	4.4.87	1		Lahti	15	Jul
5.60	Lukasz	Michalski	POL	2.8.88	1	NC	Torun	19	Jul
	(70)								
5.60	Daniel	Clemens	GER	28.4.92	2	Déca	Valence	31	Aug

410 POLE VAULT

Mark	Name		Nat	Born	Pos	Meet	Venue	Date
5.56	Sean	Young	USA	27.12.85	1		Clermont	11 May
5.55i	Eemeli	Salomäki	FIN	11.10.87	1		Lempäälä	26 Jan
5.55i	Maksym	Mazuryk	UKR	2.4.83	4		Pardubice	5 Feb
5.55Ai	Jake	Winder	USA	12.11.87	2	NC	Albuquerque	3 Mar
5.55	Victor	Weirich	USA	25.10.87	5	NCAA	Eugene	5 Jun
5.55	Dmitry	Zhelyabin	RUS	20.5.90	1		Hérouville	13 Jun
5.55	Przemyslaw	Czerwinski	POL	28.7.83	4		Plock	19 Jun
5.55	Michel	Frauen	GER	19.1.86	2		Leverkusen	26 Jun
5.55	Damiel	Dossévi	FRA	3.2.83	2	NC	Paris (C)	14 Jul
	(80)							
5.53i	Carlo	Paech	GER	18.12.92	6		Potsdam	16 Feb
5.53Ai	Logan	Cunningham	USA	30.5.91	1	WAC	Albuquerque	23 Feb
5.53i	Jax	Thoirs	GBR	7.4.93	1		Seattle	5 Dec
5.51i	Shawn	Francis	USA	16.12.85	1		Fargo	1 Feb
5.51	Kyle	Wait	USA	20.2.92	6	TexR	Austin	29 Mar
5.51	Colton	Ross	USA	4.6.92	7=	TexR	Austin	29 Mar
5.51	Joey	Uhle	USA	14.11.92	9	TexR	Austin	29 Mar
5.51i	Sam	Pribyl	USA	25.11.82	1		Jonesboro	10 May
5.51	Rens	Blom	NED	1.3.77	1		Zweibrücken	15 Aug
5.50Ai	Robbert Jan	Jansen	NED	22.7.83	1=		Reno	19 Jan
	(90)							
5.50Ai	Derick	Hinch	USA	2.2.91	1=		Flagstaff	2 Feb
5.50Ai	Chris	Swanson	USA	6.6.82	1=		Flagstaff	2 Feb
5.50Ai	Nicholas	Frawley	USA	21.6.88	2		Albuquerque	8 Feb
5.50i	Giorgio	Piantella	ITA	6.7.81	1	NC	Ancona	16 Feb
5.50i	Melker	Svärd Jacobsson	SWE-J	8.1.94	Q	EI	Göteborg	2 Mar
5.50Ai	Mark	Hollis	USA	1.12.84	6	NC	Albuquerque	3 Mar
5.50i		Yao Jie	CHN	21.9.90	1		Nanjing	6 Mar
5.50	Rob	Simmons	USA	5.2.91	2		Las Vegas	11 May
5.50	Viktor	Kozlitin	RUS	12.6.88	2		Sochi	25 May
5.50	Yevgeniy	Lukyanenko	RUS	23.1.85	3		Sochi	25 May
	(100)							
5.50	Dimitrios	Patsoukakis	GRE	18.3.87	1		Haniá	2 Jun
5.50	Jeremy	Klas	USA	5.9.89	6	NCAA	Eugene	5 Jun
5.50	Mickaël	Guillaume	FRA	8.9.89	2		Pierre-Bénite	7 Jun
5.50	Florian	Gaul	GER	21.9.91	3		Ingolstadt	21 Jun
5.50	Dídac	Salas	ESP	19.5.93	1		Zaragoza	22 Jun
5.50	Spas	Bukhalov	BUL	14.11.80	1		Plovdiv	20 Jul
5.50	Panayiótis	Láskaris	GRE	10.3.92	2	NC	Athína	21 Jul
5.50	Ilya	Mudrov	RUS	17.11.91	3	NC	Moskva	24 Jul
5.50i	Dmitriy	Sokolov	RUS	16.1.93	2		Chelyabinsk	15 De
5.50i	Gayk	Kazaryan	RUS	19.5.90	1		Moskva	22 Dec

Mark	Name		Nat	Born	Date
5.45i	Baptiste	Boirie	FRA	26.12.92	19 Jan
5.45i	Alexandre	Feger	FRA	22.1.90	26 Jan
5.45i	Aleksey	Kovalchuk	RUS	22.7.88	14 Feb
5.45i	Anatoliy	Bednyuk	RUS	30.1.89	14 Feb
5.45i	Marco	Boni	ITA	21.5.84	16 Feb
5.45i	Andrew	Sutcliffe	GBR	10.7.91	23 Feb
5.45i	Mick	Viken	USA	21.9.90	1 Mar
5.45	Germán	Chiaraviglio	ARG	16.4.87	19 Jun
5.45	Ruben	Miranda	POR	10.6.93	4 Jul
5.45	David	Moya	ESP	6.12.89	17 Jul
5.45		Zhou Bo	CHN	10.1.89	7 Sep
5.44i	Aaron	Unterberger	USA	12.7.89	2 Mar
5.42i	Joe	Wesley	USA	19.3.90	15 Feb
5.42i	Andreas	Duplantis	SWE	2.5.93	24 Feb
5.42	Josh	Dangel	USA	21.1.91	15 Jun
5.42	Chip	Heuser	USA	9.2.85	15 Jun
5.42	Tom	Konrad	GER	30.3.91	13 Jul
5.42	Alexander	Straub	GER	14.10.83	13 Jul
5.42	Rutger	Koppelaar	NED	1.5.93	21 Jul
5.41i	Dustin	Gehrke	USA	11.5.90	9 Feb
5.41i	Kevin	Lazas	USA	25.1.92	9 Feb
5.41i	Kyal	Meyers	USA	5.9.91	9 Feb
5.41i	Stephan	Munz	GER	19.10.88	23 Feb
5.41i	Cyriel	Verberne	NED	4.12.84	9 Mar
5.41	Thomas	Reinecke	USA	30.9.90	28 Mar
5.41	Chase	Wolfle	USA	.94	28 Mar
5.41	Chris	Pillow	USA	8.7.93	28 Mar
5.41	Chase	Brannon	USA	8.2.91	12 May
5.41	Leo	Lohre	GER	14.10.90	20 May
5.41	Manel	Concepción	ESP	27.3.90	13 Jul
5.41i	Arnaud	Art	BEL	28.1.93	14 Dec
5.40i	Diogo	Ferreira	POR	30.7.90	6 Jan
5.40i	Mikhail	Gelmanov	RUS	18.3.90	9 Jan
5.40i	Andrej	Poljanec	SLO	10.11.84	13 Jan
5.40i	Robert	Rasnick	USA	7.10.88	19 Jan
5.40i	Grigoriy	Gorokhov	RUS	20.4.93	26 Jan
5.40i	Matthew	Bane	USA	3.2.92	26 Jan
5.40i	Levi	Keller	USA	30.1.86	26 Jan
5.40i	Matteo	Rubbiani	ITA	31.8.78	27 Jan
5.40i	Scott	Houston	USA	11.6.90	2 Feb
5.40i	Eelco	Sintnicolaas	NED	7.4.87	10 Feb
5.40i	Nikandros	Stylianou	CYP	22.8.89	23 Feb
5.40Ai	Daniel	Gooris	USA	28.9.89	2 Mar
5.40i	Steve	Hooker	AUS	16.7.82	9 Mar
5.40i	Zach	Ziemek	USA	23.2.93	9 Mar
5.40	Daven	Murphree	USA-J	20.10.94	30 Mar
5.40	Ryo	Tanaka	JPN	11.12.92	13 Apr
5.40	Stéfanos	Koufidís	GRE	14.5.88	13 Apr
5.40	Jordan	Yamoah	USA	30.9.93	25 May
5.40	Casey	Bowen	USA	11.1.93	25 May
5.40	Reese	Watson	USA	8.10.93	25 May
5.40	Alex	Bishop	USA	17.5.91	25 May
5.40	Tyler	Porter	USA	14.12.91	5 Jun
5.40	Adam	Lisiak	POL	8.5.90	8 Jun
5.40	Timur	Skorykh	UKR	14.5.92	14 Jun
5.40	Stanislav	Tivinchik	BLR	5.3.85.	14 Jun
5.40	Baurzhan	Serikbayev	KAZ	27.10.91	15 Jun
5.40	Alexandre	Marchand	FRA	23.2.90	15 Jun
5.40		Han Do-hyun	KOR-J	28.7.94	11 Jul
5.40	Tomoki	Yamamoto	JPN	25.8.92	14 Jul
5.40	Jonas	Efferoth	GER	3.2.93	22 Jul
5.40	Lukás	Posekany	CZE	30.12.92	24 Jul
5.40	Denys	Yurchenko	UKR	27.1.78	26 Jul
5.40	Nariharu	Matsuzawa	JPN	6.1.92	4 Aug
5.40	Ilya	Shkurenov	RUS	11.1.91	11 Aug
5.40	Hiroki	Sasase	JPN	17.8.89	25 Aug

Mark		Name		Nat	Born	Pos	Meet	Venue	Date
5.40	Perttu	Korhonen	FIN	7.7.90			25 Aug
5.40		Lu Yao	CHN	19.9.87			7 Sep
5.40	Naoya	Kawaguchi	JPN	18.6.87			22 Sep
5.38i	Nico	Weiler	GER	5.4.90			23 Feb

5.38i	Nicolas	Homo	FRA	24.11.88	20 Dec
5.38i	Axel	Chapelle	FRA-J	24.4.95	20 Dec
5.38i	Theo	Chapelle	FRA	28.5.92	20 Dec
	(183)

Best outdoors

5.82	Filippídis	1 DL	Doha	10 May
5.76	Kudlicka	1 NC	Tábor	15 Jun
5.70	Scherbarth	3 NC	Ulm	7 Jul
5.70	Lewis	6 Herc	Monaco	19 Jul
5.70	Cutts	4 DL	London (OS)	27 Jul
5.65	Irwin	1	Fayetteville	30 Mar
5.65	V Lavillenie	1	Montreuil-sous-Bois	3 Jun
5.65	Xue Changrui	1	Shenyang	15 Jun
5.63	Ivakin	3	Athina	18 May
5.63	Gruber	4	Athina	18 May
5.61	Sobera	1	Lodz	18 May

5.46	Salomäki	8 Sep	5.42	Joseph	1 Aug
5.45	Clavier	30 Jun	5.40	Gehrke	12 May
5.45	Feger	14 Jul	5.40	Wurster	12 May
5.42	Hollis	13 Jul	5.40	Viken	25 May

5.60	Sawano	3 MSR	Walnut	20 Apr
5.60	G da Silva	1	São Paulo	5 May
5.60	Yeryomin	1	Kharkov	16 Jun
5.60	Menaldo	2 MedG	Mersin	28 Jun
5.52	Paech	1	Hohen Neuendorf	12 May
5.50	Woepse	2	Chula Vista	2 May
5.50	Piantella	1	Modena	1 Jun
5.50	Thoirs	2	Somero	29 Jun
5.50	Svärd Jacobsson	2	Rieti	5 Jul
5.50	Yang Yancheng	2 NG	Shenyang	7 Sep
5.50	Yao Jie	3 NG	Shenyang	7 Sep

5.40	Gorokhov	5 Jun	5.40	Sokolov	25 Jun
5.40	Kovalchuk	6 Jun	5.40	Sintnicolaas	30 Jun
5.40	Sutcliffe	8 Jun	5.40	Jansen	6 Jul
5.40	Stylianou	22 Jun	5.40	Bednyuk	24 Jul
			5.40	Zhang Wei	7 Sep

Exhibtion – slightly downhill 5.83 sq Jan Kudlicka CZE 29.4.88 1   Praha   19 Jun
5.45/2   5.65/1   5.75/2   5.83/1   5.88/xxx

JUNIORS

See main list for top 5 juniors. 13 performances by 4 men to 5.51. Additional marks and further juniors:

Barber	5.60i	1		Ypsilanti	11 Jan	5.56i	1		Akron	18 Jan
	5.60	3	NCAA	Eugene	5 Jun	5.51i	1		Blacksburg	9 Feb
	5.58i	1		Akron	3 Feb
Zhang	5.54i	6		Villeurbanne	10 Feb
Blankenship	5.60i	4	NCAA	Fayetteville	8 Mar	5.51i	1		Birmingham, AL	9 Feb
	5.55i	2	SEC	Fayetteville	24 Feb

5.40		Han Do-hyun	KOR	28.7.94	6	WUG	Kazan	11 Jul
5.38i	Axel	Chapelle	FRA	24.4.95	7=		Aulnay-sous-Bois	20 Dec
	5.32				3		Aulnay-sous-Bopis	5 Jun
5.33	Oleg	Zernikel	GER	16.4.95	1B		Landau	21 Aug
5.32i	Menno	Vloon	NED	11.5.94	5	NC	Apeldoorn	17 Feb
5.31	Eirik Greibrokk	Dolve (10)	NOR	5.5.95	1B		Kuortane	6 Jul
5.31	Leonid	Kobelev	RUS	24.6.95	1		Sankt-Peterburg	8 Jun
5.30	Hayoto	Hotta	JPN	17.11.94	1		Gifu	13 Oct
5.30i	Dmitriy	Lyubushkin	RUS	23.3.94	4		Chelyabinsk	15 Dec
	5.20				9		Sochi	25 May
5.27	Hussain Asim	Al-Hizam	KSA-Y	4.1.98	1		Riyadh	8 May
5.27	Dylan	Duvio	USA	6.4.95	2		Hammond	23 Apr
5.26	Chris	Williams	USA	5.3.94	2	Pac 12	Los Angeles	11 May
5.26	Devin	King	USA-Y	12.3.96	1		Mobile	6 Apr
5.25	Harry	Coppell	GBR-Y	11.7.96	1	WY	Donetsk	14 Jul
5.25	Rowan	May	GBR	12.8.95	4	EJ	Rieti	20 Jul
5.23i	Medhi Amar	Rouana (20)	FRA	30.3.94	2c2		Aulnay-sous-Bois	20 Dec

LONG JUMP

8.56	0.2	Aleksandr		Menkov	RUS	7.12.90	1	WCh	Moskva			16 Aug
							8.14	7.96	8.52/0.2	8.43/0.5	8.56	x
	8.42	0.9 2	WUG	Kazan		12 Jul	7.90	8.03	x	8.16	8.42	8.34/0.7
	8.39	1.7 1	Pre	Eugene		31 May	x	x	8.11	x	8.39	x
	8.36	1.9 1	ET	Gateshead		22 Jun	7.90	8.33/1.9	7.82w	8.36
	8.31i	1	EI	Göteborg		3 Mar	8.28	x	x	8.31	x	x
	8.31	-0.2 2	DL	Shanghai		18 May	7.91	x	8.09	x	x	8.31
	8.31	0.6 1	DL	London (OS)		27 Jul	x	x	7.69	x	x	8.31
	8.27	0.6 1	DL	Birmingham		30 Jun	7.80	8.14	8.08	8.27	8.22	8.26/-0.3
8.46	1.3	Luis		Rivera	MEX	21.6.87	1	WUG	Kazan			12 Jul
							x	8.08	x	8.46	8.12	x
	8.30	1.3 1	Kuso	Szczecin		15 Jun	7.92	x	8.05	8.30	x	p
	8.27	0.6 3	WCh	Moskva		16 Aug	7.92	8.16	8.17	8.03	8.27	x
8.37	1.1	Eusebio		Cáceres	ESP	10.9.91	1	EU23	Tampere			12 Jul
							x	8.08	8.09	8.37	p	p
	8.26	0.8 4	WCh	Moskva		16 Aug	8.09	8.25/0.4	8.17	x	8.26	8.20
	8.25	0.0 Q	WCh	Moskva		14 Aug	8.25	p	p
8.34	1.1			Li Jinzhe	CHN	1.9.91	1	DL	Shanghai			18 May
							7.91	7.93	8.20	8.34	p	p
	8.34	-0.6 1	NG	Shenyang		8 Sep	7.91	8.19	x	8.34	p	p
	8.31	0.1 1		Beijing		21 May	8.31	x	8.18	p	p	p

Mark	Wind	Name		Nat	Born	Pos	Meet	Venue		Date
8.32	-0.8	Zarck	Visser	RSA	15.9.89	1	WK	Zürich		29 Aug
					8.01	8.05	8.32	x	p	p
	8.29	-0.7 NC	Stellenbosch	13 Apr	8.29	x	8.11	x	7.44	x
8.31	1.4	Mauro Vinícius	da Silva	BRA	26.12.86	1	NC	São Paulo		7 Jun
					8.05	8.31	8.18	8.15w	p	p
8.30	1.9	Khotso	Mokoena	RSA	6.3.85	1		Bad Langensalza		15 Jun
					7.74	8.28w/2.5	7.86	8.09	7.64	8.30
8.29i		Michel	Tornéus	SWE	26.5.86	2	EI	Göteborg		3 Mar
					8.27	8.10	x	7.95	7.12	8.29
8.29	2.0	Alyn	Camara	GER	31.3.89	2		Bad Langensalza		15 Jun
					7.71	x	8.00	8.11w	7.91	8.29
8.29	0.4	Ignisious	Gaisah (10)	GHA/NED	20.6.83	2	WCh	Moskva		16 Aug
					8.09	8.15	8.17	8.29	x	8.16
8.28i		Marquis	Dendy	USA	17.11.92	1	NCAA	Fayetteville		8 Mar
					x	x	8.10	8.23	8.28	x
	8.25i	1 Fayetteville		23 Feb	x	8.25	8.22	p	8.24	p
8.27	1.8	Christian	Reif	GER	24.10.84	3		Bad Langensalza		15 Jun
					7.81w	7.90	p	7.97w	8.02	8.27
	8.26	1.8 1 Weinheim		25 May	x	8.26	8.07	p	x	x
8.25	1.3	Fabrice	Lapierre	AUS	17.10.83	1		Houston		20 Jun
8.25	0.5	Damar	Forbes	JAM	18.9.90	1	NC	Kingston		22 Jun
		(30/14)								
8.23	1.8	Salim	Sdiri	FRA	26.10.78	1		Pierre-Bénite		7 Jun
8.23	0.4	Loúis	Tsátoumas	GRE	12.2.82	1	NC	Athina		21 Jul
8.22	1.6	Greg	Rutherford	GBR	17.11.86	3	Pre	Eugene		31 May
8.22	2.0	Jeff	Henderson	USA	19.2.89	2	NC	Des Moines		23 Jun
8.21	1.5	Chris	Tomlinson	GBR	15.9.81	4		Bad Langensalza		15 Jun
8.19	1.9	Ron	Taylor	USA	13.8.90	1		Chula Vista		19 Jul
		(20)								
8.17	1.0	Yeóryios	Tsákonas	GRE	22.1.88	2		Dakar		12 Jun
8.17	1.6	George	Kitchens	USA	16.1.83	1		Chula Vista		5 Jul
8.16	-1.8	Sergey	Polyanskiy	RUS	29.10.89	1	NCp	Yerino		16 Jun
8.15	0.9	Mike	Hartfield	USA	29.3.90	2	TexR	Austin		29 Mar
8.15	1.2	Marcos	Chuva	POR	8.8.89	3	WUG	Kazan		12 Jul
8.13	1.8	Tyron	Stewart	USA	8.7.89	*		Chula Vista		6 Jun
8.13	1.7	Tyrone	Smith	BER	7.8.86	2	Kuso	Szczecin		15 Jun
8.11i		Eero	Haapala	FIN	10.7.89	1		Pori		26 Jan
8.11	1.7	Adrian	Vasile	ROU	9.4.86	1		Bucuresti		21 Jul
8.10A	1.8	Ndiss Kaba	Badji	SEN	21.9.83	*		El Paso		13 Apr
		(30)								
8.10	1.2	Will	Claye	USA	13.6.91	4	Pre	Eugene		31 May
8.10	-1.8	Konstantin	Safronov	KAZ	2.9.87	1		Almaty		16 Jun
8.09A	1.1	Jarvis	Gotch	USA	25.3.92	1		Levelland		4 May
8.09	1.3	Kumaravel	Prem Kumar	IND	6.2.93	1		New Delhi		5 Aug
8.08	1.7		Kim Duk-hyun	KOR	8.12.85	1		Ansan		5 May
8.08	0.3		Su Xiongfeng	CHN	21.3.87	2	NG	Shenyang		8 Sep
8.07	0.5	Julian	Howard	GER	3.4.89	2		Wesel		30 May
8.06	1.0	Kirill	Sukharev	RUS	24.5.92	1		Moskva		11 May
8.06	0.3	Wilfredo	Martínez	CUB	9.1.85	1		Salamanca		12 Jun
8.06		Sergey	Morgunov	RUS	9.2.93	1	NC	Moskva		25 Jul
		(40)								
8.05	1.4	J.J.	Jegede	GBR	3.10.85	1		Clermont, FL		13 Apr
8.05	0.4	Stefan	Brits	RSA	19.1.92	1	ACC	Raleigh		19 Apr
8.05	1.1	Tomasz	Jaszczuk	POL	9.3.92	3	Kuso	Szczecin		15 Jun
8.04i		Jeremy	Hicks	USA	19.9.86	1		Baton Rouge		15 Feb
8.04i		Daniel	Dobrev	BUL	7.4.92	1	NC	Dobrich		16 Feb
8.04	0.2	Ngonidzashe	Makusha	ZIM	11.3.87	3		Beijing		21 May
8.04	-0.2	Sebastian	Bayer	GER	11.6.86	2	NC	Ulm		6 Jul
8.03i		Tomas	Vitonis	LTU	19.9.91	1		Kuldiga		19 Jan
8.03	-0.4	Yves	Zellweger	SUI	27.3.87	1		Oberteuringen		15 Jun
8.02i			Gao Xinglong	CHN-J	12.3.94	1		Nanjing		6 Mar
		(50)								
8.02	0.3	Junior	Díaz	CUB	28.4.87	1	NC	La Habana		17 Mar
8.02	1.5	Nicolas	Gomont	FRA	15.9.86	2		Bonneuil-sur-Marne		7 Jun
8.02	1.0	Higor	Alves	BRA-J	23.2.94	1		São Paulo		29 Jun
8.02	1.3	Kafétien	Gomis	FRA	23.3.80	2	NC	Paris (C)		14 Jul
8.02	-0.9	Julian	Reid	GBR	23.9.88	2		Loughborough		23 Jul
8.01	0.9	Mitchell	Watt	AUS	25.3.88	2		Melbourne		6 Apr
8.01	1.9	Luis Felipe	Méliz	ESP	11.8.79	6		Bad Langensalza		15 Jun
8.01	2.0	Kiril	Agoyev	KAZ	13.6.90	*	NC	Almaty		20 Jul
8.01	1.4	Tommy	Evilä	FIN	6.4.80	3		Lapinlahti		21 Jul

Mark	Wind	Name		Nat	Born	Pos	Meet	Venue	Date
8.01	0.2	Christian	Taylor	USA	18.6.90	2		Zagreb	3 Sep
		(60)							
8.00i			Zhao Xiaoxi	CHN	19.3.89	2		Nanjing	6 Mar
8.00	0.5	Samson	Idiata	NGR	28.2.82	1		Castellón	23 May
8.00	1.4	Vasiliy	Kopeykin	RUS	9.3.88	1		Yerino	2 Jun
8.00	1.5		Kim Sang-su	KOR	5.6.84	2		Goseong	19 Jun
8.00		Mohammad	Arzandeh	IRI	30.10.87	1		Tehran	21 Jun
8.00	1.6	Alessio	Guarini	ITA	5.4.85	1	NC	Milano	27 Jul
7.99A	-0.4	Irving	Saladino	PAN	23.1.83	1	NC	San José, CRC	12 Mar
7.99	1.2		Tang Gongchen	CHN	24.4.89	1		Jinan	12 May
7.99		Hussein	Al-Sabee	KSA	14.11.79	1	Arab C	Doha	24 May
7.99	0.5		Zhang Yaoguang	CHN	21.6.93	1		Shenyang	15 Jun
		(70)							
7.99	0.6	Aleksandr	Petrov	RUS	9.8.86	2	NCp	Yerino	16 Jun
7.99	1.1	Pavel	Shalin	RUS	15.3.87	1		Moskva	3 Jul
7.99	-0.6	Paulo Sérgio	Oliveira	BRA	1.6.93	1		São Paulo	31 Aug
7.99	1.2		Jie Lei	CHN	8.5.89	Q	NG	Shenyang	7 Sep
7.98i		Valentin	Toboc	ROU	17.3.92	1	NC	Bucuresti	10 Feb
7.98	0.9	Povilas	Mykolaitis	LTU	23.2.83	1		Marijampole	4 Jul
7.97	1.4	Gor	Nerkaryan	ARM	24.3.93	1		Campinas	27 Apr
7.97		Jermaine	Jackson	JAM	29.5.86	1		Kingston	1 Jun
7.97	0.7	Mario	Kral	GER	15.2.89	1		Weinheim	2 Aug
7.97	-0.7		Huang Changzhou	CHN-J	20.8.94	4	NG	Shenyang	8 Sep
		(80)							
7.96i		Emanuele	Catania	ITA	3.10.88	1		Ancona	3 Feb
7.96A	w?	Rushwal	Samaai	RSA	25.9.91	1		Germiston	9 Mar
7.96	0.3		Zhang Xiaoyi	CHN	25.5.89	5	NG	Shenyang	8 Sep
7.95i		Pavel	Karavayev ¶	RUS	27.8.88	1		Moskva	11 Jan
7.95i		Raymond	Higgs	BAH	24.1.91	1		Fayetteville	11 Jan
7.95i		Stefano	Tremigliozzi	ITA	7.5.85	1	NC	Ancona	16 Feb
7.95	0.7	Jorge	McFarlane	PER	20.2.85	1	NC	Lima	2 Jun
7.95	1.4		Wang Jianan	CHN-Y	27.8.96	1	AsiC	Pune	5 Jul
7.95	-0.2	Dwight	Phillips	USA	1.10.77	Q	WCh	Moskva	14 Aug
7.94i		Maksim	Kolesnikov	RUS	28.2.91	1		Sankt-Peterburg	5 Jan
		(90)							
7.94		Hicham	Douiri	MAR	26.2.85	1		Meknès	16 Feb
7.94i		Matthew	Burton	GBR	18.12.87	1	NC	Sheffield	9 Feb
7.94		Nick	Gordon	JAM	17.9.88	1		Kingston	13 Apr
7.93i			Li Chengbin	CHN	22.2.90	4		Nanjing	6 Mar
7.93	0.4	Jarrion	Lawson	USA-J	6.5.94	1q	NCAA-W	Austin	23 May
7.93	-1.1	Mikko	Kivinen	FIN	16.1.88	1		Jämsä	29 Jun
7.93A	0.8	Jean Marie	Okutu	ESP	4.8.88	1		Monachil	29 Jun
7.93	1.4	Larona	Koosimile	BOT	14.10.85	Q	WUG	Kazan	11 Jul
7.92i		Elvijs	Misans	LAT	8.4.89	Q	EI	Göteborg	2 Mar
7.92	2.0	Rogério	Bispo	BRA	16.11.85	2		São Paulo	27 Mar
		(100)							

7.91i		Kevin	Ojiaku	ITA	20.4.89	16 Feb		7.87	1.7	Rikiya	Saruyama	JPN	15.2.84	7 Jul
7.91		Ankit	Sharma	IND	20.7.92	25 Apr		7.87	1.0	Yves	Renaux	FRA	12.6.86	7 Jul
7.91	1.1	Tiago	da Silva	BRA	23.10.93	7 Jun		7.86	1.3	James	McLachlan	GBR	12.3.92	19 Apr
7.91	0.7	Denis	Bogdanov	RUS	2.4.91	7 Jun		7.86	0.5	Yuhi	Oiwa	JPN	17.2.91	23 Jun
7.91	-0.4	Fabian	Heinle	GER-J	14.5.94	30 Jun		7.86	1.1	Edwin	Murillo	COL	31.8.91	5 Jul
7.91	0.0	Daniel	Bramble	GBR	14.10.90	13 Jul		7.86	-0.3	Elliott	Safo	GBR-J	4.2.94	19 Jul
7.91	0.3	Bradley	Pickup	GBR	4.4.89	23 Jul		7.85i		Japeth	Cato	USA	25.12.90	22 Feb
7.91	1.3	Yohei	Sugai	JPN	30.8.85	4 Oct		7.85	0.0	Basil	George	IND	1.6.89	15 Mar
7.90	0.2	Adrian	Strzalkowski	POL	28.3.90	31 May		7.85	1.7	Aaron	Hill	USA	8.4.92	23 Mar
7.90	0.7	Taras	Neledva	UKR	7.6.92	6 Jun		7.85	0.8	Reindell	Cole	USA	16.2.88	20 Apr
7.90	1.8	Anatoliy	Ryapolov	RUS-Y	21 Jun			7.85	-1.3		Zhang Yu	CHN	17.7.92	12 May
7.90	0.3	Yevgeniy	Antonov	RUS	26.4.92	3 Jul		7.85		Mohamed Fathallah Difallah	EGY	26.8.87	24 May
7.90	1.1	Michal	Rejmus	POL	8.9.91	13 Jul		7.85	-1.1	Artyom	Primak	RUS	14.1.93	25 May
7.89	0.7	Milan	Pírek	CZE	17.7.87	14 May		7.85		M.	Arshad	IND	5.1.91	5 Jun
7.89		Vartan	Pahlevanyan	ARM	27.2.88	18 Sep		7.85	0.7	Rain	Kask	EST	11.6.91	16 Jun
7.88	1.1	Emiliano	Lasa	URU	25.1.90	3 Apr		7.85A	1.1	Alberto	Álvarez	MEX	8.3.91	5 Jul
7.88	-0.3	Denis	Eradiri	BUL	24.10.83	23 May		7.85	0.2	Michael	Schrader	GER	1.7.87	10 Aug
7.88	1.5	Mihail	Mertzanídis-Despotéris GRE	21.8.87	8 Jun		7.84i		Kamal	Fuller	JAM	20.1.91	23 Feb
								7.84	-0.4		Yu Zhenwei	CHN	18.3.86	12 May
7.88	0.1	Krzysztof	Lewandowski	POL	8.11.86	15 Jun		7.84	0.9	Zlatozar	Atanasov	BUL	12.12.89	16 Jun
7.88	0.8	Matthias	Prey	GER	9.8.88	15 Jun		7.84	-1.0	Mathias	Broothaerts	BEL-J	12.7.94	19 Jul
7.88	0.2	Ronni	Ollikainen	FIN	27.8.90	27 Jul		7.84	0.9	Shin-ichiro	Shimono	JPN	10.10.90	23 Aug
7.88	0.9	Kota	Minemura	JPN	22.12.92	7 Sep		7.83i		Mamadou	Gueye	SEN	1.4.86	18 Jan
7.87i		Patrick	Rädler	GER	23.9.90	22 Feb		7.83i		Benjamin	Compaoré	FRA	5.8.87	17 Feb
7.87i		Jeffrey	Artis-Gray	USA	13.8.90	22 Feb		7.83	2.0	Janis	Leitis	LAT	13.4.89	26 May
7.87i		Taylor	Stewart	CAN	11.4.91	9 Feb		7.83	0.9		Lin Qing	CHN-J	5.4.95	12 May
7.87		Arsan	Sarkisyan	RUS	13.12.84	26 May		7.83	2.0	Laderrick	Ward	USA	28.12.92	23 May
7.87A		Elijah	Kimitei	KEN	.86	22 Jun		7.83	0.0	Douglas	da Conceição	BRA	1.6.91	25 May

Mark	Wind	Name		Nat	Born	Pos	Meet	Venue	Date
7.83	0.1	Dino	Pervan	CRO	12.1.91	11	Jul		
7.83	1.0	Yasuhiro	Moro	JPN-J	21.12.94	7	Sep		
7.82i		Malcolm	Pennix	USA	30.10.89	23	Feb		
7.82	-1.2	Maicel	Uibo	EST	27.12.92	11	Apr		
7.82	0.6	Ted	Hooper	USA	31.1.91	10	May		
7.82		Ahmad Fayez	Marzouk	KSA	6.9.79	24	May		
7.82	1.6	José Luis	Despaigne	CUB-J	1.2.95	25	May		
7.82	-0.2	Jairo	Guibert	CUB	22.2.84	15	Jun		
7.82		Fabrizio	Schembri	ITA	27.1.81	3	Jul		
7.82	1.9	Diego	Hernández	VEN-J	21.2.95	19	Sep		
7.81i		Oleksiy	Kasyanov	UKR	26.8.85	15	Feb		
7.81	0.3	Duwayne	Boer	RSA-J	6.1.95	13	Apr		
7.81	0.6		Li Jin	CHN	23.5.90	28	Apr		
7.81A		Lingo	Ubang	ETH	10.7.93	30	Jun		
7.81	-0.8	Robert	Martey	GHA	27.12.84	27	Jul		
7.81	0.6	Teddy	Tamgho	FRA	15.6.89	31	Aug		
7.80		Marquise	Cherry	USA	26.3.93	2	Mar		
7.80	1.5	Tyler	Stepp	USA	8.2.91	13	Apr		
7.80	1.7		Chen Changhang	CHN	3.10.93	12	May		
7.80	0.8	Eddy	Florian	DOM	20.2.89	22	Jun		
7.80	-0.7	Feron	Sayers	GBR-J	15.10.94	30	Jun		
7.80	0.5	Thomas	Van Der Plaetsen	BEL	24.12.90	8	Jul		
7.80		Vitaliy	Muravyov	RUS	1.10.93	4	Aug		
7.80	0.4	Gunnar	Nixon	USA	13.1.93	10	Aug		
7.80	-2.1	Henry	Dagmil	PHI	7.12.81	15	Dec		
		(180)							

Wind assisted

Mark	Wind	Name		Nat	Born	Pos	Meet	Venue	Date
8.35	2.9	Damar	Forbes	JAM	18.9.90	1	NCAA	Eugene	6 Jun
					x		8.35w	8.14w p	p	7.95
	8.34w	1 SEC	Columbia, MO		11 May		8.17w x	8.02 x	x	8.34w
8.31	3.3	Jeremy	Hicks	USA	19.9.86	1		Baton Rouge	20 Apr
					8.03		7.77 8.31w	x	p	7.93
8.29	2.3	Marquis	Dendy	USA	17.11.92	2	SEC	Columbia, MO	11 May
					8.00w		7.66 x	8.29w x		8.10w
8.24	2.3	Loúis	Tsátoumas	GRE	12.2.82	1		Göteborg	15 Jun
8.23	2.8	George	Kitchens	USA	16.1.83	1	NC	Des Moines	23 Jun
8.22	2.7		Kim Duk-hyun	KOR	8.12.85	1		Goseong	19 Jun
8.20	5.3	Ngonidzashe	Makusha	ZIM	11.3.87	1	FBK	Hengelo	8 Jun
8.18A	2.4	Jarvis	Gotch	USA	25.3.92	1		Lubbock	25 Apr
8.14	2.1	Tyron	Stewart	USA	8.7.89	1		Chula Vista	6 Jun
8.13	3.1	Rogério	Bispo	BRA	16.11.85	1		São Paulo	23 Feb
8.13	3.0	Julian	Howard	GER	3.4.89	1		Karlsruhe	23 Jun
8.12	3.1	Michel	Tornéus	SWE	26.5.86	2		Göteborg	15 Jun
8.12	3.1	Kumaravel	Prem Kumar	IND	6.2.93	2		Chula Vista	19 Jul
8.11A	2.6	Ndiss Kaba	Badji	SEN	21.9.83	1		El Paso	13 Apr
8.07	3.0	Christian	Taylor	USA	18.6.90	6	NC	Des Moines	23 Jun
8.06	2.1	Vasiliy	Kopeykin	RUS	9.3.88	1		Sotteville-lès-Rouen	8 Jul
8.04	2.4	Kiril	Agoyev	KAZ	13.6.90	1	NC	Almaty	20 Jul
8.03	2.3	Bryce	Lamb	USA	9.11.90	1	Big 12	Waco	4 May
8.03	2.3	Raymond	Higgs	BAH	24.1.91	2	NCAA	Eugene	6 Jun
8.01	2.6	Jorge	McFarlane	PER	20.2.88	2	SACh	Cartagena	5 Jul
8.00	3.7	Rain	Kask	EST	11.6.91	1		Rakvere	16 Jun
7.99	2.1	Adrian	Strzalkowski	POL	28.3.90	1	Franc	Nice	11 Sep
7.98	4.3	Rikiya	Saruyama	JPN	15.2.84	1		Hirakata	13 Jul
7.97	2.5	Dimítrios	Diamadáras-Despotéris	GRE	18.7.84	1	Veniz	Haniá	8 Jun
7.96	2.6		Li Chengbin	CHN	22.2.90	1		Hong Kong	29 Jun
7.94	3.4	Jeffrey	Artis-Gray	USA	13.8.90	2	ACC	Raleigh	19 Apr
7.92	2.4	Simon	Hechler	GER	15.6.88	15	Jun		
7.92A	3.1	Andre	Jefferson	USA-J	14.5.94	23	Aug		
7.91	2.3	Hamed	Suleman	USA	14.7.90	11	May		
7.90	2.8	Tarik	Batchelor	JAM	22.3.90	13	Apr		
7.88A	2.1	Jamal	Bowen	PAN	5.1.91	12	Mar		
7.87	3.4	Ronald	Brookins	USA	5.7.89	13	Jun		
7.87	2.1	Kyron	Blaise	TTO	3.10.89	22	Jun		
7.87	2.2	Yuhi	Oiwa	JPN	17.2.91	13	Jul		
7.86	3.0	Janis	Leitis	LAT	13.4.89	26	Apr		
7.86	3.0	Cameron	Hudson	USA-J	5.3.94	6	Jun		
7.86	3.6	Alper	Kulaksiz	TUR	6.4.92	27	Jul		
7.83	3.7	Jharyl	Bowery	CAN	28.1.90	6	Jun		
7.83	3.7	Marcin	Starzak	POL	20.10.85	12	Jun		
7.82	4.4	Guy-Elphège	Anouman	FRA	13.6.94	28	Apr		
7.82	4.8	Benoît	Maxwell	FRA	2.5.88	23	Jun		
7.81	3.4	Curtis	Beach	USA	22.7.90	5	Jun		
7.80	2.2	Seref	Osmanoglou	TUR	2.1.89	24	Aug		

Best at low altitude

Mark	Wind	Name				Venue	Date
8.01	0.2	Badji	1		Villeneuve d'Ascq		19 May
7.94	-1.5	Saladino	3	SACh	Cartagena		5 Jul
7.90	0.4	Gotch				6 Apr	
7.90	0.4	Ojiaku				2 Jun	

Best outdoors

Mark	Wind	Name				Venue	Date
8.10	1.3	Dendy	5	NC	Des Moines	23 Jun	
8.03	0.0	Hicks	*		Baton Rouge	20 Apr	
8.00	1.6	Tornéus	*		Göteborg	15 Jun	
7.98	1.4	Gao Xinglong	1	NC-j	Jiaxing	21 Apr	
7.92	2.0	Catania	1		Rieti	12 May	
7.89	1.3	Misans		22 Jun		7.81 0.4	Burton	14 Jun		7.80		Kolesnikov	3 Jul
7.84	0.0	Cato		27 Apr		7.84w 2.7		17 Aug		7.80 1.8	Stewart	12 Jul
7.83	1.8	Fuller		6 Jun		7.81 0.9	Zhao Xiaoxi	12 May				
7.92	0.0	Toboc	2		Bucuresti	25 Aug	
7.90	0.4	Ojiaku	1		Mondovi	2 Jun	
7.90	0.4	Higgs	*	NCAA	Eugene	6 Jun	
7.90	1.0	Haapala	1		Turku	16 Jun	
7.96w	2.8	1 ET-1	Dublin (S)		22 Jun		

JUNIORS

See main list for top 5 juniors. 1Q performances by 5 men to 7.92. Additional marks and further juniors:

Name	Mark	Wind			Venue		Date
Alves	7.95Aw	2.9 & 7.92A	1.2	1 PAm-J	Medellín		23 Aug
Huang	7.95	0.3 Q	NG	Shenyang		8 Sep	
Wang	7.93i	-		Fuzhou	23 Mar	7.92 -0.2 5	Beijing	21 May
Lawson	7.92i	-	4	NCAA Fayetteville	8 Mar		
7.91	-0.4	Fabian	Heinle	GER	14.5.94	1	Mannheim	30 Jun
7.90	1.8	Anatoliy	Ryapolov	RUS-Y	31.1.97	1 NC-y	Chelyabinsk	21 Jun

Mark	Wind	Name		Nat	Born	Pos	Meet	Venue	Date
7.86	-0.3	Elliott	Safo	GBR	4.2.94	1	EJ	Rieti	19 Jul
7.84	-1.0	Mathias	Broothaerts	BEL	12.7.94	2	EJ	Rieti	19 Jul
7.83	0.9	Lin Qing (10)		CHN	5.4.95	4		Jinan	12 May
7.83	1.0	Yasuhiro	Moro	JPN	21.12.94	2		Tokyo	7 Sep
7.82	1.6	José Luis	Despaigne	CUB	1.2.95	2		La Habana	25 May
7.82	1.9	Diego	Hernández	VEN	21.2.95	1		Caracas	19 Sep
7.81	0.3	Duwayne	Boer	RSA	6.1.95	3	NC	Stellenbosch	13 Apr
7.80	-0.7	Feron	Sayers	GBR	15.10.94	2		Mannheim	30 Jun
7.76A	0.2	Travonn	White	USA	3.6.95	1		Albuquerque	8 Jun
7.75i		Lamont Marcell	Jacobs	ITA	26.9.94	1	NC-j	Ancona	23 Feb
7.75	1.3	Nikólaos	Xenikákis	GRE	23.12.94	3	Veniz	Haniá	8 Jun
7.74A	-0.2	Andre	Jefferson	USA	14.5.94	*	PAm-J	Medellín	23 Aug
7.73		Angus	Gould	AUS	8.1.94	1		Sydney	14 Apr
7.72	2.0	Stephan	Hartmann (20)	GER	13.1.94	2	NC-j	Rostock	28 Jul

Wind assisted

Mark	Wind	Name		Nat	Born	Pos	Meet	Venue	Date
7.92A	3.1	Andre	Jefferson	USA	14.5.94	2	PAm-J	Medellín	23 Aug
7.86	3.0	Cameron	Hudson	USA	5.3.94	4	NCAA	Eugene	6 Jun
7.79	5.7	Shotaro	Saruyama	JPN	5.3.95	1		Sapporo	22 Sep
7.73	2.8	Zoheir	Laroussi	FRA	9.6.94	2		Pierre-Bénite	7 Jun
7.73	2.4	Natsuki	Yamakawa	JPN	24.7.95	1		Nara	13 Jun
7.72	2.8	Kodai	Sakuma	JPN-Y	29.4.96	1		Sagamihara	21 Sep

TRIPLE JUMP

Mark	Wind		Meet	Name	Born/Venue	Pos	Series					
18.04	0.3			Teddy	Tamgho	FRA	15.6.89	1	WCh	Moskva		18 Aug
							17.65/-1.5	x	x	17.68/0.2	x	18.04
17.47	0.2	2 DL	Birmingham			30 Jun	x	x	17.47	x	x	x
17.45	0.8	* NC	Paris (C)			13 Jul	17.10	x	x	17.49w	x	17.45
17.41	0.7	Q WCh	Moskva			16 Aug	x	17.41				
17.40	0.1	2 Athl	Lausanne			4 Jul	16.92	17.40	x	17.11	x	x
17.30	2.0	1	Besançon			15 Jun	x	x	x	17.19	17.30	16.34
17.30	-0.1	1 VD	Bruxelles			6 Sep	x	x	16.88	x	17.27/0.0	17.30
17.70i				Daniele	Greco	ITA	1.3.89	1	EI	Göteborg		2 Mar
							17.00	x	17.15	17.70	p	x
17.25	0.3	2 Herc	Monaco			19 Jul	x	15.58	16.74	16.54		17.25
17.69	2.0			Pedro Pablo	Pichardo	CUB	30.6.93	1	Barr	La Habana		4 Jun
							17.69	13.92	p	p	p	p
17.68	-0.2	2 WCh	Moskva			18 Aug	17.38/0.3	17.68	x	17.22	17.52/-0.1	16.98
17.58	0.5	1 Athl	Lausanne			4 Jul	17.32/1.0	x	17.43/0.1	17.24/0.3	p	17.58
17.49	1.0	1	Bilbao			21 Jun	17.49	p	p	p	p	p
17.32nwi		1	La Habana			20 Dec	17.11	17.62	x	p	p	p
17.31	0.9	1	La Habana			24 May	17.31	p	p	p	p	p
17.66	0.9			Christian	Taylor	USA	18.6.90	1	DL	Birmingham		30 Jun
							16.98	17.12	17.32/0.4	17.19	17.66	16.97
17.36	0.2	Q WCh	Moskva			16 Aug	17.36					
17.30	1.6	1 Herc	Monaco			19 Jul	17.08	17.30	x	16.72	x	17.23
17.25	0.5	1 DL	Doha			10 May	16.67	17.11	17.06	16.89	x	17.25
17.52	0.5			Will	Claye	USA	13.6.91	3	WCh	Moskva		18 Aug
							17.19	17.33/-0.1	17.52	17.38/0.1	16.94	17.46/0.5
17.47	2.0	1	Chula Vista			5 Jul	16.86	17.22	17.07	17.32/1.3	17.47	p
17.46	-1.5			Ernesto	Revé	CUB	26.2.92	1	NC	La Habana		16 Mar
							x	16.82	17.11w	17.46	x	x
17.37	0.5	1	Belém			12 May	16.52	17.37	p	x		
17.35		1	La Habana			23 Feb	17.35	p	p	x		
17.32	0.7	2 Barr	La Habana			4 Jun	16.64	16.60	17.32	p	p	p
17.45	0.9			Yoann	Rapinier	FRA	29.9.89	2	NC	Paris (C)		13 Jul
							17.00	16.37	17.30/1.1	16.76	x	17.45
17.39	0.5	Q WCh	Moskva			16 Aug	16.79	17.39				
17.36	1.4			Samyr	Laine	HAI	17.7.84	1	MSR	Walnut		20 Apr
							17.36	x	p	p	p	p
17.30i				Ruslan	Samitov	RUS	11.2.91	2	EI	Göteborg		2 Mar
							16.51	x	16.97	x	17.30	17.03
17.26	0.0			Cao Shuo (10)		CHN	8.10.91	1	NG	Shenyang		10 Sep
							16.90	16.72	17.19	17.26	16.72	p
17.24	1.7			Marian	Oprea	ROU	6.6.82	1	Balk C	Stara Zagora		28 Jul
				(31/11)			17.19	17.24	x	x	p	16.96
17.22	0.0			Ryan	Grinnell	USA	4.2.87	1		Chicago		27 Jun
17.16i					Dong Bin	CHN	22.11.88	1		Nanjing		7 Mar
17.13	-0.1			Aleksey	Fyodorov	RUS	25.5.91	1	EU23	Tampere		14 Jul
17.10	0.6			Roman	Valiyev	KAZ	27.3.84	1		Bangkok		4 May
17.09	1.3			Zlatozar	Atanasov	BUL	12.12.89	1		Burgas		19 May
17.07	1.3			Benjamin	Compaoré	FRA	5.8.87	1		Montreuil-sous-Bois		3 Jun

MEN 2013

Mark	Wind	Name		Nat	Born	Pos	Meet	Venue	Date
17.07	0.3	Gaëtan	Saku Bafuanga	FRA	22.7.91	1		La Roche-sur-Yon	24 Jul
17.05	0.7	Dimítrios	Tsiámis	GRE	12.1.82	1	NC	Athina	20 Jul
17.02i		Viktor	Kuznetsov	UKR	17.7.86	4	EI	Göteborg	2 Mar
		(20)							
16.98	0.6	Renjith	Maheswary	IND	30.1.86	1		Chennai	7 Jun
16.98	-0.3	Fabrizio	Schembri	ITA	27.1.81	1	NC	Milano	28 Jul
16.96i		Bryce	Lamb	USA	9.11.90	1	NCAA	Fayetteville	9 Mar
16.94i		Harold	Corréa	FRA	26.6.88	1	NC	Aubière	16 Feb
16.94	1.8	Jefferson	Sabino	BRA	4.11.82	1	NC	São Paulo	9 Jun
16.92	1.9	Omar	Craddock	USA	26.4.91	1	NCAA	Eugene	8 Jun
16.87i		Tosin	Oke	NGR	1.10.80	1	GBR Ch	Sheffield	9 Feb
16.86	2.0	Fabrizio	Donato	ITA	14.8.76	5	Athl	Lausanne	4 Jul
16.84i		Yuriy	Kovalyov	RUS	18.6.91	1	NC-23	Volgograd	24 Feb
16.84		Arpinder	Singh	IND	30.12.92	1		Patiala	23 Apr
		(30)							
16.84	1.7	Jonathan	Silva	BRA	21.7.91	2	NC	São Paulo	9 Jun
16.83i		Karl	Taillepierre	FRA	13.8.76	2	NC	Aubière	16 Feb
16.82	1.4	Lyukman	Adams	RUS	24.9.88	1		Sochi	26 May
16.81	1.5	Alwyn	Jones	AUS	28.2.85	1		Melbourne	6 Apr
16.79	1.1	Julian	Reid	GBR	23.9.88	1	NC	Birmingham	14 Jul
16.78	1.9	Chris	Benard	USA	4.4.90	1		Chula Vista	8 Jun
16.77	1.2	Rafeeq	Curry	USA	19.8.83	6	NC	Des Moines	20 Jun
16.76	-0.6	Igor	Spasovkhodskiy	RUS	1.8.79	2	NC	Moskva	24 Jul
16.74	1.9	Aleksey	Tsapik	BLR	4.8.88	1		Brest	24 May
16.74	1.9	Nathan	Douglas	GBR	4.12.82	2	NC	Birmingham	14 Jul
		(40)							
16.73i		Fabian	Florant	NED	1.2.83	1		Fayetteville	9 Feb
16.73	0.5	Yochai	Halevi	ISR	10.5.82	1	ET-2	Kaunas	22 Jun
16.71	1.7	Vicente	Docavo	ESP	13.2.92	1		Cáceres	11 May
16.69	0.0	Chris	Carter	USA	11.3.89	2		Beijing	21 May
16.68	1.9	Nelson	Évora	POR	20.4.84	1		Lisboa (U)	9 Jun
16.67i		Yevgen	Semenenko	UKR	17.7.84	1	NC	Sumy	14 Feb
16.67	1.8	Julien	Kapek	FRA	12.1.79	2	MSR	Walnut	20 Apr
16.67	1.9	Aleksandr	Lebedko	BLR	24.5.87	1		Brest	30 May
16.67	0.0	Artyom	Primak	RUS	14.1.93	1	NC-23	Cheboksary	26 Jun
16.67	0.4	Aleksandr	Yurchenko	RUS	30.7.92	2	NC-23	Cheboksary	26 Jun
		(50)							
16.67	0.0	Aboubacar	Bamba	FRA	20.6.91	4		Villeneuve d'Ascq	19 May
16.67	1.3		Nguyen Van Hung	VIE	4.3.89	1	SEAG	Nay Pyi Taw	19 Dec
16.66	1.8	Tareq	Bougtaïb	MAR	30.4.81	3	Franc	Nice	13 Sep
16.66	1.1	Karol	Hoffmann	POL	1.6.89	4	Franc	Nice	13 Sep
16.65i		Michele	Boni	ITA	2.4.81	1		Ancona	19 Jan
16.63	1.8	Lázaro	Martínez	CUB-Y	3.11.97	1	WY	Donetsk	13 Jul
16.62	0.5	Viktor	Yastrebov	UKR	13.1.82	1	NC	Donetsk	27 Jul
16.59i		Vladimir	Letnicov	MDA	7.10.81	1	Balk C	Istanbul	23 Feb
16.59Ai		Josh	Honeycutt	USA	7.3.89	1	NC	Albuquerque	3 Mar
16.58	0.7	Jhon Freddy	Murillo	COL	13.6.84	1	NC	Cartagena	14 Jun
		(60)							
16.58i		Georgi	Tsonov	BUL	2.5.93	Q	EI	Göteborg	1 Mar
16.57	0.8	Yevgeniy	Ektov	KAZ	1.9.86	3	WUG	Kazan	9 Jul
16.56	1.1	José Ernesto	Martínez	CUB	1.1.91	3	Barr	La Habana	4 Jun
16.55	1.0	Jadel	Gregório	BRA	16.9.80	Q	NC	São Paulo	8 Jun
16.55	0.2	Michal	Lewandowski	POL	28.8.88	1	Sidlo	Sopt	13 Jul
16.55	0.9	Dmitriy	Kolosov	RUS	19.5.86	5	NC	Moskva	24 Jul
16.54i		Hugo	Mamba-Schlick	CMR	1.2.82	3		Metz	24 Feb
16.53i		Tarik	Batchelor	JAM	22.3.90	1		Fayetteville	24 Feb
16.53	1.1	Yuriy	Opatskiy	UKR	5.11.79	2	NC	Donetsk	27 Jul
16.51	0.0	Issam	Nima	ALG	8.4.79	3		Baie Mahault	8 May
		(70)							
16.51	0.2	Maksym	Moskalenko	UKR	20.10.87	2		Yalta	7 Jun
16.51	-0.3	Askin	Karaca	TUR	20.10.90	3	Balk C	Stara Zagora	28 Jul
16.50i		Kola	Adedoyin	GBR	8.4.91	2	NC	Sheffield	9 Feb
16.50i		James	Jenkins	USA	31.3.84	2		Fayetteville	9 Feb
16.50i			Zhang Yaoguang	CHN	21.6.93	2		Nanjing	7 Mar
16.49	1.7	Roumen	Dimitrov	BUL	19.9.86	*	NC	Pravets	15 Jun
16.49	2.0	Aleksi	Tammentie	FIN	6.8.86	1	NC	Vaasa	28 Jul
16.49A	0.4	Timothy	White-Edwards	USA-J	15.7.94	1		Medellín	25 Aug
16.48	0.7		Fang Yaoqing	CHN-Y	20.4.96	2	WY	Donetsk	13 Jul
16.47	1.2	Alexandre	Hochuli	SUI	19.1.84	7	Athl	Lausanne	4 Jul
		(80)							
16.47	2.0	Louhab	Kafia	ALG	24.2.87	1		Alger	5 Jul

Mark	Wind	Name		Nat	Born	Pos	Meet	Venue		Date
16.47	0.6		Xu Xiaolong	CHN	20.12.92	1		Lanzhou		26 Jul
16.46		Sief el Islem	Temacini	ALG	5.3.88	1		Alger		27 Apr
16.46	-0.2		Huang Qiang	CHN-J	18.12.95	2	NC	Suzhou		1 Jun
16.46	-2.4	Mamadou Chérif	Dia	MLI	13.3.85	1		Aubagne		6 Jul
16.46	0.7	Igor	Syunin	EST	4.12.90	1		Kohila		31 Aug
16.45A		Elijah	Kimitei	KEN	.86	1	NC	Nairobi		22 Jun
16.45A	-1.2	Yordanis	Durañona	DMA/ex CUB	16.6.88	1	CAC	Morelia		7 Jul
16.44i		Latario	Collie-Minns	BAH-J	10.3.94	1		Lincoln		2 Feb
16.44	-0.1	Phillips	Idowu	GBR	30.12.78	7	GGala	Roma		6 Jun
		(90)								
16.44	1.9	Andreas	Graber	SUI	20.5.92	1	NC	Luzern		26 Jul
16.44			Zhang Yu	CHN	17.7.92	2		Lanzhou		26 Jul
16.44	0.6	Muhammad Hakimi	Ismail	MAS	8.4.91	2	SEAG	Nay Pyi Taw		19 Dec
16.43i		Michael	Puplampu	GBR	11.1.90	3	NC	Sheffield		9 Feb
16.43	0.0	Sheryf	El Sheryf/Osmanoglou	UKR/TUR	2.1.89	8	GGala	Roma		6 Jun
16.43	0.7	Jaanus	Uudmäe	EST	24.12.80	2		Kohila		31 Aug
16.43	-0.3		Fu Haitao	CHN	1.11.93	3	NG	Shenyang		10 Sep
16.41	1.4	Sergey	Laptev	RUS	7.2.91	4		Sochi		26 May
16.40i		Maksim	Nesterenko	BLR	1.9.92	2		Gomel		16 Feb
16.40	1.7	Takayuki	Tsunoyama	JPN	9.6.85	1		Naka		18 May
		(100)								
16.40		Rashid Ahmed	Al-Mannai	QAT	18.6.88	2	Arab C	Doha		23 May

Mark	Wind	Name		Nat	Born	Pos		Mark	Wind	Name		Nat	Born	Pos
16.39A	0.6	Alberto	Álvarez	MEX	8.3.91	7 Jul		16.31	-2.8	Jean	Rosa	BRA	1.2.90	6 Apr
16.37i		José Emilio	Bellido	ESP	25.5.87	16 Feb		16.31	-0.7		Sun Qiang	CHN	31.10.91	11 May
16.36	1.3	Yohei	Kajikawa	JPN	8.11.83	9 Jun		16.30	1.5	Yuma	Okabe	JPN	13.7.90	29 Apr
16.36	-0.4	Jules	Lechanga	FRA	19.11.86	6 Jul		16.30A	0.5	Angel	Delgado	VEN	6.1.88	19 May
16.36	0.0	Daigo	Hasegawa	JPN	27.2.90	22 Sep		16.30	0.0	Yevgeniy	Chetykbayev	KAZ	29.3.88	15 Jun
16.35	1.9	Manuel	Ziegler	GER	28.7.90	8 Jun		16.30	0.2	Dmitriy	Platnitskiy	BLR	26.8.88	18 Jul
16.35	-1.0	Andreas	Pohle	GER	6.4.81	6 Jul		16.28	0.8		Kong Guanyong	CHN	18.3.88	27 Apr
16.35	-0.1	Adrian	Swiderski	POL	26.9.86	3 Aug		16.28		Lasha	Torgvaidze	GEO	26.5.93	11 May
16.34i		Jean-Noël	Cretinoir	FRA-J	28.12.94	2 Mar		16.28	1.5	Pablo	Torrijos	ESP	12.5.92	30 Jun
16.34	1.9	Kaual Kamal	Bento	BRA	10.1.93	16 Mar		16.27	1.9	Hamed	Suleman	USA	14.7.90	29 Mar
16.33A	0.9	Roger	Haitengi	NAM	12.9.83	22 Apr		16.27	1.0	Mathias	Ström	SWE	30.12.87	8 Sep
16.33	0.8	Alexandru George	Baciu	ROU	25.2.91	13 Jul		16.26	0.5	Theerayut	Philakong	THA	27.2.84	19 Dec
16.33	-1.5	Paulo Sérgio	Oliveira	BRA	1.6.93	20 Oct		16.25i		Marquis	Dendy	USA	17.11.92	24 Feb
16.32	2.0	Chris	Hercules	TTO	14.5.79	8 Jun		16.25	1.1	Sergey	Yarmak	RUS	21.3.86	24 Jul

Wind assisted

Mark	Wind	Name		Nat	Born	Pos	Meet	Venue		Date
17.49	2.1		Tamgho			1	NC	Paris (C)		13 Jul
17.32	2.3	Marian	Oprea	ROU	6.6.82	1		Bucuresti		28 Jun
					16.88		17.32w	p	p	p
17.22	3.3	Igor	Spasovkhodskiy	RUS	1.8.79	1	ECCp	Vila Real de S.António		26 May
17.15	2.2	Omar	Craddock	USA	26.4.91	1	NC	Des Moines		20 Jun
17.01	3.3	Issam	Nima	ALG	8.4.79	1	Arab C	Doha		23 May
16.92	3.2	Chris	Carter	USA	11.3.89	4	NC	Des Moines		20 Jun
16.85	2.4	Georgi	Tsonov	BUL	2.5.93	1		Parow		16 Feb
16.85	2.1	Fabian	Florant	NED	1.2.83	1		Hilversum		7 Jul
16.82	2.2	Jean	Rosa	BRA	1.2.90	3	NC	São Paulo		9 Jun
16.82A	4.9	Jhon Freddy	Murillo	COL	13.6.84	1		Medellín		6 Oct
16.78	2.4	Josh	Honeycutt	USA	7.3.89	5	NC	Des Moines		20 Jun
16.71	3.8	Pablo	Torrijos	ESP	12.5.92	1	NC	Alcobendas		28 Jul
16.61	2.4	Roumen	Dimitrov	BUL	19.9.86	1	NC	Pravets		15 Jul
16.48	2.1	Manuel	Ziegler	GER	28.7.90	2	NCAA	Eugene		8 Jun
16.45	5.1	Kevin	Luron	FRA	8.11.91	1		Montgeron		22 Jun
16.45	2.9	Jean-Noël	Cretinoir	FRA	28.12.94	2		Antony		19 May
16.45	3.3	Yohei	Kajikawa	JPN	8.11.83	1		Hiratsuka		7 Jul
16.41	2.8	Paulo Sérgio	Oliveira	BRA	1.6.93	2		Campinas		15 Sep
16.40	2.2	Wilbert	Walker	JAM	7.1.85	21 Jun		16.25	2.4	Olu	Olamigoke	USA	19.9.90	3 May
16.37	3.3	Nkosinza	Balumbu	USA	16.3.87	20 Jun		16.25	6.0	Cameron	Parker	BAH	.90	5 May
16.28	2.7	Pávlos	Bóftsis	GRE	17.9.92	20 Jul		16.25	2.1		Kim Dong-hyun	KOR	5.6.89	6 May
16.27	2.8		Yoo Jae-hyuk	KOR	13.5.89	6 May		16.25	2.6	José Alfonso	Palomanes	ESP	2.1.89	22 Jun
16.27	4.7	Anders	Møller	DEN	5.9.77	26 May		16.25	3.7	Shoichi	Matsushita	JPN	18.4.89	7 Jul

Best outdoors

17.01	1.0	Kuznetsov		1	WUG	Kazan		9 Jul			
16.98	1.1	Dong Bin		Q	WCh	Moskva		16 Aug			
16.92	0.0	Corréa		1		Villeneuve d'Ascq		19 May			
16.67	-0.3	Florant		*		Hilversum		7 Jul			
16.64	0.5	Oke		5	DL	Doha		10 May			
16.55	0.7	Honeycutt		*	NC	Des Moines		20 Jun			

16.54	0.0	Taillepierre	1		Montgeron	12 May
16.54	0.0	Samitov	2		Sochi	26 May
16.54	0.1	Semenenko	4		Beijing	21 May
16.50	1.8	Mamba-Schlick	4	FR Ch Paris (C)	13 Jul
16.41	0.7	Collie-Minns	1	JUCO Hutchinson	17 May
16.41	-0.1	Zhang Yaoguang	4	NG Shenyang	10 Sep
16.50w	4.4	Jenkins	8	NC Des Moines	20 Jun

16.36	-1.4	Kovalyov	30 Jun		16.31	1.0	Álvarez	24 Apr
16.35	0.7	Nesterenko	18 Jul		16.26		Letnicov	2 Jun
					16.25	1.1	Bellido	11 May
					16.25	0.4	Cretinoir	19 May

Best at low altitude

16.75w	2.4	J F Murillo	1	Bol G Trujillo	26 Nov

Mark	Wind	Name		Nat	Born	Pos	Meet	Venue			Date

JUNIORS

See main list for top 5 juniors. 11 performances by 6 men to 16.30. Additional marks and further juniors:

Mark	Wind		Name		Nat	Born	Pos	Meet	Venue			Date
Martínez	16.58	1		La Habana		20 Dec		16.49A -1.8 1	PAm-J Medellín			25 Aug
	16.53	1.1 4	Barr	La Habana		4 Jun						
Fang	16.31	0.6 3	NC	Suzhou			1 Jun					
16.34i			Jean-Noël	Cretinoir	FRA	28.12.94	1		Ancona			2 Mar
	16.25	0.4					2		Antony			19 May
16.18i			Felix	Obi	USA	10.3.94	1	Big 12	Ames			24 Feb
16.14	5.0		Mateus Daniel	de Sá	BRA	21.11.95	2	SAm-J	Resistencia			20 Oct
16.10	0.8		Ryuma	Yamamoto	JPN	14.7.95	1		Tokyo (Chofu)			7 Oct
16.02	0.8		Dimitri	Antonov (10)	GER-Y	13.4.96	3	WY	Donetsk			13 Jul
16.01	1.4		Levon	Aghasyan	ARM	19.1.95	1	EJ	Rieti			21 Jul
15.98	-0.1			Wu Lianglin	CHN	15.11.95	6	NC	Suzhou			1 Jun
15.96	0.4			He Guang	CHN-Y	19.3.96	1	NC-y	Weifang			14 Apr
15.95	0.4			Li Jialei	CHN	14.9.94	8	NC	Suzhou			1 Jun
15.95	1.8		Yevgenmiy	Ognev	RUS	25.2.94	Q	NC-j	Kazan			15 Jun
15.95	-0.1		Oleksandr	Malosilov	UKR-Y	6.6.97	4	WY	Donetsk			13 Jul
15.92	0.8		Sabelo	Ndlovu	RSA	24.6.94	1	Af-J	Bambous			30 Aug
15.91	1.3		Klyvens	Delaunay	USA	16.2.94	8	NCAA	Eugene			8 Jun
15.91	-2.1		Tomás	Veszelka	SVK	9.7.95	Q	EJ	Rieti			20 Jul
15.91	2.0		Kristian	Pulli (20)	FIN	2.9.94	2	NC	Vaasa			28 Jul

Best at low altitude

| 16.18 | 1.4 | | Timothy | White-Edwards | USA | 15.7.94 | 1 | NC-j | Des Moines | | | 20 Jun |

SHOT

Mark				Name		Nat	Born	Pos	Meet	Venue			Date
22.28				Ryan	Whiting	USA	24.11.86	1	DL	Doha			10 May
					21.14		21.62	x		21.37	22.28	21.99	
	22.11	1	NC	Des Moines		23 Jun	20.54	x		22.11	x	p	p
	22.03i	1	WK	Zürich		28 Aug	20.77	21.57	21.99	22.03	21.00	21.91	
	21.88	1	Athl	Lausanne		4 Jul	21.31	x	21.88	21.38	x	x	
	21.80i	1	NC	Albuquerque		3 Mar	21.29	21.00	x	x	21.80	21.53	
	21.74	1		Kingston		4 May							
	21.65i	1	KansR	Lawrence		17 Apr	19.94	20.71	21.20	20.48	21.36	21.65	
	21.60	1	Hanz	Zagreb		3 Sep	20.87	21.06	x	21.60	x	21.19	
	21.59i	1		University Park		2 Feb	x	21.43	21.59	20.85	21.04	x	
	21.57	2	WCh	Moskva		16 Aug	21.57	x	21.35	21.20	x	21.22	
	21.51	Q	WCh	Moskva		15 Aug	21.51	p	p				
	21.45	1	VD	Bruxelles		6 Sep	x	19.78	21.45	x	x	x	
	21.38i	1		Bygoszcz		12 Feb	x	20.88	x	x	21.38	x	
	21.37	2	Drake	Des Moines		27 Apr	21.31	x	x	x	21.23	21.37	
	21.27	1	adidas	New York		25 May	20.32	x	x	21.27	x	20.39	
21.73				David	Storl	GER	27.7.90	1	WCh	Moskva			16 Aug
					21.19		21.24	x		21.73	x	x	
	21.19i	2	WK	Zürich		28 Aug	20.67	x	21.19	x	x	x	
	21.15	1		Thum		30 Aug	x	x	21.15	x	21.04	x	
21.71				Reese	Hoffa	USA	8.10.77	1	Drake	Des Moines			27 Apr
					21.12		21.71	x		21.30	x	21.57	
	21.60i	2	KansR	Lawrence		17 Apr	x	20.12	20.43	20.71	21.60	20.72	
	21.58	2	Athl	Lausanne		4 Jul	21.17	21.40	21.02	21.58	21.38	x	
	21.34	2	NC	Des Moines		23 Jun	x	21.22	21.25	21.34	p	p	
	21.33	1	FlaR	Gainesville		6 Apr	20.26	20.52	21.33	x	20.73	x	
	21.31	1	DL	Birmingham		30 Jun	20.14	21.05	x	20.65	x	21.31	
21.47				Ladislav	Prásil	CZE	17.5.90	1		Potchefstroom			20 Apr
					20.87		21.47	20.98		20.88	x	20.84	
	21.21	1		Tábor		24 Jul							
21.45				Dylan	Armstrong	CAN	15.1.81	2		Zagreb			3 Sep
					20.71		21.45	20.63		20.89	20.86	21.23	
	21.34	3	WCh	Moskva		16 Aug	20.38	21.10	20.73	20.87	21.34	20.46	
	21.19	1		Padova		1 Sep	20.03	21.19	20.78	20.86	20.97	20.80	
21.29				Justin	Rodhe	CAN	17.10.84	3	Drake	Des Moines			27 Apr
					19.90		x	20.65		20.63	21.29	x	
21.26				Germán	Lauro	ARG	2.4.84	2	DL	Doha			10 May
		(30/7)			19.82		20.07	21.26		20.69	20.59	20.95	
21.09				Ryan	Crouser	USA	18.12.92	1	Big 12	Waco			5 May
21.09				Zack	Lloyd	USA	10.10.84	3	NC	Des Moines			23 Jun
21.09				Georgi	Ivanov	BUL	13.3.85	1		Ustí nad Labem			21 Jul
		(10)											
21.05				Paul	Davis	USA	11.9.90	1		Coppell			25 May
20.98i				Cory	Martin	USA	22.5.85	2		Bydgoszcz			12 Feb
20.98				Martin	Stasek	CZE	8.4.89	1		Chodov			4 May
20.98				Kurt	Roberts	USA	20.2.88	1		Tucson			16 May

Mark	Name		Nat	Born	Pos	Meet	Venue	Date	
20.98	Maksim	Sidorov	RUS	13.5.86	1	NCp	Yerino	16	Jun
20.98	Tomasz	Majewski	POL	30.8.81	5	WCh	Moskva	16	Aug
20.97	O'Dayne	Richards	JAM	14.12.88	1	CAC	Morelia	7	Jul
20.82	Joe	Kovacs	USA	28.6.89	2		Tucson	16	May
20.80	Asmir	Kolasinac	SRB	15.10.84	1		Beograd	3	Aug
20.74	Tim	Nedow	CAN	16.10.90	1		La Jolla	27	Apr
	(20)								
20.73	Hamza	Alic	BIH	20.1.79	1		Zenica	12	Jun
20.63	Borja	Vivas	ESP	26.5.84	1		Málaga	1	Jun
20.61	Anton	Lyuboslavskiy	RUS	26.6.84	1		Sochi	26	May
20.61	Tom	Walsh	NZL	1.3.92	1	Zátopek	Melbourne	7	Dec
20.60	Aleksandr	Lesnoy	RUS	28.7.88	2		Sochi	26	May
20.59i	Jordan	Clarke	USA	10.7.90	1		Flagstaff	12	Jan
20.59	Marin	Premeru	CRO	29.8.90	1		Drazevina	28	Apr
20.55	Orazio	Cremona	RSA	1.7.89	1		Donnas	7	Jul
20.53	Russ	Winger	USA	2.8.84	1		Lisle, IL	8	Jun
20.50	Leif	Arrhenius	SWE	15.7.86	1		Hässleholm	27	Jul
	(30)								
20.46	Valeriy	Kokoyev	RUS	25.7.88	3		Sochi	26	May
20.44	Konstantin	Lyadusov	RUS	2.3.88	4		Sochi	26	May
20.37	Kemal	Mesic	BIH	4.8.85	1		Zenica	9	Jun
20.32	Jakub	Szyszkowski	POL	21.8.91	1	CISM	Warendorf	15	Sep
20.31	Jaco	Engelbrecht	RSA	8.3.87	1		Pretoria	29	Apr
20.29i	Curtis	Jensen	USA	1.11.90	1		Charleston	6	Dec
20.28	Antonin	Zalsky	CZE	7.8.80	2	Werfer	Halle	25	May
20.27i	Dmytro	Savytskyy	UKR	14.12.90	1	NC	Sumy	13	Feb
20.22	Jacob	Thormaehlen	USA	13.2.90	1		San Marcos	27	Apr
20.22	Marco	Fortes	POR	26.9.82	2		Dakar	12	Jun
	(40)								
20.20	Nedzad	Mulabegovic	CRO	4.2.81	1		Split	11	May
20.16i	Ralf	Bartels	GER	21.2.78	4	EI	Göteborg	1	Mar
20.13	Raymond	Brown	JAM	15.1.88	1		Kingston	9	Feb
20.13	Eric	Werskey	USA	17.7.87	3		La Jolla	27	Apr
20.13	Rafal	Kownatke	POL	24.3.85	2		Warszawa	3	Aug
20.13i	Christian	Cantwell	USA	30.9.80	8	WK	Zürich	28	Aug
20.12i	Derrick	Vicars	USA	8.5.89	1		Kent, OH	12	Jan
20.12	Pavel	Lyzhin	BLR	24.3.81	1		Minsk	18	Jul
20.12		Wang Guangfu	CHN	15.11.87	1	NG	Shenyang	9	Sep
20.12i	Mason	Finley	USA	7.10.90	1		Laramie	6	Dec
	(50)								
20.10	Soslan	Tsirikhov	RUS	24.11.84	3		Yerino	2	Jun
20.10	Gaëtan	Bucki	FRA	9.5.80	1		Etampes	31	Aug
20.08	Darlan	Romani	BRA	9.4.91	1		Campinas	27	Apr
20.06i	Richard	Chavez	USA	.92	1		Jonesboro	1	Dec
20.05i	Richard	Garrett	USA	21.12.90	1	WAC	Albuquerque	22	Feb
20.02i	Bozidar	Antunovic	SRB	24.7.91	2	WAC	Albuquerque	22	Feb
20.02i	Kole	Weldon	USA	25.3.92	2	NCAA	Fayetteville	8	Mar
20.02	Michael	Putman	PER	7.3.89	1		Miami (Hialeh)	9	Jun
20.00i	Dan	Block	USA	8.1.91	3	NCAA	Fayetteville	8	Mar
19.99	Chris	Reed	USA	22.7.92	1	NCAA-2	Pueblo, CO	25	May
	(60)								
19.96	Tobias	Dahm	GER	23.5.87	2	NC	Ulm	7	Jul
19.92i	Aleksandr	Bulanov	RUS	26.12.89	Q	EI	Göteborg	1	Mar
19.90	Mihaíl	Stamatóyiannis	GRE	20.5.82	1		Thíva	24	Jul
19.89i	Stephen	Mozia	USA/NGR	16.8.93	1		Ithaca	19	Jan
19.89		Chang Ming-Huang	TPE	7.8.82	3		Tucson	18	May
19.86i	Luke	Pinkelman	USA	5.5.88	1		Lincoln	2	Feb
19.85	Luka	Rujevic	SRB	14.10.85	1		Kragujevac	1	Sep
19.81i	Marco	Schmidt	GER	5.9.83	1		Sindelfingen	26	Jan
19.77i	Niklas	Arrhenius	SWE	10.9.82	2	NC	Norrköping	17	Feb
19.77		Liu Yang	CHN	29.10.86	2	NG	Shenyang	9	Sep
	(70)								
19.76i	Lajos	Kürthy	HUN	22.10.86	1		Budapest	8	Feb
19.76	Tumatai	Dauphin	FRA	12.1.88	1		Bourg-en-Bresse	13	Jun
19.74	Anton	Tikhomirov	RUS	29.4.88	4	NC	Moskva	23	Jul
19.70i	Stephen	Saenz	MEX	23.8.90	1		Fayetteville	24	Feb
19.70	Inderjeet	Singh	IND	19.4.88	2	WUG	Kazan	7	Jul
19.68	Sultan	Al-Hebshi	KSA	23.2.83	1	AsiC	Pune	3	Jul
19.67i	Kim	Christensen	DEN	1.4.84	1		Provo	12	Jan
19.63i	Robert	Golabek	USA	27.4.89	1		Geneva, OH	26	Jan
19.63i	Hayden	Baillio	USA	22.7.91	1	Big 12	Ames	24	Feb

Mark	Name		Nat	Born	Pos	Meet	Venue	Date
19.63	Dominik	Witczak	POL	10.3.92	2	EU23	Tampere	11 Jul
(80)								
19.62	Mateusz	Mikos	POL	10.4.87	1		Kraków	27 Apr
19.60i	Andriy	Semenov	UKR	4.7.84	Q	NC	Sumy	13 Feb
19.59i	Jonathan	Jones	USA	23.4.91	1		Ypsilanti	22 Feb
19.59i	Hüseyin	Atici	TUR	3.5.86	Q	EI	Göteborg	1 Mar
19.56		Ding Weiye	CHN	13.4.90	2		Shenyang	15 Jun
19.53	Andriy	Borodkin	UKR	18.4.78	1	NC	Donetsk	24 Jul
19.52i		Wang Like	CHN	2.4.89	2		Beijing	29 Mar
19.50	Sarunas	Banevicius	LTU	10.11.91	1		Kaunas	31 May
19.50	Tomás	Stanek	CZE	13.6.91	1		Pardubice	18 Sep
19.49	Willy	Irwin	USA	2.6.92	2	MSR	Walnut	20 Apr
(90)								
19.49	Michal	Bosko	POL	25.7.88	1		Bialogard	4 May
19.48i		Guo Yanxiang	CHN	29.1.87	3		Beijing	29 Mar
19.48	Raigo	Toompuu	EST	17.7.81	1		Valmiera	19 Jul
19.45	Mikhal	Abramchuk	BLR	15.11.92	1		Brest	27 Apr
19.45	Om Prakash	Singh	IND	11.1.87	3	AsiC	Pune	3 Jul
19.43		Zhang Jun	CHN	11.4.83	1		Zhaoqing	27 Apr
19.43	Nick	Vena	USA	16.4.93	1q	NCAA-E	Greensboro	24 May
19.42	Jon	Arthur	USA	.90	1		Lake Charles	11 May
19.42	Zane	Duquemin	GBR	23.9.91	2		Hässleholm	27 Jul
19.41	Yioser	Toledo	CUB/ESP	24.4.83	3	ESP Ch	Alcobendas	27 Jul
(100)								
19.39	Yasser Fathi	Ibrahim	EGY	2.5.84	1		Al Qahira	17 Apr
19.39	Chad	Wright	JAM	25.3.91	1	Big 10	Columbus	12 May
19.39	Robert	Dippl	GER	21.10.83	1		München	18 May

Mark	Name		Nat	Born	Date
19.37	Meshari Suroor	Saad	KUW	2.7.87	21 May
19.36i	Artur	Hoppe	GER	3.5.88	19 Jan
19.34	Akeem	Stewart	TTO	4.7.92	28 Apr
19.32i	Lukas	Weißhaidinger	AUT	20.2.92	31 Jan
19.32i	Ivan	Yushkov	RUS	15.1.81	13 Feb
19.31	Bobby	Grace	USA	10.10.90	27 Apr
19.31	Hendrik	Müller	GER	28.8.90	7 Jul
19.28	Jan	Marcell	CZE	4.6.85	24 Jul
19.28i	Vladislav	Tulácek	CZE	9.7.88	20 Dec
19.27	Damien	Birkinhead	AUS	8.4.93	14 Apr
19.26		Fu Qingnan	CHN	22.2.89	15 Jun
19.25i	Cody	Riffle	USA	14.4.91	26 Jan
19.24	Carlos	Tobalina	ESP	2.8.85	27 Jul
19.23	Sergey	Dementyev	UZB	1.6.90	12 Sep
19.21	Patrick	Cronie	NED	5.11.89	27 Jul
19.20	Tomás	Kozák	CZE	1.5.90	22 Sep
19.19	Martin	Novák	CZE	5.10.92	15 Jun
19.17	Max	Bedewitz	GER	18.10.90	7 Jul
19.16i	Jakob	Engel	USA	12.10.89	2 Mar
19.16	Grigoriy	Kamulya	UZB	31.1.89	4 May
19.15	Kristo	Galeta	EST	9.4.83	27 Jul
19.13i	Caleb	Whitener	USA	29.5.92	24 Feb
19.13	Darrell	Hill	USA	17.8.93	3 May
19.13	Marko	Spiler	SLO	8.1.90	13 Jul
19.12i	Tomas	Söderlund	FIN	14.5.89	27 Jan
19.12	Matt	Hoty	USA	21.10.91	12 Apr
19.08	Amin	Nikfar	IRI	2.1.81	10 May
19.07	Thomas	Schmitt	GER	23.1.89	25 May
19.07	Arttu	Kangas	FIN	13.7.93	27 Jul
19.06i	Robert	Häggblom	FIN	9.8.82	25 Jan
19.06	Eric	van Vreumingen	NED	15.6.78	8 Sep
19.05	Asinia	Miller	JAM	6.6.93	13 Apr
19.05	Chukwuewuka	Enekwechi	USA	28.1.93	24 May
19.03	Daniel	Anglés	ESP	11.4.85	27 Jul
19.02	Frank	Elemba	CGO	21.7.90	23 Mar
19.01i	Travis	Smith	USA	6.6.91	26 Jan
19.00	Matt	DeChant	USA	31.5.89	11 Jun
18.99	Mykyta	Nesterenko	UKR	15.4.91	4 May
18.95i	Andy	Dittmar	GER	5.7.74	20 Jan
18.95	Marcus	Popenfoose	USA	18.9.91	11 May
18.94		Tian Zhizhong	CHN	15.12.92	9 Sep
18.93	Abdollah	Jamshidi	IRI		26 Apr
18.93	Cody	Hunt	USA	8.2.88	10 May
18.90	Adriatik	Hoxha	ALB	9.1.90	19 Jun
18.89	Isaiah	Simmons	USA	3.12.92	19 Apr
18.89	Kevin	Farley	USA	18.7.93	5 Jun
18.88	Georgios	Arestis	CYP	27.12.81	8 Mar
18.88	Sylwester	Zielinski	POL	13.8.89	14 Jun
18.87	Aleksey	Nechypor	BLR	10.4.93	7 Jun
18.87	Jasdeep	Singh	IND	6.10.90	21 Dec
18.86i		Feng Jie	CHN	18.1.86	29 Mar
18.86	David	Pless	USA	.91	17 May
18.86	Mesud	Pezer	BIH-J	27.8.94	9 Jun
18.85	Nicolás	Martina	ARG	18.8.89	21 Nov
18.83i	Scott	Barnas	USA	9.10.86	11 Jan
18.83i	Brad	Szypka	USA	13.2.93	24 Feb
18.83	Aldo	González	BOL	5.9.84	4 May
18.83		Han Zibin	CHN	5.4.87	9 Sep
18.82i	Will	Spence	USA	.91	1 Mar
18.81i	Kamil	Zbroszczyk	POL	24.1.87	9 Feb
18.81	Tyler	Blatchley	USA	12.3.86	17 Apr
18.79	Ivan	Ivanov	KAZ	3.1.92	25 Apr
18.78i	Bob	Bertemes	LUX	24.5.93	5 Jan
18.78	Willian	Braido	BRA	18.3.92	19 May
18.78	Jacek	Wisniewski	POL	29.1.91	23 Jun
18.78	Daniel	Ståhl	SWE	27.8.92	10 Aug
18.77i	Alex	Adams	USA	6.8.89	2 Mar
18.76	Krzysztof	Brzozowski	POL	15.7.93	21 Jul
18.75i	Scott	Rider	GBR	22.9.77	10 Mar
18.74i	Maksim	Afonin	RUS	16.1.92	22 Dec
18.73i	Daniele	Secci	ITA	9.3.92	20 Jan
18.73	Milan	Jotanovic	SRB	11.1.84	1 May
18.73	Andre	Reid	JAM	26.8.82	28 Jun
18.72	Maksim	Afonin	RUS	16.1.92	24 Jun
18.71	Michal	Rasinski	POL	31.3.90	29 Jun
18.70	Nikita	Lyuboslavskiy	RUS	21.6.91	24 Apr
18.70	Edder	Moreno	COL	4.2.89	20 Jul
18.69i	Nicholas	Scarvelis	USA	2.2.93	23 Feb
18.67i		Wu Jiaxing	CHN	29.3.90	6 Mar
18.67	Gustavo	de Mendonça	BRA	10.4.84	4 May
18.67	Dennis	Lewke	GER	6.6.93	13 Jul
18.67i	Josh	Uchtman	USA	18.12.88	7 Dec
18.66	Itamar	Levi	ISR	1.11.91	23 Apr
18.66i	Ryan	Spencer-Jones	GBR	14.10.86	15 Dec
18.65i	Nick	Baatz	USA	4.1.90	25 Jan
18.65i	Matt	Babicz	USA		9 Jun
18.63i	Aleksandr	Lobynya	RUS	31.5.84	13 Feb
18.63	Timothy	Hendry-Gallagher	CAN	3.2.90	21 Jun
18.61i	Andy	Novak	USA	24.4.90	9 Feb
18.61	David	Nichols	USA	13.1.85	4 May
18.60		Jung Il-woo	KOR	28.3.86	21 Oct
18.59i	Greg	Beard	GBR	10.9.82	13 Jan
18.59i	Ryan	Smith	USA	27.1.90	9 Mar
18.58i	Andrey	Sinyakov	BLR	6.1.82	26 Jan
18.58i	Coy	Blair	USA-J	10.6.94	16 Feb
18.57	Nick	Petersen	DEN	25.4.87	8 Jun
18.57	Simon	Gustafsson	SWE	24.5.90	9 Jun
(201)		Ding Yongheng	CHN	18.7.91	9 Sep

Mark	Name	Nat	Born	Pos	Meet	Venue	Date

Best outdoors

Mark	Name		Nat/Note	Surname	Nat	Born	Pos	Meet	Venue	Date
20.67	Martin	4	NC	Des Moines		23 Jun				
20.28	Clarke	2	NCAA	Eugene		5 Jun				
20.13	Bartels	1		Ried		14 Jun				
19.86	Cantwell	7		Zagreb		3 Sep				
19.81	Bulanov	2	Znam	Zhukovskiy		30 Jun				
19.66	Schmidt	1		Bad Boll		1 May				

Mark	Name	Pos	Meet	Venue	Date
19.63	Jensen	4		Tucson	18 May
19.62	Vicars	1		Ashland, OH	3 May
19.57	Arrhenius	1	vFIN	Stockholm	8 Sep
19.55	Semenov	3	ECp-w	Castellón	17 Mar
19.53	Atici	5	Med G	Mersin	29 Jun
19.43	Weldon	1		San Diego	16 Mar

Mark	Name	Date		Mark	Name	Date		Mark	Name	Date		Mark	Name	Date
19.38	Christensen	1 Aug		19.14	Kürthy	15 Jun		18.82	Feng Jie	9 Sep		18.72	Spence	29 Mar
19.33	Wang Like	29 May		19.09	Whitener	13 Apr		18.80	Smith	6 Apr		18.72	Afonin	24 Jun
19.31	Block	12 May		19.03	Guo Yanxiang	12 May		18.80	Riffle	26 Apr		18.69	Engel	16 Mar
19.26	Garrett	27 Apr		19.08	Pinkelman	6 Apr		18.79	Saenz	29 Mar		18.64	Adams	20 Apr
19.26	Golabek	18 May		18.95	Antunovic	11 May		18.78	Dittmar	23 Jun		18.62	Söderlund	10 Jul
19.24	Jones	5 Jun		18.90	Baillio	24 May		18.78	Bertemes	10 Sep		18.57	Szypka	8 Jun
19.20	Mozia	26 Apr		18.90	Weißhaidinger	14 Jun		18.77	Zbroszczyk	3 May				

JUNIORS

Mark	Name	Surname	Nat	Born	Pos	Meet	Venue	Date
18.86	Mesud	Pezer	BIH	27.8.94	3		Zenica	9 Jun
18.58i	Coy	Blair	USA	10.6.94	2		West Lafayette	16 Feb
	18.33				5	Big 10	Columbus	12 May
18.54	Tejinder	Pal Singh	IND	13.11.94	1		Patiala	25 Dec
18.14i	Derek	Bunch	USA	11.5.94	1		Cedar Falls	24 Feb
18.10	Tyler	Schultz	USA	29.3.94	1		Fort Co9llins	27 Apr
18.02	Macklin	Tudor	USA	13.6.94	3		Ashland	27 Apr
17.75	Tibor	Rakoovszky	HUN	3.7.94	3		Budapest	15 Jun
17.73	Ethan	Cochran	USA	9.1.94	1		Stanford	20 Apr
17.58	Matti	Sivonen	FIN	28.7.94	5	vSWE	Stockholm	8 Sep

6 KG SHOT

Mark	Name	Surname	Nat	Born	Pos	Meet	Venue	Date
23.00	Jacko	Gill	NZL	10.12.94	1		Auckland	18 Aug
	22.53	1		Auckland		4 Aug		
	22.32	1		Brisbane		20 Jul		
20.93	Nelson	Fernandes	BRA	9.7.94	1	SAm-J	Resistencia	18 Oct
20.44	Mesud	Pezer	BIH	27.8.94	1	EJ	Rieti	18 Jul
	20.40	1		Balk-J Denizli		6 Jul		
20.35	Filip	Mihaljevic	CRO	31.7.94	1		Bar	1 May
20.35	Magdy Mohamed	Hamza	EGY-Y	30.8.96	1		El Maadi	5 Dec
20.25	Amrou Mohamed	Ahmed	EGY	16.12.95	2		El Maadi	5 Dec
20.20	Josh	Freeman	USA	22.8.94	1	PAm-J	Medellín	25 Aug
20.12i	Henning	Prüfer	GER-Y	7.3.96	1	v2N	Ancona	2 Mar
	19.52				1		Thum	30 Aug
20.10	Patrick	Müller	GER-Y	4.2.96	1	NC-j	Rostock	28 Jul
20.07	Andrzej	Regin (10)	POL	21.2.94	3	EJ	Rieti	18 Jul
20.00	Dawid	Krzyzan	POL	20.4.94	1	NC-j	Kraków	3 Jul
19.96	Coy	Blair	USA	10.6.94	1	NC-j	Des Moines	20 Jun
19.90	Tomas	Djurivic	MNE	14.2.94	2		Bar	1 May
19.81	Matti	Sivonen	FIN	28.7.94	5	EJ	Rieti	18 Jul
19.59	Péter	Simon	HUN	18.9.94	2	v3N	Praha	3 Jul
19.59	Ahmed Ahmed	Hassan	EGY	28.7.94	1	Af-J	Bambous	30 Aug
19.40	Tyler	Schultz	USA	29.3.94	3	NC-j	Des Moines	20 Jun
19.39	Konrad	Bukowiecki	POL-Y	17.3.97	1		Gdansk	21 Sep
19.29	Fedrick	Dacres	JAM	28.2.94	1	N.Sch	Kingston	16 Mar

6 KG SHOT secondary marks:
- 21.43i 1 Sätra 20 Apr
- 20.53 1 NC-j Auckland 23 Mar
- 9 performances by 4 men to 20.35

DISCUS

Mark	Name	Surname	Nat	Born	Pos	Meet	Venue	Date
71.84	Piotr	Malachowski	POL	7.6.83	1	FBK	Hengelo	8 Jun

65.53	x	x	67.73	71.84	x

Mark	Pos	Meet	Venue	Date						
68.53	1		Cetniewo	29 Jun	66.85	65.29	x	x	68.53	61.75
68.36	2	WCh	Moskva	13 Aug	64.49	x	65.09	67.18	68.36	67.21
68.19	2	Pre	Eugene	1 Jun	66.50	68.19	66.99	66.58	66.89	x
67.35	1	DL	London (OS)	26 Jul	x	67.04	67.35	66.79	x	x
67.34	1	DL	Shanghai	18 May	x	63.07	64.33	67.34	62.75	p
67.07	2	Skol	Warszawa	25 Aug	x	67.07	65.95	66.03	65.87	64.63
66.95	5	GS	Ostrava	26 Jun	x	x	63.07	66.95	63.46	65.17
66.87	1	NC	Torun	19 Jul	66.87	63.78	62.64	x	x	x

Mark	Name	Surname	Nat	Born	Pos	Meet	Venue	Date
69.91	Robert	Harting	GER	18.10.84	2	FBK	Hengelo	8 Jun

69.36	x	x	68.16	69.91	x

Mark	Pos	Meet	Venue	Date						
69.75	1	Pre	Eugene	1 Jun	67.16	69.75	x	67.42	68.00	x
69.11	1	WCh	Moskva	13 Aug	62.16	68.13	x	69.11	p	69.08
69.02	1	ISTAF	Berlin	1 Sep	61.89	65.00	63.70	69.02	x	x
68.85	1		Kienbaum	31 Jul						
68.60	1	Skol	Warszawa	25 Aug	68.60	68.28	x	x	x	x
68.31	1		Wiesbaden	19 May	x	x	66.30	x	68.31	x
67.95	1	NC	Ulm	7 Jul	66.34	67.44	67.73	66.72	x	67.95

MEN 2013

Mark	Name		Nat	Born	Pos	Meet	Venue	Date
67.89	1 CISM Warendorf 15 Sep			65.49 x x x x 67.89				
67.10	2 GS Ostrava 27 Jun			65.73 x x 66.09 x 67.10				
67.04	1 DL Saint Denis 6 Jul			64.97 x 66.80 x 67.04 x				
66.83	2 WK Zürich 29 Aug			65.96 x x 66.83 x x				
68.20	Benn	Harradine	AUS	14.10.82	1		Townsville	10 May
				60.77 x 68.20 62.35 61.02 p				
68.16	Julian	Wruck	AUS	6.7.91	1		Claremont	1 Jun
				68.16 66.38 x 67.93 67.14 x				
67.59	Gerd	Kanter	EST	6.5.79	1		Kohila	31 Aug
				61.42 66.05 63.07 65.23 67.59 67.08				
67.02	1 WK Zürich 29 Aug			64.49 x 67.02 64.00 65.55 63.22				
66.97	4 GS Ostrava 26 Jun			62.90 63.28 63.47 63.43 x 66.97				
67.46	Martin	Wierig	GER	10.6.87	1	GS	Ostrava	26 Jun
				63.23 62.98 x x 67.46 67.05				
66.73	2 ISTAF Berlin 1 Sep			64.33 x 63.73 66.73 x x				
66.98	Ehsan	Hadadi	IRI	21.1.85	3	GS	Ostrava	26 Jun
				61.47 65.49 66.98 65.04 x x				
66.84	Brett	Morse	GBR	11.2.89	1		Cardiff	30 Jun
	(30/8)							
				62.83 66.84 64.77 x 66.01 x				
66.16	Frank	Casañas	ESP	18.10.78	1		Villa Nova de Cerveira	24 Jul
65.98	Lois Maikel	Martínez	ex-CUB	3.6.81	1		Donnas	7 Jul
	(10)							
65.97	Viktor	Butenko	RUS	10.3.93	1		Sochi	25 May
65.94	Jason	Morgan	JAM	6.10.82	1		Ruston, LA	16 Mar
65.92	Erik	Cadée	NED	15.2.84	1		Vught	15 Sep
65.91	Rutger	Smith	NED	9.7.81	1		Azusa	11 May
65.82	Vikas	Gowda	IND	5.7.83	1		Mesa	5 Apr
65.79	Mario	Pestano	ESP	8.4.78	1		Rabat	9 Jun
65.55	Ronald	Julião	BRA	16.6.85	1		La Jolla	27 Apr
65.33	Victor	Hogan	RSA	25.7.89	2		Donnas	8 Jul
65.30	Robert	Urbanek	POL	29.4.87	2	NC	Torun	19 Jul
65.16	Gerhard	Mayer	AUT	20.5.80	1		Hainfeld	22 May
	(20)							
65.09	Jorge	Fernández	CUB	2.10.87	1		Leiria	4 Jul
65.03	Martin	Kupper	EST	31.5.89	1		Paunküla	23 Aug
64.99	Christopher	Harting	GER	4.10.90	1eA	Werfer	Halle	25 May
64.77	Ercüment	Olgundeniz	TUR	7.7.76	1		Mersin	16 Feb
64.77	Giovanni	Faloci	ITA	13.10.85	1		Tarquinia	4 Jun
64.69	Daniel	Jasinski	GER	5.8.89	1	ECp-w	Castellón	16 Mar
64.66	Virgilijus	Alekna	LTU	13.2.72	2	ECp-w	Castellón	16 Mar
64.60	Danijel	Furtula	MNE	31.7.92	1		Bar	10 Mar
64.46	Irfan	Yildirim	TUR	26.7.88	1		Ankara	30 Mar
64.46A	Niklas	Arrhenius	SWE	10.9.82	1		Provo	27 Jul
	(30)							
64.44	Markus	Münch	GER	13.6.86	3		Wiesbaden	19 May
64.25	Sultan M.	Al-Dawoodi	KSA	16.6.77	1		Warszawa	23 Jun
64.19	Oleksiy	Semenov	UKR	27.6.82	1		Kyiv	22 May
64.17	Martin	Maric	CRO	19.4.84	1		Maribor	3 Jul
64.09	Mahmoud	Samimi	IRI	18.9.88	1		Tehran	31 May
64.02	Lance	Brooks	USA	1.1.84	1q		Claremont	20 Jul
63.92	Sergiu	Ursu	ROU	26.4.80	1		Bucuresti	24 Aug
63.74	Chad	Wright	JAM	25.3.91	2	NCAA	Eugene	7 Jun
63.59	Jarred	Rome	USA	21.12.76	2		Azusa	11 May
63.58	Märt	Israel	EST	23.9.83	1		Helsingborg	7 Jul
	(40)							
63.55	Mohammed	Samimi	IRI	29.3.87	2		Tehran	31 May
63.48	Traves	Smikle	JAM	7.5.92	1		Mona	5 Apr
63.44	Casey	Malone	USA	6.4.77	2q		Claremont	20 Jul
63.29	Russ	Winger	USA	2.8.84	1		Claremont	20 Jul
63.23	Przemyslaw	Czajkowski	POL	26.10.88	1		Bonneuil-sur-Marne	7 Jun
63.16	Konrad	Szuster	POL	21.1.84	1	Sidlo	Sopot	13 Jul
63.12	Mike	Torie	USA	12.3.86	2		Claremont	1 Jun
63.09	Aleksas	Abromavicius	LTU	6.12.84	1		Madison, WI	4 May
63.09A	Leif	Arrhenius	SWE	15.7.86	1		Provo	25 Sep
63.08	Jason	Young	USA	27.5.81	1		Abilene	13 Apr
	(50)							
62.89	Jared	Schuurmans	USA	20.8.87	1		Portland	2 Jun
62.88	Rodney	Brown	USA	21.5.93	2	TexR	Austin	30 Mar
62.88	Mykyta	Nesterenko	UKR	15.4.91	1		Kyiv	22 May
62.78	Andrew	Evans	USA	25.1.91	3	NCAA	Eugene	7 Jun

Mark	Name		Nat	Born	Pos	Meet	Venue	Date	
62.76	James	Plummer	USA	19.8.90	1		New York	29	Jun
62.69	Hannes	Kirchler	ITA	22.12.78	3		Donnas	7	Jul
62.63	Luke	Bryant	USA	5.12.88	5		La Jolla	25	Apr
62.55	Gleb	Sidorchenko	RUS	15.5.86	2		Sochi	25	May
62.48	Apostolos	Parellis	CYP	24.7.85	1		Nicosia	8	Mar
62.48	Mason	Finley	USA	7.10.90	1		Laramie	3	May
	(60)								
62.46	Matej	Gasaj	SVK	27.12.81	1		Nitra	16	Sep
62.40	Andrius	Gudzius	LTU	14.2.91	1	EU23	Tampere	13	Jul
62.39	Eduardo	Albertazzi	ITA	14.9.91	1		Ancona	2	Mar
62.37	Nikolay	Sedyuk	RUS	29.4.88	1	Kuts	Moskva	15	Jul
62.03	Dmitriy	Sivakov	BLR	15.2.83	1		Brest	27	Apr
62.00	Carter	Comito	USA	26.10.90	1		Spokane	6	Apr
61.91	Rashid	Al-Dosari	QAT	8.5.81	1	Arab C	Doha	24	May
61.86	Petr	Vuklisevic	CZE	25.2.82	1		Karlovy Vary	21	Sep
61.83		Wu Tao	CHN	3.10.83	6		Wiesbaden	19	May
61.81	Philip	Milanov	BEL	6.7.91	1		Vilvoorde	17	Aug
	(70)								
61.72	Germán	Lauro	ARG	2.4.84	3		São Paulo	19	May
61.70	Lolassonn	Djouhan	FRA	18.5.91	1		Vannes	9	Mar
61.66	Axel	Härstedt	SWE	28.2.87	1eB	Werfer	Halle	25	May
61.53		Wu Jian	CHN	25.5.86	7		Wiesbaden	19	May
61.44	Jean-François	Aurokium	FRA	14.4.81	1		Marseille	31	May
61.43	Yasser Fathi	Ibrahim	EGY	2.5.84	1		El Maadi	24	Apr
61.29	Daniel	Ståhl	SWE	27.8.92	4	EU23	Tampere	13	Jul
61.24	Chase	Madison	USA	13.9.85	1		Rock Island	17	May
61.17	Nick	Jones	USA	22.6.89	1		Abilene	8	May
61.14	Ivan	Krasnoshenkov	RUS	26.3.87	3		Sochi	25	May
	(80)								
61.13	Stephen	Mozia	USA/NGR	16.8.93	2		New York	29	Jun
61.11	Andrei	Gag	ROU	7.4.91	1		Bucuresti	24	May
61.07	Dan	Block	USA	8.1.91	7		La Jolla	25	Apr
61.01	Pedro José	Cuesta	ESP	22.8.83	1		Leiria	3	Aug
61.00	Jorge	Grave	POR	5.9.82	1	NC-w	Leiria	23	Feb
60.98	Bryan	Powlen	USA	3.12.87	3		New York	29	Jun
60.95	Maarten	Persoon	NED	15.3.87	4		Donnas	7	Jul
60.92	Fredrik	Amundgård	NOR	12.1.89	3		Helsingborg	21	Jul
60.84	Stéphane	Marthély	FRA	9.9.79	1		Vannes	29	Jun
60.83	Michael	Salzer	GER	25.10.91	2eB	Werfer	Halle	25	May
	(90)								
60.82	Ahmed Mohamed	Dheeb	QAT	29.9.85	3	AsiC	Pune	4	Jul
60.71	Peter	Savanyú	HUN	26.6.87	2		Maribor	3	Jul
60.67	Andrés	Rossini	ARG	12.4.88	1		La Jolla	27	Apr
60.63	David	Wrobel	GER	13.2.91	3eB	Werfer	Halle	25	May
60.56	Zane	Duquemin	GBR	23.9.91	1	NC-23	Bedford	15	Jun
60.38	Tomás	Vonavka	CZE	4.6.90	1	NCAA	Tábor	15	Jun
60.37	Aleksandr	Tammert	EST	2.2.73	1		Tallinn	22	Sep
60.22	Aleksandr	Kirya	RUS	23.3.92	4		Sochi	26	May
60.21	Bo	Taylor	USA	5.1.88	1		Chula Vista	13	Jun
60.21	Musaeb	Al-Momani	JOR	28.8.86	5	AsiC	Pune	4	Jul
	(100)								
60.21	Eligijus	Ruskys	LTU	1.12.90	1		Siauliai	6	Jul

Mark		Name	Nat	Born		Date			Mark		Name	Nat	Born		Date
60.15	Igor	Gondor	CZE	10.3.79	13	Sep			59.28	Ryan	Crouser	USA	18.12.92	30	Mar
60.14	Sergey	Roganov	BLR	18.4.86	27	Apr			59.27A	Russel	Tucker	RSA	4.11.90	9	Mar
60.10A	Mario	Cota	MEX	11.9.90	22	Mar			59.21	Yuji	Tsutsumi	JPN	22.12.89	8	Sep
59.98	Chris	Scott	GBR	21.3.88	7	Jul			59.20	Volodomyr	Kostyuchenko	UKR	20.9.88	17	May
59.95	Dalton	Rowan	USA	6.4.93	26	Apr			59.13	Essa Mohamed Al-Zankawi		KUW	17.10.92	24	May
59.93A	John	Talbert	USA	3.7.89	24	May			59.13	Lukas	Weißhaidinger	AUT	20.2.92	30	May
59.90	Gordon	Wolf	GER	17.1.90	12	Jun			59.13	Desmine	Hilliard	USA	23.12.92	7	Jun
59.86	Nathaniel	Moses	USA	1.4.90	20	Apr			59.09	Shane	Dodd	JAM	2.10.90	26	Jan
59.84	Yevgeniy	Talanovskiy	RUS	15.4.91	26	Feb			59.06	Yevgeniy	Labutov	KAZ	17.11.84	27	Apr
59.83	Alex	Rose	SAM	7.11.91	17	May			59.05	Quincy	Wilson	TTO	3.4.91	4	May
59.82		Tulake Nuermaimaiti	CHN	8.3.82	11	Sep			59.05	Maximiliano	Alonso	CHI	10.10.86	27	Oct
59.80	Gabe	Hull	USA	1.12.93	13	Apr			59.03	Ulf	Ankarling	SWE	12.4.88	3	Aug
59.78	Antonio	James	USA	7.4.92	19	Apr			59.01	Marek	Bárta	CZE	8.12.92	15	Jun
59.68		Choi Jong-bum	KOR	22.8.81	8	Jun			58.97	Priidu	Niit	EST	27.1.90	31	Aug
59.67	Mauricio	Ortega	COL-J	4.8.94	27	Nov			58.96	András	Seres	HUN	31.1.89	28	Jul
59.59	Jouni	Waldén	FIN	9.1.82	23	Jun			58.95	Jordan	Williams	USA	22.5.90	23	Mar
59.51	Tavis	Bailey	USA	6.1.92	23	Mar			58.94	Jared	Thomas	USA	17.2.90	3	May
59.47	Pavel	Lyzhin	BLR	24.3.81	26	Jul			58.89	Zach	Lindsley	USA	24.11.90	29	Mar
59.44	Benedikt	Stienen	GER	12.1.92	2	Mar			58.89		Hong Qingbin	CHN	6.5.91	11	Sep
59.34	Dávid	Mozsdényi	HUN	17.7.86	27	Apr			58.84	Aleksey	Sysoyev	RUS	8.3.85	25	May
59.30	Fedrick	Dacres	JAM-J	28.2.94	4	May			58.83	Marin	Premeru	CRO	29.8.90	23	Jun

Mark	Name		Nat	Born		Pos	Meet	Venue		Date
58.81	Matthew	Kosecki	USA	1.7.91						30 Mar
58.80	Pawel	Pasinski	POL	6.3.93						3 Jun
58.74	Zach	Duncavage	USA	.91						4 May
58.73	Mike	Guidry	USA	29.10.79						27 Apr
58.65	Federico	Apolloni	ITA	14.3.87						28 Jul
58.48	Ivan	Panasyuk	UKR	8.10.91						5 Jun
58.46	Willy	Irwin	USA	2.6.92						19 Apr
58.42	Pyry	Niskala	FIN	6.11.90						15 Jul
58.34	Sam	Mattis	USA-J	19.3.94						5 May
58.34	Maksim	Gigashvili	RUS	22.4.92						26 Jun
58.29	Johnny	Karlsson	SWE	22.8.89						6 May
58.26		Xin Jia	CHN	1.3.88						11 May
58.26	Magnus	Aunevik-Berntsen	NOR	19.10.89						7 Jul
58.26	Filip	Mihaljevic	CRO-J	31.7.94						22 Sep
58.19	Derek	White	USA	19.11.90						13 Apr
58.11	Darian	Brown	USA	30.7.93						15 Mar
58.08A	Macklin	Tudor	USA-J	13.6.94						24 May
58.07	Austin	Gamble	USA	27.9.90						10 May
58.07	Wojciech	Praczyk	POL	10.1.93						2 Jun
58.06	Oleg	Rezanovich	BLR	17.1.91						14 Jun
58.05	Nazzareno	Di Marco	ITA	30.4.85						10 Feb
58.02	Kole	Weldon	USA	25.3.92						4 May
58.01	Matt	Stopel	AUS	4.5.90						20 Dec
(166)										

JUNIORS

Mark	Name		Nat	Born	Pos	Meet	Venue	Date
59.67	Mauricio	Ortega	COL	4.8.94	1	Bol G	Trujillo	27 Nov
57.76	3	SAm-J	Cartagena	5 Jul				
59.30	Fedrick	Dacres	JAM	28.2.94	3		Kingston	4 May
58.38	3	NC	Kingston	22 Jun				
58.34	Sam	Mattis	USA	19.3.94	1		Princeton, NJ	5 May
58.26	Filip	Mihaljevic	CRO	31.7.94	1		Bar	22 Sep
57.73	2	Zenica	12 Jun					
58.08A	Macklin	Tudor	USA	13.6.94	2	NCAA-2	Pueblo, CO	24 May
57.71	1	Ashland	3 May	9 performances by 5 men to 57.70				
57.60	Jan-Louw	Kotze	RSA	18.3.94	1		Mobile	30 Mar
57.52	Ethan	Cochran	USA	9.1.94	2		Salinas	13 Apr
57.21	Aleksandr	Dobrenshkiy	RUS	11.3.94	8		Sochi	25 May
56.91	Matthew	Denny	AUS-Y	2.6.96	2	NC	Sydney	13 Apr
56.85	Róbert	Szikszai (10)	HUN	30.9.94	1		Nyíregyháza	4 Sep
56.62	Hayden	Reed	USA	4.4.94	1		Birmingham AL	27 Apr
55.99	Reggie	Jagers	USA	13.8.94	1		Akron	6 Apr
55.08	Jason	Zahn	USA	15.2.94	6	Owens	Columbus	19 Apr
54.73	Thiago Adriano	Negreiros	BRA	12.10.94	Q	NC	São Paulo	7 Jun
54.63	Onyinchukwu	Afoaku	USA	12.3.94	12	TexR	Austin	30 Mar
54.57	Coleman	Nelson	USA	29.9.94	3		Lisle	15 Jun

1.75KG DISCUS

Mark	Name		Nat	Born	Pos	Meet	Venue	Date
64.75	Róbert	Szikszai	HUN	30.9.94	1	EJ	Rieti	21 Jul
64.04	1	Nyiregyháza	4 Sep	63.70	1	Budapest	11 May	
63.76	1	Budapest	2 Jun					
63.39	Aleksey	Khudyakov	RUS	31.3.95	1		Adler	18 Feb
62.84	Hayden	Reed	USA	4.4.94	1	NC-j	Des Moines	20 Jun
62.49A	1	PAm-J	Medellín	23 Aug	10 performances by 6 men to 62.30			
62.80	Fedric	Dacres	JAM	28.2.94	1	N.Sch	Kingston	14 Mar
62.79	Nicholas	Percy	GBR	6,12.94	1		Watford	23 Jun
62.78	Mauricio	Ortega	COL	4.8.94	1	SAm-J	Resistencia	19 Oct
62.16	Filip	Mihaljevic	CRO	31.7.94	1	NC-j	Varazdin	30 Jun
61.54	Aleksandr	Dobrenshkiy	RUS	11.3.94	3	EJ	Rieti	21 Jul
60.83	Mesud	Pezer	BIH	27.8.94	4	EJ	Rieti	21 Jul
59.98	Valeriy	Golubkovich (10)	BLR	21.1.95	1	NC-j	Brest	12 Jun
59.96	Domantas	Poska	LTU-Y	10.1.96	5	EJ	Rieti	21 Jul
59.30A	Reggie	Jagers	USA	13.8.94	3	PAm-J	Medellín	23 Aug
59.27	Denzel	Comenentia	NED	25.11.95	1	NC-j	Eindhoven	29 Jun
59.10	Jan-Louw	Kotze	RSA	18.3.94	1		Mobile	30 Mar
58.98	Maximilian	Klaus	GER-Y	7.2.98	1	NC-j	Rostock	27 Jul
58.94	Martin	Pilato	ITA	5.3.94	1	NC-j	Rieti	15 Jun
58.76	Gregory	Thompson	GBR	5.5.94	2	LI	Loughborough	19 May
58.75A	Gerhard	de Beer	RSA	5.7.94	1		Pretoria	16 Mar
58.74	Thiago Adtiano	Negreiros	BRA	12.10.94	1		São Paulo	6 Apr
58.67	Matthew	Denny (20)	AUS-Y	2.6.96	1	NC-j	Perth	13 Mar

HAMMER

82.40		Krisztián	Pars		HUN	18.2.82	1		Dubnica nad Váhom	21 Aug
					80.94	80.73	81.54	82.40		
	81.02	1	Kuso	Szczecin	15 Jun	80.25	79.45	x	x	81.02	p
	80.75	1	GS	Ostrava	26 Jun	78.31	79.68	x	79.54	x	80.75
	80.73	1	Gyulai	Budapest	10 Jul	78.63	78.42	79.08	80.73	x	x
	80.46	1		Cetniewo	29 Jun	78.84	80.46	78.99	78.44	x	78.83
	80.45	1		Velenje	4 Jun	79.18	78.60	80.45	x	p	x
	80.43	1	Skol	Warszawa	25 Aug	78.34	79.49	x	80.43	79.19	79.38
	80.41	1	NC	Budapest	27 Jul	80.41	x	79.39	79.06	77.86	x
	80.30	2	WCh	Moskva	12 Aug	80.30	79.47	79.61	78.90	79.02	x
	79.80	1		Rieti	8 Sep	72.76	78.67	79.80	x		

Mark	Name		Nat	Born	Pos	Meet	Venue	Date	Series
82.27	Pawel	Fajdek	POL	4.6.89	2		Dubnica nad Váhom	21 Aug	80.66 x 82.27 x
81.97	1	WCh					Moskva	12 Aug	81.97 80.92 x 78.41 x 79.57
79.99	3	Kuso					Szczecin	15 Jun	79.09 79.99 x x x x
79.99	1	WUG					Kazan	8 Jul	76.96 x x 79.99 x 78.65
79.92	2	Skol					Warszawa	25 Aug	x x 77.25 79.92 x 77.95
79.68	1						Biala Podlaska	31 Aug	77.05 x 79.68 79.46
80.89	Sergey	Litvinov	RUS	27.1.86	1	Kuts	Moskva	15 Jul	77.88 80.89 x p
80.71	Dilshod	Nazarov	TJK	6.5.82	1	Werfer	Halle	25 May	x 75.36 77.67 78.40 80.71 79.27
79.42	4	Kuso					Szczecin	15 Jun	75.93 75.48 77.98 79.42 79.11 79.05
80.28	Lukás	Melich	CZE	16.9.80	2	Kuso	Szczecin	15 Jun	73.16 x 76.17 76.90 80.28 79.53
80.16	2	GS					Ostrava	26 Jun	75.69 80.16 x 74.93 77.77 x
80.07	1						Castres	30 Jun	77.08 x 79.42 x 80.07 78.33
79.59	2						Cetniewo	29 Jun	75.27 77.78 79.23 77.34 77.13 79.59
79.36	3	WCh					Moskva	12 Aug	70.66 77.11 79.36 76.88 x 75.52
79.19	1						Kladno	18 May	77.81 76.48 78.11 77.75 79.19 78.74
79.70	Primoz	Kozmus	SLO	30.9.79	1	NC	Celje	28 Jul	75.81 79.54 77.63 79.70 x x
79.22	4	WCh					Moskva	12 Aug	77.80 79.21 79.22 78.26 x x
79.61	Denis	Lukyanov	RUS	11.7.89	2	Kuts	Moskva	15 Jul	77.09 78.04 76.89 79.61
79.36	Pavel	Krivitskiy	BLR	17.4.84	1		Minsk	28 Jun	x 79.36 x 77.23 x x
79.26	Aleksey	Zagornyi	RUS	31.5.78	3	Kuts	Moskva	15 Jul	76.01 76.62 79.26 x
79.16	Valeriy	Svyatokho	BLR	20.7.81	1	Klim	Minsk	18 Jun	79.16 x 77.02 p p p
	(31/10)								
79.06	Anatoliy	Pozdnyakov	RUS	1.2.87	4	Kuts	Moskva	15 Jul	
78.99	Yuriy	Shayunov	BLR	22.10.87	1	NC-w	Staiki	3 Feb	
78.79	Szymon	Ziólkowski	POL	1.7.76	5	Kuso	Szczecin	15 Jun	
78.73	Marcel	Lomnicky	SVK	6.7.87	2	WUG	Kazan	8 Jul	
78.21	Hassan Mohamed	Mahmoud	EGY	10.2.84	1		Ceska Lipa	28 Jul	
78.19	Aleksey	Korolyov	RUS	5.4.82	5	Kuts	Moskva	15 Jul	
78.03	Koji	Murofushi	JPN	8.10.74	6	WCh	Moskva	12 Aug	
78.00	Mostafa	Al-Gamal	EGY	1.10.88	1		Cairo	15 Nov	
77.99	Markus	Esser	GER	3.2.80	1		Split	11 May	
77.68	Yevgen	Vynogradov	UKR	30.4.84	1		Nikíti	14 Jul	
	(20)								
77.61	Nicola	Vizzoni	ITA	4.11.73	7	WCh	Moskva	12 Aug	
77.38	Oleksiy	Sokyrskyy	UKR	16.3.85	2		Kiev (Koncha-Zaspa)	21 May	
77.10	A.G.	Kruger	USA	18.2.79	1		Tucson	18 May	
77.00	Igor	Vinichenko	RUS	11.4.84	1		Adler	19 Feb	
76.97	Quentin	Bigot	FRA	1.12.92	1		Metz	6 Jul	
76.94	Esref	Apak ¶	TUR	3.1.82	1	NC	Izmir	1 Jun	
76.93	Ákos	Hudi	HUN	10.8.91	2		Budapest	21 Jul	
76.77	Igors	Sokolovs	LAT	17.8.74	1		Alitus	31 Jul	
76.75	Roberto	Janet	CUB	29.8.86	1		La Habana	25 May	
76.71	Javier	Cienfuegos	ESP	15.7.90	1		Leganés	17 Jul	
	(30)								
76.68	Ali Mohamed	Al-Zankawi	KUW	27.2.84	2	Is.Sol	Palembang	27 Sep	
76.48	Dmitriy	Marshin	AZE	24.2.72	2		Brest	24 May	
76.43	Markus	Johansson	SWE	8.5.90	1		Karlstad	24 Aug	
76.39	Mattias	Jons	SWE	19.11.82	1	vFIN	Stockholm	7 Sep	
76.37	Ashraf Amjad	El-Seify	QAT-J	20.2.95	1		Doha	10 Apr	
76.28	Kibwé	Johnson	USA	17.7.81	1	MSR	Walnut	20 Apr	
76.20	Jacob	Freeman	USA	5.11.80	1		Lakewood Township	17 Jul	
76.08	Zakhar	Makhrosenko	BLR	10.10.91	1	NC-w	Staiki	3 Feb	
75.98	Reinier	Mejias	CUB	22.9.90	1		La Habana	9 Mar	
75.87	Wojciech	Nowicki	POL	22.2.89	2		Bydgoszcz	8 Jun	
	(40)								
75.67	David	Söderberg	FIN	11.8.79	2		Kuortane	3 Aug	
75.66	Sergey	Kolomoyets	BLR	11.8.89	2		Brest	27 Apr	
75.62	Pavel	Boreysho	BLR	16.2.91	3	Klim	Minsk	18 Jun	
75.20		Wang Shizhu	CHN	20.2.89	1	NG	Shenyang	8 Sep	
75.14	András	Haklits	CRO	23.9.77	1		Veszprém	9 Jun	
75.11	Dmytro	Mykolaychuk	UKR	30.1.87	3		Kiev (Koncha-Zaspa)	21 May	
75.11	Alaa El-Din M.	El-Ashry	EGY	6.1.91	1		Cairo	20 Sep	
74.72	Kristóf	Németh	HUN	17.9.87	2		Szombathely	15 May	

MEN 2013

Mark	Name		Nat	Born	Pos	Meet	Venue	Date
74.63	Drew	Loftin	USA	15.9.80	2	MSR	Walnut	20 Apr
74.58	Marco	Lingua	ITA	4.6.78	4		Ponce	18 May
	(50)							
74.55	Chris	Cralle	USA	13.6.88	2	NC	Des Moines	21 Jun
74.46	Mark	Dry	GBR	11.10.87	3	MSR	Walnut	20 Apr
74.41	Sergey	Marghiev	MDA	7.11.92	1	NC	Chisinau	1 Jun
74.41	James	Steacy	CAN	29.5.84	1		Sherwood Park	20 Jul
74.35	Lorenzo	Povegliano	ITA	11.11.84	1		Savona	22 May
74.27	Alexander	Ziegler	GER	7.7.87	6	Werfer	Halle	25 May
74.19		Qi Dakai	CHN	23.5.87	3	AsiC	Pune	6 Jul
74.14	Tuomas	Seppänen	FIN	16.5.86	4		Kuortane	3 Aug
74.01	Mergen	Mamedov	TKM	24.12.90	1		Almaty	16 Jun
73.63	Libor	Charfreitag	SVK	11.9.77	4	MSR	Walnut	20 Apr
	(60)							
73.60	Roberto	Sawyers	CRC	17.10.86	1		Ciudad de Guatemala	24 Aug
73.50	Valeriy	Pronkin	RUS-J	15.6.94	4		Sochi	25 May
73.49		Wan Yong	CHN	22.7.87	2	NG	Shenyang	8 Sep
73.40	Oleg	Dubitskiy	BLR	14.10.90	5	NC-w	Staiki	3 Feb
73.27	Eivind	Henriksen	NOR	14.9.90	1		Tønsberg	4 Jul
73.15	Jérôme	Bortoluzzi	FRA	20.5.82	1		La Roche-sur-Yon	24 Jul
73.10	Sven	Möhsner	GER	30.1.86	7	Werfer	Halle	25 May
72.98		Lee Yun-chul	KOR	28.3.82	4	AsiC	Pune	6 Jul
72.57	Bruno	Boccalatte	FRA	10.11.88	1		Bertrix	10 Aug
72.54	Fatih	Eryildirim ¶	TUR	1.3.79	1		Ankara	27 Apr
	(70)							
72.49	Yevgeniy	Aydamirov	RUS	11.5.87	3		Yerino	2 Jun
72.45	Alex	Smith	GBR	6.3.88	1	LI	Loughborough	19 May
72.43	Simone	Falloni	ITA	26.9.91	4	EU23	Tampere	13 Jul
72.43	Hiroshi	Noguchi	JPN	3.5.83	1		Tokyo (Chofu)	7 Oct
72.40	Chris	Harmse	RSA	31.5.73	1	NC	Stellenbosch	12 Apr
72.31	Andrew	Frost	GBR	17.4.81	1		Livingston	7 Sep
72.07	Andy	Fryman	USA	3.2.85	1		Charlotte, NC	15 Mar
72.05	Frédéric	Pouzy	FRA	18.2.83	3		Castres	30 Jun
72.03	Yevgeniy	Korotovskiy	RUS	21.6.92	1	NC-w23	Adler	27 Feb
71.95	Arno	Laitinen	FIN	9.3.88	3	NC	Vaasa	27 Jul
	(80)							
71.92	Mohsen	Anani	EGY	25.5.85	4	Arab C	Doha	22 May
71.65	Pedro José	Martín	ESP	12.8.92	1		Madrid (Tajamar)	13 Dec
71.60	Nick	Miller	GBR	1.5.93	1q	NCAA-w	Austin	23 May
71.49	Conor	McCullough	IRL	31.1.91	6	EU23	Tampere	13 Jul
71.43	Kaveh	Mousavi	IRI	27.5.85	5	AsiC	Pune	6 Jul
71.36	Wágner	Domingos	BRA	23.6.83	1	SACh	Cartagena	6 Jul
71.24	Chris	Bennett	GBR	17.12.89	1		Grangemouth	21 Jul
71.14	Nicolas	Figère	FRA	19.5.79	1		Antony	28 Apr
71.14	Dário	Manso	POR	1.7.82	1		Leiria	3 Aug
71.01	Amir	Williamson	GBR	10.4.87	1		Abingdon	21 Jul
	(90)							
70.90	Michael	Bomba	GBR	10.10.86	1		Wakefield	6 Apr
70.84	Tomás	Kruzliak	SVK	9.2.92	1	ACC	Raleigh	20 Apr
70.82	James	Bedford	GBR	29.12.88	3	LI	Loughborough	19 May
70.76	Sukhrob	Khodjayev	UZB	21.5.93	1		Tashkent	8 Jun
70.73	Driss	Barid	MAR	12.12.86	1		Rabat	1 Jun
70.63	Juha	Kauppinen	FIN	16.8.86	1		Pori	5 Jun
70.63		Ma Liang	CHN	22.7.83	4	NG	Shenyang	8 Sep
70.61	Özkan	Baltaci	TUR-J	13.2.94	1		Ankara	24 Aug
70.55	Garland	Porter	USA	10.2.82	2		Tucson	18 May
70.49	Garrett	Grey	USA	22.2.90	1	NCAA-2	Pueblo, CO	23 May
	(100)							

70.48	Mike	Floyd	GBR	26.9.76	22 Jun	69.75	Alec	Faldermeyer	USA	9.7.92	28 Mar
70.44	Colin	Dunbar	USA	27.6.88	6 Apr	69.68	Tim	Driesen	AUS	27.3.84	12 Apr
70.41	Adonson	Shallow	VIN	17.8.86	18 Apr	69.64	Collin	Post	USA	13.2.82	2 Jun
70.38	Aurélien	Boisrond	FRA	17.2.85	8 May	69.61	Justin	Welch	USA	29.9.91	20 Apr
70.27	Michal	Fiala	CZE	22.6.85	18 May	69.59	Mirko	Micuda	CRO	22.12.89	27 Jul
70.19	Isaac	Vicente	ESP	30.4.87	5 May	69.49	Masoud	Moghaddam	IRI	22.5.88	21 Jun
70.18	Johannes	Bichler	GER	3.7.90	7 Jul	69.48	Jerrit	Lipske	GER	1.2.87	13 Jul
70.15	Olli-Pekka	Karjalainen	FIN	7.3.80	16 Jun	69.44	Paul	Hützen	GER	7.3.91	23 Jun
70.13	Noleisis	Bicet	CUB	6.2.81	8 Jun	69.40	Benjamin	Boruschewski	GER	23.4.80	7 Jul
70.10	Reza	Moghaddam	IRI	17.11.88	21 Jun	69.33	Juan Ignacio	Cerra	ARG	16.10.76	6 Jul
70.00	Oleksandr	Myakhkyh	UKR	7.5.86	21 May	69.11	Norbert	Rauhut	POL	17.1.90	16 Jul
69.98	Ilmari	Lahtinen	FIN	12.10.93	5 Jun	69.10	Andriy	Martynyuk	UKR	25.9.90	26 Jul
69.95		Zhang Dapeng	CHN	6.8.83	8 Sep	68.80	Fabián	Di Paolo	ARG	25.11.83	6 Apr
69.92	Ryan	Loughney	USA	21.8.89	9 Jul	68.80	Konstadínos	Stathelakos	CYP	30.12.87	21 Jun

Mark	Name		Nat	Born	Pos	Meet	Venue	Date
68.79	Igor	Buryi	RUS	8.4.93	27 Feb			
68.69	Nikolay	Bashan	BLR	18.11.92	27 Feb			
68.68	Jeremy	Postin	USA	7.3.90	27 Apr			
68.57	Michael	Lauro	USA	1.7.89	14 Jul			
68.50	Miroslav	Pavlícek	CZE	31.3.87	27 Jul			
68.46	Gergely	Nagy	HUN	8.4.91	24 Aug			
68.45	Mihail	Anastasákis	GRE-J	3.12.94	11 May			
68.38	Dan Zhangcheng		CHN	14.12.88	31 Mar			
68.35	Chris	Shorthouse	GBR	23.6.88	22 Jun			

Irregular conditions

71.51	Reza	Moghaddam	IRI	17.10.88	1		Tehran	31 May
69.67	Masoud	Moghaddam	IRI	22.5.88	31 May			

Drugs disqualification

68.97	Andrey	Vorontsov ¶	BLR	24.7.75	18 Jan			

Mark	Name		Nat	Born	Pos	Meet	Venue	Date
68.35	Pedro	Muñoz	VEN	24.4.82	27 Nov
68.34	Vincent	Onos	NED	8.4.86	11 May
68.30	Remy	Conatser	USA	20.7.90	6 Jun
68.25	Kai	Räsänen	FIN	29.6.90	23 Feb
68.21	Hiroaki	Doi	JPN	2.12.78	19 Oct
68.17	Kamalpreet	Singh	IND	3.11.87	30 Mar
68.04	Nicolò	Bolla	ITA	8.6.90	8 Jun
68.03	Giovanni	Sanguin	ITA	14.5.69	12 Jun
68.00	Kevin	Becker	USA	1.5.84	5 Apr
(146)					
68.62	Aleksandr	Drygol ¶	UKR	25.4.66	24 Jul

JUNIORS

Mark	Name			Nat	Born	Pos	Meet	Venue	Date
76.37	Ashraf Amjad	El-Seify		QAT	20.2.95	1		Doha	10 Apr
	73.17	2	ArabC Doha		22 May	72.88	3	Franc Nice	10 Sep
73.50	Valeriy	Pronkin		RUS	15.6.94	4		Sochi	25 May
	70.50	2	Adler		19 Feb				
70.61	Özkan	Baltaci		TUR	13.2.94	1		Ankara	24 Aug
	70.41	2	BalkC Stara Zagora		27 Jul	8 performances by 4 men over 70.00			
66.69	Bence	Pásztor		HUN-Y	5.2.95	5	NC	Budapest	27 Jul
66.63	Diego	del Real		MEX	6.3.94	1	NC	Zapopan	23 Jun
66.42	Sebastian	Nowicki		POL	26.8.94	2		Warszawa	15 Sep
65.65	Marco	Bortolato		ITA	11.2.94	1		Gorizia	7 Jul
65.59	Sergiy	Reheda		UKR	6.2.94	2	NC-w23	Yalta	28 Mar
65.03	Artem	Poleshko		UKR	13.2.94	2		Yalta	18 May
64.93	Rudy	Winkler (10)		USA	6.12.94	1		Wakefield RI	14 Jul

6KG HAMMER

Mark	Name			Nat	Born	Pos	Meet	Venue	Date
81.16	Özkan	Baltaci		TUR	13.2.94	1		Ankara	31 Jul
	79.01	1	Trabzon		20 Aug	77.81	1	BalkC Denizli	6 Jul
	78.44	1	Ankara		22 Jun				
80.70	Valeriy	Pronkin		RUS	15.6.94	1		Adler	23 Apr
	80.31	1	NC-j Kazan		15 Jun	78.34	1	EJ Rieti	19 Jul
	79.72	1	Krasnodar		16 May	78.32	1	NC-w Adler	27 Feb
79.24	Ashraf Amjad	El-Seify		QAT-Y	20.2.95	1		Doha	11 Mar
	77.60	1	Doha		2 Apr	12 performances by 4 men over 77.00			
77.35	Bence	Pásztor		HUN	5.2.95	2	EJ	Rieti	19 Jul
76.98	Sergiy	Reheda		UKR	6.2.94	1	NC-wj	Yalta	30 Feb
75.40	Mihaíl	Anastasákis		GRE	3.12.94	1	NC-j	Lárisa	29 Jun
74.80	Rudy	Winkler		USA	6.12.94	1	NC-j	Des Moines	21 Jun
74.49	Islam Ahmed	Taha		EGY	23.7.94	1	Af-J	Bambous	30 Aug
73.94	Marco	Bortolato		ITA	11.2.94	1	NC-wj	Lucca	23 Feb
73.62	Denzel	Comenentia (10)		NED	25.11.95	1	Werfer	Halle	25 May
73.60	Alexander	Larsson		SWE	10.6.94	2	Werfer	Halle	25 May
73.36	Tolgahan	Yavuz		TUR	10.8.95	1		Bursa	27 Mar
73.32	Ilyas	Terentyev		RUS	23.1.95	1		Adler	18 Feb
73.29	Matthew	Denny		AUS-Y	2.6.96	1	NC-j	Perth	14 Mar
73.05	Joaquín	Gómez		ARG-Y	14.10.96	1		Resistencia	22 Sep
72.99	Diego	del Real		MEX	6.3.94	1	PAm-J	Medellín	23 Aug
72.86	Simon	Lang		GER	14.1.94	3	Werfer	Halle	25 May
72.65	Hevert	Álvarez		CHI	17.9.94	1		Temuco	27 Apr
72.49	Callum	Brown		GBR	20.7.94	1		Watford	22 Jun
72.15	Bálint	Horváth (20)		HUN	31.5.95	1		Szombathely	19 Jun

JAVELIN

Mark					Nat	Born	Pos			Meet		Venue				Date
89.03		Tero		Pitkämaki	FIN	19.12.82	1					Bad Köstritz				25 Aug
							80.06	x	80.38	89.03	81.17	79.80				
	87.60	1	DL	Shanghai		18 May	79.75	83.43	87.60	86.54	p	p			
	87.32	1	VD	Bruxelles		6 Sep	79.75	80.34	x	87.32	p	p			
	87.07	2	WCh	Moskva		17 Aug	83.40	86.88	87.07	85.67	x	85.22			
	86.40A	1		Potchefstroom		16 Mar	85.16	83.75	86.40	82.40	84.59	83.78			
	86.38	1	vSWE	Stockholm		8 Sep	82.74	79.41	85.15	x	81.50	86.38			
	86.36	1	Hanz	Zagreb		3 Sep	85.15	84.27	86.36	85.66	83.77	85.14			
	86.13	1		Kuortane		3 Aug	83.08	x	x	79.50	86.13	82.67			
	85.70	1	NC	Vaasa		28 Jul	81.92	83.83	85.70	x	x	x			
	85.39	1	DL	Dessau		31 May	82.41	85.39	79.14	82.94	x	x			
88.84		Dmitriy		Tarabin	RUS	29.10.91	1	NC				Moskva				24 Jul
							84.49	81.25	84.34	x	83.22	88.84			
	86.23	3	WCh	Moskva		17 Aug	x	84.38	x	82.25	x	86.23			
	85.99	1	ET	Gateshead		23 Jun	x	85.99	84.69	x					

Mark	Name		Nat	Born	Pos	Meet	Venue			Date
85.63	1	NC-w Adler		28 Feb	81.77	82.89	x	85.63	x	x
85.36	3	DL Shanghai		18 May	82.41	85.36	79.14	82.94	x	x
87.68	Vitezslav	Vesely	CZE	27.2.83	1	Herc	Monaco			19 Jul
					83.58	87.68	p	p		
87.58	1	GS Ostrava		27 Jun	87.58	85.71	84.29	84.51	x	x
87.17	1	WCh Moskva		17 Aug	87.17	78.80	81.21	83.80	x	p
86.94	1	Odlozil Praha		10 Jun	86.94	85.22	p	p	p	p
86.67	2	DL Shanghai		18 May	86.67	x	x	80.06	x	x
86.67	2	VD Bruxelles		6 Sep	86.67	x	83.46	x	x	80.44
85.96	1	Bisl Oslo		13 Jun	83.98	85.96	x	x	x	x
85.09	1	DL Doha		10 May	x	81.78	85.09	x	p	p
85.96	Yukifumi	Murakami	JPN	23.12.79	1	Oda	Hiroshima			29 Apr
					x	78.89	85.96	p	p	p
85.70	Antti	Ruuskanen	FIN	21.2.84	2		Kuortane			3 Aug
					77.74	80.63	x	81.11	85.70	84.19
85.64	2	Hanz Zagreb		3 Sep	80.79	80.09	85.64	80.07	p	p
85.07	2	vSWE Stockholm		8 Sep	78.66	x	77.60	85.07	80.01	80.83
85.04	1	Tampere		25 Aug	82.71	84.18	85.04	80.33	82.21	81.14
85.59	Guillermo	Martínez	CUB	28.6.81	1	NC	La Habana			17 Mar
					73.79	85.59	p	p	p	p
85.40	Julius	Yego	KEN	4.1.89	4	WCh	Moskva			17 Aug
	(30/7)				80.60	x	81.13	x	85.40	81.20
84.65	Ari	Mannio	FIN	23.7.87	1	PNG	Turku			16 Jun
84.64	Andreas	Thorkildsen	NOR	1.4.82	1		Florø			8 Jun
84.61	Kim	Amb	SWE	31.7.90	4		Zagreb			3 Sep
	(10)									
84.58	Fatih	Avan	TUR	1.1.89	1		Yerino			2 Jun
84.48	Roman	Avramenko ¶	UKR	23.3.88	1		Bellinzona			11 Jun
84.39	Keshorn	Walcott	TTO	2.4.93	1		Port of Spain			3 May
84.20	Lars	Hamann	GER	4.4.89	1		Neukieritzsch			19 Jul
83.98	Lukasz	Grzeszczuk	POL	3.3.90	1		Bialystok			3 May
83.95	Thomas	Röhler	GER	30.9.91	3		Dessau			31 May
83.79	Ivan	Zaytsev	UZB	11.11.88	1	Sule	Tartu			28 May
83.62	Ihab Abdelrahman	Sayed	EGY	1.5.89	Q	WCh	Moskva			15 Aug
83.56	Valeriy	Iordan	RUS	14.2.92	2	NC-w	Adler			28 Feb
83.50	Riley	Dolezal	USA	16.11.85	1	NC	Des Moines			23 Jun
	(20)									
83.48	Risto	Mätas	EST	30.4.84	1		Kohila			31 Aug
83.23	Gabriel	Wallin	SWE	14.10.81	1		Hässelby			25 Jun
83.14	Sam	Humphreys	USA	12.9.90	2	NC	Des Moines			23 Jun
83.14		Zhao Qinggang	CHN	24.7.85	1	NG	Shenyang			9 Sep
83.04	Marcin	Krukowski	POL	14.6.92	1		Lodz			18 May
82.91	Teemu	Wirkkala	FIN	14.1.84	2	PNG	Turku			16 Jun
82.79	Vadims	Vasilevskis	LAT	5.1.82	2		Riga			30 May
82.77	Zigismunds	Sirmais	LAT	6.5.92	1	EU23	Tampere			12 Jul
82.54	Aleksey	Tovarnov	RUS	21.1.85	3	NC-w	Adler			28 Feb
82.49	Vladimir	Kozlov	BLR	20.4.85	2	Sule	Tartu			28 May
	(30)									
82.42	Bernhard	Seifert	GER	15.2.93	2	EU23	Tampere			12 Jul
82.39	Petr	Frydrych	CZE	13.1.88	1		Domazlice			13 Sep
82.11		Huang Shih-Feng	TPE	2.3.92	2	EAsG	Tianjin			9 Oct
81.97A	Robert	Oosthuizen	RSA	23.1.87	1		Potchefstroom			20 Apr
81.73	Tuomas	Laaksonen	FIN	9.3.90	4	PNG	Turku			16 Jun
81.68	Rolands	Strobinders	LAT	14.4.92	1		Liepaja			11 May
81.67	Sampo	Lehtola	FIN	10.5.89	1		Lapinlahti			21 Jul
81.49	Matthias	de Zordo	GER	21.2.88	4	DL	Doha			10 May
81.40	Corey	White	USA	31.1.86	1		Tucson			18 May
81.14	Hamish	Peacock	AUS	15.10.90	1		Hobart			28 Jul
	(40)									
81.07	Stuart	Farquhar	NZL	15.3.82	1		Melbourne			6 Apr
81.05	Tanel	Laanmäe	EST	29.9.89	2		Bellinzona			11 Jun
80.98	Erki	Leppik	EST	18.3.88	1		Tallinn			15 Jul
80.71	Ainars	Kovals	LAT	21.11.81	2		Viljandi			2 Jul
80.67	David	Golling	GER	13.3.90	2		Bad Köstritz			25 Aug
80.66	Gudmundur	Sverrisson	ISL	24.5.90	1	NC	Akureyri			27 Jul
80.39	Lassi	Etelätalo	FIN	30.4.88	2		Joensuu			9 Jun
80.28	Hubert	Chmielak	POL	19.6.89	1	NC	Torun			21 Jul
80.15	Roderick Genki	Dean	JPN	30.12.91	1		Tokyo			7 Apr
80.13	Igor	Janik	POL	18.1.83	3		Bellinzona			11 Jun
	(50)									
80.05	Oleksandr	Nychyporchuk	UKR	14.4.92	1	NC-w	Yalta			21 Feb

Mark	Name		Nat	Born	Pos	Meet	Venue	Date
80.04	Sean	Furey	USA	31.8.82	1		Urjala	27 Aug
79.99	Jarrod	Bannister ¶	AUS	3.10.84	3		Melbourne	6 Apr
79.98	Killian	Duréchou	FRA	15.8.92	1		Poitiers	21 Sep
79.97	Spiridon	Lebésis	GRE	30.5.87	5		Bellinzona	11 Jun
79.82	Magnus	Kirt	EST	10.4.90	1		Tallinn	24 Aug
79.80	Till	Wöschler	GER	9.6.91	2		Reims	28 Jun
79.71		Park Jae-myong	KOR	15.12.81	1	NG	Incheon	22 Oct
79.68	Julian	Weber	GER-J	29.8.94	1	EJ	Rieti	20 Jul
79.62	Dejan	Mileusnic	BIH	16.11.91	1	NC-w	Sremska Mitrovica	23 Mar
	(60)							
79.62	Sachith	Maduranga	SRI	15.6.90	2	AsiC	Pune	5 Jul
79.52	Patrik	Zenúch	SVK	30.12.90	1		Trnava	17 Aug
79.20	Viktor	Goncharov	RUS	9.5.91	2		Incheon	3 Jul
79.15	Matija	Kranjc	SLO	12.6.84	1		Leibnitz	29 Aug
79.06	Rainer	Manninen	FIN	21.3.91	1	NC-23	Raahe	31 Aug
79.03	Víctor	Fatecha	PAR	10.3.88	17q	WCh	Moskva	15 Aug
79.03A	Dayron	Márquez	COL	19.11.83	1		Medellín	6 Oct
78.90	Pawel	Rozinski	POL	11.7.87	4	ECp-w	Castellón	17 Mar
78.78	Tino	Häber	GER	6.10.82	6	Werfer	Halle	25 May
78.77A	Jayson	Henning	RSA	13.8.90	1		Potchefstroom	25 May
	(70)							
78.77	Maksym	Bohdan	UKR-J	27.2.94	2	EJ	Rieti	19 Jul
78.69	Tim	Glover	USA	1.11.90	2		Tucson	18 May
78.66	Braian	Toledo	ARG	8.9.93	1		Buenos Aires	7 Dec
78.62	Thomas	Smet	BEL	12.7.88	1		Hilversum	7 Jul
78.62	Toni	Sirviö	FIN	8.1.92	1		Joensuu	8 Sep
78.59	Jiannis [Ioannis]	Smaliós	SWE	17.2.87	6	vFIN	Stockholm	8 Sep
78.53	Sam	Crouser	USA	31.12.91	3q	NCAA-w	Austin	25 May
78.43A	Juan José	Méndez	MEX	27.4.88	1	NC	Zapopan	21 Jun
78.41	Nick	Howe	USA	17.11.89	3		Tucson	18 May
78.20	Vedran	Samac	SRB	22.1.90	1		Sremska Mitrovica	10 Mar
	(80)							
78.19	Ryohei	Arai	JPN	23.6.91	1		Tokyo	28 Jul
78.10	Matthew	Outzen	AUS	12.10.87	5		Melbourne	6 Apr
78.08	Krzysztof	Szalecki	POL	3.2.91	5	EU23	Tampere	12 Jul
78.00	Marko	Jänes	EST	29.8.76	1		Tartu	13 Jun
77.98A	Cody	Parker	CAN	27.6.92	1	NCAA-2	Pueblo, CO	25 May
77.92	Aleksandr	Ashomko	BLR	18.2.84	1		Minsk	28 Jun
77.84	Yuya	Koriki	JPN	19.10.89	3	NC	Tokyo [Chofu]	8 Jun
77.66	Aleksandr	Kharitonov	RUS	19.7.90	2		Liepaja	11 May
77.63	Pavel	Meleshko	BLR	24.11.92	1		Minsk	7 Jun
77.60		Jung Sang-jin	KOR	16.4.84	2	NG	Incheon	22 Oct
	(90)							
77.52		Zhao Pengju	CHN	6.2.88	2		Zhaoqing	28 Apr
77.50	Bobur	Shokirjanov	UZB	5.12.90	1		Chonburi	8 May
77.47	Andy	Fahringer	USA	30.5.89	1		Bethlehem, PA	20 Apr
77.46	Oleksandr	Pyatnytsya	UKR	14.7.85	1		Kiev (Koncha-Zaspa)	13 Nov
77.36	Barry	Krammes	USA	1.9.81	4	NC	Des Moines	23 Jun
77.27	Sami	Peltomäki	FIN	11.1.91	4		Joensuu	9 Jun
77.23	Júlio César	de Oliveira	BRA	4.2.86	1		Campinas	4 May
77.19	Jonas	Lohse	SWE	15.5.87	1		Borås	12 May
77.15	Rustem	Dremdzhy	UKR	3.6.91	2		Yalta	18 May
77.10	Norbert	Bonvecchio	ITA	14.8.85	1		Savona	22 May
	(100)							

Mark			Nat	Born	Date		Mark			Nat	Born	Date
76.97	Oleksandr	Chehlatyy	UKR	27.9.89	18 May		76.10		Wang Qingbo	CHN	24.5.88	16 Jun
76.89	Kim-Dominik	Seyfried	GER	23.6.92	28 Jul		75.93	Yevgeniy	Filichkin	RUS	3.3.87	24 Jul
76.88	Mykola	Shama	UKR	5.4.91	21 Feb		75.92	Matthias	Treff	GER	27.2.88	19 Apr
76.87	Leslie	Copeland	FIJ	23.4.88	5 Jun		75.88	Ahti	Peder	EST	29.8.76	24 Aug
76.86	Kyle	Nielsen	CAN	22.4.89	17 May		75.88		Chen Qi	CHN	10.3.82	9 Sep
76.86	Curtis	Moss	USA	12.4.87	1 Jul		75.86		Jiang Xingyu	CHN	16.3.87	8 May
76.77	Devender	Singh	IND	18.12.88	6 Apr		75.85	Jakub	Vadlejch	CZE	10.10.90	28 Aug
76.61	German	Komarov	RUS-J	14.12.94	3 Jul		75.83A	Chad	Herman	RSA	25.5.92	29 Apr
76.58	Luke	Cann	AUS-J	17.7.94	23 Mar		75.82	Harri	Haatainen	FIN	5.1.78	27 Jul
76.58	Johannes	Vetter	GER	26.3.93	8 Jun		75.81		Sun Jianjun	CHN	9.6.91	31 Mar
76.47	Igor	Sukhomlinov	RUS	13.2.77	19 Feb		75.80	Vipin	Kasana	IND	4.8.89	25 Apr
76.47	Kennosuke	Sogawa	JPN-J	12.7.94	12 May		75.80	Jani	Kiiskulä	FIN	28.12.89	14 Sep
76.38	Jan	Kubes	CZE-J	19.6.94	24 Jul		75.73	Mustafa	Tan	TUR	10.4.90	8 Sep
76.36	Jan Felix	Knobel	GER	16.1.89	27 Feb		75.72	Bartosz	Osewski	POL	20.3.91	18 May
76.30	David	Madeo	GER	15.2.86	16 Mar		75.63	Toni	Kuusela	FIN-J	21.1.94	16 Jun
76.30	Peerachet	Janthra	THA	9.9.90	15 Dec		75.60	Lee	Doran	GBR	5.3.85	27 Jun
76.29	Jérôme	Haeffler	FRA	12.5.82	9 Mar		75.59	Ken	Arai	JPN	22.12.81	8 Jun
76.13	Arley	Ibargüen	COL	4.12.82	7 Jul		75.56	Alex	Kiprotich	KEN-J	10.10.94	13 Aug
76.11		Xu Chaoping	CHN	21.6.87	31 Mar		75.56	Andreas	Hoffman	GER	16.12.91	21 Sep

Mark	Name		Nat	Born	Pos	Meet	Venue	Date
75.55	Tim	Van Liew	USA	25.5.90				25 May
75.52A	Carlos Alberto	Armenta	MEX	18.7.90				9 Jun
75.47	Ravinder	Singh Kharia	IND	19.3.86				8 Sep
75.43	Ville	Räsänen	FIN	18.3.77				8 Sep
75.43	Hussadin	Rodmanee	THA	13.7.88				15 Dec
75.39	Antoine	Wagner	LUX	20.10.88				17 Mar
75.39	Kacper	Oleszczuk	POL-J	15.5.94				11 May
75.36	Ben	Lincoln	USA	26.5.91				15 Mar
75.34	Mika	Aalto	FIN	11.3.82				16 Jun
75.24	Kyle	Smith	USA	9.3.90				23 Jun
75.23	Billy	Stanley	USA-J	6.2.94				12 May
75.17	Morné	Moolman	RSA-J	1.9.94				24 May
75.16	Chris	Dittelbach	GER	17.2.87				27 Apr
75.11	Lukas	Wieland	SUI-J	24.7.94				26 Jul
75.03	Samarjeet	Singh	IND	7.11.88				5 Jul
75.02	Antonio	Fent	ITA	31.3.88				27 Jul
74.98	Karol	Jakimowicz	POL	15.6.87				18 May
74.94	Joel	Karjalainen	FIN	19.7.91				6 Jun
74.94		Park Won-kil	KOR	24.2.90				1 Sep
74.93	Cyrus	Hostetler	USA	8.8.86				3 May
74.90A	Dylan	Lindsay	RSA	4.9.91				25 May
74.88	Pawel	Rakoczy	POL	15.5.87				18 May
74.88	Nikita	Petinov	RUS	29.8.90				24 Jul
74.83	Jason	Flanagan	USA	30.5.90				15 Mar
74.82A	José Gregorio	Lemus	COL	4.6.91				20 Jun
74.80	Krishnan	Kumar Patel	IND	13.5.91				5 Jun
74.80	Daan	Meyer	NED	17.2.83				29 Sep
74.78		Qin Qiang	CHN	18.4.83				9 Sep
74.76		Hu Hailong	CHN	26.8.88				31 Mar
74.75	Craig	Kinsley	USA	19.1.89				18 May
74.68	Yevgeniy	Zoteyev	RUS	24.8.91				15 Jun
74.62	Dinesh	Kumar Rao	IND	7.2.88				8 Sep
74.61		Dai Li	CHN	20.5.91				30 May
74.58	Roberto	Bertolini	ITA	9.10.85				27 Apr
74.52	Rajesh	Kumar Bind	IND-J	20.7.94				7 Dec
74.48	Yutaro	Tanemoto	JPN	30.11.84				25 Mar
74.46		Kim Ye-ram	KOR-J	2.3.94				6 Jun
74.32	Ranno	Koorep	EST	24.1.90				28 May
74.30	Tatsuya	Mine	JPN	2.2.92				22 Oct
74.28	Sho	Tanaka	JPN-J	28.2.94				29 Apr
74.28	Paulo Enrique	da Silva	BRA	28.9.93				9 Jun
74.23	Ilya	Korotkov	RUS	6.12.83				19 Feb
74.18	Yasuo	Ikeda	JPN	28.7.77				29 Apr
74.18	Caleb	Jones	CAN	17.5.91				28 Jul
74.15	Peter	Esenwein	GER	7.12.67				16 Jun
74.15	Jarolsav	Jílek	CZE	22.10.89				8 Sep
74.13	Tiago	Aperta	POR	15.1.92				15 Jun
74.11	Brent	Lagace	USA	31.5.88				8 Jun
74.11		Song Bin	CHN	30.9.90				9 Sep
74.03	Timothy	Herman	BEL	19.10.90				19 Oct
74.00	Dawid	Kosciów	POL	1.1.90				11 May
74.00	Ryan	Brandel	USA	9.5.84				14 Jun
(185)								

JUNIORS

See main list for top 2 juniors. 10 performances by 6 men over 76.50. Additional marks and further juniors:

Weber   78.17   1   Mannheim   30 Jun   77.02   Q   EJ   Rieti   18 Jul
Bohdan   77.27   Q   EJ   Rieti   18 Jul   76.89   1   Kyiv (K-Z)   13 Nov

Mark	Name		Nat	Born	Pos	Meet	Venue	Date
76.61	German	Komarov	RUS	14.12.94	2		Moskva	3 Jul
76.58	Luke	Cann	AUS	17.7.94	2		Brisbane	23 Mar
76.47	Kennosuke	Sogawa	JPN	12.7.94	1		Osaka	12 May
76.38	Jan	Kubes	CZE	19.6.94	1		Tábor	24 Jul
75.63	Toni	Kuusela	FIN	21.1.94	2		Kuortane	16 Jun
75.56	Alex	Kiprotich	KEN	10.10.94	1		Nairobi	13 Aug
75.39	Kacper	Oleszczuk	POL	15.5.94	1		Slupsk	11 May
75.23	Billy	Stanley (10)	USA	6.2.94	1	Big 10	Columbus	12 May
75.17	Morné	Moolman	RSA	1.9.94	1q	NCAA-E	Greensboro	24 May
75.11	Lukas	Wieland	SUI	24.7.94	1		Luzern	26 Jul
74.52	Rajesh	Kumar Bind	IND	20.7.94	1	NC-j	Bangalore	7 Dec
74.46		Kim Ye-ram	KOR	2.3.94	1	NC	Yeosu	6 Jun
74.28	Sho	Tanaka	JPN	28.2.94	6	Oda	Hiroshima	29 Apr
73.97	Norbert	Rivasz-Tóth	HUN-Y	6.5.96	Q	EJ	Rieti	18 Jul
73.83	Adriaan	Beukes	BOT	14.7.94	2	RSA Uns	Durban	28 Apr
73.73	Jami	Kinnunen	FIN	31.5.95	Q	NC-j	Lappeenranta	10 Aug
73.68	Joni	Karvinen	FIN	7.2.94	Q	EJ	Rieti	18 Jul
73.62	Yuriy	Kishniruk (20)	UKR	6.12.94	1	NC	Donetsk	26 Jul

DECATHLON

8809   Ashton   Eaton   USA   21.1.88   1   WCh   Moskva   11 Aug
10.35/-0.5   7.73/0.3   14.39   1.93   46.02   13.72/0.4   45.00   5.20   64.83   4:29.80

8670   Michael   Schrader   GER   1.7.87   2   WCh   Moskva   11 Aug
10.73/-0.5   7.85/0.2   14.56   1.99   47.66   14.29/0.4   46.44   5.00   65.67   4:25.38

8514   Pascal   Behrenbruch   GER   19.1.85   1   Ratingen   16 Jun
10.73W/5.4   6.94/-0.5   15.89   1.97   48.60   14.17/0.9   48.25   5.00   67.59   4:30.26

8512   Damian   Warner   CAN   4.11.89   3   WCh   Moskva   11 Aug
10.43/-0.5   7.39/0.3   14.23   2.05   48.41   13.96/0.4   44.13   4.80   64.67   4:29.97

8488w   Rico   Freimuth   GER   14.3.88   2   Ratingen   16 Jun
10.36W/5.4   7.55/0.5   14.97   1.94   48.46   13.85/0.9   49.03   4.80   57.61   4:34.69

8446   Kevin   Mayer   FRA   10.2.92   4   WCh   Moskva   11 Aug
11.23/-0.1   7.50/0.1   13.76   2.05   49.53   14.21/-0.2   45.37   5.20   66.09   4:25.04

8427   Schrader   GER   1   Ulm   23 May
10.52/1.7   7.82/0.7   14.74   1.90   49.84   14.02/1.6   45.62   4.80   62.99   4:29.50

8396w   Jan Felix   Knobel   GER   16.8.89   3   Ratingen   16 Jun
10.85W/5.4   7.36/1.0   15.82   1.91   49.19   14.59/0.9   49.21   5.00   71.61   4:51.68

8393   Carlos Eduardo   Chinin   BRA   3.5.85   1   NC   São Paulo   8 Jun
10.85/0.5   7.55/0.9   15.28   2.04   48.18   14.08/1.0   42.46   4.90   59.58   4:34.77

8391   Eelco   Sintnicolaas   NED   7.4.87   5   WCh   Moskva   11 Aug
10.85/-0.5   7.65/0.8   14.08   2.02   48.25   14.18/0.4   39.21   5.30   56.75   4:24.64

8390   Andrey   Kravchenko (10)   BLR   4.1.86   1   Firenze   3 May
11.16/0.0   7.39/0.9   14.76   2.07   49.27   14.11/0.6   46.04   5.05   60.59   4:30.11

Mark	Name	Nat	Born	Pos	Meet	Venue	Date

8390 **Mayer** — 1 ECp Tallinn 30 Jun
11.04/1.4 7.63/1.2 14.95 2.04 49.50 14.39w/2.7 44.89 4.90 60.04 4:21.95

8388 **Chinin** — 6 WCh Moskva 11 Aug
10.78/-0.1 7.54/1.0 14.49 1.96 48.80 14.05/0.4 45.84 5.10 59.98 4:36.01

8382 **Freimuth** — 7 WCh Moskva 11 Aug
10.60/-0.5 7.22/1.3 14.80 1.99 48.05 13.90/0.4 48.74 4.90 56.21 4:37.83

8380 **Kravchenko** — 1 Kladno 9 Jun
11.23/-1.7 7.64/0.9 14.96 2.09 49.17 14.14/1.1 47.11 4.82 62.52 4:41.08

8370 Ilya **Shkurenyov** RUS 11.1.91 — 8 WCh Moskva 11 Aug
10.97/-0.1 7.35/0.1 13.88 2.05 48.39 14.34/-0.1 44.06 5.40 59.46 4:36.95

8366 Kai **Kazmirek** GER 28.1.91 — 1 EU23 Tampere 12 Jul
10.81/0.8 7.58/-1.3 13.09 2.07 46.98 14.35/-0.3 44.77 5.20 52.69 4:34.46

8354 **Shkurenyov** — 1 NC Cheboksary 6 Jun
10.91/1.2 7.54/2.0 13.77 2.05 49.35 14.13/1.6 45.28 5.30 55.91 4:35.71

8350w **Kazmirek** — 4 Ratingen 16 Jun
10.61W/5.4 7.51/0.2 13.05 2.09 47.26 14.36/0.9 44.69 5.10 54.45 4:40.46

8343 Willem **Coertzen** RSA 30.12.82 — 9 WCh Moskva 11 Aug
10.95/0.1 7.44/1.8 13.88 2.05 48.32 14.30/-0.1 43.25 4.50 69.35 4:24.60

8322 **Sintnicolaas** — 1 ECp-1 Nottwil 30 Jun
10.94/-0.7 7.16/0.0 13.53 1.98 48.16 13.92/0.9 43.17 5.40 56.62 4:25.51

8317 Leonel **Suárez** CUB 1.9.87 — 10 WCh Moskva 11 Aug
11.07/-0.5 7.33/0.3 14.20 1.90 48.21 14.62/-0.2 46.41 4.90 68.61 4:23.87

8316 **Behrenbruch** — 11 WCh Moskva 11 Aug
10.95/0.1 7.19/0.6 15.86 1.99 48.40 14.46/-0.1 45.66 4.70 67.07 4:37.21

8314 **Kravchenko** — 12 WCh Moskva 11 Aug
11.19/0.1 7.39/-0.2 14.84 2.11 49.65 14.44/0.4 46.12 5.10 59.98 4:39.63

8312 Gunnar **Nixon** USA 13.1.93 — 13 WCh Moskva 11 Aug
10.84/-0.5 7.80/0.4 14.68 2.14 48.56 14.57/-0.1 42.38 4.60 57.97 4:35.82

8307 **Warner** — 1 Götzis 26 May
10.36/1.1 7.40/-0.9 13.55 2.09 49.58 13.92/-0.4 42.99 4.56 62.84 4:37.37

8293 (w) Johannes **Hock** GER 24.3.92 — 1 Big 12 Waco 4 May
10.78/1.6 7.46w/3.7 15.40 1.94 49.80 14.86/1.0 53.85 4.69 63.63 4:45.82

8291 **Eaton** — 1 NC Des Moines 22 Jun
10.48/1.2 7.59/0.3 15.00 1.90 46.89 14.68/0.0 43.99 4.60 60.36 4:34.15

8279 **Shkurenyov** — 2 EU23 Tampere 12 Jul
11.05/0.8 7.35/0.3 13.98 2.04 48.78 14.29/-0.3 45.09 5.20 56.76 4:33.0

8275 Mihail **Dudas** SRB 1.11.89 — 14 WCh Moskva 11 Aug
10.67/-0.5 7.51/0.7 13.45 1.96 47.73 14.59/-0.2 44.06 4.90 59.06 4:26.62
(30/17)

8255 Thomas **Van Der Plaetsen** BEL 24.12.90 — 15 WCh Moskva 11 Aug
11.09/0.1 7.64/0.4 13.57 2.05 49.00 14.66/0.0 41.17 5.10 65.31 4:37.93

8252 Adam **Helcelet** CZE 27.10.91 — 3 EU23 Tampere 12 Jul
11.10/0.4 7.36/0.9 14.45 2.04 49.22 14.38/-0.3 43.03 5.00 64.89 4:37.93

8251 Arthur **Abele** GER 30.7.86 — 1 NC Lage 25 Jul
11.04/-1.6 7.26/1.9 14.44 1.91 48.89 13.98/0.9 44.02 4.80 69.53 4:33.11
(20)

8239 Jeremy **Taiwo** USA 15.1.90 — 2 NCAA Eugene 6 Jun
10.84/1.4 7.42/0.7 13.70 2.17 48.11 14.16w/2.8 34.90 5.00 49.87 4:16.34

8223 Maicel **Uibo** EST 27.12.92 — 1 Athens 12 Apr
10.99/1.8 7.82/-1.2 12.73 2.05 50.94 14.93/1.2 49.14 4.95 59.21 4:30.60

8215 Matthias **Prey** GER 9.8.88 — 6 Ratingen 16 Jun
11.03/1.2 7.88/0.8 15.66 1.76 49.98 14.36w/2.2 50.63 4.50 63.64 4:32.85

8179w Norman **Müller** GER 7.8.85 — 7 Ratingen 16 Jun
10.69W/5.4 7.52w/2.9 14.09 2.12 49.51 14.79/0.9 42.44 4.60 56.07 4:27.08

8177 Artem **Lukyanenko** RUS 30.1.90 — 16 WCh Moskva 11 Aug
11.11/-0.1 7.09/0.6 14.43 1.99 49.01 14.21/0.4 44.06 5.00 61.83 4:32.97

8170 Mikk **Pahapill** EST 18.7.83 — 17 WCh Moskva 11 Aug
11.33/-0.5 7.12/0.7 14.87 1.99 49.84 14.54/-0.1 47.57 5.00 62.89 4:33.16

8157h Yordani **García** CUB 21.11.88 — 1 La Habana 10 May
10.5 7.02 14.55 2.05 49.0 14.0 42.80 4.70 61.74 4:36.30

8146 Gaël **Quérin** FRA 26.6.87 — 1 NC Paris (C) 13 Jul
11.11/1.6 7.45w/2.3 13.36 1.96 48.30 14.33/0.9 39.70 4.90 58.16 4:13.42

8125 Eduard **Mikhon** BLR 7.6.89 — 2 ECp Tallinn 30 Jun
10.85/1.4 7.47/0.9 14.38 2.01 49.05 14.59w/2.7 48.36 4.70 48.53 4:27.94

8104 (w) Marcus **Nilsson** SWE 3.5.91 — 3 NCAA Eugene 6 Jun
11.22w/2.2 7.14w/2.8 14.91 1.96 50.03 14.74/1.8 48.19 4.80 59.97 4:24.46
(30)

8098 Vasiliy **Kharlamov** RUS 8.10.86 — 2 NC Cheboksary 6 Jun
11.06/1.2 7.35/1.3 15.77 1.93 50.23 14.62/1.6 46.61 4.60 62.78 4:35.97

8086 (w) Isaac **Murphy** USA 5.10.90 — 4 NCAA Eugene 6 Jun
10.61w/2.4 7.43w/3.8 13.91 1.90 48.25 14.34w/2.1 42.73 4.90 52.86 4:33.30

Mark	Name	Nat	Born	Pos	Meet	Venue	Date
8070	Ashley Bryant	GBR	17.5.91	4	EU23	Tampere	12 Jul
	11.12/-1.0 7.53/0.2 13.76	1.95	48.22	14.45/-0.3	41.17 4.50 65.46		4:30.97
8037	Dmitriy Karpov	KAZ	23.7.81	1	AsiC	Pune	4 Jul
	11.01/0.2 7.01/1.9 16.18	1.98	49.36	14.46/-0.5	50.27 5.10 48.40		4:57.56
8022	Bastien Auzeil	FRA	22.10.89	2	NC	Paris (C)	13 Jul
	11.14/0.9 7.34w/3.3 14.61	1.96	49.48	14.56/0.9	44.22 5.00 58.58		4:45.87
8013	Romain Martin	FRA	12.7.88	6	NCAA	Eugene	6 Jun
	10.93w/2.4 7.38/1.5 14.50	2.05	49.96	14.27w/2.1	38.51 4.60 59.15		4:34.16
8011 (w)	Curtis Beach	USA	22.7.90	1	TexR	Austin	28 Mar
	10.68w/2.8 7.57w/3.0 12.57	1.99	48.21	14.76/1.1	36.37 5.10 47.01		4:17.94
8001	Dakotah Keys	USA	27.9.91	1	Pac-12	Los Angeles	5 May
	10.94/1.7 7.18/0.0 12.70	2.09	51.14	14.60/0.7	35.69 4.90 66.81		4:25.76
7990	Florian Geffrouais	FRA	5.12.88	5	ECp	Tallinn	30 Jun
	11.12/-0.2 7.00/-0.1 15.39	1.92	48.64	14.90/1.4	42.19 4.40 61.82		4:14.18
7967h	José Angel Mendieta	CUB	16.10.91	2		La Habana	10 May
	10.5 7.05 15.53	1.93	48.9	14.0	43.02 4.50 60.44		4:48.60
(40)							
7960	Andres Raja	EST	2.6.82	1	NC	Rakvere	4 Aug
	10.79w/2.6 7.53/2.0 14.58	1.93	49.25	14.32/0.5	41.70 4.65 56.14		4:46.43
7958	Luiz Alberto de Araújo	BRA	27.9.87	2	NC	São Paulo	8 Jun
	10.83/0.5 7.16/0.4 15.37	1.98	48.91	14.40/1.0	44.42 4.70 52.59		4:49.94
7939	Sergey Sviridov	RUS	20.10.90	2	WUG	Kazan	9 Jul
	11.03/-0.5 7.26/-0.4 14.23	2.01	49.31	15.43/0.3	47.06 4.50 64.59		4:47.69
7933	Kevin Lazas	USA	25.1.92	8	NCAA	Eugene	6 Jun
	10.83/1.4 7.58w/3.2 13.89	1.99	52.00	15.08/0.0	41.57 5.30 55.33		4:48.35
7918	Gray Horn	USA	18.2.90	4	NC	Des Moines	22 Jun
	10.76/1.2 7.44/-1.3 13.67	1.99	49.58	14.43/-0.3	39.26 5.00 50.43		4:41.35
7916	John Lane	GBR	29.1.89	1		Woerden	25 Aug
	10.84/-0.5 7.20w/2.2 13.97	1.99	48.17	14.58/-1.0	39.45 5.13 50.39		4:47.17
7900	Patrick Spinner	GER	28.11.85	8		Ratingen	16 Jun
	11.05/1.2 7.57/0.4 14.08	1.91	49.84	14.96/1.9	39.60 4.50 68.27		4:28.95
7880	Jérémy Lelièvre	FRA	8.2.91	7	ECp	Tallinn	30 Jun
	10.87/-0.1 6.87/0.3 14.79	1.89	47.83	14.59/2.0	44.37 4.50 51.03		4:23.19
7878	Masimo Bertocchi	CAN	27.9.85	7		Götzis	26 May
	11.07/0.2 6.86/-0.8 15.37	2.00	50.89	14.24/-0.4	49.96 4.76 55.76		5:03.74
7873 (w)	Garrett Scantling	USA	19.5.93	9	NCAA	Eugene	6 Jun
	11.06w/2.4 7.05w/2.6 13.50	2.02	49.72	14.66/1.1	43.74 4.80 61.30		4:50.74
(50)							
7872	Dominik Distelberger	AUT	16.3.90	3	NC	Paris (C)	13 Jul
	10.70/1.6 7.34/-0.5 12.23	1.96	49.41	14.51/0.9	41.28 4.80 55.61		4:37.58
7864	Maximilian Gilde	GER	5.1.90	9		Ratingen	16 Jun
	11.15/1.2 7.53/0.4 13.49	1.91	50.04	14.53w/2.2	39.07 4.80 60.90		4:35.55
7854h	Manuel González	CUB	23.3.93	3		La Habana	10 May
	11.0 7.35 14.95	2.02	51.5	14.8	35.66 4.90 59.74		4:27.30
7847w	Austin Bahner	USA	7.7.91	10	NCAA	Eugene	6 Jun
	10.75w/2.4 7.55W/4.2 13.12	1.84	49.61	15.49/1.8	48.96 4.60 57.09		4:38.45
7840	Pelle Rietveld	NED	4.2.85	21	WCh	Moskva	11 Jun
	11.15/-0.1 6.68/0.5 13.21	1.90	48.67	14.37/-0.1	38.06 5.10 64.38		4:35.94
7824	Keisuke Ushiro	JPN	24.7.86	1		Wakayama	28 Apr
	11.47/1.0 6.93/2.0 14.13	1.96	51.11	15.05/0.8	49.03 4.80 64.40		4:44.13
7813w	Terry Prentice	USA	7.1.89	1		Fayetteville	8 Apr
	10.66w/3.0 7.66W/4.4 13.71	2.03	50.75	14.26w/2.2	38.91 4.40 49.77		4:40.24
7804 (w(	Daniel Gooris	USA	28.9.89	4	vGER	Chula Vista	27 Jul
	11.30w/2.5 6.88/1.6 13.90	1.95	51.09	14.86w/2.4	41.26 5.25 52.77		4:21.11
7767	Tom Bechert	GER	2.7.87	1	IC4A	Princeton	12 May
	11.31/0.0 6.92w/3.7 13.90	2.02	50.04	14.78/0.0	42.07 5.15 49.86		4:37.69
7756	Steffen Fricke	GER	25.3.83	5	vUSA	Chula Vista	27 Jul
	11.43w/2.5 7.04/1.1 14.51	2.10	49.85	15.10w/2.4	42.62 4.35 57.343		4:34.00
(60)							
7753	Marek Lukás	CZE	16.7.91	3		Kladno	9 Jun
	11.09/-1.7 7.17/0.8 13.46	1.88	50.64	14.71/1.1	40.35 4.62 69.17		4:44.51
7750	Scott McLaren	NZL	22.2.82	1	NC	Waitakere	17 Feb
	10.99w/3.6 6.84/-0.6 14.28	1.95	49.71	15.48/1.2	43.73 4.80 56.81		4:35.65
7748	Simon Hechler	GER	15.6.88	6	vUSA	Chula Vista	27 Jul
	10.83/0.7 7.57w/2.8 13.80	1.92	51.13	17.70/1.0	38.85 4.45 59.50		4:39.46
7744	Brent Newdick	NZL	31.1.85	23	WCh	Moskva	11 Jun
	11.14/-0.5 7.28/0.2 13.84	2.02	50.25	15.19/-0.2	42.49 4.50 57.30		4:38.54
7739	Yevgeniy Sarantsev	RUS	5.8.88	4	NC	Cheboksary	6 Jun
	11.13/1.2 7.04/2.0 14.55	1.93	51.39	14.89/1.6	45.42 4.70 62.33		4:53.16
7738	Fabian Rosenquist	SWE	1.4.91	5	EU23	Tampere	12 Jul
	11.18/-1.0 7.52/0.6 12.65	2.01	48.17	14.92/-1.0	40.25 4.50 48.14		4:26.64

Mark	Name		Nat	Born	Pos	Meet	Venue	Date
7733	Matthias	Brugger	GER	6.8.92	1	NC-23	Lage	25 Aug
	11.38/-1.5 7.21/1.7 14.27 2.00 49.86 15.08/0.9 42.41 4.70 52.61 4:33.51							
7729	Alexandre	Folacci	FRA	26.3.91	1	NC-23	Cognac	30 Jun
	11.02w/2.7 7.11w/2.7 12.57 1.94 50.44 14.75/-0.1 39.42 5.01 57.05 4:35.44							
7727	Pawel	Wiesolek	POL	13.8.91	3		Firenze	3 May
	11.03/0.0 7.24/0.1 13.32 2.10 50.19 15.20/0.0 40.82 4.45 57.23 4:42.50							
7726	Ivan	Grigoryev	RUS	27.10.89	5	NC	Cheboksary	6 Jun
	10.84/1.2 7.18w/3.1 13.16 1.78 49.90 14.71/0.9 38.26 4.70 61.65 4:26.09							
(70)								
7726	Dominic	Giovannoni	USA	30.7.90	13	NCAA	Eugene	6 Jun
	11.05/1.4 7.13w/2.9 13.89 1.93 49.53 14.45/1.1 38.99 5.00 49.70 4:40.33							
7723	Akihiko	Nakamura	JPN	23.10.90	2	NC	Nagano	2 Jun
	11.12/-4.3 7.42/-3.7 11.64 2.00 47.32 14.24/0.7 34.51 4.80 42.50 4:18.96							
7721	Mikhail	Logvinenko	RUS	19.4.84	1		Adler	9 May
	11.27/0.2 7.13w/2.6 14.33 1.97 49.60 14.57/0.1 43.07 4.90 43.80 4:35.14							
7718	Wesley	Bray	USA	11.4.88	8	vGER	Chula Vista	27 Jul
	10.99/0.7 7.51w/2.6 12.65 1.95 49.90 15.09w/2.4 40.36 4.45 56.22 4:28.06							
7710	Ryan	Harlan	USA	25.4.81	9	vGER	Chula Vista	27 Jul
	11.26w/2.5 6.69/1.5 16.02 2.01 52.42 14.63/1.0 47.16 4.75 64.50 5:20.42							
7700	Tomas	Kirielius	LTU	10.6.89	14	NCAA	Eugene	6 Jun
	11.15w/2.2 6.75/1.2 13.43 2.05 49.47 14.86/1.8 45.68 4.40 60.64 4:51.48							
7697 (w)	Matt	Johnson	USA	4.10.89	15	NCAA	Eugene	6 Jun
	10.70w/2.4 7.09w/2.9 13.55 1.87 50.10 14.56w/2.1 47.80 4.50 53.79 4:52.83							
7694	René	Stauß	GER	17.9.87	10	vUSA	Chula Vista	27 Jul
	11.05/0.7 7.59/1.8 14.35 2.16 52.70 15.67w/2.4 40.40 4.65 54.54 4:55.33							
7691 (w)	Dmitriy	Zikeyev	RUS	10.1.91	6	NC	Cheboksary	6 Jun
	11.18/1.2 7.62w/3.7 14.39 1.93 50.68 15.09/1.6 43.04 4.40 59.08 4:51.75							
7689	Jake	Arnold	USA	3.1.84	1		Dallas	2 Jun
	11.27/1.6 6.37w/2.9 14.37 1.93 50.49 14.24w/2.4 46.81 5.05 58.94 5:03.35							
(80)								
7678	Clayton	Chaney	USA	16.9.89	1		Houston	10 May
	11.05/-0.3 7.31/1.0 13.60 1.99 50.30 14.44/0.4 41.73 4.40 54.60 4:47.35							
7678	Niklas	Wiberg	SWE	16.4.85	2	ECp-1	Nottwil	30 Jun
	11.51/-0.7 6.90/0.2 14.33 1.98 49.96 15.27/0.9 41.45 4.20 68.33 4:30.63							
7675	Aleksandr	Frolov	RUS	5.3.87	2		Adler	9 May
	11.34/1.9 7.05/1.9 14.92 2.03 52.96 15.63/0.1 44.72 4.80 56.48 4:37.84							
7662		Zhu Hengjun	CHN	5.2.87	1	NG	Shenyang	10 Sep
	10.85/0.2 6.99/0.4 13.16 1.94 49.59 14.32/-0.6 42.14 4.80 57.76 5:10.29							
7659	Martin	Brockman	GBR	13.11.87	2		Woerden	25 Aug
	11.42/0.0 7.12w/2.2 14.28 2.08 49.22 15.98/-0.8 39.58 4.83 47.92 4:26.74							
7658	Kaarel	Jööväli	EST	8.1.90	9	ECp	Tallinn	30 Jun
	11.02/-0.2 7.54/-0.7 13.26 2.01 49.67 14.80/1.4 38.57 4.60 49.40 4:44.66							
7647	Janis	Jansons	LAT	25.5.90	1	NC	Valmiera	2 Jun
	10.94/1.7 7.39w/2.7 15.52 2.09 51.19 14.49/-0.4 41.33 4.20 48.47 5:01.29							
7644	Niels	Pittomvils	BEL	18.7.92	7	EU23	Tampere	12 Jul
	11.34/-0.2 6.92/-0.2 12.42 1.95 49.96 15.02/-1.0 39.78 5.20 53.12 4:30.26							
7643	Petter	Olson	SWE	14.2.91	1	NC	Kalmar	15 Sep
	11.14/-1.2 7.16/0.5 12.89 1.94 48.92 14.94/0.0 38.72 4.92 54.00 4:43.84							
7640 (w)	Zach	Ziemek	USA	23.2.93	1	Big 10	Columbus	11 May
	10.60w/2.5 7.65w/4.0 12.94 1.91 50.46 15.10/1.4 40.43 5.00 53.84 5:16.40							
(90)								
7636	Darko	Pesic	MNE	30.11.92	2	Franc	Nice	12 Sep
	11.33/1.6 7.15/0.2 15.11 2.01 50.95 14.91/1.4 41.76 4.10 57.76 4:35.57							
7631 (w)	Derek	Masterson	USA	30.1.90	2		Dallas	2 Jun
	11.34w/3.2 7.02w/2.4 14.18 1.93 51.22 15.06w/2.4 44.61 4.55 62.81 4:47.67							
7621	Lars Vikan	Rise	NOR	23.11.88	1	ECp-2	Ribeira Brava	30 Jun
	11.61/-0.8 6.89/0.3 15.68 1.98 50.26 16.03/0.8 43.38 4.20 66.93 4:36.33							
7612A (w)	J Patrick	Smith	USA	28.4.91	1	NCAA-2	Pueblo, CO	24 May
	10.68w/3.0 7.50w/2.9 11.71 1.96 49.33 14.95/0.5 37.50 4.50 58.27 4:53.04							
7611	Patrick	Scherfose	GER	28.11.91	11		Ratingen	16 Jun
	11.03/0.5 7.14/1.6 13.58 1.85 50.63 14.59w/2.2 43.32 4.80 47.79 4:34.78							
7603 (w)	Rudy	Bourguignon	FRA	16.7.79	2		Grenoble	2 Jun
	11.22w/2.3 6.74w/2.2 14.99 1.91 52.29 15.62w/2.2 45.68 4.85 62.56 4:50.46							
7603	Tiago	Marto	POR	5.4.86	2	ECp-2	Ribeira Brava	30 Jun
	11.19/-0.8 7.15/0.5 13.95 1.95 50.86 14.63/0.8 41.38 4.60 51.42 4:38.84							
7593	Patrick	Arbour	CAN	17.3.88	1		Tucson	5 Apr
	11.55/-0.2 7.01/0.0 15.32 1.87 52.25 15.00/-2.0 50.82 4.40 65.32 5:03.62							
7590	Nikolay	Shubyanok	BLR	4.5.85	11	ECp	Tallinn	30 Jun
	11.57/-0.2 6.90/0.4 15.05 1.98 51.47 14.94/1.4 44.98 4.60 53.30 4:39.29							
7586	Frédéric	Xhonneux (100)	BEL	11.5.83	2		Bruxelles	30 Jun
	11.82 6.80/0.4 13.87 1.97 49.55 15.19/0.3 38.74 4.75 58.45 4:23.71							

MEN 2013

Mark	Name		Nat	Born	Pos Meet	Venue	Date
7575	Maksim	Fayzulin	RUS	18.1.92	6 Jun		
7575		Liu Haibo	CHN	17.3.87	10 Sep		
7574	Lars-Niklas	Heinke	GER	7.11.89	16 Jun		
7569	Attila	Zsivoczky-Pandel	HUN	29.4.77	15 Sep		
7563	Martin	Roe	NOR	1.4.92	20 May		
7558	Vasyl	Ivanytskyy	UKR	29.1.91	30 Jun		
7540	Pieter	Braun	NED	21.1.93	12 Jul		
7526	Rasmus	Carlsson	SWE	6.9.88	9 Jun		
7523	Christian	Loosli	SUI	12.6.92	12 Jul		
7520	Nathanael	Franks	USA	8.11.91	10 May		
7520		Qi Haifeng	CHN	7.8.81	10 Sep		
7511	Guillaume	Thierry	MRI	15.9.86	12 Sep		
7510	Peter	Glass	GBR	1.5.88	14 Jul		
7508	Ânderson	Venâncio	BRA	6.1.87	30 Mar		
7508	Yuki	Matsushita	JPN	9.9.91	7 Sep		
7506	Kazuya	Kawasaki	JPN	2.9.92	7 Sep		
7500	Michele	Calvi	ITA	7.6.90	3 May		
7490	Miller	Moss	USA	14.3.88	22 Jun		
7484	David	Gómez	ESP	13.2.81	28 Jul		
7478	Benjamin	Fenrich	FRA	11.6.90	13 Jul		
7476	Otto	Ylöstalo	FIN	4.2.91	12 Jul		
7474	Krzysztof	Plaskota	POL	6.11.85	30 Jun		
7470	Moritz	Cleve	GER	18.2.87	9 Jun		
7457	Roger	Skedd	GBR	3.9.82	12 Apr		
7457	Bas	Markies	NED	24.7.84	30 Jun		
7456	Ali	Kamé	MAD	21.5.84	12 Sep		
7454	Dino	Dodig	SRB	25.3.93	9 Jun		
7437w	Jesse	Chapman	USA	3.1.90	4 May		
7437	Jaroslav	Hedvicák	CZE	13.12.90	9 Jun		
7432w	Teran	Walford	USA	25.8.89	11 May		
7428	Jonay	Jordán	ESP	12.5.91	28 Jul		
7427 (w)	Ethan	Miller	USA	2.2.90	2 Jun		
7424	Corbin	Duer	USA	29.11.88	22 Jun		
7415		Guo Qi	CHN	28.12.90	10 Sep		
7413	Takeshi	Shimizu	JPN	21.12.93	7 Sep		
7412w	Kurt	Reichenbach	USA	3.9.89	11 May		
7411	Alex	McCune	USA	.93	10 May		
7406 (w)	Reinis	Krūgers	LAT	22.1.92	4 May		
7406	Takayoshi	Shinohara	JPN	4.6.92	7 Sep		
7403	Liam	Ramsay	GBR	18.11.92	4 Aug		
7402	Pavel	Baar	CZE	18.4.84	9 Jun		
7402	Nils	Büker	GER	12.12.86	25 Aug		
7401	Kenny	Greaves	USA	13.10.88	2 Jun		
	(143)						

Best without wind assistance

7960   Norman   Müller   GER   7.8.85   6   Götzis   24 May
11.07/0.2   7.31/0.3   14.19   2.00   49.59   14.85/0.0   43.92   4.76   55.21   4:31.59

7744   Austin   Bahner   USA   7.7.91   7   vGER   Chula Vista   28 Jul
10.87/0.7   7.66/2.0   12.84   1.83   49.70   16.02w/2.4   47.42   4.55   59.20   4:37.96

JUNIORS

7335   Abdel-Kader   Larrinaga   CUB   13.7.94   3   NC   La Habana   17 Mar
11.23/-0.5   7.05/0.0   13.73   2.07   50.50   14.81/0.8   37.52   3.80   54.61   4:49.57

7302   Wang Qunhao   CHN   3.2.95   6   NG   Shenyang   10 Sep
11.39/0.2   6.78/0.5   11.97   1.88   48.94   14.97/-0.6   38.88   4.40   56.14   4:37.94

7203   Chen Xiaohong   CHN-Y   9.2.97   4   NC   Suzhou   1 Jun
10.97/0.3   7.04/0.3   11.30   2.01   50.97   15.41/-0.1   37.85   4.20   60.32   5:05.61

7065A   Wolf   Mahler   USA   26.9.94   1   Albuquerque   8 Jun
11.39/0.2   6.78/0.5   11.97   1.88   48.94   14.97/-0.6   38.88   4.40   56.14   4:37.94

7001   Orlan   Rivero   CUB   11.2.95   4   NC   La Habana   17 Mar
11.55/-0.5   6.70/1.2   12.02   2.13   49.63   15.15/0.8   35.10   3.50   51.12   4:42.10

IAAF JUNIOR SPECIFICATION – WITH 99CM 110MH, 6KG SP, 1.75KG DT

7975   Yevgemniy   Likhanov   RUS   10.1.95   1   EJ   Rieti   21 Jul
10.94/1.3   7.54/1.3   15.36   2.13   50.20   14.23/-0.3   38.82   4.70   51.17   4:52.58

7790   Aleksey   Cherkasov   RUS   22.10.94   2   EJ   Rieti   21 Jul
10.97/0.8   6.81/0.6   14.05   2.04   49.44   14.12/-0.3   40.37   4.80   48.78   4:38.25

7612   1   Adler   10 May   8 performances by 7 men over 7580

7778   Tim   Nowak   GER   13.8.95   3   EJ   Rieti   21 Jul
11.04/1.3   7.06/0.9   15.64   1.92   49.44   14.17/-0.3   36.49   4.60   55.34   4:37.12

7762A   Felipe Vinícius   dos Santos   BRA   30.7.94   1   PAm-J   Medellín   24 Aug
10.65/1.2   7.36/0.2   14.21   1.99   48.58   14.12/1.5   42.55   4.10   51.97   5:16.09

7715   Jake   Stein   AUS   17.1.94   1   Sydney (C)   8 Dec
11.46/-1.6   7.05/1.2   16.70   2.00   52.45   14.46/1.6   53.64   4.00   60.60   5:10.56

7701h   Abdel-Kader   Larrinaga   CUB   13.7.94   1   La Habana   28 Jun
10.7/0.7   7.12/1.3   15.01   2.05   49.4   13.8/1.7   41.67   3.70   51.06   4:36.5

7604   Janek   Oiglane   EST   25.4.94   4   EJ   Rieti   21 Jul
11.50/0.7   6.96/0.9   15.15   2.01   51.73   14.52/0.7   42.88   4.10   62.56   4:45.51

7581   Axel   Martin   FRA   13.4.94   1   NC-j   Cognac   30 Jun
11.14/1.8   7.25w/3.6   12.35   1.97   50.87   14.82/-0.5   40.04   4.81   51.30   4:36.54

7573   Fredrick   Ekholm   SWE   15.6.94   5   EJ   Rieti   21 Jul
10.85/0.8   7.16/0.7   13.75   1.98   49.40   13.98/-0.3   34.87   4.60   48.28   4:53.80

7542   Fredrik   Samuelsson (10)   SWE   16.2.95   7   EJ   Rieti   21 Jul
11.19/0.7   6.92/1.0   13.42   2.04   50.37   14.86/0.7   39.98   4.50   51.53   4:37.72

7521   Jirí   Sykora   CZE   20.1.95   1   NC-j   Stará Boleslav   26 May
10.89/0.1   7.37   14.83   2.01   49.56   14.65/0.5   42.39   4.00   49.20   5:09.44

7487   Kristjan   Rosenberg   EST   16.5.94   1   NC-j   Ralvere   3 Jul
11.58/-4.0   7.14/0.8   13.56   2.03   51.83   15.07/-0.5   44.88   4.60   55.10   4:56.27

7478A   Jefferson   dos Santos   BRA   30.8.95   3   PAm-J   Medellín   24 Aug
10.98w/2.2   7.08/-1.0   14.92   2.05   53.27   14.68/1.5   47.76   4.20   51.97   5:16.09

7465h   Orlan   Rivero   CUB   11.2.95   2   La Habana   28 Jun
11.0(0.7)   6.68/0.7   14.88   2.14   49.7   14.3/1.7   45.07   3.40   49.01   4:40.8

7419   Wolf   Mahler   USA   26.9.94   1   NC-j   Des Moines   20 Jun
10.81/1.7   6.42/0.4   12.86   1.75   48.04   14.30/1.9   41.54   4.60   44.75   4:28.66

7389   Taavi   Tsernjavski   EST   4.3.95   1   Tallinn   21 Jun
11.62/-1.0   6.80w/3.3   14.61   1.89   50.31   14.98w/2.1   47.30   4.05   55.91   4:44.80

Mark	Name	Nat	Born	Pos	Meet	Venue	Date
7386	Fabian Christ	GER	18.9.95	2		Filderstadt	9 Jun
	11.24/0.0 6.81/0.2 13.00 1.93 48.67 14.50/0.2 35.34 4.70 48.65 4:43.92						
7351	David Brock	AUS	8.6.94	1	NC-j	Adelaide	17 Feb
	11.42/-1.5 6.83/1.3 13.77 2.06 51.42 15.39/-0.4 39.81 4.50 52.21 4:46.53						
7336	Vadym Adamchuk	UKR	30.5.94	9	EJ	Rieti	21 Jul
	11.31/0.7 7.36/0.5 14.95 1.95 50.44 15.24/-0.6 41.20 3.80 48.83 4:43.04						
7280	Benjamin Gföhler (20)	SUI	27.1.94	11	EJ	Rieti	21 Jul
	10.88/1.3 7.15/0.5 13.18 1.80 49.78 14.92/-0.3 40.72 4.20 44.26 4:37.40						

Wind assisted marks: w against a score shows that as per the IAAF rules up to 2009 the wind velocity in an event exceeded 4m/s and the average of the winds in the three measured events exceeded 2 m/s; (w) as per the current IAAF rules the average of the three events exceeded 2m/s but not necessarily any event over 4m/s.

4 X 100 METRES RELAY

Mark	Nat	Name	Pos	Meet	Venue	Date
37.36	JAM	Carter, Bailey Cole, Ashmeade, Bolt	1	WCh	Moskva	18 Aug
37.58	USA	'Red': Silmon, Rodgers, Salaam, Gatlin	1	Herc	Monaco	19 Jul
37.66	USA	Silmon, Rodgers, Salaam, Gatlin	2	WCh	Moskva	18 Aug
37.75	JAM	Forsythe, Bailey Cole, Weir, Bolt	1	DL	London (OS)	27 Jul
37.92	CAN	Smellie, A.Brown, Richards-Kwok, Warner	3	WCh	Moskva	18 Aug
38.04	GER	Jakubczyk, Knipphals, Reus, Keller	4	WCh	Moskva	18 Aug
38.06	USA	Silmon, Rodgers, Salaam, Gatlin	1h2	WCh	Moskva	18 Aug
38.12	GBR	Kilty, Aikines-Aryeetey, Ellington, Chambers	1h1	WCh	Moskva	18 Aug
38.13	GER	Jakubczyk, Knipphals, Reus, Keller	1		Weinheim	2 Aug
38.13	GER	Jakubczyk, Knipphals, Reus, Keller	1h3	WCh	Moskva	18 Aug
38.17	JAM	Carter, Bailey Cole, Weir, O.Bailey	2h1	WCh	Moskva	18 Aug
38.23	JPN	Kiryu, Fujimitsu, Takase, Iizuka	2h2	WCh	Moskva	18 Aug
38.26	USA	Red Rodgers, Gatlin, Patton, R.Bailey	1	Penn R	Philadelphia	27 Apr
38.26	USA	'Blue' Demps, Batson, Locke, Newman	2	Herc	Monaco	19 Jul
38.29	CAN	Smellie, A.Brown, Richards-Kwok, Warner	2h3	WCh	Moskva	18 Aug
38.33	CAN	Smellie, A.Brown, Harris, Warner	3	Herc	Monaco	19 Jul
38.37	NED	Mariano, Martina, Bonevacia, Paulina	5	WCh	Moskva	18 Aug
38.38	TTO	James, Bledman, Sorrillo, Thompson	3h1	WCh	Moskva	18 Aug
38.39	GBR	Gemili, Aikines-Aryeetey, Ellington, Dasaolu	1	ET	Gateshead	22 Jun
38.39	JPN	Kiryu, Fujimitsu, Takase, Izuka	6	WCh	Moskva	18 Aug
		(20 performances by teams from 8 nations)				
38.45	FRA	Biron, Lemaitre, Remy, Vicaut	2	DL	London (OS)	27 Jul
38.46	ESP	Viles, Ruiz, Hortelano, Rodríguez (10)	4h1	WCh	Moskva	18 Aug
38.49	ITA	Tumi, Galvan, Marani, Obou	4h3	WCh	Moskva	18 Aug
38.51	POL	Kubaczyk, Zikmniewicz, Zalewski, Krynski	5h1	WCh	Moskva	18 Aug
38.56	UKR	Perestyuk, Smelyk, Bodrov, Korzh	1	WUG	Kazan	12 Jul
38.58	SKN	Lestrod, Rogers, Adams, Clarke	5h3	WCh	Moskva	18 Aug
38.70	BAH	Griffith, Fraser, Rolle, Hart	6h3	WCh	Moskva	18 Aug
38.71	AUS	Leathart, Ross, McCabe, Geddes	4	DL	London (OS)	27 Jul
38.73	CHN	(Guangdong) Tan J, Mo Y, Su B, Liang J	1	NG	Shenyang	11 Sep
38.94	HKG	Tang YC, Lai CH, Ng KF, Tsui CH	1	AsiC	Pune	6 Jul
38.94	BAR	Hinds, Cadogan, S.Brathwaite, Gittens	4h2	WCh	Moskva	18 Aug
39.00	KOR	Oh K, Cho K, Yoo M, Kim K	6h1	WCh	Moskva	18 Aug
		(20)				
39.01	RUS	Khyutte, Petryashkov, Smirnov, Brednev	7h1	WCh	Moskva	18 Aug
39.14	VEN	Chirinos, Rivas, Cassiani, Bravo	8h1	WCh	Moskva	18 Aug
39.19	BRA	Feitosa, de Jesus, de Moraes, André	1		São Paulo	7 Jun
39.23	SWE	Brorsson, de Oliveira, Wissman, Tärnhuvud	2		Regensburg	8 Jun
39.23	CZE	Jirka, Stastny, Maslák, Desensky	5	EU23	Tampere	14 Jul
39.23	POR	Antunes, Obikwelu, Abrantes, Nascimento	1		Luzern	17 Jul
39.25	NGR	Nmalu, Imhoaperamhe, Ukale, Ogho-Ogene	1		Warri	14 Jun
39.30	THA	Sowan, Promkaew, Meenapra, Chimdee	4	WUG	Kazan	12 Jul
39.36	TPE	Wang W, Liu Y, Pan P, Yi W	3h2		Taipei	27 May
39.38A	PUR	Reeves, Lopez, Rodríguez, Llanos	4h1	CAC	Morelia	5 Jul
		(30)				

39.45	SIN	8 May	39.62	CUB-J	8 Jun	39.69	IRI	21 Jun	39.76 COL 6 Jul	39.83 LTU 21 Jun
39.58	BEL	12 Sep	39.62	ECU	28 Nov	39.72	OMA	28 Sep	39.80 FIN 14 Jul	39.94 RSA 11 Jul

Mixed nationality team

38.36	USA/CAN	Spearmon, M Mitchell, Connaughton CAN, Patton	1	TexR	Austin	30 Mar

JUNIORS

39.17A	USA	Hester, Burrell, Rese, Bromell	1	PAm-J	Medellín	25 Aug
39.42	NGR		2		Warri	14 Jun
39.62	CUB	Ramos, Ruíz, Mena, Carrero	1		La Habana	8 Jun
39.68A	JAM	Minzie, Murphy, Henry, Todd	2	PAm-J	Medellín	25 Aug
39.80	POL	Mudlaff, Kabacinski, Kalandyk, Jabłoński	1	EJ	Rieti	21 Jul
39.96	GBR	Cox, Mitchell-Blake, Riewd, Ejiakuekwu	1h3	EJ	Rieti	21 Jul

MEN 2013

Mark		Name	Nat	Born	Pos	Meet	Venue		Date
39.96	GER	Heber,Polkowsli, Ruth, Schürmann			2	EJ	Rieti		21 Jul
39.96A	BRA	do Nascimento, V da Silva, L Silva, R de Souza			3	PAm-J	Medellín		25 Aug
39.97	FRA	Rene, Zeze, Dutamby, Belocian			1h2	EJ	Rieti		21 Jul
39.97	JPN	Soyo HS Konno, Tokuyama, Nakajima, Hayashi (10)			1		Oita		30 Jul

4 X 200 METRES RELAY

1:20.75	Texas A&M University USA Bryan, Hardy, A Bailey, Webb		1	PennR	Philadelphia	27 Apr
1:21.51	St. Augustine's		2	PennR	Philadelphia	27 Apr

4 X 400 METRES RELAY

Mark	Nat	Name	Pos	Meet	Venue	Date
2:58.71	USA	Verburg 45.0, McQuay 44.1, Hall 44.87, Merritt 44.77	1	WCh	Moskva	16 Aug
2:59.85	USA	J.Harris 45.2, Verburg 44.8, Mance 45.21, Hall 44.62	1h2	WCh	Moskva	15 Aug
2:59.88	JAM	McDonald 46.0, Steele 44.3, O.Johnson 45.53, Francis 44.05	2	WCh	Moskva	16 Aug
2:59.90	RUS	Dyldin 45.4, Mosin 44.8, Petukhov 45.05, Krasnov 44.67	3	WCh	Moskva	16 Aug
3:00.41	JAM	McDonald 45.6, Bell 45.1, Steele 45.14, Francis 44.62	1h1	WCh	Moskva	15 Aug
3:00.48	TTO	Quow 45.1, Solomon 44.8, L.Gordon 45.11, Lendore 45.49	2h2	WCh	Moskva	15 Aug
3:00.50	GBR	C Williams 45.4, Bingham 45.7, Bowie 44.64, Rooney 44.77	2h1	WCh	Moskva	15 Aug
3:00.81	BEL	Gillet 46.8, J.Borlée 44.1, D.Borlée 45.96, K.Borlée 43.90	3h2	WCh	Moskva	15 Aug
3:00.88	GBR	C Williams 45.3, Rooney 44.5, Bingham 45.65, Levine 45.35	4	WCh	Moskva	16 Aug
3:00.91	USA Red	Lawrence 45.6, M.Mitchell 44.8, B.Jackson 45.7, McQuay 44.8	1	Penn R	Philadelphia	27 Apr
3:01.02	BEL	J.Borlée 45.50, K.Borlée 44.04, D.Borlée 45.74, Oyowe 45.74	5	WCh	Moskva	16 Aug
3:01.09	BRA	de Oliveira 45.9, Cardoso 45.3, Henriques 44.73, H. Sousa 45.18	4h2	WCh	Moskva	15 Aug
3:01.15	JAM	Fothergill 46.2, Hylton 45.6, L.Green 45.0, Nolan 44.3	2	Penn R	Philadelphia	27 Apr
3:01.34	Un. Florida, USA	Glass 46.0, Graham 45.4, Dukes 45.09, Hall 44.86	1	NCAA	Eugene	8 Jun
3:01.73	POL	Kozlowski 46.0, Omelko 45.3, Krawczyk 45.48, Marciniszyn 44.95	5h2	WCh	Moskva	15 Aug
3:01.74	TTO	Quow 45.6, J.Gordon 45.3, L.Gordon 45.12, Solomon 45.74	6	WCh	Moskva	16 Aug
3:01.81	RUS	Dyldin 45.5, Mosin 45.1, Petukhov 45.99, Krasnov 45.27	1h3	WCh	Moskva	15 Aug
3:01.93	San Antonio Elite USA	Betters, C.Smith, Courtney, Iglehart-Summers 45.11	1	TexR	Austin	30 Mar
3:02.04	VEN	Ramírez 46.0, Aguilar 45.4, Meléndez 45.26, Mezones 45.38	3h1	WCh	Moskva	15 Aug
3:02.19A	TTO	Quow, Mayers, Cedenio, Solomon	1	CAC	Morelia	7 Jul
3:02.19	BRA	de Oliveira 45.9, Cardoso 45.2, Henriques 45.32, H Sousa 45.73	7	WCh	Moskva	16 Aug
3:02.23	BAH	R.Miller 47.4, Mathieu 45.0, C.Brown 45.4, Newbold 44.4	3	Penn R	Philadelphia	27 Apr
	(22 performances by teams from 10 nations)					
3:02.26	AUS	Solomon 45.6, Beck 45.8, Burns 45.46, Thomas 45.36	8	WCh	Moskva	16 Aug
3:02.43	JPN	Yamazaki 46.1, Kanemaru 45.6, Hirose 44.94, Nakano 45.82	4h1	WCh	Moskva	15 Aug
3:02.53	KSA	Al-Sabyani, Al-Bishi, Al-Salhi, Al-Masrahi	1	AsiC	Pune	7 Jul
3:02.62	GER	Gollnow 46.3, Krüger 45.2, Schneider 45.37, Plass 45.75	3h3	WCh	Moskva	15 Aug
3:02.82A	DOM	Peguero, Cuesta, Sánchez, Santos	3	CAC	Morelia	7 Jul
3:03.17A	CUB	N.Ruíz, O.Rodríguez, Lescay, Acea	4	CAC	Morelia	7 Jul
3:03.88	ITA	Lorenzi 46.49, Juárez 45.67, Haliti 46.66, Galvan 45.06	5h3	WCh	Moskva	15 Aug
3:04.07	ESP	Briones 46.5, S.García 45.2, Ujakpor 45.74, Fradera 46.62	6h1	WCh	Moskva	15 Aug
3:04.26	NGR	Odeka, Onakoya, Salihu, Akwu	1		Warri	14 Jun
3:04.54	CZE	Nemecek 46.6, Maslák 44.3, Lichy 46.87, Tesar 46.75	7h3	WCh	Moskva	15 Aug
	(20)					
3:04.92	SRI	Priyashantha, Aloka, Seneviratne, Gunarathne	3	AsiC	Pune	7 Jul
3:04.98	UKR	Butrym 46.7, Knysh 45.7, Hutsol 46.68, Burakov 45.87	6h2	WCh	Moskva	15 Aug
3:05.14	CHN	(Guangdong) Cui H, Qin J, Liu X, Qu S	1	NG	Shenyang	11 Sep
3:05.22	FRA	Coulibaby, Hanné, Décimus, Chelala	1	Franc	Nice	14 Sep
3:05.26	CAN	Ayesu-Attah 47.2, Rodney 45.6, Robertson 45.9, Harper 46.6	2	WUG	Kazan	12 Jul
3:05.28	TUR	Güzel, Kocabeyoglu, Kiliç, Can	2	Med G	Mersin	29 Jun
3:05.43	COL	Perlaza, Sinisterra, Lemos, Rodríguez	1	Bol G	Trujillo	29 Nov
3:05.74	BOT	Seribe 47.1, Ngwigwa 46.2, Makwala 46.15, Ketlogetswe 46.27	8h1	WCh	Moskva	15 Aug
3:06.01	IND	Davinder Singh, Roby, Rajiv, Kunhu Muhammed	4	AsiC	Pune	7 Jul
3:06.19	RSA	Conradie 47.3, de Swardt 46.5, Beneke 46.4, Van Niekerk 46.0	3	WUG	Kazan	12 Jul
	(30)					

3:06.29A	KEN	15 Aug		3:07.27	NED	13 Jul		3:07.79	OMA	10 Apr		3:08.66	CRO	28 Jul		3:08.77A	CRC	7 Jul
3:07.21	SUI	14 Sep		3:07.71	IRL	13 Jul		3:08.07	PHI	6 Sep		3:08.73	SRB	23 Jun				

Hand timed: 3:05.1A Prisons Team, KEN   1   Nairobi   13 Jul

Best at low altitude

3:03.61	DOM	Peguero 46.5e, Cuesta 46.0e, Soriano 46.12, Santos 44.99	5h1	WCh	Moskva	15 Aug
3:04.27	CUB	Lescay 45.4e, Acea 44.8e, Rodríguez 46.27, Pellicier 47.82	6h3	WCh	Moskva	15 Aug

Mixed nationality team

3:02.21	Green & Gold Elite Hewitt TRI, Boyd USA, Henry ISV, Wariner USA 44.72	2	TexR	Austin	30 Mar

JUNIORS

3:04.87	RUS	Peremetov, Savin, Khasanov, Ivashko	1	EJ	Rieti	21 Jul
3:05.07	POL	Walczuk, Smole⊠, Ozdarski, Dobek	2	EJ	Rieti	21 Jul
3:05.14	GBR	Boyce, Hudson-Smith, Snaith, Caddick	3	EJ	Rieti	21 Jul
3:05.41	FRA	Vaillant, Jordier, Geenan, Mandrou	4	EJ	Rieti	21 Jul

Mark	Nat	Name	Pos	Meet	Venue	Date
3:05.68	JAM	L Williams, McLeod, Minzie, Francis	1	Carifta	Nassau	1 Apr
3:06.23	TTO	Guevara, Lewis, Richards, Cedenio	2	Carifta	Nassau	1 Apr
3:06.40	GER	Gladitz, Koch, Steudel, Schürmann	5	EJ	Rieti	21 Jul
3:06.57A	USA	Chamnbers, Robinson, Bruton, Green	1	PAm-J	Medellín	25 Aug
3:06.94A	BRA	Russo, Pereitra, Grachet, do Nascimento	2	PAm-J	Medellín	25 Aug
3:07.44	BAH	Williams, Cartwright, Newbold, Colebrook (10)	3	Carifta	Nassau	1 Apr
3:07.61A	CAN	George, Greem Sherwood, McBride	3	PAm-J	Medellín	25 Aug

4 X 800 METRES RELAY

Penn relays, Philadeplhia 27 Apr: 1, Penn State University USA 7:14.14, 2. Villanova University, USA 7:17.37

4 X 110 METRES HURDLES

54.23	Star Athletics	R Brathwaite BAR, Nurudeen NGR, Monrose HAI, Hyman CAY	1	FlaR	Gainesville	6 Apr
54.36	Brooks Beast	D Oliver USA, D Thomas JAM, R Wilson USA, J Porter USA	2	FlaR	Gainesville	6 Apr

3000 METRES WALK

Mark	Name		Nat	Born	Pos		Venue	Date
11:00.68	Antón	Kucmin	SVK	7.6.84	1		Dubnica nad Váhom	21 Aug
11:03.96	Matej	Tóth	SVK	10.2.83	2		Dubnica nad Váhom	21 Aug
11:11.94	Robert	Heffernan	IRL	20.2.78	1		Cork	2 Jul
11:21.32	Grzegorz	Sudol	POL	28.8.78	3		Dubnica nad Váhom	21 Aug
11:26.76	Dane	Bird-Smith	AUS	15.7.92	1		Brisbane (Nathan)	30 Nov
11:34.60	Wayne	Snyman	RSA	8.3.85	2		Cork	2 Jul
Indoors								
11:13.92		Heffernan			1		Athlone	27 Jan
11:23.99	Alex	Wright	GBR	19.12.90	2		Athlone	27 Jan
11:28.45+	Lukasz	Nowak	POL	18.12.88	1	in 3k	Spala	17 Feb

5000 METRES WALK

18:33.32	Yohann	Diniz	FRA	1.1.78	1		Reims	5 May
18:44.79	Kevin	Campion	FRA	23.5.88	1		Reims	28 Jun
18:56.96	Dane	Bird-Smith	AUS	15.7.92	1		Brisbane	6 Jul
18:57.23	Bertrand	Moulinet	FRA	6.12.87	2		Reims	28 Jun
18:59.17	Erik	Tysse	NOR	4.12.80	1	NC	Tønsberg	23 Aug
18:59.51	Hédi	Taraaoui	TUN	10.11.89	3		Reims	28 Jun
19:13.51	Benjamín	Sánchez	ESP	10.3.85	1		Avilés	15 Jun
19:14.05	Pyotr	Trofimov	RUS	28.11.83	4		Reims	28 Jun
19:16.93	Dawid	Tomala	POL	27.8.89	1		Gdansk	1 Jun
19:20.50+	Miguel Ángel	López	ESP	3.7.88	1	in 10k	Alcobendas	28 Jul
19:25.86	Álvaro	Martín	ESP-J	18.6.94	2		Avilés	15 Jun

19:27.39	Alex	Wright	GBR	19.12.90	14 Jul	19:35.68	Takuya	Yoshida	JPN	10.8.90	18 May
19:30.01	Antonin	Boyez	FRA	9.11.84	28 Jun	19:36.78	Takayuki	Tanii	JPN	14.2.83	19 May
19:30.57	Rhydian	Cowley	AUS	4.1.91	9 Feb	19:38.39	Matej	Tóth	SVK	10.2.83	11 May
19:33.11	Daisuke	Matsunaga	JPN-J	24.3.95	20 Apr	19:38.62	Tom	Bosworrth	GBR	17.1.90	14 Jul

Indoors								
18:28.54	Igor	Yerokhin	RUS	4.9.85	1		Samara	31 Jan
18:43.33	Valeriy	Borchin	RUS	11.9.86	2		Samara	31 Jan
18:55.65		Diniz			1		Reims	3 Feb
19:03.48	Grzegorz	Sudol	POL	28.8.78	1	NC	Spala	17 Feb
19:06.16	Antonin	Boyez	FRA	9.11.84	1	NC	Aubière	17 Feb
19:13.03	Robert	Heffernan	IRL	20.2.78	1	NC	Athlone	16 Feb
19:13.16	Dawid	Tomala	POL	27.8.89	2	NC	Spala	17 Feb
19:15.9	Ato	Ibáñez	SWE	14.11.85	1		Borås	23 Nov
19:18.66	Lukasz	Nowak	POL	18.12.88	3	NC	Spala	17 Feb
19:18.9	Perseus	Karlström	SWE	2.5.90	2		Borås	23 Nov
19:19.08	Alsksandr	Lyakovich	BLR	4.7.89	1		Gomel	17 Feb
19:20.89	Oleksandr	Venglovskyy	UKR	5.8.85	1		Zaporizhzhya	29 Jan
19:22.98	Rafal	Augustyn	POL	14.5.84	4	NC	Spala	17 Feb
19:24.37	Ihor	Hlavan	UKR	25.9.90	1		Kyiv	11 Jan
19:26.54	Aleksandr	Yargunkin	RUS	6.1.81	2		Novocheboksarsk	12 Jan

19:28.35	Sergey	Kirdyapkin	RUS	18.6.80	31 Jan	19:34.12	Kirill	Frolov	RUS	29.9.93	22 Dec
19:29.06	João	Vieira	POR	20.2.76	16 Feb	19:35.81	Rafal	Sikora	POL	17.2.87	17 Feb
19:31.32	Sergio	Vieira	POR	20.2.76	16 Feb	19:37.00	Aléxandros	Papamihaíl	GRE	18.9.88	10 Feb
19:32.51	Giorgio	Rubino	ITA	15.4.86	16 Feb	19:39.11	Brendan	Boyce	IRL	15.10.86	6 Jan

JUNIORS

19:33.11	Daisuke	Matsunaga	JPN	24.3.95	1	Kumagaya	20 Apr
19:47.37	Diego	García	ESP-Y	19.1.96	3	Avilés	15 Jun
19:53.73	Takteru	Kutsuna	JPN	17.2.94	2	Kumagaya	20 Apr

+ intermediate time in longer race, A made at an altitude of 1000m or higher, D made in a decathlon, h made in a heat, qf quarter-final, sf semi-final, i indoors, Q qualifying round, r race number, -J juniors, -Y youths (b. 1996 or later)

MEN 2013

Mark		Name	Nat	Born	Pos	Meet	Venue	Date	

10,000 METRES TRACK WALK

Mark	Name (first)	Name (last)	Nat	Born	Pos	Meet	Venue	Date	
38:37.02	Kevin	Campion	FRA	23.5.88	1	NC	Paris (C)	13	Jul
39:06.87	Eiki	Takahashi	JPN	19.11.92	1		Isahaya	8	Dec
39:07.58	Miguel Ángel	López	ESP	3.7.88	1	NC	Alcobendas	28	Jul
39:08.23	Daisuke	Matsunaga	JPN-J	24.3.95	1		Tama	14	Dec
39:13.38	Christopher	Linke	GER	24.10.88	1	NC	Jüterbog	22	Jun
39:27.63	Yohann	Diniz	FRA	1.1.78	2	NC	Paris (C)	13	Jul
39:37.96	Hédi	Taraaoui	TUN	10.11.89	3	FRA Ch	Paris (C)	13	Jul
39:42.38	Takaki	Matsuzaki	JPN	12.8.92	2		Tama	14	Dec
39:47.0	Matteo	Giupponi	ITA	8.10.88	1		Brusaporto	26	May
39:50.03	Bertrand	Moulinet	FRA	6.12.87	4	NC	Paris (C)	13	Jul
39:52.20	Álvaro	Martín	ESP-J	18.6.94	2	NC	Alcobendas	28	Jul
39:52.76	Igor	Lyashchenko	UKR	24.8.93	1		Yalta	17	May
39:54.33	Hagen	Pohle	GER	5.3.92	1	NC-23	Jüterbog	22	Jun
39:54.34	Nils Christopher	Gloger	GER	1.1.90	2	NC	Jüterbog	22	Jun
40:02.25	Takumi	Saito	JPN	23.3.93	1	NSF	Tokyo (Chofu)	6	Oct
40:02.78	João	Vieira	POR	20.2.76	1	NC	Leiria	27	Jul
40:02.93	Sérgio	Vieira	POR	20.2.76	2	NC	Leiria	27	Jul
40:10.73A	Érick	Barrondo	GUA	14.6.91	1		Ciudad de Guatemala	25	Oct

40:19.04	Yusuke	Suzuki	JPN	1.2.88	6 Oct	40:30.60	Jorge Estiven	Díaz	COL	2.3.87	15 Jun
40:20.64	Nils	Brembach	GER	23.2.93	22 Jun	40:32.00	Perseus	Karlström	SWE	2.5.90	7 Sep
40:24.30	Federico	Tontodonati	ITA	30.10.89	26 Jun	40:33.86	Marcel	Lehmberg	GER	1.1.92	22 Jun
40:27.89	Hiroki	Arai	JPN	18.5.88	21 Sep	40:34.49	Yuki	Sasagawa	JPN	18.11.91	6 Oct

Indoors

39:41.3	Ihor	Hlavan	UKR	25.9.90	1		Sumy	21	Dec
40:01.51	Oleksandr	Venglovskyy	UKR	5.8.85	1	NC	Sumi	13	Feb

JUNIORS

39:08.23	Daisuke	Matsunaga	JPN	24.3.95	1		Tama	14	Dec
39:52.20	Álvaro	Martín	ESP	18.6.94	2	NC	Alcobendas	28	Jul
40:36.85A	Erwin	González	MEX	7.2.94	1	PAm-J	Medellín	24	Aug
41:01.55	Pavel	Parshin	RUS	2.1.94	1	EJ	Rieti	20	Jul
41:03.82	Kota	Yamada	JPN	27.4.94	3		Tama	14	Dec
41:08.76	Vito	Minei	ITA	16.6.94	2	EJ	Rieti	20	Jul
41:11.2	Viktor	Sokolov	RUS	7.1.94	1	NC	Cheboksary	8	Jun
41:12.8	Aleksey	Sorachenkov	RUS	6.11.94	2	NC	Cheboksary	8	Jun
41:21.97A	Brian	Pintado	ECU	29.7.95	2	PAm-J	Medellín	24	Aug
41:39.62	Francesco	Fortunato (10)	ITA	13.12.94	4	NC	Milano	26	Jul
41:39.85	Richard	Vargas	VEN	28.12.94	1		Caracas	21	Sep
41:40.57A	Paulo César	Yaurivilca	PER-Y	23.4.96	1		Lima	15	Jun
41:50.88	Nikolay	Markov	RUS	1.2.95	4	EJ	Rieti	20	Jul
41:51.24	Marc	Tur	ESP	30.11.94	5	EJ	Rieti	20	Jul
41:51.4	Damir	Baybikov	RUS	5.5.94	3	NC	Cheboksary	8	Jun
41:53.80	Toshikazu	Yamanishi	JPN-Y	15.2.96	1	WY	Donetsk	13	Jul
41:53.86A	Kenny	Pérez	COL	19.11.94	3	PAm-J	Medellín	24	Aug
41:55.95	Manuel	Soto	COL	28.1.94	1	SAm-J	Resistencia	18	Oct

10 KILOMETRES ROAD WALK

Where better than track times. See also 20km list for many intermediate times

39:28	Andriy	Kovenko	UKR	25.11.73	1		Katowice	7	Sep
39:29+	Aleksandr	Ivanov	RUS	25.4.93	1	in 20k	Sochi	23	Feb
39:34	Antón	Kucmin	SVK	7.6.84	2		Katowice	7	Sep
39:54	Ato	Ibáñez	SWE	14.11.85	1	Nurmi	Turku	10	Jun
40:01	Iñaki	Gómez	CAN	16.1.88	1	NC	Moncton	22	Jun
40:02	Grzegorz	Sudol	POL	28.8.78	2	Nurmi	Turku	10	Jun
40:11	Dawid	Tomala	POL	27.8.89	3		Katowice	7	Sep

40:17	Marc	Tur	ESP-J	30.11.94	15 Dec	40:21	Jarkko	Kinnunen	FIN	19.1.84	10 Jun
40:19	Evan	Dunfee	CAN	28.9.90	22 Jun	40:25	Marius	Ziukas	LTU	29.6.85	7 Sep

JUNIORS

40:17	Marc		Tur	ESP	30.11.94	1		Getafe	15	Dec
40:43		Yao Biao	CHN-Y	15.4.96	1	NC-y	Taicang	1	Mar
40:47		Leng Xiao	CHN-Y	26.1.96	2	NC-y	Taicang	1	Mar
40:50+	Takateru	Kutsuna	JPN	17.2.94		in 20k	Kobe	17	Feb
40:51		Dai Jianxing	CHN-Y	11.8..96	3	NC-y	Taicang	1	Mar
40:55	Diego	García	ESP-Y	19.1.96	3		Getafe	15	Dec
40:58		Tong Dongliang	CHN-Y	3.4.97	4	NC-y	Taicang	1	Mar
41:06		Zhao Jianguo	CHN-Y	1.1.97	5	NC-y	Taicang	1	Mar
41:13	Nikolay	Markov	RUS	1.2.95	2	ECp-J	Dudince	19	May
41:14	Toshikazu	Yamanishi (10)	JPN-Y	15.2.96	1		Kobe	17	Feb
41:15	Kota	Yamada	JPN		2		Kobe	17	Feb

Mark		Name	Nat	Born	Pos	Meet	Venue	Date
41:19A	Manuel	Soto	COL	28.1.94	1	PAmCp	Ciudad de Guatemala	25 May
41:33A	Iván	Garrido	COL	25.1.94	3	PAmCp	Ciudad de Guatemala	25 May
41:35A	Brian	Pintado	ECU	29.7.95	4	PAmCp	Ciudad de Guatemala	25 May
41:40+	Tenta	Kawashima	JPN	10.2.95	3		Kobe	17 Feb
41:41A	Richard	Vargas	VEN	28.12.94	5	PAmCp	Ciudad de Guatemala	25 May
41:43	Zaharías	Tsamoudákis	GRE-Y	14.1.96	1		Chiasso	13 Oct
41:45A	Kenny	Pérez	COL	19.11.94	6	PAmCp	Ciudad de Guatemala	25 May

20 KILOMETRES WALK

20k	10k			Nat	Born	Pos	Meet	Venue	Date
1:18:28	39:10	Pyotr	Trofimov	RUS	28.11.83	1	NC-w	Sochi	23 Feb
1:18:34	38:43	Yusuke	Suzuki	JPN	2.1.88	1	AsiC	Nomi	10 Mar
1:18:52	40:14		Li Jianbo	CHN	14.11.86	1	NC/IAAF	Taicang	1 Mar
1:18:55	40:14		Cai Zelin	CHN	11.4.91	2	NC/IAAF	Taicang	1 Mar
1:19:02	39:23		Suzuki			1	NC	Kobe	17 Feb
1:19:06	39:10	Andrey	Ruzavin	RUS	28.3.86	2	NC-w	Sochi	23 Feb
1:19:07			Yu Wei	CHN	11.9.87	3	NC	Taicang	1 Mar
1:19:08	39:51		Wang Zhen	CHN	24.8.91	1		Lugano	17 Mar
1:19:08			Ruzavin			1	NC	Cheboksary	8 Jun
1:19:34			Bian Fongda	CHN	1.4.91	4	NC	Taicang	1 Mar
1:19:34			Liu Jianmin	CHN	9.3.88	5	NC	Taicang	1 Mar
1:19:36		Pyotr	Bogatyrev (10)	RUS	11.3.91	2	NC	Cheboksary	8 Jun
1:19:45	40:26	Eider	Arévalo	COL	9.3.93	1		Podébrady	13 Apr
1:19:51	40:26	Erik	Tysse	NOR	4.12.80	2		Podébrady	13 Apr
1:19:53	39:23	Denis	Strelkov	RUS	26.10.90	3	NC-w	Sochi	23 Feb
1:19:54			Wang Zhen			1		Shenyang	11 May
1:19:55			Sun Chenggang	CHN	11.3.91	6	NC	Taicang	1 Mar
1:20:05	39:23	Takumi	Saito	JPN	23.3.93	2	NC	Kobe	17 Feb
1:20:14	40:03	Koichiro	Morioka	JPN	2.4.85	3	NC	Kobe	17 Feb
1:20:14	40:27	Matej	Tóth	SVK	10.2.83	3		Podébrady	13 Apr
1:20:18			Cai Zelin			2		Shenyang	11 May
1:20:22		Andriy	Kovenko	UKR	25.11.73	1	NC	Yevpatoria	2 Mar
1:20:25	40:03	Eiki	Takahashi	JPN	19.11.92	4	NC	Kobe	17 Feb
1:20:25		Érick	Barrondo	GUA	14.6.91	1		Dublin	29 Jun
1:20:30	40:26	Dawid	Tomala	POL	27.8.89	1		Olomouc	30 Mar
1:20:31			Wang Gang	CHN	2.4.91	1	NG	Shenyang	12 May
1:20:38	40:36	Ruslan	Dmytrenko	UKR	22.3.86	2		Lugano	17 Mar
1:20:41	40:26	Jared	Tallent	AUS	17.10.84	3	IAAF	Taicang	1 Mar
1:20:46		Grzegorz	Sudol	POL	28.8.78	1		Zaniemysl	20 Apr
1:20:47	40:15	Takuya	Yoshida	JPN	10.8.90	5	NC	Kobe	17 Feb
1:20:47		Andrey	Krivov	RUS	14.11.85	1	WUG	Kazan	9 Jul
		(31/27)							
1:20:48		Lukasz	Nowak	POL	18.12.88	2		Zaniemysl	20 Apr
1:20:50	40:22	Isamu	Fujisawa	JPN	12.10.87	6	NC	Kobe	17 Feb
1:20:50			Zhao Qi	CHN	14.1.93	7/4	NC/IAAF	Taicang	1 Mar
		(30)							
1:20:54			Li Shijia	CHN	14.1.92	8	NC	Taicang	1 Mar
1:20:58		Aleksandr	Ivanov	RUS	25.4.93	1	WCh	Moskva	11 Aug
1:20:59		Kolothum Thodi	Irfan	IND	8.2.90	5	IAAF	Taicang	1 Mar
1:21:02	40:23	Kevin	Campion	FRA	23.5.88	3		Lugano	17 Mar
1:21:06	40:03	Takayuki	Tanii	JPN	14.2.83	7	NC	Kobe	17 Feb
1:21:07		Giorgio	Rubino	ITA	15.4.86	4		Podébrady	13 Apr
1:21:08	40:31	João	Vieira	POR	20.2.76	1		Rio Maior	6 Apr
1:21:09			Chen Ding	CHN	5.8.92	2	WCh	Moskva	11 Aug
1:21:10	40:27	Nazar	Kovalenko	UKR	9.2.89	4		Lugano	17 Mar
1:21:13	40:26	Isaac	Palma	MEX	26.10.90	5		Lugano	17 Mar
		(40)							
1:21:13		Rafal	Augustyn	POL	14.5.84	3		Zaniemysl	20 Apr
1:21:17		Gurmeet	Singh	IND	1.7.85	1	NC	Patiala	14 Feb
1:21:21		Miguel Ángel	López	ESP	3.7.88	3	WCh	Moskva	11 Aug
1:21:22			Kim Hyun-sub	KOR	31.5.85	1	NG	Incheon	22 Oct
1:21:26		Andrés	Chocho	ECU	4.11.83	4		Zaniemysl	20 Apr
1:21:28	40:03	Hiroki	Arai	JPN	18.5.88	8	NC	Kobe	17 Feb
1:21:28	39:55		Li Tianlei	CHN-J	13.1.95	2	AsiC	Nomi	10 Mar
1:21:30			Hu Wanli	CHN	27.5.92	9	NC	Taicang	1 Mar
1:21:33	40:43	Denis	Simanovich	BLR	20.4.87	2		Alytus	14 Jun
1:21:35			Xu Faguang	CHN	17.5.87	7		Lugano	17 Mar
		(50)							
1:21:38		Pedro	Gómez	MEX	31.12.90	8		Lugano	17 Mar

MEN 2013

Mark		Name		Nat	Born	Pos	Meet	Venue	Date
1:21:41			Xu Dexing	CHN	20.8.88	10	NC	Taicang	1 Mar
1:21:41			Niu Wenbin	CHN	20.1.91	4	NG	Shenyang	12 May
1:21:51	40:27	Andreas	Gustafsson	SWE	10.8.81	5		Podébrady	13 Apr
1:21:51		Luis Fernando	López	COL	3.6.79	3		La Coruña	1 Jun
1:21:52			Choi Byung-kwang	KOR	7.4.91	5	AsiC	Nomi	10 Mar
1:21:52			Chu Yafei	CHN	5.9.88	5	NG	Shenyang	12 May
1:21:53	40:39	Sérgio	Vieira	POR	20.2.76	2		Rio Maior	6 Apr
1:21:55	40:36	Ivan	Losev	UKR	26.1.86	9		Lugano	17 Mar
1:21:55			Wang Zhendong	CHN	11.1.91	6	NG	Shenyang	12 May
		(60)							
1:21:56	40:39	Diego	Flores	MEX	23.3.87	3		Rio Maior	6 Apr
1:21:59	40:28	Robert	Heffernan	IRL	20.2.78	10		Lugano	17 Mar
1:22:01	40:43	Rafal	Fedaczynski	POL	3.12.80	4		Alytus	14 Jun
1:22:02	40:26	Ever	Palma	MEX	18.3.92	11		Lugano	17 Mar
1:22:03		Dane	Bird-Smith	AUS	15.7.92	4		La Coruña	1 Jun
1:22:06	40:22	Takaki	Matsuzaki	JPN	12.8.92	9	NC	Kobe	17 Feb
1:22:14			Du Yunpeng	CHN	6.9.88	12	NC	Taicang	1 Mar
1:22:14		Caio	Bonfim	BRA	19.3.91	5		La Coruña	1 Jun
1:22:16		Quentin	Rew	NZL	16.7.84	1		Naumburg	28 Apr
1:22:16		Artur	Brzozowski	POL	29.3.85	1	NC	Torun	20 Jul
		(70)							
1:22:19		Kirill	Frolov	RUS	29.9.93	5	NC-w	Sochi	23 Feb
1:22:19	40:35	Aníbal	Paau	GUA	12.1.87	12		Lugano	17 Mar
1:22:21		Iñaki	Gómez	CAN	16.1.88	8	WCh	Moskva	11 Aug
1:22:23		Francisco	Arcilla	ESP	14.1.84	6		La Coruña	1 Jun
1:22:24	40:39	Hayato	Katsuki	JPN	28.11.90	10	NC	Kobe	17 Feb
1:22:25	40:38	Jaime	Quiyuch	GUA	24.4.88	13		Lugano	17 Mar
1:22:25		Álvaro	Martín	ESP-J	18.6.94	5		La Coruña	1 Jun
1:22:25	40:44	Ivan	Trotskiy	BLR	27.5.76	5		Alytus	14 Jun
1:22:29		Jakub	Jelonek	POL	7.7.85	2		Sesto San Giovanni	1 May
1:22:32			Jiang Jie	CHN-J	25.10.94	1	NC-j	Taicang	1 Mar
		(80)							
1:22:32		Igor	Hlavan	UKR	25.9.90	6	WUG	Kazan	9 Jul
1:22:33		Benjamín	Sánchez	ESP	10.3.85	1	NC	Murcia	3 Mar
1:22:33		Federico	Tontodonati	ITA	30.10.89	6		Podébrady	13 Apr
1:22:36		Christopher	Linke	GER	24.10.88	9	WCh	Moskva	11 Aug
1:22:37		Hagen	Pohle	GER	5.3.92	2		Naumburg	28 Apr
1:22:37		José Ignacio	Díaz	ESP	22.11.79	8		La Coruña	1 Jun
1:22:39		Máté	Helebrandt	HUN	12.1.89	7		Podébrady	13 Apr
1:22:39		Jesús Tadeo	Vega	MEX-J	23.5.94	2	NC	Boca del Rio	21 Apr
1:22:39			Xie Sichao	CHN	28.2.93	8	NG	Shenyang	12 May
1:22:40			Wang Hao	CHN	16.8.89	13	NC	Taicang	1 Mar
		(90)							
1:22:46			Tong Anqi	CHN	29.9.92	14	NC	Taicang	1 Mar
1:22:46		Evan	Dunfee	CAN	28.9.90	1		Huntington Beach, CA	17 Mar
1:22:46.5t		Juan Manuel	Cano	ARG	12.12.87	1	NC	Santa Fe	9 Jun
1:22:47		Kai	Kobayashi	JPN	28.2.93	4		Takahata	26 Oct
1:22:48		Oleksandr	Verbytskyy	UKR	28.7.92	5	NC	Yevpatoria	2 Mar
1:22:49		Benjamin	Thorne	CAN	19.3.93	2		Huntington Beach, CA	17 Mar
1:22:50.8t		Moacir	Zimmerman	BRA	30.12.83	1		Itajaí	28 Apr
1:22:53		Jarkko	Kinnunen	FIN	19.1.84	8		Podébrady	13 Apr
1:22:54			Chen Zongliang	CHN	9.1.92	4	NG	Shenyang	11 May
1:22:56			Zhang Hang	CHN	28.10.91	16	NC	Taicang	1 Mar
		(100)							

Mark	Name	Nat	Born	Date
1:22:58	Zhao Ziyang	CHN	29.7.91	1 Mar
1:23:00	Liu Xu	CHN-J	11.12.94	1 Mar
1:23:01	Takafumi Higuma	JPN	3.9.82	17 Feb
1:23:05	Wu Qianlong	CHN	30.1.90	1 Mar
1:23:05	Alex Wright	GBR	19.12.90	17 Mar
1:23:09	Wei Xubao	CHN	1.2.93	1 Mar
1:23:15	Andrey Talashko	BLR	31.5.82	14 Jun
1:23:17	Yohann Diniz	FRA	1.1.78	13 Oct
1:23:20	Luo Yadong	CHN	15.1.92	1 Mar
1:23:20	Rafal Sikora	POL	17.2.87	30 Mar
1:23:22	Ji Chunlong	CHN	25.2.88	12 May
1:23:23	Valeriy Filipchuk	RUS	30.6.91	23 Feb
1:23:27	Matteo Giupponi	ITA	8.10.88	11 Aug
1:23:28	Chandan Singh	IND	8.6.87	14 Feb
1:23:28	Omar Segura	MEX	24.3.81	21 Apr
1:23:28	Chris Erickson	AUS	1.12.81	30 Jun
1:23:30	Oleksiy Kazanin	UKR	22.5.82	15 Jun
1:23:32	Men Fuqiang	CHN	22.6.92	1 Mar
1:23:32	Carlos Sánchez	MEX	19.5.85	21 Apr
1:23:35	Wang Kaihua	CHN-J	16.2.94	1 Jun
1:23:39	Aleksey Golovin	RUS	24.12.88	23 Feb
1:23:40	Li Yajun	CHN	14.12.93	1 Mar
1:23:40	Kim Dae-ro	KOR	30.4.88	2 May
1:23:42	Zhang Zhi	CHN-J	22.7.94	1 Mar
1:23:43	Ivan Banzeruk	UKR	9.2.90	5 Oct
1:23:43	Marius Ziukas	LTU	29.6.85	27 Apr
1:23:43	José Leonardo Montaña	COL	21.3.92	27 Nov
1:23:44	Hu Enxi	CHN-J	26.3.94	1 Mar
1:23:44	Kostantyn Puzanov	UKR	19.5.91	2 Mar
1:23:44	Antón Kucmin	SVK	7.6.84	13 Apr
1:23:45	Su Guanyu	CHN-J	26.6.94	12 May
1:23:45	Yosuke Kimura	JPN	5.2.93	26 Oct
1:23:46	Antonin Boyez	FRA	9.11.84	17 Mar
1:23:46	Takeshi Okuma	JPN	14.12.83	26 Oct
1:23:48	Luke Adams	AUS	22.10.76	24 Feb
1:23:48	Aléxandros Papamihail	GRE	18.9.88	14 Jun
1:23:50	Carl Dohmann	GER	18.5.90	13 Apr
1:23:56	Daisuke Matsunaga	JPN-J	24.3.95	17 Feb

Mark	Name	Nat	Born	Date
1:23:56	Sun Song	CHN-Y	15.12.96 1	Mar
1:24:01	Babubhai Panocha	IND	10.8.78 14	Feb
1:24:01	Nils Christopher Gloger	GER	6.8.90 28	Apr
1:24:01	Rolando Saquipay	ECU	21.7.79 11	Aug
1:24:04	Richard Vargas	VEN-J	28.12.94 27	Nov
1:24:05	Ding Xianyu	CHN	27.11.93 12	May
1:24:06	Hatem Ghoula	TUN	7.6.73 1	Jun
1:24:08	Ebrahim Rahimian	IRI	29.6.81 10	Mar
1:24:09	Ma Haijun	CHN	24.11.92 1	Mar
1:24:14	Yin Jiaxing	CHN-J	16.3.94 12	May
1:24:19	Georgiy Sheyko	KAZ	24.8.89 23	Feb
1:24:20	Luis Manuel Corchete	ESP	14.5.84 3	Mar
1:24:22	Baljinder Singh	IND	18.9.86 14	Feb
1:24:22	Rhydian Cowley	AUS	4.1.91 1	Jun
1:24:24	Aleksandr Lyakhovich	BLR	4.7.89 5	Oct
1:24:28	Surender Singh	IND		14 Feb
1:24:28	Konstantin Kulagov	RUS	14.10.91 23	Feb
1:24:29	Daniele Paris	ITA	18.10.84 17	Mar
1:24:30	Dmitriy Dzlubin	BLR	12.7.90 14	Jun
1:24:31	Hitoshi Warita	JPN	26.9.91 26	Oct
1:24:35	Anatole Ibáñez	SWE	14.11.85 13	Apr
1:24:36	Geng Zhiyao	CHN	15.8.87 12	May
1:24:37	Sergey Lyubomirov	RUS	26.6.89 23	Feb
1:24:37	Zhao Yinliang	CHN	6.1.93 1	Mar
1:24:37	Qu Guanchen	CHN-J	18.12.94 12	May
1:24:38	Brendan Boyce	IRL	15.10.86 28	Apr
1:24:39	Nils Brembach	GER	23.2.93 17	Mar
1:24:42	Satoshi Maruo	JPN	28.11.91 10	Mar
1:24:42	Yerko Araya	CHI	14.2.86 11	Aug
1:24:44	Tom Bosworth	GBR	17.1.90 13	Apr
1:24:47	Kuldeep Singh	IND-J	30.12.94 24	Apr
1:24:53	Byun Young-joon	KOR	20.3.84 2	May
1:24:54	Kenma Ishida	JPN	28.9.92 10	Mar
1:24:55	Perseus Karlström	SWE	2.5.90 21	Sep
1:24:56	Denis Asanov	RUS	23.9.92 23	Feb
1:24:57	Luis Alberto Amezcua	ESP	1.5.82 3	Mar
1:24:59	Keita Shinohe	JPN	26.6.91 10	Mar
(175)				

Best track times | 1:23:04.0 Bonfim 5 May | 1:24:10.5 Saquipay 15 Jun | 1:24:36.4 Arévalo 6 Jul

Short course: At Casablanca 1 Jun: 1. Hassanine Sbaï TUN 1:19:36, 2. Hichem Mediber ALG 10.2.82 1:19:43, 3. Mohamed Ameur ALG 1.11.84 1:20:33

JUNIORS

See main list for top 4 juniors. 5 performances by 4 men to 1:23:00. Additional marks and further juniors:

Mark	Name	Nat	Born	Pos	Meet	Venue	Date
Li Tianlei	1:21:49 6		Taicang				1 Mar
1:23:00	Liu Xu	CHN	11.12.94	2	NC-j	Taicang	1 Mar
1:23:35	Wang Kaihua	CHN	16.2.94	12		La Coruña	1 Jun
1:23:42	Zhang Zhi	CHN	22.7.94	3	NC-j	Taicang	1 Mar
1:23:44	Hu Enxi	CHN	26.3.94	4	NC -j	Taicang	1 Mar
1:23:45	Su Guanyu	CHN	26.6.94	13	NG	Shenyang	12 May
1:23:56	Daisuke Matsunaga (10)	JPN-	24.3.95	12	NC	Kobe	17 Feb
1:23:56	Sun Song	CHN-Y	15.12.96	5	NC-j	Taicang	1 Mar
1:24:04	Richard Vargas	VEN	28.12.94	3	Bol G	Trujillo	27 Nov
1:24:14	Yin Jiaxing	CHN	16.3.94	17	NG	Shenyang	12 May
1:24:37	Qu Guanchen	CHN	18.12.94	20	NG	Shenyang	12 May
1:24:47	Kuldeep Singh	IND	30.12.94	2		Patiala	24 Apr
1:25:30	Lu Jiefang	CHN	7.1.95	6	NC-j	Taicang	1 Mar
1:25:41	Li Shuai	CHN	6.1.95	7	NC-j	Taicang	1 Mar
1:25:59	Hiu Ying	CHN	28.2.94	8	NC-j	Taicang	1 Mar
1:26:10	Marc Tur	ESP	30.11.94	19		La Coruña	1 Jun
1:26:17	Li Peng (20)	CHN	10.11.94	10	NC-j	Taicang	1 Mar

30-35 KILOMETRES WALK

30k	35k	Name	Nat	Born	Pos	Meet	Venue	Date
2:05:19	2:26:08	Sergey Bakulin	RUS	13.11.86	1	NC-w	Sochi	23 Feb
2:06:24	2:27:42	Aleksey Bartsaykin	RUS	22.3.89	2	NC-w	Sochi	23 Feb
2:06:26	2:28:09	Mikhail Ryzhov	RUS	17.12.91	3	NC-w	Sochi	23 Feb
2:06:54	2:29:04	Ivan Noskov	RUS	16.7.88	4	NC-w	Sochi	23 Feb
2:08:18	2:31:10	Konstantin Maksimov	RUS	17.6.82	5	NC-w	Sochi	23 Feb
	2:31:15	Igor Hlavan	UKR	25.9.90	1	NC	Yevpatoriya	2 Mar
2:09:26	2:31:26	Aleksandr Yargunkin	RUS	6.1.81	6	NC-w	Sochi	18 Feb
	2:32:13	Sergiy Budza	UKR	6.12.84	2	NC	Yevpatoriya	2 Mar
2:10:08	2:32:19	Aleksey Khimin	RUS	26.2.89	7	NC-w	Sochi	18 Feb
2:10:42	2:32:30	Edikt Khaybullin	RUS	29.5.89	8	NC-w	Sochi	18 Feb
2:10:52		Jared Tallent	AUS	17.10.84	1	in 20M 2:20:42	Canberra	9 Jun
2:11:26		Chris Erickson	AUS	1.12.81	2	in 20M 2:21:12	Canberra	9 Jun
	2:32:36	Oleksiy Kazanin	UKR	22.5.82	3	NC	Yevpatoriya	2 Mar
	2:33:06	Ivan Banzeruk	UKR	9.2.90	4	NC	Yevpatoriya	2 Mar
2:12:36		Ian Rayson	AUS	4.2.88	3	in 20M 2:22:30	Canberra	9 Jun
2:12:41	2:34:41	Jaime Quiyuch	GUA	24.4.88		in 50k	Dudince	23 Mar
2:12:44	2:34:42+	Li Jianbo	CHN	14.11.86		in 50k	Moskva	14 Aug
2:12:53+		Erik Tysse	NOR	4.12.80		in 50k	Moskva	14 Aug
2:12:10	2:35:26	Sergey Korepanov	RUS	15.7.84	9	NC-w	Sochi	18 Feb
	2:35:36	Igor Saharuk	UKR	3.6.88	5	NC	Yevpatoriya	2 Mar
2:13:57		Alex Wright	GBR	19.12.90	1	IRL Ch	Dublin	22 Dec
	2:36:18	Oleksandr Venglovskyy	UKR	5.8.85	6	NC	Yevpatoriya	2 Mar
2:14:06	2:37:20+	Koichiro Morioka	JPN	2.4.85		in 50k	Moskva	11 Aug

50 KILOMETRES WALK

50k	30k	35k	Name	Nat	Born	Pos	Meet	Venue	Date
3:37:56	2:12:17	2:33:46	Robert Heffernan	IRL	20.2.78	1	WCh	Moskva	14 Aug
3:38:58	2:12:18	2:33:47	Mikhail Ryzhov	RUS	17.12.91	2	WCh	Moskva	14 Aug
3:40:03	2:12:44	2:34:22	Jared Tallent	AUS	17.10.84	3	WCh	Moskva	14 Aug

Mark			Name		Nat	Born	Pos	Meet	Venue	Date
3:40:39	2:14:18	2:35:40	Igor	Hlavan	UKR	25.9.90	4	WCh	Moskva	14 Aug
3:41:07	2:14:06	2:36:04	Yohann	Diniz	FRA	1.1.78	1	ECp	Dudince	19 May
3:41:07	2:12:44	2:34:23	Matej	Tóth	SVK	10.2.83	5	WCh	Moskva	14 Aug
3:41:09	2:12:21	2:34:13	Érick	Barrondo	GUA	14.6.91	1		Dudince	23 Mar
3:41:20	2:12:17	2:33:53	Grzegorz	Sudol	POL	28.8.78	6	WCh	Moskva	14 Aug
3:41:36	2:12:18	2:33:48	Ivan	Noskov	RUS	16.7.88	7	WCh	Moskva	14 Aug
3:43:38	2:13:07	2:35:17	Lukasz	Nowak (10)	POL	18.12.88	8	WCh	Moskva	14 Aug
3:43:54	2:13:59	2:36:19	Yuriy	Andronov	RUS	6.11.71	1	NC	Cheboksary	9 Jun
3:44:25			Takayuki	Tanii	JPN	14.2.83	1	NC	Wajima	21 Apr
3:44:26	2:13:58	2:36:18		Tanii			9	WCh	Moskva	14 Aug
3:44:41		2:37:15		Ryzhov			2	ECp	Dudince	19 May
3:45:18	2:12:20	2:34:53		Diniz			10	WCh	Moskva	14 Aug
3:45:31		2:37:16		Noskov			3	ECp	Dudince	19 May
3:45:56	2:13:59	2:36:19	Hiroki	Arai	JPN	18.5.88	11	WCh	Moskva	11 Aug
3:46:09		2:39:08		Hlavan			4	ECp	Dudince	19 May
3:46:41		2:38:52		Sudol			5	ECp	Dudince	19 May
3:46:44		2:39:38	Jesús Ángel	García	ESP	17.10.69	12	WCh	Moskva	14 Aug
3:47:35			Ivan	Banzeruk	UKR	9.2.90	6	ECp	Dudince	19 May
3:47:36		2:38:36	Sergiy	Budza	UKR	6.12.84	13	WCh	Moskva	14 Aug
3:47:48		2:37:24	Konstantin	Maksimov	RUS	17.6.82	7	ECp	Dudince	19 May
3:47:52	2:12:44	2:34:49	Ivan	Trotskiy	BLR	27.5.76	14	WCh	Moskva	14 Aug
3:48:05		2:38:32	Marco	De Luca	ITA	12.5.81	15	WCh	Moskva	14 Aug
3:48:13		2:38:52	Rafal	Sikora (20)	POL	17.2.87	8	ECp	Dudince	19 May
3:49:24		2:38:54		Budza			9	ECp	Dudince	19 May
3:49:41		2:39:38	Chris	Erickson	AUS	1.12.81	16	WCh	Moskva	14 Aug
3:49:47			Aleksandr	Yargunkin	RUS	6.1.81	2	NC	Cheboksary	9 Jun
3:49:52				Diniz			2		Dudince	23 Mar
	(30/22)									
3:50:27			Quentin	Rew	NZL	16.7.84	17	WCh	Moskva	14 Aug
3:50:29			Claudio	Villanueva	ESP	3.8.88	18	WCh	Moskva	14 Aug
3:50:43			Omar	Zepeda	MEX	8.6.77	19	WCh	Moskva	14 Aug
3:50:48			Adrian	Blocki	POL	11.4.90	3		Dudince	23 Mar
3:50:51			Koichiro	Morioka	JPN	2.4.85	2	NC	Wajima	21 Apr
3:50:56			Jarkko	Kinnunen	FIN	19.1.84	20	WCh	Moskva	14 Aug
3:51:05			Aléxandros	Papamihail	GRE	18.9.88	10	ECp	Dudince	19 May
3:51:32			Damian	Blocki (30)	POL	28.4.89	4		Dudince	23 Mar
3:51:33			Rafal	Augustyn	POL	14.5.84	5	1 NC	Dudince	23 Mar
3:51:35				Wu Qianlong	CHN	30.1.90	1	NG	Shenyang	10 May
3:52:12				Li Jianbo	CHN	14.11.86	2	NG	Shenyang	10 May
3:52:43			Perseus	Karlström	SWE	2.5.90	1	NC	Eskilstuna	5 Oct
3:53:19				Si Tianfeng	CHN	17.6.84	3	NG	Shenyang	10 May
3:53:30				Zhao Jianguo	CHN	19.1.88	4	NG	Shenyang	10 May
3:53:38			Anatole	Ibáñez	SWE	14.11.85	22	WCh	Moskva	14 Aug
3:53:49			Mikhail	Puzakov	RUS	13.3.91	3	NC	Cheboksary	9 Jun
3:54:00			Jean-Jacques	Nkouloukidi	ITA	15.4.82	24	WCh	Moskva	14 Aug
3:54:13				Park Chil-sung	KOR	8.7.82	3	JPN Ch	Wajima	21 Apr
	(40)									
3:54:24			Brendan	Boyce	IRL	15.10.86	25	WCh	Moskva	14 Aug
3:54:40			Oleksiy	Kazanin	UKR	22.5.82	13	ECp	Dudince	19 May
3:54:47			José Ignacio	Díaz	ESP	22.11.79	14	ECp	Dudince	19 May
3:55:23A			Erik	Tysse	NOR	4.12.80	1	IAAF	Chihuahua	23 Feb
3:56:07			Oleksandr	Venglovskyy	UKR	5.8.85	6		Dudince	23 Mar
3:56:45			Teodorico	Caporaso	ITA	14.9.87	16	ECp	Dudince	19 May
3:56:56				Niu Wenbin	CHN	20.1.91	1	NC	Taicang	2 Mar
3:56:58			Jonnathan	Cáceres	ECU	20.1.90	27	WCh	Moskva	14 Aug
3:57:09			Pedro	Isidro	POR	17.7.85	17	ECp	Dudince	19 May
3:57:24			Igor	Saharuk (50)	UKR	3.6.88	1	NC	Ivano-Frankivsk	20 Oct
3:57:28			Michal	Stasiewicz	POL	28.9.88	18	ECp	Dudince	19 May
3:57:48A			Omar	Segura	MEX	24.3.81	3	IAAF	Chihuahua	23 Feb
3:57:50			Dusan	Majdan	SVK	8.9.87	29	WCh	Moskva	14 Aug
3:57:54				Xu Faguang	CHN	17.5.87	30	WCh	Moskva	14 Aug
3:57:55			Marc	Mundell	RSA	7.7.83	31	WCh	Moskva	14 Aug
3:57:58			Carl	Dohmann	GER	18.5.90	1	NC	Gleina	19 Oct
3:58:00A			Horacio	Nava	MEX	20.1.82	2	PAmCp	Ciudad de Guatemala	26 May
3:58:04			Sergey	Korepanov	RUS	15.7.84	4	NC	Cheboksary	9 Jun
3:58:20			Basant Bahadur	Rana	IND	18.1.84	33	WCh	Moskva	14 Aug

Mark	Name		Nat	Born	Pos	Meet	Venue	Date
3:58:26	Andrey (60)	Hrechkovskyy	UKR	30.8.93	2	NC	Ivano-Frankivsk	20 Oct
3:58:32	Predrag	Filipovic	SRB	5.10.78	7		Dudince	23 Mar
3:58:50	Veli-Matti	Partanen	FIN	28.10.91	1		Dublin	29 Jun
3:58:50	Andrés	Chocho	ECU	4.11.83	1	Bol G	Trujillo	29 Nov
3:59:07A	Luis	Bustamante	MEX	10.6.84	4	IAAF	Chihuahua	23 Feb
3:59:13	Jorge	Ruíz	COL	17.5.89	2	Bol G	Trujillo	29 Nov
3:59:15		Geng Zhiyao	CHN	15.8.87	5	NG	Shenyang	10 May
3:59:28	Evan	Dunfee	CAN	28.9.90	36	WCh	Moskva	14 Aug
3:59:46	Oleksandr	Romanenko	UKR	26.6.81	3	NC	Ivano-Frankivsk	20 Oct
3:59:55	Takafumi	Higuma	JPN	3.9.82	4	NC	Wajima	21 Apr
4:00:05	Mikel (70)	Odriozola	ESP	25.5.73	2	NC	Montijo	16 Mar
4:00:25		Oh Se-hyun	KOR	22.2.84	5		Wajima	21 Apr
4:00:31A	Edward	Araya	CHI	14.2.86	5	IAAF	Chihuahua	23 Feb
4:00:37	Aleksey	Arkhipov	RUS	7.12.88	4	UKR Ch	Ivano-Frankivsk	20 Oct
4:00:51	Tadas	Suskevicius	LTU	22.5.85	8		Dudince	23 Mar
4:01:40	Andreas	Gustafsson	SWE	10.8.81	39	WCh	Moskva	14 Aug
4:01:45		He Yongqiang	CHN	27.11.93	1		Changbaishan	21 Sep
4:02:07		Xu Jie	CHN	1.1.93	2	NC	Taicang	2 Mar
4:02:19	Sandeep	Kumar	IND	16.12.86	1	NC	Patiala	15 Feb
4:02:27		Guo Xiaoxin	CHN	18.1.86	3	NC	Taicang	2 Mar
4:02:46	(80)	Wang Guozhen	CHN	1.12.92	4	NC	Taicang	2 Mar
4:02:56		Wang Hao	CHN	16.8.89	7	NG	Shenyang	10 May
4:03:11		Bai Xuejin	CHN	6.6.87	5	NC	Taicang	2 Mar
4:03:59	Mario Alfonso	Bran	GUA	17.10.89	4	PAmCp	Ciudad de Guatemala	26 May
4:04:23	Marius	Cocioran	ROU	10.7.83	40	WCh	Moskva	14 Aug
4:04:23	Ferney	Rojas	COL	30.9.87	4	Bol G	Trujillo	29 Nov
4:04:42	Lukasz	Augustyn	POL	29.11.90	10		Dudince	23 Mar
4:05:27		Du Gang	CHN	26.3.92	7	NC	Taicang	2 Mar
4:05:36	Daniel	King	GBR	30.5.83	1		Tilburg	6 Oct
4:05:37	Mário	Santos	POR	28.7.88	11		Dudince	23 Mar
4:05:38	Fredy (90)	Hernández	COL	25.4.78	5	RUS Ch	Cheboksary	9 Jun
4:06:12		Liu Rusi	CHN	6.8.91	8	NG	Shenyang	10 May
4:06:12	Mário José	dos Santos	BRA	10.9.79	43	WCh	Moskva	14 Aug
4:06:44	Lorenzo	Dessi	ITA	4.5.89	20	ECp	Dudince	19 May
4:07:14A	Cristian	Berdeja	MEX	21.6.81	5	PAmCp	Ciudad de Guatemala	26 May
4:07:28		Zhang Lin	CHN	11.11.93	3		Changbaishan	21 Sep
4:07:29	Xavier	Moreno	ECU	15.11.79	44	WCh	Moskva	14 Aug
4:08:02	Michael	Doyle	IRL	17.5.87	21	ECp	Dudince	19 May
4:08:09	Cédric	Houssaye	FRA	13.12.79	22	ECp	Dudince	19 May
4:08:16		Yin Mingxing	CHN	25.10.88	9	NG	Shenyang	10 May
4:08:33	Pavel (100)	Chihuán	PER	19.1.86	5	Bol G	Trujillo	29 Nov

4:08:40A	Clemente	García	MEX	21.8.89	23 Feb		4:09:17		Wang Zhendong	CHN	11.1.91	21 Sep
4:09:02A	Omar	Sierra	COL	10.9.88	26 May		4:09:36		Wei Xubao	CHN	1.2.93	2 Mar
4:09:16	Aleksey	Terentyev	RUS	19.7.91	9 Jun		4:09:40	Xavier	Le Coz	FRA	30.12.79	19 May

| 8:50:21 | Bertrand | Mouilinet | FRA | 6.1.87 | 1 | NC | St-Thibault-les-Vignes | 5 Oct |

100 KILOMETRES WALK

Some Recent Marriages

Female	Male	
Elle Baker GBR	Steve Vernon GBR	24.8.13
Shana Cox GBR	Michael Bingham GBR	9.11.13
Hanna Knyazyeva UKR	Anatoliy Minenko ISR	.11.12
Ivet Lalova BUL	Simone Collio ITA	21.9.13
Katia Lannon GBR	Ben Hazell GBR	.6.13
Zuzana Malíková SVK	Jamie Costin IRL	24.8.13
Yekaterina Martynova RUS	Yevgeniy Sharmin RUS	
Christina Obergföll GER	Boris Henry GER	13.9.13
Svetlana Podosyenova RUS	Maksim Karamashev RUS	.9.13
Marestella Torres PHI	Eliezer Sunang PHI	.13
Jana Tucholke GER	Peter Sack GER	31.8.13

MEN 2013

Mark	Wind	Name		Nat	Born	Pos	Meet	Venue	Date	

WOMEN'S WORLD LISTS 2013

60 METRES INDOORS

Mark	Wind	Name		Nat	Born	Pos	Meet	Venue	Date	
6.99		Murielle	Ahouré	CIV	23.8.87	1	GP	Birmingham	16	Feb
7.00		Ahouré				1		Houston	26	Jan
7.03		Ahouré				1h1	GP	Birmingham	16	Feb
7.04		Shelly-Ann	Fraser-Pryce	JAM	27.12.86	1		Stockholm	21	Feb
7.06		Ahouré				1		Val-de-Reuil	12	Feb
7.07		Ahouré				1	BIG	Boston (Roxbury)	2	Feb
7.07		Myriam	Soumaré	FRA	29.10.86	1s2	EI	Göteborg	3	Mar
7.08		Ahouré				1		Düsseldorf	8	Feb
7.08A		Barbara	Pierre	USA	28.4.87	1	NC	Albuquerque	3	Mar
		(9/4)								
7.10		Mariya	Ryemyen	UKR	2.8.87	1s1	EI	Göteborg	3	Mar
7.10A		Lekeisha	Lawson	USA	3.6.87	2	NC	Albuquerque	3	Mar
7.12		Ruddy	Zang Milama	GAB	6.6.87	2		Moskva	3	Feb
7.12		Verena	Sailer	GER	16.10.85	1h1	EI	Göteborg	1	Mar
7.12		Ivet	Lalova	BUL	18.5.84	3	EI	Göteborg	3	Mar
7.13		Laverne	Jones-Ferrette	ISV	16.9.81	2		Houston	26	Jan
		(10)								
7.13		Aurieyall	Scott	USA	18.5.92	1		Birmingham, AL	24	Feb
7.13		Ezinne	Okparaebo	NOR	3.3.88	1h2	EI	Göteborg	1	Mar
7.14		Dafne	Schippers	NED	15.6.92	4	EI	Göteborg	3	Mar
7.15		Asha	Philip	GBR	25.10.90	1	NC	Sheffield	9	Feb
7.15		English	Gardner	USA	22.4.92	1h1	NCAA	Fayetteville	8	Mar
7.16		Kimberlyn	Duncan	USA	2.8.91	1r1		New York (Armory)	1	Feb
7.16		Octavious	Freeman	USA	20.4.92	3	NCAA	Fayetteville	9	Mar
7.18A		Carmelita	Jeter	USA	24.11.79	1		Albuquerque	2	Feb
7.18						4	GP	Birmingham	16	Feb
7.19		Dezerea	Bryant	USA	27.4.93	1		Clemson	11	Jan
7.19		Sheri-Ann	Brooks	JAM	11.2.83	3h1	GP	Birmingham	16	Feb
		(20)								
7.19A		Shayla	Mahan	USA	18.1.89	2h2	NC	Albuquerque	3	Mar
7.21A		Kya	Brookins	USA	28.7.89	4	NC	Albuquerque	3	Mar
7.22		Jeneba	Tarmoh	USA	27.9.89	2	Mill	New York (Armory)	16	Feb
7.23		Tatjana	Pinto	GER	2.7.92	1h1		Bielefeld	26	Jan
7.24		Katerina	Cechová	CZE	21.3.88	1	NC	Praha (Strom)	16	Feb
7.24		Lauryn	Williams	USA	11.9.83	3	Mill	New York (Armory)	16	Feb
7.24		Trisha-Ann	Hawthorne	JAM	8.11.89	4	Mill	New York (Armory)	16	Feb
7.24		Jura	Levy	JAM	4.11.90	1	NAIA	Geneva, OH	2	Mar
7.25		Montell	Douglas	GBR	14.1.86	1A2		London (Nh)	13	Feb
7.25		Hanna-Maari	Latvala	FIN	30.10.87	4h1	EI	Göteborg	1	Mar
		(30)								
7.26		Natasha	Hastings	USA	23.7.86	1		Houston	18	Jan
7.26		Gloria	Asumnu	NGR	22.5.85	4		Karlsruhe	2	Feb
7.26		Atarah	Clark	USA	.93			Levelland	16	Feb
7.26		Ashley	Collier	USA	4.2.92	2	SEC	Fayetteville	24	Feb
7.26		Jamile	Samuel	NED	24.4.92	4s2	EI	Göteborg	3	Mar
7.27A		Geronne	Black	TTO	26.10.89	1r1		Albuquerque	8	Feb
7.27		Flings	Owusu-Agyapong	GHA	16.10.88	1		Toronto	16	Feb
7.27		NyEma	Sims	USA	10.2.88	1s2	NAIA	Geneva, OH	1	Mar
7.28		Takeia	Pinckney	USA	24.7.91	3	Tyson	Fayetteville	8	Feb
7.28		Yuliya	Katsura	RUS	28.5.83	1	NC	Moskva	12	Feb
		(40)								
7.29A		Asia	Cooper	USA		2		Albuquerque	8	Feb
7.29		Yuliya	Kashina	RUS	26.2.87	2	NC	Moskva	12	Feb
7.29		Adella	King	USA	21.3.90	3	NAIA	Geneva, OH	2	Mar
7.29			Wei Yongli	CHN	11.10.91	1rA		Nanjing	6	Mar
7.29		Jenna	Prandini	USA	20.11.92	4h2	NCAA	Fayetteville	8	Mar
Drugs disqualification										
7.10		Tezdzhan	Naimova ¶	BUL	1.5.87	(1)	EI	Göteborg	3	Mar

100 METRES

Mark	Wind	Name		Nat	Born	Pos	Meet	Venue	Date	
10.71	-0.3	Shelly-Ann	Fraser-Pryce	JAM	27.12.86	1	WCh	Moskva	12	Aug
10.72	-0.3		Fraser-Pryce			1	VD	Bruxelles	6	Sep
10.77	0.7		Fraser-Pryce			1h1	DL	London (OS)	27	Jul
10.79	1.1	Blessing	Okagbare	NGR	9.10.88	1	DL	London (OS)	27	Jul
10.83	1.6	Kelly-Ann	Baptiste	TTO	14.10.86	1	NC	Port of Spain	22	Jun
10.85	2.0	Barbara	Pierre	USA	28.4.87	1s1	NC	Des Moines	21	Jun
10.85	1.8	English	Gardner	USA	22.4.92	1	NC	Des Moines	21	Jun

Mark	Wind	Name		Nat	Born	Pos	Meet	Venue	Date	
10.85	1.1		Pierre			2	DL	London (OS)	27	Jul
10.86	0.1		Okagbare			1h2	DL	London (OS)	27	Jul
10.87	1.7		Gardner			1s2	NC	Des Moines	21	Jun
10.87	1.8	Octavious	Freeman	USA	20.4.92	2	NC	Des Moines	21	Jun
10.87	-0.1		Fraser-Pryce			1s3	WCh	Moskva	12	Aug
10.90	1.7		Freeman			2s2	NC	Des Moines	21	Jun
10.90	0.1		Pierre			2h2	DL	London (OS)	27	Jul
10.91	1.7	Alexandria	Anderson	USA	28.1.87	3s2	NC	Des Moines	21	Jun
10.91	1.8		Anderson			3	NC	Des Moines	21	Jun
10.91	1.5	Murielle	Ahouré	CIV	23.8.87	1		Sotteville-lès-Rouen	8	Jul
10.92	-0.2		Fraser-Pryce			1	DL	Saint-Denis	6	Jul
10.92	1.5		Pierre			1r2		Madrid	13	Jul
10.93	0.1		Fraser-Pryce			1	DL	Shanghai	18	May
10.93	1.8	Jeneba	Tarmoh	USA	27.9.89	4	NC	Des Moines	21	Jun
10.93	-0.2		Okagbare			2	DL	Saint-Denis	6	Jul
10.93	0.7	Carmelita	Jeter	USA	24.11.79	2h1	DL	London (OS)	27	Jul
10.93	1.1		Baptiste			3	DL	London (OS)	27	Jul
10.93	-0.3		Ahouré			2	WCh	Moskva	12	Aug
10.94	1.8		Pierre			5	NC	Des Moines	21	Jun
10.94	1.1		Fraser-Pryce			4	DL	London (OS)	27	Jul
10.94	-0.5		Gardner			1h3	WCh	Moskva	11	Aug
10.94	-0.3		Jeter			3	WCh	Moskva	12	Aug
10.95	0.4		Jeter			1		George Town	8	May
10.95	1.1		Ahouré			5	DL	London (OS)	27	Jul
10.95	-0.4		Jeter			1s2	WCh	Moskva	12	Aug
10.95	-0.4		Ahouré			2s2	WCh	Moskva	12	Aug
		(33/10)								
10.96	0.9	Kerron	Stewart	JAM	16.4.84	1	NC	Kingston	21	Jun
10.96	2.0	Aurieyall	Scott	USA	18.5.92	2s1		Des Moines	21	Jun
10.98	0.5	Carrie	Russell	JAM	18.10.90	1	WK	Zürich	29	Aug
11.00	1.7	Lauryn	Williams	USA	11.9.83	5s2	NC	Des Moines	21	Jun
11.00	1.8	Muna	Lee	USA	30.10.81	7	NC	Des Moines	21	Jun
11.01	0.0	Veronica	Campbell-Brown	JAM	15.5.82	1		Kingston	4	May
11.02	1.1	Verena	Sailer	GER	16.10.85	1r1		Weinheim	2	Aug
11.03	0.9	Sherone	Simpson	JAM	12.8.84	2	NC	Kingston	21	Jun
11.04	1.2	Ivet	Lalova	BUL	18.5.84	1	Bisl	Oslo	13	Jun
11.04	1.5	Shalonda	Solomon	USA	19.12.85	2r2		Madrid	13	Jul
		(20)								
11.05	1.7	Ana Cláudia	Silva	BRA	6.11.88	1		Belém	12	May
11.06+	0.2	Allyson	Felix	USA	18.11.85	1	in 150m	Manchester	25	May
11.06	1.1	Mariya	Ryemyen	UKR	2.8.87	1		Yalta	5	Jun
11.06	1.6	Michelle-Lee	Ahye	TTO	10.4.92	2	NC	Port of Spain	22	Jun
11.07	1.2	Mandy	White	USA	23.10.88	1r2	MSR	Walnut	20	Apr
11.07	0.9	Schillonie	Calvert	JAM	27.7.88	3	NC	Kingston	21	Jun
11.07	2.0	Charonda	Williams	USA	27.3.87	4s1	NC	Des Moines	21	Jun
11.08	0.9	Kimberlyn	Duncan	USA	2.8.91	3	NCAA	Eugene	7	Jun
11.09	1.9	Cierra	White	USA	29.4.93	1		Lubbock	25	Apr
11.09	1.5	Dafne	Schippers	NED	15.6.92	1	Athl	Lausanne	4	Jul
		(30)								
11.12	2.0	Chauntae	Bayne	USA	4.4.84	1		San Marcos	6	Apr
11.13	-0.7	Franciela	Krasucki	BRA	26.4.88	1s2	NC	São Paulo	6	Jun
11.14	1.8	Tori	Bowie	USA	27.8.90	2r1	MSR	Walnut	20	Apr
11.14	1.6	Lakeisha	Lawson	USA	3.6.87	1		Azusa	11	Ma
11.14	1.1	Olesya	Povh	UKR	18.10.87	2		Yalta	5	Jun
11.14	0.9	Sheri-Ann	Brooks	JAM	11.2.83	4	NC	Kingston	21	Jun
11.15	1.7	Mikele	Barber	USA	4.10.80	2		Belém	12	Ma
11.16	2.0	Jessica	Young	USA	6.4.87	6s1	NC	Des Moines	21	Jun
11.17	0.9	Natasha	Morrison	JAM	17.11.92	6	NC	Kingston	21	Jun
11.18	0.0	Sheniqua	Ferguson	BAH	24.11.89	1	NC	Freeport	21	Jun
		(40)								
11.19	1.2	Candyce	McGrone	USA	24.3.89	2r2	MSR	Walnut	20	Apr
11.19	0.9	Aleen	Bailey	JAM	25.11.80	7	NC	Kingston	21	Jun
11.19	1.7	Tiffany	Townsend	USA	14.6.89	8s2	NC	Des Moines	21	Jun
11.20+	0.2	Anyika	Onuora	GBR	28.10.84	2		Manchester	25	Ma
11.20	2.0	Dezerea	Bryant	USA	27.4.93	8s1	NC	Des Moines	21	Jun
11.20	-0.2	Asha	Philip	GBR	25.10.90	1	NC	Birmingham	13	Jul
11.21	0.9	Samantha	Henry-Robinson	JAM	25.9.88	8	NC	Kingston	21	Jun
11.22	1.3	Tatjana	Pinto	GER	2.7.92	1		Weinheim	25	Ma
11.23	1.7	Rosângela	Santos	BRA	20.12.90	4		Belém	12	Ma

Mark	Wind	Name		Nat	Born	Pos	Meet	Venue	Date	
11.23	0.3	Anneisha	McLaughlin	JAM	6.1.86	1		Kingston	18	Ma
		(50)								
11.23	2.0	Viktoriya	Yarushkina	RUS	4.4.91	1h1		Yerino	2	Jun
11.23	1.6	Kai	Selvon	TTO	13.4.92	3	NC	Port of Spain	22	Jun
11.23	-0.3	Ezinne	Okparaebo	NOR	3.3.88	3h1	WCh	Moskva	11	Aug
11.24	1.9	Ruddy	Zang Milama	GAB	6.6.87	1		Baltimore	20	Apr
11.24	1.8	Natasha	Hastings	USA	23.7.86	6	MSR	Walnut	20	Apr
11.24	1.4	Chastity	Riggien	USA	5.7.89	1		Clermont	11	Ma
11.24A	-0.7	Danielle	Williams	JAM	14.9.92	1	NCAA II	Pueblo	25	Ma
11.24	0.3	Tawanna	Meadows	USA	4.8.86	2h2		Montverde	8	Jun
11.24A	0.1	Mariely	Sánchez	DOM	30.12.88	2	CAC	Morelia	5	Jul
11.25	0.3	Melissa	Breen	AUS	17.9.90	1		Sydney	9	Mar
		(60)								
11.25A	1.8	MaryBeth	Sant	USA-J	16.4.95	1		Denver	1	Jun
11.26	1.5	LaShauntea	Moore	USA	31.7.83	5r2		Madrid	13	Jul
11.26	1.0	Stella	Akakpo	FRA-J	28.2.94	1h1	EJ	Rieti	18	Jul
11.27	1.4	Gloria	Asumnu	NGR	22.5.85	2		Clermont	11	Ma
11.27	1.1	Natalya	Pogrebnyak	UKR	19.2.88	3		Yalta	5	Jun
11.28	0.9	Yekaterina	Gonchar	BLR	28.3.88	1		Brest	24	Ma
11.28	1.9	Semoy	Hackett	TTO	27.11.88	2s2	NC	Port of Spain	22	Jun
11.29	-0.2	Yekaterina	Kuzina	RUS	28.6.91	1	NCp	Yerino	15	Jun
11.29	-0.3	Wei Yongli		CHN	11.10.91	1	AsiC	Pune	4	Jul
11.29	1.0	Marika	Popowicz	POL	28.4.88	1h2	NC	Torun	19	Jun
		(70)								
11.30A	?	Angela	Tenorio	ECU-Y	27.1.96	1		Quito	29	Jun
11.30	1.3	Myriam	Soumaré	FRA	29.10.86	1	NC	Paris (C)	13	Jul
11.31	1.8	Jenna	Prandini	USA	20.11.92	7r1	MSR	Walnut	20	Apr
11.31	0.9	Jennifer	Madu	USA-J	23.9.94	5	NCAA	Eugene	7	Jun
11.31	1.8	Hayley	Jones	GBR	14.9.88	1		Manchester (SC)	22	Jun
11.31	0.5	Lina	Grincikaite	LTU	3.5.87	1	ET-2	Kaunas	22	Jun
11.31	0.9	Céline	Distel-Bonnet	FRA	25.7.87	1h1	NC	Paris (C)	13	Jul
11.32	1.0	Emily	Blok	USA	14.4.91	1h1		Las Vegas	10	May
11.32	1.4	Debbie	Ferguson-McKenzie	BAH	18.1.76	3		Clermont	11	May
11.32+	0.2	Jodie	Williams	GBR	28.9.93	3		Manchester	25	May
		(80)								
11.32	1.8	Nadine	Palmer	JAM	9.2.83	1		New York	30	May
11.33	0.9	Tahesia	Harrigan-Scott	IVB	15.2.82	3r1		Gainesville	20	Apr
11.33A	0.0	Ana	Holland	USA-J	16.2.95	1		Lakewood	17	May
11.33	2.0	Mahagony	Jones	USA	20.12.90	1h5	NCAA-E	Greensboro	23	May
11.33	1.7	Stephanie	Kalu	NGR	5.8.93	2h6	NCAA-W	Austin	23	May
11.33	1.1	Hrystyna	Stuy	UKR	3.2.88	4		Yalta	5	Jun
11.33	-0.8	Ky	Westbrook	USA-Y	25.2.96	1	WY	Donetsk	11	Jul
11.33	1.4	Shai-Anne	Davis	CAN	4.12.93	1r2		Weinheim	2	Aug
11.33	0.5	Ashleigh	Nelson	GBR	20.2.91	1rB	WK	Zürich	29	Aug
11.34	1.4	Cleo	VanBuren	USA	1.5.86	1r1		Arlington	22	Mar
		(90)								
11.34	1.8	Chelsea	Hayes	USA	9.2.88	2r1		Baton Rouge	20	Apr
11.34	1.6	Paris	Daniels	USA	25.1.90	2	Big12	Waco	5	May
11.34	0.2	Ashley	Marshall	USA	10.9.93	1		Northridge	11	May
11.34	0.6	Remona	Burchell	JAM	15.9.91	1		Hutchinson	18	May
11.34	-0.2	Yuliya	Kashina	RUS	26.2.87	2	NCp	Yerino	15	Jun
11.34	1.5	Katerina	Cechová	CZE	21.3.88	2	Athl	Lausanne	4	Jul
11.34	1.3	Ayodelé	Ikuesan	FRA	15.5.85	3	NC	Paris (C)	13	Jul
11.35	0.3	Ashton	Purvis	USA	12.7.92	1		Tempe	16	Mar
11.35	1.6	Shataya	Hendricks	USA	15.8.89	2r1		Coral Gables	13	Apr
11.35	1.4	Trisha-Ann	Hawthorne	JAM	8.11.89	5		Clermont	11	May
		(100)								
11.35	1.7	Irene	Ekelund	SWE-Y	8.3.97	1		Kil	8	Jun
11.35	-0.2	Yuliya	Katsura	RUS	28.5.83	3	NCp	Yerino	15	Jun
11.35A	1.2	Cache	Armbrister	BAH	26.9.89	2h2	CAC	Morelia	5	Jul
11.35	1.0	Evelyn	dos Santos	BRA	11.4.85	1h2		Bottrop	19	Jul

Mark	Wind	Name		Nat	Born	Date	
11.36	1.7	Kylie	Price	USA	1.10.93	27	Apr
11.36	1.3	Hanna-Maari	Latvala	FIN	30.10.87	25	May
11.36	1.8	Annabelle	Lewis	GBR	20.3.89	12	Jul
11.36	0.5	Bianca	Williams	GBR	18.12.93	29	Aug
11.37	0.6	Olivia	Ekponé	USA	5.1.93	27	Apr
11.37	1.7	Ashlee	Abraham	USA	24.3.90	23	May
11.37A	2.0	Eliecit	Palacios	COL	15.8.87	25	May
11.37	0.5	Andreea	Ogrăzeanu	ROU	24.3.90	28	Jun
11.38A	-0.8	Globine	Mayova	NAM	29.2.88	16	Mar
11.38	1.8	Carol	Rodríguez	PUR	16.12.85	12	May
11.38	1.7	Darshay	Davis	USA	23.9.91	23	May
11.38	1.9	Chisato	Fukushima	JPN	27.6.88	7	Jun
11.38	1.9	Ayanna	Hutchinson	TTO	18.2.78	22	Jun
11.38	-0.3	Dina	Asher-Smith	GBR-J	4.12.95	29	Jun
11.38A	1.3	Fani	Chala	DOM	2.2.93	5	Jul
11.39	1.4	Kamaria	Brown	USA	21.12.92	23	Mar
11.39	1.6	Flings	Owusu-Agyapong	GHA	16.10.88	13	Apr
11.39	0.7	Inna	Weit	GER	5.8.88	25	May
11.39	0.9	Ariana	Washington	USA-Y	4.9.96	1	Jun
11.40	-1.4	Yekaterina	Voronenkova	RUS	8.9.88	11	May
11.40	1.6	Reyare	Thomas	TTO	23.11.87	22	Jun
11.40	0.0	Crystal	Emmanuel	CAN	27.11.91	1	Jun

Mark	Wind	Name		Nat	Born	Pos	Meet	Venue		Date
11.41	-0.1	Elaine	Thompson	JAM	28.8.92					23 Feb
11.41	-0.7	Toea	Wisil	PNG	1.1.88					6 Apr
11.41	0.9	Sharika	Nelvis	USA	10.5.90					12 May
11.41	-0.7	Tianna	Bartoletta	USA	30.8.85					18 May
11.41	1.3	Nakia	Linson	USA	2.8.92					23 May
11.41A	1.8	Alleandra	Watt	USA-Y	12.3.97	1				Jun
11.41	1.6	Peace	Uko	NGR-J	26.12.95	5				Jun
11.41	1.2	Kamara	Durant	TTO	24.2.91	21				Jun
11.41	0.5	Eleni	Artymata	CYP	16.5.86	22				Jun
11.41	1.4	Yasmin	Kwadwo	GER	9.11.90	2				Aug
11.42	1.7	Dalilah	Muhammad	USA	7.2.90	4				May
11.42	1.6	Erin	Jones	USA	16.7.92	5				May
11.42	-0.8	Olga	Safronova	KAZ	5.11.91	15				May
11.42	1.7	Alexis	Faulknor	USA-J	22.9.94	23				May
11.42	2.0	Tynia	Gaither	BAH	16.3.93	23				May
11.42	1.0	Estela	García	ESP	20.3.89	12				Jun
11.42	1.5	Kadene	Vassell	NED	29.1.89	4				Jul
11.43	1.4	Porscha	Lucas	USA	18.6.88	23				Mar
11.43	2.0	Phobay	Kutu-Akoi	LBR	3.12.87	6				Apr
11.43	1.3	Émilie	Gaydu	FRA	5.2.89	13				Jul
11.44	1.8	India	Daniels	USA	23.1.93	20				Apr
11.44	0.5	Shareese	Woods	USA	20.2.85	18				May
11.44	0.6	Dominique	Kimpel	USA	6.2.93	18				May
11.44	-0.2	Natalya	Rusakova	RUS	12.12.79	15				Jun
11.44	-0.2	Marina	Panteleyeva	RUS	16.5.89	15				Jun
11.45	0.4	Takeia	Pinckney	USA	24.7.91	12				May
11.45	0.3	Audrea	Segree	JAM	5.10.90	18				May
11.45	0.9	Morolake	Akinosun	USA-J	17.5.94	7				Jun
11.45	0.4	Gloria	Hooper	ITA	3.3.92	14				Jun
11.45A	1.3	Omhunique	Browne	SKN-J	14.8.94	5				Jul
11.45	0.8	Marta	Jeschke	POL	2.6.86	13				Jul
11.46	0.1	Ashley	Spencer	USA	8.6.93	23				Mar
11.46	2.0	Nandelle	Cameron	TTO	21.10.83	24				Mar
11.46	0.5	Briana	Vaughn	USA-J	28.4.94	13				Apr
11.46	1.3	Mercedes	Jackson	USA	12.11.93	23				May
11.46	0.7	Anna-Lena	Freese	GER-J	21.1.94	15				Jun
11.46	-1.7	Anne	Zagré	BEL	13.3.90	21				Jul
11.47	1.4	Patricia	Hall	JAM	16.10.82	29				Mar
11.47	0.0	Germe	Poston	USA	7.1.92	6				Apr
11.47		Khadija	Suleman	USA	16.8.93	19				Apr
11.47	-1.0	Gabrielle	Houston	USA	12.6.90	20				Apr
11.47	1.8	Anthonique	Strachan	BAH	22.8.93	20				Apr
11.47	-0.2	Viktoriya	Pyatachenko	UKR	7.5.89	17				May
11.47	2.0	Yelizaveta	Savlinis	RUS	14.8.87	2				Jun
11.47	2.0	Yuliya	Balykina	BLR	12.4.84	14				Jun
11.47	-0.2	Yelena	Bolsun	RUS	25.6.82	15				Jun
11.47	1.2	Éva	Kaptur	HUN	15.11.87	26				Jul
11.48	1.9	Taylor	Evans	USA	7.10.89	25				Apr
11.48	1.7	Akawkaw	Ndipagbor	USA	30.4.93	27				Apr
11.48	0.3	Véronique	Mang	FRA	15.12.84	19				May
11.48	1.3	Margret	Harris	USA	15.9.89	23				May
11.48	1.7	Sophie	Papps	GBR-J	6.10.94	27				May
11.48	1.6	Geronne	Black	TTO	26.10.89	22				Jun
11.48	0.8	Weronika	Wedler	POL	17.7.89	19				Jul
11.48	0.6	Louise	Bloor	GBR	21.9.85	23				Jul
11.48	0.6	Montell	Douglas	GBR	24.1.86	23				Jul
11.48A	2.0	Arialis	Gandulla	CUB-J	22.6.95	23				Aug
11.48	0.0	Tao Yujia		CHN	16.2.87	7				Sep
11.48		Beatrice	Gyaman	GHA	17.2.87	26				Oct
11.49	-1.2	Viktoriya	Zyabkina	KAZ	4.9.92	25				Apr
11.49	-0.7	Bianca	Knight	USA	2.1.89	18				May
11.49	1.5	Cathleen	Tschirch	GER	23.7.79	25				May
11.49	1.1	Yelizaveta	Bryzgina ¶	UKR	28.11.89	5				Jun
11.49	2.0	Natalya	Shishkova	RUS	28.8.90	19				Jun
11.49	0.7	Amy	Foster	IRL	2.10.88	25				Jun
11.49	1.4	Esther	Cremer	GER	29.3.88	2				Aug
11.49	0.7	Mayumi	Watanabe	JPN	6.6.83	24				Aug
		(193)								

Wind assisted

Mark	Wind	Name		Nat	Born	Pos	Meet	Venue	Date
10.71	2.2		Fraser-Pryce			1		Pre	Eugene	1 Jun
10.75	2.2	Blessing	Okagbare	NGR	9.10.88	2	Pre	Eugene	1 Jun
10.78	2.2	Veronica	Campbell-Brown	JAM	15.5.82	3	Pre	Eugene	1 Jun
10.93	2.2	Ana Cláudia	Silva	BRA	6.11.88	1h1		Campinas	4 May
10.97	2.3	Samantha	Henry-Robinson	JAM	25.9.88	1		Montverde	1 Jun
10.97	3.0	Shalonda	Solomon	USA	19.12.85	1		Liège (NX)	10 Jul
10.98	3.6	LaShauntea	Moore	USA	31.7.83	1		Edmonton	29 Jun
11.02	2.3	Kimberlyn	Duncan	USA	2.8.91	1h3	NCAA	Eugene	5 Jun
11.04	3.6	Tori	Bowie	USA	27.8.90	2		Edmonton	29 Jun
11.08	3.6	Sheri-Ann	Brooks	JAM	11.2.83	3		Edmonton	29 Jun
11.12	2.7	Cleo	VanBuren	USA	1.5.86	1r1	TexR	Austin	30 Mar
11.12	5.3	Kandace	Thomas	USA	6.2.93	1h2		Hutchinson	17 May
11.12	2.2	Natasha	Morrison	JAM	17.11.92	2		Sundsvall	28 Jul
11.13	2.7	Porscha	Lucas	USA	18.6.88	2r1	TexR	Austin	30 Mar
11.14	2.5	Chastity	Riggien	USA	5.7.89	1h1		Clermont	11 May
11.14	2.6	Jenna	Prandini	USA	20.11.92	2s1	NCAA	Eugene	5 Jun
11.15	2.8	Ashley	Collier	USA	4.2.92	2r3	TexR	Austin	30 Mar
11.16	3.6	Crystal	Emmanuel	CAN	27.11.91	4		Edmonton	29 Jun
11.18	2.6	Jennifer	Madu	USA-J	23.9.94	3s1	NCAA	Eugene	5 Jun
11.18A	3.4	Ariana	Washington	USA-Y	4.9.96	1		Albuquerque	8 Jun
11.20	2.8	Ashton	Purvis	USA	12.7.92	3r3	TexR	Austin	30 Mar
11.20	2.7	Gloria	Asumnu	NGR	22.5.85	1h2		Clermont	11 May
11.21	2.3	Chelsea	Hayes	USA	9.2.88	3r2	TexR	Austin	30 Mar
11.21	2.2	Ezinne	Okparaebo	NOR	3.3.88	4		Sundsvall	28 Jul
11.23	3.5	Jodie	Williams	GBR	28.9.93	1	NC-23	Bedford	15 Jun
11.24	2.3	Angela	Tenorio	ECU-Y	27.1.96	1	SAm-J	Resistencia	18 Oct
11.25	2.6	Carima	Louami	FRA	12.5.79	1		Bonneuil-sur-Marne	7 Jun
11.27	4.0	Olivia	Ekponé	USA	5.1.93	1r2		Fayetteville	13 Apr
11.28	2.5	Trisha-Ann	Hawthorne	JAM	8.11.89	2h1		Clermont	11 May
11.28	2.7	Debbie	Ferguson-McKenzie	BAH	16.1.76	2h2		Clermont	11 May
11.28	4.3	Viktoriya	Pyatachenko	UKR	7.5.89	1		Istanbul	8 Jun
11.29	2.8	Morolake	Akinosun	USA-J	17.5.94	6r3	TexR	Austin	30 Mar
11.29	2.4	Tahesia	Harrigan-Scott	IVB	15.2.82	2		Miramar	29 Apr
11.29	3.8	Darshay	Davis	USA	23.9.91	2q1	NCAA-E	Greensboro	24 May
11.29	4.3	Nimet	Karakus	TUR	23.1.93	2		Istanbul	8 Jun
11.30	3.7	Erica	Peake	USA	20.2.91	1h2		Lynchburg	19 Apr
11.30	3.9	Mahagony	Jones	USA	20.12.90	2q2	NCAA-E	Greensboro	24 May
11.30	3.8	Takeia	Pinckney	USA	24.7.91	3q1	NCAA-E	Greensboro	24 May
11.30	2.9	Dina	Asher-Smith	GBR-J	4.12.95	1	NC-j	Bedford	15 Jun

WOMEN 2013

Mark	Wind	Name		Nat	Born	Pos	Meet	Venue	Date
11.30	2.3	Hayley	Jones	GBR	14.9.88	1		Wigan	7 Jul
11.31	2.7	LaQuisha	Jackson	USA-J	7.1.94	1h2		Las Vegas	10 May
11.31	3.1	Shai-Anne	Davis	CAN	4.12.93	2rB		Edmonton	29 Jun
11.32	3.0	Kylie	Price	USA	1.10.93	2h3	NCAA-W	Austin	23 May
11.32A	2.8	Arialis	Gandulla	CUB-J	22.6.95	1	PAm-J	Medellín	23 Aug
11.33A	3.5	Shavine	Hodges	JAM	22.10.91	1r1		Albuquerque	6 Apr
11.33	7.2	Jasmine	Gibbs	USA-J	15.1.94	1		Manhattan, KS	11 May
11.33	3.8	Chalonda	Goodman	USA	29.9.90	2h5	NCAA-W	Austin	23 May
11.33	3.9	Alexis	Faulknor	USA-J	22.9.94	3q2	NCAA-E	Greensboro	24 May
11.33	3.8	Katie	Wise	USA	15.10.93	4q1	NCAA-E	Greensboro	24 May
11.33	2.8	Johanna	Danois	FRA	4.4.87	2		Castres	30 Jun

Mark	Wind	Name		Nat	Born	Date		Mark	Wind	Name		Nat	Born	Date
11.34	2.7	Omhunique	Browne	SKN-J	14.8.94	17 May		11.42	2.7	Aaliyah	Brown	USA-J	6.1.95	16 May
11.34	5.3	Dominique	Kimpel	USA	6.2.93	17 May		11.42	3.4	Éva	Kaptur	HUN	15.11.87	25 May
11.34	3.8	Nakia	Linson	USA	2.8.92	24 May		11.43	3.0	Taylor	Evans	USA	7.10.89	13 Apr
11.35		Kourtni	Johnson	USA-Y	.97	26 Apr		11.43A	2.8	Isidora	Jiménez	CHI	10.8.93	25 May
11.36	4.0	Adella	King	USA	21.3.90	16 Mar		11.43	2.3	Desiree	Henry	GBR-J	26.8.95	7 Jul
11.36	2.7	Me'Lisa	Barber	USA	4.10.80	13 Apr		11.44Aw?		Claudine	van Rensburg	RSA	26.10.89	9 Feb
11.36	4.3	Stormy	Kendrick	USA	6.1.91	18 Apr		11.44	3.1	Dulaini D.	Odelín	CUB	21.8.92	22 Feb
11.36	2.3	Chisato	Fukushima	JPN	27.6.88	29 Apr		11.44A	3.7	Yolanda	Suggs	USA		23 Mar
11.36mx4.3		Sophie	Papps	GBR-J	6.10.94	8 May		11.44	w?	Lisa	Wickham	TTO-J	13.8..94	6 Apr
11.36	3.3	Jasmine	Webb	USA	10.3.92	12 May		11.44	3.1	Angela	Whyte	CAN	22.5.80	29 Jun
11.36	2.6	Émilie	Gaydu	FRA	5.2.89	7 Jun		11.45	3.9	Adenike	Pedro	USA	20.6.92	24 May
11.36	3.1	Jessica	Zelinka	CAN	3.9.81	29 Jun		11.45	2.5	Amy	Foster	IRL	2.10.88	19 Jul
11.36	4.3	Marta	Jeschke	POL	2.6.86	19 Jul		11.46	2.1	Olivia	Kizzee	NGR	3.11.88	13 Apr
11.37	3.9	Briana	Vaughn	USA-J	28.4.94	16 Mar		11.46	4.0	Gwendolyn	Flowers	USA	5.11.91	13 Apr
11.37A	3.7	Magen	Del Pino	USA	24.4.90	23 Mar		11.46	2.8	Charnell	Price	USA	14.11.91	11 May
11.37	4.0	Diamond	Dixon	USA	29.6.92	13 Apr		11.46	4.3	Ashley	Fields	USA	13.4.93	23 May
11.37	3.8	Keilah	Tyson	USA	6.11.92	24 May		11.46	3.7	Ewa	Swoboda	POL-Y	26.7.97	29 May
11.37	4.3	Olga	Kharitonova	RUS	23.8.90	8 Jun		11.46	3.8	Laura	Turner	GBR	12.8.82	29 Jun
11.37	3.5	Reyare	Thomas	TTO	23.11.87	22 Jun		11.46	2.3	Grigoría-Emmanouéla	Keramidá	GRE	25.8.90	20 Jul
11.37	3.1	Shayla	Mahan	USA	18.1.89	29 Jun		11.47	4.0	Alexis	Love	USA	24.4.91	16 Mar
11.38	2.2	Peace	Uko	NGR-J	26.12.95	5 Jun		11.47A	3.5	Samantha	Bogatz	USA		6 Apr
11.38	2.6	Sarah	Goujon	FRA	11.9.90	7 Jun		11.47	3.7	Christy	Udoh	NGR	30.9.91	20 Apr
11.38A	3.4	Hannah	Cunliffe	USA-Y	9.1.96	8 Jun		11.47A	3.4	Kaylin	Whitney	USA-Y	9.3.98	8 Jun
11.39	3.5	Kamara	Durant	TTO	24.2..91	22 Jun		11.47	3.5	Rachel	Johncock	GBR	4.10.93	15 Jun
11.39	2.8	Madiea	Ghafoor	NED	9.9.92	3 Aug		11.47	4.3	Ewelina	Ptak	POL	20.3.87	19 Jul
11.40	4.3	Shannon	Reynolds	USA	25.9.90	15 Mar		11.47	2.5	Ksenija	Balta	EST	1.11..86	27 Jul
11.40	2.5	Diandra	Gilbert	JAM	9.6.91	1 May		11.48	5.6	Tylia	Gillon	USA	16.9.92	15 Mar
11.40	2.7	Karene	King	IVB	24.10.87	11 May		11.48	2.5	Tyshonda	Hawkins	USA		16 Mar
11.40	3.2	Lenka	Krsáková	SVK	22.2.91	29 Jun		11.48	4.2	Akeyla	Mitchell	USA-J	11.11.95	29 Mar
11.41	2.7	Kineke	Alexander	VIN	21.2.86	30 Mar		11.48	3.1	Aireonna	Bailey	USA	7.9.89	5 May
11.41	2.3	Patricia	Hall	JAM	16.10.82	30 Mar		11.48	2.8	Uchechi	Anunkor	USA	19.4.91	11 May
11.41	3.8	Toshica	Sylvester	USA	3.12.91	24 May		11.48	2.2	Rebekka	Haase	GER	2.1.93	25 May
11.41	3.6	Cambrya	Jones	USA	20.9.90	1 Jun		11.48	2.8	Patricia	Buval	FRA	22.1.76	30 Jun
11.42	w?	Nandelle	Cameron	TTO	21.10.83	6 Apr		11.48	3.0	Olivia	Borlée	BEL	10.4.86	10 Jul
11.42	3.3	Khadija	Suleman	USA	16.8.93	4 May		11.49	4.9	Dariel	Jackson	USA	20.11.90	4 May
11.42	2.8	Brea	Buchanan	USA	8.1.93	11 May		11.49	3.3	Brittany	Brown	USA-J	18.4.95	18 May
11.42	3.9	Kia	Jackson	USA	15.1.92	11 May								

Best al low altitude

11.41	-1.5	D Williams	11 May	11.41	-0.8	Tenorio	11 Jul	11.44	0.0	Armbrister	22 Jun
		11.34w 2.5	16 Mar	11.41	-0.4	M Sánchez	11 Aug				

11.20w 3.1 Washington 1   Walnut   18 May

Hand timing

11.1	1.8	Arialis	Gandulla	CUB-J	22.6.95	1	NC-j	La Tunas	18 Jul
11.2A	0.2	Erika	Chávez	ECU	4.6.90	15 May	11.2	Peace Uko Alphonsus NGR	12.1.89 25 May
							11.2	Justina Sule NGR	30.7.89 25 May

Drugs disqualification

11.17w 3.9 Tedzhyan Naimova ¶ BUL 1.5.87 (1)   Parow   23 Feb

JUNIORS

See main list for top 7 juniors (& 2 wa). 7 performances by 7 women to 11.35. Additional marks and further juniors:

Mark	Wind	Name		Nat	Born	Pos	Meet	Venue	Date
11.38	-0.3	Dina	Asher-Smith	GBR	4.12.95	1		Mannheim	29 Jun
11.39	0.9	Ariana	Washington	USA-Y	4.9.96	1		Clovis	1 Jun
11.41A	1.8	Alleandra	Watt (10)	USA-Y	12.3.97	2		Denver	1 Jun
11.41	1.6	Peace	Uko	NGR	26.12.95	1r1		Port Harcourt	5 Jun
11.42	1.7	Alexis	Faulknor	USA	22.9.94	2h2	NCAA-E	Greensboro	23 May
11.45	0.9	Morolake	Akinosun	USA	17.5.94	8	NCAA	Eugene	7 Jun
11.45A	1.3	Omhunique	Browne	SKN-J	14.8.94	3h3	CAC	Morelia	5 Jul
11.46	0.5	Briana	Vaughn	USA	28.4.94	1	Towns	Athens	13 Apr
11.46	0.7	Anna-Lena	Freese	GER	21.1.94	1	NC-23	Göttingen	15 Jun
11.48	1.7	Sophie	Papps	GBR	6.10.94	2r1	BIG	Bedford	27 May
11.48A	2.0	Arialis	Gandulla	CUB	22.6.95	1h2	PAm-J	Medellín	23 Aug
11.50A	0.7	Shayna	Yon	USA	29.3.87	1r4		Albuquerque	8 Jun
11.50	0.7	Desiree	Henry (20)	GBR	26..8.95	8h1	LGP	London (OS)	27 Jul

Wind assisted: 10 performances by 6 women to 11.30w. Additional marks and further juniors to 11.45w

Madu   11.26w 2.8 5   TexR   Austin   20 Mar

Mark	Wind		Name		Nat	Born	Pos	Meet	Venue	Date
Sant	11.26wA 3.4	2	Albuquerque				8 Jun			
Akakpo	11.27 2.6	2	Bonneuil-sur-Marne				7 Jun			
Washington 2+	11.27w 2.2	1	Norwalk				24 May			
11.34	2.7	Omhunique	Browne		SKN	14.8.94	1		San Mateo	17 May
11.35		Kourtni	Johnson		USA-Y	.97	1		Abilene	26 Apr
11.36mx	4.3	Sophie	Papps		GBR	6.10.94	1mx		London (LV)	8 May
11.37	3.9	Briana	Vaughn		USA	28.4.94	1		Athens, GA	16 Mar
11.38	2.2	Peace	Uko		NGR	26.12.95	1r2		Port Harcourt	5 Jun
11.38A	3.4	Hannah	Cunliffe		USA-Y	9.1.96	3		Albuquerque	8 Jun
11.42	2.7	Aaliyah	Brown		USA	6.1.95	1		Charleston	16 May
11.43	2.3	Desiree	Henry		GBR	26.8.95	2		Wigan	7 Jul
11.44	w?	Lisa	Wickham		TTO	13.8..94	3		Port of Spain	6 Apr

150 METRES STRAIGHT

Mark	Wind		Name	Nat	Born	Pos	Venue	Date
16.36	0.2	Allyson	Felix	USA	18.11.85	1	Manchester	25 May
16.63	0.2	Anyika	Onuora	GBR	28.10.84	2	Manchester	25 May
16.64	0.2	Lauryn	Williams	USA	11.9.83	3	Manchester	25 May
16.81	0.2	Jodie	Williams	GBR	28.9.93	4	Manchester	25 May

150m Turn: Amsterdam 31 Aug: (2.0) 1. Mariya Ryemyen UKR 2.8.87 16.73, 2. Dafne Schippers NED 15.6.92 16.95

200 METRES

Mark	Wind		Name	Nat	Born	Pos	Meet	Venue	Date
22.13	1.0	Shelly-Ann	Fraser-Pryce	JAM	27.12.86	1	NC	Kingston	23 Jun
22.17	-0.3		Fraser-Pryce			1	WCh	Moskva	16 Aug
22.24	-0.5	Murielle	Ahouré	CIV	23.8.87	1	Herc	Monaco	19 Jul
22.26	-0.5	Tiffany	Townsend	USA	14.6.89	2	Herc	Monaco	19 Jul
22.28	-0.5		Fraser-Pryce			3	Herc	Monaco	19 Jul
22.30	0.0	Allyson	Felix	USA	18.11.85	1s2	WCh	Moskva	15 Aug
22.31	1.3	Blessing	Okagbare	NGR	9.10.88	1	MSR	Walnut	20 Apr
22.32	0.9	Anthonique	Strachan	BAH	22.8.93	1	NC	Freeport	22 Jun
22.32	-0.3		Ahouré			2	WCh	Moskva	16 Aug
22.32	-0.3		Okagbare			3	WCh	Moskva	16 Aug
22.35	1.3	Kimberlyn	Duncan	USA	2.8.91	1	SEC	Columbia, MO	12 May
22.36	0.3		Felix			1		Beijing	21 May
22.36	1.2		Ahouré			1	GGala	Roma	6 Jun
22.36	0.3	Kelly-Ann	Baptiste	TTO	14.10.86	1	NC	Port of Spain	23 Jun
22.38	0.5		Fraser-Pryce			1		Kingston	4 May
22.39	2.0	Anastasiya	Kapachinskaya	RUS	21.11.79	1h2		Moskva	4 Jul
22.39	0.0		Okagbare			2s2	WCh	Moskva	15 Aug
22.40	1.5	LaShauntea	Moore (10)	USA	31.7.83	1h3	NC	Des Moines	22 Jun
22.40	-0.4		Fraser-Pryce			1	WK	Zürich	29 Aug
22.41	1.6	Shalonda	Solomon	USA	19.12.85	1		Edmonton	29 Jun
22.41	-0.5		Felix			1	DL	London (OS)	27 Jul
22.45	0.9	Shaunae	Miller	BAH-J	15.4.94	2	NC	Freeport	22 Jun
22.46	1.5	Aurieyall	Scott	USA	18.5.92	2h3	NC	Des Moines	22 Jun
22.46	-0.5		Duncan			4	Herc	Monaco	19 Jul
22.46	0.0		Ahouré			1s1	WCh	Moskva	15 Aug
22.47	-0.4		Ahouré			1		Ponce	18 May
22.48	-0.1		Townsend			1		Ljubljana	13 Jul
22.50	-0.5		Solomon			2	DL	London (OS)	27 Jul
22.51	1.4	Patricia	Hall	JAM	16.10.82	1		São Paulo	19 May
22.52	1.9		Scott			1q1	NCAA-E	Greensboro	25 May
			(30/14)						
22.53	-1.3	Veronica	Campbell-Brown	JAM	15.5.82	1	adidas	New York	25 May
22.55	1.9	Octavious	Freeman	USA	20.4.92	2q1	NCAA-E	Greensboro	25 May
22.55	1.0	Sherone	Simpson	JAM	12.8.84	2	NC	Kingston	23 Jun
22.57	1.4	Chauntae	Bayne	USA	4.4.84	2		São Paulo	19 May
22.58	0.1	Lauryn	Williams	USA	11.9.83	2		Coral Gables	13 Apr
22.58	1.3	Kamaria	Brown	USA	21.12.92	2	SEC	Columbia, MO	12 May
			(20)						
22.58	1.0	Anneisha	McLaughlin	JAM	6.1.86	3	NC	Kingston	23 Jun
22.61	1.4	Ana Cláudia	Silva	BRA	6.11.88	3		São Paulo	19 May
22.61	1.4	Mariya	Ryemyen	UKR	2.8.87	1	Athl	Lausanne	4 Jul
22.62	1.1	English	Gardner	USA	22.4.92	1	Pac 12	Los Angeles	12 May
22.62A	-0.7	Danielle	Williams	JAM	14.9.92	1	NCAA II	Pueblo	25 May
22.62	-0.2	Carrie	Russell	JAM	18.10.90	1		Rieti	8 Sep
22.68	0.4	Viktoriya	Pyatachenko	UKR	7.5.89	1		Yalta	6 Jun
22.70	0.0	Jeneba	Tarmoh	USA	27.9.89	3s1	WCh	Moskva	15 Aug
22.71	0.5	Kerron	Stewart	JAM	16.4.84	2		Kingston	4 May
22.71	-0.1	Charonda	Williams	USA	27.3.87	2		Ljubljana	13 Jul
			(30)						

WOMEN 2013

Mark	Wind	Name		Nat	Born	Pos	Meet	Venue	Date	
22.72	-1.8	Yelizaveta	Bryzgina ¶	UKR	28.11.89	1	NC	Donetsk	26	Jul
22.73	1.6	Paris	Daniels	USA	25.1.90	1	Big12	Waco	5	May
22.75A	-0.7	Vashti	Thomas	USA	21.4.90	2	NCAA II	Pueblo	25	May
22.76	-0.1	Franciela	Krasucki	BRA	26.4.88	1	NC	São Paulo	9	Jun
22.77	1.1	Phyllis	Francis	USA	4.5.92	2	Pac 12	Los Angeles	12	May
22.77	1.4	Carmelita	Jeter	USA	24.11.79	5	Athl	Lausanne	4	Jul
22.78	1.2	Ivet	Lalova	BUL	18.5.84	3	GGala	Roma	6	Jun
22.78	1.6	Kimberly	Hyacinthe	CAN	28.3.89	1	WUG	Kazan	10	Jul
22.79	-0.5	Anyika	Onuora	GBR	28.10.84	4	DL	London (OS)	27	Jul
22.81	0.1	Jessica	Beard	USA	8.1.89	3		Coral Gables	13	Apr
		(40)								
22.83	0.5	Samantha	Henry-Robinson	JAM	25.9.88	4		Kingston	4	May
22.83	0.3	Myriam	Soumaré	FRA	29.10.86	3h6	WCh	Moskva	15	Aug
22.84	1.7	Shericka	Jackson	JAM-J	15.7.94	2		Nassau	1	Apr
22.84	1.0	Dafne	Schippers	NED	15.6.92	3	FBK	Hengelo	8	Jun
22.85	1.3	Candyce	McGrone	USA	24.3.89	2	MSR	Walnut	20	Apr
22.85	-1.1	Deedee	Trotter	USA	8.12.82	5s1	NC	Des Moines	23	Jun
22.86	0.4	Hrystyna	Stuy	UKR	3.2.88	2h7	WCh	Moskva	15	Aug
22.87	-1.1	Dezerea	Bryant	USA	27.4.93	6s1	NC	Des Moines	23	Jun
22.88	-0.2	Margaret	Adeoye	GBR	27.4.85	2		Rieti	8	Sep
22.89	1.8	Natasha	Hastings	USA	23.7.86	2	FlaR	Gainesville	5	Apr
		(50)								
22.89	1.6	Cierra	White	USA	29.4.93	2	Big12	Waco	5	May
22.89	1.6	Crystal	Emmanuel	CAN	27.11.91	5		Edmonton	29	Jun
22.91	-0.2	Andreea	Ogrăzeanu	ROU	24.3.90	1s1	NC	Bucuresti	29	Jun
22.91	-0.1	Lenora	Guion-Firmin	FRA	7.8.91	3h5	WCh	Moskva	15	Aug
22.92	-0.5	Jodie	Williams	GBR	28.9.93	1	EU23	Tampere	13	Jul
22.92	-0.1	Irene	Ekelund	SWE-Y	8.3.97	1	WY	Donetsk	14	Jul
22.93	1.0	Angela	Morosanu	ROU	26.7.86	1		Bucuresti	7	Jun
22.98	-0.5	Michelle-Lee	Ahye	TTO	10.4.92	1h3	NC	Port of Spain	23	Jun
22.98	0.3	Semoy	Hackett	TTO	27.11.88	2	NC	Port of Spain	23	Jun
22.98	1.6	Hanna-Maari	Latvala	FIN	30.10.87	2	WUG	Kazan	10	Jul
		(60)								
23.00	1.5	Jessica	Young	USA	6.4.87	4h3	NC	Des Moines	22	Jun
23.00A	-0.6	Kineke	Alexander	VIN	21.2.86	1	CAC	Morelia	7	Jul
23.00	0.0	Johanna	Danois	FRA	4.4.87	2h1	WCh	Moskva	15	Aug
23.01	1.9	Jasmine	Chaney	USA	25.8.88	1		San Marcos	29	Mar
23.01	1.6	Mariely	Sánchez	DOM	30.12.88	7		Edmonton	29	Jun
23.01	0.5	Antonina	Krivoshapka	RUS	21.7.87	4		Rovereto	3	Sep
23.04	0.0	Ashley	Spencer	USA	8.6.93	1r2		Tempe	6	Apr
23.04	0.2	Brianna	Rollins	USA	18.8.91	1		Raleigh	20	Apr
23.05	1.3	Kali	Davis-White	USA-J	27.10.94	1		Jacksonville	4	May
23.05	0.3	Kai	Selvon	TTO	13.4.92	3	NC	Port of Spain	23	Jun
		(70)								
23.07	1.3	Ashton	Purvis	USA	12.7.92	3	SEC	Columbia, MO	12	May
23.08A	-0.6	Aleen	Bailey	JAM	25.11.80	2	CAC	Morelia	7	Jul
23.08	1.6	Natasha	Morrison	JAM	17.11.92	1		Sundsvall	28	Jul
23.10	1.0	Ebonie	Floyd	USA	21.10.83	2		Lake Charles	13	Apr
23.10	1.5	Shareese	Woods	USA	20.2.85	5h3	NC	Des Moines	22	Jun
23.10	2.0	Inna	Weit	GER	5.8.88	1		Bottrop	19	Jul
23.10	0.0	Gloria	Hooper	ITA	3.3.92	4h1	WCh	Moskva	15	Aug
23.11	0.3	Kaliese	Spencer	JAM	6.5.87	2rB		Rovereto	3	Sep
23.12	0.4	Melissa	Breen	AUS	17.9.90	1		Sydney	9	Mar
23.12	1.6	Shai-Anne	Davis	CAN	4.12.93	4	WUG	Kazan	10	Jul
		(80)								
23.13	-0.1	Rosângela	Santos	BRA	20.12.90	3	NC	São Paulo	9	Jun
23.13	1.5	Chalonda	Goodman	USA	29.9.90	6h3	NC	Des Moines	22	Jun
23.13	-0.1	Ángela	Tenorio	ECU-Y	27.1.96	2	WY	Donetsk	14	Jul
23.14		Dina	Asher-Smith	GBR-J	4.12.95	1	LI	Loughborough	19	May
23.15	1.9	Taylor	Evans	USA	7.10.89	2r1		San Marcos	29	Mar
23.15		Lakeisha	Lawson	USA	3.6.87	1		Los Angeles	6	Apr
23.15	1.6	Le'Quisha	Parker	USA	26.5.93	2		Greensboro	4	May
23.15	1.1	Jenna	Prandini	USA	20.11.92	3	Pac 12	Los Angeles	12	May
23.15	-0.4	Eleni	Artymata	CYP	16.5.86	1	ET-2	Kaunas	23	Jun
23.16	0.3	Natalya	Pogrebnyak	UKR	19.2.88	2		Yalta	18	May
		(90)								
23.16	-0.4	Bianca	Knight	USA	2.1.89	4		Ponce	18	May
23.16	-0.1	Yelizaveta	Savlinis	RUS	14.8.87	1s2	NC	Moskva	24	Jul
23.16	0.7	Marzia	Caravelli	ITA	23.10.81	1		Milano	28	Jul
23.17	1.1	Christy	Udoh	NGR	30.9.91	1r2	FlaR	Gainesville	5	Apr
23.17	-1.2	Libania	Grenot	ITA	12.7.83	1rB		St.Martin	11	May

Mark	Wind	Name	Nat	Born	Pos	Meet	Venue	Date
23.17	0.1	Olivia Ekponé	USA	5.1.93	1q2	NCAA-W	Austin	25 May
23.17	0.9	Nivea Smith	BAH	18.2.90	3	NC	Freeport	22 Jun
23.18	0.4	María Belibasáki	GRE	19.6.91	1		Thíva	24 Jul
23.18	1.8	Ariana Washington	USA-Y	4.9.96	1		Norwalk	25 May
23.19	2.0	Felicia Brown (100)	USA	27.10.93	1r1		Nashville	20 Apr
23.19	1.9	Destinee Gause	USA-J	4.4,94	3q1	NCAA-E	Greensboro	25 May
23.19	1.5	Mahagony Jones	USA	20.12.90	3q3	NCAA-E	Greensboro	25 May
23.19	1.1	Moa Hjelmer	SWE	19.6.90	1	Bisl	Oslo	13 Jun
23.19A	1.3	Isidora Jiménez	CHI	10.8.93	1		Cali	23 Jun
23.20	-0.3	Cambrya Jones	USA	20.9.90				17 May
23.20	1.6	Muna Lee	USA	30.10.81				28 Jul
23.21	1.6	Tristie Johnson	USA	20.11.93				4 May
23.21	0.0	Olga Safronova	KAZ	5.11.91				16 May
23.21	-0.1	Evelyn dos Santos	BRA	11.4.85				9 Jun
23.21	0.2	Wei Yongli	CHN	11.10.91				16 Jun
23.21	0.0	Marina Konovalova	RUS	17.9.90				4 Aug
23.22	1.6	Ashley Fields	USA	13.4.93				5 May
23.22	0.1	Marika Popowicz	POL	28.4.88				15 Aug
23.23	0.1	LaQuisha Jackson	USA-J	7.1.94				11 May
23.23	-0.1	Vanda Gomes	BRA	7.11.88				9 Jun
23.23	0.4	Reyare Thomas	TTO	23.11.87				3 Aug
23.24	-0.5	Karene King	IVB	24.10.87				23 Jun
23.24	-1.4	Bianca Williams	GBR	18.12.93				12 Jul
23.24	0.7	Émilie Gaydu	FRA	5.2.89				14 Jul
23.24	0.4	Mujinga Kambundji	SUI	17.6.92				15 Aug
23.25	1.0	Ashley Marshall	USA	10.9.93				11 May
23.25	0.1	Emily Blok	USA	14.4.91				11 May
23.25	-0.9	Yuliya Katsura	RUS	28.5.83				26 May
23.25	1.8	Kelly Fogarty	USA	7.3.89				8 Jun
23.25	0.5	Chisato Fukushima	JPN	27.6.88				9 Jun
23.25	0.3	Denisa Rosolová	CZE	21.8.86				16 Jun
23.25	-0.5	Ashleigh Nelson	GBR	20.2.91				13 Jul
23.26	0.0	Morolake Akinosun	USA-J	17.5.94				6 Apr
23.26	1.3	Hanne Claes	BEL	4.8.91				8 Jun
23.27	0.3	Perri Shakes-Drayton	GBR	21.12.88				20 Apr
23.27	-0.5	Joanna Atkins	USA	31.1.89				11 May
23.27	0.5	Anastasiya Kocherzhova	RUS	16.10.90				16 Jun
23.27A	0.9	Arialis Gandulla	CUB-J	22.6.95				24 Aug
23.28	-0.1	Justine Palframan	RSA	4.11.93				13 Apr
23.28	2.0	Kiara Porter	USA	22.10.93				20 Apr
23.28	0.2	Porscha Lucas	USA	18.6.88				8 May
23.28A	-0.7	Kayan Robinson	JAM	27.3.89				25 May
23.28	1.0	Anna-Lena Freese	GER-J	21.1.94				30 Jun
23.29A	1.6	Ana Holland	USA-J	16.2.95				27 Apr
23.29	1.3	Tynia Gaither	BAH	16.3.93				12 May
23.29	1.9	Hayley Jones	GBR	14.9.88				7 Jul
23.30	0.8	Tianna Bartoletta	USA	30.8.85				8 May
23.30		Emily Diamond	GBR	11.6.91				19 May
23.30A	-0.7	Quanera Hayes	USA	7.3.92				25 May
23.30	1.8	Viktoriya Zyabkina	KAZ	4.9.92				9 Jun
23.30	0.6	Yelena Bolsun	RUS	25.6.82				15 Jun
23.30	1.8	Agne Serksniene	LTU	18.2.88				6 Jul
23.30	1.2	Céline Distel-Bonnet	FRA	25.7.87				14 Jul
23.31	0.1	Shataya Hendricks	USA	15.8.89				13 Apr
23.31	-2.0	Nercely Soto	VEN	23.8.90				22 Jun
23.31	1.7	Louise Bloor	GBR	21.9.85				6 Jul
23.31	1.5	Léa Sprunger	SUI	5.3.90				29 Aug
23.31	-0.6	Jiang Lan	CHN	27.6.89				10 Sep
23.32	1.2	Sheniqua Ferguson	BAH	28.11.89				20 Apr
23.32	0.5	Shericka Williams	JAM	17.9.85				4 May
23.32	0.7	Nadine Palmer	JAM	9.2.83				8 Jun
23.32	0.7	Yuliya Gushchina	RUS	4.3.83				15 Jun
23.32	1.0	Desiree Henry	GBR-J	26.8.95				30 Jun
23.33	0.5	Nadezhda Kotlyarova	RUS	12.6.89				16 Jun
23.33	-1.0	Maike Dix	GER	2.7.86				7 Jul
23.33	0.4	Grigoría-Emmanouéla Keramidá	GRE	25.8.90				21 Jul
23.34A	1.0	Globine Mayova	NAM	29.2.88				9 Mar
23.34	1.6	Gayon Evans	JAM	15.1.90				4 May
23.34	0.8	Debbie Ferguson-McKenzie	BAH	16.1.76				8 May
23.34	0.7	Jennifer Galais	FRA	7..3.92				29 Jun
23.35	-0.8	Erica Peake	USA	20.2.91				30 Mar
23.35	0.4	Mayumi Watanabe	JPN	6.6.83				3 May
23.35	2.0	Jasmine Webb	USA	10.3.92				12 May
23.35	1.8	Kamara Durant	TTO	1.1.91				19 May
23.35	1.1	Alena Tamkova	RUS	30.5.90				30 Jun
23.35	1.0	Gina Lückenkemper	GER-Y	21.11.96				30 Jun
23.36	1.0	Weronika Wedler	POL	17.7.89				27 Jun
23.37	-2.4	Stephenie Ann McPherson	JAM	25.11.88				23 Mar
23.37	1.0	Georganne Moline	USA	6.3.90				19 Apr
23.37	0.3	Tahesia Harrigan-Scott	IVB	15.2.82				20 Apr
23.37	0.0	Ky Westbrook	USA-Y	25.2.96				26 Jun
23.37	1.9	Olivia Borlée	BEL	10.4.86				13 Jul
23.37	1.0	Katarina Johnson-Thompson	GBR	9.1.93				12 Aug
23.38	0.4	Adella King	USA	21.3.90				16 Mar
23.38	1.6	Ashley McCoy	USA	22.2.91				4 May
23.38	1.6	Diamond Dixon	USA	29.6.92				5 May
23.38	1.3	Regina George (182)	NGR	17.2.91				12 May

Indoors

Mark		Name	Nat	Born	Pos	Meet	Venue	Date
22.70		Ashton Purvis	USA	12.7.92	1	SEC	Fayetteville	24 Feb
22.81		Johanna Danois	FRA	4.4.87	1	NC	Aubière	16 Feb
23.00		Regina George	NGR	17.2.91	1h1	SEC	Fayetteville	23 Feb
23.11		Trisha-Ann Hawthorne	JAM	8.11.89	1		Boston (Allston)	25 Jan
23.13		Christy Udoh	NGR	30.9.91	4r2	NCAA	Fayetteville	8 Mar
23.14		Ashley Collier	USA	4.2.92	2h3	SEC	Fayetteville	23 Feb
23.20#		Jura Levy	JAM	4.11.90	2			Mar
23.21		Yuliya Katsura	RUS	28.5.83				16 Jan
23.29#		Adella King	USA	21.3.90	2			Mar

Wind assisted

Mark	Wind	Name	Nat	Born	Pos	Meet	Venue	Date
21.80	3.2	Kimberlyn Duncan	USA	2.8.91	1	NC	Des Moines	23 Jun
21.85	3.2	Allyson Felix	USA	18.11.85	2	NC	Des Moines	23 Jun
22.04	3.5	Duncan			1	NCAA	Eugene	8 Jun
22.15	2.7	Duncan			1h2	NCAA	Eugene	6 Jun
22.15	3.2	Jeneba Tarmoh	USA	27.9.89	3	NC	Des Moines	23 Jun
22.16	3.2	Kamaria Brown	USA	21.12.92	4	NC	Des Moines	23 Jun
22.18	2.6	Veronica Campbell-Brown	JAM	15.5.82	1r1		Gainesville	20 Apr
22.21	3.5	Brown			2	NCAA	Eugene	8 Jun
22.23	5.2	Tarmoh			1h4	NCAA	Eugene	6 Jun
22.31	2.2	Duncan			1h2	NC	Des Moines	22 Jun
22.33	3.2	Shalonda Solomon	USA	13.12.85	5	NC	Des Moines	23 Jun
22.39	5.2	Chauntae Bayne	USA	4.4.84	2h4	NC	Des Moines	22 Jun
22.41	3.1	Shaunae Miller	BAH-J	15.4.94	1		Athens, GA	13 Apr
22.52	3.5	Paris Daniels	USA	25.1.90	4	NCAA	Eugene	8 Jun
22.54	3.5	Dezerea Bryant	USA	27.4.93	5	NCAA	Eugene	8 Jun
22.54	2.2	Deedee Trotter	USA	8.12.82	2h2	NC	Des Moines	22 Jun

WOMEN 2013

Mark	Wind	Name		Nat	Born	Pos	Meet	Venue	Date
22.65	3.5	Kai	Selvon	TTO	13.4.92	6	NCAA	Eugene	8 Jun
22.67	4.1	Alexandria	Anderson	USA	28.1.87	2r1		Montverde	1 Jun
22.71	2.5	Anyika	Onuora	GBR	28.10.84	1	NC	Birmingham	14 Jul
22.75	2.3	Lakeisha	Lawson	USA	3.6.87	1		Azusa	11 May
22.81	2.2	Myriam	Soumaré	FRA	29.10.86	3	DL	Doha	10 May
22.85	3.3	Karene	King	IVB	24.10.87	1		Basseterre	9 Jun
22.86	3.2	Bianca	Knight	USA	2.1.89	4h1	NC	Des Moines	22 Jun
22.91A	5.4	Quanera	Hayes	USA	7.3.92	2h1	NCAA II	Pueblo	24 May
22.91	2.2	Olivia	Ekponé	USA	5.1.93	3h1	NCAA	Eugene	6 Jun
22.93	5.2	Porscha	Lucas	USA	18.6.88	5h4	NC	Des Moines	22 Jun
22.94	6.3	Tawanna	Meadows	USA	4.8.86	2r1		Clermont	11 May
22.95	6.3	Simone	Facey	JAM	7.5.85	3r1		Clermont	11 May
22.96	3.7	Kelly	Proper	IRL	1.5.88	2		Gent	3 Aug
22.98	3.2	Ashley	Fields	USA	13.4.93	1r1		Fort Worth	15 Mar
23.01	2.2	Brooklyn	Morris	USA	27.3.86	2r1		Montverde	8 Jun
23.02	2.9	Brianna	Rollins	USA	18.8.91	1h4		Raleigh	18 Apr
23.03	3.2	Cambrya	Jones	USA	20.9.90	5h1	NC	Des Moines	22 Jun
23.03	3.7	Kadene	Vassell	NED	29.1.89	3		Gent	3 Aug
23.04	4.6	Felicia	Brown	USA	27.10.91	1h2		Knoxville	12 Apr
23.04	4.1	Reyare	Thomas	TTO	23.11.87	1		Abilene	8 May
23.04	3.0	Ana	Holland	USA-J	16.2.95	1	NC	Des Moines	21 Jun
23.05	6.3	Ashley	Kelly	IVB	25.3.91	4		Clermont	11 May
23.05	2.2	Mahagony	Jones	USA	20.12.90	4h1	NCAA	Eugene	6 Jun
23.05A	2.6	Ariana	Washington	USA-Y	4.9.96	1		Albuquerque	8 Jun
23.05	3.4	Nercely	Soto	VEN	26.8.90	2	SACh	Cartagena	6 Jul
23.07	2.5	Asha	Philip	GBR	25.10.90	2	NC	Birmingham	14 Jul
23.09	2.1	Toea	Wisil	PNG	1.1.88	1		Melbourne	6 Apr
23.09	3.6	Erica	Peake	USA	20.2.91	1h1		Lynchburg	19 Apr
23.10A	2.6	Hannah	Cunliffe	USA-Y	9.1.96	2		Albuquerque	8 Jun
23.10	3.4	Erika	Chávez	ECU	4.6.90	3	SACh	Cartagena	6 Jul
23.13	2.6	Libania	Grenot	ITA	12.7.83	5r1		Gainesville	20 Apr
23.14A	w?	Chante	van Tonder	RSA	25.5.93	1		Roodepoort	9 Feb
23.15	3.2	Veronica	Jones	USA	10.3.91	2r1		Fort Worth	15 Mar
23.18	2.6	Debbie	Ferguson-McKenzie	BAH	16.1.76	6r1		Gainesville	20 Apr
23.18	3.0	Morolake	Akinosun	USA-J	17.5.94	2	NC	Des Moines	21 Jun

Mark	Wind	Name		Nat	Born	Date		Mark	Wind	Name		Nat	Born	Pos	Date
23.20	2.5	Ashley	Collier	USA	4.2.92	20 Apr		23.27A	2.6	Ky	Westbrook	USA-Y	25.2.96		8 Jun
23.21	3.1	Tynia	Gaither	BAH	16.3.93	13 Apr		23.28	3.5	Regina	George	NGR	17.2.91		13 Apr
23.22	2.3	Dalilah	Muhammad	USA	7.2.90	11 May		23.28	4.5	Dominique	Kimpel	USA	5.2.93		18 May
23.22	5.7	Omhunique	Browne	SKN-J	14.8.94	16 Jun		23.28A	2.6	Kaylin	Whitney	USA-Y	9.3.98		8 Jun
23.23	5.5	Aireonna	Bailey	USA	7.9.89	5 Apr		23.30	2.9	Christine	Ohuruogu	GBR	17.5.84		14 Jul
23.24	4.3	Cleo	VanBuren	USA	1.5.86	15 Mar		23.33	2.8	Danielle	Dowie	JAM	5.5.92		20 Apr
23.27	3.8	Shataya	Hendricks	USA	15.8.89	23 Mar		23.33	3.6	Nakia	Linson	USA	2.8.92		6 Jun
								23.34	2.5	Akeyla	Mitchell	USA-J	11.11.95		11 May

Best at low altitude

23.27	0.8	K Alexander		27 Apr	23.33	1.3 V Thomas		20 Apr	23.30 w Whitney 24 Apr

Hand timing

Mark	Wind	Name		Nat	Born	Pos	Venue	Date
22.7		Bukola	Abogunloko	NGR-J	18.8.94	1h3	Sagamu	13 Apr
22.9		Racheal	Nachula	ZAM	14.1.90	1	Ndola	4 May

JUNIORS

See main list for top 8 juniors (& 5 wa). 10 (+1w) performances by 3 to 22.98. Additional marks and further juniors:

Name	Mark	Wind	Pos	Meet		Venue	Date
Miller	22.61	1.2	1		Auburn	20 Apr	22.74 -0.3 4 WCh Moskva 16 Aug
	22.64	0.0	2s1	WCh	Moskva	15 Aug	22.77 1.7 1 Carita Nassau 1 Apr
	22.72	0.0	1h3	WCh	Moskva	15 Aug	
Jackson	22.98	-0.1	1	N.Sch	Kingston	16 Mar	
Ekelund	22.95	0.7	1	vFIN	Stockholm	8 Sep	

Mark	Wind	Name		Nat	Born	Pos	Meet	Venue	Date
23.23	0.1	LaQuisha	Jackson	USA	7.1.94	1		Las Vegas	11 May
23.26	0.0	Morolake	Akinosun (10)	USA	17.5.94	2r2		Tempe	6 Apr
23.27A	0.9	Arialis	Gandulla	CUB	22.6.95	1	PAm-J	Medellín	24 Aug
23.28	1.0	Anna-Lena	Freese	GER	21.1.94	1		Mannheim	30 Jun
23.29A	1.6	Ana	Holland	USA	16.2.95	1		Littleton	27 Apr
23.32	1.0	Desiree	Henry	GBR	26.8.95	2		Mannheim	30 Jun
23.35	1.0	Gina	Lückenkemper	GER-Y	21.11.96	3		Mannheim	30 Jun
23.37	0.0	Ky	Westbrook	USA-Y	25.2.96	1		Edwardsville	26 Jun
23.40	0.8	Kaylin	Whitney	USA-Y	9.3.98	1		Jacksonville	3 May
23.41	0.0	Monica	Brennan	AUS	22.1.94	1		Sydney	14 Apr
23.44	-0.1	Monique	Spencer	JAM	20.10.94	2	N.Sch	Kingston	16 Mar
23.44	0.1	Hannaj	Cunliffe (20)	USA-Y	9.1.96	4	WY	Donetsk	14 Jul
23.44A	0.9	Omhunique	Browne	SKN	14.8.94	1h2	PAm-J	Medellín	24 Aug
23.44	-0.6	Kong Lingwei		CHN	28.7.95	2	NG	Shenyang	10 Sep

Wind assisted *more*

Mark	Wind	Name		Nat	Born	Pos	Venue	Date
23.22	5.7	Omhunique	Browne	SKN	14.8.94	1	Basseterre	16 Jun
23.27A	2.6	Ky	Westbrook	USA-Y	25.2.96	3	Albuquerque	8 Jun

Mark	Wind	Name		Nat	Born	Pos	Meet	Venue	Date
23.28A	2.6	Kaylin	Whitney	USA-Y	9.3.98	4		Albuquerque	8 Jun
		23.30w				1		Leto	24 Apr
23.34	2.5	Akeyla	Mitchell	USA	11.11.95	1		Austin	11 May

300 METRES

Mark	Name		Nat	Born	Pos	Meet	Venue	Date
37.04	Blessing	Okagbare	NGR	9.10.88	1		Pasadena	23 Mar
37.30	Denisa	Rosolová	CZE	21.8.86	2 Aug	37.52	Carmelita Jeter	USA 24.11.79 23 Mar
37.36	Keshia	Baker	USA	30.1.88	23 Mar	**Hand timing**		
37.36	Agne	Serksniene	LTU	18.2.88	11 May	37.2	Daysurami Bonne	CUB 9.3.88 20 Dec
37.49A	Zuzana	Hejnová	CZE	19.12.86	23 Jan			
Indoors								
36.76	Kseniya	Ustalova	RUS	14.1.88	1rA		Yekaterinburg	7 Jan
36.9+	Perri	Shakes-Drayton	GBR	21.12.88	1 in 400m		Göteborg	3 Mar
37.1+	Eilidh	Child	GBR	20.2.87	16 Feb	37.54	Kadecia Baird	USA-J 24.2.95 2 Feb

400 METRES

Mark	Name		Nat	Born	Pos	Meet	Venue	Date
49.33	Amantle	Montsho	BOT	4.7.83	1	Herc	Monaco	19 Jul
49.41	Christine	Ohuruogu	GBR	17.5.84	1	WCh	Moskva	12 Aug
49.41		Montsho			2	WCh	Moskva	12 Aug
49.56		Montsho			1s1	WCh	Moskva	11 Aug
49.57	Antonina	Krivoshapka	RUS	21.7.87	1r1	Kuts	Moskva	15 Jul
49.75		Ohuruogu			1s2	WCh	Moskva	11 Aug
49.78		Krivoshapka			3	WCh	Moskva	12 Aug
49.80	Kseniya	Ryzhova	RUS	19.4.87	1h1		Cheboksary	24 Jun
49.86	Francena	McCorory	USA	20.10.88	1s3	WCh	Moskva	11 Aug
49.87		Montsho			1	GGala	Roma	6 Jun
49.88		Montsho			1	DL	Doha	10 May
49.91		Montsho			1	adidas	New York	25 May
49.92	Stephenie Ann	McPherson	JAM	25.11.88	2	Herc	Monaco	19 Jul
49.94	Natasha	Hastings	USA	23.7.86	1	NC	Des Moines	22 Jun
49.94		Hastings			2s2	WCh	Moskva	11 Aug
49.96		McCorory			3	Herc	Monaco	19 Jul
49.99		Krivoshapka			2s3	WCh	Moskva	11 Aug
49.99		McPherson			3s3	WCh	Moskva	11 Aug
49.99		McPherson			4	WCh	Moskva	12 Aug
50.00		Ohuruogu			1	DL	London (OS)	27 Jul
50.00		McPherson			1		Rieti	8 Sep
50.01		Montsho			1	Pre	Eugene	1 Jun
50.01		McCorory			2	NC	Des Moines	22 Jun
50.01	Novlene	Williams-Mills	JAM	26.4.82	1	NC	Kingston	23 Jun
50.05		McCorory			2	GGala	Roma	6 Jun
50.13		McCorory			2	DL	London (OS)	27 Jul
50.14		Montsho			1		Abidjan	27 Apr
50.16		McPherson			1s1	NC	Kingston	22 Jun
50.19	Allyson	Felix	USA	18.11.85	2	DL	Doha	10 May
50.19	Kaliese	Spencer	JAM	6.5.87	2		Rieti	8 Sep
	(30/10)							
50.28	Ashley	Spencer	USA	8.5.93	1	NCAA	Eugene	7 Jun
50.47	Libania	Grenot	ITA	12.7.83	4s2	WCh	Moskva	11 Aug
50.50	Perri	Shakes-Drayton	GBR	21.12.88	1rA	ET	Gateshead	22 Jun
50.55	Kseniya	Zadorina	RUS	2.3.87	1	NC	Moskva	24 Jul
50.60	Kseniya	Ustalova	RUS	14.1.88	1	WUG	Kazan	9 Jul
50.70	Shaunae	Miller	BAH-J	15.4.94	2	NCAA	Eugene	7 Jun
50.71	Tatyana	Firova	RUS	10.10.82	2	NC	Moskva	24 Jul
50.77	Joanna	Atkins	USA	31.1.89	4	NC	Des Moines	22 Jun
50.84	Regina	George	NGR	17.2.91	3s1	WCh	Moskva	11 Aug
50.86	Patricia	Hall	JAM	16.10.82	1		Belém	12 May
	(20)							
50.86	Phyllis	Francis	USA	4.5.92	3	NCAA	Eugene	7 Jun
50.86	Rosemarie	Whyte	JAM	8.9.86	4	Herc	Monaco	19 Jul
50.86	Nataliya	Pygyda	UKR	30.1.81	2		Valence	31 Aug
50.91	Christine	Day	JAM	23.8.86	2h1	NC	Kingston	22 Jun
50.91	Anastasiya	Kapachinskaya	RUS	21.11.79	2h2	NC	Moskva	23 Jul
51.04	Courtney	Okolo	USA-J	15.3.94	1	NC-j	Des Moines	22 Jun
51.05	Jessica	Beard	USA	8.1.89	2		Padova	1 Sep
51.06	Yuliya	Gushchina	RUS	4.3.83	5	NC	Moskva	24 Jul
51.10	Ebonie	Floyd	USA	21.10.83	3s2	NC	Des Moines	21 Jun
51.12	Shana	Cox	GBR	22.1.85	4	DL	London (OS)	27 Ju
	(30)l							
51.15	Keshia	Baker	USA	30.1.88	1		Los Angeles (ER)	4 May

Mark	Name		Nat	Born	Pos	Meet	Venue	Date	
51.17	Alena	Tamkova	RUS	30.5.90	2	WUG	Kazan	9	Jul
51.19	Moushaumi	Robinson	USA	13.4.81	2		George Town	8	May
51.19	Anastacia	Le-Roy	JAM	8.11.87	4	NC	Kingston	23	Jun
51.32A	Kadecia	Baird	GUY-J	24.2.95	1	CAC	Morelia	6	Jul
51.38	Anyika	Onuora	GBR	28.10.84	1		Tomblaine	1	Jul
51.42	Floria	Guei	FRA	2.5.90	5s2	WCh	Moskva	11	Aug
51.43	Sanya	Richards-Ross	USA	26.2.85	1h1	NC	Des Moines	20	Jun
51.49	Bianca	Râzor	ROU-J	8.8.94	4s1	WCh	Moskva	11	Aug
51.54A	Quanera	Hayes	USA	7.3.92	1	NCAA II	Pueblo	25	May
	(40)								
51.54	Marie	Gayot	FRA	18.12.89	3rA	ET	Gateshead	22	Jun
51.56	Patrycja	Wyciszkiewicz	POL-J	8.1.94	1	EJ	Rieti	19	Jul
51.58	Mary	Wineberg	USA	3.1.80	1		Burnaby	1	Jul
51.60	Shericka	Jackson	JAM-J	15.7.94	1		Kingston	16	Mar
51.62	Monica	Hargrove	USA	30.12.82	1		Saint-Martin	11	May
51.62	Joelma	Sousa	BRA	13.7.84	2		Belém	12	May
51.62	Esther	Cremer	GER	29.3.88	1h1	NC	Ulm	6	Jul
51.62	Kineke	Alexander	VIN	21.2.86	3h1	WCh	Moskva	10	Aug
51.63A	Maureen	Maiyo	KEN	28.5.85	1	WCT	Nairobi	13	Jul
51.67	Deedee	Trotter	USA	8.12.82	3		Baie Mahault	8	May
	(50)								
51.67	Omolara	Omotosho	NGR	25.5.93	3		Belém	12	May
51.68	Lenora	Guion-Firmin	FRA	7.8.91	1	EU23	Tampere	13	Jul
51.73	Diamond	Dixon	USA	29.6.92	1	Big12	Waco	5	May
51.77	Aauri Lorena	Bokesa	ESP	14.12.88	1	NC	Alcobendas	28	Jul
51.78	Geisa	Coutinho	BRA	1.6.80	4		Belém	12	May
51.78	Rebecca	Alexander	USA	2.5.90	4s1	NC	Des Moines	21	Jun
51.82	Mikele	Barber	USA	4.10.80	1		Claremont	13	Apr
51.83	Kerron	Stewart	JAM	16.4.84	1		Auburn	6	Apr
51.83	Natalya	Nazarova	RUS	26.5.79	2h1	NC	Moskva	23	Jul
51.83	Eilidh	Child	GBR	20.2.87	8	DL	London (OS)	27	Jul
	(60)								
51.86	Shericka	Williams	JAM	17.9.85	8	NC	Kingston	23	Jun
51.87	Patience	Okon	NGR	25.11.91	2	NC	Calabar	20	Jun
51.88A	Kayan	Robinson	JAM	27.3.89	2	NCAA II	Pueblo	25	May
51.90	Zuzana	Hejnová	CZE	19.12.86	1	ET-1	Dublin	22	Jun
51.90	Tatyana	Veshkurova	RUS	23.9.81	1		Perm	29	Jun
51.93	Margaret	Adeoye	GBR	27.4.85	3	NC	Birmingham	13	Jul
51.93	Nadezhda	Kotlyarova	RUS	12.6.89	3h2	NC	Moskva	23	Jul
51.94	Nercely	Soto	VEN	26.8.90	1	Bol G	Trujillo	27	Nov
51.95	Olga	Zemlyak	UKR	16.1.90	6	GGala	Roma	6	Jun
51.97	Indira	Terrero	ex-CUB	29.11.85	1		Valencia	27	Apr
	(70)								
51.98	Alina	Logvynenko	UKR	18.7.90	2	NC	Donetsk	25	Jul
52.01	Kseniya	Karandyuk	UKR	21.6.86	1		Bar	1	May
52.01	Sadé	Sealy	BAR	18.11.91	1		Des Moines	12	May
52.01	Tjipekapora	Herunga	NAM	1.1.88	5h4	WCh	Moskva	10	Aug
52.02	Jody-Ann	Muir	JAM	1.1.91	1q2	NCAA-E	Greensboro	24	May
52.02	Muriel	Hurtis	FRA	25.3.79	2		Ninove	27	Jul
52.03	Kendall	Baisden	USA-J	5.3.95	2	NC-j	Des Moines	22	Jun
52.05	Olga	Lyakhova	UKR	18.3.92	3	NC	Donetsk	25	Jul
52.06	Chiara	Bazzoni	ITA	5.7.84	1	MedG	Mersin	28	Jun
52.06	Mirela	Lavric	ROU	17.2.91	2	EU23	Tampere	13	Jul
	(80)								
52.06	Ami Mbacké	Thiam	SEN	10.11.76	2	NC	Paris (C)	14	Jul
52.07	Erika	Rucker	USA	29.9.93	1h4	NCAA-E	Greensboro	23	May
52.08	Alicia	Brown	CAN	21.1.90	5	WUG	Kazan	9	Jul
52.10	Kamaria	Brown	USA	21.12.92	2	SEC	Columbia, MO	12	May
52.13	Olesea	Cojuhari	MDA	29.3.90	1		Bucuresti	7	Jun
52.13	Robin	Reynolds	USA-J	22.2.94	3	NC-j	Des Moines	22	Jun
52.14	Kseniya	Gusarova	RUS	29.3.89	4r1		Yerino	2	Jun
52.14	Nicky	van Leuveren	NED	20.5.90	1		Amsterdam	21	Jul
52.15		Zhao Yanmin	CHN	26.1.91	1	NG	Shenyang	8	Sep
52.16	Chris-Ann	Gordon	JAM-J	18.9.94	2		Kingston	16	Mar
	(90)								
52.16	Yekaterina	Renzhina	RUS-J	18.10.94	2r3	NCp	Yerino	15	Jun
52.16	Caitlin	Sargent	AUS	14.6.92	3s1	WUG	Kazan	8	Jul
52.17	Sparkle	McKnight	TTO	21.12.91	1		Tempe	6	Apr
52.18	Bukola	Abogunloko	NGR-J	18.8.94	3		Warri	14	Jun
52.19	Michelle	Brown	USA	24.1.92	1		Piscataway	5	May
52.19	Ilona	Usovich	BLR	14.11.82	3	Gyulai	Budapest	10	Jul

Mark	Name		Nat	Born	Pos	Meet	Venue	Date
52.22	Chizoba	Okodogbe	NGR	3.11.92	2	Pac 12	Los Angeles	12 May
52.22	Justyna	Swiety	POL	3.12.92	3	EU23	Tampere	13 Jul
52.25	Margaret	Bamgbose	USA	19.10.93	2		Piscataway	5 May
52.25	Ristananna	Tracey	JAM	5.9.92	1		Kingston	8 Jun
	(100)							
52.28	Malgorzata	Holub	POL	30.10.92	13	Jul		
52.28	Agne	Serksniene	LTU	18.2.88	10	Aug		
52.29	Jennifer	Carey	IRL	29.6.90	11	May		
52.29	Darya	Prystupa	UKR	26.11.87	25	Jul		
52.31	Turquoise	Thompson	USA	31.7.91	27	Apr		
52.31	Briana	Nelson	USA	18.7.92	5	Jun		
52.33	Felicia	Brown	USA	27.10.93	24	May		
52.33	Kiara	Porter	USA	22.10.93	24	May		
52.34	Yuliya	Baraley	UKR	25.4.90	17	May		
52.35	Josphine	Ehigwe	NGR	12.6.85	20	Jun		
52.37	Shapri	Romero	USA	13.11.91	6	Apr		
52.38	Allison	Beckford	JAM	8.5.79	27	Apr		
52.39	Moa	Hjelmer	SWE	19.6.90	10	Aug		
52.42	Emily	Diamond	GBR	11.6.91	1	Jun		
52.43	Rita	Ossai	NGR-J	21.10.95	20	Jun		
52.43	Iryna	Kornyeva	UKR	31.10.91	25	Jul		
52.43	Yenifer	Padilla	COL	1.1.90	26	Nov		
52.44	Ebony	Eutsey	USA	3.5.92	20	Jun		
52.44	Kelly	Massey	GBR	11.1.85	13	Jul		
52.44	Adelina	Pastor	ROU	5.5.93	13	Jul		
52.44	Marina	Konovalova	RUS	17.9.90	3	Aug		
52.45	Carol	Rodríguez	PUR	16.12.85	20	Apr		
52.45	Jenna	Martin	CAN	31.3.88	29	Jun		
52.46	Madiea	Ghafoor	NED	9.9.92	11	Jul		
52.47A	Gabriela	Medina	MEX	3.3.85	22	Jun		
52.48	Brittany	Wallace	USA	13.7.91	23	Mar		
52.49	Afia	Charles	ANT	22.7.92	12	May		
52.49A	Ana	Holland	USA-J	16.2.95	18	May		
52.49	Yuliya	Terekhova	RUS	20.2.90	11	Jun		
52.50	Bobby-Gaye	Wilkins-Goodden	JAM	10.9.88	22	Jun		
52.52	Haruka	Sugiura	JPN-J	8.6.95	8	Jun		
52.55	Liliane Cristina	Barbosa	BRA	8.10.87	12	May		
52.56	Raysa	Sánchez	DOM	6.5.88	20	Apr		
52.57	Kemi	Adekoya	NGR	16.1.93	18	May		
52.59A	LaSasha	Aldredge	USA	30.1.91	6	Apr		
52.59	Kala	Funderburk	USA	14.9.92	24	May		
52.59	Shamier	Little	USA-J	20.3.95	22	Jun		
52.61	Anneliese	Rubie	AUS	22.4.92	6	Apr		
52.61	Paris	Daniels	USA	25.1.90	11	May		
52.61	Nikolina	Nikolova	BUL	2.12.89	15	Jun		
52.61	Gemma	Nicol	GBR	27.7.86	3	Aug		
52.62	Victoria	Ohuruogu	GBR	28.2.93	27	Apr		
52.62	Olga	Tovarnova	RUS	11.4.85	15	Jun		
52.62	Shawna	Fermin	TTO	17.8.91	3	Aug		
52.63	Ruth Sophia	Spelmeyer	GER	19.9.90	7	Jul		
52.64	Jonnique	Lawrence	USA	5.1.91	12	May		
52.65	Brianna	Tate	USA	1.1.93	27	Apr		
52.66	Morganne	Phillips	USA	10.11.92	13	Apr		
52.66	Lanie	Whittaker	USA	21.5.91	23	May		
52.66	Maria Benedicta	Chigboglu	ITA	27.7.89	28	Jun		
52.66	Elena	Bonfanti	ITA	9.7.88	8	Jul		
52.66	Yuliya	Yurenya	BLR	27.5.92	13	Jul		
52.68A	Sage	Watson	CAN-J	20.1.94	23	Aug		
52.69	Yana	Glotova	RUS-J	8.4.95	15	Jun		
52.71	Olivia	Baker	USA-Y	12.6.96	26	Jun		
52.73	Jernail	Hayes	USA	8.7.88	5	Jul		
52.75	Dalilah	Muhammad	USA	7.2.90	6	Apr		
52.75	Machettira Raju	Poovamma	IND	5.6.90	24	Apr		
52.75	Vania	Stambolova	BUL	28.11.83	15	Jun		
52.76	Cátia	Azevedo	POR-J	9.3.94	18	Jul		
52.76	Gunta	Latiseva-Cudare	LAT-J	9.3.95	19	Jul		
52.77	Molly	Ellis	USA		5	May		
52.77	Sabrina	Bakare	GBR-Y	14.5.96	12	Jul		
52.78	Line	Kloster	NOR	27.2.90	13	Jun		
52.78	Lena	Schmidt	GER	4.8.89	7	Jul		
52.79		Chen Jingwen	CHN	8.2.90	8	Sep		
52.81	Lydia	Mashila	BOT	22.6.90	27	Jul		
52.82	Daysurami	Bonne	CUB	9.3.88	8	Feb		
52.82mx	Tamsyn	Manou	AUS	20.7.78	16	Nov		
52.85	Kirsten	McAslan	GBR	1.9.93	13	Jul		
52.86	Yuliya	Rakhmanova	KAZ	25.10.91	9	Jun		
52.86	Natalya	Danilova	RUS	28.8.91	25	Jun		
52.86	Chandrika	Subashini	SRI	20.6.87	19	Oct		
52.87	Jitka	Bartoníková	CZE	22.12.85	16	Jun		
52.87	Ada	Benjamin	NGR-J	18.5.94	30	Aug		
52.89	Vanessa	Jones	USA	1.1.93	12	May		
52.90	Agnès	Raharolahy	FRA	7.11.92	28	Jun		
52.91	Phara	Anacharsis	FRA	17.12.83	19	May		
52.92	Olivia	James	JAM-J	1.6.94	16	Mar		
52.92	Georganne	Moline	USA	6.3.90	29	Mar		
52.92	Jaílma	de Lima	BRA	31.12.86	6	Apr		
52.92	Petra	Fanty	JAM	29.1.92	27	Apr		
52.92	Alina Andreea	Panainte	ROU	7.11.88	15	Jun		
52.92	Emma	Pullen	GBR	6.8.89	29	Jun		
52.92	Lisanne	de Witte	NED	10.9.92	21	Jul		
52.95	Jordan	Lavender	USA	23.7.93	20	Apr		
52.96	Donna-Lee	Hylton	JAM	8.6.90	20	Apr		
52.96	Anna	Yagupova	RUS	10.5.84	11	Jul		
52.97	Jackie	Rose	USA	.90	27	Apr		
52.97	Lashinda	Demus	USA	10.3.83	28	Apr		
52.97	Natalie	Stewart	USA	15.3.90	24	May		
52.98	Anneisha	McLaughlin	JAM	6.1.86	9	Jun		
52.98		Nguyen Thi Oanh	VIE-Y	20.2.96	24	Sep		
52.98		Nguyen Thi Huyen	VIE	19.5.93	24	Sep		
52.99	Blessing	Mayungbe	NGR	15.4.92	20	Apr		
52.99	Kristina	Malvinova	RUS	16.7.89	1	Jun		
	(196)							

Hand timing

| 51.2 | Daysurami | Bonne | CUB | 9.3.88 | 1 | | La Habana | 18 May |

Indoors

51.27	Zuzana	Hejnová	CZE	19.12.86	2s2	EI	Göteborg	2 Mar
51.45	Eilidh	Child	GBR	20.2.87	2	EI	Göteborg	3 Mar
52.04	Moa	Hjelmer	SWE	19.6.90	3	EI	Göteborg	3 Mar
52.07	Angela	Morosanu	ROU	26.7.86	1h2	EI	Göteborg	1 Mar
52.09	Georganne	Moline	USA	6.3.90	3r2	NCAA	Fayetteville	9 Mar
52.12	Denisa	Rosolová	CZE	21.8.86	3s2	EI	Göteborg	2 Mar
52.37	Ella	Räsänen	FIN-J	27.1.94	1	Mar		
52.46	Olga	Tovarnova	RUS	11.4.85	13	Feb		
52.70	Phara	Anacharsis	FRA	17.12.83	24	Feb		
52.78	Line	Kloster	NOR	27.2.90	2	Mar		
52.80	Meghan	Beesley	GBR	15.11.89	29	Jan		
52.82#	Danielle	Dowie	JAM	5.5.92	24	Feb		
52.84	Marlena	Wesh	HAI	16.2.91	23	Feb		
52.90	Liliya	Molgacheva	RUS	2.3.90	26	Jan		

Best at low altitude

52.61 Aldredge 27 Apr   52.79 K Robinson 20 Apr

JUNIORS

See main list for top 11 juniors. 11 performances (2 Indoors) by 6 women to 51.70. Additional marks and further juniors:

Miller	50.88i	1	NCAA	Fayetteville	9 Mar	51.57	1h1	NCAA	Eugene	5 Jun
	51.14i	1h2	NCAA	Fayetteville	9 Mar	51.63	1	Carifta	Nassau	30 Mar
Razor	51.51	4h1	WCh	Moskva	10 Aug					
52.43	Rita		Ossai	NGR	21.10.95	6	NC	Calabar	20 Jun
52.49A	Ana		Holland	USA	16.2.95	1		Lakewood	18 May
52.52	Haruka		Sugiura	JPN	8.6.95	1	NC	Tokyo (Chofu)	8 Jun

Mark	Name		Nat	Born	Pos	Meet	Venue			Date
52.59	Shamier	Little	USA	20.3.95	4	NC-j	Des Moines			22 Jun
52.68A	Sage	Watson	CAN	20.1.94	3	PAm-J	Medellín			23 Aug
52.69	Yana	Glotova	RUS	8.4.95	1	NC-j	Kazan			15 Jun
52.71	Olivia	Baker	USA-Y	12.6.96	1		Edwardsville			26 Jun
52.76	Cátia	Azevedo	POR	9.3.94	2h3	EJ	Rieti			18 Jul
52.76	Gunta	Latiseva-Cudare (20)	LAT	9.3.95	4	EJ	Rieti			19 Jul
52.37	Ella	Räsänen	FIN	27.1.94	3h3	EI	Göteborg			1 Mar

600 METRES

Mark	Name		Nat	Born	Pos	Meet	Venue			Date
1:26.1	Sahily	Diago	CUB-J	26.8.95	1		La Habana			9 Apr
1:26.87	Svetlana	Usovich	BLR	14.10.80	6 Jul	1:26.9	Rose Marie	Almanza	CUB 13.7.92	19 Dec

Indoors

Mark	Name		Nat	Born	Pos	Meet	Venue			Date
1:23.59	Alysia	Montaño	USA	26.4.86	1	Mill	New York (Armory)			16 Feb
1:26.45	Ajee'	Wilson	USA-J	8.5.94	2	Mill	New York (Armory)			16 Feb
1:26.48	Erica	Moore	USA	25.3.88	3	Mill	New York (Armory)			16 Feb
1:27.28	Marina	Arzamasova	BLR 17.12.87	19 Jan	1:27.70	Ilona	Usovich	BLR	14.11.82	19 Jan
						1:27.95	Melissa	Bishop	CAN	5.8.88	16 Feb

800 METRES

Mark	Name		Nat	Born	Pos	Meet	Venue			Date
1:56.72	Francine	Niyonsaba	BDI	5.5.93	1	Pre	Eugene			1 Jun
1:57.26		Niyonsaba			1	DL	Saint-Denis			6 Jul
1:57.38	Eunice	Sum	KEN	2.9.88	1	WCh	Moskva			18 Aug
1:57.64	Malika	Akkaoui	MAR	25.12.87	2	DL	Saint-Denis			6 Jul
1:57.75	Alysia	Montaño	USA	26.4.86	3	DL	Saint-Denis			6 Jul
1:57.80	Mariya	Savinova	RUS	13.8.85	2	WCh	Moskva			18 Aug
1:57.91	Brenda	Martinez	USA	8.9.87	3	WCh	Moskva			18 Aug
1:57.95		Montaño			4	WCh	Moskva			18 Aug
1:58.05	Yekaterina	Poistogova	RUS	1.3.91	5	WCh	Moskva			18 Aug
1:58.18		Martinez			2	Pre	Eugene			1 Jun
1:58.19		Martinez			1	DL	London (OS)			26 Jul
1:58.21	Ajee'	Wilson	USA-J	8.5.94	6	WCh	Moskva			18 Aug
1:58.67		Montaño			1	NC	Des Moines			23 Jun
1:58.71	Janeth	Jepkosgei	KEN	13.12.83	3	Pre	Eugene			1 Jun
1:58.75		Savinova			1		Yerino			2 Jun
1:58.78		Martinez			2	NC	Des Moines			23 Jun
1:58.82		Sum			1	WK	Zürich			29 Aug
1:58.84		Sum			1	DNG	Stockholm			22 Aug
1:58.92		Montaño			1s1	WCh	Moskva			16 Aug
1:58.92	Caster	Semenya (10)	RSA	7.1.91	1		Rieti			8 Sep
1:58.93		Savinova			2	WK	Zürich			29 Aug
1:58.96	Margarita	Mukasheva	KAZ	4.1.86	1	WUG	Kazan			9 Jul
1:58.96		Montaño			2	DNG	Stockholm			22 Aug
1:59.03		Martinez			2s1	WCh	Moskva			16 Aug
1:59.03		Poistogova			1	Hanz	Zagreb			3 Sep
1:59.20	Abeba	Aregawi	SWE	5.7.90	1	FBK	Hengelo			8 Jun
1:59.21	Yekaterina	Kupina	RUS	2.2.86	2		Yerino			2 Jun
1:59.3A		Sum			1	WCT	Nairobi			13 Jul
1:59.30	Winny	Chebet	KEN	20.12.90	2	Hanz	Zagreb			3 Sep
1:59.34		Akkaoui			3	WK	Zürich			29 Aug
	(30/14)									
1:59.38	Halima	Hachlaf	MAR	8.9.88	1		Rabat			25 Jul
1:59.4	Rose Marie	Almanza	CUB	13.7.92	1		La Habana			27 Jul
1:59.40	Nelly	Jepkosgei	KEN	14.7.91	2		Rieti			8 Sep
1:59.43	Marilyn	Okoro	GBR	23.9.84	2h1	WCh	Moskva			15 Aug
1:59.43	Nataliya	Lupu	UKR	4.11.87	3s1	WCh	Moskva			16 Aug
1:59.47	Kate	Grace	USA	24.10.88	4	DL	Saint-Denis			6 Jul
	(20)									
1:59.51	Mary	Cain	USA-Y	3.5.96	5	Pre	Eugene			1 Jun
1:59.56	Yelena	Kotulskaya	RUS	8.8.88	1	NC	Moskva			23 Jul
1:59.56	Lenka	Masná	CZE	22.4.85	5s1	WCh	Moskva			16 Aug
1:59.60	Marina	Arzamasova	BLR	17.12.87	5h1	WCh	Moskva			15 Aug
1:59.61	Ayvika	Malanova	RUS	28.11.92	4		Yerino			2 Jun
1:59.76	Melissa	Bishop	CAN	5.8.88	1		Victoria			5 Jul
1:59.79	Mirela	Lavric	ROU	17.2.91	2	DL	London (OS)			26 Jul
1:59.82	Egle	Balciunaite	LTU	31.10.88	3	WUG	Kazan			9 Jul
1:59.85	Jessica	Judd	GBR-J	7.1.95	1	DL	Birmingham			30 Jun
1:59.91	Yekaterina	Sharmina	RUS	6.8.86	2	NCp	Yerino			16 Jun
	(30)									
1:59.93	Natoya	Goule	JAM	30.3.91	1	NC	Kingston			22 Jun
2:00.03	Angela	Smit	NZL	16.8.91	4	WUG	Kazan			9 Jul

Mark	Name		Nat	Born	Pos	Meet	Venue	Date	
2:00.04	Heather	Kampf	USA	19.1.87	1		Lignano	16	Jul
2:00.15	Siham	Hilali	MAR	2.5.86	6	DL	Saint-Denis	6	Jul
2:00.17	Yelena	Soboleva	RUS	3.10.82	2	Kuts	Moskva	15	Jul
2:00.20	Phoebe	Wright	USA	30.8.88	2		Lignano	16	Jul
2:00.23	Laura	Roesler	USA	19.12.91	5	NC	Des Moines	23	Jun
2:00.25	Fantu	Magiso	ETH	9.9.92	4	Bisl	Oslo	13	Jun
2:00.30	Lea	Wallace	USA	19.12.88	3		Lignano	16	Jul
2:00.32	Svetlana (40)	Cherkasova	RUS	20.5.78	2		Sochi	25	May
2:00.39	Hannah	England	GBR	6.3.87	4		Rieti	8	Sep
2:00.43	Jessica	Smith	CAN	11.10.89	6	WUG	Kazan	9	Jul
2:00.45	Jennifer	Simpson	USA	23.8.86	1rA		Los Angeles (ER)	17	May
2:00.49	Anita	Hinriksdottir	ISL-Y	13.1.96	1		Mannheim	30	Jun
2:00.53	Geena	Gall	USA	18.1.87	3s2	NC	Des Moines	21	Jun
2:00.58	Rabab	Arrafi	MAR	12.1.91	1		Oordegem	6	Jul
2:00.58	Rose-Anne	Galligan	IRL	9.12.87	6	DL	London (OS)	26	Jul
2:00.60	Angelika	Cichocka	POL	15.3.88	4	Hanz	Zagreb	3	Sep
2:00.61	LaTavia	Thomas	USA	17.12.88	5s2	NC	Des Moines	21	Jun
2:00.61	Marina (50)	Pospelova	RUS	23.7.90	3	NC	Moskva	23	Jul
2:00.76A	Sylvia	Chesebe	KEN	16.4.89	3		Nairobi	22	Jun
2:00.79	Olga	Lyakhova	UKR	18.3.92	1		Yalta	6	Jun
2:00.80	Laura	Muir	GBR	9.5.93	3h4	WCh	Moskva	15	Aug
2:00.81	Olena	Zhushman #	UKR	30.12.85	2		Bellinzona	11	Jun
2:00.82	Irina	Maracheva	RUS	24.9.84	4	NC	Moskva	23	Jul
2:00.82	Manal	El Bahraoui	MAR-J	6.1.94	2		Rabat	25	Jul
2:00.86	Sifan	Hassan	ETH/NED	.93	1	NA	Heusden-Zolder	13	Jul
2:00.88	Chanelle	Price	USA	22.8.90	6s2	NC	Des Moines	21	Jun
2:00.93	Tatyana	Markelova	RUS	19.12.88	4	NCp	Yerino	16	Jun
2:00.93	Zoe (60)	Buckman	AUS	21.12.88	5		Rieti	8	Sep
2:00.93	Laura	Crowe	IRL	29.11.87	6		Rieti	8	Sep
2:00.97	Justine	Fédronic	FRA	11.5.91	9	DL	Saint-Denis	6	Jul
2:00.98	Amy	Weissenbach	USA-J	16.6.94	4s1	NC	Des Moines	21	Jun
2:01.00	Olena	Sidorska	UKR-J	30.7.94	6		Yerino	2	Jul
2:01.02	Margaret	Vessey	USA	23.12.81	5s1	NC	Des Moines	21	Jun
2:01.07	Anna	Shchagina	RUS	7.12.91	5	NCp	Yerino	16	Jun
2:01.12	Diane	Cummins	CAN	19.1.74	2		Victoria	5	Jul
2:01.13	Karine	Belleau-Béliveau	CAN	29.12.83	3		Victoria	5	Jul
2:01.15	Sanne	Verstegen	NED	10.11.85	3		Oordegem	6	Jul
2:01.17A	Selah Jepleting (70)	Busienei	KEN	27.12.91	2		Nairobi	11	May
2:01.18	Alena	Glazkova	RUS	6.5.88	6	NC	Moskva	23	Jul
2:01.22	Kelly	Hetherington	AUS	10.3.89	1	NC	Sydney	14	Apr
2:01.25	Tigist	Assefa	ETH-J	.94	3		Bellinzona	11	Jun
2:01.30	Sahily	Diago	CUB-J	26.8.95	1		La Habana	28	Jun
2:01.34	Anna	Rostkowska	POL	26.7.80	7		Rieti	8	Sep
2:01.35	Helen	Crofts	CAN	28.5.90	3s1	WUG	Kazan	8	Jul
2:01.38	Gabriele	Anderson	USA	25.6.86	5r2	Pre	Eugene	31	May
2:01.40	Marta	Milani	ITA	9.3.87	4		Lignano	16	Jul
2:01.43	Clarisse	Moh	FRA	6.12.86	4		Oordegem	6	Jul
2:01.44	Anna (80)	Balakshina	RUS	22.11.86	4	Kuts	Moskva	15	Jul
2:01.47A	Hellen	Obiri	KEN	13.12.89	3		Nairobi	11	May
2:01.48	Renata	Plis	POL	5.2.85	8		Rieti	8	Sep
2:01.53	Svetlana	Podosyonova	RUS	24.5.88	6	NCp	Yerino	16	Jun
2:01.59	Natalja	Piliusina	LTU	22.10.90	5s1	WUG	Kazan	8	Jul
2:01.65	Tugba	Koyuncu	TUR	16.2.91	1	NC	Izmir	2	Jun
2:01.66	Selina	Büchel	SUI	26.7.91	4	Flame	Amsterdam	31	Aug
2:01.67	Anastasiya	Tkachuk	UKR	20.4.93	4		Bellinzona	11	Jun
2:01.67	Mary	Kuria	KEN	29.11.87	4		Rovereto	3	Sep
2:01.68	Svetlana	Rogozina	RUS	26.12.92	7	NCp	Yerino	16	Jun
2:01.70	Charlene (90)	Lipsey	USA	16.7.91	4	NCAA	Eugene	7	Jun
2:01.72	Lydia	Wafula	KEN	15.2.88	6		Rovereto	3	Sep
2:01.74	Khadija	Rahmouni	ESP	30.11.86	2		Huelva	12	Jul
2:01.84	Nicole	Sifuentes	CAN	30.6.86	1		Gent	3	Aug
2:01.87	Yvonne	Hak	NED	30.6.86	4	DL	Birmingham	30	Jun
2:01.87	Tintu	Luka	IND	26.4.89	1		Ranchi	8	Sep
2:01.96	Luiza	Gega	ALB	5.11.88	4	MedG	Mersin	29	Jun
2:01.98	Rosibel	García	COL	13.2.81	1	Bol G	Trujillo	28	Nov

Mark	Name	Nat	Born	Pos	Meet	Venue	Date
2:02.00	Katie Mackey	USA	12.11.87	2		Gent	3 Aug
2:02.04	Ibtissam Aït Elbatoul	MAR	26.11.89	2		Casablanca	7 Jul
2:02.05	Wang Chunyu	CHN-J	17.1.95	6h2	WCh	Moskva	15 Aug

(100)

Mark	Name	Nat	Born	Date
2:02.06	Megan Malasarte	USA	1.8.92	21 Jun
2:02.10	Samantha Murphy	CAN	18.3.92	7 Jun
2:02.12	Anne Kesselring	GER	4.12.89	31 May
2:02.14	Shannon Leinert	USA	30.6.87	30 May
2:02.22	Mantegbosh Melese	ETH	.88	16 Jul
2:02.30	María Kládou	GRE	19.3.85	21 Jul
2:02.36	Zhao Jing	CHN	9.7.88	9 Sep
2:02.39	Hilary Stellingwerff	CAN	7.8.81	20 Apr
2:02.39	Joanna Józwik	POL	30.1.91	8 Jun
2:02.40	Gabriela Medina	MEX	3.3.85	17 May
2:02.40	Renelle Lamote	FRA	26.12.93	1 Jul
2:02.43A	Nancy Chebet	KEN	.81	11 May
2:02.48	Cydney Ross	USA	16.3.90	7 Jun
2:02.48A	Cherono Koech	KEN	8.12.92	22 Jun
2:02.51	Anastasiya Bazdyreva	RUS	6.3.92	26 May
2:02.51	Morgan Uceny	USA	10.3.85	16 Jul
2:02.56	Rachel Aubry	CAN	18.5.90	3 Aug
2:02.58	Sarah Brown	USA	15.10.86	5 Jul
2:02.59	Anna Konovalova	RUS	4.7.88	16 Jun
2:02.61	Olga Lvova	RUS	21.9.89	4 Jul
2:02.62	Ilona Usovich	BLR	14.11.82	28 Jun
2:02.63	Lynsey Sharp	GBR	11.7.90	20 Apr
2:02.63	Shelby Houlihan	USA	8.2.93	21 Jun
2:02.64	Shannon Rowbury	USA	19.9.84	3 Sep
2:02.65	Christina Rodgers	USA	4.8.88	17 May
2:02.68	Liliya Lobanova	UKR	14.10.85	11 Jun
2:02.72	Sofia Ennaoui	POL-J	30.8.95	22 Jun
2:02.79	Svetlana Uloga	RUS	23.11.86	22 Jul
2:02.8A	Faith Kipyegon	KEN-J	10.1.94	27 Apr
2:02.83	Lemlem Ogbasilassie	CAN	10.12.87	1 Jul
2:02.84	Katarzyna Broniatowska	POL	22.2.90	8 Jun
2:02.84	Margherita Magnani	ITA	26.2.87	3 Sep
2:02.87	Élian Périz	ESP	1.4.84	17 Jul
2:02.89	Natalya Peryakova	RUS	4.3.83	26 May
2:02.89	Danuta Urbanik	POL	24.12.89	8 Jul
2:02.91	Lauren Wallace	USA	19.12.88	7 Jun
2:02.94	Flávia de Lima	BRA	1.7.93	7 Jul
2:02.96	Winnie Nanyondo	UGA	23.8.93	8 Jul
2:02.96	Ciara Everard	IRL	10.7.90	17 Jul
2:02.96	Alison Leonard	GBR	17.3.90	27 Jul
2:03.01	Annett Horna	GER	4.2.87	8 Jun
2:03.02	Elina Sujew	GER	2.11.90	2 Aug
2:03.03	Alem Gereziher	ETH-J	15.4.95	6 Jun
2:03.03	Corinna Harrer	GER	19.1.91	8 Jun
2:03.04	Carolyn Plateau	GBR	22.8.88	17 Jul
2:03.08A	Simoya Campbell	JAM-J	1.3.94	7 Jul
2:03.09	Emily Dudgeon	GBR	3.3.93	17 Jul
2:03.11	Christina Hering	GER-J	9.10.94	20 Jul
2:03.11	Sushma Devi	IND	7.5.84	8 Sep
2:03.20	Yelena Kobeleva	RUS	12.6.88	26 May
2:03.2A	Sofiya Shemsu	ETH-J	12.9.94	27 Jun
2:03.21	Kseniya Savina	UKR	4.6.89	25 Jul
2:03.25	Sara Edao	ETH-Y	8.4.96	14 Jul
2:03.26	Song Tingting	CHN	22.4.88	9 Sep
2:03.30	Heather Wilson	USA	13.6.90	13 Jul
2:03.32	Raevyn Rogers	USA-Y	7.9.96	14 Jul
2:03.34	Greta Feldman	USA	30.3.91	15 Jun
2:03.35	Tatyana Suprun	BLR	16.2.86	31 May
2:03.37	Georgia Wassall	AUS-Y	3.3.96	14 Apr
2:03.37	Florina Pierdevarã	ROU	29.3.90	24 Aug
2:03.42	Isabel Macías	ESP	11.8.84	12 Jun
2:03.43	Tatyana Myazina	RUS	18.3.88	26 May
2:03.45	Ophélie Claude-Boxberger	FRA	18.10.88	10 Aug
2:03.47	Rachel François	CAN	14.11.92	3 Aug
2:03.49	Jemma Simpson	GBR	10.2.84	21 Jun
2:03.50	Dorina Korozsi	ROU	22.5.82	28 Jun
2:03.51	Lovisa Lindh	SWE	9.7.91	11 Jul
2:03.51	Sinimole Markose	IND	24.6.83	8 Sep
2:03.52	Shelayne Oskan-Clarke	GBR	20.1.90	7 Aug
2:03.55	Andrea Ferris	PAN	21.9.87	20 Apr
2:03.59	Katharina Trost	GER-J	28.6.95	18 Jul

(171)

Indoors

Mark	Name	Nat	Born	Pos	Meet	Venue	Date
2:00.31	Alena Glazkova	RUS	6.5.88	1h3	NC	Moskva	12 Feb
2:00.32	Svetlana Podosyonova	RUS	24.5.88	2h3	NC	Moskva	12 Feb
2:01.02	Jennifer Meadows	GBR	17.4.81	1s1	EI	Göteborg	2 Mar
2:01.56	Olga Lvova	RUS	21.9.89	1h2	NC	Moskva	12 Feb
2:01.64	Selina Büchel	SUI	26.7.91	4s1	EI	Göteborg	2 Mar

2:02.42	Anastasiya Grigoryeva	RUS	23.11.88	12 Feb	2:03.57A	Bethany Praska	USA	10.6.89	3 Mar
2:02.54	Ciara Everard	IRL	10.7.90	10 Feb					

Irregular kerb: 2:01.65 Treniere Moser USA 27.10.81 3 San Diego 5 May

JUNIORS

See main list for top 10 juniors. 11 performances by 4 women to 2:00.80. Additional mark and further juniors:

Name	Mark	Pos	Meet	Venue		Date	Mark	Pos	Meet	Venue		Date
Wilson	1:59.55	3	NC	Des Moines		23 Jun	2:00.20	3	DL	London (OS)		26 Jul
	1:59.96	4	DNG	Stockholm		22 Aug	2:00.35	5	WK	Zürich		29 Aug
	2:00.00	3h3	WCh	Moskva		15 Aug						
Judd	2:00.37	1		Watford		15 May	2:00.71	1	LI	Loughborough		19 May

Mark	Name	Nat	Born	Pos	Meet	Venue	Date
2:02.72	Sofia Ennaoui	POL	30.8.95	1		Szczecin	22 Jun
2:02.8A	Faith Kipyegon	KEN	10.1.94	1		Mumias	27 Apr
2:03.03	Alem Gereziher	ETH	15.4.95	1		Montbéliard	6 Jun
2:03.08A	Simoya Campbell	JAM	1.3.94	2	CAC	Morelia	7 Jul
2:03.11	Christina Hering	GER	9.10.94	3	EJ	Rieti	20 Jul
2:03.2A	Sofiya Shemsu	ETH	12.9.94	2	NC	Assela	27 Jun
2:03.25	Sara Edao	ETH-Y	8.4.96	2	WY	Donetsk	14 Jul
2:03.32	Raevyn Rogers	USA-Y	7.9.96	3	WY	Donetsk	14 Jul
2:03.37	Georgia Wassall	AUS-Y	3.3.96	3	NC	Sydney	14 Apr
2:03.59	Katharina Trost (20)	GER	28.6.95	2h2	EJ	Rieti	18 Jul

1000 METRES

Mark	Name	Nat	Born	Pos	Meet	Venue	Date
2:35.43	Nelly Jepkosgei	KEN	14.7.91	1	VD	Bruxelles	6 Sep
2:35.73	Winny Chebet	KEN	20.12.90	2	VD	Bruxelles	6 Sep
2:36.41	Yekaterina Kupina	RUS	2.2.86	1	Skol	Warszawa	25 Aug
2:36.45	Kupina			3	VD	Bruxelles	6 Sep
2:37.30	Chebet			2	Skol	Warszawa	25 Aug
2:37.61	Morgan Uceny	USA	10.3.85	4	VD	Bruxelles	6 Sep

2:38.26 Joanna Józwik POL 30.1.91 6 Sep | 2:38.49 Laura Weightman GBR 1.7.91 6 Sep

Mark	Name		Nat	Born	Pos	Meet	Venue		Date
2:38.68	Rose-Anne	Galligan	IRL	9.12.87	6 Sep	2:38.83 Katarzyna	Broniatowska POL		22.2.90 6 Sep
2:38.71	Danuta	Urbanik	POL	24.12.89	6 Sep	2:39.00 Anna	Rostkowska POL		26.7.80 25 Aug
2:38.76	Kate	Van Buskirk	CAN	9.6.87	6 Sep	2:39.80 Renata	Plis POL		5.2.85 25 Aug
2:38.80	Angelika	Cichocka	POL	15.3.88	25 Aug	2:39.86 Malika	Akkaoui MAR		25.12.87 26 Aug
Indoors						2:40.81 Maureen	Koster NED		3.7.92 1 May
2:36.97	Yekaterina	Poistogova	RUS	1.3.91	1		Moskva		3 Feb
2:37.01	Yelena	Kotulskaya	RUS	8.8.88	2		Moskva		3 Feb
2:38.20	Marina	Pospelova	RUS	23.7.90	3 Feb	2:39.72 Svetlana	Kireyeva RUS		12.6.87 11 Jan
2:38.38	Anna	Shchagina	RUS	7.12.91	11 Jan	2:40.31 Tatyana	Markelova RUS		19.12.88 3 Feb
2:38.73	Svetlana	Podosyonova	RUS	24.5.88	3 Feb	2:40.55 Lydia	Wafula KEN		15.2.88 3 Feb
2:38.95	Ayvika	Malanova	RUS	28.11.92	11 Jan	2:40.66 Natalya	Koreyvo BLR		14.11.85 3 Feb
JUNIOR: 2:41.06	Sofia	Ennaoui	POL	30.8.95	1J		Pliezhausen		12 May
Drugs disqualification									
2:36.84i	Anzhela	Shevchenko ¶	UKR	29.10.87	(1)		Moskva		3 Feb

1500 METRES

Mark	Name		Nat	Born	Pos	Meet	Venue	Date
3:56.60	Abeba	Aregawi	SWE	5.7.90	1	DL	Doha	10 May
3:56.98	Faith	Kipyegon	KEN-J	10.1.94	2	DL	Doha	10 May
3:57.54	Genzebe	Dibaba	ETH	8.2.91	3	DL	Doha	10 May
3:58.58	Hellen	Obiri	KEN	13.12.89	1	Pre	Eugene	1 Jun
4:00.23		Aregawi			1	GGala	Roma	6 Jun
4:00.48	Jennifer	Simpson	USA	23.8.86	1	Herc	Monaco	19 Jul
4:00.76	Viola	Kibiwot	KEN	22.12.83	4	DL	Doha	10 May
4:00.93		Obiri			2	Herc	Monaco	19 Jul
4:00.94	Brenda	Martinez	USA	8.9.87	3	Herc	Monaco	19 Jul
4:01.08		Kipyegon			2	Pre	Eugene	1 Jun
4:01.28	Shannon	Rowbury	USA	19.9.84	4	Herc	Monaco	19 Jul
4:01.41	Nancy	Langat	KEN	22.8.81	3	Pre	Eugene	1 Jun
4:01.48	Gabriele	Anderson (10)	USA	25.6.86	5	Herc	Monaco	19 Jul
4:01.62		Dibaba			2	GGala	Roma	6 Jun
4:02.05	Eunice	Sum	KEN	2.9.88	5	DL	Doha	10 May
4:02.11		Aregawi			1	Athl	Lausanne	4 Jul
4:02.16	Siham	Hilali	MAR	2.5.86	4	Pre	Eugene	1 Jun
4:02.30		Simpson			3	GGala	Roma	6 Jun
4:02.50		Kibiwot			6	Herc	Monaco	19 Jul
4:02.56	Yuliya	Zaripova	RUS	26.4.86	1	NC	Moskva	25 Jul
4:02.67		Aregawi			1	WCh	Moskva	15 Aug
4:02.85	Treniere	Moser	USA	27.10.81	5	Pre	Eugene	1 Jun
4:02.96	Sheila	Reid	CAN	2.8.89	6	Pre	Eugene	1 Jun
4:02.99		Simpson			2	WCh	Moskva	15 Aug
4:03.13		Sum			7	Pre	Eugene	1 Jun
4:03.35		Simpson			1	Drake	Des Moines	26 Apr
4:03.38	Hannah	England	GBR	6.3.87	8	Pre	Eugene	1 Jun
4:03.55		Obiri			1		Rabat	9 Jun
4:03.56	Mary	Kuria	KEN	29.11.87	6	DL	Doha	10 May
4:03.63	Mimi	Belete	BRN	9.6.88	7	Herc	Monaco	19 Jul
		(30/18)						
4:03.73	Sifan	Hassan	ETH/NED	.93	2	Athl	Lausanne	4 Jul
4:03.74mp	Charlene	Thomas	GBR	6.5.82	1		Watford	4 Sep
		(20)						
4:04.01	Svetlana	Podosyonova	RUS	24.5.88	2	NC	Moskva	25 Jul
4:04.30	Yelena	Soboleva	RUS	3.10.82	9	Pre	Eugene	1 Jun
4:04.36	Gelete	Burka	ETH	15.2.86	9	Herc	Monaco	19 Jul
4:04.55	Yekaterina	Sharmina	RUS	6.8.86	3	DL	Birmingham	30 Jun
4:04.55	Senbere	Teferi	ETH-J	3.5.95	10	Herc	Monaco	19 Jul
4:04.60	Katie	Mackey	USA	12.11.87	1		Los Angeles (ER)	17 May
4:04.62	Mary	Cain	USA-Y	3.5.96	2		Los Angeles (ER)	17 May
4:04.63	Ibtissam	Lakhouad	MAR	7.12.80	10	Pre	Eugene	1 Jun
4:04.65	Nicole	Sifuentes	CAN	30.6.86	3		Los Angeles (ER)	17 May
4:04.81	Lisa	Dobriskey	GBR	23.12.83	1	Kuso	Szczecin	15 Jun
		(30)						
4:04.82	Zoe	Buckman	AUS	21.12.88	1s1	WCh	Moskva	13 Aug
4:04.97	Malika	Akkaoui	MAR	25.12.87	1		Sotteville-lès-Rouen	8 Jul
4:05.11	Luiza	Gega	ALB	5.11.88	2	Kuso	Szczecin	15 Jun
4:05.11	Meraf	Bahta	ERI	26.6.89	1	NA	Heusden-Zolder	13 Jul
4:05.13	Betlhem	Desalegn	UAE	13.11.91	8	DL	Doha	10 May
4:05.16	Axumawit	Embaye	ETH-J	18.10.94	2	NA	Heusden-Zolder	13 Jul
4:05.18	Yelena	Korobkina	RUS	25.11.90	3s1	WCh	Moskva	13 Aug
4:05.22	Rabab	Arrafi	MAR	12.1.91	9	DL	Doha	10 May
4:05.27	Sarah	Brown	USA	15.10.86	4		Los Angeles (ER)	17 May

WOMEN 2013

Mark	Name		Nat	Born	Pos	Meet	Venue	Date
4:05.36	Laura	Weightman	GBR	1.7.91	11	Pre	Eugene	1 Jun
	(40)							
4:05.38	Susan	Kuijken	NED	8.7.86	2	GS	Ostrava	27 Jun
4:05.62	Diana	Sujew	GER	2.11.90	5	NA	Heusden-Zolder	13 Jul
4:05.64	Brianna	Felnagle	USA	9.12.86	6	NA	Heusden-Zolder	13 Jul
4:05.66	Violah	Lagat	KEN	1.3.89	3	GS	Ostrava	27 Jun
4:05.69	Amela	Terzic	SRB	2.4.93	1	EU23	Tampere	14 Jul
4:05.82	Mercy	Cherono	KEN	7.5.91	2	VD	Bruxelles	6 Sep
4:05.83mp	Emma	Jackson	GBR	7.6.88	2		Watford	4 Sep
4:05.89	Julia	Lucas	USA	4.3.84	5		Los Angeles (ER)	17 May
4:05.91	Anna	Shchagina	RUS	7.12.91	4	NC	Moskva	25 Jul
4:06.19	Kalkidan	Gezahegne	ETH	8.5.91	4	GS	Ostrava	27 Jun
	(50)							
4:06.20	Natalia	Rodríguez	ESP	2.6.79	11	Herc	Monaco	19 Jul
4:06.22	Tugba	Koyuncu	TUR	16.2.91	3	MedG	Mersin	26 Jun
4:06.34	Margherita	Magnani	ITA	26.2.87	4	MedG	Mersin	26 Jun
4:06.39	Renata	Plis	POL	5.2.85	11	GGala	Roma	6 Jun
4:06.50	Maureen	Koster	NED	3.7.92	2		Nijmegen	12 Jun
4:06.60	Corinna	Harrer	GER	19.1.91	6	GS	Ostrava	27 Jun
4:06.67	Cory	McGee	USA	29.5.92	7	NA	Heusden-Zolder	13 Jul
4:06.69	Halima	Hachlaf	MAR	6.9.88	5		Rabat	9 Jun
4:06.87	Emma	Coburn	USA	19.10.90	8		Los Angeles (ER)	17 May
4:07.17	Kim	Conley	USA	14.3.86	9		Los Angeles (ER)	17 May
	(60)							
4:07.27	Gudaf	Tsegay	ETH-Y	23.1.97	1		Ninove	27 Jul
4:07.31	Maryam	Jamal	BRN	16.9.84	12	Herc	Monaco	19 Jul
4:07.32	Sonja	Roman	SLO	11.3.79	8	NA	Heusden-Zolder	13 Jul
4:07.36	Kate	Van Buskirk	CAN	9.6.87	6s2	WCh	Moskva	13 Aug
4:07.40	Kate	Grace	USA	24.10.88	1		Lignano	16 Jul
4:07.51	Hilary	Stellingwerff	CAN	7.8.81	1		Burnaby	1 Jul
4:07.63	Anna	Konovalova	RUS	4.7.88	6	NC	Moskva	25 Jul
4:07.67	Gemeda	Feyne	ETH	28.6.92	9	GS	Ostrava	27 Jun
4:07.70	Isabel	Macías	ESP	11.8.84	5		Sotteville-lès-Rouen	8 Jul
4:07.76	Laura	Muir	GBR	9.5.93	8	DL	Birmingham	30 Jun
	(70)							
4:08.09	Renee	Tomlin	USA	21.11.88	10		Los Angeles (ER)	17 May
4:08.09	Molly	Huddle	USA	31.8.84	4		Lignano	16 Jul
4:08.25	Heather	Wilson	USA	13.6.90	5		Lignano	16 Jul
4:08.30mx	Stephanie	Twell	GBR	17.8.89	1mx		Watford	21 Aug
4:08.37	Heather	Kampf	USA	19.1.87	1		Oordegem	6 Jul
4:08.43A	Tabitha	Wambui	KEN	29.12.83	4	WCT	Nairobi	13 Jul
4:08.49	Morgan	Uceny	USA	10.3.85	7	adidas	New York	25 May
4:08.51	Jemma	Simpson	GBR	10.2.84	11		Los Angeles (ER)	17 May
4:08.59	Nelly	Jepkosgei	KEN	14.7.91	3		Beijing	21 May
4:08.65	Yelena	Kobeleva	RUS	12.6.88	5	NCp	Yerino	15 Jun
	(80)							
4:08.77	Chelsea	Reilly	USA	9.5.89	6		Lignano	16 Jul
4:08.78	Tereza	Capková	CZE	24.7.87	10	GS	Ostrava	27 Jun
4:08.80	Ioana	Doagâ	ROU	5.4.92	4	EU23	Tampere	14 Jul
4:08.81	Yekaterina	Kupina	RUS	2.2.86	7	NC	Moskva	25 Jul
4:08.82	Elina	Sujew	GER	2.11.90	4		Bottrop	19 Jul
4:09.00	Dawit	Seyoum	ETH-Y	27.7.96	1		Reduit	31 Aug
4:09.06	Yuliya	Chizhenko	RUS	30.8.79	1		Sochi	25 May
4:09.06	Esma	Aydemir	TUR	1.1.92	5	MedG	Mersin	26 Jun
4:09.13	Lea	Wallace	USA	19.12.88	8		Lausanne	4 Jul
4:09.21	Elena	Romagnolo	ITA	5.10.82	7		Lignano	16 Jul
	(90)							
4:09.45	Sanae	El Otmani	MAR	20.12.86	1		Rabat	1 Jun
4:09.57	Natalja	Piliusina	LTU	22.10.90	4	Jordan	Stanford	28 Apr
4:09.64	Kerri	Gallagher	USA	31.5.89	1		Victoria	5 Jul
4:09.64	Christine	Bardelle	FRA	16.8.74	1		Gent	3 Aug
4:09.67	Eilish	McColgan	GBR	25.11.90	1	LI	Loughborough	19 May
4:09.75	Rosibel	García	COL	13.2.81	1	Bol G	Trujillo	26 Nov
4:09.79	Muriel	Coneo	COL	15.3.87	2	Bol G	Trujillo	26 Nov
4:09.90	Rosemary	Wanjiru	KEN-J	9.12.94	1		Oita	31 Jul
4:09.95	Geena	Gall	USA	18.1.87	2		Victoria	5 Jul
4:09.98	Yelena	Tumayeva	RUS	24.8.89	8	NC	Moskva	25 Jul
	(100)							

4:10.00	Danuta	Urbanik	POL	24.12.89	10 Jun		4:10.04	Katarzyna	Broniatowska	POL	22.2.90	15 Jun
4:10.00	Giulia Alessandra Viola		ITA	24.4.91	26 Jun		4:10.08	Ayako	Jinnouchi	JPN	21.1.87	3 Aug
4:10.01	Nikki	Hamblin	NZL	20.5.88	5 Jul		4:10.29	Genevieve	LaCaze	AUS	4.8.89	15 Jun

Mark	Name		Nat	Born	Pos	Meet	Venue	Date
4:10.34	Natalya	Aristarkhova	RUS	31.10.89				11 Jun
4:10.35	Janet	Achola	UGA	26.6.88				16 Jul
4:10.37	Tigist	Gashaw	ETH-Y	25.12.96				9 Jun
4:10.42	Svetlana	Belova	RUS	24.5.85				25 May
4:10.43	Josephine	Moultrie	GBR	19.11.90				16 Jul
4:10.48	Kaltoum	Bouaasayriya	MAR	23.8.82				1 Jun
4:10.49	Gulnara	Galkina	RUS	9.7.78				25 May
4:10.5A	Margaret	Muriuki	KEN	21.3.86				22 Jun
4:10.53	Rachel	Schneider	USA	18.7.91				28 Apr
4:10.55	Kelly	Hetherington	AUS	10.3.89				9 Mar
4:10.55	Anna	Rostkowska	POL	26.7.80				27 Jun
4:10.64	Perine	Nengampi	KEN	1.1.89				3 Aug
4:10.69	Olga	Golovkina ¶	RUS	17.12.86				15 Jun
4:10.77	Alfiya	Muryasova	RUS	3.10.88				11 Jun
4:10.78	Kaila	McKnight	AUS	5.5.86				6 Apr
4:10.79	Amanda	Winslow	USA	10.12.90				28 Apr
4:10.98	Annett	Horna	GER	4.2.87				27 Jun
4:11.16	Hiwot	Ayalew	ETH	6.3.90				1 Sep
4:11.27	Agata	Strausa	LAT	2.12.89				28 Apr
4:11.33	Angelika	Cichocka	POL	15.3.88				21 Jun
4:11.35	Claire	Tarplee	IRL	22.9.88				15 Jun
4:11.35	Tatyana	Gudkova	RUS	26.3.85				25 Jul
4:11.44mx	Morag	MacLarty	GBR	10.2.86				4 Jun
4:12.91								19 May
4:11.49	Yuliya	Vasilyeva	RUS	23.3.87				3 Jul
4:11.51	Emily	Infeld	USA	21.3.90				1 Sep
4:11.62	Hillary	Holt	USA	24.4.92				3 May
4:11.65	Darya	Yachmeneva	RUS	9.9.90				25 Jul
4:11.72	Angela	Smit	NZL	16.8.91				12 Jul
4:11.73	Eliza	Curnow	AUS	3.3.92				9 Mar
4:11.77	Olena	Zhushman #	UKR	30.12.85				23 Jun
4:11.80	Nicole	Schappert	USA	30.10.86				17 May
4:11.82	Ashley	Higginson	USA	17.3.89				13 Jul
4:11.94	Abbey	D'Agostino	USA	25.5.92				5 May
4:12.0A	Susan	Cherotich	KEN	.87				4 May
4:12.0A	Sheila	Keter	KEN-J	27.6.95				22 Jun
4:12.05	Sofia	Ennaoui	POL-J	30.8.95				15 Jun
4:12.06	Laura	Crowe	IRL	29.11.87				1 Sep
4:12.10	Beverly	Ramos	PUR	24.8.87				19 Apr
4:12.14	Rebecca	Tracy	USA	20.2.91				5 Jul
4:12.15	Carly	Hamilton	USA	15.2.93				27 Apr
4:12.17	Emily	Lipari	USA	19.11.92				11 Jun
4:12.32		Zhao Jing	CHN	9.7.88				8 Sep
4:12.33	Almensch	Belete	BEL	28.7.89				13 Jul
4:12.41	Anna	Balakshina	RUS	22.11.85				3 Jul
4:12.51	Maren	Kock	GER	22.6.90				15 May
4:12.54	Svetlana	Uloga	RUS	11.3.86				25 Jul
4:12.61	Janeth	Jepkosgei	KEN	13.12.83				10 May
4:12.68	Agnes	Tirop	KEN-J	23.10.95				11 Jun
4:12.68	Olesya	Mikheyeva	RUS	23.7.81				3 Jul
4:12.85	Sultana	Aït Hammou	MAR	10.5.80				1 Jun
4:12.93	Helen	Hofstede	NED	31.12.80				3 Aug
4:12.96	Elena	García	ESP	19.6.86				13 Jul
4:12.98	Ayvika	Malanova	RUS	28.11.92				26 Jun
4:13.0A	Stacy	Ndiwa	KEN	6.12.92				24 May
4:13.02	Kseniya	Kozhedub	RUS	11.8.92				2 Jun
4:13.09	Natalya	Koreyvo	BLR	14.11.85				4 Jun
4:13.12	Azemra	Gebru	ETH	5.5.92				11 Jun
4:13.21	Pilar	McShine	TTO	6.1.87				27 Jun
4:13.33	Stephanie	Garcia	USA	3.5.88				13 Jul
4:13.44	Alemitu	Hawi	ETH-Y	14.11.96				13 Jul
4:13.46	Selah	Busienei	KEN	27.12.91				15 Jun
4:13.53	Laura	Roxberg	USA	20.11.89				27 Apr
4:13.61	Kelly	Williams	USA					11 May
4:13.62	Tatyana	Suprun	BLR	16.2.86				11 Jun
4:13.63	Katrina	Coogan	USA	15.11.93				11 May
4:13.64	Shelby	Houlihan	USA	8.2.93				6 Apr
4:13.64	Kristine Eikrem	Engeset	NOR	15.11.88				27 Jul
4:13.67		Liu Chang	CHN	25.2.90				21 May
4:13.74	Alison	Leonard	GBR	17.3.90				24 Aug
4:13.75	Charlotta	Fougberg	SWE	19.6.85				15 Jun
(176)								

Indoors

Mark	Name		Nat	Born	Pos	Meet	Venue	Date
3:58.40i		Aregawi			1		Stockholm	21 Feb
4:00.83i		Dibaba			1	GP	Birmingham	16 Feb
4:02.25i		Dibaba			1		Karlsruhe	2 Feb
4:11.36	Almensch	Belete	BEL	28.7.89				10 Feb
4:11.47	Marina	Pospelova	RUS	23.7.90				14 Feb
4:12.41	Natalya	Koreyvo	BLR	14.11.85				1 Mar
4:12.48	Marusa	Mismas	SLO-J	24.10.94				29 Jan
4:13.49	Sara	Moreira	POR	17.10.85				16 Feb

Drugs disqualification

Mark	Name		Nat	Born	Pos	Meet	Venue	Date
4:09.06	Yekaterina	Ishova ¶	RUS	17.1.89	(1)	Chall	Moskva	11 Jun
4:07.65i	Anzhela	Shevchenko ¶	UKR	29.10.87	(1)		Sankt-Peterburg	24 Jan

JUNIORS

See main list for top 7 juniors. 14 performances by 5 women to 4:07.3. Additional marks and further juniors:

Kipyegon 2+	4:04.83	2s1	WCh	Moskva	13 Aug		4:05.31	7	GGala	Roma	6 Jun
	4:05.08	5	WCh	Moskva	15 Aug		4:07.00A	2	WCT	Nairobi	13 Jul
Teferi	4:05.35	3	NA	Heusden-Zolder	13 Jul						
Cain	4:05.21	4s1	WCh	Moskva	13 Aug						
Embaye	4:06.03	3		Sotteville-lès-Rouen	8 Jul		4:07.29	10	WCh	Moskva	15 Aug

Mark	Name			Nat	Born	Pos	Meet	Venue	Date
4:10.37	Tigist	Gashaw (10)		ETH-Y	25.12.96	9		Rabat	9 Jun
4:12.0A	Sheila	Keter		KEN	27.6.95	5		Nairobi	22 Jun
4:12.05	Sofia	Ennaoui		POL	30.8.95	5	Kuso	Szczecin	15 Jun
4:12.68	Agnes	Tirop		KEN	23.10.95	1		Bellinzona	11 Jun
4:13.44	Alemitu	Hawi		ETH-Y	14.11.96	2rB	KBC	Heusden-Zolder	13 Jul
4:13.81	Nataliya	Pryshchepa		UKR	11.9.94	2		Yalta	5 Jun
4:13.97	Haftamnesh	Tesfay		ETH	28.4.94	3rB	KBC	Heusden-Zolder	13 Jul
4:14.40	Georgie	Peel		GBR	26.5.94	1		Tallahassee	13 Apr
4:14.43	Jessica	Judd		GBR	7.1.95	3		Pavia	5 May
4:15.07	Elise	Cranny		USA-Y	8.5.96	3rB	Jordan	Stanford	28 Apr
4:15.91	Sara	Edeo (20)		ETH-Y	8.4.96	7		Padova	1 Sep
4:12.48i	Marusa	Mismas		SLO	24.10.94	2		Wien	29 Jan

1 MILE

Mark	Name		Nat	Born	Pos	Meet	Venue	Date
4:28.50	Nancy	Langat	KEN	22.8.81	1	PennR	Philadelphia	27 Apr
4:30.44	Brianna	Felnagle	USA	9.12.83				17 Jul
4:30.95	Hilary	Stellingwerff	CAN	7.8.81				17 Jul
4:32.89	Ioana	Doagă	ROU	5.4.92				17 Jul
4:34.47	Ashley	Higginson	USA	17.3.89				17 Jul

irregular kerb

Mark	Name		Nat	Born	Pos	Meet	Venue	Date
4:27.13	Susan	Kuijken	NED	8.7.86	1		San Diego	5 May
4:28.90	Brianna	Felnagle	USA	9.12.83	2		San Diego	5 May
4:30.60	Katie	Mackey	USA	12.11.87				5 May
4:30.76	Zoe	Buckman	AUS	21.12.88				5 May
4:32.06	Lea	Wallace	USA	19.12.88				5 May

WOMEN 2013

Mark	Name		Nat	Born	Pos	Meet	Venue	Date
Indoors								
4:27.02	Sheila	Reid	CAN	2.8.89	1	Mill	New York (Armory)	16 Feb
4:28.25	Mary	Cain	USA-Y	3.5.96	2	Mill	New York (Armory)	16 Feb
4:28.79	Kate	Grace	USA	24.10.88	3	Mill	New York (Armory)	16 Feb
4:29.86	Emma	Coburn	USA	19.10.90	4	Mill	New York (Armory)	16 Feb
4:30.03	Abbey	D'Agostino	USA	25.5.92	5	Mill	New York (Armory)	16 Feb
4:30.50	Hilary	Stellingwerff	CAN	7.8.81				16 Feb
4:31.08	Amanda	Winslow	USA	13.8.90				9 Mar
4:31.26	Sarah	Brown	USA	15.10.86				16 Feb
4:31.50	Emily	Infeld	USA	21.3.90				16 Feb
4:31.65	Nicole	Sifuentes	CAN	30.6.86				26 Jan
4:31.75 #	Geena	Gall	USA	18.1.87				9 Feb
4:32.10 #	Cory	McGee	USA	29.5.92				9 Feb
4:32.26 #	Natalja	Piliusina	LTU	22.10.90				9 Feb
4:33.06 #	Lauren	Johnson	USA	4.5.87				9 Feb
4:33.53 #	Rebecca	Tracy	USA	20.2.91				2 Mar
4:33.88	Yelena	Soboleva	RUS	3.10.82				1 Feb
4:34.06	Svetlana	Podosyonova	RUS	24.5.88				1 Feb
4:34.19	Jillian	King	USA	21.3.90				14 Feb
4:34.30	Anna	Shchagina	RUS	7.12.91				1 Feb

JUNIORS

Mark	Name		Nat	Born	Pos	Meet	Venue	Date
4:39.17	Wesley	Frazier	USA	.95	1	adidas	New York	25 May

2000 METRES

Mark	Name		Nat	Born	Pos	Meet	Venue	Date
5:38.37	Susan	Kuijken	NED	8.7.86	1	Flame	Amsterdam	31 Aug
5:38.53	Mimi	Belete	BRN	9.6.88	2	Flame	Amsterdam	31 Aug
5:39.17	Zoe	Buckman	AUS	21.12.88	3	Flame	Amsterdam	31 Aug
5:40.70	Kate	Van Buskirk	CAN	9.6.87	4	Flame	Amsterdam	31 Aug
5:44.22	Laura	Weightman	GBR	1.7.91	5	Flame	Amsterdam	31 Aug
5:45.20+	Gabriele	Anderson	USA	25.6.86	6			Jul
5:47.06+	Meseret	Defar	ETH	19.11.83	22			Aug
5:47.16+	Mercy	Cherono	KEN	7.5.91				8 Sep
5:48.38+	Tirunesh	Dibaba	ETH	1.10.85				1 Jun
Indoors								
5:37.2+	Genzebe	Dibaba	ETH	8.2.91	1	in 3000	Stockholm	21 Feb
5:44.08	Svetlana	Kireyeva	RUS	12.6.87	1		Yekaterinburg	7 Jan
5:46.36	Yelena	Soboleva	RUS	3.10.82	7 Jan			
5:46.72+	Meseret	Defar	ETH	19.11.83	2 Feb			
5:47.26+	Tirunesh	Dibaba	ETH	1.10.85				2 Feb
5:48.82	Anna	Shchagina	RUS	7.12.91				7 Jan

JUNIOR: 5:48.65 Agnes Tirop KEN-J 23.10.95 6 Flame Amsterdam 31 Aug

3000 METRES

Mark	Name		Nat	Born	Pos	Meet	Venue	Date
8:30.29	Meseret	Defar	ETH	19.11.83	1	DNG	Stockholm	22 Aug
8:31.23	Mercy	Cherono	KEN	7.5.91	2	DNG	Stockholm	22 Aug
8:32.53	Sifan	Hassan	ETH/NED	.93	3	DNG	Stockholm	22 Aug
8:33.97	Viola	Kibiwot	KEN	22.12.83	4	DNG	Stockholm	22 Aug
8:34.05	Gladys	Cherono	KEN	12.5.83	5	DNG	Stockholm	22 Aug
8:34.25	Hellen	Obiri	KEN	13.12.89	6	DNG	Stockholm	22 Aug
8:34.43	Shannon	Rowbury	USA	19.9.84	7	DNG	Stockholm	22 Aug
8:35.97		M Cherono			1		Rieti	8 Sep
8:37.00	Genzebe	Dibaba	ETH	8.2.91	8	DNG	Stockholm	22 Aug
8:37.47	Sylvia	Kibet	KEN	28.3.84	2		Rieti	8 Sep
8:39.13	Agnes	Tirop (10)	KEN-J	23.10.95	3		Rieti	8 Sep
8:39.65	Susan	Kuijken	NED	8.7.86	4		Rieti	8 Sep
8:40.42	Renata	Plis	POL	5.2.85	9	DNG	Stockholm	22 Aug
8:40.53+	Almaz	Ayana	ETH	21.11.91	1	in 5000	Saint-Denis	6 Jul
8:40.7+	Tirunesh	Dibaba	ETH	1.10.85	2	in 5000	Saint-Denis	6 Jul
8:41.43	Emily	Infeld	USA	21.3.90	5		Rieti	8 Sep
(16/15)								
8:42.64	Gabriele	Anderson	USA	25.6.86	2	DL	London (OS)	26 Jul
8:42.99	Molly	Huddle	USA	31.8.84	3	DL	London (OS)	26 Jul
8:43.46mx	Laura	Weightman	GBR	1.7.91	1		Manchester (Str)	14 May
8:44.02	Sheila	Reid	CAN	2.8.89	4	DL	London (OS)	26 Jul
8:46.89	Jordan	Hasay	USA	21.9.91	5	DL	London (OS)	26 Jul
(20)								
8:47.34	Chelsea	Reilly	USA	9.5.89	6		Rieti	8 Sep
8:47.68	Diana	Sujew	GER	2.11.90	7		Rieti	8 Sep
8:47.79	Eilish	McColgan	GBR	25.11.90	8		Rieti	8 Sep
8:47.95	Kim	Conley	USA	14.3.86	6	DL	London (OS)	26 Jul
8:48.10+	Janet	Kisa	KEN	5.3.92	+	in 5000	Oslo	13 Jun
8:48.37	Tejitu	Daba	BRN	20.8.91	1		Nijmegen	12 Jun
8:49e+	Margaret	Muriuki	KEN	21.3.86		in 5000	Oslo	13 Jun
8:49.32	Rosemary	Wanjiru	KEN-J	9.12.94	1		Oita	3 Aug
8:50.17mx	Stephanie	Twell	GBR	17.8.89	1mx		Watford	4 Sep
8:58.57					13	DL	London (OS)	26 Ju
8:50.40	Alemitu	Haroye	ETH-J	9.5.95	2		Nijmegen	12 Jur
(30)								
8:50.?+e	Hiwot	Ayalew	ETH	6.3.90		in 5000	Eugene	1 Jur
8:51.60	Perine	Nengampi	KEN	1.1.89	1		Lapinlahti	21 Ju
8:51.70	Almensch	Belete	BEL	26.7.89	9		Rieti	8 Sep

Outdoor

Mark	Name	Nat	Born	Pos	Meet	Venue	Date
8:51.73	Nadia Noujani	MAR	3.9.81	1		Fès	11 May
8:52.06	Habiba Ghribi	TUN	9.4.84	1		Franconville	28 Apr
8:52.34	Violah Lagat	KEN	1.3.89	10		Rieti	8 Sep
8:52.59	Brianna Felnagle	USA	9.12.86	8	DL	London (OS)	26 Jul
8:55.51	Salami Alima El Ouali	MAR	29.12.83	2		Fès	11 May
8:55.59	Emelia Gorecka	GBR-J	29.1.94	10	DL	London (OS)	26 Jul
8:55.89mx	Fionnuala Britton (40)	IRL	24.9.84	4		Letterkenny	18 May
8:56.20	Irene Cheptai	KEN	4.2.92	11	DL	London (OS)	26 Jul
8:56.42	Dolores Checa	ESP	27.12.82	12	DL	London (OS)	26 Jul
8:56.73	Ruti Aga	ETH-J	16.1.94	3		Nijmegen	12 Jun
8:57.56	Elina Sujew	GER	2.11.90				12 May
8:57.63mx	Laura Whittle	GBR	27.6.85				6 Aug
8:57.75	Viktoriya Pogoryelska	UKR	4.8.90				7 Jun
8:58.0	Zoe Buckman	AUS	21.12.88				21 Mar
8:58.55	Meraf Bahta	ERI	26.6.89				21 Jul
8:58.60	Julie Culley	USA	10.9.81				11 Jun
8:58.74	Lilian Rengruk	KEN-Y	3.5.97				10 Jul
8:58.90mx	Kate Avery	GBR	10.10.91				26 Jun
9:02.48							
8:59.41	Katie Mackey	USA	12.11.87				8 Sep
8:59.60	Maryiam Waithera	KEN-Y	23.12.96				8 Oct
8:59.90	Beverly Ramos	PUR	24.8.87				14 Jun
9:00.06	Berhan Demiesa	ETH-Y	3.1.97				10 Jul
9:00.25	Margherita Magnani	ITA	26.2.87				3 Jun
9:00.77	Roxana Bârca ¶	ROU	22.6.88				12 Jun
9:01.45	Yelena Korobkina	RUS	25.11.90				22 Jun
9:01.47	Susan Wairimu	KEN	11.10.92				14 Sep
9:01.56	Dominika Nowakowska	POL	25.1.85				2 Jul
9:01.63	Silenat Yismaw	ETH-Y	19.3.97				10 Jul
9:02.15mx	Katrina Wootton	GBR	2.9.85				8 May
9:02.15	Beatrice Wainaina	KEN	20.11.93				3 Jul
9:02.43	Kaltoum Bouaasayriya	MAR	23.8.82				12 Jun
9:02.73	Yuka Ando	JPN-J	16.3.94				21 Sep
9:03.20	Iris Fuentes-Pila	ESP	10.8.80				22 Jun
9:03.28	Sandra Eriksson	FIN	4.6.89				21 Jul
9:03.42	Lisa Dobriskey	GBR	23.12.83				19 May
9:03.52	Akari Okinada	JPN-J	26.1.94				21 Sep
9:03.55	Corinna Harrer	GER	19.1.91				22 Jun
9:03.73	Mary Waithera	KEN-J	12.12.94				29 Jun
9:04.67	Jip Vastenburg	NED-J	21.3.94				12 Jun

Indoors

Mark	Name	Nat	Born	Pos	Meet	Venue	Date
8:26.95	Genzebe Dibaba	ETH	8.2.91	1		Stockholm	21 Feb
8:35.28	Defar			1		Karlsruhe	2 Feb
8:38.44+	Tirunesh Dibaba	ETH	1.10.85	1	in 2M	Boston (Roxbury)	2 Feb
8:48.27	Svetlana Kireyeva	RUS	12.6.87	1	NC	Moskva	12 Feb
8:50.16	Helen Clitheroe	GBR	2.1.74	1	GP	Birmingham	16 Feb
8:50.42	Yelena Korobkina	RUS	25.11.90	2	NC	Moskva	12 Feb
8:50.76	Natalya Aristarkhova	RUS	31.10.89	3	NC	Moskva	12 Feb
8:51.04	Corinna Harrer	GER	19.1.91	2		Karlsruhe	2 Feb
8:52.00	Lauren Howarth	GBR	21.4.90	2	GP	Birmingham	16 Feb
8:52.48	Sara Moreira	POR	17.10.85	1		Eaubonne	7 Feb
8:52.86	Ancuta Bobocel	ROU	3.10.87	3	GP	Birmingham	16 Feb
8:53.12	Siham Hilali	MAR	2.5.86	4		Stockholm	21 Feb
8:54.37	Fionnuala Britton	IRL	24.9.84	5		Stockholm	21 Feb
8:55.06 #	Kate Grace	USA	24.10.88	2		Seattle	26 Jan
8:55.41 #	Abbey D'Agostino	USA	25.5.92	3		Seattle	26 Jan
8:56.06	Polina Jelizarova	LAT	1.5.89	6		Stockholm	21 Feb
8:57.01	Christine Bardelle	FRA	16.8.74				7 Feb
8:57.17	Layes Abdullayeva	AZE	29.5.91				2 Feb
8:57.80	Natalya Leontyeva	RUS	5.7.87				12 Feb
8:58.32	Rabab Arrafi	MAR	12.1.91				24 Feb
8:59.38	Emily Stewart	GBR	24.12.91				16 Feb
8:59.50	Haftamnesh Tesfay	ETH-J	28.4.94				7 Feb
8:59.98 #	Cally McCumber	USA	19.8.90				9 Feb
9:00.06	Jessica Judd	GBR-J	7.1.95				16 Feb
9:00.34	Mekdes Bekele	ETH	20.1.87				7 Feb
9:00.88	Gete Dima	ETH	10.3.92				21 Feb
9:02.10 #	Mary Cain	USA-Y	3.5.96				12 Jan
9:02.14	Dudu Karakaya	TUR	11.11.85				23 Feb
9:02.28	Nancy Chepkwemoi	KEN	8.10.93				16 Feb
9:02.35	Laura Muir	GBR	9.5.93				3 Jan
9:02.57 #	Natasha Fraser	CAN	17.12.81				9 Feb
9:02.96 #	Tara Erdmann	USA	14.6.89				12 Jan
9:03.29	Silvia Weissteiner	ITA	13.7.79				17 Feb
9:03.54 #	Treniere Moser	USA	27.10.81				12 Jan
9:03.95 #	Frances Koons	USA	2.4.86				9 Feb
9:04.40 +	Nicole Sifuentes	CAN	30.6.86				2 Feb

JUNIORS

See main list for top 5 juniors. 5 performances 5 women to 8:57.0. Additional marks and further juniors:

Mark	Name	Nat	Born	Pos	Meet	Venue	Date
8:58.74	Lilian Rengruk	KEN-Y	3.5.97	1	WY	Donetsk	10 Jul
8:59.60	Maryiam Waithera	KEN-Y	23.12.96	1		Tokyo (Chofu)	8 Oct
9:00.06	Berhan Demiesa	ETH-Y	3.1.97	2	WY	Donetsk	10 Jul
9:01.63	Silenat Yismaw	ETH-Y	19.3.97	3	WY	Donetsk	10 Jul
9:02.73	Yuka Ando (10)	JPN	16.3.94	1		Fukuroi	21 Sep
9:03.52	Akari Okinada	JPN	26.1.94	1		Kumagaya	21 Sep
9:03.73	Mary Waithera	KEN	12.12.94	1		Fukagawa	29 Jun
9:04.67	Jip Vastenburg	NED	21.3.94	5		Nijmegen	12 Jun
9:05.20	Saki Yoshimizu	JPN	13.7.95	2		Tokyo (Chofu)	8 Oct
9:06.22	Hiwot Mesfin	ETH	11.5.95	3		Dakar	12 Jun
9:06.97	Hanami Sekine	JPN-Y	26.2.96	1		Yokohama	30 Nov
9:07.11	Azusa Sumi	JPN-Y	12.8.96	1		Toyokawa	22 Sep
9:07.58	Miyuki Uehara	JPN	22.11.95	3	N.Sch	Oita	2 Aug
9:07.97	Maki Izumida	JPN-Y	22.1.96	4	N.Sch	Oita	2 Aug

Indoors

Mark	Name	Nat	Born	Pos	Meet	Venue	Date
8:59.50	Haftamnesh Tesfay	ETH	28.4.94	5		Eaubonne	7 Feb
9:00.06	Jessica Judd	GBR	7.1.95	8	GP	Birmingham	16 Feb
9:02.10 #	Mary Cain	USA-Y	3.5.96	1		Seattle	12 Jan

Mark	Name		Nat	Born	Pos	Meet	Venue			Date

2 MILES INDOORS

Mark	Name		Nat	Born	Pos	Meet	Venue			Date
9:13.17	Tirunesh	Dibaba	ETH	1.10.85	1	BIG	Boston (Roxbury)			2 Feb
9:37.97	Sheila	Reid	CAN	2.8.89	2	BIG	Boston (Roxbury)			2 Feb
9:38.68	Mary	Cain	USA-Y	3.5.96	2 Feb	9:39.48	Tara	Erdmann	USA 14.6.89	2 Feb
9:38.78	Nicole	Sifuentes	CAN	30.6.86	2 Feb	9:41.59	Sarah	Brown	USA 15.10.86	2 Feb

5000 METRES

Mark	Name		Nat	Born	Pos	Meet	Venue	Date
14:23.68	Tirunesh	Dibaba	ETH	1.10.85	1	DL	Saint-Denis	6 Ju
14:25.84	Almaz	Ayana	ETH	21.11.91	2	DL	Saint-Denis	6 Ju
14:26.90	Meseret	Defar	ETH	19.11.83	1	Bisl	Oslo	13 Jur
14:32.83		Defar			1	WK	Zürich	29 Aug
14:33.48	Viola	Kibiwot	KEN	22.12.83	2	Bisl	Oslo	13 Jur
14:34.82		T Dibaba			2	WK	Zürich	29 Aug
14:37.68	Genzebe	Dibaba	ETH	8.2.91	3	Bisl	Oslo	13 Jur
14:40.33	Mercy	Cherono	KEN	7.5.91	3	WK	Zürich	29 Aug
14:40.48	Margaret	Muriuki	KEN	21.3.86	4	Bisl	Oslo	13 Jur
14:42.01		T Dibaba			1	Pre	Eugene	1 Jur
14:42.07	Gelete	Burka	ETH	15.2.86	3	DL	Saint-Denis	6 Ju
14:42.43		M Cherono			5	Bisl	Oslo	13 Jur
14:42.51		M Cherono			2	Pre	Eugene	1 Jur
14:43.68		Muriuki			3	Pre	Eugene	1 Jur
14:45.92		G Dibaba			1	DL	Shanghai	18 May
14:46.89	Emily	Chebet	KEN	18.2.86	4	WK	Zürich	29 Aug
14:47.12	Gladys	Cherono (10)	KEN	12.5.83	5	WK	Zürich	29 Aug
14:47.76		Defar			2	DL	Shanghai	18 May
14:48.29		Kibiwot			3	DL	Shanghai	18 May
14:49.84		M Cherono			4	DL	Shanghai	18 May
14:49.92		Muriuki			5	DL	Shanghai	18 May
14:50.02	Buze	Diriba	ETH-J	9.2.94	6	Bisl	Oslo	13 Jur
14:50.19		Defar			1	WCh	Moskva	17 Aug
14:50.24		Diriba			6	DL	Shanghai	18 May
14:50.36	Agnes	Tirop	KEN-J	23.10.95	7	Bisl	Oslo	13 Jur
14:50.99	Irene	Cheptai	KEN	4.2.92	7	DL	Shanghai	18 May
14:51.15		Diriba			4	Pre	Eugene	1 Jur
14:51.22		M Cherono			2	WCh	Moskva	17 Aug
14:51.33		Ayana			3	WCh	Moskva	17 Aug
14:52.42		Ayana			1	FBK	Hengelo	8 Jur
	(30/13)							
14:56.26	Jennifer	Simpson	USA	23.8.86	7	WK	Zürich	29 Aug
14:57.02	Hiwot	Ayalew	ETH	6.3.90	6	Pre	Eugene	1 Jur
14:58.15	Molly	Huddle	USA	31.8.84	10	WK	Zürich	29 Aug
14:58.26	Sylvia	Kibet	KEN	28.3.84	11	WK	Zürich	29 Aug
14:59.74	Sule	Utura	ETH	8.2.90	4	DL	Saint-Denis	6 Ju
15:01.51	Beleynesh	Oljira	ETH	26.6.90	7	Pre	Eugene	1 Jur
15:02.56mx	Kimberly	Smith	NZL	19.11.81	1		Waltham	11 May
	(20)							
15:02.90	Azemra	Gebru	ETH	5.5.92	10	DL	Shanghai	18 May
15:02.98	Linet	Masai	KEN	5.12.89	8	Pre	Eugene	1 Jur
15:03.13	Shitaye	Eshete	BRN	21.5.90	6	FBK	Hengelo	8 Jur
15:04.36	Susan	Kuijken	NED	8.7.86	11	Bisl	Oslo	13 Jur
15:04.38	Genet	Yalew	ETH	31.12.92	12	Bisl	Oslo	13 Jur
15:05.08	Alemitu	Haroye	ETH-J	9.5.95	7	FBK	Hengelo	8 Jur
15:05.89	Janet	Kisa	KEN	5.3.92	11	DL	Shanghai	18 May
15:06.10	Shannon	Rowbury	USA	19.9.84	7	WCh	Moskva	17 Aug
15:08.11	Tejitu	Daba	BRN	20.8.91	9	FBK	Hengelo	8 Jur
15:09.57	Kim	Conley	USA	14.3.86	9	Pre	Eugene	1 Jur
	(30)							
15:09.59	Amy	Hastings	USA	21.1.84	1		Waltham	8 Jur
15:09.73	Alisha	Williams	USA	5.2.82	1		Stanford	29 Ma
15:10.14	Chelsea	Reilly	USA	9.5.89	12	WK	Zürich	29 Aug
15:11.00	Treniere	Moser	USA	27.10.81	2		Los Angeles (ER)	17 May
15:11.12	Gotytom	Gebresilase	ETH-J	15.1.95	13	DL	Shanghai	18 May
15:11.35	Abbey	D'Agostino	USA	25.5.92	1	MSR	Walnut	19 Ap
15:12.05	Betsy	Saina	KEN	30.6.88	2		Stanford	29 Ma
15:12.09	Jacqueline	Areson	AUS	31.3.88	9	DL	Saint-Denis	6 Ju
15:12.26	Almensch	Belete	BEL	26.7.89	2		Ninove	27 Ju
15:12.84	Betlhem	Desalegn	UAE	13.11.91	1	AsiC	Pune	7 Ju
	(40)							
15:13.48	Ruti	Aga	ETH-J	16.1.94	14	DL	Shanghai	18 Ma
15:14.12	Selly	Chepyego	KEN	3.10.85	1		Isahaya	22 Jur

Mark	Name		Nat	Born	Pos	Meet	Venue	Date
15:14.33	Brianna	Felnagle	USA	9.12.86	3		Los Angeles (ER)	17 May
15:14.57	Sophie	Duarte	FRA	31.7.81	10	DL	Saint-Denis	6 Jul
15:16.11	Dominika	Nowakowska	POL	25.1.85	1		Watford	30 Jun
15:16.27mx	Karoline Bjerkeli	Grøvdal	NOR	14.6.90	1mx		Oslo	8 Jul
15:27.31					14	Bisl	Oslo	13 Jun
15:17.43	Grace	Kimanzi	KEN	1.3.92	1		Kumagaya	21 Sep
15:17.51	Magdalene	Masai	KEN	4.4.93	15	DL	Shanghai	18 May
15:17.72	Dolores	Checa	ESP	27.12.82	1		Liège (NX)	10 Jul
15:18.60	Stephanie	Twell	GBR	17.8.89	11	DL	Saint-Denis	6 Jul
	(50)							
15:18.86	Aliphine	Tuliamok-Bolton	KEN	5.4.89	4		Stanford	29 Mar
15:20.38	Afera	Godfay	ETH	25.9.91	12	DL	Saint-Denis	6 Jul
15:20.42	Alfiya	Muryasova	RUS	3.10.88	1	NCp	Yerino	16 Jun
15:20.49	Susan	Wairimu	KEN	11.10.92	2		Kumagaya	21 Sep
15:21.08	Lucy	Van Dalen	NZL	18.11.88	2	MSR	Walnut	19 Apr
15:21.41	Marisol	Romero	MEX	26.11.83	5		Los Angeles (ER)	17 May
15:21.57	Felista	Wanjugu	KEN	18.2.90	1	NC	Tokyo (Chofu)	9 Jun
15:21.73	Misaki	Onishi	JPN	24.2.85	2	NC	Tokyo (Chofu)	9 Jun
15:22.23	Yelena	Nagovitsyna	RUS	7.12.82	2	NCp	Yerino	16 Jun
15:22.79	Haftamnesh	Tesfay	ETH-J	28.4.94	1		Sollentuna	27 Jun
	(60)							
15:23.12	Mary	Cullen	IRL	17.8.82	3	MSR	Walnut	19 Apr
15:23.65	Katie	Mackey	USA	12.11.87	2	Jordan	Stanford	28 Apr
15:23.77	Julia	Lucas	USA	4.3.84	3	Jordan	Stanford	28 Apr
15:25.52	Karolina	Jarzynska	POL	6.9.81	1		Portland	8 Jun
15:26.05	Riko	Matsuzaki	JPN	24.12.92	3	NC	Tokyo (Chofu)	9 Jun
15:26.51	Neely	Spence	USA	16.4.90	4	MSR	Walnut	19 Apr
15:26.61	Kasumi	Nishihara	JPN	1.3.89	1		Yokohama	30 Nov
15:26.80	Yuika	Mori	JPN	25.1.88	2		Yokohama	30 Nov
15:27.16	Mariya	Konovalova	RUS	14.8.74	2	NC	Moskva	24 Jul
15:27.39	Iris	Fuentes-Pila	ESP	10.8.80	2		Liège (NX)	10 Jul
	(70)							
15:27.58	Nicole	Sifuentes	CAN	30.6.86	5	Jordan	Stanford	28 Apr
15:28.34	Caroline	Kipkirui	KEN-J	26.5.94	13	FBK	Hengelo	8 Jun
15:28.35	Viktoriya	Pogoryelska	UKR	4.8.90	1		Yalta	5 Jun
15:29.64	Lisa	Uhl	USA	31.8.87	5		Stanford	29 Mar
15:29.72	Kate	Van Buskirk	CAN	9.6.87	6	MSR	Walnut	19 Apr
15:29.85	Shiho	Takechi	JPN	18.8.90	4	NC	Tokyo (Chofu)	9 Jun
15:30.41	Rosemary	Wanjiru	KEN-J	9.12.94	3		Yokohama	30 Nov
15:30.44+	Hitomi	Niiya	JPN	26.2.88	1+	in 10k	Moskva	11 Aug
15:30.46	Pauline	Kamulu	KEN-J	30.12.94	1		Yokohama	29 Sep
15:30.61		Wei Xiaojie	CHN	20.11.89	1		Suzhou	1 Jun
	(80)							
15:30.63	Inés	Melchor	PER	30.8.86	1	Bol G	Trujillo	28 Nov
15:30.82	Katrina	Wootton	GBR	2.9.85	1		Solihull	18 May
15:30.82	Akari	Okinada	JPN-J	26.1.94	2		Yokohama	29 Sep
15:30.89mx	Brenda	Martinez	USA	8.9.87			Pasadena	8 Jun
15:35.65					1		Fullerton	9 Mar
15:30.99	Judith	Plá	ESP	2.5.78	5		Liège (NX)	10 Jul
15:31.06	Alena	Kudashkina	RUS-J	10.4.94	1		Kazan	16 Jun
15:31.45	Ayuko	Suzuki	JPN	8.10.91	5	NC	Tokyo (Chofu)	9 Jun
15:32.45	Olga	Golovkina ¶	RUS	17.12.86	1	ET	Gateshead	23 Jun
15:32.73	Sabrina	Mockenhaupt	GER	6.12.81	1	NC	Ulm	6 Jul04
15:33.21	Miyuki	Uehara	JPN-J	22.11.95	2		Nobeoka	11 May
	(90)							
15:33.25	Yukari	Abe	JPN	21.8.89	3		Nobeoka	11 May
15:33.47	Mariam	Waithera	KEN-J	23.12.96	1		Yokohama	16 Nov
15:33.63	Megan	Goethals	USA	8.7.92	7	MSR	Walnut	19 Apr
15:34.34	Natalya	Novichkova	RUS	9.10.88	1		Sochi	26 May
15:34.85	Natsuko	Goto	JPN	4.8.87	4		Yokohama	30 Nov
15:35.24	Laura	Whittle	GBR	27.6.85	3		Watford	30 Jun
15:35.30	Carolina	Tabares	COL	18.6.86	2	Bol G	Trujillo	28 Nov
15:35.55	Nadia	Noujani	MAR	3.9.81	2		Huelva	12 Jun
15:35.73	Eina	Yokosawa	JPN	29.10.92	1		Tama	6 Oct
15:35.74	Kaoru	Nagao	JPN	26.9.89	1		Yokohama	21 Dec
	(100)							

15:35.82	Emelia	Gorecka	GBR-J	29.1.94	1 Jun	15:36.56	Amy	Van Alstine	USA	11.11.87	28 Apr
15:35.96	Trihas	Gebre	ETH	29.4.90	12 Jun	15:36.66	Chiaki	Morikawa	JPN	22.9.87	21 Dec
15:36.22	Misuzu	Nakahara	JPN-J	29.11.94	30 Nov	15:36.85	Laura	Thweatt	USA	17.12.88	29 Mar
15:36.28	Risa	Kikuchi	JPN	5.2.90	21 Sep	15:36.90	Chieko	Kido	JPN	14.3.90	11 May
15:36.45	Delilah	DiCrescenzo	USA	28.2.83	28 Apr	15:37.46	Natalya	Leontyeva	RUS	5.7.87	26 May

Mark	Name		Nat	Born	Pos	Meet	Venue		Date
15:37.55	Mai	Shoji	JPN	9.12.93				28	Apr
15:37.63	Kayo	Asaba	JPN	24.2.83				16	Nov
15:37.89	Ayumi	Uehara	JPN-J	23.11.94				17	Nov
15:38.19	Elena	Romagnolo	ITA	5.10.82				8	Jun
15:38.22	Maki	Izumida	JPN-Y	22.1.96				30	Nov
15:38.62	Natalya	Popkova	RUS	21.9.88				24	Jul
15:38.68	Khadija	Sammah	MAR	.83				12	Jun
15:38.73	Jéssica	Augusto	POR	8.11.81				10	Jul
15:39.32	Sara	Hall	USA	15.4.83				28	Apr
15:39.45	Mai	Ishibashi	JPN	2.7.89				9	Jun
15:39.54	Christine	Bardelle	FRA	16.8.74				28	Jun
15:39.80	Emily	Sisson	USA	12.10.91				19	Apr
15:39.92	Megumi	Hirai	JPN	14.2.90				30	Nov
15:40.03	Svetlana	Kireyeva	RUS	12.6.87				24	Jul
15:40.23	Rina	Yamazaki	JPN	6.5.88				29	Sep
15:40.34	Natsuki	Omori	JPN-J	22.6.94				7	Sep
15:40.58	Yuko	Mizuguchi	JPN	24.5.85				16	Nov
15:40.68	Nanako	Kanno	JPN-J	30.12.94				17	Nov
15:40.68	Rui	Aoyama	JPN	15.4.89				30	Nov
15:40.78	Sayo	Nomura	JPN	18.4.89				29	Sep
15:41.41	Julie	Culley	USA	10.9.81				28	Apr
15:41.49	Mao	Kuroda	JPN	1.11.89				29	Sep
15:41.82	Miki	Sakakibara	JPN	5.4.93				16	Nov
15:41.97	Keiko	Nogami	JPN	6.12.85				28	Apr
15:41.98	Yuki	Hidaka	JPN	22.7.92				29	Sep
15:42.16	Aki	Saito	JPN-J					16	Nov
15:42.36	Kureha	Seki	JPN-Y	15.9.96				29	Sep
15:42.39	Tara	Erdmann	USA	14.6.89				8	Jun
15:42.51		Liu Ruihuan	CHN	29.6.92				1	Jun
15:42.62	Roxana	Bârca ¶	ROU	22.6.88				7	Jun
15:42.62	Yuko	Aoki	JPN	27.9.92				29	Sep
15:42.63	Tomomi	Tanaka	JPN	25.1.88				6	Oct
15:42.65	Risa	Takenaka	JPN	6.1.90				11	May
15:42.71	Nazret	Woldu	ERI	90				27	Jun

Mark	Name		Nat	Born	Pos	Meet	Venue		Date
15:42.81	Kanako	Shimada	JPN	11.10.88				16	Nov
15:43.20	Natalya	Vlasova	RUS	19.7.88				24	Jul
15:43.51	Katie	Clark	GBR	4.2.91				19	Apr
15:43.63	Yelena	Sedova	RUS	1.3.90				24	Jul
15:43.69	Ami	Hirose	JPN-J	20.10.94				16	Nov
15:43.72mx	Tomoyo	Adachi	JPN-Y	5.2.96				30	Nov
15:43.81	Kaila	McKnight	AUS	5.5.86				28	Apr
15:43.85	Zakya	Mrisho	TAN	19.2.84				29	Sep
15:44 e+	Christelle	Daunay	FRA	5.12.74				11	Aug
15:44.06	Hannah	Kiser	USA					19	Apr
15:44.10	Shiori	Morita	JPN-J	19.9.95				16	Nov
15:44.19	Katie	Matthews	USA	19.11.90				28	Apr
15:44.19	Mao	Kiyota	JPN	12.9.93				16	Nov
15:44.30	Saori	Noda	JPN	30.3.93				30	Nov
15:44.40	Sakiko	Matsumi	JPN	7.8.88				29	Sep
15:44.41	Laura	Carleton	USA	23.9.89				19	Apr
15:44.53	Helaria	Johannes	NAM	13.8.80				2	Jun
15:44.53	Silvia	Weissteiner	ITA	13.7.79				28	Jun
15:44.78	Kellyn	Johnson	USA	22.7.86				8	Jun
15:44.79	Mayumi	Hatakeyama	JPN-Y	.97				16	Nov
15:44.97	Mai	Ito	JPN	23.5.84				7	Dec
15:44.98	Christine	Babcock	USA	19.5.90				29	Mar
15:45.00	Asahi	Takeuchi	JPN-J					16	Nov
	(167)								

Indoors

15:38.98	Natalya	Gorchakova	RUS	17.4.83				14	Feb
15:40.30	Jordan	Hasay	USA	21.9.91				8	Mar
15:41.00	Sarah	Collins	IRL-J	15.9.94				7	Dec
15:41.42	Yelena	Zadorozhnaya	RUS	3.12.77				14	Feb
15:41.75#	Diane	Nukuri-Johnson	BDI	1.12.84				9	Feb
15:42.27	Katie	Matthews	USA	19.11.90				8	Mar
15:42.60	Laura	Nagel	NZL	11.2.92				7	Dec

Unconfirmed

15:38.1	Yuliya	Zaripova	RUS	26.4.86				13	May

Drugs disqualification

15:33.64	Yekaterina	Ishova ¶	RUS	17.1.89	3	NC	Moskva	24	Jul
15:39.76	Roxana	Bârca ¶	ROU	22.6.88	(1)	WUG	Kazan	11	Jul

JUNIORS

See main list for top 13 juniors. 15 performances by 5 women to 15:12.0. Additional marks and further juniors:

Diriba 3+	14:52.89	2	FBK	Hengelo	8	Jun	15:01.44	5	DL	Saint-Denis	6	Jul
	14:56.34	8	WK	Zürich	29	Aug	15:05.38	5	WCh	Moskva	17	Aug
Tirop	14:54.12	3	FBK	Hengelo	8	Jun	14:56.49	9	WK	Zürich	29	Aug
Haroye	15:11.78	7	DL	Saint-Denis	6	Jul	15:19.14	16	DL	Shanghai	18	May

15:35.82	Emelia	Gorecka	GBR	29.1.94	1			Manchester (SC)	1	Jun
15:36.22	Misuzu	Nakahara	JPN	29.11.94	5			Yokohama	30	Nov
15:37.89	Ayumi	Uehara	JPN	23.11.94	1			Fukuroi	17	Nov
15:38.22	Maki	Izumida	JPN-Y	22.1.96	6			Yokohama	30	Nov
15:40.34	Natsuki	Omori	JPN	22.6.94	1			Tokyo	7	Sep
15:40.68	Nanako	Kanno	JPN	30.12.94	2			Fukuroi	17	Nov
15:42.16	Aki	Saito (20)	JPN		5			Yokohama	16	Nov
15:41.00i	Sarah	Collins	IRL	15.9.94	2			Boston (R)	7	Dec

10,000 METRES

30:08.06	Meseret	Defar	ETH	19.11.83	1		Sollentuna	27	Jun
30:26.67	Tirunesh	Dibaba	ETH	1.10.85	1	GS	Ostrava	27	Jun
30:29.23	Gladys	Cherono	KEN	12.5.83	2	GS	Ostrava	27	Jun
30:31.44	Belaynesh	Oljira	ETH	26.6.90	3	GS	Ostrava	27	Jun
30:35.91	Birhane	Ababel	ETH	10.6.90	4	GS	Ostrava	27	Jun
30:43.35		Dibaba			1	WCh	Moskva	11	Aug
30:45.17		Cherono			2	WCh	Moskva	11	Aug
30:46.98		Oljira			3	WCh	Moskva	11	Aug
30:47.02	Emily	Chebet	KEN	18.2.86	4	WCh	Moskva	11	Aug
30:55.50	Sule	Utura	ETH	8.2.90	5	GS	Ostrava	27	Jun
30:56.70	Hitomi	Niiya	JPN	26.2.88	5	WCh	Moskva	11	Aug
31:02.89	Linet	Masai	KEN	5.12.89	6	GS	Ostrava	27	Jun
31:04.85	Shalane	Flanagan (10)	USA	8.7.81	1		Stanford	29	Mar
31:06.67		Niiya			1	NC	Tokyo (Chofu)	7	Jun
31:08.23	Afera	Godfay	ETH	25.9.91	2		Sollentuna	27	Jun
31:13.79	Shitaye	Eshete	BRN	21.5.90	6	WCh	Moskva	11	Aug
31:16.68	Wude	Ayalew	ETH	4.7.87	7	GS	Ostrava	27	Jun
31:22.11	Selly	Chepyego	KEN	3.10.85	7	WCh	Moskva	11	Aug
31:34.83		Flanagan			8	WCh	Moskva	11	Aug
31:37.22	Betsy	Saina	KEN	30.6.88	1	Jordan	Stanford	28	Apr

Mark	Name		Nat	Born	Pos	Meet	Venue	Date	
31:42.06	Esther	Chemtai	KEN	4.6.88	8	GS	Ostrava	27	Jun
31:43.20		Flanagan			1	NC	Des Moines	20	Jun
31:43.51	Karolina	Jarzynska	POL	6.9.81	9	GS	Ostrava	27	Jun
31:44.92	Doricah	Obare	KEN	10.1.90	2	Jordan	Stanford	28	Apr
31:45.29	Ayumi	Hagiwara	JPN	1.6.92	3	Jordan	Stanford	28	Apr
31:46.37	Kimberley	Smith (20)	NZL	19.11.81	4	Jordan	Stanford	28	Apr
31:46.42-mx	Jordan	Hasay	USA	21.9.91	1mx		Portland	14	Jul
32:06.64					6	Jordan	Stanford	28	Apr
31:46.43	Marisol	Romero	MEX	26.11.83	5	Jordan	Stanford	28	Apr
31:46.64	Kara	Goucher	USA	9.7.78	2		Stanford	29	Mar
31:48.21	Muluhabt	Tsega	ETH	11.9.89	10	GS	Ostrava	27	Jun
	(30/24)								
31:51.42	Gotytom	Gebresilase	ETH-J	15.1.95	3		Sollentuna	27	Jun
31:52.55	Ana Dulce	Félix	POR	23.10.82	11	GS	Ostrava	27	Jun
31:55.66		Cao Mojie	CHN	10.4.92	1	NG	Shenyang	11	Sep
31:56.80		Liu Ruihuan	CHN	29.6.92	2	NG	Shenyang	11	Sep
31:58.34		Jiang Xiaoli	CHN	6.4.89	3	NG	Shenyang	11	Sep
32:01.83	Gulshat	Fazlitdinova	RUS	28.8.92	1	Chall	Moskva	11	Jun
	(30)								
32:02.67	Natalya	Puchkova	RUS	28.1.87	2	Chall	Moskva	11	Jun
32:02.92	Alina	Prokopeva	RUS	16.8.85	3	Chall	Moskva	11	Jun
32:02.99	Yelena	Nagovitsyna	RUS	7.12.82	4	Chall	Moskva	11	Jun
32:03.39	Trihas	Gebre	ETH	29.4.90	12	GS	Ostrava	27	Jun
32:04.44	Christelle	Daunay	FRA	5.12.74	10	WCh	Moskva	11	Aug
32:05.88	Kasumi	Nishihara	JPN	1.3.89	1		Kitami	6	Jul
32:06.70	Yuka	Takashima	JPN	12.5.88	2		Kitami	6	Jul
32:06.79	Sayuri	Oka	JPN	19.9.90	3		Kumagaya	20	Sep
32:07.20	Aliphine	Tuliamok-Bolton	KEN	5.4.89	7	Jordan	Stanford	28	Apr
32:07.41	Mai	Ito	JPN	23.5.84	3		Kitami	6	Jul
	(40)								
32:07.70	Yuko	Shimizu	JPN	13.7.85	8	Jordan	Stanford	28	Apr
32:08.73	Rei	Ohara	JPN	10.8.90	4		Kitami	6	Jul
32:09.95		Wang Xueqin	CHN	1.1.91	4	NG	Shenyang	11	Sep
32:10.15	Yuko	Mizuguchi	JPN	24.5.85	5		Kitami	6	Jul
32:10.66	Risa	Takenaka	JPN	6.1.90	6		Kumagaya	20	Sep
32:13.64	Sabrina	Mockenhaupt	GER	6.12.80	1		Pravets	8	Jun
32:15.45	Yuki	Mitsunobu	JPN	9.11.92	6		Kitami	6	Jul
32:15.51	Laura	Thweatt	USA	17.12.88	9	Jordan	Stanford	28	Apr
32:16.05	Yurie	Doi	JPN	8.12.88	8		Kumagaya	20	Sep
32:16.13	Lara	Tamsett	AUS	12.10.88	10	Jordan	Stanford	28	Apr
	(50)								
32:16.46	Miho	Ihara	JPN	4.2.88	11	Jordan	Stanford	28	Apr
32:16.77		Xiao Huimin	CHN	1.3.92	5	NG	Shenyang	11	Sep
32:17.78		Wei Xiaojie	CHN	20.11.89	6	NG	Shenyang	11	Sep
32:18.86		Zhang Meixia	CHN	20.1.91	7	NG	Shenyang	11	Sep
32:20.58	Kenza	Dahmani	ALG	18.11.80	1		Bejaia	8	Jun
32:24.16	Tara	Erdmann	USA	14.6.89	3	NC	Des Moines	20	Jun
32:24.85	Ayumi	Sakaida	JPN	7.11.85	10		Kumagaya	20	Sep
32:25.05	Hanae	Tanaka	JPN	12.2.90	12	Jordan	Stanford	28	Apr
32:26.92	Eleni	Gebrehiwot	ETH	2.1.83	1		Bremen	4	Ma
32:29.14	Mattie	Suver	USA	10.9.87	13	Jordan	Stanford	28	Apr
	(60)								
32:29.14	Diane	Nukuri-Johnson	BDI	1.12.84	1	Franc	Nice	13	Sep
32:30.41	Corinna	Harrer	GER	19.1.91	1		Regensburg	16	Mar
32:30.56	Valeria	Straneo	ITA	5.4.76	1		Ancona	18	Ma
32:31.28	Amy	Hastings	USA	21.1.84	4	NC	Des Moines	20	Jun
32:31.78	Sayo	Nomura	JPN	18.4.89	7		Kitami	6	Jul
32:32.23	Aheza	Kiros	ETH	26.3.82	4		Sollentuna	27	Jun
32:33.05	Brianne	Nelson	USA	27.10.80	4	Jordan	Stanford	28	Apr
32:34.04	Mao	Kiyota	JPN	12.9.93	1		Yokohama	21	Dec
32:34.29	Hiroko	Shoi	JPN	18.6.80	12		Kumagaya	20	Sep
32:34.38	Eri	Makikawa	JPN	22.4.93	2		Yokohama	21	Dec
	(70)								
32:38.42	Khadija	Sammah	MAR	9.7.83	2	Franc	Nice	14	Sep
32:38.62	Yuko	Watanabe	JPN	3.11.87	2		Fukagawa	29	Jun
32:38.71	Beatrice	Wainaina	KEN	23.11.93	3		Fukagawa	29	Jun
32:39.39	Alia Saeed	Mohammed	UAE	18.5.91	2	AsiC	Pune	3	Jul
32:39.90	Tomomi	Tanaka	JPN	25.1.88	7	NC	Tokyo (Chofu)	7	Jun
32:39.91	Natalya	Novichkova	RUS	9.10.88	5	Chall	Moskva	11	Jun
32:40.03	Carla Salomé	Rocha	POR	25.4.90	2		Mataró	6	Apr
32:40.80	Yuki	Hidaka	JPN	22.7.92	9		Kitami	6	Jul

Mark	Name	Nat	Born	Pos	Meet	Venue	Date
32:41.16	Rina Yamazaki	JPN	6.5.88	13		Kumagaya	20 Sep
32:41.69	Grace Kimanzi	KEN	1.3.92	3		Naka	18 Ma
(80)							
32:41.98	Lisa Uhl	USA	31.8.87	15	Jordan	Stanford	28 Apr
32:41.99	Jia Chaofeng	CHN	16.11.88	2		Suzhou	30 Ma
32:42.40	Krisztina Papp	HUN	17.12.82	1		Budapest	27 Apr
32:42.56	Kayoko Fukushi	JPN	25.3.82	4		Fukagawa	29 Jun
32:42.96	Katsuki Suga	JPN-J	1.2.94	1rB		Kumagaya	20 Sep
32:44.1A	Lucy Kabuu	KEN	24.3.84	1		Nairobi	21 Jun
32:44.13	Misaki Kato	JPN	15.6.91	2rB		Kumagaya	20 Sep
32:44.20	Natalya Leontyeva	RUS	5.7.87	6	Chall	Moskva	11 Jun
32:44.44	Sakiko Matsumi	JPN	7.8.88	2		Tokyo	20 Apr
32:45.60	Yuka Kakimi	JPN	4.4.86	3		Tokyo	20 Apr
(90)							
32:45.66	Shino Saito	JPN	7.9.88	5		Fukagawa	29 Jun
32:45.67	Misato Tanaka	JPN	21.12.89	3rB		Kumagaya	20 Sep
32:46.08	Lyudmila Lebedeva	RUS	23.5.90	7	Chall	Moskva	11 Jun
32:46.3A	Sharon Cherop	KEN	16.3.84	2		Nairobi	21 Jun
32:46.52	Yelena Khamidova	UZB	12.5.89	8	Chall	Moskva	11 Jun
32:46.96	Cruz da Silva	BRA	18.8.74	1		Piracicaba	26 Apr
32:47.14	Ding Changqin	CHN	27.11.91	9	NG	Shenyang	11 Sep
32:47.83	Chieko Kido	JPN	14.3.90	1		Oita	27 Apr
32:47.96	Zsófia Erdélyi	HUN	10.12.87	13	GS	Ostrava	27 Jun
32:48.60	Yelena Sedova	RUS	1.3.90	9	Chall	Moskva	11 Jun
(100)							

Mark	Name	Nat	Born	Date	Mark	Name	Nat	Born	Date
32:48.84	Michi Numata	JPN	6.5.89	20 Sep	32:58.00	Juliet Bottorff	USA	21.1.91	29 Mar
32:49.02	Ayuko Suzuki	JPN	8.10.91	19 May	32:58.14	Mari Ozaki	JPN	16.7.75	29 Jun
32:49.12	Kotomi Takayama	JPN	18.2.93	20 Sep	32:58.24	Galina Ivanova	RUS	11.3.76	11 Jun
32:49.59	Rika Shintaku	JPN	19.10.85	20 Sep	32:59.05	Sun Weiwei	CHN	13.1.85	11 Sep
32:50.31	Hiroko Miyauchi	JPN	9.6.83	20 Sep	32:59.2A	Pasalia Kipkoech	KEN	22.12.88	21 Jun
32:50.34	Lidia Rodríguez	ESP	26.5.86	6 Apr	32:59.30	Elvan Abeylegesse	TUR	11.9.82	26 Jun
32:51.0A	Caroline Kilel	KEN	21.3.81	21 Jun	33:02.88	Emily Sisson	USA	12.10.91	4 May
32:51.47	Kumi Ogura	JPN	24.6.85	6 Jul	33:03.36	María Azucena Díaz	ESP	19.12.82	6 Apr
32:51.53	Sairi Maeda	JPN	7.11.91	29 Jun	33:03.84	Meguimi Amako	JPN	13.12.90	27 Apr
32:52.56	Olivera Jevtic	SRB	24.7.77	8 Jun	33:04.1A	Esther Chemutai	KEN	6.6.87	25 May
32:52.57	Shiho Takechi	JPN	18.8.90	18 May	33:04.24	Yui Okada	JPN-J	15.3.94	29 Jun
32:52.60	Yukari Abe	JPN	21.8.89	6 Jul	33:04.58	Jennifer Bergman	USA	1.11.91	29 Mar
32:52.78	Megan Goethals	USA	8.7.92	29 Mar	33:05.71	Meaghan Nelson	USA	12.2.90	28 Apr
32:53.21	Yoko Miyauchi	JPN	9.6.83	6 Jul	33:07.29	Noriko Higuchi	JPN	18.5.85	17 May
32:54.03	Yuka Tokuda	JPN	1.6.88	18 May	33:07.36	Catherine White	USA	24.7.89	29 Mar
32:54.25	Mai Tsuda	JPN	21.2.93	21 Apr	33:07.75	Inés Melchor	PER	30.8.86	6 Oct
32:55.27	Sonia Bejarano	ESP	2.8.81	6 Apr	33:07.80	Gina Valgoi	USA	30.11.90	29 Mar
32:55.6A	Isabellah Ochichi	KEN	28.10.79	21 Jun	33:08.0A	Jemima Jelagat	KEN	21.12.84	4 Apr
32:56.22	Nikki Chapple	AUS	9.2.81	12 Dec	33:08.04	Nanaka Izawa	JPN	13.4.91	21 Jun
32:56.76	Aya Nagata	JPN	31.3.90	28 Apr	33:08.26	Jessica Trengove	AUS	15.8.87	12 Dec
32:57.0A	Viola Yator	KEN		21 Jun	33:08.80	Aleksandra Duliba	BLR	9.1.88	11 Jun
32:57.02	Juliet Chekwel	UGA	25.5.90	11 Aug	33:08.85	Ayaka Inoue	JPN	19.6.91	20 Sep
32:57.51	Asami Kato	JPN	12.10.90	29 Jun	33:09.14	Korei Omata	JPN	15.7.87	29 Jun
32:57.26	Kim Do-yeon	KOR	2.9.93	22 Oct	33:09.57	Natasha Wodak	CAN	17.12.81	28 Apr
32:57.78	Natasha LaBeaud	USA	5.8.87	28 Apr	(149)				

JUNIORS

Mark	Name	Nat	Born	Pos	Meet	Venue	Date
31:51.42	Gotytom Gebresilase	ETH	15.1.95	3		Sollentuna	27 Jun
32:42.96	Katsuki Suga	JPN	1.2.94	1rB		Kumagaya	20 Sep
33:19.19	1rB Fukagawa 29 Jun						
33:04.24	Yui Okada	JPN	15.3.94	12		Fukagawa	29 Jun
33:24.92	8 Kumagawa 20 Sep 8 performances by 6 women to 33:30.0						
33:16.45	Fuyuka Kimura	JPN	13.1.95	2		Tokyo	23 Nov
33:20.38	Anna Matsuda	JPN	18.4.94	4		Tokyo	23 Nov
33:27.43	Liu Zhuang	CHN	18.1.95	12	NG	Shenyang	11 Sep
33:38.4A	Ruth Aga	ETH	16.1.94	2	NC	Assela	30 Jun
33:43.96	Chika Okazaki	JPN	21.6.94	5		Tokyo	6 Sep
33:46.12	Reina Iwade	JPN	8.12.94	4rB		Fukagawa	29 Jun
33:50.15	Natsumi Saito	JPN	9.4.94	7rB		Fukagawa	29 Jun
33:50.20	Akari Okinada	JPN	26.1.94	2		Miyoshi	18 May
33:57.03	Aiko Sakata	JPN	18.3.94	1		Kyoto	12 Apr
Best European: 34:38.89	Oona Kettunen	FIN	10.2.94	1	NC	Vaasa	28 Jul

10 KILOMETRES ROAD

Mark	Name	Nat	Born	Pos	Meet	Venue	Date
30:30	Tirunesh Dibaba	ETH	1.10.85	1		Tilburg	1 Sep
30:37	Joyce Chepkirui	KEN	20.8.88	1		Berlin	13 Oct
30:38	Tadelech Bekele	ETH	11.4.91	2		Berlin	13 Oct
30:49	Dibaba			1		Manchester	26 May
31:17+	Lucy Kabuu	KEN	24.3.84		in HMar	Ra's Al-Khaymah	15 Feb

Mark	Name		Nat	Born	Pos	Meet	Venue	Date	
31:17+	Rita	Jeptoo	KEN	15.2.81		in HMar	Ra's Al-Khaymah	15	Feb
31:18+	Meselech	Melkamu	ETH	27.4.85		in HMar	Ra's Al-Khaymah	15	Feb
31:18+	Meseret	Hailu	ETH	12.9.90		in HMar	Ra's Al-Khaymah	15	Feb
31:19+	Florence	Kiplagat	KEN	27.2.87		in HMar	Ra's Al-Khaymah	15	Feb
31:19+	Helah	Kiprop	KEN	7.4.85		in HMar	Ra's Al-Khaymah	15	Feb
31:19+	Priscah	Jeptoo	KEN	26.6.84		in HMar	Ra's Al-Khaymah	15	Feb
31:20		Chepkirui			1		Utrecht	29	Sep
31:24		Chepkirui			1		Cape Elizabeth	3	Aug
31:25+	Pasalia	Kipkoech	KEN	22.12.88		in HMar	Ra's Al-Khaymah	15	Feb
31:33	Sentayehu	Ejigu	ETH	21.6.85	1		Boston	13	Oct
31:36+	Atsede	Baysa	ETH	16.4.87	1	in HMar	Barcelona	17	Feb
31:36	Gemma	Steel	GBR	12.11.85	2		Cape Elizabeth	3	Aug
31:38	Sule	Utura	ETH	8.2.90	3		Cape Elizabeth	3	Aug

Where superior to track best

31:40	Yebrwual	Melese	ETH	18.4.90	4		Cape Elizabeth	3	Aug
31:40+	Molly	Huddle	USA	31.8.84	1	in 12k	Alexandria	17	Nov
31:43+	Josephine	Chepkoech	KEN	89	2	in HMar	Barcelona	17	Feb
31:45	Mamitu	Daska	ETH	16.10.83	1		Boston	23	Jun
31:46	Malika	Asahssah	MAR	24.9.82	1		Ottawa	25	May
31:47	Emily	Infeld	USA	21.3.90	2		Boston	13	Oct
31:49	Firehiwot	Dado	ETH	9.1.84	2		Ottawa	25	May
31:49+	Flomena	Chepchirchir	KEN	1.12.81		in 10M	Zaandam	22	Sep
31:49+	Sylvia	Kibet	KEN	28.3.84		in 10M	Zaandam	22	Sep
31:51	Alice	Kimutai	KEN		1	CresC	New Orleans	30	Mar
31:52	Karoline Bjerkeli	Grøvdal	NOR	14.6.90	1		Hole	19	Oct
31:55+	Feyse	Tadesse	ETH	19.11.88		in HMar	Ra's Al-Khaymah	15	Feb
31:55	Lucy	Macharia	KEN	.91	1		Otterndorf	15	Sep
31:59	Lilian	Jelagat ¶	KEN	23.1.89	2		Paderborn	30	Mar
32:01+	Worknesh	Degefa	ETH	28.10.90		in HMar	Praha	6	Apr
32:01+	Waganesh	Mekasha	ETH	16.1.92		in HMar	Praha	6	Apr
32:02+	Isabellah	Ochichi	KEN	28.10.79		in HMar	Praha	6	Apr
32:03	Sabrina	Mockenhaupt	GER	6.12.80	1		Leverkusen	3	Mar
32:05	Hiwot	Ayalew	ETH	6.3.90	2	CresC	New Orleans	30	Mar
32:08+	Mercy	Kibarus	KEN	25.2.84		in HMar	Ostia	3	Mar
32:08	Kaltoum	Bouaasayriya	MAR	23.8.82	1		Marrakech	6	Oct
32:09+	Filomena	Cheyech	KEN	5.7.82		in HMar	Ostia	3	Mar
32:09+	Hilda	Kibet	NED	27.3.81		in HMar	Ostia	3	Mar
32:09+	Agnes	Kiprop	KEN	12.12.79		in HMar	Ostia	3	Mar
32:09dh 34m	Lineth	Chepkurui	KEN	23.2.88	1	Peach	Atlanta	4	Jul
32:10					2		San Juan	24	Feb
32:09	Mary	Davies	NZL	27.8.82	3		Ottawa	25	May
32:09	Genet	Yalew	ETH	31.12.92	3		Tilburg	1	Sep
32:10	Guteni	Shone	ETH	17.11.91	2		Bangalore	19	May
32:10dh 34m	Sharon	Cherop	KEN	16.3.84	2	Peach	Atlanta	4	Jul
32:11+	Elvan	Abeylegesse	TUR	11.9.82		in HMar	Ra's Al-Khaymah	15	Feb
32:11+	Diana	Sigei	KEN	87		in HMar	Ra's Al-Khaymah	15	Feb
32:11	Khadija	Sammah	MAR	9.7.83	1		Taroudant	10	Mar
32:12	Eleni	Gebrehiwot	ETH	2.1.83	3		Paderborn	30	Mar
32:12	Buzunesh	Deba	ETH	8.9.87	6		Cape Elizabeth	3	Aug
32:12	Risper	Gesebwa	KEN	1.1.89	3		Boston	14	Oct
32:13	Helen	Jemutai	KEN	.81	4		Ottawa	25	May
32:15+	Pamela	Lisoreng	KEN	5.8.88		in HMar	Praha	6	Apr
32:16	Valentine	Kibet	KEN	.89	2		Brunssum	7	Apr
32:18	Olga	Kimaiyo	KEN	24.7.88	4	CresC	New Orleans	30	Mar
32:19+	Tiki	Gelana	ETH	22.10.87		in HMar	Marugame	3	Feb
32:19	Pauline	Wanjiku	KEN	.88	1		Swansea	22	Sep
32:20	Joan	Chelimo	KEN	.88	2		Taroudant	10	Mar
32:21+	Philes	Ongori	KEN	19.7.86		in HMar	Berlin	7	Apr
32:21	Delam	Abere	ETH	18.1.89	2		Bristol	5	May
32:21	Jelena	Prokopcuka	LAT	21.9.76	2		Manchester	26	May
32:22	Agnes	Mutune	KEN	26.6.86	1		Würzburg	28	Apr
32:22	Fantu	Eticha	ETH	.91	1		Langueux	22	Jun
32:23	Carla Salomé	Rocha	POR	25.4.90	1		Porto	15	Dec
32:24	Cynthia	Kosgei	KEN	.93	2		Otterndorf	15	Sep
32:24	Grace	Kimanzi	KEN	1.3.92	1		Okayama	23	Dec

32:26	Katrina	Wootton	GBR	2.9.85	5 May	32:30	Etalemahu	Habtewold	ETH	.90	22 Jun
32:27	Elizeba	Cherono	KEN	6.6.88	29 Jun	32:32+	Ashu	Kasim	ETH	20.10.84	15 Feb
32:28	Sofiya	Shemsu	ETH-J	12.9.94	30 Mar	32:32	Emily	Samoei	KEN	11.110.80	10 Mar
32:28	Leonidah	Mosop	KEN	.91	22 Jun	32:32	Belaynesh	Zemedkun	ETH	23.12.87	30 Mar
32:28	Janet	Bawcom	USA	22.8.78	14 Oct	32:32	Alice	Kamunya	KEN		14 Oct
32:29	Deena	Kastor	USA	14.2.73	3 Aug	32:33	Mary	Maina	KEN		1 May

Mark	Name		Nat	Born	Pos	Meet	Venue	Date
32:33	Aster	Demissie	CAN	.83				27 Oct
32:34	Jane	Murage	KEN	.87				30 Mar
32:34	Sarah	Chepchirchir	KEN	27.7.84				8 May
32:34	Rkia	El Moukim	MAR	22.2.88				29 Dec
32:35+	Lyudmyla	Kovalenko	UKR	26.6.89				15 Sep
32:35	Clémence	Calvin	FRA	17.5.90				15 Dec
32:36	Aziza	Aliyu	ETH	20.10.85				30 Mar
32:36	Nancy	Kipron	KEN					19 May
32:36	Jane	Moraa	KEN	21.9.91				29 Jun
32:36	Beatrice	Wainaina	KEN	20.11.93				23 Dec
32:37	Millicent	Kuria	KEN					30 Mar
32:37	Cyntjia	Cherotich	KEN	.89				12 May
32:39	Alem	Fikre	ETH	22.10.88				25 Jan
32:39	Juliet	Chekwel	UGA	25.5.90				25 May
32:39dh 34m	Madaí	Pérez	MEX	2.2.80	4			Jul
32:40	Nikki	Chapple	AUS	9.2.81	20			Oct
32:41	Non	Stanford	GBR	8.1.89	10			Mar
32:41+	Ehitu	Kiros	ETH	13.1.88	6			Apr
32:41	Soud	Kanbouchia	MAR	12.8.82	3			Aug
32:41	Margherita	Mahnani	ITA	26.2.87	8			Dec
32:42	Alemitu	Abera	ETH	.86	24			Feb
32:42+	Valentine	Kipketer	KEN	5.1.93	7			Apr
32:42dh 28m	Natasha	Wodak (Fraser)	CAN	17.12.81	21			Apr
32:43+	Caroline	Chepkwony	KEN	18.4.84	15			Sep
32:43	Jéssica	Augusto	POR	8.11.81	28			Dec
32:44+	Misato	Horie	JPN	10.3.87	3			Feb
32:44+	Kumi	Ogura	JPN	24.6.85	3			Feb
32:44	Tabitha	Wambui	KEN	29.12.83	21			Apr
32:45+	Rui	Aoyama	JPN	15.4.89	3			Feb
32:45+	Eri	Hayakawa	JPN	15.11.81	3			Feb
32:45	Adrienne	Herzog	NED	30.9.85	6			Oct
32:46	Lanni	Marchant	CAN	11.4.84	25			May
32:47+	Yuka	Hakoyama	JPN	9.3.90				3 Feb
32:47+	Horoki	Miyauchi	JPN	19.6.83				3 Feb
32:47+	Mestawet	Tufa	ETH	14.9.83				19 May
32:47+	Eunice	Kirwa	KEN	20.5.84				19 May
32:47	Louise	Damen	GBR	12.10.82				15 Dec
32:48	Alice	Mogire	KEN	27.5.87				10 Mar
32:48	Riko	Mitsuzaki	JPN	24.12.92				17 Mar
32:49	Mapaseka	Makhanya	RSA	9.4.85				23 Jun
32:49	Jackline	Chepngeno	KEN	16.1.93				7 Sep
32:50+	Caroline	Rotich	KEN	13.5.84				17 Mar
32:50	Mizuki	Tanimoto	JPN-J	18.12.94				23 Dec
32:51+	Lydia	Cheromei	KEN	11.5.77				3 Mar
32:51	Amy	Van Alstine	USA	11.11.87				14 Oct
32:52	Krista	Duchene	CAN	9.1.77				25 May
32:53	Natalya	Popkova	RUS	21.9.88				7 Sep
32:54	Keiko	Nogami	JPN	6.12.85				10 Feb
32:54+	Yolanda	Caballero	COL	19.3.82				17 Mar
32:54	Clara	Santucci	USA	24.3.87				29 Sep
32:55	Maurine	Kipchumba	KEN					19 May
32:55dh 34m	Stephanie	Rothstein Bruce	USA	14.1.84				4 Jul
32:55	Samira	Raïf	MAR	4.4.74				3 Aug
32:56	Hirut	Tibedu	ETH					3 Aug
32:56A	Pasalia	Kipkoech	KEN	22.12.88				28 Apr
32:56	Alexi	Pappas	USA	28.3.90				3 Aug
32:57	Iris	Fuentes-Pila	ESP	10.8.80				16 Mar
32:57+	Kim	Conley	USA	14.3.86				17 Nov
32:58	Misaki	Onishi	JPN	24.2.85				17 Mar
32:58	Yui	Okada	JPN-J	15.3.94				17 Mar
32:58	Lisa	Stublic	CRO	18.5.84				7 Sep
32:58+	Yukiko	Akaba	JPN	18.10.79				23 Dec
32:59+	Felista	Wanjugu	KEN	18.2.90				23 Dec
32:59	Pauline	Njeri	KEN	28.7.85				31 Dec

Drugs disqualification
31:56   Lilian   Jelagat ¶   KEN   23.1.89   (1)   Appingedam   29 Jun
Excessively downhill: Dec 12, Madrid (50m): 4. Magdalene Masai KEN KEN 4.4.93 32:37; Apr 21, Rockville (60m):
1. Jane Murage KEN .87 32:20, 2. Tsehay Gebre ETH 32:22; Apr 12, Toronto (82m) 1. Lanni Marchant CAN 31:57.

JUNIORS

32:28	Sofiya	Shemsu	ETH-J	12.9.94	5	CresC	New Orleans	30 Mar
32:50	Mizuki	Tanimoto	JPN	18.12.94	4		Okayama	23 Dec
32:58	Yui	Okada	JPN	15.3.94	4		Yamaguchi	17 Mar

15 KILOMETRES ROAD

And see splits in 10 Miles, 20 Km and Half Marathon lists

48:43	Tirunesh	Dibaba	ETH	1.10.85	1		Nijmegen	17 Nov
48:48	Sara	Moreira	POR	17.10.85	1		Lisboa	13 Jan
49:02	Chaltu	Tafa	ETH	85	1		Osmangazi-Bursa	14 Apr
49:08	Getnet	Selomie	ETH	10.4.86	2		Osmangazi-Bursa	14 Apr
49:14+	Yukiko	Akaba	JPN	18.10.79		in HMar	Okayama	23 Dec
49:15	Ana Dulce	Félix	POR	23.10.82	2		Lisboa	13 Jan
49:24	Aliphine	Tuliamok-Bolton	KEN	5.4.89	1		Tulsa	26 Oct
49:36+	Eunice	Kirwa	KEN	20.5.84		in HMar	Gifu	19 May
49:44+	Elvan	Abeylegesse	TUR	11.9.82	15			Feb
49:44	Janet	Bawcom	USA	22.8.78	9			Mar
49:44	Risper	Gesebwa	KEN	1.1.89	28			Oct
49:46	Cynthia	Kosgei	KEN	.93	1			Dec
49:49+	Caroline	Chepkwony	KEN	18.4.84				15 Sep
49:51+	Lucy	Macharia	KEN	.91				20 Oct
49:52	Venenesh	Tilahun	ETH-J	.94				17 Nov
49:59	Letrebrhan	Gebreslasea	ETH	.90				17 Nov

10 MILES ROAD

10M	15k				Nat	Born	Pos		Meet/Venue	Date
51:33	48:08	Joyce	Chepkirui		KEN	20.8.88	1		Zaandam	22 Sep
51:33	48:08	Flomena	Chepchirchir		KEN	1.12.81	2		Zaandam	22 Sep
52:03+		Kimberley	Smith		NZL	19.11.81		in HMar	Boston	13 Oct
52:06	48:34	Sylvia	Kibet		KEN	28.3.84	3		Zaandam	22 Sep
52:32+		Lyudmyla	Kovalenko		UKR	26.6.89		in HMar	Philadelphia	15 Sep
52:43+		Aheza	Kiros		ETH	26.3.82		in HMar	Boston	13 Oct
52:46		Caroline	Rotich		KEN	13.5.84	1		Washington	7 Apr
52:49		Belaynesh	Oljira		ETH	26.6.90	2		Washington	7 Apr
	49:08+	Mai	Ito		JPN	23.5.84		in HMar	Okayama	23 Dec
52:51		Hilda	Kibet		NED	27.3.81	4		Zaandam	22 Sep
52:57+		Alice	Kimutai		KEN			in HMar	Boston	13 Oct
53:22		Risper	Gesebwa		KEN	1.1.89	7		Apr	
53:28		Janet	Bawcom		USA	22.8.78				7 Apr
53:28		Millicent	Kuria		KEN					7 Apr

Downhill course (30.5m)
50:38 + Priscah Jeptoo KEN 26.6.84 1 in HMar South Shields 15 Sep

---

Times at 15km in 2nd column

20 KILOMETRES ROAD

Time	15km	First	Last	Nat	DOB	Rk		Venue	Date
65:01		Sarah	Chepchirchir	KEN	27.7.84	1		Paris	13 Oct
65:07		Cynthia	Limo	KEN	18.12.89	2		Paris	13 Oct
65:55	48:55+	Waganesh	Mekasha	ETH	16.1.92		in HMar	Praha	6 Apr
66:05	+49:29d	Lyudmyla	Kovalenko	UKR	26.6.89		in HMar	New York	17 Mar
66:12		Gladys	Kipsoi	KEN	.86	3		Paris	13 Oct
66:28	49:29+	Agnes	Mutune	KEN	26.6.86		in HMar	Praha	6 Apr
66:51+		Tomomi	Tanaka	JPN	25.1.88		in HMar	New York	17 Mar
67:08		Leonodah	Mosop	KEN	.91	4		Paris	13 Oct
67:04	49:27	Kumi	Ogura	JPN	24.6.85		in HMar	Marugame	3 Feb
67:10+		Valentine	Kipketer	KEN	5.1.93		in HMar	Amsterdam	20 Oct

67:26+	Flomena	Chepchirchir	KEN	1.12.81	27 Oct	67:34+	Rita	Jeptoo	KEN	15.2.81	13 Oct
67:26+	Tirfi	Tsegaye	ETH	25.11.84	27 Oct	67:34+	Yukiko	Akaba	JPN	18.10.79	13 Oct
67:33+	Mariya	Konovalova	RUS	14.8.74	13 Oct	67:35+	Eunice	Kales	KEN	6.12.84	13 Oct

Slightly downhill course: South Shields 30.5m

HALF MARATHON

HMar	20k	15k	First	Last	Nat	DOB	Rk	GNR	Venue	Date
65:45dh	62:32	47:29	Priscah	Jeptoo	KEN	26.6.84	1	GNR	South Shields	15 Sep
66:09	62:49	47:14	Lucy	Kabuu	KEN	24.3.84	1		Ra's Al-Khaymah	15 Feb
66:09dh		47:30	Meseret	Defar	ETH	19.11.83	2	GNR	South Shields	15 Sep
66:11	62:54	47:15	P	Jeptoo			2		Ra's Al-Khaymah	15 Feb
66:27		47:14	Rita	Jeptoo	KEN	15.2.81	3		Ra's Al-Khaymah	15 Feb
66:48	63:26	47:43	Gladys	Cherono	KEN	12.5.83	1		Praha	6 Apr
66:56	63:26	47:13	Meseret	Hailu	ETH	12.9.90	4		Ra's Al-Khaymah	15 Feb
66:56dh		47:34	Tirunesh	Dibaba	ETH	1.10.85	3	GNR	South Shields	15 Sep
67:13	63:43	47:16	Florence	Kiplagat	KEN	27.2.87	5		Ra's Al-Khaymah	15 Feb
67:25				Defar			1		New Orleans	24 Feb
67:34	64:09	47:52	Atsede	Baysa	ETH	16.4.87	1		Barcelona	17 Feb
67:39	64:10	47:32	Helah	Kiprop (10)	KEN	7.4.85	6		Ra's Al-Khaymah	15 Feb
67:39		48:26	Flomena	Cheyech	KEN	5.7.82	1		Ostia	3 Mar
67:46		48:26	Agnes	Kiprop	KEN	12.12.79	2		Ostia	3 Mar
67:49		48:26	Worknesh	Degefa	ETH	28.10.90	3		Ostia	3 Mar
67:54				Kiprop			1		Berlin	7 Apr
67:59		48:26	Hilda	Kibet	NED	27.3.81	4		Ostia	3 Mar
68:00				F Kiplagat			1		New Delhi	15 Dec
68:01			Philes	Ongori	KEN	19.7.86	2		Berlin	7 Apr
68:03				G Cherono			2		New Delhi	15 Dec
68:05	64:33	47:55	Meselech	Melkamu	ETH	27.4.85	7		Ra's Al-Khaymah	15 Feb
68:08	64:33	47:56	Pasalia	Kipkoech	KEN	22.12.88	8		Ra's Al-Khaymah	15 Feb
68:10				Kabuu			3		New Delhi	15 Dec
68:12	64:34	47:45		Degefa			2		Praha	6 Apr
68:15	64:46		Joyce	Chepkirui	KEN	20.8.88	1		Valencia	20 Oct
68:18		48:24	Mercy	Kibarus	KEN	25.2.84	5		Ostia	3 Mar
68:20	64:55	48:29	Emily	Chebet (20)	KEN	18.2.86	2		Valencia	20 Oct
68:24		48:50	Selly	Chepyego	KEN	3.10.85	1		Okayama	23 Dec
68:31			Shalane	Flanagan	USA	8.7.81	2		New Orleans	24 Feb
68:35	65:03	48:36	Feyse	Tadesse	ETH	19.11.88	9		Ra's Al-Khaymah	15 Feb
68:38	65:03	48:28	Tadelech	Bekele	ETH	11.4.91	3		Valencia	20 Oct
(31/24)										
68:48			Waganesh	Mekasha	ETH	16.1.92	1		Marrakech	27 Jan
68:48	65:29		Edna	Kiplagat	KEN	15.11.79	1		Lisboa	24 Mar
68:53	65:27	48:48	Tiki	Gelana	ETH	22.10.87	1		Marugame	3 Feb
68:53	65:26	48:23	Josephine	Chepkoech	KEN	.89	2		Barcelona	17 Feb
68:56	65:31	49:08	Ashu	Kasim	ETH	20.10.84	10		Ra's Al-Khaymah	15 Feb
68:59	65:29	49:15	Yukiko	Akaba	JPN	18.10.79	1		Yamaguchi	17 Mar
(30)										
68:59	65:32		Eunice	Kirwa	KEN	20.5.84	2		Lisboa	24 Mar
68:59			Guteni	Shone	ETH	17.11.91	1		Luanda	1 Sep
68:59			Lyudmyla	Kovalenko	UKR	26.6.89	1		Philadelphia	15 Sep
69:00	65:27	48:47	Kimberley	Smith	NZL	19.11.81	2		Marugame	3 Feb
69:00			Konjit	Biruk	ETH	22.9.87	2		Philadelphia	15 Sep
69:02			Yebrwual	Melese	ETH	18.4.90	3		Yangzhou	21 Apr
69:04	65:32	49:09	Sharon	Cherop	KEN	16.3.84	11		Ra's Al-Khaymah	15 Feb
69:09	65:36	49:18d	Caroline	Rotich	KEN	13.5.84	1		New York	17 Mar
69:11			Gladys	Kipsoi	KEN	.86	1		Paris	3 Mar
69:11		49:40	Malika	Asahssah	MAR	24.9.82	6		Ostia	3 Mar
(40)										
69:12	65:37	49:26d	Diane	Nukuri-Johnson	BDI	1.12.84	2		New York	17 Mar
69:18	65:41	49:09	Diana	Sigei	KEN	.87	12		Ra's Al-Khaymah	15 Feb
69:18	65:46	49:15	Hanae	Tanaka	JPN	12.2.90	2		Yamaguchi	17 Mar
69:18	65:38	49:26d	Lisa	Stublic	CRO	18.5.84	3		New York	17 Mar

Mark			Name		Nat	Born	Pos	Meet	Venue	Date
69:20			Mariya	Konovalova	RUS	14.8.74	1		Novosibirsk	14 Sep
69:21	65:46	48:35	Isabellah	Ochichi	KEN	28.10.79	3		Praha	6 Apr
69:21			Wude	Ayalew	ETH	4.7.87	5		New Delhi	15 Dec
69:23		48:40	Valeria	Straneo	ITA	5.4.76	1		Lisboa	6 Oct
69:24A			Eunice	Kioko	KEN	.88	2		Nairobi	24 Feb
69:32	65:58	49:26	Yuko	Shimizu	JPN	13.7.85	3		Marugame	3 Feb
(50)										
69:32			Monica	Jepkoech	KEN	.85	2		Paris	3 Mar
69:36A			Hellen	Cheprugut	KEN		3		Nairobi	24 Feb
69:36	65:52	49:08	Felista	Wanjugu	KEN	18.2.90	3		Okayama	23 Dec
69:38	65:56	49:07	Ehitu	Kiros	ETH	13.1.88	5		Praha	6 Apr
69:42	66:04	49:39d	Sabrina	Mockenhaupt	GER	6.12.81	4		New York	17 Mar
69:45	66:11	49:29	Rei	Ohara	JPN	10.8.90	3		Yamaguchi	17 Mar
69:45	66:06	49:14	Reina	Iwade	JPN-J	8.12.94	4		Okayama	23 Dec
69:49	dh		Christelle	Daunay	FRA	5.12.74	4	GBR	South Shields	15 Sep
69:52A			Jacqueline	Kiplimo	KEN	84	4		Nairobi	24 Feb
69:53		49:08	Mamitu	Daska	ETH	16.10.83	1		Houston	13 Jan
(60)										
69:59			Cynthia	Limo	KEN	18.12.89	1		Rabat	7 Apr
70:00			Georgina	Rono	KEN	19.5.80	1		Santa Pola	20 Jan
70:00			Mai	Ito	JPN	23.5.84	3		Berlin	7 Apr
70:03+			Agnes	Mutune	KEN	26.6.86		in 25k	Berlin	5 Ma
70:03	66:36	49:36	Mestawet	Tufa	ETH	14.9.83	1		Gifu	19 May
70:03			Tomomi	Tanaka	JPN	25.1.88	4		Philadelphia	15 Sep
70:03			Aheza	Kiros	ETH	26.3.82	2		Boston	13 Oct
70:03	66:25	49:27	Sayo	Nomura	JPN	18.4.89	5		Okayama	23 Dec
70:04+			Esther	Chemtai	KEN	4.6.88		in 25k	Berlin	5 May
70:06			Gorreti	Jepkoech	KEN-J	7.3.94	1		Udine	22 Sep
(70)										
70:09	66:27	49:09	Pamela	Lisoreng	KEN	5.8.88	7		Praha	6 Apr
70:09			Alice	Kimutai	KEN		7		New Delhi	15 Dec
70:10	66:32	49:26	Sakiko	Matsumi	JPN	7.8.88	4		Marugame	3 Feb
70:11			Leonidah	Mosop	KEN	.91	2		Ivry-sur-Seine	21 Apr
70:11	66:29	49:16	Chieko	Kido	JPN	14.3.90	6		Okayama	23 Dec
70:13	66:32	49:27	Eri	Hayakawa	JPN	15.11.81	5		Marugame	3 Feb
70:14	dh		Jelena	Prokopcuka	LAT	21.9.76	5	GNR	South Shields	15 Sep
70:17	66:39	49:47	Grace	Kimanzi	KEN	1.3.92	4		Yamaguchi	17 Mar
70:19			Gemma	Steel	GBR	12.11.85	1		Birmingham	20 Oct
70:21			Asami	Kato	JPN	12.10.90	5		Philadelphia	15 Sep
(80)										
70:24			Caroline	Chepkwony	KEN	18.4.84	3		Paris	3 Mar
70:24			Joyce	Kiplimo	KEN	.88	2		Udine	22 Sep
70:26	66:42	49:26	Misato	Horie	JPN	10.3.87	6		Marugame	3 Feb
70:27	66:45	49:59d	Madaí	Pérez	MEX	2.2.80	6		New York	17 Mar
70:27			Jane	Moraa	KEN	21.9.91	2		Zwolle	8 Jun
70:28	66:53	49:40	Rui	Aoyama	JPN	15.4.89	7		Marugame	3 Feb
70:28			Pauline	Wanjiru	KEN	11.10.84	1		Bath	3 Mar
70:30	66:45	49:43d	Yolanda	Caballero	COL	19.3.82	7		New York	17 Mar
70:32			Mary	Ngugi	KEN	17.12.88	3		New Orleans	24 Feb
70:32			Susan	Partridge	GBR	4.1.80	2		Bath	3 Mar
(90)										
70:32			Elvan	Abeylegesse	TUR	11.9.82	1		Nice	21 Apr
70:33			Sarah	Chepchirchir	KEN	27.7.84	1		Boulogne-Billancourt	17 Nov
70:34	66:57	49:59	Nikki	Chapple	AUS	9.2.81	8		Marugame	3 Feb
70:36			Kenza	Dahmani	ALG	18.11.80	1		El Khroub	27 Apr
70:36	66:49	49:52	Mizuki	Noguchi	JPN	3.7.78	1		Sendai	12 May
70:36			Valentine	Kipketer	KEN	5.1.93	1		Sotokoto	7 Jul
70:38			Bethlehem	Moges	ETH	3.5.91	1		Olomouc	22 Jun
70:41	67:16		Sylvia	Kibet	KEN	28.3.84	4		Lisboa	24 Mar
70:42+	67:10		Alice	Timbilil	KEN	16.6.83			Amsterdam	20 Oct
70:44	67:12		Ana Dulce	Félix	POR	23.10.82	5		Lisboa	24 Mar
(100)										
70:44	dh		Misaki	Kato	JPN	15.8.91	6	GNR	South Shields	15 Sep

70:48		Pauline	Wanjiku	KEN	.88	15 Sep	70:56		Flomena	Chepchirchir	KEN	1.12.81	13 Jan
70:50	67:06	Yurie	Doi (49:51)	JPN	8.12.88	17 Mar	70:56		Merima	Hasen	ETH	10.6.92	13 Jan
70:51	67:04	Kumi	Ogura	JPN	24.6.85	3 Feb	70:56+	67:08	Buzunesh	Deba	ETH	8.9.87	13 Jan
70:51		Tigist	Tufa	ETH	81	29 Sep	70:56+	67:07	Meskerem	Assefa	ETH	20.9.85	13 Jan
70:51		Desiree	Davila	USA	26.7.83	23 Dec	70:56		Rkia	El Moukim	MAR	22.2.88	11 Nov
70:52		Krista	Duchene	CAN	9.1.77	23 Jun	71:00	67:15	Yuka	Tokuda	JPN	1.6.88	17 Mar
70:53	67:17	Stephanie	Rothstein Bruce	USA	14.1.84	17 Mar	71:01+		Belaynesh	Oljira	ETH	26.6.90	25 Jan
70:54		Krisztina	Papp	HUN	17.12.82	3 Mar	71:01+		Tirfi	Tsegaye	ETH	25.11.84	25 Jan
70:55		Isabellah	Andersson	SWE	12.11.80	24 Mar	71:01+		Amane	Gobena	ETH	1.9.82	25 Jan

Mark		Name		Nat	Born	Pos	Meet	Venue	Date
71:03	67:18	Sara	Moreira	POR	17.10.85				17 Mar
71:03		Shure	Damise	ETH					7 Apr
71:04		Tsgereda	Girma	ETH-J	.95				23 Mar
71:05		Lydia	Cheromei	KEN	11.5.77				3 Mar
71.07		Mary	Davies	NZL	27.8.82				22 Jun
71:09		Mulu	Seboka	ETH	25.9.84				6 Jan
71:09	67:29	Adriana	Nelson	USA	31.1.80				17 Mar
71:10		Lucy	Macharia	KEN	.86				7 Apr
71:10+	67:26	Caroline	Kilel	KEN	21.3.81				27 Oct
71:10+	67:26	Gelete	Burka	ETH	15.2.86				27 Oct
71:11	67:27	Doricah	Obare	KEN	10.1.90				17 Mar
71:11		Maryanne	Wangari Wanjiru	KEN	.86				30 Mar
71:12		Agnes	Cheserek	KEN	.87				27 Jan
71:13	67:20	Janet	Bawcom	USA	22.8.78				17 Mar
71:13		Alice	Kibor	KEN	.92				30 Mar
71:13+	67:26	Birhane	Dibaba	ETH	11.9.93				27 Oct
71:15+	67:34	Jemima	Jelagat	KEN	21.12.84				13 Oct
71:16	67:35	Misaki	Onishi	JPN	24.2.85				3 Feb
71:16+	67:36	Abebech	Afework	ETH	11.12.90				13 Oct
71:16+	67:35	Werknesh	Kidane	ETH	21.11.81				13 Oct
71:19		Jane	Kiptoo	KEN	8.8.82				12 Jun
71:21		Yiska	Melat	KEN	.92				6 Jan
71:21		Alyson	Dixon	GBR	24.9.78				3 Mar
71:21		Helen	Jepkurgat	KEN	21.2.89				24 Mar
71:21		Sarah	Kiptoo	KEN	.89				17 Nov
71:22	67:41	Aya	Nagata	JPN	31.3.90				17 Mar
71:23	67:37	Rika	Shintaku	JPN	19.10.85				23 Dec
71:24	67:42	Chihiro	Takato	JPN	20.7.91				3 Feb
71:24	67:38	Serena	Burla	USA	29.7.82				17 Mar
71:27		Violet	Jelagat	KEN					8 Dec
71:28		Edith	Chelimo	KEN	16.7.86				23 Mar
71:28		Noriko	Higuchi	JPN	23.5.85				12 May
71:28		Jackline	Sakilu	TAN	28.12.86				3 Nov
71:29	67:48	Yuka	Hakoyama	JPN	9.3.90				3 Feb
71:30	67:52	Yasuka	Ueno	JPN	16.1.92				17 Mar
71:30		Jane	Murage	KEN	.87				15 Sep
71:30+	67:45	Aleksandra	Duliba	BLR	9.1.88				13 Oct
71:31		Meseret	Kitata	ETH	.90				7 Apr
71:32+		Shitaye	Bedaso	ETH	.85				25 Jan
71:32+	67:50	Ryoko	Kizaki	JPN	21.6.85				10 Mar
71:32+	67:49	Genet	Getaneh	ETH	6.1.86				10 Mar
71:33		Gladys	Tarus	KEN					27 Jan
71:33		Kelly	Brinkman	USA	.81				21 Jun

Downhill course (San Diego 84m, Buffalo 306m)

Mark	Name		Nat	Born	Pos	Venue	Date
69:03	Georgina	Rono	KEN	19.5.80	2	San Diego	2 Jun
69:16	Aliphine	Tuliamok-Bolton	KEN	5.4.89	1	Santa Fe - Buffalo	15 Sep
69:46	Firehiwot	Dado	ETH	9.1.84	3	San Diego	2 Jun
69:56	Emebet	Itaa Bedada	ETH	11.1.90	4	San Diego	2 Jun

Drugs Disqualification

Mark	Name		Nat	Born	Pos	Venue	Date
68:58	Pauline	Njeri ¶	KEN	28.7.85	(1)	Paris	3 Mar

JUNIORS

Mark	Name		Nat	Born	Pos	Venue	Date
72:29	Letekidan	Gebreham	ERI	16.1.94	3	Ceske Budejovice	8 Jun
73:26	Aiko	Sakata	JPN	18.3.94	7	Matsue	17 Mar
73:26A	Naomi	Chepngeno	KEN	.94	5	Narok	5 Oct
73:33	Cynthia	Cherop	KEN	.94	2	Columbus	20 Oct

Mark		Name		Nat	Born	Date
71:34		Valentine	Kibet	KEN	..89	24 Mar
71:35+	67:51	Yoko	Miyauchi	JPN	9.6.83	10 Mar
71:35		Gladys	Chemweno	KEN	4.7.88	21 Apr
71:35		Souad	Aït Salem	ALG	6.1.79	27 Apr
71:36+	67:46	Azusa	Nojiri	JPN	6.6.82	27 Jan
71:36+	67:46	Atsede	Habtamu	ETH	26.10.87	27 Jan
71:36+	67:47	Mari	Ozaki	JPN	16.7.75	27 Jan
71:36+	67:47	Yoko	Shibui	JPN	14.3.79	27 Jan
71:36+	67:47	Kayoko	Fukushi	JPN	25.3.82	27 Jan
71:36	67:58	Kim Sung-eun		KOR	24.2.89	3 Feb
71:37		Marta	Tigabea	ETH	4.10.90	7 Apr
71:37		Lanni	Marchant	CAN	11.4.84	23 Jun
71:37		Letrebhan	Gebreslasea	ETH	.90	15 Dec
71:40+	67:55	Yuko	Watanabe	JPN	3.11.87	27 Jan
71:40+	67:55	Tetyana	Hamera-Shmyrko	UKR	1.6.83	27 Jan
71:40		Nancy	Kiprono	KEN		26 May
71:40		Adrienne	Herzog	NED	30.9.85	20 Oct
71:40		Yewbdar	Tesgome	ETH		15 Dec
71:45		Laurane	Picoche	FRA	17.7.85	10 Mar
71:46		Helen	Clitheroe	GBR	2.1.74	24 Feb
71:46		Keiko	Nogami	JPN	6.12.85	17 Mar
71:48		Barkahoum	Drici	ALG	28.3.89	27 Apr
71:48+		Yeshi	Esayias	ETH	28.12.85	27 Oct
71:49		Kara	Goucher	USA	9.7.78	24 Feb
71:49		Aziza	Aliyu	ETH	20.10.85	17 Mar
71:50+	67:52	Aberu	Kebede	ETH	12.9.89	24 Feb
71:50		Visiline	Jepkesho	KEN	.88	6 Oct
71:51		Jessica	Trengove	AUS	15.8.87	7 Jul
71:51		Freya	Ross	GBR	20.9.83	6 Oct
71:52		Purity	Kimetto	KEN	.85	13 Oct
71:55		Belaynesh	Zemedkun	ETH	23.12.87	20 Jan
71:55		Maurine	Kipchumba	KEN		18 Aug
71:56		Mattie	Suver	USA	10.9.87	21 Jun
71:56+		Sechale	Delasa Adugna	ETH	20.9.91	20 Oct
71:57A		Agnes	Tirop	KEN-J	23.10.95	6 Oct
71:57+		Getnet	Selomie	ETH	10.4.86	20 Oct
71:58+		Biruktayit	Eshetu	ETH	.82	17 Mar
71:58+		Helena	Kirop	KEN	9.9.76	17 Mar
71:58+		Sultan	Haydar	TUR	23.5.87	17 Mar
71:59		Nanami	Matsura	JPN	24.12.89	17 Mar
71:59		Lilian	Jelagat ¶	KEN	23.1.89	7 Apr
71:59+		Beatrice	Toroitich	KEN	15.12.81	20 Oct
(204)						

25 – 30 KILOMETRES ROAD

25k	30k	Name		Nat	Born	Pos	Venue	Date
1:21:37		Lucy	Kabuu	KEN	24.3.84	1	Berlin	5 May
1:23:08		Agnes	Katunga	KEN	.86	2	Berlin	5 May
1:23:18		Esther	Chemtai	KEN	4.6.88	3	Berlin	5 May
1:23:35+	1:40:29	Alice	Timbilil	KEN	16.6.83	in Mar	Amsterdam	20 Oct
1:24:10+	1:41:20	Tirfi	Tsegaye	ETH	25.11.84	in Mar	Frankfurt	27 Oct
1:24:16+	1:40:30	Florence	Kiplagat	KEN	27.2.87	in Mar	London	21 Apr
1:24:17+	1:42:28	Gelete	Burka	ETH	15.2.86	in Mar	Frankfurt	27 Oct
1:24:18+	1:41:05	Atsede	Baysa	ETH	16.4.87	in Mar	Chicago	13 Oct
1:24:21+	1:41:18	Abebech	Afework	ETH	11.12.90	in Mar	Chicago	13 Oct
1:24:26+	1:42:50	Tiki	Gelana	ETH	22.10.87	in Mar	London	21 Apr
1:24:26+		Werknesh	Kidane	ETH	21.11.81	in Mar	Chicago	13 Oct
1:24:34+		Merima	Hasen	ETH	10.6.92	in Mar	Chicago	13 Oct
1:24:42+	1:42:04	Ehitu	Kiros	ETH	13.1.88	in Mar	Chicago	13 Oct
1:24:43+	1:42:53	Isabellah	Ochichi	KEN	28.10.79	in Mar	Amsterdam	20 Oct
1:24:49+	1:42:12	Margaret	Agai	KEN	10.6.88	in Mar	Nagoya	10 Mar
1:24:49+	1:42:13	Georgina	Rono	KEN	19.5.80	in Mar	Nagoya	10 Mar
1:24:50+		Yukiko	Akaba	JPN	18.10.79	in Mar	Chicago	13 Oct
1:24:54+	1:42:37	Joyce	Chepkirui	KEN	20.8.88	in Mar	London	21 Apr

Mark		Name		Nat	Born	Pos	Meet	Venue	Date
1:24:55+	1:41:44	Mulu	Seboka	ETH	25.9.84	in Mar		Osaka	27 Jan
1:24:55+	1:41:44	Atsede	Habtamu	ETH	26.10.87	in Mar		Osaka	27 Jan
1:24:56+	1:42:17	Yoko	Shibui	JPN	14.3.79	in Mar		Osaka	27 Jan
1:24:56+		Azusa	Nojiri	JPN	6.6.82	in Mar		Osaka	27 Jan
1:24:59+		Isabellah	Andersson	SWE	12.11.80	in Mar		Berlin	29 Sep
1:25:14	1:42:18	Ashu	Kasim	ETH	20.10.84	in Mar		Roma	17 Mar
	1:42:32	Flomena	Cheyech	KEN	5.7.82	in Mar		Toronto	20 Oct
1:25:21	1:42:39	Aberu	Kebede	ETH	12.9.89	in Mar		Tokyo	24 Feb
1:25:14	1:42:56	Biruktayit	Eshetu	ETH	.82	in Mar		Roma	17 Mar

MARATHON

Mark	25k	30k	Name		Nat	Born	Pos	Meet	Venue	Date
2:19:57	1:24:19	1:40:52	Rita	Jeptoo	KEN	15.2.81	1		Chicago	13 Oct
2:20:15	1:24:17	1:40:20	Priscah	Jeptoo	KEN	26.6.84	1		London	21 Apr
2:20:48	1:24:19	1:40:52	Jemima	Jelagat	KEN	21.12.84	2		Chicago	13 Oct
2:21:06			Feyse	Tadesse	ETH	19.11.88	1		Paris	7 Apr
2:21:13	1:22:56	1:39:38	Florence	Kiplagat	KEN	27.2.87	1		Berlin	29 Sep
2:21:32	1:24:17	1:40:18	Edna	Kiplagat	KEN	15.11.79	2		London	21 Apr
2:22:28	1:22:57	1:39:40	Sharon	Cherop	KEN	16.3.84	2		Berlin	29 Sep
2:22:34	1:24:10	1:41:05	Caroline	Kilel	KEN	21.3.81	1		Frankfurt	27 Oct
2:22:46	1:24:19	1:41:07	Mariya	Konovalova	RUS	14.8.74	3		Chicago	13 Oct
2:23:00	1:24:10	1:41:05	Flomena	Chepchirchir (10)	KEN	1.12.81	2		Frankfurt	27 Oct
2:23:01	1:24:10	1:41:05	Birhane	Dibaba	ETH	11.9.93	3		Frankfurt	27 Oct
2:23:02	1:23:35	1:40:17	Valentine	Kipketer	KEN	5.1.93	1		Amsterdam	20 Oct
2:23:14			Merima	Hasen	ETH	10.6.92	2		Paris	7 Apr
2:23:23			Tirfi	Tsegaye	ETH	25.11.84	1		Dubai	25 Jan
2:23:23	1:24:10	1:41:05	Mamitu	Daska	ETH	16.10.83	4		Frankfurt	27 Oct
2:23:27				Jelagat			1		Rotterdam	14 Apr
2:23:28			Margaret	Agai	KEN	10.6.88	1		Daegu	14 Apr
2:23:28			Aberu	Kebede	ETH	12.9.89	1		Shanghai	1 Dec
2:23:34	1:24:50	1:41:58	Ryoko	Kizaki	JPN	21.6.85	1		Nagoya	10 Mar
2:23:34			Eunice	Jepkirui	KEN	20.5.84	3		Paris	7 Apr
2:23:37				Hasen			1		Houston	13 Jan
2:23:39			Ehitu	Kiros (20)	ETH	13.1.88	2		Dubai	25 Jan
2:23:43			Mulu	Seboka	ETH	25.9.84	2		Daegu	14 Apr
2:23:44	1:24:44	1:41:44	Aleksandra	Duliba	BLR	9.1.88	4		Chicago	13 Oct
2:23:45	1:24:10	1:41:05		Jepkirui			5		Frankfurt	27 Oct
2:23:50			Amane	Gobena	ETH	1.9.82	3		Dubai	25 Jan
2:23:51	1:24:49	1:41:54		Dibaba			2		Nagoya	10 Mar
2:23:58	1:24:56	1:42:00	Tetyana	Hamera-Shmyrko	UKR	1.6.83	1		Osaka	27 Jan
2:23:59			Abebech	Afework	ETH	11.12.90	2		Rotterdam	14 Apr
2:24:03			Agnes	Barsosio	KEN	5.8.82	3		Daegu	14 Apr
2:24:05	1:24:49	1:41:57	Mizuki	Noguchi	JPN	3.7.78	3		Nagoya	10 Mar
2:24:06	1:25:01	1:41:59	Yeshi	Esayias	ETH	28.12.85	6		Frankfurt	27 Oct
2:24:21	1:24:55	1:41:45	Kayoko	Fukushi	JPN	25.3.82	2		Osaka	27 Jan
2:24:26	1:24:46	1:42:15	Buzunesh	Deba (30)	ETH	8.9.87	2		Houston	13 Jan
2:24:30			Aheza	Kiros	ETH	26.3.82	4		Dubai	25 Jan
2:24:33				Kipketer			1		Mumbai	20 Jan
2:24:34			Flomena	Cheyech	KEN	5.7.82	1		Wien	14 Apr
2:24:40	1:25:14	1:42:18	Helena	Kirop	KEN	9.9.76	1		Roma	17 Mar
2:24:43	1:25:00	1:42:08	Yukiko	Akaba	JPN	18.10.79	3		London	21 Apr
2:24:54	1:25:45	1:42:46	Irina	Mikitenko (40/35)	GER	23.8.72	3		Berlin	29 Sep
2:25:01			Belaynesh	Oljira	ETH	26.6.90	5		Dubai	25 Jan
2:25:09			Dinknesh	Mekasha	ETH	.85	4		Paris	7 Apr
2:25:14	1:24:59		Atsede	Baysa	ETH	16.4.87	4		London	21 Apr
2:25:15	1:25:14	1:42:17	Getnet	Selomie	ETH	10.4.86	2		Roma	17 Mar
2:25:17	1:24:45	1:42:15	Meskerem	Assefa (40)	ETH	20.9.85	3		Houston	13 Jan
2:25:22			Agnes	Kiprop	KEN	12.12.79	5		Paris	7 Apr
2:25:44			Lisa	Stublic	CRO	18.5.84	1		Zürich	7 Apr
2:25:45			Misiker	Mekonnin	ETH	23.7.86	2		Ottawa	26 May
2:25:46	1:26:13	1:43:30	Jelena	Prokopcuka	LAT	21.9.76	4		Nagoya	10 Mar
2:25:46	1:24:17	1:40:51	Meselech	Melkamu	ETH	27.4.85	5		London	21 Apr
2:25:47			Shitaye	Bedaso	ETH	.85	6		Dubai	25 Jan
2:25:53			Emebet	Etea	ETH	11.1.90	2		Seoul	17 Mar
2:25:55			Albina	Mayorova	RUS	16.5.77	1		Yokohama	17 Nov
2:25:56	1:24:56	1:42:17	Yuko	Watanabe	JPN	3.11.87	3		Osaka	27 Jan
2:25:58			Valeria	Straneo (50)	ITA	5.4.76	2	WCh	Moskva	10 Aug

Mark			Name		Nat	Born	Pos	Meet	Venue	Date
2:26:05			Isabellah	Andersson	SWE	12.11.80	7		Dubai	25 Jan
2:26:05			Lisa Jane	Weightman	AUS	16.1.79	1		Melbourne	13 Oct
2:26:07			Aberu	Mekuria	ETH		1		Hengshui	21 Sep
2:26:15			Meseret	Legese	ETH	28.8.87	2		Hengshui	21 Sep
2:26:17	1:25:04	1:42:58	Eri	Hayakawa	JPN	15.11.81	5		Nagoya	10 Mar
2:26:17			Yeshimebet	Tadesse	ETH	.88	3		Seoul	17 Mar
2:26:20	1:25:59	1:43:39	Mestawet	Tufa	ETH	14.9.83	6		Nagoya	10 Mar
2:26:24			Melkam	Gisaw	ETH	17.9.90	1		Düsseldorf	28 Apr
2:26:32				Kim Mi-gyong	PRK	17.10.90	1		Pyongyang	14 Apr
2:26:32			Sarah	Kiptoo	KEN	.89	1		Duluth (40m dh)	22 Jun
			(60)							
2:26:34			Ashu	Kasim	ETH	20.10.84	3		Shanghai	1 Dec
2:26:41	1:24:56	1:41:59	Mari	Ozaki	JPN	16.7.75	4		Osaka	27 Jan
2:26:42	1:25:16	1:42:11	Hilda	Kibet	NED	27.3.81	3		Rotterdam	14 Apr
2:26:43		1:42:32	Sechale	Delasa	ETH	20.9.91	2		Toronto	20 Oct
2:26:45			Karolina	Jarzynska	POL	6.9.81	1		Lódz	14 Apr
2:27:00			Caroline	Rotich	KEN	13.5.84	1		Praha	12 May
2:27:01			Azalech	Masresha	ETH	4.5.88	1		Valencia	17 Nov
2:27:03			Alessandra	Aguilar	ESP	1.7.78	4		Rotterdam	14 Apr
2:27:07			Olena	Burkovska	UKR	9.8.81	1		Hannover	5 May
2:27:10	1:25:14	1:42:18	Sultan	Haydar	TUR	23.5.87	3		Roma	17 Mar
			(70)							
2:27:17	1:25:02	1:42:50	Yoko	Miyauchi	JPN	9.6.83	7		Nagoya	10 Mar
2:27:19		1:42:08	Eunice	Kales	KEN	6.12.84	2		Melbourne	13 Oct
2:27:20				Kim Sung-eun	KOR	24.2.89	4		Seoul	17 Mar
2:27:27			Caroline	Chepkwony	KEN	18.4.84	1		Ljubljana	27 Oct
2:27:35			Fatuma	Sado	ETH	11.10.91	1		Xiamen	5 Jan
2:27:44			Netsanet	Achamo	ETH	14.12.87	4		Ottawa	26 May
2:27:47			Ashete	Bekele	ETH	17.4.88	1		Kosice	6 Oct
2:27:52			Rebecca	Chesire	KEN	.89	2		Düsseldorf	28 Apr
2:27:54			Beata	Naigambo	NAM	11.3.80	9		Dubai	25 Jan
2:27:55			Anna	Hahner	GER	20.11.89	8		Frankfurt	27 Oct
			(80)							
2:28:00			Lanni	Marchant	CAN	11.4.84	3		Toronto	20 Oct
2:28:01			Serena	Burla	USA	29.7.82	2		Amsterdam	20 Oct
2:28:02	1:25:45	1:42:46	Helah	Kiprop	KEN	7.4.85	4		Berlin	29 Sep
2:28:02			Marta	Lema	ETH	90	2		Kosice	6 Oct
2:28:03			Fantu	Jimma	ETH	91	6		Paris	7 Apr
2:28:08	1:24:49	1:42:26	Genet	Getaneh	ETH	6.1.86	8		Nagoya	10 Mar
2:28:14			Christelle	Daunay	FRA	5.12.74	4		New York	3 Nov
2:28:22			Lydia	Jerotich	KEN		5		Seoul	17 Mar
2:28:23			Milka	Jerotich	KEN	24.2.78	1		Warszawa	21 Apr
2:28:30			Yoshimi	Ozaki	JPN	1.7.81	5		Tokyo	24 Feb
			(90)							
2:28:32				Kim Hye-gyong	PRK	9.3.93	2		Pyongyang	14 Apr
2:28:32			Krista	Duchene	CAN	9.1.77	4		Toronto	20 Oct
2:28:36			Janet	Rono	KEN	8.12.88	1		Köln	13 Oct
2:28:36			Alice	Timbilil	KEN	16.6.83	3		Amsterdam	20 Oct
2:28:37			Mai	Ito	JPN	23.5.84	7		London	21 Apr
2:28:47			Azusa	Nojiri	JPN	6.6.82	2		Yokohama	17 Nov
2:28:49			Kimberley	Smith	NZL	19.11.81	6		New York	3 Nov
2:28:53			Philes	Ongori	KEN	19.7.86	2		Praha	12 May
2:28:54			Faith	Cheruto	KEN	.87	2		Valencia	17 Nov
2:29:10			Sabrina	Mockenhaupt	GER	6.12.81	7		New York	3 Nov
			(100)							

Mark	Name		Nat	Born	Date
2:29:11	Jéssica	Augusto	POR	8.11.81	17 Nov
2:29:12	Eleni	Gebrehiwot	ETH	2.1.83	8 Sep
2:29:15	Desiree	Davila	USA	26.7.83	29 Sep
2:29:17	Diana	Lobacevske	LTU	7.8.80	21 Apr
2:29:22	Meseret	Mengistu	ETH	6.3.90	14 Apr
2:29:22	Beatrice	Toroitich	KEN	15.12.81	20 Oct
2:29:24	Tigist	Tufa	ETH	.81	3 Nov
2:29:30	Helaria	Johannes	NAM	13.8.80	24 Feb
2:29:30	Elvan	Abeylegesse	TUR	11.9.82	17 Nov
2:29:32	Goitetom	Haftu	ETH	.87	29 Sep
2:29:35	Edinah	Kwambai	KEN	.86	27 Oct
2:29:42	Lemelen	Berha	ETH	.92	6 Oct
2:29:42	Maja	Neuenschwander	SUI	13.2.80	27 Oct
2:29:45		Jia Chaofeng	CHN	16.11.88	18 May
2:29:47	Alice	Chelagat	KEN	27.12.76	7 Jul
2:29:52	Ehite	Bizuayehu	ETH	.91	24 Feb
2:30:01	Emily	Samoei	KEN	11.11.80	27 Oct
2:30:02	Alevtina	Biktimirova	RUS	10.9.82	21 Apr
2:30:04	Olha	Kotovska	UKR	5.12.83	6 Oct
2:30:09	Diane	Nukuri-Johnson	BDI	1.12.84	3 Nov
2:30:13	Alem	Fikre	ETH	22.10.88	17 Mar
2:30:17	Lisa	Hahner	GER	20.11.89	27 Oct
2:30:18	Abeba	Teklu	ETH	.89	29 Sep
2:30:20	Mika	Yoshikawa	JPN	16.9.84	24 Feb
2:30:20		Ding Changqin	CHN	27.11.91	18 May
2:30:21	Doreen	Kitaka	KEN	.83	22 Jun
2:30:26	Asami	Kato	JPN	12.10.90	10 Mar
2:30:27	Mizuho	Nasukawa	JPN	22.11.79	17 Nov
2:30:28	Agnieszka	Gortel	POL	20.3.77	13 Oct
2:30:36	Ruth	Wanjiru	KEN	11.9.81	26 May
2:30:38		Yang Fengxia	CHN	26.9.91	31 Mar
2:30:40	Natalya	Puchkova	RUS	28.1.87	21 Apr
2:30:40	Gelete	Burka	ETH	15.2.86	27 Oct
2:30:42	Misaki	Katsumata	JPN	26.12.85	25 Jan
2:30:45	Anastasiya	Staravoytova	BLR	4.11.82	24 Feb
2:30:46	Susan	Partridge	GBR	4.1.80	21 Apr

Mark	Name		Nat	Born	Pos	Meet	Venue		Date	
2:30:50	Esther Wanjiru	Macharia	KEN	.87	6 Oct					
2:30:52	Misato	Horie	JPN	10.3.87	10 Mar					
2:30:52	Jacqueline	Kiplimo	KEN	.84	7 Apr					
2:30:53	Annie	Bersagel	USA	30.3.83	6 Oct					
2:30:57	Asami	Furuse	JPN	17.3.88	10 Mar					
2:30:57	Lydia	Rutto	KEN		29 Sep					
2:31:00		Wei Xiaojie	CHN	20.11.89	18 May					
2:31:10	Alyson	Dixon	GBR	24.9.78	14 Apr					
2:31:11	Tetyana	Holovchenko	UKR	13.2.80	7 Apr					
2:31:14	Mercy	Kibarus	KEN	25.2.84	27 Oct					
2:31:16	Bizunesh	Urgesa	ETH	18.6.89	17 Nov					
2:31:19		Zhang Yingying	CHN	4.1.90	20 Oct					
2:31:20	Makda	Harun	ETH	.88	24 Feb					
2:31:23	Priscilla	Lorchima	KEN	.85	21 Apr					
2:31:26	Irvette	van Zyl	RSA	5.7.87	21 Apr					
2:31:27	Joan	Kigen	KEN		6 Oct					
2:31:28	Hiroko	Yoshitomi	JPN	26.12.83	24 Feb					
2:31:32		Park Ho-sun	KOR	17.11.86	3 Nov					
2:31:33	Etalemahu	Kidane	ETH	14.2.83	27 Oct					
2:31:38	Isabellah	Ochichi	KEN	28.10.79	20 Oct					
2:31:39		Jon Kyong-hui	PRK	12.12.86	14 Apr					
2:31:39	Clara	Santucci	USA	24.3.87	13 Oct					
2:31:41	Elfnesh	Melaku	ETH	20.12.85	23 Mar					
2:31:44	Desta	Girma	ETH	29.3.87	20 Jan					
2:31:44	Adriana	da Silva	BRA	22.7.81	21 Apr					
2:31:48	Gladys	Tejeda	PER	30.9.85	7 Apr					
2:31:49	Megersa	Megertu	ETH	.91	24 Feb					
2:31:49	Miranda	Boonstra	NED	29.8.72	20 Oct					
2:31:50	Radiya	Adlo	ETH	22.9.89	28 Sep					
2:31:54	Makida	Wordofa	ETH	.89	23 Mar					
2:31:54	Risa	Shigetomo	JPN	29.8.87	3 Nov					
2:31:55	Asnakech	Egigayehu	ETH	9.5.86	17 Mar					
2:32:00	Winfrida	Kwamboka	KEN	4.3.82	31 Mar					
2:32:00	Hellen	Mugo	KEN	12.12.85	6 Oct					
2:32:01	Alevtina	Ivanova	RUS	22.5.75	7 Jul					
2:32:04	Woyshinet	Girma	ETH	28.7.86	21 Sep					
2:32:11	Inés	Melchor	PER	30.8.86	7 Apr					
2:32:12		Ro Un-ok	PRK	14.11.89	4 Oct					
2:32:14	Nadezhda	Leontyeva	RUS	26.6.84	17 Mar					
2:32:16	Noriko	Higuchi	JPN	23.5.85	27 Jan					
2:32:21		Kim Kum-ok	PRK	9.12.85	24 Feb					
2:32:24	Eyerusalem	Kuma ¶	ETH	4.11.81	14 Mar					
2:32:24	Tatyana	Aryasova	RUS	2.4.79	12 May					
2:32:31	Nikki	Chapple	AUS	9.2.81	10 Mar					
2:32:33	Tigist	Abdi	ETH	.85	7 Apr					
2:32:35	Vianey	de la Rosa	MEX	4.8.86	29 Sep					
2:32:37	Melissa	White	USA	7.4.81	13 Oct					
2:32:38	Estela	Navascues	ESP	3.2.81	24 Nov					
2:32:39	Mildred	Kiminy	UGA	23.12.85	31 Mar					
2:32:39		Cao Mojie	CHN	10.4.92	18 May					
2:32:39	René	Kalmer	RSA	3.11.80	17 Nov					
2:32:41	Yuko	Shibui	JPN	14.3.79	27 Jan					
2:32:43	Shoko	Shimizu	JPN	13.10.90	24 Feb					
2:32:44	Rose	Kosgei	KEN	22.8.81	24 Feb					
2:32:46	Biruktayit	Degefa	ETH	29.9.90	22 Sep					
2:32:47	Ednah	Mukwana	KEN		16 Jun					
2:32:49	Elizabeth	Rumokol	KEN	26.3.83	23 Mar					
2:32:50	Chizuru	Ideta	JPN	15.11.86	10 Mar					
2:32:50		Liu Ruihuan	CHN	29.6.92	18 May					
2:32:54	Monica	Jepkoech	KEN	.85	7 Apr					
2:32:55	Adhana	Tsehay	ETH	8.4.85	7 Apr					
2:32:59	Wudnesh	Nega	ETH	.84	24 Feb					
2:33:00	Marina	Damantsevich	BLR	6.6.85	21 Apr					
2:33:03	Natalya (200)	Sokolova	RUS	12.3.82	20 Oct					

Exceesively Downhill   (Boston 136.29m, Los Angeles 17 Mar 122.22m, Sacramento 8 Dec 104m)

Mark	Name		Nat	Born	Pos		Venue		Date	
2:26:58 dh	Meseret	Hailu	ETH	12.9.90	2		Boston		15 Apr	
2:27:08 dh	Shalane	Flanagan	USA	8.7.81	4		Boston		15 Apr	
2:28:11 dh	Kara	Goucher	USA	9.7.78	6		Boston		15 Apr	
2:28:59 dh	Madaí	Pérez	MEX	2.2.80	7		Boston		15 Apr	
2:29:54dh	Diane	Nukuri-Johnson	BDI	1.12.84	15 Apr					
2:30:05dh	Ana Dulce	Félix	POR	23.10.82	15 Apr					
2:30:32	Zemzem	Ahmed	ETH	27.12.84	17 Mar					
2:30:41dh	Rebecca	Wade	USA	9.2.89	8 Dec					

2:32:39	Deena	Kastor	USA	14.2.73	17 Mar					

Drugs disqualification

2:31:30	Eyerusalem	Kuma ¶	ETH	4.11.81	20 Oct					
2:31:50	Yevgeniya	Danilova ¶	RUS	10.8.81	22 Sep					

100 KILOMETRES

Mark	Name		Nat	Born	Pos	Meet	Venue		Date	
7:38:52	Kajsa	Berg	SWE	16.1.79	1	EC	Belves		27 Apr	
7:40:51		Berg			1		Stockholm		4 Aug	
7:42:52	Irina	Antropova	RUS	2.6.82	2	EC	Belves		27 Apr	
7:44:06		Antropova			1		Torhout		22 Jun	
7:47:58	Marija	Vrajic	CRO	22.9.76	2		Torhout		22 Jun	
7:48:12	Susan	Harrison	GBR	6.8.71	3	EC	Belves		27 Apr	
7:49:23	Irina	Pankovskaya	RUS	10.1.86	4	EC	Belves		27 Apr	
7:53:21	Sophia	Sundberg	SWE	5.9.84	5	EC	Belves		27 Apr	
7:54:06		Vrajic			6	EC	Belves		27 Apr	
7:56:07	Oksana (10/7)	Akimenkova	RUS	15.10.86	7	EC	Belves		28 Apr	
8:03:22	Nadezhda	Shikhanova	RUS	14.5.84	1		Sankt-Peterburg		7 Sep	
8:03:26	Mariya	Aksenova	RUS	25.10.88	8	EC	Belves		28 Apr	
8:04:39	Tomoko	Hara	JPN	14.4.73	1		Nakamura		20 Oct	
8:08:45	Frida	Södermark	SWE	5.8.78	4 Aug					
8:10:39	Mai	Fujisawa	JPN	21.9.74	30 Jun					
8:10:53	Pamela	Veith	GER	10.7.73	13 Apr					
8:12:54		Mikie	Sakane	JPN	31.7.74	20 Oct				
8:15:15		Barbara	Cimarrusti	ITA	18.12.71	27 Apr				
8:16:55		Emily	Gelder	GBR	1.4.75	31 Mar				

24 HOURS

Mark	Name		Nat	Born	Pos	Meet	Venue	Date	
252.205 km	Mami	Kudo	JPN	17.7.64	1	WCh	Steenbergen	12 May	
244.669	Sabrina	Little	USA	12.7.86	2	WCh	Steenbergen	12 May	
239.564 t	Deb	Nicholl	NZL	10.2.70	1		Caboolture	21 Jul	
236.228	Suzanna	Bon	USA	28.7.64	3	WCh	Steenbergen	12 May	
234.146 t	Yudith	Hernandez Melgar	SWE	6.10.89	1		Skövde	25 Aug	
230.890	Mikie	Sakane	JPN	31.7.74	1		Tokyo	10 Nov	
229.702	Traci	Falbo	USA	12.11.71	4	WCh	Steenbergen	12 May	
229.393	Anne-Marie	Vernet	FRA	15.12.67	5	WCh	Steenbergen	12 May	
228.907	Sayuri	Oka	JPN	6.8.70	6	WCh	Steenbergen	12 May	
227.618	Cécile (10)	Nissen	FRA	21.3.72	7	WCh	Steenbergen	12 May	
226.107	Sharon	Law	GBR	9.3.75	8	WCh	Steenbergen	12 May	

Mark	Name		Nat	Born	Pos	Meet	Venue	Date
225.508 t	Ruthann	Sheahan	IRL	30.4.75	1		Belfast	20 Jul
224.932	Heike	Bergmann	GER	16.12.62	9	WCh	Steenbergen	12 May
224.664	Wilma	Dierx	NED	11.5.66	10	WCh	Steenbergen	12 May
224.471	Kiyoko	Shirakawa	JPN	22.6.66	11	WCh	Steenbergen	12 May
222.065	Traci	Falbo	USA	12.11.71	1		Morganton	1 Jan
220.911 t	Åsa	Hällstorp	SWE	20.7.73	2		Skövde	25 Aug
220.777	Torill	Fonn	SWE	1.11.67	12	WCh	Steenbergen	12 May
220.722	Christine	Tamnga	FRA	3.8.74	1		Grenoble	6 Oct
220.363	Sylvie	Peuch	FRA	22.11.61	2		Grenoble	6 Oct
	(20)							
220.221	Antje	Krause	GER	1.5.72	13	WCh	Steenbergen	12 May
220.037	Debbie	Martin-Consani	GBR	4.4.75	14	WCh	Steenbergen	12 May
219.260	Maria Luisa	Zecchino	ITA	11.12.67	15	WCh	Steenbergen	12 May
218.676	Constance	Gardner	USA	5.11.64	16	WCh	Steenbergen	12 May
218.553	Sandra	Lundqvist	SWE	5.7.77	17	WCh	Steenbergen	12 May
218.049	Szilvia	Lubics	HUN	27.5.74	18	WCh	Steenbergen	12 May

217.752 t	Jennifer	Salter	GBR	18.7.74	15 Dec		213.687	Pascale	Bouly	FRA	9.1.62	12 May
217.527	Kotomi	Suzuki	JPN	27.10.75	10 Nov		213.576	Helen	James	GBR	5.9.72	5 May
217.285	Monica	Barchetti	ITA	28.11.68	12 May		212.990	Nathalie	Zimmer	FRA	7.2.70	6 Oct
216.624 t	Fionna	Cameron	GBR	28.1.80	22 Sep		212.902	Irina	Koval	RUS	19.11.58	12 May
216.343	Bernadette	Benson	AUS	25.3.69	12 May		212.213	Emily	Gelder	GBR	1.4.75	12 May
216.304	Aleksandra	Niwinska	POL	23.1.86	20 Oct		212.045	Christine	Zanconato	FRA	23.10.62	6 Oct
215.481	Stéphanie	Dessartine	FRA	29.1.74	20 May		211.489	Tatyana	Moskaleva	RUS	13.8.90	12 May
215.344	Ulrike	Striednig	AUT	16.4.61	12 May		210.906 t	Mami	Kudo	JPN	17.7.64	8 Dec
215.115	Michaela	Dimitriadu	CZE	23.12.73	12 May		210.876	Karen	Hathaway	GBR	9.5.77	12 May
215.081 t	Kerrie	Bremner	AUS	2.12.65	6 Oct		**Best track times**					
214.179	Maibritt	Sørensen	DEN	.85	15 Sep		216.956 t	Maria Luisa	Zecchino	ITA	11.12.67	1 Dec
Indoors							210.754 t	Karen	Hathaway	GBR	9.5.77	15 Dec
220.775	Sumie	Inagaki	JPN	6.4.66	1		Espoo	24 Feb				
215.018	Annika	Nilrud	SWE	7.12.75	1 Dec		210.064	Sandra	Lundqvist	SWE	5.7.77	24 Feb
210.965	Pernilla	Johansson	SWE	20.8.71	24 Feb							

2000 METRES STEEPLECHASE

Mark	Name		Nat	Born	Pos	Meet	Venue	Date
6:12.0A	Roseline	Chepngetich	KEN-Y	17.6.97	1		Nairobi	11 Jun
6:14.60		Chepngetich			1	WY	Donetsk	14 Jul
6:15.12	Daisy	Jepkemei	KEN-Y	13.2.96	2	WY	Donetsk	14 Jul
6:16.95	Milcah	Chemos	KEN	24.2.86	1		Dubnica nad Váhom	21 Aug
6:17.33	Ruth	Chebet	KEN/BRN-Y	17.11.96	1	W.Asi-Y	Manama	29 Oct
6:17.58		Chebet			1		Amman	24 Oct
6:19.09	Bridget	Franek	USA	8.11.87	1		Eugene	16 Mar
6:19.48	Fancy	Cherotich	KEN	10.8.90	2		Dubnica nad Váhom	21 Aug
6:19.55	Oona	Kettunen	FIN-J	10.2.96	1		Kotka	13 Jul
6:24.82	Antje	Moldner-Schmidt	GER	13.6.84	1		Berlin	15 May
6:26.38	Valentyna	Zhudina	UKR	12.3.83	3		Dubnica nad Váhom	21 Aug
6:27.07	Jannika	John	GER	26.12.92	1		Pliezhausen	12 May
6:28.65	Maya	Rehberg	GER-J	28.4.94	1	NC-j	Rostock	28 Jul
6:29.38	Sanaa	Koubaa	GER	6.1.85	2		Pliezhausen	12 May
6:29.53	Natalya	Gorchakova	RUS	17.4.83	1		Moskva	12 May
More JUNIORS								
6:30.05	Woynshet	Ansa	ETH-Y	9.4.96	3	WY	Donetsk	14 Jul
6:30.64	Stella	Ruto	KEN-Y	12.12.96	2	Afr-Y	Warri	30 Mar

3000 METRES STEEPLECHASE

Mark	Name		Nat	Born	Pos	Meet	Venue	Date
9:11.65	Milcah	Chemos	KEN	24.2.86	1	WCh	Moskva	13 Aug
9:12.55	Lydia	Chepkurui	KEN	23.8.84	2	WCh	Moskva	13 Aug
9:12.84	Sofia	Assefa	ETH	14.11.87	3	WCh	Moskva	13 Aug
9:13.75		Chepkurui			1	DL	Doha	10 May
9:14.17		Chemos			1	Herc	Monaco	19 Jul
9:14.61		Assefa			2	DL	Doha	10 May
9:15.06		Chemos			1	VD	Bruxelles	6 Sep
9:15.18		Chepkurui			2	Herc	Monaco	19 Jul
9:15.25	Hiwot	Ayalew	ETH	6.3.90	4	WCh	Moskva	13 Aug
9:15.26		Assefa			2	VD	Bruxelles	6 Sep
9:15.85		Ayalew			3	VD	Bruxelles	6 Sep
9:16.14		Chemos			1	GGala	Roma	6 Jun
9:16.97	Etenesh	Diro	ETH	10.5.91	5	WCh	Moskva	13 Aug
9:17.43		Chemos			1	DL	Birmingham	30 Jun
9:17.60		Ayalew			3	DL	Doha	10 May
9:17.66		Ayalew			1	Athl	Lausanne	4 Jul
9:17.69		Assefa			2	Athl	Lausanne	4 Jul
9:17.78		Diro			4	DL	Doha	10 May

WOMEN 2013

Mark	Name		Nat	Born	Pos	Meet	Venue	Date	
9:17.92		Chemos			1	GS	Ostrava	27	Jun
9:17.97		Assefa			2	DL	Birmingham	30	Jun
9:18.10		Chepkurui			2	GGala	Roma	6	Jun
9:18.72		Ayalew			1		Rabat	9	Jun
9:18.77		Chepkurui			2		Rabat	9	Jun
9:18.83		Ayalew			3	DL	Birmingham	30	Jun
9:19.17		Chemos			5	DL	Doha	10	May
9:19.42	Purity	Kirui	KEN	13.8.91	6	DL	Doha	10	May
9:19.87		Ayalew			2	GS	Ostrava	27	Jun
9:21.24		Assefa			3	GGala	Roma	6	Jun
9:21.94		Chepkurui			4	VD	Bruxelles	6	Sep
9:22.05	Hyvin	Jepkemoi	KEN	13.1.92	6	WCh	Moskva	13	Aug
	(30/7)								
9:22.20	Habiba	Ghribi	TUN	9.4.84	7	DL	Doha	10	May
9:26.31	Lydia	Rotich	KEN	8.8.88	8	DL	Doha	10	May
9:27.49	Almaz	Ayana	ETH	21.11.91	1		Montbéliard	6	Jun
	(10)								
9:28.00	Yuliya	Zaripova	RUS	26.4.86	1	WUG	Kazan	10	Jul
9:28.04	Fancy	Cherotich	KEN	10.8.90	5	GS	Ostrava	27	Jun
9:28.26	Emma	Coburn	USA	19.10.90	1	Jordan	Stanford	28	Apr
9:29.13	Jamie	Cheever	USA	28.2.87	2	Jordan	Stanford	28	Apr
9:29.27	Antje	Möldner-Schmidt	GER	13.6.84	4h2	WCh	Moskva	10	Aug
9:30.64	Natalya	Aristarkhova	RUS	31.10.89	1	ET	Gateshead	22	Jun
9:30.72	Gulnara	Galkina	RUS	9.7.78	5		Rabat	9	Jun
9:31.81	Ruth	Bisibori	KEN	2.1.88	9	DL	Doha	10	May
9:32.26	Valentyna	Zhudina	UKR	12.3.83	1		Yalta	6	Jun
9:32.50	Kaltoum	Bouaasayriya	MAR	23.8.82	1		Fès	11	May
	(20)								
9:34.33	Agnes	Chesang	KEN	.86	1		Tampere	25	Aug
9:34.58A	Miriam	Muthoni	KEN-J	.95	1		Nairobi	13	Aug
9:35.14	Birtukan	Fente	ETH	18.6.89	3	Hanz	Zagreb	3	Sep
9:35.42	Bridget	Franek	USA	8.11.87	4	adidas	New York	25	May
9:35.66	Silvia	Danekova	BUL	7.2.83	5h2	WCh	Moskva	10	Aug
9:35.78	Ancuta	Bobocel	ROU	3.10.87	6h2	WCh	Moskva	10	Aug
9:35.82	Eilish	McColgan	GBR	25.11.90	7h2	WCh	Moskva	10	Aug
9:35.88	Salami	Alami El Ouali	MAR	29.12.83	7	GGala	Roma	6	Jun
9:36.66	Gladys	Kipkemboi	KEN	15.10.86	7	VD	Bruxelles	6	Sep
9:37.11	Gesa-Felicitas	Krause	GER	3.8.92	9	WCh	Moskva	13	Aug
	(30)								
9:37.23	Shalaya	Kipp	USA	19.8.90	4	Herc	Monaco	19	Jul
9:37.33	Svitlana	Shmidt	UKR	20.3.90	6	GS	Ostrava	27	Jun
9:37.62	Genevieve	LaCaze	AUS	4.8.89	1		Ponce	18	May
9:38.23	Colleen	Quigley	USA	20.11.92	2	NCAA	Eugene	8	Jun
9:38.30	Diana	Martín	ESP	1.4.81	11	WCh	Moskva	13	Aug
9:38.38	Sandra	Eriksson	FIN	4.5.89	1		Stockholm	8	Sep
9:38.57	Natalya	Gorchakova	RUS	17.4.83	12	WCh	Moskva	13	Aug
9:39.00	Charlotta	Fougberg	SWE	19.6.85	2	vFIN	Stockholm	8	Sep
9:39.36	Nicole	Bush	USA	4.4.86	2		Ponce	18	May
9:39.98	Lyudmila	Lebedeva	RUS	23.5.90	3	NC	Moskva	22	Jul
	(40)								
9:40.71	Amina	Bettiche	ALG	14.12.87	1	MedG	Mersin	28	Jun
9:40.84	Ruth	Chebet	KEN/BRN-Y	17.11.96	1	AsiC	Pune	5	Jul
9:40.90	Natalya	Vlasova	RUS	19.7.88	4	NC	Moskva	22	Jul
9:41.51	Mekdes	Bekele	ETH	20.1.87	8		Rabat	9	Jun
9:42.10	Yekaterina	Doseykina	RUS	30.3.90	5	NC	Moskva	22	Jul
9:42.35	Katarzyna	Kowalska	POL	7.4.85	1		Bottrop	19	Jul
9:42.91	Helen	Hofstede	NED	31.12.80	1		Ninove	27	Jul
9:43.22	Birtukan	Adamu	ETH	29.4.92	9	VD	Bruxelles	6	Sep
9:43.28	Beverly	Ramos	PUR	24.8.87	6	adidas	New York	25	May
9:43.39	Amber	Henry	USA	27.12.90	3	NCAA	Eugene	8	Jun
	(50)								
9:43.50	Yekaterina	Sokolenko	RUS	13.9.92	2		Sochi	25	May
9:43.70	Claire	Perraux	FRA	6.10.87	7	adidas	New York	25	May
9:45.22	Binnaz	Uslu	TUR	12.3.85	1		Izmir	2	Jun
9:45.51	Oona	Kettunen	FIN-J	10.2.94	1	EJ	Rieti	20	Jul
9:45.60	Sudha	Singh	IND	25.6.86	1		Chennai	6	Jun
9:45.78	Stephanie	Garcia	USA	3.5.88	9	adidas	New York	25	May
9:45.78	Ashley	Higginson	USA	17.3.89	11h2	WCh	Moskva	10	Aug
9:45.80	Gülcan	Mingir	TUR	21.5.89	1		Turku	16	Jul
9:46.56	Yevdokiya	Bukina	RUS	10.2.93	1		Chelyabinsk	25	May

Mark	Name		Nat	Born	Pos	Meet	Venue	Date
9:46.60	Lyudmila (60)	Kuzmina	RUS	13.8.87	1		Yerino	2 Jun
9:46.73	Alexi	Pappas	USA	28.3.90	1		Stanford	29 Mar
9:46.98	Fabienne	Schlumpf	SUI	17.11.90	2		Bottrop	19 Jul
9:47.23	Polina	Jelizarova	LAT	1.5.89	14	DL	Doha	10 May
9:47.58	Sara	Vaughn	USA	16.5.86	2		Los Angeles (ER)	17 May
9:48.32	Lindsey	Anderson	USA	23.5.85	3		Los Angeles (ER)	17 May
9:48.68	Svetlana	Kudzelich	BLR	7.5.87	1		Riga	30 May
9:49.84	Türkan	Özata	TUR	5.1.84	2		Izmir	2 Jun
9:50.06	Aisha	Praught	USA	14.12.89	1		Portland	8 Jun
9:50.39	Rachel	Sorna	USA	15.4.92	1		Irvine	22 May
9:50.88	Albina (70)	Chinchikeyeva	RUS	17.2.92	3		Yerino	2 Jun
9:51.15	Marusa	Mismas	SLO-J	24.10.94	2	EJ	Rieti	20 Jul
9:51.17	Chantelle	Groenewoud	CAN	3.3.89	4	WUG	Kazan	10 Jul
9:51.23	Jessica	Furlan	CAN	15.3.90	5	WUG	Kazan	10 Jul
9:51.33	Mary	Ballinger	USA	5.5.88	4		Los Angeles (ER)	17 May
9:51.42	Emily	Stewart	GBR	24.12.91	6		Ninove	27 Jul
9:51.50	Fadwa	Sidi Madane	MAR-J	20.11.94	10		Rabat	9 Jun
9:52.07	Rolanda	Bell	PAN	27.10.87	7		Ninove	27 Jul
9:52.66	Clarisse	Cruz	POR	9.7.78	1	FRA Ch	Paris (C)	12 Jul
9:52.69	Eva	Krchová	CZE	10.9.89	8	GS	Ostrava	27 Jun
9:53.17		Li Zhenzhu (80)	CHN	13.12.85	1		Tianjin	9 Oct
9:53.34	Valeriya	Mara	UKR	22.2.83	2		Joensuu	9 Jun
9:53.35	Geneviève	Lalonde	CAN	5.9.91	3	Franc	Nice	12 Sep
9:53.53	Leah	O'Connor	USA	30.8.92	1		Columbus	12 May
9:54.00	Michele	Finn	IRL	16.12.89	1		Nashville	1 Jun
9:54.02	Misaki	Sango	JPN	21.4.89	2		Tianjin	9 Oct
9:54.03	Mariya	Shatalova	UKR	3.3.89	3		Yalta	6 Jun
9:54.27	Athiná	Koíni	GRE	17.12.92	1		Sérres	15 Jun
9:54.36	Carla Salomé	Rocha	POR	25.4.90	1		Huelva	12 Jun
9:54.61	Matylda	Szlezak	POL	11.1.89	4		Bottrop	19 Jul
9:54.79	Rimma (90)	Rodko	RUS	4.11.87	4		Sochi	25 May
9:54.88	Sara	Hall	USA	15.4.83	11	adidas	New York	25 May
9:54.97	Erika	Lima	BRA	13.8.93	1	SACh	Cartagena	7 Jul
9:55.02	Courtney	Frerichs	USA	18.1.93	6	NCAA	Eugene	8 Jun
9:55.36	Julia	Webb	USA	14.2.83	3		Portland	8 Jun
9:55.91	Nicol	Traynor	USA	6.5.89	2h2	NC	Des Moines	20 Jun
9:56.19	Lennie	Waite	GBR	4.2.86	5	ET	Gateshead	22 Jun
9:56.2A	Jane	Murage	KEN	.87	5		Nairobi	22 Jun
9:56.21	Alexa	Aragon	USA	1.6.92	3h1	NCAA	Eugene	6 Jun
9:56.32	Eliane	Saholinirina	MAD	20.3.82	7		Sotteville-lès-Rouen	8 Jul
9:56.50	Maria (100)	Larsson	SWE-J	24.3.94	1		Manchester	1 Jun

9:57.12	Allix	Potratz-Lee	USA	3.5.86	8 Jun		10:03.20	Alicia	Nelson	USA	20.10.90	20 Jun
9:57.18	Grace	Heymsfield	USA	24.3.92	8 Jun		10:03.21	Andrea	Ferris	PAN	21.9.87	28 Nov
9:58.08	Virginia	Nyambura	KEN	20.7.93	6 Sep		10:03.48	Ann	Detmer	USA	1.11.85	8 Jun
9:58.22	Yoshika	Arai	JPN	26.2.82	9 Jun		10:03.6A	Mercyline	Ondieki	KEN		16 May
9:58.30	Johanna	Lehtinen	FIN	21.2.79	3 Sep		10:03.64	Marta	Tigabea	ETH	4.10.90	18 May
9:58.97	Katie	Fry	USA	9.3.93	24 May		10:03.68	Ashley	Beutler	USA	19.9.89	6 Jun
9:59.16	Yekaterina	Rogozina	RUS	21.12.89	22 Jul		10:03.72	Kara	DeWalt	USA	27.7.88	28 Apr
9:59.46	Woynshet	Ansa	ETH-Y	9.4.96	31 Aug		10:03.73	Yevgeniya	Soboleva	RUS	26.1.88	15 Jun
9:59.82	Carrie	Dimoff	USA	31.5.83	3 May		10:03.74	Linner	Cheruto	KEN-J	18.3.95	1 Sep
10:00.00	Maya	Rehberg	GER-J	28.4.94	20 Jul		10:03.84	Tigist	Mekonen	ETH-Y	7.7.97	16 Jun
10:00.09	Muriel	Coneo	COL	15.3.87	28 Nov		10:03.89	Olesya	Muratova	RUS	25.10.92	25 Jun
10:00.75	Minori	Hayakari	JPN	29.11.72	22 Sep		10:03.93	Kimber	Mattox	USA	27.11.88	28 Apr
10:01.12	Marissa	VanderMalle	USA		24 May		10:04.04	Cinthya	Paucar	PER	10.6.90	28 Nov
10:01.23	Touria	Samiri	ITA	1.2.88	28 Jun		10:04.07	Misato	Horie	JPN	10.3.87	9 Jun
10:01.59	Yelena	Orlova	RUS	30.5.80	25 May		10:04.51	Kristen	Zillmer	USA	24.11.91	24 May
10:01.93	Ángela	Figueroa	COL	28.6.84	28 Nov		10:04.54	Rini	Budiarti	INA	22.1.83	18 Dec
10:02.0A	Purity	Rionoripo	KEN	10.6.93	27 Apr		10:04.83		Pak Kum-hyang	PRK	7.10.86	9 Oct
10:02.02	Leslie	Boozer	USA	10.2.91	14 May		10:05.11	Martina	Tresch	SUI	10.6.89	24 May
10:02.40	Victoria	Mitchell	AUS	25.4.82	25 May		10:05.21	Juliane	Masciana	USA	10.6.85	8 Jun
10:02.40	Olga	Tarantinova	RUS	28.11.87	2 Jun		10:05.48	Jannika	John	GER	26.12.92	20 May
10:02.46	Marion	Kibor	KEN-J	.94	1 Sep		10:05.48	Aleksandra	Pavlyutenkova	RUS	21.3.90	22 Jul
10:02.49	Shelby	Greany	USA	1.4.91	6 Jun		10:05.53	Sarah	Benson	GBR	9.6.82	14 Jul
10:02.6A	Nancy	Kimaiyo	KEN	.84	22 Jun		10:05.53	Zulema	Arenas	PER-J	15.11.95	28 Nov
10:02.69	Natalya	Tarantinova	RUS	28.11.87	22 Jul		10:05.57	Kanako	Ushirogata	JPN	27.1.91	22 Sep
10:02.7A	Lucia	Muangi	KEN	26.6.92	9 May		10:05.6A	Caroline	Chepkwony	KEN	18.4.84	25 May
10:02.70	Vaida	Zusinaite	LTU	13.1.88	23 Jul		10:06.30	Kerry	Harty	IRL	15.7.81	19 May
10:02.9A	Veronica	Jepkosgei	KEN	.93	25 May		10:06.33	Anastasiya	Puzakova	BLR	12.12.93	26 Jul
10:03.18	Brianna	Nerud	USA-J	16.9.94	24 May		10:06.38	María	Pardaloú	GRE	21.4.84	27 Jul

Mark	Name		Nat	Born	Pos	Meet	Venue	Date
10:06.43	Mayuko	Nakamura	JPN	20.11.90	8	Sep		
10:06.45	María Teresa	Urbina	ESP	20.3.85	27	Jul		
10:06.47	Jordan	Hamric	USA	4.10.89	6	Jun		
10:06.52		Fang Xiaoyu	CHN	6.3.87	1	Jun		
10:06.74	Genna	Hartung	USA	5.8.91	24	May		
10:07.24	Nolene	Conrad	RSA	26.7.85	6	Jun		
10:07.78	Mel	Lawrence	USA	29.8.89	6	Apr		
10:07.79	Elif	Karabulut	TUR	8.8.91	26	Sep		
10:07.86	Natalie	Bower	USA	9.10.90	24	May		
10:08.10	Viktoriya	Voronko	RUS	15.5.91	24	May		
10:08.11	Bethany	Nickless	USA	4.10.85	17	May		
10:08.49	Caroline	Austin	USA	1.7.91	12	May		
10:08.73	Collier	Lawrence	USA	4.10.86	18	Apr		
10:08.77	Liberty	Miller	USA		24	May		
10:09.28	Justyna	Korytkowska	POL	12.3.86	30	Jun		
10:09.34	Bridget	Dahlberg	USA	4.12.90	10	May		
10:09.34		Zhang Xinyan	CHN-J	9.2.94	1	Jun		
10:09.65	Milly	Clark	AUS	1.3.89	2	Feb		
10:09.83	Megan	Patrignelli	USA	22.6.92	24	May		
10:09.90	Yekaterina	Ishova	RUS	17.1.89	2	Jun		
10:10.11	Jessica	Kamilos	USA	3.8.93	11	May		
10:10.11	Shannon	Klenke	USA	1.2.93	24	May		
10:10.20	Klara	Bodinson	SWE	11.6.90	28	Jun		
10:10.25	Joanna	Murphy	USA	8.3.84	12	Jun		
10:10.34	Veerle	Dejaeghere	BEL	1.8.73	10	Aug		
10:10.45	Anezka	Drahotová	CZE-J	22.7.95	25	May		
10:10.49	Rebeka	Stowe	USA	9.3.90	28	Apr		
10:10.59	Kelly	McShea	USA	19.9.92	24	May		
10:10.86	Eva	Arias	ESP	8.10.80	2	Jul		
10:10.96	Diana	Martín Hidalgo	ESP	31.7.90	21	Jun		
10:11.20	Hitomi	Nakamura	JPN	23.6.87	9	Jun		
10:11.21	Madelin	Talbert	USA-J	23.4.94	24	May		
10:11.4A	Norah	Tanui	KEN-J	2.10.95	19	Apr		
10:11.75	Sofie	Gallein	BEL	7.8.92	25	May		
10:11.94	Esther	Vermeer	CAN	17.1.90	24	May		
		(191)						

Drugs disqualification

10:02.99	Sabine	Heitling #	BRA	2.7.87	7	Jun		

JUNIORS

See main list for top 6 juniors. 10 performances by 6 women to 9:56.50. Additional marks and further juniors:

Chebet	9:52.47	2	Arab	Doha		23 May		
Kettunen	9:48.73	3		Tampere		25 Aug	9:54.67 2 NC Vaasa 27 Jul
	9:53.18	3	vSWE	Stockholm		8 Sep		

Mark	Name		Nat	Born	Pos	Meet	Venue	Date
9:59.46	Woynshet	Ansa	ETH-Y	9.4.96	1		Reduit	31 Aug
10:00.04	Maya	Rehberg	GER	28.4.94	3	EJ	Rieti	20 Jul
10:02.46	Marion	Kibor	KEN	.94	2	Af-J	Bambous	1 Sep
10:03.18	Brianna	Nerud (10)	USA	16.9.94	2h1	NCAA-E	Greensboro	24 May
10:03.74	Linner	Cheruto	KEN	18.3.95	3	AfrJ	Bambous	1 Sep
10:03.84	Tigist	Mekonen	ETH-Y	7.7.97	4	PNG	Turku	16 Jun
10:05.53	Zulema	Arenas	PER	15.11.95	5	Bol G	Trujillo	28 Nov
10:09.34		Zhang Xinyan	CHN	9.2.94	2	NC	Suzhou	1 Jun
10:10.45	Anezka	Drahotová	CZE	22.7.95	5	ECCp	Vila Real de S.Antonio	25 May
10:11.21	Madelin	Talbert	USA	23.4.94	4h2	NCAA-E	Greensboro	24 May
10:11.4A	Norah	Tanui	KEN	2.10.95	1		Nairobi	19 Apr
10:13.47	Misaki	Mishima	JPN	14.6.94	2		Tokyo	8 Sep
10:13.74	Amy-Eloise	Neale	GBR	5.8.95	3h1	EJ	Rieti	18 Jul
10:13.89	Nicole Svetlana	Reina (20)	ITA-Y	25.9.97	1	NC	Milano	28 Jul

60 METRES HURDLES INDOORS

Mark	Name		Nat	Born	Pos	Meet	Venue	Date
7.78	Brianna	Rollins	USA	18.8.91	1		Clemson	11 Jan
7.79		Rollins			1	NCAA	Fayetteville	9 Mar
7.82		Rollins			1h1	NCAA	Fayetteville	8 Mar
7.84	Yvette	Lewis	PAN	16.3.85	1	Mill	New York (Armory)	16 Feb
7.90		Rollins			1	ACC	Blacksburg	23 Feb
7.92		Rollins			1h3	ACC	Blacksburg	22 Feb
7.93		Rollins			1		New York (Armory)	1 Feb
7.93	Yuliya	Kondakova	RUS	4.12.81	1		Moskva	3 Feb
7.93A	Nia	Ali	USA	23.10.88	1	NC	Albuquerque	3 Mar
8.08					5	Mill	New York (Armory)	16 Feb
		(9/4)						
7.94	Alina	Talay	BLR	14.5.89	1	EI	Göteborg	1 Mar
7.94	Veronica	Borsi	ITA	13.6.87	2	EI	Göteborg	1 Mar
7.95	Eline	Berings	BEL	28.5.86	1r2		Gent	2 Feb
7.95	Derval	O'Rourke	IRL	28.5.81	3	EI	Göteborg	1 Mar
7.96	Beate	Schrott	AUT	15.4.88	1r2		Wien	23 Feb
7.96	Tiffani	McReynolds	USA	4.12.91	2	NCAA	Fayetteville	9 Mar
		(10)						
7.97	Janay	DeLoach Soukup	USA	12.10.85	1		Boston (Allston)	26 Jan
7.97	Virginia	Crawford	USA	7.9.83	2	Mill	New York (Armory)	16 Feb
7.97A	Kristi	Castlin	USA	7.7.88	2	NC	Albuquerque	3 Mar
8.03					3	Mill	New York (Armory)	16 Feb
7.99	Tiffany	Porter	GBR	13.11.87	2		Boston (Allston)	26 Jan
8.00	Olga	Samylova	RUS	4.1.86	1h		Sankt-Peterburg	20 Jan
8.00A	Queen	Harrison	USA	10.9.88	4	NC	Albuquerque	3 Mar
8.03					4	Mill	New York (Armory)	16 Feb
8.01	Sara	Aerts	BEL	25.1.84	1	NC	Gent	17 Feb
8.03	Lucie	Skrobáková	CZE	4.1.82	1		Karlsruhe	2 Feb
8.03	Marzia	Caravelli	ITA	23.10.81	1		Magglingen	2 Feb
8.03	Reina-Flor	Okori	FRA	2.5.80	1	NC	Aubière	16 Feb
		(20)						
8.04	Svetlana	Topylina	RUS	6.1.85	1		Samara	31 Jan

Mark		Name		Nat	Born	Pos	Meet	Venue	Date	
8.04		Christina	Manning	USA	29.5.90	4		Val-de-Reuil	12	Feb
8.04		Alice	Decaux #	FRA	10.4.85	2	NC	Aubière	16	Feb
8.05		Sharona	Bakker	NED	12.4.90	4s2	EI	Göteborg	1	Mar
8.05A		LaTisha	Holden	USA	29.8.89	3h2	NC	Albuquerque	3	Mar
8.06		Danielle	Carruthers	USA	22.12.79	4		Düsseldorf	8	Feb
8.06		Jasmin	Stowers	USA	23.9.91	1	SEC	Fayetteville	24	Feb
8.07		Aleksandra	Antonova	RUS	24.3.80	2		Samara	31	Jan
8.07		Nadine	Hildebrand	GER	20.9.87	1h2		Karlsruhe	2	Feb
8.07		Loreal	Smith	USA	12.10.85	2h2		Düsseldorf	8	Feb
		(30)								
8.07		Cindy	Billaud	FRA	11.3.86	3	NC	Aubière	16	Feb
8.07		Nooralotta	Neziri	FIN	9.11.92	1h2		Jyväskylä	17	Feb
8.08		Cassandra	Lloyd	USA	27.1.90	2		University Park	25	Jan
8.08		Angela	Whyte	CAN	22.5.80	1		Moscow, ID	1	Feb
8.08		Micol	Cattaneo	ITA	14.5.82	3s1	EI	Göteborg	1	Mar
8.08		Danielle	Williams	USA	10.10.89	1	NCAA II	Birmingham, AL	9	Mar
8.09		Tatyana	Filatova	RUS	22.1.87	2s2	NC	Moskva	12	Feb
8.11		Chelsea	Carrier-Eades	USA	21.8.89	3		University Park	25	Jan
8.11		Sarah	Claxton	GBR	23.9.79	1		Wien	29	Jan
8.11		Cindy	Roleder	GER	21.8.89	1h1	NC	Dortmund	23	Feb
		(40)								
8.11		Morgan	Snow	USA	26.7.93	2h1	NCAA	Fayetteville	8	Mar
8.11		Donique	Flemings	USA	1.11.91	4	NCAA	Fayetteville	9	Mar
8.12		Antoinette	Nana Djimou	FRA	2.8.85	1P2	EI	Göteborg	1	Mar
8.12		Brea	Buchanan	USA	8.1.93	3h2	NCAA	Fayetteville	8	Mar
8.13		Kendra	Harrison	USA	18.9.92	2	ACC	Blacksburg	23	Feb
8.13		Jade	Barber	USA	4.4.93	1		Notre Dame	1	Mar
8.13		Vashti	Thomas	USA	21.4.90	1h1	NCAA II	Birmingham, AL	8	Mar
8.14		Aisseta	Diawara	FRA	29.6.89	2h1	NC	Aubière	16	Feb
8.15		Katie	Grimes	USA	22.12.90	4h2	NCAA	Fayetteville	8	Mar
Drugs disqualification										
7.89		Nevin	Yanit ¶	TUR	16.2.86	(1)	EI	Göteborg	1	Mar

100 METRES HURDLES

Mark			Name		Nat	Born	Pos	Meet	Venue	Date	
12.26	1.2	Brianna	Rollins		USA	18.8.91	1	NC	Des Moines	22	Jun
12.39	1.7		Rollins				1	NCAA	Eugene	8	Jun
12.43	1.2	Queen	Harrison		USA	10.9.88	2	NC	Des Moines	22	Jun
12.44	-0.6		Rollins				1	WCh	Moskva	17	Aug
12.47	1.2		Rollins				1h3	NCAA	Eugene	6	Jun
12.48	1.2	Nia	Ali		USA	23.10.88	3	NC	Des Moines	22	Jun
12.48	1.0	Dawn	Harper-Nelson		USA	13.5.84	1	VD	Bruxelles	6	Sep
12.50	1.9	Lolo	Jones		USA	5.8.82	1h2	NC	Des Moines	21	Jun
12.50	-0.7	Sally	Pearson		AUS	19.9.86	1s3	WCh	Moskva	17	Aug
12.50	-0.6		Pearson				2	WCh	Moskva	17	Aug
12.53	1.2		Harper-Nelson				1	Athl	Lausanne	4	Jul
12.54	1.2	Kellie	Wells		USA	18.7.82	4	NC	Des Moines	22	Jun
12.54	0.2		Rollins				1s2	WCh	Moskva	17	Aug
12.55	1.2		Jones				5	NC	Des Moines	22	Jun
12.55	-0.8		Rollins				1h5	WCh	Moskva	16	Aug
12.55	-0.6	Tiffany	Porter		GBR	13.11.87	3	WCh	Moskva	17	Aug
12.58	1.2		Wells				2	Athl	Lausanne	4	Jul
12.59	1.1	Cindy	Billaud		FRA	11.3.86	1	NC	Paris (C)	13	Jul
12.59	-0.6		Harper-Nelson				4	WCh	Moskva	17	Aug
12.60	0.4		Harper-Nelson				1	DL	Doha	10	May
12.60	1.2		Jones				3	Athl	Lausanne	4	Jul
12.61	1.2	Kristi	Castlin (10)		USA	7.7.88	6	NC	Des Moines	22	Jun
12.61	1.8	Vashti	Thomas		USA	21.4.90	1	WUG	Kazan	10	Jul
12.61	-0.7		Harper-Nelson				2s3	WCh	Moskva	17	Aug
12.62	0.8		Harper-Nelson				1		Kingston	4	May
12.62	-0.5		Pearson				1h2	WCh	Moskva	16	Aug
12.63	1.2		Ali				4	Athl	Lausanne	4	Jul
12.63	-0.4		Rollins				1	Spitz	Luzern	17	Jul
12.63	-0.6		Porter				1s1	WCh	Moskva	17	Aug
12.63	-0.1		Harper-Nelson				1	Hanz	Zagreb	3	Sep
12.63	1.0		Pearson				2	VD	Bruxelles	6	Sep
		(31/11)									
12.66A	1.8	Angela	Whyte		CAN	22.5.80	1		Calgary	16	Jun
12.67	1.9	Virginia	Crawford		USA	7.9.83	2h1	NC	Des Moines	21	Jun
12.67	1.5	Yvette	Lewis		PAN	16.3.85	1		Lahti	17	Jul

Mark	Wind	Name		Nat	Born	Pos	Meet	Venue	Date	
12.69	0.7	Danielle	Williams	JAM	14.9.92	1	NC	Kingston	23	Jun
12.73	0.2	Yuliya	Kondakova	RUS	4.12.81	2s2	WCh	Moskva	17	Aug
12.76	0.1	Kori	Carter	USA	6.3.92	1	Pac 12	Los Angeles	12	May
12.76	0.6	Veronica	Borsi	ITA	13.6.87	1		Orvieto	2	Jun
12.77	0.1	Brea	Buchanan	USA	8.1.93	2	Pac 12	Los Angeles	12	May
12.77	1.8	Lavonne	Idlette	DOM	31.10.85	1h2		Montverde	8	Jun
		(20)								
12.78	1.8	Alina	Talay	BLR	14.5.89	2	WUG	Kazan	10	Jul
12.79	0.3	Lucie	Skrobáková	CZE	4.1.82	1	NC	Tábor	15	Jun
12.80	1.9	Jacqueline	Coward	USA	5.11.89	1h3		Montverde	8	Jun
12.82	0.8	Loreal	Smith	USA	12.10.85	2h1		Montverde	8	Jun
12.82	0.7	Andrea	Bliss	JAM	5.10.80	2	NC	Kingston	23	Jun
12.83	1.1	Reina-Flor	Okori	FRA	2.5.80	2	NC	Paris (C)	13	Jul
12.84	1.3	Sharika	Nelvis	USA	10.5.90	1h2	NCAA	Eugene	6	Jun
12.84	1.7	Anne	Zagré	BEL	13.3.90	1h2		Bruxelles	20	Jul
12.85	1.7	Doniqué	Flemings	USA	1.11.91	3	NCAA	Eugene	8	Jun
12.85	0.7	Alice	Decaux #	FRA	10.4.85	1r3		Besançon	15	Jun
		(30)								
12.85	1.1	Nadine	Hildebrand	GER	20.9.87	1r2		Mannheim	30	Jun
12.86	0.0	Jessica	Zelinka	CAN	3.9.81	2		Burnaby	1	Jul
12.87	1.8	Tenaya	Jones	USA	22.3.89	2h2		Montverde	8	Jun
12.87	0.0	Beate	Schrott	AUT	15.4.88	1		Salzburg (Rif)	15	Jun
12.88	1.7	Morgan	Snow	USA	26.7.93	4	NCAA	Eugene	8	Jun
12.88	1.7	Kendra	Harrison	USA	18.9.92	5	NCAA	Eugene	8	Jun
12.90	1.9	Cassandra	Lloyd	USA	27.1.90	4h2	NC	Des Moines	21	Jun
12.90	1.2	Chelsea	Carrier-Eades	USA	21.8.89	1H	vGER	Chula Vista	27	Jul
12.90	0.1	Sara	Aerts	BEL	25.1.84	1h1		Ninove	27	Jul
12.91	-0.7	Tatyana	Dektyareva	RUS	8.5.81	5s3	WCh	Moskva	17	Aug
		(40)								
12.93	0.7	Shermaine	Williams	JAM	4.2.90	3	NC	Kingston	23	Jun
12.93	0.7		Wu Shujiao	CHN	19.6.92	1		Tianjin	9	Oct
12.94	0.7	Delloreen	Ennis	JAM	5.5.75	4	NC	Kingston	23	Jun
12.94	1.2	Marina	Tomic	SLO	30.4.83	2rA		La Chaux-de-Fonds	7	Jul
12.95	0.0	Marzia	Caravelli	ITA	23.10.81	2		Bellinzona	11	Jun
12.97	0.2	Janay	DeLoach-Soukup	USA	12.10.85	3		Atlanta	17	May
12.97	0.7	Monique	Morgan	JAM	10.10.85	5	NC	Kingston	23	Jun
12.98	-0.1	Yekaterina	Galitskaya	RUS	24.2.87	3	NC	Moskva	24	Jul
12.99	0.7	Indira	Spence	JAM	8.9.86	6	NC	Kingston	23	Jun
13.00	0.7	Jade	Barber	USA	4.4.93	1q2	NCAA-E	Greensboro	25	May
		(50)								
13.00	1.7	Jasmin	Stowers	USA	23.9.91	7	NCAA	Eugene	8	Jun
13.00A	1.5	Lina	Florez	COL	1.11.84	1		Cali	23	Jun
13.00	0.3	Rosina	Hodde	NED	10.2.83	1		Ninove	27	Jul
13.01A	0.5	Briggit	Merlano	COL	29.4.82	2		Medellín	25	May
13.01	1.1	Aïsseta	Diawara	FRA	29.6.89	3	NC	Paris (C)	13	Jul
13.01	-0.1	Nina	Argunova	RUS	18.2.89	2h1	NC	Moskva	23	Jul
13.01	0.4		Sun Yawei	CHN	17.10.87	2	NG	Shenyang	8	Sep
13.02	0.1	Micol	Cattaneo	ITA	14.5.82	1		Lodi	11	May
13.02	-0.6	Hitomi	Shimura	JPN	8.11.90	1	NC	Tokyo (Chofu)	8	Jun
13.03	-0.1	Lauren	Smith	USA	27.8.81	2		Turlock	10	May
		(60)								
13.03	1.3	Anna	Plotitsyna	UKR	1.1.87	1		Yalta	5	Jun
13.03	-0.6	Ayako	Kimura	JPN	11.6.88	2	NC	Tokyo (Chofu)	8	Jun
13.03	0.7	LaToya	Greaves	JAM	31.5.86	7	NC	Kingston	23	Jun
13.03	0.1	Cindy	Roleder	GER	21.8.89	3h1		Ninove	27	Jul
13.04	0.2	Aleesha	Barber	TTO	16.5.87	1		George Town	8	May
13.04	0.7	Noemi	Zbären	SUI-J	12.3.94	1h1		Nottwil	30	Jun
13.04	0.5	Isabelle	Pedersen	NOR	27.1.92	2r1		Mannheim	30	Jun
13.04	0.2	Nooralotta	Neziri	FIN	9.11.92	6s2	WCh	Moskva	17	Aug
13.05	1.9	Melaine	Walker	JAM	1.1.83	1h3		Montverde	8	Jun
13.06	1.2	Evonne	Britton	USA	10.10.91	5h3	NCAA	Eugene	6	Jun
		(70)								
13.06	1.7	Janice	Jackson	JAM/USA	30.10.91	8	NCAA	Eugene	8	Jun
13.08	1.8	Nichole	Denby	USA	10.10.82	1		San Marcos	27	Apr
13.08	-0.4	Kimberley	Laing	JAM	8.1.89	2h1	NC	Kingston	23	Jun
13.08	0.0	Jessica	Ennis-Hill	GBR	28.1.86	4	DL	London (OS)	27	Jul
13.09	2.0	Kierre	Beckles	BAR	21.5.90	1		Raleigh	30	Mar
13.09	1.8	Bridgette	Owens	USA	14.3.92	1		Athens	13	Apr
13.09	1.1	Serita	Solomon	GBR	1.3.93	1h4	NC	Birmingham	13	Jul
13.09	0.3	Anastasiya	Soprunova	KAZ	14.1.86	1		Almaty	20	Jul
13.09	0.4		Wang Dou	CHN	18.5.93	3	NG	Shenyang	8	Sep

Mark	Wind	Name		Nat	Born	Pos	Meet	Venue	Date
13.10	0.2	Vonette	Dixon	JAM	26.11.75	5		Atlanta	17 May
(80)									
13.10	1.5	Katie	Grimes	USA	22.12.90	2q1	NCAA-W	Austin	25 May
13.10	0.1	Gnima	Faye	SEN	17.11.84	3h2	NC	Paris (C)	13 Jul
13.11	0.0	Eline	Berings	BEL	28.5.86	3		Bruxelles	6 Jul
13.13	1.2	Shakeia	Pinnick	USA	23.1.91	1H	NCAA	Eugene	6 Jun
13.13	1.8	Clemence	Vifquin	FRA	9.6.86	1		Vénissieux	23 Jun
13.13	1.8	Brianne	Theisen-Eaton	CAN	18.12.88	2		Tallinn	27 Jul
13.13	0.4		Zhang Rong	CHN	5.1.83	4	NG	Shenyang	8 Sep
13.14	0.5	Ugonna	Ndu	USA/NGR	27.6.91	2h1	SEC	Columbia, MO	11 May
13.15	1.4	Lutisha	Bowen	USA	9.7.90	1		Orlando	23 Mar
13.15	1.6	Kim	Francis	USA	6.1.92	1h1		Arlington	10 May
(90)									
13.15		Olga	Samylova	RUS	4.1.86	1		Sankt-Peterburg	8 Jun
13.15	1.9	Briana	Stewart	USA	13.10.90	1		Berkeley	9 Jun
13.16	1.9	Julian	Purvis	USA	8.9.90	1r2	MSR	Walnut	20 Apr
13.16	1.7	Shanique	Walker	USA	20.11.93	1		Jacksonville	11 May
13.16	0.1	Sade-Mariah	Greenidge	BAR	14.10.93	2		Houston	12 May
13.16	1.1	Rosvitha	Okou	CIV	5.9.86	5	FRA Ch	Paris (C)	13 Jul
13.18	1.7	Caridad	Jerez	ESP	23.1.91	1		Barcelona	5 Jun
13.19	0.5	Kayla	Parker	USA	12.3.92	4	SEC	Columbia, MO	12 May
13.19	0.8	Kendra	Newton	USA	3.8.87	3h1		Montverde	8 Jun
13.19	0.4		Kang Ya	CHN	18.3.90	5	NG	Shenyang	8 Sep
(100)									

Mark	Wind	Name		Nat	Born	Date
13.20	1.6	Crystal	Bardge	USA	25.9.88	20 Apr
13.21	-1.7	Belkis	Milanés	CUB	16.1.90	16 Mar
13.21	1.4	Christie	Gordon	CAN	5.10.86	12 May
13.21	-0.5	Clélia	Reuse	SUI	1.8.88	30 Jun
13.21	2.0	Fabiana	dos Santos	BRA	5.6.86	5 Jul
13.21	1.5	Nadine	Visser	NED-J	9.2.95	18 Jul
13.21	1.4	Karolina	Koleczak	POL	15.1.93	21 Jul
13.22	0.3	Lakaevia	Tyler	USA	4.4.88	16 Mar
13.22	0.4	LaTisha	Holden	USA	29.8.89	10 May
13.22	0.7	Eriko	Soma	JPN	30.9.91	9 Oct
13.23	1.1	Kendell	Williams	USA-J	14.6.95	11 May
13.23	-0.2	Samantha	Elliott	JAM	3.2.92	11 May
13.24	1.2	Deborah	John	TTO	1.1..90	22 Jun
13.24	0.3	Natalya	Ivoninskaya	KAZ	22.2.85	20 Jul
13.25	0.5	Ivanique	Kemp	BAH	11.6.91	12 May
13.25	0.5	Mulern	Jean	USA	25.9.92	25 May
13.25	0.1	Giulia	Pennella	ITA	27.10.89	8 Jun
13.26	1.9	Raven	Clay	USA	5.10.90	8 Jun
13.26	1.1	Anna	Melnychenko	UKR	24.4.83	8 Jun
13.26	1.1	Yariatou	Touré	FRA	27.12.90	13 Jul
13.26	1.6	Elisa	Leinonen	FIN	27.1.87	26 Jul
13.27	-0.2		Wang Li	CHN	24.8.89	31 May
13.27	1.3	Deanna	Latham	USA	23.2.92	6 Jun
13.27	-0.6	Airi	Ito	JPN	5.7.89	8 Jun
13.28	1.9	Natasha	Ruddock	JAM	25.12.89	27 Apr
13.28	-0.3	Eliecit	Palacios	COL	15.8.87	14 Jun
13.28	1.1	Adrianna	Lamalle	FRA	27.9.82	6 Jul
13.28	0.1	Anna	Kostina	RUS	16.12.86	24 Jul
13.29	0.1	Le'Tristan	Pledger	USA	27.8.93	25 May
13.29	0.5	Eva	Vital	POR	8.7.92	28 Jul
13.30	1.2	Allison	Reaser	USA	9.9.92	6 Jun
13.30	1.8	Shannon	McCann	AUS	20.12.88	10 Jul
13.30	1.4	Urszula	Bhebhe	POL	27.2.92	21 Jul
13.30	-0.6	Dafne	Schippers	NED	15.6.92	12 Aug
13.31	1.9	Kacey	Elphage	USA	7.10.89	27 Apr
13.31	1.6	Tatyana	Filatova	RUS	22.1.87	4 Jun
13.32	0.9	Layne	Baggett	USA	1.10.90	11 May
13.32	0.7	Nevada	Sorenson	USA	8.1.91	25 May
13.32	0.1	Sirena	Williams	USA		1 Jun
13.33	0.1	Brianna	McGhee	USA	8.11.93	12 May
13.33	1.8	Megan	Simmonds	JAM-J	18.3.94	25 May
13.33	0.5	Aleksandra	Antonova	RUS	24.3.80	15 Jul
13.34	2.0	Cindy	Ofili	USA-J	5.8.94	30 Mar
13.34	0.8	Dalilah	Muhammad	USA	7.2.90	6 Apr
13.34	0.2	Ashlea	Maddex	CAN	16.12.92	8 May
13.34	1.3	Sarah	Lavin	IRL-J	28.5.94	20 Jul
13.35	-1.7	Rojaine	Coto	CUB	18.7.88	16 Mar
13.35	1.4	Myesha	Dixon	USA	30.10.90	6 Apr
13.35	1.9	Shavon	Briscoe	USA	2.6.92	12 May
13.35	1.3	Svetlana	Topylina	RUS	6.1.85	25 May
13.35	1.5	Lauren	Blackburn	USA	18.11.91	25 May
13.35	1.8	Sonata	Tamosaityte	LTU	26.6.87	10 Jul
13.36	0.1	Samantha	Sharper	USA	26.9.90	12 May
13.36	1.3	Heloise	Kane	FRA-J	25.12.95	20 Jul
13.36	-0.6	Antoinette	Nana Djimou	FRA	2.8.85	12 Aug
13.37	1.4	Larissa	Matthews	USA	19.5.91	6 Apr
13.37	1.9	Melia	Cox	USA	23.11.92	20 Apr
13.37	1.2	Erica	Bougard	USA	26.7.93	6 Jun
13.37	1.3	Suzanne	Williams	NED	7.10.93	21 Jul
13.37	0.2		Deng Ru	CHN	21.11.89	8 Sep
13.38	0.7	Bianca	Blair	USA	9.4.89	25 May
13.38	1.7	Adja Arété	N'Diaye	SEN	24.8.86	7 Jun
13.38	0.0	Anastasiya	Pilipenko	KAZ	13.9.86	16 Jun
13.38	1.8	Solène	Hamelin	FRA	9.12.88	28 Jun
13.38	-0.2	Franziska	Hofmann	GER-J	9.7.93	19 Jul
13.38	0.1	Valentina	Kibalnikova	UZB	16.10.90	24 Jul
13.39	-0.1	Erica	Wilson	USA		11 May
13.39	1.7	Chastity	Stewart	USA		12 May
13.39	0.5	Shanekia	Hall	JAM	27.11.88	25 May
13.39	1.0	Olibia	Petsoúdi	GRE	6.12.86	5 Jun
13.39	1.0	Vanessa	Jules	USA	21.3.91	6 Jun
13.39	0.4	Giselle	de Albuquerque	BRA	11.7.88	7 Jun
13.39	1.6	Gemma	Bennett	GBR	4.1.84	23 Jun
13.39	1.0	Karla	Drew	GBR	22.5.89	29 Jun
13.39	0.5	Pamela	Dutkiewicz	GER	28.9.91	2 Aug
(175)						

Wind assisted

Mark	Wind	Name		Nat	Born	Pos	Meet	Venue	Date
12.30	2.8		Rollins			1s1	NC	Des Moines	22 Jun
12.33	2.3		Rollins			1h3	NC	Des Moines	21 Jun
12.43	2.7	Yvette	Lewis	PAN	16.3.85	1	MSR	Walnut	20 Apr
12.44	3.1		Harrison			1h4	NC	Des Moines	21 Jun
12.44	2.7	Lolo	Jones	USA	5.8.82	1s2	NC	Des Moines	22 Jun
12.44	2.7		Harrison			2s2	NC	Des Moines	22 Jun
12.47	2.8	Kellie	Wells	USA	16.7.82	2s1	NC	Des Moines	22 Jun
12.47	2.4		Rollins			1		Lapinkahti	21 Jul
12.49	3.1		Jones			1		Edmonton	29 Jun
12.52	3.1	Angela	Whyte	CAN	22.5.80	2		Edmonton	29 Jun
12.54	2.1		Rollins			1	TexR	Austin	30 Mar
12.56	2.7	Vashti	Thomas	USA	21.4.90	2	MSR	Walnut	20 Apr

WOMEN 2013

Mark	Wind		Name	Nat	Born	Pos	Meet	Venue	Date	
12.57	2.8		Ali			3s1	NC	Des Moines	22	Jun
12.60	2.1		Harper-Nelson			1h1	NC	Des Moines	21	Jun
12.61	2.7		Castlin			3s2	NC	Des Moines	22	Jun
12.65	2.6	Tenaya	Jones	USA	22.3.89	1		Montverde	1	Jun
12.66	3.1	Jessica	Zelinka	CAN	3.9.81	3		Edmonton	29	Jun
12.66	2.2	Loreal	Smith	USA	12.10.85	1		Liège (NX)	10	Jul
12.67	2.2	Jacqueline	Coward	USA	5.11.89	1		Montverde	8	Jun
12.76	2.6	Crystal	Bardge	USA	25.9.88	2		Montverde	1	Jun
12.78	4.6	Katie	Grimes	USA	22.12.90	1		Lubbock	25	Apr
12.84	2.3	Beate	Schrott	AUT	15.4.88	1h2		Weinheim	25	May
12.84	3.1	Shermaine	Williams	JAM	4.2.90	5		Edmonton	29	Jun
12.85	2.2	Sara	Aerts	BEL	25.1.84	3		Liège (NX)	10	Jul
12.87	3.1	Kendra	Harrison	USA	18.9.92	1		Auburn	6	Apr
12.88	2.1	Jasmin	Stowers	USA	23.9.91	3	TexR	Austin	30	Mar
12.88	2.6	Tatyana	Dektyareva	RUS	8.5.81	2	ET	Gateshead	23	Jun
12.91	2.6	Anna	Plotitsyna	UKR	1.1.87	3	ET	Gateshead	23	Jun
12.92	4.3	Lakaevia	Tyler	USA	4.4.88	1		Greensboro	12	May
12.92	2.3	Kendra	Newton	USA	3.8.87	5h3	NC	Des Moines	21	Jun
12.93	3.0	Monique	Morgan	JAM	10.10.85	1		Colts Neck	8	Jun
12.93	2.3	Jade	Barber	USA	4.4.93	6h3	NC	Des Moines	21	Jun
12.93	2.2	Rosina	Hodde	NED	10.2.83	4		Liège (NX)	10	Jul
12.93	2.2	Cindy	Roleder	GER	21.8.89	5		Liège (NX)	10	Jul
12.95	3.8	Kim	Francis	USA	6.1.92	1		Arlington	11	May
12.96	2.7	LaTisha	Holden	USA	29.8.89	4	MSR	Walnut	20	Apr
12.99	2.8	Janice	Jackson	JAM/USA	30.10.91	1h1	NCAA	Eugene	6	Jun
13.00	3.1	Christie	Gordon	CAN	5.10.86	6		Edmonton	29	Jun
13.01	2.2	Eline	Berings	BEL	28.5.86	7		Liège (NX)	10	Jul
13.02	2.4	Ayako	Kimura	JPN	11.6.88	1rA	Oda	Hiroshima	29	Apr
13.02A	2.7	Briana	Stewart	USA	13.10.90	2h2	NCAA II	Pueblo	24	May
13.03	3.1	Kimberley	Laing	JAM	8.1.89	3		Auburn	6	Apr
13.04	3.3	Ugonna	Ndu	NGR	27.6.91	1h5	NCAA-E	Greensboro	24	May
13.04	2.7	Shakeia	Pinnick	USA	23.1.91	1H	NC	Des Moines	20	Jun
13.06	3.1	Vonette	Dixon	JAM	26.11.75	4		Auburn	6	Apr
13.08A	4.8	Samantha	Elliott	JAM	3.2.92	1h1	NCAA II	Pueblo	24	May
13.10	3.8	Ivanique	Kemp	BAH	11.6.91	1h3	SEC	Columbia, MO	11	May
13.11	3.9	Tatyana	Filatova	RUS	22.1.87	2		Brandbu	22	May
13.15	3.1	Deanna	Latham	USA	23.2.92	2		Columbus	12	May

Mark	Wind	Name		Nat	Born	Pos	Date		Wind	Name		Nat	Born	Pos	Meet	Venue	Date	
13.16	2.8	Kayla	Parker	USA	12.3.92	6	Jun	13.33	3.3	Chene	Townsend	JAM	12.12.90			24	May
13.17	2.5	Natasha	Ruddock	JAM	25.12.89	9	Jun	13.33	2.3	Gemma	Bennett	GBR	4.1.84			24	May
13.18	2.3	Nevada	Sorenson	USA	8.1.91	24	May	13.34	2.7	Tamika	Robinson	USA	24.8.89			20	Apr
13.19	2.4	Giulia	Pennella	ITA	27.10.89	25	May	13.35	2.6	Larissa	Matthews	USA	19.5.91			5	May
13.21	4.6	Le'Tristan	Pledger	USA	27.8.93	25	Apr	13.35	2.5	Bianca	Blair	USA	9.4.89			24	May
13.22	3.3	Shanekia	Hall	JAM	27.11.88	24	May	13.35	3.0	Shericka	Ward	USA	30.3.90			8	Jun
13.23	5.5	Megan	Simmonds	JAM-J	18.3.94	3	Mar	13.37	2.3	Dinesha	Bean	USA	20.4.91			19	Apr
13.23	3.0	Yariatou	Touré	FRA	27.12.90	23	Jun	13.38A	2.7	Ackiesha	Burnette	JAM	15.11.92			24	May
13.26A	5.8	Brianna	McGhee	USA	8.11.93	23	Mar	13.38	2.8	Erin	Tucker	USA	24.11.92			24	May
13.28	2.8	Layne	Baggett	USA	1.10.90	24	May	13.38	2.4	Dedeh	Erawati	INA	25.5.79			5	Sep
13.30	3.1	Cindy	Ofili	USA-J	5.8.94	12	May	13.39	3.2	Chanice	Chase	CAN	6.8.93			11	May

Best at low altitude

12.76	-0.6	Whyte		2s1WCh	Moskva		17 Aug	13.01	0.2	Florez	5h2 WCh Moskva	17 Aug
								13.11	0.2	Merlano	2 George Town	8 May

Drugs disqualification

Mark	Wind	Name		Nat	Born	Pos	Meet	Venue	Date	
12.70	1.1	Alice	Decaux #	FRA	10.4.85	(2)	NC	Paris (C)	13	Jul

JUNIORS

Mark	Wind	Name		Nat	Born	Pos	Meet	Venue	Date	
13.04	0.7	Noemi	Zbären	SUI-J	12.3.94	1h1		Nottwil	30	Jun
	13.12	0.3 1			30 Jun		13.27	0.8 1	Zofingen	18	May
	13.17	1.3 1	EJ Rieti		20 Jul		13.29	0.4 1h1 EJ	Rieti	19	Jul
	13.20	0.7 1	Thun		26 Jun		13.31	1.9 2	Athl Lausanne	4	Jul
13.21	1.5	Nadine	Visser	NED-J	9.2.95	1H	EJ	Rieti	18	Jul
13.23	1.1	Kendell	Williams	USA-J	14.6.95	1		Albany	11	May
	13.29	-0.8 1h1	Albany		10 May	10 performances by 3 women to 13.31 (and 2 wa)						
13.33	1.8	Megan	Simmonds	JAM	18.3.94	2		Kingston	25	May
13.34	2.0	Cindy	Ofili	USA	5.8.94	2		Raleigh	30	Mar
13.34	1.3	Sarah	Lavin	IRL-J	28.5.94	2	EJ	Rieti	20	Jul
13.36	1.3	Heloise	Kane	FRA-	25.12.95	3	EJ	Rieti	20	Jul
13.38	-0.2	Franziska	Hofmann	GER	27.3.94	1s1	EJ	Rieti	19	Jul
13.40	1.7	Masumi	Aoki	JPN	16.4.94	2		Hiratsuka	22	Jun
13.43	1.8	Sasha	Wallace (10)	USA	21.9.85	1	MSR	Walnut	20	Apr
13.43	0.5	Christelle	Vertueux	FRA	17.8.94	1		Montgeron	23	Jun
13.44	0.5	Yasmin	Miller	GBR	24.5.95	1	BIG	Bedford	27	May
13.44	0.9	Reetta	Hurske	FIN	15.5.95	1h4	EJ	Rieti	19	Jul
13.45	1.5	Marjolein	Lindemans	BEL	17.2.94	1H	EJ	Rieti	19	Jul

Mark	Wind	Name		Nat	Born	Pos	Meet	Venue	Date	
13.48	1.3	Awa	Sene	FRA	24.7.94	4	EJ	Rieti	20	Jul
13.52	1.4	Trinity	Wilson	USA	4.9.94	4		Los Angeles (Ww)	6	Apr
13.53	0.7	Vanessa	Clerveaux	USA	17.6.94	6q2	NCAA-E	Greensboro	25	May
13.54	-0.1	Mollie	Williams	USA	17.6.95	1		Durham	21	Jul
13.56	1.0	Eveline	Rebsamen	SUI	8.4.94	3h3	EJ	Rieti	19	Jul
13.56	0.5	Stefani	Kerrison (20)	USA-Y	7.6.96	1	Jnr Oly	Greensboro	28	Jul
13.56A	-0.7	Alexis	Perry	USA	8.8.94	1	PAm-J	Medellín	23	Aug
Wind assisted										
13.23	5.5	Megan	Simmonds	JAM	18.3.94	1J		Kingston	3	Mar
13.30	3.1	Cindy	Ofili	USA	5.8.94	3	Big 10	Columbus	12	May
13.40	3.6	Trinity	Wilson	USA	4.9.94	2h2	Pac 12	Los Angeles	11	May
13.41	3.2	Vanessa	Clerveaux	USA	17.6.94	3h1	NCAA-E	Greensboro	24	May
13.44	2.1	Anri	Tanaka	JPN	10.7.94	1		Nara	4	Nov
13.50	3.4	Autumne	Franklin	USA	20.7.94	1		Princeton	5	May
13.52	2.6	Taije	Jordan	USA	18.8.94	1h7	TexR	Austin	29	Mar
13.52	2.5	Alaysh'A	Johnson	USA-Y	20.7..96	1		Austin	11	May

200 METRES HURDLES

Mark	Wind	Name		Nat	Born	Pos	Meet	Venue	Date	
24.8	0.4	Yadisleidis	Pedroso	ITA	28.1.87	1		Caserta	6	Apr
26.40	-0.1	Noemi	Zbären	SUI-J	12.3.94	1		Basel	11	May
26.74	-0.4	Stine	Tomb	NOR	27.8.86	1		Huddinge	14	Jun
26.94	1.2	Vilde J.	Svortevik	NOR-J	18.5.94	1		Bergen (Fana)	14	Sep

200 METRES HURDLES – STRAIGHT

Mark	Wind	Name		Nat	Born	Pos	Meet	Venue	Date	
25.74	-1.1	Perri	Shakes-Drayton	GBR	21.12.88	1		Manchester	25	May
26.23	-1.1	Natalya	Antyukh	RUS	26.6.81	2		Manchester	25	May
26.27	-1.1	Eilidh	Child	GBR	20.2.87	3		Manchester	25	May

300 METRES HURDLES

Mark	Wind	Name		Nat	Born	Pos	Meet	Venue	Date	
38.16		Zuzana	Hejnová	CZE	19.12.86	1		Cheb	2	Aug
38.75			Hejnová			1		Susice	14	May
39.09		Yadisleidis	Pedroso	ITA	28.1.87	1		Firenze	3	May
39.56		Marzia	Caravelli	ITA	23.10.81	1		Roma	25	Apr

400 METRES HURDLES

Mark	Wind	Name		Nat	Born	Pos	Meet	Venue	Date	
52.83		Zuzana	Hejnová	CZE	19.12.86	1	WCh	Moskva	15	Aug
53.07			Hejnová			1	DL	London (OS)	26	Jul
53.21		Kori	Carter	USA	6.3.92	1	NCAA	Eugene	7	Jun
53.23			Hejnová			1	DL	Saint-Denis	6	Jul
53.32			Hejnová			1	GS	Ostrava	27	Jun
53.32			Hejnová			1	WK	Zürich	29	Aug
53.52			Hejnová			1s1	WCh	Moskva	13	Aug
53.60			Hejnová			1	Bisl	Oslo	13	Jun
53.67		Perri	Shakes-Drayton	GBR	21.12.88	2	DL	London (OS)	26	Jul
53.70			Hejnová			1	Pre	Eugene	1	Jun
53.70			Hejnová			1	DNG	Stockholm	22	Aug
53.72		Georganne	Moline	USA	6.3.90	2	NCAA	Eugene	7	Jun
53.79			Hejnová			1	DL	Shanghai	18	May
53.82			Shakes-Drayton			1	DL	Birmingham	30	Jun
53.83		Dalilah	Muhammad	USA	7.2.90	1	NC	Des Moines	23	Jun
53.85		Angela	Morosanu	ROU	26.7.86	2	DL	Shanghai	18	May
53.88			Moline			2	NC	Des Moines	23	Jun
53.92			Shakes-Drayton			1s2	WCh	Moskva	13	Aug
53.96			Shakes-Drayton			2	DL	Saint-Denis	6	Jul
54.03			Shakes-Drayton			2	Bisl	Oslo	13	Jun
54.08			Muhammad			2s1	WCh	Moskva	13	Aug
54.09			Muhammad			2	WCh	Moskva	15	Aug
54.19			Moline			3	DL	Saint-Denis	6	Jul
54.21			Carter			1	Pac 12	Los Angeles	12	May
54.22		Eilidh	Child	GBR	20.2.87	2	DL	Birmingham	30	Jun
54.22		Lashinda	Demus	USA	10.3.83	2s2	WCh	Moskva	13	Aug
54.22		Kaliese	Spencer	JAM	6.5.87	2	WK	Zürich	29	Aug
54.27			Demus			3	WCh	Moskva	15	Aug
54.32			Moline			3	DL	London (OS)	26	Jul
54.32			Child			3s1	WCh	Moskva	13	Aug
		(30/9)								
54.38		Denisa	Rosolová (10)	CZE	21.8.86	4	DL	Saint-Denis	6	Jul
54.52		Ristananna	Tracey	JAM	5.9.92	1	NC	Kingston	21	Jun

WOMEN 2013

Mark	Name		Nat	Born	Pos	Meet	Venue	Date	
54.54	Yadisleidis	Pedroso	ITA	28.1.87	3	DL	Shanghai	18	May
54.56	Christine	Spence	USA	25.11.81	3	NC	Des Moines	23	Jun
54.63	Hanna	Titimets	UKR	5.3.89	3s2	WCh	Moskva	13	Aug
54.77	Vania	Stambolova	BUL	28.11.83	1		Huelva	12	Jun
54.77	Anna	Yaroshchuk	UKR	24.11.89	2	WUG	Kazan	9	Jul
54.79	Irina	Davydova	RUS	27.5.88	3	WUG	Kazan	9	Jul
54.83	T'Erea	Brown	USA	24.10.89	1		Kingston	4	May
54.94	Danielle	Dowie	JAM	5.5.92	2	NC	Kingston	21	Jun
54.94	Nickiesha (20)	Wilson	JAM	28.7.86	3	NC	Kingston	21	Jun
54.97	Meghan	Beesley	GBR	15.11.89	6s1	WCh	Moskva	13	Aug
54.99	Turquoise	Thompson	USA	31.7.91	3	NCAA	Eugene	7	Jun
55.04	Tiffany	Williams	USA	5.2.83	1		George Town	8	May
55.08	Lauren	Boden	AUS	3.8.88	1		Oordegem	6	Jul
55.10	Ajoke	Odumosu	NGR	27.10.87	1		Warri	14	Jun
55.12	Anastasiya	Korshunova ¶	RUS	17.5.92	1r1	NCp	Yerino	16	Jun
55.20	Natalya	Antyukh	RUS	26.6.81	1h2	NC	Moskva	22	Jul
55.27	Hayat	Lambarki	MAR	18.5.88	1	MedG	Mersin	27	Jun
55.30	Kemi	Adekoya	NGR	16.1.93	2		Warri	14	Jun
55.45	Cassandra (30)	Tate	USA	11.9.90	5	NC	Des Moines	23	Jun
55.49	Anastasiya	Ott	RUS	7.9.88	1		Moskva	4	Jul
55.51	Lamia	Lhabz	MAR	19.5.84	2	MedG	Mersin	27	Jun
55.54	Shevon	Stoddart	JAM	21.11.82	4		George Town	8	May
55.65	Sarah	Wells	CAN	10.11.89	1	Spitz	Luzern	17	Jul
55.70	Jennifer	Rockwell	ITA	18.5.83	1		La Chaux-de-Fonds	7	Jul
55.71	Sparkle	McKnight	TTO	21.12.91	1	SEC	Columbia, MO	12	May
55.75	Kendra	Harrison	USA	18.9.92	4	NCAA	Eugene	7	Jun
55.78	Ellen	Wortham	USA	5.1.90	3	Drake	Des Moines	27	Apr
55.80	Wenda	Theron/Nel	RSA	30.7.88	2		La Chaux-de-Fonds	7	Jul
55.83	Manuela (40)	Gentili	ITA	7.2.78	2		Milano	28	Jul
55.87A	Annerie	Ebersohn	RSA	9.8.90	1		Potchefstroom	25	May
55.89	Jernail	Hayes	USA	8.7.88	4s2	NC	Des Moines	22	Jun
55.92	Vera	Rudakova	RUS	20.3.92	1	EU23	Tampere	13	Jul
55.94	Phara	Anacharsis	FRA	17.12.83	1h2	NC	Paris (C)	13	Jul
55.96	Noelle	Montcalm	CAN	3.4.88	1		Toronto	11	Jun
55.96	Axelle	Dauwens	BEL	1.12.90	1		Bruxelles	21	Jul
56.03	LaTosha	Wallace	USA	25.3.85	1		São Paulo	19	May
56.08	Nikita	Tracey	JAM	18.9.90	2h1	NC	Kingston	20	Jun
56.12	Ugonna	Ndu	NGR	27.6.91	2	SEC	Columbia, MO	12	May
56.13	(50)	Huang Xiaoxiao	CHN	3.3.83	1		Shenyang	16	Jun
56.15	Landria	Buckley	USA	2.7.88	3h1	WUG	Kazan	8	Jul
56.25		Xia Xiao	CHN	6.6.91	1	NG	Shenyang	10	Sep
56.26	Fawn	Dorr	CAN	19.4.87	5		Atlanta	17	May
56.30	Janeive	Russell	JAM	14.11.93	5	NC	Kingston	21	Jun
56.32	Ashley	Spencer	USA	8.6.93	1		Tempe	6	Apr
56.33	Satomi	Kubokura	JPN	27.4.82	4h1	WCh	Moskva	12	Aug
56.38A	Samantha	Elliott	JAM	3.2.92	1	NCAA II	Pueblo	25	May
56.45	Christine	Merrill	SRI	20.8.87	2		Chula Vista	8	Jun
56.51	Jasmine	Chaney	USA	25.8.88	4h2	NC	Des Moines	21	Jun
56.56	Elif (60)	Yildirim ¶	TUR	11.2.90	1		Kayseri	19	May
56.56	Maris	Mägi	EST	11.8.87	1	NC	Tallinn	28	Jul
56.65	Francesca	Doveri	ITA	21.12.82	4	MedG	Mersin	27	Jun
56.73		Deng Xiaoqing	CHN	13.6.89	2		Shenyang	16	Jun
56.74	Jessie	Barr	IRL	24.7.89	1rA		Chambéry	30	Jun
56.75	Bianca	Baak	NED	25.1.92	2	EU23	Tampere	13	Jul
56.79	MacKenzie	Hill	USA	5.1.86	2		Azusa	11	May
56.80	Marina	Reznikova	RUS	10.6.91	1	NC-23	Cheboksary	25	Jun
56.80	Aurélie	Chaboudez	FRA	9.5.93	2rA		Chambéry	30	Jun
56.81	Christina	Holland	USA	5.8.91	1	Big12	Waco	5	May
56.81	Svetlana (70)	Gogoleva	RUS	11.12.86	1		Sankt-Peterburg	4	Jul
56.81A	Sage	Watson	CAN-J	20.6.94	1	PAm-J	Medellín	25	Aug
56.83	Christiane	Klopsch	GER	21.8.90	1		Regensburg	8	Jun
56.86	Joanna	Linkiewicz	POL	2.5.90	1	NC	Torun	20	Jul
56.91	Anastasiya	Lebid	UKR	30.10.93	3		Yalta	6	Jun
56.95	Dominique	Darden	USA	9.12.83	1r1		Gainesville	20	Apr
56.99	Andrea	Sutherland	JAM	26.5.88	4h1	NC	Kingston	20	Jun

Mark	Name		Nat	Born	Pos	Meet	Venue	Date
57.02	Irina	Takuncheva	RUS	14.11.90	1r2	NCp	Yerino	16 Jun
57.06	Shakeia	Pinnick	USA	23.1.91	1r1		Baton Rouge	13 Apr
57.06	Valeriya	Khramova	RUS	13.8.92	1h4	NC	Moskva	22 Jul
57.07	Sandy	Jean-Claude	USA	4.9.91	1h5	NCAA-E	Greensboro	23 May
	(80)							
57.08	Kou	Luogon	LBR	11.6.84	3r1		Azusa	19 Apr
57.10	Autumne	Franklin	USA-J	20.7.94	1	NC-j	Des Moines	22 Jun
57.13	Raasin	McIntosh	LBR	29.4.82	7		Atlanta	17 May
57.13	Stine	Tomb	NOR	27.8.86	4		Sollentuna	27 Jun
57.15	Manami	Kira	JPN	23.10.91	2	NC	Tokyo (Chofu)	9 Jun
57.17	Yadira	Moreno	COL	2.11.87	1	Bol G	Trujillo	28 Nov
57.19	Caryl	Granville	GBR	24.9.89	1		Bromley	3 Aug
57.21	Jade	Miller	USA-J	13.1.95	2	NC-j	Des Moines	22 Jun
57.21	Eseroghene	Okoro	GBR	4.7.90	4	NC	Birmingham	14 Jul
57.26	Hayley	McLean	GBR-J	9.9.94	1	EJ	Rieti	21 Jul
	(90)							
57.27	Joanna	Banach	POL	20.8.92	5	EU23	Tampere	13 Jul
57.28	Sayaka	Aoki	JPN	15.12.86	3	NC	Tokyo (Chofu)	9 Jun
57.29	Jessica	Gelibert	USA/HAI-J	8.11.94	3	USA-j	Des Moines	20 Jun
57.32	Allison	Beckford	JAM	8.5.79	5		Toronto	11 Jun
57.34	Janeil	Bellille	TTO	18.6.89	1		San Marcos	27 Apr
57.34		Jo Eun-ju	KOR	12.11.89	1h1		Ansan	3 May
57.34	Joan	Medjid	FRA-J	29.9.95	2	EJ	Rieti	21 Jul
57.38	Liliane Cristina	Barbosa	BRA	8.1.87	1		São Paulo	10 Jul
57.39	Nadezhda	Alekseyeva	RUS	16.7.88	4	NC	Moskva	24 Jul
57.40	Tyler	Brockington	USA-J	6.2.94	2h5	NCAA-E	Greensboro	23 May
	(100)							

Mark	Name		Nat	Born		Date
57.41	Stina	Troest	DEN-J	17.1.94	21 Jul
57.42	Mame Fatou	Faye	SEN	19.8.86	14 Jul
57.44	Venla	Paunonen	FIN	24.7.90	28 Jul
57.46	Alexis	Franklin	USA	9.10.93	11 May
57.46	Vilde J.	Svortevik	NOR-J	18.5.94	30 Jun
57.52	Abigayle	Fitzpatrick	GBR	10.6.93	14 Jul
57.57	Laura	Sotomayor	ESP	22.4.86	12 Jun
57.59A	Michelle	Cumberbatch	BAH	20.9.88	25 May
57.59	Lauren	Smith	USA	27.8.81	22 Jun
57.61A	Yanique	Haye	JAM	22.3.90	25 May
57.61	Petra	Fontanive	SUI	10.10.88	1 Jun
57.62	Stacia	Weatherford	USA	28.5.91	12 May
57.62	Valeriya	Znamenskaya	RUS	25.3.90	16 Jun
57.62	Laura	Wake	GBR	3.5.91	30 Jun
57.66	Jailma	de Lima	BRA	31.12.86	16 May
57.67	Egle	Staisiunaite	LTU	30.9.88	27 Jul
57.68	Jessica	Gulli	AUS	19.3.88	14 Apr
57.69		Liu Xin	CHN	26.8.92	11 May
57.72	Birsen	Engin	TUR	18.10.80	27 Jun
57.73	Émeline	Bauwe	FRA-J	1.7.95	31 May
57.74A	Sharolyn	Scott	CRC	27.10.84	7 Jul
57.74		Quach Thi Lan	VIE-J	18.10..95	20 Oct
57.76	Chante'sean	White	USA	14.10.90	27 Apr
57.76	Emilia	Ankiewicz	POL	22.11.90	8 Jun
57.78	Claudia	Wehrsen	GER	18.10.84	7 Jul
57.80	Javiera	Errázuriz	CHI	5.6.90	28 Nov
57.81	Olesya	Tsaranok	RUS	3.7.89	4 Jul
57.86	Chen	Meili	CHN	2.1.90	27 Apr
57.86	Magdalena	Mendoza	VEN	20.10.90	28 Nov
57.88	Gianna	Woodruff	USA	18.11.93	24 May
57.88	Gwendolyn	Flowers	USA	5.11.91	24 May
57.90	Kayla	Stueckle	USA	19.1.92	23 May
57.91	Amani	Bryant	USA	26.1.91	20 Apr
57.93	Ann	Nwogu	NGR-J	10.1.95	14 Jun
57.94	Frida	Persson	SWE	14.12.89	1 Jun
57.94	Christine	Salterberg	GER-J	9.6.94	20 Jul

Mark	Name		Nat	Born		Date
57.95	Emily	Bonnett	GBR	26.9.87	27 May
57.95	Haruka	Shibata	JPN	13.1.91	9 Jun
57.95	Polina	Bordyugova	RUS	18.8.91	25 Jun
57.97		Wang Jinping	CHN	14.12.88	30 May
57.97	Amaliya	Sharoyan	ARM	19.6.88	12 Aug
57.99	Kiani	Profit	USA	18.2.90	23 Mar
57.99	Agnieszka	Karczmarczyk	POL	27.4.93	30 Jun
58.00	Robine	Schürmann	SUI	31.1.89	27 Jul
58.02	Déborah	Rodríguez	URU	2.12.92	16 May
58.02	Manaho	Sugiyama	JPN	7.5.92	9 Jun
58.07	Maya	Williamson	USA	26.2.93	24 May
58.08	Özge	Akın	TUR	17.6.85	2 Jun
58.08	Helene	Swanepoel	RSA-Y	5.8.96	13 Jul
58.11	Klaudia	Żurek	POL	22.9.91	22 Jun
58.12	Fanny	Lefèvre	FRA	12.2.92	31 May
58.12A	Zudikey	Rodriguez	MEX	14.3.87	7 Jul
58.13	Frederike	Hogrebe	GER	19.2.91	16 Jun
58.13	Sanda	Belgyan	ROU	17.12.92	28 Jul
58.15	Oksana	Kalabashina	RUS	11.3.91	25 Jun
58.15	Myrnah	Bloud	FRA	31.3.87	30 Jun
58.16	Kübra	Sesli	TUR	1.11.93	26 May
58.18	Vera	Barbosa	POR	13.1.89	28 Jul
58.19	Deseree	King	USA	15.4.92	5 May
58.20	Lucie	Slanicková	SVK	8.11.88	27 Jun
58.21	Viktoriya	Nikolenko	UKR	15.6.91	5 Jun
58.21	Nisha	Desai	GBR	5.8.84	13 Jul
58.22	Camira	Haughton	JAM-J	21.8.95	15 Mar
58.22	Elisabeth	Monty	USA		10 May
58.22	Kiah	Seymour	USA-J	11.1.94	23 May
58.25	Tamera	Harris	USA	25.2.93	12 May
58.25	Elisa	Scardanzan	ITA	15.7.85	2 Jun
58.25	Agnieszka	Karpiesiuk	POL	17.4.82	19 Jul
58.28	Rachel	Watkins	USA	16.10.90	24 May
	(169)					

Hand timed

57.7A	Maureen	Maiyo	KEN	28.5.85	17 May

Best at low altitude

56.03	Ebersohn	3		Huelva	12 Jun
56.44	Elliott	6	NC	Kingston	21 Jun

57.91 Haye	6 Apr	58.20 Watson	5 Apr
58.08 Cumberbatch	27 Apr		

JUNIORS

See main list for top 7 juniors.12 performances by 9 women to 57.45. Additional marks and further juniors:

Russell	57.04	4h2	NC	Kingston	26 Jun	57.23	1s3	WJ	Barcelona	13 Jul
Adekoya	57.22	2	NC	Calabar	21 Jun					
57.41	Stina		Troest	DEN	17.1.94	3	EJ	Rieti	21 Jul
57.46	Vilde J.		Svortevik	NOR	18.5.94	2		Mannheim	30 Jun
57.73	Émeline		Bauwe (10)	FRA	1.7.95	2		Marseille	31 May
57.74			Quach Thi Lan	VIE	18.10..95	1		Kuala Lumpur	20 Oct

WOMEN 2013

Mark	Name		Nat	Born	Pos	Meet	Venue	Date
57.93	Ann	Nwogu	NGR	10.1.95	3		Warri	14 Jun
57.94	Christine	Salterberg	GER	9.6.94	2s1	EJ	Rieti	20 Jul
58.08	Helene	Swanepoel	RSA-Y	5.8.96	1	WY	Donetsk	13 Jul
58.22	Camira	Haughton	JAM	21.8.95	1	N.Sch	Kingston	15 Mar
58.22	Kiah	Seymour	USA	11.1.94	2h2	NCAA-E	Greensboro	23 May
58.33	Shona	Richards	GBR	1.9.95	5	EJ	Rieti	21 Jul
58.41	Kimone	Green	JAM	23.5.95	1		Kingston	2 Mar
58.42	Tia Adana	Belle	BAR-Y	16.6.96	2	WY	Donetsk	13 Jul
58.50	Nguyen Thi Oanh (20)		VIE	20.2.96	2	NC	Ho-Chi -Minh	22 Sep

HIGH JUMP

Mark			Name			Nat	Born	Pos	Meet	Venue	Date
2.04			Brigetta	Barrett		USA	24.12.90	1	NC	Des Moines	22 Jun
			1.84/1 1.89/1 1.92/1 1.95/1 2.00/1 2.04/2								
	2.01	1	Herc	Monaco	19 Jul	1.80/1 1.85/1 1.89/1 1.92/1 1.95/1 1.98/1 2.01/1 2.06/xxx					
	2.00	2	WCh	Moskva	17 Aug	1.89/1 1.93/1 1.97/1 2.00/1 2.03/xx 2.05/x					
	1.99	1	Pac 12	Los Angeles	11 May	1.65/1 1.70/1 1.75/1 1.78/1 1.84/1 1.87/1 1.93/1 1.99/3 2.02/xxx					
	1.98	2	DL	Saint-Denis	6 Jul	1.80/1 1.85/1 1.89/2 1.92/2 1.95/1 1.98/1 2.01/xxx					
	1.98	1		Madrid	13 Jul	1.82/1 1.89/1 1.92/1 1.95/1 1.98/2 2.01/xxxx					
2.03			Svetlana	Shkolina		RUS	9.3.86	1	WCh	Moskva	17 Aug
			1.89/1 1.93/2 1.97/1 2.00/1 2.03/1 2.05/xxp						
	2.00	1	VD	Bruxelles	6 Sep	1.90/1 1.93/1 1.96/2 1.98/1 2.00/1 2.02/xx 2.04/x					
	1.98	1=	GGala	Roma	6 Jun	1.88/1 1.92/1 1.95/1 1.98/2 2.01/xxxx 1.99/x 1.97/1					
	1.98	1	DNG	Stockholm	22 Aug	1.90/1 1.94/1 1.98/1 2.01/xxx					
2.02			Anna	Chicherova		RUS	22.7.82	1		Beijing	21 May
			1.85/1 1.89/1 1.95/1 1.98/1 2.00/2 2.02/2 2.04/xxx						
	2.01	1	DL	Saint-Denis	6 Jul	1.85/1 1.89/1 1.95/1 1.98/2 2.01/1 2.05/xxx					
	1.98	1=	GGala	Roma	6 Jun	1.84/1 1.88/1 1.95/1 1.98/2 2.01/xxxx 1.99/x 1.97/1					
	1.98	2	Herc	Monaco	19 Jul	1.85/1 1.89/1 1.92/1 1.95/1 1.98/1 2.01/xxx					
	1.98	2	DNG	Stockholm	22 Aug	1.85/1 1.90/1 1.94/2 1.98/1 2.01/xxx					
	1.98	2	VD	Bruxelles	6 Sep	1.84/1 1.90/1 1.93/2 1.96/2 1.98/1 2.00/x 2.02/xx					
2.00i			Alessia	Trost		ITA	8.3.93	1		Trinec	29 Jan
			1.76/1 1.81/1 1.85/1 1.88/1 1.91/1 1.94/1 2.00/1 2.02/xx						
	1.98i	1		Udine	20 Jan	1.85/1 1.90/1 1.95/2 1.98/3 2.00/xx					
	1.98	1	EU23	Tampere	13 Jul	1.76/1 1.80/1 1.84/1 1.87/1 1.90/3 1.92/1 1.94/1 1.98/3					
2.00			Blanka	Vlasic		CRO	8.11.83	1		Bühl	21 Jun
			1.80/1 1.87/1 1.90/1 1.93/1 1.97/1 2.00/3 2.02/xxx						
	1.98	3	DL	Saint-Denis	6 Jul	1.85/1 1.92/1 1.95/1 1.98/2 2.01/xxx					
	1.98	2		Madrid	13 Jul	1.86/1 1.92/1 1.95/1 1.98/2 2.01/xxxx					
	1.98	3	Herc	Monaco	19 Jul	1.85/1 1.92/1 1.95/1 1.98/2 2.01/xxx					
1.99i			Ruth	Beitia		ESP	1.4.79	1	EI	Göteborg	3 Mar
			1.87/1 1.92/1 1.96/1 1.99/2 2.02/xxx						
	1.98i	1		Santander	9 Feb	1.82/1 1.88/1 1.93/1 1.96/1 1.98/2 2.00/xxx					
1.99			Kamila	Stepaniuk		POL	22.3.86	1		Opole	9 Jun
			1.78/1 1.82/1 1.86/1 1.90/1 1.93/1 1.95/1 1.99/1						
1.99			Irina	Gordeyeva		RUS	9.10.86	1		Rieti	8 Sep
			1.80/1 1.85/1 1.89/1 1.93/1 1.96/1 1.99/1 2.01/xxx						
1.98i			Mariya	Kuchina		RUS	14.1.93	1	ET	Gateshead	23 Jun
			(28/9)								
			1.75/1 1.80/1 1.85/1 1.89/1 1.92/1 1.95/3 1.98/1 2.00/xxx						
1.97i			Tia	Hellebaut (10)		BEL	16.2.78	1		Eaubonne	7 Feb
1.97			Emma	Green Tregaro		SWE	8.12.84	5	WCh	Moskva	17 Aug
1.97			Justyna	Kasprzycka		POL	20.8.87	6	WCh	Moskva	17 Aug
1.96i			Ebba	Jungmark		SWE	10.3.87	2	EI	Göteborg	3 Mar
1.96			Ana	Simic		CRO	5.5.90	1	Gyulai	Budapest	10 Jul
1.96			Eleanor	Patterson		AUS-Y	22.5.96	1	N.Sch	Townsville	7 Dec
1.95i			Olena	Holosha		UKR	26.1.82	2		Eaubonne	7 Feb
1.95			Marie-Laurence	Jungfleisch		GER	7.10.90	1		Eppingen	30 May
1.95			Marina	Aitova		KAZ	13.9.82	1		Almaty	15 Jun
1.95A			Lavern	Spencer		LCA	23.8.84	1	CAC	Morelia	5 Jul
1.95			Airine	Palsyte		LTU	13.7.92	1	NC	Siauliai	27 Jul
			(20)								
1.95			Adonía	Steryíou		GRE	7.7.85	1	BalkC	Stara Zagora	28 Jul
1.94i			Anja	Iljustsenko		EST	12.10.85	3		Arnstadt	2 Feb
1.94			Mirela	Demireva		BUL	28.9.89	2	Gyulai	Budapest	10 Jul
1.94			Svetlana	Radzivil		UZB	17.1.87	1		Bangkok	4 Sep
1.93i			Venelina	Veneva-Mateeva		BUL	13.6.74	2		Hustopece	26 Jan
1.93i			Mélanie	Skotnik		FRA	8.11.82	1	NC	Aubière	16 Feb
1.93			Nadezhda	Dusanova		UZB	17.11.87	1		Colombo	12 May
1.93			Iryna	Kovalenko		UKR	17.6.86	1		Kyiv	27 Jun
1.93				Zheng Xingjuan		CHN	20.3.89	9=	WCh	Moskva	17 Aug
1.92Ai			Barbara	Szabó		HUN	17.2.90	1		Golden	8 Feb
			(30)								

Mark	Name		Nat	Born	Pos	Meet	Venue	Date
1.92i	Iryna	Herashchenko	UKR-J	10.3.95	2	NC	Sumy	15 Feb
1.92i	My	Nordström	SWE	21.4.90	3	NC	Norrköping	17 Feb
1.92	Miyuki	Fukumoto	JPN	4.1.77	1	NC	Sydney	14 Apr
1.92	Yevgeniya	Kononova	RUS	28.9.89	1	NCp	Yerino	16 Jun
1.92	Oksana	Starostina	RUS	1.4.88	2	NCp	Yerino	16 Jun
1.92	Inika	McPherson	USA	29.9.86	2	NC	Des Moines	22 Jun
1.92	Burcu	Yüksel-Ayhan	TUR	3.5.90	1	MedG	Mersin	29 Jun
1.92	Tonje	Angelsen	NOR	17.1.90	1		Trondheim	1 Jul
1.92A	Jeannelle	Scheper	LCA-J	21.11.94	2	CAC	Morelia	5 Jul
1.92	Maya	Pressley	USA	1.2.91	1		Tallahassee	13 Jul
	(40)							
1.92	Maayan	Shahaf	ISR	9.11.86	1		Tel Aviv	17 Jul
1.92	Yelena	Slesarenko	RUS	28.2.82	3	NC	Moskva	24 Jul
1.92	Oksana	Okuneva	UKR	14.3.90	1	NC	Donetsk	25 Jul
1.92	Nafissatou	Thiam	BEL-J	19.8.94	1H	WCh	Moskva	12 Aug
1.92	Wang Yang		CHN	14.2.89	2	NG	Shenyang	10 Sep
1.91i	Yuliya	Kostrova	RUS	20.8.91	1		Novocheboksarsk	13 Jan
1.91i	Esthera	Petre	ROU	13.5.90	1		Bucuresti	26 Jan
1.91i	Tatyana	Kivimyagi	RUS	23.6.84	1	NC	Moskva	13 Feb
1.91i	Daniela	Stanciu	ROU	15.10.87	2=	Balk	Istanbul	23 Feb
1.91	Doreen	Amata	NGR	6.5.88	1		Auburn	6 Apr
	(50)							
1.91		Pham Thi Diem	VIE	24.1.90	1		Taipei	27 May
1.91	Valeriya	Bogdanovich	BLR	1.5.92	1		Minsk	7 Jun
1.91	Viktoriya	Palamar	UKR	12.10.77	1		Kyiv	14 Jun
1.91	Isobel	Pooley	GBR	21.12.92	1		Bedford	18 Aug
1.90i	Yekaterina	Kuntsevich	RUS	13.7.84	1		Wien	19 Jan
1.90i	Yana	Maksimova	BLR	9.1.89	1P		Gomel	23 Jan
1.90i	Tynita	Butts	USA	10.6.90	1		University Park	25 Jan
1.90i	Alesya	Paklina	KGZ	22.6.88	1		Volgograd	26 Jan
1.90i	Eleriin	Haas	EST	4.7.92	5		Hustopece	26 Jan
1.90i	Kateryna	Tabashnyk	UKR-J	15.6.94	1P		Sumy	6 Feb
	(60)							
1.90	Viktoriya	Styopina	UKR	21.2.77	1		Mykolaiv	11 May
1.90	Sofie	Skoog	SWE	7.6.90	1		Málaga	28 May
1.90	Nataliya	Hapchuk	UKR	15.11.88	2		Riga	30 May
1.90	Nadine	Broersen	NED	29.4.90	1Tr		Salzburg	15 Jun
1.90	Sharon	Day	USA	9.6.85	1H	NC	Des Moines	20 Jun
1.90	Ariane	Friedrich	GER	10.1.84	3		Bühl	21 Jun
1.90	Oksana	Krasnokutskaya	RUS	24.9.93	1	NC-23	Cheboksary	25 Jun
1.90	Daniellys	Dutil	CUB-J	12.2.95	1		La Habana	28 Jun
1.90	Alina	Fyodorova	UKR	31.7.89	1H		Tallinn	29 Jun
1.90	Morgan	Lake	GBR-Y	12.5.97	1H	WY	Donetsk	12 Jul
	(70)							
1.90	Marina	Smolyakova	RUS	20.6.89	1		Irkutsk	3 Aug
1.90	Grete	Udras	EST	11.3.88	1		Valga	10 Aug
1.89i	Irina	Iliyeva	RUS-J	22.12.95	3		Chelyabinsk	9 Jan
1.89i	Makeba	Alcide	LCA	24.2.90	1P		Fayetteville	25 Jan
1.89i	Viktoriya	Dobrynska	UKR	18.1.80	1	NCp	Zaporizhzhya	30 Jan
1.89i	Yekaterina	Bolshova	RUS	4.2.88	1P		Volgograd	8 Feb
1.89	Yekaterina	Fedotova	RUS	3.7.92	2	NC-23	Cheboksary	25 Jun
1.89	Anastasiya	Andreyeva	RUS	11.1.92	3	NC-23	Cheboksary	25 Jun
1.89	Urszula	Gardzielewska	POL	21.7.88	2	NC	Torun	20 Jul
1.89	Valentyna	Lyashenko	UKR	30.1.81	3	NC	Donetsk	25 Jul
	(80)							
1.89	Linda	Sandblom	FIN	18.10.89	2	vSWE	Stockholm	8 Sep
1.89	Eliska	Klucinová	CZE	14.4.88	1H		Talence	14 Sep
1.88i	Hanne	Van Hessche	BEL	5.7.91	1		Gent	6 Jan
1.88i	Krystle	Schade	USA	2.7.90	1		Birmingham, AL	19 Jan
1.88i	Shanay	Briscoe	USA	7.8.92	2		Fayetteville	25 Jan
1.88i	Julia	Straub	GER	10.4.86	1		Unna	27 Jan
1.88i	Michelle	Kinsella	CAN	27.2.91	1		Geneva, OH	17 Feb
1.88	Izabela	Mikolajczyk	POL	4.9.90	1		Kalamáta	1 Jun
1.88	Sahana	Kumari	IND	6.3.81	1		Chennai	5 Jun
1.88	Nadja	Kampschulte	GER	5.9.92	1		Regensburg	8 Jun
	(90)							
1.88	Aleksandra	Yaryshkina	RUS-J	10.6.94	2	EJ	Rieti	21 Jul
1.87i	Margarita	Mazina	RUS-J	7.7.95	1		Moskva	11 Jan
1.87i	Victoria	Dronsfield	SWE	6.6.91	1		Karlstad	26 Jan
1.87i	Austra	Skujyte	LTU	12.8.79	1		Vilnius	26 Jan
1.87i	Agnieszka	Borowska	POL	21.10.91	1		Spala	2 Feb

WOMEN 2013

Mark	Name		Nat	Born	Pos	Meet	Venue	Date
1.87i	Sietske	Noorman	NED	16.7.91	4		Gent	10 Feb
1.87i	Ann	Dudley	USA	28.5.91	1P		Jonesboro	24 Feb
1.87i	Dior	Delophont	FRA-J	19.10.94	5	NCAA	Fayetteville	8 Mar
1.87	Yulimar	Rojas	VEN-J	21.10.95	1		Barquisimeto	6 Apr
1.87	Leontia	Kallenou	CYP-J	5.10.94	4	MedG	Mersin	29 Jun
	(100)							
1.87	Emma	Nuttall	GBR	23.4.92	1	NC	Birmingham	13 Jul
1.87	Nele	Hollmann	GER	18.10.92	5	EU23	Tampere	13 Jul
1.87	Chiara	Vitobello	ITA	21.10.91	8	EU23	Tampere	13 Jul
1.87		Zhang Luyu	CHN-J	18.8.94	3	NG	Shenyang	10 Sep

Mark	Name		Nat	Born		Mark	Name		Nat	Born	
1.86i	Tatyana	Mnatsakanova	RUS	23.5.83	25 Jan	1.85	Amber	Melville	USA	20.12.92	20 Apr
1.86i	Ulyana	Aleksandrova	RUS	1.1.91	8 Feb	1.85	Ilva	Bikanova	LAT	12.12.90	5 May
1.86i	Taylor	Burke	USA	4.6.93	9 Feb	1.85	Saniel	Atkinson Grier	BAH	2.7.91	11 May
1.86i	Lisa	Engman	SWE-J	27.7.94	17 Feb	1.85	Olena	Demydova	UKR	16.6.82	11 May
1.86i	Mariya	Nestserchuk	BLR	14.8.89	17 Feb	1.85A	Susan	Jackson	USA	26.7.89	12 May
1.86i	Taisa	Roslova	BLR	7.2.92	17 Feb	1.85	Laetitia	Jovien	FRA	3.11.91	19 May
1.86i	J'Lynn	Ledesma	USA	17.5.91	24 Feb	1.85	Jayne	Nisbet	GBR	17.7.88	8 Jun
1.86	Valdiléia	Martins	BRA	19.9.89	23 Feb	1.85	Priscilla	Frederick	USA	14.2.89	8 Jun
1.86	Fabiola	Ayala	MEX	31.12.86	15 Mar	1.85	Regina	Sarsekova	KAZ	7.4.93	9 Jun
1.86	Kimberley	Williamson	JAM	2.10.93	6 Apr	1.85	Brianne	Theisen-Eaton	CAN	18.12.88	21 Jun
1.86	Mônica	de Freitas	BRA	21.6.84	4 May	1.85	Elina	Smolander	FIN	11.10.89	2 Jul
1.86	Undine	Dindune	LAT-J	7.4.95	18 May	1.85		Duong Thi Viet Anh	VIE	30.12.90	20 Jul
1.86	Gintare	Nesteckyte	LTU-J	30.12.95	18 May	1.85	Elena	Vallortigara	ITA	21.9.91	27 Jul
1.86	Rachel	Machin	CAN	14.3.92	1 Jun	1.85	Sofiya	Voronina	RUS-Y	18.9.97	30 Nov
1.86	Courtney	Anderson	USA	28.8.90	8 Jun	1.84i	Alexandra	Plaza	GER-J	10.8.94	11 Jan
1.86	Patricia	Sylvester	GRN	3.2.83	11 Jun	1.84i	Molly	Bergvall	SWE-J	2.9.95	13 Jan
1.86	Romana	Dubnová	CZE	4.11.78	15 Jun	1.84i	Katarina	Mögenburg	NOR	16.6.91	23 Jan
1.86	Magdaléna	Nová	CZE	27.10.92	15 Jun	1.84i	Allison	Barwise	USA	21.7.91	22 Feb
1.86	Monika	Gollner	AUT	23.10.74	16 Jun	1.84i	Gema	Martín-Pozuelo	ESP	21.6.87	23 Feb
1.86	Svetlana	Linkevich	RUS	26.9.91	25 Jun	1.84i		Wang Lin	CHN-J	8.1.95	7 Mar
1.86		Chen Yanjun	CHN	13.1.88	4 Jul	1.84i		Zhao Jian	CHN	24.3.91	7 Mar
1.86	Tatyana	Chernova	RUS	29.1.88	10 Jul	1.84i		Shen Xin	CHN	5.11.92	7 Mar
1.86	Laura	Rautanen	FIN	13.2.88	3 Aug	1.84i		Qiao Yanrui	CHN	29.9.88	15 Mar
1.86	Yorgelis	Rodríguez	CUB-J	25.1.95	12 Aug	1.84	Elizabeth	Lamb	NZL	12.5.91	2 Mar
1.86	Anna	Melnychenko	UKR	24.4.83	12 Aug	1.84	Samantha	Balentine	USA	21.6.91	11 Apr
1.86i	Akela	Jones	BAR-J	31.12.95	3 Dec	1.84		Wu Yin	CHN-J	27.7.94	22 Apr
1.85 6'1	Cyre	Virgo	USA-Y	24.10.96	16 Apr	1.84	Israel	Ramsey	JAM	15.8.93	29 Apr
1.85 6'1	Rachel	Proteau	USA-J	18.5.95	25 May	1.84	Imke	Onnen	GER-J	17.8.94	17 May
1.85i	Yuliya	Babayeva	RUS	22.5.88	26 Jan	1.84A	Tiana	Wills	USA		25 May
1.85i	Sibel	Çinar	TUR	16.1.87	2 Feb	1.84	Ekateríni	Kiriakopoúlou	GRE	4.12.93	16 Jun
1.85i	Alfiya	Neveretdinova	RUS	5.11.93	9 Feb	1.84	Elizabeth	Evans	USA	1.12.90	22 Jun
1.85i	Ligia	Grozav	ROU-J	26.1.94	16 Feb	1.84	Nawal	Meniker	FRA-Y	9.12.97	23 Jun
1.85A	Julia	du Plessis	RSA-Y	27.5.96	28 Feb	1.84	Senni	Ronkainen	FIN	23.8.93	11 Jul
1.85	Lesyanís	Mayor	CUB	8.7.89	9 Mar	1.84	Katarina	Johnson-Thompson	GBR	9.1.93	13 Jul
1.85A	Romary	Rifka	MEX	8.4.73	16 Mar	1.84	Giovanna	Demo	SUI	29.6.87	17 Jul
1.85	Bianca	Erwee	RSA	4.3.90	13 Apr	1.84		Ye Jiaying	CHN	7.1.93	8 Sep
1.85	Sarah	Cowley	NZL	3.2.84	14 Apr		(177)				

Best outdoor marks

1.97	Beitia		3=	WCh	Moskva	17 Aug	1.89A	Szabó		1	Boulder	13 Apr
1.96	Kuchina		2	WUG	Kazan	12 Jul	1.89	Paklina		1	Orel	29 May
1.94	Iljustsenko		3	WUG	Kazan	12 Jul	1.89	Jungmark		8	Herc Monaco	19 Jul
1.91	Herashchenko (J)		1		Kharkiv	17 Jun	1.88	Alcide		1H	Fayetteville	7 Apr
1.90	Skotnik		1		Strasbourg	5 May	1.88	Kivimyagi		3=	Sochi	26 May
1.90	Veneva-Mateeva		2		Bucuresti	7 Jun	1.88	Iliyeva		1	Kazan	16 Jun
1.90	Stanciu		1	NC	Bucuresti	28 Jun	1.87	Van Hessche		7	EU23 Tampere	13 Jul
1.90	Holosha		1		Tomblaine	1 Jul	1.87	Borowska		1H	Firenze	2 May
1.90	Tabashnyk (J)		1	EJ	Rieti	21 Jul	1.87	Haas		6	EU23 Tampere	13 Jul
1.86	Kinsella		10 May		1.86	Mnatsakanova	4 Jul	1.87	Maksimova		Tr Flame Amsterdam	31 Aug
1.86	Kostrova		26 May		1.85	Schade	20 Apr	1.84	Dudley	26 Apr		1.84 Kuntsevich	8 Jun
1.86	Straub		30 May		1.85	Nordström	7 Jun	1.84	Shen Xin	11 May		1.84 Wang Lin	15 Jun
1.86	Nestserchuk	30 May		1.85	Noorman	21 Jul	1.84	Roslova	30 May		1.84 Aleksandrova	29 Jun
1.86	Dronsfield	8 Jun		1.84	Butts	20 Apr	1.84	Zhao Jian	1 Jun		1.84 Qiao Yanrui	10 Sep

JUNIORS

See main list for top 14 juniors. 12 performances (inc. 4 indoors) by 7 women to 1.90. Additional marks

Mark		Name		Nat	Born	Pos	Meet	Venue	Date
Scheper		1.91i	1		Fayetteville	9 Feb	1.90i	2 NCAA Fayetteville	8 Mar
Thiam		1.90	1H	Afr-J Bambous		18 Apr			
1.86i		Lisa	Engman	SWE	27.7.94	5	NC	Norrköping	17 Feb
1.86		Undine	Dindune	LAT	7.4.95	1		Riga	18 May
1.86		Gintare	Nesteckyte	LTU	30.12.95	1		Vidukle	18 May
1.86		Yorgelis	Rodríguez	CUB	25.1.95	3H	WCh	Moskva	12 Aug
1.86i		Akela	Jones	BAR	31.12.95	1		Shawnee	3 Dec
1.85 6'1		Cyre	Virgo (20)	USA-Y	24.10.96	1		Fleetwood	16 Apr
1.85 6'1		Rachel	Proteau	USA	18.5.95	1		Eugene	25 May
1.85i		Ligia	Grozav	ROU	26.1.94	1		Bucuresti	16 Feb

Mark	Name		Nat	Born	Pos	Meet	Venue	Date
1.85A	Julia	du Plessis	RSA-Y	27.5.96	1		Germiston	28 Feb

POLE VAULT

Mark	Name		Nat	Born	Pos	Meet	Venue	Date
5.02Ai	Jennifer	Suhr	USA	5.2.82	1	NC	Albuquerque	2 Mar
	4.65/1	4.70/1	4.80/1	4.90/1	5.02/1	5.07/xxx		
	4.91 1		Lyndonville				14 Jun	
	4.84i 1		Fort Wayne				23 Feb	
	4.60/1	4.70/1	4.84/2	5.02/xxx				
	4.82 2 WCh		Moskva				13 Aug	
	4.55/1	4.75/1	4.82/2	4.89/xxx				
	4.80 1		Allendale				10 May	
	4.55/1	4.70/1	4.80/2	5.07/xx				
	4.77 1		Lyndonville				31 May	
	4.76i 1		Boston (R)				2 Feb	
	4.55/1	4.65/2	4.76/1	4.90/xxp				
	4.73 2 DL		London (OS)				26 Jul	
	4.63/1	4.73/1	4.83/x	4.88/xx				
4.90	Yarisley	Silva	CUB	1.6.87	1	FBK	Hengelo	8 Jun
	4.05/xx	4.40/1	4.60/1	4.70/1	4.80/1	4.90/1	5.00/xxx	
	4.85 1 Drake	Des Moines	26 Apr					
	4.53/1	4.63/3	4.73/3	4.85/1	4.90/xxx			
	4.83 1 DL	London (OS)	26 Jul					
	4.53/1	4.63/2	4.73/2	4.83/1				
	4.82i 1 Drake	Des Moines	24 Apr					
	4.50/1	4.60/1	4.70/1	4.82/1	4.90/xxx			
	4.82 3 WCh	Moskva	13 Aug					
	4.55/1	4.65/3	4.75/2	4.82/3	4.89/xxx			
	4.81 1 NC	La Habana	16 Mar					
	4.50/2	4.61/1	4.81/1	4.90/xxx				
	4.81 1 Spitz	Luzern	17 Jul					
	4.51/1	4.61/1	4.71/2	4.81/2	4.91/x	5.00/x		
	4.78i 1	Stockholm	21 Feb					
	4.45/1	4.64/2	4.78/1	4.81/xxx				
	4.76i 1 Stars	Donetsk	9 Feb					
	4.45/2	4.60/2	4.65/1	4.70/1	4.76/1	4.78/xxx		
	4.73 1 DL	Birmingham	30 Jun					
	4.63/1	4.73/1	4.83/xxx					
4.89	Yelena	Isinbayeva	RUS	3.6.82	1	WCh	Moskva	13 Aug
	4.65/2	4.75/1	4.82/2	4.89/1	5.07/xxx			
	4.78 1 GS	Ostrava	27 Jun					
	4.72/1	4.78/1	4.84/xxx					
	4.75 1 NC	Moskva	23 Jul					
	4.60/2	4.75/3	4.85/xxx					
4.79	Silke	Spiegelburg	GER	17.3.86	1	WK	Zürich	29 Aug
	4.52/1	4.62/1	4.72/1	4.79/1	4.86/xxx			
	4.75 4 WCh	Moskva	13 Aug					
	4.45/1	4.55/1	4.65/1	4.75/1	4.82/xxx			
4.77i	Holly	Bleasdale	GBR	2.11.91	1	NC	Sheffield	9 Feb
	4.35/1	4.50/2	4.65/1	4.77/3	4.90/xxx			
	4.75i 1	Moskva	3 Feb					
	4.36/1	4.56/2	4.65/3	4.70/2	4.75/1	4.80/xxx		
4.76	Jirina	Svobodová	CZE	20.5.86	1		Plzen	4 Sep
	4.35/1	4.55/1	4.71/1	4.76/2	4.81/xxx			
4.75Ai	Kylie	Hutson	USA	27.11.87	2	NC	Albuquerque	2 Mar
	4.40/1	4.55/1	4.65/1	4.70/3	4.75/3	4.80/xxx		
4.75	Fabiana	Murer	BRA	16.3.81	1		Beckum	25 Aug
	4.43/1	4.55/1	4.65/2	4.75/3	4.83/xxx			
	4.73 1 NC	São Paulo	9 Jun					
	4.53/1	4.63/2	4.73/3	4.86/xxx				
4.73	Anastasiya	Savchenko	RUS	15.11.89	1	NCp	Yerino	15 Jun
	(30/9)			4.20/2	4.40/1	4.50/2	4.60/1	4.73/1
4.71	Carolin	Hingst (10)	GER	18.9.80	1		Göteborg	15 Jun
4.70	Mary	Saxer	USA	21.6.87	1		Chula Vista	6 Jun
4.70	Angelina	Krasnova	RUS	7.2.91	1	EU23	Tampere	13 Jul
4.67i	Anna	Rogowska	POL	21.5.81	2	EI	Göteborg	2 Mar
4.65	Martina	Strutz	GER	4.11.81	1	NC	Ulm	6 Jul
4.65	Nikoléta	Kiriakopoúlou	GRE	21.3.86	1	NC	Athina	20 Jul
4.65		Li Ling	CHN	6.7.89	1	NG	Shenyang	8 Sep
4.62i	Anzhelika	Sidorova	RUS	28.6.91	3	EI	Göteborg	2 Mar
4.61	Nicole	Büchler	SUI	17.12.83	3	Spitz	Luzern	17 Jul
4.61	Kristina	Gadschiew	GER	3.7.84	1		Rovereto	3 Sep
4.60i	Roberta	Bruni	ITA-J	8.3.94	1	NC	Ancona	17 Feb
	(20)							
4.60Ai	Janice	Keppler	USA	22.3.87	4	NC	Albuquerque	2 Mar
4.60	Tori	Pena	IRL	30.7.87	2		Chula Vista	6 Jun
4.60	Svetlana	Feofanova	RUS	16.7.80	2	FBK	Hengelo	8 Jun
4.60	Marion	Lotout	FRA	19.11.89	1		Grenoble	12 Jun
4.56i	Aleksandra	Kiryashova	RUS	21.8.85	1		Sankt-Peterburg	17 Feb
4.55	Becky	Holliday	USA	12.3.80	3	NC	Des Moines	23 Jun
4.55	Angelica	Bengtsson	SWE	8.7.93	3	EU23	Tampere	13 Jul
4.55	Elizaveta	Ryzih	GER	27.9.88	4		Jockgrim	23 Jul
4.53	Lacy	Janson	USA	20.2.83	5	Drake	Des Moines	26 Apr
4.53	Karla	da Silva	BRA	12.11.84	1		São Paulo	11 May
	(30)							
4.50i	Morgann	LeLeux	USA	14.11.92	1		Fayetteville	25 Jan
4.50i	Lyudmila	Yeryomina	RUS	8.8.91	1		Irkutsk	26 Jan
4.50	Alana	Boyd	AUS	10.5.84	1		Brisbane	9 Mar
4.50	April	Bennett	USA	22.4.80	2		Chula Vista	23 May
4.50	Kelsie	Hendry	CAN	29.6.82	4		Chula Vista	6 Jun
4.50	Katherine	Viuf	USA	23.5.87	5		Chula Vista	6 Jun

Mark	Name		Nat	Born	Pos	Meet	Venue	Date	
4.50	Melissa	Gergel	USA	24.4.89	1		Chula Vista	8	Jun
4.50	Stélla-Iró	Ledáki	GRE	18.7.88	1		Pátra	12	Jun
4.50	Martina	Schultze	GER	12.9.90	1		Biesigheim	24	Jul
4.50	Minna	Nikkanen	FIN	9.4.88	1		Somero	6	Aug
	(40)								
4.50i	Kaitlin	Petrillose	USA	12.10.92	1		Belton	28	Dec
4.46i	Katharina	Bauer	GER	12.6.90	Q	EI	Göteborg	1	Mar
4.46	Bethany	Buell	USA	4.12.91	1	TexR	Austin	29	Mar
4.45Ai	Ekateríni	Stefanídi	GRE	4.2.90	1		Flagstaff	1	Feb
4.45Ai	April	Kubishta	USA	5.7.85	2		Flagstaff	14	Feb
4.45i	Natalya	Bartnovskaya	RUS	7.1.89	1	NCAA	Fayetteville	9	Mar
4.45i	Jade	Riebold	USA	14.4.91	2	NCAA	Fayetteville	9	Mar
4.45	Alexis	Paine	USA	12.10.90	1		Atlanta	30	Mar
4.45	Loréla	Mánou	GRE	20.12.90	2		Pátra	12	Jun
4.45	Katie	Nageotte	USA	30.6.91	1		Knoxville	15	Jun
	(50)								
4.45	Vera	Schmitz	USA	3.12.87	2		Terre Haute	15	Jun
4.45	Elizabeth	Parnov	AUS-J	9.5.94	1J		Mannheim	29	Jun
4.45	Anjuli	Knäsche	GER	18.10.93	3	NC	Ulm	6	Jul
4.43i	Sandi	Morris	USA	8.7.92	1		Fayetteville	1	Mar
4.43	Patricia	dos Santos	BRA	13.6.84	1		Buenos Aires	25	Apr
4.43	Naroa	Agirre	ESP	15.5.79	4		Rovereto	3	Sep
4.43i	Maria Eleonor	Tavares	POR	24.9.85	3		Aulnay-sous-Bois	21	Dec
4.42i	Romana	Malácová	CZE	15.5.87	2		Praha	2	Feb
4.42	Sonia	Malavisi	ITA-J	31.10.94	1		Rieti	5	Jul
4.41	Megan	Jamerson	USA	4.5.86	1		Chula Vista	17	Jul
	(60)								
4.41	Anna Katharina	Schmid	SUI	2.12.89	8=	Spitz	Luzern	17	Jul
4.41	Annika	Roloff	GER	10.3.91	1		Holzminden	8	Aug
4.40i	Yekaterina	Kazeka	RUS	7.10.90	1		Chelyabinsk	9	Jan
4.40i	Sally	Peake	GBR	8.2.86	2		Rouen	26	Jan
4.40i	Victoria	von Eynatten	GER	6.10.91	1c2		Sindelfingen	26	Jan
4.40i	Giorgia	Benecchi	ITA	9.7.89	2	NC	Ancona	17	Feb
4.40i		Ren Mengqian	CHN	4.10.93	1		Beijing	29	Mar
4.40	Daylis	Caballero	CUB	6.3.88	1		La Habana	23	Feb
4.40A	Kayla	Caldwell	USA	19.6.91	2	NCAA II	Pueblo	23	May
4.40	Joana	Kraft	GER	27.7.91	1	NC-23	Göttingen	15	Jun
	(70)								
4.40	Marion	Buisson	FRA	19.2.88	3	MedG	Mersin	26	Jun
4.40	Lucy	Bryan	GBR-J	22.5.95	2J		Mannheim	29	Jun
4.40		Wu Sha	CHN	21.10.87	3		Mannheim	29	Jun
4.40	Vanessa	Boslak	FRA	11.6.82	2		Bron	2	Jul
4.40	Heather	Hamilton	CAN	31.3.88	1		Victoria	5	Jul
4.40A	Alysha	Newman	CAN-J	29.6.94	1	PAm-J	Medellín	25	Aug
4.40A	Robeilys	Peinado	VEN-Y	26.11.97	2	PAm-J	Medellín	25	Aug
4.40	Fanny	Smets	BEL	21.4.86	2	Franc	Nice	11	Sep
4.37	Malin	Dahlström	SWE	26.8.89	1		København	1	Aug
4.35i	Mélanie	Blouin	CAN	14.7.90	1		Montreal	26	Jan
	(80)								
4.35i	Rianna	Galiart	NED	22.11.85	1		Zoetermeer	2	Feb
4.35i	Sarah	Pappas	USA	30.3.87	1		Norman	16	Feb
4.35i	Katie	Byres	GBR	11.9.93	3	GP	Birmingham	16	Feb
4.35i	Marion	Fiack	FRA	13.10.92	2	NC	Aubière	16	Feb
4.35	MacKenzie	Fields	USA	19.1.90	1		Columbus	20	Apr
4.35	Mandissa	Marshall	USA	2.4.91	1		Ewing	27	Apr
4.35	Katrine	Haarklau	NOR	21.2.91	5	NCAA	Eugene	7	Jun
4.35	Tina	Sutej	SLO	7.11.88	1		Ljubljana	13	Jul
4.35	Caroline Bonde	Holm	DEN	19.7.90	1	NC	Aalborg	27	Jul
4.33i	Tomomi	Abiko	JPN	17.3.88	1		Kosai	23	Feb
	(90)								
4.33	Chloë	Henry	BEL	5.3.87	2		Albi	29	Jun
4.31i	Cathrine	Larsåsen	NOR	5.12.86	2		Manchester	9	Mar
4.31	Nina	Kennedy	AUS-Y	5.4.97	1		Perth	12	Mar
4.31	Christen	Gunther	USA	14.9.89	2	TexR	Austin	29	Mar
4.31	Allison	Koressel	USA	2.3.91	4	TexR	Austin	29	Mar
4.31	Stephanie	Richartz	USA	21.1.92	5	TexR	Austin	29	Mar
4.30Ai	Angela	Rummans	USA	23.3.92	1		Reno	19	Jan
4.30i	Yuliya	Golubchikova	RUS	27.3.83	1		Moskva	23	Jan
4.30i	Alayna	Lutkovskaya	RUS-Y	15.3.96	1	NC-j	Penza	1	Feb
4.30i	Olga	Mullina	RUS	1.8.92	6	NC	Moskva	12	Feb
	(100)								

Mark	Name		Nat	Born	Pos	Meet	Venue	Date
4.30i	Alina	Kakoshinskaya	RUS	16.11.86	8	NC	Moskva	12 Feb
4.30	Melinda	Owen	USA	30.10.84	3	MSR	Walnut	20 Apr
4.30	Anna	Felzmann	GER	18.1.92	1		Kaiserslautern	9 May
4.30		Xu Huiqin	CHN	4.9.93	2		Jinan	11 May
4.30		Li Caixia	CHN	23.8.87	3=		Jinan	11 May
4.30	Kristina	Bondarenko	RUS-J	10.8.95	4		Sochi	25 May
4.30	Emily	Grove	USA	22.5.93	7	NCAA	Eugene	7 Jun
4.30	Lilli	Schnitzerling	GER	5.12.93	1		Bad Meinberg	12 Jul
4.30	Femke	Pluim	NED-J	10.5.94	3	NA	Heusden-Zolder	13 Jul
4.30		Zhang Yingning	CHN	6.1.90	5	NG	Shenyang	8 Sep

Mark	Name		Nat	Born	Date
4.27	Kristen	Brown	USA	26.5.92	9 Mar
4.27	Leslie	Brost	USA	28.9.89	3 May
4.26	Kerry	Charlesworth	NZL	13.12.93	23 Feb
4.25i	Demi	Payne	USA	30.9.91	25 Jan
4.25i	Nicole	Hope	USA	4.4.90	26 Jan
4.25i	Catherine	Street	USA	9.5.90	10 Feb
4.25i	Anais	Poumarat	FRA	25.2.89	16 Feb
4.25i	Kristen	Hixson	USA	1.7.92	8 Mar
4.25	Natasha	Masterson	USA	1.8.91	7 Jun
4.25	Kiley	Tobel	USA	7.7.91	7 Jun
4.25	Tatyana	Stetsuk	RUS	24.8.92	24 Jun
4.25	Noelina	Madarieta	ARG-Y	6.7.96	29 Jun
4.25	Alessandra	Lazzari	ITA	4.5.91	13 Jul
4.24i	Reena	Koll	EST-Y	15.11.96	5 Feb
4.24i	Petra	Olsen	SWE	2.10.90	2 Mar
4.24i	Linda	Hadfield	USA	12.9.92	2 Mar
4.24	Lakan	Taylor	USA-J	21.6.95	27 Apr
4.23i	Merritt	Van Meter	USA	8.1.92	8 Feb
4.22Ai	Annie	Burlingham	USA	.86	8 Feb
4.22Ai	Shaylah	Simpson	USA	16.3.92	8 Feb
4.22i	Zoë	Brown	IRL	15.9.83	17 Feb
4.22	Robin	Bone	CAN-J	13.2.94	5 May
4.22	Sophie	Dangla	FRA	19.10.87	15 Jun
4.22	Marta	Onofre	POR	28.1.91	28 Jul
4.22	Kira	Grünberg	AUT	13.8.93	3 Aug
4.21i	Nataliya	Mazuryk	UKR	5.3.83	15 Feb
4.21i	Michelle	Favre	USA	13.6.91	2 Mar
4.21	Kat	Majester	USA	22.5.87	8 Jun
4.21	Sukanya	Chomchuendee	THA	9.9.88	15 Dec
4.20Ai	Allison	Stokke	USA	22.3.89	19 Jan
4.20i	Fanny	Berglund	SWE	8.2.88	8 Mar
4.20	Lindsey	Bergevin	CAN	14.1.89	19 Apr
4.20	Kseniya	Chertkoshvili	UKR	18.2.92	17 May
4.20		Lim Eun-ji	KOR	2.4.89	27 May
4.20	Kateryna	Kozlova	UKR	14.9.89	6 Jun
4.20	Logan	Miller	USA	21.5.91	7 Jun
4.20	Desiree	Singh	GER-J	17.8.94	22 Jun
4.20	Carla	Franch	ESP	25.10.89	2 Jul
4.20	Hanna	Sheleh	UKR	14.7.93	24 Jul
4.20	Elena	Scarpellini	ITA	14.1.87	28 Jul
4.20	Tatyana	Tretyakova	RUS	10.8.89	3 Aug
4.20i	Olga	Chigirintseva	RUS	29.6.87	22 Dec
4.20i	Tatyana	Shvydkina	RUS	8.5.90	22 Dec
4.19i	Krista	Obizajeva	LAT-Y	30.4.96	5 Feb
4.19	Desiree	Freier	USA-Y	24.7.96	11 May
4.18	Annie	Rhodes	USA-J	13.5.95	30 Mar
4.18	Alissa	Söderberg	SWE-J	12.4.94	6 Jul
4.17i	Cameron	Overstreet	USA	30.9.92	22 Feb
4.17	Stephanie	Foreman	USA	10.3.90	10 May
4.17	Maira	Silva	BRA	15.9.91	29 Jun
4.16i	Ninon	Guillon-Romarin	FRA-J	15.4.95	16 Mar
4.16	Kaitlyn	Merritt	USA-Y	27.3.97	6 Apr
4.15i	Samantha	Sonnenberg	USA	10.2.88	18 Jan
4.15Ai	Theresa	Raub	USA	4.4.88	2 Feb
4.15i	Brigitte	Gross	USA	22.11.90	8 Mar
4.15i		Zhang Yunyun	CHN	26.2.92	29 Mar
4.15	Kelsie	Ahbe	USA	6.7.91	13 Apr
4.15	Mallory	Gilbert	USA	.85	27 Apr
4.15		Shi Qiaowen	CHN	25.12.90	27 Apr
4.15	Gabriella	Duclos-Lasnier	CAN	1.3.88	2 May
4.15	Megan	Clark	USA	10.6.94	11 May
4.15	Janneke	Oosterink	NED	22.1.87	20 May
4.15	Miriam	Galli	ITA	30.10.91	26 May
4.15		Wang Hui	CHN	17.6.93	1 Jun
4.15	Shade	Weygandt	USA	24.1.91	6 Jun
4.15	Bryson	Stately	USA	22.11.86	6 Jun
4.15	Valeria	Chiaraviglio	ARG	9.4.89	6 Jul
4.15	Sirine	Ebondo	TUN	31.10.83	13 Jul
4.15	Anna María	Pinero	ESP	15.1.86	27 Jul
4.15		Sun Sinan	CHN	15.12.93	8 Sep
4.15i	Karley	King	USA	29.10.90	7 Dec

(181)

Best outdoor marks

Mark	Name			Venue	Date
4.70	Hutson	1		Terre Haute	15 Jun
4.60	Bleasdale	1		Phoenix	17 May
4.60	Sidorova	2	EU23	Tampere	13 Jul
4.60	Rogowska	1		Slupsk	17 Jul
4.50	Kiryashova	3	FBK	Hengelo	8 Jun
4.45	Bartnovskaya	1		Manhattan, KS	11 May
4.45	Yeryomina	2	NC-23	Cheboksary	24 Jun
4.45	Bauer	1		Wipperfürth	8 Aug
4.43	Keppler	8	Drake	Des Moines	26 Apr
4.41	Kubishta	2		Tempe	6 Apr
4.40	Ren Mengqian	1		Zhaoqing	27 Apr
4.40	Bruni (J)	1		Formia	29 May

4.27	Peake	31 Jul		4.21	Abiko	18 May
4.25	Hixson	10 May		4.21	Rummans	8 Jun
4.25	Kakoshinskaya	16 Jun		4.21	Z Brown	29 Jun
4.22	V von Eynatten	13 Jul		4.20	Hope	20 Apr

Irrgular pegs (75mm)

Mark	Name		Nat	Born	Pos	Meet	Venue	Date
4.26	Annie	Rhodes	USA-J	13.5.95				16 Mar
4.40	Stefanídi				7=		Chula Vista	6 Jun
4.40	Riebold				3	NCAA	Eugene	7 Jun
4.40	Kazeka				1		Chelyabinsk	5 Jul
4.36	Petrillose				1		Waco	3 May
4.35	Fiack				2		Pierre-Bénite	7 Jun
4.32	LeLeux				2		Athens	13 Apr
4.32	Tavares				2		Aulnay-sous-Bois	5 Jun
4.32	Malácová				5	GS	Ostrava	27 Jun
4.31	Galiart				1		Vught	9 May
4.30	Golubchikova				3		Sochi	25 May
4.30	Benecchi				1		Parma	29 May
4.30	Lutkovskaya (J)				1	EJ	Rieti	21 Jul
4.30	Larsåsen				1	NC	Tonsberg	23 Aug

4.20	Mullina	6 Jun	4.15	Poumarat	7 Jun
4.20	Byres	12 Jul	4.15	Overstreet	7 Jun
4.15	Zhang Yunyun	11 May	4.15	Koll	22 Jun
4.15	Mazuryk	18 May	4.15	Guillon-Romarin	21 Jul

JUNIORS

See main list for top 10 juniors. 11 performances (inc. 3 indoors) by 6 women to 4.40. Additional marks:

Mark	Name		Nat	Born	Pos	Meet	Venue	Date
Bruni	4.51i		1		Fermo	2 Feb	4.40i	1 NC-j Ancona 24 Feb
Parnov	4.40		2		Perth	16 Mar		
Malavisi	4.41		1	NC-j	Rieti	15 Jun		
4.25	Noelina	Madarieta	ARG-Y	6.7.96	1	NC-j	Buenos Aires	29 Jun
4.24i	Reena	Koll	EST-Y	15.11.96	2		Tartu	5 Feb
4.24	Lakan	Taylor	USA	21.6.95	1		Abilene	27 Apr
4.22	Robin	Bone	CAN	13.2.94	1		London. ON	5 May
4.20	Desiree	Singh	GER	17.8.94	1		Bottrop	22 Jun

Mark	Wind	Name		Nat	Born	Pos	Meet	Venue	Date
4.19i		Krista	Obizajeva	LAT-Y	30.4.96	3		Tartu	5 Feb
4.19		Desiree	Freier	USA-Y	24.7.96	1		Austin	11 May
4.18		Annie	Rhodes	USA	13.5.95	1		Austin	30 Mar
4.18		Alissa	Söderberg	SWE	12.4.94	3		Halmstad	6 Jul
4.16i		Ninon	Guillon-Romarin (20)	FRA	15.4.95	1	NC-j	Lyon	16 Mar
4.16		Kaitlyn	Merritt	USA-Y	27.3.97	1		Arcadia	6 Apr

LONG JUMP

Mark	Wind	Name		Nat	Born	Pos	Meet	Venue	Date
7.25	1.6	Brittney	Reese	USA	9.9.86	1	DL	Doha	10 May
					x　x　7.04w/2.5　7.25　x　x				
7.01	0.2 1	WCh	Moskva		11 Aug		6.50　7.01　x　x　6.95/0.2　x		
6.99	-1.0 1	GGala	Roma		6 Jun		6.94/-2.3　6.74　x　6.89/-0.1　6.99　x		
6.96	1.0 2	Athl	Lausanne		4 Jul		x　6.75　x　6.96　5.70/0.2　x		
6.85i	2	Mill	New York (Armory)		16 Feb		6.32　x　6.65　6.85　6.43　6.62		
6.94w	2.5 1	Drake	Des Moines		26 Apr		x　x　6.73w　6.56　x　6.94w		
7.04	1.5	Sosthene	Moguenara	GER	17.10.89	1		Weinheim	2 Aug
					6.76　7.04　p　p　p				
7.02	2.0	Oksana	Zhukovskaya	RUS	12.9.84	1	Kuts	Moskva	15 Jul
					6.34　4.82　6.62　7.02				
7.01i		Darya	Klishina	RUS	15.1.91	1	EI	Göteborg	2 Mar
					7.01　6.83　x　6.57　6.71　x				
6.90	0.3 1	WUG	Kazan		8 Jul		6.72　x　6.77　6.90　6.61　6.78		
7.00i		Olga	Kucherenko	RUS	5.11.85	1		Krasnodar	20 Jan
					7.00　x　x　p　6.89　6.92				
6.90i	1		Volgograd		26 Jan		6.90　x　p　6.86		
7.00	0.0	Blessing	Okagbare	NGR	6.10.88	*	Herc	Monaco	19 Jul
					6.86/1.5　7.04w　7.00/0.0　x　x　5.45				
6.99	0.2 2	WCh	Moskva		11 Aug		6.89/-0.2　6.58　6.68　6.80　6.99　6.96/0.3		
6.98	1.1 1	Athl	Lausanne		4 Jul		6.73　6.83/1.5　x　6.64　6.98　6.81w		
6.92	1.8 *	DL	Doha		10 May		6.70　7.14w　7.03w/2.4　4.98w　6.92　p		
6.99	1.8	Janay	DeLoach-Soukup	USA	12.10.85	*	DL	Doha	10 May
					6.67w　x　6.55　7.04w/2.3　7.08w　6.99				
6.97	0.5 2	GGala	Roma		6 Jun		6.72　6.88/0.6　x　x　6.97　6.65		
6.90i	1	Mill	New York (Armory)		16 Feb		6.65　6.61　6.90　x　x　5.09		
6.92	1.3	Funmilayo	Jimoh	USA	29.5.84	4	DL	Doha	10 May
					x　6.84w/3.7　6.83/1.7　6.66　6.92　x				
6.92	1.9	Shara	Proctor	GBR	16.9.88	3	Athl	Lausanne	4 Jul
					6.64　x　6.72　x　6.92　x				
6.91	0.2 3	GGala	Roma		6 Jun		6.63　6.56　6.70　6.89/0.4　6.78　6.91		
6.89	1.5 1	Bisl	Oslo		13 Jun		6.89　6.39　6.65　6.76w　6.35w　p		
6.88	-0.3 1	WK	Zürich		29 Aug		6.65　x　6.88　6.47　x　6.51		
6.85	-0.1 Q	WCh	Moskva		10 Aug		6.85		
6.84	1.7 1	NC	Birmingham		14 Jul		x　6.84　x　p　p　p		
6.91	1.0	Tori	Bowie (10)	USA	27.8.90	1		Los Angeles (Ww)	6 Apr
					6.62　6.66　5.26　6.91　p　p				
6.91	1.9	Yelena	Sokolova	RUS	23.7.86	5	DL	Doha	10 May
					x　6.85w/2.2　6.87/1.7　6.81w　x　6.91				
6.87	-1.2 4	GGala	Roma		6 Jun		6.71/1.6　6.87　6.80　6.80　x　6.59		
6.90i		Éloyse	Lesueur	FRA	15.7.88	2	EI	Göteborg	2 Mar
					6.85　x　x　6.87　6.90　x				
6.89	-0.1	Lyudmila	Kolchanova (30/13)	RUS	1.10.79	1	NC	Moskva	23 Jul
					6.80　x　x　6.89　6.44　x				
6.82	0.1	Ivana	Spanovic	SRB	10.5.90	2	WCh	Moskva	11 Aug
6.82	-0.1	Olga	Sudareva	BLR	22.2.84	4	WCh	Moskva	11 Aug
6.81	-1.2	Lynique	Prinsloo	RSA	30.3.91	1		Stellenbosch	13 Apr
6.79	0.5	Veronika	Mosina	RUS	17.10.90	1	Chall	Moskva	11 Jun
6.78	1.8	Maryna	Bekh	UKR-J	18.7.95	1		Yalta	6 Jun
6.77	1.9	Lorraine	Ugen	GBR	22.8.91	1	NCAA	Eugene	5 Jun
6.76i		Svetlana	Denyayeva (20)	RUS	10.5.91	3	NC	Moskva	13 Feb
6.76	2.0	Lena	Malkus	GER	6.8.93	1	EU23	Tampere	14 Jul
6.75	0.0	Christabel	Nettey	CAN	2.6.91	1		Tempe	6 Apr
6.75	0.1	Tori	Polk	USA	21.9.83	Q	WCh	Moskva	10 Aug
6.73	1.2	Bianca	Stuart	BAH	17.5.88	1		Dakar	12 Jun
6.72	0.9	Chelsea	Hayes	USA	9.2.88	2		Nassau	13 Apr
6.72	1.6	Lauma	Griva	LAT	27.10.84	1		Tartu	28 May
6.72	2.0	Hanna	Kornuta	UKR	10.11.88	1		Kyiv	14 Jun
6.71i		Erica	Jarder	SWE	2.4.86	3	EI	Göteborg	2 Mar
6.70	0.9	Malaika	Mihambo	GER-J	3.2.94	1	EJ	Rieti	21 Jul
6.70	1.1	Yekaterina	Levitskaya (30)	RUS	2.1.87	1		København	1 Aug

Mark	Wind	Name		Nat	Born	Pos	Meet	Venue	Date	
6.69i		Andrea	Geubelle	USA	21.6.91	1		New York (Armory)	1	Feb
6.69	0.4	Jana	Veldáková	SVK	3.6.81	1		Brno	14	May
6.68i		Melanie	Bauschke	GER	14.7.88	2		Karlsruhe	2	Feb
6.68	0.0	Vashti	Thomas	USA	21.4.90	2		Tempe	6	Apr
6.68	1.0	Anna	Jagaciak	POL	10.2.90	1	Franc	Nice	12	Sep
6.67i		Margaryta	Tverdohlib	UKR	2.6.91	1		Donetsk	23	Feb
6.67	-0.7	Francine	Simpson	JAM	1.11.89	1	Big12	Waco	4	May
6.67	1.5	Darya	Derkach	ITA	27.3.93	1		Rieti	15	Jun
6.67	1.0	Claudia	Rath	GER	25.4.86	1H	WCh	Moskva	13	Aug
6.66	0.5	Xenia	Achkinadze	GER	14.1.89	1		Wesel	30	May
		(40)								
6.66	0.5	Teresa	Dobija	POL	9.10.82	2	Franc	Nice	12	Sep
6.65Ai		Whitney	Gipson	USA	20.9.90	2	NC	Albuquerque	2	Mar
6.65	0.8	Chantel	Malone	IVB	2.12.91	1		Nassau	13	Apr
6.65	-0.4	Jana	Koresová	CZE	8.4.81	1		Tabor	15	Jun
6.64	0.7	Carla	Marais	RSA	10.12.87	2		Stellenbosch	13	Apr
6.63	0.9	Abigail	Irozuru	GBR	3.1.90	3	Chall	Moskva	11	Jun
6.63	0.5	Jazmin	Sawyers	GBR-J	21.5.94	2	EJ	Rieti	21	Jul
6.63	0.0	Alina	Rotaru	ROU	5.6.93	1		Bucuresti	25	Aug
6.62i		Anastasiya	Mokhnyuk	UKR	1.1.91	1		Kyiv	11	Jan
6.62i		Cornelia	Deiac	ROU	20.3.88	1	NC	Bucuresti	10	Feb
		(50)								
6.62	1.4	Evaggelía	Galéni	GRE	29.12.88	1		Athina	20	Jul
6.61	1.6	Krystyna	Hryshutyna	UKR	21.3.92	2	EU23	Tampere	14	Jul
6.60	0.0	Iryna	Nikolayeva	UKR	20.1.84	2		Yalta	6	Jun
6.60	1.4	Anastasiya	Mironchik-Ivanova	BLR	13.4.89	1		Minsk	28	Jun
6.59	1.1	Concepción	Montaner	ESP	14.1.81	1		Castellón	23	May
6.59	-0.3	Saeko	Okayama	JPN	12.4.82	1	NC	Tokyo (Chofu)	7	Jun
6.59	1.6	Dafne	Schippers	NED	15.6.92	3	EU23	Tampere	14	Jul
6.58	0.6	Lisa	Steinkamp	GER	17.8.90	3		Wesel	30	May
6.58	1.4	Oksana	Zubkovska	UKR	15.7.81	4		Yalta	6	Jun
6.58	1.1	María del Mar	Jover	ESP	21.4.88	1		Alicante	15	Jun
		(60)								
6.57i		Yekaterina	Bolshova	RUS	4.2.88	1P		Volgograd	8	Feb
6.57Ai		Alesha	Walker	USA	9.4.88	3	NC	Albuquerque	2	Mar
6.57	1.6	Tatyana	Chernova	RUS	29.1.88	1H	NCp	Adler	9	May
6.57	2.0	Michelle	Weitzel	GER	18.6.87	*		Weinheim	25	May
6.56	-0.6	Keila	Costa	BRA	6.2.83	1		Belém	12	May
6.56	1.1	Stephanie	Voss	GER	9.9.89	5		Wesel	30	May
6.56	1.7	Jessica	dos Reis	BRA	17.3.93	3	Kuso	Szczecin	15	Jun
6.56	0.6	Katarina	Johnson-Thompson	GBR	9.1.93	2H	WCh	Moskva	13	Aug
6.55	1.9	Eunice	Barber	FRA	17.11.74	1		Besançon	15	Jun
6.55	0.0	Sachiko	Masumi	JPN	20.12.84	1	AsiC	Pune	3	Jul
		(70)								
6.55	1.5	Viktoriya	Valyukevich	RUS	22.5.82	2	Kuts	Moskva	15	Jul
6.55	1.9	Mara	Griva	LAT	27.10.84	1	v2N	Valmiera	20	Jul
6.55	0.6	Nectaria	Panayi	CYP	20.3.90	1		Thivá	24	Jul
6.54	-0.2	Dominique	Blaize	GBR	3.10.87	1	LI	Loughborough	19	May
6.54	-1.6	Florentina	Marincu	ROU-Y	8.4.96	1		Bucuresti	1	Jun
6.54A		Caterine	Ibargüen	COL	12.2.84	1		Cali	22	Jun
6.53	1.5	Eliane	Martins	BRA	26.5.86	1		Santiago de Chile	3	Apr
6.53	0.9	Kerrie	Perkins	AUS	2.4.79	1		Melbourne	6	Apr
6.53	-0.1	Anna	Misochenko	RUS	15.4.92	1		Krasnodar	7	Jun
6.53	0.5	Snezana	Rodic	SLO	19.8.82	1		Nova Gorica	16	Jun
		(80)								
6.53	1.2	Ese	Brume	NGR-Y	17.1.96	2	NC	Calabar	21	Jun
6.53	1.8	Brooke	Stratton	AUS	12.7.93	1	Zat	Melbourne	12	Dec
6.52	1.7	Kylie	Price	USA	1.10.93	2	TexR	Austin	29	Mar
6.52	-2.0	Anastasiya	Kudinova	KAZ	27.2.88	1		Shymkent	25	Apr
6.52	0.0	Darya	Reznichenko	UZB	3.4.91	1		Bangkok	4	May
6.52	0.3	Alexis	Faulknor	USA-J	22.9.94	*		Houston	11	May
6.52	-0.1	Yelena	Sitnikova	RUS	12.11.89	1		Bryansk	19	Jun
6.52	1.2	Irène	Pusterla	SUI	21.6.88	1		Chiasso	19	Jun
6.51	1.3	Irina	Ilyina	RUS	25.5.85	2		Brno	14	May
6.51	0.0	Yekaterina	Khalyutina	RUS	16.1.91	1		Bucuresti	7	Jun
		(90)								
6.51	1.2	Polina	Yurchenko	RUS	20.8.93	1	NC-23	Cheboksary	25	Jun
6.51	-0.2	Cristina Mihaela	Sandu	ROU	4.3.90	2	BalkC	Stara Zagora	28	Jul
6.50Ai		Jessie	Gaines	USA	12.8.90	4	NC	Albuquerque	2	Mar
6.50	0.7	Tania	Vicenzino	ITA	1.4.86	1		Nembro	3	Jul
6.49	0.0	Patience	Ntshingila	RSA	26.8.89	1		Roodeport	9	Feb

Mark	Wind	Name		Nat	Born	Pos	Meet	Venue	Date
6.49	1.3	Jennifer	Clayton	USA/PAN	5.10.92	2		Houston	11 May
6.49	0.0	Mayookha	Johny	IND	4.9.88	1		Chennai	4 Jun
6.49	1.4	Karolina	Blazej	POL	21.11.86	1		Kraków	22 Jun
6.49	0.9	Nina	Kolaric	SLO	12.12.86	2	MedG	Mersin	27 Jun
6.49	-0.3	Yuliya	Pidluzhnaya	RUS	1.10.88	5	NC	Moskva	23 Jul
(100)									
6.49	0.2	Anna	Melnychenko	UKR	24.4.83	3H	WCh	Moskva	13 Aug

Mark	Wind	Name		Nat	Born	Pos	Meet	Venue	Date
6.48		Paula	Álvarez	CUB-J	11.9.95				22 Feb
6.48	1.9	Renata	Medgyesová	SVK	28.1.83				18 May
6.48	0.7	Xu Xiaoling		CHN	13.5.92				9 Sep
6.47i		Maryse	Luzolo	GER-J	13.3.95				9 Feb
6.47	0.2	Efthímia	Kolokithá	GRE	9.7.87	3			Jul
6.47	0.4	Olga	Balayeva	RUS	30.6.84	15			Jul
6.46i		Leah	Eber	USA	22.11.88				26 Jan
6.46i		Wang Wupin		CHN	18.1.91				23 Mar
6.46	2.0	Karolina	Tyminska	POL	4.10.84	1			Jun
6.45i		Karimah	Shepherd	USA	13.3.91				22 Feb
6.45i		Jiang Yanfei		CHN	5.7.92				6 Mar
6.45A	-0.3	Arantxa	King	BER	27.11.89	7			Jul
6.45	-0.1	Yurina	Hiraka	JPN	4.6.91	8			Sep
6.44	0.0	Malaina	Payton	USA	16.10.91	20			Apr
6.44	1.2	Kira	Biesenbach	GER	7.10.92	26			May
6.44	0.0	Chinazor	Amadi	NGR	12.9.87	14			Jun
6.44	-3.3	Yana	Gubar	RUS	2.7.90	15			Jun
6.44	1.8	Jaana	Sieviläinen	FIN	18.8.82	29			Jun
6.44	-0.2	Yekaterina	Koneva	RUS	25.9.88	8			Sep
6.43i		Erica	Bougard	USA	26.7.93				22 Feb
6.43i		Wang Rong		CHN-Y	1.7.96				6 Mar
6.43	-1.0	Anastasiya	Juravlyeva	UZB	9.10.81	31			May
6.43	1.9	Dana	Veldáková	SVK	3.6.81	8			Sep
6.42i		Ulyana	Aleksandrova	RUS	1.1.91				27 Feb
6.42	1.1	Maria Natalia	Londa	INA	29.10.90	28			May
6.42	1.9	Kseniya	Detsuk	BLR	23.4.86	28			Jun
6.42	1.6	Amy	Harris	GBR	14.9.87	29			Jun
6.41i		Chanice	Porter	JAM-J	25.5.94				25 Jan
6.41i		Le'Tristan	Pledger	USA	27.8.93	1			Feb
6.41i		Melissa	Norville	USA	18.11.91				22 Feb
6.41	1.8	Bohdana	Melnyk	UKR-J	25.10.94	17			Jun
6.40i		Valeriya	Zavyalova	RUS	16.1.88				16 Jan
6.40i		Viktoriya	Molchanova	UKR	26.5.82	3			Feb
6.40	1.8	Giulia	Liboà	ITA	3.6.93	2			Jun
6.40	0.3	Irisdaymi	Herrera	CUB	18.4.92	4			Jun
6.40	0.9	Juliet	Itoya	ESP	17.8.86	8			Jun
6.40	1.5	Courtney	Corrin	USA-Y	12.12.97	25			Jun
6.40	2.0	Kelly	Proper	IRL	1.5.88	3			Aug
6.39	0.3	Linda	Leverton	AUS	22.3.87	16			Feb
6.39	1.1	Macarena	Reyes	CHI	30.3.84	3			Apr
6.39	0.5	Jade	Nimmo	GBR	23.3.91	13			Apr
6.39	1.7	Keisha	Lockhart	USA	5.3.90	10			May
6.39	-0.5	Sandisha	Antoine	LCA	5.11.91	7			Jul
6.39	-1.2	Keturah	Orji	USA-Y	5.3.96	14			Jul
6.39	1.1	Marjolein	Lindemans	BEL-J	17.2.94	19			Jul
6.39	0.2	Hitomi	Nakano	JPN	23.11.90	9			Aug
6.38i		LaQue	Moen-Davis	USA	14.8.93				12 Jan
6.38i		Erin	Busbee	USA	12.1.92	1			Mar
6.38	-0.5	Fátima	Diame	ESP-Y	22.9.96	23			May
6.37i		Sevim	Serbest-Sinmez	TUR	20.4.87	3			Feb
6.37i		Ja'nia	Sears	USA		17			Feb
6.37i		Urszula	Westhof	GER	13.7.77	24			Feb
6.37	1.8	Kumiko	Imura	JPN	10.1.81	21			Apr
6.37	1.3	Tamaka	Shimizu	JPN	22.6.91	25			May
6.37	0.1	Nafissatou	Thiam	BEL-J	19.8.94	19			Jul
6.37	0.5	Brianne	Theisen-Eaton	CAN	18.12.88	13			Aug
6.36i		Veronika	Shutkova	BLR	26.5.86	6			Feb
6.36A		Zanri	van der Merwe	RSA	14.5.93	19			Mar
6.36	0.3	Hafdís	Sigurdjardóttir	ISL	12.8.87	23			May
6.36	2.0		Bae Chan-mi	KOR	24.3.91	19			Jun
6.36	2.0	Bernadett	Berecz	HUN	27.7.88	27			Jul
6.36	1.0	Sarah	Ngongoa	CMR	7.7.83	12			Sep
6.36	0.5	Corinna	Minko	AUS	13.12.89	12			Dec
6.35i		Cristina	Bujin	ROU	12.4.88	26			Jan
6.35i		Tatyana	Akmukhamedova	RUS	14.7.93	23			Feb
6.35	1.7	Sydney	Conley	USA	11.12.93	13			Apr
6.35	-3.6	Sharika	Smith	USA	23.4.90	13			Apr
6.35	1.2	Crystal	Walker	USA	23.6.91	13			Apr
6.35	0.0	Julia	Gerter	GER-J	13.7.94	30			Jun
6.35	1.2	Grit	Sadeiko	EST	29.7.89	30			Jun
6.35	0.2	Teresa	Carvalho	POR-J	30.1.95	20			Jul
(171)									

Wind assisted

Mark	Wind	Name		Nat	Born	Pos	Meet	Venue	Date
7.14	2.2	Blessing	Okagbare	NGR	9.10.88	2	DL	Doha	10 May
7.04	2.1	1					Herc	Monaco	19 Jul

See main list for series of these two marks

Mark	Wind	Name		Nat	Born	Pos	Meet	Venue	Date
7.08	2.2	Janay	DeLoach-Soukup	USA	12.10.85	3	DL	Doha	10 May

6.92 3.5 2 Drake Des Moines 26 Apr   6.68w 6.92w 6.65 x 6.67
6.89 2.2 1 NC Des Moines 22 Jun   6.89w 6.65w p p p

Mark	Wind	Name		Nat	Born	Pos	Meet	Venue	Date
6.98	2.4	Darya	Klishina	RUS	15.1.91	2	Herc	Monaco	19 Jul

6.72   6.89w 6.75 6.90w/2.2 x 6.60

Mark	Wind	Name		Nat	Born	Pos	Meet	Venue	Date
6.80	2.5	Malaika	Mihambo	GER-J	3.2.94	1		Weinheim	25 May
6.80	3.9	Tori	Polk	USA	21.9.83	2	NC	Des Moines	22 Jun
6.73	4.1	María del Mar	Jover	ESP	21.4.88	1	ECCp	Vila Real S.António	26 May
6.69	2.3	Xenia	Achkinadze	GER	14.1.89	2		Bad Langensalza	15 Jun
6.69	3.0	Irène	Pusterla	SUI	21.6.88	1		Donnas	8 Jul
6.67	2.8	Michelle	Weitzel	GER	18.6.87	1		Weinheim	25 May
6.63	4.3	Renata	Medgyesová	SVK	28.1.83	1		Trnava	30 Jun
6.62	3.8	Sachiko	Masumi	JPN	20.12.84	3		Tokyo	5 May
6.56	2.7	Alexis	Faulknor	USA-J	22.9.94	1		Houston	12 May
6.56	2.6	Dominique	Blaize	GBR	3.10.87	1		Bedford	27 May
6.55	5.3	LaQue	Moen-Davis	USA	14.8.93	1	SEC	Columbia, MO	11 May
6.55	2.9	Kylie	Price	USA	1.10.93	2	Pac 12	Los Angeles	11 May
6.54	2.9	Macarena	Reyes	CHI	30.3.84	1	SACh	Cartagena	6 Jul
6.54	3.3	Ana	Martín-Sacristán	ESP-J	15.12.94	1		Castellón	7 Jul
6.54	5.1	Fanni	Schmelcz	HUN	19.4.92	1		Budapest	28 Jul
6.54	3.8	Dana	Veldáková	SVK	3.6.81	1		Nove Mesto nad Metuj	8 Sep
6.50	3.4	Karolina	Blazej	POL	21.11.86	4	Kuso	Szczecin	15 Jun

Mark	Wind	Name		Nat	Born		Date		Mark	Wind	Name		Nat	Born		Date
6.49	2.6	Anna	Yermakova	UKR	1.10.91	27	Jun		6.39	2.7	Brianne	Theisen-Eaton	CAN	18.12.88	26	May
6.47	3.1	Claudette	Allen	JAM-J	4.4.95	13	Apr		6.39	2.2	Chelsea	Carrier-Eades	USA	21.8.89	27	Jul
6.43	2.7	Jacinda	Evans	USA	18.6.90	19	Apr		6.38	4.3	Zanri	van der Merwe	RSA	14.5.93	28	Apr
6.43	2.1	Nadja	Käther	GER	29.9.88	21	Jul		6.36		Kendell	Williams	USA-J	14.6.95	26	Apr
6.42	2.4	Denisa	Rosolová	CZE	21.8.86	8	Sep		6.36	3.4	Yorsiris	Urrutia	COL	26.6.86	6	Jul
6.41	3.0	Crystal	Walker	USA	23.6.91	5	Jun		6.35	2.7	LaToya	Powell	JAM		16	Feb
6.40	3.0	Sharika	Nelvis	USA	10.5.90	11	May		6.35	2.2		Zhou Xiaoxue	CHN	19.6.92	12	May
6.40	2.9	Kristina	Savitskaya	RUS	10.6.91	6	Jun		6.35	2.1	Akela	Jones	BAR-J	31.12.95	23	May

Mark	Wind	Name			Nat	Born	Pos	Meet	Venue	Date

Best outdoor marks

Mark	Wind	Name			Nat			Meet	Venue	Date
6.81	0.1	Kucherenko	5	WCh	Moskva					11 Aug
6.78	1.9	Lesueur	6	GGala	Roma					6 Jun
6.68	0.4	Denyayeva	1		Moskva					11 May
6.66	1.9	Jarder	7	DL	Doha					10 May

6.64	0.8	Bauschke	2	Chall	Moskva	11 Jun
6.57	1.6	Mokhnyuk	5		Yalta	6 Jun
6.53	0.7	Geubelle	2	Big12	Waco	4 May
6.53	-1.7	Tverdohlib	Q		Yalta	17 May
6.50	0.0	Deiac	2		Bucuresti	7 Jun

6.46	2.0	Gipson	29 Mar		6.38	1.4	A Walker	27 Apr		6.36	-0.3	Jiang Yanfei	16 Jun
6.45	1.8	Luzolo	27 Jul		6.51w	2.7		27 Apr		6.35	0.5	Westhof	21 Jun
6.39	1.4	Bougard	11 May	6.37			Pledger	23 May		**Best at low altitude**			
				6.36	1.8	Serbest-Sinmez		9 Jun		6.36	1.5	A King	19 Jul

JUNIORS

See main list for top 5 juniors. 10 performances by 5 women to 6.52. Additional marks and further juniors:

Mark		Wind		Name		Nat	Born			Venue	Date
Mlhambo	6.64	-0.5	Q	EJ	Rieti			21 Jul	6.60	1.0	1	NC-j	Rostock	27 Jul
	6.61	1.4	*		Mannheim			25 May	6.54	1.4	1		Wesel	30 May
Marincu	6.54	0.0	1	NC-j	Bucuresti			27 Jul						
6.48			Paula		Álvarez	CUB	11.9.95	1			La Habana	22 Feb
6.47i			Maryse		Luzolo	GER	13.3.95	1			Frankfurt	9 Feb
6.43i					Wang Rong	CHN-Y	1.7.96	2			Nanjing	6 Mar
	6.33	-0.8						1	NC		Suzhou	29 May
6.41i			Chanice		Porter	JAM	25.5.94	1			Fayetteville	25 Jan
6.41		1.8	Bohdana		Melnyk (10)	UKR	25.10.94	1	NC-j		Kharkiv	17 Jun
6.40		1.5	Courtney		Corrin	USA-Y	12.12.97	1	NC-y		Edwardsville	25 Jun
6.39		-1.2	Keturah		Orji	USA-Y	5.3.96	2	WY		Donetsk	14 Jul
6.39		1.1	Marjolein		Lindemans	BEL	17.2.94	1H	EJ		Rieti	19 Jul
6.38		-0.5	Fátima		Diame	ESP-Y	22.9.96	2			Castellón	23 May
6.37		0.1	Nafissatou		Thiam	BEL	19.8.94	2H	EJ		Rieti	19 Jul
6.35		0.0	Julia		Gerter	GER	13.7.94	3			Mannheim	30 Jun
6.35		0.2	Teresa		Carvalho	POR	30.1.95	Q	EJ		Rieti	20 Jul
6.31		0.1	Yelena		Mashinistova	RUS	29.3.94				Irkutsk	4 Aug
6.30		1.1	Callie		Ives	USA	17.8.94	1	Towns		Athens, GA	13 Apr
6.30		1.7	Annika		Gärtz (20)	GER	24.8.94	4			Mannheim	30 Jun
6.30		0.2	Anastasiya		Yeremina	RUS	14.7.95				Irkutsk	4 Aug

Wind assisted

6.47	3.1	Claudette		Allen	JAM	4.4.95	1J			Kingston	13 Apr
6.36		Kendell		Williams	USA	14.6.95	1			Fayetteville	26 Apr
6.35	2.1	Akela		Jones	BAR	31.12.95	1	NAIA		Marion	23 May

TRIPLE JUMP

Mark	Wind			Name		Nat	Born	Pos	Meet	Venue	Date
14.88i				Olga	Saladuha	UKR	4.6.83	1	EI	Göteborg	3 Mar
				14.88	x			x	14.68	x	x
	14.85	1.7	2	Pre	Eugene			1 Jun	14.48	14.72/0.5 14.65/1.9 14.85 14.70/1.6 14.69w/3.6	
	14.69	0.4	Q	WCh	Moskva			13 Aug	13.95	14.69	
	14.65	0.9	3	WCh	Moskva			15 Aug	14.42	14.65 14.33 14.51/0.7 14.60/0.7 14.49	
	14.61i		1	GP	Birmingham			16 Feb	14.37	14.61 14.48 p 14.31 x	
	14.56	0.6	2	Bisl	Oslo			13 Jun	14.01	14.30 14.56 14.28 14.34 14.26	
	14.55	0.6	3	DL	Saint-Denis		6	Jul	14.28	14.55 14.21 x 11.92 14.38	
	14.52i		1		Düsseldorf			8 Feb	14.36	14.52 14.12 14.20 14.29 x	
14.85	0.2			Caterine	Ibargüen	COL	12.2.84	1	WCh	Moskva	15 Aug
					x				14.85 14.69/0.6 14.83/0.3 x x	
	14.83	1.4	*	Pre	Eugene			1 Jun	14.47	14.43 14.30 14.83/1.4 14.93w x	
	14.81		1	Bisl	Oslo			13 Jun	14.39	14.25 14.71w/2.5 x 14.81 14.78	
	14.69	-1.1	1	DL	Shanghai			18 May	14.35	14.28 14.69 13.45 14.18 x	
	14.69	-1.3	1	DL	Saint-Denis		6	Jul	14.23	14.54/0.0 14.69 14.11 14.40 14.47	
	14.61	0.7	1	DNG	Stockholm			22 Aug	14.40	14.50/-1.0 13.80 14.37 14.46 14.61	
	14.53A	1.7	1		Medellín			25 May	14.40/0.0	14.16w/2.7 14.53 p p	
	14.52	0.5	Q	WCh	Moskva			13 Aug	14.52		
14.82	-0.2			Yekaterina	Koneva	RUS	25.9.88	1	WUG	Kazan	11 Jul
					14.39			14.59	14.03 14.72 14.82 14.58	
	14.81	0.9	2	WCh	Moskva			15 Aug	14.29	14.81 14.59/0.1 14.33 14.79/0.8 12.18	
	14.80	1.9	1		Sochi			26 May	13.76	14.62/-0.1 x 14.75/1.9 14.80 x	
	14.59	1.9	1	NCp	Yerino			16 Jun	14.42/1.9	14.59 p x p p x	
	14.57	0.6	1	Znam	Zhukovskiy			30 Jun	14.37	14.57 x 14.45	
	14.52	-0.3	1	DL	London (OS)			26 Jul	14.40	x 14.29 14.52 14.46 14.47	
	14.51	2.0	1		Ankara			24 Aug	13.48	14.52 p p p p	
14.62	0.6			Kimberly	Williams	JAM	3.11.88	4	WCh	Moskva	15 Aug
					x			13.98	14.17 14.62 x x	
14.58	2.0			Keila	Costa	BRA	6.2.83	1	NC	São Paulo	7 Jun
					14.10			14.26	x p p 14.58	
14.58	2.0			Snezana	Rodic	SLO	19.8.82	1		Nova Gorica	15 Jun
					x			14.40	14.58 p p p	
14.58	1.5			Irina	Gumenyuk	RUS	6.1.88	2	NCp	Yerino	16 Jun
					14.20			14.58	14.16 14.44/1.9 p p	

Mark	Wind	Name		Nat	Born	Pos	Meet	Venue		Date
	14.50	1 NC	Moskva	25 Jul	14.17	13.97	x	14.41	14.50	14.32
14.58	0.6	Hanna	Knyazyeva-Minenko	ISR	25.9.89	2	DL	Saint-Denis		6 Jul
					14.58	x		14.29	14.04　x	x
	14.50	1.5 1 NC	Tel Aviv	3 Jul						
14.54	1.4	Alsu	Murtazina	RUS	20.12.87	3	NCp	Yerino		16 Jun
					14.24	14.27	x	14.54	x	p
14.50i		Natalya	Kutyakova	RUS	28.11.86	Q	NC	Moskva		13 Feb
		(32/10)								
14.48	1.9	Athanasía	Pérra	GRE	2.2.83	1	MedG	Mersin		28 Jun
14.45	1.2	Mabel	Gay	CUB	5.5.83	5	WCh	Moskva		15 Aug
14.41i		Viktoriya	Dolgacheva ¶	RUS	17.4.91	2	NC	Moskva		14 Feb
14.40	1.9	Yekaterina	Chernenko	RUS	9.10.86	2		Sochi		26 May
14.40	2.0	Natalya	Vyatkina	BLR	10.2.87	1		Brest		30 May
14.40	0.4	Anna	Pyatykh	RUS	4.4.81	2	NC	Moskva		25 Jul
14.39	0.8		Xie Limei	CHN	27.6.86	1	NG	Shenyang		11 Sep
14.37	1.7	Yarianna	Martínez	CUB	20.9.84	1		La Habana		8 Jun
14.36	0.2	Viktoriya	Valyukevich	RUS	22.5.82	3	NC	Moskva		25 Jul
14.35	0.0		Li Yanmei	CHN	6.2.90	2	NG	Shenyang		11 Sep
		(20)								
14.31	0.6	Dana	Veldáková	SVK	3.6.81	4	Pre	Eugene		1 Jun
14.30i		Veronika	Mosina	RUS	17.10.90	2		Sankt-Peterburg		26 Jan
14.29i		Niki	Panétta	GRE	21.4.86	1	NC-j	Pireás		17 Feb
14.29		Baya	Rahouli	ALG	27.7.79	1		Doha		24 May
14.27	2.0	Anna	Krylova	RUS	3.10.85	4	NCp	Yerino		16 Jun
14.26i		Simona	La Mantia	ITA	14.4.83	3	EI	Göteborg		3 Mar
14.26	1.9	Ruslana	Tsyhotska	UKR	23.3.86	1		Yalta		7 Jun
14.24i		Cristina	Bujin	ROU	12.4.88	1		Bucuresti		25 Jan
14.23	-0.1	Irina	Ektova	KAZ	8.1.87	1		Almaty		19 Jul
14.21	0.3	Paraskevi	Papahrístou	GRE	17.4.89	1		Pátra		12 Jun
		(30)								
14.21	-0.4	Anna	Jagaciak	POL	10.2.90	2	WUG	Kazan		11 Jul
14.20i		Trecia	Smith	JAM	5.11.75	2	GP	Birmingham		16 Feb
14.20		Liuba M.	Zaldívar	CUB	5.4.93	1		La Habana		23 Feb
14.20	0.5	Anastasiya	Juravlyeva	UZB	9.10.81	1		Tashkent		4 May
14.19	0.7	Kseniya	Detsuk	BLR	23.4.86	2		Brest		30 May
14.18i		Andrea	Geubelle	USA	21.6.91	1	NCAA	Fayetteville		9 Mar
14.17	-0.7	Maria Natalia	Londa	INA	29.10.90	1	SEAG	Nay Pyi Taw		17 Dec
14.16	1.5	Susana	Costa	POR	22.9.84	2		Madrid		13 Jul
14.16	-0.6	Thitima	Muangjan	THA	13.4.83	2	SEAG	Nay Pyi Taw		17 Dec
14.15	1.8	Shanieka	Thomas	JAM	2.2.92	1		Las Vegas		11 May
		(40)								
14.14i		Gabriela	Petrova	BUL	29.6.92	1	NC	Dobrich		16 Feb
14.14	0.2	Carmen	Toma	ROU	28.3.89	3	WUG	Kazan		11 Jul
14.12	-0.9	Jenny	Elbe	GER	18.4.90	1		Garbsen		19 May
14.12	-1.9		Tran Hue Hoa	VIE	8.8.91	3	SEAG	Nay Pyi Taw		17 Dec
14.11i		Valeriya	Zavyalova	RUS	16.1.88	6	NC	Moskva		14 Feb
14.11	0.0	Yana	Borodina	RUS	21.4.92	1	NC-23	Cheboksary		26 Jun
14.09i			Wang Rong	CHN-Y	1.7.96	7		Nanjing		7 Mar
14.08	1.7	Yorsiris	Urrutia	COL	26.6.86	1	Bol G	Trujillo		27 Nov
14.07i		Patricia	Sarrapio	ESP	16.11.82	5	EI	Göteborg		3 Mar
14.06i			Li Xiaohong	CHN-J	8.1.95	2		Nanjing		7 Mar
		(50)								
14.06	1.5	Yamilé	Aldama	GBR	14.8.72	8	Pre	Eugene		1 Jun
14.05	0.2	Yargelis	Savigne	CUB	13.11.84	3		La Habana		8 Jun
14.04	0.2	Nataliya	Yastrebova	UKR	12.10.84	Q	NC	Donetsk		26 Jul
14.02	0.7	Dailenis	Alcántara	CUB	10.8.91	2		La Habana		4 Jun
14.02	1.3	Patrícia	Mamona	POR	21.11.88	*		Madrid		13 Jul
13.99i		Gita	Dodova	BUL	2.5.82	1		Dobrich		12 Feb
13.99	2.0	Toni	Smith	USA	13.10.84	1		Chula Vista		17 Jul
13.98	0.0	Nadezhda	Alekhina	RUS	22.9.78	Q	NC	Moskva		23 Jul
13.97A	1.8	Giselly	Landázuri	COL	8.2.92	2		Medellín		25 May
13.97	2.0	Amanda	Smock	USA	27.7.82	1		Chula Vista		5 Jul
		(60)								
13.97	0.0	Tatyana	Lebedeva	RUS	21.7.76	6	NC	Moskva		25 Jul
13.96i		Svetlana	Denyayeva	RUS	12.5.91	1		Moskva		19 Jan
13.96	-1.4	Aleksandra	Kotlyarova	UZB	10.10.88	1		Tashkent		1 Jun
13.95	1.1	Sevim	Serbest-Sinmez	TUR	20.4.87	1		Istanbul		15 Jun
13.93	1.8	Iryna	Nikolayeva	UKR	20.1.84	2		Yalta		7 Jun
13.92	1.1	Darya	Derkach	ITA	27.3.93	1		Rieti		16 Jun
13.92	0.1		Deng Lina	CHN	16.3.92	3	NG	Shenyang		11 Sep
13.92	0.0		Liu Yanan	CHN	18.1.87	4	NG	Shenyang		11 Sep

Mark	Wind	Name		Nat	Born	Pos	Meet	Venue	Date
13.91i		Kristin	Gierisch	GER	20.8.90	2		Düsseldorf	8 Feb
13.91	0.5	Theresa	N'Zola Meso	FRA	30.11.83	1		Pierre-Bénite	7 Jun
		(70)							
13.89	1.3	Nathalie	Marie-Nély	FRA	24.11.86	2		Pierre-Bénite	7 Jun
13.89	1.7	April	Sinkler	USA	1.9.89	2		Chula Vista	5 Jul
13.88	1.1	Sarah	Nambawa	UGA	23.9.85	1	NC	Calabar	19 Jun
13.87	1.4	Yosleidis	Ribalta	CUB	2.5.90	3		La Habana	25 May
13.86	2.0	Crystal	Manning	USA	15.4.86	1		Los Angeles (ER)	4 May
13.85	1.6	Ciarra	Brewer	USA	12.3.93	1	SEC	Columbia, MO	12 May
13.84i		Svetlana	Bolshakova	BEL	14.10.84	3		Gent	10 Feb
13.84	-0.6		Chen Yufei	CHN	26.1.89	2		Jinan	11 May
13.84	-1.8	Yekaterina	Ektova	KAZ	30.8.92	1		Almaty	15 May
13.84i		Irina	Kosko	RUS	1.3.90	1		Sankt-Peterburg	22 Dec
		(80)							
13.83	-0.2		Hu Guanlian	CHN	18.7.90	2		Suzhou	31 May
13.82i			Sun Yan	CHN	30.3.91	3		Nanjing	7 Mar
13.81i			Hu Qian	CHN	14.1.89	4		Nanjing	7 Mar
13.81	-2.4	Florentina	Marincu	ROU-Y	8.4.96	1		Edirne	3 Aug
13.80	0.8	Linda	Leverton	AUS	22.3.87	1		Brisbane	23 Mar
13.78	0.6	Anna	Zych	POL	15.5.88	5	Gyulai	Budapest	10 Jul
13.76	1.5	Irina	Vaskovskaya	BLR	2.4.91			Minsk	14 Jun
13.75i		Ana	Peleteiro	ESP-J	2.12.95	2	NC	Sabadell	17 Feb
13.75	0.3	Débora	Calveras	ESP	26.12.88	1		Barcelona	19 Jun
13.74	-0.1		Wang Huiqin	CHN	7.2.90	5	NG	Shenyang	11 Sep
		(90)							
13.73	0.4	Ayanna	Alexander	TTO	20.7.82	3		Kingston	4 May
13.73	2.0	Alisa	Vlasova	RUS	16.9.90	8	NCp	Yerino	16 Jun
13.73	0.8	Laura	Samuel	GBR	19.2.91	*	NC	Birmingham	13 Jul
13.72	1.1	Gisele	de Oliveira	BRA	1.8.80	*		São Paulo	23 Feb
13.71	1.6	Dovile	Dzindzalietaite	LTU	14.7.93	1		Kaunas	1 Jun
13.71	0.0	Cristina Mihaela	Sandu	ROU	4.3.90	2		Bucuresti	24 Aug
13.70	1.1	Olesya	Tikhonova	RUS	22.1.90	1		Krasnodar	7 Jun
13.69	1.2	Ottavia	Cestonaro	ITA-J	12.1.95	1		Rieti	15 Jun
13.69	1.4	Elina	Torro	FIN	22.7.86	1		Jyvaskyla	19 Jun
13.69	0.8	Keturah	Orji	USA-Y	5.3.96	3	WY	Donetsk	12 Jul
		(100)							

Mark	Wind	Name		Nat	Born	Date		Mark	Wind	Name		Nat	Born	Date
13.68	0.1	Hanna	Kornuta	UKR	10.11.88	19 May		13.44	-0.7	Noni	Mordi	GBR	25.7.87	19 May
13.68A	2.0	Yudelsy	González	VEN	23.10.92	25 May		13.44	0.8	Ariana	Gutiérrez	VEN-J	14.8.95	2 Jun
13.68	1.1	Katja	Demut	GER	21.12.83	30 May		13.44	1.6	Svitlana	Mamyeyeva	UKR	19.4.82	7 Jun
13.67i			Lai Mengqin	CHN	21.1.91	7 Mar		13.44	1.9	Sharika	Smith	USA	23.4.90	7 Jun
13.65	1.3	Maja	Bratkic	SLO	14.5.91	15 Jun		13.44	1.5	Darya	Kucherova	BLR	14.11.93	14 Jun
13.64	1.3	LaQue	Moen-Davis	USA	14.8.93	12 May		13.44	-1.2	Lyudmila	Grankovskaya	KAZ	13.2.89	16 Jun
13.64	1.7	Iryna	Pimenova	UKR	19.12.88	30 Jul		13.44	0.0	Patricia	Sylvester	GRN	3.2.83	16 Jun
13.63		Jamaa	Chnaïk	MAR	28.7.84	24 May		13.44	0.4	Sandrine	Mbumi	CMR	22.5.86	14 Sep
13.63	0.0	Hanna	Aleksandrova	UKR	11.7.93	14 Jun		13.43	0.9	NoorAmira Mohd	Nafiah	MAS	16.7.89	11 Jul
13.63	-0.1	Sanna	Nygård	FIN	22.3.88	7 Sep		13.42i		Iryna	Yanchenko	UKR	22.3.88	13 Feb
13.62	1.8	Anastasiya	Mironchik-Ivanova	BLR	13.4.89	24 May		13.41i			Qu Nuo	CHN	27.9.91	7 Mar
13.61	0.6		Yao Jiajia	CHN	7.4.88	11 May		13.41	0.7	Ellen	Pettitt	AUS	13.5.86	13 Apr
13.61	1.9	Vasylyna	Bovanko	UKR-J	11.12.94	18 Jun		13.40	1.4	Tatyana	Nagornaya	BLR	14.12.89	7 Jun
13.60	0.8	Nubia	Soares	BRA-Y	26.3.96	12 Jul		13.39	1.2	Jhanelle	McLeod	JAM	21.1.91	6 Apr
13.60	-0.5		Tang Pingping	CHN	16.2.89	24 Jul		13.38i		Angelica	Ström	SWE	15.9.81	16 Feb
13.60	-0.6	Suslaidy	Girat	CUB	19.8.87	2 Aug		13.38	0.5	Cecilia	Pacchetti	ITA	18.5.89	15 Jun
13.60	-0.7		Vu Thi Mon	VIE	10.7.90	17 Dec		13.38	1.4	Silvia	Cucchi	ITA	1.10.78	15 Jun
13.59i			Xu Tingting	CHN	12.7.89	30 Mar		13.38	2.0	Alitta	Boyd	USA	7.12.91	20 Jun
13.59		Jihad	Bakhchi	MAR	22.8.91	5 May		13.38	-0.1		Dai Liting	CHN	26.4.93	24 Jul
13.58	1.8	Mayookha	Johny	IND	4.9..88	6 Jun		13.38	1.7	Sinead	Gutzmore	GBR	9.10.86	18 Aug
13.58	-0.6	Anastasiya	Sayenko	RUS	11.11.92	26 Jun		13.38		Nellickal V.	Sheena	IND	22.11.92	28 Dec
13.57A	0.0	Paula	Álvarez	CUB-J	11.9.95	24 Aug		13.37i		Tatyana Akmukhamedova	RUS	14.7.93	24 Feb
13.56	2.0	Kateryna	Kravchenko	UKR	29.1.92	14 Jun		13.37	0.3	Darya	Shushenkova	KAZ	4.9.90	16 Jun
13.56	1.4	Nelli	Stekolnikova	RUS	23.11.93	26 Jun		13.37	0.4	Amy	Zongo-Filet	FRA	4.10.80	12 Jul
13.56	1.0	Gabriela	dos Santos	BRA-J	23.2.95	22 Sep		13.37	1.7	Essi	Lindgren	FIN	10.4.90	7 Sep
13.55	-0.2		Lin Yan	CHN	26.1.93	11 Sep		13.37	0.4		Wei Mingchen	CHN	4.1.91	10 Sep
13.54	1.2	Liadagmis	Povea	CUB-J	6.2.96	20 Jul		13.36i		Tamara	Myers	BAH	27.7.93	9 Mar
13.53i		Ruth	Ndoumbe	ESP	1.1.87	3 Feb		13.36	-0.4	Tori	Franklin	USA	7.10.92	25 May
13.53i			Chen Mudan	CHN	4.10.93	30 Mar		13.36	-0.6	Elena Andreea	Panturoiu	ROU-J	24.2.95	19 Jul
13.51	0.1	Claudine	de Jesus	BRA-J	9.9.94	22 Sep		13.35	1.8	Lucie	Májková	CZE	9.7.88	18 May
13.50	1.7	Mara	Griva	LAT	4.8.89	27 Apr		13.35		Darya	Nidbaykina	RUS-J	26.12.94	5 Jun
13.50	1.2	Yelena	Sidorkina	RUS	27.9.88	7 Jun		13.35		Yekaterina	Lutsenko	RUS	9.1.89	14 Jun
13.50	0.0	Chioma	Matthews	GBR	12.3.81	30 Jun		13.35	1.8	Eleftheria	Christofi	CYP	29.10.86	12 Jun
13.47	-0.4	Anastasiya	Baykova	UZB	26.9.93	16 Jun		13.35	1.4	Celia-Christelle M'Boua	FRA	17.4.86	12 Jul
13.47	1.4	Anna	Krasutska	UKR-J	20.7.95	18 Jun		13.34i		Francesca	Lanciano	ITA-J	3.4.94	24 Feb
13.46i		Keri	Emanuel	USA	30.6.92	24 Feb		13.34	2.0	Jeanine	Assani Issouf	FRA	17.8.92	9 Jun
13.46	1.3	Sonia	Krnjeta	CRO	4.10.85	22 Jun		13.34	1.1	Maike	Nieklauson	GER	13.11.89	22 Jun
13.45	-0.2		Liu Jiaqi	CHN	3.8.87	31 May		13.33i		Lynnika	Pitts	USA	19.5.92	24 Feb
13.44Ai		Blessing	Ufodiama	USA	28.11.81	3 Mar		13.33i		Santa	Matule	LAT	13.12.92	1 Mar

Mark	Wind	Name	Nat	Born	Pos	Meet	Venue	Date
13.33	-1.7	Dilyara Abuova	KAZ-J	6.1.94				1 Jun
13.32A	1.8	Paola Sinisterra	COL	3.8.91				25 May
13.32		Yekaterina Sariyeva	AZE	18.12.95				28 May
13.32	1.0	Kristina Poletayeva	RUS	24.2.91				26 Jun
13.31i		Dior Delophont	FRA-J	19.10.94				9 Mar
13.31	1.0	Marie-José Ebwea	FRA-Y	7.2.97				12 Jul

(184)

Wind assisted

Mark	Wind	Name	Nat	Born	Pos	Meet	Venue	Date
14.93	2.1	Caterine Ibargüen	COL	12.2.84	1	Pre	Eugene	1 Jun
14.78	2.7	Kimberly Williams	JAM	3.11.88	3	Pre	Eugene	1 Jun

x   x   14.17   x   14.25   14.78w

Mark	Wind	Name	Nat	Born	Pos	Meet	Venue	Date
14.56	2.5	Carmen Toma	ROU	28.3.89	1	BalkC	Stara Zagora	27 Jul

14.09   x   x   14.56w p   x

Mark	Wind	Name	Nat	Born	Pos	Meet	Venue	Date
14.15	3.6	Nataliya Yastrebova	UKR	12.10.84	1	NC	Donetsk	27 Jul
14.12	2.1	Valeriya Zavyalova	RUS	16.1.88	5	NCp	Yerino	16 Jun
14.07	2.3	Linda Leverton	AUS	22.3.87	1		Hobart	23 Feb
14.07	2.6	Nathalie Marie-Nély	FRA	14.11.86	1		Alger	18 Jun
14.07	2.7	Patrícia Mamona	POR	21.11.88	3		Madrid	13 Jul
14.06	3.7	Amanda Smock	USA	27.7.82	1	Drake	Des Moines	27 Apr
13.95	2.7	Theresa N'Zola-Meso	FRA	30.11.83	1	NC	Paris (C)	12 Jul
13.78	2.7	Gisele de Oliveira	BRA	1.8.80	1		São Paulo	23 Feb
13.75	2.1	Laura Samuel	GBR	19.2.91	1	NC	Birmingham	13 Jul
13.65	2.4	LaQue Moen-Davis	USA	14.8.93				12 May
13.60	4.3	Blessing Ufodiama	USA	28.11.81				20 Jun
13.58	2.9	Darya Nidbaykina	RUS-J	26.12.94				16 Jun
13.57	2.6	Blessing Ibrahim	NGR	4.4.90				19 Jun
13.56	2.2	Tori Franklin	USA	7.10.92				7 Jun
13.48	2.8	Anna Krasutska	UKR-J	20.7.95				18 Jun
13.47A	?	Ivonne Rangel	MEX	24.8.93				10 Mar
13.46	2.7	Silvana Segura	PER	6.11.90				27 Nov
13.43A	3.6	Amanda Ouédraogo	FRA	24.4.85				24 May
13.40A	2.8	Kearah Danville	JAM					24 May
13.40	4.7	Paula Álvarez	CUB-J	11.9.95				20 Jul
13.37	3.1	Aliyah Johnson	AUS-Y	16.12.96				27 Oct
13.33	2.7	Andreea Simona Lefcenco	ROU-J	10.5.95				7 Jun
13.32	2.8	Zhao Jing	CHN-Y	2.6.96				13 Apr
13.31	2.5	Natalya Yevdokimova	RUS	7.9.93				26 Jun
13.30	3.2	Amanda Alvarez	USA					25 May
13.30	2.3	Liane Pintsaar	EST	17.3.90				2 Jul

Best outdoor marks

Mark	Wind	Name			Meet	Venue	Date
14.29	0.7	Kutyakova	4		NC	Moskva	25 Jul
14.20	1.0	Panétta	2		NC	Athina	21 Jul
14.23w	2.3Q				NC	Athina	21 Jul
14.18	1.5	T Smith	2		NC	Kingston	23 Jun
14.03	-0.7	Mosina	2			Athina	28 May
13.99	0.6	Zavyalova	2			Rabat	9 Jun
13.97	1.2	La Mantia	4		MedG	Mersin	28 Jun
13.99w	2.5		3		ET	Gateshead	22 Jun
13.68	-0.3	Sun Yan					10 Sep
13.67	0.9	Gierisch					30 May
13.67	0.5	Dodova					27 Jul

Mark	Wind	Name		Date
13.63	0.2	Li Xiaohong (J)		11 Sep
13.88w	2.3			11 May
13.49	-0.5	Xu Tingting		11 May
13.45	0.1	Chen Mudan		11 May

Mark	Wind	Name		Meet	Venue	Date
13.92	0.3	Petrova	2	BalkC	Stara Zagora	27 Jul
13.96w	2.1		1	NC	Pravets	16 Jun
13.91	1.8	Bujin	2	Gyulai	Budapest	10 Jul
13.88	0.8	Sarrapio	2		Huelva	12 Jun
13.85	0.0	Geubelle	1		Atlanta	11 May
14.03w	3.4		1	NC	Des Moines	20 Jun
13.69	0.5	Wang Rong (Y)	2	WY	Donetsk	12 Jul
13.38	1.5	Ndoumbe				27 Jul
13.35	0.9	Ufodiama				1 Jun
13.32	0.3	Hu Qian				31 May
13.30w	4.0	Peleteiro				6 Jul

Best at low altitude

Mark	Wind	Name		Meet	Venue	Date
13.81	1.5	Landázuri	1	NC	Cartagena	16 Jun
13.52	?	Y González				5 Apr
13.40w	4.7	Álvarez				20 Jul

Drugs disqualification

Mark	Wind	Name		Nat	Born	Pos	Meet	Venue	Date
14.33	0.0	Viktoriya Dolgacheva ¶		RUS	17.4.91	(1)	(best out)	Cheboksary	26 Jun
13.32	-0.6	Çagdas Arslan ¶		TUR	10.3.86				1 Jun
13.39w	3.3								12 Jun

JUNIORS

See main list for top 6 juniors. 12 performances (4 Indoors) +1w by 6 women to 13.63. Additional marks:

Mark	Wind	Name	Nat	Born	Pos	Meet	Venue	Date
Wang Rong 2+	13.74	1 Beijing 30 Mar						
	13.65	0.3 1 Sydney 19 Jan						
Marincu	13.75	0.8 1 WY Donetsk 12 Jul						
	13.69	1.0 Q WY Donetsk 10 Jul						
13.61	1.9	Vasylyna Bovanko	UKR	11.12.94	1		Kharkiv	18 Jun
13.60	0.8	Nubia Soares	BRA-Y	26.3.96	4	WY	Donetsk	12 Jul
13.57A	0.0	Paula Álvarez	CUB	11.9.95	1	PAm-J	Medellín	24 Aug
13.56	1.0	Gabriela dos Santos (10)	BRA	23.2.95	1	NC-j	São Paulo	22 Sep
13.54	1.2	Liadagmis Povea	CUB-Y	6.2.96	1	NC-j	Las Tunas	20 Jul
13.51	0.1	Claudine de Jesus	BRA	9.9.94	2	NC-j	São Paulo	22 Sep
13.47	1.4	Anna Krasutska	UKR	20.7.95	*		Kharkiv	18 Jun
13.44	0.8	Ariana Gutiérrez	VEN	14.8.95	1		Barquisimeto	2 Jun
13.36	-0.6	Elena Andreea Panturoiu	ROU	24.2.95	2	EJ	Rieti	19 Jul
13.35		Darya Nidbaykina	RUS	26.12.94	1		Moskva	5 Jun
13.34i		Francesca Lanciano	ITA	3.4.94	1	NC-j	Ancona	24 Feb
13.33	-1.7	Dilyara Abuova	KAZ	6.1.94	3		Tashkent	1 Jun
13.31i		Dior Delophont (20)	FRA	19.10.94	5	NCAA	Fayetteville	9 Mar
13.31	1.0	Marie-José Ebwea	FRA-Y	7.2.97	5	WY	Donetsk	12 Jul

Best out: Li Xiaohong 13.63 0.2 8 NG Shenyang 11 Sep, 13.88w 2.3 1 Jinan 11 May

Wind assisted

Mark	Wind	Name	Nat	Born	Pos	Meet	Venue	Date
13.58	2.9	Darya Nidbaykina	RUS	26.12.94	1		Kazan	16 Jun
13.48	2.8	Anna Krasutska	UKR	20.7.95	2		Kharkiv	18 Jun
13.40	4.7	Paula Álvarez	CUB	11.9.95	2	NC-j	Las Tunas	20 Jul
13.37	3.1	Aliyah Johnson	AUS-Y	16.12.96	1		Brisbane	27 Oct
13.33	2.7	Andreea Simona Lefcenco	ROU	10.5.95	4	IntC	Bucuresti	7 Jun
13.32	2.8	Zhao Jing	CHN-Y	2.6.96	2	NCy	Weifang	13 Apr

Mark	Name	Nat	Born	Pos	Meet	Venue	Date	Series
20.98i	Valerie Adams	NZL	6.10.84	1	WK	Zürich	28 Aug	20.97 20.98 x 20.66 20.76 20.42
20.90				1	DL	London (OS)	27 Jul	20.71 20.79 20.82 20.31 20.90 20.40
20.88				1	GS	Ostrava	27 Jun	20.15 20.55 20.30 20.64 x 20.88
20.88				1	WCh	Moskva	12 Aug	20.41 20.46 20.88 x 20.76 20.32
20.76				1	Spitz	Luzern	17 Jul	19.71 19.70 20.64 20.36 x 20.76
20.75i				1		Auckland	2 Mar	19.93 x 19.94 19.58 20.07 20.75
20.62				1	DL	Saint-Denis	6 Jul	20.12 20.60 x 20.62 x x
20.58				1	ISTAF	Berlin	1 Sep	20.28 20.34 20.29 20.54 20.16 20.58
20.37				1		Auckland	23 Mar	20.18 20.37 20.20 20.25 20.29 20.20
20.30				1	DNG	Stockholm	22 Aug	20.12 20.30 20.17 x x x
20.15				1	Pre	Eugene	31 May	19.90 19.96 x 19.82 20.15 19.88
20.02				1		Sydney	9 Mar	19.45 19.97 19.93 19.79 20.02 x
19.89				Q	WCh	Moskva	11 Aug	19.89
20.41	Christina Schwanitz	GER	24.12.85	2	WCh	Moskva	12 Aug	19.22 19.72 19.61 19.42 19.74 20.41
20.20				1	DL	Shanghai	18 May	19.76 20.12 19.69 x 20.20 x
20.18				1		Bad Köstritz	25 Aug	19.40 x 19.71 x 19.56 20.18
20.10				1	Bisl	Oslo	13 Jun	19.83 19.19 20.10 19.84 x x
20.04				1		Thum	30 Aug	x 19.09 19.63 19.50 19.05 20.04
19.94				1		Praha	10 Jun	x 19.16 19.94 19.60 19.48 x
19.90				1		Binz	8 Sep	18.73 19.22 18.11 18.79 19.03 19.90
19.84				1	Werfer	Halle	25 May	19.73 19.69 19.69 19.84 19.50 x
20.24	Michelle Carter	USA	12.10.85	1	NC	Des Moines	22 Jun	19.13 19.31 18.88 18.73 20.24 x
19.94				4	WCh	Moskva	12 Aug	19.92 19.94 19.35 x 19.67 19.57
19.88i				3	WK	Zürich	28 Aug	19.34 19.86 19.11 19.85 19.80 19.88
20.12	Gong Lijiao	CHN	24.1.89	2	Pre	Eugene	31 May	19.31 19.62 20.12 20.05 19.86 19.60
19.97				1		Zhaoqing	27 Apr	
19.95				3	WCh	Moskva	12 Aug	19.16 19.95 19.74 x 19.37 19.77
19.88i				1		Beijing	29 Mar	
19.97i	Yevgeniya Kolodko	RUS	2.7.90	2	WK	Zürich	28 Aug	18.74 18.81 x 19.18 19.97 x
19.86				1	NC	Moskva	25 Jul	19.49 19.27 19.54 19.75 19.86 x
19.81				5	WCh	Moskva	12 Aug	18.97 19.49 19.40 19.81 x x
								(30/5)
19.24	Alena Kopets	BLR	14.2.88	1		Minsk	7 Jun	
19.22i	Tia Brooks	USA	2.8.90	1	NCAA	Fayetteville	9 Mar	
19.20	Irina Tarasova	RUS	15.4.87	1		Sochi	26 May	
19.15	Li Ling	CHN	7.2.85	1		Fränkisch-Crumbach	2 Aug	
18.81i	Liu Xiangrong	CHN	6.6.88	1		Nanjing	6 Mar	
								(10)
18.77	Halyna Obleshchuk	UKR	23.2.89	1		Kyiv (Koncha-Zaspa)	21 May	
18.76	Nadine Kleinert	GER	20.10.75	2	Werfer	Halle	25 May	
18.74	Anca Heltne	ROU	1.1.78	1		Bucuresti	25 May	
18.72	Olha Holodna	UKR	14.11.91	1		Kyiv	14 Jun	
18.67	Radoslava Mavrodieva	BUL	13.3.87	1		Burgas	19 May	
18.66	Anna Omarova	RUS	3.10.81	2		Sochi	26 May	
18.47	Yuliya Leontyuk	BLR	21.1.84	1		Brest	27 Apr	
18.47	Jeneva McCall	USA	28.10.89	1		Lisle	8 Jun	
18.37i	Chiara Rosa	ITA	28.1.83	4	EI	Göteborg	3 Mar	
18.36	Josephine Terlecki	GER	17.2.86	1		Rodenbach	21 Jun	
								(20)
18.34	Anna Avdeyeva ¶	RUS	6.4.85	3	NC	Moskva	25 Jul	
18.28	Natalia Ducó	CHI	31.1.89	Q	WCh	Moskva	11 Aug	
18.27	Felisha Johnson	USA	24.7.89	Q	NCAA-E	Greensboro	25 May	
18.27	Geisa Arcanjo	BRA	19.9.91	1	SACh	Cartagena	6 Jul	
18.18	Anita Márton	HUN	15.1.89	1		Drazevina	28 Apr	
18.18	Leyla Rajabi	IRI	18.4.83	2	AsiC	Pune	6 Jul	
18.15	Yaniuvis López	CUB	1.2.86	1		La Habana	20 Jul	
18.15	Ahymara Espinoza	VEN	28.5.85	1	Bol G	Trujillo	26 Nov	
18.10i	Vera Yepimashko	BLR	10.7.76	2		Mogilyov	19 Jan	
18.10	Alyssa Hasslen	USA	13.5.91	3	NC	Des Moines	22 Jun	
								(30)
18.04	Emel Dereli	TUR-Y	25.2.96	1	EJ	Rieti	20 Jul	
18.03	Sandra Lemus	COL	1.1.89	2		Uberlândia	16 May	
17.91	Yanina Provalinskaya	BLR	26.12.76	1		Minsk	14 Jun	
17.88	Alyona Dubitskaya	BLR	25.1.90	5	WUG	Kazan	11 Jul	

Mark	Name		Nat	Born	Pos	Meet	Venue	Date
18.77	Halyna	Obleshchuk	UKR	23.2.89	1		Kyiv (Koncha-Zaspa)	21 May
18.76	Nadine	Kleinert	GER	20.10.75	2	Werfer	Halle	25 May
18.74	Anca	Heltne	ROU	1.1.78	1		Bucuresti	25 May
18.72	Olha	Holodna	UKR	14.11.91	1		Kyiv	14 Jun
18.67	Radoslava	Mavrodieva	BUL	13.3.87	1		Burgas	19 May
18.66	Anna	Omarova	RUS	3.10.81	2		Sochi	26 May
18.47	Yuliya	Leontyuk	BLR	21.1.84	1		Brest	27 Apr
18.47	Jeneva	McCall	USA	28.10.89	1		Lisle	8 Jun
18.37i	Chiara	Rosa	ITA	28.1.83	4	EI	Göteborg	3 Mar
18.36	Josephine (20)	Terlecki	GER	17.2.86	1		Rodenbach	21 Jun
18.34	Anna	Avdeyeva ¶	RUS	6.4.85	3	NC	Moskva	25 Jul
18.28	Natalia	Ducó	CHI	31.1.89	Q	WCh	Moskva	11 Aug
18.27	Felisha	Johnson	USA	24.7.89	Q	NCAA-E	Greensboro	25 May
18.27	Geisa	Arcanjo	BRA	19.9.91	1	SACh	Cartagena	6 Jul
18.18	Anita	Márton	HUN	15.1.89	1		Drazevina	28 Apr
18.18	Leyla	Rajabi	IRI	18.4.83	2	AsiC	Pune	6 Jul
18.15	Yaniuvis	López	CUB	1.2.86	1		La Habana	20 Jul
18.15	Ahymara	Espinoza	VEN	28.5.85	1	Bol G	Trujillo	26 Nov
18.10i	Vera	Yepimashko	BLR	10.7.76	2		Mogilyov	19 Jan
18.10	Alyssa (30)	Hasslen	USA	13.5.91	3	NC	Des Moines	22 Jun
18.04	Emel	Dereli	TUR-Y	25.2.96	1	EJ	Rieti	20 Jul
18.03	Sandra	Lemus	COL	1.1.89	2		Uberlândia	16 May
17.91	Yanina	Provalinskaya	BLR	26.12.76	1		Minsk	14 Jun
17.88	Alyona	Dubitskaya	BLR	25.1.90	5	WUG	Kazan	11 Jul
17.87i	Yevgeniya	Solovyova ¶	RUS	28.6.86	2		Volgograd	26 Jan
17.86		Meng Qianqian	CHN	6.1.91	4	NG	Shenyang	8 Sep
17.85	Brittany	Smith	USA	25.3.91	2	NCAA	Eugene	8 Jun
17.84	Cleopatra	Borel	TTO	3.10.79	14q	WCh	Moskva	11 Aug
17.83	Úrsula	Ruíz	ESP	11.8.83	1		Leon	29 Jun
17.80	Kearsten (40)	Peoples	USA	20.12.91	1	SEC	Columbia, MO	12 May
17.79	Melissa	Boekelman	NED	11.5.89	1		Hilversum	7 Jul
17.78	Rebecca	O'Brien	USA	30.4.90	1		Providence	28 Apr
17.76		Gao Yang	CHN	1.3.93	3	AsiC	Pune	6 Jul
17.69i	Christina	Hillman	USA	6.10.93	2	NCAA	Fayetteville	9 Mar
17.66i	Shanice	Craft	GER	15.5.93	3	NC	Dortmund	23 Feb
17.63	Julie	Labonté	CAN	12.1.90	1	NC	Moncton	21 Jun
17.59		Ma Qiao	CHN	28.9.89	1		Lanzhou	25 Jul
17.58	Lena	Urbaniak	GER	31.10.92	3	NC	Ulm	6 Jul
17.57		Guo Tianqian	CHN-J	1.6.95	2		Lanzhou	25 Jul
17.52	Valentina (50)	Muzaric	CRO	23.7.92	Q	NCAA-E	Greensboro	25 May
17.50		Bian Ka	CHN	5.1.93	4		Jinan	12 May
17.48		Li Meiju	CHN	3.10.81	5	NG	Shenyang	8 Sep
17.38	Nia	Henderson	USA	21.10.86	1		Toledo	2 May
17.38	Sophie	Kleeberg	GER	30.5.90	4	Werfer	Halle	25 May
17.38		Lee Mi-young	KOR	19.8.79	1		Incheon	20 Oct
17.36	Taylor	Smith	USA	20.7.91	1		La Jolla	27 Apr
17.36	Agnieszka	Dudzinska	POL	16.3.88	1		Kalamata	1 Jun
17.35i	Anna	Jelmini	USA	15.7.90	1		Flagstaff	14 Feb
17.34i	Helena	Engman	SWE	16.6.76	9q	EI	Göteborg	2 Mar
17.31i	Annie (60)	Alexander	TTO	28.8.87	1		New York (Riverdale)	6 Dec
17.28	Kyla	Buckley	USA	22.3.91	1	TexR	Austin	29 Mar
17.25	Natalya	Troneva	RUS	24.2.93	1-23		Adler	24 Apr
17.17i	Julaika	Nicoletti	ITA	20.3.88	1		Ancona	2 Feb
17.17	Keely	Medeiros	BRA	30.4.87	3		São Paulo	19 May
17.17	Paulina	Guba	POL	14.5.91	1		Bydgoszcz	29 Jun
17.13	Dani	Bunch	USA	16.5.91	1		Columbus	11 May
17.12	Sophie	McKinna	GBR-J	31.8.94	1J	Werfer	Halle	25 May
17.07i	Skylar	White	USA	15.9.91	3	Big 12	Ames	24 Feb
17.07	Sofiya	Burkhanova	UZB	1.12.89	1		Tashkent	31 May
17.06i	Khadija (70)	Abdullah	USA	24.7.90	1		Geneva, OH	17 Feb
17.04	Cecilia	Dzul ¶	MEX	20.4.92	1		Mérida	24 Feb
17.04	Tori	Bliss	USA	1.12.92	1		Baton Rouge	13 Apr
17.04	Jessica	Cérival	FRA	20.1.82	7	DL	Saint-Denis	6 Jul
17.03i	Hilenn	James	TTO	16.3.90	7	NCAA	Fayetteville	9 Mar
16.97i	Alyssa	Wisdom	USA	.91	4		Seattle	23 Feb

Mark	Name		Nat	Born	Pos	Meet	Venue	Date
16.95i	Yekaterina	Zyuganova	RUS	18.1.91	1		Moskva	25 Jan
16.95		Lin Chia-Ying	TPE	5.11.82	2		Tianjin	7 Oct
16.89	Ányela	Rivas	COL	13.8.89	4	SACh	Cartagena	6 Jul
16.88i	Danielle	Frere	USA	27.4.90	1		Ames	9 Feb
16.87	Baillie	Gibson	USA	18.11.91	5	MSR	Walnut	20 Apr
	(80)							
16.86i	Sam	Lockhart	USA	25.8.91	1	NCAA II	Birmingham, AL	8 Mar
16.85i	Kelsey	Card	USA	20.8.92	1		Madison	1 Mar
16.84	Nieves	Berroa	CUB	16.3.90	1		La Habana	8 Feb
16.83	Anna	Wloka	POL	14.3.93	2		Bydgoszcz	29 Jun
16.82	Dani	Samuels	AUS	26.5.88	1		Sydney	3 Mar
16.80i	Ashley	Duncan	USA	16.9.86	2		West Lafayette	16 Feb
16.80	Kim	Fortney	USA	15.8.91	Q	NCAA-W	Austin	25 May
16.80	Kätlin	Piirimäe	EST-J	8.11.95	3	EJ	Rieti	20 Jul
16.78i	Anastasia	Muchkaev	ISR	18.7.91	2		Lawrence	25 Jan
16.76i		Cai Yilin	CHN	27.11.90	5		Nanjing	6 Mar
	(90)							
16.76	Annie	Jackson	USA	11.3.90	3		Columbus	11 May
16.75	Michelle	Anumba	USA	18.9.91	1		Durham	6 Apr
16.72	Nadia	Alexander	JAM	27.12.85	1		Fairfax	13 Apr
16.71	Mariam	Kevkhishvili	GEO	17.9.85	3	FlaR	Gainesville	6 Apr
16.68i	Breanna	Radford	USA	31.8.90	2		Baton Rouge	1 Mar
16.67i	Jill	Rushin	USA	18.7.91	2	SEC	Fayetteville	23 Feb
16.67	Jana	Kárníková	CZE	14.2.81	1		Olomouc	8 May
16.67	Magdalyn	Ewen	USA-J	23.9.94	1		St.Paul	8 Jun
16.67		Geng Shuang	CHN	9.7.93	7		Shenyang	15 Jun
16.65i		Dong Yangzi	CHN	22.10.92	6		Nanjing	6 Mar
	(100)							

Mark	Name		Nat	Born	Date		Mark	Name		Nat	Born	Date
16.60	Héléna	Perez	FRA	13.9.91	12 May		16.12	Carlie	Pinkelman	USA	21.11.91	11 May
16.60	Kelsey	Titzman	USA	27.10.90	8 Jun		16.11i	Torie	Owers	USA-J	6.3.94	8 Feb
16.59	Victoria	Flowers	USA	17.1.90	12 May		16.11	Te Rina	Keenan	NZL	29.9.90	11 Jul
16.59	Amashi-Ali	Kendall	USA	11.3.91	25 May		16.10	Danniel	Thomas	JAM	11.11.92	25 May
16.57	Fabienne	Digard	FRA	2.2.91	12 Jul		16.07		Rong Jun	CHN	7.4.89	12 May
16.54i	Catarina	Andersson	SWE	17.11.77	9 Feb		16.02		Wang Xiaoyun	CHN	7.12.93	7 Sep
16.52	Austra	Skujyte	LTU	12.8.79	23 Jun		16.01i	Chioma	Amaechi	USA	2.3.92	26 Jan
16.52i	Olga	Sidorina	RUS	23.8.92	22 Dec		16.01i	Hayli	Bozarth	USA	10.6.91	9 Feb
16.51i	Claire	Uke	USA	31.12.92	24 Feb		16.01	Chase	Ealey	USA-J	20.7.94	4 May
16.47	Megan	Smith	USA	31.3.93	13 Apr		16.01	Yekaterina	Burmistrova	RUS	18.8.90	26 May
16.46	Lyudmila	Morunova	RUS	27.1.85	25 Jul		16.01	Ivanna	Gallardo	CHI	20.7.93	26 Nov
16.45i		Cui Shuang	CHN	9.8.91	29 Mar		16.00i	Agnieszka	Maluskiewicz	POL	18.3.89	9 Feb
16.45	Tremanisha	Taylor	USA	10.3.92	25 Apr		16.00	Yelena	Smolyanova	UZB	16.2.86	4 May
16.45	Chelsea	Whalen	CAN	18.10.92	10 May		16.00i	Katie	Evans	USA	7.9.90	6 Dec
16.45	Trine	Mulbjerg	DEN	23.4.90	15 Jun		15.98		Sun Yuting	CHN-J	6.5.94	21 Apr
16.44	Irina	Kirichenko	RUS	18.6.87	3 Aug		15.98	Luise	Weber	GER	6.4.92	6 Jul
16.43	Assunta	Legnante	ITA	14.5.78	13 Jul		15.97i	Julia	Mächtig	GER	1.1.86	1 Mar
16.42	Yevgeniya	Smirnova	RUS	16.3.91	24 Jun		15.97	Jacquelyne	Leffler	USA	10.2.90	4 May
16.41	Rachel	Wallader	GBR	1.9.89	3 Aug		15.97	Viktoryia	Kolb	BLR	26.10.93	30 May
16.40	Renata	Severiano	BRA	2.6.90	27 Apr		15.96	Dana	LaRue	USA	30.8.90	10 May
16.39	Shaunagh	Brown	GBR	15.3.90	19 May		15.95	Wilamena	Hopkins	USA	21.10.90	25 May
16.38	Magdalena	Zebrowska	POL	11.1.91	12 Jul		15.94	Marcella	Leblanc	USA	22.6.91	11 May
16.36	Sara	Gambetta	GER	18.2.93	29 Jun		15.94	Moriah	Young	USA	25.10.91	25 May
16.34	Samira	Burkhardt	GER	9.8.90	12 Jun		15.93	Khadija	Shallow	USA	18.8.86	19 Apr
16.31i	Kayla	Kovar	USA	11.8.91	23 Feb		15.93		Qi Yueqiu	CHN-J	1.10.94	27 Apr
16.30	Olesya	Sviridova	RUS	28.10.89	1 Jun		15.93	Aaliyah	Pete	USA-J		8 Jun
16.25	Taryn	Suttie	CAN	7.12.90	30 May		15.92i	Brea	Garrett	USA	27.6.93	1 Mar
16.23i	Joh'Vonnie	Mosley	USA	8.10.92	12 Jan		15.92	Frida	Åkerström	SWE	29.11.90	29 Aug
16.23	Laura	Pulido	MEX	30.9.88	24 Apr		15.92		Xu Yang	CHN	22.4.91	7 Sep
16.22	Kerri	Simmons	USA		11 May		15.91	Andréa	Pereira Brito	BRA	8.12.73	12 May
16.21	Omotayo	Talabi	NGR	11.8.92	29 Mar		15.90	Evaggelía	Sofáni	GRE	28.1.85	1 Jun
16.21	Cassie	Wertman	USA	14.6.93	29 Mar		15.89i	Breanna	Strupp	USA	16.7.91	1 Mar
16.18	Myriam	Lixfé	FRA	29.4.89	13 Jul		15.89	Stamatia	Scarvelis	USA-J	17.8.95	20 Jun
16.18i	Jessica	Ramsey	USA	26.7.91	3 Dec		15.88	Auriole	Dongmo	CMR	3.8.88	2 Feb
16.17i	Vera	Kunova	RUS	2.4.90	25 Jan		15.87i	Kirsty	Yates	GBR	14.5.93	6 Feb
16.17	Sarah	Howard	USA	11.10.93	6 Apr		15.87	Courtney	Gapelu	USA	22.9.92	25 May
16.15	Anastasiya	Bessoltseva	RUS	18.8.90	15 Jul		15.86i	Kristin	Zaumsegel	GER	9.6.92	3 Feb
16.14i	Florentia	Kappa	CYP	29.5.88	2 Feb		15.86i	Brittany	Cox	USA	18.4.88	3 Mar
16.14	Kelsey	Samuels	USA	28.6.91	4 May			(177)				

Best outdoor marks

Mark	Name				Venue	Date		Mark	Name			Venue	Date
18.96	Brooks	Q	NCAA-W	Austin		25 May		16.80	Lockhart	1		Ashland	3 May
18.73	Liu Xiangrong	1		Beijing		21 May		16.76	Frere	7	NC	Des Moines	22 Jun
18.04	Rosa	1		Mestre		16 Jun		16.75	Nicoletti	2		Milano	28 Jul
17.66	Yepimashko	3		Brest		27 Apr		16.65	Cai Yilin	Q	NG	Shenyang	7 Sep
17.40	Hillman	2	MSR	Walnut		20 Apr		16.58	Wisdom	25 Apr		16.49	Uke	25 May
17.29	Craft	2	EU23	Tampere		12 Jul		16.56	Radford	6 Apr		16.41	Dong Yangzi	7 Sep
17.01	Jelmini	3	Pac 12	Los Angeles		11 May		16.52	Rushin	6 Apr		16.30	A Alexander	27 Apr

WOMEN 2013

Mark	Name	Nat	Born	Pos	Meet	Venue	Date

Mark	Name	Date		Mark	Name	Date		Mark	Name	Date		Mark	Name	Date
16.30	Cui Shuang	8 Sep		16.18	James	12 May		16.06	Andersson	7 Aug		15.96	Ramsey	27 Apr
16.28	Muchkaev	30 Mar		16.08	Mosley	13 Apr		16.02	Card	11 May		15.96	Maluskiewicz	13 Jul
								16.00	Sidorina	24 Jun		15.94	Amaechi	11 May

Drugs disqualification

Mark	Name		Nat	Born	Pos	Meet	Venue	Date
18.66i	Yevgeniya	Solovyova ¶	RUS	28.6.86	(2)	NC	Moskva	13 Feb
15.95	Salome	Rigishvili ¶	GEO	26.1.90	(1)	EC-3	Banská Bystrica	23 Jun

JUNIORS

See main list for top 5 juniors. 12 performances (2 indoors) by 3 women to 17.00. Additional marks and further juniors:

Name	Mark	Pos	Meet	Venue	Date		Mark	Pos	Meet	Venue	Date
Dereli	17.67	2		Burgas	19 May		17.34	2	Pavlov	Sofia	29 Jun
	17.58i	1		Istanbul	28 Dec		17.31i	1		Istanbul	21 Dec
	17.50	3	ET	Gateshead	23 Jun		17.06	1		Ankara	31 Jul
Guo Tianqian	17.30	5		Shenyang	15 Jun		17.11	3	NC	Suzhou	1 Jun
McKinna	17.09	2	EJ	Rieti	20 Jul						

Mark	Name	Nat	Born	Pos	Meet	Venue	Date
16.11i	Torie Owers	USA	6.3.94	6		Albuquerque	8 Feb
16.01	Chase Ealey	USA	20.7.94	6	Big 12	Waco	4 May
15.98	Sun Yuting	CHN	6.5.94	1	NC-j	Jiaxing	21 Apr
15.93	Qi Yueqiu	CHN	1.10.94	12	NGP	Zhaoqing	27 Apr
15.93	Aaliyah Pete (10)	USA		3		Lisle	8 Jun
15.89	Stamatia Scarvelis	USA	17.8.95	1	NC-j	Des Moines	20 Jun
15.82	Belén Toimil	ESP	5.5.94	4	EJ	Rieti	20 Jul
15.82	Fanny Roos	SWE	2.1.95	5	EJ	Rieti	20 Jul
15.78	Shelbi Vaughan	USA	24.8.94	2		Fayetteville	13 Apr
15.76i	Xu Jiaqi	CHN	3.2.95	11		Nanjing	6 Mar
15.76	Ashlie Blake	USA-Y	7.6.96	2		Greensboro	16 Jun
15.74	Saily Viart	CUB-Y	10.9.95	2		La Habana	8 Feb
15.74	Alyona Bugakova	RUS-Y	24.4.97	1		Krasnodar	15 May
15.67i	Brittany Crew	CAN	3.6.94	1		Ypsilanti	11 Jan
15.54	Itohan Aikhonbare (20)	USA	29.3.94	3	NC-j	Des Moines	20 Jun

DISCUS

Mark	Name	Nat	Born	Pos	Meet	Venue	Date	Series
68.96	Sandra Perkovic	CRO	21.6.90	1	Athl	Lausanne	4 Jul	
								x 68.96 x 66.32 67.29 65.13
68.48				1	adidas	New York	25 May	64.00 62.50 66.31 x 68.48 x
68.25				1	GGala	Roma	6 Jun	66.24 68.25 x x 65.71 67.25
68.23				1	DL	Doha	10 May	67.37 66.36 x 65.70 67.13 68.23
67.99				1	WCh	Moskva	11 Aug	67.52 67.99 x 67.80 x x
67.04				1	VD	Bruxelles	6 Sep	67.04 64.11 65.63 64.92 x 65.08
66.21				1	MedG	Mersin	29 Jun	63.78 x 62.93 66.21 65.30 x
66.12				1		Rieti	8 Sep	65.79 x x 66.12 64.89 63.90
65.77				1	ET-2	Kaunas	22 Jun	x 64.56 64.08 65.77
65.63				2	Hanz	Zagreb	3 Sep	65.63 x 62.77 x x x
65.30				1	Herc	Monaco	19 Jul	61.20 x 62.26 64.13 65.30 x
67.86	Gu Siyu	CHN	11.2.93	1		Wiesbaden	19 May	
								61.48 67.86 60.79 x x x
67.36	Yarelis Barrios	CUB	12.7.83	2	Athl	Lausanne	4 Jul	
								x 67.36 63.75 x x 63.68
65.17				2	NC	La Habana	16 Mar	65.03 65.17 63.05 x x 64.52
65.00				1		Cetniewo	29 Jun	62.02 64.46 62.95 65.00 x 64.60
64.96				3	WCh	Moskva	11 Aug	64.96 63.99 x 62.77 61.28 63.33
64.51				1		Bilbao	21 Jun	64.51 63.18 63.93 63.23 x x
66.69	Nadine Müller	GER	21.11.85	1	ECp-w	Castellón	17 Mar	
								66.69 62.39 x 61.81 64.62 63.89
66.52				1		Kienbaum	18 Feb	61.40 62.95 66.52 65.20 62.26 63.76
64.68				1		Kienbaum	31 Jul	
64.47				4	WCh	Moskva	11 Aug	64.12 64.47 x x 61.92 63.22
66.29	Gia Lewis-Smallwood	USA	1.4.79	1	Hanz	Zagreb	3 Sep	
								54.50 63.75 x 62.65 66.29 61.98
65.49				1		Tucson	18 May	63.00 62.66 65.49 58.86 63.65 65.25
65.13				1	NC	Des Moines	23 Jun	65.13 60.77 60.43 x 59.95 x
64.82				2	VD	Bruxelles	6 Sep	58.30 64.82 64.33 61.28 63.01 62.75
66.28	Melina Robert-Michon	FRA	18.7.79	2	WCh	Moskva	11 Aug	
								62.53 61.77 65.13 65.08 x 66.28
66.04	Julia Fischer	GER	1.4.90	1cA		Wiesbaden	19 May	
								64.27 x x 63.48 66.04 x
66.01	Yaimé Pérez	CUB	29.5.91	1	NC	La Habana	16 Mar	
								66.01 64.89 64.71 64.10 60.80 64.72
65.29				1		La Habana	24 May	62.38 61.86 65.29 62.17 63.60 64.06
65.97	Zinaida Sendriute (30/9)	LTU	10.6.84	1	NCp	Kaunas	12 May	
								63.85 65.97 x x 61.26 58.23
64.46	Dani Samuels (10)	AUS	26.5.88	1		Sydney	9 Mar	

Mark	Name		Nat	Born	Pos	Meet	Venue	Date	
64.40		Tan Jian	CHN	20.1.88	1		Fränkisch-Crumbach	2	Aug
64.33	Anna	Rüh	GER	17.6.93	2u23		Wiesbaden	19	May
64.30	Vera	Ganeyeva	RUS	6.11.88	1		Sochi	25	May
63.91		Li Yanfeng	CHN	15.5.79	2	NG	Shenyang	9	Sep
63.80	Yekaterina	Strokova	RUS	17.12.89	1		Moskva	4	Jul
63.47	Denia	Caballero	CUB	13.1.90	1		Leiria	4	Jul
63.32	Liz	Podominick	USA	5.12.84	1		Portland	14	Jun
63.30		Yang Yanbo	CHN	9.3.90	3	NG	Shenyang	9	Sep
63.27		Lu Xiaoxin	CHN	22.2.89	4	NG	Shenyang	9	Sep
63.04	Dragana	Tomasevic	SRB	4.6.82	1		Sremska Mitrovica	18	May
	(20)								
62.90	Zaneta	Glanc	POL	11.3.83	7	WCh	Moskva	11	Aug
62.77	Rocío	Comba	ARG	14.7.87	1		Belém	12	May
62.74	Alla	Denisenko	RUS	12.10.83	1		Brest	27	Apr
62.68	Yanisley	Collado	CUB	30.4.85	4	NC	La Habana	16	Mar
62.23	Svetlana	Serova	BLR	28.8.86	2		Brest	27	Apr
62.21	Aretha	Thurmond	USA	14.8.76	2		Tucson	16	May
62.01		Liang Yan	CHN-J	2.1.95	5	NG	Shenyang	9	Sep
61.89	Whitney	Ashley	USA	18.2.89	1		Chula Vista	17	Jul
61.67		Su Xinyue	CHN	8.11.91	1		Chonburi	8	May
61.65		Song Aimin	CHN	15.3.78	2		Zhaoqing	28	Apr
	(30)								
61.41	Nataliya	Semenova	UKR	7.7.82	5	DL	Doha	10	May
61.13	Anastasiya	Kashtonova	BLR	14.1.89	1		Brest	25	May
61.09	Svetlana	Saykina	RUS	10.7.85	1	Kuts	Moskva	15	Jul
61.04	Andressa	de Morais	BRA	21.12.90	1		Mar del Plata	22	Apr
61.02	Yelena	Panova	RUS	2.3.87	2		Sochi	25	May
60.79	Fernanda Raquel	Borges	BRA	26.7.88	1	SACh	Cartagena	5	Jul
60.77	Shanice	Craft	GER	15.5.93	3	NC	Ulm	6	Jul
60.61	Anna	Jelmini	USA	15.7.90	1		Mesa	5	Apr
60.53		Sun Taifeng	CHN	26.8.82	2		Jinan	12	May
60.53		Jiang Fengjing	CHN	28.8.87	7	NG	Shenyang	9	Sep
	(40)								
60.23	Jade	Lally	GBR	30.3.87	1	NC	Birmingham	13	Jul
59.90	Sabine	Rumpf	GER	18.3.83	1		Regensburg	30	Jun
59.76	Irina	Rodrigues	POR	5.2.91	1		Leiria	23	Feb
59.74	Kristin	Pudenz	GER	9.2.93	3u23		Wiesbaden	19	May
59.74		Yang Fei	CHN	20.7.87	8	NG	Shenyang	9	Sep
59.66	Elizabeth	Rohl	USA	7.11.90	4	NC	Des Moines	23	Jun
59.64	Joanna	Wisniewska	POL	24.5.72	4		Bilbao	21	Jun
59.60	Nicoleta	Grasu	ROU	11.9.71	1		Bucuresti	20	Jul
59.57	Karen	Gallardo	CHI	6.3.84	1		Vila Nova de Cerve	18	Jul
59.50	Yuliya	Maltseva	RUS	30.11.90	3		Moskva	4	Jul
	(50)								
59.43	Krishna	Poonia	IND	5.5.82	2		Chonburi	8	May
59.23	Heike	Koderisch	GER	27.5.85	1		Berlin	3	Feb
59.03	Suzanne	Kragbé	CIV	22.12.81	1		Blagnac	3	Jul
58.97	Allison	Randall	JAM	25.5.88	1	NC	Kingston	21	Jun
58.93	Shelbi	Vaughan	USA-J	24.8.94	1		Eugene	6	Apr
58.88	Ulrike	Giesa	GER	16.8.84	5cA		Wiesbaden	19	May
58.87	Sam	Lockhart	USA	25.8.91	1		Ashland	3	May
58.80	Vera	Cechlová	CZE	19.11.78	1		Brno	10	Jul
58.65	Sabina	Asenjo	ESP	3.8.86	1		León	1	Jun
58.40	Eliska	Stanková	CZE	11.11.84	2		Dakar	12	Jun
	(60)								
58.35	Summer	Pierson	USA	3.9.78	1c1		La Jolla	26	Apr
58.30	Jitka	Kubelová	CZE	2.10.91	7	ECp-w	Castellón	17	Mar
58.25	Te Rina	Keenan	NZL	29.9.90	1		Wanganui	22	Jan
58.18	Sofia	Larsson	SWE	22.7.88	1	vFIN	Stockholm	8	Sep
58.14		Feng Bin	CHN-J	3.4.94	10	NG	Shenyang	9	Sep
58.13A	Elizna	Naude	RSA	14.9.78	1		Pretoria	9	Feb
58.10	Rachel	Longfors	USA	6.6.83	4		Tucson	16	May
58.04	Jeré	Summers	USA	21.5.87	4		Tucson	18	May
58.01	Jessica	Maroszek	USA	26.2.92	7	NC	Des Moines	23	Jun
57.91	Siositina	Hakeai	NZL-J	1.3.94	1		Auckland (NS)	28	Sep
	(70)								
57.84	Lucie	Catouillart	FRA	21.10.91	1		Aubagne	7	Jul
57.73	Valentina	Aniballi	ITA	19.4.84	1		Tarquinia	4	Jun
57.43	Yuliya	Kurylo	UKR	3.7.91	1		Kiev (Koncha-Zaspa)	22	May
57.39	Paige	Blackburn	USA	5.3.90	1		Tallahassee	3	May
57.24	Maryke	Oberholzer	RSA	27.11.89	1		Stellenbosch	13	Apr

Mark	Name		Nat	Born	Pos	Meet	Venue	Date	
57.12	Julia	Bremser	GER	27.4.82	1		Wiesbaden	12	Jun
57.09	Becky	Famurewa	USA-J	24.2.94	1		Louisville	13	Apr
57.08	Tetyana	Yuryeva	UKR-J	21.1.95	2		Kiev (Koncha-Zaspa)	22	May
56.99	Sanna	Kämäräinen	FIN	8.2.86	1		Kokemaki	28	Jun
56.96		Lin Xiaojing	CHN	8.1.86	9		Zhaoqing	28	Apr
	(80)								
56.87	Jessica	Kolotzei	GER	6.4.85	3		Osterode	12	Jun
56.79	Julie	Labonté	CAN	12.1.90	2	Pac 12	Los Angeles	12	May
56.77	Subenrat	Insaeng	THA-J	10.2.94	1	SEAG	Nay Pyi Taw	19	Dec
56.55	Hrisoúla	Anagnostopoúlou	GRE	27.8.91	1	Veniz	Haniá	8	Jun
56.48	Laura	Bordignon	ITA	26.3.81	2		Tarquinia	4	Jun
56.43	Anita	Márton	HUN	15.1.89	2	ET-1	Dublin	22	Jun
56.37	Seema	Antil	IND	27.7.83	1		Lucknow	30	Nov
56.34		Xie Yuchen	CHN-Y	12.5.96	1	WY	Donetsk	10	Jul
56.27	Alexandra	Collatz	USA	25.5.93	1c3		La Jolla	25	Apr
56.13	Valarie	Allman	USA-J	23.2.95	1J	TexR	Austin	29	Mar
	(90)								
56.12	Viktoriya	Klochko	UKR	2.9.92	2	NC	Donetsk	24	Jul
56.09	Katerina	Klausová	CZE	28.2.89	3cB	Werfer	Halle	25	May
55.90	Emily	Pendleton	USA	16.4.89	6		Tucson	16	May
55.88	Izabela	da Silva	BRA-J	2.8.95	1	SAm-J	Resistencia	18	Oct
55.87	Johana	Martínez	COL	9.9.86	1	NC	Cartagena	15	Jun
55.83	Katri	Hirvonen	FIN	25.6.90	1		Tampere	25	Aug
55.80	Pauline	Pousse	FRA	17.9.87	1		Hérouville	13	Jun
55.76	Alix	Kennedy	AUS	22.1.92	2	NC	Sydney	14	Apr
55.75		Li Wen-Hua (Li Tsai-Yi)	TPE	3.12.89	1		Taipei	22	Oct
55.70	Salome	Rigishvili ¶	GEO	26.1.90	1		Tbilisi	9	Jun
	(100)								

55.68	Kellion	Knibb	JAM	25.12.93	11 May		54.59	Julia	Agawu	USA	20.4.91	10 May
55.66	Kirsty	Law	GBR	11.10.86	8 Sep		54.57		Li Shanshan	CHN	6.1.92	9 Sep
55.57	Anna	Salvini	ITA	9.7.78	29 Jun		54.55	Julie	Hartwig	GER-J	30.6.94	25 May
55.53	Alexis	Cooks	USA	11.9.93	23 May		54.50	Irène	Donzelot	FRA	8.12.88	25 Jun
55.42	Marike	Steinacker	GER	4.3.92	19 May		54.44	Yekaterina	Burmistrova	RUS	18.8.90	25 May
55.42	Natalya	Shirobokova	RUS-J	18.1.94	25 May		54.43	Kelsey	Card	USA	20.8.92	26 Apr
55.39	Mariah	Garcia	USA	26.12.93	13 Apr		54.39A	Elizabeth	Johnson	USA	29.3.90	27 Apr
55.38	Gokce	Çelenk	TUR	22.7.88	16 Feb		54.33		Xi Shangxue	CHN	27.1.89	9 Sep
55.37		Liu Jing	CHN	1.1.91	9 Sep		54.29	Gleneve	Grange	JAM-J	6.7.95	25 Apr
55.35	Marie-Christin	Lehm	GER	19.6.83	19 May		54.25	Luz	Montaño	COL	20.12.88	15 Jun
55.31	Jasmine	Burrell	USA	27.2.92	10 May		54.22	Mélanie	Pingeon	FRA	4.11.86	25 Jun
55.20	Gabriella	Dixson	USA	24.8.81	25 May		54.17	Ayumi	Takahashi	JPN	31.8.89	3 May
55.19	Majesty	Tutson	USA	2.5.91	26 Apr		54.17	Erica	Brand	USA	1.8.92	10 May
55.18	Olga	Abramchuk	UKR	12.4.91	22 May		54.10	Androniki	Lada	CYP	19.4.91	19 Apr
55.17	Rosalia	Vázquez	CUB-J	11.10.95	8 Feb		54.08	Taylor	Smith	USA	20.7.91	30 Mar
55.17	Larissa	Richards	USA	6.8.88	13 Apr		54.08	Melissa	Boekelman	NED	11.5.89	2 Jun
55.16	Skylar	White	USA	15.9.91	13 Apr		54.07	Julia	Wiberg	SWE	8.1.92	11 May
55.13A	Kiah	Hicks	USA	21.2.93	3 May		54.05	Jeneva	McCall	USA	28.10.89	20 Apr
55.11	Stephanie	Brown Trafton	USA	1.12.79	26 Apr		54.05	Kearsten	Peoples	USA	20.12.91	11 May
55.07	Andzelika	Przybylska	POL	14.10.92	21 Jul		53.97	Devene	Brown	JAM		26 Apr
55.06		Weng Chunxia	CHN	29.8.92	28 Apr		53.95	Morgan	Wilken	USA	15.4.90	13 Apr
55.01	Baillie	Gibson	USA	18.11.91	12 May		53.89	Ilaria	Marchetti	ITA	24.6.91	2 Mar
54.95	Cecilia	Barnes	USA	24.7.80	20 Jul		53.80	Brittany	Smith	USA	25.3.91	23 Mar
54.90	Taylor	Freeman	USA	28.1.90	6 Apr		53.69	Janae	Allen	USA	28.9.90	6 Jun
54.83	Rebecca	Hammar	USA	28.1.93	20 Apr		53.68	Sharae	Robinson	USA	6.8.91	11 May
54.81	Taja	Moore	USA	16.5.92	6 Jun		53.62		Ling Shan	CHN-J	8.3.95	21 Apr
54.79	Taryn	Gollshewsky	AUS	18.5.93	9 Mar		53.59	Chinwe	Okoro	NGR	20.6.89	10 May
54.79	Karolina	Makul	POL-J	23.8.94	1 Sep		53.54A	Paulina	Flores	MEX	4.2.89	21 Mar
54.78	Danniel	Thomas	JAM	11.11.92	6 Jun		53.54	Marie-Francine	Mvoto Abeng	FRA	3.1.87	30 Jun
54.76		Kim Min	KOR	9.4.86	17 Apr			(163)				
54.71	Magdalyn	Ewen	USA-J	23.9.94	22 Jun		**Drugs disqualification**					
54.70	Kimberley	Mulhall	AUS	9.1.91	9 Mar		55.45	Dilek	Esmer ¶	TUR	15.1.88	2 Jun
54.70		Wang Bin	CHN	7.1.87	31 May		54.31	Semra	Akdogan ¶	TUR	1.1.90	12 May
54.65	Elisângela	Adriano	BRA	27.7.72	2 Mar							

JUNIORS

See main list for top 10 juniors. 12 performances by 4 women to 57.50. Additional marks and further juniors:

Liang Yan	59.12	4		Chonburi	8 May		57.67	7		Zhaoqing	28 Apr
	58.85	5		Shenyang	16 Jun		57.67	1		Colombo	12 May
Vaughan	57.69	1		San Marcos	26 Apr		57.50	1		Arlington	23 Mar
Hakeai	57.81	1	NCpj	Auckland	24 Mar		57.55	2		Hamilton	9 Feb
55.42	Natalya	Shirobokova	RUS	18.1.94	4					Sochi	25 May
55.17	Rosalia	Vázquez	CUB	11.10.95	3					La Habana	8 Feb
54.79	Karolina	Makul	POL	23.8.94	1	Sep					
54.71	Magdalyn	Ewen	USA	23.9.94	1	NC-j			Des Moines	22 Jun
54.55	Julie	Hartwig	GER	30.6.94	1-J	Werfer			Halle	25 May
54.29	Gleneve	Grange	JAM	6.7.95	1-HSPennR				Philadelphia	25 Apr

Mark	Name		Nat	Born	Pos	Meet	Venue	Date
53.62		Ling Shan	CHN	8.3.95	9	NC-j	Jiaxing	21 Apr
52.95	Nwanneka	Okwelogu	USA	5.5.95	1		Clovis	1 Jun
52.59	Claudine	Vita	GER-Y	19.9.96	2	WY	Donetsk	10 Jul
52.34	Salla	Sipponen (20)	FIN	13.3.95	1	Nord-J	Espoo	17 Aug

HAMMER

Mark	Name		Nat	Born	Pos	Meet	Venue	Date
78.80	Tatyana	Lysenko	RUS	9.10.83	1	WCh	Moskva	16 Aug
				77.58	77.33	76.34	78.80	76.90 74.49
78.15	1	NC Moskva		24 Jul	77.27	78.15	p	p p p
74.89	2	ISTAF Berlin		1 Sep	x	74.53	73.15	74.10 74.89 74.39
78.46	Anita	Wlodarczyk	POL	8.8.85	2	WCh	Moskva	16 Aug
				70.75	74.21	77.79	78.46	72.85 71.39
78.22	1	Dubnica nad Vahom		21 Aug	74.79	76.16	x	78.22
77.15	1	ISTAF Berlin		1 Sep	x	74.03	73.68	75.16 76.05 77.15
76.93	1	NC Torun		19 Jul	75.66	76.93	75.66	73.30 74.37 75.33
76.57	1	Rieti		8 Sep	73.04	75.14	75.07	76.57
76.18	Q	WCh Moskva		14 Aug	x	76.18		
76.06	2	Kuso Szczecin		15 Jun	62.47	74.28	74.50	74.80 74.91 76.06
75.78	1	Skol Warszawa		25 Aug	69.94	75.78	75.48	75.03 74.55 73.97
75.62	1	Franc Nice		13 Sep	71.25	73.24	75.62	x x x
75.28	1	Cetniewo		29 Jun	72.60	74.76	75.28	75.21 74.36 71.49
74.98	2	GS Ostrava		26 Jun	72.91	74.25	x	74.98 71.37 x
77.13	Oksana	Kondratyeva	RUS	22.11.85	1	Znam	Zhukovskiy	30 Jun
				x	77.13	63.14	74.64	
74.82	1	NCp Yerino		15 Jun	x	71.39	71.68	70.94 74.82 72.84
76.48	Betty	Heidler	GER	14.10.83	1	Kuso	Szczecin	15 Jun
				74.32	73.28	76.10	75.44	73.29 76.48
75.80	1	Mont Dore		9 Mar	73.27	73.37	74.15	75.80 x 74.91
75.24	1	GS Ostrava		26 Jun	73.32	x	71.60	x 72.84 75.24
75.21	1	Pre Eugene		31 May	71.20	74.30	74.24	73.42 75.21 69.72
74.92	1	Werfer Halle		25 May	74.92	73.09	x	73.48 71.23 x
76.17	Anna	Bulgakova	RUS	17.1.88	2	NC	Moskva	24 Jul
				x	72.31	73.67	76.17	x 73.94
74.83	Q	WCh Moskva		14 Aug	68.86	74.83		
75.73	Amanda	Bingson	USA	20.2.90	1	NC	Des Moines	22 Jun
				72.58	74.92	75.73	72.41	x x
75.58		Zhang Wenxiu	CHN	22.3.86	3	WCh	Moskva	16 Aug
				74.62	73.60	75.08	75.58	72.70 x
75.15	Q	WCh Moskva		14 Aug	71.99	75.15		
75.45	Oksana	Menkova	BLR	28.3.82	1		Brest	27 Apr
				75.45	72.86	70.42	70.11	73.07 x
75.09	Yelena	Rigert	RUS	2.12.83	1	Kuts	Moskva	15 Jul
				71.19	72.06	75.09	x	
75.02	Gulfiya	Khanafeyeva (10)	RUS	4.6.82	2	Kuts	Moskva	15 Jul
				67.40	73.98	75.02	72.82	
74.90		Wang Zheng	CHN	14.12.87	4	WCh	Moskva	16 Aug
	(30/11)			68.46	74.90	x	73.94	x 72.35
74.77	Jeneva	McCall	USA	28.10.89	2		Dubnica nad Vahom	21 Aug
74.16	Yipsi	Moreno	CUB	19.11.80	6	WCh	Moskva	16 Aug
73.81	Gwen	Berry	USA	29.6.89	1		Lisle	8 Jun
73.64	Rosa	Rodríguez	VEN	2.7.86	1		Barquisimeto	16 May
73.58	Jessica	Cosby Toruga	USA	31.5.82	1		Tucson	16 May
73.44	Éva	Orbán	HUN	29.11.84	2	Werfer	Halle	25 May
73.03	Amber	Campbell	USA	5.6.81	3	NC	Des Moines	22 Jun
72.97	Sophie	Hitchon	GBR	11.7.91	3	ET	Gateshead	23 Jun
72.64	Jennifer	Dahlgren	ARG	21.4.84	1		Mar del Plata	22 Apr
	(20)							
72.57	Kathrin	Klaas	GER	6.2.84	2		Fränkisch-Crumbach	19 May
72.41	Martina	Hrasnová	SVK	21.3.83	1		Banská Bystrica	11 May
71.70	Mariya	Bespalova	RUS	21.5.86	5	Kuts	Moskva	15 Jul
71.57	Sultana	Frizell	CAN	24.10.84	1	MSR	Walnut	20 Apr
71.57	Bianca	Perie	ROU	1.6.90	1		Bucuresti	24 Aug
71.02	Kivilcim	Salman-Kaya ¶	TUR	27.3.92	2	ECCp	Vila Real S.António	26 May
70.88	Barbara	Spiler	SLO	2.1.92	1	NC-23	Koper	29 Jun
70.82	Tracey	Andersson	SWE	5.12.84	3	ECp-w	Castellón	17 Mar
70.79	Alexandra	Tavernier	FRA	13.12.93	1		Annecy	9 Jun
70.46	Ariannis	Vichy	CUB	18.5.89	1		La Habana	1 Mar
	(30)							
70.40	Iryna	Novozhylova	UKR	7.1.86	2		Brest	27 Apr
70.21	Tereza	Kralová	CZE	22.10.89	1		Kladno	18 May

Mark	Name		Nat	Born	Pos	Meet	Venue	Date
70.07	Chelsea	Cassulo	USA	10.6.90	Q	NCAA-W	Austin	23 May
70.00	Iryna	Sekachova	UKR	21.7.76	1		Kiev (Koncha-Zaspa)	21 May
69.83		Liu Tingting	CHN	29.10.90	6	Werfer	Halle	25 May
69.78	Stéphanie	Falzon	FRA	7.1.83	1	NC	Paris (C)	14 Jul
69.75	Britney	Henry	USA	17.10.84	2	MSR	Walnut	20 Apr
69.68	Silvia	Salis	ITA	17.9.85	7	Werfer	Halle	25 May
69.59	Laura	Redondo	ESP	3.7.88	1		Barcelona	20 Jan
69.39		Wang Lu	CHN	22.12.91	1		Zhaoqing	27 Apr
	(40)							
69.38	Merja	Korpela	FIN	15.5.81	1		Vaasa	28 Jul
69.20	Tugce	Sahutoglu ¶	TUR	1.5.88	1		Mersin	17 Feb
69.05	Jessika	Guéhaseim	FRA	23.8.89	1		Eaubonne	12 Jun
68.92	Joanna	Fiodorow	POL	4.3.89	4	ECp-w	Castellón	17 Mar
68.84	Natalya	Polyakova	RUS	9.12.90	1		Orel	29 May
68.80	Julia	Ratcliffe	NZL	14.7.93	1		Princeton	19 Apr
68.64	Yurisleydi	Ford	CUB	18.8.91	1		La Habana	15 Feb
68.63	Aysegul	Alniaçik	TUR	15.4.87	1		Tokat	3 May
68.63	Carolin	Paesler	GER	16.12.90	1		Fränkisch-Crumbach	4 Aug
68.53	Ashley	Harbin	USA	15.2.86	5		Tucson	16 May
	(50)							
68.51	Brittany	Smith	USA	25.3.91	2	NCAA	Eugene	5 Jun
68.44	Hanna	Skydan	UKR	14.5.92	2		Yalta	20 Feb
68.35	Alexia	Sedykh	FRA	13.9.93	3		Reims	28 Jun
68.22	Alena	Krechyk	BLR	20.7.87	3	NCAA	Eugene	5 Jun
68.05	Ida	Storm	SWE	11.10.91	5	MSR	Walnut	20 Apr
68.00	Zlata	Tarasova	RUS	2.12.86	5		Adler	19 Feb
67.99	Johana	Moreno	COL	15.4.85	1		Bogotà	20 Jul
67.96		Hao Shuai	CHN	19.7.87	1		Suzhou	31 May
67.88	Nikola	Lomnická	SVK	16.9.88	2	NC	Trnava	29 Jun
67.73	Amy	Haapanen	USA	23.3.84	5		Tucson	18 May
	(60)							
67.70	Sarah	Holt	GBR	17.4.87	2		Stanford	28 Apr
67.59	Yelizaveta	Tsareva	RUS	15.3.93	Q	EU23	Tampere	12 Jul
67.49	Nina	Volkova	RUS	26.8.84	6	NC	Moskva	24 Jul
67.45	Alina	Kostrova	BLR	2.3.90	1		Minsk	28 Jun
67.20	Berta	Castells	ESP	24.1.84	1		Mataró	3 Jul
67.18	Josefin	Berg	SWE	27.12.85	1		Torsby	29 Mar
67.13	Eleni	Larsson	SWE	4.4.93	Q	EU23	Tampere	12 Jul
67.09		Luo Na	CHN	8.10.93	4		Chengdu	31 Mar
67.03	Natalya	Zolotuhina	UKR	4.1.85	1		Kiev (Koncha-Zaspa)	30 Jul
67.02	Fruzsina	Fertig	HUN	2.9.93	2	NC	Budapest	27 Jul
	(70)							
66.99	Brooke	Pleger	USA	21.6.92	1		Akron	5 Apr
66.96	Kristin	Smith	USA	23.12.87	8	NC	Des Moines	22 Jun
66.73	Caressa	Sims	USA	7.3.86	6		Tucson	16 May
66.64	Alena	Lysenko	RUS	3.2.88	6		Sochi	25 May
66.62	Yana	Kleshchevnikova	RUS	24.7.88	2		Yerino	2 Jun
66.60	Jenny	Ozorai	HUN	3.12.90	1		Culver City	27 Apr
66.36	Hanna	Zinchuk	BLR-J	4.2.94	1		Zhirovich	6 Jul
66.11	Malwina	Kopron	POL-J	16.11.94	7	Kuso	Szczecin	15 Jun
66.10	Alena	Novogrodskaya	BLR	11.5.93	6	EU23	Tampere	13 Jul
66.08	Brittany	Funk	USA	13.5.92	2		Akron	5 Apr
	(80)							
66.06	Shaunagh	Brown	GBR	15.3.90	2	LI	Loughborough	19 May
66.01	Alyona	Shamotina	UKR-J	27.12.95	4		Yalta	20 Feb
65.81	Johanna	Salmela	FIN	6.11.90	2		Tampere	15 Jun
65.61	Marissa	Minderler	USA	7.5.89	7		Tucson	16 May
65.58	Amy	Sène	SEN	6.4.85	23q	WCh	Moskva	14 Aug
65.48	Alexis	Thomas	USA	25.12.90	2		Columbus	20 Apr
65.43	Katerina	Safránková	CZE	8.6.89	11	ECp-w	Castellón	17 Mar
65.36	Chandra	Andrews	USA	4.9.83	1		Warrensburg	21 Apr
65.33	Laëtitia	Bambara	BUR	30.3.84	2		Chelles	15 May
65.27	Heather	Steacy	CAN	14.4.88	1		Sherwood Park	20 Jul
	(90)							
65.18	DeAnna	Price	USA	8.6.93	2		Des Moines	10 May
65.03	Masumi	Aya	JPN	1.1.80	1		Amagasaki	18 May
65.03	Emma	Johannesson	SWE	16.1.84	1		Göteborg	24 Aug
65.01	Réka	Gyurétz	HUN-Y	31.5.96	2	EJ	Rieti	20 Jul
64.97	Erin	Atkinson	USA	30.1.92	1		Austin	13 Apr
64.89	Karina	Frolova	RUS	2.3.90	10		Adler	19 Feb
64.78	Victoria	Flowers	USA	17.1.90	2		Princeton	19 Apr

Mark	Name		Nat	Born	Pos	Meet	Venue	Date
64.74	Kim	Fortney	USA	15.8.91	Q	NCAA-W	Austin	23 May
64.70	Jillian	Weir	CAN	9.2.93	4	Pac12	Los Angeles	11 May
64.65	Francesca	Massobrio	ITA	9.7.93	1		Rieti	16 Jun
(100)								

Mark	Name		Nat	Born	Date
64.49	Taylor	Bush	USA	26.11.89	16 May
64.33	Anastasiya	Shatybelko	BLR-J	20.5.94	22 Nov
64.30	Daina	Levy	JAM	27.5.93	22 Jun
64.30	Jenni	Penttilä	FIN	9.3.91	29 Jun
64.23	Zsófia	Bácskay	HUN-Y	18.3.97	10 Mar
64.22	Hassana	Divó	CUB-J	15.8.95	17 Mar
64.21	Cintia	Gergelics	HUN	16.11.91	3 Jul
64.15	Tatyana	Timofeychuk	BLR	6.3.86	27 Apr
64.11	Sara	Savatovic	SRB	5.1.93	3 May
64.09	Jessica	Rowland	USA	25.2.90	3 May
64.08	Vânia	Silva	POR	8.6.80	5 May
64.02	Micaela	Mariani	ITA	11.2.88	22 May
63.96	Karolina	Pedersen	SWE	16.4.87	24 Aug
63.95	Odette	Palma	CHI	7.8.82	6 Oct
63.89	Beatrix	Banga	HUN-J	30.10.95	20 Jul
63.88	Iliána	Korosídou	GRE-J	14.1.95	5 Jun
63.81	Carys	Parry	GBR	24.7.81	9 May
63.80	Dagmara	Stala	POL	9.12.91	12 Jul
63.79	Queen	Obisesan	NGR	15.9.82	1 Jun
63.78	Amélie	Perrin	FRA	30.3.80	10 Feb
63.77	Magdalena	Szewa	POL	20.9.90	11 May
63.68	Baillie	Gibson	USA	18.11.91	11 May
63.50	Dan Dongxue		CHN	23.3.92	31 Mar
63.46	Kristýna	Krouzková	CZE	5.3.90	18 May
63.35	Emily	Hunsucker	USA	20.4.91	23 May
63.35	Daniela	Manz	GER	19.9.86	26 May
63.33	Annabelle	Rolnin	FRA	28.12.87	26 Jun
63.31	Sarah	Bensaad	TUN	27.1.87	28 Apr
63.29	Hayli	Bozarth	USA	10.6.91	3 May
63.29	Li Juan		CHN	6.2.88	31 May
63.15	Zuleima	Mina	ECU	5.6.90	15 Jun
63.14	Irina	Sarvilova	RUS	11.11.91	25 May
63.07	Carly	Fehringer	USA	9.11.91	13 Apr
63.07	Wang Lamei		CHN	15.1.90	7 Sep
63.01	Tatyana	Kachegina	RUS	6.2.89	29 May
62.96	Elisa	Magni	ITA	22.6.91	13 Jul
62.93	Trude	Raad	NOR	27.4.90	16 Jun
62.77	Kang Na-ru		KOR	25.4.83	2 May
62.68	Bianca	Lazãr	ROU	24.2.93	28 Jun
62.65	Susan	McKelvie	GBR	15.6.85	2 Jul
62.63	Katarzyna	Furmanek	POL-Y	19.2.96	4 May
62.60	Xia Youlian		CHN	4.8.93	31 Mar
62.57	Reta	Woodard	USA	8.8.91	8 Mar
62.48	Helga	Völgyi	HUN-Y	12.2.96	3 Jul
62.42	Heavin	Warner	USA		27 Apr
62.41	Elisa	Palmieri	ITA	18.9.83	4 Jun
62.38	Hanna	Nesterenko	BLR	9.2.91	30 May
62.32	Liz	Murphy	USA	23.4.90	23 May
62.26	Meagan	McKee	USA	6.12.91	11 May
62.22	Jonna	Miettinen	FIN	7.12.90	29 Jun
62.18	Valeria	Chiliquinga	ECU	27.2.91	15 Jun
62.17	Sandra	Malinowska	POL	31.7.93	3 May
62.14	Lisa	Wilson	USA	29.3.88	4 May
62.14	Agápi	Proskinitopoúlou	GRE	3.9.93	14 Jul
62.01	Anjulie	Vester	GER	25.9.91	16 Jun
61.98	Elianne	Despaigne	CUB-Y	1.1.97	17 Mar
61.98	Elizabeth	Tepe	USA	31.10.87	10 May
61.98	Kristin	Obrochta	CAN	20.10.89	18 May
61.95	Paraskevi	Theodorou	CYP	15.3.86	25 May
61.89	Viktoriya	Sadova	RUS	18.3.93	26 Feb
61.83	Rachel	Gair	GBR	12.9.86	26 May
61.79	Charlene	Woitha	GER	21.8.93	19 May
61.70	Jessika	Byrd	USA	.93	4 May
61.70	Yan Ni		CHN	7.2.93	31 May
61.66	Katja	Vangsnes	NOR	16.11.91	25 May
61.63	Malin	Johansson	SWE	28.4.92	28 May
61.63	Aline	Salut	FRA	30.7.92	21 Jun
61.59	Carla	Michel	BRA	18.1.88	12 May
61.58	Denise	Hinton	USA	17.12.91	10 May
61.54	Aoife	Hickey	IRL	7.4.91	12 Apr
61.54	Nicole	Zihlmann	SUI	30.7.86	26 Jul
61.53	Shelby	Ashe	USA	13.3.93	20 Apr
61.48	Lauren	Stuart	CAN	16.11.91	27 Apr
61.48	Sam	Lockhart	USA	25.8.91	3 May
61.46	Daramola	Feyisayo	NGR	19.1.80	1 Jun
61.44	Petra	Jakeljic	CRO-J	2.5.95	14 Apr
61.43	Mélanie	Fromentin	FRA	10.10.81	21 Jun
61.39	Zeliha	Uzunbilek	TUR	10.6.91	18 May
61.39	Anna Paula	Pereira	BRA	7.8.86	5 Jul
61.27	Karen	Henning	USA	7.5.92	28 Mar
61.25	Lachel	Milander	USA	27.11.89	13 Apr
61.23	Megann	Rodhe	CAN	27.8.85	23 Jun
61.17	Rachel	Peña	PUR/USA		11 May
61.17	Heli	Rinnekari	FIN-J	30.9.94	11 Aug
61.16	Sarah	Lippold	GER	11.5.91	19 May
61.07	Lacey	Craker	USA		4 May
61.07	Lidiya	Provozina	UKR	13.2.86	6 Jun
61.05	Meiken	Greve	DEN	7.11.80	17 Jul
61.01	Wang Yingying		CHN	16.5.93	11 May
61.00	Iryna	Klymets	UKR-J	4.10.94	8 May
(190)					

Drugs disqualification

Mark	Name		Nat	Born	Pos	Venue	Date
74.28	Zalina	Marghieva ¶	MDA	5.2.88	(1)	Chisinau	9 Feb
72.10	Tugce	Sahutoglu ¶	TUR	1.5.88	1	Izmir	1 Jun

JUNIORS

See main list for top 4 juniors. 10 performances by 4 women to 64.50. Additional marks and further juniors:

Zinchuk 65.44 1 EJ Rieti 20 Jul — 64.83 2 Brest 24 May
65.00 1 NC-j Brest 11 Jun
Kopron 65.09 1 NC-j Kraków 4 Jul — 65.06 1 Chorzów 7 Sep
Shamotina 64.50 2 ECp-23 Castellón 17 Mar

Mark	Name		Nat	Born	Pos	Meet	Venue	Date
64.33	Anastasiya	Shatybelko	BLR-J	20.5.94	1		Novopolotsk	22 Nov
64.23	Zsófia	Bácskay	HUN-Y	18.3.97	1		Budapest	10 Mar
64.22	Hassana	Divó	CUB-J	15.8.95	4	NC	La Habana	17 Mar
63.89	Beatrix	Banga	HUN-J	30.10.95	3	EJ	Rieti	20 Jul
63.88	Iliána	Korosídou	GRE-J	14.1.95	1	NC-23	Sérres	5 Jun
62.63	Katarzyna	Furmanek (10)	POL-Y	19.2.96	2		Poznań	4 May
62.48	Helga	Völgyi	HUN-Y	12.2.96	2		Szombathely	3 Jul
61.98	Elianne	Despaigne	CUB-Y	1.1.97	1	NC	La Habana	17 Mar
61.44	Petra	Jakeljic	CRO	2.5.95	1		Split	14 Apr
61.17	Heli	Rinnekari	FIN	30.9.94	1	NC-j	Lappeenranta	11 Aug
61.00	Iryna	Klymets	UKR	4.10.94	1		Yalta	8 May
60.83	Louisa	James	GBR	5.7.94	1		Crawley	25 May
60.45	Sanni	Saarinen	FIN	29.12.94	5		Kaustinen	29 Jun
60.29	Susen	Küster	GER	27.7.94	2J	Werfer	Halle	25 May
59.71	Marinda	Petersson	SWE	3.2.95	3J	Werfer	Halle	25 May
59.69	Kimberley	Reed (20)	GBR	18.2.95	1		Birmingham	8 Sep

WOMEN 2013

Mark			Name	Nat	Born	Pos	Meet	Venue			Date

JAVELIN

Mark			Name	Nat	Born	Pos	Meet	Venue			Date
70.53			Mariya Abakumova	RUS	15.1.86	1	ISTAF	Berlin			1 Sep
						68.82	x	66.51	70.53	65.51	69.04
	69.75	1	Berlin (Elstal)	25 Aug	69.75	68.22	x	69.35	x	x	
	69.34	1	ECp-w Castellón	16 Mar	57.95	65.58	66.33	x	64.75	69.34	
	69.09	Q	WCh Moskva	16 Aug	69.09						
	68.94	1	WK Zürich	29 Aug	64.90	65.29	68.94	66.91	66.26	x	
	68.59	1	DNG Stockholm	22 Aug	62.73	68.59	65.79	63.34	66.09	65.84	
	65.99	1	NC Moskva	25 Jul	64.56	x	65.99	63.33	63.20	60.42	
	65.94	1	Chall Moskva	11 Jun	65.94	60.45	p	p	p	p	
	65.12	1	WUG Kazan	9 Jul	62.65	65.12	59.24	x	x	x	
	65.09	3	WCh Moskva	18 Aug	65.09	63.78	64.33	x	60.99	58.71	
	64.52	1	Tallinn	4 Sep	63.20	64.52	x	x	x	63.73	
	64.48	2	DL London (OS)	27 Jul	x	61.62	64.48	60.67	63.17	x	
69.05			Christina Obergföll	GER	22.8.81	1	WCh	Moskva			18 Aug
						64.63	69.05	64.02	62.93	x	x
	67.70	1	Pre Eugene	31 May	x	61.93	63.95	67.70	x	59.96	
	66.45	1	GGala Roma	6 Jun	62.43	66.45	x	x	60.81	x	
	65.82	2	Berlin (Elstal)	25 Aug	x	65.82	x	x	61.31	63.39	
	65.61	1	DL London (OS)	27 Jul	65.61	63.80	x	x	x	61.93	
	65.33	1	adidas New York	25 May	x	60.65	60.18	65.33	61.71	x	
	64.74	1	DL Saint-Denis	6 Jul	64.74	62.82	p	p	p	p	
	64.53	1	Rehlingen	20 May	x	60.14	59.18	64.53	x	x	
66.60			Kimberley Mickle	AUS	28.12.84	2	WCh	Moskva			18 Aug
						60.43	66.25	64.18	64.29	x	66.60
	65.73	Q	WCh Moskva	16 Aug	59.92	65.73					
65.76			Linda Stahl	GER	2.10.85	1	Werfer	Halle			25 May
						63.23.	62.42	61.26	62.15	61.71	65.76
	65.35	2	ISTAF Berlin	1 Sep	60.38	62.97	63.32	62.92	61.18	65.35	
	65.24	1	Spitz Luzern	17 Jul	60.64	61.81	62.44	62.79	63.46	65.24	
	64.78	4	WCh Moskva	18 Aug	64.78	62.58	x	x	x	61.81	
	64.51	Q	WCh Moskva	16 Aug	64.51						
65.62			Lu Huihui	CHN	26.6.89	1		Zhaoqing			27 Apr
	64.48	1	Chengdu	18 Mar							
64.51			Sunette Viljoen	RSA	6.1.83	Q	WCh	Moskva			16 Aug
		(30/6)				64.51					
64.51			Sinta Ozolina-Kovale	LAT	26.2.88	1		Riga			30 May
64.38			Vira Rebryk	UKR	25.2.89	1		Yalta			17 May
64.30			Kathryn Mitchell	AUS	10.7.82	5	WCh	Moskva			18 Aug
63.77			Katharina Molitor	GER	8.11.83	2	Werfer	Halle			25 May
		(10)									
63.55			Li Lingwei	CHN	26.1.89	1	NG	Shenyang			9 Sep
63.06			Yuki Ebihara	JPN	28.10.85	1	Oda	Hiroshima			29 Apr
62.83			Viktoriya Sudarushkina	RUS	2.9.90	1		Liepaja			11 May
62.77			Madara Palameika	LAT	18.6.87	1		Valmiera			19 Jul
62.72			Tatjana Jelaca	SRB	10.8.90	Q	WCh	Moskva			16 Aug
62.68			Martina Ratej	SLO	2.11.81	1	ET-2	Kaunas			22 Jun
62.60			Liina Laasma	EST	13.1.92	1		Kohila			31 Aug
62.50			Barbora Spotáková	CZE	30.6.81	1		Domazlice			13 Sep
62.33			Zhang Li	CHN	17.1.89	2	NG	Shenyang			9 Sep
62.07			Marharyta Dorozhon	UKR	4.9.87	1	NC	Donetsk			26 Jul
62.01			(20)								
61.98			Jucilene de Lima	BRA	14.9.90	1	NC	São Paulo			8 Jun
61.97			Lina Muze	LAT	4.12.92	1		Jekabpils			26 Jul
61.96			Sofi Flink	SWE-J	8.7.95	Q	WCh	Moskva			16 Aug
61.37			Yang Xinli	CHN	7.2.88	1		Jinan			11 May
61.18			Hanna Hatsko	UKR	3.10.90	2	NC	Donetsk			26 Jul
60.98			Hanna Habina	UKR	26.10.92	2		Yalta			20 Feb
60.91			Brittany Borman	USA	1.7.89	1	NC	Des Moines			20 Jun
60.90			Chang Chunfeng	CHN	4.5.88	3	NG	Shenyang			9 Sep
60.80			Eliza-Raluca Toader	ROU	12.5.90	1		Argos Orestikó			3 Jul
60.64			B.L.Nadeeka Lakmali	SRI	18.9.81	1		Colombo			17 Jul
		(30)									
60.56			Oona Sormunen	FIN	2.8.89	1		Kuortane			3 Aug
60.23			Flor Denis Ruiz	COL	29.1.91	1	SACh	Cartagena			6 Jul
60.23			Liu Shiying	CHN	24.9.93	4	NG	Shenyang			9 Sep
60.15			Krista Woodward	CAN	22.11.84	3		Tokyo			5 May
59.97			Asdis Hjalmsdóttir	ISL	28.10.85	2		Sollentuna			27 Jun
59.91			Laila Ferrer e Silva	BRA	30.7.82	2	NC	São Paulo			8 Jun
59.81			Nora Aída Bicet	ESP	29.10.77	3		Rabat			9 Jun

Mark	Name		Nat	Born	Pos	Meet	Venue	Date	
59.76	Mercedes	Chilla	ESP	19.1.80	4		Rabat	9	Jun
59.37	Tatyana	Kholodovich	BLR	21.6.91	1		Brest	27	Apr
59.35	Sanni	Utriainen	FIN	5.2.91	2		Kuortane	3	Aug
	(40)								
59.29	Lismania	Muñoz	CUB	28.2.93	1	NC	La Habana	16	Mar
59.21		Song Xiaodan	CHN	23.1.93	4		Jinan	11	May
59.03		Liu Chunhua	CHN	1.10.86	5	NG	Shenyang	9	Sep
58.98	Kihou	Kuze	JPN-J	28.3.95	2	NC	Tokyo (Chofu)	7	Jun
58.97	Vanda	Juhász	HUN	6.6.89	1	NC	Budapest	27	Jul
58.64		Liu Beibei	CHN	5.10.90	7	NG	Shenyang	9	Sep
58.59	Yekaterina	Starygina	RUS-J	26.8.95	1		Yerino	2	Jun
58.58	Kelsey-Lee	Roberts	AUS	21.9.91	2	NC	Sydney	13	Apr
58.55	Christin	Hussong	GER-J	17.4.94	5		Berlin (Elstal)	25	Aug
58.32	Risa	Miyashita	JPN	26.4.84	1		Kumatori	25	May
	(50)								
58.14	Mareike	Rittweg	GER	1.6.84	1		Sulz	8	Sep
58.08	Desiree	Schwarz	GER	24.4.92	1		Göttingen	16	Jun
58.00	Oksana	Gromova	RUS	23.9.80	2		Adler	28	Feb
57.83		Wang Ping	CHN	28.7.90	3		Suzhou	30	May
57.79	Sara	Kolak	CRO-J	22.6.95	3	EJ	Rieti	21	Jul
57.74		Song Dan	CHN	5.7.90	5		Jinan	11	May
57.69	Barbara	Madejczyk	POL	30.9.76	1	NC	Torun	20	Jul
57.48A	Coralys	Ortiz	PUR	16.4.85	1	CAC	Morelia	7	Jul
57.47	Susanne	Rosenbauer	GER	2.8.84	7	Spitz	Luzern	17	Jul
57.38	Mizuki	Murakami	JPN	3.5.91	1		Osaka	12	May
	(60)								
57.32A	Gundega	Griva	LAT	8.4.91	1		Potchefsroom	21	Apr
57.30	Tetyana	Fetiskina	UKR-J	11.9.94	2		Yalta	17	May
57.30	Marina	Maksimova	RUS	20.5.85	1		Sochi	26	May
57.12	Kara	Patterson	USA	10.4.86	1		Lisle	20	Jul
57.10	Yainelis	Riviaux	CUB	30.12.87	1		La Habana	15	Feb
56.98	Eva	Vivod	SLO-J	7.8.94	1		Nova Gorica	2	Jun
56.85	Sarah	Mayer	GER	20.5.91	1u23		Kienbaum	18	Feb
56.83		Sui Liping	CHN	1.5.91	4		Zhaoqing	27	Apr
56.76	Marina	Saito	JPN-J	15.10.95	1	NC-j	Nagoya	18	Oct
56.74	Tove Beate	Dahle	NOR	6.4.88	1		Nadderud	15	Jun
	(70)								
56.72		Suh Hae-an	KOR	1.7.85	1		Goseong	19	Jun
56.66	Ariana	Ince	USA	14.3.89	2	NC	Des Moines	20	Jun
56.55	Silvia	Cruz	POR	29.12.80	1		Leiria	27	Jun
56.31	Izzy	Jeffs	GBR	3.2.92	1	LI	Loughborough	19	May
56.20	Nikola	Ogrodníková	CZE	18.8.90	1		Prerov	1	May
56.20	Marcelina	Witek	POL-J	2.6.95	1		Kolobrzeg	20	Sep
56.17	Matilde	Andraud	FRA	28.4.89	1		St.Denis, Reunion	20	Apr
56.17		Xue Juan	CHN	10.2.86	5		Shenyang	15	Jun
56.13	Irena	Sedivá	CZE	19.1.92	1B	ECp-23	Castellón	16	Mar
56.10	Indre	Jakubaityte	LTU	24.1.76	1		Ventspils	21	Jul
	(80)								
56.04	Annu	Rani	IND	29.8.92	1		Kochi	20	Dec
56.03	Brianna	Bain	USA	23.6.93	1		Stanford	20	Apr
56.01	Minami	Kajihara	JPN-Y	24.8.96	1	NC-y	Nagoya	18	Oct
56.00A	María Lucelly	Murillo	COL	5.5.91	2		Cali	22	Jun
55.98	Sávva	Líka	GRE	27.6.70	1	NC	Athina	21	Jul
55.90	Sephora	Bissoly	FRA	6.11.81	1		Bertrix	10	Aug
55.89	Nicoleta	Anghelescu	ROU	3.1.92	2		Bucuresti	7	Jun
55.81	Anikó	Ormay	HUN	22.1.91	2	NC	Budapest	27	Jul
55.77		Wu You	CHN	18.12.92	5		Chengdu	31	Mar
55.73	Ai	Yamauchi	JPN-J	6.12.94	2	Oda	Hiroshima	29	Apr
	(90)								
55.68	Leryn	Franco	PAR	1.3.82	2		São Paulo	11	May
55.62	Jenni	Kangas	FIN	3.7.92	1		Mikkeli	27	May
55.60	Marija	Vucenovic	SRB	3.4.93	2		Sremska Mitrovica	15	Jun
55.59	Hitomi	Sukenaga	JPN	4.5.88	1		Kumatori	13	Apr
55.46	Yu	Kawanobe	JPN	22.11.91	3	Oda	Hiroshima	29	Apr
55.46	Ester	Eisenlauer	GER	29.10.77	1		Kaiserslautern	9	May
55.36		Kim Kyong-ae	KOR	5.3.88	2	NG	Incheon	21	Oct
55.35	Sara	Jemai	ITA	12.4.92	1		Rieti	14	Jun
55.15	Kim	Hamilton	USA	28.11.85	4	NC	Des Moines	20	Jun
55.10	Kateryna	Derun	UKR	24.9.93	3		Yalta	20	Feb
	(100)								

Mark	Name		Nat	Born	Pos Meet	Venue	Date
55.04	Tiffany	Matteazzi	CAN	13.9.91			11 Jun
55.02	Elisabeth	Eberl	AUT	25.3.88			9 Jul
54.99	Alexia	Kogut-Kobiak	FRA	22.1.88			19 May
54.98	Lilian	Seibert	BRA	23.7.89			4 May
54.95	Freya	Jones	GBR	13.11.93			5 Jun
54.94	Hiroko	Takigawa	JPN-J	25.7.94			4 Apr
54.92	Anita	Fitzgibbon	IRL	21.2.83			27 Jul
54.84	Leigh	Petranoff	USA	16.5.89			6 Jul
54.81A	Gezelle	Bernard	RSA	15.9.91			25 May
54.77	Kisumi	Miyamoto	JPN	4.5.91			7 Jun
54.68	Yuka	Sato	JPN	21.7.92			6 Sep
54.62	Antoinette	Nana Djimou	FRA	2.8..85			15 Jun
54.56	Heidi	Nokelainen	FIN	30.9.90			25 Aug
54.52	Lidia	Parada	ESP	11.6.93			13 Jul
54.51	Urszula	Jakimowicz	POL	11.6.88			31 Aug
54.49	Prescilla	Lecurieux	FRA	1.12.92			16 Mar
54.39	Jenna	Higgins	USA	23.2.91			26 Apr
54.37	Sofía	Ifantídou	GRE	10.1.85			29 Jun
54.31	Kateema	Riettie	JAM	12.5.73			23 Jun
54.26	Aleksandra	Spikina	RUS	16.1.89			28 Feb
54.20	Marta	Kakol	POL	25.2.92			1 Jun
54.15	Laura	Loht	USA	30.6.92			20 Jun
54.13	Liz	Gleadle	CAN	5.12.88			6 Apr
54.11	María Paz	Ríos	CHI	13.10.89			6 Apr
54.09	Magdalena	Czenska	POL	14.6.81			20 Jul
54.08	Maria Børstad	Jensen	NOR-J	12.12.94			15 Jun
54.04	Lyubov	Zhatkina	RUS	30.3.90			21 May
54.02	Lauren	Kenney	USA	7.9.92			25 May
54.02	Bárbara	López	ARG	5.4.91			8 Jun
53.99		Zhang Ying	CHN	5.1.88			18 Mar
53.93A	Megan	Glasmann	USA-J	3.1.95			25 Aug
53.92	Dilhani	Lekamge	SRI	14.1.87			15 Jun
53.89	Orie	Ushiro	JPN	24.8.90			7 Jun
53.77	Piia	Pyykkinen	FIN	2.4.91			27 Jun
53.74	Luziana	Tomé	BRA	1.9.85			19 Oct
53.72	Arantxa	Moreno	ESP-J	16.1.95			27 Jul
53.66		Chang Ya-Ching	TPE	5.9.89			20 Oct
53.60	Karolina	Bołdysz	POL	21.4.93			8 Jun
53.53		Heo Hyo-jung	KOR-J	19.12.94			7 Jun
53.52	Olga	Shestakova	RUS	4.12.93			26 Jun
53.49	Liveta	Jasiunaite	LTU-J	26.7.94			1 Jun
53.42	Elia	Pascual	ESP	4.7.89			27 Jul
53.39	Charlotte	Müller	GER	14.9.93			20 Apr
53.39	Tatyana	Korzh	BLR	17.3.93			27 Apr
53.34	Berivan	Sakır	TUR	22.9.93			26 May
53.30	Gülsüm	Özdemir	TUR	7.10.91			8 May
53.28	Petra	Andrejsková	CZE	25.6.92			16 Jun
53.26	Felicia	Moldovan	ROU	29.9.67			8 Jun
53.25	Franziska	Krebs	GER	11.10.85			16 Jun
53.21	Maria	Negoiță	ROU	6.12.86			25 Aug
53.17	Agnieszka	Lewandowska	POL	10.9.88			1 Jun
53.14	Nina	Otto	DEN	22.6.92			13 Jul
53.14	Shiori	Toma	JPN-Y	7.2.96			6 Oct
53.12	Nicole	Prenner	AUT-J	6.9.94			11 May
53.10	Anouk	Vetter	NED	4.2.93			3 May
53.07	Miho	Nakajima	JPN-J	28.7..94			18 May
53.07	Aleksandra	Mickiewicz	POL-J	24.3.95			4 Aug
53.03	Anne Maheshi	de Silva	SRI	15.11.77			15 Jun
53.03	Tetyana	Lyahovych	UKR	20.5.79			26 Jul
(159)							

Drugs disqualification

53.78	Maroya	Yakovenko ¶	RUS	6.1.82			26 May

JUNIOR

See main list for top 11 juniors. 11 performances by 4 women to 58.00. Additional marks and further juniors:

Name	Mark	Pos	Meet	Venue	Date		Mark	Pos	Meet	Venue	Date
Flink	60.96	1		Sollentuna	27 Jun		59.66	5	DNG	Stockholm	22 Aug
	60.66	1	vFIN	Stockholm	7 Sep		59.52	10	WCh	Moskva	18 Aug
	59.84	6	WK	Zürich	29 Aug		58.14	1	NC-j	Västerås	11 Aug
Hussong	58.44	1	NC-j	Rostock	27 Jul						

Mark	Name		Nat	Born	Pos Meet	Venue	Date
54.94	Hiroko	Takigawa	JPN	25.7.94	2	Osaka	4 Apr
54.08	Maria Børstad	Jensen	NOR	12.12.94	1	Nadderud	15 Jun
53.93A	Megan	Glasmann	USA	3.1.95	1 PAm-J	Medellín	25 Aug
53.72	Arantxa	Moreno	ESP	16.1.95	3 NC	Alcobendas	27 Jul
53.53		Heo Hyo-jung	KOR	19.12.94	2 NC	Yeosu	7 Jun
53.49	Liveta	Jasiunaite	LTU	26.7.94	1 NCp	Kaunas	1 Jun
53.14	Shiori	Toma	JPN-Y	7.2.96	3	Chofu	6 Oct
53.12	Nicole	Prenner	AUT	6.9.94	1	Südstadt	11 May
53.07	Miho	Nakajima (20)	JPN	28.7..94	1	Nagoya	18 May
53.07	Aleksandra	Mickiewicz	POL	24.3.95	3	Chojnice	4 Aug

HEPTATHLON

Score	Name		Nat	Born	Pos	Meet	Venue	Date
6623	Tatyana	Chernova	RUS	29.1.88	1	WUG	Kazan	11 Jul
	13.63/0.8	1.86	13.92	23.93/-0.2	6.48/0.9	47.90	2:11.58	
6586	Anna	Melnychenko	UKR	24.4.83	1	WCh	Moskva	13 Aug
	13.29/-0.6	1.86	13.85	23.87/0.0	6.49/0.2	41.87	2:09.85	
6550	Sharon	Day	USA	9.6.85	1	NC	Des Moines	21 Jun
	13.54/1.7	1.90	13.77	24.02/1.0	6.16w/2.6	47.38	2:12.12	
6530	Brianne	Theisen-Eaton	CAN	18,12.88	2	WCh	Moskva	13 Aug
	13.17/-0.6	1.83	13.07	24.18/0.0	6.37/0.5	45.64	2:09.03	
6477	Dafne	Schippers	NED	15.6.92	3	WCh	Moskva	13 Aug
	13.30/-0.6	1.77	12.91	22.84/0.0	6.35/1.3	41.47	2:08.62	
6462	Claudia	Rath	GER	25.4.86	4	WCh	Moskva	13 Aug
	13.55/-0.6	1.83	12.88	24.27/0.0	6.67/1.0	39.04	2:06.43	
6449	Katarina	Johnson-Thompson	GBR	9.1.93	5	WCh	Moskva	13 Aug
	13.49/-0.6	1.83	11.52	23.37/0.0	6.56/0.6	40.86	2:07.64	
6430	Julia	Mächtig	GER	1.6.86	1		Ratingen	16 Jun
	14.12/1.4	1.75	15.79	24.89/0.3	6.31/0.8	51.58	2:14.12	
6416		Melnychenko			1		Kladno	9 Jun
	13.26/1.1	1.80	13.71	23.85/1.0	6.46/0.7	38.63	2:12.54	
6407		Day			6		Moskva	13 Aug
	13.51/-0.2	1.83	14.35	24.28/0.0	5.79/0.9	47.17	2:08.94	
6376		Theisen-Eaton			1		Götzis	26 May
	13.19/0.6	1.84	13.00	24.17/-0.5	6.39w/2.7	42.95	2:17.02	
6360	Karolina	Tyminska	POL	4.10.84	2		Kladno	9 Jun
	13.47/1.1	1.74	14.32	23.69/1.0	6.34/0.8	39.11	2:09.62	

Mark	Name		Nat	Born	Pos	Meet	Venue	Date
6347		Tyminska			1	ECp	Tallinn	30 Jun
	13.60/0.0	1.66 14.48 23.77w/2.2			6.41w/2.6	42.40	2:08.60	
6345	Nadine	Broersen (10)	NED	29.4.90	2		Götzis	26 May
	13.53/1.1	1.84 13.70 25.22/-0.7			6.08/0.8	52.37	2:18.17	
6332	Eliska	Klucinová	CZE	14.4.88	7	WCh	Moskva	13 Aug
	13.97/-0.6	1.86 14.19 24.91/-0.2			6.12/0.6	45.76	2:12.50	
6326	Antoinette	Nana Djimou	FRA	2.8.85	8	WCh	Moskva	13 Aug
	13.36/-0.6	1.77 14.54 24.95/-0.2			5.97/0.8	52.47	2:18.44	
6321	Laura	Ikauniece	LAT	31.5.92	2	WUG	Kazan	11 Jul
	13.85/1.6	1.80 12.88 24.08/0.8			6.20/0.4	48.67	2:14.10	
6317		Rath			2		Ratingen	16 Jun
	13.46/1.4	1.75 12.97 24.26/-0.3			6.50/0.6	40.30	2:08.68	
6308		Melnychenko			1		Talence	15 Sep
	13.29/-0.1	1.80 13.08 24.22/-0.8			6.43/1.0	39.78	2:13.94	
6298	Nafissatou	Thiam	BEL-J	19.8.94	1	EJ	Rieti	19 Jul
	13.87/1.2	1.89 14.26 25.15/-0.6			6.37/0.1	46.94	2:24.89	
6288		Tyminska			2		Talence	15 Sep
	13.83/-0.1	1.74 14.13 24.31/-0.8			6.36/1.5	40.71	2:08.61	
6287		Schippers			3		Götzis	26 May
	13.51/0.6	1.75 13.71 23.08/-1.5			6.56w/2.3	37.72	2:19.90	
6284		Chernova			4		Götzis	26 May
	13.83/0.6	1.72 14.09 24.31/-1.5			6.57w/2.6	45.45	2:18.14	
6270		Tyminska			9	WCh	Moskva	13 Aug
	13.48/-0.6	1.68 13.74 24.13/0.0			6.32/0.9	40.61	2:06.64	
6269	Györgyi	Farkas-Zsivoczky	HUN	13.2.85	3	WUG	Kazan	11 Jul
	13.97/1.8	1.83 13.60 25.43/0.8			6.32/1.2	49.23	2:17.26	
6260		Melnychenko			2	ECp	Tallinn	30 Jun
	13.40/0.0	1.81 13.69 24.16w/ 2.2			6.33w/2.2	36.67	2:13.86	
6252		Theisen-Eaton			3		Talence	15 Sep
	13.26/-0.1	1.80 12.66 24.24/-0.8			6.20/2.3	42.24	2:14.30	
6238		Broersen			1	ECp-1	Nottwil	30 Jun
	13.51/0.2	1.81 14.34 25.53/-2.2			6.20/1.3	44.60	2:16.33	
6235		Rath			4		Talence	15 Sep
	13.78/-0.1	1.80 12.62 24.69/-0.8			6.50/0.9	39.62	2:10.14	
6233		Theisen-Eaton			1	NC	Moncton	22 Jun
	13.78/-2.9	1.85 12.50 24.76/-3.3			6.14w/2.9	43.85	2:11.32	
	(30/15)							
6221	Grit	Sadeiko	EST	29.7.89	3	ECp	Tallinn	30 Jun
	13.62/-0.4	1.78 12.00 24.21/1.7			6.35/1.2	46.75	2:17.58	
6214	Ida	Marcussen	NOR	1.11.87	6		Talence	15 Sep
	14.16/0.3	1.74 13.07 25.22/0.7			6.26/0.9	50.16	2:10.08	
6210	Kristina	Savitskaya	RUS	10.6.91	1	NC	Cheboksary	6 Jun
	13.82/1.8	1.75 14.02 25.15/1.0			6.40w/2.9	46.83	2:18.21	
6194	Yana	Maksimova	BLR	9.1.89	5		Götzis	26 May
	13.89/0.4	1.87 14.09 25.48/0.0			5.97w/2.1	43.46	2:13.38	
6186	Yorgelis	Rodríguez	CUB-J	25.1.95	1	NC	La Habana	17 Mar
	13.97/-1.6	1.82 13.17 24.58/0.0			6.00/1.1	48.70	2:18.05	
	(20)							
6185	Kira	Biesenbach	GER	7.10.92	3		Ratingen	16 Jun
	13.71/1.4	1.78 12.95 23.76/0.3			6.42/1.2	36.53	2:14.32	
6133	Kiani	Profit	USA	18.2.90	1		Chula Vista	28 Jul
	13.52/1.2	1.69 12.32 23.98/1.3			6.11w/2.3	42.94	2:09.37	
6086	Lindsay	Vollmer	USA	10.9.92	1	NCAA	Eugene	7 Jun
	13.58/1.0	1.75 11.97 24.27/1.3			6.16w/3.3	46.18	2:19.36	
6081	Sofia	Linde	SWE-J	12.1.95	2	EJ	Rieti	19 Jul
	13.68/1.5	1.80 14.46 25.15/-0.6			5.99/1.1	42.85	2:20.78	
6081	Ellen	Sprunger	SUI	5.8.86	13	WCh	Moskva	13 Aug
	13.68/-0.2	1.68 12.86 23.39/0.0			6.16/0.9	40.41	2:14.83	
6057	Linda	Züblin	SUI	21.3.86	17	WCh	Moskva	13 Aug
	13.51/-0.4	1.65 12.51 25.01/-0.1			6.23/0.5	49.64	2:17.50	
6050	Makeba	Alcide	LCA	24.2.90	2	NCAA	Eugene	7 Jun
	13.52/1.0	1.81 12.35 24.18w/2.3			6.05w/2.7	34.65	2:12.05	
6024	Yusleidys	Mendieta	CUB-J	17.2.94	2	NC	La Habana	17 Mar
	14.61/-1.6	1.79 13.76 24.15/0.0			5.99/1.6	48.63	2:26.31	
6018	Bettie	Wade	USA	11.9.86	2	NC	Des Moines	21 Jun
	13.75/1.7	1.81 13.49 24.95/0.1			6.06/0.9	38.54	2:17.68	
6002	Mari	Klaup	EST	27.2.90	6	ECp	Tallinn	30 Jun
	14.09/0.0	1.81 12.81 25.62w/2.2			5.83w/2.2	49.92	2:18.67	
	(30)							
5999	Chelsea	Carrier-Eades	USA	21.8.89	2	vGER	Chula Vista	28 Jul
	12.90/1.2	1.66 11.62 23.55/1.3			6.39w/2.2	32.03	2:14.01	

WOMEN 2013

514 HEPTATHLON

Mark	Name		Nat	Born	Pos	Meet	Venue	Date
5993	Aleksandra	Butvina	RUS	14.2.86	2	NC	Cheboksary	6 Jun
	14.04/1.8	1.69 14.38 25.00/1.0		6.13w/2.9	39.85		2:13.23	
5990w	Erica	Bougard	USA	26.7.93	3	NC	Des Moines	21 Jun
	13.53w/4.9	1.78 10.37 23.56/0.1		6.22w/2.6	34.60		2:12.25	
5989	Yekaterina	Netsvetayeva	BLR	26.6.89	8		Talence	15 Sep
	13.96/0.3	1.71 14.23 25.28/-0.8		5.82/0.8	43.00		2:11.13	
5984(w)	Shakeia	Pinnick	USA	23.1.91	3	NCAA	Eugene	7 Jun
	13.13/1.2	1.66 11.07 23.60w/2.3		6.07w/3.1	38.13		2:10.89 & 5981 with 6.06/1.9	
5983	Yasmina	Omrami	ALG	1.1.88	20	WCh	Moskva	13 Aug
	13.57/-0.4	1.77 13.32 24.75/-0.1		5.82/0.9	39.26		2:14.81	
5980	Lindsay	Schwartz	USA	23.4.90	3	vGER	Chula Vista	28 Jul
	13.78/1.2	1.66 11.94 24.06/1.8		6.15/1.5	42.47		2:12.85	
5972	Carolin	Schäfer	GER	5.12.91	5		Ratingen	16 Jun
	13.54/1.4	1.75 12.37 24.67/0.3		6.00/0.9	46.41		2:24.17	
5957	Ryann	Krais	USA	21.3.90	4	NC	Des Moines	21 Jun
	13.76/1.7	1.78 11.87 24.98/0.4		5.84/0.8	39.90		2:08.74	
5945(w)	Heather	Miller	USA	30.3.87	5	NC	Des Moines	21 Jun
	13.75w/4.9	1.75 11.66 24.08/0.1		6.00/0.1	38.38		2:13.30	
(40)								
5941	Anastasiya	Mokhnyuk	UKR	1.1.91	8	ECp	Tallinn	30 Jun
	13.45/1.0	1.81 12.55 25.29/1.1		6.31/1.6	34.77		2:20.22	
5916	Ulyana	Aleksandrova	RUS	1.1.91	9	ECp	Tallinn	30 Jun
	14.34/-0.4	1.84 13.18 25.98/1.7		6.33w/3.3	43.32		2:26.74	
5899(w)	Tanya	Friesen	USA	23.6.91	5	NCAA	Eugene	7 Jun
	13.83w/2.2	1.78 11.00 24.45w/2.8		6.02/1.6	41.80		2:17.89	
5899	Katerina	Cachová	CZE	26.2.90	4		Nottwil	30 Jun
	13.73/-0.1	1.78 10.88 24.93/-1.4		5.91/0.4	42.67		2:13.95	
5897	Sami	Spenner	USA	21.3.91	4	vGER	Chula Vista	28 Jul
	14.31/0.7	1.72 11.94 23.67/1.3		6.16w/3.1	36.30		2:13.18	
5896	Xénia	Krizsán	HUN	13.1.93	14		Götzis	26 May
	13.86/1.1	1.69 12.65 25.50/0.0		6.04w/2.6	47.59		2:19.05	
5894	Sofía	Ifantídou	GRE	10.1.85	23	WCh	Moskva	13 Aug
	13.93/-0.4	1.65 12.89 25.94/-0.2		5.85/1.0	53.66		2:17.74	
5888	Lisa	Linnell	SWE	30.4.91	4	EU23	Tampere	14 Jul
	13.97/0.5	1.72 12.58 24.77/0.0		6.10/-0.1	39.80		2:16.27	
5874	Ivona	Dadic	AUT	29.12.93	5	EU23	Tampere	14 Jul
	14.74/0.3	1.69 13.57 24.63/0.2		5.87/0.8	44.82		2:14.49	
5872	Anouk	Vetter	NED	4.2.93	1		Firenze	3 May
	14.12/0.0	1.75 13.86 24.95/-1.0		5.55/0.6	53.10		2:30.69	
(50)								
5865(w)	Vanessa	Jules	USA	21.3.91	6	NCAA	Eugene	7 Jun
	13.39/1.0	1.75 11.21 24.47w/2.3		6.26w/4.0	35.41		2:19.63	
5863	Anna	Maiwald	GER	21.7.90	6		Ratingen	16 Jun
	13.73/1.4	1.63 12.78 24.39/-1.4		5.72/0.6	46.05		2:16.70	
5856	Valérie	Reggel	SUI	3.1.87	1	NC	Landquart	18 Aug
	14.29/-0.5	1.69 13.42 24.53/1.6		5.90/0.8	40.57		2:14.90	
5853	Lucie	Ondraschková	CZE	12.10.89	7	NCAA	Eugene	7 Jun
	13.75w/2.2	1.72 11.82 24.81w/2.8		6.10/0.8	39.06		2:16.04	
5834	Nadja	Casadei	SWE	3.4.83	5	ECp-1	Nottwil	30 Jun
	14.15/-0.1	1.66 13.58 25.29/-1.4		6.04/0.8	39.24		2:12.44	
5831	Marjolein	Lindemans	BEL-J	17.2.94	3	EJ	Rieti	19 Jul
	13.45/1.5	1.83 10.38 24.74/-0.6		6.39/1.1	32.04		2:21.34	
5818	Wassanee	Winatho	THA	30.6.80	1	AsiC	Pune	6 Jul
	13.90/0.6	1.82 11.98 25.06/-0.6		5.98/0.6	35.45		2:17.50	
5817	Grace	Clements	GBR	2.5.84	11	ECp	Tallinn	30 Jun
	14.60/-1.8	1.69 14.12 26.03/1.3		5.93/1.4	45.07		2:15.19	
5814	Tamara	de Souza	BRA	8.9.93	1	NC	São Paulo	7 Jun
	14.03/0.4	1.79 14.14 24.63/0.6		5.78/1.1	45.57		2:38.30	
5814	Beatrice	Puiu	ROU	1.1.86	1	NC	Bucuresti	23 Jul
	13.71/-0.7	1.76 12.48 25.87		6.28/1.1	37.42		2:21.05	
(60)								
5813	Allison	Reaser	USA	9.9.92	8	NCAA	Eugene	7 Jun
	13.30/1.2	1.60 11.98 23.88w/2.3		5.79/0.6	37.81		2:12.08	
5796	Yelena	Molodchinina	RUS	16.4.91	12	ECp	Tallinn	30 Jun
	13.91/1.0	1.72 11.57 25.21/1.1		6.21/1.6	37.24		2:14.75	
5792	Alina	Fyodorova	UKR	31.7.89	1	NC	Donetsk	25 Jul
	14.54/1.6	1.81 14.44 26.13/-0.3		6.12/0.0	37.35		2:22.90	
5788	Aisha	Adams	USA	24.9.87	2		Santa Barbara	6 Apr
	13.90/-1.3	1.73 12.08 24.78/0.4		5.72/0.2	42.00		2:17.35	
5785		Wang Qingling	CHN	14.1.93	1	NG	Shenyang	8 Sep
	13.59/0.2	1.75 11.54 25.19/-0.4		6.34/0.5	34.85		2:21.24	

Mark	Name		Nat	Born	Pos	Meet	Venue	Date
5774(w)	Portia	Bing	NZL	17.4.93	1	NC	Waitakere	17 Feb
	13.87/2.0	1.76 11.59 24.19/1.5		5.92w/3.5		36.04	2:19.10	
5774w	Niki	Oudenaarden	CAN-J	14.1.94	2	MSR	Azusa	18 Apr
	14.43/1.2	1.59 13.46 24.73w/2.3		6.10w/2.1		44.63	2:19.81	
5774	Nadine	Visser	NED-J	9.2.95	4	EJ	Rieti	19 Jul
	13.21/1.5	1.77 12.58 24.53/-0.6		5.83/-0.2		33.02	2:23.36	
5772	Myrte	Goor	NED	3.4.89	6	ECp-1	Nottwil	30 Jun
	14.23/-0.1	1.72 13.11 25.06/-1.4		5.79/0.4		37.94	2:13.29	
5767	Alina	Biesenbach	GER	27.4.92	7		Ratingen	16 Jun
	14.66/1.9 (70)	1.78 13.11 26.36/-1.4		6.02/1.0		43.24	2:18.78	
5761	Breanna	Leslie	USA	11.8.91	3		Azusa	18 Apr
	13.88/1.3	1.71 11.42 24.27w/2.4		5.88/2.0		36.66	2:14.16	
5735	Laura	Arteil	FRA	9.10.93	1		Cognac	30 Jun
	14.28w/2.7	1.61 13.09 24.72/1.7		6.11/0.7		42.19	2:20.89	
5733	Ana Camila	Pirelli	PAR	10.1.89	1	Bol G	Trujillo	29 Nov
	13.96/0.3	1.67 13.36 25.11/0.9		5.48/0.0		42.72	2:15.28	
5729	Lindsay	Lettow	USA	6.6.90	11	NC	Des Moines	21 Jun
	13.92/1.7	1.72 11.95 24.70/0.1		5.74/1.7		37.75	2:15.08	
5726	Yana	Panteleyeva	RUS	16.6.88	5	NC	Cheboksary	6 Jun
	14.30/1.8	1.75 13.13 26.10/1.0		5.97/1.3		44.18	2:24.59	
5717	Marisa	De Aniceto	FRA	11.11.86	18		Götzis	26 May
	14.00/0.8	1.72 12.10 25.89/0.0		5.61/1.0		49.21	2:21.15	
5717	Michelle	Zeltner	SUI	22.12.91	2	NC	Landquart	18 Aug
	14.43/-0.5	1.78 14.19 25.37/1.6		5.75/1.3		36.39	2:20.69	
5715A	Bianca	Erwee	RSA	4.3.90	1		Germiston	23 Mar
	14.50/0.1	1.83 11.02 25.58/2.0		6.00/0.5		40.06	2:18.41	
5702	Jo	Rowland	GBR	29.12.89	1		Arona	2 Jun
	14.59/1.5	1.67 13.38 24.85/0.0		5.82/-0.4		40.53	2:17.27	
5694	Ellinore	Hallin	SWE	12.8.87	19		Götzis	26 May
	13.55/0.8 (80)	1.66 14.14 24.84/-0.7		5.46/0.7		36.27	2:17.63	
5691(w)	Tatum	Souza	USA	20.4.92	9	NCAA	Eugene	7 Jun
	13.86w/2.7	1.69 12.76 25.26w/2.8		5.74/1.2		39.30	2:17.91	
5681	Amanda	Spiljard	NED	18.9.89	8	ECp-1	Nottwil	30 Jun
	14.64/-0.2	1.69 13.29 25.85/-1.5		5.99/0.7		44.45	2:22.25	
5676(w)	Jess	Tappin	GBR	17.5.90	1		Bedford	2 Jun
	13.49w/2.6	1.68 11.39 24.57/0.5		5.77w/3.0		34.43	2:14.17	
5664	Yana	Cherepanova	RUS	1.2.81	1	NCp	Adler	9 May
	13.82/1.2	1.74 13.24 24.90/0.8		5.75/-0.1		31.98	2:19.55	
5649	Lucia	Mokrásová	SVK-J	27.3.94	5	EJ	Rieti	19 Jul
	13.96/1.5	1.68 11.79 24.36/-0.6		5.96/0.8		36.67	2:21.66	
5636	Rokhaya	Mbaye	FRA	12.3.92	9	EU23	Tampere	14 Jul
	14.05/0.7	1.72 12.92 25.36/0.0		5.66/-0.6		47.55	2:33.47	
5629(w)	Dorcas	Akinniyi	USA	23.1.90	10	NCAA	Eugene	7 Jun
	13.81w/2.7	1.75 13.13 25.48w/2.8		5.88w/2.8		36.09	2:27.58	
5601A	Rachael	McIntosh	CAN	17.1.91	1		Calgary	12 May
	14.52/-1.3	1.69 12.05 25.17/-0.4		5.90/1.3		36.28	2:14.30	
5599	Yekaterina	Voronina	UZB	16.2.92	2	AsiC	Pune	6 Jul
	16.09/-0.7	1.73 12.62 25.93/-0.5		6.02/1.0		50.63	2:23.86	
5598(w)	Chari	Hawkins	USA	21.5.91	11	NCAA	Eugene	7 Jun
	13.74w/2.7 (90)	1.75 10.30 25.05w/2.8		5.84w/3.4		41.03	2:25.70	
5586w	Agnieszka	Borowska	POL	21.10.91	1		Opole	2 Jun
	14.21w/2.4	1.81 11.25 26.81/-1.5		6.13/1.5		36.50	2:20.58	
5582	Inna	Poltavets	RUS	6.11.90	6	NC	Cheboksary	6 Jun
	14.79/0.0	1.78 11.65 26.55/1.0		5.70/1.6		47.84	2:22.17	
5580	Sun Lu		CHN	19.2.88	2	NG	Shenyang	8 Sep
	13.54/0.2	1.69 11.42 25.28/0.1		5.91/-1.1		35.64	2:21.42	
5576(w)	Madelaine	Buttinger	CAN	3.11.89	1		Charlottesville	11 May
	14.53w/2.7	1.76 12.39 25.30w/2.3		5.67w/3.1		34.92	2:16.14	
5574w	Deanna	Latham	USA	23.2.92	12	NCAA	Eugene	7 Jun
	13.37/1.2	1.54 11.43 24.31w/2.8		5.78w/2.1		39.76	2:20.32	
5572A	Kendell	Williams	USA-J	14.6.95	2	PAm-J	Medellín	25 Aug
	13.48/0/2	1.77 10.49 24.84/0.6		6.15/1.2		31.40	2:28.43	
5564	Chie	Kiriyama	JPN	2.8.91	1	NC	Nagano	2 Jun
	13.90/-1.5	1.57 11.58 24.47w/2.1		6.07/0.7		41.53	2:26.87	
5563	Joenisha	Vinson	USA	18.4.90	13	NCAA	Eugene	7 Jun
	13.76w/2.7	1.63 12.68 24.84/1.3		5.93/1.3		36.73	2:26.47	
5562	Mary	Nall	USA	22.4.92	14	NCAA	Eugene	7 Jun
	13.77w/2.2	1.63 9.90 24.90/1.3		5.77w/2.2		43.12	2:17.76	

Mark	Name		Nat	Born	Pos	Meet	Venue		Date
5560	Camille	Le Joly	FRA	1.3.92	2	NC	Paris (C)		13 Jul
	14.24/0.9	1.70 10.68 25.58/1.2		5.72/1.7	40.45		2:13.73		
	(100)								
5559	Mariya	Shumilova	RUS	10.1.90	26 May		5473	Alena	Galertová	CZE	18.8.92	26 May
5558	Merryl	Mbeng	FRA	5.11.91	13 Jul		5470(w)	Carly	Loeffel	USA	20.8.92	7 Jun
5557w	Crystal	Ruiz	MEX	1.1.88	5 Apr		5469	Élodie	Jakob	SUI	8.10.93	29 Sep
5556	Sophie	Stanwell	AUS	8.6.91	10 Feb		5467	Yilian	Durruthy	CUB	30.1.90	17 Mar
5551	Darya	Khramtsova	RUS	7.1.90	9 May		5467	Sarah	Chauchard	FRA	13.3.91	13 Jul
5551	Jesse	Labreck	USA	31.1.90	11 May		5464	Judit	Nagy	ROU	14.9.89	30 Jun
5547	Lucija	Cvitanovic	CRO	17.9.91	30 Jun		5463	Xenia	Rahn	GER	9.3.91	10 May
5547(w)	Sandra	Jacmaire	FRA	4.1.91	30 Jun		5460	Elizabeth	Kline	USA	13.6.91	4 May
5545	Jennifer	Cotten	CAN	14.10.87	27 Aug		5459	Laura	Ginés	ESP	11.6.86	11 Jul
5535	Karla	Drew	GBR	22.3.89	30 Jun		5459	Michelle	Weitzel	GER	18.6.87	25 Jul
5531w	Jena	Hemann	USA	16.10.92	28 Mar		5456	Olha	Pushkina	UKR	23.3.89	25 Jul
5528	Tine	Ejlersen	DEN	25.7.85	30 Jun		5454		Yu Xiaoxuan	CHN	30.10.91	8 Sep
5524	Miia	Kurppa	FIN	30.1.88	30 Jun		5452	Tanja	Mayer	SUI	2.7.93	14 Jul
5522w	Danessa	Lyssy	USA	10.10.90	9 May		5452(w)	Fiorella	Chiappe	ARG-Y	1.1.96	20 Oct
5514	Anaelle	Nyabeu Djapa	FRA	15.9.92	30 Jun		5442	Annie	Kunz	USA	16.2.93	28 Mar
5509		Li Weijian	CHN	19.10/93	8 Sep		5442	Kelly	Proper	IRL	1.5.88	3 May
5505		Wang Yunhan	CHN	20.2.93	12 May		5442	Elise	Malmberg	SWE-J	13.7.95	9 Jun
5500	Anna	Petrich	RUS	17.2.92	9 May		5430	Tiffeny	Parker	USA	8.6.88	10 May
5499	Guillercy	González	VEN	7.5.88	11 May		5429(w)	Yelna	Yermolina	RUS	2.2.89	26 May
5493A	Georgia	Ellenwood	CAN-J	5.8.95	25 Aug		5428	Shana	Woods	USA	7.7.88	8 Jun
5492	Ali	Worthen	USA	21.9.89	12 Apr		5426	Victoria	Joäng	SWE	17.10.89	15 Sep
5491	Rachel	Machin	CAN	14.3.92	25 Aug		5417	Fumie	Takehara	JPN	14.7.87	2 Jun
5487	Ana	Lorenzo	DOM	6.7.81	6 Apr		5414	Anne	Martin	USA	16.4.91	7 Jun
5481	Carolina	Bianchi	ITA	7.2.88	30 Jun		5409	Anouk	Forafo	FRA	23.10.85	13 Jul
5479	Sveinbjörg	Zophoníasdóttir	ISL	27.4.92	30 Jun		5408	Karolina	Kedzia	POL	8.7.90	9 Jun
5476w	Paige	Knodle	USA	15.8.93	11 May		5406	Lara	Groenewold	GER-Y	21.4.97	18 May

Best without excess wind assistance

5976	Erica	Bougard	USA	26.7.93	4	NCAA	Eugene		7 Jun
	13.37/1.2	1.75 11.07 23.84w/2.3		6.25/0.4	34.28		2:13.75		
5716	Niki	Oudenaarden	CAN-J	14.1.94	2	MSR	Azusa		18 Apr
	14.82/0.1	1.67 14.04 24.79/0/8		5.74/-0.8	45.35		2:22.63		

Best al low altitude

5481   K Williams (J) 20 Jun | 5461   Ellenwood   14 Jul | 5467A Ruiz   6 Jul | 5426A Chiappe   25 Aug

Drugs disqualification

5826	Yunna	Dmitriyeva ¶	RUS	7.7.88	(1)	NCp	Adler		9 May
	3.99/0.7	1.71 12.59 25.48/0.8		5.89/1.5	42.63		2:14.38		

JUNIORS

See main list for top 9 juniors. 11 performances by 5 women to 5830. Additional marks and further juniors:

Thiam	6070	14	WCh	Moskva	13 Aug	6021	1	Réduit	19 Apr
Rodríguez	6148	12	WCh	Moskva	13 Aug	5947	1	PAmCp Ottawa	2 Jun
Linde	5950	13	Götzis		26 May				
5493A	Georgia	Ellenwood (10)	CAN	5.8.95	3	PAm-J	Medellín		25 Aug
	14.43.0.2	1.74 10.44 24.87/0.6		5.81/0.6	35.61		2:18.80		
5452(w)	Fiorella	Chiappe	ARG-Y	1.1.96	1	SAm-J	Resistencia		20 Oct
	14.31/2.0	1.73 10.68 25.42w/2.7		5.91w/3.5	32.46		2:17.46		
5442	Elise	Malmberg	SWE	13.7.95	2	v2N	Huddinge		9 Jun
	14.22/-1.1	1.68 11.07 24.67/-2.5		6.03/-1.0	31.90		2:23.53		
5406	Lara	Groenewold	GER-Y	21.4.97	1		Kreuztal		18 May
	15.22/0.1	1.75 11.85 25.90/-0.5		6.02/0.7	40.96		2:31.20		
5383	Ana Stefania	Gudmundsdóttir	ISL	1.9.95	6	EJ	Rieti		19 Jul
	14.14/1.2	1.71 9.89 24.69/-0.8		5.36/0.7	39.01		2:20.85		
5381	Frida	Thorsås	NOR	31.1.94	1	v2N	Huddinge		9 Jun
	14.54/1.4	1.62 12.63 25.60/0.7		5.24/0.0	36.31		2:10.30		
5366	Leike	Muller	NED	3.11.94	7	EJ	Rieti		19 Jul
	14.66/1.2	1.71 13.12 25.41/0.1		5.68/0.5	37.79		2:33.58		
5362	Caroline	Klein	GER-Y	4.3.96	2		Kreutzel		18 May
	14.69/0.1	1.66 12.35 26.37/-0.5		5.63/0.0	46.85		2:30.44		
5359	Yelizaveta	Kolokolchikova	RUS-Y	7.6.96	1	NCp-j	Adler		10 May
	14.79/1.2	1.74 11.99 25.33/1.9		5.58/-0.1	34.20		2:22.46		
5323	Flavia	Nasella	ITA	18.6.94	8	EJ	Rieti		19 Jul
	14.66/-0.5	1.68 9.98 24.57/-0.6		5.56/1.5	38.13		2:21.49		
5304	Ottavia	Cestonaro (20)	ITA	12.1.95	1	NC-j	Busto Arsizio		2 Jun
	14.41/-2.4	1.72 11.14 25.09/-0.3		6.07w/2.5	25.63		2:25.07		

4 X 100 METRES RELAY

41.29	JAM	Russell, Stewart, Calvert, Fraser-Pryce		1	WCh	Moskva	18 Aug
41.67	USA	Pierre, Anderson, Townsend, C Williams		1	WK	Zürich	29 Aug
41.75	USA Red	Freeman, Felix, Gardner, Jeter		1	Herc	Monaco	19 Jul
41.78	USA Blue	Tarmoh, Anderson, Pierre, Scott		2	Herc	Monaco	19 Jul
41.78	JAM	Russell, Stewart, Morrison, Fraser-Pryce		2	WK	Zürich	29 Aug

Mark	Name	Nat	Born	Pos	Meet	Venue	Date
41.82	USA Tarmoh, Anderson, Gardner, Freeman			1h3	WCh	Moskva	18 Aug
41.87	JAM Russell, Stewart, Calvert, Brooks			1h1	WCh	Moskva	18 Aug
42.25	FRA Distel-Bonnet, Ikuesan, Soumaré, Akakpo			2h1	WCh	Moskva	18 Aug
42.29	BRA E dos Santos, Silva, Krasucki, R Santos			2h3	WCh	Moskva	18 Aug
42.42	JAM Simpson, Stewart, McLaughlin, Fraser-Pryce			1	PennR	Philadelphia	27 Apr
42.56	Texas A&M USA L Stewart, Ash. Purvis, K Brown, Collier			1	TexR	Austion	30 Mar
42.62	UKR Povh, Pyatachenko, Ryemyen, Pogrebnyak			1rA	ET	Gateshead	22 Jun
42.65	USA Blue M White, Anderson, Pierre. Lucas			2	PennR	Philadelphia	27 Apr
42.65	GER Kwadwo, Weit, Pinto, Sailer			3h1	WCh	Moskva	18 Aug
42.66	USA Red Bartoletta, Felix, Knight, Tarmoh			3	PennR	Philadelphia	27 Apr
42.69	GBR Asher-Smith, Onuora, Lewis, Nelson			1	DL	London (OS)	26 Jul
42.71	UKR Ryemyen, Pogrebnyak, Stuy, Puayachenko			1	ET	Gateshead	22 Jun
42.75	GBR Asher-Smith, Nelson, Lewis, Jones			1h2	WCh	Moskva	18 Aug
42.75	USA Tarmoh, Anderson, Gardner, Freeman			2	WCh	Moskva	18 Aug
42.77	UKR Povh, Pogrebnyak, Ryemyen, Pyatachenko			3	WK	Zürich	29 Aug
	20 perfromances by teams from 7 nations						
42.93	RUS Belkina, Rusakova, Savlinis, Bolsun			5	WCh	Moskva	18 Aug
42.99	CAN Emmanuel, Hyacinthe, S Davis, Bingham			2h2	WCh	Moskva	18 Aug
43.01	TTO Durant, Ayhe, R Thomas, Selvon			4h3	WCh	Moskva	18 Aug
	(10)						
43.18	POL Popowicz, Wedler, Ptak, Jeschke			5h3	WCh	Moskva	18 Aug
43.21	SUI Kambundji, Lavanchy, E.Sprunger, L.Sprunger			3h2	WCh	Moskva	18 Aug
43.26	NED Vassell, Schippers, Ghafoor, Samuel			4h1	WCh	Moskva	18 Aug
43.28	DOM M Sánchez, Chala, Mejía, Manzueta			5h1	WCh	Moskva	18 Aug
43.44	CHN (Jiangsu) Xu Meiling, Zhu Yayun, Jiang Lan, Yuan Qiqi			1	NG	Shenyang	11 Sep
43.52	NGR Asumnu, George, Kizzee, Okagbare			4	PennR	Philadelphia	27 Apr
43.65	COL Hinestroza, Idrobo, Obregón, E Palacios			6h3	WCh	Moskva	18 Aug
43.67	CUB Montes, Gandulla, Guillén, Odelín			1		La Habana	8 Jun
43.86	ITA Gamba, Siragusa, Amidei, Hooper			2	EU23	Tampere	14 Jul
43.88	ECU Angulo, Chávez, Cevallos, Tenorio			2		La Habana	8 Jun
	(20)						
43.90	BAH .Ferguson, Smith, Cox, Strachan			6	PennR	Philadelphia	27 Apr
44.06	AUS Brennan, Breen, Pearson, Whittaker			1		Chonburi	8 May
44.10	CZE Mazácová, Schmidová, Procházková, Cechová			4	Herc	Monaco	19 Jul
44.16	VEN Hidalgo, Álvarez, Vargas, Soto			2	Bol G	Trujillo	28 Nov
44.37	FIN Rasanen, Latvala, Berghem, Leppakoski			1	vSWE	Stockholm	7 Aug
44.38	BLR Astoshko, Talay, Shumak, Gpnchar			2rB	ET	Gateshead	22 Jun
44.38	JPN Kitazake, Fukushima, Watanabe, Fujimori			2	AsiC	Pune	6 Jul
44.42	THA Jaksuninkorn, Klomdee, Wannakit, Sanrat			1	SEAG	Nay Pyi Taw	16 Dec

44.65	IVB	1 Jun	44.73	SLO	22 Jun	44.84	LTU	22 Jun	44.99	VIE	16 Dec	45.06	ESP	22 Jun
44.69	IRL	1 Jun	44.79	CYP	28 Jun	44.88	KAZ	15 Jun	45.03	IND	6 Jul	45.07	TUR	22 Jun
44.70	BEL	12 Sep	44.79	SWE	14 Jul	44.98	POR	20 Apr	45.04	POR	22 Jun			

Mixed nation team

41.79	Team Jet USA M Whote, Jeter, L Williams, Okagbare NGR			1	MSR	Walnut	20 Apr

JUNIORS

Mark	Name	Nat	Born	Pos	Meet	Venue	Date
43.81	GBR Miller, Asher-Smith, S Wilson, Henry			1	EJ	Rieti	21 Jul
43.89	GBR Miller, Asher-Smith, S Wilson, Henry			1h2	EJ	Rieti	21 Jul
43.97A	USA Atkinsont, Madu, Faulknor,Holland			1	PAm-J	Medellín	25 Aug
44.00	FRA Compper, Akakpo, Ntiamoah, Sananes			2	EJ	Rieti	21 Jul
44.22	NED van Agt, van Schagen, Sedney, Boone			3	EJ	Rieti	21 Jul
44.24	NGR Odeyemi, Francis, Uko, Bassey			1		Warri	14 Jun
44.56	GER Bechthold, Burghardt, Drazek, Freese			2r2		Mannheim	30 Jun
44.73	BEL Missinne, Grillet,Depuydt, Mehuys			4	EJ	Rieti	21 Jul
44.77	BAH Charlton, Cox, Miller, Albury			1	Carifta	Nassau	31 Mar
44.82	JAM Bonner, Thompson, Devilds, D Johnson			1	PennR	Philadelphia	26 Apr
44.99	SUI Strebel, Atcho, C Keller, M Keller			3h1	EJ	Rieti	21 Jul
45.07	JPN Sugiyma, Doi, Nobayashi, Matsumoto			1		Fukuroi	2 Nov

4 X 200 METRES RELAY

1:29.98	Texas, A&M Ash.Purvis, Collier, Ekpone, K.Brown			1	PennR	Philadelphia	27 Apr

4 X 400 METRES RELAY

Mark	Name	Nat		Pos	Meet	Venue	Date
3:20.19	RUS Gushchina 51.0e, Firova 49,6e, Ryzhova 50.23, Krivoshapka 49.40			1	WCh	Moskva	17 Aug
3:20.41	USA Beard 50.6, Hastings 50.1, Spencer 50.44, McCorory 49.25			2	WCh	Moskva	17 Aug
3:22.61	GBR Child 51.9, Cox 50.3, Adeoye 51.01, Ohuruogu 49.43			2	WCh	Moskva	17 Aug
3:22.66	USA Red Beard 51.5, Hastings 49.9, Trotter 51.0, McCorory 50.3			1	PennR	Philadelphia	27 Apr
3:22.68	GBR Child 51.6, Cox 50.4, Ohuruogu 50.4, Shakes-Drayton 50.3			2	PennR	Philadelphia	27 Apr
3:23.51	RUS Gushchina 51.0, Firova 50.4, Antyukh 50.78, Ryzhova 51.27			1h3	WCh	Moskva	16 Aug
3:24.11	JAM S Williams 51.9, Williams-Mills 50.0, Day 51.0, Spencer 51.2			3	PennR	Philadelphia	27 Apr

Mark	Name	Nat	Born	Pos	Meet	Venue	Date
3:24.21	FRA	Gayot 51.54, Guion-Firmin 50.26, Hurtis 51.74, Guei 50.67		4	WCh	Moskva	17 Aug
3:25.18	USA	Spencer 51.7, Beard 50.0, Atkins 51.89, McCorory 51.63		1h1	WCh	Moskva	16 Aug
3:25.39	GBR	Child 51.7, Cox 50.9, Adeoye 51.31, Ohuruogu 51.43		1h2	WCh	Moskva	16 Aug
3:26.26	USA Blue	Floyd 52.9, Wineberg 51.5, Atkins 50.3, Baker 51.6		4	PennR	Philadelphia	27 Apr
3:26.61	RUS	Tamkova, Kotlyarova, Renzhina, Ustalova		1	WUG	Kazan	12 Jul
3:27.38	UKR	Prystyupa 52.5e, Lyakhova 51.2e, Logvynenko 52.50, Pygyda 51.18	5	WCh	Moskva	17 Aug
3:27.39	NGR	P George 52.2e, Abogunloko 53.5e, Omotosho 51.76, R George 49.93		2h2	WCh	Moskva	16 Aug
3:27.43	Univ of Florida USA	Reynolss, Whittaker, Gause, Eutsey		2	FlaR	Gainesville	6 Apr
3:27.57	NGR	Omotosho 52.4e, P George 51.2e, Abogunloko 54.29, R George 49.67		6	WCh	Moskva	17 Aug
(16/7)							
3:28.40	ROU	Pastor 52.7e, Lavric 51.8e, Belgyan 53.08, Razor 50.85		7	WCh	Moskva	17 Aug
3:29.62	ITA	Bazzoni 52.7e, Milani 52.4e, Chigbolu 53.66, Grenot 50.86		2h1	WCh	Moskva	16 Aug
3:29.74	POL	Gorzkowska, Holub, Karczmarczyk, Swiety		1	EU23	Tampere	14 Jul
(10)							
3:30.28	BLR	Reishal 53.6e, Khlyustova 52.5e, Yurenya 51.84, I Usovich 52.34		4h3	WCh	Moskva	16 Aug
3:30.48	CZE	Rosolová 52.5e, Bartonícková 52.1e, Slaninová 54.78, Hejnová 51.10		4h1	WCh	Moskva	16 Aug
3:30.64A	TTO	Fermin, McKnight, Modeste, Brooks		1	CAC	Morelia	7 Jul
3:30.82	BRA	J Sousa, J de Lima, Barbosa, Coutinho		1		São Paulo	18 May
3:31.09	CAN	Brown 54.1e, Wells 52.1e, Montcalm 52.54, Martin 52.39		5h3	WCh	Moskva	16 Aug
3:31.21	CHN (Guangdong)	Tang Xiaoyin, Li Xueji, Chen Yanmei, Chen Jingwen		1	NG	Shenyang	11 Sep
3:31.83	GER	Cremer 52.9, L Schmidt 52.9, Klopsch 53.40, Spelmeyer 52.50		6	ET	Gateshead	23 Jun
3:32.26	IND	Sheoran, Luka, Jose, Poovamma		1	AsiC	Pune	7 Jul
3:32.90	BAH	Amertil, Jones, Martin, Clarke		6	PennR	Philadelphia	27 Apr
3:34.35	COL	Moreno, R García, Florez, Padilla		1	Bol G	Trujillo	29 Nov
(20)							
3:34.52A	MEX	Espinosa, Rodríguez, Soberanes, Medina		2	CAC	Morelia	7 Jul
3:35.03	JPN-J	Aoyama, Sugiura, Oki, Jumpo		1		Fukuroi	2 Nov
3:35.11	LTU	Misiunaite, Balciunaite, Morauskaite, Serksniene		1	ET-2	Kaunas	22 Jun
3:35.39	KAZ	Maslenko, Yurchenko, Yermak, Mukasheva		1	NC	Almaty	19 Jul
3:35.78	AUS	Sargent, Rubie, Doyle, Boden		1		Brisbane	23 Mar
3:36.05	RSA	van der Merwe, Nienaber, Palframan, Ebersohn		2	WUG	Kazan	12 Jul

3:36.68	THA	19 Dec	3:37.56	CUB	17 Mar	3:38.95	SVK	23 Jun	3:39.14	ISL	23 Jun	3:39.54	SRI	7 Jul
3:36.89	TUR	23 Jun	3:38.13A	PUR	7 Jul	3:38.96	BOT	16 Aug	3:39.19	NED	23 Jun	3:39.57	SLO	22 Jun
3:36.92	VIE	19 Dec	3:38.43	IRL	23 Jun	3:39.05	ESP	23 Jun	3:39.27	CHI	9 Jun	3:39.82	POR	23 Jun
3:37.48	MAR	14 Sep	3:38.49	CRO	28 Jul	3:39.11	SWE	8 Sep	3:29.48	BEL	23 Jun			

Best al low altitude

3:33.50	TTO	Fermin 53.0e, McKnight 53.0e, D Williams 53.99, Modeste 53.55		5h2	WCh	Moskva	16 Aug

Mixed nation teams

3:24.58	One Goal Athletics		1	FlaR	Gainesville	6 Apr
	M Robinson, N Williams-Mills JAM, D Trotter, N Hastings					
3:26.73	Univ of Oregon USA		1U	PennR	Philadelphia	27 Apr
	Gardner 52.5, Okodogbe NGR 52.3, Roesler 52.0, Francis 49.9					
3:27.09	Univ of Arkansas USA		1	NCAA	Eugene	8 Jun

Indoors

3:28.49	CZE	Rosolová, Bartonícková, Masná, Hejnová		3	EI	Göteborg	3 Mar

Disqualified

3:27.39	ITA	Bazzoni 52.2e, Milani 51.4e, Spacca 52.66, Grenot 51.13		(6)	WCh	Moskva	17 Aug

JUNIORS

3:30.01	JAM	Vere Tach.		1	N.Sch	Kingston	16 Mar
3:31.21	NGR			2		Warri	14 Jun
3:32.83	POL	Curylo, Dabrowska, Janowicz, Wyciszkiewicz		1	EJ	Rieti	21 Jul
3:33.36	RUS	Glotova, Parfyonova, Aslanidi, Renzhina		2	EJ	Rieti	21 Jul
3:33.40	GER	Müller, Schachtschneider, Kohlmann, Hering		3	EJ	Rieti	21 Jul
3:35.03	JPN	Aoyama, Sugiura, Oki, Jumpo		1		Fukuroi	2 Nov
3:36.31	UKR	Ralko, Sidorska, Shevchenko, Klymyuk		4	EJ	Rieti	21 Jul
3:36.48A	USA	Reynolds, Baisden, C Williams, Okolo		1	PAm-J	Medellín	25 Aug
3:37.61	ITA	Vitale, Morelli, Lukudo, Pasquale		5	EJ	Rieti	21 Jul
3:38.57	ROU	Timofei, Carasila, Ene, Razor		6	EJ	Rieti	21 Jul
3:40.21	FRA	Sananes, Medjid, Ntia,oah, Bauwe		7	EJ	Rieti	21 Jul

4 X 800 METRES RELAY

8:04.31	USA Red	L Wallace 2:02.0, Martinez 2:00.6, Wilson 2:03.1, Montaño 1:58.6	1	PennR	Philadelphia	27 Apr
8:07.58	KEN	Jepkosgei 2:02.1, W Chebet 2:01.2, Obiri 2:02.8, Sum 2:01.5	2	PennR	Philadelphia	27 Apr
8:10.99	USA Blue	Wright 2:01.8, Gall 2:02.7, Schmidt 2:02.8, L Thomas 2:03.7	3	PennR	Philadelphia	27 Apr
8:13.46	GBR	M Okoro 2:01.8, J Simpson 2:03.9, Sharp 2:02.8, Bird 2:05.0	4	PennR	Philadelphia	27 Apr
8:14.85	CAN	Bishop 2:02.2, Belleau-Béliveau 2:03.2, Cummins 2:02.9, Ogbasilassie 2:06.6	5	PennR	Philadelphia	27 Apr
8:18.96	AUS	Buckman 2:03.3, Laman 2:03.7, Gregson 2:05.6, Kajan 2:06.4	6	PennR	Philadelphia	27 Apr

Mark	Name		Nat	Born	Pos	Meet	Venue		Date

4 X 100 METRES HURDLES

50.78	USA Boogie Tast TC Ali, Castlin, Y Lewis, Q Harrison			1	FlaR	Gainesville	6 Apr
52.29	Mixed team Carruthers USA, Schott AUT, Porter GBR, Pedersen NOR			2	FlaR	Gainesville	6 Apr
52.38	Star Athletics USA Coward, Wells, T Jones, Idlette DOM			3	FlaR	Gainesville	6 Apr

3000 METRES WALK

Mark	Name		Nat	Born	Pos		Meet	Venue		Date
12:27.73mx	Tanya	Holliday	AUS	21.9.88	1			Adelaide		19 Jan
12:31.4	Yevdokiya	Korotkova	RUS	28.2.79	1			Yerino		2 Jun
12:31.6	Hanna	Drabenya	BLR	15.8.87	2			Yerino		2 Jun
12:33.1	Nadezhda	Leontyeva	RUS-J	6.11.94	3			Yerino		2 Jun
12:38.2	Agnieszka	Szwarnóg	POL	28.12.86	2 Jun	12:42.15	Emilie	Tissot	FRA 11.4.93	5 May
12:40.3	Olga	Yakovenko	UKR	1.6.87	2 Jun	12:44.2+	Elisa	Rigaudo	ITA 17.6.80	1 May
Indoors										
11:57.86	Olga	Kaniskina	RUS	19.1.85	1			Samara		31 Jan
12:21.40	Katarzyna	Kwoka	POL	29.6.85	1	NC		Spala		17 Feb
12:21.56	Ana	Cabecinha	POR	29.4.84	1	NC		Pombal		16 Feb
12:24.41	Brigita	Virbalyte	LTU	1.2.85	1			Kaunas		2 Feb
12:25.36	Inês	Henriques	POR	1.5.80	2	NC		Pombal		16 Feb
12:31.62	Paulina	Buziak	POL	16.12.86	2	NC		Spala		17 Feb
12:38.0	Olga	Shargina	RUS-Y	.96	1			Chelyabinsk		6 Jan
12:38.16	Rachel	Seaman	CAN	14.1.86	21 Dec	12:38.43	Lyudmila	Olyanovska	UKR 20.2.93	11 Jan

5000 METRES WALK

Mark	Name		Nat	Born	Pos		Meet	Venue		Date
20:46.12	Eleonora	Giorgi	ITA	14.9.89	1			Milano		24 Apr
21:03.15	Agnese	Pastare	LAT	27.10.88	1	v2N		Valmiera		20 Jul
21:07.97	Julia	Takacs	ESP	29.6.89	1			Avilés		15 Jun
21:10.6+	Elisa	Rigaudo	ITA	17.6.80	1	in 10k		Mondovi		1 May
21:21.43	Maríaa José	Poves	ESP	16.3.78	2			Avilés		15 Jun
21:21.51mx	Tanya	Holliday	AUS	21.9.88	1			Sydney		9 Mar
21:28.92mx	Jessica	Rothwell	AUS	18.6.89	2			Sydney		9 Mar
21:31.22	Raquel	González	ESP	16.11.89	1			Mataró		3 Jul
21:37.09	Lorena	Luaces	ESP	29.2.84	15 Jun	21:50.13mx	Kelly	Ruddick	AUS 19.4.73	1 Mar
21:40.4	Federica	Ferraro	ITA	18.8.88	31 Aug	21:53.42	Sibilla	Di Vincenzo	ITA 22.1.83	8 Jul
21:41.79	Kumi	Otoshi	JPN	29.7.85	18 May	21:53.93	Agnieszka	Szwarnóg	POL 28.12.86	25 May
21:46.33	Beatriz	Pascual	ESP	9.5.82	8 Jun	21:54.07mx	Masumi	Fuchise	JPN 2.9.86	19 May
						21:55.81	Ainhoa	Pinedo	ESP 17.2.83	8 Jun
Indoors										
21:04.9	Lyudmila	Olyanovska	UKR	20.2.93	1			Sumy		21 Dec
21:12.00	Irina	Yumanova	RUS	6.11.90	1			Novocheboksarsk		12 Jun
21:24.7	Inna	Kashyna	UKR	27.9.91	2			Sumy		21 Dec
21:37.09	Olga	Suranova	RUS	7.12.86	12 Jan	21:52.0	Natalya	Makarova	RUS 17.4.87	6 Jan
21:40.41	Marina	Pandakova	RUS	1.3.89	12 Jan	21:54.0mx	Anezka	Drahotová	CZE-J 22.7.95	27 Dec

10 KILOMETRES WALK

See also 20km list for many intermediate times. t = 10,000m track time

Mark	Name		Nat	Born	Pos		Meet	Venue		Date
42:29.06 t	Elisa	Rigaudo	ITA	17.6.80	1			Mondovi		1 May
42:32.74 t	Julia	Takacs	ESP	29.6.89	1	NC		Alcobendas		27 Jul
43:31.29 t	Inês	Henriques	POR	1.5.80	1	NC		Leiria		27 Jul
43:33.75 t	María José	Poves	ESP	16.3.78	2	NC		Alcobendas		27 Jul
43:36	Olga	Suranova	RUS	7.12.86	1			Podolsk		9 May
43:39.42 t	Beatriz	Pascual	ESP	9.5.82	3	NC		Alcobendas		27 Jul
43:44.96 t		Rigaudo			1	NC		Milano		26 Jul
43:50	Yekaterina	Medvedyeva ¶	RUS-J	29.3.94	1	NC-wj		Sochi		23 Feb
43:53	Federica	Ferraro	ITA	18.8.88	1			Katowice		7 Sep
43:53.65 t	Ana	Cabecinha	POR	29.4.84	2	NC		Leiria		27 Jul
43:55		Ferraro			1			Bacúch		28 Sep
44:01	Brigita	Virbalyte	LTU	1.2.85	2			Katowice		7 Sep
44:03	Tatyana	Korotkova	RUS	31.5.82	2			Podolsk		9 May
44:08	Ayman	Kozhakhmetova ¶	KAZ	23.4.91	3			Podolsk		9 May
44:15.87 t	Anezka	Drahotová	CZE-J	22.7.95	1	EJ		Rieti		18 Jul
44:21.03 t	Oksana	Golyatkina	RUS-J	13.3.,95	2	EJ		Rieti		18 Jul
44:22.56tmx	Kumi	Otoshi	JPN	29.7.85	1			Kumagaya		21 Sep
44:25 mx t	Rachel	Seaman	CAN	14.1.86	1			Pharr		29 Dec
44:33.56 t	Eleonora	Giorgi	ITA	14.9.89	2	NC		Milano		26 Jul
44:40	Agnieszka	Dygacz	POL	18.7.85	3			Katowice		7 Sep
44:42+	Mirna	Ortiz	GUA	28.2.87		in 20k		Dublin		28 Jun
44:45+	Natalya	Kholodilina	RUS	21.7.89		in 20k		Cheboksary		8 Jun
44:45.27 t	Eliska	Drahotová	CZE-J	22.7.95	3	EJ		Rieti		18 Jul
44:50	Laura	Reynolds	IRL	20.1.89	1			Dublin		28 Jun
44:56	Nadezhda	Leontyeva	RUS-J	6.11.94	2	NC-wj		Sochi		23 Feb

WOMEN 2013

Mark	Name		Nat	Born	Pos	Meet	Venue	Date
44:56.03 t	Vera	Santos	POR	3.12.81	3	NC	Leiria	27 Jul
44:59	Paulina	Buziak	POL	16.12.86	4		Katowice	7 Sep
45:00+		Zhou Tongmei	CHN	4.4.88		in 20k	La Coruña	1 Jun
45:07	Viktória	Madarász	HUN	12.5.85	3		Bacúch	28 Sep
45:10	Antonella	Palmisano	ITA	6.8.91	1		Voronovo	14 Sep
45:11.4 t	Agnese	Pastare	LAT	27.10.88	1		Murjani	20 Apr
45:13+	Mayra Carolina	Herrera	GUA	20.12.88		in 20k	Dublin	28 Jun
45:21.72 t	Anastasiya	Yatsevich	BLR	18.1.85	1		Brest	24 May
45:21.90tmx	Ai	Michiguchi	JPN	3.6.88	2		Kumagaya	21 Sep
45:22	Yevdokiya	Korotkova	RUS	28.2.79	4		Podolsk	9 May
45:30	Irina	Shushina	RUS	30.10.86	5		Podolsk	9 May
45:31	Tatyana	Akulinushkina #	RUS-J	6.4.94	4	NC-wj	Sochi	23 Feb

Mark	Name		Nat	Born	Date
45:33	Rei	Inoue	JPN	23.7.91	21 Apr
45:36	Kelly	Ruddick	AUS	19.4.73	10 Oct
45:38+		Qieyang Shenjie	CHN	11.11.90	13 Aug
45:42	Sholpan	Kozhakhmetova	KAZ	23.4.91	9 May
45:43.2 t	Inna	Kashyna	UKR	27.9.91	2 Nov
45:44+	Lyudmyla	Olyanovska	UKR	20.2.93	13 Aug
45:49	Anne	Halkivaha	FIN	9.2.86	21 Apr
45:49.93t	Lorena	Luaces	ESP	29.2.84	27 Jul
45:50	Natalya	Kopliyenko	RUS-J	30.6.94	23 Feb
45:51+	Ainhoa	Pinedo	ESP	17.2.83	6 Apr
45:51+	Kristina	Saltanovic	LTU	20.2.75	6 Apr
45:54	Tomomi	Maekawa	JPN	28.9.91	21 Apr
45:55+	Olga	Yakovenko	UKR	1.6.87	19 May
46:00.54t	Lorena	Arenas	COL	17.9.93	15 Jun
46:02	Neringa	Aidietyte	LTU	5.6.83	7 Sep
46:04	Olga	Nacharkina	RUS-J	13.10.94	23 Feb
46:06.21t	Valentina	Trapletti	ITA	12.7.85	26 Jul
46:15+	Regan	Lamble	AUS	14.10.91	28 Jun
46:18+	Paola	Pérez	ECU	21.12.89	13 Aug
46:18+	Lizbeth	Silva	MEX	30.9.89	13 Aug
46:27.35t	Dariya	Balkunets	BLR	4.3.93	24 May
46:29.89t	Chiaki	Asada	JPN	21.1.91	21 Sep

Best track times

Mark	Name		Nat	Born	Pos	Meet	Venue	Date
45:08.81 t	Federica	Ferraro	ITA	18.8.88	3	NC	Milano	26 Jul
45:23.95 t	Nadezhda	Leontyeva	RUS-J	6.11.94	4	EJ	Rieti	18 Jul
45:39.04t	Mirna	Ortiz	GUA	21.7.89	25 Oct
45:43.84 t	Hiroi	Maeda	JPN	1.6.91	7 Oct
45:57.53 +t	Lucie	Pelantová	CZE	7.5.86	8 Jun
46:03.15 tmx	Masumi	Fuchise	JPN	2.9.86	21 Sep
46:23.82 tmx	Rei	Inoue	JPN	23.7.91	21 Sep

Drugs disqualification

Mark	Name		Nat	Born	Date
45:49.3 t	Tatyana	Akulishkina #	RUS-J	6.4.94	8 Jun

JUNIORS

See main list for top juniors. 7 performances by 5 women to 45:15. Additional marks and further juniors:

	Mark			Pos	Meet	Venue	Date
Golyatkina	44:50.0 t			1	NC	Cheboksary	8 Jun
Leontyeva	45:14			1		Lugano	17 Mar
45:50	Natalya	Kopliyenko	RUS	30.6.94	5	NC-wj	Sochi	23 Feb
46:04	Olga	Nacharkina	RUS	13.10.94	6	NC-wj	Sochi	23 Feb

20 KILOMETRES WALK

Mark		Name		Nat	Born	Pos	Meet	Venue	Date
1:25:49	43:54	Yelena	Lashmanova	RUS	9.4.92	1	NC-w	Sochi	23 Feb
1:25:59	43:55	Anisya	Kirdyapkina	RUS	23.10.89	2	NC-w	Sochi	23 Feb
1:26:00	43:56	Vera	Sokolova	RUS	8.6.87	3	NC-w	Sochi	23 Feb
1:27:00	43:59	Irina	Yumanova	RUS	6.11.90	4	NC-w	Sochi	23 Feb
1:27:06	44:15		Liu Hong	CHN	12.5.87	1		Lugano	17 Mar
1:27:08	45:26		Lashmanova			1	WCh	Moskva	13 Aug
1:27:11	45:26		Kirdyapkina			2	WCh	Moskva	13 Aug
1:27:36	45:03		Sun Huanhuan	CHN	15.3.90	1	NC	Taicang	1 Mar
1:27:39	43:58	Marina	Pandakova	RUS	1.3.89	5	NC-w	Sochi	23 Feb
1:27:40			Li Yanfei	CHN	12.1.90	2	NC	Taicang	1 Mar
1:27:42			He Qin	CHN	23.3.92	3	NC	Taicang	1 Mar
1:27:53			Lu Xiuzhi (10)	CHN	26.10.93	1	NG	Shenyang	11 May
1:27:53			Liu Hong			2	NG	Shenyang	11 May
1:27:58	45:06		Lu Xiuzhi			4	NC	Taicang	1 Mar
1:28:03			Li Yanfei			3	NG	Shenyang	11 May
1:28:05			Qieyang Shenjie	CHN	11.11.90	4	NG	Shenyang	11 May
1:28:10	45:34		Liu Hong			3	WCh	Moskva	13 Aug
1:28:16			Sun Huanhuan			5	NG	Shenyang	11 May
1:28:19	44:51		Lashmanova			1		Rio Maior	6 Apr
1:28:27	45:05		Qieyang Shenjie			5	NC	Taicang	1 Mar
1:28:32	44:51	Mirna	Ortiz	GUA	28.2.87	2		Rio Maior	6 Apr
1:28:32	45:36		Sun Huanhuan			4	WCh	Moskva	13 Aug
1:28:33			Nie Jingjing	CHN	1.3.88	6	NC	Taicang	1 Mar
1:28:39	44:07		Kirdyapkina			1	ECp	Dudince	19 May
1:28:41	45:20	Elisa	Rigaudo	ITA	17.6.80	5	WCh	Moskva	13 Aug
1:28:42	44:24	Lina	Bikulova	RUS	1.10.88	1	NC	Cheboksary	8 Jun
1:28:44	44:08	Julia	Takacs	ESP	29.6.89	1	NC	Murcia	3 Mar
1:28:54	44:28		Ortiz			2		Lugano	17 Mar
1:28:58	44:16		Bikulova			3		Lugano	17 Mar
1:29:00	45:38	Beatriz	Pascual	ESP	9.5.82	6	WCh	Moskva	13 Aug
:		(30/17)							

Mark		Name		Nat	Born	Pos	Meet	Venue	Date	
1:29:03	44:06	Nina	Ochotnikova	RUS	11.3.91	6	NC-w	Sochi	23	Feb
1:29:05	45:20	Anezka	Drahotová	CZE-J	22.7.95	7	WCh	Moskva	13	Aug
1:29:17	45:38	Ana	Cabecinha	POR	29.4.84	8	WCh	Moskva	13	Aug
		(20)								
1:29:21	44:28	Katarzyna	Kwoka	POL	29.6.85	4		Lugano	17	Mar
1:29:30			Wang Shanshan	CHN	16.6.87	7	NC	Taicang	1	Mar
1:29:30	44:57	Inês	Henriques	POR	1.5.80	1		La Coruña	1	Jun
1:29:42	46:03		Ding Huiqin	CHN	5.2.90	8	NC	Taicang	1	Mar
1:29:48	45:42		Yang Mingxia	CHN	13.1.90	9	NC	Taicang	1	Mar
1:29:49	44:47	Natalya	Kholodilina	RUS	21.7.89	8	NC-w	Sochi	23	Feb
1:29:54	44:40	Natalya	Makarova	RUS	17.4.87	9	NC-w	Sochi	23	Feb
1:29:55		Agnese	Pastare	LAT	27.10.88	1		Gdansk	31	Aug
1:29:56	44:24	Svetlana	Vasilyeva	RUS	24.7.92	2	NC	Cheboksary	8	Jun
1:29:58	45:13	María José	Poves	ESP	16.3.78	1		Dublin	28	Jun
		(30)								
1:29:59			Bo Yanmin	CHN	29.6.87	10	NC	Taicang	1	Mar
1:30:00			Xu Liqin	CHN	6.2.90	11	NC	Taicang	1	Mar
1:30:01	45:44	Eleonora	Giorgi	ITA	14.9.89	10	WCh	Moskva	13	Aug
1:30:11	45:00	Raquel	González	ESP	16.11.89	3		La Coruña	1	Jun
1:30:15	45:28	Paulina	Buziak	POL	16.12.86	5		Lugano	17	Mar
1:30:19	44:41	Natalya	Serezhkina	RUS	7.5.92	10	NC-w	Sochi	23	Feb
1:30:24			Shi Tianshu	CHN	7.6.88	3		Shenyang	12	May
1:30:25			Liu Huan	CHN	24.2.93	12	NC	Taicang	1	Mar
1:30:26		Lyudmyla	Olyanovska	UKR	20.2.93	1	NC-23	Yevpatoriya	2	Mar
1:30:27	44:42	Masumi	Fuchise	JPN	2.9.86	1		Nomi	10	Mar
		(40)								
1:30:28			Zhou Tongmei	CHN	4.4.88	13	NC	Taicang	1	Mar
1:30:31			Li Li	CHN	18.6.87	7	NG	Shenyang	11	May
1:30:33			Pei Mowen	CHN-J	17.9.95	1	NC-j	Taicang	1	Mar
1:30:38		Olga	Yakovenko	UKR	1.6.87	2	NC	Yevpatoriya	2	Mar
1:30:45		Kumi	Otoshi	JPN	29.7.85	1	NC	Kobe	17	Feb
1:30:50	45:46	Antonella	Palmisano	ITA	6.8.91	13	WCh	Moskva	13	Aug
1:30:55			Li Hua	CHN	15.1.91	14	NC	Taicang	1	Mar
1:30:55	45:10	Brigita	Virbalyte	LTU	1.2.85	1		Alytus	14	Jun
1:30:58			Zhou Kang	CHN	24.12.89	15	NC	Taicang	1	Mar
1:30:58	45:12	Yanelli	Caballero	MEX	29.5.93	2		Dublin	28	Jun
		(50)								
1:30:58		Agnieszka	Dygacz	POL	18.7.85	1	NC	Torun	20	Jul
1:30:59		Mayra Carolina	Herrera	GUA	20.12.88	14	WCh	Moskva	13	Aug
1:31:00			Liu Shuyu	CHN	13.12.93	16	NC	Taicang	1	Mar
1:31:00	45:00	Vera	Santos	POR	3.12.81	4		La Coruña	1	Jun
1:31:03			Luo Xingcai	CHN-J	18.7.94	2	NC-j	Taicang	1	Mar
1:31:03	46:05		Gao Ni	CHN	14.9.91	17	NC	Taicang	1	Mar
1:31:09	45:16	Monica	Equihua	MEX	23.9.82	5		Rio Maior	6	Apr
1:31:12			Chen Shuangyan	CHN	14.8.91	18	NC	Taicang	1	Mar
1:31:16	46:14	Hanna	Drabenya	BLR	15.8.87	16	WCh	Moskva	13	Aug
1:31:19			Kang Jinzi	CHN	25.1.90	19	NC	Taicang	1	Mar
		(60)								
1:31:20		Federica	Ferraro	ITA	18.8.88	1		Chiasso	13	Oct
1:31:32	45:35	Lorena	Luaces	ESP	29.2.84	3	NC	Murcia	3	Mar
1:31:33	44:33	Agnieszka	Szwarnóg	POL	28.12.86	1		Dudince	23	Mar
1:31:49			He Dan	CHN	22.7.84	21	NC	Taicang	1	Mar
1:31:54	45:50	Olena	Shumkina	UKR	24.1.88	19	WCh	Moskva	13	Aug
1:31:57			Mao Yanxue	CHN-J	15.2.94	3	NC-j	Taicang	1	Mar
1:32:01			Wang Yingliu	CHN	1.3.92	22	NC	Taicang	1	Mar
1:32:07			Zhang Xuhong	CHN-J	2.1.94	4	NC-j	Taicang	1	Mar
1:32:07			Su Qiuyue	CHN-J	1.2.95	5	NG	Shenyang	12	May
1:32:07	45:10	Lucie	Pelantová	CZE	7.5.86	5		La Coruña	1	Jun
		(70)								
1:32:11	45:54	Kristina	Saltanovic	LTU	20.2.75	21	WCh	Moskva	13	Aug
1:32:20	46:00	Ainhoa	Pinedo	ESP	17.2.83	9		Lugano	17	Mar
1:32:22	45:45	Kumiko	Okada	JPN	17.10.91	2	NC	Kobe	17	Feb
1:32:25	45:33	Hiroi	Maeda	JPN	1.6.91	2		Nomi	10	Mar
1:32:25	46:14	Lorena	Arenas	COL	17.9.93	22	WCh	Moskva	13	Aug
1:32:28			Chen Zhen	CHN-J	3.11.94	6	NC-j	Taicang	1	Mar
1:32:31	45:44	Anastasiya	Yatsevich	BLR	18.1.85	24	WCh	Moskva	13	Aug
1:32:33			Wang Min	CHN	2.12.91	23	NC	Taicang	1	Mar
1:32:37		Katarzyna	Golba	POL	21.12.89	4		Zaniemysl	20	Apr
1:32:43	45:32	Dariya	Balkunets	BLR	4.34.93	2		Alytus	14	Jun
		(80)								
1:32:45	46:39		Duan Dandan	CHN-J	23.5.95	7		La Coruña	1	Jun

522　20 KILOMETRES WALK

Mark		Name		Nat	Born	Pos	Meet	Venue	Date
1:32:53		Paola	Pérez	ECU	21.12.89	2		Dudince	23 Mar
1:32:58		Inna	Kashyna	UKR	27.9.91	4		Yevpatoriya	2 Mar
1:32:59	45:37	Galina	Kichigina	KAZ	14.7.88	11	RUS-w	Sochi	23 Feb
1:32:59		Érica	de Sena	BRA	3..5.85	3		Dudince	23 Mar
1:33:10			Shi Yang	CHN	24.1.83	8	NG	Shenyang	11 May
1:33:11			Sun Xueping	CHN	10.12.88	24	NC	Taicang	1 Mar
1:33:11		Jamy	Franco	GUA	1.7.91	11		Lugano	17 Mar
1:33:15		Kelly	Ruddick	AUS	19.4.73	1		Launceston	1 Sep
1:33:21		Viktória	Madarász	HUN	12.5.85	2		Chiasso	13 Oct
(90)									
1:33:24			Zhao Jing	CHN	18.2.92	10	NG	Shenyang	11 May
1:33:25	46:40		Hou Yongbo	CHN-J	15.9.94	8		La Coruña	1 Jun
1:33:30			Wang Xiaolan	CHN	5.2.90	25	NC	Taicang	1 Mar
1:33:31		Laura	Reynolds	IRL	20.1.89	6	WUG	Kazan	10 Jul
1:33:34			Gao Shan	CHN-J	8.4.95	8	NC-j	Taicang	1 Mar
1:33:40			Tong Lingling	CHN	25.1.92	27	NC	Taicang	1 Mar
1:33:42	46:14	Antigóni	Drisbióti	GRE	21.3.84	31	WCh	Moskva	13 Aug
1:33:43	46:18	Neringa	Aidietyte	LTU	5.6.83	5		Alytus	14 Jun
1:33:48			Xu Yaozhi	CHN	20.5.90	28	NC	Taicang	1 Mar
1:33:48			Wang Di	CHN	30.8.92	11	NG	Shenyang	11 May
(100)									

Mark	Name		Nat	Born	Date
1:33:49	Sandra	Galvis (46:25)	COL	28.6.86	13 Aug
1:33:51	Maria	Michta	USA	23.8.86	13 Aug
1:33:55		Wang Tingting	CHN	18.1.87	1 Mar
1:33:57	Kimberley	García (46:36)	PER	19.10.93	13 Aug
1:33:58		Xiao Junying	CHN	16.6.92	1 Mar
1:34:03	Regan	Lamble (46:10)	AUS	14.10.91	1 Mar
1:34:07		Liu Ke	CHN	2.10.90	1 Mar
1:34:07	Laura	Polli	SUI	7.9.83	13 Aug
1:34:11		Zhang Xin	CHN	17.8.89	1 Mar
1:34:11		Xie Lijuan	CHN	14.5.93	12 May
1:34:13	Jessica	Rothwell	AUS	18.6.89	1 May
1:34:18	Olga S	uranova (45:28)	RUS	7.12.86	23 Feb
1:34:23	Olga	Dubrovina	RUS	11.6.93	23 Feb
1:34:27		Huang Jing	CHN	28.2.88	1 Mar
1:34:28	Khushbir	Kaur (46:42)	IND	9.7.93	13 Aug
1:34:29	(46:33)	Jeon Yong-eun	KOR	24.5.88	13 Aug
1:34:32	Tanya	Holliday	AUS	21.9.88	24 Feb
1:34:34		Zhu Dan	CHN	27.1.93	1 Mar
1:34:36		Song Meiying	CHN	8.9.89	1 Mar
1:34:37	Anita	Kazemaka	LAT	30.5.90	13 Aug
1:34:38	Erin	Gray (46:33)	USA	15.5.87	13 Aug
1:34:53	Rachel	Tallent	AUS	20.2.93	1 Mar
1:34:57	Alina	Matveyuk	BLR	29.7.90	13 Apr
1:34:58	Irina	Shushina	RUS	30.10.86	23 Feb
1:35:03		Dong Genmiao	CHN-J	16.7.94	1 Mar
1:35:03		Saw Mar Lar Nwe	MYA	6.1.81	15 Dec
1:35:05A	Grace	Wanjiru	KEN	10.1.79	11 May
1:35:08		Mao Jie	CHN-J	12.2.94	1 Mar
1:35:10		Li Ping	CHN-J	7.1.94	1 Mar
1:35:17	Anne	Halkivaha	FIN	9.2.86	28 Apr
1:35:19		He Qinqin	CHN	21.6.90	1 Mar
1:35:22		Ma Faying	CHN	30.8.93	1 Mar
1:35:26	Nguyen	Thi Thanh Phuc	VIE	12.8.90	10 Mar
1:35:28	Tomomi	Maekawa	JPN	28.9.91	17 Feb
1:35:29		Ma Yimei	CHN-J	29.4.94	1 Mar
1:35:30	Maria	Czaková	SVK	2.10.88	17 Mar
1:35:34	Anna	Krakhmaleva	RUS	1.5.92	23 Feb
1:35:37A	Wendy	Cornejo	BOL	7.1.93	25 May
1:35:39	Ai	Michiguchi	JPN	3.6.88	17 Mar
1:35:39	Galina	Kireyeva	RUS	11.10.91	23 Feb
1:35:43		Yang Lei	CHN-J	29.11.95	1 Mar
1:35:44	Lizbeth	Silva	MEX	30.9.89	21 Apr
1:35:46	Cheryl	Webb	AUS	3.10.76	24 Feb
1:35:47		Weon Ases-byeol	KOR	8.4.90	1 Mar
1:35:54		Xu Haiyang	CHN	19.3.93	1 Mar
1:35:58	Halyna	Yakovchuk	UKR	21.2.92	2 Mar
1:35:58	Rei	Inoue	JPN	23.7.91	10 Mar
1:35:58	Ángela	Castro	BOL	21.2.93	28 Nov
1:36:06		Li Maocuo	CHN	20.10.92	1 Mar
1:36:14	Anna	Yeremina	RUS	24.6.93	8 Jun
1:36:16A	Arabelly	Orjuela	COL	24.7.88	23 Feb
1:36:22		Yang Kaixuan	CHN	2.8.92	1 Mar
1:36:26		Kim Mi-jung	KOR	10.6.79	22 Oct
1:36:31	Marie	Polli	SUI	28.10.80	13 Aug
1:36:37	Ayman	Kozhakhmetova ¶	KAZ	23.4.91	10 Jul
1:36:38	Émilie	Tissot	FRA	11.4.93	19 May
1:36:42		Kang Bin	CHN	8.1.92	1 Mar
1:36:50	Claudia	Stef	ROU	25.2.78	23 Mar
1:36:51	Chiaki	Asada	JPN	21.1.91	17 Feb
1:36:52	Valentina	Trapletti	ITA	12.7.85	13 Apr
1:36:58	Maria	Gáliková	SVK	21.8.80	13 Apr
1:37:00		Yang Peili	CHN-J	7.8.94	1 Mar
1:37:00	Georgiana	Enache	ROU	19.2.91	23 Mar
1:37:02	Eva María	Iglesias	ESP	10.6.85	3 Mar
1:37:02	María Guadaloupe González	MEX	9.1.89	21 Apr
1:37:03		Zhang Shasha	CHN	4.12.92	1 Mar
1:37:05	Nadyezhda	Dorozhuk	BLR	23.1.90	13 Apr
1:37:07	Magaly	Bonilla	ECU	8.2.92	28 Nov
1:37:08		Wang Chen	CHN-J	18.2.94	1 Mar
1:37:08		Yang Liu	CHN	26.2.92	1 Mar
1:37:09		Wang Jiaojiao	CHN	11.12.93	1 Mar
1:37:12		Li Wanfang	CHN	5.1.93	1 Mar
1:37:13		Wang Zhenzhen	CHN-J	3.2.95	1 Mar
1:37:15		Cao Hua	CHN-J	14.6.95	1 Mar
1:37:16		Zhuang Chunli	CHN-J	7.3.94	1 Mar
1:37:16		Mu Juan	CHN	20.6.89	1 Mar
1:37:21A	Rosalía	Ortiz	MEX	3.9.87	23 Feb
1:37:25		Wang Yalan	CHN	19.2.93	20 Sep
1:37:27		Geng Shasha	CHN-Y	7.2.96	1 Mar
1:37:33		Ma Yue	CHN-J	2.2.94	1 Mar
1:37:34	Federica	Curiazzi	ITA	14.8.92	10 Jul
1:37:38.8t	Violaine	Averous	FRA	15.3.85	11 Nov
1:37:39	Sibilla	Di Vincenzo	ITA	22.1.83	1 Jun
1:37:47	Yumi	Nemoto	JPN	14.12.93	17 Feb
1:37:48	Lyudmyla	Shelest	UKR	4.10.74	2 Mar
1:37:51	Cristina	López	ESA	19.9.82	20 Jan
1:37:52	Déspina	Zapounídou	GRE	5.10.85	30 Mar
1:37:53A	Yeseida	Carrillo	COL	22.10.93	25 May
1:37:54A	Emily	Ngii	KEN	13.8.86	11 May
1:37:55		Yang Yawei	CHN	16.10.83	12 May
1:37:58	Miranda	Melville	USA	20.3.89	17 Mar
(191)					

Best track times

Mark		Name		Nat	Born	Pos	Meet	Venue	Date
1:32:31.7At		Lorena	Arenas	COL	17.9.93	1		Medellín	6 Oct
1:37:37.7At		Wendy	Cornejo	BOL	7.1.93	1	NC	Cochabamba	4 May

Unofficial

Mark	Name		Nat	Born	Date
1:34:38	Lizbeth	Silva	MEX	30.9.89	25 Apr
1:36:04	Alejandra	Ortega	MEX-J	8.7.94	25 Apr

Drugs disqualification

Mark	Name		Nat	Born	Pos	Meet	Venue	Date
1:33:00	Ayman	Kozhakhmetova ¶	KAZ	23.4.91	(27)	WCh	Moskva	13 Aug

Mark	Name	Nat	Born	Pos	Meet	Venue	Date

JUNIORS

See main list for top 10 juniors. 10 performances by 8 women to 1:33:00. Additional marks and further juniors:

Mark		Name	Nat	Born	Pos	Meet	Venue	Date
A Drahotová	1:30:54 7	Lugano		17 Mar				
Su Yingqiu	1:32:15 5	NC-j		Taicang		1 Mar		
Mao Yanxue	1:32:24 9	NG Shenyang				11 May		
1:35:03		Dong Genmiao	CHN	16.7.94	10	NC-j	Taicang	1 Mar
1:35:08		Mao Jie	CHN	12.2.94	11	NC-j	Taicang	1 Mar
1:35:10		Li Ping	CHN	7.1.94	12	NC-j	Taicang	1 Mar
1:35:29		Ma Yimei	CHN	29.4. 94	13	NC-j	Taicang	1 Mar
1:35:43		Yang Lei	CHN	29.11.95	14u2	NC	Taicang	1 Mar
1:37:00		Yang Peili	CHN	7.8.94	15	NC-j	Taicang	1 Mar
1:37:08		Wang Chen	CHN	18.2.94	16	NC-j	Taicang	1 Mar
1:37:13		Wang Zhenzhen	CHN	3.2.95	17	NC-j	Taicang	1 Mar
1:37:15		Cao Hua	CHN	14.6.95	18	NC-j	Taicang	1 Mar
1:37:16	(20)	Zhuang Chunli	CHN	7.3.94	19	NC	Taicang	1 Mar

Transfer of Nationality/Allegiance

Name	From	To	Noted	Eligible
Men				
Annouar Assila	MAR	FRA	5.9.13	21.10.13
Zelalem Bacha (Regasa)	ETH	BRN	13.2.13	12.2.14
Ray Bobrownicki	USA	GBR	11.3.14	
Josphat Boit	KEN	USA	28.9.12	21.3.14
Jamel Chatbi	MAR	ITA	16.10.10	19.7.13
Abdelhadi El Hachimi	MAR	BEL	1,6,12	31.5.13
Takeshi Fujiwara	ESA	JPN	8.3.13	
Ignisious Gaisah	GHA	NED	12.6.13	26.7.13
Marouane Habti	MAR	BRN	23.4.13	22.4.14
Sébastien Hoffelt	BEL	LUX	22..3.12	27.11.13
Dimítrios Hondroúkis	GRE	CYP	25.5.12	26.11.13
Isaac Korir Kedikou	KEN	BRN	14.2.13	13.2.14
Nelson Cherutich Kipkogei	KEN	BRN	13.2.13	12.2.14
Linus Kiplagat	KEN	BRN	13.2.13	12.2.14
Eddie Lovett	USA	IVB	6.7.13	
Ion Luchianov	MDA	RUS	.12.13	
Kevin Moore	AUS	MLT	27.5.13	
Stephan Mozia	USA	NGR	2.3.14	
Aron Rono	KEN	USA	26.2.13	14.6.13
Albert Rop	KEN	BRN	2.4.13	1.4.14
Abraham Kipchirchir Rotich	KEN	BRN	2.4.13	1.4.14
Benson Seurei	KEN	BRN	2.4.13	1.4.14
Homiyu Tesfaye	ETH	GER	28.6.13	
Delano Williams	TKS	GBR	18.6.13	
John Woods	USA	AUS	28.2.12	21.6.13
Alex Wright	GBR	IRL	2.1.14	1.1.15
Rabah Yousif	SUD	GBR	23.1.13	13.6.13
Liam Zamel Paez	AUS	IRL	31.1.14	31.1.15
Women				
Jackie Areson	USA	AUS	30.6.13	
Meraf Bahta	ERI	SWE	14.1.14	20.1.14
Jenifer Clayton	USA	PAN	1.6.13	
Nichole Denby	USA	NGR	2.3.14	
Dariya Derkach	UKR	ITA	28.3.13	4.6.13
Eleni Gebrehiwot	ETH	GER	.2.14	
Jessica Gelibert	USA	HAI	1.8.13	
Sifan Hassan	ETH	NED	19.11.13	29.11.13
Tameka Jameson	USA	NGR	2.3.14	
Hanna Knyazyeva	UKR	ISR	12.5.13	12.6.13
Yvette Lewis	USA	PAN	25.10.12	
Anaelle Nyabeu Djapa	CMR	FRA	5.2.13	
Yadisleidy Pedroso	CUB	ITA	7.2.13	13.12.13
Jennifer Rockwell	USA	ITA		

Recent women's name changes

Original	Married name
Linda Allen AUS	Leverton
Gabriele Anderson USA	Grunewald
Burcu Ayhan TUR	Yüksel
Sirine Balti TUN	Ebondo
Molly Beckwith USA	Ludlow
Olga Bludova KAZ	Safronova
Lauren Boden AUS	Wells
Desiree Davila USA	Linden
Sharon Day USA	Monroe
Svetlana Denyayeva RUS	Biryukova
Maauan Furman ISR	Shahaf
Yekaterina Gorbunova RUS	Ishova
Clara Grandt USA	Santucci
Johanna Jackson GBR	Atkinson
Yekaterina Kayukova RUS	Chernenko
Jarmila Klimesová CZE	Junkovicová
Sophie Krauel GER	Poser
Sabrina Moran USA	Little
Claire Navez FRA	Perraux
Vera Neuenswander USA	Schmitz
Svetlana Podosyonova RUS	Karamasheva
Wenda Theron RSA	Nel
Kseniya Vdovina RUS	Ryzhova
Anna Yaroshchuk UKR	Ryzhykova
Angelina Zhuk RUS	Krasnova

See also list of recent marriages on page 443

Change of name and nationality

Men

Sheryf El-Sheryf UKR	Seref Osmanoglu TUR	3.6.13	2.6.14
Ivan Hryshyn UKR	Irfan Yildirim TUR	15.8.11	12.3.13
Stanley Kiprotich Mukche KEN	Ali Kaya TUR	6.6.13	20.6.13
Amir Shaker SWE	Aneed Ameer Shakir IRQ	24.2.14	
Ioánnis-Yeóryios Smaliós GRE	Jiannios Smalios SWE	29.7.13	

WOMEN 2013

WORLD LIST TRENDS – MEN

This table shows the 10th and 100th bests in the year lists for the last seven years and 2004, with previous bests.

Men 10th Bests	Pre 2004	2004	2007	2008	2009	2010	2011	2012	2013
100m	9.98- 97	10.01	10.02	9.95	9.97	9.95	**9.89**	9.94	9.96
200m	**20.03**- 00	20.17	20.06	20.17	20.17	20.11	20.16	20.10	20.10
400m	**44.51**- 96	44.72	44.62	44.70	44.81	44.81	44.78	44.77	44.82
800m	**1:43.66**- 96	1:44.09	1:44.27	1:44.10	1:43.82	1:43.89	1:44.07	1:43.71	1:43.87
1500m	3:31.49- 01	**3:31.10**	3:32.13	3:32.16	3:31.90	3:32.20	3:31.84	3:31.61	3:31.94
5000m	**12:54.99**- 03	12:59.04	13:02.89	13:03.04	12:58.16	12:55.95	12:59.15	12:55.99	13:01.64
10000m	27:14.61- 03	27:05.14	**27:00.30**	27:08.06	27:15.94	27:17.61	26:52.84	27:03.49	27:21.50
Half Mar	60:20- 02	60:22	59:32	59:37	59:30	59:40	59:39	**59:15**	59:54
Marathon	2:06:48- 03	2:07:43	2:07:19	2:06:25	2:06:14	2:05:52	2:05:45!	**2:04:54**	2:05:16
3000mSt	**8:08.14**- 02	8:11.44	8:09.72	8:12.72	8:10.63	8:09.87	8:08.43	8:10.20	8:08.83
110mh	13.20- 98	13.22	13.19	13.24	13.21	13.28	13.23	13.13	13.18
400mh	48.25- 02	48.16	48.26	48.52	48.30	48.47	48.47	48.41	48.46
HJ	**2.36**- 88	2.32	2.34	2.34	2.33	2.32	2.33	2.32	2.34
PV	**5.90**- 98	5.81	5.83	5.81	5.80	5.80	5.80	5.73	5.80
LJ	**8.35**- 97	8.28	8.26	8.25	8.30	8.25	8.27	8.26	8.29
TJ	**17.48**- 85	17.41	17.39	17.43	17.41	17.29	17.35	17.31	17.26
SP	**21.63**- 84	21.14	20.87	21.19	20.99	21.29	21.16	21.14	21.09
DT	**68.20**- 82	66.73	66.61	67.91	66.19	66.90	67.21	67.50	65.98
HT	**81.88**- 88	80.90	80.00	80.58	79.48	78.73	79.27	79.56	79.16
JT	**87.12**- 96/97	85.83	84.35	85.05	84.24	85.12	84.81	84.72	84.61
Decathlon	**8526**- 98	8285	8298	8372	8406	8253	8288	8322	8390
20kmW	**1:18:30**- 05	1:19:30	1:19:34	1:19:15	1:19:55	1:20:36	1:19:57	1:19:20	1:19:36
50kmW	**3:41:30**- 05	3:44:42	3:44:26	3:45:21	3:41:55	3:47:54	3:44:03	**3:41:24**	3:43:38

Peak years shown in bold.

Men 100th Bests		2004	2007	2008	2009	2010	2011	2012	2013
100m	10.24- 00	10.26	10.25	10.23	10.22	10.26	10.21	**10.20**	10.21
200m	20.66- 99/00	20.67	20.66	20.67	20.68	20.71	20.63	**20.57**	20.60
400m	**45.78**- 00	45.86	45.91	45.89	45.86	45.92	45.91	45.79	45.87
800m	1:46.54- 99	1:46.67	1:46.99	1:46.70	1:46.88	1:46.76	1:46.50	1:46.56	**1:46.44**
1500m	3:38.42- 97	3:38.50	3:38.66	3:38.57	3:38.60	3:38.47	3:37.77	**3:36.84**	3:37.77
5000m	13:28.62- 00	13:25.52	13:27.48	13:25.05	13:26.90	13:25.88	13:26.29	**13:23.58**	13:27.29
10000m	28:15.98- 00	28:21.4	28:10.73	**28:04.47**	28:18.00	28:21.00	28:15.79	28:06.74	28:18.68
Half Mar	62:00- 00	62:06	61:54	61:50	**61:28**	61:38	61:31	**61:19**	61:25
Marathon	2:10:38- 03	2:11:13	2:10:43	2:10:22	2:09:53	2:09:31	2:09:19!	**2:08:32**	2:09:06
3000mSt	8:33.58- 03	**8:31.06**	8:32.94	8:32.12	8:35.21	8:35.29	8:35.45	8:31.2	8:34.42
110mh	13.72- 96	13.70	13.72	13.67	13.71	13.68	13.67	**13.66**	13.67
400mh	**50.06**- 00	50.14	50.28	50.33	50.35	50.41	50.28	50.15	50.16
HJ	**2.24**- 84/88/89/92/96	2.23	2.23	2.23	2.23	2.23	**2.24**	**2.24**	**2.24**
PV	**5.55**- 00	5.50	5.50	5.50	5.46	5.42	5.45	5.50	5.50
LJ	7.94- 96	**7.96**	7.90	7.93	7.94	7.91	7.94	7.93	7.92
TJ	**16.60**- 88	16.55	16.44	16.53	16.46	16.46	16.53	16.49	16.40
SP	19.48- 84	19.28	19.22	19.21	19.15	19.08	19.18	**19.51**	19.41
DT	**60.96**- 84	60.05	59.75	60.77	60.00	59.77	59.98	60.95	60.21
HT	**73.06**- 84	71.12	70.58	70.89	70.66	70.78	70.44	71.22	70.49
JT	77.14- 91	76.31	75.66	76.28	77.03	76.71	77.38	**77.78**	77.10
Decathlon	**7702**- 88	7572	7545	7594	7623	7526	7678	7648	7586
20kmW	**1:22:48**- 05	1:23:25	1:23:55	1:23:32	1:23:57	1:24:24	1:23:40	1:23:10	1:22:56
50kmW	4:03:49- 99	4:05:13	4:04:52	4:05:05	4:09:24	4:08:08	4:06:15	**4:03:04**	4:08:33

! From 2011 main marathon lists no longer include Boston or other such excessively downhill races

Number of athletes achieving base level standards for world lists:

Men		2008	2009	2010	2011	2012	2013			2008	2009	2010	2011	2012	2013
100m	10.29	154	161	133	166	198	188	HJ	2.20	180	184	194	192	216	197
200m	20.79	165	174	140	175	227	198	PV	5.40	153	151	138	139	177	179
400m	46.19	150	163	154	151	184	178	LJ	7.80	191	182	173	186	183	180
800m	1:47.59	173	154	169	198	220	190	TJ	16.30	167	123	139	142	144	120
1500m	3:39.99	139	141	152	170	201	185	SP	18.50	170	171	168	163	203	217
5000m	13:37.0	178	181	177	193	203	180	DT	58.00	172	164	156	155	177	166
10000m	28:35.0	227	159	157	172	199	168	HT	68.00	155	149	158	149	158	146
HMar	61:59	112	158	145	147	199	171	JT	74.00	152	166	168	173	199	190
Mar	2:10:59	129	160	175	215	233	212	Dec	7400	155	150	136	165	173	143
3000St	8:39.9	166	140	135	147	184	141	20kmW	1:25:00	147	136	124	154	175	175
110mh	13.89	172	171	196	194	214	199	50kmW	4:10:00	123	105	103	110	132	106
400mh	50.79	165	152	155	171	186	177	TOTAL		3695	3595	3545	3827	4386	4006

The 2013 numbers compared to those of 2012: for 10th best 4-17, 100th best -1-19 (1 tie), base level 2-20 (1 tie)

WORLD LIST TRENDS – WOMEN

This table shows the 10th and 100th bests in the year lists for the last seven years and 2004, with previous bests.

10th Bests	Pre 2004	2004	2007	2008	2009	2010	2011	2012	2013
100m	**10.92**- 88	11.04	11.04	10.95	11.04	11.08	11.01	10.99	10.93
200m	**22.24**- 88	22.46	22.49	22.43	22.45	22.49	22.55	22.37	22.40
400m	**49.74**- 84	50.19	50.16	50.11	50.27	50.43	50.67	50.06	50.19
800m	**1:56.91**- 88	1:57.96	1:58.61	1:57.9	1:58.80	1:58.67	1:58.21	1:57.77	1:58.92
1500m	**3:58.07**- 97	4:01.29	4:02.8	4:02.44	4:00.86	4:00.25	4:01.73	3:59.71	4:01.48
5000m	14:45.35- 00	14:44.81	14:45.22	14:43.89	14:41.62	**14:38.64**	14:39.44	14:50.80	14:47.12
10000m	31:01.07- 03	31:04.34	31:22.80	**30:39.96**	30:51.92	31:29:03	31:10.02	30:59.19	31:04.85
Half Mar	68:23- 00	68:52	68:28	68:51	68:14	67:52	68:07	67:42	**67:39**
Marathon	2:23:33- 02	2:24:27	2:24:23	2:24:14	2:25:06	2:23:44	2:22:43!	**2:20:57**	2:23:00
3000mSt	9:44:95- 03	9:39.84	9:26.63	9:21.76	**9:18.54**	9:24.84	9:25.96	9:23.52	9:27.49
100mh	12.67- 98	12.60	12.67	**12.58**	12.67	12.65	12.73	12.62	12.81
400mh	54.15- 99	**53.99**	54.14	54.45	54.49	54.58	54.69	54.21	54.38
HJ	**2.01**- 03	2.00	1.97	1.98	1.98	1.97	1.96	1.96	1.97
PV	4.60- 02/03	4.60	4.70	4.70	4.65	4.66	**4.71**	4.70	**4.71**
LJ	**7.07**- 88	6.83	6.89	6.89	6.87	6.89	6.88	6.97	6.91
TJ	14.76- 03	14.78	14.69	**14.84**	14.62	14.48	14.57	14.60	14.50
SP	**20.85**- 87	19.29	19.13	19.29	19.38	19.47	19.26	19.60	18.81
DT	**70.34**- 88	65.25	64.87	64.10	63.89	64.04	63.91	64.45	64.46
HT	71.12- 03	72.57	73.94	74.40	73.07	73.40	72.65	**75.59**	75.02
JT	64.89- 00	63.07	63.58	63.24	63.89	63.36	63.50	**64.91**	63.55
Heptathlon	**6540**- 88	6287	6327	6465	6323	6204	6338	6466	6345
20kmW	1:27:55- 01	1:27:52	1:28:51	1:27:18	1:28:50	1:29:20	1:28:41	**1:27:08**	1:27:53

Women 100th Bests									
100m	11.36- 00	11.38	11.37	11.36	11.41	11.40	11.36	**11.34**	11.35
200m	23.21- 00	23.20	23.27	**23.17**	23.26	23.27	23.21	**23.10**	23.19
400m	52.25- 00	52.14	52.14	**52.08**	52.44	52.52	52.33	52.16	52.25
800m	2:01.50- 84	2:01.98	2:02.25	2:02.50	2:02.13	2:02.14	2:01.86	**2:01.48**	2:02.05
1500m	4:10.22- 84	4:10.34	4:11.67	4:11.64	4:11.06	4:10.50	4:09.88	**4:09.06**	4:09.98
5000m	15:29.36- 00	**15:27.20**	15:33.90	15:27.50	15:37.31	15:37.45	15:31.67	15:32.88	15:35.74
10000m	32:32.47- 00	32:37.88	32:46.28	**32:30.10**	32:54.64	32:57.59	32:53.44	32:38.95	32:48.60
Half Mar	71:29- 01	71:44	71:15	71:19	70:57	70:59	71:06	70:48	**70:44**
Marathon	2:31:05- 01	2:31:53	2:31:25	2:29:53	2:30:08	2:29:36	2:28:32	**2:28:01**	2:29:10
3000mSt	10:23.76- 01	10:18.55	10:03.2	9:56.48	10:02.94	10:03.50	9:59.44	**9:53.79**	9:56.50
100mh	13.22- 00	13.26	13.25	13.22	13.28	13.23	13.16	**13.11**	13.19
400mh	57.48- 00	57.33	57.21	57.46	57.45	57.22	57.26	**57.14**	57.40
HJ	**1.88**- 86/87/88/92/93	1.87	1.87	1.86	1.86	1.87	1.86	1.87	1.87
PV	4.15- 03	4.20	4.22	4.25	4.21	4.25	4.30	**4.31**	4.30
LJ	6.53- 88	6.50	6.49	6.52	6.49	6.51	6.50	**6.55**	6.49
TJ	13.68- 00	13.70	13.64	**13.75**	13.65	13.67	13.70	13.71	13.69
SP	**17.19**- 87	16.76	16.54	16.49	16.43	16.46	16.60	16.82	16.65
DT	**58.50**- 92	55.15	55.92	55.43	56.06	55.05	56.12	56.94	55.70
HT	63.23- 03	63.73	64.34	64.81	63.77	64.12	64.79	**65.78**	64.65
JT	55.55- 00	55.09	55.07	54.81	55.16	54.98	55.34	**55.97**	55.10
Heptathlon	**5741**- 88	5631	5674	5687	5586	5568	5591	5702	5560
20kmW	1:34:11- 05	1:34:32	1:35:57	1:34:30	1:35:54	1:36:32	1:34:52	**1:33:43**	1:33:48

All-time record levels indicated in bold.

! From 2011 main marathon lists no longer include Boston or other such excessively downhill races.

Number of athletes achieving base level standards for world lists:

Women		2008	2009	2010	2011	2012	2013	Women		2008	2009	2010	2011	2012	2013
100m	11.50	202	185	171	195	217	208	400mh	58.44	177	179	169	181	228	193
200m	23.39	166	140	135	146	185	187	HJ	1.85	144	136	142	172	164	155
400m	52.99	199	169	167	187	210	196	PV	4.15	163	153	156	176	189	181
800m	2:03.50	147	153	153	176	196	166	LJ	6.35	205	181	180	185	212	171
1500m	4:13.5	124	154	152	161	197	167	TJ	13.30	189	183	182	191	199	184
5000m	15:45.0	178	136	139	163	201	167	SP	15.85	160	159	159	163	180	177
10000m	33:15.0	160	144	133	146	200	153	DT	53.65	154	139	144	153	172	159
HMar	72:00	143	173	156	174	199	204	HT	61.00	179	163	167	181	205	190
Mar	2:32:00	137	143	152	165	212	170	JT	53.00	158	154	151	160	177	159
3000mSt	10:12.0	150	147	144	177	200	191	Hep	5450	155	137	126	146	157	140
100mh	13.39	156	140	154	177	198	175	20kmW	1:38:00	155	137	123	167	173	191
								TOTAL		3654	3405	3355	3742	4270	3884

The 2013 numbers compared with those of 2012: for 10th best 4-17 (1 tie), 100th best 0-20 (1 tie), base level 3-19

Name		Nat	Born	Ht/Wt	Event	2013 Mark	Pre-2013 Best

Athletes included are those ranked in the top 100s at standard (World Championships) events (plus shorter lists for 1000m, 1M, 2000m and 3000m). Those with detailed biographical profiles are indicated in first column by:
* in this year's Annual, ^ featured in a previous year's Annual.

	Name	First	Nat	Born	Ht/Wt	Event	2013 Mark	Pre-2013 Best
	Abate	Emanuele	ITA	8.7.85	190/75	110h	13.49	13.28- 12
	Abbas	Ali Khamis	BRN-J	30.6.95	175/65	400	45.65	
	Abbott	Joe	USA	3.3.90	180/73	800	1:45.04	1:46.84- 11
	Abda	Harun	USA	1.1.90	178/64	800	1:46.38	1:46.65- 12
	Abdi	Bashir	BEL	10.2.89	168/59	10k	27:43.99	28:18.50- 12
	Abdi	Youcef	AUS	7.12.77	178/66	3kSt	8:33.74	8:16.36- 08
	Abe	Takatoshi	JPN	12.11.91	182/68	400h	49.57	49.46- 10
	Abele	Arthur	GER	30.7.86	184/80	Dec	8251	8269- 07
	Abera	Mulaku	ETH-J	20.4.94	177/61	10k	27:54.74	
	Abera	Tesfaye	ETH	31.3.92		HMar	61:06	60:32- 12
	Abinet	Abiyot	ETH	10.5.89	168/54	1500	3:34.06	3:36.07- 10
	Aboud	Rabah	ALG	1.1.81	169/54	5000	13:24.08	13:19.00- 11
	Abramchuk	Mikhal	BLR	15.11.92		SP	19.45	18.62- 12
	Abromavicius	Aleksas	LTU	6.12.84	197/115	DT	63.09	63.32- 10
*	Abshero	Ayele	ETH	28.12.90	167/52	Mar	2:06:57	2:04:23- 12
	Acea	Raidel	CUB	31.10.90	188/77	800	1:46.05	1:45.62- 11
	Adams	Antoine	SKN	31.8.88	180/79	100	10.01, 10.00w	10.10- 12
						200	20.13A, 20.47, 20.25w	20.43, 20.41w- 12
^	Adams	Harry	USA	27.11.89	182/81	100	10.22, 9.97w	9.96- 12
						200	20.44w	20.10- 12
	Adams	Liam	AUS	4.9.86	178/65	10k	28:16.18	28:11.76- 12
*	Adams	Lyukman	RUS	24.9.88	194/87	TJ	16.82	17.53- 12
	Adams	Spencer	USA	10.9.89	188/84	110H	13.40, 13.24w	13.39, 13.38w- 12
	Adedoyin	Kola	GBR	8.4.91	183/73	TJ	16.50i	16.25- 12
	Adhana	Gebretsadik	ETH	16.7.92		Mar	2:09:00	2:06:21- 12
	Agbaje	Frederick	NGR	26.6.88	182/73	100	10.16w	10.39- 10
	Agoyev	Kiril	KAZ	13.6.90	170/69	LJ	8.01, 8.04w	7.71- 11
	Ahmed	Mohammed	CAN	5.1.91	180/61	10k	27:35.76	27:34.64- 12
	Aikines-Aryeetey	Harry	GBR	29.8.88	176/86	100	10.08	10.10 - 08, 10.09w- 11
*	Akdag	Tarik Langat	TUR	16.6.88	176/60	3kSt	8:20.08	8:08.59- 11
	Akins	Tyrone	USA	6.1.86	180/79	110h	13.50, 13.49w	13.25- 08, 13.2w- 10
	Akwu	Noah	NGR	23.9.90	179/73	400	45.59	45.95- 11
	Al-Dawoodi	Sultan M.	KSA	16.6.77	180/110	DT	64.25	65.08- 12
	Al-Dosari	Rashid	QAT	8.5.81	197/123	DT	61.91	64.43- 02
	Al-Gamal	Mostafa	EGY	1.10.88	191/96	HT	78.19	77.14- 12
	Al-Garni	Mohamed	QAT	1.7.92	178/66	1500	3:35.88	3:34.61- 11
	Al-Hebshi	Sultan	KSA	23.2.83	180/103	SP	19.68	21.13- 09
	Al-Mandeel	Abdulaziz	KUW	22.5.89	175/66	110h	13.66	13.58, 13.50w- 12
	Al-Mannai	Rashid Ahmed	QAT	18.6.88	187/75	TJ	16.40	16.02- 10
*	Al-Masrahi	Youssef	KSA	31.12.87	176/76	400	44.61	45.43- 12
	Al-Momani	Musaeb	JOR	28.8.86	184/110	DT	60.21	62.64- 12
^	Al-Sabee	Hussein	KSA	14.11.79	189/88	LJ	7.99	8.35, 8.41w- 04
	Al-Subaie	Fahad Mohamed	KSA-J	4.2.94		200	20.74, 20.55w	21.29, 21.03- 12
*	Al-Zankawi	Ali Mohamed	KUW	27.2.84	186/87	HT	76.68	79.74- 09
	Alaiz	Roberto	ESP	20.7.90	182/63	3kSt	8:25.34	8:24.53- 12
*	Alamirew	Yenew	ETH	27.5.90	175/57	3000	7:32.64	7:27.26- 11
						5000	12:54.95	12:48.77- 12
	Albertazzi	Eduardo	ITA	14.9.91	201/118	DT	62.39	62.80- 12
	Alejandro	Eric	PUR	15.4.86	180/70	400h	49.44	49.15- 12
*	Alekna	Virgilijus	LTU	13.2.72	200/130	DT	64.66	73.88- 00
	Alemayehu	Zebene	ETH	4.9.92	175/57	1500	3:33.73	3:34.59- 11
	Ali	Ahmed	USA	15.11.93	180/80	100	10.23, 10.12w	10.45w- 12
	Alic	Hamza	BIH	20.1.79	192/108	SP	20.73	20.56- 08
	Alonso	Carlos	ESP	15.9.89	180/63	1500	3:37.77	3:42.14- 12
	Alves	Higor	BRA-J	23.2.94		LJ	8.02	7.59, 7.96w- 12
*	Aman	Mohammed	ETH-J	10.1.94	169/55	800	1:42.37	1:42.53- 12
	Amb	Kim	SWE	31.7.90	180/85	JT	84.61	81.84- 12
	Amels	Douwe	NED	16.9.91	193/68	HJ	2.28	2.22i, 2.21- 12
	Ames	Brendan	USA	6.10.88	190/79	110h	13.62A, 13.77, 13.40w	13.39, 13.34w- 11
^	Amos	Nijel	BOT-J	15.3.94	179/60	400	45.66A	45.94- 12
						800	1:44.71	1:41.73- 12
	Amundgård	Fredrik	NOR	12.1.89	210/140	DT	60.92	63.72- 10
	Ananenko	Anis	BLR	29.11.85	176/65	800	1:44.43	1:45.59- 11
	Anani	Mohsen	EGY	25.5.85	187/117	HT	71.92	77.36- 10
*	Anderson	Jeshua	USA	22.6.89	187/84	400h	49.14	47.93- 11
	Anderson	Kenroy	JAM	27.6.87	172/64	100	10.16	10.18, 10.15w- 11

Name		Nat	Born	Ht/Wt	Event	2013 Mark	Pre-2013 Best
Anderson	Malcolm	USA	18.9.89	188/77	110h	13.57	13.65- 12
Anderson	Sabiel	JAM	21.6.88	198/82	110h	13.66A	14.04, 13.93Aw- 12
					400h	49.49A	49.82- 10
Andrade	Jordin	USA	5.5.92	183/73	400h	50.11	51.54- 12
* Andronov	Yuriy	RUS	6.11.71	180/68	50kW	3:43:54	3:40:46- 12
Anishchenkov	Nikita	RUS	25.7.92	188/80	HJ	2.25i	2.30- 11
Anne	Mame-Ibra	FRA	7.11.89	181/73	400	45.73	46.23- 12
Anou	Abderrahmane	ALG	29.1.91	172/60	1500	3:36.90	3:35.2 - 11
Antmanis	Vladimir	RUS	12.3.84	188/77	400h	49.47	49.71- 12
Antunovic	Bozidar	SRB	24.7.91	198/110	SP	20.02i, 18.95	19.85- 12
^ Apak ¶	Esref	TUR	3.1.82	185/115	HT	76.94	81.45- 05
April	Lusapho	RSA	24.5.82		Mar	2:08:32	2:09:25- 11
Arai	Hiroki	JPN	18.5.88	179/61	20kW	1:21:28	1:21:10- 12
					50kW	3:45:56	3:47:08- 12
Arai	Ryohei	JPN	23.6.91	182/86	JT	78.19	78.21- 11
* Araptany	Jacob	UGA	11.2.92	168/58	3kSt	8:16.43	8:14.48- 12
Arastu	Ali	USA	18.6.92	188/77	400h	49.37	49.43- 12
de Araújo	Luiz Alberto	BRA	27.9.87	190/90	Dec	7958	8276- 12
Araya	Edward	CHI	14.2.86	175/60	50kW	4:00:31A	4:02:03A- 12
Arbour	Patrick	CAN	17.3.88	195/97	Dec	7593	7088- 12
Arcilla	Francisco	ESP	14.1.84	171/62	20kW	1:22:23	1:23:06- 08
Arents	Mareks	LAT	6.6.86	190/90	PV	5.62	5.60- 12
Arévalo	Eider	COL	9.3.93	165/58	20kW	1:19:45	1:21:49- 12
* Arikan	Polat Kemboi	TUR	12.12.90	170/55	10k	28:17.26	27:38.81- 12
Arkhipov	Aleksey	RUS	7.12.88		50kW	4:00:37	4:17:44- 11
* Armstrong	Dylan	CAN	15.1.81	190/125	SP	21.45	22.21- 11
^ Arnold	Jake	USA	3.1.84	191/91	Dec	7689	8253- 10
Arnold	Mike	USA	13.8.90	190/84	PV	5.70	5.53A- 12
Arrhenius	Leif	SWE	15.7.86	192/120	SP	20.50	20.03- 12
					DT	63.09A	64.46- 11
Arrhenius	Niklas	SWE	10.9.82	192/125	SP	19.77i, 19.57	19.91i- 04, 19.79- 11
					DT	64.46A	66.22- 11
Arthur	Jon	USA	.90		SP	19.42	18.55- 12
Artis-Gray	Jeffrey	USA	13.8.90	184/77	LJ	7.87i, 7.94w	7.60- 12
Arzandeh	Mohammad	IRI	30.10.87	180/76	LJ	8.00	8.17- 12
* Ashmeade	Nickel	JAM	7.4.90	184/87	100	9.90	9.93- 12
					200	19.93	19.85- 12
Ashomko	Aleksandr	BLR	18.2.84	186/92	JT	77.92	84.27- 08
Asmerom	Yared	ERI	3.2.79	171/58	Mar	2:08:22	2:07:27- 11
Assefa	Abrhe Milaw	ETH	.88		Mar	2:09:00	2:20:54- 11
Assefa	Habtamu	ETH	29.3.85		HMar	61:05	61:09-12
					Mar	2:08:28	2:10:55- 12
Atanasov	Zlatozar	BUL	12.12.89	191/77	TJ	17.09	16.73- 12
Atici	Hüseyin	TUR	3.5.86	188/118	SP	19.59i, 19,53	20.42- 12
^ Atkins	Derrick	BAH	5.1.84	185/84	100	10.06	9.91, 9.83w- 07
Atnafu	Yitayal	ETH	20.1.93	172/55	5000	13:19.45	13:04.18i, 13:08.13- 12
Augustyn	Lukasz	POL	29.11.90	180/70	50kW	4:04:42	-0-
Augustyn	Rafal	POL	14.5.84	178/71	20kW	1:21:13	1:20:53- 12
					50kW	3:51:33	3:46:56- 11
Aurokium	Jean-François	FRA	14.4.81	192/92	DT	61.44	62.38- 10
Austin	Justin	USA	8.10.89	186/80	200	20.53, 20.33w	20.46, 20.31w- 11
Auzeil	Bastien	FRA	22.10.89	190/82	Dec	8022	8008- 12
* Avan	Fatih	TUR	1.1.89	183/90	JT	84.58	85.60- 12
^ Avramenko ¶	Roman	UKR	23.3.88	185/90	JT	84.48	84.30- 11
Ayalew	Aweke	BRN	23.3.93		5000	13:05.00	14:18.8A- 11
Aydamirov	Yevgeniy	RUS	11.5.87	183/100	HT	72.49	74.92- 10
Ayeko	Thomas	UGA	10.2.92	168/58	10k	27:40.96	27:43.22- 12
Ayele	Abayneh	ETH	4.11,87	175/57	10k	27:57.51	-0-
^ Bába	Jaroslav	CZE	2.9.84	196/82	HJ	2.31i, 2.27	2.37i, 2.36- 05
Bacha	Megersa	ETH	18.1.85		Mar	2:06:56	2:08:55- 11
Bacha Regassa	Zelalem	BRN	10.1.88		5000	13:17.89	13:38.58- 11
^ Badji	Ndiss Kaba	SEN	21.9.83	192/79	LJ	8.10A, 8.01, 8.11Aw	8.32- 09
Bahner	Austin	USA	7.7.91	188/81	Dec	7847w, 7744	7188- 12
Bai Xuejin		CHN	6.6.87	176/63	50kW	4:03:11	3:54:41- 05
Bailey	Oshane	JAM	9.8.89	168/64	100	10.12	10.11- 10, 10.06w- 12
* Bailey	Ryan	USA	13.4.89	193/100	100	10.10, 10.00w	9.88- 10
* Bailey-Cole	Kemar	JAM	10.1.92	193/83	100	9.93	9.97- 12
Baillio	Hayden	USA	22.7.91	186/141	SP	19.63i, 18.90	19.92- 12
Baji	Balázs	HUN	9.6.89	192/84	110h	13.36	13.50- 12
Balla	Abdulrahman Musaeb	QAT	19.3.89	175/60	800	1:43.93	1:45.19- 12
Balner	Michal	CZE	12.9.82	193/78	PV	5.68	5.76i, 5.73- 10

Name		Nat	Born	Ht/Wt	Event	2013 Mark	Pre-2013 Best
Balnuweit	Erik	GER	21.9.88	189/75	110h	13.44, 13.32w	13.46- 11
Baloyes	Bernardo	COL-J	6.1.94	177/66	200	20.46A, 20.71, 20.54w	20.48A, 20.87- 12
Baltaci	Özkan	TUR-J	13.2.94	187/111	HT	70.61	68.55- 11
Bamba	Aboubacar	FRA	20.6.91	190/70	TJ	16.67	16.43- 12
Banevicius	Sarunas	LTU	10.11.91	188/105	SP	19.50	18.44i, 17.89- 11
* Baniótis	Konstadínos	GRE	6.11.86	202/80	HJ	2.34	2.32i- 11, 2.28- 09
^ Bannister ¶	Jarrod	AUS	3.10.84	190/100	JT	79.99	89.02- 08
Banzeruk	Ivan	UKR	9.2.90	177/65	50kW	3:47:35	3:56:20- 12
Barák	Václav	CZE	22.10.90	178/73	400h	49.95	50.04- 12
Barber	Shawn	CAN-J	27.5.94	190/82	PV	5.71	5.58i, 5.57- 12
Barid	Driss	MAR	12.12.86		HT	70.73	70.12- 11
Barnaby	Daundre	CAN	9.12.90	189/75	400	45.47	45.67- 12
Barnes	Winston	JAM	7.11.88	178/73	100	10.14	10.16- 09
Barr	Thomas	IRL	24.7.92	183/73	400h	49.78	50.06- 11
Barrett	DeWayne	JAM	26.9.81	185/75	400	45.75	45.63- 11
Barrios	Juan Luis	MEX	24.6.83	175/63	3000	7:45.12	7:37.64- 06
10k	27:57.69		27:28.82- 12		HMar	61:21	61:48- 08
* Barrondo	Érick	GUA	14.6.91	172/60	20kW	1:20:25	1:18:25- 12
					50kW	3:41:09	3:44:59- 12
* de Barros	Bruno	BRA	7.1.87	178/70	100	10.22, 10.17w	10.16- 09, 10.1- 06
					200	20.24	20.16- 11
Barry	Trevor	BAH	14.6.83	190/77	HJ	2.25	2.32- 11
* Barshim	Mutaz Essa	QAT	24.6.91	192/70	HJ	2.40	2.39- 12
* Barsoton	Leonard	KEN-J	21.10.94	166/56	5000	13:19.04	13:26.84- 12
					10k	27:33.13	
^ Bartels	Ralf	GER	21.2.78	186/138	SP	20.16i, 20.13	21.44i- 10, 21.37- 09
Barusei	Geoffrey	KEN-J	.94	164/53	1500	3:37.05	3:33.39- 12
2000	4:59.52				3000	7:44.32+	7:52.02- 12
Bascou	Dimitri	FRA	20.7.87	182/79	110h	13.51	13.34- 12, 13.26w- 11
Bat-Ochir	Serod	MGL	7.10.81	169.59	Mar	2:09:00	2:11:05- 12
Batchelor	Tarik	JAM	22.3.90	188/82	TJ	16.53i	16.52- 11
Batson	Diondre	USA	13.7.92	188/75	100	10.06, 10.10w	10.27, 10.10w- 12
					200	20.52, 20.35w	20.50- 12
Bayer	Andrew	USA	3.2.90	180/60	1500	3:34.47	3:37.24- 12
1M	3:52.90	3:57.75i- 11	2000	4:59.99		-0-	3000	7:43.84	7:48.35i- 11
* Bayer	Sebastian	GER	11.6.86	189/79	LJ	8.04	8.71i, 8.49- 09
Beach	Curtis	USA	22.7.90	183/76	Dec	8011 (w)	8083- 11
Bean	Cameron	USA	17.12.86		3kSt	8:32.57	8:37.28- 12
Bechert	Tom	GER	2.7.87	190/89	Dec	7767	7528- 11
Bedford	James	GBR	29.12.88	186/110	HT	70.82	70.68- 12
Behailu	Ketema	ETH			HMar	60:53	
* Behrenbruch	Pascal	GER	19.1.85	196/96	Dec	8514	8558- 12
Bekele	Alemu	BRN	23.3.90	163/50	5000	13:18.00	13:21.54- 12
Bekele	Feyisa	ETH	4.8.83	170/55	Mar	2:09:05	2:06:26- 12
* Bekele	Kenenisa	ETH	13.6.82	162/54	5000	13:07.88	12:37.35- 04
10k	27:12.08		26:17.53- 05		HMar	60.09dh	-0-
* Bekele	Tariku	ETH	21.1.87	168/52	3000	7:43.98	7:28.70- 10
5000	13:13.61		12:52.45- 08		10k	27:38.15	27:03.24- 12
* Bekric	Emir	SRB	14.3.91	196/87	400h	48.05	49.21- 12
Belay	Shimelis	ETH			HMar	60:58	-0-
Belharbazi	Othmane	FRA	3.11.88	174/57	1500	3:35.93	3:36.09- 11
Bell	Javere	JAM	20.9.92	184/73	400	45.08	45.78- 12
Bellani	Hicham	MAR	15.9.79	180/64	5000	13:26.31	12:55.52- 06
Ben-Yahia	Amor	TUN	1.7.85	176/54	3kSt	8:14.05	8:22.70- 12
Benard	Chris	USA	4.4.90	190/74	TJ	16.78	16.74- 12
Benedetti	Giordano	ITA	22.5.89	189/67	800	1:44.67	1:45.34- 12
Beneke	Piet C	RSA	18.7.90	190/79	400h	49.18	50.30A- 12, 50.42- 11
Benferare	Mohamed Amine	MAR	16.2.91		800	1:46.07	1:47.89- 12
Benhanbel	Nader	MAR-J	1.7.94		800	1:45.69	1:49.32- 12
Bennett	Chris	GBR	17.12.89	188/115	HT	71.24	68.84- 11
Bensghir	Yassine	MAR	3.1.83	170/68	1500	3:35.51	3:33.04- 07
Berch	Rolando	JAM	8.9.90	190/73	400	45.82A	46.83- 12
Berdeja	Cristian	MEX	21.6.81	169/58	50kW	4:07:14A	3:52:18A- 12
Berger	Dominic	USA	19.5.86	181/79	110h	13.44, 13.33w	13.32- 11
Bergius	Jere	FIN	4.4.87	182/72	PV	5.60	5.72- 12
Bernard	Koech	KEN	31.1.88		HMar	59:54	59:10- 12
Berry	Brien	USA	23.4.93		100	10.19w	10.36- 12
Berry	Michael	USA	10.12.91	184/73	400	45.14	44.75- 12
Bertocchi	Masimo	CAN	27.9.85	195/85	Dec	7878	8053- 09
Beshir	Anas	EGY	19.7.93	188/77	400	45.79	
* Bett	Emmanuel	KEN	30.3.83	170/55	10k	27:28.71	26:51.16- 12

Name		Nat	Born	Ht/Wt	Event	2013 Mark			Pre-2013 Best
* Bett	Josphat	KEN	12.6.90	173/60	5000	13:19.46			12:57.43- 09
					10k	27:44.26A			26:48.99- 11
Bett	Nicholas	KEN	.92		400h	49.70A			50.39- 11
Bett	Reuben	KEN	6.11.84	180/70	800	1:46.40			1:44.79- 09
^ Bezabeh	Alemayehu	ESP	22.9.86	182/53	5000	13:14.91			12:57.25- 10
Bian Fongda		CHN	1.4.91	170/58	20kW	1:19:34			1:22:42- 11
Bigot	Quentin	FRA	1.12.92	179/95	HT	76.97			78.28- 12
Bingham	Michael	GBR	13.4.86	183/75	400	45.37			44.74- 09
Bird-Smith	Dane	AUS	15.7.92		20kW	1:22:03			1:23:15- 12
* Birech	Jairus	KEN	15.12.92	165/54	3000	7:41.83			
					3kSt	8:08.72			8:03.43- 12
* Birgen	Bethwel	KEN	6.8.88	178/64	1500	3:30.77			3:31.00- 12
1M	3:50.42				3:50.43- 12	3000	7:37.15		7:39.65- 10
Birmingham	Collis	AUS	27.12.84	189/71	1500	3:37.18			3:35.50- 10
3000	7:41.02	7:35.45- 12			10k	27:56.22	27:29.73- 09	HMar	60:56	61:25dh- 12
Bispo	Rogério	BRA	16.11.85	180/75	LJ	7.92, 8.13w			8.21, 8.32Aw- 06
Biwott	Robert	KEN-Y	28.1.96		1500	3:36.77			
* Biwott	Stanley	KEN	21.4.86		HMar	58:56			59:44- 12
					Mar	2:08:39			2:05:12- 12
Biwott	Yusuf	KEN	12.11.86	175/64	HMar	60:33			-0-
Black	Ronnie	USA	2.8.90		HJ	2.26i, 2.25			2.22i, 2.21- 12
Blackwood	Jodi-Rae	JAM	6.3.91	181/73	400h	50.16			51.47- 12
Blair	Montez	USA	23.10.90	190/77	HJ	2.27i, 2.25			2.22i- 11, 2.22- 12
Blankenship	Ben	USA	15.12.88	173/61	1500	3:37.03			3:37.23- 11
Blankenship	Jake	USA-J	15.3.94	180/75	PV	5.61			5.34i- 12, 5.20- 11
* Bledman	Keston	TTO	8.3.88	183/75	100	10.02, 9.86w			9.86, 9.85w- 12
Block	Dan	USA	8.1.91	193/109	SP	20.00i, 19.31			18.91i, 18.38- 12
					DT	61.07			59.64- 12
Blocki	Adrian	POL	11.4.90	173/63	50kW	3:50:48			3:54:41- 12
Blocki	Damian	POL	28.4.89	180/65	50kW	3:51:32			3:55:51- 12
Blom	Rens	NED	1.3.77	178/75	PV	5.51			5.81- 04
Boccalatte	Bruno	FRA	10.11.88	182/105	HT	72.57			69.70- 12
Bochenek	Dominik	POL	14.5.87	182/70	110h	13.72, 13.65w			13.44- 11, 13.3w- 10
Bogatyrev	Pyotr	RUS	11.3.91		20kW	1:19:36			1:20:18- 11
Bohdan	Maksym	UKR-J	27.2.94		JT	78.77			67.94- 12
Bojic	Nik	AUS	18.1.92		HJ	2.28			2.15- 12
Bolarinwa	David	GBR	20.10.93	178/72	200	20.60			20.69- 12
Bolas	John	USA	1.11.87	183/72	1500	3:35.54			3:36.33- 12
Bologo	Innocent	BUR	5.9.89	172/73	100	10.05w			10.42- 11
* Bolt	Usain	JAM	21.8.86	196/88	100	9.77			9.58- 09
					200	19.66			19.19- 09
Bomba	Michael	GBR	10.10.86	188/110	HT	70.90			68.74- 12
Bonavacia	Liemarvin	CUR	5.4.89	190/79	400	45.84			45.60- 12
* Bondarenko	Bogdan	UKR	30.8.89	197/80	HJ	2.41			2.31- 12
Bonfim	Caio	BRA	19.3.91	170/58	20kW	1:22:14			1:20:58.5t- 11
Boni	Michele	ITA	2.4.81	194/86	TJ	16.65i, 16.23			16.61- 07
Bonvecchio	Norbert	ITA	14.8.85	183/82	JT	77.10			79.22- 12
Bor	Hillary	KEN	22.11.89	168/57	3kSt	8:32.41			8:35.12- 09
Boreysho	Pavel	BLR	16.2.91	193/105	HT	75.62			72.25- 12
* Borges	Lázaro	CUB	19.6.86	173/70	PV	5.71			5.90- 11
* Borlée	Dylan	BEL	20.9.92	179/66	400	45.80			47.93- 12
* Borlée	Jonathan	BEL	22.2.88	180/70	200	20.38			20.31- 12
					400	44.54			44.43- 12
* Borlée	Kévin	BEL	22.2.88	180/71	400	44.73			44.56- 12
Borodkin	Andriy	UKR	18.4.78	202/135	SP	19.53			20.38- 04
Bortoluzzi	Jérôme	FRA	20.5.82	180/111	HT	73.15			78.26- 12
* Borzakovskiy	Yuriy	RUS	12.4.81	182/72	800	1:45.24			1:42.47- 01
Bosko	Michal	POL	25.7.88	190/110	SP	19.49			19.26- 12
* Bosse	Pierre-Ambroise	FRA	11.5.92	185/68	800	1:43.76			1:44.97- 12
Bouchicha	Hichem	ALG	19.5.89		3kSt	8:20.11			8:35.69- 12
Bougtaïb	Tareq	MAR	30.4.81	180/75	TJ	16.66			17.37- 07
Boulama	Mohammed	MAR	31.12.93		3kSt	8:21.62			8:33.21- 12
Bouqantar	Soufiyan	MAR	30.8.93	173/54	5000	13:20.98			13:19.59- 12
Bourguignon	Rudy	FRA	16.7.79	185/82	Dec	7603 (w)			8025- 05
Bowen	Francis K.	KEN	12.10.73		Mar	2:08:53			2:08:01- 11
Boyce	Brendan	IRL	15.10.86	183/76	50kW	3:54:04			3:55:01- 12
Boyd	Marcus	USA	3.3.89	185/75	400	45.69			45.42- 11
Boylan-Pett	Liam	USA	11.9.85	180/64	1500	3:37.31			3:37.05- 12
* Bracy	Marvin	USA	15.12.93	178/74	100	10.09			10.25- 12, 10.05w- 11
Bran	Mario Alfonso	GUA	17.10.89		50kW	4:03:59			4:23:42- 12

Name		Nat	Born	Ht/Wt	Event	2013 Mark	Pre-2013 Best
Brannen	Nathan	CAN	8.9.82	175/59	1500	3:36.59	3:34.22- 12
					2000	4:59.56	
* Brathwaite	Ryan	BAR	6.6.88	186/75	110h	13.14, 13.13w	13.14, 13.05w- 09
Brathwaite	Shane	BAR	8.2.90	185/75	110h	13.44, 13.43w	13.31A, 13.46, 13.43w- 12
Braun	Aaron	USA	28.5.87	183/65	5000	13:22.37	13:20.25- 12
					10k	27:44.58	27:41.54- 12
Bray	Wesley	USA	11.4.88	180/80	Dec	7718	7932(w)- 12
* Braz da Silva	Thiago	BRA	16.12.93	193/84	PV	5.83	5.55- 12
Brits	Stefan	RSA	19.1.92		LJ	8.05	7.74A- 08
Brockman	Martin	GBR	13.11.87	197/92	Dec	7659	7712- 10
Bromell	Trayvon	USA-J	10.7.95	175/71	100	10.27, 9.99Aw	10.40- 12
Brookins	Ronald	USA	5.7.89	185/75	110h	13.61	13.42- 11
Brooks	Lance	USA	1.1.84	198/123	DT	64.02	65.15- 12
Broothaerts	Damien	BEL	12.11.84	180/74	110h	13.70, 13.63w	13.62- 09, 13.53w- 11
Brown	Aaron	CAN	27.5.92	185/79	100	10.05, 10.01w	10.18, 10.09w- 12
					200	20.44, 20.26w	20.42- 12
* Brown	Chris	BAH	15.10.78	178/68	400	45.18	44.40- 08
Brown	Jermaine	JAM	4.7.91	183/80	200	20.49	20.72- 12
^ Brown	Joel	USA	31.1.80	180/73	110h	13.51,13.44w	13.20- 11,13.18w- 09,13.1w- 10
Brown	Raymond	JAM	15.1.88	180/120	SP	20.13	19.41- 12
Brown	Rodney	USA	21.5.93	183/109	DT	62.88	58.12- 12
Brown	Russell	USA	3.3.85	188/77	1500	3:36.79	3:34.11- 12
Brown	Trevor	USA	24.3.92	183/79	110h	13.78, 13.55w	13.75- 12
Brown-Stewart	Cass	USA	2.8.92	173/66	400	45.62	46.17- 12
Broz	Michal	CZE	16.6.92	186/73	400h	49.78	50.91- 12
Brugger	Matthias	GER	6.8.92	192/93	Dec	7733	7942- 12
Bruintjies	Henricho	RSA	16.7.93	182/73	100	10.06w	
Brunson	Andrew	USA	4.4.86	182/75	110h	13.73, 13.50w	13.33- 08
Bryant	Ashley	GBR	17.5.91	180/82	Dec	8070	7837- 12
Bryant	Luke	USA	5.12.88	188/110	DT	62.63	62.70- 12
Brzozowski	Artur	POL	29.3.85	172/65	20kW	1:22:16	1:22:23- 09
Bubeniík	Matus	SVK	14.11.89	196/77	HJ	2.26i, 2.24	2.25i, 2.20- 12
Bucki	Gaëtan	FRA	9.5.80	195/135	SP	20.10	20.39i, 19.87- 11
Budza	Sergiy	UKR	6.12.84	180/72	50kW	3:47:36	3:53:02- 12
Bühler	Matthias	GER	2.9.86	189/74	110h	13.45	13.34- 12, 13.2w- 10
Bukhalov	Spas	BUL	14.11.80	186/85	PV	5.50	5.82- 07
Bulanov	Aleksandr	RUS	26.12.89	193/120	SP	19.92i, 19.81	19.47- 11
Bumbalough	Andrew	USA	14.3.87	173/64	3000	7:40.02	7:44.45i, 7:44.71 - 12
2M	8:13.02i	8:21.65- 11		5000	13:12.01	13:16.26- 12	10k	27:56.78	-0-
Buraas	Sindre	NOR	8.5.89	183/64	5000	13:15.91	13:28.07- 11
Burrell	Cameron	USA-J	11.9.94	173/68	100	10.07w	10.42- 12
Burton	Matthew	GBR	18.12.87	193/82	LJ	7.94i, 7.81, 7.84w	7.83- 12
Burya	Artem	RUS	11.4.86	185/82	PV	5.60	5.60- 12
Bustamante	Luis	MEX	10.6.84		50kW	3:59:07A	3:59:17A- 12
Bustos	David	ESP	25.8.90	182/65	1500	3:35.69	3:34.77- 12
					1M	3:53.40	
Butenko	Viktor	RUS	10.3.93	196/116	DT	65.97	57.32- 12
Butler	Kind	USA	8.4.89	183/75	400	45.50	45.43- 12
Butler	LaShawn	USA	3.2.87	178/77	200	20.50w	20.54, 20.52w- 11
Bybyk	Taras	UKR	27.3.92	179/64	800	1:46.20	1:48.51- 12
Bychkov	Igor	ESP	7.3.87	189/80	PV	5.65	5.60- 11
Byram	Brandon	USA	11.9.88	188/82	200	20.54, 20.12w	20.31- 10
Cabello	Diego	ESP	14.1.88	185/66	400h	49.96	50.48A, 50.49- 12
Cabral	Donn	USA	12.12.89	175/60	3kSt	8:34.23	8:19.14-12
Cabral	Johnathan	USA	31.12.92	193/82	110h	13.47, 13.33w	13.45- 12
* Cáceres	Eusebio	ESP	10.9.91	176/69	LJ	8.37	8.27- 10, 8.31w- 12
Cáceres	Jonnathan	ECU	20.1.90		50kW	3:56:58	4:14:45- 12
Cackett	Greg	GBR	14.11.89	178/75	200	20.78, 20.56w	21.07- 12
* Cadée	Erik	NED	15.2.84	200/110	DT	65.92	67.30- 12
* Cai Zelin		CHN	11.4.91	172/55	20kW	1:18:55	1:18:47- 11
Callender	Emmanuel	TTO	10.5.84	184/79	100	10.20w	10.05- 09
Camara	Alyn	GER	31.3.89	195/85	LJ	8.29	8.20- 12
Campion	Kevin	FRA	23.5.88	183/63	20kW	1:21:02	1:22:48- 11
Cano	Juan Manuel	ARG	12.12.87	168/57	20kW	1:22:46.5	1:22:10- 12
* Cantwell	Christian	USA	30.9.80	193/154	SP	20.13i, 19.86	22.54- 04
Cao Shuo		CHN	8.10.91	183/69	TJ	17.26	17.35- 12
Caporaso	Teodorico	ITA	14.9.87	166/60	50kW	3:56:45	3:59:19- 12
Capotosti	Leonardo	ITA	24.7.88	192/78	400h	50.06	50.49- 11
Cardoso	Wágner	BRA	20.3.89	182/73	400	45.80	46.42- 10
Carter	Chris	USA	11.3.89	186/80	TJ	16.69, 16.92w	16.86- 11
Carter	Deuce	JAM	28.9.90	182/75	110h	13.53	13.72- 11

Name		Nat	Born	Ht/Wt	Event	2013 Mark	Pre-2013 Best
* Carter	Nesta	JAM	11.10.85	178/70	100	9.87	9.78- 10
Carter	Ryan	USA	24.7.89		200	20.54w	20.88- 11
Carvalho	Florian	FRA	9.3.89	182/69	1500	3:33.47	3:33.60- 11
					3000	7:45.77i	7:48.62i- 12
Casado	Arturo	ESP	26.1.83	187/71	1500	3:36.33	3:32.70- 10
* Casañas	Frank	ESP	18.10.78	187/115	DT	66.16	67.91- 08
Castillejo	Carles	ESP	18.8.78	171/60	10k	27:57.92	27:39.79- 08
					HMar	61:18	62:37- 12
Castillo	Maurys Surel	CUB	19.10.84	182/60	800	1:45.10	1:44.89- 12
					1500	3:37.51	3:35.03- 12
Castro	Luis Joel	PUR	28.1.91	195/72	HJ	2.25	2.25A, 2.22- 12
Catania	Emanuele	ITA	3.10.88	182/68	LJ	7.96i, 7.92	7.85- 11
Cato	Roxroy	JAM	1.5.88	175/66	400h	49.15	49.03- 12
* Centrowitz	Matthew	USA	18.10.89	175/61	800	1:45.86	1:47.72- 12
1500	3:33.58		3:31.96- 12		1M	3:51.79, 3:51.34i	3:57.44- 12
Chalá	Emerson	ECU	2.8.91	175/68	400h	49.76	50.82A, 51.11- 12
Chalyy	Timothy	RUS-J	7.4.94	190/79	400h	49.23	50.80- 12
^ Chambers	Dwain	GBR	5.4.78	180/83	100	10.04, 10.02w	9.97- 99, 9.87dq- 02
Chaney	Clayton	USA	16.9.89	180/79	Dec	7678	7475- 12
Chang Ming-Huang		TPE	7.8.82	194/130	SP	19.89	20.58- 11
^ Charfreitag	Libor	SVK	11.9.77	191/117	HT	73.63	81.81- 03
Chatbi	Jamel	ITA	30.4.84	178/62	5000	13:27.08	13:41.93- 12
					3kSt	8:25.37	8:08.86- 09
Chavez	Richard	USA	.92	178/115	SP	20.06i	18.43- 12
Chávez	Arturo	PER	12.1.90	190/78	HJ	2.25	2.16A- 12
Chavkin	Nikolay	RUS	22.4.84	183/70	3kSt	8:31.84	8:22.81- 12
* Chebet	Wilson	KEN	12.7.85	174/59	Mar	2:05:36	2:05:27- 11
Chebii	Ezekiel	KEN	3.1.91		HMar	61:00	59:05- 12
* Cheboi	Collins	KEN	25.9.87	175/64	1500	3:31.53	3:32.08- 12
					1M	3:51.44	3:51.44- 12
Chelanga	Samuel	KEN	23.2.85	168/57	5000	13:20.07	13:09.67- 12
10k	27:46.06		27:08.39- 10		HMar	61:04	61:19- 12
Chelimo	Elijah	KEN	10.3.84	175/57	3kSt	8:19.07	8:10.63- 09
Chemlal	Jaouad	MAR-J	11.4.94		3kSt	8:19.22	8:25.98- 12
Chemlany	Stephen	KEN	9.8.82	175/59	Mar	2:07:44	2:07:55- 11
Chemosin	Robert	KEN	1.2.89		HMar	59:19	60:23- 12
Chemut	Anthony	KEN	17.12.92	170/57	800	1:44.33A	1:43.96A- 12
Chen Chieh		TPE	8.5.92	174/55	400h	49.90	49.68- 12
* Chen Ding		CHN	5.8.92	180/62	20kW	1:21:09	1:17:40- 12
Chen Ke		CHN	14.9.89		400h	50.11	50.36- 11
Chen Zongliang		CHN	9.1.92		20kW	1:22:54	1:22:30- 12
Cheng Wen		CHN	18.3.92	187/77	400h	49.66	49.28- 11
* Chepkok	Vincent	KEN	5.7.88	174/60	5000	13:15.51	12:51.45- 10
					10k	27:17.30	26:51.68- 12
Chepkwony	Frankline	KEN	15.6.84		HMar	60:11	
					Mar	2:06:59	2:06:11- 12
Cheprot	Simon	KEN	2.7.93	183/62	HMar	59:20	61:07- 12
* Chepseba	Nixon	KEN	12.12.90	185/66	1500	3:33.15	3:29.77- 12
					1M	3:50.95	3:53.36- 11
Cheroben	Abreham	KEN	10.11.92		HMar	60:38	63:53- 12
Cheru	Tesfaye	ETH	2.3.93	171/55	1500	3:35.67	3:35.71- 11
					3000	7:43.47i	7:54.76i- 12
* Cheruiyot	Ferguson	KEN	30.11.89	183/73	800	1:43.22	
Chesani	Silvano	ITA	17.7.88	190/75	HJ	2.33i, 2.13	2.31i- 12, 2.28- 11
Chesari	Jacob	KEN	6.4.84	170/55	Mar	2:07:46	-0-
Chesebe	Abednego	KEN	20.6.82	172/57	800	1:45.49A	
					1500	3:36.35	3:35.02A- 12
Chihuán	Pavel	PER	19.1.86		50kW	4:08:33	
* Chimsa	Deressa	ETH	21.11.86	175/62	Mar	2:07:05	2:05:42- 12
* Chinin	Carlos Eduardo	BRA	3.5.85	195/83	Dec	8393	8068- 11
Chmielak	Hubert	POL	19.6.89	188/88	JT	80.28	78.45- 12
Chocho	Andrés	ECU	4.11.83	167/57	20kW	1:21:26	1:20:23.8t- 11
					50kW	3:58:50	3:49:32- 11
* Choge	Augustine	KEN	21.1.87	162/53	1500	3:33.21	3:29.47- 09
1M	3:50.01		3:50.14- 10		3000	7:37.707:28.00i, 7:28.76- 11	5000	13:05.31	12:53.66- 05
Choi Byung-kwang		KOR	7.4.91	185/72	20kW	1:21:52	1:23:45- 12
Christensen	Kim	DEN	1.4.84	187/115	SP	19.67i, 19.38	20.39i, 20.06- 11
* Chu Yafei		CHN	5.9.88	172/55	20kW	1:21:52	1:18:38- 11
Churyla	Andrey	BLR	19.5.93	190/72	HJ	2.25	2.28- 12
Chuva	Marcos	POR	8.8.89	182/75	LJ	8.15	8.34- 11
Cienfuegos	Javier	ESP	15.7.90	193/134	HT	76.71	76.21- 12

Name		Nat	Born	Ht/Wt	Event	2013 Mark	Pre-2013 Best
* Cisneros	Omar	CUB	19.11.89	186/80	400h	47.93	47.99A- 11, 48.21- 10
Clark	Charles	USA	10.8.87	178/74	200	20.52	20.22- 08, 20.00w- 09
Clarke	Chris	GBR	25.1.90	176/70	200	20.22	20.65, 20.60w- 12
Clarke	Everton	JAM	.92	172/70	100	10.21	10.79- 12
Clarke	Jordan	USA	10.7.90	193/125	SP	20.59i, 20.28	20.86i, 20.40- 12
Clarke	Lerone	JAM	2.10.81	174/66	100	10.13w	9.99- 09, 9.90w- 11
^ Clavier	Jérôme	FRA	3.5.83	185/73	PV	5.62i	5.81i- 11, 5.75- 08
* Claye	Will	USA	13.6.91	180/68	LJ	8.10	8.29- 11
					TJ	17.52	17.70i, 17.62- 12
Cleaver	Matt	USA	7.11.89	175/64	3kSt	8:31.28	8:41.86- 12
Clemens	Daniel	GER	28.4.92	181/74	PV	5.60	5.50- 11
* Clement	Kerron	USA	31.10.85	188/84	400	45.74	44.48- 07
					400h	48.06	47.24- 05
Clemons	Kyle	USA	27.8.90	181/73	400	45.10	45.44- 12
Cobbo	Guilherme	BRA	1.10.87	185/65	HJ	2.25	2.28- 12
Cochrane	Mike	NZL	13.8.91	188/82	400h	50.07	50.62- 11
Cocioran	Marius	ROU	10.7.83	178/66	50kW	4:04:23	3:57:52- 12
* Coertzen	Willem	RSA	30.12.82	186/80	Dec	8343	8244- 12
Collazo	William	CUB	31.8.86	174/72	400	45.5	44.93- 09
Collie-Minns	Latario	BAH-J	10.3.94		TJ	16.44i, 16.41	16.64, 16.66w- 12
Collins	Davion	USA	3.10.92	176/73	200	20.53, 20.42w	21.26- 12
* Collins	Kim	SKN	5.4.76	175/64	100	9.97	9.98- 02, 9.92w- 03
Comito	Carter	USA	26.10.90	193/120	DT	62.00	59.41- 11
* Compaoré	Benjamin	FRA	5.8.87	189/86	TJ	17.07	17.31- 11
Connaughton	Jared	CAN	20.7.85	175/77	100	10.15w	10.15- 08, 10.04w- 11
Coover	Jeff	USA	1.12.87	185/77	PV	5.60	5.50i- 10, 5.50- 11
Copello	Yasmani	CUB	15.4.87	196/86	400h	49.89	49.56- 09
Corréa	Harold	FRA	26.6.88	190/78	TJ	16.94i, 16.92	16.76- 12
Cotton	Terrel	USA	19.7.88	182/73	200	20.41w	20.48A, 20.39Aw, 20.66- 12
Coulibaly	Toumany	FRA	6.1.88	190/80	400	45.84	45.74- 12
Cowart	Donnie	USA	24.10.85	170/60	3kSt	8:30.02	8:26.38- 11
Craddock	Kevin	USA	25.6.87	193/84	110h	13.42	13.42- 12, 13.41w- 08
Craddock	Omar	USA	26.4.91	178/79	TJ	16.92, 17.15w	16.75i, 16.71, 16.92w- 12
Cralle	Chris	USA	13.6.88	183/109	HT	74.55	74.36- 12
Cremona	Orazio	RSA	1.7.89	197/130	SP	20.55	19.76- 12
Cretinoir	Jean-Noël	FRA	28.12.94	178/64	TJ	16.34i, 16.25, 16.45w	15.78- 12
* Cronje	Johan	RSA	13.4.82	182/69	800	1:45.64	1:45.77- 06
1500	3:31.93		3:33.63- 09		1M	3:54.86	3:54.84- 09
Cross	Caleb	USA	31.5.91	181/73	400h	50.14	50.30- 12
* Crouser	Ryan	USA	18.12.92	201/109	SP	21.09	20.29i, 19.32- 12
Crouser	Sam	USA	31.12.91	196/102	JT	78.53	80.80- 12
Cuesta	Gustavo	DOM	14.11.88	183/80	400	45.45A, 45.87	45.78- 10
Cuesta	Pedro José	ESP	22.8.83	187/108	DT	61.01	61.95- 11
Cuevas	Winder	DOM	1.8.88	170/65	400h	49.66	49.20A- 11, 49.71- 10
* Culson	Javier	PUR	25.7.84	198/79	400h	48.14	47.72- 10
Cunningham	Logan	USA	30.5.91	183/80	PV	5.53Ai	5.53- 12
Curry	Rafeeq	USA	19.8.83	183/68	TJ	16.77	17.22- 08
Curtis	Bobby	USA	28.11.84	182/68	5000	13:24.15	13:18.97- 10
* Cutts	Luke	GBR	13.2.88	188/82	PV	5.71i, 5.70	5.62i, 5.60- 09
Czajkowski	Przemyslaw	POL	26.10.88	197/108	DT	63.23	65.61- 12
Czerwinski	Przemyslaw	POL	28.7.83	185/80	PV	5.55	5.82i- 10, 5.80- 06
D'Hoedt	Jeroen	BEL	10.1.90	182/59	1500	3:37.25	3:36.07- 11
Daba	Demma	ETH	18.7.89	171/53	5000	13:18.72	13:34.00- 09
Dabo	Rasul	POR	14.2.89	183/73	110h	13.52, 13.41w	13.64- 12, 13.60w- 11
Dahm	Tobias	GER	23.5.87	203/117	SP	19.96	19.56- 12
Dame	Tasama	ETH	12.10.87	173/57	5000	13:12.64	13:28.19- 10
* Dasaolu	James	GBR	5.9.87	180/75	100	9.91	10.09- 09, 10.06w- 10
Dauphin	Tumatai	FRA	12.1.88	188/138	SP	19.76	19.33- 12
Davide	Kléberson	BRA	20.7.85	175/67	800	1:44.84	1:44.21- 11
Davis	Geoffrey	USA	8.8.90	193/79	HJ	2.26i, 2.24	2.24- 11
Davis	Paul	USA	11.9.90	190/79	SP	21.05	19.11- 12
Davis	Wayne	TTO	22.8.91	178/72	110h	13.38, 13.14w	13.37, 13.26w- 12
De Borger (Seghers)	Dario	BEL	20.3.92	179/70	110h	13.59	13.79- 12
De Grasse	André	CAN-J	10.11.94	180/73	100	10.25, 9.96w	10.59- 12
					200	20.74A, 20.57w	
De Luca	Marco	ITA	12.5.81	189/72	50kW	3:48:05	3:46:31- 09
de Swardt	Jacques	RSA	12.8.92	184/78	400	45.87A	46.06- 12
de Vries	Ruan	RSA	1.2.86	187/80	110h	13.59A, 13.67 13.62A- 06, 13.77, 13.72w- 11	
* de Zordo	Matthias	GER	21.2.88	190/98	JT	81.49	88.36- 11
Dean	Roderick Genki	JPN	30.12.91	182/88	JT	80.15	84.28- 12
Debele	Dereje	ETH	26.7.86		Mar	2:07:48	2:09:08- 09

Name		Nat	Born	Ht/Wt	Event	2013 Mark	Pre-2013 Best
Dechase	Shumi	ETH	28.5.89		Mar	2:07:11	2:07:56- 12
Décimus	Yoan	FRA	30.11.87	182/62	400h	49.52	50.09- 12
Degefa	Abebe	ETH	20.5.84		Mar	2:08:46	2:09:52- 09
Deghelt	Adrien	BEL	10.5.85	188/78	110h	13.43	13.42- 12
DeLeo	Dustin	USA	3.1.86	185/82	PV	5.60	5.53- 12
Demczyszak	Mateusz	POL	18.1.86	176/62	3kSt	8:26.30	8:26.31- 10
* Demelash	Yigrem	ETH-J	28.1.94	167/52	5000	13:13.18	13:03.30- 12
					10k	27:15.51	26:57.56- 12
Demonte	Enrico	ITA	25.9.88	180/73	200	20.45	20.97- 10
^ Demps	Jeffrey	USA	8.1.90	175/77	100	10.11, 9.99w	10.01- 08, 9.96w- 10
Demyanyuk	Dmytro	UKR	30.6.83	195/75	HJ	2.25i, 2.25	2.35- 11
Dendy	Marquis	USA	17.11.92	190/75	LJ	8.28i, 8.10, 8.29w	8.06i. 7.81- 12
Denecker	Émile	FRA	28.3.92	197/82	PV	5.62i	5.63- 11
Denissel	Simon	FRA	22.5.90	181/60	1500	3:34.54	3:38.70- 11
Derevyagin	Aleksandr	RUS	24.3.79	178/80	400h	50.08	49.00- 08
Derrick	Chris	USA	17.10.90	180/64	3000	7:44.01	7:46.81i, 7:54.31- 12
5000	13:08.04	13:19.58i- 12, 13:29.74- 11			10k	28:04.54	27:31.38- 12
* Desisa	Lelisa	ETH	14.1.90	170/52	HMar	60:34	59:30- 11
					Mar	2:04:45	-0-
Dessi	Lorenzo	ITA	4.5.89		50kW	4:06:44	3:57:32- 11
Dewhurst	Ian	AUS	13.11.90	185/73	400h	49.89	51.05- 12
Dheeb	Ahmed Mohamed	QAT	29.9.85	195/113	DT	60.82	63.70. 64.56dq- 10
Dia	Mamadou Chérif	MLI	13.3.85		TJ	16.46	15.71- 07
Diamadáras-Despotéris	Dimítrios	GRE	18.7.84	180/65	LJ	7.88, 7.97w	8.12- 05
Diarra	Abdoulaye	FRA/MLI	27.5.88	184/82	HJ	2.24i, 2.20	2.27i- 09, 2.25- 12
Díaz	José Ignacio	ESP	22.11.79	168/53	20kW	1:22:37	1:21:48- 06
					50kW	3:54:47	3:51:09- 05
* Díaz	Junior	CUB	28.4.87	193/80	LJ	8.02	7.75- 07
Dilla	Karsten	GER	17.7.89	189/81	PV	5.72	5.73i, 5.72- 11
Dimitrov	Denis	BUL-J	10.2.94	181/73	100	10.16	10.71- 10
Dimitrov	Roumen	BUL	19.9.86		TJ	16.49, 16.16w	16.61, 16.74w- 12
Ding Weiye		CHN	13.4.90		SP	19.56	19.14- 12
* Diniz	Yohann	FRA	1.1.78	185/69	50kW	3:41:07	3:38:45- 09
Dirisa	Teshome	ETH-J	25.4.94	175/56	1500	3:35.47	3:34.55- 12
Distelberger	Dominik	AUT	16.3.90	182/77	Dec	7872	7840- 11
* Dix	Walter	USA	31.1.86	178/84	100	9.99	9.88- 10, 9.80w- 08
					200	20.12	19.53- 11
Djouhan	Lolassonn	FRA	18.5.91	188/118	DT	61.70	60.05- 12
* Dmitrik	Aleksey	RUS	12.4.84	191/69	HJ	2.36i, 2.30	2.36- 11
* Dmytrenko	Ruslan	UKR	22.3.86	180/62	20kW	1:20:38	1:20:17- 12
Dobrev	Daniel	BUL	7.4.92	183/75	LJ	8.04i	7.86- 12
Docavo	Vicente	ESP	13.2.92	182/72	TJ	16.71	16.72- 12
Dodson	Jeremy	USA	30.8.87	184/75	100	10.25A, 10.00Aw	10.27, 10.03Aw- 11
					200	20.49, 20.37Aw, 20.40w	20.33, 20.07w- 11
Dohmann	Carl	GER	18.5.90	182/60	50kW	3:57:58	-0-
Dolezal	Riley	USA	16.11.85	188/100	JT	83.50	72.60- 12
Domingos	Wágner	BRA	23.6.83	183/126	HT	71.36	72.78- 12
* Donato	Fabrizio	ITA	14.8.76	189/82	TJ	16.86 17.73i- 11, 17.60- 00, 17.63w- 12	17.38- 12
Dong Bin		CHN	22.11.88	179/67	TJ	17.16i, 16.98	17.38- 12
Donisan	Mihai	ROU	24.7.88	193/74	HJ	2.31	2.30- 11
^ Dossévi	Damiel	FRA	3.2.83	182/82	PV	5.55	5.75- 05
^ Doucouré	Ladji	FRA	28.3.83	183/75	110h	13.60	12.97- 05
^ Douglas	Nathan	GBR	4.12.82	183/71	TJ	16.74	17.64- 05
Douiri	Hicham	MAR	26.2.85		LJ	7.94	7.89- 10
Douvalídis	Konstadínos	GRE	10.3.87	184/78	110h	13.34	13.37- 12
Downing	Quincy	USA	16.1.93	185/75	400	45.87	46.18- 12
Doyle	Michael	IRL	17.5.87	176/62	50kW	4:08:02	
Dremdzhy	Rustem	UKR	3.6.91	180/85	JT	77.15	73.03- 11
Dreyer	Hannes	RSA	13.1.85	178/75	100	10.21 10.23A-12, 10.27,10.17w- 11, 10.0A- 06	
* Drouin	Derek	CAN	6.3.90	195/80	HJ	2.38	2.33i- 11, 2.31- 12
Dry	Mark	GBR	11.10.87	184/110	HT	74.46	74.82- 12
Du Gang		CHN	26.3.92		50kW	4:05:27	4:17:12- 12
Du Yunpeng		CHN	6.9.88	186/70	20kW	1:22:14	1:23:04- 11
Dubitskiy	Oleg	BLR	14.10.90	184/100	HT	73.40	73.62- 12
* Dudas	Mihail	SRB	1.11.89	182/85	Dec	8275	8256- 11
Dukes	Dedric	USA	4.2.92	180/70	200	20.45, 20.34w	20.47- 12
Dunfee	Evan	CAN	28.9.90	183/62	20kW	1:22:46	1:23:45- 11
					50kW	3:59:28	3:59:58- 12
Duquemin	Zane	GBR	23.9.91	185/110	SP	19.42	18.48- 12
					DT	60.56	63.46- 12
Durañona	Yordanis	DMA/ex CUB	16.6.88	188/75	TJ	16.45A	17.02, 17.28w- 09

Name		Nat	Born	Ht/Wt	Event	2013 Mark	Pre-2013 Best
Duréchou	Killian	FRA	15.8.92	183/86	JT	79.98	75.06- 12
Durham	Adam	USA	30.8.85	186/79	400h	49.88	50.15- 10
* Dutch	Johnny	USA	20.1.89	180/82	110h	13.51	13.50,13.30w- 10
					400h	48.02	47.63- 10
* Dutra de Oliveira	Augusto	BRA	16.7.90	180/70	PV	5.82	5.45- 12
Dwyer	Rasheed	JAM	29.1.89	188/80	100	10.20	10.24- 12, 10.20w- 11
					200	20.15	20.20- 11
Dyldin	Maksim	RUS	19.5.87	185/78	400	45.55	45.01- 12
* Eaton	Ashton	USA	21.1.88	186/86	400	45.64	45.68- 12
110h	13.64, 13.37w	13.35- 11, 13.34w- 12			Dec	8809	9039- 12
* Edris	Muktar	ETH-J	14.1.94	172/57	5000	13:03.69	13:04.34- 12
^ Edward	Alonso	PAN	8.12.89	183/73	100	10.13	10.09, 9.97w- 09
					200	20.37, 20.32w	19.81- 09
Effah	Sam	CAN	29.12.88	173/55	100	10.14, 10.09w	10.06- 10
Eichberger	James	MEX	4.8.90	175/68	800	1:45.88	1:47.42- 10
Ekelund-Arenander	Nick	DEN	23.1.89	179/73	400	45.50	46.24- 12
Ektov	Yevgeniy	KAZ	1.9.86	186/72	TJ	16.57	17.22- 12
El Abbassi	El Hassan	MAR	15.7.79		HMar	61:09	61:13- 11
El Aziz	Mustapha	MAR	.85		Mar	2:07:55	2:13:54- 11
El Goumri	Othmane	MAR	28.5.92	171/57	5000	13:13.72	13:17.66- 12
El Kaam	Fouad	MAR	27.5.88	177/62	1500	3:33.71	3:34.01- 11
El Manaoui	Amine	MAR	20.11.91	183/65	800	1:44.96	1:45.00- 12
^ El Sheryf/Osmanoglou	Sheryf	UKR/TUR	2.1.89	176/64	TJ	16.43	17.72- 11
El-Ashry	Alaa El-Din M.	EGY	6.1.91		HT	75.11	71.95- 12
El-Seify	Ashraf Amjad	QAT-J	20.2.95	183/93	HT	76.37	-0-
Ellington	James	GBR	6.9.85	180/75	100	10.17	10.23- 10, 10.12w- 11
					200	20.42	20.52- 11
Elliott	Matt	USA	8.9.85	183/70	1500	3:36.61	3:40.52- 11
Emanuel	Lee	GBR	24.1.85	178/64	1500	3:36.55	3:37.25- 09
					1M	3:54.75	3:57.62i- 10, 3:59.69- 12
Engel	Roscoe	RSA	6.3.89	174/68	100	10.22, 10.20w	10.19- 11
Engelbrecht	Jaco	RSA	8.3.87	200/125	SP	20.31	19.75- 12
English	Mark	IRL	18.3.93	184/73	800	1:44.84	1:45.77- 12
Erickson	Chris	AUS	1.12.81	175/62	50kW	3:49:41	3:51:57- 11
Eriguchi	Masashi	JPN	17.12.88	170/62	100	10.29, 10.15w	10.07- 09
Ernest	Aaron	USA	8.11.93	183/75	100	10.18, 10.04w	10.17, 10.15w- 12
					200	20.38, 20.36w	20.53, 20.39w- 12
Eryildirim ¶	Fatih	TUR	1.3.79	183/89	HT	72.54	75.90- 08
Essalhi	Younès	MAR	20.2.93		1500	3:35.52	3:38.89- 12
					5000	13:16.07	13:41.69- 12
* Esser	Markus	GER	3.2.80	180/105	HT	77.99	81.10- 06
Estévez	Alejandro	ESP	21.1.92	183/68	800	1:46.00	1:48.02- 12
Estrada	Diego	MEX	12.12.89	180/61	5000	13:15.33	13:26.94- 11
Etelätalo	Lassi	FIN	30.4.88	193/80	JT	80.39	84.41- 11
Eto	Takashi	JPN	5.2.91	182/69	HJ	2.27	2.24- 11
Evans	Andrew	USA	25.1.91	198/105	DT	62.78	58.91- 12
Evilä	Tommy	FIN	6.4.80	194/83	LJ	8.01	8.22- 08, 8.41w- 07
* Évora	Nelson	POR	20.4.84	181/64	TJ	16.68	17.74- 07, 17.82w- 09
Ezzine	Hamid	MAR	5.10.83	174/60	3kSt	8:13.27	8:09.72- 07
* Fahringer	Andy	USA	30.5.89	183/86	JT	77.47	75.19- 12
* Fajdek	Pawel	POL	4.6.89	186/118	HT	82.27	81.39- 12
Falloni	Simone	ITA	26.9.91	190/108	HT	72.43	71.48- 12
Faloci	Giovanni	ITA	13.10.85	193/108	DT	64.77	64.24- 12
Fang Yaoqing		CHN-Y	20.4.96		TJ	16.48	16.17- 12
* Farah	Mohamed	GBR	23.3.83	175/65	1500	3:28.81	3:33.98- 09
3000	7:36.85	7:34.47i- 09, 7:38.15- 06			5000	13:05.88	12:53.11- 11
10k	27:21.71	26:46.57- 11			HMar	60:10dh	60:23- 11
Farnosov	Andrey	RUS	9.7.80	182/66	3kSt	8:31.34	8:21.95- 11
^ Farquhar	Stuart	NZL	15.3.82	187/98	JT	81.07	86.31- 12
Fassinotti	Marco	ITA	29.4.89	188/75	HJ	2.27i, 2.27	2.29i- 11, 2.28- 10
Fatecha	Víctor	PAR	10.3.88	190/98	JT	79.03	78.01- 07
Favretto	Vincent	FRA	5.4.84	188/73	PV	5.60	5.65- 06
Fearon	Joel	GBR	11.10.88	175/77	100	10.10	10.25, 10.22w- 12
Fedaczynski	Rafal	POL	3.12.80	168/61	20kW	1:22:01	1:21:21- 12
Feitosa	Ailson	BRA	13.8.88	183/73	100	10.19w	10.32- 09
Feleke	Getu	ETH	28.11.86		HMar	60:26	59:56- 10
					Mar	2:06:45	2:04:50- 12
* Fernández	Jorge	CUB	2.10.87	190/100	DT	65.09	66.05- 12
Ferrín	Diego	ECU	21.3.88	180/68	HJ	2.28	2.30A- 11
Fida	Soresa	ETH	27.5.93	168/55	1500	3:36.73	3:34.72- 11
Fifa	Illias	MAR	16.5.89	174/55	5000	13:25.62	13:25.55- 11

Name		Nat	Born	Ht/Wt	Event	2013 Mark	Pre-2013 Best
Figère	Nicolas	FRA	19.5.79	177/100	HT	71.14	80.88- 01
Filipovic	Predrag	SRB	5.10.78	182/72	50kW	3:58:32	3:57:22- 10
* Filippídis	Konstadinos	GRE	26.11.86	190/78	PV	5.83i, 5.82	5.80-12
Filippov	Nikita	KAZ	7.10.91	194/84	PV	5.60	5.60- 12
Finley	Mason	USA	7.10.90	203/150	SP	20.12i	20.71i- 11, 19.89- 12
					DT	62.48	61.40- 12
Fisher	Andrew	JAM	15.12.91	168/64	100	10.07A, 10.28, 10.16w	10.39- 12
Fisher	Kawayne	JAM	25.10.86	177/75	100	10.04w	10.15- 09
Flannery	Niall	GBR	26.4.91	178/70	400h	49.62	49.76- 11
Fleet	Mac	USA	17.10.90	190/77	800	1:46.32	1:49.19- 10
Fleischhauer	Georg	GER	21.10.88	191/82	400h	49.73	48.72- 11
Florant	Fabian	NED	1.2.83	176/73	TJ	16.73i, 16.67, 16.85w	16.75i- 12, 16.65- 09
Flores	Diego	MEX	23.3.87	160/55	20kW	1:21:56	1:23:53- 11
Floriani	Yuri	ITA	25.12.81	180/64	3kSt	8:24.62	8:22.62- 12
Folacci	Alexandre	FRA	26.3.91	182/79	Dec	7729	7564- 12
Fontenot	Ryan	USA	4.5.86	188/75	110h	13.44	13.48- 10, 13.39w- 12
* Forbes	Damar	JAM	18.9.90	185/77	LJ	8.25, 8.35w	8.23- 11
Forbes	Ronald	CAY	5.4.85	186/79	110h	13.65, 13.31w	13.50, 13.24w- 11
Forsythe	Mario	JAM	30.10.85	173/68	200	20.27	20.29- 11
Forte	Julian	JAM	1.7.93	186/73	100	10.12, 9.98w	10.19- 12
					200	20.79, 20.22w	20.36- 12
* Fortes	Marco	POR	26.9.82	189/139	SP	20.22	21.02- 12
Forys	Craig	USA	13.7.89	176/64	3kSt	8:33.22	8:28.90- 12
^ Fourie	Lehann	RSA	16.2.87	196/98	110h	13.43	13.24- 12
Francis	Javon	JAM-J	14.12.94	183/73	400	45.24	46.06- 12
Francis	Miguel	ANT-J	28.2.95	186/75	200	20.60, 20.58w	
Francis	Samuel	QAT	27.3.87	190/80	100	10.08, 10.0	9.99- 07
Francis	Shawn	USA	16.12.85	178/75	PV	5.51i	5.40- 10
François	Mickaël	FRA	12.3.88	182/72	400h	49.35	50.20- 09
Frankis	Gianni	GBR	16.4.88	190/77	110h	13.54, 13.53w	13.57- 09
Fraser	Rory	GBR	25.4.87	188/70	5000	13:24.07	13:27.70- 12
Fraser	Warren	BAH	8.7.91	172/73	100	10.24, 10.19Aw	10.18- 12
^ Frater	Michael	JAM	6.10.82	170/67	100	10.20w	9.88, 9.86w- 11
Frauen	Michel	GER	19.1.86	179/76	PV	5.55	5.53- 09
Frawley	Nicholas	USA	21.6.88	178/70	PV	5.50Ai	5.53- 12
* Fredericks	Cornel	RSA	3.3.90	178/70	400h	48.78	48.14- 11
Freeman	Jacob	USA	5.11.80	193/129	HT	76.20	76.86- 09
* Freimuth	Rico	GER	14.3.88	198/93	Dec	8488w, 8382	8322- 12
Fricke	Steffen	GER	25.3.83	188/80	Dec	7756	7845(w), 7610- 11
Frolov	Aleksandr	RUS	5.3.87		Dec	7675	7592- 12
Frolov	Kirill	RUS	29.9.93		20kW	1:22:19	-0-
Frost	Andrew	GBR	17.4.81	189/115	HT	72.31	72.79- 11
^ Frydrych	Petr	CZE	13.1.88	198/99	JT	82.39	88.23- 10
Fryman	Andy	USA	3.2.85	188/130	HT	72.07	73.23- 12
Fu Haitao		CHN	1.11.93		TJ	16.43	16.56- 11
Fueki	Yasuhiro	JPN	20.12.85	181/70	400h	49.31	49.71- 12
Fujimutsu	Kenji	JPN	1.5.86	185/80	200	20.48	20.38- 10
Fujisawa	Isamu	JPN	12.10.87	164/56	20kW	1:20:50	1:20:12- 10
Fujiwara	Masakazu	JPN	6.3.81	167/54	Mar	2:08:51	2:08:12- 03
Furey	Sean	USA	31.8.82	190/95	JT	80.04	82.73- 12
Furtula	Danijel	MNE	31.7.92	195/115	DT	64.60	63.79- 12
Furukawa	Yutaro	JPN	3.6.85	177/60	110h	13.65, 13.62w	13.71- 10
* Fyodorov	Aleksey	RUS	25.5.91	184/73	TJ	17.13	17.19- 12
Gabius	Arne	GER	22.3.81	188/68	5000	13:12.50	13:13.43- 12
Gag	Andrei	ROU	7.4.91	190/92	DT	61.11	57.99- 12
Gagnon	Brian	USA	8.5.87	185/70	800	1:45.45	1:46.40- 12
* Gaisah	Ignisious	GHA/NED	20.6.83	186/70	LJ	8.29	8.43, 8.51w- 06
Gakémé	Antoine	BDI	24.12.91	170/57	800	1:45.39	1:52.81- 09
Gallimore	Javan	JAM	7.8.93	182/75	400h	49.76	50.45- 12
Galvan	Matteo	ITA	24.8.88	174/73	200	20.50	20.62- 09
					400	45.35	45.86- 09
Gandu	Benjamin	KEN	21.5.90	169/57	HMar	61:21	61:06- 12
Gao Xinglong		CHN-J	12.3.94		LJ	8.02i, 7.98	7.27- 12
* García	Jesús Ángel	ESP	17.10.69	172/64	50kW	3:46:44	3:39:54- 97
García	Yordani	CUB	21.11.88	193/88	Dec	8157h	8496- 09
* Gari	Roba	ETH	12.4.82	181/60	3kSt	8:12.22	8:06.16- 12
Garrett	Richard	USA	21.12.90	186/118	SP	20.05i	18.96- 12
Garrido	Lucirio	VEN	4.10.88		400h	49.74	50.65- 12
Gasaj	Matej	SVK	27.12.81	205/130	DT	62.46	61.26- 12
^ Gathimba	Gideon	KEN	9.3.80	179/64	3000	7:42.18	7:39.70i- 12, 7:40.10- 11
* Gatlin	Justin	USA	10.2.82	185/83	100	9.85	9.79- 12, 9.77dq- 06
					200	20.21	20.00- 05, 19.86w- 01, 19.86dq- 02

Name		Nat	Born	Ht/Wt	Event	2013 Mark	Pre-2013 Best
Gaul	Florian	GER	21.9.91	182/78	PV	5.50	5.43- 12
Gauntlett	Akheem	JAM	26.8.90	184/70	200	20.55	20.45- 12
					400	45.48	45.13- 12
* Gay ¶ ?	Tyson	USA	9.8.82	183/73	100	9.75dq?, 9.86	9.69- 09, 9.68w- 08
					200	19.74, 19.79w	19.58- 09
* Gaymon	Justin	USA	13.12.86	175/70	400h	48.46	48.46- 08
* Gebremariam	Gebre-egziabher	ETH	10.9.84	178/56	HMar	61:00	60:25- 10
* Gebremedhin	Mekonnen	ETH	11.10.88	180/64	1500	3:32.43	3:31.45- 12
1M	3:54.04				3:49.70- 11	3000	7:41.59i	7:41.42- 11
* Gebremeskel	Dejen	ETH	24.11.89	178/53	3000	7:43.32i	7:34.14i- 12, 7:45.9- 10
5000	13:31.02				12:46.81- 12	10k	26:51.02	-0-
* Gebrhiwet	Hagos	ETH-J	11.5.94	167/65	3000	7:30.36	7:44.08i- 12, 7:45.11- 11
					5000	12:55.73	12:47.53- 12
* Gebrselassie	Haile	ETH	18.4.73	164/53	HMar	60:41	58:55- 06
Gebrselassie	Leul	ETH	20.9.93		10k	28:05.66	28:10.49- 12
Geffrouais	Florian	FRA	5.12.88	183/78	Dec	7990	8118- 12
Gelant	Elroy	RSA	25.8.86	174/55	3000	7:44.83	7:41.38- 12
5000	13:15.87				13:25.09- 11	10k	27:41.30	29:07.02A- 12
Gemeda	Haile	ETH	22.10.88		Mar	2:08:35	2:09:20- 11
* Gemili	Adam	GBR	6.10.93	178/73	100	10.06	10.05- 12
					200	19.98	20.38- 12
Genest	Alexandre	CAN	30.6.86	175/57	3kSt	8:23.43	8:19.33- 11
Geng Zhiyao		CHN	15.8.87	182/67	50kW	3:59:15	3:53:26- 11
George	Winston	GUY	19.5.87	174/66	200	20.59	21.43, 20.84w- 11
Getachew	Limenih	ETH	30.4.90		Mar	2:07:35	2:07:39- 12
Ghasemi	Reza	IRI	24.7.87	179/76	100	10.16	10.24- 12
Ghebrselassie	Ghirmay	ERI-J	14.11.95		HMar	60:09	-0-
^ Gibilisco	Giuseppe	ITA	5.1.79	183/79	PV	5.70	5.90- 03
Gibson	Jeffrey	BAH	15.8.90	186/79	400h	49.39	50.27A, 50.69- 12
Gilde	Maximilian	GER	5.1.90	180/75	Dec	7864	7720- 12
Giovannoni	Dominic	USA	30.7.90	190/86	Dec	7726	7117- 11
Giraldo	Gerald	COL	21.3.89		3kSt	8:28.6	8:44.48- 11
Girma	Abraham	ETH	.86		Mar	2:08:20	2:06:48- 12
Girma	Berhanu	ETH	22.11.86		Mar	2:06:06	2:12:25- 12
Girma	Gezahegn	ETH	28.11.83	158/48	Mar	2:07:41	2:09:16- 11
Gitau	Daniel	KEN	1.10.87	175/57	10k	27:54.35	27:42.91- 12
Gitau	Joseph	KEN	3.1.88	167/49	Mar	2:09:00	2:06:58- 12
Gittens	Ramon	BAR	20.7.87	178/69	100	10.02	10.18- 10
Glass	Najee	USA-J	12.6.94	188/77	400	45.71	46.06i- 12, 46.43- 11
Glover	Tim	USA	1.11.90	185/86	JT	78.69	81.69- 12
Gogochuri	Zurab	GEO	22.3.90		HJ	2.24	2.26- 12
Golabek	Robert	USA	27.4.89	178/116	SP	19.63i, 19.26	19.75- 12
Golling	David	GER	13.3.90	193/94	JT	80.67	77.33- 12
Gollnow	David	GER	8.4.89	180/69	400	45.72	46.60- 11
Gomes	Diego	BRA	19.4.85	184/73	800	1:45.88	1:45.62- 12
Gomes	Hélio	POR	27.12.84	191/73	1500	3:37.50	3:38.49- 12
Gómez	Iñaki	CAN	16.1.88	172/58	20kW	1:22:21	1:20:58- 12
Gómez	Pedro	MEX	31.12.90		20kW	1:21:38	1:22:17- 09
^ Gomis	Kafétien	FRA	23.3.80	183/67	LJ	8.02	8.24- 10
Gomont	Nicolas	FRA	15.9.86	193/89	LJ	8.02	8.08i, 8.00- 12, 8.07w- 11
Goncharov	Viktor	RUS	9.5.91	178/84	JT	79.20	80.34- 11
González	Andy	CUB	17.10.87	183/70	800	1:45.72	1:45.3 - 08, 1:45.41- 09
González	Manuel	CUB	23.3.93	188/84	Dec	7854h	7161- 12
Gooris	Daniel	USA	28.9.89	188/84	Dec	7804 (w(	7629- 12
* Gordon	Jehue	TTO	15.12.91	190/80	400h	47.69	47.96- 12
* Gordon	Lalonde	TTO	25.11.88	188/83	200	20.26	20.62, 20.58i- 12
					400	45.67	44.52- 12
Gordon	Nick	JAM	17.9.88	174/73	LJ	7.94	8.11- 09, 8.14w- 11
Gotch	Jarvis	USA	25.3.92	185/73	LJ	8.09A, 7.90, 8.18Aw	7.79A- 12
* Gowda	Vikas	IND	5.7.83	196/115	DT	65.82	66.28- 12
* Grabarz	Robbie	GBR	3.10.87	192/87	HJ	2.31i, 2.13	2.37- 12
Graber	Andreas	SUI	20.5.92		TJ	16.44	15.66, 15.84w- 12
Graham	Hugh	USA	10.10.92	184/75	400	45.19	46.18i, 46.37- 12
Grave	Jorge	POR	5.9.82	187/104	DT	61.00	60.89- 12
Gray	Cordero	USA	9.5.89	173/68	100	10.09w	10.11, 10.09w- 12
Greaux	Kyle	TTO	26.4.88	190/80	200	20.57	
* Greco	Daniele	ITA	1.3.89	184/75	TJ	17.70i, 17.25	17.47, 17.67w- 12
* Green	Leford	JAM	14.11.86	186/79	400h	48.84	48.47- 10
* Greene	Dai	GBR	11.4.86	183/75	400h	48.66	47.84- 12
Greer	Elijah	USA	24.10.90	185/66	800	1:45.04	1:45.06- 11
Gregan	Brian	IRL	31.12.89	190/85	400	45.53	45.61- 12

Name		Nat	Born	Ht/Wt	Event	2013 Mark	Pre-2013 Best
^ Gregório	Jadel	BRA	16.9.80	202/102	TJ	16.55	17.90- 07
^ Gregson	Ryan	AUS	26.4.90	184/68	1500	3:35.25	3:31.06- 10
					1M	3:55.97i, 3:57.08	3:52.24- 10
Grey	Garrett	USA	22.2.90		HT	70.49	65.05- 12
Grice	Charlie	GBR	7.11.93	180/63	1M	3:54.61	3:57.90- 12
Griffith	Adrian	BAH	11.11.84	178/75	100	10.29, 10.09w	10.19- 10, 10.16w- 11
Grigoryev	Ivan	RUS	27.10.89		Dec	7726	7828- 12
Grillas	Hugo	FRA	28.2.89	180/68	400h	49.92	49.76- 11
Grinnell	Ryan	USA	4.2.87	188/82	TJ	17.22	16.60i- 12, 16.58- 11
^ Gripich	Aleksandr	RUS	21.9.86	190/80	PV	5.60	5.75- 09
Gruber	Hendrik	GER	28.9.86	192/86	PV	5.75i, 5.63	5.70- 10
Grzeszczuk	Lukasz	POL	3.3.90	189/95	JT	83.98	80.58- 11
Guarini	Alessio	ITA	5.4.85	183/70	LJ	8.00	7.84- 09
Gudzius	Andrius	LTU	14.2.91	198/125	DT	62.40	63.39- 12
Guillaume	Mickaël	FRA	8.9.89	182/72	PV	5.50	5.41- 12
^ Guliyev	Ramil	TUR	29.5.90	187/73	200	20.46	20.04- 09
Günther	Martin	GER	8.10.86	188/74	HJ	2.24	2.30i- 10, 2.24- 08
Guo Xiaoxin		CHN	18.1.86	179/60	50kW	4:02:27	3:57:48- 10
Guo Yanxiang		CHN	29.1.87	190/110	SP	19.48i, 19.03	19.40- 08
Gustafsson	Andreas	SWE	10.8.81	180/67	20kW	1:21:51	1:23:20- 12
					50kW	4:01:40	3:54:08- 11
Haapala	Eero	FIN	10.7.89	193/87	LJ	8.11i, 7.90, 7.96w	7.87, 7.89w- 12
Häber	Tino	GER	6.10.82	185/76	JT	78.78	83.46- 09
* Hadadi	Ehsan	IRI	21.1.85	193/125	DT	66.98	69.32- 08
Hadj Lazib	Othman	ALG	10.5.83	186/85	110h	13.50	13.46- 11
Hadnot	Trey	USA	7.3.92	173/70	200	20.49, 20.48i	20.80- 11
^ Haklits	András	CRO	23.9.77	189/103	HT	75.14	80.41- 05
Halevi	Yochai	ISR	10.5.82	184/78	TJ	16.73	16.81, 16.86w- 12
Haliti	Eusebio	ITA	1.1.91	183/75	400h	49.85	50.47- 11
* Hall	Arman	USA-J	14.2.94	188/77	400	44.82	45.39- 12
Hall-Thompson	Elijah	USA-J	22.8.94	181/73	200	20.60	20.86- 12
Hamada	Mohamed Ahmed	EGY	22.10.92	179/65	800	1:45.71	1:44.98- 12
Hamann	Lars	GER	4.4.89	187/88	JT	84.20	79.55- 12
Hamer	Chris	AUS	2.8.88		10k	28:18.26	29:51.54- 11
Hamilton	Jermaine	JAM	22.10.84	178/70	100	10.15	10.41- 12
Hanany	Mickaël	FRA	25.3.83	198/84	HJ	2.31	2.32- 08
Hancock	Jerrell	USA	7.6.89	178/70	200	20.49	21.21, 20.92w- 12
* Hann	Mamadou Kassé	SEN	10.10.86	190/73	400h	48.50	48.80- 12
Hannes	Pieter Jan	BEL	30.10.92	186/72	1500	3:35.97	3:39.55- 12
Hara	Shota	JPN	18.7.92		200	20.57w	21.16- 12
Hardy	Jeremy	USA	10.8.89	173/64	100	10.17	10.50- 12, 10.38w- 11
Hardy	Prezel	USA	1.6.92	168/60	100	10.11w	10.11, 10.03w- 12
					200	20.78, 20.54w	20.33- 12
Harlan	Ryan	USA	25.4.81	190/93	Dec	7710	8171- 04
Harmse	Chris	RSA	31.5.73	184/118	HT	72.40	80.63- 05
* Harradine	Benn	AUS	14.10.82	198/115	DT	68.20	67.53- 12
Harris	Adam	GUY	21.7.87	178/77	100	10.16, 10.09w	10.21, 10.09w- 09
					200	20.60A	20.67- 09, 20.66w- 10
Harris	Aleec	USA	31.10.90	185/77	110h	13.55w	13.65, 13.55w- 11
Harris	James	USA	19.9.91	196/88	400	45.23	45.58- 12
					HJ	2.26i, 2.24	2.27i- 12, 2.23- 11
Harris	Tremaine	CAN	10.2.92	181/79	200	20.54, 20.53w	20.22A, 20.63, 20.42w- 12
Härstedt	Axel	SWE	28.2.87	196/115	DT	61.66	61.57- 12
Hart	Shavez	BAH	9.6.92	176/70	100	10.16A, 10.24, 10.08w	10.28, 10.16w- 12
					200	20.56w	21.02A, 20.24w- 12, 21.12- 11
Hartfield	Mike	USA	29.3.90	190/77	LJ	8.15	7.96- 12
Harting	Christopher	GER	4.10.90	205/117	DT	64.99	62.12- 11
* Harting	Robert	GER	18.10.84	201/126	DT	69.91	70.66- 12
Harvey	Jacques	JAM	5.4.89	182/73	100	10.04	10.08- 12, 10.03w- 11
					200	20.44	20.99- 11
Harvey	Jason	IRL	9.8.91	190/82	400h	50.13	50.65- 11
Hashimoto	Akiyuki	JPN-J	18.11.94	175/80	200	20.35	20.81- 12
Hathat	Yassine	MAR	30.7.91	180/68	800	1:46.09	1:49.22- 12
Haverney	Matthias	GER	21.7.85	198/78	HJ	2.26i, 2.22	2.28- 11
Hayes	Keith	USA	16.2.90	186/77	110h	13.66, 13.30w	13.65- 11
He Yongqiang		CHN	27.11.93		50kW	4:01:45	3:50:47- 12
Heath	Garrett	USA	3.11.85	178/65	1500	3:34.12	3:36.03- 12
1M	3:53.15		3:55.24i, 3:56.21- 12	3000	7:44.87	7:45.80i, 7:51.34- 12 5000 13:20.01	13:27.07- 12
Hechler	Simon	GER	15.6.88	189/79	Dec	7748	8058- 11
* Heffernan	Robert	IRL	20.2.78	173/55	20kW	1:21:59	1:19:22- 08
					50kW	3:37:56	3:37:54- 12

Name		Nat	Born	Ht/Wt	Event	2013 Mark	Pre-2013 Best
Helcelet	Adam	CZE	27.10.91	187/86	Dec	8252	8064- 12
Helebrandt	Máté	HUN	12.1.89	174/60	20kW	1:22:39	1:23:32- 12
Henderson	Jeff	USA	19.2.89	168/64	100	10.18A, 10.25, 10.20w	10.25- 11
					LJ	8.22	8.15u, 8.19w- 09, 7.94- 10
Henning	Jayson	RSA	13.8.90	188/87	JT	78.77A	77.08- 12
Henriksen	Eivind	NOR	14.9.90	191/116	HT	73.27	75.57- 12
* Henriques	Anderson	BRA	3.3.92	187/80	400	44.95	45.59- 12
Heriot	Blake	USA	26.9.91	178/70	200	20.52	20.66, 20.55w- 12
					400	45.46	46.28- 12
Hernández	Fredy	COL	25.4.78	173/60	50kW	4:05:38	3:56:00- 12
Herron	Jeffery	USA	22.4.90		HJ	2.24	2.24- 12
Hester	Tevin	USA-J	10.1.94	170/66	100	10.21	10.50- 12
* Hicks	Antwon	USA	12.3.83	187/79	110h	13.25	13.09- 08
Hicks	Jeremy	USA	19.9.86	178/75	LJ	8.04i, 8.03, 8.31w	8.11- 12, 8.20Aw- 10
Higgs	Raymond	BAH	24.1.91	188/75	LJ	7.95i, 7.90, 8.03w	8.15- 11, 8.36w- 12
Higuma	Takafumi	JPN	3.9.82		50kW	3:59:55	3:52:53 - 12
Hill	Devon	USA	26.10.89	185/75	110h	13.38, 13.32w	13.35- 12
Hill	Ryan	USA	31.1.90	176/60	1M	3:54.89i	3:56.78- 12
3000	7:42.32		7:43.08i- 12		5000	13:14.22	13:26.34- 12
Hill	Tyreek	USA-J	1.3.94	178/79	100	9.98w, 10.23w?	10.19- 12
Hinch	Derick	USA	2.2.91	186/80	PV	5.50Ai	5.50- 12
Hinds	Andrew	BAR	25.4.84	172/72	100	10.13A, 10.24, 10.22w	10.03- 09
Hitrane	Jamal	MAR	1.9.89	175/57	2000	4:59.97	
* Hlavan	Igor	UKR	25.9.90	172/62	20kW	1:22:32	1:25:58- 11
					50kW	3:40:39	3:48:07- 12
Hochuli	Alexandre	SUI	19.1.84		TJ	16.47	16.37- 10
Hock	Johannes	GER	24.3.92	185/86	Dec	8293 (w)	7884- 12
* Hoffa	Reese	USA	8.10.77	181/133	SP	21.71	22.43- 07
Hoffmann	Karol	POL	1.6.89	196/78	TJ	16.66	17.09- 12
* Hogan	Victor	RSA	25.7.89	198/108	DT	65.33	62.76- 12
Hollis	Mark	USA	1.12.84	190/84	PV	5.50Ai, 5.42	5.75- 08
* Holzdeppe	Raphael	GER	28.9.89	181/78	PV	5.91	5.91- 12
Honeycutt	Josh	USA	7.3.89	182/73	TJ	16.59Ai, 16.55, 16.78w	16.09- 11, 16.39w- 09
Horák	Peter	SVK	7.12.83	197/83	HJ	2.24i, 2.24	2.30i- 07, 2.28- 09
Horn	Gray	USA	18.2.90	191/91	Dec	7918	7954- 12
Horn	Joe	USA	.86	178/73	200	20.59Aw	21.25- 09
Hortelano	Bruno	ESP	18.9.91	181/72	200	20.47	20.64A, 20.87- 12
Horvat	Dario	CRO	25.2.92	174/70	100	10.20, 10.18w	10.41- 11
Horvat	Ivan	CRO	17.8.93	188/77	PV	5.62	5.60- 12
Hoshi	Sota	JPN	6.1.88	173/56	10k	28:15.92	28:24.68- 12
Houssaye	Cédric	FRA	13.12.79	178/65	50kW	4:08:09	3:53:24- 11
Howard	Julian	GER	3.4.89	176/75	LJ	8.07.8.13w	7.88- 11
Howe	Nick	USA	17.11.89	190/93	JT	78.41	70.49- 11
Hrechkovskyy	Andrey	UKR	30.8.93		50kW	3:58:26	-0-
Hu Wanli		CHN	27.5.92		20kW	1:21:30	1:23:46- 11
Huang Shih-Feng		TPE	2.3.92	181/88	JT	82.11	76.54- 12
Huang Changzhou		CHN-J	20.8.94		LJ	7.97	7.79- 12
Huang Qiang		CHN-J	18.12.95		TJ	16.46	15.48- 12
Hubbard	Jamil	USA	12.5.86	170/64	200	20.54w	20.67- 12
Hudi	Ákos	HUN	10.8.91	185/95	HT	76.93	73.55- 12
Hughes	Joey	USA	26.10.90	178/70	400	45.84	45.05- 11
Hughes	Matt	CAN	3.8.89	180/64	3kSt	8:11.64	8:24.87- 11
Huling	Dan	USA	16.7.83	185/70	3000	7:44.42	7:46.97- 10
5000	13:18.42		13:24.72- 10		3kSt	8:21.92	8:13.29- 10
Humphreys	Sam	USA	12.9.90	201/115	JT	83.14	81.86- 12
Hussein	Kariem	SUI	1.4.89	190/77	400h	49.78	49.61- 12
Huyler	Garrett	USA	15.1.87	196/86	HJ	2.24i	2.21- 09
Hyatt	Dane	JAM	22.1.84	182/77	400	45.41A, 45.99	44.83- 12
Hylton	Riker	JAM	13.12.88	190/73	400	45.67	45.30- 11
Hyman	Kemar	CAY	11.10.89	178/74	100	10.02	9.95- 12
Ibáñez	Anatole	SWE	14.11.85	176/67	50kW	3:53:38	4:03:20- 12
Ibrahim	Yasser Fathi	EGY	2.5.84	185/127	DT	61.43	63.37i- 10, 63.30- 11
* Ibrahimov	Hayle	AZE	18.1.90	168/58	3000	7:34.57	7:41.88i, 7:45.92- 12
					5000	13:23.59	13:11.34- 12
Idiata	Samson	NGR	28.2.82	186/75	LJ	8.00	7.98, 8.02w- 12
^ Idowu	Phillips	GBR	30.12.78	192/86	TJ	16.44	17.81- 10
Idris	Ali Mohamed Younes	SUD	15.9.89	191/75	HJ	2.25	2.25- 11
Iglehart-Summers	Quentin	USA	15.6.87	193/80	400	45.72	45.46A- 08, 45.62- 07
* Iguider	Abdelati	MAR	25.3.87	170/52	1500	3:33.29	3:31.47- 09
1M	3:55.93		3:51.78- 12		3000	7:34.92i	7:41.95- 07
Iizuka	Shota	JPN	25.6.91	185/80	200	20.21	20.45- 12

Name		Nat	Born	Ht/Wt	Event	2013 Mark	Pre-2013 Best
Ilyichev	Ivan	RUS	14.10.86		HJ	2.27i. 2.26	2.28i- 07, 2.26- 08
Imazeki	Yuta	JPN	6.11.87	173/55	400h	49.42	49.27- 11
Imedio	Alberto	ESP	24.5.91	170/56	1500	3:37.68	3:38.96- 12
* Ingebrigtsen	Henrik	NOR	24.2.91	180/69	1500	3:33.95	3:35.43- 12
1M	3:54.53		3:54.28- 12		3000	7:42.19	7:58.15- 10
Ingraham	Ryan	BAH	2.11.93	194/73	HJ	2.30	2.28- 12
Inocêncio	Matheus	BRA	17.5.81	192/94	110h	13.58, 13.43w	13.33- 04
Iordan	Valeriy	RUS	14.2.92	192/95	JT	83.56	83.23- 12
Irfan	Kolothum Thodi	IND	8.2.90		20kW	1:20:59	1:20:21- 12
Irwin	Andrew	USA	23.1.93	190/84	PV	5.70i, 5.65	5.72- 12
Irwin	Willy	USA	2.6.92	188/107	SP	19.49	18.51- 12
Ishitsuka	Yusuke	JPN	19.6.87	179/72	400	45.87	46.02- 09
Isidro	Pedro	POR	17.7.85	175/58	50kW	3:57:09	3:58:00- 12
Ismail	Muhammad Hakimi	MAS	8.4.91		TJ	16.44	16.15- 11
^ Israel	Märt	EST	23.9.83	190/119	DT	63.58	66.98- 11
Ivakin	Anton	RUS	3.2.91	178/73	PV	5.65i, 5.63	5.60- 12
* Ivanov	Aleksandr	RUS	25.4.93		20kW	1:20:58	-0-
* Ivanov	Georgi	BUL	13.3.85	187/130	SP	21.09	20.33- 12
Ivanyuk	Ilya	RUS	9.3.93	183/75	HJ	2.27i, 2.26	2.23i, 2.21- 12
Ivashko	Pavel	RUS-J	16.11.94	185/75	400	45.81	
* Jackson	Bershawn	USA	8.5.83	173/69	400h	48.09	47.30- 05
Jackson	Jermaine	JAM	29.5.86		LJ	7.97	7.76- 12
Jackson	Kenny	USA	.91	178/75	100	10.16w	10.52, 10.49w- 09
Jackson	Marcus	USA	8.7.91	201/82	HJ	2.29i, 2.27	2.24- 12
* Jager	Evan	USA	8.3.89	186/66	1500	3:36.34	3:38.33- 09
3000	7:43.36, 7:39.98+i		7:35.16- 12		2M	8:14.95i	8:47.59- 07
5000	13:02.40		13:22.18- 09		3kSt	8:08.60	8:06.81- 12
Jakubczyk	Lucas	GER	28.4.85	183/73	100	10.21	10.20, 10.16w- 12
Jaleta	Habtamu	ETH	19.4.93		3kSt	8:24.90	8:29.03- 12
Jamaa	Samir	MAR	9.2.90	175/61	800	1:45.47	1:46.61- 12
James	Jamol	TTO	16.7.92	175/70	100	10.08w	10.17- 12
* James	Kirani	GRN	1.9.92	185/74	400	43.96	43.94- 12
Jänes	Marko	EST	29.8.76	186/83	JT	78.00	80.33- 11
Janet	Roberto	CUB	29.8.86	187/95	HT	76.75	77.08- 12
^ Janik	Igor	POL	18.1.83	200/112	JT	80.13	84.76- 08
Jansen	Robbert Jan	NED	22.7.83	175/67	PV	5.50Ai, 5.40	5.62- 12
Jansons	Janis	LAT	25.5.90	191/98	Dec	7647	7128- 10
* Jarso	Yakob	ETH	5.2.88	173/54	HMar	60:39	60:07- 10
Jasinski	Daniel	GER	5.8.89	207/125	DT	64.69	64.37- 12
Jaszczuk	Tomasz	POL	9.3.92	195/83	LJ	8.05	8.11- 11
Jegede	J.J.	GBR	3.10.85	179/73	LJ	8.05	8.11- 12
Jelonek	Jakub	POL	7.7.85	184/71	20kW	1:22:29	1:21:05- 12
Jeng	Alhaji	SWE	13.12.81	185/77	PV	5.65	5.81i- 09, 5.80- 06
Jenkins	Eric	USA	24.11.91	170/61	5000	13:18.57	14:09.67- 11
Jenkins	James	USA	31.3.84	188/77	TJ	16.50i, 16.50w	16.28, 16.79w- 09
Jensen	Curtis	USA	1.11.90	193/130	SP	20.29i, 19.63	18.74- 12
* Jeylan	Ibrahim	ETH	12.6.89	168/57	5000	13:09.38- 06	13:09.38- 06
					10k	27:22.23	27:02.81- 06
Ji Wei		CHN	5.2.84	194/83	110h	13.65	13.40- 07
Jiang Fan		CHN	16.9.89	188/75	110h	13.50	13.47- 11
Jiang Jie		CHN-J	25.10.94		20kW	1:22:32	1:24:33- 12
Jie Lei		CHN	8.5.89		LJ	7.99	7.83- 12
Jin Min-sup		KOR	2.9.92	185/75	PV	5.64	5.51- 12
* Jobodwana	Anaso	RSA	30.7.92	187/71	100	10.10	10.34, 10.24w- 12
					200	20.13, 20.00w	20.27- 12
Jock	Charles	USA	23.11.89	188/73	800	1:45.01	1:44.67- 11
Jöeväli	Kaarel	EST	8.1.90		Dec	7658	7342- 11
Johansson	Markus	SWE	8.5.90	183/110	HT	76.43	73.33- 12
John	Alexander	GER	3.5.86	185/77	110h	13.49	13.35- 09
John	Mwangangi	KEN	1.11.90		HMar	60:37	59:45- 11
* Johnson	Brandon	USA	6.3.85	175/68	800	1:43.84	1:46.23- 12
^ Johnson	Kibwé	USA	17.7.81	189/108	HT	76.28	80.31- 11
Johnson	Matt	USA	4.10.89	188/84	Dec	7697 (w)	7721(w)- 12
Johnson	Omar	JAM	25.11.88	183/75	200	20.48w	20.80- 12
					400	45.50	46.30- 11
Johnson	Taffawee	JAM	10.3.88	180/73	100	10.20, 10.19w	10.30- 12
* Jonas	Dusty	USA	19.4.86	198/84	HJ	2.34i, 2.31	2.36A- 08, 2.33- 10
Jones	Alwyn	AUS	28.2.85	189/72	TJ	16.81	16.83- 09
Jones	Jermaine	USA	24.5.91	190/91	200	20.57A	
Jones	Jonathan	USA	23.4.91	183/127	SP	19.59i	15.79i- 11
Jones	Nick	USA	22.6.89	188/109	DT	61.17	61.95A- 12

Name		Nat	Born	Ht/Wt	Event	2013 Mark	Pre-2013 Best
Jons	Mattias	SWE	19.11.82	182/108	HT	76.39	76.12- 12
Jørgensen	Rasmus W	DEN	23.1.89	180/75	PV	5.65	5.53i- 12, 5.50- 10
Joseph	Stanley	FRA	24.10.91	181/66	PV	5.62i	5.55- 12
Joseph	Vanier	USA	9.9.91	185/79	110h	13.59	14.14, 14.03w- 10
Jufar	Tariku	ETH	18.7.84	173/55	Mar	2:08:05	2:06:51- 12
Julião	Ronald	BRA	16.6.85	194/113	DT	65.55	65.41- 12
Julmis	Jeffrey	HAI	6.1.87	183/80	110h	13.67A, 13.63w	13.50, 13.38w- 11
Jung Sang-jin		KOR	16.4.84	184/82	JT	77.60	82.05- 12
Kaan	James	AUS	17.9.90	178/64	1500	3:37.02	3:38.04- 12
Kabelka	Michal	SVK	4.2.85	192/77	HJ	2.26i	2.31i, 2.24- 12
Kafia	Louhab	ALG	24.2.87		TJ	16.47	15.50- 11
Kajikawa	Yohei	JPN	8.11.83	185/70	TJ	16.36, 16.45w	16.45- 05
Kamathi	Joseph	KEN-Y	23.11.96	175/56	10k	28:16.27	
Kanda	Lukas	KEN	.87		Mar	2:08:50	2:08:04- 12
Kanemaru	Yuzo	JPN	18.9.87	177/75	400	45.56	45.16- 09
Kangogo	Cornelius	KEN	31.12.93	166/62	3000	7:41.90	7:39.73- 12
					5000	13:15.26	
* Kanter	Gerd	EST	6.5.79	196/125	DT	67.59	73.38- 06
Kapek	Julien	FRA	12.1.79	178/70	TJ	16.67	17.38- 06
Karaca	Askin	TUR	20.10.90		TJ	16.51	16.10- 09
Karavayev ¶	Pavel	RUS	27.8.88	185/74	LJ	7.95i	8.08- 11
Karlström	Perseus	SWE	2.5.90	184/72	50kW	3:52:43	
* Karoki	Bidan	KEN	21.8.90	169/53	3000	7:37.68	7:49.38- 10
5000	13:15.75		13:15.76- 11		10k	27:13.12	27:05.50- 12
* Karpov	Dmitriy	KAZ	23.7.81	198/94	Dec	8037	8725- 04
Karukawa	Maina	KEN	19.6.91	171/58	10k	28:13.23	28:33.32- 11
Kask	Rain	EST	11.6.91		LJ	7.85, 8.00w	7.69- 12
Kassaw	Abere	ETH-J	8.12.94		HMar	61:07	-0-
Kassaye	Meresa	ETH-Y	23.5.96		3kSt	8:29.92	8:36.13- 12
Kato	Nobuya	JPN-J	16.4.95	183/63	400	45.69	47.92- 12
Katsuki	Hayato	JPN	28.11.90	168/58	20kW	1:22:24	1:21:14- 12
Kauppinen	Juha	FIN	16.8.86	182/103	HT	70.63	74.38- 09
Kawauchi	Yuki	JPN	5.3.87	172/59	Mar	2:08:14	2:08:37- 11
Kazanin	Oleksiy	UKR	22.5.82	170/58	50kW	3:54:40	3:50:17- 12
Kazaryan	Gayk	RUS	19.5.90	184/80	PV	5.50i	5.40- 11
Kazi	Tamás	HUN	16.5.85	179/70	800	1:45.37	1:45.55- 09
* Kazmirek	Kai	GER	28.1.91	189/86	Dec	8366, 8350w	8130- 12
* Kebede	Tsegaye	ETH	15.1.87	158/50	Mar	2:06:04	2:04:38- 12
* Kebenei	Stanley	KEN	6.11.89	170/61	3kSt	8:24.45	8:45.81- 11
Keddo	Eric	JAM	1.7.84	186/77	110h	13.62A, 13.72	13.49- 11, 13.0- 10
Kedi	Aman	ETH	.93		1500	3:37.54	
^ Keflezighi	Mebrahtom	USA	5.5.75	170/58	HMar	61:22	61:00- 09
Keiner	Sebastian	GER	22.8.89	183/65	800	1:46.18	1:45.98- 08
					1500	3:37.75	3:39.96- 12
Keller	Martin	GER	26.9.86	180/80	100	10.07, 9.99w	10.23, 10.15w- 08
Kemboi	Clement	KEN	1.2.92		3kSt	8:17.18	8:25.67- 12
Kemboi	Elijah	KEN	10.9.84		Mar	2:07:34	2:07:51- 12
* Kemboi	Ezekiel	KEN	25.5.82	175/62	3kSt	7:59.03	7:55.76- 11
Kemboi	Hillary	KEN	.86		3kSt	8:29.2 A	8:29.8A- 12
Kemboi	Lawrence	KEN	.93		3kSt	8:25.0 A	8:31.2A- 12
^ Kemboi	Nicholas	QAT	25.11.83	163/50	HMar	60:27	60:31- 03
					Mar	2:08:51	2:08:01- 11
Kendagor	Jacob	KEN	19.9.84		HMar	59:36	61:15- 12
Kendricks	Sam	USA	7.9.92	189/79	PV	5.81	5.50- 12
Kenesi	Geoffrey	KEN	.90		HMar	61:21	61:14- 12
Keny	Felix	KEN	25.12.85		Mar	2:07:14	2:07:31- 12
Kering	Alfred	KEN	.80	172/57	Mar	2:08:42	2:07:11- 10
Keys	Dakotah	USA	27.9.91	188/79	Dec	8001	7793- 12
Kgosimang	Kabelo Mmono	BOT	7.1.86	184/70	HJ	2.29A	2.34A- 08, 2.30- 06
Kharitonov	Aleksandr	RUS	19.7.90	186/88	JT	77.66	77.37- 10
Kharlamov	Vasiliy	RUS	8.10.86	184/94	Dec	8098	8166- 11
Khodjayev	Sukhrob	UZB	21.5.93	186/105	HT	70.76	74.20- 12
Kibet	Alex	KEN/QAT	20.10.90		5000	13:20.57	13:48.09- 12
					3kSt	8:33.18	8:31.4A- 12
Kibet	Moses	KEN-J	20.11.94	177/60	800	1:45.83	1:47.4A- 12
Kibet	Sammy	KEN	2.2.82		Mar	2:08:50	2:08:17- 11
* Kibet	Stephen	KEN	9.11.86	172/55	HMar	59:59	58:54- 12
Kibet	Vincent	KEN	.91		1500	3:35.62	3:40.51A- 12
Kibiwott	Francis	KEN	15.9.78		Mar	2:08:31	2:07:32- 12
Kiecana	Szymon	POL	26.3.89	193/67	HJ	2.31	2.28- 12
Kifle	Goitom	ERI	3.12.93	178/60	10k	27:32.00	
					HMar	61:18	62:46- 12

Name		Nat	Born	Ht/Wt	Event	2013 Mark	Pre-2013 Best
* Kigen	Mike	KEN	15.1.86	170/54	Mar	2:08:24	-0-
* Kilty	Richard	GBR	2.9.89	184/79	100	10.10	10.23, 10.15w- 12
					200	20.34	20.50- 12
Kim Byung-jun		KOR	15.8.91	190/80	110h	13.61	13.79- 12
Kim Duk-hyun		KOR	8.12.85	180/68	LJ	8.08, 8.22w	8.20, 8.41w- 09
* Kim Hyun-sub		KOR	31.5.85	176/56	20kW	1:21:22	1:19:31- 11
Kim Kuk-young		KOR	19.4.91	172/60	100	10.20w	10.23, 10.17w- 10
Kim Sang-su		KOR	5.6.84	187/74	LJ	8.00	7.88- 10
Kim Yoo-suk		KOR	19.1.82	191/87	PV	5.60	5.66- 07
Kimani	Bernard	KEN	10.9.93	172/54	5000	13:22.15	
* Kimetto	Dennis	KEN	22.1.84	172/57	Mar	2:03:45	2:04:16- 12
Kimitei	Elijah	KEN	.86		TJ	16.45A	16.66A, 16.28- 12
* Kimmons	Trell	USA	13.7.85	178/77	100	10.22, 10.02w	9.95, 9.92w- 10
Kimurer	Joel	KEN	21.1.88		HMar	60:02	59:36- 12
					Mar	2:07:48	2:08:18- 12
Kimutai	Kennedy	KEN	18.6.90		HMar	61:00	61:08- 12
Kimutai	Philip Sanga	KEN	10.9.83	170/60	Mar	2:06:57	2:06:07- 11
King	Daniel	GBR	30.5.83	178/64	50kW	4:05:36	4:04:49- 08
Kinnunen	Jarkko	FIN	19.1.84	187/69	20kW	1:22:53	1:23:13- 12
					50kW	3:50:56	3:46:25- 12
Kino	Tomoharu	JPN	4.8.89	177/67	400h	49.94	49.57- 10
Kinyor	Job	KEN	2.9.90	176/68	800	1:44.24	1:43.76- 12
Kipchirchir	Victor	KEN	5.12.87		HMar	60:27	59:31- 12
* Kipchoge	Eliud	KEN	5.11.84	167/52	HMar	60:04	59:25- 12
					Mar	2:04:05	-0-
Kipchumba	Hillary	KEN	25.11.92		HMar	61:02	62:42- 12
Kipkemboi	Nicholas	KEN	5.7.86		HMar	60:24	60:15- 12
					Mar	2:06:33	-0-
* Kipkemoi	Kenneth	KEN	2.8.84	169.55	5000	13:13.91	13:03.37- 12
10k	27:28.50		26:52.65- 12		HMar	59:55	59:11- 12
Kipketer	Alfred	KEN-Y	26.12.96		800	1:46.2 A	
* Kipkoech	John	KEN	29.12.91	160/52	3000	7:37.40	7:32.72- 10
					5000	13:01.64	12:49.50- 12
Kipkorir	Evans	KEN	.85	174/61	800	1:46.09	1:45.91- 12
Kipkosgei	Nelson	KEN	9.3.93		3kSt	8:32.72	8:22.24- 12
Kiplagat	Abraham	KEN	8.9.84	182/72	800	1:45.71	1:43.77- 10
* Kiplagat	Benjamin	UGA	4.3.89	186/61	3kSt	8:13.07	8:03.81- 10
Kiplagat	Evans	KEN	5.3.88		HMar	60:28	59:56- 09
Kiplagat	Henry	KEN	16.12.82		HMar	60:21	60:01- 12
* Kiplagat	Silas	KEN	20.8.89	170/57	1500	3:30.13	3:29.27- 10
					1M	3:49.48	3:49.39- 11
Kiplangat	Cornelius	KEN	21.12.92	168/55	800	1:45.47A	1:46.4A- 12
Kipngetich	Gideon	KEN	.90		800	1:46.38	1:47.58- 12
* Kiprop	Asbel	KEN	30.6.89	186/70	800	1:44.8 A	1:43.15- 11
1500	3:27.72		3:28.88- 12		1M	3:49.53	3:48.50- 09
* Kiprop	Wilson	KEN	14.4.87	179/62	10k	28:18.0 A	27:01.98- 12
					HMar	59:15	59:15- 12
* Kiprotich	Stephen	UGA	27.2.89	172/56	HMar	61:15	63:32+- 12
					Mar	2:08:05	2:07:20- 11
Kiprotich ¶	Abraham	FRA	17.8.85		Mar	2:08:33	2:08:35- 12
* Kipruto	Brimin	KEN	31.7.85	176/54	3kSt	8:06.86	7:53.64- 11
* Kipruto	Conseslus	KEN-J	8.12.94	174/55	3kSt	8:01.16	8:03.49- 12
Kipruto	Silas	KEN	26.9.84	184/66	HMar	60:12	59:39- 10
Kipruto	Vincent	KEN	13.9.87	172/57	HMar	60:39	60:46- 12
					Mar	2:06:15	2:05:13- 10
Kipsang	Emmanuel	KEN	13.6.91		10k	27:59.7 A	
* Kipsang	Geoffrey	KEN	28.11.92	168/54	10k	28:17.0 A	27:06.35- 11
HMar	58:54		59:26- 12		Mar	2:06:26	2:06:12- 12
* Kipsang	Wilson	KEN	15.3.82	178/59	HMar	61:02	58:59- 09
					Mar	2:03:23	2:03:42- 11
* Kipsiro	Moses	UGA	2.9.86	174/59	5000	13:11.56	12:50.72- 07
					10k	27:04.53	27:04.48- 12
Kiptoo	Edwin	KEN	28.12.87		HMar	61:19	62:01- 12
* Kiptoo	Mark	KEN	21.6.76	175/64	5000	13:20.51	12:53.46- 10
HMar	60:42		60:29- 11		Mar	2:06:16	
Kiptoo	Solomon	KEN	27.8.87		Mar	2:08:34	2:08:30- 12
* Kipyego	Bernard	KEN	16.7.86	160/50	Mar	2:07:19	2:06:29- 11
Kipyego	Edwin	KEN	16.11.90		HMar	60:04	60:55- 12
* Kipyego	Michael	KEN	2.10.83	168/59	Mar	2:06:58	2:06:48- 11
Kipyegon	Bernard	KEN-J	.94	181/65	800	1:46.0 A	
Kipyeko	Phillip	UGA-J	10.1.95		5000	13:16.92	13:45.52- 12

Name		Nat	Born	Ht/Wt	Event	2013 Mark	Pre-2013 Best
Kirchler	Hannes	ITA	22.12.78	191/105	DT	62.69	65.01- 07
Kirielius	Tomas	LTU	10.6.89	196/91	Dec	7700	7508- 10
Kirongo	Sammy	KEN-J	4.2.94	176/62	800	1:45.38	1:49.1A- 11
Kirop	Pius	KEN	8.1.90		HMar	60:18	59:25- 12
Kirt	Magnus	EST	10.4.90	191/87	JT	79.82	76.97- 12
Kirui	Geoffrey	KEN	16.2.93	158/50	3000	7:42.26	
					5000	13:16.68	13:20.54 - 11
* Kirui	Gilbert	KEN-J	22.1.94	172/55	3kSt	8:06.96	8:11.27- 12
Kirwa	Edwin	KEN			3kSt	8:25.2 A	8:34.8A- 12
Kirwa	Gilbert	KEN	20.12.85	178/59	Mar	2:08:17	2:06:14- 09
* Kirwa Yego	Alfred	KEN	28.11.86	175/56	800	1:46.43	1:42.67- 09
Kirya	Aleksandr	RUS	23.3.92		DT	60.22	57.00- 12
Kiryu	Yoshihide	JPN-J	15.12.95	175/66	100	10.01	10.19- 12
					200	20.41	20.70- 12
Kishimoto	Takayuki	JPN	6.5.90	170/59	400h	49.08	48.41- 12
Kishoyan	Alphas	KEN-J	12.10.94	162/56	400	45.76A, 45.5A	45.64A, 46.10- 12
Kiss	Dániel	HUN	12.2.82	195/73	110h	13.65	13.32, 13.20w- 10
Kitchens	George	USA	16.1.83	183/77	LJ	8.17, 8.23w	8.21, 8.27w- 12
Kitonyi	Daniel	KEN-J	12.1.94	163/51	10k	28:02.79	28:28.42- 12
Kitum	Silas	KEN	25.5.90	167/52	3kSt	8:27.36	8:12.17- 11
* Kitum	Timothy	KEN-J	20.11.94	172/60	800	1:44.45	1:42.53- 12
Kitur	Felix	KEN	17.4.87	178/66	800	1:45.13	1:46.75- 08
* Kitwara	Sammy	KEN	26.11.86		Mar	2:05:16	2:05:54- 12
Kiumbani	Johnson	KEN	27.1.93	168/56	10k	28:01.87	28:02.26- 12
Kivinen	Mikko	FIN	16.1.88	183/70	LJ	7.93	8.02- 12
^ Kivuva	Jackson	KEN	11.8.88	172/59	800	1:46.3 A	1:43.72- 10
Kiyeng	David	KEN	22.4.83		Mar	2:08:30	2:06:26- 09
Kjerpeset	Øyvind	NOR	12.12.91	186/77	400h	49.95	51.16- 11
Klas	Jeremy	USA	5.9.89	190/82	PV	5.50	5.43i- 12, 5.25- 10
Knipphals	Sven	GER	20.9.85	190/85	100	10.20	10.23- 11
* Knobel	Jan Felix	GER	16.1.89	189/89	Dec	8396w	8288- 11
Kobayashi	Kai	JPN	28.2.93		20kW	1:22:47	-0-
Kobayashi	Yuichi	JPN	25.8.89	172/60	200	20.46	20.59- 11 , 20.52w- 10
* Koech	Bernard	KEN	31.1.88	165/50	Mar	2:04:53	-0-
* Koech	Isiah	KEN	19.12.93	178/60	3000	7:36.28	7:30.43- 12
					5000	12:56.08	12:48.64- 12
Koech	John	KEN-J	23.8.95		3kSt	8:16.96	8:47.1A- 12
Koech	Josphat	KEN	.82		3kSt	8:31.75	9:01.27- 12
* Koech	Paul Kipsiele	KEN	10.11.81	168/57	3000	7:38.35i	7:32.78i- 10, 7:33.93- 05
					3kSt	8:02.63	7:54.31- 12
Koffi Hua	Wilfried	CIV	24.9.89	186/80	100	10.21	10.31- 12
					200	20.57	20.82- 11
* Kogo	Micah	KEN	3.6.86	170/60	Mar	2:06:56	-0-
Kokoyev	Valeriy	RUS	25.7.88	197/118	SP	20.46	20.42i- 11, 20.20- 09
* Kolasinac	Asmir	SRB	15.10.84	185/130	SP	20.80	20.85- 12
Kolesnikov	Maksim	RUS	28.2.91		LJ	7.94i, 7.80	7.78- 12
Kolomoyets	Sergey	BLR	11.8.89	191/110	HT	75.66	77.52- 11
Kolosov	Dmitriy	RUS	19.5.86		TJ	16.55	16.89- 11, 17.00w- 08
* Komen	Daniel Kipchirchir	KEN	27.11.84	175/60	1500	3:33.05	3:29.02- 06
1M	3:51.28				3000	7:42.21, 7:41.16i	7:31.41- 11
				3:48.28- 07			
Komen	Willy	KEN	22.12.87	168/55	3kSt	8:32.37	8:11.18- 07
* Komon	Leonard Patrick	KEN	10.1.88	175/52	10k	27:53.85A	26:55.29- 11
Königsmark	Varg	GER	28.4.92	193/84	400h	49.62	49.54- 12
Konishi	Yuta	JPN	31.7.90	176/60	400h	49.94	49.41- 11
Koosimile	Larona	BOT	14.10.85	177/70	LJ	7.93	7.70-10, 8.00w- 12
Kopeykin	Vasiliy	RUS	9.3.88		LJ	8.00, 8.06w	7.84, 7.92w- 11
Korchmid	Oleksandr	UKR	22.1.82	188/89	PV	5.70	5.81- 05
Korepanov	Sergey	RUS	15.7.84		50kW	3:58:04	3:56:16- 08
Koriki	Yuya	JPN	19.10.89	174/91	JT	77.84	76.02- 12
Korir	Fredrick	KEN	17.4.87		800	1:46.30A	1:52.8A- 05
Korir	Leonard	KEN	10.12.86	173/61	5000	13:15.45	13:19.54i- 12, 13:35.71- 11
					HMar	61:19	61:19- 12
Korir	Mark	KEN	10.1.85		HMar	60:49	61:19- 12
					Mar	2:07:08	-0-
Kornegay-Gober	Kris	USA	6.10.91		HJ	2.24i, 2.20	2.24i, 2.21- 12
Korolyov	Aleksey	RUS	5.4.82		HT	78.19	79.36- 08
Korotovskiy	Yevgeniy	RUS	21.6.92		HT	72.03	70.00- 12
Kosgei	David	KEN	.85		HMar	60:50	61:54- 12
Kotut	Cyprian	KEN	.92		HMar	59:59	62:25- 12
* Kovacs	Joe	USA	28.6.89	188/114	SP	20.82	21.08- 12
Kovalenko	Nazar	UKR	9.2.89	177/65	20kW	1:21:10	1:19:55- 12

Name		Nat	Born	Ht/Wt	Event	2013 Mark	Pre-2013 Best
^ Kovals	Ainars	LAT	21.11.81	192/105	JT	80.71	86.64- 08
Kovalyov	Andriy	UKR	11.6.92	197/78	HJ	2.24	2.20i– 11, 2.20- 12
Kovalyov	Yuriy	RUS	18.6.91		TJ	16.84i, 16.36	17.06- 11
Kovenko	Andriy	UKR	25.11.73	174/64	20kW	1:20:22	1:20:51- 12
Kowal	Yoann	FRA	28.5.87	172/58	3kSt	8:12.53	8:21.66- 12
Kownatke	Rafal	POL	24.3.85	189/133	SP	20.13	19.51i- 10, 19.30- 11
Kozlitin	Viktor	RUS	12.6.88	190/80	PV	5.50	5.66- 11
Kozlov	Vladimir	BLR	20.4.85	183/87	JT	82.49	82.86- 12
* Kozmus	Primoz	SLO	30.9.79	188/106	HT	79.70	82.58- 09
Kral	Mario	GER	15.2.89	187/80	LJ	7.97	7.99- 10
Krammes	Barry	USA	1.9.81	190/102	JT	77.36	78.97- 08
Kranjc	Matija	SLO	12.6.84	183/91	JT	79.15	79.72- 11
Krasnoshenkov	Ivan	RUS	26.3.87	199/120	DT	61.14	57.58- 12
Krasnov	Vladimir	RUS	19.8.90	190/70	400	45.49	45.12- 10
Krauss	Simon	FRA	12.2.92	182/75	110h	13.55, 13.41w	13.97- 12
* Kravchenko	Andrey	BLR	4.1.86	187/84	Dec	8390	8617- 07
^ Krimarenko	Yuriy	UKR	11.8.83	187/65	HJ	2.34	2.34i- 07, 2.33- 05
* Krivitskiy	Pavel	BLR	17.4.84	184/115	HT	79.36	80.67- 11
* Krivov	Andrey	RUS	14.11.85	185/72	20kW	1:20:47	1:18:25- 12
Kruger	A.G.	USA	18.2.79	193/118	HT	77.10	79.26- 04
Krüger	Eric	GER	21.3.88	178/72	400	45.77	45.97- 12
Krukowski	Marcin	POL	14.6.92	182/92	JT	83.04	82.58- 12
Kruzliak	Tomás	SVK	9.2.92	186/95	HT	70.84	67.60- 12
* Kszczot	Adam	POL	2.9.89	178/68	800	1:44.76	1:43.30- 11
Kubista	Ján	CZE	23.9.90	190/75	800	1:46.16	1:47.59- 12
Kubota	Shinobu	JPN	12.12.91	167/53	10k	28:07.54	28:07.01- 12
Kucera	Martin	SVK	10.5.90	193/80	400h	49.79	50.73- 12
^ Kucheranyu	Sergey	RUS	30.6.85	185/75	PV	5.71	5.81- 08
* Kudlicka	Jan	CZE	29.4.88	184/76	PV	5.77i, 5.76, 5.83ex	5.81ex- 11, 5.73- 12
Kudryavtsev	Denis	RUS	13.4.92		400h	49.40	51.45- 11
Kuira	Paul	KEN	25.1.90	172/53	10k	27:54.00	27:40.60- 11
Kuki	Takumi	JPN	18.5.92	170/64	100	10.19	10.23- 12
* Kuma	Abera	ETH	31.8.90	160/50	10k	26:52.85	27:18.39- 12
					HMar	61:09	60:19- 12
Kumar	Sandeep	IND	16.12.86	183/68	50kW	4:02:19	4:03:45- 12
Kupper	Martin	EST	31.5.89	195/108	DT	65.03	62.32- 12
Kurgat	Nixson	KEN	7.11.87		Mar	2:08:29	2:08:36- 11
Kürthy	Lajos	HUN	22.10.86	190/125	SP	19.76i, 19.14	20.78- 08
* Kuznetsov	Viktor	UKR	17.7.86	190/75	TJ	17.02i, 17.01	17.29- 10
* Kwambai	James	KEN	28.2.83	162/52	Mar	2:06:25	2:04:27--09
Kwambai	Robert	KEN	22.11.85		HMar	60:31	61:47- 11
* Kynard	Eric	USA	3.2.91	193/86	HJ	2.37	2.34- 12
Laaksonen	Tuomas	FIN	9.3.90	182/90	JT	81.73	72.86- 11
Laanmäe	Tanel	EST	29.9.89	184/89	JT	81.05	81.96- 09
Labäli	Abdelhadi	MAR	26.4.93	174/62	1500	3:35.95	3:37.59- 12
Lafi	Sami	ALG	25.4.90	170/60	1500	3:37.45	3:43.11- 12
* Lagat	Bernard	USA	12.12.74	174/61	1500	3:36.36	3:26.34- 01
3000	7:46.39, 7:34.71i	7:29.00- 10	2M	8:09.49i		8:12.45- 08 5000 12:58.99	12:53.60- 11
Lagat	Haron	KEN	15.8.83	174/57	5000	13:26.57	13:30.59- 11
					3kSt	8:22.95	8:15.80- 11
Lahbabi	Aziz	MAR	3.2.91	178/62	5000	13:09.45	13:04.06- 12
Laine	Samyr	HAI	17.7.84	188/82	TJ	17.36	17.39A, 17.45w- 09, 17.09- 11
Laitinen	Arno	FIN	9.3.88	187/95	HT	71.95	72.37- 11
* Lalang	Lawi	KEN	15.6.91	168/58	1500	3:33.20	3:36.77- 12
1M	3:54.56i		3:55.09i- 12		3000	7:41.9+	7:44.48i- 12
5000	13:00.95	13:08.28i, 13:18.88- 12			10k	28:14.63	-0-
Lamb	Bryce	USA	9.11.90	183/80	LJ	8.03w	8.15- 11
					TJ	16.96i	16.56- 12
Landry	Christopher	USA	29.4.86		10k	27:59.22	28:18.62- 12
Lane	John	GBR	29.1.89	185/88	Dec	7916	7534- 12
Lange	Andreas	GER	29.1.91	187/74	800	1:45.69	1:47.56- 12
Langowski	Artur	BRA	8.5.91	183/77	400h	49.77	50.22- 12
^ Lapierre	Fabrice	AUS	17.10.83	179/66	LJ	8.25	8.40, 8.78w- 10
Laptev	Sergey	RUS	7.2.91	176/70	TJ	16.41	16.63- 11
Láskaris	Panayiótis	GRE	10.3.92	180/70	PV	5.50	5.40- 11
* Lauro	Germán	ARG	2.4.84	190/110	SP	21.26	20.84- 12
					DT	61.72	63.55- 12
* Lavillenie	Renaud	FRA	18.9.86	177/69	PV	6.02	6.03i- 11, 6.01- 09
Lavillenie	Valentin	FRA	16.7.91	170/65	PV	5.70i	5.52- 12
Law	James	USA	8.10.80		100	10.14w	10.33- 10
Lawrence	Brijesh BJ	SKN	27.12.89	181/75	200	20.79, 20.53w	20.59- 11

Name		Nat	Born	Ht/Wt	Event	2013 Mark	Pre-2013 Best
Lawrence	Torrin	USA	11.4.89	186/77	400	45.33	45.40- 12
Lawson	Jarrion	USA-J	6.5.94	188/75	LJ	7.93	7.82, 7.89w- 12
Lazas	Kevin	USA	25.1.92	178/84	Dec	7933	7955- 12
le Roux	Wouter	RSA	17.1.86	186/77	400h	49.85A, 50.06	49.25A- 05
Lebedko	Aleksandr	BLR	24.5.87		TJ	16.67	16.80- 09
Lebésis	Spiridon	GRE	30.5.87	192/94	JT	79.97	83.02- 12
Lee	Beejay	USA	5.3.93	168/72	100	10.07	10.28, 10.26w- 12
Lee	Dexter	JAM	18.1.91	186/77	100	10.19	10.06- 11
Lee Yun-chul		KOR	28.3.82	188/110	HT	72.98	71.79- 08
Leer	Will	USA	15.4.85	184/70	1500	3:35.27	3:36.33- 11
3000	7:39.38			7:49.73- 10	5000	13:21.55	13:36.15- 12
Legesse	Berhanu	ETH	.93	168/55	5000	13:15.32	
Lehata	Mosito	LES	8.4.89	177/69	200	20.37	20.63- 12
Lehtola	Sampo	FIN	10.5.89	188/82	JT	81.67	83.77- 11
Lelei	Henry	KEN	31.12.88	180/64	3kSt	8:23.16	8:38.90- 12
Lelièvre	Jérémy	FRA	8.2.91	186/80	Dec	7880	7911- 12
* Lemaitre	Christophe	FRA	11.6.90	189/74	100	10.00, 9.98w	9.92- 11
					200	20.07	19.80- 11
Lemma	Sisay	ETH	12.12.90		Mar	2:09:02	2:11:58- 12
* Lendore	Deon	TTO	28.10.92	179/75	400	44.94	45.13- 12
Leppik	Erki	EST	18.3.88	183/86	JT	80.98	76.99- 11
Lescay	Yoandys	CUB-J	5.1.94	183/75	400	45.29	46.17- 12
Leslie	Cory	USA	24.10.89	175/60	1500	3:34.93	3:39.00- 12
1M	3:55.85	3:56.85i, 3:59.17- 12			3kSt	8:20.08	8:31.08- 12
* Lesnoy	Aleksandr	RUS	28.7.88	194/116	SP	20.60	20.05- 12
Letnicov	Vladimir	MDA	7.10.81	174/68	TJ	16.59i, 16.26	17.06- 02
Letting	Vincent	KEN	.93		1500	3:37.5 A	3:36.61A- 12
Levine	Nigel	GBR	30.4.89	175/68	400	45.23	45.11- 12
Levins	Cameron	CAN	28.3.89	181/68	1500	3:36.88	3:42.61- 12
3000	7:41.74+i			7:45.75i- 12	2M	8:14.69i	
5000	13:15.19			13:18.29- 12	10k	27:47.89	27:27.96- 12
Lewandowski	Marcin	POL	13.6.87	180/64	800	1:43.79	1:43.84- 09
Lewandowski	Michal	POL	28.8.88	200/84	TJ	16.55	16.32- 12, 16.43w- 11
Lewis	Reggie	USA	18.8.93	180/73	100	10.22, 10.07w	10.48- 12
* Lewis	Steve	GBR	20.5.86	191/83	PV	5.71i, 5.70	5.82- 12
^ Lewis-Francis	Mark	GBR	4.9.82	180/85	100	10.19	10.04- 02, 9.97w? -01
Li Chengbin		CHN	22.2.90		LJ	7.93i, 7.96w	7.78- 11
* Li Jianbo		CHN	14.11.86	176/57	20kW	1:18:52	1:19:10- 09
					50kW	3:52:12	3:39:01- 12
* Li Jinzhe		CHN	1.9.89	188/64	LJ	8.34	8.25- 12, 8.29w- 10
Li Shijia		CHN	14.1.92		20kW	1:20:54	1:22:15- 12
Li Tianlei		CHN-J	13.1.95	173/63	20kW	1:21:28	1:21:01- 12
Li Zhilong		CHN	9.3.88	185/75	400h	49.96	49.47- 11
Licciardi	Devis	ITA	21.7.86		3kSt	8:30.78	8:46.54- 12
* Lilesa	Feyisa	ETH	1.2.90	158/50	HMar	59:25	59:22- 12
					Mar	2:07:46	2:04:52- 12
Limaa	Ruben	KEN	.87		HMar	60:53	
Limo	Daniel Kiprop	KEN	10.12.83		HMar	60:42	59:55- 12
Limo	Philemon	KEN	2.8.85	180/62	HMar	60:38	59:32- 12
^ Lingua	Marco	ITA	4.6.78	179/112	HT	74.58	79.97- 08
Linke	Christopher	GER	24.10.88	191/64	20kW	1:22:36	1:20:41- 12
Linnik	Aleksandr	BLR	28.1.91	190/82	110h	13.53	
Lisek	Piotr	POL	16.8.92	188/85	PV	5.60	5.20, 5.30dq- 12
* Litvinov	Sergey	RUS	27.1.86	185/105	HT	80.89	80.98- 12
Liu Jianmin		CHN	9.3.88	183/68	20kW	1:19:34	1:22:41- 12
Liu Rusi		CHN	6.8.91		50kW	4:06:12	4:09:50- 11
Liu Yang		CHN	29.10.86	190/110	SP	19.77	18.87- 12
Livermore	Jason	JAM	25.4.88	178/77	100	10.07	10.31- 11
					200	20.13	20.73- 11
Llanos	Enrique	PUR	7.5.80	186/79	110h	13.56	13.52A- 11, 13.64, 13.57dq- 08
Lloyd	Zack	USA	10.10.84	191/141	SP	21.09	21.03- 08
Locke	Dentarius	USA	12.12.89	170/68	100	9.96, 9.91w	10.18- 12, 10.12w- 11
Loftin	Drew	USA	15.9.80	190/102	HT	74.63	76.11- 12
Logvinenko	Mikhail	RUS	19.4.84	186/83	Dec	7721	8004- 11
Lohse	Jonas	SWE	15.5.87	202/110	JT	77.19	81.40- 08
Lomerinyang	Julius	KEN	15.7.83		HMar	61:15	-0-
* Lomnicky	Marcel	SVK	6.7.87	177/106	HT	78.73	77.43- 12
Lomong	Lopez	USA	1.1.85	178/67	1500	3:34.55	3:32.20- 10
1M	3:51.45, 3:51.21i	3:53.18- 10			5000	13:07.00i	13:11.63- 12
* Longosiwa	Thomas	KEN	14.1.82	175/57	3000	7:32.01	7:30.09- 09
					5000	12:59.81	12:49.04- 12

Name		Nat	Born	Ht/Wt	Event	2013 Mark	Pre-2013 Best
Lonyangat	Paul	KEN	12.12.92	170/55	Mar	2:07:44	-0-
López	Francisco Javier	ESP	29.12.89	181/70	110h	13.64, 13.62w	13.74- 10, 13.69Aw- 12
López	Kevin	ESP	12.6.90	172/60	800	1:43.93	1:43.74- 12
* López	Luis Fernando	COL	3.6.79	173/60	20kW	1:21:51	1:20:03- 09
* López	Miguel Ángel	ESP	3.7.88	181/70	20kW	1:21:21	1:19:49- 12
Losev	Ivan	UKR	26.1.86	176/65	20kW	1:21:55	1:20:48- 12
Lotiang	John Kipsang	KEN	.91		HMar	60:16	61:50- 12
Lovett	Eddie	USA/ISV	25.6.92	181/73	110h	13.39, 13.29w	13.49- 12
Loxsom	Casimir	USA	17.3.91	183/64	800	1:45.75	1:45.28- 11
Lozano ¶	Alberto	ESP	23.2.87		5000	13:20.34	14:14.70- 09
Lu Anye		CHN	12.3.90	183/69	110h	13.67	13.89- 12
Luchianov	Ion	MDA	31.1.81	178/67	3kSt	8:19.64	8:18.97- 08
Lucindo	Jefferson	BRA	17.10.90	185/80	100	10.17	10.36, 10.22w- 12
Lukáš	Marek	CZE	16.7.91	180/75	Dec	7753	7448- 12
Lukyanenko	Artem	RUS	30.1.90	193/84	Dec	8177	8080- 12
^ Lukyanenko	Yevgeniy	RUS	23.1.85	190/80	PV	5.50	6.01- 08
Lukyanov	Denis	RUS	11.7.89	190/115	HT	79.61	74.84- 12
Luron	Kevin	FRA	8.11.91	184/80	TJ	16.48w	16.26- 12
Lyadusov	Konstantin	RUS	2.3.88	190/125	SP	20.44	19.75i, 19.48- 12
Lynsha	Maksim	BLR	6.4.85	190/72	110h	13.62	13.36- 12
Lyuboslavskiy	Anton	RUS	26.6.84	190/137	SP	20.61	20.78- 12
* Lyzhin	Pavel	BLR	24.3.81	189/110	SP	20.12	21.21- 10
Ma Liang		CHN	22.7.83	186/100	HT	70.63	74.11- 09
Maazouzi	Zakaria	MAR	15.6.85	171/62	1500	3:31.94	3:39.87- 08
Macharinyang	Hosea	KEN	12.6.85	160/45	10k	28:03.5 A	27:58.41- 07
Mackey ¶	Trevorvano	BAH	5.1.92	188/84	100	10.10w	10.31, 10.25w- 12
					200	20.60	20.52A, 20.68- 12
Madison	Chase	USA	13.9.85	192/130	DT	61.24	62.85- 08
Maduranga	Sachith	SRI	15.6.90		JT	79.62	77.80- 12
Maeda	Kazuhiro	JPN	19.4.81	167/56	Mar	2:08:00	2:08:38- 12
Magakwe	Simon	RSA	25.5.85	177/73	100	9.9	10.06A, 10.11- 12
Mägi	Rasmus	EST	4.5.92	186/75	400h	49.19	49.54- 12
Magut	James	KEN	20.7.90	180/64	1500	3:35.2 A	3:33.31- 12
					1M	3:50.93	3:50.68- 12
Maheswary	Renjith	IND	30.1.86	177/72	TJ	16.98	17.07- 10, 17.19w- 07
Mahmoud	Hassan Mohamed	EGY	10.2.84	188/132	HT	78.21	76.69- 12
Mahoney	Travis	USA	25.7.90	172/61	3kSt	8:30.87	8:36.10- 11
Maia	Edi	POR	10.11.87	176/75	PV	5.70	5.64i- 12, 5.60- 11
Maina	Johana	KEN	24.12.90	170/54	10k	28:05.13	28:04.25- 12
Mainy	Ahmed	MAR	20.8.86	172/62	800	1:46.25	1:47.43- 12
					1500	3:36.80	3:41.83- 12
Maitland	Nicholas	JAM	27.11.89	185/73	400	45.63	46.07- 12
Majdan	Dusan	SVK	8.9.87	180/67	50kW	3:57:50	3:59:05- 12
* Majewski	Tomasz	POL	30.8.81	204/140	SP	20.98	21.95- 09
* Makhloufi	Taoufik	ALG	29.4.88	181/66	1500	3:36.30+	3:30.80- 12
					1M	3:52.94	
Makhrosenko	Zakhar	BLR	10.10.91		HT	76.08	73.02- 12
Makinde	Oluwasegun	CAN	6.7.91	179/82	200	20.48w	20.71A, 20.62w- 12, 20.72- 11
Maksimov	Konstantin	RUS	17.6.82	178/67	50kW	3:47:48	3:48:18- 12
* Makusha	Ngonidzashe	ZIM	11.3.87	178/73	LJ	8.04, 8.20w	8.40- 11
Makwala	Isaac	BOT	29.9.86	183/73	200	20.21	20.73- 09
					400	45.86	45.25- 12
* Malachowski	Piotr	POL	7.6.83	193/130	DT	71.84	69.83- 10
Malel	William	KEN-J	1.3.94	165/52	5000	13:19.83	13:25.82- 12
					10k	27:48.55	28:29.3A- 12
Malone	Casey	USA	6.4.77	203/109	DT	63.44	68.49A- 09
Mamba-Schlick	Hugo	CMR	1.2.82	195/85	TJ	16.54i, 16.50	17.14- 10
Mamedov	Mergen	TKM	24.12.90	187/108	HT	74.01	70.70- 12
* Mance	Josh	USA	21.3.92	191/82	400	45.08	44.83- 12
Manenti	Davide	ITA	16.4.89	175/77	200	20.60	20.76- 12
Manninen	Rainer	FIN	21.3.91	189/84	JT	79.06	73.28- 11
* Mannio	Ari	FIN	23.7.87	185/104	JT	84.65	85.70- 09
Manso	Dário	POR	1.7.82	183/117	HT	71.14	71.81- 12
* Manzano	Leonel	USA	12.9.84	165/57	800	1:46.28	1:44.56- 10
					1500	3:33.14	3:32.37- 10
Maraba	Wilson	KEN	2.12.86		3kSt	8:28.21	8:16.96- 12
Marco	Luis Alberto	ESP	20.8.86	183/70	800	1:45.44	1:45.14- 12
Marghiev	Sergey	MDA	7.11.92	195/93	HT	74.41	75.20- 12
Maric	Martin	CRO	19.4.84	196/115	DT	64.17	66.53- 12
Maritim	Anthony	KEN	.86		HMar	61:24	61:27- 10
Márquez	Dayron	COL	19.11.83	181/93	JT	79.03A	80.61A- 12, 82.20Au- 08

Name		Nat	Born	Ht/Wt	Event	2013 Mark		Pre-2013 Best
Marshin	Dmitriy	AZE	24.2.72	180/100	HT	76.48		79.56- 12
Marthély	Stéphane	FRA	9.9.79	193/104	DT	60.84		58.34- 12
* Martin	Cory	USA	22.5.85	196/125	SP	20.98i, 20.67		22.10- 10
Martin	Romain	FRA	12.7.88	198/86	Dec	8013		7977- 12
Martín	Álvaro	ESP-J	18.6.94	181/62	20kW	1:22:25		1:22:12- 12
Martín	Pedro José	ESP	12.8.92	188/100	HT	71.65		68.43- 11
* Martina	Churandy	NED	3.7.84	180/68	100	10.03		9.91- 12, 9.76Aw- 06
					200	20.01		19.85- 12
* Martínez	Guillermo	CUB	28.6.81	185/100	JT	85.59		87.20A- 11
Martínez	José Ernesto	CUB	1.1.91	175/73	TJ	16.56		16.39, 16.70w- 12
Martínez	Lázaro	CUB-Y	3.11.97	192/83	TJ	16.63		15.38- 12
Martínez	Lois Maikel	ex-CUB	3.6.81	185/90	DT	65.98		67.45- 05
^ Martínez	Wilfredo	CUB	9.1.85	180/82	LJ	8.06		8.31A- 08, 8.20- 10
* Martinot Lagarde	Pascal	FRA	22.9.91	190/80	110h	13.12		13.41, 13.30w- 12
Martinot Lagarde	Thomas	FRA	7.2.88	186/78	110h	13.26		13.56- 10
Marto	Tiago	POR	5.4.86	184/85	Dec	7603		7624- 10
Martos	Sebastián	ESP	20.6.89	178/63	3kSt	8:22.97		8:23.02- 11
Maru	David	KEN			HMar	60:41		63:53- 12
Maruyama	Fumihiro	JPN	1.7.90	163/46	HMar	61:15		63:29- 10
Masai	Denis	KEN	1.12.91	168/52	5000	13:23.32		13:23.53- 11
* Maslák	Pavel	CZE	21.2.91	176/67	200	20.49		20.59- 12
					400	44.84		44.91- 12
Mason	Jamele	PUR	19.10.89	190/85	400h	50.12		48.89- 12
Mason	Michael	CAN	30.9.86	186/67	HJ	2.31		2.31- 12
Masterson	Derek	USA	30.1.90	188/84	Dec	7631 (w)		7558- 12
Mástoras	Adónios	GRE	6.1.91	198/77	HJ	2.29i, 2.26		2.25- 12
Maswai	Samuel	KEN	29.3.88		Mar	2:08:52		2:11:46- 12
* Mätas	Risto	EST	30.4.84	190/87	JT	83.48		82.10- 12
Matebor	Albert	KEN	20.12.80	174/57	Mar	2:08:17		2:05:23- 11
Mateelong	Peter	KEN	26.11.89		3kSt	8:29.5 A		8:29.7A- 12
* Mathathi	Martin	KEN	25.12.85	167/52	10k	27:52.65		26:59.88- 09
HMar	60:54	59:48- 10, 58:56dh- 11			Mar	2:07:16		-0-
Mathieu	Michael	BAH	24.6.83	180/78	200	20.35		20.16- 12
					400	45.21		45.06- 12
Matsumoto	Aoi	JPN	7.9.87	177/60	3kSt	8:33.82		8:30.49- 10
Matsushita	Yuki	JPN	9.9.91	175/68	400h	49.71		51.78- 12
Matsuzaki	Takaki	JPN	12.8.92		20kW	1:22:06		1:23:47- 12
May	Anthony	USA	19.9.90	180/73	HJ	2.24		2.24- 12
Mayer	Gerhard	AUT	20.5.80	191/100	DT	65.16		65.24- 10
* Mayer	Kevin	FRA	10.2.92	186/77	Dec	8446		8447w/8415- 12
Mayers	Emanuel	TTO	9.3.89	178/70	400h	49.72A, 50.34		49.65- 10
Mazác	Martin	CZE	6.5.90	187/74	110h	13.48		13.64- 10
^ Mazuryk	Maksym	UKR	2.4.83	190/85	PV	5.55i		5.88i- 11, 5.82- 08
Mbow	El Hadji Seth	SEN	2.4.85	183/74	400h	49.86A, 50.09		50.39- 12
Mbuvi	Boniface	KEN	20.12.86		Mar	2:09:06		2:08:39- 12
McBride	Brandon	CAN-J	15.6.94		800	1:46.38		1:46.07- 12
McClain	Remontay	USA	21.9.92	188/85	200	20.54, 20.32w		20.57, 20.33w- 12
McCoy	Reuben	USA	16.3.86	186/75	400h	49.75		48.37- 08
McCullough	Conor	IRL	31.1.91	186/102	HT	71.49		75.09- 12
McDonald	Rusheen	JAM	17.8.92	175/73	400	45.28		45.10- 12
McFarlane	Jorge	PER	20.2.88	176/70	110h	13.61, 13.53Aw		13.72A- 11, 13.75- 10
					LJ	7.95, 8.01w		8.10A- 09, 7.95- 11
McKenzie	Ramone	JAM	15.11.90	184/82	100	10.21, 10.02w		10.10, 10.05w- 12
McLaren	Scott	NZL	22.2.82	190/89	Dec	7750		7733- 12
McLeod	Omar	JAM-J	25.4.94	184/79	400h	49.98		51.16- 12
McNamara	Jordan	USA	7.3.87	178/64	1500	3:34.00		3:35.63- 12
					1M	3:52.42		3:54.89- 11
* McQuay	Tony	USA	16.4.90	178/64	200	20.60		20.60- 12
					400	44.40		44.49- 12
Mead	Hassan	USA	28.8.89	174/61	5000	13:11.80		13:28.45- 09
Mechaal	Adel	ESP	5.12.90		1500	3:36.78		3:42.77- 11
Mecheso	Girma	ETH/USA	16.1.88	162/50	10k	27:52.38		28:16.97- 12
* Medhin	Teklemariam	ERI	24.6.89	178/57	10k	27:19.97		27:16.69- 11
Mejias	Reinier	CUB	22.9.90	180/96	HT	75.98		73.86- 12
Mekashaw	Kassa	ETH	19.3.84	167/54	10k	28:01.01		
* Mekhissi-Benabbad	Mahiedine	FRA	15.3.85	190/75	1500	3:33.12		3:33.86- 11
2000	4:56.85	5:00.17- 11		3000	7:43.72i	7:44.98- 10	3kSt	8:00.09	8:02.09- 11
Meléndez	José	VEN	19.5.93	182/73	400	45.82		46.45- 12
Meleshko	Pavel	BLR	24.11.92		JT	77.63		78.08- 11
* Melich	Lukás	CZE	16.9.80	186/110	HT	80.28		79.44- 12
Méliz	Luis Felipe	ESP	11.8.79	182/80	LJ	8.01		8.43- 00

Name		Nat	Born	Ht/Wt	Event	2013 Mark	Pre-2013 Best
Melly	Edwin	KEN-J	23.4.94	178/60	800	1:44.49	1:43.81- 12
Menaldo	Kévin	FRA	12.7.92	176/66	PV	5.65i, 5.60	5.50- 11
Mendes	Jonathan	BRA	14.4.90	187/80	110h	13.61, 13.55w	13.96- 12
Méndez	Juan José	MEX	27.4.88	180/80	JT	78.43A	78.23- 11
Mendieta	José Angel	CUB	16.10.91	187/84	Dec	7967h	7833- 12
Mengistu	Azmeraw	ETH	15.9.92	170/54	10k	27:59.96	28:19.40- 12
* Menjo	Josephat Kiprono	KEN	20.8.79	168/50	10k	28:03.0 A	26:56.74- 10
* Menkov	Aleksandr	RUS	7.12.90	178/74	LJ	8.56	8.29- 12
* Merga	Imane	ETH	15.10.88	174/61	5000	13:09.17	12:53.58- 10
					10k	26:57.33	26:48.35- 11
* Merritt	Aries	USA	24.7.85	182/74	110h	13.09	12.80- 12
* Merritt	LaShawn	USA	27.6.86	188/82	200	20.26	19.98- 07, 19.80w- 08
					400	43.74	43.75- 08
Merzougui	Abdelaziz	MAR	30.8.91	177/62	3kSt	8:22.68	8:18.03- 12
Mesel	Amanuel	ERI	29.12.90	175/57	HMar	60:10	61:20- 11
					Mar	2:08:17	
Mesic	Kemal	BIH	4.8.85	196/110	SP	20.37	20.71- 12
^ Mesnil	Romain	FRA	13.6.77	188/80	PV	5.62i	5.95- 03
Metu	Obinna	NGR	12.7.88	185/75	200	20.55	20.54- 12, 20.5- 07
Meucci	Daniele	ITA	7.10.85	178/62	3000	7:45.31	7:41.74- 12
10k	28:06.74		27:32.86- 12		HMar	61:06	62:30- 11
* Michalski	Lukasz	POL	2.8.88	190/85	PV	5.60	5.85- 11
Mikhon	Eduard	BLR	7.6.89	194/85	Dec	8125	8152- 11
Mikhou	Sadik	MAR	25.7.90	174/61	1500	3:33.31	
Mikos	Mateusz	POL	10.4.87	196/107	SP	19.62	19.40- 12
Milanov	Philip	BEL	6.7.91		DT	61.81	57.66- 12
Mileusnic	Dejan	BIH	16.11.91	183/84	JT	79.62	77.45- 12
Milion	Zewdie	ETH	24.1.89	171/53	5000	13:20.73	13:35.38- 12
					10k	28:02.86	27:54.52- 12
Miller	Brunson	USA	10.2.91	183/77	400	45.86	46.90- 12
Miller	Craig	USA	3.8.87	185/72	1500	3:35.48	3:36.35- 12
Miller	Nick	GBR	1.5.93	185/105	HT	71.60	67.56- 12
Miller	Ramon	BAH	17.2.87	180/73	400	44.93	44.87- 12
Milne	Taylor	CAN	14.6.81	180/66	3kSt	8:31.48	-0-
Milus	Ryan	USA	19.9.90	178/70	100	10.19, 10.14w	10.21- 12, 10.07w- 11
Misans	Elvijs	LAT	8.4.89	182/73	LJ	7.92i	8.00i- 11, 7.96- 12
Misganaw	Abraraw	ETH	.90		HMar	61:17	63:06- 12
Missirov	Lev	RUS	4.8.90		HJ	2.26	2.21i, 2.21- 12
* Mitchell	Curtis	USA	11.3.89	188/79	200	19.97	19.99- 10
Mitchell	Manteo	USA	6.7.87	178/73	400	45.25	44.96- 12
* Mitchell	Maurice	USA	22.12.89	178/73	100	10.20w	10.00- 11
					200	20.32	20.13- 12, 19.99w- 11
Mitchell	Sheldon	JAM	19.7.90	181/75	100	10.11	10.14- 12
Miyao	Kotaro	JPN	12.7.91	172/72	400h	50.10	49.88- 12
Miyawaki	Chihiro	JPN	28.8.91	175/55	10k	27:57.90	27:41.57- 11
Moffatt	Keith	USA	20.6.84	203/84	HJ	2.28	2.30- 06
Mohamed	Abdulaziz	KSA	7.1.91	184/70	800	1:43.86	1:45.52- 12
Mohammed	Mukhtar	GBR	1.12.90	175/59	800	1:45.67	1:45.90- 11
* Mohr	Malte	GER	24.7.86	192/84	PV	5.86	5.91- 12
Möhsner	Sven	GER	30.1.86	190/115	HT	73.10	73.82- 09
Mokdel	Lyès	ALG	20.6.90	195/84	110h	13.63	13.64- 12, 13.5- 10
* Mokoena	Khotso	RSA	6.3.85	190/73	LJ	8.30	8.50- 09
Mokoka	Stephen	RSA	31.1.85	156/50	5000	13:25.94	13:27.22- 10
					10k	28:09.70	27:40.73- 12
Molepo	Edwin	RSA	31.5.87	175/65	3kSt	8:33.06	8:26.82- 11
Momoh	Leoman	NGR	30.3.91	188/74	800	1:46.07i	1:48.73- 12
Moogas	Tasama	ISR	2.2.88	165/52	10k	28:12.58	28:12.87- 12
Morales	Ignacio	CUB	28.1.87	183/69	110h	13.48, 13.4	13.51- 09, 13.1- 08
Moreira	José Carlos	BRA	28.9.83	168/63	100	10.16	10.15- 09, 10.0- 08
Moreno	Xavier	ECU	15.11.79	168.60	50kW	4:07:29	3:52:07- 07
Morgan	Jason	JAM	6.10.82	186/114	DT	65.94	67.15- 12
* Morgunov	Sergey	RUS	9.2.93	178/70	LJ	8.06	8.35- 12
^ Morioka	Koichiro	JPN	2.4.85	184/65	20kW	1:20:14	1:20:43- 10
					50kW	3:50:51	3:43:14- 12
Morris	Joe	USA	4.10.89	180/68	100	10.24, 10.09Aw	10.37A- 11,10.42, 10.31w- 12
					200	20.45Aw	20.77A, 20.82, 20.77w- 12
Morse	Brett	GBR	11.2.89	191/114	DT	66.84	66.06- 11
Mosin	Lev	RUS	7.12.92	185/75	400	45.51	46.64- 12
Moskalenko	Maksym	UKR	20.10.87	188/68	TJ	16.51	16.26i, 16.16- 08
Mossberg	Nick	USA	5.4.86	178/77	PV	5.60	5.55- 11
Mousavi	Kaveh	IRI	27.5.85	196/105	HT	71.43	75.26- 11

Name		Nat	Born	Ht/Wt	Event	2013 Mark	Pre-2013 Best
* Moustaoui	Mohammed	MAR	2.4.85	174/60	1500	3:32.08	3:31.84- 11
					1M	3:52.42	3:50.08- 08
Mozia	Stephen	USA/NGR	16.8.93	193/102	SP	19.89i, 19.20	19.10i, 18.81- 12
					DT	61.13	53.22- 12
Mucheru	Boniface	KEN	2.5.92	185/75	400h	49.59A	49.45- 12
Mudrov	Ilya	RUS	17.11.91		PV	5.50	5.50- 12
* Mudrov	Sergey	RUS	8.9.90	190/79	HJ	2.35i, 2.31	2.31- 12
Mukono	Moses	KEN-J	27.11.95		3000	7:44.61	
^ Mulabegovic	Nedzad	CRO	4.2.81	190/120	SP	20.20	20.66- 12
Mulder	Tyler	USA	15.2.87	189/77	800	1:44.34	1:44.75- 12
Müller	Norman	GER	7.8.85	195/84	Dec	8179w, 7960	8295- 09
Mullera	Angel	ESP	20.4.84	175/62	3kSt	8:19.26 drugs?	8:13.71- 12
Mullett	Rob	GBR	31.7.87	183/68	3kSt	8:32.68	8:31.62- 12
Mumba	Prince	ZAM	28.8.84	167/67	800	1:46.20	1:46.14- 11
Münch	Markus	GER	13.6.86	207/117	DT	64.44	66.87- 11
Mundell	Marc	RSA	7.7.83	189/86	50kW	3:57:55	3:55:32- 12
* Murakami	Yukifumi	JPN	23.12.79	186/102	JT	85.96	83.95- 12
Murayama	Kenta	JPN	23.2.93	175/53	10k	28:18.11	28:14.27- 12
					HMar	61:19	62:46- 12
Murillo	Jhon Freddy	COL	13.6.84		TJ	16.58, 16.82Aw, 16.75w	16.37A, 16.32- 12
* Murofushi	Koji	JPN	8.10.74	187/103	HT	78.03	84.86- 03
Murphy	Isaac	USA	5.10.90	188/83	Dec	8086 (w)	8067- 12
Musagala	Ronald	UGA	16.12.92	176/61	800	1:45.71A	1:50.76A- 11
* Mutai	Abel	KEN	2.10.88	172/73	3kSt	8:08.83	8:01.67- 12
* Mutai	Emmanuel	KEN	12.10.84	168/54	Mar	2:03:52	2:04:40- 11
* Mutai	Geoffrey	KEN	7.10.81	170/54	10k	27:55.3 A	27:27.79A- 10
HMar	58:58		59:30- 09		Mar	2:08:24	2:04:15- 12, 2:03:02wdh- 11
Mutai	Jeremiah	KEN	27.12.92	173/60	800	1:43.9 A	1:48.1A- 09
Mutunga	Patrick	KEN-J	20.11.94	174/57	5000	13:19.96	13:19.13- 11
					10k	27:28.67	27:30.32- 12
Mutunga	William	KEN	17.9.93	178/70	400h	49.82A	50.95A- 12
Mvumuvre	Gabriel	ZIM	23.4.88	172/75	100	9.98	10.23, 10.10w- 11
Mwaka	Patrick	KEN	2.11.92	165/45	5000	13:23.20	13:21.45- 10
					10k	27:51.10	27:33.14- 11
Mwangangi	John	KEN	1.11.90		10k	28:08.5 A	28:47.4A- 11
Mwangi	Alex	KEN	14.6.90	158/50	10k	27:58.02	27:42.20- 10
Mwangi	James	KEN	23.6.84	178/58	Mar	2:08:48	2:08:38- 11
Mykolaitis	Povilas	LTU	23.2.83	187/79	LJ	7.98	8.15- 11
Mykolaychuk	Dmytro	UKR	30.1.87	192/89	HT	75.11	75.24- 11
Mzazi	Gladwin	RSA	28.8.88	160/48	HMar	61:12	61:38- 12
* Nakamoto	Kentaro	JPN	7.12.82	174/57	Mar	2:08:35	2:08:53- 12
Nakamura	Akihiko	JPN	23.10.90	180/73	400h	49.77	49.38- 12
					Dec	7723	7710- 12
Nakamura	Shogo	JPN	16.9.92	172/52	10k	28:05.79	28:22.59- 12
Nakano	Hiroyuki	JPN	9.12.88	173/69	400	45.62	45.81- 12
Nall	Donte	USA	27.1.88	188/77	HJ	2.25	2.24i- 12, 2.23- 11
Naoki	Masafumi	JPN	19.11.93	173/63	100	10.20w	10.62- 12
Nasti	Patrick	ITA	30.8.89	188/73	3kSt	8:30.28	8:29.08- 12
Naumovich	Artyom	BLR	19.2.91		HJ	2.25	2.21- 12
^ Nava	Horacio	MEX	20.1.82	175/62	50kW	3:58:00A	3:45:21- 08
* Nazarov	Dilshod	TJK	6.5.82	187/115	HT	80.71	80.30- 11
Ndiaye	Amadou	SEN	6.12.92	180/71	400h	49.74	50.95- 12
Ndiema	Eric	KEN	28.12.92		Mar	2:06:34	2:06:07- 11
* Ndiku	Caleb	KEN	9.10.92	183/68	1500	3:29.50	3:32.02- 11
1M	3:50.46	3:49.77- 11			3000	7:33.92, 7:31.66i	7:30.99- 12 5000 13:03.80 13:18.96- 10
^ Ndiku	Jonathan	KEN	18.9.91	173/60	5000	13:14.97	13:11.99- 09
					3kSt	8:18.78	8:07.75- 11
Ndirangu	Macharia	KEN-J	9.9.94	168/49	10k	27:59.11	
Ndungu	Geoffrey	KEN	11.3.87		Mar	2:08:42	2:08:35- 11
Nebebew	Birhan	ETH-J	14.8.94	172/55	5000	13:14.60	
Nedow	Tim	CAN	16.10.90	198/125	SP	20.74	20.51i, 20.21- 12
Negesse	Endeshaw	ETH	13.3.88	170/54	Mar	2:04:52	2:09:59- 12
Negewo	Abebe	ETH	20.5.84		HMar	60:40	62:25- 09
* Nellum	Bryshon	USA	1.5.89	183/79	200	20.23, 19.99w	20.43- 07
					400	44.73	44.80- 12
Nelson	Billy	USA	11.9.84	167/55	3kSt	8:29.10	8:17.27- 11
Németh	Kristóf	HUN	17.9.87	190/97	HT	74.72	76.45- 10
Nerkaryan	Gor	ARM	24.3.93		LJ	7.97	7.62A- 11
Nesterenko	Maksim	BLR	1.9.92		TJ	16.40i, 16.35	15.56- 12
Nesterenko	Mykyta	UKR	15.4.91	202/97	DT	62.88	65.31- 08
Nevers	Adolphus	JAM	19.3.90	180/70	200	20.58	21.30- 12

Name		Nat	Born	Ht/Wt	Event	2013 Mark	Pre-2013 Best
Newdick	Brent	NZL	31.1.85	189/89	Dec	7744	8114- 11
Newman	Calesio	USA	20.8.86	172/66	100	10.08, 10.05w	10.07- 12
					200	20.37, 20.33w	20.28, 20.17w- 12
Neymour	Wesley	BAH	1.9.88	193/82	400	45.54	46.18- 12
* Nganga	Bernard Mbugua	KEN	17.1.85	170/55	3kSt	8:19.14	8:05.88- 11
Ngatia	Hiram	KEN-Y	.96		5000	13:26.73	13:49.04- 12
Ngetich	Hillary	KEN-J	15.9.95		1500	3:35.87	3:36.15- 12
Nguyen Van Hung		VIE	4.3.89	172/62	TJ	16.67	16.41- 10
Nilsson	Marcus	SWE	3.5.91	185/90	Dec	8104 (w)	7823- 12
^ Nima	Issam	ALG	8.4.79	186/74	TJ	16.51, 17.01w	16.89- 12
Ninov	Viktor	BUL	19.6.88	197/82	HJ	2.30i, 2.24	2.29- 11
Niu Wenbin		CHN	20.1.91		20kW	1:21:41	1:22:13- 12
					50kW	3:56:56	3:54:19- 11
^ Nixon	Greg	USA	12.9.81	183/75	200	20.60	20.39- 09
* Nixon	Gunnar	USA	13.1.93	190/77	Dec	8312	7892- 12
Njiru	Kennedy	KEN	.87		3kSt	8:31.4 A	8:33.5A- 12
Njui	Cyrus	KEN	11.2.86	171/52	10k	28:11.81	27:56.63- 07
					HMar	61:08	61:03- 09
Nkanata	Carvin	USA	6.5.91	183/73	200	20.32, 20.29w	20.99w- 12
Nkouloukidi	Jean-Jacques	ITA	15.4.82	172/56	50kW	3:54:00	3:52:35- 11
Nkrumah	Keith	GHA	28.11.90	188/79	110h	13.63	13.68- 12
* Noga	Artur	POL	2.5.88	196/82	110h	13.26	13.27- 12, 13.20w- 10
Noguchi	Hiroshi	JPN	3.5.83	176/115	HT	72.43	71.58- 10
Nolan	Errol	JAM	18.8.91	178/73	400	45.72i, 45.88	45.25- 12
Norwood	Vernon	USA	10.4.92	187/77	400	45.56A, 45.67	45.72A, 45.98- 12
* Noskov	Ivan	RUS	16.7.88	177/62	50kW	3:41:36	3:55:16- 12
Nossmy	Philip	SWE	6.12.82	189/87	110h	13.49	13.47- 12
* Nowak	Lukasz	POL	18.12.88	194/77	20kW	1:20:48	1:21:12- 12
					50kW	3:43:38	3:42:47- 12
Nowicki	Wojciech	POL	22.2.89	196/112	HT	75.87	73.52- 12
Nozawa	Keisuke	JPN	7.6.91	175/57	400h	49.86	49.15- 12
Nugent	Barrett	USA	29.1.90	186/77	110h	13.48	13.32A- 12, 13.35- 10, 13.19w- 11
Nurudeen	Selim	NGR	1.2.83	183/75	110h	13.52	13.51- 12
Nychyporchuk	Oleksandr	UKR	14.4.92	185/84	JT	80.05	81.65- 12
O'Farrill	Yordan	CUB	9.2.93	185/77	110h	13.44	13.91- 12
O'Hare	Chris	GBR	23.11.90	173/60	1500	3:35.37	3:37.95- 12
					1M	3:52.98i	3:56.48i, 3:58.77- 11
O'Lionáird	Ciarán	IRL	11.4.88	180/64	1500	3:36.85i	3:34.46- 11
					1M	3:52.10i	3:54.76i, 3:57.02- 12
O'Shea	Daniel	NZL	11.2.89	187/80	400h	50.16	51.62- 11
^ Odriozola	Mikel	ESP	25.5.73	180/62	50kW	4:00:05	3:41:47- 05
Ogho-Oghene	Egweru	NGR	26.11.88	171/66	100	10.16	10.06- 11, 10.0- 08
Ogita	Hiroki	JPN	30.12.87	185/78	PV	5.70	5.65- 12
Oh Se-hyun		KOR	22.2.84	178/64	50kW	4:00:25	3:54:20- 11
^ Oke	Tosin	NGR	1.10.80	178/77	TJ	16.87i, 16.64	17.23- 12
Okello	Tony	UGA	26.12.83	167/52	10k	27:55.07	28:12.95- 12
Okutu	Jean Marie	ESP	4.8.88	179/68	LJ	7.93A	7.94- 09, 8.05w- 12
Olgundeniz	Ercüment	TUR	7.7.76	203/120	DT	64.77	67.50- 12
de Oliveira	Júlio César	BRA	4.2.86	185/97	JT	77.23	80.05, 80.29 irreg- 09
de Oliveira	Nil	SWE	3.9.86	186/74	200	20.53	20.62- 12
Oliveira	Paulo Sérgio	BRA	1.6.93		LJ	7.99	7.67- 12
					TJ	16.33, 16.41w	16.14- 12
de Oliveira	Pedro	BRA	17.2.92	188/85	400	45.62	45.52- 12
* Oliver	David	USA	24.4.82	188/93	110h	13.00	12.89- 10
Olivier	André	RSA	29.12.89	192/72	800	1:44.37	1:44.29- 12
Oloisunga	Benson	KEN	.86		HMar	61:16	61:07- 12
Olson	Petter	SWE	14.2.91	183/81	Dec	7643	7857- 12
Omelko	Rafal	POL	16.1.89	195/75	400	45.69	46.30- 12
Omuro	Hideki	JPN	25.7.90	179/65	110h	13.58	13.54- 12
Omwamba	Enoch	KEN	4.4.93	168/54	10k	28:15.80	28:18.93- 12
					HMar	61:15	-0-
Onakoya	Abiola	NGR	10.10.90	194/79	400	45.79	45.89- 11
Ondoro	Pius	KEN	.88		Mar	2:08:00	2:12:10- 12
Oosthuizen	Robert	RSA	23.1.87	188/101	JT	81.97A	86.80- 08
Opatskiy	Yuriy	UKR	5.11.79	180/75	TJ	16.53	16.48- 01, 16.53w- 12
* Oprea	Marian	ROU	6.6.82	190/80	TJ	17.24, 17.32w	17.81- 05
* Ortega	Orlando	CUB	29.7.91	185/70	110h	13.08	13.09- 12
* Osaghae	Omo	USA	18.5.88	184/75	110h	13.35, 13.13w	13.23, 13.18w- 11
* Osagie	Andrew	GBR	19.2.88	189/72	800	1:44.36	1:43.77- 12
Osako	Suguru	JPN	23.5.91	170/53	5000	13:20.80	13:31.27- 11
					10k	27:38.31	27:56.94- 12

Name		Nat	Born	Ht/Wt	Event	2013 Mark	Pre-2013 Best
Osei	Philip	CAN	30.10.90	176/64	400	45.71	45.51A, 46.16- 12
Osman	Abrar	ERI-J	1.1.94	173/55	3000	7:39.70	7:40.89- 11
					5000	13:20.79	13:17.32- 12
Ostrowski	Cameron	USA	15.6.92	200/84	HJ	2.24	2.20- 12
* Otto	Björn	GER	16.10.77	188/84	PV	5.90	6.01- 12
Oualich	Hamid	FRA	26.4.88	184/68	800	1:45.91	1:45.96- 12
Ouhadi	Aziz	MAR	24.7.84	175/73	100	10.27, 10.12w	10.09- 11, 9.9- 09
					200	20.81, 20.46w	20.50- 12
Outzen	Matthew	AUS	12.10.87	185/100	JT	78.10	79.41- 10
Özbilen	Ilham Tanui	TUR	5.3.90	177/60	800	1:44.00	1:44.25- 11
1500	3:31.30			3:31.37- 11	1M	3:52.30	3:49.29- 09
Paau	Aníbal	GUA	12.1.87	174/62	20kW	1:22:19	1:24:06- 11
Paech	Carlo	GER	18.12.92	190/84	PV	5.53i, 5.52	5.50i- 11, 5.40- 12
Page	Cameron	AUS	12.6.91	177/64	1M	3:54.77	
^ Pahapill	Mikk	EST	18.7.83	196/93	Dec	8170	8398- 11
Pai Long		CHN	8.10.89		HJ	2.26	2.28- 12
Palma	Ever	MEX	18.3.92	176/66	20kW	1:22:02	1:21:02- 11
Palma	Isaac	MEX	26.10.90	174/59	20kW	1:21:13	1:21:14- 12
Papamihail	Aléxandros	GRE	18.9.88	178/63	50kW	3:51:05	3:49:56- 12
* Parchment	Hansle	JAM	17.6.90	196/90	110h	13.05	13.12- 12
Parellis	Apostolos	CYP	24.7.85	186/110	DT	62.48	65.36- 12
Park Chil-sung		KOR	8.7.82	173/61	50kW	3:54:13	3:45:55- 12
Park Jae-myong		KOR	15.12.81	180/95	JT	79.71	83.99- 04
Parker	Cody	CAN	27.6.92	184/91	JT	77.98A	73.50- 11
Parros	Clayton	USA	11.12.90	178/70	400	45.73	45.71- 09
* Pars	Krisztián	HUN	18.2.82	188/113	HT	82.40	82.45- 06
Parsons	Tom	GBR	5.5.84	192/80	HJ	2.28	2.31i- 11, 2.30- 08
Parszczynski	Lukasz	POL	4.5.85	180/64	3kSt	8:25.01	8:15.47- 11
Partanen	Veli-Matti	FIN	28.10.91	178/62	50kW	3:58:50	-0-
Patrakov	Andrey	RUS	7.11.89	196/80	HJ	2.27i, 2.14	2.30i- 12, 2.21- 11
Patsoukakis	Dimitrios	GRE	18.3.87	180/70	PV	5.50	5.55- 09
^ Patton	Darvis	USA	4.12.77	183/75	100	10.07, 9.75w	9.89, 9.84w- 08
Paulo	Alberto	POR	3.10.85	178/62	3kSt	8:33.09	8:22.41- 11
* Payne	David	USA	24.7.82	185/81	110h	13.30, 13.22w	13.02- 07
Peacock	Hamish	AUS	15.10.90	186/96	JT	81.14	79.33- 12
Peltomäki	Sami	FIN	11.1.91	180/87	JT	77.27	76.71- 12
Peña	José Gregorio	VEN	12.1.87	163/60	3kSt	8:20.87	8:24.06- 12
Persoon	Maarten	NED	15.3.87	190/110	DT	60.95	61.28- 11
Pesic	Darko	MNE	30.11.92	189/89	Dec	7636	7307- 12
* Pestano	Mario	ESP	8.4.78	195/120	DT	65.79	69.50- 08
Peter	Some	KEN	5.6.90		HMar	60:21	61:34- 10
Peters	Richard	GBR	18.2.90	183/64	1500	3:37.67	3:42.69- 12
Petrov	Aleksandr	RUS	9.8.86	187/79	LJ	7.99	8.20- 11
^ Phillips	Dwight	USA	1.10.77	181/82	LJ	7.95	8.74- 09
^ Phillips	Isa	JAM	22.4.84	193/84	400h	49.28	48.05- 09
Phiri	Gerald	ZAM	6.10.88	184/80	100	10.00w	10.06- 11, 10.03Aw- 08
Piantella	Giorgio	ITA	6.7.81	181/75	PV	5.50i, 5.50	5.60- 10
* Pichardo	Pedro Pablo	CUB	30.6.93	185/71	TJ	17.69	16.79- 12
Pinkelman	Luke	USA	5.5.88	190/114	SP	19.86i	20.07i- 11, 20.02- 12
* Pitkämaki	Tero	FIN	19.12.82	195/92	JT	89.03	91.53- 05
Pittomvils	Niels	BEL	18.7.92	198/88	Dec	7644	7597- 12
Plummer	James	USA	19.8.90	194/125	DT	62.76	60.43- 11
Pohle	Hagen	GER	5.3.92	177/64	20kW	1:22:37	1:23:18- 12
Pollitt	Don	USA	1.10.91	181/75	110h	13.64, 13.52w	14.18- 11, 14.06w- 12
Polyanskiy	Sergey	RUS	29.10.89	180/75	LJ	8.16	8.01- 12, 8.18w- 11
Poore	Andrew	USA	3.12.88	178/64	3kSt	8:26.82	8:35.77- 12
Porter	Garland	USA	10.2.82	193/118	HT	70.55	72.99- 11
* Porter	Jeff	USA	27.11.85	183/84	110h	13.35	13.08- 12
Portilla	Jhoanis	CUB	24.7.90	181/70	110h	13.46	13.62, 13.1w- 11, 13.3- 10
Pouzy	Frédéric	FRA	18.2.83	184/88	HT	72.05	77.05- 12
Povegliano	Lorenzo	ITA	11.11.84	187/102	HT	74.35	79.08- 12
* Powell	Asafa	JAM	23.11.82	190/88	100	9.88	9.72- 08
Powlen	Bryan	USA	3.12.87	193/120	DT	60.98	61.09- 12
Pozdnyakov	Anatoliy	RUS	1.2.87	184/101	HT	79.06	76.59- 11
Prader	John	USA	10.2.91	178/73	PV	5.67	5.35- 12
* Prásil	Ladislav	CZE	17.5.90	198/125	SP	21.47	20.14- 12
Prem Kumar	Kumaravel	IND	6.2.93		LJ	8.09, 8.12w	7.94- 12
Premeru	Marin	CRO	29.8.90	186/115	SP	20.59	20.45- 12
Prentice	Terry	USA	7.1.89	178/77	Dec	7813w	7585- 12
Prey	Matthias	GER	9.8.88	192/89	Dec	8215	7923(w)- 11, 7863- 12
Prezelj	Rozle	SLO	26.9.79	193/73	HJ	2.28	2.32- 12

Name		Nat	Born	Ht/Wt	Event	2013 Mark	Pre-2013 Best
Pribyl	Sam	USA	25.11.82	188/	PV	5.51i	5.40- 06
Primak	Artyom	RUS	14.1.93	190/77	TJ	16.67	16.76- 12
Pronkin	Valeriy	RUS-J	15.6.94	195/115	HT	73.50	64.78- 12
* Protsenko	Andriy	UKR	20.5.88	190/65	HJ	2.32	2.31- 11
Przybylko	Mateusz	GER	9.3.92	194/72	HJ	2.24	2.20- 11
Puplampu	Michael	GBR	11.1.90	176/73	TJ	16.43i	16.19, 16.59w- 12
Putman	Michael	PER	7.3.89	180/118	SP	20.02	19.20i- 12, 18.90- 11
Puzakov	Mikhail	RUS	13.3.91		50kW	3:53:49	
* Pyatnytsya	Oleksandr	UKR	14.7.85	186/90	JT	77.46	86.12- 12
Qi Dakai		CHN	23.5.87	185/120	HT	74.19	72.49- 09
Quérin	Gaël	FRA	26.6.87	182/76	Dec	8146	8098- 12
Quigley	Sean	USA	8.2.85	170/59	10k	27:50.78	28:03.72- 08
Quiñónez	Alex	ECU	11.8.89	176/65	100	10.09A, 10.22, 10.0	10.27A, 10.33- 12
					200	20.44	20.28- 12
Quiyuch	Jaime	GUA	24.4.88	178/57	20kW	1:22:25	
^ Quow	Renny	TTO	25.8.87	170/66	400	45.65	44.53- 09
Rahmani	Miloud	ALG	13.12.83	175/70	400h	49.34	50.48- 11
Raja	Andres	EST	2.6.82	187/80	Dec	7960	8119- 09
Rana	Basant Bahadur	IND	18.1.84	171/59	50kW	3:58:20	3:56:48- 12
* Rapinier	Yoann	FRA	29.9.89	182/70	TJ	17.45	17.23i- 11, 16.76- 12
Redouane	Benabbad	MAR	9.10.91		3kSt	8:33.72	
Reed	Chris	USA	22.7.92	193/140	SP	19.99	18.91- 12
Regassa	Dejene	BRN	18.4.89	173/55	5000	13:25.21	13:20.43- 12
Regassa	Tilahun	ETH	18.1.90	170/54	Mar	2:05:38	2:05:27- 12
Reid	Julian	GBR	23.9.88	186/77	LJ	8.02	8.08- 11, 8.18w- 09
					TJ	16.79	16.98, 17.10w- 09
* Reif	Christian	GER	24.10.84	196/84	LJ	8.27	8.47- 10
Renaudie	Paul	FRA	2.4.90	192/78	800	1:46.42	1:45.85- 12
Renner	Robert	SLO-J	8.3.94	182/75	PV	5.62i	5.50- 12
Repcík	Jozef	SVK	3.8.86	186/72	800	1:46.11	1:44.94- 08
Reus	Julian	GER	29.4.88	177/73	100	10.08, 10.00w	10.09- 12
					200	20.36	20.58- 12
* Revé	Ernesto	CUB	26.2.92	181/65	TJ	17.46	17.40- 11
Revenko	Vladislav	UKR	15.11.84	181/71	PV	5.70	5.80- 05
Rew	Quentin	NZL	16.7.84	175/63	20kW	1:22:16	1:27:47- 11
					50kW	3:50:27	3:55:03- 12
Reynolds	Ben	IRL	26.9.90	188/77	110h	13.49	13.75- 11
Richards	O'Dayne	JAM	14.12.88	180/114	SP	20.97	20.31- 12
Richards-Kwok	Dontae	CAN	1.3.89	174/66	100	10.12	10.32- 11
* Richardson	Jason	USA	4.4.86	186/73	110h	13.20, 13.17w	12.98- 12
Ricks	Keith	USA	9.10.90	183/75	100	10.13	10.21- 12
Rietveld	Pelle	NED	4.2.85	184/75	Dec	7840	8073- 12
* Riley	Andrew	JAM	6.9.88	188/80	110h	13.14	13.19- 12
^ Rimmer	Michael	GBR	3.2.86	180/71	800	1:44.97	1:43.89- 10
Ringer	Richard	GER	27.2.89	180/64	5000	13:27.29	13:43.07- 12
Rise	Lars Vikan	NOR	23.11.88	184/86	Dec	7621	7942- 11
^ Ritzenhein	Dathan	USA	30.12.82	170/52	3000	7:44.68	7:39.03- 07
5000	13:09.53 12:56.27- 09			10k	27:37.90	27:22.28- 09	HMar	61:10	60:00- 09
Rivera	Edgar	MEX	13.2.91	191/80	HJ	2.28	2.28- 11
* Rivera	Luis	MEX	21.6.87	183/82	LJ	8.46	8.22- 12
Roach	Kimmari	JAM	21.9.90	175/73	100	10.15	10.13- 10
Roberts	Gil	USA	15.3.89	183/75	200	20.62, 20.33w	20.54A- 12, 20.65- 11
					400	45.73	44.84- 12
* Roberts	Kurt	USA	20.2.88	191/127	SP	20.98	21.14- 12
Robertson	Andrew	GBR	17.12.90	174/72	100	10.14	10.29- 11, 10.24w- 12
Robertson	Jake	NZL	14.11.89	180/65	5000	13:15.54	13:22.38- 11
					10k	27:45.46	-0-
Robertson	Ricky	USA	19.9.90	178/70	HJ	2.29i	2.32- 12
Robertson	Zane	NZL	14.11.89	180/65	1500	3:35.45	3:36.53- 12
					5000	13:13.83	13:58.37- 11
Robi	Deribe	ETH	26.9.84		Mar	2:08:10	2:08:40- 11
Robinson	Brett	AUS	8.5.91	173/57	5000	13:18.96	13:40.98- 12
Robinson	Jeron	USA	30.4.91	193/73	HJ	2.26	2.23- 11
Robinson	Paul	IRL	24.5.91	175/64	800	1:45.86	1:47.02- 12
					1500	3:35.22	3:37.91- 12
* Robles	Dayron	CUB	19.11.86	191/91	110h	13.18	12.87- 08
Rodger	Sebastian	GBR	29.6.91	181/73	400h	49.19	50.50- 12
* Rodgers	Michael	USA	24.4.85	178/73	100	9.90	9.85- 11
Rodhe	Justin	CAN	17.10.84	188/125	SP	21.29	21.11- 12
Rodney	Brendon	CAN	9.4.92	183/75	200	20.60, 20.58w	21.51- 11, 21.48w- 10
Rodríguez	Alejandro	ESP	1.5.89	190/75	800	1:45.97	1:48.68- 12

Name		Nat	Born	Ht/Wt	Event	2013 Mark	Pre-2013 Best
Rodríguez	Ángel David	ESP	25.4.80	178/66	100	10.15	10.14- 08
					200	20.52w	20.61- 08, 20.34w- 11
Rodríguez	Rafith	COL	1.6.89	187/73	400	45.62	45.9A, 46.20A, 46.38- 12
					800	1:44.33	1:44.31- 11
Rogers	Jason	SKN	31.8.91	173/66	100	10.01	10.06A, 10.24- 12
* Röhler	Thomas	GER	30.9.91	195/83	JT	83.95	80.79- 12
Rojas	Ferney	COL	30.9.87		50kW	4:04:23	4:06:24A- 12
Roland	Lestrod	SKN	5.9.92	173/66	200	20.60	20.67- 12
Rolle	Jamial	BAH	16.4.80	177/75	100	10.20w	10.26- 11, 10.18w- 10
					200	20.51	20.62- 08, 20.60w- 11
Romanenko	Oleksandr	UKR	26.6.81	168/60	50kW	3:59:46	3:58:31- 12
Romani	Darlan	BRA	9.4.91	183/127	SP	20.08	20.48- 12
Romaniw	Anthony	CAN	15.9.91	178/68	800	1:45.60	1:47.89- 12
Rome	Jarred	USA	21.12.76	194/140	DT	63.59	68.76- 11
Rono	Daniel	KEN	13.7.78		Mar	2:07:20	2:06:58- 08
Rono	Geoffrey	KEN	21.4.87	175/60	800	1:45.0 A	1:45.13- 08
Rono	Philemon	KEN	8.2.91		HMar	60:39	60:58- 12
* Rooney	Martyn	GBR	3.4.87	198/78	400	45.05	44.60- 08
* Rop	Albert	KEN/BRN	17.7.92	176/55	3000	7:35.53	7:35.66- 11
					5000	12:51.96	13:01.91- 12
Rosa	Jean	BRA	1.2.90		TJ	16.31, 16.82w	16.53- 12
Rosenquist	Fabian	SWE	1.4.91	186/80	Dec	7738	7619- 12
Ross	Colton	USA	4.6.92	184/73	PV	5.51	5.18- 10
Ross	Joshua	AUS	9.2.81	185/81	100	10.25, 10.20w	10.08- 07
					200	20.57	20.53, 20.51w- 07
Ross	Nick	USA	8.8.91	188/75	HJ	2.28	2.28- 12
Rossini	Andrés	ARG	12.4.88	188/102	DT	60.67	57.80- 11
* Rotich	Abraham	BRN	26.6.93	183/64	800	1:44.57	1:43.13- 12
Rotich	Anthony	KEN		174/60	3kSt	8:21.19	8:41.14- 12
Rotich	Edwin	KEN			HMar	61:25	63:56- 12
Rotich	Luka	KEN	7.8.88	171/57	HMar	60:14	61:39- 12
					Mar	2:08:12	
Rotich	Milton	KEN	.84		Mar	2:08:55	
Rowe	Alex	AUS	8.7.92	181/70	800	1:45.44	1:46.28- 11
Royster	Chris	USA	26.1.92	176/75	100	10.17w	10.35, 10.34w- 12
Rozinski	Pawel	POL	11.7.87	198/91	JT	78.90	78.83- 11
* Rubino	Giorgio	ITA	15.4.86	176/55	20kW	1:21:07	1:19:37- 09
* Rudisha	David	KEN	17.12.88	188/73	400	45.2A	45.50- 10
					800	1:43.87	1:40.91- 12
Ruell	Kim	BEL	27.4.87	176/60	1500	3:37.62	3:38.85- 10
Ruíz	Jorge	COL	17.5.89	167/57	50kW	3:59:13	4:14:04A- 12
Ruíz	Sergio	ESP	21.10.89	184/75	200	20.51	20.97- 12
Rujevic	Luka	SRB	14.10.85	200/132	SP	19.85	20.46- 09
Rungaru	James	KEN	14.1.93	174/58	10k	28:17.85	27:22.53- 11
* Rupp	Galen	USA	8.5.86	180/62	1500	3:36.69+, 3.34.78i	3:34.75- 12
1M	3:52.11, 3:50.92i	3:56.22i, 3:57.72- 10			3000	7:45.1+, 7:30.16i	7:42.40i, 7:43.24- 10
5000	13:01.37		12:58.90- 12		10k	27:24.39	26:48.00- 11
Ruskys	Eligijus	LTU	1.12.90		DT	60.21	56.56- 11
* Rutherford	Greg	GBR	17.11.86	188/84	LJ	8.22	8.35- 12
Rutt	Michael	USA	28.10.87	175/64	800	1:45.08	1:45.20- 12
Rutto	Cyrus	KEN	21.4.92		3000	7:37.57	
					5000	13:12.91	13:45.3A- 11
* Ruuskanen	Antti	FIN	21.2.84	189/86	JT	85.70	87.79- 12, 87.88dh- 07
* Ruzavin	Andrey	RUS	28.3.86	175/70	20kW	1:19:06	1:17:47- 12
* Ryzhov	Mikhail	RUS	17.12.91	180/65	50kW	3:38:58	3:53:49- 12
Sabino	Jefferson	BRA	4.11.82	192/94	TJ	16.94	17.28- 08
Saenz	Stephen	MEX	23.8.90	188/116	SP	19.70i, 18.79	20.08i, 19.91- 12
Safiulin	Ilgizar	RUS	9.12.92	191/70	3kSt	8:28.65	8:29.59- 12
Safo-Antwi	Sean	GBR	31.10.90	171/69	100	10.10w	10.52, 10.19w- 12
Safronov	Konstantin	KAZ	2.9.87	184/70	LJ	8.10	8.06- 10
Saharuk	Igor	UKR	3.6.88		50kW	3:57:24	3:54:40- 12
* Saidy Ndure	Jaysuma	NOR	1.1.84	192/72	100	10.07, 9.95w	9.99- 11, 9.98w- 10
					200	20.23, 20.12w	19.89- 07
Saint-Jean	Fabrice	FRA	21.11.80	190/84	HJ	2.25	2.28- 12
Saito	Hitoshi	JPN	9.10.86	180/70	200	20.56	20.42- 09
Saito	Takumi	JPN	23.3.93	178/61	20kW	1:20:05	1:21:01- 12
Saku Bafuanga	Gaëtan	FRA	22.7.91	181/75	TJ	17.07	16.87- 12
Salaam	Rakieem Mookie	USA	5.4.90	180/73	100	10.01, 9.86w	9.97- 11
* Saladino	Irving	PAN	23.1.83	183/70	LJ	7.99A, 7.94	8.73- 08
Salas	Dídac	ESP	19.5.93	187/75	PV	5.50	5.55- 12
Salel	Daniel	KEN	11.12.90	173/57	HMar	60:41	-0-

Name		Nat	Born	Ht/Wt	Event	2013 Mark	Pre-2013 Best
Salomäki	Eemeli	FIN	11.10.87	182/71	PV	5.55i	5.60- 09
Salzer	Michael	GER	25.10.91	200/88	DT	60.83	59.40- 12
Samaai	Rushwal	RSA	25.9.91		LJ	7.96A	7.94A- 12, 7.75- 11
Samac	Vedran	SRB	22.1.90	183/90	JT	78.20	77.76- 12
Sambu	Stephen	KEN	3.7.88	169/55	HMar	60:41	-0-
Samimi	Mahmoud	IRI	18.9.88	190/105	DT	64.09	64.67- 09
Samimi	Mohammed	IRI	29.3.87	188/104	DT	63.55	65.41- 10
* Samitov	Ruslan	RUS	11.2.91	187/77	TJ	17.30i, 16.54	17.25- 12
Samoylenko	Vitaliy	UKR	22.5.84	196/74	HJ	2.25i	2.24i- 09, 2.23- 07
Sánchez	Benjamín	ESP	10.3.85	185/72	20kW	1:22:33	1:20:48- 08
* Sánchez	Félix	DOM	30.8.77	178/73	400h	48.10	47.25- 03
Sánchez ¶	Sergio	ESP	1.10.82	178/64	5000	13:12.97	13:19.21- 10
Sancho	Miguel Ángel	ESP	24.4.90	180/67	HJ	2.25	2.27i- 09, 2.26- 11
Sanford	Donald	ISR	5.2.87	193/84	400	45.65	45.21- 10
Sanneh	Su'Waibou	GAM	30.10.90	178/77	100	10.16	10.18- 12
* Santos	Luguelín	DOM	12.11.93	173/61	200	20.55A	20.73- 12
					400	44.52	44.45- 12
Santos	Mário	POR	28.7.88		50kW	4:05:37	
dos Santos	Mário José	BRA	10.9.79	172/59	50kW	4:06:12	3:58:30- 08
dos Santos	Rafael	BRA	10.10.91		HJ	2.25	2.21- 11
Sarantsev	Yevgeniy	RUS	5.8.88		Dec	7739	7861- 12
Saruyama	Rikiya	JPN	15.2.84	175/68	LJ	7.87, 7.98w	8.05- 11
Sato	Hiroyuki	JPN	6.8.90	184/67	110h	13.61	13.62, 13.59w- 12
Sato	Yuki	JPN	26.11.86	178/59	5000	13:13.60	13:23.57- 06
					10k	27:39.50	27:38.25- 09
Savanyú	Peter	HUN	26.6.87	189/103	DT	60.71	60.07- 11
Savytskyy	Dmytro	UKR	14.12.90	196/125	SP	20.27i, 18.50	20.38- 12
^ Sawano	Daichi	JPN	16.9.80	183/75	PV	5.60i, 5.60	5.83- 05
Sawyers	Roberto	CRC	17.10.86		HT	73.60	72.74- 12
Sayed	Ihab Abdelrahman	EGY	1.5.89	194/96	JT	83.62	82.25- 12
Scantling	Garrett	USA	19.5.93	190/86	Dec	7873 (w)	7410- 12
Schembera	Robin	GER	1.10.88	186/67	800	1:46.01	1:45.63- 09
Schembri	Fabrizio	ITA	27.1.81	183/74	TJ	16.98	17.27- 09
Scherbarth	Tobias	GER	17.8.85	195/84	PV	5.75i, 5.70	5.76i- 09, 5.71- 10
Scherfose	Patrick	GER	28.11.91	186/86	Dec	7611	7420- 11
Schirrmeister	Silvio	GER	7.12.88	195/80	400h	49.15	49.21- 12
Schlangen	Carsten	GER	31.12.80	189/68	1500	3:35.07	3:33.64- 12
Schmidt	Marco	GER	5.9.83	202/106	SP	19.81i, 19.66	20.58i- 10, 20.51- 11
* Schrader	Michael	GER	1.7.87	183/83	Dec	8670	8522- 09
Schuurmans	Jared	USA	20.8.87	198/118	DT	62.89	61.15- 12
^ Scott	Jeremy	USA	21.5.81	206/91	PV	5.65	5.82i, 5.75- 09
Scott	Jordan	USA	22.2.88	188/84	PV	5.61	5.72- 12
^ Sdiri	Salim	FRA	26.10.78	185/80	LJ	8.23	8.42- 09
Seddon	Zak	GBR-J	28.6.94		3kSt	8:34.42	8:38.07- 12
Sedoc	Gregory	NED	16.10.81	179/74	110h	13.50	13.37- 07, 13.1w- 10
Sedyuk	Nikolay	RUS	29.4.88	198/115	DT	62.37	64.72- 08
See	Jeff	USA	6.6.86	186/72	1500	3:37.54	3:35.21- 12
* Sefir	Dino	ETH	28.5.88	172/59	HMar	60:30	59:42- 11
Segura	Omar	MEX	24.3.81	170/57	50kW	3:57:48A	-0-
Seifert	Bernhard	GER	15.2.93	190/88	JT	82.42	78.55- 11
Semenenko	Yevgen	UKR	17.7.84	178/67	TJ	16.67i, 16.54	17.16- 09
Semenov	Andriy	UKR	4.7.84	204/117	SP	19.60i, 19.55	20.63- 11
Semenov	Oleksiy	UKR	27.6.82	204/115	DT	64.19	65.96- 12
Semyonov	Dmitriy	RUS	2.8.92	195/77	HJ	2.30i, 2.24	2.26- 12
Senesca	Gerkenz	USA	6.4.90	183/82	110h	13.65, 13.54w	13.81- 12
Seppänen	Tuomas	FIN	16.5.86	180/107	HT	74.14	75.31- 11
Seurei	Benson	BRN	27.3.84	172/62	800	1:46.18	1:45.67- 12
1000	2:16.44	2:16.39- 12		1500	3:33.04	3:31.61- 12 3000 7:40.56	7:48.96i, 7:56.82- 12
Sghaier	Mohamed	TUN	18.7.88		400h	49.82	50.05A- 10, 50.37- 11
Shabanov	Konstandin	RUS	17.11.89	184/75	110h	13.38	13.35- 11
Shablyuyev	Ivan	RUS	17.4.88	189/82	400h	49.65	50.37- 11
Shalin	Pavel	RUS	15.3.87	175/73	LJ	7.99	8.25- 10, 8.33w- 11
Shami	Abdullah Dawit	ETH	16.7.84	167/50	Mar	2:08:02	2:05:42- 12
Shapoval	Viktor	UKR	17.10.79	198/75	HJ	2.24i, 2.20	2.34- 09
* Sharman	William	GBR	12.9.84	188/82	110h	13.26	13.30- 09, 12.9w- 10
* Shayunov	Yuriy	BLR	22.10.87	189/120	HT	78.99	80.72- 09
^ Shi Dongpeng		CHN	6.1.84	192/85	110h	13.48	13.19- 07
* Shiferaw	Berhanu	ETH	31.5.93	165/52	Mar	2:04:48	2:08:51- 12
Shinoto	Jun	JPN	2.4.85	171/54	3kSt	8:32.89	8:33.44- 06
Shitara	Keita	JPN	18.12.91	169/50	10k	27:51.54	28:15.90- 12
Shitara	Yuta	JPN	18.12.91	167/44	10k	27:54.82	28:12.82- 12

Name		Nat	Born	Ht/Wt	Event	2013 Mark	Pre-2013 Best
* Shkurenyov	Ilya	RUS	11.1.91	191/82	Dec	8370	8219- 12
Shokirjanov	Bobur	UZB	5.12.90	190/84	JT	77.50	79.31- 09
* Shubenkov	Sergey	RUS	4.10.90	190/75	110h	13.16, 13.10w	13.09- 12
Shubyanok	Nikolay	BLR	4.5.85	190/75	Dec	7590	8055- 12
* Shustov	Aleksandr	RUS	29.6.84	188/80	HJ	2.32	2.36- 11
* Si Tianfeng		CHN	17.6.84	181/67	50kW	3:53:19	3:37:16- 12
Sidorchenko	Gleb	RUS	15.5.86	197/110	DT	62.55	61.68- 12
* Sidorov	Maksim	RUS	13.5.86	190/126	SP	20.98	21.51- 12
Sigueni	Hicham	MAR	30.1.93	172/61	3kSt	8:29.82	8:21.78- 12
Sikora	Rafal	POL	17.2.87	187/76	50kW	3:48:13	3:46:16- 11
* Silmon	Charles	USA	4.7.91	175/72	100	9.98, 9.85w	10.05, 10.04w- 12
					200	20.23	20.56A, 20.60- 11, 20.58w- 10
* Silnov	Andrey	RUS	9.9.84	198/83	HJ	2.32i	2.38- 08
^ Silva	Fábio Gomes da	BRA	4.8.83	178/74	PV	5.70i, 5.60	5.80- 11
Silva	Jonathan	BRA	21.7.91	185/75	TJ	16.84	17.39- 12
da Silva	Aldemir	BRA	8.6.92	186/73	200	20.44	20.38, 20.33w- 12
* da Silva	Mauro Vinícius	BRA	26.12.86	183/69	LJ	8.31	8.28i- 12, 8.27- 11
Simanovich	Denis	BLR	20.4.87	179/58	20kW	1:21:33	1:20:42- 12
Simmons	Cale	USA	5.2.91	178/70	PV	5.61	5.53A, 5.40- 12
Simmons	Rob	USA	5.2.91	178/70	PV	5.50	5.40iA- 12, 5.10- 11
Singh	Arpinder	IND	30.12.92	186/77	TJ	16.84	16.63- 11
Singh	Gurmeet	IND	1.7.85		20kW	1:21:17	1:20:22.52t- 12
Singh	Inderjeet	IND	19.4.88	191/125	SP	19.70	16.90- 10
Singh	Om Prakash	IND	11.1.87	196/125	SP	19.45	20.69- 12
* Sintnicolaas	Eelco	NED	7.4.87	186/78	Dec	8391	8506- 12
* Sirmais	Zigismunds	LAT	6.5.92	191/90	JT	82.77	84.69- 11
Sirviö	Toni	FIN	8.1.92	190/93	JT	78.62	74.54- 12
Sivakov	Dmitriy	BLR	15.2.83	190/120	DT	62.03	64.83- 08
Skorobogatko	Aleksandr	RUS-J	7.8.94	186/78	400h	49.93	53.23- 12
Sleboda	Piotr	POL	22.1.87	185/62	HJ	2.28	2.27- 11
Slobodenyuk	Vadym	UKR	17.3.81	189/74	3kSt	8:26.24	8:22.19- 12
Smaïl	Noureddine	FRA	6.2.87	181/64	5000	13:26.67	13:32.15- 10
					3kSt	8:15.89	8:22.67- 10
Smaliós	Jiannis [Ioannis]	SWE	17.2.87	192/90	JT	78.59	80.77- 10
Smellie	Gavin	CAN	26.6.86	180/75	100	10.20, 10.17w	10.14- 12, 10.11w- 11
Smelyk	Sergiy	UKR	19.4.87	178/72	100	10.21, 10.20w	10.28, 10.24w- 12
					200	20.39	20.63- 12
Smet	Koen	NED	9.8.92	186/74	110h	13.58, 13.52w	13.81- 12
Smet	Thomas	BEL	12.7.88	185/83	JT	78.62	79.14- 09
Smikle	Traves	JAM	7.5.92	201/95	DT	63.48	67.12- 12
Smirnov	Valentin	RUS	13.2.86	177/62	1500	3:37.55i, 3:39.21	3:36.14- 11
Smith	Alex	GBR	6.3.88	184/105	HT	72.45	75.63- 12
Smith	Allan	GBR	6.11.92	198/84	HJ	2.26	2.15- 12
Smith	Calvin	USA	10.12.87	180/75	400	45.33	44.81- 10
Smith	J Patrick	USA	28.4.91	185/84	Dec	7612A (w)	7366- 12
Smith	Johnathan	USA	15.9.92	183/73	100	10.23, 10.20w	10.53, 10.51w- 12
* Smith	Rutger	NED	9.7.81	197/129	DT	65.91	67.77- 11
Smith	Teray	BAH-J	28.9.94	185/77	200	20.58w	20.79- 12
Smith	Tyrone	BER	7.8.86	183/70	LJ	8.13	8.22- 10
Sobera	Robert	POL	19.1.91	183/67	PV	5.71i, 5.61	5.42- 12
Söderberg	David	FIN	11.8.79	185/100	HT	75.67	78.83- 03
* Soi	Edwin	KEN	3.3.86	168/53	3000	7:36.53	7:27.55- 11
					5000	12:51.34	12:52.40- 06
Sokolov	Dmitriy	RUS	16.1.93		PV	5.50i, 5.40	5.30i, 5.20- 12
^ Sokolovs	Igors	LAT	17.8.74	187/110	HT	76.77	80.14- 09
* Sokyrskyy	Oleksiy	UKR	16.3.85	185/108	HT	77.38	78.91- 12
Solinsky	Chris	USA	5.12.84	185/73	5000	13:23.62	12:55.53- 10
* Solomon	Duane	USA	28.12.84	191/77	800	1:43.27	1:42.82- 12
Solomon	Jarrin	TTO	11.1.86	173/73	400	45.19	45.31- 12
Some	Peter	KEN	5.6.90		Mar	2:05:38	2:08:29- 12
Somerville	Terence	USA	5.11.89	184/75	110h	13.49, 13.37w	13.44- 11
^ Sorrillo	Rondell	TTO	21.1.86	178/62	100	10.21, 9.99w	10.03- 12
* Souleiman	Ayanleh	DJI	3.12.92	172/60	800	1:43.63	1:47.45- 12
1000	2:15.77		-0-		1500	3:31.64	3:30.31- 12
1M	3:50.07		3:50.21- 12		3000	7:39.81i	7:42.22- 12
de Sousa	Hugo	BRA	5.3.87	188/77	400	45.31	46.52- 12
Sousa	João Gabriel	BRA	6.11.84	182/75	PV	5.61	5.46- 09
Sowinski	Erik	USA	21.12.89	186/70	800	1:45.21	1:45.90 - 12
^ Spasovkhodskiy	Igor	RUS	1.8.79	191/91	TJ	16.76, 17.22w	17.44- 01
* Spearmon	Wallace	USA	24.12.84	190/80	100	10.29, 9.92w	9.96- 07
					200	20.10	19.65- 06

Name		Nat	Born	Ht/Wt	Event	2013 Mark	Pre-2013 Best
Spinner	Patrick	GER	28.11.85	186/77	Dec	7900	7818- 11
Spratling	Brycen	USA	10.3.92	175/68	400	45.71	45.82i, 45.93- 12
St. Lawrence	Ben	AUS	7.11.81	176/62	3000	7:40.48	7:42.94- 10
5000	13:10.83		13:10.08- 11		10k	27:37.55	27:24.95- 11
Ståhl	Daniel	SWE	27.8.92	200/155	DT	61.29	62.16- 12
Stamatóyiannis	Mihaíl	GRE	20.5.82	188/112	SP	19.90	20.36i- 10, 20.17- 11
Stanek	Tomás	CZE	13.6.91	190/127	SP	19.50	18.52- 12
Stanys	Raivydas	LTU	3.2.87	184/77	HJ	2.28	2.31- 12
Starc	Brandon	AUS	24.11.93	188/73	HJ	2.28	2.20- 11
* Starodubtsev	Dmitriy	RUS	3.1.86	191/79	PV	5.70i	5.90i- 11, 5.75- 08
Stasek	Martin	CZE	8.4.89	190/127	SP	20.98	19.23- 12
Stasiewicz	Michal	POL	28.9.88	181/63	50kW	3:57:28	3:52:45- 12
Stauß	René	GER	17.9.87	190/75	Dec	7694	7534- 12
Steacy	James	CAN	29.5.84	189/115	HT	74.41	79.13- 08
Stecchi	Claudio Michel	ITA	23.11.91	184/82	PV	5.60	5.60- 12
Steele	Edino	JAM	6.1.87	175/68	200	20.39	20.58, 20.37w- 07
					400	45.53	45.38- 12
Stewart	Keiron	JAM	21.11.89	180/73	110h	13.51w	13.44- 11, 13.36w- 12
Stewart	Ray	USA	5.4.89	183/79	110h	13.43	13.48- 11
Stewart	Tyron	USA	8.7.89	180/70	LJ	8.13, 8.14w	8.21- 12
Stigler	Michael	USA	5.4.92	178/70	400h	49.19	49.45- 12
* Storl	David	GER	27.7.90	199/115	SP	21.73	21.88i, 21.86- 12
Strachan	Richard	GBR	18.11.86	175/73	400	45.48	45.70- 11
* Strelkov	Denis	RUS	26.10.90	185/75	20kW	1:19:53	1:20:19- 10
Strobinders	Rolands	LAT	14.4.92	193/90	JT	81.68	81.20- 12
Strzalkowski	Adrian	POL	28.3.90	178/64	LJ	7.90, 7.99w	7.88- 11
Su Bingtian		CHN	29.8.89	185/65	100	10.06	10.16- 11, 10.04w- 12
Su Xiongfeng		CHN	21.3.87	183/70	LJ	8.08	8.27i- 11, 8.19- 11
* Suárez	Leonel	CUB	1.9.87	181/76	Dec	8317	8654- 09
* Sudol	Grzegorz	POL	28.8.78	174/64	20kW	1:20:46	1:20:50- 10
					50kW	3:41:20	3:42:24- 10
Suguimati	Mahau	BRA	13.11.84	184/78	400h	48.79	48.67- 09
Sugut	Henry	KEN	4.5.85	180/54	Mar	2:08:19	2:06:58- 12
Sukharev	Kirill	RUS	24.5.92		LJ	8.06	7.87- 12
Summers	Harry	AUS	19.5.90		10k	28:16.05	28:13.23- 12
Sumner	Ben	GBR	16.8.83	188/80	400h	49.58	49.57- 12
Sun Chenggang		CHN	11.3.91		20kW	1:19:55	1:22:25- 12
Sun Zhao		CHN	8.2.90		HJ	2.24i, 2.24	2.25- 12
Suskevicius	Tadas	LTU	22.5.85	175/65	50kW	4:00:51	3:52:31- 10
* Suzuki	Yusuke	JPN	2.1.88	169/56	20kW	1:18:34	1:20:06- 10
Svärd Jacobsson	Melker	SWE-J	8.1.94	187/82	PV	5.50i, 5.50	5.48- 12
Sverrisson	Gudmundur	ISL	24.5.90		JT	80.66	74.09- 12
* Sviridov	Sergey	RUS	20.10.90	192/85	Dec	7939	8365- 12
Svyatokho	Valeriy	BLR	20.7.81	186/112	HT	79.16	81.49- 06
Swanson	Chris	USA	6.6.82	188/77	PV	5.50Ai	5.60- 12
Swaray	Josh	GBR	2.2.86	180/77	100	10.20	10.37, 10.29w- 10
Swift	Greggmar	BAR	16.2.91	183/68	110h	13.48	13.52, 13.49w- 12
* Symmonds	Nick	USA	30.12.83	178/73	800	1:43.03	1:42.95- 12
					1500	3:34.55	3:36.04- 12
Syunin	Igor	EST	4.12.90	173/70	TJ	16.46	16.86- 10
Szalecki	Krzysztof	POL	3.2.91	191/92	JT	78.08	76.62- 11
Szuster	Konrad	POL	21.1.84	192/115	DT	63.16	63.40- 12
Szymkowiak	Tomasz	POL	5.7.83	176/58	3kSt	8:26.77	8:18.23- 10
Szyszkowski	Jakub	POL	21.8.91	187/105	SP	20.32	19.59- 12
Tabti	Bilal	ALG	7.6.93		3kSt	8:32.32	8:32.08- 12
* Tadese	Zersenay	ERI	8.2.82	158/52	HMar	60:10	58:23- 10
Tadesse	Abraham	ERI	12.8.86		Mar	2:07:45	2:09:24- 10
Tadesse	Dereje	ETH	24.1.87		Mar	2:08:46	2:10:42- 11
Taffe	Ayodele	TTO-J	13.9.94	173/66	100	10.19w	10.71- 11
Taftian	Hassan	IRI	4.5.93	178/75	100	10.15	10.41, 10.39w- 12
^ Taher	Tareq Mubarak	BRN	24.3.84	178/68	3kSt	8:34.32	8:06.13- 09
* Tahri	Bouabdellah	FRA	20.12.78	191/68	1500	3:32.73	3:34.65- 09
3000	7:36.96		7:33.18- 09		5000	13:17.42	13:12.29- 07
^ Taillepierre	Karl	FRA	13.8.76	176/64	TJ	16.83i, 16.54	17.45- 05
Taiwo	Jeremy	USA	15.1.90	196/85	HJ	2.25i	2.11- 11
					Dec	8239	7742- 11
Tajadura	Tomás	ESP	25.6.85	170/58	3kSt	8:32.51	8:19.00- 11
Takahari	Hiromi	JPN	13.11.87	182/64	HJ	2.25	2.24- 10
Takahashi	Eiki	JPN	19.11.92	175/58	20kW	1:20:25	1:22:33- 12
Takahira	Shinji	JPN	18.7.84	180/62	200	20.52	20.22- 09
Takase	Kei	JPN	25.11.88	179/62	200	20.48	20.42- 12

Name		Nat	Born	Ht/Wt	Event	2013 Mark	Pre-2013 Best
Takeda	Tsuyoshi	JPN	22.1.87	178/56	3kSt	8:33.48	8:35.27- 12
Talbot	Danny	GBR	1.5.91	184/73	200	20.45	20.52- 12
Taleb	Brahim	MAR	16.2.85	182/70	3kSt	8:30.05	8:07.02- 07
* Tallent	Jared	AUS	17.10.84	178/60	20kW	1:20:41	1:19:15- 10
					50kW	3:40:03	3:36:53- 12
Tamberi	Gianmarco	ITA	1.6.92	192/77	HJ	2.30i, 2.25	2.31- 12
* Tamgho	Teddy	FRA	15.6.89	187/82	TJ	18.04	17.98- 10
Tammentie	Aleksi	FIN	6.8.86	185/75	TJ	16.49	16.44, 16.46w- 12
Tammert	Aleksandr	EST	2.2.73	196/125	DT	60.37	70.82- 06
Tang Gongchen		CHN	24.4.89	185/71	LJ	7.99	8.03i- 12, 7.97- 08
Taniguchi	Kotaro	JPN-J	3.11.94		200	20.63, 20.56w	21.10- 12
Tanii	Takayuki	JPN	14.2.83	167/57	20kW	1:21:06	1:20:39- 04
					50kW	3:44:25	3:43:56- 12
* Tanui	Paul	KEN	22.12.90	172/54	5000	13:16.57	13:04.65- 11
					10k	27:21.50	26:50.63- 11
* Tarabin	Dmitriy	RUS	29.10.91	176/85	JT	88.84	85.10- 11
Taylor	Bo	USA	5.1.88	190/116	DT	60.21	58.44- 11
* Taylor	Christian	USA	18.6.90	190/75	LJ	8.01, 8.07w	8.19- 10
					TJ	17.66	17.96- 11
Taylor	Fred	USA	17.8.89	183/75	200	20.75, 20.57Aw	21.12, 20.87w- 11
Taylor	James	USA	30.6.90	190/80	200	20.63, 20.58w	20.71- 12
Taylor	Ron	USA	13.8.90	182/73	LJ	8.19	7.93- 12
Teimet	Sylvester Kimeli	KEN	4.6.84		Mar	2:08:15	2:06:49- 10
Tekele	Adugna	ETH	26.12.89		HMar	60:35	61:39- 11
Temacini	Sief el Islem	ALG	5.3.88	180/65	TJ	16.46	16.88- 11
Terer	Patrick	KEN	6.7.89	178/60	Mar	2:08:52	2:10:34- 12
Terfa	Negari	ETH	12.6.83	166/52	Mar	2:07:32	2:07:41- 09
Tesfaldet	Nguse	ERI	10.11.86	180/56	10k	27:29.21	27:28.10- 12
					HMar	60:46	61:39- 12
Tesfaye	Homiyu	GER	23.6.93	183/66	800	1:46.40	1:47.40- 12
					1500	3:34.18	3:38.56- 12
Tesfaye Nebebew	Birhan	ETH-J	14.8.94	172/55	10k	27:14.34	
Theiner	Wojciech	POL	25.6.86	187/74	HJ	2.28	2.30- 10
Thoirs	Jax	GBR	7.4.93	198/88	PV	5.53i, 5.50	5.20i, 5.10- 12
Thomas	Chris	USA	9.2.81	178/76	110h	13.67, 13.55w	13.45- 12
* Thomas	Donald	BAH	1.7.84	190/75	HJ	2.32	2.35- 07
* Thomas	Dwight	JAM	23.9.80	185/82	110h	13.27	13.15- 11, 13.10w- 10
Thomas	Mikel	TTO	23.11.87	182/77	110h	13.19	13.48, 13.31w- 12
Thomas	Tristan	AUS	23.5.86	184/70	400h	49.56	48.68- 09
Thompson	Chris	GBR	17.4.81	176/70	3000	7:45.52	7:43.34- 10
5000	13:24.06		13:11.51- 10		10k	27:40.81	27:27.36- 11
* Thompson	Richard	TTO	7.6.85	187/79	100	10.14, 9.91w	9.85- 11
* Thorkildsen	Andreas	NOR	1.4.82	188/90	JT	84.64	91.59- 06
Thormaehlen	Jacob	USA	13.2.90	193/118	SP	20.22	20.50i, 20.31- 12
Thorne	Benjamin	CAN	19.3.93	180/57	20kW	1:22:49	1:21:55- 12
Thuku	Karemi	KEN-J	7.7.94	176/62	5000	13:24.50	13:36.09- 12
					10k	27:33.38	28:38.52- 12
Tikhomirov	Anton	RUS	29.4.88		SP	19.74	19.56i, 19.40- 12
* Tinsley	Michael	USA	21.4.84	185/74	200	20.34w	20.66- 09
					400h	47.70	47.91- 12
Tiouali	Mohammed Ayoub	MAR	26.5.91	175/60	800	1:46.32	1:48.12- 11
					1500	3:36.98	3:34.52- 12
Tobe	Naoto	JPN	31.3.92	194/71	HJ	2.28	2.24- 10
Toboc	Valentin	ROU	17.3.92	188/73	LJ	7.98i, 7.92	7.91i, 7.79- 12
Togom	Nicholas	KEN	17.2.92		HMar	61:02	61:37- 12
Tola	Seboka	ETH	10.11.87	172/53	Mar	2:07:26	2:06:17- 12
* Tola	Tadesse	ETH	31.10.87	178/60	Mar	2:04:49	2:05:10- 12
Toledo	Braian	ARG	8.9.93	182/86	JT	78.66	79.87- 12
Toledo	Yoiser	ex-CUB	24.4.83	196/100	SP	19.41	19.29- 11
Tomala	Dawid	POL	27.8.89	182/65	20kW	1:20:30	1:20:50- 12
* Tomlinson	Chris	GBR	15.9.81	197/84	LJ	8.21	8.35- 11
Tong Anqi		CHN	29.9.92		20kW	1:22:46	1:26:34- 12
Tontodonati	Federico	ITA	30.10.89	169/55	20kW	1:22:33	1:22:00- 12
Too	Silas	KEN	.89		1000	2:17.33	2:20.81- 12
Toompuu	Raigo	EST	17.7.81	188/118	SP	19.48	20.20- 10
Torie	Mike	USA	12.3.86	186/110	DT	63.12	59.15- 12
* Tornéus	Michel	SWE	26.5.86	184/70	LJ	8.29i, 8.00, 8.12w	8.22- 12
Toroitich	Timothy	UGA	10.10.91		10k	27:31.07	
					3kSt	8:24.59	8:23.61- 12
Torrance	Jamaal	USA	20.7.83	168/64	400	45.85	44.80- 10
Torrence	David	USA	26.11.85	175/61	1500	3:33.23	3:34.25- 10
1M	3:52.74		3:52.01- 12		3000	7:40.78	7:47.80- 12

Name		Nat	Born	Ht/Wt	Event	2013 Mark	Pre-2013 Best
Torrijos	Pablo	ESP	12.5.92	187/78	TJ	16.71w	16.16i- 11, 16.08, 16.47w- 12
Torro	Osku	FIN	21.8.79	183/68	HJ	2.26i	2.33i- 11, 2.28- 12
* Tóth	Matej	SVK	10.2.83	185/72	20kW	1:20:14	1:20:16- 11
					50kW	3:41:07	3:39:46- 11
Touil	Abdelmadjed	ALG	11.2.89	172/62	3kSt	8:15.93	8:31.01- 12
Touil	Imad	ALG	11.2.89	172/62	1500	3:36.71	3:35.82- 12
Tovarnov	Aleksey	RUS	21.1.85	183/86	JT	82.54	81.21- 09
Townsend	Fred	USA	19.2.82	188/82	110h	13.53	13.39- 12
Traber	Gregor	GER	2.12.92	189/77	110h	13.49	13.47- 12
Trafeh	Mohamed	USA	7.5.85	172/57	HMar	61:17	60:39- 10
Trajkovic	Milan	CYP	17.9.92	187/77	110h	13.67	14.09- 12
^ Trammell	Terrence	USA	23.11.78	188/84	110h	13.86, 13.60w	12.95- 07
Tremigliozzi	Stefano	ITA	7.5.85	178/68	LJ	7.95i	8.01- 10
Trofimov	Pyotr	RUS	28.11.83	174/63	20kW	1:18:28	1:19:02- 09
^ Trotskiy	Ivan	BLR	27.5.76	167/50	20kW	1:22:25	1:19:40- 03
					50kW	3:47:52	3:46:09- 12
True	Ben	USA	29.12.85	183/70	3000	7:36.59	7:44.40- 12
					5000	13:11.59	13:20.53- 12
Tsákonas	Likoúrgos-Stéfanos	GRE	8.3.90	184/67	200	20.45	20.52- 12
Tsákonas	Yeóryios	GRE	22.1.88	190/78	LJ	8.17	8.25- 12
Tsapik	Aleksey	BLR	4.8.88		TJ	16.74	16.86i, 16.82, 16.97w- 12
* Tsátoumas	Loúis	GRE	12.2.82	187/76	LJ	8.23, 8.24w	8.66- 07
Tsegay	Atsedu	ETH	17.12.91		10k	27:28.11	-0-
					HMar	59:12	58:47- 12
Tsenov	Mitko	BUL	13.6.93		3kSt	8:27.09	8:52.24- 12
Tsiámis	Dimítrios	GRE	12.1.82	178/67	TJ	17.05	17.55- 06
Tsirikhov	Soslan	RUS	24.11.84	195/125	SP	20.10	20.76- 11
Tsonov	Georgi	BUL	2.5.93	172/66	TJ	16.58i, 16.85w	16.04, 16.10w- 12
Tsumurai	Akihiko	JPN	10.7.84	168/51	10k	28:16.99	28:35.99- 12
Tsunoyama	Takayuki	JPN	9.6.85	178/70	TJ	16.40	16.26- 09
* Tsyplakov	Daniyil	RUS	29.7.92	190/75	HJ	2.30i, 2.30	2.31- 12
Tuemay	Tsegay	ERI-J	20.12.95		5000	13:20.89	13:29.36- 12
Tufa	Alexandru	ROU	28.5.89	192/77	HJ	2.27i, 2.22	2.23- 12
Tugumisirize	Emmnuel	UGA	30.11.88	174/64	400	45.82	46.77- 11
Tuka	Amel	BIH	9.1.91	183/68	800	1:46.29	1:48.31- 12
Tum	Stephen	KEN	12.7.86		Mar	2:06:35	2:07:17- 12
Tumi	Michael	ITA	12.2.90	178/76	100	10.19	10.35- 11, 10.27w- 12
Turner	De'Sean	USA	16.9.88	175/62	3kSt	8:25.56	8:36.39- 12
^ Tysse	Erik	NOR	4.12.80	184/59	20kW	1:19:51	1:19:11- 08
					50kW	3:55:23A	3:45:08- 08
Ueno	Yuichiro	JPN	29.7.85	180/60	10k	28:09.56	28:12.37- 12
Ugachi	Tsuyoshi	JPN	27.4.87	163/49	10k	27:50.79	27:40.69- 11
					HMar	61:16	60:58- 11
Uhle	Joey	USA	14.11.92	185/75	PV	5.51	5.35- 12
Uibo	Maicel	EST	27.12.92	188/86	Dec	8223	7548- 12
Ukaoma	Miles	USA	21.7.92	183/75	400h	49.57	49.23- 12
* Ukhov	Ivan	RUS	29.3.86	192/83	HJ	2.35	2.40i- 09, 2.39- 12
Uliczka	Steffen	GER	17.7.84	179/65	3kSt	8:23.57	8:22.93- 12
* Urbanek	Robert	POL	29.4.87	200/115	DT	65.30	66.93- 12
Ursu	Sergiu	ROU	26.4.80	202/127	DT	63.92	64.74- 10
Ushiro	Keisuke	JPN	24.7.86	196/86	Dec	7824	8076w, 8073- 11
Uudmäe	Jaanus	EST	24.12.80	188/75	TJ	16.43	17.06i- 09, 16.60, 17.00w- 08
Vail	Ryan	USA	19.3.86	173/59	10k	27:44.05	27:51.07- 12
Valiyev	Roman	KAZ	27.3.84	190/73	TJ	17.10	17.20- 12
Valle	Amaurys	CUB	18.1.90	186/80	400h	50.02A	49.19- 12
Van Den Broeck	Jan	BEL	11.3.89	179/70	800	1:46.44	1:47.01- 11
* Van Der Plaetsen	Thomas	BEL	24.12.90	188/82	Dec	8255	8157- 11
van Deventer	Juan	RSA	26.3.83	184/70	1500	3:36.84	3:34.30- 09
van Niekerk	Wayde	RSA	15.7.92	178/68	400	45.09	46.43- 12
* van Zyl	Louis 'L.J'	RSA	20.7.85	186/75	400h	49.11	47.66- 11
Vasile	Adrian	ROM	9.4.86	190/72	LJ	8.11	7.89i- 11, 7.87- 12, 7.88w- 10
* Vasilevskis	Vadims	LAT	5.1.82	188/101	JT	82.79	90.73- 07
Vaughn	Clayton	USA	15.5.92	173/74	100	10.13w	10.33- 12
Vázquez	Wesley	PUR-J	27.3.94	184/73	800	1:45.94	1:45.29- 12
Vega	Jesús Tadeo	MEX-J	23.5.94		20kW	1:22:39	-0-
Vena	Nick	USA	16.4.93	194/120	SP	19.43	19.51- 12
Venglovskyy	Oleksandr	UKR	5.8.85	184/66	50kW	3:56:07	4:00:55- 12
Verburg	David	USA	14.5.91	168/64	400	44.75	45.06- 12
Verbytskyy	Oleksandr	UKR	28.7.92		20kW	1:22:48	1:23:39- 12
Vernon	Andrew	GBR	7.1.86	175/64	3000	7:45.75	7:49.84i- 10, 7:55.41-08
Veryovkin	Mikhail	RUS	28.6.91		HJ	2.25i	2.10- 11

	Name		Nat	Born	Ht/Wt	Event	2013 Mark	Pre-2013 Best
*	Vesely	Vitezslav	CZE	27.2.83	186/94	JT	87.68	88.34- 12
	Vicars	Derrick	USA	8.5.89	188/114	SP	20.12i, 19.62	19.83- 12
*	Vicaut	Jimmy	FRA	27.2.92	188/83	100	9.95	10.02- 12
						200	20.30	20.58- 12
*	Vieira	João	POR	20.2.76	174/58	20kW	1:21:08	1:20:09- 06
	Vieira	Sérgio	POR	20.2.76	174/58	20kW	1:21:53	1:20:58- 97
	Villanueva	Claudio	ESP	3.8.88	166/55	50kW	3:50:29	4:00:52- 11
	Vinichenko	Igor	RUS	11.4.84	196/119	HT	77.00	80.00- 07
*	Visser	Zarck	RSA	15.9.89	178/70	LJ	8.32	8.15A, 8.07, 8.21w- 12
	Vitonis	Tomas	LTU	19.9.91	193/77	LJ	8.03i	7.75- 12
	Vivas	Borja	ESP	26.5.84	203/140	SP	20.63	20.18i- 11, 20.06- 12
*	Vizzoni	Nicola	ITA	4.11.73	193/126	HT	77.61	80.50- 01
	Vojta	Andreas	AUT	9.6.89	184/68	1500	3:36.36	3:37.82- 11
						1M	3:53.95	
	Vonavka	Tomás	CZE	4.6.90		DT	60.38	61.74- 12
	Vrublevskiy	Vadim	RUS	18.3.93		HJ	2.24	2.20- 12
	Vuklisevic	Petr	CZE	25.2.82	187/100	DT	61.86	59.97- 12
	Vynogradov	Yevgen	UKR	30.4.84	195/98	HT	77.68	80.58- 08
	Wait	Kyle	USA	20.2.92	183/79	PV	5.51	5.35- 12
*	Walcott	Keshorn	TTO	2.4.93	184/90	JT	84.39	84.58- 12
*	Walker	Brad	USA	21.6.81	188/86	PV	5.83	6.04- 08
	Wallin	Gabriel	SWE	14.10.81	193/95	JT	83.23	81.45- 12
*	Walsh	Tom	NZL	1.3.92	186/123	SP	20.61	19.33- 12
	Wan Yong		CHN	22.7.87	188/97	HT	73.49	70.42- 09
	Wang Chen		CHN	27.2.90	193/65	HJ	2.25	2.26- 09
	Wang Gang		CHN	2.4.91		20kW	1:20:31	1:22:18- 11
	Wang Guangfu		CHN	15.11.87	192/110	SP	20.12	20.20- 12
	Wang Guozhen		CHN	1.12.92		50kW	4:02:46	4:13:13- 12
*	Wang Hao		CHN	16.8.89	180/65	20kW	1:22:40	1:18:13- 09
						50kW	4:02:56	3:41:55- 09
	Wang Jianan		CHN-Y	27.8.96		LJ	7.95	8.04- 12
	Wang Like		CHN	2.4.89	190/120	SP	19.52i, 19.33	19.61- 11
	Wang Shizhu		CHN	20.2.89	/90	HT	75.20	69.62- 12
	Wang Yu		CHN	18.8.91	192/73	HJ	2.33	2.28- 11
*	Wang Zhen		CHN	24.8.91	180/62	20kW	1:19:08	1:17:36- 12
	Wang Zhendong		CHN	11.1.91		20kW	1:21:55	1:21:59- 12
	Wanjiru	Daniel	KEN	26.5.92		HMar	61:10	61:19- 12
	Wanjuki	Jacob	KEN	16.1.86	178/52	10k	27:50.07	27:48.74- 11
						HMar	60:55	60:32- 10
	Ware	Torian	USA	17.12.92	193/80	HJ	2.26i	2.12, 2.13i- 12
	Warga	Sahle	ETH	30.1.84	182/64	Mar	2:08:19	2:09:48dh- 10
						HMar	60:39	61:32- 10
*	Wariner	Jeremy	USA	31.1.84	183/70	400	45.35	43.45- 07
*	Warner	Damian	CAN	4.11.89	185/83	110h	13.64	13.61- 12
						Dec	8512	8442- 12
	Warner	Justyn	CAN	28.6.87	174/70	100	10.19, 10.16w	10.09- 12
	Wasehun	Mule	ETH	.93		HMar	60:35	-0-
	Watanabe	Kazuya	JPN	20.7.88	170/60	400	45.71	46.43- 11
*	Watt	Mitchell	AUS	25.3.88	184/83	LJ	8.01	8.54- 11
	Waweru	Edward	KEN	3.10.90	178/58	5000	13:22.96	13:13.80- 11
						10k	27:30.51	27:13.94- 10
	Webb	Ameer	USA	19.3.91	175/75	100	10.14, 10.07w	10.17, 10.05w- 12
						200	20.20, 20.05w	20.46, 20.39i, 20.20w- 12
	Weber	Julian	GER-J	29.8.94	190/94	JT	79.68	71.12- 12
*	Weir	Warren	JAM	31.10.89	178/75	100	10.02	10.50- 09
						200	19.79	19.84- 12
	Weirich	Victor	USA	25.10.87	188/86	PV	5.55	5.50Ai- 11, 5.50- 12
	Weldesilasie	Dawit	ERI-J	10.12.94		5000	13:27.10	
						HMar	61:07	-0-
	Weldon	Kole	USA	25.3.92	193/114	SP	20.02i, 19.43	18.10- 12
	Werskey	Eric	USA	17.7.87	188/120	SP	20.13	19.83- 11
	Wesh	Darrell	USA	21.1.92	173/70	100	10.14	10.15- 12
^	Wheating	Andrew	USA	21.11.87	195/77	1500	3:37.03	3:30.90- 10
	White	Corey	USA	31.1.86	185/91	JT	81.40	82.97- 09
	White	James	USA	22.1.92	179/61	HJ	2.27i	2.28- 09
	White	Steven	USA	27.7.91	170/64	400h	49.32	50.07- 12
	White-Edwards	Timothy	USA-J	15.7.94	181/82	TJ	16.49A	15.53- 12
	Whitfield	Levonte	USA	8.10.93	175/76	100	10.15w	10.31- 11, 10.21w- 12
*	Whiting	Ryan	USA	24.11.86	190/134	SP	22.28	22.00i- 12, 21.97- 10
	Whitt	Jack	USA	12.4.90	193/84	PV	5.70	5.72i- 12, 5.65- 11
	Whyte	Annsert	JAM	10.4.87	185/75	400h	49.17	-0-

Name		Nat	Born	Ht/Wt	Event	2013 Mark	Pre-2013 Best
Wiberg	Niklas	SWE	16.4.85	193/84	Dec	7678	8406- 09
Wieczorek	Mark	USA	25.12.84	178/68	800	1:45.36	1:45.62- 12
Wielart	Jürgen	NED	17.1.92	180/73	400	45.83	46.65- 12
* Wierig	Martin	GER	10.6.87	202/108	DT	67.46	68.33- 12
Wiesolek	Pawel	POL	13.8.91	194/84	Dec	7727	7342- 12
Wijesekara	Manjula Kumara	SRI	30.1.84	183/73	HJ	2.24	2.27- 04
Wilkinson	James	GBR	13.7.90		3kSt	8:28.74	8:34.00- 12
Wilks	Terrell	USA	30.12.89	188/82	100	9.99w	10.15- 09, 10.11w- 11
Williams	Akeem	JAM	7.11.90	178/72	200	20.41w	20.68, 20.63w- 12
Williams	Conrad	GBR	20.3.82	182/76	400	45.59	45.08- 12
Williams	Delano	TKS/GBR	23.12.93	183/72	200	20.27	20.48- 12
* Williams	Jesse	USA	27.12.83	184/75	HJ	2.31	2.37- 11
Williams	Kendal	USA-J	23.9.95	183/75	100	10.18w	10.48- 12
Williams	LaToy	BAH	28.5.88	190/77	400	45.26	44.73- 09
* Williams	Rhys	GBR	27.2.84	183/73	400h	48.84	48.96- 10
Williamson	Amir	GBR	10.4.87	183/100	HT	71.01	69.72- 10
* Willis	Nick	NZL	25.4.83	183/68	1500	3:32.57	3:30.35- 12
1M	3:55.70		3:50.66- 08		3000	7:40.62	7:44.90i- 04, 7:45.97- 05
Wilson	Alex	SUI	19.9.90	179/77	100	10.12	10.26- 12
					200	20.60	20.51- 11, 20.43w- 12
Wilson	Jamal	BAH	1.9.88	188/68	HJ	2.28	2.24Ai- 11, 2.23A- 08
* Wilson	Ryan	USA	19.12.80	188/81	110h	13.08	13.02- 07
Winder	Jake	USA	12.11.87	183/79	PV	5.55Ai	5.50- 09, 5.50-10
Winger	Russ	USA	2.8.84	191/120	SP	20.53	21.29i- 08, 21.25- 10
					DT	63.29	66.04- 11
Winter	Chris	CAN	22.7.86	185/66	3kSt	8:28.92	8:28.46- 11
Winters	David	USA-J	19.2.94	175/66	200	20.59w	20.72- 12
* Wirkkala	Teemu	FIN	14.1.84	187/85	JT	82.91	87.23- 09
^ Wissman	Johan	SWE	2.11.82	180/75	200	20.59w	20.30- 07, 20.26w- 05
Witczak	Dominik	POL	10.3.92	192/120	SP	19.63	18.74- 12
Woepse	Mike	USA	29.5.91	185/79	PV	5.60Ai, 5.50	5.55- 12
Wolde	Dawit	ETH	19.5.91	175/62	1500	3:34.64	3:33.82- 12
					1M	3:54.51	3:57.48- 12
Woodson	Markesh	USA	6.9.93	168/64	100	10.18, 10.11w	10.51A- 10
Worku	Gemechu	ETH	.85		Mar	2:08:53	2:07:43- 12
Wöschler	Till	GER	9.6.91	196/110	JT	79.80	84.38- 11
* Wote	Aman	ETH	18.4.84	181/64	800	1:44.99	
1500	3:32.65		3:35.38- 12		1M	3:49.88	3:53.02- 12
Wote	Aman	ETH	18.4.84	181/64	3000	7:43.99i	7:48.65- 01
Wright	Chad	JAM	25.3.91	188/110	DT	63.74	62.88- 12
Wright	Ed	USA	3.3.86	188/79	HJ	2.26i	2.25- 10
Wright	Josh	AUS	3.5.91	186/73	1500	3:37.10	3:41.68- 12
Wrobel	David	GER	13.2.91	195/100	DT	60.63	57.39- 12
* Wruck	Julian	AUS	6.7.91	198/125	DT	68.16	65.74- 11
Wu Jian		CHN	25.5.86	189/95	DT	61.53	63.54- 11
Wu Qianlong		CHN	30.1.90	176/62	50kW	3:51:35	3:57:56- 09
Wu Tao		CHN	3.10.83	191/100	DT	61.83	64.28- 05
Wurster	Jason	CAN	23.9.84	185/82	PV	5.60i	5.51- 12
Wyatt	Reggie	USA	17.9.90	195/86	400h	48.58	49.11- 12
Xhonneux	Frédéric	BEL	11.5.83	184/79	Dec	7586	8142- 08
Xie Sichao		CHN	28.2.93		20kW	1:22:39	1:22:34- 11
Xie Wenjun		CHN	11.7.90	186/74	110h	13.28	13.34- 12
Xie Zhenye		CHN	17.8.93	183/72	200	20.55	20.54- 12
Xu Dexing		CHN	20.8.88	183/60	20kW	1:21:41	1:21:57- 11
Xu Faguang		CHN	17.5.87	178/69	20kW	1:21:35	1:20:26- 08
					50kW	3:57:54	3:42:20- 11
Xu Jie		CHN	1.1.93		50kW	4:02:07	-0-
Xu Xiaolong		CHN	20.12.92		TJ	16.47	16.27- 12
* Xue Changrui		CHN	31.5.91	183/60	PV	5.75i, 5.65	5.60- 12
Yakovenko	Dmytro	UKR	17.9.92	191/72	HJ	2.24i	2.20- 12
Yamada	Atsushi	JPN	3.7.91	173/61	400h	49.96	50.47- 11
Yamagata	Ryota	JPN	10.6.92	176/70	100	10.11, 10.04w	10.07- 12
					200	20.41	20.62- 11
Yamamoto	Ryo	JPN	18.5.84	173/60	10k	28:13.23	28:22.84- 11
					Mar	2:09:06	2:08:44- 12
Yamamoto	Seito	JPN	11.3.92	178/67	PV	5.75	5.65- 12
Yamashita	Minato	JPN	15.11.88	169/54	3kSt	8:33.57	8:34.95- 12
Yami	Dadi	ETH	.82		Mar	2:07:55	2:05:41- 12
Yáñez	Eure	VEN	20.5.93		HJ	2.25	2.23- 12
Yang Yancheng		CHN	5.1.88	189/75	PV	5.80i, 5.50	5.75- 10
Yao Jie		CHN	21.9.90	188/85	PV	5.50i, 5.50	5.30- 12

Name		Nat	Born	Ht/Wt	Event	2013 Mark	Pre-2013 Best
Yargunkin	Aleksandr	RUS	6.1.81	182/68	50kW	3:49:47	3:50:53- 12
Yashin Hasen	Agato	ETH	19.1.86	175/58	10k	27:46.35	27:51.71- 12
Yastrebov	Viktor	UKR	13.1.82	185/73	TJ	16.62	17.32- 04
Yates	Richard	GBR	26.1.86	185/77	400h	49.49	49.06- 08
Yazawa	Wataru	JPN	2 .7.91	180/62	110h	13.59	13.69- 11
* Yego	Hillary	KEN	2.4.92	178/60	3kSt	8:03.57	8:07.71- 11
* Yego	Julius	KEN	4.1.89	175/85	JT	85.40	81.81- 12
Yeryomin	Ivan	UKR	30.5.89	192/74	PV	5.60i, 5.60	5.55- 12
Yildirum	Irfan	TUR	26.7.88	202/100	DT	64.46	64.96- 11
Yin Mingxing		CHN	25.10.88		50kW	4:08:16	4:10:01- 11
Yoroizaka	Tetsuya	JPN	20.3.90	166/52	10k	27:53.34	27:44.30- 11
Yoshida	Kazuaki	JPN	31.8.87	180/72	400h	50.09	49.45-09
Yoshida	Takuya	JPN	10.8.90		20kW	1:20:47	1:22:42- 12
* Young	Isiah	USA	5.1.90	183/75	100	9.99, 9.93w	10.09, 10.08w- 12
					200	19.86	20.33, 20.16w- 12
* Young	Jason	JAM	21.3.91	180/68	100	10.18	10.06- 12
					200	19.98, 19,96w	19.86- 12
^ Young	Jason	USA	27.5.81	185/116	DT	63.08	69.90- 10
Young	Sean	USA	27.12.85	182/78	PV	5.56	5.46- 12
Yu Wei		CHN	11.9.87	180/60	20kW	1:19:07	1:20:06- 12
Yurchenko	Aleksandr	RUS	30.7.92		TJ	16.67	16.56- 12
Zaghou	Mounatcer	MAR	1.1.89		3kSt	8:23.84	8:29.78- 12
* Zagornyi	Aleksey	RUS	31.5.78	197/135	HT	79.26	83.43- 02
Zalewski	Karol	POL	7.8.93	185/73	200	20.41	20.54- 12
Zalewski	Krystian	POL	11.4.89	185/67	3kSt	8:23.31	8:25.50- 12
Zalsky	Antonin	CZE	7.8.80	200/128	SP	20.28	20.71- 04
Zamel-Paez	Liam	AUS	4.8.88	180/68	HJ	2.29	2.26- 10
Zasimovich	Sergey	KAZ	11.3.86	185/73	HJ	2.24i	2.30- 07
Zavacky	Adam	SVK	27.6.88	177/73	100	10.21	10.56- 12
Zawude	Tebalu	ETH	2.11.87		HMar	60:33	62:07- 12
Zaytsev	Ivan	UZB	11.11.88	190/98	JT	83.79	85.03- 12
Zebrowski	Krzysztof	POL	9.7.90	177/62	1500	3:35.07	3:39.47- 12
Zellweger	Yves	SUI	27.3.87	188/86	LJ	8.03	7.85- 10
Zenúch	Patrik	SVK	30.12.90		JT	79.52	78.89- 12
Zepeda	Omar	MEX	8.6.77	177/68	50kW	3:50:43	3:48:38A- 12
Zerrifi	Abdelhamid	ALG	20.6.86		3kSt	8:25.96	8:32.23- 09
Zhang Guowei		CHN	4.6.91	200/77	HJ	2.32i, 2.29	2.31- 11
Zhang Hang		CHN	28.10.91		20kW	1:22:56	1:23:52- 12
Zhang Jun		CHN	11.4.83	186/125	SP	19.43	20.41- 09
Zhang Lin		CHN	11.11.93		50kW	4:07:28	
* Zhang Peimeng		CHN	13.3.87	186/78	100	10.00	10.21- 11
					200	20.47	20.64- 11
Zhang Wei		CHN-J	22.3.94		PV	5.62i	5.50- 12
Zhang Xiaoyi		CHN	25.5.89	186/65	LJ	7.96	8.27- 09
Zhang Yaoguang		CHN	21.6.93		LJ	7.99	7.83- 11
					TJ	16.50i, 16.41	15.92- 10
Zhang Yu		CHN	17.7.92		TJ	16.44	15.83- 11
Zhao Jianguo		CHN	19.1.88	175/55	50kW	3:53:30	3:50:18- 11
Zhao Pengju		CHN	6.2.88		JT	77.52	76.28- 09
Zhao Qi		CHN	14.1.93		20kW	1:20:50	1:19:58- 12
Zhao Qinggang		CHN	24.7.85	184/75	JT	83.14	81.74- 12
Zhao Xiaoxi		CHN	19.3.89	173/75	LJ	8.00i, 7.81	8.00, 8.09w- 12
Zhelyabin	Dmitry	RUS	20.5.90	187/75	PV	5.55	5.65- 12
Zhu Hengjun		CHN	5.2.87	194/77	Dec	7662	7708- 09
Ziegler	Alexander	GER	7.7.87	180/98	HT	74.27	75.78- 12
Ziegler	Manuel	GER	28.7.90	183/75	TJ	16.35, 16.48w	16.26- 12
Ziemek	Zach	USA	23.2.93	190/77	Dec	7640 (w)	7042- 12
Zikeyev	Dmitriy	RUS	10.1.91		Dec	7691 (w)	7387- 12
Zimmerman	Moacir	BRA	30.12.83	170/52	20kW	1:22:50.8t	1:21:02.5t- 11
* Ziólkowski	Szymon	POL	1.7.76	192/120	HT	78.79	83.38- 01
Zumer	Jan	SLO	9.6.82	189/75	200	20.59	20.76- 08
Zwicker	Patrick	GER-J	13.7.94	188/75	800	1:46.04	1:47.74- 12

	Name		Nat	Born	Ht/Wt	Event	2013 Mark	Pre-2013 Best

WOMEN'S INDEX 2013

Athletes included are those ranked in the top 100s at standard (World Champs) events (plus shorter lists for 1000m, 1M, 2000m and 3000m). Those with detailed biographical profiles are indicated in first column by:
* in this year's Annual, ^ featured in a previous year's Annual

	Name		Nat	Born	Ht/Wt	Event	2013 Mark	Pre-2013 Best
	Ababel	Birhane	ETH	10.6.90	157/42	10k	30:35.91	34:10.0A- 11
*	Abakumova	Mariya	RUS	15.1.86	180/80	JT	70.53	71.99- 11
	Abdullah	Khadija	USA	24.7.90		SP	17.06i	17.12- 12
	Abdullayeva	Layes	AZE	29.5.91	170/54	3000	8:57.17i	8:49.65i, 8:55.33- 10
	Abe	Yukari	JPN	21.8.89	154/48	5000	15:33.25	15:53.03- 08
*	Abeylegesse	Elvan	TUR	11.9.82	159/40	HMar	70:32	67:07- 10
	Abiko	Tomomi	JPN	17.3.88	175/33	PV	4.33i	4.40- 12
	Abogunloko	Bukola	NGR-J	18.8.94	173/55	200	22.7	23.19- 12
						400	52.18	51.57- 12
	Achamo	Netsanet	ETH	14.12.87	167/53	Mar	2:27:44	2:24:12- 12
	Achkinadze	Xenia	GER	14.1.89	174/58	LJ	6.66, 6.69w	6.56i, 6.52, 6.72w- 12
	Adams	Aisha	USA	24.9.87	168/64	Hep	5788	5861- 12
*	Adams	Valerie	NZL	6.10.84	193/123	SP	20.98i, 20.90	21.24- 11
^	Adamu	Birtukan	ETH	29.4.92	164/49	3kSt	9:43.22	9:20.37- 11
	Adekoya	Kemi	NGR	16.1.93	168/57	400h	55.30	57.16- 12
	Adeoye	Margaret	GBR	27.4.85	175/64	200	22.88	22.94- 12
						400	51.93	53.43- 12
	Aerts	Sara	BEL	25.1.84	182/64	100h	12.90, 12.85w	12.94- 12
	Afework	Abebech	ETH	11.12.90	152/42	Mar	2:23:59	
	Aga	Ruti	ETH-J	16.1.94	159/45	3000	8:56.73	9:03.00- 12
						5000	15:13.48	15:21.36mx- 12
	Agai	Margaret	KEN	10.6.88		Mar	2:23:28	2:24:17- 12
^	Agirre	Naroa	ESP	15.5.79	177/64	PV	4.43	4.56i- 07, 4.50- 06
	Aguilar	Alessandra	ESP	1.7.78	165/50	Mar	2:27:03	2:27:00- 11
*	Ahouré	Murielle	CIV	23.8.87	167/57	100	10.91	10.99- 12, 10.86w- 11
						200	22.24	22.42- 12, 22.31w- 11
	Ahye	Michelle-Lee	TTO	10.4.92	168/59	100	11.06	11.19- 11, 11.15w- 11
						200	22.98	23.13- 12
	Aidietyte	Neringa	LTU	5.6.83	177/64	20kW	1:33:43	1:33:05- 12
	Aït Elbatoul	Ibtissam	MAR	26.11.89		800	2:02.04	2:09.67- 11
*	Aitova	Marina	KAZ	13.9.82	180/60	HJ	1.95	1.99- 09
^	Akaba	Yukiko	JPN	18.10.79	158/43	HMar	68:59	68:11- 08
						Mar	2:24:43	2:24:09- 11
	Akakpo	Stella	FRA-J	28.2.94	158/50	100	11.26	11.61- 12
	Akinniyi	Dorcas	USA	23.1.90	170/59	Hep	5629(w)	5733- 12
	Akinosun	Morolake	USA-J	17.5.94	165/54	100	11.45, 11.29w	11.41- 12
						200	23.26, 23.18w	23.49, 23.44w?- 11
*	Akkaoui	Malika	MAR	25.12.87	160/46	800	1:57.64	1:59.01i, 1:59.54- 12
						1500	4:04.97	4:04.96- 11
	Alami El Ouali	Salami	MAR	29.12.83	167/53	3kSt	9:35.88	9:31.03- 12
	Alcántara	Dailenis	CUB	10.8.91	163/56	TJ	14.02	14.58- 12
	Alcide	Makeba	LCA	24.2.90	175/62	HJ	1.89i, 1.88	1.79- 11
^	Aldama	Yamilé	GBR	14.8.72	173/62	TJ	14.06	15.29- 03
^	Alekhina	Nadezhda	RUS	22.9.78	176/62	TJ	13.98	15.14- 09
	Aleksandrova	Ulyana	RUS	1.1.91	182/63	Hep	5916	5693- 12
	Alekseyeva	Nadezhda	RUS	16.7.88		400h	57.39	58.85- 11
	Alexander	Annie	TTO	28.8.87	175/91	SP	17.31i, 16.30	17.70i- 12, 17.66- 11
	Alexander	Ayanna	TTO	20.7.82	172/65	TJ	13.73	14.15- 12
	Alexander	Kineke	VIN	21.2.86	178/65	200	23.00A, 23.27	23.58- 06
						400	51.62	51.35- 06
	Alexander	Nadia	JAM	27.12.85	165/66	SP	16.72	16.68- 09
	Alexander	Rebecca	USA	2.5.90	168/55	400	51.78	51.13A, 51.20- 12
*	Ali	Nia	USA	23.10.88	170/64	100h	12.48	12.73, 12.63w- 11
	Alima El Ouali	Salami	MAR	29.12.83	167/53	3000	8:55.51	9:18.37- 10
	Allman	Valarie	USA-J	23.2.95	183/70	DT	56.13	50.91- 12
	Almanza	Rose Marie	CUB	13.7.92	166/53	800	1:59.4	1:59.55- 12
	Alniaçik	Aysegul	TUR	15.4.87	165/70	HT	68.63	66.93- 12
^	Amata	Doreen	NGR	6.5.88	185/55	HJ	1.91	1.95- 08
	Anacharsis	Phara	FRA	17.12.83	177/60	400h	55.94	55.97- 13
	Anagnostopoúlou	Hrisoúla	GRE	27.8.91	176/79	DT	56.55	57.10- 12
*	Anderson	Alexandria	USA	28.1.87	175/60	100	10.91	11.01- 11, 10.88w- 12
						200	22.67w	22.80- 09
	Anderson/Grunewald	Gabriele	USA	25.6.86	168/55	800	2:01.38	2:02.83- 12
		1500	4:01.48		4:04.84- 12	3000	8:42.64	8:43.52- 12
	Anderson	Lindsey	USA	23.5.85	163/52	3kSt	9:48.32	9:30.75- 08
^	Andersson	Isabellah	SWE	12.11.80	167/51	Mar	2:26:05	2:23:41- 11

Name		Nat	Born	Ht/Wt	Event	2013 Mark	Pre-2013 Best
Andersson	Tracey	SWE	5.12.84	167/80	HT	70.82	70.33- 12
Andraud	Matilde	FRA	28.4.89	172/68	JT	56.17	56.96- 12
Andrews	Chandra	USA	4.9.83	170/73	HT	65.36	66.72- 12
Andreyeva	Anastasiya	RUS	11.1.92		HJ	1.89	1.86- 11
^ Angelsen	Tonje	NOR	17.1.90	179/62	HJ	1.92	1.97- 12
Anghelescu	Nicoleta	ROU	3.1.92	160/70	JT	55.89	54.32- 12
Aniballi	Valentina	ITA	19.4.84	176/64	DT	57.73	57.51- 09
Antil	Seema	IND	27.7.83	183/85	DT	56.37	64.84- 04
* Antyukh	Natalya	RUS	26.6.81	182/73	400h	55.20	52.70- 12
Anumba	Michelle	USA	18.9.91	165/77	SP	16.75	17.18- 12
Aoki	Sayaka	JPN	15.12.86	163/51	400h	57.28	55.94- 08
Aoyama	Rui	JPN	15.4.89	157/45	HMar	70:28	72:16- 12
Aragon	Alexa	USA	1.6.92		3kSt	9:56.21	10:25.82- 12
Arcanjo	Geisa	BRA	19.9.91	180/92	SP	18.27	19.02- 12
* Aregawi	Abeba	SWE	5.7.90	169/48	800	1:59.20	1:59.39- 12
					1500	3:56.60	3:56.54- 12
Arenas	Lorena	COL	17.9.93		20kW	1:32:25, 1:32:31.7t	1:32:36- 12
Areson	Jacqueline	AUS	31.3.88	150/45	5000	15:12.09	15:14.31- 12
Argunova	Nina	RUS	18.2.89	172/62	100h	13.01	13.02- 11
Aristarkhova	Natalya	RUS	31.10.89	163/46	3000	8:50.76i	9:11.55- 12
					3kSt	9:30.64	9:31.93- 12
Armbrister	Cache	BAH	26.9.89	170/54	100	11.35A	11.65- 08
Arrafi	Rabab	MAR	12.1.91	177/64	800	2:00.58	2:04.60- 12
					1500	4:05.22	4:05.80- 12
Arteil	Laura	FRA	9.10.93	171/60	Hep	5735	5319- 12
Artymata	Eleni	CYP	16.5.86	178/58	200	23.15	22.61- 10
* Arzamasova	Marina	BLR	17.1.87	173/57	800	1:59.60	1:59.30- 11
Asahssah	Malika	MAR	24.9.82	173/56	HMar	69:11	69:54- 12
Asenjo	Sabina	ESP	3.8.86	181/95	DT	58.65	56.74- 12
Asher-Smith	Dina	GBR-J	4.12.95	165/55	100	11.38, 11.30w	11.54- 12
					200	23.14	23.49- 12
Ashley	Whitney	USA	18.2.89	178/80	DT	61.89	59.99- 12
Assefa	Meskerem	ETH	20.9.85	155/43	Mar	2:25:17	
* Assefa	Sofia	ETH	14.11.87	171/58	3kSt	9:12.84	9:09.00- 12
Assefa	Tigist	ETH-J	.94	170/55	800	2:01.25	
Asumnu	Gloria	NGR	22.5.85	163/52	100	11.27, 11.20w	11.03- 08
Atkins	Joanna	USA	31.1.89	175/61	400	50.77	50.39- 09
Atkinson	Erin	USA	30.1.92	178/79	HT	64.97	62.20- 12
Avdeyeva ¶	Anna	RUS	6.4.85	171/100	SP	18.34	20.07- 09
Aya	Masumi	JPN	1.1.80	165/75	HT	65.03	67.26- 06
* Ayalew	Hiwot	ETH	6.3.90	173/51	3000	8:50.?+e	
5000	14:57.02		14:49.36- 12		3kSt	9:15.25	9:09.61- 12
* Ayalew	Wude	ETH	4.7.87	150/44	10k	31:16.68	30:11.87- 09
					HMar	69:21	67:58- 09
* Ayana	Almaz	ETH	21.11.91	165/50	3000	8:40.53+	8:49.64- 12
5000	14:25.84		14:57.97- 12		3kSt	9:27.49	9:22.51- 10
Aydemir	Esma	TUR	1.1.92	163/45	1500	4:09.06	4:09.06- 12
Baak	Bianca	NED	25.1.92	174/56	400h	56.75	58.33- 11
Bahta	Meraf	ERI	26.6.89	175/57	1500	4:05.11	4:12.52- 08
^ Bailey	Aleen	JAM	25.11.80	170/64	100	11.19	11.04- 04
					200	23.08A	22.33- 04
Bain	Brianna	USA	23.6.93	178/75	JT	56.03	54.93- 12
Baird	Kadecia	GUY-J	24.2.95	167/52	400	51.32A	51.04- 12
Baisden	Kendall	USA-J	5.3.95	168/54	400	52.03	52.59- 10
Baker	Keshia	USA	30.1.88	170/61	400	51.15	50.76- 10
Balakshina	Anna	RUS	22.11.86		800	2:01.44	2:00.19- 10
Balciunaite	Egle	LTU	31.10.88	175/60	800	1:59.82	1:59.29- 10
Balkunets	Dariya	BLR	4.34.93		20kW	1:32:43	1:41:44- 11
Ballinger	Mary	USA	5.5.88		3kSt	9:51.33	10:22.98- 09
Bambara	Laëtitia	BUR	30.3.84	180/75	HT	65.33	68.53- 11
Bamgbose	Margaret	USA	19.10.93	162/52	400	52.25	
Banach	Joanna	POL	20.8.92	176/65	400h	57.27	58.37- 12
* Baptiste	Kelly-Ann	TTO	14.10.86	160/54	100	10.83	10.84- 10
					200	22.36	22.60- 09, 22.23w- 12
Barber	Aleesha	TTO	16.5.87	153/57	100h	13.04	12.85- 10, 12.83w- 08
Barber	Eunice	FRA	17.11.74	175/68	LJ	6.55	7.05- 03
Barber	Jade	USA	4.4.93	170/64	100h	13.00, 12.93w	13.55, 13.34w- 12
^ Barber	Mikele	USA	4.10.80	159/50	100	11.15	11.02- 07, 10.96w- 11
					400	51.82	50.63- 01
Barbosa	Liliane Cristina	BRA	8.1.87		400h	57.38	57.79- 12
Bardelle	Christine	FRA	16.8.74	160/48	1500	4:09.64	4:13.79- 03
					3000	8:57.01i	9:00.64i- 11, 9:01.67- 07

Name		Nat	Born	Ht/Wt	Event	2013 Mark	Pre-2013 Best
Bardge	Crystal	USA	25.9.88	158/52	100h	13.20, 12.76w	13.09- 12
Barr	Jessie	IRL	24.7.89	178/60	400h	56.74	55.93- 12
* Barrett	Brigetta	USA	24.12.90	183/64	HJ	2.04	2.03- 12
* Barrios	Yarelis	CUB	12.7.83	172/98	DT	67.36	68.03- 12
Barsosio	Agnes	KEN	5.8.82	159/44	Mar	2:24:03	2:24:27- 12
Bartnovskaya	Natalya	RUS	7.1.89	163/	PV	4.45i, 4.45	4.30i- 11, 4.21A- 12
Bauer	Katharina	GER	12.6.90	178/66	PV	4.46i, 4.45	4.42- 12
Bauschke	Melanie	GER	14.7.88	179/63	LJ	6.68i, 6.64	6.83- 09
Bayne	Chauntae	USA	4.4.84	164/54	100	11.12	11.15A- 06, 11.24- 07
					200	22.57, 22.39w	22.72i, 22.87A- 06, 22.95- 07
* Baysa	Atsede	ETH	16.4.87	160/42	HMar	67:34	68:42- 10
					Mar	2:25:14	2:22:03- 12
Bazzoni	Chiara	ITA	5.7.84	172/60	400	52.06	52.62- 12
* Beard	Jessica	USA	8.1.89	168/57	200	22.81	22.95i, 23.02- 11
					400	51.05	50.56- 09
Beckford	Allison	JAM	8.5.79	175/60	400h	57.32	55.12- 03
Beckles	Kierre	BAR	21.5.90	169/54	100h	13.09	13.01- 11, 12.97w- 12
Bedaso	Shitaye	ETH	.85		Mar	2:25:47	2:25:09- 11
Beesley	Meghan	GBR	15.11.89	165/63	400h	54.97	55.69- 11
* Beitia	Ruth	ESP	1.4.79	192/71	HJ	1.99i, 1.97	2.02- 07
Bekele	Ashete	ETH	17.4.88		Mar	2:27:47	2:31:23- 12
Bekele	Mekdes	ETH	20.1.87	180/58	3kSt	9:41.51	9:20.23- 08
Bekele	Tadelech	ETH	11.4.91	156/42	HMar	68:38	70:54- 12
Bekh	Maryna	UKR-J	18.7.95	172.61	LJ	6.78	6.47- 11
Belete	Almensch	BEL	26.7.89	156/44	3000	8:51.70	8:51.76- 09
					5000	15:12.26	15:03.63- 11
* Belete	Mimi	BRN	9.6.88	164/62	1500	4:03.63	4:00.25- 10
					2000	5:38.53	
Belibasáki	María	GRE	19.6.91	174/54	200	23.18	23.28- 12
Bell	Rolanda	PAN	27.10.87	160/48	3kSt	9:52.07	10:07.77- 12
Belleau-Béliveau	Karine	CAN	29.12.83	168/52	800	2:01.13	2:02.04- 12
Bellille	Janeil	TTO	18.6.89	172/60	400h	57.34	55.80- 11
Benecchi	Giorgia	ITA	9.7.89	164/55	PV	4.40i, 4.30	4.36i- 10, 4.35, 12, 4.40ex- 11
* Bengtsson	Angelica	SWE	8.7.93	164/51	PV	4.55	4.63i- 11, 4.58- 12
Bennett	April	USA	22.4.80	175/58	PV	4.50	4.63- 08
Berg	Josefin	SWE	27.12.85	174/72	HT	67.18	64.63- 12
Berings	Eline	BEL	28.5.86	162/53	100h	13.11, 13.01w	12.94- 09
Berroa	Nieves	CUB	16.3.90	175/72	SP	16.84	17.10- 11
Berry	Gwen	USA	29.6.89	165/68	HT	73.81	71.95- 12
* Bespalova	Mariya	RUS	21.5.86	183/85	HT	71.70	76.72- 12
Bettiche	Amina	ALG	14.12.87	161/44	3kSt	9:40.71	9:57.46- 12
Bian Ka		CHN	5.1.93		SP	17.50	16.97- 12
Bicet	Nora Aída	ESP	29.10.77	178/78	JT	59.81	63.32- 04
Biesenbach	Alina	GER	27.4.92	180/68	Hep	5767	5677- 12
Biesenbach	Kira	GER	7.10.92	186/70	Hep	6185	5878- 12
* Bikulova	Lina	RUS	1.10.88	165/51	20kW	1:28:42	1:31:01- 12
* Billaud	Cindy	FRA	11.3.86	167/59	100h	12.59	12.93- 11
Bing	Portia	NZL	17.4.93	182/64	Hep	5774(w)	5653- 12
* Bingson	Amanda	USA	20.2.90	170/89	HT	75.73	71.78- 12
Biruk	Konjit	ETH	22.9.87		HMar	69:00	
Bishop	Melissa	CAN	5.8.88	173/58	800	1:59.76	1:59.82- 12
^ Bisibori	Ruth	KEN	2.1.88	170/55	3kSt	9:31.81	9:13.16- 09
Bissoly	Sephora	FRA	6.11.81	168/66	JT	55.90	59.52- 06
Blackburn	Paige	USA	5.3.90	180/82	DT	57.39	53.24- 12
Blaize	Dominique	GBR	3.10.87	168/54	LJ	6.54, 6.56w	6.45- 12, 6.51w- 11
Blazej	Karolina	POL	21.11.86	169/50	LJ	6.49, 6.50w	6.21- 11
* Bleasdale	Holly	GBR	2.11.91	175/68	PV	4.77i, 4.60	4.87i, 4.71- 12
Bliss	Andrea	JAM	5.10.80	173/63	100h	12.82	12.83- 05
Bliss	Tori	USA	1.12.92	183/91	SP	17.04	15.73- 12
Blok	Emily	USA	14.4.91	166/59	100	11.32	11.58A, 11.73- 11; 11.53w- 12
Blouin	Mélanie	CAN	14.7.90	175/64	PV	4.35i	4.40- 12
Bo Yanmin		CHN	29.6.87	170/51	20kW	1:29:59	1:27:37- 05
Bobocel	Ancuta	ROU	3.10.87	163/52	3000	8:52.86i	8:54.08i- 10, 9:10.58- 07
					3kSt	9:35.78	9:25.70- 12
Boden/Wells	Lauren	AUS	3.8.88	179/66	400h	55.08	55.25- 10
Boekelman	Melissa	NED	11.5.89	177/82	SP	17.79	18.17- 10
Bogdanovich	Valeriya	BLR	1.5.92	184/56	HJ	1.91	1.88- 11
Bokesa	Aauri Lorena	ESP	14.12.88	183/68	400	51.77	52.23- 12
^ Bolshakova	Svetlana	BEL	14.10.84	178/68	TJ	13.84i	14.55- 10
* Bolshova	Yekaterina	RUS	4.2.88	178/66	HJ	1.89i	1.92i, 1.91- 12
					LJ	6.57i	6.52i, 6.45- 12

Name		Nat	Born	Ht/Wt	Event	2013 Mark	Pre-2013 Best
Bondarenko	Kristina	RUS-J	10.8.95		PV	4.30	4.25- 12
Bonne	Daysurami	CUB	9.3.88	173/56	400	51.2, 52.82	51.69A- 11, 51.81- 09
Bordignon	Laura	ITA	26.3.81	180/78	DT	56.48	59.21- 08
^ Borel	Cleopatra	TTO	3.10.79	168/93	SP	17.84	19.48i- 04, 19.42- 11
Borges	Fernanda Raquel	BRA	26.7.88	165/65	DT	60.79	60.91- 11
Borman	Brittany	USA	1.7.89	180/77	JT	60.91	61.51- 12
Borodina	Yana	RUS	21.4.92	167/52	TJ	14.11	14.41- 12
Borowska	Agnieszka	POL	21.10.91	187/64	HJ	1.87i, 1.87	1.84- 12
					Hep	5586w	5505- 12
Borsi	Veronica	ITA	13.6.87	168/51	100h	12.76	13.05, 13.03w- 12
^ Boslak	Vanessa	FRA	11.6.82	170/57	PV	4.40	4.70- 06
Bouaasayriya	Kaltoum	MAR	23.8.82	157/46	3kSt	9:32.50	9:40.69- 12
Bougard	Erica	USA	26.7.93	168/57	Hep	5990w, 5976	5547- 12
Bowen	Lutisha	USA	9.7.90	159/52	100h	13.15	13.65- 12
Bowie	Tori	USA	27.8.90	175/61	100	11.14, 11.04w	11.28- 12
					LJ	6.91	6.78- 12
Boyd	Alana	AUS	10.5.84	171/61	PV	4.50	4.76- 12
Breen	Melissa	AUS	17.9.90	174/66	100	11.25	11.27- 12, 11.22w- 09
					200	23.12	23.30- 12
Bremser	Julia	GER	27.4.82	176/78	DT	57.12	59.84--11
Brewer	Ciarra	USA	12.3.93	158/52	TJ	13.85	13.65- 11
Briscoe	Shanay	USA	7.8.92		HJ	1.88i	1.92- 12
Britton	Evonne	USA	10.10.91	167/55	100h	13.06	13.11- 11
* Britton	Fionnuala	IRL	24.9.84	158/45	3000	8:55.89mx,8:54.37i	8:55.01mx-12,9:02.11- 11
Brockington	Tyler	USA-J	6.2.94	169/55	400h	57.40	
* Broersen	Nadine	NED	29.4.90	171/62	HJ	1.90	1.87- 11
					Hep	6345	6319- 12
^ Brooks	Sheri-Ann	JAM	11.2.83	170/64	100	11.14, 11.08w	11.05- 07
* Brooks	Tia	USA	2.8.90	183/109	SP	19.22i, 18.96	19.00i, 18.47- 12
Brown	Alicia	CAN	21.1.90	165/58	400	52.08	54.16- 12
Brown	Felicia	USA	27.10.93	168/57	200	23.19, 23.04w	23.78- 12
Brown	Kamaria	USA	21.12.92	164/55	200	22.58, 22.16w	23.53- 10, 22.86i- 12
					400	52.10	52.60i- 12, 52.99- 10
Brown	Michelle	USA	24.1.92	170/57	400	52.19	52.91- 09
Brown	Sarah	USA	15.10.86	170/52	1500	4:05.27	4:05.67- 09
Brown	Shaunagh	GBR	15.3.90	182/82	HT	66.06	61.13- 12
* Brown	T'Erea	USA	24.10.89	178/59	400h	54.83	54.21- 12
Brume	Ese	NGR-Y	17.1.96		LJ	6.53	
Bruni	Roberta	ITA-J	8.3.94	170/54	PV	4.60i, 4.40	4.35- 12
Bryan	Lucy	GBR-J	22.5.95	162/48	PV	4.40	4.11i- 12, 4.10- 11
Bryant	Dezerea	USA	27.4.93	157/50	100	11.20	11.29- 12
					200	22.87, 22.54w	22.97- 12
^ Bryzgina ¶	Yelizaveta	UKR	28.11.89	172/56	200	22.72	22.44- 10
Buchanan	Brea	USA	8.1.93	170/57	100h	12.77	13.45- 12
Büchel	Selina	SUI	26.7.91	168/58	800	2:01.66, 2:01.64i	2:04.02- 12
Büchler	Nicole	SUI	17.12.83	161/56	PV	4.61	4.60- 12
Buckley	Kyla	USA	22.3.91	168/86	SP	17.28	16.98- 12
Buckley	Landria	USA	2.7.88	166/53	400h	56.15	56.79- 11
* Buckman	Zoe	AUS	21.12.88	172/55	800	2:00.93	2:02.19- 12
1500	4:04.82		4:05.03- 12		1M	4:30.76irr	4:30.86- 12
2000	5:39.17				3000	8:58.0	
Buell	Bethany	USA	4.12.91	163/59	PV	4.46	4.40- 12
Buisson	Marion	FRA	19.2.88	176/61	PV	4.40	4.50- 08
^ Bujin	Cristina	ROU	12.4.88	171/52	TJ	14.24i, 13.91	14.42- 09
Bukina	Yevdokiya	RUS	10.2.93	165/54	3kSt	9:46.56	9:56.46- 12
* Bulgakova	Anna	RUS	17.1.88	173/90	HT	76.17	74.02- 12
Bunch	Dani	USA	16.5.91	178/95	SP	17.13	16.65i, 16.46- 12
Burchell	Remona	JAM	15.9.91	166/52	100	11.34	11.55A, 11.52w- 12
* Burka	Gelete	ETH	15.2.86	165/45	1500	4:04.36	3:58.79- 09
					5000	14:42.07	14:31.20- 07
Burkhanova	Sofiya	UZB	1.12.89	170/60	SP	17.07	17.44- 12
Burkovska	Olena	UKR	9.8.81	158/50	Mar	2:27:07	2:28:31- 10
Burla	Serena	USA	29.7.82		Mar	2:28:01	2:28:27- 12
Bush	Nicole	USA	4.4.86	159/50	3kSt	9:39.36	9:39.38- 09
Busienei	Selah Jepleting	KEN	27.12.91	170/59	800	2:01.17A	2:02.99A- 12
Buttinger	Madelaine	CAN	3.11.89		Hep	5576(w)	5403- 11
Butts	Tynita	USA	10.6.90		HJ	1.90i, 1.84	1.87i- 10, 1.87- 12
Butvina	Aleksandra	RUS	14.2.86	181/71	Hep	5993	6110- 12
Buziak	Paulina	POL	16.12.86	170/52	20kW	1:30:15	1:29:44- 12
Byres	Katie	GBR	11.9.93	171/63	PV	4.35i	4.52i, 4.36- 12
Caballero	Daylis	CUB	6.3.88	166/59	PV	4.40	4.51- 11

Name		Nat	Born	Ht/Wt	Event	2013 Mark			Pre-2013 Best
Caballero	Denia	CUB	13.1.90	175/73	DT	63.47			65.60- 12
Caballero	Yanelli	MEX	29.5.93	161/43	20kW	1:30:58			
Caballero	Yolanda	COL	19.3.82	155/46	HMar	70:30			72:35- 11
* Cabecinha	Ana	POR	29.4.84	168/52	20kW	1:29:17			1:27:46- 08
Cachová	Katerina	CZE	26.2.90	176/64	Hep	5899			6123- 11
Cai Yilin		CHN	27.11.90	178/90	SP	16.76i, 16.65			16.62- 08
* Cain	Mary	USA-Y	3.5.96	170/50	800	1:59.51			2:03.34- 12
1500	4:04.62	4:11.01- 12		1M		4:28.25i		4:39.28- 12	2M	9:38.68i	-0-
Caldwell	Kayla	USA	19.6.91	163/57	PV	4.40A			4.10- 10
Calveras	Débora	ESP	26.12.88	174/61	TJ	13.75	13.26, 13.56w- 11, 13.31i- 12		
* Calvert	Schillonie	JAM	27.7.88	166/57	100	11.07			11.05- 11
Campbell	Amber	USA	5.6.81	170/91	HT	73.03			72.59- 11
* Campbell-Brown	Veronica	JAM	15.5.82	163/61	100	11.01, 10.78w			10.76- 11
					200	22.53, 22.18w			21.74- 08
Cao Mojie		CHN	10.4.92		10k	31:55.66			33:10.19- 12
Capková	Tereza	CZE	24.7.87	162/53	1500	4:08.78			4:08.27- 12
Caravelli	Marzia	ITA	23.10.81	176/64	200	23.16	23.42, 23.1- 11		
					100h	12.95			12.85- 12
Card	Kelsey	USA	20.8.92	173/90	SP	16.85i, 16.02			16.98i, 15.94- 12
Carrier-Eades	Chelsea	USA	21.8.89	168/59	100h	12.90			12.78- 12
					Hep	5999			5927w- 11, 5839- 12
* Carter	Kori	USA	6.3.92	165/52	100h	12.76			12.99- 12
					400h	53.21			57.10- 11
* Carter	Michelle	USA	12.10.85	175/110	SP	20.24			19.86- 11
Casadei	Nadja	SWE	3.4.83	174/66	Hep	5834			5905- 09
Cassulo	Chelsea	USA	10.6.90	173/77	HT	70.07			66.50- 12
Castells	Berta	ESP	24.1.84	174/59	HT	67.20			69.59- 12
* Castlin	Kristi	USA	7.7.88	170/57	100h	12.61	12.56, 12.48w- 12		
Catouillart	Lucie	FRA	21.10.91	171/75	DT	57.84			54.00- 11
Cattaneo	Micol	ITA	14.5.82	178/68	100h	13.02			12.98- 08
^ Cechlová	Vera	CZE	19.11.78	178/78	DT	58.80			67.71- 03
Cechová	Katerina	CZE	21.3.88	170/52	100	11.34			11.32- 12
Cérival	Jessica	FRA	20.1.82	185/120	SP	17.04	17.99i- 11, 17.87- 09		
Cestonaro	Ottavia	ITA-J	12.1.95	162/55	TJ	13.69			13.32- 12
Chaboudez	Aurélie	FRA	9.5.93	173/60	400h	56.80			57.14- 12
Chaney	Jasmine	USA	25.8.88	160/52	200	23.01	23.16i- 11, 23.55- 10, 23.18w- 12		
					400h	56.51			55.22- 11
Chang Chunfeng		CHN	4.5.88	179/75	JT	60.90			61.61- 07
Chapple	Nikki	AUS	9.2.81	179/58	HMar	70:34			68:37- 10
Chávez	Erika	ECU	4.6.90	170/56	200	23.10w			23.09A- 12
* Chebet	Emily	KEN	18.2.86	157/45	5000	14:46.89			
10k	30:47.02		31:30.22- 11		HMar	68:20			72:00- 11
Chebet	Ruth	KEN/BRN-Y	17.11.96		3kSt	9:40.84			
Chebet	Winny	KEN	20.12.90	165/50	800	1:59.30			1:59.37- 12
					1000	2:35.73			
^ Checa	Dolores	ESP	27.12.82	168/52	3000	8:56.42			8:37.78- 08
					5000	15:17.72			14:46.30- 11
Cheever	Jamie	USA	28.2.87	175/55	3kSt	9:29.13			9:51.42- 12
* Chemos	Milcah	KEN	24.2.86	163/48	3kSt	9:11.65			9:07.14- 12
Chemtai	Esther	KEN	4.6.88	156/44	10k	31:42.06			
					HMar	70:04+			
Chen Shuangyan		CHN	14.8.91		20kW	1:31:12			1:32:36- 12
Chen Yufei		CHN	26.1.89	170/63	TJ	13.84			14.11- 09
Chen Zhen		CHN-J	3.11.94		20kW	1:32:28			1:35:57- 12
Chepchirchir	Flomena	KEN	1.12.81	165/43	Mar	2:23:00			2:24:21- 11
Chepchirchir	Sarah	KEN	27.7.84		HMar	70:33			68:07- 11
* Chepkirui	Joyce	KEN	20.8.88		HMar	68:15			67:03- 12
Chepkoech	Josephine	KEN	.89		HMar	68:53			70:42- 12
* Chepkurui	Lydia	KEN	23.8.84	170/52	3kSt	9:12.55			9:14.98- 12
Chepkwony	Caroline	KEN	18.4.84		HMar	70:24			68:36- 12
					Mar	2:27:27			2:30:34- 12
Cheprugut	Hellen	KEN			HMar	69:36A			
Cheptai	Irene	KEN	4.2.92	160/45	3000	8:56.20			9:22.05- 07
					5000	14:50.99			16:02.0A- 12
Chepyego	Selly	KEN	3.10.85	160/42	5000	15:14.12			15:06.26- 06
10k	31:22.11		31:27.98- 11		HMar	68:24			69:58- 11
Cherepanova	Yana	RUS	1.2.81		Hep	5664			5696- 12
Cherkasova	Svetlana	RUS	20.5.78	171/55	800	2:00.32			1:56.93- 05
Chernenko (Kayukova)	Yekaterina	RUS	9.10.86	175/61	TJ	14.40			14.64- 09
* Chernova	Tatyana	RUS	29.1.88	189/63	LJ	6.57			6.82- 11
					Hep	6623			6880- 11

Name		Nat	Born	Ht/Wt	Event	2013 Mark		Pre-2013 Best
Cherono	Gladys	KEN	12.5.83	158/46	3000	8:34.05		9:17.80- 04
5000	14:47.12	15:39.5A- 12		10k	30:29.23	32:41.40- 12	HMar	66:48	68:18- 12
* Cherono	Mercy	KEN	7.5.91	168/54	1500	4:05.82		4:02.31- 11
3000	8:31.23		8:38.51- 12		5000	14:40.33		14:35.13- 11
* Cherop	Sharon	KEN	16.3.84	157/45	10k	32:46.3A		32:03.0A- 11
HMar	69:04		67:08- 11		Mar	2:22:28		2:22:39- 12
Cherotich	Fancy	KEN	10.8.90	173/54	3kSt	9:28.04		9:35.03- 12
Cheruto	Faith	KEN	.87		Mar	2:28:54		2:31:10- 12
Chesang	Agnes	KEN	.86		3kSt	9:34.33		9:53.7A- 12
Chesebe	Sylvia	KEN	16.4.89	167/52	800	2:00.76A		2:01.21A- 12
Chesire	Rebecca	KEN	.89		Mar	2:27:52		
Cheyech	Flomena	KEN	5.7.82	165/49	HMar	67:39		68:44- 09
					Mar	2:24:34		2:34:13- 12
* Chicherova	Anna	RUS	22.7.82	180/57	HJ	2.02		2.07- 11
* Child	Eilidh	GBR	20.2.87	172/59	400	51.83, 51.45i		52.28- 11
					400h	54.22		54.96- 12
Chilla	Mercedes	ESP	19.1.80	170/60	JT	59.76		64.07- 10
Chinchikeyeva	Albina	RUS	17.2.92		3kSt	9:50.88		10:14.41- 10
^ Chizhenko	Yuliya	RUS	30.8.79	173/63	1500	4:09.06		3:55.68- 06
Cichocka	Angelika	POL	15.3.88	169/54	800	2:00.60		2:00.20- 11
Clayton	Jennifer	USA/PAN	5.10.92	170/57	LJ	6.49		6.37- 09, 6.41w- 10
Clements	Grace	GBR	2.5.84	170/64	Hep	5817		5819- 10
Clitheroe	Helen	GBR	2.1.74	168/57	3000	8:50.16i		8:39.81i- 11, 8:51.82- 10
Coburn	Emma	USA	19.10.90	173/54	1500	4:06.87		4:09.42- 12
1M	4:29.86i		4:33.24i- 12		3kSt	9:28.26		9:23.54- 12
Cojuhari	Olesea	MDA	29.3.90	170/58	400	52.13		52.00- 12
Collado	Yanisley	CUB	30.4.85	178/74	DT	62.68		64.10- 09
Collatz	Alexandra	USA	25.5.93		DT	56.27		55.09- 10
Collier	Ashley	USA	4.2.92	172/60	100	11.15w		11.01- 12
					200	23.14i, 23.20		22.89- 12
Comba	Rocío	ARG	14.7.87	175/78	DT	62.77		59.99- 12
Coneo	Muriel	COL	15.3.87	160/49	1500	4:09.79		4:18.74- 12
Conley	Kim	USA	14.3.86	160/49	1500	4:07.17		4:12.05- 11
3000	8:47.95		8:56.38- 12		5000	15:09.57		15:14.48- 12
* Cosby Toruga	Jessica	USA	31.5.82	173/77	HT	73.58		74.19- 12
^ Costa	Keila	BRA	6.2.83	170/62	LJ	6.56		6.88- 07
					TJ	14.58		14.57, 15.10w- 07
Costa	Susana	POR	22.9.84	178/65	TJ	14.16		14.19- 12
Coutinho	Geisa	BRA	1.6.80	160/53	400	51.78		51.08- 11
Coward	Jacqueline	USA	5.11.89	167/55	100h	12.80, 12.67w		12.81- 12, 12.79w- 11
Cox	Shana	GBR	22.1.85	171/57	400	51.12		50.84- 08
Craft	Shanice	GER	15.5.93	185/89	SP	17.66i, 17.29		17.15- 12
					DT	60.77		62.92- 12
* Crawford	Virginia	USA	7.9.83	178/63	100h	12.67		12.45- 07
Cremer	Esther	GER	29.3.88	170/55	400	51.62		51.76- 12
Crofts	Helen	CAN	28.5.90	178/59	800	2:01.35		2:03.12- 11
Crowe	Laura	IRL	29.11.87		800	2:00.93		2:05.41- 11
Cruz	Clarisse	POR	9.7.78	170/54	3kSt	9:52.66		9:30.06- 12
Cruz	Silvia	POR	29.12.80	175/85	JT	56.55		59.76- 08
Cullen	Mary	IRL	17.8.82	165/54	5000	15:23.12		15:19.04- 07
^ Cummins	Diane	CAN	19.1.74	165/50	800	2:01.12		1:58.39- 01
Cunliffe	Hannah	USA-Y	1.9.96	169/55	200	23.10wA		23.74- 12
D'Agostino	Abbey	USA	25.5.92	158/48	1500	4:30.03i		4:37.41i- 12
3000	8:55.41i		9:02.15i, 9:24.64- 12		5000	15:11.35		15:19.98- 12
Daba	Tejitu	BRN	20.8.91	162/44	3000	8:48.37		8:53.75i- 12, 9:01.22- 10
					5000	15:08.11		15:05.59- 12
Dadic	Ivona	AUT	29.12.93	183/60	Hep	5874		5959- 12
* Dado	Firehiwot	ETH	9.1.84	165/	HMar	69:46dh		68:35- 12
Dahle	Tove Beate	NOR	6.4.88	170/75	JT	56.74		54.23- 11
* Dahlgren	Jennifer	ARG	21.4.84	180/115	HT	72.64		73.74- 10
Dahlström	Malin	SWE	26.8.89	171/60	PV	4.37		4.50i- 11, 4.50- 12
Dahmani	Kenza	ALG	18.11.80	162/44	10k	32:20.58		32:48.44- 09
					HMar	70:36		
Danekova	Silvia	BUL	7.2.83	165/50	3kSt	9:35.66		9:42.72- 12
Daniels	Paris	USA	25.1.90	163/52	100	11.34		11.28, 11.23w- 12
					200	22.73, 22.52w		22.89, 22.65w- 12
Danois	Johanna	FRA	4.4.87	169/53	200	23.00, 22.81i		22.86- 12
Darden	Dominique	USA	9.12.83	165/54	400h	56.95		54.88- 06
* Daska	Mamitu	ETH	16.10.83	165/	HMar	69:53		68:07- 09
					Mar	2:23:23		2:21:59- 11
Daunay	Christelle	FRA	5.12.74	163/43	10k	32:04.44		31:35.81- 12
HMar	69:49dh		68:34- 10		Mar	2:28:14		2:24:22- 10

Name		Nat	Born	Ht/Wt	Event	2013 Mark	Pre-2013 Best
Dauwens	Axelle	BEL	1.12.90	171.62	400h	55.96	56.60- 12
Davis	Darshay	USA	23.9.91	173/62	100	11.29w	11.30- 12
Davis	Shai-Anne	CAN	4.12.93	167/59	100	11.33, 11.31w	11.39- 12
					200	23.12	23.24- 12
Davis-White	Kali	USA-J	27.10.94	170/55	200	23.05	23.61, 23.57w- 12
* Davydova	Irina	RUS	27.5.88	170/65	400h	54.79	53.77- 12
Day	Christine	JAM	23.8.86	168/51	400	50.91	50.85- 12
* Day-Monroe	Sharon	USA	9.6.85	175/70	HJ	1.90	1.95- 09
					Hep	6550	6343- 12
De Aniceto	Marisa	FRA	11.11.86	162/57	Hep	5717	6182- 12
Deba	Buzunesh	ETH	8.9.87	162/45	Mar	2:24:26	2:23:19- 11
Decaux #	Alice	FRA	10.4.85	165/61	100h	12.85, 12.70 dq	12.88- 12
* Defar	Meseret	ETH	19.11.83	155/42	3000	8:30.29	8:23.72i, 8:24.51- 07
5000	14:26.90	14:12.88- 08			10k	30:08.06	29:59.20- 09 HMar 66:09dh 67:45- 10
Degefa	Worknesh	ETH	28.10.90	159/42	HMar	67:49	76:48- 12
Deiac	Cornelia	ROU	20.3.88	171/55	LJ	6.62i, 6.50	6.70- 10
* Dektyareva	Tatyana	RUS	8.5.81	174/60	100h	12.91, 12.88w	12.68- 10
Delasa	Sechale	ETH	20.9.91		Mar	2:26:43	2:26:27- 12
* DeLoach-Soukup	Janay	USA	12.10.85	165/59	100h	12.97	13.27- 12, 13.23w- 10
					LJ	6.99, 7.08w	7.03, 7.15w- 12
Delophont	Dior	FRA-J	19.10.94	184/65	HJ	1.87i	1.86- 12
Demireva	Mirela	BUL	28.9.89	180/50	HJ	1.94	1.95- 12
* Demus	Lashinda	USA	10.3.83	170/62	400h	54.22	52.47- 11
^ Denby	Nichole	USA	10.10.82	163/52	100h	13.08	12.54- 08
Deng Lina		CHN	16.3.92	165/44	TJ	13.92	13.89- 11
Deng Xiaoqing		CHN	13.6.89	165/58	400h	56.73	56.82- 12
Denisenko	Alla	RUS	12.10.83		DT	62.74	58.74- 12
* Denyayeva	Svetlana	RUS	10.5.91	167/52	LJ	6.76i, 6.68	6.72, 6.85w- 12
(now Biryukova)					TJ	13.96i	13.68- 11, 14.00w- 12
Dereli	Emel	TUR-Y	25.2.96	167/90	SP	18.04	16.87- 12
Derkach	Darya	ITA	27.3.93	165/50	LJ	6.67	6.55- 11
					TJ	13.92	13.56- 11, 13.64w- 12
Derun	Kateryna	UKR	24.9.93	168/73	JT	55.10	56.31- 11
Desalegn	Betlhem	UAE	13.11.91	164/52	1500	4:05.13	4:08.87- 12
					5000	15:12.84	15:36.61- 11
Detsuk	Kseniya	BLR	23.4.86	177/56	TJ	14.19	14.76, 14.81w- 12
Diago	Sahily	CUB-J	26.8.95	168/49	800	2:01.30	2:00.9- 12
Diawara	Aïsseta	FRA	29.6.89	169/54	100h	13.01	12.88- 12
* Dibaba	Birhane	ETH	11.9.93	159/44	Mar	2:23:01	2:29:22- 12
* Dibaba	Genzebe	ETH	8.2.91	168/52	1500	3:57.54	3:57.77- 12
2000	5:37.2i+		3000	8:37.00, 8:26.95i		8:47.01i, 8:48.35- 10 5000 14:37.68 14:37.56- 11	
* Dibaba	Tirunesh	ETH	1.10.85	160/47	3000	8:40.7+, 8:38.44+i	8:29.55- 06
2M	9:12.23i- 10			9:13.17i		5000	14:23.68 14:11.15- 08
10k	30:26.67			29:54.66- 08		HMar	66:56dh 67:35dh- 12
Ding Changqin		CHN	27.11.91		10k	32:47.14	32:44.86- 11
Ding Huiqin		CHN	5.2.90		20kW	1:29:42	1:30:14- 12
Diriba	Buze	ETH-J	9.2.94	160/43	5000	14:50.02	14:53.06- 12
* Diro	Etenesh	ETH	10.5.91	169/47	3kSt	9:16.97	9:14.07- 12
Distel-Bonnet	Céline	FRA	25.7.87	170/60	100	11.31	11.32, 11.30w- 12
Dixon	Diamond	USA	29.6.92	168/55	400	51.73	50.88- 12
^ Dixon	Vonette	JAM	26.11.75	170/62	100h	13.10, 13.06w	12.64- 07
Dmitriyeva ¶	Yunna	RUS	7.7.88		Hep	5826 dq	5578- 10
Doagâ	Ioana	ROU	5.4.92	174/58	1500	4:08.80	4:09.19- 12
Dobija	Teresa	POL	9.10.82	175/62	LJ	6.66	6.78- 11
^ Dobriskey	Lisa	GBR	23.12.83	171/56	1500	4:04.81	3:59.50- 09
Dobrynska	Viktoriya	UKR	18.1.80	176/65	HJ	1.89i	1.93- 12
Dodova	Gita	BUL	2.5.82	182/60	TJ	13.99i, 13.67	14.24- 08
Doi	Yurie	JPN	8.12.88	163/47	10k	32:16.05	
Dolgacheva ¶	Viktoriya	RUS	17.4.91	174/60	TJ	14.41i, 14.33dq	14.35- 12
Dong Yangzi		CHN	22.10.92		SP	16.65i, 16.41	16.70- 11
Dorozhon	Marharyta	UKR	4.9.87	180/75	JT	62.01	61.84- 12
Dorr	Fawn	CAN	19.4.87	162/52	400h	56.26	55.57- 10
Doseykina	Yekaterina	RUS	30.3.90		3kSt	9:42.10	10:16.24- 12
Doveri	Francesca	ITA	21.12.82	179/64	400h	56.65	57.39- 12
Dowie	Danielle	JAM	5.5.92	173/60	400h	54.94	56.10- 12
Drabenya	Hanna	BLR	15.8.87	153/46	20kW	1:31:16	1:31:58- 12
* Drahotová	Anezka	CZE-J	22.7.95		20kW	1:29:05	-0-
Drisbióti	Antigóni	GRE	21.3.84	162/52	20kW	1:33:42	1:38:04- 12
Dronsfield	Victoria	SWE	6.6.91	170/52	HJ	1.87i, 1.86	1.88- 12
Duan Dandan		CHN-J	23.5.95		20kW	1:32:45	1:36:47- 12
* Duarte	Sophie	FRA	31.7.81	170/54	5000	15:14.57	-0-

Name		Nat	Born	Ht/Wt	Event	2013 Mark	Pre-2013 Best
Dubitskaya	Alyona	BLR	25.1.90	182/77	SP	17.88	17.95- 09
Duchene	Krista	CAN	9.1.77		Mar	2:28:32	2:32:06- 12
Ducó	Natalia	CHI	31.1.89	177/95	SP	18.28	18.80- 12
Dudley	Ann	USA	28.5.91	180/62	HJ	1.87i	1.84- 12
Dudzinska	Agnieszka	POL	16.3.88	178/86	SP	17.36	17.00- 12
Duliba	Aleksandra	BLR	9.1.88	168/54	Mar	2:23:44	
Duncan	Ashley	USA	16.9.86	175/84	SP	16.80i	17.57i- 12, 16.80- 08
* Duncan	Kimberlyn	USA	2.8.91	173/59	100	11.08, 11.02w	10.96, 10.94w- 12
					200	22.35, 21.80w	22.19, 22.12w- 12
Dusanova	Nadezhda	UZB	17.11.87	174/56	HJ	1.93	1.96i, 1.95- 09
Dutil	Daniellys	CUB-J	12.2.95	175/56	HJ	1.90	1.87- 12
Dygacz	Agnieszka	POL	18.7.85	160/51	20kW	1:30:58	1:30:56- 11
Dzindzalietaite	Dovile	LTU	14.7.93	168/58	TJ	13.71	14.17- 12
Dzul ¶	Cecilia	MEX	20.4.92	182/88	SP	17.04	15.59- 12
Ebersohn	Annerie	RSA	9.8.90	167/55	400h	55.87A, 56.03	57.11A, 58.11A- 12
Ebihara	Yuki	JPN	28.10.85	164/66	JT	62.83	62.36- 12
Eisenlauer	Ester	GER	29.10.77	180/75	JT	55.46	61.04- 10
Ekelund	Irene	SWE-Y	8.3.97	167/52	100	11.35	11.73, 11.71w- 12
					200	22.92	24.04- 12
Ekponé	Olivia	USA	5.1.93	172/59	100	11.27w	11.58- 10, 11.57w- 12
					200	23.17, 22.91w	23.15- 12
Ektova	Irina	KAZ	8.1.87	173/61	TJ	14.23	14.48- 11
Ektova	Yekaterina	KAZ	30.8.92	170/60	TJ	13.84	13.36- 09
El Bahraoui	Manal	MAR-J	6.1.94	159/49	800	2:00.82	2:03.03- 12
El Otmani	Sanae	MAR	20.12.86		1500	4:09.45	4:12.38- 11
Elbe	Jenny	GER	18.4.90	180/60	TJ	14.12	14.06- 12
Elliott	Samantha	JAM	3.2.92	164/52	100h	13.23, 13.08wA	13.32A,13.12Aw-12,13.42- 10
					400h	56.38A, 56.44	59.10- 12
Embaye	Axumawit	ETH-J	18.10.94	160/50	1500	4:05.16	4:12.92- 12
Emmanuel	Crystal	CAN	27.11.91	170/50	100	11.40, 11.16w	11.34, 11.30Aw- 12
					200	22.89	22.90- 11
* England	Hannah	GBR	6.3.87	177/54	800	2:00.39	1:59.56- 12
					1500	4:03.38	4:01.89- 11
Engman	Helena	SWE	16.6.76	171/94	SP	17.34i	18.17- 10
Ennis	Delloreen	JAM	5.5.75	178/67	100h	12.94	12.50- 07
* Ennis-Hill	Jessica	GBR	28.1.86	164/57	100h	13.08	12.54- 12
Equihua	Monica	MEX	23.9.82	167/53	20kW	1:31:09	1:32:28- 12
Erdélyi	Zsófia	HUN	10.12.87	163/53	10k	32:47.96	33:18.75- 10
Erdmann	Tara	USA	14.6.89	155/45	2M	9:39.48i	
					10k	32:24.16	32:09.15- 12
Eriksson	Sandra	FIN	4.5.89	163/48	3kSt	9:38.38	9:43.38- 12
Erwee	Bianca	RSA	4.3.90	174/57	Hep	5715A	5432- 12
Esayias	Yeshi	ETH	28.12.85	160/48	Mar	2:24:06	2:26:00- 12
* Eshete	Shitaye	BRN	21.5.90	159/56	5000	15:03.13	15:05.48- 12
					10k	31:13.79	30:47.25- 12
Espinoza	Ahymara	VEN	28.5.85		SP	18.15	17.07- 12
Etea	Emebet	ETH	11.1.90	163/49	Mar	2:25:53	2:34:43- 12
Evans	Taylor	USA	7.10.89	168/52	200	23.15	23.23, 23.02w- 12
Ewen	Magdalyn	USA-J	23.9.94		SP	16.67	14.78- 12
^ Facey	Simone	JAM	7.5.85	162/53	200	22.95w	22.25- 08
* Falzon	Stéphanie	FRA	7.1.83	170/75	HT	69.78	73.40- 08
Famurewa	Becky	USA-J	24.2.94	180/86	DT	57.09	48.93- 12
Farkas-Zsivoczky	Györgyi	HUN	13.2.85	170/58	Hep	6269	6068- 11
Faulknor	Alexis	USA-J	22.9.94	165/52	LJ	6.52, 6.56w	6.04, 6.17w- 12
Faye	Gnima	SEN	17.11.84	169/61	100h	13.10	13.17- 12
Fazlitdinova	Gulshat	RUS	28.8.92	165/48	10k	32:01.83	33:06.96- 12
Fedotova	Yekaterina	RUS	3.7.92		HJ	1.89	1.90- 11
Fédronic	Justine	FRA	11.5.91	168/54	800	2:00.97	2:03.54- 12
* Felix	Allyson	USA	18.11.85	168/57	100	11.06+	10.89- 12
	200	22.30, 21.85w		21.69- 12	400	50.19	49.59- 11
Félix	Ana Dulce	POR	23.10.82	165/53	10k	31:52.55	31:30.90*- 09, 31:33.42- 11
					HMar	70:44	68:33- 11
Felnagle	Brianna	USA	9.12.86	170/57	1500	4:05.64	4:08.54- 08
					1M	4:30.44, 4:28.90irr	4:32.17i- 09, 4:36.21- 07
					5000	15:14.33	15:22.39- 12
	3000	8:52.59		8:51.38- 12	PV	4.30	4.00- 12
Felzmann	Anna	GER	18.1.92	166/49	DT	58.14	55.94- 11
Feng Bin		CHN-J	3.4.94		3kSt	9:35.14	9:28.27- 11
Fente	Birtukan	ETH	18.6.89	167/52	PV	4.60	4.88- 04
* Feofanova	Svetlana	RUS	16.7.80	164/53	100	11.18	11.07- 12
Ferguson	Sheniqua	BAH	24.11.89	170/57	100	11.32, 11.28w	10.91- 02
^ Ferguson-McKenzie	Debbie	BAH	18.1.76	170/57	200	23.34, 23.18w	22.19- 99

Name		Nat	Born	Ht/Wt	Event	2013 Mark	Pre-2013 Best
Ferraro	Federica	ITA	18.8.88	168/51	20kW	1:31:20	1:31:45- 12
Ferrer e Silva	Laila	BRA	30.7.82	180/80	JT	59.91	60.21- 12
Fertig	Fruzsina	HUN	2.9.93	175/80	HT	67.02	65.52- 12
Fetiskina	Tetyana	UKR-J	11.9.94		JT	57.30	53.36- 12
Feyne	Gemeda	ETH	28.6.92	159/50	1500	4:07.67	4:06.66- 12
Fiack	Marion	FRA	13.10.92	170/60	PV	4.35i, 4.35	4.42i- 12, 4.15- 11
Fields	Ashley	USA	13.4.93	175/59	200	23.22, 22.98w	23.76- 10, 23.66w- 09
Fields	MacKenzie	USA	19.1.90	165/54	PV	4.35	4.21i, 4.16- 11
Filatova	Tatyana	RUS	22.1.87	165/55	100h	13.31, 13.11w	13.18- 08
Finn	Michele	IRL	16.12.89		3kSt	9:54.00	10:13.15- 12
* Fiodorow	Joanna	POL	4.3.89	169/69	HT	68.92	74.18- 12
* Firova	Tatyana	RUS	10.10.82	174/59	400	50.71	49.72- 12
* Fischer	Julia	GER	1.4.90	192/85	DT	66.04	64.22- 12
* Flanagan	Shalane	USA	8.7.81	165/50	10k	31:04.85	30:22.22- 08
HMar	68:31			68:37- 10	Mar	2:27:08dh	2:25:38- 12
Flemings	Doniqué	USA	1.11.91	164/54	100h	12.85	13.00, 12.87w- 12
Flink	Sofi	SWE-J	8.7.95	168.69	JT	61.96	61.40- 12
Florez	Lina	COL	1.11.84	170/58	100h	13.00A, 13.01	12.94- 11
Flowers	Victoria	USA	17.1.90	173/89	HT	64.78	63.24- 12
Floyd	Ebonie	USA	21.10.83	168/57	200	23.10	22.32- 07
					400	51.10	51.25- 08
Ford	Yurisleydi	CUB	18.8.91	168/69	HT	68.64	68.45- 12
Fortney	Kim	USA	15.8.91	174/82	SP	16.80	16.28i, 16.20- 12
					HT	64.74	59.50- 12
Fougberg	Charlotta	SWE	19.6.85	160/48	3kSt	9:39.00	10:09.05- 11
Francis	Kim	USA	6.1.92	170/50	100h	13.15, 12.95w	13.40, 13.21w- 12
Francis	Phyllis	USA	4.5.92	178/61	200	22.77	23.03- 12
					400	50.86	51.22- 12
Franco	Jamy	GUA	1.7.91	170/48	20kW	1:33:11	1:30:57- 12
Franco	Leryn	PAR	1.3.82	174/54	JT	55.68	57.77- 12
Franek	Bridget	USA	8.11.87	160/50	3kSt	9:35.42	9:29.53- 12
Franklin	Autumne	USA-J	20.7.94	162/54	400h	57.10	59.63- 11
* Fraser-Pryce	Shelly-Ann	JAM	27.12.86	160/52	100	10.71	10.70- 12
					200	22.13	22.09- 12
* Freeman	Octavious	USA	20.4.92	169/57	100	10.87	11.09- 12
					200	22.55	22.74- 12
Frere	Danielle	USA	27.4.90		SP	16.88i, 16.76	17.47i- 12, 16.79- 11
Frerichs	Courtney	USA	18.1.93	167/52	3kSt	9:55.02	10:34.48- 12
^ Friedrich	Ariane	GER	10.1.84	179/57	HJ	1.90	2.06- 09
Friesen	Tanya	USA	23.6.91	170/59	Hep	5899(w)	5472- 12
* Frizell	Sultana	CAN	24.10.84	183/110	HT	71.57	75.04- 12
Frolova	Karina	RUS	2.3.90		HT	64.89	66.61- 12
^ Fuchise	Masumi	JPN	2.9.86	161/51	20kW	1:30:27	1:28:03- 09
Fuentes-Pila	Iris	ESP	10.8.80	169/53	5000	15:27.39	-0-
Fukumoto	Miyuki	JPN	4.1.77	172/53	HJ	1.92	1.92- 04
* Fukushi	Kayoko	JPN	25.3.82	160/45	10k	32:42.56	30:51.81- 02
					Mar	2:24:21	2:24:38- 11
Funk	Brittany	USA	13.5.92	172/86	HT	66.08	58.65- 12
Furlan	Jessica	CAN	15.3.90	165/54	3kSt	9:51.23	10:03.70- 12
Furman/Shahaf	Maayan	ISR	9.11.86	184/62	HJ	1.92	1.92- 11
* Fyodorova	Alina	UKR	31.7.89	174/63	HJ	1.90	1.86- 11
					Hep	5792	6126- 12
* Gadschiew	Kristina	GER	3.7.84	170/62	PV	4.61	4.66i- 11, 4.60- 10
Gaines	Jessie	USA	12.8.90	164/52	LJ	6.50Ai, 6.46	6.48- 12
Galéni	Evaggelía	GRE	29.12.88	172/51	LJ	6.62	6.44- 12
Galiart	Rianna	NED	22.11.85	168/56	PV	4.35i, 4.31	4.33i, 4.32- 12
Galitskaya	Yekaterina	RUS	24.2.87	174/63	100h	12.98	12.78- 12
* Galkina	Gulnara	RUS	9.7.78	174/56	3kSt	9:30.72	8:58.81- 08
Gall	Geena	USA	18.1.87	168.52	800	2:00.53	1:59.24- 12
					1500	4:09.95	4:12.23- 11
Gallagher	Kerri	USA	31.5.89	169/52	1500	4:09.64	4:16.07- 12
Gallardo	Karen	CHI	6.3.84	175/95	DT	59.57	60.48- 11
Galligan	Rose-Anne	IRL	9.12.87	173/57	800	2:00.58	2:01.76- 10
Gandulla	Arialis	CUB-J	22.6.95	170/65	100	11.32wA, 11.1	11.67, 11.57w- 12
Ganeyeva	Vera	RUS	6.11.88	172/87	DT	64.30	64.20- 12
Gao Ni		CHN	14.9.91	163/51	20kW	1:31:03	1:28:06- 12
Gao Shan		CHN-J	8.4.95		20kW	1:33:34	1:45:30- 11
Gao Yang		CHN	1.3.93		SP	17.76	17.07- 12
Garcia	Stephanie	USA	3.5.88	168/52	3kSt	9:45.78	9:41.12- 11
García	Rosibel	COL	13.2.81	171/62	800	2:01.98	1:59.38- 08
					1500	4:09.75	4:15.78- 07

Name		Nat	Born	Ht/Wt	Event	2013 Mark	Pre-2013 Best
* Gardner	English	USA	22.4.92	162/50	100	10.85	11.03- 11, 11.00w- 12
					200	22.62	22.82- 12
Gardzielewska	Urszula	POL	21.7.88	178/53	HJ	1.89	1.89- 12
Gause	Destinee	USA-J	4.4,94		200	23.19	24.09, 23.50w- 11
* Gay	Mabel	CUB	5.5.83	185/69	TJ	14.45	14.67- 11
Gayot	Marie	FRA	18.12.89	171/58	400	51.54	51.60- 12
Gebre	Trihas	ETH	29.4.90	163/48	10k	32:03.39	
Gebrehiwot	Eleni	ETH	2.1.83	157/45	10k	32:26.92	
Gebresilase	Gotytom	ETH-J	15.1.95	152/42	5000	15:11.12	15:46.49- 12
					10k	31:51.42	33:52.2A- 11
Gebru	Azemra	ETH	5.5.92		5000	15:02.90	15:39.01- 12
Gega	Luiza	ALB	5.11.88	166/56	800	2:01.96	2:02.94- 11
					1500	4:05.11	4:08.65mx, 4:09.76- 12
* Gelana	Tiki	ETH	22.10.87	165/48	HMar	68:53	67:48dh- 12
Gelibert	Jessica	USA/HAI-J	8.11.94	173/57	400h	57.29	59.54- 12
Geng Shuang		CHN	9.7.93		SP	16.67	16.15- 12
Gentili	Manuela	ITA	7.2.78	163/52	400h	55.83	55.54- 12
George	Regina	NGR	17.2.91	176/61	200	23.00i, 23.38, 23.28w	23.20- 12
					400	50.84	51.11- 12
Gergel	Melissa	USA	24.4.89	170/62	PV	4.50	4.46- 12
Getaneh	Genet	ETH	6.1.86	163/49	Mar	2:28:08	2:25:38- 12
Geubelle	Andrea	USA	21.6.91	165/57	LJ	6.69i, 6.53	6.50, 6.52w- 12
					TJ	14.18i, 13.85, 14.03w	13.84, 14.17w- 12
* Gezahegne	Kalkidan	ETH	8.5.91	163/44	1500	4:06.19	4:02.98- 09
* Ghribi	Habiba	TUN	9.4.84	173/52	3000	8:52.06	8:56.22- 11
					3kSt	9:22.20	9:08.37- 12
Gibson	Baillie	USA	18.11.91	175/89	SP	16.87	17.35- 12
Gierisch	Kristin	GER	20.8.90	177/57	TJ	13.91i, 13.67	14.19i- 12, 14.02- 09
Giesa	Ulrike	GER	16.8.84	183/93	DT	58.88	60.63- 05
* Giorgi	Eleonora	ITA	14.9.89	162/52	20kW	1:30:01	1:29:48- 12
Gipson	Whitney	USA	20.9.90	168/57	LJ	6.65Ai, 6.46	6.97- 12
Gisaw	Melkam	ETH	17.9.90		Mar	2:26:24	2:26:52- 11
* Glanc	Zaneta	POL	11.3.83	187/86	DT	62.90	65.34- 12
Glazkova	Alena	RUS	6.5.88		800	2:01.18, 2:00.31i	2:00.39- 12
^ Gobena	Amane	ETH	1.9.82	163/48	Mar	2:23:50	2:24:13- 10
Godfay	Afera	ETH	25.9.91	162/48	5000	15:20.38	15:01.20- 12
					10k	31:08.23	34:30.23- 12
Goethals	Megan	USA	8.7.92	165/52	5000	15:33.63	15:46.82- 12
Gogoleva	Svetlana	RUS	11.12.86		400h	56.81	56.38- 12
Golba	Katarzyna	POL	21.12.89	180/52	20kW	1:32:37	1:36:20- 12
Golovkina ¶	Olga	RUS	17.12.86	170/50	5000	15:32.45	15:05.26- 12
^ Golubchikova	Yuliya	RUS	27.3.83	175/57	PV	4.30i, 4.30	4.75- 08
Gonchar	Yekaterina	BLR	30.8.88	167/64	100	11.28	11.43- 11
* Gong Lijiao		CHN	24.1.89	174/110	SP	20.12	20.35- 09
González	Raquel	ESP	16.11.89	176/55	20kW	1:30:11	1:36:32- 12
Goodman	Chalonda	USA	29.9.90	175/59	200	23.13	22.85- 12
Goor	Myrte	NED	3.4.89	179/68	Hep	5772	5634- 11
Gorchakova	Natalya	RUS	17.4.83	167/55	3kSt	9:38.57	9:35.55- 12
* Gordeyeva	Irina	RUS	9.10.86	183/52	HJ	1.99	2.04- 12
Gordon	Chris-Ann	JAM-J	18.9.94	164/52	400	52.16	51.62- 11
Gordon	Christie	CAN	5.10.86	172/62	100h	13.21, 13.00w	13.20A,13.33- 11, 13.28w- 12
Gorecka	Emelia	GBR-J	29.1.94	172/52	3000	8:55.59	8:55.11- 12
Goto	Natsuko	JPN	4.8.87	165/47	5000	15:34.85	15:55.38mx- 09
* Goucher	Kara	USA	9.7.78	170/57	10k	31:46.64	30:55.16- 08
					Mar	2:28:11dh	2:24:52wdh- 11, 2:25:53- 08
Goule	Natoya	JAM	30.3.91	160/50	800	1:59.93	2:01.45- 11
Grace	Kate	USA	24.10.88	171/55	800	1:59.47	2:01.63- 12
	1500	4:07.40	4:10.57- 12	1M	4:28.79i	4:39.52i- 11	3000	8:55.06i
Granville	Caryl	GBR	24.9.89		400h	57.19	57.61- 11
^ Grasu	Nicoleta	ROU	11.9.71	176/88	DT	59.60	68.80- 99
Greaves	LaToya	JAM	31.5.86	171/62	100h	13.03	12.77- 12
* Green Tregaro	Emma	SWE	8.12.84	180/62	HJ	1.97	2.01- 10
Greenidge	Sade-Mariah	BAR	14.10.93	170/60	100h	13.16	13.38- 12
* Grenot	Libania	ITA	12.7.83	175/65	200	23.17, 23.13w	22.85, 22.45w- 12
					400	50.47	50.30- 09
Grimes	Katie	USA	22.12.90	168/60	100h	13.10, 12.78w	13.20, 12.99w- 12
Grincikaite	Lina	LTU	3.5.87	167/62	100	11.31	11.19- 12
Griva	Gundega	LAT	8.4.91	168/62	JT	57.32A	53.61- 12
Griva	Lauma	LAT	27.10.84	180/64	LJ	6.72	6.86- 11
Griva	Mara	LAT	27.10.84	170/55	LJ	6.55	6.59, 6.70w- 11
Groenewoud	Chantelle	CAN	3.3.89	172/57	3kSt	9:51.17	9:54.70- 12

Name		Nat	Born	Ht/Wt	Event	2013 Mark	Pre-2013 Best
Gromova	Oksana	RUS	23.9.80	178/75	JT	58.00	61.12- 03
Grøvdal	Karoline Bjerkeli	NOR	14.6.90	167/52	5000	15:16.27mx, 15:27.31	15:24.86- 12
Grove	Emily	USA	22.5.93	168/61	PV	4.30	4.32- 12
* Gu Siyu		CHN	11.2.93	182/80	DT	67.86	60.59- 12
Guba	Paulina	POL	14.5.91	184/90	SP	17.17	17.79i, 17.47- 12
Guéhaseim	Jessika	FRA	23.8.89	176/79	HT	69.05	70.44- 12
Guei	Floria	FRA	2.5.90	166/53	400	51.42	51.96- 12
Guion-Firmin	Lenora	FRA	7.8.91	172/60	200	22.91	23.51, 23.49w- 12
					400	51.68	52.20- 12
* Gumenyuk	Irina	RUS	6.1.88	176/59	TJ	14.58	14.24i, 14.18w- 12, 14.14- 11
Gunther	Christen	USA	14.9.89	168/57	PV	4.31	4.30i, 4.25- 12
Guo Tianqian		CHN-J	1.6.95		SP	17.57	17.10- 12
Gusarova	Kseniya	RUS	29.3.89		400	52.14	52.77- 12
* Gushchina	Yuliya	RUS	4.3.83	175/63	400	51.06	49.28- 12
Gyurétz	Réka	HUN-Y	31.5.96	175/70	HT	65.01	62.03- 12
Haapanen	Amy	USA	23.3.84	172/79	HT	67.73	70.63- 12
Haarklau	Katrine	NOR	21.2.91	177/68	PV	4.35	4.20- 12
Haas	Eleriin	EST	4.7.92	180/60	HJ	1.90i, 1.87	1.92- 12
Habina	Hanna	UKR	26.10.92	167/70	JT	60.98	57.77- 12
* Hachlaf	Halima	MAR	8.9.88	167/56	800	1:59.38	1:58.27- 11
					1500	4:06.69	4:07.63- 12
Hackett	Semoy	TTO	27.11.88	173/70	100	11.28	11.10, 11.04dq- 12, 10.98w- 11
					200	22.98	22.55- 12, 22.41w- 11
Hagiwara	Ayumi	JPN	1.6.92	155/41	10k	31:45.29	32:00.73- 12
Hahner	Anna	GER	20.11.89	164/47	Mar	2:27:55	2:30:14- 12
* Hailu	Meseret	ETH	12.9.90	170/54	HMar	66:56	68:55- 12
					Mar	2:26:58dh	2:21:09- 12
Hak	Yvonne	NED	30.6.86	177/57	800	2:01.87	1:58.85- 10
Hakeai	Siositina	NZL-J	1.3.94	182/105	DT	57.91	56.62- 12
Hall	Patricia	JAM	16.10.82	165/58	200	22.51	22.88i, 22.69w- 12, 23.07- 11
					400	51.56	50.71- 12
Hall	Sara	USA	15.4.83	163/48	3kSt	9:54.88	9:39.48- 11
Hallin	Ellinore	SWE	12.8.87	173/70	Hep	5694	5801- 12
* Hamera-Shmyrko	Tetyana	UKR	1.6.83	170/51	Mar	2:23:58	2:24:32- 12
Hamilton	Heather	CAN	31.3.88	178/68	PV	4.40	4.30- 10
Hamilton	Kim	USA	28.11.85	170/70	JT	55.15	58.04- 12
Hao Shuai		CHN	19.7.87	178/65	HT	67.96	69.37- 11
Hapchuk	Nataliya	UKR	15.11.88	182/62	HJ	1.90	1.93- 12
Harbin	Ashley	USA	15.2.86	170/91	HT	68.53	65.62- 11
Hargrove	Monica	USA	30.12.82	173/58	400	51.62	50.39- 09
Haroye	Alemitu	ETH-J	9.5.95	160/44	3000	8:50.40	9:04.53- 11
					5000	15:05.08	15:55.36- 12
* Harper-Nelson	Dawn	USA	13.5.84	168/61	100h	12.48	12.37- 12, 12.36w- 09
Harrer	Corinna	GER	19.1.91	167/55	1500	4:06.60	4:04.30- 12
	3000	8:51.04i, 9:03.55		8:55.47- 12		10k	32:30.41	33:13.62- 12
^ Harrigan-Scott	Tahesia	IVB	15.2.82	157/54	100	11.33,11.29w	11.13,11.02w- 06, 10.89wdq- 11
Harrison	Kendra	USA	18.9.92	163/52	100h	12.88, 12.87w	13.03, 13.02w- 12
					400h	55.75	56.72- 12
* Harrison	Queen	USA	10.9.88	170/60	100h	12.43	12.61, 12.44w- 10
Hasay	Jordan	USA	21.9.91	163/45	3000	8:46.89	9:03.95i- 12, 9:15.78- 10
					10k	31:46.42mx, 32:02.64	-0-
Hasen	Merima	ETH	10.6.92	154/41	Mar	2:23:14	2:23:06- 10
* Hassan	Sifan	ETH/NED	.93	166/52	800	2:00.86	
	1500	4:03.73		4:08.24- 12		3000	8:32.53	9:08.10- 12
Hasslen	Alyssa	USA	13.5.91	180/91	SP	18.10	18.35- 12
Hastings	Amy	USA	21.1.84	163/46	5000	15:09.59	15:14.31- 11
					10k	32:31.28	31:10.69- 11
* Hastings	Natasha	USA	23.7.86	173/63	100	11.24	11.38, 11.34w- 12
	200	22.89		22.61- 07		400	49.94	49.84- 07
Hatsko	Hanna	UKR	3.10.90	175/70	JT	61.18	61.46- 12
Hawkins	Chari	USA	21.5.91	170/57	Hep	5598(w)	5159- 11
Hawthorne	Trisha-Ann	JAM	8.11.89	165/57	100	11.35, 11.28w	11.22- 12
					200	23.11i	23.22- 11
Hayakawa	Eri	JPN	15.11.81	160/42	HMar	70:13	70:14- 05
					Mar	2:26:17	2:28:11- 04
Haydar	Sultan	TUR	23.5.87	170/55	Mar	2:27:10	2:25:09- 12
Hayes	Chelsea	USA	9.2.88	168/55	100	11.34, 11.21w	11.15, 11.09w- 12
					LJ	6.72	7.10- 12
Hayes	Jernail	USA	8.7.88	163/65	400h	55.89	56.30- 12
Hayes	Quanera	USA	7.3.92	172/59	200	23.30A, 22.91wA	23.62, 23.46Aw- 12
					400	51.54A	54.18A- 12

Name		Nat	Born	Ht/Wt	Event	2013 Mark	Pre-2013 Best
He Dan		CHN	22.7.84	167/58	20kW	1:31:49	1:28:20- 06
He Qin		CHN	23.3.92		20kW	1:27:42	1:29:01- 12
* Heidler	Betty	GER	14.10.83	174/80	HT	76.48	79.42- 11
* Hejnová	Zuzana	CZE	19.12.86	170/54	400	51.90, 51.27i	52.61- 09
					400h	52.83	53.29- 11
^ Hellebaut	Tia	BEL	16.2.78	182/62	HJ	1.97i	2.05i- 07, 2.05- 08
Heltne	Anca	ROU	1.1.78	175/80	SP	18.74	19.90i- 10, 19.08- 09
Henderson	Nia	USA	21.10.86		SP	17.38	16.88- 12
Hendricks	Shataya	USA	15.8.89	160/57	100	11.35	11.30- 07
Hendry	Kelsie	CAN	29.6.82	170/59	PV	4.50	4.60Ai- 12, 4.55- 08
* Henriques	Inês	POR	1.5.80	158/46	20kW	1:29:30	1:29:36- 10
Henry	Amber	USA	27.12.90	173/59	3kSt	9:43.39	9:53.94- 12
Henry	Britney	USA	17.10.84	178/84	HT	69.75	71.27- 10
Henry	Chloë	BEL	5.3.87	170/58	PV	4.33	4.29- 12
Henry-Robinson	Samantha	JAM	25.9.88	160/52	100	11.21, 10.97w	11.11, 10.94w- 12
					200	22.83	22.77, 22.50w- 12
Herashchenko	Iryna	UKR-J	10.3.95	181/60	HJ	1.92i, 1.91	1.90- 12
Herrera	Mayra Carolina	GUA	20.12.88	158/55	20kW	1:30:59	1:31:03- 12
Herunga	Tjipekapora	NAM	1.1.88	167/51	400	52.01	51.24A- 12, 51.84- 11
Hetherington	Kelly	AUS	10.3.89	168/54	800	2:01.22	2:02.46- 12
Hidaka	Yuki	JPN	22.7.92	156/41	10k	32:40.80	33:15.94- 12
Higginson	Ashley	USA	17.3.89	167/62	3kSt	9:45.78	9:34.49- 12
Hilali	Siham	MAR	2.5.86	161/58	800	2:00.15	2:02.04- 11
1500	4:02.16		4:01.33- 11		3000	8:53.12i	8:46.17i- 12, 9:03.16- 04
Hildebrand	Nadine	GER	20.9.87	158/51	100h	12.85	12.94- 12, 12.91w- 11
Hill	MacKenzie	USA	5.1.86	166/54	400h	56.79	56.73- 11
Hillman	Christina	USA	6.10.93	178/84	SP	17.69i, 17.40	17.36i, 16.41- 12
* Hingst	Carolin	GER	18.9.80	174/60	PV	4.71	4.72- 10
Hinriksdottir	Anita	ISL-Y	13.1.96	161/50	800	2:00.49	2:03.15- 12
Hirvonen	Katri	FIN	25.6.90	176/89	DT	55.83	54.64- 12
Hitchon	Sophie	GBR	11.7.91	167/74	HT	72.97	71.98- 12
Hjalmsdóttir	Asdis	ISL	28.10.85	175/65	JT	59.97	62.77- 12
Hjelmer	Moa	SWE	19.6.90	172/60	200	23.19	23.20, 23.16w- 11
					400	52.39, 52.04i	51.13- 12
Hodde	Rosina	NED	10.2.83	171/59	100h	13.00, 12.93w	13.35- 06
Hofstede	Helen	NED	31.12.80	172/57	3kSt	9:42.91	9:55.44- 12
Holden	LaTisha	USA	29.8.89	170/61	100H	13.22, 12.96w	12.95- 12, 12.89w- 11
Holland	Ana	USA-J	16.2.95	162/52	100	11.33A	11.85A, 11.90w- 12
					200	23.29A, 23.04w	
Holland	Christina	USA	5.8.91	165/55	400h	56.81	56.87- 12
Holliday	Becky	USA	12.3.80	160/52	PV	4.55	4.60- 10, 4.61dh- 11
Hollmann	Nele	GER	18.10.92	190/75	HJ	1.87	1.85- 11
Holm	Caroline Bonde	DEN	19.7.90	178/68	PV	4.35	4.42i, 4.36- 12
Holodna	Olha	UKR	14.11.91		SP	18.72	17.47- 12
Holosha	Olena	UKR	26.1.82	162/56	HJ	1.95i, 1.90	1.96- 12
Holt	Sarah	GBR	17.4.87	183/76	HT	67.70	68.80- 12
Hooper	Gloria	ITA	3.3.92	175/63	200	23.10	22.95- 12
Horie	Misato	JPN	10.3.87	168/49	HMar	70:26	70:37- 12
Hou Yongbo		CHN-J	15.9.94		20kW	1:33:25	1:36:37- 12
Howarth	Lauren	GBR	21.4.90		3000	8:52.00i	9:10.10mx- 11, 9:10.32- 12
* Hrasnová	Martina	SVK	21.3.83	180/100	HT	72.41	76.90- 09
Hryshutyna	Krystyna	UKR	21.3.92		LJ	6.61	6.65- 12
Hu Guanlian		CHN	18.7.90		TJ	13.83	13.69i, 13.67, 13.69w- 12
Hu Qian		CHN	14.1.89	177/59	TJ	13.81i, 13.32	14.18- 12
Huang Xiaoxiao		CHN	3.3.83	175/65	400h	56.13	54.00- 07
* Huddle	Molly	USA	31.8.84	163/48	1500	4:08.09	4:09.22- 12
3000	8:42.99		8:53.6+- 10		5000	14:58.15	14:44.76- 10
Hurtis	Muriel	FRA	25.3.79	180/68	400	52.02	51.41- 10
Hussong	Christin	GER-J	17.4.94	187/82	JT	58.55	59.74- 11
* Hutson	Kylie	USA	27.11.87	165/57	PV	4.75Ai, 4.70	4.70i, 4.65- 11
Hyacinthe	Kimberly	CAN	28.3.89	179/61	200	22.78	23.15- 09
* Ibargüen	Caterine	COL	12.2.84	181/65	LJ	6.54A	6.73A, 6.63, 6.87Aw, 6.66w- 12
					TJ	14.85, 14.93w	14.99A, 14.84- 11
Idlette	Lavonne	DOM	31.10.85	167/54	100h	12.77	12.96- 11
Ifantídou	Sofía	GRE	10.1.85	164/53	Hep	5894	6109- 12
Ihara	Miho	JPN	4.2.88	154/40	10k	32:16.46	32:18.00mx- 11, 32:21.80- 12
* Ikauniece	Laura	LAT	31.5.92	179/60	Hep	6321	6414- 12
Ikuesan	Ayodelé	FRA	15.5.85	176/60	100	11.34	
Iliyeva	Irina	RUS-J	22.12.95	180/58	HJ	1.89i, 1.88	1.85i, 1.81- 12
* Iljustsenko	Anja	EST	12.10.85	168/49	HJ	1.94i, 1.94	1.96- 11
Ilyina	Irina	RUS	25.5.85		LJ	6.51	6.45- 10

Name		Nat	Born	Ht/Wt	Event	2013 Mark	Pre-2013 Best
Ince	Ariana	USA	14.3.89	180/75	JT	56.66	53.48- 12
Infeld	Emily	USA	21.3.90	162/48	3000	8:41.43	9:00.13i- 12
Insaeng	Subenrat	THA-J	10.2.94	180/85	DT	56.77	54.88- 12
Irozuru	Abigail	GBR	3.1.90	170/61	LJ	6.63	6.80- 12
Ishova ¶	Yekaterina	RUS	17.1.89	164/52	1500	4:09.06 dq	3:59.89dq- 12, 4:07.04- 11
					5000	15:33.64 dq	15:19.94- 11
* Isinbayeva	Yelena	RUS	3.6.82	174/66	PV	4.89	5.06- 09
Itaa Bedada	Emebet	ETH	11.1.90		HMar	69:56dh	70:01- 12
Ito	Mai	JPN	23.5.84	156/41	10k	32:07.41	32:14.43mx- 10, 32:27.04- 09
HMar	70:00		70:03- 11		Mar	2:28:37	2:25:26- 12
Iwade	Reina	JPN-J	8.12.94	154/42	HMar	69:45	
Jackson	Annie	USA	11.3.90		SP	16.76	15.96- 11
Jackson	Emma	GBR	7.6.88	173/63	1500	4:05.83mp	4:11.54- 12
Jackson	Janice	JAM/USA	30.10.91	170/55	100h	13.06, 12.99w	13.24- 12
Jackson	LaQuisha	USA-J	7.1.94	168/59	100	11.31w	
Jackson	Shericka	JAM-J	15.7.94	174/59	200	22.84	23.32- 11
					400	51.60	52.94- 11
Jagaciak	Anna	POL	10.2.90	177/59	LJ	6.68	6.74- 10
					TJ	14.21	14.25- 11
Jakubaityte	Indre	LTU	24.1.76	177/70	JT	56.10	63.65- 07
* Jamal	Maryam	BRN	16.9.84	170/54	1500	4:07.31	3:56.18- 06
Jamerson	Megan	USA	4.5.86	175/59	PV	4.41	4.25Ai- 10, 4.23, 4.36irr- 12
James	Hilenn	TTO	16.3.90	193/105	SP	17.03i, 16.18	16.54- 12
^ Janson	Lacy	USA	20.2.83	178/68	PV	4.53	4.66i, 4.60A- 10
Jarder	Erica	SWE	2.4.86	173/59	LJ	6.71i, 6.66	6.48- 12
Jarzynska	Karolina	POL	6.9.81	165/54	5000	15:25.52	15:26.97- 10
10k	31:43.51		32:44.40- 10		Mar	2:26:45	2:27:16- 11
Jean-Claude	Sandy	USA	4.9.91	175/59	400h	57.07	58.84- 11
Jeffs	Izzy	GBR	3.2.92	166/64	JT	56.31	55.79- 12
Jelaca	Tatjana	SRB	10.8.90	178/76	JT	62.68	60.89- 12
* Jelagat	Jemima	KEN	21.12.84	158/45	Mar	2:20:48	2:28:32- 11
Jelizarova	Polina	LAT	1.5.89	155/47	3000	8:56.06i	9:22.74i- 06, 9:22.8- 07
					3kSt	9:47.23	9:27.21- 12
Jelmini	Anna	USA	15.7.90	176/86	SP	17.35i, 17.01	17.63- 10
					DT	60.61	60.80- 10
Jemai	Sara	ITA	12.4.92	174/64	JT	55.35	52.43- 12
* Jepkemoi	Hyvin	KEN	13.1.92	156/45	3kSt	9:22.05	9:23.53- 12
Jepkirui	Eunice	KEN	20.5.84	158/45	Mar	2:23:34	2:21:41- 12
Jepkoech	Gorreti	KEN-J	7.3.94		HMar	70:06	
Jepkoech	Monica	KEN	.85	160/48	HMar	69:32	69:12- 12
Jepkosgei	Janeth	KEN	13.12.83	167/47	800	1:58.71	1:56.04- 07
Jepkosgei	Nelly	KEN	14.7.91	164/53	800	1:59.40	2:02.48A- 11
1000	2:35.43				1500	4:08.59	4:08.10- 11
* Jeptoo	Priscah	KEN	26.6.84	165/49	HMar	65:45dh	70:26- 11
					Mar	2:20:15	2:20:14- 12
* Jeptoo	Rita	KEN	15.2.81	165/48	HMar	66:27	67:08- 07
					Mar	2:19:57	2:22:04- 12
Jerez	Caridad	ESP	23.1.91	170/57	100h	13.18	13.59- 12
Jerotich	Lydia	KEN			Mar	2:28:22	2:39:10- 12
Jerotich	Milka	KEN	24.2.78		Mar	2:28:23	2:29:33- 12
* Jeter	Carmelita	USA	24.11.79	163/63	100	10.93	10.64- 09
					200	22.77	22.11- 12
Jia Chaofeng		CHN	16.11.88	164/47	10k	32:41.99	31:45.67- 09
Jiang Fengjing		CHN	28.8.87	180/75	DT	60.53	62.56- 11
Jiang Xiaoli		CHN	6.4.89		10k	31:58.34	32:53.62- 11
Jiménez	Isidora	CHI	10.8.93	170/54	200	23.19A	23.42- 12
Jimma	Fantu	ETH	.91		Mar	2:28:03	2:30:25- 11
* Jimoh	Funmilayo	USA	29.5.84	173/64	LJ	6.92	6.96- 09
Jo Eun-ju		KOR	12.11.89	166/58	400h	57.34	58.35- 12
Johannesson	Emma	SWE	16.1.84		HT	65.03	65.78- 12
Johnson	Felisha	USA	24.7.89	185/105	SP	18.27	17.47i, 17.35- 12
* Johnson-Thompson	Katarina	GBR	9.1.93	183/70	LJ	6.56	6.51, 6.81w- 12
					Hep	6449	6267- 12
Johny	Mayookha	IND	4.9.88	171/55	LJ	6.49	6.64- 10
Jones	Cambrya	USA	20.9.90	171/64	200	23.20, 23.03w	22.72- 12
Jones	Hayley	GBR	14.9.88	161/50	100	11.31, 11.30w	11.42- 12
* Jones	Lolo	USA	5.8.82	175/60	100h	12.50, 12.44w	12.43, 12.29w- 08
Jones	Mahagony	USA	20.12.90	167/55	100	11.33, 11.30w	11.69, 11,60w- 09
					200	23.19, 23.05w	24.13- 09
Jones	Tenaya	USA	22.3.89	162/53	100h	12.87, 12.65w	13.20- 10, 13.05w- 11
Jones	Veronica	USA	10.3.91	158/50	200	23.15w	23.90, 23.75w- 09

Name		Nat	Born	Ht/Wt	Event	2013 Mark	Pre-2013 Best
Jover	María del Mar	ESP	21.4.88	161/51	LJ	6.58, 6.73w	6.69A, 6.57- 12
Judd	Jessica	GBR-J	7.1.95	178/60	800	1:59.85	2:00.96- 12
Juhász	Vanda	HUN	6.6.89	172/71	JT	58.97	59.31- 12
Jules	Vanessa	USA	21.3.91	180/62	Hep	5865(w)	5216- 12
Jungfleisch	Marie-Laurence	GER	7.10.90	181/68	HJ	1.95	1.95- 12
* Jungmark	Ebba	SWE	10.3.87	179/57	HJ	1.96i, 1.89	1.96i, 1.94- 11
Juravlyeva	Anastasiya	UZB	9.10.81	172/57	TJ	14.20	14.55- 05
* Kabuu	Lucy	KEN	24.3.84	155/41	10k	32:44.1A	30:39.96- 08
					HMar	66:09	67:04- 11
Kajihara	Minami	JPN-Y	24.8.96		JT	56.01	49.31- 12
Kakimi	Yuka	JPN	4.4.86	159/43	10k	32:45.60	33:54.48- 11
Kakoshinskaya	Alina	RUS	16.11.86		PV	4.30i, 4.25	4.20i- 10, 4.20- 12
Kales	Eunice	KEN	6.12.84	160/45	Mar	2:27:19	
Kallenou	Leontia	CYP-J	5.10.94	180/58	HJ	1.87	1.80- 10
Kalu	Stephanie	NGR	5.8.93		100	11.33	11.69- 12, 11.56w- 11
Kämäräinen	Sanna	FIN	8.2.86	182/82	DT	56.99	57.30- 11
Kampf	Heather	USA	19.1.87	162/53	800	2:00.04	2:00.41- 11
					1500	4:08.37	4:12.09- 11
Kampschulte	Nadja	GER	5.9.92	186/66	HJ	1.88	1.91i- 12, 1.88- 11
Kamulu	Pauline	KEN-J	30.12.94	154/40	5000	15:30.46	16:30.6A- 10
Kang Jinzi		CHN	25.1.90		20kW	1:31:19	1:33:28- 12
Kang Ya		CHN	18.3.90	168/50	100h	13.19	13.23- 11
Kangas	Jenni	FIN	3.7.92	178/68	JT	55.62	53.19- 11
* Kapachinskaya	Anastasiya	RUS	21.11.79	176/65	200	22.39	22.38- 03
					400	50.91	49.35- 11
Karakus	Nimet	TUR	23.1.93	168/64	100	11.29w	11.33- 12
Karandyuk	Kseniya	UKR	21.6.86	178/60	400	52.01	52.19- 06, 51.9- 11
Kárníková	Jana	CZE	14.2.81	187/75	SP	16.67	17.30i- 10, 17.29- 08
Kashina	Yuliya	RUS	26.2.87	174/60	100	11.34	11.34, 11.16w- 10
Kashtonova	Anastasiya	BLR	14.1.89	173/70	DT	61.13	57.87- 12
Kashyna	Inna	UKR	27.9.91		20kW	1:32:58	1:37:37- 12
Kasim	Ashu	ETH	20.10.84	172/54	HMar	68:56	70:05- 09
					Mar	2:26:34	2:23:09- 12
* Kasprzycka	Justyna	POL	20.8.87	183/62	HJ	1.97	1.88- 10
Kato	Asami	JPN	12.10.90	156/38	HMar	70:21	71:12- 12
Kato	Misaki	JPN	15.6.91	155/40	10k	32:44.13	33:54.08- 11
					HMar	70:44dh	
Katsura	Yuliya	RUS	28.5.83	168/55	100	11.35	11.22- 10
Kawanobe	Yu	JPN	22.11.91	162/67	JT	55.46	54.77- 12
Kazeka	Yekaterina	RUS	7.10.90		PV	4.40i, 4.40	4.40i, 4.25- 11
* Kebede	Aberu	ETH	12.9.89	163/50	Mar	2:23:28	2:20:30- 12
Keenan	Te Rina	NZL	29.9.90	180/84	DT	58.25	56.45- 12
Kelly	Ashley	IVB	25.3.91		200	23.05w	23.49- 11
Kemp	Ivanique	BAH	11.6.91	164/53	100h	13.25, 13.10w	13.13- 12
Kennedy	Alix	AUS	22.1.92	181/80	DT	55.76	54.38- 12
Kennedy	Nina	AUS-Y	5.4.97	166/57	PV	4.31	4.10- 12
Keppler	Janice	USA	22.3.87	178/68	PV	4.60Ai, 4.43	4.42- 11
Kettunen	Oona	FIN-J	10.2.94	164/45	3kSt	9:45.51	9:59.38- 12
Kevkhishvili	Mariam	GEO	17.9.85	185/84	SP	16.71	18.59i, 18.46- 10
Khalyutina	Yekaterina	RUS	16.1.91		LJ	6.51	6.50- 11
Khamidova	Yelena	UZB	12.5.89		10k	32:46.52	
* Khanafeyeva	Gulfiya	RUS	4.6.82	173/84	HT	75.02	77.26- 06, 77.36dq- 07
Kholodilina	Natalya	RUS	21.7.89		20kW	1:29:49	1:33:20- 12
Kholodovich	Tatyana	BLR	21.6.91		JT	59.37	59.15- 12
Khramova	Valeriya	RUS	13.8.92		400h	57.06	57.82- 12
Kibarus	Mercy	KEN	25.2.84	155/42	HMar	68:18	72:39- 08
^ Kibet	Hilda	NED	27.3.81	168/46	HMar	67:59	68:39- 10
					Mar	2:26:42	2:24:27- 11
* Kibet	Sylvia	KEN	28.3.84	157/44	3000	8:37.47	8:37.48- 10
5000	14:58.26		14:31.91- 10		HMar	70:41	69:51- 09
* Kibiwot	Viola	KEN	22.12.83	157/45	1500	4:00.76	3:59.25- 12
3000	8:33.97		8:40.14- 03		5000	14:33.48	14:34.86- 11
Kichigina	Galina	KAZ	14.7.88	167/53	20kW	1:32:59	1:35:09- 12
Kido	Chieko	JPN	14.3.90	161/48	10k	32:47.83	33:17.81- 10
					HMar	70:11	71:38- 12
Kilel	Caroline	KEN	21.3.81	172/54	Mar	2:22:34	2:22:36dh- 11, 2:23:25- 10
Kim Hye-gyong		PRK	9.3.93	152/41	Mar	2:28:32	2:31:29- 12
Kim Kyong-ae		KOR	5.3.88	163/62	JT	55.36	58.76- 08
Kim Mi-gyong		PRK	17.10.90	160/50	Mar	2:26:32	2:30:41- 12
Kim Sung-eun		KOR	24.2.89	164/47	Mar	2:27:20	2:29:27- 10
Kimanzi	Grace	KEN	1.3.92	161/48	5000	15:17.43	15:32.23- 12
10k	32:41.69				HMar	70:17	

Name		Nat	Born	Ht/Wt	Event	2013 Mark	Pre-2013 Best
Kimura	Ayako	JPN	11.6.88	167/52	100h	13.03, 13.02w	13.04- 12
Kimutai	Alice	KEN			HMar	70:09	
King	Karene	IVB	24.10.87	163/54	200	23.24, 22.85w	23.43, 23.27w- 12
Kinsella	Michelle	CAN	27.2.91		HJ	1.88i, 1.86	1.86- 12
Kioko	Eunice	KEN	.88		HMar	69:24A	
Kipkemboi	Gladys	KEN	15.10.86	163/51	3kSt	9:36.66	9:13.22- 10
* Kipketer	Valentine	KEN	5.1.93	150/40	HMar	70:36	68:21- 11
					Mar	2:23:02	2:28:02- 12
Kipkirui	Caroline	KEN-J	26.5.94	153/44	5000	15:28.34	15:24.66- 11
Kipkoech	Pasalia	KEN	22.12.88	153/42	HMar	68:08	67:17- 12
* Kiplagat	Edna	KEN	15.11.79	171/54	HMar	68:48	67:41dh- 12
					Mar	2:21:32	2:19:50- 12
* Kiplagat	Florence	KEN	27.2.87	155/42	HMar	67:13	66:38- 12
					Mar	2:21:13	2:19:44- 11
Kiplimo	Jacqueline	KEN	84		HMar	69:52A	
Kiplimo	Joyce	KEN	.88		HMar	70:24	72:34- 11
Kipp	Shalaya	USA	19.8.90	170/58	3kSt	9:37.23	9:35.73- 12
Kiprop	Agnes	KEN	12.12.79	162/45	HMar	67:46	67:22- 12
					Mar	2:25:22	2:23:54- 11
Kiprop	Helah	KEN	7.4.85	164/48	HMar	67:39	68:26- 12
					Mar	2:28:02	
Kipsoi	Gladys	KEN	.86	160/45	HMar	69:11	69:22- 12
Kiptoo	Sarah	KEN	.89		Mar	2:26:32	2:46:36- 12
* Kipyegon	Faith	KEN-J	10.1.94	157/42	1500	3:56.98	4:03.82- 12
Kira	Manami	JPN	23.10.91	174/62	400h	57.15	57.73- 12
* Kirdyapkina	Anisya	RUS	23.10.89	165/51	20kW	1:25:59	1:25:09- 11
Kireyeva	Svetlana	RUS	12.6.87		2000	5:44.08i	
					3000	8:48.27i	9:02.55i, 9:02.97- 11
* Kiriakopoúlou	Nikoléta	GRE	21.3.86	167/54	PV	4.65	4.71- 11
Kiriyama	Chie	JPN	2.8.91	174/54	Hep	5564	5463- 11
Kirop	Helena	KEN	9.9.76	165/48	Mar	2:24:40	2:23:37- 11
Kiros	Aheza	ETH	26.3.82	152/42	10k	32:32.23	31:06.93- 08
HMar	70:03		69:10- 11		Mar	2:24:30	2:33:21- 12
Kiros	Ehitu	ETH	13.1.88	162/50	HMar	69:38	71:58- 12
					Mar	2:23:39	2:33:43- 12
* Kirui	Purity	KEN	13.8.91	166/50	3kSt	9:19.42	9:35.61- 12
Kirwa	Eunice	KEN	20.5.84	158/45	HMar	68:59	68:39- 12
* Kiryashova	Aleksandra	RUS	21.8.85	168/55	PV	4.56i, 4.50	4.65i- 10, 4.65- 11
Kisa	Janet	KEN	5.3.92	160/48	3000	8:48.10+	8:51.63- 12
					5000	15:05.89	14:57.68- 12
Kivimyagi	Tatyana	RUS	23.6.84	184/64	HJ	1.91i, 1.88	1.98- 04
Kiyota	Mao	JPN	12.9.93		10k	32:34.04	
Kizaki	Ryoko	JPN	21.6.85	157/44	Mar	2:23:34	2:26:32- 11
* Klaas	Kathrin	GER	6.2.84	168/72	HT	72.57	76.05- 12
Klaup	Mari	EST	27.2.90	180/58	Hep	6002	5743(w)- 11, 5739- 10
Klausová	Katerina	CZE	28.2.89		DT	56.09	55.06- 12
Kleeberg	Sophie	GER	30.5.90	182/82	SP	17.38	17.92- 11
Kleinert	Nadine	GER	20.10.75	190/90	SP	18.76	20.20- 09
Kleshchevnikova	Yana	RUS	24.7.88		HT	66.62	67.67- 12
* Klishina	Darya	RUS	15.1.91	180/57	LJ	7.01i, 6.90, 6.98w	7.05- 11
Klochko	Viktoriya	UKR	2.9.92	187/112	DT	56.12	55.67- 12
Klopsch	Christiane	GER	21.8.90	175/58	400h	56.83	56.97- 11
* Klucinová	Eliska	CZE	14.4.88	177/68	HJ	1.89	1.85- 12
					Hep	6332	6283- 12
Knäsche	Anjuli	GER	18.10.93	169/61	PV	4.45	4.31- 12
* Knight	Bianca	USA	2.1.89	163/60	200	23.16, 22.86w	22.35- 11, 22.25w- 08
* Knyazyeva-Minenko	Hanna	ISR	25.9.89	178/61	TJ	14.58	14.71- 12
Kobeleva	Yelena	RUS	12.6.88	173/57	1500	4:08.65	4:18.62- 11
Koderisch	Heike	GER	27.5.85	188/87	DT	59.23	61.18- 12
Koíni	Athiná	GRE	17.12.92	177/55	3kSt	9:54.27	9:59.96- 12
Kolak	Sara	CRO-J	22.6.95	168/70	JT	57.79	55.69- 10
Kolaric	Nina	SLO	12.12.86	175/60	LJ	6.49	6.78- 08
* Kolchanova	Lyudmila	RUS	1.10.79	175/60	LJ	6.89	7.21- 07
* Kolodko	Yevgeniya	RUS	2.7.90	188/85	SP	19.97i, 19.86	20.48- 12
Kolotzei	Jessica	GER	6.4.85	186/86	DT	56.87	60.31- 08
Kondakova	Yuliya	RUS	4.12.81	170/57	100h	12.73	12.79- 08
Kondratyeva	Oksana	RUS	22.11.85	180/80	HT	77.13	73.31- 12
* Koneva	Yekaterina	RUS	25.9.88	170/55	TJ	14.82	14.60i- 12, 14.46- 11
Kononova	Yevgeniya	RUS	28.9.89	175/53	HJ	1.92	1.92- 12
Konovalova	Anna	RUS	4.7.88	170/55	1500	4:07.63	4:03.92- 11
* Konovalova	Mariya	RUS	14.8.74	179/58	5000	15:27.16	14:38.09- 08
HMar	69:20		69:56- 12		Mar	2:22:46	2:23:50- 10

Name		Nat	Born	Ht/Wt	Event	2013 Mark	Pre-2013 Best
* Kopets	Alena	BLR	14.2.88	178/84	SP	19.24	18.90i- 12, 17.99- 10
Kopron	Malwina	POL-J	16.11.94	170/63	HT	66.11	64.88- 12
Koresová	Jana	CZE	8.4.81	168/57	LJ	6.65	6.65- 09
Koressel	Allison	USA	2.3.91	168/57	PV	4.31	4.15- 11
Kornuta	Hanna	UKR	10.11.88	168/57	LJ	6.72	6.43- 12
Korobkina	Yelena	RUS	25.11.90	163/47	1500	4:05.18	4:06.73- 12
					3000	8:50.42i, 9:01.45	8:51.41- 10
Korpela	Merja	FIN	15.5.81	170/75	HT	69.38	69.56- 09
Korshunova ¶	Anastasiya	RUS	17.5.92	168/60	400h	55.12	56.63- 12
Kosko	Irina	RUS	1.3.90		TJ	13.84i	13.52- 12
Koster	Maureen	NED	3.7.92	175/56	1500	4:06.50	4:13.48- 12
Kostrova	Alina	BLR	2.3.90	181/79	HT	67.45	70.31- 12
Kostrova	Yuliya	RUS	20.8.91	174/59	HJ	1.91i, 1.86	1.92- 11
Kotlyarova	Aleksandra	UZB	10.10.88	170/64	TJ	13.96	14.35- 11
Kotlyarova	Nadezhda	RUS	12.6.89	176/64	400	51.93	53.13- 12
* Kotulskaya	Yelena	RUS	8.8.88	174/61	800	1:59.56	1:57.77- 12
					1000	2:37.01i	2:37.58i- 12
Kovalenko	Iryna	UKR	17.6.86	181/53	HJ	1.93	1.95i- 03, 1.93- 04
Kovalenko	Lyudmyla	UKR	26.6.89	170/63	HMar	68:59	73:35- 12
Kowalska	Katarzyna	POL	7.4.85	177/55	3kSt	9:42.35	9:26.93- 09
Koyuncu	Tugba	TUR	16.2.91	168/55	800	2:01.65	2:01.78- 11
					1500	4:06.22	4:03.41- 11
Kozhakhmetova ¶	Ayman	KAZ	23.4.91	165/60	20kW	1:33:00dq	1:31:55- 12
Kraft	Joana	GER	27.7.91	172/57	PV	4.40	4.45i, 4.35- 10
Kragbé	Suzanne	CIV	22.12.81	177/92	DT	59.03	59.32- 11
Krais	Ryann	USA	21.3.90	173/61	Hep	5957	6030- 11
Kralová	Tereza	CZE	22.10.89	175/85	HT	70.21	69.20- 12
Krasnokutskaya	Oksana	RUS	24.9.93		HJ	1.90	1.87- 12
* Krasnova (Zhuk)	Angelina	RUS	7.2.91	168/55	PV	4.70	4.40- 12
Krasucki	Franciela	BRA	26.4.88	172/59	100	11.13	11.35- 06
					200	22.76	23.36- 11
* Krause	Gesa-Felicitas	GER	3.8.92	167/55	3kSt	9:37.11	9:23.52- 12
Krchová	Eva	CZE	10.9.89	182/67	3kSt	9:52.69	9:54.71- 11
Krechyk	Alena	BLR	20.7.87	174/73	HT	68.22	69.02- 12
* Krivoshapka	Antonina	RUS	21.7.87	168/60	200	23.01	23.03- 12
					400	49.57	49.16- 12
Krizsán	Xénia	HUN	13.1.93	171/62	Hep	5896	5957- 12
* Krylova	Anna	RUS	3.10.85	170/61	TJ	14.27	14.40- 12
Kubelová	Jitka	CZE	2.10.91	176/82	DT	58.30	57.57- 12
Kubishta	April	USA	5.7.85	165/57	PV	4.45Ai, 4.41	4.40- 12
Kubokura	Satomi	JPN	27.4.82	160/52	400h	56.33	55.34- 11
* Kucherenko	Olga	RUS	5.11.85	172/59	LJ	7.00i, 6.81	7.13- 10
* Kuchina	Mariya	RUS	14.1.93	182/60	HJ	1.98i, 1.96	1.97i, 1.95- 11
Kudashkina	Alena	RUS-J	10.4.94	157/42	5000	15:31.06	15:45.80- 12
Kudinova	Anastasiya	KAZ	27.2.88	176/59	LJ	6.52	6.50- 11
Kudzelich	Svetlana	BLR	7.5.87	170/52	3kSt	9:48.68	9:39.43- 12
Kuijken	Susan	NED	8.7.86	170/54	1500	4:05.38	4:05.86- 09
1M	4:27.13 irr					4:34.11i- 09	
3000	8:39.65				2000	5:38.37	
					5000	15:04.36	16:20.30- 06
						9:28.45- 05	
Kumari	Sahana	IND	6.3.81		HJ	1.88	1.92- 12
Kuntsevich	Yekaterina	RUS	13.7.84	175/60	HJ	1.90i, 1.84	1.94- 08
Kupina	Yekaterina	RUS	2.2.86	172/59	800	1:59.21	1:59.85- 12
1000	2:36.41				1500	4:08.81	4:20.42- 11
						2:38.97i- 12	
Kuria	Mary	KEN	29.11.87	157/48	800	2:01.67	
					1500	4:03.56	4:03.18- 12
Kurylo	Yuliya	UKR	3.7.91	187/100	DT	57.43	59.05- 12
Kutyakova	Natalya	RUS	28.11.86	181/62	TJ	14.50i, 14.29	14.67- 11
Kuze	Kihou	JPN-J	28.3.95	165/58	JT	58.98	56.84- 12
Kuzina	Yekaterina	RUS	28.6.91	170/58	100	11.29	11.58- 11
Kuzmina	Lyudmila	RUS	13.8.87	158/49	3kSt	9:46.60	9:26.03- 11
Kwoka	Katarzyna	POL	29.6.85	168/55	20kW	1:29:21	1:31:25- 12
* La Mantia	Simona	ITA	14.4.83	177/65	TJ	14.26i, 13.97,13.99w	14.69- 05, 14.71w- 04
Laasma	Liina	EST	13.1.92	178/77	JT	62.50	57.82- 11
Labonté	Julie	CAN	12.1.90	183/91	SP	17.63	18.31- 11
					DT	56.79	54.02A- 12
LaCaze	Genevieve	AUS	4.8.89	164/53	3kSt	9:37.62	9:37.90- 12
Lagat	Violah	KEN	1.3.89	165/49	1500	4:05.66	4:13.30- 12
					3000	8:52.34	
Laing	Kimberley	JAM	8.1.89	167/55	100h	13.08, 13.03w	12.97- 12, 12.92w- 10
Lake	Morgan	GBR-Y	12.5.97	174/59	HJ	1.90	1.80- 12
* Lakhouad	Ibtissam	MAR	7.12.80	172/55	1500	4:04.63	3:59.35- 10

Name		Nat	Born	Ht/Wt	Event	2013 Mark	Pre-2013 Best
Lakmali	B.L.Nadeeka	SRI	18.9.81	165/60	JT	60.64	58.48- 07
Lally	Jade	GBR	30.3.87	183/81	DT	60.23	60.76- 11
Lalonde	Geneviève	CAN	5.9.91	167/47	3kSt	9:53.35	9:55.01- 11
* Lalova	Ivet	BUL	18.5.84	168/56	100	11.04	10.77- 04
					200	22.78	22.51, 22.36w- 04
Lambarki	Hayat	MAR	18.5.88	168/62	400h	55.27	55.41- 12
Landázuri	Giselly	COL	8.2.92		TJ	13.97A, 13.81	13.64A, 13.31- 12
* Langat	Nancy	KEN	22.8.81	153/49	1500	4:01.41	4:00.13- 10
					1M	4:28.50	-0-
Larsåsen	Cathrine	NOR	5.12.86	172/59	PV	4.31i, 4.30	4.41i- 12, 4.40- 11
Larsson	Eleni	SWE	4.4.93	186/100	HT	67.13	66.19- 12
Larsson	Maria	SWE-J	24.3.94		3kSt	9:56.50	10:48.79- 12
Larsson	Sofia	SWE	22.7.88	174/82	DT	58.18	58.65- 09
* Lashmanova	Yelena	RUS	9.4.92	170/48	20kW	1:25:49	1:25:02- 12
Latham	Deanna	USA	23.2.92	168/59	100h	13.27, 13.15w	13.66- 12
					Hep	5574w	5606- 12
Latvala	Hanna-Maari	FIN	30.10.87	170/59	200	22.98	23.38- 12
Lavric	Mirela	ROU	17.2.91	162/45	400	52.06	52.11- 12
					800	1:59.79	1:59.74- 12
Lawson	Lakeisha	USA	3.6.87	168/57	100	11.14	11.31- 12, 11.26w- 10
					200	23.15, 22.75w	23.27, 23.19w- 12
Le Joly	Camille	FRA	1.3.92	174/56	Hep	5560	5342- 11
Le-Roy	Anastacia	JAM	8.11.87	168/55	400	51.19	51.09- 08
Lebedeva	Lyudmila	RUS	23.5.90	165/48	10k	32:46.08	33:41.03- 12
					3kSt	9:39.98	9:42.58- 12
^ Lebedeva	Tatyana	RUS	21.7.76	171/61	TJ	13.97	15.34- 04
Lebid	Anastasiya	UKR	30.10.93	165/52	400h	56.91	58.13- 12
Ledáki	Stélla-Iró	GRE	18.7.88	170/58	PV	4.50	4.50- 12
Lee	Muna	USA	30.10.81	172/50	100	11.00	10.85- 08
Lee Mi-young		KOR	19.8.79	174/97	SP	17.38	17.62- 05
Legese	Meseret	ETH	28.8.87		Mar	2:26:15	2:28:01dh- 12, 2:29:05- 11
LeLeux	Morgann	USA	14.11.92	170/61	PV	4.50i, 4.32	4.44- 12
Lema	Marta	ETH	90		Mar	2:28:02	
Lemus	Sandra	COL	1.1.89	170/102	SP	18.03	17.56- 12
Leontyeva	Natalya	RUS	5.7.87	168/48	3000	8:57.80i	9:08.75- 12
					10k	32:44.20	34:49.82- 09
Leontyuk	Yuliya	BLR	21.1.84	185/80	SP	18.47	19.79- 08
Leslie	Breanna	USA	11.8.91	172/61	Hep	5761	5369- 12
* Lesueur	Éloyse	FRA	15.7.88	179/65	LJ	6.90i, 6.78	6.91- 11, 7.04w- 12
Lettow	Lindsay	USA	6.6.90	175/62	Hep	5729	5807- 12
Leverton	Linda	AUS	22.3.87	178/65	TJ	13.80, 14.07w	13.82- 11
Levitskaya	Yekaterina	RUS	2.1.87		LJ	6.70	6.68- 12
* Lewis	Yvette	PAN	16.3.85	173/62	100h	12.67, 12.43w	12.76, 12.74w- 11
* Lewis-Smallwood	Gia	USA	1.4.79	183/93	DT	66.29	65.58- 10
Lhabz	Lamia	MAR	19.5.84	178/59	400h	55.51	56.07A- 08, 56.18- 07
Li Caixia		CHN	23.8.87	172/60	PV	4.30	4.50- 10
Li Hua		CHN	15.1.91	165/50	20kW	1:30:55	1:33:54- 11
Li Li		CHN	18.6.87	164/50	20kW	1:30:31	1:30:27- 12
Li Ling		CHN	6.7.89	185/70	PV	4.65	4.50i- 12, 4.45- 08
* Li Ling		CHN	7.2.85	183/84	SP	19.15	19.95- 12
Li Lingwei		CHN	26.1.89	172/75	JT	63.06	65.11- 12
^ Li Meiju		CHN	3.10.81	172/100	SP	17.48	19.38- 09
Li Wen-Hua (Li Tsai-Yi)		TPE	3.12.89	180/130	DT	55.75	60.23- 12
Li Xiaohong		CHN-J	8.1.95		TJ	14.06i, 13.63, 13.88w	13.85- 12
Li Yanfei		CHN	12.1.90	168/55	20kW	1:27:40	1:28:43- 11
* Li Yanfeng		CHN	15.5.79	179/90	DT	63.91	67.98- 11
Li Yanmei		CHN	6.2.90	171/56	TJ	14.35	14.35- 11
Li Zhenzhu		CHN	13.12.85	168/45	3kSt	9:53.17	9:32.35- 07
Liang Yan		CHN-J	2.1.95		DT	62.01	60.50- 12
Líka	Sávva	GRE	27.6.70	173/68	JT	55.98	63.13- 07
Lima	Erika	BRA	13.8.93		3kSt	9:54.97	10:05.73- 12
de Lima	Jucilene	BRA	14.9.90	172/63	JT	61.98	57.85- 12
Limo	Cynthia	KEN	18.12.89		HMar	69:59	70:06- 12
Lin Chia-Ying		TPE	5.11.82	168/82	SP	16.95	17.43- 12
Lin Xiaojing		CHN	8.1.86	178/82	DT	56.96	57.95- 06
Linde	Sofia	SWE-J	12.1.95	174/66	Hep	6081	5872- 12
Lindemans	Marjolein	BEL-J	17.2.94	175/62	Hep	5831	5306- 12
Linkiewicz	Joanna	POL	2.5.90	172/55	400h	56.86	57.38- 11
Linnell	Lisa	SWE	30.4.91		Hep	5888	5383- 11
Lipsey	Charlene	USA	16.7.91	168/57	800	2:01.70	2:01.40- 12
Lisoreng	Pamela	KEN	5.8.88		HMar	70:09	71:33- 10

Name		Nat	Born	Ht/Wt	Event	2013 Mark	Pre-2013 Best
Liu Beibei		CHN	5.10.90	169/63	JT	58.64	57.90- 12
Liu Chunhua		CHN	1.10.86	164/65	JT	59.03	62.81- 12
* Liu Hong		CHN	12.5.87	161/48	20kW	1:27:06	1:25:46- 12
Liu Huan		CHN	24.2.93		20kW	1:30:25	1:35:10- 12
Liu Ruihuan		CHN	29.6.92		10k	31:56.80	33:51.73- 12
Liu Shiying		CHN	24.9.93		JT	60.23	59.20- 12
Liu Shuyu		CHN	13.12.93		20kW	1:31:00	1:33:43- 12
Liu Tingting		CHN	29.10.90	174/75	HT	69.83	69.46- 11
* Liu Xiangrong		CHN	6.6.88	185/119	SP	18.81i, 18.73	19.24- 12
Liu Yanan		CHN	18.1.87		TJ	13.92	14.09- 09
Lloyd	Cassandra	USA	27.1.90	163/54	100h	12.90	13.17- 12
Lockhart	Sam	USA	25.8.91	175/82	SP	16.86i, 16.80	16.60i, 15.88- 12
					DT	58.87	57.11- 12
Logvynenko	Alina	UKR	18.7.90	180/68	400	51.98	51.19- 12
Lomnická	Nikola	SVK	16.9.88	166/70	HT	67.88	66.90- 10
Londa	Maria Natalia	INA	29.10.90		TJ	14.17	13.73- 11
Longfors	Rachel	USA	6.6.83	183/82	DT	58.10	58.05- 12
López	Yaniuvis	CUB	1.2.86	180/71	SP	18.15	18.81- 09
Lotout	Marion	FRA	19.11.89	165/54	PV	4.60	4.50- 11
Louami	Carima	FRA	12.5.79	165/50	100	11.25w	11.28- 11, 11.21w- 12
* Lu Huihui		CHN	26.6.89	171/68	JT	65.62	64.95- 12
Lu Xiaoxin		CHN	22.2.89		DT	63.27	59.64- 12
* Lu Xiuzhi		CHN	26.10.93	167/52	20kW	1:27:53	1:27:01- 12
Luaces	Lorena	ESP	29.2.84	161/48	20kW	1:31:32	1:31:50- 12
Lucas	Julia	USA	4.3.84	174/60	1500	4:05.89	4:07.23- 12
					5000	15:23.77	15:08.52- 12
Lucas	Porscha	USA	18.6.88	170/56	100	11.43, 11.13w	11.12- 09, 11.02w- 12
					200	23.28, 22.93w	22.29A- 08, 22.38- 09
Luka	Tintu	IND	26.4.89	157/50	800	2:01.87	1:59.17- 10
Luo Na		CHN	8.10.93		HT	67.09	63.61- 12
Luo Xingcai		CHN-J	18.7.94		20kW	1:31:03	1:31:49- 12
Luogon	Kou	LBR	11.6.84	174/60	400h	57.08	55.55- 09
* Lupu	Nataliya	UKR	4.11.87	170/50	800	1:59.43	1:58.46- 12
Lutkovskaya	Alayna	RUS-Y	15.3.96		PV	4.30i, 4.30	4.20- 12
Lvova	Olga	RUS	21.9.89		800	2:02.61, 2:01.56i	2:02.12- 12
Lyakhova	Olga	UKR	18.3.92	170/59	400	52.05	54.20- 12
					800	2:00.79	2:00.55- 12
Lyashenko	Valentyna	UKR	30.1.81		HJ	1.89	1.91- 12
Lysenko	Alena	RUS	3.2.88		HT	66.64	67.96- 12
* Lysenko	Tatyana	RUS	9.10.83	180/84	HT	78.80	78.51- 12, 78.61dq- 07
Ma Qiao		CHN	28.9.89	185/150	SP	17.59	17.50- 10
Mächtig	Julia	GER	1.6.86	187/80	Hep	6430	6345- 12
Macías	Isabel	ESP	11.8.84	167/55	1500	4:07.70	4:04.84- 12
Mackey	Katie	USA	12.11.87	165/52	800	2:02.00	2:02.23- 12
	1500	4:04.60	4:06.67- 12	1M	4:30.60irr	4:28.62- 07	5000	15:23.65	15:31.59- 12
Madarász	Viktória	HUN	12.5.85	153/46	20kW	1:33:21	1:33:34- 12
^ Madejczyk	Barbara	POL	30.9.76	180/81	JT	57.69	64.08- 06
Madu	Jennifer	USA-J	23.9.94	160/52	100	11.31, 11.18w	11.46- 12
Maeda	Hiroi	JPN	1.6.91	161/48	20kW	1:32:25	1:35:01- 12
Mägi	Maris	EST	11.8.87	168/54	400h	56.56	57.91- 08
* Magiso	Fantu	ETH	9.9.92	178/60	800	2:00.25	1:57.48- 12
Magnani	Margherita	ITA	26.2.87	161/45	1500	4:06.34	4:08.94- 12
Maiwald	Anna	GER	21.7.90	176/62	Hep	5863	5696- 12
Maiyo	Maureen	KEN	28.5.85	157/58	400	51.63A	52.46A- 11
Makarova	Natalya	RUS	17.4.87		20kW	1:29:54	1:30:27- 12
Makikawa	Eri	JPN	22.4.93		10k	32:34.38	
Maksimova	Marina	RUS	20.5.85	177/80	JT	57.30	60.73- 11
Maksimova	Yana	BLR	9.1.89	182/70	HJ	1.90i, 1.87	1.91- 12
					Hep	6194	6198- 12
Malácová	Romana	CZE	15.5.87	164/57	PV	4.42i, 4.32	4.41sq- 10
Malanova	Ayvika	RUS	28.11.92	167/55	800	1:59.61	2:03.59- 11
Malavisi	Sonia	ITA-J	31.10.94	172/65	PV	4.42	4.05- 12
Malkus	Lena	GER	6.8.93	180/74	LJ	6.76	6.72, 6.80w- 12
Malone	Chantel	IVB	2.12.91	175/62	LJ	6.65	6.56- 10, 6.66w- 12
Maltseva	Yuliya	RUS	30.11.90		DT	59.50	58.16- 12
* Mamona	Patrícia	POR	21.11.88	168/53	TJ	14.02, 14.07w	14.52- 12
Manning	Crystal	USA	15.4.86	173/64	TJ	13.86	13.96- 10
Mánou	Loréla	GRE	20.12.90	167/52	PV	4.45	4.40- 12
Mao Yanxue		CHN-J	15.2.94	162/44	20kW	1:31:57	1:30:25- 12
Mara	Valeriya	UKR	22.2.83	163/50	3kSt	9:53.34	9:38.91- 10
Maracheva	Irina	RUS	24.9.84	165/50	800	2:00.82	1:58.82- 12

Name		Nat	Born	Ht/Wt	Event	2013 Mark	Pre-2013 Best
Marais	Carla	RSA	10.12.87	166/55	LJ	6.64	6.28, 6.40w- 12
Marchant	Lanni	CAN	11.4.84		Mar	2:28:00	2:31:51- 12
Marcussen	Ida	NOR	1.11.87	173/67	Hep	6214	6226- 07
^ Marghieva ¶	Zalina	MDA	5.2.88		HT	74.28dq	74.47- 12
Marie-Nély	Nathalie	FRA	24.11.86	175/66	TJ	13.89, 14.07w	14.03- 12, 14.18w- 11
Marincu	Florentina	ROU-Y	8.4.96	178/60	LJ	6.54	6.07- 11
					TJ	13.81	12.64- 11
Markelova	Tatyana	RUS	19.12.88	166/59	800	2:00.93	1:58.55- 12
Maroszek	Jessica	USA	26.2.92	175/91	DT	58.01	56.73- 12
Marshall	Ashley	USA	10.9.93	160/52	100	11.34	11.87, 11.70w- 11
Marshall	Mandissa	USA	2.4.91	173/61	PV	4.35	4.30- 12
Martín	Diana	ESP	1.4.81	162/50	3kSt	9:38.30	9:35.77- 12
Martín-Sacristán	Ana	ESP-J	15.12.94	163/53	LJ	6.54w	5.99, 6.19w- 12
* Martinez	Brenda	USA	8.9.87	163/52	800	1:57.91	1:59.14- 12
1500	4:00.94				4:06.96- 12	5000	15:30.89 mx, 15:35.65	16:23.75- 12
Martínez	Johana	COL	9.9.86	180/84	DT	55.87	52.84- 12
Martínez	Yarianna	CUB	20.9.84	167/56	TJ	14.37	14.42- 11
Martins	Eliane	BRA	26.5.86		LJ	6.53	6.66A- 07, 6.61- 09
Márton	Anita	HUN	15.1.89	171/84	SP	18.18	18.48- 12
					DT	56.43	56.62- 10
* Masai	Linet	KEN	5.12.89	170/55	5000	15:02.98	14:31.14- 10
					10k	31:02.89	30:26.50- 08
Masai	Magdalene	KEN	4.4.93	160/48	5000	15:17.51	15:17.75- 12
Masná	Lenka	CZE	22.4.85	170/56	800	1:59.56	1:59.71- 10
Masresha	Azalech	ETH	4.5.88		Mar	2:27:01	2;25:34- 10
Massobrio	Francesca	ITA	9.7.93	184/91	HT	64.65	61.19- 11
Masumi	Sachiko	JPN	20.12.84	176/62	LJ	6.55, 6.62w	6.65- 09
Matsumi	Sakiko	JPN	7.8.88	159/41	10k	32:44.44	33:53.63- 12
					HMar	70:10	72:13- 09
Matsuzaki	Riko	JPN	24.12.92	157/44	5000	15:26.05	15:34.69- 12
Mavrodieva	Radoslava	BUL	13.3.87	178/86	SP	18.67	18.20- 12
Mayer	Sarah	GER	20.5.91	170/60	JT	56.85	59.29- 11
Mayorova	Albina	RUS	16.5.77	167/50	Mar	2:25:55	2:23:52- 12
Mazina	Margarita	RUS-J	7.7.95		HJ	1.87i	1.80- 12
Mbaye	Rokhaya	FRA	12.3.92	166/59	Hep	5636	5500- 12
* McCall	Jeneva	USA	28.10.89	178/102	SP	18.47	19.10i, 17.89- 12
					HT	74.77	69.55- 11
McColgan	Eilish	GBR	25.11.90	176/59	1500	4:09.67	4:11.78mx, 4:13.19- 12
3000	8:47.79		8:58.83mx, 9:11.35- 12			3kSt	9:35.82	9:38.45- 12
* McCorory	Francena	USA	20.10.88	170/60	400	49.86	50.06- 12
McGee	Cory	USA	29.5.92	168/52	1500	4:06.67	4:12.61- 12
McGrone	Candyce	USA	24.3.89	160/59	100	11.19	11.08, 11.07w- 11
					200	22.85	22.81- 11
McIntosh	Raasin	LBR	29.4.82	170/59	400h	57.13	54.16- 04
McIntosh	Rachael	CAN	17.1.91	174/62	Hep	5601A	5477A- 12
McKinna	Sophie	GBR-J	31.8.94	167/79	SP	17.12	16.23- 12
McKnight	Sparkle	TTO	21.12.91	165/55	400	52.17	52.44- 12
					400h	55.71	57.42- 12
* McLaughlin	Anneisha	JAM	6.1.86	163/54	100	11.23	11.24- 12
					200	22.58	22.54- 10
McLean	Hayley	GBR-J	9.9.94	170/59	400h	57.26	58.57- 12
McPherson	Inika	USA	29.9.86	168/55	HJ	1.92	1.95- 12
* McPherson	Stephenie Ann	JAM	25.11.88	168/55	400	49.92	51.64- 10
* Meadows	Jennifer	GBR	17.4.81	156/48	800	2:01.02i	1:57.93- 09
Meadows	Tawanna	USA	4.8.86	168/55	100	11.24	11.27, 11.13w- 08, 11.1w- 10
					200	22.94w	23.14-0 08
Medeiros	Keely	BRA	30.4.87	178/90	SP	17.17	17.26- 11
Medgyesová	Renata	SVK	28.1.83	172/53	LJ	6.63w	6.79- 10
Medjid	Joan	FRA-J	29.9.95	173/60	400h	57.34	61.06- 12
Mekasha	Dinknesh	ETH	.85	160/48	Mar	2:25:09	2:29:56- 12
Mekasha	Waganesh	ETH	16.1.92	159/45	HMar	68:48	71:11- 12
Mekonnin	Misiker	ETH	23.7.86		Mar	2:25:45	2:25:21dh- 12
Mekuria	Aberu	ETH			Mar	2:26:07	2:27:20- 12
Melchor	Inés	PER	30.8.86	158/55	5000	15:30.63	16:00.41A- 09
Melese	Yebrwual	ETH	18.4.90	164/45	HMar	69:02	69:45- 12
* Melkamu	Meselech	ETH	27.4.85	158/48	HMar	68:05	70:25- 12
					Mar	2:25:46	2:21:01- 12
* Melnychenko	Anna	UKR	24.4.83	178/59	LJ	6.49	6.74- 12
					Hep	6586	6445- 09
Mendieta	Yusleidys	CUB	17.2.94	180/66	Hep	6024	5702h- 12
Meng Qianqian		CHN	6.1.91	178/65	SP	17.86	18.31- 11

Name		Nat	Born	Ht/Wt	Event	2013 Mark	Pre-2013 Best
* Menkova	Oksana	BLR	28.3.82	183/91	HT	75.45	78.69- 12
Merlano	Briggit	COL	29.4.82	174/64	100h	13.01A, 13.11	12.89- 11
Merrill	Christine	SRI	20.8.87	167/57	400h	56.45	56.83- 11
* Mickle	Kimberley	AUS	28.12.84	169/69	JT	66.60	64.12- 12
Mihambo	Malaika	GER-J	3.2.94	170/52	LJ	6.70, 6.80w	6.32, 6.50w- 12
* Mikitenko	Irina	GER	23.8.72	162/47	Mar	2:24:54	2:19:19- 08
Mikolajczyk	Izabela	POL	4.9.90	175/59	HJ	1.88	1.92- 12
Milani	Marta	ITA	9.3.87	175/60	800	2:01.40	2:01.35- 12
Miller	Heather	USA	30.3.87	173/63	Hep	5945(w)	5779- 12
Miller	Jade	USA-J	13.1.95	168/57	400h	57.21	-0-
* Miller	Shaunae	BAH-J	15.4.94	185/69	200	22.45, 22.41w	22.70- 12
					400	50.70	51.25- 12
Minderler	Marissa	USA	7.5.89	178/77	HT	65.61	67.35- 12
^ Mingir	Gülcan	TUR	21.5.89	165/52	3kSt	9:45.80	9:13.53- 12
* Mironchik-Ivanova	Anastasiya	BLR	13.4.89	171/54	LJ	6.60	7.08, 7.22w- 12
Mismas	Marusa	SLO-J	24.10.94	164/52	3kSt	9:51.15	0
Misochenko	Anna	RUS	15.4.92		LJ	6.53	6.33i- 11, 6.27- 10
* Mitchell	Kathryn	AUS	10.7.82	168/75	JT	63.77	64.34- 12
Mitsunobu	Yuki	JPN	9.11.92	161/47	10k	32:15.45	32:31.33- 12
Miyashita	Risa	JPN	26.4.84	171/71	JT	58.32	60.08- 11
Miyauchi	Yoko	JPN	9.6.83	153441	Mar	2:27:17	2:26:23- 12
Mizuguchi	Yuko	JPN	24.5.85	164/43	10k	32:10.15	32:30.33- 12
^ Mockenhaupt	Sabrina	GER	6.12.81	156/45	5000	15:32.73	14:59.88mx- 09, 15:03.47- 04
10k	32:13.64	31:14.21- 08		HMar	69:42	68:45- 09 Mar 2:29:10	2:26:21- 10
Moen-Davis	LaQue	USA	14.8.93	173/62	LJ	6.55w	6.29- 12
Moges	Bethlehem	ETH	3.5.91		HMar	70:38	71:51- 12
* Moguenara	Sosthene	GER	17.10.89	182/68	LJ	7.04	6.88- 12
Moh	Clarisse	FRA	6.12.86	163/54	800	2:01.43	2:02.14- 12
Mohammed	Alia Saeed	UAE	18.5.91	160/45	10k	32:39.39	34:23.72- 12
Mokhnyuk	Anastasiya	UKR	1.1.91	175/67	LJ	6.62i, 6.57	6.52- 12
					Hep	5941	5830- 12
Mokrásová	Lucia	SVK-J	27.3.94		Hep	5649	5610- 12
* Möldner-Schmidt	Antje	GER	13.6.84	173/56	3kSt	9:29.27	9:18.54- 09
* Moline	Georganne	USA	6.3.90	178/59	400	52.09i, 52.92	52.92- 12
					400h	53.72	53.92- 12
* Molitor	Katharina	GER	8.11.83	182/76	JT	63.55	64.67- 11
Molodchinina	Yelena	RUS	16.4.91	174/65	Hep	5796	5757- 12
^ Montaner	Concepción	ESP	14.1.81	170/56	LJ	6.59	6.92- 05
* Montaño	Alysia	USA	26.4.86	170/61	800	1:57.75	1:57.34- 10
Montcalm	Noelle	CAN	3.4.88	168/3	400h	55.96	56.87A, 57.21- 12
* Montsho	Amantle	BOT	4.7.83	173/57	400	49.33	49.54- 12
* Moore	LaShauntea	USA	31.7.83	170/62	100	11.26, 10.98w	10.97- 10, 10.93w- 12
					200	22.40	22.46- 07
Moraa	Jane	KEN	21.9.91		HMar	70:27	
de Morais	Andressa	BRA	21.12.90	178/100	DT	61.04	64.21- 12
^ Moreira	Sara	POR	17.10.85	168/51	3000	8:52.48i	8:42.69- 10
Moreno	Johana	COL	15.4.85	175/78	HT	67.99	69.80- 09
Moreno	Yadira	COL	2.11.87		400h	57.17	59.20A- 12
* Moreno	Yipsi	CUB	19.11.80	171/81	HT	74.16	76.62- 08
Morgan	Monique	JAM	10.10.85	168/60	100h	12.97, 12.93w	13.09- 07
Mori	Yuika	JPN	25.1.88	157/47	5000	15:26.80	
* Morosanu	Angela	ROU	26.7.86	178/57	200	22.93	22.91- 06
400	52.07i	51.93i- 07, 52.48- 05			400h	53.86	53.95- 09
Morris	Brooklyn	USA	27.3.86	167/57	200	23.01w	23.03- 06
Morris	Sandi	USA	8.7.92	163/54	PV	4.43i	4.30- 11
Morrison	Natasha	JAM	17.11.92	170/57	100	11.17, 11.12w	11.42- 11
					200	23.08	23.89- 12
Moser	Treniere	USA	27.10.81	159/50	800	2:01.65 irr	1:59.15- 07
1500	4:02.85		4:03.32- 06		5000	15:11.00	15:34.56- 07
Mosina	Veronika	RUS	17.10.90	172/57	LJ	6.79	6.71i, 6.46- 12
					TJ	14.30i, 14.03	14.50- 12
Mosop	Leonidah	KEN	.91		HMar	70:11	71:00- 12
Muangjan	Thitima	THA	13.4.83	168/53	TJ	14.16	14.08- 09
Muchkaev	Anastasia	ISR	18.7.91	185/93	SP	16.78i, 16.28	17.22- 12
* Muhammad	Dalilah	USA	7.2.90	170/62	400h	53.83	56.04- 11
Muir	Jody-Ann	JAM	1.1.91	163/54	400	52.02	52.00- 12
Muir	Laura	GBR	9.5.93	162/54	800	2:00.80	2:07.3mx, 2:07.52- 12
					1500	4:07.76	4:14.52mx, 4:17.81- 12
Mukasheva	Margarita	KAZ	4.1.86	166/50	800	1:58.96	1:59.20- 12
* Müller	Nadine	GER	21.11.85	193/90	DT	66.69	68.89- 12
Mullina	Olga	RUS	1.8.92		PV	4.30i, 4.20	4.20- 12

Name		Nat	Born	Ht/Wt	Event	2013 Mark	Pre-2013 Best
Muñoz	Lismania	CUB	28.2.93	171/63	JT	59.29	56.33- 12
Murage	Jane	KEN	.87		3kSt	9:56.2A	10:00.69A- 09
Murakami	Mizuki	JPN	3.5.91	159/64	JT	57.38	51.20- 12
* Murer	Fabiana	BRA	16.3.81	172/64	PV	4.75	4.85- 10
Murillo	María Lucelly	COL	5.5.91	176/65	JT	56.00A	57.16A- 10
* Muriuki	Margaret	KEN	21.3.86	158/45	3000	8:49e+	8:37.97- 10
					5000	14:40.48	14:48.94- 10
Murtazina	Alsu	RUS	20.12.87	175/59	TJ	14.54	14.55- 11, 14.63w- 10
Muryasova	Alfiya	RUS	3.10.88	167/53	5000	15:20.42	15:26.31- 11
Muthoni	Miriam	KEN-J	.95		3kSt	9:34.58A	
Mutune	Agnes	KEN	26.6.86		HMar	70:03+	70:05- 09
Muzaric	Valentina	CRO	23.7.92	178/86	SP	17.52	16.82- 12
Muze	Lina	LAT	4.12.92	182/75	JT	61.97	61.04- 12
N'Zola Meso	Theresa	FRA	30.11.83	169/53	TJ	13.91, 13.95w	14.69- 07
Nachula	Racheal	ZAM	14.1.90	164/60	200	22.9	23.41A- 08
Nageo	Kaoru	JPN	26.9.89	160/45	5000	15:35.74	15:43.78- 11
Nageotte	Katie	USA	30.6.91	168/59	PV	4.45	4.00i- 11, 3.96- 09
Nagovitsyna	Yelena	RUS	7.12.82	165/55	5000	15:22.23	15:02.80- 12
					10k	32:02.99	32:08.00- 11
Naigambo	Beata	NAM	11.3.80	160/47	Mar	2:27:54	2:29:20- 12
^ Naimova ¶	Tedzhyan	BUL	1.5.87	166/58	100	11.17w dq	11.04- 07, 11.0- 12
Nall	Mary	USA	22.4.92	165/54	Hep	5562	5195- 11
Nambawa	Sarah	UGA	23.9.85	165/64	TJ	13.88	14.06- 11
* Nana Djimou	Antoinette	FRA	2.8.85	174/69	Hep	6326	6576- 12
^ Naude	Elizna	RSA	14.9.78	180/105	DT	58.13A	64.87- 07
Nazarova	Natalya	RUS	26.5.79	166/57	400	51.83	49.85- 04
Ndu	Ugonna	USA/NGR	27.6.91	169/54	100h	13.14, 13.04w	13.37- 12
					400h	56.12	57.59- 12
Nelson	Ashleigh	GBR	20.2.91	175/69	100	11.33	11.36- 09
Nelson	Brianne	USA	27.10.80	161/47	10k	32:33.05	
Nelvis	Sharika	USA	10.5.90	178/64	100h	12.84	13.22, 12.99w- 12
Nengampi	Perine	KEN	1.1.89		3000	8:51.60	8:53.26- 12
Netsvetayeva	Yekaterina	BLR	26.6.89	174/64	Hep	5989	5940- 12
Nettey	Christabel	CAN	2.6.91	162/59	LJ	6.75	6.58- 12
Newman	Alysha	CAN-J	29.6.94	172/66	PV	4.40A	4.06- 12
Newton	Kendra	USA	3.8.87		100h	13.19, 12.92w	13.32- 12
Neziri	Nooralotta	FIN	9.11.92	174/60	100h	13.04	13.10- 12
Ngugi	Mary	KEN	17.12.88		HMar	70:32	70:54- 12
Nicoletti	Julaika	ITA	20.3.88	178/90	SP	17.17i, 16.75	17.13i, 17.09- 12
Nie Jingjing		CHN	1.3.88	168/45	20kW	1:28:33	1:28:26- 12
* Niiya	Hitomi	JPN	26.2.88	165/44	5000	15:30.44+	15:10.20- 12
					10k	30:56.70	30:59.19- 12
Nikkanen	Minna	FIN	9.4.88	169/52	PV	4.50	4.60i- 11, 4.46- 09
Nikolayeva	Iryna	UKR	20.1.84	170/55	LJ	6.60	6.49- 04
					TJ	13.93	13.38- 04
Nishihara	Kasumi	JPN	1.3.89	161/46	5000	15:26.61	15:23.80- 11
					10k	32:05.88	32:22.93- 10
* Niyonsaba	Francine	BDI	5.5.93	161/56	800	1:56.72	1:56.59- 12
Njeri	Pauline	KEN	28.7.85		HMar	68:58dq	67:55- 12
* Noguchi	Mizuki	JPN	3.7.78	150/41	HMar	70:36	67:43- 06
					Mar	2:24:05	2:19:12- 05
Nojiri	Azusa	JPN	6.6.82	156/43	Mar	2:28:47	2:24:57- 12
Nomura	Sayo	JPN	18.4.89	157/48	10k	32:31.78	32:27.41- 09
					HMar	70:03	70:34- 12
Noorman	Sietske	NED	16.7.91	184/80	HJ	1.87i, 1.85	1.87- 12
Nordström	My	SWE	21.4.90	180/66	HJ	1.92i, 1.85	1.85- 12
Noujani	Nadia	MAR	3.9.81	164/46	3000	8:51.73	9:07.83- 11
					5000	15:35.55	15:16.50- 12
Novichkova	Natalya	RUS	9.10.88	171/58	5000	15:34.34	15:40.53- 12
					10k	32:39.91	32:40.89- 12
Novogrodskaya	Alena	BLR	11.5.93	180/96	HT	66.10	67.13- 12
Novozhylova	Iryna	UKR	7.1.86	175/71	HT	70.40	74.10- 12
Nowakowska	Dominika	POL	25.1.85	172/56	5000	15:16.11	15:58.32- 12
Ntshingila	Patience	RSA	26.8.89	175/61	LJ	6.49	6.60- 12
Nukuri-Johnson	Diane	BDI	1.12.84	175/54	10k	32:29.14	32:45.96- 12
					HMar	69:12	70:55- 12
Nuttall	Emma	GBR	23.4.92		HJ	1.87	1.86- 12
O'Brien	Rebecca	USA	30.4.90	173/86	SP	17.78	17.59- 12
O'Connor	Leah	USA	30.8.92	174/81	3kSt	9:53.53	10:03.40- 12
Obare	Doricah	KEN	10.1.90	162/48	10k	31:44.92	31:37.07- 10
* Obergföll	Christina	GER	22.8.81	175/79	JT	69.05	70.20- 07

Name		Nat	Born	Ht/Wt	Event	2013 Mark	Pre-2013 Best
Oberholzer	Maryke	RSA	27.11.89	175/85	DT	57.24	55.09- 12
* Obiri	Hellen	KEN	13.12.89	155/45	800	2:01.47A	2:00.54- 11
1500	3:58.58		3:59.68- 12		3000	8:34.25	8:35.35i- 12
Obleshchuk	Halyna	UKR	23.2.89	176/88	SP	18.77	19.23- 12
^ Ochichi	Isabellah	KEN	28.10.79	162/48	HMar	69:21	68:38- 01
Ochotnikova	Nina	RUS	11.3.91	162/46	20kW	1:29:03	1:28:16- 12
* Odumosu	Ajoke	NGR	27.10.87	168/59	400h	55.10	54.40- 12
Ogrâzeanu	Andreea	ROU	24.3.90	179/62	200	22.91	23.29- 09
Ogrodníková	Nikola	CZE	18.8.90	175/73	JT	56.20	54.48- 08
Ohara	Rei	JPN	10.8.90	165/47	10k	32:08.73	32:30.45- 12
					HMar	69:45	70:50- 11
* Ohuruogu	Christine	GBR	17.5.84	173/70	400	49.41	49.61- 07
Oka	Sayuri	JPN	19.9.90	156/43	10k	32:06.79	32:45.65- 11
Okada	Kumiko	JPN	17.10.91	158/44	20kW	1:32:22	1:34:27- 12
* Okagbare	Blessing	NGR	9.10.88	180/68	100	10.79, 10,75w	10.92- 12, 10.7wA- 10
200	22.31		22.63- 12		LJ	7.00, 7.14w	6.97- 12
Okayama	Saeko	JPN	12.4.82	180/63	LJ	6.59	6.56- 11, 6.67w- 12
Okinada	Akari	JPN-J	26.1.94	157/43	5000	15:30.82	15:44.53- 12
Okodogbe	Chizoba	NGR	3.11.92	170/60	400	52.22	52.71- 11
Okolo	Courtney	USA-J	15.3.94	168/54	400	51.04	52.40- 12
Okon	Patience	NGR	25.11.91	171/64	400	51.87	52.49- 12
Okori	Reina-Flor	FRA	2.5.80	163/56	100h	12.83	12.65- 08
Okoro	Eseroghene	GBR	4.7.90	170/59	400h	57.21	57.60- 12
^ Okoro	Marilyn	GBR	23.9.84	167/60	800	1:59.43	1:58.45- 08
Okou	Rosvitha	CIV	5.9.86	165/62	100h	13.16	13.13- 11
Okparaebo	Ezinne	NOR	3.3.88	164/56	100	11.23, 11.21w	11.10- 12
Okuneva	Oksana	UKR	14.3.90	175/61	HJ	1.92	1.94- 11
de Oliveira	Gisele	BRA	1.8.80	160/57	TJ	13.72, 13.78w	14.28, 14.31w- 08
* Oljira	Belaynesh	ETH	26.6.90	165/49	10k	30:31.44	30:26.70- 12
Mar	2:25:01		-0-		5000	15:01.51	14:58.16- 10
Olyanovska	Lyudmyla	UKR	20.2.93		20kW	1:30:26	-
^ Omarova	Anna	RUS	3.10.81	180/103	SP	18.66	19.69- 07
Omotosho	Omolara	NGR	25.5.93	152/50	400	51.67	51.28- 12
Omrami	Yasmina	ALG	1.1.88	183/67	Hep	5983	5979- 10
Ondraschková	Lucie	CZE	12.10.89	168/59	Hep	5853	5487- 10
* Ongori	Philes	KEN	19.7.86	158/47	HMar	68:01	67:38- 09
					Mar	2:28:53	2:24:20- 11
Onishi	Misaki	JPN	24.2.85	164/47	5000	15:21.73	15:32.88- 12
Onuora	Anyika	GBR	28.10.84	175/69	100	11.20+	11.18- 11
200	22.79, 22.17w		22.93- 11		400	51.38	-0-
* Orbán	Éva	HUN	29.11.84	173/75	HT	73.44	71.33- 11
Orji	Keturah	USA-Y	5.3.96		TJ	13.69	12.46, 12.51w- 12
Ormay	Anikó	HUN	22.1.91		JT	55.81	52.06- 12
Ortiz	Coralys	PUR	16.4.85	176/61	JT	57.48A	54.62- 12
Ortiz	Mirna	GUA	28.2.87	158/44	20kW	1:28:32	1:28:54- 12
Otoshi	Kumi	JPN	29.7.85	161/46	20kW	1:30:45	1:29:11- 11
Ott	Anastasiya	RUS	7.9.88	175/61	400h	55.49	54.74- 08
Oudenaarden	Niki	CAN-J	14.1.94	178/65	Hep	5774w, 5716	
Owen/Withrow	Melinda	USA	30.10.84	165/62	PV	4.30	4.55Ai- 11, 4.52- 10
Owens	Bridgette	USA	14.3.92	163/52	100h	13.09	12.71- 12
^ Ozaki	Mari	JPN	16.7.75	162/46	Mar	2:26:41	2:23:30- 03
^ Ozaki	Yoshimi	JPN	1.7.81	155/41	Mar	2:28:30	2:23:30- 08
Özata	Türkan	TUR	5.1.84	174/50	3kSt	9:49.84	9:28.84- 09
Ozolina-Kovale	Sinta	LAT	26.2.88	185/72	JT	64.38	62.53- 12
Ozorai	Jenny	HUN	3.12.90	164/70	HT	66.60	68.08- 12
Paesler	Carolin	GER	16.12.90	167/77	HT	68.63	65.18- 12
Paine	Alexis	USA	12.10.90	168/60	PV	4.45	4.20- 12
Paklina	Alesya	KGZ	22.6.88		HJ	1.90i, 1.89	1.89- 12
^ Palamar	Viktoriya	UKR	12.10.77	187/66	HJ	1.91	2.01- 03
* Palameika	Madara	LAT	18.6.87	185/76	JT	62.72	64.51-09
Palmer	Nadine	JAM	9.2.83	173/68	100	11.32	11.36- 00
Palmisano	Antonella	ITA	6.8.91	166/49	20kW	1:30:50	1:34:27- 12
Palsyte	Airine	LTU	13.7.92	186/62	HJ	1.95	1.96- 11
Panayi	Nectaria	CYP	20.3.90	165/48	LJ	6.55	6.56- 12
Pandakova	Marina	RUS	1.3.89		20kW	1:27:39	1:28:29- 12
Panétta	Niki	GRE	21.4.86	171/54	TJ	14.29i, 14.20, 14.23w	14.55- 11
Panova	Yelena	RUS	2.3.87	185/95	DT	61.02	57.97- 12
Panteleyeva	Yana	RUS	16.6.88	170/60	Hep	5726	6430- 08
* Papahrístou	Paraskevi	GRE	17.4.89	170/53	TJ	14.21	14.72- 11, 14.77w- 12
Papp	Krisztina	HUN	17.12.82	170/54	10k	32:42.40	31:46.47- 10
Pappas	Alexi	USA	28.3.90	166/52	3kSt	9:46.73	9:55.89- 12

Name		Nat	Born	Ht/Wt	Event	2013 Mark	Pre-2013 Best
Pappas	Sarah	USA	30.3.87		PV	4.35i	4.18- 11
Parker	Kayla	USA	12.3.92	163/52	100h	13.19, 13.16w	13.72- 12
Parker	Le'Quisha	USA	26.5.93	170/59	200	23.15	
Parnov	Elizabeth	AUS-J	9.5.94	178/57	PV	4.45	4.50- 12
Partridge	Susan	GBR	4.1.80	170/55	HMar	70:32	71:10- 12
* Pascual	Beatriz	ESP	9.5.82	163/53	20kW	1:29:00	1:27:44- 08
Pastare	Agnese	LAT	27.10.88	178/70	20kW	1:29:55	1:31:25- 10
Patterson	Eleanor	AUS-Y	22.5.96	180/62	HJ	1.96	1.87- 12
Patterson	Kara	USA	10.4.86	175/76	JT	57.12	66.67- 10
Peake	Erica	USA	20.2.91	165/52	100	11.30w	11.71- 12
					200	23.35, 23.09w	23.58- 12
Peake	Sally	GBR	8.2.86	164/57	PV	4.40i, 4.27	4.42i- 12, 4.35- 11
* Pearson	Sally	AUS	19.9.86	166/60	100h	12.50	12.28- 11
Pedersen	Isabelle	NOR	27.1.92	168/54	100h	13.04	13.21- 11
Pedroso	Yadisleidis	ITA	28.1.87	168/51	400h	54.54	54.89- 12
Pei Mowen		CHN-J	17.9.95		20kW	1:30:33	1:32:23- 12
Peinado	Robeilys	VEN-Y	26.11.97	168/62	PV	4.40A	4.15- 12
Pelantová	Lucie	CZE	7.5.86	168/60	20kW	1:32:07	1:32:53- 12
Peleteiro	Ana	ESP-J	2.12.95	160/40	TJ	13.75i	14.17- 12
Pena	Tori	IRL	30.7.87	167/57	PV	4.60	4.52- 12
Pendleton	Emily	USA	16.4.89	172/82	DT	55.90	55.85- 07
Peoples	Kearsten	USA	20.12.91	181/105	SP	17.80	18.22- 12
^ Pérez	Madaí	MEX	2.2.80	158/44	HMar	70:27	69:45- 10
					Mar	2:28:59dh	2:22:59- 06
Pérez	Paola	ECU	21.12.89	148/55	20kW	1:32:53	1:32:01- 12
* Pérez	Yaimé	CUB	29.5.91	174/78	DT	66.01	62.50- 12
* Perie	Bianca	ROU	1.6.90	170/70	HT	71.57	73.52- 10
Perkins	Kerrie	AUS	2.4.79	174/59	LJ	6.53	6.66- 06, 6.70w- 12
* Perkovic	Sandra	CRO	21.6.90	183/80	DT	68.96	69.11- 12, 69.99dq- 11
Pérra	Athanasía	GRE	2.2.83	167/55	TJ	14.48	14.71- 12
Perrauix	Claire	FRA	6.10.87	170/50	3kSt	9:43.70	9:44.11- 12
^ Petre	Esthera	ROU	13.5.90	175/60	HJ	1.91i	1.98- 11
Petrillose	Kaitlin	USA	12.10.92	168/57	PV	4.50i, 4.36	4.30i- 12, 4.16- 11
Petrova	Gabriela	BUL	29.6.92	167/61	TJ	14.14i, 13.92, 13.96w	13.45- 12
Pham Thi Diem		VIE	24.1.90		HJ	1.91	1.88- 12
Philip	Asha	GBR	25.10.90	163/54	100	11.20	11.37- 07
					200	23.07w	24.82- 11
Pidluzhnaya	Yuliya	RUS	1.10.88	180/63	LJ	6.49	6.84- 10, 6.85w- 11
* Pierre	Barbara	USA	28.4.87	160/64	100	10.85	11.14- 11
Pierson	Summer	USA	3.9.78	180/84	DT	58.35	61.19, 61.25dh- 09
Piirimäe	Kätlin	EST-J	8.11.95		SP	16.80	15.22- 12
Piliusina	Natalja	LTU	22.10.90	170/60	800	2:01.59	2:02.12- 12
					1500	4:09.57	4:09.51- 12
Pinckney	Takeia	USA	24.7.91	163/52	100	11.45, 11.30w	11.26- 10
Pinedo	Ainhoa	ESP	17.2.83	171/60	20kW	1:32.20	1:33:41- 12
Pinnick	Shakeia	USA	23.1.91	165/55	100h	13.13, 13.04w	13.34- 12
	400h	57.06		57.34- 12	Hep	5984(w)	5761- 12
Pinto	Tatjana	GER	2.7.92	170/56	100	11.22	11.19- 12
Pirelli	Ana Camila	PAR	10.1.89	167/62	Hep	5733	5479- 12
Plá	Judith	ESP	2.5.78	168/53	5000	15:30.99	15:20.39- 12
Pleger	Brooke	USA	21.6.92	171/77	HT	66.99	61.22- 12
Plis	Renata	POL	5.2.85	165/51	800	2:01.48	2:00.45- 10
	1500	4:06.39		4:03.50- 11	3000	8:40.42	8:59.3+l, 9:08.94- 10
Plotitsyna	Anna	UKR	1.1.87	182/65	100h	13.03, 12.91w	13.27- 12
Pluim	Femke	NED-J	10.5.94	180/62	PV	4.30	3.80- 12
Podominick	Liz	USA	5.12.84	188/86	DT	63.32	60.96- 12
Podosyonova	Svetlana	RUS	24.5.88	167/52	800	2:01.53, 2:00.32i	2:00.69- 12
(now Karamasheva)					1500	4:04.01	3:59.61- 12
Pogoryelska	Viktoriya	UKR	4.8.90	170/50	3000	8:57.75	9:01.25- 11
					5000	15:28.35	15:46.25- 12
Pogrebnyak	Natalya	UKR	19.2.88	171/62	100	11.27	11.17- 11
					200	23.16	23.40- 12
* Poistogova	Yekaterina	RUS	1.3.91	175/65	800	1:58.05	1:57.53- 12
					1000	2:36.97i	2:38.94i- 12
* Polk	Tori	USA	21.9.83	173/62	LJ	6.75, 6.80w	6.75- 11
Poltavets	Inna	RUS	6.11.90		Hep	5582	5679- 12
Polyakova	Natalya	RUS	9.12.90		HT	68.84	67.08- 12
Pooley	Isobel	GBR	21.12.92	190/68	HJ	1.91	1.90- 12
* Poonia	Krishna	IND	5.5.82	182/80	DT	59.43	64.76- 12
Popowicz	Marika	POL	28.4.88	163/53	100	11.29	11.38- 09
* Porter	Tiffany	GBR	13.11.87	172/62	100h	12.55	12.56- 11, 12.47w- 12

Name		Nat	Born	Ht/Wt	Event	2013 Mark	Pre-2013 Best
Pospelova	Marina	RUS	23.7.90	164/53	800	2:00.61	1:59.45i, 1:59.70- 12
Pousse	Pauline	FRA	17.9.87	184/84	DT	55.80	55.78- 11
^ Poves	María José	ESP	16.3.78	168/52	20kW	1:29:58	1:28:15- 12
* Povh	Olesya	UKR	18.10.87	169/58	100	11.14	11.08- 12
Prandini	Jenna	USA	20.11.92	172/59	100	11.31, 11.14w	11.34- 10
					200	23.15	23.75, 23.51w- 11
Praught	Aisha	USA	14.12.89	173/55	3kSt	9:50.06	9:51.30- 12
Pressley	Maya	USA	1.2.91	175/60	HJ	1.92	1.85- 11
Price	Chanelle	USA	22.8.90	166/53	800	2:00.88	2:00.15- 12
Price	DeAnna	USA	8.6.93		HT	65.18	62.62- 12
Price	Kylie	USA	1.10.93	178/64	100	11.36, 11.32w	11.68- 10
					LJ	6.52, 6.55w	6.43- 12
Prinsloo	Lynique	RSA	30.3.91	165/54	LJ	6.81	6.38- 12
* Proctor	Shara	GBR	16.9.88	174/56	LJ	6.92	6.95- 12
Profit	Kiani	USA	18.2.90	163/55	Hep	6133	5695- 12
^ Prokopcuka	Jelena	LAT	21.9.76	168/51	HMar	70:14dh	68:09dh- 12
					Mar	2:25:46	2:22:56- 05
Prokopeva	Alina	RUS	16.8.85	157/42	10k	32:02.92	31:57.38- 12
Proper	Kelly	IRL	1.5.88	164/58	200	22.96w	23.67- 10
Provalinskaya	Yanina	BLR	26.12.76	186/85	SP	17.91	20.61- 01
Puchkova	Natalya	RUS	28.1.87	154/47	10k	32:02.67	32:42.67- 11
Pudenz	Kristin	GER	9.2.93	190/92	DT	59.74	57.74- 12
Puiu	Beatrice	ROU	1.1.86		Hep	5814	5549- 12
Purvis	Ashton	USA	12.7.92	173/60	100	11.35, 11.20w	11.17- 10
					200	23.07, 22.70e	22.86- 12
Purvis	Julian	USA	8.9.90	172/50	100h	13.16	13.29- 11
Pusterla	Irène	SUI	21.6.88	176/64	LJ	6.52, 6.69w	6.84- 11
Pyatachenko	Viktoriya	UKR	7.5.89	170/57	100	11.47, 11.28w	11.30- 12
					200	22.68	22.71- 12
* Pyatykh	Anna	RUS	4.4.81	176.64	TJ	14.40	15.02, 15.17w- 06
Pygyda	Nataliya	UKR	30.1.81	167/54	400	50.86	51.09- 12
* Qieyang Shenjie		CHN	11.11.90	160/50	20kW	1:28:05	1:25:16- 12
Quigley	Colleen	USA	20.11.92	176/60	3kSt	9:38.23	10:02.53- 12
Radford	Breanna	USA	31.8.90		SP	16.68i, 16.56	15.79- 12
* Radzivil	Svetlana	UZB	17.1.87	184/61	HJ	1.94	1.97- 12
Rahmouni	Khadija	ESP	30.11.86	165/52	800	2:01.74	2:04.32- 12
^ Rahouli	Baya	ALG	27.7.79	174/61	TJ	14.29	14.98- 05
Rajabi	Leyla	IRI	18.4.83	185/95	SP	18.18	18.06- 06
Ramos	Beverly	PUR	24.8.87	163/51	3kSt	9:43.28	9:39.33- 12
Randall	Allison	JAM	25.5.88	180/95	DT	58.97	61.21- 12
Rani	Annu	IND	29.8.92		JT	56.04	53.95- 12
Ratcliffe	Julia	NZL	14.7.93	171/66	HT	68.80	67.00- 12
* Ratej	Martina	SLO	2.11.81	178/64	JT	62.60	67.16- 10
* Rath	Claudia	GER	25.4.86	175/58	LJ	6.67	6.50- 10
					Hep	6462	6210- 12
Râzor	Bianca	ROU-J	8.8.94	169/54	400	51.49	51.96- 11
Reaser	Allison	USA	9.9.92	171/61	Hep	5813	5753- 12
* Rebryk	Vira	UKR	25.2.89	176/65	JT	64.30	66.86- 12
Redondo	Laura	ESP	3.7.88	165/80	HT	69.59	69.15- 12
* Reese	Brittney	USA	9.9.86	173/64	LJ	7.25	7.23i- 12, 7.19- 11
Reggel	Valérie	SUI	3.1.87	174/64	Hep	5856	5794- 12
Reid	Sheila	CAN	2.8.89	166/52	1500	4:02.96	4:07.07- 12
1M	4:27.02i	4:35.30i- 11		3000	8:44.02	8:56.92i- 11	2M 9:37.97i
Reilly	Chelsea	USA	9.5.89	167/52	1500	4:08.77	4:24.49- 11
3000	8:47.34		9:00.86i- 12		5000	15:10.14	15:57.53- 12
dos Reis	Jessica	BRA	17.3.93	160/50	LJ	6.56	6.58- 12
Ren Mengqian		CHN	4.10.93	175/62	PV	4.40i, 4.40	4.15- 11
Renzhina	Yekaterina	RUS-J	18.10.94	172/57	400	52.16	52.92- 12
Reyes	Macarena	CHI	30.3.84	165/58	LJ	6.54w	6.60- 12
Reynolds	Laura	IRL	20.1.89	173/57	20kW	1:33:31	1:31:02- 12
Reynolds	Robin	USA-J	22.2.94	162/50	400	52.13	52.15- 09
Reznichenko	Darya	UZB	3.4.91		LJ	6.52	6.60- 12
Reznikova	Marina	RUS	10.6.91		400h	56.80	57.89- 12
Ribalta	Yosleidis	CUB	2.5.90	183/74	TJ	13.87	14.61- 11
* Richards-Ross	Sanya	USA	26.2.85	172/63	400	51.43	48.70- 06
Richartz	Stephanie	USA	21.1.92	170/59	PV	4.31	4.34- 12
Riebold	Jade	USA	14.4.91		PV	4.45i, 4.40	4.31- 12
* Rigaudo	Elisa	ITA	17.6.80	168/56	20kW	1:28:41	1:27:12- 08
Rigert	Yelena	RUS	2.12.83	167/73	HT	75.09	71.92- 08
Riggien	Chastity	USA	5.7.89	157/52	100	11.24, 11.14w	11.20, 11.09w- 12
Rigishvili ¶	Salome	GEO	26.1.90	186/85	DT	55.70	58.90- 12

Name		Nat	Born	Ht/Wt	Event	2013 Mark	Pre-2013 Best
Rittweg	Mareike	GER	1.6.84	173/78	JT	58.14	60.63- 07
Rivas	Ányela	COL	13.8.89	180/82	SP	16.89	17.53- 12
Riviaux	Yainelis	CUB	30.12.87	163/57	JT	57.10	63.18- 09
* Robert-Michon	Melina	FRA	18.7.79	180/85	DT	66.28	65.78- 02
Roberts	Kelsey-Lee	AUS	21.9.91	170/68	JT	58.58	52.01- 11
Robinson	Kayan	JAM	27.3.89	167/57	400	51.88A, 52.79	52.53A- 12, 53.45- 06
Robinson	Moushaumi	USA	13.4.81	170/59	400	51.19	50.38- 05
Rocha	Carla Salomé	POR	25.4.90	158/48	10k	32:40.03	32:40.86- 12
					3kSt	9:54.36	9:51.91- 12
Rockwell	Jennifer	ITA	18.5.83	175/62	400h	55.70	55.51- 10
* Rodic	Snezana	SLO	19.8.82	180/66	LJ	6.53	6.51- 08
					TJ	14.58	14.47, 14.52w- 10
Rodko	Rimma	RUS	4.11.87	163/54	3kSt	9:54.79	10:10.09- 11
Rodrigues	Irina	POR	5.2.91	182/81	DT	59.76	62.91- 12
* Rodríguez	Natalia	ESP	2.6.79	164/49	1500	4:06.20	3:59.51- 05
Rodríguez	Rosa	VEN	2.7.86	179/78	HT	73.64	72.83- 12
Rodríguez	Yorgelis	CUB-J	25.1.95	173/60	Hep	6186	5994- 12
Roesler	Laura	USA	19.12.91	168/54	800	2:00.23	2:02.09- 12
* Rogowska	Anna	POL	21.5.81	171/53	PV	4.67i, 4.60	4.85i- 11, 4.83- 05
Rogozina	Svetlana	RUS	26.12.92	165/52	800	2:01.68	2:01.99- 12
Rohl	Elizabeth	USA	7.11.90	175/82	DT	59.66	57.82- 12
Rojas	Yulimar	VEN-J	21.10.95		HJ	1.87	1.81- 11
Roleder	Cindy	GER	21.8.89	175/62	100h	13.03, 12.93w	12.91- 11
* Rollins	Brianna	USA	18.8.91	164/55	200	23.04, 23.02w	24.13- 12
					100h	12.26	12.70, 12.60Aw- 12
Roloff	Annika	GER	10.3.91	166/54	PV	4.41	4.42i- 12, 4.40- 11
Romagnolo	Elena	ITA	5.10.82	163/47	1500	4:09.21	4:06.03- 10
Roman	Sonja	SLO	11.3.79	165/54	1500	4:07.32	4:02.13- 09
Romero	Marisol	MEX	26.11.83	155/42	5000	15:21.41	15:27.94- 11
					10k	31:46.43	32:45.05- 11
Rono	Georgina	KEN	19.5.80	165/46	HMar	70:00, 69:03dh	67:58- 12
Rono	Janet	KEN	8.12.88		Mar	2:28:36	2:33:42- 11
^ Rosa	Chiara	ITA	28.1.83	178/112	SP	18.37i, 18.04	19.15- 07
Rosenbauer	Susanne	GER	2.8.84	173/69	JT	57.47	58.83- 09
* Rosolová	Denisa	CZE	21.8.86	175/63	400	52.12i	50.84- 11
					400h	54.38	54.24- 12
Rostkowska	Anna	POL	26.7.80	174/54	800	2:01.34	1:58.62- 08
Rotaru	Alina	ROU	5.6.93	175/54	LJ	6.63	6.57, 6.58w- 12
Rotich	Caroline	KEN	13.5.84	161/45	HMar	69:09	68:52- 11
					Mar	2:27:00	2:23:22- 12
* Rotich	Lydia	KEN	8.8.88	158/45	3kSt	9:26.31	9:18.03- 10
* Rowbury	Shannon	USA	19.9.84	166/52	1500	4:01.28	4:00.33- 08
3000	8:34.43		8:31.38- 10		5000	15:06.10	15:00.51- 10
Rowland	Jo	GBR	29.12.89		Hep	5702	5381- 12
Rucker	Erika	USA	29.9.93	168.57	400	52.07	51.10- 12
Rudakova	Vera	RUS	20.3.92	175/57	400h	55.92	56.47- 12
Ruddick	Kelly	AUS	19.4.73		20kW	1:38:32- 12	
Ruddock	Natasha	JAM	25.12.89	176/64	100h	13.28, 13.17w	12.87- 10
* Rüh	Anna	GER	17.6.93	186/78	DT	64.33	63.38- 12
Ruiz	Flor Denis	COL	29.1.91	171/67	JT	60.23	59.32A- 12
Ruíz	Úrsula	ESP	11.8.83	170/83	SP	17.83	17.99- 12
Rummans	Angela	USA	23.3.92	168/57	PV	4.30Ai, 4.21	4.40- 12
Rumpf	Sabine	GER	18.3.83	176/95	DT	59.90	62.21- 10
Rushin	Jill	USA	18.7.91		SP	16.67i, 16.52	16.23i, 16.07- 12
* Russell	Carrie	JAM	18.10.90	171/68	100	10.98	11.05- 11
					200	22.62	23.86- 12, 23.75w- 06
Russell	Janeive	JAM	14.11.93	169/57	400h	56.30	56.62- 12
* Ryemyen	Mariya	UKR	2.8.87	171/62	100	11.06	11.20- 12, 11.18w- 11
					200	22.61	22.58- 12
* Ryzhova (Vdovina)	Kseniya	RUS	19.4.87	172/62	400	49.80	50.43- 12
* Ryzih	Elizaveta 'Lisa"	GER	27.9.88	179/59	PV	4.55	4.65- 10
Sadeiko	Grit	EST	29.7.89	172/62	Hep	6221	6134- 11
Sado	Fatuma	ETH	11.10.91	165/48	Mar	2:27:35	2:25:39dh- 12, 2:28:01- 11
Safránková	Katerina	CZE	8.6.89	191/105	HT	65.43	71.16- 12
Saholinirina	Eliane	MAD	20.3.82	155/43	3kSt	9:56.32	9:47.57- 12
Sahutoglu ¶	Tugce	TUR	1.5.88	180/115	HT	69.20, 72.10dq	74.17- 12
* Sailer	Verena	GER	16.10.85	166/50	100	11.02	11.05- 12
Saina	Betsy	KEN	30.6.88	163/48	5000	15:12.05	15:36.09i- 12. 15:50.74- 11
					10k	31:37.22	31:15.97- 12
Saito	Marina	JPN-J	15.10.95	163/61	JT	56.76	53.47- 12
Saito	Shino	JPN	7.9.88	153/42	10k	32:45.66	32:33.99- 10

Name		Nat	Born	Ht/Wt	Event	2013 Mark			Pre-2013 Best
Sakaida	Ayumi	JPN	7.11.85	157/44	10k	32:24.85			32:29.28- 12
* Saladuha	Olga	UKR	4.6.83	175/55	TJ	14.88im, 15.85			14.99- 12, 15.06w- 11
Salis	Silvia	ITA	17.9.85	179/74	HT	69.68			71.93- 11
Salman-Kaya ¶	Kivilcim	TUR	27.3.92	166/85	HT	71.02			72.55- 12
Salmela	Johanna	FIN	6.11.90	172/76	HT	65.81			64.10- 12
Saltanovic	Kristina	LTU	20.2.75	163/54	20kW	1:32:11			1:30:44- 02
Sammah	Khadija	MAR	9.7.83		10k	32:38.42			
Samuel	Laura	GBR	19.2.91	165/65	TJ	13.73, 13.75w			13.75- 10, 13.77w- 11
* Samuels	Dani	AUS	26.5.88	182/82	SP	16.82			16.65- 12
					DT	64.46			65.84- 10
Samylova	Olga	RUS	4.1.86	163/50	100h	13.15			12.82- 12
Sánchez	Mariely	DOM	30.12.88	168/57	100	11.24A, 11.4111.49A- 11, 11.49, 11.41w- 12			
					200	23.01			23.02A- 11, 23.20- 12
Sandblom	Linda	FIN	18.10.89	176/62	HJ	1.89			1.83- 12
Sandu	Cristina-Mihaela	ROU	4.3.90	172/58	LJ	6.51			6.57, 6.70w- 12
					TJ	13.71			13.61- 09
Sango	Misaki	JPN	21.4.89	165/46	3kSt	9:54.02			10:26.20- 11
Sant	MaryBeth	USA-J	16.4.95	155/45	100	11.25A			11.65A, 11.86- 12
dos Santos	Evelyn	BRA	11.4.85	172/52	100	11.35			11.36- 12
dos Santos	Patricia	BRA	13.6.84	168/58	PV	4.43			4.25- 10
Santos	Rosângela	BRA	20.12.90	165/55	100	11.23			11.17, 11.07w- 12
					200	23.13			22.92- 12
* Santos	Vera	POR	3.12.81	164/57	20kW	1:31:00			1:28:14- 08
Sargent	Caitlin	AUS	14.6.92	168/59	400	52.16			53.18- 11
Sarrapio	Patricia	ESP	16.11.82	168/58	TJ	14.07i, 13.88			14.10- 10, 14.30w- 11
* Savchenko	Anastasiya	RUS	15.11.89	175/65	PV	4.73			4.60- 12
* Savigne	Yargelis	CUB	13.11.84	168/59	TJ	14.05			15.28- 07
* Savinova	Mariya	RUS	13.8.85	172/60	800	1:57.80			1:55.87- 11
* Savitskaya	Kristina	RUS	10.6.91	180/72	Hep	6210			6681- 12
Savlinis	Yelizaveta	RUS	14.8.87	178/65	200	23.16			22.62- 11
Sawyers	Jazmin	GBR-J	21.5.94	167/52	LJ	6.63			6.67- 12
* Saxer	Mary	USA	21.6.87	166/57	PV	4.70			4.62Ai- 12, 4.60- 11
Saykina	Svetlana	RUS	10.7.85	177/82	DT	61.09			63.42- 08
Schade	Krystle	USA	2.7.90		HJ	1.88i			1.88i, 1.87- 12
Schäfer	Carolin	GER	5.12.91	176/56	Hep	5972			6072- 12
Scheper	Jeannelle	LCA-J	21.11.94	180/58	HJ	1.92A			1.85- 12
* Schippers	Dafne	NED	15.6.92	179/68	100	11.09			11.19, 11.13w- 11
	200	22.84	22.69- 11	LJ		6.59	6.54- 12	Hep	6477	6360- 12
Schlumpf	Fabienne	SUI	17.11.90	170/54	3kSt	9:46.98			9:55.50- 12
Schmelcz	Fanni	HUN	19.4.92		LJ	6.54w			5.83- 12
Schmid	Anna Katharina	SUI	2.12.89	165/56	PV	4.41			4.45- 11
Schmitz (Neuenswander)	Vera	USA	3.12.87	168/57	PV	4.45			4.37- 12
Schnitzerling	Lilli	GER	5.12.93	157/49	PV	4.30			4.30- 12
Schrott	Beate	AUT	15.4.88	177/68	100h	12.87, 12.84w			12.82- 12
Schultze	Martina	GER	12.9.90	172/62	PV	4.50			4.40- 10
* Schwanitz	Christina	GER	24.12.85	180/103	SP	20.41			19.68i, 19.31- 08
Schwartz	Lindsay	USA	23.4.90	178/64	Hep	5980			5614- 12
Schwarz	Desiree	GER	24.4.92	171/70	JT	58.08			56.93- 12
Scott	Aurieyall	USA	18.5.92	170/60	100	10.96			11.12- 11
					200	22.46			22.68, 22.56w- 12
Sealy	Sadé	BAR	18.11.91	173/61	400	52.01			53.16- 12
Seboka	Mulu	ETH	25.9.84	158/45	Mar	2:23:43			2:25:45- 12
Sedivá	Irena	CZE	19.1.92		JT	56.13			57.41- 12
Sedova	Yelena	RUS	1.3.90	169/50	10k	32:48.60			33:13.44- 12
Sedykh	Alexia	FRA	13.9.93	173/70	HT	68.35			67.98- 12
Sekachova	Iryna	UKR	21.7.76	165/72	HT	70.00			74.52- 08
Selomie	Getnet	ETH	10.4.86	172/52	Mar	2:25:15			2:31:15- 09
Selvon	Kai	TTO	13.4.92	165/59	100	11.23			11.21- 12, 11.19w- 11
					200	23.05, 22.65w			22.85, 22.66w- 12
^ Semenova	Nataliya	UKR	7.7.82	178/85	DT	61.41			64.70- 08
* Semenya	Caster	RSA	7.1.91	170/64	800	1:58.92			1:55.45- 09
de Sena	Érica	BRA	3..5.85	152/52	20kW	1:32:59			1:31:53- 12
* Sendriute	Zinaida	LTU	10.6.84	188/89	DT	65.97			64.03- 12
Sène	Amy	SEN	6.4.85	174/70	HT	65.58			69.10- 12
Serbest-Sinmez	Sevim	TUR	20.4.87	173/62	TJ	13.95			13.53i, 13.44, 13.52w- 12
Serezhkina	Natalya	RUS	7.5.92		20kW	1:30:19			1:34:40- 12
Serova	Svetlana	BLR	28.8.86	178.92	DT	62.23			60.90- 12
Seyoum	Dawit	ETH-Y	27.7.96		1500	4:09.00			
* Shakes-Drayton	Perri	GBR	21.12.88	170/67	400	50.50			51.26- 12
					400h	53.67			53.77- 12
da Silva	Cruz	BRA	18.8.74	160/47	10k	32:46.96			32:15.72- 12

Name		Nat	Born	Ht/Wt	Event	2013 Mark	Pre-2013 Best
da Silva	Izabela	BRA-J	2.8.95		DT	55.88	48.79- 12
da Silva	Karla	BRA	12.11.84	168/58	PV	4.53	4.35- 11
Shamotina	Alyona	UKR-J	27.12.95	178/98	HT	66.01	62.35- 12
* Sharmina	Yekaterina	RUS	6.8.86	172/59	800	1:59.91	1:59.17- 11
					1500	4:04.55	3:59.49- 12
(née Martynova)					3kSt	9:54.03	9:44.91- 12
Shatalova	Mariya	UKR	3.3.89				
Shchagina	Anna	RUS	7.12.91	166.54	800	2:01.07	2:03.03- 12
					1500	4:05.91	4:13.63- 12
Shevchenko ¶	Anzhela	UKR	29.10.87	177/55	1000	2:36.84idq	2:40.01i- 12
					1500	4:07.65idq	4:05.96dq- 12
Shi Tianshu		CHN	7.6.88	174/55	20kW	1:30:24	1:31:22- 12
Shi Yang		CHN	24.1.83	168/55	20kW	1:33:10	1:29:39- 08
Shimizu	Yuko	JPN	13.7.85	158/42	10k	32:07.70	32:14.71- 11
					HMar	69:32	70:58- 12
Shimura	Hitomi	JPN	8.11.90	167/53	100h	13.02	13.15- 12
* Shkolina	Svetlana	RUS	9.3.86	187/66	HJ	2.03	2.03- 12
Shmidt	Svitlana	UKR	20.3.90	167/52	3kSt	9:37.33	9:31.16- 12
Shoi	Hiroko	JPN	18.6.80	152/40	10k	32:34.29	32:17.39mx- 11, 32:23.98- 12
Shone	Guteni	ETH	17.11.91		HMar	68:59	70:07- 12
Shumkina	Olena	UKR	24.1.88	153/47	20kW	1:31:54	1:25:32- 09
Sidi Madane	Fadwa	MAR-J	20.11.94	162/50	3kSt	9:51.50	10:44.04- 11
* Sidorova	Anzhelika	RUS	28.6.91	170/52	PV	4.62i, 4.60	4.50- 12
Sidorska	Olena	UKR-J	30.7.94		800	2:01.00	2:03.69- 12
Sifuentes	Nicole	CAN	30.6.86	173/57	800	2:01.84	2:01.30- 12
	1500	4:04.65	4:04.76- 12	2M	9:38.78i	5000	15:27.58 15:27.84- 11
Sigei	Diana	KEN	.87		HMar	69:18	68:08- 12
Silva	Ana Claúdia	BRA	6.11.88	158/55	100	11.05, 10.93w	11.15- 10
					200	22.61	22.48- 11
da Silva	Cruz	BRA	18.8.74	160/47	10k	32:46.96	32:15.72- 12
da Silva	Izabela	BRA-J	2.8.95		DT	55.88	48.79- 12
da Silva	Karla	BRA	12.11.84	168/58	PV	4.53	4.35- 11
* Silva	Yarisley	CUB	1.6.87	169/68	PV	4.90	4.75A- 11
Simic	Ana	CRO	5.5.90	177/58	HJ	1.96	1.92- 10
Simpson	Francine	JAM	1.11.89	170/62	LJ	6.67	6.57, 6.67w- 12
^ Simpson	Jemma	GBR	10.2.84	168/58	1500	4:08.51	4:06.39- 10
* Simpson	Jennifer	USA	23.8.86	165/54	800	2:00.45	2:01.20- 11
	1500	4:00.48		3:59.90- 09	5000	14:56.26	15:01.70i, 15:05.25- 09
* Simpson	Sherone	JAM	12.8.84	175/59	100	11.03	10.82- 06
					200	22.55	22.00- 06
Sims	Caressa	USA	7.3.86	168/79	HT	66.73	65.21- 10
Singh	Sudha	IND	25.6.86	163/52	3kSt	9:45.60	9:47.70- 12
Sinkler	April	USA	1.9.89	170/57	TJ	13.89	13.51- 12
Sitnikova	Yelena	RUS	12.11.89		LJ	6.52	6.36, 6.58w- 12
Skoog	Sofie	SWE	7.6.90	180/64	HJ	1.90	1.80- 12
^ Skotnik	Mélanie	FRA	8.11.82	182/61	HJ	1.93i, 1.90	1.97i, 1.96- 07
Skrobáková	Lucie	CZE	4.1.82	170/62	100h	12.79	12.73- 09
* Skujyte	Austra	LTU	12.8.79	188/80	HJ	1.87i	1.92- 12
Skydan	Hanna	UKR	14.5.92	183/114	HT	68.44	74.21- 12
* Slesarenko	Yelena	RUS	28.2.82	178/57	HJ	1.92	2.06- 04
Smets	Fanny	BEL	21.4.86	173/59	PV	4.40	4.30sq, 4.25- 12
Smit	Angela	NZL	16.8.91	164/55	800	2:00.03	2:00.67- 12
Smith	Brittany	USA	25.3.91	178/89	SP	17.85	17.92- 12
					HT	68.51	68.45- 12
Smith	Jessica	CAN	11.10.89	172/54	800	2:00.43	1:59.86- 12
* Smith	Kimberley	NZL	19.11.81	166/48	10k	31:46.37	30:35.54- 08
	HMar	69:00	67:11- 11	Mar	2:28:49	2:25:21- 10	5000	15:02.56mx, 14:45.93- 08
Smith	Kristin	USA	23.12.87	168/75	HT	66.96	68.25- 12
Smith	Lauren	USA	27.8.81	158/50	100h	13.03	13.00, 12.94w- 07
Smith	Loreal	USA	12.10.85	162/57	100h	12.82, 12.66w	12.81, 12.64w- 11
Smith	Nivea	BAH	18.2.90	176/62	200	23.17	22.71- 10, 22.44w- 11
Smith	Taylor	USA	20.7.91	168/86	SP	17.36	16.30i, 16.25- 12
Smith	Toni	USA	13.10.84	168/59	TJ	13.99	13.99- 08, 14.02w- 10
Smith	Trecia	JAM	5.11.75	181/79	TJ	14.20i, 14.18	15.16- 04
Smock	Amanda	USA	27.7.82	170/57	TJ	13.97, 14.06w	14.18- 11
Smolyakova	Marina	RUS	20.6.89		HJ	1.90	1.85- 11
Snow	Morgan	USA	26.7.93	161/52	100h	12.88	13.13, 13.04w- 12
* Soboleva	Yelena	RUS	3.10.82	176/66	800	2:00.17	1:57.28- 06
					1500	4:04.30	3:56.43- 06
Sokolenko	Yekaterina	RUS	13.9.92		3kSt	9:43.50	10:04.26- 12
* Sokolova	Vera	RUS	8.6.87	151/51	20kW	1:26:00	1:25:08- 11
* Sokolova	Yelena	RUS	23.7.86	173/66	LJ	6.91	7.07- 12

Name		Nat	Born	Ht/Wt	Event	2013 Mark	Pre-2013 Best
Solomon	Serita	GBR	1.3.93	165/59	100h	13.09	13.27- 11, 13.26w- 12
* Solomon	Shalonda	USA	19.12.85	169/56	100	11.04, 10.97w	10.90- 10
					200	22.41, 22.33w	22.15- 11
Solovyova ¶	Yevgeniya	RUS	28.6.86	185/90	SP	17.87i, 18.66idq	18.71i, 18.03- 12
Song Aimin		CHN	15.3.78	178/95	DT	61.65	65.44- 09
Song Dan		CHN	5.7.90		JT	57.74	60.68- 08
Song Xiaodan		CHN	23.1.93		JT	59.21	56.56- 12
Soprunova	Anastasiya	KAZ	14.1.86	165/52	100h	13.09	12.95- 12
Sorenson	Nevada	USA	8.1.91	174/62	100h	13.32, 13.18w	15.52- 10
Sormunen	Oona	FIN	2.8.89	168/72	JT	60.56	59.14- 12
Sorna	Rachel	USA	15.4.92		3kSt	9:50.39	10:13.18- 12
Soto	Nercely	VEN	26.8.90	169/55	200	23.31, 23.05w	22.53dt- 12
					400	51.94	53.45- 12
* Soumaré	Myriam	FRA	29.10.86	167/57	100	11.30	11.07- 12
					200	22.83, 22.81w	22.32- 10
Sousa	Joelma	BRA	13.7.84	174/51	400	51.62	51.54- 12
de Souza	Tamara	BRA	8.9.93	185/76	Hep	5814	5900- 12
Souza	Tatum	USA	20.4.92	168/57	Hep	5691(w)	5350- 12
* Spanovic	Ivana	SRB	10.5.90	176/67	LJ	6.82	6.78- 10
Spence	Christine	USA	25.11.81	174/64	400h	54.56	54.21- 08
Spence	Indira	JAM	8.9.86	171/62	100h	12.99	12.92, 12.80Aw, 12.80w- 12
Spence	Neely	USA	16.4.90	163/50	5000	15:26.51	15:27.72- 11
* Spencer	Ashley	USA	8.6.93	168/54	200	23.04	22.99- 12
400	50.28				400h	56.32	59.43- 12
* Spencer	Kaliese	JAM	6.5.87	173/59	200	23.11	23.62- 12
400	50.19				400h	54.22	52.79- 11
* Spencer	Lavern	LCA	23.8.84	180/54	HJ	1.95A	1.98- 10
Spenner	Sami	USA	21.3.91	168/59	Hep	5897	5593- 12
* Spiegelburg	Silke	GER	17.3.86	173/64	PV	4.79	4.82- 12
Spiler	Barbara	SLO	2.1.92	184/79	HT	70.88	71.25- 12
Spiljard	Amanda	NED	18.9.89		Hep	5681	5534- 08
* Spotáková	Barbora	CZE	30.6.81	182/80	JT	62.33	72.28- 08
Sprunger	Ellen	SUI	5.8.86	172/62	Hep	6081	6124- 12
* Stahl	Linda	GER	2.10.85	174/72	JT	65.76	66.81- 10
* Stambolova	Vania	BUL	28.11.83	173/63	400h	54.77	53.68- 11
Stanciu	Daniela	ROU	15.10.87	175/57	HJ	1.91i, 1.90	1.88- 11
Stanková	Eliska	CZE	11.11.84		DT	58.40	58.70- 12
Starostina	Oksana	RUS	1.4.88		HJ	1.92	1.92- 12
Starygina	Yekaterina	RUS-J	26.8.95	177/73	JT	58.59	51.81- 11
Steacy	Heather	CAN	14.4.88	175/73	HT	65.27	72.16- 12
Steel	Gemma	GBR	12.11.85		HMar	70:19	70:46dh- 12
Stefanídi	Ekateríni	GRE	4.2.90	172/63	PV	4.45Ai, 4.40	4.51- 12
Steinkamp	Lisa	GER	17.8.90	178/58	LJ	6.58	6.38- 12
Stellingwerff	Hilary	CAN	7.8.81	160/48	1500	4:07.51	4:05.08- 12
					1M	4:30.95, 4:30.50i	4:28.62- 07
* Stepaniuk/Licwinko	Kamila	POL	22.3.86	183/66	HJ	1.99	1.93- 09
Steryíou	Adonía	GRE	7.7.85	180/58	HJ	1.95	1.97- 08
Stewart	Briana	USA	13.10.90	174/62	100h	13.15, 13.02Aw	13.57- 12
Stewart	Emily	GBR	24.12.91		3kSt	9:51.42	9:53.47- 12
* Stewart	Kerron	JAM	16.4.84	175/61	100	10.96	10.75- 09
200	22.71		21.99- 08		400	51.83	52.08- 08
Stoddart	Shevon	JAM	21.11.82	165/52	400h	55.54	54.47- 05
Storm	Ida	SWE	11.10.91	189/86	HT	68.05	66.48- 12
Stowers	Jasmin	USA	23.9.91	175/64	100h	13.00, 12.88w	12.88, 12.86w- 11
* Strachan	Anthonique	BAH	22.8.93	168/57	200	22.32	22.53- 12
* Straneo	Valeria	ITA	5.4.76	168/44	10k	32:30.56	32:15.87- 12
HMar	69:23		67:46- 12		Mar	2:25:58	2:23:44- 12
Stratton	Brooke	AUS	12.7.93		LJ	6.53	6.60- 11
Straub	Julia	GER	10.4.86	180/60	HJ	1.88i, 1.86	1.93i- 07, 1.91- 06
Strokova	Yekaterina	RUS	17.12.89	184/80	DT	63.80	63.52- 12
* Strutz	Martina	GER	4.11.81	160/57	PV	4.65	4.80- 11
Stuart	Bianca	BAH	17.5.88	168/52	LJ	6.73	6.81, 6.91w- 11
Stublic	Lisa	CRO	18.5.84	158/44	HMar	69:18	70:31- 12
					Mar	2:25:44	2:30:46- 11
Stuy	Hrystyna	UKR	3.2.88	168/57	100	11.33	11.32- 10
					200	22.86	22.66- 12
^ Styopina	Viktoriya	UKR	21.2.77	178/58	HJ	1.90	2.02- 04
Su Xinyue		CHN	8.11.91	179/70	DT	61.67	60.32- 12
Su Yingqiu		CHN-J	1.2.95		20kW	1:32:07	1:40:25- 12
* Sudareva	Olga	BLR	22.2.84	176/63	LJ	6.82	6.85- 12
Sudarushkina	Viktoriya	RUS	2.9.90	176/76	JT	62.77	60.59- 12

Name		Nat	Born	Ht/Wt	Event	2013 Mark	Pre-2013 Best
Suga	Katsuki	JPN-J	1.2.94	153/33	10k	32:42.96	
Suh Hae-an		KOR	1.7.85	181/93	JT	56.72	57.61- 10
* Suhr	Jennifer	USA	5.2.82	180/64	PV	5.02Ai, 4.91	4.92- 08
Sui Liping		CHN	1.5.91	174/65	JT	56.83	56.27- 11
Sujew	Diana	GER	2.11.90	166/52	1500	4:05.62	4:05.71- 12
					3000	8:47.68	-0-
Sujew	Elina	GER	2.11.90	164/51	1500	4:08.82	4:07.36- 12
					3000	8:57.56	-0-
Sukenaga	Hitomi	JPN	4.5.88	168/76	JT	55.59	54.35- 09
* Sum	Eunice	KEN	2.9.88	168/54	800	1:57.38	1:59.13- 12
					1500	4:02.05	4:04.26- 12
Summers	Jeré	USA	21.5.87	172/84	DT	58.04	59.59- 12
* Sun Huanhuan		CHN	15.3.90	161/50	20kW	1:27:36	1:29:46- 11
Sun Lu		CHN	19.2.88		Hep	5580	5506- 12
Sun Taifeng		CHN	26.8.82	185/105	DT	60.53	64.98- 07
Sun Xueping		CHN	10.12.88	160/48	20kW	1:33:11	1:32:46- 12
Sun Yan		CHN	30.3.91		TJ	13.82i, 13.68	14.00- 10
Sun Yawei		CHN	17.10.87	169/55	100h	13.01	12.94- 11
* Sutej	Tina	SLO	7.11.88	173/58	PV	4.35	4.61- 11
Sutherland	Andrea	JAM	26.5.88		400h	56.99	56.44- 11
Suver	Mattie	USA	10.9.87	163/48	10k	32:29.14	33:37.73- 09
Suzuki	Ayuko	JPN	8.10.91	153/38	5000	15:31.45	15:34.15- 12
* Svobodová	Jirina	CZE	20.5.86	175/69	PV	4.76	4.72- 12
Swiety	Justyna	POL	3.12.92	170/56	400	52.22	52.81- 12
Szabó	Barbara	HUN	17.2.90	175/59	HJ	1.92Ai, 1.89A	1.88Ai, 1.86- 12
Szlezak	Matylda	POL	11.1.89	165/54	3kSt	9:54.61	9:39.87- 12
Szwarnóg	Agnieszka	POL	28.12.86	167/59	20kW	1:31:33	1:30:56- 12
Tabares	Carolina	COL	18.6.86		5000	15:35.30	16:29.69A- 12
Tabashnyk	Kateryna	UKR-J	15.6.94	178/60	HJ	1.90i, 1.90	1.87- 12
* Tadesse	Feyse	ETH	19.11.88	167/53	HMar	68:35	68:44- 11
					Mar	2:21:06	2:23:07- 12
Tadesse	Yeshimebet	ETH	.88	173/54	Mar	2:26:17	2:27:45- 10
* Takacs	Julia	ESP	29.6.89	171/55	20kW	1:28:44	1:30:14- 10
Takashima	Yuka	JPN	12.5.88	153/42	10k	32:06.70	32:22.93- 10
Takechi	Shiho	JPN	18.8.90	159/44	5000	15:29.85	15:40.64- 09
Takenaka	Risa	JPN	6.1.90	159/41	10k	32:10.66	
Takuncheva	Irina	RUS	14.11.90		400h	57.02	58.06- 12
* Talay	Alina	BLR	14.5.89	164/54	100h	12.78	12.71- 12
Tamkova	Alena	RUS	30.5.90	168/58	400	51.17	53.93- 12
Tamsett	Lara	AUS	12.10.88	161/47	10k	32:16.13	32:01.60- 12
* Tan Jian		CHN	20.1.88	179/80	DT	64.40	64.45- 12
Tanaka	Hanae	JPN	12.2.90	160/48	10k	32:25.05	32:27.56- 11
					HMar	69:18	
Tanaka	Misato	JPN	21.12.89	155/44	10k	32:45.67	
Tanaka	Tomomi	JPN	25.1.88	154/40	10k	32:39.90	32:27.70- 12
					HMar	70:03	69:47- 12
Tappin	Jess	GBR	17.5.90		Hep	5676(w)	5288- 12
* Tarasova	Irina	RUS	15.4.87	183/110	SP	19.20	19.35- 12
Tarasova	Zlata	RUS	2.12.86	172/77	HT	68.00	67.63- 12
* Tarmoh	Jeneba	USA	27.9.89	165/59	100	10.93	11.07- 12, 10.94w- 11
					200	22.70, 22.15w	22.28- 11
Tate	Cassandra	USA	11.9.90	174/64	400h	55.45	55.22- 12
Tavares	Maria Eleonor	POR	24.9.85	164/55	PV	4.43i, 4.32	4.50- 11
Tavernier	Alexandra	FRA	13.12.93	170/75	HT	70.79	70.62- 12
Teferi	Senbere	ETH-J	3.5.95	159/45	1500	4:04.55	4:06.06- 12
Tenorio	Angela	ECU-Y	27.1.96	167/59	100	11.30A, 11.41, 11.24w	11.59A- 12
					200	23.13	23.74A- 12
Terlecki	Josephine	GER	17.2.86	183/84	SP	18.36	18.87- 12
Terrero	Indira	ex-CUB	29.11.85	161/52	400	51.97	50.98A, 50.5- 08, 51.00- 07
Terzic	Amela	SRB	2.4.93	169/50	1500	4:05.69	4:07.59- 12
Tesfay	Haftamnesh	ETH-J	28.4.94	162/48	5000	15:22.79	16:20.0A- 11
* Theisen-Eaton	Brianne	CAN	18.12.88	180/64	100h	13.13	13.09A, 13.30- 12
					Hep	6530	6440- 12
Theron/Nel	Wenda	RSA	30.7.88	169/52	400h	55.80	55.36A, 55.79- 12
Thiam	Ami Mbacké	SEN	10.11.76	183/70	400	52.06	49.86- 01
Thiam	Nafissatou	BEL-J	19.8.94	184/68	HJ	1.92	1.88- 12
					Hep	6298	5916- 12
Thomas	Alexis	USA	25.12.90	167/72	HT	65.48	64.62- 12
Thomas	Charlene	GBR	6.5.82	166/52	1500	4:03.74mp	4:05.06- 10
Thomas	Kandace	USA	6.2.93		100	11.12w	
Thomas	LaTavia	USA	17.12.88	173/	800	2:00.61	1:59.67- 11

Name		Nat	Born	Ht/Wt	Event	2013 Mark	Pre-2013 Best
Thomas	Reyare	TTO	23.11.87	169/59	200	23.23, 23.04w	23.36- 12
Thomas	Shanieka	JAM	2.2.92	180/64	TJ	14.15	13.64, 13.96w- 12
* Thomas	Vashti	USA	21.4.90	175/60	200	22.75A, 23.33 24.29i, 24.20w- 12, 24.45- 10	
100h	12.61, 12.56w	13.03- 07, 13.02w- 12			LJ	6.68	6.97- 12
Thompson	Turquoise	USA	31.7.91	178/66	400h	54.99	55.28- 12
^ Thurmond	Aretha	USA	14.8.76	181/98	DT	62.21	65.86- 04, 66.23dh- 03
Thweatt	Laura	USA	17.12.88	165/54	10k	32:15.51	33:49.00- 11
Tikhonova	Olesya	RUS	22.1.90		TJ	13.70	13.89- 12
^ Timbilil	Alice	KEN	16.6.83	155/45	HMar	70:42+	68:56- 07
					Mar	2:28:36	2:25:03- 10
Tirop	Agnes	KEN-J	23.10.95	159/44	3000	8:39.13	
					5000	14:50.36	15:36.74- 12
* Titimets	Hanna	UKR	5.3.89	173/62	400h	54.63	54.69- 11
Tkachuk	Anastasiya	UKR	20.4.93	168/56	800	2:01.67	2:00.37- 11
Toader	Eliza-Raluca	ROU	12.5.90	170/54	JT	60.80	56.61- 12
Toma	Carmen	ROU	28.3.89	168/50	TJ	14.14, 14.56w	14.29- 09
* Tomasevic	Dragana	SRB	4.6.82	175/80	DT	63.04	63.63- 06
Tomb	Stine	NOR	27.8.86	170/61	400h	57.13	56.38- 11
Tomic	Marina	SLO	30.4.83	167/55	100h	12.94	13.04- 12
Tomlin	Renee	USA	21.11.88	160/52	1500	4:08.09	4:11.31- 12
Tong Lingling		CHN	25.1.92		20kW	1:33:40	1:31:32- 12
Torro	Elina	FIN	22.7.86	166/50	TJ	13.69	13.72- 09
Townsend	Tiffany	USA	14.6.89	163/50	100	11.19	11.13- 09, 11.09w- 11
					200	22.26	22.58- 11
Tracey	Nikita	JAM	18.9.90	173/63	400h	56.08	56.89- 10
Tracey	Ristananna	JAM	5.9.92	170/61	400	52.25	51.95- 11
					400h	54.52	54.58- 11
Tran Hue Hoa		VIE	8.8.91		TJ	14.12	13.76- 11
Traynor	Nicol	USA	6.5.89	170/54	3kSt	9:55.91	10:02.94- 11
Troneva	Natalya	RUS	24.2.93	181/84	SP	17.25	16.76i- 12, 16.74- 11
* Trost	Alessia	ITA	8.3.93	188/68	HJ	2.00i, 1.98	1.92- 12
* Trotter	Deedee	USA	8.12.82	180/63	200	22.85, 22.54w	23.04- 06
					400	51.67	49.64- 07
					HT	67.59	60.82- 12
Tsareva	Yelizaveta	RUS	15.3.93				
Tsega	Muluhabt	ETH	11.9.89	165/54	10k	31:48.21	
Tsegay	Gudaf	ETH-Y	23.1.97		1500	4:07.27	
* Tsegaye	Tirfi	ETH	25.11.84	165/54	Mar	2:23:23	2:21:19- 12
Tsyhotska	Ruslana	UKR	23.3.86	166/49	TJ	14.26	14.53- 12
Tufa	Mestawet	ETH	14.9.83	157/49	HMar	70:03	68:48- 10
					Mar	2:26:20	
Tuliamok-Bolton	Aliphine	KEN	5.4.89	161/50	5000	15:18.86	15:26.07- 12
10k	32:07.20		32:39.35- 12		HMar	69:16dh	
Tumayeva	Yelerna	RUS	24.8.89		1500	4:09.98	4:15.40- 12
Tverdohlib	Margaryta	UKR	2.6.91	179/70	LJ	6.67i, 67.53	6.80- 12
^ Twell	Stephanie	GBR	17.8.89	168/54	1500	4:08.30mx	4:02.54- 10
3000	8:50.17mx, 8:58.57	8:42.75mx-10, 8:50.89- 08			5000	15:18.60	14:54.08- 10
Tyler	Lakaevia	USA	4.4.88		100h	12.92w	13.52- 11
* Tyminska	Karolina	POL	4.10.84	176/64	Hep	6360	6544- 11
* Uceny	Morgan	USA	10.3.85	168/55	1000	2:37.61	2:38.44i- 12
					1500	4:08.49	4:00.06- 11
Udoh	Christy	NGR	30.9.91	173/58	200	23.17, 23.13i	22.72- 12
Udras	Grete	EST	11.3.88	180/59	HJ	1.90	1.92i- 11, 1.89- 09
Uehara	Miyuki	JPN-J	22.11.95	153/38	5000	15:33.21	15:47.88- 12
Ugen	Lorraine	GBR	22.8.91	178/64	LJ	6.77	6.74, 6.83w- 12
Uhl	Lisa	USA	31.8.87	163/50	5000	15:29.64	14:55.74- 10
					10k	32:41.98	31:12.80- 12
Urbaniak	Lena	GER	31.10.92	175/95	SP	17.58	17.21i- 12, 16.65- 11
Urrutia	Yorsiris	COL	26.6.86		TJ	14.08	12.94- 10
Uslu	Binnaz	TUR	12.3.85	165/55	3kSt	9:45.22	9:24.06- 11
^ Usovich	Ilona	BLR	14.11.82	170/60	400	52.19	50.31- 07
* Ustalova	Kseniya	RUS	14.1.88	177/65	400	50.60	49.92- 10
Utriainen	Sanni	FIN	5.2.91	170/64	JT	59.35	59.31- 12
Utura	Sule	ETH	8.2.90	169/50	5000	14:59.74	14:44.21- 10
					10k	30:55.50	31:41.54- 12
* Valyukevich	Viktoriya	RUS	22.5.82	177/63	LJ	6.55	6.72- 07
					TJ	14.36	14.85- 08
Van Buskirk	Kate	CAN	9.6.87	178/63	1500	4:07.36	4:11.45- 12
2000	5:40.70				5000	15:29.72	
Van Dalen	Lucy	NZL	18.11.88	168/53	5000	15:21.08	15:23.54- 12
Van Hessche	Hanne	BEL	5.7.91	180/60	HJ	1.88i, 1.87	1.87- 09
van Leuveren	Nicky	NED	20.5.90	165/55	400	52.14	53.87- 10

Name		Nat	Born	Ht/Wt	Event	2013 Mark	Pre-2013 Best
van Tonder	Chante	RSA	25.5.93		200	23.14Aw?	24.05- 12
VanBuren	Cleo	USA	1.5.86	175/60	100	11.34, 11.12w	11.10- 06
Vasilyeva	Svetlana	RUS	24.7.92		20kW	1:29:56	1:28:30- 12
Vaskovskaya	Irina	BLR	2.4.91		TJ	13.76	13.55- 11
Vassell	Kadene	NED	29.1.89	173/56	200	23.03w	23.49- 12
Vaughan	Shelbi	USA-J	24.8.94	185/91	DT	58.93	60.59- 12
Vaughn	Sara	USA	16.5.86	155/48	3kSt	9:47.58	
* Veldáková	Dana	SVK	3.6.81	179/60	LJ	6.43, 6.54w	6.56- 08
					TJ	14.31	14.51- 08, 14.59w- 10
Veldáková	Jana	SVK	3.6.81	177/59	LJ	6.69	6.72- 08, 6.88w- 10
* Veneva-Mateeva	Venelina	BUL	13.6.74	179/61	HJ	1.93i, 1.90	2.04- 01
Verstegen	Sanne	NED	10.11.85	164/54	800	2:01.15	2:02.17- 12
Veshkurova	Tatyana	RUS	23.9.81	180/70	400	51.90	49.99- 06
^ Vessey	Margaret	USA	23.12.81	172/53	800	2:01.02	1:57.84- 09
Vetter	Anouk	NED	4.2.93	177/62	Hep	5872	5764- 12
Vicenzino	Tania	ITA	1.4.86	168/59	LJ	6.50	6.57, 6.65w- 12
Vichy	Ariannis	CUB	18.5.89	170/70	HT	70.46	71.50- 12
Vifquin	Clemence	FRA	9.6.86	169/59	100h	13.13	13.25- 11
* Viljoen	Sunette	RSA	6.1.83	170/70	JT	64.51	69.35- 12
Vinson	Joenisha	USA	18.4.90		Hep	5563	5227- 11
Virbalyte	Brigita	LTU	1.2.85	165/50	20kW	1:30:55	1:31:08- 12
Visser	Nadine	NED-J	9.2.95	175/63	Hep	5774	5475- 12
Vitobello	Chiara	ITA	21.10.91	173/59	HJ	1.87	1.89- 12
Viuf	Katherine	USA	23.5.87	175/61	PV	4.50	4.50- 12
Vivod	Eva	SLO-J	7.8.94	174/65	JT	56.98	50.79- 12
* Vlasic	Blanka	CRO	8.11.83	192/75	HJ	2.00	2.08- 09
Vlasova	Alisa	RUS	16.9.90		TJ	13.73	13.86i- 10, 13.60- 08
Vlasova	Natalya	RUS	19.7.88	164/48	3kSt	9:40.90	9:37.41- 12
Volkova	Nina	RUS	26.8.84	168/70	HT	67.49	67.82- 12
Vollmer	Lindsay	USA	10.9.92	168/59	Hep	6086	5517- 12
von Eynatten	Victoria	GER	6.10.91	174/54	PV	4.40i, 4.22	4.37i- 12, 4.30- 11
Voronina	Yekaterina	UZB	16.2.92		Hep	5599	5287- 11
Voss	Stephanie	GER	9.9.89	173/60	LJ	6.56	6.49- 12
Vucenovic	Marija	SRB	3.4.93	172/70	JT	55.60	57.12- 12
Vyatkina	Natalya	BLR	10.2.87	176/50	TJ	14.40	14.32- 11
Wade	Bettie	USA	11.9.86	178/64	Hep	6018	6143- 12
Wafula	Lydia	KEN	15.2.88		800	2:01.72	2:00.27- 12
Wainaina	Beatrice	KEN	23.11.93	161/45	10k	32:38.71	
Wairimu	Susan	KEN	11.10.92	160/40	5000	15:20.49	15:23.9- 11
Waite	Lennie	GBR	4.2.86	173/60	3kSt	9:56.19	9:48.35- 12
Waithera	Mariam	KEN-J	23.12.96	162/44	5000	15:33.47	
Walker	Alesha	USA	9.4.88	167/61	LJ	6.57Ai, 6.38, 6.51w	6.50- 08
* Walker	Melaine	JAM	1.1.83	173/58	100h	13.05	12.75- 06
Walker	Shanique	USA	20.11.93		100h	13.16	13.64- 12
Wallace	LaTosha	USA	25.3.85	173/60	400h	56.03	55.18- 12
Wallace	Lea	USA	19.12.88	163/52	800	2:00.30	2:01.33- 12
					1500	4:09.13	4:10.77- 11
Wambui	Tabitha	KEN	29.12.83	162/52	1500	4:08.43A	4:14.67A- 09
Wang Chunyu		CHN-J	17.1.95		800	2:02.05	2:01.34- 11
Wang Di		CHN	30.8.92		20kW	1:33:48	1:38:58- 12
Wang Dou		CHN	18.5.93	167/56	100h	13.09	13.40- 12, 13.36w- 11
Wang Huiqin		CHN	7.2.90	168/52	TJ	13.74	14.16- 12
Wang Lu		CHN	22.12.91	178/83	HT	69.39	65.80- 12
Wang Min		CHN	2.12.91		20kW	1:32:33	1:35:14- 11
Wang Ping		CHN	28.7.90		JT	57.83	59.14- 12
Wang Qingling		CHN	14.1.93		Hep	5785	5668- 12
Wang Rong		CHN-Y	1.7.96		TJ	14.09i, 13.69	13.76- 12
Wang Shanshan		CHN	16.6.87	168/50	20kW	1:29:30	1:29:43- 12
Wang Xiaolan		CHN	5.2.90		20kW	1:33:30	1:37:57- 11
Wang Xueqin		CHN	1.1.91		10k	32:09.95	31:55.31- 11
Wang Yang		CHN	14.2.89	185/65	HJ	1.92	1.92- 12
Wang Yingliu		CHN	1.3.92		20kW	1:32:01	1:33:52- 12
* Wang Zheng		CHN	14.12.87	174/108	HT	74.90	71.19- 10
Wanjiru	Pauline	KEN	11.10.84		HMar	70:28	75:47- 11
Wanjiru	Rosemary	KEN-J	9.12.94	158/45	1500	4:09.90	4:18.15- 12
3000	8:49.32		8:51.97- 12		5000	15:30.41	15:26.07mx- 11, 15:40.35- 12
Wanjugu	Felista	KEN	18.2.90	158/46	5000	15:21.57	15:02.28mx, 15:23.69- 08
					HMar	69:36	
Washington	Ariana	USA-Y	4.9.96	175/59	100	11.39, 11.18wA, 11.20w	11.45- 12
					200	23.18, 23.05Aw	23.41- 12
Watanabe	Yuko	JPN	3.11.87	151/41	10k	32:38.62	32:27.89mx- 11, 32:52.91- 12
					Mar	2:25:56	2:29:20- 12

	Name		Nat	Born	Ht/Wt	Event	2013 Mark	Pre-2013 Best
	Watson	Sage	CAN-J	20.6.94		400h	56.81A, 58.20	58.04- 12
	Webb	Julia	USA	14.2.83	176/61	3kSt	9:55.36	10:15.58- 11
	Wei Xiaojie		CHN	20.11.89		5000	15:30.61	15:52.57- 12
						10k	32:17.78	33:25.69- 11
	Wei Yongli		CHN	11.10.91	168/55	100	11.29	11.36- 11
	Weightman	Laura	GBR	1.7.91	172/56	1500	4:05.36	4:02.99- 12
	2000	5:44.22				3000	8:43.46mx	9:02.62- 12
	Weightman	Lisa Jane	AUS	16.1.79	157/44	Mar	2:26:05	2:27:32- 12
	Weir	Jillian	CAN	9.2.93	177/78	HT	64.70	
	Weissenbach	Amy	USA-J	16.6.94	171/57	800	2:00.98	2:02.04- 11
	Weit	Inna	GER	5.8.88	171/58	200	23.10	23.08- 12
	Weitzel	Michelle	GER	18.6.87	181/63	LJ	6.57. 6.687w	6.64- 11
*	Wells	Kellie	USA	18.7.82	163/57	100h	12.54, 12.47w	12.48- 12, 12.35w- 11
	Wells	Sarah	CAN	10.11.89	163/56	400h	55.65	55.71A, 55.97- 12
	Westbrook	Ky	USA-Y	25.2.96	175/64	100	11.33	11.63, 11.42w- 12
	White	Cierra	USA	29.4.93	165/52	100	11.09	11.57, 11.34w- 12
						200	22.89	23.44- 12
	White	Mandy	USA	23.10.88	170/60	100	11.07	11.44- 12, 11.39w- 11
	White	Skylar	USA	15.9.91	170/86	SP	17.07i	17.42i- 12, 17.16- 11
	Whittle	Laura	GBR	27.6.85	169/55	3000	8:57.63mx	8:50.37- 09
						5000	15:35.24	15:26.96- 08
*	Whyte	Angela	CAN	22.5.80	170/56	100h	12.66A, 12.76, 12.52w	12.63, 12.55w- 07
*	Whyte	Rosemarie	JAM	8.9.86	175/66	400	50.86	49.84- 11
	Williams	Alisha	USA	5.2.82	167/52	5000	15:09.73	15:24.82- 12
*	Williams	Charonda	USA	27.3.87	167/55	100	11.07	11.13, 10.95w- 12
						200	22.71	22.52- 12, 22.39w- 09
	Williams	Danielle	JAM	14.9.92	168/59	100	11.24A, 11.41, 11.35w	11.54, 11.46w- 11
						200	22.62A	24.42- 10, 24.39w- 11
	Williams	Jodie	GBR	28.9.93	170/55	100	11.32+, 11.23w	11.18- 11
						200	22.92	22.79- 10
	Williams	Kendell	USA-J	14.6.95		Hep	5572A	5578- 12
*	Williams	Kimberly	JAM	3.11.88	169/66	TJ	14.62, 14.78w	14.53- 12
^	Williams	Lauryn	USA	11.9.83	157/57	100	11.00	10.88- 05, 10.86w- 08
						200	22.58	22.27- 05
*	Williams	Shericka	JAM	17.9.85	170/64	400	51.86	49.32- 09
	Williams	Shermaine	JAM	4.2.90	174/62	100h	12.93, 12.84w	12.78, 12.65w- 12
	Williams	Tiffany	USA	5.2.83	158/57	400h	55.04	53.28- 07
	Williams	Danielle	JAM	14.9.92	168/60	100h	12.69	13.32, 13.13w- 11
*	Williams-Mills	Novlene	JAM	26.4.82	170/57	400	50.01	49.63- 06
*	Wilson	Ajee'	USA-J	8.5.94	169/55	800	1:58.21	2:00.91- 12
	Wilson	Heather	USA	13.6.90	169/55	1500	4:08.25	4:18.14- 12
*	Wilson	Nickiesha	JAM	28.7.86	173/64	400h	54.94	53.97- 07
	Winatho	Wassanee	THA	30.6.80	170/57	Hep	5818	5889- 07
^	Wineberg	Mary	USA	3.1.80	178/61	400	51.58	50.24- 07
	Wisdom	Alyssa	USA	.91	170/73	SP	16.97i, 16.58	15.79- 12
	Wisil	Toea	PNG	1.1.88	168/63	200	23.09w	23.46- 12
^	Wisniewska	Joanna	POL	24.5.72	178/84	DT	59.64	63.97- 99
	Witek	Marcelina	POL-J	2.6.95	168/58	JT	56.20	51.97- 12
*	Wlodarczyk	Anita	POL	8.8.85	178/95	HT	78.46	78.30- 10
	Wloka	Anna	POL	14.3.93	176/80	SP	16.83	16.28- 11
^	Woods	Shareese	USA	20.2.85	165/57	200	23.10	22.71- 10, 22.70w- 06
	Woodward	Krista	CAN	22.11.84	163.59	JT	60.15	59.34- 12
	Wootton	Katrina	GBR	2.9.85	165/54	5000	15:30.82	15:33.38- 12
	Wortham	Ellen	USA	5.1.90	174/61	400h	55.78	55.55- 12
	Wright	Phoebe	USA	30.8.88	170/57	800	2:00.20	1:58.22- 10
	Wu Sha		CHN	21.10.87	172/64	PV	4.40	4.40- 09
	Wu Shujiao		CHN	19.6.92	159/48	100h	12.93	12.98- 12
	Wu You		CHN	18.12.92		JT	55.77	53.51- 12
	Wyciszkiewicz	Patrycja	POL-J	8.1.94	164/46	400	51.56	52.76- 12
	Xia Xiao		CHN	6.6.91		400h	56.25	57.71- 12
	Xiao Huimin		CHN	1.3.92		10k	32:16.77	32:23.49- 11
*	Xie Limei		CHN	27.6.86	173/57	TJ	14.39	14.90- 07
	Xie Yuchen		CHN-Y	12.5.96	179/79	DT	56.34	49.46- 11
	Xu Huiqin		CHN	4.9.93		PV	4.30	4.40- 11
	Xu Liqin		CHN	6.2.90	170/55	20kW	1:30:00	1:35:50- 10
	Xu Yaozhi		CHN	20.5.90		20kW	1:33:48	1:36:59- 12
	Xue Juan		CHN	10.2.86	174/65	JT	56.17	62.93- 03
	Yakovenko	Olga	UKR	1.6.87	159/46	20kW	1:30:38	1:32:07- 12
	Yalew	Genet	ETH	31.12.92	159/44	5000	15:04.38	14:48.43- 12
	Yamauchi	Ai	JPN-J	6.12.94	167/	JT	55.73	52.84- 12
	Yamazaki	Rina	JPN	6.5.88	162/50	10k	32:41.16	32:56.28- 12

Name		Nat	Born	Ht/Wt	Event	2013 Mark	Pre-2013 Best
Yang Fei		CHN	20.7.87	186/90	DT	59.74	60.43- 12
Yang Mingxia		CHN	13.1.90	163/44	20kW	1:28:48	1:28:56- 08
Yang Xinli		CHN	7.2.88		JT	61.37	59.88- 12
Yang Yanbo		CHN	9.3.90		DT	63.30	63.32- 12
* Yaroshchuk	Anna	UKR	24.11.89	176/67	400h	54.77	54.35- 12
Yarushkina	Viktoriya	RUS	4.4.91	164/50	100	11.23	11.64- 11
Yaryshkina	Aleksandra	RUS-J	10.6.94		HJ	1.88	1.85i, 1.79- 11
Yastrebova	Nataliya	UKR	12.10.84	175/57	TJ	14.04, 14.15w	14.50- 11
Yatsevich	Anastasiya	BLR	18.1.85		20kW	1:32:31	1:29:30- 11
Yepimashko	Vera	BLR	10.7.76	181/74	SP	18.10i, 17.66	18.95- 10
Yeryomina	Lyudmila	RUS	8.8.91	171/60	PV	4.50i, 4.45	4.40i- 12, 4.30- 11
Yildirim ¶	Elif	TUR	11.2.90	170/55	400h	56.56	57.33- 12
Yokosawa	Eina	JPN	29.10.92	157/41	5000	15:35.73	15:37.27- 12
Young	Jessica	USA	6.4.87	160/50	100	11.16	11.14, 11.08w- 11
					200	23.00	22.99- 11
Yüksel-Ayhan	Burcu	TUR	3.5.90	182/58	HJ	1.92	1.94- 11
Yumanova	Irina	RUS	6.11.90		20kW	1:27:00	1:26:47- 12
Yurchenko	Polina	RUS	20.8.93		LJ	6.51	6.47- 12
Yuryeva	Tetyana	UKR-J	21.1.95		DT	57.08	53.55- 12
* Zadorina	Kseniya	RUS	2.3.87	173/59	400	50.55	50.87- 10
Zagré	Anne	BEL	13.3.90	178/69	100h	12.84	12.79- 12
Zaldívar	Liuba M.	CUB	5.4.93	161/54	TJ	14.20	13.91, 14.18w- 12
Zang Milama	Ruddy	GAB	6.6.87	156/46	100	11.24	11.03- 12
* Zaripova	Yuliya	RUS	26.4.86	172/54	1500	4:02.56	4:01.70- 12
					3kSt	9:28.00	9:05.02- 12
Zavyalova	Valeriya	RUS	16.1.88	172/82	TJ	14.11i, 13.99, 14.12w	14.37- 12
Zbären	Noemi	SUI-J	12.3.94	177/65	100h	13.04	13.15- 12
* Zelinka	Jessica	CAN	3.9.81	172/62	100h	12.86, 12.66w	12.65- 12
Zeltner	Michelle	SUI	22.12.91	184/72	Hep	5717	5442w, 5399- 11
Zemlyak	Olga	UKR	16.1.90	165/55	400	51.95	51.82- 12
Zhang Li		CHN	17.1.89	174/65	JT	62.07	64.74- 12
Zhang Luyu		CHN-J	18.8.94		HJ	1.87	1.80- 12
Zhang Meixia		CHN	20.1.91		10k	32:18.86	33:39.43- 11
Zhang Rong		CHN	5.1.83	174/65	100h	13.13	13.06- 11
* Zhang Wenxiu		CHN	22.3.86	182/108	HT	75.58	76.99- 12
Zhang Xuhong		CHN-J	2.1.94		20kW	1:32:07	1:44:41- 12
Zhang Yingning		CHN	6.1.90	170/42	PV	4.30	4.46i- 07, 4.45- 06
Zhao Jing		CHN	18.2.92		20kW	1:33:24	1:32:45- 11
Zhao Yanmin		CHN	26.1.91	168/55	400	52.15	52.62- 11
Zheng Xingjuan		CHN	20.3.89	184/60	HJ	1.93	1.95- 09, 1.94i- 10
Zhou Kang		CHN	24.12.89	165/54	20kW	1:30:58	1:31:49- 09
Zhou Tongmei		CHN	4.4.88		20kW	1:30:28	1:30:35- 05
Zhudina	Valentyna	UKR	12.3.83	160/49	3kSt	9:32.26	9:27.26- 08
Zhukovskaya	Oksana	RUS	12.9.84		LJ	7.02	6.77A- 07, 6.64- 12, 6.95w- 11
Zhushman #	Olena	UKR	30.12.85	172/58	800	2:00.81	1:59.32- 12
Zinchuk	Hanna	BLR-J	4.2.94		HT	66.36	63.54- 12
Zolotuhina	Natalya	UKR	4.1.85	180/76	HT	67.03	72.22- 11
Zubkovska	Oksana	UKR	15.7.81	175/62	LJ	6.58	6.71- 07
Züblin	Linda	SUI	21.3.86	171/60	Hep	6057	6018- 08
Zych	Anna	POL	15.5.88	166/55	TJ	13.78	13.59- 12
Zyuganova	Yekaterina	RUS	18.1.91		SP	16.95i	17.03- 12

Top women athletes who gave birth in 2013 included

Tatyana Arkhipova, Christine Arron, Stephanie Brown Trafton, Vivian Cheruiyot, Elegayehu Dibaba, Aleksandra Fedoriva, Lauren Fleshman, Yevgeniya Isakova, Bianca Kappler, Mary Keitany, Lucia Klocová, Viktoriya Klyugina, Yekaterina Kosketskaya, Ingvill Måkestad Bovim, Lee McConnell, Cydonie Mothersill, Priscilla Lopes-Schliep, Chaunté Lowe, Anna Mishchenko, Sara Moreira, Anna Nazarova, Jo Pavey, Anastasiya Potapova, Monika Pyrek, Olga Rypakova, Melanie Seeger, Liliya Shobukhova, Barbora Spotáková, Olga Tereshkova, Tatyana Tomashova, Biljana Topic, Dire Tune, Anita Weyermann.
Jan 2014: Marestella Torres PHI.

WORLD INDOOR LISTS 2014 – MEN

60 METRES

! In late 2013, # Oversized track (over 200m)

Mark	First	Last	Nat	DOB	Pos	Meet	Venue	Date
6.47	James	Dasaolu	GBR	5.9.87	1h2	GP	Birmingham	15 Feb
6.48	Jimmy	Vicaut	FRA	27.2.92	1h1	GP	Birmingham	15 Feb
6.48A	Marvin	Bracy	USA	15.12.93	1	NC	Albuquerque	23 Feb
6.49	Yuniel	Pérez	CUB	16.2.85	1	Winter	Moskva	2 Feb
6.49A	Trell	Kimmons	USA	13.7.85	2	NC	Albuquerque	23 Feb
6.49	Kim	Collins	SKN	5.4.76	1		Praha (O2)	25 Feb
6.49	Richard	Kilty	GBR	2.9.89	1	WI	Sopot	8 Mar
6.50A	Tosin	Ogunode	QAT	2.3.94	1		Flagstaff	25 Jan
6.50		Dasaolu			1	v3N	Glasgow	25 Jan
6.50		Pérez			1		Düsseldorf	30 Jan
6.50		Dasaolu			1	NC	Sheffield	8 Feb
6.50		Dasaolu			1	GP	Birmingham	15 Feb
6.50	Nesta	Carter	JAM	11.10.85	1s1	WI	Sopot	8 Mar
6.51A	Femi	Ogunode (10)	QAT	15.5.91	2		Flagstaff	25 Jan
6.51A	Mike	Rodgers	USA	24.4.85	1h4	NC	Albuquerque	22 Feb
6.52	Jason	Rogers	SKN	31.8.91	1		Toronto	15 Feb
6.52A	D'Angelo	Cherry	USA	1.8.90	1s2	NC	Albuquerque	23 Feb
6.52A	Joe	Morris	USA	4.10.89	3	NC	Albuquerque	23 Feb
6.52	Dwain	Chambers	GBR	5.4.78	2		Praha (O2)	25 Feb
6.52		Su Bingtian	CHN	29.8.89	4	WI	Sopot	8 Mar
6.52	Gerald	Phiri	ZAM	6.10.88	5	WI	Sopot	8 Mar
6.52A	Dentarius	Locke	USA	12.12.89	1	NCAA	Albuquerque	15 Mar
6.54	Warren	Fraser	BAH	8.7.91	1		Birmingham AL	18 Jan
6.54A	Diondre	Batson (20)	USA	13.7.92	1h1	NCAA	Albuquerque	14 Mar
6.54A	Cameron	Burrell	USA	11.9.94	1h2	NCAA	Albuquerque	14 Mar
6.55	Clayton	Vaughn	USA	15.5.92	1		Lincoln NE	8 Feb
6.55A	Aaron	Brown	CAN	27.5.92	1		Albuquerque	15 Feb
6.55	Adam	Harris	GUY	21.7.87	1		Allendale	21 Feb
6.55A	Sean	McLean	USA	23.3.92	4	NC	Albuquerque	23 Feb
6.55	Kimmari	Roach	JAM	21.9.90	2s2	WI	Sopot	8 Mar
6.56	Prezel	Hardy	USA	1.6.92	1		College Station	18 Jan
6.56A	Keith	Ricks	USA	9.10.90	2s1	NC	Albuquerque	23 Feb
6.56	Lucas	Jakubczyk	GER	28.4.85	2	ISTAF	Berlin	1 Mar
6.57A	Ryan	Milus (30)	USA	19.9.90	2	NCAA	Albuquerque	15 Mar
6.58	Sam	Effah	CAN	29.12.88	1		Edmonton	18 Jan
6.58A	Mark	Jelks	USA	10.4.84	1		Air Force Academy	15 Feb
6.58A	Jeffrey	Henderson	USA	19.2.89	2h3	NC	Albuquerque	22 Feb
6.58	Reza	Ghasemi	IRI	24.7.87	2h4	WI	Sopot	7 Mar
6.58	Dariusz	Kuc	POL	24.4.86	2h5	WI	Sopot	7 Mar

Mark	First	Last	Nat	DOB	Date		Mark	First	Last	Nat	DOB	Date
6.59	Sean	Safo-Antwi	GBR	31.10.90	18 Jan		6.60A	Antwan	Wright	USA	17.11.93	14 Mar
6.59A	Tatum	Benard-Taylor	USA	8.9.94	25 Jan		6.61	Christophe	Lemaitre	FRA	11.6.90	1 Feb
6.59	Alex	Schaf	GER	28.4.87	8 Feb		6.61	Devin	Jenkins	USA	16.2.94	1 Feb
6.59	Chijindu	Ujah	GBR	5.3.94	8 Feb		6.61	Samuel	Francis	QAT	27.3.87	15 Feb
6.59	Yoshihide	Kiryu (40)	JPN-J	15.12.95	9 Feb		6.61	Christian	Blum	GER	10.3.87	22 Feb
6.60	Leshon	Collins	USA	11.12.93	11 Jan		6.61A	Nic	Bowens	USA	28.6.93	1 Mar
6.60	Rion	Pierre	GBR	24.11.87	26 Jan		6.61	Dontae	Richards-Kwok	CAN	1.3.89	6 Mar
6.60A	Raymond	Bozmans	USA	16.12.94	1 Feb		6.62	Marcus	Rowland	USA	11.3.90	18 Jan
6.60	Tevin	Hester	USA	10.1.94	7 Feb		6.62A	Jermaine	Brown (60)	JAM	4.7.91	24 Jan
6.60	Markesh	Woodson	USA	6.9.93	7 Feb		6.62	Dominique	Hubert	USA	4.11.90	1 Feb
6.60A	Gavin	Smellie	CAN	26.6.86	8 Feb		6.62	Jalen	Miller	USA-J	17.6.95	7 Feb
6.60	T.J.	Lawrence	CAN	26.2.91	15 Feb		6.62A	B.J.	Lawrence	SKN	27.12.89	8 Feb
6.60A	Cordero	Gray	USA	9.5.89	22 Feb		6.62	Danny	Talbot	GBR	1.5.91	8 Feb
6.60A	Jeremy	Dodson	USA	30.8.87	22 Feb		6.62	Nickel	Ashmeade	JAM	7.4.90	8 Feb
6.60A	Ryan	Bailey (50)	USA	13.4.89	23 Feb		6.62	Hugh	Graham	USA	10.10.92	28 Feb
6.60	Gabriel	Mvumvure	ZIM	23.4.88	8 Mar		6.62	Bolade	Ajomale	CAN-J	31.8.95	1 Mar

Best at low altitude

6.50	Bracy	1	Mill	New York (Arm)	15 Feb
6.54	Rodgers	1		Houston	1 Feb
6.54	Cherry	2	Mill	New York (Arm)	15 Feb
6.55	Morris	2		Boston (R)	8 Feb

6.55	F Ogunode	1s2	WI	Sopot	8 Mar
6.57	Burrell	1		Fayetteville	14 Feb
6.59	A Brown	18 Jan		6.61	Locke	14 Feb
6.59	Ricks	30 Jan		6.62	Kimmons	11 Jan
6.61	Batson	1 Feb		6.62	R Bailey	1 Feb
				6.62	Milus	1 Mar

55m:	6.11	Odean	Skeen	JAM	28.8.94	1s2		Lubbock	31 Jan
100m:	10.19	Jaysuma	Saidy Ndure	NOR	1.1.84	1		Florø	15 Feb

200 METRES

Mark	First	Last	Nat	DOB	Pos	Meet	Venue	Date
20.32A	Diondre	Batson	USA	13.7.92	1r1	NCAA	Albuquerque	14 Mar
20.34A	Dedric	Dukes	USA	2.4.92	1r2	NCAA	Albuquerque	14 Mar
20.51	Wallace	Spearmon	USA	24.12.84	1	Tyson	Fayetteville	15 Feb
20.52	Pavel	Maslák	CZE	21.2.91	1	NC	Praha (Strom)	16 Feb
20.52A	Carvin	Nkanata	USA	6.5.91	2r1	NCAA	Albuquerque	14 Mar
20.53A	Aaron	Brown	CAN	27.5.92	1r1		Albuquerque	14 Feb

20.55A	Arman	Hall		USA	14.2.94	3r1	NCAA	Albuquerque			14 Mar
20.56	Robin	Erewa		GER	24.6.91	1r1	NC	Leipzig			23 Feb
20.57A	Tyreek	Hill		USA	1.3.94	2r2	NCAA	Albuquerque			14 Mar
20.58	Christophe	Lemaitre (10)		FRA	11.6.90	1		Metz			28 Feb
20.59A	Jermaine	Brown		JAM	4.7.91	1r6		Albuquerque			14 Feb

20.62	Sebastian	Ernst	GER	11.10.84	23 Feb		20.70	Prezel	Hardy	USA	1.6.92	18 Jan
20.63	Marek	Niit	EST	9.8.87	15 Feb		20.70	Lalonde	Gordon	TTO	25.11.88	8 Feb
20.66	Shavez	Hart	BAH	9.6.92	1 Mar		20.75A	Bruno	Hortelano (20)	ESP	18.9.91	14 Mar
20.66A	Aldrich	Bailey	USA	6.2.94	14 Mar		**Oversized track**					
20.68	Deon	Lendore	TTO	28.10.92	8 Feb		20.73	Raheem	Mostert	USA	9.4.92	1 Mar
20.68	Chris	Clarke	GBR	25.1.90	9 Feb		20.74	Wayne	Gordon	USA	20.12.93	1 Mar

Best at low altitude

20.55	Dukes	1h1	SEC	College Station	28 Feb		20.69	A Bailey	1 Mar
20.58	Hall	1h4	SEC	College Station	28 Feb		20.74	Brown	8 Feb

300 METRES

32.15	Pavel	Maslák		CZE	21.2.91	1	Flanders	Gent			9 Feb
32.47	Lalonde	Gordon		TTO	25.11.88	1	Mill	New York (Arm)			15 Feb
32.59	Manteo	Mitchell		USA	6.7.87	2	Mill	New York (Arm)			15 Feb
32.71	Renny	Quow	TTO	25.8.87	15 Feb		32.82	Karol	Zalewski	POL	7.8.93	9 Feb

400 METRES

45.03	Deon	Lendore		TTO	28.10.92	1r1	SEC	College Station			1 Mar
45.17	Lalonde	Gordon		TTO	25.11.88	1		Boston (A)			8 Feb
45.21A		Lendore				1r1	NCAA	Albuquerque			15 Mar
45.24	Pavel	Maslák		CZE	21.2.91	1	WI	Sopot			8 Mar
45.28	Arman	Hall		USA	14.2.94	2r2	SEC	College Station			1 Mar
45.39	Vernon	Norwood		USA	10.4.92	1r2	SEC	College Station			1 Mar
45.58	Chris	Brown		BAH	15.10.78	2	WI	Sopot			8 Mar
45.60A	Kyle	Clemons		USA	27.8.90	1r1	NC	Albuquerque			23 Feb
45.62A	David	Verburg		USA	14.5.91	1r2	NC	Albuquerque			23 Feb
45.64A	Mike	Berry		USA	10.12.91	3r1	NCAA	Albuquerque			15 Mar
45.71	Nigel	Levine (10)		GBR	30.4.89	1	GP	Birmingham			15 Feb
45.74A	Chris	Giesting		USA	10.12.92	2r2	NCAA	Albuquerque			15 Mar
45.84A	Kind	Butler		USA	8.4.89	2r2	NC	Albuquerque			23 Feb
45.89	Luguelín	Santos		DOM	12.11.93	2	XLG	Stockholm			6 Feb
45.90A	James	Harris		USA	19.9.91	1h1	NCAA	Albuquerque			14 Mar
45.91A	Calvin	Smith		USA	10.12.87	2	NC	Albuquerque			23 Feb
45.92A	Clayton	Parros		USA	11.12.90	3r3	NC	Albuquerque			23 Feb
45.94	Hugh	Graham		USA	10.10.92	2r2	SEC	College Station			1 Mar

45.95	Gustavo	Cuesta	DOM	14.11.88	8 Feb		46.15	Michael	Bingham	GBR	13.4.86	15 Feb
45.95	Najee	Glass	USA	12.6.94	1 Mar		46.16	Luke	Lennon-Ford	GBR	5.5.89	15 Feb
45.96	Neil	Braddy (20)	USA	18.10.91	14 Feb		46.18	Akheem	Gauntlett	JAM	26.8.90	14 Feb
46.05A	Pat	Feeney	USA	29.12.91	14 Mar		46.21	Quincy	Downing	USA	16.1.93	1 Mar
46.06A	Brycen	Spratling	USA	10.3.92	14 Mar		46.22A	Emmanuel	Tugumisirize (30)	UGA	30.11.88	14 Mar
46.09	Richard	Buck	GBR	14.11.86	15 Feb		46.24A	Jermaine	Brown	JAM	4.7.91	8 Feb
46.10	Marek	Niit	EST	9.8.87	14 Feb		46.25	Aldrich	Bailey	USA	6.2.94	1 Mar
46.11	Edino	Steele	JAM	6.1.87	25 Feb		46.25	Nery	Brenes	CRC	25.9.85	7 Mar

Best at low altitude

45.74	Clemons	3	WI	Sopot	8 Mar		46.20	Harris	1 Feb		46.21	Verburg	8 Mar

Oversized track

45.57	Brycen	Spratling		USA	10.3.92	1		Geneva OH			15 Feb
46.03	Zack	Bilderback	USA		1 Mar		46.24	Steven	Solomon	AUS	16.5.93	1 Mar
46.05	Emmanuel	Tugumisirize	UGA	30.11.88	25 Jan							

600 METRES

1:15.31	Mohamed	Aman		ETH	10.1.94	1	Winter	Moskva			2 Feb
1:15.75	Adam	Kszczot		POL	2.9.89	2	Winter	Moskva			2 Feb
1:15.83	Abdulrahman Musaeb	Balla		QAT	19.3.89	3	Winter	Moskva			2 Feb
1:16.08	Stepan	Poistogov		RUS	14.12.86	4	Winter	Moskva			2 Feb
1:16.11	Erik	Sowinski	USA	21.12.89	2 Feb	1:16.48	Guy	Learmonth	GBR	24.4.92	25 Jan

500 METRES: 1:00.36 Pavel Maslák   CZE 21.2.91   1   Praha (O2)   25 Feb

800 METRES

1:44.52	Mohamed	Aman		ETH	10.1.94	1	GP	Birmingham			15 Feb
1:44.99	André	Olivier		RSA	29.12.89	2	GP	Birmingham			15 Feb
1:45.08		Aman				1	XLG	Stockholm			6 Feb
1:45.22	Adam	Kszczot		POL	2.9.89	3	GP	Birmingham			15 Feb
1:45.22	Andrew	Osagie		GBR	19.2.88	4	GP	Birmingham			15 Feb
1:45.42		Kszczot				1		Düsseldorf			30 Jan
1:45.56	Marcin	Lewandowski		POL	13.6.87	2	XLG	Stockholm			6 Feb
1:45.69	Kevin	López		ESP	12.6.90	3	XLG	Stockholm			6 Feb
1:45.98#	Edward	Kemboi		KEN	12.12.91	1		Ames			15 Feb
1:46.30	Abraham	Rotich		BRN	26.6.93	1		Karlsruhe			1 Feb
1:46.52	Drew	Windle		USA	22.7.92	1		Allendale			14 Feb
1:46.53	Stepan	Poistogov (10)		RUS	14.12.86	1	NC	Moskva			18 Feb
1:46.55	Thijmen	Kupers		NED	4.10.91	3h2	WI	Sopot			7 Mar

1:46.71	Michael	Rutt	USA	28.10.87	1		Boston (A)	7 Feb

1:46.77	Jeremiah	Mutai	KEN	27.12.92	6 Feb
1:46.82	Mark	English	IRL	18.3.93	2 Feb
1:46.82	Abdulrahman Musaeb Balla		QAT	19.3.89	6 Feb
1:46.84	Erik	Sowinski	USA	21.12.89	30 Jan
1:46.98	Brian	Gagnon	USA	8.5.87	7 Feb

1:47.07	Robby	Andrews	USA	29.3.91	7 Feb
1:47.18	Ivan	Nesterov	RUS	10.2.85	18 Feb
1:47.29	Nick	Symmonds (20)	USA	30.12.83	7 Mar
1:47.43	Guy	Learmonth	GBR	24.4.92	15 Feb
1:47.45	Brannon	Kidder	USA	18.11.93	8 Feb

1000 METRES

2:15.96	Ilham Tanui	Özbilen	TUR	5.3.90	1		Istanbul	20 Feb
2:16.76	David	Torrence	USA	26.11.85	1		Boston(A)	2 Mar
2:16.87	Nate	Brannen	CAN	8.9.82	2		Boston(A)	2 Mar
2:17.63	Pierre-Ambroise	Bosse	FRA	11.5.92	1	Mill	New York (Arm)	15 Feb
2:17.67	Marcin	Lewandowski	POL	13.6.87	1		Metz	28 Feb

2:18.55	Richard	Peters	GBR	18.2.90	2 Mar
2:18.63	Erik	Sowinski	USA	21.12.89	15 Feb

2:18.87	Nick	Symmonds	USA	30.12.83	15 Feb
2:19.24	Nader	Belhanbel	MAR	1.7.94	28 Feb

1500 METRES

3:35.0	Mohamed	Moustaoui	MAR	2.4.85	1	XLG	Stockholm	6 Feb
3:35.2	Ayanleh	Souleiman	DJI	3.12.92	2	XLG	Stockholm	6 Feb
3:35.3	Bethwel	Birgen	KEN	6.8.88	3	XLG	Stockholm	6 Feb
3:35.85	Silas	Kiplagat	KEN	20.8.89	1	Winter	Moskva	2 Feb
3:36.10		Birgen			2	Winter	Moskva	2 Feb
3:36.4	Aman	Wote	ETH	18.4.84	4	XLG	Stockholm	6 Feb
3:36.41	Collins	Cheboi	KEN	25.9.87	3	Winter	Moskva	2 Feb
3:36.8	Caleb	Ndiku	KEN	9.10.92	5	XLG	Stockholm	6 Feb
3:37.02	Nixon	Chepseba	KEN	12.12.90	1		Karlsruhe	1 Feb
3:37.3	Fouad	El Kaam	MAR	27.5.88	6	XLG	Stockholm	6 Feb
3:37.35	Homiyu	Tesfaye (10)	GER	23.6.93	2	GP	Birmingham	15 Feb
3:37.37	Marcin	Lewandowski	POL	13.6.87	3	GP	Birmingham	15 Feb
3:37.42	Mekonnen	Gebremedhin	ETH	11.10.88	2		Karlsruhe	1 Feb
3:37.42+	Lawi	Lalang	KEN	15.6.91	1	in 1M	New York	15 Feb
3:37.49	Johan	Cronje	RSA	13.4.82	3		Karlsruhe	1 Feb
3:37.62+	Nick	Willis	NZL	25.4.83	2	in 1M	New York	15 Feb

3:37.63	Zakaria	Maazouzi	MAR	15.6.85	15 Feb
3:37.83	Abdelaati	Iguider	MAR	25.3.87	7 Mar
3:37.89+	Will	Leer	USA	15.4.85	15 Feb
3:38.22	Ilham Tanui	Özbilen	TUR	5.3.90	2 Feb
3:38.28+	Chris	O'Hare (20)	GBR	23.11.90	15 Feb
3:38.79	Jakub	Holusa	CZE	20.2.88	2 Feb
3:38.88+	Craig	Miller	USA	3.8.87	15 Feb

3:38.89+	Garrett	Heath	USA	3.11.85	25 Jan
3:38.99+	Lee	Emanuel	GBR	24.1.85	25 Jan
3:39.01+	Nate	Brannen	CAN	8.9.82	15 Feb
3:39.14	David	McCarthy	IRL	3.8.88	2 Feb
3:39.21	Bernard	Koros	KEN	7.5.94	9 Feb
3:39.22+	Leonel	Manzano	USA	12.9.84	15 Feb
3:39.36	Adel	Mechaal	ESP	5.12.90	15 Feb

1 MILE

3:52.47	Will	Leer	USA	15.4.85	1	Mill	New York (Arm)	15 Feb
3:52.88	Lawi	Lalang	KEN	15.6.91	2	Mill	New York (Arm)	15 Feb
3:53.02	Nick	Willis	NZL	25.4.83	3	Mill	New York (Arm)	15 Feb
3:54.30	Lee	Emanuel	GBR	24.1.85	1		New York (Arm)	25 Jan
3:54.32	Nate	Brannen	CAN	8.9.82	4	Mill	New York (Arm)	15 Feb
3:54.59	Garrett	Heath	USA	3.11.85	2		New York (Arm)	25 Jan
3:54.66	Chris	O'Hare	GBR	23.11.90	5	Mill	New York (Arm)	15 Feb
3:55.09	Craig	Miller	USA	3.8.87	6	Mill	New York (Arm)	15 Feb

3:56.73	Leonel	Manzano	USA	12.9.84	15 Feb
3:56.84#	Jordan	Williamsz (10)	AUS	21.8.92	15 Feb
3:57.00#	Matt	Hillenbrand	USA	8.5.92	15 Feb
3:57.25#	Jeremy	Rae	CAN	19.5.91	8 Feb

3:57.27	Richard	Peters	GBR	18.2.90	8 Feb
3:57.29	Chris	Gowell	GBR	26.9.85	8 Feb
3:57.48#	Frezer	Legesse	USA	4.6.90	15 Feb
3:57.71#	Luc	Bruchet	CAN	23.2.91	1 Feb

2000 METRES

4:54.74	Bernard	Lagat	USA	12.12.74	1	Mill	New York (Arm)	15 Feb
4:55.35	Cam	Levins	CAN	28.3.89	2	Mill	New York (Arm)	15 Feb
4:56.99	David	Torrence	USA	26.11.85	3	Mill	New York (Arm)	15 Feb
4:57.17	Abiyot	Abinet	ETH	10.5.89	1		Metz	28 Feb
4:57.35	Andrew	Bumbalough	USA	14.3.87	4	Mill	New York (Arm)	15 Feb
4:57.56	Evan	Jager	USA	8.3.89	5	Mill	New York (Arm)	15 Feb

5:00.18	Donn	Cabral	USA	12.12.89	15 Feb

5:00.84	Soufiyan	Bouqantar	MAR	30.8.93	28 Feb

3000 METRES

7:34.13	Hagos	Gebrhiwet	ETH	11.5.94	1		Boston (R)	8 Feb
7:34.68+	Galen	Rupp	USA	8.5.86	1	in 2M	Boston (A)	25 Jan
7:34.70	Dejen	Gebremeskel	ETH	24.11.89	2		Boston (R)	8 Feb
7:34.87	Ryan	Hill	USA	31.1.90	3		Boston (R)	8 Feb
7:35.73		Gebrhiwet			1	GP	Birmingham	15 Feb
7:36.27	Caleb	Ndiku	KEN	9.10.92	1		Karlsruhe	1 Feb
7:36.53		Gebremeskel			2	GP	Birmingham	15 Feb
7:37.10	Yenew	Alamirew	ETH	27.5.90	3	GP	Birmingham	15 Feb
7:37.11	Augustine	Choge	KEN	21.1.87	4	GP	Birmingham	15 Feb
7:37.17+	Bethwel	Birgen	KEN	6.8.88	2	in 2M	Boston (A)	25 Jan
7:37.22	Paul Kipsiele	Koech	KEN	10.11.81	5	GP	Birmingham	15 Feb
7:37.40	Garrett	Heath (10)	USA	3.11.85	4		Boston (R)	8 Feb

7:37.62	Andrew	Bumbalough	USA	14.3.87	5		Boston (R)	8 Feb
7:38.51	Bernard	Lagat	USA	12.12.74	4		Karlsruhe	1 Feb
7:38.77	Albert	Rop	BRN	17.7.92	1	Flanders	Gent	9 Feb
7:39.14	Isiah	Koech	KEN	19.12.93	3	Flanders	Gent	9 Feb
7:39.55	Elroy	Gelant	RSA	25.8.86	4	Flanders	Gent	9 Feb
7:39.56	Abdelaati	Iguider	MAR	25.3.87	5	Flanders	Gent	9 Feb
7:39.73	Hayle	Ibrahimov	AZE	18.1.90	6		Boston (R)	8 Feb
7:40.00	Mohamed	Moustaoui	MAR	2.4.85	3		Düsseldorf	30 Jan
7:40.85	Ayanleh	Souleiman	DJI	3.12.92	4		Düsseldorf	30 Jan
7:41.59	Cam	Levins (20)	CAN	28.3.89	7		Boston (R)	8 Feb
7:42.05	Yomif	Kejelcha	ETH-Y	1.8.97	1		Bordeaux	26 Jan
7:42.95	Will	Leer	USA	15.4.85	8		Boston (R)	8 Feb
7:43.61	Ali	Kaya	TUR	20.4.94	6		Düsseldorf	30 Jan
7:44.16	Zane	Robertson	NZL	14.11.89	6h2	WI	Sopot	7 Mar
7:44.20#	Lawi	Lalang	KEN	15.6.91	1		Seattle	1 Feb
7:44.73	Othmane	El Goumri	MAR	28.5.92	2		Bordeaux	26 Jan
7:44.78	Edwin	Soi	KEN	3.3.86	7		Düsseldorf	30 Jan
7:44.87	Soufiyan	Bouqantar	MAR	30.8.93	1		Mondeville	1 Feb
7:44.88	Hassan	Mead	USA	28.8.89	9		Boston (R)	8 Feb
7:45.12	Lee	Emanuel (30)	GBR	24.1.85	7	GP	Birmingham	15 Feb
7:45.21	Samuel	Chelanga	KEN	23.2.85	10		Boston (R)	8 Feb
7:45.49	Andrew	Vernon	GBR	7.1.86	4h1	WI	Sopot	7 Mar
7:45.62	Abdelhadi	Labäli	MAR	26.4.93	3		Mondeville	1 Feb
7:46.15	Collis	Birmingham	AUS	27.12.84	6h1	WI	Sopot	7 Mar
7:46.36	Antonio	Abadía	ESP	2.7.90	7h2	WI	Sopot	7 Mar
7:46.55	Ben	Blankenship	USA	15.12.88	11		Boston (R)	8 Feb
7:46.73	Jonathan	Mellor	GBR	27.12.86	8	GP	Birmingham	15 Feb

7:47.20#	Edward	Cheserek	KEN	2.2.94	1	Mar		7:49.05	Craig	Miller	USA	3.8.87	8 Feb
7:47.50	Youness	Essalhi (40)	MAR	20.2.93	26	Jan		7:49.26	Łukasz	Parszczynski	POL	4.5.85	23 Feb
7:47.54	Thomas	Farrell	GBR	23.3.91	15	Feb		7:49.36	Yoann	Kowal	FRA	28.5.87	26 Jan
7:48.32	Hiss Bachir	Youssouf	DJI	87	1	Feb		7:49.99	Yegor	Nikolayev	RUS	12.2.88	25 Feb
7:48.60	Abdellah	Haidane	ITA	28.3.89	8	Feb		7:50.31	Andrew	Poore	USA	3.12.88	15 Feb

2 MILES   8:07.41 Galen Rupp   USA   8.5.86   1   Boston (A)   25 Jan:

5000 METRES

Boston (A) 16 Jan: 1. Galen Rupp USA 13:01.26, 2. Samuel Chelanga KEN 13:04.35, 3, Cam Levins CAN 13:19.16

60 METRES HURDLES

7.45	Pascal	Martinot-Lagarde	FRA	22.9.91	1		Mondeville	1 Feb
7.45	Omo	Osaghae	USA	18.5.88	1	WI	Sopot	9 Mar
7.46	Jeff	Porter	USA	27.11.85	2		Mondeville	1 Feb
7.46		Martinot-Lagarde			2	WI	Sopot	9 Mar
7.47	Garfield	Darien	FRA	22.12.87	3	WI	Sopot	9 Mar
7.49		Martinot-Lagarde			1h2		Mondeville	1 Feb
7.49		Martinot-Lagarde			1	NC	Bordeaux	22 Feb
7.50		Osaghae			1s1	WI	Sopot	9 Mar
7.50		Martinot-Lagarde			2s1	WI	Sopot	9 Mar
7.51	Dayron	Robles	CUB	19.11.86	1		Praha (O2)	25 Feb
7.53	William	Sharman	GBR	12.9.84	3s1	WI	Sopot	9 Mar
7.53	Andy	Pozzi	GBR	15.5.92	4	WI	Sopot	9 Mar
7.54	Jarret	Eaton	USA	24.6.89	1		Karlsruhe	1 Feb
7.54	Erik	Balnuweit	GER	21.9.88	4s1	WI	Sopot	9 Mar
7.55	Sergey	Shubenkov (10)	RUS	4.10.90	1h2	Winter	Moskva	2 Feb
7.56	Konstantin	Shabanov	RUS	17.11.89	3	Winter	Moskva	2 Feb
7.56A	Dominic	Berger	USA	19.5.86	2	NC	Albuquerque	23 Feb
7.56A	Terrence	Trammell	USA	23.11.78	3	NC	Albuquerque	23 Feb
7.56	Gregor	Traber	GER	2.12.92	5	WI	Sopot	9 Mar
7.57A	Omar	McLeod	JAM	25.4.94	1h1	NCAA	Albuquerque	14 Mar
7.57A	Eddie	Lovett	ISV	25.6.92	1h2	NCAA	Albuquerque	14 Mar
7.58	Kevin	Craddock	USA	25.6.87	2		Karlsruhe	1 Feb
7.59	Andrew	Riley	JAM	6.9.88	4s2	WI	Sopot	9 Mar
7.60A	Aleec	Harris	USA	31.10.90	1		Albuquerque	15 Feb
7.60	Paolo	Dal Molin (20)	ITA	31.7.87	1	NC	Ancona	22 Feb
7.60A	Terence	Somerville	USA	5.11.89	5	NC	Albuquerque	23 Feb
7.60	Konstadínos	Douvalídis	GRE	10.3.87	2=		Praha (O2)	25 Feb

7.61	Ashton	Eaton	USA	21.1.88	1	Feb		7.64	Martin	Mazác	CZE	6.5.90	15 Mar
7.61	Dapo	Akinmoladun	USA	28.2.94	1	Mar		7.65	Demoye	Bogle	USA	8.11.91	10 Jan
7.61A	Wayne	Davis II	TTO	22.8.91	15	Mar		7.65	Donovan	Robertson	USA	8.11.93	1 Mar
7.62	Ladji	Doucouré	FRA	28.3.83	1	Feb		7.65A	Johnathan	Cabral	USA	31.12.92	15 Mar
7.63	Dominik	Bochenek	POL	14.5.87	8	Feb		7.66A	Brendan	Ames	USA	6.10.88	11 Jan
7.63A	Andrew	Brunson	USA	4.4.86	23	Feb		7.66	Rasul	Dabo	POR	14.2.89	28 Feb
7.63	Balázs	Baji	HUN	9.6.89	8	Mar		7.67	Gregory	Sedoc	NED	16.10.81	1 Feb
7.64	Greggmar	Swift (30)	BAR	16.2.91	1	Feb		7.67	Simon	Krauss	FRA	12.2.92	12 Feb

7.67		Xie Wenjun	CHN	11.7.90	15 Feb		7.69	Dimitri	Bascou	FRA	20.7.87	26 Jan
7.67	Koen	Smet (40)	NED	9.8.92	23 Feb		7.69	Damian	Warner	CAN	4.11.89	15 Feb
7.67A	Milan	Ristic	SRB	8.8.91	14 Mar		7.69A	Ray	Stewart	USA	5.4.89	23 Feb
7.68	Chris	Caldwell	USA	6.4.94	14 Feb		7.70	Jordan	Moore	USA	13.12.93	14 Feb
7.68A	Artie	Burns	USA-J	1.5.95	15 Feb		7.70	Aleksey	Dryomin	RUS	10.5.89	18 Feb
7.69	Thomas	Martinot-Lagarde	FRA	7.2.88	18 Jan		7.70	Maksim	Lynsha (50)	BLR	6.4.85	22 Feb

Best at low altitude

| 7.57 | Trammell | 1 | Mill New York (Arm) | 15 Feb |
| 7.57 | Berger | 2 | Mill New York (Arm) | 15 Feb |

7.64	Harris	22 Feb
7.65	Lovett	28 Feb
7.66	Somerville	15 Feb

55mh: 7.05 Omo Osaghae
USA 1h1 Lubbock 14 Feb

HIGH JUMP

Mark	First	Last	Nat	DOB		Pos	Meet	Venue	Date
2.42	Ivan	Ukhov	RUS	29.3.86		1		Praha (O2)	25 Feb
2.41		Ukhov				1		Chelyabinsk	16 Jan
2.40		Ukhov				1		Arnstadt	8 Feb
2.40	Aleksey	Dmitrik	RUS	12.4.84		2		Arnstadt	8 Feb
2.38		Ukhov				1		Novocheboksarsk	11 Jan
2.38		Ukhov				1	NC	Moskva	18 Feb
2.38	Mutaz Essa	Barshim	QAT	24.6.91		1	WI	Sopot	9 Mar
2.38		Ukhov				2	WI	Sopot	9 Mar
2.36		Ukhov				1		Moskva	28 Jan
2.36		Ukhov				1	Winter	Moskva	2 Feb
2.36		Barshim				1	AsiC	Hangzhou	16 Feb
2.36	Andriy	Protsenko	UKR	20.5.88		3	WI	Sopot	9 Mar
2.35		Barshim				1		Malmö	26 Jan
2.34	Erik	Kynard	USA	3.2.91		1	GP	Birmingham	15 Feb
2.34	Daniyil	Tsyplakov	RUS	29.7.92		2	NC	Moskva	18 Feb
2.34	Marco	Fassinotti	ITA	29.4.89		1	NC	Ancona	23 Feb
2.34		Kynard				1	GP	Birmingham	15 Feb
2.33	Lev	Missirov	RUS	4.8.90		3		Arnstadt	8 Feb
2.33	Donald	Thomas	BAH	1.7.84		4		Arnstadt	8 Feb
2.33	(10)	Zhang Guowei	CHN	4.6.91		1	NGP	Beijing	21 Mar
2.32!	Andrey	Silnov	RUS	9.9.84		1		Rostov	21 Dec
	2.29					2=		Chelyabinsk	16 Ja
2.32	Mihai	Donisan	ROU	24.7.88		1	NC	Bucuresti	15 Feb
2.32	Sergey	Mudrov	RUS	8.9.90		3	NC	Moskva	18 Feb
2.32A	James	Harris	USA	19.9.91		1	NCAA	Albuquerque	14 Mar
2.31A	Nick	Ross	USA	8.8.91		1		Albuquerque	24 Jan
2.30	Ivan	Ilyichev	RUS	14.10.86		1		Moskva	12 Jan
2.30	Tom	Parsons	GBR	5.5.84		1		Solihull	19 Jan
2.30	Dusty	Jonas	USA	19.4.86		1		Lincoln NE	24 Jan
2.30	Ricky	Robertson	USA	19.9.90		1		Nashville	24 Jan
2.30	Michael	Mason (20)	CAN	30.9.86		1	Mill	New York (Arm)	15 Feb
2.29	Yevgeniy	Korshunov	RUS	11.4.86		2=		Chelyabinsk	16 Jan
2.29	Derek	Drouin	CAN	6.3.90		1H		Bloomington	24 Jan
2.29A	Marcus	Jackson	USA	8.7.91		3	NCAA	Albuquerque	14 Mar
2.28	Ali Mohamed	Younes Idris	SUD	15.9.89		1	NC	Bordeaux	23 Feb
2.28	Martin	Günther	GER	8.10.86		1	NC	Leipzig	23 Feb
2.27	Dmitriy	Semyonov	RUS	2.8.92		1		Belgorod	22 Jan
2.27	Robbie	Grabarz	GBR	3.10.87		3	GP	Birmingham	15 Feb
2.27	Adónios	Mástoras	GRE	6.1.91		1	BalkC	Istanbul	22 Feb
2.27A	Darius	Purcell	USA	10.1.89		2	NC	Albuquerque	22 Feb

2.26	Aleksandr	Shustov (30)	RUS	29.6.84	16 Jan		2.24	Andrey	Patrakov	RUS	7.11.89	28 Jan
2.26	Mickaël	Hanany	FRA	25.3.83	18 Jan		2.24	Mikhail	Andreyev	RUS	4.4.91	30 Jan
2.26A	Edgar	Rivera	MEX	13.2.91	7 Feb		2.24	Giulio	Ciotti	ITA	5.10.76	1 Feb
2.26	Naoto	Tobe	JPN	31.3.92	11 Feb		2.24	Nikita	Anishchenkov	RUS	25.7.92	2 Feb
2.26	Donte	Nall	USA	27.1.88	22 Feb		2.24	Lukáš	Beer (50)	SVK	23.8.89	4 Feb
2.26	Jaroslav	Bába	CZE	2.9.84	15 Mar		2.24	Matús	Bubeník	SVK	14.11.89	4 Feb
2.25!	Mikhail	Veryovkin	RUS	28.6.91	8 Dec		2.24	Mikhail	Akimenko	RUS-J	6.12.95	8 Feb
	2.24				11 Jan		2.24	Maalik	Reynolds	USA	26.4.92	8 Feb
2.25	Trevor	Barry	BAH	14.6.83	1 Feb		2.24	Luís Joel	Castro	PUR	28.1.91	8 Feb
2.25	Yuriy	Krymarenko	UKR	11.8.83	21 Feb		2.24	Vadim	Vrublevskiy	RUS	18.3.93	8 Feb
2.25	Fernand	Djoumessi	CMR	5.9.89	23 Feb		2.24	Raúl	Spank	GER	13.7.88	8 Feb
2.25		Wang Yu (40)	CHN	18.8.91	8 Mar		2.24	Chris	Baker	GBR	2.2.91	9 Feb
2.24	Arseniy	Rasov	RUS	20.6.92	7 Jan		2.24	Allan	Smith	GBR	6.11.92	9 Feb
2.24	Ryan	Ingraham	BAH	2.11.93	18 Jan		2.24	Montez	Blair	USA	23.10.90	22 Feb
2.24	David	Smith	GBR	14.7.91	25 Jan		2.24	Mateusz	Przybylko (60)	GER	9.3.92	23 Feb
2.24	Garrett	Huyler	USA	15.1.87	25 Jan		2.24	Peter	Horák	SVK	7.12.83	23 Feb
2.24	Wojciech	Theiner	POL	25.6.86	27 Jan		2.24		Guo Jinqi	CHN	21.9.92	8 Mar
							2.24		Sun Zhao	CHN	8.2.90	8 Mar

POLE VAULT

Mark	First	Last	Nat	DOB		Pos	Meet	Venue	Date
6.16	Renaud	Lavillenie	FRA	18.9.86		1	Stars	Donetsk	15 Feb
6.08		Lavillenie				1	Pedros	Bydgoszcz	31 Jan
6.04		Lavillenie				1		Rouen	25 Jan
5.93!		Lavillenie				1		Aulnay-sous-Bois	21 Dec
5.90	Malte	Mohr	GER	24.7.86		1	ISTAF	Berlin	1 Mar
5.84		Lavillenie				1		Aubière	11 Jan

Mark			Nat	DOB	Pos	Meet	Place	Date
5.84		Mohr			1	NC	Leipzig	23 Feb
5.83	Luke	Cutts	GBR	13.2.88	2		Rouen	25 Jan
5.81		Cutts			2	Stars	Donetsk	15 Feb
5.80	Konstadínos	Filippídis	GRE	26.11.86	1	WI	Sopot	8 Mar
5.80	Jan	Kudlicka	CZE	29.4.88	3	WI	Sopot	8 Mar
5.77	Piotr	Lisek	POL	16.8.92	1		Bad Oeynhausen	1 Mar
5.76	Pawel	Wojciechowski	POL	6.6.89	1		Orléans	18 Jan
5.76		Xue Changrui	CHN	31.5.91	1		Nice	8 Feb
5.76	Jérôme	Clavier	FRA	3.5.83	2		Nice	8 Feb
5.76	Thiago	Braz da Silva (10)	BRA	16.12.93	3	Stars	Donetsk	15 Feb
5.75	Kévin	Menaldo	FRA	12.7.92	2		Aubière	11 Jan
5.75	Robert	Sobera	POL	19.1.91	2	Pedros	Bydgoszcz	31 Jan
5.75A	Shawn	Barber	CAN	27.5.94	1	NCAA	Albuquerque	15 Mar
5.71	Alhaji	Jeng	SWE	13.12.81	3		Dessau	27 Feb
5.70!	Dmitriy	Starodubtsev	RUS	3.1.86	1		Chelyabinsk	15 Dec
5.70	Edi	Maia	POR	10.11.87	3		Orléans	18 Jan
5.70A	Sam	Kendricks	USA	7.9.92	1		Albuquerque	14 Feb
5.66		Yang Yancheng	CHN	5.1.88	1cB		Aubière	11 Jan
5.66	Valentin	Lavillenie	FRA	16.7.91	3		Nice	8 Feb
5.66	Damiel	Dossévi (20)	FRA	3.2.83	4		Nice	8 Feb
5.65	Michal	Balner	CZE	12.9.82	2		Praha (Strom)	1 Feb
5.65	Karsten	Dilla	GER	17.7.89	3		Karlsruhe	1 Feb
5.65	Mark	Hollis	USA	1.12.84	1		Blacksburg	8 Feb
5.65	Melker	Svärd-Jacobsson	SWE	8.1.94	3		Potsdam	15 Feb
5.65	Augusto	Dutra de Oliveira	BRA	16.7.90	7	WI	Sopot	8 Mar
5.61	Jack	Whitt	USA	12.4.90	1		Akron	5 Jan
5.60	Anatoliy	Bednyuk	RUS	30.1.89	1		Chelyabinsk	16 Jan
5.60A	Mike	Arnold	USA	13.8.90	3		Reno	17 Jan
5.60	Björn	Otto	GER	16.10.77	1		Cottbus	22 Jan
5.60	Przemyslaw	Czerwinski (30)	POL	28.7.83	5	Pedros	Bydgoszcz	31 Jan
5.60	Łukasz	Michalski	POL	2.8.88	2		Spala	8 Feb
5.60 ·	Andrew	Irwin	USA	23.1.93	1	Tyson	Fayetteville	15 Feb
5.60	Ilya	Mudrov	RUS	17.11.91	1	NC	Moskva	19 Feb
5.60	Anton	Ivakin	RUS	3.2.91	1	NC	Mogilyov	21 Feb
5.60	Igor	Bychkov	ESP	7.3.87	1		Madrid	1 Mar

Mark			Nat	DOB	Date		Mark			Nat	DOB	Date
5.55	Max	Eaves	GBR	31.5.88	11 Jan		5.50A	Victor	Weirich	USA	25.10.87	11 Jan
5.55	Stanley	Joseph	FRA	24.10.91	18 Jan		5.50	Dmitriy	Zhelyabin	RUS	20.5.90	16 Jan
5.55	Eemeli	Salomäki	FIN	11.10.87	25 Jan		5.50A	Hiroki	Ogita	JPN	30.12.87	17 Jan
5.55	Japheth	Cato	USA	25.12.90	15 Feb		5.50	Arnaud	Art	BEL	28.1.93	18 Jan
5.55A	Shawn	Francis (40)	USA	16.12.85	22 Feb		5.50	Vincent	Favretto	FRA	5.4.84	18 Jan
5.55A	Nicholas	Frawley	USA	21.6.88	22 Feb		5.50A	Braydon	Bringhurst	USA		18 Jan
5.55	Theo	Chapelle	FRA	28.5.92	16 Mar		5.50	Dmitriy	Sokolov	RUS	16.1.93	19 Jan
5.53!	Jax	Thoirs	GBR	7.4.93	5 Dec		5.50	Aleksandr	Gripich	RUS	21.9.86	25 Jan
		5.50A			7 Feb		5.50	Nicolas	Homo (60)	FRA	24.11.88	8 Feb
5.52	Mareks	Arents	LAT	6.6.86	18 Jan		5.50	Daichi	Sawano	JPN	16.9.80	9 Feb
5.52	Jake	Blankenship	USA	15.3.94	18 Jan		5.50A	Mike	Woepse	USA	29.5.91	14 Feb
5.51	Rutger	Koppelaar	NED	1.5.93	7 Feb		5.50	Jeff	Coover	USA	1.12.87	15 Feb
5.51	Daniel	Clemens	GER	28.4.92	7 Feb		5.50	Adam	Pasiak	CZE	18.7.90	16 Feb
5.51	Max	Babits	USA	30.5.92	22 Feb		5.50	Artem	Burya	RUS	11.4.86	19 Feb
5.50!	Gayk	Kazaryan	RUS	19.5.90	22 Dec		5.50	Dídac	Salas	ESP	19.5.93	22 Feb
5.50	Jake	Winder (50)	USA	12.11.87	5 Jan		5.50	Florian	Gaul	GER	21.9.91	23 Feb
5.50	Oleksandr	Korchmid	UKR	22.1.82	10 Jan		5.50A	Pauls	Pujats	LAT	6.8.91	15 Mar

LONG JUMP

Mark			Nat	DOB	Pos	Meet	Place	Date
8.39A	Jarrion	Lawson	USA	6.5.94	1	NCAA	Albuquerque	14 Mar
8.30	Aleksandr	Menkov	RUS	7.12.90	1	Winter	Moskva	2 Feb
8.28	Mauro	da Silva	BRA	26.12.86	1	WI	Sopot	8 Mar
8.23	Loúis	Tsátoumas	GRE	12.2.82	1	NC	Pireás	8 Feb
8.23		Li Jinzhe	CHN	1.9.89	2	WI	Sopot	8 Mar
8.22A	Tyron	Stewart	USA	8.7.89	1	NC	Albuquerque	22 Feb
8.22	Corey	Crawford	USA		1		New York (Arm)	28 Feb
8.21	Michel	Tornéus	SWE	26.5.86	3	WI	Sopot	8 Mar
8.18	Ngonidzashe	Makusha	ZIM	11.3.87	1	XLG	Stockholm	6 Feb
8.18	Adrian	Strzalkowski (10)	POL	28.3.90	Q	WI	Sopot	7 Mar
8.13	Christian	Reif	GER	24.10.84	Q	WI	Sopot	7 Mar
8.11	Irving	Saladino	PAN	23.1.83	3	XLG	Stockholm	6 Feb
8.10A	Chris	Benard	USA	4.4.90	1		Albuquerque	14 Feb
8.08	Pavel	Shalin	RUS	15.3.87	1	Mosc Ch	Moskva	23 Jan
8.06A	Jeremy	Hicks	USA	19.9.86	3	NC	Albuquerque	22 Feb
8.06A	Jeffrey	Henderson	USA	19.2.89	4	NC	Albuquerque	22 Feb
8.06	Stefano	Tremigliozzi	ITA	7.5.85	1	NC	Ancona	23 Feb
8.03		Gao Xinglong	CHN	12.3.94	1	NGP	Nanjing	8 Mar
8.02		Wang Jianan	CHN-J	27.8.96	2	NGP	Nanjing	8 Mar
8.01	Luis	Rivera (20)	MEX	21.6.87	Q	WI	Sopot	7 Mar
8.00	Greg	Rutherford	GBR	17.11.86	3	GP	Birmingham	15 Feb

Mark	First	Last	Nat	DOB	Pos	Meet	Venue	Date
7.99	Raymond	Higgs	BAH	24.1.91				14 Feb
7.99	Dino	Pervan	CRO	12.1.91				15 Feb
7.99	Ignisious	Gaisah	NED	20.7.83				7 Mar
7.98	J.J.	Jegede	GBR	3.10.85				28 Jan
7.98	Julian	Howard	GER	3.4.89				22 Feb
7.97A	Ron	Taylor	USA	13.8.90				14 Feb
7.96	Marcos	Chuva	POR	8.8.89				26 Jan
7.96	Tomasz	Jaszczuk	POL	9.3.92				23 Feb
7.95	Aleksandr	Petrov (30)	RUS	19.8.86				23 Jan
7.94	Vasiliy	Kopeykin	RUS	9.3.88				8 Feb
7.94	Saleh Abdelaziz	Al-Haddad	KUW	7.4.86				15 Feb
7.93	Zarck	Visser	RSA	15.9.89				7 Mar
7.91	Guillaume	Victorin	FRA	26.5.90				28 Feb
7.90	Kafétien	Gomis	FRA	23.3.80				23 Feb

Best at low altitude

Mark	Name	Pos	Meet	Venue	Date
8.00	Stewart	9q	WI	Sopot	7 Mar
7.94	Hicks	1		New York (Arm)	7 Feb

TRIPLE JUMP

Mark	First	Last	Nat	DOB	Pos	Meet	Venue	Date
17.37	Lyukman	Adams	RUS	24.9.88	1	WI	Sopot	9 Mar
17.33	Ernesto	Revé	CUB	26.2.92	2	WI	Sopot	9 Mar
17.32	Pedro Pablo	Pichardo	CUB	30.6.93	1		Praha (O2)	25 Feb
17.30	Marian	Oprea	ROU	6.6.82	1	NC	Bucuresti	15 Feb
17.24		Pichardo			3	WI	Sopot	9 Mar
17.21		Oprea			4	WI	Sopot	9 Mar
17.15A	Chris	Carter	USA	11.3.89	1	NC	Albuquerque	23 Feb
17.04	Will	Claye	USA	13.6.91	1		New York (Arm)	25 Jan
16.99A	Chris	Benard	USA	4.4.90	2	NC	Albuquerque	23 Feb
16.89	Karol	Hoffmann	POL	1.6.89	5	WI	Sopot	9 Mar
16.87	Julian	Reid	GBR	23.9.88	1	NC	Sheffield	8 Feb
16.84A	Troy	Doris (10)	USA	12.4.89	3	NC	Albuquerque	23 Feb
16.80	Gaëtan	Saku Bafuanga	FRA	22.7.91	1		Eaubonne	9 Feb
16.80	Latario	Collie-Minns	BAH	10.3.94	1	JUCO	New York	8 Mar
16.78	Fabrizio	Schembri	ITA	27.1.81	1	NC	Ancona	22 Feb
16.74	Dmitriy	Sorokin	RUS	27.9.92	2	NC	Moskva	18 Feb
16.72	Aleksey	Fyodorov	RUS	25.5.91	1		Samara	30 Jan
16.69	Aboubacar	Bamba	FRA	20.6.91	2		Eaubonne	9 Feb
16.65	Daniele	Greco	ITA	1.3.89	1		Ancona	1 Feb
16.63	Igor	Spasovkhodskiy	RUS	1.8.79	3	NC	Moskva	18 Feb
16.61A	Omar	Craddock	USA	26.4.91				23 Feb
16.60	Aleksey	Tsapik (20)	BLR	4.8.88				25 Jan
16.59A	Felix	Obi	USA	15.6.94				15 Mar
16.58	Fabrizio	Donato	ITA	14.8.76				1 Feb
16.55	Pablo	Torrijos	ESP	12.5.92				22 Feb
16.55		Cao Shuo	CHN	8.10.91				9 Mar
16.54	Viktor	Kuznetsov	UKR	17.7.86				21 Feb

Best at low altitude

Mark	Name	Pos	Meet	Venue	Date
16.81	Doris	2		New York (Arm)	25 Jan
16.76	Benard	3		New York (Arm)	25 Jan
16.74	Carter	6	WI	Sopot	9 Mar

SHOT

Mark	First	Last	Nat	DOB	Pos	Meet	Venue	Date
22.23	Ryan	Whiting	USA	24.11.86	1	NC	Albuquerque	23 Feb
22.05		Whiting			1	WI	Sopot	7 Mar
21.79	David	Storl	GER	27.7.90	2	WI	Sopot	7 Mar
21.50	Kurt	Roberts	USA	20.2.88	2	NC	Albuquerque	23 Feb
21.46	Joe	Kovacs	USA	28.6.89	3	NC	Albuquerque	23 Feb
21.37		Whiting			1	Pedros	Bydgoszcz	31 Jan
21.35		Kovacs			1		Boston (R)	8 Feb
21.33		Storl			1		Karlsruhe	1 Feb
21.26	Tom	Walsh	NZL	1.3.92	3	WI	Sopot	7 Mar
21.23	Ryan	Crouser	USA	18.12.92	1		Albuquerque	8 Feb
21.04	Germán	Lauro	ARG	2.4.84	1		Praha (O2)	25 Feb
21.04	Tomasz	Majewski	POL	30.8.81	4	WI	Sopot	7 Mar
21.02	Georgi	Ivanov	BUL	13.3.85	5	WI	Sopot	7 Mar
20.82	Ladislav	Prásil (10)	CZE	17.5.90	1		Jablonec nad Nisou	22 Jan
20.79	Stephen	Mozia	NGR	16.8.93	1		Hanover NH	1 Mar
20.78	Maksim	Sidorov	RUS	13.5.86	1	NC	Moskva	18 Feb
20.78	Jordan	Clarke	USA	10.7.90	4	NC	Albuquerque	23 Feb
20.67	Asmir	Kolasinac	SRB	15.10.84	1		Novi Sad	1 Mar
20.63	Cory	Martin	USA	22.5.85	3		Boston (R)	8 Feb
20.58	Valeriy	Kokoyev	RUS	25.7.88	1	Mosc Ch	Moskva	23 Jan
20.51	Aleksandr	Lesnoy	RUS	28.7.88	2	NC	Moskva	18 Feb
20.51	Borja	Vivas	ESP	26.5.84	1	NC	Sabadell	22 Feb
20.49	Orazio	Cremona	RSA	1.7.89	7	WI	Sopot	7 Mar
20.41	Marco	Fortes (20)	POR	26.9.82	1	NC	Pombal	16 Feb
20.39	Tomás	Stanek	CZE	13.6.91	4		Praha (O2)	25 Feb
20.29!	Curtis	Jensen	USA	1.11.90	1		Charleston	6 Dec
19.77					1		Champaign	22 Feb
20.29	Pavel	Lyzhyn	BLR	24.3.81	1	NC	Mogilyov	21 Feb
20.20	Mason	Finley	USA	7.10.90	1		Laramie	21 Feb
20.17	Andrei	Gag	ROU	7.4.91	2	BalkC	Istanbul	22 Feb
20.15	Anton	Tikhomirov	RUS	29.4.88	1		Sankt Peterburg	8 Feb
20.11	Kole	Weldon	USA	25.3.92	2		Albuquerque	8 Feb
20.07	Chris	Reed	USA	22.7.92	1		Mankato	1 Feb
20.06!	Richard	Chavez	USA	,92	1		Jonesboro	1 Dec
19.98					1		Jonesboro	24 Jan
20.05	Jan	Marcell (30)	CZE	4.6.85	1		Otrokovice	27 Feb
20.02	Carlos	Tobalina	ESP	2.8.85	1		San Sebastián	15 Feb
20.02	Kemal	Mesic	BIH	4.8.85	1		Blacksburg	22 Feb

20.01	Eric		Werskey	USA	17.7.87	3		Albuquerque	8 Feb
20.00	Zack		Lloyd	USA	10.10.84	1		Nampa	15 Feb
19.95	Jonathan	Jones	USA	23.4.91	15 Feb	19.59	Amin	Nikfar	IRI	2.1.81	25 Jan
19.94	Aleksandr	Shapran	RUS	23.6.93	18 Jan	19.56	Arttu	Kangas (50)	FIN	13.7.93	8 Feb
19.93	Antonio	James	USA	7.4.92	28 Feb	19.55	Hüseyin	Atici	TUR	3.5.86	8 Feb
19.90	Bobby	Grace	USA	10.10.90	15 Mar	19.55	Dan	Block	USA	8.1.91	21 Feb
19.89	Paul	Davis	USA	11.9.90	31 Jan	19.51	Leif	Arrhenius	SWE	15.7.86	15 Feb
19.83	Mikhail	Abramchuk (40)	BLR	15.11.92	25 Jan	19.51	Brad	Szypka	USA	13.2.93	15 Mar
19.80	Rafal	Kownatke	POL	24.3.85	22 Feb	19.50	Wesley	Lavong	USA	27.1.91	15 Mar
19.77	O'Dayne	Richards	JAM	14.12.88	7 Mar	19.45	Konstantin	Lyadusov	RUS	2.3.88	18 Feb
19.75	Aleksandr	Bulanov	RUS	26.12.89	25 Jan	19.43	Marco	Schmidt	GER	5.9.83	12 Jan
19.72	Luke	Pinkelman	USA	5.5.88	8 Feb	19.43	Matt	Babicz	USA		1 Feb
19.70	Marin	Premeru	CRO	29.8.90	22 Feb	19.43	Tobias	Dahm	GER	23.5.87	1 Feb
19.68	Jakub	Szyszkowski	POL	21.8.91	27 Feb	19.43	Josh	Freeman (60)	USA	22.8.94	21 Feb
19.65	Tim	Nedow	CAN	16.10.90	16 Feb	19.40	Andy	Novak	USA		14 Feb
19.63	Luka	Rujevic	SRB	14.10.85	1 Mar	19.38	Martin	Stasek	CZE	8.4.89	27 Feb

DISCUS
Berlin 1 Mar ISTAF: 1. Martin Wierig GER 10.6.87 64.82, 2. Piotr Malachowski POL 7.6.83 63.73
3. Robert Urbanek POL 29.4.87 62.27, 4. Robert Harting GER 18.10.84 62.20

WEIGHT

24.27	Michael		Lihrman	USA	6.12.91	1		Madison	21 Feb
24.00	A.G.		Kruger	USA	18.2.79	1		Akron	8 Feb
23.78			Lihrman			1	Big 10	Geneva OH	1 Mar
23.70			Kruger			1	NC	Albuquerque	22 Feb
23.62	Chukwuebuka		Enekwechi	USA/NGR	28.1.93	1		Findlay	31 Jan
23.22	Pawel		Fajdek	POL	4.6.89	1	Pedros	Bydgoszcz	31 Jan
23.07	Nick		Miller	GBR	1.5.93	2	NCAA	Albuquerque	14 Mar
23.05	J.C.		Lambert	USA	12.4.90	2	NC	Albuquerque	22 Feb
22.98	Jon		Lehman	USA	13.12.90	1		Minneapolis	21 Feb
22.80	Jacob		Freeman	USA	5.11.80	3	NC	Albuquerque	22 Feb
22.74	Antonio		James	USA	7.4.92	1		Notre Dame	25 Jan
22.72	Wojciech		Nowicki (10)	POL	22.2.89	2	Pedros	Bydgoszcz	31 Jan
22.27	Justin		Welch	USA	29.9.91	1	NCAA-II	Winston-Salem	14 Mar
22.15	Joe	Frye	USA	20.7.88	24 Jan	22.10	Matthias	Tayala	USA	27.4.93	14 Feb
22.15	Andy	Fryman	USA	3.2.85	22 Feb	21.81	Jordan	Young	CAN	21.6.93	14 Feb
22.14	Markus	Johansson	SWE	8.5.90	23 Feb	21.66	Akil	Mills	USA	8.6.92	14 Feb

HEPTATHLON

6632	Ashton		Eaton	USA	21.1.88	1	WI	Sopot		8 Mar
		6.66	7.78	14.88	2.06		7.64	5.20	2:34.72	
6303	Andrey		Kravchenko	BLR	4.1.86	2	WI	Sopot		8 Mar
		7.12	7.46	15.42	2.21		8.10	5.00	2:41.88	
6259	Thomas		Van Der Plaetsen	BEL	24.12.90	3	WI	Sopot		8 Mar
		7.13	7.67	14.32	2.12		8.16	5.20	2:40.50	
6242	Eelco		Sintnicolaas	NED	7.4.87	1	NC	Apeldoorn		16 Feb
		7.04	7.59	14.66	2.02		8.16	5.40	2:42.21	
6198			Sintnicolaas			4	WI	Sopot		8 Mar
		7.01	7.14	14.39	2.03		8.16	5.40	2:42.21	
6190A	Curtis		Beach	USA	22.7.90	1	NCAA	Albuquerque		15 Mar
		7.06	7.67	12.11	2.06		8.12	5.05	2:28.76	
6188			Van Der Plaetsen			2		Apeldoorn		16 Feb
		7.24	7.78	14.14	2.08		8.16	5.30	2:44.64	
6176	Oleksiy		Kasyanov	UKR	26.8.85	5	WI	Sopot		8 Mar
		6.88	7.54	15.41	2.03		7.85	4.50	2:39.44	
6173	Kai		Kazmirek	GER	28.1.91	6	WI	Sopot		8 Mar
		7.02	7.44	14.06	2.03		8.07	5.20	2:39.51	
6129	Damian		Warner	CAN	4.11.89	7	WI	Sopot		8 Mar
		6.75	7.31	13.86	2.00		7.70	4.60	2:37.98	
6071A	Gray		Horn	USA	18.2.90	1	NC	Albuquerque		22 Feb
		6.96	7.69	13.36	2.07		8.03	4.90	2:48.51	
6044A	Maicel		Uibo (10)	EST	27.12.92	2	NCAA	Albuquerque		15 Mar
		7.16	7.37	13.77	2.12		8.25	5.05	2:43.06	
6039	Gunnar		Nixon	USA	13.1.93	1		Birmingham AL		8 Feb
6022	Pavel		Rudnev	RUS	26.10.92	1	NC	Novocheboksarsk		15 Feb
5996	Ilya		Shkurenyov	RUS	11.1.91	1		Krasnodar		19 Jan
5982	John		Lane	GBR	29.1.89	1	v4N	Sheffield		26 Jan
5973A	Kevin		Lazas	USA	25.1.92	3	NCAA	Albuquerque		15 Mar
5962	Eduard		Mikhon	BLR	7.6.89	1		Gomel		13 Feb
5959	Trey		Hardee	USA	7.2.84	3	NC	Apeldoorn		16 Feb
5951	Carlos Eduardo		Chinin	BRA	3.5.85	1		Tallinn		8 Feb
5942A	Dakotah		Keys	USA	27.9.91	4	NCAA	Albuquerque		15 Mar

5913A	Zach	Ziemek (20)	USA	23.2.93	15 Mar	5864	Alex	McCune	USA	.93	8 Feb
5910	Bastien	Auzeil	FRA	22.10.89	23 Feb	5863	Dominik	Distelberger	AUT	16.3.90	8 Feb
5905	Maksim	Fayzulin	RUS	18.1.92	15 Feb	5863	Artem	Lukyanenko	RUS	30.1.90	8 Feb
5904	Petter	Olson	SWE	14.2.91	9 Feb	5856	Yevgeniy	Sarantsev	RUS	5.8.88	15 Feb
5892	Romain	Martin	FRA	12.7.88	23 Feb	5853	Kaarel	Jõeväli	EST	8.1.90	8 Feb

5837	Japheth	Cato (30)	USA	25.12.90	1 Mar	5766A	Mike	Morgan	USA		15 Mar
5813	Andres	Raja	EST	2.6.82	8 Feb	5765	Felipe	dos Santos	BRA	30.7.94	8 Feb
5805	Richard	Reeks	GBR	6.12.85	26 Jan	5765	Nick	Lebron	USA		15 Mar
5769	Pawel	Wiesiolek	POL	13.8.91	8 Feb	5764	Ben	Gregory	GBR	21.11.90	26 Jan
5768	Jorge	Ureña	ESP	8.10.93	23 Feb	5760A	Marcus	Nilsson	SWE	3.5.91	15 Mar
						5752	Dmitriy	Karpov (40)	KAZ	23.7.81	16 Feb

3000 METRES WALK

| 11:17.66 | Quentin | Rew | NZL | 16.7.84 | 1 | | Sheffield | 5 Jan |
| 11:20.48 | Erik | Tysse | NOR | 4.12.80 | 1 | | Bergen | 18 Jan |

5000 METRES WALK

18:15.54	Andrey	Ruzavin	RUS	28.3.86	1		Samara	30 Jan
18:21.76	Ruslan	Dmytrenko	UKR	22.3.86	2		Samara	30 Jan
18:26.51		Ruzavin			1		Novocheboksarsk	11 Jan
18:29.44	Yohann	Diniz	FRA	1.1.78	1		Reims	26 Jan
18:46.02	Matej	Tóth	SVK	10.2.83	1		Wien	8 Feb
18:57.37	Aleksandr	Yargunkin	RUS	6.1.81	2		Novocheboksarsk	11 Jan
19:00.48	Pyotr	Trofimov	RUS	28.12.83	3		Novocheboksarsk	11 Jan
19:03.05	Anatole	Ibáñez	SWE	14.11.85	2		Wien	8 Feb
19:08.27	Marius	Ziukas	LTU	29.6.85	1	NCp	Vilnius	1 Feb
19:09.86	Mikhail	Ryzhov	RUS	17.12.91	3		Samara	30 Jan

19:13.08	Lukasz	Nowak (10)	POL	18.12.88	23 Feb	19:16.06	Perseus	Karlström	SWE	2.5.90	8 Feb
19:13.25	Aléxandros	Papamihaíl	GRE	18.9.88	2 Feb	19:16.51	Rafal	Augustyn	POL	14.5.84	23 Feb
19:13.77	Rafal	Sikora	POL	17.2.87	23 Feb	19:21.07	João	Vieira	POR	20.2.76	15 Mar
19:14.06	Erik	Tysse	NOR	4.12.80	5 Feb	19:24.59	Sérgio	Vieira	POR	20.2.76	15 Mar

10,000 METRES WALK

Mogilyov 21 Feb NC: 1. Aleksandr Lyakhovich BLR 4.7.89 39:47.97, 2. Ivan Trotskiy BLR 27.5.76 39:53.70

WORLD INDOOR LISTS 2014 – WOMEN

60 METRES

6.98	Shelly-Ann	Fraser-Pryce	JAM	27.12.86	1	WI	Sopot	9 Mar
7.01	Murielle	Ahouré	CIV	23.8.87	2	WI	Sopot	9 Mar
7.03		Ahouré			1		Houston	1 Feb
7.05		Ahouré			1		Houston	17 Jan
7.06		Ahouré			1s1	WI	Sopot	9 Mar
7.06	Tianna	Bartoletta	USA	30.8.85	3	WI	Sopot	9 Mar
7.08A		Bartoletta			1	NC	Albuquerque	23 Feb
7.08		Fraser-Pryce			1s3	WI	Sopot	9 Mar
7.09	Asha	Philip	GBR	25.10.90	1	NC	Sheffield	8 Feb
7.09A	Lekeisha	Lawson	USA	3.6.87	2	NC	Albuquerque	23 Feb
7.10A	Barbara	Pierre	USA	28.4.87	3	NC	Albuquerque	23 Feb
7.10	Michelle-Lee	Ahye	TTO	10.4.92	3s3	WI	Sopot	9 Mar
7.11A	Kya	Brookins	USA	28.7.89	4	NC	Albuquerque	23 Feb
7.11	Gloria	Asumnu	NGR	22.5.85	2s1	WI	Sopot	9 Mar
7.11A	Remona	Burchell (10)	JAM	15.9.91	1	NCAA	Albuquerque	15 Mar
7.12	Verena	Sailer	GER	16.10.85	1	ISTAF	Berlin	1 Mar
7.12A	Dezerea	Bryant	USA	27.4.93	2	NCAA	Albuquerque	15 Mar
7.13	Veronica	Campbell-Brown	JAM	15.5.82	5	WI	Sopot	9 Mar
7.14	Tori	Bowie	USA	27.8.90	2	Mill	New York (Arm)	15 Feb
7.16A	Chauntae	Bayne	USA	4.4.84	5	NC	Albuquerque	23 Feb
7.16A	Jasmine	Todd	USA	23.12.93	3	NCAA	Albuquerque	15 Mar
7.17	Dafne	Schippers	NED	15.6.92	4	GP	Birmingham	15 Feb
7.17	Ruddy	Zang Milama	GAB	6.6.87	1		Praha (O2)	25 Feb
7.17	Tahesia	Harrigan-Scott	IVB	15.2.82	2	ISTAF	Berlin	1 Mar
7.18	Ezinne	Okparaebo (20)	NOR	3.3.88	3		Karlsruhe	1 Feb
7.18A	Shayla	Sanders	USA	6.1.94	2h1	NCAA	Albuquerque	14 Mar
7.19	Franciela	Krasucki	BRA	26.4.88	1r2		São Caetano do Sul	16 Feb

7.21A	Kenyanna	Wilson	USA	27.10.88	22 Feb	7.23	Khamica	Bingham	CAN	15.6.94	22 Feb
7.22	Muna	Lee	USA	30.10.81	1 Feb	7.24	Jenna	Prandini	USA	20.11.92	18 Jan
7.22	Dina	Asher-Smith	GBR-J	4.12.95	8 Feb	7.24	Nataliya	Pogrebnyak	UKR	19.2.88	1 Feb
7.22	Bianca	Knight	USA	2.1.89	8 Feb	7.24	Takeia	Pinckney	USA	24.7.91	1 Feb
7.22	Sophie	Papps	GBR	6.10.94	15 Feb	7.25	Samantha	Henry-Robinson	JAM	25.9.88	1 Feb
7.22	Aleen	Bailey	JAM	25.11.80	25 Feb	7.25	Jessica	Young	USA	6.4.87	8 Feb
7.22	Desiree	Henry	GBR-J	26.8.95	25 Feb	7.25	Olivia	Ekponé	USA	5.1.93	28 Feb
7.23A	Morolake	Akinosun (30)	USA	17.5.94	8 Feb	7.25	Jennifer	Madu	USA	23.9.94	28 Feb
7.23	Flings	Owusu-Agyapong	GHA	16.10.88	15 Feb	7.25	Sheniqua	Ferguson (40)	BAH	24.11.89	9 Mar
						7.25A	Katie	Wise	USA	15.10.93	14 Mar

Best at low altitude						7.18	Lawson		3s1	WI	Sopot		9 Mar
7.16	Bryant	1	Tyson Fayetteville		14 Feb	7.20	Todd		18 Jan		7.25	Brookins	18 Jan
7.18	Bayne	2	Karslruhe		1 Feb	7.24	Sanders		28 Feb		7.25	Akinosun	14 Feb
						7.24	Burchell		1 Mar				

200 METRES

22.50	Kamaria	Brown	USA	21.12.92	1r1	SEC	College Station	1 Mar
22.51		Brown			1h6	SEC	College Station	28 Feb
22.69A	Dezerea	Bryant	USA	27.4.93	1r2	NCAA	Albuquerque	14 Mar

22.79A	Kyra	Jefferson	USA	23.9.94	1r1	NCAA	Albuquerque		14 Mar
22.92A	Phyllis	Francis	USA	4.5.92	1		Albuquerque		14 Feb
22.93A	Mahagony	Jones	USA	20.12.90	2r1	NCAA	Albuquerque		14 Mar
23.06	Regine	Williams	USA-J	5.9.95	1		Fayetteville		31 Jan
23.10	Olivia	Ekponé	USA	5.1.93	2r2	SEC	College Station		1 Mar
23.11	Patricia	Hall	JAM	16.10.82	1		College Station		8 Feb
23.11A	Ashton	Purvis	USA	12.7.92	2r2	NCAA	Albuquerque		14 Mar
23.15	Dina	Asher-Smith (10)	GBR-J	4.12.95	1	NC-j	Sheffield		2 Mar

223.17	Rebekka	Haase	GER	2.1.93	23 Feb	
23.21	Felecia	Majors	USA	11.2.95	28 Feb	
23.22A	Destinee	Gause	USA	4.4.94	14 Mar	
23.24	Shannon	Hylton	GBR-J	19.12.96	9 Feb	
23.24	Anna	Kielbasinska	POL	26.6.90	23 Feb	
23.25A	Tynia	Gaither	BAH	16.3.93	14 Mar	
23.26	Maike	Dix	GER	2.7.86	8 Feb	
23.27A	Shayla	Sanders	USA	6.1.94	14 Mar	
23.28	Jessica	Beard	USA	8.1.89	15 Feb	
23.30A	Jenna	Prandini (20)	USA	20.11.92	14 Feb	

Best at low altitude

22.87		Jefferson	2r1	SEC	College Station		1 Mar
23.23		Purvis	15 Feb	23.30	Gause		28 Feb

300 METRES

36.10	Shaunae	Miller	BAH	15.4.94	1	Mill	New York (Arm)		15 Feb
36.50	Francena	McCorory	USA	20.10.88	2	Mill	New York (Arm)		15 Feb

37.04	Denisa	Rosolová	CZE	21.8.86	25 Feb			
37.23	Kseniya	Ryzhova	RUS	19.4.87	12 Jan			
37.26	Kadecia	Baird	GUY-J	24.2.95	25 Jan		
37.27	Marina	Chernova	RUS	17.4.91	7 Jan		

400 METRES

550.46A	Phyllis	Francis	USA	4.5.92	1r2	NCAA	Albuquerque		15 Mar
50.85A	Francena	McCorory	USA	20.10.88	1	NC	Albuquerque		23 Feb
50.94	Kamaria	Brown	USA	21.12.92	1r1	SEC	College Station		1 Mar
51.03	Kseniya	Ryzhova	RUS	19.4.87	1	NC	Moskva		18 Feb
51.13A	Joanna	Atkins	USA	31.1.89	2	NC	Albuquerque		23 Feb
51.34A	Natasha	Hastings	USA	23.7.86	3	NC	Albuquerque		23 Feb
51.54	Kaliese	Spencer	JAM	6.5.87	2	WI	Sopot		8 Mar
51.60	Regina	George	NGR	17.2.91	1h1	WI	Sopot		7 Mar
51.63	Shaunae	Miller	BAH	15.4.94	3s2	WI	Sopot		7 Mar
51.71A	Ashley	Spencer (10)	USA	8.6.93	2r2	NCAA	Albuquerque		15 Mar
51.77	Robin	Reynolds	USA	22.2.94	2r1	SEC	College Station		1 Mar
51.82A	Deedee	Trotter	USA	8.12.82	1		Albuquerque		24 Jan
51.86	Shamier	Little	USA-J	20.3.95	3r1	SEC	College Station		1 Mar
51.97A	Courtney	Okolo	USA	15.3.94	2r1	NCAA	Albuquerque		15 Mar
52.00	Patricia	Hall	JAM	16.10.82	1		College Station		15 Feb
52.01A	Kendall	Baisden	USA-J	5.3.95	3r1	NCAA	Albuquerque		15 Mar
52.13	Justyna	Swiety	POL	3.12.92	2h1	WI	Sopot		7 Mar

5252.37	Denisa	Rosolová	CZE	21.8.86	7 Mar	
52.39	Irina	Davydova	RUS	27.5.88	2 Feb	
52.40	Alena	Tamkova (20)	RUS	30.5.90	17 Feb	
52.40A	Cassandra	Tate	USA	11.9.90	23 Feb	
52.44	Esther	Cremer	GER	29.3.88	22 Feb	
52.47A	Akawkaw	Ndipagbor	USA	30.4.93	14 Mar	
52.49	Eilidh	Child	GBR	20.2.87	15 Feb	
52.49	Nicky	van Leuveren	NED	20.5.90	23 Feb	
52.50	Kiara	Porter	USA	22.10.93	2 Mar	
52.52A	Monica	Hargrove	USA	30.12.82	23 Feb	
52.58	Janeil	Bellille	TTO	18.6.89	1 Mar	
52.58A	Kyah	Seymour	USA	11.1.94	14 Mar	
52.59	Jordan	Lavender (30)	USA	23.7.93	14 Feb	
52.61	Lisanne	de Witte	NED	10.9.92	7 Mar	
52.65	Felecia	Majors	USA-J	11.2.95	1 Mar	
52.68	Yuliya	Terekhova	RUS	20.2.90	17 Feb	

Best at low altitude

51.69	Hastings		1	Winter	Moskva		2 Feb
52.33	A Spencer	14 Feb	52.55	Atkins			8 Mar
52.54	Okolo	14 Feb	52.57	Trotter			7 Mar

Oversized track

51.54	Ashley	Spencer	USA	8.6.93	1	Big 12	Ames		1 Mar
51.56	Courtney	Okolo	USA	15.3.94	2	Big 12	Ames		1 Mar
52.20	Diamond	Dixon	USA	29.6.92	1 Mar	52.53	Kyah	Seymour	USA	11.1.94	1 Mar

600 METRES 1:25.76 Regina George   NGR 17.2.91 1   Fayetteville 10 Jan

800 METRES

2:00.09	Chanelle	Price	USA	22.8.90	1	WI	Sopot		9 Mar
2:00.37	Angelika	Cichocka	POL	15.3.88	1h1	WI	Sopot		7 Mar
2:00.43A	Ajee'	Wilson	USA	8.5.94	1	NC	Albuquerque		23 Feb
2:00.65	Nataliya	Lupu	UKR	4.11.87	1h2	WI	Sopot		7 Mar
2:00.79	Marina	Arzamasova	BLR	17.12.87	3	WI	Sopot		9 Mar
2:00.93	Selina	Büchel	SUI	26.7.91	1h3	WI	Sopot		7 Mar
2:00.94	Laura	Muir	GBR	9.5.93	1	v3N	Glasgow		25 Jan
2:01.25	Lenka	Masná	CZE	22.4.85	3h3	WI	Sopot		7 Mar
2:01.29	Anna	Shchagina	RUS	7.12.91	1	NC	Moskva		18 Feb
2:01.32#	Laura	Roesler (10)	USA	19.12.91	1		Lexington		25 Jan
2:01.46	Yekaterina	Kupina	RUS	2.2.86	2	NC	Moskva		18 Feb
2:01.53	Svetlana	Karamysheva	RUS	24.5.88	1	Mosc Ch	Moskva		24 Jan
2:01.67	Jennifer	Meadows	GBR	17.4.81	1		Praha (O2)		25 Feb

2:01.81	Aníta	Hinriksdóttir	ISL-J	13.1.96	19 Jan	
2:01.87A	Molly	Beckwith-Ludlow	USA	4.8.87	23 Feb	
2:01.89	Jenna	Westaway	CAN	19.6.94	15 Feb	
2:01.89	Natoya	Goule	JAM	30.3.91	7 Mar	
2:02.15	Stephanie	Charnigo	USA	25.7.88	7 Feb	
2:02.29	Tatyana	Myazina	RUS	18.3.88	17 Feb	
2:02.34	Yekaterina	Poistogova (20)	RUS	1.3.91	2 Feb	
2:02.39	Melissa	Bishop	CAN	5.8.88	28 Feb	
2:02.42#	Anastasiya	Tkachuk	UKR	20.4.93	1 Feb	
2:02.71	Olha	Lyakhova	UKR	18.3.92	7 Mar	
2:02.89	Yelena	Kobeleva	RUS	12.6.88	18 Feb	
2:02.90	Yevgeniya	Zinurova	RUS	16.11.82	2 Feb	
2:02.95	Stina	Troest	DEN	17.1.94	7 Mar	

1000 METRES
Boston (R) 8 Feb: 1. Mary Cain USA-J 3.5.96 2:35.80, 2. Chanelle Price USA 22.8.90 2:36.63, 3. Sarah Brown USA 15.10.86 2:36.90, Molly Beckwith-Ludlow USA 4.8.87 2:37.19, 5. Treniere Moser USA 27.10.81 2:37.88

2:39.16	Svetlana	Karamysheva	RUS	24.5.88	12 Jan	2:39.77	Melissa	Bishop	CAN	5.8.88	8 Feb
						2:39.94	Margherita	Magnani	ITA	26.2.87	26 Jan

1500 METRES

3:55.17	Genzebe	Dibaba	ETH	8.2.91	1		Karlsruhe		1 Feb
3:57.91	Abeba	Aregawi	SWE	5.7.90	1	XLG	Stockholm		6 Feb
4:00.61		Aregawi			1	WI	Sopot		8 Mar
4:05.32	Laura	Muir	GBR	9.5.93	1	GP	Birmingham		15 Feb
4:05.34	Sifan	Hassan	NED	.93	2	GP	Birmingham		15 Feb
4:05.70+	Kim	Conley	USA	14.3.86	1		New York (Arm)		25 Jan
4:05.78	Yelena	Korobkina	RUS	25.11.90	3	GP	Birmingham		15 Feb
4:05.82	Hellen	Obiri	KEN	13.12.89	4	GP	Birmingham		15 Feb
4:06.63+	Mary	Cain	USA-J	3.5.96	1		Boston (A)		24 Jan
4:07.12	Axumawit	Embaye	ETH	18.10.94	2	WI	Sopot		8 Mar
4:07.61	Nicole	Sifuentes (10)	CAN	30.6.86	3	WI	Sopot		8 Mar
4:07.62	Siham	Hilali	MAR	2.5.86	4	WI	Sopot		8 Mar
4:07.84	Luiza	Gega	ALB	5.11.88	1	BalkC	Istanbul		22 Feb
4:07.84	Treniere	Moser	USA	27.10.81	5	WI	Sopot		8 Mar
4:07.94	Gamze	Bulut	TUR	3.8.92	1		Istanbul		15 Feb
4:08.15	Angelika	Cichocka	POL	15.3.88	2		Karlsruhe		1 Feb
4:08.47	Gudaf	Tsegay	ETH-Y	23.1.97	2	XLG	Stockholm		6 Feb
4:08.66+	Jordan	Hasay	USA	21.9.91	2		Boston (A)		24 Jan
4:08.79	Betlhem	Desalegn	UAE	13.11.91	3	XLG	Stockholm		6 Feb
4:09.01	Katarzyna	Broniatowska	POL	22.2.90	5	GP	Birmingham		15 Feb
4:09.08	Dawit	Seyoum (20)	ETH-J	27.7.96	1		Praha (O2)		25 Feb
4:09.15	Rabab	Arrafi	MAR	12.1.91	2		Praha (O2)		25 Feb
4:09.19	Renata	Plis	POL	5.2.85	4	XLG	Stockholm		6 Feb
4:09.22	Isabel	Macías	ESP	11.8.84	6	GP	Birmingham		15 Feb
4:09.27	Margherita	Magnani	ITA	26.2.87	4		Karlsruhe		1 Feb
4:09.77+	Abbey	D'Agostino	USA	25.5.92	3		Boston (A)		24 Jan

4:10.07	Danuta	Urbanik	POL	24.12.89	6 Feb	4:11.37	Senbera	Teferi	ETH-J	3.5.95	25 Feb
4:10.91	Svetlana	Karamysheva	RUS	24.5.88	7 Mar	4:11.59	Jemma	Simpson	GBR	10.2.84	15 Feb
4:11.18+	Morgan	Uceny	USA	10.3.85	25 Jan	4:12.10	Mimi	Belete	BRN	9.6.88	6 Feb
4:11.27+	Sarah	Brown	USA	15.10.86	25 Jan	4:12.51	Natalya	Aristarkhova	RUS	31.10.89	19 Feb
4:11.27	Heather	Kampf (30)	USA	19.1.87	7 Mar	4:12.76	Gabe	Grunewald	USA	25.6.86	25 Jan

1 MILE

4:24.11	Mary	Cain	USA	3.5.96	1		Boston (A)		24 Jan
4:24.54	Kim	Conley	USA	14.3.86	1		New York (Arm)		25 Jan
4:26.28	Amanda	Winslow	USA	10.12.90	1		Boston ()		7 Feb
4:28.31	Abbey	D'Agostino	USA	25.5.92	2		Boston (A)		24 Jan
4:28.37	Jordan	Hasay	USA	21.9.91	3		Boston (A)		24 Jan
4:28.86	Treniere	Moser	USA	27.10.81	2	Mill	New York (Arm)		15 Feb
4:28.97	Nicole	Sifuentes	CAN	30.6.86	3	Mill	New York (Arm)		15 Feb
4:29.62	Sarah	Brown	USA	15.10.86	3		New York (Arm)		25 Jan

4:30.14	Heather	Kampf	USA	19.1.87	25 Jan	4:32.15	Alexa	Efraimson	USA-Y	20.2.97	15 Feb
4:30.57	Morgan	Uceny (10)	USA	10.3.85	25 Jan	4:32.20	Yelena	Korobkina	RUS	25.11.90	8 Feb
4:31.30	Lauren	Penney	USA	1.5.90	7 Feb	4:32.37	Nicole	Schappert	USA	30.10.86	7 Feb
4:32.01	Emma	Coburn	USA	19.10.90	15 Feb	4:32.61	Lucy	Van Dalen	NZL	18.11.88	25 Jan

2000m: 5:37.2+ Genzebe Dibaba   ETH   8.2.91   1   in 3000   Stockholm   21 Feb

3000 METRES

8:16.60	Genzebe	Dibaba	ETH	8.2.91	1	XLG	Stockholm		6 Feb
8:24.85+		G Dibaba			1	in 2M	Birmingham		15 Feb
8:29.99	Hellen	Obiri	KEN	13.12.89	2	XLG	Stockholm		6 Feb
8:40.75	Irene	Jelagat	KEN	10.12.88	3	XLG	Stockholm		6 Feb
8:43.16	Maryam	Jamal	BRN	16.9.84	1	AsiC	Hangzhou		16 Feb
8:43.29+	Hiwot	Ayalew	ETH	6.3.90	2	in 2M	Birmingham		15 Feb
8:43.42	Viola	Kibiwot	KEN	22.12.83	4	XLG	Stockholm		6 Feb
8:43.47	Almaz	Ayana	ETH	21.11.91	5	XLG	Stockholm		6 Feb
8:44.28+	Jenny	Simpson	USA	23.8.86	1	in 2M	Boston (R)		8 Feb
8:44.69+	Sally	Kipyego	KEN	19.12.85	2	in 2M	Boston (R)		8 Feb
8:45.32	Sifan	Hassan (10)	NED	.93	1		Karlsruhe		1 Feb
8:46.54	Betlhem	Desalegn	UAE	13.11.91	2	AsiC	Hangzhou		16 Feb
8:47.94	Senbera	Teferi	ETH-J	3.5.95	6	XLG	Stockholm		6 Feb
8:48.27	Alia Mohamed	Saeed	UAE	18.5.91	7	XLG	Stockholm		6 Feb
8:48.35	Kim	Conley	USA	14.3.86	1	Mill	New York (Arm)		15 Feb

8:50.60	Betsy	Saina	KEN	30.6.88	15 Feb	8:53.95	Lucy	Van Dalen	NZL	18.11.88	15 Feb
8:51.48	Yelena	Korobkina	RUS	25.11.90	17 Feb	8:54.30+	Jordan	Hasay	USA	21.9.91	8 Feb
8:51.81	Margherita	Magnani	ITA	26.2.87	15 Feb	8:55.21	Lydia	Chepkurui	KEN	23.8.84	6 Feb
8:51.91	Abbey	D'Agostino	USA	25.5.92	15 Feb	8:56.20	Kate	Avery	GBR	10.10.91	15 Feb
8:53.74	Renata	Plis	POL	5.2.85	9 Feb	8:56.37#	Amanda	Winslow	USA	10.12.90	1 Feb
8:53.87	Gabe	Grunewald (20)	USA	25.6.86	15 Feb	8:56.44#	Lauren	Penney	USA	1.5.90	1 Feb

| 8:57.03 | Natalya | Aristarkhova | RUS | 31.10.89 | 17 Feb | 8:58.79 | Yelena | Nagovitsyna | RUS | 7.12.82 | 11 Jan |
| 8:57.20# | Jessica | O'Connell | CAN | 10.2.89 | 1 Feb | 8:58.85 | Shannon | Rowbury (30) | USA | 19.9.84 | 7 Mar |

2 MILES

9:00.48	Genzebe	Dibaba	ETH	8.2.91	1	GP	Birmingham	15 Feb
9:21.04	Sally	Kipyego	KEN	19.12.85	1		Boston (R)	8 Feb
9:21.59	Hiwot	Ayalew	ETH	6.3.90	2	GP	Birmingham	15 Feb
9:26.19	Jenny	Simpson	USA	23.8.86	2		Boston (R)	8 Feb
9:36.00	Jordan	Hasay	USA	21.9.91	3		Boston (R)	8 Feb

5000 METRES

15:13.86	Molly	Huddle	USA	31.8.84	1		Boston(A)	2 Mar
15:28.84#	Betsy	Saina	KEN	30.6.88	1		Seattle	31 Jan
15:30.52	Alla	Kulyatina	RUS	9.6.90	19 Feb	15:33.68	Yelena	Nagovitsyna RUS 7.12.82			

2000 METRES STEEPLECHASE

Novocheboksarsk 11 Jan: 1. Albina Chinchikeyeva RUS 17.2.92 6:11.57, 2. Viktoriya Ivanova RUS 21.11.91 6:12.03 3. Lyudmila Lebedeva RUS 23.5.90 6:12.73, 4. Yelena Orlova RUS 30.5.80 6:13.71

60 METRES HURDLES

7.79	Sally		Pearson	AUS	19.9.86	1h1	ISTAF	Berlin	1 Mar
7.79			Pearson			1h1	WI	Sopot	7 Mar
7.80A	Nia		Ali	USA	23.10.88	1	NC	Albuquerque	23 Feb
7.80			Pearson			1	ISTAF	Berlin	1 Mar
7.80			Ali			1	WI	Sopot	8 Mar
7.81			Pearson			1s1	WI	Sopot	8 Mar
7.82A	Janay		DeLoach Soukup	USA	12.10.85	2	NC	Albuquerque	23 Feb
7.85			Pearson			2	WI	Sopot	8 Mar
7.86	Tiffany		Porter	GBR	13.11.87	3	WI	Sopot	8 Mar
7.87	Cindy		Billaud	FRA	11.3.86	1h3	WI	Sopot	7 Mar
7.88A	Kristi		Castlin	USA	7.7.88	3	NC	Albuquerque	23 Feb
7.91	Nadine		Hildebrand	GER	20.9.87	1		Karlsruhe	1 Feb
7.91	Yvette		Lewis	PAN	16.3.85	2h2	WI	Sopot	7 Mar
7.93	Yekaterina		Galitskaya	RUS	24.2.87	1	NC	Moskva	18 Feb
7.93A	Sharika		Nelvis (10)	USA	10.5.90	1	NCAA	Albuquerque	15 Mar
7.93A	Tiffani		McReynolds	USA	4.12.91	2	NCAA	Albuquerque	15 Mar
7.94	Kendra		Harrison	USA	18.9.92	1	SEC	College Station	1 Mar
7.94A	Jasmin		Stowers	USA	23.9.91	3	NCAA	Albuquerque	15 Mar
7.95	Cindy		Roleder	GER	21.8.89	2	NC	Leipzig	22 Feb
7.95	Eline		Berings	BEL	28.5.86	2h1	WI	Sopot	7 Mar
7.97	Marzia		Caravelli	ITA	23.10.81	3h2	WI	Sopot	7 Mar
7.98A	Janice		Jackson	USA	30.10.91	2h1	NCAA	Albuquerque	14 Mar
8.00A	Candice		Price	USA	26.10.85	1		Flagstaff	8 Feb

8.02A	Jessica	Zelinka	CAN	3.9.81	8 Feb	8.07	Rosina	Hodde	NED	10.2.83	7 Mar
8.02		Wu Shujiao (20)	CHN	19.6.92	15 Feb	8.07A	Cindy	Ofili (30)	USA	5.8.94	15 Mar
8.02	Alina	Talay	BLR	14.5.89	22 Feb	8.08	Kellie	Wells	USA	16.7.82	1 Feb
8.02A	Vashti	Thomas	USA	21.4.90	23 Feb	8.08	Angela	Whyte	CAN	22.5.80	7 Feb
8.03	Yuliya	Kondakova	RUS	4.12.81	8 Mar	8.08A	Sasha	Wallace	USA-J	21.9.95	14 Mar
8.04	Giulia	Pennella	ITA	27.10.89	22 Feb	8.09A	Jade	Barber	USA	4.4.93	1 Feb
8.05	Marina	Tomic	SLO	30.4.83	1 Feb	8.09	Nooralotta	Neziri	FIN	9.11.92	23 Feb
8.05	Sara	Aerts	BEL	25.1.84	7 Mar	8.09	Andrea	Ivancevic	CRO	21.8.84	8 Mar
8.06	Jacqueline	Coward	USA	5.11.89	14 Feb	8.10	Evonne	Britton	USA	10.10.91	1 Mar
8.07A	LeTristan	Pledger	USA	27.8.93	8 Feb	8.10	Monique	Morgan	JAM	14.10.85	7 Mar

HIGH JUMP

2.01	Mariya	Kuchina	RUS	14.1.93	1	XLG	Stockholm	6 Feb
2.00		Kuchina			1		Chelyabinsk	16 Jan
2.00	Kamila	Licwinko	POL	22.3.86	1		Arnstadt	8 Feb
2.00	Ruth	Beitia	ESP	1.4.79	1	NC	Sabadell	22 Feb
2.00		Licwinko			1	NC	Sopot	22 Feb
2.00	Blanka	Vlasic	CRO	8.11.83	1		Praha (O2)	25 Feb
2.00		Kuchina			1=	WI	Sopot	8 Mar
2.00		Licwinko			1=	WI	Sopot	8 Mar
2.00		Beitia			3	WI	Sopot	8 Mar
1.97	Emma	Green Tregaro	SWE	8.12.84	1		Trinec	29 Jan
1.97	Marie-Laurence	Jungfleisch	GER	7.10.90	2		Arnstadt	8 Feb
1.97	Airine	Palsyte	LTU	13.7.92	1	NC	Klaipeda	21 Feb
1.97	Justyna	Kasprzycka	POL	20.8.87	4	WI	Sopot	8 Mar
1.96	Alessia	Trost	ITA	8.3.93	1P		Padova	11 Jan
1.96	Katarina	Johnson-Thompson (10)	GBR	9.1.93	1	NC	Sheffield	8 Feb
1.96	Svetlana	Radzivil	UZB	17.1.87	1	AsiC	Hangzhou	16 Feb
1.95	Iryna	Herashchenko	UKR-J	10.3.95	1	NC	Sumy	21 Feb
1.95	Levern	Spencer	LCA	23.6.84	Q	WI	Sopot	7 Mar
1.95		Zheng Xingjuan	CHN	20.3.89	1	NGP	Nanjing	9 Mar
1.94	Irina	Gordeyeva	RUS	9.10.86	1		Bordeaux	26 Jan
1.94	Ana	Simic	CRO	5.5.90	3		Hustopece	1 Feb

1.94	Nadezhda	Dusanova	UZB	17.11.87	3		Arnstadt	8 Feb
1.94	Nafissatou	Thiam	BEL	19.8.94	1	Flanders	Gent	9 Feb
1.94	Inika	McPherson	USA	29.9.86	1		Houston	14 Feb
1.93	Yana	Maksimova (20)	BLR	9.1.89	1	NC	Mogilyov	21 Feb
1.93	Nadine	Broersen	NED	29.4.90	1P	WI	Sopot	7 Mar
1.92	Daniela	Stanciu	ROU	15.10.87	1	NC	Bucuresti	16 Feb
1.92	Oksana	Okuneva	UKR	14.3.90	2	NC	Sumy	21 Feb
1.92	Anna	Iljustsenko	EST	12.10.85	1	NC	Tartu	22 Feb
1.91	Oksana	Starostina	RUS	1.4.88	9			Jan

1.91	Adonía	Steryíou	GRE	7.7.85	25 Jan
1.91	Venelina	Veneva-Mateeva	BUL	13.6.74	1 Feb
1.91	Barbara	Szabó	HUN	17.2.90	15 Feb
1.90	Oksana	Krasnokutskaya	RUS	24.9.93	4 Jan
1.90	Jeannelle	Scheper (30)	LCA	21.11.94	18 Jan
1.90	Yekaterina	Kuntsevich	RUS	13.7.84	28 Jan
1.90	Valentyna	Lyashenko	UKR	30.1.81	11 Feb
1.90	Mariya	Nesterchuk	BLR	14.8.89	21 Feb
1.90	Urszula	Gardzielewska	POL	21.7.88	22 Feb
1.90	Leontia	Kallenou	CYP	5.10.94	1 Mar
1.89	Yuliya	Kostrova	RUS	20.8.91	11 Jan

1.89	Tatyana	Mnatsakanova	RUS	25.5.83	23 Jan
1.89	Olena	Holosha	UKR	26.1.82	21 Feb
1.88	Alesya	Paklina	KGZ	22.6.88	25 Jan
1.88	Erika	Wiklund (40)	SWE	10.3.88	1 Feb
1.88	Sofie	Skoog	SWE	7.6.90	6 Feb
1.88	Grete	Udras	EST	11.3.88	11 Feb
1.88	Tatyana	Kivimyagi	RUS	23.6.84	19 Feb
1.88A	Sharon	Day-Monroe	USA	9.6.85	21 Feb
1.88A	Tiana	Wills	USA		23 Feb
1.88	Morgan	Lake	GBR-Y	12.5.97	2 Mar
1.88	Emma	Nuttall	GBR	23.4.92	8 Mar
1.88A	Kendell	Williams	USA-J	14.6.95	15 Mar

POLE VAULT

4.76	Anna	Rogowska	POL	21.5.81	1	Flanders	Gent	9 Feb
4.73	Holly	Bleasdale	GBR	2.11.91	1	NC	Sheffield	8 Feb
4.73	Jenn	Suhr	USA	5.2.82	1		Jonesboro	27 Feb
4.72	Silke	Spiegelburg	GER	17.3.86	1	XLG	Stockholm	6 Feb
4.72	Nikolía	Kiriakopoúlou	GRE	21.3.86	2	XLG	Stockholm	6 Feb
4.72	Anzhelika	Sidorova	RUS	28.6.91	1	NC	Moskva	17 Feb
4.71	Jirina	Svobodová	CZE	20.5.86	1=		Dresden	31 Jan
4.71	Tina	Sutej	SLO	7.11.88	1	Winter	Moskva	2 Feb

4.71 also Spiegelburg 18 Jan, Bleasdale 31 Jan & 15 Feb, Sidorova 11 Feb, Suhr 15 Feb

4.71A	Mary	Saxer	USA	21.6.87	1	NC	Albuquerque	23 Feb
4.70	Yarisley	Silva (10)	CUB	1.6.87	1	WI	Sopot	9 Mar
4.70	Fabiana	Murer	BRA	16.3.81	4	WI	Sopot	9 Mar
4.66A	Kylie	Hutson	USA	27.11.87	3	NC	Albuquerque	23 Feb
4.63	Nicole	Büchler	SUI	17.12.83	2		Bad Oeynhausen	28 Feb
4.62	Angelica	Bengtsson	SWE	8.7.93	1		Nice	8 Feb
4.61	Marion	Fiack	FRA	13.10.92	1		Orléans	18 Jan
4.61	Lisa	Ryzih	GER	27.9.88	1		Zweibrücken	7 Feb
4.61	Kristina	Gadschiew	GER	3.7.84	2	NC	Leipzig	22 Feb
4.60A	Kaitlin	Petrillose	USA	12.10.92	1	NCAA	Albuquerque	14 Mar
4.56	Lyudmila	Yeryomina	RUS	8.8.91	2	NC	Moskva	17 Feb
4.56	Marion	Lotout (20)	FRA	19.11.89	1	NC	Bordeaux	22 Feb
4.55A	Ekateríni	Stefanídi	GRE	4.2.90	2		Flagstaff	25 Jan
4.55	Minna	Nikkanen	FIN	9.4.88	1	v3N	Tampere	8 Feb
4.52	Becky	Holliday	USA	12.3.80	1		Jonesboro	30 Jan
4.52	Malin	Dahlström	SWE	26.8.89	3		Dresden	31 Jan
4.52	Hanna	Sheleh	UKR	14.7.93	6	Stars	Donetsk	15 Feb
4.51	Vanessa	Boslak	FRA	11.6.82	3		Aubière	11 Jan
4.51	Katharina	Bauer	GER	12.6.90	4	NC	Leipzig	22 Feb
4.51A	Sandi	Morris	USA	8.7.92	4	NC	Albuquerque	23 Feb
4.51A	Kat	Majester	USA	22.5.87	5	NC	Albuquerque	23 Feb
4.51A	Emily	Grove (30)	USA	22.5.93	6	NC	Albuquerque	23 Feb
4.50	Angelina	Krasnova	RUS	7.2.91	1		Moskva	12 Jan
4.50	Alayna	Lutkovskaya	RUS-J	15.3.96	3	NC	Moskva	17 Feb
4.50	Anastasiya	Savchenko	RUS	15.11.89	4	NC	Moskva	17 Feb

4.46	Joana	Kraft	GER	27.7.91	8 Feb
4.46	Martina	Strutz	GER	4.11.81	22 Feb
4.45A	April	Steiner Bennett	USA	22.4.80	11 Jan
4.45	Romana	Malácová	CZE	15.5.87	25 Feb
4.45A	Annika	Roloff	GER	10.3.91	14 Mar
4.44	Maria Eleonor	Tavares	POR	24.9.85	16 Feb
4.43	Caroline Bonde	Holm (40)	DEN	19.7.90	28 Feb
4.41A	Katie	Nageotte	USA	30.6.91	17 Jan
4.40	Tatyana	Stetsyuk	RUS	27.8.92	12 Jan
4.40	Yekaterina	Kazeka	RUS	7.10.90	16 Jan
4.40	Kayla	Caldwell	USA	19.6.91	3 Feb

4.40	Aleksandra	Kiryashova	RUS	21.8.85	8 Feb
4.40	Tatyana	Shvydkina	RUS	8.5.90	17 Feb
4.40	Naroa	Agirre	ESP	15.5.79	1 Mar
4.40	Martina	Schultze	GER	12.9.90	1 Mar
4.40	Megan	Clark	USA	10.6.94	1 Mar
4.40A	Bethany	Firsick (50)	USA	4.12.91	14 Mar
4.38	Morgann	LeLeux	USA	14.11.92	28 Feb
4.36	Loréla	Mánou	GRE	20.12.90	22 Feb
4.35	Alexis	Paine	USA	12.10.90	8 Feb
4.35	Alysha	Newman	CAN	29.6.94	1 Mar
4.35	Kristen	Hixson	USA	1.7.92	2 Mar

LONG JUMP

6.98	Svetlana	Biryukova	RUS	1.4.91	1		Moskva	12 Jan
6.98		Biryukova			1		Volgograd	25 Jan
6.95	Tori	Bowie	USA	27.8.90	1		Naperville	25 Jan
6.92	Ivana	Spanovic	SRB	10.5.90	1	BalkC	Istanbul	22 Feb
6.87		Biryukova			1	NC	Moskva	18 Feb
6.86	Éloyse	Lesueur	FRA	15.7.88	1	Mill	New York (Arm)	15 Feb
6.85		Lesueur			1	WI	Sopot	9 Mar

6.81	Katarina	Johnson-Thompson	GBR	9.1.93	2	WI	Sopot	9 Mar
6.76	Darya	Klishina	RUS	15.1.91	Q	WI	Sopot	8 Mar
6.75	Yuliya	Pidluzhnaya	RUS	1.10.88	1		Chelyabinsk	19 Jan
6.73A	Lorraine	Ugen	GBR	22.8.91	1	NCAA	Albuquerque	14 Mar
6.70A	Tori	Polk	USA	21.9.83	1	NC	Albuquerque	22 Feb
6.69	Olga	Kucherenko (10)	RUS	5.11.85	2		Volgograd	25 Jan
6.69	Shara	Proctor	GBR	16.9.88	Q	WI	Sopot	8 Mar
6.68	Nadja	Käther	GER	29.9.88	1		Hamburg	26 Jan
6.68	Teresa	Dobija	POL	9.10.82	1	Pedros	Bydgoszcz	31 Jan
6.68	Alina	Rotaru	ROU	5.6.93	1	NC	Bucuresti	16 Feb
6.67	Florentina	Marincu	ROU	8.4.96	2	NC	Bucuresti	16 Feb
6.66	Olga	Sudareva	BLR	22.2.84	1	NCp	Gomel	8 Feb
6.62A	Christabel	Nettey	CAN	2.6.91	1		Albuquerque	14 Feb
6.61	Sosthene	Moguenara	GER	17.10.89	3		Karlsruhe	1 Feb
6.61A	Andrea	Geubelle	USA	21.6.91	3	NC	Albuquerque	22 Feb

6.57	Funmi	Jimoh (20)	USA	29.5.84	30 Jan		6.51	Iryna	Nikolayeva	UKR	20.1.84	27 Jan
6.57	Erica	Jarder	SWE	2.4.86	6 Feb		6.51	Cornelia	Deiac	ROU	20.3.88	16 Feb
6.56	Yekaterina	Koneva	RUS	25.9.88	25 Jan		6.50	Anna	Misochenko	RUS	15.4.92	9 Feb
6.56A	Chelsea	Hayes	USA	9.2.88	22 Feb		6.50A	Jasmine	Todd (30)	USA	23.12.93	14 Feb
6.53A	Janay	DeLoach Soukup	USA	12.10.85	24 Jan		6.50	Aiga	Grabuste	LAT	24.3.88	21 Feb
6.53	Anna	Kornuta	UKR	10.11.88	21 Feb		**Best at low altitude**					
6.52	Olga	Balayeva	RUS	31.7.84	30 Jan		6.59	Ugen		1	Ames	28 Feb

TRIPLE JUMP

14.65	Yekaterina	Koneva	RUS	25.9.88	1		Samara	30 Jan
14.65	Olga	Saladuha	UKR	4.6.83	1	NC	Sumy	21 Feb
14.60		Saladuha			1		Eaubonne	11 Feb
14.46		Koneva			1	WI	Sopot	8 Mar
14.45		Saladuha			2	WI	Sopot	8 Mar
14.39	Kimberly	Williams	JAM	3.11.88	3	WI	Sopot	8 Mar
14.36	Patrícia	Mamona	POR	21.11.88	1		Pombal	22 Feb
14.34	Kseniya	Detsuk	BLR	23.4.86	1	NCp	Gomel	8 Feb
14.24	Kristin	Gierisch	GER	20.8.90	1		Chemnitz	19 Jan
14.19		Li Yanmei	CHN	6.2.90	5	WI	Sopot	8 Mar
14.10	Dana	Veldáková	SVK	3.6.81	Q	WI	Sopot	7 Mar
14.09	Veronika	Mosina	RUS	17.10.90	1		Sankt Peterburg	8 Feb
14.04	Yarianna	Martínez (10)	CUB	20.9.84	Q	WI	Sopot	7 Mar
13.98	Alsu	Murtazina	RUS	20.12.87	2	NC	Moskva	19 Feb
13.98	Dovilė	Dzindzaletaite	LTU	14.7.93	1	NC	Klaipeda	22 Feb
13.97A	Shanieka	Thomas	JAM	2.2.92	1	NCAA	Albuquerque	15 Mar
13.96	Irina	Kosko	RUS	1.3.90	3	NC	Moskva	19 Feb
13.94	Nataliya	Yastrebova	UKR	12.10.84	1		Kyiv	11 Jan

13.93	Elena Andreea	Panturoiu	ROU-J	24.2.95	15 Feb		13.78	Irina	Vaskovskaya	BLR	2.4.91	21 Feb
13.91	Ana	Peleteiro	ESP-J	2.12.95	23 Feb		13.77	Anastasiya	Juravlyeva	UZB	9.10.81	24 Jan
13.88	Patricia	Sarrapio	ESP	16.11.82	23 Feb		13.77	Jeanine	Assani Issouf	FRA	17.8.92	22 Feb
13.83	Cristina	Sandu	ROU	4.3.90	15 Feb		13.76	Susana	Costa	POR	22.9.84	22 Feb
13.83	Jenny	Elbe (20)	GER	18.4.90	22 Feb		13.73	Irina	Gumenyuk	RUS	6.1.88	17 Feb
13.81A	Amanda	Smock	USA	27.7.82	23 Feb		13.73	Simona	La Mantia	ITA	14.4.83	22 Feb
13.79	Viktoriya	Valyukevich	RUS	22.5.82	24 Jan		13.73	Nathalie	Marie-Nély (30)	FRA	24.11.86	22 Feb
13.78	Iryna	Nikolayeva	UKR	20.1.84	28 Jan		13.73		Li Xiaohong	CHN-J	8.1.95	9 Mar

SHOT

20.67	Valerie	Adams	NZL	6.10.84	1	WI	Sopot	8 Mar
20.11		Adams			Q	WI	Sopot	8 Mar
20.05	Christina	Schwanitz	GER	24.12.85	1		Rochlitz	2 Feb
19.94		Schwanitz			2	WI	Sopot	8 Mar
19.93		Schwanitz			1		Düsseldorf	30 Jan
19.89		Schwanitz			1	NC	Leipzig	22 Feb
19.79		Schwanitz			1		Saßnitz	18 Jan
19.73		Schwanitz			Q	WI	Sopot	8 Mar
19.27		Schwanitz			1		Gammertingen	12 Jan
19.24		Gong Lijiao	CHN	24.1.89	3	WI	Sopot	8 Mar
19.11	Yevgeniya	Kolodko	RUS	2.7.90	4	WI	Sopot	8 Mar
19.10	Michelle	Carter	USA	12.10.85	5	WI	Sopot	8 Mar
18.88	Anca	Heltne	ROU	1.1.78	1	NC	Bucuresti	15 Feb
18.85	Yuliya	Leontyuk	BLR	31.1.84	Q	WI	Sopot	8 Mar
18.74	Alena	Kopets	BLR	14.2.88	1	NC	Mogilyov	21 Feb
18.63	Anita	Márton	HUN	15.1.89	Q	WI	Sopot	8 Mar
18.51	Tia	Brooks (10)	USA	2.8.90	1		Seattle	1 Feb
18.45	Jeneva	McCall	USA	28.10.89	1		New York	14 Feb
18.34	Alena	Dubitskaya	BLR	25.1.90	3	NCp	Gomel	8 Feb
18.31	Irina	Tarasova	RUS	15.4.87	2	NC	Moskva	19 Feb
18.31	Halyna	Obleshchuk	UKR	23.2.89	1	NC	Sumy	19 Feb
18.23	Chiara	Rosa	ITA	28.1.83	1	NC	Ancona	22 Feb
18.22	Vera	Yepimashko	BLR	10.7.76	1		Minsk	17 Jan

18.15	Olha		Holodna		UKR	14.11.91	1	NCp	Zaporizhzhya		27 Jan
18.15	Christina		Hillman		USA	6.10.93	1	NCAA	Albuquerque		15 Mar
18.08	Felisha		Johnson		USA	24.7.89	1		Notre Dame		7 Feb
17.89	Valentina		Muzaric (20)		CRO	23.7.92	2	NCAA	Albuquerque		15 Mar

17.81	Kearsten	Peoples	USA	20.12.91	28 Feb	17.36	Becky	O'Brien	USA	30.4.90	23 Feb
17.70	Brittany	Smith	USA	25.3.91	23 Feb	17.35	Shanice	Craft	GER	15.5.93	2 Feb
17.69	Josephine	Terlecki	GER	17.2.86	2 Feb	17.31!	Annie	Alexander (30)	TTO	28.8.87	6 Dec
17.65	Úrsula	Ruiz	ESP	11.8.83	15 Feb	17.30	Mary	Theisen	USA	3.11.90	1 Feb
17.63	Radoslava	Mavrodieva	BUL	13.3.87	22 Feb	17.27	Jessica	Cérival	FRA	20.1.82	22 Feb
17.58!	Emel	Dereli	TUR-J	25.2.96	28 Dec	17.26	Raven	Saunders	USA-J	15.5.96	15 Mar
	17.40				1 Feb	17.24	Natalia	Ducó	CHI	31.1.89	8 Mar
17.37	Kelsey	Card	USA	20.8.92	21 Feb	17.22	Whitney	Ashley	USA	18.2.89	1 Feb

20 LB WEIGHT

24.39	Gwen		Berry		USA	29.6.89	1		Lawrence		24 Jan
23.86			Berry				1	Mill	New York (Arm)		15 Feb
23.82	Jeneva		McCall		USA	28.10.89	2		Lawrence		24 Jan
23.82			Berry				1	NC	Albuquerque		22 Feb
23.68	Amber		Campbell		USA	5.6.81	2	NC	Albuquerque		22 Feb
22.95	Felisha		Johnson		USA	24.7.89	1		Notre Dame		7 Feb
22.66	Brea		Garrett		USA	27.6.93	1		College Station		8 Feb
22.53	Denise		Hinton		USA	17.12.91	1	SEC	College Station		1 Mar
22.42	Amanda		Bingson		USA	20.2.90	5	NC	Albuquerque		22 Feb
22.35	Dani		Bunch		USA	16.5.91	1		Minneapolis		18 Jan

21.96	Chelsea	Cassulo	USA	10.6.90	22 Feb	21.77	Brittany	Funk	USA	13.5.92	17 Jan
21.95	Kayla	Padgett (10)	USA		31 Jan	21.75	Chioma	Amaechi	USA	2.3.92	14 Feb
21.90	Ida	Storm	SWE	11.10.91	14 Mar	21.37	Kiah	Hicks	USA	21.2.93	28 Feb
21.80	La'Shantena	Rounds	USA	20.2.91	14 Mar	21.36	Jayla	Bostic	USA		1 Mar

PENTATHLON

484830	Nadine		Broersen		NED	29.4.90	1	WI	Sopot		7 Mar
	8.32		1.93			14.59	6.17	2:14.97			
4805A	Sharon		Day-Monroe		USA	9.6.85	1	NC	Albuquerque		21 Feb
	8.44		1.88			15.59	6.09	2:13.19			
4768	Brianne		Theisen-Eaton		CAN	18.12.88	2	WI	Sopot		7 Mar
	8.13		1.84			13.86	6.13	2:10.07			
4724	Alina		Fyodorova		UKR	31.7.89	3	WI	Sopot		7 Mar
	8.52		1.84			15.05	6.26	2:15.31			
4718			Day-Monroe				4	WI	Sopot		7 Mar
	8.43		1.84			14.95	5.94	2:09.80			
4686	Yana		Maksimova		BLR	9.1.89	1	NC	Gomel		8 Feb
	8.51		1.86			14.43	6.14	2:12.86			
4681	Claudia		Rath		GER	25.4.86	5	WI	Sopot		7 Mar
	8.43		1.78			13.66	6.37	2:10.29			
4635A	Kendell		Williams		USA	14.6.95	1	NCAA	Albuquerque		15 Mar
	8.21		1.88			12.05	6.32	2:17.31			
4587	Hanna		Melnychenko		UKR	24.4.83	7	WI	Sopot		7 Mar
	8.18		1.81			13.02	6.27	2:18.40			
4586A	Erica		Bougard		USA	26.7.93	2	NCAA	Albuquerque		15 Mar
	8.31		1.79			12.51	6.29	2:12.63			
4557	Karolina		Tyminska (10)		POL	4.10.84	8	WI	Sopot		7 Mar
	8.50		1.75			14.36	6.07	2:12.03			
4549	Aleksandra		Butvina		RUS	14.2.86	1		Tallinn		8 Feb
4498A	Sami		Spenner		USA	21.3.91	2	NC	Albuquerque		21 Feb
4496	Laura		Ikauniece		LAT	31.5.92	3		Tallinn		8 Feb
4444	Sofia		Linde		SWE-J	12.1.95	1		Växjö		9 Feb
4415			Wang Qingling		CHN	14.1.93	1	NGP	Beijing		22 Mar
4406A	Barbara		Nwaba		USA	18.1.89	3	NC	Albuquerque		21 Feb

4369	Michelle	Zeltner	SUI	22.12.91	23 Feb	4253A	Deanna	Latham	USA	23.2.92	15 Mar
4330	Myrte	Goor	NED	3.4.89	16 Feb	4246	Makeba	Alcide	LCA	24.2.90	31 Jan
4287A	Brittany	Harrell	USA	.91	15 Mar	4230	Kira	Biesenbach	GER	7.10.92	2 Feb
4284	Morgan	Lake (20)	GBR-J	12.5.97	8 Feb	4229A	Sarah	Chauchard	FRA	13.3.91	15 Mar
4284A	Lindsay	Lettow	USA	6.6.90	21 Feb	4226	Alina	Biesenbach	GER	27.4.92	2 Feb
4268	Nadine	Visser	NED	9.2.95	25 Jan	4222	Thea	Lafond	DMA	5.4.94	27 Feb
4268A	Lucie	Ondraschková	CZE	12.10.89	15 Mar	4210	Agnieszka	Borowska (30)	USA	1.9.92	15 Mar

3000 METRES WALK

11:50.08	Eleonora		Giorgi		ITA	14.9.89	1	NC	Ancona			22 Feb
11:56.59	Irina		Yumanova		RUS	6.11.90	1		Novocheboksarsk			11 Jan
11:57.66	Anisya		Kirdyapkina		RUS	23.10.89	1		Samara			30 Jan
11:57.71	Svetlana		Vasilyeva		RUS	24.7.92	2		Novocheboksarsk			11 Jan
11:57.89	Marina		Pandakova		RUS	1.3.89	3		Novocheboksarsk			11 Jan
11:58.44	Vera		Sokolova		RUS	8.6.87	4		Novocheboksarsk			11 Jan
12:07.19	Brigita		Virbalyte-Dimsiene	LTU	1.2.85	1		Wien			8 Feb
12:23.84	Rachel	Seaman	CAN	14.1.86	9 Feb	12:29.72	Ana	Cabecinha	POR	29.4.84	15 Feb

5000 Metres Walk: 21:54.0!   Anezka Drahotová   CZE 22.7.95   1   Jablonec   27 Dec